Business
Statistics
of the United States

Sixth Edition, 2000

D1524627

Business Statistics
of the United States

Sixth Edition, 2000

Editors
Linz Audain
Cornelia J. Strawser

Associate Editor
Katherine DeBrandt

BERNAN

ISBN: 0-89059-282-9

ISSN: 1086-8488

Printed by Automated Graphic Systems, Inc., White Plains, MD, on acid-free paper that meets the American National Standards Institute Z39-48 standard.

2002 2001   4 3 2 1

BERNAN
4611-F Assembly Drive
Lanham, MD 20706
800-274-4447
email: info@bernan.com
www.bernan.com

CONTENTS

ACKNOWLEDGEMENTS

The editors are profoundly grateful to all those at Bernan who assisted in the preparation of the sixth edition of *Business Statistics of the United States.* This volume would not have been possible without the careful and reliable work of the analysts who maintain the database, prepare the data tables, and review and fact-check all the material. Over the past year this team included: Katherine DeBrandt, Susan Huestis, Shanon Venegas, Alex Venezia, Michele Venezia, and Rebekah Venezia.

Copy editing was done by Bernan's editorial department, under the direction of Tamera Wells-Lee. Layout and graphics preparation were done by Bernan's production department, under the direction of Dan Parham. Lorrent Smith prepared the graphics, and Kara Gottschlich coordinated the production assignments. Dan, Lorrent, and Kara capably handled all production aspects of the volume.

Finally, special thanks are due to the many federal agency personnel who, as always, responded generously to our frequent need for assistance in obtaining data and background information.

PREFACE

Business Statistics of the United States is a basic desk reference for everyone requiring recent or historical information about the U.S. economy. It contains some 2,000 economic time series, predominantly from federal government sources, presenting a rich selection of the data most needed for analysis of economic trends and patterns. Of equal importance to the data themselves are the extensive background notes that enable the user to understand the data, use them appropriately, and, if desired, seek additional information from the source agencies.

THE 2000 EDITION

As always, each table in the 2000 edition of Business Statistics has been updated through the latest year available and all historical revisions to the data have been incorporated. All the standard features that have made earlier editions a must-have for every business reference shelf have been maintained. These include:

- Approximately 2,000 data series covering virtually every aspect of the U.S. economy, including GDP, employment, production, prices, productivity, international trade, money supply, and interest rates;

- Statistical profiles of each major industry group, from mining through retail trade and services, as well as statistical profiles of Federal, state and local governments;

- Tables presenting 30 years of annual data and 4 years of monthly or 9 years of quarterly data;

- An introductory chapter that summarizes critical developments with respect to the subject matter of each of the first 21 chapters of Business Statistics;

- Additional historical data back to 1963 for quarterly data and 1972 for monthly data for selected key series;

- Annual time series covering personal income and employment for each state and region;

- Detailed background notes providing definitions, data revision schedules, and sources of additional information.

USING THIS BOOK

Time period coverage. The 2000 edition of Business Statistics contains annual data for 1970 through 1999; quarterly data for 1991 through 1999; and monthly data for 1996 through 1999. Part III contains selected quarterly and monthly data for earlier time periods. In general, these quarterly data begin with 1963, and the monthly data, with 1972.

Annual data for certain series that are particularly important to an understanding of the U.S. economy are also included even though monthly or quarterly data are not available. This is the case for example for the data in Chapter 2, the chapter on income distribution and poverty. These data are annual time series through 1999. Other examples are the inclusion of available data from the Census Bureau's Annual Capital Expenditure Survey (Chapter 5) and Annual Survey of Services (Chapter 20).

Subject matter coverage. Part I covers the U.S. economy as a whole. It contains 12 chapters:

Chapter 1: National Product and Income and Cyclical Indicators
Chapter 2: Income Distribution and Poverty
Chapter 3: Consumer Income and Spending
Chapter 4: Industrial Production and Capacity Utilization
Chapter 5: Saving and Investment; Business Sales and Inventories
Chapter 6: Prices
Chapter 7: Employment Costs, Productivity, and Profits
Chapter 8: Employment, Hours, and Earnings
Chapter 9: Energy
Chapter 10: Money and Financial Markets
Chapter 11: U.S. Foreign Trade and Finance
Chapter 12: International Comparisons

Part II presents data by major industry group, following the structure of the Standard Industrial Classification (SIC) system. Basic data are repeated from Part I and are supplemented by additional industry detail. The user thus has the convenience of a profile of the industry in a single location. The industry groups covered are:

Chapter 13: Mining, Oil, and Gas
Chapter 14: Construction and Housing
Chapter 15: Manufacturing
Chapter 16: Durable Goods Manufacturing (nine two-digit industries)
Chapter 17: Nondurable Goods Manufacturing (ten two-digit industries)
Chapter 18: Transportation, Communications, and Utilities
Chapter 19: Retail and Wholesale Trade
Chapter 20: Finance, Insurance, Real Estate, and Private Services
Chapter 21: Government

Part III, as noted, contains additional historical data for selected series. Part IV contains annual data (1970 through 1999) for each state and region. The state data cover personal income and its major components, as well as employment and population. Unless otherwise noted, in this volume, the presence of an ellipsis (. . .) in the body of any given table implies that the data was not available from the relevant government agency or other source at press time.

Special features. Each chapter in Parts I and II begins with a chart and brief text highlighting some of the major trends reflected in the data. The text of each chapter has been reproduced in the introductory article "Business Statistics 2000 at a Glance" that appears after this Preface.

The reader is referred to two excellent introductory articles that appeared in the 1999 edition of Business Statistics. The first article, "The 1990s: Prosperous Prelude to the Twenty-First Century," described overall trends in the U.S. economy during the period covered by Business Statistics, with particular emphasis on the most recent few years. This analysis is carried through the first half of 1999. The second article, "Current Issues in Economic Measurement," described important recent developments in federal statistical programs. It discussed the recent comprehensive revision of the National Income and Product Accounts; the measurement of prices and productivity; different approaches to the measurement of saving; the differences between the two basic measures of employment—total civilian employment and nonfarm payroll employment; and the impact of alternative definitions on the measurement of income and poverty. Many of the issues discussed in that article have been dealt with in recent comprehensive data revisions, and are dealt with and revisited in the notes of the 2000 edition of Business Statistics.

The notes. The background notes contain definitions, descriptions of recent data revisions, information about data availability and release schedules, and references to sources of additional technical information. They are arranged in the order in which the data appear in the book, with references to the data pages and the subject to which they pertain shown at the beginning of each group of notes.

THE HISTORY OF BUSINESS STATISTICS

The history of Business Statistics begins with the publication, many years ago, by the U.S. Commerce Department's Bureau of Economic Analysis (BEA) of the first edition of a volume of the same name and general purpose. After 27 periodic editions, the last of which appeared in 1992, the BEA found it necessary, for budgetary and other reasons, to discontinue not only that publication but also maintenance of the database from which the publication was derived.

The individual statistical series in Business Statistics are publicly available. However, the task of gathering them from a number of sources within the government, plus a few private sources, and assembling them into one coherent database is highly impractical for most data users.

Even when current data are more or less readily available, obtaining the full historical time series often is time-consuming and difficult. Believing that a Business Statistics compilation was too valuable to be lost to the public, Bernan Press published the first edition of the present publication in 1995. The first edition received a warm welcome among users of economic data, and the volume's popularity has been sustained through four subsequent editions.

The great majority of the statistical data in this book is from federal government sources and is in the public domain. A few series are from private sources and further use may be subject to copyright restrictions. Sources for all the data are given in the notes.

The data in this volume meet the publication standards of the federal statistical agencies from which they were obtained. Every effort has been made to select data that are accurate, meaningful, and useful. All statistical data are subject to error arising from sampling variability, reporting errors, incomplete coverage, imputation, and other causes. The responsibility of the editors and publisher of this volume is limited to reasonable care in the reproduction and presentation of data obtained from established sources.

Linz Audain and Cornelia J. Strawser have edited the 2000 edition of Business Statistics. In this volume, both editors have attempted to maintain the tradition of excellence begun by the prior editor of Business Statistics, Dr. Courtenay M. Slater. Dr. Audain is a Senior Economic Consultant to Bernan. He has taught economics and statistics at the undergraduate and graduate level at seven different colleges and universities. He is an economist and an attorney. He is also a physician at the George Washington University Medical Center. He has published widely on economic, legal and medical issues in various journals. Dr. Strawser is a Senior Economic Consultant to Bernan. She was formerly Senior Economist at the U.S. House of Representatives Budget Committee and also has served at the Senate Budget Committee, the Congressional Budget Office, and the Federal Reserve Board, specializing in analysis of current economic developments and issues of economic measurement. Dr. Strawser outlined the scope of the publication, supervised data preparation, reviewed the data, and prepared the background notes. Dr. Audain reviewed the data and notes and prepared the introductory sections to each chapter and to the volume. Associate Editor Katherine DeBrandt was responsible for all of the database and table preparation.

BUSINESS STATISTICS 2000 AT A GLANCE

In this, as in prior volumes of Business Statistics, each chapter opens with a few observations regarding the data to be presented in the chapter. Because these observations often reflect some of the more current developments in business statistics, we have reproduced them below, organized by chapter, so that the reader might have access to them in one place.

CHAPTER 1: NATIONAL INCOME AND PRODUCT AND CYCLICAL INDICATORS

The comprehensive revision of the National Income and Product Accounts has revealed faster economic growth in recent periods. Growth from the last business cycle peak in 1990 to the end of 1999 was 3.2 percent per year, faster than in the 1980s and 1970s, though still below the 3.6 percent growth rate registered in the shorter business cycle from 1969 to 1973.

Inflation, however, decelerated over the same period, from 7.8 percent in the 1970s to 2.1 percent in the period from 1990 to 1999.

In 1999, imports of goods and services (in constant 1996 dollars) exceeded exports by $322 billion, compared with $221 billion in 1998. This was largely a result of a sharp 10.7 percent increase in the real volume of imports. The cost of imports, however, measured in the current dollars of each year, rose by 11.34 percent, suggesting an increase in the price of imports during 1999.

Real government consumption expenditures increased by $50 billion in 1999 (in constant 1996 dollars) to $1,536 billion from $1,486 billion. Federal government consumption expenditures increased by $13 billion, reflecting increases in both defense and nondefense spending, while state and local government consumption expenditures increased by $36 billion to $995.6 billion.

CHAPTER 2: INCOME DISTRIBUTION AND POVERTY

Real median household income in 1999 increased to an all-time high of $40,816. Median earnings of year-round full-time male workers increased to $36,476, the highest since 1989. Year-round, full-time female worker earnings rose to a record high of $26,324.

The poverty rate in 1999 was 11.8 percent, the lowest level since 1979. The rate for people in households with a female head declined to 30.4 percent, the lowest level in at least 40 years.

Income inequality (as measured by the Gini coefficient) increased slightly in 1999, based on the official definition of income, and it remained near its 31-year high reached in 1997. Adjusted for taxes and transfer payments, inequality was lower than in the official definition but still increasing in 1999.

CHAPTER 3: CONSUMER INCOME AND SPENDING

Total wage and salary payments rose at an 8.4 percent annual rate from 1971 to 1999; the service industries were the leading sector with a 10.2 percent rate, while manufacturing trailed with a growth rate of 5.6 percent.

Personal saving was 2.2 percent of disposable personal income in 1999, the lowest rate since the 1930s. For a discussion of the statistical and economic significance of recent low and negative measured saving rates, see "Current Issues in Economic Measurement" in the 1999 edition of this book.

Adjusted for inflation, disposable personal income rose at a 3.1 percent annual rate from 1971 to 1999, while personal consumption expenditures rose at a 3.3 percent rate. With population rising at a rate of 1.0 percent, the increase in real per capita income was 2.1 percent per year.

CHAPTER 4: INDUSTRIAL PRODUCTION AND CAPACITY UTILIZATION

In contrast to declining plant capacity utilization, manufacturing labor force utilization (measured as 100 minus the unemployment rate for workers last employed in manufacturing) rose to 96.4 percent in 1999, the highest since 1968 and 1969, when it was 96.7 percent.

The 42 percent rise in manufacturing production from 1992 to 1999 was concentrated primarily in durable goods industries, where production rose 72 percent during the seven years. Production of nondurable goods was up 12 percent overall even though in 1999 there was a decline in the production of apparel, leather products, and printing and publishing, with a significant 11 percent decline in the production of tobacco products.

Among major market categories, production of electronic and business equipment has shown by far the strongest gains since 1992, with 1999 production of computers and office equipment more than ten times its 1992 level. In 1999, production of semiconductors was more than 11 times its 1992 level.

CHAPTER 5: SAVING AND INVESTMENT; BUSINESS SALES AND INVENTORIES

The 1999 revisions to the National Income and Product Accounts created a new category in the business and government investment component of GDP termed "Equipment and Software." That category replaces the old "Producers' Durable Equipment" category. Starting in 1999, software that is separate from (i.e., not "embedded" within) the computer is being recognized as an investment because of its long useful life. A comparison of the two categories shows that the new category "Equipment and Software" has grown more rapidly than the older, narrower "Producers' Durable Equipment" category, contributing to the upward revision in recent GDP growth.

Other major components of business fixed investment also increased, if less dramatically. Total real (nonresidential) business fixed investment grew 11 percent per year from 1994 to 1999.

Real residential investment grew rather slowly from 1994 to 1997, but moved ahead 8.3 percent in 1998, with the strongest rise occurring in single family housing. In 1999 there was a more modest increase in real residential investment of 6.4 percent.

The emergence of a federal budget surplus contributed to a rise in economy-wide gross saving (personal, business and government) to 18.8 and 18.5 percent of gross national product in 1998 and 1999 respectively. These were the highest percentages since 1988, but still well below the averages of the 1970s and early 1980s.

CHAPTER 6: PRICES

The recent U.S. record of essential price stability was extended in 1999, when consumer prices rose only 2.2 percent, marking the eighth consecutive year in which consumer prices rose 3 percent or less.

Producer prices for finished goods increased 1.7 percent in 1999, the result of a 4.9 percent increase in energy prices coupled with a 1.3 percent rise in prices of finished goods other than energy.

Prices received by farmers fell for the third consecutive year in 1999, bringing the prices received index 14.3 percent below its 1996 peak. Thus, even though prices paid by farmers changed little over the three years, the ratio of prices received to prices paid fell to 83 percent of its 1990–1992 base.

CHAPTER 7: EMPLOYMENT, COSTS, PRODUCTIVITY, AND PROFITS

For all nonfarm business, from 1990 to 1999, annual average gains in labor productivity exceeded the annual average gains achieved from 1973 to 1990. The annual average gains from 1990 to 1999, however, were less than the strong gains of 1969 to 1973. In manufacturing, however, 1990s labor productivity gains have been even more rapid than those gains from 1969 to 1973.

Productivity gains in 1999 were especially strong—2.9 percent for all nonfarm business and 6.2 percent for manufacturing.

Employment cost increases remained moderate in 1999, with the index for total compensation for all civilian workers rising 3.4 percent from the fourth quarter of 1998 to the fourth quarter of 1999.

Productivity gains offset much of the rise in compensation per hour, and unit labor costs for nonfarm business were up only 1.9 percent, consistent with the continued low rate of price inflation.

After-tax corporate profits in manufacturing reached a record high of $260,995 million in 1999, surpassing the previous high of 1997 and maintaining the string of high-profit years that began in 1994.

CHAPTER 8: EMPLOYMENT, HOURS, AND EARNINGS

The 1999 unemployment rate of 4.2 percent was the lowest recorded in 30 years. The rates for Blacks and Hispanics remained higher, but each fell to its lowest point since these data first became available in the mid-1970s.

1999 saw 64.3 percent of the civilian noninstitutional population holding jobs, an all-time record. The labor force participation rate (i.e., labor force as a percent of population) of 67.1 percent was also a record, unchanged from that of 1997 and 1998.

Nonfarm payroll employment grew by 2.9 million to 128.8 million in 1999. Of the 2.9 million net new jobs created, 2.85 million were in the service-producing industries. The industry group with the most rapid job growth was Business Services, which includes both computer and temporary job (i.e., "help supply") services.

Adjusted for inflation using the CPI-W, average hourly earnings of production or nonsupervisory workers declined during and after the 1990–1991 recession. Beginning in 1996, however, hourly wages started an upward trend that continued through 1999. From 1995 to 1999, real wages increased an average of 1.6 percent per year. This increase, however, lagged behind the 2.5 percent nonfarm productivity growth over the same period.

CHAPTER 9: ENERGY

The decline in energy consumption per dollar of GDP slowed during the late 1980s and early 1990s, but accelerated again in 1998 and 1999.

Industrial energy use has shown the greatest decline relative to GDP. In absolute amount (measured in Btu's), industrial energy use in 1999 was about equal to 1979, even though industrial production rose 67 percent over this period.

While the ratio of petroleum and natural gas to GDP declined rapidly in the late 1980s, the ratio of other energy use to GDP was little changed. In contrast, these two ratios fell at similar rates from 1996 to 1999.

CHAPTER 10: MONEY AND FINANCIAL MARKETS

Short- and long-term interest rates roughly tracked the rate of price inflation from 1970 to 1980, though they did not match the inflationary spike of 1974–1975. During the 1980s, short-term rates fell faster than long-term, and inflation fell faster than either. As a result, rates of return were positive after adjustment for inflation; these positive real rates have continued into the 1990s.

Currency was 22.7 percent of M1 in 1970; by 1999, it had risen to 45.9 percent. Demand deposits were 76.8 percent of M1 in 1970, but by 1999 had fallen to 31.6 percent. Other checkable deposits, which include credit union share draft balances and demand deposits at thrift institutions, grew rapidly, from less than a tenth of one percent in 1970 to 21.7 percent of M1 by 1999.

Credit market debt outstanding grew over 15 times from 1970 to 1999. The fastest growth took place in the domestic financial sectors, increasing by a factor of 60. In this category, the federal government related debt (credit agencies such as FNMA and mortgage pools) was 89 times higher than it had been in 1970, while private debt was 44 times higher.

Credit market debt owed by the domestic private nonfinancial sectors, which accounts for two-thirds of total debt outstanding, was about 12 times higher in 1999 than in 1970. Household debt increased the most in this category, growing 14.5 times.

CHAPTER 11: U.S. FOREIGN TRADE AND FINANCE

U.S. imports of goods and services exceeded exports by a record $264 billion in 1999.

The current-account deficit, which also includes net income payments or receipts and unilateral transfers and which must be financed by equal financial inflows from abroad, expanded to $331 billion, also a record.

In 1999, the trade surplus in services rose slightly. In 1998 it had declined for the first time since 1985, due to slower growth in exports of services and an increase in imports. In 1999, at $80.6 billion, the services surplus offset 23 percent of the deficit on trade in goods compared to a 32 percent offset in 1998.

Total goods exports increased 2.1 percent in 1999, while imports increased 12.3 percent. Exports of goods to major Asian trading partners rebounded from declines in 1998 while exports to Europe and the Americas continued to grow.

As a percentage of GDP, exports of goods and services have nearly doubled from 1970 to 1999, from 5.4 percent to 10.3 percent. Over this same period, imports have gained even more, from 5.2 percent to 13.1 percent.

CHAPTER 12: INTERNATIONAL COMPARISONS

Consumer prices were remarkably stable in all the major industrial countries in 1999, varying from a 0.3 percent decline in Japan to a 2.2 percent rise in the U.S.

Unemployment rates in six of the seven countries declined in 1999. The exception was Japan, which had an increase from 4.1 percent in 1998 to 4.7 percent in 1999.

CHAPTER 13: MINING, OIL, AND GAS

The mining industries boomed in the late 1970s and peaked in 1981, stimulated by rising prices and shortages of petroleum and other natural resources. Subsequently, production subsided to near its 1970 level. Employment fell to the lowest level in the 30 years shown.

In oil and gas extraction, the largest of the mining industries, production in 1999 was below 1970, despite an employment increase of 19 percent, illustrating the increasing difficulty of finding and extracting crude oil within the U.S.

The trends in coal mining have been just the opposite. The fastest-growing of the mining industries from 1970 to 1999, coal production rose 74 percent. Increasing mechanization made this increase possible, with a 41 percent decline in employment.

A similar rate of productivity growth occurred in metal mining, with output up 26 percent while employment declined 52 percent.

Nonmetallic minerals except fuels (stone and earth minerals) had an output increase of 39 percent from 1970 to 1999, while employment fell 3 percent.

CHAPTER 14: CONSTRUCTION AND HOUSING

The construction industry serves several different markets, with different reactions to the general business cycle. In 1999, private residential and public (i.e., government) construction spending rose, while spending for the nonresidential and utilities sectors fell. A fall in industrial construction was responsible for the weakness in the nonresidential construction spending.

Residential spending has been the most volatile sector, falling steeply just before and during recessions but responding swiftly to interest-rate reductions.

Construction workers were relatively well-paid, averaging $17.18 per hour in 1999. Hourly pay was up 3.4 percent in 1999, exceeding the rate of consumer price increase.

Other indicators confirmed the strength of the residential housing market in 1999. With the exception of mobile home shipments, in 1999, housing starts, building permits, mobile home shipments, sales of new and existing homes, and median sales prices all increased.

CHAPTER 15: MANUFACTURING

U.S. manufacturers received $659 billion worth of new orders for nondefense capital goods (roughly equivalent to business equipment) in 1999, up 6.3 percent from 1998 and continuing the steep upward trend that began in 1994. Orders for defense capital goods increased in 1998 and 1999 after declining from 1986 through 1997. Defense accounted for 23 percent of U.S. capital goods orders in 1970 but only 10.5 percent of orders in 1999.

Production at primary processing industries (such as primary metals) rose 83 percent from 1970 to 1999, and capacity utilization rose from 79.9 percent to 83 percent—still well below earlier highs. Production at advanced processing industries (such as machinery) rose 210 percent, but capacity rose so rapidly that utilization, at 78.8 percent, was a little higher than in the recession year 1970.

While total manufacturing production was up 160 percent from 1970 to 1999, payroll employment was lower in 1999 than in 1970. The average factory workweek, however, was 41.7 hours in 1999 compared with 39.8 hours in 1970.

CHAPTER 16: DURABLE GOODS MANUFACTURING (NINE TWO-DIGIT INDUSTRIES)

Over the past 29 years, by far the greatest growth in production has been in industries directly affected by the "high-tech" revolution—electronic and electric machinery and equipment, industrial machinery (which includes computers), and instruments. Production of electronic equipment was up nearly 1,400 percent; industrial machinery 460 percent; and instruments over 200 percent.

No durable goods industry has shown much growth in employment, and some have shown declines. Within the industrial machinery industry group, employment in computer and office equipment grew 32 percent from 1970 to 1999, accounting for much of this industry's total employment gain. The largest decline was in primary metals, with a 44 percent drop in employment.

Measured from the 1989 business cycle peak, the employment picture has been mixed for durable goods. Lumber and wood products; furniture and fixtures; fabricated metals; and industrial machinery all have seen growth in employment. Stone, clay, and glass products; primary metals; electronic equipment; transportation equipment; and instruments have seen declines.

CHAPTER 17: NONDURABLE GOODS MANUFACTURING (TEN TWO-DIGIT INDUSTRIES)

Among the nondurable goods industries, rubber and plastics products had the most rapid increase in production, rising fourfold from 1970 to 1999. Chemicals was second, growing 140.7 percent. Paper and paper products and printing and publishing followed, both doubling their respective production rates.

Leather and leather products was the only nondurable goods industry to show a drop in production (70 percent) from 1970 to 1999.

Employment increased in rubber and plastics (63.1 percent) and in printing and publishing (40.7 percent) from 1970 to 1999, but fell in every other nondurable goods industry. Leather goods had the largest drop of all industries in nondurables (75.6 percent), followed by tobacco (54.2 percent).

Food and food products remained the largest industry in nondurables measured by employment, with 1,677,000 workers in 1999. Printing and publishing, with 1,553,000 workers, was the second-largest industry.

CHAPTER 18: TRANSPORTATION, COMMUNICATIONS, AND UTILITIES

From 1989 to 1999, employment in air transportation and in trucking and warehousing grew 37 and 31 percent, respectively, with both well above the average for all private nonfarm employment.

Employment rose at a fairly steady rate from 1970 to 1999 in the communications and transportation industries. In electric, gas, and sanitary services, however, employment increased from 1970 to 1991, but (with the exception of 1999) has fallen thereafter.

Electricity generation more than doubled between 1970 and 1999, with even greater growth in nuclear and hydro production.

Output of gas utilities, on the other hand, has declined 20 percent since 1970.

CHAPTER 19: RETAIL AND WHOLESALE TRADE

The 1970 to 1999 time period saw employment in retail trade more than double and employment in wholesale grow by 73 percent. In 1999 employment in retail trade increased by 2.2 percent to 22.8 million. Employment in wholesale trade grew by 1.8 percent to 6.9 million. Fully a third of the increase in retail in 1999 came from eating and drinking establishments, reflecting a long-standing trend of much more rapid growth in this sector.

Average weekly earnings of nonsupervisory workers in retail trade averaged $263.32 in 1999, up 3.9 percent from 1998, reflecting a 3.6 percent increase in hourly wages. Low weekly earnings in this industry reflect both low hourly wages and a short average workweek.

Average weekly earnings of nonsupervisory workers in wholesale trade grew to $558.41, reflecting a 3.6 percent increase in average hourly earnings.

The value of retail sales increased by 9.1 percent in 1999. Durable goods sales increased by more than 10 percent, with particularly strong growth for automotive dealers. Sales of nondurable goods increased by 8.1 percent.

Though most nondurable goods stores recorded larger increases, food stores, with over 25 percent of the nondurable total, only grew by 5.3 percent in 1999. This was the smallest increase in retail sales registered by a category of nondurable goods store. Drug and proprietary stores registered the largest increase with retail sales of 13 percent.

Beginning in 1999, total retail sales as reported by the Census Bureau included e-commerce sales of goods but not services. Although such sales are a small segment of total retail sales, they have increased over the past year with e-commerce accounting for 0.78 percent of total retail sales in the third quarter of 2000, compared with 0.63 percent in the fourth quarter of 1999.

CHAPTER 20: FINANCE, INSURANCE, REAL ESTATE, AND PRIVATE SERVICES

Finance, insurance, real estate, business services, health services, and other private services all grew strongly from 1970 to 1999. The strongest employment growth was in business services, a large and heterogeneous category that ranges from janitors and temporary help ("help supply") to computer and data processing services.

Since the last business cycle employment peak in 1989, total finance, insurance, and real estate payroll employment rose, but employment in the subindustry of depository institutions fell by 9.3 percent.

From 1989 to 1999 the fastest-growing service industry continued to be business services. In total, employment in the industry grew 87.6 percent in the period, buoyed by growth in help supply of 165 percent and computer and data processing services of 149 percent.

Hourly earnings for those employed in help supply averaged $10.56 per hour in 1999, 20 percent below the average for all private nonfarm industries. Hourly earnings for nonsupervisory workers in computer services, on the other hand, averaged $22.38 in 1999.

CHAPTER 21: GOVERNMENT

Federal government employment declined slightly in 1999 and was lower than it had been in 1970. Job growth continued at the state and local levels. Local governments added 5.6 million jobs over the 1970–1999 period, 58 percent of which were accounted for by education. State governments added over 2 million jobs from 1970 to 1999, 42 percent of which were due to education.

In 1999, for the second consecutive year and the second time since 1969, the federal government achieved a budget surplus. The surplus of $124.4 billion for FY 1999 exceeded the surplus of $69.2 billion in 1998. The surplus was used mainly to repay debt held by the public (also the second time since 1969) and the ratio of debt to GDP dropped to 39.9 percent. Even excluding the "off-budget" (Social Security) surplus, the budget still registered a small surplus in FY 1999. On the national income and product accounts (NIPA) basis, the federal government displayed a similar swing to surplus in calendar year 1999.

State and local governments have had substantial and growing surpluses of receipts over current expenditures for almost the entire 1970–1999 period. Their investment spending, which is outside their NIPA current budget, also has grown; it greatly exceeds their current surplus and is substantially greater than federal investment.

PART I

THE U.S. ECONOMY

CHAPTER 1: NATIONAL INCOME AND PRODUCT AND CYCLICAL INDICATORS

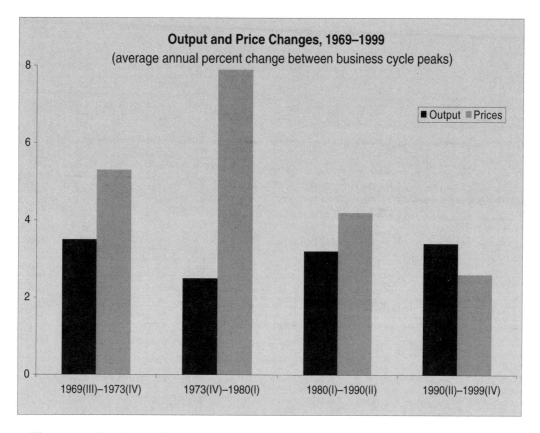

Output and Price Changes, 1969–1999
(average annual percent change between business cycle peaks)

- The comprehensive revision of the National Income and Product Accounts has revealed faster economic growth in recent periods. Growth from the last business cycle peak in 1990 to the end of 1999 was 3.2 percent per year, faster than in the 1980s and 1970s, though still below the 3.6 growth rate registered in the shorter business cycle from 1969 to 1973.

- Inflation, however, decelerated over the same period, from 7.8 percent in the 1970s to 2.1 percent in the period from 1990 to 1999.

- In 1999, imports of goods and services (in constant 1996 dollars) exceeded exports by $322 billion, compared with $221 billion in 1998. This was largely a result of a sharp 10.7 percent increase in the real volume of imports. The cost of imports, however, measured in the current dollars of each year, rose by 11.34 percent, suggesting an increase in the price of imports during 1999.

- Real government consumption expenditures increased by $50 billion in 1999 (in constant 1996 dollars) to $1,536 billion from $1,486 billion. Federal government consumption expenditures increased by $13 billion, reflecting increases in both defense and nondefense spending, while state and local government consumption expenditures increased by $36 billion to $995.6 billion.

Table 1-1. Gross Domestic Product

(Billions of dollars, quarterly data are at seasonally adjusted annual rates.)

Year and quarter	Gross domestic product	Personal consumption expenditures	Gross private domestic investment						Exports and imports of goods and services			Government consumption expenditures and gross investment		
			Total	Fixed investment		Change in private inventories			Net exports	Exports	Imports	Total	Federal	State and local
				Nonresidential	Residential	Nonfarm	Farm							
1970	1 039.7	648.9	152.4	109.0	41.4	2.8	-0.8	1.2	57.0	55.8	237.1	116.4	120.7
1971	1 128.6	702.4	178.2	114.1	55.8	6.6	1.7	-3.0	59.3	62.3	251.0	117.6	133.5
1972	1 240.4	770.7	207.6	128.8	69.7	8.8	0.3	-8.0	66.2	74.2	270.1	125.6	144.4
1973	1 385.5	852.5	244.5	153.3	75.3	14.4	1.5	0.6	91.8	91.2	287.9	127.8	160.1
1974	1 501.0	932.4	249.4	169.5	66.0	16.8	-2.8	-3.1	124.3	127.5	322.4	138.2	184.2
1975	1 635.2	1 030.3	230.2	173.7	62.7	-9.6	3.4	13.6	136.3	122.7	361.1	152.1	209.0
1976	1 823.9	1 149.8	292.0	192.4	82.5	18.0	-0.8	-2.3	148.9	151.1	384.5	160.6	223.9
1977	2 031.4	1 278.4	361.3	228.7	110.3	17.8	4.5	-23.7	158.8	182.4	415.3	176.0	239.3
1978	2 295.9	1 430.4	436.0	278.6	131.6	24.4	1.4	-26.1	186.1	212.3	455.6	191.9	263.8
1979	2 566.4	1 596.3	490.6	331.6	141.0	14.4	3.6	-24.0	228.7	252.7	503.5	211.6	291.8
1980	2 795.6	1 762.9	477.9	360.9	123.2	-0.2	-6.1	-14.9	278.9	293.8	569.7	245.3	324.4
1981	3 131.3	1 944.2	570.8	418.4	122.6	21.0	8.8	-15.0	302.8	317.8	631.4	281.8	349.6
1982	3 259.2	2 079.3	516.1	425.3	105.7	-20.7	5.8	-20.5	282.6	303.2	684.4	312.8	371.6
1983	3 534.9	2 286.4	564.2	417.4	152.5	9.6	-15.4	-51.7	277.0	328.6	735.9	344.4	391.5
1984	3 932.7	2 498.4	735.5	490.3	179.8	59.7	5.7	-102.0	303.1	405.1	800.8	376.4	424.4
1985	4 213.0	2 712.6	736.3	527.6	186.9	16.1	5.8	-114.2	303.0	417.2	878.3	413.4	464.9
1986	4 452.9	2 895.2	747.2	522.5	218.1	8.0	-1.5	-131.9	320.3	452.2	942.3	438.7	503.6
1987	4 742.5	3 105.3	781.5	526.7	227.6	33.6	-6.4	-142.3	365.6	507.9	997.9	460.4	537.5
1988	5 108.3	3 356.6	821.1	568.4	234.2	30.4	-11.9	-106.3	446.9	553.2	1 036.9	462.6	574.3
1989	5 489.1	3 596.7	872.9	613.4	231.8	27.7	0.0	-80.7	509.0	589.7	1 100.2	482.6	617.7
1990	5 803.2	3 831.5	861.7	630.3	216.8	12.2	2.4	-71.4	557.2	628.6	1 181.4	508.4	673.0
1991	5 986.2	3 971.2	800.2	608.9	191.5	0.9	-1.1	-20.7	601.6	622.3	1 235.5	527.4	708.1
1992	6 318.9	4 209.7	866.6	626.1	225.5	10.1	5.0	-27.9	636.8	664.6	1 270.5	534.5	736.0
1993	6 642.3	4 454.7	955.1	682.2	251.8	27.0	-5.9	-60.5	658.0	718.5	1 293.0	527.3	765.7
1994	7 054.3	4 716.4	1 097.1	748.6	286.0	51.8	10.8	-87.1	725.1	812.1	1 327.9	521.1	806.8
1995	7 400.5	4 969.0	1 143.8	825.1	285.6	42.2	-9.2	-84.3	818.6	902.8	1 372.0	521.5	850.5
1996	7 813.2	5 237.5	1 242.7	899.4	313.3	22.1	7.9	-89.0	874.2	963.1	1 421.9	531.6	890.4
1997	8 318.4	5 529.3	1 390.5	999.4	328.2	59.9	2.9	-89.3	966.4	1 055.8	1 487.9	538.2	949.7
1998	8 790.2	5 850.9	1 549.9	1 107.5	365.4	76.4	0.6	-151.5	966.0	1 117.5	1 540.9	540.6	1 000.3
1999	9 299.2	6 268.7	1 650.1	1 203.1	403.8	43.5	-0.2	-254.0	990.2	1 244.2	1 634.4	568.6	1 065.8
1991													
1st quarter	5 886.3	3 904.6	786.5	616.8	185.0	-15.6	0.3	-33.4	577.1	610.5	1 228.6	530.3	698.3
2nd quarter	5 962.0	3 958.6	780.5	611.7	186.6	-17.3	-0.4	-12.6	602.5	615.1	1 235.5	532.2	703.3
3rd quarter	6 015.9	3 998.2	801.5	605.9	194.5	11.7	-10.7	-22.3	602.3	624.5	1 238.4	526.9	711.5
4th quarter	6 080.7	4 023.6	832.1	601.1	200.0	24.7	6.3	-14.5	624.5	639.0	1 239.5	520.1	719.4
1992													
1st quarter	6 183.6	4 123.1	810.9	600.1	211.8	-7.8	6.8	-7.7	629.5	637.3	1 257.3	527.1	730.2
2nd quarter	6 276.6	4 171.5	867.2	621.5	223.9	13.8	8.0	-27.1	633.4	660.5	1 265.1	530.5	734.5
3rd quarter	6 345.8	4 225.7	878.7	633.0	226.6	15.4	3.7	-36.4	637.2	673.6	1 277.8	540.6	737.2
4th quarter	6 469.8	4 318.3	909.8	649.9	239.7	18.9	1.3	-40.1	647.0	687.1	1 281.8	539.9	741.9
1993													
1st quarter	6 521.6	4 350.6	938.0	659.3	242.7	41.6	-5.5	-46.5	646.4	692.9	1 279.5	528.9	750.5
2nd quarter	6 596.7	4 421.3	943.6	675.2	244.1	29.0	-4.6	-57.3	660.6	717.9	1 289.1	525.3	763.9
3rd quarter	6 655.5	4 488.2	943.0	683.2	252.9	19.1	-12.2	-72.0	646.4	718.3	1 296.2	526.9	769.3
4th quarter	6 795.5	4 558.7	995.8	711.4	267.3	18.3	-1.3	-66.2	678.8	744.9	1 307.1	528.0	779.1
1994													
1st quarter	6 887.8	4 613.8	1 042.0	721.7	276.4	28.8	15.0	-71.3	683.8	755.1	1 303.3	515.8	787.5
2nd quarter	7 015.7	4 677.5	1 106.4	738.2	288.4	64.3	15.5	-84.2	714.5	798.7	1 316.1	515.9	800.2
3rd quarter	7 096.0	4 753.0	1 094.0	752.7	289.3	42.5	9.6	-99.1	736.1	835.2	1 348.1	532.5	815.6
4th quarter	7 217.7	4 821.3	1 146.1	781.8	289.8	71.5	3.1	-93.8	765.8	859.6	1 344.0	520.0	824.0
1995													
1st quarter	7 297.5	4 868.6	1 162.8	812.5	287.6	67.0	-4.3	-94.5	787.7	882.2	1 360.6	523.4	837.1
2nd quarter	7 342.6	4 943.7	1 133.1	820.3	276.9	47.4	-11.5	-109.0	802.5	911.5	1 374.9	525.5	849.4
3rd quarter	7 432.8	5 005.2	1 123.5	825.2	284.9	31.7	-18.2	-74.2	834.1	908.3	1 378.3	525.0	853.3
4th quarter	7 529.3	5 058.4	1 155.6	842.3	293.1	22.8	-2.7	-59.3	850.0	909.3	1 374.5	512.3	862.2
1996													
1st quarter	7 629.6	5 130.5	1 172.4	865.1	300.5	5.8	1.0	-75.8	853.3	929.1	1 402.6	530.6	872.0
2nd quarter	7 782.7	5 218.0	1 231.5	885.4	316.3	18.6	11.1	-89.8	864.7	954.5	1 423.0	537.2	885.7
3rd quarter	7 859.0	5 263.7	1 282.6	913.6	319.0	34.0	16.0	-110.6	865.6	976.1	1 423.4	529.1	894.3
4th quarter	7 981.4	5 337.9	1 284.3	933.7	317.2	30.2	3.3	-79.7	913.1	992.8	1 438.9	529.4	909.4
1997													
1st quarter	8 124.2	5 429.9	1 324.2	955.5	320.0	50.1	-1.3	-89.2	927.8	1 017.1	1 459.2	529.2	930.0
2nd quarter	8 279.8	5 470.8	1 397.7	984.3	325.7	87.4	0.2	-75.0	966.8	1 041.7	1 486.3	543.4	942.9
3rd quarter	8 390.9	5 575.9	1 405.7	1 026.0	329.8	41.8	8.1	-88.6	988.7	1 077.3	1 498.0	541.3	956.6
4th quarter	8 478.6	5 640.6	1 434.5	1 031.8	337.5	60.5	4.6	-104.6	982.4	1 087.0	1 508.2	538.9	969.3
1998													
1st quarter	8 634.7	5 712.6	1 532.1	1 073.0	346.7	106.9	5.4	-117.5	975.0	1 092.6	1 507.6	528.0	979.6
2nd quarter	8 722.0	5 811.4	1 523.9	1 105.8	359.6	60.8	-2.3	-151.8	962.8	1 114.7	1 538.6	544.9	993.7
3rd quarter	8 829.1	5 893.4	1 553.0	1 110.5	371.9	76.5	-5.9	-167.6	947.8	1 115.4	1 550.3	541.4	1 008.9
4th quarter	8 974.9	5 986.0	1 590.8	1 140.7	383.4	61.3	5.3	-169.0	978.3	1 147.3	1 567.2	548.0	1 019.2
1999													
1st quarter	9 104.5	6 095.3	1 609.8	1 165.3	395.3	47.0	2.2	-196.1	957.3	1 153.4	1 595.5	554.1	1 041.4
2nd quarter	9 191.5	6 213.2	1 607.9	1 188.0	405.4	13.4	1.2	-240.4	973.0	1 213.4	1 610.9	558.3	1 052.6
3rd quarter	9 340.9	6 319.9	1 659.1	1 216.8	405.6	42.0	-5.3	-280.5	999.5	1 280.0	1 642.4	570.4	1 072.1
4th quarter	9 559.7	6 446.2	1 723.7	1 242.2	408.8	71.8	0.9	-299.1	1 031.0	1 330.1	1 688.8	591.6	1 097.3

Table 1-2. Real Gross Domestic Product

(Billions of chained [1996] dollars, quarterly data are at seasonally adjusted annual rates.)

Year and quarter	Gross domestic product	Personal consumption expenditures	Gross private domestic investment						Exports and imports of goods and services			Government consumption expenditures and gross investment		
			Total	Fixed investment		Change in private inventories			Net exports	Exports	Imports	Total	Federal	State and local
				Nonresidential	Residential	Nonfarm	Farm							
1970	3 578.0	2 317.5	436.2	...	...	8.3	-3.0	...	159.3	223.1	931.1	...	...
1971	3 697.7	2 405.2	485.8	...	...	19.1	4.3	...	160.4	235.0	913.8	...	...
1972	3 898.4	2 550.5	543.0	...	...	24.7	0.2	...	173.5	261.3	914.9	...	...
1973	4 123.4	2 675.9	606.5	...	...	37.3	0.9	...	211.4	273.4	908.3	...	...
1974	4 099.0	2 653.7	561.7	...	...	35.4	-5.3	...	231.6	267.2	924.8	...	...
1975	4 084.4	2 710.9	462.2	...	...	-19.4	6.8	...	230.0	237.5	942.5	...	...
1976	4 311.7	2 868.9	555.5	...	...	34.6	-0.8	...	243.6	284.0	943.3	...	...
1977	4 511.8	2 992.1	639.4	...	...	32.5	7.6	...	249.7	315.0	952.7	...	...
1978	4 760.6	3 124.7	713.0	...	...	41.7	3.1	...	275.9	342.3	982.2	...	...
1979	4 912.1	3 203.2	735.4	...	...	21.7	4.0	...	302.4	347.9	1 001.1	...	...
1980	4 900.9	3 193.0	655.3	...	...	0.3	-8.2	...	334.8	324.8	1 020.9	...	...
1981	5 021.0	3 236.0	715.6	...	...	25.9	10.6	...	338.6	333.4	1 030.0	...	...
1982	4 919.3	3 275.5	615.2	...	...	-24.6	8.4	...	314.6	329.2	1 046.0	...	...
1983	5 132.3	3 454.3	673.7	...	...	11.1	-18.9	...	306.9	370.7	1 081.0	...	...
1984	5 505.2	3 640.6	871.5	...	...	68.7	7.5	...	332.6	461.0	1 118.4	...	...
1985	5 717.1	3 820.9	863.4	...	...	18.6	8.3	...	341.6	490.7	1 190.5	...	...
1986	5 912.4	3 981.2	857.7	...	...	10.8	-1.4	...	366.8	531.9	1 255.2	...	...
1987	6 113.3	4 113.4	879.3	572.5	290.7	38.7	-9.8	-156.2	408.0	564.2	1 292.5	597.8	695.6
1988	6 368.4	4 279.5	902.8	603.6	289.2	33.7	-14.2	-112.1	473.5	585.6	1 307.5	586.9	721.4
1989	6 591.8	4 393.7	936.5	637.0	277.3	29.9	0.1	-79.4	529.4	608.8	1 343.5	594.7	749.5
1990	6 707.9	4 474.5	907.3	641.7	253.5	13.8	2.6	-56.5	575.7	632.2	1 387.3	606.8	781.1
1991	6 676.4	4 466.6	829.5	610.1	221.1	1.4	-2.3	-15.8	613.2	629.0	1 403.4	604.9	798.9
1992	6 880.0	4 594.5	899.8	630.6	257.2	10.7	6.1	-19.8	651.0	670.8	1 410.0	595.1	815.3
1993	7 062.6	4 748.9	977.9	683.6	276.0	28.6	-7.9	-59.1	672.7	731.8	1 398.8	572.0	827.0
1994	7 347.7	4 928.1	1 107.0	744.6	302.7	53.6	13.0	-86.5	732.8	819.4	1 400.1	551.3	848.9
1995	7 543.8	5 075.6	1 140.6	817.5	291.7	42.6	-12.3	-78.4	808.2	886.6	1 406.4	536.5	869.9
1996	7 813.2	5 237.5	1 242.7	899.4	313.3	22.1	7.9	-89.0	874.2	963.1	1 421.9	531.6	890.4
1997	8 159.5	5 423.9	1 393.3	1 009.3	319.7	60.6	3.2	-113.3	981.5	1 094.8	1 455.4	529.6	925.8
1998	8 515.7	5 678.7	1 566.8	1 140.3	346.1	78.7	1.2	-221.0	1 003.6	1 224.6	1 486.4	526.9	959.2
1999	8 875.8	5 978.8	1 669.7	1 255.3	368.3	44.9	0.0	-322.4	1 033.0	1 355.3	1 536.1	540.1	995.6
1991													
1st quarter	6 631.4	4 437.5	815.1	616.2	214.7	-15.3	-0.4	-18.2	584.5	602.7	1 404.7	612.6	792.6
2nd quarter	6 668.5	4 469.9	808.8	611.9	215.6	-18.1	-1.6	-10.7	613.3	623.9	1 408.9	613.4	796.0
3rd quarter	6 684.9	4 484.3	829.8	607.7	223.4	12.7	-13.1	-23.9	616.9	640.8	1 403.0	602.7	800.6
4th quarter	6 720.9	4 474.8	864.2	604.6	230.6	26.5	5.7	-10.4	638.3	648.7	1 397.0	591.0	806.3
1992													
1st quarter	6 783.3	4 544.8	843.8	603.6	245.0	-8.2	7.8	-6.7	643.9	650.6	1 407.6	591.8	816.1
2nd quarter	6 846.8	4 566.7	901.8	626.1	256.6	14.6	9.8	-23.0	647.1	670.1	1 405.7	591.1	814.9
3rd quarter	6 899.7	4 600.5	912.1	637.6	257.9	16.4	5.0	-22.0	650.8	672.9	1 413.1	598.3	815.1
4th quarter	6 990.6	4 665.9	941.6	655.0	269.2	20.2	1.9	-27.3	662.2	689.5	1 413.7	599.1	814.9
1993													
1st quarter	6 988.7	4 674.9	964.8	661.7	269.5	44.0	-7.0	-44.4	661.4	705.8	1 396.4	579.6	817.1
2nd quarter	7 031.2	4 721.5	967.0	676.6	268.6	30.7	-6.6	-51.7	674.4	726.1	1 398.0	572.2	826.1
3rd quarter	7 062.0	4 776.9	964.1	684.2	275.7	20.6	-14.7	-72.3	660.8	733.1	1 398.4	568.9	829.7
4th quarter	7 168.7	4 822.3	1 015.6	711.8	290.1	19.2	-3.3	-67.9	694.3	762.2	1 402.2	567.3	835.1
1994													
1st quarter	7 229.4	4 866.6	1 057.3	720.0	296.5	30.2	16.5	-80.1	696.7	776.8	1 388.0	550.9	837.3
2nd quarter	7 330.2	4 907.9	1 118.5	734.1	307.5	66.8	18.6	-86.2	725.1	811.3	1 390.4	545.2	845.4
3rd quarter	7 370.2	4 944.5	1 101.8	747.2	305.2	44.0	12.7	-92.2	742.4	834.6	1 417.5	563.2	854.4
4th quarter	7 461.1	4 993.6	1 150.5	777.1	301.8	73.2	4.2	-87.7	767.1	854.8	1 404.5	546.1	858.5
1995													
1st quarter	7 488.7	5 011.6	1 162.4	806.4	295.8	67.9	-5.6	-92.5	780.6	873.1	1 407.3	544.1	863.3
2nd quarter	7 503.3	5 059.6	1 128.5	811.4	283.5	47.3	-14.9	-97.5	788.9	886.4	1 414.0	544.3	869.7
3rd quarter	7 561.4	5 099.2	1 119.1	816.7	290.4	31.9	-23.3	-67.3	821.9	889.1	1 410.8	540.4	870.4
4th quarter	7 621.9	5 132.1	1 152.4	835.5	297.3	23.4	-5.2	-56.4	841.4	897.8	1 393.5	517.1	876.4
1996													
1st quarter	7 676.4	5 174.3	1 172.3	861.6	303.6	6.1	-0.3	-75.0	846.1	921.1	1 404.8	529.1	875.7
2nd quarter	7 802.9	5 229.5	1 233.4	885.6	318.1	18.6	11.7	-90.4	860.1	950.4	1 430.4	540.2	890.2
3rd quarter	7 841.9	5 254.3	1 281.4	914.3	317.3	34.1	16.7	-115.9	867.0	982.9	1 422.0	529.5	892.5
4th quarter	7 931.3	5 291.9	1 283.7	936.2	314.0	29.8	3.3	-74.6	923.5	998.1	1 430.6	527.6	903.0
1997													
1st quarter	8 016.4	5 350.7	1 325.4	960.8	314.7	50.4	-1.1	-94.0	940.3	1 034.3	1 434.6	521.7	912.8
2nd quarter	8 131.9	5 375.7	1 400.6	992.7	318.7	88.3	0.3	-100.6	979.2	1 079.8	1 457.0	534.8	922.2
3rd quarter	8 216.6	5 462.1	1 408.6	1 037.0	320.3	42.4	8.7	-119.6	1 004.2	1 123.8	1 464.8	533.4	931.4
4th quarter	8 272.9	5 507.1	1 438.5	1 047.0	324.9	61.3	4.8	-139.2	1 002.1	1 141.2	1 465.3	528.4	936.8
1998													
1st quarter	8 404.9	5 572.4	1 545.1	1 096.0	332.4	109.7	7.6	-175.3	1 004.5	1 179.8	1 461.6	515.9	945.5
2nd quarter	8 465.6	5 651.6	1 540.8	1 136.4	342.4	62.5	-1.7	-219.8	996.8	1 216.6	1 487.6	531.8	955.7
3rd quarter	8 537.6	5 711.0	1 571.4	1 146.3	350.9	79.2	-6.9	-244.1	988.8	1 232.9	1 492.9	527.5	965.1
4th quarter	8 654.5	5 779.8	1 609.9	1 182.3	358.5	63.5	5.9	-244.9	1 024.1	1 269.0	1 503.3	532.4	970.7
1999													
1st quarter	8 730.0	5 860.2	1 623.2	1 209.4	365.7	49.2	-1.6	-279.8	1 003.3	1 283.1	1 517.1	529.5	987.2
2nd quarter	8 783.2	5 940.2	1 623.1	1 237.5	370.9	14.1	-1.1	-314.6	1 017.6	1 332.2	1 519.9	532.1	987.5
3rd quarter	8 905.8	6 013.8	1 680.8	1 272.5	368.0	43.5	-5.0	-342.6	1 042.6	1 385.2	1 537.8	541.0	996.4
4th quarter	9 084.1	6 101.0	1 751.6	1 301.8	368.5	73.0	7.9	-352.5	1 068.4	1 420.9	1 569.5	558.1	1 011.2

Table 1-3. Chain-type Price Indexes for Gross Domestic Product and Domestic Purchases

(Index numbers, 1996=100.)

Year and quarter	Gross domestic product											Gross domestic purchases
	Gross domestic product	Personal consumption expenditures		Private fixed investment			Exports and imports of goods and services		Government consumption expenditures and gross investment			
		Total	Excluding food and energy	Total	Nonresi-dential	Residen-tial	Exports	Imports	Total	Federal	State and local	
1970	29.1	28.0	28.6	34.0	38.8	24.6	35.8	25.0	25.4	26.0	25.0	28.4
1971	30.5	29.2	30.0	35.7	40.7	26.0	37.0	26.5	27.4	28.2	26.8	29.8
1972	31.8	30.2	30.9	37.2	42.1	27.6	38.2	28.4	29.5	30.8	28.4	31.2
1973	33.6	31.9	32.1	39.3	43.7	30.0	43.4	33.3	31.7	33.0	30.6	33.0
1974	36.6	35.1	34.4	43.2	48.0	33.1	53.7	47.7	34.8	35.8	33.9	36.4
1975	40.0	38.0	37.2	48.6	54.6	36.2	59.2	51.7	38.3	39.4	37.3	39.7
1976	42.3	40.1	39.4	51.4	57.6	38.5	61.1	53.2	40.7	42.1	39.5	41.9
1977	45.0	42.7	42.0	55.5	61.5	42.4	63.6	57.9	43.6	45.3	42.1	44.8
1978	48.2	45.8	44.8	60.2	65.7	47.6	67.5	62.0	46.4	48.2	44.8	48.0
1979	52.2	49.8	48.0	65.7	71.1	53.0	75.6	72.6	50.3	51.9	48.8	52.3
1980	57.1	55.2	52.4	71.8	77.4	58.7	83.3	90.5	55.8	57.5	54.3	57.8
1981	62.4	60.1	56.9	78.6	84.9	63.5	89.4	95.3	61.3	63.1	59.7	63.1
1982	66.3	63.5	60.8	82.9	89.7	66.9	89.8	92.1	65.4	67.5	63.6	66.7
1983	68.9	66.2	63.9	82.8	88.9	68.4	90.2	88.7	68.1	70.0	66.4	69.1
1984	71.4	68.6	66.5	83.4	88.8	70.4	91.1	87.9	71.6	74.1	69.4	71.5
1985	73.7	71.0	69.2	84.5	89.6	72.2	88.7	85.0	73.8	75.7	72.1	73.6
1986	75.3	72.7	71.8	86.5	91.2	75.2	87.3	85.0	75.1	76.1	74.1	75.2
1987	77.6	75.5	74.8	88.1	92.0	78.3	89.6	90.0	77.2	77.0	77.3	77.7
1988	80.2	78.4	77.9	90.5	94.2	81.0	94.4	94.5	79.3	78.8	79.6	80.4
1989	83.3	81.9	81.2	92.8	96.3	83.6	96.2	96.9	81.9	81.1	82.4	83.5
1990	86.5	85.6	84.7	94.7	98.2	85.5	96.8	99.4	85.2	83.8	86.2	86.9
1991	89.7	88.9	88.2	96.1	99.8	86.6	98.1	98.9	88.0	87.2	88.6	89.8
1992	91.9	91.6	91.4	96.1	99.3	87.7	97.8	99.1	90.1	89.8	90.3	92.0
1993	94.1	93.8	93.8	97.5	99.8	91.2	97.8	98.2	92.4	92.2	92.6	94.1
1994	96.0	95.7	95.9	98.9	100.5	94.5	98.9	99.1	94.8	94.5	95.0	96.1
1995	98.1	97.9	98.2	100.1	100.9	97.9	101.3	101.8	97.6	97.2	97.8	98.2
1996	100.0	100.0	100.0	100.0	100.0	100.0	100.0	100.0	100.0	100.0	100.0	100.0
1997	102.0	101.9	101.9	99.9	99.0	102.7	98.5	96.4	102.2	101.6	102.6	101.6
1998	103.2	103.0	103.5	99.2	97.1	105.6	96.3	91.3	103.7	102.6	104.3	102.5
1999	104.8	104.9	105.1	99.1	95.8	109.6	95.9	91.8	106.4	105.3	107.1	104.1
1991												
1st quarter	88.8	88.0	87.0	96.2	100.1	86.2	98.7	101.2	87.5	86.6	88.1	89.1
2nd quarter	89.4	88.6	87.8	96.2	100.0	86.5	98.2	98.6	87.7	86.8	88.4	89.5
3rd quarter	90.0	89.2	88.5	96.2	99.7	87.1	97.6	97.4	88.3	87.4	88.9	90.0
4th quarter	90.5	89.9	89.4	95.9	99.4	86.8	97.8	98.5	88.7	88.0	89.2	90.6
1992												
1st quarter	91.2	90.7	90.4	95.8	99.4	86.5	97.8	98.0	89.3	89.1	89.5	91.3
2nd quarter	91.7	91.4	91.1	95.9	99.3	87.3	97.9	98.6	90.0	89.8	90.1	91.8
3rd quarter	92.0	91.9	91.6	96.1	99.3	87.9	97.9	100.1	90.4	90.4	90.4	92.3
4th quarter	92.6	92.6	92.4	96.4	99.2	89.1	97.7	99.7	90.7	90.1	91.0	92.8
1993												
1st quarter	93.3	93.1	92.9	97.0	99.6	90.1	97.7	98.2	91.6	91.3	91.9	93.4
2nd quarter	93.8	93.7	93.6	97.4	99.8	90.9	98.0	98.9	92.2	91.8	92.5	94.0
3rd quarter	94.3	94.0	94.0	97.6	99.9	91.8	97.8	98.0	92.7	92.6	92.7	94.3
4th quarter	94.8	94.5	94.6	97.8	99.9	92.2	97.8	97.7	93.2	93.1	93.3	94.8
1994												
1st quarter	95.3	94.8	94.9	98.4	100.2	93.3	98.2	97.2	93.9	93.6	94.1	95.2
2nd quarter	95.7	95.3	95.5	98.7	100.6	93.8	98.6	98.5	94.7	94.6	94.7	95.7
3rd quarter	96.3	96.1	96.3	99.2	100.7	94.8	99.2	100.1	95.1	94.6	95.5	96.4
4th quarter	96.7	96.6	96.7	99.4	100.6	96.1	99.8	100.6	95.7	95.2	96.0	96.9
1995												
1st quarter	97.5	97.2	97.4	99.8	100.8	97.2	100.9	101.1	96.7	96.2	97.0	97.5
2nd quarter	97.9	97.7	97.9	100.2	101.1	97.7	101.7	102.8	97.2	96.5	97.7	98.0
3rd quarter	98.3	98.2	98.5	100.3	101.0	98.1	101.5	102.2	97.7	97.1	98.0	98.4
4th quarter	98.8	98.6	98.9	100.3	100.8	98.6	101.0	101.3	98.6	99.0	98.4	98.9
1996												
1st quarter	99.4	99.2	99.4	100.0	100.4	99.0	100.8	100.9	99.8	100.3	99.6	99.4
2nd quarter	99.7	99.8	99.8	99.8	100.0	99.4	100.5	100.4	99.5	99.5	99.5	99.7
3rd quarter	100.2	100.2	100.2	100.1	99.9	100.5	99.8	99.3	100.1	99.9	100.2	100.2
4th quarter	100.6	100.9	100.7	100.1	99.7	101.0	98.9	99.4	100.6	100.4	100.7	100.7
1997												
1st quarter	101.4	101.5	101.3	100.0	99.4	101.7	98.7	98.3	101.7	101.4	101.9	101.3
2nd quarter	101.8	101.8	101.9	99.9	99.1	102.2	98.7	96.4	102.0	101.6	102.3	101.5
3rd quarter	102.1	102.1	102.1	99.9	98.9	103.0	98.5	95.8	102.3	101.5	102.7	101.7
4th quarter	102.5	102.4	102.5	99.9	98.6	103.9	98.0	95.2	102.9	102.0	103.5	102.1
1998												
1st quarter	102.8	102.5	102.8	99.5	97.9	104.3	97.1	92.6	103.2	102.4	103.6	102.1
2nd quarter	103.0	102.8	103.2	99.2	97.3	105.1	96.6	91.6	103.4	102.5	104.0	102.3
3rd quarter	103.4	103.2	103.7	99.1	96.9	106.0	95.9	90.5	103.9	102.6	104.6	102.6
4th quarter	103.7	103.6	104.1	99.0	96.5	107.0	95.5	90.4	104.3	102.9	105.0	102.9
1999												
1st quarter	104.3	104.0	104.6	99.1	96.3	108.1	95.4	89.9	105.2	104.7	105.5	103.4
2nd quarter	104.6	104.6	104.9	99.1	96.0	109.3	95.6	91.1	106.0	105.0	106.6	103.9
3rd quarter	104.9	105.1	105.3	99.1	95.6	110.2	95.9	92.5	106.8	105.5	107.6	104.3
4th quarter	105.3	105.7	105.7	99.1	95.4	110.9	96.5	93.7	107.6	106.0	108.5	104.8

Table 1-4. Implicit Price Deflators for Gross Domestic Product

(Index numbers, 1996=100.)

Year and quarter	Gross domestic product	Personal consumption expenditures	Private fixed investment			Exports and imports of goods and services		Government consumption expenditures and gross investments		
			Total	Nonresi-dential	Residential	Export	Imports	Total	Federal	State and local
1970	29.1	28.0	34.0	38.8	24.6	35.8	25.0	25.5	26.0	25.0
1971	30.5	29.2	35.7	40.7	26.0	37.0	26.5	27.5	28.3	26.8
1972	31.8	30.2	37.2	42.1	27.6	38.2	28.4	29.5	30.9	28.4
1973	33.6	31.9	39.3	43.7	30.0	43.4	33.3	31.7	33.0	30.6
1974	36.6	35.1	43.2	47.9	33.1	53.7	47.7	34.9	35.9	33.9
1975	40.0	38.0	48.6	54.6	36.2	59.2	51.7	38.3	39.5	37.3
1976	42.3	40.1	51.4	57.6	38.5	61.1	53.2	40.8	42.2	39.5
1977	45.0	42.7	55.5	61.5	42.4	63.6	57.9	43.6	45.4	42.1
1978	48.2	45.8	60.2	65.7	47.6	67.5	62.0	46.4	48.2	44.8
1979	52.3	49.8	65.7	71.1	53.0	75.6	72.6	50.3	52.0	48.8
1980	57.0	55.2	71.8	77.4	58.7	83.3	90.5	55.8	57.5	54.3
1981	62.4	60.1	78.6	84.9	63.5	89.4	95.3	61.3	63.1	59.7
1982	66.3	63.5	82.9	89.7	66.9	89.8	92.1	65.4	67.5	63.6
1983	68.9	66.2	82.8	88.9	68.4	90.2	88.7	68.1	70.0	66.4
1984	71.4	68.6	83.4	88.8	70.4	91.1	87.9	71.6	74.1	69.4
1985	73.7	71.0	84.5	89.6	72.2	88.7	85.0	73.8	75.7	72.1
1986	75.3	72.7	86.5	91.2	75.2	87.3	85.0	75.1	76.1	74.1
1987	77.6	75.5	88.1	92.0	78.3	89.6	90.0	77.2	77.0	77.3
1988	80.2	78.4	90.5	94.2	81.0	94.4	94.5	79.3	78.8	79.6
1989	83.3	81.9	92.8	96.3	83.6	96.2	96.9	81.9	81.1	82.4
1990	86.5	85.6	94.7	98.2	85.5	96.8	99.4	85.2	83.8	86.2
1991	89.7	88.9	96.1	99.8	86.6	98.1	98.9	88.0	87.2	88.6
1992	91.8	91.6	96.1	99.3	87.7	97.8	99.1	90.1	89.8	90.3
1993	94.1	93.8	97.5	99.8	91.2	97.8	98.2	92.4	92.2	92.6
1994	96.0	95.7	98.9	100.5	94.5	98.9	99.1	94.8	94.5	95.0
1995	98.1	97.9	100.1	100.9	97.9	101.3	101.8	97.6	97.2	97.8
1996	100.0	100.0	100.0	100.0	100.0	100.0	100.0	100.0	100.0	100.0
1997	102.0	101.9	99.9	99.0	102.7	98.5	96.4	102.2	101.6	102.6
1998	103.2	103.0	99.2	97.1	105.6	96.3	91.3	103.7	102.6	104.3
1999	104.8	104.9	99.1	95.8	109.6	95.9	91.8	106.4	105.3	107.1
1991										
1st quarter	88.8	88.0	96.2	100.1	86.2	98.7	101.3	87.5	86.6	88.1
2nd quarter	89.4	88.6	96.2	100.0	86.5	98.3	98.6	87.7	86.8	88.4
3rd quarter	90.0	89.2	96.2	99.7	87.1	97.6	97.5	88.3	87.4	88.9
4th quarter	90.5	89.9	95.9	99.4	86.7	97.9	98.5	88.7	88.0	89.2
1992										
1st quarter	91.2	90.7	95.8	99.4	86.5	97.8	98.0	89.3	89.1	89.5
2nd quarter	91.7	91.4	95.9	99.3	87.3	97.9	98.6	90.0	89.8	90.1
3rd quarter	92.0	91.9	96.1	99.3	87.9	97.9	100.1	90.4	90.4	90.4
4th quarter	92.6	92.6	96.4	99.2	89.0	97.7	99.7	90.7	90.1	91.0
1993										
1st quarter	93.3	93.1	97.0	99.6	90.1	97.7	98.2	91.6	91.3	91.9
2nd quarter	93.8	93.6	97.4	99.8	90.9	98.0	98.9	92.2	91.8	92.5
3rd quarter	94.2	94.0	97.6	99.9	91.7	97.8	98.0	92.7	92.6	92.7
4th quarter	94.8	94.5	97.8	99.9	92.2	97.8	97.7	93.2	93.1	93.3
1994										
1st quarter	95.3	94.8	98.3	100.2	93.2	98.1	97.2	93.9	93.6	94.1
2nd quarter	95.7	95.3	98.7	100.6	93.8	98.6	98.5	94.7	94.6	94.7
3rd quarter	96.3	96.1	99.2	100.7	94.8	99.2	100.1	95.1	94.6	95.5
4th quarter	96.7	96.6	99.4	100.6	96.1	99.8	100.6	95.7	95.2	96.0
1995										
1st quarter	97.5	97.2	99.8	100.8	97.2	100.9	101.0	96.7	96.2	97.0
2nd quarter	97.9	97.7	100.2	101.1	97.7	101.7	102.8	97.2	96.5	97.7
3rd quarter	98.3	98.2	100.3	101.0	98.1	101.5	102.2	97.7	97.1	98.0
4th quarter	98.8	98.6	100.2	100.8	98.6	101.0	101.3	98.6	99.1	98.4
1996										
1st quarter	99.4	99.2	100.0	100.4	99.0	100.9	100.9	99.8	100.3	99.6
2nd quarter	99.7	99.8	99.8	100.0	99.4	100.5	100.4	99.5	99.5	99.5
3rd quarter	100.2	100.2	100.1	99.9	100.5	99.8	99.3	100.1	99.9	100.2
4th quarter	100.6	100.9	100.1	99.7	101.0	98.9	99.5	100.6	100.3	100.7
1997										
1st quarter	101.3	101.5	100.0	99.5	101.7	98.7	98.3	101.7	101.4	101.9
2nd quarter	101.8	101.8	99.9	99.2	102.2	98.7	96.5	102.0	101.6	102.3
3rd quarter	102.1	102.1	99.9	98.9	103.0	98.5	95.9	102.3	101.5	102.7
4th quarter	102.5	102.4	99.9	98.6	103.9	98.0	95.2	102.9	102.0	103.5
1998										
1st quarter	102.7	102.5	99.5	97.9	104.3	97.1	92.6	103.1	102.4	103.6
2nd quarter	103.0	102.8	99.2	97.3	105.0	96.6	91.6	103.4	102.5	104.0
3rd quarter	103.4	103.2	99.1	96.9	106.0	95.9	90.5	103.8	102.6	104.5
4th quarter	103.7	103.6	99.0	96.5	107.0	95.5	90.4	104.3	102.9	105.0
1999										
1st quarter	104.3	104.0	99.2	96.4	108.1	95.4	89.9	105.2	104.7	105.5
2nd quarter	104.7	104.6	99.1	96.0	109.3	95.6	91.1	106.0	104.9	106.6
3rd quarter	104.9	105.1	99.1	95.6	110.2	95.9	92.4	106.8	105.4	107.6
4th quarter	105.2	105.7	99.1	95.4	110.9	96.5	93.6	107.6	106.0	108.5

Table 1-5. Final Sales

(Billions of dollars, quarterly data are at seasonally adjusted annual rates.)

Year and quarter	Final sales of domestic product			Final sales to domestic purchasers		
	Billions of dollars	Billions of chained (1996) dollars	Chain-type price index, 1996=100	Billions of dollars	Billions of chained (1996) dollars	Chain-type price index, 1996=100
1970	1 037.7	3 588.6	28.9	1 036.5	3 671.1	28.2
1971	1 120.3	3 688.1	30.4	1 123.3	3 782.0	29.7
1972	1 231.3	3 887.7	31.7	1 239.3	3 993.5	31.0
1973	1 369.7	4 094.3	33.4	1 369.0	4 167.4	32.8
1974	1 487.0	4 080.7	36.4	1 490.2	4 118.2	36.2
1975	1 641.4	4 118.5	39.8	1 627.9	4 119.6	39.5
1976	1 806.8	4 288.8	42.1	1 809.1	4 331.1	41.8
1977	2 009.1	4 478.8	44.8	2 032.7	4 553.3	44.6
1978	2 270.1	4 722.9	48.1	2 296.2	4 797.0	47.9
1979	2 548.4	4 894.4	52.1	2 572.4	4 938.4	52.1
1980	2 801.9	4 928.1	56.9	2 816.8	4 890.3	57.6
1981	3 101.5	4 989.5	62.2	3 116.5	4 958.6	62.8
1982	3 274.1	4 954.9	66.1	3 294.7	4 951.7	66.5
1983	3 540.7	5 154.5	68.7	3 592.3	5 215.9	68.9
1984	3 867.3	5 427.9	71.2	3 969.3	5 569.5	71.3
1985	4 191.2	5 698.8	73.6	4 305.4	5 865.0	73.4
1986	4 446.3	5 912.6	75.2	4 578.2	6 096.6	75.1
1987	4 715.3	6 088.8	77.4	4 857.6	6 261.9	77.6
1988	5 089.8	6 352.6	80.1	5 196.1	6 474.0	80.3
1989	5 461.4	6 565.4	83.2	5 542.1	6 648.3	83.4
1990	5 788.7	6 695.6	86.5	5 860.1	6 752.6	86.8
1991	5 986.4	6 681.5	89.6	6 007.1	6 693.5	89.8
1992	6 303.9	6 867.7	91.8	6 331.7	6 884.1	92.0
1993	6 621.2	7 043.8	94.0	6 681.7	7 101.8	94.1
1994	6 991.8	7 285.8	96.0	7 078.9	7 372.2	96.0
1995	7 367.5	7 512.2	98.1	7 451.7	7 590.3	98.2
1996	7 783.2	7 783.2	100.0	7 872.1	7 872.1	100.0
1997	8 255.5	8 095.2	102.0	8 344.8	8 207.3	101.7
1998	8 713.2	8 435.2	103.3	8 864.7	8 647.2	102.5
1999	9 255.9	8 826.9	104.9	9 509.9	9 130.3	104.2
1991						
1st quarter	5 901.6	6 652.5	88.7	5 935.0	6 666.4	89.0
2nd quarter	5 979.7	6 692.5	89.4	5 992.4	6 698.8	89.4
3rd quarter	6 014.8	6 689.2	89.9	6 037.1	6 710.1	90.0
4th quarter	6 049.6	6 692.0	90.4	6 064.1	6 698.5	90.5
1992						
1st quarter	6 184.5	6 788.9	91.1	6 192.3	6 791.3	91.2
2nd quarter	6 254.8	6 827.1	91.6	6 281.9	6 847.0	91.8
3rd quarter	6 326.7	6 882.7	91.9	6 363.1	6 901.4	92.2
4th quarter	6 449.6	6 972.4	92.5	6 489.7	6 996.8	92.8
1993						
1st quarter	6 485.5	6 953.6	93.3	6 532.0	6 996.2	93.4
2nd quarter	6 572.4	7 008.8	93.8	6 629.7	7 059.1	93.9
3rd quarter	6 648.5	7 057.9	94.2	6 720.5	7 129.6	94.3
4th quarter	6 778.5	7 154.8	94.8	6 844.6	7 222.0	94.8
1994						
1st quarter	6 844.0	7 187.1	95.2	6 915.2	7 266.9	95.2
2nd quarter	6 936.0	7 250.2	95.7	7 020.2	7 336.2	95.7
3rd quarter	7 044.0	7 318.5	96.2	7 143.1	7 410.8	96.4
4th quarter	7 143.1	7 387.2	96.7	7 236.9	7 474.8	96.8
1995						
1st quarter	7 234.8	7 427.3	97.4	7 329.3	7 520.0	97.5
2nd quarter	7 306.8	7 469.6	97.8	7 415.8	7 567.4	98.0
3rd quarter	7 419.4	7 549.7	98.3	7 493.6	7 616.2	98.4
4th quarter	7 509.1	7 602.5	98.8	7 568.3	7 657.8	98.8
1996						
1st quarter	7 622.8	7 669.6	99.4	7 698.6	7 744.1	99.4
2nd quarter	7 752.9	7 773.4	99.7	7 842.7	7 863.6	99.7
3rd quarter	7 809.0	7 792.1	100.2	7 919.6	7 908.0	100.2
4th quarter	7 947.9	7 897.6	100.6	8 027.6	7 972.7	100.7
1997						
1st quarter	8 075.4	7 966.4	101.4	8 164.6	8 060.6	101.3
2nd quarter	8 192.1	8 043.2	101.9	8 267.1	8 143.4	101.5
3rd quarter	8 341.1	8 164.9	102.2	8 429.6	8 282.8	101.8
4th quarter	8 413.5	8 206.3	102.5	8 518.0	8 342.7	102.1
1998						
1st quarter	8 522.4	8 289.4	102.8	8 639.9	8 459.3	102.1
2nd quarter	8 663.5	8 402.7	103.1	8 815.3	8 613.9	102.3
3rd quarter	8 758.5	8 463.4	103.5	8 926.1	8 697.1	102.6
4th quarter	8 908.3	8 585.0	103.8	9 077.3	8 818.6	102.9
1999						
1st quarter	9 055.3	8 680.3	104.3	9 251.4	8 946.5	103.4
2nd quarter	9 177.0	8 764.9	104.7	9 417.4	9 061.5	103.9
3rd quarter	9 304.2	8 861.8	105.0	9 584.7	9 182.8	104.4
4th quarter	9 486.9	9 000.5	105.4	9 786.1	9 330.4	104.9

Table 1-6. Gross Domestic Product, Gross and Net National Product, and National Income

(Billions of dollars, quarterly data are at seasonally adjusted annual rates.)

Year and quarter	Gross domestic product	Plus: Income receipts from rest of world	Less: Income payments to rest of world	Equals: Gross national product	Less: Consumption of fixed capital	Equals: Net national product	Less			Plus: Subsidies less current surplus of government enterprises	Equals: National income
							Indirect business taxes and nontaxes	Business transfer payments	Statistical discrepancy		
1970	1 039.7	13.0	6.6	1 046.1	109.1	937.0	94.3	3.2	6.9	4.8	837.5
1971	1 128.6	14.1	6.4	1 136.2	118.9	1 017.3	103.6	3.4	11.3	4.9	903.9
1972	1 240.4	16.4	7.7	1 249.1	130.9	1 118.2	111.4	3.9	8.7	6.1	1 000.4
1973	1 385.5	23.8	11.1	1 398.2	142.9	1 255.3	121.0	4.5	8.0	5.6	1 127.4
1974	1 501.0	30.3	14.6	1 516.7	164.8	1 351.9	129.3	5.0	10.0	4.2	1 211.9
1975	1 635.2	28.2	14.9	1 648.4	190.9	1 457.5	140.0	5.2	17.7	7.7	1 302.2
1976	1 823.9	32.9	15.7	1 841.0	209.0	1 632.1	151.6	6.5	24.5	6.9	1 456.4
1977	2 031.4	37.9	17.2	2 052.1	231.6	1 820.5	165.5	7.3	21.6	9.7	1 635.8
1978	2 295.9	47.4	25.3	2 318.0	261.5	2 056.5	177.8	8.2	21.0	10.6	1 860.2
1979	2 566.4	70.4	37.5	2 599.3	300.4	2 298.9	188.7	9.9	35.7	11.0	2 075.6
1980	2 795.6	81.8	46.5	2 830.8	345.2	2 485.6	212.0	11.2	33.9	14.5	2 243.0
1981	3 131.3	95.6	60.9	3 166.1	394.8	2 771.2	249.3	13.4	27.5	16.1	2 497.1
1982	3 259.2	102.4	65.9	3 295.7	436.5	2 859.2	256.7	15.2	2.5	18.1	2 603.0
1983	3 534.9	102.5	65.6	3 571.8	456.1	3 115.7	280.3	16.2	47.0	24.3	2 796.5
1984	3 932.7	122.9	87.6	3 968.1	482.4	3 485.7	309.1	18.6	18.6	22.9	3 162.3
1985	4 213.0	113.1	87.8	4 238.4	516.5	3 721.9	329.4	20.7	11.7	20.4	3 380.4
1986	4 452.9	111.1	95.6	4 468.3	551.6	3 916.8	346.8	23.8	43.9	23.6	3 525.8
1987	4 742.5	122.9	109.2	4 756.2	586.1	4 170.1	369.3	24.2	3.3	30.1	3 803.4
1988	5 108.3	151.8	133.4	5 126.8	627.4	4 499.4	392.6	25.3	-42.2	27.4	4 151.1
1989	5 489.1	177.2	156.8	5 509.4	677.2	4 832.2	420.7	25.8	16.3	22.6	4 392.1
1990	5 803.2	188.3	159.3	5 832.2	711.3	5 120.9	447.3	26.1	30.6	25.3	4 642.1
1991	5 986.2	167.7	143.0	6 010.9	748.0	5 262.8	482.3	25.9	19.6	21.5	4 756.6
1992	6 318.9	151.1	127.6	6 342.3	787.5	5 554.9	510.6	28.1	43.7	22.4	4 994.9
1993	6 642.3	154.4	130.1	6 666.7	812.8	5 853.9	540.1	27.8	63.8	29.6	5 251.9
1994	7 054.3	184.3	167.5	7 071.1	874.9	6 196.2	575.3	30.8	58.5	25.2	5 556.8
1995	7 400.5	232.3	211.9	7 420.9	911.7	6 509.1	594.6	33.5	26.5	22.2	5 876.7
1996	7 813.2	245.6	227.5	7 831.2	956.2	6 875.0	620.0	34.4	32.8	22.6	6 210.4
1997	8 318.4	281.3	274.2	8 325.4	1 013.3	7 312.1	646.2	36.8	29.7	19.1	6 618.4
1998	8 790.2	285.4	288.9	8 786.7	1 077.3	7 709.3	679.6	38.0	-24.8	21.5	7 038.1
1999	9 299.2	305.9	316.9	9 288.2	1 161.0	8 127.1	718.1	39.7	-71.9	28.4	7 469.7
1991											
1st quarter	5 886.3	186.2	153.3	5 919.1	738.6	5 180.5	468.3	25.7	6.4	23.4	4 703.5
2nd quarter	5 962.0	167.3	145.8	5 983.6	744.1	5 239.5	477.2	25.8	20.3	21.0	4 737.1
3rd quarter	6 015.9	160.8	142.7	6 034.0	749.7	5 284.3	487.9	25.8	18.8	21.1	4 773.0
4th quarter	6 080.7	156.4	130.3	6 106.8	759.7	5 347.0	495.9	26.1	33.0	20.7	4 812.6
1992											
1st quarter	6 183.6	153.7	128.7	6 208.6	758.2	5 450.4	500.8	27.4	7.7	20.6	4 935.1
2nd quarter	6 276.6	156.1	131.6	6 301.1	765.3	5 535.8	503.2	28.1	30.4	21.4	4 995.5
3rd quarter	6 345.8	148.0	126.5	6 367.3	844.8	5 522.5	511.9	28.5	52.6	22.4	4 951.9
4th quarter	6 469.8	146.5	123.9	6 492.4	781.6	5 710.8	526.3	28.3	84.2	25.2	5 097.2
1993											
1st quarter	6 521.6	150.9	120.5	6 552.0	801.7	5 750.3	524.6	27.7	78.8	30.9	5 150.2
2nd quarter	6 596.7	153.3	129.4	6 620.6	803.4	5 817.2	535.2	27.5	51.3	29.3	5 232.6
3rd quarter	6 655.5	156.2	126.6	6 685.1	822.0	5 863.1	542.0	27.7	63.7	29.7	5 259.4
4th quarter	6 795.5	157.3	143.8	6 809.1	824.1	5 985.0	558.5	28.3	61.2	28.5	5 365.5
1994											
1st quarter	6 887.8	164.0	143.3	6 908.5	915.2	5 993.3	565.3	29.5	52.7	27.6	5 373.4
2nd quarter	7 015.7	175.2	158.5	7 032.4	848.5	6 183.9	572.2	30.3	81.3	25.1	5 525.2
3rd quarter	7 096.0	191.1	176.0	7 111.1	861.5	6 249.6	578.7	31.2	54.6	23.6	5 608.7
4th quarter	7 217.7	206.8	191.9	7 232.6	874.6	6 358.0	584.9	32.1	45.3	24.3	5 719.9
1995											
1st quarter	7 297.5	224.2	202.8	7 318.9	889.6	6 429.2	589.3	33.0	53.7	21.8	5 775.0
2nd quarter	7 342.6	234.5	209.2	7 367.9	904.1	6 463.8	594.1	33.1	24.9	22.0	5 833.7
3rd quarter	7 432.8	231.6	220.4	7 444.1	915.9	6 528.2	593.6	33.9	3.1	22.5	5 920.0
4th quarter	7 529.3	238.7	215.3	7 552.7	937.4	6 615.3	601.3	34.0	24.4	22.5	5 978.1
1996											
1st quarter	7 629.6	239.1	212.3	7 656.5	938.4	6 718.1	606.8	33.6	34.4	23.3	6 066.6
2nd quarter	7 782.7	237.7	220.0	7 800.3	948.6	6 851.7	613.2	34.3	49.6	22.9	6 177.5
3rd quarter	7 859.0	245.6	234.1	7 870.5	962.5	6 908.0	615.7	34.6	25.1	22.0	6 254.5
4th quarter	7 981.4	259.8	243.5	7 997.7	975.3	7 022.4	644.3	35.2	22.3	22.2	6 342.9
1997											
1st quarter	8 124.2	268.1	260.4	8 131.8	989.7	7 142.1	632.0	35.7	40.6	21.1	6 454.8
2nd quarter	8 279.8	282.6	270.6	8 291.8	1 005.2	7 286.6	643.8	36.7	69.5	19.2	6 555.8
3rd quarter	8 390.9	289.5	282.8	8 397.7	1 021.0	7 376.6	654.1	37.2	26.9	18.0	6 676.4
4th quarter	8 478.6	285.0	283.2	8 480.4	1 037.4	7 443.1	655.0	37.6	-18.0	18.2	6 786.7
1998											
1st quarter	8 634.7	289.3	283.8	8 640.3	1 050.9	7 589.4	664.4	37.1	16.4	17.8	6 889.3
2nd quarter	8 722.0	292.6	289.6	8 725.0	1 067.1	7 657.9	671.9	37.9	-20.8	17.8	6 986.7
3rd quarter	8 829.1	277.2	291.4	8 814.9	1 086.0	7 728.8	679.2	38.2	-63.7	18.0	7 093.0
4th quarter	8 974.9	282.6	290.9	8 966.6	1 105.3	7 861.3	702.7	38.8	-31.0	32.4	7 183.2
1999											
1st quarter	9 104.5	281.9	289.2	9 097.2	1 124.9	7 972.3	697.2	38.9	-53.6	22.9	7 312.7
2nd quarter	9 191.5	295.9	305.6	9 181.8	1 148.8	8 033.0	707.9	39.3	-76.8	29.7	7 392.3
3rd quarter	9 340.9	314.4	328.0	9 327.3	1 181.8	8 145.5	721.6	39.9	-89.5	19.5	7 493.1
4th quarter	9 559.7	331.2	344.6	9 546.3	1 188.5	8 357.7	745.5	40.6	-67.8	41.4	7 680.7

Table 1-7. National Income by Type of Income

(Billions of dollars, quarterly data are at seasonally adjusted annual rates.)

Year and quarter	National income	Compensation of employees			Proprietors' income with IVA [1] and CCAdj [2]			Rental income of persons with CCAdj [2]	Corporate profits					Net interest
		Total	Wage and salary accruals	Supplements to wages and salaries	Total	Farm	Nonfarm		Total with IVA [1] and CCAdj [2]	Profits before tax	Profits after tax			
											Total	Dividends	Undistributed profits	
1970	837.5	617.2	551.5	65.7	79.8	14.3	65.5	20.3	81.6	80.6	46.2	24.3	21.9	38.4
1971	903.9	658.8	584.5	74.4	86.1	14.9	71.2	21.2	95.1	92.4	54.7	25.0	29.7	42.6
1972	1 000.4	725.1	638.7	86.5	97.7	18.8	78.9	21.6	109.8	107.3	65.5	26.8	38.6	46.2
1973	1 127.4	811.2	708.6	102.6	115.2	30.7	84.5	23.1	123.9	134.2	84.9	29.9	55.0	53.9
1974	1 211.9	890.2	772.2	118.0	115.5	25.2	90.3	23.0	114.5	146.8	95.0	33.2	61.8	68.8
1975	1 302.2	949.0	814.7	134.4	121.6	23.5	98.1	22.0	133.0	144.8	93.9	33.0	60.9	76.6
1976	1 456.4	1 059.3	899.6	159.7	134.3	18.7	115.6	21.5	160.6	178.6	114.4	39.0	75.4	80.8
1977	1 635.8	1 180.4	994.0	186.4	148.3	17.5	130.8	20.4	190.9	209.0	136.0	44.8	91.2	95.7
1978	1 860.2	1 336.0	1 121.0	215.0	170.1	21.5	148.5	22.4	217.2	244.9	161.4	50.8	110.6	114.5
1979	2 075.6	1 500.8	1 255.6	245.2	183.7	23.7	160.0	24.5	222.5	270.1	182.1	57.5	124.6	144.2
1980	2 243.0	1 651.7	1 377.4	274.3	177.6	13.1	164.5	31.3	198.5	251.4	166.6	64.1	102.6	183.9
1981	2 497.1	1 825.7	1 517.3	308.5	186.2	20.3	165.9	39.6	219.0	240.9	159.8	73.8	86.0	226.5
1982	2 603.0	1 926.0	1 593.4	332.6	179.9	14.4	165.4	39.6	201.2	195.5	132.4	76.2	56.2	256.3
1983	2 796.5	2 042.7	1 684.3	358.5	195.5	7.2	188.3	36.9	254.1	231.4	154.1	83.6	70.5	267.2
1984	3 162.3	2 255.9	1 854.8	401.1	247.5	21.6	225.9	39.5	309.8	266.0	172.0	91.0	81.0	309.6
1985	3 380.4	2 425.2	1 995.2	430.0	267.0	21.5	245.5	39.1	322.4	255.2	158.7	97.7	61.0	326.7
1986	3 525.8	2 570.7	2 114.4	456.3	278.6	23.0	255.6	32.2	300.7	243.4	136.9	106.3	30.6	343.6
1987	3 803.4	2 755.6	2 270.2	485.4	303.9	29.0	274.8	35.8	346.6	314.6	187.5	112.2	75.3	361.5
1988	4 151.1	2 973.8	2 452.7	521.1	338.8	26.0	312.7	44.1	405.0	381.9	244.8	129.6	115.2	389.4
1989	4 392.1	3 151.0	2 596.8	554.2	361.8	32.2	329.6	40.5	395.7	376.7	235.3	155.0	80.2	443.1
1990	4 642.1	3 351.0	2 754.6	596.4	381.0	31.1	349.9	49.1	408.6	401.5	260.9	165.6	95.3	452.4
1991	4 756.6	3 454.9	2 824.2	630.7	384.2	26.4	357.8	56.4	431.2	416.1	282.6	178.4	104.1	429.8
1992	4 994.9	3 644.8	2 966.8	677.9	434.3	32.7	401.7	63.3	453.1	451.6	308.4	185.5	122.9	399.5
1993	5 251.9	3 814.4	3 091.6	722.8	461.8	30.1	431.7	90.9	510.5	510.4	345.0	203.1	141.9	374.3
1994	5 556.8	4 016.2	3 254.3	761.9	476.6	31.9	444.6	110.3	573.2	573.4	386.7	234.9	151.8	380.5
1995	5 876.7	4 202.5	3 441.1	761.4	497.7	22.2	475.5	117.9	668.8	668.5	457.5	254.2	203.3	389.8
1996	6 210.4	4 395.6	3 630.1	765.4	544.7	34.3	510.5	129.7	754.0	726.3	502.7	297.7	205.0	386.3
1997	6 618.4	4 651.3	3 886.0	765.3	581.2	29.7	551.5	128.3	833.8	792.4	555.2	335.2	220.0	423.9
1998	7 038.1	4 984.2	4 192.8	791.4	620.7	25.4	595.2	135.4	815.0	758.2	513.6	351.5	162.1	482.7
1999	7 469.7	5 299.8	4 475.1	824.6	663.5	25.3	638.2	143.4	856.0	823.0	567.1	370.7	196.4	507.1
1991														
1st quarter	4 703.5	3 403.5	2 786.7	616.8	373.3	26.5	346.7	53.9	432.9	410.9	281.1	172.9	108.2	440.0
2nd quarter	4 737.1	3 436.2	2 810.7	625.5	383.0	27.7	355.4	56.4	429.0	410.2	277.9	178.2	99.7	432.5
3rd quarter	4 773.0	3 471.0	2 835.7	635.3	385.0	23.8	361.3	57.6	428.3	417.0	280.9	181.3	99.6	430.9
4th quarter	4 812.6	3 509.0	2 863.7	645.3	395.4	27.5	367.9	57.8	434.7	426.4	290.3	181.4	108.9	415.7
1992														
1st quarter	4 935.1	3 574.8	2 913.3	661.4	420.6	31.4	389.2	59.3	469.8	458.6	314.2	178.8	135.4	410.6
2nd quarter	4 995.5	3 625.4	2 952.4	673.0	432.7	33.6	399.1	63.8	468.6	471.0	320.9	179.5	141.4	405.0
3rd quarter	4 951.9	3 668.0	2 984.0	683.9	436.7	33.2	403.5	53.2	401.4	410.7	281.9	186.7	95.2	392.7
4th quarter	5 097.2	3 710.9	3 017.4	693.4	447.4	32.5	414.9	76.8	472.5	466.0	316.8	197.0	119.8	389.6
1993														
1st quarter	5 150.2	3 750.6	3 044.8	705.9	455.9	29.5	426.4	84.7	472.4	476.6	325.6	192.4	133.2	386.6
2nd quarter	5 232.6	3 795.5	3 077.3	718.2	464.4	34.4	430.0	90.3	503.6	506.3	340.8	198.4	142.4	378.8
3rd quarter	5 259.4	3 835.1	3 107.0	728.1	455.5	22.9	432.5	90.8	508.5	505.8	343.5	206.5	137.0	369.5
4th quarter	5 365.5	3 876.3	3 137.4	738.9	471.6	33.7	437.9	97.6	557.6	552.8	370.1	215.3	154.9	362.4
1994														
1st quarter	5 373.4	3 943.5	3 190.2	753.3	468.4	40.6	427.9	98.0	498.8	514.8	349.4	220.0	129.4	364.6
2nd quarter	5 525.2	3 994.9	3 233.4	761.5	479.5	33.9	445.6	112.0	569.3	562.7	379.8	229.7	150.1	369.6
3rd quarter	5 608.7	4 032.8	3 267.7	765.1	475.8	27.7	448.1	116.2	598.5	595.4	401.0	240.5	160.5	385.4
4th quarter	5 719.9	4 093.6	3 325.9	767.7	482.5	25.5	457.0	115.2	626.2	620.7	416.6	249.4	167.1	402.5
1995														
1st quarter	5 775.0	4 142.7	3 379.6	763.1	488.6	21.4	467.2	116.9	630.0	643.2	440.1	248.6	191.5	396.8
2nd quarter	5 833.7	4 178.8	3 417.2	761.6	491.4	19.6	471.8	115.1	655.5	665.3	456.6	251.1	205.5	392.8
3rd quarter	5 920.0	4 224.3	3 463.6	760.7	499.7	20.5	479.2	116.6	692.8	683.5	464.8	252.1	212.7	386.7
4th quarter	5 978.1	4 264.1	3 503.8	760.2	511.1	27.3	483.9	123.2	696.7	681.8	468.5	265.0	203.4	383.0
1996														
1st quarter	6 066.6	4 297.4	3 537.4	760.0	525.9	31.1	494.8	128.4	736.7	713.2	493.5	286.2	207.3	378.2
2nd quarter	6 177.5	4 367.8	3 604.6	763.2	546.6	36.3	510.3	129.0	748.6	726.3	501.0	290.7	210.3	385.5
3rd quarter	6 254.5	4 427.8	3 660.9	766.8	553.5	38.0	515.5	130.1	755.0	724.9	500.9	302.7	198.2	388.1
4th quarter	6 342.9	4 489.4	3 717.6	771.8	553.0	31.7	521.4	131.4	775.8	741.0	515.4	311.3	204.1	393.3
1997														
1st quarter	6 454.8	4 553.7	3 786.5	767.2	570.0	30.6	539.4	130.4	798.5	757.7	530.7	321.4	209.3	402.2
2nd quarter	6 555.8	4 607.8	3 845.0	762.8	576.0	29.6	546.4	128.9	825.6	781.2	549.4	331.8	217.5	417.5
3rd quarter	6 676.4	4 675.8	3 912.7	763.0	586.0	29.8	556.2	127.4	858.3	819.0	573.8	340.6	233.2	429.0
4th quarter	6 786.7	4 767.9	3 999.7	768.2	592.7	28.9	563.8	126.7	852.7	811.6	566.9	347.1	219.8	446.8
1998														
1st quarter	6 889.3	4 867.5	4 087.0	780.5	606.2	25.3	580.9	126.7	824.5	763.5	519.4	348.8	170.6	464.4
2nd quarter	6 986.7	4 943.1	4 155.5	787.6	613.3	23.3	590.0	132.8	814.0	766.7	520.9	349.8	171.1	483.5
3rd quarter	7 093.0	5 023.4	4 228.3	795.1	619.5	21.2	598.4	138.8	818.0	760.1	511.1	351.4	159.7	493.3
4th quarter	7 183.2	5 102.7	4 300.3	802.4	643.7	32.0	611.7	143.5	803.4	742.3	502.9	356.1	146.9	489.8
1999														
1st quarter	7 312.7	5 181.6	4 369.4	812.2	644.1	25.0	619.1	144.9	852.0	797.6	549.9	361.1	188.7	490.1
2nd quarter	7 392.3	5 255.4	4 435.5	819.9	660.4	29.0	631.4	145.7	836.8	804.5	553.7	367.2	186.5	494.1
3rd quarter	7 493.1	5 340.9	4 512.2	828.7	659.7	15.5	644.2	136.6	842.0	819.0	564.8	373.9	190.9	513.8
4th quarter	7 680.7	5 421.1	4 583.5	837.7	689.6	31.7	657.9	146.2	893.2	870.7	599.9	380.6	219.3	530.6

1. Inventory valuation adjustment.
2. Capital consumption adjustment.

Table 1-8. Gross Product and Domestic Income of Nonfinancial Corporate Business

(Billions of dollars, quarterly data are at seasonally adjusted annual rates.)

Year and quarter	Gross product	Less: Consumption of fixed capital	Equals: Net product	Less: Indirect business taxes plus business transfer payments less subsidies	Equals: Domestic income	Components of domestic income									
						Compensation of employees	Corporate profits								Net interest
							Total with IVA and CCAdj [2]	Profits before tax	Profits tax liability	Profits after tax			Inventory valuation adjustment	Capital consumption adjustment	
										Total	Dividends	Undistributed profits			
1970	562.0	48.5	513.5	59.0	454.6	378.1	59.4	58.5	27.2	31.4	18.5	12.8	-6.6	7.4	17.1
1971	606.9	53.1	553.8	64.6	489.1	401.2	69.8	67.3	29.9	37.4	18.5	18.9	-4.6	7.1	18.1
1972	673.9	58.4	615.6	69.4	546.2	445.9	81.1	79.0	33.8	45.3	20.1	25.2	-6.6	8.7	19.2
1973	755.6	63.8	691.8	76.6	615.2	504.5	88.2	99.0	40.2	58.8	21.1	37.8	-19.6	8.8	22.5
1974	816.7	74.7	742.0	81.9	660.1	555.1	76.7	109.6	42.2	67.4	21.7	45.7	-38.2	5.3	28.3
1975	883.0	89.2	793.8	88.0	705.8	578.6	98.5	110.5	41.5	69.0	24.8	44.2	-10.5	-1.4	28.7
1976	997.1	98.9	898.2	95.9	802.4	655.0	119.9	137.9	53.0	84.9	28.0	56.9	-14.1	-3.8	27.5
1977	1 127.8	111.0	1 016.9	104.9	912.0	740.0	141.3	159.2	59.9	99.3	31.5	67.8	-15.7	-2.3	30.7
1978	1 285.0	126.8	1 158.2	114.4	1 043.8	851.0	156.5	184.4	67.1	117.3	36.4	80.9	-23.7	-4.2	36.3
1979	1 431.5	147.0	1 284.6	123.3	1 161.3	966.2	150.1	197.1	69.6	127.5	38.1	89.4	-40.1	-6.9	45.0
1980	1 556.6	169.4	1 387.2	139.5	1 247.8	1 056.9	132.7	183.6	67.0	116.6	45.3	71.3	-42.1	-8.8	58.1
1981	1 770.1	195.9	1 574.2	168.1	1 406.1	1 169.9	164.4	184.2	63.9	120.3	53.3	67.0	-24.6	4.8	71.8
1982	1 831.4	216.8	1 614.6	169.7	1 444.9	1 216.1	146.3	136.9	46.3	90.7	53.3	37.4	-7.5	16.9	82.5
1983	1 953.3	225.1	1 728.2	185.3	1 542.9	1 279.9	186.4	160.7	59.4	101.3	64.2	37.1	-7.4	33.1	76.6
1984	2 194.8	237.3	1 957.5	205.4	1 752.1	1 421.4	242.9	195.3	73.7	121.6	67.8	53.8	-4.0	51.7	87.7
1985	2 329.3	253.9	2 075.4	219.0	1 856.4	1 522.3	243.7	172.3	69.9	102.3	72.3	30.1	0.0	71.4	90.4
1986	2 414.4	270.3	2 144.1	231.2	1 912.9	1 603.8	210.7	147.9	75.6	72.3	73.9	-1.6	7.1	55.8	98.4
1987	2 595.3	283.8	2 311.6	241.9	2 069.7	1 716.3	248.3	209.5	93.5	116.0	75.9	40.1	-16.2	55.0	105.1
1988	2 814.5	302.0	2 512.5	256.3	2 256.2	1 844.1	288.6	257.3	101.9	155.5	79.8	75.7	-22.2	53.4	123.6
1989	2 961.4	322.8	2 638.6	275.9	2 362.7	1 946.6	264.2	235.6	98.9	136.7	104.2	32.6	-16.3	45.0	151.8
1990	3 096.2	338.4	2 757.9	290.6	2 467.3	2 052.7	258.5	237.2	95.8	141.4	119.2	22.2	-12.9	34.3	156.0
1991	3 150.6	354.9	2 795.7	313.1	2 482.6	2 086.9	252.8	221.6	85.5	136.1	125.8	10.3	4.9	26.3	143.0
1992	3 288.0	369.6	2 918.5	332.0	2 586.5	2 194.2	278.9	258.0	91.2	166.8	135.0	31.9	-2.8	23.7	113.3
1993	3 457.6	386.4	3 071.3	349.3	2 721.9	2 290.7	325.3	305.8	105.2	200.5	149.3	51.2	-4.0	23.6	105.9
1994	3 737.2	414.5	3 322.7	382.1	2 940.6	2 430.2	402.5	381.4	128.9	252.6	158.6	94.0	-12.4	33.5	107.9
1995	3 945.9	437.5	3 508.4	397.3	3 111.0	2 552.7	442.5	422.1	136.7	285.4	179.3	106.0	-18.3	38.7	115.8
1996	4 159.5	462.7	3 696.9	411.9	3 284.9	2 667.1	509.1	460.2	150.1	310.1	201.9	108.2	3.1	45.8	108.7
1997	4 435.1	493.0	3 942.1	431.4	3 510.7	2 835.1	555.6	496.1	158.3	337.7	218.1	119.6	8.4	51.1	120.0
1998	4 728.1	526.8	4 201.3	456.5	3 744.9	3 055.1	560.4	489.9	159.4	330.5	240.5	90.0	17.0	53.5	129.4
1999	5 048.8	569.6	4 479.3	482.5	3 996.8	3 267.0	588.5	539.5	166.6	373.0	250.9	122.1	-9.1	58.0	141.3
1991															
1st quarter	3 116.4	352.1	2 764.2	303.3	2 460.9	2 056.1	252.9	215.4	82.8	132.6	121.5	11.1	11.4	26.0	152.0
2nd quarter	3 138.3	354.1	2 784.3	309.5	2 474.8	2 074.9	253.1	218.6	84.4	134.2	126.5	7.7	8.6	25.9	146.8
3rd quarter	3 164.1	355.9	2 808.2	317.0	2 491.2	2 097.4	252.4	224.9	87.1	137.9	126.1	11.8	1.4	26.1	141.3
4th quarter	3 183.5	357.5	2 826.0	322.5	2 503.5	2 119.0	252.8	227.5	87.8	139.7	128.9	10.7	-1.7	27.0	131.7
1992															
1st quarter	3 227.6	360.2	2 867.4	325.6	2 541.8	2 151.0	268.6	238.7	84.8	153.9	123.9	30.0	2.2	27.7	122.3
2nd quarter	3 267.8	363.3	2 904.5	326.9	2 577.6	2 181.8	280.1	263.3	93.6	169.7	129.4	40.3	-10.6	27.4	115.7
3rd quarter	3 298.5	383.6	2 914.9	332.8	2 582.1	2 208.6	264.0	253.7	89.1	164.6	135.3	29.2	-3.4	13.7	109.5
4th quarter	3 358.3	371.2	2 987.0	342.7	2 644.3	2 235.6	302.9	276.5	97.4	179.1	151.2	27.9	0.4	25.9	105.9
1993															
1st quarter	3 365.3	378.9	2 986.5	338.3	2 648.2	2 250.8	288.0	273.0	93.3	179.7	145.8	33.8	-6.1	21.1	109.4
2nd quarter	3 434.4	382.3	3 052.1	344.9	2 707.2	2 279.8	321.1	304.6	104.9	199.7	146.0	53.7	-6.3	22.9	106.3
3rd quarter	3 472.3	391.7	3 080.6	350.0	2 730.6	2 303.0	323.6	301.4	103.7	197.7	148.9	48.8	0.4	21.7	104.0
4th quarter	3 558.4	392.6	3 165.8	364.1	2 801.7	2 329.3	368.6	344.0	118.9	225.1	156.7	68.4	-4.1	28.6	103.9
1994															
1st quarter	3 633.5	425.6	3 207.9	371.9	2 836.0	2 376.6	357.3	352.3	119.7	232.5	148.4	84.2	-8.3	13.3	102.1
2nd quarter	3 700.7	404.3	3 296.5	379.4	2 917.1	2 413.7	398.9	370.8	125.1	245.7	158.5	87.3	-10.2	38.3	104.5
3rd quarter	3 763.3	410.9	3 352.4	385.8	2 966.6	2 442.7	414.0	389.3	131.1	258.2	158.1	100.1	-15.7	40.3	109.9
4th quarter	3 851.3	417.3	3 434.0	391.2	3 042.8	2 487.6	439.9	413.3	139.6	273.7	169.3	104.4	-15.6	42.2	115.3
1995															
1st quarter	3 875.9	425.3	3 450.5	394.8	3 055.7	2 517.8	420.9	414.1	134.4	279.6	172.7	107.0	-32.5	39.4	117.0
2nd quarter	3 911.4	433.9	3 477.5	397.2	3 080.3	2 538.5	424.7	414.5	134.1	280.4	173.5	106.9	-28.2	38.4	117.2
3rd quarter	3 979.8	440.7	3 539.1	396.0	3 143.1	2 566.7	460.6	431.3	139.5	291.8	183.2	108.5	-9.8	39.2	115.8
4th quarter	4 016.5	450.0	3 566.4	401.4	3 165.0	2 587.9	463.8	428.7	139.0	289.7	188.0	101.7	-2.6	37.7	113.3
1996															
1st quarter	4 056.5	453.1	3 603.3	405.4	3 197.9	2 600.0	491.1	445.9	144.9	300.9	198.9	102.0	2.1	43.1	106.9
2nd quarter	4 130.9	458.9	3 672.0	410.7	3 261.3	2 649.2	504.0	460.2	150.0	310.2	195.0	115.2	-1.7	45.5	108.0
3rd quarter	4 187.6	465.9	3 721.7	412.0	3 309.6	2 689.1	511.4	460.1	150.0	310.1	203.8	106.3	4.7	46.6	109.1
4th quarter	4 263.3	472.9	3 790.4	419.5	3 370.9	2 730.1	529.8	474.7	155.5	319.2	210.1	109.1	7.1	48.0	111.0
1997															
1st quarter	4 319.1	480.1	3 839.0	421.6	3 417.4	2 768.9	534.5	473.9	150.9	323.0	210.4	112.6	10.4	50.2	113.9
2nd quarter	4 389.6	488.6	3 901.0	432.2	3 468.8	2 805.3	544.7	481.6	153.4	328.2	214.0	114.2	12.1	51.1	118.8
3rd quarter	4 479.0	497.4	3 981.6	435.4	3 546.2	2 850.1	573.9	517.0	165.5	351.5	218.9	132.6	5.6	51.3	122.2
4th quarter	4 552.6	505.8	4 046.8	436.2	3 610.5	2 916.1	569.2	511.8	163.6	348.2	229.1	119.1	5.7	51.8	125.2
1998															
1st quarter	4 619.1	512.9	4 106.2	445.6	3 660.6	2 979.7	555.3	480.0	155.3	324.7	234.4	90.3	22.6	52.7	125.6
2nd quarter	4 681.7	521.6	4 160.1	452.4	3 707.7	3 027.6	550.9	490.2	159.3	330.9	239.9	91.0	7.7	53.0	129.3
3rd quarter	4 773.0	531.3	4 241.7	453.2	3 788.5	3 080.3	576.8	505.6	165.3	340.2	239.9	100.3	17.7	53.6	131.5
4th quarter	4 838.5	541.3	4 297.2	474.6	3 822.6	3 132.7	558.5	483.8	157.7	326.1	247.8	78.3	19.9	54.8	131.4
1999															
1st quarter	4 923.1	550.6	4 372.6	469.3	3 903.3	3 183.5	586.6	517.2	158.5	358.6	237.6	121.0	11.4	58.0	133.1
2nd quarter	4 999.7	564.5	4 435.2	477.3	3 958.0	3 236.5	586.0	538.1	167.2	370.9	256.3	114.6	-8.9	56.9	135.5
3rd quarter	5 080.6	579.2	4 501.4	482.3	4 019.0	3 295.8	579.1	539.9	167.1	372.8	252.1	120.6	-19.7	58.9	144.1
4th quarter	5 191.9	584.0	4 607.9	501.1	4 106.8	3 352.2	602.0	563.0	173.5	389.5	257.5	132.0	-19.2	58.2	152.6

1. Inventory valuation adjustment.
2. Capital consumption adjustment.

Table 1-9. Per Capita Product and Income and U.S. Population

(Dollars, except as noted; quarterly data are at seasonally adjusted annual rates.)

Year and quarter	Current dollars							Chained (1996) dollars						Population (mid-period, thousands)
	Gross domestic product	Personal income	Dispos-able personal income	Personal consumption expenditures				Gross domestic product	Dispos-able personal income	Personal consumption expenditures				
				Total	Durable goods	Nondur-able goods	Services			Total	Durable goods	Nondur-able goods	Services	
1970	5 069	4 101	3 591	3 164	414	1 326	1 424	17 446	12 823	11 300	899	4 169	6 220	205 089
1971	5 434	4 358	3 860	3 382	467	1 375	1 541	17 804	13 218	11 581	977	4 191	6 376	207 692
1972	5 909	4 736	4 138	3 671	526	1 467	1 678	18 570	13 692	12 149	1 089	4 329	6 656	209 924
1973	6 537	5 254	4 619	4 022	583	1 619	1 821	19 456	14 496	12 626	1 190	4 428	6 904	211 939
1974	7 017	5 730	5 013	4 359	572	1 798	1 989	19 163	14 268	12 407	1 098	4 299	6 989	213 898
1975	7 571	6 166	5 470	4 771	618	1 948	2 205	18 911	14 393	12 551	1 087	4 320	7 157	215 981
1976	8 363	6 765	5 960	5 272	728	2 102	2 442	19 771	14 873	13 155	1 214	4 487	7 423	218 086
1977	9 221	7 432	6 519	5 803	823	2 257	2 724	20 481	15 256	13 583	1 314	4 550	7 674	220 289
1978	10 313	8 302	7 253	6 425	906	2 472	3 047	21 383	15 845	14 035	1 369	4 670	7 954	222 629
1979	11 401	9 247	8 033	7 091	952	2 774	3 365	21 821	16 120	14 230	1 349	4 742	8 121	225 106
1980	12 276	10 205	8 869	7 741	940	3 057	3 744	21 521	16 063	14 021	1 229	4 680	8 161	227 726
1981	13 614	11 301	9 773	8 453	1 006	3 299	4 148	21 830	16 265	14 069	1 232	4 688	8 200	230 008
1982	14 035	11 922	10 364	8 954	1 034	3 392	4 528	21 184	16 328	14 105	1 221	4 688	8 261	232 218
1983	15 085	12 576	11 036	9 757	1 200	3 547	5 010	21 902	16 673	14 741	1 389	4 801	8 589	234 332
1984	16 636	13 853	12 215	10 569	1 383	3 742	5 444	23 288	17 799	15 401	1 579	4 948	8 873	236 394
1985	17 664	14 738	12 941	11 373	1 523	3 894	5 956	23 970	18 229	16 020	1 719	5 038	9 254	238 506
1986	18 501	15 425	13 555	12 029	1 667	3 982	6 379	24 565	18 641	16 541	1 859	5 171	9 478	240 682
1987	19 529	16 317	14 246	12 787	1 728	4 181	6 878	25 174	18 870	16 938	1 874	5 248	9 798	242 842
1988	20 845	17 433	15 312	13 697	1 837	4 419	7 441	25 987	19 522	17 463	1 965	5 367	10 109	245 061
1989	22 188	18 593	16 235	14 539	1 891	4 711	7 937	26 646	19 833	17 760	1 987	5 461	10 291	247 387
1990	23 215	19 614	17 176	15 327	1 871	4 985	8 472	26 834	20 058	17 899	1 948	5 479	10 466	249 981
1991	23 691	20 126	17 710	15 717	1 753	5 061	8 902	26 423	19 919	17 677	1 800	5 398	10 495	252 677
1992	24 741	21 105	18 616	16 482	1 843	5 180	9 459	26 938	20 318	17 989	1 875	5 441	10 688	255 403
1993	25 735	21 735	19 121	17 259	1 989	5 328	9 942	27 363	20 384	18 399	2 008	5 542	10 858	258 107
1994	27 068	22 593	19 820	18 097	2 152	5 518	10 428	28 194	20 709	18 910	2 140	5 698	11 074	260 616
1995	28 131	23 571	20 613	18 888	2 242	5 692	10 955	28 676	21 055	19 294	2 218	5 812	11 265	263 073
1996	29 428	24 660	21 385	19 727	2 322	5 929	11 476	29 428	21 385	19 727	2 322	5 929	11 476	265 504
1997	31 029	25 876	22 262	20 625	2 397	6 123	12 105	30 436	21 838	20 232	2 452	6 042	11 739	268 087
1998	32 489	27 317	23 359	21 625	2 565	6 311	12 749	31 474	22 672	20 989	2 688	6 227	12 084	270 560
1999	34 063	28 534	24 314	22 962	2 789	6 760	13 414	32 512	23 191	21 901	2 996	6 518	12 421	272 996
1991														
1st quarter	23 390	19 868	17 480	15 515	1 746	5 038	8 732	26 351	19 866	17 633	1 799	5 400	10 449	251 659
2nd quarter	23 631	20 072	17 668	15 690	1 749	5 077	8 863	26 432	19 950	17 717	1 800	5 425	10 508	252 295
3rd quarter	23 776	20 196	17 779	15 802	1 774	5 078	8 949	26 420	19 940	17 723	1 819	5 412	10 506	253 025
4th quarter	23 965	20 366	17 910	15 858	1 744	5 051	9 063	26 489	19 918	17 636	1 785	5 356	10 516	253 728
1992														
1st quarter	24 315	20 749	18 332	16 213	1 805	5 132	9 275	26 673	20 207	17 871	1 843	5 431	10 613	254 315
2nd quarter	24 614	20 989	18 529	16 359	1 817	5 134	9 408	26 850	20 284	17 908	1 848	5 408	10 670	255 004
3rd quarter	24 809	21 075	18 581	16 521	1 854	5 184	9 482	26 975	20 229	17 986	1 885	5 427	10 689	255 782
4th quarter	25 222	21 605	19 020	16 835	1 897	5 268	9 669	27 253	20 551	18 190	1 925	5 498	10 779	256 510
1993														
1st quarter	25 365	21 258	18 754	16 921	1 896	5 273	9 752	27 182	20 151	18 183	1 927	5 485	10 784	257 111
2nd quarter	25 595	21 709	19 106	17 154	1 969	5 317	9 868	27 281	20 403	18 319	1 992	5 531	10 805	257 735
3rd quarter	25 751	21 784	19 146	17 365	2 015	5 338	10 012	27 324	20 378	18 482	2 030	5 564	10 895	258 458
4th quarter	26 225	22 184	19 476	17 593	2 076	5 384	10 133	27 665	20 602	18 610	2 083	5 586	10 946	259 124
1994														
1st quarter	26 526	22 004	19 326	17 768	2 104	5 429	10 236	27 841	20 385	18 742	2 106	5 643	10 997	259 662
2nd quarter	26 956	22 518	19 705	17 972	2 127	5 475	10 369	28 164	20 676	18 857	2 120	5 677	11 064	260 268
3rd quarter	27 193	22 745	19 969	18 214	2 158	5 556	10 499	28 244	20 774	18 948	2 137	5 713	11 101	260 948
4th quarter	27 592	23 099	20 276	18 431	2 217	5 609	10 605	28 522	21 000	19 090	2 195	5 759	11 136	261 587
1995														
1st quarter	27 839	23 309	20 441	18 573	2 206	5 630	10 738	28 569	21 041	19 119	2 176	5 777	11 167	262 129
2nd quarter	27 949	23 460	20 489	18 818	2 225	5 680	10 913	28 561	20 970	19 259	2 198	5 806	11 257	262 714
3rd quarter	28 219	23 637	20 670	19 002	2 264	5 705	11 034	28 707	21 058	19 359	2 242	5 815	11 302	263 400
4th quarter	28 515	23 877	20 849	19 157	2 272	5 751	11 134	28 866	21 153	19 436	2 256	5 850	11 331	264 047
1996														
1st quarter	28 841	24 212	21 072	19 394	2 292	5 820	11 282	29 018	21 252	19 560	2 275	5 874	11 412	264 542
2nd quarter	29 354	24 551	21 261	19 681	2 343	5 919	11 418	29 430	21 308	19 724	2 340	5 921	11 463	265 134
3rd quarter	29 564	24 817	21 517	19 801	2 320	5 939	11 542	29 499	21 478	19 765	2 325	5 938	11 502	265 834
4th quarter	29 948	25 057	21 687	20 029	2 332	6 035	11 662	29 761	21 500	19 857	2 348	5 981	11 528	266 504
1997														
1st quarter	30 416	25 430	21 929	20 329	2 378	6 090	11 861	30 012	21 609	20 032	2 402	6 011	11 620	267 105
2nd quarter	30 928	25 696	22 129	20 435	2 332	6 078	12 024	30 376	21 744	20 080	2 378	6 007	11 694	267 713
3rd quarter	31 259	25 997	22 351	20 772	2 430	6 158	12 183	30 609	21 895	20 348	2 498	6 079	11 774	268 433
4th quarter	31 508	26 377	22 637	20 961	2 446	6 165	12 350	30 743	22 102	20 465	2 530	6 072	11 866	269 096
1998														
1st quarter	32 025	26 818	22 976	21 188	2 487	6 203	12 498	31 173	22 412	20 667	2 583	6 130	11 959	269 623
2nd quarter	32 281	27 164	23 254	21 509	2 551	6 273	12 685	31 332	22 615	20 917	2 662	6 204	12 059	270 188
3rd quarter	32 594	27 485	23 483	21 756	2 557	6 342	12 858	31 518	22 756	21 083	2 683	6 254	12 154	270 882
4th quarter	33 051	27 799	23 720	22 044	2 664	6 427	12 953	31 871	22 903	21 285	2 823	6 319	12 163	271 548
1999														
1st quarter	33 464	28 037	23 946	22 403	2 698	6 566	13 140	32 087	23 022	21 539	2 877	6 427	12 261	272 070
2nd quarter	33 716	28 353	24 196	22 791	2 774	6 696	13 321	32 218	23 133	21 789	2 973	6 474	12 374	272 619
3rd quarter	34 176	28 643	24 384	23 123	2 807	6 805	13 511	32 584	23 203	22 003	3 023	6 535	12 480	273 315
4th quarter	34 892	29 098	24 728	23 528	2 875	6 972	13 681	33 156	23 404	22 268	3 109	6 636	12 567	273 980

Table 1-10. Composite Indexes of Economic Activity and Selected Index Components

Year and month	Cyclical composite indexes, 1996=100				Selected components of leading index			Selected components of lagging index	
	Leading	Coincident	Lagging	Ratio, coincident to lagging	Vendor performance (slower deliveries diffusion index, percent)	Interest rate spread, 10-year Treasury bonds less federal funds [1]	Index of consumer expecta-tions [1,2]	Change in manufac-turing labor cost per unit of output [3]	Consumer installment credit outstanding (percent of personal income)
1970	82.5	53.0	96.2	55.1	50.3	0.17	73.7	4.4	15.4
1971	85.0	53.8	93.7	57.4	48.0	1.50	77.1	0.0	15.5
1972	88.3	56.7	92.4	61.4	62.7	1.78	87.3	0.2	15.8
1973	88.9	59.9	95.4	62.8	88.0	-1.89	67.6	4.9	16.2
1974	85.3	60.2	98.8	60.9	65.8	-2.95	56.0	12.1	16.1
1975	84.3	58.3	95.7	60.9	30.2	2.16	65.5	9.6	15.0
1976	88.3	61.1	92.5	66.1	54.4	2.57	82.7	3.5	14.5
1977	90.0	64.2	92.9	69.1	55.7	1.88	81.3	4.7	14.9
1978	90.3	67.8	95.1	71.3	60.5	0.48	69.3	5.2	15.4
1979	89.0	70.2	98.5	71.3	57.9	-1.75	52.8	9.7	15.8
1980	87.4	70.0	99.3	70.4	40.6	-1.90	56.8	11.1	15.0
1981	87.9	71.0	98.3	72.2	46.3	-2.47	65.0	7.2	13.8
1982	87.7	69.6	97.1	71.7	43.5	0.74	62.7	5.3	13.6
1983	92.4	70.8	93.5	75.7	56.8	2.02	84.7	-3.4	13.7
1984	94.1	75.6	96.8	78.1	57.3	2.21	92.7	2.1	14.5
1985	94.9	77.9	99.2	78.6	48.0	2.52	86.5	1.9	15.9
1986	96.2	79.8	99.9	79.9	50.6	0.88	85.8	-0.6	16.8
1987	97.6	82.4	99.5	82.8	57.4	1.73	81.3	-1.6	16.6
1988	98.0	85.4	100.1	85.3	57.7	1.28	85.2	2.7	16.4
1989	97.4	87.6	101.8	86.1	47.6	-0.72	85.3	2.2	16.5
1990	97.1	88.6	101.5	87.2	47.9	0.45	70.2	2.8	16.1
1991	97.0	87.5	99.1	88.4	47.3	2.17	70.3	2.5	15.4
1992	98.0	88.8	95.2	93.3	50.2	3.49	70.3	0.2	14.5
1993	98.4	90.8	94.6	95.9	51.6	2.85	72.8	0.7	14.3
1994	99.3	94.2	95.5	98.6	60.1	2.88	83.8	-1.8	15.3
1995	98.9	97.2	99.0	98.2	52.8	0.74	83.2	-2.4	16.6
1996	100.0	100.0	100.0	100.0	50.5	1.14	85.7	-3.6	17.6
1997	101.8	104.0	100.5	103.5	53.9	0.89	97.7	-3.1	17.5
1998	103.3	108.1	101.9	106.1	51.1	-0.09	98.3	0.4	17.1
1999	105.2	111.9	102.8	108.8	53.2	0.67	99.3	-0.6	17.4
1996									
January	98.7	98.0	99.9	98.1	47.8	0.09	78.7	-6.2	17.4
February	99.4	98.7	99.9	98.8	49.5	0.59	77.8	-3.7	17.4
March	99.5	98.9	99.8	99.1	49.6	0.96	86.2	-2.9	17.4
April	99.7	99.2	99.8	99.4	49.4	1.29	83.0	-3.5	17.5
May	100.0	99.7	99.9	99.8	49.9	1.50	79.2	-4.5	17.5
June	100.2	100.0	99.8	100.2	52.8	1.64	84.0	-4.7	17.6
July	100.3	100.2	100.2	100.0	50.8	1.47	86.5	-2.9	17.7
August	100.3	100.6	100.0	100.6	51.9	1.42	87.3	-3.7	17.7
September	100.4	100.8	100.1	100.7	50.0	1.53	90.1	-4.2	17.6
October	100.4	101.0	100.1	100.9	50.9	1.29	89.9	-3.3	17.6
November	100.5	101.4	100.1	101.3	51.2	0.89	93.9	-2.7	17.7
December	100.6	101.5	100.3	101.2	52.0	1.01	91.8	-1.3	17.6
1997									
January	100.9	101.9	100.2	101.7	49.6	1.33	91.3	-1.3	17.6
February	101.2	102.5	100.1	102.4	52.1	1.23	94.9	-1.7	17.6
March	101.3	102.8	100.3	102.5	53.0	1.30	93.6	-2.8	17.5
April	101.2	103.1	100.4	102.7	53.4	1.38	92.5	-3.6	17.6
May	101.5	103.4	100.6	102.8	54.9	1.21	96.6	-3.8	17.6
June	101.6	103.8	100.5	103.3	54.7	0.93	98.9	-5.7	17.6
July	102.0	104.2	100.3	103.9	54.7	0.70	102.6	-5.7	17.5
August	102.1	104.4	100.4	104.0	55.2	0.76	100.3	-5.1	17.5
September	102.3	104.9	100.4	104.5	54.8	0.67	100.7	-4.1	17.4
October	102.4	105.3	100.6	104.7	54.9	0.53	102.8	-2.6	17.4
November	102.5	105.6	100.9	104.7	55.1	0.36	102.3	-1.3	17.3
December	102.4	106.0	100.8	105.2	54.1	0.31	96.1	0.4	17.3
1998									
January	102.6	106.4	101.1	105.2	52.9	-0.02	102.2	1.1	17.2
February	102.9	106.7	101.4	105.2	52.8	0.06	104.2	2.5	17.1
March	103.0	107.1	101.7	105.3	52.7	0.16	101.9	3.6	17.2
April	103.1	107.3	101.5	105.7	52.5	0.19	104.3	1.8	17.2
May	103.1	107.6	101.6	105.9	51.5	0.16	101.7	1.3	17.1
June	103.0	107.9	102.1	105.7	51.1	-0.06	99.3	2.0	17.1
July	103.3	108.1	102.2	105.8	50.3	-0.08	100.0	0.7	17.1
August	103.4	108.6	102.2	106.3	50.2	-0.21	98.3	-1.7	17.1
September	103.2	108.9	102.3	106.4	50.8	-0.70	93.9	-0.9	17.2
October	103.4	109.2	102.4	106.6	49.9	-0.54	87.5	-1.5	17.2
November	103.9	109.7	102.2	107.3	50.2	0.00	94.3	-1.3	17.1
December	104.1	110.0	102.0	107.8	48.6	-0.03	91.9	-2.4	17.2
1999									
January	104.5	110.1	102.3	107.6	51.0	0.09	95.7	-1.3	17.3
February	104.7	110.6	102.4	108.0	50.9	0.24	103.6	-0.4	17.3
March	104.8	110.9	102.5	108.2	52.1	0.42	99.0	-2.0	17.4
April	104.7	111.0	102.7	108.1	49.5	0.44	97.4	-0.2	17.3
May	105.0	111.3	102.7	108.4	52.0	0.80	97.6	-0.9	17.4
June	105.3	111.9	102.4	109.3	53.1	1.14	99.8	-0.2	17.3
July	105.6	112.2	102.9	109.0	54.2	0.80	99.2	0.0	17.4
August	105.5	112.4	103.0	109.1	51.2	0.87	98.4	0.2	17.4
September	105.4	112.3	103.2	108.8	55.7	0.70	101.5	0.9	17.4
October	105.5	112.9	103.1	109.5	56.4	0.91	97.1	0.0	17.2
November	105.7	113.3	103.2	109.8	56.1	0.61	101.0	-1.3	17.3
December	106.1	113.6	103.5	109.8	56.7	0.98	101.1	-2.4	17.4

1. Not seasonally adjusted.
2. Copyright, University of Michigan, Survey Research Center, first quarter 1966=100.
3. Monthly data are six-month percent change at annual rate; annual data are for the six-month period ending in September.

CHAPTER 2: INCOME DISTRIBUTION AND POVERTY

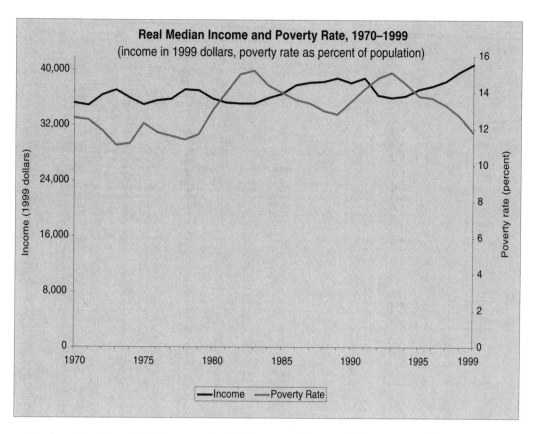

Real Median Income and Poverty Rate, 1970–1999
(income in 1999 dollars, poverty rate as percent of population)

- Real median household income in 1999 increased to an all-time high of $40,816. Median earnings of year-round full-time male workers increased to $36,476, the highest since 1989. Year-round, full-time female worker earnings rose to a record high of $26,324.

- The poverty rate in 1999 was 11.8 percent, the lowest level since 1979. The rate for people in households with a female head declined to 30.4 percent, the lowest level in at least 40 years.

- Income inequality as measured by the Gini coefficient increased slightly in 1999, based on the official definition of income, and it remained near its 31-year high reached in 1997. Adjusted for taxes and transfer payments, inequality was lower than in the official definition but still increasing in 1999.

Table 2-1. Median Income and Earnings

(1999 dollars.)

Year	Median household income						Median family income						Median earnings of year-round, full-time workers	
	All races	White		Black	Asian and Pacific Islander	Hispanic	All families	Married couples			Male house-holder [1]	Female house-holder [1]	Male workers	Female workers
		Total	Not Hispanic					Total	Wife in workforce	Wife not in workforce				
1967	32 783	34 188	. . .	19 850	. . .	. . .	36 409	38 740	45 693	34 931	31 273	19 707	32 962	19 047
1968	34 217	35 627	. . .	21 008	. . .	. . .	38 145	40 408	47 222	36 303	32 352	19 784	33 868	19 696
1969	35 473	37 020	. . .	22 377	. . .	. . .	39 887	42 288	49 172	37 544	35 265	20 389	35 752	21 045
1970	35 232	36 696	. . .	22 336	. . .	. . .	39 802	42 420	49 520	37 531	36 353	20 545	36 168	21 472
1971	34 897	36 502	. . .	21 561	. . .	. . .	39 756	42 481	49 682	37 665	33 714	19 768	36 331	21 619
1972	36 385	38 172	38 716	22 280	. . .	28 806	41 710	44 663	52 145	39 609	38 667	20 045	38 280	22 150
1973	37 104	38 886	39 229	22 890	. . .	28 745	42 536	45 984	53 781	40 302	37 916	20 461	39 483	22 360
1974	35 943	37 589	37 910	22 355	. . .	28 589	41 416	44 693	52 070	39 262	37 422	20 827	38 081	22 374
1975	34 980	36 580	36 856	21 961	. . .	26 280	40 669	44 072	51 098	37 802	38 523	20 288	37 820	22 245
1976	35 581	37 271	38 032	22 163	. . .	26 838	41 953	45 445	52 535	39 072	36 069	20 225	37 738	22 716
1977	35 777	37 622	38 368	22 201	. . .	28 066	42 201	46 437	53 428	39 707	38 271	20 469	38 555	22 718
1978	37 180	38 651	39 379	23 228	. . .	29 131	43 538	47 734	54 568	39 875	39 406	21 071	38 824	23 078
1979	37 060	38 856	39 403	22 813	. . .	29 362	44 097	48 244	55 971	39 862	37 841	22 243	38 305	22 854
1980	35 851	37 822	38 492	21 790	. . .	27 634	42 557	46 844	54 411	38 405	35 464	21 069	37 676	22 666
1981	35 269	37 264	37 802	20 911	. . .	28 290	41 397	46 347	54 079	37 582	36 776	20 266	37 462	22 191
1982	35 152	36 800	37 418	20 857	. . .	26 451	40 836	45 343	52 876	37 117	35 098	20 013	36 731	22 679
1983	35 157	36 857	37 577	20 864	. . .	26 419	41 272	45 641	53 705	36 615	36 540	19 719	36 600	23 276
1984	35 942	37 917	38 704	21 601	. . .	27 246	42 385	47 482	55 589	37 813	37 401	20 529	37 230	23 699
1985	36 568	38 565	39 433	22 945	. . .	27 041	42 943	48 153	56 407	38 021	35 026	21 150	37 462	24 191
1986	37 845	39 788	40 692	22 922	. . .	27 897	44 779	49 866	58 289	39 222	37 944	20 744	38 391	24 674
1987	38 220	40 268	41 376	22 984	. . .	28 357	45 419	51 152	59 763	39 069	36 969	21 533	38 051	24 801
1988	38 340	40 532	41 649	23 105	45 441	28 672	45 334	51 246	60 146	38 333	37 780	21 612	37 539	24 794
1989	38 836	40 852	41 731	24 295	48 505	29 452	45 967	51 790	60 817	38 623	37 414	22 091	36 721	25 217
1990	38 168	39 809	40 720	23 805	49 012	28 463	45 064	50 853	59 625	38 578	37 024	21 583	35 281	25 267
1991	36 850	38 615	39 537	23 005	44 584	27 756	43 961	50 145	58 920	36 788	34 679	20 418	35 988	25 140
1992	36 379	38 246	39 530	22 270	44 887	26 386	43 428	49 742	59 106	35 830	32 745	20 216	35 858	25 382
1993	36 019	38 001	39 399	22 521	44 211	26 386	42 612	49 582	59 035	34 840	30 515	20 111	35 058	25 073
1994	36 270	38 253	39 487	23 638	45 507	26 329	43 597	50 541	59 928	35 047	31 196	20 500	34 685	24 963
1995	37 251	39 099	40 642	24 480	44 397	24 990	44 395	51 447	61 024	35 392	33 187	21 526	34 431	24 594
1996	37 686	39 459	41 185	24 934	45 952	26 445	44 916	52 780	61 990	35 834	33 554	21 142	34 132	25 176
1997	38 411	40 453	42 119	26 002	46 969	27 640	46 262	53 552	62 975	37 396	34 213	21 822	34 954	25 922
1998	39 744	41 816	43 376	25 911	47 667	28 956	47 769	55 377	65 159	37 982	36 469	22 652	36 126	26 433
1999	40 816	42 504	44 366	27 910	51 205	30 735	48 950	56 676	66 529	38 626	37 396	23 732	36 476	26 324

1. No spouse present.

Table 2-2. Shares of Aggregate Household Income by Race and Hispanic Origin

Year, race and Hispanic origin	Number of house-holds (thou-sands)	Share of aggregate income (percent)						Mean household income (1999 dollars)						Gini coefficient
		Lowest fifth	Second fifth	Third fifth	Fourth fifth	Highest fifth	Top five percent	Lowest fifth	Second fifth	Third fifth	Fourth fifth	Highest fifth	Top five percent	
ALL RACES														
1967	60 813	4.0	10.8	17.3	24.2	43.8	17.5	7 463	20 345	32 485	45 450	82 364	131 284	0.399
1968	62 214	4.2	11.1	17.5	24.4	42.8	16.6	8 096	21 397	33 934	47 342	82 911	128 366	0.388
1969	62 874	4.1	10.9	17.5	24.5	43.0	16.6	8 275	22 055	35 244	49 363	86 767	133 559	0.391
1970	64 374	4.1	10.8	17.4	24.5	43.3	16.6	8 185	21 763	35 047	49 403	87 471	134 260	0.394
1971	66 676	4.1	10.6	17.3	24.5	43.5	16.7	8 218	21 372	34 654	49 265	87 293	133 887	0.396
1972	68 251	4.1	10.5	17.1	24.5	43.9	17.0	8 690	22 131	36 115	51 845	93 078	144 263	0.401
1973	69 859	4.2	10.5	17.1	24.6	43.6	16.6	9 064	22 470	36 716	52 783	93 610	142 658	0.397
1974	71 163	4.4	10.6	17.1	24.7	43.1	15.9	9 344	22 383	35 971	51 941	90 712	133 758	0.395
1975	72 867	4.4	10.5	17.1	24.8	43.2	15.9	8 994	21 356	34 942	50 742	88 366	130 256	0.397
1976	74 142	4.4	10.4	17.1	24.8	43.3	16.0	9 194	21 821	35 794	51 946	90 648	134 079	0.398
1977	76 030	4.4	10.3	17.0	24.8	43.6	16.1	9 261	21 856	36 038	52 769	92 503	136 528	0.402
1978	77 330	4.3	10.3	16.9	24.8	43.7	16.2	9 396	22 490	37 047	54 250	95 742	142 227	0.402
1979	80 776	4.2	10.3	16.9	24.7	44.0	16.4	9 262	22 561	37 136	54 467	96 786	144 530	0.404
1980	82 368	4.3	10.3	16.9	24.9	43.7	15.8	9 075	21 901	36 047	53 075	93 225	134 853	0.403
1981	83 527	4.2	10.2	16.8	25.0	43.8	15.6	8 942	21 429	35 393	52 720	92 346	131 459	0.406
1982	83 918	4.1	10.1	16.6	24.7	44.5	16.2	8 719	21 327	35 193	52 326	94 390	137 576	0.412
1983	85 290	4.1	10.0	16.5	24.7	44.7	16.4	8 763	21 404	35 302	52 969	95 850	140 411	0.414
1984	86 789	4.1	9.9	16.4	24.7	44.9	16.5	8 989	21 862	36 153	54 428	98 850	145 320	0.415
1985	88 458	4.0	9.7	16.3	24.6	45.3	17.0	8 976	22 188	36 750	55 266	101 943	153 201	0.419
1986	89 479	3.9	9.7	16.2	24.5	45.7	17.5	9 035	22 742	37 970	57 188	106 922	163 323	0.425
1987	91 124	3.8	9.6	16.1	24.3	46.2	18.2	9 044	22 855	38 211	57 757	109 840	173 053	0.426
1988	92 830	3.8	9.6	16.0	24.3	46.3	18.3	9 159	22 979	38 433	58 097	110 915	174 930	0.427
1989	93 347	3.8	9.5	15.8	24.0	46.8	18.9	9 433	23 379	38 862	58 784	114 912	185 658	0.431
1990	94 312	3.9	9.6	15.9	24.0	46.6	18.6	9 171	22 982	37 961	57 234	111 071	176 869	0.428
1991	95 669	3.8	9.6	15.9	24.2	46.5	18.1	8 884	22 200	36 876	56 215	107 801	168 229	0.428
1992	96 426	3.8	9.4	15.8	24.2	46.9	18.6	8 654	21 589	36 373	55 835	108 189	171 715	0.434
1993	97 107	3.6	9.0	15.1	23.5	48.9	21.0	8 546	21 509	36 055	56 032	116 739	200 363	0.454
1994	98 990	3.6	8.9	15.0	23.4	49.1	21.2	8 726	21 611	36 406	56 652	119 099	205 770	0.456
1995	99 627	3.7	9.1	15.2	23.3	48.7	21.0	9 128	22 298	37 284	57 314	119 605	206 422	0.450
1996	101 018	3.7	9.0	15.1	23.3	49.0	21.4	9 127	22 401	37 680	58 317	122 655	213 660	0.455
1997	102 528	3.6	8.9	15.0	23.2	49.4	21.7	9 209	22 938	38 590	59 770	127 430	223 624	0.459
1998	103 874	3.6	9.0	15.0	23.2	49.2	21.4	9 427	23 802	39 828	61 597	130 346	227 192	0.456
1999	104 705	3.6	8.9	14.9	23.2	49.4	21.5	9 940	24 436	40 879	63 555	135 401	235 392	0.457
WHITE														
1967	54 188	4.1	11.2	17.4	24.0	43.3	17.3	8 036	21 855	33 885	46 786	84 287	134 588	0.391
1968	55 394	4.4	11.4	17.6	24.3	42.3	16.5	8 741	22 922	35 366	48 672	84 939	132 118	0.381
1969	56 248	4.3	11.3	17.6	24.3	42.5	16.4	8 956	23 671	36 855	50 885	89 063	137 614	0.383
1970	57 575	4.2	11.1	17.5	24.3	42.9	16.5	8 834	23 219	36 503	50 823	89 569	137 867	0.387
1971	59 463	4.3	11.0	17.4	24.4	43.0	16.5	8 856	22 849	36 196	50 714	89 469	137 451	0.389
1972	60 618	4.3	10.8	17.2	24.3	43.4	16.8	9 396	23 789	37 871	53 458	95 607	148 244	0.393
1973	61 965	4.4	10.8	17.3	24.5	43.1	16.4	9 784	24 108	38 473	54 519	96 056	146 626	0.389
1974	62 984	4.6	11.0	17.2	24.6	42.6	15.7	10 112	23 956	37 596	53 572	92 936	136 782	0.387
1975	64 392	4.6	10.8	17.2	24.7	42.7	15.7	9 735	22 808	36 542	52 322	90 572	133 434	0.390
1976	65 353	4.6	10.7	17.3	24.7	42.8	15.9	9 943	23 332	37 510	53 612	93 063	137 866	0.391
1977	66 934	4.5	10.6	17.2	24.7	43.0	15.8	10 025	23 469	38 157	54 551	94 828	139 738	0.394
1978	68 028	4.5	10.6	17.1	24.6	43.2	16.1	10 233	24 013	38 799	55 913	98 097	145 806	0.394
1979	70 766	4.4	10.6	17.0	24.6	43.4	16.2	10 154	24 204	38 962	56 223	99 359	148 364	0.396
1980	71 872	4.5	10.6	17.1	24.7	43.1	15.5	10 014	23 583	37 889	54 883	95 567	137 891	0.394
1981	72 845	4.5	10.5	17.0	24.8	43.2	15.3	9 905	23 073	37 299	54 571	94 831	134 621	0.397
1982	73 182	4.4	10.4	16.8	24.6	43.9	15.9	9 637	22 970	36 962	54 234	96 903	140 488	0.403
1983	74 170	4.4	10.4	16.6	24.6	44.1	16.1	9 797	23 103	37 132	54 846	98 376	143 719	0.404
1984	75 328	4.3	10.3	16.6	24.6	44.2	16.2	9 961	23 581	38 063	56 344	101 427	148 858	0.405
1985	76 576	4.2	10.2	16.5	24.4	44.7	16.8	9 911	23 849	38 614	57 212	104 781	157 228	0.411
1986	77 284	4.1	10.1	16.4	24.3	45.1	17.2	10 096	24 516	39 975	59 246	109 766	167 621	0.415
1987	78 519	4.1	10.0	16.3	24.2	45.5	17.9	10 181	24 758	40 354	59 873	112 698	177 708	0.415
1988	79 734	4.1	10.0	16.2	24.1	45.6	18.0	10 292	24 903	40 535	60 138	113 932	179 897	0.416
1989	80 163	4.1	9.8	16.0	23.8	46.3	18.7	10 559	25 158	40 814	60 820	118 239	191 387	0.422
1990	80 968	4.2	10.0	16.0	23.9	46.0	18.3	10 303	24 699	39 737	59 220	114 080	181 959	0.419
1991	81 675	4.1	9.9	16.0	24.1	45.8	17.9	10 016	23 917	38 783	58 303	110 751	172 661	0.418
1992	81 795	4.1	9.7	15.9	24.1	46.2	18.4	9 768	23 402	38 413	58 065	111 413	176 900	0.423
1993	82 387	3.9	9.3	15.3	23.3	48.2	20.7	9 613	23 262	38 146	58 220	120 350	206 922	0.444
1994	83 737	3.8	9.2	15.1	23.2	48.6	21.1	9 708	23 216	38 310	58 806	123 144	213 929	0.448
1995	84 511	4.0	9.3	15.3	23.3	48.1	20.7	10 099	23 845	39 111	59 429	122 940	211 392	0.442
1996	85 059	3.9	9.2	15.2	23.2	48.4	21.1	10 109	23 974	39 607	60 416	126 011	219 009	0.446
1997	86 106	3.8	9.1	15.0	23.0	49.1	21.7	10 138	24 457	40 504	62 076	132 236	233 697	0.453
1998	87 212	3.8	9.2	15.1	23.1	48.8	21.5	10 489	25 471	41 937	63 849	135 273	237 992	0.450
1999	87 671	3.9	9.1	15.0	23.1	49.0	21.5	10 954	25 926	42 729	65 620	139 313	244 129	0.451

NOTE: An updating of survey methodology affected the reported income of higher income households and the Gini coefficient beginning in 1993. The increases in both would have been less sharp without this change. See Notes for explanation of the Gini coefficient.

Table 2-2. Shares of Aggregate Household Income by Race and Hispanic Origin—*Continued*

Year, race and Hispanic origin	Number of house-holds (thou-sands)	Share of aggregate income (percent)						Mean household income (1999 dollars)						Gini coefficient
		Lowest fifth	Second fifth	Third fifth	Fourth fifth	Highest fifth	Top five percent	Lowest fifth	Second fifth	Third fifth	Fourth fifth	Highest fifth	Top five percent	
BLACK														
1967	5 728	3.8	9.3	15.9	24.3	46.7	18.2	4 668	11 497	19 707	30 121	57 865	90 074	0.432
1968	5 870	4.0	9.8	16.3	25.1	44.9	15.9	5 091	12 506	20 823	32 145	57 386	81 497	0.412
1969	6 053	3.9	9.7	16.5	25.1	44.7	15.9	5 197	12 905	21 916	33 312	59 164	84 370	0.411
1970	6 180	3.7	9.3	16.3	25.2	45.5	16.4	5 059	12 743	22 166	34 353	62 062	89 512	0.422
1971	6 578	4.0	9.4	16.1	25.1	45.4	16.4	5 330	12 489	21 565	33 536	60 718	87 560	0.419
1972	6 809	3.9	9.2	15.8	24.9	46.2	16.9	5 527	12 900	22 217	35 065	65 034	94 846	0.427
1973	7 040	4.1	9.4	16.0	25.1	45.5	16.6	5 810	13 353	22 692	35 632	64 639	94 358	0.419
1974	7 263	4.2	9.4	16.2	25.2	45.0	15.7	5 820	13 107	22 461	35 015	62 615	87 004	0.414
1975	7 489	4.2	9.1	16.0	25.5	45.3	15.9	5 692	12 418	21 925	34 950	62 090	86 940	0.419
1976	7 776	4.3	9.2	15.8	25.5	45.2	15.7	6 033	12 997	22 393	36 184	64 071	89 086	0.421
1977	7 977	4.2	9.2	15.5	24.9	46.3	16.7	5 931	13 038	22 048	35 413	65 810	94 762	0.425
1978	8 066	4.0	8.7	15.6	25.3	46.4	16.3	5 862	12 975	23 220	37 590	68 805	97 011	0.431
1979	8 586	3.9	8.8	15.5	25.4	46.3	16.1	5 633	12 948	22 752	37 242	67 822	94 458	0.433
1980	8 847	3.7	8.7	15.4	25.3	46.9	16.6	5 279	12 283	21 741	35 763	66 357	93 942	0.439
1981	8 961	3.8	8.6	15.3	25.4	46.9	16.1	5 188	11 804	21 007	34 916	64 491	88 359	0.440
1982	8 916	3.6	8.6	15.3	25.5	47.0	16.9	4 937	11 782	21 053	35 023	64 425	92 893	0.442
1983	9 243	3.6	8.3	15.2	25.2	47.8	16.9	4 936	11 583	21 068	34 988	66 386	93 779	0.448
1984	9 480	3.6	8.4	15.0	24.7	48.3	17.4	5 190	12 127	21 584	35 643	69 525	100 261	0.450
1985	9 797	3.5	8.3	15.2	25.0	48.0	17.5	5 263	12 492	22 716	37 372	71 861	105 021	0.450
1986	9 922	3.2	8.0	15.0	25.1	48.8	18.2	4 843	12 329	23 040	38 555	75 032	112 136	0.464
1987	10 192	3.3	7.9	14.8	24.4	49.7	19.3	5 036	12 191	22 950	37 833	77 161	119 459	0.468
1988	10 561	3.3	7.7	14.6	24.7	49.7	18.7	5 222	12 256	23 076	39 084	78 722	118 562	0.468
1989	10 486	3.2	8.0	15.0	24.9	48.9	18.2	5 096	12 893	24 235	40 147	78 833	117 261	0.461
1990	10 671	3.1	7.9	15.0	25.1	49.0	18.5	4 897	12 438	23 773	39 632	77 430	117 144	0.464
1991	11 083	3.1	7.8	15.0	25.2	48.9	18.3	4 729	12 016	23 019	38 553	74 876	112 401	0.464
1992	11 269	3.1	7.8	14.7	24.8	49.7	19.1	4 656	11 757	22 215	37 431	75 064	115 697	0.470
1993	11 281	3.0	7.7	14.3	23.7	51.3	21.1	4 758	12 007	22 460	37 205	80 548	132 152	0.484
1994	11 655	3.0	7.9	14.3	24.3	50.5	20.1	4 999	12 911	23 594	39 955	83 030	132 013	0.477
1995	11 577	3.2	8.2	14.8	24.2	49.6	20.2	5 263	13 635	24 643	40 130	82 491	133 977	0.468
1996	12 109	3.1	8.0	14.5	23.7	50.7	21.7	5 361	13 802	24 902	40 846	87 422	149 690	0.479
1997	12 474	3.2	8.5	15.1	24.5	48.7	19.1	5 462	14 515	25 883	41 956	83 275	130 687	0.458
1998	12 579	3.1	8.2	14.8	24.4	49.5	19.1	5 309	14 346	25 820	42 590	86 400	133 263	0.466
1999	12 849	3.1	8.3	14.7	24.0	50.0	20.0	5 889	15 864	28 166	46 146	96 174	153 428	0.470
HISPANIC														
1972	2 655	5.3	11.2	17.2	24.0	42.3	16.2	8 626	18 341	28 247	39 425	69 417	106 087	0.373
1973	2 722	5.1	11.1	17.1	24.7	42.0	15.0	8 626	18 795	28 830	41 692	70 777	101 262	0.371
1974	2 897	5.2	10.9	17.2	24.7	42.0	15.1	8 535	18 056	28 444	40 950	69 635	100 066	0.376
1975	2 948	4.8	10.7	16.9	24.9	42.9	15.8	7 426	16 627	26 297	38 825	66 904	98 605	0.388
1976	3 081	4.7	10.5	16.9	25.1	42.8	15.2	7 519	16 576	26 735	39 863	67 919	96 645	0.387
1977	3 304	4.9	10.8	16.9	24.7	42.8	15.4	8 106	17 820	27 958	40 838	70 918	102 264	0.383
1978	3 291	4.7	10.7	16.9	24.9	42.8	15.4	8 081	18 444	29 048	42 916	73 598	105 940	0.385
1979	3 684	4.6	10.5	16.6	24.6	43.7	15.9	8 134	18 720	29 535	43 694	77 633	112 709	0.396
1980	3 906	4.4	10.2	16.4	24.9	44.1	16.0	7 391	17 223	27 729	41 972	74 535	107 701	0.405
1981	3 980	4.5	10.3	16.7	24.8	43.6	15.3	7 681	17 544	28 444	42 221	74 077	104 039	0.398
1982	4 085	4.2	9.6	16.2	24.7	45.3	16.7	6 873	15 742	26 384	40 292	73 984	108 869	0.417
1983	4 666	4.2	9.7	16.3	24.9	44.9	16.0	6 784	15 681	26 447	40 211	72 710	103 354	0.413
1984	4 883	3.9	9.5	16.2	25.0	45.3	16.6	6 666	16 168	27 480	42 299	76 822	112 515	0.420
1985	5 213	4.1	9.5	16.1	24.8	45.6	16.5	6 980	15 983	27 156	41 862	76 978	111 260	0.418
1986	5 418	4.0	9.5	15.9	24.8	45.8	16.5	6 960	16 731	27 956	43 764	80 766	116 267	0.424
1987	5 642	3.7	9.1	15.5	24.1	47.6	19.2	6 755	16 616	28 084	43 731	86 601	139 692	0.441
1988	5 910	3.7	9.3	15.6	24.2	47.2	19.0	6 718	17 085	28 598	44 220	86 440	138 889	0.437
1989	5 933	3.8	9.5	15.7	24.4	46.6	18.1	7 090	17 950	29 617	45 898	87 591	136 518	0.430
1990	6 220	4.0	9.5	15.9	24.3	46.3	17.9	7 193	16 879	28 398	43 240	82 595	127 743	0.425
1991	6 379	4.0	9.4	15.8	24.3	46.5	17.7	7 037	16 662	27 857	42 881	82 175	125 299	0.427
1992	7 153	4.0	9.4	15.7	24.1	46.9	18.1	6 757	16 101	26 820	41 272	80 192	123 611	0.430
1993	7 362	3.9	9.1	15.1	23.1	48.7	20.4	6 831	15 899	26 406	40 399	85 129	142 687	0.447
1994	7 735	3.7	8.7	14.8	23.3	49.6	21.0	6 539	15 445	26 285	41 273	88 012	149 200	0.459
1995	7 939	3.8	8.9	14.8	23.3	49.3	20.8	6 430	15 201	25 178	39 653	84 082	142 022	0.455
1996	8 225	3.8	9.0	14.7	23.1	49.5	21.5	6 873	16 155	26 452	41 670	89 384	154 966	0.457
1997	8 590	3.6	8.9	14.9	23.1	49.5	21.5	6 758	16 651	27 672	42 960	92 213	160 143	0.458
1998	9 060	3.6	8.9	14.8	22.9	49.7	21.9	7 043	17 502	28 972	44 809	97 303	171 653	0.460
1999	9 319	4.1	9.5	15.2	23.4	47.9	19.9	8 206	19 184	30 660	47 314	96 895	160 798	0.438

NOTE: An updating of survey methodology affected the reported income of higher income households and the Gini coefficient beginning in 1993. The increases in both would have been less sharp without this change. See Notes for explanation of the Gini coefficient.

Table 2-3. Average Poverty Thresholds by Family Size

(Dollars.)

Year	Unrelated individuals			Families of 2 persons			Families, all ages								CPI-U, all items (1982-1984 = 100)
	All ages	Under age 65	Age 65 and older	All ages	Householder under age 65	Householder age 65 and older	3 persons	4 persons	5 persons	6 persons	7 persons or more (before 1980)	7 persons	8 persons	9 persons	
1959	1 467	1 503	1 397	1 894	1 952	1 761	2 324	2 973	3 506	3 944	4 849	. . .	. . .	. . .	29.2
1960	1 490	1 526	1 418	1 924	1 982	1 788	2 359	3 022	3 560	4 002	4 921	. . .	. . .	. . .	29.6
1961	1 506	1 545	1 433	1 942	2 005	1 808	2 383	3 054	3 597	4 041	4 967	. . .	. . .	. . .	29.9
1962	1 519	1 562	1 451	1 962	2 027	1 828	2 412	3 089	3 639	4 088	5 032	. . .	. . .	. . .	30.3
1963	1 539	1 581	1 470	1 988	2 052	1 850	2 442	3 128	3 685	4 135	5 092	. . .	. . .	. . .	30.6
1964	1 558	1 601	1 488	2 015	2 079	1 875	2 473	3 169	3 732	4 193	5 156	. . .	. . .	. . .	31.0
1965	1 582	1 626	1 512	2 048	2 114	1 906	2 514	3 223	3 797	4 264	5 248	. . .	. . .	. . .	31.5
1966	1 628	1 674	1 556	2 107	2 175	1 961	2 588	3 317	3 908	4 388	5 395	. . .	. . .	. . .	32.5
1967	1 675	1 722	1 600	2 168	2 238	2 017	2 661	3 410	4 019	4 516	5 550	. . .	. . .	. . .	33.4
1968	1 748	1 797	1 667	2 262	2 333	2 102	2 774	3 553	4 188	4 706	5 789	. . .	. . .	. . .	34.8
1969	1 840	1 893	1 757	2 383	2 458	2 215	2 924	3 743	4 415	4 958	6 101	. . .	. . .	. . .	36.7
1970	1 954	2 010	1 861	2 525	2 604	2 348	3 099	3 968	4 680	5 260	6 468	. . .	. . .	. . .	38.8
1971	2 040	2 098	1 940	2 633	2 716	2 448	3 229	4 137	4 880	5 489	6 751	. . .	. . .	. . .	40.5
1972	2 109	2 168	2 005	2 724	2 808	2 530	3 339	4 275	5 044	5 673	6 983	. . .	. . .	. . .	41.8
1973	2 247	2 307	2 130	2 895	2 984	2 688	3 548	4 540	5 358	6 028	7 435	. . .	. . .	. . .	44.4
1974	2 495	2 562	2 364	3 211	3 312	2 982	3 936	5 038	5 950	6 699	8 253	. . .	. . .	. . .	49.3
1975	2 724	2 797	2 581	3 506	3 617	3 257	4 293	5 500	6 499	7 316	9 022	. . .	. . .	. . .	53.8
1976	2 884	2 959	2 730	3 711	3 826	3 445	4 540	5 815	6 876	7 760	9 588	. . .	. . .	. . .	56.9
1977	3 075	3 152	2 906	3 951	4 072	3 666	4 833	6 191	7 320	8 261	10 216	. . .	. . .	. . .	60.6
1978	3 311	3 392	3 127	4 249	4 383	3 944	5 201	6 662	7 880	8 891	11 002	. . .	. . .	. . .	65.2
1979	3 689	3 778	3 479	4 725	4 878	4 390	5 784	7 412	8 775	9 914	12 280	. . .	. . .	. . .	72.6
1980	4 190	4 290	3 949	5 363	5 537	4 983	6 565	8 414	9 966	11 269	13 955	12 761	14 199	16 896	82.4
1981	4 620	4 729	4 359	5 917	6 111	5 498	7 250	9 287	11 007	12 449	. . .	14 110	15 655	18 572	90.9
1982	4 901	5 019	4 626	6 281	6 487	5 836	7 693	9 862	11 684	13 207	. . .	15 036	16 719	19 698	96.5
1983	5 061	5 180	4 775	6 483	6 697	6 023	7 938	10 178	12 049	13 630	. . .	15 500	17 170	20 310	99.6
1984	5 278	5 400	4 979	6 762	6 983	6 282	8 277	10 609	12 566	14 207	. . .	16 096	17 961	21 247	103.9
1985	5 469	5 593	5 156	6 998	7 231	6 503	8 573	10 989	13 007	14 696	. . .	16 656	18 512	22 083	107.6
1986	5 572	5 701	5 255	7 138	7 372	6 630	8 737	11 203	13 259	14 986	. . .	17 049	18 791	22 497	109.6
1987	5 778	5 909	5 447	7 397	7 641	6 872	9 056	11 611	13 737	15 509	. . .	17 649	19 515	23 105	113.6
1988	6 022	6 155	5 674	7 704	7 958	7 157	9 435	12 092	14 304	16 146	. . .	18 232	20 253	24 129	118.3
1989	6 310	6 451	5 947	8 076	8 343	7 501	9 885	12 674	14 990	16 921	. . .	19 162	21 328	25 480	124.0
1990	6 652	6 800	6 268	8 509	8 794	7 905	10 419	13 359	15 792	17 839	. . .	20 241	22 582	26 848	130.7
1991	6 932	7 086	6 532	8 865	9 165	8 241	10 860	13 924	16 456	18 587	. . .	21 058	23 582	27 942	136.2
1992	7 143	7 299	6 729	9 137	9 443	8 487	11 186	14 335	16 952	19 137	. . .	21 594	24 053	28 745	140.3
1993	7 363	7 518	6 930	9 414	9 728	8 740	11 522	14 763	17 449	19 718	. . .	22 383	24 838	29 529	144.5
1994	7 547	7 710	7 108	9 661	9 976	8 967	11 821	15 141	17 900	20 235	. . .	22 923	25 427	30 300	148.2
1995	7 763	7 929	7 309	9 933	10 259	9 219	12 158	15 569	18 408	20 804	. . .	23 552	26 237	31 280	152.4
1996	7 995	8 163	7 525	10 233	10 564	9 491	12 516	16 036	18 952	21 389	. . .	24 268	27 091	31 971	156.9
1997	8 183	8 350	7 698	10 473	10 805	9 712	12 802	16 400	19 380	21 886	. . .	24 802	27 593	32 566	160.5
1998	8 316	8 480	7 818	10 634	10 972	9 862	13 003	16 660	19 680	22 228	. . .	25 257	28 166	33 339	163.0
1999	8 501	8 667	7 990	10 869	11 214	10 075	13 290	17 029	20 127	22 727	. . .	25 912	28 967	34 417	166.6

Table 2-4. Poverty Status of Persons by Family Relationship, Race and Hispanic Origin

(Thousands of persons, percent of population.)

Year, race and Hispanic origin	All persons			Married couple families [1]			Female householder, no spouse present			Unrelated individuals		
	Population	Below poverty level		Population	Below poverty level		Population	Below poverty level		Population	Below poverty level	
		Number	Percent		Number	Percent		Number	Percent		Number	Percent
ALL RACES												
1959	176 557	39 490	22.4	39 335	...	...	...	7 014	49.4	10 699	4 928	46.1
1960	179 503	39 851	22.2	39 624	...	...	...	7 247	48.9	10 888	4 926	45.2
1961	181 277	39 628	21.9	40 405	...	...	...	7 252	48.1	11 146	5 119	45.9
1962	184 276	38 625	21.0	40 923	...	...	...	7 781	50.3	11 013	5 002	45.4
1963	187 258	36 436	19.5	41 311	...	...	...	7 646	47.7	11 182	4 938	44.2
1964	189 710	36 055	19.0	41 648	...	...	...	7 297	44.4	12 057	5 143	42.7
1965	191 413	33 185	17.3	42 107	...	...	16 371	7 524	46.0	12 132	4 827	39.8
1966	193 388	28 510	14.7	42 553	...	...	17 240	6 861	39.8	12 271	4 701	38.3
1967	195 672	27 769	14.2	43 292	...	...	17 788	6 898	38.8	13 114	4 998	38.1
1968	197 628	25 389	12.8	43 842	...	...	18 048	6 990	38.7	13 803	4 694	34.0
1969	199 517	24 147	12.1	44 436	...	...	17 995	6 879	38.2	14 626	4 972	34.0
1970	202 183	25 420	12.6	44 739	...	...	19 673	7 503	38.1	15 491	5 090	32.9
1971	204 554	25 559	12.5	45 752	...	...	20 153	7 797	38.7	16 311	5 154	31.6
1972	206 004	24 460	11.9	46 314	...	...	21 264	8 114	38.2	16 811	4 883	29.0
1973	207 621	22 973	11.1	46 812	2 482	5.3	21 823	8 178	37.5	18 260	4 674	25.6
1974	209 362	23 370	11.2	47 069	2 474	5.3	23 165	8 462	36.5	18 926	4 553	24.1
1975	210 864	25 877	12.3	47 318	2 904	6.1	23 580	8 846	37.5	20 234	5 088	25.1
1976	212 303	24 975	11.8	47 497	2 606	5.5	24 204	9 029	37.3	21 459	5 344	24.9
1977	213 867	24 720	11.6	47 385	2 524	5.3	25 404	9 205	36.2	23 110	5 216	22.6
1978	215 656	24 497	11.4	47 692	2 474	5.2	26 032	9 269	35.6	24 585	5 435	22.1
1979	222 903	26 072	11.7	49 112	2 640	5.4	26 927	9 400	34.9	26 170	5 743	21.9
1980	225 027	29 272	13.0	49 294	3 032	6.2	27 565	10 120	36.7	27 133	6 227	22.9
1981	227 157	31 822	14.0	49 630	3 394	6.8	28 587	11 051	38.7	27 714	6 490	23.4
1982	229 412	34 398	15.0	49 908	3 789	7.6	28 834	11 701	40.6	27 908	6 458	23.1
1983	231 700	35 303	15.2	50 081	3 815	7.6	30 049	12 072	40.2	29 158	6 740	23.1
1984	233 816	33 700	14.4	50 350	3 488	6.9	30 844	11 831	38.4	30 268	6 609	21.8
1985	236 594	33 064	14.0	50 933	3 438	6.7	30 878	11 600	37.6	31 351	6 725	21.5
1986	238 554	32 370	13.6	51 537	3 123	6.1	31 152	11 944	38.3	31 679	6 846	21.6
1987	240 982	32 221	13.4	51 675	3 011	5.8	31 893	12 148	38.1	32 992	6 857	20.8
1988	243 530	31 745	13.0	52 100	2 897	5.6	32 164	11 972	37.2	34 340	7 070	20.6
1989	245 992	31 528	12.8	52 137	2 931	5.6	32 525	11 668	35.9	35 185	6 760	19.2
1990	248 644	33 585	13.5	52 147	2 981	5.7	33 795	12 578	37.2	36 056	7 446	20.7
1991	251 179	35 708	14.2	52 457	3 158	6.0	34 790	13 824	39.7	36 839	7 773	21.1
1992	256 549	38 014	14.8	53 090	3 385	6.4	36 446	14 205	39.0	36 842	8 075	21.9
1993	259 278	39 265	15.1	53 181	3 481	6.5	37 861	14 636	38.7	38 038	8 388	22.1
1994	261 616	38 059	14.5	53 865	3 272	6.1	37 253	14 380	38.6	38 538	8 287	21.5
1995	263 733	36 425	13.8	53 570	2 982	5.6	38 908	14 205	36.5	39 484	8 247	20.9
1996	266 218	36 529	13.7	53 604	3 010	5.6	38 584	13 796	35.8	40 727	8 452	20.8
1997	268 480	35 574	13.3	54 321	2 821	5.2	38 412	13 494	35.1	41 672	8 687	20.8
1998	271 059	34 476	12.7	54 778	2 879	5.3	39 000	12 907	33.1	42 539	8 478	19.9
1999	273 493	32 258	11.8	55 315	2 673	4.8	38 223	11 607	30.4	43 432	8 305	19.1
WHITE												
1959	156 956	28 484	18.1	36 217	...	...	...	4 232	40.2	9 154	4 041	44.1
1966	170 247	19 290	11.3	39 007	...	...	12 261	3 646	29.7	10 686	3 860	36.1
1970	177 376	17 484	9.9	41 092	...	...	13 226	3 761	28.4	13 500	4 161	30.8
1971	179 398	17 780	9.9	42 039	...	...	13 502	4 099	30.4	14 214	4 214	29.6
1972	180 125	16 203	9.0	42 585	...	...	13 739	3 770	27.4	14 495	3 935	27.1
1973	181 185	15 142	8.4	43 805	2 306	5.3	14 303	4 003	28.0	15 761	3 730	23.7
1974	182 376	15 736	8.6	43 049	1 977	4.6	15 433	4 278	27.7	16 295	3 555	21.8
1975	183 164	17 770	9.7	43 311	2 363	5.5	15 577	4 577	29.4	17 503	3 972	22.7
1976	184 165	16 713	9.1	43 397	2 071	4.8	15 941	4 463	28.0	18 594	4 213	22.7
1977	185 254	16 416	8.9	43 423	2 028	4.7	16 721	4 474	26.8	19 869	4 051	20.4
1978	186 450	16 259	8.7	43 636	2 033	4.7	16 877	4 371	25.9	21 257	4 209	19.8
1979	191 742	17 214	9.0	44 751	2 099	4.7	17 349	4 375	25.2	22 587	4 452	19.7
1980	192 912	19 699	10.2	44 860	2 437	5.4	17 642	4 940	28.0	23 370	4 760	20.4
1981	194 504	21 553	11.1	45 007	2 712	6.0	18 795	5 600	29.8	23 913	5 061	21.2
1982	195 919	23 517	12.0	45 252	3 104	6.9	18 374	5 686	30.9	24 300	5 041	20.7
1983	197 496	23 984	12.1	45 470	3 125	6.9	19 256	6 017	31.2	25 206	5 189	20.6
1984	198 941	22 955	11.5	45 643	2 858	6.3	19 727	5 866	29.7	26 094	5 181	19.9
1985	200 918	22 860	11.4	45 924	2 815	6.1	20 105	5 990	29.8	27 067	5 299	19.6
1986	202 282	22 183	11.0	46 410	2 591	5.6	20 163	6 171	30.6	27 143	5 198	19.2
1987	203 605	21 195	10.4	46 510	2 382	5.1	20 244	5 989	29.6	28 290	5 174	18.3
1988	205 235	20 715	10.1	46 877	2 294	4.9	20 396	5 950	29.2	29 315	5 314	18.1
1989	206 853	20 785	10.0	46 981	2 329	5.0	20 362	5 723	28.1	29 993	5 063	16.9
1990	208 611	22 326	10.7	47 014	2 386	5.1	20 845	6 210	29.8	30 833	5 739	18.6
1991	210 121	23 747	11.3	47 124	2 573	5.5	21 604	6 806	31.5	31 201	5 872	18.8
1992	213 060	25 259	11.9	47 383	2 677	5.7	22 453	6 907	30.8	31 170	6 147	19.7
1993	214 899	26 226	12.2	47 452	2 757	5.8	23 224	7 199	31.0	32 112	6 443	20.1
1994	216 460	25 379	11.7	47 905	2 629	5.5	22 713	7 228	31.8	32 569	6 292	19.3

1. These numbers and rates refer to families rather than persons; data on persons were not available.

Table 2-4. Poverty Status of Persons by Family Relationship, Race and Hispanic Origin—*Continued*

(Thousands of persons, percent of population.)

Year, race and Hispanic origin	All persons			Married couple families [1]			Female householder, no spouse present			Unrelated individuals		
	Population	Below poverty level		Population	Below poverty level		Population	Below poverty level		Population	Below poverty level	
		Number	Percent		Number	Percent		Number	Percent		Number	Percent
WHITE—*Continued*												
1995	218 028	24 423	11.2	47 877	2 443	5.1	23 732	7 047	29.7	33 399	6 336	19.0
1996	219 656	24 650	11.2	47 650	2 416	5.1	23 744	7 073	29.8	34 247	6 463	18.9
1997	221 200	24 396	11.0	48 070	2 312	4.8	23 773	7 296	30.7	34 858	6 593	18.9
1998	222 837	23 454	10.5	48 461	2 400	5.0	24 211	6 674	27.6	35 563	6 386	18.0
1999	224 373	21 922	9.8	48 794	2 161	4.4	23 895	5 891	24.7	36 151	6 375	17.6
BLACK												
1959	18 013	9 927	55.1	. . .	. . .	. . .	. . .	2 416	70.6	1 430	815	57.0
1966	21 206	8 867	41.8	. . .	. . .	. . .	. . .	3 160	65.3	. . .	777	54.4
1970	22 515	7 548	33.5	3 301	. . .	. . .	6 225	3 656	58.7	1 791	865	48.3
1971	22 784	7 396	32.5	3 289	. . .	. . .	6 398	3 587	56.1	1 884	866	46.0
1972	23 144	7 710	33.3	3 233	. . .	. . .	7 125	4 139	58.1	2 028	870	42.9
1973	23 512	7 388	31.4	3 360	. . .	. . .	7 188	4 064	56.5	2 183	828	37.9
1974	23 699	7 182	30.3	3 357	435	13.0	7 483	4 116	55.0	2 359	927	39.3
1975	24 089	7 545	31.3	3 352	479	14.3	7 679	4 168	54.3	2 402	1 011	42.1
1976	24 399	7 595	31.1	3 406	450	13.2	7 926	4 415	55.7	2 559	1 019	39.8
1977	24 710	7 726	31.3	3 260	429	13.1	8 315	4 595	55.3	2 860	1 059	37.0
1978	24 956	7 625	30.6	3 244	366	11.3	8 689	4 712	54.2	2 929	1 132	38.6
1979	25 944	8 050	31.0	3 433	453	13.2	9 065	4 816	53.1	3 127	1 168	37.3
1980	26 408	8 579	32.5	3 392	474	14.0	9 338	4 984	53.4	3 208	1 314	41.0
1981	26 834	9 173	34.2	3 535	543	15.4	9 214	5 222	56.7	3 277	1 296	39.6
1982	27 216	9 697	35.6	3 486	543	15.6	9 699	5 698	58.8	3 051	1 229	40.3
1983	27 678	9 882	35.7	3 454	535	15.5	10 059	5 736	57.0	3 287	1 338	40.7
1984	28 087	9 490	33.8	3 469	479	13.8	10 384	5 666	54.6	3 501	1 255	35.8
1985	28 485	8 926	31.3	3 680	447	12.2	10 041	5 342	53.2	3 641	1 264	34.7
1986	28 871	8 983	31.1	3 742	403	10.8	10 175	5 473	53.8	3 714	1 431	38.5
1987	29 362	9 520	32.4	3 681	439	11.9	10 701	5 789	54.1	3 977	1 471	37.0
1988	29 849	9 356	31.3	3 722	421	11.3	10 794	5 601	51.9	4 095	1 509	36.8
1989	30 332	9 302	30.7	3 750	443	11.8	11 190	5 530	49.4	4 180	1 471	35.2
1990	30 806	9 837	31.9	3 569	448	12.6	11 866	6 005	50.6	4 244	1 491	35.1
1991	31 312	10 242	32.7	3 631	399	11.0	11 959	6 557	54.8	4 505	1 590	35.3
1992	32 411	10 827	33.4	3 777	490	13.0	12 591	6 799	54.0	4 410	1 569	35.6
1993	32 910	10 877	33.1	3 715	458	12.3	13 132	6 955	53.0	4 608	1 541	33.4
1994	33 353	10 196	30.6	3 842	336	8.7	12 926	6 489	50.2	4 649	1 617	34.8
1995	33 740	9 872	29.3	3 713	314	8.5	13 604	6 553	48.2	4 756	1 551	32.6
1996	34 110	9 694	28.4	3 851	352	9.1	13 193	6 123	46.4	4 989	1 606	32.2
1997	34 458	9 116	26.5	3 921	312	8.0	13 218	5 654	42.8	5 316	1 645	31.0
1998	34 877	9 091	26.1	3 979	290	7.3	13 156	5 629	42.8	5 390	1 752	32.5
1999	35 373	8 360	23.6	4 144	294	7.1	12 644	5 179	41.0	5 619	1 552	27.6
HISPANIC												
1973	10 795	2 366	21.9	1 876	239	12.7	1 534	881	57.4	526	157	29.9
1974	11 201	2 575	23.0	1 926	278	14.4	1 723	915	53.1	617	201	32.6
1975	11 117	2 991	26.9	1 896	335	17.7	1 842	1 053	57.2	645	236	36.6
1976	11 269	2 783	24.7	1 978	312	15.8	1 766	1 000	56.6	716	266	37.2
1977	12 046	2 700	22.4	2 104	280	13.3	1 901	1 077	56.7	797	237	29.8
1978	12 079	2 607	21.6	2 089	248	11.9	1 817	1 024	56.4	886	264	29.8
1979	13 371	2 921	21.8	2 282	298	13.1	2 058	1 053	51.2	991	286	28.8
1980	13 600	3 491	25.7	2 365	363	15.3	2 421	1 319	54.5	970	312	32.2
1981	14 021	3 713	26.5	2 414	366	15.1	2 622	1 465	55.9	1 005	313	31.1
1982	14 385	4 301	29.9	2 448	465	19.0	2 664	1 601	60.1	1 018	358	35.1
1983	16 544	4 633	28.0	2 752	437	17.7	3 032	1 670	55.1	1 364	457	33.5
1984	16 916	4 806	28.4	2 824	469	16.6	3 139	1 764	56.2	1 481	545	36.8
1985	18 075	5 236	29.0	2 962	505	17.0	3 561	1 983	55.7	1 602	532	33.2
1986	18 758	5 117	27.3	3 118	518	16.6	3 631	1 921	52.9	1 685	553	32.8
1987	19 395	5 422	28.0	3 196	556	17.4	3 678	2 045	55.6	1 933	598	31.0
1988	20 064	5 357	26.7	3 398	547	16.1	3 734	2 052	55.0	1 864	597	32.0
1989	20 746	5 430	26.2	3 395	549	16.2	3 763	1 902	50.6	2 045	634	31.0
1990	21 405	6 006	28.1	3 454	605	17.5	3 993	2 115	53.0	2 254	774	34.3
1991	22 068	6 339	28.7	3 532	674	19.1	4 326	2 282	52.7	2 145	667	31.1
1992	25 646	7 592	29.6	3 940	743	18.8	4 806	2 474	51.5	2 577	881	34.2
1993	26 559	8 126	30.6	4 038	770	19.1	5 333	2 837	53.2	2 717	972	35.8
1994	27 442	8 416	30.7	4 236	827	19.5	5 328	2 920	54.8	2 798	926	33.1
1995	28 344	8 574	30.3	4 247	803	18.9	5 785	3 053	52.8	2 947	1 092	37.0
1996	29 614	8 697	29.4	4 520	815	18.0	5 641	3 020	53.5	2 985	1 066	35.7
1997	30 637	8 308	27.1	4 804	836	17.4	5 718	2 911	50.9	2 976	1 017	34.2
1998	31 515	8 070	25.6	4 945	775	15.7	6 074	2 837	46.7	3 218	1 097	34.1
1999	32 669	7 439	22.8	5 133	728	14.2	6 113	2 488	40.7	3 207	991	30.9

1. These numbers and rates refer to families rather than persons; data on persons were not available.

Table 2-5. Poverty Status of Persons by Sex and Age

(Thousands of persons, percent of population.)

Year	Poverty status of persons by sex				Poverty status of persons by age					
	Males below poverty level		Females below poverty level		Children under 18 below poverty level		Persons 18 to 64 years old below poverty level		Persons 65 years and older below poverty level	
	Number (thousands)	Poverty rate	Number (thousands)	Poverty rate	Number (thousands)	Poverty rate	Number (thousands)	Poverty rate	Number (thousands)	Poverty rate
1959	. . .	. . .	. . .	. . .	17 552	27.3	16 457	17.0	5 481	35.2
1966	12 225	13.0	16 265	16.3	12 389	17.6	11 007	10.5	5 114	28.5
1967	11 813	12.5	15 951	15.8	11 656	16.6	10 725	10.0	5 388	29.5
1968	10 793	11.3	14 578	14.3	10 954	15.6	9 803	9.0	4 632	25.0
1969	10 292	10.6	13 978	13.6	9 691	14.0	9 669	8.7	4 787	25.3
1970	10 879	11.1	14 632	14.0	10 440	15.1	10 187	9.0	4 793	24.6
1971	10 708	10.8	14 841	14.1	10 551	15.3	10 735	9.3	4 273	21.6
1972	10 190	10.2	14 258	13.4	10 284	15.1	10 438	8.8	3 738	18.6
1973	9 642	9.6	13 316	12.5	9 642	14.4	9 977	8.3	3 354	16.3
1974	10 313	10.2	13 881	12.9	10 156	15.4	10 132	8.3	3 085	14.6
1975	10 908	10.7	14 970	13.8	11 104	17.1	11 456	9.2	3 317	15.3
1976	10 373	10.1	14 603	13.4	10 273	16.0	11 389	9.0	3 313	15.0
1977	10 340	10.0	14 381	13.0	10 288	16.2	11 316	8.8	3 177	14.1
1978	10 017	9.6	14 480	13.0	9 931	15.9	11 332	8.7	3 233	14.0
1979	10 535	10.0	14 810	13.2	10 377	16.4	12 014	8.9	3 682	15.2
1980	12 207	11.2	17 065	14.7	11 543	18.3	13 858	10.1	3 871	15.7
1981	13 360	12.1	18 462	15.8	12 505	20.0	15 464	11.1	3 853	15.3
1982	14 842	13.4	19 556	16.5	13 647	21.9	17 000	12.0	3 751	14.6
1983	15 182	13.5	20 084	16.8	13 911	22.3	17 767	12.4	3 625	13.8
1984	14 537	12.8	19 163	15.9	13 420	21.5	16 952	11.7	3 330	12.4
1985	14 140	12.3	18 923	15.6	13 010	20.7	16 598	11.3	3 456	12.6
1986	13 721	11.8	18 649	15.2	12 876	20.5	16 017	10.8	3 477	12.4
1987	14 029	12.0	18 518	15.0	12 843	20.3	15 815	10.6	3 563	12.5
1988	13 599	11.5	18 146	14.5	12 455	19.5	15 809	10.5	3 481	12.0
1989	13 366	11.2	18 162	14.4	12 590	19.6	15 575	10.2	3 363	11.4
1990	14 211	11.7	19 373	15.2	13 431	20.6	16 496	10.7	3 658	12.2
1991	15 082	12.3	20 626	16.0	14 341	21.8	17 585	11.4	3 781	12.4
1992	16 222	12.9	21 792	16.6	15 294	22.3	18 793	11.9	3 928	12.9
1993	16 900	13.3	22 365	16.9	15 727	22.7	19 781	12.4	3 755	12.2
1994	16 316	12.8	21 744	16.3	15 289	21.8	19 107	11.9	3 663	11.7
1995	15 683	12.2	20 742	15.4	14 665	20.8	18 442	11.4	3 318	10.5
1996	15 611	12.0	20 918	15.4	14 463	20.5	18 638	11.4	3 428	10.8
1997	15 187	11.6	20 387	14.9	14 113	19.9	18 084	10.9	3 376	10.5
1998	14 714	11.1	19 764	14.3	13 467	18.9	17 624	10.5	3 386	10.5
1999	13 813	10.3	18 445	13.2	12 109	16.9	16 982	10.0	3 167	9.7

Table 2-6. Poverty Status of Persons Inside and Outside Metropolitan Areas, and Persons In and Near Poverty

(Thousands of persons, percent of population.)

| Year | Inside metropolitan areas | | | | | | Outside metropolitan areas | | Total in and near poverty (income below 1.25 times the poverty level) | | Near-poor (income between 1 and 1.25 times poverty level) | |
| | Number (thousands) | Poverty rate | Central city | | Outside central city | | Number (thousands) | Poverty rate | Number (thousands) | Percent | Number (thousands) | Percent |
			Number (thousands)	Poverty rate	Number (thousands)	Poverty rate						
1959	17 019	15.3	10 437	18.3	6 582	12.2	21 747	33.2	54 942	31.1	15 452	8.7
1960	...	...	...	...	...	...	...	...	54 560	30.4	14 709	8.2
1961	...	...	...	...	...	...	...	...	54 280	30.0	14 652	8.1
1962	...	...	...	...	...	...	...	...	53 119	28.8	14 494	7.9
1963	...	...	...	...	...	...	...	...	50 778	27.1	14 342	7.7
1964	...	...	...	...	...	...	...	...	49 819	26.3	13 764	7.3
1965	...	...	...	...	...	...	...	...	46 163	24.1	12 978	6.8
1966	...	...	...	...	...	...	...	...	41 267	21.3	12 757	6.6
1967	13 832	10.9	8 649	15.0	5 183	7.5	13 936	20.2	39 206	20.0	11 437	5.8
1968	12 871	10.0	7 754	13.4	5 117	7.3	12 518	18.0	35 905	18.2	10 516	5.3
1969	13 084	9.5	7 993	12.7	5 091	6.8	11 063	17.9	34 665	17.4	10 518	5.3
1970	13 317	10.2	8 118	14.2	5 199	7.1	12 103	16.9	35 624	17.6	10 204	5.0
1971	14 561	10.4	8 912	14.2	5 649	7.2	10 999	17.2	36 501	17.8	10 942	5.3
1972	14 508	10.3	9 179	14.7	5 329	6.8	9 952	15.3	34 653	16.8	10 193	4.9
1973	13 759	9.7	8 594	14.0	5 165	6.4	9 214	14.0	32 828	15.8	9 855	4.7
1974	13 851	9.7	8 373	13.7	5 477	6.7	9 519	14.2	33 666	16.1	10 296	4.9
1975	15 348	10.8	9 090	15.0	6 259	7.6	10 529	15.4	37 182	17.6	11 305	5.4
1976	15 229	10.7	9 482	15.8	5 747	6.9	9 746	14.0	35 509	16.7	10 534	5.0
1977	14 859	10.4	9 203	15.4	5 657	6.8	9 861	13.9	35 659	16.7	10 939	5.1
1978	15 090	10.4	9 285	15.4	5 805	6.8	9 407	13.5	34 155	15.8	9 658	4.5
1979	16 135	10.7	9 720	15.7	6 415	7.2	9 937	13.8	36 616	16.4	10 544	4.7
1980	18 021	11.9	10 644	17.2	7 377	8.2	11 251	15.4	40 658	18.1	11 386	5.1
1981	19 347	12.6	11 231	18.0	8 116	8.9	12 475	17.0	43 748	19.3	11 926	5.3
1982	21 247	13.7	12 696	19.9	8 551	9.3	13 152	17.8	46 520	20.3	12 122	5.3
1983	21 750	13.8	12 872	19.8	8 878	9.6	13 516	18.3	47 150	20.3	11 847	5.1
1984	...	...	...	...	...	...	...	...	45 288	19.4	11 588	5.0
1985	23 275	12.7	14 177	19.0	9 097	8.4	9 789	18.3	44 166	18.7	11 102	4.7
1986	22 657	12.3	13 295	18.0	9 362	8.4	9 712	18.1	43 486	18.2	11 116	4.7
1987	23 054	12.3	13 697	18.3	9 357	8.3	9 167	17.0	43 032	17.9	10 811	4.5
1988	23 059	12.2	13 615	18.1	9 444	8.3	8 686	16.0	42 551	17.5	10 806	4.4
1989	22 917	12.0	13 592	18.1	9 326	8.0	8 611	15.7	42 653	17.3	11 125	4.5
1990	24 510	12.7	14 254	19.0	10 255	8.7	9 075	16.3	44 837	18.0	11 252	4.5
1991	26 827	13.7	15 314	20.2	11 513	9.6	8 881	16.1	47 527	18.9	11 819	4.7
1992	28 380	14.2	16 346	20.9	12 034	9.9	9 634	16.9	50 592	19.7	12 578	4.9
1993	29 615	14.6	16 805	21.5	12 810	10.3	9 650	17.2	51 801	20.0	12 536	4.8
1994	29 610	14.2	16 098	20.9	13 511	10.3	8 449	16.0	50 401	19.3	12 342	4.7
1995	28 342	13.4	16 269	20.6	12 072	9.1	8 083	15.6	48 761	18.5	12 336	4.7
1996	28 211	13.2	15 645	19.6	12 566	9.4	8 318	15.9	49 310	18.5	12 781	4.8
1997	27 273	12.6	15 018	18.8	12 255	9.0	8 301	15.9	47 853	17.8	12 279	4.6
1998	26 997	12.3	14 921	18.5	12 076	8.7	7 479	14.4	46 036	17.0	11 560	4.3
1999	24 816	11.2	13 123	16.4	11 693	8.3	7 442	14.3	44 286	16.2	12 028	4.4

Table 2-7. Poor Persons 16 Years and Over by Work Experience

(Thousands of persons, percent of total poor persons.)

Year	Total number of poor persons	Worked		Worked year-round, full-time		Worked less than year-round or full-time		Did not work	
		Number	Percent of total poor	Number	Percent of total poor	Number	Percent of total poor	Number	Percent of total poor
1978	16 914	6 599	39.0	1 309	7.7	5 290	31.3	10 315	61.0
1979	16 803	6 601	39.3	1 394	8.3	5 207	31.0	10 202	60.7
1980	18 892	7 674	40.6	1 644	8.7	6 030	31.9	11 218	59.4
1981	20 571	8 524	41.4	1 881	9.1	6 643	32.3	12 047	58.6
1982	22 100	9 013	40.8	1 999	9.0	7 014	31.7	13 087	59.2
1983	22 741	9 329	41.0	2 064	9.1	7 265	31.9	13 412	59.0
1984	21 541	8 999	41.8	2 076	9.6	6 923	32.1	12 542	58.2
1985	21 243	9 008	42.4	1 972	9.3	7 036	33.1	12 235	57.6
1986	20 688	8 743	42.3	2 007	9.7	6 736	32.6	11 945	57.7
1987	20 546	8 258	40.2	1 821	8.9	6 437	31.3	12 288	59.8
1988	20 323	8 363	41.2	1 929	9.5	6 434	31.7	11 960	58.8
1989	19 952	8 376	42.0	1 908	9.6	6 468	32.4	11 576	58.0
1990	21 242	8 716	41.0	2 076	9.8	6 640	31.3	12 526	59.0
1991	22 530	9 208	40.9	2 103	9.3	7 105	31.5	13 322	59.1
1992	23 951	9 739	40.6	2 211	9.2	7 528	31.4	14 212	59.3
1993	24 832	10 144	40.8	2 408	9.7	7 736	31.2	14 688	59.1
1994	24 108	9 829	40.8	2 520	10.5	7 309	30.3	14 279	59.2
1995	23 077	9 484	41.1	2 418	10.5	7 066	30.6	13 593	58.9
1996	23 472	9 586	40.8	2 263	9.6	7 323	31.2	13 886	59.2
1997	22 754	9 444	41.5	2 345	10.3	7 099	31.2	13 310	58.5
1998	22 255	9 133	41.0	2 804	12.6	6 329	28.4	13 122	59.0
1999	21 382	9 113	42.6	2 499	11.7	6 614	30.9	12 269	57.4

Table 2-8. Median Household Income and Poverty Rate for Persons, Based on Alternative Definitions of Income

Year	Definition 1: Money income excluding capital gains (current official measure)				Definition 4: Money income before taxes and transfers, plus health insurance supplements			
	Median income (1999 dollars)	Poverty rate (percent)		Gini coefficient	Median income (1999 dollars)	Poverty rate (percent)		Gini coefficient
		Official threshold	CPI-U-X1 threshold			Official threshold	CPI-U-X1 threshold	
1979	37 059	11.7	10.6	0.403	36 528	18.8	17.8	0.460
1980	35 850	13.0	11.5	0.401	34 648	20.1	19.0	0.462
1981	35 269	14.0	12.2	0.404	33 856	21.1	19.8	0.466
1982	35 152	15.0	13.2	0.409	33 391	22.0	20.6	0.475
1983	35 157	15.2	13.7	0.412	33 812	21.8	20.6	0.478
1984	35 942	14.4	12.8	0.413	34 813	20.8	19.5	0.477
1985	36 019	14.0	12.5	0.418	34 390	20.4	19.1	0.486
1986	36 568	13.6	12.2	0.423	35 379	19.9	18.7	0.505
1987	37 845	13.4	12.0	0.424	36 802	19.7	18.7	0.488
1988	38 220	13.0	11.7	0.425	36 954	19.7	18.6	0.489
1989	38 341	12.8	11.4	0.429	37 283	19.4	18.3	0.492
1990	38 837	13.5	12.1	0.426	37 787	19.9	18.8	0.487
1991	38 168	14.2	12.7	0.425	36 593	21.1	20.0	0.490
1992	36 850	14.8	13.4	0.430	35 218	22.1	20.9	0.497
1993	36 379	15.1	13.7	0.448	34 672	22.6	21.4	0.514
1994	36 270	14.5	13.2	0.450	35 043	22.0	20.8	0.515
1995	37 251	13.8	12.3	0.444	35 877	21.1	19.9	0.509
1996	37 686	13.7	12.2	0.447	36 500	20.8	19.5	0.511
1997	38 411	13.3	11.8	0.448	37 343	20.3	19.1	0.513
1998	39 744	12.7	11.3	0.446	38 505	19.3	18.1	0.509
1999	40 816	11.8	10.6	0.445	39 791	18.5	17.4	0.508

Year	Definition 14: Income after all taxes and transfers				Definition 15: Income after all taxes and transfers, plus net imputed return on equity in own home			
	Median income (1999 dollars)	Poverty rate (percent)		Gini coefficient	Median income (1999 dollars)	Poverty rate (percent)		Gini coefficient
		Official threshold	CPI-U-X1 threshold			Official threshold	CPI-U-X1 threshold	
1979	33 977	8.9	7.9	0.359	36 222	7.5	6.7	0.352
1980	32 828	10.1	8.6	0.354	36 192	8.2	7.0	0.347
1981	32 052	11.5	9.8	0.358	37 499	8.7	7.3	0.350
1982	32 306	12.3	10.6	0.366	36 668	9.9	8.5	0.359
1983	32 801	12.7	11.0	0.374	36 471	10.4	9.0	0.368
1984	33 355	12.0	10.4	0.378	37 364	9.9	8.6	0.372
1985	35 044	11.7	10.1	0.385	36 999	9.9	8.6	0.381
1986	33 908	11.3	9.8	0.409	37 423	10.1	8.6	0.404
1987	35 310	11.0	9.5	0.382	37 996	9.7	8.3	0.380
1988	35 700	10.8	9.5	0.385	38 890	9.4	8.2	0.384
1989	35 624	10.4	8.9	0.389	38 828	9.1	7.7	0.387
1990	36 159	10.9	9.5	0.382	39 072	9.8	8.5	0.381
1991	35 455	11.4	9.9	0.380	37 851	10.3	8.9	0.379
1992	34 773	11.9	10.5	0.385	37 354	10.7	9.5	0.381
1993	34 879	12.1	10.7	0.398	36 990	11.2	9.8	0.395
1994	35 471	11.1	9.8	0.400	37 644	10.0	8.8	0.395
1995	36 409	10.3	9.0	0.394	38 544	9.4	8.1	0.388
1996	36 653	10.2	8.9	0.398	38 608	9.3	8.1	0.392
1997	37 223	10.0	8.8	0.403	39 053	9.2	8.0	0.397
1998	38 505	9.5	8.2	0.405	40 176	10.0	7.6	0.399
1999	39 264	8.8	7.6	0.409	41 100	8.1	6.9	0.402

See Notes for explanation of alternative definitions and thresholds, and of the Gini coefficient.

Table 2-9. Median Income and Poverty Rate by State

State	Median household income (1999 dollars)							Poverty rate						
	1994	1995	1996	1997	1998	1999	Standard error [1], 1999	1994	1995	1996	1997	1998	1999	Standard error [1], 1999
United States	36 270	37 251	37 686	38 411	39 744	40 816	192	14.5	13.8	13.7	13.3	12.7	11.8	0.20
Alabama	30 573	28 413	32 175	33 153	37 067	36 213	1 185	16.4	20.1	14.0	15.7	14.5	15.1	1.74
Alaska	51 000	52 422	56 042	49 818	51 812	51 509	2 198	10.2	7.1	8.2	8.8	9.4	7.6	1.32
Arizona	35 178	33 739	33 593	33 984	37 909	37 119	1 206	15.9	16.1	20.5	17.2	16.6	12.0	1.48
Arkansas	28 739	28 219	28 800	27 156	28 276	29 762	1 062	15.3	14.9	17.2	19.7	14.7	14.7	1.73
California	39 718	40 457	41 211	41 203	41 838	43 744	697	17.9	16.7	16.9	16.6	15.4	13.8	0.69
Colorado	42 530	44 499	43 482	44 876	47 628	48 346	1 490	9.0	8.8	10.6	8.2	9.2	8.3	1.32
Connecticut	46 199	43 993	44 723	45 657	47 535	50 798	2 333	10.8	9.7	11.7	8.6	9.5	7.1	1.43
Delaware	40 327	38 182	41 739	44 669	42 374	46 839	2 318	8.3	10.3	8.6	9.6	10.3	10.4	1.67
District of Columbia	33 855	33 613	33 942	33 071	34 171	38 686	1 625	21.2	22.2	24.1	21.8	22.3	14.9	2.02
Florida	32 931	32 517	32 535	33 688	35 680	35 876	641	14.9	16.2	14.2	14.3	13.1	12.4	0.85
Georgia	35 374	37 276	34 505	38 056	39 519	39 433	1 382	14.0	12.1	14.8	14.5	13.5	12.9	1.45
Hawaii	47 501	46 844	44 354	42 490	41 729	44 373	1 750	8.7	10.3	12.1	13.9	10.9	10.9	1.70
Idaho	35 451	35 721	36 855	34 674	37 490	35 906	1 405	12.0	14.5	11.9	14.7	13.0	13.9	1.64
Illinois	39 437	41 618	41 999	42 852	44 132	46 392	1 029	12.4	12.4	12.1	11.2	10.1	9.9	0.88
Indiana	31 317	36 496	37 320	40 367	40 608	40 929	1 721	13.7	9.6	7.5	8.8	9.4	6.7	1.24
Iowa	37 186	38 829	35 262	35 067	37 837	41 238	1 125	10.7	12.2	9.6	9.6	9.1	7.5	1.34
Kansas	31 838	33 168	34 600	37 857	37 522	37 476	2 123	14.9	10.8	11.2	9.7	9.6	12.2	1.66
Kentucky	29 897	32 588	34 417	34 723	37 053	33 901	1 497	18.5	14.7	17.0	15.9	13.5	12.1	1.62
Louisiana	28 864	30 553	32 133	34 524	32 436	32 695	1 255	25.7	19.7	20.5	16.3	19.1	19.2	1.89
Maine	34 080	37 013	36 841	34 018	36 427	38 932	1 328	9.4	11.2	11.2	10.1	10.4	10.6	1.70
Maryland	44 065	44 865	46 713	48 459	51 121	52 310	2 212	10.7	10.1	10.3	8.4	7.2	7.3	1.38
Massachusetts	45 528	42 168	41 936	43 620	43 280	44 192	2 088	9.7	11.0	10.1	12.2	8.7	11.7	1.19
Michigan	39 665	39 820	41 650	40 214	42 745	46 238	1 031	14.1	12.2	11.2	10.3	11.0	9.7	0.91
Minnesota	37 821	41 467	43 525	44 182	48 984	47 240	1 565	11.7	9.2	9.8	9.6	10.3	7.2	1.27
Mississippi	28 554	29 011	28 326	29 582	29 763	32 540	1 402	19.9	23.5	20.6	16.7	17.6	16.1	1.80
Missouri	33 938	38 070	36 383	37 942	41 089	41 466	1 231	15.6	9.4	9.5	11.8	9.8	11.6	1.63
Montana	31 062	30 343	30 457	30 322	32 274	31 244	961	11.5	15.3	17.0	15.6	16.6	15.6	1.75
Nebraska	35 741	35 997	36 117	36 011	37 217	38 787	1 380	8.8	9.6	10.2	9.8	12.3	10.9	1.60
Nevada	40 325	39 446	40 923	40 331	40 634	41 680	1 880	11.1	11.1	8.1	11.0	10.6	11.3	1.54
New Hampshire	39 621	42 821	41 843	42 556	45 951	46 167	1 963	7.7	5.3	6.4	9.1	9.8	7.7	1.50
New Jersey	47 529	48 017	50 403	49 846	50 926	49 930	1 390	9.2	7.8	9.2	9.3	8.6	7.8	0.87
New Mexico	30 245	28 413	26 637	31 229	32 240	32 475	1 761	21.1	25.3	25.5	21.2	20.4	20.7	1.95
New York	35 859	36 105	37 599	37 159	38 220	40 058	882	17.0	16.5	16.7	16.5	16.7	14.1	0.78
North Carolina	33 853	34 959	37 802	37 202	36 630	37 340	1 016	14.2	12.6	12.2	11.4	14.0	13.5	1.23
North Dakota	31 789	31 799	33 416	32 864	30 973	32 877	1 349	10.4	12.0	11.0	13.6	15.1	13.0	1.75
Ohio	35 810	38 197	36 176	37 507	39 785	39 617	986	14.1	11.5	12.7	11.0	11.2	12.0	0.99
Oklahoma	30 342	28 763	29 133	32 543	34 472	32 919	1 559	16.7	17.1	16.6	13.7	14.1	12.7	1.60
Oregon	35 361	39 763	37 686	38 663	39 930	40 713	1 242	11.8	11.2	11.8	11.6	15.0	12.6	1.70
Pennsylvania	36 047	37 741	37 057	38 943	39 877	37 995	1 207	12.5	12.2	11.6	11.2	11.3	9.4	0.85
Rhode Island	35 892	38 654	39 273	36 119	41 585	42 936	2 012	10.3	10.6	11.0	12.7	11.6	9.9	1.68
South Carolina	33 552	31 780	36 808	35 564	34 002	36 563	1 746	13.8	19.9	13.0	13.1	13.7	11.7	1.69
South Dakota	33 425	32 334	31 351	30 823	33 510	35 982	917	14.5	14.5	11.8	16.5	10.8	7.7	1.34
Tennessee	32 195	31 719	32 694	31 800	34 844	36 536	1 326	14.6	15.5	15.9	14.3	13.4	11.9	1.62
Texas	34 573	35 024	35 117	36 408	36 573	38 978	1 025	19.1	17.4	16.6	16.7	15.1	15.0	0.90
Utah	40 150	39 879	39 328	44 401	45 277	46 094	1 631	8.0	8.4	7.7	8.9	9.0	5.7	1.06
Vermont	40 247	36 976	34 358	36 385	40 242	41 630	1 422	7.6	10.3	12.6	9.3	9.9	9.7	1.65
Virginia	42 321	39 597	41 635	44 590	44 312	45 750	1 787	10.7	10.2	12.3	12.7	8.8	7.9	1.28
Washington	37 696	38 882	38 943	46 256	48 468	45 639	2 027	11.7	12.5	11.9	9.2	8.9	9.5	1.52
West Virginia	26 490	27 198	26 808	28 533	27 294	29 433	1 140	18.6	16.7	18.5	16.4	17.8	15.7	1.75
Wisconsin	39 782	44 771	42 474	41 100	42 240	45 825	1 883	9.0	8.5	8.8	8.2	8.8	8.6	1.36
Wyoming	37 255	34 467	32 867	34 693	36 029	37 395	1 298	9.3	12.2	11.9	13.5	10.6	11.6	1.63

1. See Notes for an explanation of standard errors.

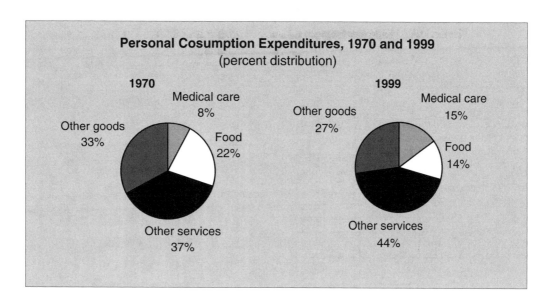

Personal Cosumption Expenditures, 1970 and 1999
(percent distribution)

- The amount of money devoted to medical care, expressed as a percentage of Personal Consumption Expenditure, doubled from 1970 to 1999. It should be noted, however, that these medical care payments include medical care payments made by government and private insurance, as well as direct consumer payments. The share of PCE attributed to other services also grew, while the shares of food and other goods fell.

- Total wage and salary payments rose at an 8.4 percent annual rate from 1971 to 1999; the service industries were the leading sector with a 10.2 percent rate, while manufacturing trailed with a growth rate of 5.6 percent.

- Personal saving was 2.2 percent of disposable personal income in 1999, the lowest rate since the 1930s. For a discussion of the statistical and economic significance of recent low and negative measured saving rates, see "Current Issues in Economic Measurement" in the 1999 edition of this book.

- Adjusted for inflation, disposable personal income rose at a 3.1 percent annual rate from 1971 to 1999, while personal consumption expenditures rose at a 3.3 percent rate. With population rising at a rate of 1.0 percent, the increase in real per capita income was 2.1 percent per year.

Table 3-1. Personal Income by Source

(Billions of dollars, monthly data are at seasonally adjusted annual rates.)

Year and month	Total	Wage and salary disbursements							Other labor income
		Total	Private industries					Government	
			Total	Goods-producing industries		Distributive industries	Service industries		
				Total	Manufacturing				
1970	841.1	551.5	434.3	203.7	158.4	131.2	99.4	117.1	41.9
1971	905.1	583.9	457.4	209.1	160.5	140.4	107.9	126.5	48.0
1972	994.3	638.7	501.2	228.2	175.6	153.3	119.7	137.4	55.3
1973	1 113.4	708.7	560.0	255.9	196.6	170.3	133.9	148.7	62.8
1974	1 225.6	772.6	611.8	276.5	211.8	186.8	148.6	160.9	73.3
1975	1 331.7	814.6	638.6	277.1	211.6	198.1	163.4	176.0	87.6
1976	1 475.4	899.5	710.8	309.7	238.0	219.5	181.6	188.6	105.3
1977	1 637.1	993.9	791.6	346.1	266.7	242.7	202.8	202.3	125.3
1978	1 848.3	1 120.7	901.2	392.6	300.1	274.9	233.7	219.6	143.4
1979	2 081.5	1 255.8	1 018.7	442.3	335.2	308.5	267.8	237.1	162.6
1980	2 323.9	1 377.5	1 116.2	472.3	356.2	336.7	307.2	261.3	185.4
1981	2 599.4	1 517.2	1 231.7	514.5	387.6	368.5	348.6	285.6	204.8
1982	2 768.4	1 593.4	1 286.1	514.6	385.7	385.9	385.6	307.3	222.8
1983	2 946.9	1 684.7	1 359.8	527.7	400.7	405.7	426.4	325.0	238.6
1984	3 274.8	1 854.6	1 507.0	586.1	445.4	445.2	475.6	347.6	262.1
1985	3 515.0	1 995.4	1 621.7	620.2	468.5	476.5	524.9	373.8	282.3
1986	3 712.4	2 114.4	1 717.8	636.8	480.7	501.6	579.3	396.6	298.4
1987	3 962.5	2 270.2	1 848.0	660.1	496.9	535.4	652.4	422.2	319.1
1988	4 272.1	2 452.7	2 001.8	706.7	529.9	575.1	720.1	450.9	336.5
1989	4 599.8	2 596.8	2 117.1	732.2	547.9	606.5	778.5	479.7	360.5
1990	4 903.2	2 754.6	2 237.9	754.4	561.4	633.6	849.9	516.7	390.0
1991	5 085.4	2 824.2	2 278.6	746.3	562.5	646.3	886.0	545.6	415.6
1992	5 390.4	2 982.6	2 414.9	765.7	583.5	680.2	969.0	567.7	449.5
1993	5 610.0	3 085.2	2 500.3	780.6	592.4	697.3	1 022.4	584.9	482.8
1994	5 888.0	3 236.7	2 632.8	824.0	620.3	738.4	1 070.4	603.9	507.5
1995	6 200.9	3 424.7	2 802.0	863.6	647.5	782.1	1 156.3	622.7	497.0
1996	6 547.4	3 626.5	2 985.5	908.2	673.7	822.4	1 254.9	641.0	490.0
1997	6 937.0	3 888.9	3 224.7	975.1	718.4	879.6	1 369.9	664.3	475.4
1998	7 391.0	4 190.7	3 498.0	1 038.6	756.6	949.1	1 510.3	692.7	485.5
1999	7 789.6	4 470.0	3 745.6	1 089.2	782.4	1 020.3	1 636.0	724.4	501.0
1996									
January	6 352.5	3 499.8	2 868.4	871.4	648.4	794.2	1 202.8	631.4	490.5
February	6 413.2	3 541.6	2 906.9	887.3	660.6	804.9	1 214.7	634.7	489.9
March	6 449.7	3 559.8	2 923.1	887.6	659.1	811.3	1 224.2	636.8	489.5
April	6 472.0	3 574.7	2 936.8	897.2	667.8	809.3	1 230.3	637.9	489.2
May	6 506.8	3 597.2	2 957.2	902.5	670.7	814.9	1 239.8	640.0	489.1
June	6 549.5	3 631.1	2 991.0	909.3	674.8	825.7	1 255.9	640.1	489.1
July	6 563.5	3 632.1	2 990.7	912.9	677.5	821.0	1 256.8	641.4	489.3
August	6 595.9	3 657.6	3 014.4	917.9	680.2	828.6	1 267.9	643.1	489.6
September	6 631.9	3 682.2	3 037.4	921.9	682.8	835.4	1 280.1	644.8	490.0
October	6 643.4	3 688.4	3 042.5	923.7	683.0	835.1	1 283.7	645.9	490.4
November	6 676.4	3 713.1	3 065.8	929.7	686.9	840.6	1 295.5	647.3	491.3
December	6 713.8	3 740.3	3 091.7	936.4	692.9	847.8	1 307.5	648.6	492.5
1997									
January	6 754.8	3 758.6	3 103.4	944.8	698.6	848.6	1 310.0	655.2	486.1
February	6 792.1	3 791.8	3 134.5	951.0	701.3	855.9	1 327.5	657.4	482.7
March	6 830.4	3 817.9	3 159.8	958.3	706.3	864.6	1 336.9	658.1	479.4
April	6 850.2	3 828.9	3 169.1	961.0	708.8	865.8	1 342.3	659.8	477.1
May	6 877.5	3 847.1	3 186.6	965.2	710.4	869.3	1 352.1	661.0	475.0
June	6 909.5	3 867.1	3 204.3	968.2	712.9	872.8	1 363.4	662.8	473.4
July	6 937.4	3 885.8	3 220.8	972.9	716.1	877.7	1 370.3	665.0	472.3
August	6 982.4	3 921.4	3 255.0	981.2	722.3	888.7	1 385.0	666.5	471.6
September	7 016.0	3 939.7	3 271.7	985.7	724.8	892.7	1 393.3	668.0	471.3
October	7 058.0	3 969.9	3 299.2	996.2	733.7	898.6	1 404.4	670.7	470.7
November	7 103.1	4 011.1	3 338.5	1 004.7	740.1	910.8	1 423.0	672.6	471.7
December	7 132.7	4 026.8	3 352.8	1 012.4	745.0	909.5	1 431.0	674.0	473.5
1998									
January	7 186.5	4 057.9	3 378.9	1 018.4	746.3	918.2	1 442.4	679.0	477.9
February	7 233.7	4 089.0	3 406.7	1 021.8	748.8	926.1	1 458.8	682.3	480.1
March	7 272.0	4 107.8	3 423.9	1 025.1	751.4	927.9	1 471.0	683.9	481.9
April	7 299.3	4 125.5	3 439.3	1 028.4	752.3	931.9	1 479.0	686.2	482.5
May	7 344.2	4 160.3	3 471.1	1 033.5	755.7	942.4	1 495.2	689.1	483.8
June	7 375.0	4 174.4	3 483.3	1 033.3	753.6	944.2	1 505.8	691.2	485.0
July	7 410.8	4 196.4	3 503.1	1 032.3	749.6	951.1	1 519.7	693.3	486.3
August	7 451.5	4 233.9	3 536.8	1 045.8	760.1	959.0	1 532.0	697.2	487.5
September	7 473.0	4 248.3	3 548.7	1 050.7	765.1	963.3	1 534.7	699.6	488.6
October	7 508.1	4 273.2	3 571.4	1 053.6	764.2	967.7	1 550.1	701.7	489.6
November	7 575.2	4 302.5	3 598.9	1 057.6	765.2	977.5	1 563.8	703.7	490.8
December	7 562.6	4 318.9	3 613.8	1 063.1	766.8	979.8	1 571.0	705.1	492.2
1999									
January	7 595.3	4 340.7	3 627.7	1 062.2	766.1	984.7	1 580.8	712.9	493.8
February	7 632.1	4 370.1	3 654.5	1 067.3	768.1	995.8	1 591.5	715.5	495.1
March	7 656.9	4 382.1	3 664.6	1 069.7	770.1	995.9	1 599.0	717.4	496.4
April	7 690.1	4 407.8	3 689.1	1 076.2	773.2	1 004.5	1 608.4	718.7	497.4
May	7 716.0	4 428.6	3 708.5	1 081.0	777.0	1 007.9	1 619.7	720.1	498.7
June	7 783.0	4 454.8	3 732.5	1 087.7	782.0	1 017.2	1 627.6	722.3	500.0
July	7 797.4	4 484.8	3 760.1	1 094.8	787.0	1 024.6	1 640.7	724.8	501.4
August	7 841.1	4 508.5	3 780.8	1 095.6	788.0	1 031.7	1 653.5	727.7	502.8
September	7 847.0	4 527.7	3 797.8	1 103.0	792.1	1 033.4	1 661.3	729.9	504.3
October	7 945.7	4 559.6	3 827.4	1 110.7	797.5	1 041.7	1 675.0	732.2	505.8
November	7 977.0	4 572.6	3 838.2	1 109.6	793.4	1 046.5	1 682.1	734.4	507.4
December	7 994.3	4 602.7	3 865.9	1 113.2	794.3	1 060.1	1 692.6	736.9	509.0

Table 3-1. Personal Income by Source—*Continued*

(Billions of dollars, monthly data are at seasonally adjusted annual rates.)

Year and month	Proprietors' income [1]			Rental Income of persons [2]	Personal dividend income	Personal interest income	Transfer payments to persons				Less: personal contributions for social insurance
	Total	Farm	Nonfarm				Total	Social Security and Medicare	Unemployment insurance benefits	Other transfers	
1970	79.8	14.3	65.5	20.3	24.3	71.5	74.3	38.5	4.0	31.9	22.5
1971	86.1	14.9	71.2	21.2	25.0	77.5	88.2	44.5	5.8	38.0	24.7
1972	97.7	18.8	78.9	21.6	26.8	84.2	98.0	49.6	5.7	42.7	28.0
1973	115.2	30.7	84.5	23.1	29.9	97.6	111.9	60.4	4.4	47.1	35.7
1974	115.5	25.2	90.3	23.0	33.2	116.1	132.3	70.1	6.8	55.4	40.5
1975	121.6	23.5	98.1	22.0	32.9	128.0	167.5	81.4	17.6	68.5	42.6
1976	134.3	18.7	115.6	21.5	39.0	140.5	182.3	92.9	15.8	73.7	46.9
1977	148.3	17.5	130.8	20.4	44.7	161.9	194.6	104.9	12.7	77.0	52.0
1978	170.1	21.5	148.5	22.4	50.7	191.3	209.3	116.2	9.7	83.4	59.7
1979	183.7	23.7	160.0	24.5	57.4	233.5	234.2	131.8	9.8	92.6	70.2
1980	177.6	13.1	164.5	31.3	64.0	286.4	279.0	154.2	16.1	108.8	77.2
1981	186.2	20.3	165.9	39.6	73.6	352.7	317.2	182.0	15.9	119.4	92.1
1982	179.9	14.4	165.4	39.6	76.1	401.6	354.2	204.5	25.2	124.4	99.1
1983	195.5	7.2	188.3	36.9	83.5	431.6	382.2	221.7	26.3	134.3	106.1
1984	247.5	21.6	225.9	39.5	90.8	505.3	393.4	235.7	15.9	141.9	118.4
1985	267.0	21.5	245.5	39.1	97.5	546.4	420.9	253.4	15.7	151.8	133.6
1986	278.6	23.0	255.6	32.2	106.1	579.2	449.0	269.2	16.3	163.5	145.6
1987	303.9	29.0	274.8	35.8	112.1	609.7	468.6	282.9	14.5	171.2	156.8
1988	338.8	26.0	312.7	44.1	129.4	650.5	496.9	300.5	13.2	183.3	176.8
1989	361.8	32.2	329.6	40.5	154.8	736.5	540.4	325.2	14.3	200.9	191.6
1990	381.0	31.1	349.9	49.1	165.4	772.4	594.4	352.1	18.0	224.3	203.7
1991	384.2	26.4	357.8	56.4	178.3	771.8	669.9	382.4	26.6	260.9	215.1
1992	434.3	32.7	401.7	63.3	185.3	750.1	751.7	414.0	38.9	298.9	226.6
1993	461.8	30.1	431.7	90.9	203.0	725.5	798.6	444.4	34.1	320.1	237.8
1994	476.6	31.9	444.6	110.3	234.7	742.4	833.9	473.0	23.6	337.2	254.1
1995	497.7	22.2	475.5	117.9	254.0	792.5	885.9	508.0	21.5	356.5	268.8
1996	544.7	34.3	510.5	129.7	297.4	810.6	928.8	537.6	22.1	369.1	280.4
1997	581.2	29.7	551.5	128.3	334.9	864.0	962.2	565.8	19.9	376.5	297.9
1998	620.7	25.4	595.2	135.4	351.1	940.8	983.0	578.0	19.5	385.4	316.2
1999	663.5	25.3	638.2	143.4	370.3	963.7	1 016.2	588.0	20.3	407.9	338.5
1996											
January	516.2	29.6	486.6	127.7	280.1	796.2	914.6	524.6	23.5	366.5	272.6
February	526.8	31.0	495.7	128.6	286.6	796.8	918.1	528.4	22.9	366.9	275.2
March	534.7	32.6	502.1	129.1	291.1	798.6	923.3	533.4	22.4	367.5	276.3
April	539.3	35.1	504.2	128.8	289.1	803.0	925.2	533.3	23.3	368.6	277.2
May	549.3	36.5	512.9	129.0	289.3	805.9	925.5	534.7	21.9	368.9	278.5
June	551.1	37.4	513.7	129.3	292.8	808.8	928.1	536.8	21.9	369.4	280.7
July	553.7	38.6	515.1	129.7	297.5	811.5	930.5	538.7	22.0	369.8	280.7
August	551.8	38.2	513.6	130.1	302.7	814.6	931.8	540.6	20.9	370.3	282.3
September	554.8	37.0	517.8	130.5	307.0	817.8	933.4	541.2	21.6	370.6	283.8
October	552.9	32.7	520.2	131.0	308.5	821.2	935.1	542.9	21.7	370.5	284.1
November	552.3	31.4	520.9	131.4	310.7	824.6	938.7	547.0	21.0	370.7	285.7
December	553.8	30.9	522.9	131.8	313.6	828.2	941.0	549.2	21.8	370.0	287.4
1997											
January	566.1	31.1	535.0	130.9	317.4	830.1	955.6	560.5	20.8	374.3	289.9
February	570.9	30.5	540.3	130.4	321.0	834.4	952.9	557.1	20.7	375.2	292.1
March	573.0	30.1	542.9	129.9	324.8	839.8	959.3	562.5	20.6	376.2	293.7
April	573.3	29.8	543.5	129.4	328.1	847.9	959.8	563.5	20.5	375.8	294.4
May	575.6	29.6	546.0	128.9	331.5	854.2	960.1	565.4	19.7	375.1	295.5
June	579.2	29.5	549.7	128.4	334.9	860.3	962.9	566.2	20.1	376.7	296.7
July	583.4	29.9	553.6	127.7	337.6	865.2	963.0	567.2	19.4	376.3	297.7
August	584.6	29.8	554.8	127.3	340.3	871.7	965.3	569.7	18.8	376.8	299.9
September	589.9	29.6	560.3	127.0	343.0	878.9	967.1	569.2	20.0	378.0	300.9
October	594.0	29.6	564.5	126.8	345.2	887.4	966.7	570.0	18.8	377.9	302.7
November	589.9	29.0	561.0	126.6	347.0	895.1	966.9	569.2	19.4	378.2	305.2
December	594.0	28.1	565.9	126.6	348.1	902.7	967.0	569.1	19.8	378.1	305.9
1998											
January	601.3	26.3	575.1	125.8	348.1	910.1	974.2	575.5	18.8	379.9	308.9
February	605.4	25.2	580.2	126.5	348.4	917.7	977.1	576.8	19.2	381.1	310.5
March	611.8	24.4	587.5	127.8	348.8	925.3	980.0	578.8	19.5	381.6	311.5
April	610.8	23.9	586.8	130.8	349.1	934.3	978.7	577.4	18.8	382.5	312.4
May	611.6	23.3	588.3	132.8	349.3	940.9	980.0	577.8	19.2	383.0	314.4
June	617.4	22.6	594.8	134.8	349.7	946.5	982.2	578.1	19.3	384.8	315.1
July	621.2	21.5	599.8	137.3	350.1	952.1	983.9	579.2	20.1	384.6	316.4
August	617.9	21.1	596.8	138.9	350.8	955.7	985.4	579.0	20.5	386.0	318.6
September	619.5	21.0	598.5	140.1	352.1	955.8	988.0	580.4	19.7	387.9	319.4
October	630.8	23.7	607.1	140.8	354.1	953.3	987.2	578.3	18.9	390.0	320.9
November	661.6	50.3	611.3	147.5	355.7	950.3	989.5	577.9	20.3	391.3	322.7
December	638.8	22.1	616.7	142.3	357.3	947.2	989.8	577.4	20.1	392.3	323.8
1999											
January	639.6	24.0	615.5	144.2	359.0	945.2	1 002.5	583.0	20.4	399.0	329.5
February	644.3	26.2	618.1	145.3	360.7	944.7	1 003.5	582.9	20.3	400.3	331.6
March	648.4	24.7	623.7	145.2	362.6	945.5	1 009.1	584.5	20.6	404.0	332.4
April	653.8	25.6	628.2	145.2	364.7	947.5	1 008.0	585.4	19.2	403.4	334.2
May	649.2	22.3	626.9	144.3	366.8	950.8	1 013.3	585.8	21.9	405.6	335.7
June	678.2	39.1	639.1	147.6	368.9	955.6	1 015.3	587.0	20.7	407.7	337.5
July	659.2	17.6	641.6	141.7	371.2	963.2	1 015.4	588.1	19.4	407.9	339.5
August	665.0	16.0	649.0	141.2	373.5	969.4	1 021.7	589.9	21.0	410.8	341.1
September	655.1	13.0	642.0	127.0	375.8	975.8	1 023.8	591.0	20.2	412.7	342.4
October	688.9	39.7	649.2	146.5	378.0	984.4	1 027.0	593.1	20.5	413.4	344.6
November	698.8	39.6	659.1	148.0	380.2	989.5	1 026.0	591.3	20.3	414.4	345.5
December	681.2	15.8	665.5	144.1	382.4	993.1	1 029.2	593.9	19.6	415.7	347.5

1. Includes inventory valuation and capital consumption adjustments.
2. Includes capital consumption adjustment.

Table 3-2. Disposition of Personal Income

(Billions of dollars, except as noted; monthly data are at seasonally adjusted annual rates.)

Year and month	Total personal income	Less: Personal tax and nontax payments	Equals: Disposable personal income	Less: Personal outlays — Total	Personal consumption expenditures	Interest paid by persons	Personal transfer payments to the rest of the world	Equals: Personal saving — Billions of dollars	Percent of disposable personal income	Disposable personal income — Total, chained (1996) dollars	Per capita (dollars) — Current dollars	Per capita (dollars) — Chained (1996) dollars	Population (thousands)
1970	841.1	104.6	736.5	667.0	648.9	16.8	1.3	69.5	9.4	2 630.0	3 591	12 823	205 089
1971	905.1	103.4	801.7	721.6	702.4	17.8	1.3	80.1	10.0	2 745.3	3 860	13 218	207 692
1972	994.3	125.6	868.6	791.7	770.7	19.6	1.4	76.9	8.9	2 874.3	4 138	13 692	209 924
1973	1 113.4	134.5	979.0	876.5	852.5	22.4	1.5	102.5	10.5	3 072.3	4 619	14 496	211 939
1974	1 225.6	153.3	1 072.3	957.9	932.4	24.2	1.3	114.3	10.7	3 051.9	5 013	14 268	213 898
1975	1 331.7	150.3	1 181.4	1 056.2	1 030.3	24.5	1.3	125.2	10.6	3 108.5	5 470	14 393	215 981
1976	1 475.4	175.5	1 299.9	1 177.8	1 149.8	26.6	1.3	122.1	9.4	3 243.5	5 960	14 873	218 086
1977	1 637.1	201.2	1 436.0	1 310.4	1 278.4	30.7	1.3	125.6	8.7	3 360.7	6 519	15 256	220 289
1978	1 848.3	233.5	1 614.8	1 469.4	1 430.4	37.5	1.5	145.4	9.0	3 527.5	7 253	15 845	222 629
1979	2 081.5	273.3	1 808.2	1 642.4	1 596.3	44.5	1.6	165.8	9.2	3 628.6	8 033	16 120	225 106
1980	2 323.9	304.2	2 019.8	1 814.1	1 762.9	49.4	1.8	205.6	10.2	3 658.0	8 869	16 063	227 726
1981	2 599.4	351.5	2 247.9	2 004.2	1 944.2	54.6	5.5	243.7	10.8	3 741.1	9 773	16 265	230 008
1982	2 768.4	361.6	2 406.8	2 144.6	2 079.3	58.8	6.5	262.2	10.9	3 791.7	10 364	16 328	232 218
1983	2 946.9	360.9	2 586.0	2 358.2	2 286.4	65.0	6.8	227.8	8.8	3 906.9	11 036	16 673	234 332
1984	3 274.8	387.2	2 887.6	2 581.1	2 498.4	75.0	7.7	306.5	10.6	4 207.6	12 215	17 799	236 394
1985	3 515.0	428.5	3 086.5	2 803.9	2 712.6	83.2	8.1	282.6	9.2	4 347.8	12 941	18 229	238 506
1986	3 712.4	449.9	3 262.5	2 994.7	2 895.2	90.6	9.0	267.8	8.2	4 486.6	13 555	18 641	240 682
1987	3 962.5	503.0	3 459.5	3 206.7	3 105.3	91.5	9.9	252.8	7.3	4 582.5	14 246	18 870	242 842
1988	4 272.1	519.7	3 752.4	3 460.1	3 356.6	92.9	10.6	292.3	7.8	4 784.1	15 312	19 522	245 061
1989	4 599.8	583.5	4 016.3	3 714.4	3 596.7	106.4	11.4	301.8	7.5	4 906.5	16 235	19 833	247 387
1990	4 903.2	609.6	4 293.6	3 959.3	3 831.5	115.8	12.0	334.3	7.8	5 014.2	17 176	20 058	249 981
1991	5 085.4	610.5	4 474.8	4 103.2	3 971.2	118.9	13.0	371.7	8.3	5 033.0	17 710	19 919	252 677
1992	5 390.4	635.8	4 754.6	4 340.9	4 209.7	118.7	12.5	413.7	8.7	5 189.3	18 616	20 318	255 403
1993	5 610.0	674.6	4 935.3	4 584.5	4 454.7	115.4	14.4	350.8	7.1	5 261.3	19 121	20 384	258 107
1994	5 888.0	722.6	5 165.4	4 849.9	4 716.4	117.9	15.6	315.5	6.1	5 397.2	19 820	20 709	260 616
1995	6 200.9	778.3	5 422.6	5 120.2	4 969.0	134.7	16.5	302.4	5.6	5 539.1	20 613	21 055	263 073
1996	6 547.4	869.7	5 677.7	5 405.6	5 237.5	149.9	18.2	272.1	4.8	5 677.7	21 385	21 385	265 504
1997	6 937.0	968.8	5 968.2	5 715.3	5 529.3	164.8	21.2	252.9	4.2	5 854.5	22 262	21 838	268 087
1998	7 391.0	1 070.9	6 320.0	6 054.7	5 850.9	179.8	24.0	265.4	4.2	6 134.1	23 359	22 672	270 560
1999	7 789.6	1 152.0	6 637.7	6 490.1	6 268.7	194.8	26.6	147.6	2.2	6 331.0	24 314	23 191	272 996
1996													
January	6 352.5	819.4	5 533.1	5 251.6	5 090.9	143.3	17.4	281.5	5.1	5 593.4	20 930	21 158	264 369
February	6 413.2	832.6	5 580.6	5 303.3	5 141.8	144.2	17.4	277.3	5.0	5 629.4	21 096	21 280	264 535
March	6 449.7	840.2	5 609.5	5 321.7	5 158.8	145.5	17.4	287.8	5.1	5 643.3	21 190	21 318	264 723
April	6 472.0	896.4	5 575.6	5 372.1	5 207.7	146.4	18.0	203.5	3.7	5 594.0	21 046	21 116	264 921
May	6 506.8	855.3	5 651.5	5 389.1	5 223.1	148.1	18.0	262.4	4.6	5 661.3	21 316	21 353	265 130
June	6 549.5	865.7	5 683.8	5 390.4	5 223.2	149.2	18.0	293.4	5.2	5 692.7	21 420	21 454	265 351
July	6 563.5	868.7	5 694.8	5 408.6	5 239.9	150.4	18.2	286.2	5.0	5 691.9	21 442	21 431	265 588
August	6 595.9	877.4	5 718.5	5 438.2	5 268.2	151.7	18.2	280.3	4.9	5 710.8	21 511	21 482	265 836
September	6 631.9	885.8	5 746.1	5 454.3	5 282.8	153.3	18.2	291.8	5.1	5 726.3	21 596	21 521	266 079
October	6 643.4	890.1	5 753.3	5 487.9	5 314.8	153.7	19.3	265.4	4.6	5 715.0	21 604	21 460	266 311
November	6 676.4	898.0	5 778.4	5 507.7	5 332.9	155.5	19.3	270.7	4.7	5 727.9	21 681	21 492	266 515
December	6 713.8	906.3	5 807.5	5 542.3	5 365.9	157.1	19.3	265.2	4.6	5 746.8	21 777	21 549	266 687
1997													
January	6 754.8	926.1	5 828.7	5 587.9	5 410.2	157.5	20.3	240.7	4.1	5 755.4	21 837	21 562	266 924
February	6 792.1	936.0	5 856.0	5 612.6	5 433.3	159.0	20.3	243.4	4.2	5 767.5	21 925	21 593	267 099
March	6 830.4	943.1	5 887.3	5 627.0	5 446.3	160.4	20.3	260.2	4.4	5 792.6	22 026	21 671	267 293
April	6 850.2	946.8	5 903.4	5 644.3	5 461.8	162.1	20.4	259.1	4.4	5 802.2	22 069	21 691	267 498
May	6 877.5	954.8	5 922.7	5 637.4	5 454.1	162.9	20.4	285.3	4.8	5 822.2	22 124	21 748	267 709
June	6 909.5	963.1	5 946.5	5 680.5	5 496.4	163.7	20.4	265.9	4.5	5 839.3	22 194	21 794	267 933
July	6 937.4	969.6	5 967.8	5 746.9	5 560.8	164.8	21.2	220.9	3.7	5 853.1	22 253	21 825	268 180
August	6 982.4	980.1	6 002.3	5 764.1	5 576.6	166.3	21.2	238.2	4.0	5 882.1	22 360	21 912	268 437
September	7 016.0	986.9	6 029.0	5 780.0	5 590.2	168.6	21.2	249.0	4.1	5 896.5	22 439	21 946	268 681
October	7 058.0	996.0	6 062.0	5 809.5	5 616.5	170.2	22.9	252.5	4.2	5 919.9	22 543	22 015	268 904
November	7 103.1	1 008.2	6 094.9	5 833.5	5 640.2	170.4	22.9	261.4	4.3	5 950.4	22 649	22 112	269 099
December	7 132.7	1 014.8	6 117.9	5 859.9	5 665.0	172.0	22.9	258.1	4.2	5 972.2	22 719	22 178	269 284
1998													
January	7 186.5	1 028.3	6 158.2	5 874.0	5 678.5	173.0	22.6	284.1	4.6	6 008.8	22 854	22 300	269 458
February	7 233.7	1 038.3	6 195.3	5 910.1	5 713.5	174.0	22.6	285.3	4.6	6 042.9	22 978	22 413	269 618
March	7 272.0	1 040.9	6 231.1	5 943.6	5 745.9	175.1	22.6	287.5	4.6	6 076.7	23 096	22 523	269 793
April	7 299.3	1 044.8	6 254.5	5 963.2	5 763.4	175.8	24.1	291.2	4.7	6 087.9	23 166	22 549	269 982
May	7 344.2	1 058.0	6 286.3	6 021.5	5 820.5	176.9	24.1	264.7	4.2	6 111.2	23 267	22 619	270 183
June	7 375.0	1 066.5	6 308.5	6 053.8	5 850.3	179.4	24.1	254.7	4.0	6 131.8	23 330	22 677	270 398
July	7 410.8	1 073.6	6 337.2	6 067.0	5 862.0	180.8	24.3	270.2	4.3	6 146.9	23 416	22 713	270 636
August	7 451.5	1 086.9	6 364.6	6 099.4	5 893.3	181.8	24.3	265.2	4.2	6 165.1	23 495	22 759	270 885
September	7 473.0	1 091.6	6 381.5	6 132.2	5 924.9	183.0	24.3	249.3	3.9	6 180.5	23 537	22 796	271 124
October	7 508.1	1 098.0	6 410.0	6 167.7	5 957.7	184.9	25.1	242.3	3.8	6 195.5	23 623	22 832	271 350
November	7 575.2	1 108.5	6 466.7	6 187.3	5 975.9	186.2	25.1	279.4	4.3	6 245.5	23 814	22 999	271 552
December	7 562.6	1 115.9	6 446.7	6 236.4	6 024.5	186.8	25.1	210.3	3.3	6 216.6	23 724	22 877	271 743
1999													
January	7 595.3	1 106.9	6 488.4	6 262.6	6 049.1	187.9	25.6	225.8	3.5	6 240.4	23 862	22 950	271 914
February	7 632.1	1 116.5	6 515.6	6 304.5	6 089.3	189.6	25.6	211.1	3.2	6 264.4	23 949	23 025	272 065
March	7 656.9	1 116.1	6 540.8	6 363.9	6 147.5	190.8	25.6	176.9	2.7	6 286.3	24 027	23 092	272 230
April	7 690.1	1 121.1	6 569.0	6 405.2	6 187.3	191.2	26.7	163.9	2.5	6 280.8	24 114	23 056	272 413
May	7 716.0	1 132.9	6 583.1	6 419.8	6 200.4	192.7	26.7	163.4	2.5	6 294.3	24 148	23 089	272 613
June	7 783.0	1 146.1	6 636.9	6 473.3	6 251.8	194.8	26.7	163.6	2.5	6 344.7	24 326	23 255	272 832
July	7 797.4	1 159.1	6 638.3	6 499.6	6 277.4	195.5	26.6	138.7	2.1	6 331.3	24 310	23 185	273 071
August	7 841.1	1 154.3	6 686.8	6 547.4	6 323.4	197.4	26.6	139.4	2.1	6 366.4	24 465	23 293	273 318
September	7 847.0	1 178.6	6 668.3	6 583.0	6 358.9	197.5	26.6	85.3	1.3	6 327.6	24 377	23 131	273 556
October	7 945.7	1 185.6	6 760.0	6 625.5	6 399.3	198.6	27.6	134.5	2.0	6 403.8	24 691	23 390	273 782
November	7 977.0	1 195.4	6 781.6	6 660.9	6 433.2	200.2	27.6	120.7	1.8	6 420.7	24 752	23 435	273 984
December	7 994.3	1 210.9	6 783.4	6 735.7	6 506.3	201.8	27.6	47.7	0.7	6 412.0	24 741	23 387	274 174

Table 3-2. Disposition of Personal Income—*Continued*

(Billions of dollars, except as noted; monthly data are at seasonally adjusted annual rates.)

Year and month	Personal consumption expenditures											
	Current dollars				Chained (1996) dollars				Chain-type price indexes for personal consumption expenditures (1996=100)			
	Total	Durable goods	Nondurable goods	Services	Total	Durable goods	Nondurable goods	Services	Total	Durable goods	Nondurable goods	Services
1970	648.9	85.0	272.0	292.0	2 317.5	...	...	...	28.0	46.1	31.8	22.9
1971	702.4	96.9	285.5	320.0	2 405.2	...	...	...	29.2	47.8	32.8	24.2
1972	770.7	110.4	308.0	352.3	2 550.5	...	...	...	30.2	48.3	33.9	25.2
1973	852.5	123.5	343.1	385.9	2 675.9	...	...	...	31.9	49.0	36.6	26.4
1974	932.4	122.3	384.5	425.5	2 653.7	...	...	...	35.1	52.1	41.8	28.5
1975	1 030.3	133.5	420.7	476.1	2 710.9	...	...	...	38.0	56.8	45.1	30.8
1976	1 149.8	158.9	458.3	532.6	2 868.9	...	...	...	40.1	60.0	46.8	32.9
1977	1 278.4	181.2	497.2	600.0	2 992.1	...	...	...	42.7	62.6	49.6	35.5
1978	1 430.4	201.7	550.2	678.4	3 124.7	...	...	...	45.8	66.2	52.9	38.3
1979	1 596.3	214.4	624.4	757.4	3 203.2	...	...	...	49.8	70.6	58.5	41.4
1980	1 762.9	214.2	696.1	852.7	3 193.0	...	...	...	55.2	76.5	65.3	45.9
1981	1 944.2	231.3	758.9	954.0	3 236.0	...	...	...	60.1	81.6	70.4	50.6
1982	2 079.3	240.2	787.6	1 051.5	3 275.5	...	...	...	63.5	84.8	72.3	54.8
1983	2 286.4	281.2	831.2	1 174.0	3 454.3	...	...	...	66.2	86.4	73.9	58.3
1984	2 498.4	326.9	884.7	1 286.9	3 640.6	...	...	...	68.6	87.6	75.6	61.4
1985	2 712.6	363.3	928.8	1 420.6	3 820.9	...	...	...	71.0	88.6	77.3	64.4
1986	2 895.2	401.3	958.5	1 535.4	3 981.2	...	...	...	72.7	89.7	77.0	67.3
1987	3 105.3	419.7	1 015.3	1 670.3	4 113.4	455.2	1 274.5	2 379.3	75.5	92.2	79.7	70.2
1988	3 356.6	450.2	1 082.9	1 823.5	4 279.5	481.5	1 315.1	2 477.2	78.4	93.5	82.3	73.6
1989	3 596.7	467.8	1 165.4	1 963.5	4 393.7	491.7	1 351.0	2 546.0	81.9	95.1	86.3	77.1
1990	3 831.5	467.6	1 246.1	2 117.8	4 474.5	487.1	1 369.6	2 616.2	85.6	96.0	91.0	81.0
1991	3 971.2	443.0	1 278.8	2 249.4	4 466.6	454.9	1 364.0	2 651.8	88.9	97.4	93.8	84.8
1992	4 209.7	470.8	1 322.9	2 415.9	4 594.5	479.0	1 389.7	2 729.7	91.6	98.3	95.2	88.5
1993	4 454.7	513.4	1 375.2	2 566.1	4 748.9	518.3	1 430.3	2 802.5	93.8	99.1	96.2	91.6
1994	4 716.4	560.8	1 438.0	2 717.6	4 928.1	557.7	1 485.1	2 886.2	95.7	100.6	96.8	94.2
1995	4 969.0	589.7	1 497.3	2 882.0	5 075.6	583.5	1 529.0	2 963.4	97.9	101.1	97.9	97.3
1996	5 237.5	616.5	1 574.1	3 047.0	5 237.5	616.5	1 574.1	3 047.0	100.0	100.0	100.0	100.0
1997	5 529.3	642.5	1 641.6	3 245.2	5 423.9	657.3	1 619.9	3 147.0	101.9	97.8	101.3	103.1
1998	5 850.9	693.9	1 707.6	3 449.3	5 678.7	727.3	1 684.8	3 269.4	103.0	95.4	101.4	105.5
1999	6 268.7	761.3	1 845.5	3 661.9	5 978.8	817.8	1 779.4	3 390.8	104.9	93.1	103.7	108.0
1996												
January	5 073.3	622.2	1 497.6	2 953.5	5 146.4	593.5	1 545.6	3 007.6	98.9	100.9	98.8	98.6
February	5 114.8	642.4	1 508.3	2 964.1	5 186.7	608.5	1 557.6	3 020.6	99.1	100.7	99.0	98.9
March	5 136.4	632.4	1 514.6	2 989.4	5 189.9	603.3	1 558.5	3 028.3	99.4	100.7	99.4	99.1
April	5 189.9	649.3	1 538.3	3 002.3	5 224.9	621.9	1 567.9	3 035.1	99.7	100.4	100.0	99.4
May	5 210.4	653.3	1 540.3	3 016.8	5 232.1	626.3	1 569.7	3 036.0	99.8	100.0	100.1	99.7
June	5 196.6	639.4	1 535.2	3 021.9	5 231.4	613.0	1 572.0	3 046.4	99.8	100.0	99.9	99.8
July	5 231.0	638.9	1 540.4	3 051.8	5 237.2	611.9	1 572.6	3 052.7	100.1	99.8	100.0	100.1
August	5 242.0	647.6	1 540.2	3 054.1	5 261.1	622.7	1 579.0	3 059.4	100.1	99.7	99.9	100.4
September	5 254.4	641.1	1 550.2	3 063.1	5 264.6	619.6	1 584.1	3 060.8	100.4	99.8	100.2	100.6
October	5 292.0	652.8	1 563.8	3 075.4	5 279.5	626.1	1 592.2	3 061.2	100.7	99.6	100.6	100.9
November	5 309.4	651.0	1 567.4	3 090.9	5 286.3	624.6	1 593.2	3 068.5	100.9	99.4	100.9	101.2
December	5 338.4	649.4	1 573.6	3 115.4	5 309.7	626.4	1 596.4	3 086.9	101.1	99.0	101.2	101.4
1997												
January	5 410.2	637.4	1 623.7	3 149.1	5 342.1	644.5	1 602.3	3 095.5	101.3	98.9	101.3	101.7
February	5 433.3	631.1	1 627.3	3 174.9	5 351.2	636.8	1 605.0	3 109.4	101.5	99.1	101.4	102.1
March	5 446.3	636.8	1 629.4	3 180.1	5 358.7	643.2	1 609.4	3 106.3	101.6	99.0	101.2	102.4
April	5 461.8	625.3	1 628.2	3 208.2	5 368.2	635.8	1 606.4	3 125.7	101.7	98.3	101.4	102.6
May	5 454.1	614.5	1 620.6	3 218.9	5 361.5	626.8	1 601.9	3 132.0	101.7	98.0	101.2	102.8
June	5 496.4	633.3	1 633.0	3 230.1	5 397.4	647.0	1 616.3	3 134.1	101.8	97.9	101.0	103.1
July	5 560.8	653.3	1 646.8	3 260.8	5 454.0	669.2	1 629.5	3 156.0	102.0	97.6	101.1	103.3
August	5 576.6	654.8	1 654.5	3 267.3	5 464.9	673.7	1 633.0	3 159.2	102.0	97.2	101.3	103.4
September	5 590.2	649.0	1 658.2	3 283.1	5 467.3	668.6	1 632.7	3 166.6	102.3	97.0	101.6	103.7
October	5 616.5	647.1	1 656.8	3 312.5	5 484.8	668.1	1 630.9	3 186.0	102.4	96.8	101.6	104.0
November	5 640.2	662.8	1 660.3	3 317.2	5 506.5	686.1	1 635.3	3 186.4	102.4	96.6	101.5	104.1
December	5 665.0	664.9	1 659.9	3 340.1	5 530.0	688.6	1 636.0	3 206.5	102.4	96.5	101.5	104.2
1998												
January	5 678.5	670.7	1 665.1	3 342.7	5 540.8	695.5	1 641.7	3 205.0	102.5	96.4	101.4	104.3
February	5 713.5	670.9	1 673.5	3 369.0	5 573.0	696.7	1 653.0	3 224.5	102.5	96.3	101.2	104.5
March	5 745.9	669.8	1 678.8	3 397.3	5 603.5	696.9	1 663.8	3 243.8	102.5	96.1	100.9	104.7
April	5 763.4	675.1	1 683.0	3 405.3	5 609.8	701.6	1 667.0	3 242.6	102.7	96.2	101.0	105.0
May	5 820.5	695.1	1 696.3	3 429.1	5 658.4	725.8	1 676.4	3 258.9	102.9	95.7	101.2	105.2
June	5 850.3	697.6	1 705.0	3 447.7	5 686.4	730.6	1 685.5	3 273.1	102.9	95.4	101.2	105.3
July	5 862.0	680.1	1 713.7	3 468.2	5 685.9	711.5	1 692.0	3 283.6	103.1	95.6	101.3	105.6
August	5 893.3	692.4	1 716.3	3 484.5	5 708.7	725.5	1 691.0	3 294.2	103.2	95.4	101.5	105.8
September	5 924.9	705.1	1 723.8	3 496.1	5 738.4	742.9	1 699.5	3 299.3	103.3	94.9	101.4	106.0
October	5 957.7	715.8	1 733.5	3 508.5	5 758.3	756.9	1 705.0	3 301.0	103.5	94.5	101.7	106.3
November	5 975.9	720.1	1 744.1	3 511.7	5 771.5	764.5	1 716.6	3 296.1	103.5	94.2	101.6	106.6
December	6 024.5	734.4	1 758.1	3 532.0	5 809.5	778.6	1 726.3	3 311.2	103.7	94.3	101.9	106.7
1999												
January	6 049.1	715.0	1 777.1	3 557.0	5 817.9	759.2	1 738.6	3 324.7	104.0	94.2	102.2	107.0
February	6 089.3	733.4	1 788.4	3 567.5	5 854.5	781.6	1 751.5	3 328.3	104.0	93.8	102.1	107.2
March	6 147.5	753.3	1 793.7	3 600.5	5 908.4	807.2	1 755.5	3 354.3	104.1	93.3	102.2	107.3
April	6 187.3	760.7	1 815.0	3 611.6	5 915.8	813.3	1 753.1	3 358.6	104.6	93.5	103.5	107.5
May	6 200.4	741.8	1 827.8	3 630.8	5 928.4	794.6	1 767.7	3 373.1	104.6	93.3	103.4	107.6
June	6 251.8	766.4	1 833.2	3 652.1	5 976.6	823.6	1 774.2	3 388.6	104.6	93.1	103.3	107.8
July	6 277.4	758.2	1 842.0	3 677.3	5 987.1	815.3	1 777.3	3 402.9	104.9	93.0	103.7	108.1
August	6 323.4	768.9	1 860.7	3 693.9	6 020.4	828.3	1 789.0	3 412.8	105.0	92.8	104.0	108.2
September	6 358.9	774.7	1 877.3	3 706.8	6 033.9	834.8	1 791.9	3 417.6	105.4	92.8	104.8	108.5
October	6 399.3	778.2	1 891.1	3 730.0	6 062.1	840.0	1 801.6	3 431.2	105.6	92.6	105.0	108.7
November	6 433.2	786.9	1 899.3	3 747.0	6 090.8	850.6	1 810.9	3 441.2	105.6	92.5	104.9	108.9
December	6 506.3	797.6	1 940.2	3 768.4	6 150.0	864.8	1 841.7	3 456.8	105.8	92.2	105.4	109.0

Table 3-3. Personal Consumption Expenditures by Major Type of Product

(Billions of dollars, quarterly data are seasonally adjusted annual rates.)

Year and quarter	Total	Durable goods				Nondurable goods					
		Total	Motor vehicles and parts	Furniture and household equipment	Other	Total	Food	Clothing and shoes	Gasoline and oil	Fuel oil and coal	Other
1970	648.9	85.0	35.5	35.7	13.7	272.0	143.8	47.8	21.9	4.4	54.1
1971	702.4	96.9	44.5	37.8	14.6	285.5	149.7	51.7	23.2	4.6	56.4
1972	770.7	110.4	51.1	42.4	16.9	308.0	161.4	56.4	24.4	5.1	60.8
1973	852.5	123.5	56.1	47.9	19.5	343.1	179.6	62.5	28.1	6.3	66.6
1974	932.4	122.3	49.5	51.5	21.3	384.5	201.8	66.0	36.1	7.8	72.7
1975	1 030.3	133.5	54.8	54.5	24.2	420.7	223.2	70.8	39.7	8.4	78.5
1976	1 149.8	158.9	71.3	60.2	27.4	458.3	242.5	76.6	43.0	10.1	86.0
1977	1 278.4	181.2	83.5	67.2	30.5	497.2	262.7	84.1	46.9	11.1	92.4
1978	1 430.4	201.7	93.1	74.3	34.3	550.2	289.6	94.3	50.1	11.5	104.7
1979	1 596.3	214.4	93.5	82.7	38.2	624.4	324.7	101.2	66.2	14.4	118.0
1980	1 762.9	214.2	87.0	86.7	40.5	696.1	356.0	107.3	86.7	15.4	130.6
1981	1 944.2	231.3	95.8	92.1	43.4	758.9	383.5	117.2	97.9	15.8	144.5
1982	2 079.3	240.2	102.9	93.4	43.9	787.6	403.4	120.5	94.1	14.5	155.2
1983	2 286.4	281.2	126.9	106.6	47.7	831.2	423.8	130.9	93.1	13.6	169.8
1984	2 498.4	326.9	152.5	119.0	55.4	884.7	447.4	142.5	94.6	13.9	186.3
1985	2 712.6	363.3	175.7	128.5	59.0	928.8	467.6	152.1	97.2	13.6	198.2
1986	2 895.2	401.3	192.4	143.0	66.0	958.5	492.0	163.1	80.1	11.3	211.9
1987	3 105.3	419.7	193.1	153.4	73.2	1 015.3	515.3	174.4	85.4	11.2	229.1
1988	3 356.6	450.2	206.1	163.6	80.5	1 082.9	553.5	185.5	87.7	11.7	244.5
1989	3 596.7	467.8	211.4	171.4	84.9	1 165.4	591.9	198.9	97.0	11.9	265.7
1990	3 831.5	467.6	206.4	171.4	89.8	1 246.1	636.9	204.1	107.3	12.9	285.0
1991	3 971.2	443.0	182.8	171.5	88.7	1 278.8	657.6	208.7	102.5	12.4	297.8
1992	4 209.7	470.8	200.2	178.7	91.9	1 322.9	669.3	221.9	104.9	12.2	314.7
1993	4 454.7	513.4	222.1	192.4	98.9	1 375.2	697.9	231.1	106.6	12.9	326.8
1994	4 716.4	560.8	242.3	211.2	107.2	1 438.0	728.2	240.7	109.0	13.5	346.6
1995	4 969.0	589.7	249.3	225.0	115.4	1 497.3	755.8	247.8	113.3	14.1	366.4
1996	5 237.5	616.5	256.3	236.9	123.3	1 574.1	786.0	258.6	124.2	15.6	389.8
1997	5 529.3	642.5	264.2	248.9	129.4	1 641.6	812.2	271.7	128.1	15.1	414.5
1998	5 850.9	693.9	288.8	266.1	139.0	1 707.6	845.8	286.4	115.2	12.8	447.4
1999	6 268.7	761.3	320.7	288.5	152.0	1 845.5	897.8	307.0	128.3	14.4	498.0
1991											
1st quarter	3 904.6	439.4	180.5	169.3	89.6	1 267.8	649.7	205.6	106.2	12.8	293.5
2nd quarter	3 958.6	441.4	179.1	173.1	89.2	1 281.0	661.2	209.9	101.8	11.7	296.4
3rd quarter	3 998.2	448.9	187.3	173.2	88.4	1 284.9	661.8	210.9	100.7	12.6	299.1
4th quarter	4 023.6	442.5	184.5	170.3	87.7	1 281.5	657.6	208.3	101.2	12.3	302.2
1992											
1st quarter	4 123.1	459.0	193.7	175.6	89.7	1 305.2	667.1	216.1	101.2	11.5	309.4
2nd quarter	4 171.5	463.3	196.6	176.3	90.4	1 309.2	661.3	219.3	103.2	13.2	312.3
3rd quarter	4 225.7	474.2	201.4	179.6	93.3	1 326.0	667.1	224.3	106.7	11.9	316.1
4th quarter	4 318.3	486.6	209.2	183.2	94.2	1 351.4	681.9	227.7	108.4	12.2	321.1
1993											
1st quarter	4 350.6	487.6	206.3	185.9	95.4	1 355.7	686.9	226.1	108.1	12.4	322.2
2nd quarter	4 421.3	507.5	219.9	189.9	97.6	1 370.4	695.1	230.0	106.4	12.6	326.4
3rd quarter	4 488.2	520.8	225.1	194.7	101.0	1 379.6	701.4	232.5	104.7	13.3	327.7
4th quarter	4 558.7	537.9	237.3	199.1	101.6	1 395.0	708.3	235.6	107.1	13.1	331.0
1994											
1st quarter	4 613.8	546.2	241.4	202.1	102.7	1 409.7	714.6	237.2	105.7	14.5	337.7
2nd quarter	4 677.5	553.6	239.0	208.6	106.0	1 425.1	725.4	237.9	104.8	12.9	344.1
3rd quarter	4 753.0	563.2	240.2	214.3	108.8	1 449.9	733.1	241.5	111.5	13.8	350.1
4th quarter	4 821.3	580.0	248.8	219.9	111.3	1 467.2	739.6	246.3	113.8	13.0	354.6
1995											
1st quarter	4 868.6	578.2	245.0	220.4	112.9	1 475.8	745.5	244.5	113.9	13.2	358.7
2nd quarter	4 943.7	584.4	248.2	221.9	114.3	1 492.2	753.6	246.0	114.3	14.4	364.0
3rd quarter	5 005.2	596.2	252.3	227.0	116.9	1 502.6	758.8	249.3	112.7	14.2	367.6
4th quarter	5 058.4	600.0	251.7	231.0	117.3	1 518.5	765.3	251.2	112.2	14.6	375.3
1996											
1st quarter	5 130.5	606.4	256.3	230.4	119.7	1 539.6	773.9	253.0	117.7	16.1	378.9
2nd quarter	5 218.0	621.3	259.2	238.2	123.8	1 569.4	781.8	259.0	127.0	15.1	386.4
3rd quarter	5 263.7	616.7	255.4	237.7	123.6	1 578.8	788.8	259.3	123.3	15.0	392.3
4th quarter	5 337.9	621.5	254.2	241.2	126.1	1 608.4	799.3	263.0	128.6	16.0	401.6
1997											
1st quarter	5 429.9	635.1	264.5	243.1	127.5	1 626.8	806.9	266.6	132.0	15.3	405.9
2nd quarter	5 470.8	624.4	251.0	246.4	127.0	1 627.3	808.2	267.8	125.1	15.3	410.8
3rd quarter	5 575.9	652.4	270.1	251.4	130.9	1 653.1	817.4	274.8	127.3	15.1	418.6
4th quarter	5 640.6	658.3	271.0	254.9	132.4	1 659.0	816.2	277.6	128.1	14.6	422.5
1998											
1st quarter	5 712.6	670.5	275.2	260.2	135.0	1 672.5	825.4	282.3	119.5	12.8	432.4
2nd quarter	5 811.4	689.3	288.9	262.5	137.8	1 694.8	838.9	285.1	115.7	13.1	441.9
3rd quarter	5 893.4	692.5	283.5	268.3	140.7	1 717.9	851.5	286.5	114.0	13.0	452.9
4th quarter	5 986.0	723.4	307.7	273.2	142.6	1 745.2	867.2	291.7	111.8	12.3	462.3
1999											
1st quarter	6 095.3	733.9	307.6	279.4	146.9	1 786.4	878.1	301.1	110.7	12.9	483.5
2nd quarter	6 213.2	756.3	321.8	284.7	149.8	1 825.3	886.6	306.1	127.3	14.0	491.3
3rd quarter	6 319.9	767.2	323.2	291.0	153.0	1 860.0	900.4	308.7	133.4	15.1	502.4
4th quarter	6 446.2	787.6	330.3	298.8	158.5	1 910.2	926.1	311.9	142.0	15.6	514.6

Table 3-3. Personal Consumption Expenditures by Major Type of Product—*Continued*

(Billions of dollars, quarterly data are seasonally adjusted annual rates.)

Year and quarter	Services								
	Total	Housing	Household operation			Transportation	Medical care	Recreation	Other
			Total	Electricity and gas	Other household operation				
1970	292.0	94.0	37.9	15.3	22.6	23.7	50.4	15.1	70.9
1971	320.0	102.7	41.3	16.9	24.4	27.1	56.9	16.3	75.7
1972	352.3	112.1	45.7	18.8	26.9	29.8	63.9	17.6	83.3
1973	385.9	122.7	50.2	20.4	29.8	31.2	71.5	19.7	90.5
1974	425.5	134.1	56.0	24.0	32.0	33.3	80.4	22.5	99.1
1975	476.1	147.0	64.3	29.2	35.2	35.7	93.4	25.4	110.3
1976	532.6	161.5	73.1	33.2	40.0	41.3	106.5	28.4	121.7
1977	600.0	179.5	82.7	38.5	44.3	49.2	122.6	31.4	134.6
1978	678.4	201.7	92.1	43.0	49.1	53.5	140.0	34.5	156.7
1979	757.4	226.5	101.0	47.8	53.2	59.1	158.1	38.3	174.5
1980	852.7	255.1	114.2	57.5	56.7	64.7	181.2	42.8	194.6
1981	954.0	287.7	127.3	64.8	62.5	68.7	213.0	49.3	208.0
1982	1 051.5	313.0	143.0	74.2	68.8	70.9	239.3	54.9	230.4
1983	1 174.0	338.7	157.6	82.4	75.2	79.4	267.9	61.7	268.9
1984	1 286.9	370.3	169.8	86.5	83.3	90.0	294.6	67.9	294.4
1985	1 420.6	406.8	182.2	90.8	91.4	100.0	322.5	75.6	333.6
1986	1 535.4	442.0	188.9	89.2	99.7	107.3	346.8	81.5	368.9
1987	1 670.3	476.4	196.9	90.9	106.0	118.2	381.8	87.7	409.3
1988	1 823.5	511.9	208.4	96.3	112.2	129.9	429.9	99.0	444.4
1989	1 963.5	546.4	221.3	101.0	120.2	136.6	479.2	110.1	469.9
1990	2 117.8	585.6	227.6	101.0	126.5	141.8	540.6	120.8	501.5
1991	2 249.4	616.0	238.6	107.4	131.2	142.8	591.0	126.4	534.5
1992	2 415.9	641.3	248.3	108.9	139.4	155.0	652.6	139.1	579.5
1993	2 566.1	666.5	268.9	118.6	150.4	166.2	700.6	151.2	612.6
1994	2 717.6	704.7	284.0	119.8	164.2	180.9	737.3	160.0	650.7
1995	2 882.0	740.8	298.1	122.5	175.6	197.7	780.7	176.0	688.7
1996	3 047.0	772.5	317.3	128.7	188.5	214.2	814.4	191.1	737.5
1997	3 245.2	810.5	333.0	130.4	202.7	234.4	854.6	206.2	806.5
1998	3 449.3	858.2	345.6	128.5	217.1	244.5	898.6	218.7	883.7
1999	3 661.9	906.2	360.2	128.9	231.3	256.5	943.6	237.1	958.4
1991									
1st quarter	2 197.4	605.1	231.8	104.0	127.8	141.2	571.9	123.9	523.7
2nd quarter	2 236.2	612.6	241.1	110.7	130.4	141.8	582.7	125.3	532.7
3rd quarter	2 264.4	619.3	241.5	108.5	132.9	143.0	596.2	127.0	537.4
4th quarter	2 299.5	626.9	240.1	106.4	133.7	145.4	613.3	129.6	544.2
1992									
1st quarter	2 358.9	633.4	241.7	104.4	137.3	151.3	630.5	134.5	567.5
2nd quarter	2 399.1	638.5	248.9	108.4	140.5	154.1	646.3	137.7	573.5
3rd quarter	2 425.4	643.4	243.5	108.9	134.6	152.7	661.0	140.4	584.5
4th quarter	2 480.3	649.9	259.1	113.8	145.3	161.9	672.8	143.8	592.7
1993									
1st quarter	2 507.3	655.9	259.8	115.0	144.8	163.0	686.2	146.7	595.7
2nd quarter	2 543.4	662.5	264.0	115.3	148.7	164.8	695.7	149.7	606.8
3rd quarter	2 587.8	669.6	274.7	122.1	152.5	166.9	706.3	153.5	616.8
4th quarter	2 625.8	678.2	277.2	121.8	155.5	170.3	714.1	154.7	631.3
1994									
1st quarter	2 657.9	690.7	275.3	121.3	154.0	174.3	723.4	156.4	637.7
2nd quarter	2 698.8	700.1	287.5	123.3	164.2	179.1	732.3	158.5	641.3
3rd quarter	2 739.8	709.6	286.7	118.7	168.0	183.1	741.5	161.5	657.5
4th quarter	2 774.0	718.6	286.4	115.9	170.5	186.9	752.0	163.7	666.5
1995									
1st quarter	2 814.7	727.7	287.8	116.2	171.6	190.4	767.6	168.6	672.7
2nd quarter	2 867.1	736.9	295.7	121.8	173.9	195.5	776.2	174.5	688.3
3rd quarter	2 906.3	744.9	304.6	127.3	177.3	200.8	784.8	178.1	693.1
4th quarter	2 939.9	753.7	304.2	124.7	179.6	204.2	794.3	182.7	700.7
1996									
1st quarter	2 984.4	760.4	314.6	131.3	183.3	206.5	798.2	185.0	719.7
2nd quarter	3 027.4	768.1	318.3	130.0	188.4	211.7	810.7	189.1	729.5
3rd quarter	3 068.2	776.6	313.4	124.6	188.9	215.9	817.9	193.7	750.7
4th quarter	3 107.9	785.1	322.7	129.1	193.6	222.6	831.0	196.5	750.0
1997									
1st quarter	3 168.0	794.6	325.9	128.7	197.1	229.1	839.6	201.9	776.9
2nd quarter	3 219.1	805.0	329.0	128.8	200.2	232.9	850.0	205.4	796.8
3rd quarter	3 270.4	815.7	332.9	128.1	204.8	236.2	860.8	207.3	817.5
4th quarter	3 323.3	826.7	344.4	135.8	208.6	239.5	868.1	210.0	834.6
1998									
1st quarter	3 369.7	839.3	336.6	125.0	211.6	240.9	885.4	214.3	853.3
2nd quarter	3 427.4	852.2	346.7	131.8	214.9	244.0	893.9	216.4	874.3
3rd quarter	3 482.9	864.4	353.7	134.1	219.6	245.8	902.5	220.4	896.2
4th quarter	3 517.4	877.1	345.4	122.9	222.5	247.4	912.4	224.0	911.1
1999									
1st quarter	3 575.0	888.7	353.9	127.5	226.4	250.8	924.5	228.6	928.4
2nd quarter	3 631.5	900.8	357.2	127.4	229.7	254.7	935.9	234.8	948.0
3rd quarter	3 692.7	911.6	366.7	133.7	232.9	258.1	950.0	240.5	965.8
4th quarter	3 748.5	923.5	363.0	126.7	236.3	262.3	964.0	244.5	991.2

Table 3-4. Real Personal Consumption Expenditures by Major Type of Product

(Billions of chained [1996] dollars, quarterly data are at seasonally adjusted annual rates.)

Year and quarter	Total	Durable goods				Nondurable goods					
		Total	Motor vehicles and parts	Furniture and household equipment	Other	Total	Food	Clothing and shoes	Gasoline and oil	Fuel oil and coal	Other
1970	2 317.5	...	...	...	...	...	...	...	...	...	...
1971	2 405.2	...	...	...	...	...	...	...	...	...	...
1972	2 550.5	...	...	...	...	...	...	...	...	...	...
1973	2 675.9	...	...	...	...	...	...	...	...	...	...
1974	2 653.7	...	...	...	...	...	...	...	...	...	...
1975	2 710.9	...	...	...	...	...	...	...	...	...	...
1976	2 868.9	...	...	...	...	...	...	...	...	...	...
1977	2 992.1	...	...	...	...	...	...	...	...	...	...
1978	3 124.7	...	...	...	...	...	...	...	...	...	...
1979	3 203.2	...	...	...	...	...	...	...	...	...	...
1980	3 193.0	...	...	...	...	...	...	...	...	...	...
1981	3 236.0	...	...	...	...	...	...	...	...	...	...
1982	3 275.5	...	...	...	...	...	...	...	...	...	...
1983	3 454.3	...	...	...	...	...	...	...	...	...	...
1984	3 640.6	...	...	...	...	...	...	...	...	...	...
1985	3 820.9	...	...	...	...	...	...	...	...	...	...
1986	3 981.2	...	...	...	...	...	...	...	...	...	...
1987	4 113.4	455.2	242.4	133.3	88.9	1 274.5	664.6	182.4	112.8	14.2	303.4
1988	4 279.5	481.5	254.9	142.3	93.8	1 315.1	690.7	187.8	114.9	14.7	309.9
1989	4 393.7	491.7	253.9	149.9	95.7	1 351.0	703.5	198.6	116.4	14.4	319.9
1990	4 474.5	487.1	246.1	150.9	96.7	1 369.6	722.4	197.2	113.1	13.1	326.7
1991	4 466.6	454.9	211.8	152.7	92.6	1 364.0	721.4	197.8	109.4	12.9	325.1
1992	4 594.5	479.0	225.7	161.5	94.1	1 389.7	725.6	208.8	112.5	13.2	331.2
1993	4 748.9	518.3	242.2	177.4	100.7	1 430.3	745.1	218.5	115.4	14.0	338.5
1994	4 928.1	557.7	255.1	196.3	107.6	1 485.1	764.9	231.6	117.4	15.0	356.8
1995	5 075.6	583.5	253.4	215.4	115.0	1 529.0	777.0	244.3	120.2	15.7	372.0
1996	5 237.5	616.5	256.3	236.9	123.3	1 574.1	786.0	258.6	124.2	15.6	389.8
1997	5 423.9	657.3	264.8	261.9	130.8	1 619.9	794.5	271.6	128.1	15.0	410.8
1998	5 678.7	727.3	291.7	294.4	141.5	1 684.8	812.8	292.2	131.2	14.0	434.9
1999	5 978.8	817.8	323.0	338.7	157.3	1 779.4	845.9	318.5	134.2	15.5	466.0
1991											
1st quarter	4 437.5	452.6	210.8	149.7	94.5	1 358.9	718.0	196.9	108.9	12.4	325.7
2nd quarter	4 469.9	454.0	208.2	153.5	93.9	1 368.7	724.0	200.0	109.9	12.7	324.6
3rd quarter	4 484.3	460.2	216.1	154.5	91.8	1 369.4	724.5	199.2	109.8	13.8	324.8
4th quarter	4 474.8	452.8	211.9	152.8	90.1	1 358.9	719.2	195.3	109.1	12.9	325.3
1992											
1st quarter	4 544.8	468.7	221.6	157.5	92.1	1 381.2	726.8	203.5	110.8	12.6	329.7
2nd quarter	4 566.7	471.4	222.4	158.8	92.5	1 379.1	718.7	206.8	111.7	14.4	329.1
3rd quarter	4 600.5	482.1	225.9	162.9	95.5	1 388.1	721.3	211.1	113.5	12.8	330.7
4th quarter	4 665.9	493.8	233.1	166.7	96.4	1 410.3	735.6	213.8	113.8	13.2	335.4
1993											
1st quarter	4 674.9	495.4	228.6	170.8	97.6	1 410.2	738.6	212.6	113.4	13.3	333.9
2nd quarter	4 721.5	513.3	241.1	174.9	99.4	1 425.5	743.2	218.0	115.2	13.6	336.9
3rd quarter	4 776.9	524.7	244.0	180.0	102.7	1 438.1	747.9	220.2	116.8	14.6	339.8
4th quarter	4 822.3	539.9	255.0	184.1	103.2	1 447.4	750.8	223.3	116.3	14.5	343.6
1994											
1st quarter	4 866.6	546.9	258.2	187.1	103.9	1 465.3	756.0	227.6	116.6	15.9	349.9
2nd quarter	4 907.9	551.7	253.3	193.1	106.7	1 477.6	764.7	227.3	117.3	14.3	354.9
3rd quarter	4 944.5	557.7	251.4	198.6	108.8	1 490.9	767.2	232.2	117.6	15.2	359.3
4th quarter	4 993.6	574.3	257.5	206.4	111.2	1 506.5	771.6	239.2	118.3	14.5	363.2
1995											
1st quarter	5 011.6	570.4	250.7	207.7	112.5	1 514.3	773.4	240.1	119.5	14.8	366.8
2nd quarter	5 059.6	577.4	252.2	211.1	114.5	1 525.3	776.0	242.4	120.0	16.1	371.2
3rd quarter	5 099.2	590.7	256.4	218.1	116.6	1 531.7	778.0	246.3	120.0	15.7	371.9
4th quarter	5 132.1	595.7	254.4	224.6	116.7	1 544.6	780.6	248.4	121.5	16.3	378.1
1996											
1st quarter	5 174.3	601.7	257.0	226.1	118.7	1 553.9	784.5	250.7	121.9	16.6	380.2
2nd quarter	5 229.5	620.4	259.6	237.2	123.6	1 569.9	785.5	257.8	124.4	15.3	386.9
3rd quarter	5 254.3	618.1	255.2	238.7	124.1	1 578.6	785.3	261.6	124.5	15.5	391.7
4th quarter	5 291.9	625.7	253.4	245.5	126.7	1 593.9	788.5	264.3	125.9	14.9	400.4
1997											
1st quarter	5 350.7	641.5	262.9	250.5	128.1	1 605.6	794.0	267.1	126.6	14.2	403.7
2nd quarter	5 375.7	636.5	250.8	257.6	128.5	1 608.2	792.8	265.2	128.3	15.2	406.7
3rd quarter	5 462.1	670.5	271.8	266.5	132.3	1 631.7	797.8	275.0	128.7	15.4	414.8
4th quarter	5 507.1	680.9	273.7	273.2	134.3	1 634.1	793.2	279.1	128.9	15.1	418.1
1998											
1st quarter	5 572.4	696.4	278.3	281.9	136.6	1 652.8	798.3	287.0	129.4	13.6	424.9
2nd quarter	5 651.6	719.4	292.6	286.9	140.0	1 676.3	809.2	291.3	130.7	14.1	431.3
3rd quarter	5 711.0	726.7	284.9	299.1	143.6	1 694.2	816.8	292.0	132.2	14.3	439.2
4th quarter	5 779.8	766.7	311.1	309.9	146.0	1 716.0	827.0	298.7	132.2	14.0	444.2
1999											
1st quarter	5 860.2	782.7	311.0	320.9	151.5	1 748.5	832.7	313.3	132.5	15.0	455.6
2nd quarter	5 940.2	810.5	325.3	331.7	154.1	1 765.0	838.0	316.5	134.3	15.7	461.3
3rd quarter	6 013.8	826.2	324.9	343.9	158.9	1 786.1	846.7	322.1	133.6	16.0	468.5
4th quarter	6 101.0	851.8	330.9	358.2	164.9	1 818.1	866.0	322.1	136.2	15.3	478.7

Table 3-4. Real Personal Consumption Expenditures by Major Type of Product—*Continued*

(Billions of chained [1996] dollars, quarterly data are at seasonally adjusted annual rates.)

Year and quarter	Services								
	Total	Housing	Household operation			Transportation	Medical care	Recreation	Other
			Total	Electricity and gas	Other household operation				
1970	...	...	...	...	...	...	...	...	...
1971	...	...	...	...	...	...	...	...	...
1972	...	...	...	...	...	...	...	...	...
1973	...	...	...	...	...	...	...	...	...
1974	...	...	...	...	...	...	...	...	...
1975	...	...	...	...	...	...	...	...	...
1976	...	...	...	...	...	...	...	...	...
1977	...	...	...	...	...	...	...	...	...
1978	...	...	...	...	...	...	...	...	...
1979	...	...	...	...	...	...	...	...	...
1980	...	...	...	...	...	...	...	...	...
1981	...	...	...	...	...	...	...	...	...
1982	...	...	...	...	...	...	...	...	...
1983	...	...	...	...	...	...	...	...	...
1984	...	...	...	...	...	...	...	...	...
1985	...	...	...	...	...	...	...	...	...
1986	...	...	...	...	...	...	...	...	...
1987	2 379.3	644.8	238.0	106.9	130.9	164.6	631.0	120.2	578.7
1988	2 477.2	663.4	248.2	112.3	135.7	172.8	659.9	130.7	600.6
1989	2 546.0	679.9	257.2	114.7	142.3	174.6	678.5	139.2	614.7
1990	2 616.2	696.2	259.8	112.8	146.9	173.4	710.9	145.0	630.6
1991	2 651.8	709.8	262.9	116.3	146.4	164.7	734.4	144.5	636.1
1992	2 729.7	719.3	267.6	115.7	151.8	171.1	765.4	154.5	653.0
1993	2 802.5	728.1	282.3	122.2	160.0	176.6	775.4	163.0	677.6
1994	2 886.2	749.1	293.0	122.8	170.2	189.0	783.1	169.3	702.9
1995	2 963.4	763.7	304.0	125.3	178.7	201.0	797.7	181.7	715.3
1996	3 047.0	772.6	317.3	128.7	188.5	214.2	814.4	191.1	737.5
1997	3 147.0	787.2	327.4	127.5	199.9	226.4	835.4	200.0	770.4
1998	3 269.4	807.7	343.0	130.0	213.0	233.1	859.8	206.8	818.6
1999	3 390.8	828.3	358.0	130.9	226.9	241.2	881.7	217.8	863.1
1991									
1st quarter	2 629.6	703.5	257.4	112.7	144.6	165.4	724.9	143.9	635.1
2nd quarter	2 651.1	708.0	266.7	120.6	146.0	164.8	729.5	143.6	638.5
3rd quarter	2 658.3	712.5	265.7	117.8	147.7	163.9	736.7	144.3	635.6
4th quarter	2 668.3	715.0	261.8	114.3	147.4	164.6	746.5	146.2	635.1
1992									
1st quarter	2 698.9	716.7	262.7	112.2	150.5	167.2	755.7	151.5	646.4
2nd quarter	2 720.9	718.0	269.3	115.8	153.4	169.3	764.0	153.4	648.0
3rd quarter	2 734.1	720.0	261.9	115.6	146.2	173.8	769.7	155.2	655.0
4th quarter	2 765.0	722.5	276.3	119.2	157.0	174.0	772.3	158.0	662.6
1993									
1st quarter	2 772.7	723.7	276.3	120.7	155.5	173.5	774.2	160.1	665.6
2nd quarter	2 784.9	725.0	277.9	118.9	159.0	175.3	774.2	161.8	671.2
3rd quarter	2 816.0	729.4	286.9	124.9	161.9	177.4	776.3	165.0	681.2
4th quarter	2 836.4	734.2	288.3	124.4	163.8	180.3	776.8	164.9	692.1
1994									
1st quarter	2 855.4	741.9	284.9	124.0	160.8	183.8	778.5	166.0	701.0
2nd quarter	2 879.6	746.1	296.8	126.4	170.5	187.4	782.0	168.0	699.3
3rd quarter	2 896.8	752.1	295.3	121.7	173.6	190.7	784.3	170.8	703.8
4th quarter	2 912.9	756.5	294.9	119.2	175.7	194.2	787.7	172.2	707.6
1995									
1st quarter	2 927.3	759.8	293.9	118.8	175.1	196.7	791.1	176.1	709.9
2nd quarter	2 957.4	762.6	302.2	125.1	177.2	198.8	795.6	180.8	717.4
3rd quarter	2 977.0	764.9	310.5	130.3	180.3	202.5	799.8	183.4	715.8
4th quarter	2 992.0	767.6	309.3	127.2	182.1	206.0	804.5	186.7	717.9
1996									
1st quarter	3 018.8	768.7	317.6	132.8	184.9	210.2	804.1	187.6	730.6
2nd quarter	3 039.2	770.8	319.1	130.5	188.6	212.7	812.7	189.9	733.8
3rd quarter	3 057.7	773.6	312.3	123.8	188.5	215.3	816.3	192.7	747.4
4th quarter	3 072.2	777.0	320.1	127.9	192.2	218.5	824.6	194.0	738.0
1997									
1st quarter	3 103.7	781.1	319.6	124.6	195.0	223.6	825.9	198.1	755.3
2nd quarter	3 130.6	784.7	324.1	126.8	197.3	225.3	832.5	199.9	764.0
3rd quarter	3 160.6	789.1	327.7	125.9	201.9	227.8	839.3	200.0	776.5
4th quarter	3 193.0	793.9	338.4	132.9	205.5	228.8	844.0	202.0	785.9
1998									
1st quarter	3 224.5	800.0	333.9	125.5	208.4	230.4	855.2	204.3	800.2
2nd quarter	3 258.2	806.1	343.1	132.6	210.7	233.4	857.7	204.9	812.7
3rd quarter	3 292.4	810.3	351.3	136.2	215.2	233.7	861.5	207.9	827.4
4th quarter	3 302.8	814.4	343.6	125.8	217.6	235.1	864.8	210.2	833.9
1999									
1st quarter	3 335.8	820.4	351.9	130.3	221.5	237.3	870.5	212.9	842.2
2nd quarter	3 373.4	825.7	355.9	130.2	225.6	239.7	878.1	216.3	857.1
3rd quarter	3 411.1	830.7	364.7	135.5	229.1	242.7	885.6	220.1	867.0
4th quarter	3 443.0	836.5	359.3	127.7	231.2	245.0	892.8	222.2	886.1

CHAPTER 4: INDUSTRIAL PRODUCTION AND CAPACITY UTILIZATION

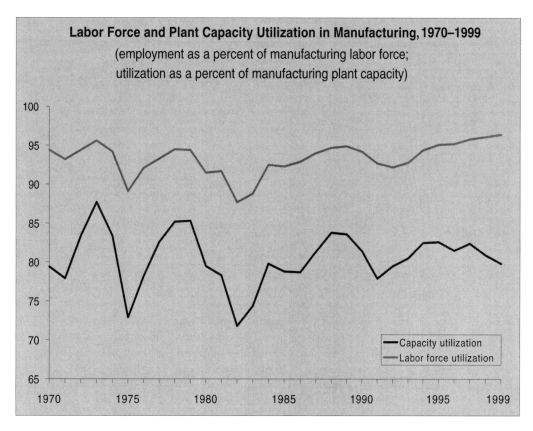

Labor Force and Plant Capacity Utilization in Manufacturing, 1970–1999
(employment as a percent of manufacturing labor force; utilization as a percent of manufacturing plant capacity)

- Despite a 4.3 percent rise in output, manufacturing plant capacity utilization declined in 1999; at 79.8 percent, the plant utilization rate was down from a high point four years earlier and substantially below its peaks in 1973 and 1979.

- In contrast to declining plant capacity utilization, manufacturing labor force utilization (measured as 100 minus the unemployment rate for workers last employed in manufacturing) rose to 96.4 percent in 1999, the highest since 1968 and 1969, when it was 96.7 percent.

- The 42 percent rise in manufacturing production from 1992 to 1999 was concentrated primarily in durable goods industries, where production rose 72 percent during the seven years. Production of nondurable goods was up 12 percent overall even though in 1999 there was a decline in the production of apparel, leather products, and printing and publishing with a significant 11 percent decline in the production of tobacco products.

- Among major market categories, production of electronic and business equipment has shown by far the strongest gains since 1992, with 1999 production of computers and office equipment more than ten times its 1992 level. In 1999, production of semiconductors was more than 11 times its 1992 level.

Table 4-1. Industrial Production and Capacity Utilization Summary

(Seasonally adjusted.)

Year and month	Industrial production indexes (1992=100)											Capacity utilization (output as a percent of capacity)					
	Total indus-trial produc-tion	Major market groups					Major industry groups					Total industry	Manufacturing			Mining	Utilities
		Products				Mater-ials	Manufacturing			Mining	Utilities		Total	Primary process-ing	Ad-vanced process-ing		
		Total	Con-sumer goods	Business equip-ment	Con-struction supplies		Total	Primary process-ing	Advanced processing								
1970	58.7	57.2	60.8	45.3	70.8	60.5	54.8	67.2	48.9	101.8	66.5	81.1	79.4	79.9	78.9	88.8	96.2
1971	59.5	58.0	64.3	43.1	73.0	61.4	55.6	68.7	49.4	99.3	69.6	79.4	77.9	78.7	77.1	87.3	94.6
1972	65.3	63.4	69.5	49.1	82.9	67.7	61.5	77.3	54.3	101.4	74.1	84.4	83.4	85.5	82.2	90.3	95.2
1973	70.6	68.0	72.6	57.5	88.7	74.2	66.9	84.6	59.0	102.3	77.0	88.4	87.7	90.5	86.2	92.3	93.5
1974	69.6	67.2	70.3	60.0	83.1	72.6	65.9	82.0	58.6	101.8	76.1	84.3	83.4	85.1	82.5	92.3	87.3
1975	63.5	62.8	67.7	53.6	71.4	63.8	59.4	71.4	53.8	99.5	76.8	74.6	72.9	72.1	73.3	89.7	84.4
1976	69.3	67.6	74.3	55.5	79.8	71.3	65.4	80.3	58.6	100.3	79.9	79.3	78.2	79.2	77.6	89.8	85.2
1977	74.9	73.2	79.5	62.0	87.0	76.9	71.2	86.7	64.0	103.4	82.0	83.5	82.6	83.8	81.9	90.9	85.0
1978	79.3	77.8	82.6	69.3	92.1	81.0	75.8	90.7	68.9	106.5	84.4	85.8	85.2	85.9	84.8	90.9	85.4
1979	82.0	80.2	81.5	77.3	93.1	83.9	78.5	92.5	72.0	108.3	86.8	86.0	85.3	86.0	84.9	91.4	86.6
1980	79.7	78.9	79.6	76.7	84.9	80.3	75.5	84.4	71.4	111.5	87.3	81.5	79.5	77.2	80.8	93.4	85.9
1981	81.0	80.4	80.1	78.0	82.3	81.4	76.7	85.2	72.8	115.6	85.0	80.8	78.3	77.2	78.8	93.9	82.5
1982	76.7	77.7	78.8	70.6	75.7	75.1	72.1	75.7	70.5	111.2	82.3	74.5	71.8	68.6	73.5	86.3	79.3
1983	79.5	80.2	83.2	68.3	84.2	78.3	76.3	82.1	73.6	106.6	83.7	75.7	74.4	74.5	74.4	80.4	79.7
1984	86.6	86.9	86.7	79.2	90.4	85.9	83.8	88.4	81.7	113.9	86.7	80.8	79.8	80.0	79.7	86.0	81.9
1985	88.0	89.2	87.6	82.5	93.5	86.3	85.7	88.4	84.5	111.0	88.8	79.8	78.8	79.1	78.6	84.3	83.5
1986	89.3	90.9	90.7	82.0	98.4	86.3	88.1	90.0	87.2	102.6	86.4	78.7	78.7	79.9	78.1	77.6	80.6
1987	93.2	95.1	93.7	85.1	104.7	90.4	92.8	95.3	91.6	102.1	89.4	81.3	81.3	84.5	79.9	80.3	82.5
1988	97.4	99.0	96.7	93.5	106.3	95.1	97.1	99.0	96.2	104.7	93.9	84.0	83.8	86.8	82.3	85.2	84.9
1989	99.1	100.6	97.7	98.8	105.5	97.0	99.0	99.9	98.6	103.2	97.1	84.1	83.6	86.1	82.5	86.9	86.3
1990	98.9	100.1	97.3	98.2	102.9	97.2	98.5	99.3	98.2	104.8	98.3	82.3	81.4	83.9	80.3	89.8	85.7
1991	97.0	97.6	97.0	95.7	96.2	95.9	96.2	95.7	96.4	102.6	100.4	79.3	77.9	79.6	77.2	88.4	86.3
1992	100.0	100.0	100.0	100.0	100.0	100.0	100.0	100.0	100.0	100.0	100.0	80.2	79.4	82.3	78.3	86.4	84.5
1993	103.4	103.2	103.6	104.6	103.3	103.8	103.7	103.5	103.7	100.0	103.9	81.3	80.5	84.0	79.0	86.0	87.2
1994	109.1	107.3	108.0	111.4	110.6	111.9	110.0	109.8	110.1	102.5	105.3	83.1	82.5	87.1	80.6	87.5	87.4
1995	114.4	110.7	110.8	119.4	112.5	120.3	115.8	112.1	117.7	102.1	109.0	83.3	82.6	86.5	81.0	86.8	89.2
1996	119.4	114.2	112.4	130.2	117.7	127.8	121.3	114.3	124.7	103.7	112.6	82.5	81.5	85.4	79.9	88.5	90.4
1997	127.1	119.7	115.1	145.7	122.6	138.6	130.1	119.5	135.1	105.9	112.7	83.3	82.4	86.1	81.0	89.2	89.7
1998	132.4	124.1	116.2	161.2	128.0	145.7	136.4	121.2	144.0	103.8	114.4	81.8	80.9	84.0	79.8	86.4	90.8
1999	137.1	126.5	116.9	171.6	133.4	154.8	142.3	123.3	151.8	98.0	115.6	80.6	79.8	83.0	78.8	81.5	90.7
1996																	
January	115.6	110.8	110.1	123.5	112.2	123.1	117.0	111.2	119.7	100.3	113.1	81.8	80.9	84.4	79.3	85.8	91.5
February	116.9	112.4	111.5	126.3	113.3	124.1	118.3	111.5	121.5	101.9	114.7	82.4	81.4	84.4	80.0	87.2	92.6
March	116.6	112.1	111.0	124.7	115.6	123.8	117.8	112.5	120.3	103.4	114.6	81.8	80.6	84.9	78.7	88.5	92.5
April	118.0	112.9	111.5	128.0	114.4	125.9	119.4	112.6	122.7	104.0	113.7	82.4	81.3	84.7	79.8	89.0	91.6
May	119.0	113.7	112.0	129.0	116.8	127.4	120.5	113.6	123.9	103.9	114.6	82.7	81.6	85.2	80.0	88.9	92.1
June	119.8	114.6	112.8	130.6	119.1	128.1	121.5	114.8	124.8	105.3	113.1	82.9	81.8	85.9	80.1	90.0	90.7
July	119.9	114.7	112.7	131.3	118.5	128.2	122.0	114.8	125.5	104.8	109.2	82.6	81.8	85.6	80.1	89.6	87.5
August	120.7	115.0	112.8	131.3	119.9	129.8	122.8	115.6	126.3	104.8	110.7	82.8	81.9	86.0	80.2	89.5	88.6
September	121.2	115.9	113.6	133.1	120.9	129.8	123.5	116.2	127.0	104.5	110.9	82.8	82.0	86.2	80.2	89.1	88.6
October	121.2	115.4	112.9	133.2	119.6	130.4	123.4	116.3	126.8	104.1	111.4	82.4	81.6	86.0	79.7	88.7	88.9
November	122.1	116.4	113.7	134.7	122.1	131.1	124.3	116.5	128.2	103.8	112.9	82.7	81.8	85.9	80.1	88.4	90.1
December	122.4	116.7	113.9	136.3	119.6	131.5	124.8	116.5	128.9	103.4	112.5	82.6	81.7	85.6	80.2	87.9	89.7
1997																	
January	123.0	116.9	113.5	137.7	119.4	132.7	125.3	116.5	129.7	104.2	113.3	82.6	81.7	85.4	80.2	88.4	90.2
February	124.0	117.7	114.1	139.4	122.0	134.2	126.5	117.9	130.8	106.0	111.7	83.0	82.1	86.1	80.5	89.9	88.9
March	124.5	118.2	114.4	141.0	123.0	134.6	127.1	117.9	131.8	106.6	110.0	83.0	82.1	85.9	80.7	90.3	87.5
April	125.2	118.4	113.9	142.3	122.6	136.2	127.8	118.8	132.4	105.6	113.0	83.1	82.1	86.3	80.6	89.3	89.9
May	125.8	118.9	114.4	143.7	122.5	136.8	128.4	118.9	133.3	106.8	112.1	83.1	82.1	86.1	80.7	90.2	89.2
June	126.6	119.5	114.9	145.7	122.9	137.9	129.5	119.1	134.8	105.9	110.9	83.2	82.4	86.0	81.1	89.4	88.2
July	127.2	119.5	114.8	145.5	122.4	139.6	130.1	119.8	135.4	106.0	112.6	83.3	82.4	86.1	81.0	89.3	89.6
August	128.0	120.5	115.6	148.3	122.8	140.1	131.1	120.0	136.9	105.9	111.5	83.4	82.6	86.0	81.5	89.1	88.7
September	128.8	120.8	115.6	149.1	122.2	141.7	131.8	120.9	137.5	106.3	113.8	83.6	82.7	86.4	81.4	89.3	90.6
October	129.6	121.8	116.8	150.4	122.9	142.2	132.7	121.0	138.7	106.0	115.4	83.7	82.8	86.2	81.6	88.9	91.9
November	130.2	122.2	116.8	152.3	124.3	143.0	133.5	121.9	139.5	105.6	114.2	83.7	82.8	86.5	81.5	88.5	90.9
December	130.6	122.4	116.4	153.5	124.3	143.8	134.0	122.1	140.2	105.5	114.3	83.5	82.6	86.3	81.4	88.3	91.0
1998																	
January	130.9	123.1	117.3	154.5	125.7	143.4	134.5	122.0	141.0	107.7	109.4	83.3	82.5	86.0	81.3	90.0	87.1
February	130.7	122.8	116.2	155.1	126.2	143.7	134.3	121.7	141.0	107.4	109.8	82.7	81.9	85.5	80.7	89.7	87.4
March	131.1	123.1	116.5	156.1	125.6	144.0	134.5	121.6	141.3	105.8	113.8	82.5	81.5	85.1	80.3	88.2	90.6
April	131.7	123.7	117.1	157.2	126.3	144.6	135.3	122.1	142.2	105.5	113.0	82.4	81.5	85.1	80.2	87.9	89.8
May	132.4	124.1	117.1	158.2	127.1	146.0	135.9	121.9	143.3	106.0	116.0	82.4	81.3	84.7	80.2	88.3	92.2
June	131.5	123.7	116.0	159.9	126.9	144.1	134.8	120.8	142.2	104.2	117.8	81.3	80.1	83.7	78.9	86.7	93.6
July	131.3	123.4	115.4	159.6	128.7	144.0	134.7	120.9	142.0	103.1	117.0	80.8	79.7	83.5	78.3	85.7	92.9
August	133.6	125.3	116.9	165.1	128.7	147.1	137.4	120.6	146.2	103.2	117.3	81.9	80.8	83.0	80.2	85.8	93.0
September	133.5	124.9	115.5	167.0	128.2	147.8	137.3	120.3	146.3	101.7	119.1	81.5	80.4	82.6	79.7	84.5	94.4
October	134.1	125.8	116.0	168.4	129.8	147.6	138.3	120.7	147.5	101.6	115.6	81.5	80.5	82.7	79.9	84.3	91.5
November	133.8	125.1	115.6	167.0	130.3	147.9	138.3	120.8	147.5	101.5	110.8	80.9	80.2	82.6	79.4	84.2	87.6
December	133.8	124.9	115.1	166.3	132.2	148.5	138.4	121.9	147.2	98.1	112.5	80.6	79.9	83.1	78.8	81.4	88.9
1999																	
January	134.1	125.4	116.3	165.9	133.3	148.2	138.6	122.2	147.2	98.0	114.5	80.4	79.6	83.1	78.4	81.3	90.3
February	134.5	125.8	117.2	166.3	132.5	148.7	139.3	122.1	148.4	97.4	112.6	80.4	79.7	82.8	78.7	80.9	88.7
March	135.1	126.0	116.7	167.5	131.7	150.3	139.7	122.4	148.8	96.7	116.8	80.5	79.6	82.9	78.5	80.9	91.9
April	135.5	126.2	116.5	169.4	131.3	150.8	140.2	122.2	149.6	96.7	116.3	80.4	79.5	82.6	78.5	80.4	91.4
May	136.2	126.8	116.8	171.2	132.9	151.7	141.0	122.5	150.7	97.4	116.1	80.5	79.7	82.7	78.7	81.0	91.1
June	136.6	126.8	117.0	171.2	132.6	153.1	141.4	122.7	151.2	97.1	117.4	80.5	79.6	82.7	78.6	80.7	92.1
July	137.4	126.9	116.8	172.6	133.2	155.0	142.0	123.3	151.8	97.8	119.8	80.7	79.7	82.9	78.8	81.3	93.9
August	137.7	127.6	117.6	173.9	132.9	154.6	142.5	123.4	152.6	98.5	117.8	80.7	79.7	82.8	78.8	81.9	92.2
September	138.1	127.6	117.1	173.7	134.1	155.7	142.9	123.6	153.1	98.3	117.7	80.6	79.7	82.8	78.7	81.8	92.0
October	139.1	128.5	118.2	174.8	135.4	156.8	144.2	124.8	154.5	99.2	115.2	81.0	80.2	83.4	79.1	82.6	89.9
November	139.4	128.0	117.6	175.0	134.3	158.8	145.0	125.6	155.2	99.7	110.9	80.9	80.3	83.8	79.2	83.0	86.5
December	140.1	128.5	118.1	175.5	134.9	159.7	145.6	125.9	155.9	99.5	113.5	81.1	80.3	83.9	79.2	82.8	88.4

Table 4-2. Industrial Production Indexes by Market Groups

(Seasonally adjusted, 1992=100.)

Year and month	Total industrial production	Products										
		Total	Final products									
			Total	Total consumer goods	Durable consumer goods							
					Total	Automotive products					Other consumer durables	
						Total	Total autos and trucks	Autos	Trucks	Auto parts and allied products	Total	Household appliances
1970	58.7	57.2	56.7	60.8	52.6	49.7	49.3	...	14.2	51.3	54.6	63.3
1971	59.5	58.0	57.2	64.3	59.6	63.3	67.7	...	20.0	55.1	57.7	65.5
1972	65.3	63.4	62.0	69.5	66.7	68.4	72.3	130.9	25.8	61.2	66.1	74.6
1973	70.6	68.0	66.7	72.6	71.8	75.2	82.8	140.8	33.6	62.8	70.0	84.4
1974	69.6	67.2	66.4	70.3	64.4	65.0	66.1	102.0	31.5	61.7	64.7	79.6
1975	63.5	62.8	62.6	67.7	58.7	61.8	60.7	94.7	28.5	61.6	56.9	64.2
1976	69.3	67.6	67.0	74.3	68.8	76.3	82.8	126.5	40.1	65.4	63.8	72.2
1977	74.9	73.2	72.4	79.5	77.9	87.2	95.4	136.2	50.1	73.6	71.8	80.2
1978	79.3	77.8	77.2	82.6	80.7	89.6	97.8	133.6	55.7	75.8	74.9	82.2
1979	82.0	80.2	79.7	81.5	76.7	81.4	87.5	123.1	45.8	70.4	73.6	84.2
1980	79.7	78.9	79.3	79.6	66.9	62.3	61.5	97.1	24.6	59.3	69.7	79.3
1981	81.0	80.4	81.2	80.1	67.2	61.6	61.2	93.7	26.8	58.3	70.7	79.7
1982	76.7	77.7	78.3	78.8	62.5	59.1	57.2	78.3	34.0	57.4	64.4	69.7
1983	79.5	80.2	80.0	83.2	73.8	74.3	79.9	111.0	45.9	64.7	73.1	82.0
1984	86.6	86.9	87.0	86.7	84.1	89.4	96.0	127.1	60.8	77.8	80.1	91.5
1985	88.0	89.2	89.3	87.6	84.7	95.4	103.9	134.9	68.2	81.6	77.3	85.4
1986	89.0	90.9	90.3	90.7	88.7	97.5	104.1	132.7	70.8	85.8	82.6	90.4
1987	93.2	95.1	93.3	93.7	93.9	100.7	104.0	123.9	80.1	94.1	89.1	95.7
1988	97.4	99.0	97.9	96.7	99.8	107.1	111.1	131.1	87.0	99.3	94.5	100.2
1989	99.1	100.6	99.9	97.7	101.3	108.9	114.0	131.5	92.5	99.2	95.9	101.7
1990	98.9	100.1	99.5	97.3	98.0	100.9	103.3	115.2	88.4	96.1	96.0	98.2
1991	97.0	97.6	97.7	97.0	93.0	90.3	89.6	94.5	83.4	91.6	95.2	91.9
1992	100.0	100.0	100.0	100.0	100.0	100.0	100.0	100.0	100.0	100.0	100.0	100.0
1993	103.4	103.2	103.4	103.6	112.0	111.3	114.7	108.0	123.3	105.5	112.4	109.6
1994	109.1	107.3	107.7	108.0	124.1	122.9	131.5	123.9	141.2	109.5	125.0	123.7
1995	114.4	110.7	111.6	110.8	128.4	122.6	129.2	118.2	142.6	112.2	132.7	116.6
1996	119.4	114.2	115.3	112.4	130.8	123.5	128.3	109.9	149.4	115.7	136.6	118.8
1997	127.1	119.6	121.1	115.1	135.4	130.7	136.2	108.3	167.0	121.9	138.9	114.2
1998	132.4	123.7	125.4	116.2	142.7	134.7	138.4	103.5	175.7	128.6	149.0	122.0
1999	137.1	126.5	128.0	116.9	152.6	144.7	151.8	102.6	202.4	133.9	158.6	131.4
1996												
January	115.6	110.8	111.9	110.1	124.6	116.2	118.0	102.0	136.6	113.3	131.3	112.8
February	116.9	112.4	113.7	111.5	127.4	121.7	125.9	109.6	144.9	115.0	131.7	114.8
March	116.6	112.1	113.0	111.0	122.9	110.7	106.0	84.4	130.2	118.1	132.8	118.2
April	118.0	112.9	114.2	111.5	130.1	124.4	131.5	116.1	149.9	113.0	134.5	117.3
May	119.0	113.7	114.8	112.0	132.1	124.9	131.2	118.4	146.8	114.8	137.7	118.4
June	119.8	114.6	115.7	112.8	136.1	129.3	136.2	122.0	153.4	118.0	141.4	127.0
July	119.9	114.7	115.9	112.7	134.9	131.8	142.8	121.9	166.7	114.4	137.0	119.0
August	120.7	115.0	116.0	112.8	133.8	126.7	134.4	116.9	154.7	114.5	139.3	122.8
September	121.2	115.9	116.9	113.6	133.3	126.2	131.9	116.5	150.2	116.9	138.8	120.7
October	121.2	115.4	116.4	112.9	130.1	120.3	122.3	97.9	149.1	116.9	138.0	117.2
November	122.1	116.4	117.3	113.7	131.9	123.9	127.9	108.1	150.4	117.5	138.2	116.5
December	122.4	116.7	117.9	113.9	132.9	125.6	131.6	105.3	160.5	115.9	138.6	120.5
1997												
January	123.0	116.9	117.9	113.5	131.7	128.0	133.8	107.6	162.7	118.7	134.3	113.4
February	124.0	117.7	118.8	114.1	133.3	129.3	134.6	110.8	161.3	120.7	136.2	113.4
March	124.5	118.2	119.5	114.4	135.1	130.8	137.1	110.7	166.4	120.9	138.1	117.5
April	125.2	118.4	119.5	113.9	131.5	123.2	124.9	104.6	147.8	120.4	138.0	114.2
May	125.8	118.9	120.2	114.4	133.5	125.8	128.8	107.6	152.8	120.8	139.5	113.0
June	126.6	119.5	121.0	114.9	136.5	131.0	136.9	108.6	168.1	121.8	140.7	114.7
July	127.2	119.5	120.8	114.8	133.0	123.0	122.9	103.3	145.4	122.4	141.1	114.3
August	128.0	120.5	122.2	115.6	136.8	133.6	139.8	111.8	170.8	123.7	138.9	111.4
September	128.8	120.8	122.4	115.6	137.0	135.8	144.6	111.7	180.5	122.2	137.4	111.6
October	129.6	121.8	123.5	116.8	136.3	133.2	140.4	106.2	177.3	121.8	138.4	114.2
November	130.2	122.2	124.0	116.8	140.9	139.4	147.8	110.8	187.5	126.3	141.5	117.9
December	130.6	122.4	124.1	116.4	139.4	135.3	143.1	105.5	183.2	123.0	142.4	114.4
1998												
January	130.9	123.1	125.1	117.3	141.9	135.2	142.1	108.7	178.2	124.0	147.2	121.1
February	130.7	122.8	124.5	116.2	141.4	133.2	138.8	102.1	177.8	124.1	148.0	120.4
March	131.1	123.1	124.9	116.5	142.8	134.3	138.9	100.3	179.6	126.7	149.6	117.0
April	131.7	123.7	125.5	117.1	143.9	136.3	141.9	102.6	183.4	127.1	149.9	119.3
May	132.4	124.1	125.8	117.1	144.7	136.9	141.6	103.6	181.9	129.0	151.0	124.8
June	131.5	123.7	125.4	116.0	137.7	123.1	118.3	88.4	150.2	128.8	150.0	117.5
July	131.3	123.4	124.8	115.4	130.9	108.0	92.2	68.6	117.2	129.0	150.9	121.4
August	133.6	125.3	127.2	116.9	147.1	143.5	151.7	116.1	190.3	131.2	149.3	121.0
September	133.5	124.9	126.7	115.5	144.6	139.3	145.4	120.2	174.4	129.9	148.3	120.7
October	134.1	125.8	127.5	116.0	146.2	143.4	151.4	113.5	191.9	131.5	147.6	125.9
November	133.8	125.1	126.8	115.6	145.4	142.0	150.2	109.3	193.3	129.9	147.3	127.1
December	133.8	124.9	126.0	115.1	146.0	141.7	148.2	108.4	190.2	131.8	148.8	127.3
1999												
January	134.1	125.4	126.6	116.3	149.1	143.7	149.4	104.7	195.9	134.8	152.8	128.9
February	134.5	125.8	127.3	117.2	150.9	142.0	148.7	100.2	198.5	131.8	158.0	134.6
March	135.1	126.0	127.3	116.7	149.9	140.0	147.0	101.6	194.1	129.3	157.8	128.8
April	135.5	126.2	127.6	116.5	152.0	142.0	149.0	102.3	197.3	131.4	160.0	134.2
May	136.2	126.8	128.2	116.8	152.8	145.4	153.2	99.9	207.4	133.6	158.3	125.6
June	136.6	126.8	128.3	117.0	154.0	147.4	157.5	101.8	214.2	132.5	158.8	131.0
July	137.4	126.9	128.6	116.8	153.4	143.7	148.9	102.4	197.2	135.3	161.1	132.3
August	137.7	127.6	129.5	117.6	155.5	150.6	162.9	105.0	221.6	132.8	158.7	127.7
September	138.1	127.6	129.1	117.1	153.5	145.5	152.8	105.5	201.9	134.4	159.7	122.2
October	139.1	128.5	130.2	118.2	157.4	147.9	155.1	103.9	207.8	136.7	165.0	134.3
November	139.4	128.0	129.8	117.6	154.4	146.2	154.3	107.2	203.6	133.8	160.7	138.6
December	140.1	128.5	130.3	118.1	155.7	144.4	148.7	99.8	199.0	137.1	164.9	138.0

Table 4-2. Industrial Production Indexes by Market Groups—*Continued*

(Seasonally adjusted, 1992=100.)

Year and month	Durable consumer goods—Continued — Other consumer durables—Continued			Nondurable consumer goods								
				Total	Nonenergy products					Energy products		
	Home electronics	Carpeting and furniture	Miscel- laneous home goods		Total	Foods and tobacco	Clothing	Chemical products	Paper products	Total	Fuels	Utilities
1970	...	64.2	70.5	64.2	62.8	62.3	95.9	45.9	58.9	72.1	81.8	62.7
1971	...	69.1	74.3	66.0	64.4	64.2	95.5	48.5	60.1	75.5	85.1	66.0
1972	...	83.3	83.3	70.3	68.6	67.8	103.9	53.0	60.6	79.8	89.3	69.9
1973	...	88.5	84.1	72.4	70.6	69.8	104.4	57.0	60.8	83.2	93.6	72.7
1974	...	80.4	78.7	72.4	70.7	70.2	99.3	59.7	62.1	82.3	90.4	72.8
1975	...	70.2	73.7	71.0	68.7	70.2	92.0	57.9	59.2	85.2	91.6	76.1
1976	...	79.3	82.5	76.2	74.3	74.3	103.8	63.2	63.4	86.8	97.2	76.0
1977	...	89.7	91.2	79.8	78.2	77.0	108.8	65.9	71.4	88.0	102.6	77.0
1978	...	95.8	92.7	82.9	81.6	80.0	111.4	70.1	76.1	89.8	102.6	79.7
1979	...	96.4	88.3	82.9	81.7	80.8	106.7	71.6	77.2	88.9	99.1	81.0
1980	...	88.9	83.4	83.8	83.4	82.4	107.5	75.0	77.9	85.8	91.1	82.7
1981	...	87.8	86.3	84.3	84.1	83.9	107.1	73.3	80.4	85.1	90.0	82.3
1982	21.6	78.8	81.2	84.2	84.1	84.7	105.8	71.0	82.1	85.2	89.1	83.3
1983	33.9	87.8	82.6	86.2	86.4	86.6	107.9	73.4	85.9	85.3	87.8	84.3
1984	39.9	94.2	88.6	87.5	87.5	88.2	106.4	73.5	90.1	87.7	91.6	86.0
1985	38.1	92.9	85.9	88.5	88.5	90.6	100.8	74.5	92.1	88.5	91.2	87.3
1986	48.6	98.3	86.8	91.3	91.5	92.8	102.1	80.3	94.7	90.7	95.4	88.8
1987	55.2	103.5	94.2	93.6	93.8	95.3	104.2	83.0	96.4	92.7	95.6	91.3
1988	70.7	103.4	97.5	95.9	95.7	96.9	102.2	87.6	98.3	97.0	97.9	96.5
1989	73.3	103.5	99.0	96.7	96.4	97.4	100.1	89.7	100.2	98.3	98.2	98.2
1990	78.9	100.8	99.4	97.1	97.1	98.3	96.6	92.4	100.6	97.7	98.5	97.2
1991	93.1	94.5	97.3	98.1	97.8	98.5	97.6	95.1	99.6	100.4	99.0	100.9
1992	100.0	100.0	100.0	100.0	100.0	100.0	100.0	100.0	100.0	100.0	100.0	100.0
1993	150.7	104.9	106.4	101.5	100.9	99.3	102.4	102.8	102.5	105.2	102.5	106.3
1994	218.1	108.8	111.1	104.0	103.8	103.5	105.0	105.2	101.8	105.1	101.9	106.3
1995	313.9	109.3	113.0	106.5	106.3	106.0	104.5	109.7	103.7	107.7	104.3	109.0
1996	355.3	110.9	113.4	107.8	107.1	106.3	102.1	114.0	103.3	112.3	106.8	114.6
1997	378.9	113.2	115.2	110.1	109.9	108.3	100.5	119.5	107.7	111.5	109.3	112.1
1998	549.7	117.9	115.2	109.9	109.5	108.6	95.2	120.9	105.6	112.6	110.5	113.1
1999	805.5	121.7	114.7	108.7	108.0	107.3	90.6	121.8	102.3	114.0	111.3	115.0
1996												
January	313.9	107.2	112.4	106.4	105.5	105.0	99.0	112.4	101.5	112.9	105.2	116.2
February	310.5	107.1	112.9	107.6	106.5	105.8	102.4	112.4	102.8	114.8	107.3	118.0
March	305.1	111.7	112.1	108.0	107.0	107.0	101.9	112.4	102.5	114.8	107.1	118.2
April	341.5	108.7	112.5	106.9	105.9	105.9	102.1	109.9	102.7	113.8	106.3	117.1
May	358.7	112.3	114.3	107.0	106.0	105.4	102.5	111.3	103.0	113.7	106.5	116.9
June	366.2	115.5	115.8	107.1	106.3	106.6	102.2	110.3	102.3	112.7	106.4	115.5
July	356.5	107.2	115.7	107.2	107.0	105.8	102.2	114.7	102.9	108.6	106.0	109.5
August	359.4	113.3	115.1	107.7	107.3	105.8	103.4	114.8	103.9	110.1	106.9	111.3
September	375.0	112.9	113.5	108.7	108.4	107.8	102.5	115.9	103.8	110.3	106.2	111.9
October	396.3	111.8	111.6	108.5	108.2	106.4	102.6	117.7	104.2	110.9	108.1	111.9
November	400.9	112.2	111.5	109.2	108.6	107.1	102.5	117.5	104.8	112.8	108.5	114.6
December	379.1	111.2	113.6	109.2	108.8	107.2	101.5	118.3	105.1	112.1	107.3	114.0
1997												
January	343.6	106.1	114.4	109.0	108.7	107.6	101.1	118.5	103.6	111.1	106.0	113.3
February	343.8	111.5	114.7	109.3	109.3	108.1	100.6	118.7	105.4	109.7	106.9	110.7
March	343.4	114.0	115.7	109.3	109.5	109.1	101.2	116.3	106.6	107.7	108.5	106.9
April	362.4	113.3	115.0	109.6	109.2	107.3	101.2	119.0	106.7	112.1	109.0	113.3
May	384.6	112.0	116.4	109.7	109.2	107.2	101.0	118.6	107.7	113.2	111.0	114.0
June	379.6	114.1	117.3	109.6	109.6	107.4	100.3	119.7	108.6	109.4	110.9	108.3
July	387.6	113.5	117.9	110.2	110.2	108.4	100.6	119.7	108.8	110.3	108.1	110.9
August	382.4	114.5	114.8	110.4	110.3	107.9	100.6	121.8	108.5	110.7	110.1	110.5
September	376.6	113.8	113.0	110.3	110.1	108.5	100.2	119.5	108.4	111.8	111.2	111.7
October	390.5	113.1	113.5	112.0	111.6	110.3	100.4	121.6	109.1	114.7	111.4	115.8
November	404.5	117.9	113.9	110.9	110.6	109.1	99.4	119.8	110.3	113.1	107.9	115.0
December	447.6	114.2	115.4	110.8	110.3	108.4	99.5	120.7	108.9	114.1	110.6	115.3
1998												
January	487.7	117.9	116.7	111.4	111.7	111.0	99.2	121.3	108.9	108.6	110.9	107.1
February	508.4	117.3	117.1	110.0	110.5	109.4	97.3	121.2	107.7	106.9	110.4	105.0
March	545.7	117.5	117.9	110.1	109.7	108.8	97.3	120.2	106.3	112.8	111.3	113.1
April	550.9	117.4	117.5	110.6	110.4	109.4	96.9	122.0	106.2	112.0	111.3	111.9
May	535.7	118.7	117.9	110.5	110.1	109.6	95.6	121.1	105.6	113.6	110.4	114.6
June	547.1	117.6	118.2	110.7	109.8	109.0	96.2	121.4	105.0	117.1	111.2	119.3
July	564.4	118.9	116.9	111.3	110.4	109.5	95.7	122.8	105.9	117.2	112.4	119.0
August	554.9	118.0	115.5	109.8	108.8	107.5	94.5	120.6	106.1	116.9	111.5	118.9
September	570.4	117.5	113.5	108.6	107.5	106.0	93.9	119.1	105.0	116.9	109.2	120.0
October	549.6	120.2	110.5	108.9	108.2	108.0	92.5	119.1	104.4	113.8	108.1	116.0
November	567.1	117.7	110.1	108.6	108.9	108.4	91.3	122.0	103.4	106.3	109.6	104.7
December	614.9	115.9	111.0	107.9	107.7	107.2	91.3	120.2	102.9	108.6	110.1	107.6
1999												
January	683.5	121.1	111.0	108.7	108.1	108.4	91.7	119.7	101.5	113.1	112.2	113.3
February	747.5	122.8	113.6	109.3	109.2	109.4	92.0	122.8	100.4	109.9	113.4	108.2
March	770.2	119.6	115.7	108.9	108.0	108.4	91.3	121.6	98.8	115.4	110.7	117.2
April	778.1	120.2	116.9	108.3	107.3	107.8	91.8	118.7	99.9	115.1	111.5	116.4
May	757.9	121.0	117.2	108.4	107.6	107.7	90.2	120.5	100.3	114.7	110.9	116.1
June	764.3	121.0	116.2	108.4	107.5	107.4	90.2	120.2	101.5	115.3	109.9	117.4
July	815.1	124.1	115.9	108.3	106.9	106.7	89.2	119.4	102.0	118.6	111.1	121.7
August	789.7	122.1	115.4	108.9	107.8	106.5	90.1	122.7	103.2	116.6	110.0	119.3
September	871.7	124.1	114.4	108.7	107.5	106.2	89.9	120.9	104.7	117.6	112.0	119.7
October	983.3	124.8	114.8	109.3	108.5	106.8	89.4	123.1	106.3	114.5	112.4	114.9
November	868.6	117.4	115.0	109.1	109.4	107.3	90.6	126.0	105.1	106.7	110.1	104.3
December	924.4	123.0	116.7	109.5	109.1	107.4	89.1	126.5	103.1	112.0	111.7	111.6

Table 4-2. Industrial Production Indexes by Market Groups—*Continued*

(Seasonally adjusted, 1992=100.)

Year and month	Final products—Continued											Intermediate products		
	Equipment											Total	Construction supplies	Business supplies
	Total	Business equipment							Defense and space	Oil and gas well drilling	Manufactured homes			
		Total	Information processing and related		Industrial equipment	Transit		Other business equipment						
			Total	Computer and office equipment		Total	Autos and trucks							
1970	52.5	45.3	15.3	2.7	100.9	57.3	39.4	63.0	64.8	85.2	96.5	59.2	70.8	51.7
1971	49.2	43.1	14.2	2.3	94.4	55.3	46.7	64.7	58.2	81.8	118.6	61.0	73.0	53.2
1972	53.8	49.1	16.6	2.8	104.7	60.4	50.1	79.7	56.6	93.9	146.6	68.1	82.9	58.5
1973	60.1	57.5	19.6	3.5	120.0	72.8	59.7	93.9	55.3	101.9	144.0	72.5	88.7	61.9
1974	62.0	60.0	21.8	4.1	126.0	70.3	54.2	92.9	54.5	126.4	101.7	69.9	83.1	61.4
1975	56.8	53.6	20.5	3.7	109.5	64.2	50.5	77.4	53.5	143.4	81.5	63.1	71.4	57.8
1976	58.8	55.5	22.3	4.5	108.8	61.8	61.5	86.9	54.3	144.1	107.1	69.5	79.8	62.9
1977	64.3	62.0	26.0	6.0	118.2	65.8	71.4	94.9	54.4	175.0	118.7	75.7	87.0	68.4
1978	71.0	69.3	31.8	8.9	125.3	76.7	74.9	97.4	55.9	196.4	126.0	79.9	92.1	72.0
1979	77.6	77.3	38.6	12.2	130.8	88.1	70.9	106.0	57.7	190.7	121.2	82.0	93.1	74.9
1980	79.1	76.7	43.3	16.4	126.5	81.3	53.6	95.7	63.2	236.8	99.6	77.7	84.9	73.2
1981	82.8	78.0	48.1	21.7	126.5	74.6	55.5	94.9	64.5	315.6	101.8	77.6	82.3	74.7
1982	77.7	70.6	51.2	25.2	103.7	62.0	49.3	84.1	72.6	296.0	89.3	75.8	75.8	75.8
1983	76.4	68.3	56.0	33.4	87.3	58.4	64.2	85.3	80.4	257.6	110.5	81.0	84.2	79.1
1984	87.6	79.2	67.9	48.6	98.1	67.0	80.9	95.2	89.5	296.1	104.7	86.9	90.4	84.9
1985	91.8	82.5	74.9	58.8	97.4	73.0	91.6	90.5	103.8	259.9	102.5	89.1	93.5	86.4
1986	90.0	82.0	73.8	58.9	95.6	74.6	92.2	91.8	113.0	143.3	102.5	92.7	98.4	89.3
1987	92.9	85.1	78.9	67.3	95.4	75.4	92.5	98.4	117.5	130.7	106.4	100.7	104.7	98.4
1988	99.9	93.5	86.3	77.9	105.2	84.9	94.1	105.5	117.1	150.0	103.1	102.5	106.3	100.3
1989	103.7	98.8	90.7	88.4	109.6	94.4	96.0	109.5	117.4	139.9	96.3	102.9	105.5	101.3
1990	103.2	98.2	90.5	84.1	107.3	95.2	93.7	108.7	115.9	151.1	94.0	101.9	102.9	101.4
1991	98.8	95.7	91.1	79.9	100.9	96.4	91.6	98.2	106.7	128.6	84.5	97.5	96.2	98.3
1992	100.0	100.0	100.0	100.0	100.0	100.0	100.0	100.0	100.0	100.0	100.0	100.0	100.0	100.0
1993	103.2	104.6	105.4	107.1	106.5	98.2	108.6	107.8	93.7	122.5	115.3	102.5	103.3	102.0
1994	107.2	111.4	113.7	123.3	116.5	97.7	123.4	113.4	86.8	126.9	127.0	106.3	110.6	103.7
1995	112.8	119.4	126.4	158.1	126.9	94.4	123.0	119.2	84.0	126.4	135.8	108.1	112.5	105.4
1996	120.4	130.2	148.7	228.9	131.0	98.8	115.7	122.4	78.9	137.9	144.6	110.8	117.7	106.7
1997	132.1	145.7	173.5	322.2	135.5	116.0	121.4	137.1	75.9	149.3	157.7	115.3	122.6	111.0
1998	142.7	161.2	205.7	526.9	139.0	130.0	123.3	139.8	75.4	134.6	166.3	118.8	128.0	113.4
1999	148.9	171.6	248.6	840.1	135.3	126.9	131.4	131.4	74.4	106.8	155.2	122.1	133.4	115.3
1996														
January	115.0	123.5	136.6	182.6	129.4	92.2	109.1	118.7	78.3	134.3	138.8	107.4	112.2	104.5
February	117.4	126.3	139.9	185.7	131.8	96.0	116.0	119.3	79.0	136.8	135.7	108.3	113.3	105.3
March	116.2	124.7	141.6	193.4	130.9	87.2	97.0	119.4	79.7	132.6	142.8	109.4	115.6	105.6
April	118.8	128.0	143.9	203.9	131.0	97.9	120.6	119.8	79.1	139.7	143.2	109.0	114.4	105.7
May	119.6	129.0	145.5	214.2	131.4	98.8	121.1	120.9	78.9	141.5	144.1	110.2	116.8	106.3
June	120.7	130.6	148.6	222.3	131.0	102.0	124.7	119.5	78.5	139.7	147.3	111.2	119.1	106.5
July	121.3	131.3	148.8	229.8	131.0	103.3	125.1	123.3	79.2	139.1	144.2	111.0	118.5	106.6
August	121.4	131.3	150.3	239.9	130.4	101.3	119.4	124.4	79.3	138.1	148.7	111.8	119.9	107.1
September	122.7	133.1	154.4	253.6	131.1	102.5	118.5	123.1	79.6	138.1	149.5	112.5	120.9	107.5
October	122.6	133.2	157.1	267.4	131.4	97.7	106.2	124.2	78.7	138.1	150.3	112.1	119.6	107.7
November	123.6	134.7	157.7	276.4	131.6	102.8	114.3	124.9	78.3	137.9	148.2	113.4	122.1	108.3
December	124.8	136.3	159.7	277.6	131.5	104.4	115.7	131.0	78.3	139.4	142.2	113.1	119.6	109.3
1997														
January	125.5	137.7	160.7	275.7	132.8	106.5	118.3	132.3	76.7	138.9	148.6	113.6	119.4	110.1
February	127.0	139.4	162.9	277.1	133.7	109.1	120.8	132.6	76.8	143.2	151.9	114.2	122.0	109.6
March	128.4	141.0	164.3	286.2	134.3	112.1	122.5	134.8	76.5	149.6	154.3	114.4	123.0	109.2
April	129.3	142.3	168.7	300.8	135.1	109.9	113.2	135.1	76.1	149.6	158.8	114.9	122.6	110.3
May	130.3	143.7	170.5	315.9	135.2	112.7	117.5	136.2	76.1	149.5	158.7	114.9	122.5	110.4
June	131.8	145.7	174.3	327.3	134.7	115.4	121.7	138.1	75.9	150.0	158.9	114.7	122.9	109.9
July	131.4	145.5	176.4	333.2	134.5	111.8	114.6	138.3	74.6	150.8	162.0	115.4	122.4	111.2
August	133.8	148.3	176.4	332.6	136.1	120.7	125.2	139.5	75.9	152.0	161.2	115.1	122.8	110.5
September	134.3	149.1	177.8	331.9	136.2	123.0	127.3	137.6	75.6	152.1	160.0	116.0	122.6	112.1
October	135.1	150.4	180.7	336.9	137.3	121.4	124.1	140.2	75.3	150.6	159.6	116.7	122.9	113.0
November	136.6	152.3	183.4	357.9	137.5	125.3	128.6	140.4	75.1	152.6	160.4	116.8	124.3	112.4
December	137.5	153.5	186.3	390.9	138.8	124.5	122.9	140.2	75.5	152.2	159.9	117.3	124.3	113.2
1998														
January	138.5	154.5	189.9	416.0	137.9	125.7	123.8	139.0	75.4	155.6	163.6	117.1	125.7	112.0
February	139.1	155.1	193.4	445.1	137.3	124.4	120.4	137.7	75.6	157.6	166.1	117.2	126.2	111.9
March	139.5	156.1	194.0	449.1	138.6	125.0	120.3	139.8	75.2	151.8	164.6	117.6	125.6	112.9
April	140.1	157.2	195.4	445.9	138.2	127.5	122.9	141.5	75.2	147.7	164.9	118.0	126.3	113.1
May	140.8	158.2	197.6	447.7	137.6	130.1	124.1	140.4	75.2	146.3	165.6	118.7	127.1	113.7
June	141.7	159.9	201.3	478.1	141.5	125.3	109.7	143.2	75.3	136.3	162.3	118.2	126.9	113.0
July	141.3	159.6	206.6	527.1	141.0	116.2	88.0	147.2	75.2	130.5	170.1	119.0	128.7	113.3
August	145.3	165.1	212.4	575.8	140.7	137.7	135.6	132.7	76.1	124.6	164.3	119.3	128.7	113.6
September	146.4	167.0	217.5	608.7	139.2	136.9	134.9	142.1	75.3	123.0	166.0	119.0	128.2	113.6
October	147.5	168.4	220.1	628.6	139.7	138.8	134.9	141.4	76.3	119.2	168.5	120.4	129.8	114.9
November	146.3	167.0	219.4	642.8	138.1	137.2	133.8	139.7	75.8	116.0	171.2	120.0	130.3	113.9
December	145.2	166.3	220.9	657.8	138.6	134.8	131.0	133.0	75.2	105.2	172.5	121.1	132.2	114.5
1999														
January	144.6	165.9	223.0	677.5	137.0	132.8	130.9	132.6	75.0	99.8	173.3	121.4	133.3	114.3
February	144.9	166.3	224.5	703.1	135.8	131.2	128.9	139.9	75.4	97.4	169.2	121.3	132.5	114.7
March	145.9	167.5	229.2	736.1	135.2	129.5	129.0	143.0	75.6	100.8	168.8	121.6	131.7	115.6
April	147.0	169.4	236.9	773.0	136.0	129.4	130.7	135.7	75.1	97.2	164.7	121.7	131.3	116.1
May	148.4	171.2	244.3	805.8	135.3	128.9	131.2	134.0	75.2	99.8	161.3	122.3	132.9	116.1
June	148.3	171.2	248.2	830.2	133.7	128.2	132.2	130.2	74.6	100.1	158.9	121.7	132.6	115.3
July	149.3	172.6	253.8	851.9	135.4	127.5	131.2	123.8	74.5	102.0	151.5	121.5	133.2	114.6
August	150.5	173.9	259.9	892.8	133.6	128.1	135.3	123.2	74.7	107.1	151.3	121.7	132.9	115.1
September	150.2	173.7	261.3	926.9	133.9	124.0	132.0	126.4	73.6	111.3	144.4	122.6	134.1	115.8
October	151.2	174.8	265.6	950.5	134.9	122.3	133.4	125.1	73.7	115.7	142.6	123.2	135.4	115.9
November	151.4	175.0	266.7	970.0	134.6	121.2	134.2	127.5	73.0	121.3	139.3	122.4	134.3	115.2
December	151.8	175.5	270.1	985.6	135.0	118.5	127.8	128.1	72.4	124.3	138.3	123.1	134.9	116.0

Table 4-2. Industrial Production Indexes by Market Groups—Continued

(Seasonally adjusted, 1992=100.)

Year and month	Special aggregates								Materials, excluding energy
	Total excluding				Consumer goods excluding		Business equipment excluding		
	Autos and trucks	Motor vehicles and parts	Computer and office equipment	Computers and semiconductors	Autos and trucks	Energy	Autos and trucks	Computer and office equipment	
1970	59.3	59.3	62.6	65.7	61.9	59.5	45.8	63.4	51.3
1971	59.7	59.5	63.7	66.8	64.2	63.1	43.3	61.1	52.2
1972	65.5	65.3	69.7	72.9	69.4	68.3	49.4	68.9	58.5
1973	70.6	70.3	75.3	78.5	71.9	71.3	57.7	80.4	65.5
1974	70.0	69.8	73.9	77.1	70.8	69.0	60.8	82.8	64.3
1975	63.8	63.9	67.4	70.4	68.3	65.9	54.1	73.8	54.8
1976	69.2	69.0	73.4	76.5	73.7	72.9	55.5	75.0	62.7
1977	74.6	74.2	79.1	82.6	78.5	78.5	61.4	81.4	68.6
1978	79.1	78.6	83.3	86.8	81.6	81.7	69.0	88.6	73.4
1979	82.0	81.8	85.6	88.9	81.1	80.6	77.8	96.8	76.4
1980	80.2	80.4	82.8	85.7	80.5	78.8	78.4	93.0	71.4
1981	81.5	81.8	83.7	86.4	81.0	79.4	79.7	91.9	73.8
1982	77.1	77.6	78.9	81.0	79.9	78.0	72.2	80.7	66.0
1983	79.6	79.9	81.3	83.3	83.2	82.9	68.6	74.9	71.8
1984	86.5	86.6	88.0	89.7	86.1	86.6	79.0	84.1	80.9
1985	87.8	87.7	89.1	90.8	86.6	87.5	81.8	85.8	81.6
1986	88.8	88.8	90.0	91.6	89.9	90.7	81.2	85.2	83.3
1987	93.0	93.1	94.0	95.4	93.0	93.8	84.5	87.3	88.5
1988	97.2	97.3	97.9	99.2	95.8	96.7	93.5	95.3	94.0
1989	98.9	99.1	99.5	100.5	96.7	97.6	99.2	99.8	96.2
1990	98.9	99.1	99.3	100.1	97.0	97.3	98.6	99.6	96.1
1991	97.2	97.4	97.2	97.7	97.5	96.7	96.2	97.4	94.3
1992	100.0	100.0	100.0	100.0	100.0	100.0	100.0	100.0	100.0
1993	103.2	103.0	103.1	102.8	103.0	103.4	104.2	104.4	105.2
1994	108.6	108.1	108.5	107.3	106.7	108.4	110.2	110.4	115.2
1995	114.1	113.5	113.2	110.2	109.8	111.2	119.1	116.4	125.8
1996	119.4	118.8	117.4	112.4	111.5	112.4	131.8	123.2	135.2
1997	127.0	126.4	124.2	116.9	113.9	115.5	148.5	134.7	150.1
1998	132.4	131.9	128.1	118.7	115.0	116.7	165.6	142.6	160.2
1999	137.0	136.4	131.1	119.3	115.0	117.3	176.2	143.8	172.0
1996									
January	115.6	114.9	114.0	109.9	109.7	109.8	125.1	118.9	129.5
February	116.8	116.2	115.3	111.1	110.7	111.1	127.5	121.7	130.4
March	117.0	116.9	115.0	110.6	111.3	110.6	127.8	119.5	129.7
April	117.7	117.0	116.2	111.7	110.4	111.3	128.9	122.3	132.5
May	118.7	118.0	117.0	112.3	110.9	111.8	129.9	122.7	134.4
June	119.5	118.9	117.8	112.9	111.5	112.8	131.3	123.8	135.2
July	119.5	118.9	117.8	112.8	111.0	113.1	132.1	124.2	135.9
August	120.5	119.9	118.5	113.2	111.6	113.2	132.7	123.7	137.9
September	121.1	120.7	118.9	113.5	112.5	114.0	134.8	124.9	137.9
October	121.4	121.0	118.7	113.2	112.3	113.1	136.3	124.3	138.7
November	122.1	121.6	119.5	113.9	112.9	113.8	137.0	125.5	139.6
December	122.4	122.0	119.9	114.1	112.9	114.1	138.7	127.1	140.3
1997									
January	122.9	122.3	120.5	114.6	112.4	113.8	139.9	128.7	141.6
February	124.0	123.4	121.6	115.3	112.9	114.6	141.5	130.3	143.4
March	124.4	123.9	122.0	115.5	113.1	115.1	143.1	131.6	144.1
April	125.5	124.9	122.5	116.0	113.3	114.2	145.6	132.2	146.3
May	125.9	125.4	122.9	116.1	113.6	114.6	146.7	133.0	147.0
June	126.5	125.9	123.6	116.4	113.7	115.5	148.4	134.4	148.8
July	127.5	126.8	124.2	116.8	114.3	115.3	149.0	134.0	150.8
August	127.9	127.2	125.0	117.4	114.3	116.2	150.9	136.8	151.7
September	128.7	127.9	125.8	118.1	114.0	116.0	151.6	137.7	153.4
October	129.6	128.9	126.6	118.8	115.5	117.1	153.4	138.7	154.2
November	130.0	129.3	127.0	119.1	115.1	117.2	155.0	139.8	155.6
December	130.6	129.8	127.2	119.2	114.9	116.7	157.0	139.7	156.6
1998									
January	130.9	130.3	127.2	119.1	115.9	118.3	158.1	139.8	156.1
February	130.8	130.3	126.8	118.7	114.9	117.2	159.1	139.2	156.5
March	131.2	130.7	127.1	118.9	115.2	116.9	160.2	140.0	156.6
April	131.7	131.2	127.7	119.2	115.7	117.7	161.2	141.2	157.5
May	132.5	131.8	128.4	119.7	115.8	117.6	162.1	142.1	158.9
June	132.0	132.0	127.3	118.3	115.8	116.0	165.8	142.7	156.6
July	132.6	132.6	126.9	117.6	116.4	115.2	168.1	140.9	156.7
August	133.3	132.5	128.9	119.4	115.1	117.0	168.4	144.8	160.9
September	133.4	132.7	128.7	119.1	113.9	115.4	170.6	145.8	161.6
October	133.9	133.3	129.2	119.3	114.2	116.3	172.2	146.5	161.7
November	133.6	133.1	128.8	118.7	113.8	116.7	170.8	144.8	162.4
December	133.7	133.2	128.7	118.6	113.4	115.9	170.3	143.7	163.3
1999									
January	133.9	133.5	128.8	118.7	114.6	116.7	169.9	142.7	162.9
February	134.4	133.9	129.1	118.9	115.5	118.0	170.6	142.4	163.6
March	135.1	134.6	129.5	119.1	115.1	116.9	171.9	142.6	165.5
April	135.4	134.9	129.7	119.0	114.8	116.7	173.8	143.4	166.3
May	136.1	135.6	130.2	119.4	114.8	117.0	175.7	144.2	167.4
June	136.4	135.9	130.6	119.3	114.8	117.2	175.7	143.6	169.5
July	137.3	136.7	131.2	119.7	115.1	116.6	177.4	144.4	171.6
August	137.4	137.1	131.4	119.8	115.2	117.7	178.3	144.6	171.3
September	138.0	137.2	131.5	119.9	115.2	117.1	178.5	143.6	173.0
October	138.9	138.3	132.4	120.5	116.3	118.7	179.5	144.0	174.7
November	139.3	138.7	132.7	120.5	115.6	118.8	179.7	143.7	177.4
December	140.2	139.5	133.2	120.8	116.4	118.8	181.1	143.8	178.6

Table 4-2. Industrial Production Indexes by Market Groups—*Continued*

(Seasonally adjusted, 1992=100.)

Year and month	Special aggregates								
	Total excluding				Consumer goods excluding		Business equipment excluding		Materials, excluding energy
	Autos and trucks	Motor vehicles and parts	Computer and office equipment	Computers and semiconductors	Autos and trucks	Energy	Autos and trucks	Computer and office equipment	
1970	59.3	59.3	62.6	65.7	61.9	59.5	45.8	63.4	51.3
1971	59.7	59.5	63.7	66.8	64.2	63.1	43.3	61.1	52.2
1972	65.5	65.3	69.7	72.9	69.4	68.3	49.4	68.9	58.5
1973	70.6	70.3	75.3	78.5	71.9	71.3	57.7	80.4	65.5
1974	70.0	69.8	73.9	77.1	70.8	69.0	60.8	82.8	64.3
1975	63.8	63.9	67.4	70.4	68.3	65.9	54.1	73.8	54.8
1976	69.2	69.0	73.4	76.5	73.7	72.9	55.5	75.0	62.7
1977	74.6	74.2	79.1	82.6	78.5	78.5	61.4	81.4	68.6
1978	79.1	78.6	83.3	86.8	81.6	81.7	69.0	88.6	73.4
1979	82.0	81.8	85.6	88.9	81.1	80.6	77.8	96.8	76.4
1980	80.2	80.4	82.8	85.7	80.5	78.8	78.4	93.0	71.4
1981	81.5	81.8	83.7	86.4	81.0	79.4	79.7	91.9	73.8
1982	77.1	77.6	78.9	81.0	79.9	78.0	72.2	80.7	66.0
1983	79.6	79.9	81.3	83.3	83.2	82.9	68.6	74.9	71.8
1984	86.5	86.6	88.0	89.7	86.1	86.6	79.0	84.1	80.9
1985	87.8	87.7	89.1	90.8	86.6	87.5	81.8	85.8	81.6
1986	88.8	88.8	90.0	91.6	89.9	90.7	81.2	85.2	83.3
1987	93.0	93.1	94.0	95.4	93.0	93.8	84.5	87.3	88.5
1988	97.2	97.3	97.9	99.2	95.8	96.7	93.5	95.3	94.0
1989	98.9	99.1	99.5	100.5	96.7	97.6	99.2	99.8	96.2
1990	98.9	99.1	99.3	100.1	97.0	97.3	98.6	99.6	96.1
1991	97.2	97.4	97.2	97.7	97.5	96.7	96.2	97.4	94.3
1992	100.0	100.0	100.0	100.0	100.0	100.0	100.0	100.0	100.0
1993	103.2	103.0	103.1	102.8	103.0	103.4	104.2	104.4	105.2
1994	108.6	108.1	108.5	107.3	106.7	108.4	110.2	110.4	115.2
1995	114.1	113.5	113.2	110.2	109.8	111.2	119.1	116.4	125.8
1996	119.4	118.8	117.4	112.4	111.5	112.4	131.8	123.2	135.2
1997	127.0	126.4	124.2	116.9	113.9	115.5	148.5	134.7	150.1
1998	132.4	131.9	128.1	118.7	115.0	116.7	165.6	142.6	160.2
1999	137.0	136.4	131.1	119.3	115.0	117.3	176.2	143.8	172.0
1996									
January	115.6	114.9	114.0	109.9	109.7	109.8	125.1	118.9	129.5
February	116.8	116.2	115.3	111.1	110.7	111.1	127.5	121.7	130.4
March	117.0	116.9	115.0	110.6	111.3	110.6	127.8	119.5	129.7
April	117.7	117.0	116.2	111.7	110.4	111.3	128.9	122.3	132.5
May	118.7	118.0	117.0	112.3	110.9	111.8	129.9	122.7	134.4
June	119.5	118.9	117.8	112.9	111.5	112.8	131.3	123.8	135.2
July	119.5	118.9	117.8	112.8	111.0	113.1	132.1	124.2	135.9
August	120.5	119.9	118.5	113.2	111.6	113.2	132.7	123.7	137.9
September	121.1	120.7	118.9	113.5	112.5	114.0	134.8	124.9	137.9
October	121.4	121.0	118.7	113.2	112.3	113.1	136.3	124.3	138.7
November	122.1	121.6	119.5	113.9	112.9	113.8	137.0	125.5	139.6
December	122.4	122.0	119.9	114.1	112.9	114.1	138.7	127.1	140.3
1997									
January	122.9	122.3	120.5	114.6	112.4	113.8	139.9	128.7	141.6
February	124.0	123.4	121.6	115.3	112.9	114.6	141.5	130.3	143.4
March	124.4	123.9	122.0	115.5	113.1	115.1	143.1	131.6	144.1
April	125.5	124.9	122.5	116.0	113.3	114.2	145.6	132.2	146.3
May	125.9	125.4	122.9	116.1	113.6	114.6	146.7	133.0	147.0
June	126.5	125.9	123.6	116.4	113.7	115.5	148.4	134.4	148.8
July	127.5	126.8	124.2	116.8	114.3	115.3	149.0	134.0	150.8
August	127.9	127.2	125.0	117.4	114.3	116.2	150.9	136.8	151.7
September	128.7	127.9	125.8	118.1	114.0	116.0	151.6	137.7	153.4
October	129.6	128.9	126.6	118.8	115.5	117.1	153.4	138.7	154.2
November	130.0	129.3	127.0	119.1	115.1	117.2	155.0	139.8	155.6
December	130.6	129.8	127.2	119.2	114.9	116.7	157.0	139.7	156.6
1998									
January	130.9	130.3	127.2	119.1	115.9	118.3	158.1	139.8	156.1
February	130.8	130.3	126.8	118.7	114.9	117.2	159.1	139.2	156.5
March	131.2	130.7	127.1	118.9	115.2	116.9	160.2	140.0	156.6
April	131.7	131.2	127.7	119.2	115.7	117.7	161.2	141.2	157.5
May	132.5	131.8	128.4	119.7	115.8	117.6	162.1	142.1	158.9
June	132.0	132.0	127.3	118.3	115.8	116.0	165.8	142.7	156.6
July	132.6	132.6	126.9	117.6	116.4	115.2	168.1	140.9	156.7
August	133.3	132.5	128.9	119.4	115.1	117.0	168.4	144.8	160.9
September	133.4	132.7	128.7	119.1	113.9	115.4	170.6	145.8	161.6
October	133.9	133.3	129.2	119.3	114.2	116.3	172.2	146.5	161.7
November	133.6	133.1	128.8	118.7	113.8	116.7	170.8	144.8	162.4
December	133.7	133.2	128.7	118.6	113.4	115.9	170.3	143.7	163.3
1999									
January	133.9	133.5	128.8	118.7	114.6	116.7	169.9	142.7	162.9
February	134.4	133.9	129.1	118.9	115.5	118.0	170.6	142.4	163.6
March	135.1	134.6	129.5	119.1	115.1	116.9	171.9	142.6	165.5
April	135.4	134.9	129.7	119.0	114.8	116.7	173.8	143.4	166.3
May	136.1	135.6	130.2	119.4	114.8	117.0	175.7	144.2	167.4
June	136.4	135.9	130.6	119.3	114.8	117.2	175.7	143.6	169.5
July	137.3	136.7	131.2	119.7	115.1	116.6	177.4	144.4	171.6
August	137.4	137.1	131.4	119.8	115.2	117.7	178.3	144.6	171.3
September	138.0	137.2	131.5	119.9	115.2	117.1	178.5	143.6	173.0
October	138.9	138.3	132.4	120.5	116.3	118.7	179.5	144.0	174.7
November	139.3	138.7	132.7	120.5	115.6	118.8	179.7	143.7	177.4
December	140.2	139.5	133.2	120.8	116.4	118.8	181.1	143.8	178.6

Table 4-3. Industrial Production Indexes by Industry Groups

(1992=100, seasonally adjusted.)

Year and month	Total	Manufacturing Total	Primary processing	Advanced processing	Durable goods manufacturing Total	Lumber and products	Furniture and fixtures	Stone, clay, and glass products	Primary metals Total	Iron and steel Total	Iron and steel Raw steel	Nonferrous
1970	58.7	54.8	67.2	48.9	52.7	68.6	56.2	74.8	111.2	139.0	139.2	75.9
1971	59.5	55.6	68.7	49.4	52.4	70.4	58.6	78.5	104.9	126.3	127.1	76.6
1972	65.3	61.5	77.3	54.3	58.5	80.6	70.7	86.9	118.3	141.5	143.9	87.0
1973	70.6	66.9	84.6	59.0	65.3	80.9	75.4	93.9	134.1	161.0	164.3	98.1
1974	69.6	65.9	82.0	58.6	64.0	73.4	70.1	92.4	129.7	155.7	163.1	94.8
1975	63.5	59.4	71.4	53.8	56.1	68.3	60.0	81.8	103.4	125.1	128.6	74.3
1976	69.3	65.4	80.3	58.6	61.8	77.8	67.0	91.5	115.7	137.9	140.9	85.7
1977	74.9	71.2	86.7	64.0	68.1	86.1	74.8	98.3	119.0	138.0	139.3	93.0
1978	79.3	75.8	90.7	68.9	73.6	87.5	80.4	106.0	128.0	147.5	154.9	101.1
1979	82.0	78.5	92.5	72.0	77.4	86.3	80.5	106.8	130.0	148.4	154.4	104.6
1980	79.7	75.5	84.4	71.4	73.4	80.4	79.1	96.5	108.0	119.0	126.9	92.4
1981	81.0	76.7	85.2	72.8	74.6	78.1	78.4	94.3	113.9	126.6	138.5	96.1
1982	76.7	72.1	75.7	70.5	68.2	70.3	74.6	84.2	80.5	80.5	82.6	80.7
1983	79.5	76.3	82.1	73.6	72.2	83.3	80.2	91.2	88.2	90.0	94.1	85.9
1984	86.6	83.8	88.4	81.7	82.7	89.9	88.6	98.6	98.7	98.9	102.6	98.6
1985	88.0	85.7	88.4	84.5	85.6	92.0	88.9	98.0	98.4	98.8	97.7	98.2
1986	89.0	88.1	90.0	87.2	87.4	99.6	93.3	101.7	91.2	86.8	89.7	97.6
1987	93.2	92.8	95.3	91.6	92.0	104.9	100.9	104.8	97.8	95.4	98.8	101.2
1988	97.4	97.1	99.0	96.2	98.1	105.1	101.1	107.5	106.2	107.6	111.2	104.6
1989	99.1	99.0	99.9	98.6	100.5	104.3	102.4	107.4	104.9	106.2	107.2	103.2
1990	98.9	98.5	99.3	98.2	99.0	101.6	100.9	105.0	104.0	106.4	108.3	100.9
1991	97.0	96.2	95.7	96.4	95.5	94.5	94.8	97.2	96.7	96.0	96.2	97.7
1992	100.0	100.0	100.0	100.0	100.0	100.0	100.0	100.0	100.0	100.0	100.0	100.0
1993	103.4	103.7	103.5	103.7	105.4	100.8	104.9	102.1	105.1	106.1	103.0	104.0
1994	109.1	110.0	109.8	110.1	114.3	105.9	108.1	107.8	113.8	114.4	107.5	113.0
1995	114.4	115.8	112.1	117.7	123.9	107.9	111.4	110.9	116.2	116.5	112.0	115.7
1996	119.4	121.3	114.3	124.7	134.0	110.1	113.1	118.0	119.6	118.9	111.9	120.5
1997	127.1	130.1	119.5	135.1	148.0	115.0	118.0	122.0	126.7	125.6	115.5	128.1
1998	132.4	136.4	121.2	144.0	160.7	118.5	122.0	126.8	125.6	122.6	115.3	129.4
1999	137.1	142.3	123.3	151.8	172.8	121.6	125.5	130.5	126.6	123.2	113.3	130.9
1996												
January	115.6	117.0	111.2	119.7	127.6	106.9	110.7	114.4	115.3	116.4	111.4	113.8
February	116.9	118.3	111.5	121.5	129.6	106.6	110.5	113.6	116.2	114.6	110.3	118.1
March	116.6	117.8	112.5	120.3	128.1	109.8	109.7	115.0	118.1	117.0	111.7	119.3
April	118.0	119.4	112.6	122.7	131.6	110.2	110.8	114.3	117.6	115.9	110.7	119.6
May	119.0	120.5	113.6	123.9	133.3	110.3	114.2	117.2	118.6	117.0	111.4	120.6
June	119.8	121.5	114.8	124.8	134.9	112.1	112.6	119.1	119.8	119.4	114.4	120.2
July	119.9	122.0	114.8	125.5	135.3	109.7	111.7	121.6	118.2	118.2	113.1	118.1
August	120.7	122.8	115.6	126.3	136.5	111.2	116.2	119.1	121.3	120.8	113.0	121.9
September	121.2	123.5	116.2	127.0	137.1	111.6	114.8	121.1	122.1	119.6	112.3	125.2
October	121.2	123.4	116.3	126.8	137.0	110.6	115.6	120.9	123.2	123.6	112.6	122.5
November	122.1	124.3	116.5	128.2	138.5	112.3	115.7	120.2	122.4	122.4	110.2	122.3
December	122.4	124.8	116.5	128.9	139.0	109.7	115.2	118.8	122.9	121.6	113.3	124.5
1997												
January	123.0	125.3	116.5	129.7	140.1	110.9	114.7	121.1	121.1	121.6	111.9	120.4
February	124.0	126.5	117.9	130.8	142.0	113.6	116.0	121.1	123.6	122.0	112.2	125.5
March	124.5	127.1	117.9	131.8	143.1	114.6	116.5	120.2	122.2	118.6	113.7	126.5
April	125.2	127.8	118.8	132.4	144.5	115.0	118.4	121.7	125.2	125.3	114.0	125.1
May	125.8	128.4	118.9	133.3	145.8	115.7	117.6	120.2	126.1	124.6	113.7	127.9
June	126.6	129.5	119.1	134.8	147.9	116.2	117.8	121.3	128.0	126.5	114.5	129.8
July	127.2	130.1	119.8	135.4	148.4	116.3	119.5	122.2	127.4	125.7	115.0	129.5
August	128.0	131.1	120.0	136.9	150.5	115.0	118.1	121.7	127.3	123.8	115.6	131.6
September	128.8	131.8	120.9	137.5	151.5	114.9	118.2	123.0	128.9	128.8	118.1	128.9
October	129.6	132.7	121.0	138.7	152.3	115.0	118.3	122.8	129.6	129.3	118.6	130.0
November	130.2	133.5	121.9	139.5	154.3	116.4	120.1	124.2	131.5	131.1	121.5	131.9
December	130.6	134.0	122.1	140.2	155.3	116.2	120.8	124.8	129.6	129.5	120.1	129.6
1998												
January	130.9	134.5	122.0	141.0	155.9	116.3	120.3	124.2	130.7	130.5	122.6	130.8
February	130.7	134.3	121.7	141.0	156.4	117.2	120.7	124.4	130.6	130.8	123.3	130.2
March	131.1	134.5	121.6	141.3	157.0	116.9	121.9	125.2	128.9	129.1	119.1	128.5
April	131.7	135.3	122.1	142.2	158.1	117.6	122.0	125.5	128.9	127.4	121.3	130.8
May	132.4	135.9	121.9	143.3	159.6	117.5	121.0	125.7	128.3	127.0	120.0	129.9
June	131.5	134.8	120.8	142.2	158.0	117.9	122.1	125.8	123.5	121.4	115.6	126.0
July	131.3	134.7	120.9	142.0	157.3	118.6	122.0	126.8	123.8	121.6	116.7	126.5
August	133.6	137.4	120.6	146.2	164.2	119.6	120.5	127.2	124.9	122.3	119.3	128.2
September	133.5	137.3	120.3	146.3	164.6	118.7	122.6	127.0	122.2	115.7	112.2	130.3
October	134.1	138.3	120.7	147.5	165.8	119.8	124.2	128.4	122.5	116.2	110.0	130.4
November	133.8	138.3	120.8	147.5	165.4	119.9	123.7	130.1	120.5	112.1	101.6	130.9
December	133.8	138.4	121.9	147.2	166.2	122.5	123.3	131.8	122.5	116.5	102.7	130.0
1999												
January	134.1	138.6	122.2	147.2	166.3	122.6	122.7	133.2	122.9	118.1	106.8	128.9
February	134.5	139.3	122.1	148.4	166.8	122.3	124.6	132.2	120.1	114.6	106.8	127.0
March	135.1	139.7	122.4	148.8	168.1	121.7	125.8	130.8	124.0	118.1	108.3	131.4
April	135.5	140.2	122.2	149.6	169.4	121.5	123.8	128.8	123.9	119.4	109.3	129.4
May	136.2	141.0	122.5	150.7	170.8	123.9	124.4	128.5	123.9	120.1	111.4	128.6
June	136.6	141.4	122.7	151.2	172.2	122.2	124.4	127.8	127.4	124.5	110.7	130.8
July	137.4	142.0	123.3	151.8	173.8	121.5	125.7	129.3	128.0	126.2	111.1	130.2
August	137.7	142.5	123.4	152.6	174.4	120.2	126.4	130.2	129.6	127.6	115.9	132.1
September	138.1	142.9	123.6	153.1	175.0	119.7	127.9	129.6	128.3	125.9	112.4	131.4
October	139.1	144.2	124.8	154.5	176.5	120.5	127.0	131.2	129.0	124.9	121.8	134.0
November	139.4	145.0	125.6	155.2	177.4	119.8	125.2	132.4	131.1	130.7	124.0	131.7
December	140.1	145.6	125.9	155.9	178.4	121.4	128.6	131.4	132.8	131.7	124.2	134.1

Table 4-3. Industrial Production Indexes by Industry Groups—*Continued*

(1992=100, seasonally adjusted.)

Year and month	Fabricated metal products	Industrial machinery and equiment		Electrical machinery		Transportation equipment				Instruments	Miscellaneous
							Motor vehicles and parts		Aerospace and miscellaneous		
		Total	Computer and office equipment	Total	Semiconductors	Total	Total	Autos and light trucks			
1970	77.7	41.1	2.3	26.2	. . .	54.1	52.0	. . .	62.3	36.2	72.1
1971	77.3	38.2	2.0	26.3	. . .	58.5	65.2	. . .	55.9	37.9	72.4
1972	84.8	44.3	2.4	30.1	. . .	62.4	71.1	. . .	57.7	42.5	84.6
1973	94.3	51.8	2.9	34.3	. . .	71.1	82.8	. . .	63.8	48.5	85.7
1974	90.5	55.2	3.5	33.9	. . .	64.6	71.4	. . .	62.0	51.4	81.9
1975	78.4	47.8	3.2	29.2	. . .	58.2	61.0	. . .	59.3	48.9	76.0
1976	86.9	50.2	3.9	32.8	. . .	66.3	80.0	. . .	56.6	53.7	82.5
1977	94.7	56.6	5.1	38.1	. . .	71.9	92.4	84.2	55.6	60.1	92.6
1978	98.2	63.3	7.5	42.2	. . .	77.5	96.8	87.5	62.2	66.2	92.7
1979	101.6	70.2	10.3	46.9	. . .	78.7	89.0	80.1	71.1	71.7	92.1
1980	94.4	70.5	13.9	48.6	. . .	70.3	65.8	58.1	74.3	73.6	86.9
1981	93.0	74.7	18.4	51.0	. . .	66.9	62.8	59.3	70.5	75.4	89.6
1982	84.9	65.8	21.3	51.7	. . .	63.0	56.9	54.4	68.3	76.3	85.5
1983	87.2	65.2	29.5	55.9	. . .	70.5	72.1	74.7	69.3	77.7	83.2
1984	95.2	78.9	42.0	66.7	. . .	80.5	87.3	90.7	75.1	86.0	87.6
1985	96.5	81.2	50.3	68.4	. . .	88.8	95.0	99.1	83.7	89.3	82.2
1986	95.6	81.8	53.7	71.0	42.9	94.1	94.2	99.2	94.2	88.8	83.5
1987	101.9	86.0	62.2	75.6	50.6	96.1	94.9	98.7	97.5	93.8	93.5
1988	106.1	97.1	74.6	82.5	57.3	101.1	100.2	103.1	102.1	97.2	99.8
1989	104.8	103.0	83.0	85.8	64.2	105.1	101.2	106.5	109.4	98.2	100.3
1990	101.2	100.1	81.4	87.7	71.7	102.3	95.3	99.3	109.8	98.4	100.0
1991	96.2	95.4	82.3	89.6	80.8	96.5	88.5	91.0	105.0	99.8	98.4
1992	100.0	100.0	100.0	100.0	100.0	100.0	100.0	100.0	100.0	100.0	100.0
1993	104.4	110.1	121.2	109.4	114.8	103.5	113.0	111.3	93.9	100.8	105.7
1994	112.2	125.6	152.9	130.5	153.2	107.5	130.6	125.4	84.9	99.8	110.0
1995	116.4	143.7	208.8	165.7	245.5	106.7	133.2	122.4	81.0	103.6	113.0
1996	120.1	159.6	296.0	206.6	368.2	107.6	131.8	121.1	83.9	107.6	116.5
1997	126.1	178.3	403.9	260.0	558.3	117.1	140.6	127.1	94.2	109.6	119.6
1998	128.8	206.4	675.1	315.1	799.5	121.6	141.7	127.8	101.7	112.6	122.0
1999	128.7	230.1	1 061.4	390.2	1 180.9	122.4	151.0	137.8	94.9	116.5	124.7
1996											
January	117.4	150.2	238.0	185.1	305.6	104.0	128.6	111.3	79.9	106.0	114.7
February	118.8	151.8	238.6	191.5	317.2	106.0	131.5	118.9	81.2	107.8	115.8
March	118.4	152.8	248.5	193.7	325.4	95.9	110.5	98.9	81.5	108.2	116.1
April	118.3	154.8	264.0	196.4	332.8	108.8	136.6	124.7	81.7	107.7	115.2
May	119.0	158.1	278.9	200.4	345.3	109.9	138.2	124.9	82.3	107.5	116.2
June	120.0	159.6	288.9	205.5	357.3	110.3	138.6	129.6	82.8	108.2	117.0
July	120.6	160.1	297.3	208.2	371.8	111.6	139.8	134.8	84.2	107.0	116.4
August	121.7	162.4	309.5	212.9	388.9	110.6	137.3	127.3	84.6	107.2	117.0
September	121.9	163.5	327.9	216.6	401.3	109.0	132.4	125.3	86.1	108.1	117.5
October	121.7	165.4	346.8	219.5	413.8	105.7	125.2	114.3	86.7	107.9	116.6
November	121.7	167.5	357.7	223.3	424.2	109.4	131.9	120.6	87.5	107.0	116.9
December	121.6	168.5	355.9	226.0	434.8	109.6	131.2	123.0	88.4	108.3	118.7
1997											
January	122.6	168.9	348.9	229.1	445.2	112.4	136.6	125.2	88.7	107.3	118.8
February	124.1	169.9	347.8	236.4	469.9	112.9	136.6	126.4	89.8	108.3	119.2
March	124.3	171.7	359.0	242.8	494.0	113.9	137.1	128.3	91.2	107.8	118.7
April	125.3	175.9	378.9	245.7	502.1	112.6	133.0	117.5	92.5	108.7	118.3
May	125.6	178.0	398.8	251.6	524.6	113.5	134.2	121.2	93.1	108.8	118.8
June	125.0	178.4	412.1	259.7	554.7	116.7	140.6	127.7	93.4	109.7	119.2
July	126.3	179.0	417.5	266.6	578.1	114.1	135.3	115.8	93.2	109.7	120.0
August	127.0	180.4	415.4	270.6	605.4	119.8	144.1	130.5	96.0	110.6	119.8
September	127.1	180.1	413.0	274.4	617.7	122.1	147.4	134.3	97.3	110.1	119.6
October	128.1	182.6	418.7	277.1	624.0	120.7	144.4	130.0	97.5	111.7	120.1
November	128.6	185.5	445.3	282.2	635.8	123.2	148.9	136.6	98.1	111.4	120.7
December	130.0	189.0	491.1	284.4	648.3	123.8	148.7	131.9	99.4	110.7	122.2
1998											
January	129.4	193.5	533.9	287.4	660.1	121.7	143.7	131.7	100.0	111.1	122.3
February	129.3	196.3	574.6	289.6	669.6	120.8	141.9	127.9	100.0	111.2	122.9
March	129.2	199.1	585.1	291.9	682.2	120.4	140.6	127.5	100.3	111.9	123.3
April	129.4	199.2	584.5	298.0	706.1	121.9	143.3	130.3	100.8	111.7	123.4
May	129.9	201.1	589.8	303.5	734.2	124.1	146.6	130.3	101.8	112.8	122.7
June	129.2	205.9	625.8	311.7	773.7	113.2	123.2	109.2	102.6	112.0	122.4
July	127.7	209.9	681.5	319.0	812.3	105.6	106.9	85.1	102.8	112.2	122.5
August	127.2	211.7	734.5	323.3	842.5	129.1	155.8	140.7	103.1	113.3	122.0
September	127.7	213.0	767.4	331.9	880.4	126.9	152.4	136.8	102.0	114.3	121.6
October	128.1	215.0	786.8	338.2	921.5	127.1	151.1	139.9	103.6	114.4	120.5
November	128.6	215.3	805.3	341.7	949.2	124.9	148.0	138.1	102.3	113.0	119.5
December	129.8	216.6	832.2	344.8	962.1	123.9	147.1	136.4	101.2	112.8	120.8
1999											
January	129.0	217.5	868.1	346.7	961.0	122.7	146.5	136.5	99.4	113.3	120.6
February	128.4	221.7	907.1	347.5	966.9	123.2	147.8	135.0	99.3	112.9	121.8
March	128.5	224.6	947.6	354.0	1 009.4	122.6	148.1	134.0	97.9	113.7	122.9
April	128.0	227.0	987.5	366.4	1 062.8	122.1	148.4	135.7	96.5	115.1	124.3
May	127.2	228.4	1 021.6	373.3	1 091.7	122.8	150.6	138.3	96.0	116.7	125.5
June	128.3	228.2	1 048.2	384.2	1 155.2	123.5	152.9	142.0	95.2	117.0	124.5
July	128.6	230.0	1 075.1	399.2	1 212.5	122.9	152.2	135.8	94.7	117.2	125.2
August	128.5	231.4	1 123.7	401.3	1 224.7	122.9	152.2	146.8	94.7	117.7	125.2
September	128.4	235.5	1 167.5	402.1	1 243.7	123.1	155.6	139.4	92.2	117.2	125.1
October	128.8	238.3	1 196.6	412.6	1 294.0	122.3	155.7	140.7	90.6	118.3	125.0
November	129.7	239.7	1 222.8	418.1	1 373.2	121.8	155.8	141.0	89.5	118.9	125.0
December	129.0	241.8	1 244.6	426.4	1 420.3	120.4	152.7	135.0	89.7	119.7	126.4

Table 4-3. Industrial Production Indexes by Industry Groups—*Continued*

(1992=100, seasonally adjusted.)

Year and month	Nondurable goods manufacturing										
	Total	Foods	Tobacco products	Textile mill products	Apparel products	Paper and products	Printing and publishing	Chemicals and products	Petroleum products	Rubber and plastics products	Leather and products
1970	58.0	60.6	94.3	71.8	81.8	56.7	54.4	48.8	80.8	33.0	235.0
1971	60.3	62.5	93.1	75.8	82.9	59.1	54.8	51.9	83.5	35.9	225.7
1972	65.7	65.8	96.6	83.1	87.9	64.3	58.5	58.4	87.4	43.7	234.2
1973	69.0	67.1	101.7	86.5	88.5	68.8	60.1	63.9	92.2	49.0	217.9
1974	68.5	68.0	99.4	78.7	84.5	68.2	59.1	66.2	89.0	47.9	207.2
1975	64.2	67.5	101.7	75.0	77.4	59.4	55.4	60.3	88.0	41.6	206.6
1976	70.7	71.4	106.8	83.3	91.1	67.4	60.5	67.5	93.6	48.1	205.1
1977	75.7	74.6	102.8	88.3	98.0	70.1	66.3	72.4	101.5	56.0	200.6
1978	78.9	77.2	107.4	88.6	100.4	73.4	70.1	76.4	104.9	59.3	201.6
1979	79.9	77.9	106.9	91.5	95.3	76.0	72.0	79.2	103.9	58.7	184.4
1980	78.3	79.7	108.5	89.0	95.4	75.2	72.4	75.9	95.9	53.3	181.6
1981	79.5	81.4	109.9	86.3	97.3	76.6	74.3	77.3	91.2	57.5	176.0
1982	77.7	82.4	106.2	80.1	96.3	74.3	77.5	71.0	86.6	56.8	163.1
1983	81.9	84.6	101.6	89.9	100.3	81.0	81.4	76.0	86.9	64.0	158.3
1984	85.3	86.4	101.7	90.4	102.2	85.0	87.0	79.3	89.9	72.1	141.9
1985	86.0	88.9	101.8	86.5	98.6	83.8	90.2	79.4	89.5	73.8	126.1
1986	89.1	91.2	100.3	90.5	101.8	88.3	93.4	82.4	95.7	78.2	115.0
1987	93.8	93.5	104.7	96.3	105.5	90.9	102.5	87.0	97.0	86.0	112.4
1988	96.0	94.9	106.5	95.0	103.5	93.8	103.4	92.2	98.8	88.2	112.0
1989	97.3	95.9	105.4	96.5	100.3	95.4	103.5	95.1	99.3	91.2	111.9
1990	97.9	97.0	105.4	93.2	97.2	96.0	103.1	97.3	100.3	92.2	107.8
1991	97.0	98.4	98.9	92.7	97.8	96.8	99.1	96.4	99.1	90.7	98.4
1992	100.0	100.0	100.0	100.0	100.0	100.0	100.0	100.0	100.0	100.0	100.0
1993	101.8	102.0	84.1	105.3	102.4	104.0	100.7	101.6	102.9	106.9	101.0
1994	105.2	103.7	104.4	110.6	106.3	108.4	100.7	104.8	102.7	116.5	93.6
1995	107.1	105.8	111.8	110.2	107.1	109.6	101.3	107.4	104.5	119.7	86.9
1996	107.8	105.4	113.5	108.7	104.1	108.8	101.3	109.8	106.8	123.3	87.5
1997	111.2	107.8	112.9	111.9	102.1	114.3	105.2	114.6	110.8	128.4	83.6
1998	111.6	109.3	106.2	110.9	96.6	114.9	105.1	115.1	113.3	133.2	77.1
1999	111.8	110.1	94.3	110.9	90.7	116.2	104.4	117.5	114.7	137.7	69.8
1996											
January	105.6	104.7	108.6	103.3	101.5	106.2	99.0	107.7	105.1	120.3	85.7
February	106.2	105.2	112.3	105.7	104.7	104.6	100.2	107.6	106.0	120.4	86.9
March	106.7	105.6	116.7	109.5	103.7	106.2	100.1	107.6	105.7	121.2	87.3
April	106.5	105.2	113.2	107.4	104.6	108.4	100.4	106.8	105.3	120.5	87.5
May	106.9	104.6	111.5	108.7	104.8	108.3	101.2	107.9	106.0	122.6	87.2
June	107.4	105.0	118.2	111.0	104.7	109.2	100.5	107.9	106.4	124.1	88.7
July	107.9	104.9	113.0	109.0	104.2	110.0	101.2	110.4	105.5	124.1	88.2
August	108.3	104.6	113.3	110.2	105.6	108.9	102.1	110.8	107.6	125.3	88.3
September	109.1	106.0	119.7	109.7	104.9	109.7	102.1	111.5	108.0	125.9	88.3
October	109.0	105.8	110.3	109.9	104.1	109.7	102.6	112.9	109.1	124.3	87.4
November	109.4	106.3	113.3	110.3	103.9	111.6	102.9	112.6	108.7	124.5	86.9
December	109.9	106.7	111.6	109.2	103.1	112.6	103.1	113.6	108.5	125.9	87.5
1997											
January	109.8	106.3	117.3	108.9	102.6	111.4	103.2	114.1	107.4	125.0	87.5
February	110.4	107.6	112.3	110.3	102.2	113.2	103.8	113.8	108.7	126.8	85.5
March	110.6	107.7	120.2	110.7	103.5	113.7	104.0	112.7	109.0	127.2	86.7
April	110.6	107.2	109.1	111.6	102.6	113.4	104.6	114.6	110.5	126.2	85.6
May	110.6	107.4	106.7	109.6	102.8	113.9	105.1	113.7	112.6	127.1	85.0
June	110.7	107.4	108.9	111.2	102.6	113.0	104.6	113.9	112.7	127.8	83.9
July	111.4	108.8	107.2	113.2	101.9	114.3	105.7	114.5	110.4	128.1	84.3
August	111.5	108.0	107.9	112.2	101.7	114.9	105.3	115.1	110.6	130.2	81.2
September	111.9	107.9	112.6	112.9	101.7	116.2	105.7	115.4	112.1	130.1	80.9
October	112.8	107.6	129.4	113.2	101.6	115.3	107.1	116.1	112.6	129.8	81.9
November	112.4	108.6	113.8	114.6	100.9	116.3	107.0	115.4	110.1	131.2	80.8
December	112.5	108.7	109.7	114.1	100.8	115.9	106.5	116.4	112.4	131.0	80.4
1998											
January	113.0	109.9	118.6	114.7	100.4	115.2	106.0	116.3	112.1	131.8	79.8
February	112.2	109.3	111.8	112.2	98.9	115.4	105.7	115.7	111.1	131.7	80.7
March	112.0	109.4	106.2	112.5	98.7	114.5	105.5	115.5	113.9	132.1	80.0
April	112.5	109.4	110.3	112.7	97.7	115.5	105.5	116.2	113.2	133.5	78.8
May	112.2	109.5	111.2	113.6	96.8	115.1	105.5	115.6	112.0	133.3	78.2
June	111.6	108.9	109.6	112.3	97.0	114.7	104.2	114.9	112.6	132.8	76.4
July	112.0	108.4	116.1	112.0	96.9	115.9	104.4	115.5	114.5	132.8	77.0
August	111.0	107.7	107.2	110.6	96.3	114.7	104.5	114.0	115.0	132.7	76.0
September	110.4	108.4	95.0	109.9	95.8	114.2	104.3	113.9	113.0	133.2	75.7
October	111.2	109.5	100.7	106.6	94.8	115.8	105.1	114.4	112.5	133.6	75.0
November	111.6	110.9	96.0	107.0	93.3	112.8	105.1	116.2	114.8	134.9	75.1
December	111.1	110.3	91.1	106.4	93.2	114.9	105.3	114.7	114.8	135.6	73.2
1999											
January	111.3	111.0	94.8	108.0	92.3	115.7	104.3	114.5	117.2	135.4	71.9
February	112.3	111.4	99.2	110.5	92.2	115.9	104.3	116.6	117.0	135.6	71.5
March	111.8	110.9	95.4	110.1	91.8	115.9	103.7	116.8	114.9	135.8	71.3
April	111.5	110.6	94.2	111.4	92.4	115.0	104.2	115.6	114.6	136.2	70.6
May	111.9	110.6	95.4	110.9	91.2	114.6	104.1	117.0	114.2	137.4	70.9
June	111.4	110.0	94.5	110.8	90.7	115.7	103.5	116.3	113.4	136.4	71.3
July	111.0	108.9	96.0	112.3	89.8	115.0	102.8	115.8	115.1	138.0	69.1
August	111.5	108.9	94.8	111.7	89.2	115.8	103.6	117.7	114.1	137.6	70.2
September	111.8	109.6	90.9	110.8	89.0	117.2	104.6	117.4	114.6	139.3	69.5
October	113.0	110.1	91.9	112.7	89.1	118.0	106.0	119.8	114.5	138.9	68.2
November	113.6	110.3	93.1	111.4	89.1	118.1	105.7	122.7	112.8	139.3	67.7
December	113.7	110.0	94.7	110.1	89.1	117.7	105.3	122.9	114.9	141.4	65.4

Table 4-3. Industrial Production Indexes by Industry Groups—*Continued*

(1992=100, seasonally adjusted.)

Year and month	Mining					Utilities			Special aggregates		
									Manufacturing excluding:		
	Total	Metal mining	Coal mining	Oil and gas extraction	Stone and earth minerals	Total	Electric	Gas	Motor vehicles and parts	Computer and office equipment	Computers and semi-conductors
1970	101.8	77.1	62.3	116.5	89.5	66.5	51.0	130.5	. . .	. . .	. . .
1971	99.3	68.6	57.3	115.2	89.9	69.6	53.9	134.4	. . .	. . .	. . .
1972	101.4	66.3	61.3	117.2	93.9	74.1	58.4	136.5	. . .	. . .	. . .
1973	102.3	70.0	60.7	116.6	102.5	77.0	62.3	134.4	. . .	. . .	. . .
1974	101.8	68.0	61.6	115.8	102.1	76.1	61.9	131.2	. . .	. . .	. . .
1975	99.5	63.5	66.2	113.1	91.9	76.8	64.0	125.2	. . .	. . .	. . .
1976	100.3	69.2	68.9	111.2	97.2	79.9	67.1	127.1	. . .	. . .	. . .
1977	103.4	61.1	70.6	116.8	99.4	82.0	70.7	120.7	. . .	. . .	. . .
1978	106.5	69.5	67.6	121.1	104.7	84.4	73.3	122.6	. . .	. . .	. . .
1979	108.3	72.2	78.6	119.5	107.1	86.8	75.2	126.6	. . .	. . .	. . .
1980	111.5	65.2	83.4	124.4	97.9	87.3	76.4	124.8	. . .	. . .	. . .
1981	115.6	73.5	82.9	129.7	94.1	85.0	78.0	109.3	. . .	. . .	. . .
1982	111.2	54.8	84.5	125.6	78.7	82.3	76.7	102.4	. . .	. . .	. . .
1983	106.6	52.8	79.0	120.2	84.0	83.7	79.2	100.4	. . .	. . .	. . .
1984	113.9	57.2	90.2	126.9	94.7	86.7	82.4	102.6	. . .	. . .	. . .
1985	111.0	56.6	89.1	123.0	97.9	88.8	84.6	104.3	. . .	. . .	. . .
1986	102.6	59.3	89.7	111.0	96.6	86.4	86.2	87.0	87.8	89.2	91.1
1987	102.1	61.9	92.5	108.9	100.9	89.4	89.4	89.0	92.7	93.7	95.4
1988	104.7	74.3	95.4	110.4	103.2	93.9	93.6	94.5	97.0	97.7	99.3
1989	103.2	85.6	98.9	106.1	101.8	97.1	96.8	98.1	98.9	99.4	100.7
1990	104.8	93.1	103.7	106.4	103.3	98.3	99.2	94.4	98.7	98.9	99.9
1991	102.6	93.3	100.1	104.7	96.7	100.4	101.2	97.3	96.7	96.5	97.0
1992	100.0	100.0	100.0	100.0	100.0	100.0	100.0	100.0	100.0	100.0	100.0
1993	100.0	98.8	94.0	101.1	102.3	103.9	103.8	104.3	103.1	103.3	103.0
1994	102.5	100.5	103.0	101.7	108.6	105.3	105.5	104.6	108.8	109.2	107.9
1995	102.1	101.6	102.6	100.5	112.9	109.0	109.5	107.2	114.8	114.4	110.9
1996	103.7	104.0	105.0	101.8	114.9	112.6	112.7	112.3	120.6	118.9	113.1
1997	105.9	110.3	108.2	103.1	120.1	112.7	113.3	110.6	129.2	126.5	118.2
1998	103.8	109.1	109.7	99.5	123.4	114.4	116.9	103.2	135.9	131.0	120.4
1999	98.0	97.1	108.1	92.5	124.4	115.6	118.2	104.6	141.7	135.3	121.6
1996											
January	100.3	98.0	94.4	100.8	107.7	113.1	112.8	114.1	116.3	115.2	110.4
February	101.9	97.4	99.3	101.5	112.6	114.7	114.3	116.0	117.5	116.5	111.5
March	103.4	102.3	106.9	101.3	113.9	114.6	114.4	115.6	118.2	115.9	110.8
April	104.0	100.8	105.5	102.6	114.2	113.7	113.2	115.8	118.4	117.3	112.1
May	103.9	103.3	105.7	102.1	114.7	114.6	114.8	114.0	119.5	118.3	112.8
June	105.3	104.4	108.2	103.1	117.3	113.1	113.7	110.7	120.5	119.2	113.5
July	104.8	106.8	108.2	102.3	116.4	109.2	110.2	105.3	120.9	119.6	113.7
August	104.8	106.8	109.0	102.2	116.0	110.7	111.4	107.9	122.0	120.3	114.2
September	104.5	107.4	105.7	102.5	114.8	110.9	111.0	110.6	122.9	120.8	114.5
October	104.1	106.8	105.8	101.6	118.3	111.4	111.4	111.5	123.3	120.5	114.0
November	103.8	105.5	106.2	101.3	117.8	112.9	112.7	113.9	123.9	121.4	114.8
December	103.4	108.0	105.7	100.8	115.0	112.5	112.7	112.1	124.4	121.8	115.1
1997											
January	104.2	111.9	106.2	101.8	112.2	113.3	113.6	112.1	124.6	122.4	115.5
February	106.0	109.7	109.7	102.8	121.6	111.7	112.0	110.7	125.9	123.6	116.4
March	106.6	109.5	108.3	103.7	123.7	110.0	111.4	104.1	126.6	124.2	116.6
April	105.6	108.8	106.2	103.4	118.2	113.0	113.4	111.7	127.6	124.7	117.0
May	106.8	109.7	114.1	103.4	119.0	112.1	110.8	118.0	128.1	125.1	117.2
June	106.0	112.1	108.1	102.7	122.6	110.9	110.7	111.9	128.9	126.1	117.7
July	106.0	111.5	107.6	103.5	118.5	112.6	113.4	108.9	129.8	126.6	118.0
August	105.9	112.0	107.5	103.0	121.2	111.5	112.0	109.0	130.4	127.7	118.8
September	106.3	109.3	107.1	103.8	121.9	113.8	114.9	108.7	131.0	128.4	119.4
October	106.0	112.3	106.1	103.3	121.2	115.4	116.7	109.9	132.1	129.2	120.1
November	105.6	112.5	106.5	102.8	120.5	114.2	115.0	111.1	132.6	129.8	120.6
December	105.5	104.6	110.9	102.6	120.2	114.3	115.2	110.5	133.2	130.0	120.7
1998											
January	107.7	109.2	113.4	104.2	124.1	109.4	110.9	102.9	134.0	130.2	120.8
February	107.4	118.7	106.0	104.5	123.5	109.8	111.6	102.0	134.0	129.8	120.3
March	105.8	105.2	109.3	103.0	121.1	113.8	115.8	105.2	134.3	129.9	120.3
April	105.5	104.5	107.7	102.7	123.5	113.0	115.2	102.9	134.9	130.7	120.8
May	106.0	108.8	112.8	102.1	123.2	116.0	119.2	101.8	135.4	131.3	121.1
June	104.2	109.6	108.7	100.2	123.6	117.8	120.3	106.6	135.6	129.9	119.4
July	103.1	109.1	108.1	99.0	122.0	117.0	118.7	110.0	136.5	129.6	118.8
August	103.2	114.3	107.9	98.7	122.9	117.3	119.0	109.8	136.3	131.9	120.9
September	101.7	108.0	110.3	96.7	121.6	119.1	122.0	106.1	136.5	131.7	120.4
October	101.6	106.5	110.9	96.4	122.6	115.6	119.0	100.1	137.6	132.5	121.0
November	101.5	109.4	112.4	94.7	128.9	110.8	114.7	93.3	137.8	132.5	120.7
December	98.1	106.6	109.2	91.5	124.1	112.5	115.9	97.5	138.0	132.5	120.7
1999											
January	98.0	102.9	107.7	91.2	129.4	114.5	115.8	108.8	138.2	132.4	120.6
February	97.4	101.3	108.9	90.7	127.1	112.6	114.9	102.5	138.9	133.0	121.1
March	97.5	98.5	103.9	92.1	126.6	116.8	119.1	106.4	139.3	133.1	121.0
April	96.7	100.5	107.3	90.8	121.8	116.3	118.6	105.7	139.8	133.4	120.9
May	97.4	100.2	106.1	91.8	123.9	116.1	118.4	105.8	140.5	134.1	121.3
June	97.1	98.9	107.0	91.4	123.3	117.4	119.6	107.5	140.8	134.3	121.2
July	97.8	96.2	110.0	92.3	120.5	119.8	122.6	107.4	141.4	134.8	121.4
August	98.5	93.0	110.7	93.2	123.0	117.8	120.0	108.2	142.0	135.1	121.6
September	98.3	91.4	109.4	93.0	125.5	117.7	119.8	108.5	142.3	135.3	121.7
October	99.2	94.2	108.8	94.0	126.3	115.2	116.9	107.9	143.6	136.5	122.6
November	99.7	94.5	110.0	94.5	125.0	110.9	115.8	88.2	144.5	137.1	122.9
December	99.5	95.2	109.5	94.6	122.4	113.5	116.9	98.1	145.2	137.6	123.1

Table 4-4. Capacity Utilization

(Output as a percent of capacity, seasonally adjusted.)

Year and month	Total industry	Manufacturing												
		Total	Primary process-ing	Advanced process-ing	Durable goods									
					Total	Lumber and products	Furniture and fixtures	Stone, clay, and glass products	Primary metals					
									Total	Iron and steel		Nonferrous		
										Total	Raw steel	Total	Primary copper	Primary aluminum
1970	81.1	79.4	79.9	78.9	77.2	80.5	81.0	73.9	80.8	84.9	83.4	74.3	88.4	97.4
1971	79.4	77.9	78.7	77.1	74.7	80.0	80.7	75.6	74.8	76.6	76.0	71.7	74.9	88.1
1972	84.4	83.4	85.5	82.2	81.4	88.2	93.0	81.7	83.7	86.2	85.6	79.2	85.1	87.4
1973	88.4	87.7	90.5	86.2	88.0	85.5	93.9	86.0	94.5	98.0	97.1	88.1	85.0	94.0
1974	84.3	83.4	85.1	82.5	83.1	75.8	82.9	81.9	90.7	94.7	96.0	83.7	73.0	100.2
1975	74.6	72.9	72.1	73.3	70.6	69.5	68.9	70.3	71.7	75.9	75.2	64.1	61.9	78.4
1976	79.3	78.2	79.2	77.6	75.7	78.2	75.7	77.2	79.0	82.4	80.7	72.9	67.9	83.1
1977	83.5	82.6	83.8	81.9	80.8	85.7	82.1	81.8	80.1	80.7	78.6	79.4	63.2	87.4
1978	85.8	85.2	85.9	84.8	84.4	86.1	84.5	86.5	86.6	86.5	87.6	86.9	67.9	92.3
1979	86.0	85.3	86.0	84.9	85.6	83.8	81.0	85.5	88.4	88.6	88.3	88.0	71.8	95.7
1980	81.5	79.5	77.2	80.8	78.4	77.7	77.2	76.3	73.5	71.6	73.4	76.9	56.7	95.0
1981	80.8	78.3	77.2	78.8	76.8	74.9	74.7	75.0	77.6	76.4	80.5	79.1	72.0	90.3
1982	74.5	71.8	68.6	73.5	68.0	66.6	70.2	67.5	54.5	48.9	48.3	65.6	54.0	65.9
1983	75.7	74.4	74.5	74.4	70.1	78.8	74.9	73.1	61.7	56.9	57.4	69.6	56.8	67.4
1984	80.8	79.8	80.0	79.7	77.6	84.0	81.4	78.3	71.9	66.5	66.4	81.0	66.9	83.6
1985	79.8	78.8	79.1	78.6	76.8	84.0	79.5	76.3	73.2	68.9	65.8	80.3	71.9	74.9
1986	78.7	78.7	79.9	78.1	75.7	89.0	81.5	78.3	70.1	64.1	63.9	80.3	74.4	71.9
1987	81.3	81.3	84.5	79.9	77.9	92.1	86.0	79.8	79.2	76.2	77.7	84.1	77.2	84.1
1988	84.0	83.8	86.8	82.3	81.7	91.1	84.0	81.6	87.4	87.4	88.9	87.5	78.4	97.4
1989	84.1	83.6	86.1	82.5	82.0	88.7	83.1	81.1	85.2	84.7	84.1	85.9	76.3	98.6
1990	82.3	81.4	83.9	80.3	79.0	85.1	80.1	78.6	83.4	83.6	84.5	83.1	77.8	98.3
1991	79.3	77.9	79.6	77.2	74.7	78.5	74.7	72.2	77.6	75.7	75.8	80.1	81.3	99.6
1992	80.2	79.4	82.3	78.1	76.6	82.7	78.2	74.3	80.7	80.5	80.7	81.2	85.6	97.0
1993	81.3	80.5	84.0	79.0	78.8	82.6	80.2	75.8	85.4	87.0	86.9	83.4	92.8	88.8
1994	83.1	82.5	87.2	80.5	81.5	84.8	80.9	79.5	91.1	92.2	91.7	89.7	87.5	79.0
1995	83.3	82.6	86.6	80.8	81.7	83.6	80.5	80.5	90.7	91.9	92.8	89.4	94.7	80.7
1996	82.5	81.5	85.4	79.9	80.8	82.5	78.2	83.2	89.4	90.2	90.3	88.5	82.7	85.1
1997	83.3	82.4	86.1	81.0	82.1	83.2	78.4	83.3	90.5	91.2	89.1	89.7	90.5	85.8
1998	81.8	80.9	84.0	79.8	80.9	83.1	78.4	84.2	86.9	85.2	83.4	89.1	86.9	88.4
1999	80.6	79.8	83.0	78.8	79.9	82.7	78.8	83.9	85.1	82.0	79.5	89.1	79.5	90.0
1996														
January	81.8	80.9	84.4	79.3	80.2	81.4	78.0	81.9	88.4	90.5	90.8	86.0	88.9	84.5
February	82.4	81.4	84.4	80.0	80.9	81.0	77.5	81.1	88.8	88.8	89.7	88.9	86.3	84.9
March	81.8	80.6	84.9	78.7	79.3	83.2	76.7	82.0	89.8	90.2	90.7	89.3	83.2	85.0
April	82.4	81.3	84.7	79.8	80.8	83.2	77.2	81.2	89.0	89.0	89.7	89.0	84.2	85.3
May	82.7	81.6	85.2	80.0	81.2	83.0	79.3	83.0	89.3	89.4	90.1	89.3	82.6	85.1
June	82.9	81.8	85.9	80.1	81.5	84.1	77.9	84.1	89.7	90.8	92.3	88.5	82.2	84.9
July	82.6	81.8	85.6	80.1	81.2	82.1	77.1	85.6	88.1	89.5	91.1	86.5	82.2	84.6
August	82.8	81.9	86.0	80.2	81.4	83.0	79.8	83.6	89.9	91.1	90.8	88.7	77.5	85.3
September	82.8	82.0	86.2	80.2	81.2	83.0	78.7	84.8	90.1	89.7	90.0	90.6	80.0	85.3
October	82.4	81.6	86.0	79.7	80.6	82.0	78.9	84.4	90.4	92.4	90.0	88.2	83.1	85.4
November	82.7	81.8	85.9	80.1	80.9	83.0	78.7	83.7	89.4	91.0	87.8	87.7	78.5	85.5
December	82.6	81.7	85.6	80.2	80.7	80.8	78.2	82.5	89.5	90.1	90.0	88.8	83.2	85.4
1997														
January	82.6	81.7	85.4	80.2	80.8	81.5	77.6	83.9	87.8	89.8	88.5	85.5	86.4	85.5
February	83.0	82.1	86.1	80.5	81.3	83.2	78.2	83.6	89.3	89.8	88.4	88.8	85.4	85.8
March	83.0	82.1	85.9	80.7	81.4	83.7	78.3	82.7	88.0	87.0	89.2	89.3	88.4	85.9
April	83.1	82.1	86.3	80.6	81.7	83.8	79.3	83.6	90.0	91.6	89.0	88.0	88.0	85.5
May	83.1	82.1	86.1	80.7	81.8	84.1	78.5	82.3	90.4	90.9	88.4	89.8	82.3	85.3
June	83.2	82.4	86.0	81.1	82.4	84.2	78.4	82.9	91.5	92.0	88.5	90.9	90.3	85.6
July	83.3	82.4	86.1	81.0	82.1	84.1	79.3	83.3	90.8	91.2	88.4	90.5	93.8	85.5
August	83.4	82.6	86.0	81.5	82.7	82.9	78.2	82.8	90.6	89.6	88.1	91.8	92.0	85.5
September	83.6	82.7	86.4	81.4	82.7	82.6	78.0	83.4	91.5	92.9	89.8	89.8	95.9	85.5
October	83.7	82.8	86.2	81.6	82.5	82.5	77.8	83.1	91.8	92.9	89.7	90.4	96.0	86.2
November	83.7	82.8	86.5	81.5	82.9	83.2	78.8	83.9	92.9	93.9	91.3	91.7	92.7	86.3
December	83.5	82.6	86.3	81.4	82.8	82.9	79.0	84.1	91.3	92.5	89.8	90.0	95.1	86.6
1998														
January	83.3	82.5	86.0	81.3	82.4	82.7	78.5	83.5	91.9	92.8	91.1	90.7	88.9	86.7
February	82.7	81.9	85.5	80.7	81.9	83.2	78.5	83.5	91.5	92.7	91.1	90.2	89.6	86.8
March	82.5	81.5	85.1	80.3	81.5	82.7	79.0	83.8	90.1	91.1	87.5	88.8	86.1	87.3
April	82.4	81.5	85.1	80.2	81.3	83.0	78.9	83.8	89.8	89.4	88.6	90.3	88.0	88.2
May	82.4	81.3	84.7	80.2	81.3	82.7	78.0	83.8	89.1	88.8	87.1	89.6	84.7	88.5
June	81.3	80.1	83.7	78.9	79.7	82.8	78.5	83.7	85.5	84.5	83.5	86.8	85.5	88.7
July	80.8	79.7	83.5	78.3	78.7	83.1	78.3	84.2	85.5	84.3	83.9	87.0	85.9	89.3
August	81.9	80.8	83.0	80.2	81.5	83.6	77.1	84.2	86.0	84.3	85.4	88.1	89.3	89.4
September	81.5	80.4	82.6	79.7	81.1	82.7	78.3	83.9	83.9	79.4	80.0	89.4	84.1	90.1
October	81.5	80.5	82.7	79.9	81.1	83.3	79.1	84.6	83.9	79.4	78.1	89.4	88.3	88.3
November	80.9	80.2	82.6	79.4	80.3	83.1	78.6	85.5	82.2	76.3	71.9	89.6	89.4	88.9
December	80.6	79.9	83.1	78.8	80.1	84.8	78.2	86.4	83.4	79.0	72.5	88.9	82.7	88.7
1999														
January	80.4	79.6	83.1	78.4	79.6	84.6	77.7	87.0	83.5	79.8	75.2	88.1	80.6	88.5
February	80.4	79.7	82.8	78.7	79.3	84.2	78.7	86.2	81.4	77.1	75.1	86.7	87.1	88.9
March	80.5	79.6	82.9	78.5	79.5	83.6	79.3	85.0	83.8	79.2	76.0	89.6	91.3	89.2
April	80.4	79.5	82.6	78.5	79.6	83.2	78.0	83.5	83.6	79.9	76.7	88.2	91.7	89.3
May	80.5	79.7	82.7	78.7	79.7	84.7	78.2	83.0	83.5	80.1	78.0	87.6	80.9	89.4
June	80.5	79.6	82.7	78.6	79.9	83.3	78.1	82.3	85.6	82.8	77.4	89.1	76.7	89.6
July	80.7	79.7	82.9	78.6	80.3	82.7	78.8	83.1	85.9	83.7	77.7	88.6	72.5	89.5
August	80.7	79.7	82.8	78.8	80.2	81.6	79.1	83.4	86.8	84.4	81.0	89.9	74.7	90.9
September	80.6	79.7	82.8	78.7	80.0	81.0	79.9	82.7	85.8	83.0	78.5	89.3	72.1	90.4
October	81.0	80.2	83.4	79.1	80.3	81.4	79.3	83.5	86.1	82.1	85.0	91.1	76.7	90.6
November	80.9	80.3	83.8	79.2	80.3	80.7	78.0	84.0	87.4	85.7	86.5	89.4	75.7	91.5
December	81.1	80.3	83.9	79.2	80.3	81.6	80.1	83.2	88.3	86.1	86.6	91.0	73.8	91.7

Table 4-4. Capacity Utilization—*Continued*

(Output as a percent of capacity, seasonally adjusted.)

Year and month	Fabricated metal products	Durable goods manufacturing—*Continued*								
		Industrial machinery and equiment		Electrical machinery	Transportation equipment				Instruments	Miscellaneous
		Total	Computer and office equipment		Total	Motor vehicles and parts		Aerospace and miscellaneous		
						Total	Autos and light trucks			
1970	75.0	81.3	90.9	76.6	70.5	66.6	. . .	76.7	77.4	77.9
1971	73.7	73.0	70.9	73.5	74.2	79.5	. . .	68.7	76.3	74.3
1972	79.9	82.5	79.2	81.1	76.8	82.5	. . .	70.6	81.4	82.7
1973	86.8	93.0	86.3	88.0	84.7	91.6	. . .	77.3	87.6	79.9
1974	80.9	94.6	91.7	81.9	75.0	76.4	. . .	73.9	86.5	73.5
1975	68.6	78.4	74.0	67.0	65.8	63.1	. . .	69.6	77.1	66.9
1976	74.6	78.8	75.6	72.8	72.7	80.2	. . .	65.3	80.5	71.8
1977	79.9	83.9	78.1	80.1	76.4	90.3	89.8	63.2	86.1	79.5
1978	81.0	88.2	87.3	83.9	80.7	91.0	88.3	70.2	89.5	78.2
1979	82.0	91.6	89.3	87.7	80.2	82.0	78.3	78.4	90.6	76.1
1980	74.9	85.9	88.2	84.0	70.9	61.3	57.8	79.1	87.2	70.6
1981	73.2	84.8	85.7	81.2	66.1	59.3	60.3	72.2	84.8	72.4
1982	66.9	70.5	74.3	76.7	60.9	52.8	53.5	67.8	81.7	69.1
1983	68.4	66.2	78.7	77.8	66.7	66.2	71.9	67.2	79.7	67.3
1984	74.3	75.7	86.1	85.8	74.1	79.0	81.6	70.0	84.6	70.7
1985	74.9	72.8	80.0	80.5	77.9	83.1	81.5	73.8	83.6	65.9
1986	73.6	70.3	72.5	77.8	78.6	78.7	76.7	78.5	79.1	66.6
1987	78.1	72.1	74.6	78.7	77.5	76.8	74.7	78.1	80.2	74.0
1988	81.1	79.6	79.5	82.3	80.6	81.2	79.2	80.0	80.8	78.2
1989	80.0	83.4	81.2	81.3	81.8	79.5	79.8	84.4	79.8	77.4
1990	77.3	79.4	73.7	78.9	77.7	71.6	71.0	84.0	78.5	75.6
1991	73.4	74.2	68.8	76.3	71.8	64.1	64.6	80.8	78.7	73.2
1992	77.0	75.5	75.4	79.7	73.0	69.4	69.0	77.2	77.4	73.3
1993	79.7	79.1	77.1	81.8	75.0	76.3	76.9	73.5	77.0	76.2
1994	83.3	83.2	78.2	86.4	76.0	83.3	83.6	67.4	75.5	78.1
1995	82.4	86.2	83.6	87.7	73.0	79.1	78.0	65.1	76.5	78.4
1996	80.4	86.1	85.6	82.7	73.0	76.4	80.5	68.3	78.6	78.8
1997	80.1	84.6	79.4	83.5	78.3	79.5	84.0	76.8	79.7	80.0
1998	76.8	84.9	84.5	78.9	78.9	77.3	80.8	81.1	80.6	80.8
1999	74.9	82.1	83.3	78.8	78.9	82.0	88.1	74.9	80.7	81.2
1996										
January	80.4	85.6	81.7	84.4	70.6	75.0	72.2	64.8	77.5	78.4
February	81.0	85.7	79.7	85.1	72.0	76.6	77.5	65.9	78.8	79.0
March	80.4	85.4	80.7	83.9	65.1	64.3	64.8	66.2	79.0	79.0
April	80.0	85.7	83.3	83.0	73.9	79.4	82.1	66.4	78.6	78.2
May	80.1	86.6	85.4	82.5	74.6	80.3	82.6	67.0	78.5	78.7
June	80.5	86.5	85.9	82.6	74.9	80.4	86.1	67.5	79.0	79.1
July	80.6	86.0	85.7	82.0	75.7	81.1	89.9	68.6	78.1	78.6
August	81.0	86.4	86.5	82.2	75.0	79.5	85.2	69.0	78.3	78.8
September	80.8	86.1	88.8	82.1	73.9	76.6	84.1	70.3	78.9	79.0
October	80.4	86.2	91.0	81.7	71.6	72.3	76.9	70.8	78.8	78.3
November	80.1	86.4	90.9	81.6	74.1	76.1	81.3	71.4	78.2	78.4
December	79.6	86.0	87.6	81.1	74.1	75.6	82.9	72.2	79.1	79.5
1997										
January	79.9	85.3	83.1	80.9	76.0	78.5	84.3	72.5	78.4	79.5
February	80.6	84.9	80.1	82.1	76.2	78.3	85.1	73.4	79.1	79.8
March	80.3	84.8	80.0	82.9	76.7	78.4	86.2	74.5	78.6	79.4
April	80.6	85.9	81.6	82.5	75.7	75.9	78.7	75.6	79.3	79.1
May	80.4	85.9	83.0	83.1	76.2	76.3	80.9	76.1	79.3	79.5
June	79.6	85.1	82.9	84.3	78.2	79.7	84.8	76.2	79.9	79.7
July	80.0	84.5	81.1	85.2	76.3	76.4	76.5	76.1	79.8	80.2
August	80.1	84.3	77.9	85.1	79.9	81.1	85.8	78.3	80.4	80.1
September	79.7	83.2	74.8	84.8	81.2	82.7	87.8	79.2	80.0	79.9
October	79.8	83.4	73.1	84.1	80.1	80.7	84.5	79.2	81.1	80.2
November	79.7	83.8	75.0	84.0	81.5	82.9	88.3	79.6	80.7	80.6
December	80.1	84.4	79.7	82.9	81.6	82.4	84.8	80.5	80.1	81.5
1998										
January	79.3	85.3	83.5	81.9	80.0	79.4	84.3	80.8	80.3	81.5
February	78.8	85.5	86.5	80.6	79.2	78.1	81.4	80.6	80.3	81.8
March	78.3	85.6	84.8	79.4	78.7	77.2	80.9	80.6	80.6	82.0
April	78.0	84.5	81.6	79.0	79.5	78.4	82.4	80.8	80.4	82.0
May	77.9	84.2	79.2	78.4	80.7	80.1	82.2	81.4	81.1	81.4
June	77.1	85.1	80.8	78.5	73.4	67.2	68.8	81.8	80.3	81.1
July	75.8	85.7	84.7	78.6	68.3	58.1	53.5	81.8	80.3	81.0
August	75.2	85.5	87.7	78.1	83.4	84.6	88.5	81.8	80.9	80.6
September	75.3	85.0	88.1	78.6	81.8	82.7	86.1	80.8	81.5	80.2
October	75.2	84.8	86.9	78.5	81.9	81.9	88.0	81.9	81.4	79.4
November	75.3	84.0	85.4	77.9	80.4	80.1	87.0	80.8	80.2	78.6
December	75.9	83.5	84.8	77.2	79.7	79.6	86.0	79.9	79.8	79.4
1999										
January	75.3	82.8	85.0	76.3	78.9	79.3	86.2	78.4	79.9	79.2
February	74.8	83.4	85.3	75.2	79.2	80.0	85.4	78.3	79.4	79.9
March	74.9	83.5	85.6	75.5	78.8	80.1	84.9	77.2	79.7	80.5
April	74.5	83.4	85.7	77.0	78.5	80.3	86.1	76.2	80.4	81.3
May	74.1	82.9	85.2	77.4	79.0	81.5	88.0	75.8	81.3	82.1
June	74.7	81.8	83.9	78.7	79.4	82.7	90.5	75.2	81.2	81.4
July	74.9	81.5	82.7	80.9	79.1	82.3	86.6	74.9	81.1	81.8
August	74.9	81.1	83.0	80.5	79.1	82.3	93.8	75.0	81.1	81.7
September	74.9	81.6	82.9	79.8	79.3	84.1	89.1	73.1	80.5	81.5
October	75.1	81.6	81.6	81.1	78.8	84.2	90.1	71.9	81.0	81.4
November	75.7	81.1	80.1	81.3	78.5	84.2	90.3	71.2	81.1	81.4
December	75.3	80.7	78.3	82.0	77.6	82.5	86.5	71.4	81.4	82.2

Table 4-4. Capacity Utilization—*Continued*

(Output as a percent of capacity, seasonally adjusted.)

| Year and month | Nondurable goods manufacturing | | | | | | | | | | |
| | Total | Foods | Textile mill products | Apparel products | Paper and products | | Printing and publishing | Chemicals | | | Petroleum products |
					Total	Pulp and paper		Total	Plastics materials	Synthetic fibers	
1970	82.8	83.6	83.5	78.9	86.5	92.2	86.9	77.7	82.3	81.9	93.9
1971	82.6	83.6	84.7	78.6	87.4	93.3	85.3	77.5	81.3	87.6	91.8
1972	86.4	85.5	88.6	82.0	91.9	95.8	88.3	82.3	98.5	87.6	92.8
1973	87.3	85.0	89.7	81.4	95.4	96.1	87.7	85.5	98.5	91.5	94.2
1974	83.9	83.6	80.5	76.5	91.9	93.5	83.9	84.4	93.8	89.9	87.1
1975	76.3	80.4	76.1	69.3	78.1	79.4	77.0	73.3	64.8	76.3	83.7
1976	81.8	82.4	83.6	80.3	87.0	89.8	82.6	78.4	74.5	77.7	85.2
1977	85.3	83.5	87.2	84.8	90.1	90.8	89.4	80.8	80.6	81.1	87.6
1978	86.4	83.6	86.0	85.9	92.5	92.4	91.7	82.7	85.3	86.5	87.6
1979	84.9	82.0	87.7	80.5	92.6	94.6	89.5	83.7	86.7	91.4	84.1
1980	81.0	81.6	84.8	79.4	88.4	92.2	85.8	78.4	75.2	65.3	74.7
1981	80.4	81.2	81.6	80.6	87.2	91.3	83.9	78.1	76.9	81.2	70.7
1982	77.5	80.2	75.5	79.7	83.1	86.2	83.8	70.7	71.2	68.6	70.1
1983	80.8	80.9	85.3	82.6	89.5	91.7	85.2	75.2	82.3	84.9	73.4
1984	82.9	81.5	85.8	84.1	92.1	93.4	87.7	77.4	86.3	85.4	77.8
1985	81.5	82.2	81.5	80.4	88.2	90.4	86.4	75.6	85.7	78.4	78.4
1986	82.8	82.9	85.4	82.3	90.3	94.0	85.6	77.6	89.4	86.3	83.7
1987	85.9	84.1	90.5	85.2	90.8	95.7	91.0	81.3	98.7	92.1	83.5
1988	86.4	84.4	88.0	83.6	92.2	95.6	89.5	84.0	95.5	91.7	85.3
1989	85.7	84.3	87.9	80.9	91.0	93.9	87.7	83.7	90.3	94.8	87.0
1990	84.4	83.9	83.5	78.3	88.9	93.9	85.2	83.0	87.1	86.7	87.6
1991	81.9	83.4	81.7	78.7	86.7	91.7	80.8	80.1	81.4	85.6	86.6
1992	82.8	83.0	87.3	80.1	87.5	92.0	81.4	80.2	88.8	85.9	88.6
1993	82.5	83.2	89.6	81.3	88.8	93.1	81.7	78.7	87.0	87.6	92.3
1994	83.7	83.2	91.2	83.5	91.1	94.9	81.3	79.2	95.6	85.8	90.9
1995	83.7	83.1	88.3	82.8	90.0	93.9	81.6	79.4	92.3	86.5	91.9
1996	82.4	80.8	85.3	79.9	87.5	91.1	81.1	78.6	90.7	87.3	93.4
1997	83.1	80.8	86.0	78.0	89.9	94.2	83.1	79.7	91.9	81.8	94.9
1998	81.3	80.1	84.4	73.3	87.3	92.3	81.5	77.8	89.4	81.2	94.5
1999	80.2	79.2	84.3	68.9	86.1	92.5	80.5	78.2	91.2	81.1	93.7
1996											
January	81.6	81.1	81.8	78.0	85.9	89.0	79.6	78.3	90.0	83.8	92.5
February	81.9	81.3	83.6	80.4	84.5	88.1	80.5	78.0	90.5	83.6	93.2
March	82.2	81.5	86.5	79.6	85.7	88.8	80.4	77.8	90.8	83.9	92.9
April	81.8	81.0	84.7	80.3	87.3	91.1	80.5	76.9	90.4	83.9	92.5
May	82.0	80.4	85.6	80.4	87.2	90.7	81.1	77.5	91.8	87.0	93.0
June	82.3	80.6	87.2	80.3	87.8	90.5	80.6	77.3	92.0	87.4	93.2
July	82.5	80.4	85.6	79.9	88.4	92.1	81.1	78.8	90.7	89.7	92.3
August	82.6	80.0	86.4	81.0	87.5	91.7	81.7	79.0	91.3	88.9	94.0
September	83.1	80.9	85.8	80.5	88.0	91.4	81.6	79.3	91.2	88.0	94.1
October	82.9	80.6	85.9	79.8	87.9	92.1	82.0	80.0	90.9	93.1	94.9
November	83.0	80.9	86.0	79.7	89.4	93.1	82.1	79.6	89.4	89.7	94.4
December	83.2	81.0	85.0	79.1	90.0	94.3	82.2	80.2	89.8	89.0	94.0
1997											
January	83.0	80.6	84.6	78.7	88.9	92.9	82.2	80.4	90.9	90.0	93.0
February	83.3	81.4	85.6	78.3	90.2	94.6	82.6	80.0	91.3	83.1	93.9
March	83.3	81.3	85.7	79.3	90.4	94.8	82.6	79.1	92.2	82.4	94.0
April	83.1	80.8	86.2	78.6	89.9	93.6	83.0	80.2	91.3	88.0	95.2
May	82.9	80.8	84.4	78.7	90.0	93.9	83.2	79.4	91.2	78.9	96.7
June	82.8	80.7	85.5	78.5	89.1	92.8	82.7	79.4	91.4	77.2	96.7
July	83.1	81.5	86.9	77.9	89.8	93.8	83.4	79.6	92.8	82.0	94.6
August	83.0	80.8	86.0	77.7	90.0	94.5	82.9	79.9	91.7	79.4	94.5
September	83.1	80.5	86.4	77.6	90.7	95.4	83.1	79.8	92.5	80.6	95.6
October	83.6	80.1	86.6	77.6	89.7	94.7	84.0	80.1	91.8	79.7	95.8
November	83.1	80.7	87.5	76.9	90.2	94.4	83.9	79.4	92.9	78.5	93.5
December	83.0	80.7	87.1	76.8	89.6	94.6	83.3	79.9	92.6	81.8	95.2
1998											
January	83.2	81.4	87.4	76.4	88.8	94.1	82.8	79.6	92.0	82.0	94.7
February	82.4	80.8	85.5	75.2	88.6	93.5	82.4	78.9	88.5	83.7	93.7
March	82.1	80.7	85.7	75.0	87.7	92.7	82.1	78.6	88.5	84.0	95.8
April	82.2	80.6	85.8	74.2	88.2	93.4	82.0	78.9	90.5	84.7	95.0
May	81.9	80.5	86.5	73.5	87.7	92.6	81.8	78.3	89.2	82.7	93.7
June	81.2	79.9	85.4	73.5	87.2	92.7	80.7	77.6	85.7	81.5	93.9
July	81.4	79.4	85.2	73.4	87.9	93.4	80.8	77.8	90.4	81.8	95.3
August	80.5	78.8	84.2	72.9	86.8	92.0	80.8	76.6	85.6	81.4	95.6
September	80.0	79.1	83.7	72.6	86.2	91.4	80.6	76.4	87.1	81.7	93.7
October	80.4	79.8	81.2	71.8	87.3	92.0	81.1	76.7	89.5	79.1	93.0
November	80.5	80.6	81.5	70.7	84.8	89.5	81.1	77.7	93.9	78.2	94.8
December	80.1	80.1	81.0	70.6	86.3	90.7	81.2	76.6	91.8	73.7	94.6
1999											
January	80.2	80.4	82.2	70.0	86.7	91.7	80.4	76.4	89.0	78.3	96.4
February	80.7	80.6	84.1	69.9	86.7	91.6	80.4	77.7	92.0	80.9	96.0
March	80.3	80.1	83.8	69.6	86.5	92.1	79.9	77.8	90.2	80.9	94.3
April	80.0	79.8	84.8	70.2	85.7	92.6	80.3	76.9	90.1	81.3	93.9
May	80.2	79.7	84.4	69.3	85.2	91.6	80.3	77.8	90.5	81.5	93.4
June	79.7	79.1	84.2	68.9	85.9	92.5	79.9	77.3	89.5	83.5	92.6
July	79.5	78.1	85.3	68.3	85.2	91.7	79.4	76.9	90.9	81.0	93.9
August	79.7	78.0	84.8	68.0	85.6	92.3	80.0	78.1	87.8	82.0	93.0
September	79.9	78.4	84.1	67.9	86.4	93.1	80.8	77.8	90.5	77.3	93.3
October	80.6	78.7	85.5	68.0	86.9	93.5	81.9	79.4	94.0	79.7	93.2
November	81.0	78.7	84.5	68.1	86.7	93.3	81.7	81.3	95.4	86.8	91.7
December	81.0	78.3	83.5	68.2	86.3	93.5	81.5	81.3	94.9	80.2	93.3

Table 4-4. Capacity Utilization—*Continued*

(Output as a percent of capacity, seasonally adjusted.)

Year and month	Nondurable goods manufacturing—*Continued*		Mining						Utilites		
	Rubber and plastics products	Leather and products	Total	Metal mining	Coal mining	Oil and gas extraction		Stone and earth minerals	Total	Electric	Gas
						Total	Oil and gas well drilling				
1970	81.2	81.8	88.8	93.6	95.8	87.7	69.7	87.2	96.2	98.9	91.9
1971	82.6	79.9	87.3	83.2	86.0	88.5	68.6	85.9	94.6	96.5	92.3
1972	91.6	84.2	90.3	80.7	89.2	92.3	79.1	87.8	95.2	97.0	92.5
1973	93.3	79.6	92.3	84.6	85.7	94.8	85.2	92.8	93.5	95.4	90.7
1974	84.9	77.4	92.3	82.1	84.2	96.1	98.9	89.6	87.3	87.3	88.6
1975	70.1	79.7	89.7	76.4	87.5	93.8	99.2	79.1	84.4	84.8	84.8
1976	78.5	81.7	89.8	81.0	88.9	92.1	91.5	83.0	85.2	85.1	86.6
1977	88.3	83.3	90.9	69.4	88.2	94.2	101.7	85.4	85.0	86.0	83.2
1978	89.2	86.8	90.9	78.5	80.3	94.7	100.0	89.2	85.4	85.3	85.5
1979	84.2	82.2	91.4	81.4	88.8	92.8	88.2	90.6	86.6	85.3	89.5
1980	73.9	84.1	93.4	72.8	90.3	95.8	95.7	82.7	85.9	84.7	89.3
1981	77.9	83.9	93.9	79.1	86.7	96.1	98.0	79.8	82.5	84.3	79.1
1982	74.4	80.7	86.3	57.5	86.1	88.2	70.3	67.4	79.3	81.3	74.9
1983	79.2	82.8	80.4	57.9	79.1	81.7	52.6	72.6	79.7	82.3	74.4
1984	84.3	78.6	86.0	63.3	88.6	86.7	63.4	81.8	81.9	84.0	77.1
1985	82.1	74.1	84.3	62.7	85.7	84.9	58.5	84.4	83.5	84.7	79.8
1986	82.9	71.9	77.6	65.9	84.7	76.4	34.3	82.7	80.6	84.9	67.6
1987	89.0	74.7	80.3	70.9	85.7	79.3	38.4	85.7	82.5	86.1	69.9
1988	87.8	78.7	85.2	80.5	86.8	85.0	56.0	86.9	84.9	87.8	73.7
1989	87.4	82.5	86.9	85.4	88.3	87.0	63.7	85.2	86.2	89.4	75.7
1990	84.6	82.7	89.8	85.7	90.7	90.3	75.6	86.3	85.7	89.6	72.9
1991	80.3	78.8	88.4	82.9	85.7	90.4	69.4	81.1	86.3	89.1	75.1
1992	84.8	83.0	86.4	87.1	84.6	87.0	55.3	84.0	84.5	86.8	77.2
1993	86.1	86.1	86.1	84.7	79.6	88.2	67.7	82.6	87.1	88.7	80.4
1994	89.7	81.4	87.5	87.0	84.7	88.6	70.7	85.3	87.4	89.2	80.3
1995	88.4	77.0	87.0	88.2	83.3	87.8	71.2	86.8	89.2	91.0	82.1
1996	87.5	78.9	88.5	89.1	84.2	89.8	78.9	85.7	90.4	91.6	84.8
1997	86.8	76.7	89.2	92.2	86.0	90.1	85.4	85.9	89.7	91.6	82.1
1998	85.6	72.4	86.4	89.2	87.0	86.1	75.5	85.4	90.8	94.4	75.7
1999	84.1	68.4	81.5	80.0	85.4	80.3	60.4	84.4	90.7	94.3	75.9
1996											
January	87.0	76.9	85.8	84.6	76.4	88.7	76.4	81.6	91.5	92.5	86.9
February	86.8	78.0	87.2	83.9	80.3	89.4	78.0	85.2	92.6	93.5	88.3
March	87.1	78.4	88.5	88.1	86.3	89.3	75.7	85.9	92.5	93.4	87.9
April	86.4	78.7	89.0	86.7	85.0	90.5	79.8	86.0	91.6	92.3	87.8
May	87.6	78.6	88.9	88.7	85.0	90.1	80.9	86.0	92.1	93.4	86.3
June	88.3	80.0	90.0	89.6	86.8	91.0	79.9	87.7	90.7	92.3	83.7
July	88.1	79.6	89.6	91.5	86.7	90.3	79.7	86.8	87.5	89.4	79.4
August	88.6	79.8	89.5	91.4	87.1	90.1	79.2	86.2	88.6	90.3	81.3
September	88.7	79.9	89.1	91.7	84.4	90.4	79.2	85.0	88.6	89.8	83.2
October	87.2	79.2	88.7	91.1	84.4	89.5	79.3	87.3	88.9	90.1	83.7
November	87.0	78.8	88.4	89.8	84.6	89.2	79.2	86.6	90.1	91.1	85.4
December	87.6	79.4	87.9	91.8	84.1	88.7	80.1	84.2	89.7	91.0	83.9
1997											
January	86.6	79.6	88.4	94.9	84.5	89.5	79.8	81.9	90.2	91.8	83.8
February	87.5	77.9	89.9	92.8	87.1	90.3	82.3	88.4	88.9	90.5	82.6
March	87.4	79.1	90.3	92.4	86.1	91.0	85.9	89.6	87.5	90.0	77.6
April	86.3	78.2	89.3	91.6	84.3	90.6	85.9	85.3	89.9	91.6	83.1
May	86.6	77.7	90.2	92.0	90.7	90.5	85.8	85.5	89.2	89.5	87.8
June	86.7	76.9	89.4	93.8	85.8	89.8	86.0	87.8	88.2	89.5	83.1
July	86.5	77.4	89.3	93.0	85.5	90.4	86.3	84.6	89.6	91.8	80.8
August	87.5	74.7	89.1	93.1	85.4	89.9	86.9	86.2	88.7	90.7	80.8
September	87.1	74.5	89.3	90.7	85.2	90.5	86.9	86.4	90.6	93.0	80.5
October	86.5	75.6	88.9	92.9	84.3	90.0	85.8	85.7	91.9	94.5	81.3
November	87.0	74.7	88.5	92.8	84.7	89.4	86.8	84.9	90.9	93.1	82.1
December	86.5	74.4	88.3	86.2	88.2	89.2	86.4	84.5	91.0	93.3	81.6
1998											
January	86.7	74.0	90.0	89.7	90.1	90.5	88.1	87.0	87.1	89.8	75.9
February	86.2	75.0	89.7	97.3	84.3	90.7	89.0	86.3	87.4	90.4	75.1
March	86.2	74.5	88.2	86.1	86.8	89.3	85.6	84.5	90.6	93.7	77.4
April	86.7	73.5	87.9	85.4	85.6	89.0	83.0	85.9	89.8	93.3	75.6
May	86.2	73.1	88.3	88.9	89.6	88.4	82.1	85.5	92.2	96.4	74.8
June	85.6	71.6	86.7	89.5	86.3	86.8	76.3	85.6	93.6	97.2	78.3
July	85.2	72.4	85.7	89.0	85.8	85.7	73.0	84.3	92.9	95.8	80.6
August	84.8	71.5	85.8	93.3	85.5	85.3	70.6	84.7	93.0	96.0	80.5
September	84.8	71.5	84.5	88.1	87.4	83.6	68.6	83.7	94.4	98.4	77.7
October	84.7	71.0	84.3	86.9	87.8	83.4	66.5	84.2	91.5	95.9	73.2
November	85.2	71.4	84.2	89.3	89.0	82.0	64.7	88.4	87.6	92.2	68.2
December	85.3	69.8	81.4	87.1	86.4	79.2	58.7	84.9	88.9	93.1	71.2
1999											
January	84.8	68.8	81.3	84.2	85.1	79.0	55.8	88.3	90.3	93.0	79.4
February	84.5	68.7	80.9	82.9	86.1	78.5	54.5	86.6	88.7	92.1	74.7
March	84.3	68.8	80.9	80.7	82.1	79.8	56.6	86.2	91.9	95.4	77.4
April	84.2	68.4	80.4	82.4	84.7	78.8	54.7	82.8	91.4	94.9	76.9
May	84.5	69.0	81.0	82.3	83.8	79.7	56.3	84.1	91.1	94.6	76.9
June	83.5	69.6	80.7	81.3	84.4	79.3	56.6	83.6	92.1	95.5	78.1
July	84.1	67.8	81.3	79.2	86.8	80.2	57.9	81.6	93.9	97.7	77.9
August	83.6	69.2	81.9	76.8	87.3	81.0	61.0	83.2	92.2	95.5	78.4
September	84.2	68.8	81.8	75.5	86.3	80.9	63.7	84.8	92.0	95.2	78.6
October	83.6	67.9	82.6	78.0	85.8	81.8	66.4	85.2	89.9	92.8	78.1
November	83.4	67.7	83.0	78.3	86.7	82.3	69.9	84.3	86.5	91.8	63.8
December	84.3	65.6	82.8	79.0	86.3	82.4	71.8	82.5	88.4	92.6	70.9

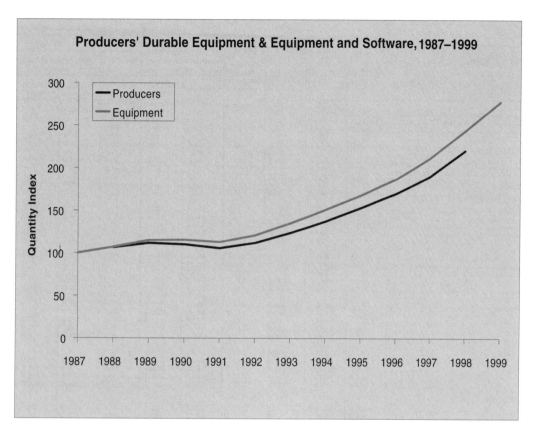

- The 1999 revisions to the National Income and Product Accounts created a new category in the business and government investment component of GDP termed "Equipment and Software." That category replaces the old "Producers' Durable Equipment" category. Starting in 1999, software that is separate from (i.e., not "embedded" within) the computer is being recognized as an investment because of its long useful life. A comparison of the two categories shows that the new category "Equipment and Software" has grown more rapidly than the older, narrower "Producers' Durable Equipment" category, contributing to the upward revision in recent GDP growth.

- Other major components of business fixed investment also increased, if less dramatically. Total real (nonresidential) business fixed investment grew 11 percent per year from 1994 to 1999.

- Real residential investment grew rather slowly from 1994 to 1997, but moved ahead 8.3 percent in 1998, with the strongest rise occurring in single family housing. In 1999 there was a more modest increase in real residential investment of 6.4 percent.

- The emergence of a federal budget surplus contributed to a rise in economy-wide gross saving (personal, business, and government) to 18.8 and 18.5 percent of gross national product in 1998 and 1999 respectively. These were the highest percentages since 1988, but still well below the averages of the 1970s and early 1980s.

Table 5-1. Gross Saving and Investment

(Billions of dollars, quarterly data are at seasonally adjusted annual rates.)

Year and quarter	Total	Private[1] Total	Personal	Undistributed corporate profits[2]	Consumption of fixed capital Corporate	Noncorporate	Government Total	Consumption of fixed capital Federal	State and local	Current surplus or deficit (-) Federal	State and local
1970	194.3	174.3	69.5	23.0	50.5	31.4	20.0	16.7	10.6	-14.4	7.1
1971	211.4	202.6	80.1	32.4	55.4	34.4	8.8	17.4	11.8	-26.8	6.4
1972	241.6	217.0	76.9	41.1	60.9	38.5	24.6	18.7	12.9	-22.5	15.6
1973	294.6	256.4	102.5	44.8	66.8	42.3	38.2	19.5	14.3	-11.2	15.7
1974	304.0	270.7	114.3	29.5	78.5	48.4	33.3	20.2	17.7	-13.9	9.3
1975	298.4	323.5	125.2	49.1	94.0	55.2	-25.1	21.6	20.2	-69.3	2.4
1976	342.7	344.0	122.1	57.3	104.5	60.0	-1.3	23.2	21.3	-53.0	7.3
1977	398.2	383.1	125.6	73.1	117.5	66.9	15.1	24.6	22.6	-45.2	13.1
1978	481.6	439.1	145.4	82.9	134.5	76.2	42.5	26.3	24.4	-26.9	18.7
1979	544.9	487.8	165.8	77.0	156.4	88.5	57.1	28.0	27.4	-11.4	13.0
1980	555.5	537.8	205.6	49.6	181.1	101.5	17.7	30.9	31.7	-53.8	8.8
1981	656.5	631.7	243.7	64.1	210.1	113.7	24.8	34.7	36.3	-53.7	7.5
1982	625.7	681.6	262.2	61.9	233.4	124.0	-55.9	39.5	39.5	-132.6	-2.3
1983	608.0	693.8	227.8	93.2	244.4	128.3	-85.7	42.4	40.9	-173.9	4.8
1984	769.4	824.8	306.5	124.7	260.2	133.4	-55.4	46.4	42.4	-168.1	23.8
1985	772.5	833.4	282.6	128.3	280.9	141.7	-60.9	49.3	44.7	-177.1	22.3
1986	735.9	806.5	267.8	88.0	302.1	148.7	-70.5	52.9	47.9	-192.1	20.8
1987	810.4	838.3	252.8	107.3	320.8	157.4	-27.9	56.3	51.5	-147.9	12.2
1988	936.2	943.0	292.3	138.3	344.3	168.1	-6.7	60.2	54.9	-137.4	15.6
1989	967.6	955.1	301.8	99.2	370.6	183.4	12.5	64.4	58.8	-130.0	19.3
1990	977.7	1 016.2	334.3	102.4	391.1	188.4	-38.6	68.7	63.1	-173.0	2.6
1991	1 015.8	1 098.9	371.7	119.2	411.2	196.8	-83.2	73.0	66.9	-215.3	-7.8
1992	1 007.4	1 164.6	413.7	124.4	427.9	214.3	-157.2	75.4	69.9	-297.5	-4.9
1993	1 039.4	1 159.4	350.8	142.0	448.5	211.6	-120.0	78.7	73.9	-274.1	1.5
1994	1 155.9	1 199.3	315.5	151.6	482.7	231.9	-43.4	81.4	78.9	-212.3	8.6
1995	1 257.5	1 266.0	302.4	203.6	512.1	231.5	-8.5	84.0	84.1	-192.0	15.3
1996	1 349.3	1 290.4	272.1	232.7	543.5	238.5	58.9	85.3	88.9	-136.8	21.4
1997	1 502.3	1 343.7	252.9	261.3	581.5	250.9	158.6	86.8	94.2	-53.3	31.0
1998	1 654.4	1 375.7	265.4	218.9	624.3	265.1	278.7	88.4	99.5	49.0	41.7
1999	1 717.6	1 343.5	147.6	229.4	676.9	284.5	374.0	92.8	106.8	124.4	50.0
1991											
1st quarter	1 056.3	1 094.6	363.2	130.2	407.8	193.4	-38.3	71.7	65.6	-160.1	-15.6
2nd quarter	1 005.5	1 090.4	367.1	118.4	410.2	194.6	-84.9	72.6	66.6	-213.5	-10.6
3rd quarter	989.7	1 087.9	368.3	111.0	412.5	196.2	-98.3	73.6	67.4	-234.6	-4.7
4th quarter	1 011.7	1 122.9	388.1	117.3	414.5	203.0	-111.2	74.2	68.0	-253.2	-0.3
1992											
1st quarter	1 018.1	1 168.6	406.7	146.6	417.7	197.6	-150.5	74.4	68.6	-288.3	-5.1
2nd quarter	1 025.8	1 181.6	421.9	138.9	421.2	199.4	-155.7	75.1	69.5	-291.8	-8.5
3rd quarter	1 002.2	1 181.3	396.5	85.9	442.0	256.9	-179.2	75.6	70.3	-316.5	-8.5
4th quarter	983.3	1 126.9	429.6	126.3	430.5	203.5	-143.6	76.4	71.2	-293.5	2.3
1993											
1st quarter	1 029.6	1 192.8	340.0	129.0	439.2	212.5	-163.2	77.5	72.4	-300.8	-12.4
2nd quarter	1 047.6	1 166.9	373.7	139.7	443.7	207.9	-119.4	78.2	73.5	-267.2	-4.0
3rd quarter	1 022.0	1 141.4	331.5	139.7	454.4	213.9	-119.4	79.3	74.4	-275.5	2.4
4th quarter	1 058.5	1 136.5	358.2	159.6	456.6	212.3	-78.0	79.8	75.4	-253.1	19.9
1994											
1st quarter	1 122.4	1 200.9	274.3	113.4	491.4	265.4	-78.5	80.4	78.0	-237.5	0.6
2nd quarter	1 145.7	1 170.3	319.5	156.7	471.7	217.6	-24.6	81.2	77.8	-190.5	6.9
3rd quarter	1 151.1	1 193.1	324.1	163.6	480.0	220.8	-42.0	81.5	79.3	-212.0	9.2
4th quarter	1 204.6	1 233.0	344.2	172.6	407.8	223.8	-28.4	82.5	80.6	-209.4	17.8
1995											
1st quarter	1 238.0	1 264.9	346.0	178.4	497.5	226.7	-26.8	83.3	82.2	-208.3	15.9
2nd quarter	1 233.1	1 240.2	291.5	195.6	507.8	228.9	-7.0	83.9	83.5	-188.9	14.6
3rd quarter	1 260.1	1 271.3	285.9	222.0	516.3	230.8	-11.2	84.1	84.8	-197.6	17.5
4th quarter	1 298.5	1 287.6	286.3	218.4	527.0	239.6	10.9	84.8	86.1	-173.2	13.3
1996											
1st quarter	1 295.6	1 282.7	282.2	230.8	531.5	234.6	12.9	85.0	87.3	-176.5	17.0
2nd quarter	1 328.2	1 264.6	253.1	232.6	538.7	236.6	63.5	85.1	88.3	-137.0	27.2
3rd quarter	1 372.8	1 305.6	286.1	228.4	547.5	240.1	67.2	85.5	89.5	-130.1	22.3
4th quarter	1 400.5	1 308.6	267.1	238.9	556.2	242.7	92.0	85.7	90.7	-103.7	19.3
1997											
1st quarter	1 422.1	1 306.8	248.1	250.1	565.6	245.9	115.3	86.2	92.1	-86.5	23.5
2nd quarter	1 492.9	1 354.2	270.1	261.9	576.0	249.1	138.7	86.6	93.6	-68.0	26.6
3rd quarter	1 528.4	1 345.1	236.0	272.5	587.0	252.6	183.3	86.8	94.7	-33.7	35.5
4th quarter	1 565.8	1 368.8	257.3	260.8	597.6	256.0	197.0	87.5	96.3	-25.0	38.3
1998											
1st quarter	1 634.3	1 385.3	285.6	231.6	606.8	259.2	248.9	87.5	97.4	25.9	38.1
2nd quarter	1 633.1	1 371.4	270.2	218.4	617.8	262.8	261.7	87.9	98.5	41.9	33.4
3rd quarter	1 676.7	1 378.3	261.6	217.6	630.1	267.0	298.4	88.7	100.3	71.9	37.5
4th quarter	1 673.5	1 367.9	244.0	208.0	642.5	271.3	305.7	89.5	102.1	56.4	57.7
1999											
1st quarter	1 715.5	1 383.2	204.6	243.1	654.4	276.0	332.3	90.9	103.7	89.7	47.9
2nd quarter	1 691.7	1 338.5	163.6	218.7	670.7	280.3	353.3	92.0	105.8	117.5	38.0
3rd quarter	1 716.8	1 321.1	121.1	214.0	687.7	293.1	395.7	93.4	107.7	147.3	47.4
4th quarter	1 746.3	1 331.4	101.0	241.7	694.8	288.7	414.9	95.0	109.9	143.3	66.6

1. Includes wage and salary accruals less disbursements, not shown separately.
2. Includes inventory valuation and capital consumption adjustments.

Table 5-1. Gross Saving and Investment—*Continued*

(Billions of dollars, quarterly data are at seasonally adjusted annual rates.)

| Year and quarter | Gross investment | | | | Statistical discrepancy [1] | Gross saving as a percent of GNP |
	Total	Private domestic	Government	Net foreign		
1970	201.2	152.4	44.8	4.0	6.9	18.6
1971	222.7	178.2	44.0	0.6	11.3	18.6
1972	250.3	207.6	46.3	-3.6	8.7	19.3
1973	302.6	244.5	49.4	8.7	8.0	21.1
1974	314.0	249.4	57.4	7.1	10.0	20.0
1975	316.1	230.2	64.5	21.4	17.7	18.1
1976	367.2	292.0	66.4	8.9	24.5	18.6
1977	419.8	361.3	67.5	-9.0	21.6	19.4
1978	502.6	436.0	77.1	-10.4	21.0	20.8
1979	580.6	490.6	88.5	1.4	35.7	21.0
1980	589.5	477.9	100.3	11.4	33.9	19.6
1981	684.0	570.8	106.9	6.3	27.5	20.7
1982	628.2	516.1	112.3	-0.2	2.5	19.0
1983	655.0	564.2	122.8	-32.0	47.0	17.0
1984	787.9	735.5	139.4	-87.0	18.6	19.4
1985	784.2	736.3	158.8	-110.9	11.7	18.2
1986	779.8	747.2	173.2	-140.6	43.9	16.5
1987	813.8	781.5	184.3	-152.0	3.3	17.0
1988	894.0	821.1	186.2	-113.2	-42.2	18.3
1989	983.9	872.9	197.7	-86.7	16.3	17.6
1990	1 008.2	861.7	215.8	-69.2	30.6	16.8
1991	1 035.4	800.2	220.3	14.9	19.6	16.9
1992	1 051.1	866.6	223.1	-38.7	43.7	15.9
1993	1 103.2	955.1	220.9	-72.9	63.8	15.6
1994	1 214.4	1 097.1	225.6	-108.3	58.5	16.3
1995	1 284.0	1 143.8	238.2	-98.0	26.5	16.9
1996	1 382.1	1 242.7	250.1	-110.7	32.8	17.2
1997	1 532.1	1 390.5	264.6	-123.1	29.7	18.0
1998	1 629.6	1 549.9	278.8	-199.1	-24.8	18.8
1999	1 645.6	1 650.1	308.7	-313.2	-71.9	18.5
1991						
1st quarter	1 062.8	786.5	216.4	59.8	6.4	17.8
2nd quarter	1 025.8	780.5	221.3	24.0	20.3	16.8
3rd quarter	1 008.4	801.5	222.0	-15.1	18.8	16.4
4th quarter	1 044.7	832.1	221.5	-9.0	33.0	16.6
1992						
1st quarter	1 025.8	810.9	227.1	-12.2	7.7	16.4
2nd quarter	1 056.3	867.2	224.6	-35.5	30.4	16.3
3rd quarter	1 054.7	878.7	221.3	-45.3	52.6	15.7
4th quarter	1 067.5	909.8	219.4	-61.7	84.2	15.1
1993						
1st quarter	1 108.3	938.0	217.6	-47.3	78.8	15.7
2nd quarter	1 098.9	943.6	222.5	-67.3	51.3	15.8
3rd quarter	1 085.7	943.0	220.3	-77.6	63.7	15.3
4th quarter	1 119.7	995.8	223.3	-99.3	61.2	15.5
1994						
1st quarter	1 175.1	1 042.0	215.7	-82.6	52.7	16.2
2nd quarter	1 227.0	1 106.4	222.2	-101.6	81.3	16.3
3rd quarter	1 205.7	1 094.0	233.3	-121.6	54.6	16.2
4th quarter	1 249.9	1 146.1	231.1	-127.3	45.3	16.7
1995						
1st quarter	1 291.7	1 162.8	236.4	-107.5	53.7	16.9
2nd quarter	1 258.0	1 133.1	241.0	-116.1	24.9	16.7
3rd quarter	1 263.3	1 123.5	236.4	-96.7	3.1	16.9
4th quarter	1 322.9	1 155.6	238.9	-71.6	24.4	17.2
1996						
1st quarter	1 330.0	1 172.4	248.3	-90.7	34.4	16.9
2nd quarter	1 377.7	1 231.5	253.0	-106.7	49.6	17.0
3rd quarter	1 397.9	1 282.6	249.9	-134.5	25.1	17.4
4th quarter	1 422.8	1 284.3	249.4	-111.0	22.3	17.5
1997						
1st quarter	1 462.8	1 324.2	256.0	-117.5	40.6	17.5
2nd quarter	1 562.4	1 397.7	264.8	-100.2	69.5	18.0
3rd quarter	1 555.4	1 405.7	269.8	-120.2	26.9	18.2
4th quarter	1 547.8	1 434.5	267.7	-154.4	-18.0	18.5
1998						
1st quarter	1 650.6	1 532.1	269.9	-151.3	16.4	18.9
2nd quarter	1 612.3	1 523.9	277.6	-189.3	-20.8	18.7
3rd quarter	1 613.0	1 553.0	284.7	-224.7	-63.7	19.0
4th quarter	1 642.6	1 590.8	283.1	-231.3	-31.0	18.7
1999						
1st quarter	1 661.9	1 609.8	298.9	-246.8	-53.6	18.9
2nd quarter	1 614.9	1 607.9	303.5	-296.5	-76.8	18.4
3rd quarter	1 627.3	1 659.1	308.0	-339.8	-89.5	18.4
4th quarter	1 678.5	1 723.7	324.4	-369.6	-67.8	18.3

1. Includes wage and salary accruals less disbursements, not shown separately.
2. Includes inventory valuation and capital consumption adjustments.

Table 5-2. Gross Private Fixed Investment by Type

(Billions of dollars, quarterly data are at seasonally adjusted annual rates.)

Year and quarter	Total	Nonresidential										
		Total	Structures					Equipment and software				
			Total	Nonresidential buildings including farm	Utilities	Mining exploration, shafts, and wells	Other structures	Total	Information processing equipment and software			
									Computers and peripheral equipment [1]	Software	Other	
1970	150.4	109.0	40.3	25.4	11.1	2.8	1.0	68.7	2.7	2.3	11.6
1971	169.9	114.1	42.7	27.1	11.9	2.7	1.0	71.5	2.8	2.4	12.1
1972	198.5	128.8	47.2	30.1	13.1	3.1	0.9	81.7	3.5	2.8	13.1
1973	228.6	153.3	55.0	35.5	15.0	3.5	1.0	98.3	3.5	3.2	16.3
1974	235.4	169.5	61.2	38.3	16.5	5.2	1.2	108.2	3.9	3.9	19.0
1975	236.5	173.7	61.4	35.6	17.1	7.4	1.3	112.4	3.6	4.8	19.9
1976	274.8	192.4	65.9	35.9	20.0	8.6	1.4	126.4	4.4	5.2	22.8
1977	339.0	228.7	74.6	39.9	21.5	11.5	1.8	154.1	5.7	5.5	27.5
1978	410.2	278.6	91.4	49.7	24.1	15.4	2.2	187.2	7.6	6.6	34.2
1979	472.7	331.6	114.9	65.7	27.5	19.0	2.6	216.7	10.2	8.7	39.8
1980	484.2	360.9	133.9	73.7	30.2	27.4	2.6	227.0	12.5	10.7	46.4
1981	541.0	418.4	164.6	86.3	33.0	42.5	2.8	253.8	17.1	12.9	52.3
1982	531.0	425.3	175.0	94.5	32.5	44.8	3.2	250.3	18.9	15.4	54.6
1983	570.0	417.4	152.7	90.5	28.7	30.0	3.5	264.7	23.9	18.0	58.9
1984	670.1	490.3	176.0	110.0	30.0	31.3	4.7	314.3	31.6	22.1	68.0
1985	714.5	527.6	193.3	128.0	30.6	27.9	6.8	334.3	33.7	25.6	71.5
1986	740.7	522.5	175.8	123.3	31.2	15.7	5.7	346.8	33.4	27.8	76.4
1987	754.3	526.7	172.1	126.0	26.5	13.1	6.5	354.7	35.8	31.4	74.8
1988	802.7	568.4	181.6	133.8	26.6	15.7	5.5	386.8	38.0	36.7	81.2
1989	845.2	613.4	193.4	142.7	29.5	14.9	6.2	420.0	43.1	44.4	85.5
1990	847.2	630.3	202.5	149.1	28.4	17.9	7.2	427.8	38.6	50.2	87.3
1991	800.4	608.9	183.4	124.2	33.7	18.5	6.9	425.4	37.7	56.6	87.1
1992	851.6	626.1	172.2	113.2	36.7	14.2	8.2	453.9	43.6	60.8	93.1
1993	934.0	682.2	179.4	119.3	34.8	17.7	7.7	502.8	47.2	69.4	98.4
1994	1 034.6	748.6	187.5	129.0	34.0	17.4	7.0	561.1	51.3	75.5	106.9
1995	1 110.7	825.1	204.6	144.3	35.8	17.2	7.3	620.5	64.6	83.5	113.8
1996	1 212.7	899.4	225.0	161.7	36.0	21.1	6.2	674.4	70.9	95.1	121.3
1997	1 327.7	999.4	255.8	182.7	36.1	30.1	7.0	743.6	79.6	116.5	129.2
1998	1 472.9	1 107.5	283.2	202.3	44.5	29.3	7.1	824.3	84.9	144.1	138.4
1999	1 606.8	1 203.1	285.6	208.5	45.0	24.3	7.8	917.4	94.3	180.1	158.6
1991											
1st quarter	801.8	616.8	194.5	134.8	31.7	21.3	6.7	422.3	36.4	54.7	85.0
2nd quarter	798.3	611.7	189.7	129.0	33.3	20.8	6.7	421.9	36.5	56.2	87.0
3rd quarter	800.5	605.9	177.6	119.5	34.5	16.4	7.1	428.4	37.6	56.9	88.3
4th quarter	801.1	601.1	172.0	113.7	35.4	15.7	7.2	429.1	40.4	58.5	88.0
1992											
1st quarter	811.8	600.1	170.2	112.8	36.2	13.8	7.4	429.8	40.0	58.7	89.8
2nd quarter	845.4	621.5	170.7	112.3	36.8	13.3	8.4	450.7	43.9	60.0	91.0
3rd quarter	859.6	633.0	172.6	112.7	36.8	14.1	9.0	460.4	45.2	61.3	96.4
4th quarter	889.6	649.9	175.4	114.9	36.9	15.5	8.2	474.5	45.1	63.2	95.1
1993											
1st quarter	901.9	659.3	176.7	115.7	35.9	16.9	8.2	482.6	47.1	66.0	95.2
2nd quarter	919.3	675.2	177.5	118.0	34.7	16.8	8.0	497.7	46.0	68.2	96.3
3rd quarter	936.1	683.2	179.2	120.5	34.1	17.5	7.2	503.9	48.4	70.7	100.6
4th quarter	978.8	711.4	184.2	122.8	34.3	19.7	7.3	527.3	47.1	72.8	101.7
1994											
1st quarter	998.1	721.7	178.0	120.5	34.0	16.8	6.7	543.7	48.7	73.9	104.6
2nd quarter	1 026.6	738.2	188.2	131.1	33.5	16.8	6.8	550.0	50.3	75.0	105.7
3rd quarter	1 042.0	752.7	189.9	130.8	34.0	17.5	7.6	562.8	51.3	75.9	107.4
4th quarter	1 071.6	781.8	193.9	133.7	34.5	18.7	7.0	587.9	54.8	77.1	110.0
1995											
1st quarter	1 100.1	812.5	200.5	140.2	35.4	17.6	7.3	612.0	57.7	78.8	114.0
2nd quarter	1 097.2	820.3	204.8	144.7	36.1	16.5	7.5	615.5	64.3	81.8	115.0
3rd quarter	1 110.1	825.2	206.2	145.2	36.2	17.0	7.7	619.0	65.6	85.0	112.5
4th quarter	1 135.4	842.3	207.0	147.2	35.5	17.8	6.5	635.3	70.7	88.6	113.9
1996											
1st quarter	1 165.6	865.1	213.4	151.8	35.8	19.0	6.8	651.7	70.5	91.7	117.8
2nd quarter	1 201.7	885.4	220.0	157.4	35.5	20.7	6.3	665.4	69.6	94.0	119.8
3rd quarter	1 232.6	913.6	226.3	163.2	35.5	21.6	5.9	687.3	71.6	96.1	123.2
4th quarter	1 250.9	933.7	240.3	174.2	37.3	23.0	5.8	693.4	71.7	98.9	124.2
1997											
1st quarter	1 275.5	955.5	246.9	178.5	34.9	27.8	5.7	708.6	74.8	106.2	126.0
2nd quarter	1 310.0	984.3	247.7	177.1	35.2	29.5	5.8	736.6	78.8	113.5	126.7
3rd quarter	1 355.8	1 026.0	260.6	187.6	36.4	30.1	6.4	765.4	83.0	120.1	132.4
4th quarter	1 369.3	1 031.8	267.9	187.4	37.8	32.8	9.9	764.0	81.9	126.0	131.6
1998											
1st quarter	1 419.7	1 073.0	275.1	194.6	42.9	30.7	6.9	797.9	85.4	131.9	136.3
2nd quarter	1 465.4	1 105.8	286.3	202.1	44.4	32.4	7.3	819.5	85.5	140.0	137.4
3rd quarter	1 482.4	1 110.5	283.9	202.6	45.2	29.2	6.8	826.6	84.0	148.5	138.8
4th quarter	1 524.1	1 140.7	287.6	209.9	45.6	24.9	7.2	853.1	85.0	155.9	141.0
1999											
1st quarter	1 560.6	1 165.3	287.2	212.9	44.7	22.3	7.3	878.1	88.1	165.4	148.2
2nd quarter	1 593.4	1 188.0	283.7	207.7	44.5	23.2	8.4	904.3	92.8	173.3	157.5
3rd quarter	1 622.4	1 216.8	281.2	204.7	45.1	23.8	7.6	935.6	97.6	184.7	163.2
4th quarter	1 651.0	1 242.2	290.4	208.7	45.8	27.8	8.1	951.8	98.9	196.8	165.7

1. New computers and peripheral equipment only.

Table 5-2. Gross Private Fixed Investment by Type—*Continued*

(Billions of dollars, quarterly data are at seasonally adjusted annual rates.)

| Year and quarter | Nonresidential | | | Residential | | | | | |
| | Equipment and software | | | | Structures | | | | |
	Industrial equipment	Transportation equipment	Other equipment	Total	Total	Single family	Multifamily	Other structures	Equipment
1970	20.2	16.2	15.6	41.4	40.2	17.5	9.5	13.2	1.1
1971	19.4	18.4	16.4	55.8	54.5	25.8	12.9	15.8	1.3
1972	21.3	21.8	19.2	69.7	68.1	32.8	17.2	18.0	1.5
1973	25.9	26.6	22.8	75.3	73.6	35.2	19.4	19.0	1.7
1974	30.5	26.3	24.6	66.0	64.1	29.7	13.7	20.7	1.9
1975	31.1	25.2	27.9	62.7	60.8	29.6	6.7	24.5	1.9
1976	33.9	30.0	30.1	82.5	80.4	43.9	6.9	29.6	2.1
1977	39.2	39.3	37.1	110.3	107.9	62.2	10.0	35.7	2.4
1978	47.4	47.3	44.1	131.6	128.9	72.8	12.8	43.3	2.7
1979	55.9	53.6	48.6	141.0	137.9	72.3	17.0	48.6	3.2
1980	60.4	48.4	48.6	123.2	119.9	53.0	16.7	50.2	3.4
1981	65.2	50.6	55.6	122.6	119.0	52.0	17.5	49.5	3.6
1982	62.3	46.8	52.3	105.7	102.0	41.5	15.5	45.0	3.7
1983	58.4	53.7	51.8	152.5	148.3	72.2	22.4	53.7	4.2
1984	67.6	64.8	60.2	179.8	175.1	85.6	28.2	61.3	4.7
1985	71.9	69.7	61.8	186.9	181.9	86.1	28.5	67.2	5.1
1986	74.8	71.8	62.6	218.1	212.6	102.2	31.0	79.4	5.5
1987	76.1	70.4	66.2	227.6	221.8	114.5	25.5	81.9	5.8
1988	83.5	76.1	71.3	234.2	228.2	116.6	22.3	89.2	6.1
1989	92.7	71.4	83.0	231.8	225.7	116.9	22.3	86.5	6.1
1990	91.5	75.7	84.5	216.8	210.8	108.7	19.3	82.9	6.0
1991	88.7	79.5	75.8	191.5	185.8	95.4	15.1	75.2	5.7
1992	92.4	86.1	77.9	225.5	219.6	116.5	13.1	90.0	5.9
1993	101.8	98.1	87.9	251.8	245.4	133.3	10.8	101.3	6.4
1994	113.3	117.8	96.3	286.0	279.1	153.8	14.1	111.2	6.9
1995	128.7	126.1	103.7	285.6	278.3	145.0	17.9	115.4	7.3
1996	136.4	138.9	111.8	313.3	305.6	159.1	20.3	126.2	7.7
1997	141.0	151.4	126.0	328.2	320.4	163.2	22.9	134.3	7.9
1998	148.9	168.2	139.8	365.4	357.1	185.8	24.6	146.8	8.3
1999	150.7	193.5	140.2	403.8	394.9	207.2	27.3	160.4	8.9
1991									
1st quarter	89.9	79.6	76.7	185.0	179.2	87.8	17.3	74.1	5.8
2nd quarter	88.5	77.7	76.0	186.6	180.7	89.9	15.3	75.6	5.8
3rd quarter	88.7	81.7	75.1	194.5	188.8	100.3	14.0	74.4	5.8
4th quarter	87.8	79.1	75.3	200.0	194.4	103.7	14.0	76.7	5.6
1992									
1st quarter	88.5	77.1	75.7	211.8	205.9	109.0	13.3	83.6	5.9
2nd quarter	90.4	89.6	75.8	223.9	218.0	115.9	15.1	87.1	5.9
3rd quarter	93.6	84.7	79.1	226.6	220.7	117.8	12.5	90.4	5.9
4th quarter	97.0	93.0	81.1	239.7	233.7	123.3	11.6	98.7	6.0
1993									
1st quarter	98.4	90.8	85.0	242.7	236.5	127.3	10.6	98.7	6.1
2nd quarter	99.3	100.7	87.1	244.1	237.9	128.5	10.3	99.0	6.3
3rd quarter	101.3	94.7	88.3	252.9	246.4	133.8	11.2	101.4	6.5
4th quarter	108.0	106.3	91.4	267.3	260.8	143.6	11.0	106.2	6.5
1994									
1st quarter	109.4	114.0	93.0	276.4	269.9	150.4	11.7	107.7	6.6
2nd quarter	110.5	112.8	95.7	288.4	281.6	156.9	13.3	111.4	6.8
3rd quarter	114.5	116.4	97.4	289.3	282.4	155.0	15.1	112.2	6.9
4th quarter	119.0	127.8	99.2	289.8	282.7	153.0	16.2	113.5	7.2
1995									
1st quarter	124.7	134.0	102.9	287.6	280.3	149.1	17.2	114.1	7.2
2nd quarter	128.9	122.4	103.1	276.9	269.8	140.1	17.1	112.6	7.2
3rd quarter	130.8	121.8	103.4	284.9	277.5	142.4	18.4	116.6	7.4
4th quarter	130.4	126.4	105.3	293.1	285.7	148.4	18.9	118.3	7.5
1996									
1st quarter	135.0	129.1	107.6	300.5	293.0	152.9	19.9	120.3	7.5
2nd quarter	137.7	134.6	109.8	316.3	308.7	160.2	21.7	126.8	7.7
3rd quarter	135.9	146.5	114.0	319.0	311.3	162.9	19.5	129.0	7.7
4th quarter	137.2	145.5	115.9	317.2	309.4	160.5	20.2	128.7	7.8
1997									
1st quarter	135.7	145.3	120.6	320.0	312.1	160.1	21.9	130.1	7.8
2nd quarter	141.0	151.7	124.9	325.7	317.9	162.2	22.9	132.8	7.8
3rd quarter	142.9	157.8	129.2	329.8	321.9	163.5	22.4	136.0	7.9
4th quarter	144.5	150.9	129.1	337.5	329.5	167.0	24.3	138.2	7.9
1998									
1st quarter	147.0	161.1	136.3	346.7	338.6	172.8	25.0	140.7	8.1
2nd quarter	148.6	166.7	141.3	359.6	351.4	182.0	23.9	145.5	8.2
3rd quarter	149.7	162.6	143.0	371.9	363.6	190.5	24.2	148.9	8.3
4th quarter	150.2	182.3	138.8	383.4	375.0	197.8	25.2	152.0	8.5
1999									
1st quarter	146.5	185.5	144.5	395.3	386.7	203.9	27.2	155.5	8.6
2nd quarter	148.3	191.6	140.8	405.4	396.5	207.2	27.1	162.3	8.8
3rd quarter	151.8	200.3	137.9	405.6	396.6	206.1	27.5	163.1	9.0
4th quarter	156.3	196.5	137.6	408.8	399.6	211.5	27.3	160.9	9.2

1. New computers and peripheral equipment only.

Table 5-3. Real Gross Private Fixed Investment by Type

(Billions of chained [1996] dollars, quarterly data are at seasonally adjusted annual rates.)

Year and quarter	Total	Nonresidential	Structures					Equipment and software			
		Total	Total	Nonresidential buildings including farm	Utilities	Mining exploration, shafts, and wells	Other structures	Total	Information processing and related equipment		
									Computers and peripheral equipment [1]	Software	Other
1970	...	...	...	...	...	...	...	...	...	...	...
1971	...	...	...	...	...	...	...	...	...	...	...
1972	...	...	...	...	...	...	...	...	...	...	...
1973	...	...	...	...	...	...	...	...	...	...	...
1974	...	...	...	...	...	...	...	...	...	...	...
1975	...	...	...	...	...	...	...	...	...	...	...
1976	...	...	...	...	...	...	...	...	...	...	...
1977	...	...	...	...	...	...	...	...	...	...	...
1978	...	...	...	...	...	...	...	...	...	...	...
1979	...	...	...	...	...	...	...	...	...	...	...
1980	...	...	...	...	...	...	...	...	...	...	...
1981	...	...	...	...	...	...	...	...	...	...	...
1982	...	...	...	...	...	...	...	...	...	...	...
1983	...	...	...	...	...	...	...	...	...	...	...
1984	...	...	...	...	...	...	...	...	...	...	...
1985	...	...	...	...	...	...	...	...	...	...	...
1986	...	...	...	...	...	...	...	...	...	...	...
1987	856.0	572.5	224.3	162.6	34.9	18.6	8.2	360.0	10.3	27.9	78.0
1988	887.1	603.6	227.1	166.5	33.6	20.4	6.8	386.9	11.8	32.4	83.5
1989	911.2	637.0	232.7	171.4	35.4	18.4	7.5	414.0	14.4	40.1	86.8
1990	894.6	641.7	236.1	173.6	33.0	21.3	8.3	415.7	14.2	45.9	87.6
1991	832.5	610.1	210.1	142.7	38.9	20.8	7.8	407.2	15.4	51.4	86.4
1992	886.5	630.6	197.3	129.2	41.8	17.2	9.2	437.5	20.8	58.7	91.5
1993	958.4	683.6	198.9	131.7	38.4	20.5	8.5	487.1	26.4	66.8	96.4
1994	1 045.9	744.6	200.5	137.2	36.1	19.8	7.6	544.9	32.6	74.3	104.9
1995	1 109.2	817.5	210.1	147.6	36.8	18.2	7.5	607.6	49.2	82.0	113.1
1996	1 212.7	899.4	225.0	161.7	36.0	21.1	6.2	674.4	70.9	95.1	121.3
1997	1 328.6	1 009.3	245.4	177.0	35.3	26.2	6.8	764.2	102.9	119.0	129.8
1998	1 485.3	1 140.3	263.0	189.1	43.0	24.4	6.7	879.0	149.3	151.0	140.7
1999	1 621.4	1 255.3	259.2	187.4	43.5	21.5	7.3	1 003.1	217.3	188.0	163.1
1991											
1st quarter	833.1	616.2	222.3	155.1	36.7	22.9	7.6	402.8	13.9	49.3	84.3
2nd quarter	829.5	611.9	216.6	148.1	38.4	22.6	7.5	403.4	14.4	50.8	86.3
3rd quarter	832.1	607.7	202.9	136.7	39.7	18.5	8.0	410.9	15.7	51.8	87.6
4th quarter	835.4	604.6	198.5	130.6	40.7	19.2	8.1	411.7	17.7	53.9	87.2
1992											
1st quarter	847.4	603.6	196.5	129.8	41.6	16.9	8.3	412.3	17.7	55.6	88.6
2nd quarter	881.4	626.1	196.2	128.6	42.0	16.2	9.3	434.1	20.5	57.8	89.7
3rd quarter	894.4	637.6	197.5	128.5	41.8	17.1	10.0	444.1	22.2	59.5	94.3
4th quarter	922.8	655.0	199.1	129.8	41.7	18.6	9.1	459.4	23.0	61.7	93.3
1993											
1st quarter	929.9	661.7	198.6	129.4	40.4	19.8	9.1	466.3	24.7	63.5	93.3
2nd quarter	944.3	676.6	197.6	131.0	38.3	19.5	8.9	481.4	25.3	65.5	94.3
3rd quarter	958.7	684.2	197.8	132.5	37.5	20.1	7.9	488.5	27.7	67.9	98.4
4th quarter	1 000.6	711.8	201.5	133.8	37.4	22.5	8.1	512.2	28.1	70.2	99.5
1994											
1st quarter	1 014.9	720.0	193.2	130.2	36.5	19.3	7.3	527.4	29.7	72.2	102.3
2nd quarter	1 039.9	734.1	202.9	140.7	35.7	19.2	7.4	532.6	31.2	73.7	103.4
3rd quarter	1 050.9	747.2	202.3	138.5	36.0	19.7	8.2	545.7	32.8	74.9	105.4
4th quarter	1 078.0	777.1	203.8	139.6	36.1	20.8	7.4	573.7	36.7	76.3	108.6
1995											
1st quarter	1 101.9	806.4	208.1	144.5	36.9	19.1	7.7	598.5	40.5	77.5	112.8
2nd quarter	1 095.0	811.4	211.0	148.3	37.3	17.6	7.8	600.7	47.0	80.1	113.9
3rd quarter	1 107.1	816.7	210.9	148.1	37.0	17.9	7.9	606.0	50.8	83.3	111.9
4th quarter	1 132.7	835.5	210.4	149.4	36.0	18.4	6.6	625.0	58.4	87.2	113.8
1996											
1st quarter	1 165.2	861.6	215.9	153.4	36.1	19.6	6.8	645.8	63.1	90.7	117.8
2nd quarter	1 203.7	885.6	221.3	158.3	35.7	21.0	6.4	664.3	67.9	93.6	119.7
3rd quarter	1 231.6	914.3	225.4	162.4	35.5	21.5	5.9	688.9	73.9	96.4	123.3
4th quarter	1 250.2	936.2	237.3	172.4	36.8	22.3	5.7	698.8	78.5	99.8	124.3
1997											
1st quarter	1 275.4	960.8	241.1	175.4	34.4	25.5	5.6	719.6	87.2	107.7	126.5
2nd quarter	1 311.1	992.7	239.3	172.8	34.4	26.1	5.7	753.7	98.1	115.3	127.4
3rd quarter	1 356.7	1 037.0	248.5	180.9	35.5	25.7	6.2	788.9	110.5	123.0	132.8
4th quarter	1 371.3	1 047.0	252.7	178.8	36.7	27.4	9.5	794.5	115.8	130.1	132.5
1998											
1st quarter	1 427.4	1 096.0	257.5	184.5	41.5	25.1	6.6	839.4	131.8	137.8	137.7
2nd quarter	1 477.6	1 136.4	266.2	190.1	43.0	26.2	7.0	871.3	144.0	146.7	139.7
3rd quarter	1 496.4	1 146.3	263.0	188.6	43.6	24.6	6.5	885.2	153.4	155.7	141.6
4th quarter	1 539.7	1 182.3	265.1	193.2	44.0	21.7	6.9	920.0	168.0	163.9	143.9
1999											
1st quarter	1 574.0	1 209.4	262.9	193.6	43.3	19.7	6.9	950.9	186.1	173.3	151.4
2nd quarter	1 607.1	1 237.5	258.7	187.7	43.2	20.6	7.9	985.0	208.5	181.1	161.3
3rd quarter	1 637.8	1 272.5	254.6	183.2	43.6	21.3	7.1	1 026.6	230.9	192.5	168.1
4th quarter	1 666.6	1 301.8	260.6	185.1	44.0	24.6	7.5	1 050.1	243.8	205.3	171.6

Table 5-3. Real Gross Private Fixed Investment by Type—*Continued*

(Billions of chained [1996] dollars, quarterly data are at seasonally adjusted annual rates.)

| Year and quarter | Nonresidential—*Continued* | | | Total | Residential | | | | |
| | Equipment and software—*Continued* | | | | Structures | | | | |
	Industrial equipment	Transportation equipment	Other equipment		Total	Single family	Multifamily	Other structures	Equipment
1970	...	...	...	...	...	...	...	...	...
1971	...	...	...	...	...	...	...	...	...
1972	...	...	...	...	...	...	...	...	...
1973	...	...	...	...	...	...	...	...	...
1974	...	...	...	...	...	...	...	...	...
1975	...	...	...	...	...	...	...	...	...
1976	...	...	...	...	...	...	...	...	...
1977	...	...	...	...	...	...	...	...	...
1978	...	...	...	...	...	...	...	...	...
1979	...	...	...	...	...	...	...	...	...
1980	...	...	...	...	...	...	...	...	...
1981	...	...	...	...	...	...	...	...	...
1982	...	...	...	...	...	...	...	...	...
1983	...	...	...	...	...	...	...	...	...
1984	...	...	...	...	...	...	...	...	...
1985	...	...	...	...	...	...	...	...	...
1986	...	...	...	...	...	...	...	...	...
1987	99.9	88.0	83.8	290.7	284.7	149.5	29.3	104.9	6.1
1988	104.9	93.6	87.7	289.2	283.0	146.9	25.0	110.5	6.3
1989	112.4	84.9	98.1	277.3	271.0	142.0	24.9	103.4	6.4
1990	105.8	87.4	96.2	253.5	247.3	128.6	21.7	96.4	6.2
1991	99.0	87.7	83.6	221.1	215.1	112.3	16.8	85.6	5.9
1992	100.8	92.3	84.1	257.2	251.0	135.7	14.2	100.9	6.1
1993	109.6	103.4	93.3	276.0	269.4	148.0	11.5	109.9	6.5
1994	119.6	120.4	100.6	302.7	295.8	163.2	14.8	117.7	6.9
1995	131.3	128.2	106.2	291.7	284.4	147.7	18.4	118.3	7.4
1996	136.4	138.9	111.8	313.3	305.6	159.1	20.3	126.2	7.7
1997	140.0	150.5	124.7	319.7	311.8	158.6	21.9	131.3	7.9
1998	146.9	168.0	136.7	346.1	337.7	175.9	21.7	140.2	8.3
1999	147.8	191.8	135.6	368.3	359.2	187.6	23.2	148.5	9.1
1991									
1st quarter	100.6	88.8	85.2	214.7	208.6	103.6	19.3	85.1	5.9
2nd quarter	99.3	86.2	84.1	215.6	209.4	105.9	16.9	86.1	6.1
3rd quarter	99.1	90.0	82.6	223.4	217.4	117.5	15.4	84.3	5.9
4th quarter	97.3	86.0	82.4	230.6	224.7	122.2	15.4	86.9	5.8
1992									
1st quarter	97.4	83.1	82.4	245.0	238.9	128.8	14.6	95.3	6.1
2nd quarter	99.0	96.0	82.1	256.6	250.5	135.8	16.4	98.1	6.1
3rd quarter	101.5	90.9	85.0	257.9	251.8	136.9	13.5	101.2	6.1
4th quarter	105.5	99.2	86.9	269.2	263.0	141.4	12.4	109.1	6.2
1993									
1st quarter	106.8	96.1	90.8	269.5	263.1	143.8	11.2	108.1	6.4
2nd quarter	107.2	106.3	92.4	268.6	262.1	143.9	11.0	107.2	6.5
3rd quarter	108.9	99.8	93.4	275.7	269.0	147.8	12.0	109.2	6.7
4th quarter	115.6	111.4	96.6	290.1	283.4	156.6	11.7	115.2	6.7
1994									
1st quarter	116.7	117.4	97.9	296.5	289.8	162.4	12.4	115.0	6.7
2nd quarter	117.1	115.0	99.9	307.5	300.6	168.3	14.1	118.2	6.9
3rd quarter	120.5	118.2	101.3	305.2	298.2	163.6	15.9	118.6	7.0
4th quarter	124.3	131.1	103.3	301.8	294.6	158.6	16.9	119.1	7.2
1995									
1st quarter	129.3	137.3	106.6	295.8	288.5	152.7	17.7	118.1	7.3
2nd quarter	131.8	124.7	105.9	283.5	276.3	143.0	17.6	115.7	7.2
3rd quarter	132.7	123.3	105.6	290.4	283.0	144.8	18.9	119.3	7.4
4th quarter	131.6	127.5	106.7	297.3	289.7	150.3	19.3	120.1	7.5
1996									
1st quarter	135.6	130.2	108.3	303.6	296.1	154.5	20.2	121.4	7.5
2nd quarter	138.0	134.7	110.2	318.1	310.4	161.5	21.9	127.1	7.7
3rd quarter	135.7	145.8	113.8	317.3	309.7	161.8	19.3	128.5	7.7
4th quarter	136.5	144.9	115.0	314.0	306.3	158.7	19.9	127.6	7.8
1997									
1st quarter	134.9	144.5	119.5	314.7	307.0	157.2	21.4	128.3	7.8
2nd quarter	140.2	150.8	123.7	318.7	310.8	158.7	22.2	130.0	7.8
3rd quarter	141.8	156.2	128.0	320.3	312.4	158.2	21.3	132.9	7.9
4th quarter	143.2	150.3	127.5	324.9	316.9	160.2	22.7	134.0	8.0
1998									
1st quarter	145.5	161.1	133.9	332.4	324.3	165.6	22.6	136.1	8.1
2nd quarter	146.9	167.1	138.4	342.4	334.1	173.6	21.3	139.4	8.3
3rd quarter	147.6	162.3	139.5	350.9	342.6	179.9	21.1	141.7	8.4
4th quarter	147.7	181.6	134.8	358.5	350.0	184.7	21.7	143.7	8.5
1999									
1st quarter	143.7	183.1	140.1	365.7	356.9	187.6	23.4	146.0	8.8
2nd quarter	145.7	189.0	136.2	370.9	361.9	188.5	23.1	150.4	9.0
3rd quarter	148.9	199.1	133.3	368.0	358.8	185.6	23.3	150.1	9.2
4th quarter	152.8	195.9	132.8	368.5	359.2	188.8	23.0	147.5	9.3

Table 5-4. Inventories to Sales Ratios

(Seasonally adjusted, ratio of inventories at end of quarter to monthly rate of sales during the quarter, annual data are for fourth quarter.)

Year and quarter	Total private inventories to final sales of domestic business		Nonfarm inventories to:			
			Final sales of domestic business		Final sales of goods and structures	
	Current dollars	Chained (1996) dollars	Current dollars	Chained (1996) dollars	Current dollars	Chained (1996) dollars
1970	3.05	2.73	2.51	2.29	3.76	4.03
1971	3.02	2.70	2.44	2.26	3.68	3.99
1972	3.01	2.60	2.37	2.19	3.53	3.82
1973	3.30	2.64	2.55	2.26	3.78	3.94
1974	3.61	2.81	3.01	2.45	4.56	4.43
1975	3.27	2.66	2.69	2.28	4.09	4.11
1976	3.22	2.65	2.72	2.30	4.17	4.15
1977	3.18	2.66	2.69	2.29	4.13	4.12
1978	3.25	2.61	2.68	2.27	4.07	4.02
1979	3.44	2.63	2.84	2.27	4.32	4.04
1980	3.45	2.59	2.91	2.27	4.50	4.09
1981	3.39	2.70	2.92	2.35	4.59	4.25
1982	3.21	2.65	2.74	2.27	4.46	4.18
1983	2.99	2.46	2.59	2.16	4.21	3.94
1984	3.03	2.53	2.64	2.23	4.31	4.02
1985	2.85	2.49	2.50	2.18	4.17	3.98
1986	2.64	2.42	2.34	2.12	3.94	3.86
1987	2.68	2.42	2.39	2.16	4.08	3.95
1988	2.65	2.35	2.37	2.13	4.07	3.90
1989	2.62	2.36	2.35	2.14	4.06	3.92
1990	2.60	2.38	2.34	2.16	4.11	4.00
1991	2.46	2.38	2.24	2.17	4.03	4.06
1992	2.36	2.30	2.13	2.09	3.85	3.89
1993	2.30	2.28	2.09	2.08	3.79	3.85
1994	2.34	2.33	2.13	2.11	3.86	3.89
1995	2.33	2.31	2.15	2.13	3.91	3.88
1996	2.25	2.26	2.06	2.08	3.76	3.77
1997	2.19	2.28	2.01	2.10	3.68	3.76
1998	2.12	2.30	1.98	2.12	3.58	3.75
1999	2.11	2.25	1.96	2.08	3.56	3.65
1991						
1st quarter	2.56	2.39	2.29	2.17	4.05	4.02
2nd quarter	2.48	2.36	2.24	2.14	3.97	4.00
3rd quarter	2.46	2.36	2.23	2.15	3.99	4.03
4th quarter	2.46	2.38	2.24	2.17	4.03	4.06
1992						
1st quarter	2.42	2.34	2.18	2.12	3.93	3.97
2nd quarter	2.41	2.34	2.18	2.12	3.94	3.97
3rd quarter	2.40	2.33	2.16	2.11	3.93	3.95
4th quarter	2.36	2.30	2.13	2.09	3.85	3.89
1993						
1st quarter	2.39	2.33	2.15	2.12	3.90	3.96
2nd quarter	2.37	2.32	2.14	2.12	3.88	3.93
3rd quarter	2.34	2.31	2.12	2.11	3.87	3.93
4th quarter	2.30	2.28	2.09	2.08	3.79	3.85
1994						
1st quarter	2.31	2.29	2.09	2.09	3.80	3.87
2nd quarter	2.32	2.31	2.11	2.10	3.83	3.89
3rd quarter	2.31	2.31	2.11	2.10	3.84	3.88
4th quarter	2.34	2.33	2.13	2.11	3.86	3.89
1995						
1st quarter	2.38	2.34	2.17	2.14	3.93	3.91
2nd quarter	2.38	2.34	2.19	2.15	3.99	3.95
3rd quarter	2.35	2.32	2.16	2.13	3.95	3.92
4th quarter	2.33	2.31	2.15	2.13	3.91	3.88
1996						
1st quarter	2.30	2.28	2.12	2.11	3.85	3.84
2nd quarter	2.28	2.27	2.09	2.09	3.79	3.79
3rd quarter	2.29	2.28	2.09	2.10	3.79	3.80
4th quarter	2.25	2.26	2.06	2.08	3.76	3.77
1997						
1st quarter	2.23	2.26	2.04	2.08	3.70	3.75
2nd quarter	2.22	2.28	2.03	2.10	3.71	3.79
3rd quarter	2.20	2.26	2.02	2.08	3.66	3.73
4th quarter	2.19	2.28	2.01	2.10	3.68	3.76
1998						
1st quarter	2.20	2.31	2.02	2.12	3.67	3.79
2nd quarter	2.17	2.30	2.00	2.11	3.65	3.77
3rd quarter	2.15	2.31	2.00	2.13	3.64	3.80
4th quarter	2.12	2.30	1.98	2.12	3.58	3.75
1999						
1st quarter	2.12	2.29	1.96	2.12	3.55	3.73
2nd quarter	2.11	2.27	1.96	2.10	3.54	3.69
3rd quarter	2.12	2.26	1.97	2.09	3.57	3.68
4th quarter	2.11	2.25	1.96	2.08	3.56	3.65

Table 5-5. Manufacturing and Trade Sales

(Millions of dollars.)

Year and month	Total		Seasonally adjusted								
			Manufacturing			Retail trade			Merchant wholesalers		
	Not seasonally adjusted	Seasonally adjusted	Total	Durable goods industries	Nondurable goods industries	Total	Durable goods stores	Nondurable goods stores	Total	Durable goods establishments	Nondurable goods establishments
1970	1 298 651	1 298 651	633 663	337 876	295 787	374 989	114 586	260 403	289 999	133 778	156 221
1971	1 402 745	1 402 745	670 877	359 089	311 788	413 969	135 113	278 856	317 899	147 761	170 138
1972	1 572 976	1 572 976	756 321	407 844	348 477	458 267	155 937	302 330	358 388	168 879	189 509
1973	1 844 121	1 844 121	875 173	475 621	399 552	511 570	176 817	334 753	457 378	208 554	248 824
1974	2 134 949	2 134 949	1 017 477	530 074	487 403	541 686	172 497	369 189	575 786	255 863	319 923
1975	2 186 375	2 186 375	1 039 065	523 178	515 887	587 704	185 479	402 225	559 606	235 723	323 883
1976	2 449 803	2 449 803	1 185 563	607 475	578 088	655 859	219 908	435 951	608 381	263 605	344 776
1977	2 754 158	2 754 158	1 358 416	710 017	648 399	722 109	249 078	473 031	673 633	304 721	368 912
1978	3 123 838	3 123 838	1 522 858	812 776	710 082	804 019	280 899	523 120	796 961	372 176	424 785
1979	3 572 409	3 572 409	1 727 234	911 124	816 110	896 561	306 561	590 000	948 614	436 254	512 360
1980	3 926 797	3 926 797	1 852 689	929 027	923 662	956 921	298 618	658 303	1 117 187	486 509	630 678
1981	4 269 863	4 269 863	2 017 544	1 004 725	1 012 819	1 038 163	324 211	713 952	1 214 156	525 607	688 549
1982	4 171 496	4 171 496	1 960 214	950 541	1 009 673	1 068 747	335 587	733 160	1 142 535	480 318	662 217
1983	4 431 432	4 431 432	2 070 564	1 025 770	1 044 794	1 170 163	390 849	779 314	1 190 705	523 080	667 625
1984	4 921 490	4 921 490	2 288 184	1 175 276	1 112 908	1 286 914	454 481	832 433	1 346 392	622 361	724 031
1985	5 070 990	5 070 990	2 334 456	1 215 352	1 119 104	1 375 027	498 125	876 902	1 361 507	651 864	709 643
1986	5 165 031	5 165 031	2 335 881	1 238 859	1 097 022	1 449 636	540 688	908 948	1 379 514	681 691	697 823
1987	5 492 818	5 492 818	2 475 906	1 297 532	1 178 374	1 541 299	575 863	965 436	1 475 613	730 592	745 021
1988	5 965 883	5 965 883	2 695 432	1 421 501	1 273 931	1 656 202	629 154	1 027 048	1 614 249	801 751	812 498
1989	6 324 469	6 324 469	2 840 375	1 477 900	1 362 475	1 758 971	657 154	1 101 817	1 725 123	851 550	873 573
1990	6 550 911	6 550 911	2 912 228	1 485 313	1 426 915	1 844 611	668 835	1 175 776	1 794 072	880 767	913 305
1991	6 513 777	6 513 777	2 878 167	1 451 998	1 426 169	1 855 937	649 974	1 205 963	1 779 673	860 138	919 535
1992	6 806 114	6 806 114	3 004 727	1 541 866	1 462 861	1 951 589	703 604	1 247 985	1 849 798	908 917	940 881
1993	7 147 540	7 147 540	3 127 625	1 630 635	1 496 990	2 082 112	781 921	1 300 191	1 937 803	993 449	944 354
1994	7 669 951	7 669 951	3 348 019	1 789 576	1 558 443	2 248 198	886 653	1 361 545	2 073 734	1 098 457	375 277
1995	8 219 785	8 219 785	3 594 663	1 927 029	1 667 634	2 359 013	947 347	1 411 666	2 266 109	1 207 906	1 058 203
1996	8 617 357	8 617 357	3 715 460	2 004 159	1 711 301	2 502 365	1 018 994	1 483 371	2 399 532	1 262 698	1 136 834
1997	9 041 337	9 041 337	3 929 419	2 159 699	1 770 720	2 610 562	1 063 229	1 547 333	2 501 356	1 334 672	1 166 684
1998	9 352 958	9 352 958	4 052 248	2 275 987	1 776 261	2 745 593	1 136 387	1 609 206	2 555 117	1 381 390	1 173 187
1999	9 996 943	9 996 943	4 259 532	2 407 473	1 852 059	2 994 929	1 254 996	1 739 966	2 742 482	1 481 780	1 260 702
1996											
January	634 566	695 735	300 389	161 326	139 063	201 391	81 369	120 022	193 955	102 879	91 076
February	668 392	700 314	302 541	163 002	139 539	203 647	82 990	120 657	194 126	102 697	91 429
March	717 033	703 323	301 083	160 941	140 142	205 534	84 213	121 321	196 706	104 227	92 479
April	707 274	711 229	307 672	164 906	142 766	206 506	83 864	122 642	197 051	103 509	93 542
May	737 372	717 805	312 489	169 351	143 138	207 519	84 726	122 793	197 797	104 509	93 288
June	733 606	714 217	308 248	167 004	141 244	207 920	85 003	122 917	198 049	104 342	93 707
July	690 958	719 587	310 576	167 129	143 447	208 293	85 098	123 195	200 718	104 317	96 401
August	736 765	721 805	312 153	168 808	143 345	207 754	84 264	123 490	201 898	104 746	97 152
September	734 245	724 971	313 159	170 292	142 867	210 545	86 240	124 305	201 267	105 804	95 463
October	754 630	728 649	313 737	168 855	144 882	212 290	86 614	125 676	202 622	106 309	96 313
November	730 765	734 102	317 744	171 970	145 774	212 197	85 954	126 243	204 161	107 998	96 163
December	760 014	729 295	313 779	169 204	144 575	212 907	85 852	127 055	202 609	106 658	95 951
1997											
January	674 348	738 592	319 150	172 304	146 846	214 362	86 774	127 588	205 080	107 587	97 493
February	696 983	746 801	321 274	174 534	146 740	216 017	88 195	127 822	209 510	110 819	98 691
March	760 684	744 645	320 700	175 504	145 196	216 289	88 320	127 969	207 656	108 845	98 811
April	741 676	748 467	325 639	178 523	147 116	215 573	87 688	127 885	207 255	110 686	96 569
May	757 845	742 728	322 260	175 749	146 511	212 634	85 152	127 482	207 834	110 355	97 479
June	775 896	750 494	326 118	180 038	146 080	216 262	87 931	128 331	208 114	111 287	96 827
July	730 004	758 243	331 331	183 484	147 847	218 834	89 284	129 550	208 078	112 421	95 657
August	759 941	756 217	328 250	180 554	147 696	220 112	90 069	130 043	207 855	111 016	96 839
September	784 233	764 556	333 422	184 966	148 456	220 354	90 005	130 349	210 780	113 525	97 255
October	788 634	762 089	332 321	183 225	149 096	219 836	89 580	130 256	209 932	113 018	96 914
November	747 289	761 132	331 404	182 791	148 613	220 905	90 469	130 436	208 823	112 658	96 165
December	807 604	768 111	336 424	186 007	150 417	221 753	91 348	130 405	209 934	112 814	97 120
1998											
January	692 927	765 347	331 937	182 303	149 634	222 108	91 443	130 665	211 302	114 336	96 966
February	720 192	769 681	335 883	187 298	148 585	222 574	91 185	131 389	211 224	114 511	96 713
March	797 710	775 568	338 991	189 998	148 993	223 975	92 117	131 858	212 602	115 408	97 194
April	771 370	774 889	335 553	186 843	148 710	226 183	94 050	132 133	213 153	116 092	97 061
May	777 715	773 935	333 622	185 789	147 833	227 791	94 334	133 457	212 522	115 051	97 471
June	813 712	777 165	335 110	186 536	148 574	230 046	96 195	133 851	212 009	115 176	96 833
July	748 807	777 069	335 380	186 907	148 473	228 231	93 746	134 485	213 458	116 026	97 432
August	777 164	776 190	336 445	188 789	147 656	228 078	93 384	134 694	211 667	115 262	96 405
September	803 255	783 932	340 481	192 842	147 639	230 610	95 330	135 280	212 841	114 842	97 999
October	807 722	786 998	340 133	193 818	146 315	233 751	97 530	136 221	213 114	114 427	98 687
November	779 603	790 432	341 423	194 823	146 600	235 251	98 112	137 139	213 758	114 630	99 128
December	843 090	797 812	344 247	195 531	148 716	237 116	99 247	137 869	216 449	116 027	100 422
1999											
January	574 497	796 003	341 673	194 091	147 582	239 154	99 641	139 513	215 176	116 397	98 779
February	606 390	803 573	343 724	194 465	149 259	241 580	101 280	140 300	218 269	119 570	98 699
March	697 371	812 182	349 065	198 292	150 773	242 316	101 367	140 949	220 801	119 826	100 975
April	661 565	814 099	347 568	197 246	150 322	244 556	101 905	142 651	221 975	119 882	102 093
May	676 783	823 887	350 624	199 425	151 199	247 325	103 821	143 504	225 938	121 964	103 974
June	711 145	831 662	354 702	200 990	153 712	247 826	103 798	144 028	229 134	123 265	105 869
July	652 661	836 625	357 301	203 268	154 033	249 816	105 028	144 788	229 508	124 172	105 336
August	695 678	846 499	361 844	205 709	156 135	253 030	106 730	146 300	231 625	124 485	107 140
September	704 324	845 425	358 709	201 895	156 814	253 748	106 391	147 357	232 968	125 303	107 665
October	697 137	850 386	360 201	202 306	157 895	254 959	106 743	148 216	235 226	126 603	108 623
November	700 132	861 000	364 971	204 430	160 541	257 489	108 640	148 849	238 540	128 091	110 449
December	767 201	871 172	367 872	206 480	161 392	261 628	109 545	152 083	241 672	130 720	110 952

Table 5-6. Manufacturing and Trade Inventories

(Block value, end of period; millions of dollars.)

Year and month	Total		Seasonally adjusted								
			Manufacturing			Retail trade			Merchant wholesalers		
	Not seasonally adjusted	Seasonally adjusted	Total	Durable goods industries	Nondurable goods industries	Total	Durable goods stores	Nondurable goods stores	Total	Durable goods establish-ments	Nondurable goods establish-ments
1980	. . .	. . .	. . .	. . .	. . .	121 078	55 799	65 279	122 631	79 372	43 259
1981	. . .	. . .	. . .	. . .	. . .	132 719	61 050	71 669	129 654	85 856	43 798
1982	566 523	573 908	311 852	200 444	111 408	134 628	61 316	73 312	127 428	85 222	42 206
1983	582 494	590 287	312 379	199 854	112 525	147 833	68 856	78 977	130 075	85 180	44 895
1984	640 467	649 780	339 516	221 330	118 186	167 812	79 074	88 738	142 452	95 474	46 978
1985	654 899	664 039	334 749	218 193	116 556	181 881	88 315	93 566	147 409	97 371	50 038
1986	653 299	662 738	322 654	211 997	110 657	186 510	89 983	96 527	153 574	102 349	51 225
1987	700 139	709 848	338 109	220 799	117 310	207 836	105 481	102 355	163 903	108 112	55 791
1988	757 952	767 222	369 374	242 468	126 906	219 047	112 453	106 594	178 801	117 045	61 756
1989	805 579	815 455	391 212	257 513	133 699	237 234	121 347	115 887	187 009	122 237	64 772
1990	830 883	840 663	405 073	263 209	141 864	239 815	121 194	118 621	195 775	880 767	69 362
1991	824 764	834 715	390 950	250 019	140 931	243 389	119 189	124 200	200 376	127 342	73 034
1992	832 779	842 939	382 510	238 105	144 405	252 185	123 152	129 033	208 244	131 458	76 786
1993	859 636	870 316	384 039	239 334	144 705	269 303	135 088	134 215	216 974	137 042	79 932
1994	922 771	934 342	404 877	253 624	151 253	294 052	153 019	141 033	235 413	150 928	84 485
1995	982 528	994 826	430 985	268 353	162 632	310 276	165 108	145 168	253 565	163 474	90 091
1996	1 000 439	1 013 201	436 729	273 815	162 914	320 601	170 849	149 752	255 871	166 185	89 686
1997	1 047 582	1 060 326	456 133	286 372	169 761	330 308	176 483	153 825	273 885	177 746	96 139
1998	1 085 669	1 095 042	466 798	295 344	171 454	340 760	181 070	159 690	287 484	187 734	99 750
1999	1 136 555	1 150 554	470 377	295 034	175 343	372 252	202 474	169 778	307 925	202 274	105 651
1996											
January	996 180	1 001 065	433 597	270 707	162 890	311 076	165 914	145 162	256 392	165 956	90 436
February	1 003 299	1 001 442	434 023	271 111	162 912	311 360	165 945	145 415	256 059	165 726	90 333
March	998 801	998 435	434 157	271 251	162 906	308 750	163 913	144 837	255 528	165 163	90 365
April	1 007 780	1 002 387	433 815	271 153	162 662	308 847	163 714	145 133	259 725	166 502	93 223
May	1 003 397	1 003 784	432 518	270 995	161 523	311 246	165 791	145 455	260 020	166 172	93 848
June	990 487	1 003 059	432 102	270 682	161 420	311 887	166 561	145 326	259 070	165 978	93 092
July	997 283	1 008 159	432 854	271 759	161 095	315 792	168 678	147 114	259 513	166 842	92 671
August	998 957	1 010 176	433 794	272 684	161 110	317 499	170 175	147 324	258 883	167 439	91 444
September	1 005 168	1 009 579	434 864	273 092	161 772	318 049	170 779	147 270	256 666	167 946	88 720
October	1 036 703	1 014 637	436 428	274 146	162 282	320 678	172 242	148 436	257 531	167 617	89 914
November	1 041 852	1 014 731	437 606	274 896	162 710	319 248	170 354	148 894	257 877	168 299	89 578
December	1 000 439	1 014 340	436 729	273 815	162 914	319 985	170 775	149 210	257 626	168 163	89 463
1997											
January	1 013 132	1 018 811	438 641	275 517	163 124	319 929	170 836	149 093	260 241	169 323	90 918
February	1 024 685	1 023 014	440 915	277 080	163 835	321 834	172 197	149 637	260 265	169 481	90 784
March	1 024 278	1 023 326	441 676	277 399	164 277	319 982	171 311	148 671	261 668	170 927	90 741
April	1 034 925	1 028 394	444 714	279 880	164 834	321 523	171 621	149 902	262 157	171 724	90 433
May	1 033 484	1 033 508	446 888	281 143	165 745	322 784	172 546	150 238	263 836	173 240	90 596
June	1 028 336	1 040 577	447 947	282 013	165 934	324 100	173 655	150 445	268 530	177 363	91 167
July	1 032 930	1 043 543	449 657	283 723	165 934	326 268	175 048	151 220	267 618	175 749	91 869
August	1 033 977	1 045 241	451 737	284 982	166 755	324 792	174 249	150 543	268 712	176 052	92 660
September	1 046 326	1 051 084	452 224	284 660	167 564	327 606	175 633	151 973	271 254	178 386	92 868
October	1 078 034	1 055 893	455 553	286 654	168 899	328 313	176 197	152 116	272 027	177 758	94 269
November	1 087 299	1 059 714	457 766	287 949	169 817	327 947	175 689	152 258	274 001	178 409	95 592
December	1 047 582	1 061 815	456 133	286 372	169 761	329 542	176 349	153 193	276 140	180 391	95 749
1998											
January	1 059 154	1 065 249	458 197	288 086	170 111	330 854	176 009	154 845	276 198	181 479	94 719
February	1 073 624	1 072 016	461 178	290 153	171 025	331 537	176 466	155 071	279 301	183 693	95 608
March	1 078 506	1 076 464	461 948	290 887	171 061	333 756	177 445	156 311	280 760	185 010	95 750
April	1 087 341	1 079 636	464 668	293 393	171 275	334 933	177 852	157 081	280 035	185 164	94 871
May	1 080 789	1 080 689	465 729	294 375	171 354	332 404	175 676	156 728	282 556	186 163	96 393
June	1 070 018	1 082 465	466 701	295 143	171 558	333 131	174 760	158 371	282 633	185 543	97 090
July	1 073 605	1 084 628	467 636	295 669	171 967	334 043	175 248	158 795	282 949	185 723	97 226
August	1 077 499	1 089 101	468 445	296 913	171 532	334 878	175 992	158 886	285 778	187 912	97 866
September	1 088 730	1 093 987	468 552	296 757	171 795	337 819	178 277	159 542	287 616	188 868	98 748
October	1 119 913	1 097 577	471 031	298 561	172 470	338 726	179 702	159 024	287 820	189 767	98 053
November	1 129 782	1 101 149	471 000	297 981	173 019	341 165	182 257	158 908	288 984	189 706	99 278
December	1 085 669	1 100 166	466 798	295 344	171 454	343 197	183 630	159 567	290 171	191 054	99 117
1999											
January	1 093 980	1 101 132	464 867	293 563	171 304	346 158	185 402	160 756	290 107	191 543	98 564
February	1 104 965	1 103 951	464 198	294 030	170 168	347 792	186 926	160 866	291 961	192 456	99 505
March	1 111 225	1 108 649	463 578	293 391	170 187	352 287	190 241	162 046	292 784	192 781	100 003
April	1 119 058	1 110 716	463 194	292 415	170 779	354 556	192 171	162 385	292 966	191 947	101 019
May	1 114 291	1 113 924	463 742	292 403	171 339	355 826	193 264	162 562	294 356	193 404	100 952
June	1 105 679	1 118 449	462 690	291 645	171 045	360 166	196 472	163 694	295 593	194 756	100 837
July	1 109 741	1 122 570	465 043	293 505	171 538	359 060	195 601	163 459	298 467	196 441	102 026
August	1 112 131	1 126 111	464 351	292 461	171 890	361 854	197 054	164 800	299 906	196 166	103 740
September	1 124 379	1 130 313	465 669	292 901	172 768	363 134	197 581	165 553	301 510	197 549	103 961
October	1 157 867	1 134 646	467 522	293 448	174 074	363 553	197 333	166 220	303 570	199 080	104 490
November	1 175 112	1 144 815	469 836	294 970	174 866	368 079	199 811	168 268	306 900	201 858	105 042
December	1 136 555	1 150 554	470 377	295 034	175 343	372 252	202 474	169 778	307 925	202 274	105 651

Table 5-7. Manufacturing and Trade Inventory to Sales Ratios

(Seasonally adjusted, annual figures are averages of seasonally adjusted monthly ratios.)

Year and month	Total	Manufacturing			Retail trade			Merchant wholesalers		
		Total	Durable goods industries	Nondurable goods industries	Total	Durable goods stores	Nondurable goods stores	Total	Durable goods establishments	Nondurable goods establishments
1970	...	...	...	...	...	...	...	...	...	...
1971	...	...	...	...	...	...	...	...	...	...
1972	...	...	...	...	...	...	...	...	...	...
1973	...	...	...	...	...	...	...	...	...	...
1974	...	...	...	...	...	...	...	...	...	...
1975	...	...	...	...	...	...	...	...	...	...
1976	...	...	...	...	...	...	...	...	...	...
1977	...	...	...	...	...	...	...	...	...	...
1978	...	...	...	...	...	...	...	...	...	...
1979	...	...	...	...	...	...	...	...	...	...
1980	...	...	...	...	...	...	...	...	...	...
1981					1.48	2.18	1.16	1.25	1.88	0.76
1982	1.67	1.95	2.60	1.34	1.49	2.17	1.18	1.36	2.15	0.77
1983	1.56	1.78	2.30	1.27	1.44	1.98	1.17	1.28	1.89	0.78
1984	1.53	1.73	2.16	1.27	1.49	1.96	1.23	1.23	1.74	0.78
1985	1.55	1.73	2.18	1.25	1.52	2.02	1.25	1.28	1.77	0.82
1986	1.55	1.68	2.08	1.22	1.56	2.07	1.26	1.32	1.77	0.87
1987	1.50	1.59	1.99	1.16	1.55	2.08	1.24	1.29	1.72	0.86
1988	1.49	1.57	1.95	1.15	1.54	2.05	1.23	1.30	1.71	0.89
1989	1.52	1.63	2.06	1.16	1.58	2.18	1.22	1.28	1.70	0.86
1990	1.52	1.65	2.12	1.16	1.56	2.17	1.20	1.29	1.70	0.88
1991	1.53	1.65	2.12	1.18	1.54	2.18	1.20	1.33	1.76	0.92
1992	1.48	1.54	1.90	1.17	1.52	2.06	1.22	1.32	1.70	0.96
1993	1.44	1.47	1.76	1.17	1.51	1.98	1.23	1.32	1.62	1.00
1994	1.41	1.41	1.65	1.13	1.50	1.95	1.21	1.31	1.58	1.00
1995	1.43	1.41	1.64	1.15	1.55	2.05	1.22	1.32	1.59	1.00
1996	1.40	1.40	1.63	1.14	1.51	1.98	1.19	1.29	1.59	0.97
1997	1.38	1.37	1.57	1.13	1.49	1.96	1.17	1.28	1.57	0.95
1998	1.39	1.38	1.56	1.16	1.46	1.86	1.18	1.33	1.62	1.00
1999	1.35	1.31	1.46	1.12	1.44	1.86	1.13	1.31	1.59	0.97
1996										
January	1.44	1.44	1.68	1.17	1.55	2.03	1.21	1.32	1.61	0.99
February	1.43	1.43	1.66	1.17	1.53	1.99	1.21	1.32	1.61	0.99
March	1.41	1.44	1.69	1.16	1.50	1.94	1.20	1.30	1.58	0.98
April	1.41	1.41	1.64	1.14	1.49	1.95	1.18	1.32	1.61	1.00
May	1.40	1.38	1.60	1.13	1.50	1.95	1.18	1.31	1.59	1.01
June	1.41	1.40	1.62	1.14	1.51	1.98	1.19	1.31	1.59	0.99
July	1.40	1.39	1.63	1.12	1.52	1.99	1.20	1.29	1.60	0.96
August	1.40	1.39	1.62	1.12	1.53	2.01	1.20	1.28	1.60	0.94
September	1.39	1.39	1.60	1.13	1.51	1.99	1.19	1.28	1.59	0.93
October	1.39	1.39	1.62	1.12	1.51	1.99	1.18	1.27	1.58	0.93
November	1.38	1.38	1.60	1.12	1.51	1.98	1.18	1.26	1.56	0.93
December	1.39	1.39	1.62	1.13	1.50	1.99	1.18	1.27	1.58	0.93
1997										
January	1.38	1.37	1.60	1.11	1.49	1.95	1.17	1.27	1.57	0.93
February	1.36	1.37	1.59	1.12	1.48	1.93	1.17	1.24	1.53	0.92
March	1.37	1.38	1.58	1.13	1.47	1.93	1.16	1.26	1.57	0.92
April	1.38	1.37	1.57	1.12	1.50	1.97	1.18	1.26	1.55	0.94
May	1.39	1.39	1.60	1.13	1.52	2.02	1.18	1.27	1.57	0.93
June	1.39	1.37	1.57	1.14	1.50	1.99	1.17	1.29	1.59	0.94
July	1.38	1.36	1.55	1.12	1.49	1.97	1.17	1.29	1.56	0.96
August	1.38	1.38	1.58	1.13	1.48	1.93	1.16	1.29	1.59	0.96
September	1.38	1.36	1.54	1.13	1.49	1.96	1.17	1.29	1.57	0.95
October	1.39	1.37	1.56	1.13	1.49	1.97	1.17	1.30	1.57	0.97
November	1.39	1.38	1.58	1.14	1.49	1.95	1.17	1.31	1.58	0.99
December	1.39	1.36	1.54	1.13	1.49	1.93	1.18	1.32	1.60	0.99
1998										
January	1.39	1.38	1.58	1.14	1.49	1.90	1.19	1.31	1.59	0.98
February	1.39	1.37	1.55	1.15	1.48	1.90	1.18	1.32	1.60	0.99
March	1.39	1.36	1.53	1.15	1.49	1.91	1.19	1.32	1.60	0.99
April	1.39	1.38	1.57	1.15	1.48	1.89	1.19	1.31	1.59	0.98
May	1.40	1.40	1.58	1.16	1.46	1.85	1.18	1.33	1.62	0.99
June	1.39	1.39	1.58	1.15	1.45	1.82	1.19	1.33	1.61	1.00
July	1.39	1.39	1.58	1.16	1.46	1.86	1.18	1.33	1.60	1.00
August	1.40	1.39	1.57	1.16	1.46	1.86	1.18	1.35	1.63	1.02
September	1.40	1.38	1.54	1.16	1.47	1.86	1.18	1.35	1.64	1.01
October	1.39	1.38	1.54	1.18	1.45	1.83	1.17	1.35	1.66	0.99
November	1.39	1.38	1.53	1.18	1.44	1.84	1.16	1.35	1.65	1.00
December	1.38	1.36	1.51	1.15	1.44	1.82	1.16	1.34	1.65	0.99
1999										
January	1.39	1.36	1.51	1.16	1.45	1.86	1.15	1.35	1.65	1.00
February	1.38	1.35	1.51	1.14	1.44	1.85	1.15	1.34	1.61	1.01
March	1.37	1.33	1.48	1.13	1.45	1.88	1.15	1.33	1.61	0.99
April	1.37	1.33	1.48	1.14	1.45	1.89	1.14	1.32	1.60	0.99
May	1.35	1.32	1.47	1.13	1.44	1.86	1.13	1.30	1.59	0.97
June	1.35	1.30	1.45	1.11	1.45	1.88	1.14	1.29	1.58	0.95
July	1.35	1.30	1.44	1.11	1.44	1.85	1.13	1.30	1.58	0.97
August	1.33	1.28	1.42	1.10	1.43	1.84	1.13	1.29	1.58	0.97
September	1.34	1.30	1.45	1.10	1.43	1.86	1.12	1.29	1.58	0.97
October	1.34	1.30	1.45	1.10	1.43	1.85	1.12	1.29	1.57	0.96
November	1.34	1.29	1.44	1.09	1.43	1.84	1.13	1.29	1.58	0.95
December	1.32	1.28	1.43	1.09	1.42	1.85	1.12	1.27	1.55	0.95

Table 5-8. Real Manufacturing and Trade Sales and Inventories

(Billions of chained [1996] dollars, except as noted; seasonally adjusted; annual figures for sales are averages of seasonally adjusted monthly data; annual figures for inventories and inventory-sales ratio are as of end of December.)

Year and month	Sales				Inventories (Book value, end of period)				Inventory-sales ratios (Based on chained [1996] dollars)			
	Total	Manufac-turing	Retail trade	Merchant wholesalers	Total	Manufac-turing	Retail trade	Merchant wholesalers	Total	Manufac-turing	Retail trade	Merchant wholesalers
1970	330.9	167.9	94.1	70.0	458.4	258.3	109.6	83.7	1.37	1.54	1.15	1.17
1971	346.2	172.6	100.5	74.0	476.1	255.2	124.3	90.5	1.33	1.43	1.19	1.17
1972	376.9	188.7	109.1	80.2	498.1	262.2	133.8	96.0	1.24	1.29	1.16	1.12
1973	408.3	203.8	114.8	90.6	531.4	281.6	144.4	98.7	1.28	1.37	1.31	1.00
1974	405.8	199.0	109.4	97.3	561.4	302.8	142.3	108.4	1.47	1.66	1.37	1.15
1975	376.2	179.0	110.1	87.5	540.7	295.2	135.3	102.1	1.41	1.60	1.20	1.17
1976	403.5	195.4	117.4	91.4	572.9	309.3	145.7	109.8	1.36	1.52	1.20	1.15
1977	431.8	211.2	123.2	98.0	601.1	317.9	153.9	121.5	1.35	1.46	1.23	1.18
1978	458.5	221.3	129.1	108.4	639.4	332.5	164.1	135.3	1.35	1.46	1.23	1.22
1979	469.5	224.2	131.3	114.0	660.1	345.3	164.1	142.5	1.42	1.58	1.25	1.23
1980	454.9	211.5	126.5	116.4	662.8	345.7	159.5	149.4	1.42	1.59	1.26	1.22
1981	457.7	213.1	127.0	117.1	679.3	350.3	168.4	153.1	1.55	1.73	1.35	1.36
1982	439.1	202.9	125.8	110.3	657.5	334.6	164.5	151.7	1.52	1.71	1.27	1.41
1983	460.7	212.4	135.1	113.5	670.0	334.2	177.9	152.6	1.37	1.47	1.26	1.27
1984	499.3	229.3	144.8	125.4	736.1	363.2	199.7	168.2	1.45	1.56	1.36	1.32
1985	513.8	233.5	151.2	129.4	751.5	356.9	215.1	176.9	1.45	1.53	1.40	1.35
1986	533.6	237.6	159.6	136.6	759.2	353.1	218.5	185.9	1.38	1.46	1.30	1.33
1987	553.2	248.0	164.2	141.3	796.5	361.6	239.7	194.5	1.42	1.43	1.43	1.36
1988	579.1	259.4	171.3	148.6	830.0	378.5	247.4	203.1	1.39	1.41	1.41	1.33
1989	590.5	261.9	175.6	153.1	862.4	392.7	261.9	207.0	1.45	1.51	1.48	1.32
1990	593.9	261.4	177.3	155.3	878.2	401.6	260.2	215.2	1.52	1.60	1.50	1.41
1991	586.4	257.1	174.0	155.3	876.7	394.9	260.8	220.4	1.50	1.55	1.50	1.40
1992	607.7	266.4	179.9	161.5	885.4	390.1	265.4	229.5	1.42	1.41	1.44	1.39
1993	632.7	274.5	188.7	169.4	911.1	393.7	280.8	236.3	1.41	1.40	1.44	1.40
1994	670.3	290.1	201.0	179.2	958.8	405.8	301.4	251.5	1.38	1.34	1.47	1.35
1995	699.5	301.1	208.2	190.2	996.4	419.9	313.6	262.9	1.40	1.38	1.47	1.34
1996	726.0	309.5	218.5	198.0	1 016.4	430.0	321.0	265.4	1.38	1.37	1.44	1.31
1997	767.9	329.3	227.5	211.0	1 066.1	445.2	332.3	288.7	1.35	1.31	1.43	1.35
1998	811.8	346.5	242.0	223.3	1 126.4	470.8	347.1	308.7	1.34	1.32	1.38	1.34
1999	866.2	363.9	262.8	239.4	1 163.9	470.9	368.0	324.8	1.30	1.26	1.34	1.31
1996												
January	706.9	300.7	212.4	193.8	1 000.9	423.3	313.4	264.2	1.42	1.41	1.48	1.36
February	713.2	303.9	215.4	193.9	1 000.6	423.3	313.7	263.5	1.40	1.39	1.46	1.36
March	713.6	302.1	216.3	195.2	997.1	424.2	309.9	263.0	1.40	1.40	1.43	1.35
April	720.0	308.1	217.1	194.8	1 002.4	424.5	311.3	266.6	1.39	1.38	1.43	1.37
May	725.5	311.6	218.6	195.3	1 002.2	423.2	313.0	266.0	1.38	1.36	1.43	1.36
June	722.0	307.9	218.0	196.1	1 001.7	423.3	313.8	264.5	1.39	1.38	1.44	1.35
July	727.7	310.8	218.5	198.5	1 006.0	424.6	316.6	264.8	1.38	1.37	1.45	1.33
August	730.2	311.9	219.0	199.3	1 008.0	425.4	318.5	264.1	1.38	1.36	1.45	1.33
September	732.5	312.3	220.7	199.5	1 009.4	426.8	319.6	262.9	1.38	1.37	1.45	1.32
October	738.2	313.1	222.2	203.0	1 013.9	428.9	320.8	264.2	1.37	1.37	1.44	1.30
November	743.7	317.5	221.6	204.5	1 016.5	430.7	320.7	265.1	1.37	1.36	1.45	1.30
December	738.3	313.7	222.2	202.4	1 016.4	430.0	321.0	265.4	1.38	1.37	1.44	1.31
1997												
January	747.8	319.2	223.3	205.3	1 020.9	431.6	320.7	268.6	1.37	1.35	1.44	1.31
February	756.9	321.9	224.5	210.5	1 025.7	433.7	322.8	269.1	1.36	1.35	1.44	1.28
March	755.1	321.6	224.8	208.7	1 025.4	434.4	320.1	271.0	1.36	1.35	1.42	1.30
April	760.3	326.8	224.5	208.9	1 033.0	437.3	324.0	271.7	1.36	1.34	1.44	1.30
May	755.7	323.6	222.0	210.1	1 038.4	439.3	325.4	273.7	1.37	1.36	1.47	1.30
June	766.3	328.1	226.3	211.9	1 043.5	440.2	324.4	279.0	1.36	1.34	1.43	1.32
July	775.9	334.2	229.2	212.6	1 047.3	441.7	327.1	278.6	1.35	1.32	1.43	1.31
August	772.1	330.4	230.5	211.1	1 047.5	442.6	324.9	280.1	1.36	1.34	1.41	1.33
September	780.0	335.5	230.6	213.9	1 052.7	442.5	327.6	282.8	1.35	1.32	1.42	1.32
October	778.2	335.2	230.3	212.7	1 058.7	445.2	330.0	283.6	1.36	1.33	1.43	1.33
November	778.8	334.6	231.7	212.4	1 062.9	446.2	330.9	285.9	1.37	1.33	1.43	1.35
December	787.7	340.7	232.8	214.1	1 066.1	445.2	332.3	288.7	1.35	1.31	1.43	1.35
1998												
January	789.6	338.2	233.5	217.9	1 071.6	448.4	334.0	289.3	1.36	1.33	1.43	1.33
February	796.4	343.3	234.5	218.6	1 081.2	452.7	335.5	293.2	1.36	1.32	1.43	1.34
March	805.1	347.2	236.7	221.2	1 088.4	454.7	338.6	295.2	1.35	1.31	1.43	1.34
April	804.4	343.4	239.0	222.1	1 094.5	457.9	341.8	294.9	1.36	1.33	1.43	1.33
May	803.9	341.1	240.8	222.1	1 097.8	459.8	340.3	297.8	1.37	1.35	1.41	1.34
June	809.5	343.3	243.5	222.7	1 098.9	462.0	338.9	298.2	1.36	1.35	1.39	1.34
July	809.2	343.9	241.4	223.9	1 104.6	465.8	340.1	299.0	1.37	1.35	1.41	1.34
August	811.2	346.2	241.3	223.8	1 109.1	467.2	339.7	302.5	1.37	1.35	1.41	1.35
September	820.5	350.6	244.5	225.3	1 114.8	468.0	342.1	305.0	1.36	1.34	1.40	1.35
October	823.9	351.0	247.6	225.1	1 120.5	471.9	343.4	305.7	1.36	1.34	1.39	1.36
November	829.3	353.1	249.4	226.7	1 126.5	473.5	346.0	307.3	1.36	1.34	1.39	1.36
December	838.8	357.1	251.5	230.2	1 126.4	470.8	347.1	308.7	1.34	1.32	1.38	1.34
1999												
January	836.6	354.5	253.5	228.4	1 130.1	470.0	351.3	308.8	1.35	1.33	1.39	1.35
February	847.7	357.7	256.8	233.2	1 131.6	470.0	350.8	310.9	1.34	1.31	1.37	1.33
March	855.3	362.4	257.7	235.1	1 134.8	470.5	352.6	311.8	1.33	1.30	1.37	1.33
April	850.7	358.6	257.7	234.4	1 131.8	469.4	350.7	311.8	1.33	1.31	1.36	1.33
May	859.5	360.6	260.7	238.1	1 134.7	469.9	351.7	313.2	1.32	1.30	1.35	1.32
June	867.1	364.6	261.1	241.4	1 136.2	468.2	353.6	314.5	1.31	1.28	1.35	1.30
July	870.6	366.2	263.1	241.2	1 141.7	470.1	354.4	317.3	1.31	1.28	1.35	1.32
August	876.7	369.4	266.0	241.2	1 143.1	468.9	355.8	318.4	1.30	1.27	1.34	1.32
September	871.0	364.3	265.8	240.8	1 146.2	469.0	357.5	319.6	1.32	1.29	1.35	1.33
October	876.1	365.5	267.1	243.5	1 151.4	469.7	360.3	321.3	1.31	1.29	1.35	1.32
November	887.2	370.5	270.0	246.6	1 157.6	471.1	362.2	324.2	1.31	1.27	1.34	1.32
December	895.5	372.9	273.9	248.6	1 163.9	470.9	368.0	324.8	1.30	1.26	1.34	1.31

Table 5-9. Capital Expenditures, 1996–1998

(Millions of dollars.)

Capital expenditures	All companies			Companies with employees			Companies without employees		
	1996	1997	1998	1996	1997	1998	1996	1997	1998
TOTAL	807 070	871 765	973 587	707 110	772 343	879 041	99 960	99 422	94 546
Structures	243 427	273 298	328 146	204 345	236 166	290 353	39 082	37 132	37 793
New	223 588	254 451	283 526	191 867	225 107	250 814	31 721	29 344	32 712
Used	19 839	18 849	44 620	12 478	11 060	39 539	7 361	7 789	5 081
Equipment	563 641	598 466	645 441	502 762	536 177	588 687	60 878	62 289	56 753
New	526 016	562 019	609 864	481 785	515 965	564 769	44 231	46 054	45 095
Used	37 625	36 447	35 576	20 977	20 212	23 919	16 648	16 235	11 658
Not distributed as structures or equipment	2	...	...	2	...	...	...	...	...
CAPITAL LEASE AND CAPITALIZED INTEREST EXPENSES [1]									
Capital leases	15 675	16 066	16 533	13 023	14 549	15 323	2 652	1 517	1 210
Capitalized interest	...	...	...	6 827	7 273	8 965	...	...	...

1. Included in data shown above.

Table 5-10. Capital Expenditures for Companies with Employees, Selected Industries, 1996–1998

(Millions of current dollars.)

SIC code	Industry	1996			1997			1998		
		Total	New	Used	Total	New	Used	Total	New	Used
- - -	**TOTAL EXPENDITURES**	707 110	673 655	33 455	772 343	741 072	31 272	879 041	815 583	63 458
10-14	**Mining**	30 155	28 066	2 089	38 957	36 867	2 091	40 346	37 269	3 077
15-17	**Construction**	13 806	10 992	2 814	15 531	12 903	2 628	18 292	14 717	3 575
20-39	**Manufacturing**	191 762	183 580	8 182	192 345	186 932	5 413	207 304	200 178	7 125
24, 25, 32-39	Durable goods industries [1]	109 898	105 457	4 441	108 405	105 104	3 300	118 991	115 118	3 873
24	Wood and lumber products	5 294	4 806	488	4 138	3 708	430	3 609	3 241	368
25	Furniture and fixtures	1 719	1 607	111	1 618	1 593	26	2 082	1 987	95
32	Stone, clay, glass, and concrete products	5 079	4 909	170	6 816	6 520	296	6 884	6 623	262
331	Steel works, blast furnaces, and rolling mills	4 256	4 109	148	4 354	4 274	80	5 838	5 599	239
333-335	Nonferrous metal products	2 149	2 086	63	2 586	2 491	94	2 268	2 201	66
332,336,339	Miscellaneous primary metal products	2 225	2 161	65	1 599	1 536	64	1 963	1 893	69
34	Fabricated metal products	8 995	8 160	835	8 586	8 138	448	9 278	8 953	326
357	Computer and office equipment	6 099	5 291	(2)	5 995	5 540	(2)	7 552	7 205	346
351-356, 358, 359	Industrial and commercial machinery	11 309	10 798	511	13 403	12 913	490	11 929	11 151	779
36	Communications equipment and electronic components	31 949	31 408	541	27 683	27 217	466	27 972	27 488	484
371	Motor vehicles and equipment	17 897	17 762	135	18 317	18 242	75	24 401	24 114	287
372	Aircraft and parts	2 713	(2)	65	3 472	3 358	113	3 924	3 755	169
376	Missiles and space vehicles	515	(2)	(2)	745	741	4	876	873	2
373-375, 379	Miscellaneous transportation equipment	1 224	1 193	31	1 371	1 330	40	1 721	1 663	58
38	Instruments and related products	5 930	5 841	89	6 036	5 902	134	6 688	6 411	277
39	Miscellaneous manufactured products	2 546	2 187	359	1 686	1 600	(2)	2 004	1 960	44
20-23, 26-31	Nondurable goods industries [1]	81 864	78 123	3 742	83 940	81 827	2 112	88 312	85 060	3 252
208	Beverages	4 169	4 146	24	4 923	4 865	57	5 407	5 171	236
201-207, 209	Food products (excluding beverages)	14 088	13 118	971	14 259	13 685	574	13 419	12 767	653
21	Tobacco products	816	815	(2)	805	802	2	468	450	18
22	Textile mill products	3 658	3 386	273	3 921	3 819	101	3 981	3 828	153
23	Apparel and finished textile products	1 558	1 482	76	1 497	1 449	48	1 525	1 462	62
26	Paper and allied products	10 071	9 353	718	10 153	9 839	314	9 623	9 046	577
27	Printing and publishing (including commercial)	7 799	7 328	470	8 811	8 264	546	9 690	9 099	591
283	Drugs	5 797	5 769	28	6 262	6 231	31	7 243	7 165	78
281, 282, 284-287, 289	Chemical products	20 462	19 573	(2)	19 860	19 650	210	21 563	21 094	469
29	Petroleum refining and related products	5 513	5 436	77	4 635	4 573	62	5 077	4 842	235
30	Rubber and miscellaneous plastics products	7 753	7 541	212	8 552	8 393	160	10 102	9 928	174
31	Leather and leather products	181	178	3	264	256	7	215	210	6
40-42, 44-49	**Transportation** [1]	36 698	32 082	4 616	45 045	41 165	3 880	51 843	46 450	5 393
40	Railroad transportation	7 416	6 462	954	8 092	7 834	258	9 608	9 311	297
42	Motor freight transportation; warehousing	11 383	10 350	1 034	14 835	14 204	632	13 876	12 393	1 483
45	Air transportation	10 754	8 646	(2)	13 612	11 359	(2)	18 000	15 199	2 801
48	**Communications**	57 133	56 484	649	68 467	67 412	1 054	78 491	77 451	1 040
49	**Utilities**	36 744	35 588	1 156	38 719	37 380	1 339	42 319	41 014	1 306
50-59	**Wholesale and retail trade**	81 857	77 835	4 022	84 715	80 649	4 066	94 227	87 272	6 956
60-62, 67	**Finance**	87 144	85 620	1 524	91 328	89 374	1 955	110 064	99 686	10 378
63-35	**Insurance and real estate**	23 410	21 662	1 747	29 270	27 637	1 633	50 325	34 935	15 391
07-09, 70, 72, 73, 75, 76, 78, 79	**Rental and business services**	78 064	74 678	3 386	86 789	83 757	3 033	93 308	88 951	4 357
80	**Health services**	34 176	32 748	1 428	36 974	34 712	2 262	41 616	38 968	2 648
81-84, 86, 87, 89	**Membership organizations, educational and miscellaneous services**	33 657	31 878	1 778	41 211	39 366	1 845	47 514	45 384	2 130
- - -	**Structures and equipment expenditures serving multiple industries**	2 503	2 442	61	2 992	2 919	74	3 392	3 308	85

1. Includes industries not shown separately.
2. Not published.

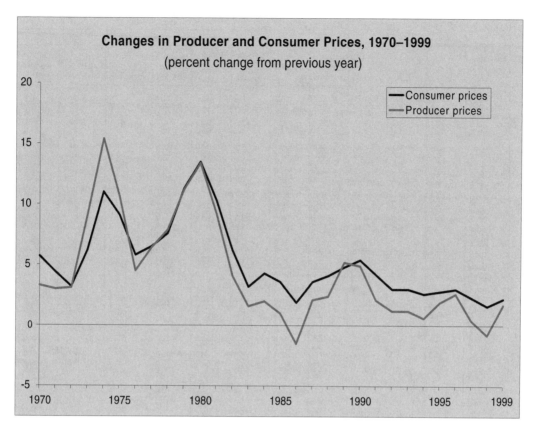

Changes in Producer and Consumer Prices, 1970–1999
(percent change from previous year)

- The recent U.S. record of essential price stability was extended in 1999, when consumer prices rose only 2.2 percent, marking the eighth consecutive year in which consumer prices rose 3 percent or less.

- Producer prices for finished goods increased 1.7 percent in 1999, the result of a 4.9 percent increase in energy prices coupled with a 1.3 percent rise in prices of finished goods other than energy.

- Prices received by farmers fell for the third consecutive year in 1999, bringing the prices received index 14.3 percent below its 1996 peak. Thus, even though prices paid by farmers changed little over the three years, the ratio of prices received to prices paid fell to 83 percent of its 1990–1992 base.

Table 6-1. Consumer Price Indexes

(All urban consumers, 1982–1984=100, seasonally adjusted, except as noted.)

Year and month	All items Not seasonally adjusted	Seasonally adjusted Index	Percent change	Total	Total food	Food at home Total	Cereals and bakery products	Meats, poultry, fish, and eggs	Dairy and related products	Fruits and vegetables	Non-alcoholic beverages	Other food at home	Food away from home	Alcoholic beverages
1970	38.8	38.8	5.7	40.1	39.2	39.9	37.1	44.6	44.7	37.8	27.1	32.9	37.5	52.1
1971	40.5	40.5	4.4	41.4	40.4	40.9	38.8	44.1	46.1	39.7	28.1	34.3	39.4	54.2
1972	41.8	41.8	3.2	43.1	42.1	42.7	39.0	48.0	46.8	41.6	28.0	34.6	41.0	55.4
1973	44.4	44.4	6.2	48.8	48.2	49.7	43.5	60.9	51.2	47.4	30.1	36.7	44.2	56.8
1974	49.3	49.3	11.0	55.5	55.1	57.1	56.5	62.2	60.7	55.2	35.9	47.8	49.8	61.1
1975	53.8	53.8	9.1	60.2	59.8	61.8	62.9	67.0	62.6	56.9	41.3	55.4	54.5	65.9
1976	56.9	56.9	5.8	62.1	61.6	63.1	61.5	68.0	67.7	58.4	49.4	56.4	58.2	68.1
1977	60.6	60.6	6.5	65.8	65.5	66.8	62.5	67.4	69.5	63.8	74.4	68.4	62.6	70.0
1978	65.2	65.2	7.6	72.2	72.0	73.8	68.1	77.6	74.2	70.9	78.7	73.6	68.3	74.1
1979	72.6	72.6	11.3	79.9	79.9	81.8	74.9	89.0	82.8	76.6	82.6	79.0	75.9	79.9
1980	82.4	82.4	13.5	86.7	86.8	88.4	83.9	92.0	90.9	82.1	91.4	88.4	83.4	86.4
1981	90.9	90.9	10.3	93.5	93.6	94.8	92.3	96.0	97.4	92.0	95.3	94.9	90.9	92.5
1982	96.5	96.5	6.2	97.3	97.4	98.1	96.5	99.6	98.8	97.0	97.9	97.3	95.8	96.7
1983	99.6	99.6	3.2	99.5	99.4	99.1	99.6	99.2	100.0	97.3	99.8	99.5	100.0	100.4
1984	103.9	103.9	4.3	103.2	103.2	102.8	103.9	101.3	101.3	105.7	102.3	103.1	104.2	103.0
1985	107.6	107.6	3.6	105.6	105.6	104.3	107.9	100.1	103.2	108.4	104.3	105.7	108.3	106.4
1986	109.6	109.6	1.9	109.1	109.0	107.3	110.9	104.5	103.3	109.4	110.4	109.4	112.5	111.1
1987	113.6	113.6	3.6	113.5	113.5	111.9	114.8	110.5	105.9	119.1	107.5	110.5	117.0	114.1
1988	118.3	118.3	4.1	118.2	118.2	116.6	122.1	114.3	108.4	128.1	107.5	113.1	121.8	118.6
1989	124.0	124.0	4.8	124.9	125.1	124.2	132.4	121.3	115.6	138.0	111.3	119.1	127.4	123.5
1990	130.7	130.7	5.4	132.1	132.4	132.3	140.0	130.0	126.5	149.0	113.5	123.4	133.4	129.3
1991	136.2	136.2	4.2	136.8	136.3	135.8	145.8	132.6	125.1	155.8	114.1	127.3	137.9	142.8
1992	140.3	140.3	3.0	138.7	137.9	136.8	151.5	130.9	128.5	155.4	114.3	128.8	140.7	147.3
1993	144.5	144.5	3.0	141.6	140.9	140.1	156.6	135.5	129.4	159.0	114.6	130.5	143.2	149.6
1994	148.2	148.2	2.6	144.9	144.3	144.1	163.0	137.2	131.7	165.0	123.2	135.6	145.7	151.5
1995	152.4	152.4	2.8	148.9	148.4	148.8	167.5	138.8	132.8	177.7	131.7	140.8	149.0	153.9
1996	156.9	156.9	3.0	153.7	153.3	154.3	174.0	144.8	142.1	183.9	128.6	142.9	152.7	158.5
1997	160.5	160.5	2.3	157.7	157.3	158.1	177.6	148.5	145.5	187.5	133.4	147.3	157.0	162.8
1998	163.0	163.0	1.6	161.1	160.7	161.1	181.1	147.3	150.8	198.2	133.0	150.8	161.1	165.7
1999	166.6	166.6	2.2	164.6	164.1	164.2	185.0	147.9	159.6	203.1	134.3	153.5	165.1	169.7
1996														
January	154.4	154.7	-0.5	150.7	150.5	150.7	171.7	142.0	136.3	175.7	129.8	141.5	150.6	155.7
February	154.9	155.1	0.3	151.2	150.9	151.2	171.8	142.1	137.2	177.9	129.2	141.4	150.9	156.5
March	155.7	155.7	0.4	151.9	151.5	152.1	172.4	142.2	136.7	182.2	129.1	142.0	151.2	157.1
April	156.3	156.2	0.3	152.5	152.2	152.9	173.0	142.0	137.0	186.6	129.3	142.3	151.6	157.6
May	156.6	156.6	0.3	152.5	152.2	152.6	173.6	142.0	137.6	183.2	129.1	142.6	152.0	158.0
June	156.7	156.8	0.1	153.5	153.2	154.1	173.7	144.0	139.8	186.1	128.5	142.8	152.3	158.4
July	157.0	157.2	0.3	154.0	153.7	154.7	174.2	144.7	142.0	186.0	128.1	143.0	152.8	158.7
August	157.3	157.3	0.1	154.4	154.1	155.1	174.4	145.6	144.6	184.3	128.8	143.1	153.1	159.2
September	157.8	157.8	0.3	155.1	154.8	156.0	174.8	147.0	146.7	184.4	127.8	143.5	153.5	159.6
October	158.3	158.3	0.3	155.9	155.7	157.0	175.3	147.6	149.3	186.4	127.6	143.8	154.2	160.2
November	158.6	158.7	0.3	156.4	156.3	157.6	176.2	148.1	149.3	187.9	127.6	144.1	154.7	160.4
December	158.6	159.1	0.3	156.6	156.4	157.6	176.4	149.2	148.6	186.0	128.0	144.4	155.0	160.8
1997														
January	159.1	159.4	0.2	156.2	155.9	156.7	176.6	148.8	147.8	181.3	128.2	144.5	155.3	161.2
February	159.6	159.8	0.3	156.9	156.6	157.5	176.5	148.6	146.2	187.8	127.7	144.8	155.6	161.6
March	160.0	160.0	0.1	156.9	156.7	157.4	177.1	147.6	146.1	188.2	128.9	145.0	156.0	161.8
April	160.2	160.1	0.1	156.9	156.7	157.3	176.6	148.2	145.7	185.1	131.2	146.3	156.2	162.0
May	160.1	160.1	0.0	157.2	156.9	157.6	176.9	148.6	145.4	185.3	133.2	146.9	156.3	162.5
June	160.3	160.4	0.2	157.5	157.2	157.9	177.6	148.8	144.1	186.0	134.8	147.7	156.6	162.6
July	160.5	160.6	0.1	157.8	157.5	158.1	177.7	149.0	143.3	186.2	136.8	148.6	157.1	163.1
August	160.8	160.8	0.1	158.3	158.0	158.7	178.0	148.9	143.4	189.7	137.0	148.6	157.4	163.5
September	161.2	161.3	0.3	158.5	158.2	158.8	178.3	148.8	143.5	189.4	136.7	148.9	157.8	163.6
October	161.6	161.6	0.2	158.8	158.6	159.1	178.6	148.5	145.7	190.0	136.7	149.0	158.2	163.8
November	161.5	161.7	0.1	159.1	158.9	159.4	178.8	148.5	147.0	191.1	135.2	148.5	158.6	163.9
December	161.3	161.8	0.1	159.2	158.9	159.2	179.1	147.6	147.8	190.7	134.3	148.5	159.0	164.3
1998														
January	161.6	162.0	0.1	159.7	159.4	159.9	179.1	147.6	148.3	196.3	134.0	148.6	159.2	164.7
February	161.9	162.1	0.1	159.7	159.4	159.7	179.5	147.3	147.7	195.0	133.9	148.9	159.6	164.8
March	162.2	162.2	0.1	159.9	159.7	159.9	180.0	147.1	148.4	195.2	133.5	149.5	159.9	164.8
April	162.5	162.5	0.2	160.0	159.7	159.8	180.0	146.7	148.5	195.8	133.1	149.3	160.2	165.0
May	162.8	162.8	0.2	160.7	160.4	160.7	180.4	146.8	148.1	202.9	132.7	149.5	160.6	164.9
June	163.0	163.0	0.1	160.7	160.4	160.6	180.9	146.8	148.1	199.9	132.8	150.4	160.7	165.4
July	163.2	163.3	0.2	161.1	160.8	161.1	181.2	147.2	148.2	201.1	132.7	151.2	161.1	165.8
August	163.4	163.5	0.1	161.5	161.3	161.5	182.1	147.7	150.5	199.8	132.2	151.9	161.5	165.9
September	163.6	163.6	0.1	161.6	161.3	161.3	182.1	146.9	152.9	196.4	132.3	152.5	162.1	166.4
October	164.0	163.9	0.2	162.5	162.2	162.6	182.5	147.4	155.0	202.2	132.8	152.8	162.3	166.7
November	164.0	164.2	0.2	162.8	162.5	162.9	182.9	147.0	155.9	201.7	133.3	153.8	162.6	167.1
December	163.9	164.4	0.1	162.8	162.6	162.7	183.0	146.6	157.6	201.0	132.9	153.2	163.0	167.4
1999														
January	164.3	164.7	0.2	163.4	163.1	163.2	184.2	145.7	161.2	203.0	133.4	152.9	163.5	167.6
February	164.5	164.8	0.1	163.7	163.4	163.5	183.7	146.8	162.3	201.6	133.6	153.1	163.8	168.4
March	165.0	165.1	0.2	163.5	163.3	163.1	183.9	146.7	161.5	199.2	133.7	152.9	164.2	168.2
April	166.2	166.2	0.7	163.7	163.4	163.1	184.6	147.1	156.1	201.8	133.6	153.4	164.5	168.6
May	166.2	166.2	0.0	164.1	163.9	163.8	185.0	147.3	156.2	205.8	134.0	153.5	164.6	169.0
June	166.2	166.2	0.0	164.2	163.9	163.8	185.0	147.6	156.1	205.0	134.3	153.6	164.6	169.5
July	166.7	166.7	0.3	164.4	164.1	163.9	185.6	147.5	155.7	204.9	134.7	153.8	165.1	170.0
August	167.1	167.2	0.3	164.8	164.4	164.2	184.3	148.0	156.5	205.7	134.8	154.1	165.6	170.4
September	167.9	167.8	0.4	165.2	164.9	164.7	185.4	148.6	158.7	205.7	134.4	154.1	165.8	170.8
October	168.2	168.1	0.2	165.6	165.3	165.2	185.5	148.6	164.1	204.9	134.8	153.8	166.2	170.6
November	168.3	168.4	0.2	166.0	165.6	165.5	185.7	149.5	164.6	204.2	134.5	154.1	166.5	171.5
December	168.3	168.8	0.2	166.1	165.8	165.6	186.6	149.1	162.1	205.1	136.0	154.2	166.8	172.0

Table 6-1. Consumer Price Indexes—*Continued*

(All urban consumers; 1982–1984=100, except as noted; seasonally adjusted.)

Year and month	Total	Housing												
		Shelter						Fuels and utilities				Household furnishings and operations	
		Total	Rent of shelter[1]	Rent of primary residence	Lodging away from home[2]	Owners' equivalent rent of primary residence[1]	Tenants' and household insurance[2]	Total	Fuels		Water and sewer and trash collection services[2]	Total	Household operations[2]
									Fuel oil and other fuels	Gas (piped) and electricity			
1970	36.4	35.5	...	46.5	...	...	...	29.1	17.0	25.4	...	46.8	...
1971	38.0	37.0	...	48.7	...	...	...	31.1	18.2	27.1	...	48.6	...
1972	39.4	38.7	...	50.4	...	...	...	32.5	18.3	28.5	...	49.7	...
1973	41.2	40.5	...	52.5	...	...	...	34.3	21.1	29.9	...	51.1	...
1974	45.8	44.4	...	55.2	...	...	...	40.7	33.2	34.5	...	56.8	...
1975	50.7	48.8	...	58.0	...	...	...	45.4	36.4	40.1	...	63.4	...
1976	53.8	51.5	...	61.1	...	...	...	49.4	38.8	44.7	...	67.3	...
1977	57.4	54.9	...	64.8	...	...	...	54.7	43.9	50.5	...	70.4	...
1978	62.4	60.5	...	69.3	...	...	...	58.5	46.2	55.0	...	74.7	...
1979	70.1	68.9	...	74.3	...	...	...	64.8	62.4	61.0	...	79.9	...
1980	81.1	81.0	...	80.9	...	...	...	75.4	86.1	71.4	...	86.3	...
1981	90.4	90.5	...	87.9	...	...	...	86.4	104.6	81.9	...	93.0	...
1982	96.9	96.9	...	94.6	...	...	...	94.9	103.4	93.2	...	98.0	...
1983	99.5	99.1	102.7	100.1	...	102.5	...	100.2	97.2	101.5	...	100.2	...
1984	103.6	104.0	107.7	105.3	...	107.3	...	104.8	99.4	105.4	...	101.9	...
1985	107.7	109.8	113.9	111.8	...	113.2	...	106.5	95.9	107.1	...	103.8	...
1986	110.9	115.8	120.2	118.3	...	119.4	...	104.1	77.6	105.7	...	105.2	...
1987	114.2	121.3	125.9	123.1	...	124.8	...	103.0	77.9	103.8	...	107.1	...
1988	118.5	127.1	132.0	127.8	...	131.1	...	104.4	78.1	104.6	...	109.4	...
1989	123.0	132.8	138.0	132.8	...	137.4	...	107.8	81.7	107.5	...	111.2	...
1990	128.5	140.0	145.5	138.4	...	144.8	...	111.6	99.3	109.3	...	113.3	...
1991	133.6	146.3	152.1	143.3	...	150.4	...	115.3	94.6	112.6	...	116.0	...
1992	137.5	151.2	157.3	146.9	...	155.5	...	117.8	90.7	114.8	...	118.0	...
1993	141.2	155.7	162.0	150.3	...	160.5	...	121.3	90.3	118.5	...	119.3	...
1994	144.8	160.5	167.0	154.0	...	165.8	...	122.8	88.8	119.2	...	121.0	...
1995	148.5	165.7	172.4	157.8	...	171.3	...	123.7	88.1	119.2	...	123.0	...
1996	152.8	171.0	178.0	162.0	...	176.8	...	127.5	99.2	122.1	...	124.7	...
1997	156.8	176.3	183.4	166.7	...	181.9	...	130.8	99.8	125.1	...	125.4	...
1998	160.4	182.1	189.6	172.1	109.0	187.8	99.8	128.5	90.0	121.2	101.6	126.6	101.5
1999	163.9	187.3	195.0	177.5	112.3	192.9	101.3	128.8	91.4	120.9	104.0	126.7	104.5
1996													
January	150.8	168.5	175.7	159.9	...	174.6	...	125.3	95.2	119.3	...	124.3	...
February	151.1	168.8	176.0	160.3	...	174.9	...	125.7	94.8	120.2	...	124.1	...
March	151.5	169.3	176.5	160.6	...	175.4	...	126.2	97.2	119.8	...	124.4	...
April	151.8	169.6	176.9	160.9	...	175.7	...	126.7	100.9	120.9	...	124.5	...
May	152.2	170.1	177.3	161.3	...	176.2	...	127.4	99.5	121.4	...	124.2	...
June	152.3	170.4	177.6	161.8	...	176.5	...	126.9	95.7	120.4	...	124.4	...
July	152.9	171.2	178.5	162.3	...	177.0	...	127.4	94.8	121.7	...	124.6	...
August	153.3	171.5	178.8	162.5	...	177.4	...	128.0	95.1	122.3	...	124.7	...
September	153.6	171.9	179.0	162.9	...	177.8	...	128.3	98.2	122.2	...	124.9	...
October	153.9	172.2	179.4	163.2	...	178.2	...	128.8	104.1	122.0	...	124.9	...
November	154.3	172.7	179.9	163.6	...	178.6	...	129.2	105.6	122.3	...	124.9	...
December	154.6	172.9	180.2	163.9	...	179.0	...	130.0	108.9	123.2	...	125.2	...
1997													
January	155.2	173.5	180.8	164.3	...	179.4	...	131.3	108.8	125.5	...	125.0	...
February	155.6	174.0	181.3	164.7	...	179.9	...	131.7	106.4	126.4	...	125.1	...
March	155.7	174.3	181.8	165.1	...	180.2	...	130.9	103.3	125.2	...	125.1	...
April	155.9	174.8	182.2	165.6	...	180.7	...	130.2	100.9	123.8	...	125.3	...
May	156.1	175.3	182.6	166.1	...	181.2	...	129.7	100.3	122.7	...	125.6	...
June	156.5	175.7	183.1	166.5	...	181.6	...	130.4	99.2	123.8	...	125.6	...
July	156.8	176.2	183.7	166.9	...	182.2	...	130.5	97.3	123.9	...	125.5	...
August	156.9	176.7	184.2	167.3	...	182.7	...	129.9	96.4	122.9	...	125.1	...
September	157.3	177.1	184.4	167.8	...	183.1	...	130.7	96.2	124.2	...	125.2	...
October	157.7	177.6	185.0	168.2	...	183.4	...	130.9	96.4	124.4	...	125.3	...
November	158.2	178.0	185.5	168.6	...	183.9	...	131.7	96.2	125.7	...	125.4	...
December	158.3	178.7	186.2	169.0	100.0	184.5	100.0	130.4	95.8	123.1	100.0	125.3	100.0
1998													
January	158.5	179.2	186.7	169.4	100.5	185.0	100.3	129.5	94.0	122.1	100.1	125.8	100.1
February	158.7	179.6	187.2	169.8	100.9	185.5	100.2	128.4	92.4	120.8	100.5	126.1	100.3
March	159.1	180.1	187.6	170.3	100.7	186.0	100.3	128.6	92.5	120.9	100.8	126.2	100.3
April	159.6	180.6	188.2	170.8	101.1	186.6	100.4	128.9	91.7	121.2	101.1	126.6	100.7
May	159.9	181.2	188.8	171.3	102.1	187.1	99.6	128.9	91.6	121.1	101.3	126.5	101.0
June	160.1	181.6	189.3	171.8	101.8	187.6	99.1	128.5	90.7	120.7	101.4	126.5	101.7
July	160.4	181.9	189.7	172.3	101.1	188.1	99.3	128.4	90.3	120.5	101.7	127.1	101.9
August	160.7	182.6	190.3	172.9	102.0	188.6	99.2	127.8	89.4	119.9	101.8	126.8	102.0
September	161.0	183.2	191.0	173.4	103.3	189.1	99.2	127.2	88.2	119.1	102.1	126.4	102.2
October	161.3	183.7	191.5	173.9	103.4	189.6	99.7	126.8	87.4	118.7	102.2	126.7	102.4
November	161.7	184.2	192.0	174.3	104.7	190.0	99.9	127.1	86.4	119.1	102.4	126.9	102.8
December	161.9	184.5	192.4	174.8	103.8	190.5	99.9	127.0	84.8	119.0	102.7	127.0	103.0
1999													
January	162.0	184.7	192.5	175.2	102.4	190.9	99.7	126.9	84.4	118.8	102.9	127.0	103.1
February	162.2	185.0	192.8	175.5	102.0	191.3	100.1	127.1	83.7	119.2	103.0	126.7	103.3
March	162.6	185.6	193.4	176.0	103.8	191.6	100.2	127.4	84.5	119.3	103.3	126.6	103.7
April	163.1	186.2	194.1	176.5	105.1	192.1	100.3	127.6	86.7	119.3	103.6	126.8	104.0
May	163.3	186.5	194.4	176.9	104.9	192.5	100.5	127.4	87.5	119.0	103.6	126.6	104.1
June	163.6	186.9	194.9	177.2	105.6	192.8	102.2	127.6	88.5	119.1	103.8	126.6	104.3
July	163.9	187.3	195.3	177.6	105.9	193.1	102.1	128.2	90.1	119.7	103.8	126.6	104.3
August	164.2	187.6	195.6	178.0	105.9	193.5	102.2	128.7	92.0	120.0	104.0	126.8	105.0
September	164.7	188.1	196.1	178.4	107.0	193.8	102.3	129.9	96.5	121.1	104.2	126.9	105.2
October	164.8	188.3	196.3	178.8	106.6	194.0	102.2	130.1	98.7	121.0	104.5	126.7	105.2
November	165.3	188.9	196.8	179.6	106.7	194.6	102.1	130.5	100.1	121.4	104.6	126.7	105.8
December	165.4	189.1	197.2	180.1	105.9	195.0	102.2	129.8	104.6	120.2	104.7	126.8	106.0

1. December 1982=100.
2. December 1997=100.

Table 6-1. Consumer Price Indexes—*Continued*

(All urban consumers; 1982–1984=100, except as noted; seasonally adjusted.)

Year and month	Apparel					Transportation								
							Private transportation							
								New and used motor vehicles			Motor fuel			
	Total	Men's and boys' apparel	Women's and girls' apparel	Infants' and toddlers' apparel	Footwear	Total	Total	Total [1]	New vehicles	Used cars and trucks	Total	Gasoline (all types)	Motor vehicle parts and equipment	Motor vehicle maintenance and repair
1970	59.2	62.2	71.8	39.2	56.8	37.5	37.5	...	53.1	31.2	27.9	27.9	...	36.6
1971	61.1	63.9	74.4	40.0	58.6	39.5	39.4	...	55.3	33.0	28.1	28.1	...	39.3
1972	62.3	64.7	76.2	41.1	60.3	39.9	39.7	...	54.8	33.1	28.4	28.4	...	41.1
1973	64.6	67.1	78.8	42.5	62.8	41.2	41.0	...	54.8	35.2	31.2	31.2	...	43.2
1974	69.4	72.4	83.5	54.2	66.6	45.8	46.2	...	58.0	36.7	42.2	42.2	...	47.6
1975	72.5	75.5	85.5	64.5	69.6	50.1	50.6	...	63.0	43.8	45.1	45.1	...	53.7
1976	75.2	78.1	87.9	68.0	72.3	55.1	55.6	...	67.0	50.3	47.0	47.0	...	57.6
1977	78.6	81.7	90.6	74.6	75.7	59.0	59.7	...	70.5	54.7	49.7	49.7	...	61.9
1978	81.4	83.5	92.4	77.4	79.0	61.7	62.5	...	75.9	55.8	51.8	51.8	77.6	67.0
1979	84.9	85.4	94.0	79.0	85.3	70.5	71.7	...	81.9	60.2	70.1	70.2	85.1	73.7
1980	90.9	89.4	96.0	85.5	91.8	83.1	84.2	...	88.5	62.3	97.4	97.5	95.3	81.5
1981	95.3	94.2	97.5	92.9	96.7	93.2	93.8	...	93.9	76.9	108.5	108.5	101.0	89.2
1982	97.8	97.6	98.5	96.3	99.1	97.0	97.1	...	97.5	88.8	102.8	102.8	103.6	96.0
1983	100.2	100.3	100.2	101.1	99.8	99.3	99.3	...	99.9	98.7	99.4	99.4	100.7	100.3
1984	102.1	102.1	101.3	102.6	101.1	103.7	103.6	...	102.6	112.5	97.9	97.8	95.6	103.8
1985	105.0	105.0	104.9	107.2	102.3	106.4	106.2	...	106.1	113.7	98.7	98.6	95.9	106.8
1986	105.9	106.2	104.0	111.8	101.9	102.3	101.2	...	110.6	108.8	77.1	77.0	95.4	110.3
1987	110.6	109.1	110.4	112.1	105.1	105.4	104.2	...	114.4	113.1	80.2	80.1	96.1	114.8
1988	115.4	113.4	114.9	116.4	109.9	108.7	107.6	...	116.5	118.0	80.9	80.8	97.9	119.7
1989	118.6	117.0	116.4	119.1	114.4	114.1	112.9	...	119.2	120.4	88.5	88.5	100.2	124.9
1990	124.1	120.4	122.6	125.8	117.4	120.5	118.8	...	121.4	117.6	101.2	101.0	100.9	130.1
1991	128.7	124.2	127.6	128.9	120.9	123.8	121.9	...	126.0	118.1	99.4	99.2	102.2	136.0
1992	131.9	126.5	130.4	129.3	125.0	126.5	124.6	...	129.2	123.2	99.0	99.0	103.1	141.3
1993	133.7	127.5	132.6	127.1	125.9	130.4	127.5	91.8	132.7	133.9	98.0	97.7	101.6	145.9
1994	133.4	126.4	130.9	128.1	126.0	134.3	131.4	95.5	137.6	141.7	98.5	98.2	101.4	150.2
1995	132.0	126.2	126.9	127.2	125.4	139.1	136.3	99.4	141.0	156.5	100.0	99.8	102.1	154.0
1996	131.7	127.7	124.7	129.7	126.6	143.0	140.0	101.0	143.7	157.0	106.3	105.9	102.2	158.4
1997	132.9	130.1	126.1	129.0	127.6	144.3	141.0	100.5	144.3	151.1	106.2	105.8	101.9	162.7
1998	133.0	131.8	126.0	126.1	128.0	141.6	137.9	100.1	143.4	150.6	92.2	91.6	101.1	167.1
1999	131.3	131.1	123.3	129.0	125.7	144.4	140.5	100.1	142.9	152.0	100.7	100.1	100.5	171.9
1996														
January	132.7	127.0	127.6	131.5	124.8	140.0	137.7	100.7	142.3	157.9	100.7	100.5	102.3	156.2
February	132.1	127.5	125.4	134.4	126.4	140.8	138.1	100.9	142.7	157.5	101.3	101.0	102.2	156.6
March	132.7	128.3	125.7	133.3	128.0	141.7	138.9	101.0	142.9	157.3	104.4	104.2	102.3	156.9
April	131.9	127.6	124.8	133.7	126.4	143.3	140.7	101.1	143.0	157.4	109.9	109.5	102.3	157.2
May	131.8	127.7	124.7	130.4	126.8	143.8	141.1	101.2	143.2	157.6	110.7	110.3	102.2	157.5
June	131.6	127.8	124.0	129.1	127.4	143.6	140.8	101.4	143.6	157.2	108.6	108.5	102.6	157.7
July	131.3	127.5	123.7	125.7	127.0	143.4	140.5	101.5	143.9	156.9	106.8	106.5	102.0	158.1
August	130.5	127.7	122.6	125.1	126.3	143.1	140.2	101.6	144.1	156.6	105.0	104.6	102.0	158.6
September	131.3	127.2	123.5	131.4	126.8	143.6	140.6	101.8	144.5	157.0	104.7	104.1	102.1	160.0
October	131.4	127.2	124.1	128.5	126.2	144.0	140.8	101.8	144.5	157.0	105.3	104.5	102.2	160.5
November	131.6	129.0	123.9	126.7	126.5	144.5	141.3	101.8	144.5	156.5	107.5	106.8	102.0	160.5
December	131.9	128.3	125.4	126.9	126.5	145.3	142.0	101.8	144.7	155.6	110.0	109.4	102.1	160.6
1997														
January	132.2	129.2	125.5	127.9	126.5	145.1	142.1	101.5	144.5	154.7	110.8	110.3	102.1	161.1
February	132.8	128.4	127.0	127.2	127.0	145.3	142.5	101.5	144.6	154.4	111.6	111.1	102.3	161.2
March	132.4	128.4	125.9	129.7	127.2	145.4	142.2	101.6	144.7	154.4	109.7	109.1	102.1	161.5
April	133.1	129.8	126.3	133.7	127.5	145.0	141.7	101.6	144.7	154.3	107.3	106.7	102.0	161.9
May	133.3	130.0	126.5	133.8	127.8	143.8	140.4	101.4	144.4	153.9	103.0	102.5	101.9	162.2
June	133.1	129.7	126.7	132.9	126.6	143.7	140.5	101.0	144.3	151.8	103.6	103.2	101.9	162.6
July	133.3	130.5	126.5	131.3	127.2	143.6	140.2	100.8	144.4	149.9	102.1	101.6	102.5	162.9
August	132.5	130.5	125.2	127.3	127.7	144.1	141.1	100.5	144.2	148.5	106.1	105.8	101.9	163.3
September	133.0	131.4	126.0	126.7	127.5	144.6	141.6	100.4	144.0	148.2	107.8	107.6	101.7	163.5
October	132.8	131.0	125.4	126.2	128.7	144.5	141.0	100.3	143.9	147.9	105.7	105.5	101.4	163.9
November	132.8	130.8	126.0	126.0	127.8	143.6	140.5	100.2	143.8	147.6	104.0	103.5	101.4	164.0
December	133.1	131.8	125.7	125.8	128.7	143.3	140.2	100.0	143.4	147.9	103.1	102.5	101.2	164.7
1998														
January	133.0	132.1	125.2	124.8	129.1	142.9	139.6	100.1	143.5	148.1	99.9	99.3	101.0	165.0
February	132.9	132.0	125.7	123.1	127.5	142.6	139.1	100.2	143.6	148.4	97.3	96.8	101.1	165.5
March	132.9	132.9	126.0	124.4	126.8	141.9	138.2	100.1	143.7	147.3	93.7	93.1	101.1	165.7
April	132.5	131.6	125.6	126.6	126.1	141.8	138.1	100.2	143.8	148.2	92.9	92.3	100.7	165.7
May	132.8	131.4	126.1	126.9	127.1	141.5	138.0	100.2	143.1	150.0	92.5	92.0	100.9	165.9
June	133.1	131.7	126.7	124.7	128.6	141.5	138.1	100.1	142.7	150.9	93.0	92.6	101.2	166.5
July	132.7	131.9	126.0	122.0	128.2	141.8	138.2	100.5	143.4	151.3	92.3	91.7	101.3	166.8
August	134.3	132.3	128.7	124.4	129.1	141.5	137.8	100.8	144.0	151.1	90.1	89.5	101.3	167.3
September	133.0	131.2	126.7	124.9	128.7	141.0	137.4	100.7	143.6	151.9	88.7	88.1	101.1	168.3
October	133.0	131.9	125.4	130.2	128.4	141.2	137.7	100.7	143.1	153.0	89.6	89.1	101.4	169.0
November	132.9	131.9	124.8	131.3	128.7	141.2	137.8	101.0	143.3	154.0	88.9	88.4	101.1	169.5
December	132.1	130.8	124.4	129.6	127.9	140.7	137.3	100.9	143.4	153.1	87.1	86.7	101.0	169.6
1999														
January	131.1	130.3	122.8	130.0	127.3	140.6	137.0	100.5	143.5	150.6	86.9	86.4	100.9	169.8
February	130.7	131.1	122.0	126.4	125.8	140.3	136.5	99.8	143.0	148.3	86.5	86.2	100.6	170.4
March	130.7	130.7	122.6	125.6	126.9	141.1	137.0	99.6	142.7	147.4	89.1	88.6	100.1	170.6
April	131.9	131.6	123.6	128.2	127.4	144.5	140.5	99.8	142.8	148.3	102.2	101.7	100.5	170.9
May	131.8	131.7	123.8	127.6	126.3	143.8	139.9	100.0	142.8	149.6	99.3	98.7	100.5	171.3
June	131.4	132.1	123.3	126.8	125.8	143.2	139.6	100.2	142.7	150.9	97.5	96.9	100.3	171.7
July	130.4	130.8	121.4	127.4	126.3	144.7	140.7	100.4	142.7	152.3	101.0	100.3	100.2	172.1
August	130.0	128.8	122.4	128.3	125.0	145.8	142.1	100.5	142.6	153.8	105.9	105.2	100.5	172.1
September	131.2	130.7	124.1	129.9	124.7	146.7	143.2	101.0	142.9	155.7	108.6	107.9	100.5	172.8
October	132.0	131.8	125.0	132.4	124.3	147.1	143.2	101.1	142.9	156.4	108.3	107.7	100.5	173.2
November	131.5	131.0	124.0	132.6	124.7	147.2	143.3	101.2	142.9	156.1	108.0	107.4	100.9	173.6
December	131.5	132.0	123.8	133.0	124.1	148.4	144.6	101.1	142.9	155.0	113.4	112.7	100.6	173.8

1. December 1997=100.

Table 6-1. Consumer Price Indexes—*Continued*

(All urban consumers; 1982–1984=100, except as noted; seasonally adjusted.)

Year and month	Transportation—Continued		Medical care					Recreation		Education and communication				
					Medical care services						Education			
	Public transportation	Transportation services	Medical care	Medical care commodities	Total	Professional services	Hospital and related services	Total[1]	Video and audio[1]	Total[1]	Total[1]	Educational books and supplies	Tuition, other school fees, and childcare
1970	35.2	40.2	34.0	46.5	32.3	37.0	. . .	. . .	. . .	. . .	. . .	38.8	. . .
1971	37.8	43.4	36.1	47.3	34.7	39.4	. . .	. . .	. . .	. . .	. . .	41.4	. . .
1972	39.3	44.4	37.3	47.4	35.9	40.8	. . .	. . .	. . .	. . .	. . .	44.2	. . .
1973	39.7	44.7	38.8	47.5	37.5	42.2	. . .	. . .	. . .	. . .	. . .	45.6	. . .
1974	40.6	46.3	42.4	49.2	41.4	45.8	. . .	. . .	. . .	. . .	. . .	47.2	. . .
1975	43.5	49.8	47.5	53.3	46.6	50.8	. . .	. . .	. . .	. . .	. . .	50.3	. . .
1976	47.8	56.9	52.0	56.5	51.3	55.5	. . .	. . .	. . .	. . .	. . .	53.7	. . .
1977	50.0	61.5	57.0	60.2	56.4	60.0	. . .	. . .	. . .	. . .	. . .	56.9	. . .
1978	51.5	64.4	61.8	64.4	61.2	64.5	55.1	. . .	. . .	. . .	. . .	61.6	59.8
1979	54.9	69.5	67.5	69.0	67.2	70.1	61.0	. . .	. . .	. . .	. . .	65.7	64.7
1980	69.0	79.2	74.9	75.4	74.8	77.9	69.2	. . .	. . .	. . .	. . .	71.4	71.2
1981	85.6	88.6	82.9	83.7	82.8	85.9	79.1	. . .	. . .	. . .	. . .	80.3	79.9
1982	94.9	96.1	92.5	92.3	92.6	93.2	90.3	. . .	. . .	. . .	. . .	91.0	90.5
1983	99.5	99.1	100.6	100.2	100.7	99.8	100.5	. . .	. . .	. . .	. . .	100.3	99.7
1984	105.7	104.8	106.8	107.5	106.7	107.0	109.2	. . .	. . .	. . .	. . .	108.7	109.8
1985	110.5	110.0	113.5	115.2	113.2	113.5	116.1	. . .	. . .	. . .	. . .	118.2	119.7
1986	117.0	116.3	122.0	122.8	121.9	120.8	123.1	. . .	. . .	. . .	. . .	128.1	129.6
1987	121.1	121.9	130.1	131.0	130.0	128.8	131.6	. . .	. . .	. . .	. . .	138.1	140.0
1988	123.3	128.0	138.6	139.9	138.3	137.5	143.9	. . .	. . .	. . .	. . .	148.1	151.0
1989	129.5	135.6	149.3	150.8	148.9	146.4	160.5	. . .	. . .	. . .	. . .	158.0	162.7
1990	142.6	144.2	162.8	163.4	162.7	156.1	178.0	. . .	. . .	. . .	. . .	171.3	175.7
1991	148.9	151.2	177.0	176.8	177.1	165.7	196.1	. . .	. . .	. . .	. . .	180.3	191.4
1992	151.4	155.7	190.1	188.1	190.5	175.8	214.0	. . .	. . .	. . .	. . .	190.3	208.5
1993	167.0	162.9	201.4	195.0	202.9	184.7	231.9	90.7	96.5	85.5	78.4	197.6	225.3
1994	172.0	168.6	211.0	200.7	213.4	192.5	245.6	92.7	95.4	88.8	83.3	205.5	239.8
1995	175.9	175.9	220.5	204.5	224.2	201.0	257.8	94.5	95.1	92.2	88.0	214.4	253.8
1996	181.9	180.5	228.2	210.4	232.4	208.3	269.5	97.4	96.6	95.3	92.7	226.9	267.1
1997	186.7	185.0	234.6	215.3	239.1	215.4	278.4	99.6	99.4	98.4	97.3	238.4	280.4
1998	190.3	187.9	242.1	221.8	246.8	222.2	287.5	101.1	101.1	100.3	102.1	250.8	294.2
1999	197.7	190.7	250.6	230.7	255.1	229.2	299.5	102.0	100.7	101.2	107.0	261.7	308.4
1996													
January	171.6	176.2	225.4	207.9	229.2	205.2	264.4	96.0	94.8	94.1	91.0	222.0	261.2
February	177.4	178.0	225.9	208.3	229.7	205.8	265.2	96.7	95.2	94.4	91.4	223.1	262.4
March	178.9	178.0	226.4	208.7	230.3	206.2	266.3	96.8	95.5	94.8	91.8	224.2	263.5
April	179.3	178.8	227.0	209.3	230.9	206.7	267.1	97.0	95.8	94.5	92.2	225.1	264.8
May	180.2	179.4	227.6	209.6	231.5	207.4	268.1	97.0	96.0	95.2	92.5	225.4	265.7
June	182.2	180.2	228.2	210.2	232.1	207.7	269.5	97.2	96.4	95.6	92.9	225.9	266.8
July	182.7	180.7	228.8	210.6	232.8	208.5	270.5	97.4	97.3	95.8	93.3	226.3	267.9
August	181.4	181.0	229.3	211.0	233.3	209.1	271.1	97.5	97.2	96.0	93.6	228.6	268.7
September	184.6	182.4	229.9	211.5	233.9	209.8	271.9	97.8	97.4	96.2	93.9	229.4	269.5
October	187.2	183.0	230.5	212.6	234.4	210.5	272.6	98.0	97.8	96.6	94.3	230.2	270.7
November	187.3	183.2	231.2	212.3	235.3	211.4	273.4	98.3	97.9	96.8	94.7	231.0	271.8
December	189.9	183.8	231.4	212.3	235.6	211.7	274.1	98.5	98.2	97.1	95.1	232.0	272.9
1997													
January	185.8	182.9	232.1	213.0	236.2	212.4	274.8	98.7	98.3	97.4	95.5	232.7	274.2
February	182.4	182.8	232.4	213.8	236.5	212.9	275.3	99.0	98.6	97.6	95.8	233.6	275.1
March	188.1	184.5	233.2	214.6	237.3	213.9	276.1	99.3	98.7	97.9	96.2	234.4	276.2
April	189.8	185.2	233.7	214.9	237.8	214.3	277.1	99.2	98.0	98.1	96.5	235.4	277.1
May	188.1	184.9	234.3	215.5	238.4	214.8	277.8	99.3	98.8	98.4	97.0	236.6	278.5
June	186.6	184.9	234.7	215.6	238.8	215.2	278.3	99.7	99.5	98.7	97.4	238.5	279.6
July	189.4	186.0	234.9	215.6	239.1	215.7	278.4	99.6	99.9	98.9	97.9	239.5	280.8
August	183.4	184.8	235.3	215.4	239.7	216.2	278.9	99.8	99.9	98.9	98.3	241.0	282.1
September	186.0	185.5	235.9	215.5	240.3	216.6	279.7	99.9	100.2	99.2	98.7	241.1	283.4
October	190.9	186.8	236.3	215.9	240.8	217.1	280.5	100.0	100.2	99.5	99.2	241.9	284.7
November	185.9	185.7	237.1	216.3	241.6	217.6	281.6	100.0	100.6	99.7	99.5	242.5	285.8
December	184.3	185.6	237.9	217.1	242.4	218.3	282.8	100.0	100.5	100.0	100.0	243.6	287.1
1998													
January	187.1	186.7	238.4	217.9	242.8	218.7	282.6	100.2	100.8	100.0	100.4	243.3	288.3
February	191.2	187.7	239.1	218.4	243.6	219.4	283.8	100.4	100.8	99.9	100.7	245.1	289.0
March	193.7	188.4	239.6	218.4	244.3	220.1	284.5	100.7	101.0	100.2	101.1	246.5	290.3
April	193.4	188.3	240.6	219.8	245.1	220.7	285.7	100.8	101.0	100.4	101.6	248.4	291.7
May	190.4	187.8	241.5	221.3	245.8	221.3	286.1	100.8	101.1	100.7	102.1	249.6	293.1
June	188.2	187.3	242.2	221.7	246.6	222.2	286.7	101.0	101.1	100.8	102.4	250.0	293.8
July	192.0	188.1	242.7	221.7	247.3	222.5	288.5	100.9	101.1	100.8	102.8	251.0	295.0
August	192.2	188.2	243.6	222.9	248.1	223.2	289.3	101.1	101.1	100.3	103.0	250.2	295.9
September	190.2	187.8	244.4	224.1	248.7	223.9	289.6	101.3	101.7	100.5	103.4	253.4	296.8
October	189.9	188.1	245.0	224.5	249.4	224.5	290.7	101.0	101.4	100.6	103.8	256.3	297.8
November	187.4	187.9	245.5	225.1	249.8	224.9	291.2	101.1	101.1	100.9	104.2	257.1	299.0
December	188.4	188.1	246.0	225.9	250.3	225.4	291.7	101.2	101.2	100.7	104.7	257.9	300.4
1999													
January	190.4	188.4	246.8	226.3	251.2	226.1	293.4	101.6	101.6	101.0	105.0	256.6	301.5
February	193.1	189.1	247.5	226.9	251.9	226.5	294.7	101.5	101.1	101.0	105.6	259.5	303.0
March	198.8	190.6	248.2	227.7	252.6	227.1	295.8	101.5	100.8	101.1	106.1	260.4	304.3
April	201.4	191.0	249.0	228.9	253.2	227.8	296.4	101.8	100.7	101.1	106.5	260.9	305.5
May	198.4	190.4	249.6	229.2	253.9	228.2	297.5	102.0	100.8	101.0	106.9	262.3	306.7
June	192.6	189.5	250.4	230.0	254.7	229.0	298.6	102.0	100.6	101.1	107.3	263.5	307.9
July	200.8	191.3	251.2	231.2	255.4	229.5	299.7	102.0	100.6	101.3	107.8	264.5	309.4
August	197.1	190.6	252.0	232.3	256.1	230.0	301.1	102.0	100.8	101.5	108.1	265.7	310.1
September	194.7	190.5	252.8	233.1	256.9	230.6	302.5	101.6	100.4	101.5	108.5	266.7	311.2
October	201.5	191.7	253.4	233.5	257.5	231.2	303.5	101.6	100.4	101.8	108.9	268.2	312.5
November	202.2	192.3	254.1	234.3	258.2	231.9	304.4	101.8	100.4	102.1	109.0	255.6	313.8
December	201.2	192.5	255.0	234.9	259.2	232.6	306.6	102.0	100.6	102.3	109.4	256.5	315.0

1. December 1997=100.

Table 6-1. Consumer Price Indexes—*Continued*

(All urban consumers; 1982–1984=100, except as noted; seasonally adjusted.)

Year and month	Education and communication—*Continued*					Other goods and services				
	Communication							Personal care		
		Information and Information processing								
				Information and information processing other than telephone services						
	Total [1]	Total [1]	Telephone services [1]	Total [2]	Personal computers and peripheral equipment [1]	Total	Tobacco and smoking products	Total	Personal care products	Personal care services
1970	...	...	...	...	...	40.9	43.1	43.5	42.7	44.2
1971	...	...	...	...	...	42.9	44.9	44.9	44.0	45.7
1972	...	...	...	...	...	44.7	47.4	46.0	45.2	46.8
1973	...	...	...	...	...	46.4	48.7	48.1	46.4	49.7
1974	...	...	...	...	...	49.8	51.1	52.8	51.5	53.9
1975	...	...	...	...	...	53.9	54.7	57.9	58.0	57.7
1976	...	...	...	...	...	57.0	57.0	61.7	61.3	61.9
1977	...	...	...	...	...	60.4	59.8	65.7	64.7	66.4
1978	...	...	...	...	...	64.3	63.0	69.9	68.2	71.3
1979	...	...	...	...	...	68.9	66.8	75.2	72.9	77.2
1980	...	...	...	...	...	75.2	72.0	81.9	79.6	83.7
1981	...	...	...	...	...	82.6	77.8	89.1	87.8	90.2
1982	...	...	...	...	...	91.1	86.5	95.4	95.1	95.7
1983	...	...	...	...	...	101.1	103.4	100.3	100.7	100.0
1984	...	...	...	...	...	107.9	110.1	104.3	104.2	104.4
1985	...	...	...	...	...	114.5	116.7	108.3	107.6	108.9
1986	...	...	...	...	...	121.4	124.7	111.9	111.3	112.5
1987	...	...	...	...	...	128.5	133.6	115.1	113.9	116.2
1988	...	...	...	...	...	137.0	145.8	119.4	118.1	120.7
1989	...	...	...	96.3	...	147.7	164.4	125.0	123.2	126.8
1990	...	...	...	93.5	...	159.0	181.5	130.4	128.2	132.8
1991	...	...	...	88.6	...	171.6	202.7	134.9	132.8	137.0
1992	...	...	...	83.7	...	183.3	219.8	138.3	136.5	140.0
1993	96.7	97.7	...	78.8	...	192.9	228.4	141.5	139.0	144.0
1994	97.6	98.6	...	72.0	...	198.5	220.0	144.6	141.5	147.9
1995	98.8	98.7	...	63.8	...	206.9	225.7	147.1	143.1	151.5
1996	99.6	99.5	...	57.2	...	215.4	232.8	150.1	144.3	156.6
1997	100.3	100.4	...	50.1	...	224.8	243.7	152.7	144.2	162.4
1998	98.7	98.5	100.7	39.9	78.2	237.7	274.8	156.7	148.3	166.0
1999	96.0	95.5	100.1	30.5	53.5	258.3	355.8	161.1	151.8	171.4
1996										
January	99.0	98.9	...	60.7	...	212.5	229.3	149.1	143.7	155.0
February	99.1	99.0	...	61.0	...	213.2	229.8	149.3	144.1	155.2
March	99.5	99.4	...	60.4	...	213.9	230.8	149.4	144.0	155.3
April	98.1	97.9	...	58.9	...	214.5	230.5	149.7	144.2	155.7
May	99.3	99.2	...	58.0	...	215.7	233.1	150.3	145.3	155.8
June	99.8	99.7	...	58.2	...	215.9	232.9	149.6	143.9	155.9
July	99.7	99.7	...	55.8	...	216.6	233.3	150.0	144.4	156.3
August	99.9	99.8	...	55.0	...	217.2	233.4	150.5	145.0	156.5
September	100.0	100.0	...	55.3	...	217.8	234.1	150.8	145.1	157.2
October	100.2	100.2	...	55.2	...	218.4	235.3	150.9	144.6	157.9
November	100.2	100.2	...	54.4	...	219.3	236.2	151.2	144.7	158.6
December	100.3	100.3	...	53.9	...	219.2	234.3	150.5	142.8	159.2
1997										
January	100.5	100.5	...	53.5	...	220.5	236.4	151.6	143.6	160.7
February	100.5	100.6	...	53.2	...	221.3	237.4	151.5	143.3	160.7
March	100.6	100.7	...	52.4	...	222.3	238.2	151.8	143.6	161.2
April	100.6	100.6	...	51.4	...	223.9	243.2	152.7	144.5	162.0
May	100.6	100.6	...	50.8	...	224.7	243.8	152.6	144.1	162.3
June	100.7	100.8	...	49.9	...	225.0	241.3	152.8	144.2	162.6
July	100.6	100.7	...	49.1	...	225.6	242.0	152.6	143.7	162.5
August	99.8	99.8	...	48.2	...	226.7	243.4	152.5	143.5	162.7
September	99.8	99.8	...	48.5	...	227.6	246.5	152.7	143.7	162.8
October	100.0	100.0	...	48.9	...	229.1	250.2	153.3	144.5	163.4
November	100.1	100.1	...	47.6	...	230.0	250.7	154.3	146.1	163.5
December	100.0	100.0	100.0	47.4	100.0	230.6	251.2	154.0	145.3	163.9
1998										
January	99.6	99.6	99.9	46.2	96.9	231.8	253.8	154.6	146.1	164.3
February	99.2	99.1	100.0	44.3	91.3	233.7	261.2	155.0	146.7	164.3
March	99.3	99.3	100.4	43.4	88.7	233.0	254.1	155.5	147.3	164.7
April	99.3	99.2	100.5	42.8	86.6	235.2	263.5	155.9	147.3	165.2
May	99.4	99.3	101.1	41.5	82.7	237.2	270.0	156.6	149.3	165.4
June	99.4	99.3	101.4	40.6	80.0	236.9	266.9	156.8	149.2	165.3
July	99.1	99.0	101.5	39.1	75.2	238.4	273.2	157.0	149.1	166.1
August	97.9	97.7	100.4	37.6	71.1	238.5	273.7	157.1	148.5	166.6
September	97.9	97.7	100.7	36.7	68.5	240.9	283.5	157.5	149.1	167.1
October	97.8	97.6	100.7	36.1	67.5	241.9	284.9	158.1	149.4	167.5
November	97.8	97.6	101.1	35.3	65.6	241.0	281.3	158.0	148.8	167.6
December	97.1	96.9	100.3	34.8	64.2	250.9	331.2	158.3	148.7	168.3
1999										
January	97.3	96.9	100.7	33.8	61.4	256.0	354.2	158.9	149.9	168.8
February	96.9	96.5	100.4	33.3	59.7	255.5	348.7	159.4	149.8	169.3
March	96.6	96.1	100.2	32.4	57.6	253.9	335.9	160.0	150.8	169.9
April	96.3	95.8	100.0	32.1	56.8	256.7	349.9	160.2	150.9	170.3
May	95.7	95.2	99.6	30.9	55.7	256.4	345.5	160.7	150.9	171.0
June	95.5	94.9	99.7	29.8	54.5	256.5	343.2	161.1	152.6	170.9
July	95.5	94.9	99.5	30.0	52.9	258.9	356.0	161.1	152.0	171.4
August	95.6	95.0	99.8	29.8	50.9	258.1	350.1	161.4	152.3	171.9
September	95.3	94.7	99.6	29.3	49.7	263.2	373.8	161.8	153.0	172.1
October	95.3	94.7	99.8	28.7	48.2	263.8	373.3	162.4	153.4	172.9
November	95.9	95.3	100.6	28.2	47.0	263.6	369.8	162.8	153.3	173.9
December	95.9	95.4	100.7	28.2	47.2	263.6	369.1	162.9	152.5	174.3

1. December 1997=100.
2. December 1988=100.

Table 6-1. Consumer Price Indexes—*Continued*

(All urban consumers; 1982–1984=100, except as noted; seasonally adjusted, except as noted.)

Year and month	Commodities Total	Commodities less food and beverages Total	Durables	Non-durables	Services	Energy	All items less: Food	Energy	Food and energy	CPI-U-X1 [1]	CPI-U-RS [2]	Consumer Price Index, urban wage earners and clerical workers (CPI-W)
1970	41.7	43.1	44.1	40.8	35.0	25.5	39.0	40.3	40.8	41.3	...	39.0
1971	43.2	44.7	46.0	42.1	37.0	26.5	40.8	42.0	42.7	43.1	...	40.7
1972	44.5	45.8	46.9	43.5	38.4	27.2	42.0	43.4	44.0	44.4	...	42.1
1973	47.8	47.3	48.1	47.5	40.1	29.4	43.7	46.1	45.6	47.2	...	44.7
1974	53.5	52.4	51.5	54.0	43.8	38.1	48.0	50.6	49.4	51.9	...	49.6
1975	58.2	57.3	57.4	58.3	48.0	42.1	52.5	55.1	53.9	56.2	...	54.1
1976	60.7	60.2	60.9	60.5	52.0	45.1	56.0	58.2	57.4	59.4	...	57.2
1977	64.2	63.6	64.4	64.0	56.0	49.4	59.6	61.9	61.0	63.2	...	60.9
1978	68.8	67.3	68.6	68.6	60.8	52.5	63.9	66.7	65.5	67.5	104.3	65.6
1979	76.6	75.2	75.4	77.2	67.5	65.7	71.2	73.4	71.9	74.0	114.1	73.1
1980	86.0	85.7	83.0	87.6	77.9	86.0	81.5	81.9	80.8	82.3	126.8	82.9
1981	93.2	93.1	89.6	95.2	88.1	97.7	90.4	90.1	89.2	90.1	138.7	91.4
1982	97.0	96.9	95.1	97.8	96.0	99.2	96.3	96.1	95.8	95.6	146.9	96.9
1983	99.8	100.0	99.8	99.7	99.4	99.9	99.7	99.6	99.6	99.6	152.9	99.8
1984	103.2	103.1	105.1	102.5	104.6	100.9	104.0	104.3	104.6	103.9	159.1	103.3
1985	105.4	105.2	106.8	104.8	109.9	101.6	108.0	108.4	109.1	107.6	164.4	106.9
1986	104.4	101.4	106.6	103.5	115.4	88.2	109.8	112.6	113.5	109.6	167.4	108.6
1987	107.7	104.0	108.2	107.5	120.2	88.6	113.6	117.2	118.2	113.6	173.1	112.5
1988	111.5	107.3	110.4	111.8	125.7	89.3	118.3	122.3	123.4	118.3	179.4	117.0
1989	116.7	111.6	112.2	118.2	131.9	94.3	123.7	128.1	129.0	124.0	187.2	122.6
1990	122.8	117.0	113.4	126.0	139.2	102.1	130.3	134.7	135.5	130.7	196.6	129.0
1991	126.6	120.4	116.0	130.3	146.3	102.5	136.1	140.9	142.1	136.2	203.8	134.3
1992	129.1	123.2	118.6	132.8	152.0	103.0	140.8	145.4	147.3	140.3	209.2	138.2
1993	131.5	125.3	121.3	135.1	157.9	104.2	145.1	150.0	152.2	144.5	214.6	142.1
1994	133.8	126.9	124.8	136.8	163.1	104.6	149.0	154.1	156.5	148.2	219.3	145.6
1995	136.4	128.9	128.0	139.3	168.7	105.2	153.1	158.7	161.2	152.4	224.8	149.8
1996	139.9	131.5	129.4	143.5	174.1	110.1	157.5	163.1	165.6	156.9	231.0	154.1
1997	141.8	132.2	128.7	146.4	179.4	111.5	161.1	167.1	169.5	160.5	236.0	157.6
1998	141.9	130.5	127.6	146.9	184.2	102.9	163.4	170.9	173.4	163.0	239.2	159.7
1999	144.4	132.5	126.0	151.2	188.8	106.6	167.0	174.4	177.0	166.6	244.2	163.2
1996												
January	138.0	130.3	129.0	141.2	171.5	106.0	155.3	161.2	163.8	154.4	227.4	151.9
February	138.3	130.4	129.1	141.4	172.1	106.7	155.7	161.6	164.2	154.9	228.3	152.3
March	139.0	131.2	129.4	142.4	172.5	108.1	156.3	162.1	164.7	155.7	229.4	152.9
April	139.8	132.0	129.2	143.1	172.9	111.4	156.8	162.4	164.9	156.3	230.2	153.5
May	139.8	132.1	129.2	143.5	173.5	111.8	157.2	162.7	165.3	156.6	230.7	153.9
June	139.9	131.7	129.3	143.6	173.8	110.2	157.3	163.1	165.6	156.7	230.9	154.0
July	140.0	131.4	129.3	143.8	174.5	109.9	157.7	163.5	166.0	157.0	231.2	154.3
August	139.9	131.1	129.4	143.5	174.9	109.4	157.8	163.8	166.2	157.3	231.5	154.5
September	140.4	131.5	129.7	144.0	175.4	109.4	158.2	164.3	166.7	157.8	232.3	155.0
October	140.9	131.7	129.5	144.5	175.8	109.9	158.6	164.8	167.1	158.3	232.9	155.4
November	141.3	132.2	129.5	145.4	176.3	111.1	159.0	165.2	167.4	158.6	233.3	155.9
December	141.7	132.6	129.6	145.7	176.7	112.9	159.4	165.4	167.6	158.6	233.3	156.2
1997												
January	141.7	132.9	129.4	146.0	177.2	114.3	159.9	165.5	167.9	159.1	234.0	156.5
February	142.1	133.2	129.5	146.3	177.7	114.9	160.3	166.0	168.3	159.6	234.7	156.9
March	141.9	132.8	129.8	146.1	178.2	113.3	160.4	166.3	168.7	160.0	235.2	157.0
April	141.8	132.7	129.3	145.8	178.5	111.4	160.6	166.7	169.2	160.2	235.4	157.1
May	141.5	132.1	129.3	145.7	178.8	108.9	160.6	166.9	169.5	160.1	235.4	157.1
June	141.5	131.9	129.0	145.9	179.3	109.7	160.8	167.2	169.6	160.3	235.7	157.3
July	141.5	131.6	128.5	146.1	179.8	108.9	161.0	167.5	170.0	160.5	235.9	157.5
August	141.8	131.9	128.3	146.6	179.9	110.2	161.2	167.6	170.0	160.8	236.3	157.8
September	142.2	132.3	128.1	147.0	180.5	111.6	161.7	168.0	170.4	161.2	237.0	158.2
October	142.1	132.1	128.0	146.8	181.0	110.7	162.0	168.4	170.8	161.6	237.5	158.4
November	142.1	131.8	127.7	147.0	181.4	110.5	162.1	168.6	171.0	161.5	237.4	158.5
December	142.0	131.7	127.6	146.9	181.6	108.9	162.2	168.8	171.3	161.3	237.0	158.6
1998												
January	142.0	131.3	127.8	146.7	182.0	106.9	162.3	169.3	171.8	161.6	237.4	158.7
February	141.8	131.1	127.9	146.5	182.4	105.0	162.4	169.6	172.2	161.9	237.7	158.7
March	141.5	130.5	127.9	146.2	182.9	103.4	162.5	169.9	172.5	162.2	238.2	158.7
April	141.6	130.6	127.9	145.9	183.4	103.2	162.8	170.3	172.9	162.5	238.7	159.1
May	141.8	130.6	127.6	146.7	183.8	103.0	163.1	170.7	173.3	162.8	239.0	159.4
June	141.8	130.6	127.5	147.0	184.1	103.0	163.3	170.8	173.5	163.0	239.2	159.5
July	142.0	130.7	127.8	147.1	184.5	102.5	163.6	171.2	173.8	163.2	239.4	159.8
August	142.1	130.6	127.8	147.3	184.8	101.2	163.7	171.6	174.2	163.4	239.8	160.0
September	141.9	130.3	127.3	147.0	185.2	100.1	163.8	171.9	174.5	163.6	240.1	160.1
October	142.3	130.4	127.1	147.4	185.5	100.3	164.1	172.2	174.7	164.0	240.6	160.4
November	142.3	130.2	127.2	147.5	186.0	100.2	164.3	172.5	175.0	164.0	240.5	160.7
December	142.5	130.6	127.0	147.8	186.2	99.2	164.6	172.9	175.5	163.9	240.3	161.0
1999												
January	142.8	130.7	126.7	148.4	186.5	99.0	164.8	173.3	175.8	164.3	240.9	161.3
February	142.5	130.1	126.2	148.3	186.9	99.0	164.9	173.3	175.8	164.5	241.2	161.3
March	142.5	130.2	125.9	148.5	187.6	100.3	165.2	173.5	176.1	165.0	242.0	161.5
April	144.3	132.7	125.9	150.6	188.1	106.3	166.5	174.0	176.7	166.2	243.6	162.7
May	144.0	132.2	125.8	150.6	188.3	104.9	166.5	174.2	176.8	166.2	243.6	162.7
June	143.9	131.9	125.8	150.7	188.5	104.2	166.5	174.3	177.0	166.2	243.7	162.7
July	144.4	132.5	125.8	151.4	189.1	106.1	167.1	174.7	177.4	166.7	244.4	163.3
August	144.9	133.1	125.9	152.0	189.4	108.5	167.5	174.9	177.5	167.1	245.1	163.7
September	145.8	134.3	126.1	153.1	189.8	110.4	168.2	175.4	178.1	167.9	246.1	164.5
October	146.0	134.4	126.0	153.3	190.2	110.4	168.5	175.8	178.4	168.2	246.7	164.8
November	145.9	134.1	125.7	153.4	190.8	110.5	168.8	176.1	178.7	168.3	246.7	165.1
December	146.5	134.8	125.5	153.9	191.1	112.5	169.2	176.3	178.9	168.3	246.7	165.5

1. See Notes for definition; not seasonally adjusted.
2. December 1977=100; not seasonally adjusted; see Notes for more information.

Table 6-2. Producer Price Indexes

(1982=100, seasonally adjusted.)

Year and month	Finished goods Total	Finished goods Percent change from previous period	Finished consumer goods Total	Finished consumer foods Total	Finished consumer foods Crude	Finished consumer foods Processed	Finished consumer goods, except foods Total	Finished consumer goods, except foods Durable goods	Finished consumer goods, except foods Nondurable goods less foods	Capital equipment Total	Capital equipment Manufacturing industries	Capital equipment Nonmanufacturing industries
1970	39.3	3.3	39.1	43.8	46.0	43.9	37.4	47.2	32.5	40.1	38.1	41.3
1971	40.5	3.0	40.2	44.5	45.8	44.7	38.7	48.9	33.5	41.7	39.6	43.0
1972	41.8	3.1	41.5	46.9	48.0	47.2	39.4	50.0	34.1	42.8	40.5	44.2
1973	45.6	9.1	46.0	56.5	63.6	55.8	41.2	50.9	36.1	44.2	42.2	45.3
1974	52.6	15.4	53.1	64.4	71.6	63.9	48.2	55.5	44.0	50.5	48.8	51.2
1975	58.2	10.6	58.2	69.8	71.7	70.3	53.2	61.0	48.9	58.2	56.5	58.9
1976	60.8	4.5	60.4	69.6	76.7	69.0	56.5	63.7	52.4	62.1	60.3	62.9
1977	64.7	6.4	64.3	73.3	79.5	72.7	60.6	67.4	56.8	66.1	64.5	66.8
1978	69.8	7.9	69.4	79.9	85.8	79.4	64.9	73.6	60.0	71.3	70.1	71.8
1979	77.6	11.2	77.5	87.3	92.3	86.8	73.5	80.8	69.3	77.5	77.1	77.7
1980	88.0	13.4	88.6	92.4	93.9	92.3	87.1	91.0	85.1	85.8	86.0	85.7
1981	96.1	9.2	96.6	97.8	104.4	97.2	96.1	96.4	95.8	94.6	94.9	94.4
1982	100.0	4.1	100.0	100.0	100.0	100.0	100.0	100.0	100.0	100.0	100.0	100.0
1983	101.6	1.6	101.3	101.0	102.4	100.9	101.2	102.8	100.5	102.8	102.3	103.0
1984	103.7	2.1	103.3	105.4	111.4	104.9	102.2	104.5	101.1	105.2	104.9	105.4
1985	104.7	1.0	103.8	104.6	102.9	104.8	103.3	106.5	101.7	107.5	107.4	107.6
1986	103.2	-1.5	101.4	107.3	105.6	107.4	98.5	108.9	93.3	109.7	109.7	109.7
1987	105.4	2.1	103.6	109.5	107.1	109.6	100.7	111.5	94.9	111.7	111.8	111.6
1988	108.0	2.4	106.2	112.6	109.8	112.7	103.1	113.8	97.3	114.3	115.5	113.9
1989	113.6	5.2	112.1	118.7	119.6	118.6	108.9	117.6	103.8	118.8	120.3	118.2
1990	119.2	4.9	118.2	124.4	123.0	124.4	115.3	120.4	111.5	122.9	124.5	122.2
1991	121.7	2.1	120.5	124.1	119.3	124.4	118.7	123.9	115.0	126.7	127.8	126.3
1992	123.2	1.2	121.7	123.3	107.6	124.4	120.8	125.7	117.3	129.1	129.3	129.0
1993	124.7	1.2	123.0	125.7	114.4	126.5	121.7	128.0	117.6	131.4	131.2	131.4
1994	125.5	0.6	123.3	126.8	111.3	127.9	121.6	130.9	116.2	134.1	133.2	134.3
1995	127.9	1.9	125.6	129.0	118.8	129.8	124.0	132.7	118.8	136.7	135.8	137.0
1996	131.3	2.6	129.5	133.6	129.2	133.8	127.6	134.2	123.3	138.3	137.2	138.6
1997	131.8	0.4	130.2	134.5	126.6	135.1	128.2	133.7	124.3	138.2	137.7	138.4
1998	130.7	-0.8	128.9	134.3	127.2	134.8	126.4	132.9	122.2	137.6	137.9	137.4
1999	133.0	1.7	132.0	135.1	125.5	135.9	130.5	133.0	127.9	137.6	138.5	137.3
1996												
January	129.7	0.2	127.6	131.1	125.8	131.5	125.9	133.7	121.1	138.1	137.1	138.3
February	129.7	0.0	127.5	130.9	122.2	131.5	125.9	133.8	121.1	138.0	137.1	138.3
March	130.5	0.6	128.6	132.3	146.1	131.2	126.9	133.9	122.4	138.1	137.1	138.4
April	130.8	0.2	128.9	131.7	134.7	131.4	127.6	133.8	123.4	138.1	137.0	138.5
May	130.9	0.1	129.0	131.3	117.9	132.3	127.9	134.4	123.6	138.3	137.1	138.6
June	131.3	0.3	129.5	133.7	131.9	133.8	127.6	134.7	123.0	138.4	137.2	138.7
July	131.3	0.0	129.5	133.8	125.3	134.4	127.4	134.4	123.0	138.4	137.2	138.8
August	131.6	0.2	129.8	134.5	120.0	135.5	127.7	134.7	123.2	138.6	137.3	139.0
September	131.8	0.2	130.1	135.1	124.7	135.9	127.8	134.5	123.3	138.4	137.3	138.8
October	132.4	0.5	130.9	136.4	135.7	136.5	128.4	134.2	124.4	138.4	137.3	138.7
November	132.6	0.2	131.1	136.2	135.6	136.3	128.8	134.3	124.9	138.4	137.3	138.7
December	132.8	0.2	131.5	135.3	129.0	135.7	129.7	134.3	126.1	138.4	137.4	138.7
1997												
January	132.9	0.1	131.6	134.7	130.2	135.0	130.1	134.4	126.6	138.7	137.7	138.9
February	132.6	-0.2	131.2	134.2	132.2	134.3	129.8	134.4	126.2	138.5	137.7	138.7
March	132.6	0.0	131.2	135.7	140.8	135.3	129.1	134.6	125.2	138.5	137.8	138.7
April	131.8	-0.6	130.1	135.0	124.9	135.7	127.9	134.3	123.7	138.4	137.8	138.6
May	131.4	-0.3	129.7	134.8	124.6	135.6	127.3	133.9	123.0	138.2	137.6	138.4
June	131.3	-0.1	129.6	134.0	118.4	135.1	127.5	133.8	123.3	138.3	137.6	138.5
July	131.0	-0.2	129.2	133.8	117.0	135.0	127.1	133.0	123.1	138.1	137.6	138.3
August	131.4	0.3	129.7	133.9	115.7	135.2	127.7	133.4	123.8	138.2	137.7	138.3
September	131.8	0.3	130.1	134.1	120.7	135.1	128.2	133.4	124.5	138.3	137.8	138.3
October	131.9	0.1	130.0	135.1	133.4	135.2	128.3	133.6	124.4	137.9	137.6	138.0
November	131.6	-0.2	130.1	134.6	129.3	135.0	128.0	133.1	124.3	137.8	137.6	137.9
December	131.2	-0.3	129.6	134.1	129.5	134.4	127.5	132.7	123.7	137.7	137.6	137.7
1998												
January	130.6	-0.5	128.8	133.6	127.4	134.1	126.5	132.9	122.3	137.7	137.8	137.5
February	130.5	-0.1	128.7	134.0	129.2	134.4	126.2	132.8	121.9	137.6	137.8	137.5
March	130.6	0.1	128.7	133.9	130.9	134.1	126.4	132.9	122.1	137.7	137.9	137.6
April	130.6	0.0	128.9	134.5	135.6	134.4	126.3	132.8	122.1	137.6	137.7	137.4
May	130.5	-0.1	128.7	133.3	122.7	134.2	126.6	132.5	122.6	137.4	137.9	137.2
June	130.5	0.0	128.7	133.7	120.4	134.8	126.4	132.3	122.4	137.4	137.9	137.1
July	130.8	0.2	129.1	134.5	129.7	134.9	126.6	132.8	122.4	137.5	137.9	137.2
August	130.4	-0.3	128.7	134.4	121.0	135.5	126.0	132.6	121.7	137.3	137.9	137.1
September	130.6	0.2	128.8	134.8	124.5	135.6	126.1	133.0	121.6	137.6	138.0	137.4
October	131.0	0.3	129.4	135.5	135.0	135.5	126.6	133.2	122.3	137.6	138.0	137.4
November	130.8	-0.2	129.0	134.9	126.2	135.5	126.3	133.4	121.8	137.8	138.1	137.5
December	131.1	0.2	129.5	134.3	127.3	134.9	127.3	133.1	123.3	137.6	138.1	137.3
1999												
January	131.6	0.4	130.2	136.3	137.4	136.2	127.4	132.8	123.6	137.6	138.3	137.3
February	131.1	-0.4	129.5	134.6	123.4	135.5	127.1	132.9	123.1	137.7	138.4	137.3
March	131.6	0.4	130.1	135.2	132.0	135.5	127.7	132.7	124.1	137.5	138.4	137.1
April	132.2	0.5	130.9	134.1	131.5	134.3	129.3	132.9	126.2	137.6	138.4	137.3
May	132.3	0.1	131.0	134.2	126.8	134.8	129.5	133.0	126.4	137.7	138.4	137.3
June	132.4	0.1	131.3	135.0	127.9	135.6	129.5	132.8	126.6	137.5	138.4	137.0
July	132.7	0.2	131.7	134.4	122.3	135.3	130.4	132.6	127.9	137.3	138.5	136.9
August	133.5	0.6	132.7	135.1	122.6	136.1	131.5	132.8	129.3	137.4	138.4	137.0
September	134.6	0.8	134.1	136.1	123.7	137.1	133.1	133.2	131.4	137.6	138.4	137.2
October	134.6	0.0	134.0	135.7	118.6	137.1	133.2	133.7	131.3	137.9	138.6	137.6
November	134.7	0.1	134.2	135.4	119.0	136.7	133.5	133.5	131.9	137.8	138.6	137.5
December	134.9	0.1	134.4	135.4	124.0	136.3	133.8	133.6	132.3	138.0	138.8	137.7

Table 6-2. Producer Price Indexes—*Continued*

(1982=100, seasonally adjusted.)

Year and month	Total	Materials and components for manufacturing					Materials and components for construction	Processed fuels and lubricants			Containers, non-returnable	Supplies	
		Total	Materials for food manufacturing	Materials for nondurable manufacturing	Materials for durable manufacturing	Components for manufacturing		Total	Manufacturing industries	Nonmanufacturing industries		Total	Manufacturing industries
1970	35.4	38.0	44.3	36.5	37.0	40.6	38.3	17.7	21.5	15.2	39.0	39.7	41.4
1971	36.8	38.9	45.7	37.0	38.1	41.9	40.8	19.5	23.6	16.6	40.8	40.8	42.5
1972	38.2	40.4	47.0	38.5	39.9	42.9	43.0	20.1	24.5	16.9	42.7	42.5	43.3
1973	42.4	44.1	57.2	42.6	43.1	44.3	46.5	22.2	26.4	19.4	45.2	51.7	45.6
1974	52.5	56.0	82.0	54.6	55.4	51.1	55.0	33.6	35.5	32.7	53.3	56.8	53.3
1975	58.0	61.7	82.1	61.4	60.8	57.8	60.1	39.4	41.9	38.0	60.0	61.8	59.4
1976	60.9	64.0	70.6	64.8	64.8	60.8	64.1	42.3	44.8	41.1	63.1	65.8	62.6
1977	64.9	67.4	71.9	66.8	70.2	64.5	69.3	47.7	51.0	46.2	65.9	69.3	66.6
1978	69.5	72.0	81.0	69.2	76.2	69.2	76.5	49.9	53.7	48.1	71.0	72.9	71.2
1979	78.4	80.9	89.9	78.3	87.3	75.8	84.2	61.6	64.3	60.4	79.4	80.2	78.1
1980	90.3	91.7	103.7	91.2	97.1	84.6	91.3	85.0	85.5	84.7	89.1	89.9	87.2
1981	98.6	98.7	102.1	100.5	100.7	94.7	97.9	100.6	100.2	101.0	96.7	96.9	95.2
1982	100.0	100.0	100.0	100.0	100.0	100.0	100.0	100.0	100.0	100.0	100.0	100.0	100.0
1983	100.6	101.2	101.3	98.5	103.0	102.4	102.8	95.4	96.2	94.9	100.4	101.8	101.5
1984	103.1	104.1	106.3	102.1	104.9	105.0	105.6	95.7	97.1	94.6	105.9	104.1	105.0
1985	102.7	103.3	101.5	100.5	103.3	106.4	107.3	92.8	93.8	92.0	109.0	104.4	107.3
1986	99.1	102.2	98.4	98.1	101.2	107.5	108.1	72.7	75.1	71.2	110.3	105.6	108.3
1987	101.5	105.3	100.8	102.2	106.2	108.8	109.8	73.3	75.9	71.7	114.5	107.7	110.0
1988	107.1	113.2	106.0	112.9	118.7	112.3	116.1	71.2	73.3	69.9	120.1	113.7	114.8
1989	112.0	118.1	112.7	118.5	123.6	116.4	121.3	76.4	78.3	75.3	125.4	118.1	119.8
1990	114.5	118.7	117.9	118.0	120.7	119.0	122.9	85.9	87.3	85.0	127.7	119.4	122.1
1991	114.4	118.1	115.3	116.7	117.2	121.0	124.5	85.3	88.4	83.4	128.1	121.4	124.4
1992	114.7	117.9	113.9	115.4	117.2	122.0	126.5	84.5	87.5	82.6	127.7	122.7	125.9
1993	116.2	118.9	115.6	115.5	119.1	123.0	132.0	84.7	88.1	82.6	126.4	125.0	128.5
1994	118.5	122.1	118.5	119.2	125.2	124.3	136.6	83.1	86.1	81.1	129.7	127.0	130.7
1995	124.9	130.4	119.5	135.1	135.6	126.5	142.1	84.2	87.1	82.3	148.8	132.1	137.0
1996	125.7	128.6	125.3	130.5	131.3	126.9	143.6	90.0	92.4	88.4	141.1	135.9	138.7
1997	125.6	128.3	123.2	129.6	132.8	126.4	146.5	89.3	92.0	87.6	136.0	135.9	139.4
1998	123.0	126.1	123.2	126.7	128.0	125.9	146.8	81.1	85.8	78.1	140.8	134.8	140.6
1999	123.2	124.6	120.8	124.9	125.1	125.7	148.9	84.6	87.9	82.5	142.5	134.2	140.7
1996													
January	125.5	129.5	121.3	133.3	132.2	127.3	142.0	86.9	89.2	85.4	148.1	135.2	138.3
February	125.1	129.0	121.4	132.4	131.0	127.3	142.1	85.9	89.1	83.9	146.1	135.2	138.4
March	125.3	128.6	121.0	131.4	131.0	127.1	142.3	88.2	90.7	86.6	144.6	135.3	138.4
April	125.7	128.3	121.9	130.4	131.1	126.8	142.4	91.2	93.3	89.8	143.0	135.6	138.4
May	126.2	128.7	126.3	130.1	132.4	126.7	143.4	91.6	94.4	89.8	141.6	136.2	138.7
June	125.8	128.7	128.0	129.8	132.6	126.6	143.9	89.3	92.2	87.5	140.1	136.1	138.8
July	125.5	128.3	128.1	129.5	130.7	126.7	143.6	89.0	91.3	87.5	139.7	136.4	138.9
August	125.6	128.3	128.4	129.6	130.6	126.8	144.1	89.6	91.9	88.1	138.5	136.5	139.0
September	126.1	128.7	128.9	130.1	131.2	126.8	144.7	90.5	92.4	89.2	138.5	136.8	139.1
October	125.9	128.4	129.2	129.7	130.5	126.7	144.3	91.6	93.6	90.3	137.9	136.0	138.8
November	125.8	128.1	125.0	129.6	130.9	126.7	145.0	91.5	94.1	89.9	137.5	135.5	138.8
December	126.3	128.3	123.9	129.9	131.5	126.8	144.9	93.9	96.3	92.4	137.8	135.5	138.8
1997													
January	126.6	128.4	123.6	130.1	131.9	126.8	145.1	95.0	97.6	93.3	137.7	135.4	138.7
February	126.5	128.4	123.4	129.8	132.5	126.7	145.8	94.2	96.2	92.8	136.9	135.4	138.8
March	126.1	128.5	124.7	129.3	133.3	126.7	146.3	91.3	93.2	90.1	136.1	135.8	138.8
April	125.6	128.3	124.2	128.9	133.3	126.6	146.7	88.8	91.2	87.3	135.1	136.0	139.0
May	125.4	128.3	123.4	129.0	133.4	126.5	147.1	87.5	89.9	86.0	134.6	136.2	139.1
June	125.4	128.2	122.5	129.0	133.7	126.4	146.9	88.0	90.3	86.4	134.2	136.0	139.1
July	125.2	128.2	121.9	129.3	133.3	126.4	147.1	86.9	89.4	85.3	134.2	135.9	139.4
August	125.3	128.3	122.0	129.8	133.2	126.2	147.0	87.8	90.3	86.1	133.4	135.8	139.5
September	125.5	128.3	122.8	129.9	133.0	126.2	146.8	88.0	91.2	86.0	135.4	136.2	139.6
October	125.4	128.1	122.4	129.9	132.3	126.0	146.5	88.5	91.8	86.4	136.4	135.8	140.0
November	125.6	128.2	122.4	130.1	132.2	126.0	146.6	88.5	92.0	86.2	138.0	136.1	140.2
December	125.3	128.0	123.2	130.3	131.4	126.0	146.5	87.2	90.6	85.0	139.8	136.0	140.2
1998													
January	124.5	127.5	120.4	129.9	130.5	126.0	146.4	84.8	88.4	82.5	141.4	135.4	140.3
February	124.2	127.3	122.0	129.1	130.3	125.9	146.5	83.6	87.6	81.0	141.9	135.3	140.4
March	123.8	127.0	121.5	128.6	129.8	126.0	146.8	82.0	86.2	79.4	141.7	135.4	140.5
April	123.7	126.9	122.2	128.1	129.9	125.9	147.0	82.1	86.8	79.2	141.0	135.0	140.7
May	123.6	126.7	123.4	127.8	129.1	125.9	146.8	82.2	86.6	79.5	141.7	134.8	140.7
June	123.2	126.3	122.8	127.3	128.0	125.9	146.6	81.3	86.1	78.4	141.4	134.8	140.6
July	123.1	126.0	122.7	126.9	127.8	125.8	147.0	81.1	86.1	78.0	141.3	135.1	140.7
August	122.8	125.9	123.9	126.4	127.8	125.8	147.3	79.9	85.0	76.8	140.8	134.7	140.6
September	122.4	125.5	124.7	125.1	127.2	125.9	147.3	79.4	84.6	76.3	140.6	134.3	140.6
October	122.2	125.0	125.3	124.4	126.0	125.9	146.7	80.2	85.0	77.3	139.4	134.1	140.6
November	121.9	124.7	125.5	123.9	125.1	125.9	146.6	79.4	84.8	76.1	139.3	134.3	140.6
December	121.2	124.2	123.9	123.4	124.2	125.8	146.7	76.8	82.9	73.1	138.6	134.3	140.7
1999													
January	121.1	123.9	124.9	123.0	123.6	125.7	147.0	77.6	83.1	74.2	138.3	134.0	140.2
February	120.8	123.5	122.6	122.5	123.2	125.7	147.4	76.7	82.1	73.5	138.0	133.8	140.1
March	121.1	123.4	121.9	122.5	123.2	125.6	147.9	78.6	83.3	75.7	138.5	133.6	140.3
April	121.9	123.2	118.6	122.6	123.2	125.7	147.9	82.6	85.8	80.5	140.5	133.8	140.4
May	122.3	123.7	119.3	123.2	124.2	125.6	148.4	82.9	86.6	80.6	141.6	133.8	140.4
June	122.7	124.0	119.9	123.7	124.8	125.7	149.4	83.2	86.7	81.0	142.2	133.9	140.5
July	123.5	124.6	118.8	124.8	126.1	125.7	150.3	85.5	88.5	83.6	142.1	134.0	140.5
August	124.1	125.0	120.4	125.5	126.2	125.6	150.3	87.7	90.0	86.1	143.7	134.2	140.9
September	124.7	125.4	121.6	126.5	126.2	125.7	149.5	89.4	91.6	87.8	145.8	134.5	140.9
October	124.9	126.0	122.2	127.8	126.5	125.8	149.1	88.6	91.2	86.8	146.3	134.9	141.3
November	125.2	126.0	121.0	127.9	126.7	125.8	149.5	90.2	92.9	88.4	146.4	135.0	141.4
December	125.6	126.0	118.1	128.2	127.2	125.8	150.0	91.5	92.7	90.6	146.4	135.1	141.5

Table 6-2. Producer Price Indexes—*Continued*

(1982=100, seasonally adjusted.)

Year and month	Intermediate materials, supplies, and components—*Continued*			Crude materials for further processing									
	Supplies—*Continued*			Total	Foodstuffs and feedstuffs	Nonfood materials							
	Nonmanufacturing industries					Total	Nonfood materials except fuel			Crude fuel		
	Total	Feeds	Other supplies				Total	Manu-facturing	Construc-tion	Total	Manu-facturing industries	Nonmanu-facturing industries
1970	38.9	49.9	37.6	35.2	45.2	23.8	29.1	28.3	42.1	13.8	11.3	16.6
1971	39.9	50.4	38.9	36.0	46.1	24.7	29.4	28.4	44.1	15.7	12.6	19.3
1972	42.0	56.1	39.8	39.9	51.5	27.0	32.3	31.5	45.0	16.8	13.5	20.6
1973	54.7	97.3	42.7	54.5	72.6	34.3	42.9	42.7	46.2	18.6	14.8	22.9
1974	58.4	90.2	50.5	61.4	76.4	44.1	54.5	55.0	50.0	24.8	19.1	31.8
1975	62.9	84.0	58.9	61.6	77.4	43.7	50.0	49.7	55.9	30.6	24.4	38.0
1976	67.3	95.1	62.0	63.4	76.8	48.2	54.9	54.7	59.6	34.5	29.0	40.5
1977	70.7	99.3	65.2	65.5	77.5	51.7	56.3	56.0	63.1	42.0	37.2	47.4
1978	73.8	95.5	69.7	73.4	87.3	57.5	61.9	61.5	68.7	48.2	43.1	53.8
1979	81.2	106.9	76.3	85.9	100.0	69.6	75.5	75.6	76.6	57.3	53.1	62.0
1980	91.1	110.6	87.5	95.3	104.6	84.6	91.8	92.3	87.9	69.4	66.7	72.5
1981	97.8	111.3	95.4	103.0	103.9	101.8	109.8	110.9	96.8	84.8	83.6	86.2
1982	100.0	100.0	100.0	100.0	100.0	100.0	100.0	100.0	100.0	100.0	100.0	100.0
1983	102.0	109.1	101.0	101.3	101.8	100.7	98.8	98.6	100.1	105.1	105.8	104.4
1984	103.7	104.2	103.7	103.5	104.7	102.2	101.0	100.8	103.1	105.1	105.6	104.6
1985	103.0	86.6	105.3	95.8	94.8	96.9	94.3	93.1	105.7	102.7	102.7	102.5
1986	104.2	90.5	106.2	87.7	93.2	81.6	76.0	72.6	106.5	92.2	91.1	93.6
1987	106.6	94.6	108.3	93.7	96.2	87.9	88.5	84.7	114.8	84.1	82.1	86.3
1988	113.2	115.0	112.7	96.0	106.1	85.5	85.9	81.5	126.5	82.1	80.1	84.5
1989	117.2	114.4	117.5	103.1	111.2	93.4	95.8	91.0	136.9	85.3	83.9	87.0
1990	118.0	102.8	120.2	108.9	113.1	101.5	107.3	102.5	145.2	84.8	82.9	87.0
1991	119.9	101.3	122.5	101.2	105.5	94.6	97.5	92.2	147.5	82.9	82.3	84.1
1992	121.1	103.0	123.7	100.4	105.1	93.5	94.2	87.9	162.1	84.0	83.1	85.2
1993	123.2	105.4	125.8	102.4	108.4	94.7	94.1	85.6	193.6	87.1	85.9	88.6
1994	125.1	105.8	127.9	101.8	106.5	94.8	97.0	88.3	199.1	82.4	81.7	83.6
1995	129.5	103.4	133.2	102.7	105.8	96.8	105.8	97.3	201.7	72.1	72.5	72.9
1996	134.4	133.1	134.6	113.8	121.5	104.5	105.7	97.6	195.7	92.6	90.7	94.3
1997	134.1	129.1	134.8	111.1	112.2	106.4	103.5	95.0	201.4	101.3	98.4	103.3
1998	132.2	100.2	136.2	96.8	103.9	88.4	84.5	76.7	196.0	86.7	84.8	88.5
1999	131.4	89.2	136.5	98.2	98.7	94.3	91.1	83.0	195.7	91.2	90.0	92.9
1996												
January	133.6	126.9	134.6	109.6	116.8	100.9	104.0	95.6	198.9	86.1	85.0	87.5
February	133.6	126.3	134.6	111.6	116.5	104.3	102.7	94.3	198.5	97.1	94.8	99.0
March	133.8	128.2	134.6	110.3	117.2	101.8	104.1	95.9	196.0	88.2	86.8	89.7
April	134.2	132.3	134.5	114.8	120.9	106.5	108.0	100.1	191.2	93.9	91.8	95.6
May	134.9	137.1	134.6	115.3	126.5	103.7	105.9	97.9	193.0	90.1	88.5	91.6
June	134.8	136.9	134.5	112.8	128.1	98.6	102.6	94.6	192.7	82.3	81.5	83.5
July	135.1	138.5	134.6	114.7	129.0	101.1	102.5	94.4	192.9	89.2	87.6	90.8
August	135.2	139.0	134.7	114.8	126.8	102.7	104.4	96.3	194.2	90.2	88.6	91.7
September	135.7	141.9	134.8	112.3	123.4	100.8	107.1	99.0	196.1	80.5	80.0	81.6
October	134.5	133.1	134.7	111.5	119.8	102.0	109.8	101.6	197.4	79.1	78.7	80.2
November	133.8	128.4	134.5	115.3	118.5	109.0	108.0	99.8	198.4	100.4	97.6	102.4
December	133.8	128.3	134.6	122.3	114.8	122.8	109.4	101.2	199.0	134.1	127.6	137.5
1997												
January	133.8	127.2	134.7	127.4	114.8	131.1	113.0	104.7	200.7	149.8	141.6	153.9
February	133.7	127.7	134.6	116.8	112.8	115.1	108.0	99.5	201.5	116.6	112.0	119.3
March	134.2	132.6	134.5	108.0	115.4	99.2	103.8	95.2	201.9	82.1	81.4	83.3
April	134.5	134.3	134.5	108.4	118.2	97.9	103.2	94.7	201.9	79.6	79.2	80.7
May	134.8	136.7	134.5	109.7	115.8	101.7	105.1	96.6	202.7	86.3	85.1	87.7
June	134.5	133.6	134.6	106.5	110.0	100.3	100.6	92.0	202.1	90.4	88.7	92.0
July	134.0	128.7	134.8	106.2	109.9	99.9	101.3	92.7	202.3	88.0	86.5	89.5
August	133.9	127.6	134.8	106.3	108.8	100.8	102.1	93.5	201.9	88.9	87.3	90.5
September	134.5	131.4	135.0	108.0	109.3	103.2	101.0	92.4	201.9	97.1	94.5	99.0
October	133.6	122.3	135.2	112.9	110.4	110.5	102.9	94.5	200.2	112.9	108.7	115.5
November	134.0	123.8	135.4	115.2	111.1	113.6	102.1	93.6	200.0	122.7	117.4	125.7
December	133.9	123.1	135.4	108.4	109.9	103.4	99.2	90.7	200.1	100.9	97.9	103.0
1998												
January	133.1	115.4	135.4	102.6	107.6	95.6	93.3	85.0	201.1	91.1	89.8	92.8
February	132.8	111.1	135.6	100.7	106.8	92.9	92.9	84.6	202.7	85.5	83.4	87.3
March	133.0	106.9	136.3	99.9	107.7	90.9	87.3	79.3	202.7	88.5	86.8	90.2
April	132.5	101.6	136.3	100.8	107.1	92.8	88.2	80.1	203.5	91.8	89.8	93.6
May	132.2	99.5	136.2	99.8	104.8	92.8	88.2	80.1	200.3	91.8	89.9	93.6
June	132.1	99.0	136.2	97.0	104.9	88.1	84.7	76.9	196.1	85.7	83.4	87.4
July	132.5	101.4	136.4	97.2	101.8	90.5	85.1	77.4	192.5	90.7	88.6	92.5
August	132.1	98.0	136.3	93.2	100.8	84.6	79.9	72.4	192.9	84.4	83.4	86.0
September	131.6	92.9	136.3	91.6	100.0	82.4	82.8	75.2	191.8	75.3	74.3	76.7
October	131.4	90.4	136.3	94.2	104.0	84.0	80.6	73.1	190.5	81.9	80.0	83.6
November	131.6	92.9	136.3	93.7	102.6	84.3	77.8	70.5	189.4	86.4	83.8	88.2
December	131.6	93.2	136.3	90.2	97.8	81.8	72.7	65.6	188.5	87.7	84.2	89.6
1999												
January	131.3	92.8	136.0	91.1	103.3	79.4	75.6	68.3	189.5	78.3	77.6	79.8
February	131.0	90.9	135.9	88.9	99.9	78.1	73.6	66.4	191.7	78.1	75.9	79.7
March	130.8	87.6	136.0	89.6	100.2	79.0	77.7	70.3	192.3	74.6	72.3	76.2
April	131.0	88.4	136.2	91.5	96.5	84.8	83.3	75.6	194.1	80.0	77.5	81.7
May	130.9	87.6	136.1	96.7	98.2	92.2	87.4	79.5	195.1	91.6	90.2	93.3
June	131.1	88.0	136.3	96.9	98.2	92.4	88.7	80.7	194.8	90.1	88.4	91.9
July	131.2	87.1	136.5	97.1	94.4	95.4	92.7	84.5	195.2	91.6	90.5	93.3
August	131.4	87.8	136.7	102.1	97.8	101.3	96.0	87.7	196.8	100.5	99.7	102.4
September	131.7	88.8	136.8	106.8	99.1	108.2	102.4	93.7	197.5	107.6	107.6	109.5
October	132.1	90.3	137.1	104.2	99.2	103.9	100.8	92.2	199.2	99.8	99.6	101.6
November	132.2	90.7	137.2	109.6	100.2	112.1	105.2	96.3	200.5	112.6	112.3	114.6
December	132.3	90.3	137.4	104.2	98.2	104.5	109.5	100.4	201.2	89.5	89.2	91.1

Table 6-2. Producer Price Indexes—*Continued*

(1982=100, seasonally adjusted.)

Year and month	Finished energy goods	Finished goods excluding: Foods	Finished goods excluding: Energy	Finished goods excluding: Foods and energy	Finished consumer goods excluding: Energy	Finished consumer goods excluding: Foods and energy	Intermediate materials: Foods and feeds	Intermediate materials: Energy goods	Intermediate materials less: Foods and feeds	Intermediate materials less: Energy	Intermediate materials less: Foods and energy	Crude materials: Energy materials	Crude materials: Less energy	Crude materials: Nonfood materials less energy
1970	...	38.2	...	...	...	...	45.6	...	34.8	...	...	...	...	...
1971	...	39.6	...	...	...	...	46.7	...	36.2	...	...	...	...	...
1972	...	40.4	...	...	...	...	49.5	...	37.7	...	...	...	...	...
1973	...	42.0	...	48.1	...	50.4	70.3	...	40.6	...	44.3	...	...	70.8
1974	26.2	48.8	...	53.6	58.7	55.5	83.6	33.1	50.5	56.2	54.0	27.8	78.4	83.3
1975	30.7	54.7	62.4	59.7	63.9	60.6	81.6	38.7	56.6	61.7	60.2	33.3	75.9	69.3
1976	34.3	58.1	64.8	63.1	65.7	63.7	77.4	41.5	60.0	64.7	63.8	35.3	77.6	80.2
1977	39.7	62.2	68.6	66.9	69.4	67.3	79.6	46.8	64.1	68.5	67.6	40.4	78.1	79.8
1978	42.3	66.7	74.0	71.9	74.9	72.2	84.8	49.1	68.6	73.4	72.5	45.2	87.5	87.8
1979	57.1	74.6	80.7	78.3	81.7	78.8	94.5	61.1	77.4	81.7	80.7	54.9	101.5	106.2
1980	85.2	86.7	88.4	87.1	89.3	87.8	105.5	84.9	89.4	91.4	90.3	73.1	106.5	113.1
1981	101.5	95.6	95.4	94.6	95.7	94.6	104.6	100.5	98.2	98.2	97.7	97.7	105.7	111.7
1982	100.0	100.0	100.0	100.0	100.0	100.0	100.0	100.0	100.0	100.0	100.0	100.0	100.0	100.0
1983	95.2	101.8	102.5	103.0	102.4	103.1	103.6	95.3	100.5	101.7	101.6	98.7	102.6	105.3
1984	91.2	103.2	105.5	105.5	105.6	105.7	105.7	95.5	103.0	104.6	104.7	98.0	106.3	111.7
1985	87.6	104.6	107.2	108.1	107.0	108.4	97.3	92.6	103.0	104.7	105.2	93.3	97.0	104.9
1986	63.0	101.9	109.7	110.6	109.7	111.1	96.2	72.6	99.3	104.5	104.9	71.8	95.4	103.1
1987	61.8	104.0	112.3	113.3	112.5	114.2	99.2	73.0	101.7	107.3	107.8	75.0	100.9	115.7
1988	59.8	106.5	115.8	117.0	116.3	118.5	109.5	70.9	106.9	114.6	115.2	67.7	112.6	133.0
1989	65.7	111.8	121.2	122.1	122.1	124.0	113.8	76.1	111.9	119.5	120.2	75.9	117.7	137.9
1990	75.0	117.4	126.0	126.6	127.2	128.8	113.3	85.5	114.5	120.4	120.9	85.9	118.6	136.3
1991	78.1	120.9	129.1	131.1	130.0	133.7	111.1	85.1	114.6	120.8	121.4	80.4	110.9	128.2
1992	77.8	123.1	131.1	134.2	131.8	137.3	110.7	84.3	114.9	121.3	122.0	78.8	110.7	128.4
1993	78.0	124.4	132.9	135.8	133.5	138.5	112.7	84.6	116.4	123.2	123.8	76.7	116.3	140.2
1994	77.0	125.1	134.2	137.1	134.2	139.0	114.8	83.0	118.7	126.3	127.1	72.1	119.3	156.2
1995	78.1	127.5	136.9	140.0	136.9	141.9	114.8	84.1	125.5	134.0	135.2	69.4	123.5	173.6
1996	83.2	130.5	139.6	142.0	140.1	144.3	128.1	89.8	125.6	133.6	134.0	85.0	130.0	155.8
1997	83.4	130.9	140.2	142.4	141.0	145.1	125.4	89.0	125.7	133.7	134.2	87.3	123.5	156.5
1998	75.1	129.5	141.1	143.7	142.5	147.7	116.2	80.8	123.4	132.4	133.5	68.6	113.6	142.1
1999	78.8	132.3	143.0	146.1	145.2	151.7	111.1	84.3	123.9	131.7	133.1	78.5	107.9	135.2
1996														
January	80.1	129.3	138.5	141.5	138.7	143.6	123.3	86.7	125.7	134.1	134.8	78.1	128.4	162.4
February	79.8	129.2	138.5	141.6	138.8	143.8	123.3	85.8	125.2	133.7	134.4	82.7	128.0	162.0
March	82.2	129.9	138.9	141.6	139.3	143.8	123.6	88.0	125.4	133.5	134.1	80.6	127.6	158.3
April	84.0	130.5	138.8	141.6	139.0	143.7	125.5	90.9	125.7	133.3	133.8	87.3	129.8	156.8
May	83.6	130.7	139.0	142.0	139.3	144.4	130.0	91.4	126.0	133.8	134.0	83.3	134.0	157.6
June	82.6	130.5	139.8	142.2	140.4	144.6	131.1	89.2	125.5	133.8	133.9	77.6	134.4	154.7
July	82.4	130.4	139.8	142.2	140.4	144.6	131.7	88.9	125.1	133.5	133.6	81.8	134.3	152.2
August	82.8	130.7	140.1	142.3	140.7	144.7	132.1	89.5	125.3	133.6	133.6	83.8	132.8	152.5
September	83.1	130.7	140.2	142.2	140.9	144.6	133.3	90.3	125.7	134.0	134.0	81.0	130.7	153.5
October	84.5	131.1	140.6	142.2	141.5	144.7	130.7	91.4	125.7	133.5	133.7	82.7	128.0	153.1
November	85.5	131.4	140.5	142.2	141.4	144.6	126.4	91.3	125.8	133.3	133.7	91.9	127.0	152.9
December	87.3	132.0	140.3	142.3	141.1	144.8	125.6	93.6	126.4	133.4	133.9	109.6	124.5	153.6
1997														
January	88.1	132.4	140.2	142.5	140.9	144.9	125.1	94.8	126.7	133.5	134.1	119.4	125.4	157.0
February	87.5	132.1	140.1	142.4	140.7	144.8	125.1	93.9	126.6	133.6	134.1	98.0	124.5	158.6
March	85.4	131.6	140.6	142.6	141.5	145.1	127.5	91.1	126.0	133.8	134.2	77.1	126.4	158.9
April	82.6	130.8	140.4	142.5	141.2	145.2	127.7	88.6	125.5	133.7	134.1	76.4	127.5	155.8
May	81.5	130.3	140.2	142.4	141.1	145.0	127.9	87.2	125.3	133.8	134.2	80.8	126.3	157.5
June	81.8	130.4	140.0	142.4	140.8	145.1	126.3	87.7	125.4	133.7	134.2	79.2	122.0	156.9
July	81.4	130.1	139.8	142.2	140.5	144.7	124.4	86.6	125.2	133.6	134.2	79.1	121.5	155.3
August	82.4	130.6	139.9	142.3	140.7	145.0	124.0	87.5	125.4	133.7	134.3	79.7	121.2	156.9
September	83.0	131.0	140.2	142.6	141.0	145.4	125.8	87.7	125.5	133.8	134.3	83.2	121.2	155.8
October	82.9	130.9	140.4	142.6	141.5	145.5	122.7	88.2	125.6	133.6	134.3	92.8	121.9	155.7
November	82.5	130.7	140.2	142.4	141.2	145.4	124.5	88.2	125.7	133.8	134.4	97.1	122.4	155.4
December	81.4	130.2	140.0	142.3	140.9	145.2	123.5	86.9	125.4	133.7	134.4	84.3	121.0	153.6
1998														
January	78.9	129.6	139.9	142.4	140.8	145.4	119.1	84.5	124.8	133.3	134.3	74.9	118.6	151.1
February	77.8	129.4	140.1	142.5	141.1	145.7	118.8	83.3	124.5	133.2	134.1	71.7	118.0	150.7
March	76.2	129.5	140.6	143.3	141.8	146.9	117.2	81.7	124.1	133.1	134.1	69.6	118.1	148.7
April	75.7	129.4	140.9	143.4	142.2	147.2	115.9	81.9	124.1	132.9	134.1	72.7	117.3	147.2
May	76.0	129.5	140.6	143.5	141.9	147.4	116.1	82.0	124.0	132.8	133.9	72.7	115.5	146.9
June	75.6	129.4	140.7	143.5	142.1	147.5	115.5	81.0	123.6	132.5	133.6	66.9	115.3	146.1
July	75.3	129.5	141.1	143.7	142.6	147.8	116.2	80.8	123.5	132.5	133.6	70.9	112.4	143.4
August	73.7	129.1	141.1	143.8	142.7	148.0	116.0	79.6	123.2	132.4	133.4	64.5	110.6	139.4
September	73.3	129.3	141.5	144.1	143.1	148.4	114.9	79.2	122.8	132.0	133.1	62.2	109.6	137.6
October	74.3	129.6	141.7	144.2	143.5	148.6	114.6	80.0	122.6	131.6	132.7	65.6	111.4	133.5
November	73.4	129.5	141.7	144.3	143.3	148.7	115.5	79.2	122.3	131.4	132.4	66.9	109.6	130.9
December	71.7	130.1	142.6	145.8	144.6	151.3	114.5	76.5	121.5	131.1	132.2	64.2	105.6	128.9
1999														
January	72.5	130.2	143.0	145.6	145.2	150.9	115.0	77.3	121.5	130.9	131.9	61.0	109.8	129.4
February	71.8	130.0	142.5	145.7	144.5	151.0	112.9	76.5	121.2	130.6	131.8	58.8	107.7	130.9
March	73.2	130.4	142.7	145.6	144.8	151.0	111.4	78.3	121.7	130.7	131.9	60.5	107.6	129.6
April	76.9	131.5	142.4	145.7	144.4	151.0	109.3	82.3	122.6	130.7	132.1	68.1	104.6	128.9
May	77.1	131.6	142.5	145.8	144.5	151.1	109.5	82.6	123.0	131.0	132.4	77.1	106.5	131.1
June	77.0	131.6	142.7	145.8	144.9	151.3	110.1	82.9	123.4	131.4	132.8	77.1	106.7	131.8
July	79.1	132.1	142.5	145.7	144.7	151.3	109.0	85.2	124.3	131.9	133.4	80.4	104.4	133.7
August	81.7	132.9	142.7	145.8	145.0	151.3	110.4	87.3	124.9	132.2	133.7	87.3	107.6	136.2
September	83.4	134.1	143.7	146.7	146.2	152.7	111.5	89.0	125.4	132.5	133.9	95.4	109.2	138.7
October	83.1	134.2	143.8	147.0	146.2	153.0	112.4	88.3	125.6	132.9	134.2	88.7	110.1	142.0
November	84.0	134.4	143.6	146.9	146.1	152.9	111.7	89.9	126.0	133.0	134.4	98.9	111.2	143.4
December	84.6	134.7	143.7	147.0	146.1	153.1	109.6	91.2	126.5	133.1	134.6	87.9	110.7	147.0

Table 6-2. Producer Price Indexes and Purchasing Power of the Dollar—*Continued*

(1982=100, except as noted; not seasonally adjusted.)

Year and month	Finished goods Total	Finished consumer goods Total	Foods	Consumer goods except foods Total	Durable	Nondurable	Capital equipment	Intermediate materials, supplies, and components	Crude materials for further processing	Producer prices for finished goods (1982–1984 =$1.00) [1]	Consumer prices (1982–1984 =$1.00)
1970	39.3	39.1	43.8	37.4	47.2	32.5	40.1	35.4	35.2	2.590	2.577
1971	40.5	40.2	44.5	38.7	48.9	33.5	41.7	36.8	36.0	2.513	2.469
1972	41.8	41.5	46.9	39.4	50.0	34.1	42.8	38.2	39.9	2.435	2.392
1973	45.6	46.0	56.5	41.2	50.9	36.1	44.2	42.4	54.5	2.232	2.252
1974	52.6	53.1	64.4	48.2	55.5	44.0	50.5	52.5	61.4	1.935	2.028
1975	58.2	58.2	69.8	53.2	61.0	48.9	58.2	58.0	61.6	1.749	1.859
1976	60.8	60.4	69.6	56.5	63.7	52.4	62.1	60.9	63.4	1.674	1.757
1977	64.7	64.3	73.3	60.6	67.4	56.8	66.1	64.9	65.5	1.573	1.650
1978	69.8	69.4	79.9	64.9	73.6	60.0	71.3	69.5	73.4	1.458	1.534
1979	77.6	77.5	87.3	73.5	80.8	69.3	77.5	78.4	85.9	1.311	1.377
1980	88.0	88.6	92.4	87.1	91.0	85.1	85.8	90.3	95.3	1.156	1.214
1981	96.1	96.6	97.8	96.1	96.4	95.8	94.6	98.6	103.0	1.059	1.100
1982	100.0	100.0	100.0	100.0	100.0	100.0	100.0	100.0	100.0	1.018	1.036
1983	101.6	101.3	101.0	101.2	102.8	100.5	102.8	100.6	101.3	1.002	1.004
1984	103.7	103.3	105.4	102.2	104.5	101.1	105.2	103.1	103.5	0.981	0.962
1985	104.7	103.8	104.6	103.3	106.5	101.7	107.5	102.7	95.8	0.972	0.929
1986	103.2	101.4	107.3	98.5	108.9	93.3	109.7	99.1	87.7	0.986	0.912
1987	105.4	103.6	109.5	100.7	111.5	94.9	111.7	101.5	93.7	0.966	0.880
1988	108.0	106.2	112.6	103.1	113.8	97.3	114.3	107.1	96.0	0.942	0.845
1989	113.6	112.1	118.7	108.9	117.6	103.8	118.8	112.0	103.1	0.896	0.806
1990	119.2	118.2	124.4	115.3	120.4	111.5	122.9	114.5	108.9	0.854	0.765
1991	121.7	120.5	124.1	118.7	123.9	115.0	126.7	114.4	101.2	0.836	0.734
1992	123.2	121.7	123.3	120.8	125.7	117.3	129.1	114.7	100.4	0.826	0.713
1993	124.7	123.0	125.7	121.7	128.0	117.6	131.4	116.2	102.4	0.816	0.692
1994	125.5	123.3	126.8	121.6	130.9	116.2	134.1	118.5	101.8	0.811	0.675
1995	127.9	125.6	129.0	124.0	132.7	118.8	136.7	124.9	102.7	0.796	0.656
1996	131.3	129.5	133.6	127.6	134.2	123.3	138.3	125.7	113.8	0.775	0.637
1997	131.8	130.2	134.5	128.2	133.7	124.3	138.2	125.6	111.1	0.772	0.623
1998	130.7	128.9	134.3	126.4	132.9	122.2	137.6	123.0	96.8	0.779	0.614
1999	133.0	132.0	135.1	130.5	133.0	127.9	137.6	123.2	98.2	0.765	0.600
1996											
January	129.4	127.1	130.7	125.4	134.2	120.1	138.3	125.2	108.8	0.785	0.648
February	129.4	127.0	130.7	125.3	134.3	119.9	138.4	124.7	111.1	0.785	0.645
March	130.1	128.0	132.0	126.1	134.3	121.2	138.3	124.9	110.0	0.780	0.642
April	130.6	128.7	131.2	127.4	134.0	123.1	138.3	125.4	114.4	0.778	0.640
May	131.1	129.3	131.5	128.2	134.2	124.1	138.2	126.2	115.9	0.777	0.639
June	131.7	130.0	133.6	128.3	134.4	124.2	138.2	126.2	113.3	0.775	0.638
July	131.5	129.9	133.9	128.0	133.8	124.0	138.1	125.9	115.6	0.775	0.637
August	131.9	130.4	135.3	128.1	133.7	124.2	138.2	126.1	116.0	0.773	0.636
September	131.8	130.4	135.6	128.0	132.4	124.6	137.3	126.7	112.9	0.772	0.634
October	132.7	131.2	136.6	128.8	135.2	124.5	138.9	126.0	111.3	0.769	0.632
November	132.6	131.1	136.1	128.8	135.2	124.5	138.7	125.7	114.8	0.767	0.631
December	132.7	131.2	135.5	129.2	135.0	125.2	138.7	126.0	121.6	0.766	0.631
1997											
January	132.6	131.0	134.1	129.5	134.9	125.7	139.0	126.3	126.3	0.766	0.628
February	132.2	130.6	133.8	129.0	135.0	124.9	138.9	126.1	116.1	0.767	0.626
March	132.1	130.4	135.2	128.2	135.0	123.8	138.8	125.6	107.6	0.767	0.625
April	131.6	129.8	134.3	127.7	134.5	123.2	138.6	125.3	107.9	0.772	0.624
May	131.6	130.0	135.2	127.6	133.6	123.5	138.1	125.4	110.4	0.775	0.625
June	131.6	130.0	134.0	128.1	133.4	124.4	138.1	125.8	107.1	0.775	0.624
July	131.3	129.7	134.0	127.6	132.4	124.1	137.8	125.5	107.1	0.777	0.623
August	131.7	130.3	134.9	128.1	132.3	124.8	137.7	125.8	107.5	0.775	0.622
September	131.8	130.5	134.7	128.6	131.4	125.8	137.2	126.0	108.5	0.772	0.620
October	132.3	130.7	135.1	128.7	134.7	124.6	138.5	125.5	112.7	0.772	0.619
November	131.7	130.1	134.6	128.0	134.1	123.9	138.3	125.5	114.7	0.773	0.619
December	131.1	129.4	134.4	127.2	133.4	123.0	137.9	125.0	107.8	0.776	0.620
1998											
January	130.3	128.3	133.1	126.1	133.4	121.5	137.9	124.2	101.7	0.779	0.619
February	130.2	128.2	133.6	125.6	133.4	120.8	137.9	123.8	100.1	0.780	0.618
March	130.1	128.1	133.4	125.6	133.2	120.9	137.9	123.3	99.4	0.779	0.617
April	130.4	128.5	133.8	126.0	133.0	121.5	137.7	123.3	100.3	0.779	0.615
May	130.6	128.9	133.6	126.7	132.3	122.8	137.3	123.5	100.5	0.780	0.614
June	130.7	129.1	133.8	127.0	131.8	123.4	137.2	123.5	97.6	0.780	0.614
July	131.0	129.4	134.7	127.0	132.0	123.3	137.1	123.5	98.1	0.778	0.613
August	130.7	129.2	135.2	126.4	131.5	122.7	136.8	123.2	94.3	0.780	0.612
September	130.6	129.1	135.4	126.3	131.0	122.8	136.7	122.9	92.1	0.779	0.611
October	131.4	129.8	135.5	127.1	134.4	122.5	138.1	122.3	94.0	0.777	0.610
November	130.9	129.0	134.9	126.4	134.4	121.4	138.2	121.8	93.6	0.778	0.610
December	131.1	129.4	134.5	127.1	133.8	122.7	137.9	120.9	89.8	0.776	0.610
1999											
January	131.4	129.7	135.6	127.1	133.3	122.9	137.8	120.9	90.1	0.773	0.608
February	130.8	129.0	134.1	126.6	133.5	122.2	138.0	120.4	88.2	0.776	0.608
March	131.1	129.4	134.7	127.0	133.1	122.9	137.7	120.7	89.0	0.773	0.606
April	131.9	130.4	133.4	129.0	133.1	125.7	137.8	121.6	91.1	0.770	0.602
May	132.4	131.2	134.5	129.6	132.8	126.6	137.6	122.2	97.4	0.769	0.602
June	132.7	131.7	135.1	130.0	132.3	127.5	137.2	123.0	97.4	0.769	0.602
July	132.9	132.1	134.6	130.8	131.7	128.9	137.0	123.9	97.9	0.767	0.600
August	133.7	133.2	135.9	131.9	131.6	130.4	136.9	124.6	103.1	0.762	0.598
September	134.7	134.6	136.7	133.5	131.2	132.8	136.7	125.3	107.3	0.756	0.596
October	135.1	134.5	135.8	133.7	134.9	131.5	138.5	125.0	104.0	0.756	0.594
November	134.9	134.3	135.4	133.6	134.6	131.6	138.3	125.2	109.2	0.756	0.594
December	134.9	134.3	135.6	133.6	134.4	131.7	138.3	125.4	103.5	0.754	0.594

1. Calculations by the editors.

Table 6-3. Prices Received and Paid by Farmers

(1990–1992=100, not seasonally adjusted.)

Year and month	All farm prod-ucts	Prices received by farmers														Food com-mod-ities	Prices paid by farmers [1]		Ratio of prices re-ceived to prices paid
		Crops									Livestock and products								
		Total	Food grains	Feed grains and hay	Cotton	Tobac-co	Oil-bearing crops	Fruit and nuts	Com-mercial vege-tables	Pota-toes and dry beans	Total	Meat animals	Dairy prod-ucts	Poultry and eggs			All items	Pro-duction items	
1975	73	88	128	112	68	56	93	46	66	78	62	56	67	83	69	47	55	158
1976	75	87	105	105	99	63	97	45	67	75	64	57	74	83	71	50	59	150
1977	73	83	83	87	100	66	119	54	70	71	64	56	74	81	71	53	61	138
1978	83	89	102	88	91	72	110	72	74	73	78	75	81	87	83	58	67	144
1979	94	98	121	100	96	75	121	77	79	65	90	90	92	90	95	66	76	144
1980	98	107	136	115	114	80	118	73	80	93	89	84	100	91	96	75	85	131
1981	100	111	138	122	111	94	122	76	99	126	89	82	105	94	97	82	92	121
1982	94	98	119	103	92	99	103	78	92	88	90	86	104	89	93	86	94	109
1983	98	108	120	125	104	96	118	71	96	89	88	81	104	95	95	86	92	113
1984	101	111	117	127	108	98	125	85	97	111	91	83	103	109	98	89	94	114
1985	91	98	108	105	93	92	96	84	95	87	86	78	97	97	89	86	91	106
1986	87	87	89	84	91	82	89	83	92	81	88	80	96	105	87	85	86	103
1987	89	86	83	72	98	83	90	93	105	89	91	90	96	87	91	87	87	102
1988	99	104	113	102	95	86	126	96	104	88	93	91	93	98	99	91	90	108
1989	104	109	127	109	98	96	118	99	103	131	100	94	104	111	104	96	95	108
1990	104	103	100	105	107	97	105	97	102	133	105	105	105	105	104	99	99	105
1991	100	101	94	101	108	102	99	112	100	99	99	101	94	99	99	100	100	99
1992	98	101	113	98	88	101	100	99	111	88	97	96	100	97	99	101	101	97
1993	101	102	105	99	89	101	108	93	116	107	100	100	98	105	102	104	104	97
1994	100	105	119	106	109	101	110	90	109	110	95	90	99	106	98	106	106	94
1995	102	112	134	112	127	103	104	99	121	107	92	85	98	107	99	109	108	93
1996	112	127	157	146	122	105	128	118	111	114	99	87	114	120	108	115	115	98
1997	107	115	128	117	112	104	131	109	118	90	98	92	102	113	105	118	119	91
1998	101	106	103	100	107	104	107	111	121	99	97	79	119	117	101	115	113	88
1999	96	96	91	86	85	102	83	115	108	101	95	83	110	111	96	115	112	83
1996																		
January	108	121	158	133	126	109	120	95	94	111	94	82	108	117	102	113	113	96
February	106	123	159	140	125	118	125	95	111	116	93	82	106	113	101	113	113	94
March	109	129	161	146	127	100	125	104	147	125	94	83	106	112	105	114	114	96
April	108	129	168	159	130	92	132	100	122	132	93	81	106	112	102	115	115	94
May	112	131	184	169	127	. . .	137	114	103	138	97	84	109	116	106	116	116	97
June	118	140	175	166	127	. . .	133	134	116	140	100	85	113	122	113	115	116	103
July	119	137	159	170	121	92	136	130	99	138	102	89	118	122	113	116	117	103
August	117	133	153	166	119	100	138	131	116	103	104	91	122	123	113	116	117	101
September	116	126	147	147	118	109	125	144	102	95	105	92	126	123	113	116	117	100
October	112	119	140	124	118	110	119	140	109	91	103	91	126	121	111	115	115	97
November	110	117	137	116	115	111	120	125	112	89	102	90	116	126	109	115	115	96
December	108	113	137	115	114	111	124	103	96	86	103	90	109	128	106	115	115	94
1997																		
January	107	115	137	118	112	111	127	93	111	84	98	90	103	119	105	117	117	91
February	105	113	134	118	112	110	131	90	105	85	98	90	103	116	102	117	117	90
March	108	118	136	123	114	111	142	97	118	86	99	92	104	113	105	118	118	92
April	106	116	140	127	112	. . .	146	89	113	85	99	94	101	111	104	118	119	90
May	107	117	139	124	113	. . .	149	106	106	94	100	97	97	112	106	119	120	90
June	107	118	120	118	111	. . .	145	127	112	85	97	94	93	111	106	118	119	91
July	107	114	111	112	111	91	134	127	112	99	99	95	93	118	106	118	119	91
August	107	116	122	114	111	92	128	126	122	107	99	94	97	117	107	118	119	91
September	107	114	126	113	115	101	113	131	119	87	99	92	100	116	106	119	120	90
October	107	115	124	112	115	103	112	121	145	85	97	89	108	108	106	118	118	91
November	106	113	123	112	112	106	120	109	122	90	98	88	113	112	105	119	119	89
December	105	112	119	112	105	110	120	92	136	94	98	87	113	107	103	119	119	88
1998																		
January	103	109	116	113	101	110	119	81	120	97	95	84	113	106	100	117	116	88
February	101	109	117	113	103	110	117	87	114	104	94	82	114	104	98	117	116	86
March	102	111	118	113	105	104	114	94	123	109	95	82	111	108	100	116	114	88
April	104	115	114	109	105	97	112	100	153	108	95	84	107	109	103	116	114	90
May	103	112	109	106	105	. . .	112	111	126	111	96	87	102	108	102	116	114	89
June	102	107	96	104	115	. . .	111	121	107	106	98	86	109	116	101	115	113	89
July	102	107	89	101	112	94	111	131	119	102	97	80	109	123	101	115	113	89
August	101	103	85	91	109	93	98	136	112	95	99	78	119	131	102	114	112	89
September	100	101	87	86	109	103	96	130	111	89	98	73	129	128	100	113	110	88
October	99	100	100	85	109	107	95	127	131	82	98	75	136	126	101	114	110	87
November	99	101	105	86	107	109	101	113	113	89	97	72	137	124	100	114	111	87
December	99	100	101	89	100	110	102	95	117	94	97	66	139	119	99	114	110	87
1999																		
January	97	97	102	91	96	111	96	92	105	97	96	75	133	115	97	115	111	84
February	96	98	101	91	92	113	88	96	111	98	94	77	116	110	95	115	111	83
March	97	99	99	92	91	104	83	98	119	103	95	79	116	109	96	115	111	84
April	96	103	96	92	92	86	83	106	129	108	91	81	96	107	96	115	111	83
May	98	103	90	93	91	. . .	81	119	118	106	93	83	97	111	98	115	111	85
June	98	100	87	91	90	. . .	80	134	110	110	95	84	100	114	98	115	111	85
July	95	95	78	84	89	86	75	135	104	123	95	81	106	113	96	115	111	83
August	99	100	87	85	87	94	78	138	105	107	98	85	116	112	100	115	111	86
September	96	95	88	81	76	101	83	129	104	90	98	84	120	109	98	115	112	83
October	91	88	87	76	76	105	80	131	97	84	96	87	114	104	93	116	113	78
November	93	89	89	77	74	105	82	115	99	94	98	87	110	116	97	116	113	80
December	91	88	85	81	71	110	82	91	97	93	95	88	93	110	92	117	114	78

1. Includes commodities, services, taxes, and wage rates.

CHAPTER 7: EMPLOYMENT, COSTS, PRODUCTIVITY, AND PROFITS

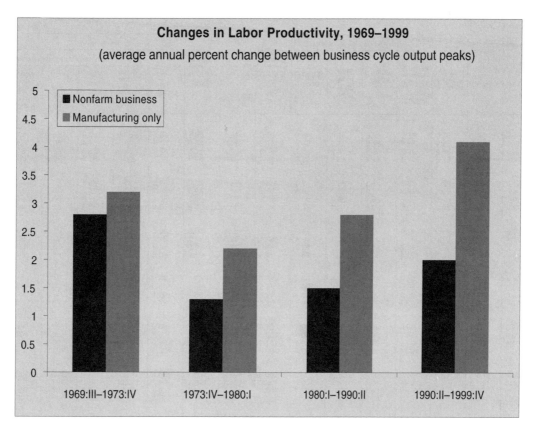

- For all nonfarm business, from 1990 to 1999, annual average gains in labor productivity exceeded the annual average gains achieved from 1973 to 1990. The annual average gains from 1990 to 1999, however, were less than the strong gains of 1969 to 1973. In manufacturing, however, 1990s labor productivity gains have been even more rapid than those gains from 1969 to 1973.

- Productivity gains in 1999 were especially strong—2.9 percent for all nonfarm business and 6.2 percent for manufacturing.

- Employment cost increases remained moderate in 1999, with the index for total compensation for all civilian workers rising 3.4 percent from the fourth quarter of 1998 to the fourth quarter of 1999.

- Productivity gains offset much of the rise in compensation per hour, and unit labor costs for nonfarm business were up only 1.9 percent, consistent with the continued low rate of price inflation.

- After-tax corporate profits in manufacturing reached a record high of $260,995 million in 1999, surpassing the previous high of 1997 and maintaining the string of high-profit years that began in 1994.

Table 7-1. Employment Cost Indexes—Total Compensation

(June 1989 [not seasonally adjusted] =100, indexes are seasonally adjusted, except as noted.)

Year and quarter	All civilian workers [1]	State and local government workers	All private industry workers	Private industry workers excluding sales occupations [2]	By occupational group			By industry division									
					White-collar occupations	Blue-collar occupations	Service occupations	Goods-producing industries			Service-producing industries						Non-manufacturing industries
								Total	Construction	Manufacturing	Total	Transportation and utilities	Wholesale trade	Retail trade	Finance, insurance, and real estate	Services	
1985																	
1st quarter	84.5	81.2	85.0	85.2	83.6	86.6	85.9	86.6	86.2	86.1	83.7	87.5	83.0	85.6	83.1	81.2	84.2
2nd quarter	85.4	82.2	85.9	85.8	84.6	87.3	86.7	87.2	86.9	86.8	84.8	88.3	84.4	86.5	83.0	82.4	85.1
3rd quarter	86.4	83.5	86.9	86.9	85.6	88.2	88.1	87.9	87.5	87.5	86.0	89.6	85.2	88.0	84.6	83.6	86.3
4th quarter	87.1	84.6	87.5	87.3	86.6	88.6	88.5	88.4	88.4	88.0	86.7	90.2	85.9	89.0	85.9	84.1	87.1
1986																	
1st quarter	87.9	85.6	88.3	88.3	87.3	89.3	89.0	89.2	88.6	88.7	87.5	91.1	86.5	89.3	86.7	85.1	87.8
2nd quarter	88.5	86.8	89.0	88.9	88.2	89.8	89.8	90.1	89.7	89.7	88.2	91.3	87.0	89.7	87.4	86.1	88.5
3rd quarter	89.1	87.8	89.6	89.6	88.7	90.5	90.5	90.6	90.5	90.2	88.7	91.8	87.8	90.4	87.9	86.6	89.1
4th quarter	89.9	88.9	90.2	90.2	89.6	91.1	91.2	91.2	90.9	90.9	89.5	92.2	88.8	91.0	88.6	87.8	89.9
1987																	
1st quarter	90.6	89.8	90.9	91.0	90.5	91.2	91.9	91.5	91.6	90.9	90.5	92.9	89.8	91.5	90.9	88.9	90.9
2nd quarter	91.4	90.9	91.6	91.7	91.1	92.1	92.6	92.1	92.5	91.7	91.2	93.8	90.8	92.3	90.0	89.8	91.5
3rd quarter	92.2	91.5	92.5	92.7	92.1	92.9	92.9	93.0	93.3	92.6	92.0	94.3	91.6	92.8	90.2	91.1	92.3
4th quarter	93.1	92.8	93.3	93.4	92.9	93.9	93.4	94.0	94.2	93.7	92.8	95.0	92.3	93.2	90.4	92.3	93.1
1988																	
1st quarter	94.4	94.2	94.5	94.9	93.8	95.3	94.5	95.5	95.3	95.1	93.8	95.8	93.2	94.7	91.5	93.5	94.1
2nd quarter	95.5	95.3	95.7	95.9	95.0	96.3	95.7	96.5	96.2	96.1	95.0	96.6	94.4	96.1	92.8	94.8	95.4
3rd quarter	96.5	96.5	96.6	96.9	96.1	97.1	97.1	97.2	97.1	96.9	96.1	97.4	95.5	97.1	92.9	96.2	96.4
4th quarter	97.7	98.1	97.8	97.7	97.5	98.1	98.2	98.1	98.2	97.8	97.6	97.8	96.3	98.6	96.2	97.6	97.7
1989																	
1st quarter	98.8	99.3	98.9	99.0	98.8	98.7	99.1	98.9	99.1	98.7	98.9	98.7	98.7	99.3	98.3	98.9	98.8
2nd quarter	100.0	100.8	100.0	100.0	99.9	99.9	100.1	100.0	99.8	99.9	100.0	99.8	99.8	99.8	100.0	100.3	99.9
3rd quarter	101.4	102.7	101.2	101.2	101.3	101.1	101.1	101.2	101.1	101.2	101.2	100.6	102.5	100.9	100.4	101.6	101.2
4th quarter	102.7	104.2	102.4	102.1	102.6	102.1	102.5	102.3	102.6	102.4	102.5	101.5	104.7	101.8	101.4	103.0	102.5
1990																	
1st quarter	104.0	105.7	103.8	103.9	104.0	103.4	103.8	103.8	103.2	103.8	103.8	103.0	105.0	103.2	102.6	104.9	103.8
2nd quarter	105.4	107.3	105.1	105.1	105.4	104.6	105.0	105.1	104.1	105.1	105.1	103.1	105.2	104.6	104.4	106.7	105.0
3rd quarter	106.6	108.8	106.2	106.3	106.6	105.6	105.7	106.2	105.0	106.4	106.2	104.1	105.8	105.3	105.4	107.9	106.1
4th quarter	107.7	110.3	107.2	107.1	107.6	106.6	107.4	107.2	105.8	107.5	107.2	105.4	106.6	106.3	105.5	109.4	107.1
1991																	
1st quarter	108.9	111.7	108.4	108.6	108.9	107.8	108.2	108.4	107.5	108.4	108.4	105.9	107.9	107.5	108.3	110.7	108.4
2nd quarter	110.2	112.7	109.7	109.8	110.2	108.9	110.0	109.7	108.4	109.9	109.7	107.6	109.3	108.7	109.5	111.7	109.7
3rd quarter	111.2	113.3	110.9	111.1	111.4	110.2	111.5	110.8	109.1	111.2	110.9	108.9	110.7	109.9	109.7	113.0	110.8
4th quarter	112.2	114.2	111.9	112.0	112.4	111.2	112.5	112.0	110.1	112.4	111.8	110.0	111.3	110.7	110.0	114.1	111.7
1992																	
1st quarter	113.3	115.2	113.0	113.3	113.3	112.4	113.5	113.3	110.7	113.8	112.7	111.0	112.6	111.0	111.7	115.2	112.6
2nd quarter	114.1	116.4	113.7	114.1	114.1	113.3	114.3	114.1	111.6	114.7	113.5	111.8	113.2	111.9	110.8	116.6	113.5
3rd quarter	115.0	117.2	114.7	115.0	115.0	114.3	115.4	115.2	112.9	115.7	114.3	112.8	113.2	112.7	111.1	117.7	114.3
4th quarter	116.1	118.5	115.7	115.9	116.1	115.2	115.9	116.2	114.0	116.8	115.3	113.8	114.5	113.6	111.3	119.0	115.4
1993																	
1st quarter	117.2	119.3	116.9	117.5	117.3	116.5	117.2	117.8	115.1	118.5	116.3	114.6	115.4	114.8	112.6	120.0	116.2
2nd quarter	118.2	120.1	117.9	118.5	118.2	117.6	118.1	118.8	115.8	119.6	117.2	116.0	116.1	115.4	113.1	121.0	117.1
3rd quarter	119.2	120.8	118.9	119.5	119.3	118.6	118.9	119.7	116.5	120.6	118.3	116.7	116.6	116.0	115.7	122.2	118.3
4th quarter	120.1	121.7	119.9	120.2	120.4	119.5	119.5	120.6	116.8	121.6	119.4	117.8	118.0	116.9	116.4	123.2	119.2
1994																	
1st quarter	121.2	122.7	120.9	121.4	121.4	120.3	120.5	121.8	118.8	122.4	120.3	119.0	118.0	117.7	117.7	124.3	120.2
2nd quarter	122.3	123.6	121.9	122.3	122.4	121.1	121.0	123.0	120.0	123.4	121.2	119.8	119.4	119.0	117.7	125.0	121.2
3rd quarter	123.3	124.6	123.0	123.4	123.4	122.2	121.7	123.9	121.1	124.5	122.2	121.3	120.6	120.1	118.5	125.8	122.1
4th quarter	124.0	125.3	123.7	123.9	124.3	122.8	122.8	124.6	121.1	125.3	123.0	122.4	121.7	120.4	118.9	126.7	122.8
1995																	
1st quarter	124.9	126.4	124.5	125.0	125.2	123.5	123.3	125.5	121.3	126.1	124.0	123.8	123.3	121.0	120.2	127.4	123.6
2nd quarter	125.8	127.4	125.4	125.7	126.2	124.3	123.9	126.2	121.8	126.8	125.0	124.8	124.6	121.7	121.8	128.3	124.6
3rd quarter	126.5	128.3	126.2	126.5	126.9	125.0	124.5	126.9	122.8	127.3	125.8	125.9	126.1	122.3	122.7	128.8	125.4
4th quarter	127.3	129.1	126.9	127.1	127.8	125.8	125.0	127.8	123.7	128.4	126.5	126.8	127.2	123.0	123.1	129.5	126.1
1996																	
1st quarter	128.3	129.9	127.9	128.3	128.9	126.6	125.6	128.5	124.5	129.1	127.6	127.7	127.6	124.6	124.5	130.6	127.2
2nd quarter	129.3	130.8	128.9	129.2	130.0	127.5	126.3	129.6	125.1	130.3	128.6	128.5	129.1	124.7	126.3	131.8	128.2
3rd quarter	130.1	131.5	129.8	130.2	131.0	128.0	127.1	130.4	125.6	131.2	129.5	129.3	129.9	125.9	126.7	132.6	129.0
4th quarter	131.0	132.5	130.6	130.8	131.8	129.2	128.6	131.2	126.7	132.1	130.4	130.6	131.0	127.7	126.0	133.5	130.0
1997																	
1st quarter	131.9	133.2	131.6	131.9	133.1	129.7	129.5	131.7	127.4	132.5	131.6	131.1	133.0	128.6	128.6	134.6	131.1
2nd quarter	132.9	133.9	132.7	133.0	134.1	130.7	130.6	132.9	128.5	133.6	132.6	131.8	133.6	129.6	129.4	135.8	132.1
3rd quarter	133.9	134.6	133.7	134.1	135.1	131.6	132.7	133.8	129.4	134.5	133.7	132.9	134.6	130.8	130.5	136.9	133.2
4th quarter	135.2	135.4	135.1	135.2	136.8	132.4	133.8	134.3	130.0	135.3	135.5	134.3	135.2	132.0	134.5	138.6	134.8
1998																	
1st quarter	136.2	136.5	136.2	136.4	138.1	133.2	134.9	135.2	130.8	136.2	136.6	135.6	137.8	133.2	136.7	139.3	136.0
2nd quarter	137.4	137.5	137.3	137.5	139.4	134.2	135.6	136.3	132.5	137.1	137.8	137.2	138.5	134.2	138.4	140.4	137.2
3rd quarter	138.7	138.6	138.8	138.8	141.0	135.1	136.9	137.2	133.1	138.2	139.5	138.4	140.8	135.6	141.0	141.7	138.8
4th quarter	139.6	139.5	139.7	139.4	142.0	136.0	137.7	137.9	134.6	138.8	140.5	139.4	142.9	135.9	142.5	142.8	139.8
1999																	
1st quarter	140.3	140.4	140.3	140.5	142.4	137.0	139.1	139.0	135.8	139.8	140.9	139.6	142.8	137.0	141.5	143.5	140.4
2nd quarter	141.8	141.6	141.8	141.9	144.2	138.1	140.2	139.9	136.7	140.8	142.7	141.0	144.5	138.9	145.8	144.7	142.0
3rd quarter	143.0	142.7	143.1	143.2	145.5	139.3	140.6	141.1	137.6	142.0	144.0	141.7	146.3	139.6	147.6	146.0	143.2
4th quarter	144.4	144.2	144.5	144.5	146.9	140.6	142.2	142.6	139.0	143.6	145.4	142.4	148.6	141.1	148.3	147.5	144.6

1. Includes private industry and state and local government workers. Federal government workers are not included.
2. Not seasonally adjusted.

Table 7-2. Employment Cost Indexes—Wages and Salaries

(June 1989 [not seasonally adjusted] =100, indexes are seasonally adjusted, except as noted.)

Year and quarter	All civilian workers [1]	State and local government workers	Private industry workers															
					By occupational group				By industry division								
									Goods-producing industries			Service-producing industries						
			All private industry workers	Private industry workers excluding sales occupations [2]	White-collar occupations	Blue-collar occupations	Service occupations	Total	Construction	Manufacturing	Total	Transportation and utilities	Wholesale trade	Retail trade	Finance, Insurance, and real estate [2]	Services	Non-manufacturing industry
1985																	
1st quarter	85.3	82.1	85.9	86.0	84.3	87.7	87.5	87.4	88.0	87.2	84.6	89.9	83.1	86.0	84.0	82.1	85.2
2nd quarter	86.3	83.1	86.9	86.9	85.2	88.6	88.5	88.2	88.5	88.1	85.7	90.8	84.7	86.9	83.8	83.4	86.1
3rd quarter	87.3	84.4	87.9	88.1	86.3	89.7	89.8	89.0	88.9	88.8	87.0	92.1	85.7	88.5	85.5	84.6	87.4
4th quarter	88.0	85.5	88.5	88.4	87.2	89.9	89.9	89.4	89.7	89.2	87.8	92.7	86.3	89.6	87.1	85.1	88.1
1986																	
1st quarter	88.9	86.6	89.4	89.3	88.0	90.7	90.5	90.3	90.0	90.3	88.5	93.3	87.1	90.1	87.2	86.2	88.7
2nd quarter	89.6	87.7	90.0	90.0	89.0	91.2	91.0	91.2	90.9	91.1	89.2	93.6	87.8	90.5	88.2	87.2	89.4
3rd quarter	90.2	89.0	90.5	90.6	89.5	91.9	91.6	91.7	91.5	91.6	89.7	94.0	88.5	91.1	88.8	87.3	90.0
4th quarter	91.0	90.1	91.2	91.2	90.2	92.4	92.3	92.2	91.9	92.1	90.4	94.4	89.5	91.5	89.5	88.5	90.7
1987																	
1st quarter	91.9	91.0	92.0	92.1	91.4	92.8	93.1	92.8	92.6	92.7	91.5	94.7	90.7	92.2	91.9	89.8	91.7
2nd quarter	92.5	92.1	92.6	92.7	91.8	93.5	93.8	93.3	93.1	93.3	92.1	95.5	91.8	93.0	90.6	90.9	92.3
3rd quarter	93.3	92.6	93.5	93.8	92.9	94.3	94.1	94.3	94.0	94.2	92.9	96.0	92.4	93.6	90.8	92.2	93.2
4th quarter	94.1	93.9	94.2	94.5	93.5	95.1	94.5	95.1	94.9	95.2	93.5	96.4	93.1	93.9	90.6	93.2	93.8
1988																	
1st quarter	95.0	95.0	95.0	95.4	94.4	95.9	95.4	96.0	95.8	96.0	94.3	97.1	93.5	95.1	91.5	94.1	94.5
2nd quarter	96.1	96.0	96.1	96.3	95.5	96.8	96.5	96.9	96.9	96.8	95.5	97.8	94.8	96.3	92.9	95.2	95.8
3rd quarter	97.0	97.0	96.9	97.3	96.6	97.4	97.7	97.4	97.6	97.3	96.5	98.5	96.1	97.5	92.9	96.6	96.8
4th quarter	98.1	98.5	98.0	98.0	97.9	98.1	98.6	98.1	98.4	98.1	97.9	98.8	96.6	98.7	96.3	97.9	97.9
1989																	
1st quarter	99.2	99.5	99.1	99.1	99.0	99.0	99.4	99.0	99.3	99.0	99.2	99.5	99.2	99.4	98.3	99.0	99.1
2nd quarter	100.2	100.8	100.0	100.0	99.9	100.0	100.1	100.0	99.9	100.0	100.0	99.9	99.7	99.7	100.0	100.3	100.0
3rd quarter	101.4	102.4	101.1	101.1	101.3	101.0	100.9	100.9	101.0	100.9	101.2	100.6	102.8	100.9	100.6	101.3	101.3
4th quarter	102.5	103.7	102.2	101.9	102.5	101.7	102.2	101.9	101.8	101.9	102.3	101.4	105.3	101.8	101.3	102.5	102.3
1990																	
1st quarter	103.6	105.1	103.2	103.2	103.6	102.8	103.1	103.1	102.2	103.3	103.3	102.6	104.9	103.0	101.8	104.1	103.2
2nd quarter	104.8	106.5	104.4	104.4	104.8	103.9	104.3	104.2	102.8	104.5	104.6	103.1	105.0	104.1	103.5	106.0	104.5
3rd quarter	105.8	107.9	105.4	105.4	105.9	104.7	104.8	105.1	103.3	105.4	105.6	104.0	105.3	104.8	104.9	106.9	105.3
4th quarter	106.8	109.3	106.2	106.2	106.7	105.4	106.4	105.8	103.9	106.2	106.4	104.8	106.3	105.5	104.8	108.4	106.2
1991																	
1st quarter	107.9	110.6	107.3	107.4	107.9	106.6	106.9	107.0	105.3	107.4	107.5	105.4	107.6	106.6	107.0	109.4	107.3
2nd quarter	109.0	111.6	108.4	108.4	109.0	107.4	108.4	108.0	105.8	108.4	108.7	106.5	109.0	107.7	108.1	110.2	108.4
3rd quarter	109.8	112.2	109.2	109.4	110.0	108.2	109.7	108.8	106.1	109.3	109.6	107.6	110.3	108.7	108.0	111.3	109.2
4th quarter	110.6	113.1	110.1	110.2	110.8	108.9	110.6	109.7	106.9	110.3	110.3	108.9	110.3	109.4	108.4	112.2	109.9
1992																	
1st quarter	111.5	113.8	111.0	111.1	111.7	109.8	111.2	110.7	107.4	111.5	111.1	109.7	111.7	109.7	109.5	113.1	110.7
2nd quarter	112.2	114.9	111.6	111.8	112.2	110.6	111.7	111.4	107.8	112.2	111.7	110.5	112.2	110.3	108.2	114.2	111.3
3rd quarter	112.7	115.3	112.1	112.5	112.8	111.3	112.4	112.2	108.5	112.9	112.2	111.2	111.9	111.1	108.3	115.0	111.8
4th quarter	113.7	116.5	113.0	113.2	113.8	111.9	112.8	112.9	109.0	113.7	113.1	111.9	113.5	111.9	108.3	116.2	112.7
1993																	
1st quarter	114.5	117.2	113.9	114.2	114.7	112.7	113.5	113.8	109.7	114.7	113.9	112.8	114.2	112.9	109.3	116.9	113.4
2nd quarter	115.2	118.1	114.6	115.0	115.4	113.4	114.2	114.6	110.3	115.5	114.7	114.0	114.8	113.6	109.3	117.8	114.2
3rd quarter	116.2	118.8	115.6	115.9	116.6	114.4	114.8	115.4	111.1	116.3	115.8	114.7	115.2	114.3	112.3	118.8	115.3
4th quarter	117.1	119.5	116.5	116.6	117.6	115.0	115.2	116.2	111.3	117.3	116.7	115.5	116.4	115.1	112.9	119.7	116.2
1994																	
1st quarter	117.7	120.4	117.1	117.5	118.3	115.8	116.3	117.0	112.4	118.0	117.3	116.3	116.5	115.4	113.7	120.7	116.8
2nd quarter	118.7	121.3	118.1	118.3	119.2	116.7	116.9	118.0	113.5	119.0	118.2	117.2	118.0	116.8	113.2	121.4	117.7
3rd quarter	119.6	122.3	119.0	119.4	120.1	117.8	117.5	119.0	114.4	120.0	119.1	118.9	119.0	117.7	113.8	122.1	118.6
4th quarter	120.4	123.2	119.7	120.0	121.0	118.2	118.7	119.6	114.9	120.8	119.8	119.7	119.9	118.1	114.2	123.1	119.2
1995																	
1st quarter	121.3	124.3	120.6	121.0	121.7	119.2	119.4	120.5	115.0	121.9	120.7	121.1	121.1	118.9	115.0	123.8	120.0
2nd quarter	122.2	125.3	121.5	121.8	122.7	120.3	120.0	121.4	115.5	122.9	121.6	122.1	122.4	119.4	117.0	124.5	120.9
3rd quarter	123.1	126.1	122.4	122.6	123.5	121.1	120.8	122.1	116.5	123.5	122.5	122.9	124.0	120.2	118.0	125.2	121.8
4th quarter	123.9	127.0	123.2	123.4	124.4	121.7	121.4	122.9	117.6	124.3	123.3	123.7	125.5	120.9	118.4	126.1	122.6
1996																	
1st quarter	125.1	127.8	124.4	124.7	125.8	122.8	122.2	123.9	118.5	125.4	124.7	124.5	126.3	122.9	119.8	127.5	123.9
2nd quarter	126.2	128.8	125.6	125.7	127.0	123.9	123.0	125.1	119.4	126.5	125.8	125.1	127.8	123.0	121.9	128.8	125.1
3rd quarter	127.0	129.7	126.5	126.8	127.9	124.5	124.1	126.1	120.1	127.7	126.6	125.9	128.5	124.1	122.2	129.7	125.8
4th quarter	128.0	130.6	127.4	127.5	128.8	125.4	125.7	126.8	121.0	128.4	127.6	127.0	129.6	126.1	122.2	130.5	126.9
1997																	
1st quarter	129.1	131.4	128.5	128.6	130.2	126.2	126.6	127.6	122.2	129.1	129.0	128.1	131.6	127.2	124.5	131.7	128.2
2nd quarter	130.2	132.2	129.7	129.9	131.3	127.5	127.6	128.9	123.4	130.3	130.1	129.0	132.1	128.3	125.3	133.1	129.3
3rd quarter	131.4	133.2	131.0	131.2	132.6	128.4	129.9	129.9	124.4	131.3	131.4	130.0	133.0	129.6	126.4	134.7	130.6
4th quarter	132.7	134.1	132.4	132.4	134.3	129.3	131.1	130.6	125.1	132.2	133.2	131.3	133.5	130.9	130.6	136.2	132.2
1998																	
1st quarter	133.9	135.1	133.7	133.7	135.7	130.4	132.1	132.0	126.2	133.7	134.4	132.0	136.4	132.0	132.6	137.1	133.4
2nd quarter	135.1	136.1	134.9	134.8	137.0	131.4	133.0	133.3	127.9	134.6	135.6	133.0	137.1	133.1	134.8	138.4	134.7
3rd quarter	136.6	137.1	136.5	136.3	138.9	132.6	134.4	134.4	128.2	136.0	137.5	134.2	139.2	134.9	138.1	140.0	136.4
4th quarter	137.6	138.2	137.5	136.9	139.9	133.3	135.3	135.2	129.6	136.8	138.5	135.1	141.1	135.1	139.8	140.8	137.5
1999																	
1st quarter	138.3	139.1	138.1	138.2	140.4	134.5	136.7	136.3	131.0	137.9	138.9	135.3	140.9	136.4	137.2	142.1	137.9
2nd quarter	139.9	140.4	139.7	139.6	142.1	135.8	137.8	137.4	131.7	139.0	140.8	137.0	142.4	138.1	142.4	143.3	139.8
3rd quarter	141.1	141.7	140.9	140.8	143.4	137.0	138.0	138.6	132.7	140.2	142.0	137.4	144.2	138.6	144.5	144.5	140.9
4th quarter	142.4	143.1	142.2	142.0	144.8	137.9	139.6	139.7	133.9	141.5	143.3	137.9	146.3	139.9	145.2	145.9	142.2

1. Includes private industry and state and local government workers. Federal government workers are not included.
2. Not seasonally adjusted.

Table 7-3. Productivity and Related Data

(1992=100, seasonally adjusted.)

Year and quarter	Business sector								Nonfarm business sector							
	Output per hour of all persons	Output	Hours of all persons	Compensation per hour	Real compensation per hour	Unit labor costs	Unit nonlabor payments	Implicit price deflator	Output per hour of all persons	Output	Hours of all persons	Compensation per hour	Real compensation per hour	Unit labor costs	Unit nonlabor payments	Implicit price deflator
1970	67.0	49.4	73.7	23.5	78.9	35.1	31.6	33.9	68.9	49.5	71.8	23.7	79.5	34.4	31.3	33.3
1971	69.9	51.3	73.3	25.0	80.4	35.8	34.4	35.3	71.8	51.4	71.5	25.3	81.1	35.2	33.9	34.7
1972	72.2	54.7	75.7	26.6	82.7	36.8	35.8	36.5	74.2	54.9	73.9	26.9	83.6	36.2	34.9	35.8
1973	74.5	58.5	78.5	28.9	84.5	38.8	37.7	38.4	76.6	58.9	76.9	29.1	85.1	38.0	35.3	37.0
1974	73.2	57.6	78.6	31.7	83.5	43.2	40.0	42.1	75.4	58.0	77.0	32.0	84.2	42.4	38.0	40.8
1975	75.8	57.0	75.2	34.9	84.4	46.1	46.1	46.1	77.4	57.0	73.6	35.2	85.0	45.5	44.6	45.1
1976	78.5	60.9	77.6	38.0	86.8	48.4	48.6	48.5	80.3	61.1	76.1	38.2	87.3	47.6	47.5	47.6
1977	79.8	64.3	80.6	41.0	87.9	51.4	51.5	51.4	81.5	64.6	79.2	41.3	88.5	50.7	50.6	50.6
1978	80.7	68.3	84.7	44.6	89.5	55.3	54.8	55.1	82.6	68.8	83.3	45.0	90.2	54.5	53.4	54.1
1979	80.7	70.6	87.5	48.9	89.7	60.7	58.3	59.8	82.3	70.9	86.3	49.3	90.3	59.9	56.5	58.7
1980	80.4	69.8	86.8	54.2	89.5	67.4	61.5	65.2	82.0	70.2	85.6	54.6	90.0	66.5	60.5	64.3
1981	82.0	71.7	87.4	59.4	89.5	72.4	69.2	71.2	83.0	71.6	86.2	59.9	90.3	72.1	67.7	70.5
1982	81.7	69.6	85.2	63.8	90.9	78.2	70.3	75.3	82.5	69.4	84.1	64.3	91.6	77.9	69.4	74.8
1983	84.6	73.3	86.6	66.5	91.0	78.6	76.4	77.8	86.3	73.8	85.6	67.1	91.8	77.8	76.2	77.2
1984	87.0	79.7	91.6	69.5	91.3	79.8	80.4	80.0	88.1	80.0	90.7	70.0	92.0	79.4	79.3	79.4
1985	88.7	83.1	93.6	72.9	92.7	82.1	82.2	82.2	89.3	83.0	93.0	73.2	93.2	82.0	81.6	81.9
1986	91.4	86.1	94.2	76.7	95.8	83.9	82.8	83.5	92.0	86.2	93.8	77.0	96.3	83.7	82.4	83.2
1987	91.9	89.2	97.0	79.7	96.3	86.7	83.6	85.6	92.3	89.3	96.7	80.0	96.6	86.6	83.2	85.4
1988	93.0	92.9	100.0	83.5	97.3	89.8	85.7	88.3	93.3	93.3	100.0	83.6	97.5	89.4	85.4	87.9
1989	93.9	96.2	102.4	85.8	95.9	91.3	91.8	91.5	94.2	96.5	102.4	85.8	95.9	91.1	91.3	91.2
1990	95.2	97.6	102.6	90.7	96.5	95.3	93.9	94.8	95.3	97.8	102.7	90.5	96.3	95.0	93.6	94.5
1991	96.3	96.5	100.2	95.0	97.5	98.7	97.0	98.1	96.4	96.6	100.2	95.0	97.5	98.5	97.1	98.0
1992	100.0	100.0	100.0	100.0	100.0	100.0	100.0	100.0	100.0	100.0	100.0	100.0	100.0	100.0	100.0	100.0
1993	100.5	103.1	102.6	102.5	99.9	101.9	102.5	102.2	100.5	103.3	102.9	102.2	99.6	101.7	103.0	102.2
1994	101.9	108.1	106.1	104.5	99.7	102.6	106.4	104.0	101.8	108.2	106.2	104.3	99.5	102.5	106.9	104.1
1995	102.6	111.5	108.7	106.7	99.3	104.1	109.4	106.0	102.8	111.8	108.8	106.6	99.2	103.7	110.4	106.1
1996	105.4	116.4	110.4	110.1	99.7	104.5	113.3	107.7	105.4	116.7	110.7	109.8	99.5	104.2	113.5	107.6
1997	107.6	122.5	113.8	113.3	100.4	105.3	117.1	109.7	107.3	122.7	114.3	112.9	100.0	105.1	118.0	109.8
1998	110.5	128.6	116.4	119.3	104.3	107.9	115.2	110.6	110.2	129.0	117.1	118.6	103.8	107.7	116.3	110.8
1999	114.0	134.8	118.3	125.2	107.3	109.9	115.1	111.8	113.4	135.1	119.2	124.4	106.5	109.7	116.8	112.3
1991																
1st quarter	95.1	95.7	100.6	93.1	96.3	97.9	95.9	97.1	95.3	95.8	100.5	93.1	96.3	97.7	96.0	97.1
2nd quarter	96.2	96.4	100.2	94.5	97.4	98.3	97.0	97.8	96.4	96.5	100.1	94.6	97.4	98.1	97.0	97.7
3rd quarter	96.4	96.6	100.2	95.5	97.7	99.0	97.3	98.4	96.7	96.8	100.1	95.5	97.7	98.8	97.7	98.4
4th quarter	97.3	97.2	99.9	96.7	98.2	99.4	97.8	98.8	97.4	97.3	99.9	96.7	98.2	99.3	97.9	98.8
1992																
1st quarter	99.2	98.5	99.3	98.8	99.8	99.6	99.1	99.4	99.2	98.5	99.3	98.7	99.7	99.6	99.1	99.4
2nd quarter	99.7	99.6	99.9	99.3	99.5	99.6	100.1	99.8	99.7	99.6	99.8	99.3	99.6	99.6	100.1	99.8
3rd quarter	99.7	99.8	100.2	100.6	100.2	100.9	98.7	100.1	99.6	99.8	100.2	100.6	100.2	100.9	98.6	100.1
4th quarter	101.4	102.1	100.7	101.4	100.2	99.9	102.1	100.7	101.5	102.2	100.7	101.4	100.2	99.9	102.2	100.7
1993																
1st quarter	100.2	101.7	101.5	101.7	100.0	101.4	101.4	101.4	100.2	101.8	101.6	101.5	99.8	101.3	101.9	101.5
2nd quarter	100.2	102.5	102.3	102.4	99.9	102.2	101.6	101.9	100.1	102.6	102.6	102.1	99.7	102.0	101.8	101.9
3rd quarter	100.2	103.1	102.9	102.8	99.9	102.5	102.0	102.3	100.4	103.6	103.2	102.4	99.5	102.0	102.8	102.3
4th quarter	101.4	105.1	103.7	103.1	99.5	101.6	105.1	102.9	101.3	105.3	104.0	102.7	99.2	101.4	105.3	102.9
1994																
1st quarter	101.6	106.0	104.3	104.4	100.5	102.7	104.2	103.3	101.5	105.9	104.4	104.1	100.2	102.6	104.2	103.2
2nd quarter	101.9	107.9	106.0	104.2	99.7	102.3	106.0	103.7	101.9	108.0	106.0	104.1	99.6	102.2	106.4	103.7
3rd quarter	101.6	108.5	106.7	104.4	99.1	102.7	107.1	104.3	101.6	108.5	106.9	104.2	98.9	102.6	107.9	104.5
4th quarter	102.4	110.1	107.6	105.1	99.3	102.7	108.3	104.8	102.4	110.3	107.7	105.0	99.2	102.5	100.2	104.9
1995																
1st quarter	102.0	110.5	108.3	105.5	99.1	103.5	108.9	105.5	102.2	110.8	108.4	105.4	99.0	103.1	110.0	105.6
2nd quarter	102.3	110.8	108.2	106.4	99.1	104.0	109.2	105.9	102.6	111.1	108.3	106.2	99.0	103.6	110.4	106.0
3rd quarter	102.5	111.8	109.1	107.1	99.3	104.5	109.4	106.3	102.8	112.2	109.2	106.9	99.1	104.0	110.4	106.3
4th quarter	103.4	112.9	109.2	108.0	99.5	104.4	110.3	106.6	103.6	113.3	109.4	107.7	99.3	104.0	110.9	106.5
1996																
1st quarter	104.5	114.0	109.2	108.6	99.4	104.0	112.3	107.0	104.6	114.4	109.4	108.4	99.2	103.7	112.7	106.9
2nd quarter	105.6	116.1	110.0	109.7	99.5	103.9	113.7	107.5	105.6	116.4	110.3	109.4	99.3	103.7	113.8	107.3
3rd quarter	105.6	116.8	110.7	110.7	99.9	104.8	113.3	108.0	105.5	117.2	111.0	110.3	99.6	104.5	113.4	107.7
4th quarter	106.0	118.4	111.7	111.5	99.9	105.2	113.7	108.4	105.9	118.7	112.1	111.1	99.6	104.9	114.2	108.3
1997																
1st quarter	106.3	119.9	112.8	112.0	99.8	105.4	115.3	109.1	106.1	120.2	113.3	111.7	99.5	105.2	115.9	109.1
2nd quarter	107.3	122.0	113.7	112.3	99.8	104.7	118.0	109.6	107.1	122.2	114.1	112.0	99.5	104.5	118.8	109.7
3rd quarter	108.3	123.5	114.1	113.5	100.4	104.8	118.5	109.9	108.0	123.6	114.5	113.0	100.0	104.7	119.5	110.1
4th quarter	108.5	124.4	114.7	115.3	101.5	106.3	116.8	110.2	108.1	124.7	115.3	114.7	101.0	106.1	117.8	110.4
1998																
1st quarter	109.7	126.8	115.6	117.1	102.9	106.7	116.4	110.3	109.3	127.1	116.3	116.4	102.3	106.5	117.4	110.5
2nd quarter	110.0	127.7	116.1	118.5	103.8	107.7	115.1	110.5	109.8	128.1	116.7	117.9	103.2	107.5	116.3	110.7
3rd quarter	110.6	128.9	116.6	120.0	104.7	108.5	114.6	110.7	110.3	129.2	117.2	119.4	104.2	108.3	115.8	111.0
4th quarter	111.6	131.0	117.4	121.4	105.5	108.8	114.6	110.9	111.2	131.4	118.1	120.8	104.9	108.5	115.8	111.2
1999																
1st quarter	112.6	132.3	117.5	123.0	106.4	109.3	115.1	111.4	112.0	132.6	118.4	122.1	105.7	109.0	116.7	111.8
2nd quarter	112.8	133.1	118.0	124.5	106.9	110.4	114.1	111.8	112.1	133.4	118.9	123.6	106.1	110.2	115.7	112.2
3rd quarter	114.2	135.3	118.5	126.1	107.6	110.5	114.3	111.9	113.6	135.6	119.4	125.2	106.8	110.3	116.1	112.4
4th quarter	116.3	138.5	119.1	127.3	107.8	109.5	116.8	112.2	115.8	138.9	120.0	126.5	107.2	109.3	118.6	112.7

Table 7-3. Productivity and Related Data—*Continued*

(1992=100, seasonally adjusted.)

Year and quarter	Nonfinancial corporations										Manufacturing					
	Output per hour of all employees	Output	Employee hours	Compensation per hour	Real compensation per hour	Unit costs			Unit profits	Implicit price deflator	Output per hour of all persons	Output	Hours of all persons	Compensation per hour	Real compensation per hour	Unit labor costs
						Total	Labor costs	Nonlabor costs								
1970	70.4	48.0	68.1	25.3	84.7	34.8	35.9	31.9	44.4	35.6	54.3	56.7	104.4	23.7	79.5	43.7
1971	73.3	49.9	68.0	26.9	86.3	35.8	36.7	33.4	50.2	37.0	58.0	58.3	100.5	25.2	80.8	43.4
1972	75.3	53.8	71.5	28.4	88.4	36.6	37.8	33.5	54.1	38.1	60.5	63.5	105.1	26.5	82.3	43.8
1973	76.1	57.0	74.9	30.7	89.9	38.9	40.4	35.1	55.5	40.3	61.7	68.1	110.4	28.5	83.4	46.2
1974	74.5	56.0	75.2	33.7	88.7	43.9	45.2	40.5	49.2	44.4	61.5	66.3	107.9	31.6	83.4	51.5
1975	77.3	55.1	71.3	37.0	89.3	47.3	47.9	45.9	64.1	48.8	64.5	62.7	97.2	35.5	85.6	55.0
1976	79.8	59.5	74.6	40.0	91.4	49.0	50.2	45.9	72.3	51.0	67.2	68.4	101.9	38.4	87.8	57.2
1977	81.6	63.8	78.2	43.2	92.5	51.4	52.9	47.4	79.4	53.8	69.9	74.2	106.1	41.8	89.6	59.8
1978	82.1	68.1	82.9	46.8	93.9	55.1	57.0	50.0	82.5	57.4	70.6	78.1	110.6	45.2	90.6	64.0
1979	81.5	70.2	86.1	51.1	93.8	60.7	62.7	55.1	76.7	62.0	70.0	79.0	112.7	49.6	90.9	70.8
1980	81.1	69.2	85.3	56.4	93.1	68.4	69.6	65.1	68.8	68.4	70.3	75.5	107.5	55.6	91.7	79.1
1981	82.6	71.5	86.5	61.6	92.9	74.6	74.6	74.8	82.4	75.3	70.9	75.8	107.0	61.1	92.1	86.1
1982	83.4	70.0	83.9	66.1	94.1	80.0	79.2	82.3	75.0	79.6	74.4	72.9	97.9	67.0	95.4	89.9
1983	85.9	73.3	85.3	68.4	93.6	80.1	79.6	81.5	91.2	81.1	76.9	76.1	98.9	68.8	94.2	89.5
1984	88.2	80.2	91.0	71.2	93.6	80.9	80.7	81.1	108.6	83.2	79.7	83.9	105.3	71.2	93.6	89.4
1985	89.9	83.8	93.2	74.4	94.7	82.7	82.7	82.4	104.2	84.5	82.5	86.3	104.6	75.1	95.6	91.0
1986	91.6	85.9	93.7	78.0	97.5	85.3	85.1	85.7	88.0	85.5	86.3	88.9	103.0	78.5	98.1	91.0
1987	94.7	90.7	95.8	81.7	98.7	86.0	86.2	85.3	98.1	87.0	88.6	91.9	103.8	80.7	97.5	91.1
1988	95.5	95.8	100.3	83.8	97.7	87.6	87.7	87.4	108.0	89.4	90.3	96.2	106.6	84.0	97.9	93.0
1989	94.6	97.4	102.9	86.2	96.3	92.0	91.1	94.6	97.3	92.5	90.5	96.9	107.1	86.6	96.8	95.8
1990	95.4	98.3	103.0	90.8	96.6	95.9	95.2	98.0	94.3	95.8	92.9	97.4	104.8	90.8	96.6	97.7
1991	97.6	97.5	99.9	95.2	97.8	98.8	97.5	102.1	93.0	98.3	95.0	95.4	100.4	95.6	98.1	100.6
1992	100.0	100.0	100.0	100.0	100.0	100.0	100.0	100.0	100.0	100.0	100.0	100.0	100.0	100.0	100.0	100.0
1993	100.8	103.0	102.2	102.1	99.6	101.0	101.3	100.2	113.2	102.1	102.0	103.4	101.4	102.7	100.2	100.7
1994	103.2	109.6	106.2	104.3	99.5	101.1	101.0	101.3	131.7	103.7	105.2	109.0	103.6	105.6	100.8	100.4
1995	104.3	114.2	109.5	106.2	98.9	102.0	101.9	102.2	139.0	105.1	109.3	113.7	104.0	107.9	100.4	98.7
1996	107.6	119.9	111.4	109.1	98.8	101.2	101.4	100.6	152.2	105.5	113.1	117.3	103.7	109.3	99.0	96.6
1997	110.2	127.2	115.4	112.0	99.3	101.4	101.6	100.8	156.7	106.1	117.6	124.0	105.5	111.4	98.8	94.8
1998	114.2	135.5	118.6	117.4	102.7	102.2	102.8	100.8	148.3	106.1	123.9	130.3	105.2	117.3	102.6	94.6
1999	119.2	144.0	120.9	123.2	105.5	102.9	103.4	101.7	146.5	106.6	131.6	136.0	103.3	123.2	105.5	93.6
1991																
1st quarter	96.7	97.1	100.3	93.4	96.6	98.0	96.5	102.1	93.4	97.7	93.3	94.0	100.8	93.7	97.0	100.5
2nd quarter	97.6	97.3	99.7	94.9	97.7	98.5	97.2	102.2	93.3	98.1	94.0	94.3	100.3	95.0	97.8	101.0
3rd quarter	97.9	97.7	99.7	95.8	98.1	99.1	97.9	102.3	92.7	98.5	95.8	96.3	100.5	96.3	98.5	100.5
4th quarter	98.4	98.0	99.6	97.0	98.5	99.4	98.5	101.6	92.5	98.8	96.8	96.9	100.2	97.3	98.8	100.5
1992																
1st quarter	99.7	99.0	99.3	98.8	99.7	99.4	99.0	100.2	97.3	99.2	98.3	97.8	99.5	98.4	99.4	100.2
2nd quarter	99.6	99.6	100.0	99.4	99.7	99.7	99.8	99.3	100.8	99.8	99.6	100.1	100.1	99.6	99.9	100.0
3rd quarter	100.0	100.1	100.0	100.6	100.3	100.8	100.6	101.3	94.6	100.2	100.8	100.7	99.9	100.7	100.3	99.9
4th quarter	100.7	101.3	100.6	101.3	100.1	100.2	100.5	99.3	107.2	100.8	101.3	101.7	100.4	101.2	100.1	100.0
1993																
1st quarter	99.5	100.8	101.2	101.3	99.7	101.5	101.8	100.7	102.5	101.6	101.8	102.6	100.8	101.5	99.9	99.7
2nd quarter	100.7	102.6	101.8	102.0	99.6	100.8	101.3	99.7	112.2	101.8	101.9	103.1	101.2	102.3	99.9	100.5
3rd quarter	100.8	103.4	102.6	102.3	99.4	101.2	101.5	100.4	112.2	102.1	101.6	103.1	101.5	103.1	100.2	101.5
4th quarter	101.8	105.4	103.5	102.6	99.0	100.6	100.7	100.2	125.4	102.7	102.7	104.8	102.0	104.0	100.4	101.3
1994																
1st quarter	102.9	107.1	104.1	104.1	100.1	101.6	101.1	103.1	119.6	103.2	103.6	105.9	102.2	105.1	101.1	101.4
2nd quarter	102.9	108.9	105.8	104.0	99.5	100.8	101.0	100.1	131.4	103.4	105.1	108.3	103.0	105.2	100.7	100.1
3rd quarter	103.0	110.1	106.9	104.1	98.9	101.1	101.1	101.0	134.8	103.9	105.7	109.9	104.0	105.8	100.5	100.1
4th quarter	103.7	112.3	108.2	104.7	99.0	101.0	101.0	100.9	140.5	104.3	106.4	111.8	105.1	106.5	100.6	100.1
1995																
1st quarter	103.1	112.5	109.0	105.2	98.8	102.1	102.0	102.3	134.2	104.8	107.7	113.2	105.1	106.8	100.3	99.2
2nd quarter	103.7	113.2	109.2	105.9	98.7	102.3	102.2	102.8	134.5	105.1	108.9	113.2	104.0	107.8	100.4	99.0
3rd quarter	104.7	115.0	109.8	106.5	98.7	101.7	101.7	101.6	143.6	105.3	109.8	113.8	103.7	108.4	100.5	98.7
4th quarter	105.4	116.0	110.1	107.1	98.7	101.7	101.6	102.0	143.3	105.3	110.7	114.5	103.4	108.6	100.1	98.1
1996																
1st quarter	106.2	117.0	110.1	107.6	98.5	101.3	101.3	101.3	150.5	105.5	111.6	114.5	102.6	108.4	99.2	97.2
2nd quarter	107.1	119.1	111.2	108.6	98.5	101.2	101.4	100.7	151.8	105.5	112.5	116.8	103.8	108.9	98.8	96.8
3rd quarter	107.9	120.7	111.9	109.5	98.9	101.2	101.5	100.3	151.9	105.5	113.9	118.5	104.1	109.6	98.9	96.2
4th quarter	108.9	122.9	112.9	110.2	98.8	100.9	101.2	100.2	154.6	105.5	114.5	119.4	104.2	110.3	98.9	96.3
1997																
1st quarter	108.8	124.0	113.9	110.8	98.7	101.4	101.8	100.5	154.6	105.9	115.2	121.0	105.0	110.4	98.3	95.8
2nd quarter	109.3	125.8	115.1	111.1	98.7	101.6	101.6	101.4	155.3	106.1	116.3	122.8	105.6	110.5	98.1	95.0
3rd quarter	110.8	128.4	115.8	112.1	99.2	101.1	101.2	100.8	160.3	106.1	118.7	125.0	105.3	111.5	98.6	93.9
4th quarter	111.6	130.5	116.9	113.7	100.1	101.5	101.9	100.4	156.5	106.1	120.1	127.3	106.0	113.3	99.8	94.4
1998																
1st quarter	112.3	132.4	117.9	115.2	101.2	102.0	102.6	100.5	150.4	106.1	121.3	128.5	106.0	115.2	101.2	95.0
2nd quarter	113.4	134.2	118.3	116.6	102.1	102.3	102.8	100.9	147.2	106.1	122.7	129.5	105.6	116.6	102.1	95.1
3rd quarter	114.9	136.6	118.9	118.0	103.0	102.1	102.7	100.2	151.4	106.2	125.1	130.7	104.5	118.1	103.0	94.4
4th quarter	115.8	138.6	119.6	119.3	103.7	102.6	103.0	101.6	144.5	106.2	126.8	132.6	104.5	119.4	103.7	94.1
1999																
1st quarter	117.1	140.6	120.0	120.9	104.6	102.5	103.2	100.7	149.7	106.5	128.9	133.4	103.5	120.7	104.4	93.6
2nd quarter	118.2	142.5	120.5	122.4	105.1	103.0	103.5	101.4	147.5	106.7	130.4	135.0	103.5	122.4	105.1	93.8
3rd quarter	119.7	145.0	121.1	124.0	105.8	103.2	103.6	102.1	143.3	106.6	131.9	136.5	103.5	124.1	105.9	94.1
4th quarter	121.5	148.1	122.0	125.3	106.1	103.0	103.1	102.5	145.7	106.6	135.1	138.9	102.8	125.5	106.4	92.9

Table 7-4. Corporate Profits

(Income after income taxes, millions of dollars.)

Year and quarter	Total	Manufacturing											
		Nondurable goods											
		Total	Food and tobacco [1]	Textiles	Apparel (including leather)	Paper	Printing	Chemicals				Petroleum and coal products	Rubber and plastics products
								Total	Industrial chemicals and synthetics	Drugs	Other chemicals		
1970	28 572	...	2 549	413	...	719	...	3 434	...	...	...	5 893	...
1971	31 038	...	2 754	558	...	501	...	3 780	...	...	...	5 829	...
1972	36 467	...	3 021	659	...	941	...	4 499	...	...	...	5 151	...
1973	48 259	...	3 723	831	...	1 427	...	5 670	...	...	...	7 759	...
1974	58 747	...	4 601	780	...	2 287	...	7 175	...	...	...	14 483	...
1975	49 135	...	5 154	409	...	1 801	...	6 703	...	...	...	9 307	...
1976	64 519	...	5 826	809	...	2 270	...	7 610	...	...	...	11 725	...
1977	70 366	...	5 575	828	...	2 367	...	8 060	...	...	...	12 179	...
1978	81 148	...	6 213	1 170	...	2 598	...	9 117	...	...	...	12 805	...
1979	98 698	...	7 340	1 340	...	3 723	...	10 896	...	...	...	21 936	...
1980	92 579	...	8 222	977	...	2 789	...	11 578	...	...	...	25 133	...
1981	101 302	...	9 109	1 157	...	3 110	...	12 973	...	...	...	23 733	...
1982	71 028	...	8 383	851	...	1 460	...	10 324	...	...	...	19 666	...
1983	85 834	...	9 436	1 599	...	2 327	...	11 644	...	...	...	19 297	...
1984	107 648	...	9 760	1 635	...	3 015	...	13 883	...	...	...	17 154	...
1985	87 648	...	12 798	1 200	...	2 880	...	9 542	...	...	...	12 739	...
1986	83 121	...	13 292	1 706	...	3 280	...	12 900	...	...	...	8 823	...
1987	115 498	...	4 966	1 882	...	5 505	...	16 572	...	...	...	10 867	...
1988	153 764	86 813	20 591	1 493	1 853	8 021	7 407	23 448	10 129	7 367	...	21 087	2 911
1989	135 141	79 611	16 482	670	2 071	6 981	7 799	23 994	9 017	7 741	...	19 366	2 246
1990	110 128	69 441	15 997	345	1 260	4 846	5 110	22 710	7 448	9 309	...	17 811	1 365
1991	66 407	59 255	19 576	691	1 896	2 134	3 921	19 527	4 406	10 185	...	10 786	724
1992	22 085	46 043	17 502	1 991	3 473	1 176	4 792	12 446	-2 962	9 487	5 921	3 142	1 522
1993	83 156	55 713	15 811	1 449	2 430	-255	5 492	15 198	3 873	10 196	1 128	12 970	2 621
1994	174 874	87 816	21 913	1 754	1 963	5 168	8 350	29 608	8 069	13 340	8 197	14 880	4 176
1995	198 151	103 889	24 806	893	1 956	11 784	9 978	36 007	10 516	15 468	10 024	13 929	4 540
1996	224 869	118 785	26 432	1 844	1 925	6 249	11 181	39 843	8 063	16 431	15 349	26 640	4 675
1997	244 505	123 119	26 615	1 883	3 247	3 606	10 889	41 981	9 391	17 732	14 858	29 447	5 452
1998	234 386	106 549	26 844	2 083	2 533	4 728	13 978	42 542	7 725	22 697	12 121	8 315	5 527
1999	260 995	116 924	28 269	770	2 103	6 963	14 754	41 803	7 615	22 982	11 205	17 771	4 491
1991													
1st quarter	18 011	16 619	4 957	-55	318	852	684	5 084	1 735	2 243	...	4 833	-53
2nd quarter	22 793	15 231	5 163	148	335	812	696	5 253	1 196	2 158	...	2 512	311
3rd quarter	17 298	16 257	5 469	177	802	846	1 515	5 240	601	3 097	...	1 573	634
4th quarter	8 305	11 148	3 987	421	441	-376	1 026	3 950	874	2 687	...	1 868	-168
1992													
1st quarter	-44 377	-4 160	3 113	254	748	-509	124	-3 213	-5 832	1 472	1 147	-3 934	-743
2nd quarter	29 596	18 503	5 924	502	441	864	1 670	6 023	1 824	2 688	1 511	2 181	898
3rd quarter	27 449	18 588	4 584	568	1 711	720	1 775	6 088	1 500	2 825	1 763	2 331	811
4th quarter	9 417	13 112	3 881	667	573	101	1 223	3 548	-454	2 502	1 500	2 564	556
1993													
1st quarter	10 998	12 683	2 910	227	642	714	962	4 226	1 474	3 014	-261	2 593	408
2nd quarter	24 961	15 690	4 813	597	574	803	1 622	3 031	1 911	2 611	-1 491	3 243	1 008
3rd quarter	24 729	13 251	4 459	321	883	-1 757	1 147	4 582	-39	3 273	1 347	2 961	658
4th quarter	22 468	14 089	3 629	304	331	-15	1 761	3 359	527	1 298	1 533	4 173	547
1994													
1st quarter	35 085	18 939	5 505	336	176	661	1 914	7 418	2 015	3 891	1 511	2 265	663
2nd quarter	46 557	19 977	4 635	526	679	1 000	2 277	6 936	2 019	2 790	2 127	2 609	1 314
3rd quarter	46 452	24 165	5 799	661	731	1 275	2 248	8 027	2 471	3 111	2 445	4 255	1 168
4th quarter	46 780	24 735	5 974	231	377	2 232	1 911	7 227	1 564	3 548	2 114	5 751	1 031
1995													
1st quarter	51 960	25 968	5 851	339	403	2 452	3 473	8 934	3 388	3 299	2 247	3 331	1 185
2nd quarter	57 023	28 007	6 675	388	196	3 192	2 079	10 303	3 855	3 909	2 539	3 755	1 419
3rd quarter	50 291	29 622	6 655	194	893	3 474	1 940	10 348	2 515	5 003	2 831	5 029	1 092
4th quarter	38 877	20 292	5 625	-28	464	2 666	2 486	6 422	758	3 257	2 407	1 814	844
1996													
1st quarter	50 749	28 163	6 368	213	195	2 125	2 886	9 913	3 380	3 437	3 096	5 148	1 315
2nd quarter	58 871	27 996	6 176	596	254	1 555	1 942	7 755	-344	4 163	3 937	8 079	1 639
3rd quarter	62 063	34 473	6 810	657	815	1 721	2 936	13 678	3 305	4 453	5 920	6 456	1 401
4th quarter	53 186	28 153	7 078	378	661	848	3 417	8 497	1 722	4 378	2 396	6 957	320
1997													
1st quarter	60 589	33 558	6 053	418	870	1 102	2 980	12 998	3 405	5 221	4 371	7 871	1 266
2nd quarter	66 877	30 532	7 231	650	912	1 033	2 840	8 572	3 853	1 208	3 512	7 353	1 941
3rd quarter	62 498	33 017	8 067	506	1 164	1 568	2 611	11 054	2 174	4 351	4 530	6 639	1 408
4th quarter	54 541	26 012	5 264	309	301	-97	2 458	9 357	-41	6 952	2 445	7 584	837
1998													
1st quarter	74 680	29 867	6 747	587	765	1 325	3 180	11 697	2 884	5 222	3 592	3 968	1 598
2nd quarter	54 723	28 950	6 226	530	732	1 590	3 022	11 860	2 704	5 333	3 823	3 107	1 883
3rd quarter	61 198	33 084	9 397	663	991	1 395	4 163	10 540	1 334	5 664	3 542	4 879	1 055
4th quarter	43 785	14 648	4 474	303	45	418	3 613	8 445	803	6 478	1 164	-3 639	991
1999													
1st quarter	60 059	26 513	6 686	205	222	1 073	3 098	12 001	1 870	6 277	3 854	1 980	1 247
2nd quarter	66 847	27 110	6 021	150	311	1 646	4 199	9 480	2 413	3 465	3 601	3 909	1 393
3rd quarter	68 283	33 484	7 800	285	1 099	1 901	3 419	11 359	1 879	7 161	2 319	6 678	944
4th quarter	65 806	29 817	7 762	130	471	2 343	4 038	8 963	1 453	6 079	1 431	5 204	907

1. The tobacco industry is included beginning with the data for 1985.

Table 7-4. Corporate Profits—Continued

(Income after income taxes, millions of dollars.)

Year and quarter		Manufacturing—Continued										
		Durable goods										
				Primary metals					Transportation equipment			
	Total	Stone, clay, and glass products	Total	Iron and steel	Nonferrous metals	Fabricated metal products	Machinery (except electrical)	Electrical and electronic equipment	Total	Motor vehicles and equipment	Aircraft, missiles, parts	Instruments
1970	...	627	...	692	1 297	1 066	2 689	2 349	...	1 424	...	...
1971	...	853	...	748	621	1 070	2 489	2 563	...	3 097	...	...
1972	...	1 060	...	1 022	687	1 569	3 481	2 999	...	3 639	...	...
1973	...	1 266	...	1 695	1 343	2 207	4 936	3 883	...	4 122	...	...
1974	...	1 204	...	3 149	2 035	2 837	5 648	2 940	...	1 957	...	...
1975	...	968	...	2 280	663	2 523	6 311	2 564	...	1 737	...	...
1976	...	1 447	...	2 085	913	3 196	7 889	4 073	...	5 099	...	...
1977	...	1 686	...	864	873	3 458	9 131	5 383	...	6 133	...	...
1978	...	2 353	...	2 124	1 362	3 815	10 746	6 500	...	6 211	...	...
1979	...	2 373	...	2 185	2 691	4 431	11 530	7 386	...	4 382	...	...
1980	...	1 833	...	2 334	2 768	3 967	11 459	7 114	...	-3 424	...	...
1981	...	1 627	...	3 507	2 124	4 235	12 580	7 872	...	-209	...	...
1982	...	408	...	-3 705	-333	2 320	8 038	6 449	...	734	...	...
1983	...	1 002	...	-3 746	-288	2 693	7 680	6 367	...	7 168	...	...
1984	...	1 870	...	-379	-84	4 646	11 963	8 616	...	10 575	...	...
1985	...	1 627	...	-1 349	-1 000	3 388	9 676	6 886	...	9 087	...	...
1986	...	2 120	...	-3 372	760	3 232	6 551	7 619	...	8 363	...	...
1987	...	2 907	...	1 353	1 065	4 428	10 205	9 585	...	10 642	...	...
1988	66 948	2 443	5 177	984	4 195	5 334	13 758	11 137	17 468	12 454	4 880	7 728
1989	55 532	1 950	5 223	1 491	3 733	5 506	9 666	9 643	13 108	8 799	3 860	6 069
1990	40 686	1 049	3 084	544	2 541	4 577	11 127	6 390	4 576	-566	4 491	6 697
1991	7 152	-1 568	-523	-1 482	958	3 341	-2 763	4 686	-4 827	-7 602	2 477	6 680
1992	-23 960	-427	-2 440	-1 245	-1 195	4 036	-9 261	8 356	-32 394	-30 720	-1 839	4 250
1993	27 442	1 052	-775	-235	-538	2 773	-6 774	12 552	7 756	2 738	4 603	5 758
1994	87 061	1 837	4 786	2 488	2 297	5 499	15 624	18 308	22 764	16 484	5 594	11 504
1995	94 261	2 825	8 150	2 716	5 436	5 493	16 168	26 354	21 364	15 404	4 301	9 349
1996	106 086	3 593	5 396	1 677	3 718	9 249	22 932	26 201	23 845	14 986	7 125	8 319
1997	121 385	3 066	6 563	2 765	3 798	10 130	24 044	34 220	27 734	19 132	7 222	7 729
1998	127 837	4 200	5 400	1 826	3 575	10 169	22 407	28 802	43 356	34 221	7 715	6 136
1999	144 071	6 120	3 457	428	3 029	10 631	28 957	38 637	37 203	24 445	10 197	10 702
1991												
1st quarter	1 392	-559	270	-268	537	499	-1 250	1 870	-1 011	-1 975	951	1 486
2nd quarter	7 562	144	342	-62	404	1 485	76	2 242	211	-1 292	1 364	2 211
3rd quarter	1 041	239	256	7	249	1 083	-325	-1 324	-1 595	-1 679	-39	1 844
4th quarter	-2 843	-1 392	-1 391	-1 159	-232	274	-1 264	1 898	-2 432	-2 656	201	1 139
1992												
1st quarter	-40 217	-1 112	-2 918	-1 131	-1 787	918	-3 919	631	-33 975	-28 471	-5 493	-539
2nd quarter	11 092	506	676	251	425	1 621	1 150	2 932	1 124	-79	1 076	1 974
3rd quarter	8 860	508	862	384	478	1 498	-460	2 720	37	-1 227	1 192	2 243
4th quarter	-3 695	-329	-1 060	-749	-311	-1	-6 032	2 073	420	-943	1 386	572
1993												
1st quarter	-1 684	-766	-1 358	-787	-570	701	-1 085	2 065	-2 276	-3 560	1 180	1
2nd quarter	9 271	1 445	939	680	259	1 596	-7 068	4 045	4 242	2 633	1 380	2 568
3rd quarter	11 476	709	197	40	157	1 310	369	3 369	1 966	689	1 147	2 046
4th quarter	8 379	-336	-553	-168	-384	-834	1 010	3 073	3 824	2 976	896	1 143
1994												
1st quarter	16 147	-484	713	421	291	1 507	2 112	3 939	4 540	3 182	1 265	2 419
2nd quarter	26 581	1 020	1 179	660	518	1 892	5 308	5 024	7 110	5 408	1 488	3 185
3rd quarter	22 288	873	1 307	712	596	1 706	3 458	5 217	4 569	3 023	1 369	2 983
4th quarter	22 045	428	1 587	695	892	394	4 746	4 128	6 545	4 871	1 472	2 917
1995												
1st quarter	25 991	235	2 412	842	1 571	1 808	4 702	5 547	6 582	5 012	1 230	3 459
2nd quarter	29 015	683	2 055	618	1 437	2 109	6 317	6 679	6 212	4 830	918	3 361
3rd quarter	20 669	1 299	2 047	728	1 320	1 342	1 992	6 792	4 046	2 002	1 587	2 022
4th quarter	18 586	608	1 636	528	1 108	234	3 157	7 336	4 524	3 560	566	507
1996												
1st quarter	22 587	377	1 334	232	1 103	2 134	3 840	6 155	5 596	3 327	1 512	1 910
2nd quarter	30 875	1 206	1 776	675	1 101	2 413	6 434	6 447	8 177	5 584	2 099	2 537
3rd quarter	27 590	1 433	1 443	626	817	3 146	5 839	6 030	5 471	3 293	1 801	2 277
4th quarter	25 034	577	843	144	697	1 556	6 819	7 569	4 601	2 782	1 713	1 595
1997												
1st quarter	27 031	-818	1 703	595	1 108	2 367	5 475	8 303	6 885	4 807	1 792	1 471
2nd quarter	36 344	1 277	2 130	920	1 210	2 898	7 213	9 464	8 778	6 094	2 175	2 125
3rd quarter	29 481	1 693	1 640	637	1 003	2 909	4 567	8 363	5 820	3 257	2 240	2 364
4th quarter	28 529	914	1 090	613	477	1 956	6 789	8 090	6 251	4 974	1 015	1 769
1998												
1st quarter	44 813	515	1 796	652	1 145	2 805	6 160	6 404	23 804	21 837	1 615	1 840
2nd quarter	25 774	1 776	1 497	692	805	3 294	3 593	3 865	8 107	5 458	2 106	1 317
3rd quarter	28 113	2 018	1 449	437	1 012	2 658	5 938	8 246	4 585	1 952	2 133	1 312
4th quarter	29 137	-109	658	45	613	1 412	6 716	10 287	6 860	4 974	1 861	1 667
1999												
1st quarter	33 546	825	666	-48	715	2 418	6 567	7 933	11 279	6 790	3 761	1 761
2nd quarter	39 737	1 950	1 256	346	910	3 130	8 940	8 013	11 159	7 161	3 129	2 546
3rd quarter	34 799	2 042	931	99	832	3 410	6 939	9 839	6 904	4 732	1 613	2 648
4th quarter	35 989	1 303	604	31	572	1 673	6 511	12 852	7 861	5 762	1 694	3 747

1. The tobacco industry is included beginning with the data for 1985.

Table 7-4. Corporate Profits and Dividends Paid, All Manufacturing—*Continued*

(Income after income taxes, millions of dollars.)

| Year and quarter | Durable goods manufacturing—*Continued* | | | | Mining | Wholesale trade | | | Retail trade | | | | Dividends paid, all manu-facturing |
| | Other durable goods | | | | | Total | Durable goods | Nondurable goods | Total | General merchan-dise stores | Food stores | All others | |
	Total	Lumber and wood products	Furniture and fixtures	Miscel-laneous manufac-turing									
1970	...	...	...	...	...	...	...	...	...	...	...	...	15 070
1971	...	...	...	...	...	...	...	...	...	...	...	...	15 252
1972	...	...	...	...	...	...	...	...	...	...	...	...	16 110
1973	...	...	...	...	...	...	...	...	...	...	...	...	17 734
1974	...	...	...	...	...	...	...	...	...	...	...	...	19 467
1975	...	...	...	...	...	...	...	...	...	...	...	...	19 968
1976	...	...	...	...	...	...	...	...	...	...	...	...	22 763
1977	...	...	...	...	...	...	...	...	...	...	...	...	26 585
1978	...	...	...	...	...	...	...	...	...	...	...	...	28 932
1979	...	...	...	...	...	...	...	...	...	...	...	...	32 491
1980	...	...	...	...	...	...	...	...	...	...	...	...	36 495
1981	...	...	...	...	...	...	...	...	...	...	...	...	40 317
1982	...	...	...	...	...	...	...	...	...	...	...	...	41 259
1983	...	...	...	...	...	...	...	...	...	...	...	...	41 624
1984	...	...	...	...	...	...	...	...	...	...	...	...	45 102
1985	...	...	...	...	...	...	...	...	...	...	...	...	45 517
1986	...	...	...	...	...	...	...	...	...	...	...	...	46 044
1987	...	...	...	...	...	...	...	...	...	...	...	...	49 512
1988	3 901	...	...	...	584	7 583	3 532	4 051	10 961	5 685	1 491	3 785	57 064
1989	4 370	...	...	...	1 613	7 275	2 731	4 543	8 380	3 560	540	4 281	65 243
1990	3 186	...	...	...	2 469	4 415	519	3 896	7 192	3 285	1 013	2 897	62 201
1991	2 125	...	...	...	759	3 916	333	3 584	6 798	2 747	1 601	2 450	60 231
1992	3 921	1 753	955	1 213	-240	5 121	1 355	3 766	6 170	2 288	1 007	2 872	63 061
1993	5 095	2 357	1 339	1 401	1 476	6 717	2 069	4 649	11 357	6 281	1 672	3 402	66 756
1994	6 738	3 274	1 593	1 870	820	5 698	1 433	4 266	18 144	7 468	2 981	7 693	69 977
1995	4 560	2 095	1 061	1 404	863	11 245	4 779	6 464	14 855	6 654	3 228	4 974	80 866
1996	6 552	2 619	2 284	1 648	5 828	13 371	5 538	7 833	18 197	6 902	3 627	7 668	95 517
1997	7 898	3 731	2 744	1 422	5 288	16 810	7 187	9 624	21 231	7 923	3 796	9 512	108 029
1998	8 363	3 983	2 804	1 578	2 027	17 455	7 472	6 409	31 687	9 636	4 397	12 573	119 959
1999	7 366	2 606	3 140	1 620	-3 720	14 021	...	...	28 595	...	...	...	103 193
1991													
1st quarter	87	...	...	...	443	671	-264	935	731	388	331	12	14 722
2nd quarter	850	...	...	...	340	1 015	-58	1 073	1 887	658	654	575	14 982
3rd quarter	861	...	...	...	241	1 335	204	1 132	1 394	468	455	472	14 647
4th quarter	327	...	...	...	-265	895	451	444	2 786	1 233	161	1 391	15 880
1992													
1st quarter	698	380	138	181	-684	621	-170	792	-735	-1 220	264	221	14 765
2nd quarter	1 109	465	260	384	142	1 470	232	1 238	2 411	1 433	435	542	15 533
3rd quarter	1 453	562	423	468	170	1 447	423	1 024	1 551	719	292	539	15 519
4th quarter	661	346	134	180	132	1 583	870	712	2 943	1 356	16	1 570	17 244
1993													
1st quarter	1 035	541	342	153	241	674	-167	841	1 511	1 020	-149	639	16 137
2nd quarter	1 501	746	348	407	779	2 474	908	1 566	3 661	1 927	670	1 064	16 982
3rd quarter	1 508	640	322	546	362	1 268	503	766	2 609	1 234	518	857	16 246
4th quarter	1 051	430	327	295	94	2 301	825	1 476	3 576	2 100	633	842	17 391
1994													
1st quarter	1 401	716	217	468	-538	2 149	794	1 355	2 704	816	624	1 264	16 269
2nd quarter	1 863	991	475	396	694	2 535	1 312	1 223	4 143	1 563	851	1 729	17 187
3rd quarter	2 173	1 020	570	584	556	-890	-1 841	951	3 805	1 398	783	1 623	17 533
4th quarter	1 301	547	331	422	108	1 904	1 168	737	7 492	3 691	723	3 077	18 988
1995													
1st quarter	1 247	621	289	337	244	2 594	956	1 637	3 201	1 353	767	1 081	18 292
2nd quarter	1 599	733	594	272	646	2 606	874	1 731	3 621	1 422	894	1 306	20 646
3rd quarter	1 129	362	505	262	-438	2 930	1 437	1 493	3 593	1 284	706	1 603	20 980
4th quarter	585	379	-327	533	411	3 115	1 512	1 603	4 440	2 595	861	984	20 948
1996													
1st quarter	1 239	368	413	459	794	3 388	1 473	1 915	2 943	941	888	1 114	20 048
2nd quarter	1 888	926	544	416	1 435	3 277	1 242	2 035	3 916	1 466	925	1 525	27 067
3rd quarter	1 949	957	616	376	2 074	3 464	1 968	1 496	4 858	1 665	875	2 318	23 387
4th quarter	1 476	368	711	397	1 525	3 242	855	2 387	6 480	2 830	939	2 711	25 015
1997													
1st quarter	1 644	883	455	307	2 082	3 822	1 483	2 339	3 651	1 224	893	1 533	21 815
2nd quarter	2 459	1 219	797	442	1 432	4 568	1 710	2 858	3 826	1 111	766	1 950	25 734
3rd quarter	2 125	945	784	395	1 697	4 982	2 168	2 814	4 974	1 443	878	2 653	25 586
4th quarter	1 670	684	708	278	77	3 438	1 826	1 613	8 780	4 145	1 259	3 376	34 894
1998													
1st quarter	1 438	618	629	192	568	4 734	1 067	2 061	12 062	1 636	958	2 956	31 131
2nd quarter	2 085	1 040	587	459	1 295	5 072	1 586	2 227	5 960	2 173	1 177	2 974	28 145
3rd quarter	2 743	1 381	835	526	301	4 255	3 198	969	7 051	1 343	1 044	2 962	27 123
4th quarter	2 097	944	753	401	-137	3 394	1 621	1 152	6 614	4 484	1 218	3 681	33 560
1999													
1st quarter	1 645	406	807	432	-4 790	2 837	...	...	9 872	...	...	...	25 151
2nd quarter	1 907	589	746	572	-26	4 216	...	...	5 261	...	...	...	26 849
3rd quarter	2 325	1 011	911	403	471	3 840	...	...	7 912	...	...	...	23 804
4th quarter	1 489	600	676	213	625	3 128	...	...	5 550	...	...	...	27 389

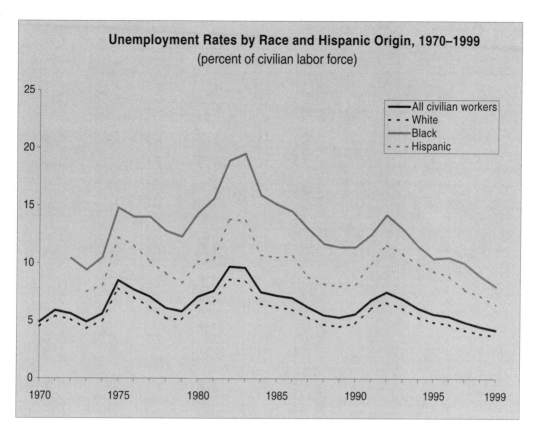

Unemployment Rates by Race and Hispanic Origin, 1970–1999
(percent of civilian labor force)

- The 1999 unemployment rate of 4.2 percent was the lowest recorded in 30 years. The rates for Blacks and Hispanics remained higher, but each fell to its lowest point since these data first became available in the mid-1970s.

- 1999 saw 64.3 percent of the civilian noninstitutional population holding jobs, an all-time record. The labor force participation rate (i.e., labor force as a percent of population) of 67.1 percent was also a record, unchanged from that of 1997 and 1998.

- Nonfarm payroll employment grew by 2.9 million to 128.8 million in 1999. Of the 2.9 million net new jobs created, 2.85 million were in the service-producing industries. The industry group with the most rapid job growth was Business Services, which includes both computer and temporary job (i.e., "help supply") services.

- Adjusted for inflation using the CPI-W, average hourly earnings of production or non-supervisory workers declined during and after the 1990–1991 recession. Beginning in 1996, however, hourly wages started an upward trend that continued through 1999. From 1995 to 1999, real wages increased an average 1.6 percent per year. This increase lagged behind, however, the 2.5 percent nonfarm productivity growth over the same period.

Table 8-1. Civilian Population and Labor Force [1]

(Thousands of persons, 16 years of age and over.)

Year and month	Not seasonally adjusted				Civilian labor force (seasonally adjusted)					Not in labor force, want a job, seasonally adjusted
	Civilian noninstitutional population	Civilian labor force			Total		Persons 20 years and over		Both sexes, 18 to 19 years	
		Total	Employed	Unemployed	Thousands of persons	Participation rate [2]	Men	Women		
1970	137 085	82 771	78 678	4 093	82 771	60.4	47 220	28 301	7 249	3 907
1971	140 216	84 382	79 367	5 016	84 382	60.2	48 009	28 904	7 470	4 441
1972	144 126	87 034	82 153	4 882	87 034	60.4	49 079	29 901	8 054	4 476
1973	147 096	89 429	85 064	4 365	89 429	60.8	49 932	30 991	8 507	4 474
1974	150 120	91 949	86 794	5 156	91 949	61.3	50 879	32 201	8 871	4 541
1975	153 153	93 775	85 846	7 929	93 775	61.2	51 494	33 410	8 870	5 292
1976	156 150	96 158	88 752	7 406	96 158	61.6	52 288	34 814	9 056	5 217
1977	159 033	99 009	92 017	6 991	99 009	62.3	53 348	36 310	9 351	5 777
1978	161 911	102 251	96 048	6 202	102 251	63.2	54 471	38 128	9 652	5 459
1979	164 863	104 962	98 824	6 137	104 962	63.7	55 615	39 708	9 638	5 439
1980	167 745	106 940	99 303	7 637	106 940	63.8	56 455	41 106	9 378	5 682
1981	170 130	108 670	100 397	8 273	108 670	63.9	57 197	42 485	8 988	5 819
1982	172 271	110 204	99 526	10 678	110 204	64.0	57 980	43 699	8 526	6 563
1983	174 215	111 550	100 834	10 717	111 550	64.0	58 744	44 636	8 171	6 484
1984	176 383	113 544	105 005	8 539	113 544	64.4	59 701	45 900	7 943	6 054
1985	178 206	115 461	107 150	8 312	115 461	64.8	60 277	47 283	7 901	5 908
1986	180 587	117 834	109 597	8 237	117 834	65.3	61 320	48 589	7 926	5 848
1987	182 753	119 865	112 440	7 425	119 865	65.6	62 095	49 783	7 988	5 721
1988	184 613	121 669	114 968	6 701	121 669	65.9	62 768	50 870	8 031	5 370
1989	186 393	123 869	117 342	6 528	123 869	66.5	63 704	52 212	7 954	5 312
1990	189 164	125 840	118 793	7 047	125 840	66.5	64 916	53 131	7 792	5 481
1991	190 925	126 346	117 718	8 628	126 346	66.2	65 374	53 708	7 265	5 745
1992	192 805	128 105	118 492	9 613	128 105	66.4	66 213	54 796	7 096	6 172
1993	194 838	129 200	120 259	8 940	129 200	66.3	66 642	55 388	7 170	6 346
1994	196 814	131 056	123 060	7 996	131 056	66.6	66 921	56 655	7 481	6 218
1995	198 584	132 304	124 900	7 404	132 304	66.6	67 324	57 215	7 765	5 670
1996	200 591	133 943	126 708	7 236	133 943	66.8	68 044	58 094	7 806	5 451
1997	203 133	136 297	129 558	6 739	136 297	67.1	69 166	59 198	7 932	4 941
1998	205 220	137 673	131 463	6 210	137 673	67.1	69 715	59 702	8 256	4 812
1999	207 753	139 368	133 488	5 880	139 368	67.1	70 194	60 840	8 333	4 568
1996										
January	199 634	131 396	123 126	8 270	132 668	66.5	67 417	57 518	7 733	5 583
February	199 773	131 995	124 137	7 858	133 002	66.6	67 706	57 587	7 709	5 720
March	199 921	132 692	124 992	7 700	133 198	66.6	67 829	57 692	7 677	5 520
April	200 101	132 513	125 388	7 124	133 403	66.7	67 780	57 844	7 779	5 413
May	200 278	133 558	126 391	7 166	133 674	66.7	67 977	57 875	7 822	5 459
June	200 459	135 083	127 706	7 377	133 690	66.7	68 087	57 863	7 740	5 614
July	200 641	136 272	128 579	7 693	134 265	66.9	68 215	58 192	7 858	5 381
August	200 847	135 011	128 143	6 868	134 043	66.7	68 089	58 233	7 721	5 472
September	201 061	134 230	127 529	6 700	134 486	66.9	68 217	58 336	7 933	5 359
October	201 273	135 015	128 439	6 577	134 881	67.0	68 387	58 518	7 976	5 403
November	201 463	134 973	128 157	6 816	134 953	67.0	68 399	58 690	7 864	5 296
December	201 636	134 583	127 903	6 680	135 071	67.0	68 368	58 818	7 885	5 133
1997										
January	202 285	134 317	126 384	7 933	135 576	67.0	68 849	58 791	7 936	5 034
February	202 389	134 535	126 887	7 647	135 496	66.9	68 805	58 708	7 983	5 160
March	202 513	135 524	128 125	7 399	135 958	67.1	69 019	58 991	7 948	5 074
April	202 674	135 181	128 629	6 551	136 043	67.1	69 083	58 977	7 983	4 843
May	202 832	135 963	129 565	6 398	136 061	67.1	69 016	59 123	7 922	5 205
June	203 000	137 557	130 463	7 094	136 218	67.1	69 183	59 164	7 871	4 916
July	203 166	138 331	131 350	6 981	136 421	67.1	69 170	59 289	7 962	4 922
August	203 364	137 460	130 865	6 594	136 590	67.2	69 286	59 398	7 906	4 817
September	203 570	136 375	129 972	6 403	136 612	67.1	69 269	59 484	7 859	4 846
October	203 767	136 665	130 671	5 995	136 547	67.0	69 275	59 401	7 871	4 783
November	203 941	136 912	130 999	5 914	136 860	67.1	69 443	59 374	8 043	4 850
December	204 098	136 742	130 785	5 957	137 097	67.2	69 474	59 676	7 947	4 798
1998										
January	204 238	135 951	128 882	7 069	137 225	67.2	69 491	59 567	8 167	4 916
February	204 400	136 286	129 482	6 804	137 263	67.2	69 499	59 594	8 170	4 820
March	204 547	136 967	130 150	6 816	137 333	67.1	69 448	59 662	8 223	4 889
April	204 731	136 379	130 735	5 643	137 216	67.0	69 625	59 503	8 088	4 874
May	204 899	137 240	131 476	5 764	137 329	67.0	69 637	59 552	8 140	4 693
June	205 085	138 798	132 265	6 534	137 449	67.0	69 591	59 528	8 330	4 767
July	205 270	139 336	132 769	6 567	137 476	67.0	69 754	59 496	8 226	4 878
August	205 479	138 379	132 206	6 173	137 565	66.9	69 536	59 727	8 302	4 932
September	205 699	137 903	131 864	6 039	138 156	67.2	69 869	59 859	8 428	4 915
October	205 919	138 255	132 424	5 831	138 189	67.1	69 967	59 883	8 339	4 879
November	206 104	138 288	132 577	5 711	138 230	67.1	70 029	59 935	8 266	4 571
December	206 270	138 297	132 732	5 565	138 545	67.2	70 044	60 118	8 383	4 607
1999										
January	206 719	137 943	131 339	6 604	139 232	67.4	70 202	60 691	8 339	4 693
February	206 873	138 202	131 639	6 563	139 137	67.3	70 111	60 591	8 435	4 630
March	207 036	138 418	132 299	6 119	138 804	67.0	69 934	60 554	8 316	4 606
April	207 236	138 240	132 552	5 688	139 086	67.1	69 992	60 765	8 329	4 740
May	207 427	138 919	133 411	5 507	139 013	67.0	69 978	60 708	8 327	4 658
June	207 632	140 666	134 395	6 271	139 332	67.1	70 116	60 988	8 228	4 770
July	207 828	141 119	134 800	6 319	139 336	67.0	70 167	60 852	8 317	4 575
August	208 038	140 090	134 264	5 826	139 372	67.0	70 240	60 904	8 228	4 497
September	208 265	139 217	133 555	5 661	139 475	67.0	70 328	60 860	8 287	4 352
October	208 483	139 761	134 390	5 372	139 697	67.0	70 339	60 955	8 403	4 331
November	208 666	139 895	134 515	5 380	139 834	67.0	70 388	61 052	8 394	4 429
December	208 832	139 941	134 696	5 245	140 108	67.1	70 529	61 154	8 425	4 467

1. Changes in survey design, population estimates, and methodology in 1994 and several other years affect year-to-year comparisons. See Notes for more information.
2. Labor force as a percent of population.

Table 8-2. Civilian Employment and Unemployment [1]

(Thousands of persons, 16 years and over, except as noted; seasonally adjusted.)

Year and month	Employment						Unemployment						
	Total		By age and sex			By industry		Total	Long-term [3]	Persons 20 years and over		Both sexes, 16 to 19 years	Average weeks unem-ployed	Median weeks unem-ployed
	Thousands of persons	Ratio: employ-ment to popu-lation [2]	Persons 20 years and over		Both sexes, 16 to 19 years	Agricul-tural	Nonagri-cultural							
			Men	Women						Men	Women			
1970	78 678	57.4	45 581	26 952	6 144	3 463	75 215	4 093	663	1 638	1 349	1 107	8.6	4.9
1971	79 367	56.6	45 912	27 246	6 208	3 394	75 972	5 016	1 187	2 097	1 658	1 263	11.3	6.3
1972	82 153	57.0	47 130	28 276	6 746	3 484	78 669	4 882	1 167	1 948	1 625	1 310	12.0	6.2
1973	85 064	57.8	48 310	29 484	7 271	3 470	81 594	4 365	826	1 624	1 507	1 237	10.0	5.2
1974	86 794	57.8	48 922	30 424	7 448	3 515	83 279	5 156	955	1 957	1 777	1 423	9.8	5.2
1975	85 846	56.1	48 018	30 726	7 104	3 408	82 438	7 929	2 505	3 476	2 684	1 768	14.2	8.4
1976	88 752	56.8	49 190	32 226	7 336	3 331	85 421	7 406	2 366	3 098	2 588	1 719	15.8	8.2
1977	92 017	57.9	50 555	33 775	7 688	3 283	88 734	6 991	1 942	2 794	2 535	1 662	14.0	7.0
1978	96 048	59.3	52 143	35 836	8 070	3 387	92 661	6 202	1 414	2 328	2 292	1 583	12.0	6.0
1979	98 824	59.9	53 308	37 434	8 083	3 347	95 477	6 137	1 241	2 308	2 276	1 554	11.0	5.0
1980	99 303	59.2	53 101	38 492	7 710	3 364	95 938	7 637	1 871	3 353	2 615	1 668	11.9	6.5
1981	100 397	59.0	53 582	39 590	7 225	3 368	97 030	8 273	2 285	3 615	2 895	1 762	13.7	6.9
1982	99 526	57.8	52 891	40 086	6 549	3 401	96 125	10 678	3 485	5 089	3 613	1 976	15.6	8.7
1983	100 834	57.9	53 487	41 004	6 342	3 383	97 450	10 717	4 210	5 257	3 632	1 829	20.0	10.1
1984	105 005	59.5	55 769	42 793	6 444	3 321	101 685	8 539	2 737	3 932	3 107	1 500	18.2	7.9
1985	107 150	60.1	56 562	44 154	6 434	3 179	103 971	8 312	2 305	3 715	3 129	1 469	15.6	6.8
1986	109 597	60.7	57 569	45 556	6 472	3 163	106 434	8 237	2 232	3 751	3 032	1 454	15.0	6.9
1987	112 440	61.5	58 726	47 074	6 640	3 208	109 232	7 425	1 983	3 369	2 709	1 347	14.5	6.5
1988	114 968	62.3	59 781	48 383	6 805	3 169	111 800	6 701	1 610	2 987	2 487	1 226	13.5	5.9
1989	117 342	63.0	60 837	49 745	6 759	3 199	114 142	6 528	1 375	2 867	2 467	1 194	11.9	4.8
1990	118 793	62.8	61 678	50 535	6 581	3 223	115 570	7 047	1 525	3 239	2 596	1 212	12.0	5.3
1991	117 718	61.7	61 178	50 634	5 906	3 269	114 449	8 628	2 357	4 195	3 074	1 359	13.7	6.8
1992	118 492	61.5	61 496	51 328	5 669	3 247	115 245	9 613	3 408	4 717	3 469	1 427	17.7	8.7
1993	120 259	61.7	62 355	52 099	5 805	3 115	117 144	8 940	3 094	4 287	3 288	1 365	18.0	8.3
1994	123 060	62.5	63 294	53 606	6 161	3 409	119 651	7 996	2 860	3 627	3 049	1 320	18.8	9.2
1995	124 900	62.9	64 085	54 396	6 419	3 440	121 460	7 404	2 363	3 239	2 819	1 346	16.6	8.3
1996	126 708	63.2	64 897	55 311	6 500	3 443	123 264	7 236	2 316	3 146	2 783	1 306	16.7	8.3
1997	129 558	63.8	66 284	56 613	6 661	3 399	126 159	6 739	2 062	2 882	2 585	1 271	15.8	8.0
1998	131 463	64.1	67 135	57 278	7 051	3 378	128 085	6 210	1 637	2 580	2 424	1 205	14.5	6.7
1999	133 488	64.3	67 761	58 555	7 172	3 281	130 207	5 880	1 480	2 433	2 285	1 162	13.4	6.4
1996														
January	125 152	62.7	64 192	54 592	6 368	3 486	121 666	7 516	2 372	3 225	2 926	1 365	16.2	8.3
February	125 672	62.9	64 411	54 855	6 406	3 555	122 117	7 330	2 304	3 295	2 732	1 303	16.4	7.8
March	125 875	63.0	64 510	55 000	6 365	3 490	122 385	7 323	2 456	3 319	2 692	1 312	17.3	8.3
April	126 002	63.0	64 475	55 074	6 453	3 396	122 606	7 401	2 438	3 305	2 770	1 326	17.5	8.6
May	126 229	63.0	64 678	55 040	6 511	3 476	122 753	7 445	2 403	3 299	2 835	1 311	17.0	8.6
June	126 598	63.2	64 938	55 170	6 490	3 418	123 180	7 092	2 347	3 149	2 693	1 250	17.6	8.3
July	126 942	63.3	65 064	55 360	6 518	3 434	123 508	7 323	2 298	3 151	2 832	1 340	16.8	8.3
August	127 172	63.3	65 225	55 523	6 424	3 402	123 770	6 871	2 269	2 864	2 710	1 297	17.3	8.4
September	127 513	63.4	65 160	55 656	6 697	3 448	124 065	6 973	2 224	3 057	2 680	1 236	16.8	8.5
October	127 863	63.5	65 451	55 737	6 675	3 465	124 398	7 018	2 275	2 936	2 781	1 301	16.3	8.3
November	127 732	63.4	65 310	55 877	6 545	3 353	124 379	7 221	2 169	3 089	2 813	1 319	15.9	7.6
December	127 831	63.4	65 422	55 837	6 572	3 431	124 400	7 240	2 134	2 946	2 981	1 313	15.6	7.8
1997														
January	128 387	63.5	65 734	56 045	6 608	3 459	124 928	7 189	2 166	3 115	2 746	1 328	16.0	7.8
February	128 350	63.4	65 778	55 977	6 595	3 358	124 992	7 146	2 133	3 027	2 731	1 388	15.8	8.1
March	128 922	63.7	65 978	56 296	6 648	3 422	125 500	7 036	2 114	3 041	2 695	1 300	15.6	7.9
April	129 191	63.7	66 103	56 370	6 718	3 468	125 723	6 852	2 160	2 980	2 607	1 265	15.6	8.3
May	129 383	63.8	66 276	56 451	6 656	3 434	125 949	6 678	2 125	2 740	2 672	1 266	15.4	7.9
June	129 417	63.8	66 295	56 567	6 555	3 398	126 019	6 801	2 059	2 888	2 597	1 316	15.5	8.0
July	129 812	63.9	66 418	56 786	6 608	3 421	126 391	6 609	2 122	2 752	2 503	1 354	16.4	8.3
August	129 987	63.9	66 520	56 833	6 634	3 359	126 628	6 603	2 011	2 766	2 565	1 272	16.0	7.8
September	129 982	63.9	66 486	56 900	6 596	3 400	126 582	6 630	2 062	2 783	2 584	1 263	15.8	8.2
October	130 121	63.9	66 495	56 947	6 679	3 309	126 812	6 426	1 959	2 780	2 454	1 192	16.1	7.7
November	130 577	64.0	66 737	56 991	6 849	3 375	127 202	6 283	1 837	2 706	2 383	1 194	15.4	7.6
December	130 646	64.0	66 621	57 197	6 828	3 395	127 251	6 451	1 918	2 853	2 479	1 119	15.9	7.5
1998														
January	130 819	64.1	66 822	56 961	7 036	3 334	127 485	6 406	1 833	2 669	2 606	1 131	15.6	7.3
February	130 911	64.0	66 877	57 064	6 970	3 354	127 557	6 352	1 795	2 622	2 530	1 200	15.3	7.0
March	130 854	64.0	66 708	57 141	7 005	3 180	127 674	6 479	1 767	2 740	2 521	1 218	14.6	6.8
April	131 255	64.1	67 146	57 109	7 000	3 341	127 914	5 961	1 482	2 479	2 394	1 088	14.6	6.6
May	131 278	64.1	67 137	57 195	6 946	3 347	127 931	6 051	1 504	2 500	2 357	1 194	14.8	6.0
June	131 234	64.0	67 014	57 130	7 090	3 345	127 889	6 215	1 613	2 577	2 398	1 240	14.0	6.8
July	131 274	64.0	67 087	57 160	7 027	3 408	127 866	6 202	1 586	2 667	2 336	1 199	14.2	6.8
August	131 381	63.9	66 997	57 319	7 065	3 498	127 883	6 184	1 637	2 539	2 408	1 237	13.8	6.7
September	131 922	64.1	67 267	57 483	7 172	3 499	128 423	6 234	1 636	2 602	2 376	1 256	14.4	6.7
October	131 950	64.1	67 456	57 459	7 035	3 585	128 365	6 239	1 585	2 511	2 424	1 304	14.0	5.9
November	132 156	64.1	67 573	57 538	7 045	3 340	128 816	6 074	1 605	2 456	2 397	1 221	14.4	6.7
December	132 517	64.2	67 528	57 776	7 213	3 241	129 276	6 028	1 572	2 516	2 342	1 170	14.0	6.8
1999														
January	133 225	64.4	67 771	58 373	7 081	3 297	129 928	6 007	1 491	2 431	2 318	1 258	13.5	6.8
February	133 029	64.3	67 527	58 261	7 241	3 328	129 701	6 108	1 539	2 584	2 330	1 194	13.8	6.9
March	132 976	64.2	67 628	58 216	7 132	3 290	129 686	5 828	1 467	2 306	2 338	1 184	13.6	6.8
April	133 054	64.2	67 562	58 336	7 156	3 341	129 713	6 032	1 474	2 430	2 429	1 173	13.2	6.1
May	133 190	64.2	67 470	58 483	7 237	3 290	129 900	5 823	1 519	2 508	2 225	1 090	13.4	6.6
June	133 398	64.2	67 645	58 647	7 106	3 330	130 068	5 934	1 634	2 471	2 341	1 122	14.3	6.3
July	133 399	64.2	67 703	58 477	7 219	3 278	130 121	5 937	1 511	2 464	2 375	1 098	13.5	5.8
August	133 530	64.2	67 768	58 648	7 114	3 234	130 296	5 842	1 463	2 472	2 256	1 114	13.2	6.4
September	133 650	64.2	67 943	58 630	7 077	3 179	130 471	5 825	1 412	2 385	2 230	1 210	13.0	5.9
October	133 940	64.2	67 898	58 800	7 242	3 238	130 702	5 757	1 434	2 441	2 155	1 161	13.2	6.3
November	134 098	64.3	68 037	58 838	7 223	3 310	130 788	5 736	1 401	2 351	2 214	1 171	13.0	6.2
December	134 420	64.4	68 197	58 958	7 265	3 279	131 141	5 688	1 388	2 332	2 196	1 160	12.8	5.9

1. Changes in survey design, population estimates, and methodology in 1994 and several other years affect year-to-year comparisions. See Notes for more information.
2. Civilian employment as a percent of the civilian noninstitutional population.
3. Fifteen weeks and over.

Table 8-3. Unemployment Rates [1]

(Percent of the civilian labor force in group, seasonally adjusted.)

Year and month	All civilian workers	By age and sex			By race		Persons of Hispanic origin	By marital status			By industry of last job		
		20 years and over		Both sexes, 16 to 19 years	White	Black		Married men, spouse present	Married women, spouse present	Women who maintain families	Private nonagricultural wage and salary workers		
		Men	Women								Total	Construction	Manufacturing, total
1970	4.9	3.5	4.8	15.3	4.5	. . .	. . .	2.6	4.9	5.4	5.2	9.7	5.6
1971	5.9	4.4	5.7	16.9	5.4	. . .	. . .	3.2	5.7	7.3	6.2	10.4	6.8
1972	5.6	4.0	5.4	16.2	5.1	10.4	. . .	2.8	5.4	7.2	5.7	10.3	5.6
1973	4.9	3.3	4.9	14.5	4.3	9.4	7.5	2.3	4.7	7.1	4.9	8.9	4.4
1974	5.6	3.8	5.5	16.0	5.0	10.5	8.1	2.7	5.3	7.0	5.7	10.7	5.8
1975	8.5	6.8	8.0	19.9	7.8	14.8	12.2	5.1	7.9	10.0	9.1	18.0	10.9
1976	7.7	5.9	7.4	19.0	7.0	14.0	11.5	4.2	7.1	10.1	7.9	15.5	7.9
1977	7.1	5.2	7.0	17.8	6.2	14.0	10.1	3.6	6.5	9.4	7.1	12.7	6.7
1978	6.1	4.3	6.0	16.4	5.2	12.8	9.1	2.8	5.5	8.5	5.9	10.6	5.5
1979	5.8	4.2	5.7	16.1	5.1	12.3	8.3	2.8	5.1	8.3	5.8	10.3	5.6
1980	7.1	5.9	6.4	17.8	6.3	14.3	10.1	4.2	5.8	9.2	7.4	14.1	8.5
1981	7.6	6.3	6.8	19.6	6.7	15.6	10.4	4.3	6.0	10.4	7.7	15.6	8.3
1982	9.7	8.8	8.3	23.2	8.6	18.9	13.8	6.5	7.4	11.7	10.1	20.0	12.3
1983	9.6	8.9	8.1	22.4	8.4	19.5	13.7	6.5	7.0	12.2	9.9	18.4	11.2
1984	7.5	6.6	6.8	18.9	6.5	15.9	10.7	4.6	5.7	10.4	7.4	14.3	7.5
1985	7.2	6.2	6.6	18.6	6.2	15.1	10.5	4.3	5.6	10.4	7.2	13.1	7.7
1986	7.0	6.1	6.2	18.3	6.0	14.5	10.6	4.4	5.2	9.8	7.0	13.1	7.1
1987	6.2	5.4	5.4	16.9	5.3	13.0	8.8	3.9	4.3	9.2	6.2	11.6	6.0
1988	5.5	4.8	4.9	15.3	4.7	11.7	8.2	3.3	3.9	8.1	5.5	10.6	5.3
1989	5.3	4.5	4.7	15.0	4.5	11.4	8.0	3.0	3.7	8.1	5.3	10.0	5.1
1990	5.6	5.0	4.9	15.5	4.8	11.4	8.2	3.4	3.8	8.3	5.8	11.1	5.8
1991	6.8	6.4	5.7	18.7	6.1	12.5	10.0	4.4	4.5	9.3	7.1	15.5	7.3
1992	7.5	7.1	6.3	20.1	6.6	14.2	11.6	5.1	5.0	10.0	7.8	16.8	7.8
1993	6.9	6.4	5.9	19.0	6.1	13.0	10.8	4.4	4.6	9.7	7.1	14.4	7.2
1994	6.1	5.4	5.4	17.6	5.3	11.5	9.9	3.7	4.1	8.9	6.3	11.8	5.6
1995	5.6	4.8	4.9	17.3	4.9	10.4	9.3	3.3	3.9	8.0	5.8	11.5	4.9
1996	5.4	4.6	4.8	16.7	4.7	10.5	8.9	3.0	3.6	8.2	5.5	10.1	4.8
1997	4.9	4.2	4.4	16.0	4.2	10.0	7.7	2.7	3.1	8.1	5.0	9.0	4.2
1998	4.5	3.7	4.1	14.6	3.9	8.9	7.2	2.3	2.9	7.2	4.6	7.5	3.9
1999	4.2	3.5	3.8	13.9	3.7	8.0	6.4	2.2	2.7	6.4	4.3	7.0	3.6
1996													
January	5.7	4.8	5.1	17.7	4.9	10.6	9.4	3.2	3.9	8.0	5.8	10.6	5.0
February	5.5	4.9	4.7	16.9	4.9	10.0	9.6	3.1	3.7	7.4	5.6	11.0	4.8
March	5.5	4.9	4.7	17.1	4.8	10.6	9.7	3.1	3.5	7.3	5.8	10.2	5.3
April	5.5	4.9	4.8	17.0	4.8	10.7	9.5	3.0	3.7	7.6	5.7	10.5	4.8
May	5.6	4.9	4.9	16.8	4.9	10.2	9.5	3.0	3.7	8.6	5.8	10.3	5.1
June	5.3	4.6	4.7	16.1	4.6	10.4	8.8	3.0	3.5	7.8	5.4	9.7	4.9
July	5.5	4.6	4.9	17.1	4.7	10.6	8.8	3.0	3.5	9.1	5.6	10.1	4.6
August	5.1	4.2	4.7	16.8	4.4	10.6	8.8	2.9	3.4	8.5	5.3	8.8	4.6
September	5.2	4.5	4.6	15.6	4.5	10.6	8.2	3.0	3.4	8.4	5.2	9.3	4.3
October	5.2	4.3	4.8	16.3	4.4	10.7	8.0	2.9	3.6	8.5	5.3	9.6	4.7
November	5.4	4.5	4.8	16.8	4.6	10.6	8.5	3.1	3.6	8.6	5.5	10.5	4.8
December	5.4	4.3	5.1	16.7	4.6	10.5	7.4	2.9	3.8	8.6	5.4	9.2	4.7
1997													
January	5.3	4.5	4.7	16.7	4.5	10.8	8.3	2.8	3.3	8.9	5.4	9.9	4.5
February	5.3	4.4	4.7	17.4	4.5	10.7	8.2	2.8	3.3	8.8	5.3	9.2	4.5
March	5.2	4.4	4.6	16.4	4.4	10.5	8.5	2.8	3.3	8.6	5.3	9.6	4.5
April	5.0	4.3	4.4	15.8	4.3	10.1	8.1	2.7	3.1	7.8	5.1	8.9	4.5
May	4.9	4.0	4.5	16.0	4.1	10.3	7.7	2.7	3.2	7.7	5.1	8.5	4.3
June	5.0	4.2	4.4	16.7	4.2	10.8	7.5	2.7	3.1	8.1	5.0	8.6	4.2
July	4.8	4.0	4.2	17.0	4.2	9.5	7.0	2.7	3.1	7.7	4.9	8.9	4.2
August	4.8	4.0	4.3	16.1	4.2	9.4	7.2	2.6	3.0	8.1	4.9	8.9	4.0
September	4.9	4.0	4.3	16.1	4.2	9.4	7.4	2.6	3.2	7.7	4.9	8.5	4.0
October	4.7	4.0	4.1	15.1	4.1	9.5	7.7	2.6	2.9	7.8	4.8	8.8	3.7
November	4.6	3.9	4.0	14.8	3.9	9.5	7.0	2.4	2.8	8.0	4.7	8.0	3.7
December	4.7	4.1	4.2	14.1	3.9	10.0	7.3	2.5	2.9	7.8	4.7	8.9	3.8
1998													
January	4.7	3.8	4.4	13.8	4.0	9.5	7.1	2.5	3.0	7.7	4.7	8.0	3.8
February	4.6	3.8	4.2	14.7	4.0	9.3	7.0	2.5	3.0	7.5	4.7	7.9	3.8
March	4.7	3.9	4.2	14.8	4.1	9.2	7.2	2.5	3.3	7.5	4.7	8.7	4.0
April	4.3	3.6	4.0	13.5	3.7	9.1	6.7	2.2	2.8	7.5	4.4	6.5	4.0
May	4.4	3.6	4.0	14.7	3.8	9.0	6.9	2.3	2.8	7.5	4.5	7.9	3.7
June	4.5	3.7	4.0	14.9	3.9	8.7	7.4	2.3	2.9	7.0	4.6	7.8	3.6
July	4.5	3.8	3.9	14.6	3.8	9.4	7.2	2.3	2.8	6.9	4.6	6.9	4.2
August	4.5	3.7	4.0	14.9	3.9	8.9	7.4	2.3	3.1	6.8	4.7	7.2	3.8
September	4.5	3.7	4.0	14.9	3.9	8.9	7.2	2.3	2.8	7.5	4.7	8.8	3.9
October	4.5	3.6	4.0	15.6	3.9	8.5	7.1	2.3	2.8	6.9	4.6	6.7	3.9
November	4.4	3.5	4.0	14.8	3.8	8.6	7.2	2.3	2.9	6.9	4.5	7.5	3.8
December	4.4	3.6	3.9	14.0	3.8	7.8	7.8	2.3	2.8	6.3	4.4	6.1	3.9
1999													
January	4.3	3.5	3.8	15.1	3.8	7.8	6.7	2.3	2.8	6.3	4.3	7.3	3.5
February	4.4	3.7	3.8	14.2	3.8	8.2	6.8	2.4	2.8	6.5	4.4	7.4	3.7
March	4.2	3.3	3.9	14.2	3.6	8.0	6.0	2.1	2.7	6.6	4.3	7.0	3.5
April	4.3	3.5	4.0	14.1	3.8	7.8	6.8	2.3	2.9	7.1	4.4	7.3	3.4
May	4.2	3.6	3.7	13.1	3.7	7.6	6.7	2.3	2.6	6.0	4.3	7.2	3.5
June	4.3	3.5	3.8	13.6	3.8	7.6	6.6	2.2	2.7	6.5	4.4	7.3	3.7
July	4.3	3.5	3.9	13.2	3.7	8.6	6.3	2.3	2.8	6.4	4.4	6.9	3.5
August	4.2	3.5	3.7	13.5	3.7	7.8	6.5	2.3	2.7	6.3	4.2	7.6	3.8
September	4.2	3.4	3.7	14.6	3.6	8.3	6.6	2.2	2.6	6.4	4.3	6.9	3.9
October	4.1	3.5	3.5	13.8	3.5	8.3	6.3	2.2	2.5	6.0	4.2	6.7	3.7
November	4.1	3.3	3.6	14.0	3.5	8.0	6.1	2.1	2.5	6.0	4.2	5.7	3.7
December	4.1	3.3	3.6	13.8	3.5	7.9	5.9	2.2	2.5	6.2	4.1	6.6	3.6

1. Changes in survey design, population estimates, and methodology in 1994 and several other years affect year-to-year comparisons. See Notes for more information.

Table 8-3. Unemployment Rates [1]—*Continued*

(Percent of the civilian labor force in group, seasonally adjusted, except as noted.)

Year and month	By industry of last job—Continued								By occupation						Augmented unemployment rate [3]
	Private nonagricultural wage and salary workers—Continued						Government workers	Agricultural wage and salary workers	Managerial and professional speciality	Technical, sales, and administrative support	Precision production, craft, and repair	Operators, fabricators, and laborers	Farming, forestry, fishing	Service occupations [2]	
	Manufacturing		Transportation and utilities	Wholesale and retail trade	Finance, insurance, real estate	Services									
	Durable goods	Nondurable goods													
1970	5.7	5.4	3.2	5.3	2.8	4.7	2.2	7.5	...	...	...	...	...	...	9.2
1971	7.0	6.5	3.8	6.4	3.3	5.6	2.9	7.9	...	...	...	...	...	...	10.6
1972	5.5	5.7	3.5	6.4	3.4	5.3	2.9	7.7	...	...	...	...	...	...	10.2
1973	3.9	4.9	3.0	5.6	2.7	4.8	2.7	7.0	...	...	...	...	...	...	9.4
1974	5.4	6.2	3.2	6.4	3.1	5.2	3.0	7.5	...	...	...	...	...	...	10.0
1975	11.3	10.4	5.6	8.7	4.9	7.1	4.1	10.4	...	...	...	...	...	...	13.3
1976	7.7	8.1	5.0	8.6	4.4	7.2	4.4	11.8	...	...	...	...	...	...	12.5
1977	6.2	7.4	4.7	8.0	3.9	6.6	4.2	11.2	...	...	...	...	...	...	12.2
1978	5.0	6.3	3.7	6.9	3.1	5.7	3.9	8.9	...	...	...	...	...	...	10.8
1979	5.0	6.4	3.7	6.5	3.0	5.5	3.7	9.3	...	...	...	...	...	...	10.5
1980	8.9	7.9	4.9	7.4	3.4	5.9	4.1	11.0	...	...	...	...	...	...	11.8
1981	8.2	8.4	5.2	8.1	3.5	6.6	4.7	12.1	...	...	...	...	...	...	12.3
1982	13.3	10.8	6.9	10.0	4.7	7.6	4.9	14.7	3.3	6.1	10.6	16.7	8.5	10.8	14.8
1983	12.1	10.0	7.4	10.0	4.5	7.9	5.3	16.0	3.3	6.3	10.6	15.5	10.0	10.9	14.6
1984	7.2	7.8	5.5	8.0	3.7	6.6	4.5	13.5	2.6	5.0	7.4	11.5	8.4	9.1	12.2
1985	7.6	7.8	5.2	7.7	3.5	6.2	3.9	13.2	2.4	4.8	7.2	11.3	8.3	8.8	11.7
1986	6.9	7.4	5.1	7.6	3.5	6.1	3.6	12.5	2.4	4.7	7.2	10.9	7.8	8.6	11.4
1987	5.8	6.3	4.5	6.9	3.1	5.4	3.5	10.5	2.3	4.3	6.1	9.4	7.1	7.7	10.5
1988	5.0	5.7	3.9	6.2	3.0	4.9	2.8	10.6	1.9	4.0	5.4	8.3	7.0	6.9	9.5
1989	4.8	5.5	3.9	6.0	3.1	4.8	2.7	9.6	2.0	3.9	5.2	8.0	6.4	6.5	9.2
1990	5.8	5.8	3.9	6.4	3.0	5.0	2.7	9.8	2.1	4.3	5.9	8.7	6.4	6.6	9.5
1991	7.5	6.9	5.3	7.6	4.0	5.8	3.3	11.8	2.8	5.2	8.0	10.6	7.9	7.6	10.9
1992	8.0	7.6	5.5	8.4	4.6	6.6	3.6	12.5	3.1	5.9	8.9	11.1	8.3	8.2	11.8
1993	7.1	7.4	5.1	7.8	4.1	6.1	3.3	11.7	3.0	5.4	7.9	10.0	8.4	7.7	11.3
1994	5.2	6.0	4.8	7.4	3.6	5.9	3.4	11.3	2.6	5.0	6.3	9.0	8.4	8.0	10.4
1995	4.4	5.7	4.5	6.5	3.3	5.4	2.9	11.1	2.4	4.5	6.0	8.2	7.9	7.5	9.5
1996	4.5	5.2	4.1	6.4	2.7	5.4	2.9	10.2	2.3	4.5	5.5	7.9	7.6	7.2	9.1
1997	3.5	5.1	3.5	6.2	3.0	4.6	2.6	9.1	2.0	4.1	4.8	7.5	7.1	6.7	8.3
1998	3.4	4.6	3.4	5.6	2.5	4.5	2.3	8.3	1.8	3.9	4.2	6.7	6.5	6.4	7.7
1999	3.5	3.9	3.0	5.2	2.4	4.1	2.2	8.8	1.9	3.7	4.0	6.2	6.7	5.7	7.3
1996															
January	4.4	5.9	3.9	6.6	2.7	5.7	2.8	10.6	2.4	4.5	5.4	8.4	7.9	8.1	9.5
February	5.1	4.4	3.9	6.3	2.4	5.6	2.9	10.7	2.3	4.5	6.0	8.1	7.5	7.4	9.4
March	5.1	5.7	4.1	6.8	2.5	5.5	2.8	10.2	2.4	4.4	5.8	8.3	7.7	7.5	9.3
April	4.8	5.0	4.4	6.7	2.4	5.7	3.0	10.7	2.3	4.4	5.7	8.2	8.0	7.6	9.2
May	4.9	5.5	4.3	6.6	2.7	5.7	3.2	10.5	2.3	4.8	5.4	8.4	9.1	7.2	9.3
June	4.5	5.5	4.5	6.3	2.7	5.0	2.8	9.4	2.4	4.1	5.3	8.1	7.2	7.3	9.1
July	4.2	5.2	4.3	6.4	2.8	5.5	3.0	9.5	2.4	4.6	5.4	7.7	6.9	7.5	9.1
August	3.7	5.9	3.9	6.3	2.5	5.2	2.7	8.7	2.2	4.4	5.1	7.8	6.7	6.9	8.8
September	4.1	4.5	3.9	6.1	3.0	5.2	2.9	10.9	2.3	4.5	5.4	7.2	7.4	6.8	8.8
October	4.5	5.0	4.4	6.2	2.8	5.0	3.0	10.0	2.2	4.5	5.4	7.7	7.0	6.9	8.9
November	4.5	5.2	3.7	6.3	2.8	5.2	3.0	11.1	2.3	4.6	5.8	7.7	7.9	7.0	8.9
December	4.6	4.9	4.0	6.2	3.0	5.1	3.2	9.8	2.3	4.6	5.2	7.6	7.3	6.3	8.8
1997															
January	4.3	5.0	4.1	6.4	3.3	5.0	2.9	8.4	2.1	4.3	5.2	8.1	7.2	7.5	8.7
February	4.1	5.1	4.1	6.4	3.1	4.9	2.9	8.8	2.1	4.3	4.9	8.1	7.3	7.5	8.7
March	3.8	5.4	4.0	6.4	3.2	4.8	2.8	8.9	2.1	4.2	5.0	8.1	7.2	7.1	8.6
April	3.7	5.7	3.0	6.4	3.4	4.7	2.5	9.3	2.0	4.2	4.9	7.6	6.9	6.7	8.3
May	3.6	5.3	3.7	6.2	3.3	4.6	2.3	7.3	2.1	4.0	4.6	7.3	6.5	6.9	8.4
June	3.5	5.1	3.0	6.3	2.6	4.6	2.8	10.5	2.0	4.2	4.8	7.5	7.6	7.1	8.3
July	3.3	5.5	3.3	6.1	3.2	4.3	2.6	8.4	2.0	4.1	4.8	7.3	6.3	6.4	8.2
August	3.3	5.0	3.6	6.2	2.9	4.5	2.7	9.8	2.0	4.2	4.5	7.4	7.8	6.3	8.1
September	3.1	5.2	3.8	6.1	3.1	4.6	2.6	9.2	2.0	4.0	4.7	7.5	6.8	6.6	8.1
October	3.2	4.5	3.1	6.1	2.8	4.4	2.4	10.3	1.8	3.9	5.3	7.0	8.0	6.3	7.9
November	3.2	4.4	3.1	6.1	2.2	4.4	2.4	8.9	1.7	4.0	4.5	7.0	6.8	6.1	7.9
December	3.1	4.7	3.3	5.8	2.6	4.6	2.2	10.0	1.9	4.0	4.7	6.8	6.9	5.7	7.9
1998															
January	3.3	4.6	3.9	5.9	2.6	4.4	2.4	10.0	2.0	4.1	4.7	6.2	6.6	6.5	8.0
February	3.0	4.9	3.2	5.8	2.6	4.7	2.3	8.2	2.0	4.0	4.3	6.6	6.2	6.4	7.9
March	3.8	4.4	3.3	5.5	2.6	4.7	2.8	9.1	1.8	4.0	4.5	7.0	6.9	6.9	8.0
April	3.5	4.6	3.3	5.3	2.2	4.4	2.0	7.9	1.8	3.6	3.8	6.4	6.0	6.1	7.6
May	3.0	4.7	3.1	5.3	2.2	4.7	2.2	7.6	1.7	4.0	4.3	6.5	6.2	5.7	7.6
June	2.9	4.6	3.6	5.6	2.2	4.6	2.1	8.2	1.7	3.9	4.2	7.0	6.1	6.5	7.7
July	3.9	4.7	3.3	5.6	2.1	4.5	2.3	8.3	1.7	3.8	4.3	6.9	6.7	6.6	7.8
August	3.5	4.4	3.5	5.6	2.6	4.6	2.2	7.3	1.9	3.7	4.4	6.6	6.0	6.7	7.8
September	3.5	4.5	3.5	5.7	2.4	4.4	2.3	8.4	1.8	3.9	4.2	6.8	7.8	6.5	7.8
October	3.3	4.8	3.3	5.7	2.5	4.7	2.2	7.1	1.9	3.9	4.0	6.7	5.8	6.6	7.8
November	3.1	4.7	3.1	5.2	2.7	4.6	2.2	7.8	1.8	3.7	4.1	6.6	6.3	6.4	7.5
December	3.4	4.8	3.1	5.5	2.8	4.1	2.1	9.1	1.8	3.7	3.3	6.6	7.6	5.6	7.4
1999															
January	3.3	3.9	2.6	5.3	2.4	4.2	2.2	9.1	1.9	3.7	3.6	6.0	7.5	5.9	7.4
February	3.3	4.3	3.1	5.2	2.4	4.1	2.3	10.8	1.9	3.9	4.3	6.1	7.6	5.6	7.5
March	3.1	4.2	2.9	5.4	2.0	4.2	2.1	9.4	1.9	3.7	3.7	6.1	6.9	5.8	7.3
April	3.2	3.9	2.9	5.4	3.2	4.1	2.4	9.5	1.9	3.8	3.8	6.5	7.1	5.7	7.5
May	3.4	3.8	3.2	5.3	2.2	4.0	2.5	10.1	2.0	3.4	4.0	6.4	7.6	5.6	7.3
June	3.5	4.0	2.9	5.3	2.4	4.2	2.3	9.3	2.0	3.6	4.7	6.1	7.1	6.2	7.4
July	3.7	3.1	3.4	5.2	2.4	4.4	2.2	9.0	1.9	3.9	3.9	6.3	6.5	5.9	7.3
August	3.7	4.1	3.0	4.8	2.4	4.0	2.1	9.6	1.8	3.6	4.5	6.2	6.4	5.6	7.2
September	4.0	3.9	2.8	5.2	2.3	4.1	2.0	5.7	1.8	3.5	3.9	6.4	5.3	5.9	7.1
October	3.5	4.0	3.1	4.9	2.3	4.0	2.1	7.7	1.8	3.5	4.0	6.3	5.8	5.7	7.0
November	3.7	3.7	3.3	5.3	2.3	3.9	2.0	8.3	1.8	3.6	3.7	6.2	6.7	5.4	7.0
December	3.6	3.5	3.0	5.2	2.1	3.8	2.1	7.1	1.7	3.6	4.0	6.1	5.8	4.9	7.0

1. Changes in survey design, population estimates, and methodology in 1994 and several other years affect year-to-year comparisions. See Notes for more information.
2. Not seasonally adjusted.
3. See Notes.

Table 8-4. Insured Unemployment [1]

(Weekly averages, thousands of persons.)

Year and month	State programs (seasonally adjusted)			Federal programs (not seasonally adjusted)					
				Initial claims		Persons claiming benefits			
	Initial claims	Insured unemployment	Insured unemployment rate [2]	Federal employees	Newly discharged veterans	Federal employees	Newly discharged veterans	Railroad retirement	Extended benefits
1970	296	1 805	3.4	...	...	...	...	...	...
1971	295	2 150	4.1	...	...	...	...	...	...
1972	261	1 848	3.5	...	...	...	...	...	...
1973	247	1 632	2.7	...	...	...	...	...	...
1974	363	2 262	3.5	...	...	...	...	...	...
1975	478	3 986	6.0	...	...	...	...	...	...
1976	386	2 991	4.6	...	...	...	...	...	...
1977	375	2 655	3.9	...	...	...	...	...	...
1978	346	2 359	3.3	...	...	...	...	...	...
1979	388	2 434	2.9	...	...	...	...	...	...
1980	488	3 350	3.9	...	...	...	...	...	...
1981	460	3 047	3.5	...	...	...	...	...	...
1982	583	4 059	4.6	...	...	...	...	...	...
1983	438	3 395	3.9	...	...	...	...	...	...
1984	377	2 475	2.8	...	...	...	...	...	...
1985	397	2 617	2.9	...	...	...	...	...	...
1986	378	2 643	2.8	2.13	2.52	20.24	17.11	...	...
1987	328	2 300	2.4	2.19	2.57	21.29	17.71	...	8.64
1988	310	2 081	2.0	2.32	2.74	22.91	18.13	13.28	1.21
1989	330	2 158	2.1	2.14	2.31	22.17	15.09	10.37	0.60
1990	388	2 522	2.4	2.45	2.54	23.89	18.43	10.56	2.23
1991	447	3 342	3.2	2.55	2.93	30.50	22.12	10.73	32.05
1992	408	3 245	3.1	2.75	4.95	32.10	60.25	8.77	4.63
1993	341	2 751	2.6	2.55	3.94	32.06	54.90	7.40	8.02
1994	340	2 670	2.5	2.54	3.02	32.21	37.65	6.21	31.23
1995	357	2 572	2.3	4.57	2.51	31.68	29.78	5.48	14.31
1996	356	2 595	2.3	7.33	2.13	29.84	24.30	5.40	5.51
1997	323	2 323	2.0	2.01	1.75	23.58	19.66	4.00	5.07
1998	320	2 220	1.9	1.64	1.41	19.60	15.68	3.17	6.31
1999	297	2 185	1.8	...	...	...	...	...	...
1996									
January	368	2 629	2.3	66.18	2.50	49.79	28.61	9.50	10.99
February	370	2 676	2.4	4.39	2.22	36.15	28.53	9.50	9.39
March	383	2 648	2.4	1.82	2.15	32.26	26.84	8.00	3.04
April	360	2 601	2.3	2.28	2.02	27.94	25.09	6.00	3.25
May	347	2 572	2.3	1.80	1.97	24.84	23.86	4.50	5.11
June	350	2 552	2.3	2.39	2.08	24.26	22.66	4.00	11.75
July	334	2 515	2.2	2.96	2.23	26.63	22.61	4.00	13.88
August	326	2 504	2.2	1.98	2.30	27.40	22.74	4.20	8.27
September	341	2 470	2.2	2.03	2.23	25.76	22.68	4.00	0.23
October	338	2 477	2.2	2.95	2.15	27.40	22.99	3.75	0.11
November	338	2 453	2.2	2.32	1.84	28.07	22.49	3.80	0.09
December	354	2 508	2.2	2.07	1.91	29.50	23.14	4.00	0.06
1997									
January	336	2 477	2.1	2.59	2.05	29.47	23.79	6.50	0.06
February	314	2 402	2.1	1.83	1.87	27.40	23.72	7.50	0.18
March	313	2 309	2.0	1.42	1.79	24.16	22.12	6.60	2.45
April	329	2 284	2.0	1.62	1.66	21.19	20.57	5.00	2.69
May	328	2 276	2.0	1.61	1.57	18.52	19.02	3.40	1.96
June	335	2 298	2.0	2.06	1.68	18.59	18.16	2.75	1.38
July	321	2 305	2.0	2.69	1.87	21.31	18.04	2.50	0.38
August	324	2 282	2.0	1.75	2.10	23.00	19.01	2.80	0.11
September	313	2 233	1.9	1.82	1.71	22.10	18.38	2.50	8.43
October	310	2 232	1.9	2.85	1.79	24.40	18.21	2.50	15.10
November	319	2 244	1.9	2.15	1.43	26.14	17.52	2.80	18.19
December	315	2 261	2.0	2.00	1.56	27.37	17.59	3.25	9.94
1998									
January	318	2 267	1.9	2.27	1.71	27.40	18.36	4.60	0.44
February	309	2 197	1.8	1.43	1.48	24.53	17.73	5.00	0.24
March	308	2 170	1.8	1.28	1.50	21.98	16.87	4.25	7.29
April	311	2 136	1.8	1.34	1.35	19.09	15.82	3.25	14.59
May	316	2 112	1.8	1.29	1.26	15.99	14.94	2.00	19.90
June	353	2 235	1.9	1.64	1.38	15.42	14.41	2.00	14.57
July	325	2 372	2.0	2.16	1.50	17.10	14.78	2.00	0.27
August	305	2 230	1.9	1.31	1.42	18.31	15.21	2.00	0.05
September	301	2 166	1.8	1.46	1.39	16.90	14.89	2.00	0.03
October	313	2 195	1.8	1.98	1.33	18.28	14.83	2.40	...
November	320	2 238	1.9	1.73	1.21	19.09	14.74	3.50	6.21
December	323	2 262	1.9	1.70	1.33	20.75	15.40	5.50	13.40
1999									
January	316	2 254	1.9	...	...	...	...	...	...
February	292	2 204	1.8	...	...	...	...	...	...
March	296	2 180	1.8	...	...	...	...	...	...
April	308	2 180	1.8	...	...	...	...	...	...
May	306	2 189	1.8	...	...	...	...	...	...
June	305	2 216	1.8	...	...	...	...	...	...
July	295	2 211	1.8	...	...	...	...	...	...
August	289	2 201	1.8	...	...	...	...	...	...
September	295	2 187	1.8	...	...	...	...	...	...
October	289	2 140	1.7	...	...	...	...	...	...
November	286	2 132	1.8	...	...	...	...	...	...
December	285	2 129	1.7	...	...	...	...	...	...

1. Updated materials for federal programs were not available at press time.
2. Insured unemployed as a percent of employment covered by state programs.

Table 8-5. Nonfarm Employment

(Wage and salary workers on nonfarm payrolls, thousands.)

Year and month	Not seasonally adjusted		Seasonally adjusted		Diffusion index, 6-month span, private industry [1]	Goods-producing industries (seasonally adjusted)			Manufacturing			
	Total	Private sector	Total	Private sector		Total	Mining [2]	Construc- tion [2]	Total	Production workers	Durable goods	
											Total	Total, produc- tion workers
1970	70 880	58 325	70 880	58 325	. . .	23 578	623	3 588	19 367	14 044	11 176	8 088
1971	71 211	58 331	71 211	58 331	. . .	22 935	609	3 704	18 623	13 544	10 604	7 697
1972	73 675	60 341	73 675	60 341	. . .	23 668	628	3 889	19 151	14 045	11 022	8 025
1973	76 790	63 058	76 790	63 058	. . .	24 893	642	4 097	20 154	14 834	11 863	8 699
1974	78 265	64 095	78 265	64 095	. . .	24 794	697	4 020	20 077	14 638	11 897	8 634
1975	76 945	62 259	76 945	62 259	. . .	22 600	752	3 525	18 323	13 043	10 662	7 532
1976	79 382	64 511	79 382	64 511	. . .	23 352	779	3 576	18 997	13 638	11 051	7 888
1977	82 471	67 344	82 471	67 344	79.7	24 346	813	3 851	19 682	14 135	11 570	8 280
1978	86 697	71 026	86 697	71 026	76.2	25 585	851	4 229	20 505	14 734	12 245	8 777
1979	89 823	73 876	89 823	73 876	57.9	26 461	958	4 463	21 040	15 068	12 730	9 082
1980	90 406	74 166	90 406	74 166	37.5	25 658	1 027	4 346	20 285	14 214	12 159	8 416
1981	91 152	75 121	91 152	75 121	58.0	25 497	1 139	4 188	20 170	14 020	12 082	8 270
1982	89 544	73 707	89 544	73 707	36.8	23 812	1 128	3 904	18 780	12 742	11 014	7 290
1983	90 152	74 282	90 152	74 282	78.2	23 330	952	3 946	18 432	12 528	10 707	7 095
1984	94 408	78 384	94 408	78 384	72.6	24 718	966	4 380	19 372	13 280	11 476	7 715
1985	97 387	80 992	97 387	80 992	57.6	24 842	927	4 668	19 248	13 084	11 458	7 618
1986	99 344	82 651	99 344	82 651	57.6	24 533	777	4 810	18 947	12 864	11 195	7 399
1987	101 958	84 948	101 958	84 948	69.5	24 674	717	4 958	18 999	12 952	11 154	7 409
1988	105 209	87 823	105 209	87 823	66.3	25 125	713	5 098	19 314	13 193	11 363	7 582
1989	107 884	90 105	107 884	90 105	53.7	25 254	692	5 171	19 391	13 230	11 394	7 594
1990	109 403	91 098	109 403	91 098	43.4	24 905	709	5 120	19 076	12 947	11 109	7 363
1991	108 249	89 847	108 249	89 847	43.8	23 745	689	4 650	18 406	12 434	10 569	6 967
1992	108 601	89 956	108 601	89 956	57.4	23 231	635	4 492	18 104	12 287	10 277	6 822
1993	110 713	91 872	110 713	91 872	66.0	23 352	610	4 668	18 075	12 341	10 221	6 849
1994	114 163	95 036	114 163	95 036	69.7	23 908	601	4 986	18 321	12 632	10 448	7 104
1995	117 191	97 885	117 191	97 885	60.0	24 265	581	5 160	18 524	12 826	10 683	7 317
1996	119 608	100 189	119 608	100 189	64.5	24 493	580	5 418	18 495	12 776	10 789	7 386
1997	122 690	103 133	122 690	103 133	67.1	24 962	596	5 691	18 675	12 907	11 010	7 553
1998	125 865	106 042	125 865	106 042	61.4	25 414	590	6 020	18 805	12 952	11 205	7 666
1999	128 786	108 616	128 786	108 616	59.7	25 482	535	6 404	18 543	12 739	11 103	7 590
1996												
January	116 210	96 957	118 049	98 727	62.5	24 247	573	5 210	18 464	12 763	10 724	7 342
February	117 146	97 486	118 538	99 179	64.6	24 367	576	5 300	18 491	12 777	10 746	7 354
March	117 952	98 158	118 774	99 377	65.6	24 358	578	5 327	18 453	12 734	10 715	7 321
April	118 779	99 017	118 949	99 558	64.6	24 399	579	5 354	18 466	12 750	10 754	7 357
May	119 922	100 092	119 293	99 861	64.5	24 445	581	5 381	18 483	12 763	10 776	7 376
June	120 589	101 111	119 557	100 147	64.5	24 491	582	5 418	18 491	12 775	10 793	7 392
July	119 558	101 204	119 753	100 352	67.3	24 514	581	5 440	18 493	12 767	10 794	7 387
August	119 829	101 586	120 031	100 610	65.7	24 567	582	5 472	18 513	12 786	10 818	7 404
September	120 569	101 347	120 182	100 749	65.2	24 586	580	5 495	18 511	12 784	10 822	7 410
October	121 287	101 565	120 430	101 007	67.1	24 628	581	5 524	18 523	12 798	10 831	7 419
November	121 740	101 830	120 696	101 271	66.0	24 657	583	5 544	18 530	12 797	10 844	7 426
December	121 716	101 911	120 913	101 475	67.4	24 676	584	5 555	18 537	12 804	10 858	7 434
1997												
January	119 166	99 784	121 116	101 659	66.3	24 683	586	5 549	18 548	12 813	10 873	7 451
February	120 017	100 262	121 411	101 949	67.0	24 762	590	5 604	18 568	12 827	10 893	7 466
March	120 903	101 040	121 758	102 290	66.6	24 833	592	5 644	18 597	12 842	10 916	7 480
April	121 879	102 018	122 052	102 557	66.3	24 846	594	5 644	18 608	12 854	10 932	7 493
May	122 970	103 058	122 311	102 801	65.6	24 889	597	5 669	18 623	12 874	10 951	7 511
June	123 615	104 004	122 537	102 997	67.1	24 922	598	5 670	18 654	12 892	10 982	7 533
July	122 662	104 141	122 833	103 252	66.3	24 956	599	5 690	18 667	12 903	11 009	7 552
August	122 714	104 312	122 904	103 321	68.5	25 028	600	5 720	18 708	12 928	11 058	7 588
September	123 703	104 329	123 335	103 754	69.0	25 070	601	5 747	18 722	12 939	11 069	7 599
October	124 575	104 658	123 653	104 030	70.4	25 118	601	5 753	18 764	12 977	11 109	7 629
November	124 969	104 900	123 945	104 309	69.7	25 180	600	5 772	18 808	13 006	11 152	7 660
December	125 103	105 088	124 269	104 625	70.4	25 247	601	5 809	18 837	13 021	11 178	7 677
1998												
January	122 554	102 974	124 559	104 901	69.8	25 335	602	5 865	18 868	13 045	11 215	7 706
February	123 335	103 358	124 752	105 068	67.4	25 356	604	5 883	18 869	13 047	11 225	7 713
March	124 050	103 965	124 934	105 241	65.2	25 346	604	5 862	18 880	13 037	11 237	7 709
April	125 097	105 006	125 178	105 457	61.8	25 416	598	5 937	18 881	13 034	11 247	7 713
May	126 171	106 000	125 531	105 756	62.9	25 419	597	5 948	18 874	13 013	11 248	7 703
June	126 847	106 995	125 748	105 966	61.4	25 445	596	5 991	18 858	12 996	11 239	7 690
July	125 770	107 012	125 847	106 041	59.0	25 305	589	6 028	18 688	12 813	11 093	7 540
August	126 007	107 325	126 225	106 351	58.4	25 453	586	6 061	18 806	12 925	11 224	7 660
September	126 817	107 127	126 469	106 571	57.4	25 466	582	6 083	18 801	12 930	11 221	7 665
October	127 591	107 372	126 677	106 751	59.7	25 451	578	6 120	18 753	12 895	11 198	7 652
November	128 000	107 578	126 939	106 987	59.3	25 444	572	6 165	18 707	12 856	11 168	7 628
December	128 143	107 789	127 286	107 311	59.1	25 512	570	6 253	18 689	12 844	11 158	7 624
1999												
January	125 413	105 489	127 463	107 461	60.0	25 470	557	6 246	18 667	12 830	11 139	7 610
February	126 410	106 039	127 883	107 808	58.0	25 514	551	6 337	18 626	12 792	11 127	7 597
March	127 125	106 627	128 054	107 955	57.6	25 479	549	6 328	18 602	12 784	11 123	7 603
April	128 201	107 717	128 282	108 175	58.6	25 493	539	6 380	18 574	12 763	11 106	7 591
May	129 031	108 528	128 377	108 274	54.4	25 436	532	6 364	18 540	12 741	11 091	7 584
June	129 767	109 573	128 630	108 507	59.7	25 432	529	6 388	18 515	12 711	11 083	7 572
July	128 845	109 745	128 898	108 735	60.4	25 488	528	6 408	18 552	12 753	11 125	7 620
August	128 851	109 845	129 057	108 846	62.1	25 430	526	6 401	18 503	12 706	11 097	7 590
September	129 614	109 589	129 265	109 042	64.0	25 460	527	6 439	18 494	12 700	11 090	7 580
October	130 381	109 833	129 523	109 275	62.8	25 483	529	6 470	18 484	12 702	11 083	7 581
November	130 839	110 126	129 788	109 517	65.2	25 527	527	6 516	18 484	12 702	11 085	7 579
December	130 952	110 275	130 038	109 730	64.6	25 561	530	6 552	18 479	12 701	11 087	7 579

1. See Notes for definition.
2. Additional industry detail available in individual industry profile sections.

Table 8-5. Nonfarm Employment—*Continued*

(Wage and salary workers on nonfarm payrolls; thousands, seasonally adjusted.)

Year and month	Manufacturing—*Continued*									
	Durable goods—*Continued*									
	Lumber and wood products	Furniture and fixtures	Stone, clay, and glass products	Primary metal industries [1]	Fabricated metal products	Industrial machinery and equipment [1]	Electronic and electrical equipment	Transportation equipment [1]	Instruments and related products	Miscellaneous manufacturing
1970	658	440	610	1 260	1 559	2 003	1 584	1 833	804	426
1971	681	444	611	1 171	1 479	1 834	1 477	1 743	753	412
1972	740	483	645	1 173	1 541	1 909	1 535	1 777	786	433
1973	774	507	680	1 259	1 645	2 111	1 667	1 915	851	454
1974	727	489	673	1 289	1 632	2 230	1 666	1 853	885	452
1975	627	417	598	1 139	1 453	2 076	1 442	1 700	804	407
1976	693	444	613	1 155	1 505	2 085	1 503	1 785	840	429
1977	736	464	636	1 182	1 577	2 195	1 591	1 857	895	438
1978	770	494	664	1 215	1 667	2 347	1 699	1 987	952	452
1979	782	498	674	1 254	1 713	2 508	1 793	2 059	1 006	445
1980	704	466	629	1 142	1 609	2 517	1 771	1 881	1 022	418
1981	680	464	606	1 122	1 586	2 521	1 774	1 879	1 041	408
1982	610	432	548	922	1 424	2 264	1 701	1 718	1 013	382
1983	671	448	541	832	1 368	2 053	1 704	1 730	990	370
1984	718	486	562	857	1 462	2 218	1 869	1 883	1 040	382
1985	711	493	557	808	1 464	2 195	1 859	1 960	1 045	367
1986	724	498	554	751	1 422	2 074	1 790	2 003	1 018	361
1987	754	515	554	746	1 399	2 028	1 750	2 028	1 011	370
1988	767	527	567	770	1 428	2 089	1 764	2 036	1 031	383
1989	756	524	568	772	1 445	2 125	1 744	2 052	1 026	381
1990	733	506	556	756	1 419	2 095	1 673	1 989	1 006	375
1991	675	475	522	723	1 355	2 000	1 591	1 890	974	366
1992	680	478	513	695	1 329	1 929	1 528	1 830	929	368
1993	709	487	517	683	1 339	1 931	1 526	1 756	896	378
1994	754	505	532	698	1 388	1 990	1 571	1 761	861	389
1995	769	510	540	712	1 437	2 067	1 625	1 790	843	390
1996	778	504	544	711	1 449	2 115	1 661	1 785	855	388
1997	796	512	552	711	1 479	2 168	1 689	1 845	866	392
1998	814	533	562	715	1 509	2 206	1 707	1 893	873	395
1999	828	548	563	700	1 517	2 141	1 670	1 884	856	395
1996										
January	766	506	534	713	1 440	2 106	1 648	1 773	849	389
February	773	505	539	712	1 442	2 106	1 651	1 778	851	389
March	771	503	540	711	1 440	2 112	1 651	1 745	853	389
April	775	502	540	709	1 438	2 111	1 655	1 783	854	387
May	776	503	542	711	1 442	2 113	1 658	1 786	857	388
June	780	503	543	712	1 447	2 115	1 661	1 787	857	388
July	781	505	543	706	1 450	2 116	1 664	1 786	856	387
August	783	506	546	713	1 454	2 116	1 665	1 791	857	387
September	783	505	547	713	1 456	2 115	1 667	1 792	857	387
October	784	504	549	708	1 458	2 119	1 668	1 795	859	387
November	787	506	549	708	1 460	2 120	1 669	1 798	859	388
December	784	507	551	707	1 461	2 125	1 670	1 804	860	389
1997										
January	784	507	551	708	1 462	2 132	1 670	1 811	858	390
February	787	508	551	708	1 463	2 139	1 672	1 815	859	391
March	790	509	551	708	1 466	2 145	1 674	1 824	859	390
April	793	509	551	708	1 470	2 152	1 675	1 821	862	391
May	796	510	551	708	1 474	2 156	1 676	1 826	862	392
June	796	512	551	708	1 477	2 162	1 684	1 835	865	392
July	797	514	553	707	1 474	2 169	1 690	1 844	868	393
August	799	513	553	712	1 484	2 177	1 696	1 864	868	392
September	800	513	554	713	1 487	2 181	1 700	1 860	869	392
October	800	516	555	714	1 492	2 193	1 707	1 868	871	393
November	802	518	554	716	1 497	2 200	1 713	1 887	873	392
December	804	520	555	717	1 501	2 206	1 718	1 888	875	394
1998										
January	805	523	562	720	1 506	2 214	1 725	1 889	876	395
February	807	526	561	719	1 507	2 216	1 725	1 895	873	396
March	808	528	559	719	1 508	2 219	1 725	1 897	877	397
April	811	531	560	719	1 510	2 218	1 723	1 902	877	396
May	812	533	559	718	1 512	2 219	1 720	1 902	877	396
June	812	533	562	718	1 510	2 218	1 718	1 897	876	395
July	813	534	560	708	1 493	2 210	1 709	1 795	875	396
August	815	535	563	717	1 513	2 208	1 702	1 903	873	395
September	817	536	563	717	1 514	2 202	1 697	1 907	872	396
October	818	536	563	711	1 514	2 194	1 689	1 912	869	392
November	820	538	564	706	1 511	2 183	1 681	1 908	866	391
December	823	540	566	706	1 513	2 173	1 677	1 905	864	391
1999										
January	826	541	564	704	1 518	2 156	1 672	1 903	864	391
February	827	543	566	704	1 516	2 155	1 668	1 892	864	392
March	828	544	563	703	1 516	2 149	1 668	1 898	862	392
April	827	544	564	701	1 516	2 144	1 667	1 889	860	394
May	827	546	563	699	1 515	2 141	1 666	1 883	857	394
June	827	547	562	698	1 515	2 139	1 667	1 878	856	394
July	829	554	563	701	1 517	2 142	1 675	1 890	859	395
August	829	551	563	699	1 515	2 135	1 669	1 887	854	395
September	830	551	563	697	1 518	2 133	1 670	1 880	852	396
October	831	553	562	697	1 519	2 130	1 672	1 873	849	397
November	831	553	564	698	1 520	2 131	1 670	1 870	850	398
December	831	552	565	698	1 521	2 132	1 673	1 867	849	399

1. Additional data available in individual industry profile sections.

Table 8-5. Nonfarm Employment—*Continued*

(Wage and salary workers on nonfarm payrolls, thousands, seasonally adjusted.)

Year and month	Manufacturing—*Continued*											
	Nondurable goods											
	Total	Total, production workers	Food and products	Tobacco products	Textile mill products	Apparel and other textile products	Paper and products	Printing and publishing	Chemicals and products	Petroleum and coal products	Rubber and miscellaneous plastics products	Leather and products
1970	8 190	5 956	1 786	83	975	1 364	701	1 104	1 049	191	617	320
1971	8 019	5 847	1 766	77	955	1 343	677	1 081	1 011	194	617	299
1972	8 129	6 022	1 745	75	986	1 383	679	1 094	1 009	195	667	296
1973	8 291	6 138	1 715	78	1 010	1 438	694	1 111	1 038	193	731	284
1974	8 181	6 004	1 707	77	965	1 363	696	1 111	1 061	197	733	271
1975	7 661	5 510	1 658	76	868	1 243	633	1 083	1 015	194	643	248
1976	7 946	5 750	1 689	77	919	1 318	666	1 099	1 043	199	675	263
1977	8 112	5 855	1 711	71	910	1 316	682	1 141	1 074	202	750	255
1978	8 259	5 956	1 724	71	899	1 332	689	1 192	1 096	208	793	257
1979	8 310	5 986	1 733	70	885	1 304	697	1 235	1 109	210	821	246
1980	8 127	5 798	1 708	69	848	1 264	685	1 252	1 107	198	764	233
1981	8 089	5 751	1 671	70	823	1 244	681	1 266	1 109	214	772	238
1982	7 766	5 451	1 636	69	749	1 161	655	1 272	1 075	201	729	219
1983	7 725	5 433	1 614	68	741	1 163	654	1 298	1 043	196	743	205
1984	7 896	5 565	1 611	64	746	1 185	674	1 375	1 049	189	813	189
1985	7 790	5 466	1 601	64	702	1 120	671	1 426	1 044	179	818	165
1986	7 752	5 465	1 607	59	703	1 100	667	1 456	1 021	169	823	149
1987	7 845	5 543	1 617	55	725	1 097	674	1 503	1 025	164	842	143
1988	7 951	5 611	1 626	54	728	1 085	689	1 543	1 057	160	866	143
1989	7 997	5 636	1 644	50	720	1 076	696	1 556	1 074	156	888	138
1990	7 968	5 584	1 661	49	691	1 036	697	1 569	1 086	157	888	133
1991	7 837	5 467	1 667	49	670	1 006	688	1 536	1 076	160	862	124
1992	7 827	5 466	1 663	48	674	1 007	690	1 507	1 084	158	878	120
1993	7 854	5 492	1 680	44	675	989	692	1 517	1 081	152	909	117
1994	7 873	5 528	1 678	43	676	974	692	1 537	1 057	149	953	113
1995	7 841	5 508	1 692	42	663	936	693	1 546	1 038	145	980	106
1996	7 706	5 390	1 692	41	627	868	684	1 540	1 034	142	983	96
1997	7 665	5 354	1 685	41	616	824	683	1 552	1 036	141	996	91
1998	7 600	5 287	1 683	41	598	766	677	1 565	1 043	139	1 005	84
1999	7 440	5 149	1 677	38	560	692	668	1 553	1 034	134	1 006	78
1996												
January	7 740	5 421	1 701	42	631	884	687	1 542	1 035	143	976	99
February	7 745	5 423	1 702	42	635	888	685	1 541	1 035	143	975	99
March	7 738	5 413	1 705	41	631	881	684	1 543	1 037	143	975	98
April	7 712	5 393	1 696	42	627	877	681	1 539	1 035	142	976	97
May	7 707	5 387	1 696	41	627	872	682	1 538	1 034	142	978	97
June	7 698	5 383	1 688	41	627	868	683	1 538	1 033	142	982	96
July	7 699	5 380	1 687	41	626	867	682	1 539	1 034	142	985	96
August	7 695	5 382	1 688	41	625	861	681	1 540	1 034	142	988	95
September	7 689	5 374	1 685	42	622	859	683	1 541	1 033	142	988	94
October	7 692	5 379	1 688	42	624	856	683	1 543	1 032	141	989	94
November	7 686	5 371	1 687	42	621	852	685	1 541	1 032	142	992	92
December	7 679	5 370	1 686	42	621	848	685	1 541	1 032	141	989	94
1997												
January	7 675	5 362	1 688	42	621	844	684	1 541	1 033	141	988	93
February	7 675	5 361	1 687	42	619	843	684	1 543	1 033	141	990	93
March	7 681	5 362	1 690	42	621	838	685	1 545	1 035	140	992	93
April	7 676	5 361	1 688	41	618	833	684	1 551	1 035	141	993	92
May	7 672	5 363	1 685	41	616	830	684	1 553	1 036	141	994	92
June	7 672	5 359	1 686	41	617	826	683	1 556	1 036	141	995	91
July	7 658	5 351	1 683	42	616	820	683	1 555	1 034	141	994	90
August	7 650	5 340	1 679	41	614	819	681	1 555	1 033	141	997	90
September	7 653	5 340	1 682	41	613	813	682	1 555	1 037	141	1 000	89
October	7 655	5 348	1 682	41	612	812	682	1 556	1 038	141	1 002	89
November	7 656	5 346	1 684	41	612	807	682	1 558	1 040	141	1 003	88
December	7 659	5 344	1 685	41	612	803	682	1 561	1 041	142	1 004	88
1998												
January	7 653	5 339	1 684	41	610	799	682	1 563	1 040	140	1 007	87
February	7 644	5 334	1 683	41	608	791	681	1 564	1 041	140	1 008	87
March	7 643	5 328	1 682	42	607	789	681	1 563	1 042	141	1 010	86
April	7 634	5 321	1 684	42	606	781	680	1 565	1 042	140	1 009	85
May	7 626	5 310	1 685	41	605	774	679	1 566	1 044	140	1 007	85
June	7 619	5 306	1 686	40	601	770	678	1 568	1 045	141	1 006	84
July	7 595	5 273	1 684	40	595	766	676	1 567	1 045	139	999	84
August	7 582	5 265	1 679	40	594	759	676	1 565	1 045	138	1 003	83
September	7 580	5 265	1 684	40	593	755	676	1 565	1 043	138	1 004	82
October	7 555	5 243	1 679	40	589	743	675	1 565	1 043	137	1 002	82
November	7 539	5 228	1 683	40	584	734	672	1 563	1 042	137	1 002	82
December	7 531	5 220	1 685	40	580	731	672	1 560	1 042	138	1 002	81
1999												
January	7 528	5 220	1 692	40	578	725	671	1 560	1 040	136	1 005	81
February	7 499	5 195	1 684	40	573	713	672	1 558	1 040	136	1 003	80
March	7 479	5 181	1 682	38	569	710	671	1 556	1 036	135	1 003	79
April	7 468	5 172	1 679	38	565	705	670	1 554	1 037	135	1 006	79
May	7 449	5 157	1 677	38	562	699	669	1 551	1 035	134	1 006	78
June	7 432	5 139	1 674	39	560	693	668	1 551	1 033	133	1 003	78
July	7 427	5 133	1 674	38	557	688	668	1 552	1 032	134	1 008	76
August	7 406	5 116	1 667	36	556	681	667	1 552	1 030	132	1 008	77
September	7 404	5 120	1 673	38	552	678	666	1 551	1 031	133	1 005	77
October	7 401	5 121	1 673	38	550	674	665	1 551	1 032	133	1 008	77
November	7 399	5 123	1 675	38	552	672	665	1 549	1 031	132	1 009	76
December	7 392	5 122	1 674	38	549	669	665	1 548	1 030	132	1 011	76

Table 8-5. Nonfarm Employment—*Continued*

(Wage and salary workers on nonfarm payrolls; thousands, seasonally adjusted.)

Year and month	Service-producing industries												
	Total	Transportation and public utilities [1]	Wholesale trade	Retail trade [1]					Finance, insurance, and real estate				
				Total	General merchandise stores	Food stores	Automotive dealers and service stations	Eating and drinking places	Total	Finance		Insurance	Real estate
										Total	Depository institutions		
1970	47 302	4 515	4 006	11 034	. . .	1 731	1 617	2 575	3 645	. . .	. . .	. . .	. . .
1971	48 278	4 476	4 014	11 338	. . .	1 752	1 642	2 700	3 772	. . .	. . .	. . .	. . .
1972	50 007	4 541	4 127	11 822	2 149	1 805	1 723	2 860	3 908	1 778	. . .	1 373	756
1973	51 897	4 656	4 291	12 315	2 229	1 856	1 778	3 054	4 046	1 866	. . .	1 401	778
1974	53 471	4 725	4 447	12 539	2 210	1 948	1 666	3 231	4 148	1 936	. . .	1 434	778
1975	54 345	4 542	4 430	12 630	2 113	2 007	1 677	3 380	4 165	1 964	. . .	1 442	760
1976	56 030	4 582	4 562	13 193	2 155	2 039	1 744	3 656	4 271	2 026	. . .	1 468	776
1977	58 125	4 713	4 723	13 792	2 204	2 106	1 801	3 949	4 467	2 113	. . .	1 528	826
1978	61 113	4 923	4 985	14 556	2 308	2 199	1 861	4 277	4 724	2 233	. . .	1 591	900
1979	63 363	5 136	5 221	14 972	2 287	2 297	1 812	4 513	4 975	2 369	. . .	1 643	963
1980	64 748	5 146	5 292	15 018	2 245	2 384	1 689	4 626	5 160	2 483	. . .	1 688	989
1981	65 655	5 165	5 375	15 171	2 230	2 448	1 653	4 749	5 298	2 593	. . .	1 713	992
1982	65 732	5 081	5 295	15 158	2 184	2 477	1 632	4 829	5 340	2 647	. . .	1 723	970
1983	66 821	4 952	5 283	15 587	2 165	2 556	1 674	5 038	5 466	2 741	. . .	1 728	997
1984	69 690	5 156	5 568	16 512	2 267	2 636	1 798	5 381	5 684	2 852	. . .	1 765	1 067
1985	72 544	5 233	5 727	17 315	2 323	2 774	1 889	5 699	5 948	2 974	. . .	1 840	1 135
1986	74 811	5 247	5 761	17 880	2 365	2 896	1 941	5 902	6 273	3 145	. . .	1 944	1 184
1987	77 284	5 362	5 848	18 422	2 411	2 958	2 001	6 086	6 533	3 264	. . .	2 027	1 242
1988	80 084	5 512	6 030	19 023	2 472	3 074	2 071	6 258	6 630	3 274	2 255	2 075	1 280
1989	82 630	5 614	6 187	19 475	2 544	3 164	2 092	6 402	6 668	3 283	2 273	2 090	1 296
1990	84 497	5 777	6 173	19 601	2 540	3 215	2 063	6 509	6 709	3 268	2 251	2 126	1 315
1991	84 504	5 755	6 081	19 284	2 453	3 204	1 984	6 476	6 646	3 187	2 164	2 161	1 299
1992	85 370	5 718	5 997	19 356	2 451	3 180	1 966	6 609	6 602	3 160	2 096	2 152	1 290
1993	87 361	5 811	5 981	19 773	2 488	3 224	2 014	6 821	6 757	3 238	2 089	2 197	1 322
1994	90 256	5 984	6 162	20 507	2 583	3 291	2 116	7 078	6 896	3 299	2 066	2 236	1 361
1995	92 925	6 132	6 378	21 187	2 681	3 366	2 190	7 354	6 806	3 231	2 025	2 225	1 351
1996	95 115	6 253	6 482	21 597	2 702	3 436	2 267	7 517	6 911	3 303	2 019	2 226	1 382
1997	97 727	6 408	6 648	21 966	2 701	3 478	2 311	7 646	7 109	3 424	2 027	2 264	1 421
1998	100 451	6 611	6 800	22 295	2 730	3 484	2 332	7 768	7 389	3 588	2 046	2 335	1 465
1999	103 304	6 826	6 924	22 788	2 771	3 495	2 369	7 940	7 569	3 691	2 061	2 371	1 507
1996													
January	93 802	6 189	6 420	21 345	2 675	3 404	2 226	7 441	6 831	3 256	2 020	2 217	1 358
February	94 171	6 203	6 423	21 398	2 685	3 407	2 234	7 455	6 851	3 265	2 020	2 217	1 369
March	94 416	6 207	6 431	21 441	2 689	3 410	2 241	7 474	6 857	3 269	2 017	2 216	1 372
April	94 550	6 227	6 440	21 448	2 678	3 410	2 249	7 483	6 870	3 280	2 017	2 217	1 373
May	94 848	6 239	6 456	21 532	2 708	3 424	2 258	7 495	6 889	3 289	2 017	2 223	1 377
June	95 066	6 264	6 474	21 572	2 710	3 431	2 269	7 501	6 906	3 301	2 019	2 225	1 380
July	95 239	6 282	6 476	21 625	2 710	3 439	2 278	7 524	6 919	3 307	2 017	2 228	1 384
August	95 464	6 283	6 500	21 658	2 704	3 444	2 282	7 539	6 936	3 320	2 017	2 228	1 388
September	95 596	6 281	6 518	21 687	2 705	3 451	2 286	7 538	6 948	3 324	2 018	2 234	1 390
October	95 802	6 280	6 542	21 774	2 717	3 459	2 290	7 582	6 964	3 335	2 020	2 234	1 395
November	96 039	6 288	6 551	21 806	2 712	3 465	2 294	7 586	6 975	3 340	2 018	2 237	1 398
December	96 237	6 299	6 557	21 861	2 719	3 469	2 297	7 596	6 989	3 350	2 018	2 238	1 401
1997													
January	96 433	6 332	6 565	21 842	2 688	3 471	2 299	7 609	7 000	3 357	2 018	2 240	1 403
February	96 649	6 354	6 582	21 833	2 674	3 472	2 301	7 616	7 016	3 366	2 019	2 243	1 407
March	96 925	6 379	6 600	21 892	2 698	3 472	2 305	7 626	7 033	3 376	2 021	2 246	1 411
April	97 206	6 397	6 613	21 905	2 698	3 475	2 306	7 631	7 057	3 390	2 022	2 251	1 416
May	97 422	6 407	6 624	21 911	2 692	3 476	2 307	7 632	7 074	3 403	2 025	2 252	1 419
June	97 615	6 417	6 636	21 937	2 697	3 479	2 306	7 641	7 087	3 412	2 026	2 258	1 417
July	97 877	6 422	6 656	21 938	2 699	3 481	2 309	7 628	7 113	3 425	2 028	2 264	1 424
August	97 876	6 280	6 670	21 990	2 704	3 479	2 315	7 654	7 137	3 441	2 029	2 269	1 427
September	98 265	6 454	6 682	22 022	2 701	3 478	2 318	7 671	7 154	3 452	2 028	2 273	1 429
October	98 535	6 478	6 706	22 061	2 711	3 482	2 320	7 672	7 183	3 469	2 032	2 281	1 433
November	98 765	6 481	6 715	22 119	2 722	3 481	2 322	7 690	7 207	3 485	2 036	2 288	1 434
December	99 022	6 489	6 726	22 146	2 735	3 476	2 322	7 690	7 236	3 505	2 041	2 299	1 432
1998													
January	99 224	6 504	6 755	22 145	2 711	3 481	2 322	7 704	7 257	3 513	2 036	2 304	1 440
February	99 396	6 528	6 761	22 140	2 708	3 477	2 319	7 716	7 281	3 527	2 038	2 309	1 445
March	99 588	6 546	6 774	22 154	2 705	3 477	2 321	7 721	7 317	3 546	2 041	2 318	1 453
April	99 762	6 560	6 786	22 163	2 709	3 473	2 321	7 719	7 342	3 559	2 043	2 324	1 459
May	100 112	6 584	6 797	22 240	2 723	3 480	2 328	7 745	7 365	3 572	2 046	2 331	1 462
June	100 303	6 597	6 799	22 261	2 724	3 479	2 332	7 749	7 384	3 585	2 047	2 335	1 464
July	100 542	6 620	6 798	22 306	2 729	3 490	2 334	7 762	7 408	3 600	2 048	2 340	1 468
August	100 772	6 641	6 809	22 345	2 737	3 485	2 334	7 782	7 425	3 612	2 049	2 344	1 469
September	101 003	6 654	6 821	22 391	2 752	3 490	2 338	7 797	7 439	3 617	2 047	2 348	1 474
October	101 226	6 675	6 821	22 414	2 756	3 489	2 342	7 815	7 461	3 635	2 052	2 351	1 475
November	101 495	6 692	6 833	22 466	2 761	3 492	2 344	7 836	7 481	3 642	2 052	2 357	1 482
December	101 774	6 725	6 850	22 509	2 760	3 492	2 348	7 858	7 497	3 652	2 056	2 358	1 487
1999													
January	101 993	6 736	6 847	22 560	2 771	3 485	2 352	7 871	7 518	3 662	2 059	2 361	1 495
February	102 369	6 755	6 870	22 662	2 778	3 495	2 361	7 904	7 524	3 666	2 061	2 362	1 496
March	102 575	6 772	6 877	22 702	2 790	3 497	2 361	7 909	7 536	3 675	2 063	2 366	1 495
April	102 789	6 782	6 892	22 744	2 793	3 497	2 363	7 930	7 546	3 681	2 062	2 367	1 498
May	102 941	6 797	6 898	22 763	2 781	3 496	2 364	7 932	7 559	3 689	2 061	2 370	1 500
June	103 198	6 817	6 905	22 810	2 777	3 494	2 365	7 965	7 573	3 693	2 060	2 373	1 507
July	103 410	6 834	6 927	22 833	2 774	3 495	2 368	7 958	7 583	3 700	2 060	2 374	1 509
August	103 627	6 848	6 946	22 841	2 768	3 498	2 369	7 958	7 590	3 704	2 063	2 375	1 511
September	103 805	6 866	6 962	22 844	2 757	3 495	2 372	7 956	7 589	3 702	2 063	2 376	1 511
October	104 040	6 875	6 973	22 863	2 752	3 496	2 377	7 950	7 599	3 704	2 063	2 378	1 517
November	104 261	6 898	6 989	22 893	2 752	3 498	2 380	7 966	7 604	3 707	2 061	2 375	1 522
December	104 477	6 911	7 002	22 936	2 766	3 501	2 386	7 986	7 613	3 710	2 059	2 378	1 525

1. Additional data available in individual industry profile sections.

Table 8-5. Nonfarm Employment—*Continued*

(Wage and salary workers on nonfarm payrolls, thousands, seasonally adjusted.)

Year and month	Total	Hotels and other lodging places	Personal services	Business services Total	Personnel supply Total	Personnel supply Help supply	Computer and data processing	Auto repair, services, and parking	Amusement and recreation	Health services Total	Offices and clinics of medical doctors	Nursing and personal care facilities	Hospitals
1970	11 548	...	898	1 397	...	...	...	...	...	3 053	...	...	1 863
1971	11 797	...	848	1 402	...	...	...	...	...	3 239	...	...	1 935
1972	12 276	813	828	1 491	214	...	107	399	...	3 412	467	591	1 980
1973	12 857	854	823	1 610	247	...	120	422	...	3 641	519	659	2 051
1974	13 441	878	807	1 686	257	...	135	430	...	3 887	567	708	2 160
1975	13 892	898	782	1 697	242	...	143	439	...	4 134	608	759	2 274
1976	14 551	929	790	1 806	293	...	159	466	...	4 350	644	809	2 363
1977	15 302	956	806	1 958	357	...	187	498	...	4 584	681	860	2 465
1978	16 252	988	827	2 181	438	...	224	549	...	4 792	720	911	2 538
1979	17 112	1 060	821	2 410	508	...	271	575	...	4 993	761	951	2 608
1980	17 890	1 076	818	2 564	543	...	304	571	...	5 278	802	997	2 750
1981	18 615	1 119	828	2 700	585	...	337	574	...	5 562	845	1 029	2 904
1982	19 021	1 133	844	2 722	541	417	365	589	...	5 811	887	1 067	3 014
1983	19 664	1 172	869	2 948	619	488	416	619	...	5 986	934	1 106	3 037
1984	20 746	1 263	918	3 353	797	643	474	682	...	6 118	977	1 147	3 004
1985	21 927	1 331	957	3 679	891	732	542	730	...	6 293	1 028	1 198	2 997
1986	22 957	1 378	991	3 957	990	837	588	762	...	6 528	1 081	1 245	3 037
1987	24 110	1 464	1 027	4 278	1 177	989	629	794	...	6 794	1 139	1 283	3 142
1988	25 504	1 540	1 056	4 638	1 350	1 126	673	834	977	7 105	1 200	1 311	3 294
1989	26 907	1 596	1 086	4 941	1 455	1 216	736	884	1 033	7 463	1 268	1 356	3 439
1990	27 934	1 631	1 104	5 139	1 535	1 288	772	914	1 076	7 814	1 338	1 415	3 549
1991	28 336	1 589	1 112	5 086	1 485	1 268	797	882	1 122	8 183	1 405	1 493	3 655
1992	29 052	1 576	1 116	5 315	1 629	1 411	836	881	1 188	8 490	1 463	1 533	3 750
1993	30 197	1 596	1 137	5 735	1 906	1 669	893	925	1 258	8 756	1 506	1 585	3 779
1994	31 579	1 631	1 140	6 281	2 272	2 017	959	968	1 334	8 992	1 545	1 649	3 763
1995	33 117	1 668	1 163	6 812	2 476	2 189	1 090	1 020	1 417	9 230	1 609	1 691	3 772
1996	34 454	1 715	1 180	7 293	2 654	2 352	1 228	1 080	1 476	9 478	1 678	1 730	3 812
1997	36 040	1 746	1 186	7 988	2 985	2 656	1 409	1 120	1 552	9 703	1 739	1 756	3 860
1998	37 533	1 789	1 201	8 618	3 278	2 926	1 615	1 145	1 594	9 853	1 806	1 772	3 930
1999	39 027	1 848	1 233	9 267	3 601	3 228	1 831	1 184	1 660	9 989	1 877	1 785	3 982
1996													
January	33 695	1 681	1 169	6 988	2 489	2 196	1 162	1 052	1 435	9 351	1 647	1 713	3 791
February	33 937	1 691	1 173	7 102	2 555	2 258	1 175	1 060	1 446	9 388	1 655	1 717	3 798
March	34 083	1 701	1 176	7 143	2 573	2 274	1 187	1 066	1 458	9 414	1 661	1 722	3 803
April	34 174	1 706	1 178	7 184	2 596	2 298	1 198	1 070	1 471	9 430	1 668	1 724	3 804
May	34 300	1 714	1 182	7 221	2 625	2 324	1 206	1 073	1 469	9 448	1 672	1 728	3 808
June	34 440	1 733	1 182	7 266	2 655	2 355	1 212	1 078	1 474	9 472	1 678	1 732	3 808
July	34 536	1 719	1 181	7 318	2 678	2 376	1 229	1 084	1 479	9 491	1 683	1 734	3 811
August	34 666	1 717	1 182	7 384	2 709	2 404	1 243	1 090	1 488	9 506	1 689	1 734	3 811
September	34 729	1 720	1 183	7 413	2 725	2 419	1 257	1 092	1 481	9 527	1 692	1 736	3 820
October	34 819	1 723	1 185	7 418	2 692	2 391	1 274	1 097	1 497	9 548	1 695	1 739	3 823
November	34 994	1 731	1 186	7 514	2 755	2 449	1 289	1 099	1 501	9 571	1 700	1 741	3 829
December	35 093	1 735	1 184	7 568	2 775	2 469	1 306	1 102	1 506	9 587	1 703	1 743	3 833
1997													
January	35 237	1 738	1 184	7 632	2 807	2 503	1 323	1 104	1 520	9 613	1 711	1 745	3 835
February	35 402	1 742	1 185	7 722	2 851	2 538	1 341	1 110	1 528	9 629	1 720	1 747	3 841
March	35 553	1 744	1 184	7 801	2 894	2 576	1 359	1 114	1 535	9 646	1 720	1 748	3 848
April	35 739	1 748	1 182	7 878	2 932	2 609	1 377	1 119	1 541	9 667	1 726	1 753	3 849
May	35 896	1 746	1 189	7 939	2 959	2 634	1 392	1 121	1 557	9 686	1 735	1 758	3 853
June	35 998	1 740	1 184	7 991	2 987	2 655	1 406	1 116	1 563	9 692	1 736	1 756	3 856
July	36 167	1 738	1 184	8 049	3 023	2 690	1 418	1 121	1 566	9 716	1 741	1 758	3 862
August	36 216	1 735	1 186	8 045	3 007	2 670	1 430	1 121	1 556	9 728	1 742	1 760	3 866
September	36 372	1 744	1 187	8 123	3 045	2 707	1 446	1 124	1 558	9 739	1 747	1 760	3 871
October	36 484	1 755	1 190	8 146	3 062	2 721	1 460	1 126	1 559	9 757	1 755	1 762	3 876
November	36 607	1 754	1 194	8 220	3 110	2 767	1 471	1 128	1 558	9 771	1 761	1 764	3 883
December	36 781	1 757	1 186	8 304	3 150	2 803	1 492	1 131	1 568	9 792	1 771	1 766	3 888
1998													
January	36 905	1 768	1 183	8 369	3 181	2 827	1 506	1 132	1 565	9 794	1 773	1 763	3 895
February	37 002	1 765	1 189	8 404	3 197	2 844	1 521	1 128	1 569	9 802	1 778	1 766	3 897
March	37 104	1 767	1 192	8 435	3 203	2 849	1 538	1 130	1 572	9 808	1 782	1 766	3 902
April	37 190	1 775	1 195	8 465	3 215	2 862	1 558	1 131	1 577	9 816	1 788	1 769	3 912
May	37 351	1 783	1 207	8 531	3 241	2 889	1 580	1 138	1 582	9 837	1 794	1 771	3 921
June	37 480	1 790	1 202	8 609	3 289	2 933	1 603	1 144	1 581	9 848	1 800	1 772	3 929
July	37 604	1 796	1 203	8 645	3 281	2 932	1 630	1 148	1 594	9 856	1 806	1 772	3 937
August	37 678	1 799	1 206	8 687	3 306	2 956	1 647	1 153	1 600	9 867	1 814	1 773	3 943
September	37 800	1 803	1 205	8 704	3 305	2 953	1 664	1 156	1 615	9 885	1 823	1 776	3 950
October	37 929	1 806	1 207	8 776	3 334	2 978	1 687	1 157	1 613	9 897	1 830	1 777	3 957
November	38 071	1 808	1 212	8 841	3 366	3 014	1 710	1 162	1 627	9 906	1 836	1 778	3 959
December	38 218	1 815	1 216	8 910	3 400	3 046	1 730	1 165	1 632	9 917	1 839	1 778	3 962
1999													
January	38 330	1 826	1 221	8 970	3 441	3 086	1 752	1 169	1 632	9 920	1 847	1 782	3 963
February	38 483	1 830	1 218	9 032	3 478	3 121	1 772	1 176	1 633	9 939	1 853	1 783	3 971
March	38 589	1 835	1 220	9 081	3 507	3 149	1 786	1 179	1 637	9 953	1 859	1 785	3 975
April	38 718	1 838	1 225	9 133	3 530	3 169	1 800	1 183	1 639	9 967	1 865	1 783	3 978
May	38 821	1 837	1 223	9 183	3 554	3 189	1 815	1 185	1 640	9 975	1 871	1 785	3 980
June	38 970	1 845	1 228	9 242	3 585	3 216	1 831	1 185	1 649	9 983	1 875	1 785	3 983
July	39 070	1 851	1 233	9 303	3 618	3 244	1 846	1 185	1 650	9 994	1 880	1 784	3 983
August	39 191	1 857	1 237	9 339	3 626	3 251	1 857	1 185	1 664	10 008	1 885	1 786	3 987
September	39 321	1 863	1 243	9 404	3 678	3 298	1 866	1 186	1 672	10 015	1 888	1 785	3 989
October	39 482	1 863	1 247	9 465	3 712	3 327	1 874	1 191	1 691	10 027	1 893	1 785	3 992
November	39 606	1 868	1 252	9 502	3 734	3 343	1 880	1 191	1 701	10 041	1 898	1 785	3 992
December	39 707	1 868	1 257	9 538	3 748	3 358	1 888	1 192	1 703	10 053	1 903	1 787	3 997

1. Additional data available in individual industry profile sections.

Table 8-5. Nonfarm Employment—*Continued*

(Wage and salary workers on nonfarm payrolls; thousands, seasonally adjusted.)

| Year and month | Services (private)—Continued | | | | | Government | | | | | |
	Legal services	Educational services	Social services	Membership organizations	Engineering and management services	Total	Federal	State Total	State Education	Local Total	Local Education
1970	. . .	940	. . .	. . .	. . .	12 554	2 731	2 664	1 104	7 158	4 004
1971	. . .	948	. . .	. . .	. . .	12 881	2 696	2 747	1 149	7 437	4 188
1972	271	958	553	1 403	. . .	13 334	2 684	2 859	1 188	7 790	4 363
1973	296	975	552	1 410	. . .	13 732	2 663	2 923	1 205	8 146	4 537
1974	326	990	625	1 438	. . .	14 170	2 724	3 039	1 267	8 407	4 692
1975	341	1 001	690	1 452	. . .	14 686	2 748	3 179	1 323	8 758	4 834
1976	364	1 013	763	1 487	. . .	14 871	2 733	3 273	1 371	8 865	4 899
1977	394	1 031	855	1 495	. . .	15 127	2 727	3 377	1 385	9 023	4 974
1978	427	1 062	991	1 502	. . .	15 672	2 753	3 474	1 367	9 446	5 075
1979	460	1 090	1 081	1 516	. . .	15 947	2 773	3 541	1 378	9 633	5 107
1980	498	1 138	1 134	1 539	. . .	16 241	2 866	3 610	1 398	9 765	5 210
1981	532	1 179	1 149	1 527	. . .	16 031	2 772	3 640	1 420	9 619	5 216
1982	565	1 199	1 149	1 526	. . .	15 837	2 739	3 640	1 433	9 458	5 169
1983	602	1 225	1 188	1 510	. . .	15 869	2 774	3 662	1 450	9 434	5 139
1984	645	1 270	1 222	1 504	. . .	16 024	2 807	3 734	1 488	9 482	5 196
1985	692	1 359	1 325	1 517	. . .	16 394	2 875	3 832	1 540	9 687	5 344
1986	747	1 421	1 406	1 536	. . .	16 693	2 899	3 893	1 561	9 901	5 484
1987	801	1 449	1 454	1 614	. . .	17 010	2 943	3 967	1 586	10 100	5 598
1988	845	1 567	1 552	1 740	2 230	17 386	2 971	4 076	1 621	10 339	5 722
1989	880	1 647	1 644	1 836	2 389	17 779	2 988	4 182	1 668	10 609	5 875
1990	908	1 661	1 734	1 946	2 478	18 304	3 085	4 305	1 730	10 914	6 042
1991	912	1 710	1 845	1 982	2 433	18 402	2 966	4 355	1 768	11 081	6 136
1992	914	1 678	1 959	1 973	2 471	18 645	2 969	4 408	1 799	11 267	6 220
1993	924	1 711	2 070	2 035	2 521	18 841	2 915	4 488	1 834	11 438	6 353
1994	924	1 850	2 200	2 082	2 579	19 128	2 870	4 576	1 882	11 682	6 479
1995	921	1 965	2 336	2 146	2 731	19 305	2 822	4 635	1 919	11 849	6 606
1996	928	2 030	2 413	2 201	2 844	19 419	2 757	4 606	1 911	12 056	6 748
1997	944	2 104	2 518	2 277	2 988	19 557	2 699	4 582	1 904	12 276	6 918
1998	971	2 178	2 646	2 372	3 139	19 823	2 686	4 612	1 922	12 525	7 084
1999	997	2 276	2 800	2 425	3 254	20 170	2 669	4 695	1 968	12 806	7 272
1996											
January	921	1 988	2 370	2 172	2 790	19 322	2 782	4 613	1 907	11 927	6 646
February	924	2 002	2 385	2 178	2 798	19 359	2 782	4 626	1 918	11 951	6 660
March	924	2 009	2 390	2 181	2 815	19 397	2 778	4 625	1 920	11 994	6 688
April	924	2 014	2 398	2 184	2 810	19 391	2 773	4 622	1 920	11 996	6 701
May	926	2 018	2 408	2 195	2 831	19 432	2 770	4 622	1 921	12 040	6 712
June	927	2 030	2 415	2 199	2 843	19 410	2 762	4 617	1 919	12 031	6 728
July	928	2 044	2 422	2 199	2 845	19 401	2 756	4 606	1 912	12 039	6 741
August	930	2 045	2 429	2 213	2 858	19 421	2 751	4 600	1 914	12 070	6 761
September	929	2 038	2 431	2 217	2 870	19 433	2 743	4 596	1 908	12 094	6 776
October	931	2 051	2 438	2 221	2 878	19 423	2 733	4 584	1 900	12 106	6 790
November	933	2 060	2 445	2 227	2 891	19 425	2 728	4 580	1 897	12 117	6 802
December	933	2 063	2 448	2 231	2 901	19 438	2 723	4 580	1 897	12 135	6 812
1997											
January	936	2 070	2 459	2 235	2 904	19 457	2 727	4 575	1 895	12 155	6 829
February	936	2 074	2 469	2 238	2 925	19 462	2 713	4 578	1 898	12 171	6 845
March	939	2 079	2 481	2 245	2 933	19 468	2 709	4 570	1 891	12 189	6 857
April	942	2 089	2 494	2 256	2 954	19 495	2 706	4 579	1 898	12 210	6 869
May	942	2 092	2 504	2 265	2 963	19 510	2 703	4 580	1 904	12 227	6 871
June	943	2 099	2 517	2 272	2 976	19 540	2 699	4 578	1 907	12 263	6 902
July	945	2 109	2 542	2 283	2 992	19 581	2 695	4 604	1 919	12 282	6 917
August	945	2 114	2 544	2 291	3 011	19 583	2 701	4 579	1 904	12 303	6 933
September	949	2 123	2 549	2 296	3 023	19 581	2 685	4 579	1 905	12 317	6 951
October	950	2 128	2 557	2 305	3 044	19 623	2 684	4 587	1 908	12 352	6 967
November	952	2 131	2 560	2 309	3 054	19 636	2 686	4 587	1 908	12 363	6 972
December	955	2 134	2 568	2 324	3 071	19 644	2 684	4 580	1 905	12 380	6 978
1998											
January	957	2 143	2 577	2 335	3 085	19 658	2 678	4 579	1 902	12 401	6 995
February	959	2 149	2 586	2 344	3 098	19 684	2 675	4 577	1 901	12 432	7 018
March	961	2 156	2 598	2 354	3 111	19 693	2 671	4 581	1 903	12 441	7 024
April	964	2 159	2 609	2 359	3 118	19 721	2 672	4 588	1 906	12 461	7 039
May	967	2 165	2 626	2 364	3 133	19 775	2 674	4 601	1 914	12 500	7 056
June	970	2 171	2 646	2 369	3 141	19 782	2 675	4 601	1 920	12 506	7 063
July	974	2 177	2 666	2 374	3 149	19 806	2 675	4 624	1 928	12 507	7 080
August	976	2 174	2 656	2 381	3 150	19 874	2 689	4 630	1 934	12 555	7 111
September	979	2 191	2 682	2 387	3 159	19 898	2 694	4 644	1 945	12 560	7 105
October	983	2 210	2 689	2 395	3 164	19 926	2 711	4 636	1 936	12 579	7 118
November	983	2 215	2 700	2 399	3 176	19 952	2 722	4 635	1 933	12 595	7 138
December	985	2 224	2 712	2 405	3 181	19 975	2 701	4 652	1 945	12 622	7 149
1999											
January	986	2 223	2 724	2 413	3 189	20 002	2 700	4 650	1 939	12 652	7 170
February	989	2 242	2 738	2 420	3 198	20 075	2 710	4 674	1 960	12 691	7 197
March	991	2 250	2 750	2 428	3 205	20 099	2 705	4 678	1 963	12 716	7 216
April	994	2 260	2 764	2 423	3 219	20 107	2 684	4 686	1 968	12 737	7 222
May	995	2 270	2 775	2 419	3 232	20 103	2 664	4 684	1 963	12 755	7 238
June	997	2 278	2 799	2 427	3 246	20 123	2 662	4 673	1 950	12 788	7 257
July	996	2 285	2 790	2 419	3 265	20 163	2 656	4 691	1 967	12 816	7 273
August	999	2 292	2 808	2 426	3 276	20 211	2 655	4 698	1 972	12 858	7 305
September	1 000	2 294	2 823	2 430	3 283	20 223	2 655	4 714	1 978	12 854	7 299
October	1 003	2 299	2 845	2 431	3 300	20 248	2 647	4 722	1 979	12 879	7 308
November	1 005	2 305	2 868	2 434	3 310	20 271	2 646	4 723	1 980	12 902	7 323
December	1 007	2 309	2 884	2 438	3 327	20 308	2 646	4 727	1 983	12 935	7 343

1. Additional industry detail available in individual industry profile sections.

Table 8-6. Average Weekly Hours

(Production or nonsupervisory workers on private nonfarm payrolls; seasonally adjusted, except as noted.)

Year and month	All industries		Goods-producing industries [1]	Mining	Construc-tion	Total manufacturing		Durable goods manufacturing					
								Total		Lumber and products	Furniture and fixtures	Stone, clay, and glass products	Primary metal industries
	Not seasonally adjusted	Seasonally adjusted				Average weekly hours	Overtime hours	Average weekly hours	Overtime hours				
1970	37.1	37.1	39.4	42.7	37.3	39.8	3.0	40.3	3.0	39.6	39.2	41.2	40.4
1971	36.9	36.9	39.4	42.4	37.2	39.9	2.9	40.3	2.9	39.8	39.8	41.6	40.1
1972	37.0	37.0	39.9	42.6	36.5	40.5	3.5	41.2	3.6	40.4	40.2	42.0	41.4
1973	36.9	36.9	40.0	42.4	36.8	40.7	3.8	41.4	4.1	40.0	40.0	41.9	42.3
1974	36.5	36.5	39.5	41.9	36.6	40.0	3.3	40.6	3.4	39.2	39.1	41.3	41.6
1975	36.1	36.1	39.0	41.9	36.4	39.5	2.6	39.9	2.6	38.8	38.0	40.4	40.0
1976	36.1	36.1	39.6	42.4	36.8	40.1	3.1	40.6	3.2	39.9	38.8	41.1	40.8
1977	36.0	36.0	39.8	43.4	36.5	40.3	3.5	41.0	3.7	39.9	39.0	41.3	41.3
1978	35.8	35.8	39.9	43.4	36.8	40.4	3.6	41.1	3.8	39.8	39.3	41.6	41.8
1979	35.7	35.7	39.7	43.0	37.0	40.2	3.3	40.8	3.5	39.5	38.7	41.5	41.4
1980	35.3	35.3	39.3	43.3	37.0	39.7	2.8	40.1	2.8	38.6	38.1	40.8	40.1
1981	35.2	35.2	39.5	43.7	36.9	39.8	2.8	40.2	2.8	38.7	38.4	40.6	40.5
1982	34.8	34.8	38.7	42.7	36.7	38.9	2.3	39.3	2.2	38.1	37.2	40.1	38.6
1983	35.0	35.0	39.7	42.5	37.1	40.1	3.0	40.7	3.0	40.1	39.4	41.5	40.5
1984	35.2	35.2	40.2	43.3	37.8	40.7	3.4	41.4	3.6	39.9	39.7	42.0	41.7
1985	34.9	34.9	40.0	43.4	37.7	40.5	3.3	41.2	3.5	39.9	39.4	41.9	41.5
1986	34.8	34.8	40.1	42.2	37.4	40.7	3.4	41.3	3.5	40.4	39.8	42.2	41.9
1987	34.8	34.8	40.3	42.4	37.8	41.0	3.7	41.5	3.8	40.6	40.0	42.3	43.1
1988	34.7	34.7	40.4	42.3	37.9	41.1	3.9	41.8	4.1	40.1	39.4	42.3	43.5
1989	34.6	34.6	40.3	43.0	37.9	41.0	3.8	41.6	3.9	40.1	39.5	42.3	43.0
1990	34.5	34.5	40.3	44.1	38.2	40.8	3.6	41.3	3.7	40.2	39.1	42.0	42.7
1991	34.3	34.3	40.3	44.4	38.1	40.7	3.6	41.1	3.5	40.0	38.9	41.7	42.2
1992	34.4	34.4	40.5	43.9	38.0	41.0	3.8	41.5	3.7	40.6	39.7	42.2	43.0
1993	34.5	34.5	40.9	44.3	38.5	41.4	4.1	42.1	4.3	40.8	40.1	42.7	43.7
1994	34.7	34.7	41.4	44.8	38.9	42.0	4.7	42.9	5.0	41.2	40.4	43.4	44.7
1995	34.5	34.5	41.0	44.7	38.9	41.6	4.4	42.4	4.7	40.6	39.6	43.0	44.0
1996	34.4	34.4	41.1	45.3	39.0	41.6	4.5	42.4	4.8	40.8	39.4	43.3	44.2
1997	34.6	34.6	41.3	45.4	39.0	42.0	4.8	42.8	5.1	41.0	40.2	43.3	44.9
1998	34.6	34.6	41.0	43.9	38.9	41.7	4.6	42.3	4.8	41.1	40.5	43.5	44.2
1999	34.5	34.5	41.0	43.8	39.1	41.7	4.6	42.2	4.8	41.2	40.3	43.5	44.2
1996													
January	33.4	34.0	39.6	44.1	37.9	40.0	4.2	41.0	4.5	39.0	36.0	42.1	43.3
February	34.1	34.4	41.0	45.3	39.0	41.5	4.4	42.2	4.6	40.7	39.2	43.6	44.0
March	34.2	34.5	40.9	45.8	38.9	41.4	4.3	42.0	4.5	40.7	39.4	43.5	43.8
April	34.1	34.4	41.1	45.2	39.0	41.6	4.5	42.4	4.8	40.9	39.4	43.5	43.9
May	34.3	34.4	41.0	45.1	38.6	41.7	4.6	42.5	4.9	41.1	39.6	43.3	44.2
June	34.9	34.6	41.3	45.7	39.1	41.8	4.6	42.6	4.9	41.2	39.7	43.6	44.3
July	34.6	34.4	41.1	45.0	38.7	41.7	4.5	42.5	4.8	41.1	39.8	43.3	44.3
August	34.8	34.5	41.2	45.2	39.0	41.8	4.6	42.6	4.9	41.1	39.7	43.4	44.3
September	34.9	34.6	41.2	45.6	39.0	41.9	4.6	42.7	4.9	41.2	39.8	43.4	44.5
October	34.5	34.5	41.1	45.3	39.0	41.7	4.5	42.5	4.8	41.1	39.8	43.4	44.4
November	34.5	34.5	41.1	45.3	39.0	41.7	4.5	42.5	4.8	41.0	39.9	43.2	44.0
December	34.9	34.6	41.3	45.6	39.0	41.9	4.6	42.6	4.9	41.0	40.2	43.0	44.5
1997													
January	33.9	34.4	40.9	44.7	38.1	41.7	4.7	42.5	5.0	40.5	39.6	42.2	44.4
February	34.5	34.6	41.2	46.1	38.8	41.9	4.7	42.7	5.0	40.8	39.4	43.1	44.7
March	34.6	34.7	41.5	46.5	39.2	42.1	4.9	42.9	5.2	41.1	40.3	43.3	44.8
April	34.4	34.7	41.6	45.5	39.2	42.2	5.0	43.1	5.4	41.3	40.2	43.3	45.1
May	34.5	34.7	41.5	45.8	39.5	42.0	4.9	42.9	5.2	41.2	40.3	43.4	44.8
June	34.9	34.5	41.3	45.5	39.1	41.9	4.7	42.7	5.0	41.1	40.0	43.1	44.7
July	34.8	34.6	41.3	45.3	39.1	41.9	4.8	42.8	5.1	41.2	40.0	43.2	44.8
August	35.0	34.7	41.3	45.5	38.9	42.0	4.8	42.8	5.1	41.0	40.2	43.1	44.9
September	34.8	34.6	41.3	45.1	39.3	41.9	4.7	42.7	5.0	41.1	40.5	43.3	45.0
October	34.7	34.6	41.3	45.0	38.9	42.0	4.8	42.7	5.1	41.0	40.3	43.1	45.2
November	34.8	34.6	41.2	45.2	38.3	42.1	4.9	42.8	5.2	41.1	40.6	42.8	45.1
December	34.8	34.6	41.4	45.0	38.9	42.1	4.9	42.9	5.2	41.0	40.8	43.5	45.2
1998													
January	34.2	34.7	41.5	45.7	39.1	42.2	4.9	42.9	5.2	41.1	41.0	43.6	45.4
February	34.6	34.7	41.3	44.4	39.2	42.0	4.8	42.7	5.1	41.1	41.0	43.7	44.8
March	34.5	34.6	41.2	44.2	38.9	41.8	4.8	42.5	5.0	41.1	40.8	43.4	44.6
April	34.2	34.6	41.0	44.0	38.9	41.6	4.6	42.2	4.8	41.2	40.7	43.3	44.1
May	34.6	34.7	41.1	44.1	39.0	41.8	4.6	42.4	4.8	41.1	40.7	43.5	44.3
June	34.7	34.6	41.0	43.7	38.7	41.8	4.6	42.3	4.8	41.1	40.9	43.4	44.3
July	34.8	34.6	41.1	43.8	39.2	41.7	4.6	42.2	4.8	41.1	40.6	43.5	44.0
August	35.2	34.6	41.1	43.6	39.2	41.7	4.6	42.2	4.7	41.1	40.6	43.6	44.0
September	34.3	34.5	40.9	43.3	38.8	41.6	4.5	42.1	4.6	40.8	40.0	43.4	43.8
October	34.6	34.6	41.1	43.6	39.2	41.7	4.5	42.3	4.6	41.1	40.5	43.4	43.8
November	34.7	34.6	41.1	43.5	39.1	41.7	4.5	42.3	4.7	41.2	40.3	43.4	43.9
December	34.7	34.6	41.1	43.3	39.5	41.7	4.5	42.3	4.6	41.5	40.2	43.7	43.7
1999													
January	34.0	34.5	41.1	43.0	39.5	41.6	4.5	42.1	4.6	41.6	40.4	43.8	43.7
February	34.3	34.6	41.0	43.2	39.1	41.6	4.5	42.1	4.6	40.9	40.3	43.4	43.8
March	34.2	34.5	40.8	43.0	38.7	41.6	4.5	42.1	4.6	41.3	40.3	43.1	44.0
April	34.3	34.5	41.0	43.7	39.0	41.7	4.4	42.2	4.5	41.2	40.3	43.4	44.0
May	34.6	34.5	41.0	43.9	39.0	41.7	4.6	42.2	4.7	41.2	40.3	43.4	44.2
June	34.6	34.5	41.1	43.9	39.3	41.8	4.7	42.3	4.8	41.2	40.4	43.5	44.3
July	34.7	34.5	41.1	44.5	39.0	41.8	4.6	42.4	4.8	41.1	40.5	43.5	44.4
August	35.1	34.5	41.1	44.1	39.0	41.8	4.6	42.3	4.8	41.2	40.3	43.5	44.4
September	34.3	34.5	41.2	44.3	39.3	41.8	4.7	42.4	4.9	41.1	40.4	43.5	44.5
October	34.6	34.5	41.1	44.1	39.1	41.8	4.7	42.3	4.8	41.1	40.1	43.5	44.3
November	34.5	34.5	41.3	44.2	40.1	41.7	4.7	42.2	4.8	41.1	39.9	43.8	44.3
December	34.6	34.5	41.0	44.3	38.9	41.7	4.7	42.2	4.8	41.0	40.2	43.5	44.4

1. Includes mining, construction, and manufacturing. Additional industry detail available in individual industry profile sections.

Table 8-6. Average Weekly Hours—Continued

(Production or nonsupervisory workers on private nonfarm payrolls; seasonally adjusted, except as noted.)

Year and month	Durable goods manufacturing—Continued						Nondurable goods manufacturing					
	Fabricated metal products	Industrial machinery and equipment[1]	Electronic and electrical equipment	Transportation equipment[1]	Instruments and related products	Miscellaneous manufacturing	Total		Food and products	Tobacco products	Textile mill products	Apparel and other textile products
							Average weekly hours	Overtime hours				
1970	40.7	41.1	...	40.3	...	38.7	39.1	3.0	40.5	37.8	39.9	35.3
1971	40.4	40.6	...	40.7	...	38.9	39.3	3.0	40.3	37.8	40.6	35.6
1972	41.2	42.1	...	41.7	...	39.5	39.7	3.3	40.5	37.6	41.3	36.0
1973	41.6	42.8	...	42.1	...	39.0	39.6	3.4	40.4	38.6	40.9	35.9
1974	40.8	42.1	...	40.5	...	38.7	39.1	3.0	40.4	38.3	39.5	35.2
1975	40.1	40.8	...	40.4	...	38.5	38.8	2.7	40.3	38.2	39.3	35.2
1976	40.8	41.2	...	41.7	...	38.8	39.4	3.0	40.5	37.5	40.1	35.8
1977	41.0	41.5	...	42.5	...	38.8	39.4	3.2	40.0	37.8	40.4	35.6
1978	41.0	42.0	...	42.2	...	38.8	39.4	3.2	39.7	38.1	40.4	35.6
1979	40.7	41.7	...	41.1	...	38.8	39.3	3.1	39.9	38.0	40.4	35.3
1980	40.4	41.0	...	40.6	...	38.7	39.0	2.8	39.7	38.1	40.1	35.4
1981	40.3	40.9	...	40.9	...	38.8	39.2	2.8	39.7	38.8	39.6	35.7
1982	39.2	39.7	...	40.5	...	38.4	38.4	2.5	39.4	37.8	37.5	34.7
1983	40.6	40.5	...	42.1	...	39.1	39.4	3.0	39.5	37.4	40.4	36.2
1984	41.4	41.9	...	42.7	...	39.4	39.7	3.1	39.8	38.9	39.9	36.4
1985	41.3	41.5	...	42.6	...	39.4	39.6	3.1	40.0	37.2	39.7	36.4
1986	41.3	41.6	...	42.3	...	39.6	39.9	3.3	40.0	37.4	41.1	36.7
1987	41.6	42.2	...	42.0	...	39.4	40.2	3.6	40.2	39.0	41.8	37.0
1988	41.9	42.7	41.0	42.7	41.4	39.2	40.2	3.6	40.3	39.8	41.0	37.0
1989	41.6	42.4	40.8	42.4	41.1	39.4	40.2	3.6	40.7	38.6	40.9	36.9
1990	41.3	41.9	40.8	42.0	41.1	39.5	40.0	3.6	40.8	39.2	39.9	36.4
1991	41.2	41.7	40.7	41.9	41.0	39.7	40.2	3.7	40.6	39.1	40.6	37.0
1992	41.6	42.2	41.2	41.8	41.1	39.9	40.4	3.8	40.6	38.6	41.1	37.2
1993	42.1	43.0	41.8	43.0	41.1	39.8	40.6	4.0	40.7	37.4	41.4	37.2
1994	42.9	43.7	42.2	44.3	41.7	40.0	40.9	4.3	41.3	39.3	41.6	37.5
1995	42.4	43.4	41.6	43.8	41.4	39.9	40.5	4.0	41.1	39.6	40.8	37.0
1996	42.4	43.1	41.5	44.0	41.7	39.7	40.5	4.1	41.0	40.0	40.6	37.0
1997	42.6	43.6	42.0	44.5	42.0	40.4	40.9	4.4	41.3	38.9	41.4	37.3
1998	42.3	42.8	41.4	43.4	41.3	39.9	40.9	4.3	41.7	38.3	41.0	37.3
1999	42.2	42.2	41.4	43.8	41.5	39.8	40.9	4.4	41.8	40.0	40.9	37.5
1996												
January	41.0	42.0	40.4	42.5	40.2	37.8	38.7	3.8	39.7	36.9	36.3	33.7
February	42.2	43.1	41.7	43.2	41.7	39.5	40.5	4.1	41.1	39.5	40.5	36.9
March	42.1	43.1	41.5	42.1	41.7	39.7	40.5	4.0	41.1	40.3	40.7	36.9
April	42.4	43.2	41.3	44.1	41.6	39.7	40.5	4.1	41.1	40.1	40.2	36.8
May	42.5	43.2	41.5	44.2	41.7	39.8	40.6	4.1	41.0	39.9	40.8	37.3
June	42.6	43.2	41.6	44.4	42.0	39.8	40.7	4.1	41.1	40.0	41.0	37.5
July	42.6	43.1	41.4	44.4	41.6	39.7	40.6	4.1	40.9	39.9	41.0	37.3
August	42.6	43.1	41.7	44.5	41.7	39.8	40.7	4.1	40.9	40.3	41.0	37.5
September	42.5	43.2	41.7	44.6	41.9	40.0	40.7	4.1	41.1	40.8	41.0	37.4
October	42.4	43.0	41.5	44.0	41.8	39.8	40.7	4.1	41.2	39.9	40.9	37.4
November	42.4	43.1	41.5	44.1	41.8	40.0	40.7	4.2	41.2	40.3	41.2	37.4
December	42.4	43.3	41.7	44.3	42.2	40.4	40.9	4.3	41.2	40.9	41.5	37.4
1997												
January	42.4	43.3	41.2	44.8	41.7	40.1	40.7	4.2	41.0	39.8	41.1	37.2
February	42.5	43.4	41.9	44.4	42.0	40.3	40.7	4.3	41.3	40.4	40.7	37.0
March	42.7	43.6	42.2	44.8	42.0	40.2	40.9	4.4	41.3	40.1	41.3	37.4
April	43.0	44.0	42.5	44.8	42.0	40.6	41.0	4.4	41.3	39.2	41.5	37.5
May	42.6	43.7	42.2	44.4	42.0	40.3	40.8	4.4	41.3	38.6	41.4	37.2
June	42.5	43.4	42.0	44.5	41.9	40.2	40.7	4.2	41.0	38.3	41.3	37.3
July	42.5	43.5	42.1	44.2	41.8	40.4	40.7	4.3	41.2	36.4	41.4	37.1
August	42.5	43.5	41.9	44.5	42.1	40.2	40.8	4.3	41.3	38.0	41.3	37.1
September	42.5	43.5	41.7	43.8	42.0	40.4	40.8	4.3	41.2	38.4	41.6	37.3
October	42.5	43.5	41.8	44.2	42.0	40.4	40.9	4.4	41.4	38.7	41.4	37.3
November	42.7	43.7	42.0	44.0	42.2	40.6	41.0	4.4	41.5	38.8	41.5	37.3
December	42.8	43.7	42.0	44.3	42.1	40.7	41.0	4.4	41.6	39.1	41.6	37.5
1998												
January	42.9	43.6	41.9	44.0	41.9	40.5	41.1	4.4	41.7	38.6	41.7	37.6
February	42.6	43.4	41.8	43.6	42.0	40.5	40.9	4.4	41.5	38.7	41.5	37.3
March	42.4	43.3	41.4	43.5	41.6	40.4	40.9	4.4	41.6	38.0	41.3	37.2
April	42.4	42.8	41.3	42.9	41.4	40.0	40.7	4.2	41.4	38.4	40.9	37.4
May	42.4	43.0	41.3	43.4	41.4	40.0	40.9	4.4	41.7	38.9	41.1	37.3
June	42.4	43.2	41.4	42.9	41.4	40.0	40.9	4.3	41.7	39.0	41.2	37.3
July	42.3	42.9	41.3	42.9	41.3	39.9	40.9	4.4	41.7	39.2	41.0	37.4
August	42.2	42.8	41.5	43.0	41.3	39.9	40.9	4.4	41.7	39.1	41.0	37.5
September	42.1	42.6	41.3	43.6	41.1	39.6	40.9	4.3	41.8	37.6	40.7	37.3
October	42.3	42.5	41.4	43.8	41.2	39.7	40.9	4.3	41.6	38.2	41.0	37.4
November	42.2	42.4	41.5	44.1	41.1	39.4	40.8	4.3	41.7	37.9	40.8	37.4
December	42.3	42.1	41.2	44.2	41.1	39.5	40.9	4.3	42.0	36.3	40.9	37.3
1999												
January	42.1	42.1	41.1	43.4	41.2	39.6	40.8	4.4	41.9	38.1	40.8	37.1
February	42.0	42.1	41.3	43.9	41.4	39.7	40.8	4.3	41.8	38.4	40.5	37.5
March	42.1	42.0	40.9	43.7	41.3	39.8	40.9	4.4	41.8	39.1	40.4	37.4
April	42.1	42.0	41.2	43.9	41.5	39.8	40.9	4.3	41.8	39.7	40.8	37.5
May	42.1	42.1	41.4	43.6	41.5	40.1	41.0	4.4	41.8	39.7	40.9	37.7
June	42.2	42.1	41.5	44.1	41.5	39.9	41.0	4.5	41.8	39.3	40.7	37.6
July	42.3	42.3	41.5	44.2	41.6	39.9	41.0	4.4	41.9	40.1	41.1	37.5
August	42.3	42.3	41.6	43.9	41.5	40.0	41.0	4.4	41.7	39.8	41.0	37.4
September	42.3	42.4	41.6	44.0	41.5	39.9	41.0	4.4	41.7	40.2	40.9	37.4
October	42.2	42.3	41.6	43.8	41.5	39.8	41.0	4.5	41.9	40.8	41.2	37.5
November	42.1	42.2	41.4	43.6	41.5	39.7	41.0	4.5	41.8	41.9	41.3	37.4
December	42.1	42.2	41.5	43.4	41.5	39.7	40.9	4.5	41.7	42.3	41.2	37.5

1. Additional industry detail available in individual industry profile sections.

Table 8-6. Average Weekly Hours—*Continued*

(Production or nonsupervisory workers on private nonfarm payrolls; seasonally adjusted, except as noted.)

Year and month	Nondurable goods manufacturing—*Continued*						Service-producing industries					
	Paper and products	Printing and publishing	Chemicals and products	Petroleum and coal products [1]	Rubber and miscellaneous plastics products	Leather and products	Total	Transportation and public utilities	Wholesale trade	Retail trade	Finance, insurance, real estate [1]	Services
1970	41.9	37.7	41.6	42.8	40.3	37.2	35.8	40.5	39.9	33.8	36.7	34.4
1971	42.1	37.5	41.6	42.8	40.4	37.7	35.5	40.1	39.4	33.7	36.6	33.9
1972	42.8	37.7	41.7	42.7	41.2	38.3	35.4	40.4	39.4	33.4	36.6	33.9
1973	42.9	37.7	41.8	42.4	41.2	37.8	35.2	40.5	39.2	33.1	36.6	33.8
1974	42.2	37.5	41.5	42.1	40.6	36.9	34.9	40.2	38.8	32.7	36.5	33.6
1975	41.6	36.9	41.0	41.2	39.9	37.1	34.7	39.7	38.6	32.4	36.5	33.5
1976	42.5	37.5	41.6	42.1	40.7	37.4	34.4	39.8	38.7	32.1	36.4	33.3
1977	42.9	37.7	41.7	42.7	41.1	36.9	34.2	39.9	38.8	31.6	36.4	33.0
1978	42.9	37.6	41.9	43.6	40.9	37.1	33.9	40.0	38.8	31.0	36.4	32.8
1979	42.6	37.5	41.9	43.8	40.6	36.5	33.7	39.9	38.8	30.6	36.2	32.7
1980	42.2	37.1	41.5	41.8	40.0	36.7	33.5	39.6	38.4	30.2	36.2	32.6
1981	42.5	37.3	41.6	43.2	40.3	36.7	33.5	39.4	38.5	30.1	36.3	32.6
1982	41.8	37.1	40.9	43.9	39.6	35.6	33.3	39.0	38.3	29.9	36.2	32.6
1983	42.6	37.6	41.6	43.9	41.2	36.8	33.3	39.0	38.5	29.8	36.2	32.7
1984	43.1	37.9	41.9	43.7	41.7	36.8	33.3	39.4	38.5	29.8	36.5	32.6
1985	43.1	37.8	41.9	43.0	41.1	37.2	33.1	39.5	38.4	29.4	36.4	32.5
1986	43.2	38.0	41.9	43.8	41.4	36.9	32.9	39.2	38.3	29.2	36.4	32.5
1987	43.4	38.0	42.3	44.0	41.6	38.2	32.9	39.2	38.1	29.2	36.3	32.5
1988	43.3	38.0	42.2	44.4	41.7	37.5	32.8	38.2	38.1	29.1	35.9	32.6
1989	43.3	37.9	42.4	44.3	41.4	37.9	32.7	38.3	38.0	28.9	35.8	32.6
1990	43.3	37.9	42.6	44.6	41.1	37.4	32.7	38.4	38.1	28.8	35.8	32.5
1991	43.3	37.7	42.9	44.1	41.1	37.5	32.5	38.1	38.1	28.6	35.7	32.4
1992	43.6	38.1	43.1	43.8	41.7	38.0	32.7	38.3	38.2	28.8	35.8	32.5
1993	43.6	38.3	43.1	44.2	41.8	38.6	32.7	39.3	38.2	28.8	35.8	32.5
1994	43.9	38.6	43.2	44.4	42.2	38.5	32.8	39.7	38.4	28.9	35.8	32.5
1995	43.1	38.2	43.2	43.7	41.5	38.0	32.7	39.4	38.3	28.8	35.9	32.4
1996	43.3	38.2	43.2	43.6	41.5	38.1	32.7	39.6	38.3	28.8	35.9	32.4
1997	43.7	38.5	43.2	43.1	41.8	38.4	32.9	39.7	38.4	28.9	36.1	32.6
1998	43.4	38.3	43.2	43.6	41.7	37.6	32.9	39.5	38.3	29.0	36.4	32.6
1999	43.5	38.2	43.0	43.1	41.7	37.8	32.8	38.7	38.3	29.0	36.2	32.6
1996												
January	41.6	37.1	42.5	43.1	40.4	35.2	32.4	39.1	38.0	28.5	35.7	32.2
February	43.2	38.2	43.2	42.8	41.3	37.6	32.6	39.6	38.2	28.8	35.8	32.3
March	43.1	38.2	43.1	42.9	41.4	37.9	32.7	39.8	38.3	28.9	35.9	32.4
April	43.4	38.2	43.0	43.3	41.5	37.9	32.6	39.4	38.2	28.7	35.8	32.3
May	43.4	38.3	43.2	42.6	41.6	38.4	32.7	39.5	38.3	28.8	35.8	32.4
June	43.5	38.3	43.4	44.7	41.6	38.6	32.7	39.6	38.4	28.8	36.0	32.5
July	43.4	38.3	43.3	44.3	41.5	38.4	32.6	39.5	38.2	28.7	35.8	32.3
August	43.5	38.3	43.2	43.9	41.7	38.6	32.7	39.7	38.3	28.8	35.9	32.4
September	43.4	38.3	43.1	44.2	41.8	38.7	32.8	39.8	38.4	28.9	36.2	32.5
October	43.4	38.2	43.1	43.6	41.5	38.7	32.7	39.8	38.3	28.8	35.9	32.4
November	43.5	38.2	43.3	43.9	41.4	38.9	32.7	39.8	38.3	28.9	36.0	32.4
December	43.7	38.4	43.5	43.9	41.7	38.7	32.8	39.7	38.4	28.9	36.1	32.5
1997												
January	43.7	38.3	43.1	44.9	41.5	38.4	32.7	39.5	38.2	28.9	36.0	32.4
February	43.7	38.4	43.3	43.4	41.7	38.5	32.8	39.5	38.4	28.9	36.0	32.6
March	43.9	38.7	43.2	43.0	41.8	38.7	32.9	39.9	38.4	29.0	36.0	32.6
April	43.9	38.5	43.3	42.4	42.1	38.6	32.8	39.6	38.4	28.9	36.1	32.6
May	43.8	38.5	43.3	42.4	41.7	38.4	32.8	39.6	38.5	28.9	36.1	32.6
June	43.5	38.4	43.1	42.9	41.5	38.3	32.7	39.4	38.4	28.8	36.1	32.5
July	43.5	38.4	43.1	42.8	41.7	38.5	32.8	39.3	38.4	28.9	36.1	32.6
August	43.5	38.4	43.2	43.0	41.8	38.0	32.9	40.1	38.4	29.0	36.2	32.6
September	43.6	38.6	43.2	43.3	41.7	38.5	32.9	40.0	38.4	28.9	36.1	32.6
October	43.7	38.7	43.3	43.3	41.9	38.4	32.9	39.9	38.4	29.0	36.1	32.6
November	43.9	38.7	43.3	43.3	42.1	38.0	32.9	39.9	38.5	29.0	36.2	32.6
December	43.8	38.6	43.2	42.2	42.0	38.3	32.8	39.9	38.3	28.9	35.9	32.6
1998												
January	43.7	38.5	43.5	44.5	42.0	38.5	32.9	39.9	38.4	29.0	36.3	32.7
February	43.5	38.5	43.4	42.2	41.8	38.5	32.9	39.9	38.4	29.0	36.3	32.6
March	43.5	38.5	43.4	43.1	41.6	37.8	32.9	39.7	38.3	29.0	36.3	32.6
April	42.6	38.2	43.2	42.8	41.7	37.3	32.9	39.6	38.3	29.0	36.3	32.6
May	43.5	38.4	43.1	42.9	41.8	37.2	33.0	39.7	38.4	29.1	36.4	32.7
June	43.5	38.4	43.2	43.2	41.9	37.5	32.9	39.5	38.3	29.0	36.3	32.6
July	43.6	38.3	43.1	44.8	41.8	37.2	32.9	39.5	38.3	29.1	36.3	32.7
August	43.4	38.5	43.1	44.0	41.7	37.6	32.9	39.3	38.4	29.0	36.3	32.7
September	43.6	38.2	43.1	43.2	41.6	37.5	32.9	39.3	38.2	29.1	36.3	32.6
October	43.5	38.1	43.1	44.0	41.8	37.5	32.9	39.4	38.3	29.1	36.3	32.7
November	43.5	38.1	42.9	43.9	41.7	37.6	32.9	39.3	38.4	29.1	36.3	32.6
December	43.4	38.1	42.7	44.7	41.8	37.6	32.9	39.1	38.3	29.0	36.3	32.7
1999												
January	43.5	38.2	42.8	43.9	41.4	37.5	32.8	39.3	38.3	29.0	36.2	32.6
February	43.4	38.1	42.9	43.3	41.7	37.8	32.9	39.2	38.3	29.2	36.3	32.6
March	43.7	38.0	42.8	43.7	41.9	37.7	32.8	39.1	38.2	29.0	36.2	32.6
April	43.7	38.1	43.0	42.8	41.7	37.9	32.9	39.0	38.4	29.1	36.2	32.6
May	43.4	38.2	43.0	42.6	41.8	38.2	32.8	38.9	38.3	29.0	36.1	32.6
June	43.6	38.3	43.0	43.0	41.8	37.9	32.8	38.9	38.3	29.1	36.2	32.6
July	43.5	38.3	43.1	43.4	41.7	37.9	32.9	38.8	38.4	29.1	36.5	32.6
August	43.6	38.3	43.2	42.6	41.7	37.9	32.8	38.8	38.3	29.0	36.3	32.6
September	43.4	38.3	43.2	43.2	41.8	37.5	32.8	38.6	38.4	28.8	36.4	32.6
October	43.5	38.3	43.0	43.2	41.5	37.6	32.9	38.4	38.6	29.0	36.4	32.7
November	43.4	38.3	43.0	43.0	41.5	37.7	32.8	38.3	38.4	29.0	36.2	32.7
December	43.3	38.3	43.0	43.1	41.5	37.4	32.9	38.4	38.5	29.1	36.3	32.7

1. Not seasonally adjusted.

Table 8-7. Indexes of Aggregate Weekly Hours

(Production or nonsupervisory workers on private nonfarm payrolls, 1982=100, seasonally adjusted.)

Year and month	Total private	Goods-producing industries									
		Total	Mining	Construction	Manufacturing						
					Total	Durable goods					
						Total	Lumber and wood products	Furniture and fixtures	Stone, clay, and glass products	Primary metal industries [1]	Fabricated metal products
1970	86.3	107.8	57.6	101.3	112.8	113.0	117.9	111.0	120.9	152.9	120.3
1971	85.8	105.0	54.9	103.6	108.8	107.4	123.8	114.0	122.2	140.5	113.2
1972	89.2	110.5	57.8	107.9	114.8	115.4	136.1	126.6	131.1	146.3	121.9
1973	93.2	116.9	58.8	113.7	121.7	125.8	140.6	132.0	138.4	161.8	131.8
1974	93.2	113.7	63.4	109.5	118.1	122.4	128.2	123.4	134.5	162.4	127.4
1975	88.8	99.9	68.3	92.7	103.8	104.9	107.8	100.7	115.6	134.3	108.4
1976	92.3	105.4	71.5	94.0	110.3	111.9	123.5	111.0	120.8	140.0	115.3
1977	96.0	110.3	76.5	100.2	115.0	118.4	132.0	117.2	125.9	144.2	121.9
1978	100.7	116.5	79.0	112.2	120.1	125.9	138.3	125.6	132.1	151.3	129.3
1979	104.0	119.9	88.2	119.9	122.1	129.1	138.6	123.5	132.8	154.8	131.4
1980	102.8	112.9	94.1	115.1	113.8	117.8	119.9	112.4	119.8	133.4	119.8
1981	104.1	111.6	104.8	109.3	112.5	116.1	115.1	112.7	114.1	132.5	117.1
1982	100.0	100.0	100.0	100.0	100.0	100.0	100.0	100.0	100.0	100.0	100.0
1983	101.5	100.5	81.5	102.2	101.4	100.7	117.7	110.3	103.2	95.2	100.3
1984	107.7	109.0	84.9	116.8	109.0	111.5	126.3	121.6	109.5	102.9	111.0
1985	110.5	108.7	81.4	125.3	106.9	109.5	124.9	121.9	108.1	96.1	111.2
1986	112.3	107.3	65.7	128.2	105.7	106.8	129.2	124.2	108.7	89.8	107.8
1987	115.6	109.0	61.8	132.7	107.0	107.4	134.9	129.5	109.7	91.8	107.1
1988	119.3	111.4	61.7	136.9	109.3	110.5	135.6	130.1	113.3	97.2	110.5
1989	122.1	111.7	60.5	138.9	109.3	110.1	132.6	129.6	113.5	96.0	110.6
1990	123.0	109.5	63.9	138.0	106.4	106.1	128.2	122.8	109.7	93.0	107.1
1991	120.4	103.4	62.0	122.8	102.1	99.3	116.9	113.9	101.4	87.2	101.4
1992	121.2	102.1	56.2	118.4	101.7	98.2	119.9	117.6	101.2	85.6	100.7
1993	124.6	104.2	54.3	125.4	103.1	100.0	126.1	121.3	102.9	86.2	103.3
1994	130.0	109.2	54.6	136.3	107.0	105.5	135.9	127.0	107.9	90.9	110.5
1995	133.4	110.3	54.1	140.8	107.5	107.5	135.8	125.6	108.8	92.1	113.6
1996	136.7	111.5	55.6	148.7	107.2	109.2	138.0	123.4	110.8	92.6	114.5
1997	141.5	114.6	58.3	156.2	109.4	112.9	142.1	128.6	112.4	94.5	118.1
1998	145.1	115.6	56.0	164.7	109.0	112.4	145.4	135.3	115.4	93.7	119.5
1999	148.1	115.8	50.3	175.7	107.2	111.1	148.0	138.4	115.6	91.6	119.5
1996											
January	132.6	106.4	52.8	139.1	103.0	104.9	129.5	112.9	105.4	90.9	110.0
February	135.1	110.8	54.9	146.0	106.9	108.4	136.4	122.6	110.2	92.4	113.2
March	135.6	110.2	55.9	145.7	106.2	107.3	136.0	122.9	110.2	92.0	112.9
April	135.5	110.9	55.3	146.8	106.9	108.8	137.5	122.3	110.4	91.7	113.5
May	136.2	111.2	55.4	146.1	107.3	109.4	138.4	123.6	110.5	92.8	114.2
June	137.0	112.0	56.4	149.0	107.8	109.9	140.1	124.2	111.5	93.2	115.0
July	136.6	111.6	55.3	148.1	107.4	109.6	139.3	124.5	110.7	92.2	115.6
August	137.4	112.2	55.8	150.2	107.8	110.1	139.9	124.8	111.5	93.2	115.6
September	138.0	112.4	56.2	150.9	107.9	110.3	140.1	125.1	112.0	93.6	115.6
October	138.0	112.4	56.0	151.6	107.6	109.9	140.4	125.1	112.3	92.9	115.4
November	138.4	112.5	56.2	152.4	107.7	110.0	140.5	125.4	111.8	92.1	115.6
December	138.9	113.0	56.7	152.9	108.2	110.6	139.8	126.7	111.3	93.1	115.6
1997											
January	138.6	112.0	56.0	148.9	107.8	110.4	138.1	125.1	109.4	92.9	115.7
February	139.7	113.4	58.3	154.3	108.3	111.1	139.6	124.8	111.8	93.7	116.2
March	140.6	114.3	59.0	155.9	109.0	112.0	141.3	127.6	112.6	93.7	117.0
April	140.9	114.6	58.1	155.8	109.5	112.8	142.6	127.6	112.3	94.5	118.1
May	141.2	114.7	58.9	157.7	109.1	112.4	142.7	128.3	112.8	93.9	117.4
June	140.9	114.2	58.7	156.0	108.9	112.3	142.6	127.9	111.8	93.7	117.5
July	141.6	114.4	58.5	156.6	109.0	112.6	142.7	128.3	112.8	93.9	117.7
August	141.8	114.7	58.8	156.6	109.4	113.3	142.4	128.9	112.6	94.8	118.2
September	142.4	115.1	58.5	159.1	109.4	113.2	143.0	129.9	113.1	95.0	118.4
October	142.8	115.3	58.3	157.6	109.9	113.8	142.9	129.9	113.1	95.8	118.9
November	143.1	115.3	58.4	155.5	110.4	114.5	143.6	131.5	112.3	95.9	119.7
December	143.4	116.2	58.5	159.2	110.7	115.0	143.5	132.7	113.9	96.3	120.5
1998											
January	144.3	116.9	59.7	161.9	110.9	115.3	144.3	134.4	116.0	97.2	121.1
February	144.2	116.7	58.3	163.5	110.4	114.9	144.3	135.0	115.7	95.9	120.6
March	144.1	115.8	57.9	160.1	110.0	114.3	144.5	135.0	114.4	95.5	119.9
April	144.2	115.6	57.1	162.4	109.4	113.7	145.3	135.6	114.4	94.5	120.1
May	145.1	116.0	57.1	163.4	109.6	113.9	144.9	136.3	114.9	94.5	119.9
June	144.9	115.8	56.3	163.1	109.5	113.6	145.2	136.3	114.7	94.5	119.6
July	145.2	114.9	55.9	166.4	107.7	111.0	145.4	135.3	114.7	92.2	118.7
August	145.6	115.8	55.3	166.9	108.7	112.9	145.4	135.9	115.7	93.7	119.3
September	145.6	115.4	54.3	166.0	108.5	112.7	144.5	134.2	115.4	93.1	119.2
October	146.2	115.8	54.2	168.9	108.4	112.9	145.8	135.6	115.4	92.3	119.7
November	146.3	115.6	53.5	169.3	108.1	112.5	146.6	135.2	115.7	91.9	119.2
December	146.8	116.3	53.1	173.9	108.0	112.4	148.3	136.2	116.8	91.4	119.6
1999											
January	146.8	115.9	51.4	173.9	107.6	111.8	149.1	137.2	116.8	91.1	119.4
February	147.5	116.0	50.8	175.6	107.3	111.7	146.8	136.8	116.0	91.3	118.8
March	147.1	115.2	50.4	171.8	107.2	111.6	148.5	137.5	114.6	91.4	119.0
April	147.7	115.6	50.1	174.3	107.2	111.7	147.7	137.5	115.7	91.2	118.9
May	147.6	115.5	49.8	174.2	107.1	111.6	147.7	137.8	115.7	91.5	118.9
June	148.2	115.8	49.6	176.2	107.1	111.8	147.7	138.4	115.7	91.3	119.1
July	148.5	116.1	50.3	175.3	107.6	112.7	147.8	140.1	115.7	92.2	120.5
August	148.4	115.5	49.7	174.6	107.1	112.1	147.9	139.0	115.4	92.1	119.5
September	148.6	116.0	50.2	177.5	107.1	112.1	147.8	139.4	115.4	91.9	119.6
October	149.3	116.0	50.3	177.5	107.0	111.8	148.2	139.0	115.2	91.7	119.5
November	149.6	116.8	50.2	183.3	106.8	111.5	148.0	138.0	116.5	91.5	119.3
December	149.8	116.0	50.5	178.6	106.7	111.5	147.6	139.0	116.0	91.9	119.4

1. Additional industry detail available in individual industry profile sections.

Table 8-7. Indexes of Aggregate Weekly Hours—*Continued*

(Production or nonsupervisory workers on private nonfarm payrolls, 1982=100, seasonally adjusted.)

| Year and month | Manufacturing—*Continued* | | | | | | | | | | |
| | Durable goods—*Continued* | | | | | Nondurable goods | | | | | |
	Industrial machinery and equipment	Electronic and electrical equipment	Transportation equipment[1]	Instruments and related products	Miscellaneous manufacturing	Total	Food and products	Tobacco products	Textile mill products	Apparel and other textile products[1]	Paper and products
1970	101.2	...	114.1	...	119.8	112.4	110.2	129.2	141.8	123.9	110.2
1971	89.5	...	112.6	...	116.2	110.8	109.3	118.7	141.3	122.9	106.4
1972	97.8	...	118.4	...	126.2	114.1	108.7	115.9	148.9	127.8	110.3
1973	111.8	...	129.1	...	130.9	116.0	106.3	124.0	150.7	131.7	112.7
1974	116.1	...	117.9	...	128.8	112.1	106.0	120.9	138.5	121.3	111.2
1975	101.6	...	106.8	...	112.5	102.1	101.8	118.1	122.9	110.2	96.8
1976	102.6	...	117.9	...	120.1	108.1	104.4	118.2	133.3	119.3	104.7
1977	109.8	...	125.6	...	122.2	110.2	104.6	106.8	132.9	117.9	107.6
1978	119.4	...	133.6	...	125.9	112.0	105.1	106.1	131.6	119.5	109.0
1979	126.9	...	134.1	...	123.8	112.3	107.0	104.4	129.3	115.6	110.5
1980	122.1	...	114.6	...	113.9	108.1	105.1	101.2	122.7	112.2	106.9
1981	120.2	...	114.2	...	110.5	107.6	102.8	105.1	117.3	111.0	106.8
1982	100.0	...	100.0	...	100.0	100.0	100.0	100.0	100.0	100.0	100.0
1983	90.1	...	105.7	...	98.1	102.4	99.1	96.3	107.4	104.5	102.1
1984	103.8	...	118.9	...	102.9	105.5	100.3	93.5	107.0	107.2	106.8
1985	101.0	...	122.7	...	97.8	103.4	100.6	88.4	100.1	100.7	106.8
1986	94.7	...	123.3	...	97.5	104.2	101.7	81.6	103.8	99.7	106.9
1987	93.8	...	124.3	...	99.9	106.6	103.7	80.1	109.4	100.1	108.5
1988	98.8	113.1	125.8	89.9	103.5	107.7	105.0	80.1	107.7	99.0	108.9
1989	100.3	111.5	125.3	89.6	103.0	108.2	107.8	70.6	105.6	98.3	109.9
1990	97.5	106.5	119.1	87.6	101.1	106.8	109.7	70.6	98.4	92.9	110.4
1991	91.8	100.7	113.3	84.0	98.1	105.9	110.2	70.2	97.0	91.3	109.3
1992	89.6	99.1	110.9	80.2	99.4	106.6	110.9	68.2	98.6	92.2	110.5
1993	92.7	100.9	111.4	77.0	101.6	107.4	112.6	60.7	98.9	90.4	110.9
1994	99.3	105.7	118.5	75.2	104.2	109.2	114.6	64.1	99.4	89.7	112.3
1995	103.5	107.8	121.6	73.7	103.3	107.6	115.5	62.8	94.9	84.2	110.5
1996	105.0	108.5	123.1	75.4	102.1	104.3	115.9	63.3	89.2	77.2	109.5
1997	109.6	111.1	129.2	76.7	104.4	104.6	116.6	61.4	89.8	73.7	111.0
1998	109.9	109.9	127.0	76.7	103.5	104.2	117.5	59.7	86.3	67.4	109.3
1999	105.0	107.0	126.8	76.5	102.5	101.7	117.9	55.8	80.6	60.7	107.3
1996											
January	102.2	105.3	118.1	72.2	97.8	100.3	112.5	58.5	80.1	72.0	105.7
February	104.8	108.8	120.4	74.9	102.2	104.8	116.6	62.6	90.2	79.0	109.3
March	104.8	108.3	114.3	75.1	102.4	104.7	116.7	63.9	90.1	78.3	108.8
April	104.9	108.1	123.4	75.1	102.0	104.3	116.2	63.5	88.4	77.8	109.2
May	105.0	108.7	123.9	75.6	102.6	104.5	116.1	63.2	89.7	78.3	109.2
June	105.0	109.0	124.8	76.0	102.3	104.8	115.8	63.4	90.1	78.4	109.6
July	105.0	108.5	124.5	74.9	101.3	104.4	115.2	63.2	89.9	77.8	109.2
August	105.0	109.2	125.0	75.6	101.5	104.6	115.4	63.9	89.9	77.6	109.9
September	105.2	109.2	125.5	76.0	102.4	104.6	115.8	64.7	89.6	77.2	110.0
October	104.9	108.7	124.1	76.1	101.9	104.5	116.3	63.2	90.1	76.8	110.2
November	105.4	108.7	124.3	76.1	102.8	104.5	116.2	65.9	89.9	76.4	110.7
December	106.1	109.0	125.6	77.0	104.2	104.9	116.4	66.9	90.5	76.1	111.2
1997											
January	106.7	107.7	127.8	75.8	103.8	104.2	116.0	63.1	89.8	75.4	111.0
February	107.3	109.8	126.7	76.5	104.3	104.4	116.5	64.0	88.6	74.9	111.2
March	108.3	110.7	128.3	76.3	103.7	104.8	116.6	63.5	90.3	75.3	111.7
April	109.9	111.5	128.1	76.3	104.7	104.9	116.7	60.2	90.4	75.0	111.7
May	109.3	110.7	127.6	76.3	104.7	104.6	116.3	61.2	90.0	74.1	111.5
June	108.9	110.7	128.5	76.5	104.0	104.2	115.7	58.8	89.6	74.0	110.5
July	109.5	111.4	128.3	76.3	104.6	104.1	116.1	57.7	90.0	73.1	110.3
August	110.0	111.3	130.8	76.7	104.0	104.0	116.1	60.2	89.1	72.6	110.1
September	110.4	111.0	128.7	76.9	104.2	104.2	116.1	60.9	89.9	72.5	110.3
October	110.8	111.8	130.5	76.9	104.9	104.6	116.8	61.3	89.4	72.4	110.8
November	111.8	112.9	131.1	77.4	105.1	104.8	117.0	61.5	89.5	71.9	111.3
December	112.1	113.3	131.8	77.6	105.7	104.7	117.3	62.0	89.9	71.8	111.0
1998											
January	112.3	113.3	130.8	77.8	105.6	104.9	117.6	61.2	89.6	71.4	111.2
February	112.0	112.8	130.0	77.9	105.6	104.3	117.1	61.3	89.0	70.2	110.3
March	111.7	111.4	129.4	77.4	105.7	104.1	117.2	62.1	88.2	69.5	110.3
April	110.4	110.8	127.5	77.2	104.7	103.5	116.8	62.8	87.3	69.0	107.8
May	110.9	110.5	128.5	77.2	104.3	103.8	117.7	61.7	87.6	68.0	109.9
June	111.5	110.6	126.3	77.0	104.3	103.8	117.9	59.9	87.3	67.8	109.6
July	110.3	109.5	114.5	76.6	104.0	103.1	117.1	60.2	85.9	67.6	109.5
August	110.0	109.4	125.1	76.8	103.6	103.0	116.9	60.0	85.5	67.1	109.0
September	109.4	108.6	127.6	76.4	102.5	102.8	117.9	57.8	84.7	66.5	109.3
October	108.7	108.2	129.0	76.3	101.6	102.4	117.2	58.6	84.8	65.3	108.8
November	107.8	108.0	129.1	75.9	100.9	102.0	117.7	58.2	83.7	64.3	108.4
December	106.5	106.9	129.2	75.9	100.8	102.0	118.7	55.7	83.4	63.9	107.9
1999											
January	105.6	106.3	126.5	76.3	101.0	101.8	119.1	58.5	82.9	63.0	108.0
February	105.5	106.3	127.3	76.6	101.3	101.4	118.4	57.1	81.4	62.7	107.5
March	105.1	105.7	127.2	76.5	101.9	101.2	118.3	56.2	80.9	62.1	108.2
April	104.8	106.6	127.1	76.8	102.3	101.1	118.0	56.2	81.0	62.0	108.2
May	105.0	106.9	125.8	76.8	103.0	100.9	117.9	57.0	80.7	61.7	107.3
June	104.7	106.9	127.0	76.7	102.5	100.6	117.6	56.5	79.8	60.9	107.6
July	105.7	108.3	128.1	76.8	102.5	100.6	117.9	55.6	80.6	60.2	107.1
August	104.8	107.7	127.6	76.5	103.2	100.1	116.5	49.3	80.1	59.5	107.3
September	104.9	107.5	127.5	76.1	102.9	100.2	117.4	53.7	79.5	59.1	106.9
October	104.5	107.4	126.4	76.3	103.0	100.3	118.0	54.6	79.9	58.9	106.7
November	104.4	106.8	125.5	76.3	102.8	100.3	117.9	56.0	80.0	58.6	106.6
December	104.5	106.8	125.0	75.8	103.1	100.2	117.7	56.6	79.6	58.7	106.4

1. Additional industry detail available in individual industry profile sections.

Table 8-7. Indexes of Aggregate Weekly Hours—*Continued*

(Production or nonsupervisory workers on private nonfarm payrolls, 1982=100, seasonally adjusted.)

Year and month	Nondurable goods manufacturing—*Continued*					Service-producing industries					
	Printing and publishing	Chemicals and products	Petroleum and coal products	Rubber and miscellaneous plastics products	Leather and products	Total	Transportation and public utilities	Wholesale trade	Retail trade	Finance, insurance, real estate	Services
1970	98.9	102.5	96.2	86.3	156.4	76.7	96.9	81.7	83.4	73.0	65.3
1971	95.3	99.8	100.9	87.5	148.7	77.2	95.1	80.4	85.3	74.3	65.6
1972	96.5	100.9	101.5	97.8	150.7	79.6	97.3	82.5	88.2	76.5	68.0
1973	97.4	104.2	99.9	107.9	142.3	82.5	99.9	85.6	90.9	78.9	71.3
1974	95.5	105.7	100.9	105.8	131.8	84.0	100.4	87.6	91.0	79.8	73.9
1975	88.9	97.1	96.3	89.0	121.3	83.9	94.6	86.4	90.6	79.9	76.0
1976	90.3	102.0	102.3	96.1	130.6	86.4	95.5	89.1	93.9	81.5	78.8
1977	94.1	105.0	106.6	109.2	123.9	89.5	97.9	92.5	96.5	85.4	82.0
1978	97.5	107.4	112.2	115.3	125.5	93.6	101.3	97.7	100.0	90.3	86.3
1979	101.0	108.3	114.0	118.2	117.1	96.9	104.9	102.0	101.5	94.4	90.2
1980	100.1	106.0	99.1	106.7	110.7	98.3	104.1	101.9	100.1	97.8	94.3
1981	100.6	106.8	110.0	109.0	113.6	100.8	103.3	103.3	100.6	105.5	98.2
1982	100.0	100.0	100.0	100.0	100.0	100.0	100.0	100.0	100.0	100.0	100.0
1983	103.3	98.3	98.4	107.2	96.8	102.0	97.3	99.9	102.7	101.6	103.6
1984	110.9	99.8	92.5	119.6	89.3	107.1	102.8	105.3	108.2	106.4	108.2
1985	114.9	98.9	88.7	117.6	78.1	111.3	104.6	108.4	111.7	110.9	114.0
1986	119.6	97.3	88.1	119.6	69.5	114.6	104.0	108.5	114.3	116.7	119.2
1987	123.2	99.3	89.4	123.1	70.3	118.5	106.5	109.4	117.9	120.1	124.9
1988	126.7	102.9	88.1	127.3	67.9	122.8	108.2	113.3	121.0	119.2	132.2
1989	126.2	104.5	85.7	129.6	66.4	126.8	111.1	116.1	122.9	119.5	139.3
1990	127.5	104.3	87.2	127.9	62.8	129.1	114.5	115.7	123.0	120.2	144.2
1991	123.3	101.6	86.7	123.2	57.7	128.0	113.4	113.7	119.5	118.3	145.3
1992	122.3	100.0	86.0	127.8	56.6	129.7	113.6	112.8	120.6	118.1	149.3
1993	123.9	100.9	83.1	133.2	55.6	133.7	118.2	112.8	123.4	121.2	155.4
1994	125.9	102.0	81.4	141.9	53.0	139.3	122.4	116.9	128.6	124.0	162.9
1995	125.0	102.5	77.9	143.4	48.3	143.8	123.9	121.1	132.2	122.9	170.5
1996	124.0	101.5	76.3	143.2	43.3	148.0	127.5	122.9	134.6	125.0	177.4
1997	126.0	101.2	76.1	146.4	40.6	153.6	130.5	126.1	137.7	129.6	186.6
1998	124.8	103.4	76.0	147.3	35.6	158.3	132.3	127.9	140.0	136.3	194.2
1999	122.1	102.7	72.2	147.4	33.6	162.5	134.1	129.9	143.1	138.6	201.3
1996											
January	120.7	101.1	75.6	138.5	41.6	144.4	124.4	120.9	131.5	122.8	172.4
February	124.3	102.6	75.4	141.2	44.5	146.0	126.5	121.6	133.4	123.5	174.3
March	124.5	102.1	75.7	141.6	44.2	146.9	127.2	122.1	134.2	124.0	175.6
April	124.0	101.6	75.6	142.1	43.7	146.5	126.3	121.9	133.3	124.0	175.5
May	124.2	101.5	75.2	142.6	43.7	147.4	126.9	122.5	134.3	124.3	176.7
June	124.2	102.1	78.5	143.4	43.9	148.2	127.7	123.1	134.5	125.3	177.9
July	124.2	101.6	77.1	143.6	43.1	147.9	127.8	122.5	134.4	124.9	177.3
August	124.3	101.5	76.8	144.7	43.3	148.7	128.3	123.2	135.0	125.5	178.6
September	124.2	100.9	76.6	145.0	42.8	149.5	128.7	124.0	135.7	126.8	179.4
October	124.0	100.6	75.6	144.2	42.8	149.5	128.7	124.1	135.9	126.1	179.3
November	123.9	100.8	75.9	144.4	42.4	150.0	128.9	124.3	136.5	126.6	180.1
December	124.7	101.3	76.3	144.9	43.4	150.6	128.5	124.6	136.7	127.2	181.2
1997											
January	124.0	100.2	77.3	143.8	42.5	150.6	128.7	124.2	136.8	127.0	181.3
February	124.5	100.7	77.1	145.1	42.0	151.5	129.1	125.1	136.8	127.4	183.3
March	125.6	100.4	76.4	145.6	42.2	152.3	131.0	125.5	137.6	127.6	184.1
April	125.7	100.8	76.0	146.8	41.5	152.7	130.4	125.5	137.2	128.4	185.1
May	126.6	100.8	76.7	145.6	41.3	153.1	130.6	126.0	137.2	128.8	185.9
June	126.3	100.6	76.2	145.1	40.6	152.9	130.0	125.9	136.9	129.0	185.9
July	126.1	100.6	75.2	145.8	40.2	153.7	129.7	126.2	137.3	129.5	187.5
August	125.8	101.1	76.0	146.3	39.7	153.9	127.9	126.4	138.1	130.3	187.7
September	126.2	101.5	75.9	146.4	39.6	154.6	131.9	126.5	137.9	130.4	188.5
October	126.8	102.1	75.9	147.5	39.5	155.1	131.7	126.8	138.6	130.9	189.0
November	127.0	102.4	76.6	148.4	39.1	155.6	131.7	127.3	138.9	131.8	189.6
December	126.8	102.4	74.9	148.0	38.8	155.7	131.5	126.9	138.5	131.3	190.4
1998											
January	126.2	103.4	76.4	148.4	39.0	156.6	131.8	127.6	139.0	133.4	191.6
February	126.2	103.6	74.2	148.1	39.0	156.6	131.8	127.7	139.0	133.9	191.5
March	125.9	103.9	75.6	147.7	37.7	156.8	131.4	127.4	139.0	134.7	191.9
April	124.9	103.6	75.2	148.1	36.7	157.0	131.4	127.6	139.1	135.2	192.4
May	125.6	103.6	76.1	148.1	36.6	158.1	132.4	128.2	140.1	136.0	193.8
June	125.6	104.0	76.6	148.2	36.9	157.9	131.9	127.9	139.6	136.1	193.9
July	124.9	103.7	77.0	146.3	36.0	158.8	132.6	127.6	140.4	136.5	195.2
August	125.4	103.6	76.3	146.9	35.8	159.0	132.7	128.3	140.1	136.8	195.7
September	124.3	103.4	75.8	146.6	35.2	159.1	132.8	127.9	140.8	137.0	195.6
October	123.8	103.2	75.6	146.9	35.2	159.8	133.7	128.3	140.9	137.5	196.8
November	123.4	102.7	75.8	146.6	35.2	160.0	133.7	128.8	141.2	137.9	196.8
December	123.0	102.2	76.6	146.9	35.2	160.5	133.6	129.0	141.0	138.1	198.1
1999											
January	123.4	102.3	73.9	146.1	34.6	160.7	134.7	128.7	141.4	138.2	198.0
February	122.7	102.5	74.4	146.8	34.8	161.6	134.7	129.3	143.1	138.6	198.8
March	121.9	102.1	74.6	147.3	34.2	161.5	134.6	129.0	142.4	138.3	199.3
April	121.8	102.8	72.9	147.3	34.4	162.0	134.4	129.9	143.3	138.4	199.9
May	121.9	102.6	72.3	147.3	34.6	162.1	134.2	129.6	142.9	138.2	200.4
June	122.1	102.4	72.3	146.9	33.8	162.7	134.5	129.8	143.7	138.7	201.1
July	122.0	102.7	72.1	147.3	32.6	163.1	134.3	130.4	143.9	140.0	201.6
August	122.0	102.6	71.4	147.7	33.8	163.2	134.6	130.3	143.5	139.2	202.3
September	121.8	103.3	71.3	147.7	32.8	163.2	134.3	130.8	142.5	139.6	202.9
October	122.0	103.0	71.3	147.4	32.9	164.3	133.8	131.8	143.6	139.6	204.6
November	121.8	103.5	70.1	147.6	32.4	164.4	133.8	131.3	143.7	138.9	205.2
December	121.8	103.5	69.1	147.9	32.2	165.0	134.4	132.0	144.6	139.4	205.7

Table 8-8. Average Hourly Earnings

(Average earnings per hour of production or nonsupervisory workers on private nonfarm payrolls; dollars, seasonally adjusted)

Year and month	Total private Current dollars	Total private 1982 dollars	Goods Total	Mining [1]	Construction [1]	Mfg Total [1]	Mfg Excluding overtime	Service Total [1]	Transportation and public utilities [1]	Wholesale	Retail trade [1]	Finance, insurance, and real estate [1]	Services [1]
1970	3.23	8.03	3.67	3.85	5.24	3.35	3.23	2.95	3.85	3.43	2.44	3.07	2.81
1971	3.45	8.21	3.94	4.06	5.69	3.57	3.45	3.15	4.21	3.64	2.60	3.22	3.04
1972	3.70	8.53	4.22	4.44	6.06	3.82	3.66	3.38	4.65	3.85	2.75	3.36	3.27
1973	3.94	8.55	4.50	4.75	6.41	4.09	3.91	3.59	5.02	4.07	2.91	3.53	3.47
1974	4.24	8.28	4.84	5.23	6.81	4.42	4.25	3.87	5.41	4.38	3.14	3.77	3.75
1975	4.53	8.12	5.27	5.95	7.31	4.83	4.67	4.14	5.88	4.72	3.36	4.06	4.02
1976	4.86	8.24	5.65	6.46	7.71	5.22	5.02	4.43	6.45	5.02	3.57	4.27	4.31
1977	5.25	8.36	6.10	6.94	8.10	5.68	5.44	4.77	6.99	5.39	3.85	4.54	4.65
1978	5.69	8.40	6.64	7.67	8.66	6.17	5.91	5.17	7.57	5.88	4.20	4.89	4.99
1979	6.16	8.17	7.21	8.49	9.27	6.70	6.43	5.58	8.16	6.39	4.53	5.27	5.36
1980	6.66	7.78	7.83	9.17	9.94	7.27	7.02	6.06	8.87	6.95	4.88	5.79	5.85
1981	7.25	7.69	8.57	10.04	10.82	7.99	7.72	6.59	9.70	7.55	5.25	6.31	6.41
1982	7.68	7.68	9.16	10.77	11.63	8.49	8.25	7.02	10.32	8.08	5.48	6.78	6.92
1983	8.02	7.79	9.48	11.28	11.94	8.83	8.52	7.37	10.79	8.54	5.74	7.29	7.31
1984	8.32	7.80	9.83	11.63	12.13	9.19	8.82	7.62	11.12	8.88	5.85	7.63	7.59
1985	8.57	7.77	10.19	11.98	12.32	9.54	9.16	7.86	11.40	9.15	5.94	7.94	7.90
1986	8.76	7.81	10.39	12.46	12.48	9.73	9.34	8.08	11.70	9.34	6.03	8.36	8.18
1987	8.98	7.73	10.58	12.54	12.71	9.91	9.48	8.32	12.03	9.59	6.12	8.73	8.49
1988	9.28	7.69	10.88	12.80	13.08	10.19	9.73	8.64	12.24	9.98	6.31	9.06	8.88
1989	9.66	7.64	11.22	13.26	13.54	10.48	10.02	9.04	12.57	10.39	6.53	9.53	9.38
1990	10.01	7.52	11.56	13.68	13.77	10.83	10.37	9.42	12.92	10.79	6.75	9.97	9.83
1991	10.32	7.45	11.86	14.19	14.00	11.18	10.71	9.77	13.20	11.15	6.94	10.39	10.23
1992	10.57	7.41	12.09	14.54	14.15	11.46	10.95	10.04	13.43	11.39	7.12	10.82	10.54
1993	10.83	7.39	12.37	14.60	14.38	11.74	11.18	10.30	13.55	11.74	7.29	11.35	10.78
1994	11.12	7.40	12.71	14.88	14.73	12.07	11.43	10.56	13.78	12.06	7.49	11.83	11.04
1995	11.43	7.39	13.04	15.30	15.09	12.37	11.74	10.88	14.13	12.43	7.69	12.32	11.39
1996	11.82	7.43	13.47	15.62	15.47	12.77	12.12	11.26	14.45	12.87	7.99	12.80	11.79
1997	12.28	7.55	13.92	16.15	16.04	13.17	12.45	11.73	14.92	13.45	8.33	13.34	12.28
1998	12.78	7.75	14.34	16.91	16.61	13.49	12.79	12.27	15.31	14.07	8.74	14.07	12.84
1999	13.24	7.86	14.84	17.09	17.18	13.91	13.18	12.73	15.69	14.58	9.08	14.62	13.36
1996													
January	11.63	7.42	13.31	15.43	15.34	12.62	12.00	11.08	14.28	12.62	7.84	12.59	11.61
February	11.64	7.40	13.26	15.45	15.24	12.58	11.95	11.09	14.31	12.65	7.85	12.63	11.62
March	11.67	7.40	13.24	15.46	15.27	12.54	11.92	11.14	14.35	12.74	7.88	12.70	11.66
April	11.72	7.40	13.39	15.48	15.32	12.72	12.06	11.16	14.37	12.75	7.90	12.72	11.68
May	11.75	7.40	13.39	15.55	15.36	12.72	12.07	11.19	14.41	12.78	7.94	12.75	11.71
June	11.81	7.43	13.45	15.63	15.42	12.77	12.11	11.25	14.48	12.88	8.01	12.78	11.76
July	11.83	7.43	13.49	15.65	15.48	12.80	12.15	11.26	14.44	12.87	7.99	12.82	11.80
August	11.87	7.45	13.54	15.70	15.53	12.84	12.18	11.30	14.49	12.92	8.02	12.84	11.84
September	11.91	7.44	13.57	15.71	15.59	12.87	12.20	11.34	14.53	12.99	8.03	12.87	11.89
October	11.93	7.44	13.57	15.63	15.59	12.86	12.21	11.38	14.51	12.97	8.09	12.91	11.94
November	11.99	7.45	13.64	15.76	15.67	12.92	12.25	11.43	14.58	13.08	8.12	13.00	11.99
December	12.02	7.46	13.67	15.89	15.62	12.98	12.29	11.46	14.61	13.12	8.16	12.97	12.02
1997													
January	12.06	7.47	13.74	16.09	15.82	13.02	12.33	11.50	14.69	13.15	8.18	13.00	12.07
February	12.10	7.47	13.77	16.00	15.88	13.02	12.33	11.53	14.65	13.22	8.21	13.02	12.10
March	12.14	7.49	13.80	15.98	15.83	13.07	12.36	11.58	14.76	13.27	8.24	13.09	12.14
April	12.16	7.50	13.82	16.02	15.89	13.08	12.34	11.60	14.78	13.32	8.25	13.08	12.16
May	12.21	7.53	13.85	16.12	15.93	13.10	12.37	11.65	14.82	13.36	8.28	13.22	12.20
June	12.23	7.54	13.87	16.19	15.98	13.11	12.42	11.69	14.89	13.38	8.30	13.27	12.23
July	12.27	7.55	13.88	16.15	16.00	13.12	12.42	11.73	14.97	13.44	8.33	13.34	12.26
August	12.33	7.57	13.95	16.12	16.07	13.19	12.48	11.79	15.02	13.56	8.36	13.50	12.33
September	12.37	7.58	13.98	16.20	16.13	13.20	12.50	11.83	14.98	13.56	8.40	13.54	12.37
October	12.43	7.60	14.06	16.27	16.20	13.30	12.57	11.88	15.07	13.61	8.45	13.59	12.42
November	12.48	7.63	14.10	16.39	16.24	13.35	12.62	11.94	15.10	13.73	8.50	13.63	12.48
December	12.52	7.65	14.16	16.39	16.32	13.39	12.65	11.96	15.13	13.74	8.50	13.65	12.52
1998													
January	12.54	7.66	14.18	16.49	16.35	13.39	12.66	11.99	15.18	13.76	8.55	13.69	12.53
February	12.60	7.69	14.24	16.77	16.40	13.43	12.70	12.06	15.21	13.85	8.57	13.79	12.61
March	12.64	7.71	14.26	16.83	16.44	13.46	12.74	12.10	15.22	13.89	8.62	13.84	12.66
April	12.69	7.73	14.28	16.75	16.48	13.46	12.76	12.17	15.26	13.91	8.67	13.94	12.74
May	12.73	7.74	14.30	16.73	16.49	13.48	12.77	12.21	15.27	14.02	8.70	13.99	12.79
June	12.76	7.75	14.29	16.76	16.53	13.46	12.76	12.25	15.28	14.05	8.72	14.05	12.84
July	12.79	7.76	14.32	16.85	16.61	13.44	12.74	12.29	15.31	14.11	8.76	14.07	12.88
August	12.85	7.78	14.39	17.01	16.69	13.51	12.80	12.35	15.34	14.19	8.80	14.15	12.93
September	12.87	7.79	14.41	17.07	16.64	13.56	12.86	12.37	15.36	14.18	8.84	14.17	12.97
October	12.91	7.80	14.45	17.16	16.75	13.56	12.87	12.41	15.40	14.25	8.83	14.24	13.00
November	12.95	7.81	14.49	17.32	16.79	13.59	12.89	12.45	15.43	14.30	8.86	14.33	13.05
December	12.99	7.82	14.53	17.22	16.83	13.61	12.91	12.49	15.50	14.30	8.89	14.42	13.08
1999													
January	13.04	7.83	14.56	17.15	16.86	13.65	12.95	12.55	15.52	14.36	8.93	14.46	13.16
February	13.06	7.84	14.59	17.05	16.87	13.68	12.98	12.57	15.53	14.42	8.95	14.51	13.19
March	13.10	7.86	14.64	17.05	16.96	13.73	13.02	12.61	15.55	14.43	8.97	14.52	13.24
April	13.14	7.83	14.71	16.94	17.02	13.80	13.08	12.64	15.62	14.47	9.01	14.57	13.27
May	13.19	7.86	14.77	17.11	17.11	13.85	13.13	12.68	15.66	14.52	9.03	14.60	13.31
June	13.23	7.88	14.85	17.07	17.18	13.93	13.19	12.71	15.67	14.56	9.07	14.62	13.35
July	13.27	7.88	14.89	17.26	17.20	13.98	13.24	12.76	15.72	14.61	9.10	14.68	13.39
August	13.30	7.87	14.91	17.16	17.21	14.01	13.27	12.78	15.73	14.65	9.13	14.65	13.42
September	13.35	7.86	14.96	17.14	17.26	14.04	13.29	12.83	15.79	14.70	9.16	14.71	13.46
October	13.38	7.87	14.99	17.09	17.33	14.06	13.31	12.86	15.79	14.75	9.18	14.73	13.51
November	13.41	7.87	15.03	17.00	17.37	14.07	13.33	12.89	15.84	14.76	9.21	14.76	13.53
December	13.44	7.87	15.05	17.04	17.44	14.10	13.36	12.93	15.94	14.83	9.25	14.78	13.57

1. Additional industry data available in individual industry profile sections.

Table 8-8. Average Hourly Earnings—*Continued*

(Average earnings per hour of production or nonsupervisory workers on private nonfarm payrolls; dollars, not seasonally adjusted.)

| Year and month | Total private | Goods-producing industries | | | Manufacturing | | | | | | |
| | | Total | Mining | Construction | Total | Durable goods | | | | | |
						Total	Lumber and wood products	Furniture and fixtures	Stone, clay, and glass products	Primary metal industries [1]
1970	3.23	3.67	3.85	5.24	3.35	3.55	2.97	2.77	3.40	3.93
1971	3.45	3.94	4.06	5.69	3.57	3.79	3.18	2.90	3.67	4.23
1972	3.70	4.22	4.44	6.06	3.82	4.07	3.34	3.08	3.94	4.66
1973	3.94	4.50	4.75	6.41	4.09	4.35	3.62	3.29	4.22	5.04
1974	4.24	4.84	5.23	6.81	4.42	4.70	3.90	3.53	4.54	5.60
1975	4.53	5.27	5.95	7.31	4.83	5.15	4.28	3.78	4.92	6.18
1976	4.86	5.65	6.46	7.71	5.22	5.57	4.74	3.99	5.33	6.77
1977	5.25	6.10	6.94	8.10	5.68	6.06	5.11	4.34	5.81	7.40
1978	5.69	6.64	7.67	8.66	6.17	6.58	5.62	4.68	6.32	8.20
1979	6.16	7.21	8.49	9.27	6.70	7.12	6.08	5.06	6.85	8.98
1980	6.66	7.83	9.17	9.94	7.27	7.75	6.57	5.49	7.50	9.77
1981	7.25	8.57	10.04	10.82	7.99	8.53	7.02	5.91	8.27	10.81
1982	7.68	9.16	10.77	11.63	8.49	9.03	7.46	6.31	8.87	11.33
1983	8.02	9.48	11.28	11.94	8.83	9.38	7.82	6.62	9.27	11.35
1984	8.32	9.83	11.63	12.13	9.19	9.73	8.05	6.84	9.57	11.47
1985	8.57	10.19	11.98	12.32	9.54	10.09	8.25	7.17	9.84	11.67
1986	8.76	10.39	12.46	12.48	9.73	10.28	8.37	7.46	10.04	11.86
1987	8.98	10.58	12.54	12.71	9.91	10.43	8.43	7.67	10.25	11.94
1988	9.28	10.88	12.80	13.08	10.19	10.71	8.59	7.95	10.56	12.16
1989	9.66	11.22	13.26	13.54	10.48	11.01	8.84	8.25	10.82	12.43
1990	10.01	11.56	13.68	13.77	10.83	11.35	9.08	8.52	11.12	12.92
1991	10.32	11.86	14.19	14.00	11.18	11.75	9.24	8.76	11.36	13.33
1992	10.57	12.09	14.54	14.15	11.46	12.02	9.44	9.01	11.60	13.66
1993	10.83	12.37	14.60	14.38	11.74	12.33	9.61	9.27	11.85	13.99
1994	11.12	12.71	14.88	14.73	12.07	12.68	9.84	9.55	12.13	14.34
1995	11.43	13.04	15.30	15.09	12.37	12.94	10.12	9.82	12.41	14.62
1996	11.82	13.47	15.62	15.47	12.77	13.33	10.44	10.15	12.82	14.97
1997	12.28	13.92	16.15	16.04	13.17	13.73	10.76	10.55	13.18	15.22
1998	12.78	14.34	16.90	16.59	13.49	13.98	11.10	10.90	13.60	15.49
1999	13.24	14.84	17.09	17.18	13.91	14.40	11.47	11.23	13.87	15.83
1996										
January	11.70	13.27	15.63	15.26	12.66	13.17	10.28	10.01	12.60	14.84
February	11.68	13.19	15.61	15.16	12.57	13.12	10.23	9.95	12.56	14.70
March	11.68	13.17	15.50	15.16	12.54	13.05	10.29	10.00	12.60	14.73
April	11.74	13.36	15.55	15.22	12.73	13.28	10.33	10.06	12.77	14.99
May	11.72	13.38	15.45	15.30	12.70	13.27	10.35	10.08	12.74	14.82
June	11.75	13.45	15.59	15.35	12.75	13.32	10.45	10.11	12.82	14.91
July	11.73	13.54	15.55	15.52	12.79	13.35	10.47	10.13	12.94	15.08
August	11.76	13.55	15.52	15.58	12.79	13.38	10.54	10.19	12.92	15.02
September	11.96	13.66	15.74	15.77	12.89	13.51	10.57	10.27	12.99	15.18
October	11.96	13.62	15.56	15.77	12.83	13.41	10.56	10.28	12.91	15.09
November	12.01	13.63	15.69	15.64	12.92	13.48	10.57	10.28	12.96	15.18
December	12.07	13.73	15.97	15.68	13.07	13.64	10.62	10.42	12.93	15.15
1997										
January	12.12	13.68	16.20	15.76	13.03	13.61	10.58	10.38	12.99	15.12
February	12.15	13.67	16.09	15.72	13.01	13.57	10.61	10.34	13.04	15.09
March	12.18	13.73	16.01	15.71	13.07	13.63	10.61	10.43	13.02	15.16
April	12.18	13.78	16.08	15.78	13.08	13.63	10.65	10.42	13.06	15.15
May	12.18	13.83	16.00	15.86	13.08	13.63	10.71	10.47	13.12	15.09
June	12.18	13.86	16.13	15.91	13.09	13.64	10.77	10.51	13.13	15.16
July	12.17	13.94	16.05	16.04	13.10	13.61	10.82	10.53	13.20	15.28
August	12.23	13.97	15.96	16.13	13.14	13.69	10.80	10.60	13.21	15.16
September	12.41	14.08	16.24	16.31	13.23	13.79	10.86	10.70	13.27	15.27
October	12.45	14.12	16.19	16.34	13.28	13.88	10.87	10.67	13.32	15.33
November	12.54	14.13	16.38	16.30	13.36	13.95	10.90	10.70	13.36	15.38
December	12.53	14.21	16.49	16.39	13.47	14.06	10.92	10.79	13.39	15.43
1998										
January	12.61	14.11	16.60	16.28	13.40	13.95	10.89	10.75	13.38	15.48
February	12.66	14.12	16.85	16.23	13.41	13.95	10.90	10.78	13.45	15.46
March	12.68	14.18	16.85	16.31	13.47	14.01	10.94	10.81	13.46	15.53
April	12.70	14.24	16.80	16.37	13.46	13.95	10.98	10.86	13.62	15.66
May	12.71	14.29	16.68	16.45	13.47	13.97	11.05	10.80	13.58	15.55
June	12.68	14.29	16.69	16.48	13.44	13.93	11.09	10.82	13.58	15.54
July	12.68	14.36	16.77	16.68	13.38	13.77	11.17	10.91	13.58	15.56
August	12.76	14.42	16.90	16.79	13.45	13.92	11.18	10.96	13.61	15.44
September	12.90	14.49	17.13	16.81	13.60	14.06	11.17	10.99	13.80	15.60
October	12.94	14.52	17.10	16.91	13.54	14.02	11.22	11.00	13.66	15.31
November	13.01	14.51	17.31	16.85	13.60	14.07	11.24	11.00	13.64	15.34
December	13.01	14.58	17.33	16.91	13.69	14.16	11.34	11.12	13.68	15.35
1999										
January	13.11	14.48	17.27	16.78	13.66	14.11	11.29	11.12	13.64	15.38
February	13.10	14.47	17.12	16.70	13.66	14.12	11.26	11.07	13.61	15.39
March	13.12	14.55	17.06	16.83	13.73	14.19	11.31	11.11	13.68	15.51
April	13.16	14.66	16.98	16.90	13.80	14.27	11.38	11.15	13.73	15.60
May	13.20	14.77	17.05	17.06	13.85	14.34	11.43	11.14	13.84	15.74
June	13.15	14.85	16.98	17.13	13.90	14.40	11.46	11.16	13.91	15.90
July	13.16	14.93	17.17	17.27	13.91	14.38	11.53	11.25	13.97	16.02
August	13.20	14.95	17.05	17.31	13.95	14.47	11.54	11.28	13.94	15.98
September	13.38	15.08	17.13	17.46	14.11	14.62	11.56	11.33	14.10	16.18
October	13.41	15.07	17.05	17.54	14.03	14.55	11.60	11.33	14.00	16.01
November	13.43	15.05	17.01	17.42	14.08	14.58	11.60	11.36	14.04	16.12
December	13.46	15.11	17.19	17.47	14.20	14.73	11.64	11.47	13.97	16.17

1. Additional industry data available in individual industry profile sections.

Table 8-8. Average Hourly Earnings—*Continued*

(Average earnings per hour of production or nonsupervisory workers on private nonfarm payrolls; dollars, not seasonally adjusted.)

Year and month	Manufacturing—*Continued*										
	Durable goods—*Continued*						Nondurable goods				
	Fabricated metal products	Industrial machinery and equipment [1]	Electronic and electronic equipment	Transportation equipment [1]	Instruments and products	Miscellaneous manufacturing	Total	Food and products	Tobacco products	Textile mill products	Apparel and other textile products [1]
1970	3.53	3.77	...	4.06	...	2.83	3.08	3.16	2.91	2.45	2.39
1971	3.77	4.02	...	4.45	...	2.97	3.27	3.38	3.16	2.57	2.49
1972	4.05	4.32	...	4.81	...	3.11	3.48	3.60	3.47	2.75	2.60
1973	4.29	4.60	...	5.15	...	3.29	3.70	3.85	3.76	2.95	2.76
1974	4.61	4.94	...	5.54	...	3.53	4.01	4.19	4.12	3.20	2.97
1975	5.05	5.37	...	6.07	...	3.81	4.37	4.61	4.55	3.42	3.17
1976	5.50	5.79	...	6.62	...	4.04	4.71	4.98	4.98	3.69	3.40
1977	5.91	6.26	...	7.29	...	4.36	5.11	5.37	5.54	3.99	3.62
1978	6.35	6.78	...	7.91	...	4.69	5.54	5.80	6.13	4.30	3.94
1979	6.85	7.32	...	8.53	...	5.03	6.01	6.27	6.67	4.66	4.23
1980	7.45	8.00	...	9.35	...	5.46	6.56	6.85	7.74	5.07	4.56
1981	8.20	8.81	...	10.39	...	5.97	7.19	7.44	8.88	5.52	4.97
1982	8.77	9.26	...	11.11	...	6.42	7.75	7.92	9.79	5.83	5.20
1983	9.12	9.56	...	11.67	...	6.81	8.09	8.19	10.38	6.18	5.38
1984	9.40	9.97	...	12.20	...	7.05	8.39	8.39	11.22	6.46	5.55
1985	9.71	10.30	...	12.71	...	7.30	8.72	8.57	11.96	6.70	5.73
1986	9.89	10.58	...	12.81	...	7.55	8.95	8.75	12.88	6.93	5.84
1987	10.01	10.73	...	12.94	...	7.76	9.19	8.93	14.07	7.17	5.94
1988	10.29	11.08	9.79	13.29	10.60	8.00	9.45	9.12	14.67	7.38	6.12
1989	10.57	11.40	10.05	13.67	10.83	8.29	9.75	9.38	15.31	7.67	6.35
1990	10.83	11.77	10.30	14.08	11.29	8.61	10.12	9.62	16.23	8.02	6.57
1991	11.19	12.15	10.70	14.75	11.64	8.85	10.44	9.90	16.77	8.30	6.77
1992	11.42	12.41	11.00	15.20	11.89	9.15	10.73	10.20	16.92	8.60	6.95
1993	11.69	12.73	11.24	15.80	12.23	9.39	10.98	10.45	16.89	8.88	7.09
1994	11.93	13.00	11.50	16.51	12.47	9.67	11.24	10.66	19.07	9.13	7.34
1995	12.13	13.24	11.69	16.74	12.71	10.05	11.58	10.93	19.41	9.41	7.64
1996	12.50	13.59	12.18	17.19	13.13	10.38	11.97	11.20	19.35	9.69	7.96
1997	12.78	14.07	12.70	17.55	13.52	10.60	12.34	11.48	19.24	10.03	8.25
1998	13.06	14.47	13.09	17.53	13.81	10.89	12.76	11.80	18.55	10.39	8.52
1999	13.48	15.02	13.46	18.04	14.17	11.30	13.16	12.09	19.07	10.71	8.86
1996											
January	12.38	13.44	11.95	16.88	13.00	10.30	11.91	11.08	18.38	9.56	7.87
February	12.32	13.40	11.88	16.95	12.94	10.25	11.79	11.03	18.13	9.55	7.82
March	12.32	13.36	11.91	16.64	12.96	10.24	11.83	11.10	19.34	9.55	7.86
April	12.46	13.44	12.01	17.22	13.03	10.33	11.93	11.19	20.40	9.65	7.95
May	12.45	13.45	12.09	17.19	13.03	10.34	11.88	11.18	21.06	9.62	7.94
June	12.51	13.52	12.19	17.22	13.08	10.33	11.92	11.22	21.40	9.68	7.99
July	12.50	13.55	12.25	17.28	13.17	10.37	12.00	11.25	20.98	9.69	7.95
August	12.52	13.64	12.28	17.27	13.15	10.37	11.95	11.16	20.24	9.72	7.94
September	12.65	13.77	12.35	17.43	13.29	10.47	12.01	11.19	18.39	9.78	7.99
October	12.53	13.71	12.33	17.23	13.24	10.47	12.00	11.16	17.75	9.73	8.02
November	12.59	13.81	12.35	17.32	13.30	10.52	12.11	11.38	18.65	9.78	8.01
December	12.76	13.98	12.54	17.55	13.36	10.59	12.23	11.45	18.68	9.93	8.14
1997											
January	12.72	13.92	12.46	17.43	13.35	10.58	12.20	11.41	18.58	9.94	8.12
February	12.71	13.90	12.41	17.36	13.35	10.55	12.19	11.32	18.59	9.90	8.18
March	12.74	13.95	12.49	17.48	13.42	10.55	12.25	11.40	19.46	9.93	8.23
April	12.75	13.96	12.55	17.44	13.43	10.52	12.26	11.45	20.34	9.95	8.21
May	12.74	13.94	12.55	17.43	13.48	10.51	12.26	11.47	20.75	9.95	8.22
June	12.72	13.97	12.59	17.41	13.52	10.50	12.27	11.44	21.12	9.98	8.25
July	12.65	14.03	12.68	17.19	13.51	10.51	12.37	11.52	20.93	10.02	8.19
August	12.75	14.04	12.74	17.42	13.50	10.58	12.34	11.51	19.79	10.02	8.23
September	12.80	14.20	12.84	17.55	13.65	10.66	12.41	11.51	18.26	10.10	8.33
October	12.85	14.24	12.90	17.86	13.62	10.65	12.40	11.45	18.00	10.11	8.33
November	12.92	14.31	12.98	17.91	13.69	10.73	12.49	11.59	17.80	10.16	8.33
December	13.02	14.42	13.11	18.05	13.71	10.82	12.58	11.71	18.63	10.25	8.42
1998											
January	12.98	14.35	12.98	17.72	13.67	10.81	12.57	11.66	18.36	10.26	8.42
February	12.97	14.38	12.95	17.74	13.71	10.80	12.58	11.63	18.12	10.26	8.38
March	12.99	14.38	13.04	17.88	13.76	10.80	12.64	11.69	18.42	10.29	8.43
April	12.88	14.34	13.06	17.67	13.78	10.77	12.72	11.74	18.84	10.39	8.48
May	13.03	14.38	13.03	17.60	13.78	10.79	12.72	11.77	20.23	10.37	8.47
June	13.01	14.42	13.06	17.40	13.75	10.82	12.70	11.76	20.81	10.36	8.50
July	12.89	14.44	13.13	16.84	13.78	10.84	12.81	11.80	20.53	10.36	8.48
August	13.05	14.46	13.10	17.27	13.79	10.84	12.75	11.75	18.95	10.38	8.54
September	13.18	14.55	13.24	17.46	13.89	10.96	12.92	11.95	17.94	10.48	8.63
October	13.19	14.57	13.13	17.43	13.87	11.00	12.83	11.81	16.98	10.45	8.65
November	13.23	14.64	13.18	17.48	13.91	11.01	12.90	11.95	17.32	10.52	8.64
December	13.36	14.73	13.27	17.52	14.01	11.09	12.98	12.01	17.07	10.56	8.71
1999											
January	13.31	14.70	13.26	17.42	13.92	11.13	12.98	11.93	17.15	10.63	8.68
February	13.31	14.73	13.26	17.45	13.94	11.14	12.96	11.90	17.84	10.60	8.64
March	13.36	14.82	13.29	17.60	13.98	11.16	13.02	11.92	19.39	10.63	8.78
April	13.39	14.86	13.32	17.82	14.07	11.22	13.07	12.06	19.91	10.69	8.83
May	13.47	14.97	13.39	17.92	14.11	11.21	13.10	12.10	20.47	10.69	8.81
June	13.49	14.99	13.42	18.14	14.13	11.26	13.14	12.15	20.69	10.76	8.89
July	13.47	15.08	13.49	17.88	14.25	11.29	13.21	12.15	21.09	10.71	8.83
August	13.52	15.14	13.52	18.17	14.28	11.31	13.17	12.07	20.86	10.72	8.88
September	13.64	15.24	13.64	18.50	14.29	11.43	13.33	12.18	18.90	10.78	9.01
October	13.52	15.18	13.60	18.41	14.36	11.45	13.25	12.09	17.82	10.73	8.99
November	13.59	15.22	13.61	18.39	14.34	11.41	13.31	12.19	18.02	10.80	8.98
December	13.72	15.36	13.73	18.72	14.41	11.54	13.39	12.28	18.03	10.84	9.04

1. Additional industry data available in individual industry profile sections.

Table 8-8. Average Hourly Earnings—*Continued*

(Average earnings per hour of production or nonsupervisory workers on private nonfarm payrolls; dollars, not seasonally adjusted.)

Year and month	Manufacturing—*Continued* Nondurable goods—*Continued*						Service-producing industries					
	Paper and products	Printing and publishing	Chemicals and products	Petroleum and coal products	Rubber and miscellaneous plastics products	Leather and products	Total	Transportation and public utilities [1]	Wholesale trade	Retail trade [1]	Finance insurance, and real estate [1]	Services [1]
1970	3.44	3.92	3.69	4.28	3.21	2.49	2.95	3.85	3.43	2.44	3.07	2.81
1971	3.67	4.20	3.97	4.57	3.41	2.59	3.15	4.21	3.64	2.60	3.22	3.04
1972	3.95	4.51	4.26	4.96	3.63	2.68	3.38	4.65	3.85	2.75	3.36	3.27
1973	4.20	4.75	4.51	5.28	3.84	2.79	3.59	5.02	4.07	2.91	3.53	3.47
1974	4.53	5.03	4.88	5.68	4.09	2.99	3.87	5.41	4.38	3.14	3.77	3.75
1975	5.01	5.38	5.39	6.48	4.42	3.21	4.14	5.88	4.72	3.36	4.06	4.02
1976	5.47	5.71	5.91	7.21	4.71	3.40	4.43	6.45	5.02	3.57	4.27	4.31
1977	5.96	6.12	6.43	7.83	5.21	3.61	4.77	6.99	5.39	3.85	4.54	4.65
1978	6.52	6.51	7.02	8.63	5.57	3.89	5.17	7.57	5.88	4.20	4.89	4.99
1979	7.13	6.94	7.60	9.36	6.02	4.22	5.58	8.16	6.39	4.53	5.27	5.36
1980	7.84	7.53	8.30	10.10	6.58	4.58	6.06	8.87	6.95	4.88	5.79	5.85
1981	8.60	8.19	9.12	11.38	7.22	4.99	6.59	9.70	7.55	5.25	6.31	6.41
1982	9.32	8.74	9.96	12.46	7.70	5.33	7.02	10.32	8.08	5.48	6.78	6.92
1983	9.93	9.11	10.58	13.28	8.06	5.54	7.37	10.79	8.54	5.74	7.29	7.31
1984	10.41	9.41	11.07	13.44	8.35	5.71	7.62	11.12	8.88	5.85	7.63	7.59
1985	10.83	9.71	11.56	14.06	8.60	5.83	7.86	11.40	9.15	5.94	7.94	7.90
1986	11.18	9.99	11.98	14.19	8.79	5.92	8.08	11.70	9.34	6.03	8.36	8.18
1987	11.43	10.28	12.37	14.58	8.98	6.08	8.32	12.03	9.59	6.12	8.73	8.49
1988	11.69	10.53	12.71	14.97	9.19	6.28	8.64	12.24	9.98	6.31	9.06	8.88
1989	11.96	10.88	13.09	15.41	9.46	6.59	9.04	12.57	10.39	6.53	9.53	9.38
1990	12.31	11.24	13.54	16.24	9.76	6.91	9.42	12.92	10.79	6.75	9.97	9.83
1991	12.72	11.48	14.04	17.04	10.07	7.18	9.77	13.20	11.15	6.94	10.39	10.23
1992	13.07	11.74	14.51	17.90	10.36	7.42	10.04	13.43	11.39	7.12	10.82	10.54
1993	13.42	11.93	14.82	18.53	10.57	7.63	10.30	13.55	11.74	7.29	11.35	10.78
1994	13.77	12.14	15.13	19.07	10.70	7.97	10.56	13.78	12.06	7.49	11.83	11.04
1995	14.23	12.33	15.62	19.36	10.91	8.17	10.88	14.13	12.43	7.69	12.32	11.39
1996	14.67	12.65	16.17	19.32	11.24	8.57	11.26	14.45	12.87	7.99	12.80	11.79
1997	15.05	13.06	16.57	20.20	11.57	8.97	11.73	14.92	13.45	8.33	13.34	12.28
1998	15.51	13.45	17.12	20.92	11.89	9.32	12.27	15.31	14.06	8.73	14.06	12.85
1999	15.94	13.84	17.38	21.39	12.36	9.77	12.73	15.69	14.58	9.08	14.62	13.36
1996												
January	14.58	12.49	16.08	19.41	11.13	8.51	11.18	14.32	12.66	7.89	12.61	11.73
February	14.43	12.49	15.96	19.54	11.14	8.41	11.18	14.34	12.68	7.87	12.69	11.72
March	14.44	12.53	16.00	19.21	11.15	8.46	11.18	14.33	12.69	7.90	12.73	11.72
April	14.61	12.53	16.15	19.32	11.20	8.40	11.20	14.40	12.78	7.92	12.75	11.71
May	14.58	12.54	16.04	18.98	11.20	8.43	11.16	14.35	12.75	7.92	12.74	11.67
June	14.63	12.54	16.11	18.88	11.16	8.48	11.18	14.41	12.88	7.98	12.76	11.66
July	14.78	12.63	16.16	19.01	11.25	8.44	11.13	14.45	12.83	7.93	12.69	11.61
August	14.69	12.70	16.22	18.98	11.23	8.63	11.15	14.50	12.85	7.95	12.72	11.63
September	14.73	12.82	16.26	19.34	11.30	8.71	11.37	14.59	13.04	8.06	12.91	11.90
October	14.73	12.81	16.29	19.34	11.28	8.73	11.38	14.51	12.95	8.11	12.88	11.94
November	14.85	12.82	16.38	19.61	11.33	8.74	11.45	14.59	13.07	8.13	12.99	12.04
December	14.93	12.90	16.45	20.25	11.51	8.85	11.51	14.63	13.21	8.15	13.04	12.16
1997												
January	14.82	12.86	16.37	20.11	11.48	8.86	11.61	14.75	13.19	8.24	13.02	12.19
February	14.76	12.89	16.49	20.39	11.45	8.94	11.65	14.69	13.27	8.24	13.17	12.24
March	14.92	13.01	16.42	20.48	11.50	8.89	11.67	14.74	13.29	8.26	13.22	12.24
April	14.98	12.98	16.42	19.94	11.53	8.89	11.64	14.80	13.35	8.27	13.12	12.19
May	14.97	12.93	16.48	19.96	11.50	8.92	11.62	14.76	13.34	8.27	13.21	12.16
June	14.97	12.90	16.53	19.92	11.52	8.94	11.62	14.81	13.38	8.27	13.26	12.14
July	15.16	13.01	16.58	20.02	11.57	8.77	11.58	14.98	13.39	8.26	13.21	12.06
August	15.11	13.07	16.57	19.99	11.57	8.89	11.64	15.03	13.50	8.29	13.38	12.12
September	15.17	13.22	16.62	20.27	11.64	9.11	11.83	15.04	13.55	8.44	13.48	12.36
October	15.18	13.20	16.64	20.32	11.64	9.15	11.88	15.07	13.59	8.46	13.56	12.41
November	15.22	13.25	16.84	20.42	11.64	9.13	12.00	15.17	13.79	8.50	13.73	12.57
December	15.28	13.31	16.91	20.58	11.76	9.21	11.97	15.15	13.76	8.50	13.64	12.61
1998												
January	15.19	13.28	16.88	20.66	11.74	9.31	12.11	15.24	13.81	8.61	13.71	12.66
February	15.21	13.34	16.92	20.95	11.77	9.28	12.18	15.25	13.89	8.60	13.95	12.75
March	15.28	13.38	16.96	21.20	11.78	9.30	12.19	15.21	13.90	8.64	13.98	12.77
April	15.45	13.34	17.13	21.01	11.84	9.27	12.20	15.24	13.93	8.69	13.98	12.77
May	15.50	13.33	17.09	20.81	11.86	9.33	12.18	15.18	14.00	8.69	13.99	12.75
June	15.46	13.34	17.02	20.72	11.82	9.35	12.14	15.20	13.95	8.68	13.94	12.70
July	15.63	13.45	17.15	20.81	11.92	9.16	12.14	15.28	14.07	8.69	13.94	12.67
August	15.53	13.48	17.10	20.78	11.86	9.30	12.22	15.31	14.19	8.72	14.12	12.75
September	15.82	13.66	17.25	20.81	12.00	9.39	12.38	15.43	14.17	8.88	14.11	12.97
October	15.58	13.62	17.16	21.04	11.91	9.48	12.41	15.40	14.23	8.84	14.20	13.00
November	15.62	13.57	17.21	20.92	12.00	9.49	12.52	15.50	14.36	8.86	14.43	13.13
December	15.76	13.69	17.24	21.19	12.11	9.48	12.50	15.52	14.32	8.88	14.41	13.16
1999												
January	15.70	13.67	17.16	21.18	12.24	9.69	12.67	15.59	14.42	9.00	14.48	13.29
February	15.67	13.68	17.11	21.38	12.20	9.62	12.67	15.58	14.44	8.98	14.56	13.30
March	15.75	13.74	17.09	21.53	12.25	9.61	12.66	15.53	14.37	8.99	14.54	13.31
April	15.80	13.73	17.17	21.42	12.28	9.66	12.68	15.60	14.49	9.03	14.62	13.30
May	15.88	13.75	17.30	20.98	12.27	9.67	12.69	15.57	14.58	9.03	14.73	13.32
June	15.95	13.74	17.26	21.06	12.30	9.65	12.60	15.59	14.45	9.02	14.51	13.21
July	16.02	13.81	17.39	21.28	12.41	9.69	12.60	15.69	14.57	9.03	14.54	13.18
August	15.95	13.83	17.41	21.21	12.37	9.86	12.65	15.69	14.65	9.05	14.62	13.23
September	16.24	13.98	17.67	21.55	12.51	9.95	12.82	15.80	14.68	9.19	14.64	13.45
October	16.09	13.98	17.61	21.62	12.42	9.91	12.87	15.78	14.74	9.21	14.69	13.51
November	16.08	14.02	17.64	21.76	12.46	9.93	12.90	15.90	14.76	9.22	14.74	13.57
December	16.12	14.12	17.67	21.76	12.57	10.02	12.94	15.96	14.85	9.26	14.76	13.65

1. Additional industry data available in individual industry profile sections.

Table 8-9. Average Weekly Earnings

(Average earnings per week of production or nonsupervisory workers on private nonfarm payrolls; dollars, not seasonally adjusted, except as noted.)

Year and month	Total private		Goods-producing [1]	Mining [2]	Construc-tion [2]	Manufacturing					
	Seasonally adjusted	Not seasonally adjusted				Total	Durable goods				
							Total	Lumber and wood products	Furniture and fixtures	Stone, clay and glass products	Primary metal industries [2]
1970	119.83	119.83	144.60	164.40	195.45	133.33	143.07	117.61	108.58	140.08	158.77
1971	127.31	127.31	155.24	172.14	211.67	142.44	152.74	126.56	115.42	152.67	169.62
1972	136.90	136.90	168.38	189.14	221.19	154.71	167.68	134.94	123.82	165.48	192.92
1973	145.39	145.39	180.00	201.40	235.89	166.46	180.09	144.80	131.60	176.82	213.19
1974	154.76	154.76	191.18	219.14	249.25	176.80	190.82	152.88	138.02	187.50	232.96
1975	163.53	163.53	205.53	249.31	266.08	190.79	205.49	166.06	143.64	198.77	247.20
1976	175.45	175.45	223.74	273.90	283.73	209.32	226.14	189.13	154.81	219.06	276.22
1977	189.00	189.00	242.78	301.20	295.65	228.90	248.46	203.89	169.26	239.95	305.62
1978	203.70	203.70	264.94	332.88	318.69	249.27	270.44	223.68	183.92	262.91	342.76
1979	219.91	219.91	286.24	365.07	342.99	269.34	290.50	240.16	195.82	284.28	371.77
1980	235.10	235.10	307.72	397.06	367.78	288.62	310.78	253.60	209.17	306.00	391.78
1981	255.20	255.20	338.52	438.75	399.26	318.00	342.91	271.67	226.94	335.76	437.81
1982	267.26	267.26	354.49	459.88	426.82	330.26	354.88	284.23	234.73	355.69	437.34
1983	280.70	280.70	376.36	479.40	442.97	354.08	381.77	313.58	260.83	384.71	459.68
1984	292.86	292.86	395.17	503.58	458.51	374.03	402.82	321.20	271.55	401.94	478.30
1985	299.09	299.09	407.60	519.93	464.46	386.37	415.71	329.18	282.50	412.30	484.31
1986	304.85	304.85	416.64	525.81	466.75	396.01	424.56	338.15	296.91	423.69	496.93
1987	312.50	312.50	426.37	531.70	480.44	406.31	432.85	342.26	306.80	433.58	514.61
1988	322.02	322.02	439.55	541.44	495.73	418.81	447.68	344.46	313.23	446.69	528.96
1989	334.24	334.24	452.17	570.18	513.17	429.68	458.02	354.48	325.88	457.69	534.49
1990	345.35	345.35	465.87	603.29	526.01	441.86	468.76	365.02	333.13	467.04	551.68
1991	353.98	353.98	477.96	630.04	533.40	455.03	482.93	369.60	340.76	473.71	562.53
1992	363.61	363.61	489.65	638.31	537.70	469.86	498.83	383.26	357.70	489.52	587.38
1993	373.64	373.64	505.93	646.78	553.63	486.04	519.09	392.09	371.73	506.00	611.36
1994	385.86	385.86	526.19	666.62	573.00	506.94	543.97	405.41	385.82	526.44	641.00
1995	394.34	394.34	534.64	683.91	587.00	514.59	548.66	410.87	388.87	533.63	643.28
1996	406.61	406.61	553.62	707.59	603.33	531.23	565.19	425.95	399.91	555.11	661.67
1997	424.89	424.89	574.90	733.21	625.56	553.14	587.64	441.16	424.11	569.38	683.38
1998	442.19	442.19	587.94	741.91	643.69	562.53	591.35	456.21	442.54	591.60	684.66
1999	456.78	456.78	608.44	748.54	671.74	580.05	607.68	472.56	452.57	603.35	699.69
1996											
January	395.42	390.78	521.51	686.16	560.04	503.87	538.65	396.81	359.36	515.34	644.06
February	400.42	398.29	536.83	704.01	579.11	519.14	552.35	407.15	384.07	532.54	648.27
March	402.62	399.46	536.02	697.50	577.60	517.90	548.10	415.72	390.00	538.02	645.17
April	403.17	400.33	543.75	698.20	587.49	524.48	557.76	420.43	389.32	551.66	653.56
May	404.20	402.00	548.58	696.80	595.17	528.32	562.65	426.42	394.13	555.46	653.56
June	408.63	410.08	556.83	717.14	607.86	534.23	568.76	434.72	399.35	565.36	660.51
July	406.95	405.86	552.43	696.64	617.70	525.67	556.70	426.13	398.11	562.89	657.49
August	409.52	409.25	560.97	701.50	621.64	534.62	568.65	436.36	408.62	568.48	662.38
September	412.09	417.40	570.99	724.04	627.65	545.25	582.28	439.71	414.91	575.46	680.06
October	411.59	412.62	565.23	714.20	629.22	537.58	572.61	437.18	413.26	568.04	670.00
November	413.66	414.35	564.28	712.33	606.83	543.93	578.29	433.37	416.34	563.76	675.51
December	415.89	421.24	573.91	734.62	605.25	559.40	594.70	437.54	433.47	558.58	686.30
1997											
January	414.86	410.87	552.67	716.04	573.66	540.75	574.34	418.97	407.93	531.29	672.84
February	418.66	419.18	557.74	733.70	589.50	541.22	576.73	426.52	402.23	547.68	673.01
March	421.26	421.43	565.68	731.66	603.26	548.94	584.73	431.83	416.16	553.35	679.17
April	421.95	418.99	567.74	725.21	612.26	546.74	582.00	438.78	411.59	560.27	677.21
May	423.69	420.21	572.56	734.40	629.64	548.05	583.36	442.32	416.71	573.34	674.52
June	421.94	425.08	573.80	738.75	630.04	549.78	583.79	446.96	419.35	572.47	679.17
July	424.54	423.52	571.54	723.86	643.20	539.72	570.26	441.46	415.94	571.56	670.79
August	427.85	428.05	579.76	727.78	641.97	551.88	584.56	446.04	429.30	578.60	677.65
September	428.00	431.87	589.95	738.92	654.03	560.95	594.35	450.69	440.84	586.53	691.73
October	430.08	432.02	588.80	733.41	650.33	560.42	596.84	451.11	435.34	584.75	691.38
November	431.81	436.39	584.98	746.93	617.77	569.14	604.04	451.26	440.84	575.82	699.79
December	433.19	436.04	596.82	747.00	631.02	579.21	617.23	449.90	454.26	585.14	711.32
1998											
January	435.14	431.26	577.10	748.66	610.50	561.46	594.27	437.78	437.53	565.97	702.79
February	437.22	438.04	577.51	739.72	616.74	559.20	592.88	441.45	436.59	572.97	691.06
March	437.34	437.46	579.96	731.29	619.78	561.70	595.43	445.26	436.72	573.40	691.09
April	439.07	434.34	572.45	729.12	623.70	549.17	576.14	447.98	431.14	584.30	679.64
May	441.73	439.77	588.75	740.59	646.49	563.05	593.73	456.37	433.08	597.52	691.98
June	441.50	440.00	588.75	734.36	646.02	561.79	590.63	461.34	441.46	596.16	689.98
July	442.53	441.26	587.32	737.88	670.54	549.92	571.46	460.20	439.67	594.80	670.64
August	444.61	449.15	596.99	741.91	674.96	560.87	587.42	465.09	449.36	601.56	676.27
September	444.02	442.47	586.85	736.59	630.38	564.40	587.71	452.39	436.30	607.20	683.28
October	446.69	447.72	602.58	752.40	676.40	567.33	595.85	465.63	449.90	603.77	667.52
November	448.07	451.45	597.81	759.91	650.41	573.92	600.79	466.46	449.90	597.43	678.03
December	449.45	451.45	607.99	755.59	661.18	583.19	613.13	472.88	461.48	600.55	684.61
1999											
January	449.88	445.74	586.44	730.52	635.96	564.16	591.21	459.50	445.91	579.70	673.64
February	451.88	449.33	586.04	731.02	634.60	564.16	591.63	454.90	440.59	575.70	672.54
March	451.95	448.70	589.28	719.93	636.17	568.42	595.98	461.45	444.40	577.30	680.89
April	453.33	451.39	599.59	735.23	654.03	574.08	602.19	468.86	447.12	594.51	687.96
May	455.06	456.72	607.05	753.61	670.46	577.55	606.58	473.20	443.37	607.58	698.86
June	456.44	454.99	613.31	750.52	681.77	581.02	610.56	476.74	449.75	612.04	707.55
July	457.82	456.65	610.64	767.50	689.07	573.09	598.21	475.04	452.25	611.89	698.47
August	458.85	463.32	618.93	758.73	692.40	583.11	612.08	482.37	459.10	614.75	704.72
September	460.58	458.93	616.77	758.86	673.96	588.39	615.50	472.80	456.60	620.40	716.77
October	461.61	463.99	625.41	758.73	701.60	589.26	618.38	480.24	458.87	616.00	709.24
November	462.65	463.34	624.58	758.65	688.09	594.18	622.57	480.24	458.94	620.57	720.56
December	463.68	465.72	627.07	763.24	677.84	603.50	634.86	480.73	471.42	604.90	732.50

1. Includes mining, construction, and manufacturing.
2. Additional industry detail available in individual industry profile sections.

Table 8-9. Average Weekly Earnings—*Continued*

(Average earnings per week of production or nonsupervisory workers on private nonfarm payrolls; dollars, not seasonally adjusted.)

Year and month	Manufacturing—*Continued*										
	Durable goods—*Continued*						Nondurable goods				
	Fabricated metal products	Industrial machinery and equipment	Electronic and electric equipment	Transportation equipment	Instruments and products	Miscellaneous manufacturing	Total	Food and products	Tobacco	Textile mill products	Apparel and other textile products
1970	143.67	154.95	154.95	163.62	163.62	109.52	120.43	127.98	110.00	97.76	84.37
1971	152.31	163.21	163.21	181.12	181.12	115.53	128.51	136.21	119.45	104.34	88.64
1972	166.86	181.87	181.87	200.58	200.58	122.85	138.16	145.80	130.47	113.58	93.60
1973	178.46	196.88	196.88	216.82	216.82	128.31	146.52	155.54	145.14	120.66	99.08
1974	188.09	207.97	207.97	224.37	224.37	136.61	156.79	169.28	157.80	126.40	104.54
1975	202.51	219.10	219.10	245.23	245.23	146.69	169.56	185.78	173.81	134.41	111.58
1976	224.40	238.55	238.55	276.05	276.05	156.75	185.57	201.69	186.75	147.97	121.72
1977	242.31	259.79	259.79	309.83	309.83	169.17	201.33	214.80	209.41	161.20	128.87
1978	260.35	284.76	284.76	333.80	333.80	181.97	218.28	230.26	233.55	173.72	140.26
1979	278.80	305.24	305.24	350.58	350.58	195.16	236.19	250.17	253.46	188.26	149.32
1980	300.98	328.00	328.00	379.61	379.61	211.30	255.84	271.95	294.89	203.31	161.42
1981	330.46	360.33	360.33	424.95	424.95	231.64	281.85	295.37	344.54	218.59	177.43
1982	343.78	367.62	367.62	449.96	449.96	246.53	297.60	312.05	370.06	218.63	180.44
1983	370.27	387.18	387.18	491.31	491.31	266.27	318.75	323.51	388.21	249.67	194.76
1984	389.16	417.74	417.74	520.94	520.94	277.77	333.08	333.92	436.46	257.75	202.02
1985	401.02	427.45	427.45	541.45	541.45	287.62	345.31	342.80	444.91	265.99	208.57
1986	408.46	440.13	440.13	541.86	541.86	298.98	357.11	350.00	481.71	284.82	214.33
1987	416.42	452.81	452.81	543.48	543.48	305.74	369.44	358.99	548.73	299.71	219.78
1988	431.15	473.12	401.39	567.48	438.84	313.60	379.89	367.54	583.87	302.58	226.44
1989	439.71	483.36	410.04	579.61	445.11	326.63	391.95	381.77	590.97	313.70	234.32
1990	447.28	493.16	420.24	591.36	464.02	340.10	404.80	392.50	636.22	320.00	239.15
1991	461.03	506.66	435.49	618.03	477.24	351.35	419.69	401.94	655.71	336.98	250.49
1992	475.07	523.70	453.20	635.36	488.68	365.09	433.49	414.12	653.11	353.46	258.54
1993	492.15	547.39	469.83	679.40	502.65	373.72	445.79	425.32	631.69	367.63	263.75
1994	511.80	568.10	485.30	731.39	520.00	386.80	459.72	440.26	749.45	379.81	275.25
1995	514.31	574.62	486.30	733.21	526.19	401.00	468.99	449.22	768.64	383.93	282.68
1996	530.00	585.73	505.47	756.36	547.52	412.09	484.79	459.20	774.00	393.41	294.52
1997	544.43	613.45	533.40	780.98	567.84	428.24	504.71	474.12	748.44	415.24	307.73
1998	552.44	619.32	541.93	760.80	570.35	434.51	521.88	492.06	710.47	425.99	317.80
1999	568.86	633.84	557.24	790.15	588.06	449.74	538.24	505.36	762.80	438.04	332.25
1996											
January	506.34	568.51	482.78	714.02	525.20	386.25	457.34	435.44	658.00	344.16	262.07
February	517.44	580.22	494.21	733.94	540.89	402.83	472.78	445.61	701.63	383.91	287.78
March	516.21	578.49	494.27	703.87	543.02	407.55	476.75	449.55	762.00	388.69	290.82
April	520.83	573.89	490.01	757.68	538.14	405.97	477.20	449.84	801.72	386.97	289.38
May	526.64	578.35	496.90	764.96	540.75	408.43	479.95	455.03	840.29	390.57	296.16
June	535.43	585.42	507.10	766.29	549.36	410.10	486.34	458.90	877.40	400.75	302.82
July	520.00	574.52	497.35	737.86	539.97	402.36	482.40	459.00	809.83	389.54	292.56
August	533.35	582.43	510.85	765.06	547.04	412.73	488.76	463.14	809.60	401.44	299.34
September	543.95	596.24	518.70	786.09	558.18	422.99	496.01	472.22	772.38	404.89	300.42
October	535.03	588.16	514.16	761.57	552.11	420.89	490.80	464.26	731.30	399.90	301.55
November	541.37	597.97	519.94	770.74	561.26	427.11	498.93	475.68	768.38	407.83	301.18
December	556.34	620.71	537.97	800.28	574.48	435.25	508.77	480.90	782.69	417.06	308.51
1997											
January	535.51	602.74	513.35	777.38	556.70	418.97	494.10	464.39	728.34	407.54	299.63
February	537.63	606.04	518.74	769.05	560.70	423.06	492.48	460.72	726.87	399.96	301.02
March	541.45	611.01	527.08	786.60	566.32	425.17	498.58	463.98	760.89	410.11	308.63
April	540.60	608.66	525.85	779.57	560.03	422.90	496.53	462.58	781.06	411.93	304.59
May	541.45	606.39	524.59	779.12	562.12	420.40	497.76	470.27	803.03	409.94	305.78
June	541.87	606.30	528.78	774.75	566.49	421.05	499.39	466.75	827.90	416.17	311.03
July	526.24	600.48	522.42	728.86	556.61	415.15	499.75	473.47	738.83	406.81	299.75
August	541.88	605.12	531.26	771.71	568.35	426.37	504.71	481.12	748.06	416.83	307.80
September	550.40	620.54	540.56	777.47	574.67	434.93	513.77	486.87	719.44	424.20	312.38
October	551.27	616.59	540.51	794.77	570.68	434.52	509.64	478.61	712.80	418.55	313.21
November	559.44	629.64	554.25	797.00	583.19	443.15	518.34	487.94	703.10	425.70	313.21
December	572.88	646.02	566.35	823.08	588.16	447.95	525.84	496.50	747.06	431.53	320.80
1998											
January	552.95	627.10	542.56	776.14	572.77	432.40	514.11	482.72	694.01	426.82	314.07
February	548.63	625.53	538.72	771.69	577.19	435.24	510.75	475.67	677.69	421.69	310.90
March	548.18	625.53	538.55	781.36	573.79	437.40	514.45	478.12	683.38	423.95	313.60
April	526.79	600.85	527.62	731.54	560.85	425.42	508.80	474.30	697.08	417.68	309.52
May	553.78	619.78	536.84	769.12	569.11	430.52	518.98	488.46	788.97	426.21	316.78
June	554.23	622.94	540.68	746.46	569.25	431.72	519.43	488.04	830.32	429.94	321.30
July	536.22	610.81	533.08	690.44	560.85	424.93	520.09	490.88	806.83	418.54	312.91
August	550.71	616.00	543.65	739.16	568.15	432.52	522.75	492.33	746.63	427.66	321.10
September	548.29	608.19	542.84	754.27	563.93	430.73	529.72	507.88	670.96	424.44	316.72
October	561.89	617.77	544.90	770.41	570.06	441.10	527.31	496.02	663.92	429.50	325.24
November	566.24	625.13	554.88	779.61	577.27	440.40	532.77	506.68	673.75	432.37	325.73
December	581.16	636.34	561.32	798.91	588.42	445.82	539.97	514.03	638.42	437.18	330.11
1999											
January	556.36	620.34	543.66	754.29	573.50	434.07	526.99	496.29	639.70	432.64	319.42
February	556.36	620.13	544.99	764.31	578.51	440.03	524.88	489.09	661.86	426.12	322.27
March	558.45	623.92	542.23	772.64	578.77	446.40	528.61	489.91	738.76	428.39	328.37
April	563.72	627.09	547.45	785.86	583.91	447.68	531.95	496.87	764.54	437.22	332.01
May	567.09	631.73	553.01	786.69	584.15	449.52	535.79	503.36	814.71	437.22	333.02
June	571.98	631.08	556.93	798.16	586.40	449.27	538.74	506.66	829.67	442.24	338.71
July	560.35	628.84	550.39	754.54	584.25	442.57	537.65	507.87	849.93	434.83	326.71
August	571.90	637.39	562.43	794.03	591.19	452.40	539.97	506.94	836.49	440.59	333.00
September	571.52	635.51	563.33	812.15	587.32	453.77	546.53	512.78	754.11	438.75	331.57
October	574.60	640.60	568.48	810.04	594.50	459.15	547.23	512.62	753.79	445.30	338.92
November	580.29	646.85	572.98	811.00	600.85	459.82	551.03	518.08	774.86	449.28	337.65
December	594.08	663.55	582.15	838.66	612.43	466.22	557.02	520.67	793.32	453.11	343.52

1. Additional industry detail available in individual industry profile sections.

Table 8-9. Average Weekly Earnings—*Continued*

(Average earnings per week of production or nonsupervisory workers on private nonfarm payrolls; dollars, not seasonally adjusted.)

| Year and month | Manufacturing—*Continued* | | | | | | Service-producing industries | | | | | |
| | Nondurable goods—*Continued* | | | | | | | | | | | |
	Paper and products	Printing and publishing	Chemicals and products	Petroleum and coal products	Rubber and miscellaneous plastics products	Leather and products	Total	Transportation and public utilities	Whole-sale trade	Retail trade	Finance, insur-ance, real estate	Services
1970	144.14	147.78	153.50	183.18	129.36	92.63	105.37	155.93	136.86	82.47	112.67	96.66
1971	154.51	157.50	165.15	195.60	137.76	97.64	111.84	168.82	143.42	87.62	117.85	103.06
1972	169.06	170.03	177.64	211.79	149.56	102.64	119.65	187.86	151.69	91.85	122.98	110.85
1973	180.18	179.08	188.52	223.87	158.21	105.46	126.37	203.31	159.54	96.32	129.20	117.29
1974	191.17	188.63	202.52	239.13	166.05	110.33	135.06	217.48	169.94	102.68	137.61	126.00
1975	208.42	198.52	220.99	266.98	176.36	119.09	143.66	233.44	182.19	108.86	148.19	134.67
1976	232.48	214.13	245.86	303.54	191.70	127.16	152.39	256.71	194.27	114.60	155.43	143.52
1977	255.68	230.72	268.13	334.34	214.13	133.21	163.13	278.90	209.13	121.66	165.26	153.45
1978	279.71	244.78	294.14	376.27	227.81	144.32	175.26	302.80	228.14	130.20	178.00	163.67
1979	303.74	260.25	318.44	409.97	244.41	154.03	188.05	325.58	247.93	138.62	190.77	175.27
1980	330.85	279.36	344.45	422.18	263.20	168.09	203.01	351.25	266.88	147.38	209.60	190.71
1981	365.50	305.49	379.39	491.62	290.97	183.13	220.77	382.18	290.68	158.03	229.05	208.97
1982	389.58	324.25	407.36	546.99	304.92	189.75	233.77	402.48	309.46	163.85	245.44	225.59
1983	423.02	342.54	440.13	582.99	332.07	203.87	245.42	420.81	328.79	171.05	263.90	239.04
1984	448.67	356.64	463.83	587.33	348.20	210.13	253.75	438.13	341.88	174.34	278.50	247.43
1985	466.77	367.04	484.36	604.58	353.46	216.88	260.17	450.30	351.36	174.64	289.00	256.75
1986	482.98	379.62	501.96	621.52	363.91	218.45	265.83	458.64	357.72	176.08	304.30	265.85
1987	496.06	390.64	523.25	641.52	373.57	232.26	273.73	471.58	365.38	178.70	316.90	275.93
1988	506.18	400.14	536.36	664.67	383.22	235.50	283.39	467.57	380.24	183.62	325.25	289.49
1989	517.87	412.35	555.02	682.66	391.64	249.76	295.61	481.43	394.82	188.72	341.17	305.79
1990	533.02	426.00	576.80	724.30	401.14	258.43	308.03	496.13	411.10	194.40	356.93	319.48
1991	550.78	432.80	602.32	751.46	413.88	269.25	317.53	502.92	424.82	198.48	370.92	331.45
1992	569.85	447.29	625.38	784.02	432.01	281.96	328.31	514.37	435.10	205.06	387.36	342.55
1993	585.11	456.92	638.74	819.03	441.83	294.52	336.81	532.52	448.47	209.95	406.33	350.35
1994	604.50	468.60	653.62	846.71	451.54	306.85	346.37	547.07	463.10	216.46	423.51	358.80
1995	613.31	471.01	674.78	846.03	452.77	310.46	355.78	556.72	476.07	221.47	442.29	369.04
1996	635.21	483.23	698.54	842.35	466.46	326.52	368.20	572.22	492.92	230.11	459.52	382.00
1997	657.69	502.81	715.82	870.62	483.63	344.45	385.92	592.32	516.48	240.74	481.57	400.33
1998	673.13	515.14	739.58	912.11	494.98	350.43	403.68	604.75	539.90	253.17	511.78	418.91
1999	693.39	528.69	747.34	921.91	515.41	369.31	417.54	607.20	558.41	263.32	529.24	435.54
1996												
January	607.99	458.38	681.79	836.57	448.54	294.45	356.64	551.32	476.02	216.98	447.66	373.01
February	617.60	473.37	687.88	836.31	460.08	312.01	362.23	563.56	481.84	221.93	453.03	377.38
March	618.03	478.65	689.60	824.11	460.50	319.79	363.35	564.60	483.49	225.15	454.46	377.38
April	626.77	474.89	691.22	836.56	460.32	315.00	362.88	563.04	486.92	224.93	453.90	377.06
May	626.94	476.52	689.72	808.55	465.92	322.03	362.70	563.96	487.05	227.30	453.54	375.77
June	634.94	475.27	699.17	843.94	465.37	331.57	371.18	577.84	499.74	234.61	465.74	382.45
July	638.50	479.94	691.65	842.14	459.00	318.19	366.18	573.67	488.82	233.14	451.76	377.33
August	637.55	490.22	695.84	833.22	467.17	335.71	367.95	581.45	493.44	234.53	455.38	380.30
September	648.12	497.42	704.06	854.83	475.73	341.43	375.21	587.98	503.34	234.55	471.22	387.94
October	642.23	493.19	702.10	843.22	469.25	341.34	370.99	576.05	495.99	232.76	459.82	386.86
November	654.89	496.13	715.81	860.88	471.33	343.48	373.27	580.68	500.58	232.52	465.04	390.10
December	664.39	503.10	730.38	888.98	490.33	347.81	379.83	583.74	511.23	238.80	478.57	397.63
1997												
January	649.12	486.11	705.55	902.94	475.27	334.02	373.84	573.78	499.90	229.90	464.81	390.08
February	637.63	491.11	710.72	884.93	475.18	337.93	383.29	580.26	510.90	236.49	483.34	400.25
March	649.02	503.49	709.34	880.64	480.70	342.27	383.94	583.70	511.67	237.06	482.53	399.02
April	650.13	497.13	706.06	845.46	480.80	338.71	379.46	581.64	511.31	236.52	471.01	394.96
May	649.70	492.63	710.29	846.30	479.55	340.74	379.97	580.07	513.59	238.18	474.24	393.98
June	649.70	490.20	712.44	854.57	480.38	346.87	384.62	590.92	517.81	243.14	486.64	398.19
July	656.43	495.68	707.97	856.86	474.37	331.51	383.30	591.71	512.84	244.50	474.24	395.57
August	655.77	504.50	712.51	859.57	482.47	341.38	387.61	608.72	519.75	246.21	483.02	398.75
September	669.00	518.22	722.97	877.69	488.88	356.20	388.02	606.11	520.32	244.76	482.58	401.70
October	664.88	513.48	720.51	879.86	487.72	353.19	389.66	599.79	525.86	243.65	486.80	404.57
November	675.77	520.73	735.91	884.19	494.70	351.51	396.00	612.87	533.67	244.80	503.89	412.30
December	683.02	521.75	744.04	868.48	505.68	357.35	393.81	602.97	528.38	248.20	489.68	411.09
1998												
January	663.80	504.64	732.59	919.37	491.91	350.99	393.58	598.93	526.16	241.94	494.93	410.18
February	654.03	509.59	732.64	884.09	489.63	351.71	401.94	608.48	534.77	246.82	517.55	418.20
March	658.57	515.13	736.06	913.72	488.87	350.61	401.05	599.27	533.76	247.97	514.46	416.30
April	656.63	504.25	733.16	899.23	485.44	338.36	397.72	595.88	527.95	249.40	504.68	413.75
May	671.15	507.87	733.16	892.75	496.93	348.94	399.50	599.61	534.80	252.01	505.04	414.38
June	672.51	506.92	733.56	895.10	496.44	356.24	400.62	601.92	534.29	254.32	501.84	415.29
July	672.09	512.45	732.31	932.29	489.91	337.09	403.05	606.62	536.07	258.96	503.23	416.84
August	669.34	520.33	735.30	914.32	492.19	356.19	409.37	610.87	549.15	260.73	521.03	423.30
September	697.66	527.28	748.65	898.99	498.00	349.31	404.83	606.40	538.46	258.41	507.96	418.93
October	679.29	523.01	741.31	925.76	497.84	356.45	407.05	605.22	543.59	255.48	512.62	423.80
November	685.72	525.16	743.47	918.39	505.20	360.62	413.16	615.35	557.17	256.05	532.47	430.66
December	698.17	531.17	749.94	947.19	517.10	361.19	411.25	606.83	548.46	259.30	521.64	429.02
1999												
January	682.95	515.36	734.45	929.80	505.51	355.62	410.51	603.33	545.08	252.90	521.28	429.27
February	672.24	517.10	730.60	925.75	506.30	358.83	414.31	607.62	548.72	256.83	528.53	432.25
March	683.55	520.75	731.45	940.86	512.05	362.30	411.45	602.56	543.19	257.11	523.44	431.24
April	688.88	523.11	731.44	916.78	513.30	366.11	413.37	602.16	552.07	259.16	524.86	430.92
May	686.02	522.50	740.44	893.75	515.34	370.36	417.50	604.12	562.79	262.77	536.17	435.56
June	693.83	520.75	742.18	905.58	516.60	371.53	414.54	608.01	553.44	265.19	522.36	430.65
July	688.86	526.16	742.55	923.55	510.05	363.38	418.32	610.34	556.57	270.00	527.80	432.30
August	690.64	531.07	750.37	903.55	512.12	381.58	423.78	618.19	565.49	270.60	540.94	439.24
September	709.69	539.63	765.11	930.96	520.42	372.13	417.93	608.30	560.78	264.67	528.50	434.44
October	704.74	539.63	758.99	933.98	516.67	374.60	422.14	605.95	567.40	266.17	530.31	441.78
November	704.30	543.98	765.58	935.68	523.32	378.33	421.83	608.97	566.78	264.61	530.64	443.74
December	712.50	550.68	772.18	937.86	532.97	375.75	424.43	612.86	570.24	271.32	534.31	444.99

1. Additional industry detail available in individual industry profile sections.

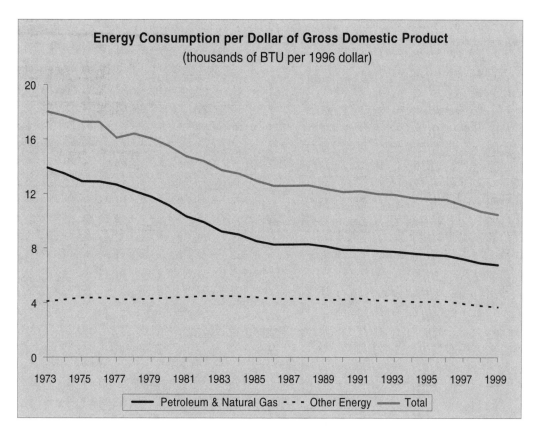

Energy Consumption per Dollar of Gross Domestic Product
(thousands of BTU per 1996 dollar)

- The decline in energy consumption per dollar of GDP slowed during the late 1980s and early 1990s, but accelerated again in 1998 and 1999.

- Industrial energy use has shown the greatest decline relative to GDP. In absolute amount (measured in Btu's), industrial energy use in 1999 was about equal to 1979, even though industrial production rose 67 percent over this period.

- While the ratio of petroleum and natural gas to GDP declined rapidly in the late 1980s, the ratio of other energy use to GDP was little changed. In contrast, these two ratios fell at similar rates from 1996 to 1999.

Table 9-1. Energy Supply and Consumption

(Quadrillion Btu.)

Year and month	Imports	Exports	Production, by source									Consumption, by end-use sector			
			Total	Coal	Natural gas	Crude oil	Natural gas plant liquids	Nuclear electric power	Hydro-electric power	Geothermal energy	Other	Total	Residential and commercial	Industrial	Transportation
1970	8.385	2.662	. . .	14.607	21.666	20.401	2.512	0.239	2.634	0.011	. . .	67.858	22.120	29.649	16.092
1971	9.585	2.176	. . .	13.186	22.280	20.033	2.544	0.413	2.824	0.012	. . .	69.314	22.981	29.614	16.722
1972	11.460	2.138	. . .	14.092	22.208	20.041	2.598	0.583	2.864	0.031	. . .	72.758	24.074	30.975	17.712
1973	14.731	2.051	62.059	13.992	22.187	19.493	2.569	0.910	2.861	0.043	0.003	74.282	24.136	31.528	18.612
1974	14.413	2.223	60.835	14.074	21.210	18.575	2.471	1.272	3.177	0.053	0.003	72.543	23.723	30.694	18.119
1975	14.111	2.359	59.860	14.989	19.640	17.729	2.374	1.900	3.155	0.070	0.002	70.546	23.899	28.402	18.244
1976	16.837	2.188	59.891	15.654	19.480	17.262	2.327	2.111	2.976	0.078	0.003	74.362	25.019	30.236	19.099
1977	20.090	2.071	60.218	15.755	19.565	17.454	2.327	2.702	2.333	0.077	0.005	76.289	25.384	31.077	19.820
1978	19.254	1.931	61.103	14.910	19.485	18.434	2.245	3.024	2.937	0.064	0.003	78.089	26.081	31.392	20.615
1979	19.616	2.870	63.801	17.540	20.076	18.104	2.286	2.776	2.931	0.084	0.005	78.898	25.809	32.616	20.471
1980	15.971	3.723	64.761	18.598	19.908	18.249	2.254	2.739	2.900	0.110	0.005	75.955	25.654	30.606	19.696
1981	13.975	4.329	64.422	18.377	19.699	18.146	2.307	3.008	2.758	0.123	0.004	73.990	25.242	29.240	19.506
1982	12.092	4.633	63.963	18.639	18.319	18.309	2.191	3.131	3.266	0.105	0.003	70.848	25.629	26.145	19.069
1983	12.027	3.717	61.279	17.247	16.593	18.392	2.184	3.203	3.527	0.129	0.004	70.524	25.621	25.759	19.141
1984	12.767	3.804	65.962	19.719	18.008	18.848	2.274	3.553	3.386	0.165	0.009	74.144	26.466	27.867	19.808
1985	12.103	4.231	64.871	19.325	16.980	18.992	2.241	4.149	2.970	0.198	0.015	73.981	26.700	27.214	20.071
1986	14.438	4.055	64.349	19.509	16.541	18.376	2.149	4.471	3.071	0.219	0.012	74.297	26.846	26.630	20.818
1987	15.764	3.853	64.952	20.141	17.136	17.675	2.215	4.906	2.635	0.229	0.016	76.894	27.614	27.826	21.456
1988	17.564	4.415	66.106	20.738	17.599	17.279	2.260	5.661	2.334	0.217	0.017	80.219	28.917	28.985	22.313
1989	18.950	4.767	. . .	21.346	17.847	16.117	2.158	. . .	2.798	0.197	0.021	81.377	29.427	29.371	22.569
1990	18.946	4.865	67.873	22.456	18.362	15.571	2.175	6.162	2.945	0.181	0.022	81.323	28.815	29.956	22.540
1991	18.489	5.157	67.509	21.594	18.229	15.701	2.306	6.580	2.908	0.170	0.021	81.330	29.542	29.637	22.128
1992	19.568	4.957	66.899	21.629	18.375	15.223	2.363	6.608	2.510	0.169	0.022	82.408	29.258	30.676	22.469
1993	21.489	4.283	65.199	20.249	18.584	14.494	2.408	6.520	2.765	0.158	0.021	84.201	30.438	30.872	22.895
1994	22.713	4.075	67.502	22.111	19.348	14.103	2.391	6.838	2.547	0.145	0.021	85.952	30.680	31.753	23.520
1995	22.532	4.536	67.813	22.029	19.101	13.887	2.442	7.177	3.061	0.099	0.017	87.553	31.538	32.036	23.974
1996	23.985	4.657	69.021	22.684	19.363	13.723	2.530	7.168	3.424	0.110	0.020	90.417	32.940	32.948	24.521
1997	25.516	4.574	69.097	23.211	19.394	13.658	2.495	6.678	3.525	0.115	0.021	90.977	33.087	33.066	24.823
1998	26.857	4.344	69.130	23.719	19.288	13.235	2.420	7.157	3.182	0.109	0.021	91.231	33.158	32.722	25.357
1999	27.573	3.827	68.302	23.219	19.239	12.451	2.528	7.736	3.074	0.036	0.021	92.939	33.509	33.332	26.094
1996															
January	2.010	0.389	5.766	1.784	1.634	1.168	0.201	0.669	0.301	0.007	0.002	8.480	3.671	2.813	1.995
February	1.714	0.376	5.548	1.799	1.544	1.106	0.184	0.594	0.311	0.008	0.001	7.865	3.307	2.661	1.898
March	1.947	0.359	5.909	1.946	1.635	1.182	0.212	0.589	0.336	0.007	0.002	7.908	3.049	2.812	2.049
April	1.934	0.378	5.701	1.897	1.612	1.121	0.209	0.535	0.318	0.008	0.001	7.119	2.493	2.610	2.018
May	2.131	0.378	5.836	1.906	1.641	1.150	0.212	0.591	0.331	0.005	0.001	7.142	2.322	2.691	2.130
June	2.034	0.387	5.668	1.804	1.597	1.124	0.208	0.611	0.315	0.008	0.002	7.084	2.346	2.729	2.008
July	2.094	0.396	5.834	1.900	1.634	1.140	0.214	0.648	0.286	0.012	0.002	7.347	2.542	2.617	2.185
August	2.129	0.381	5.944	2.024	1.633	1.144	0.218	0.653	0.259	0.012	0.002	7.453	2.523	2.717	2.208
September	1.912	0.428	5.589	1.868	1.572	1.128	0.212	0.580	0.216	0.010	0.002	6.796	2.197	2.655	1.942
October	2.093	0.425	5.779	2.017	1.600	1.165	0.224	0.538	0.221	0.011	0.002	7.236	2.218	2.847	2.171
November	1.935	0.412	5.569	1.850	1.578	1.127	0.217	0.554	0.229	0.011	0.002	7.476	2.685	2.772	2.019
December	2.029	0.399	5.777	1.850	1.618	1.170	0.220	0.607	0.300	0.010	0.002	8.135	3.275	2.824	2.036
1997															
January	2.102	0.402	5.960	1.973	1.669	1.151	0.208	0.626	0.323	0.009	0.002	8.545	3.697	2.871	1.978
February	1.855	0.344	5.503	1.880	1.512	1.058	0.197	0.538	0.310	0.006	0.002	7.554	3.091	2.615	1.850
March	2.100	0.378	5.923	1.973	1.679	1.160	0.219	0.536	0.346	0.009	0.002	7.694	2.890	2.748	2.059
April	2.082	0.366	5.612	1.879	1.600	1.121	0.206	0.477	0.317	0.010	0.002	7.205	2.451	2.703	2.053
May	2.266	0.371	5.904	2.014	1.661	1.164	0.212	0.500	0.341	0.010	0.002	7.147	2.282	2.735	2.132
June	2.189	0.367	5.652	1.847	1.573	1.121	0.206	0.553	0.341	0.008	0.002	7.133	2.342	2.695	2.095
July	2.138	0.382	5.829	1.896	1.634	1.152	0.212	0.609	0.313	0.011	0.002	7.676	2.713	2.730	2.227
August	2.230	0.444	5.819	1.907	1.631	1.141	0.214	0.649	0.265	0.011	0.002	7.517	2.591	2.739	2.182
September	2.169	0.388	5.700	1.970	1.593	1.129	0.208	0.559	0.229	0.010	0.002	7.054	2.343	2.664	2.045
October	2.287	0.419	5.785	2.019	1.638	1.163	0.211	0.499	0.242	0.010	0.002	7.298	2.367	2.793	2.137
November	2.098	0.366	5.472	1.779	1.587	1.124	0.195	0.544	0.231	0.010	0.002	7.470	2.694	2.743	2.035
December	2.047	0.418	5.877	2.026	1.616	1.174	0.207	0.589	0.252	0.011	0.002	8.346	3.329	2.886	2.131
1998															
January	2.190	0.414	6.070	2.081	1.688	1.176	0.211	0.615	0.287	0.010	0.002	8.333	3.496	2.826	2.014
February	1.937	0.324	5.442	1.850	1.493	1.052	0.196	0.542	0.300	0.008	0.001	7.441	2.990	2.599	1.855
March	2.144	0.366	5.978	2.042	1.669	1.152	0.217	0.571	0.316	0.010	0.002	7.921	3.056	2.764	2.104
April	2.273	0.375	5.699	1.955	1.610	1.128	0.211	0.505	0.281	0.007	0.002	7.235	2.451	2.683	2.106
May	2.327	0.406	5.835	1.926	1.674	1.141	0.214	0.547	0.324	0.006	0.002	7.223	2.393	2.685	2.146
June	2.240	0.377	5.771	1.962	1.604	1.091	0.198	0.592	0.316	0.007	0.001	7.385	2.574	2.679	2.129
July	2.467	0.371	5.809	1.931	1.636	1.114	0.185	0.653	0.279	0.009	0.002	7.859	2.869	2.729	2.256
August	2.374	0.333	5.805	1.944	1.647	1.115	0.201	0.641	0.243	0.010	0.002	7.820	2.807	2.785	2.223
September	2.176	0.351	5.559	2.034	1.499	1.007	0.194	0.608	0.205	0.010	0.002	7.250	2.499	2.655	2.092
October	2.305	0.359	5.798	2.063	1.620	1.104	0.204	0.610	0.184	0.011	0.002	7.294	2.364	2.743	2.188
November	2.223	0.313	5.565	1.920	1.562	1.068	0.200	0.609	0.195	0.010	0.002	7.269	2.514	2.722	2.036
December	2.201	0.354	5.799	2.011	1.586	1.087	0.189	0.664	0.251	0.009	0.002	8.197	3.144	2.853	2.203
1999															
January	2.255	0.307	5.862	1.946	1.663	1.072	0.192	0.695	0.284	0.009	0.002	8.596	3.721	2.821	2.056
February	2.077	0.252	5.520	1.969	1.507	0.969	0.181	0.608	0.277	0.007	0.002	7.552	3.020	2.626	1.909
March	2.297	0.292	5.971	2.102	1.661	1.058	0.207	0.622	0.310	0.008	0.002	8.075	3.104	2.787	2.187
April	2.382	0.357	5.480	1.889	1.577	1.024	0.203	0.513	0.263	0.009	0.002	7.328	2.528	2.706	2.097
May	2.436	0.305	5.577	1.802	1.638	1.056	0.208	0.593	0.278	*	0.002	7.253	2.375	2.653	2.226
June	2.306	0.321	5.670	1.913	1.589	1.002	0.210	0.659	0.294	*	0.002	7.455	2.515	2.752	2.184
July	2.480	0.322	5.747	1.870	1.617	1.042	0.221	0.710	0.285	*	0.002	7.929	2.885	2.751	2.286
August	2.404	0.334	5.804	1.975	1.601	1.039	0.217	0.725	0.245	*	0.002	7.961	2.808	2.856	2.291
September	2.250	0.308	5.612	1.968	1.568	1.010	0.215	0.648	0.201	*	0.002	7.336	2.416	2.804	2.114
October	2.303	0.349	5.593	1.901	1.613	1.069	0.227	0.591	0.191	*	0.002	7.474	2.367	2.844	2.262
November	2.159	0.324	5.622	1.938	1.577	1.037	0.219	0.645	0.203	*	0.002	7.439	2.511	2.803	2.126
December	2.223	0.356	5.844	1.947	1.627	1.071	0.227	0.726	0.243	*	0.002	8.535	3.258	2.929	2.349

* Less than 0.5 trillion Btu.

Table 9-2. Energy Consumption per Dollar of Real Gross Domestic Product

(Seasonally adjusted annual rate.)

Year and quarter	Consumption (quadrillion Btu)			Gross domestic product (billions of chained [1996] dollars)	Energy consumption per dollar of GDP (thousand Btu per chained [1996] dollar)		
	Total	Petroleum and natural gas	Other energy		Total	Petroleum and natural gas	Other energy
1970	67.858	. . .	. . .	3 397.6	19.97	. . .	. . .
1971	69.314	. . .	. . .	3 510.0	19.75	. . .	. . .
1972	72.758	. . .	. . .	3 702.3	19.65	. . .	. . .
1973	74.282	57.352	16.930	4 123.4	18.01	13.91	4.11
1974	72.543	55.187	17.356	4 099.0	17.70	13.46	4.23
1975	70.546	52.678	17.867	4 084.4	17.27	12.90	4.37
1976	74.362	55.520	18.842	4 311.7	17.25	12.88	4.37
1977	76.289	57.053	19.236	4 511.8	16.91	12.65	4.26
1978	78.089	57.966	20.123	4 760.6	16.40	12.18	4.23
1979	78.898	57.789	21.108	4 912.1	16.06	11.76	4.30
1980	75.955	54.596	21.359	4 900.9	15.50	11.14	4.36
1981	73.990	51.859	22.131	5 021.0	14.74	10.33	4.41
1982	70.848	48.736	22.111	4 919.3	14.40	9.91	4.49
1983	70.524	47.411	23.114	5 132.3	13.74	9.24	4.50
1984	74.144	49.558	24.586	5 505.2	13.47	9.00	4.47
1985	73.981	48.756	25.225	5 717.1	12.94	8.53	4.41
1986	74.297	48.904	25.393	5 912.4	12.57	8.27	4.29
1987	76.894	50.609	26.285	6 113.3	12.58	8.28	4.30
1988	80.219	52.774	27.444	6 368.4	12.60	8.29	4.31
1989	81.377	53.595	27.782	6 591.8	12.35	8.13	4.21
1990	81.323	52.849	28.474	6 707.9	12.12	7.88	4.24
1991	81.330	52.452	28.879	6 676.4	12.18	7.86	4.33
1992	82.408	53.657	28.751	6 880.0	11.98	7.80	4.18
1993	84.201	54.668	29.533	7 062.6	11.92	7.74	4.18
1994	85.952	55.958	29.994	7 347.7	11.70	7.62	4.08
1995	87.553	56.717	30.836	7 543.8	11.61	7.52	4.09
1996	90.417	58.316	32.101	7 813.2	11.57	7.46	4.11
1997	90.977	58.795	32.182	8 159.5	11.15	7.21	3.94
1998	91.231	58.855	32.377	8 515.7	10.71	6.91	3.80
1999	92.939	60.156	32.782	8 875.8	10.47	6.78	3.69
1991							
1st quarter	80.611	52.249	28.362	6 047.5	13.33	8.64	4.69
2nd quarter	81.122	51.976	29.146	6 074.7	13.35	8.56	4.80
3rd quarter	81.453	52.712	28.741	6 090.1	13.37	8.66	4.72
4th quarter	81.268	52.860	28.409	6 105.3	13.31	8.66	4.65
1992							
1st quarter	81.808	53.676	28.132	6 175.7	13.25	8.69	4.56
2nd quarter	82.583	54.051	28.532	6 214.2	13.29	8.70	4.59
3rd quarter	81.131	52.840	28.291	6 260.7	12.96	8.44	4.52
4th quarter	83.055	54.066	28.989	6 327.1	13.13	8.55	4.58
1993							
1st quarter	84.575	55.300	29.275	6 327.9	13.37	8.74	4.63
2nd quarter	83.235	53.653	29.581	6 359.9	13.09	8.44	4.65
3rd quarter	83.581	54.487	29.094	6 393.5	13.07	8.52	4.55
4th quarter	84.066	55.231	28.835	6 476.9	12.98	8.53	4.45
1994							
1st quarter	87.845	57.900	29.944	6 524.5	13.46	8.87	4.59
2nd quarter	85.756	55.837	29.918	6 600.3	12.99	8.46	4.53
3rd quarter	84.829	55.655	29.174	6 629.5	12.80	8.40	4.40
4th quarter	84.159	54.924	29.235	6 688.6	12.58	8.21	4.37
1995							
1st quarter	86.395	56.537	29.859	6 717.5	12.86	8.42	4.44
2nd quarter	87.141	57.101	30.040	6 724.2	12.96	8.49	4.47
3rd quarter	87.649	56.813	30.836	6 779.5	12.93	8.38	4.55
4th quarter	87.570	56.854	30.716	6 825.8	12.83	8.33	4.50
1996							
1st quarter	90.910	59.282	31.628	6 882.0	13.21	8.61	4.60
2nd quarter	90.558	58.591	31.967	6 983.9	12.97	8.39	4.58
3rd quarter	88.650	57.442	31.208	7 020.0	12.63	8.18	4.45
4th quarter	90.063	58.392	31.671	7 093.1	12.70	8.23	4.47
1997							
1st quarter	90.826	58.618	32.208	7 166.7	12.62	8.18	4.44
2nd quarter	90.931	59.407	31.524	7 236.5	12.58	8.21	4.37
3rd quarter	90.345	59.038	31.307	7 311.2	12.39	8.08	4.31
4th quarter	90.462	58.617	31.845	7 364.6	12.28	7.96	4.32
1998							
1st quarter	90.711	57.846	32.865	8 404.9	10.79	6.88	3.91
2nd quarter	92.321	59.616	32.706	8 465.6	10.91	7.04	3.86
3rd quarter	92.400	60.043	32.356	8 537.6	10.82	7.03	3.79
4th quarter	89.473	57.898	31.575	8 654.5	10.34	6.69	3.65
1999							
1st quarter	92.748	60.430	32.319	8 730.0	10.62	6.92	3.70
2nd quarter	93.079	60.124	32.955	8 783.2	10.60	6.85	3.75
3rd quarter	93.362	60.401	32.962	8 905.8	10.48	6.78	3.70
4th quarter	92.539	59.653	32.886	9 084.1	10.19	6.57	3.62

CHAPTER 10: MONEY AND FINANCIAL MARKETS

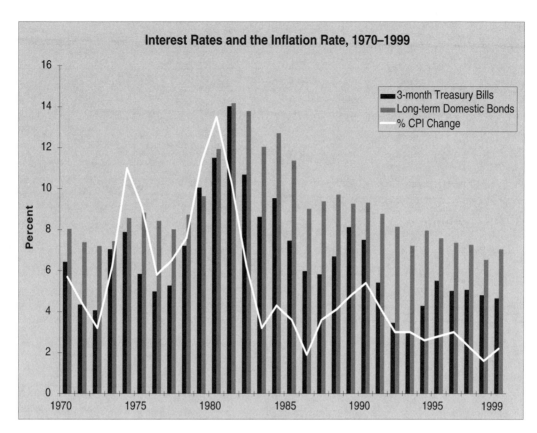

- Short- and long-term interest rates roughly tracked the rate of price inflation from 1970 to 1980, though they did not match the inflationary spike of 1974–1975. During the 1980s, short-term rates fell faster than long-term, and inflation fell faster than either. As a result, rates of return were positive after adjustment for inflation; these positive real rates have continued into the 1990s.

- Currency was 22.7 percent of M1 in 1970; by 1999, it had risen to 45. 9 percent. Demand deposits were 76.8 percent of M1 in 1970, but by 1999 had fallen to 31.6 percent. Other checkable deposits, which include credit union share draft balances and demand deposits at thrift institutions, grew rapidly, from less than a tenth of one percent in 1970 to 21.7 percent of M1 by 1999.

- Credit market debt outstanding grew over 15 times from 1970 to 1999. The fastest growth took place in the domestic financial sectors, increasing by a factor of 60. In this category, the federal government-related debt (credit agencies such as FNMA and mortgage pools) was 89 times higher than it had been in 1970, while private debt was 44 times higher.

- Credit market debt owed by the domestic private nonfinancial sectors, which accounts for two-thirds of total debt outstanding, stood about 12 times higher in 1999 than in 1970. Household debt increased the most in this category, growing 14.5 times.

Table 10-1. Money Stock, Liquid Assets, and Debt [1]

(Billions of dollars, annual data are for December.)

| Year and month | Money stock measures (monthly data are averages of daily figures) | | | | | | Debt (monthly average, seasonally adjusted) | |
| | Seasonally adjusted | | | Not seasonally adjusted | | | | |
	M1	M2	M3	M1	M2	M3	Federal	Non-federal
1970	214.3	626.4	677.0	220.1	627.8	678.2	298.0	1 115.4
1971	228.2	710.1	775.9	234.5	711.2	776.6	320.1	1 227.0
1972	249.1	802.1	885.8	256.1	803.1	886.2	337.3	1 366.2
1973	262.7	855.3	984.9	270.2	856.5	985.2	344.8	1 544.6
1974	274.0	902.2	1 070.0	281.8	903.8	1 071.1	355.7	1 706.7
1975	286.8	1 016.4	1 171.7	295.3	1 018.3	1 173.8	439.8	1 810.4
1976	305.9	1 152.3	1 311.9	314.5	1 154.1	1 314.2	509.9	1 985.4
1977	330.5	1 270.7	1 472.3	340.0	1 273.8	1 477.0	564.5	2 247.0
1978	356.9	1 366.5	1 646.1	367.9	1 371.8	1 653.5	620.2	2 579.7
1979	381.4	1 474.3	1 809.7	393.2	1 480.2	1 816.4	652.2	2 936.0
1980	408.1	1 600.4	1 996.3	419.5	1 606.2	2 002.2	728.5	3 201.5
1981	436.2	1 756.1	2 254.9	447.0	1 761.8	2 260.1	813.3	3 527.2
1982	474.3	1 911.2	2 460.9	485.8	1 919.8	2 470.0	966.7	3 809.0
1983	520.8	2 127.8	2 699.2	533.3	2 139.1	2 710.9	1 159.3	4 195.1
1984	551.2	2 311.8	2 992.8	564.6	2 324.4	3 007.2	1 352.2	4 788.5
1985	619.3	2 497.6	3 209.7	633.4	2 510.3	3 224.0	1 573.3	5 492.4
1986	724.2	2 734.5	3 501.2	740.0	2 747.9	3 516.2	1 794.4	6 134.8
1987	749.6	2 833.4	3 692.2	765.5	2 846.1	3 705.2	1 945.2	6 724.2
1988	786.3	2 996.9	3 935.5	803.3	3 010.0	3 948.5	2 098.9	7 363.4
1989	792.5	3 161.3	4 091.4	810.9	3 175.1	4 104.5	2 247.5	7 910.7
1990	824.4	3 281.0	4 155.8	843.2	3 294.9	4 167.8	2 491.3	8 333.5
1991	896.3	3 381.0	4 208.2	916.0	3 396.6	4 222.8	2 765.0	8 536.3
1992	1 024.3	3 435.7	4 219.2	1 046.0	3 453.7	4 236.1	3 069.8	8 757.2
1993	1 129.7	3 490.8	4 280.0	1 153.8	3 511.5	4 299.3	3 329.5	9 081.5
1994	1 150.1	3 505.4	4 354.1	1 174.6	3 527.0	4 373.1	3 499.0	9 500.3
1995	1 126.8	3 650.1	4 617.5	1 152.6	3 673.8	4 638.8	3 645.9	10 059.5
1996	1 081.1	3 822.9	4 952.4	1 105.1	3 845.2	4 973.4	3 787.9	10 652.5
1997	1 073.9	4 041.9	5 403.2	1 097.7	4 065.0	5 427.2	3 805.8	11 426.0
1998	1 097.4	4 396.8	5 996.7	1 121.3	4 422.0	6 026.3	3 754.9	12 524.8
1999	1 122.9	4 655.4	6 477.0	1 147.4	4 683.7	6 512.0	3 663.1	13 717.5
1996								
January	1 122.6	3 667.0	4 647.8	1 130.0	3 671.6	4 652.6	3 634.4	10 101.4
February	1 117.7	3 682.0	4 676.3	1 105.6	3 667.2	4 669.2	3 655.5	10 132.5
March	1 122.5	3 708.2	4 711.1	1 117.8	3 714.7	4 720.9	3 698.1	10 175.1
April	1 124.3	3 718.2	4 726.6	1 131.6	3 741.3	4 745.4	3 699.5	10 236.8
May	1 116.2	3 729.8	4 762.3	1 105.7	3 709.8	4 743.7	3 692.1	10 292.1
June	1 115.3	3 744.4	4 786.8	1 114.9	3 741.2	4 782.1	3 698.1	10 349.5
July	1 112.9	3 759.1	4 810.1	1 110.7	3 756.1	4 801.4	3 708.3	10 401.5
August	1 102.5	3 767.2	4 828.0	1 097.6	3 765.1	4 823.0	3 730.9	10 438.0
September	1 096.7	3 776.9	4 854.4	1 091.8	3 767.9	4 841.6	3 736.1	10 492.8
October	1 084.3	3 789.2	4 892.0	1 078.2	3 775.8	4 881.2	3 740.9	10 547.0
November	1 081.1	3 804.0	4 914.4	1 086.9	3 808.4	4 922.3	3 771.4	10 597.9
December	1 081.1	3 822.9	4 952.4	1 105.1	3 845.2	4 973.4	3 787.9	10 652.5
1997								
January	1 080.5	3 837.2	4 978.8	1 086.9	3 842.3	4 984.5	3 773.4	10 695.4
February	1 076.3	3 848.4	5 011.5	1 065.8	3 837.5	5 010.3	3 783.0	10 731.1
March	1 072.3	3 865.7	5 049.2	1 068.1	3 875.9	5 065.1	3 815.4	10 778.2
April	1 066.9	3 881.4	5 085.5	1 073.7	3 909.2	5 109.3	3 810.3	10 856.5
May	1 062.6	3 895.5	5 111.4	1 054.3	3 874.6	5 093.0	3 781.3	10 928.5
June	1 066.5	3 914.2	5 140.4	1 064.7	3 906.2	5 129.9	3 766.2	10 982.8
July	1 068.4	3 932.3	5 191.8	1 066.0	3 925.6	5 176.1	3 759.9	11 039.8
August	1 072.2	3 962.4	5 238.9	1 069.4	3 960.7	5 231.2	3 774.3	11 098.1
September	1 066.7	3 982.4	5 274.4	1 059.9	3 970.4	5 256.6	3 780.4	11 175.0
October	1 064.7	4 000.6	5 313.2	1 057.9	3 986.0	5 299.9	3 774.4	11 259.7
November	1 068.2	4 020.3	5 355.4	1 074.4	4 025.3	5 364.7	3 792.1	11 341.6
December	1 073.9	4 041.9	5 403.2	1 097.7	4 065.0	5 427.2	3 805.8	11 426.0
1998								
January	1 073.7	4 067.2	5 452.0	1 080.2	4 074.3	5 460.7	3 792.5	11 501.8
February	1 076.1	4 099.6	5 488.3	1 066.3	4 091.8	5 492.8	3 795.3	11 578.5
March	1 080.3	4 129.1	5 557.5	1 076.0	4 142.6	5 578.7	3 820.7	11 668.0
April	1 081.7	4 153.2	5 595.0	1 087.8	4 184.9	5 624.3	3 800.5	11 771.1
May	1 076.5	4 175.2	5 638.5	1 070.9	4 154.4	5 622.3	3 765.9	11 871.7
June	1 077.9	4 200.4	5 682.7	1 075.3	4 187.4	5 666.4	3 755.3	11 968.1
July	1 076.9	4 219.0	5 703.6	1 074.4	4 208.1	5 678.9	3 740.8	12 055.1
August	1 073.1	4 243.0	5 762.2	1 069.5	4 237.8	5 747.4	3 749.6	12 131.9
September	1 078.2	4 285.8	5 824.3	1 070.9	4 272.9	5 801.7	3 743.4	12 223.1
October	1 084.7	4 327.2	5 887.7	1 077.6	4 311.5	5 869.8	3 727.8	12 324.6
November	1 093.7	4 364.2	5 945.0	1 098.2	4 367.4	5 955.2	3 746.6	12 427.8
December	1 097.4	4 396.8	5 996.7	1 121.3	4 422.0	6 026.3	3 754.9	12 524.8
1999								
January	1 096.0	4 422.2	6 028.6	1 103.9	4 432.8	6 043.0	3 736.6	12 615.1
February	1 094.3	4 447.6	6 077.9	1 085.2	4 443.0	6 091.2	3 721.8	12 705.5
March	1 101.4	4 463.5	6 087.7	1 097.4	4 481.3	6 115.6	3 741.2	12 818.2
April	1 107.2	4 490.4	6 123.8	1 113.5	4 528.4	6 160.1	3 717.1	12 938.0
May	1 101.7	4 513.0	6 156.3	1 096.3	4 489.0	6 137.4	3 674.2	13 036.1
June	1 100.1	4 530.9	6 187.3	1 098.2	4 515.2	6 167.7	3 662.8	13 125.4
July	1 099.5	4 552.8	6 211.0	1 097.6	4 538.7	6 177.9	3 652.2	13 205.3
August	1 098.7	4 570.5	6 229.1	1 093.5	4 560.6	6 207.2	3 665.8	13 295.3
September	1 096.1	4 590.1	6 255.9	1 087.2	4 573.8	6 226.2	3 655.8	13 416.3
October	1 101.3	4 607.1	6 306.5	1 095.2	4 592.4	6 286.0	3 635.5	13 525.5
November	1 109.5	4 627.3	6 384.7	1 112.9	4 629.6	6 396.3	3 641.7	13 616.4
December	1 122.9	4 655.4	6 477.0	1 147.4	4 683.7	6 512.0	3 663.1	13 717.5

1. See Notes for definitions of M1, M2, M3, and debt.

Table 10-2. Selected Components of the Money Stock

(Billions of dollars, monthly data are averages of daily figures, annual data are for December.)

Year and month	Seasonally adjusted									
	Currency	Demand deposits	Other checkable deposits	Repurchase agreements	Eurodollars	Money market funds		Savings deposits	Small time deposits	Large time deposits
						Retail	Institutional			
1970	48.6	164.7	0.1	3.0	2.4	. . .	. . .	260.9	151.2	45.1
1971	52.0	175.1	0.2	5.2	2.9	. . .	. . .	292.2	189.8	57.6
1972	56.2	191.6	0.2	6.6	3.8	. . .	. . .	321.4	231.7	73.3
1973	60.8	200.3	0.3	12.8	5.8	0.1	. . .	326.7	265.8	111.0
1974	67.0	205.1	0.4	14.5	8.5	1.7	0.2	338.6	287.9	144.7
1975	72.8	211.3	0.9	15.0	10.2	2.8	0.5	388.8	337.8	129.7
1976	79.5	221.5	2.7	25.5	15.4	2.5	0.6	453.2	390.7	118.1
1977	87.4	236.4	4.2	33.5	21.9	2.6	1.0	492.2	445.5	145.2
1978	96.0	249.5	8.5	45.2	35.3	6.7	3.5	481.9	520.9	195.6
1979	104.8	256.6	16.8	49.2	52.8	34.9	10.4	423.8	634.2	223.1
1980	115.3	261.2	28.1	58.2	61.5	63.5	16.0	400.2	728.5	260.2
1981	122.5	231.4	78.7	67.8	88.9	152.9	38.2	343.9	823.1	303.9
1982	132.5	234.1	104.1	71.8	104.3	185.9	48.8	400.1	850.9	324.9
1983	146.2	238.5	132.1	97.3	116.6	138.1	40.9	684.9	784.0	316.5
1984	156.1	243.4	147.4	107.3	108.9	167.2	61.6	704.7	888.8	403.2
1985	167.8	266.8	179.8	121.2	104.2	177.3	64.4	815.2	885.7	422.4
1986	180.6	302.8	235.6	145.8	115.7	211.0	85.1	940.9	858.4	420.2
1987	196.8	287.5	259.5	178.0	121.5	225.4	92.2	937.4	921.0	467.0
1988	212.2	287.0	280.9	196.5	131.7	247.2	92.0	926.3	1 037.1	518.3
1989	222.6	278.6	285.1	169.1	109.4	323.8	110.1	893.7	1 151.4	541.5
1990	247.0	276.8	293.7	151.5	103.3	360.2	138.0	923.0	1 173.4	482.1
1991	267.5	289.5	332.3	131.1	92.3	375.3	186.2	1 043.8	1 065.6	417.6
1992	292.6	339.8	384.3	141.6	79.5	356.9	208.0	1 186.5	868.1	354.5
1993	322.1	385.5	414.6	172.6	72.8	359.8	209.4	1 219.2	782.0	334.5
1994	354.4	383.6	404.1	196.3	86.3	389.0	201.9	1 149.9	816.3	364.2
1995	372.5	389.2	356.6	198.4	94.0	457.7	254.3	1 134.2	931.4	420.5
1996	394.3	402.3	276.1	210.7	114.6	524.4	312.0	1 270.6	946.9	492.2
1997	424.8	395.3	245.8	256.0	150.7	602.8	380.8	1 397.1	968.2	573.9
1998	459.5	379.3	250.3	300.8	152.6	749.2	518.4	1 598.6	951.7	628.2
1999	515.5	355.2	244.0	334.7	173.5	842.9	607.4	1 734.4	955.2	705.9
1996										
January	373.2	394.6	346.3	200.4	96.7	462.3	259.9	1 150.0	932.2	423.8
February	372.5	396.9	339.9	201.0	98.0	468.7	267.2	1 162.3	933.3	428.2
March	374.6	402.5	336.7	200.3	97.7	478.6	272.6	1 174.9	932.1	432.2
April	376.0	405.4	334.1	202.3	99.2	481.1	273.9	1 181.1	931.7	433.0
May	377.5	407.6	322.3	216.5	98.5	486.9	276.0	1 195.7	931.0	441.5
June	380.1	409.9	316.0	213.5	100.8	493.9	280.4	1 204.5	930.6	447.8
July	383.0	411.0	309.1	211.9	99.4	499.8	286.7	1 213.5	932.9	453.1
August	385.6	406.0	301.2	210.3	97.9	501.5	292.8	1 226.0	937.3	459.8
September	387.8	406.0	293.6	212.7	100.6	504.4	298.3	1 235.0	940.8	466.0
October	390.0	401.1	284.3	215.9	107.2	510.9	300.2	1 250.3	943.8	479.6
November	391.9	402.8	277.9	212.3	108.5	515.8	305.8	1 261.2	945.9	483.9
December	394.3	402.3	276.1	210.7	114.6	524.4	312.0	1 270.6	946.9	492.2
1997										
January	396.6	402.3	273.4	213.0	117.9	528.5	314.2	1 280.1	948.2	496.6
February	398.7	401.3	268.0	216.2	120.1	532.9	321.5	1 289.6	949.6	505.3
March	401.3	400.7	261.9	215.5	123.8	540.5	329.2	1 302.1	950.8	515.0
April	403.2	396.5	258.9	220.4	126.9	549.9	331.1	1 311.3	953.3	525.7
May	406.1	395.6	252.5	220.5	131.8	551.3	335.2	1 323.2	958.3	528.4
June	408.4	398.1	250.9	219.8	128.9	556.1	341.8	1 329.0	962.8	535.6
July	410.8	399.4	248.6	229.9	131.5	563.4	350.5	1 334.9	965.7	547.6
August	413.1	401.2	248.6	232.4	135.7	575.9	356.3	1 347.3	967.0	552.2
September	415.7	393.3	248.7	230.1	137.9	585.3	364.3	1 362.9	967.4	559.6
October	418.2	391.3	246.6	243.7	136.6	590.1	370.0	1 377.7	968.1	562.4
November	421.4	393.4	245.3	253.4	140.3	598.7	372.4	1 385.7	967.8	569.0
December	424.8	395.3	245.8	256.0	150.7	602.8	380.8	1 397.1	968.2	573.9
1998										
January	427.3	392.5	245.9	265.1	152.8	612.2	389.7	1 411.3	969.9	577.3
February	429.9	392.3	245.9	258.1	146.2	623.3	393.1	1 430.8	969.4	591.3
March	431.8	390.7	249.7	273.9	141.3	634.9	402.9	1 445.4	968.4	610.3
April	433.8	388.8	251.0	276.7	140.6	643.3	416.4	1 460.6	967.6	608.1
May	435.8	386.8	245.7	277.2	143.2	655.4	428.9	1 476.5	966.8	613.9
June	438.8	384.5	245.8	273.8	144.2	666.3	440.2	1 488.8	967.3	624.1
July	442.2	379.6	245.9	276.6	147.9	670.9	446.6	1 506.3	964.9	613.4
August	445.0	374.4	244.8	283.5	153.3	684.0	458.6	1 523.8	962.1	623.8
September	450.0	375.7	243.9	288.2	154.6	706.2	472.7	1 541.1	960.2	623.1
October	453.8	376.7	245.7	289.1	157.4	723.9	491.7	1 559.7	959.0	622.3
November	456.7	379.2	249.6	293.1	155.0	736.1	507.1	1 578.7	955.6	625.6
December	459.5	379.3	250.3	300.8	152.6	749.2	518.4	1 598.6	951.7	628.2
1999										
January	463.0	374.0	250.8	300.6	150.7	761.5	523.3	1 617.8	946.9	631.7
February	467.4	371.3	247.4	315.1	154.1	773.6	533.2	1 638.6	941.1	627.8
March	471.5	371.9	249.7	305.7	158.7	777.6	535.9	1 647.2	937.3	624.0
April	475.6	371.6	251.8	300.9	161.5	785.7	544.4	1 662.4	935.1	626.5
May	480.0	365.9	247.5	305.0	162.3	793.2	550.1	1 684.4	933.8	625.8
June	483.5	360.6	247.2	312.8	164.8	799.5	553.9	1 699.9	931.4	624.8
July	487.3	360.1	243.0	312.7	163.0	803.8	556.1	1 718.0	931.5	626.4
August	491.2	356.5	242.0	313.3	158.0	808.7	563.8	1 729.6	933.4	623.5
September	495.3	351.3	240.8	313.5	155.8	814.9	566.9	1 741.4	937.6	629.6
October	499.3	353.3	240.3	313.4	155.2	820.4	577.7	1 743.1	942.3	653.1
November	504.2	355.9	241.2	321.5	163.9	827.9	592.1	1 740.8	949.2	679.9
December	515.5	355.2	244.0	334.7	173.5	842.9	607.4	1 734.4	955.2	705.9

Table 10.3. Aggregate Reserves of Depository Institutions and Monetary Base [1]

(Millions of dollars, adjusted for seasonality and changes in reserve requirements, annual data are for December.)

| Year and month | Reserves | | | | Monetary base |
	Total	Non-borrowed	Non-borrowed plus extended credit	Required	
1970	14 558	14 225	14 225	14 309	65 013
1971	15 230	15 104	15 104	15 049	69 108
1972	16 645	15 595	15 595	16 361	75 167
1973	17 021	15 723	15 723	16 717	81 073
1974	17 550	16 823	16 970	17 292	87 535
1975	17 822	17 692	17 704	17 556	93 887
1976	18 388	18 335	18 335	18 115	101 515
1977	18 990	18 420	18 420	18 800	110 324
1978	19 753	18 885	18 885	19 521	120 445
1979	20 720	19 248	19 248	20 279	131 143
1980	22 015	20 325	20 328	21 501	142 004
1981	22 443	21 807	21 956	22 124	149 021
1982	23 600	22 966	23 152	23 100	160 127
1983	25 367	24 593	24 595	24 806	175 467
1984	26 912	23 726	26 330	26 078	187 235
1985	31 558	30 240	30 739	30 495	203 547
1986	38 826	37 999	38 302	37 652	223 415
1987	38 896	38 118	38 602	37 876	239 836
1988	40 435	38 719	39 963	39 373	256 875
1989	40 469	40 204	40 223	39 528	267 710
1990	41 748	41 422	41 445	40 083	293 249
1991	45 495	45 303	45 303	44 506	317 550
1992	54 395	54 272	54 272	53 242	350 935
1993	60 541	60 459	60 459	59 471	386 561
1994	59 433	59 224	59 224	58 274	418 218
1995	56 470	56 212	56 212	55 180	434 327
1996	50 173	50 018	50 018	48 757	451 617
1997	46 868	46 543	46 543	45 183	479 171
1998	45 189	45 073	45 073	43 676	512 749
1999	41 742	41 422	41 422	40 434	591 188
1996					
January	55 869	55 831	55 831	54 405	434 700
February	54 621	54 586	54 586	53 764	432 674
March	55 301	55 280	55 280	54 162	435 859
April	55 181	55 091	55 091	54 058	437 037
May	54 042	53 915	53 915	53 136	437 681
June	54 146	53 760	53 760	53 037	440 098
July	53 381	53 014	53 014	52 363	442 625
August	52 161	51 827	51 827	51 203	444 727
September	51 295	50 927	50 927	50 248	446 160
October	50 032	49 745	49 745	49 025	446 855
November	49 783	49 569	49 569	48 732	448 620
December	50 173	50 018	50 018	48 757	451 617
1997					
January	49 669	49 624	49 624	48 445	453 317
February	48 711	48 669	48 669	47 680	454 507
March	47 851	47 695	47 695	46 686	456 378
April	47 349	47 088	47 088	46 340	458 016
May	46 639	46 396	46 396	45 376	459 724
June	46 908	46 541	46 541	45 594	462 298
July	46 733	46 323	46 323	45 516	464 818
August	46 895	46 298	46 298	45 641	466 982
September	46 219	45 781	45 781	44 918	469 356
October	45 958	45 688	45 688	44 543	471 888
November	46 428	46 275	46 275	44 760	475 607
December	46 868	46 543	46 543	45 183	479 171
1998					
January	46 679	46 469	46 469	44 886	481 804
February	45 741	45 684	45 684	44 209	483 208
March	45 859	45 817	45 817	44 508	485 011
April	46 129	46 057	46 057	44 741	487 176
May	45 520	45 367	45 367	44 247	489 009
June	45 417	45 166	45 166	43 801	491 955
July	44 893	44 635	44 635	43 522	494 690
August	44 874	44 603	44 603	43 343	497 728
September	44 524	44 274	44 274	42 829	502 274
October	44 568	44 394	44 394	42 995	506 437
November	44 637	44 554	44 554	43 018	509 459
December	45 189	45 073	45 073	43 676	512 749
1999					
January	45 499	45 294	45 294	44 012	517 418
February	44 885	44 769	44 769	43 689	521 163
March	43 876	43 811	43 811	42 603	524 387
April	43 856	43 689	43 689	42 695	528 718
May	44 381	44 254	44 254	43 159	533 813
June	42 758	42 613	42 613	41 463	536 549
July	42 035	41 726	41 726	40 911	540 488
August	41 910	41 566	41 566	40 750	544 354
September	41 772	41 434	41 434	40 563	550 333
October	41 339	41 058	41 058	40 189	557 847
November	41 560	41 325	41 325	40 231	569 432
December	41 742	41 422	41 422	40 434	591 188

1. Monthly data are averages of daily figures.

Table 10-4. Assets and Liabilities of Commercial Banks [1]

(All commercial banks in the United States, billions of dollars, seasonally adjusted, annual data are for December.)

Year and month	Assets — Bank credit								
	Total	Securities in bank credit			Loans and leases in bank credit				
		Total	U.S. government securities	Other securities	Total	Commercial and industrial	Real estate		
							Total	Revolving home equity	Other
1970	...	...	...	...	...	...	...	...	...
1971	...	...	...	...	...	...	...	...	...
1972	...	...	...	...	...	...	...	...	...
1973	660.4	180.5	90.5	90.1	479.9	167.3	123.3	...	123.3
1974	725.4	185.6	88.7	96.9	539.8	198.7	136.7	...	136.7
1975	758.8	221.8	119.8	102.1	537.0	188.9	141.9	...	141.9
1976	818.5	245.3	140.1	105.2	573.2	191.5	156.0	...	156.0
1977	905.7	253.4	140.4	112.9	652.4	211.3	183.8	...	183.8
1978	1 021.6	259.4	141.7	117.8	762.2	246.2	220.9	...	220.9
1979	1 133.3	266.6	148.1	118.5	866.7	285.6	252.6	...	252.6
1980	1 226.4	300.8	174.3	126.4	925.7	317.1	272.9	...	272.9
1981	1 319.0	313.8	182.4	131.4	1 005.2	356.0	294.5	...	294.5
1982	1 424.0	339.1	204.5	134.6	1 085.0	397.5	309.1	...	309.1
1983	1 573.7	402.9	261.7	141.2	1 170.8	419.7	337.5	...	337.5
1984	1 743.5	406.8	263.1	143.7	1 336.7	480.1	383.4	...	383.4
1985	1 925.2	453.8	272.7	181.0	1 471.4	505.7	432.3	...	432.3
1986	2 106.5	506.5	310.4	196.2	1 599.9	541.9	500.8		500.8
1987	2 252.0	534.0	338.6	195.4	1 718.0	570.5	590.7	31.0	559.7
1988	2 430.3	562.6	367.6	195.0	1 867.7	611.1	675.3	42.7	632.6
1989	2 604.6	585.2	400.8	184.3	2 019.5	642.8	771.4	53.7	717.7
1990	2 751.5	634.3	456.4	177.9	2 117.2	645.5	858.7	66.5	792.2
1991	2 857.7	746.0	566.5	179.5	2 111.7	624.0	884.5	74.5	810.1
1992	2 956.6	841.6	665.0	176.7	2 115.0	600.3	906.9	78.6	828.3
1993	3 115.3	915.3	730.7	184.6	2 200.0	590.7	948.2	78.1	870.0
1994	3 321.5	940.1	722.2	217.9	2 381.4	650.7	1 011.3	80.6	930.8
1995	3 604.1	984.6	702.4	282.2	2 619.5	724.7	1 090.2	84.5	1 005.8
1996	3 759.6	978.1	699.6	278.5	2 781.5	787.9	1 142.1	90.7	1 051.4
1997	4 099.3	1 084.1	748.4	335.7	3 015.2	855.2	1 247.4	104.7	1 142.6
1998	4 536.1	1 222.4	792.8	429.6	3 313.8	949.2	1 337.1	103.8	1 233.4
1999	4 762.2	1 263.7	804.1	459.6	3 498.5	1 001.2	1 471.2	102.0	1 369.2
1996									
January	3 624.8	984.2	696.0	288.2	2 640.7	730.5	1 095.8	84.9	1 010.9
February	3 643.7	994.9	707.7	287.2	2 648.8	732.8	1 100.3	85.3	1 015.0
March	3 640.7	984.7	699.4	285.3	2 656.0	735.5	1 104.0	85.3	1 018.7
April	3 658.6	985.7	695.9	289.8	2 672.9	740.7	1 105.3	85.4	1 019.9
May	3 663.1	993.6	700.8	292.8	2 669.5	745.4	1 107.5	85.2	1 022.3
June	3 675.4	988.3	699.2	289.1	2 687.0	750.3	1 112.0	84.8	1 027.2
July	3 691.7	987.6	702.9	284.8	2 704.1	755.5	1 113.9	85.7	1 028.2
August	3 686.7	979.0	700.7	278.3	2 707.8	758.4	1 118.9	86.8	1 032.1
September	3 701.8	972.6	700.8	271.8	2 729.2	768.6	1 123.1	87.7	1 035.4
October	3 717.5	971.5	701.0	270.5	2 745.9	775.6	1 125.7	88.9	1 036.8
November	3 739.4	976.5	702.2	274.3	2 762.9	779.8	1 134.2	89.8	1 044.4
December	3 759.6	978.1	699.6	278.5	2 781.5	787.9	1 142.1	90.7	1 051.4
1997									
January	3 796.2	998.6	700.1	298.5	2 797.6	791.5	1 147.1	91.1	1 056.0
February	3 835.0	1 018.5	699.9	318.6	2 816.5	798.7	1 150.8	91.9	1 058.9
March	3 853.0	1 016.1	705.5	310.7	2 836.9	803.3	1 162.7	93.5	1 069.2
April	3 892.2	1 031.6	715.2	316.4	2 860.7	810.7	1 177.2	95.5	1 081.7
May	3 907.1	1 020.8	716.3	304.5	2 886.3	817.9	1 187.4	97.1	1 090.3
June	3 937.3	1 021.6	722.3	299.3	2 915.7	823.7	1 200.8	98.7	1 102.1
July	3 982.3	1 045.2	726.7	318.5	2 937.1	826.2	1 208.7	100.0	1 108.6
August	3 994.8	1 042.3	720.8	321.6	2 952.5	835.1	1 213.1	101.1	1 111.9
September	4 011.1	1 040.9	728.3	312.6	2 970.2	841.0	1 224.3	102.4	1 121.9
October	4 037.9	1 050.1	735.0	315.1	2 987.8	844.6	1 232.5	103.2	1 129.3
November	4 074.1	1 075.2	744.5	330.6	2 998.9	847.0	1 241.7	104.1	1 137.7
December	4 099.3	1 084.1	748.4	335.7	3 015.2	855.2	1 247.4	104.7	1 142.6
1998									
January	4 151.6	1 109.7	760.7	349.0	3 041.9	867.7	1 247.4	105.3	1 142.0
February	4 183.1	1 114.1	766.8	347.3	3 068.9	874.0	1 262.4	105.4	1 157.0
March	4 220.8	1 127.6	777.9	349.7	3 093.2	877.5	1 274.8	105.4	1 169.4
April	4 225.5	1 116.0	765.8	350.2	3 109.5	874.4	1 281.8	105.3	1 176.5
May	4 245.4	1 128.1	770.4	357.6	3 117.3	887.0	1 279.1	105.0	1 174.1
June	4 272.5	1 129.5	759.2	370.3	3 143.0	900.8	1 280.6	104.4	1 176.1
July	4 295.3	1 136.4	763.8	372.6	3 158.9	906.8	1 286.2	104.4	1 181.8
August	4 350.7	1 158.3	774.1	384.2	3 192.5	915.0	1 294.5	104.4	1 190.0
September	4 398.5	1 174.2	770.5	403.6	3 224.3	921.1	1 297.2	105.0	1 192.2
October	4 484.1	1 214.7	776.3	438.4	3 269.5	941.4	1 301.3	104.1	1 197.2
November	4 517.2	1 216.5	789.9	426.6	3 300.7	949.7	1 323.3	104.4	1 219.0
December	4 536.1	1 222.4	792.8	429.6	3 313.8	949.2	1 337.1	103.8	1 233.4
1999									
January	4 524.3	1 213.0	795.7	417.3	3 311.3	950.0	1 343.6	103.4	1 240.3
February	4 514.5	1 206.4	794.6	411.8	3 308.1	948.7	1 346.6	103.0	1 243.6
March	4 494.1	1 191.0	801.4	389.5	3 303.2	953.0	1 347.8	103.3	1 244.5
April	4 504.0	1 192.2	802.6	389.6	3 311.8	957.6	1 352.5	104.6	1 248.0
May	4 516.0	1 191.4	802.0	389.4	3 324.6	955.7	1 363.0	105.7	1 257.3
June	4 559.8	1 214.4	811.7	402.7	3 345.3	963.2	1 370.3	104.7	1 265.6
July	4 563.6	1 232.5	815.3	417.2	3 331.1	964.9	1 373.9	99.1	1 274.7
August	4 592.9	1 244.2	818.7	425.5	3 348.8	971.2	1 385.8	100.2	1 285.6
September	4 617.0	1 245.1	817.6	427.4	3 372.0	976.4	1 404.4	100.2	1 304.2
October	4 632.7	1 250.0	813.3	436.7	3 382.7	980.4	1 421.2	100.1	1 321.1
November	4 686.6	1 243.2	799.1	444.1	3 443.4	996.0	1 434.4	100.8	1 333.6
December	4 762.2	1 263.7	804.1	459.6	3 498.5	1 001.2	1 471.2	102.0	1 369.2

1. Monthly data are prorated averages of Wednesday figures.

Table 10-4. Assets and Liabilities of Commercial Banks ¹—Continued

(All commercial banks in the United States, billions of dollars, seasonally adjusted, annual data are for December.)

Year and month	Assets—Continued						
	Bank credit—Continued			Interbank loans	Cash assets	Other assets	Total assets
	Loans and leases in bank credit—Continued						
	Consumer	Security	Other				
1970	...	...	...	...	...	...	...
1971	...	...	...	...	...	...	...
1972	...	...	...	...	...	...	...
1973	100.9	10.9	77.5	35.3	90.2	36.4	816.5
1974	104.8	10.4	89.2	39.4	98.9	48.5	905.7
1975	107.4	12.4	86.4	37.5	101.0	51.0	942.0
1976	119.0	17.3	89.5	45.8	110.7	46.7	1 014.8
1977	141.4	20.3	95.5	53.0	119.7	49.1	1 120.1
1978	168.3	19.0	107.9	56.5	138.1	59.8	1 267.6
1979	188.8	17.1	122.6	74.8	162.4	78.9	1 440.0
1980	182.1	16.8	136.8	100.6	177.9	99.8	1 594.3
1981	185.0	19.6	150.1	109.5	168.3	134.8	1 720.4
1982	190.9	22.9	164.4	116.9	187.0	146.8	1 862.3
1983	215.7	25.5	172.4	109.3	188.2	150.7	2 008.9
1984	256.6	32.7	183.8	126.9	192.3	157.8	2 204.3
1985	296.6	40.8	196.0	149.8	206.6	161.7	2 424.3
1986	316.1	36.7	204.4	164.1	226.4	175.9	2 650.6
1987	330.2	34.9	191.7	162.8	214.3	177.0	2 766.5
1988	354.5	39.8	187.0	160.8	222.2	189.9	2 940.8
1989	374.8	40.4	190.0	182.7	226.9	195.1	3 143.4
1990	380.5	44.5	188.0	195.0	212.8	209.0	3 303.4
1991	363.5	53.8	185.8	168.3	212.8	211.8	3 386.9
1992	355.9	63.9	187.9	163.3	212.4	212.9	3 483.1
1993	387.3	88.1	185.7	154.6	218.9	218.2	3 648.3
1994	447.8	77.5	194.1	175.9	209.5	227.4	3 877.9
1995	491.0	84.1	229.5	202.0	223.8	247.0	4 220.4
1996	512.4	76.4	262.7	205.5	231.9	266.4	4 407.0
1997	502.3	96.2	314.1	211.6	262.0	299.1	4 815.4
1998	497.2	148.3	381.9	219.1	251.8	341.5	5 290.6
1999	489.7	153.1	383.3	229.5	287.5	377.8	5 597.2
1996							
January	492.4	85.6	236.3	208.4	231.6	246.5	4 254.6
February	492.9	85.4	237.3	194.9	220.8	246.0	4 248.6
March	495.2	83.1	238.1	200.3	218.1	244.7	4 246.9
April	498.6	84.0	244.3	205.1	221.7	246.7	4 275.2
May	497.0	76.3	243.2	206.4	221.1	247.5	4 281.4
June	501.0	77.7	246.0	205.4	220.5	254.5	4 299.1
July	506.5	77.2	251.0	199.4	224.0	259.1	4 317.2
August	507.2	72.1	251.1	201.4	225.0	263.6	4 319.6
September	510.3	74.1	253.0	206.5	226.9	264.9	4 343.0
October	511.7	74.1	258.9	204.6	226.5	257.9	4 350.0
November	512.1	76.2	260.6	211.2	230.2	264.2	4 388.7
December	512.4	76.4	262.7	205.5	231.9	266.4	4 407.0
1997							
January	513.3	79.1	266.6	203.7	230.6	263.0	4 437.3
February	512.5	81.9	272.6	207.8	232.3	268.5	4 487.7
March	508.7	85.8	276.4	212.2	236.3	275.4	4 521.0
April	506.6	88.2	278.0	208.7	241.9	278.1	4 564.5
May	509.1	87.9	284.1	214.2	241.0	282.8	4 588.7
June	511.9	91.1	288.2	188.3	245.1	287.9	4 602.0
July	514.4	92.9	294.9	181.3	245.6	287.6	4 640.1
August	514.4	93.4	296.6	190.1	257.1	289.3	4 674.6
September	510.5	95.8	298.6	194.8	253.7	288.9	4 691.8
October	505.4	101.3	303.9	196.4	261.6	296.3	4 735.7
November	504.7	97.5	308.0	199.8	272.8	301.3	4 791.4
December	502.3	96.2	314.1	211.6	262.0	299.1	4 815.4
1998							
January	497.8	114.5	314.6	206.2	260.5	299.5	4 861.2
February	494.7	117.8	320.0	202.8	265.0	303.9	4 898.1
March	493.3	120.1	327.6	212.5	275.7	298.4	4 950.7
April	496.6	120.5	336.1	211.8	268.1	309.5	4 957.7
May	495.6	120.7	334.9	201.7	250.2	312.4	4 952.3
June	494.4	127.6	339.6	217.4	250.9	312.5	4 995.8
July	490.0	131.6	344.3	212.0	249.1	316.1	5 014.9
August	490.1	137.3	355.7	208.3	252.3	323.5	5 077.6
September	493.1	143.9	369.1	219.7	255.8	330.4	5 147.0
October	495.2	153.7	377.9	221.5	246.6	332.0	5 226.4
November	497.2	148.9	381.6	220.7	251.4	340.2	5 271.7
December	497.2	148.3	381.9	219.1	251.8	341.5	5 290.6
1999							
January	497.9	142.1	377.6	224.4	258.9	347.3	5 297.0
February	496.7	136.3	379.8	226.9	255.1	350.8	5 289.1
March	495.6	123.5	383.3	218.7	258.1	346.0	5 258.5
April	496.4	122.9	382.3	216.3	258.4	342.0	5 262.1
May	493.0	128.1	384.7	224.9	260.7	343.8	5 286.5
June	488.9	130.7	392.2	223.2	261.9	346.9	5 332.9
July	482.0	123.5	386.9	222.5	259.9	348.7	5 336.3
August	481.6	123.4	386.8	218.1	254.2	348.7	5 355.1
September	482.1	118.3	390.7	213.5	264.5	359.1	5 395.0
October	481.3	109.6	390.3	225.8	269.1	362.5	5 431.0
November	482.2	133.6	397.2	224.9	274.7	368.8	5 495.7
December	489.7	153.1	383.3	229.5	287.5	377.8	5 597.2

1. Monthly data are prorated averages of Wednesday figures.

Table 10-4. Assets and Liabilities of Commercial Banks [1]—Continued

(All commercial banks in the United States, billions of dollars, seasonally adjusted, annual data are for December.)

| Year and month | Deposits | | | | | Borrowings | | | Net due foreign offices | Other liabilities | Total liabilities | Residual (assets less liabilities) |
| | Total | Trans-action | Nontransaction | | | Total | From banks in the U.S. | From nonbanks in the U.S. | | | | |
			Total	Large time	Other							
1970	...	...	...	...	...	...	...	...	...	...	...	...
1971	...	...	...	...	...	...	...	...	...	...	...	...
1972	...	...	...	...	...	...	...	...	...	...	...	...
1973	650.5	280.2	370.3	114.7	255.6	71.0	44.1	26.9	3.8	26.8	752.1	64.4
1974	717.4	288.5	428.9	137.9	291.0	76.6	47.8	28.8	3.9	35.6	833.6	72.1
1975	757.9	295.8	462.0	143.3	318.8	72.5	45.3	27.3	2.1	32.6	865.0	76.9
1976	813.7	316.6	497.1	142.9	354.2	96.5	56.8	39.8	1.7	27.7	939.7	75.2
1977	897.3	344.9	552.3	161.2	391.1	113.7	62.8	50.9	2.0	31.5	1 044.5	75.7
1978	994.3	371.4	622.9	191.4	431.5	141.6	74.2	67.5	6.9	46.3	1 189.1	78.5
1979	1 067.0	391.0	676.0	213.2	462.8	176.1	96.9	79.2	15.5	77.4	1 336.0	104.0
1980	1 178.9	406.9	772.1	254.3	517.8	212.2	117.7	94.4	13.9	94.1	1 499.1	95.1
1981	1 245.1	343.7	901.4	302.1	599.3	255.9	142.1	113.8	-0.9	98.3	1 598.4	122.0
1982	1 362.8	347.6	1 015.2	333.6	681.6	281.7	153.6	128.1	-10.9	108.8	1 742.5	119.9
1983	1 475.9	356.2	1 119.7	326.2	793.6	281.6	148.5	133.1	-7.8	117.1	1 866.8	142.2
1984	1 605.5	464.7	1 140.8	345.7	795.0	314.8	164.7	150.1	-6.5	122.2	2 036.0	168.3
1985	1 751.6	516.1	1 235.5	363.8	871.7	371.0	191.5	179.4	-1.1	117.7	2 239.2	185.2
1986	1 911.8	598.3	1 313.5	377.9	935.6	408.6	212.4	196.2	3.7	122.6	2 446.7	203.9
1987	1 972.9	586.0	1 386.9	411.7	975.2	425.8	221.4	204.4	23.9	131.5	2 554.1	212.4
1988	2 112.1	607.9	1 504.2	440.4	1 063.8	489.0	250.9	238.0	11.9	137.0	2 749.9	190.9
1989	2 237.1	608.6	1 628.4	473.5	1 155.0	550.7	281.8	268.9	13.4	140.9	2 942.1	201.3
1990	2 338.4	610.5	1 727.9	448.6	1 279.2	574.5	295.4	279.1	38.1	138.8	3 089.8	213.6
1991	2 465.8	649.2	1 816.7	444.9	1 371.8	496.5	221.8	274.8	42.6	133.5	3 138.5	248.4
1992	2 499.7	745.0	1 754.7	379.1	1 375.6	498.8	212.5	286.3	70.9	130.3	3 199.6	283.5
1993	2 532.8	817.3	1 715.5	346.9	1 368.6	535.9	213.7	322.2	128.9	133.1	3 330.7	317.6
1994	2 533.7	797.3	1 736.4	356.4	1 380.0	621.9	256.3	365.5	225.5	176.9	3 558.0	319.9
1995	2 666.9	774.3	1 892.6	415.1	1 477.5	696.3	287.6	408.8	258.8	238.1	3 860.2	360.2
1996	2 863.9	714.7	2 149.3	532.6	1 616.7	726.5	298.5	427.9	237.2	221.4	4 049.1	357.9
1997	3 116.4	687.7	2 428.7	648.7	1 779.9	852.5	306.4	546.1	201.7	254.1	4 424.6	390.8
1998	3 331.9	671.1	2 660.8	710.9	1 949.9	1 019.4	320.3	699.0	211.6	304.2	4 867.1	423.5
1999	3 524.5	630.2	2 894.3	828.1	2 066.2	1 116.6	346.8	769.8	221.1	302.4	5 164.6	432.7
1996												
January	2 696.3	780.7	1 915.6	417.0	1 498.6	690.1	286.2	403.9	270.1	237.5	3 893.9	360.6
February	2 690.2	766.7	1 923.5	421.0	1 502.6	693.9	283.9	410.0	271.1	237.2	3 892.4	356.2
March	2 702.1	763.8	1 938.3	423.7	1 514.7	695.1	286.2	408.9	264.0	228.8	3 890.0	357.0
April	2 711.1	760.9	1 950.3	428.5	1 521.7	707.0	290.1	416.9	260.9	231.3	3 910.3	364.8
May	2 725.0	755.4	1 969.6	439.5	1 530.1	712.0	290.4	421.5	257.7	226.1	3 920.7	360.7
June	2 734.6	748.8	1 985.8	443.4	1 542.3	717.4	291.2	426.3	255.1	231.2	3 938.3	360.8
July	2 749.4	744.3	2 005.1	450.2	1 554.9	721.1	291.3	429.8	256.8	232.0	3 959.3	357.9
August	2 764.1	736.7	2 027.4	457.6	1 569.7	724.0	292.4	431.6	246.0	226.0	3 960.1	359.5
September	2 781.8	727.6	2 054.2	473.0	1 581.2	724.0	293.5	430.6	250.6	221.4	3 977.9	365.1
October	2 822.6	722.1	2 100.5	515.5	1 585.0	721.5	289.4	432.1	256.7	204.4	4 005.2	344.8
November	2 837.9	717.6	2 120.3	521.4	1 599.0	737.7	295.9	441.8	246.6	213.7	4 035.9	352.8
December	2 863.9	714.7	2 149.3	532.6	1 616.7	726.5	298.5	427.9	237.2	221.4	4 049.1	357.9
1997												
January	2 872.5	709.0	2 163.4	541.8	1 621.7	735.6	297.0	438.6	236.8	237.1	4 081.9	355.4
February	2 890.0	702.4	2 187.6	557.1	1 630.5	752.2	297.7	454.5	231.2	254.3	4 127.6	360.0
March	2 915.7	694.7	2 221.0	567.5	1 653.5	763.5	305.3	458.2	225.9	245.5	4 150.5	370.5
April	2 941.9	693.3	2 248.6	584.3	1 664.3	792.4	314.7	477.7	221.9	245.3	4 201.5	363.0
May	2 945.4	687.1	2 258.3	586.1	1 672.3	792.7	312.0	480.7	239.4	246.5	4 224.0	364.7
June	2 981.6	689.3	2 292.4	599.8	1 692.5	774.4	285.9	488.6	229.1	248.5	4 233.6	368.4
July	3 018.5	689.1	2 329.4	615.3	1 714.1	777.7	281.3	496.3	222.5	260.8	4 279.5	360.6
August	3 049.8	699.3	2 350.5	627.1	1 723.4	791.7	291.7	500.0	213.1	261.7	4 316.3	358.3
September	3 060.8	685.1	2 375.6	636.3	1 739.4	805.4	295.3	510.0	211.6	244.1	4 321.8	370.1
October	3 077.4	687.9	2 389.6	639.1	1 750.5	834.8	295.1	539.7	195.9	249.5	4 357.6	378.1
November	3 106.5	693.8	2 412.6	648.8	1 763.9	847.6	300.3	547.2	191.6	257.5	4 403.1	388.3
December	3 116.4	687.7	2 428.7	648.7	1 779.9	852.5	306.4	546.1	201.7	254.1	4 424.6	390.8
1998												
January	3 117.8	677.9	2 439.9	649.1	1 790.7	862.0	292.4	569.6	230.5	263.5	4 473.8	387.4
February	3 152.5	686.7	2 465.8	662.1	1 803.7	867.3	293.1	574.2	215.6	267.3	4 502.7	395.4
March	3 191.4	691.4	2 500.0	684.3	1 815.7	889.5	303.2	586.3	206.0	263.2	4 550.2	400.5
April	3 199.9	688.9	2 511.0	686.4	1 824.6	909.6	302.5	607.1	187.7	264.9	4 562.1	395.6
May	3 207.4	683.2	2 524.2	692.9	1 831.3	898.3	281.4	616.9	181.8	268.0	4 555.5	396.8
June	3 232.8	677.8	2 555.0	706.0	1 848.9	908.1	290.6	617.5	180.8	272.8	4 594.4	401.4
July	3 219.6	666.9	2 552.7	690.5	1 862.2	917.0	292.1	624.9	193.5	281.1	4 611.2	403.7
August	3 255.5	668.7	2 586.8	704.8	1 882.0	920.8	293.4	627.4	205.4	294.5	4 676.3	401.3
September	3 275.7	675.6	2 600.2	708.8	1 891.4	947.9	302.5	645.4	206.4	302.0	4 732.0	415.0
October	3 294.6	671.9	2 622.7	716.9	1 905.8	989.1	313.8	675.3	221.6	314.9	4 820.2	406.2
November	3 322.4	671.8	2 650.6	721.9	1 928.7	1 019.4	322.2	697.2	213.6	300.7	4 856.1	415.6
December	3 331.9	671.1	2 660.8	710.9	1 949.9	1 019.4	320.3	699.0	211.6	304.2	4 867.1	423.5
1999												
January	3 356.3	668.3	2 688.1	715.1	1 973.0	1 006.6	317.2	689.4	205.8	303.2	4 871.8	425.1
February	3 360.2	658.2	2 702.0	723.4	1 978.7	994.1	313.7	680.4	205.4	294.5	4 854.2	434.8
March	3 362.4	662.0	2 700.5	719.3	1 981.1	986.6	315.4	671.2	201.7	271.0	4 821.8	436.7
April	3 373.1	654.7	2 718.4	726.5	1 991.9	986.3	308.7	677.6	201.9	272.4	4 833.7	428.4
May	3 381.4	649.9	2 731.6	729.6	2 002.0	1 002.2	321.2	681.0	202.9	268.4	4 855.0	431.4
June	3 383.5	651.1	2 732.3	723.1	2 009.3	1 023.3	333.7	689.6	217.4	277.5	4 901.6	431.3
July	3 397.2	644.8	2 752.3	727.7	2 024.6	1 023.6	335.8	687.7	215.4	274.4	4 910.6	425.8
August	3 404.3	636.2	2 768.2	729.6	2 038.6	1 028.8	333.2	695.5	219.9	280.2	4 933.1	422.0
September	3 414.3	634.7	2 779.6	741.0	2 038.6	1 045.5	335.8	709.7	218.3	283.3	4 961.5	433.5
October	3 448.4	630.8	2 817.6	772.4	2 045.2	1 050.3	348.0	702.3	220.4	291.3	5 010.4	420.6
November	3 481.8	624.9	2 856.9	801.8	2 055.1	1 059.8	349.6	710.2	223.9	297.7	5 063.2	432.5
December	3 524.5	630.2	2 894.3	828.1	2 066.2	1 116.6	346.8	769.8	221.1	302.4	5 164.6	432.7

1. Monthly data are prorated averages of Wednesday figures.

Table 10-5. Credit Market Debt Outstanding, Household Debt Burden, and Delinquency Rates

(Billions of dollars, except as noted; end of period; not seasonally adjusted, except as noted.)

Year and quarter	Total	Credit market debt outstanding Owed by: Domestic financial sectors			Domestic nonfinancial sectors				
		Total	Federal government-related	Private	Total	Federal government Total	Treasury securities	Budget agency securities and mortgages	Households
1970	1 602.1	127.8	43.6	84.2	1 422.3	299.5	289.9	9.6	445.3
1971	1 752.9	138.9	49.6	89.3	1 557.5	324.4	315.9	8.5	487.1
1972	1 937.4	162.8	58.0	104.8	1 713.5	339.4	330.1	9.3	544.5
1973	2 175.2	209.8	77.9	131.9	1 898.0	346.3	336.7	9.6	614.1
1974	2 411.8	258.3	98.6	159.7	2 072.3	358.2	348.8	9.4	663.5
1975	2 620.7	260.4	108.9	151.5	2 264.7	443.9	434.9	9.0	715.3
1976	2 908.3	283.9	123.1	160.8	2 508.3	513.1	503.7	9.3	802.3
1977	3 296.8	337.8	145.5	192.3	2 829.6	569.4	561.0	8.4	934.6
1978	3 784.6	412.5	182.6	229.9	3 214.5	621.9	614.9	7.0	1 094.1
1979	4 284.4	504.9	231.8	273.1	3 606.5	657.7	652.1	5.6	1 258.5
1980	4 733.2	578.1	276.6	301.5	3 957.9	735.0	730.0	5.0	1 374.1
1981	5 269.4	682.4	324.0	358.4	4 366.4	820.5	815.9	4.6	1 480.8
1982	5 779.0	778.1	388.9	389.2	4 788.3	981.8	978.1	3.7	1 547.7
1983	6 477.4	882.8	456.7	426.1	5 364.9	1 167.0	1 163.4	3.6	1 706.2
1984	7 441.7	1 052.4	531.2	521.2	6 151.2	1 364.2	1 360.8	3.4	1 918.4
1985	8 630.9	1 258.3	632.7	625.6	7 133.3	1 589.9	1 586.6	3.3	2 235.9
1986	9 809.7	1 593.6	810.3	783.3	7 975.1	1 805.9	1 802.2	3.6	2 489.0
1987	10 822.5	1 896.5	978.6	917.9	8 678.6	1 949.8	1 944.6	5.2	2 743.3
1988	11 862.2	2 145.8	1 098.4	1 047.4	9 461.7	2 104.9	2 082.3	22.6	3 011.3
1989	12 830.5	2 399.3	1 247.9	1 151.4	10 166.3	2 251.2	2 227.0	24.2	3 280.8
1990	13 755.3	2 615.8	1 418.4	1 197.4	10 850.6	2 498.1	2 465.8	32.4	3 554.3
1991	14 403.2	2 786.7	1 564.2	1 222.5	11 312.5	2 776.4	2 757.8	18.6	3 723.0
1992	15 205.0	3 046.3	1 720.0	1 326.3	11 839.9	3 080.3	3 061.6	18.8	3 893.3
1993	16 170.7	3 346.1	1 885.2	1 460.9	12 436.0	3 336.5	3 309.9	26.6	4 108.0
1994	17 198.7	3 822.2	2 172.7	1 649.5	13 001.5	3 492.3	3 465.6	26.7	4 426.7
1995	18 445.3	4 278.8	2 376.8	1 902.0	13 712.9	3 636.7	3 608.5	28.2	4 782.9
1996	19 811.0	4 824.6	2 608.3	2 216.3	14 444.2	3 781.8	3 755.1	26.6	5 105.3
1997	21 300.2	5 445.2	2 821.1	2 624.1	15 247.0	3 804.9	3 778.3	26.5	5 442.8
1998	23 460.4	6 519.1	3 292.0	3 227.1	16 289.9	3 752.2	3 723.7	28.5	5 924.6
1999	25 729.5	7 607.0	3 884.0	3 723.0	17 445.6	3 681.0	3 652.8	28.3	6 469.1
1991									
1st quarter	13 859.3	2 645.8	1 452.1	1 193.7	10 910.7	2 548.8	2 522.4	26.4	3 563.6
2nd quarter	14 016.0	2 680.0	1 482.8	1 197.3	11 046.8	2 591.9	2 567.1	24.8	3 626.9
3rd quarter	14 183.6	2 715.6	1 522.9	1 192.7	11 174.2	2 687.2	2 669.6	17.6	3 660.8
4th quarter	14 403.2	2 786.7	1 564.2	1 222.5	11 312.5	2 776.4	2 757.8	18.6	3 723.0
1992									
1st quarter	14 566.9	2 843.6	1 590.3	1 253.3	11 429.1	2 859.8	2 844.0	15.8	3 736.1
2nd quarter	14 770.6	2 913.2	1 641.6	1 271.5	11 547.8	2 923.3	2 907.5	15.9	3 767.6
3rd quarter	14 994.4	2 988.7	1 683.5	1 305.1	11 689.0	2 998.9	2 980.7	18.1	3 825.9
4th quarter	15 205.0	3 046.3	1 720.0	1 326.3	11 839.9	3 080.3	3 061.6	18.8	3 893.3
1993									
1st quarter	15 334.9	3 088.9	1 755.8	1 333.1	11 915.6	3 140.2	3 120.6	19.6	3 881.2
2nd quarter	15 575.4	3 137.7	1 774.5	1 363.2	12 090.3	3 201.2	3 180.6	20.6	3 944.2
3rd quarter	15 860.4	3 247.6	1 845.7	1 401.9	12 235.9	3 247.3	3 222.6	24.7	4 022.6
4th quarter	16 170.7	3 346.1	1 885.2	1 460.8	12 436.0	3 336.5	3 309.9	26.6	4 108.0
1994									
1st quarter	16 404.4	3 474.9	1 963.0	1 511.9	12 564.3	3 387.7	3 361.4	26.3	4 140.5
2nd quarter	16 615.6	3 576.8	2 032.7	1 544.1	12 680.2	3 395.4	3 368.0	27.4	4 224.0
3rd quarter	16 867.9	3 682.1	2 093.3	1 588.9	12 823.0	3 432.3	3 404.1	28.2	4 318.6
4th quarter	17 198.7	3 822.2	2 172.7	1 649.5	13 001.5	3 492.3	3 465.6	26.8	4 426.7
1995									
1st quarter	17 458.9	3 910.0	2 196.2	1 713.8	13 188.5	3 539.5	3 531.5	26.4	4 510.1
2nd quarter	17 789.2	4 013.3	2 247.1	1 766.2	13 402.9	3 600.4	3 556.7	26.8	4 600.3
3rd quarter	18 087.8	4 131.6	2 300.1	1 831.5	13 561.6	3 623.8	3 576.5	27.0	4 699.8
4th quarter	18 445.3	4 278.8	2 376.8	1 902.0	13 712.9	3 636.7	3 608.5	28.2	4 782.9
1996									
1st quarter	18 740.3	4 384.0	2 414.0	1 970.0	13 915.3	3 690.3	3 689.6	27.7	4 880.9
2nd quarter	19 095.6	4 551.2	2 489.4	2 061.8	14 102.2	3 717.6	3 665.6	28.2	4 945.6
3rd quarter	19 422.1	4 663.9	2 545.1	2 118.8	14 286.6	3 758.3	3 705.7	27.4	5 035.2
4th quarter	19 811.0	4 824.6	2 608.3	2 216.3	14 444.2	3 781.8	3 755.1	26.6	5 105.3
1997									
1st quarter	20 076.8	4 927.4	2 634.7	2 292.7	14 624.3	3 798.7	3 803.5	26.3	5 198.0
2nd quarter	20 403.2	5 083.2	2 706.2	2 377.0	14 800.1	3 795.1	3 734.3	26.3	5 275.4
3rd quarter	20 768.9	5 207.8	2 746.5	2 461.3	15 019.5	3 807.7	3 745.1	26.1	5 366.1
4th quarter	21 300.2	5 445.2	2 821.0	2 624.2	15 247.0	3 804.9	3 778.3	26.5	5 442.8
1998									
1st quarter	21 818.9	5 687.3	2 878.0	2 809.3	15 522.3	3 800.3	3 804.8	25.9	5 565.1
2nd quarter	22 329.0	5 929.5	2 981.4	2 948.1	15 796.2	3 795.0	3 723.4	25.6	5 674.9
3rd quarter	22 815.2	6 195.2	3 121.7	3 073.5	16 023.5	3 768.5	3 694.7	25.5	5 792.6
4th quarter	23 460.4	6 519.1	3 292.0	3 227.1	16 289.9	3 752.2	3 723.7	28.5	5 924.6
1999									
1st quarter	24 073.7	6 826.3	3 434.1	3 392.2	16 611.2	3 731.4	3 731.6	28.1	6 063.9
2nd quarter	24 511.1	7 075.1	3 580.7	3 494.4	16 846.1	3 706.8	3 623.4	28.3	6 194.4
3rd quarter	25 125.3	7 341.2	3 745.9	3 595.3	17 171.7	3 688.9	3 604.5	28.3	6 341.7
4th quarter	25 729.5	7 607.0	3 884.0	3 723.0	17 445.6	3 681.0	3 652.8	28.3	6 469.1

Table 10-5. Credit Market Debt Outstanding, Household Debt Burden, and Delinquency Rates—Continued

(Billions of dollars, except as noted; end of period; not seasonally adjusted, except as noted.)

Year and quarter	Credit market debt outstanding, owed by:						Household debt-service payments as a percent of disposable personal income, seasonally adjusted			Household debt deliquency rates (percent of loans serviced)	
	Domestic nonfinancial sectors—Continued					Foreign credit market debt held in United States					
	Nonfinancial business				State and local governments		Total	Consumer	Mortgage	Credit card accounts held at banks	Mortgage (90 days)
	Total	Corporate	Nonfarm noncorporate	Farm							
1970	527.2	367.4	112.2	47.6	150.3	52.1	...	...	...	...	...
1971	579.2	395.6	132.1	51.6	166.7	56.6	...	...	...	...	...
1972	649.0	433.0	159.2	56.8	180.7	61.1	...	...	...	...	...
1973	742.8	497.0	180.4	65.4	194.8	67.4	...	...	...	...	...
1974	842.4	554.6	214.4	73.3	208.2	81.2	...	...	...	...	...
1975	886.2	575.2	228.9	82.1	219.4	95.6	...	...	...	...	...
1976	955.2	614.2	248.7	92.2	237.8	116.0	...	...	...	...	...
1977	1 069.5	687.6	275.9	105.9	256.2	129.4	...	...	...	...	...
1978	1 203.0	761.6	319.1	122.2	295.6	157.6	...	...	...	...	...
1979	1 368.2	845.4	377.0	145.7	322.2	172.9	...	...	...	...	0.51
1980	1 504.3	911.6	431.2	161.5	344.4	197.2	12.41	7.99	4.42	...	0.62
1981	1 693.0	1 028.6	486.6	177.8	372.1	220.7	12.34	7.62	4.72	...	0.64
1982	1 845.0	1 117.9	542.6	184.5	413.8	212.6	12.32	7.47	4.85	...	0.84
1983	2 030.5	1 228.8	613.4	188.4	461.1	229.8	12.33	7.46	4.88	...	0.86
1984	2 355.0	1 434.8	732.2	188.0	513.6	238.0	12.83	7.80	5.03	...	0.92
1985	2 629.6	1 613.1	843.1	173.4	677.9	239.3	13.74	8.29	5.44	...	0.96
1986	2 928.1	1 835.0	937.2	156.0	752.1	241.0	14.18	8.50	5.69	...	0.99
1987	3 144.5	2 008.0	992.1	144.4	841.0	247.4	13.71	7.92	5.79	...	0.89
1988	3 450.5	2 218.3	1 098.5	133.7	895.0	254.8	13.35	7.58	5.77	...	0.83
1989	3 689.1	2 402.2	1 152.5	134.4	945.1	265.0	13.51	7.57	5.94	...	0.75
1990	3 805.8	2 522.5	1 147.9	135.4	992.3	288.9	13.25	7.11	6.14	...	0.73
1991	3 735.5	2 470.6	1 130.1	134.8	1 077.7	304.0	12.57	6.51	6.05	5.33	0.81
1992	3 764.5	2 513.9	1 115.3	135.3	1 101.8	318.8	11.70	6.03	5.67	4.69	0.76
1993	3 823.6	2 567.2	1 118.5	137.9	1 167.9	388.6	11.60	6.13	5.46	3.92	0.75
1994	3 960.8	2 696.8	1 121.8	142.2	1 121.7	375.0	12.01	6.52	5.49	3.31	0.72
1995	4 223.0	2 925.5	1 152.4	145.1	1 070.2	453.7	12.70	7.05	5.65	3.99	0.69
1996	4 493.7	3 107.7	1 236.1	149.9	1 063.4	542.2	13.09	7.44	5.65	4.68	0.59
1997	4 879.9	3 372.7	1 351.1	156.1	1 119.5	608.0	13.17	7.47	5.70	4.88	0.61
1998	5 413.3	3 788.5	1 460.9	163.8	1 199.8	651.4	13.29	7.57	5.72	4.83	0.60
1999	6 043.3	4 302.2	1 572.0	169.0	1 252.1	676.9	13.51	7.58	5.93	4.65	0.56
1991											
1st quarter	3 792.5	2 516.2	1 144.6	131.8	1 005.8	302.8	13.12	6.96	6.16	5.33	0.78
2nd quarter	3 806.0	2 529.1	1 142.3	134.7	1 021.9	289.2	12.89	6.77	6.12	5.36	0.78
3rd quarter	3 774.9	2 501.2	1 137.3	136.4	1 051.2	293.8	12.75	6.64	6.10	5.44	0.81
4th quarter	3 735.5	2 470.6	1 130.1	134.8	1 077.7	304.0	12.57	6.51	6.05	5.33	0.81
1992											
1st quarter	3 751.9	2 490.4	1 128.5	133.0	1 081.4	294.1	12.32	6.38	5.94	5.32	0.81
2nd quarter	3 763.1	2 504.2	1 122.9	136.0	1 093.8	309.7	12.10	6.25	5.86	4.96	0.83
3rd quarter	3 755.5	2 501.8	1 118.0	135.8	1 108.8	316.7	11.99	6.18	5.81	5.04	0.82
4th quarter	3 764.5	2 513.9	1 115.3	135.3	1 101.8	318.8	11.70	6.03	5.67	4.69	0.76
1993											
1st quarter	3 773.5	2 526.1	1 115.3	132.1	1 120.8	330.4	11.89	6.15	5.74	4.64	0.79
2nd quarter	3 795.9	2 544.9	1 114.4	136.5	1 149.0	347.4	11.67	6.08	5.60	4.33	0.78
3rd quarter	3 800.5	2 546.9	1 114.8	138.9	1 165.5	376.9	11.71	6.12	5.59	4.15	0.77
4th quarter	3 823.6	2 567.2	1 118.5	137.9	1 167.9	388.6	11.60	6.13	5.46	3.92	0.75
1994											
1st quarter	3 871.3	2 617.7	1 117.0	136.6	1 164.9	365.2	11.78	6.28	5.49	3.62	0.77
2nd quarter	3 908.8	2 650.3	1 116.5	142.0	1 151.9	358.5	11.72	6.29	5.43	3.19	0.80
3rd quarter	3 932.8	2 671.2	1 117.6	143.9	1 139.3	362.8	11.85	6.41	5.44	3.30	0.74
4th quarter	3 960.8	2 696.8	1 121.8	142.2	1 121.7	375.0	12.01	6.52	5.49	3.31	0.72
1995											
1st quarter	4 031.8	2 760.8	1 128.7	139.6	1 107.1	392.6	12.14	6.56	5.58	3.49	0.72
2nd quarter	4 108.1	2 830.9	1 133.4	144.7	1 094.1	406.2	12.44	6.78	5.66	3.58	0.76
3rd quarter	4 160.7	2 875.3	1 139.2	147.3	1 077.3	430.5	12.59	6.92	5.67	3.89	0.79
4th quarter	4 223.0	2 925.5	1 152.4	145.1	1 070.2	453.7	12.70	7.05	5.65	3.99	0.69
1996											
1st quarter	4 278.8	2 958.5	1 174.7	143.0	1 065.3	469.2	12.84	7.21	5.62	4.04	0.70
2nd quarter	4 377.8	3 033.3	1 196.8	148.5	1 061.2	481.5	13.00	7.38	5.62	4.11	0.63
3rd quarter	4 440.0	3 076.4	1 214.7	149.7	1 053.2	514.1	13.04	7.42	5.62	4.53	0.60
4th quarter	4 493.7	3 107.7	1 236.1	149.9	1 063.4	542.2	13.09	7.44	5.65	4.68	0.59
1997											
1st quarter	4 560.7	3 151.5	1 258.5	148.2	1 066.9	550.5	13.12	7.47	5.65	4.67	0.57
2nd quarter	4 651.5	3 210.4	1 288.5	153.5	1 078.1	569.6	13.21	7.55	5.67	4.53	0.58
3rd quarter	4 748.4	3 274.5	1 319.4	155.2	1 097.3	593.9	13.21	7.52	5.69	4.74	0.57
4th quarter	4 879.9	3 372.7	1 351.1	156.1	1 119.5	608.0	13.17	7.47	5.70	4.88	0.61
1998											
1st quarter	5 015.5	3 479.5	1 378.3	155.3	1 141.4	634.8	13.24	7.53	5.70	4.69	0.61
2nd quarter	5 163.4	3 598.2	1 405.1	161.0	1 163.0	660.6	13.32	7.60	5.72	4.54	0.61
3rd quarter	5 281.8	3 687.6	1 431.7	163.1	1 180.6	657.7	13.31	7.59	5.72	4.78	0.61
4th quarter	5 413.3	3 788.5	1 460.9	163.8	1 199.8	651.4	13.29	7.57	5.72	4.83	0.60
1999											
1st quarter	5 596.3	3 946.2	1 485.2	162.4	1 219.7	659.1	13.34	7.59	5.75	4.61	0.61
2nd quarter	5 714.3	4 038.9	1 510.2	166.1	1 230.6	653.0	13.39	7.60	5.79	4.30	0.59
3rd quarter	5 897.4	4 188.4	1 540.9	168.6	1 243.7	672.3	13.45	7.59	5.87	4.65	0.59
4th quarter	6 043.3	4 302.2	1 572.0	169.0	1 252.1	676.9	13.51	7.58	5.93	4.65	0.56

Table 10-6. Consumer Installment Credit

(Outstanding at end of period, billions of dollars.)

Year and month	Seasonally adjusted			Not seasonally adjusted						
	Total	By major credit type		Total	By major holder					
		Revolving	Non-revolving		Commercial banks	Finance companies	Credit unions	Savings institutions	Non-financial businesses	Asset pools [1]
1970	131.6	5.0	126.6	133.7	65.6	27.6	13.0	4.4	23.0	0.0
1971	146.9	8.2	138.7	149.2	74.3	29.2	14.8	4.7	26.2	0.0
1972	166.2	9.4	156.8	168.8	87.0	31.9	17.0	5.1	27.8	0.0
1973	190.1	11.3	178.7	193.0	99.6	35.4	19.6	8.5	29.8	0.0
1974	198.9	13.2	185.7	201.9	103.0	36.1	21.9	9.1	31.8	0.0
1975	204.0	14.5	189.5	207.0	106.1	32.6	25.7	10.1	32.6	0.0
1976	225.7	16.5	209.2	229.0	118.0	33.7	31.2	10.8	35.2	0.0
1977	260.1	37.4	222.6	264.4	140.3	37.3	37.6	11.8	37.4	0.0
1978	305.2	45.7	259.5	310.4	166.5	44.4	45.2	13.1	41.2	0.0
1979	347.1	53.6	293.5	353.1	185.7	55.4	47.4	20.0	44.6	0.0
1980	349.3	55.0	294.3	355.4	180.2	62.2	44.1	22.7	46.2	0.0
1981	366.5	60.9	305.6	373.1	184.2	70.1	46.7	24.0	48.1	0.0
1982	383.5	66.3	317.1	390.3	190.9	75.3	48.8	26.6	48.7	0.0
1983	432.5	79.0	353.5	440.3	213.7	83.3	56.1	31.5	55.7	0.0
1984	511.8	100.4	411.4	521.0	258.8	89.9	67.9	44.2	60.2	0.0
1985	593.0	124.5	468.5	603.8	297.2	111.7	74.0	57.6	63.3	0.0
1986	646.6	141.1	505.6	658.2	320.2	134.0	77.1	62.9	64.0	0.0
1987	676.3	160.9	515.5	688.6	334.1	140.0	81.0	65.3	68.1	0.0
1988	718.8	184.6	534.2	732.0	360.8	144.7	88.3	66.8	71.4	0.0
1989	778.7	211.2	567.5	793.3	383.3	138.9	91.7	62.5	69.6	47.3
1990	789.1	238.6	550.5	805.1	382.0	133.4	91.6	49.6	71.9	76.7
1991	777.1	263.8	513.3	794.5	370.2	121.6	90.3	42.2	67.3	103.0
1992	782.2	278.4	503.7	800.6	362.9	118.1	91.7	37.4	70.3	120.3
1993	838.8	309.9	528.8	859.0	395.7	116.1	101.6	37.9	77.2	130.5
1994	960.4	365.6	594.9	983.9	458.8	134.4	119.6	38.5	86.6	146.1
1995	1 095.8	443.1	652.7	1 122.8	502.0	152.1	131.9	40.1	85.1	211.6
1996	1 182.6	499.4	683.1	1 211.6	526.8	152.4	144.1	44.7	77.7	265.8
1997	1 234.5	531.2	703.3	1 264.1	512.6	160.0	152.4	47.2	78.9	313.1
1998	1 301.0	560.5	740.5	1 331.7	508.9	168.5	155.4	51.6	74.9	372.4
1999	1 393.7	595.6	798.0	1 426.2	499.8	181.6	167.9	61.5	80.3	435.1
1996										
January	1 103.1	447.0	656.0	1 111.6	493.2	152.1	131.5	40.2	80.7	213.9
February	1 114.2	453.6	660.6	1 109.0	490.4	153.9	131.2	40.4	78.1	215.0
March	1 123.4	459.7	663.7	1 113.2	490.4	152.5	131.5	40.7	76.7	221.4
April	1 132.7	466.0	666.6	1 123.2	498.1	154.3	132.8	41.1	73.7	223.0
May	1 141.8	471.8	670.1	1 131.9	498.3	156.1	134.6	41.6	74.1	227.2
June	1 151.2	475.3	675.9	1 144.5	503.3	153.9	136.1	42.1	72.0	237.2
July	1 161.5	480.6	680.9	1 154.8	507.4	155.8	137.9	43.0	69.9	240.8
August	1 168.0	483.5	684.5	1 168.3	513.4	154.7	140.0	44.0	71.0	245.3
September	1 170.7	485.7	685.0	1 173.5	513.4	154.6	140.9	44.9	68.5	251.2
October	1 173.3	489.0	684.3	1 176.8	517.9	151.4	143.0	44.9	68.0	251.7
November	1 180.9	495.2	685.7	1 186.6	520.0	151.0	143.3	44.8	69.8	257.8
December	1 182.6	499.4	683.1	1 211.6	526.8	152.4	144.1	44.7	77.7	265.8
1997										
January	1 190.8	504.9	685.9	1 199.6	521.4	153.5	144.2	45.1	73.6	261.8
February	1 196.0	508.5	687.4	1 190.5	512.9	153.3	143.4	45.5	70.6	264.8
March	1 197.4	508.9	688.5	1 186.4	504.3	153.8	143.9	45.9	70.0	268.5
April	1 205.9	511.8	694.1	1 195.6	510.3	152.7	145.6	46.1	69.3	271.6
May	1 210.1	515.4	694.7	1 199.3	511.6	154.9	146.7	46.3	67.7	272.1
June	1 212.1	516.8	695.3	1 205.0	510.7	156.7	147.6	46.5	68.0	275.6
July	1 216.2	521.5	694.7	1 209.6	514.5	156.4	148.8	47.2	67.6	275.2
August	1 219.8	523.9	695.9	1 220.7	516.2	157.2	149.3	47.8	68.6	281.6
September	1 224.0	527.0	697.1	1 226.7	507.5	158.4	150.0	48.5	68.7	293.5
October	1 228.9	529.0	700.0	1 232.5	506.3	156.9	150.6	48.0	68.5	302.2
November	1 228.4	530.3	698.1	1 234.5	506.5	156.4	150.6	47.6	70.5	302.9
December	1 234.5	531.2	703.3	1 264.1	512.6	160.0	152.4	47.2	78.9	313.1
1998										
January	1 235.0	532.2	702.8	1 244.0	499.3	159.5	151.5	47.1	75.4	311.1
February	1 239.3	534.7	704.5	1 234.2	492.5	155.7	150.8	47.1	72.8	315.3
March	1 247.7	539.7	708.0	1 236.0	492.1	156.5	150.7	47.1	72.7	316.8
April	1 251.9	541.8	710.1	1 241.1	500.1	154.3	151.1	47.5	65.1	323.1
May	1 254.3	541.9	712.4	1 243.1	497.3	153.6	152.2	47.9	65.2	326.9
June	1 264.3	545.3	719.0	1 256.8	491.4	154.3	152.4	48.3	65.3	345.1
July	1 268.9	543.8	725.0	1 262.4	491.4	156.1	153.5	49.0	65.5	346.9
August	1 274.9	548.4	726.5	1 276.4	498.2	159.6	153.6	49.6	66.0	349.4
September	1 284.0	551.9	732.1	1 286.6	497.9	159.1	154.3	50.3	65.5	359.4
October	1 294.0	557.6	736.4	1 297.6	502.1	165.6	155.0	51.0	66.0	358.0
November	1 297.9	556.4	741.5	1 304.5	498.8	166.6	155.2	51.6	66.6	365.6
December	1 301.0	560.5	740.5	1 331.7	508.9	168.5	155.4	51.6	74.9	372.4
1999										
January	1 315.4	564.9	750.6	1 324.7	508.6	167.0	155.9	52.3	70.9	370.0
February	1 324.3	566.7	757.6	1 319.3	500.4	169.0	155.6	53.0	67.9	373.3
March	1 331.7	567.3	764.5	1 319.3	494.0	167.8	155.8	53.6	67.1	380.9
April	1 333.4	570.3	763.2	1 322.1	494.7	170.1	156.9	54.8	67.1	378.5
May	1 343.4	572.9	770.5	1 331.3	492.9	168.5	158.1	56.0	68.1	387.8
June	1 348.4	578.6	769.9	1 340.4	477.8	173.6	158.2	57.2	68.0	405.6
July	1 356.1	582.6	773.5	1 349.2	477.9	173.4	159.5	58.1	68.2	412.0
August	1 364.5	584.1	780.4	1 366.3	476.6	177.3	164.4	59.1	68.9	420.1
September	1 366.3	584.4	781.9	1 368.9	472.5	173.0	162.9	60.1	67.5	433.0
October	1 371.6	585.2	786.4	1 375.5	474.0	174.1	164.4	60.5	68.0	434.5
November	1 382.7	589.0	793.8	1 389.7	480.8	175.3	166.0	61.0	70.3	436.4
December	1 393.7	595.6	798.0	1 426.2	499.8	181.6	167.9	61.5	80.3	435.1

1. Outstanding balances of pools upon which securities have been issued; these balances are no longer carried on the balance sheets of the loan originators.

Table 10-7. Selected Interest Rates and Bond Yields

(Percent per annum.)

Year and month	Short-term rates							
	Federal funds	Federal Reserve discount rate [1]	Eurodollar deposits, one-month	U.S. Treasury bills, 3-month	U.S. Treasury bills, 6-month	Bankers acceptances, 3-month	CDs (secondary market), 3-month	Bank prime rate
1970	7.17	5.95	. . .	6.43	6.53	7.23	7.55	7.91
1971	4.67	4.88	6.40	4.35	4.51	4.67	5.00	5.73
1972	4.44	4.50	5.00	4.07	4.47	4.33	4.66	5.25
1973	8.74	6.45	9.25	7.04	7.18	8.27	9.30	8.03
1974	10.51	7.83	10.79	7.89	7.93	9.74	10.29	10.81
1975	5.82	6.25	6.35	5.84	6.12	6.33	6.44	7.86
1976	5.05	5.50	5.26	4.99	5.27	5.08	5.27	6.84
1977	5.54	5.46	5.75	5.27	5.52	5.53	5.63	6.83
1978	7.94	7.46	8.36	7.22	7.58	8.05	8.21	9.06
1979	11.20	10.29	11.66	10.05	10.02	10.97	11.20	12.67
1980	13.35	11.77	13.77	11.51	11.37	12.67	13.02	15.26
1981	16.39	13.42	16.72	14.03	13.78	15.34	15.93	18.87
1982	12.24	11.01	12.74	10.69	11.08	11.89	12.27	14.85
1983	9.09	8.50	9.38	8.63	8.75	8.91	9.07	10.79
1984	10.23	8.80	10.45	9.53	9.77	10.17	10.39	12.04
1985	8.10	7.69	8.12	7.47	7.64	7.91	8.04	9.93
1986	6.80	6.32	6.78	5.98	6.03	6.38	6.51	8.33
1987	6.66	5.66	6.88	5.82	6.05	6.75	6.87	8.21
1988	7.57	6.20	7.69	6.69	6.92	7.56	7.73	9.32
1989	9.21	6.93	9.16	8.12	8.04	8.87	9.09	10.87
1990	8.10	6.98	8.15	7.51	7.47	7.93	8.15	10.01
1991	5.69	5.45	5.81	5.42	5.49	5.70	5.83	8.46
1992	3.52	3.25	3.62	3.45	3.57	3.62	3.68	6.25
1993	3.02	3.00	3.07	3.02	3.14	3.13	3.17	6.00
1994	4.21	3.60	4.34	4.29	4.66	4.56	4.63	7.15
1995	5.83	5.21	5.86	5.51	5.59	5.81	5.92	8.83
1996	5.30	5.02	5.32	5.02	5.09	5.31	5.39	8.27
1997	5.46	5.00	5.52	5.07	5.18	5.54	5.62	8.44
1998	5.35	4.92	5.45	4.81	4.85	5.39	5.47	8.35
1999	4.97	4.62	5.15	4.66	4.76	5.24	5.33	8.00
1996								
January	5.56	5.24	5.45	5.02	4.97	5.31	5.39	8.50
February	5.22	5.00	5.20	4.87	4.79	5.07	5.15	8.25
March	5.31	5.00	5.26	4.96	4.96	5.21	5.29	8.25
April	5.22	5.00	5.32	4.99	5.08	5.28	5.36	8.25
May	5.24	5.00	5.30	5.02	5.12	5.29	5.36	8.25
June	5.27	5.00	5.33	5.11	5.26	5.38	5.46	8.25
July	5.40	5.00	5.31	5.17	5.32	5.45	5.53	8.25
August	5.22	5.00	5.28	5.09	5.17	5.32	5.40	8.25
September	5.30	5.00	5.35	5.15	5.29	5.39	5.51	8.25
October	5.24	5.00	5.26	5.01	5.12	5.32	5.41	8.25
November	5.31	5.00	5.26	5.03	5.07	5.29	5.38	8.25
December	5.29	5.00	5.48	4.87	5.02	5.35	5.44	8.25
1997								
January	5.25	5.00	5.33	5.05	5.11	5.34	5.43	8.25
February	5.19	5.00	5.27	5.00	5.05	5.29	5.37	8.25
March	5.39	5.00	5.40	5.14	5.24	5.44	5.53	8.30
April	5.51	5.00	5.56	5.17	5.35	5.62	5.71	8.50
May	5.50	5.00	5.56	5.13	5.35	5.62	5.70	8.50
June	5.56	5.00	5.56	4.92	5.14	5.59	5.66	8.50
July	5.52	5.00	5.54	5.07	5.12	5.53	5.60	8.50
August	5.54	5.00	5.50	5.13	5.17	5.53	5.60	8.50
September	5.54	5.00	5.58	4.97	5.11	5.54	5.60	8.50
October	5.50	5.00	5.52	4.95	5.09	5.57	5.65	8.50
November	5.52	5.00	5.56	5.15	5.17	5.66	5.74	8.50
December	5.50	5.00	5.82	5.16	5.24	5.75	5.80	8.50
1998								
January	5.56	5.00	5.51	5.09	5.07	5.48	5.54	8.50
February	5.51	5.00	5.48	5.11	5.07	5.46	5.54	8.50
March	5.49	5.00	5.56	5.03	5.04	5.50	5.58	8.50
April	5.45	5.00	5.54	5.00	5.08	5.48	5.58	8.50
May	5.49	5.00	5.52	5.03	5.15	5.48	5.59	8.50
June	5.56	5.00	5.53	4.99	5.12	5.50	5.60	8.50
July	5.54	5.00	5.51	4.96	5.03	5.50	5.59	8.50
August	5.55	5.00	5.51	4.94	4.97	5.49	5.58	8.50
September	5.51	5.00	5.43	4.74	4.75	5.38	5.41	8.49
October	5.07	4.86	5.21	4.08	4.15	5.12	5.21	8.12
November	4.83	4.63	5.13	4.44	4.43	5.15	5.24	7.89
December	4.68	4.50	5.42	4.42	4.43	5.08	5.14	7.75
1999								
January	4.63	4.50	4.86	4.34	4.36	4.80	4.89	7.75
February	4.76	4.50	4.81	4.45	4.43	4.79	4.90	7.75
March	4.81	4.50	4.81	4.48	4.52	4.82	4.91	7.75
April	4.74	4.50	4.80	4.28	4.36	4.80	4.88	7.75
May	4.74	4.50	4.78	4.51	4.55	4.86	4.92	7.75
June	4.76	4.50	4.93	4.59	4.81	5.04	5.13	7.75
July	4.99	4.50	5.07	4.60	4.62	5.16	5.24	8.00
August	5.07	4.56	5.20	4.76	4.88	5.30	5.41	8.06
September	5.22	4.75	5.31	4.73	4.91	5.37	5.50	8.25
October	5.20	4.75	5.32	4.88	4.98	6.02	6.13	8.25
November	5.42	4.86	5.49	5.07	5.17	5.94	6.00	8.37
December	5.30	5.00	6.30	5.23	5.43	6.00	6.05	8.50

1. Maturities of more than ten years.

Table 10-7. Selected Interest Rates and Bond Yields—*Continued*

(Percent per annum.)

Year and month	U.S. Treasury securities				Bond yields			Fixed-rate first mortgages
	One-year	Ten-year	Thirty-year	Long-term composite [1]	Domestic corporate (Moody's)		State and local bonds (Bond Buyer)	
					Aaa	Baa		
1970	6.90	7.35	. . .	. . .	8.04	9.11	6.33	. . .
1971	4.89	6.16	. . .	. . .	7.39	8.56	5.47	. . .
1972	4.95	6.21	. . .	. . .	7.21	8.16	5.26	7.38
1973	7.32	6.85	. . .	. . .	7.44	8.24	5.19	8.04
1974	8.20	7.56	. . .	. . .	8.57	9.50	6.17	9.19
1975	6.78	7.99	. . .	. . .	8.83	10.61	7.05	9.04
1976	5.88	7.61	. . .	. . .	8.43	9.75	6.64	8.86
1977	6.08	7.42	7.75	. . .	8.02	8.97	5.68	8.84
1978	8.34	8.41	8.49	. . .	8.73	9.49	6.02	9.63
1979	10.65	9.43	9.28	. . .	9.63	10.69	6.52	11.19
1980	12.00	11.43	11.27	. . .	11.94	13.67	8.59	13.77
1981	14.80	13.92	13.45	13.43	14.17	16.04	11.33	16.63
1982	12.27	13.01	12.76	12.23	13.79	16.11	11.66	16.08
1983	9.58	11.10	11.18	10.84	12.04	13.55	9.51	13.23
1984	10.91	12.46	12.41	12.00	12.71	14.19	10.10	13.87
1985	8.42	10.62	10.79	10.75	11.37	12.72	9.10	12.42
1986	6.45	7.67	7.78	8.14	9.02	10.39	7.32	10.18
1987	6.77	8.39	8.59	8.64	9.38	10.58	7.64	10.20
1988	7.65	8.85	8.96	8.98	9.71	10.83	7.68	10.34
1989	8.53	8.49	8.45	8.58	9.26	10.18	7.23	10.32
1990	7.89	8.55	8.61	8.74	9.32	10.36	7.27	10.13
1991	5.86	7.86	8.14	8.16	8.77	9.80	6.92	9.25
1992	3.89	7.01	7.67	7.52	8.14	8.98	6.44	8.40
1993	3.43	5.87	6.59	6.45	7.22	7.93	5.60	7.33
1994	5.32	7.09	7.37	7.41	7.97	8.63	6.18	8.35
1995	5.94	6.57	6.88	6.93	7.59	8.20	5.95	7.95
1996	5.52	6.44	6.71	6.80	7.37	8.05	5.76	7.80
1997	5.63	6.35	6.61	6.67	7.27	7.87	5.52	7.60
1998	5.05	5.26	5.58	5.69	6.53	7.22	5.09	6.94
1999	5.08	5.65	5.87	6.14	7.05	7.88	5.43	7.43
1996								
January	5.09	5.65	6.05	6.07	6.81	7.47	5.43	7.03
February	4.94	5.81	6.24	6.28	6.99	7.63	5.43	7.08
March	5.34	6.27	6.60	6.72	7.35	8.03	5.79	7.62
April	5.54	6.51	6.79	6.94	7.50	8.19	5.94	7.93
May	5.64	6.74	6.93	7.08	7.62	8.30	5.98	8.07
June	5.81	6.91	7.06	7.20	7.71	8.40	6.02	8.32
July	5.85	6.87	7.03	7.13	7.65	8.35	5.92	8.25
August	5.67	6.64	6.84	6.94	7.46	8.18	5.76	8.00
September	5.83	6.83	7.03	7.13	7.66	8.35	5.87	8.23
October	5.55	6.53	6.81	6.87	7.39	8.07	5.72	7.92
November	5.42	6.20	6.48	6.55	7.10	7.79	5.59	7.62
December	5.47	6.30	6.55	6.63	7.20	7.89	5.64	7.60
1997								
January	5.61	6.58	6.83	6.89	7.42	8.09	5.72	7.82
February	5.53	6.42	6.69	6.76	7.31	7.94	5.63	7.65
March	5.80	6.69	6.93	7.03	7.55	8.18	5.76	7.90
April	5.99	6.89	7.09	7.18	7.73	8.34	5.88	8.14
May	5.87	6.71	6.94	7.00	7.58	8.20	5.70	7.94
June	5.69	6.49	6.77	6.82	7.41	8.02	5.53	7.69
July	5.54	6.22	6.51	6.55	7.14	7.75	5.35	7.50
August	5.56	6.30	6.58	6.64	7.22	7.82	5.41	7.48
September	5.52	6.21	6.50	6.54	7.15	7.70	5.39	7.43
October	5.46	6.03	6.33	6.37	7.00	7.57	5.38	7.29
November	5.46	5.88	6.11	6.18	6.87	7.42	5.33	7.21
December	5.53	5.81	5.99	6.06	6.76	7.32	5.19	7.10
1998								
January	5.24	5.54	5.81	5.87	6.61	7.19	5.06	6.99
February	5.31	5.57	5.89	5.94	6.67	7.25	5.10	7.04
March	5.39	5.65	5.95	6.00	6.72	7.32	5.21	7.13
April	5.38	5.64	5.92	5.98	6.69	7.33	5.23	7.14
May	5.44	5.65	5.93	5.99	6.69	7.30	5.20	7.14
June	5.41	5.50	5.70	5.78	6.53	7.13	5.12	7.00
July	5.36	5.46	5.68	5.76	6.55	7.15	5.14	6.95
August	5.21	5.34	5.54	5.64	6.52	7.14	5.10	6.92
September	4.71	4.81	5.20	5.34	6.40	7.09	4.99	6.72
October	4.12	4.53	5.01	5.24	6.37	7.18	4.93	6.71
November	4.53	4.83	5.25	5.43	6.41	7.34	5.03	6.87
December	4.52	4.65	5.06	5.29	6.22	7.23	4.98	6.72
1999								
January	4.51	4.72	5.16	5.39	6.24	7.29	5.01	6.79
February	4.70	5.00	5.37	5.60	6.40	7.39	5.03	6.81
March	4.78	5.23	5.58	5.81	6.62	7.53	5.10	7.04
April	4.69	5.18	5.55	5.77	6.64	7.48	5.08	6.92
May	4.85	5.54	5.81	6.04	6.93	7.72	5.18	7.15
June	5.10	5.90	6.04	6.31	7.23	8.02	5.37	7.55
July	5.03	5.79	5.98	6.22	7.19	7.95	5.36	7.63
August	5.20	5.94	6.07	6.37	7.40	8.15	5.58	7.94
September	5.25	5.92	6.07	6.43	7.39	8.20	5.69	7.82
October	5.43	6.11	6.26	6.60	7.55	8.38	5.92	7.85
November	5.55	6.03	6.15	6.42	7.36	8.15	5.86	7.74
December	5.84	6.28	6.35	6.63	7.55	8.19	5.95	7.91

1. Maturities of more than ten years.

Table 10-8. Common Stock Prices and Yields

Year and month	Dow Jones industrials (30 stocks)	Standard and Poor's composite (500 stocks) [1]	Composite	Industrial	Transportation	Utility (Dec.31, 1965=100)	Finance	Stock dividend-price ratio, Standard and Poor's composite (percent)
1970	753.20	83.22	45.72	48.03	32.14	74.48	60.00	3.83
1971	884.76	98.29	54.22	57.92	44.35	79.04	70.38	3.14
1972	950.71	109.20	60.29	65.73	50.17	76.96	78.35	2.84
1973	923.88	107.43	57.42	63.08	37.74	75.38	70.12	3.06
1974	759.37	82.85	43.84	48.08	31.89	59.58	49.67	4.47
1975	802.49	86.16	45.73	50.52	31.10	63.00	47.14	4.31
1976	974.92	102.01	54.46	60.44	39.57	73.94	52.94	3.77
1977	894.62	98.20	53.69	57.86	41.08	81.84	55.25	4.62
1978	820.23	96.02	53.70	58.23	43.50	78.44	56.65	5.28
1979	844.40	103.01	58.32	64.75	47.34	76.40	61.42	5.47
1980	891.41	118.78	68.10	78.70	60.61	74.70	64.25	5.26
1981	932.92	128.04	74.02	85.44	72.61	77.82	73.52	5.20
1982	884.36	119.71	68.93	78.18	60.41	79.48	71.99	5.81
1983	1 190.34	160.41	92.63	107.45	89.36	94.00	95.34	4.40
1984	1 178.48	160.46	92.46	108.01	85.63	92.88	89.28	4.64
1985	1 328.23	186.84	108.09	123.78	104.10	113.48	114.21	4.25
1986	1 792.76	236.34	136.00	155.85	119.87	142.72	147.20	3.48
1987	2 275.99	286.83	161.70	195.31	140.39	148.59	146.48	3.08
1988	2 060.82	265.79	149.91	180.95	134.12	143.53	127.26	3.64
1989	2 508.91	322.84	180.02	216.23	175.28	174.87	151.88	3.45
1990	2 678.94	334.59	183.46	225.78	158.62	181.20	133.26	3.61
1991	2 929.33	376.17	206.33	258.14	173.99	185.32	150.82	3.24
1992	3 284.29	415.74	229.01	284.62	201.09	198.91	179.26	2.99
1993	3 522.06	451.41	249.58	299.99	242.49	228.90	216.42	2.78
1994	3 793.77	460.42	254.12	315.25	247.29	209.06	209.73	2.82
1995	4 493.76	541.72	291.15	367.34	269.41	220.30	238.45	2.56
1996	5 742.89	670.50	358.17	453.98	327.33	249.77	303.89	2.19
1997	7 441.15	873.43	456.54	574.52	414.60	283.82	424.48	1.77
1998	8 625.52	1 085.50	550.26	681.57	468.69	378.12	516.35	1.49
1999	10 464.88	1 327.33	619.16	774.78	491.60	473.73	530.86	1.25
1996								
January	5 179.37	614.42	329.22	412.71	300.03	254.07	273.73	2.31
February	5 518.73	649.54	346.46	435.92	315.29	257.80	290.97	2.22
March	5 612.24	647.07	346.73	439.56	324.76	245.77	290.45	2.22
April	5 579.86	647.17	347.50	441.99	326.42	244.87	287.92	2.24
May	5 616.71	661.23	354.84	452.63	334.66	249.73	290.43	2.21
June	5 671.51	668.50	358.32	458.30	331.57	247.20	294.42	2.21
July	5 496.26	644.07	345.52	438.58	316.66	245.31	287.89	2.28
August	5 685.50	662.68	354.59	449.41	321.61	244.74	302.95	2.22
September	5 804.01	674.88	360.96	459.69	323.12	242.25	308.16	2.20
October	5 996.21	701.46	373.54	473.98	332.93	249.61	324.42	2.11
November	6 318.36	735.67	388.75	490.60	348.32	258.85	345.30	2.01
December	6 435.87	743.25	391.61	494.38	352.28	257.09	350.01	2.01
1997								
January	6 707.03	766.22	403.58	509.84	359.40	263.91	361.45	1.95
February	6 917.48	798.39	418.57	524.30	364.15	271.36	388.75	1.89
March	6 901.12	792.16	416.72	523.08	372.87	264.78	387.21	1.91
April	6 657.50	763.93	401.00	506.69	366.67	253.18	364.25	1.98
May	7 242.36	833.09	433.36	549.65	395.50	268.18	392.32	1.85
June	7 599.60	876.29	457.07	578.57	410.94	280.48	419.12	1.77
July	7 990.65	925.29	480.94	610.42	433.75	288.51	441.59	1.66
August	7 948.43	927.74	481.53	609.54	439.71	287.63	446.93	1.65
September	7 866.59	937.02	489.74	617.94	451.63	291.87	459.86	1.65
October	7 875.82	951.16	499.25	625.22	466.04	302.83	476.70	1.61
November	7 677.36	938.92	492.08	615.57	453.49	307.52	465.29	1.65
December	7 909.82	962.37	504.66	623.57	461.04	325.60	490.30	1.62
1998								
January	7 808.35	963.36	504.13	624.61	458.49	332.50	479.81	1.62
February	8 323.61	1 023.74	532.15	660.91	485.73	341.91	508.97	1.55
March	8 709.47	1 076.83	560.70	693.13	508.06	367.48	539.47	1.48
April	9 037.44	1 112.20	578.05	711.89	523.73	378.92	563.07	1.43
May	9 080.07	1 108.42	574.46	712.39	505.02	372.62	551.28	1.45
June	8 872.96	1 108.39	569.76	704.14	492.98	376.51	548.57	1.45
July	9 097.14	1 156.58	586.39	718.54	503.89	388.78	579.67	1.39
August	8 478.52	1 074.62	539.16	665.66	441.36	372.48	511.22	1.48
September	7 909.79	1 020.64	506.56	629.51	408.75	372.33	454.28	1.59
October	8 164.47	1 032.47	511.49	636.62	396.61	390.17	448.12	1.59
November	9 005.75	1 144.43	564.26	704.46	442.95	412.59	501.45	1.43
December	9 018.68	1 190.05	576.05	717.00	456.70	431.14	510.31	1.37
1999								
January	9 345.86	1 248.77	595.43	741.43	479.72	449.50	523.38	1.30
February	9 322.94	1 246.58	588.70	736.20	477.47	436.49	514.75	1.32
March	9 753.63	1 281.66	603.69	751.93	491.25	436.23	544.08	1.30
April	10 443.50	1 334.76	627.75	780.84	523.08	456.96	564.99	1.24
May	10 853.87	1 332.07	635.62	791.72	537.88	470.40	562.66	1.24
June	10 704.02	1 322.55	629.53	783.96	520.66	482.71	546.43	1.25
July	11 052.22	1 380.99	648.83	809.33	528.72	501.00	557.92	1.20
August	10 935.47	1 327.49	621.03	778.82	492.13	483.68	521.59	1.25
September	10 714.03	1 318.17	607.87	769.47	462.33	475.42	493.37	1.27
October	10 396.88	1 300.01	599.04	753.94	450.13	478.19	490.92	1.28
November	10 809.80	1 391.00	634.22	791.41	474.75	502.59	539.20	1.21
December	11 246.36	1 428.68	638.17	808.28	461.04	511.64	510.99	1.18

1. 1941–1943=10.

CHAPTER 11: U.S. FOREIGN TRADE AND FINANCE

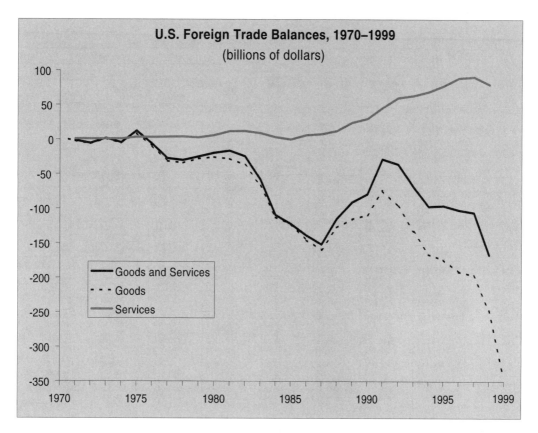

- U.S. imports of goods and services exceeded exports by a record $264 billion in 1999.

- The current-account deficit, which also includes net income payments or receipts and unilateral transfers and which must be financed by equal financial inflows from abroad, expanded to $331 billion, also a record.

- In 1999, the trade surplus in services rose slightly. In 1998 it had declined for the first time since 1985, due to slower growth in exports of services and an increase in imports. In 1999, at $80.6 billion, the services surplus offset 23 percent of the deficit on trade in goods compared to a 32 percent offset in 1998.

- Total goods exports increased 2.1 percent in 1999, while imports increased 12.3 percent. Exports of goods to major Asian trading partners rebounded from declines in 1998 while exports to Europe and the Americas continued to grow.

- As a percentage of GDP, exports of goods and services have nearly doubled from 1970 to 1999, from 5.4 percent to 10.3 percent. Over this same period, imports have gained even more, from 5.2 percent to 13.1 percent.

Table 11-1. U.S. International Transactions

(Millions of dollars, seasonally adjusted.)

Year and quarter	Current account									
	Exports of goods and services and income receipts									
						Income receipts				
							Income receipts on U.S. assets abroad			Compensation of employees
	Total	Exports of goods and services	Exports of goods	Exports of services	Income receipts Total	Total	Direct investment receipts	Other private receipts	U.S. government receipts	
1970	68 387	56 640	42 469	14 171	11 748	11 748	8 169	2 671	907	...
1971	72 384	59 677	43 319	16 358	12 707	12 707	9 160	2 641	906	...
1972	81 986	67 222	49 381	17 841	14 765	14 765	10 949	2 949	866	...
1973	113 050	91 242	71 410	19 832	21 808	21 808	16 542	4 330	936	...
1974	148 484	120 897	98 306	22 591	27 587	27 587	19 157	7 356	1 074	...
1975	157 936	132 585	107 088	25 497	25 351	25 351	16 595	7 644	1 112	...
1976	172 090	142 716	114 745	27 971	29 375	29 375	18 999	9 043	1 332	...
1977	184 655	152 301	120 816	31 485	32 354	32 354	19 673	11 057	1 625	...
1978	220 516	178 428	142 075	36 353	42 088	42 088	25 458	14 788	1 843	...
1979	287 965	224 131	184 439	39 692	63 834	63 834	38 183	23 356	2 295	...
1980	344 440	271 834	224 250	47 584	72 606	72 606	37 146	32 898	2 562	...
1981	380 928	294 398	237 044	57 354	86 529	86 529	32 549	50 300	3 680	...
1982	366 983	275 236	211 157	64 079	91 747	91 747	29 469	58 160	4 118	...
1983	356 106	266 106	201 799	64 307	90 000	90 000	31 750	53 418	4 832	...
1984	399 913	291 094	219 926	71 168	108 819	108 819	35 325	68 267	5 227	...
1985	387 612	289 070	215 915	73 155	98 542	98 542	35 410	57 633	5 499	...
1986	407 098	310 033	223 344	86 689	97 064	96 156	36 938	52 806	6 413	908
1987	457 053	348 869	250 208	98 661	108 184	107 190	46 288	55 592	5 311	994
1988	567 862	431 149	320 230	110 919	136 713	135 718	58 445	70 571	6 703	995
1989	650 494	489 207	362 120	127 087	161 287	160 270	61 981	92 638	5 651	1 017
1990	708 881	537 139	389 307	147 832	171 742	170 570	65 973	94 072	10 525	1 172
1991	730 387	581 174	416 913	164 261	149 214	147 924	58 718	81 186	8 019	1 290
1992	749 324	617 268	440 352	176 916	132 056	130 631	57 538	65 977	7 115	1 425
1993	776 933	642 773	456 832	185 941	134 159	132 725	67 246	60 353	5 126	1 434
1994	868 867	703 429	502 398	201 031	165 438	163 895	77 344	82 423	4 128	1 543
1995	1 006 576	795 074	575 845	219 229	211 502	209 741	95 260	109 768	4 713	1 761
1996	1 075 874	852 064	612 057	240 007	223 810	222 054	102 505	114 958	4 591	1 756
1997	1 194 283	936 937	679 702	257 235	257 346	255 544	115 536	136 449	3 559	1 802
1998	1 191 422	932 977	670 324	262 653	258 445	256 511	106 407	146 503	3 601	1 934
1999	1 232 407	956 242	684 358	271 884	276 165	273 957	118 802	151 958	3 197	2 208
1991										
1st quarter	181 383	139 236	101 345	37 891	42 147	41 829	16 541	22 679	2 609	318
2nd quarter	182 482	145 274	104 529	40 745	37 208	36 889	14 552	20 486	1 851	319
3rd quarter	181 141	145 592	103 732	41 860	35 549	35 224	13 459	19 821	1 944	325
4th quarter	185 387	151 073	107 307	43 766	34 314	33 986	14 169	18 200	1 617	328
1992										
1st quarter	186 161	152 390	108 344	44 046	33 771	33 433	14 714	17 083	1 636	338
2nd quarter	187 443	153 066	109 025	44 041	34 377	34 031	15 548	16 678	1 805	346
3rd quarter	186 386	154 131	109 593	44 538	32 255	31 892	14 263	15 771	1 858	363
4th quarter	189 333	157 681	113 390	44 291	31 652	31 274	13 013	16 445	1 816	378
1993										
1st quarter	190 710	157 810	111 862	45 948	32 900	32 560	16 199	15 040	1 321	340
2nd quarter	193 624	160 629	114 185	46 444	32 995	32 645	16 739	14 575	1 331	350
3rd quarter	192 131	158 154	111 429	46 725	33 977	33 612	17 158	15 124	1 330	365
4th quarter	200 466	166 179	119 356	46 823	34 287	33 908	17 150	15 614	1 144	379
1994										
1st quarter	203 393	166 881	118 382	48 499	36 512	36 146	17 799	17 301	1 046	366
2nd quarter	212 324	173 180	123 025	50 155	39 144	38 769	18 176	19 605	988	375
3rd quarter	221 478	178 475	127 629	50 846	43 003	42 610	20 207	21 437	966	393
4th quarter	231 674	184 896	133 362	51 534	46 778	46 369	21 160	24 080	1 129	409
1995										
1st quarter	242 285	191 219	139 016	52 203	51 066	50 627	22 577	26 855	1 195	439
2nd quarter	248 714	195 268	142 103	53 165	53 446	53 006	24 412	27 225	1 369	440
3rd quarter	254 995	202 342	145 909	56 433	52 653	52 211	23 502	27 677	1 032	442
4th quarter	260 578	206 242	148 817	57 425	54 336	53 896	24 769	28 011	1 116	440
1996										
1st quarter	262 540	207 983	150 438	57 545	54 557	54 118	24 915	27 935	1 268	439
2nd quarter	266 135	212 085	152 612	59 473	54 050	53 612	24 563	27 942	1 107	438
3rd quarter	266 709	210 799	151 991	58 808	55 910	55 470	25 183	29 008	1 279	440
4th quarter	280 484	221 193	157 016	64 177	59 291	58 852	27 840	30 073	939	439
1997										
1st quarter	286 666	225 252	162 670	62 582	61 414	60 963	28 446	31 655	862	451
2nd quarter	299 955	235 074	170 614	64 460	64 881	64 431	29 842	33 623	966	450
3rd quarter	305 537	239 319	173 957	65 362	66 218	65 767	30 251	34 635	881	451
4th quarter	302 129	237 295	172 461	64 834	64 834	64 384	26 998	36 536	850	450
1998										
1st quarter	301 732	235 736	170 609	65 127	65 996	65 531	28 213	36 464	854	465
2nd quarter	298 857	232 351	166 054	66 297	66 506	66 031	28 011	37 099	921	475
3rd quarter	291 341	228 872	164 378	64 494	62 469	61 979	24 025	37 066	888	490
4th quarter	299 489	236 015	169 283	66 732	63 474	62 970	26 159	35 874	937	504
1999										
1st quarter	293 717	230 321	163 949	66 372	63 396	62 861	26 946	35 004	911	535
2nd quarter	300 994	234 297	166 443	67 854	66 697	66 149	28 804	36 535	810	548
3rd quarter	313 084	241 969	173 881	68 088	71 115	70 556	31 361	38 449	746	559
4th quarter	324 612	249 653	180 085	69 568	74 959	74 393	31 691	41 970	732	566

Table 11-1. U.S. International Transactions—Continued

(Millions of dollars, seasonally adjusted.)

Year and quarter	Current account—Continued									
	Imports of goods and services and income payments [1]									
	Total	Imports of goods and services	Imports of goods	Imports of services	Income payments					Compensation of employees
					Total	Income payments on foreign-owned assets in the U.S.				
						Total	Direct investment payments	Other private payments	U.S. government payments	
1970	-59 901	-54 386	-39 866	-14 520	-5 515	-5 515	-875	-3 617	-1 024	. . .
1971	-66 414	-60 979	-45 579	-15 400	-5 435	-5 435	-1 164	-2 428	-1 844	. . .
1972	-79 237	-72 665	-55 797	-16 868	-6 572	-6 572	-1 284	-2 604	-2 684	. . .
1973	-98 997	-89 342	-70 499	-18 843	-9 655	-9 655	-1 610	-4 209	-3 836	. . .
1974	-137 274	-125 190	-103 811	-21 379	-12 084	-12 084	-1 331	-6 491	-4 262	. . .
1975	-132 745	-120 181	-98 185	-21 996	-12 564	-12 564	-2 234	-5 788	-4 542	. . .
1976	-162 109	-148 798	-124 228	-24 570	-13 311	-13 311	-3 110	-5 681	-4 520	. . .
1977	-193 764	-179 547	-151 907	-27 640	-14 217	-14 217	-2 834	-5 841	-5 542	. . .
1978	-229 870	-208 191	-176 002	-32 189	-21 680	-21 680	-4 211	-8 795	-8 674	. . .
1979	-281 657	-248 696	-212 007	-36 689	-32 961	-32 961	6 357	-15 481	-11 122	. . .
1980	-333 774	-291 241	-249 750	-41 491	-42 532	-42 532	-8 635	-21 214	-12 684	. . .
1981	-364 196	-310 570	-265 067	-45 503	-53 626	-53 626	-6 898	-29 415	-17 313	. . .
1982	-355 975	-299 391	-247 642	-51 749	-56 583	-56 583	-2 114	-35 187	-19 282	. . .
1983	-377 488	-323 874	-268 901	-54 973	-53 614	-53 614	-4 120	-30 501	-18 993	. . .
1984	-473 923	-400 166	-332 418	-67 748	-73 756	-73 756	-8 443	-44 158	-21 155	. . .
1985	-483 769	-410 950	-338 088	-72 862	-72 819	-72 819	-6 945	-42 745	-23 129	. . .
1986	-530 142	-448 572	-368 425	-80 147	-81 571	-78 893	-6 856	-47 412	-24 625	-2 678
1987	-594 443	-500 552	-409 765	-90 787	-93 891	-91 553	-7 676	-57 659	-26 218	-2 338
1988	-663 741	-545 715	-447 189	-98 526	-118 026	-116 179	-12 150	-72 314	-31 715	-1 847
1989	-721 307	-579 844	-477 365	-102 479	-141 463	-139 177	-7 045	-93 768	-38 364	-2 286
1990	-759 189	-615 996	-498 337	-117 659	-143 192	-139 728	-3 450	-95 508	-40 770	-3 464
1991	-734 524	-609 440	-490 981	-118 459	-125 084	-121 058	2 266	-82 452	-40 872	-4 026
1992	-762 035	-652 934	-536 458	-116 476	-109 101	-104 349	-2 189	-63 079	-39 081	-4 752
1993	-821 977	-711 722	-589 441	-122 281	-110 255	-105 123	-7 943	-57 804	-39 376	-5 132
1994	-949 212	-800 468	-668 590	-131 878	-148 744	-142 792	-22 150	-76 450	-44 192	-5 952
1995	-1 081 976	-891 021	-749 574	-141 447	-190 955	-184 692	-30 318	-97 004	-57 370	-6 263
1996	-1 159 111	-954 177	-803 327	-150 850	-204 934	-198 634	-33 093	-97 901	-67 640	-6 300
1997	-1 294 029	-1 042 869	-876 367	-166 502	-251 160	-244 494	-43 601	-112 843	-88 050	-6 666
1998	-1 364 531	-1 099 875	-917 178	-182 697	-264 656	-257 547	-38 679	-127 749	-91 119	-7 109
1999	-1 515 861	-1 221 213	-1 029 917	-191 296	-294 648	-287 059	-56 098	-135 830	-95 131	-7 589
1991										
1st quarter	-183 982	-149 942	-120 141	-29 801	-34 040	-33 141	858	-23 549	-10 450	-899
2nd quarter	-182 297	-150 365	-120 705	-29 660	-31 932	-30 951	203	-20 934	-10 220	-981
3rd quarter	-183 831	-152 679	-123 479	-29 200	-31 152	-30 129	-69	-19 794	-10 266	-1 023
4th quarter	-184 419	-156 455	-126 656	-29 799	-27 964	-26 838	1 273	-18 175	-9 936	-1 126
1992										
1st quarter	-183 209	-155 587	-126 284	-29 303	-27 622	-26 445	679	-17 333	-9 791	-1 177
2nd quarter	-190 705	-162 325	-133 277	-29 048	-28 380	-27 194	-1 220	-16 152	-9 822	-1 186
3rd quarter	-192 155	-165 165	-136 887	-28 278	-26 990	-25 816	-1 040	-14 996	-9 780	-1 174
4th quarter	-195 968	-169 858	-140 010	-29 848	-26 110	-24 894	-608	-14 598	-9 688	-1 216
1993										
1st quarter	-196 153	-170 725	-141 069	-29 656	-25 428	-24 218	-33	-14 483	-9 702	-1 210
2nd quarter	-205 027	-177 868	-147 571	-30 297	-27 159	-25 888	-2 375	-13 826	-9 687	-1 271
3rd quarter	-205 196	-178 459	-147 926	-30 533	-26 737	-25 454	-1 614	-13 878	-9 962	-1 283
4th quarter	-215 604	-184 671	-152 875	-31 796	-30 933	-29 564	-3 922	-15 617	-10 025	-1 369
1994										
1st quarter	-218 887	-187 420	-155 009	-32 411	-31 467	-30 024	-3 806	-16 032	-10 186	-1 443
2nd quarter	-231 617	-196 519	-163 852	-32 667	-35 098	-33 604	-4 913	-18 112	-10 579	-1 494
3rd quarter	-244 516	-205 325	-171 977	-33 348	-39 191	-37 695	-6 330	-20 225	-11 140	-1 496
4th quarter	-254 193	-211 206	-177 752	-33 454	-42 987	-41 469	-7 101	-22 081	-12 287	-1 518
1995										
1st quarter	-263 321	-217 626	-183 093	-34 533	-45 695	-44 144	-6 930	-23 914	-13 300	-1 551
2nd quarter	-272 874	-225 775	-190 539	-35 236	-47 099	-45 538	-7 041	-24 391	-14 106	-1 561
3rd quarter	-273 522	-223 742	-188 077	-35 665	-49 780	-48 219	-8 954	-24 413	-14 852	-1 561
4th quarter	-272 260	-223 880	-187 865	-36 015	-48 380	-46 791	-7 393	-24 286	-15 112	-1 589
1996										
1st quarter	-277 301	-229 726	-193 038	-36 688	-47 575	-46 065	-7 318	-23 596	-15 151	-1 510
2nd quarter	-287 269	-237 890	-200 763	-37 127	-49 379	-47 819	-8 022	-23 974	-15 823	-1 560
3rd quarter	-294 421	-241 574	-203 196	-38 378	-52 847	-51 277	-8 859	-24 767	-17 651	-1 570
4th quarter	-300 121	-244 988	-206 330	-38 658	-55 133	-53 473	-8 894	-25 564	-19 015	-1 660
1997										
1st quarter	-311 988	-252 299	-212 153	-40 146	-59 689	-58 083	-11 215	-26 559	-20 309	-1 606
2nd quarter	-320 660	-258 649	-217 884	-40 765	-62 011	-60 361	-10 690	-27 637	-22 034	-1 650
3rd quarter	-329 383	-264 599	-222 114	-42 485	-64 784	-63 102	-11 735	-28 513	-22 854	-1 682
4th quarter	-331 999	-267 324	-224 216	-43 108	-64 675	-62 948	-9 961	-30 134	-22 853	-1 727
1998										
1st quarter	-334 328	-269 349	-225 255	-44 094	-64 979	-63 244	-9 493	-31 068	-22 683	-1 735
2nd quarter	-340 233	-273 959	-228 675	-45 284	-66 274	-64 524	-9 915	-31 649	-22 960	-1 750
3rd quarter	-341 992	-275 206	-228 942	-46 264	-66 786	-64 995	-9 278	-32 940	-22 777	-1 791
4th quarter	-347 980	-281 363	-234 306	-47 057	-66 617	-64 784	-9 993	-32 092	-22 699	-1 833
1999										
1st quarter	-349 513	-282 997	-236 973	-46 024	-66 516	-64 636	-10 916	-31 051	-22 669	-1 880
2nd quarter	-368 439	-297 597	-250 427	-47 170	-70 842	-68 962	-14 106	-31 701	-23 155	-1 880
3rd quarter	-391 337	-314 687	-266 199	-48 488	-76 650	-74 749	-15 660	-34 942	-24 147	-1 901
4th quarter	-406 575	-325 933	-276 318	-49 615	-80 642	-78 712	-15 416	-38 136	-25 160	-1 930

1. A minus sign indicates imports of goods and services, or payments of income.

Table 11-1. U.S. International Transactions—*Continued*

(Millions of dollars, seasonally adjusted.)

Year and quarter	Current account—*Continued* Unilateral current transfers, net [1]				Capital account transactions, net [1]	Financial account U.S.-owned assets abroad, net [1]					
	Total	U.S. government Grants	U.S. government Pensions and other transfers	Private remittances and other transfers		Total	U.S. official reserve assets, net Total	Gold	Special drawing rights	Reserve position in the IMF	Foreign currencies
1970	-6 156	-4 449	-611	-1 096	...	-8 470	3 348	787	16	389	2 156
1971	-7 402	-5 589	-696	-1 117	...	-11 758	3 066	866	468	1 350	382
1972	-8 544	-6 665	-770	-1 109	...	-13 787	706	547	7	153	-1
1973	-6 913	-4 748	-915	-1 250	...	-22 874	158	...	9	-33	182
1974	-9 249	-7 293	-939	-1 017	...	-34 745	-1 467	...	-172	-1 265	-30
1975	-7 075	-5 101	-1 068	-906	...	-39 703	-849	...	-66	-466	-317
1976	-5 686	-3 519	-1 250	-917	...	-51 269	-2 558	...	-78	-2 212	-268
1977	-5 226	-2 990	-1 378	-859	...	-34 785	-375	-118	-121	-294	158
1978	-5 788	-3 412	-1 532	-844	...	-61 130	732	-65	1 249	4 231	-4 683
1979	-6 593	-4 015	-1 658	-920	...	-64 915	6	-65	3	-189	257
1980	-8 349	-5 486	-1 818	-1 044	...	-85 815	-7 003	...	1 136	-1 667	-6 472
1981	-11 702	-5 145	-2 041	-4 516	...	-113 054	-4 082	...	-730	-2 491	-861
1982	-16 544	-6 087	-2 251	-8 207	199	-127 882	-4 965	...	-1 371	-2 552	-1 041
1983	-17 310	-6 469	-2 207	-8 635	209	-66 373	-1 196	...	-66	-4 434	3 304
1984	-20 335	-8 696	-2 159	-9 479	235	-40 376	-3 131	...	-979	-995	-1 156
1985	-21 998	-11 268	-2 138	-8 593	315	-44 752	-3 858	...	-897	908	-3 869
1986	-24 132	-11 883	-2 372	-9 877	301	-111 723	312	...	-246	1 501	-942
1987	-23 265	-10 309	-2 409	-10 548	365	-79 296	9 149	...	-509	2 070	7 588
1988	-25 274	-10 537	-2 709	-12 028	493	-106 573	-3 912	...	127	1 025	-5 064
1989	-26 169	-10 860	-2 775	-12 534	336	-175 383	-25 293	...	-535	471	-25 229
1990	-26 654	-10 359	-3 224	-13 070	-6 579	-81 234	-2 158	...	-192	731	-2 697
1991	10 752	29 193	-3 775	-14 665	-4 479	-64 388	5 763	...	-177	-367	6 307
1992	-35 013	-16 320	-4 043	-14 650	612	-74 410	3 901	...	2 316	-2 692	4 277
1993	-37 637	-17 036	-4 104	-16 497	-88	-200 552	-1 379	...	-537	-44	-797
1994	-38 260	-14 978	-4 556	-18 726	-469	-176 056	5 346	...	-441	494	5 293
1995	-34 057	-11 190	-3 451	-19 416	372	-352 376	-9 742	...	-808	-2 466	-6 468
1996	-40 081	-15 401	-4 466	-20 214	693	-413 923	6 668	...	370	-1 280	7 578
1997	-40 794	-12 472	-4 191	-24 131	350	-488 940	-1 010	...	-350	-3 575	2 915
1998	-44 029	-13 270	-4 305	-26 454	637	-335 436	-6 783	...	-147	-5 119	-1 517
1999	-48 025	-13 774	-4 401	-29 850	-3 500	-430 187	8 747	...	10	5 484	3 253
1991											
1st quarter	15 004	19 444	-869	-3 571	-941	-10 570	-353	...	31	-341	-43
2nd quarter	3 780	8 285	-877	-3 628	73	745	1 014	...	-190	72	1 132
3rd quarter	-2 812	1 730	-880	-3 662	-3 786	-15 900	3 877	...	6	-114	3 986
4th quarter	-5 224	-267	-1 150	-3 807	175	-38 664	1 225	...	-23	17	1 232
1992											
1st quarter	-7 545	-3 040	-907	-3 598	152	-11 428	-1 057	...	-172	111	-996
2nd quarter	-8 418	-3 532	-1 197	-3 689	111	-16 235	1 464	...	-168	1	1 631
3rd quarter	-7 837	-3 161	-1 021	-3 655	173	-13 570	1 952	...	-173	-118	2 243
4th quarter	-11 214	-6 586	-919	-3 709	176	-33 177	1 542	...	2 829	-2 685	1 398
1993											
1st quarter	-7 905	-3 007	-904	-3 994	-459	-21 491	-983	...	-140	-228	-615
2nd quarter	-8 576	-3 468	-1 068	-4 040	147	-45 843	822	...	-166	313	675
3rd quarter	-9 339	-4 097	-1 071	-4 171	83	-52 975	-545	...	-118	-48	-378
4th quarter	-11 816	-6 463	-1 061	-4 292	141	-80 243	-673	...	-113	-80	-480
1994											
1st quarter	-7 971	-2 488	-964	-4 519	152	-39 740	-59	...	-101	-3	45
2nd quarter	-8 482	-2 946	-974	-4 562	-704	-43 072	3 537	...	-108	251	3 394
3rd quarter	-9 610	-3 323	-1 555	-4 732	-70	-30 985	-165	...	-111	273	-327
4th quarter	-12 194	-6 221	-1 063	-4 910	153	-62 261	2 033	...	-121	-27	2 181
1995											
1st quarter	-8 577	-2 964	-762	-4 851	146	-64 950	-5 318	...	-867	-526	-3 925
2nd quarter	-8 080	-2 491	-980	-4 609	272	-117 959	-2 722	...	-156	-786	-1 780
3rd quarter	-8 460	-2 698	-973	-4 789	-299	-46 759	-1 893	...	362	-991	-1 264
4th quarter	-8 939	-3 037	-736	-5 166	253	-122 706	191	...	-147	-163	501
1996											
1st quarter	-10 519	-4 509	-1 157	-4 853	156	-80 936	17	...	-199	-849	1 065
2nd quarter	-8 744	-2 566	-1 103	-5 075	173	-68 512	-523	...	-133	-220	-170
3rd quarter	-8 940	-2 780	-1 111	-5 049	178	-91 675	7 489	...	848	-183	6 824
4th quarter	-11 878	-5 546	-1 095	-5 237	186	-172 797	-315	...	-146	-28	-141
1997											
1st quarter	-9 054	-2 281	-1 027	-5 746	138	-153 009	4 480	...	72	1 055	3 353
2nd quarter	-9 280	-2 308	-1 071	-5 901	68	-93 350	-236	...	-133	54	-157
3rd quarter	-9 561	-2 476	-1 024	-6 061	41	-119 826	-730	...	-139	-463	-128
4th quarter	-12 902	-5 407	-1 069	-6 426	103	-122 757	-4 524	...	-150	-4 221	-153
1998											
1st quarter	-9 794	-2 365	-1 080	-6 349	149	-68 887	-444	...	-182	-85	-177
2nd quarter	-10 099	-2 209	-1 094	-6 796	157	-141 617	-1 945	...	73	-1 032	-986
3rd quarter	-10 658	-2 882	-1 055	-6 721	155	-53 027	-2 025	...	189	-2 078	-136
4th quarter	-13 474	-5 814	-1 075	-6 585	176	-71 904	-2 369	...	-227	-1 924	-218
1999											
1st quarter	-10 831	-2 574	-1 066	-7 191	157	-21 555	4 068	...	562	3	3 503
2nd quarter	-11 537	-3 097	-1 074	-7 366	165	-170 842	1 159	...	-190	1 413	-64
3rd quarter	-11 396	-2 847	-1 080	-7 469	171	-122 909	1 951	...	-184	2 268	-133
4th quarter	-14 260	-5 256	-1 181	-7 823	-3 993	-114 882	1 569	...	-178	1 800	-53

1. A minus sign indicates net unilateral transfers to foreigners, capital or financial outflows, or increases in U.S. official assets.

Table 11-1. U.S. International Transactions—*Continued*

(Millions of dollars, seasonally adjusted.)

Year and quarter	Financial account—*Continued*								
	U.S. assets abroad, net [1]—*Continued*								
	U.S. government assets other than official reserve assets, net				U.S. private assets, net				
								U.S. claims	
	Total	U.S. credits and other long-term assets	Repayments on U.S. credits and other long-term assets	U.S. foreign currency holdings and short-term assets, net	Total	Direct investment	Foreign securities	On unaffiliated foreigners reported by U.S. nonbanking concerns	Reported by U.S. banks, not included elsewhere
1970	-1 589	-3 293	1 721	-16	-10 229	-7 590	-1 076	-596	-967
1971	-1 884	-4 181	2 115	182	-12 940	-7 618	-1 113	-1 229	-2 980
1972	-1 568	-3 819	2 086	165	-12 925	-7 747	-618	-1 054	-3 506
1973	-2 644	-4 638	2 596	-602	-20 388	-11 353	-671	-2 383	-5 980
1974	366	-5 001	4 826	541	-33 643	-9 052	-1 854	-3 221	-19 516
1975	-3 474	-5 941	2 475	-9	-35 380	-14 244	-6 247	-1 357	-13 532
1976	-4 214	-6 943	2 596	133	-44 498	-11 949	-8 885	-2 296	-21 368
1977	-3 693	-6 445	2 719	33	-30 717	-11 890	-5 460	-1 940	-11 427
1978	-4 660	-7 470	2 941	-131	-57 202	-16 056	-3 626	-3 853	-33 667
1979	-3 746	-7 697	3 926	25	-61 176	-25 222	-4 726	-5 014	-26 213
1980	-5 162	-9 860	4 456	242	-73 651	-19 222	-3 568	-4 023	-46 838
1981	-5 097	-9 674	4 413	164	-103 875	-9 624	-5 699	-4 377	-84 175
1982	-6 131	-10 063	4 292	-360	-116 786	-4 556	-7 983	6 823	-111 070
1983	-5 006	-9 967	5 012	-51	-60 172	-12 528	-6 762	-10 954	-29 928
1984	-5 489	-9 599	4 490	-379	-31 757	-16 407	-4 756	533	-11 127
1985	-2 821	-7 657	4 719	117	-38 074	-18 927	-7 481	-10 342	-1 323
1986	-2 022	-9 084	6 089	973	-110 014	-23 995	-4 271	-21 773	-59 975
1987	1 006	-6 506	7 625	-113	-89 450	-35 034	-5 251	-7 046	-42 119
1988	2 967	-7 680	10 370	277	-105 628	-22 528	-7 980	-21 193	-53 927
1989	1 233	-5 608	6 725	115	-151 323	-43 447	-22 070	-27 646	-58 160
1990	2 317	-8 410	10 856	-130	-81 393	-37 183	-28 765	-27 824	12 379
1991	2 924	-12 879	16 776	-974	-73 075	-37 889	-45 673	11 097	-610
1992	-1 667	-7 408	5 807	-66	-76 644	-48 266	-49 166	-387	21 175
1993	-351	-6 311	6 270	-310	-198 822	-83 950	-146 253	766	30 615
1994	-390	-5 383	5 088	-95	-181 012	-80 167	-60 309	-36 336	-4 200
1995	-984	-4 859	4 125	-250	-341 650	-98 750	-122 506	-45 286	-75 108
1996	-989	-5 025	3 930	106	-419 602	-91 885	-149 829	-86 333	-91 555
1997	68	-5 417	5 438	47	-487 998	-105 016	-118 976	-122 888	-141 118
1998	-422	-4 678	4 111	145	-328 231	-146 052	-135 995	-10 612	-35 572
1999	2 751	-6 175	9 560	-634	-441 685	-150 901	-128 594	-92 328	-69 862
1991									
1st quarter	549	-2 018	2 630	-63	-10 766	-14 318	-9 960	-40	13 552
2nd quarter	-423	-1 061	840	-202	154	-1 230	-12 021	7 902	5 503
3rd quarter	3 256	-8 724	12 417	-437	-23 034	-9 356	-12 550	3 341	-4 469
4th quarter	-459	-1 077	890	-272	-39 431	-12 987	-11 142	-106	-15 196
1992									
1st quarter	-259	-1 517	1 326	-68	-10 112	-20 695	-8 668	7 562	11 689
2nd quarter	-302	-1 247	1 084	-139	-17 397	-10 268	-8 196	-6 620	7 687
3rd quarter	-392	-1 980	1 359	229	-15 130	-5 157	-13 059	-3 737	6 823
4th quarter	-715	-2 664	2 038	-89	-34 004	-12 145	-19 243	2 408	-5 024
1993									
1st quarter	487	-945	1 763	-331	-20 995	-14 982	-28 208	-6 130	28 325
2nd quarter	-304	-773	891	-422	-46 361	-23 264	-29 833	-725	7 461
3rd quarter	-194	-1 668	2 036	-562	-52 237	-13 155	-51 940	5 896	6 962
4th quarter	-340	-2 925	1 580	1 005	-79 230	-32 550	-36 272	1 725	-12 133
1994									
1st quarter	399	-757	1 120	36	-40 080	-28 554	-19 540	-2 215	10 229
2nd quarter	477	-1 006	1 648	-165	-47 086	-14 932	-9 229	-20 966	-1 959
3rd quarter	-323	-1 372	1 383	-334	-30 497	-17 316	-12 405	-960	184
4th quarter	-943	-2 248	937	368	-63 351	-19 367	-19 135	-12 195	-12 654
1995									
1st quarter	-553	-1 622	1 072	-3	-59 079	-19 325	-8 775	-2 631	-28 348
2nd quarter	-225	-862	649	-12	-115 012	-15 078	-27 834	-24 580	-47 520
3rd quarter	252	-1 028	1 522	-242	-45 118	-21 772	-41 564	13 729	4 489
4th quarter	-458	-1 347	882	7	-122 439	-42 573	-44 333	-31 804	-3 729
1996									
1st quarter	-210	-1 076	1 013	-147	-80 743	-23 759	-44 043	-15 210	2 269
2nd quarter	-568	-1 512	683	261	-67 421	-15 096	-30 968	-22 000	643
3rd quarter	105	-1 192	1 214	83	-99 269	-23 129	-33 273	-9 090	-33 777
4th quarter	-316	-1 245	1 020	-91	-172 166	-29 898	-41 545	-40 033	-60 690
1997									
1st quarter	-76	-1 170	1 119	-25	-157 413	-29 565	-23 836	-38 887	-65 125
2nd quarter	-298	-1 616	1 329	-11	-92 816	-24 924	-31 739	-9 578	-26 575
3rd quarter	377	-1 426	1 832	-29	-119 473	-21 281	-51 297	-22 652	-24 243
4th quarter	65	-1 205	1 158	112	-118 298	-29 248	-12 104	-51 771	-25 175
1998									
1st quarter	-80	-1 192	1 134	-22	-68 363	-47 658	-20 798	4 890	-4 797
2nd quarter	-483	-1 156	699	-26	-139 189	-45 252	-44 229	-21 521	-28 187
3rd quarter	188	-1 286	1 336	138	-51 190	-19 483	6 201	-9 579	-28 329
4th quarter	-47	-1 044	942	55	-69 488	-33 658	-77 169	15 598	25 741
1999									
1st quarter	118	-1 314	1 554	-122	-25 741	-41 112	1 107	-14 223	28 487
2nd quarter	-392	-2 167	1 887	-112	-171 609	-32 958	-71 131	-25 734	-41 786
3rd quarter	-686	-1 595	1 026	-117	-124 174	-43 552	-41 420	-27 943	-11 259
4th quarter	3 711	-1 099	5 093	-283	-120 162	-33 280	-17 150	-24 428	-45 304

1. A minus sign indicates financial outflows.

Table 11-1. U.S. International Transactions—*Continued*

(Millions of dollars, seasonally adjusted.)

Year and quarter	Total	Financial account—Continued											
		Foreign-owned assets in the United States, net [1]											
		Foreign official assets in the United States, net							Other foreign assets in the United States, net				
		Total	U.S. government securities			Other U.S. government liabilities	U.S. liabilities reported by U.S. banks, not included elsewhere	Other foreign official assets	Total	Direct investment	U.S. Treasury securities	U.S. securities other than Treasury securities	U.S. currency
			Total	U.S. Treasury securities	Other								
1970	6 359	6 908	9 439	9 411	28	-456	-2 075	...	-550	1 464	81	2 189	...
1971	22 970	26 879	26 570	26 578	-8	-510	819	...	-3 909	367	-24	2 289	...
1972	21 461	10 475	8 470	8 213	257	182	1 638	185	10 986	949	-39	4 507	...
1973	18 388	6 026	641	59	582	936	4 126	323	12 362	2 800	-216	4 041	...
1974	35 341	10 546	4 172	3 270	902	301	5 818	254	24 796	4 760	697	378	1 100
1975	17 170	7 027	5 563	4 658	905	1 517	-2 158	2 104	10 143	2 603	2 590	2 503	1 500
1976	38 018	17 693	9 892	9 319	573	4 627	969	2 205	20 326	4 347	2 783	1 284	1 500
1977	53 219	36 816	32 538	30 230	2 308	1 400	773	2 105	16 403	3 728	534	2 437	1 900
1978	67 036	33 678	24 221	23 555	666	2 476	5 551	1 430	33 358	7 897	2 178	2 254	3 000
1979	40 852	-13 665	-21 972	-22 435	463	-40	7 213	1 135	54 516	11 877	4 060	1 351	3 000
1980	62 612	15 497	11 895	9 708	2 187	615	-159	3 145	47 115	16 918	2 645	5 457	4 500
1981	86 232	4 960	6 322	5 019	1 303	-338	-3 670	2 646	81 272	25 195	2 927	6 905	3 200
1982	96 589	3 593	5 085	5 779	-694	605	-1 747	-350	92 997	12 635	7 027	6 085	4 000
1983	88 694	5 845	6 496	6 972	-476	602	545	-1 798	82 849	10 372	8 689	8 164	5 400
1984	117 752	3 140	4 703	4 690	13	739	555	-2 857	114 612	24 468	23 001	12 568	4 100
1985	146 115	-1 119	-1 139	-838	-301	844	645	-1 469	147 233	19 742	20 433	50 962	5 200
1986	230 009	35 648	33 150	34 364	-1 214	2 195	1 187	-884	194 360	35 420	3 809	70 969	4 100
1987	248 634	45 387	44 802	43 238	1 564	-2 326	3 918	-1 007	203 247	58 470	-7 643	42 120	5 400
1988	246 522	39 758	43 050	41 741	1 309	-467	-319	-2 506	206 764	57 735	20 239	26 353	5 800
1989	224 928	8 503	1 532	149	1 383	160	4 976	1 835	216 425	68 274	29 618	38 767	5 900
1990	141 571	33 910	30 243	29 576	667	1 868	3 385	-1 586	107 661	48 494	-2 534	1 592	18 800
1991	110 808	17 389	16 147	14 846	1 301	1 367	-1 484	1 359	93 420	23 171	18 826	35 144	15 400
1992	170 663	40 477	22 403	18 454	3 949	2 191	16 571	-688	130 186	19 823	37 131	30 043	13 400
1993	282 040	71 753	53 014	48 952	4 062	1 313	14 841	2 585	210 287	51 362	24 381	80 092	18 900
1994	305 989	39 583	36 827	30 750	6 077	1 564	3 665	-2 473	266 406	46 121	34 274	56 971	23 400
1995	465 684	109 880	72 712	68 977	3 735	-105	34 008	3 265	355 804	57 776	99 548	96 367	12 300
1996	571 706	126 724	120 679	115 671	5 008	-982	5 704	1 323	444 982	86 502	154 996	130 240	17 362
1997	756 962	18 876	-2 161	-6 690	4 529	-1 041	22 286	-208	738 086	106 032	146 433	197 892	24 782
1998	482 235	-20 127	-3 589	-9 921	6 332	-3 550	-9 501	-3 487	502 362	186 316	48 581	218 075	16 622
1999	753 564	42 864	32 527	12 177	20 350	-3 255	12 692	900	710 700	275 533	-20 464	331 523	22 407
1991													
1st quarter	8 347	5 569	126	155	-29	769	3 908	766	2 778	4 076	4 739	5 023	4 800
2nd quarter	12 678	-4 914	-3 764	-3 545	-219	253	-1 517	115	17 591	13 378	13 461	14 872	2 200
3rd quarter	33 236	3 854	6 095	5 621	474	771	-3 107	95	29 382	-1 354	-1 196	10 310	4 200
4th quarter	56 549	12 879	13 690	12 615	1 075	-426	-768	383	43 670	7 072	1 822	4 939	4 200
1992													
1st quarter	31 079	20 988	15 380	14 916	464	-73	5 568	113	10 091	2 086	686	4 569	1 300
2nd quarter	50 304	20 879	12 950	11 251	1 699	518	7 486	-75	29 425	5 916	10 231	10 467	1 100
3rd quarter	35 469	-7 524	593	-319	912	607	-7 724	-1 000	42 993	2 898	4 908	2 531	6 100
4th quarter	53 809	6 133	-6 520	-7 394	874	1 138	11 241	274	47 676	8 922	21 306	12 476	4 900
1993													
1st quarter	25 099	10 937	1 745	1 080	665	-469	8 257	1 404	14 162	8 060	13 363	9 694	3 000
2nd quarter	59 038	17 466	6 750	5 668	1 082	132	9 485	1 099	41 572	11 386	-292	15 205	5 900
3rd quarter	85 694	19 073	20 443	19 098	1 345	932	-2 486	184	66 621	11 688	3 258	17 782	6 400
4th quarter	112 210	24 277	24 076	23 106	970	718	-415	-102	87 933	20 229	8 052	37 411	3 600
1994													
1st quarter	90 280	10 568	1 074	897	177	659	9 588	-753	79 712	5 883	9 912	21 070	5 500
2nd quarter	56 842	9 455	8 282	5 922	2 360	-5	2 143	-965	47 387	5 767	-7 098	12 352	6 300
3rd quarter	81 934	19 358	18 697	16 475	2 222	284	1 177	-800	62 576	13 709	5 661	13 389	4 700
4th quarter	76 933	202	8 774	7 456	1 318	626	-9 243	45	76 731	20 762	25 799	10 160	6 900
1995													
1st quarter	103 250	21 956	11 258	10 132	1 126	-562	10 995	265	81 294	9 924	30 011	15 734	6 400
2nd quarter	128 905	37 072	26 560	25 234	1 326	54	7 510	2 948	91 833	11 888	30 439	20 606	1 900
3rd quarter	124 277	39 302	21 116	20 598	518	-504	18 918	-228	84 975	16 764	37 295	32 128	1 900
4th quarter	109 252	11 550	13 778	13 013	765	907	-3 415	280	97 702	19 200	1 803	27 899	2 100
1996													
1st quarter	91 377	51 771	55 839	55 685	154	-554	-3 303	-211	39 606	28 518	18 031	29 391	-2 391
2nd quarter	111 001	13 503	-1 934	-3 378	1 444	-65	14 217	1 285	97 498	16 184	26 967	31 179	4 542
3rd quarter	148 205	23 020	26 135	24 908	1 227	147	-1 677	-1 585	125 185	15 257	38 727	35 118	7 382
4th quarter	221 122	38 430	40 639	38 456	2 183	-510	-3 533	1 834	182 692	26 542	71 271	34 552	7 829
1997													
1st quarter	183 682	27 751	23 105	22 351	754	-167	8 123	-3 310	155 931	25 450	33 050	45 364	3 484
2nd quarter	151 459	-6 046	-11 411	-12 373	962	-313	4 643	1 035	157 505	21 512	37 928	54 286	4 822
3rd quarter	183 959	23 461	10 316	7 604	2 712	-575	12 817	903	160 498	21 564	40 133	63 131	6 576
4th quarter	237 862	-26 290	-24 171	-24 272	101	14	-3 297	1 164	264 152	37 506	35 322	35 111	9 900
1998													
1st quarter	86 840	10 967	13 946	11 336	2 610	-1 059	-964	-956	75 873	21 758	-2 535	76 983	746
2nd quarter	167 085	-10 235	-20 051	-20 305	254	-760	9 744	832	177 320	19 818	25 814	70 552	2 349
3rd quarter	82 790	-46 651	-30 917	-32 823	1 906	-292	-12 948	-2 494	129 441	23 635	918	21 136	7 277
4th quarter	145 520	25 792	33 433	31 871	1 562	-1 439	-5 333	-869	119 728	121 105	24 384	49 404	6 250
1999													
1st quarter	102 780	4 274	6 793	800	5 993	-1 485	-1 139	105	98 506	26 779	-7 505	62 815	2 440
2nd quarter	272 008	-1 096	-916	-6 708	5 792	-1 099	1 436	-517	273 104	143 802	-5 407	80 838	3 057
3rd quarter	194 210	12 191	14 798	12 963	1 835	-760	-2 032	185	182 019	55 563	9 639	95 620	4 697
4th quarter	184 567	27 495	11 852	5 122	6 730	89	14 427	1 127	157 072	49 390	-17 191	92 250	12 213

1. A minus sign indicates financial outflows or decrease in foreign official assets in the United States.

Table 11-1. U.S. International Transactions—*Continued*

(Millions of dollars, seasonally adjusted.)

Year and quarter	Financial account—*Continued*		Statistical discrepancy [2]		Balance on:						
	Other foreign assets in the U.S., net [1]—*Continued*										
	U.S. liabilities										
	To unaffiliated foreigners reported by U.S. nonbanking concerns	Reported by U.S. banks not included elsewhere	Total	Seasonal adjustment discrepancy	Goods	Services	Goods and services	Income	Goods, services, and income	Unilateral current transfers	Current account
1970	2 014	-6 298	-219	...	2 603	-349	2 254	6 233	8 487	-6 156	2 331
1971	369	-6 911	-9 779	...	-2 260	957	-1 303	7 272	5 969	-7 402	-1 433
1972	815	4 754	-1 879	...	-6 416	973	-5 443	8 192	2 749	-8 544	-5 795
1973	1 035	4 702	-2 654	...	911	989	1 900	12 153	14 053	-6 913	7 140
1974	1 844	16 017	-2 558	...	-5 505	1 213	-4 292	15 503	11 211	-9 249	1 962
1975	319	628	4 417	...	8 903	3 501	12 404	12 787	25 191	-7 075	18 116
1976	-578	10 990	8 955	...	-9 483	3 401	-6 082	16 063	9 981	-5 686	4 295
1977	1 086	6 719	-4 099	...	-31 091	3 845	-27 246	18 137	-9 109	-5 226	-14 335
1978	1 889	16 141	9 236	...	-33 927	4 164	-29 763	20 408	-9 355	-5 788	-15 143
1979	1 621	32 607	24 349	...	-27 568	3 003	-24 565	30 873	6 308	-6 593	-285
1980	6 852	10 743	20 886	...	-25 500	6 093	-19 407	30 073	10 666	-8 349	2 317
1981	917	42 128	21 792	...	-28 023	11 852	-16 172	32 903	16 731	-11 702	5 030
1982	-2 383	65 633	36 630	...	-36 485	12 329	-24 156	35 164	11 008	-16 544	-5 536
1983	-118	50 342	16 162	...	-67 102	9 335	-57 767	36 386	-21 381	-17 310	-38 691
1984	16 626	33 849	16 733	...	-112 492	3 419	-109 073	35 063	-74 010	-20 335	-94 344
1985	9 851	41 045	16 478	...	-122 173	294	-121 880	25 723	-96 157	-21 998	-118 155
1986	3 325	76 737	28 590	...	-145 081	6 543	-138 538	15 494	-123 044	-24 132	-147 177
1987	18 363	86 537	-9 048	...	-159 557	7 874	-151 684	14 293	-137 391	-23 265	-160 655
1988	32 893	63 744	-19 289	...	-126 959	12 393	-114 566	18 687	-95 879	-25 274	-121 153
1989	22 086	51 780	47 101	...	-115 245	24 607	-90 638	19 824	-70 814	-26 169	-96 982
1990	45 133	-3 824	23 204	...	-109 030	30 173	-78 857	28 550	-50 307	-26 654	-76 961
1991	-3 115	3 994	-48 557	...	-74 068	45 802	-28 266	24 130	-4 136	10 752	6 616
1992	13 573	16 216	-49 141	...	-96 106	60 440	-35 666	22 954	-12 712	-35 013	-47 724
1993	10 489	25 063	1 281	...	-132 609	63 660	-68 949	23 904	-45 045	-37 637	-82 681
1994	1 302	104 338	-10 859	...	-166 192	69 153	-97 039	16 694	-80 345	-38 260	-118 605
1995	59 637	30 176	-4 223	...	-173 729	77 782	-95 947	20 547	-75 400	-34 057	-109 457
1996	39 404	16 478	-35 158	...	-191 270	89 157	-102 113	18 876	-83 237	-40 081	-123 318
1997	113 921	149 026	-127 832	...	-196 665	90 733	-105 932	6 186	-99 746	-40 794	-140 540
1998	-7 001	39 769	69 702	...	-246 854	79 956	-166 898	-6 211	-173 109	-44 029	-217 138
1999	34 298	67 403	11 602	...	-345 559	80 588	-264 971	-18 483	-283 454	-48 025	-331 479
1991											
1st quarter	-586	-15 274	-9 241	4 665	-18 796	8 090	-10 706	8 107	-2 599	15 004	12 405
2nd quarter	-2 549	-23 771	-17 461	104	-16 176	11 085	-5 091	5 276	185	3 780	3 965
3rd quarter	4 761	12 661	-8 048	-6 032	-19 747	12 660	-7 087	4 397	-2 690	-2 812	-5 502
4th quarter	-4 741	30 378	-13 804	1 266	-19 349	13 967	-5 382	6 350	968	-5 224	-4 256
1992											
1st quarter	5 689	-4 239	-15 210	4 424	-17 940	14 743	-3 197	6 149	2 952	-7 545	-4 593
2nd quarter	3 954	-2 243	-22 500	451	-24 252	14 993	-9 259	5 997	-3 262	-8 418	-11 680
3rd quarter	4 854	21 702	-8 466	-6 232	-27 294	16 260	-11 034	5 265	-5 769	-7 837	-13 606
4th quarter	-924	996	-2 959	1 363	-26 620	14 443	-12 177	5 542	-6 635	-11 214	-17 849
1993											
1st quarter	-215	-19 740	10 199	5 522	-29 207	16 292	-12 915	7 472	-5 443	-7 905	-13 348
2nd quarter	6 531	2 842	6 637	59	-33 386	16 147	-17 239	5 836	-11 403	-8 576	-19 979
3rd quarter	288	27 205	-10 398	-6 249	-36 497	16 192	-20 305	7 240	-13 065	-9 339	-22 404
4th quarter	3 885	14 756	-5 154	671	-33 519	15 027	-18 492	3 354	-15 138	-11 816	-26 954
1994											
1st quarter	5 856	31 491	-27 227	3 921	-36 627	16 088	-20 539	5 045	-15 494	-7 971	-23 465
2nd quarter	4 269	25 797	14 709	-208	-40 827	17 488	-23 339	4 046	-19 293	-8 482	-27 775
3rd quarter	-1 620	26 737	-18 231	-6 807	-44 348	17 498	-26 850	3 812	-23 038	-9 610	-32 648
4th quarter	-7 203	20 313	19 888	3 092	-44 390	18 080	-26 310	3 791	-22 519	-12 194	-34 713
1995											
1st quarter	17 764	1 461	-8 833	4 742	-44 077	17 670	-26 407	5 371	-21 036	-8 577	-29 613
2nd quarter	11 864	15 136	21 022	357	-48 436	17 929	-30 507	6 347	-24 160	-8 080	-32 240
3rd quarter	13 493	-16 605	-50 232	-7 545	-42 168	20 768	-21 400	2 873	-18 527	-8 460	-26 987
4th quarter	16 516	30 184	33 822	2 448	-39 048	21 410	-17 638	5 956	-11 682	-8 939	-20 621
1996											
1st quarter	-557	-33 386	14 683	5 000	-42 600	20 857	-21 743	6 982	-14 761	-10 519	-25 280
2nd quarter	16 367	2 259	-12 784	-676	-48 151	22 346	-25 805	4 671	-21 134	-8 744	-29 878
3rd quarter	25 629	3 072	-20 056	-9 258	-51 205	20 430	-30 775	3 063	-27 712	-8 940	-36 652
4th quarter	-2 035	44 533	-16 996	4 939	-49 314	25 519	-23 795	4 158	-19 637	-11 878	-31 515
1997											
1st quarter	28 049	20 534	3 565	5 563	-49 483	22 436	-27 047	1 725	-25 322	-9 054	-34 376
2nd quarter	6 231	32 726	-28 192	-1 760	-47 270	23 695	-23 575	2 870	-20 705	-9 280	-29 985
3rd quarter	24 013	5 081	-30 767	-11 491	-48 157	22 877	-25 280	1 434	-23 846	-9 561	-33 407
4th quarter	55 628	90 685	-72 436	7 690	-51 755	21 726	-30 029	159	-29 870	-12 902	-42 772
1998											
1st quarter	27 863	-48 942	24 288	5 720	-54 646	21 033	-33 613	1 017	-32 596	-9 794	-42 390
2nd quarter	24 919	33 868	25 850	-1 578	-62 621	21 013	-41 608	232	-41 376	-10 099	-51 475
3rd quarter	1 161	75 314	31 391	-11 014	-64 564	18 230	-46 334	-4 317	-50 651	-10 658	-61 309
4th quarter	-60 944	-20 471	-11 827	6 872	-65 023	19 675	-45 348	-3 143	-48 491	-13 474	-61 965
1999											
1st quarter	27 928	-13 951	-14 755	5 514	-73 024	20 348	-52 676	-3 120	-55 796	-10 831	-66 627
2nd quarter	13 663	37 151	-22 349	-1 511	-83 984	20 684	-63 300	-4 145	-67 445	-11 537	-78 982
3rd quarter	-8 085	24 585	18 177	-9 739	-92 318	19 600	-72 718	-5 535	-78 253	-11 396	-89 649
4th quarter	792	19 618	30 531	5 738	-96 233	19 953	-76 280	-5 683	-81 963	-14 260	-96 223

1. A minus sign indicates financial outflows or decrease in foreign official assets in the United States.
2. Sum of credits and debits with the sign reversed.

Table 11-2. International Investment Position of the United States at Year End

(Millions of dollars.)

Year	U.S. net international investment position		U.S.-owned assets abroad									
	Direct investment at current cost	Direct investment at market value	Total, direct investment at current cost	Total, direct investment at market value	Official reserve assets	Other U.S. government assets	Direct investment — Current cost	Direct investment — Market value	Foreign bonds	Foreign corporate stocks	U.S. nonbank claims	U.S. bank claims
1976	164 832	...	456 964	...	44 094	44 978	222 283	...	34 704	9 453	20 317	81 135
1977	171 440	...	512 278	...	53 376	48 567	246 078	...	39 329	10 110	22 256	92 562
1978	206 423	...	621 227	...	69 450	53 187	285 005	...	42 148	11 236	29 385	130 816
1979	316 926	...	786 701	...	143 260	58 851	336 301	...	41 966	14 803	34 491	157 029
1980	360 838	...	929 806	...	171 412	65 573	388 072	...	43 524	18 930	38 429	203 866
1981	339 767	...	1 001 667	...	124 568	70 893	407 804	...	45 675	16 467	42 752	293 508
1982	328 954	235 947	1 108 436	961 015	143 445	76 903	374 059	226 638	56 604	17 442	35 405	404 578
1983	298 304	257 393	1 210 974	1 129 673	123 110	81 664	355 643	274 342	58 569	26 154	131 329	434 505
1984	160 695	134 088	1 204 900	1 127 132	105 040	86 945	348 342	270 574	62 810	25 994	130 138	445 631
1985	54 343	96 886	1 287 396	1 302 712	117 930	89 792	371 036	386 352	75 020	44 383	141 872	447 363
1986	-36 209	100 782	1 469 396	1 594 652	139 875	91 850	404 818	530 074	85 724	72 399	167 392	507 338
1987	-80 007	50 529	1 646 527	1 758 711	162 370	90 681	478 062	590 246	93 889	94 700	177 368	549 457
1988	-178 470	10 466	1 829 665	2 008 365	144 179	87 892	513 761	692 461	104 187	128 662	197 757	653 227
1989	-259 506	-46 987	2 070 868	2 350 235	168 714	86 643	553 093	832 460	116 949	197 345	234 307	713 817
1990	-245 347	-164 495	2 178 978	2 294 085	174 664	84 344	616 655	731 762	144 717	197 596	265 315	695 687
1991	-309 259	-260 819	2 286 456	2 470 629	159 223	81 422	643 364	827 537	176 774	278 976	256 295	690 402
1992	-431 198	-452 305	2 331 696	2 466 496	147 435	83 022	663 830	798 630	200 817	314 266	254 303	668 023
1993	-306 956	-178 020	2 753 648	3 057 669	164 945	83 382	723 526	1 027 547	309 666	543 862	242 022	686 245
1994	-311 872	-170 505	2 998 633	3 279 871	163 394	83 908	786 565	1 067 803	321 208	627 460	322 980	693 118
1995	-514 637	-418 648	3 451 983	3 873 632	176 061	85 064	885 506	1 307 155	392 827	776 809	367 567	768 149
1996	-596 554	-542 751	4 008 872	4 548 579	160 739	86 123	986 536	1 526 243	465 057	1 002 928	449 978	857 511
1997	-970 503	-1 065 480	4 557 945	5 277 399	134 836	86 198	1 058 735	1 778 189	543 396	1 207 787	544 891	982 102
1998	-1 111 806	-1 407 663	5 079 063	6 045 551	146 006	86 768	1 207 059	2 173 547	576 745	1 476 184	565 473	1 020 828
1999	-1 082 508	-1 473 685	5 889 028	7 173 373	136 418	84 226	1 331 187	2 615 532	556 748	2 026 638	643 747	1 110 064

Year	Foreign-owned assets in the United States										
	Total, direct investment at current cost	Total, direct investment at market value	Foreign official assets	Direct investment in the U.S. — Current cost	Direct investment in the U.S. — Market value	U.S. Treasury securities	U.S. currency	Corporate and other bonds	Corporate stocks	U.S. nonbank liabilities	U.S. bank liabilities
1976	292 132	...	104 445	47 528	...	7 028	11 792	11 964	42 949	12 961	53 465
1977	340 838	...	140 867	55 413	...	7 562	13 656	11 456	39 779	11 921	60 184
1978	414 804	...	173 057	68 976	...	8 910	16 569	11 457	42 097	16 019	77 719
1979	469 775	...	159 852	88 579	...	14 210	19 552	10 269	48 318	18 669	110 326
1980	568 968	...	176 062	127 105	...	16 113	24 079	9 545	64 569	30 426	121 069
1981	661 900	...	180 425	164 623	...	18 505	27 295	10 694	64 391	30 606	165 361
1982	779 482	725 068	189 109	184 842	130 428	25 758	31 265	16 709	76 279	27 532	227 988
1983	912 670	872 280	194 468	193 708	153 318	33 846	36 776	17 454	96 357	61 731	278 330
1984	1 044 205	993 044	199 678	223 538	172 377	62 121	40 797	32 421	96 056	77 415	312 179
1985	1 233 053	1 205 826	202 482	247 223	219 996	87 954	46 036	82 290	125 578	86 993	354 497
1986	1 505 605	1 493 870	241 226	284 701	272 966	96 078	50 122	140 863	168 940	90 703	432 972
1987	1 726 534	1 708 182	283 058	334 552	316 200	82 588	55 584	166 089	175 643	110 187	518 833
1988	2 008 135	1 997 899	322 036	401 766	391 530	100 877	61 261	191 314	200 978	144 548	585 355
1989	2 330 374	2 397 222	341 746	467 886	534 734	166 541	67 118	231 673	251 191	167 093	637 126
1990	2 424 325	2 458 580	373 293	505 346	539 601	152 452	85 933	238 903	221 741	213 406	633 251
1991	2 595 715	2 731 448	398 538	533 404	669 137	170 295	101 317	274 136	271 872	208 908	637 245
1992	2 762 894	2 918 801	437 263	540 270	696 177	197 739	114 804	299 287	300 160	220 666	652 705
1993	3 060 604	3 235 689	509 422	593 313	768 398	221 501	133 734	355 822	340 627	229 038	677 147
1994	3 310 505	3 450 376	535 217	617 982	757 853	235 684	157 185	368 077	371 618	239 817	784 925
1995	3 966 620	4 292 280	671 710	680 066	1 005 726	358 537	169 484	481 214	490 142	300 424	815 043
1996	4 605 426	5 091 330	798 368	743 214	1 229 118	502 562	186 846	588 044	611 417	346 727	828 248
1997	5 528 448	6 342 879	835 800	825 334	1 639 765	662 228	211 628	715 196	863 498	443 789	970 975
1998	6 190 869	7 453 214	837 701	928 645	2 190 990	729 738	228 250	902 155	1 110 276	437 973	1 016 131
1999	6 971 536	8 647 058	869 334	1 125 214	2 800 736	660 722	250 657	1 063 730	1 445 592	473 825	1 082 462

Table 11-3. U.S. Exports and Imports of Goods and Services

(Balance of payments basis; millions of dollars, seasonally adjusted.)

Year and month	Goods and services			Goods			Services		
	Exports	Imports	Balance	Exports	Imports	Balance	Exports	Imports	Balance
1970	56 640	54 386	2 254	42 469	39 866	2 603	14 171	14 520	-349
1971	59 677	60 979	-1 302	43 319	45 579	-2 260	16 358	15 400	958
1972	67 222	72 665	-5 443	49 381	55 797	-6 416	17 841	16 868	973
1973	91 242	89 342	1 900	71 410	70 499	911	19 832	18 843	989
1974	120 897	125 190	-4 293	98 306	103 811	-5 505	22 591	21 379	1 212
1975	132 585	120 181	12 404	107 088	98 185	8 903	25 497	21 996	3 501
1976	142 716	148 798	-6 082	114 745	124 228	-9 483	27 971	24 570	3 401
1977	152 301	179 547	-27 246	120 816	151 907	-31 091	31 485	27 640	3 845
1978	178 428	208 191	-29 763	142 075	176 002	-33 927	36 353	32 189	4 164
1979	224 131	248 696	-24 565	184 439	212 007	-27 568	39 692	36 689	3 003
1980	271 834	291 241	-19 407	224 250	249 750	-25 500	47 584	41 491	6 093
1981	294 398	310 570	-16 172	237 044	265 067	-28 023	57 354	45 503	11 851
1982	275 236	299 391	-24 156	211 157	247 642	-36 485	64 079	51 749	12 330
1983	266 106	323 874	-57 767	201 799	268 901	-67 102	64 307	54 973	9 334
1984	291 094	400 166	-109 073	219 926	332 418	-112 492	71 168	67 748	3 420
1985	289 070	410 950	-121 880	215 915	338 088	-122 173	73 155	72 862	293
1986	309 694	450 260	-140 566	223 344	368 425	-145 081	86 350	81 835	4 515
1987	348 801	502 114	-153 313	250 208	409 765	-159 557	98 593	92 349	6 244
1988	431 298	547 154	-115 856	320 230	447 189	-126 959	111 068	99 965	11 103
1989	489 353	581 550	-92 197	362 120	477 365	-115 245	127 233	104 185	23 048
1990	537 229	618 358	-81 129	389 307	498 337	-109 030	147 922	120 021	27 901
1991	581 246	612 177	-30 931	416 913	490 981	-74 068	164 333	121 196	43 137
1992	617 268	652 934	-35 666	440 352	536 458	-96 106	176 916	116 476	60 440
1993	642 773	711 722	-68 949	456 832	589 441	-132 609	185 941	122 281	63 660
1994	703 429	800 468	-97 039	502 398	668 590	-166 192	201 031	131 878	69 153
1995	795 074	891 021	-98 947	575 845	749 574	-173 729	219 229	141 447	77 782
1996	852 064	954 177	-102 113	612 057	803 327	-191 270	240 007	150 850	89 157
1997	936 937	1 042 869	-105 931	679 702	876 367	-196 664	257 235	166 502	90 733
1998	932 977	1 099 875	-166 897	670 324	917 178	-246 853	262 653	182 697	79 956
1999	956 242	1 221 213	-264 971	684 358	1 029 917	-345 559	271 884	191 296	80 588
1996									
January	68 352	76 184	-7 832	49 579	64 102	-14 523	18 773	12 082	6 691
February	69 796	76 257	-6 462	50 835	63 911	-13 077	18 961	12 346	6 615
March	69 834	77 285	-7 451	50 023	65 025	-15 002	19 811	12 260	7 551
April	69 869	78 396	-8 527	50 502	66 076	-15 574	19 367	12 320	7 047
May	71 040	80 264	-9 223	50 884	67 718	-16 833	20 156	12 546	7 610
June	71 176	79 230	-8 053	51 226	66 969	-15 742	19 950	12 261	7 689
July	69 303	79 636	-10 332	49 883	66 687	-16 803	19 420	12 949	6 471
August	10 893	80 904	-10 011	51 159	68 111	-16 952	19 734	12 793	6 941
September	70 603	81 035	-10 432	50 949	68 399	-17 450	19 654	12 636	7 018
October	73 919	80 639	-6 720	52 407	67 747	-15 340	21 512	12 892	8 620
November	74 455	81 556	-7 101	52 841	68 660	-15 819	21 614	12 896	8 718
December	72 819	82 793	-9 974	51 768	69 923	-18 155	21 051	12 870	8 181
1997									
January	73 047	83 457	-10 410	52 346	70 103	-17 757	20 701	13 354	7 347
February	75 152	83 976	-8 824	54 392	70 565	-16 173	20 760	13 411	7 349
March	77 053	84 866	-7 813	55 932	71 485	-15 553	21 121	13 381	7 740
April	77 858	85 676	-7 818	56 667	72 288	-15 621	21 191	13 388	7 803
May	78 064	86 638	-8 574	56 499	73 039	-16 540	21 565	13 599	7 966
June	79 152	86 335	-7 183	57 448	72 557	-15 109	21 704	13 778	7 926
July	80 647	87 535	-6 888	58 902	73 565	-14 663	21 745	13 970	7 775
August	79 109	87 980	-8 871	57 198	73 875	-16 677	21 911	14 105	7 806
September	79 564	89 084	-9 520	57 858	74 674	-16 816	21 706	14 410	7 296
October	79 609	89 062	-9 453	57 722	74 899	-17 177	21 887	14 163	7 724
November	78 443	88 262	-9 819	56 993	73 833	-16 840	21 450	14 429	7 021
December	79 243	89 999	-10 757	57 746	75 483	-17 738	21 497	14 516	6 981
1998									
January	79 167	89 457	-10 290	57 480	74 926	-17 446	21 687	14 531	7 156
February	77 874	88 640	-10 765	56 416	73 811	-17 394	21 458	14 829	6 629
March	78 695	91 253	-12 558	56 713	76 519	-19 806	21 982	14 734	7 248
April	77 769	91 672	-13 902	55 298	76 586	-21 287	22 471	15 086	7 385
May	77 313	91 758	-14 444	55 205	76 757	-21 551	22 108	15 001	7 107
June	77 269	90 529	-13 260	55 551	75 332	-19 781	21 718	15 197	6 521
July	76 058	90 594	-14 535	54 611	75 235	-20 623	21 447	15 359	6 088
August	75 566	92 166	-16 600	54 083	76 799	-22 716	21 483	15 367	6 116
September	77 248	92 446	-15 198	55 684	76 908	-21 224	21 564	15 538	6 026
October	79 406	94 630	-15 223	57 013	78 684	-21 670	22 393	15 946	6 447
November	78 760	94 256	-15 496	56 720	78 624	-21 904	22 040	15 632	6 408
December	77 849	92 477	-14 628	55 550	76 998	-21 448	22 299	15 479	6 820
1999									
January	77 035	92 981	-15 946	54 966	77 863	-22 897	22 069	15 118	6 951
February	76 240	94 598	-18 358	54 296	79 400	-25 104	21 944	15 198	6 746
March	77 046	95 418	-18 372	54 687	79 710	-25 023	22 359	15 708	6 651
April	77 864	96 821	-18 956	55 403	81 255	-25 851	22 461	15 566	6 895
May	77 753	98 756	-21 003	55 343	83 096	-27 753	22 410	15 660	6 750
June	78 679	102 021	-23 342	55 696	86 077	-30 381	22 983	15 944	7 039
July	79 004	103 744	-24 740	56 385	87 612	-31 227	22 619	16 132	6 487
August	81 108	105 039	-23 931	58 402	88 920	-30 518	22 706	16 119	6 587
September	81 857	105 904	-24 047	59 094	89 667	-30 573	22 763	16 237	6 526
October	82 349	107 259	-24 910	59 193	90 769	-31 576	23 156	16 490	6 666
November	83 198	108 909	-25 712	59 682	92 082	-32 401	23 516	16 827	6 689
December	84 107	109 764	-25 657	61 211	93 466	-32 255	22 896	16 298	6 598

Table 11-4. U.S. Exports of Goods by Selected Countries and Regions

(Census basis, except as noted; millions of dollars, not seasonally adjusted.)

Year and month	Total: Balance of payments basis	Net adjustments	Total: Census basis	Total	Canada	Mexico	Total [2]	Argentina	Brazil	Chile	Colombia	Dominican Republic	Venezuela
1970	42 469	...	...	11 300	9 596	1 704	...	...	841	...	...	...	759
1971	43 319	...	...	12 523	10 903	1 620	...	...	966	...	...	...	787
1972	49 381	...	...	15 052	13 070	1 982	...	...	1 243	...	...	...	924
1973	71 410	...	...	19 083	16 146	2 937	...	...	1 916	...	...	...	1 033
1974	98 306	...	...	26 136	21 281	4 855	...	...	3 088	...	...	...	1 768
1975	107 088	...	...	28 089	22 948	5 141	...	...	3 056	...	...	...	2 243
1976	114 745	...	...	30 667	25 677	4 990	...	...	2 809	...	...	...	2 628
1977	120 816	...	...	32 544	27 738	4 806	...	...	2 490	...	...	...	3 171
1978	142 075	...	...	37 220	30 540	6 680	...	...	2 981	...	...	...	3 728
1979	184 439	...	...	47 446	37 599	9 847	...	...	3 442	...	...	...	3 934
1980	224 250	...	...	55 476	40 331	15 145	...	2 625	4 344	...	1 736	...	4 573
1981	237 044	...	...	62 391	44 602	17 789	...	2 192	3 798	...	1 771	...	5 445
1982	211 157	...	...	49 704	37 887	11 817	...	1 294	3 423	...	1 903	...	5 206
1983	201 799	91	201 708	52 427	43 345	9 082	...	965	2 557	...	1 514	...	2 811
1984	219 926	1 183	218 743	63 769	51 777	11 992	...	900	2 640	...	1 450	...	3 377
1985	215 915	3 294	212 621	66 922	53 287	13 635	...	721	3 140	...	1 468	...	3 399
1986	223 344	-3 127	226 471	67 904	55 512	12 392	...	944	3 885	...	1 319	...	3 141
1987	250 208	-3 696	253 904	74 396	59 814	14 582	...	1 090	4 040	...	1 412	...	3 586
1988	320 230	-3 105	323 335	92 250	71 622	20 628	...	1 054	4 267	...	1 754	...	4 612
1989	362 120	-1 716	363 836	103 791	78 809	24 982	...	1 039	4 804	...	1 924	...	3 025
1990	389 307	-3 617	392 924	112 241	83 866	28 375	...	1 179	5 062	...	2 029	...	3 107
1991	416 913	-4 851	421 764	118 427	85 150	33 277	...	2 045	6 148	1 839	1 952	1 743	4 656
1992	440 352	-7 809	448 161	131 186	90 594	40 592	35 204	3 223	5 751	2 466	3 286	2 100	5 444
1993	456 832	-8 258	465 090	142 025	100 444	41 581	36 842	3 776	6 058	2 599	3 235	2 350	4 590
1994	502 398	-10 228	512 626	165 283	114 439	50 844	41 708	4 462	8 102	2 774	4 064	2 799	4 039
1995	575 845	-8 897	584 742	173 518	127 226	46 292	49 992	4 189	11 439	3 615	4 624	3 015	4 640
1996	612 057	-13 018	625 075	191 002	134 210	56 792	52 599	4 517	12 718	4 140	4 714	3 191	4 750
1997	679 702	-9 480	689 182	223 155	151 767	71 388	63 021	5 810	15 915	4 368	5 197	3 924	6 602
1998	670 324	-11 813	682 138	235 376	156 603	78 773	63 395	5 886	15 142	3 979	4 816	3 944	6 516
1999	684 358	-11 439	695 797	253 509	166 600	86 909	55 153	4 950	13 203	3 078	3 560	4 100	5 354
1996													
January	47 072	-695	47 767	14 578	10 301	4 276	3 773	311	829	287	380	209	332
February	50 322	-791	51 112	15 476	11 212	4 265	3 965	327	858	390	402	247	335
March	54 048	-904	54 952	16 059	11 600	4 459	4 100	346	941	280	373	259	412
April	51 029	-843	51 872	15 858	11 500	4 359	4 015	334	879	309	403	256	376
May	52 230	-1 130	53 359	16 196	11 456	4 740	4 396	383	990	308	407	294	466
June	50 939	-882	51 821	15 881	11 320	4 560	4 404	439	1 116	296	395	237	393
July	46 158	-1 440	47 598	14 214	9 647	4 567	4 463	387	1 033	403	377	271	378
August	50 223	-1 352	51 575	15 765	10 935	4 830	4 614	389	1 239	323	385	297	453
September	49 289	-1 309	50 598	16 623	11 673	4 950	4 447	395	1 203	317	387	262	371
October	55 042	-1 065	56 107	17 747	12 120	5 627	4 905	404	1 238	379	447	306	436
November	53 737	-1 279	55 016	17 261	12 145	5 116	4 773	421	1 244	356	386	305	440
December	51 980	-1 316	53 295	15 344	10 302	5 041	4 745	380	1 147	492	372	247	359
1997													
January	52 346	-558	52 904	16 651	11 733	4 917	4 327	407	1 013	300	382	259	433
February	54 392	-685	55 077	17 431	12 102	5 330	4 360	378	1 049	309	364	311	384
March	55 932	-999	56 931	18 425	13 001	5 425	5 179	448	1 323	442	418	320	483
April	56 667	-698	57 365	19 010	13 289	5 721	5 065	424	1 208	363	470	345	513
May	56 499	-1 001	57 500	18 397	12 977	5 420	5 332	498	1 341	349	476	343	569
June	57 448	-841	58 289	18 419	12 506	5 913	5 278	477	1 335	331	445	329	581
July	58 902	-688	59 590	17 097	11 113	5 984	5 232	430	1 315	334	434	334	603
August	57 198	-1 054	58 251	18 527	12 256	6 271	5 444	545	1 372	339	455	346	623
September	57 858	-748	58 605	19 733	13 407	6 326	5 394	509	1 440	368	403	323	609
October	57 722	-1 043	58 765	21 258	14 093	7 165	6 103	527	1 568	387	508	380	684
November	56 993	-664	57 657	19 485	12 867	6 618	5 769	610	1 485	369	420	323	621
December	57 746	-502	58 247	18 721	12 422	6 299	5 540	558	1 466	478	423	310	500
1998													
January	57 480	-635	58 115	18 352	12 118	6 234	4 944	468	1 123	330	401	262	608
February	56 416	-806	57 223	19 345	12 924	6 421	5 001	425	1 078	311	416	318	609
March	56 713	-881	57 593	21 484	14 573	6 911	5 722	517	1 294	294	496	370	665
April	55 298	-649	55 948	20 317	13 921	6 396	5 336	474	1 217	326	439	321	573
May	55 205	-747	55 952	19 951	13 543	6 408	5 548	496	1 311	515	407	331	624
June	55 551	-897	56 448	19 828	13 379	6 449	5 368	607	1 283	321	471	327	573
July	54 611	-966	55 577	16 659	10 517	6 142	5 409	539	1 205	311	367	375	571
August	54 083	-1 314	55 397	18 305	12 124	6 181	5 262	499	1 296	278	360	355	446
September	55 684	-943	56 627	20 151	13 255	6 896	4 759	462	1 198	352	323	284	426
October	57 013	-1 200	58 213	21 279	14 010	7 269	5 643	524	1 471	303	408	380	528
November	56 720	-1 598	58 318	20 555	13 576	6 979	5 196	434	1 330	250	356	322	488
December	55 550	-1 177	56 727	19 149	12 664	6 486	5 208	443	1 336	389	371	300	405
1999													
January	54 966	-952	55 918	18 155	12 134	6 021	4 508	384	1 107	262	284	320	436
February	54 296	-1 105	55 401	19 064	13 048	6 017	4 312	382	916	249	285	316	489
March	54 687	-1 023	55 710	21 894	14 984	6 910	4 677	385	980	236	310	381	524
April	55 403	-985	56 388	20 775	14 127	6 648	4 556	372	1 072	228	326	353	411
May	55 343	-1 136	56 479	20 809	14 151	6 659	4 570	408	1 084	234	285	361	460
June	55 696	-1 197	56 893	21 636	14 567	7 069	4 584	406	1 068	264	279	338	414
July	56 385	-1 033	57 418	18 640	11 519	7 121	4 483	359	1 091	228	258	340	642
August	58 402	-857	59 259	21 290	13 815	7 475	4 460	414	1 134	259	255	331	385
September	59 094	-1 147	60 241	2 228	14 423	7 805	4 470	512	1 134	226	283	330	356
October	59 193	-850	60 043	23 285	14 824	8 461	5 054	459	1 342	261	327	354	439
November	59 682	-263	59 945	23 301	15 099	8 202	4 737	407	1 217	266	301	340	384
December	61 211	-891	62 102	22 431	13 908	8 523	4 742	463	1 059	366	367	337	414

1. Includes Caribbean.
2. Includes countries not shown separately. See Notes for list of included countries.

Table 11-4. U.S. Exports of Goods by Selected Countries and Regions—*Continued*

(Census basis, except as noted; millions of dollars, not seasonally adjusted.)

Year and month	Total¹	Western Europe — European Union									
		Total¹	Belgium	France	Germany	Ireland	Italy	Nether-lands	Spain	Sweden	United Kingdom
1970	...	...	...	1 483	2 741	...	1 353	...	...	...	2 536
1971	...	...	...	1 373	2 831	...	1 314	...	...	...	2 369
1972	...	...	...	1 609	2 808	...	1 434	...	...	...	2 658
1973	...	...	...	2 263	3 756	...	2 119	...	...	...	3 564
1974	28 639	28 268	...	2 942	4 985	...	2 752	3 979	...	...	4 574
1975	29 939	22 862	...	3 031	5 194	...	2 867	4 183	...	...	4 527
1976	32 401	25 406	...	3 446	5 731	...	3 071	4 645	...	...	4 801
1977	33 752	26 476	...	3 503	5 989	...	2 790	4 796	...	...	5 951
1978	39 936	32 051	...	4 166	6 957	...	3 361	5 683	...	...	7 116
1979	54 331	42 582	...	5 587	8 478	...	4 362	6 907	...	...	10 635
1980	67 512	53 679	...	7 485	10 960	...	5 511	8 669	3 340	1 767	12 694
1981	65 377	52 363	...	7 341	10 277	...	5 360	8 595	3 563	1 842	12 439
1982	60 054	47 932	...	7 110	9 291	...	4 616	8 604	3 590	1 689	10 645
1983	55 980	44 311	...	5 961	8 737	...	3 908	7 767	2 915	1 581	10 621
1984	58 019	46 976	...	6 037	9 084	...	4 375	7 554	2 561	1 542	12 210
1985	56 763	48 994	...	6 096	9 050	...	4 625	7 269	2 524	1 925	11 273
1986	61 642	53 154	...	7 216	10 561	...	4 838	7 848	2 615	1 871	11 418
1987	69 718	60 575	...	7 943	11 748	...	5 530	8 217	3 148	1 894	14 114
1988	87 858	75 755	...	9 970	14 348	...	6 775	10 117	4 215	2 700	18 364
1989	100 165	86 331	...	11 579	16 862	...	7 215	11 364	4 796	3 138	20 837
1990	112 975	98 027	...	13 652	18 693	...	7 987	13 016	5 213	3 405	23 484
1991	118 682	103 123	10 572	15 346	21 302	2 681	8 570	13 511	5 474	3 287	22 046
1992	117 100	102 958	9 775	14 593	21 249	2 862	8 721	13 752	5 537	2 845	22 800
1993	113 681	96 973	8 878	13 267	18 932	2 728	6 464	12 839	4 168	2 354	26 438
1994	118 177	102 818	10 939	13 619	19 229	3 419	7 183	13 582	4 622	2 518	26 900
1995	134 863	123 671	12 466	14 245	22 394	4 109	8 862	16 558	5 526	3 080	28 857
1996	141 543	127 710	12 532	14 455	23 495	3 669	8 797	16 662	5 500	3 431	30 962
1997	155 384	140 773	13 420	15 965	24 458	4 642	8 995	19 827	5 539	3 314	36 425
1998	162 571	149 035	13 918	17 729	26 657	5 647	8 991	18 978	5 454	3 822	39 058
1999	165 952	151 814	12 381	18 877	26 800	6 384	10 091	19 437	6 133	4 251	38 407
1996											
January	10 993	10 208	978	1 204	1 903	334	745	1 249	589	257	2 342
February	11 727	10 729	1 087	1 221	1 932	317	900	1 374	535	276	2 481
March	12 869	11 285	1 048	1 313	2 169	327	807	1 593	502	307	2 613
April	12 590	11 367	1 004	1 252	1 964	342	871	1 231	428	268	3 346
May	12 771	11 483	1 085	1 154	2 044	332	756	1 340	499	277	3 150
June	11 971	10 613	1 000	1 157	1 927	247	734	1 377	432	251	2 708
July	9 805	8 775	890	953	1 662	225	602	1 025	363	221	2 155
August	11 169	10 042	1 087	1 106	1 853	253	613	1 322	362	254	2 620
September	11 125	9 868	1 051	1 112	1 907	303	614	1 238	373	268	2 360
October	12 620	11 412	1 102	1 346	2 043	336	733	1 826	465	313	2 467
November	12 031	11 013	1 067	1 316	2 086	299	694	1 554	466	379	2 410
December	11 873	10 916	1 134	1 322	2 007	355	730	1 533	484	360	2 310
1997											
January	11 261	10 424	1 099	1 233	1 838	345	684	1 445	498	262	2 466
February	12 928	11 834	1 064	1 213	2 034	325	750	1 659	525	249	3 331
March	15 014	13 210	1 218	1 433	2 300	336	811	1 682	526	315	3 838
April	13 753	12 150	1 070	1 377	2 370	375	842	1 610	457	297	3 124
May	13 513	11 919	1 137	1 314	2 010	427	753	1 760	463	286	3 113
June	13 220	11 533	1 125	1 331	1 964	391	752	1 494	449	250	3 204
July	11 567	10 450	1 010	1 232	1 813	349	690	1 433	374	234	2 749
August	11 824	10 820	1 128	1 233	1 990	385	646	1 513	335	252	2 599
September	12 519	11 605	1 087	1 284	2 007	345	687	1 867	385	272	2 934
October	13 525	12 521	1 176	1 466	2 137	425	811	1 932	544	302	2 906
November	12 627	11 746	1 192	1 391	2 008	466	769	1 669	482	287	2 841
December	13 634	12 563	1 115	1 460	1 989	473	800	1 764	501	309	3 320
1998											
January	13 042	12 054	1 208	1 501	1 980	519	813	1 707	537	253	2 951
February	13 481	12 616	1 240	1 478	2 139	462	758	1 679	461	289	3 313
March	15 305	14 164	1 392	1 722	2 329	478	822	1 749	503	340	3 964
April	13 041	11 957	1 179	1 544	2 193	500	732	1 452	475	291	2 981
May	13 740	12 682	1 123	1 521	2 148	484	690	1 468	423	330	3 749
June	13 496	12 431	1 197	1 368	2 291	497	751	1 580	436	279	3 256
July	12 042	11 030	1 084	1 243	2 047	382	693	1 417	366	238	2 752
August	12 915	11 805	1 165	1 267	2 033	419	604	1 557	350	268	3 361
September	13 481	12 457	1 106	1 379	2 264	421	743	1 378	400	404	3 594
October	14 566	12 964	1 132	1 542	2 559	500	830	1 583	495	430	3 230
November	13 707	12 234	1 029	1 438	2 217	468	765	1 738	518	419	3 003
December	13 755	12 641	1 062	1 725	2 458	517	791	1 671	490	282	2 906
1999											
January	13 161	12 302	949	1 709	1 989	572	739	1 505	473	331	3 268
February	13 583	12 643	1 121	1 605	2 171	485	734	1 647	481	368	3 312
March	15 187	14 119	1 197	1 768	2 793	643	819	1 673	472	318	3 352
April	14 161	12 806	1 097	1 530	2 337	460	1 063	1 545	422	395	3 216
May	13 664	12 692	1 084	1 678	2 192	446	762	1 534	652	401	3 295
June	13 340	12 163	966	1 614	2 079	544	766	1 618	477	357	3 110
July	12 101	11 214	862	1 275	1 966	427	882	1 356	336	316	3 077
August	13 104	12 014	939	1 298	2 163	576	691	1 687	396	327	3 270
September	13 634	12 185	994	1 457	2 009	551	771	1 651	449	352	2 999
October	14 676	13 446	1 111	1 651	2 535	568	1 063	1 661	468	354	3 297
November	14 327	12 822	1 002	1 373	2 209	537	816	1 761	784	388	3 168
December	15 015	13 410	1 059	1 920	2 357	574	985	1 800	725	345	3 043

1. Includes countries not shown separately. See Notes for list of included countries.

Table 11-4. U.S. Exports of Goods by Selected Countries and Regions—*Continued*

(Census basis, except as noted; millions of dollars, not seasonally adjusted.)

Year and month	Western Europe—*Continued* European Free Trade Association			Eastern Europe and former Soviet Republics					Near and Middle Eastern countries		
	Total[1]	Norway	Switzerland	Total[1]	Hungary	Poland	Former Soviet Republics Total[1]	Russia	Israel	Saudi Arabia	Turkey
1970	...	...	...	...	...	...	119	...	...	...	...
1971	...	...	...	...	...	...	161	...	...	...	...
1972	...	...	...	...	...	...	542	...	...	...	...
1973	...	...	...	...	...	...	1 194	...	...	...	...
1974	...	...	...	1 432	...	...	609	...	...	835	...
1975	...	...	...	2 788	...	...	1 835	...	...	1 502	...
1976	...	...	...	3 502	...	...	2 310	...	...	2 774	...
1977	...	...	...	2 544	...	...	1 628	...	...	3 575	...
1978	...	...	...	3 679	...	...	2 252	...	...	4 370	...
1979	...	...	...	5 683	...	...	3 607	...	...	4 875	...
1980	...	843	3 781	3 860	80	714	1 513	...	...	5 769	...
1981	...	892	3 022	4 338	78	681	2 431	...	...	7 327	...
1982	...	950	2 707	3 610	68	295	2 587	...	...	9 026	...
1983	...	813	2 960	2 891	110	324	2 003	...	...	7 903	...
1984	...	859	2 562	4 188	88	318	3 284	...	...	5 564	...
1985	...	666	2 288	3 215	94	238	2 423	...	...	4 474	...
1986	...	937	2 976	1 989	98	151	1 248	...	...	3 449	...
1987	...	842	3 151	2 200	95	239	1 480	...	...	3 373	...
1988	...	929	4 196	3 650	76	304	2 769	...	...	3 776	...
1989	...	1 037	4 911	5 307	122	413	4 284	...	...	3 574	...
1990	...	1 281	4 943	4 263	156	406	3 088	...	...	4 035	...
1991	12 507	1 489	5 557	4 787	256	459	3 578	...	3 911	6 557	2 468
1992	10 837	1 279	4 540	4 069	295	641	2 764	2 112	4 077	7 167	2 735
1993	12 704	1 212	6 806	6 104	435	912	3 984	2 970	4 429	6 661	3 429
1994	11 975	1 267	5 624	5 301	309	625	3 562	2 578	4 996	6 013	2 752
1995	7 706	1 293	6 227	5 701	295	776	3 807	2 823	5 621	6 155	2 768
1996	10 198	1 559	8 373	7 267	331	968	5 078	3 346	6 012	7 311	2 847
1997	10 220	1 721	8 307	7 889	486	1 170	5 191	3 365	5 995	8 438	3 540
1998	9 201	1 709	7 247	12 367	483	882	4 930	3 553	6 983	10 520	3 506
1999	10 117	1 439	8 371	9 394	504	826	3 511	2 060	7 691	7 912	3 217
1996											
January	513	106	393	491	25	69	323	243	443	428	219
February	650	126	509	757	31	63	596	355	531	501	266
March	1 258	137	1 044	620	28	78	448	330	540	732	257
April	903	118	769	590	29	73	401	277	475	565	257
May	997	113	867	544	25	94	363	273	524	561	227
June	1 072	146	908	498	25	65	328	238	554	449	202
July	795	125	653	504	23	98	316	232	448	787	192
August	817	125	670	743	24	69	575	323	486	734	251
September	911	100	792	532	27	81	360	248	424	609	271
October	946	156	774	666	26	80	488	282	488	658	195
November	720	191	510	748	42	120	491	272	574	710	236
December	617	118	484	573	27	78	389	272	524	578	274
1997											
January	516	113	387	524	33	63	377	234	464	439	241
February	726	141	571	509	39	68	331	222	458	510	261
March	1 356	208	1 128	774	47	77	480	262	564	795	381
April	1 296	199	1 079	738	43	127	468	325	514	560	257
May	1 108	175	916	715	39	163	398	259	498	640	421
June	1 287	114	1 156	717	48	184	407	245	532	529	335
July	745	138	589	536	35	67	377	264	462	563	284
August	669	140	513	640	27	88	447	255	503	513	288
September	618	111	495	646	39	82	453	309	407	749	239
October	650	122	514	742	40	93	519	294	479	550	287
November	538	112	412	765	47	83	547	445	455	587	263
December	710	149	548	584	50	77	388	251	661	2 003	284
1998											
January	664	139	448	878	35	80	341	247	570	944	254
February	559	122	422	908	43	78	362	257	698	831	235
March	622	151	455	1 599	40	89	678	557	574	960	415
April	741	164	561	1 129	47	71	423	297	516	767	242
May	735	141	577	1 256	36	73	495	363	511	674	261
June	623	122	488	1 465	40	69	634	460	680	823	382
July	640	103	520	1 216	42	76	507	345	519	628	315
August	792	147	630	970	41	60	403	288	564	656	266
September	787	167	606	591	34	59	212	109	546	897	171
October	1 123	142	965	878	41	75	337	246	557	779	419
November	1 101	165	922	796	41	88	290	209	583	1 651	316
December	813	146	654	683	42	64	250	176	666	909	232
1999											
January	636	106	515	436	36	66	141	78	665	598	167
February	690	104	571	571	38	60	178	89	748	820	192
March	669	150	505	737	41	75	216	111	603	1 078	321
April	950	141	730	982	64	71	385	113	662	523	337
May	617	135	463	650	40	65	222	126	696	587	292
June	701	125	559	590	42	57	208	114	725	388	415
July	592	100	474	698	33	75	255	145	568	627	218
August	802	135	635	771	37	57	308	197	581	475	226
September	1 174	94	1 060	1 496	43	65	654	487	577	385	217
October	899	119	749	955	38	70	385	297	548	465	233
November	1 116	106	993	714	50	92	255	162	581	410	321
December	1 273	125	1 119	793	41	74	305	142	737	1 557	279

1. Includes countries not shown separately. See Notes for list of included countries.

Table 11-4. U.S. Exports of Goods by Selected Countries and Regions—*Continued*

(Census basis, except as noted; millions of dollars, not seasonally adjusted.)

Year and month	Selected Asian and Oceanic countries											
	Australia	China	Hong Kong	India	Indonesia	Japan	South Korea	Malaysia	Philippines	Singapore	Thailand	Taiwan
1970	. . .	. . .	. . .	. . .	. . .	4 652	. . .	. . .	. . .	. . .	. . .	. . .
1971	. . .	. . .	. . .	. . .	. . .	4 055	. . .	. . .	. . .	. . .	. . .	. . .
1972	. . .	. . .	. . .	. . .	. . .	4 963	. . .	. . .	. . .	. . .	. . .	. . .
1973	. . .	. . .	. . .	. . .	. . .	8 313	. . .	. . .	. . .	. . .	. . .	. . .
1974	2 157	807	882	. . .	. . .	10 679	. . .	. . .	. . .	988	. . .	1 427
1975	1 816	304	808	. . .	. . .	9 563	. . .	. . .	. . .	994	. . .	1 660
1976	2 185	135	1 115	. . .	. . .	10 145	. . .	. . .	. . .	965	. . .	1 635
1977	2 356	171	1 292	. . .	. . .	10 529	. . .	. . .	. . .	1 172	. . .	1 798
1978	2 910	824	1 625	. . .	. . .	12 885	. . .	. . .	. . .	1 462	. . .	2 340
1979	3 617	1 724	2 083	. . .	. . .	17 581	. . .	. . .	. . .	2 331	. . .	3 271
1980	4 093	3 755	2 686	. . .	1 545	20 790	. . .	. . .	. . .	3 033	. . .	4 337
1981	5 242	3 603	2 635	. . .	1 302	21 823	. . .	. . .	. . .	3 003	. . .	4 305
1982	4 535	2 912	2 453	. . .	2 025	20 966	. . .	. . .	. . .	3 214	. . .	4 367
1983	3 954	2 173	2 564	. . .	1 466	21 894	. . .	. . .	. . .	3 759	. . .	4 667
1984	4 793	3 004	3 062	. . .	1 216	23 575	. . .	. . .	. . .	3 675	. . .	5 003
1985	5 441	3 856	2 786	. . .	795	22 631	5 956	. . .	. . .	3 476	. . .	4 700
1986	5 551	3 106	3 030	. . .	946	26 882	6 355	. . .	. . .	3 380	. . .	5 524
1987	5 495	3 497	3 983	. . .	767	28 249	8 099	. . .	. . .	4 053	. . .	7 413
1988	6 973	5 021	5 687	. . .	1 059	37 725	11 232	. . .	. . .	5 768	. . .	12 129
1989	8 331	5 755	6 246	. . .	1 247	44 494	13 478	. . .	. . .	7 345	. . .	11 335
1990	8 535	4 807	6 841	. . .	1 897	48 585	14 399	. . .	. . .	8 019	. . .	11 482
1991	8 404	6 278	8 137	1 999	1 891	48 125	15 505	3 900	2 265	8 804	3 753	13 182
1992	8 876	7 418	9 077	1 917	2 779	47 813	14 639	4 363	2 759	9 626	3 989	15 250
1993	8 277	8 763	9 874	2 778	2 770	47 892	14 782	6 064	3 529	11 678	3 766	16 168
1994	9 781	9 282	11 441	2 294	2 809	53 488	18 025	6 969	3 886	13 020	4 865	17 109
1995	10 789	11 754	14 232	3 296	3 360	64 343	25 380	8 816	5 295	15 333	6 665	19 290
1996	12 008	11 993	13 966	3 328	3 977	67 607	26 621	8 546	6 142	16 720	7 198	18 460
1997	12 063	12 862	15 117	3 608	4 522	65 549	25 046	10 780	7 417	17 696	7 349	20 366
1998	11 918	14 241	12 925	3 564	2 299	57 831	16 486	8 957	6 737	15 694	5 239	18 165
1999	11 818	13 111	12 652	3 688	2 038	57 466	22 958	9 060	7 222	16 247	4 985	19 131
1996												
January	1 013	929	996	250	336	5 222	1 925	832	469	1 276	527	1 571
February	966	1 147	970	252	307	5 875	2 067	665	455	1 439	710	1 341
March	1 076	1 093	1 192	298	350	6 412	2 567	765	496	1 713	565	1 606
April	952	841	1 126	242	386	5 440	2 144	687	617	1 340	678	1 613
May	1 099	882	1 267	257	290	5 903	2 195	693	518	1 349	535	1 719
June	946	772	1 228	229	327	5 644	2 260	649	467	1 540	664	1 432
July	950	998	997	259	281	5 432	2 053	677	460	1 437	505	1 440
August	1 062	778	1 215	250	281	5 741	2 419	605	503	1 335	524	1 400
September	957	753	1 129	273	240	5 359	2 025	580	475	1 250	480	1 422
October	1 025	928	1 392	387	311	5 810	2 221	868	569	1 309	670	1 484
November	1 019	1 586	1 197	390	339	5 372	2 269	792	575	1 393	467	1 612
December	943	1 286	1 257	240	531	5 398	2 476	733	539	1 341	873	1 821
1997												
January	873	938	1 054	250	310	5 073	1 986	725	557	1 497	583	1 444
February	882	913	1 092	285	361	5 435	1 986	706	563	1 207	602	1 429
March	1 094	1 022	1 351	395	360	6 184	2 482	821	679	1 673	639	1 770
April	880	965	1 306	309	329	5 389	2 460	968	672	1 350	674	1 541
May	1 008	1 057	1 307	327	493	5 655	2 403	1 142	618	1 536	566	1 565
June	1 258	920	1 339	283	409	5 775	2 239	947	675	1 437	558	1 735
July	1 029	1 097	1 244	261	358	5 409	2 342	941	607	1 559	539	1 790
August	1 053	938	1 344	367	327	5 519	1 916	832	620	1 674	589	1 750
September	1 044	1 040	1 231	296	323	5 038	1 707	861	578	1 527	751	1 608
October	1 009	1 439	1 289	280	361	5 424	2 069	1 200	649	1 432	677	1 856
November	965	1 301	1 250	287	422	5 433	1 822	800	607	1 391	648	1 685
December	968	1 233	1 310	269	470	5 216	1 634	837	593	1 416	523	2 193
1998												
January	927	1 271	1 025	241	283	5 161	1 089	903	583	1 203	561	1 655
February	1 093	1 019	1 036	208	163	4 636	1 127	654	579	1 359	410	1 597
March	1 133	1 034	1 147	322	159	5 228	1 289	972	573	1 378	464	1 636
April	963	985	1 072	277	161	4 869	1 395	992	574	1 177	420	1 509
May	975	911	1 240	273	133	4 753	1 238	813	543	1 248	383	1 445
June	939	1 283	1 115	311	168	4 756	1 190	640	566	1 412	363	1 326
July	990	1 101	934	275	181	4 968	1 211	729	565	1 346	356	1 288
August	1 060	870	991	325	155	4 770	1 219	595	540	1 306	328	1 335
September	901	1 215	1 198	371	153	4 572	1 299	609	530	1 337	345	1 320
October	1 082	1 855	1 051	267	178	4 965	1 504	787	598	1 207	380	1 660
November	948	1 317	1 009	221	148	4 499	1 542	615	523	1 177	370	1 711
December	907	1 380	1 108	473	418	4 656	2 383	649	564	1 545	859	1 683
1999												
January	829	781	889	331	126	4 624	1 544	651	571	1 475	329	1 444
February	807	924	889	233	114	4 836	1 416	636	549	1 102	327	1 216
March	922	1 076	1 218	364	166	5 294	1 910	676	607	1 321	383	1 457
April	881	1 035	978	280	164	4 785	2 089	686	595	1 219	341	1 502
May	929	1 114	1 000	249	163	4 271	1 819	736	566	1 222	513	1 620
June	992	1 442	1 039	350	215	4 536	1 963	854	609	1 311	380	1 567
July	900	1 074	1 058	316	161	4 444	1 863	862	635	1 303	362	1 667
August	951	1 151	1 050	300	175	4 696	2 251	733	674	1 639	378	1 654
September	1 143	1 325	1 176	369	172	4 650	2 021	763	575	1 495	376	1 527
October	1 379	1 069	1 104	266	202	5 086	1 973	812	616	1 372	579	1 920
November	1 094	1 026	1 057	299	183	5 185	1 810	823	604	1 280	434	1 534
December	991	1 094	1 193	332	198	5 059	2 301	828	622	1 509	582	2 025

Table 11-4. U.S. Exports of Goods by Selected Countries and Regions—*Continued*

(Census basis, except as noted; millions of dollars, not seasonally adjusted.)

Year and month	Selected African countries				Special country groupings [1]					
	Angola	Egypt	Nigeria	South Africa	ASEAN [2]	MERCOSUR [3]	Central American Common Market	Newly industrialized Pacific Rim countries	OPEC [4]	Pacific Rim Countries
1970	...	...	...	563	...	...	...	...	...	...
1971	...	...	...	622	...	...	...	...	...	...
1972	...	...	...	603	...	...	...	...	...	...
1973	...	...	...	746	...	...	...	...	...	...
1974	...	...	286	1 160	...	...	...	...	6 723	...
1975	...	...	536	1 302	...	...	...	...	10 767	...
1976	...	...	770	1 348	...	...	...	...	12 566	...
1977	...	...	958	1 054	...	...	...	...	14 019	...
1978	...	...	985	1 080	...	...	...	...	16 655	...
1979	...	...	632	1 413	...	...	...	...	15 051	...
1980	...	1 874	1 150	2 464	...	...	...	...	17 759	...
1981	...	2 159	1 523	2 912	...	...	...	...	21 533	...
1982	...	2 875	1 295	2 368	...	...	...	...	22 863	...
1983	...	2 813	864	2 129	...	...	...	...	16 905	...
1984	...	2 704	577	2 265	...	...	...	...	14 387	...
1985	...	2 323	676	1 205	...	...	...	16 918	12 480	...
1986	...	1 982	409	1 158	...	...	...	18 289	10 844	...
1987	...	2 210	295	1 281	...	...	...	23 548	11 058	...
1988	...	2 332	357	1 688	...	...	...	34 816	13 994	...
1989	...	2 612	490	1 659	...	...	...	38 404	13 196	...
1990	...	2 249	552	1 732	...	...	...	40 741	13 679	...
1991	186	2 720	831	2 113	20 775	8 783	3 287	45 628	19 054	117 767
1992	158	3 088	1 001	2 434	23 969	9 620	4 300	48 592	21 960	124 451
1993	174	2 768	895	2 188	28 281	10 609	4 777	52 502	19 500	131 595
1994	197	2 855	509	2 174	31 925	13 663	5 351	59 595	17 868	147 779
1995	260	2 985	603	2 751	39 659	17 016	6 023	74 234	19 533	180 552
1996	268	3 153	818	3 112	42 958	18 616	6 362	75 768	22 275	188 243
1997	281	3 835	813	2 997	47 943	23 186	7 463	78 225	25 526	193 740
1998	355	3 059	817	3 628	39 048	22 405	8 402	63 269	25 154	167 367
1999	252	3 001	628	2 586	39 639	19 162	8 455	70 989	20 166	173 774
1996										
January	20	212	68	268	3 453	1 245	487	5 768	1 512	14 719
February	47	294	56	253	3 622	1 283	471	5 816	1 572	15 415
March	19	239	68	275	4 050	1 409	527	7 078	1 944	17 587
April	14	223	60	243	3 795	1 318	497	6 223	1 708	15 388
May	20	201	57	236	3 394	1 498	506	6 530	1 777	16 086
June	17	216	47	286	3 657	1 676	530	6 460	1 886	15 419
July	13	293	75	250	3 370	1 576	534	5 928	2 124	14 882
August	26	320	74	294	3 258	1 734	527	6 368	1 936	15 524
September	17	269	79	285	3 029	1 708	555	5 826	1 801	14 343
October	32	231	67	257	3 733	1 757	591	6 406	2 027	16 084
November	22	287	122	222	3 571	1 779	594	6 471	1 950	16 320
December	23	370	46	245	4 028	1 631	542	6 896	2 038	16 477
1997										
January	13	288	49	228	3 675	1 544	553	5 980	1 534	14 615
February	28	218	46	227	3 444	1 538	577	5 714	1 623	14 705
March	33	380	71	254	4 181	1 910	618	7 277	2 082	17 595
April	30	199	56	254	3 999	1 754	613	6 657	1 950	16 024
May	21	355	74	262	4 393	1 954	625	6 810	2 286	16 984
June	24	265	58	243	4 035	1 931	642	6 749	1 927	16 996
July	22	479	62	223	4 060	1 865	605	6 935	2 188	16 610
August	22	560	136	277	4 057	2 039	638	6 684	2 074	16 179
September	21	300	72	284	4 051	2 077	598	6 074	2 288	15 132
October	25	254	57	269	4 326	2 233	663	6 647	2 047	17 011
November	21	235	56	219	3 876	2 209	709	6 148	2 101	15 862
December	21	303	78	258	3 848	2 134	621	6 553	3 425	16 028
1998										
January	43	317	65	236	3 538	1 691	633	4 972	2 376	14 291
February	31	195	65	223	3 169	1 586	652	5 119	1 975	13 415
March	22	225	92	275	3 551	1 961	773	5 449	2 476	14 744
April	34	232	48	265	3 329	1 825	742	5 152	1 878	13 831
May	18	163	52	264	3 164	1 895	708	5 170	1 829	13 469
June	20	210	71	444	3 156	1 994	679	5 042	2 107	13 531
July	39	214	63	272	3 182	1 852	677	4 779	1 801	13 449
August	17	319	71	279	2 927	1 915	711	4 851	1 628	13 030
September	38	236	61	254	2 978	1 788	664	5 154	1 829	13 299
October	33	270	104	269	3 154	2 126	744	5 422	2 152	15 219
November	28	362	56	398	2 837	1 884	739	5 439	2 912	13 625
December	32	316	69	450	4 061	1 889	679	6 720	2 191	15 463
1999										
January	24	222	87	194	3 160	1 591	672	5 352	1 534	13 086
February	18	191	56	188	2 739	1 357	713	4 623	1 786	12 637
March	20	290	45	233	3 165	1 442	778	5 906	2 112	14 803
April	22	248	47	194	3 012	1 531	713	5 787	1 423	14 060
May	19	303	40	195	3 206	1 596	717	5 661	1 534	13 577
June	18	253	58	217	3 376	1 565	727	5 880	1 359	14 665
July	24	284	61	214	3 331	1 539	652	5 891	1 767	14 110
August	22	182	48	225	3 604	1 628	670	6 594	1 328	15 124
September	22	236	57	224	3 387	1 726	680	6 218	1 306	15 160
October	20	275	37	257	3 587	1 886	730	6 369	1 458	15 777
November	22	212	41	227	3 329	1 710	727	5 680	1 480	14 774
December	21	305	50	218	3 744	1 591	678	7 028	3 080	16 002

1. See Notes for list of countries included in each group.
2. Association of Southeast Asian Nations.
3. Argentina, Brazil, Paraguay, and Uruguay.
4. Organization of Petroleum Exporting Countries.

Table 11-5. U.S. Imports of Goods by Selected Countries and Regions

(Census basis, except as noted; millions of dollars, not seasonally adjusted.)

Year and month	Total: Balance of payments basis	Net adjust-ments	Total: Census basis	Total	Canada	Mexico	Total [2]	Argentina	Brazil	Chile	Colombia	Dominican Republic	Venezuela
				North America			Central and South America [1]						
1970	39 866	...	...	12 311	11 092	1 219	...	...	670	...	...	...	1 082
1971	45 579	...	...	13 954	12 692	1 262	...	...	762	...	...	...	1 216
1972	55 797	...	...	16 559	14 927	1 632	...	...	942	...	...	...	1 298
1973	70 499	...	...	20 021	17 715	2 306	...	...	1 189	...	...	...	1 787
1974	103 811	...	...	25 314	21 924	3 390	...	...	1 700	...	...	...	4 671
1975	98 185	...	...	24 806	21 747	3 059	...	...	1 464	...	...	...	3 624
1976	124 228	...	...	29 835	26 237	3 598	...	...	1 737	...	...	...	3 574
1977	151 907	...	...	34 293	29 599	4 694	...	...	2 241	...	...	...	4 084
1978	176 002	...	...	39 619	33 525	6 094	...	...	2 826	...	...	...	3 545
1979	212 007	...	...	46 846	38 046	8 800	...	...	3 118	...	...	...	5 166
1980	249 750	...	...	53 975	41 455	12 520	...	741	3 715	...	1 248	...	5 297
1981	265 067	...	...	60 179	46 414	13 765	...	1 125	4 475	...	822	...	5 566
1982	247 642	...	...	62 043	46 477	15 566	...	1 128	4 285	...	801	...	4 768
1983	268 901	7 178	261 723	68 906	52 130	16 776	...	853	4 946	...	970	...	4 938
1984	332 418	1 908	330 510	84 498	66 478	18 020	...	954	7 621	...	1 146	...	6 543
1985	338 088	1 705	336 383	88 138	69 006	19 132	...	1 069	7 526	...	1 331	...	6 537
1986	368 425	2 753	365 672	85 555	68 253	17 302	...	856	6 813	...	1 874	...	5 097
1987	409 765	3 482	406 283	91 356	71 085	20 271	...	1 080	7 865	...	2 232	...	5 579
1988	447 189	5 263	441 926	104 658	81 398	23 260	...	1 436	9 294	...	2 161	...	5 157
1989	477 365	3 718	473 647	115 115	87 953	27 162	...	1 391	8 410	...	2 555	...	6 771
1990	498 337	2 357	495 980	121 544	91 372	30 172	...	1 511	7 976	...	3 168	...	9 446
1991	490 981	2 529	488 452	122 194	91 064	31 130	...	1 287	6 717	1 302	2 736	2 008	8 179
1992	536 458	3 795	532 663	133 841	98 630	35 211	33 531	1 256	7 609	1 388	2 837	2 373	8 181
1993	589 441	8 783	580 658	151 133	111 216	39 917	34 456	1 206	7 479	1 462	3 032	2 672	8 140
1994	668 590	5 334	663 256	177 900	128 406	49 494	38 461	1 725	8 683	1 821	3 171	3 091	8 371
1995	749 574	6 031	743 543	207 033	145 349	61 684	42 255	1 761	8 830	1 931	3 751	3 399	9 721
1996	803 327	8 037	795 289	230 190	155 893	74 297	49 547	2 279	8 773	2 262	4 424	3 575	13 173
1997	876 366	6 662	869 704	254 138	168 201	85 938	53 697	2 228	9 626	2 293	4 737	4 327	13 477
1998	917 178	5 282	911 896	267 885	173 256	94 629	50 266	2 231	10 102	2 453	4 656	4 441	9 181
1999	1 029 917	5 299	1 024 618	308 432	198 711	109 721	58 465	2 598	11 314	2 953	6 259	4 287	11 335
1996													
January	62 184	275	61 910	17 819	12 211	5 607	3 734	195	741	211	301	178	956
February	60 968	388	60 580	17 978	12 396	5 582	3 444	122	633	207	302	275	802
March	64 577	1 213	63 364	18 462	12 761	5 701	3 817	158	686	210	403	277	914
April	66 277	1 613	64 664	19 041	13 047	5 994	4 104	184	716	253	374	290	1 058
May	68 104	1 247	66 857	20 169	13 749	6 420	4 325	206	723	195	350	309	1 223
June	65 070	874	64 196	19 645	13 479	6 166	3 925	207	737	181	335	307	990
July	68 107	425	67 682	17 636	11 595	6 041	4 341	176	729	172	386	354	1 160
August	68 795	770	68 025	19 635	13 163	6 472	4 148	205	859	162	344	328	1 030
September	68 616	307	68 309	19 985	13 488	6 497	4 353	250	732	143	379	306	1 262
October	74 433	315	74 118	20 617	13 501	7 116	4 595	233	706	136	437	356	1 314
November	68 304	289	68 016	20 376	13 773	6 603	4 087	152	747	162	384	284	1 108
December	67 805	235	67 570	18 828	12 729	6 099	4 674	192	764	229	429	313	1 357
1997													
January	67 529	257	67 272	19 954	13 767	6 187	4 317	161	870	259	297	211	1 263
February	65 525	434	65 091	20 092	13 558	6 534	4 235	223	707	222	387	324	960
March	72 068	1 461	70 606	21 106	14 148	6 958	4 414	180	750	221	417	343	1 097
April	72 196	1 026	71 169	21 324	14 227	7 097	4 296	180	815	220	377	377	990
May	72 332	902	71 430	21 526	14 414	7 112	4 682	188	886	186	415	379	1 190
June	72 475	899	71 576	21 004	13 895	7 108	4 459	180	804	157	358	378	1 109
July	75 050	234	74 816	19 478	12 455	7 023	4 744	166	946	173	409	405	1 064
August	73 177	252	72 925	20 916	13 637	7 279	4 502	185	837	188	413	387	1 078
September	77 017	266	76 751	22 261	14 554	7 707	4 677	201	762	171	393	396	1 259
October	81 608	258	81 349	23 503	15 045	8 458	4 711	211	786	161	428	407	1 207
November	72 295	245	72 050	21 783	14 265	7 518	4 098	167	722	140	406	325	1 135
December	75 096	427	74 669	21 192	14 236	6 957	4 562	189	739	197	440	395	1 125
1998													
January	70 805	581	70 224	20 234	13 229	7 006	4 049	207	799	205	447	204	918
February	68 621	228	68 394	20 926	13 967	6 960	3 968	168	702	219	361	357	793
March	78 606	511	78 096	23 718	15 392	8 326	4 218	184	780	245	371	397	769
April	76 068	325	75 744	22 794	14 981	7 813	4 165	225	839	236	372	388	783
May	74 289	291	73 998	22 712	14 769	7 943	4 205	186	873	186	375	387	806
June	77 276	358	76 918	22 353	14 371	7 983	4 350	186	936	181	372	411	758
July	76 698	361	76 337	19 612	12 266	7 346	4 336	178	913	180	368	432	757
August	76 712	699	76 014	21 714	13 753	7 961	4 190	176	901	177	375	387	726
September	78 983	549	78 434	23 493	15 158	8 335	4 149	168	869	199	384	359	710
October	84 303	592	83 712	24 694	15 714	8 980	4 394	190	855	183	428	399	817
November	78 541	522	78 020	23 390	15 190	8 200	4 042	166	788	217	386	365	736
December	76 274	267	76 007	22 245	14 467	7 779	4 200	198	848	224	417	354	610
1999													
January	71 937	171	71 766	21 993	14 550	7 443	3 883	199	768	282	438	182	644
February	74 062	213	73 849	23 225	15 295	7 930	3 993	168	756	259	363	336	575
March	84 299	226	84 072	26 404	17 100	9 304	4 507	235	860	304	452	402	626
April	80 251	271	79 980	24 551	16 121	8 431	4 545	193	895	265	426	367	862
May	81 178	213	80 965	25 284	16 344	8 940	4 640	202	933	193	511	339	925
June	88 157	277	87 880	26 682	17 132	9 550	4 826	207	1 053	216	487	397	839
July	86 972	197	86 775	23 793	14 632	9 161	5 101	228	963	208	547	382	1 066
August	90 338	589	89 749	26 909	17 237	9 672	5 384	242	1 066	205	602	386	1 134
September	91 197	953	90 244	27 168	17 325	9 844	5 407	210	1 042	237	578	394	1 188
October	94 974	514	94 460	27 806	17 787	10 019	5 355	217	1 000	294	609	364	1 111
November	94 502	922	93 581	28 178	18 176	10 001	5 278	233	980	247	577	379	1 146
December	92 049	753	91 296	26 438	17 012	9 426	5 545	265	1 000	244	671	360	1 221

1. Includes Caribbean.
2. Includes countries not shown separately. See Notes for list of included countries.

Table 11-5. U.S. Imports of Goods by Selected Countries and Regions—*Continued*

(Census basis; millions of dollars, not seasonally adjusted.)

Year and month	Total¹	Western Europe European Union Total¹	Belgium	France	Germany	Ireland	Italy	Netherlands	Spain	Sweden	United Kingdom
1970	...	...	...	942	3 127	...	1 316	...	...	...	2 194
1971	...	...	...	1 088	3 651	...	1 406	...	...	...	2 499
1972	...	...	...	1 369	4 250	...	1 757	...	...	...	2 987
1973	...	...	...	1 732	5 345	...	2 002	...	...	...	3 657
1974	23 522	19 035	...	2 257	6 324	...	2 585	1 433	...	...	4 061
1975	20 735	16 610	...	2 137	5 382	...	2 397	1 083	...	...	3 784
1976	22 784	17 848	...	2 509	5 592	...	2 530	1 080	...	...	4 254
1977	27 417	22 087	...	3 032	7 238	...	3 037	1 477	...	...	5 141
1978	36 485	29 009	...	4 051	9 962	...	4 102	1 603	...	...	6 514
1979	41 684	33 295	...	4 768	10 955	...	4 918	1 852	...	...	8 028
1980	46 416	35 958	...	5 247	11 681	...	4 313	1 910	1 230	1 631	9 755
1981	51 855	41 624	...	5 851	11 379	...	5 189	2 366	1 537	1 714	12 835
1982	52 346	42 509	...	5 545	11 975	...	5 301	2 494	1 508	1 992	13 095
1983	53 884	43 892	...	6 025	12 695	...	5 455	2 970	1 536	2 429	12 470
1984	71 153	57 360	...	8 113	16 996	...	7 935	4 069	2 391	3 244	14 492
1985	79 756	67 822	...	9 482	20 239	...	9 674	4 081	2 515	4 124	14 937
1986	89 825	75 736	...	10 129	25 124	...	10 607	4 066	2 702	4 419	15 396
1987	95 496	81 188	...	10 730	27 069	...	11 040	3 964	2 839	4 758	17 341
1988	100 443	84 939	...	12 509	26 362	...	11 576	4 559	3 204	4 985	17 976
1989	101 764	85 153	...	13 013	24 832	...	11 933	4 810	3 317	4 892	18 319
1990	108 901	91 868	...	13 124	28 109	...	12 723	4 972	3 311	4 937	20 288
1991	102 262	86 481	3 929	13 333	26 137	1 948	11 764	4 811	2 848	4 524	18 413
1992	110 727	93 993	4 476	14 797	28 820	2 262	12 314	5 300	3 002	4 716	20 093
1993	115 557	97 941	5 149	15 279	28 562	2 519	13 216	5 443	2 992	4 534	21 730
1994	130 730	110 875	6 354	16 699	31 744	2 894	14 802	6 007	3 555	5 041	25 058
1995	145 320	131 871	6 054	17 209	36 844	4 079	16 348	6 405	3 880	6 256	26 930
1996	157 601	142 947	6 776	18 646	38 945	4 804	18 325	6 583	4 280	7 153	28 979
1997	172 957	157 528	7 912	20 636	43 122	5 867	19 408	7 293	4 606	7 299	32 659
1998	191 971	176 380	8 440	24 016	49 842	8 401	20 959	7 599	4 780	7 848	34 838
1999	212 969	195 227	9 196	25 709	55 228	10 994	22 357	8 475	5 059	8 103	39 237
1996											
January	11 960	10 862	494	1 294	2 914	455	1 526	457	315	567	2 182
February	11 899	10 773	532	1 354	2 857	345	1 420	501	333	581	2 217
March	13 306	12 018	577	1 679	3 312	366	1 537	568	353	623	2 328
April	13 276	11 958	566	1 491	3 225	394	1 466	544	371	636	2 470
May	13 595	12 346	575	1 607	3 423	412	1 476	578	360	643	2 583
June	12 674	11 474	548	1 560	2 970	389	1 536	533	328	593	2 364
July	14 267	12 974	682	1 621	3 613	381	1 785	560	403	629	2 475
August	12 637	11 503	422	1 533	3 268	378	1 680	542	335	338	2 329
September	12 236	11 061	570	1 531	2 958	430	1 204	554	302	565	2 246
October	14 404	13 067	692	1 815	3 448	399	1 598	636	419	682	2 624
November	13 353	12 077	556	1 509	3 404	450	1 537	558	378	639	2 366
December	13 994	12 835	562	1 653	3 555	407	1 560	553	381	658	2 795
1997											
January	12 549	11 400	543	1 430	3 082	393	1 373	534	369	497	2 544
February	12 655	11 544	589	1 471	3 234	396	1 450	461	334	574	2 405
March	14 749	13 363	676	1 686	3 772	486	1 681	585	367	714	2 674
April	14 483	13 302	742	1 636	3 820	450	1 547	561	391	671	2 731
May	14 650	13 226	677	1 622	3 735	415	1 582	607	405	610	2 799
June	14 162	12 904	622	1 770	3 486	469	1 664	640	404	631	2 469
July	15 973	14 555	802	2 057	3 771	569	1 948	692	412	656	2 866
August	13 347	12 241	484	1 655	3 354	434	1 661	583	419	392	2 557
September	13 856	12 589	723	1 783	3 199	565	1 305	674	309	590	2 730
October	16 202	14 804	738	2 008	3 883	545	1 808	718	384	696	3 208
November	14 372	13 046	648	1 629	3 667	599	1 634	553	399	588	2 603
December	15 959	14 553	668	1 891	4 119	547	1 755	685	414	681	3 073
1998											
January	13 759	12 589	626	1 661	3 291	624	1 558	565	381	507	2 659
February	13 798	12 678	695	1 675	3 510	503	1 579	536	349	572	2 550
March	16 984	15 620	780	2 061	4 692	667	1 888	605	404	663	3 003
April	16 228	14 829	663	1 976	4 315	742	1 674	646	419	642	2 991
May	15 405	14 054	675	1 957	4 047	606	1 637	580	427	615	2 816
June	16 432	15 143	728	2 193	4 022	736	1 833	668	447	641	3 012
July	17 321	15 850	844	2 234	4 291	801	2 034	673	430	740	2 921
August	14 926	13 889	472	1 816	4 030	719	1 834	620	381	472	2 780
September	15 407	14 170	766	1 978	3 759	874	1 376	619	301	692	2 982
October	17 933	16 444	773	2 348	4 643	807	1 894	790	374	778	3 124
November	16 718	15 321	734	2 109	4 323	727	1 831	639	425	716	2 990
December	17 061	15 793	685	2 007	4 918	595	1 821	659	444	810	3 011
1999											
January	14 492	13 403	737	1 872	3 551	591	1 604	600	415	496	2 760
February	15 673	14 492	679	1 932	4 053	962	1 652	535	391	561	2 885
March	18 296	16 739	960	2 178	4 852	734	1 956	730	443	724	3 239
April	17 115	15 777	791	2 069	4 471	749	1 760	652	398	683	3 240
May	17 107	15 670	743	2 114	4 548	638	1 842	620	423	670	3 195
June	18 407	16 778	796	2 096	4 756	929	2 004	695	429	759	3 323
July	19 032	17 443	786	2 229	4 987	1 147	2 037	736	428	704	3 437
August	17 518	16 150	597	2 338	4 569	955	1 983	664	466	494	3 188
September	17 109	15 658	739	2 031	4 315	1 007	1 658	673	347	647	3 404
October	19 411	17 630	879	2 254	4 853	1 284	1 905	819	422	799	3 454
November	19 794	18 083	765	5 379	5 085	1 295	1 973	849	458	799	3 563
December	19 016	17 405	725	2 216	5 189	704	1 983	903	438	768	3 550

1. Includes countries not shown separately. See Notes for list of included countries.

Table 11-5. U.S. Imports of Goods by Selected Countries and Regions—*Continued*

(Census basis; millions of dollars, not seasonally adjusted.)

Year and month	Western Europe—*Continued* European Free Trade Association			Eastern Europe and former Soviet Republics					Near and Middle Eastern countries		
	Total [1]	Norway	Switzerland	Total [1]	Hungary	Poland	Former Soviet Republics Total [1]	Russia	Israel	Saudi Arabia	Turkey
1970	...	...	...	...	...	...	72	...	...	...	...
1971	...	...	...	...	...	...	57	...	...	...	...
1972	...	...	...	...	...	...	95	...	...	...	...
1973	...	...	...	...	...	...	220	...	...	...	...
1974	...	...	...	890	...	...	350	...	...	...	...
1975	...	...	...	731	...	...	254	...	...	...	...
1976	...	...	...	856	...	...	220	...	...	...	...
1977	...	...	...	914	...	...	453	...	...	...	...
1978	...	...	...	1 503	...	...	539	...	...	...	...
1979	...	...	...	1 865	...	...	874	...	...	...	...
1980	...	2 633	2 796	1 433	107	417	453	...	...	...	...
1981	...	2 478	2 448	1 555	129	365	348	...	...	...	...
1982	...	1 973	2 340	1 067	133	212	228	...	...	...	...
1983	...	1 358	2 494	1 359	158	189	347	...	...	...	...
1984	...	1 904	3 117	2 154	221	220	554	...	...	...	...
1985	...	1 164	3 476	1 936	218	220	409	...	...	1 907	...
1986	...	1 079	5 253	2 001	225	233	558	...	...	3 612	...
1987	...	1 404	4 249	1 923	279	296	425	...	...	4 433	...
1988	...	1 446	4 611	2 163	293	377	586	...	...	5 620	...
1989	...	1 991	4 714	2 064	328	387	710	...	...	7 181	...
1990	...	1 830	5 587	2 275	348	408	1 065	...	...	9 974	...
1991	14 302	1 624	5 576	1 800	367	357	813	...	3 484	10 900	1 006
1992	15 021	1 969	5 645	1 551	347	375	658	481	3 816	10 371	1 110
1993	15 816	1 958	5 973	3 526	401	454	2 094	1 743	4 420	7 708	1 198
1994	17 665	2 353	6 373	5 832	470	651	3 848	3 245	5 229	7 688	1 575
1995	11 039	3 087	7 594	7 020	547	664	4 896	4 030	5 709	8 377	1 798
1996	12 112	3 993	7 792	6 987	676	628	4 690	3 577	6 434	10 467	1 778
1997	12 504	3 752	8 405	8 483	1 079	696	5 350	4 319	7 326	9 365	2 121
1998	12 072	2 872	8 690	17 991	1 567	784	7 089	5 747	8 640	6 241	2 543
1999	14 162	4 043	9 539	19 360	1 893	816	7 539	5 921	9 864	8 254	2 629
1996											
January	885	260	592	416	44	54	244	184	538	747	154
February	908	242	646	466	44	47	297	237	507	571	151
March	1 078	322	721	468	48	48	301	232	486	750	152
April	1 091	400	663	581	49	50	414	340	434	910	163
May	1 051	353	668	564	52	60	389	288	534	911	140
June	1 023	370	633	538	47	48	366	254	494	635	120
July	1 079	398	654	519	54	53	323	232	661	916	148
August	927	344	553	663	59	53	467	357	498	932	140
September	994	337	638	588	59	51	392	299	565	1 068	126
October	1 095	377	687	714	67	61	509	394	613	939	161
November	1 046	323	697	685	77	51	438	331	567	823	166
December	936	268	641	784	78	52	551	430	538	1 265	156
1997											
January	893	284	580	660	62	54	423	286	642	765	181
February	881	251	606	537	62	45	339	260	543	641	177
March	1 120	381	715	656	71	54	437	377	565	779	198
April	928	242	658	657	84	49	412	318	526	782	191
May	1 145	413	705	713	104	62	445	368	613	889	200
June	1 033	299	710	660	93	55	403	325	528	699	162
July	1 179	354	795	728	102	65	440	353	723	736	166
August	878	257	597	795	94	62	490	390	556	823	173
September	1 040	303	709	827	99	64	549	446	731	869	162
October	1 132	310	784	758	102	68	457	376	615	838	194
November	1 108	324	746	614	91	52	369	310	640	777	155
December	1 168	334	799	876	115	66	587	510	642	768	163
1998											
January	880	240	614	1 311	91	73	498	419	732	713	215
February	868	193	638	1 243	88	59	487	405	652	481	182
March	1 039	255	743	1 386	112	87	533	441	761	609	227
April	1 098	223	836	1 572	113	63	645	542	662	584	228
May	1 069	267	758	1 449	122	57	582	474	689	551	208
June	978	241	698	1 810	125	62	745	616	710	461	227
July	1 165	317	809	1 552	134	67	605	459	880	534	201
August	772	188	554	1 490	122	60	591	445	644	510	184
September	967	227	694	1 705	177	68	674	548	729	451	190
October	1 126	235	846	1 513	157	66	582	464	709	489	273
November	1 067	237	778	1 513	146	69	598	501	792	406	259
December	1 044	249	725	1 448	180	54	550	435	681	453	149
1999											
January	835	168	626	953	112	59	334	233	801	454	188
February	939	200	693	1 370	118	58	543	468	682	421	171
March	1 199	282	860	1 557	162	76	603	498	765	508	279
April	1 067	282	737	1 829	137	66	756	658	653	524	196
May	1 160	304	798	1 548	138	66	613	495	698	646	197
June	1 334	403	890	1 800	182	68	701	539	846	631	217
July	1 294	429	823	1 567	152	69	601	409	930	753	217
August	1 104	340	723	1 617	163	60	627	482	821	802	179
September	1 176	363	758	1 421	169	77	522	348	818	857	199
October	1 396	442	899	1 839	172	68	727	561	899	851	298
November	1 384	468	874	1 771	176	74	694	554	955	854	244
December	1 275	363	858	2 087	213	77	819	677	968	952	244

1. See Notes for list of countries included in each group.

Table 11-5. U.S. Imports of Goods by Selected Countries and Regions—*Continued*

(Census basis; millions of dollars, not seasonally adjusted.)

Year and month	Selected Asian and Oceanic countries											
	Australia	China	Hong Kong	India	Indonesia	Japan	South Korea	Malaysia	Philippines	Singapore	Thailand	Taiwan
1970	...	...	...	...	...	5 875	...	...	...	...	...	...
1971	...	...	...	...	...	7 259	...	...	...	...	...	...
1972	...	...	...	...	...	9 064	...	...	...	...	...	...
1973	...	...	...	...	...	9 676	...	...	...	...	...	...
1974	...	...	...	...	...	12 338	...	...	...	...	...	...
1975	...	...	...	...	...	11 268	...	...	...	...	...	...
1976	...	...	...	...	...	15 504	...	...	...	...	...	...
1977	...	...	...	...	...	18 550	...	...	...	...	...	...
1978	...	...	...	...	...	24 458	...	...	...	...	...	...
1979	...	...	...	...	...	26 248	...	...	...	...	...	...
1980	...	...	...	...	5 183	30 701	...	...	...	...	...	...
1981	...	...	...	...	6 022	37 612	...	...	...	...	...	...
1982	...	...	...	...	4 224	37 744	...	...	...	...	...	...
1983	...	...	...	...	5 285	41 183	...	...	...	...	...	...
1984	...	...	...	...	5 461	57 135	...	...	...	...	...	...
1985	2 837	3 862	8 396	...	4 569	68 783	10 031	...	...	4 260	...	16 396
1986	2 632	4 771	8 891	...	3 312	81 911	12 729	...	...	4 725	...	19 791
1987	3 007	6 294	9 854	...	3 394	84 575	16 987	...	...	6 201	...	24 622
1988	3 541	8 511	10 238	...	3 150	89 519	20 105	...	...	7 973	...	24 714
1989	3 898	11 989	9 739	...	3 529	93 586	19 742	...	...	8 950	...	24 326
1990	4 442	15 224	9 488	...	3 341	89 655	18 493	...	...	9 839	...	22 667
1991	3 988	18 969	9 279	3 193	3 241	91 511	17 019	6 102	3 471	9 957	6 122	23 023
1992	3 688	25 728	9 793	3 780	4 529	97 414	16 682	8 294	4 355	11 313	7 529	24 596
1993	3 297	31 540	9 554	4 554	5 435	107 246	17 118	10 563	4 894	12 798	8 542	25 102
1994	3 202	38 787	9 696	5 310	6 547	119 156	19 629	13 982	5 719	15 358	10 306	26 706
1995	3 323	45 543	10 291	5 726	7 435	123 479	24 184	17 455	7 007	18 560	11 348	28 972
1996	3 869	51 513	9 865	6 170	8 250	115 187	22 655	17 829	8 161	20 343	11 336	29 907
1997	4 602	62 558	10 288	7 322	9 188	121 663	23 173	18 027	10 445	20 075	12 602	32 629
1998	5 387	71 169	10 538	8 237	9 341	121 845	23 942	19 000	11 947	18 356	13 436	33 125
1999	5 280	81 788	10 528	9 071	9 525	130 864	31 179	21 424	12 353	18 191	14 330	35 204
1996												
January	255	3 658	912	489	617	8 955	2 268	1 504	663	1 665	937	2 453
February	289	3 540	720	471	629	9 575	1 996	1 301	636	1 417	829	2 252
March	283	2 864	640	495	567	10 241	1 940	1 423	657	1 980	915	2 165
April	277	3 248	669	514	630	9 913	1 919	1 426	569	1 699	890	2 304
May	303	3 954	806	474	593	9 082	1 937	1 443	615	1 713	817	2 476
June	302	4 111	763	446	679	8 964	1 660	1 348	655	1 611	900	2 467
July	315	4 817	953	564	751	9 781	1 816	1 500	726	1 695	1 004	2 648
August	353	5 496	889	584	736	9 453	1 770	1 596	733	1 699	1 008	2 567
September	325	5 481	902	590	715	9 205	1 725	1 638	767	1 801	1 000	2 731
October	365	5 813	1 017	638	898	10 741	1 912	1 685	783	1 759	1 110	2 818
November	407	4 585	835	479	715	9 620	1 826	1 496	655	1 601	997	2 493
December	396	3 947	758	426	722	9 657	1 887	1 469	704	1 704	931	2 533
1997												
January	345	4 668	904	556	765	9 433	1 793	1 362	737	1 567	952	2 531
February	244	4 262	623	540	633	9 721	1 506	1 199	732	1 332	868	2 301
March	343	3 629	605	624	608	10 948	1 801	1 420	866	1 669	973	2 428
April	351	4 445	683	577	679	10 344	1 916	1 415	739	1 699	976	2 577
May	408	4 795	711	536	777	9 167	1 908	1 398	831	1 713	955	2 617
June	367	5 214	848	583	755	9 895	1 985	1 509	807	1 717	1 022	2 735
July	444	5 777	995	651	860	10 528	2 216	1 557	939	1 711	1 150	2 819
August	423	6 074	972	639	807	10 063	1 943	1 670	951	1 812	1 149	2 873
September	425	6 561	1 113	741	930	10 141	2 094	1 702	1 020	1 875	1 180	2 968
October	463	6 607	1 079	795	882	11 203	2 113	1 737	967	1 773	1 172	3 068
November	387	5 426	906	516	760	9 790	1 880	1 515	932	1 528	1 056	2 756
December	403	5 101	848	566	734	10 432	2 019	1 543	925	1 679	1 150	2 958
1998												
January	354	5 453	960	652	799	9 426	1 954	1 417	914	1 490	1 033	2 755
February	437	4 560	649	641	666	9 910	1 726	1 319	945	1 341	977	2 327
March	475	4 798	708	760	680	10 986	1 950	1 524	1 065	1 715	1 131	2 699
April	473	5 263	750	684	733	10 327	1 924	1 511	924	1 540	987	2 653
May	482	5 539	789	632	707	9 655	1 895	1 462	889	1 530	1 001	2 580
June	483	6 020	948	689	765	9 971	2 101	1 489	1 022	1 616	1 136	2 780
July	445	6 556	1 016	748	867	10 210	2 023	1 576	1 041	1 514	1 187	2 841
August	442	6 780	1 059	784	846	9 890	1 998	1 754	1 143	1 516	1 221	2 900
September	434	7 125	1 058	774	880	9 736	2 062	1 747	1 105	1 589	1 233	2 947
October	489	7 378	978	757	902	10 924	2 097	1 887	1 048	1 537	1 265	2 949
November	402	6 374	840	569	778	10 334	2 102	1 720	955	1 433	1 165	2 869
December	472	5 322	784	547	718	10 476	2 110	1 596	898	1 537	1 100	2 826
1999												
January	397	5 654	805	664	787	9 213	2 066	1 502	887	1 397	1 074	2 670
February	344	5 563	727	668	654	9 999	2 023	1 438	838	1 230	950	2 471
March	345	5 204	701	824	739	11 799	2 360	1 640	956	1 544	1 102	2 836
April	417	5 819	699	745	711	10 408	2 325	1 636	829	1 423	1 090	2 763
May	467	6 363	744	660	715	9 476	2 457	1 786	933	1 527	1 023	2 856
June	496	7 117	918	679	861	10 897	2 711	1 816	1 154	1 562	1 237	3 083
July	442	7 406	992	796	803	11 109	2 654	1 857	1 177	1 719	1 252	3 010
August	509	8 022	1 042	893	879	10 801	2 687	2 020	1 193	1 512	1 316	3 091
September	495	8 198	1 054	876	898	11 271	2 797	1 967	1 167	1 517	1 327	3 007
October	443	8 208	1 038	875	886	12 126	2 888	1 922	1 115	1 598	1 382	2 994
November	445	7 544	924	735	831	11 579	3 059	1 956	1 097	1 590	1 308	3 171
December	479	6 690	883	659	761	12 185	3 151	1 886	1 009	1 572	1 269	3 255

Table 11-5. U.S. Imports of Goods by Selected Countries and Regions—*Continued*

(Census basis; millions of dollars, not seasonally adjusted.)

Year and month	Selected African countries				Special country groupings [1]					
	Angola	Egypt	Nigeria	South Africa	ASEAN [2]	MERCOSUR [3]	Central American Common Market	Newly indus-trialized Pacific Rim countries	OPEC [4]	Pacific Rim Countries
1970	. . .	. . .	. . .	290	. . .	. . .	. . .	. . .	. . .	. . .
1971	. . .	. . .	. . .	287	. . .	. . .	. . .	. . .	. . .	. . .
1972	. . .	. . .	. . .	325	. . .	. . .	. . .	. . .	. . .	. . .
1973	. . .	. . .	. . .	377	. . .	. . .	. . .	. . .	. . .	. . .
1974	. . .	. . .	. . .	609	. . .	. . .	. . .	. . .	. . .	. . .
1975	. . .	. . .	. . .	841	. . .	. . .	. . .	. . .	. . .	. . .
1976	. . .	. . .	. . .	925	. . .	. . .	. . .	. . .	. . .	. . .
1977	. . .	. . .	. . .	1 261	. . .	. . .	. . .	. . .	. . .	. . .
1978	. . .	. . .	. . .	2 259	. . .	. . .	. . .	. . .	. . .	. . .
1979	. . .	. . .	. . .	2 616	. . .	. . .	. . .	. . .	. . .	. . .
1980	. . .	459	. . .	3 321	. . .	. . .	. . .	. . .	. . .	. . .
1981	. . .	397	. . .	2 445	. . .	. . .	. . .	. . .	. . .	. . .
1982	. . .	547	. . .	1 967	. . .	. . .	. . .	. . .	. . .	. . .
1983	. . .	303	. . .	2 027	. . .	. . .	. . .	. . .	. . .	. . .
1984	. . .	169	. . .	2 488	. . .	. . .	. . .	. . .	. . .	. . .
1985	. . .	79	3 002	2 071	. . .	. . .	. . .	. . .	22 800	. . .
1986	. . .	112	2 530	2 365	. . .	. . .	. . .	. . .	19 750	. . .
1987	. . .	465	3 573	1 346	. . .	. . .	. . .	. . .	23 953	. . .
1988	. . .	220	3 279	1 513	. . .	. . .	. . .	. . .	22 962	. . .
1989	. . .	226	5 226	1 529	. . .	. . .	. . .	. . .	30 601	. . .
1990	. . .	398	5 977	1 701	. . .	. . .	. . .	. . .	38 017	. . .
1991	1 775	206	5 168	1 728	28 918	8 004	2 972	59 277	32 644	188 407
1992	2 303	434	5 103	1 727	36 050	8 865	3 727	62 384	33 200	208 424
1993	2 092	613	5 301	1 845	42 262	8 685	4 266	64 572	31 739	229 552
1994	2 061	549	4 430	2 031	51 957	10 408	4 804	71 388	31 685	261 153
1995	2 232	606	4 931	2 208	61 844	10 591	5 862	82 008	35 197	288 685
1996	2 902	680	5 978	2 323	65 968	11 052	6 774	82 770	44 285	290 033
1997	2 779	658	6 349	2 510	70 392	12 124	8 421	86 164	44 025	315 368
1998	2 241	660	4 194	3 049	72 291	12 622	9 252	85 961	33 925	327 743
1999	2 418	618	4 385	3 194	76 805	14 159	11 046	95 102	41 978	359 743
1996										
January	197	62	549	146	5 392	936	454	7 298	3 280	23 163
February	165	56	405	156	4 815	755	537	6 385	2 809	22 534
March	128	62	367	191	5 544	844	547	6 725	2 964	22 930
April	224	81	484	239	5 216	900	538	6 591	3 555	22 842
May	278	46	552	215	5 184	929	565	6 933	3 896	23 162
June	214	47	523	165	5 196	944	550	6 501	3 401	22 763
July	204	79	667	223	5 679	905	617	7 113	4 090	25 243
August	270	42	499	204	5 777	1 064	580	6 925	3 835	25 516
September	293	32	648	184	5 925	982	586	7 159	4 235	25 498
October	353	58	523	194	6 241	939	619	7 505	4 263	27 996
November	289	65	414	226	5 468	899	565	6 756	3 643	24 420
December	287	51	349	180	5 532	956	618	6 882	4 313	23 967
1997										
January	247	52	621	184	5 388	1 048	551	6 795	3 877	24 326
February	349	44	388	140	4 769	946	646	5 762	3 175	22 744
March	271	41	523	175	5 538	950	724	6 503	3 409	24 513
April	268	69	639	210	5 510	1 024	658	6 874	3 590	25 093
May	168	41	667	215	5 679	1 108	721	6 950	3 935	24 561
June	236	43	529	202	5 815	1 007	725	7 284	3 644	26 105
July	227	67	494	239	6 223	1 142	789	7 741	3 690	28 105
August	134	50	619	198	6 393	1 047	677	7 599	3 746	27 825
September	215	52	514	257	6 713	983	745	8 050	3 998	29 074
October	277	70	571	231	6 536	1 017	751	8 031	4 038	30 115
November	250	51	405	228	5 794	905	647	7 071	3 520	26 053
December	138	78	381	231	6 035	950	789	7 504	3 402	26 854
1998										
January	242	58	414	229	5 657	1 037	629	7 158	3 252	25 769
February	183	55	301	239	5 256	892	763	6 044	2 587	24 074
March	182	63	449	247	6 120	983	846	7 070	2 908	26 811
April	204	50	463	287	5 702	1 083	704	6 867	3 038	26 318
May	201	53	474	231	5 594	1 079	734	6 794	2 944	25 736
June	180	55	388	282	6 059	1 140	818	7 444	2 740	27 493
July	201	56	339	263	6 211	1 110	810	7 393	2 915	28 410
August	180	76	343	274	6 491	1 114	799	7 473	2 943	28 623
September	187	57	253	258	6 589	1 068	775	7 655	2 737	28 972
October	127	53	295	222	6 647	1 078	801	7 561	2 988	30 452
November	216	38	279	259	6 087	973	728	7 244	2 574	28 060
December	139	48	195	261	5 879	1 065	846	7 258	2 300	27 025
1999										
January	149	42	288	255	5 721	984	706	6 938	2 543	25 623
February	121	47	211	203	5 183	939	921	6 451	2 214	25 524
March	108	57	329	269	6 077	1 112	960	7 441	2 771	28 381
April	164	51	370	226	5 761	1 106	863	7 210	3 075	27 319
May	224	49	349	233	6 046	1 162	877	7 584	3 277	27 592
June	187	47	381	288	6 702	1 282	926	8 274	3 341	30 930
July	178	56	334	239	6 916	1 210	985	8 375	3 704	31 503
August	214	52	529	296	7 000	1 328	956	8 332	4 213	32 029
September	326	56	433	285	6 970	1 275	958	8 376	4 184	32 693
October	304	54	357	355	7 025	1 240	959	8 518	4 191	33 554
November	244	51	449	232	6 845	1 237	932	8 743	4 183	32 473
December	199	57	357	315	6 560	1 284	1 004	8 861	4 282	32 122

1. See Notes for list of countries included in each group.
2. Association of Southeast Asian Nations.
3. Argentina, Brazil, Paraguay, and Uruguay.
4. Organization of Petroleum Exporting Countries.

Table 11-6. U.S. Exports of Goods by Principal End-Use Category

(Census basis, except as noted; billions of dollars, seasonally adjusted.)

| Year and month | Total exports of goods | | | Foods, feeds, and beverages | Industrial supplies and materials | | Capital goods, except automotive | Automotive vehicles, engines, and parts | Consumer goods (nonfood) except automotive | Other goods |
	Total: Balance of payments basis	Net adjustments	Total: Census basis		Total	Petroleum and products				
1970	42.47	...	...	...	...	...	...	...	...	...
1971	43.32	...	...	...	...	...	...	...	...	...
1972	49.38	...	...	...	...	...	...	...	...	...
1973	71.41	...	...	...	...	...	...	...	...	...
1974	98.31	...	...	...	...	...	...	...	...	...
1975	107.09	...	...	...	...	...	...	...	...	...
1976	114.75	...	...	...	...	...	...	...	...	...
1977	120.82	...	...	...	...	...	...	...	...	...
1978	142.08	...	...	25.57	39.05	...	46.81	14.56	11.20	...
1979	184.44	...	...	30.26	57.30	...	58.71	16.56	13.58	...
1980	224.25	...	...	36.01	70.59	...	74.65	15.98	17.31	...
1981	237.04	...	...	38.57	67.79	...	82.47	18.23	17.26	...
1982	211.16	...	...	31.96	62.13	...	75.03	15.94	15.75	...
1983	201.80	0.09	201.71	31.83	57.43	...	70.02	17.02	14.50	...
1984	219.93	1.18	218.74	31.93	62.59	...	75.41	20.99	14.64	...
1985	215.92	3.29	212.62	24.42	59.17	...	76.89	22.99	14.01	...
1986	223.34	-3.13	226.47	22.84	61.89	...	79.47	22.16	15.86	...
1987	250.21	-3.70	253.90	24.74	67.84	...	90.66	25.74	19.76	...
1988	320.23	-3.11	323.34	32.86	86.73	...	115.42	30.21	26.00	...
1989	362.12	-1.72	363.84	37.06	99.33	...	138.71	34.94	36.57	...
1990	389.31	-3.62	392.92	34.95	104.92	7.65	152.12	36.50	42.78	20.73
1991	416.91	-4.85	421.76	35.74	109.57	7.59	165.96	40.01	46.86	23.66
1992	440.35	-7.81	448.16	40.27	109.14	7.62	175.92	47.03	51.42	24.39
1993	456.83	-8.26	465.09	40.63	111.81	7.50	181.70	52.40	54.66	23.89
1994	502.40	-10.23	512.63	41.96	121.40	6.97	205.02	57.78	59.98	26.50
1995	575.85	-8.90	584.74	50.47	146.25	8.10	233.05	61.83	64.43	28.72
1996	612.06	-13.02	621.90	55.76	147.66	9.63	253.58	65.01	70.05	33.85
1997	679.70	-9.48	689.18	51.51	158.23	10.42	294.55	74.03	77.37	33.51
1998	670.32	-11.81	682.14	46.40	148.27	8.08	299.61	73.16	79.26	35.44
1999	684.36	-11.44	695.80	45.53	147.00	8.62	311.41	75.76	80.77	35.34
1996										
January	49.58	-0.70	49.37	4.68	11.77	0.79	19.71	5.43	5.62	2.16
February	50.84	-0.79	50.96	4.61	12.03	0.73	20.66	5.38	5.81	2.47
March	50.02	-0.88	50.36	4.82	12.40	0.65	20.08	4.80	5.69	2.57
April	50.50	-0.85	50.80	4.53	12.63	0.68	20.46	5.04	5.72	2.43
May	50.88	-1.13	51.52	4.51	12.33	0.62	20.62	5.41	5.73	2.93
June	51.23	-0.89	51.79	4.57	12.24	0.72	20.64	5.46	5.81	3.06
July	49.88	-1.45	51.29	4.55	11.72	0.78	20.62	5.56	5.68	3.16
August	51.16	-1.36	52.67	4.40	12.44	0.88	21.30	5.59	5.86	3.07
September	50.95	-1.32	52.83	4.51	12.38	1.09	21.00	5.90	5.95	3.09
October	52.41	-1.07	54.34	4.75	12.66	0.85	22.78	5.36	6.04	2.76
November	52.84	-1.28	55.43	5.07	12.42	0.95	23.18	5.65	6.05	3.07
December	51.77	-1.32	54.55	4.78	12.64	...	22.52	5.43	6.09	3.08
1997										
January	52.35	-0.56	52.90	4.31	12.16	0.88	21.97	5.87	6.13	2.46
February	54.39	-0.69	55.08	4.38	12.80	0.80	23.19	5.87	6.33	2.51
March	55.93	-1.00	56.93	4.19	13.49	0.82	24.17	5.86	6.38	2.85
April	56.67	-0.70	57.37	4.36	13.51	0.86	24.55	6.01	6.37	2.56
May	56.50	-1.00	57.50	4.23	13.34	0.78	24.66	5.93	6.50	2.85
June	57.45	-0.84	58.29	4.20	13.79	0.84	24.59	6.37	6.61	2.74
July	58.90	-0.69	59.59	3.98	13.26	0.92	26.09	6.66	6.54	3.06
August	57.20	-1.05	58.25	4.26	13.37	0.93	24.86	6.26	6.53	2.98
September	57.86	-0.75	58.61	4.45	13.27	0.88	25.18	6.24	6.43	3.05
October	57.72	-1.04	58.77	4.46	13.15	0.90	25.21	6.44	6.61	2.90
November	56.99	-0.66	57.66	4.41	12.93	0.82	24.72	6.51	6.50	2.59
December	57.75	-0.50	58.25	4.29	13.16	0.99	25.38	6.02	6.45	2.95
1998										
January	57.48	-0.64	58.12	4.17	13.23	0.87	25.08	6.45	6.63	2.56
February	56.42	-0.81	57.22	4.24	12.67	0.72	24.85	6.32	6.45	2.70
March	56.71	-0.88	57.59	3.98	12.76	0.74	24.80	6.51	6.51	3.03
April	55.30	-0.65	55.95	3.79	12.44	0.71	24.12	6.29	6.55	2.76
May	55.21	-0.75	55.95	3.82	12.49	0.72	24.25	5.98	6.58	2.84
June	55.55	-0.90	56.45	3.89	12.20	0.66	24.94	5.82	6.77	2.83
July	54.61	-0.97	55.58	3.77	11.95	0.63	25.13	5.12	6.77	2.84
August	54.08	-1.31	55.40	3.67	12.12	0.67	23.87	5.80	6.68	3.27
September	55.68	-0.94	56.63	3.41	12.09	0.63	25.54	6.13	6.67	2.80
October	57.01	-1.20	58.21	3.95	12.34	0.59	26.08	6.17	6.55	3.13
November	56.72	-1.60	58.32	3.78	12.25	0.53	25.78	6.40	6.60	3.50
December	55.55	-1.18	56.73	3.94	11.73	0.61	25.18	6.17	6.51	3.18
1999										
January	54.97	-0.95	55.92	3.64	11.22	0.58	25.44	6.12	6.58	2.91
February	54.30	-1.11	55.40	3.53	11.33	0.48	24.74	6.10	6.67	3.03
March	54.69	-1.02	55.71	3.56	11.52	0.56	25.10	6.02	6.58	2.93
April	55.40	-0.99	56.39	3.73	11.62	0.66	25.27	6.28	6.71	2.78
May	55.34	-1.14	56.48	3.71	11.72	0.69	25.24	6.17	6.54	3.09
June	55.70	-1.20	56.89	3.82	11.85	0.70	25.21	6.33	6.62	3.07
July	56.39	-1.03	57.42	3.88	11.64	0.66	25.95	6.29	6.72	2.94
August	58.40	-0.86	59.26	3.95	12.53	0.77	26.79	6.70	6.57	2.73
September	59.09	-1.15	60.24	4.13	13.10	0.76	26.70	6.37	6.89	3.06
October	59.19	-0.85	60.04	3.99	13.18	0.90	26.79	6.39	6.79	2.89
November	59.68	-0.26	59.95	3.75	13.72	0.86	26.38	6.40	6.92	2.79
December	61.21	-0.89	62.10	3.85	13.56	1.00	27.78	6.60	7.19	3.12

Table 11-7. U.S. Imports of Goods by Principal End-Use Category

(Census basis, except as noted; billions of dollars, seasonally adjusted.)

Year and month	Total imports of goods			Foods, feeds, and beverages	Industrial supplies and materials		Capital goods, except automotive	Automotive vehicles, engines, and parts	Consumer goods (nonfood) except automotive	Other goods
	Total: Balance of payments basis	Net adjustments	Total: Census basis		Total	Petroleum and products				
1970	39.87	...	...	...	...	...	...	...	...	...
1971	45.58	...	...	...	...	...	...	...	...	...
1972	55.80	...	...	...	...	...	...	...	...	...
1973	70.50	...	...	...	...	...	...	...	...	...
1974	103.81	...	...	...	...	...	...	...	...	...
1975	98.19	...	...	...	...	...	...	...	...	...
1976	124.23	...	...	...	...	...	...	...	...	...
1977	151.91	...	...	...	...	...	...	...	...	...
1978	176.00	...	...	15.84	79.26	...	19.29	25.11	29.40	...
1979	212.01	...	...	18.01	102.67	...	24.49	26.51	31.22	...
1980	249.75	...	...	18.55	124.96	...	30.72	28.13	34.22	...
1981	265.07	...	...	18.53	131.10	...	36.86	30.80	38.30	...
1982	247.64	...	...	17.47	107.82	...	38.22	34.26	39.66	...
1983	268.90	7.18	261.72	18.56	105.63	...	42.61	42.04	46.59	...
1984	332.42	1.91	330.51	21.92	122.72	...	60.15	56.77	61.19	...
1985	338.09	1.71	336.38	21.89	112.48	...	60.81	65.21	66.43	...
1986	368.43	2.75	365.67	24.40	101.37	...	71.86	78.25	79.43	...
1987	409.77	3.48	406.28	24.81	110.67	...	84.77	85.17	88.82	...
1988	447.19	5.26	441.93	24.93	118.06	...	101.79	87.95	96.42	...
1989	477.37	3.72	473.65	25.08	132.40	...	112.45	87.38	102.26	...
1990	498.34	2.36	495.98	26.65	143.41	62.16	116.04	87.69	105.29	16.09
1991	490.98	2.53	488.45	26.21	131.38	51.78	120.80	84.94	107.78	15.94
1992	536.46	3.80	532.66	27.61	138.64	51.60	134.25	91.79	122.66	17.71
1993	589.44	8.78	580.66	27.87	145.61	51.50	152.37	102.42	134.02	18.39
1994	668.59	5.33	663.26	27.87	145.61	51.28	152.37	102.42	134.02	18.39
1995	749.57	6.03	743.54	33.18	181.85	56.16	221.43	123.80	159.91	23.39
1996	803.33	8.04	796.77	35.74	204.43	72.75	228.07	128.95	172.00	26.11
1997	876.37	6.66	869.70	39.69	213.77	71.77	253.28	139.81	193.81	29.34
1998	917.18	5.28	911.90	41.24	200.14	50.90	269.56	149.05	216.52	35.39
1999	1 029.92	5.30	1 024.62	43.58	222.02	67.81	297.11	179.39	239.47	43.05
1996										
January	64.10	0.28	63.04	2.83	16.35	5.21	17.80	10.47	13.55	2.04
February	63.91	0.39	62.91	2.82	15.78	4.57	18.00	10.41	13.78	2.12
March	65.03	1.22	63.23	2.90	16.06	4.88	18.24	10.07	13.81	2.14
April	66.08	1.62	63.56	2.85	16.52	6.00	18.05	10.38	13.56	2.21
May	67.72	1.25	66.08	2.92	17.17	6.29	18.56	11.17	14.08	2.18
June	66.97	0.88	66.56	2.98	17.48	6.27	18.76	10.94	14.18	2.21
July	66.69	0.43	67.03	3.00	17.58	6.24	18.92	11.14	14.19	2.21
August	68.11	0.78	68.18	3.14	17.52	5.91	19.45	11.30	14.64	2.13
September	68.40	0.32	68.47	3.07	17.60	6.74	19.65	11.00	14.92	2.23
October	67.75	0.32	67.89	3.00	17.52	6.98	19.96	10.23	15.01	2.18
November	68.66	0.30	69.25	3.02	16.98	6.33	20.82	11.23	14.93	2.28
December	69.92	0.24	70.57	3.22	17.87	7.34	21.33	10.61	15.37	2.18
1997										
January	70.10	0.26	69.85	3.06	18.33	6.78	19.49	11.67	15.17	2.13
February	70.57	0.43	70.13	3.14	17.85	6.39	19.66	11.76	15.26	2.46
March	71.49	1.46	70.02	3.21	17.80	6.22	20.15	11.33	15.30	2.24
April	72.29	1.03	71.26	3.28	17.46	5.78	20.78	11.34	15.94	2.46
May	73.04	0.90	72.14	3.36	17.92	6.21	20.91	11.58	16.00	2.36
June	72.56	0.90	71.66	3.24	17.39	5.71	20.94	11.72	15.93	2.43
July	73.57	0.23	73.33	3.43	17.37	5.56	21.76	12.08	16.21	2.48
August	73.88	0.25	73.62	3.39	17.90	5.93	21.73	11.74	16.36	2.51
September	74.67	0.27	74.41	3.47	18.26	6.08	21.95	11.58	16.67	2.48
October	74.90	0.26	74.64	3.38	18.20	6.22	22.11	11.60	16.65	2.70
November	73.83	0.25	73.59	3.32	17.80	5.67	21.35	11.52	17.06	2.55
December	75.48	0.43	75.06	3.41	17.49	5.22	22.47	11.90	17.26	2.53
1998										
January	74.93	0.58	74.35	3.32	17.25	4.98	21.91	11.73	17.44	2.70
February	73.81	0.23	73.58	3.51	16.78	4.43	22.01	11.84	16.85	2.59
March	76.52	0.51	76.01	3.44	16.70	4.19	22.78	12.39	18.07	2.63
April	76.59	0.33	76.26	3.40	17.29	4.59	22.27	12.25	18.16	2.89
May	76.76	0.29	76.47	3.41	17.25	4.52	22.79	12.36	18.05	2.61
June	75.33	0.36	74.97	3.52	16.83	4.25	22.18	11.73	18.08	2.63
July	75.24	0.36	74.87	3.47	16.62	4.26	22.26	11.05	18.32	3.16
August	76.80	0.70	76.10	3.41	16.76	4.21	22.25	12.31	18.21	3.17
September	76.91	0.55	76.36	3.42	16.38	3.96	22.48	12.76	18.18	3.15
October	78.68	0.59	78.09	3.45	16.64	4.27	22.99	13.32	18.48	3.22
November	78.62	0.52	78.10	3.44	16.25	3.98	23.05	13.57	18.48	3.31
December	77.00	0.27	76.73	3.47	15.38	3.27	22.60	13.76	18.20	3.33
1999										
January	77.86	0.17	77.69	3.56	15.40	3.43	23.01	13.60	18.81	3.32
February	79.40	0.21	79.19	3.52	15.32	3.31	23.54	14.18	19.35	3.28
March	79.71	0.23	79.48	3.44	16.07	3.79	23.27	14.26	18.92	3.53
April	81.26	0.27	80.98	3.56	17.06	4.78	23.56	13.87	19.43	3.51
May	83.10	0.21	82.88	3.63	17.98	5.61	24.11	14.56	19.10	3.51
June	86.08	0.28	85.80	3.72	18.22	5.56	25.31	15.23	19.75	3.57
July	87.61	0.20	87.42	3.66	18.90	6.11	25.47	15.58	20.30	3.50
August	88.92	0.59	88.33	3.66	19.99	6.75	25.07	15.57	20.27	3.77
September	89.67	0.95	88.72	3.69	20.35	7.05	25.10	15.54	20.31	3.72
October	90.77	0.51	90.26	3.63	20.65	7.15	25.86	15.36	20.89	3.87
November	92.08	0.92	91.16	3.75	20.82	7.11	26.23	15.52	21.13	3.72
December	93.47	0.75	92.71	3.77	21.27	7.17	26.59	16.12	21.20	3.76

Table 11-8. U.S. Exports and Imports of Goods by Principal End-Use Category in Constant Dollars

(Census basis; billions of 1996 dollars, except as noted; seasonally adjusted.)

Year and month	Exports							Imports						
	Total	Foods, feeds, and beverages	Industrial supplies and materials	Capital goods, except auto-motive	Auto-motive vehicles, engines, and parts	Consumer goods (nonfood) except automotive	Other goods	Total	Foods, feeds, and beverages	Industrial supplies and materials	Capital goods, except auto-motive	Auto-motive vehicles, engines, and parts	Consumer goods (nonfood) except automotive	Other goods
1970	...	...	...	...	...	...	...	...	...	...	...	...	...	...
1971	...	...	...	...	...	...	...	...	...	...	...	...	...	...
1972	...	...	...	...	...	...	...	...	...	...	...	...	...	...
1973	...	...	...	...	...	...	...	...	...	...	...	...	...	...
1974	...	...	...	...	...	...	...	...	...	...	...	...	...	...
1975	...	...	...	...	...	...	...	...	...	...	...	...	...	...
1976	...	...	...	...	...	...	...	...	...	...	...	...	...	...
1977	...	...	...	...	...	...	...	...	...	...	...	...	...	...
1978	...	...	...	...	...	...	...	...	...	...	...	...	...	...
1979	...	...	...	...	...	...	...	...	...	...	...	...	...	...
1980	...	...	...	...	...	...	...	...	...	...	...	...	...	...
1981	...	...	...	...	...	...	...	...	...	...	...	...	...	...
1982	...	...	...	...	...	...	...	...	...	...	...	...	...	...
1983	...	...	...	...	...	...	...	...	...	...	...	...	...	...
1984	...	...	...	...	...	...	...	...	...	...	...	...	...	...
1985														
1986 [1]	227.20	22.30	57.30	75.80	21.70	...	...	365.40	24.40	101.30	71.80	78.20	79.40	...
1987 [1]	254.10	24.30	66.70	86.20	24.60	...	...	406.20	24.80	111.00	84.50	85.00	88.70	...
1988 [1]	322.40	32.30	85.10	109.20	29.30	...	...	441.00	24.80	118.30	101.40	87.70	95.90	...
1989 [1]	363.80	37.20	99.30	138.80	34.80	...	...	473.20	25.10	132.30	113.30	86.10	102.90	...
1990 [1]	393.60	35.10	104.40	152.70	37.40	39.22	18.70	495.30	26.60	146.20	116.40	87.30	105.70	14.46
1991 [1]	421.70	35.70	109.70	166.70	40.00	40.42	21.11	488.50	26.50	131.60	120.70	85.70	108.00	14.15
1992 [1]	448.20	40.30	109.10	175.90	47.00	43.60	21.71	532.70	27.60	138.60	134.30	91.80	122.70	15.46
1993 [1]	471.17	40.19	111.08	190.02	51.93	54.03	23.91	591.45	28.03	151.26	160.16	100.73	132.92	18.35
1994 [1]	522.29	40.43	114.17	225.76	56.54	58.97	26.41	675.05	29.52	168.80	199.56	112.13	144.22	20.82
1994	518.60	50.80	131.90	187.00	59.10	61.60	28.30	676.00	31.80	188.10	161.70	122.40	149.30	22.70
1995	569.90	57.80	138.60	216.60	62.70	65.40	29.00	730.10	32.40	193.00	194.80	125.00	161.00	23.90
1996	625.00	55.65	147.17	253.30	65.12	69.92	33.84	794.39	35.61	203.73	228.98	129.03	171.03	26.01
1997	711.87	55.80	160.15	311.98	73.36	76.95	33.63	914.22	38.91	219.64	290.80	139.43	195.87	29.57
1998	730.04	56.12	159.90	326.18	72.40	78.97	36.46	1 021.49	41.56	241.42	331.74	148.49	221.84	36.45
1999	761.52	58.58	160.70	350.50	74.68	80.49	36.57	1 148.50	45.30	246.80	387.31	177.17	247.46	44.47
1996														
January	48.85	4.67	11.71	19.25	5.46	5.60	2.15	62.59	2.84	16.36	17.57	10.33	13.46	2.02
February	50.75	4.57	11.96	20.58	5.38	5.80	2.47	62.56	2.81	15.67	17.82	10.42	13.72	2.14
March	50.18	4.83	12.33	19.95	4.80	5.70	2.57	62.74	2.89	15.84	18.03	10.08	13.77	2.13
April	50.85	4.53	12.65	20.50	5.04	5.71	2.42	63.52	2.86	16.63	17.96	10.41	13.47	2.20
May	51.54	4.46	12.30	20.69	5.42	5.75	2.92	66.25	2.91	17.39	18.49	11.22	14.05	2.18
June	51.87	4.61	12.18	20.74	5.45	5.82	3.06	65.88	2.94	17.13	18.58	10.89	14.10	2.24
July	51.42	4.58	11.75	20.68	5.56	5.69	3.16	66.93	3.00	17.67	18.87	11.13	14.06	2.20
August	52.64	4.44	12.46	21.22	5.60	5.84	3.07	68.19	3.13	17.53	19.41	11.37	14.60	2.14
September	52.81	4.58	12.28	21.02	5.91	5.92	3.09	68.44	3.05	17.62	19.62	11.11	14.83	2.22
October	54.26	4.66	12.64	22.81	5.39	6.00	2.76	67.89	2.98	17.46	20.10	10.27	14.91	2.17
November	55.30	5.05	12.34	23.15	5.65	6.02	3.08	69.12	3.03	16.82	20.92	11.24	14.86	2.27
December	54.54	4.65	12.56	22.72	5.45	6.07	3.09	70.28	3.18	17.61	21.61	10.57	15.19	2.12
1997														
January	54.34	4.70	12.24	22.99	5.83	6.10	2.48	71.12	3.11	17.26	21.72	11.65	15.24	2.13
February	56.51	4.65	12.89	24.34	5.83	6.29	2.52	72.08	3.13	17.39	21.99	11.75	15.35	2.47
March	58.36	4.39	13.62	25.33	5.81	6.36	2.86	72.69	3.06	17.95	22.66	11.31	15.45	2.25
April	58.90	4.57	13.66	25.79	5.95	6.35	2.57	74.84	3.22	18.18	23.54	11.33	16.09	2.48
May	59.20	4.47	13.46	26.07	5.88	6.47	2.85	75.88	3.25	18.65	23.83	11.60	16.16	2.38
June	60.16	4.55	13.94	26.04	6.31	6.58	2.75	75.36	3.11	18.14	23.87	11.71	16.08	2.45
July	61.44	4.35	13.36	27.58	6.59	6.51	3.06	77.49	3.34	18.30	24.92	12.05	16.38	2.50
August	60.28	4.67	13.48	26.47	6.19	6.49	2.99	77.87	3.32	18.67	25.09	11.70	16.56	2.53
September	60.77	4.86	13.43	26.86	6.18	6.38	3.06	78.90	3.37	19.08	25.51	11.54	16.89	2.51
October	61.15	4.97	13.34	26.98	6.37	6.57	2.92	79.26	3.34	18.86	25.94	11.53	16.86	2.73
November	59.93	4.86	13.16	26.41	6.45	6.46	2.60	78.29	3.29	18.49	25.18	11.44	17.32	2.58
December	60.83	4.78	13.58	27.13	5.95	6.40	2.98	80.47	3.37	18.66	26.55	11.83	17.49	2.56
1998														
January	61.18	4.77	13.90	26.93	6.38	6.58	2.60	80.98	3.28	19.31	26.25	11.66	17.72	2.75
February	60.43	4.94	13.27	26.81	6.25	6.41	2.75	81.05	3.55	19.25	26.68	11.77	17.14	2.65
March	60.88	4.67	13.49	26.70	6.45	6.47	3.10	84.20	3.50	19.69	27.58	12.31	18.43	2.70
April	59.29	4.50	13.15	26.07	6.23	6.52	2.82	84.78	3.38	20.54	27.15	12.18	18.57	2.96
May	59.38	4.52	13.30	26.18	5.92	6.55	2.90	85.20	3.44	20.48	27.80	12.32	18.48	2.68
June	60.27	4.65	13.05	27.13	5.76	6.77	2.90	84.05	3.53	20.35	27.23	11.70	18.54	2.71
July	59.33	4.45	12.89	27.26	5.06	6.76	2.91	84.56	3.46	20.49	27.50	11.02	18.83	3.26
August	59.88	4.55	13.26	26.29	5.74	6.66	3.38	86.42	3.53	20.92	27.64	12.31	18.74	3.29
September	61.32	4.35	13.33	28.03	6.07	6.65	2.90	86.41	3.46	20.16	28.04	12.76	18.73	3.26
October	63.34	5.11	13.70	28.65	6.10	6.53	3.26	88.04	3.44	20.35	28.64	13.29	19.00	3.33
November	63.19	4.73	13.58	28.34	6.33	6.58	3.64	88.50	3.49	20.22	28.93	13.50	18.95	3.41
December	61.57	4.89	12.98	27.79	6.11	6.51	3.30	87.29	3.51	19.66	28.29	13.67	18.72	3.44
1999														
January	60.74	4.43	12.44	28.22	6.06	6.57	3.01	88.70	3.57	19.99	28.92	13.49	19.31	3.42
February	60.33	4.43	12.54	27.54	6.02	6.66	3.13	90.29	3.68	19.59	29.74	14.03	19.86	3.39
March	60.87	4.56	12.82	27.93	5.95	6.57	3.05	90.67	3.59	20.18	29.65	14.12	19.47	3.66
April	61.76	4.80	12.89	28.27	6.20	6.70	2.88	91.93	3.69	20.36	30.45	13.73	20.07	3.63
May	61.93	4.77	12.93	28.40	6.09	6.54	3.21	93.48	3.71	20.65	31.35	14.36	19.77	3.63
June	62.52	4.93	13.09	28.50	6.24	6.59	3.18	97.05	3.88	20.96	33.03	15.03	20.45	3.70
July	63.21	5.18	12.70	29.39	6.19	6.68	3.06	98.33	3.83	20.85	33.62	15.37	21.04	3.62
August	65.11	5.15	13.66	30.31	6.61	6.55	2.83	98.57	3.85	21.26	33.20	15.35	21.02	3.90
September	66.36	5.40	14.44	30.21	6.28	6.86	3.18	97.99	3.90	20.90	33.02	15.35	21.00	3.83
October	65.47	5.17	14.01	30.30	6.27	6.75	2.97	99.56	3.86	20.79	34.15	15.14	21.63	3.99
November	65.50	4.80	14.76	29.92	6.28	6.87	2.87	100.53	3.93	20.79	34.83	15.30	21.85	3.83
December	67.74	4.96	14.44	31.50	6.49	7.14	3.21	101.41	3.82	20.50	35.36	15.89	21.98	3.86

Table 11-9. U.S. Exports of Services

(Balance of payments basis, millions of dollars, seasonally adjusted.)

Year and month	Total	Travel	Passenger fares	Other transportation	Royalties and license fees	Other private services	Transfers under U.S. military sales contracts [1]	U.S. government miscellaneous services
1970	14 171	2 331	544	3 125	2 331	1 294	4 214	332
1971	16 358	2 534	615	3 299	2 545	1 546	5 472	347
1972	17 841	2 817	699	3 579	2 770	1 764	5 856	357
1973	19 832	3 412	975	4 465	3 225	1 985	5 369	401
1974	22 591	4 032	1 104	5 697	3 821	2 321	5 197	419
1975	25 497	4 697	1 039	5 840	4 300	2 920	6 256	446
1976	27 971	5 742	1 229	6 747	4 353	3 584	5 826	489
1977	31 485	6 150	1 366	7 090	4 920	3 848	7 554	557
1978	36 353	7 183	1 603	8 136	5 885	4 717	8 209	620
1979	39 692	8 441	2 156	9 971	6 184	5 439	6 981	520
1980	47 584	10 588	2 591	11 618	7 085	6 276	9 029	398
1981	57 354	12 913	3 111	12 560	7 284	10 250	10 720	517
1982	64 079	12 393	3 174	12 317	5 603	17 444	12 572	576
1983	64 307	10 947	3 610	12 590	5 778	18 192	12 524	666
1984	71 168	17 177	4 067	13 809	6 177	19 255	9 969	714
1985	73 155	17 762	4 411	14 674	6 678	20 035	8 718	878
1986	86 350	20 385	5 582	15 438	8 113	27 687	8 549	595
1987	98 593	23 563	7 003	17 027	10 183	29 186	11 106	526
1988	111 068	29 434	8 976	19 311	12 146	31 253	9 284	664
1989	127 233	36 205	10 657	20 526	13 818	36 875	8 564	587
1990	147 922	43 007	15 298	22 042	16 634	40 341	9 932	668
1991	164 333	48 385	15 854	22 631	17 819	47 821	11 135	690
1992	176 916	54 742	16 618	21 531	20 841	49 956	12 387	841
1993	185 941	57 875	16 528	21 958	21 695	53 532	13 471	883
1994	201 031	58 417	16 997	23 754	26 712	61 477	12 787	887
1995	219 229	63 395	18 909	26 081	30 289	65 094	14 643	818
1996	240 007	69 809	20 422	26 074	32 470	73 858	16 446	928
1997	257 235	73 426	20 868	27 006	33 639	84 505	16 836	955
1998	262 653	71 286	20 098	25 604	36 197	90 914	17 628	926
1999	271 884	74 881	19 776	27 033	36 467	96 508	16 334	885
1996								
January	18 773	5 442	1 624	2 110	2 633	5 722	1 136	106
February	18 961	5 434	1 644	2 035	2 639	5 849	1 248	112
March	19 811	5 938	1 747	2 118	2 639	6 036	1 226	107
April	19 367	5 487	1 566	2 203	2 622	6 050	1 368	71
May	20 156	6 218	1 787	2 166	2 629	6 060	1 234	62
June	19 950	6 017	1 722	2 121	2 647	6 083	1 300	60
July	19 420	5 309	1 604	2 106	2 704	6 140	1 481	76
August	19 734	5 493	1 663	2 203	2 734	6 159	1 406	76
September	19 654	5 392	1 633	2 129	2 760	6 212	1 454	74
October	21 512	6 419	1 831	2 311	2 820	6 432	1 639	60
November	21 614	6 508	1 852	2 304	2 828	6 550	1 512	60
December	21 051	6 152	1 749	2 267	2 815	6 562	1 442	64
1997								
January	20 701	6 156	1 711	2 203	2 773	6 535	1 238	85
February	20 760	6 026	1 715	2 219	2 752	6 639	1 321	88
March	21 121	6 169	1 758	2 279	2 744	6 755	1 329	87
April	21 191	6 025	1 722	2 284	2 771	6 868	1 450	71
May	21 565	6 076	1 711	2 273	2 781	7 011	1 644	69
June	21 704	6 175	1 746	2 204	2 799	7 105	1 605	70
July	21 745	6 111	1 729	2 220	2 874	7 231	1 501	79
August	21 911	6 176	1 727	2 249	2 880	7 256	1 541	82
September	21 706	6 308	1 778	2 222	2 869	7 171	1 275	83
October	21 887	6 154	1 765	2 354	2 797	7 366	1 369	82
November	21 450	6 081	1 772	2 242	2 791	7 300	1 183	81
December	21 497	5 969	1 734	2 259	2 810	7 267	1 380	78
1998								
January	21 687	6 138	1 702	2 205	2 913	7 325	1 338	66
February	21 458	5 985	1 658	2 094	2 945	7 363	1 347	66
March	21 982	5 775	1 600	2 086	2 967	7 509	1 977	68
April	22 471	6 307	1 788	2 143	2 988	7 670	1 492	83
May	22 108	6 041	1 720	2 121	2 988	7 584	1 570	84
June	21 718	5 831	1 671	2 029	2 976	7 719	1 409	83
July	21 447	5 728	1 689	2 092	2 903	7 608	1 359	68
August	21 483	5 780	1 696	2 134	2 916	7 566	1 323	68
September	21 564	5 776	1 693	2 102	2 968	7 631	1 323	71
October	22 393	5 907	1 607	2 261	3 189	7 697	1 643	89
November	22 040	5 869	1 626	2 204	3 227	7 588	1 435	91
December	22 299	6 149	1 648	2 134	3 215	7 652	1 412	89
1999								
January	22 069	5 947	1 562	2 135	3 073	7 664	1 615	73
February	21 944	6 061	1 604	2 133	3 032	7 800	1 247	67
March	22 359	6 132	1 648	2 247	3 009	7 882	1 378	63
April	22 461	6 149	1 621	2 220	3 053	7 867	1 490	61
May	22 410	6 166	1 628	2 201	3 047	7 892	1 415	61
June	22 983	6 249	1 653	2 271	3 040	8 013	1 656	101
July	22 619	6 181	1 672	2 189	3 044	8 106	1 350	77
August	22 706	6 167	1 681	2 299	3 035	8 057	1 386	81
September	22 763	6 347	1 752	2 240	3 027	8 108	1 208	81
October	23 156	6 577	1 672	2 355	3 035	8 228	1 213	76
November	23 516	6 731	1 693	2 398	3 034	8 412	1 175	73
December	22 896	6 174	1 590	2 344	3 038	8 478	1 201	71

1. Contains goods that cannot be separately identified.

Table 11-10. U.S. Imports of Services

(Balance of payments basis, millions of dollars, seasonally adjusted.)

Year and month	Total	Travel	Passenger fares	Other transportation	Royalties and license fees	Other private services	Direct defense expenditures [1]	U.S. government miscellaneous services
1970	14 520	3 980	1 215	2 843	224	827	4 855	576
1971	15 400	4 373	1 290	3 130	241	956	4 819	592
1972	16 868	5 042	1 596	3 520	294	1 043	4 784	589
1973	18 843	5 526	1 790	4 694	385	1 180	4 629	640
1974	21 379	5 980	2 095	5 942	346	1 262	5 032	722
1975	21 996	6 417	2 263	5 708	472	1 551	4 795	789
1976	24 570	6 856	2 568	6 852	482	2 006	4 895	911
1977	27 640	7 451	2 748	7 972	504	2 190	5 823	951
1978	32 189	8 475	2 896	9 124	671	2 573	7 352	1 099
1979	36 689	9 413	3 184	10 906	831	2 822	8 294	1 239
1980	41 491	10 397	3 607	11 790	724	2 909	10 851	1 214
1981	45 503	11 479	4 487	12 474	650	3 562	11 564	1 287
1982	51 749	12 394	4 772	11 710	795	8 159	12 460	1 460
1983	54 973	13 149	6 003	12 222	943	8 001	13 087	1 568
1984	67 748	22 913	5 735	14 843	1 168	9 040	12 516	1 534
1985	72 862	24 558	6 444	15 643	1 170	10 203	13 108	1 735
1986	81 835	25 913	6 505	17 766	1 401	14 834	13 730	1 686
1987	92 349	29 310	7 283	19 010	1 857	18 047	14 950	1 893
1988	99 965	32 114	7 729	20 891	2 601	19 106	15 604	1 921
1989	104 185	33 416	8 249	22 172	2 528	20 636	15 313	1 871
1990	120 021	37 349	10 531	24 966	3 135	24 590	17 531	1 919
1991	121 196	35 322	10 012	24 975	4 035	28 328	16 409	2 116
1992	116 476	38 552	10 603	23 767	5 161	22 296	13 835	2 263
1993	122 281	40 713	11 410	24 524	5 032	26 261	12 086	2 255
1994	131 878	43 782	13 062	26 019	5 852	30 386	10 217	2 560
1995	141 447	44 916	14 663	27 034	6 919	35 249	10 043	2 623
1996	150 850	48 078	15 809	27 403	7 837	37 975	11 061	2 687
1997	166 502	52 051	18 138	28 959	9 614	43 280	11 698	2 762
1998	182 697	56 509	19 971	30 363	11 713	49 051	12 241	2 849
1999	191 296	59 351	21 405	34 137	13 275	46 657	13 650	2 821
1996								
January	12 082	3 854	1 256	2 236	607	3 005	907	217
February	12 346	4 106	1 340	2 101	596	3 065	918	220
March	12 260	3 989	1 271	2 189	591	3 079	920	221
April	12 320	3 883	1 274	2 354	607	3 091	894	217
May	12 546	3 991	1 334	2 371	604	3 132	895	219
June	12 261	3 853	1 286	2 265	601	3 133	902	221
July	12 949	4 007	1 317	2 375	978	3 113	930	229
August	12 793	4 113	1 354	2 326	708	3 123	938	231
September	12 636	4 020	1 331	2 290	605	3 215	943	232
October	12 892	4 057	1 345	2 387	635	3 304	937	227
November	12 896	4 144	1 367	2 225	646	3 349	938	227
December	12 870	4 061	1 334	2 283	660	3 367	939	226
1997								
January	13 354	4 332	1 449	2 359	726	3 318	948	222
February	13 411	4 276	1 431	2 398	742	3 397	946	221
March	13 381	4 287	1 426	2 364	747	3 396	938	223
April	13 388	4 201	1 523	2 405	711	3 421	898	229
May	13 599	4 294	1 543	2 442	725	3 463	900	232
June	13 778	4 345	1 563	2 378	758	3 583	916	235
July	13 970	4 341	1 558	2 320	870	3 665	975	241
August	14 105	4 389	1 572	2 315	898	3 688	1 001	242
September	14 410	4 420	1 600	2 478	904	3 747	1 022	239
October	14 163	4 284	1 447	2 471	848	3 819	1 066	228
November	14 429	4 478	1 529	2 418	842	3 887	1 049	226
December	14 516	4 404	1 497	2 613	843	3 896	1 039	224
1998								
January	14 531	4 604	1 556	2 472	846	3 836	992	225
February	14 829	4 576	1 551	2 407	1 230	3 865	976	224
March	14 734	4 590	1 543	2 525	864	4 023	966	223
April	15 086	4 734	1 679	2 490	896	4 111	958	218
May	15 001	4 631	1 646	2 482	907	4 149	965	221
June	15 197	4 731	1 656	2 484	932	4 182	984	228
July	15 359	4 695	1 728	2 498	957	4 191	1 041	249
August	15 367	4 694	1 698	2 542	966	4 148	1 062	257
September	15 538	4 775	1 713	2 527	987	4 202	1 075	259
October	15 946	4 949	1 739	2 718	1 033	4 187	1 067	253
November	15 632	4 769	1 735	2 640	1 047	4 118	1 074	249
December	15 479	4 761	1 727	2 579	1 049	4 039	1 081	243
1999								
January	15 118	4 710	1 671	2 524	1 026	3 864	1 089	234
February	15 198	4 772	1 708	2 591	1 025	3 774	1 098	230
March	15 708	5 078	1 836	2 669	1 030	3 763	1 106	226
April	15 566	4 910	1 754	2 637	1 066	3 871	1 107	221
May	15 660	4 876	1 746	2 692	1 075	3 925	1 122	224
June	15 944	4 932	1 774	2 858	1 083	3 923	1 144	230
July	16 132	4 973	1 792	2 876	1 086	3 945	1 206	254
August	16 119	4 906	1 768	3 030	1 101	3 842	1 215	257
September	16 237	4 920	1 788	3 047	1 127	3 895	1 205	255
October	16 490	5 175	1 874	2 990	1 194	3 890	1 134	233
November	16 827	5 236	1 898	3 142	1 221	3 986	1 115	229
December	16 298	4 863	1 796	3 082	1 241	3 979	1 109	228

1. Contains goods that cannot be separately identified.

Table 11-11. U.S. Export and Import Price Indexes

(1995=100, not seasonally adjusted.)

Year and month	Exports			Imports		
	All commodities	Agricultural	Nonagricultural	All commodities	Petroleum [1]	Nonpetroleum
1970	. . .	. . .	. . .	. . .	. . .	. . .
1971	. . .	. . .	. . .	. . .	. . .	. . .
1972	. . .	. . .	. . .	. . .	. . .	. . .
1973	. . .	. . .	. . .	. . .	. . .	. . .
1974	. . .	. . .	. . .	. . .	. . .	. . .
1975	. . .	. . .	. . .	. . .	. . .	. . .
1976	. . .	. . .	. . .	. . .	. . .	. . .
1977	. . .	. . .	. . .	. . .	. . .	. . .
1978	. . .	. . .	. . .	. . .	. . .	. . .
1979	. . .	. . .	. . .	. . .	. . .	. . .
1980	. . .	. . .	. . .	. . .	. . .	. . .
1981	. . .	. . .	. . .	. . .	. . .	. . .
1982	. . .	. . .	. . .	. . .	. . .	. . .
1983	. . .	. . .	. . .	. . .	. . .	. . .
1984	. . .	. . .	. . .	. . .	. . .	. . .
1985	. . .	. . .	. . .	. . .	. . .	. . .
1986	. . .	. . .	. . .	. . .	. . .	. . .
1987	. . .	. . .	. . .	. . .	. . .	. . .
1988	. . .	. . .	. . .	. . .	. . .	. . .
1989	91.1	92.8	90.5	90.6	102.3	89.5
1990	91.9	88.3	92.1	93.5	126.3	90.5
1991	92.6	86.9	93.1	93.7	112.6	92.0
1992	92.7	86.1	93.4	94.3	105.3	93.3
1993	93.2	87.7	93.9	94.0	96.5	93.8
1994	95.2	91.9	95.6	95.7	90.8	96.2
1995	100.0	100.0	100.0	100.0	100.0	100.0
1996	100.5	111.4	99.2	101.0	118.9	99.2
1997	99.2	101.3	98.9	98.5	110.4	97.1
1998	95.9	91.4	96.4	92.6	74.9	93.7
1999	94.7	85.0	95.8	93.4	100.5	92.4
1996						
January	101.0	110.6	99.7	100.6	105.5	100.2
February	100.8	110.4	99.5	100.4	104.0	100.1
March	100.6	111.9	99.2	101.0	112.9	99.9
April	101.2	117.3	99.2	101.9	122.5	99.8
May	101.6	120.9	99.1	101.2	118.0	99.5
June	101.4	118.3	99.2	100.1	111.1	99.1
July	100.9	116.0	99.0	100.0	113.2	98.7
August	100.7	115.8	98.8	100.1	115.7	98.6
September	99.9	107.4	99.0	101.3	124.4	99.0
October	99.7	104.6	99.0	101.8	133.2	98.7
November	99.3	102.2	99.0	101.6	132.1	98.6
December	99.3	101.3	99.1	101.9	134.7	98.7
1997						
January	99.4	101.4	99.1	101.6	135.5	98.3
February	99.6	103.5	99.1	100.7	124.5	98.2
March	99.7	105.1	99.0	99.4	113.7	97.8
April	99.7	104.7	99.0	98.3	105.4	97.3
May	99.4	103.4	99.0	98.3	106.6	97.2
June	99.3	101.3	99.1	98.2	104.5	97.3
July	99.3	100.2	99.1	98.0	103.1	97.1
August	99.3	100.3	99.1	97.9	105.5	96.8
September	99.0	100.2	98.8	97.8	105.7	96.8
October	98.6	98.4	98.6	98.0	111.6	96.5
November	98.6	99.1	98.5	97.6	107.7	96.3
December	98.2	98.3	98.1	96.6	100.4	95.9
1998						
January	97.5	95.6	97.7	95.3	90.4	95.3
February	97.2	94.2	97.5	94.4	84.5	94.9
March	96.9	93.7	97.2	93.6	76.9	94.6
April	96.5	92.2	97.0	93.3	77.2	94.3
May	96.6	93.1	96.9	93.2	77.6	94.1
June	96.1	93.1	96.4	92.6	74.2	93.7
July	95.8	93.4	96.0	91.8	70.2	93.3
August	95.3	89.6	95.9	91.4	69.8	92.9
September	94.8	87.0	95.7	91.6	74.3	92.7
October	94.7	87.1	95.6	91.8	76.0	92.8
November	94.9	88.6	95.6	91.3	68.6	92.9
December	94.8	89.2	95.4	90.4	59.5	92.7
1999						
January	94.8	89.2	95.4	90.8	62.0	92.8
February	94.6	87.1	95.5	90.7	61.7	92.8
March	94.2	84.5	95.3	90.9	70.3	92.3
April	94.4	84.9	95.5	91.9	84.6	92.1
May	94.5	85.2	95.5	92.5	90.8	92.3
June	94.5	85.0	95.6	92.4	91.2	92.1
July	94.4	83.1	95.7	93.3	103.5	92.0
August	94.7	84.7	95.8	94.3	115.6	92.1
September	94.8	84.6	95.9	95.2	125.2	92.3
October	95.1	84.5	96.3	95.4	127.3	92.3
November	95.3	83.7	96.6	96.2	132.5	92.7
December	95.2	83.1	96.6	96.8	140.9	92.7

1. Petroleum and petroleum products.

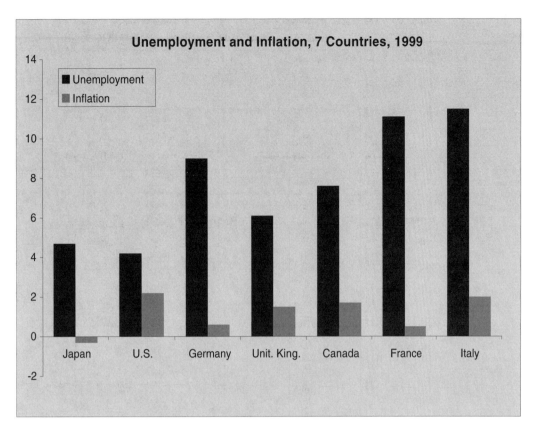

- Consumer prices were remarkably stable in all the major industrial countries in 1999, varying from a 0.3 percent decline in Japan to a 2.2 percent rise in the United States.

- Unemployment rates in six of the seven countries declined in 1999. The exception was Japan, which had an increase from 4.1 percent in 1998 to 4.7 percent in 1999.

Table 12-1. Industrial Production Indexes [1]

(1992=100, seasonally adjusted.)

Year and month	United States	Japan	Germany [2]	France	United Kingdom	Italy	Canada
1970	58.7	47.2	71.5	66.4	75.7	59.7	59.5
1971	59.5	48.4	72.1	70.7	75.4	59.5	62.8
1972	65.3	52.0	74.8	74.6	76.7	62.1	68.4
1973	70.6	59.7	79.7	79.7	83.6	68.1	76.2
1974	69.6	57.3	78.2	81.6	81.9	71.2	77.3
1975	63.5	51.1	73.4	75.7	77.4	64.6	71.6
1976	69.3	56.7	78.3	82.4	80.0	72.7	76.2
1977	74.9	59.0	80.3	83.7	84.1	73.5	78.9
1978	79.3	62.8	78.9	85.6	86.5	74.9	82.2
1979	82.0	67.4	82.9	89.4	89.8	79.9	86.2
1980	79.7	70.5	82.9	91.3	84.0	84.3	83.5
1981	81.0	71.2	81.3	90.5	81.3	82.4	84.0
1982	76.7	71.4	78.7	89.8	82.9	79.9	77.4
1983	79.5	73.8	79.2	89.2	85.9	78.1	81.4
1984	86.6	80.6	81.6	89.5	86.0	80.6	91.7
1985	88.0	83.6	85.5	91.3	90.7	80.7	96.6
1986	89.0	83.5	87.0	91.9	92.9	84.0	96.0
1987	93.2	86.4	87.4	93.1	96.6	86.2	100.2
1988	97.4	94.5	90.5	97.3	101.3	92.1	106.3
1989	99.1	99.9	95.1	100.9	103.4	95.7	105.8
1990	98.9	104.1	99.9	102.4	103.1	101.7	102.9
1991	97.0	106.1	102.3	101.2	99.7	101.3	98.9
1992	100.0	100.0	100.0	100.0	100.0	100.0	100.0
1993	103.5	96.5	92.4	96.1	102.2	97.9	104.5
1994	109.1	97.7	95.6	100.0	107.7	103.9	111.3
1995	114.4	100.9	96.8	102.0	109.5	109.2	116.3
1996	119.5	103.2	97.4	102.2	110.7	107.1	118.3
1997	126.8	107.0	100.8	106.2	111.8	111.2	124.8
1998	131.3	99.9	105.0	111.0	112.6	112.3	127.7
1995							
January	113.4	99.2	96.3	103.2	108.7	108.4	117.5
February	113.4	101.1	97.3	101.8	109.0	107.0	117.3
March	113.6	101.8	97.1	103.7	109.6	108.8	116.6
April	113.4	102.0	97.3	100.8	109.5	107.1	116.4
May	113.8	100.7	98.3	103.0	110.0	109.4	116.5
June	114.3	101.0	97.3	103.3	109.1	108.7	116.1
July	113.9	98.0	97.2	102.7	109.2	107.9	115.9
August	115.1	101.7	96.2	102.7	109.9	111.0	115.9
September	115.4	100.1	97.2	102.1	110.1	109.7	115.9
October	115.5	101.0	94.8	100.3	109.3	110.3	115.9
November	115.7	101.8	95.8	101.4	109.9	109.9	116.1
December	115.8	102.4	96.1	100.0	110.2	112.0	115.6
1996							
January	115.5	103.1	97.0	101.8	110.5	110.6	116.9
February	117.0	104.7	95.3	102.3	110.2	110.0	116.8
March	116.8	99.2	96.7	101.6	111.2	108.8	116.2
April	118.2	102.0	96.5	101.3	109.6	106.2	117.0
May	119.2	102.8	97.3	102.7	111.1	107.3	117.4
June	120.0	100.2	97.5	101.9	110.5	106.9	117.9
July	120.3	103.8	97.4	102.7	110.7	107.3	119.1
August	120.9	102.8	98.8	102.7	110.6	108.0	119.3
September	121.1	103.7	98.5	102.7	111.2	105.6	119.5
October	121.2	106.0	97.3	102.8	110.5	107.0	119.0
November	121.9	105.4	98.5	102.6	111.3	106.4	121.1
December	122.3	105.8	98.4	102.6	111.5	105.7	119.3
1997							
January	123.0	109.7	98.2	102.2	112.6	106.3	121.6
February	123.9	107.4	98.9	103.0	111.8	109.0	122.2
March	124.4	106.1	99.8	102.4	110.6	108.3	121.7
April	125.1	106.2	100.3	106.2	111.6	111.6	123.5
May	125.5	109.3	99.1	105.1	111.4	110.6	124.3
June	126.1	107.2	102.0	105.3	111.7	111.2	123.8
July	127.0	107.9	104.1	108.1	113.5	112.9	126.9
August	127.8	106.4	100.8	108.1	112.0	112.8	125.9
September	128.5	108.4	100.8	107.6	111.5	112.7	126.0
October	129.3	107.5	102.3	109.8	111.9	114.8	126.8
November	129.9	102.8	102.5	107.4	111.6	113.5	126.7
December	130.3	104.8	103.6	109.8	111.6	114.8	127.7
1998							
January	130.3	106.0	104.7	109.2	111.7	113.2	125.1
February	130.2	102.2	104.7	109.6	111.7	113.6	127.9
March	130.7	101.4	106.1	111.2	112.4	113.3	128.9
April	131.3	99.9	105.2	110.7	113.5	114.4	127.6
May	131.9	97.3	105.6	111.3	112.3	113.9	127.7
June	130.6	99.9	104.8	111.8	113.7	113.6	126.9
July	130.5	98.8	108.0	111.5	113.6	115.0	124.6
August	132.4	98.4	106.9	111.5	113.3	111.4	128.5
September	131.9	100.1	104.3	111.2	112.7	113.9	128.1
October	132.4	98.9	105.2	111.4	112.5	112.7	127.8
November	132.2	98.1	103.4	111.4	112.3	113.2	129.1
December	132.4	98.1	104.3	110.7	111.9	109.7	130.0

1. This table is reproduced from the 1999 edition of *Business Statistics of the United States*. Updated data were not available at press time.
2. Data prior to 1991 are for West Germany only.

Table 12-2. Consumer Price Indexes

(1982–1984=100, not seasonally adjusted; percent changes are from previous year's average for annual data, from the same month of the previous year for monthly data.)

Year and month	United States		Japan		Germany [1]		France		United Kingdom		Italy		Canada	
	Index	Percent change	Index	Percent change	Index	Percent change	Index	Percent change	Index	Percent change	Index	Percent change	Index	Percent change
1970	38.8	5.7	38.5	6.6	52.8	3.4	28.8	5.7	21.8	6.3	17.3	5.0	35.1	3.4
1971	40.5	4.4	40.9	6.3	55.6	5.3	30.3	5.5	23.8	9.4	18.2	4.9	36.2	2.9
1972	41.8	3.2	42.9	4.9	58.7	5.5	32.2	6.2	25.5	7.1	19.2	5.7	37.9	4.8
1973	44.4	6.2	47.9	11.7	62.8	6.9	34.6	7.3	27.9	9.2	21.3	10.8	40.7	7.5
1974	49.3	11.0	59.1	23.2	67.2	7.0	39.3	13.7	32.3	16.0	25.4	19.1	45.2	10.9
1975	53.8	9.1	66.0	11.7	71.2	6.0	43.9	11.8	40.1	24.2	29.7	17.0	50.1	10.8
1976	56.9	5.8	72.2	9.4	74.2	4.3	48.2	9.6	46.8	16.5	34.6	16.8	53.8	7.5
1977	60.6	6.5	78.1	8.1	77.0	3.7	52.7	9.4	54.2	15.8	41.0	18.4	58.1	8.0
1978	65.2	7.6	81.4	4.2	79.0	2.7	57.5	9.1	58.7	8.3	46.0	12.1	63.3	9.0
1979	72.6	11.3	84.4	3.7	82.3	4.1	63.6	10.8	66.6	13.4	52.8	14.8	69.1	9.1
1980	82.4	13.5	90.9	7.7	86.7	5.4	72.3	13.6	78.5	18.0	64.0	21.2	76.1	10.1
1981	90.9	10.3	95.4	4.9	92.2	6.3	82.0	13.4	87.9	11.9	75.4	17.8	85.6	12.5
1982	96.5	6.2	98.0	2.8	97.1	5.3	91.7	11.8	95.4	8.6	87.8	16.5	94.9	10.8
1983	99.6	3.2	99.8	1.9	100.3	3.3	100.5	9.6	99.8	4.6	100.7	14.7	100.4	5.8
1984	103.9	4.3	102.1	2.3	102.7	2.4	107.9	7.4	104.8	5.0	111.5	10.8	104.7	4.4
1985	107.6	3.6	104.2	2.0	104.8	2.1	114.2	5.8	111.1	6.1	121.8	9.2	108.9	4.0
1986	109.6	1.9	104.8	0.6	104.7	-0.1	117.2	2.7	114.9	3.4	129.0	5.9	113.4	4.1
1987	113.6	3.6	104.9	0.1	104.9	0.2	120.9	3.1	119.7	4.2	135.1	4.7	118.4	4.4
1988	118.3	4.1	105.7	0.7	106.3	1.3	124.2	2.7	125.6	4.9	141.9	5.0	123.2	4.1
1989	124.0	4.8	108.1	2.3	109.2	2.8	128.6	3.6	135.4	7.8	150.8	6.3	129.3	5.0
1990	130.7	5.4	111.4	3.1	112.1	2.7	132.8	3.3	148.2	9.5	160.5	6.5	135.5	4.8
1991	136.2	4.2	115.1	3.3	116.2	3.7	137.1	3.2	156.9	5.9	170.6	6.3	143.1	5.6
1992	140.3	3.0	117.0	1.7	120.9	4.0	140.4	2.4	162.7	3.7	179.4	5.2	145.3	1.5
1993	144.5	3.0	118.6	1.3	125.2	3.6	143.3	2.1	165.3	1.6	187.5	4.5	147.9	1.8
1994	148.2	2.6	119.4	0.7	128.6	2.7	145.7	1.7	169.3	2.4	195.0	4.0	148.2	0.2
1995	152.4	2.8	119.2	-0.1	130.7	1.6	148.2	1.7	175.2	3.5	205.1	5.2	151.4	2.1
1996	156.9	3.0	119.4	0.1	132.4	1.3	151.2	2.0	179.4	2.4	213.4	4.0	153.8	1.6
1997	160.5	2.3	121.5	1.8	134.8	1.9	153.0	1.2	185.1	3.1	217.7	2.0	156.2	1.6
1998	163.0	1.6	122.2	0.6	136.0	0.9	154.1	0.7	191.4	3.4	221.8	1.9	157.7	0.9
1999	166.6	2.2	121.9	-0.3	136.9	0.7	154.9	0.5	194.3	1.5	225.5	1.7	160.5	1.7
1996														
January	154.4	2.7	118.8	-0.5	...	...	149.8	2.0	176.5	2.9	209.0	5.6	152.3	1.6
February	154.9	2.7	118.5	-0.4	...	...	150.3	2.0	177.3	2.7	209.6	5.0	152.4	1.2
March	155.7	2.8	118.8	-0.1	...	...	151.3	2.3	178.0	2.7	210.2	4.5	153.0	1.4
April	156.3	2.9	119.5	0.2	...	...	151.5	2.4	179.3	2.4	211.4	4.5	153.4	1.4
May	156.6	2.9	119.7	0.2	...	...	151.8	2.4	179.6	2.2	212.2	4.3	153.8	1.4
June	156.7	2.8	119.4	0.0	...	...	151.7	2.3	179.8	2.1	212.7	4.0	153.8	1.4
July	157.0	3.0	119.3	0.4	...	...	151.4	2.3	179.1	2.2	212.2	3.7	153.8	1.2
August	157.3	2.9	119.1	0.2	...	...	151.0	1.6	179.9	2.1	212.4	3.4	153.8	1.3
September	157.8	3.0	119.6	0.0	...	...	151.5	1.6	180.7	2.1	213.1	3.5	154.1	1.5
October	158.3	3.0	119.9	0.5	...	...	151.9	1.8	180.7	2.7	213.3	3.0	154.4	1.7
November	158.6	3.3	119.5	0.5	...	...	151.8	1.6	180.8	2.7	213.9	2.6	155.2	2.0
December	158.6	3.3	119.6	0.6	...	...	152.1	1.7	181.4	2.5	214.1	2.6	155.2	2.1
1997														
January	159.1	3.0	119.5	0.6	...	...	152.5	1.8	181.4	2.8	...	...	155.4	2.1
February	159.6	3.0	119.3	0.6	...	...	152.7	1.6	182.1	2.7	...	...	155.7	2.2
March	160.0	2.8	119.4	0.5	...	...	152.9	1.1	182.6	2.6	...	...	156.0	2.0
April	160.2	2.5	121.8	1.9	...	...	152.9	0.9	183.6	2.4	...	...	156.0	1.7
May	160.1	2.2	122.0	1.9	...	...	153.1	0.9	184.3	2.6	...	...	156.2	1.5
June	160.3	2.3	122.0	2.2	...	...	153.1	1.0	185.1	2.9	...	...	156.5	1.7
July	160.5	2.2	121.5	1.9	...	...	152.9	1.0	185.1	3.3	...	...	156.5	1.7
August	160.8	2.2	121.6	2.1	...	...	153.3	1.5	186.2	3.5	...	...	156.8	1.9
September	161.2	2.2	122.5	2.4	...	...	153.5	1.3	187.2	3.6	...	...	156.6	1.6
October	161.6	2.1	122.8	2.5	...	...	153.5	1.0	187.4	3.7	...	...	156.8	1.5
November	161.5	1.8	122.0	2.1	...	...	153.8	1.3	187.5	3.7	...	...	156.5	0.8
December	161.3	1.7	121.8	1.8	...	...	153.8	1.1	188.0	3.6	...	...	156.3	0.7
1998														
January	161.6	1.6	121.6	1.8	...	...	153.4	0.6	187.4	3.3	...	...	157.2	1.1
February	161.9	1.4	121.5	1.9	...	...	153.9	0.8	188.3	3.4	...	...	157.3	1.0
March	162.2	1.4	122.0	2.2	...	...	154.2	0.9	188.9	3.5	...	...	157.5	0.9
April	162.5	1.4	122.2	0.4	...	...	154.5	1.1	191.0	4.0	...	...	157.3	0.8
May	162.8	1.7	122.6	0.5	...	...	154.5	0.9	192.1	4.2	...	...	157.9	1.1
June	163.0	1.7	122.1	0.1	...	...	154.7	1.0	192.0	3.7	...	...	158.1	1.0
July	163.2	1.7	121.4	-0.1	...	...	154.2	0.9	191.5	3.5	...	...	158.1	1.0
August	163.4	1.6	121.3	-0.3	...	...	154.2	0.6	192.3	3.3	...	...	158.1	0.8
September	163.6	1.5	122.2	-0.2	...	...	154.2	0.4	193.2	3.2	...	...	157.8	0.7
October	164.0	1.5	123.1	0.2	...	...	154.2	0.4	193.3	3.1	...	...	158.4	1.0
November	164.0	1.5	123.0	0.8	...	...	154.0	0.2	193.2	3.0	...	...	158.4	1.2
December	163.9	1.6	122.5	0.6	...	...	154.2	0.3	193.2	2.7	...	...	157.9	1.0
1999														
January	164.3	1.6	...	...	...	...	...	...	...	...	...	...	...	...
February	164.5	1.6	...	...	...	...	...	...	...	...	...	...	...	...
March	165.0	1.7	...	...	...	...	...	...	...	...	...	...	...	...
April	166.2	2.2	...	...	...	...	...	...	...	...	...	...	...	...
May	166.2	2.0	...	...	...	...	...	...	...	...	...	...	...	...
June	166.2	1.9	...	...	...	...	...	...	...	...	...	...	...	...
July	166.7	2.1	...	...	...	...	...	...	...	...	...	...	...	...
August	167.1	2.2	...	...	...	...	...	...	...	...	...	...	...	...
September	167.9	2.6	...	...	...	...	...	...	...	...	...	...	...	...
October	168.2	2.5	...	...	...	...	...	...	...	...	...	...	...	...
November	168.3	2.6	...	...	...	...	...	...	...	...	...	...	...	...
December	168.3	2.6	...	...	...	...	...	...	...	...	...	...	...	...

1. Former West Germany only.

Table 12-3. Unemployment Rates and Civilian Labor Forces [1]

(Quarterly data, seasonally adjusted.)

Year and quarter	United States Unemployment rate	United States Labor force (thousands)	Japan Unemployment rate	Japan Labor force (thousands)	Germany [2] Unemployment rate	Germany [2] Labor force (thousands)	France Unemployment rate	France Labor force (thousands)	United Kingdom Unemployment rate	United Kingdom Labor force (thousands)	Italy Unemployment rate	Italy Labor force (thousands)	Canada Unemployment rate	Canada Labor force (thousands)
1970	4.9	82 771	1.2	50 730	0.5	26 240	2.5	20 800	3.1	25 110	3.2	19 720	5.7	8 395
1971	5.9	84 382	1.3	51 120	0.6	26 380	2.8	21 000	3.9	24 950	3.3	19 660	6.2	8 639
1972	5.6	87 034	1.4	51 320	0.7	26 470	2.9	21 150	4.2	25 190	3.8	19 450	6.2	8 897
1973	4.9	89 429	1.3	52 590	0.7	26 780	2.8	21 430	3.2	25 440	3.7	19 590	5.5	9 276
1974	5.6	91 949	1.4	52 440	1.6	26 660	2.9	21 660	3.1	25 470	3.1	19 900	5.3	9 639
1975	8.5	93 775	1.9	52 530	3.4	26 430	4.2	21 770	4.6	25 730	3.4	20 090	6.9	9 974
1976	7.7	96 158	2.0	53 100	3.4	26 290	4.6	22 050	5.9	25 900	3.9	20 290	7.0	10 514
1977	7.1	99 009	2.0	53 820	3.4	26 330	5.2	22 380	6.4	26 050	4.1	20 510	8.0	10 774
1978	6.1	102 251	2.3	54 610	3.3	26 520	5.4	22 540	6.3	26 260	4.1	20 570	8.3	11 138
1979	5.8	104 962	2.1	55 210	2.9	26 860	6.1	22 780	5.4	26 350	4.4	20 850	7.5	11 521
1980	7.1	106 940	2.0	55 740	2.8	27 260	6.5	22 930	7.0	26 520	4.4	21 120	7.5	11 860
1981	7.6	108 670	2.2	56 320	4.0	27 540	7.6	23 090	10.5	26 590	4.9	21 320	7.6	12 222
1982	9.7	110 204	2.4	56 980	5.6	27 710	8.3	23 320	11.3	26 560	5.4	21 410	11.0	12 296
1983	9.6	111 550	2.7	58 110	6.9	27 670	8.6	23 400	11.8	26 610	5.9	21 590	11.9	12 523
1984	7.5	113 544	2.8	58 480	7.1	27 800	10.0	23 560	11.7	27 110	5.9	21 670	11.3	12 739
1985	7.2	115 461	2.6	58 820	7.2	28 020	10.5	23 620	11.2	27 350	6.0	21 800	10.7	13 002
1986	7.0	117 834	2.8	59 410	6.6	28 240	10.6	23 760	11.2	27 550	7.5	22 290	9.6	13 257
1987	6.2	119 865	2.9	60 050	6.3	28 390	10.8	23 890	10.3	27 870	7.9	22 350	8.8	13 512
1988	5.5	121 669	2.5	60 860	6.3	28 610	10.3	23 980	8.6	28 270	7.9	22 660	7.8	13 779
1989	5.3	123 869	2.3	61 920	5.7	28 840	9.6	24 170	7.2	28 580	7.8	22 530	7.5	14 047
1990	5.6	125 840	2.1	63 050	5.0	29 410	9.1	24 300	6.9	28 730	7.0	22 670	8.1	14 241
1991	6.8	126 346	2.1	64 280	5.6	39 130	9.6	24 490	8.8	28 610	6.9	22 940	10.3	14 330
1992	7.5	128 105	2.2	65 040	6.7	39 040	10.4	24 550	10.1	28 410	7.3	22 910	11.2	14 362
1993	6.9	129 200	2.5	65 470	7.9	39 140	11.8	24 650	10.5	28 310	10.2	22 570	11.4	14 505
1994	6.1	131 056	2.9	65 780	8.5	39 210	12.3	24 760	9.7	28 280	11.2	22 450	10.4	14 627
1995	5.6	132 304	3.2	65 990	8.2	39 100	11.8	24 820	8.7	28 480	11.8	22 460	9.4	14 750
1996	5.4	133 943	3.4	66 450	8.9	39 180	12.5	25 090	8.2	28 620	11.7	22 570	9.6	14 900
1997	4.9	136 297	3.4	67 200	9.9	39 450	12.4	25 180	7.0	28 760	11.9	22 680	9.1	15 153
1998	4.5	137 673	4.1	67 240	9.4	39 430	11.8	25 360	6.3	28 870	12.0	22 960	8.3	15 418
1999	4.2	139 368	4.7	67 100	9.0	. . .	11.1	25 590	6.1	29 090	11.5	23 130	7.6	15 721
1991														
1st quarter	6.6	. . .	2.1	. . .	4.4	. . .	9.1	. . .	7.8	. . .	6.9	. . .	10.2	. . .
2nd quarter	6.8	. . .	2.1	. . .	4.3	. . .	9.5	. . .	8.6	. . .	7.0	. . .	10.4	. . .
3rd quarter	6.9	. . .	2.2	. . .	4.3	. . .	9.8	. . .	9.2	. . .	6.8	. . .	10.4	. . .
4th quarter	7.1	. . .	2.1	. . .	4.3	. . .	9.9	. . .	9.5	. . .	6.9	. . .	10.5	. . .
1992														
1st quarter	7.4	. . .	2.1	. . .	4.3	. . .	10.1	. . .	9.7	. . .	7.1	. . .	10.8	. . .
2nd quarter	7.6	. . .	2.1	. . .	4.4	. . .	10.3	. . .	9.9	. . .	7.0	. . .	11.3	. . .
3rd quarter	7.6	. . .	2.2	. . .	4.6	. . .	10.5	. . .	10.1	. . .	7.0	. . .	11.6	. . .
4th quarter	7.4	. . .	2.3	. . .	4.9	. . .	10.8	. . .	10.5	. . .	8.3	. . .	11.6	. . .
1993														
1st quarter	7.2	. . .	2.4	. . .	7.4	. . .	11.2	. . .	10.6	. . .	9.2	. . .	11.1	. . .
2nd quarter	7.1	. . .	2.5	. . .	7.8	. . .	11.6	. . .	10.5	. . .	10.2	. . .	11.7	. . .
3rd quarter	6.8	. . .	2.6	. . .	8.2	. . .	12.0	. . .	10.4	. . .	10.5	. . .	11.5	. . .
4th quarter	6.6	. . .	2.8	. . .	8.5	. . .	12.4	. . .	10.2	. . .	10.9	. . .	11.3	. . .
1994														
1st quarter	6.6	. . .	2.9	. . .	8.6	. . .	12.5	. . .	10.0	. . .	10.9	. . .	11.0	. . .
2nd quarter	6.2	. . .	2.9	. . .	8.6	. . .	12.5	. . .	9.8	. . .	11.1	. . .	10.6	. . .
3rd quarter	6.0	. . .	3.0	. . .	8.4	. . .	12.3	. . .	9.5	. . .	11.1	. . .	10.1	. . .
4th quarter	5.6	. . .	2.9	. . .	8.2	. . .	12.0	. . .	9.1	. . .	11.6	. . .	9.7	. . .
1995														
1st quarter	5.5	. . .	3.0	. . .	8.0	. . .	12.0	. . .	8.9	. . .	11.9	. . .	9.6	. . .
2nd quarter	5.7	. . .	3.2	. . .	8.1	. . .	11.7	. . .	8.8	. . .	11.6	. . .	9.5	. . .
3rd quarter	5.7	. . .	3.2	. . .	8.2	. . .	11.6	. . .	8.7	. . .	11.9	. . .	9.5	. . .
4th quarter	5.6	. . .	3.4	. . .	8.4	. . .	11.8	. . .	8.5	. . .	11.6	. . .	9.3	. . .
1996														
1st quarter	5.6	. . .	3.4	. . .	8.8	. . .	12.3	. . .	8.4	. . .	11.7	. . .	9.5	. . .
2nd quarter	5.5	. . .	3.5	. . .	8.8	. . .	12.5	. . .	8.3	. . .	11.8	. . .	9.4	. . .
3rd quarter	5.3	. . .	3.4	. . .	8.9	. . .	12.6	. . .	8.1	. . .	11.8	. . .	9.7	. . .
4th quarter	5.3	. . .	3.3	. . .	9.2	. . .	12.6	. . .	7.9	. . .	11.7	. . .	9.9	. . .
1997														
1st quarter	5.3	. . .	3.3	. . .	9.8	. . .	12.4	. . .	7.4	. . .	11.9	. . .	9.4	. . .
2nd quarter	5.0	. . .	3.4	. . .	9.8	. . .	12.5	. . .	7.3	. . .	11.9	. . .	9.3	. . .
3rd quarter	4.8	. . .	3.4	. . .	10.0	. . .	12.5	. . .	6.9	. . .	11.7	. . .	8.9	. . .
4th quarter	4.7	. . .	3.5	. . .	10.0	. . .	12.3	. . .	6.6	. . .	11.9	. . .	8.8	. . .
1998														
1st quarter	4.7	. . .	3.7	. . .	9.9	. . .	12.0	. . .	6.4	. . .	11.8	. . .	8.6	. . .
2nd quarter	4.4	. . .	4.2	. . .	9.5	. . .	11.7	. . .	6.3	. . .	12.0	. . .	8.3	. . .
3rd quarter	4.5	. . .	4.3	. . .	9.1	. . .	11.7	. . .	6.3	. . .	12.0	. . .	8.2	. . .
4th quarter	4.4	. . .	4.5	. . .	9.1	. . .	11.5	. . .	6.3	. . .	12.0	. . .	8.1	. . .
1999														
1st quarter	4.3	. . .	4.7	. . .	9.0	. . .	11.3	. . .	6.3	. . .	11.9	. . .	7.9	. . .
2nd quarter	4.3	. . .	4.8	. . .	9.0	. . .	11.2	. . .	6.1	. . .	11.6	. . .	7.8	. . .
3rd quarter	4.2	. . .	4.8	. . .	9.1	. . .	11.0	. . .	5.9	. . .	11.6	. . .	7.6	. . .
4th quarter	4.1	. . .	4.7	. . .	9.0	. . .	10.6	. . .	5.9	. . .	11.1	. . .	7.0	. . .

1. Data for other countries adjusted to approximate U.S. concepts.
2. Data prior to 1991 are for West Germany only.

Table 12-4. Stock Price Indexes [1]

(Averages of daily closing values.)

Year and month	United States (S&P 500)	Canada (TSE 300)	Brazil (Bovespa)	France (CAC 40)	Germany (DAX)	United Kingdom (FTSE 100)	Hong Kong (Hang Seng)	Japan (Nikkei 225)	Singapore (Straits Times)
1970	83.22	...	...	...	...	...	...	...	...
1971	98.29	...	...	...	...	...	...	...	...
1972	109.20	...	...	...	...	...	...	...	...
1973	107.43	...	...	...	...	...	...	...	...
1974	82.85	...	...	...	...	...	...	...	...
1975	86.16	...	...	...	...	...	...	...	...
1976	102.01	...	...	...	...	...	...	...	...
1977	98.20	...	...	...	...	...	...	...	...
1978	96.02	...	...	...	...	...	...	...	...
1979	103.01	...	...	...	...	...	...	...	...
1980	118.78	...	...	...	...	...	...	...	...
1981	128.04	...	...	...	...	...	...	...	...
1982	119.71	...	...	...	...	...	...	...	...
1983	160.41	...	...	...	...	...	...	...	...
1984	160.46	...	...	...	...	...	...	10 556.59	...
1985	186.84	2 683.55	...	...	...	1 307.15	...	12 552.14	...
1986	236.34	2 999.33	...	...	...	1 588.21	...	16 482.73	...
1987	286.83	3 590.67	...	...	...	2 035.85	2 908.02	23 249.64	...
1988	265.79	3 288.66	...	...	...	1 803.11	2 555.63	27 046.97	1 000.38
1989	322.84	3 775.62	...	...	...	2 175.55	2 792.82	34 058.49	1 290.32
1990	334.59	3 464.71	...	...	...	2 225.18	3 032.66	29 436.93	1 396.03
1991	376.17	3 457.64	...	1 766.31	1 579.37	2 466.46	3 798.10	24 295.57	1 428.99
1992	415.74	3 405.84	...	1 850.49	1 635.87	2 559.42	5 479.33	18 108.70	1 439.72
1993	451.41	3 856.50	...	2 021.17	1 808.59	2 962.10	7 459.14	19 100.00	1 876.13
1994	460.33	4 274.27	3 164.83	2 058.20	2 120.32	3 140.55	9 532.10	19 936.03	2 270.05
1995	541.64	4 423.47	3 901.76	1 869.74	2 137.91	3 351.10	9 010.28	17 329.66	2 118.97
1996	670.83	5 217.73	5 868.95	2 078.83	2 566.39	3 828.35	11 474.44	21 088.34	2 263.06
1997	873.72	6 473.35	10 386.05	2 759.94	3 721.07	4 696.36	13 375.56	18 397.16	1 961.82
1998	1 085.50	6 792.23	9 261.00	3 693.37	5 016.31	5 628.29	9 418.33	15 362.35	1 254.02
1995									
January	465.25	4 122.72	3 874.05	1 841.13	2 055.68	3 028.30	7 454.47	18 948.26	2 096.21
February	481.92	4 104.28	3 339.67	1 833.66	2 100.62	3 051.68	8 002.67	18 065.00	2 103.26
March	493.15	4 213.04	2 941.23	1 795.59	1 997.59	3 078.24	8 370.70	16 447.59	2 089.51
April	507.91	4 277.73	3 325.06	1 895.04	1 981.74	3 198.38	8 501.81	16 322.05	2 067.51
May	523.81	4 349.58	3 951.95	1 968.42	2 070.01	3 288.31	8 932.72	16 265.90	2 139.47
June	539.35	4 503.74	3 720.52	1 913.09	2 126.81	3 351.55	9 280.05	15 039.32	2 139.42
July	557.37	4 625.90	3 883.38	1 928.78	2 184.73	3 426.50	9 476.98	16 188.62	2 155.76
August	559.11	4 593.87	4 254.61	1 943.60	2 241.76	3 486.96	9 131.52	17 410.74	2 106.05
September	578.77	4 551.47	4 653.20	1 853.68	2 257.55	3 534.27	9 503.62	18 097.15	2 119.73
October	582.92	4 443.95	4 438.71	1 778.55	2 164.81	3 531.80	9 833.22	17 951.57	2 114.83
November	595.53	4 599.85	4 057.71	1 860.97	2 197.41	3 580.31	9 539.33	18 109.35	2 094.05
December	614.57	4 698.47	4 271.68	1 843.99	2 268.54	3 649.20	9 902.50	19 417.90	2 201.55
1996									
January	614.42	4 833.76	4 825.05	1 944.18	2 376.43	3 716.69	10 717.38	20 497.21	2 393.10
February	649.54	5 006.85	5 270.72	1 971.76	2 431.31	3 738.08	11 341.84	20 628.55	2 453.87
March	647.07	4 962.09	4 929.24	1 986.76	2 477.10	3 697.50	10 927.46	20 424.35	2 386.85
April	647.17	5 066.41	5 016.65	2 095.12	2 521.55	3 792.32	10 936.64	21 828.67	2 387.17
May	661.23	5 195.73	5 482.18	2 113.97	2 518.07	3 758.41	10 906.83	21 770.76	2 357.37
June	668.50	5 094.69	5 788.47	2 113.26	2 554.47	3 734.02	11 012.58	22 185.45	2 302.31
July	644.07	4 995.16	6 271.87	2 030.68	2 519.99	3 707.21	10 837.12	21 558.52	2 193.62
August	662.68	5 096.06	6 249.36	1 999.89	2 540.95	3 841.75	11 203.53	20 870.27	2 135.63
September	674.89	5 233.30	6 434.24	2 056.10	2 596.70	3 927.10	11 406.33	20 823.68	2 143.58
October	701.46	5 486.12	6 626.82	2 151.19	2 694.68	4 020.99	12 274.82	21 118.95	2 090.17
November	735.67	5 845.10	6 611.45	2 236.06	2 759.32	3 969.54	12 986.34	21 040.70	2 157.08
December	743.25	5 845.25	6 841.42	2 268.10	2 849.49	4 038.89	13 201.13	20 147.25	2 195.69
1997									
January	766.22	6 027.55	7 595.45	2 395.16	2 963.56	4 164.11	13 456.78	18 050.37	2 235.62
February	798.38	6 177.99	8 604.95	2 587.07	3 192.48	4 316.57	13 398.15	18 562.55	2 222.39
March	792.16	6 147.12	9 253.79	2 634.17	3 358.09	4 349.78	12 974.13	18 244.10	2 139.64
April	763.93	5 824.88	9 596.71	2 568.47	3 340.01	4 312.51	12 460.71	18 177.90	2 051.08
May	833.09	6 266.27	10 598.60	2 690.96	3 579.74	4 622.62	14 021.83	20 046.00	2 064.43
June	876.29	6 477.56	11 934.29	2 750.06	3 727.82	4 649.40	14 673.64	20 505.62	2 014.74
July	925.29	6 678.76	12 712.77	2 963.03	4 161.70	4 842.85	15 416.92	20 148.09	1 965.23
August	927.74	6 772.29	11 637.57	2 941.45	4 191.36	4 945.56	15 945.12	19 090.57	1 919.76
September	937.02	6 868.27	11 396.55	2 939.77	4 044.67	5 010.36	14 454.28	18 248.45	1 897.53
October	951.16	7 032.88	11 898.52	2 936.96	4 078.99	5 145.13	12 609.09	17 274.77	1 783.15
November	938.92	6 748.83	9 168.65	2 782.29	3 824.86	4 846.24	10 327.41	16 103.22	1 678.88
December	962.37	6 647.23	9 707.05	2 899.71	4 133.70	5 087.53	10 806.98	15 917.10	1 620.56
1998									
January	963.36	6 521.09	9 658.71	3 000.93	4 284.11	5 242.10	9 248.06	15 929.63	1 288.97
February	1 023.74	6 918.26	10 275.00	3 250.75	4 575.55	5 656.07	10 646.23	16 797.79	1 537.52
March	1 076.83	7 382.42	11 521.41	3 616.91	4 915.28	5 861.80	11 314.71	16 840.45	1 616.75
April	1 112.20	7 675.83	11 824.16	3 857.15	5 244.45	5 974.51	11 014.92	15 941.41	1 528.71
May	1 108.42	7 678.67	10 568.65	4 006.74	5 397.79	5 936.72	9 680.72	15 514.28	1 342.95
June	1 108.39	7 336.74	9 793.86	4 124.77	5 719.69	5 846.84	8 318.89	15 231.29	1 115.37
July	1 156.58	7 300.99	10 529.77	4 266.48	6 001.07	5 989.37	8 323.92	16 370.17	1 081.03
August	1 074.62	6 332.50	8 428.71	3 960.53	5 390.41	5 555.77	7 398.00	15 243.98	964.99
September	1 020.64	5 806.89	6 389.05	3 543.34	4 746.55	5 169.88	7 652.51	14 140.69	887.25
October	1 032.47	5 735.72	6 696.57	3 301.96	4 343.36	5 063.84	9 195.26	13 486.91	1 043.87
November	1 144.43	6 401.03	8 256.25	3 693.25	4 828.34	5 595.58	10 298.70	14 525.88	1 297.11
December	1 190.05	6 364.69	7 282.75	3 761.75	4 752.13	5 686.26	10 146.01	14 320.69	1 386.94

1. This table is reproduced from the 1999 edition of *Business Statistics of the United States*. Updated data were not available at press time.

Table 12-5. Exchange Rates [1]

(Not seasonally adjusted.)

Year and month	Foreign currency per U.S. dollar						Trade-weighted exchange indexes of value of U.S. dollar					
							Nominal				Price-adjusted	
	European currency unit	Japanese yen	German mark	French franc	British pound	Canadian dollar	G-10 countries (March 1973=100)	Broad (January 1997=100)	Major currency (March 1973=100)	Other important trading partners (January 1997=100)	Broad (January 1997=100)	Other important trading partners (January 1997=100)
1970	. . .	. . .	. . .	. . .	. . .	. . .	121.07	. . .	. . .	. . .	. . .	. . .
1971	. . .	348.05	3.4818	5.5108	0.4092	1.0099	117.81	. . .	. . .	. . .	. . .	. . .
1972	. . .	303.11	3.1889	5.0448	0.4005	0.9908	109.07	. . .	. . .	. . .	. . .	. . .
1973	. . .	271.40	2.6719	4.4549	0.4084	1.0002	99.14	28.71	100.26	1.64	98.96	96.96
1974	. . .	291.94	2.5873	4.8104	0.4277	0.9781	101.41	29.56	101.85	1.75	95.24	87.57
1975	. . .	296.77	2.4614	4.2885	0.4521	1.0173	98.50	30.77	102.19	2.01	93.43	87.01
1976	. . .	296.48	2.5184	4.7805	0.5567	0.9861	105.63	32.81	105.47	2.34	92.85	85.01
1977	. . .	268.38	2.3225	4.9149	0.5733	1.0635	103.35	34.04	105.31	2.68	91.07	84.80
1978	. . .	210.46	2.0090	4.5101	0.5214	1.1408	92.39	32.59	96.67	2.88	85.61	83.88
1979	. . .	219.21	1.8331	4.2545	0.4720	1.1716	88.07	33.07	95.46	3.14	87.00	84.54
1980	. . .	226.58	1.8183	4.2269	0.4304	1.1694	87.38	34.13	95.35	3.48	89.13	85.14
1981	. . .	220.45	2.2606	5.4349	0.4978	1.1989	103.26	37.75	104.04	3.96	95.53	87.06
1982	. . .	249.05	2.4281	6.5761	0.5727	1.2339	116.50	43.93	114.67	5.14	104.75	97.43
1983	. . .	237.45	2.5545	7.6221	0.6601	1.2326	125.32	49.53	118.56	6.93	108.69	105.66
1984	. . .	237.59	2.8483	8.7439	0.7521	1.2952	138.34	56.57	126.27	9.18	115.54	111.76
1985	. . .	238.47	2.9443	8.9870	0.7792	1.3659	143.24	63.65	131.08	12.44	120.66	119.54
1986	. . .	168.50	2.1711	6.9258	0.6821	1.3898	112.27	59.56	107.89	15.63	105.95	123.27
1987	. . .	144.62	1.7976	6.0110	0.6117	1.3262	96.95	58.25	95.47	19.15	97.55	120.64
1988	. . .	128.14	1.7561	5.9565	0.5621	1.2309	92.75	59.12	88.74	23.39	91.03	110.69
1989	. . .	138.00	1.8792	6.3753	0.6111	1.1841	98.52	65.25	92.36	29.11	92.46	105.68
1990	. . .	144.82	1.6159	5.4449	0.5630	1.1670	89.05	70.05	88.39	39.21	90.04	104.77
1991	. . .	134.51	1.6585	5.6388	0.5667	1.1460	89.73	73.14	86.91	45.79	88.59	103.94
1992	. . .	126.75	1.5624	5.2956	0.5699	1.2088	86.64	76.38	85.45	53.05	86.73	100.66
1993	. . .	111.23	1.6537	5.6644	0.6662	1.2902	93.16	84.42	87.73	65.96	87.59	98.14
1994	. . .	102.19	1.6219	5.5467	0.6531	1.3659	91.32	90.42	86.25	80.51	87.25	97.79
1995	. . .	94.11	1.4331	4.9889	0.6337	1.3727	84.30	92.52	81.40	92.51	84.69	97.14
1996	. . .	108.78	1.5049	5.1158	0.6407	1.3637	87.34	97.40	84.60	98.26	86.63	94.40
1997	. . .	121.06	1.7348	5.8393	0.6106	1.3849	96.35	104.44	91.24	104.67	91.24	95.58
1998	. . .	130.99	1.7597	5.8995	0.6034	1.4836	98.82	116.48	95.79	126.03	99.25	108.20
1999	0.9387	113.73	1.8359	6.1575	0.6184	1.4858	. . .	116.87	94.06	129.94	98.66	107.44
1996												
January	. . .	105.75	1.4635	5.0117	0.6541	1.3669	86.23	96.34	83.78	97.05	86.49	96.24
February	. . .	105.79	1.4669	5.0440	0.6510	1.3752	86.42	96.50	83.97	97.13	86.29	95.22
March	. . .	105.94	1.4776	5.0583	0.6548	1.3656	86.58	96.47	83.89	97.20	86.32	95.13
April	. . .	107.20	1.5044	5.1049	0.6596	1.3592	87.46	96.76	84.40	97.09	86.33	94.35
May	. . .	106.34	1.5324	5.1855	0.6600	1.3693	88.28	97.24	84.80	97.60	86.49	94.13
June	. . .	108.96	1.5282	5.1787	0.6487	1.3658	88.16	97.74	85.08	98.32	86.85	94.43
July	. . .	109.19	1.5025	5.0881	0.6439	1.3697	87.25	97.63	84.71	98.64	86.82	94.66
August	. . .	107.87	1.4826	5.0636	0.6452	1.3722	86.54	97.22	84.19	98.47	86.25	93.72
September	. . .	109.93	1.5080	5.1307	0.6413	1.3694	87.46	97.75	84.88	98.66	86.62	93.50
October	. . .	112.41	1.5277	5.1652	0.6304	1.3508	87.98	98.23	85.21	99.27	87.07	93.93
November	. . .	112.30	1.5118	5.1156	0.6016	1.3381	86.97	97.91	84.42	99.75	86.69	93.97
December	. . .	113.98	1.5525	5.2427	0.6010	1.3622	88.71	98.97	85.91	99.93	87.32	93.52
1997												
January	. . .	117.91	1.6047	5.4145	0.6030	1.3494	91.01	100.00	87.48	100.00	88.11	93.13
February	. . .	122.96	1.6747	5.6536	0.6152	1.3556	94.52	101.80	90.06	100.34	89.45	92.64
March	. . .	122.77	1.6946	5.7154	0.6213	1.3725	95.60	102.56	90.80	101.02	90.25	93.42
April	. . .	125.64	1.7119	5.7672	0.6138	1.3942	96.39	103.37	91.94	101.23	90.66	93.33
May	. . .	119.19	1.7048	5.7482	0.6127	1.3804	95.29	102.36	90.30	101.29	89.47	92.95
June	. . .	114.29	1.7277	5.8293	0.6079	1.3843	95.42	102.01	89.76	101.26	89.07	92.68
July	. . .	115.38	1.7939	6.0511	0.5990	1.3775	97.48	103.25	90.78	102.58	90.16	93.73
August	. . .	117.93	1.8400	6.2010	0.6236	1.3905	99.96	105.10	92.65	104.07	91.68	94.82
September	. . .	120.89	1.7862	6.0031	0.6245	1.3872	98.29	105.68	92.29	105.94	91.91	95.85
October	. . .	121.06	1.7575	5.8954	0.6124	1.3869	97.07	106.39	91.72	108.38	92.58	98.03
November	. . .	125.38	1.7323	5.8001	0.5921	1.4128	96.37	108.22	92.38	111.62	94.01	100.42
December	. . .	129.73	1.7788	5.9542	0.6025	1.4271	98.82	112.51	94.58	118.32	97.48	105.96
1998												
January	. . .	129.55	1.8165	6.0832	0.6116	1.4409	100.52	116.54	95.74	126.19	100.42	111.51
February	. . .	125.85	1.8123	6.0744	0.6095	1.4334	99.93	114.89	94.78	123.72	98.47	107.94
March	. . .	129.08	1.8272	6.1257	0.6017	1.4166	100.48	114.60	95.21	122.27	98.08	106.35
April	. . .	131.75	1.8132	6.0782	0.5980	1.4298	100.30	114.35	95.73	120.89	97.77	104.93
May	. . .	134.90	1.7753	5.9528	0.6104	1.4452	99.61	115.30	96.12	122.54	98.47	106.18
June	. . .	140.33	1.7928	6.0118	0.6059	1.4655	100.91	117.96	97.85	126.15	100.70	108.96
July	. . .	140.79	1.7976	6.0280	0.6084	1.4869	101.38	118.27	98.47	125.89	101.05	108.50
August	. . .	144.68	1.7869	5.9912	0.6119	1.5346	101.80	120.23	100.03	128.09	102.68	110.12
September	. . .	134.48	1.6990	5.6969	0.5944	1.5218	97.17	119.02	96.08	131.74	100.93	111.53
October	. . .	121.05	1.6381	5.4925	0.5902	1.5452	93.68	115.85	92.74	129.59	98.02	109.22
November	. . .	120.29	1.6827	5.6422	0.6020	1.5404	95.46	115.73	93.53	127.90	97.60	106.99
December	. . .	117.07	1.6698	5.5981	0.5985	1.5433	94.60	114.98	92.73	127.42	96.83	106.15
1999												
January	0.8627	113.29	1.6874	5.6592	0.6061	1.5194	. . .	115.16	91.77	129.55	97.03	107.30
February	0.8926	116.67	1.7458	5.8552	0.6144	1.4977	. . .	116.84	93.18	131.31	98.09	107.82
March	0.9186	119.47	1.7966	6.0257	0.6168	1.5176	. . .	118.22	95.11	131.40	99.43	108.31
April	0.9345	119.77	1.8277	6.1299	0.6215	1.4881	. . .	117.57	95.22	129.60	99.37	107.63
May	0.9407	122.00	1.8399	6.1708	0.6190	1.4611	. . .	117.34	95.25	128.96	99.02	106.91
June	0.9637	120.72	1.8848	6.3213	0.6270	1.4695	. . .	117.93	96.07	129.03	99.55	107.02
July	0.9643	119.33	1.8860	6.3255	0.6349	1.4890	. . .	117.97	96.31	128.73	99.87	107.01
August	0.9430	113.23	1.8443	6.1854	0.6227	1.4932	. . .	117.00	94.31	129.73	99.00	107.72
September	0.9527	106.88	1.8632	6.2490	0.6155	1.4771	. . .	116.38	92.92	130.60	98.46	108.11
October	0.9341	105.97	1.8269	6.1270	0.6034	1.4776	. . .	115.88	91.94	131.06	97.94	108.10
November	0.9682	104.65	1.8937	6.3512	0.6171	1.4674	. . .	116.08	92.87	129.93	98.11	106.96
December	0.9891	102.58	1.9345	6.4882	0.6199	1.4722	. . .	116.09	93.23	129.34	98.05	106.39

1. Annual data are averages of monthly values.

PART II

INDUSTRY PROFILES

CHAPTER 13: MINING, OIL, AND GAS

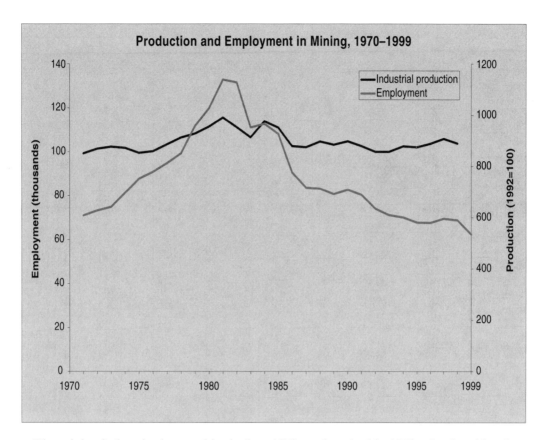

- The mining industries boomed in the late 1970s and peaked in 1981, stimulated by rising prices and shortages of petroleum and other natural resources. Subsequently, production subsided to near its 1970 level. Employment fell to the lowest level in the 30 years shown.

- In oil and gas extraction, the largest of the mining industries, production in 1999 was below 1970, despite an employment increase of 19 percent, illustrating the increasing difficulty of finding and extracting crude oil within the United States.

- The trends in coal mining have been just the opposite. The fastest-growing of the mining industries from 1970 to 1999, coal production rose 74 percent. Increasing mechanization made this increase possible with a 41 percent decline in employment.

- A similar rate of productivity growth occurred in metal mining, with output up 26 percent while employment declined 52 percent.

- Nonmetallic minerals except fuels (stone and earth minerals) had an output increase of 39 percent from 1970 to 1999 while employment fell 3 percent.

Table 13-1. Mining Industries—Industrial Production

(Seasonally adjusted, 1992=100.)

| Year and month | Total mining | Metal mining | Coal mining | Oil and gas extraction | | | | Natural gas liquids | Oil and gas well drilling | Stone and earth minerals |
| | | | | Total | Crude oil and natural gas | | | | | |
					Total	Crude oil	Natural gas			
1970	101.8	77.1	62.3	116.5	130.0	137.7	117.6	93.6	85.2	89.5
1971	99.3	68.6	57.3	115.2	128.7	135.2	120.6	94.8	81.8	89.9
1972	101.4	66.3	61.3	117.2	128.9	135.1	121.4	97.5	93.9	93.9
1973	102.3	70.0	60.7	116.6	126.6	131.6	122.0	98.0	101.9	102.5
1974	101.8	68.0	61.6	115.8	120.9	125.7	116.6	95.3	126.4	102.1
1975	99.5	63.5	66.2	113.1	114.3	119.9	107.5	92.0	143.4	91.9
1976	100.3	69.2	68.9	111.2	111.5	116.5	106.2	91.7	144.1	97.2
1977	103.4	61.1	70.6	116.8	112.3	116.8	107.5	93.2	175.0	99.4
1978	106.5	69.5	67.6	121.1	115.4	122.8	106.3	90.7	196.4	104.7
1979	108.3	72.2	78.6	119.5	113.7	120.3	105.8	94.1	190.7	107.1
1980	111.5	65.2	83.4	124.4	115.1	120.5	109.0	93.8	236.8	97.9
1981	115.6	73.5	82.9	129.7	114.5	120.0	108.4	92.9	315.6	94.1
1982	111.2	54.8	84.5	125.6	111.7	120.9	99.5	90.3	296.0	78.7
1983	106.6	52.8	79.0	120.2	108.4	121.4	90.3	90.5	257.6	84.0
1984	113.9	57.2	90.2	126.9	112.9	124.1	97.6	92.6	296.1	94.7
1985	111.0	56.6	89.1	123.0	111.4	125.1	92.3	90.5	259.9	97.9
1986	102.6	59.3	89.7	111.0	108.2	121.1	90.1	87.6	143.3	96.6
1987	102.1	61.9	92.5	108.9	106.6	116.5	93.0	91.4	130.7	100.9
1988	104.7	74.3	95.4	110.4	106.1	113.9	95.3	93.5	150.0	103.2
1989	103.2	85.6	98.9	106.1	102.5	106.5	97.0	90.0	139.9	101.8
1990	104.8	93.1	103.7	106.4	101.6	102.9	99.7	90.8	151.1	103.3
1991	102.6	93.3	100.1	104.7	101.9	103.8	99.3	97.8	128.6	96.7
1992	100.0	100.0	100.0	100.0	100.0	100.0	100.0	100.0	100.0	100.0
1993	100.0	98.8	94.0	101.1	98.0	95.2	101.7	102.1	122.5	102.3
1994	102.5	100.5	103.0	101.7	98.1	92.6	105.6	101.5	126.9	108.6
1995	102.1	101.6	102.6	100.5	96.5	90.6	104.5	103.8	126.4	112.9
1996	103.7	104.0	105.0	101.8	95.9	88.9	105.6	108.7	137.9	114.9
1997	105.9	110.3	108.2	103.1	95.7	87.8	106.6	109.4	149.3	120.1
1998	103.8	109.1	109.7	99.5	94.2	85.4	106.4	103.8	134.6	123.4
1999	98.0	97.1	108.1	92.5	90.6	80.0	105.3	109.0	106.8	124.4
1996										
January	100.3	98.0	94.4	100.8	95.5	89.2	104.4	103.5	134.3	107.7
February	101.9	97.4	99.3	101.5	96.3	89.6	105.6	98.8	136.8	112.6
March	103.4	102.3	106.9	101.3	96.2	90.0	105.0	106.1	132.6	113.9
April	104.0	100.8	105.5	102.6	96.6	88.6	107.8	108.5	139.7	114.2
May	103.9	103.3	105.7	102.1	95.7	88.0	106.4	107.8	141.5	114.7
June	105.3	104.4	108.2	103.1	97.2	89.7	107.5	109.3	139.7	117.3
July	104.8	106.8	108.2	102.3	96.3	88.6	107.0	108.7	139.1	116.4
August	104.8	106.8	109.0	102.2	96.1	88.6	106.7	110.8	138.1	116.0
September	104.5	107.4	105.7	102.5	96.5	89.6	106.1	110.8	138.1	114.8
October	104.1	106.8	105.8	101.6	95.3	88.6	104.7	113.2	138.1	118.3
November	103.8	105.5	106.2	101.3	95.0	88.4	104.2	112.5	137.9	117.8
December	103.4	108.0	105.7	100.8	94.2	88.5	102.1	114.0	139.4	115.0
1997										
January	104.2	111.9	106.2	101.8	95.6	87.5	106.9	110.4	138.9	112.2
February	106.0	109.7	109.7	102.8	96.1	88.1	107.2	112.4	143.2	121.6
March	106.6	109.5	108.3	103.7	96.3	87.9	108.0	112.1	149.6	123.7
April	105.6	108.8	106.2	103.4	96.2	88.4	106.9	108.4	149.6	118.2
May	106.8	109.7	114.1	103.4	96.1	87.8	107.7	109.4	149.5	119.0
June	105.9	112.1	108.1	102.7	95.2	87.6	105.6	110.0	150.0	122.6
July	106.0	111.5	107.6	103.5	95.9	88.0	107.0	110.4	150.8	118.5
August	105.9	112.0	107.5	103.0	95.1	87.0	106.4	110.4	152.0	121.2
September	106.3	109.3	107.1	103.8	96.1	88.0	107.3	110.7	152.1	121.9
October	106.0	112.3	106.1	103.3	95.9	87.7	107.2	108.2	150.6	121.2
November	105.6	112.5	106.5	102.8	95.2	87.8	105.5	101.4	152.6	120.5
December	105.5	104.6	110.9	102.6	94.6	87.9	104.0	108.5	152.2	120.2
1998										
January	107.7	109.2	113.4	104.2	95.9	87.5	107.5	110.9	155.6	124.0
February	107.4	118.7	106.0	104.5	95.9	87.9	107.0	110.2	157.6	123.5
March	105.8	105.2	109.3	103.0	95.3	87.4	106.3	107.3	151.8	121.1
April	105.5	104.5	107.7	102.7	95.5	87.5	106.6	108.7	147.7	123.5
May	106.0	108.8	112.8	102.1	95.0	86.8	106.3	108.8	146.3	123.2
June	104.2	109.6	108.7	100.2	94.8	86.1	107.0	103.3	136.3	123.6
July	103.1	109.1	108.1	99.0	95.0	86.7	106.4	93.8	130.5	122.0
August	103.2	114.3	107.9	98.6	94.8	86.0	107.0	101.8	126.4	122.9
September	101.7	108.0	110.3	96.7	93.0	82.8	107.0	100.9	123.0	121.6
October	101.6	106.5	110.9	96.4	93.3	83.3	107.1	101.6	119.2	122.6
November	101.5	109.4	112.4	94.7	91.9	82.2	105.2	101.7	116.0	128.9
December	98.1	106.6	109.2	91.5	90.1	80.3	103.8	96.1	105.2	124.1
1999										
January	98.0	102.9	107.7	91.2	90.6	80.9	104.0	100.4	99.8	129.4
February	97.4	101.3	108.9	90.7	90.3	80.3	104.3	100.7	97.4	127.1
March	97.5	98.5	103.9	92.1	91.3	81.6	104.9	103.5	100.8	126.6
April	96.7	100.5	107.3	90.8	90.4	80.2	104.5	104.4	97.2	121.8
May	97.4	100.2	106.1	91.8	91.0	80.8	105.1	106.4	99.8	123.9
June	97.1	98.9	107.0	91.4	90.2	79.6	105.0	109.4	100.1	123.3
July	97.8	96.2	110.0	92.3	90.9	80.2	105.9	111.9	102.0	120.5
August	98.5	93.0	110.7	93.2	91.3	80.4	106.4	110.3	107.1	123.0
September	98.3	91.4	109.4	93.0	90.2	78.4	106.5	113.0	111.3	125.5
October	99.2	94.2	108.8	94.0	90.6	78.9	106.9	114.6	115.7	126.3
November	99.7	94.5	110.0	94.5	90.4	79.5	105.6	113.8	121.3	125.0
December	99.5	95.2	109.5	94.6	89.8	79.2	104.4	119.0	124.3	122.4

Table 13-2. Mining Industries—Capacity Utilization and Producer Prices

Year and month	Capacity utilization (Output as a percent of capacity, seasonally adjusted)						Producer Prices (December 1984=100, except as noted; not seasonally adjusted)						
	Total mining	Metal mining	Coal mining	Oil and gas extraction		Stone and earth minerals	Total mining	Metal mining	Coal mining [1]	Oil and gas extraction [1]	Crude materials [2]		Nonmetallic minerals, except fuels
				Total	Oil and gas well drilling						Natural gas	Crude petroleum	
1970	88.8	93.6	95.8	87.7	69.7	87.2	. . .	. . .	. . .	. . .	7.9	14.5	. . .
1971	87.3	83.2	86.0	88.5	68.6	85.9	. . .	. . .	. . .	. . .	8.4	15.6	. . .
1972	90.3	80.7	89.2	92.3	79.1	87.8	. . .	. . .	. . .	. . .	9.0	15.5	. . .
1973	92.3	84.6	85.7	94.8	85.2	92.8	. . .	. . .	. . .	. . .	9.8	17.2	. . .
1974	92.3	82.1	84.2	96.1	98.9	89.6	. . .	. . .	. . .	. . .	11.6	28.9	. . .
1975	89.7	76.4	87.5	93.8	99.2	79.1	. . .	. . .	. . .	. . .	16.1	33.5	. . .
1976	89.8	81.0	88.9	92.1	91.5	83.0	. . .	. . .	. . .	. . .	21.8	34.6	. . .
1977	90.9	69.4	88.2	94.2	101.7	85.4	. . .	. . .	. . .	. . .	30.8	37.4	. . .
1978	90.9	78.5	80.3	94.7	100.0	89.2	. . .	. . .	. . .	. . .	36.5	40.9	. . .
1979	91.4	81.4	88.8	92.8	88.2	90.6	. . .	. . .	. . .	. . .	47.6	51.3	. . .
1980	93.4	72.8	90.3	95.8	95.7	82.7	. . .	. . .	. . .	. . .	63.3	75.9	. . .
1981	93.9	79.1	86.7	96.1	98.0	79.8	. . .	. . .	. . .	. . .	82.1	109.6	. . .
1982	86.3	57.5	86.1	88.2	70.3	67.4	. . .	. . .	. . .	. . .	100.0	100.0	. . .
1983	80.4	57.9	79.1	81.7	52.6	72.6	. . .	. . .	. . .	. . .	106.6	92.9	. . .
1984	86.0	63.3	88.6	86.7	63.4	81.8	. . .	. . .	. . .	. . .	106.1	91.3	. . .
1985	84.3	62.7	85.7	84.9	58.5	84.4	. . .	. . .	. . .	. . .	102.9	84.5	102.8
1986	77.6	65.9	84.7	76.4	34.3	82.7	77.0	91.2	99.5	76.9	89.6	46.9	104.2
1987	80.3	70.9	85.7	79.3	38.4	85.7	75.0	100.1	96.0	74.3	79.5	55.5	105.1
1988	85.2	80.5	86.8	85.0	56.0	86.9	70.6	100.7	94.6	68.5	77.4	46.2	108.0
1989	86.9	85.4	88.3	87.0	63.7	85.2	76.4	100.3	94.3	75.7	82.0	56.3	111.2
1990	89.8	85.7	90.7	90.3	75.6	86.3	81.8	93.4	96.5	82.7	80.4	71.0	113.7
1991	88.4	82.9	85.7	90.4	69.4	81.1	78.4	82.2	96.3	77.9	79.1	61.9	116.3
1992	86.4	87.1	84.6	87.0	55.3	84.0	76.9	76.6	94.0	76.5	80.6	58.0	117.5
1993	86.1	84.7	79.6	88.2	67.7	82.6	76.4	69.7	93.3	76.2	84.7	51.4	118.8
1994	87.5	87.0	84.7	88.6	70.7	85.3	73.3	81.4	93.2	71.1	78.8	47.1	120.5
1995	87.0	88.2	83.3	87.8	71.2	86.8	71.0	101.4	91.6	66.6	66.6	51.1	123.8
1996	88.5	89.1	84.2	89.8	78.9	85.7	84.4	92.1	91.4	84.8	91.2	62.6	127.1
1997	89.2	92.2	86.0	90.1	85.4	85.9	86.1	85.8	92.2	87.5	101.7	57.5	128.8
1998	86.4	89.2	87.0	86.1	75.5	85.4	70.8	73.2	89.5	68.3	83.9	35.7	132.2
1999	81.5	80.0	85.4	80.3	60.4	84.5	78.0	70.3	87.3	78.5	91.2	50.3	134.0
1996													
January	85.8	84.6	76.4	88.7	76.4	81.6	79.1	98.2	89.9	78.0	83.5	56.0	125.9
February	87.2	83.9	80.3	89.4	78.0	85.2	83.4	97.5	91.9	82.6	96.5	52.8	126.4
March	88.5	88.1	86.3	89.3	75.7	85.9	80.9	96.7	92.2	79.2	85.8	57.7	126.7
April	89.0	86.7	85.0	90.5	79.8	86.0	86.0	96.4	91.1	86.2	92.8	66.0	127.1
May	88.9	88.7	85.0	90.1	80.9	86.0	82.9	97.1	93.1	81.8	88.0	61.0	127.6
June	90.0	89.6	86.8	91.0	79.9	87.7	78.1	93.3	91.7	75.9	78.9	57.7	128.1
July	89.6	91.5	86.7	90.3	79.7	86.8	81.0	89.2	90.5	80.7	87.3	59.9	127.2
August	89.5	91.4	87.1	90.1	79.2	86.2	82.6	87.5	92.6	82.7	88.2	62.0	127.2
September	89.1	91.7	84.4	90.4	79.2	85.0	81.3	86.8	90.9	81.3	76.6	67.2	127.5
October	88.7	91.1	84.4	89.5	79.3	87.3	83.0	86.6	90.5	83.7	75.2	72.0	127.3
November	88.4	89.8	84.6	89.2	79.2	86.6	90.4	88.4	91.3	93.4	100.6	68.5	127.3
December	87.9	91.8	84.1	88.7	80.1	84.2	104.2	87.3	90.7	112.1	140.7	70.9	127.1
1997													
January	88.4	94.9	84.5	89.5	79.8	81.9	111.3	89.9	92.9	121.1	159.5	73.4	127.6
February	89.9	92.8	87.1	90.3	82.3	88.4	95.1	88.5	91.3	99.6	119.9	64.5	127.7
March	90.3	92.4	86.1	91.0	85.9	89.6	78.8	90.9	92.8	77.3	78.5	56.3	127.7
April	89.3	91.6	84.3	90.6	85.9	85.3	77.6	87.7	95.0	75.5	75.5	56.1	128.1
May	90.2	92.0	90.7	90.5	85.8	85.5	80.8	89.7	91.7	80.2	83.7	60.2	128.3
June	89.4	93.8	85.8	89.8	86.0	87.8	79.9	89.4	92.6	78.9	88.7	51.8	128.9
July	89.3	93.0	85.5	90.4	86.3	84.6	79.5	85.7	91.5	78.8	85.8	54.9	129.2
August	89.1	93.1	85.4	89.9	86.9	86.2	80.2	86.4	91.6	79.7	87.1	54.9	129.2
September	89.3	90.7	85.2	90.5	86.9	86.4	82.9	84.0	91.9	83.5	96.9	53.3	129.3
October	88.9	92.9	84.3	90.0	85.8	85.7	90.2	83.2	91.3	93.4	115.7	57.3	129.6
November	88.5	92.8	84.7	89.4	86.8	84.9	93.2	78.9	91.0	98.0	127.3	56.4	129.7
December	88.3	86.2	88.2	89.2	86.4	84.5	83.2	74.8	93.2	84.5	101.4	50.8	129.9
1998													
January	90.0	89.7	90.1	90.5	88.1	87.0	76.4	73.5	88.2	76.2	90.9	43.4	130.6
February	89.7	97.3	84.3	90.7	89.0	86.3	73.6	74.2	90.2	72.0	81.9	43.2	131.0
March	88.2	86.1	86.9	89.3	85.6	84.5	72.2	74.6	89.7	70.2	86.4	35.8	131.4
April	87.9	85.4	85.6	89.0	83.0	85.9	74.1	76.6	90.7	72.3	90.1	38.1	132.2
May	88.3	88.9	89.6	88.4	82.1	85.5	74.2	75.5	90.2	72.6	90.5	38.3	132.2
June	86.7	89.5	86.3	86.8	76.3	85.6	69.6	73.9	90.2	66.6	81.9	33.6	132.5
July	85.7	89.0	85.8	85.7	73.0	84.3	72.3	74.7	89.9	70.1	89.0	35.9	132.6
August	85.8	93.3	85.5	85.3	70.6	84.7	67.7	71.6	87.6	64.6	82.1	30.4	132.8
September	84.5	88.1	87.4	83.6	68.6	83.7	65.7	72.4	87.3	61.8	69.8	36.0	132.9
October	84.3	86.9	87.8	83.4	66.5	84.2	67.9	71.0	88.8	64.6	77.6	35.2	132.9
November	84.2	89.3	89.0	82.0	64.7	88.4	68.9	71.0	89.6	65.9	83.1	32.7	132.8
December	81.4	87.1	86.4	79.2	58.7	84.9	66.8	69.5	91.4	62.9	83.4	26.1	132.7
1999													
January	81.3	84.2	85.1	79.0	55.8	88.3	64.1	68.2	85.5	60.3	74.7	30.2	133.0
February	80.9	82.9	86.1	78.5	54.5	86.6	62.5	69.3	89.2	57.3	71.9	26.2	133.5
March	80.9	80.7	82.1	79.8	56.6	86.2	63.4	68.3	89.3	58.6	67.0	33.3	133.6
April	80.4	82.4	84.7	78.8	54.7	82.8	68.9	69.8	89.9	65.7	74.0	42.4	133.8
May	81.0	82.3	83.8	79.7	56.3	84.1	76.5	69.7	87.8	76.3	91.4	47.2	133.8
June	80.7	81.3	84.4	79.3	56.6	83.6	76.3	67.3	88.2	76.2	89.0	48.8	134.2
July	81.3	79.2	86.8	80.2	57.9	81.6	78.7	68.8	86.9	79.6	91.9	53.7	134.2
August	81.9	76.8	87.3	81.0	61.0	83.2	84.7	69.3	86.9	87.6	104.3	57.2	134.2
September	81.8	75.5	86.3	80.9	63.7	84.8	91.5	70.4	85.9	96.9	114.9	65.5	134.3
October	82.6	78.0	85.8	81.8	66.4	85.2	87.7	76.3	86.0	91.2	104.1	60.9	134.4
November	83.0	78.3	86.7	82.3	69.9	84.3	95.1	73.4	86.1	101.6	121.5	66.7	134.4
December	82.8	79.0	86.3	82.4	71.8	82.5	86.7	72.6	85.4	90.4	90.0	71.0	134.4

1. December 1985=100.
2. 1982=100.

Table 13-3. Mining Industries—Employment, Hours, and Earnings

Year and month	Total mining (seasonally adjusted)						Total mining (not seasonally adjusted)					
	Total payroll employees (thousands)	Production workers					Total payroll employees (thousands)	Production workers				
		Employees (thousands)	Average weekly hours	Aggregate weekly hours index (1982=100)	Average earnings (dollars)			Employees (thousands)	Average weekly hours	Aggregate weekly hours index (1982=100)	Average earnings (dollars)	
					Hourly	Weekly					Hourly	Weekly
1970	623	473	42.7	57.6	3.85	164.40	623	473	42.7	57.6	3.85	164.40
1971	609	455	42.4	54.9	4.06	172.14	609	455	42.4	54.9	4.06	172.14
1972	628	475	42.6	57.8	4.44	189.14	628	475	42.6	57.8	4.44	189.14
1973	642	486	42.4	58.8	4.75	201.40	642	486	42.4	58.8	4.75	201.40
1974	697	530	41.9	63.4	5.23	219.14	697	530	41.9	63.4	5.23	219.14
1975	752	571	41.9	68.3	5.95	249.31	752	571	41.9	68.3	5.95	249.31
1976	779	592	42.4	71.5	6.46	273.90	779	592	42.4	71.5	6.46	273.90
1977	813	618	43.4	76.5	6.94	301.20	813	618	43.4	76.5	6.94	301.20
1978	851	638	43.4	79.0	7.67	332.88	851	638	43.4	79.0	7.67	332.88
1979	958	719	43.0	88.2	8.49	365.07	958	719	43.0	88.2	8.49	365.07
1980	1 027	762	43.3	94.1	9.17	397.06	1 027	762	43.3	94.1	9.17	397.06
1981	1 139	841	43.7	104.8	10.04	438.75	1 139	841	43.7	104.8	10.04	438.75
1982	1 128	821	42.7	100.0	10.77	459.88	1 128	821	42.7	100.0	10.77	459.88
1983	952	673	42.5	81.5	11.28	479.40	952	673	42.5	81.5	11.28	479.40
1984	966	686	43.3	84.9	11.63	503.58	966	686	43.3	84.9	11.63	503.58
1985	927	658	43.4	81.4	11.98	519.93	927	658	43.4	81.4	11.98	519.93
1986	777	545	42.2	65.7	12.46	525.81	777	545	42.2	65.7	12.46	525.81
1987	717	511	42.4	61.8	12.54	531.70	717	511	42.4	61.8	12.54	531.70
1988	713	512	42.3	61.7	12.81	540.85	713	512	42.3	61.7	12.80	541.44
1989	692	493	43.0	60.5	13.26	570.18	692	493	43.0	60.5	13.26	570.18
1990	709	509	44.1	63.9	13.68	603.29	709	509	44.1	63.9	13.68	603.29
1991	689	489	44.4	62.0	14.19	630.04	689	489	44.4	62.0	14.19	630.04
1992	635	448	43.9	56.2	14.54	638.31	635	448	43.9	56.2	14.54	638.31
1993	610	431	44.3	54.3	14.60	646.78	610	431	44.3	54.3	14.60	646.78
1994	601	427	44.8	54.6	14.88	666.62	601	427	44.8	54.6	14.88	666.62
1995	581	424	44.7	54.1	15.30	683.91	581	424	44.7	54.1	15.30	683.91
1996	580	430	45.3	55.6	15.62	707.59	580	430	45.3	55.6	15.62	707.59
1997	596	450	45.4	58.3	16.15	733.21	596	450	45.4	58.3	16.15	733.21
1998	590	447	43.9	56.0	16.91	742.35	590	447	43.9	56.0	16.91	742.35
1999	535	402	43.8	50.3	17.09	748.54	535	402	43.8	50.3	17.09	748.54
1996												
January	573	420	44.1	52.8	15.43	680.46	562	410	43.9	51.3	15.63	686.16
February	576	425	45.3	54.9	15.45	699.89	563	413	45.1	53.2	15.61	704.01
March	578	428	45.8	55.9	15.46	708.07	566	418	45.0	53.7	15.50	697.50
April	579	429	45.2	55.3	15.48	699.70	572	423	44.9	54.1	15.55	698.20
May	581	431	45.1	55.4	15.55	701.31	579	429	45.1	55.3	15.45	696.80
June	582	433	45.7	56.4	15.63	714.29	587	437	46.0	57.3	15.59	717.14
July	581	431	45.0	55.3	15.65	704.25	591	439	44.8	56.1	15.55	696.64
August	582	433	45.2	55.8	15.70	709.64	592	442	45.2	57.0	15.52	701.50
September	580	432	45.6	56.2	15.71	716.38	587	438	46.0	57.5	15.74	724.04
October	581	433	45.3	56.0	15.63	708.04	587	439	45.9	57.4	15.56	714.20
November	583	435	45.3	56.2	15.76	713.93	588	440	45.4	57.0	15.69	712.33
December	584	436	45.6	56.7	15.89	724.58	584	436	46.0	57.2	15.97	734.62
1997												
January	586	439	44.7	56.0	16.09	719.22	576	429	44.2	54.0	16.20	716.04
February	590	443	46.1	58.3	16.00	737.60	577	431	45.6	56.1	16.09	733.70
March	592	445	46.5	59.0	15.98	743.07	580	436	45.7	56.9	16.01	731.66
April	594	448	45.5	58.1	16.02	728.91	587	441	45.1	56.7	16.08	725.21
May	597	451	45.8	58.9	16.12	738.30	595	449	45.9	58.8	16.00	734.40
June	598	452	45.5	58.7	16.19	736.65	603	456	45.8	59.6	16.13	738.75
July	599	453	45.3	58.5	16.15	731.60	608	461	45.1	59.4	16.05	723.86
August	600	453	45.5	58.8	16.12	733.46	609	462	45.6	60.1	15.96	727.78
September	601	455	45.1	58.5	16.20	730.62	608	461	45.5	59.9	16.24	738.92
October	601	454	45.0	58.3	16.27	732.15	608	461	45.3	59.6	16.19	733.41
November	600	453	45.2	58.4	16.39	740.83	604	458	45.6	59.6	16.38	746.93
December	601	456	45.0	58.5	16.39	737.55	602	456	45.3	58.9	16.49	747.00
1998												
January	602	458	45.7	59.7	16.49	753.59	593	448	45.1	57.6	16.60	748.66
February	604	460	44.4	58.3	16.77	744.59	592	448	43.9	56.1	16.85	739.72
March	604	459	44.2	57.9	16.83	743.89	592	449	43.4	55.6	16.85	731.29
April	598	455	44.0	57.1	16.75	737.00	592	449	43.4	55.6	16.80	729.12
May	597	454	44.1	57.1	16.73	737.79	594	452	44.4	57.2	16.68	740.59
June	596	452	43.7	56.3	16.76	732.41	600	456	44.0	57.2	16.69	734.36
July	589	447	43.8	55.9	16.85	738.03	598	455	44.0	57.1	16.77	737.88
August	586	445	43.6	55.3	17.01	741.64	597	454	43.9	56.9	16.90	741.91
September	582	440	43.3	54.3	17.07	739.13	589	446	43.0	54.7	17.13	736.59
October	578	436	43.6	54.2	17.16	748.18	585	443	44.0	55.5	17.10	752.40
November	572	431	43.5	53.5	17.32	753.42	577	437	43.9	54.7	17.31	759.91
December	570	430	43.3	53.1	17.22	745.63	569	431	43.6	53.7	17.33	755.59
1999												
January	557	419	43.0	51.4	17.15	737.45	547	410	42.3	49.5	17.27	730.52
February	551	412	43.2	50.8	17.05	736.56	539	401	42.7	48.9	17.12	731.02
March	549	411	43.0	50.4	17.05	733.15	539	402	42.2	48.4	17.06	719.93
April	539	402	43.7	50.1	16.94	740.28	533	396	43.3	48.9	16.98	735.23
May	532	398	43.9	49.8	17.11	751.13	531	396	44.2	49.9	17.05	753.61
June	529	396	43.9	49.6	17.07	749.37	534	399	44.2	50.3	16.98	750.52
July	528	396	44.5	50.3	17.26	768.07	537	403	44.7	51.4	17.17	767.50
August	526	395	44.1	49.7	17.16	756.76	535	403	44.5	51.1	17.05	758.73
September	527	397	44.3	50.2	17.14	759.30	535	405	44.3	51.2	17.13	758.86
October	529	400	44.1	50.3	17.09	753.67	534	406	44.5	51.6	17.05	758.73
November	527	398	44.2	50.2	17.00	751.40	531	404	44.6	51.4	17.01	758.65
December	530	400	44.3	50.5	17.04	754.87	529	400	44.4	50.6	17.19	763.24

Table 13-3. Mining Industries—Employment, Hours, and Earnings—*Continued*

(Not seasonally adjusted.)

Year and month	Metal mining					Coal mining				
	Total payroll employees (thousands)	Production workers				Total payroll employees (thousands)	Production workers			
		Employees (thousands)	Average weekly hours	Average earnings (dollars) Hourly	Weekly		Employees (thousands)	Average weekly hours	Average earnings (dollars) Hourly	Weekly
1970	93	75	43.1	3.88	167.23	145	127	40.5	4.54	183.87
1971	87	69	42.8	4.12	176.34	146	123	40.3	4.78	192.63
1972	83	66	41.4	4.56	188.78	161	140	40.7	5.27	214.49
1973	87	69	41.7	4.84	201.83	162	140	39.8	5.70	226.86
1974	95	76	41.4	5.44	225.22	180	154	37.7	6.22	234.49
1975	94	73	40.7	6.13	249.49	213	182	39.5	7.21	284.80
1976	94	73	41.0	6.76	277.16	225	192	39.8	7.74	308.05
1977	90	68	40.8	7.28	297.02	225	192	41.9	8.25	345.68
1978	94	72	41.3	8.23	339.90	210	173	40.5	9.51	385.16
1979	101	77	41.2	9.27	381.92	259	216	40.7	10.28	418.40
1980	98	74	40.5	10.26	415.53	246	204	40.1	10.86	435.49
1981	104	78	40.5	11.55	467.78	225	186	40.5	11.91	482.36
1982	73	53	39.3	12.31	483.78	237	194	39.9	12.69	506.33
1983	56	41	39.3	12.58	494.39	194	156	39.9	13.73	547.83
1984	55	40	40.5	13.05	528.53	196	158	40.7	14.82	603.17
1985	46	34	40.9	13.38	547.24	187	153	41.1	15.24	626.36
1986	41	31	41.1	13.19	542.11	176	144	40.6	15.40	625.24
1987	44	33	41.9	12.94	542.19	162	132	42.0	15.76	661.92
1988	50	39	42.3	13.24	560.05	151	123	42.2	16.06	677.73
1989	56	44	42.8	13.58	581.22	144	116	43.4	16.26	705.68
1990	58	46	42.8	14.05	601.34	147	119	44.0	16.71	735.24
1991	56	44	43.0	14.87	639.41	136	110	44.6	17.06	760.88
1992	53	42	42.9	15.26	654.65	127	103	44.0	17.15	754.60
1993	50	40	43.1	15.29	659.00	109	86	44.4	17.27	766.79
1994	49	39	43.5	16.08	699.48	112	90	45.2	17.76	802.75
1995	51	41	43.8	16.77	734.53	104	84	44.9	18.45	828.41
1996	54	42	44.0	17.35	763.40	98	80	45.8	18.74	858.29
1997	54	41	44.4	17.82	791.21	96	79	45.4	19.01	863.05
1998	50	38	44.5	18.24	811.68	92	75	44.7	19.17	856.90
1999	45	35	44.6	18.21	812.17	85	71	44.8	19.34	866.43
1996										
January	52	41	44.4	16.97	753.47	98	81	44.7	18.92	845.72
February	52	41	44.6	16.92	754.63	98	80	47.0	18.79	883.13
March	52	42	44.0	17.14	754.16	98	80	46.7	18.77	876.56
April	53	42	44.7	17.31	773.76	97	80	45.5	18.70	850.85
May	54	42	43.2	17.30	747.36	97	80	45.6	18.61	848.62
June	55	44	43.9	17.25	757.28	98	80	46.7	18.65	870.96
July	55	44	43.6	17.29	753.84	99	80	43.6	18.64	812.70
August	55	44	43.0	17.41	748.63	98	80	45.3	18.59	842.13
September	54	42	44.8	17.58	787.58	97	80	46.1	18.73	863.45
October	54	42	43.6	17.46	761.26	97	79	45.8	18.56	850.05
November	54	42	43.5	17.76	772.56	97	80	46.0	18.80	864.80
December	54	42	44.4	17.80	790.32	97	79	46.2	19.11	882.88
1997										
January	54	41	45.0	17.53	788.85	97	79	46.6	19.20	894.72
February	53	41	45.1	17.71	798.72	96	80	46.7	19.21	897.11
March	53	41	45.1	17.66	796.47	96	79	46.4	19.02	882.53
April	53	41	44.1	17.87	788.07	97	80	45.1	18.83	849.23
May	54	42	44.0	17.89	787.16	97	80	45.4	18.74	850.80
June	55	42	44.2	17.77	785.43	97	80	45.6	18.91	862.30
July	55	42	44.3	17.70	784.11	96	79	44.1	18.97	836.58
August	55	42	43.8	17.70	775.26	96	78	45.0	18.85	848.25
September	54	41	44.7	17.84	797.45	96	78	45.5	18.94	861.77
October	53	40	43.6	17.94	782.18	95	78	45.0	18.93	851.85
November	53	40	44.4	18.29	812.08	95	78	45.2	19.11	863.77
December	52	39	44.5	18.02	801.89	94	78	44.8	19.47	872.26
1998										
January	51	39	43.8	17.94	785.77	94	77	45.1	19.30	870.43
February	50	38	44.5	17.97	799.67	94	77	45.3	19.12	866.14
March	50	38	44.9	18.17	815.83	94	77	45.0	19.11	859.95
April	50	38	45.7	18.26	834.48	93	76	44.2	19.11	844.66
May	50	38	44.3	18.24	808.03	93	76	44.5	19.07	848.62
June	50	38	44.2	18.20	804.44	92	75	44.9	19.15	859.84
July	50	38	45.0	18.20	819.00	90	74	42.8	18.97	811.92
August	49	38	45.0	18.30	823.50	91	75	44.5	19.04	847.28
September	48	37	45.4	18.52	840.81	90	74	44.0	19.24	846.56
October	48	37	43.5	18.45	802.58	90	74	45.0	19.17	862.65
November	47	36	44.4	18.46	819.62	91	75	45.7	19.28	881.10
December	47	36	43.8	18.22	798.04	91	75	45.7	19.45	888.87
1999										
January	47	35	43.8	18.21	797.60	89	74	45.2	19.30	872.36
February	46	35	43.7	18.14	792.72	88	73	45.3	19.16	867.95
March	46	35	43.6	18.19	793.08	88	73	45.1	19.18	865.02
April	45	34	44.4	18.09	803.20	87	72	44.7	19.16	856.45
May	45	35	44.1	18.01	794.24	86	71	45.0	19.22	864.90
June	46	35	44.7	18.03	805.94	86	71	45.0	19.42	873.90
July	45	35	45.8	18.18	832.64	85	70	43.5	19.56	850.86
August	44	34	44.4	17.95	796.98	84	70	45.2	19.39	876.43
September	45	34	46.4	18.29	848.66	83	69	44.4	19.39	860.92
October	44	34	44.7	18.43	823.82	83	68	44.3	19.36	857.65
November	45	35	44.9	18.40	826.16	83	69	45.1	19.43	876.29
December	45	34	44.4	18.62	826.73	83	69	44.3	19.50	863.85

Table 13-3. Mining Industries—Employment, Hours, and Earnings—*Continued*

(Not seasonally adjusted.)

Year and month	Oil and gas extraction					Nonmetalic minerals, except fuel				
	Total payroll employees (thousands)	Production workers				Total payroll employees (thousands)	Production workers			
		Employees (thousands)	Average weekly hours	Average earnings (dollars)			Employees (thousands)	Average weekly hours	Average earnings (dollars)	
				Hourly	Weekly				Hourly	Weekly
1970	270	178	43.2	3.57	154.22	115	94	44.7	3.47	155.11
1971	264	173	43.2	3.78	163.30	115	93	44.9	3.70	166.13
1972	268	177	43.4	4.04	175.34	116	93	44.7	3.95	176.57
1973	274	182	43.0	4.33	186.19	119	95	45.5	4.22	192.01
1974	300	203	43.8	4.87	213.31	122	98	45.0	4.50	202.50
1975	329	223	43.7	5.38	235.11	117	92	43.5	4.95	215.33
1976	346	237	44.1	5.85	257.99	115	90	44.2	5.36	236.91
1977	381	267	44.7	6.37	284.74	116	92	44.6	5.81	259.13
1978	429	299	45.0	7.01	315.45	119	94	44.8	6.33	283.58
1979	474	327	44.4	7.72	342.77	124	98	45.0	6.90	310.50
1980	560	389	45.4	8.59	389.99	123	96	43.6	7.52	327.87
1981	692	486	45.6	9.50	433.20	119	91	43.0	8.28	356.04
1982	708	491	44.2	10.25	453.05	110	83	42.7	8.90	380.03
1983	598	398	43.6	10.67	465.21	104	79	43.6	9.31	405.92
1984	606	405	44.4	10.72	475.97	109	83	44.7	9.87	441.19
1985	583	387	44.2	11.06	488.85	110	84	44.5	10.18	453.01
1986	450	287	42.6	11.61	494.59	110	83	44.5	10.38	461.91
1987	402	261	41.7	11.53	480.80	110	85	45.4	10.60	481.24
1988	400	265	41.3	11.85	489.41	112	85	45.5	10.94	497.77
1989	381	248	42.0	12.50	525.00	111	85	45.6	11.25	513.00
1990	395	261	43.9	12.94	568.07	110	83	45.3	11.58	524.57
1991	393	258	44.5	13.53	602.09	105	78	44.5	11.93	530.89
1992	353	228	43.8	14.01	613.64	102	76	44.9	12.26	550.47
1993	350	228	43.8	14.14	619.33	102	76	46.1	12.70	585.47
1994	337	220	44.2	14.13	624.55	104	78	46.5	13.11	609.62
1995	320	218	44.2	14.52	641.78	105	80	46.6	13.39	623.97
1996	322	227	44.7	14.87	664.69	106	81	47.1	13.75	647.63
1997	339	248	45.0	15.64	703.80	108	82	47.3	14.19	671.19
1998	339	251	42.7	16.80	717.36	110	83	46.4	14.67	680.69
1999	293	212	42.4	17.02	721.65	112	85	46.3	15.01	694.96
1996										
January	314	216	43.8	14.79	647.80	97	72	42.5	13.53	575.03
February	314	218	44.6	14.89	664.09	98	74	45.0	13.40	603.00
March	315	220	44.2	14.67	648.41	102	77	46.3	13.50	625.05
April	316	221	44.0	14.81	651.64	105	80	46.9	13.58	636.90
May	320	224	44.7	14.65	654.86	108	83	47.1	13.68	644.33
June	324	228	45.3	14.87	673.61	110	85	48.2	13.80	665.16
July	326	230	44.0	14.83	652.52	110	85	48.5	13.87	672.70
August	328	234	44.5	14.76	656.82	111	85	48.5	13.91	674.64
September	324	232	45.1	15.04	678.30	110	85	48.9	14.02	685.58
October	326	234	45.4	14.83	673.28	110	84	48.6	13.92	676.51
November	328	236	45.2	14.93	674.84	109	82	46.8	13.85	648.18
December	328	236	45.9	15.34	704.11	105	79	46.7	13.81	644.93
1997										
January	327	234	43.9	15.62	685.72	99	73	42.2	13.76	580.67
February	328	236	45.5	15.43	702.07	100	74	45.1	13.84	624.18
March	327	238	45.4	15.37	697.80	103	78	46.5	14.02	651.93
April	330	240	44.6	15.59	695.31	107	81	47.1	14.00	659.40
May	334	244	45.3	15.48	701.24	110	84	48.8	14.17	691.50
June	338	248	45.3	15.68	710.30	112	86	48.2	14.19	683.96
July	344	254	44.4	15.52	689.09	112	86	48.8	14.30	697.84
August	346	255	45.1	15.40	694.54	112	86	48.5	14.29	693.07
September	346	256	44.5	15.78	702.21	112	85	48.9	14.49	708.56
October	349	258	44.6	15.76	702.90	111	84	48.6	14.34	696.92
November	348	257	45.6	15.96	727.78	109	83	46.8	14.31	669.71
December	350	259	45.1	16.05	723.86	106	80	46.6	14.36	669.18
1998										
January	348	258	45.3	16.27	737.03	100	74	44.7	14.24	636.53
February	347	258	43.1	16.76	722.36	100	75	45.2	14.27	645.00
March	345	256	42.3	16.69	705.99	104	78	44.8	14.50	649.60
April	341	252	41.8	16.64	695.55	109	83	46.4	14.54	674.66
May	340	253	43.4	16.46	714.36	111	85	47.1	14.62	688.60
June	344	256	42.5	16.44	698.70	113	86	47.5	14.70	698.25
July	344	255	42.9	16.65	714.29	114	87	47.8	14.81	707.92
August	342	253	42.3	16.81	711.06	114	88	47.9	14.84	710.84
September	336	248	41.2	17.15	706.58	114	87	46.1	14.76	680.44
October	332	246	42.6	17.10	728.46	114	87	47.1	14.87	700.38
November	326	241	42.6	17.42	742.09	112	86	45.8	14.86	680.59
December	322	237	42.3	17.41	736.44	110	83	45.9	14.86	682.07
1999										
January	309	224	40.6	17.28	701.57	102	76	44.1	14.79	652.24
February	301	216	41.0	17.12	701.92	104	77	44.7	14.71	657.54
March	300	215	40.3	16.99	684.70	106	80	44.2	14.80	654.16
April	289	205	41.4	16.93	700.90	112	85	46.4	14.88	690.43
May	285	203	42.6	17.06	726.76	115	87	47.2	15.00	708.00
June	286	204	42.3	16.85	712.76	116	89	47.7	15.01	715.98
July	290	209	43.7	17.18	750.77	117	90	47.3	15.08	713.28
August	290	210	43.1	17.01	733.13	117	89	47.3	15.09	713.76
September	291	213	43.0	17.08	734.44	116	89	46.8	15.16	709.49
October	292	215	43.7	16.90	738.53	115	88	46.8	15.20	711.36
November	290	214	43.7	16.76	732.41	113	87	46.7	15.18	708.91
December	292	215	43.9	17.03	747.62	108	82	45.4	15.13	686.90

Table 13-4. Petroleum and Petroleum Products—Imports and Stocks

(Not seasonally adjusted.)

Year and month	Total energy-related petroleum products Quantity (thousands of barrels)	Value (millions of dollars)	Crude petroleum Quantity (thousands of barrels) Total	Average per day	Value (millions of dollars)	Unit price (dollars per barrel)	Stocks (end of period, millions of barrels) All oils	Crude petroleum Total	Strategic petroleum reserve
1970	...	...	...	...	...	...	1 018	276	...
1971	...	...	...	...	...	...	1 044	260	...
1972	...	...	...	...	...	...	959	246	...
1973	...	...	...	...	...	...	1 008	242	...
1974	...	...	...	...	...	...	1 074	265	...
1975	...	...	...	...	...	...	1 133	271	...
1976	...	...	...	...	...	...	1 112	285	...
1977	...	...	...	...	...	...	1 312	348	7
1978	...	...	...	...	...	...	1 278	376	67
1979	...	...	...	...	...	...	1 341	430	91
1980	...	...	...	...	...	...	1 392	466	108
1981	...	...	...	...	...	...	1 484	594	230
1982	...	...	...	...	...	...	1 430	644	294
1983	...	...	...	...	...	...	1 454	723	379
1984	...	...	...	...	...	...	1 556	796	451
1985	...	...	...	...	...	...	1 519	814	493
1986	...	...	...	...	...	...	1 593	843	512
1987	...	...	...	...	...	...	1 607	890	541
1988	...	...	...	...	...	...	1 597	890	560
1989	...	...	...	...	...	...	1 581	921	580
1990	...	...	...	...	...	...	1 621	908	586
1991	2 828 953	50 646	2 146 064	5 880	37 463	17.46	1 617	893	569
1992	2 947 582	50 537	2 294 570	6 269	38 553	16.80	1 592	893	575
1993	3 257 008	50 210	2 543 374	6 968	38 469	15.13	1 647	922	587
1994	3 416 045	49 533	2 704 196	7 409	38 479	14.23	1 653	929	592
1995	3 361 882	53 835	2 767 312	7 582	43 750	15.81	1 563	895	592
1996	3 622 385	70 199	2 893 647	7 906	54 931	18.98	1 507	850	566
1997	3 802 574	69 288	3 069 430	8 409	54 226	17.67	1 560	868	563
1998	4 088 027	49 132	3 242 711	8 884	37 252	11.49	1 647	895	571
1999	4 081 181	65 931	3 228 092	8 844	50 890	15.76	1 493	852	567
1996									
January	306 887	5 196	238 990	7 709	3 927	16.43	1 544	895	592
February	252 634	4 181	198 120	6 832	3 189	16.10	1 500	893	592
March	255 345	4 544	201 663	6 505	3 492	17.31	1 482	889	589
April	297 886	5 861	238 198	7 940	4 589	19.27	1 502	890	586
May	323 841	6 274	261 641	8 440	4 945	18.90	1 520	890	586
June	309 546	5 637	253 014	8 434	4 544	17.96	1 546	899	584
July	339 099	6 221	275 225	8 878	4 998	18.16	1 550	891	583
August	307 806	5 844	250 957	8 095	4 681	18.65	1 545	891	578
September	316 593	6 402	260 375	8 679	5 200	19.97	1 551	876	574
October	314 661	6 842	250 694	8 087	5 367	21.41	1 538	882	574
November	275 355	5 998	216 953	7 232	4 638	21.38	1 522	869	570
December	322 733	7 199	247 816	7 994	5 361	21.63	1 507	850	566
1997									
January	295 029	6 624	224 135	7 230	4 900	21.86	1 501	864	563
February	270 487	5 683	211 073	7 538	4 324	20.48	1 482	860	563
March	315 042	6 048	245 623	7 923	4 608	18.76	1 512	876	563
April	309 804	5 473	250 947	8 365	4 298	17.13	1 518	882	563
May	343 544	6 079	278 223	8 975	4 745	17.06	1 561	889	563
June	313 136	5 431	254 232	8 474	4 285	16.85	1 575	883	563
July	325 451	5 494	266 293	8 590	4 369	16.41	1 559	873	563
August	333 875	5 857	280 897	9 061	4 762	16.95	1 570	864	563
September	335 430	5 823	274 565	9 152	4 593	16.73	1 592	867	563
October	341 352	6 163	280 555	9 050	4 968	17.71	1 598	879	563
November	308 491	5 472	252 757	8 425	4 361	17.25	1 600	887	563
December	310 934	5 141	250 131	8 069	4 014	16.05	1 560	868	563
1998									
January	332 557	4 877	271 208	8 749	3 881	14.31	1 570	880	563
February	292 678	3 983	230 593	8 235	3 002	13.02	1 569	881	563
March	330 542	4 099	263 407	8 497	3 129	11.88	1 587	897	563
April	357 373	4 415	289 968	9 666	3 412	11.77	1 614	914	563
May	356 929	4 467	282 846	9 124	3 337	11.80	1 652	914	563
June	341 622	4 026	271 314	9 044	3 018	11.12	1 651	895	563
July	366 139	4 165	289 718	9 346	3 122	10.78	1 661	901	563
August	374 808	4 136	300 227	9 685	3 166	10.55	1 669	892	563
September	330 636	3 787	259 951	8 665	2 857	10.99	1 652	873	563
October	342 903	4 183	263 149	8 489	3 069	11.66	1 649	894	564
November	337 814	3 811	267 953	8 932	2 890	10.79	1 672	904	569
December	324 027	3 181	252 378	8 141	2 368	9.38	1 647	895	571
1999									
January	349 000	3 362	280 356	9 044	2 581	9.21	1 642	904	572
February	302 085	2 957	234 298	8 368	2 221	9.48	1 635	906	572
March	339 876	3 715	271 574	8 760	2 851	10.50	1 620	917	572
April	341 124	4 587	262 378	8 746	3 379	12.88	1 624	908	572
May	367 964	5 521	289 457	9 337	4 226	14.60	1 658	914	574
June	357 634	5 320	278 274	9 276	4 040	14.52	1 642	907	575
July	364 520	6 029	288 932	9 320	4 654	16.11	1 644	908	576
August	361 349	6 668	283 813	9 155	5 073	17.88	1 622	890	575
September	335 339	6 787	267 600	8 920	5 270	19.69	1 615	879	575
October	335 459	7 062	267 574	8 631	5 556	20.76	1 585	876	572
November	318 537	6 827	254 862	8 495	5 365	21.05	1 571	867	569
December	308 292	7 096	248 974	8 031	5 673	22.79	1 493	852	567

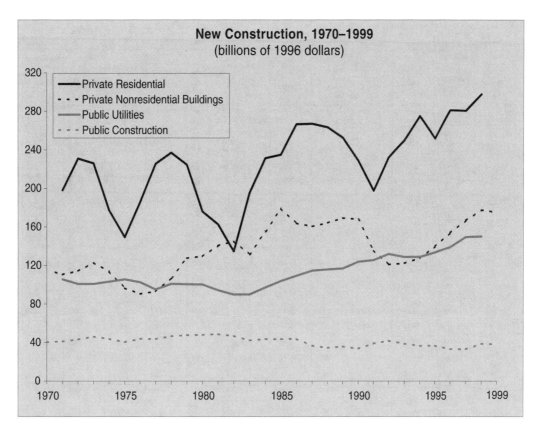

New Construction, 1970–1999
(billions of 1996 dollars)

- Private Residential
- Private Nonresidential Buildings
- Public Utilities
- Public Construction

- The construction industry serves several different markets, with different reactions to the general business cycle. In 1999, private residential and public (i.e., government) construction spending rose, while spending for the nonresidential and utilities sectors fell. A fall in industrial construction was responsible for the weakness in the nonresidential construction spending.

- Residential spending has been the most volatile sector, falling steeply just before and during recessions but responding swiftly to interest-rate reductions.

- Construction workers were relatively well-paid, averaging $17.18 per hour in 1999. Hourly pay was up 3.4 percent in 1999, exceeding the rate of consumer price increase.

- Other indicators confirmed the strength of the residential housing market in 1999. With the exception of mobile home shipments, in 1999, housing starts, building permits, mobile home shipments, sales of new and existing homes, and median sales prices all increased.

Table 14-1. Construction Costs, Prices, Employment, Hours, and Earnings

Year and month	Construction cost indexes (1996=100)		Producer price indexes (June 1986=100, not seasonally adjusted)			Employment, hours, and earnings (seasonally adjusted)								
						Employment (thousands)					Construction workers			
						All construction		General building contractors	Heavy construction except building	Special trade contractors			Average earnings (dollars)	
	Fixed weight index	Implicit deflator	Inputs to construction industries	Maintenance and repair construction	New construction	Total	Construction workers				Average weekly hours	Aggregate weekly hours index (1982=100)	Hourly	Weekly
1970	23.2	23.2	. . .	. . .	. . .	3 588	2 990	1 066	. . .	. . .	37.3	101.3	5.24	195.45
1971	24.5	24.5	. . .	. . .	. . .	3 704	3 071	1 102	. . .	. . .	37.2	103.6	5.69	211.67
1972	26.2	26.3	. . .	. . .	. . .	3 889	3 257	1 165	774	1 951	36.5	107.9	6.06	221.19
1973	28.8	28.8	. . .	. . .	. . .	4 097	3 405	1 221	790	2 087	36.8	113.7	6.41	235.89
1974	31.7	31.7	. . .	. . .	. . .	4 020	3 294	1 192	799	2 029	36.6	109.5	6.81	249.25
1975	34.5	34.5	. . .	. . .	. . .	3 525	2 808	1 012	734	1 779	36.4	92.7	7.31	266.08
1976	36.7	36.7	. . .	. . .	. . .	3 576	2 814	1 022	747	1 806	36.8	94.0	7.71	283.73
1977	41.1	40.6	. . .	. . .	. . .	3 851	3 021	1 108	760	1 983	36.5	100.2	8.10	295.65
1978	46.2	46.1	. . .	. . .	. . .	4 229	3 354	1 229	828	2 173	36.8	112.2	8.66	318.69
1979	52.1	51.7	. . .	. . .	. . .	4 463	3 565	1 272	898	2 293	37.0	119.9	9.27	342.99
1980	58.0	57.0	. . .	. . .	. . .	4 346	3 421	1 173	895	2 278	37.0	115.1	9.94	367.78
1981	62.1	61.0	. . .	. . .	. . .	4 188	3 261	1 094	865	2 229	36.9	109.3	10.82	399.26
1982	63.3	62.8	. . .	. . .	. . .	3 904	2 998	990	795	2 119	36.7	100.0	11.63	426.82
1983	65.1	64.5	. . .	. . .	. . .	3 946	3 031	1 019	753	2 174	37.1	102.2	11.94	442.97
1984	68.1	67.0	. . .	. . .	. . .	4 380	3 404	1 161	758	2 462	37.8	116.8	12.13	458.51
1985	69.8	68.3	. . .	. . .	. . .	4 668	3 655	1 251	765	2 652	37.7	125.3	12.32	464.46
1986	73.4	71.4	. . .	. . .	. . .	4 810	3 770	1 289	750	2 771	37.4	128.2	12.48	466.75
1987	76.8	74.7	101.5	101.3	101.6	4 958	3 870	1 318	739	2 901	37.8	132.7	12.71	480.44
1988	79.5	77.7	106.1	106.0	106.1	5 098	3 980	1 350	743	3 005	37.9	136.9	13.08	495.73
1989	82.2	80.8	111.0	110.9	111.0	5 171	4 035	1 332	767	3 072	37.9	138.9	13.54	513.17
1990	84.6	83.4	113.4	113.6	113.3	5 120	3 974	1 298	770	3 051	38.2	138.0	13.77	526.01
1991	84.8	84.1	114.8	115.1	114.6	4 650	3 549	1 140	727	2 783	38.1	122.8	14.00	533.40
1992	85.8	85.8	116.7	116.2	116.9	4 492	3 431	1 077	711	2 704	38.0	118.4	14.15	537.70
1993	90.0	90.0	121.4	119.4	122.2	4 668	3 589	1 120	713	2 836	38.5	124.4	14.38	553.63
1994	94.1	94.0	125.0	122.3	125.9	4 986	3 858	1 188	740	3 058	38.9	136.4	14.73	573.00
1995	98.1	98.1	129.1	127.1	129.8	5 160	3 993	1 207	752	3 201	38.9	140.9	15.09	587.00
1996	100.0	100.0	131.2	129.3	131.8	5 418	4 199	1 257	777	3 384	39.0	148.7	15.47	603.33
1997	102.9	102.9	133.8	131.5	134.6	5 691	4 415	1 310	799	3 582	39.0	156.2	16.04	625.56
1998	105.6	105.6	133.5	131.3	134.3	6 020	4 669	1 377	840	3 804	38.9	164.7	16.61	646.13
1999	110.4	110.4	136.1	133.3	137.0	6 404	4 953	1 450	869	4 084	39.1	175.7	17.18	671.74
1996														
January	98.8	98.8	129.4	127.8	129.9	5 210	4 040	1 223	737	3 250	37.9	139.1	15.34	581.39
February	99.0	99.0	129.4	127.8	130.0	5 300	4 122	1 235	763	3 302	39.0	146.0	15.24	594.36
March	99.1	99.1	129.8	128.2	130.4	5 327	4 123	1 240	774	3 313	38.9	145.7	15.27	594.00
April	99.0	99.0	130.3	128.7	130.9	5 354	4 146	1 245	772	3 337	39.0	146.8	15.32	597.48
May	99.2	99.2	131.3	129.5	132.0	5 381	4 167	1 253	771	3 357	38.6	146.1	15.36	592.90
June	99.6	99.6	131.5	129.5	132.2	5 418	4 195	1 260	780	3 378	39.1	149.0	15.42	602.92
July	100.2	100.2	131.2	129.4	131.9	5 440	4 214	1 259	782	3 399	38.7	148.1	15.48	599.08
August	100.4	100.4	131.6	129.7	132.3	5 472	4 240	1 268	785	3 419	39.0	150.2	15.53	605.67
September	100.7	100.7	132.3	130.2	133.1	5 495	4 260	1 271	787	3 437	39.0	150.9	15.59	608.01
October	100.9	100.9	132.0	130.1	132.7	5 524	4 281	1 275	791	3 458	39.0	151.6	15.59	608.01
November	100.9	101.0	132.6	130.4	133.3	5 544	4 302	1 281	790	3 473	39.0	152.4	15.67	611.13
December	101.3	101.3	132.5	130.4	133.3	5 555	4 317	1 289	788	3 478	39.0	152.9	15.62	609.18
1997														
January	101.7	101.8	132.9	130.7	133.7	5 549	4 303	1 286	794	3 469	38.1	148.9	15.82	602.74
February	101.8	101.8	133.4	131.1	134.2	5 604	4 379	1 296	800	3 508	38.8	154.3	15.88	616.14
March	102.2	102.3	133.6	131.2	134.5	5 644	4 379	1 304	801	3 539	39.2	155.9	15.83	620.54
April	102.5	102.5	134.0	131.6	134.8	5 644	4 376	1 301	795	3 548	39.2	155.8	15.89	622.89
May	102.7	102.7	134.3	131.8	135.2	5 669	4 397	1 304	800	3 565	39.5	157.7	15.93	629.24
June	102.9	102.9	134.2	131.7	135.0	5 670	4 393	1 303	793	3 574	39.1	156.0	15.98	624.82
July	103.3	103.3	134.2	131.7	135.0	5 690	4 410	1 309	792	3 589	39.1	156.6	16.00	625.60
August	103.5	103.6	134.2	131.9	135.1	5 720	4 433	1 312	798	3 610	38.9	156.6	16.07	625.12
September	103.9	103.9	134.1	131.8	134.9	5 747	4 458	1 314	804	3 629	39.3	159.1	16.13	633.91
October	104.2	104.2	133.7	131.5	134.5	5 753	4 461	1 317	802	3 634	38.9	157.6	16.20	630.18
November	104.7	104.7	133.8	131.5	134.6	5 772	4 472	1 326	800	3 646	38.3	155.5	16.24	621.99
December	104.8	104.8	133.5	131.3	134.3	5 809	4 506	1 337	810	3 662	38.9	159.2	16.32	634.85
1998														
January	104.9	105.0	133.2	131.0	134.0	5 865	4 558	1 340	823	3 702	39.1	161.9	16.35	639.29
February	104.7	104.9	133.3	131.0	134.1	5 883	4 594	1 344	817	3 722	39.2	163.5	16.40	642.88
March	104.8	104.9	133.3	131.0	134.1	5 862	4 533	1 345	820	3 697	38.9	160.1	16.44	639.52
April	105.0	105.0	133.6	131.3	134.4	5 937	4 597	1 357	831	3 749	38.9	162.4	16.48	641.07
May	105.3	105.2	133.6	131.5	134.4	5 948	4 614	1 364	833	3 751	39.0	163.4	16.49	643.11
June	105.9	105.8	133.5	131.3	134.2	5 991	4 642	1 373	837	3 781	38.7	163.1	16.53	639.71
July	106.2	106.1	133.8	131.6	134.6	6 028	4 673	1 381	844	3 803	39.2	166.4	16.61	651.11
August	106.5	106.4	133.9	131.5	134.8	6 061	4 689	1 388	847	3 826	39.2	166.9	16.69	654.25
September	106.6	106.6	133.8	131.5	134.6	6 083	4 710	1 391	843	3 849	38.8	166.0	16.64	645.63
October	106.9	107.0	133.5	131.3	134.2	6 120	4 743	1 400	847	3 873	39.2	168.9	16.75	656.60
November	107.3	107.4	133.3	131.1	134.0	6 165	4 769	1 405	855	3 905	39.1	169.3	16.79	656.49
December	107.9	107.9	133.1	130.9	133.8	6 253	4 848	1 418	875	3 960	39.5	173.9	16.83	664.79
1999														
January	108.4	108.5	133.6	131.2	134.4	6 246	4 849	1 420	871	3 955	39.5	173.9	16.86	665.97
February	108.6	108.6	133.9	131.4	134.8	6 337	4 946	1 436	872	4 029	39.1	175.6	16.87	659.62
March	109.0	108.9	134.5	131.8	135.4	6 328	4 889	1 441	865	4 022	38.7	171.8	16.96	656.35
April	109.3	109.3	135.1	132.6	136.0	6 380	4 922	1 442	879	4 059	39.0	174.3	17.02	663.78
May	109.7	109.8	135.7	132.9	136.7	6 364	4 918	1 444	861	4 059	39.0	174.2	17.11	667.29
June	110.4	110.4	136.6	133.4	137.7	6 388	4 938	1 447	866	4 075	39.3	176.2	17.18	675.17
July	110.6	110.6	137.5	134.2	138.7	6 408	4 949	1 451	867	4 090	39.0	175.3	17.20	670.80
August	110.8	110.8	137.7	134.5	138.8	6 401	4 931	1 447	865	4 089	39.0	174.6	17.21	671.19
September	110.9	110.9	137.2	134.4	138.2	6 439	4 973	1 458	866	4 115	39.3	177.5	17.26	678.32
October	111.4	111.4	136.6	134.1	137.5	6 470	5 000	1 464	872	4 134	39.1	177.5	17.33	677.60
November	112.0	111.9	136.9	134.4	137.8	6 516	5 034	1 470	876	4 170	40.1	183.3	17.37	696.54
December	112.3	112.3	137.3	134.9	138.2	6 552	5 055	1 474	882	4 196	38.9	178.6	17.44	678.42

Table 14-2. Employment, Hours, and Earnings of Construction Workers

(Not seasonally adjusted.)

Year and month	General building contractors				Heavy construction, except building				Special trade contractors			
	Employment (thousands)	Average weekly hours	Average earnings (dollars)		Employment (thousands)	Average weekly hours	Average earnings (dollars)		Employment (thousands)	Average weekly hours	Average earnings (dollars)	
			Hourly	Weekly			Hourly	Weekly			Hourly	Weekly
1970	910	36.3	5.02	182.23	. . .	. . .	. . .	. . .	. . .	. . .	. . .	. . .
1971	936	36.1	5.33	192.41	. . .	. . .	. . .	. . .	. . .	. . .	. . .	. . .
1972	976	35.7	5.58	199.21	666	39.3	5.57	218.90	1 615	35.8	6.58	235.56
1973	1 009	35.8	5.87	210.15	665	39.9	5.85	233.42	1 731	36.1	6.97	251.62
1974	967	35.9	6.24	224.02	663	39.7	6.31	250.51	1 663	35.8	7.36	263.49
1975	799	35.9	6.78	243.40	593	39.2	6.81	266.95	1 416	35.5	7.85	278.68
1976	800	36.4	7.15	260.26	597	39.3	7.31	287.28	1 417	36.0	8.20	295.20
1977	865	36.3	7.52	272.98	594	38.8	7.56	293.33	1 562	35.8	8.65	309.67
1978	955	35.8	8.00	286.40	669	40.1	8.10	324.81	1 730	36.2	9.26	335.21
1979	989	35.9	8.61	309.10	743	40.2	8.65	347.73	1 833	36.4	9.90	360.36
1980	900	36.1	9.22	332.84	720	40.3	9.20	370.76	1 802	36.2	10.63	384.81
1981	825	36.0	9.85	354.60	693	40.1	10.31	413.43	1 743	36.1	11.50	415.15
1982	734	36.2	10.53	381.19	631	40.0	11.45	458.00	1 632	35.7	12.20	435.54
1983	751	36.6	10.73	392.72	604	40.4	11.86	479.14	1 676	36.2	12.53	453.59
1984	862	37.1	10.89	404.02	618	41.5	11.90	493.85	1 925	36.8	12.78	470.30
1985	935	37.1	11.23	416.63	629	41.4	12.08	500.11	2 092	36.9	12.89	475.64
1986	953	37.0	11.43	422.91	623	40.8	12.00	489.60	2 194	36.7	13.09	480.40
1987	963	37.3	11.72	437.16	618	41.5	12.07	500.91	2 290	37.0	13.31	492.47
1988	989	37.5	12.18	456.75	621	41.5	12.46	517.09	2 370	37.1	13.64	506.04
1989	969	37.5	12.71	476.63	639	41.5	13.19	547.39	2 427	37.1	13.98	518.66
1990	938	37.7	13.01	490.48	643	42.0	13.34	560.28	2 393	37.4	14.20	531.08
1991	811	37.6	13.27	498.95	600	41.6	13.77	572.83	2 137	37.4	14.35	536.69
1992	761	37.5	13.45	504.38	588	41.6	13.96	580.74	2 083	37.2	14.47	538.28
1993	790	37.7	13.64	514.23	593	42.1	14.10	593.61	2 206	37.8	14.73	556.79
1994	843	38.1	13.97	532.26	618	42.6	14.44	615.14	2 397	38.3	15.08	577.56
1995	856	38.3	14.33	548.84	626	42.5	14.65	622.63	2 511	38.1	15.47	589.41
1996	888	38.2	14.68	560.78	649	42.8	15.10	646.28	2 662	38.3	15.83	606.29
1997	924	38.2	15.23	581.79	667	42.5	15.58	662.15	2 824	38.4	16.42	630.53
1998	965	38.0	15.92	604.96	704	42.4	16.11	683.06	3 000	38.3	16.95	649.19
1999	1 009	38.1	16.52	629.41	726	42.9	16.77	719.43	3 219	38.5	17.48	672.98
1996												
January	803	36.7	14.67	538.39	498	39.8	14.52	577.90	2 320	36.1	15.65	564.97
February	798	38.1	14.57	555.12	517	41.2	14.35	591.22	2 339	37.6	15.57	585.43
March	811	37.9	14.58	552.58	558	41.4	14.35	594.09	2 393	37.5	15.57	583.88
April	846	38.4	14.56	559.10	623	42.4	14.70	623.28	2 534	37.8	15.58	588.92
May	884	38.2	14.61	558.10	674	42.2	14.91	629.20	2 665	38.3	15.64	599.01
June	926	38.6	14.50	559.70	704	43.7	15.20	664.24	2 767	38.9	15.68	609.95
July	944	38.6	14.58	562.79	717	44.2	15.45	682.89	2 846	39.1	15.84	619.34
August	951	38.6	14.61	563.95	727	44.2	15.50	685.10	2 870	39.2	15.92	624.06
September	934	38.5	14.87	572.50	734	44.5	15.68	697.76	2 849	39.0	16.08	627.12
October	930	38.6	14.79	570.89	731	44.5	15.69	698.21	2 850	39.2	16.10	631.12
November	924	38.1	14.84	565.40	689	42.4	15.23	645.75	2 807	38.2	16.01	611.58
December	906	38.1	15.00	571.50	616	41.5	14.76	612.54	2 704	38.1	16.14	614.93
1997												
January	854	36.2	15.04	544.45	535	38.3	15.01	574.88	2 496	36.1	16.18	584.10
February	849	37.5	15.09	565.88	553	39.6	15.09	597.56	2 511	37.1	16.08	596.57
March	859	38.0	15.05	571.90	581	41.3	15.01	619.91	2 574	37.9	16.10	610.19
April	888	38.4	15.05	577.92	642	42.2	15.24	643.13	2 702	38.1	16.17	616.08
May	919	38.7	15.06	582.82	702	44.1	15.44	680.90	2 837	38.9	16.24	631.74
June	955	38.6	14.95	577.07	715	43.5	15.59	678.17	2 930	39.0	16.31	636.09
July	979	38.8	15.04	583.55	725	44.6	15.76	702.90	3 009	39.5	16.43	648.99
August	981	38.6	15.17	585.56	736	44.1	15.79	696.34	3 032	39.1	16.53	646.32
September	959	38.9	15.39	598.67	744	44.8	16.08	720.38	3 006	39.3	16.66	654.74
October	958	38.7	15.55	601.79	742	44.2	16.09	711.18	2 996	39.1	16.66	651.41
November	950	37.6	15.58	585.81	695	39.4	15.70	618.58	2 947	37.6	16.68	627.17
December	935	38.3	15.69	600.93	632	40.9	15.55	636.00	2 850	38.1	16.82	640.84
1998												
January	889	37.1	15.64	580.24	556	39.6	15.23	603.11	2 680	37.1	16.72	620.31
February	882	37.7	15.67	590.76	563	41.5	15.31	635.37	2 678	37.3	16.64	620.67
March	884	37.5	15.76	591.00	594	41.3	15.40	636.02	2 692	37.4	16.71	624.95
April	923	37.6	15.84	595.58	673	41.3	15.64	645.93	2 873	37.5	16.72	627.00
May	954	38.1	15.76	600.46	731	43.4	15.92	690.93	2 992	38.7	16.81	650.55
June	1 001	38.1	15.68	597.41	757	42.8	16.04	686.51	3 100	38.7	16.85	652.10
July	1 029	38.8	15.85	614.98	774	44.6	16.46	734.12	3 186	39.5	17.00	671.50
August	1 032	38.8	16.00	620.80	784	44.7	16.56	740.23	3 211	39.5	17.10	675.45
September	1 004	36.8	16.10	592.48	782	40.5	16.50	668.25	3 172	37.1	17.12	635.15
October	1 009	38.8	16.22	629.34	787	44.6	16.71	745.27	3 182	39.3	17.18	675.17
November	995	37.9	16.21	614.36	750	41.2	16.43	676.92	3 150	38.2	17.16	655.51
December	981	38.5	16.27	626.40	692	41.2	16.26	669.91	3 088	38.8	17.26	669.69
1999												
January	934	37.2	16.25	604.50	594	41.0	16.02	656.82	2 867	37.5	17.13	642.38
February	935	37.6	16.18	608.37	606	41.2	15.90	655.08	2 909	37.4	17.06	638.04
March	943	37.4	16.35	611.49	626	40.3	16.05	646.82	2 938	37.3	17.17	640.44
April	973	38.1	16.34	622.55	710	41.9	16.35	685.07	3 109	38.1	17.21	655.70
May	1 003	38.5	16.41	631.79	751	42.9	16.75	718.58	3 230	38.8	17.35	673.18
June	1 049	38.6	16.35	631.11	780	44.2	16.90	746.98	3 337	39.2	17.43	683.26
July	1 073	38.6	16.43	634.20	791	43.9	17.12	751.57	3 414	39.4	17.57	692.26
August	1 064	38.9	16.56	644.18	796	44.4	17.09	758.80	3 422	39.4	17.60	693.44
September	1 042	37.6	16.77	630.55	799	43.1	17.34	747.35	3 387	37.9	17.70	670.83
October	1 042	38.5	16.83	647.96	798	44.5	17.38	773.41	3 385	39.4	17.80	701.32
November	1 036	38.3	16.77	642.29	764	43.5	16.95	737.33	3 368	39.0	17.74	691.86
December	1 013	37.8	16.91	639.20	693	41.6	16.57	689.31	3 259	38.5	17.85	687.23

Table 14-3. New Construction Put in Place

(Billions of dollars, not seasonally adjusted.)

Year and month	Total	Private [1]										Public [1]				
		Total	Residential		Nonresidential buildings [1]					Public utilities		Total	Housing and redevelopment	Industrial	Military facilities	Highways and streets
			Total	New housing units	Total	Industrial	Office	Hotels, motels	Other commercial buildings	Total	Telecommunications					
1970	105.9	78.0	35.9	27.1	28.2	9.3	(2)	1.5	11.6	11.1	3.0	27.9	1.1	0.3	0.7	10.0
1971	122.4	92.7	48.5	38.7	29.3	7.8	(2)	1.5	13.8	12.0	3.0	29.7	1.1	0.4	0.9	10.7
1972	139.1	109.1	60.7	50.1	32.4	6.7	6.8	2.2	9.8	13.3	3.3	30.0	0.9	0.4	1.1	10.4
1973	153.8	121.4	65.1	54.6	37.6	9.0	7.8	2.5	11.4	15.3	4.0	32.3	0.9	0.5	1.2	10.5
1974	155.2	117.0	56.0	43.4	39.9	11.5	8.0	1.8	11.8	16.9	4.3	38.1	1.0	0.6	1.2	12.1
1975	152.6	109.3	51.6	36.3	35.4	11.7	6.5	1.2	9.5	17.6	3.8	43.3	1.4	0.7	1.4	13.1
1976	172.1	128.2	68.3	50.8	34.6	10.5	6.3	1.0	9.7	20.2	3.9	44.0	1.3	0.7	1.6	12.4
1977	200.5	157.4	92.0	72.2	38.2	11.3	7.0	1.1	11.6	21.4	4.5	43.1	1.5	0.8	1.4	12.5
1978	239.9	189.7	109.8	85.6	48.8	16.2	8.7	1.3	14.7	24.6	5.6	50.1	1.4	0.9	1.5	14.2
1979	272.9	216.2	116.4	89.3	64.8	22.0	12.6	2.5	19.0	28.0	6.9	56.6	1.7	1.1	1.6	17.1
1980	273.9	210.3	100.4	69.6	72.5	20.5	17.8	3.4	20.5	30.9	7.8	63.6	2.0	1.4	1.9	18.2
1981	289.1	224.4	99.2	69.4	85.6	25.4	23.5	4.3	20.8	33.7	8.2	64.7	2.3	1.7	2.0	18.4
1982	279.3	216.3	84.7	57.0	92.7	26.1	31.3	4.8	17.8	33.9	8.5	63.1	2.3	1.6	2.2	17.3
1983	311.9	248.4	125.8	95.0	87.1	19.5	28.3	6.1	18.9	30.8	7.6	63.5	2.6	1.8	2.5	17.9
1984	370.2	300.0	155.0	114.6	107.7	20.9	35.6	8.0	28.0	32.2	8.1	70.2	2.7	1.8	2.8	21.6
1985	403.4	325.6	160.5	115.9	127.5	24.1	43.6	8.7	35.7	32.7	8.4	77.8	2.9	2.0	3.2	23.7
1986	433.5	348.9	190.7	135.2	120.9	21.0	39.4	8.9	35.8	32.9	9.1	84.6	3.0	1.7	3.9	25.3
1987	446.6	356.0	199.7	142.7	123.2	21.2	36.9	8.9	37.3	27.9	9.2	90.6	3.3	1.5	4.3	27.1
1988	462.0	367.3	204.5	142.4	130.9	23.2	39.3	8.3	38.9	27.4	9.6	94.7	3.3	1.4	3.6	29.1
1989	477.5	379.3	204.3	143.2	140.0	28.8	40.1	9.3	39.8	30.1	9.6	98.2	3.4	1.3	3.5	28.7
1990	476.8	369.3	191.1	132.1	143.5	33.6	35.1	10.7	40.0	28.9	9.8	107.5	3.8	1.4	2.7	32.1
1991	432.6	322.5	166.3	114.6	116.6	31.4	26.0	6.9	29.4	34.0	9.0	110.1	3.6	1.8	1.8	32.0
1992	463.7	347.8	199.4	135.1	105.6	29.0	20.3	3.7	29.2	36.8	9.0	115.8	4.1	1.9	2.5	33.1
1993	493.3	377.3	225.1	150.9	110.6	26.5	20.9	4.6	32.5	34.9	9.6	116.0	4.0	1.7	2.5	34.3
1994	539.2	419.0	258.6	176.4	120.3	29.0	22.2	4.6	37.6	34.1	10.1	120.2	3.8	1.5	2.3	37.4
1995	555.6	425.7	247.4	171.4	136.5	34.0	25.6	7.1	42.7	35.9	11.1	129.9	4.7	1.5	3.0	37.6
1996	613.5	474.3	281.1	191.1	153.9	36.2	27.9	10.9	48.2	33.2	11.8	139.3	5.0	1.4	2.6	39.5
1997	656.6	501.7	289.0	198.1	173.0	36.7	34.3	12.9	51.8	33.6	12.4	154.9	5.2	1.0	2.6	44.1
1998	711.8	552.2	314.6	224.0	190.7	40.5	42.2	14.8	53.6	40.0	13.3	159.5	5.1	1.0	2.5	48.5
1999	764.2	591.6	348.8	249.5	195.8	34.9	46.6	15.9	57.1	39.6	15.2	172.7	5.6	0.9	2.1	53.5
1996																
January	39.2	30.7	17.2	12.4	10.6	2.7	1.8	0.7	3.2	...	0.8	8.5	0.4	0.1	0.3	1.7
February	37.6	29.8	16.5	11.9	10.8	2.7	1.9	0.8	3.3	...	0.8	7.9	0.3	0.1	0.2	1.7
March	42.2	33.6	19.7	14.0	11.1	2.8	1.9	0.8	3.4	...	0.9	8.6	0.3	0.1	0.2	1.8
April	47.6	37.5	22.2	15.2	12.0	2.9	2.1	0.9	3.7	...	1.0	10.1	0.3	0.1	0.2	2.6
May	52.1	40.3	24.6	16.3	12.4	2.8	2.4	0.8	4.0	...	1.0	11.8	0.4	0.1	0.2	3.4
June	55.7	43.3	26.6	17.5	13.2	3.1	2.5	0.9	4.1	...	0.9	12.4	0.4	0.1	0.2	3.8
July	57.1	43.6	27.2	18.1	13.0	2.9	2.4	0.9	4.1	...	0.9	13.4	0.4	0.1	0.2	4.5
August	59.5	45.5	27.9	18.5	13.8	2.9	2.5	1.0	4.6	...	1.1	14.1	0.4	0.1	0.2	4.5
September	59.7	44.7	26.9	18.2	14.3	3.3	2.6	1.0	4.6	...	1.0	15.0	0.6	0.2	0.3	4.7
October	59.1	45.0	26.5	17.8	14.8	3.6	2.6	1.0	4.7	...	1.1	14.1	0.5	0.1	0.2	4.7
November	55.4	42.7	24.9	17.0	14.3	3.4	2.6	1.0	4.4	...	1.1	12.8	0.5	0.1	0.2	3.4
December	48.3	37.7	20.9	14.3	13.5	3.2	2.5	1.1	4.0	...	1.3	10.6	0.5	0.1	0.2	2.5
1997																
January	43.1	33.8	18.6	13.0	12.6	2.8	2.5	0.9	3.8	...	0.9	9.4	0.4	0.1	0.2	1.8
February	42.4	32.9	17.9	12.7	12.8	2.8	2.6	1.0	3.8	...	0.8	9.6	0.4	0.1	0.2	1.8
March	47.2	36.5	21.1	14.9	13.0	2.7	2.5	1.0	3.9	...	0.9	10.6	0.4	0.1	0.2	2.2
April	51.6	39.8	23.2	15.7	13.6	2.8	2.5	1.1	4.1	...	1.0	11.7	0.4	0.1	0.2	3.0
May	55.7	42.8	25.4	16.8	14.1	2.9	2.6	1.2	4.3	...	1.0	12.9	0.5	0.1	0.2	3.8
June	59.3	44.9	26.8	17.6	14.6	3.0	2.8	1.2	4.5	...	1.1	14.3	0.4	0.1	0.2	4.5
July	61.7	46.5	27.3	18.2	15.3	3.2	3.0	1.2	4.7	...	1.1	15.1	0.4	0.1	0.2	4.9
August	63.6	47.7	27.8	18.7	15.8	3.3	3.1	1.1	4.9	...	1.1	15.9	0.4	0.1	0.2	5.3
September	63.0	47.1	27.0	18.8	15.9	3.4	3.1	1.1	4.9	...	1.2	15.9	0.5	0.1	0.3	5.0
October	61.8	46.8	27.0	18.6	15.8	3.4	3.3	1.1	4.7	...	1.2	15.0	0.5	0.1	0.2	4.9
November	56.7	43.7	25.3	17.8	15.0	3.2	3.2	1.1	4.3	...	1.0	13.0	0.4	0.1	0.2	4.0
December	50.6	39.3	21.5	15.3	14.5	3.3	3.1	1.1	4.0	...	1.1	11.3	0.4	0.1	0.2	2.9
1998																
January	45.4	35.7	19.6	14.2	13.5	2.9	3.1	1.0	3.6	...	0.9	9.7	0.4	0.1	0.2	2.1
February	44.3	34.8	18.7	13.7	13.6	3.0	3.1	1.0	3.6	...	1.0	9.5	0.4	0.1	0.2	2.0
March	50.4	40.0	22.4	16.3	14.6	3.3	3.2	1.1	4.0	...	1.2	10.4	0.4	0.1	0.2	2.5
April	55.6	43.8	24.7	17.4	15.5	3.3	3.4	1.2	4.2	...	1.1	11.8	0.4	0.1	0.2	3.3
May	59.0	46.4	26.8	18.4	15.6	3.3	3.5	1.1	4.4	...	1.1	12.6	0.4	0.1	0.2	3.8
June	66.3	51.2	28.9	19.9	16.8	3.5	3.8	1.3	4.8	...	1.2	15.2	0.5	0.1	0.2	5.0
July	67.0	51.1	30.0	21.1	16.4	3.3	3.5	1.3	4.9	...	1.1	15.8	0.5	0.1	0.3	5.2
August	69.1	52.7	30.7	21.4	17.0	3.6	3.5	1.4	5.0	...	1.1	16.5	0.4	0.1	0.2	5.8
September	68.7	51.7	30.0	21.5	17.1	3.7	3.6	1.4	4.9	...	1.2	17.0	0.5	0.1	0.2	5.9
October	66.7	51.2	29.8	21.3	17.3	3.6	3.8	1.4	5.0	...	1.3	15.5	0.4	0.1	0.2	5.7
November	62.9	49.3	28.6	20.7	17.0	3.5	3.9	1.3	4.8	...	1.1	13.6	0.4	0.1	0.2	4.2
December	56.3	44.3	24.6	18.0	16.3	3.4	3.8	1.3	4.4	...	1.2	12.0	0.4	0.1	0.2	3.1
1999																
January	50.8	40.4	22.5	16.7	14.6	2.9	3.5	1.3	3.9	...	0.9	10.4	0.4	0.1	0.1	2.4
February	50.8	40.0	21.4	16.0	15.0	2.8	3.7	1.4	4.0	...	1.0	10.8	0.4	0.1	0.2	2.5
March	57.5	45.8	25.7	19.1	15.9	3.0	3.8	1.4	4.4	...	1.4	11.8	0.4	0.1	0.2	3.0
April	61.0	47.7	28.0	20.0	16.1	2.9	3.8	1.4	4.5	...	1.4	13.2	0.5	0.1	0.2	3.8
May	64.7	50.6	30.6	21.2	16.4	2.9	3.9	1.4	4.8	...	1.1	14.1	0.5	0.1	0.2	4.5
June	69.0	53.2	32.6	22.4	16.7	3.0	3.9	1.3	5.0	...	1.2	15.8	0.5	0.1	0.2	5.2
July	70.7	54.3	33.1	23.1	16.8	3.0	3.8	1.4	5.1	...	1.3	16.4	0.5	0.1	0.2	5.5
August	72.6	55.0	33.5	23.4	17.1	3.0	4.1	1.3	5.1	...	1.4	17.6	0.5	0.1	0.1	6.1
September	71.2	53.6	32.3	23.2	17.1	2.9	4.2	1.2	5.2	...	1.3	17.6	0.5	0.1	0.2	6.1
October	69.2	52.8	32.1	22.8	16.9	2.8	4.1	1.2	5.2	...	1.3	16.3	0.5	0.0	0.1	5.6
November	66.7	51.6	30.7	22.2	17.0	2.8	4.0	1.3	5.3	...	1.4	15.2	0.5	0.1	0.2	4.8
December	60.1	46.5	26.4	19.5	16.2	2.9	3.7	1.3	4.8	...	1.5	13.6	0.4	0.1	0.2	3.8

1. Includes categories not shown separately.
2. Included in "Other commercial buildings."

Table 14-3. New Construction Put in Place—*Continued*

(Billions of dollars, monthly data are at seasonally adjusted annual rates.)

Year and month	Total	Private [1]									Public [1]				
		Total	Residential		Nonresidential buildings [1]					Tele-commun-ications	Total	Housing and redevel-opment	Industrial	Military facilities	Highways and streets
			Total	New housing units	Total	Industrial	Office	Hotels, motels	Other commer-cial buildings						
1970	105.9	78.0	35.9	27.1	28.2	9.3	(2)	1.5	11.6	3.0	27.9	1.1	0.3	0.7	10.0
1971	122.4	92.7	48.5	38.7	29.3	7.8	(2)	1.5	13.8	3.0	29.7	1.1	0.4	0.9	10.7
1972	139.1	109.1	60.7	50.1	32.4	6.7	6.8	2.2	9.8	3.3	30.0	0.9	0.4	1.1	10.4
1973	153.8	121.4	65.1	54.6	37.6	9.0	7.8	2.5	11.4	4.0	32.3	0.9	0.5	1.2	10.5
1974	155.2	117.0	56.0	43.4	39.9	11.5	8.0	1.8	11.8	4.3	38.1	1.0	0.6	1.2	12.1
1975	152.6	109.3	51.6	36.3	35.4	11.7	6.5	1.2	9.5	3.8	43.3	1.4	0.7	1.4	13.1
1976	172.1	128.2	68.3	50.8	34.6	10.5	6.3	1.0	9.7	3.9	44.0	1.3	0.7	1.6	12.4
1977	200.5	157.4	92.0	72.2	38.2	11.3	7.0	1.1	11.6	4.5	43.1	1.5	0.8	1.4	12.5
1978	239.9	189.7	109.8	85.6	48.8	16.2	8.7	1.3	14.7	5.6	50.1	1.4	0.9	1.5	14.2
1979	272.9	216.2	116.4	89.3	64.8	22.0	12.6	2.5	19.0	6.9	56.6	1.7	1.1	1.6	17.1
1980	273.9	210.3	100.4	69.6	72.5	20.5	17.8	3.4	20.5	7.8	63.6	2.0	1.4	1.9	18.2
1981	289.1	224.4	99.2	69.4	85.6	25.4	23.5	4.3	20.8	8.2	64.7	2.3	1.7	2.0	18.4
1982	279.3	216.3	84.7	57.0	92.7	26.1	31.3	4.8	17.8	8.5	63.1	2.3	1.6	2.2	17.3
1983	311.9	248.4	125.8	95.0	87.1	19.5	28.3	6.1	18.9	7.6	63.5	2.6	1.8	2.5	17.9
1984	370.2	300.0	155.0	114.6	107.7	20.9	35.6	8.0	28.0	8.1	70.2	2.7	1.8	2.8	21.6
1985	403.4	325.6	160.5	115.9	127.5	24.1	43.6	8.7	35.7	8.4	77.8	2.9	2.0	3.2	23.7
1986	433.5	348.9	190.7	135.2	120.9	21.0	39.4	8.9	35.8	9.1	84.6	3.0	1.7	3.9	25.3
1987	446.6	356.0	199.7	142.7	123.2	21.2	36.9	8.9	37.3	9.2	90.6	3.3	1.5	4.3	27.1
1988	462.0	367.3	204.5	142.4	130.9	23.2	39.3	8.3	38.9	9.6	94.7	3.3	1.4	3.6	29.1
1989	477.5	379.3	204.3	143.2	140.0	28.8	40.1	9.3	39.8	9.6	98.2	3.4	1.3	3.5	28.7
1990	476.8	369.3	191.1	132.1	143.5	33.6	35.1	10.7	40.0	9.8	107.5	3.8	1.4	2.7	32.1
1991	432.6	322.5	166.3	114.6	116.6	31.4	26.0	6.9	29.4	9.0	110.1	3.6	1.8	1.8	32.0
1992	463.7	347.8	199.4	135.1	105.6	29.0	20.3	3.7	29.2	9.0	115.8	4.1	1.9	2.5	33.1
1993	493.3	377.3	225.1	150.9	110.6	26.5	20.9	4.6	32.5	9.6	116.0	4.0	1.7	2.5	34.3
1994	539.2	419.0	258.6	176.4	120.3	29.0	22.2	4.6	37.6	10.1	120.2	3.8	1.5	2.3	37.4
1995	555.6	425.7	247.4	171.4	136.5	34.0	25.6	7.1	42.7	11.1	129.9	4.7	1.5	3.0	37.6
1996	613.5	474.3	281.1	191.1	153.9	36.2	27.9	10.9	48.2	11.8	139.3	5.0	1.4	2.6	39.5
1997	656.6	501.7	289.0	198.1	173.0	36.7	34.3	12.9	51.8	12.4	154.9	5.2	1.0	2.6	44.1
1998	711.8	552.2	314.6	224.0	190.7	40.5	42.2	14.8	53.6	13.3	159.5	5.1	1.0	2.5	48.5
1999	764.2	591.6	348.8	249.5	195.8	34.9	46.6	15.9	57.1	15.2	172.7	5.6	0.9	2.1	53.5
1996															
January	581.8	447.3	260.9	179.8	144.5	36.4	23.3	9.7	46.1	11.8	134.6	4.9	1.3	3.4	38.4
February	578.9	450.6	265.9	182.8	144.0	35.5	23.6	9.8	46.4	11.5	128.4	4.3	1.3	3.1	39.0
March	580.3	451.3	269.1	185.4	142.4	34.8	24.0	10.0	45.3	10.9	129.0	4.0	1.5	2.4	37.6
April	600.1	465.4	277.6	190.8	147.3	35.7	25.3	11.0	47.2	11.5	134.7	3.8	1.5	2.8	39.3
May	606.2	467.7	281.8	193.0	147.2	34.1	27.0	9.7	47.4	11.5	138.5	4.6	1.5	2.7	38.9
June	612.4	477.9	285.7	195.7	154.0	36.2	30.1	10.4	46.6	10.8	134.6	4.3	1.6	2.5	38.6
July	611.9	473.7	286.3	194.6	150.6	34.6	28.8	10.0	46.5	10.7	138.2	5.1	1.5	2.3	40.1
August	617.8	480.5	287.2	194.5	154.6	33.8	28.9	11.5	49.2	11.8	137.3	5.2	1.6	2.3	37.6
September	630.5	484.0	287.2	193.5	159.1	36.8	30.0	11.8	49.1	11.5	146.5	6.0	1.7	2.6	40.8
October	638.0	491.2	286.3	193.2	165.7	40.4	29.9	11.5	51.4	11.9	146.9	5.9	0.8	2.6	41.1
November	643.5	493.4	286.9	192.9	167.3	39.3	30.8	12.4	51.1	12.8	150.1	6.3	1.0	2.4	40.1
December	637.8	491.4	285.8	191.2	165.7	36.4	31.5	12.7	50.6	14.4	146.4	5.7	1.1	2.3	41.2
1997															
January	641.5	493.9	284.0	190.3	170.2	36.7	31.6	12.3	54.2	12.0	147.6	5.3	1.1	2.6	40.0
February	648.1	494.1	288.7	195.6	172.6	37.2	33.8	12.5	53.4	11.9	154.0	5.6	1.1	2.5	41.8
March	645.8	487.6	287.5	195.2	166.1	33.7	31.5	12.5	51.8	11.7	158.3	5.4	1.1	2.2	43.1
April	649.1	494.2	289.1	196.4	166.8	34.9	30.1	12.7	51.4	12.6	154.9	5.4	1.4	2.4	44.1
May	651.4	496.9	290.1	198.5	167.7	35.0	30.4	13.5	51.7	12.1	154.5	5.6	0.9	2.6	44.0
June	650.2	495.7	287.2	196.0	169.2	35.9	33.0	13.3	51.0	12.4	154.5	5.0	1.1	2.6	44.8
July	661.0	505.1	287.1	196.1	177.4	38.6	35.6	13.3	53.2	13.0	155.9	5.2	1.1	2.7	45.1
August	661.9	506.0	287.1	197.3	177.6	37.8	35.9	13.3	52.9	12.2	155.9	5.0	1.0	2.8	45.3
September	664.8	509.6	289.3	199.9	177.4	38.1	35.8	12.6	51.7	13.3	155.2	4.9	0.9	2.6	43.9
October	670.0	513.8	292.8	203.3	177.0	37.7	37.6	13.1	50.6	12.7	156.1	5.8	0.7	2.9	42.2
November	662.8	508.4	292.5	202.4	175.3	36.8	37.7	13.0	49.9	12.4	154.4	5.0	0.8	2.7	46.8
December	666.4	511.7	293.8	204.3	178.0	38.0	38.4	12.8	50.6	12.5	154.7	4.6	0.8	2.2	45.5
1998															
January	675.8	520.5	297.4	207.2	182.5	38.9	40.5	13.0	51.4	12.6	155.3	4.7	1.0	2.5	46.8
February	677.4	522.2	300.1	210.1	182.5	39.2	39.9	12.7	51.0	13.7	155.1	4.8	1.1	2.8	47.0
March	685.1	529.8	302.7	212.9	185.9	42.1	39.6	12.8	52.8	14.4	155.3	5.0	1.2	2.7	48.2
April	698.7	542.7	306.4	217.5	189.7	40.7	40.9	13.7	53.5	13.0	156.0	5.1	1.0	2.6	48.3
May	693.8	541.5	305.8	216.9	186.5	40.0	41.2	13.3	52.7	13.8	152.3	4.9	1.0	2.4	45.6
June	728.2	565.3	310.5	221.6	194.7	41.4	44.1	14.9	54.9	13.1	163.0	5.4	0.9	2.6	50.1
July	717.3	554.9	315.6	226.6	190.7	39.9	41.7	15.0	55.0	12.9	162.4	6.0	1.1	3.2	47.4
August	719.6	559.2	318.2	226.8	191.7	42.0	40.6	15.9	53.4	13.1	160.4	5.2	1.1	2.8	48.9
September	724.2	561.0	322.5	230.5	190.8	41.1	41.3	16.7	52.2	13.3	163.3	4.8	1.0	2.1	49.7
October	726.3	565.6	325.6	233.7	194.8	40.5	44.6	16.7	54.0	13.9	160.7	4.9	0.8	2.3	50.5
November	733.3	572.0	329.6	236.6	198.1	40.6	45.6	16.5	55.6	13.1	161.3	5.2	1.1	2.2	48.8
December	741.5	577.1	334.4	240.1	199.3	39.2	46.7	16.0	56.0	12.9	164.4	5.3	0.9	2.3	48.7
1999															
January	760.2	591.3	340.1	243.0	198.5	38.6	46.4	17.6	55.1	13.8	168.9	5.2	0.9	2.0	54.2
February	776.3	597.2	341.7	245.3	201.4	37.5	47.5	18.2	56.6	14.0	179.1	5.2	0.9	2.6	59.8
March	778.0	602.5	346.8	248.8	201.0	38.0	46.2	17.2	58.0	16.6	175.5	5.7	1.0	2.2	56.5
April	766.5	591.5	347.7	249.0	196.3	35.7	45.3	16.4	57.3	16.0	175.0	5.8	0.9	2.3	55.8
May	758.9	590.0	349.6	249.5	195.7	35.3	45.5	16.3	57.7	14.1	168.9	6.2	1.0	2.1	53.6
June	755.6	587.5	350.5	249.5	193.3	35.0	46.1	14.9	56.8	14.0	168.1	5.5	0.8	2.1	50.1
July	759.8	590.4	348.7	248.7	195.3	36.3	45.6	15.9	56.8	15.7	169.4	5.7	1.0	2.3	51.9
August	755.3	584.0	348.1	248.4	191.3	34.3	47.2	14.9	54.7	15.5	171.2	6.1	0.9	1.6	51.5
September	753.1	582.5	347.6	248.8	191.2	32.7	48.5	14.4	55.4	14.7	170.6	5.8	1.0	1.9	52.4
October	756.9	584.9	350.0	249.6	191.5	31.4	48.1	14.7	55.8	15.2	172.0	5.7	0.6	2.1	50.6
November	776.5	596.9	353.9	253.8	197.4	32.2	46.4	15.7	60.9	15.2	179.5	5.2	0.9	1.9	56.5
December	791.7	605.8	358.2	259.8	199.7	33.3	46.2	15.8	61.0	16.9	185.9	5.4	1.0	2.3	60.2

1. Includes categories not shown separately.
2. Included in "Other commercial buildings."

Table 14-3. New Construction Put in Place—*Continued*

(Billions of 1996 dollars, monthly data are at seasonally adjusted annual rates.)

Year and month	Total	Private [1] Total	Residential Total	Residential New housing units	Nonresidential buildings [1] Total	Nonresidential Industrial	Nonresidential Office	Nonresidential Hotels, motels	Nonresidential Other commercial buildings	Public utilities Total	Public utilities Tele-communications	Public [1] Total	Housing and redevelopment	Industrial	Military facilities	Highways and streets
1970	429.0	321.9	155.1	117.1	115.4	38.1	(2)	6.0	47.3	40.3	7.6	107.1	4.8	1.3	2.7	35.8
1971	465.6	360.0	198.0	157.8	110.5	29.3	(2)	5.7	52.0	41.0	7.6	105.6	4.7	1.5	3.2	35.6
1972	498.5	397.7	231.1	190.7	114.2	23.7	24.1	7.6	34.6	43.0	8.1	100.8	3.3	1.4	3.7	33.5
1973	506.6	405.8	226.1	189.8	122.7	29.4	25.4	8.3	37.1	46.0	8.9	100.8	3.3	1.5	3.6	31.1
1974	449.4	346.3	177.1	137.4	113.6	32.6	22.8	5.3	33.7	43.7	8.4	103.2	3.2	1.6	3.2	31.0
1975	404.1	298.6	149.4	105.2	96.4	31.7	17.8	3.3	25.8	40.2	7.2	105.6	3.9	1.9	3.4	29.0
1976	435.3	332.8	185.8	138.1	90.5	27.4	16.4	2.7	25.3	43.8	7.1	102.5	3.4	1.8	3.8	26.2
1977	470.4	375.3	225.5	176.9	92.9	27.5	17.0	2.6	28.2	43.4	7.7	95.1	3.6	2.0	3.2	26.0
1978	505.4	404.5	237.1	184.8	107.0	35.4	19.1	3.0	32.1	46.4	9.0	100.9	3.0	2.1	3.1	27.1
1979	513.8	413.2	224.7	172.3	127.4	43.4	24.7	4.9	37.2	47.6	9.8	100.5	3.2	2.2	3.0	27.8
1980	464.1	364.1	175.8	122.0	129.3	36.6	31.7	6.1	36.6	47.8	9.8	100.0	3.5	2.6	2.9	25.1
1981	455.3	361.1	162.7	113.9	140.6	41.7	38.6	7.1	34.2	48.5	10.2	94.2	3.8	2.7	2.8	23.7
1982	423.7	333.9	134.6	90.6	145.1	40.8	48.9	7.6	27.9	46.7	10.4	89.8	3.6	2.6	3.1	22.6
1983	465.1	375.2	195.0	147.2	131.3	29.4	42.7	9.3	28.5	42.0	9.7	89.9	4.1	2.7	3.6	24.1
1984	534.6	437.3	231.4	171.1	155.3	30.1	51.3	11.6	40.4	43.5	10.7	97.2	4.0	2.6	4.0	29.0
1985	567.7	463.9	235.0	169.6	178.9	33.9	61.2	12.3	50.1	43.3	10.8	103.8	4.2	2.8	4.3	29.9
1986	588.8	479.6	266.5	188.9	163.7	28.4	53.3	12.1	48.4	43.7	12.0	109.2	4.2	2.2	4.9	30.6
1987	585.1	470.6	267.1	190.8	160.4	27.6	48.0	11.6	48.6	36.5	11.9	114.5	4.4	1.9	5.4	32.5
1988	583.4	467.6	263.4	183.4	164.2	29.1	49.3	10.4	48.7	34.4	12.3	115.8	4.2	1.8	4.3	34.0
1989	579.6	463.5	252.7	177.3	169.2	34.8	48.5	11.2	48.1	35.7	11.3	116.0	4.3	1.6	4.1	32.7
1990	560.8	437.0	228.9	158.3	167.9	39.4	41.0	12.5	46.8	33.5	11.3	123.8	4.6	1.7	3.1	35.9
1991	503.7	378.2	197.5	136.1	135.4	36.5	30.1	8.1	34.1	38.8	10.3	125.5	4.3	2.1	2.1	35.4
1992	533.3	401.6	232.1	157.3	120.9	33.2	23.2	4.2	33.4	41.7	10.3	131.8	4.8	2.1	2.8	37.4
1993	546.8	418.0	249.8	167.5	122.2	29.3	23.1	5.0	35.8	38.7	10.9	128.7	4.5	1.9	2.7	38.6
1994	574.3	445.5	275.0	187.6	127.6	30.7	23.5	4.9	39.8	36.4	11.2	128.8	4.1	1.6	2.5	40.9
1995	567.9	434.5	251.9	174.6	139.7	34.8	26.2	7.3	43.6	36.7	11.6	133.5	4.8	1.5	3.1	39.0
1996	613.5	474.3	281.2	191.2	153.9	36.2	27.9	10.9	48.2	33.1	11.8	139.1	5.0	1.4	2.6	39.4
1997	635.8	486.3	280.7	192.4	166.8	35.4	33.1	12.4	49.9	32.9	12.2	149.5	5.1	1.0	2.5	42.5
1998	670.9	520.6	297.9	212.1	177.6	37.7	39.3	13.8	49.9	38.6	13.0	150.2	4.9	0.9	2.4	45.9
1999	692.5	535.6	315.8	225.9	175.0	31.2	41.6	14.3	51.1	38.2	15.1	156.9	5.1	0.8	1.9	48.8
1996																
January	589.0	452.8	264.0	181.9	146.4	36.9	23.6	9.8	46.8	. . .	11.9	136.2	5.0	1.3	3.4	38.8
February	584.8	455.3	268.6	184.7	145.6	35.9	23.9	9.9	47.0	. . .	11.6	129.6	4.3	1.4	3.1	39.3
March	585.7	455.9	272.1	187.4	143.7	35.1	24.2	10.1	45.7	. . .	10.9	129.9	4.1	1.5	2.5	37.7
April	606.3	470.5	281.0	193.2	148.7	36.0	25.5	11.1	47.7	. . .	11.6	135.8	3.8	1.5	2.8	39.5
May	611.2	471.8	284.7	195.0	148.2	34.4	27.2	9.8	47.7	. . .	11.5	139.4	4.7	1.5	2.7	39.0
June	614.6	479.6	286.8	196.5	154.5	36.3	30.2	10.4	46.7	. . .	10.9	135.0	4.3	1.6	2.5	38.7
July	610.8	472.7	285.5	194.0	150.5	34.6	28.8	10.0	46.5	. . .	10.7	138.1	5.1	1.5	2.3	40.1
August	615.2	478.4	285.7	193.6	154.2	33.7	28.8	11.5	49.1	. . .	11.7	136.8	5.2	1.6	2.3	37.5
September	625.9	480.7	285.5	192.3	157.8	36.5	29.8	11.7	48.8	. . .	11.3	145.2	6.0	1.7	2.6	40.4
October	632.3	486.8	284.1	191.7	164.1	40.0	29.6	11.4	50.9	. . .	11.8	145.5	5.9	0.8	2.5	40.8
November	637.2	488.4	284.1	191.0	165.4	38.8	30.4	12.2	50.5	. . .	12.6	148.8	6.2	1.0	2.4	40.0
December	629.7	485.0	282.1	188.8	163.4	35.9	31.0	12.5	49.9	. . .	14.2	144.7	5.6	1.0	2.3	40.9
1997																
January	630.2	485.2	279.0	186.9	167.0	36.1	31.0	12.0	53.2	. . .	11.8	145.0	5.2	1.1	2.6	39.4
February	636.4	485.4	283.6	192.2	169.4	36.5	33.2	12.3	52.4	. . .	11.8	150.9	5.5	1.0	2.5	41.0
March	631.5	477.6	282.4	191.7	161.9	32.9	30.7	12.2	50.5	. . .	11.6	153.9	5.3	1.1	2.1	42.0
April	633.4	483.2	283.4	192.6	162.3	34.0	29.3	12.3	50.0	. . .	12.3	150.3	5.3	1.4	2.3	42.7
May	634.2	484.7	284.2	194.4	162.5	33.9	29.4	13.1	50.1	. . .	11.8	149.5	5.5	0.8	2.5	42.5
June	631.8	482.3	280.2	191.3	163.8	34.7	31.9	12.9	49.4	. . .	12.1	149.5	4.9	1.1	2.5	43.3
July	639.9	489.4	279.0	190.6	170.7	37.1	34.3	12.8	51.2	. . .	12.8	150.5	5.0	1.1	2.6	43.6
August	639.0	488.8	278.2	191.2	170.3	36.2	34.4	12.8	50.7	. . .	12.0	150.2	4.8	1.0	2.7	43.8
September	639.6	490.2	278.7	192.6	169.6	36.4	34.3	12.1	49.4	. . .	13.0	149.3	4.8	0.9	2.5	42.5
October	642.7	493.0	281.2	195.3	168.9	35.9	35.9	12.5	48.3	. . .	12.4	149.7	5.6	0.7	2.7	40.4
November	632.8	486.0	280.5	194.0	166.3	34.9	35.7	12.3	47.3	. . .	12.1	146.8	4.8	0.8	2.6	44.3
December	636.1	489.1	281.7	195.9	168.9	36.1	36.5	12.2	48.0	. . .	12.1	147.1	4.4	0.8	2.1	43.1
1998																
January	643.9	496.3	284.8	198.5	172.5	36.8	38.3	12.3	48.5	. . .	12.2	147.6	4.5	0.9	2.4	44.4
February	646.3	498.6	288.0	201.7	172.5	37.1	37.7	12.0	48.2	. . .	13.2	147.7	4.6	1.0	2.6	44.8
March	653.4	505.6	290.5	204.3	175.5	39.8	37.4	12.1	49.9	. . .	13.9	147.9	4.8	1.1	2.6	46.0
April	665.3	516.9	293.5	208.3	178.4	38.3	38.5	12.9	50.3	. . .	12.6	148.5	4.9	1.0	2.5	46.2
May	659.1	514.6	292.3	207.3	174.8	37.5	38.6	12.5	49.4	. . .	13.5	144.5	4.6	0.9	2.2	43.6
June	687.9	533.9	294.6	210.2	181.5	38.5	41.1	13.9	51.1	. . .	12.9	154.0	5.1	0.8	2.4	47.7
July	675.6	522.6	298.3	214.1	177.4	37.1	38.8	13.9	51.2	. . .	12.7	153.0	5.7	1.0	3.0	45.1
August	676.0	525.6	300.4	214.2	177.6	38.9	37.6	14.7	49.5	. . .	12.9	150.4	4.9	1.0	2.6	46.1
September	679.1	526.5	304.2	217.5	176.5	38.0	38.2	15.4	48.3	. . .	13.1	152.6	4.6	0.9	2.0	46.6
October	678.7	528.7	305.7	219.5	179.7	37.3	41.2	15.4	49.8	. . .	13.7	150.0	4.6	0.7	2.1	47.3
November	683.0	532.4	307.7	220.9	182.3	37.4	42.0	15.1	51.1	. . .	12.9	150.5	4.9	1.0	2.0	45.7
December	687.5	534.4	310.2	222.7	182.7	36.0	42.8	14.7	51.3	. . .	12.6	153.1	4.9	0.9	2.1	45.6
1999																
January	701.4	544.6	313.5	223.9	180.8	35.1	42.2	16.0	50.2	. . .	13.5	156.7	4.8	0.8	1.8	50.7
February	715.5	549.5	314.7	225.9	183.1	34.1	43.2	16.5	51.4	. . .	13.8	166.0	4.8	0.8	2.4	56.0
March	714.5	552.5	318.5	228.5	181.9	34.4	41.8	15.6	52.5	. . .	16.2	161.9	5.2	0.9	2.0	52.6
April	701.3	540.6	317.8	227.6	177.2	32.2	40.8	14.8	51.7	. . .	15.9	160.8	5.3	0.8	2.1	51.6
May	691.4	537.2	318.4	227.2	176.0	31.8	40.9	14.7	51.9	. . .	14.1	154.2	5.6	0.9	1.9	49.2
June	684.3	531.9	317.5	226.0	172.8	31.2	41.2	13.4	50.8	. . .	13.9	152.4	5.0	0.8	1.9	45.5
July	686.7	533.1	314.5	224.2	174.2	32.4	40.7	14.2	50.7	. . .	15.7	153.6	5.1	0.9	2.0	47.3
August	681.2	526.4	313.6	223.8	170.2	30.5	42.0	13.2	48.7	. . .	15.4	154.8	5.5	0.8	1.5	46.9
September	678.9	524.6	312.9	223.9	170.1	29.1	43.2	12.8	49.3	. . .	14.6	154.3	5.2	0.9	1.7	47.7
October	679.4	524.7	313.9	223.9	169.4	27.7	42.6	13.0	49.4	. . .	15.2	154.7	5.1	0.6	1.9	45.7
November	693.8	533.1	315.9	226.6	173.7	28.4	40.8	13.8	53.6	. . .	15.2	160.7	4.6	0.8	1.7	50.8
December	705.2	539.3	318.7	231.2	175.2	29.2	40.5	13.9	53.5	. . .	16.9	165.9	4.8	0.9	2.1	53.9

1. Includes categories not shown separately.
2. Included in "Other commercial buildings."

Table 14-4. Housing Starts and Building Permits; Home Sales and Prices

Year and month	Housing starts and building permits								Home sales and prices				
	New private housing units (thousands)						Manufacturers' shipments of manufactured homes (thousands)		New homes			Existing homes	
	Started (not seasonally adjusted)		Seasonally adjusted annual rate						Seasonally adjusted		Median sales price (dollars)	Sold (thousands, seasonally adjusted annual rate)	Median sales price (dollars)
			Started		Authorized by building permits¹				Sold (thousands annual rate)	For sale, end-of-period (thousands)			
	Total	One-family structures	Total	One-family structures	Total	One-family structures	Not seasonally adjusted	Seasonally adjusted annual rate					
1970	1 433.6	812.9	1 434	813	1 352	647	401	401	485	227	23 400	1 612	23 000
1971	2 052.2	1 151.0	2 052	1 151	1 925	906	497	497	656	294	25 200	2 018	24 800
1972	2 356.6	1 309.2	2 357	1 309	2 219	1 033	576	576	718	416	27 600	2 252	26 700
1973	2 045.3	1 132.0	2 045	1 132	1 820	882	567	567	634	422	32 500	2 334	28 900
1974	1 337.7	888.1	1 338	888	1 074	644	329	329	519	350	35 900	2 272	32 000
1975	1 160.4	892.2	1 160	892	939	676	213	213	549	316	39 300	2 476	35 300
1976	1 537.5	1 162.4	1 538	1 162	1 296	894	246	246	646	358	44 200	3 064	38 100
1977	1 987.1	1 450.9	1 987	1 451	1 690	1 126	277	277	819	408	48 800	3 650	42 900
1978	2 020.3	1 433.3	2 020	1 433	1 800	1 183	276	276	817	419	55 700	3 986	48 700
1979	1 745.1	1 194.1	1 745	1 194	1 552	982	277	277	709	402	62 900	3 827	55 700
1980	1 292.2	852.2	1 292	852	1 191	710	222	222	545	342	64 600	2 973	62 200
1981	1 084.2	705.4	1 084	705	986	564	241	241	436	278	68 900	2 419	66 400
1982	1 062.2	662.6	1 062	663	1 000	546	240	240	412	255	69 300	1 990	67 800
1983	1 703.0	1 067.6	1 703	1 068	1 605	902	296	296	623	304	75 300	2 697	70 300
1984	1 749.5	1 084.2	1 750	1 084	1 682	922	296	296	639	358	79 900	2 829	72 400
1985	1 741.8	1 072.4	1 742	1 072	1 733	957	284	284	688	350	84 300	3 134	75 500
1986	1 805.4	1 179.4	1 805	1 179	1 769	1 078	244	244	750	361	92 000	3 474	80 300
1987	1 620.5	1 146.4	1 621	1 146	1 535	1 024	233	233	671	370	104 500	3 436	85 600
1988	1 488.1	1 081.3	1 488	1 081	1 456	994	218	218	676	371	112 500	3 513	89 300
1989	1 376.1	1 003.3	1 376	1 003	1 338	932	198	198	650	366	120 000	3 346	93 100
1990	1 192.7	894.8	1 193	895	1 111	794	188	188	534	321	122 900	3 211	95 500
1991	1 013.9	840.4	1 014	840	949	754	171	171	509	284	120 000	3 220	100 300
1992	1 199.7	1 029.9	1 200	1 030	1 095	911	210	210	610	267	121 500	3 520	103 700
1993	1 287.6	1 125.7	1 288	1 126	1 199	987	254	254	666	295	126 500	3 802	106 800
1994	1 457.0	1 198.4	1 457	1 198	1 372	1 069	304	304	670	340	130 000	3 916	107 200
1995	1 354.1	1 076.2	1 354	1 076	1 333	997	340	340	667	374	133 900	3 888	110 500
1996	1 476.8	1 160.9	1 477	1 161	1 426	1 070	363	362	757	326	140 000	4 196	115 800
1997	1 474.0	1 133.7	1 474	1 133	1 441	1 062	354	354	804	287	146 000	4 382	121 800
1998	1 616.9	1 271.4	1 617	1 271	1 612	1 188	373	374	886	300	152 500	4 970	128 400
1999	1 666.5	1 334.9	1 667	1 335	1 664	1 247	348	348	907	326	160 000	5 197	133 300
1996													
January	90.7	68.9	1 467	1 143	1 387	1 051	27	355	714	369	131 900	4 100	113 000
February	95.9	74.2	1 491	1 158	1 420	1 085	27	344	769	355	139 400	4 210	111 100
March	116.0	96.9	1 424	1 147	1 437	1 108	30	365	721	368	137 000	4 160	113 200
April	146.6	117.9	1 516	1 211	1 463	1 108	33	369	736	368	140 000	4 340	114 100
May	143.9	111.6	1 504	1 156	1 457	1 096	34	363	746	361	136 400	4 400	115 100
June	138.0	115.0	1 467	1 192	1 429	1 089	31	371	721	355	140 000	4 030	119 700
July	137.5	109.1	1 472	1 151	1 450	1 074	29	364	770	350	144 200	4 300	118 600
August	144.2	115.6	1 557	1 252	1 413	1 061	34	369	826	342	137 000	4 240	118 700
September	128.7	99.3	1 475	1 148	1 392	1 037	32	372	770	330	139 000	4 030	115 900
October	130.8	101.0	1 392	1 113	1 358	1 010	36	367	720	328	143 800	4 180	114 600
November	111.5	82.6	1 489	1 121	1 412	1 031	28	358	771	330	143 500	4 180	115 600
December	93.1	68.8	1 370	1 060	1 411	1 015	23	341	805	322	144 900	4 130	116 900
1997													
January	82.2	66.6	1 355	1 108	1 382	1 046	27	347	830	308	145 000	4 340	117 600
February	94.7	75.1	1 486	1 181	1 445	1 070	26	350	801	301	143 000	4 280	115 400
March	120.4	96.1	1 457	1 130	1 436	1 031	29	351	831	288	148 000	4 060	117 600
April	142.3	109.5	1 492	1 124	1 421	1 054	33	365	744	290	150 000	4 190	118 600
May	136.3	106.2	1 442	1 105	1 414	1 046	31	353	760	287	141 000	4 350	120 900
June	140.4	108.8	1 494	1 120	1 402	1 057	31	355	793	288	145 000	4 210	124 500
July	134.6	107.4	1 437	1 133	1 440	1 050	29	356	805	289	145 900	4 370	124 200
August	126.5	98.8	1 390	1 100	1 449	1 061	31	356	815	287	144 000	4 430	125 600
September	139.2	108.3	1 546	1 205	1 494	1 091	31	354	840	284	146 300	4 560	123 800
October	139.0	99.2	1 520	1 127	1 499	1 098	34	351	800	284	141 500	4 700	122 100
November	112.4	83.7	1 510	1 154	1 469	1 093	26	352	864	281	145 000	4 390	122 400
December	106.0	73.9	1 566	1 149	1 456	1 080	25	354	793	281	145 900	4 640	123 900
1998													
January	91.2	72.3	1 525	1 227	1 555	1 158	27	361	872	282	148 000	4 640	124 300
February	101.1	78.9	1 584	1 237	1 647	1 191	28	370	866	281	156 000	4 840	122 400
March	132.6	107.2	1 567	1 221	1 605	1 162	32	370	836	284	152 700	4 990	124 600
April	144.9	117.3	1 540	1 230	1 547	1 157	33	369	866	287	148 000	4 940	125 800
May	143.3	114.4	1 536	1 212	1 554	1 165	31	372	887	287	153 200	4 860	128 900
June	159.6	128.7	1 641	1 275	1 551	1 148	33	366	923	286	148 000	5 030	131 300
July	156.0	120.5	1 698	1 300	1 610	1 181	31	380	876	285	149 900	5 100	131 900
August	147.5	115.1	1 614	1 274	1 654	1 196	32	371	846	286	154 900	4 850	130 800
September	141.5	112.4	1 582	1 262	1 577	1 187	33	373	864	289	155 000	4 970	129 400
October	155.5	113.5	1 715	1 298	1 719	1 217	35	379	893	293	154 500	5 010	128 100
November	124.2	101.3	1 660	1 383	1 672	1 248	30	389	995	292	151 000	5 010	129 400
December	119.6	89.8	1 792	1 412	1 742	1 317	27	382	949	294	152 500	5 300	128 500
1999													
January	108.0	82.1	1 804	1 393	1 745	1 269	28	390	918	295	152 500	5 100	130 300
February	112.2	89.1	1 738	1 379	1 748	1 308	29	381	893	296	159 900	5 140	128 100
March	149.3	122.9	1 737	1 377	1 681	1 255	34	383	881	298	155 000	5 320	129 600
April	146.5	118.8	1 577	1 248	1 595	1 223	33	368	930	301	160 000	5 240	130 700
May	155.6	130.4	1 649	1 368	1 639	1 253	31	365	896	305	154 800	5 040	132 800
June	152.4	127.9	1 562	1 269	1 696	1 266	33	355	948	305	158 300	5 590	136 900
July	155.2	123.4	1 704	1 348	1 673	1 263	26	336	936	306	157 900	5 310	136 000
August	155.0	119.7	1 657	1 285	1 658	1 233	31	340	914	307	154 900	5 300	137 400
September	143.3	112.5	1 628	1 290	1 553	1 200	29	320	848	311	162 000	5 150	134 400
October	145.4	115.8	1 636	1 343	1 636	1 204	28	321	906	314	160 000	4 880	132 500
November	127.9	102.1	1 663	1 344	1 678	1 238	26	316	895	317	172 900	5 150	133 200
December	115.7	90.2	1 769	1 441	1 683	1 266	22	304	916	320	165 000	5 140	133 700

1. Data beginning with 1994 cover 19,000 permit issuing places; 1984–1993: 17,000 places; 1978–1983: 16,000 places; 1972–1977: 14,000 places; 1971: 13,000 places.

CHAPTER 15: MANUFACTURING

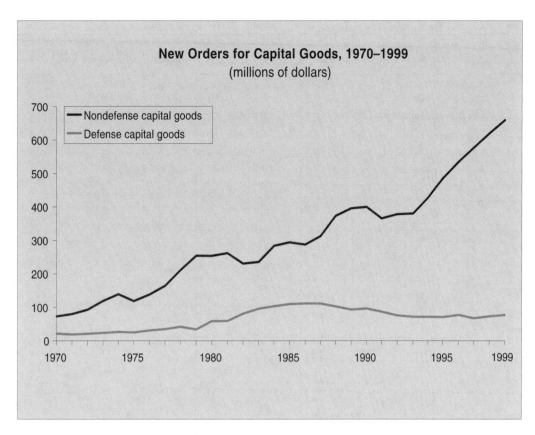

New Orders for Capital Goods, 1970–1999
(millions of dollars)

- U.S. manufacturers received $659 billion worth of new orders for nondefense capital goods (roughly equivalent to business equipment) in 1999, up 6.3 percent from 1998 and continuing the steep upward trend that began in 1994. Orders for defense capital goods, increased in 1998 and 1999 after declining from 1986 through 1997. Defense accounted for 23 percent of U.S. capital goods orders in 1970 but only 10.5 percent of orders in 1999.

- Production at primary processing industries (such as primary metals) rose 83 percent from 1970 to 1999, and capacity utilization rose from 79.9 percent to 83 percent—still well below earlier highs. Production at advanced processing industries (such as machinery) rose 210 percent, but capacity rose so rapidly that utilization, at 78.8 percent, was little higher than in the recession year 1970.

- While total manufacturing production was up 160 percent from 1970 to 1999, payroll employment was lower in 1999 than in 1970. However, the average factory workweek was 41.7 hours in 1999 compared with 39.8 in 1970.

Table 15-1. Total Manufacturing—Production, Capacity Utilization, and Prices

(Seasonally adjusted, except as noted.)

Year and month	Industrial production (1992=100)					Capacity utilization (output as a percent of capacity)					Producer price index, total manufacturing industries [1]
	Total manufacturing	Primary processing	Advanced processing	Durable goods	Nondurable goods	Total manufacturing	Primary processing	Advanced processing	Durable goods	Nondurable goods	
1970	54.8	67.2	48.9	52.7	58.0	79.4	79.9	78.9	77.2	82.8	...
1971	55.6	68.7	49.4	52.4	60.3	77.9	78.7	77.1	74.7	82.6	...
1972	61.5	77.3	54.3	58.5	65.7	83.4	85.5	82.2	81.4	86.4	...
1973	66.9	84.6	59.0	65.3	69.0	87.7	90.5	86.2	88.0	87.3	...
1974	65.9	82.0	58.6	64.0	68.5	83.4	85.1	82.5	83.1	83.9	...
1975	59.4	71.4	53.8	56.1	64.2	72.9	72.1	73.3	70.6	76.3	...
1976	65.4	80.3	58.6	61.8	70.7	78.2	79.2	77.6	75.7	81.8	...
1977	71.2	86.7	64.0	68.1	75.7	82.6	83.8	81.9	80.8	85.3	...
1978	75.8	90.7	68.9	73.6	78.9	85.2	85.9	84.8	84.4	86.4	...
1979	78.5	92.5	72.0	77.4	79.9	85.3	86.0	84.9	85.6	84.9	...
1980	75.5	84.4	71.4	73.4	78.3	79.5	77.2	80.8	78.4	81.0	...
1981	76.7	85.2	72.8	74.6	79.5	78.3	77.2	78.8	76.8	80.4	...
1982	72.1	75.7	70.5	68.2	77.7	71.8	68.6	73.5	68.0	77.5	...
1983	76.3	82.1	73.6	72.2	81.9	74.4	74.5	74.4	70.1	80.8	...
1984	83.8	88.4	81.7	82.7	85.3	79.8	80.0	79.7	77.6	82.9	...
1985	85.7	88.4	84.5	85.6	86.0	78.8	79.1	78.6	76.8	81.5	...
1986	88.1	90.0	87.2	87.4	89.1	78.7	79.9	78.1	75.7	82.8	98.4
1987	92.8	95.3	91.6	92.0	93.8	81.3	84.5	79.9	77.9	85.9	100.9
1988	97.1	99.0	96.2	98.1	96.0	83.8	86.8	82.3	81.7	86.4	104.4
1989	99.0	99.9	98.6	100.5	97.3	83.6	86.1	82.5	82.0	85.7	109.6
1990	98.5	99.3	98.2	99.0	97.9	81.4	83.9	80.3	79.0	84.4	114.5
1991	96.2	95.7	96.4	95.5	97.0	77.9	79.6	77.2	74.7	81.9	115.9
1992	100.0	100.0	100.0	100.0	100.0	79.5	82.3	78.3	76.7	82.8	117.4
1993	103.7	103.5	103.7	105.4	101.8	80.5	84.0	79.0	78.8	82.4	119.1
1994	110.0	109.8	110.1	114.3	105.2	82.5	87.1	80.6	81.7	83.6	120.7
1995	115.8	112.1	117.7	123.9	107.1	82.7	86.5	81.0	82.0	83.5	124.2
1996	121.3	114.3	124.7	134.0	107.8	81.5	85.4	79.9	80.8	82.4	127.1
1997	130.1	119.5	135.1	148.0	111.2	82.4	86.1	81.0	82.1	83.1	127.5
1998	136.4	121.2	144.0	160.7	111.6	80.9	84.0	79.8	80.9	81.3	126.2
1999	142.3	123.3	151.8	172.8	111.8	79.8	83.0	78.8	79.9	80.2	128.3
1996											
January	117.0	111.2	119.7	127.6	105.6	80.9	84.4	79.3	80.2	81.6	125.8
February	118.3	111.5	121.5	129.6	106.2	81.4	84.4	80.0	80.9	81.9	125.7
March	117.8	112.5	120.3	128.1	106.7	80.6	84.9	78.7	79.3	82.2	126.0
April	119.4	112.6	122.7	131.6	106.5	81.3	84.7	79.8	80.8	81.8	126.8
May	120.5	113.6	123.9	133.3	106.9	81.6	85.2	80.0	81.2	82.0	127.4
June	121.5	114.8	124.8	134.9	107.4	81.8	85.9	80.1	81.5	82.3	127.1
July	122.0	114.8	125.5	135.3	107.9	81.8	85.6	80.1	81.2	82.5	127.1
August	122.8	115.6	126.3	136.5	108.3	81.9	86.0	80.2	81.4	82.6	127.4
September	123.5	116.2	127.0	137.1	109.1	82.0	86.2	80.2	81.2	83.1	127.5
October	123.4	116.3	126.8	137.0	109.0	81.6	86.0	79.7	80.6	82.9	128.2
November	124.3	116.5	128.2	138.5	109.4	81.8	85.9	80.1	80.9	83.0	128.0
December	124.8	116.5	128.9	139.0	109.9	81.7	85.6	80.2	80.7	83.2	128.0
1997											
January	125.3	116.5	129.7	140.1	109.8	81.7	85.4	80.2	80.8	83.0	128.1
February	126.5	117.9	130.8	142.0	110.4	82.1	86.1	80.5	81.3	83.3	127.9
March	127.1	117.9	131.8	143.1	110.6	82.1	85.9	80.7	81.4	83.3	127.8
April	127.8	118.8	132.4	144.5	110.6	82.1	86.3	80.6	81.7	83.1	127.7
May	128.4	118.9	133.3	145.8	110.6	82.1	86.1	80.7	81.8	82.9	127.6
June	129.5	119.1	134.8	147.9	110.7	82.4	86.0	81.1	82.4	82.8	127.2
July	130.1	119.8	135.4	148.4	111.4	82.4	86.1	81.0	82.1	83.1	126.9
August	131.1	120.0	136.9	150.5	111.5	82.6	86.0	81.5	82.7	83.0	127.4
September	131.8	120.9	137.5	151.5	111.9	82.7	86.4	81.4	82.7	83.1	127.3
October	132.7	121.0	138.7	152.3	112.8	82.8	86.2	81.6	82.5	83.6	127.6
November	133.5	121.9	139.5	154.3	112.4	82.8	86.5	81.5	82.9	83.1	127.5
December	134.0	122.1	140.2	155.3	112.5	82.6	86.3	81.4	82.8	83.0	127.0
1998											
January	134.5	122.0	141.0	155.9	113.0	82.5	86.0	81.3	82.4	83.2	126.4
February	134.3	121.7	141.0	156.4	112.2	81.9	85.5	80.7	81.9	82.4	126.1
March	134.5	121.6	141.3	157.0	112.0	81.5	85.1	80.3	81.5	82.1	125.9
April	135.3	122.1	142.2	158.1	112.5	81.5	85.1	80.2	81.3	82.2	126.2
May	135.9	121.9	143.3	159.6	112.2	81.3	84.7	80.2	81.3	81.9	126.4
June	134.8	120.8	142.2	158.0	111.6	80.1	83.7	78.9	79.7	81.2	126.2
July	134.7	120.9	142.0	157.3	112.0	79.7	83.5	78.3	78.7	81.4	126.2
August	137.4	120.6	146.2	164.2	111.0	80.8	83.0	80.2	81.5	80.5	126.0
September	137.3	120.3	146.3	164.6	110.4	80.4	82.6	79.7	81.1	80.0	125.9
October	138.3	120.7	147.5	165.8	111.2	80.5	82.7	79.9	81.1	80.4	126.4
November	138.3	120.8	147.5	165.4	111.6	80.2	82.6	79.4	80.3	80.5	126.2
December	138.4	121.9	147.2	166.2	111.1	79.9	83.1	78.8	80.1	80.1	125.9
1999											
January	138.6	122.2	147.2	166.3	111.3	79.6	83.1	78.4	79.6	80.2	126.2
February	139.3	122.1	148.4	166.8	112.3	79.7	82.8	78.7	79.3	80.7	125.9
March	139.7	122.4	148.8	168.1	111.8	79.6	82.9	78.5	79.5	80.3	126.3
April	140.2	122.2	149.6	169.4	111.5	79.5	82.6	78.5	79.6	80.0	127.4
May	141.0	122.5	150.7	170.8	111.9	79.7	82.7	78.7	79.7	80.2	127.7
June	141.4	122.7	151.2	172.2	111.4	79.6	82.7	78.6	79.9	79.7	127.8
July	142.0	123.3	151.8	173.8	111.0	79.7	82.9	78.6	80.3	79.5	128.3
August	142.5	123.4	152.6	174.4	111.5	79.7	82.8	78.8	80.2	79.7	129.0
September	142.9	123.6	153.1	175.0	111.8	79.7	82.8	78.7	80.0	79.9	129.7
October	144.2	124.8	154.5	176.5	113.0	80.2	83.4	79.1	80.3	80.6	130.2
November	145.0	125.6	155.2	177.4	113.6	80.3	83.8	79.2	80.3	81.0	130.3
December	145.6	125.9	155.9	178.4	113.7	80.3	83.9	79.2	80.3	81.0	130.5

1. December 1984=100, not seasonally adjusted.

Table 15-2. Total Manufacturing—Employment and Hours

| Year and month | Employment (thousands, seasonally adjusted) | | | | | | Hours (production workers—seasonally adjusted) | | | | | |
| | Total payroll employees | | | Production workers | | | Average weekly hours | | | Average overtime hours | | |
	Total manufacturing	Durable goods	Nondurable goods	Total manufacturing	Durable goods	Nondurable goods	Total manufacturing	Durable goods	Nondurable goods	Total manufacturing	Durable goods	Nondurable goods
1970	19 367	11 176	8 190	14 044	8 088	5 956	39.8	40.3	39.1	3.0	3.0	3.0
1971	18 623	10 604	8 019	13 544	7 697	5 847	39.9	40.3	39.3	2.9	2.9	3.0
1972	19 151	11 022	8 129	14 045	8 025	6 022	40.5	41.2	39.7	3.5	3.6	3.3
1973	20 154	11 863	8 291	14 834	8 699	6 138	40.7	41.4	39.6	3.8	4.1	3.4
1974	20 077	11 897	8 181	14 638	8 634	6 004	40.0	40.6	39.1	3.3	3.4	3.0
1975	18 323	10 662	7 661	13 043	7 532	5 510	39.5	39.9	38.8	2.6	2.6	2.7
1976	18 997	11 051	7 946	13 638	7 888	5 750	40.1	40.6	39.4	3.1	3.2	3.0
1977	19 682	11 570	8 112	14 135	8 280	5 855	40.3	41.0	39.4	3.5	3.7	3.2
1978	20 505	12 245	8 259	14 734	8 777	5 956	40.4	41.1	39.4	3.6	3.8	3.2
1979	21 040	12 730	8 310	15 068	9 082	5 986	40.2	40.8	39.3	3.3	3.5	3.1
1980	20 285	12 159	8 127	14 214	8 416	5 798	39.7	40.1	39.0	2.8	2.8	2.8
1981	20 170	12 082	8 089	14 020	8 270	5 751	39.8	40.2	39.2	2.8	2.8	2.8
1982	18 780	11 014	7 766	12 742	7 290	5 451	38.9	39.3	38.4	2.3	2.2	2.5
1983	18 432	10 707	7 725	12 528	7 095	5 433	40.1	40.7	39.4	3.0	3.0	3.0
1984	19 372	11 476	7 896	13 280	7 715	5 565	40.7	41.4	39.7	3.4	3.6	3.1
1985	19 248	11 458	7 790	13 084	7 618	5 466	40.5	41.2	39.6	3.3	3.5	3.1
1986	18 947	11 195	7 752	12 864	7 399	5 465	40.7	41.3	39.9	3.4	3.5	3.3
1987	18 999	11 154	7 845	12 952	7 409	5 543	41.0	41.5	40.2	3.7	3.8	3.6
1988	19 314	11 363	7 951	13 193	7 582	5 611	41.1	41.8	40.2	3.9	4.1	3.6
1989	19 391	11 394	7 997	13 230	7 594	5 636	41.0	41.6	40.2	3.8	3.9	3.6
1990	19 076	11 109	7 968	12 947	7 363	5 584	40.8	41.3	40.0	3.6	3.7	3.6
1991	18 406	10 569	7 837	12 434	6 967	5 467	40.7	41.1	40.2	3.6	3.5	3.7
1992	18 104	10 277	7 827	12 287	6 822	5 466	41.0	41.5	40.4	3.8	3.7	3.8
1993	18 075	10 221	7 854	12 341	6 849	5 492	41.4	42.1	40.6	4.1	4.3	4.0
1994	18 321	10 448	7 873	12 632	7 104	5 528	42.0	42.9	40.9	4.7	5.0	4.3
1995	18 524	10 683	7 841	12 826	7 317	5 508	41.6	42.4	40.5	4.4	4.7	4.0
1996	18 495	10 789	7 706	12 776	7 386	5 390	41.6	42.4	40.5	4.5	4.8	4.1
1997	18 675	11 010	7 665	12 907	7 553	5 354	42.0	42.8	40.9	4.8	5.1	4.4
1998	18 805	11 205	7 600	12 952	7 666	5 287	41.7	42.3	40.9	4.6	4.8	4.3
1999	18 543	11 103	7 440	12 739	7 590	5 149	41.7	42.2	40.9	4.6	4.8	4.4
1996												
January	18 464	10 724	7 740	12 763	7 342	5 421	40.0	41.0	38.7	4.2	4.5	3.8
February	18 491	10 746	7 745	12 777	7 354	5 423	41.5	42.2	40.5	4.4	4.6	4.1
March	18 453	10 715	7 738	12 734	7 321	5 413	41.4	42.0	40.5	4.3	4.5	4.0
April	18 466	10 754	7 712	12 750	7 357	5 393	41.6	42.4	40.5	4.5	4.8	4.1
May	18 483	10 776	7 707	12 763	7 376	5 387	41.7	42.5	40.6	4.6	4.9	4.1
June	18 491	10 793	7 698	12 775	7 392	5 383	41.8	42.6	40.7	4.6	4.9	4.1
July	18 493	10 794	7 699	12 767	7 387	5 380	41.7	42.5	40.6	4.5	4.8	4.1
August	18 513	10 818	7 695	12 786	7 404	5 382	41.8	42.6	40.7	4.6	4.9	4.1
September	18 511	10 822	7 689	12 784	7 410	5 374	41.9	42.7	40.7	4.6	4.9	4.1
October	18 523	10 831	7 692	12 798	7 419	5 379	41.7	42.5	40.7	4.5	4.8	4.1
November	18 530	10 844	7 686	12 797	7 426	5 371	41.7	42.5	40.7	4.5	4.8	4.2
December	18 537	10 858	7 679	12 804	7 434	5 370	41.9	42.6	40.9	4.6	4.9	4.3
1997												
January	18 548	10 873	7 675	12 813	7 451	5 362	41.7	42.5	40.7	4.7	5.0	4.2
February	18 568	10 893	7 675	12 827	7 466	5 361	41.9	42.7	40.7	4.7	5.0	4.3
March	18 597	10 916	7 681	12 842	7 480	5 362	42.1	42.9	40.9	4.9	5.2	4.4
April	18 608	10 932	7 676	12 854	7 493	5 361	42.2	43.1	41.0	5.0	5.4	4.4
May	18 623	10 951	7 672	12 874	7 511	5 363	42.0	42.9	40.8	4.9	5.2	4.4
June	18 654	10 982	7 672	12 892	7 533	5 359	41.9	42.7	40.7	4.7	5.0	4.2
July	18 667	11 009	7 658	12 903	7 552	5 351	41.9	42.8	40.7	4.8	5.1	4.3
August	18 708	11 058	7 650	12 928	7 588	5 340	42.0	42.8	40.8	4.8	5.1	4.3
September	18 722	11 069	7 653	12 939	7 599	5 340	41.9	42.7	40.8	4.7	5.0	4.3
October	18 764	11 109	7 655	12 977	7 629	5 348	42.0	42.7	40.9	4.8	5.1	4.4
November	18 808	11 152	7 656	13 006	7 660	5 346	42.1	42.8	41.0	4.9	5.2	4.4
December	18 837	11 178	7 659	13 021	7 677	5 344	42.1	42.9	41.0	4.9	5.2	4.4
1998												
January	18 868	11 215	7 653	13 045	7 706	5 339	42.2	42.9	41.1	4.9	5.2	4.4
February	18 869	11 225	7 644	13 047	7 713	5 334	42.0	42.7	40.9	4.8	5.1	4.4
March	18 880	11 237	7 643	13 037	7 709	5 328	41.8	42.5	40.9	4.8	5.0	4.4
April	18 881	11 247	7 634	13 034	7 713	5 321	41.6	42.2	40.7	4.6	4.8	4.2
May	18 874	11 248	7 626	13 013	7 703	5 310	41.8	42.4	40.9	4.6	4.8	4.4
June	18 858	11 239	7 619	12 996	7 690	5 306	41.8	42.3	40.9	4.6	4.8	4.3
July	18 688	11 093	7 595	12 813	7 540	5 273	41.7	42.2	40.9	4.6	4.8	4.4
August	18 806	11 224	7 582	12 925	7 660	5 265	41.7	42.2	40.9	4.6	4.7	4.4
September	18 801	11 221	7 580	12 930	7 665	5 265	41.6	42.1	40.9	4.5	4.6	4.3
October	18 753	11 198	7 555	12 895	7 652	5 243	41.7	42.3	40.9	4.5	4.6	4.3
November	18 707	11 168	7 539	12 856	7 628	5 228	41.7	42.3	40.8	4.5	4.7	4.3
December	18 689	11 158	7 531	12 844	7 624	5 220	41.7	42.3	40.9	4.5	4.6	4.3
1999												
January	18 667	11 139	7 528	12 830	7 610	5 220	41.6	42.1	40.8	4.5	4.6	4.4
February	18 626	11 127	7 499	12 792	7 597	5 195	41.6	42.1	40.8	4.5	4.6	4.3
March	18 602	11 123	7 479	12 784	7 603	5 181	41.6	42.1	40.9	4.5	4.6	4.4
April	18 574	11 106	7 468	12 763	7 591	5 172	41.7	42.2	40.9	4.4	4.5	4.3
May	18 540	11 091	7 449	12 741	7 584	5 157	41.7	42.2	41.0	4.6	4.7	4.4
June	18 515	11 083	7 432	12 711	7 572	5 139	41.8	42.3	41.0	4.7	4.8	4.5
July	18 552	11 125	7 427	12 753	7 620	5 133	41.8	42.4	41.0	4.6	4.8	4.4
August	18 503	11 097	7 406	12 706	7 590	5 116	41.8	42.3	41.0	4.6	4.8	4.4
September	18 494	11 090	7 404	12 700	7 580	5 120	41.8	42.4	41.0	4.7	4.9	4.4
October	18 484	11 083	7 401	12 702	7 581	5 121	41.8	42.3	41.0	4.7	4.8	4.5
November	18 484	11 085	7 399	12 702	7 579	5 123	41.7	42.2	41.0	4.7	4.8	4.5
December	18 479	11 087	7 392	12 701	7 579	5 122	41.7	42.2	40.9	4.7	4.8	4.5

Table 15-3. Total Manufacturing—Hours and Earnings

(Production workers)

Year and month	Aggregate weekly hours index (seasonally adjusted, 1982=100)			Average hourly earnings (dollars)					Average weekly earnings (dollars, not seasonally adjusted)		
				Seasonally adjusted		Not seasonally adjusted					
	Total manufacturing	Durable goods	Nondurable goods	Total	Excluding overtime	Total manufacturing	Durable goods	Nondurable goods	Total manufacturing	Durable goods	Nondurable goods
1970	112.8	113.0	112.4	3.35	3.23	3.35	3.55	3.08	133.33	143.07	120.43
1971	108.8	107.4	110.8	3.57	3.45	3.57	3.79	3.27	142.44	152.74	128.51
1972	114.8	115.4	114.1	3.82	3.66	3.82	4.07	3.48	154.71	167.68	138.16
1973	121.7	125.8	116.0	4.09	3.91	4.09	4.35	3.70	166.46	180.09	146.52
1974	118.1	122.4	112.1	4.42	4.25	4.42	4.70	4.01	176.80	190.82	156.79
1975	103.8	104.9	102.1	4.83	4.67	4.83	5.15	4.37	190.79	205.49	169.56
1976	110.3	111.9	108.1	5.22	5.02	5.22	5.57	4.71	209.32	226.14	185.57
1977	115.0	118.4	110.2	5.68	5.44	5.68	6.06	5.11	228.90	248.46	201.33
1978	120.1	125.9	112.0	6.17	5.91	6.17	6.58	5.54	249.27	270.44	218.28
1979	122.1	129.1	112.3	6.70	6.43	6.70	7.12	6.01	269.34	290.50	236.19
1980	113.8	117.8	108.1	7.27	7.02	7.27	7.75	6.56	288.62	310.78	255.84
1981	112.5	116.1	107.6	7.99	7.72	7.99	8.53	7.19	318.00	342.91	281.85
1982	100.0	100.0	100.0	8.49	8.25	8.49	9.03	7.75	330.26	354.88	297.60
1983	101.4	100.7	102.4	8.83	8.52	8.83	9.38	8.09	354.08	381.77	318.75
1984	109.0	111.5	105.5	9.19	8.82	9.19	9.73	8.39	374.03	402.82	333.08
1985	106.9	109.5	103.4	9.54	9.16	9.54	10.09	8.72	386.37	415.71	345.31
1986	105.7	106.8	104.2	9.73	9.34	9.73	10.28	8.95	396.01	424.56	357.11
1987	107.0	107.4	106.6	9.91	9.48	9.91	10.43	9.19	406.31	432.85	369.44
1988	109.3	110.5	107.7	10.19	9.73	10.19	10.71	9.45	418.81	447.68	379.89
1989	109.3	110.1	108.2	10.48	10.02	10.48	11.01	9.75	429.68	458.02	391.95
1990	106.4	106.1	106.8	10.83	10.37	10.83	11.35	10.12	441.86	468.76	404.80
1991	102.1	99.3	105.9	11.18	10.71	11.18	11.75	10.44	455.03	482.93	419.69
1992	101.7	98.2	106.6	11.46	10.95	11.46	12.02	10.73	469.86	498.83	433.49
1993	103.1	100.0	107.4	11.74	11.18	11.74	12.33	10.98	486.04	519.09	445.79
1994	107.0	105.5	109.2	12.07	11.43	12.07	12.68	11.24	506.94	543.97	459.72
1995	107.5	107.5	107.6	12.37	11.74	12.37	12.94	11.58	514.59	548.66	468.99
1996	107.2	109.2	104.3	12.77	12.12	12.77	13.33	11.97	531.23	565.19	484.79
1997	109.4	112.9	104.6	13.17	12.45	13.17	13.73	12.34	553.14	587.64	504.71
1998	109.0	112.4	104.2	13.49	12.79	13.49	13.98	12.76	562.53	591.35	521.88
1999	107.2	111.1	101.7	13.91	13.18	13.91	14.40	13.16	580.05	607.68	538.24
1996											
January	103.0	104.9	100.3	12.62	12.00	12.66	13.17	11.91	503.87	538.65	457.34
February	106.9	108.4	104.8	12.58	11.95	12.57	13.12	11.79	519.14	552.35	472.78
March	106.2	107.3	104.7	12.54	11.92	12.54	13.05	11.83	517.90	548.10	476.75
April	106.9	108.8	104.3	12.72	12.06	12.73	13.28	11.93	524.48	557.76	477.20
May	107.3	109.4	104.5	12.72	12.07	12.70	13.27	11.88	528.32	562.65	479.95
June	107.8	109.9	104.8	12.77	12.11	12.75	13.32	11.92	534.23	568.76	486.34
July	107.4	109.6	104.4	12.80	12.15	12.79	13.35	12.00	525.67	556.70	482.40
August	107.8	110.1	104.6	12.84	12.18	12.79	13.38	11.95	534.62	568.65	488.76
September	107.9	110.3	104.6	12.87	12.20	12.89	13.51	12.01	545.25	582.28	496.01
October	107.6	109.9	104.5	12.86	12.21	12.83	13.41	12.00	537.58	572.61	490.80
November	107.7	110.0	104.5	12.92	12.25	12.92	13.48	12.11	543.93	578.29	498.93
December	108.2	110.6	104.9	12.98	12.29	13.07	13.64	12.23	559.40	594.70	508.77
1997											
January	107.8	110.4	104.2	13.02	12.33	13.03	13.61	12.20	540.75	574.34	494.10
February	108.3	111.1	104.4	13.02	12.33	13.01	13.57	12.19	541.22	576.73	492.48
March	109.0	112.0	104.8	13.07	12.36	13.07	13.63	12.25	548.94	584.73	498.58
April	109.5	112.8	104.9	13.08	12.34	13.08	13.63	12.26	546.74	582.00	496.53
May	109.1	112.4	104.6	13.10	12.37	13.08	13.63	12.26	548.05	583.36	497.76
June	108.9	112.3	104.2	13.11	12.42	13.09	13.64	12.27	549.78	583.79	499.39
July	109.0	112.6	104.1	13.12	12.42	13.10	13.61	12.37	539.72	570.26	499.75
August	109.4	113.3	104.0	13.19	12.48	13.14	13.69	12.34	551.88	584.56	504.71
September	109.4	113.2	104.2	13.20	12.50	13.23	13.79	12.41	560.95	594.35	513.77
October	109.9	113.8	104.6	13.30	12.57	13.28	13.88	12.40	560.42	596.84	509.64
November	110.4	114.5	104.8	13.35	12.62	13.36	13.95	12.49	569.14	604.04	518.34
December	110.7	115.0	104.7	13.39	12.65	13.47	14.06	12.58	579.21	617.23	525.84
1998											
January	110.9	115.3	104.9	13.39	12.66	13.40	13.95	12.57	561.46	594.27	514.11
February	110.4	114.9	104.3	13.43	12.70	13.41	13.95	12.58	559.20	592.88	510.75
March	110.0	114.3	104.1	13.46	12.74	13.47	14.01	12.64	561.70	595.43	514.45
April	109.4	113.7	103.5	13.46	12.76	13.46	13.95	12.72	549.17	576.14	508.80
May	109.6	113.9	103.8	13.48	12.77	13.47	13.97	12.72	563.05	593.73	518.98
June	109.5	113.6	103.8	13.46	12.76	13.44	13.93	12.70	561.79	590.63	519.43
July	107.7	111.0	103.1	13.44	12.74	13.38	13.77	12.81	549.92	571.46	520.09
August	108.7	112.9	103.0	13.51	12.80	13.45	13.92	12.75	560.87	587.42	522.75
September	108.5	112.7	102.8	13.56	12.86	13.60	14.06	12.92	564.40	587.71	529.72
October	108.4	112.9	102.4	13.56	12.87	13.54	14.02	12.83	567.33	595.85	527.31
November	108.1	112.5	102.0	13.59	12.89	13.60	14.07	12.90	573.92	600.79	532.77
December	108.0	112.4	102.0	13.61	12.91	13.69	14.16	12.98	583.19	613.13	539.97
1999											
January	107.6	111.8	101.8	13.65	12.95	13.66	14.11	12.98	564.16	591.21	526.99
February	107.3	111.7	101.4	13.68	12.98	13.66	14.12	12.96	564.16	591.63	524.88
March	107.2	111.6	101.2	13.73	13.02	13.73	14.19	13.02	568.42	595.98	528.61
April	107.2	111.7	101.1	13.80	13.08	13.80	14.27	13.07	574.08	602.19	531.95
May	107.1	111.6	100.9	13.85	13.13	13.85	14.34	13.10	577.55	606.58	535.79
June	107.1	111.8	100.6	13.93	13.19	13.90	14.40	13.14	581.02	610.56	538.74
July	107.6	112.7	100.6	13.98	13.24	13.91	14.38	13.21	573.09	598.21	537.65
August	107.1	112.1	100.1	14.01	13.27	13.95	14.47	13.17	583.11	612.08	539.97
September	107.1	112.1	100.2	14.04	13.29	14.11	14.62	13.33	588.39	615.50	546.53
October	107.0	111.8	100.3	14.06	13.31	14.03	14.55	13.25	589.26	618.38	547.23
November	106.8	111.5	100.3	14.07	13.33	14.08	14.58	13.31	594.18	622.57	551.03
December	106.7	111.5	100.2	14.10	13.36	14.20	14.73	13.39	603.50	634.86	557.02

Table 15-4. Manufacturers' Shipments

(Millions of dollars, adjusted for trading-day and calendar-month variation, but without seasonal adjustment.)

Year and month	Total	Durable goods industries									
		Total [1]	Stone, clay, and glass products	Primary metals		Fabricated metal products	Industrial machinery and equipment	Electronic and electric equipment	Transportation equipment		Instruments and products
				Total	Blast furnaces, steel mills				Total	Motor vehicles and parts	
1970	633 663	337 876	16 454	51 995	25 189	44 210	56 893	41 408	74 539	42 538	18 367
1971	670 877	359 089	18 220	51 585	25 791	45 478	56 445	42 377	88 857	58 247	18 613
1972	756 321	407 844	20 875	58 490	28 712	51 487	66 156	47 502	94 706	63 923	21 043
1973	875 173	475 621	23 141	72 791	36 301	58 804	78 207	54 569	110 587	74 799	23 627
1974	1 017 477	530 074	25 503	95 686	49 718	67 212	93 041	58 684	108 244	68 631	27 454
1975	1 039 065	523 178	26 233	80 890	42 281	68 411	96 354	56 068	113 503	70 033	29 547
1976	1 185 563	607 475	29 618	93 082	46 764	77 560	105 847	65 151	141 028	95 380	33 238
1977	1 358 416	710 017	34 209	103 267	50 670	89 938	122 749	77 845	166 954	117 747	38 803
1978	1 522 858	812 776	40 238	118 175	59 228	101 245	143 919	88 679	188 773	131 999	44 655
1979	1 727 234	911 124	44 287	137 488	67 414	113 494	167 014	102 361	201 623	131 378	50 702
1980	1 852 689	929 027	44 473	134 057	61 612	116 071	180 564	112 864	186 516	104 560	59 825
1981	2 017 544	1 004 725	46 220	142 072	70 254	123 535	201 102	122 084	205 223	116 981	66 613
1982	1 960 214	950 541	43 515	104 874	46 928	119 236	186 773	125 728	201 347	112 270	74 918
1983	2 070 564	1 025 770	47 697	109 240	46 398	123 083	178 446	136 138	245 392	148 296	79 637
1984	2 288 184	1 175 276	53 101	120 315	51 978	138 107	211 075	162 362	284 593	181 993	89 398
1985	2 334 456	1 215 352	55 821	112 265	48 904	143 268	218 408	163 951	307 380	193 445	96 207
1986	2 335 881	1 238 859	59 254	107 865	45 718	143 063	213 574	164 811	322 688	198 811	100 798
1987	2 475 906	1 297 532	61 477	120 248	51 815	147 367	217 671	171 287	332 936	205 923	107 325
1988	2 695 432	1 421 501	63 145	149 837	64 294	159 505	244 365	187 301	354 849	222 353	116 009
1989	2 840 375	1 477 900	63 729	155 718	64 783	164 073	256 212	194 598	369 675	233 232	121 523
1990	2 912 228	1 485 313	63 728	148 787	62 826	165 064	259 367	195 898	370 328	217 295	127 978
1991	2 878 167	1 451 998	59 957	136 378	57 267	159 760	247 508	199 278	367 235	209 210	132 836
1992	3 004 727	1 541 866	62 521	138 287	58 449	166 532	258 662	216 764	399 270	238 384	134 941
1993	3 127 625	1 630 635	65 610	142 685	62 466	175 118	278 063	233 622	414 694	267 365	137 387
1994	3 348 019	1 789 576	71 230	161 188	69 887	190 544	313 047	266 405	450 809	314 637	138 400
1995	3 594 663	1 927 029	75 932	180 314	74 927	204 384	353 338	301 447	461 806	327 908	144 719
1996	3 715 460	2 004 159	82 442	178 297	74 552	214 007	381 795	320 616	465 173	329 155	151 017
1997	3 929 419	2 158 699	90 221	188 916	77 023	226 078	408 860	351 554	502 301	346 606	162 981
1998	4 052 248	2 275 987	96 193	180 973	72 767	239 667	442 316	375 970	536 896	359 560	168 952
1999	4 259 532	2 407 473	103 773	178 466	68 766	245 517	455 140	413 204	583 559	399 807	174 661
1996											
January	271 260	142 767	5 769	13 886	5 935	15 922	25 858	22 427	33 464	25 531	10 878
February	300 080	163 354	5 976	14 921	6 331	17 264	31 337	25 286	40 460	30 165	12 204
March	315 500	173 307	6 454	15 258	6 261	17 761	36 959	27 932	38 317	26 135	13 229
April	305 310	163 709	6 910	15 291	6 351	17 889	29 840	24 788	40 220	29 747	11 699
May	314 171	170 574	7 187	15 546	6 407	18 522	30 983	25 733	42 409	30 850	12 626
June	330 105	183 002	7 554	15 308	6 476	19 026	36 898	29 070	42 175	29 620	13 803
July	279 199	141 349	6 964	13 558	5 743	15 888	26 516	22 953	27 451	18 236	11 330
August	314 384	167 129	7 463	14 915	6 271	18 720	30 052	25 752	39 136	27 997	12 473
September	334 219	183 757	7 469	15 256	6 444	19 160	35 929	29 839	42 890	29 806	13 608
October	323 005	173 001	7 801	15 382	6 479	19 122	30 940	27 400	40 498	29 728	12 369
November	317 989	171 489	6 991	14 948	6 057	18 154	30 701	29 102	40 261	28 442	13 079
December	310 238	170 721	5 904	14 028	5 797	16 579	35 782	30 334	37 892	22 898	13 719
1997											
January	287 787	151 887	6 200	14 808	6 301	18 297	27 167	23 048	36 552	27 495	11 351
February	318 634	175 038	6 882	16 105	6 689	18 491	31 924	27 331	43 165	31 279	13 159
March	335 871	188 904	7 174	16 217	6 614	18 255	38 750	31 270	43 317	29 386	14 197
April	323 369	177 387	7 710	16 430	6 682	18 953	32 421	26 477	43 600	30 579	12 809
May	323 477	176 488	7 718	16 066	6 450	18 401	32 621	27 598	42 090	29 397	12 916
June	349 240	197 434	8 090	16 656	6 784	18 755	40 108	32 148	44 901	30 065	14 985
July	298 607	156 192	7 762	14 462	5 915	18 932	29 766	25 162	31 610	19 687	12 342
August	329 999	178 322	8 044	15 695	6 334	18 995	31 849	29 146	41 490	29 419	13 134
September	356 369	200 122	8 261	16 379	6 538	19 283	39 131	34 583	44 609	30 386	15 477
October	342 277	187 885	8 305	16 264	6 590	19 274	33 894	30 031	44 797	32 999	13 858
November	331 406	181 893	7 381	15 420	6 139	19 143	32 592	30 891	43 769	29 904	13 735
December	332 383	187 147	6 694	14 414	5 987	19 299	38 637	33 869	42 401	26 010	15 018
1998											
January	298 705	159 937	6 674	15 000	6 339	17 312	30 254	24 951	36 878	26 100	12 181
February	333 973	188 429	7 262	16 331	6 764	19 980	35 503	30 112	46 542	33 024	13 908
March	357 033	205 948	7 690	16 362	6 710	20 575	43 739	33 177	48 839	32 955	15 181
April	332 551	184 959	8 113	16 098	6 583	19 748	35 439	27 883	45 528	31 657	13 226
May	333 343	185 809	8 258	15 551	6 355	20 167	35 449	28 523	45 533	31 928	13 510
June	358 824	204 742	8 712	15 842	6 425	20 951	44 856	33 909	43 265	27 659	15 641
July	302 131	158 992	8 249	13 580	5 460	18 129	32 255	27 019	28 518	16 637	12 608
August	337 377	186 058	8 424	14 961	6 058	20 575	34 028	30 345	44 265	30 383	13 346
September	364 324	209 036	8 608	15 402	6 003	21 460	40 690	36 667	49 441	32 753	15 714
October	350 525	199 125	8 757	14 935	5 851	21 391	35 476	32 427	51 680	35 596	13 698
November	341 167	194 672	8 044	13 914	5 319	20 227	34 464	33 995	49 747	32 539	14 516
December	342 295	198 280	7 402	12 997	4 900	19 152	40 163	36 962	46 660	28 329	15 423
1999											
January	307 582	170 448	7 119	13 586	5 236	18 557	30 345	27 811	42 646	30 104	12 284
February	341 000	194 919	7 961	14 635	5 776	20 585	35 722	31 196	50 526	35 628	13 874
March	369 208	215 480	8 418	15 242	5 905	21 274	43 579	35 501	53 786	36 601	15 738
April	343 780	194 694	8 575	14 731	5 693	20 541	35 872	30 994	49 661	34 451	13 463
May	349 625	198 773	8 629	14 894	5 780	20 751	36 517	32 345	50 363	34 588	13 940
June	380 057	219 424	9 324	15 501	5 933	21 800	44 097	37 380	52 128	36 080	16 166
July	320 282	171 249	8 641	13 574	5 169	18 208	34 097	30 909	32 697	20 450	12 834
August	363 407	203 223	9 358	15 298	5 897	21 368	36 108	34 123	51 079	35 318	13 975
September	384 195	219 306	9 456	15 852	5 949	21 576	41 716	40 421	51 593	35 918	16 386
October	369 691	206 861	9 442	15 539	6 024	21 336	38 305	34 795	51 055	36 628	14 506
November	364 779	203 877	8 893	15 167	5 817	20 654	36 757	36 912	49 461	33 932	15 110
December	365 926	209 219	7 957	14 447	5 587	18 867	42 025	40 817	48 564	30 109	16 385

1. Includes categories not shown separately.

Table 15-4. Manufacturers' Shipments—*Continued*

(Millions of dollars, adjusted for trading-day and calendar-month variation, but without seasonal adjustment.)

Year and month	Nondurable goods industries							
	Total [1]	Food and products	Tobacco products	Textile mill products	Paper and products	Chemicals and products	Petroleum and coal products	Rubber and plastics products
1970	295 787	98 535	5 350	22 614	24 573	49 195	24 200	16 754
1971	311 788	103 637	5 528	24 034	25 182	51 681	26 198	18 409
1972	348 477	115 054	5 919	28 065	28 004	58 130	27 918	21 662
1973	399 552	135 585	6 341	31 073	32 495	66 003	33 903	25 191
1974	487 403	161 884	7 139	32 790	41 514	85 387	57 229	28 828
1975	515 887	172 054	8 058	31 065	41 497	91 710	67 496	28 128
1976	578 088	180 830	8 786	36 387	47 939	106 467	80 022	32 880
1977	648 399	192 913	9 051	40 550	51 881	120 905	94 702	40 944
1978	710 082	215 989	9 951	42 281	56 777	132 262	100 967	44 823
1979	816 110	235 976	10 602	45 137	64 957	151 887	144 156	48 694
1980	923 662	256 191	12 194	47 256	72 553	168 220	192 969	49 157
1981	1 012 819	272 140	13 130	50 260	79 970	186 909	217 681	55 178
1982	1 009 673	280 529	16 061	47 516	79 698	176 254	203 404	57 307
1983	1 044 794	289 314	16 268	53 733	84 817	189 552	187 788	62 870
1984	1 112 908	304 584	17 473	56 336	95 525	205 963	184 488	72 938
1985	1 119 104	308 606	18 559	54 605	94 679	204 790	176 574	75 590
1986	1 097 022	318 203	19 146	57 188	99 865	205 711	122 605	78 379
1987	1 178 374	329 725	20 757	62 787	108 989	229 546	130 414	86 634
1988	1 273 931	354 084	23 809	64 627	122 882	261 238	131 682	95 485
1989	1 362 475	380 160	25 875	67 265	131 896	283 196	146 487	101 236
1990	1 426 915	391 728	29 856	65 533	132 424	292 802	173 389	105 250
1991	1 426 169	397 893	31 943	65 440	130 131	298 545	159 144	105 804
1992	1 462 861	406 964	35 198	70 753	133 201	305 420	150 227	113 593
1993	1 496 990	422 220	28 383	73 955	133 263	314 907	144 834	122 777
1994	1 558 443	430 963	30 021	78 027	143 649	333 905	143 328	135 145
1995	1 667 634	446 961	32 984	79 874	173 716	361 391	151 439	145 739
1996	1 711 301	461 297	34 482	80 243	160 661	367 674	174 284	150 467
1997	1 770 720	470 447	38 693	83 871	161 992	389 189	177 314	156 599
1998	1 776 261	490 365	41 625	80 624	165 429	391 700	145 673	158 156
1999	1 852 059	500 901	50 551	78 357	164 558	413 277	171 149	164 654
1996								
January	128 493	35 484	2 526	5 425	13 283	28 548	11 842	11 041
February	136 726	36 914	2 719	6 341	13 892	29 432	12 372	12 324
March	142 193	38 205	2 954	7 007	13 748	31 234	13 029	12 978
April	141 601	37 217	2 728	6 269	13 279	31 354	15 081	12 949
May	143 597	38 555	2 850	6 719	13 424	31 411	15 286	13 254
June	147 103	38 619	2 869	7 754	13 897	32 026	14 870	13 579
July	137 850	37 150	2 937	6 002	13 065	29 479	14 560	11 769
August	147 255	39 425	3 119	7 095	13 471	30 737	15 049	12 982
September	150 462	40 607	2 814	7 520	13 553	31 813	15 359	13 126
October	150 004	40 862	3 012	6 982	13 375	31 193	15 995	13 053
November	146 500	40 110	2 957	6 840	12 993	30 182	15 627	12 244
December	139 517	38 149	2 997	6 289	12 681	30 265	15 214	11 168
1997								
January	135 900	36 107	3 048	5 913	12 638	30 628	14 436	11 977
February	143 596	37 802	2 847	6 841	13 249	31 730	14 295	13 049
March	146 967	39 473	3 282	7 409	13 087	33 324	13 742	13 368
April	145 982	38 097	2 912	6 723	13 193	33 822	14 477	13 745
May	146 989	39 547	3 345	7 010	13 077	33 058	15 297	13 281
June	151 806	39 884	3 218	7 624	13 832	34 126	15 172	13 704
July	142 415	37 782	3 179	6 357	13 108	30 988	14 871	12 138
August	151 677	40 045	3 323	7 346	13 635	31 909	16 116	13 121
September	156 247	40 822	3 335	7 828	14 229	33 821	15 437	13 713
October	154 392	40 655	3 430	7 312	14 311	32 330	15 454	13 814
November	149 513	40 600	3 627	7 138	13 706	31 173	14 419	12 615
December	145 236	39 633	3 147	6 370	13 927	32 280	13 598	12 074
1998								
January	138 768	38 163	2 923	6 283	13 576	31 326	11 944	12 171
February	145 544	39 466	3 480	6 791	13 906	32 013	11 807	13 334
March	151 085	41 268	3 492	7 381	14 092	34 428	11 809	13 753
April	147 592	39 670	3 215	6 486	13 717	33 541	12 725	13 636
May	147 534	40 236	3 431	6 773	13 801	32 920	13 175	13 478
June	154 082	41 619	3 677	7 255	14 452	34 935	12 965	13 817
July	143 139	39 068	3 357	6 292	13 580	30 935	12 428	12 150
August	151 319	41 924	3 611	7 040	14 037	31 647	12 364	13 451
September	155 288	43 044	3 522	7 129	13 981	34 084	12 436	13 875
October	151 400	42 783	3 659	6 836	13 735	31 536	12 267	13 796
November	146 495	42 172	3 346	6 533	13 265	31 044	11 080	12 688
December	144 015	40 952	3 912	5 825	13 287	33 291	10 673	12 007
1999								
January	137 134	38 810	3 820	5 769	12 931	30 801	9 819	12 207
February	146 081	40 346	4 069	6 268	13 749	32 585	10 137	13 907
March	153 728	42 543	4 491	6 734	13 495	35 471	11 434	14 404
April	149 086	39 627	3 840	6 311	13 138	34 533	13 221	13 910
May	150 852	41 560	4 072	6 610	13 258	33 721	13 758	13 865
June	160 633	43 209	4 501	7 019	14 038	36 988	14 467	14 495
July	149 033	39 577	4 157	6 045	13 208	33 033	15 083	12 292
August	160 184	42 498	4 319	6 912	14 220	34 532	16 227	14 131
September	164 889	44 064	4 132	7 130	14 250	36 521	16 642	14 291
October	162 830	43 792	4 522	7 003	14 081	35 055	16 531	14 358
November	160 902	43 223	4 612	6 590	14 095	34 579	16 755	13 816
December	156 707	41 652	4 016	5 966	14 095	35 458	17 075	12 978

1. Includes categories not shown separately.

Table 15-4. Manufacturers' Shipments—*Continued*

(Millions of dollars, seasonally adjusted.)

Year and month	Total	Durable goods industries									
		Total [1]	Stone, clay, and glass products	Primary metals		Fabricated metal products	Industrial machinery and equipment	Electronic and electric equipment	Transportation equipment		Instruments and products
				Total	Blast furnaces, steel mills				Total	Motor vehicles and parts	
1970	633 663	337 876	16 454	51 995	25 189	44 210	56 893	41 408	74 539	42 538	18 367
1971	670 877	359 089	18 220	51 585	25 791	45 478	56 445	42 377	88 857	58 247	18 613
1972	756 321	407 844	20 875	58 490	28 712	51 487	66 156	47 502	94 706	63 923	21 043
1973	875 173	475 621	23 141	72 791	36 301	58 804	78 207	54 569	110 587	74 799	23 627
1974	1 017 477	530 074	25 503	95 686	49 718	67 212	93 041	58 684	108 244	68 631	27 454
1975	1 039 065	523 178	26 233	80 890	42 281	68 411	96 354	56 068	113 503	70 033	29 547
1976	1 185 563	607 475	29 618	93 082	46 764	77 560	105 847	65 151	141 028	95 380	33 238
1977	1 358 416	710 017	34 209	103 267	50 670	89 938	122 749	77 845	166 954	117 747	38 803
1978	1 522 858	812 776	40 238	118 175	59 228	101 245	143 919	88 679	188 773	131 999	44 655
1979	1 727 234	911 124	44 287	137 488	67 414	113 494	167 014	102 361	201 623	131 378	50 702
1980	1 852 689	929 027	44 473	134 057	61 612	116 071	180 564	112 864	186 516	104 560	59 825
1981	2 017 544	1 004 725	46 220	142 072	70 254	123 535	201 102	122 084	205 223	116 981	66 613
1982	1 960 214	950 541	43 515	104 874	46 928	119 236	186 773	125 728	201 347	112 270	74 918
1983	2 070 564	1 025 770	47 697	109 240	46 398	123 083	178 446	136 138	245 392	148 296	79 637
1984	2 288 184	1 175 276	53 101	120 315	51 978	138 107	211 075	162 362	284 593	181 993	89 398
1985	2 334 456	1 215 352	55 821	112 265	48 904	143 268	218 408	163 951	307 380	193 445	96 207
1986	2 335 881	1 238 859	59 254	107 865	45 718	143 063	213 574	164 811	322 688	198 811	100 798
1987	2 475 906	1 297 532	61 477	120 248	51 815	147 367	217 671	171 287	332 936	205 923	107 325
1988	2 695 432	1 421 501	63 145	149 837	64 294	159 505	244 365	187 301	354 849	222 353	116 009
1989	2 840 375	1 477 900	63 729	155 718	64 783	164 073	256 212	194 598	369 675	233 232	121 523
1990	2 912 228	1 485 313	63 728	148 787	62 826	165 064	259 367	195 898	370 328	217 295	127 978
1991	2 878 167	1 451 998	59 957	136 378	57 267	159 760	247 508	199 278	367 235	209 210	132 836
1992	3 004 727	1 541 866	62 521	138 287	58 449	166 532	258 662	216 764	399 270	238 384	134 941
1993	3 127 625	1 630 635	65 610	142 685	62 466	175 118	278 063	233 622	414 694	267 365	137 387
1994	3 348 019	1 789 576	71 230	161 188	69 887	190 544	313 047	266 405	450 809	314 637	138 400
1995	3 594 663	1 927 029	75 932	180 314	74 927	204 384	353 338	301 447	461 806	327 908	144 719
1996	3 715 460	2 004 159	82 442	178 297	74 552	214 007	381 795	320 616	465 173	329 155	151 017
1997	3 929 419	2 158 699	90 221	188 916	77 023	226 078	408 860	351 554	502 301	346 606	162 981
1998	4 052 248	2 275 987	96 193	180 973	72 767	239 667	442 316	375 970	536 896	359 560	168 952
1999	4 259 532	2 407 473	103 773	178 466	68 766	245 517	455 140	413 204	583 559	399 807	174 661
1996											
January	300 389	161 326	6 735	14 600	6 106	17 391	30 678	26 038	36 997	27 170	12 297
February	302 541	163 002	6 440	14 518	6 083	17 248	32 109	25 996	37 850	27 190	12 396
March	301 083	160 941	6 625	14 661	6 031	17 084	31 379	26 375	35 525	24 361	12 360
April	307 672	164 906	6 697	14 853	6 187	17 794	31 189	26 424	38 430	27 702	12 270
May	312 489	169 351	6 983	15 104	6 216	18 159	31 656	26 456	40 578	28 646	12 759
June	308 248	167 004	6 954	14 538	6 194	17 861	31 696	26 583	39 002	27 690	12 543
July	310 576	167 129	6 966	14 955	6 295	17 864	31 431	26 474	39 028	28 728	12 688
August	312 153	168 808	6 968	14 914	6 274	18 215	32 116	26 228	39 600	27 894	12 797
September	313 159	170 292	6 912	14 790	6 309	18 122	32 371	26 715	40 866	28 670	12 482
October	313 737	168 855	7 205	14 998	6 297	18 051	32 024	27 209	38 581	27 284	12 616
November	317 744	171 970	7 112	15 224	6 266	18 302	32 172	28 185	39 759	27 771	13 006
December	313 779	169 204	6 770	15 240	6 330	17 846	32 690	27 370	38 704	26 350	12 852
1997											
January	319 150	172 304	7 193	15 552	6 470	18 297	32 400	27 031	40 687	29 411	12 827
February	321 274	174 534	7 402	15 670	6 429	18 491	32 565	28 076	40 442	28 202	13 323
March	320 700	175 504	7 365	15 596	6 388	18 255	32 862	29 456	40 211	27 447	13 242
April	325 639	178 523	7 476	15 906	6 481	18 953	33 688	28 345	41 809	28 491	13 414
May	322 260	175 749	7 476	15 606	6 260	18 401	33 401	28 464	40 515	27 390	13 081
June	326 118	180 038	7 483	15 786	6 461	18 755	34 360	29 329	41 641	28 281	13 642
July	331 331	183 484	7 683	15 904	6 475	18 932	35 124	29 104	43 673	30 472	13 777
August	328 250	180 554	7 555	15 749	6 376	18 995	34 116	29 736	42 022	29 318	13 473
September	333 422	184 966	7 687	15 904	6 416	19 283	35 234	30 809	42 379	29 126	14 172
October	332 321	183 225	7 670	15 858	6 413	19 274	35 090	29 855	42 289	29 936	14 101
November	331 404	182 791	7 574	15 741	6 366	19 143	34 343	29 842	43 285	29 240	13 712
December	336 424	186 007	7 651	15 713	6 513	19 299	35 698	30 495	43 558	30 002	14 100
1998											
January	331 937	182 303	7 696	15 715	6 484	19 109	35 936	29 532	41 542	28 133	13 760
February	335 883	187 298	7 789	15 838	6 491	19 766	36 209	30 714	43 577	29 678	14 025
March	338 991	189 998	7 872	15 660	6 439	19 742	36 864	30 838	45 208	30 607	14 137
April	335 553	186 843	7 899	15 523	6 358	19 570	36 898	30 056	43 863	29 730	13 836
May	333 622	185 789	7 982	15 176	6 200	19 745	36 561	29 767	43 562	29 461	13 787
June	335 110	186 536	8 033	15 049	6 124	19 755	37 915	30 882	40 857	26 760	14 209
July	335 380	186 907	8 104	14 968	6 006	20 309	37 810	31 216	40 556	27 092	14 042
August	336 445	188 789	8 014	15 056	6 104	20 114	36 711	31 228	44 403	30 017	13 749
September	340 481	192 842	8 077	14 951	5 909	20 235	36 775	32 422	46 588	31 061	14 298
October	340 133	193 818	8 149	14 590	5 729	20 176	37 011	32 219	48 017	31 586	14 040
November	341 423	194 823	8 236	14 286	5 551	20 415	36 623	32 634	48 324	31 581	14 517
December	344 247	195 531	8 317	14 222	5 359	20 523	36 880	33 006	47 908	32 169	14 371
1999											
January	341 673	194 091	8 220	14 312	5 396	20 520	36 513	32 830	47 236	31 970	14 011
February	343 724	194 465	8 456	14 224	5 553	20 391	36 756	32 235	47 502	32 118	14 046
March	349 065	198 292	8 494	14 505	5 637	20 416	36 972	33 032	49 267	33 281	14 553
April	347 568	197 246	8 376	14 225	5 509	20 416	37 464	33 655	47 755	32 209	14 210
May	350 624	199 425	8 431	14 526	5 626	20 411	37 519	33 836	48 891	32 717	14 309
June	354 702	200 990	8 579	14 677	5 615	20 544	37 308	34 196	49 781	34 813	14 611
July	357 301	203 268	8 578	14 903	5 681	20 394	39 434	35 373	48 816	34 550	14 340
August	361 844	205 709	8 859	15 204	5 824	20 781	38 691	35 339	50 980	34 669	14 474
September	358 709	201 895	8 867	15 298	5 814	20 377	37 742	35 307	48 555	33 908	14 797
October	360 201	202 306	8 873	15 191	5 893	20 281	39 471	34 860	47 659	32 898	14 834
November	364 971	204 430	9 003	15 574	6 059	20 713	39 075	35 605	48 326	33 239	14 992
December	367 872	206 480	8 900	15 763	6 094	20 385	38 698	36 281	50 125	34 189	15 169

1. Includes categories not shown separately.

Table 15-4. Manufacturers' Shipments—*Continued*

(Millions of dollars, seasonally adjusted.)

Year and month	Nondurable goods industries							
	Total [1]	Food and products	Tobacco products	Textile mill products	Paper and products	Chemicals and products	Petroleum and coal products	Rubber and plastics products
1970	295 787	98 535	5 350	22 614	24 573	49 195	24 200	16 754
1971	311 788	103 637	5 528	24 034	25 182	51 681	26 198	18 409
1972	348 477	115 054	5 919	28 065	28 004	58 130	27 918	21 662
1973	399 552	135 585	6 341	31 073	32 495	66 003	33 903	25 191
1974	487 403	161 884	7 139	32 790	41 514	85 387	57 229	28 828
1975	515 887	172 054	8 058	31 065	41 497	91 710	67 496	28 128
1976	578 088	180 830	8 786	36 387	47 939	106 467	80 022	32 880
1977	648 399	192 913	9 051	40 550	51 881	120 905	94 702	40 944
1978	710 082	215 989	9 951	42 281	56 777	132 262	100 967	44 823
1979	816 110	235 976	10 602	45 137	64 957	151 887	144 156	48 694
1980	923 662	256 191	12 194	47 256	72 553	168 220	192 969	49 157
1981	1 012 819	272 140	13 130	50 260	79 970	186 909	217 681	55 178
1982	1 009 673	280 529	16 061	47 516	79 698	176 254	203 404	57 307
1983	1 044 794	289 314	16 268	53 733	84 817	189 552	187 788	62 870
1984	1 112 908	304 584	17 473	56 336	95 525	205 963	184 488	72 938
1985	1 119 104	308 606	18 559	54 605	94 679	204 790	176 574	75 590
1986	1 097 022	318 203	19 146	57 188	99 865	205 711	122 605	78 379
1987	1 178 374	329 725	20 757	62 787	108 989	229 546	130 414	86 634
1988	1 273 931	354 084	23 809	64 627	122 882	261 238	131 682	95 485
1989	1 362 475	380 160	25 875	67 265	131 896	283 196	146 487	101 236
1990	1 426 915	391 728	29 856	65 533	132 424	292 802	173 389	105 250
1991	1 426 169	397 893	31 943	65 440	130 131	298 545	159 144	105 804
1992	1 462 861	406 964	35 198	70 753	133 201	305 420	150 227	113 593
1993	1 496 990	422 220	28 383	73 955	133 263	314 907	144 834	122 777
1994	1 558 443	430 963	30 021	78 027	143 649	333 905	143 328	135 145
1995	1 667 634	446 961	32 984	79 874	173 716	361 391	151 439	145 739
1996	1 711 301	461 297	34 482	80 243	160 661	367 674	174 284	150 467
1997	1 770 720	470 447	38 693	83 871	161 992	389 189	177 314	156 599
1998	1 776 261	490 365	41 625	80 624	165 429	391 700	145 673	158 156
1999	1 852 059	500 901	50 551	78 357	164 558	413 277	171 149	164 654
1996								
January	139 063	38 360	2 799	6 330	13 829	29 969	13 151	11 875
February	139 539	37 868	2 788	6 538	13 841	29 802	13 366	12 276
March	140 142	37 723	2 807	6 604	13 582	29 633	14 097	12 394
April	142 766	38 237	2 887	6 538	13 589	30 190	15 103	12 576
May	143 138	38 332	2 741	6 680	13 489	30 861	14 697	12 761
June	141 244	37 639	2 846	6 965	13 310	30 256	14 136	12 659
July	143 447	38 669	2 971	6 737	13 436	31 038	14 264	12 743
August	143 345	38 721	2 982	6 695	13 227	30 972	14 319	12 693
September	142 867	38 601	2 854	6 753	13 090	30 747	14 729	12 586
October	144 882	39 372	2 966	6 683	13 096	31 636	15 247	12 585
November	145 774	39 312	2 823	6 764	13 101	31 451	15 388	12 741
December	144 575	38 524	3 027	6 909	13 089	31 191	15 484	12 518
1997								
January	146 846	38 858	3 397	6 883	13 148	32 025	15 879	12 904
February	146 740	38 854	2 870	7 054	13 216	32 167	15 504	12 946
March	145 196	39 006	3 146	6 971	12 968	31 695	14 946	12 823
April	147 116	39 084	3 116	7 020	13 455	32 547	14 532	13 321
May	146 511	39 276	3 167	6 969	13 168	32 460	14 701	12 811
June	146 080	38 960	3 215	6 842	13 248	32 365	14 518	12 791
July	147 847	39 164	3 225	7 117	13 464	32 513	14 614	13 078
August	147 696	39 310	3 194	6 959	13 408	32 220	15 311	12 880
September	148 456	38 970	3 358	7 031	13 733	32 662	14 791	13 155
October	149 096	39 315	3 346	6 998	13 987	32 695	14 638	13 301
November	148 613	39 763	3 399	7 050	13 847	32 469	14 139	13 118
December	150 417	40 116	3 252	7 012	14 364	33 092	13 836	13 536
1998								
January	149 634	40 821	3 260	7 254	14 105	32 697	13 198	13 119
February	148 585	40 556	3 474	6 962	13 880	32 514	12 883	13 185
March	148 993	40 669	3 336	6 891	13 957	32 717	12 913	13 190
April	148 710	40 604	3 393	6 806	13 937	32 380	12 782	13 203
May	147 833	40 143	3 421	6 745	13 938	32 501	12 599	13 045
June	148 574	40 645	3 561	6 640	13 879	32 981	12 416	13 001
July	148 473	40 562	3 444	6 940	13 929	32 468	12 153	13 104
August	147 656	41 117	3 479	6 694	13 761	32 204	11 759	13 196
September	147 639	41 272	3 523	6 491	13 518	32 616	11 885	13 282
October	146 315	41 351	3 466	6 551	13 421	31 960	11 500	13 249
November	146 600	41 387	3 398	6 498	13 489	32 533	11 043	13 209
December	148 716	41 585	3 817	6 472	13 669	33 581	11 060	13 400
1999								
January	147 582	41 319	4 017	6 581	13 443	32 305	11 040	13 207
February	149 259	41 479	4 088	6 426	13 662	33 196	11 262	13 718
March	150 773	41 659	4 149	6 363	13 404	33 577	12 380	13 708
April	150 322	40 733	4 071	6 561	13 387	33 575	13 042	13 442
May	151 199	41 494	4 063	6 533	13 394	33 580	13 045	13 484
June	153 712	42 055	4 230	6 447	13 460	34 483	13 703	13 609
July	154 033	41 309	4 265	6 540	13 575	34 569	14 563	13 376
August	156 135	41 767	4 257	6 514	13 949	35 028	15 218	13 839
September	156 814	42 142	4 275	6 502	13 777	35 040	15 663	13 701
October	157 895	42 292	4 500	6 638	13 781	35 552	15 627	13 811
November	160 541	42 363	4 475	6 545	14 268	35 937	16 634	14 339
December	161 392	42 176	4 324	6 615	14 376	35 636	17 414	14 400

1. Includes categories not shown separately.

Table 15-4. Manufacturers' Shipments—Continued

(Millions of dollars, seasonally adjusted.)

Year and month	By market category [1]						Supplementary series			
	Home goods and apparel	Consumer staples	Machinery and equipment	Automotive equipment	Construction materials and supplies	Other materials, supplies, and intermediate products	Household durables	Capital goods industries		
								Total	Nondefense	Defense
1970	59 987	136 616	96 531	23 038	41 945	210 904	24 259	102 285	78 907	23 378
1971	63 664	143 858	103 931	31 257	45 559	219 088	25 682	98 643	79 148	19 495
1972	72 839	158 995	117 214	34 568	54 119	249 670	29 968	107 198	87 762	19 436
1973	79 588	183 532	137 154	39 808	62 228	295 929	33 285	124 912	103 997	20 915
1974	81 310	225 831	152 937	36 687	69 146	360 524	34 445	143 828	122 674	21 154
1975	81 417	246 958	158 401	37 803	66 984	349 019	34 003	149 687	126 363	23 324
1976	91 278	269 428	176 828	50 088	77 948	408 132	39 178	162 172	135 540	26 632
1977	104 862	294 653	206 927	60 310	91 883	471 894	45 450	185 541	155 956	29 585
1978	113 615	326 611	239 871	67 007	106 017	530 773	50 495	217 165	186 427	30 738
1979	119 089	378 177	278 174	67 095	118 024	605 503	54 211	254 754	222 069	32 685
1980	125 155	437 351	294 260	54 491	118 429	635 014	56 392	287 132	246 797	40 335
1981	132 756	477 864	319 877	60 680	122 875	692 053	59 258	317 191	269 411	47 780
1982	132 734	486 398	304 358	59 108	115 697	640 173	56 080	311 837	251 851	59 986
1983	142 154	491 032	309 492	77 246	127 742	685 041	60 096	315 482	241 867	73 615
1984	152 300	510 760	354 074	93 242	141 355	774 504	65 765	360 211	278 124	82 087
1985	153 426	517 924	372 271	97 330	146 889	765 771	67 107	388 164	293 102	95 062
1986	159 323	503 246	373 070	101 336	153 957	759 499	70 257	395 325	289 599	105 726
1987	162 421	531 263	383 867	104 551	165 109	824 036	69 418	404 229	294 961	109 268
1988	168 393	568 275	426 981	112 474	175 607	926 722	73 535	437 623	333 233	104 390
1989	173 634	615 522	453 994	118 364	180 222	971 154	78 018	449 943	350 357	99 586
1990	174 762	658 106	471 148	109 913	180 459	973 637	78 288	472 738	370 416	102 322
1991	175 076	667 412	470 659	106 157	171 707	953 725	77 951	468 536	370 718	97 818
1992	185 626	677 695	500 089	120 860	184 344	1 000 318	82 226	481 005	388 969	92 036
1993	195 354	691 146	523 514	134 125	199 062	1 048 126	88 415	484 512	399 983	84 529
1994	205 719	705 797	568 643	155 522	217 523	1 154 637	95 026	505 845	428 424	77 421
1995	210 586	741 899	613 109	160 413	228 276	1 284 161	98 626	548 724	475 113	73 611
1996	210 165	780 048	651 871	162 272	237 900	1 306 404	98 395	582 683	510 748	71 935
1997	220 872	809 637	711 111	169 499	252 517	1 382 832	105 872	638 093	562 795	75 298
1998	227 683	831 179	774 197	173 972	260 109	1 392 982	112 671	702 593	623 052	79 541
1999	239 985	885 889	817 878	195 791	276 880	1 440 156	125 349	740 450	661 082	79 368
1996										
January	16 684	63 533	51 018	13 248	19 095	106 949	8 040	45 495	39 410	6 085
February	17 063	63 094	53 489	13 412	18 643	106 950	7 906	47 868	42 010	5 858
March	17 529	63 747	52 414	12 316	18 956	106 109	8 278	47 768	41 684	6 084
April	17 511	65 079	53 255	13 649	19 417	108 207	8 241	47 271	41 416	5 855
May	17 707	64 923	55 070	14 124	19 946	110 122	8 335	48 843	42 821	6 022
June	17 528	63 742	54 440	13 594	19 944	108 560	8 226	48 752	42 665	6 087
July	17 500	65 271	53 750	13 974	20 278	109 399	8 183	47 263	41 568	5 695
August	17 576	65 364	54 972	13 651	20 420	109 598	8 219	49 182	43 156	6 026
September	17 437	65 320	56 228	14 183	20 230	109 286	8 120	49 906	43 849	6 057
October	17 702	66 963	54 971	13 493	20 498	110 078	8 273	48 752	43 079	5 673
November	18 142	66 846	56 259	13 642	20 489	111 180	8 321	50 628	44 312	6 316
December	17 786	66 166	56 005	12 986	19 984	109 966	8 253	50 955	44 778	6 177
1997										
January	17 812	67 660	55 266	14 316	20 563	112 439	8 300	49 088	43 100	5 988
February	18 215	66 548	56 480	13 767	20 795	113 702	8 530	50 681	44 305	6 376
March	17 830	66 239	57 917	13 423	20 542	113 682	8 621	51 774	45 713	6 061
April	18 520	66 654	58 641	13 834	21 248	115 335	8 620	52 905	46 555	6 350
May	18 102	67 355	58 157	13 283	20 806	113 141	8 588	52 594	46 351	6 243
June	18 266	67 207	59 493	13 856	20 973	114 321	8 947	53 901	47 363	6 538
July	18 515	67 636	61 466	14 908	21 393	115 485	8 828	54 588	48 339	6 249
August	18 221	68 019	59 632	14 272	21 215	115 156	8 633	53 405	47 274	6 131
September	18 793	67 732	61 447	14 237	21 553	117 726	9 156	55 056	49 036	6 020
October	18 569	68 051	60 241	14 524	21 283	117 339	8 984	54 088	47 737	6 351
November	18 795	68 088	59 915	14 272	20 994	116 704	9 147	54 690	47 784	6 906
December	19 234	68 448	62 456	14 807	21 152	117 802	9 518	55 323	49 238	6 085
1998										
January	19 127	68 815	61 409	13 669	21 050	115 681	9 246	55 821	49 403	6 418
February	19 122	68 668	62 924	14 326	21 401	117 343	9 427	56 941	50 408	6 533
March	18 996	69 077	64 548	14 834	21 608	117 342	9 378	58 223	51 593	6 630
April	19 157	69 101	63 225	14 343	21 403	115 859	9 302	57 305	50 560	6 745
May	18 899	68 662	63 150	14 259	21 428	114 748	9 258	57 144	50 586	6 558
June	18 978	69 586	64 527	13 216	21 852	114 775	9 482	58 709	52 405	6 304
July	19 329	69 212	63 235	13 344	22 063	115 782	9 629	57 811	51 316	6 495
August	18 928	69 369	63 815	14 777	21 656	115 493	9 247	57 910	51 222	6 688
September	18 656	69 893	66 513	15 157	21 705	116 267	9 231	60 025	53 419	6 606
October	18 496	68 901	66 717	15 238	21 719	116 349	9 244	60 938	53 870	7 068
November	18 692	69 370	66 847	15 221	21 914	116 623	9 416	61 154	54 200	6 954
December	19 303	70 525	67 287	15 588	22 310	116 720	9 811	60 612	54 070	6 542
1999										
January	19 772	69 658	65 946	15 564	22 012	115 910	10 053	59 694	52 954	6 740
February	19 741	70 814	65 797	15 796	22 437	116 189	10 279	59 501	52 772	6 729
March	19 795	72 057	68 018	16 217	22 685	117 152	10 169	60 890	54 217	6 673
April	20 303	72 015	67 513	15 614	22 750	116 771	10 499	61 257	54 731	6 526
May	19 986	72 565	68 250	15 936	22 860	117 873	10 418	62 212	55 543	6 669
June	19 645	74 050	68 232	16 967	23 303	119 435	10 262	60 750	54 472	6 278
July	20 035	74 010	69 036	16 809	23 376	120 549	10 585	62 679	56 095	6 584
August	20 051	75 085	70 348	16 909	23 594	122 294	10 642	63 755	57 287	6 468
September	19 711	75 589	67 932	16 584	23 372	121 904	10 277	61 346	54 891	6 455
October	20 070	76 119	68 807	16 092	23 253	122 043	10 521	62 864	56 295	6 569
November	20 223	77 015	68 160	16 403	23 637	124 544	10 776	62 394	55 238	7 156
December	20 653	76 912	69 839	16 900	23 601	125 492	10 868	63 108	56 587	6 521

1. Defense products and business supplies not shown.

Table 15-5. Manufacturers' Inventories [1]

(Book value, end of period; millions of dollars.)

Year and month	Not seasonally adjusted			Seasonally adjusted										
					Durable goods industries									
	Total [1]	Durable goods industries	Nondura-ble goods	Total	Total [2]	Stone, clay, and glass products	Primary metals		Fabricated metal products	Industrial machinery and equipment	Electronic and electric equipment	Transportation equipment		Instru-ments and products
							Total	Blast furnaces, steel mills				Total	Motor vehicles and parts	
1970	101 246	66 187	35 059	101 599	66 651	2 239	8 995	4 990	7 907	14 500	8 410	14 648	4 178	4 196
1971	102 267	65 664	36 603	102 567	66 136	2 302	9 084	4 926	8 098	14 344	8 058	13 799	4 173	4 201
1972	107 900	69 583	38 317	108 121	70 067	2 430	9 617	5 387	8 408	15 142	8 528	14 775	4 670	4 435
1973	124 327	80 608	43 719	124 499	81 192	2 712	10 034	5 302	9 864	18 411	10 532	16 458	5 708	5 233
1974	157 595	100 763	56 832	157 625	101 493	3 403	13 447	6 820	13 387	24 189	12 231	19 197	6 688	6 486
1975	159 844	101 958	57 886	159 708	102 590	3 594	15 742	8 597	13 091	24 156	11 110	19 620	6 101	6 547
1976	174 867	111 366	63 501	174 636	111 988	3 841	17 699	10 035	14 304	25 245	12 594	20 886	7 814	7 214
1977	188 435	120 131	68 304	188 378	120 877	4 095	18 261	10 004	15 527	27 282	13 922	22 423	9 078	8 185
1978	209 113	136 015	73 098	211 691	138 181	4 710	19 420	10 719	17 296	32 086	16 163	26 170	10 357	9 682
1979	239 101	158 146	80 955	242 157	160 734	5 183	22 446	12 012	19 145	37 464	19 566	31 638	10 978	11 415
1980	261 700	171 864	89 836	265 215	174 788	5 674	23 055	12 153	19 532	40 958	21 838	35 900	9 864	13 376
1981	279 453	183 268	96 185	283 413	186 443	6 106	25 794	13 359	20 209	43 652	23 608	37 527	9 047	14 760
1982	307 212	196 663	110 549	311 852	200 444	6 506	24 174	12 556	21 440	47 908	25 100	43 005	8 534	17 038
1983	307 675	196 002	111 673	312 379	199 854	6 628	22 308	11 065	21 752	44 586	26 922	43 791	10 433	17 769
1984	334 236	217 049	117 187	339 516	221 330	7 042	22 444	11 087	23 330	48 760	31 636	50 770	11 680	20 206
1985	329 555	213 978	115 577	334 749	218 193	7 040	19 974	9 709	22 880	46 526	30 549	52 634	11 809	21 569
1986	317 567	207 865	109 702	322 654	211 997	7 093	18 436	8 567	22 094	42 409	28 632	53 363	11 445	22 461
1987	332 619	216 343	116 276	338 109	220 799	7 154	19 076	8 620	22 920	43 141	29 859	56 461	11 937	23 692
1988	363 300	237 510	125 790	369 374	242 468	7 496	22 422	10 495	24 950	47 707	31 645	63 202	12 310	25 346
1989	384 539	252 058	132 481	391 212	257 513	7 792	22 838	10 942	25 427	50 342	33 623	70 968	12 503	26 541
1990	397 850	257 363	140 487	405 073	263 209	8 205	22 560	11 045	25 044	49 673	32 913	77 640	13 504	26 552
1991	383 509	244 121	139 388	390 950	250 019	7 928	20 703	10 236	23 922	47 880	30 981	73 019	13 163	25 778
1992	374 906	232 318	142 588	382 510	238 105	8 006	19 981	9 809	23 815	47 075	30 722	63 290	13 081	24 685
1993	375 982	233 306	142 676	384 039	239 334	7 607	20 132	9 836	23 838	48 602	31 863	60 950	14 099	23 211
1994	395 974	247 001	148 973	404 877	253 664	7 874	22 588	10 697	25 597	52 905	35 847	61 354	15 692	22 965
1995	421 285	261 138	160 147	430 985	268 353	8 567	24 021	11 560	27 003	59 158	39 413	59 735	16 293	24 990
1996	427 130	266 547	167 365	436 729	273 815	8 898	24 289	11 912	27 894	57 944	39 335	64 596	16 369	25 266
1997	446 131	278 766	167 365	456 133	286 372	9 050	24 680	11 727	29 579	60 304	40 488	69 323	16 145	25 903
1998	456 330	287 415	168 915	466 798	295 344	9 331	24 679	12 057	30 855	60 532	39 786	75 701	17 419	26 515
1999	460 048	287 124	172 924	470 377	295 034	9 888	24 255	11 507	31 401	60 406	43 611	69 069	17 982	27 180
1996														
January	431 902	269 366	162 536	433 597	270 707	8 572	24 084	11 671	27 092	60 045	39 776	60 633	16 537	25 083
February	436 768	273 116	163 652	434 023	271 111	8 609	24 022	11 620	27 386	60 046	39 377	61 056	16 366	25 203
March	433 182	270 291	162 891	434 157	271 251	8 638	24 192	11 827	27 236	59 851	39 099	61 740	16 740	25 331
April	435 707	272 416	163 291	433 815	271 153	8 604	24 043	11 637	27 188	60 061	39 322	61 574	16 489	25 422
May	436 240	274 049	162 191	432 518	270 995	8 537	23 975	11 498	27 132	59 749	39 135	61 778	16 327	25 449
June	430 010	269 373	160 637	432 102	270 682	8 570	24 071	11 529	26 958	58 917	39 331	62 407	16 175	25 212
July	434 354	273 306	161 048	432 854	271 759	8 545	23 898	11 524	27 378	59 172	39 098	63 016	16 483	25 538
August	437 214	275 648	161 566	433 794	272 684	8 627	23 807	11 579	27 592	59 309	39 206	63 093	16 311	25 632
September	434 505	272 469	162 036	434 864	273 092	8 654	24 076	11 758	27 528	58 849	39 367	63 384	16 334	25 624
October	437 488	274 314	163 174	436 428	274 146	8 740	23 969	11 760	27 643	58 708	39 428	64 217	16 513	25 845
November	437 936	275 308	162 628	437 606	274 896	8 778	24 085	11 867	27 746	58 884	39 636	64 721	16 219	25 373
December	427 130	266 547	167 365	436 729	273 815	8 898	24 289	11 912	27 894	57 944	39 335	64 596	16 369	25 266
1997														
January	437 097	274 261	162 836	438 641	275 517	8 987	24 089	11 755	28 124	58 425	39 024	65 808	16 317	25 483
February	443 876	279 216	164 660	440 915	277 080	9 019	24 228	11 773	28 340	58 512	39 064	66 796	16 547	25 493
March	440 894	276 613	164 281	441 676	277 399	9 003	24 472	11 905	28 595	58 503	38 942	66 827	16 477	25 386
April	446 775	281 269	165 506	444 714	279 880	8 989	24 277	11 824	28 747	59 268	39 422	67 771	16 657	25 566
May	450 616	284 200	166 416	446 888	281 143	9 049	24 278	11 876	28 771	59 462	39 610	68 298	16 943	25 578
June	445 734	280 596	165 138	447 947	282 013	9 093	24 384	11 801	29 012	59 426	39 532	68 637	16 553	25 811
July	451 052	285 204	165 848	449 657	283 723	9 006	24 423	11 715	29 089	59 808	40 120	69 174	16 610	25 959
August	455 123	287 937	167 186	451 737	284 982	9 009	24 544	11 753	29 132	59 842	40 088	69 677	16 246	26 026
September	451 811	283 984	167 827	452 224	284 660	9 065	24 398	11 725	29 360	59 658	39 950	69 534	16 671	25 929
October	456 570	286 770	169 800	455 553	286 654	8 933	24 439	11 718	29 480	60 075	40 052	70 761	16 341	25 909
November	458 113	288 424	169 689	457 766	287 949	9 042	24 474	11 732	29 590	60 093	40 278	71 183	16 163	26 180
December	446 131	278 766	167 365	456 133	286 372	9 050	24 680	11 727	29 579	60 304	40 488	69 323	16 145	25 903
1998														
January	456 534	286 702	169 832	458 197	288 086	9 097	24 720	11 770	29 775	60 135	40 801	70 371	16 259	26 047
February	464 331	292 368	171 963	461 178	290 153	9 101	24 388	11 767	30 069	61 122	41 250	70 844	16 281	26 113
March	461 334	290 205	171 129	461 948	290 887	9 131	24 241	11 806	30 405	61 011	41 364	70 958	16 721	26 363
April	467 122	295 053	172 069	464 668	293 393	9 067	24 340	11 852	30 580	61 247	41 378	72 542	16 450	26 530
May	469 773	297 637	172 136	465 729	294 375	9 092	24 465	11 986	30 460	61 081	41 236	73 398	16 686	26 797
June	464 495	293 750	170 745	466 701	295 143	9 110	24 612	12 168	30 749	60 900	40 818	74 597	17 046	26 676
July	469 220	297 154	172 066	467 636	295 669	9 112	24 763	12 335	30 939	60 903	40 345	75 032	16 790	26 659
August	471 596	299 838	171 758	468 445	296 913	9 164	24 859	12 437	30 944	60 958	40 526	75 812	16 511	26 651
September	467 407	295 733	171 674	468 552	296 757	9 237	24 898	12 398	31 050	60 938	40 172	75 702	16 701	26 577
October	471 645	298 510	173 135	471 031	298 561	9 235	24 825	12 312	31 093	60 811	40 589	76 999	16 755	26 667
November	471 705	298 755	172 950	471 000	297 981	9 320	24 817	12 175	31 134	60 974	40 315	76 452	17 240	26 679
December	456 330	287 415	168 915	466 798	295 344	9 331	24 679	12 057	30 855	60 532	39 786	75 701	17 419	26 515
1999														
January	462 588	291 608	170 980	464 867	293 563	9 381	24 438	11 924	30 920	60 658	39 581	73 852	17 101	26 443
February	466 680	295 766	170 914	464 198	294 030	9 263	24 216	11 776	30 849	60 673	40 133	73 972	16 978	26 757
March	462 645	292 680	169 965	463 578	293 391	9 258	23 734	11 603	30 819	60 817	40 356	73 415	17 424	26 706
April	465 450	294 019	171 431	463 194	292 415	9 237	23 651	11 574	30 887	60 643	40 542	72 458	17 082	26 810
May	467 701	295 610	172 091	463 742	292 403	9 388	23 758	11 599	31 006	60 331	40 825	71 788	17 233	26 644
June	460 432	290 135	170 297	462 690	291 645	9 395	23 674	11 468	30 740	59 867	40 997	71 596	17 597	26 587
July	466 518	294 993	171 525	465 043	293 505	9 473	23 693	11 396	31 005	59 791	41 221	72 403	17 677	26 930
August	467 794	295 746	172 048	464 351	292 461	9 726	23 660	11 317	31 028	59 990	41 204	70 868	17 569	27 060
September	465 082	292 311	172 771	465 669	292 901	9 724	23 652	11 250	31 182	60 139	41 518	70 749	17 420	27 098
October	468 752	293 439	175 313	467 522	293 448	9 854	23 884	11 325	31 359	59 936	42 091	70 411	17 638	27 058
November	470 921	295 759	175 162	469 836	294 970	9 824	24 091	11 414	31 378	60 495	42 665	70 417	17 916	27 062
December	460 048	287 124	172 924	470 377	295 034	9 888	24 255	11 507	31 401	60 406	43 611	69 069	17 982	27 180

1. Data prior to 1982 are not comparable to subsequent periods due to change in inventory valuation methods; see Notes.
2. Includes categories not shown separately.

Table 15-5. Manufacturers' Inventories [1]—Continued

(Book value, end of period; millions of dollars, seasonally adjusted.)

Year and month	Durable goods industries by stage of fabrication			Nondurable goods industries										
	Materials and supplies	Work in process	Finished goods	Total [2]	Food and products	Tobacco products	Textile mill products	Paper and products	Chemicals and products	Petroleum and coal products	Rubber and plastics products	By stage of fabrication		
												Materials and supplies	Work in process	Finished goods
1970	19 149	29 745	17 757	34 948	8 738	2 052	3 676	2 735	6 749	2 161	2 386	13 168	5 271	16 509
1971	19 679	28 550	17 907	36 431	9 258	2 099	3 866	2 828	6 923	2 260	2 453	13 686	5 678	17 067
1972	20 807	30 713	18 547	38 054	9 673	2 355	4 056	2 896	7 079	2 142	2 695	14 677	5 998	17 379
1973	25 944	35 490	19 758	43 307	11 627	2 426	4 592	3 317	7 553	2 476	3 103	18 147	6 729	18 431
1974	35 070	42 530	23 893	56 132	14 625	3 024	5 044	4 816	11 579	3 945	4 023	23 744	8 189	24 199
1975	33 903	43 227	25 460	57 118	14 467	3 290	4 794	4 849	12 073	4 426	4 085	23 565	8 834	24 719
1976	37 457	46 074	28 457	62 648	15 695	3 416	5 232	5 299	13 319	4 711	4 581	25 847	9 929	26 872
1977	40 186	50 226	30 465	67 501	16 329	3 511	5 649	5 667	14 633	5 439	5 116	27 387	10 961	29 153
1978	45 198	58 848	34 135	73 510	18 073	3 669	5 935	6 114	16 018	5 330	5 801	29 619	12 085	31 806
1979	52 670	69 325	38 739	81 423	19 879	3 517	6 148	6 926	17 690	7 458	6 399	32 814	13 910	34 699
1980	55 173	76 945	42 670	90 427	21 710	3 721	6 648	7 802	20 066	9 693	6 435	36 606	15 884	37 937
1981	57 998	80 998	47 447	96 970	21 483	4 436	6 896	8 593	22 438	10 420	6 968	38 165	16 194	42 611
1982	59 136	86 707	54 601	111 408	23 016	6 873	6 723	9 022	24 448	17 009	7 748	44 039	18 612	48 757
1983	60 325	86 899	52 630	112 525	23 609	6 746	7 514	9 192	24 698	14 843	8 070	44 816	18 691	49 018
1984	66 031	98 251	57 048	118 186	24 182	6 533	7 827	10 299	26 420	14 260	8 904	45 692	19 328	53 166
1985	63 904	98 162	56 127	116 556	24 015	5 943	7 439	10 140	26 119	13 975	9 213	44 106	19 442	53 008
1986	61 331	97 000	53 666	110 657	23 884	5 449	7 191	10 254	25 743	8 791	9 285	42 335	18 124	50 198
1987	63 562	102 393	54 844	117 310	24 860	5 331	7 939	11 163	26 585	9 973	10 065	45 319	19 270	52 721
1988	69 611	112 958	59 899	126 906	27 122	5 286	8 384	12 495	29 792	9 196	11 367	49 396	20 559	56 951
1989	72 435	122 251	62 827	133 699	28 459	5 570	8 721	13 404	31 725	10 743	11 533	50 674	21 653	61 372
1990	73 559	124 130	65 520	141 864	29 714	5 974	8 732	13 640	34 001	13 432	12 292	52 645	22 817	66 402
1991	70 834	114 960	64 225	140 931	30 099	6 342	8 484	13 796	34 529	11 671	12 121	53 011	22 815	65 105
1992	69 459	104 424	64 222	144 405	30 996	6 668	8 710	14 010	35 720	11 350	12 541	54 007	23 532	66 866
1993	72 590	102 468	64 276	144 705	31 201	6 322	9 264	13 972	35 771	10 265	12 821	55 072	23 371	66 262
1994	78 468	107 037	68 119	151 253	32 332	5 782	9 804	14 463	37 024	11 121	14 232	58 157	24 638	68 458
1995	85 577	107 209	75 567	162 632	34 527	5 775	10 308	17 352	39 913	11 304	15 220	62 324	26 007	74 301
1996	86 438	111 289	76 088	162 914	35 697	5 904	9 915	16 032	41 110	12 520	15 728	60 416	26 621	75 877
1997	89 844	117 236	79 292	169 761	37 026	5 797	10 184	16 240	44 249	12 218	16 455	61 233	29 498	79 030
1998	91 740	121 246	82 358	171 454	37 299	5 867	10 180	16 362	46 217	10 254	16 766	62 306	29 344	79 804
1999	95 780	113 607	85 647	175 343	39 033	5 101	10 163	16 068	47 603	12 247	17 589	62 302	30 737	82 304
1996														
January	86 514	108 133	76 060	162 890	34 524	5 776	10 226	17 307	39 985	11 490	15 198	62 320	26 276	74 294
February	86 936	108 179	75 996	162 912	34 707	5 725	10 202	17 316	39 945	11 594	15 217	62 127	26 181	74 604
March	86 872	108 720	75 659	162 906	34 842	5 716	10 102	17 241	40 202	11 959	15 294	61 513	26 325	75 068
April	87 038	108 966	75 149	162 662	35 154	5 612	10 042	16 943	40 377	12 044	15 206	61 436	26 388	74 838
May	86 835	109 053	75 107	161 523	35 028	5 604	9 992	16 633	40 228	11 991	15 138	60 948	26 269	74 306
June	85 718	109 702	75 262	161 420	35 084	5 616	9 916	16 485	40 319	11 942	15 240	60 480	26 477	74 463
July	86 818	109 636	75 305	161 095	35 198	5 502	9 899	16 429	40 157	12 077	15 286	60 403	26 393	74 299
August	86 751	109 850	76 083	161 110	35 175	5 608	9 948	16 457	40 293	12 015	15 335	60 306	26 616	74 188
September	86 946	109 862	76 284	161 772	35 496	5 713	9 908	16 369	40 569	12 252	15 493	60 305	26 562	74 905
October	86 475	111 060	76 611	162 282	35 573	5 783	9 907	16 257	40 670	12 289	15 580	60 712	26 654	74 916
November	86 736	111 659	76 501	162 710	35 756	5 871	9 941	16 144	40 654	12 344	15 619	60 658	26 669	75 383
December	86 438	111 289	76 088	162 914	35 697	5 904	9 915	16 032	41 110	12 520	15 728	60 416	26 621	75 877
1997														
January	86 626	111 940	76 951	163 124	35 422	5 829	9 956	15 926	41 105	13 039	15 855	60 350	26 924	75 850
February	86 655	112 681	77 744	163 835	35 737	5 796	9 911	15 812	41 328	12 888	15 917	60 822	27 137	75 876
March	87 530	113 067	76 802	164 277	35 866	5 770	9 967	15 918	41 389	12 923	16 031	60 721	27 344	76 212
April	87 649	113 947	78 284	164 834	36 038	5 835	10 060	15 797	41 778	12 656	16 085	60 660	27 586	76 588
May	88 017	114 443	78 683	165 745	36 097	5 836	10 048	15 829	41 883	12 919	16 269	60 843	28 042	76 860
June	88 514	114 629	78 870	165 934	36 248	5 790	10 105	15 682	42 151	12 623	16 281	60 675	27 846	77 413
July	89 322	115 402	78 999	165 934	36 136	5 814	10 121	15 728	42 365	12 338	16 305	60 545	27 994	77 395
August	89 036	116 214	79 732	166 755	36 179	5 779	10 178	15 794	42 471	12 657	16 395	60 577	28 363	77 815
September	89 841	115 538	79 281	167 564	36 331	5 680	10 197	16 016	43 101	12 621	16 348	61 115	28 562	77 887
October	90 147	116 574	79 933	168 899	36 742	5 798	10 213	15 982	43 673	12 559	16 386	61 388	29 053	78 458
November	90 004	117 998	79 947	169 817	36 940	5 890	10 197	16 054	44 324	12 489	16 466	60 770	29 464	79 583
December	89 844	117 236	79 292	169 761	37 026	5 797	10 184	16 240	44 249	12 218	16 455	61 233	29 498	79 030
1998														
January	90 779	117 542	79 765	170 111	37 359	5 962	10 172	16 351	44 797	11 449	16 562	61 732	29 348	79 031
February	91 428	118 362	80 363	171 025	37 647	5 864	10 217	16 317	45 310	11 478	16 587	62 130	29 622	79 273
March	91 922	118 438	80 527	171 061	37 512	5 882	10 219	16 320	45 368	11 405	16 509	62 364	29 390	79 307
April	92 470	120 494	80 429	171 275	37 488	5 772	10 224	16 363	45 611	11 400	16 484	62 086	29 746	79 443
May	92 778	121 101	80 496	171 354	37 503	5 779	10 254	16 388	45 821	11 169	16 571	61 926	29 800	79 628
June	93 198	121 420	80 525	171 558	37 427	5 716	10 253	16 498	46 061	10 936	16 697	62 374	29 828	79 356
July	93 445	121 367	80 857	171 967	37 424	5 665	10 285	16 584	46 382	10 906	16 650	62 673	29 678	79 616
August	93 042	122 862	81 009	171 532	37 115	5 563	10 245	16 643	46 535	10 759	16 699	62 627	29 275	79 630
September	93 291	122 063	81 403	171 795	37 112	5 783	10 307	16 527	46 313	10 770	16 607	62 838	29 164	79 793
October	93 345	123 446	81 770	172 470	37 459	6 020	10 286	16 511	46 356	10 832	16 678	62 691	29 402	80 377
November	93 115	122 509	82 357	173 019	37 264	5 939	10 194	16 483	46 875	10 965	16 857	62 747	29 795	80 477
December	91 740	121 246	82 358	171 454	37 299	5 867	10 180	16 362	46 217	10 254	16 766	62 306	29 344	79 804
1999														
January	91 974	119 364	82 225	171 304	37 658	5 682	10 078	16 180	46 425	10 239	16 780	62 041	29 441	79 822
February	92 436	119 250	82 344	170 168	37 773	5 513	10 025	16 078	46 295	10 040	16 710	61 503	29 457	79 208
March	92 298	118 609	82 484	170 187	37 699	5 363	10 080	16 073	45 918	10 545	16 659	61 090	29 786	79 311
April	91 722	117 829	82 864	170 779	37 978	5 343	10 086	15 994	46 362	10 688	16 794	61 027	30 347	79 405
May	91 677	117 183	83 543	171 339	38 182	5 308	10 051	16 023	46 929	10 706	16 902	61 166	30 610	79 563
June	92 031	116 056	83 558	171 045	38 037	5 208	10 107	16 070	46 581	10 814	16 902	60 921	30 553	79 571
July	92 918	116 737	83 850	171 538	38 019	5 160	10 026	16 009	46 848	11 144	17 050	60 997	30 336	80 205
August	92 531	115 260	84 670	171 890	38 018	5 149	10 030	15 928	46 619	11 588	17 261	60 895	29 972	81 023
September	92 990	115 393	84 518	172 768	38 139	5 177	10 112	16 133	46 546	11 887	17 492	61 160	30 194	81 414
October	92 872	115 659	84 917	174 074	38 769	5 164	10 071	16 125	46 903	12 052	17 714	61 192	30 559	82 323
November	94 477	115 411	85 082	174 866	38 797	5 075	10 101	16 137	47 421	12 174	17 769	61 738	30 814	82 314
December	95 780	113 607	85 647	175 343	39 033	5 101	10 163	16 068	47 603	12 247	17 589	62 302	30 737	82 304

1. Data prior to 1982 are not comparable to subsequent periods due to change in inventory valuation methods; see Notes.
2. Includes categories not shown separately.

Table 15-5. Manufacturers' Inventories [1]—*Continued*

(Book value, end of period; millions of dollars, seasonally adjusted.)

Year and month	By market category [2]						Supplementary series			
	Home goods and apparel	Consumer staples	Machinery and equipment	Automotive equipment	Construction materials and supplies	Other materials, supplies, and intermediate products	Household durables	Capital goods industries		
								Total	Nondefense	Defense
1970	10 162	14 176	24 032	2 355	6 867	34 271	4 711	27 859	22 810	5 049
1971	10 642	14 865	23 978	2 387	7 145	34 562	4 829	26 587	22 455	4 132
1972	11 498	15 596	25 239	2 703	7 603	36 142	5 311	27 667	23 337	4 330
1973	13 398	17 990	29 787	3 174	8 696	41 134	6 319	32 032	27 460	4 572
1974	14 470	23 571	37 403	3 695	11 076	54 267	7 393	39 605	34 583	5 022
1975	13 586	24 083	37 041	3 455	11 267	55 960	6 649	40 181	34 289	5 892
1976	15 324	25 758	37 766	4 163	12 540	63 175	7 453	41 046	34 449	6 597
1977	16 556	27 541	41 529	4 795	13 509	68 042	8 070	44 014	37 781	6 233
1978	18 715	30 063	49 266	5 353	15 100	75 494	9 161	52 237	45 660	6 577
1979	19 157	33 648	58 623	5 630	16 908	87 232	9 533	63 816	55 393	8 423
1980	20 106	37 689	66 157	5 145	17 513	94 117	9 967	74 531	63 692	10 839
1981	21 591	39 589	69 413	4 814	18 328	101 503	10 565	81 112	67 616	13 496
1982	21 738	48 183	76 522	4 865	18 580	106 625	10 926	92 601	73 748	18 853
1983	22 682	47 337	72 066	5 494	19 309	107 999	10 845	89 562	68 420	21 142
1984	24 999	48 555	79 058	6 192	20 552	115 702	12 270	102 615	75 466	27 149
1985	24 229	48 134	75 592	6 214	20 555	111 881	11 704	102 843	71 763	31 080
1986	23 647	44 983	70 923	5 930	20 348	108 766	11 325	99 104	67 631	31 473
1987	25 379	47 186	72 400	6 322	21 158	113 976	12 190	103 167	68 734	34 433
1988	26 723	50 289	81 687	6 448	22 925	125 688	12 948	114 207	77 448	36 759
1989	27 255	54 029	90 697	6 479	23 326	131 807	13 541	124 850	86 897	37 953
1990	27 153	58 161	95 055	6 934	23 714	134 811	13 446	128 997	90 894	38 103
1991	26 303	58 657	93 404	6 559	22 509	130 000	12 678	121 629	88 958	32 671
1992	26 819	60 706	89 589	6 708	22 779	128 441	12 515	110 261	84 351	25 910
1993	28 671	60 225	89 537	6 934	23 979	129 268	13 038	107 012	83 446	23 566
1994	30 826	62 085	95 906	7 508	25 455	139 030	14 452	110 770	90 184	20 586
1995	31 892	66 038	103 724	7 828	26 898	150 711	15 368	116 387	98 241	18 146
1996	29 468	68 270	108 129	8 035	27 222	152 604	14 813	118 829	101 852	16 977
1997	30 671	71 825	115 519	8 134	28 188	157 059	15 193	126 376	108 820	17 556
1998	32 246	72 825	117 856	8 669	28 706	158 957	16 390	130 002	110 184	19 818
1999	31 861	76 594	115 566	8 829	30 556	159 841	16 597	125 501	106 269	19 232
1996										
January	31 840	66 439	105 512	7 926	26 906	151 400	15 351	117 625	99 785	17 840
February	31 820	66 499	105 734	7 957	26 839	151 477	15 469	117 867	99 929	17 938
March	31 106	66 978	105 700	8 124	26 747	151 747	15 184	117 653	99 497	18 156
April	30 844	67 045	106 465	8 159	26 522	151 236	15 129	118 172	100 300	17 872
May	30 475	66 891	106 639	8 146	26 560	150 468	15 007	118 055	100 317	17 738
June	30 145	66 943	106 395	8 065	26 571	150 504	14 859	117 842	99 911	17 931
July	29 703	66 871	107 162	8 281	26 646	150 768	14 481	118 354	100 494	17 860
August	29 795	66 976	107 953	8 235	26 731	150 795	14 760	118 997	101 259	17 738
September	29 898	67 611	107 916	8 205	26 837	151 273	14 918	118 846	101 329	17 517
October	29 845	67 705	108 584	8 240	26 923	151 676	14 889	119 517	102 035	17 482
November	29 634	68 077	109 135	8 070	27 121	151 918	14 858	120 509	103 084	17 425
December	29 468	68 270	108 129	8 035	27 222	152 604	14 813	118 829	101 852	16 977
1997										
January	29 512	68 055	109 645	8 043	27 310	152 604	14 806	120 540	103 224	17 316
February	29 488	68 691	111 002	8 115	27 407	152 900	14 761	121 443	104 468	16 975
March	29 481	68 837	111 208	8 102	27 459	153 348	14 715	121 551	104 785	16 766
April	29 716	69 530	112 767	8 220	27 571	153 540	14 835	122 999	106 154	16 845
May	29 896	69 843	113 413	8 387	27 729	154 114	14 933	123 486	106 762	16 724
June	30 179	69 877	114 392	8 303	27 844	154 072	15 011	124 161	107 658	16 503
July	30 556	69 897	115 481	8 287	27 937	154 315	15 252	125 384	108 751	16 633
August	30 738	69 952	116 125	8 090	28 133	155 137	15 315	126 257	109 616	16 641
September	30 672	70 461	115 181	8 376	28 230	155 216	15 234	125 396	108 456	16 940
October	30 887	71 410	117 298	8 202	28 235	155 594	15 343	127 109	110 425	16 684
November	30 811	71 884	118 194	8 086	28 337	156 350	15 407	127 983	111 299	16 684
December	30 671	71 825	115 519	8 134	28 188	157 059	15 193	126 376	108 820	17 556
1998										
January	30 747	72 310	116 292	8 180	28 268	157 568	15 322	127 156	109 301	17 855
February	30 933	72 851	117 039	8 166	28 240	158 818	15 432	128 269	110 270	17 999
March	31 163	72 833	116 856	8 331	28 269	159 124	15 566	127 587	109 574	18 013
April	31 136	72 886	118 836	8 277	28 383	159 407	15 623	129 474	111 365	18 109
May	31 205	72 887	119 143	8 410	28 395	159 707	15 767	129 766	111 412	18 354
June	31 308	72 821	119 419	8 532	28 377	160 034	15 819	130 294	111 859	18 435
July	31 564	73 016	119 846	8 535	28 542	159 350	16 041	130 798	111 963	18 835
August	31 724	72 611	120 861	8 330	28 752	159 287	16 164	131 975	112 969	19 006
September	32 107	72 651	120 647	8 287	28 820	159 067	16 393	131 612	112 839	18 773
October	32 345	73 416	121 725	8 364	28 973	159 129	16 556	132 785	113 708	19 077
November	32 512	73 913	120 435	8 577	28 946	159 468	16 633	131 623	112 381	19 242
December	32 246	72 825	117 856	8 669	28 706	158 957	16 390	130 002	110 184	19 818
1999										
January	31 839	73 427	117 346	8 585	28 844	158 253	16 445	128 262	109 680	18 582
February	31 578	73 309	118 149	8 516	28 741	157 575	16 279	129 050	110 270	18 780
March	31 410	73 313	118 433	8 772	28 755	156 466	16 234	128 950	110 417	18 533
April	31 133	74 088	117 710	8 595	28 802	156 486	16 165	128 115	109 749	18 366
May	31 342	74 620	116 955	8 652	29 130	156 748	16 348	127 232	108 806	18 426
June	31 431	74 284	116 397	8 817	29 218	156 281	16 239	126 199	107 909	18 290
July	31 515	74 397	116 962	8 876	29 438	157 300	16 308	126 998	108 390	18 608
August	31 452	74 649	115 663	8 786	29 592	157 744	16 248	125 949	107 353	18 596
September	31 591	74 899	116 051	8 740	29 746	157 778	16 289	126 331	107 465	18 866
October	31 539	75 785	116 218	8 903	30 109	158 500	16 359	125 743	107 299	18 444
November	31 665	76 051	117 040	8 944	30 290	159 173	16 501	126 614	108 074	18 540
December	31 861	76 594	115 566	8 829	30 556	159 841	16 597	125 501	106 269	19 232

1. Data prior to 1982 are not comparable to subsequent periods due to change in inventory valuation methods; see Notes.
2. Defense products and business supplies not shown.

Table 15-6. Manufacturers' New Orders

(Net, millions of dollars.)

Year and month	Not seasonally adjusted			Seasonally adjusted									
					Durable goods industries								
						Primary metals						Transportation equipment	
	Total	Durable goods industries	Nondurable goods industries	Total	Total [1]	Total	Blast furnaces, steel mills	Nonferrous and other primary metal	Fabricated metal products	Industrial machinery and equipment	Electronic and electrical equipment	Total	Aircraft, missiles, and parts
1970	624 263	328 079	296 184	624 263	328 079	51 793	25 521	21 883	43 990	55 322	41 117	67 380	17 417
1971	671 051	358 856	312 195	671 051	358 856	51 284	25 571	20 704	44 305	55 886	42 639	89 900	22 459
1972	770 181	420 455	349 726	770 181	420 455	61 447	30 996	24 607	52 879	70 941	48 702	96 501	20 963
1973	912 039	511 525	400 514	912 039	511 525	78 395	39 413	31 417	64 733	89 162	58 275	118 194	26 669
1974	1 047 924	562 339	485 585	1 047 924	562 339	98 831	51 047	38 394	74 281	106 101	58 884	114 081	29 934
1975	1 021 662	503 485	518 177	1 021 662	503 485	75 034	38 611	27 864	64 349	92 863	54 610	109 050	26 869
1976	1 194 151	615 680	578 471	1 194 151	615 680	94 491	47 212	37 378	76 372	107 595	66 864	143 502	31 851
1977	1 381 302	732 422	648 880	1 381 302	732 422	105 689	52 103	42 400	92 028	126 235	80 010	175 446	40 625
1978	1 579 542	867 335	712 207	1 579 542	867 335	124 741	62 648	48 319	105 182	154 051	92 781	213 539	54 600
1979	1 771 243	953 796	817 447	1 771 243	953 796	139 783	66 968	58 420	117 428	174 660	107 314	223 226	67 818
1980	1 876 304	952 701	923 603	1 876 304	952 701	134 416	62 473	60 399	116 195	179 750	115 335	202 584	72 514
1981	2 016 298	1 003 845	1 012 453	2 016 298	1 003 845	137 286	67 457	57 545	123 245	201 576	123 053	203 482	63 530
1982	1 945 684	936 764	1 008 920	1 945 684	936 764	98 445	43 013	46 942	113 399	169 274	127 630	209 325	73 365
1983	2 105 410	1 057 677	1 047 733	2 105 410	1 057 677	113 884	49 123	55 566	122 760	178 879	142 131	261 359	86 952
1984	2 314 549	1 201 964	1 112 585	2 314 549	1 201 964	118 354	50 719	56 030	141 650	212 109	165 541	295 202	91 620
1985	2 348 477	1 228 268	1 120 209	2 348 477	1 228 268	112 276	49 079	52 275	142 300	218 395	163 352	311 482	100 889
1986	2 342 444	1 243 761	1 098 683	2 342 444	1 243 761	108 218	46 408	51 294	143 541	208 567	164 282	327 541	107 993
1987	2 512 663	1 329 712	1 182 951	2 512 663	1 329 712	125 989	54 763	60 302	150 716	221 171	173 210	348 224	114 835
1988	2 739 240	1 464 916	1 274 324	2 739 240	1 464 916	152 578	64 002	75 997	158 170	250 055	189 211	389 635	137 443
1989	2 874 861	1 512 664	1 362 197	2 874 861	1 512 664	152 814	62 752	77 249	160 037	257 051	192 482	411 434	153 430
1990	2 934 086	1 507 001	1 427 085	2 934 086	1 507 001	149 338	63 369	72 944	163 285	258 894	195 748	395 737	150 329
1991	2 865 665	1 438 187	1 427 478	2 865 665	1 438 187	134 657	56 366	66 778	158 401	243 450	197 659	363 366	132 645
1992	2 978 548	1 515 694	1 462 854	2 978 548	1 515 694	136 849	58 002	67 337	165 793	258 608	217 966	377 147	110 830
1993	3 092 381	1 596 974	1 495 407	3 092 381	1 596 974	144 018	63 604	67 112	172 121	277 416	233 991	386 643	88 070
1994	3 356 797	1 794 508	1 562 289	3 356 797	1 794 508	167 685	70 960	81 963	191 099	325 788	266 386	440 817	90 217
1995	3 607 586	1 941 378	1 666 208	3 607 586	1 941 378	178 702	75 811	87 857	205 388	358 910	307 634	465 839	106 062
1996	3 749 299	2 036 536	1 712 763	3 749 299	2 036 536	180 362	74 885	88 773	215 791	383 749	319 157	495 239	129 688
1997	3 952 025	2 180 708	1 771 317	3 952 025	2 180 708	193 987	79 481	96 513	228 567	409 215	356 557	507 667	124 151
1998	4 033 676	2 259 693	1 773 983	4 033 676	2 259 693	175 482	69 444	88 067	238 751	443 332	380 470	524 963	124 111
1999	4 279 186	2 425 161	1 854 025	4 279 186	2 425 161	180 740	70 364	92 741	244 831	461 926	439 085	567 357	129 183
1996													
January	286 149	156 914	129 235	308 317	168 878	14 703	6 206	7 087	17 327	31 612	25 968	43 577	12 550
February	302 670	165 945	136 725	303 937	164 611	14 886	6 073	7 338	17 365	32 943	25 401	38 151	8 597
March	321 424	179 273	142 151	307 487	167 984	14 245	5 842	7 143	17 223	30 709	26 594	43 753	16 791
April	305 634	163 470	142 164	306 699	163 658	15 059	6 154	7 535	17 843	31 310	26 221	36 960	6 919
May	314 773	170 925	143 848	314 604	171 396	15 539	6 607	7 587	18 507	32 034	25 506	42 770	11 705
June	329 384	181 990	147 394	311 107	169 721	15 347	6 392	7 410	18 045	31 508	26 315	41 891	9 549
July	285 490	147 098	138 392	314 708	171 122	15 492	6 509	7 564	17 959	32 293	27 701	40 788	9 514
August	310 699	163 782	146 917	310 229	166 859	15 470	6 387	7 623	18 299	32 549	26 122	37 359	6 909
September	332 620	182 676	149 944	316 296	173 282	14 820	6 335	7 086	18 442	32 075	26 104	44 565	12 659
October	330 625	181 262	149 363	319 016	173 994	14 761	6 188	7 369	18 264	31 936	30 268	41 009	11 792
November	319 054	171 947	147 107	320 367	173 773	14 814	5 938	7 493	18 444	32 007	28 414	42 246	11 322
December	310 777	171 254	139 523	314 191	169 492	15 262	6 206	7 614	18 049	32 398	23 912	41 869	10 904
1997													
January	298 991	162 982	136 009	323 321	176 705	15 786	6 497	7 833	18 435	32 911	28 241	42 548	10 530
February	324 279	180 882	143 397	325 819	179 495	15 879	6 362	8 086	18 863	33 468	30 792	40 362	9 845
March	334 621	186 591	148 030	320 729	174 950	15 878	6 195	8 274	18 419	32 862	29 140	39 289	8 812
April	323 346	176 921	146 425	324 449	177 171	16 582	6 898	8 221	19 360	34 184	27 419	39 251	8 494
May	322 077	174 987	147 090	322 213	175 823	16 133	6 516	8 182	18 433	33 279	30 276	38 590	8 494
June	346 439	194 270	152 169	326 998	180 714	15 866	6 709	7 700	19 225	32 985	30 269	41 800	10 703
July	298 815	155 332	143 483	328 799	180 460	16 780	6 781	8 468	19 205	35 411	25 247	41 606	8 457
August	333 072	182 130	150 942	333 083	185 624	16 139	6 442	8 239	19 038	34 420	34 068	42 280	10 746
September	352 126	196 429	155 697	334 091	185 557	17 192	6 683	8 930	19 559	35 499	31 118	41 445	8 479
October	347 068	193 365	153 703	334 576	185 410	15 926	6 754	7 701	19 521	34 991	29 718	44 351	10 429
November	340 579	191 215	149 364	342 310	193 621	16 272	6 881	7 710	19 320	34 395	29 227	53 485	20 719
December	330 612	185 604	145 008	334 974	184 635	15 716	6 803	7 236	19 190	34 853	30 258	42 964	8 043
1998													
January	310 926	172 138	138 788	336 432	187 048	15 272	6 112	7 707	19 328	35 766	31 417	44 520	13 720
February	333 699	188 167	145 532	334 446	186 033	15 996	6 584	7 722	19 774	36 552	30 714	42 431	9 986
March	351 066	199 682	151 384	334 712	185 963	14 696	6 285	6 688	19 704	37 448	30 850	42 204	8 527
April	336 909	189 159	147 750	337 502	188 921	15 451	6 095	7 891	20 001	36 889	31 707	44 431	12 827
May	327 550	180 165	147 385	330 233	182 777	14 940	6 286	7 168	19 630	36 244	29 144	42 422	10 760
June	349 890	196 102	153 788	331 188	182 986	14 453	5 850	7 325	19 722	36 922	30 072	39 349	8 480
July	306 253	162 637	143 616	334 821	186 617	14 273	5 382	7 521	20 132	37 636	32 840	39 768	10 172
August	335 916	185 341	150 575	337 815	190 304	14 413	5 523	7 298	19 693	37 450	31 116	46 745	13 106
September	359 884	205 297	154 587	340 388	192 783	13 917	5 347	7 186	19 930	38 983	32 870	45 101	9 109
October	347 900	197 533	150 367	334 663	188 523	13 343	4 912	6 927	20 095	35 503	33 348	44 870	9 637
November	333 218	186 550	146 668	335 930	189 193	14 587	5 572	7 447	20 235	35 593	31 933	45 024	9 962
December	340 465	196 922	143 543	343 982	195 574	14 087	5 331	7 323	20 460	38 246	33 859	46 166	7 848
1999													
January	325 593	188 008	137 585	349 314	201 708	13 660	4 957	7 199	20 735	37 164	34 895	52 396	15 535
February	339 552	193 524	146 028	343 046	193 786	14 601	5 882	7 346	20 421	37 037	32 651	45 421	10 978
March	367 859	214 181	153 678	349 722	199 366	14 539	5 817	7 355	20 391	38 338	34 264	47 558	10 369
April	345 401	196 132	149 269	344 915	194 674	14 767	5 846	7 410	20 071	39 556	34 364	41 616	7 219
May	344 067	192 553	151 514	348 259	196 609	14 811	5 862	7 589	20 210	37 780	34 067	45 728	10 377
June	370 797	209 554	161 243	351 128	197 084	15 206	5 885	7 921	20 284	36 435	35 158	46 253	9 117
July	328 590	178 540	150 050	359 903	205 532	15 730	5 872	8 237	20 286	40 257	37 976	47 235	10 302
August	365 069	204 162	160 907	364 440	207 446	15 659	6 065	7 962	20 814	39 110	38 616	49 000	11 415
September	380 404	216 720	163 684	360 886	204 349	15 461	5 931	8 085	20 168	39 077	38 734	46 593	9 480
October	373 387	210 891	162 496	360 725	202 442	15 440	6 027	7 958	20 060	39 666	35 884	46 800	10 408
November	361 933	200 811	161 122	365 612	204 799	15 540	6 315	7 863	20 619	39 347	39 352	44 899	8 629
December	376 534	220 085	156 449	379 485	218 167	15 346	5 896	7 851	20 880	38 716	41 524	55 650	15 354

1. Includes categories not shown separately.

Table 15-6. Manufacturers' New Orders—*Continued*

(Net, millions of dollars, seasonally adjusted.)

Year and month	Nondurable goods industries		By market category [1]						Supplementary series		
	Total	Industries with unfilled orders	Home goods and apparel	Consumer staples	Machinery and equipment	Automotive equipment	Construction materials and supplies	Other materials, supplies, and intermediate products	Household durables	Capital goods industries	
										Nondefense	Defense
1970	296 184	50 600	60 053	136 650	90 920	22 920	41 976	208 527	24 360	72 866	21 311
1971	312 195	56 915	63 910	143 889	104 615	31 325	44 769	219 246	25 887	80 185	18 787
1972	349 726	66 492	73 471	159 032	121 439	34 668	54 858	256 608	30 564	92 943	20 467
1973	400 514	84 626	80 190	183 637	151 221	40 271	65 713	310 891	33 804	119 108	23 409
1974	485 585	84 323	80 399	225 842	168 767	36 721	71 972	367 873	33 582	139 131	26 033
1975	518 177	75 168	81 682	247 066	151 278	37 452	64 582	339 984	34 140	118 635	24 765
1976	578 471	97 470	91 453	269 537	179 180	50 230	76 851	411 296	39 289	137 875	30 616
1977	648 880	102 986	105 613	294 776	214 944	60 614	92 881	480 457	46 181	164 168	34 624
1978	712 207	119 786	114 334	326 735	261 585	67 579	107 563	552 092	51 123	211 056	41 511
1979	817 447	137 565	119 157	378 236	305 432	66 949	118 946	619 405	54 117	253 844	33 795
1980	923 603	146 334	124 929	437 370	299 968	54 244	118 449	636 198	56 099	253 619	58 256
1981	1 012 453	150 227	132 987	477 650	312 509	60 834	122 619	688 321	59 342	261 666	58 881
1982	1 008 920	131 116	132 729	486 180	285 408	58 757	112 605	629 399	56 055	230 555	81 415
1983	1 047 733	154 780	143 390	491 092	303 922	77 638	128 440	702 743	60 924	235 489	96 105
1984	1 112 585	172 990	151 993	510 701	359 604	92 714	141 669	776 636	65 706	284 022	103 504
1985	1 120 209	170 565	153 711	518 109	374 954	97 164	147 149	763 711	66 904	294 544	109 505
1986	1 098 683	188 688	159 615	503 299	371 101	101 263	154 725	761 205	70 749	287 786	111 879
1987	1 182 951	240 165	163 728	531 778	400 962	105 265	165 396	838 571	69 526	313 127	111 639
1988	1 274 324	258 834	168 005	569 099	462 470	112 298	176 043	936 836	73 599	373 294	102 728
1989	1 362 197	262 552	174 574	616 054	496 955	118 385	179 546	970 570	78 242	395 855	93 398
1990	1 427 085	264 493	175 162	658 631	500 441	110 181	180 616	972 911	77 946	399 966	96 638
1991	1 427 478	269 579	175 921	667 789	462 856	106 058	172 621	956 041	78 314	365 655	87 213
1992	1 462 854	276 163	185 713	678 613	491 195	120 525	184 385	997 722	82 175	378 293	76 155
1993	1 495 407	273 285	194 976	691 346	505 542	134 526	198 463	1 045 795	88 914	380 329	71 904
1994	1 562 289	289 335	205 505	706 182	567 922	155 702	219 305	1 166 985	95 500	428 364	71 683
1995	1 666 208	313 763	211 040	742 360	624 687	160 887	228 242	1 287 097	98 500	486 134	70 903
1996	1 712 763	294 352	209 912	780 545	672 605	162 310	239 060	1 314 471	97 963	535 575	77 283
1997	1 771 317	310 549	222 405	809 563	729 607	169 310	253 766	1 392 871	107 403	577 978	67 706
1998	1 773 983	297 071	226 721	830 983	774 254	174 795	259 859	1 384 476	111 784	620 400	73 169
1999	1 854 025	294 971	240 005	888 027	815 394	195 553	277 167	1 462 362	125 491	659 457	77 328
1996											
January	139 439	24 591	16 810	63 591	57 150	13 297	19 098	107 276	8 113	45 933	7 374
February	139 326	24 378	17 165	63 087	56 122	13 407	18 895	106 231	7 945	44 532	5 081
March	139 503	23 739	17 810	63 675	56 653	12 286	18 946	104 552	8 462	46 136	9 695
April	143 041	24 014	17 574	65 118	52 317	13 639	19 389	108 252	8 275	40 417	5 516
May	143 208	24 084	17 546	64 986	57 149	14 120	19 945	110 402	8 234	45 054	5 846
June	141 386	24 226	17 358	63 716	54 822	13 576	19 976	109 546	8 097	42 638	7 836
July	143 586	24 365	17 190	65 453	56 506	14 021	20 404	111 825	7 938	45 160	4 621
August	143 370	24 390	17 562	65 344	53 280	13 673	20 511	110 492	8 204	41 240	4 845
September	143 014	24 537	17 457	65 254	59 110	14 208	20 431	110 358	8 032	47 118	5 194
October	145 022	24 677	17 847	66 858	57 751	13 445	20 406	113 425	8 419	47 413	4 915
November	146 594	25 497	17 525	66 999	55 433	13 684	20 341	112 890	7 702	44 370	8 315
December	144 699	25 621	17 636	66 203	55 272	12 979	20 478	108 900	8 310	44 169	8 003
1997											
January	146 616	25 391	17 490	67 733	58 211	14 397	20 722	114 307	8 219	45 919	5 472
February	146 324	24 975	18 183	66 262	59 242	13 795	20 798	116 468	8 698	47 009	5 974
March	145 779	25 558	17 799	66 419	57 428	13 475	20 516	113 852	8 666	45 288	6 032
April	147 278	25 720	18 563	66 741	57 425	13 837	21 582	114 966	8 709	44 763	6 103
May	146 390	25 599	18 357	67 354	57 295	13 267	20 792	114 570	8 849	45 110	5 198
June	146 284	25 803	18 434	67 285	59 773	13 861	21 131	115 062	9 137	47 617	5 904
July	148 339	26 295	19 020	67 727	61 149	14 915	21 681	112 948	9 291	47 731	5 536
August	147 459	26 058	18 086	67 964	60 747	14 302	21 270	119 761	8 460	47 903	5 327
September	148 534	26 136	19 099	67 686	61 767	14 229	21 548	118 772	9 345	49 303	5 247
October	149 166	26 206	18 654	68 004	64 017	14 545	21 521	117 011	8 940	50 450	4 705
November	148 689	26 282	19 287	67 984	71 330	14 216	20 975	116 947	9 486	58 759	5 915
December	150 339	26 204	19 284	68 463	60 418	14 835	21 187	118 234	9 445	47 027	6 496
1998											
January	149 384	25 954	18 768	68 819	64 672	13 649	21 143	116 171	8 995	52 302	7 455
February	148 413	25 782	18 908	68 675	62 503	14 307	21 585	116 803	9 299	50 436	5 978
March	148 749	25 538	18 556	69 182	63 334	14 819	21 559	116 032	9 028	50 502	5 385
April	148 581	25 409	18 826	69 103	64 295	14 277	21 601	116 922	9 050	51 240	6 865
May	147 456	25 032	18 891	68 622	63 803	14 256	21 424	112 079	9 271	50 834	5 397
June	148 202	24 660	19 020	69 623	63 470	13 212	21 781	112 336	9 509	51 053	5 655
July	148 204	24 391	19 105	69 283	62 709	13 276	21 986	116 895	9 373	50 763	5 522
August	147 511	24 246	19 141	69 360	67 303	14 733	21 523	115 035	9 388	55 371	4 933
September	147 605	24 212	18 792	69 884	67 815	15 223	21 391	114 382	9 285	53 540	7 042
October	146 140	24 037	18 786	68 776	63 403	15 241	21 655	114 849	9 387	50 138	6 353
November	146 737	24 174	18 988	69 552	63 839	15 257	21 783	115 050	9 465	50 675	5 657
December	148 408	23 866	19 341	70 561	64 980	15 644	22 331	117 922	9 854	52 005	7 449
1999											
January	147 606	23 890	19 681	69 755	69 858	15 686	22 111	117 883	10 033	56 863	8 018
February	149 260	23 891	19 940	70 782	65 715	15 726	22 578	116 581	10 429	53 233	5 499
March	150 356	23 474	20 022	72 156	66 834	16 200	22 781	117 305	10 446	53 299	7 769
April	150 241	23 393	20 341	72 008	65 183	15 584	22 767	117 812	10 481	52 525	5 060
May	151 650	23 844	19 610	72 661	66 065	15 944	22 723	118 779	10 052	53 041	6 019
June	154 044	24 176	19 580	74 127	64 842	16 986	23 502	120 118	10 258	50 948	5 209
July	154 371	24 514	20 081	74 014	68 011	16 797	23 499	124 063	10 652	55 030	6 476
August	156 994	25 373	20 041	75 285	69 020	16 945	23 479	127 300	10 545	56 423	5 048
September	156 537	25 096	19 854	75 552	69 418	16 559	23 017	123 815	10 322	56 050	5 485
October	158 283	25 484	20 281	76 217	68 364	16 136	23 350	121 321	10 746	56 291	7 671
November	160 813	25 756	20 261	77 112	67 545	16 337	23 577	126 746	10 761	54 385	6 090
December	161 318	25 682	20 576	76 958	75 620	16 945	23 643	129 099	10 958	62 639	8 863

1. Defense products and business supplies not shown.

Table 15-7. Manufacturers' Unfilled Orders

(End of period, millions of dollars.)

Year and month	Not seasonally adjusted			Seasonally adjusted									
					Durable goods industries								
						Primary metals						Transportation equipment	
	Total	Durable goods industries	Nondurable goods industries	Total [1]	Total	Total	Blast furnaces, steel mills	Nonferrous and other primary metals	Fabricated metal products	Industrial machinery and equipment	Electronic and electric equipment	Total	Aircraft, missiles, and parts
1970	104 683	100 139	4 544	105 008	100 412	7 796	4 617	2 663	14 877	21 737	11 881	34 720	26 198
1971	104 857	99 906	4 951	105 247	100 225	7 478	4 380	2 552	13 688	21 170	12 148	35 793	26 259
1972	118 717	112 517	6 200	119 349	113 034	10 470	6 681	3 116	15 077	25 968	13 376	37 627	26 151
1973	155 583	148 421	7 162	156 561	149 204	16 129	9 794	4 962	21 019	36 959	17 111	45 248	27 842
1974	186 030	180 686	5 344	187 043	181 519	19 225	11 054	5 952	28 100	50 084	17 319	51 118	30 506
1975	168 627	160 993	7 634	169 546	161 664	13 266	7 345	4 015	24 008	46 580	15 857	46 633	28 244
1976	177 215	169 198	8 017	178 128	169 857	14 684	7 776	4 891	22 810	48 321	17 584	49 078	29 421
1977	200 101	191 603	8 498	202 024	193 323	17 298	9 435	5 483	25 152	52 026	19 999	57 101	37 325
1978	256 785	246 162	10 623	259 169	248 281	23 969	12 932	7 393	29 137	62 233	24 219	81 782	54 417
1979	300 794	288 834	11 960	303 593	291 321	26 320	12 485	9 457	33 131	69 844	29 261	103 555	74 034
1980	324 409	312 508	11 901	327 416	315 202	26 815	13 418	10 096	33 296	68 979	31 751	119 700	88 051
1981	323 163	311 628	11 535	326 547	314 707	22 024	10 589	8 784	33 036	69 405	32 718	118 008	86 794
1982	308 633	297 851	10 782	311 887	300 798	15 500	6 574	7 418	27 117	51 864	34 639	125 879	93 703
1983	343 479	329 758	13 721	347 273	333 114	20 400	9 431	9 594	26 752	52 351	40 794	141 637	105 504
1984	369 844	356 446	13 398	373 529	359 651	18 362	8 103	8 694	30 254	53 466	43 967	152 189	117 923
1985	383 865	369 362	14 503	387 196	372 097	18 331	8 248	8 361	29 197	53 516	43 366	156 155	127 282
1986	390 428	374 264	16 164	393 515	376 699	18 590	8 897	7 783	29 633	48 416	42 793	161 145	133 565
1987	427 185	406 444	20 741	430 426	408 688	24 340	11 828	10 300	32 973	48 416	44 741	176 588	144 987
1988	470 993	449 859	21 134	474 154	452 150	27 079	11 508	12 974	31 661	57 583	46 702	211 575	174 721
1989	505 479	484 623	20 856	508 849	487 098	24 120	9 479	11 824	27 629	58 369	44 616	253 517	217 557
1990	527 337	506 311	21 026	531 131	509 124	24 768	10 120	11 258	25 859	57 872	44 501	279 082	242 208
1991	514 835	492 500	22 335	519 199	495 802	23 075	9 290	10 609	24 516	53 812	42 988	275 260	242 798
1992	488 656	466 328	22 328	492 893	469 381	21 636	8 897	9 925	23 725	53 651	44 348	253 076	222 194
1993	453 412	432 667	20 745	457 810	436 017	23 068	10 163	9 623	20 731	52 952	44 784	225 256	194 154
1994	462 190	437 599	24 591	466 699	440 998	29 661	11 303	14 535	21 290	65 608	44 941	215 171	180 969
1995	475 113	451 948	23 165	479 674	455 459	27 993	12 183	12 195	22 329	71 179	51 470	219 101	186 848
1996	508 952	484 325	24 627	513 062	487 441	29 996	12 432	13 167	24 159	73 042	49 943	249 119	215 171
1997	531 558	506 334	25 224	536 131	509 927	35 160	14 905	14 656	26 649	73 419	55 174	254 579	217 998
1998	512 986	490 040	22 946	519 038	495 172	29 554	11 430	12 666	25 894	74 458	60 530	243 205	204 434
1999	532 691	507 779	24 912	538 217	512 535	31 912	13 084	14 089	25 204	81 298	85 466	227 461	191 416
1996													
January	490 002	466 095	23 907	487 602	463 011	28 096	12 283	12 051	22 265	72 113	51 400	225 681	192 279
February	492 592	468 686	23 906	488 998	464 620	28 464	12 273	12 216	22 382	72 947	50 805	225 982	193 115
March	498 516	474 652	23 864	495 402	471 663	28 048	12 084	12 001	22 521	72 277	51 024	234 210	201 821
April	498 840	474 413	24 427	494 429	470 415	28 254	12 051	12 199	22 570	72 398	50 821	232 740	200 862
May	499 442	474 764	24 678	496 544	472 460	28 689	12 442	12 264	22 918	72 776	49 871	234 932	203 497
June	498 721	473 752	24 969	499 403	475 177	29 498	12 640	12 670	23 102	72 588	49 603	237 821	204 867
July	505 012	479 501	25 511	503 535	479 170	30 035	12 854	12 967	23 197	73 450	50 830	239 581	206 685
August	501 327	476 154	25 173	501 611	477 221	30 591	12 967	13 321	23 281	73 883	50 724	237 340	204 607
September	499 728	475 073	24 655	504 748	480 211	30 621	12 993	13 305	23 601	73 587	50 113	241 039	208 275
October	507 348	483 334	24 014	510 027	485 350	30 384	12 884	13 308	23 814	73 499	53 172	243 467	211 491
November	508 413	483 792	24 621	512 650	487 153	29 974	12 556	13 177	23 956	73 334	53 401	245 954	213 658
December	508 952	484 325	24 627	513 062	487 441	29 996	12 432	13 167	24 159	73 042	49 943	249 119	215 171
1997													
January	520 156	495 420	24 736	517 233	491 842	30 230	12 459	13 290	24 297	73 553	51 153	250 980	216 913
February	525 801	501 264	24 537	521 778	496 803	30 439	12 392	13 493	24 669	74 456	53 869	250 900	217 447
March	524 551	498 951	25 600	521 807	496 249	30 721	12 199	13 879	24 833	74 456	53 553	249 978	216 300
April	524 528	498 485	26 043	520 617	494 897	31 397	12 616	14 082	25 240	74 952	52 627	247 420	214 262
May	523 128	496 984	26 144	520 570	494 971	31 924	12 872	14 265	25 272	74 830	54 439	245 495	212 481
June	520 327	493 820	26 507	521 450	495 647	32 004	13 120	13 998	25 742	73 455	55 379	245 654	212 954
July	520 535	492 960	27 575	518 918	492 623	32 880	13 426	14 463	26 015	73 742	51 522	243 587	210 968
August	523 608	496 768	26 840	523 751	497 693	33 270	13 492	14 730	26 058	74 046	55 854	243 845	211 773
September	519 365	493 075	26 290	524 420	498 284	34 558	13 759	15 601	26 334	74 311	56 163	242 911	210 030
October	524 156	498 555	25 601	526 675	500 469	34 626	14 100	15 338	26 581	74 212	56 026	244 973	210 861
November	533 329	507 877	25 452	537 581	511 299	35 157	14 615	15 092	26 758	74 264	55 411	255 173	220 532
December	531 558	506 334	25 224	536 131	509 927	35 160	14 905	14 656	26 649	73 419	55 174	254 579	217 998
1998													
January	543 779	518 535	25 244	540 626	514 672	34 717	14 533	14 590	26 868	73 249	57 059	257 557	220 894
February	543 505	518 273	25 232	539 189	513 407	34 875	14 626	14 546	26 876	73 592	57 059	256 411	219 861
March	537 538	512 007	25 531	534 910	509 372	33 911	14 472	13 594	26 838	74 176	57 071	253 407	217 113
April	541 896	516 207	25 689	536 859	511 450	33 839	14 209	13 833	27 269	74 167	58 722	253 975	218 831
May	536 103	510 563	25 540	533 470	508 438	33 603	14 295	13 504	27 154	73 850	58 099	252 835	218 389
June	527 169	501 923	25 246	529 548	504 888	33 007	14 021	13 356	27 121	72 857	57 289	251 327	216 211
July	531 291	505 568	25 723	528 989	504 598	32 312	13 397	13 384	26 944	72 683	58 913	250 539	215 817
August	529 830	504 851	24 979	530 359	506 113	31 669	12 816	13 203	26 523	73 422	58 801	252 881	217 854
September	525 390	501 112	24 278	530 266	506 054	30 635	12 254	12 854	26 218	75 630	59 249	251 394	215 042
October	522 765	499 520	23 245	524 796	500 759	29 388	11 437	12 410	26 137	74 122	60 378	248 247	211 882
November	514 816	491 398	23 418	519 303	495 129	29 689	11 458	12 637	25 957	73 092	59 677	244 947	208 629
December	512 986	490 040	22 946	519 038	495 172	29 554	11 430	12 666	25 894	74 458	60 530	243 205	204 434
1999													
January	530 997	507 600	23 397	526 677	502 787	28 902	10 991	12 474	26 109	75 109	62 595	248 365	207 714
February	529 549	506 205	23 344	525 999	502 108	29 279	11 320	12 676	26 139	75 390	63 011	246 284	206 485
March	528 200	504 906	23 294	526 656	503 182	29 313	11 500	12 711	26 114	76 756	64 243	244 575	204 756
April	529 821	506 344	23 477	524 003	500 610	29 855	11 837	12 900	25 769	78 848	64 952	238 436	199 727
May	524 263	500 124	24 139	521 638	497 794	30 140	12 073	13 093	25 568	79 109	65 183	235 273	197 363
June	515 003	490 254	24 749	518 064	493 888	30 669	12 343	13 488	25 308	78 236	66 145	231 745	195 163
July	523 311	497 545	25 766	520 666	496 152	31 496	12 534	14 069	25 200	79 059	68 748	230 164	194 586
August	525 024	498 535	26 489	523 262	497 889	31 951	12 775	14 205	25 233	79 478	72 025	228 184	193 193
September	521 233	495 949	25 284	525 439	500 343	32 114	12 892	14 346	25 024	80 813	75 452	226 222	191 783
October	524 929	499 979	24 950	525 963	500 479	32 363	13 026	14 474	24 803	81 008	76 476	225 363	190 698
November	522 083	496 913	25 170	526 604	500 848	32 329	13 282	14 332	24 709	81 280	80 223	221 936	187 850
December	532 691	507 779	24 912	538 217	512 535	31 912	13 084	14 089	25 204	81 298	85 466	227 461	191 416

1. Includes categories not shown separately.

Table 15-7. Manufacturers' Unfilled Orders—Continued

(End of period, millions of dollars, seasonally adjusted.)

Year and month	Nondurable goods industries	By market category [1]						Supplementary series		
		Home goods and apparel	Consumer staples	Machinery and equipment	Automotive equipment	Construction materials and supplies	Other materials, supplies, and intermediate products	Household durables	Capital goods industries	
									Nondefense	Defense
1970	4 596	2 245	284	42 704	714	8 880	30 991	2 078	46 544	18 804
1971	5 022	2 509	314	43 386	785	8 073	31 149	2 292	47 576	18 158
1972	6 315	3 168	355	47 635	886	8 810	38 198	2 914	52 781	19 261
1973	7 357	3 831	466	61 767	1 354	12 311	53 339	3 471	67 947	21 756
1974	5 524	2 891	480	77 672	1 400	15 125	60 751	2 582	84 495	26 558
1975	7 882	3 179	596	70 549	1 058	12 694	51 673	2 740	76 773	27 936
1976	8 271	3 376	708	72 941	1 209	11 592	54 856	2 862	79 121	31 826
1977	8 701	4 670	846	81 172	1 481	12 821	63 498	4 135	87 552	36 692
1978	10 888	5 493	978	103 005	2 046	14 408	85 040	4 864	112 277	47 425
1979	12 272	5 547	1 036	130 361	1 899	15 360	99 144	4 754	144 114	48 656
1980	12 214	5 226	1 054	136 142	1 656	15 410	100 488	4 388	150 973	66 636
1981	11 840	5 668	1 113	128 411	1 742	15 213	96 356	4 729	142 802	77 793
1982	11 089	5 784	1 140	109 196	1 563	11 981	84 771	4 860	121 082	99 052
1983	14 159	7 131	1 047	103 626	2 406	12 673	103 680	5 810	114 280	121 177
1984	13 878	6 890	1 083	108 659	2 172	13 102	105 750	5 603	119 424	142 324
1985	15 099	6 996	1 177	111 055	2 036	13 124	103 383	5 253	120 687	156 188
1986	16 816	7 357	1 171	108 830	2 159	13 677	104 644	5 815	118 429	161 705
1987	21 738	8 735	1 148	125 209	2 397	14 140	119 288	5 842	136 171	163 786
1988	22 004	7 999	1 431	160 441	2 220	14 557	129 322	5 703	176 069	161 878
1989	21 751	8 893	1 438	202 960	1 887	13 992	127 879	5 854	221 152	155 314
1990	22 007	9 067	1 276	231 612	1 531	14 021	126 374	5 215	250 314	149 844
1991	23 397	9 810	1 324	224 767	1 705	14 828	128 935	5 498	246 093	139 666
1992	23 512	9 763	1 437	215 353	1 609	14 706	126 420	5 047	234 817	124 047
1993	21 793	9 043	1 507	196 380	1 916	13 980	123 987	5 438	214 248	112 062
1994	25 701	8 430	1 664	195 078	2 218	15 754	136 735	5 788	213 268	106 548
1995	24 215	8 843	1 878	206 290	2 314	15 730	139 058	5 580	224 059	103 880
1996	25 621	8 158	2 113	225 985	2 377	16 649	146 806	4 916	247 491	109 186
1997	26 204	9 542	2 100	243 676	2 552	17 855	156 870	6 289	261 575	101 797
1998	23 866	8 979	2 364	241 602	2 474	17 506	148 367	5 522	257 382	95 947
1999	25 682	9 260	3 100	240 198	2 527	17 650	169 041	5 856	257 025	93 786
1996										
January	24 591	8 969	1 937	212 421	2 363	15 733	139 385	5 653	230 582	105 169
February	24 378	9 071	1 929	215 055	2 358	15 985	138 667	5 692	233 104	104 392
March	23 739	9 352	1 857	219 294	2 328	15 974	137 111	5 876	237 556	108 003
April	24 014	9 415	1 896	218 356	2 317	15 946	137 158	5 910	236 557	107 664
May	24 084	9 254	1 960	220 435	2 313	15 945	137 438	5 809	238 790	107 488
June	24 226	9 085	1 933	220 817	2 296	15 977	138 423	5 680	238 763	109 237
July	24 365	8 775	2 115	223 573	2 342	16 103	140 849	5 435	242 355	108 163
August	24 390	8 760	2 095	221 881	2 364	16 195	141 743	5 420	240 439	106 982
September	24 537	8 780	2 028	224 764	2 389	16 395	142 816	5 332	243 708	106 119
October	24 677	8 926	1 923	227 544	2 342	16 303	146 161	5 478	248 042	105 361
November	25 497	8 309	2 076	226 718	2 384	16 155	147 871	4 859	248 100	107 360
December	25 621	8 158	2 113	225 985	2 377	16 649	146 806	4 916	247 491	109 186
1997										
January	25 391	7 837	2 186	228 930	2 457	16 808	148 674	4 835	250 310	108 670
February	24 975	7 805	1 900	231 692	2 486	16 811	151 440	5 003	253 014	108 268
March	25 558	7 774	2 080	231 204	2 538	16 785	151 609	5 048	252 589	108 239
April	25 720	7 817	2 167	229 988	2 540	17 119	151 242	5 137	250 797	107 992
May	25 599	8 071	2 166	229 125	2 525	17 105	152 672	5 398	249 556	106 947
June	25 803	8 240	2 245	229 405	2 530	17 263	153 411	5 588	249 810	106 313
July	26 295	8 744	2 336	229 088	2 537	17 551	150 875	6 051	249 202	105 600
August	26 058	8 609	2 280	230 203	2 568	17 606	155 480	5 878	249 831	104 796
September	26 136	8 915	2 234	230 523	2 560	17 601	156 525	6 067	250 098	104 023
October	26 206	9 000	2 187	234 298	2 581	17 839	156 198	6 023	252 811	102 377
November	26 282	9 492	2 084	245 713	2 525	17 820	156 440	6 362	263 786	101 386
December	26 204	9 542	2 100	243 676	2 552	17 855	156 870	6 289	261 575	101 797
1998										
January	25 954	9 183	2 104	246 939	2 532	17 948	157 359	6 038	264 474	102 834
February	25 782	8 968	2 111	246 519	2 514	18 132	156 818	5 910	264 502	102 279
March	25 538	8 528	2 217	245 305	2 499	18 083	155 507	5 560	263 411	101 034
April	25 409	8 198	2 219	246 375	2 433	18 281	156 569	5 308	264 091	101 154
May	25 032	8 189	2 179	247 027	2 431	18 276	153 902	5 321	264 339	99 993
June	24 660	8 232	2 216	245 970	2 426	18 205	151 463	5 348	262 987	99 344
July	24 391	8 007	2 288	245 443	2 358	18 129	152 575	5 092	262 434	98 371
August	24 246	8 219	2 279	248 931	2 314	17 996	152 118	5 233	266 583	96 616
September	24 212	8 356	2 271	250 233	2 380	17 682	150 231	5 287	266 704	97 052
October	24 037	8 646	2 146	246 919	2 382	17 618	148 732	5 430	262 972	96 337
November	24 174	8 941	2 328	243 910	2 418	17 486	147 162	5 479	259 447	95 040
December	23 866	8 979	2 364	241 602	2 474	17 506	148 367	5 522	257 382	95 947
1999										
January	23 890	8 888	2 461	245 513	2 596	17 605	150 339	5 502	261 289	97 225
February	23 891	9 087	2 428	245 431	2 526	17 746	150 732	5 652	261 750	95 995
March	23 474	9 314	2 527	244 248	2 508	17 841	150 886	5 929	260 832	97 091
April	23 393	9 351	2 520	241 918	2 479	17 858	151 926	5 911	258 626	95 625
May	23 844	8 975	2 616	239 733	2 486	17 721	152 835	5 545	256 124	94 975
June	24 176	8 911	2 693	236 343	2 505	17 919	153 518	5 541	252 600	93 906
July	24 514	8 956	2 697	235 318	2 493	18 042	157 033	5 608	251 535	93 798
August	25 373	8 946	2 897	233 990	2 529	17 926	162 039	5 511	250 671	92 378
September	25 096	9 089	2 860	235 476	2 505	17 572	163 949	5 556	251 830	91 408
October	25 484	9 300	2 958	235 032	2 549	17 668	163 228	5 781	251 826	92 510
November	25 756	9 338	3 055	234 417	2 482	17 608	165 431	5 766	250 973	91 444
December	25 682	9 260	3 100	240 198	2 527	17 650	169 041	5 856	257 025	93 786

1. Defense products and business supplies not shown.

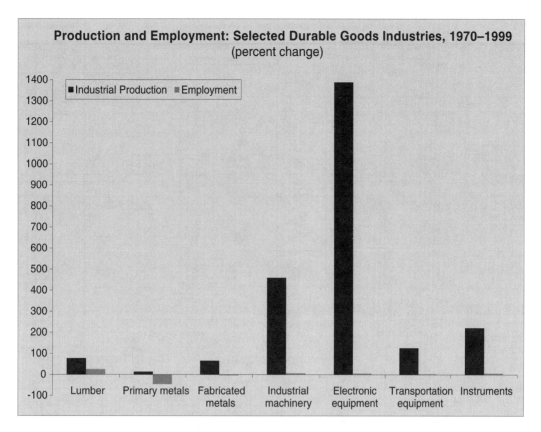

- Over the past 29 years, by far the greatest growth in production has been in industries directly affected by the "high-tech" revolution—electronic and electric machinery and equipment, industrial machinery (which includes computers), and instruments. Production of electronic equipment was up nearly 1,400 percent; industrial machinery 460 percent; and instruments over 200 percent.

- No durable goods industry has shown much growth in employment, and some have shown declines. Within the industrial machinery industry group, employment in computer and office equipment grew 32 percent from 1970 to 1999, accounting for much of this industry's total employment gain. The largest decline was in primary metals, with a 44 percent drop in employment.

- Measured from the 1989 business cycle peak, the employment picture has been mixed for durable goods. Lumber and wood products; furniture and fixtures; fabricated metals; and industrial machinery all have seen growth in employment. Stone, clay, and glass products; primary metals; electronic equipment; transportation equipment; and instruments have seen declines.

Table 16-1. Lumber and Wood Products—Production, Capacity Utilization, and Prices

Year and month	Industrial production (1992=100, seasonally adjusted)							Capacity utilization (output as a percent of capacity, seasonally adjusted)	Producer prices (1982=100, except as noted, not seasonally adjusted)		
	Total	Logging and lumber		Lumber products					Lumber and wood products industry (December 1984=100)	Lumber and wood products commodities	Intermediate materials
		Total	Logging	Total	Millwork and plywood		Manufactured homes				Softwood lumber
					Total	Plywood					
1970	68.6	75.0	70.6	65.8	56.0	70.5	. . .	80.5	. . .	39.9	35.2
1971	70.4	71.4	62.2	71.9	62.9	80.1	. . .	80.0	. . .	44.7	44.0
1972	80.6	83.2	74.4	81.3	72.9	88.7	146.6	88.2	. . .	50.7	52.1
1973	80.9	80.8	75.6	83.5	76.0	88.9	144.0	85.5	. . .	62.2	66.6
1974	73.4	79.3	81.7	71.2	64.1	77.6	101.7	75.8	. . .	64.5	65.7
1975	68.3	75.5	76.6	65.1	62.1	75.7	81.5	69.5	. . .	62.1	62.4
1976	77.8	83.6	82.5	75.6	70.5	86.5	107.1	78.2	. . .	72.2	77.1
1977	86.1	88.6	95.4	84.3	81.3	92.3	118.7	85.7	. . .	83.0	92.5
1978	87.5	87.8	91.0	87.5	84.4	95.1	126.0	86.1	. . .	96.9	107.6
1979	86.3	86.9	93.1	86.0	82.0	90.4	121.2	83.8	. . .	105.5	118.1
1980	80.4	83.6	112.2	77.9	74.8	84.4	99.6	77.7	. . .	101.5	107.3
1981	78.1	78.2	104.3	77.9	74.4	85.7	101.8	74.9	. . .	102.8	106.6
1982	70.3	70.0	89.9	70.4	65.7	80.0	89.3	66.6	. . .	100.0	100.0
1983	83.3	82.0	104.8	84.1	80.3	92.5	110.5	78.8	. . .	107.9	115.0
1984	89.9	88.3	112.0	90.8	89.8	95.2	104.7	84.0	. . .	108.0	110.0
1985	92.0	91.9	109.1	92.0	93.9	97.8	102.5	84.0	100.3	106.6	107.4
1986	99.6	102.4	118.6	97.7	102.9	109.3	102.5	89.0	101.5	107.2	108.4
1987	104.9	105.8	117.7	104.2	111.8	116.0	106.4	92.1	105.3	112.8	116.1
1988	105.1	106.7	115.0	103.9	111.5	115.6	103.1	91.1	109.2	118.9	120.0
1989	104.3	105.0	113.9	103.7	109.3	111.8	96.3	88.7	115.3	126.7	127.1
1990	101.6	100.5	103.7	102.2	105.4	107.3	94.0	85.1	117.0	129.7	123.8
1991	94.5	95.6	98.2	93.8	95.2	98.1	84.5	78.5	119.4	132.1	125.7
1992	100.0	100.0	100.0	100.0	100.0	100.0	100.0	82.7	129.7	146.6	148.6
1993	100.8	96.1	96.3	104.3	101.9	99.3	115.3	82.6	148.3	174.0	193.0
1994	105.9	99.8	96.5	110.6	108.4	101.0	127.0	84.9	154.4	180.0	198.1
1995	107.9	101.6	96.1	112.7	108.2	102.0	135.8	83.9	154.1	178.1	178.5
1996	110.1	102.0	94.0	116.2	111.0	98.6	144.6	82.5	153.5	176.1	189.5
1997	115.0	107.2	96.9	120.9	112.8	96.0	157.7	83.2	158.9	183.8	206.5
1998	118.5	107.8	92.8	126.7	119.1	96.7	166.3	83.1	157.0	179.1	182.7
1999	121.6	112.2	92.2	128.8	124.1	95.1	155.2	82.7	161.8	183.6	196.0
1996											
January	106.9	100.1	96.2	112.1	106.6	101.5	138.8	81.4	150.6	172.9	169.2
February	106.6	100.3	95.7	111.5	107.6	99.8	135.7	81.0	150.7	173.0	170.6
March	109.8	103.9	96.1	114.4	108.5	100.4	142.8	83.2	150.9	172.8	174.6
April	110.2	102.6	97.3	116.0	110.6	101.3	143.2	83.2	151.0	171.9	178.5
May	110.3	102.2	94.5	116.4	111.8	102.8	144.1	83.0	153.8	175.8	192.1
June	112.1	102.5	95.9	119.3	113.5	101.0	147.3	84.1	154.5	176.8	196.8
July	109.7	100.0	93.2	117.1	112.7	100.7	144.2	82.1	153.3	175.0	191.6
August	111.2	102.5	91.3	117.8	113.1	99.9	148.7	83.0	154.4	177.0	196.6
September	111.6	102.2	90.6	118.7	113.1	94.7	149.5	83.0	156.6	180.2	203.9
October	110.6	100.6	91.3	118.2	113.1	96.1	150.3	82.0	154.6	177.8	193.7
November	112.3	104.7	93.9	118.2	111.8	95.7	148.2	83.0	156.2	180.2	204.4
December	109.7	102.2	93.3	115.4	109.7	88.0	142.2	80.8	155.9	179.7	202.4
1997											
January	110.9	104.7	95.3	115.6	109.5	93.4	148.6	81.5	156.4	180.6	202.6
February	113.6	105.5	95.8	119.7	112.5	102.4	151.9	83.2	158.2	183.4	209.5
March	114.6	107.4	95.6	120.1	113.1	100.1	154.3	83.7	159.3	184.8	210.5
April	115.0	106.5	95.9	121.5	112.6	96.6	158.8	83.8	159.9	185.4	215.0
May	115.7	108.3	97.3	121.4	112.6	95.3	158.7	84.1	160.7	186.8	219.6
June	116.2	108.5	96.3	122.1	113.0	96.4	158.9	84.2	159.8	185.4	211.5
July	116.3	108.0	96.7	122.7	113.1	94.4	162.0	84.1	160.1	185.9	212.6
August	115.0	107.2	94.8	121.0	111.4	92.2	161.2	82.9	159.6	185.0	209.1
September	114.9	106.6	97.0	121.2	112.8	95.2	160.0	82.6	158.9	183.7	201.9
October	115.0	106.5	97.5	121.5	114.1	96.2	159.6	82.5	157.3	181.1	194.4
November	116.4	108.5	97.7	122.4	114.7	95.6	160.4	83.2	158.2	181.8	196.2
December	116.2	108.4	100.8	122.1	113.9	93.3	159.9	82.9	157.9	181.5	194.8
1998											
January	116.3	106.6	93.1	123.6	116.1	96.1	163.6	82.7	157.4	181.1	190.9
February	117.2	107.2	94.0	124.8	117.8	93.9	166.1	83.2	158.2	182.2	192.9
March	116.9	106.2	93.5	125.0	116.7	94.6	164.6	82.7	158.2	182.4	193.7
April	117.6	106.7	93.1	125.1	117.3	97.6	164.9	83.0	158.5	182.5	193.4
May	117.5	106.3	94.0	125.9	117.8	95.4	165.6	82.7	157.4	180.4	187.0
June	117.9	106.8	93.5	126.2	119.0	96.2	162.3	82.8	155.6	177.5	177.1
July	118.6	107.7	93.9	126.9	119.8	98.0	170.1	83.1	157.0	178.5	181.6
August	119.6	110.0	93.2	126.9	119.0	96.9	164.3	83.6	158.2	179.7	183.4
September	118.7	107.4	91.9	127.1	119.5	97.4	166.0	82.7	157.3	178.0	175.2
October	119.8	109.3	92.8	127.7	119.5	96.4	168.5	83.3	155.3	175.5	171.9
November	119.9	107.2	92.1	129.4	121.5	98.4	171.2	83.1	155.2	175.2	170.3
December	122.5	110.9	92.8	131.3	124.9	99.3	172.5	84.8	155.7	175.9	175.1
1999											
January	122.6	111.3	95.5	131.2	123.8	97.5	173.3	84.6	156.7	177.2	181.0
February	122.3	111.4	91.5	130.6	124.0	99.2	169.2	84.2	158.3	179.8	187.4
March	121.7	110.6	92.2	130.1	123.5	96.1	168.8	83.6	160.1	181.6	193.4
April	121.5	110.0	91.1	130.2	124.3	95.4	164.7	83.2	160.2	181.6	192.5
May	123.9	117.3	91.6	129.1	123.7	96.0	161.3	84.7	161.9	183.7	197.3
June	122.2	113.4	93.0	129.0	123.4	94.4	158.9	83.3	165.2	187.8	205.9
July	121.5	112.3	91.2	128.6	123.7	94.6	151.5	82.7	168.5	192.0	217.5
August	120.2	109.9	91.9	128.0	124.3	93.8	151.3	81.6	166.9	189.6	207.0
September	119.7	110.8	90.9	126.5	123.7	93.1	144.4	81.0	163.1	184.9	197.4
October	120.5	111.8	91.6	127.2	124.8	95.4	142.6	81.4	160.0	181.0	188.8
November	119.8	111.8	93.8	126.0	124.4	94.5	139.3	80.7	159.6	181.6	190.5
December	121.4	114.3	93.1	126.9	122.9	90.7	138.3	81.6	160.6	182.7	192.8

Table 16-2. Lumber and Wood Products—Prices, Employment, Hours, and Earnings

Year and month	Producer prices (1982=100, not seasonally adjusted)			Employment (thousands, seasonally adjusted)		Production workers			
	Intermediate materials—Continued		Crude materials: Logs and timber	Total payroll employees	Production workers	Average weekly hours, seasonally adjusted	Aggregate weekly hours index (1982=100), seasonally adjusted	Average earnings (dollars, not seasonally adjusted)	
	Millwork	Plywood						Hourly	Weekly
1970	41.5	46.7	. . .	658	564	39.6	117.9	2.97	117.61
1971	43.2	49.4	. . .	681	588	39.8	123.8	3.18	126.56
1972	46.0	56.3	. . .	740	637	40.4	136.1	3.34	134.94
1973	51.6	66.9	. . .	774	665	40.0	140.6	3.62	144.80
1974	56.2	69.4	. . .	727	618	39.2	128.2	3.90	152.88
1975	57.4	69.4	. . .	627	526	38.8	107.8	4.28	166.06
1976	63.3	80.6	. . .	693	585	39.9	123.5	4.74	189.13
1977	69.3	91.4	. . .	736	626	39.9	132.0	5.11	203.89
1978	84.3	101.5	. . .	770	657	39.8	138.3	5.62	223.68
1979	91.0	107.9	. . .	782	664	39.5	138.6	6.08	240.16
1980	93.2	106.2	. . .	704	587	38.6	119.9	6.57	253.60
1981	97.8	105.9	. . .	680	563	38.7	115.1	7.02	271.67
1982	100.0	100.0	100.0	610	497	38.1	100.0	7.46	284.23
1983	108.2	105.2	96.6	671	555	40.1	117.7	7.82	313.58
1984	110.2	104.1	97.0	718	598	39.9	126.3	8.05	321.20
1985	111.7	99.6	96.0	711	592	39.9	124.9	8.25	329.18
1986	113.7	101.4	92.3	724	605	40.4	129.2	8.37	338.15
1987	117.7	102.6	101.8	754	628	40.6	134.9	8.43	342.26
1988	121.9	103.4	117.7	767	639	40.1	135.6	8.59	344.46
1989	127.3	115.9	131.9	756	626	40.1	132.6	8.84	354.48
1990	130.4	114.2	142.8	733	603	40.2	128.2	9.08	365.02
1991	135.5	114.3	144.1	675	553	40.0	116.9	9.24	369.60
1992	143.3	133.3	164.8	680	558	40.6	119.9	9.44	383.26
1993	156.6	152.8	212.3	709	584	40.8	126.1	9.61	392.09
1994	162.4	158.6	219.1	754	623	41.2	135.9	9.84	405.41
1995	163.8	165.3	220.4	769	632	40.6	135.8	10.12	410.87
1996	166.6	156.4	206.8	778	640	40.8	138.0	10.44	425.95
1997	170.9	159.3	214.4	796	655	41.0	142.1	10.76	441.16
1998	171.1	157.3	208.1	814	669	41.1	145.4	11.10	456.21
1999	174.7	176.4	202.0	828	679	41.2	148.0	11.47	472.56
1996									
January	163.6	154.0	214.5	766	628	39.0	129.5	10.28	396.81
February	163.8	154.2	214.0	773	634	40.7	136.4	10.23	407.15
March	164.1	152.1	209.3	771	632	40.7	136.0	10.29	415.72
April	164.6	151.6	200.2	775	636	40.9	137.5	10.33	420.43
May	165.8	158.3	202.8	776	637	41.1	138.4	10.35	426.42
June	166.7	155.8	201.5	780	643	41.2	140.1	10.45	434.72
July	167.0	154.0	201.7	781	641	41.1	139.3	10.47	426.13
August	167.9	157.4	203.6	783	644	41.1	139.9	10.54	436.36
September	168.7	166.7	206.0	783	643	41.2	140.1	10.57	439.71
October	168.7	160.1	208.8	784	646	41.1	140.4	10.56	437.18
November	169.3	157.9	209.8	787	648	41.0	140.5	10.57	433.37
December	169.3	155.3	209.5	784	645	41.0	139.8	10.62	437.54
1997									
January	170.1	154.5	213.0	784	645	40.5	138.1	10.58	418.97
February	170.3	158.8	215.9	787	647	40.8	139.6	10.61	426.52
March	170.4	163.6	216.2	790	650	41.1	141.3	10.61	431.83
April	170.8	159.1	215.7	793	653	41.3	142.6	10.65	438.78
May	171.2	158.2	216.6	796	655	41.2	142.7	10.71	442.32
June	171.4	162.7	215.2	796	656	41.1	142.6	10.77	446.96
July	171.5	162.6	215.4	797	655	41.2	142.7	10.82	441.46
August	171.4	161.6	214.8	799	657	41.0	142.4	10.80	446.04
September	171.3	162.6	214.7	800	658	41.1	143.0	10.86	450.69
October	171.0	156.0	211.3	800	659	41.0	142.9	10.87	451.11
November	170.8	157.9	212.1	802	661	41.1	143.6	10.90	451.26
December	171.0	153.6	212.3	804	662	41.0	143.5	10.92	449.90
1998									
January	170.9	152.9	214.3	805	664	41.1	144.3	10.89	437.78
February	170.8	153.3	216.4	807	664	41.1	144.3	10.90	441.45
March	170.9	151.3	217.0	808	665	41.1	144.5	10.94	445.26
April	171.0	152.4	217.3	811	667	41.2	145.3	10.98	447.98
May	171.2	151.4	213.3	812	667	41.1	144.9	11.05	456.37
June	171.1	151.1	209.0	812	668	41.1	145.2	11.09	461.34
July	170.9	159.1	204.2	813	669	41.1	145.4	11.17	460.20
August	170.8	167.6	204.7	815	669	41.1	145.4	11.18	465.09
September	171.5	170.0	202.9	817	670	40.8	144.5	11.17	452.39
October	171.7	156.7	201.0	818	671	41.1	145.8	11.22	465.63
November	171.5	160.9	199.4	820	673	41.2	146.6	11.24	466.46
December	171.4	161.1	197.9	823	676	41.5	148.3	11.33	472.46
1999									
January	171.5	161.6	198.6	826	678	41.6	149.1	11.29	459.50
February	171.6	169.3	200.6	827	679	40.9	146.8	11.26	454.90
March	172.3	173.0	200.4	828	680	41.3	148.5	11.31	461.45
April	173.3	170.2	201.1	827	678	41.2	147.7	11.38	468.86
May	174.1	179.1	201.2	827	678	41.2	147.7	11.43	473.20
June	175.6	196.9	200.4	827	678	41.2	147.7	11.46	476.74
July	176.7	208.3	201.0	829	680	41.1	147.8	11.53	475.04
August	177.3	202.1	202.2	829	679	41.2	147.9	11.54	482.37
September	177.0	177.8	202.9	830	680	41.1	147.8	11.56	472.80
October	175.9	158.7	204.5	831	682	41.1	148.2	11.60	480.24
November	175.5	159.5	205.6	831	681	41.1	148.0	11.60	480.24
December	175.5	160.8	205.9	831	681	41.0	147.6	11.64	480.73

Table 16-3. Furniture and Fixtures—Production, Capacity Utilization, Prices, Employment, Hours and Earnings

Year and month	Industrial production (1992=100, seasonally adjusted)		Capacity utilization (output as a percent of capacity seasonally adjusted)	Producer prices (1982=100, except as noted; not seasonally adjusted)				Employment (thousands, seasonally adjusted)		Production workers			
				Furniture and fixtures industry (December 1984=100)	Finished goods		Public building furniture (December 1984=100)			Average weekly hours, seasonally adjusted	Aggregate weekly hours index (1982=100), seasonally adjusted	Average earnings (dollars, not seasonally adjusted)	
	Total	Household furniture			Household furniture	Commercial furniture		Total payroll employees	Production workers			Hourly	Weekly
1970	56.2	69.2	81.0	...	48.6	41.6	...	440	362	39.2	111.6	2.77	108.58
1971	58.6	73.9	80.7	...	50.0	42.9	...	444	365	39.8	114.0	2.90	115.42
1972	70.7	90.1	93.0	...	51.0	43.6	...	483	400	40.2	126.6	3.08	123.82
1973	75.4	95.0	93.9	...	53.5	47.0	...	507	420	40.0	132.0	3.29	131.60
1974	70.1	87.5	82.9	...	59.4	55.3	...	489	402	39.1	123.4	3.53	138.02
1975	60.0	75.3	68.9	...	63.6	60.5	...	417	337	38.0	100.7	3.78	143.64
1976	67.0	84.4	75.7	...	66.8	63.0	...	444	364	38.8	111.0	3.99	154.81
1977	74.8	91.8	82.1	...	70.6	67.5	...	464	382	39.0	117.2	4.34	169.26
1978	80.4	98.5	84.5	...	75.5	73.1	...	494	406	39.3	125.6	4.68	183.92
1979	80.5	96.4	81.0	...	81.0	80.5	...	498	406	38.7	123.5	5.06	195.82
1980	79.1	90.0	77.2	...	89.1	85.7	...	466	376	38.1	112.4	5.49	209.17
1981	78.4	90.3	74.7	...	95.4	93.5	...	464	374	38.4	112.7	5.91	226.94
1982	74.6	79.6	70.2	...	100.0	100.0	...	432	342	37.2	100.0	6.31	234.73
1983	80.2	86.8	74.9	...	102.1	103.9	...	448	356	39.4	110.3	6.62	260.83
1984	88.6	92.7	81.4	...	105.3	107.8	...	486	390	39.7	121.6	6.84	271.55
1985	88.9	91.1	79.5	101.9	108.5	111.9	102.0	493	394	39.4	121.9	7.17	282.50
1986	93.3	96.6	81.5	103.9	110.3	115.3	105.2	498	397	39.8	124.2	7.46	296.91
1987	100.9	103.0	86.0	106.4	113.0	118.6	106.7	515	412	40.0	129.5	7.67	306.80
1988	101.1	102.5	84.0	111.4	117.6	124.2	109.6	527	420	39.4	130.1	7.95	313.23
1989	102.4	103.0	83.1	115.6	121.8	129.0	113.7	524	418	39.5	129.6	8.25	325.88
1990	100.9	100.9	80.1	119.1	125.1	133.4	116.5	506	400	39.1	122.8	8.52	333.13
1991	94.8	96.7	74.7	121.6	128.0	136.2	117.7	475	373	38.9	113.9	8.76	340.76
1992	100.0	100.0	78.2	122.9	130.0	138.1	119.2	478	377	39.7	117.6	9.01	357.70
1993	104.9	104.5	80.3	125.4	133.4	140.5	122.4	487	385	40.1	121.3	9.27	371.73
1994	108.1	109.3	80.9	129.7	138.0	144.7	131.0	505	400	40.4	127.0	9.55	385.82
1995	111.4	109.9	81.6	133.3	141.8	148.2	134.6	510	403	39.6	125.6	9.82	388.87
1996	113.1	111.6	78.2	136.2	144.5	151.7	138.9	504	398	39.4	123.4	10.15	399.91
1997	118.0	114.0	78.4	138.2	146.2	154.3	141.4	512	407	40.2	128.6	10.55	424.11
1998	122.0	118.3	78.4	139.7	148.4	155.2	141.6	533	425	40.5	135.3	10.90	441.45
1999	125.5	120.9	78.8	141.3	150.5	156.6	142.6	548	437	40.3	138.4	11.23	452.57
1996													
January	110.7	110.3	78.0	135.2	143.6	150.6	136.8	506	399	36.0	112.9	10.01	359.36
February	110.5	108.8	77.5	135.7	143.8	151.4	137.4	505	398	39.2	122.6	9.95	384.07
March	109.7	108.4	76.7	135.6	144.1	150.9	138.0	503	397	39.4	122.9	10.00	390.00
April	110.8	110.6	77.2	135.8	144.2	151.3	137.1	502	395	39.4	122.3	10.06	389.32
May	114.2	115.1	79.3	135.7	144.4	150.7	137.1	503	397	39.6	123.6	10.08	394.13
June	112.6	112.1	77.9	135.9	144.5	151.1	138.1	503	398	39.7	124.2	10.11	399.35
July	111.7	108.9	77.1	136.2	144.6	151.8	139.6	505	398	39.8	124.5	10.13	398.11
August	116.2	115.2	79.8	136.1	144.5	151.5	140.1	506	400	39.7	124.8	10.19	408.62
September	114.8	113.4	78.7	136.4	144.7	151.8	139.5	505	400	39.8	125.1	10.27	414.91
October	115.6	113.2	78.9	137.1	144.9	153.0	140.4	504	400	39.8	125.1	10.28	413.26
November	115.7	112.7	78.7	137.3	145.2	153.2	141.0	506	400	39.9	125.4	10.28	416.34
December	115.2	110.5	78.2	137.4	145.2	153.4	141.0	507	401	40.2	126.7	10.42	433.47
1997													
January	114.7	109.0	77.6	137.5	145.4	153.6	140.5	507	402	39.6	125.1	10.38	407.93
February	116.0	113.5	78.2	137.6	145.7	153.4	140.3	508	403	39.4	124.8	10.34	402.23
March	116.5	113.1	78.3	137.7	145.9	153.2	141.0	509	403	40.3	127.6	10.43	416.16
April	118.4	115.2	79.3	138.0	146.0	153.9	140.5	509	404	40.2	127.6	10.42	411.59
May	117.6	113.3	78.5	138.2	146.0	154.3	141.7	510	405	40.3	128.3	10.47	416.71
June	117.8	113.2	78.4	138.2	146.1	154.2	141.6	512	407	40.0	127.9	10.51	419.35
July	119.5	115.9	79.3	138.5	146.4	154.7	141.3	514	408	40.0	128.3	10.53	415.94
August	118.1	114.0	78.2	138.3	146.3	154.3	141.5	513	408	40.2	128.9	10.60	429.30
September	118.2	114.6	78.0	138.6	146.6	154.7	142.1	513	408	40.5	129.9	10.70	440.84
October	118.3	114.0	77.8	138.6	146.6	154.6	141.9	516	410	40.3	129.9	10.67	435.34
November	120.1	116.3	78.8	138.9	146.9	155.0	141.8	518	412	40.6	131.5	10.70	440.84
December	120.8	116.4	79.0	138.9	146.8	155.2	142.1	520	414	40.8	132.7	10.79	454.26
1998													
January	120.3	116.0	78.5	139.1	147.4	154.7	140.6	523	417	41.0	134.4	10.75	437.53
February	120.7	118.4	78.5	139.3	147.6	155.2	141.0	526	419	41.0	135.0	10.78	436.59
March	121.9	119.0	79.0	139.4	147.8	155.2	141.1	528	421	40.8	135.0	10.81	436.72
April	122.0	118.4	78.9	139.4	147.9	155.0	141.6	531	424	40.7	135.6	10.86	431.14
May	121.0	117.3	78.0	139.7	148.2	155.6	141.8	533	426	40.7	136.3	10.80	433.08
June	122.1	118.8	78.5	139.6	148.2	155.3	141.9	533	424	40.9	136.3	10.82	441.46
July	122.0	118.0	78.3	139.6	148.4	155.2	142.0	534	424	40.6	135.3	10.91	439.67
August	120.5	117.0	77.1	139.7	148.5	155.2	141.9	535	426	40.6	135.9	10.96	449.36
September	122.6	119.2	78.3	139.7	148.6	155.2	142.1	536	427	40.0	134.2	10.99	436.30
October	124.2	120.2	79.1	140.1	149.2	155.5	142.1	536	426	40.5	135.6	11.00	449.90
November	123.7	118.8	78.6	140.0	149.2	155.4	141.6	538	427	40.3	135.2	11.00	449.90
December	123.3	118.7	78.2	140.2	149.6	155.4	141.8	540	431	40.2	136.2	11.12	461.48
1999													
January	122.7	117.6	77.7	140.5	149.8	155.8	142.0	541	432	40.4	137.2	11.12	445.91
February	124.6	120.7	78.7	140.5	150.0	155.8	142.1	543	432	40.3	136.8	11.07	440.59
March	125.8	119.7	79.3	140.6	150.1	155.9	142.3	544	434	40.3	137.5	11.11	444.40
April	123.8	118.3	78.0	140.7	150.1	155.9	142.5	544	434	40.3	137.5	11.15	447.12
May	124.4	119.3	78.2	140.9	150.1	156.2	142.3	546	435	40.3	137.8	11.14	443.37
June	124.4	119.9	78.1	141.1	150.2	156.7	142.9	547	436	40.4	138.4	11.16	449.75
July	125.7	121.3	78.8	141.3	150.4	156.7	142.8	554	440	40.5	140.1	11.25	452.25
August	126.4	122.0	79.1	141.6	150.5	157.0	142.8	551	439	40.4	139.0	11.28	459.10
September	127.9	124.0	79.9	141.8	150.8	157.1	142.9	551	439	40.4	139.4	11.33	456.60
October	127.0	122.0	79.3	142.0	151.3	157.2	142.9	553	441	40.1	139.0	11.33	458.87
November	125.2	121.5	78.0	142.0	151.2	157.2	142.8	553	440	39.9	138.0	11.36	458.94
December	128.6	124.3	80.1	142.1	151.4	157.2	142.9	552	440	40.2	139.0	11.47	471.42

Table 16-4. Stone, Clay, and Glass Products—Production, Capacity Utilization, Shipments, and Inventories

(Seasonally adjusted.)

| Year and month | Industrial production (1992=100) | | | | | | Capacity utilization (output as a percent of capacity) | Manufacturers' shipments and inventories (millions of dollars) | |
| | Total | Pressed and blown glass | | Cement | Structural clay products | Concrete and miscellaneous | | Shipments | Inventories (book value, end of period) |
		Total	Glass containers						
1970	74.8	81.5	121.3	102.1	110.4	76.2	73.9	16 454	2 239
1971	78.5	83.4	118.6	110.5	113.8	78.6	75.6	18 220	2 302
1972	86.9	88.8	120.3	117.1	120.9	88.4	81.7	20 875	2 430
1973	93.9	95.0	125.3	125.5	128.4	95.4	86.0	23 141	2 712
1974	92.4	95.8	128.0	115.5	123.2	95.6	81.9	25 503	3 403
1975	81.8	90.2	128.2	97.5	104.8	83.7	70.3	26 233	3 594
1976	91.5	97.9	136.6	102.4	113.7	93.3	77.2	29 618	3 841
1977	98.3	102.2	137.5	110.4	123.3	100.9	81.8	34 209	4 095
1978	106.0	108.0	139.1	117.0	131.2	108.9	86.5	40 238	4 710
1979	106.8	110.0	135.7	118.0	130.4	111.2	85.5	44 287	5 183
1980	96.5	109.2	131.4	100.9	111.1	99.2	76.3	44 473	5 674
1981	94.3	111.3	129.0	102.6	102.5	95.0	75.0	46 220	6 106
1982	84.2	101.4	128.6	89.6	81.5	84.0	67.5	43 515	6 506
1983	91.2	101.8	122.1	99.2	96.8	92.1	73.1	47 697	6 628
1984	98.6	102.8	118.3	110.1	111.2	100.6	78.3	53 101	7 042
1985	98.0	97.0	108.8	109.7	105.3	100.8	76.3	55 821	7 040
1986	101.7	100.4	111.4	111.5	111.8	104.4	78.3	59 254	7 093
1987	104.8	99.1	106.9	113.3	113.4	107.9	79.8	61 477	7 154
1988	107.5	101.8	106.9	113.3	115.2	111.3	81.6	63 145	7 496
1989	107.4	103.3	108.2	111.8	118.7	110.2	81.1	63 729	7 792
1990	105.0	102.4	106.8	110.5	114.2	107.0	78.6	63 728	8 205
1991	97.2	96.7	99.2	96.0	100.3	98.3	72.2	59 957	7 928
1992	100.0	100.0	100.0	100.0	100.0	100.0	74.0	62 521	8 006
1993	102.1	98.5	93.1	97.2	101.6	102.5	75.5	65 610	7 607
1994	107.8	102.4	92.6	106.2	112.1	107.7	80.0	71 230	7 874
1995	110.9	102.0	85.5	112.4	114.4	112.3	79.8	75 932	8 567
1996	118.0	104.2	83.9	114.4	118.9	120.1	83.2	82 442	8 898
1997	122.0	106.6	83.4	118.8	120.8	123.8	83.3	90 221	9 050
1998	126.8	109.6	85.4	120.9	119.3	130.1	84.2	96 193	9 331
1999	130.5	110.7	85.0	122.0	121.5	134.3	83.9	103 773	9 888
1996									
January	114.4	103.4	85.5	112.6	106.1	117.0	81.9	6 735	8 572
February	113.6	102.8	83.9	113.2	104.6	115.3	81.1	6 440	8 609
March	115.0	102.7	83.8	112.6	106.4	118.2	82.0	6 625	8 638
April	114.3	104.2	85.1	120.3	110.7	115.4	81.2	6 697	8 604
May	117.2	107.8	92.4	117.5	115.6	118.3	83.0	6 983	8 537
June	119.1	101.8	82.1	115.8	119.9	122.8	84.1	6 954	8 570
July	121.6	106.8	83.6	114.3	123.3	124.6	85.6	6 966	8 545
August	119.1	104.3	84.1	117.0	125.8	120.0	83.6	6 968	8 627
September	121.1	105.3	82.2	112.0	127.4	123.9	84.8	6 912	8 654
October	120.9	103.5	80.9	115.0	128.4	122.9	84.4	7 205	8 740
November	120.2	103.7	82.3	111.7	129.0	122.6	83.7	7 112	8 778
December	118.8	103.8	79.8	109.7	129.4	120.9	82.5	6 770	8 898
1997									
January	121.1	105.1	83.7	114.3	129.4	123.1	83.9	7 193	8 987
February	121.1	106.1	83.4	119.9	128.6	123.0	83.6	7 402	9 019
March	120.2	102.8	79.1	122.4	127.0	121.9	82.7	7 365	9 003
April	121.7	107.0	81.2	119.2	124.8	122.6	83.6	7 476	8 989
May	120.2	104.4	80.9	116.5	122.4	122.3	82.3	7 476	9 049
June	121.3	104.5	82.7	117.4	120.4	123.8	82.9	7 483	9 093
July	122.2	107.2	82.7	118.2	118.6	124.0	83.3	7 683	9 006
August	121.7	104.8	83.0	117.9	117.2	123.7	82.8	7 555	9 009
September	123.0	109.1	85.8	122.5	116.0	124.2	83.4	7 687	9 065
October	122.8	104.9	83.0	120.3	115.1	124.1	83.1	7 670	8 933
November	124.2	108.1	85.8	118.7	114.7	126.6	83.9	7 574	9 042
December	124.8	114.7	92.9	120.3	114.8	125.9	84.1	7 651	9 050
1998									
January	124.2	107.2	84.1	128.3	115.3	126.2	83.5	7 696	9 097
February	124.4	106.4	84.1	120.0	116.3	127.8	83.5	7 789	9 101
March	125.2	107.6	84.6	119.5	117.5	128.0	83.8	7 872	9 131
April	125.5	109.6	84.7	120.9	118.8	127.5	83.8	7 899	9 067
May	125.7	107.4	84.3	120.7	119.9	128.0	83.8	7 982	9 092
June	125.8	109.8	83.7	118.2	120.4	128.1	83.7	8 033	9 110
July	126.8	109.3	85.1	120.4	120.4	130.7	84.2	8 104	9 112
August	127.2	108.4	85.1	117.8	119.9	131.5	84.2	8 014	9 164
September	127.0	110.9	86.2	119.9	119.2	130.8	83.9	8 077	9 237
October	128.4	110.7	86.7	117.5	119.1	133.1	84.6	8 149	9 235
November	130.1	113.1	88.7	125.2	120.6	133.8	85.5	8 236	9 320
December	131.8	115.3	88.2	131.9	123.9	135.3	86.4	8 317	9 331
1999									
January	133.2	113.0	87.6	130.9	127.0	137.3	87.0	8 220	9 381
February	132.2	113.1	86.2	134.1	127.2	135.4	86.2	8 456	9 263
March	130.8	113.3	87.9	124.1	123.3	133.6	85.0	8 494	9 258
April	128.8	110.9	84.9	122.0	117.4	132.3	83.5	8 376	9 237
May	128.5	108.9	84.7	120.1	113.4	133.0	83.0	8 431	9 388
June	127.8	110.3	84.7	117.9	113.8	131.2	82.3	8 579	9 395
July	129.3	110.1	84.2	114.8	116.9	133.9	83.1	8 578	9 473
August	130.2	110.3	85.0	118.8	119.9	134.3	83.4	8 859	9 726
September	129.6	109.4	82.2	114.0	120.4	134.5	82.7	8 867	9 724
October	131.2	106.9	81.7	119.3	124.3	136.3	83.5	8 873	9 854
November	132.4	111.4	87.7	134.6	126.5	134.3	84.0	9 003	9 824
December	131.4	108.5	83.8	129.7	127.0	134.3	83.2	8 900	9 888

Table 16-5. Stone, Clay, and Glass Products—Prices, Employment, Hours, and Earnings

Year and month	Producer prices (1982=100, except as noted; not seasonally adjusted)						Employment (thousands, seasonally adjusted)		Production workers			
	Stone, clay, and glass products industry (Dec. 1984 =100)	Intermediate materials				Crude materials: Construc-tion sand, gravel, and crushed stone	Total payroll employees	Production workers	Average weekly hours, seasonally adjusted	Aggregate weekly hours index (1982=100), seasonally adjusted	Average earnings (dollars, not seasonally adjusted)	
		Flat glass	Cement	Concrete products	Glass containers						Hourly	Weekly
1970	. . .	52.2	. . .	37.7	33.9	40.9	610	485	41.2	120.9	3.40	140.08
1971	. . .	55.6	36.8	40.5	37.0	42.8	611	486	41.6	122.2	3.67	152.67
1972	. . .	55.3	. . .	42.2	38.0	43.7	645	516	42.0	131.1	3.94	165.48
1973	. . .	54.8	. . .	44.2	39.1	44.9	680	546	41.9	138.4	4.22	176.82
1974	. . .	58.2	. . .	50.9	43.7	48.6	673	539	41.3	134.5	4.54	187.50
1975	. . .	62.8	57.1	57.3	50.5	54.3	598	473	40.4	115.6	4.92	198.77
1976	. . .	67.7	62.9	60.5	55.0	57.9	613	486	41.1	120.8	5.33	219.06
1977	. . .	72.6	67.6	64.4	60.2	61.3	636	505	41.3	125.9	5.81	239.95
1978	. . .	78.0	74.3	71.9	68.7	66.7	664	525	41.6	132.1	6.32	262.91
1979	. . .	83.0	83.7	82.0	73.4	74.4	674	529	41.5	132.8	6.85	284.28
1980	. . .	88.7	91.9	92.0	82.3	85.3	629	486	40.8	119.8	7.50	306.00
1981	. . .	96.0	97.4	97.8	92.5	94.0	606	465	40.6	114.1	8.27	335.76
1982	. . .	100.0	100.0	100.0	100.0	100.0	548	413	40.1	100.0	8.87	355.69
1983	. . .	103.7	100.4	101.4	99.1	101.7	541	412	41.5	103.2	9.27	384.71
1984	. . .	101.4	104.0	103.9	101.4	106.0	562	431	42.0	109.5	9.57	401.94
1985	102.1	101.7	106.1	107.5	106.8	110.7	557	427	41.9	108.1	9.84	412.30
1986	103.8	104.5	104.2	109.2	111.9	114.2	554	426	42.2	108.7	10.04	423.69
1987	104.5	107.2	101.9	109.4	113.0	118.1	554	429	42.3	109.7	10.25	433.58
1988	105.8	109.7	102.2	110.0	112.3	120.6	567	443	42.3	113.3	10.56	446.69
1989	107.9	109.7	102.1	111.2	115.2	122.8	568	444	42.3	113.5	10.82	457.69
1990	110.0	107.5	103.7	113.5	120.4	125.4	556	432	42.0	109.7	11.12	467.04
1991	112.3	105.9	106.8	116.6	125.4	128.6	522	403	41.7	101.4	11.36	473.71
1992	112.8	106.5	106.3	117.2	125.1	130.6	513	396	42.2	101.2	11.60	489.52
1993	115.4	107.3	111.7	120.2	125.8	134.0	517	399	42.7	102.9	11.85	506.00
1994	119.6	110.5	119.5	124.6	127.5	137.9	532	411	43.4	107.9	12.13	526.44
1995	124.3	113.2	128.1	129.4	130.5	142.3	540	418	43.0	108.8	12.41	533.63
1996	125.8	110.0	134.0	133.2	129.1	145.6	544	423	43.3	110.8	12.82	555.11
1997	127.4	108.4	139.4	136.0	125.7	148.2	552	431	43.2	112.4	13.18	569.38
1998	129.3	107.1	145.7	140.0	125.9	152.8	562	438	43.5	115.4	13.59	591.17
1999	132.6	106.4	150.6	143.7	125.9	157.2	563	440	43.5	115.6	13.87	603.35
1996												
January	125.1	112.0	129.3	131.5	130.2	144.5	534	414	42.1	105.4	12.60	515.34
February	125.3	111.9	130.1	132.0	130.2	144.4	539	418	43.6	110.2	12.56	532.54
March	125.3	110.8	130.1	132.4	129.2	144.9	540	419	43.5	110.2	12.60	538.02
April	125.4	110.0	133.3	132.8	129.7	145.5	540	420	43.5	110.4	12.77	551.66
May	125.5	109.4	134.8	133.0	129.6	145.6	542	422	43.3	110.5	12.74	555.46
June	125.5	109.3	135.0	133.2	129.6	145.5	543	423	43.6	111.5	12.82	565.36
July	125.8	109.5	135.0	133.6	129.6	145.9	543	423	43.3	110.7	12.94	562.89
August	125.9	109.4	135.3	133.5	129.6	145.6	546	425	43.4	111.5	12.92	568.48
September	126.3	109.2	136.3	133.8	129.3	146.1	547	427	43.4	112.0	12.99	575.46
October	126.2	109.2	136.4	133.8	127.4	146.1	549	428	43.4	112.3	12.91	568.04
November	126.6	109.6	136.4	134.5	127.4	146.3	549	428	43.2	111.8	12.96	563.76
December	126.5	109.9	135.9	134.7	127.4	146.3	551	428	43.0	111.3	12.93	558.58
1997												
January	126.8	108.8	136.4	135.0	126.0	147.2	551	429	42.2	109.4	12.99	531.29
February	126.9	108.7	136.7	135.2	126.0	147.0	551	429	43.1	111.8	13.04	547.68
March	127.1	108.2	136.4	135.4	125.9	147.4	551	430	43.3	112.6	13.02	553.35
April	127.5	108.3	139.2	135.9	125.9	148.0	551	429	43.3	112.3	13.06	560.27
May	127.6	108.2	139.6	136.1	125.5	148.4	551	430	43.4	112.8	13.12	573.34
June	127.4	108.1	140.3	135.8	125.5	148.6	551	429	43.1	111.8	13.13	572.47
July	127.4	108.1	140.4	136.2	125.5	148.7	553	432	43.2	112.8	13.20	571.56
August	127.5	108.5	140.9	136.1	125.5	148.6	553	432	43.1	112.6	13.21	578.60
September	127.5	108.2	140.6	136.1	125.7	148.6	554	432	43.3	113.1	13.27	586.53
October	127.8	108.4	140.9	136.5	125.7	148.7	555	434	43.1	113.1	13.32	584.75
November	127.8	108.5	140.6	136.7	125.9	148.7	554	434	42.8	112.3	13.36	575.82
December	127.7	108.5	140.7	136.5	125.9	149.0	555	433	43.5	113.9	13.39	585.14
1998												
January	127.6	108.0	140.6	136.9	125.9	150.2	562	440	43.6	116.0	13.38	565.97
February	127.8	107.3	141.0	137.4	125.9	150.8	561	438	43.7	115.7	13.45	572.97
March	127.9	107.0	141.2	137.6	125.9	151.2	559	436	43.4	114.4	13.46	573.40
April	128.7	106.8	145.4	139.5	125.9	152.4	560	437	43.3	114.4	13.62	584.30
May	129.0	107.4	145.7	139.9	125.9	152.8	559	437	43.5	114.9	13.58	597.52
June	129.4	107.2	146.9	140.7	125.5	153.3	562	437	43.4	114.7	13.58	596.16
July	129.9	107.9	147.6	141.3	125.5	153.6	560	436	43.5	114.7	13.58	594.80
August	130.1	106.7	147.8	141.3	126.2	153.6	563	439	43.6	115.7	13.61	601.56
September	130.2	106.7	147.9	141.4	126.0	153.6	563	440	43.4	115.4	13.80	607.20
October	130.4	106.9	147.8	141.3	126.0	153.7	563	440	43.4	115.4	13.66	603.77
November	130.3	106.9	148.0	141.4	126.0	153.7	564	441	43.4	115.7	13.64	597.43
December	130.2	106.8	148.0	141.4	126.0	154.2	566	442	43.7	116.8	13.68	600.55
1999												
January	130.7	104.9	148.9	142.2	125.9	155.3	564	441	43.8	116.8	13.64	579.70
February	131.5	107.4	149.0	142.6	125.9	155.8	566	442	43.4	116.0	13.61	575.70
March	131.7	105.8	149.4	142.8	125.9	156.0	563	440	43.1	114.6	13.68	577.30
April	132.1	105.7	150.6	143.5	126.0	156.5	564	441	43.4	115.7	13.73	594.51
May	132.5	106.0	151.4	144.1	126.0	156.6	563	441	43.4	115.7	13.84	607.58
June	132.7	106.3	151.4	143.9	126.3	157.2	562	440	43.5	115.7	13.91	612.04
July	132.7	106.9	151.2	143.8	126.1	157.6	563	440	43.5	115.7	13.97	611.89
August	133.1	107.1	151.3	143.8	125.9	157.8	563	439	43.5	115.4	13.94	614.75
September	133.2	106.7	151.3	144.2	125.7	158.2	563	439	43.5	115.4	14.10	620.40
October	133.6	107.3	150.9	144.4	125.7	158.3	562	438	43.5	115.2	14.00	616.00
November	133.7	106.4	150.9	144.5	125.7	158.7	564	440	43.8	116.5	14.04	620.57
December	133.5	106.5	150.4	144.3	125.7	158.7	565	441	43.5	116.0	13.97	604.90

Table 16-6. Primary Metals—Production

(Seasonally adjusted.)

Year and month	Total	Industrial production (1992=100)											
		Iron and steel											Iron and steel foundries
		Total	Basic steel and mill products										
			Total	Basic iron and steel			Steel mill products						
				Total	Pig iron	Raw steel	Total	Consumer durable steel	Equipment steel	Construction steel	Can and closure steel	Miscellaneous steel	
1970	111.2	139.0	132.6	170.3	178.2	139.2	112.6	130.7	189.3	167.2	186.3	67.5	167.5
1971	104.9	126.3	118.0	152.5	156.9	127.1	99.8	141.5	182.9	137.8	166.2	54.9	164.0
1972	118.3	141.5	133.0	169.5	172.8	143.9	113.4	164.1	206.0	148.4	164.9	64.8	180.7
1973	134.1	161.0	152.2	191.3	196.0	164.3	131.0	196.0	229.2	174.8	182.8	74.7	201.6
1974	129.7	155.7	148.7	185.8	185.4	163.1	128.6	160.8	234.3	181.0	194.3	77.1	187.8
1975	103.4	125.1	119.4	153.0	154.8	128.6	101.4	134.6	205.1	135.2	160.1	55.8	151.9
1976	115.7	137.9	131.2	164.9	166.9	140.9	112.9	186.5	231.0	123.5	171.1	57.7	168.5
1977	119.0	138.0	126.3	158.8	157.1	139.3	108.7	178.6	233.9	117.0	159.1	54.9	180.3
1978	128.0	147.5	137.5	168.6	170.0	154.9	120.6	184.3	265.0	134.3	159.3	64.9	182.4
1979	130.0	148.4	138.4	170.7	168.3	154.4	120.8	159.5	268.9	140.5	156.9	70.3	182.4
1980	108.0	119.0	112.8	139.2	133.5	126.9	98.5	105.9	236.7	119.4	128.3	60.8	138.5
1981	113.9	126.6	121.4	145.7	142.0	138.5	108.6	120.4	252.6	125.8	124.3	70.0	142.0
1982	80.5	80.5	75.9	88.2	83.6	82.6	69.8	81.8	132.9	84.6	108.8	47.0	94.8
1983	88.2	90.0	85.5	95.1	94.3	94.1	81.5	109.7	118.4	91.4	113.9	61.9	104.7
1984	98.7	98.9	92.8	104.0	99.6	102.6	88.1	113.2	132.3	90.1	106.6	70.3	118.9
1985	98.4	98.8	95.0	99.7	96.8	97.7	93.3	124.5	121.1	99.9	104.9	77.1	110.7
1986	91.2	86.8	87.5	88.8	85.0	89.7	87.2	108.6	102.6	93.5	102.9	76.3	85.8
1987	97.8	95.4	93.5	97.7	93.6	98.8	92.3	102.1	106.9	91.9	107.0	86.0	102.5
1988	106.2	107.6	106.4	111.0	107.9	111.2	105.0	115.5	126.0	96.3	113.8	99.3	111.9
1989	104.9	106.2	104.9	109.5	108.0	107.2	103.5	107.3	117.2	102.3	112.6	99.5	110.9
1990	104.0	106.4	106.5	108.5	106.3	108.3	106.0	100.0	123.9	108.0	114.3	103.2	106.0
1991	96.7	96.0	95.7	95.7	93.8	96.2	95.7	87.9	97.9	93.7	109.9	96.6	96.9
1992	100.0	100.0	100.0	100.0	100.0	100.0	100.0	100.0	100.0	100.0	100.0	100.0	100.0
1993	105.1	106.1	106.0	101.5	101.5	103.0	107.3	113.1	106.9	111.5	106.6	105.2	106.3
1994	113.8	114.4	114.2	104.6	104.7	107.5	117.0	132.2	113.4	126.3	110.2	112.5	115.4
1995	116.2	116.5	115.9	107.7	107.4	112.0	118.3	123.0	118.0	127.1	99.1	117.0	118.8
1996	119.6	118.9	118.4	105.8	104.7	111.9	122.1	130.9	125.2	136.3	105.3	118.0	120.4
1997	126.7	125.6	123.8	106.9	105.7	115.5	128.8	132.1	128.6	148.8	108.1	125.9	131.4
1998	125.6	122.6	119.8	103.9	102.6	115.3	124.5	128.7	116.0	151.7	98.1	122.1	131.5
1999	126.6	123.2	122.0	100.9	98.7	113.3	128.2	140.6	102.8	154.5	100.6	127.1	127.5
1996													
January	115.3	116.4	116.2	107.6	107.8	111.4	118.7	122.8	123.0	141.1	91.7	115.0	117.1
February	116.2	114.6	113.5	105.9	105.7	110.3	115.7	117.0	117.6	127.9	98.7	114.3	118.4
March	118.1	117.0	117.4	106.8	106.5	111.7	120.5	118.6	124.7	134.7	104.7	119.0	115.8
April	117.6	115.9	116.1	105.1	104.0	110.7	119.4	129.2	123.2	130.3	100.1	115.8	115.1
May	118.6	117.0	117.4	104.8	102.9	111.4	121.2	131.4	123.9	130.3	101.3	118.0	115.5
June	119.8	119.4	121.8	108.5	107.8	114.4	125.7	136.3	128.2	140.3	102.2	121.9	111.5
July	118.2	118.2	120.0	106.9	105.8	113.1	123.9	145.1	128.8	135.4	117.0	116.1	112.2
August	121.3	120.8	120.3	106.5	105.1	113.0	124.3	138.9	134.0	138.6	114.6	117.1	122.7
September	122.1	119.6	119.3	105.3	103.7	112.3	123.4	137.8	130.1	135.2	107.7	117.7	120.4
October	123.2	123.6	121.4	105.0	103.2	112.6	126.3	135.9	131.0	139.1	113.5	121.8	130.8
November	122.4	122.4	118.9	102.9	100.9	110.2	123.6	133.2	123.9	143.5	109.0	118.9	133.7
December	122.9	121.6	118.8	104.7	102.4	113.3	123.0	132.5	114.5	138.9	103.7	120.9	130.9
1997													
January	121.1	121.6	119.1	103.7	101.3	111.9	123.6	133.4	121.2	140.6	111.2	119.7	129.9
February	123.6	122.0	120.4	105.6	104.4	112.2	124.8	132.2	127.9	141.4	109.8	120.8	127.0
March	122.2	118.6	116.6	105.7	104.0	113.7	119.8	127.7	120.8	141.4	100.0	115.4	125.3
April	125.2	125.3	123.2	105.8	104.4	114.0	128.4	130.1	129.8	149.3	113.0	125.3	132.0
May	126.1	124.6	122.6	106.3	105.6	113.7	127.4	129.6	131.2	150.1	109.5	123.6	131.4
June	128.0	126.5	124.0	106.1	105.1	114.5	129.2	129.4	135.5	149.5	111.0	126.0	134.7
July	127.4	125.7	123.7	105.1	103.3	115.0	129.1	132.8	127.9	148.6	102.0	127.2	132.2
August	127.3	123.8	122.1	105.5	103.6	115.1	127.0	124.9	124.5	147.3	105.9	126.1	129.6
September	128.9	128.8	127.5	109.0	108.0	118.1	132.9	136.1	131.3	151.9	111.7	130.8	133.1
October	129.6	129.3	128.2	109.2	108.0	118.6	133.8	140.0	129.2	156.2	113.4	130.7	132.8
November	131.5	131.1	130.0	111.1	110.2	121.5	135.6	135.2	131.7	156.5	104.2	135.1	134.5
December	129.6	129.5	128.2	110.1	110.1	120.1	133.5	136.7	133.2	151.7	108.2	131.4	133.9
1998													
January	130.7	130.5	127.8	111.0	111.5	122.6	132.7	127.8	131.0	155.9	108.3	131.9	139.6
February	130.6	130.8	130.4	109.4	108.8	123.3	136.5	135.1	131.8	160.1	104.5	135.8	132.4
March	128.9	129.1	127.5	107.9	108.0	119.1	133.3	137.0	130.3	156.7	104.3	130.6	134.6
April	128.9	127.4	125.1	108.5	107.4	121.3	130.0	132.5	126.8	154.3	101.3	127.4	134.9
May	128.3	127.0	124.9	107.7	106.1	120.0	129.9	131.6	123.7	156.6	98.7	127.8	134.0
June	123.5	121.4	118.4	104.1	102.0	115.6	122.7	114.6	116.3	149.0	101.0	122.5	131.3
July	123.8	121.6	119.3	105.0	103.4	116.7	123.6	111.2	114.2	161.8	100.3	123.0	129.4
August	124.9	122.3	120.4	106.5	105.2	119.3	124.6	129.0	113.1	152.7	96.7	122.2	128.6
September	122.2	115.7	111.3	100.1	97.8	112.2	114.6	124.5	106.3	141.8	94.5	109.9	129.8
October	122.5	116.2	112.4	99.4	97.6	110.0	116.2	133.3	103.3	144.8	94.6	110.2	128.6
November	120.5	112.1	108.4	92.6	89.8	101.6	113.0	128.8	92.2	140.7	97.7	108.5	124.2
December	122.5	116.5	112.2	94.9	93.5	102.7	117.3	138.5	100.5	146.9	79.2	112.0	130.4
1999													
January	122.9	118.1	114.7	95.8	93.2	106.0	120.3	134.8	101.7	156.9	109.7	113.8	128.9
February	120.1	114.6	111.2	95.8	93.4	106.8	115.8	135.7	94.5	139.7	102.3	110.9	125.4
March	124.0	118.1	116.1	96.8	94.3	108.3	121.7	140.2	99.3	143.2	104.1	118.2	124.9
April	123.9	119.4	116.8	98.8	96.9	109.3	122.1	136.8	97.5	147.7	103.4	119.3	128.1
May	123.9	120.1	118.6	99.7	97.3	111.4	124.1	138.6	98.5	148.6	101.9	122.0	125.5
June	127.4	124.5	122.4	99.0	96.2	110.7	129.3	145.4	99.5	155.0	103.3	127.6	131.7
July	128.0	126.2	124.5	100.1	98.4	111.1	131.7	143.8	104.8	160.2	99.4	130.4	132.2
August	129.6	127.6	128.3	102.6	100.1	115.9	135.8	150.0	109.1	161.9	102.2	134.5	126.6
September	128.3	125.9	126.3	100.1	97.6	112.4	134.1	146.8	110.3	156.4	100.2	133.3	125.4
October	129.0	124.9	124.9	107.5	105.9	121.8	130.0	133.8	105.4	154.8	90.9	131.7	125.6
November	131.1	130.7	132.4	107.1	104.2	124.0	139.8	141.7	107.8	157.2	106.3	144.2	126.6
December	132.8	131.7	132.8	108.9	107.3	124.2	139.8	146.7	106.4	172.7	86.5	141.8	129.6

Table 16-7. Primary Metals—Production and Capacity Utilization

(Seasonally adjusted.)

Year and month	Industrial production (1992=100)—Continued								Capacity utilization (output as a percent of capacity)					
	Nonferrous metals									Iron and steel		Nonferrous metals		
	Total	Primary nonferrous metals			Nonferrous products			Nonferrous foundries	Total	Total	Raw steel	Total	Primary copper	Primary aluminum
		Total	Copper	Aluminum	Total	Nonferrous mill products								
						Total	Aluminum							
1970	75.9	107.2	108.7	89.5	77.5	79.3	67.0	76.3	80.8	84.9	83.4	74.3	88.4	97.4
1971	76.6	101.4	93.2	88.3	78.9	82.4	74.5	72.5	74.8	76.6	76.0	71.7	74.9	88.1
1972	87.0	107.8	107.4	92.5	90.7	93.9	84.9	86.0	83.7	86.2	85.6	79.2	85.1	87.4
1973	98.1	113.6	107.4	101.9	105.2	108.8	106.4	100.1	94.5	98.0	97.1	88.1	85.0	94.0
1974	94.8	112.9	92.9	110.3	101.1	105.5	111.8	93.8	90.7	94.7	96.0	83.7	73.0	100.2
1975	74.3	93.9	82.2	87.3	76.2	79.4	78.9	70.8	71.7	75.9	75.2	64.1	61.9	78.4
1976	85.7	103.1	93.2	95.4	89.9	94.3	92.6	81.6	79.0	82.4	80.7	72.9	67.9	83.1
1977	93.0	101.9	85.5	102.2	98.7	104.8	102.1	86.0	80.1	80.7	78.6	79.4	63.2	87.4
1978	101.1	108.2	91.2	108.2	108.4	115.4	116.3	93.9	86.6	86.5	87.6	86.9	67.9	92.3
1979	104.6	116.1	98.0	113.1	110.0	116.2	118.5	97.3	88.4	88.6	88.3	88.0	71.8	95.7
1980	92.4	106.4	75.9	115.2	95.5	104.8	107.3	74.4	73.5	71.6	73.4	76.9	56.7	95.0
1981	96.1	107.5	91.1	111.4	100.0	110.0	110.3	77.5	77.6	76.4	80.5	79.1	72.0	90.3
1982	80.7	84.4	66.1	81.2	85.3	93.6	86.2	66.8	54.5	48.9	48.3	65.6	54.0	65.9
1983	85.9	86.9	68.6	83.2	92.9	100.7	98.8	75.6	61.7	56.9	57.4	69.6	56.8	67.4
1984	98.6	95.5	77.6	101.5	107.5	109.4	101.1	103.1	71.9	66.5	66.4	81.0	66.9	83.6
1985	98.2	92.2	79.7	86.9	107.4	106.6	97.0	110.0	73.2	68.9	65.8	80.3	71.9	74.9
1986	97.6	80.4	79.4	75.4	108.2	107.1	103.0	111.9	70.1	64.1	63.9	80.3	74.4	71.9
1987	101.2	83.8	80.1	83.0	111.3	112.1	110.6	109.2	79.2	76.2	77.7	84.1	77.2	84.1
1988	104.6	97.3	80.0	97.6	109.2	107.5	107.7	115.0	87.4	87.4	88.9	87.5	78.4	97.4
1989	103.2	98.7	79.0	100.0	106.0	104.1	106.2	112.5	85.2	84.7	84.1	85.9	76.3	98.6
1990	100.9	96.4	81.6	100.4	102.7	102.1	104.0	104.7	83.4	83.6	84.5	83.1	77.8	98.3
1991	97.7	103.2	88.3	102.2	97.4	97.2	102.0	98.0	77.6	75.7	75.8	80.1	81.3	99.6
1992	100.0	100.0	100.0	100.0	100.0	100.0	100.0	100.0	80.7	80.5	80.8	81.2	85.7	97.0
1993	104.0	101.8	116.7	91.7	104.9	104.2	98.7	107.2	85.7	87.6	87.7	83.4	93.6	88.8
1994	113.0	97.6	111.7	81.8	115.4	113.1	106.8	122.9	90.6	91.8	90.8	89.1	87.7	79.1
1995	115.7	101.8	121.9	83.7	116.4	111.6	103.1	132.2	90.5	92.7	94.1	87.9	95.4	80.7
1996	120.5	100.4	103.5	88.5	123.5	118.6	103.3	139.5	89.4	90.2	90.3	88.5	82.7	85.1
1997	128.1	104.8	111.0	89.4	131.3	124.7	114.5	153.4	90.5	91.2	89.1	89.7	90.5	85.8
1998	129.4	105.9	107.2	92.1	131.3	124.4	114.2	154.1	86.9	85.2	83.4	89.1	86.9	88.4
1999	130.9	104.3	96.4	93.7	133.5	126.5	121.3	156.6	85.1	82.0	79.5	89.1	79.5	90.0
1996														
January	113.8	104.3	114.3	87.7	114.1	107.7	87.8	135.8	88.4	90.5	90.8	86.0	88.9	84.4
February	118.1	102.3	110.5	88.2	120.6	115.6	98.5	137.4	88.8	88.8	89.7	88.9	86.3	84.9
March	119.3	100.3	106.1	88.3	122.4	118.7	106.4	134.8	89.8	90.2	90.7	89.3	83.2	85.0
April	119.6	100.9	106.7	88.7	122.2	118.1	103.3	136.0	89.0	89.0	89.7	89.0	84.2	85.3
May	120.6	99.6	104.1	88.5	124.3	120.2	103.8	137.8	89.3	89.4	90.1	89.3	82.6	85.1
June	120.2	98.8	103.0	88.3	123.5	118.6	102.0	139.7	89.7	90.8	92.3	88.5	82.2	84.9
July	118.1	100.9	102.5	88.0	120.6	116.1	96.9	135.6	88.1	89.5	91.1	86.5	82.2	84.6
August	121.9	97.6	96.2	88.8	125.7	121.0	107.8	141.1	89.9	91.1	90.8	88.7	77.5	85.3
September	125.2	99.8	98.8	88.8	129.2	125.1	110.6	142.6	90.1	89.7	90.0	90.6	80.0	85.3
October	122.5	99.8	102.2	89.0	125.4	120.0	105.6	143.2	90.4	92.4	90.0	88.2	83.1	85.4
November	122.3	100.5	96.2	89.1	125.1	119.2	105.8	144.4	89.4	91.0	87.8	87.7	78.5	85.5
December	124.5	100.4	101.7	88.9	128.8	123.3	111.5	146.5	89.5	90.1	90.0	88.8	83.2	85.4
1997														
January	120.4	102.8	105.4	89.1	123.5	116.6	99.3	145.9	87.8	89.8	88.5	85.5	86.4	85.5
February	125.5	103.4	104.2	89.4	129.2	123.2	112.0	148.7	89.3	89.8	88.4	88.8	85.4	85.8
March	126.5	104.4	107.8	89.5	130.1	124.2	117.2	149.4	88.0	87.0	89.2	89.3	88.4	85.9
April	125.1	104.1	107.4	89.1	127.6	120.0	107.4	152.5	90.0	91.6	89.0	88.0	88.0	85.5
May	127.9	103.0	100.5	88.9	130.8	123.9	116.5	153.3	90.4	90.9	88.4	89.8	82.3	85.3
June	129.8	106.2	110.5	89.3	132.7	126.4	119.7	153.1	91.5	92.0	88.5	90.9	90.3	85.6
July	129.5	105.3	115.0	89.1	132.5	127.0	118.1	150.4	90.8	91.2	88.4	90.5	93.8	85.5
August	131.6	106.4	113.0	89.1	135.4	128.9	121.0	156.8	90.6	89.6	88.1	91.8	92.0	85.5
September	128.9	102.4	118.0	89.1	133.2	126.1	117.1	156.6	91.5	92.9	89.8	89.8	95.9	85.5
October	130.0	106.9	118.3	89.9	133.3	126.0	114.3	157.2	91.8	92.9	89.7	90.4	96.0	86.2
November	131.9	106.7	114.5	89.9	135.7	129.1	121.5	157.5	92.9	93.9	91.3	91.7	92.7	86.3
December	129.6	106.1	117.5	90.3	132.3	124.4	109.6	158.4	91.3	92.5	89.8	90.0	95.1	86.6
1998														
January	130.8	105.5	110.0	90.3	133.7	126.3	112.3	158.4	91.9	92.8	91.1	90.7	88.9	86.7
February	130.2	104.9	110.9	90.4	132.7	125.2	113.2	157.6	91.5	92.7	91.1	90.2	89.6	86.8
March	128.5	104.8	106.6	90.9	130.2	122.4	105.9	156.4	90.1	91.1	87.5	88.8	86.1	87.3
April	130.8	106.7	108.9	91.9	133.2	126.8	115.4	154.8	89.8	89.4	88.6	90.3	88.0	88.2
May	129.9	105.5	104.8	92.2	131.9	125.4	114.2	154.2	89.1	88.8	87.1	89.6	84.7	88.5
June	126.0	102.6	105.8	92.5	127.5	121.5	109.4	147.8	85.5	84.5	83.5	86.8	85.5	88.7
July	126.5	108.7	106.1	93.1	126.6	121.6	115.2	143.8	85.5	84.3	83.9	87.0	85.9	89.3
August	128.2	107.0	110.2	93.1	129.4	121.7	109.4	155.2	86.0	84.3	85.4	88.1	89.3	89.4
September	130.3	105.8	103.6	93.8	132.4	125.4	114.6	156.2	83.9	79.4	80.0	89.4	84.1	90.1
October	130.4	106.7	108.6	92.0	132.9	125.6	119.7	157.8	83.9	79.4	78.1	89.4	88.3	88.3
November	130.9	105.8	109.8	92.7	133.4	126.3	120.3	157.3	82.2	76.3	71.9	89.6	89.4	88.9
December	130.0	106.3	101.5	92.4	132.4	125.1	121.0	157.3	83.4	79.0	72.5	88.9	82.7	88.7
1999														
January	128.9	103.3	98.6	92.2	131.2	123.9	119.4	156.0	83.5	79.8	75.2	88.1	80.6	88.5
February	127.0	105.1	106.4	92.6	127.8	119.6	111.3	155.7	81.4	77.1	75.1	86.7	87.1	88.9
March	131.4	107.3	111.4	93.0	133.6	127.3	122.4	155.1	83.8	79.2	76.0	89.6	91.3	89.2
April	129.4	106.5	111.7	93.1	131.1	123.3	117.0	157.6	83.6	79.9	76.7	88.2	91.7	89.3
May	128.6	103.9	98.3	93.2	131.0	123.0	115.5	158.1	83.5	80.1	78.0	87.6	80.9	89.4
June	130.8	103.1	93.0	93.3	133.4	125.9	122.0	158.8	85.6	82.8	77.4	89.1	76.7	89.6
July	130.2	102.1	87.7	93.2	132.8	125.3	118.0	158.2	85.9	83.7	77.7	88.6	72.5	89.5
August	132.1	103.6	90.3	94.7	135.5	129.3	125.6	156.7	86.8	84.4	81.0	89.3	74.7	90.9
September	131.4	102.9	86.9	94.2	134.8	128.6	122.0	155.9	85.8	83.0	78.5	89.3	72.1	90.4
October	134.0	105.4	92.3	94.4	137.3	131.8	130.9	156.7	86.1	82.1	85.0	91.1	76.7	90.6
November	131.7	105.0	90.9	95.3	134.8	128.9	123.1	155.1	87.4	85.7	86.5	89.4	75.7	91.5
December	134.1	104.0	88.5	95.5	137.8	132.5	128.4	156.4	88.3	86.1	86.6	91.0	73.8	91.7

Table 16-8. Primary Metals—Shipments, Inventories, and Orders

(Seasonally adjusted.)

Year and month	Manufacturers' shipments, inventories, and orders (millions of dollars)									
	Shipments		Inventories (book value, end of period)		New orders, net			Unfilled orders, end of period		
	Total	Blast furnaces, steel mills	Total	Blast furnaces, steel mills	Total [1]	Blast furnaces, steel mills	Nonferrous and other primary metals	Total [1]	Blast furnaces, steel mills	Nonferrous and other primary metals
1970	51 995	25 189	8 995	4 990	51 793	25 521	21 883	7 796	4 617	2 663
1971	51 585	25 791	9 084	4 926	51 284	25 571	20 704	7 478	4 380	2 552
1972	58 490	28 712	9 617	5 387	61 447	30 996	24 607	10 470	6 681	3 116
1973	72 791	36 301	10 034	5 302	78 395	39 413	31 417	16 129	9 794	4 962
1974	95 686	49 718	13 447	6 820	98 831	51 047	38 394	19 225	11 054	5 952
1975	80 890	42 281	15 742	8 597	75 034	38 611	27 864	13 266	7 345	4 015
1976	93 082	46 764	17 699	10 035	94 491	47 212	37 378	14 684	7 776	4 891
1977	103 267	50 670	18 261	10 004	105 689	52 103	42 400	17 298	9 435	5 483
1978	118 175	59 228	19 420	10 719	124 741	62 648	48 319	23 969	12 932	7 393
1979	137 488	67 414	22 446	12 012	139 783	66 968	58 420	26 320	12 485	9 457
1980	134 057	61 612	23 055	12 153	134 416	62 473	60 399	26 815	13 418	10 096
1981	142 072	70 254	25 794	13 359	137 286	67 457	57 545	22 024	10 589	8 784
1982	104 874	46 928	24 174	12 556	98 445	43 013	46 942	15 500	6 574	7 418
1983	109 240	46 398	22 308	11 065	113 884	49 123	55 566	20 400	9 431	9 594
1984	120 315	51 978	22 444	11 087	118 354	50 719	56 030	18 362	8 103	8 694
1985	112 265	48 904	19 974	9 709	112 276	49 079	52 275	18 331	8 248	8 361
1986	107 865	45 718	18 436	8 567	108 218	46 408	51 294	18 590	8 897	7 783
1987	120 248	51 815	19 076	8 620	125 989	54 763	60 302	24 340	11 828	10 300
1988	149 837	64 294	22 422	10 495	152 578	64 002	75 997	27 079	11 508	12 974
1989	155 718	64 783	22 838	10 942	152 814	62 752	77 249	24 120	9 479	11 824
1990	148 787	62 826	22 560	11 045	149 338	63 369	72 944	24 768	10 120	11 258
1991	136 378	57 267	20 703	10 236	134 657	56 366	66 778	23 075	9 290	10 609
1992	138 287	58 449	19 981	9 809	136 849	58 002	67 337	21 636	8 897	9 925
1993	142 685	62 466	20 132	9 836	144 018	63 604	67 112	23 068	10 163	9 623
1994	161 188	69 887	22 588	10 697	167 685	70 960	81 963	29 661	11 303	14 535
1995	180 314	74 927	24 021	11 560	178 702	75 811	87 857	27 993	12 183	12 195
1996	178 395	74 588	24 289	11 912	180 398	74 837	88 849	29 996	12 432	13 167
1997	188 985	77 048	24 680	11 727	194 149	79 521	96 580	35 160	14 905	14 656
1998	181 034	72 754	24 679	12 057	175 428	69 279	88 203	29 554	11 430	12 666
1999	178 402	68 701	24 255	11 507	180 760	70 355	92 776	31 912	13 084	14 089
1996										
January	14 600	6 106	24 084	11 671	14 703	6 206	7 087	28 096	12 283	12 051
February	14 518	6 083	24 022	11 620	14 886	6 073	7 338	28 464	12 273	12 216
March	14 661	6 031	24 192	11 827	14 245	5 842	7 143	28 048	12 084	12 001
April	14 853	6 187	24 043	11 637	15 059	6 154	7 535	28 254	12 051	12 199
May	15 104	6 216	23 975	11 498	15 539	6 607	7 587	28 689	12 442	12 264
June	14 538	6 194	24 071	11 529	15 347	6 392	7 410	29 498	12 640	12 670
July	14 955	6 295	23 898	11 524	15 492	6 509	7 564	30 035	12 854	12 967
August	14 914	6 274	23 807	11 579	15 470	6 387	7 623	30 591	12 967	13 321
September	14 790	6 309	24 076	11 758	14 820	6 335	7 086	30 621	12 993	13 305
October	14 998	6 297	23 969	11 760	14 761	6 188	7 369	30 384	12 884	13 308
November	15 224	6 266	24 085	11 867	14 814	5 938	7 493	29 974	12 556	13 177
December	15 240	6 330	24 289	11 912	15 262	6 206	7 614	29 996	12 432	13 167
1997										
January	15 552	6 470	24 089	11 755	15 786	6 497	7 833	30 230	12 459	13 290
February	15 670	6 429	24 228	11 773	15 879	6 362	8 086	30 439	12 392	13 493
March	15 596	6 388	24 472	11 905	15 878	6 195	8 274	30 721	12 199	13 879
April	15 906	6 481	24 277	11 824	16 582	6 898	8 221	31 397	12 616	14 082
May	15 606	6 260	24 278	11 876	16 133	6 516	8 182	31 924	12 872	14 265
June	15 786	6 461	24 384	11 801	15 866	6 709	7 700	32 004	13 120	13 998
July	15 904	6 475	24 423	11 715	16 780	6 781	8 468	32 880	13 426	14 463
August	15 749	6 376	24 544	11 753	16 139	6 442	8 239	33 270	13 492	14 730
September	15 904	6 416	24 398	11 725	17 192	6 683	8 930	34 558	13 759	15 601
October	15 858	6 413	24 439	11 718	15 926	6 754	7 701	34 626	14 100	15 338
November	15 741	6 366	24 474	11 732	16 272	6 881	7 710	35 157	14 615	15 092
December	15 713	6 513	24 680	11 727	15 716	6 803	7 236	35 160	14 905	14 656
1998										
January	15 715	6 484	24 720	11 770	15 272	6 112	7 707	34 717	14 533	14 590
February	15 838	6 491	24 388	11 767	15 996	6 584	7 722	34 875	14 626	14 546
March	15 660	6 439	24 241	11 806	14 696	6 285	6 688	33 911	14 472	13 594
April	15 523	6 358	24 340	11 852	15 451	6 095	7 891	33 839	14 209	13 833
May	15 176	6 200	24 465	11 986	14 940	6 286	7 168	33 603	14 295	13 504
June	15 049	6 124	24 612	12 168	14 453	5 850	7 325	33 007	14 021	13 356
July	14 968	6 006	24 763	12 335	14 273	5 382	7 521	32 312	13 397	13 384
August	15 056	6 104	24 859	12 437	14 413	5 523	7 298	31 669	12 816	13 203
September	14 951	5 909	24 898	12 398	13 917	5 347	7 186	30 635	12 254	12 854
October	14 590	5 729	24 825	12 312	13 343	4 912	6 927	29 388	11 437	12 410
November	14 286	5 551	24 817	12 175	14 587	5 572	7 447	29 689	11 458	12 637
December	14 222	5 359	24 679	12 057	14 087	5 331	7 323	29 554	11 430	12 666
1999										
January	14 312	5 396	24 438	11 924	13 660	4 957	7 199	28 902	10 991	12 474
February	14 224	5 553	24 176	11 776	14 601	5 882	7 346	29 279	11 320	12 676
March	14 505	5 637	23 734	11 603	14 539	5 817	7 355	29 313	11 500	12 711
April	14 225	5 509	23 651	11 574	14 767	5 846	7 410	29 855	11 837	12 900
May	14 526	5 626	23 758	11 599	14 811	5 862	7 589	30 140	12 073	13 093
June	14 677	5 615	23 674	11 468	15 206	5 885	7 921	30 669	12 343	13 488
July	14 903	5 681	23 693	11 396	15 730	5 872	8 237	31 496	12 534	14 069
August	15 204	5 824	23 660	11 317	15 659	6 065	7 962	31 951	12 775	14 205
September	15 298	5 814	23 652	11 250	15 461	5 931	8 085	32 114	12 892	14 346
October	15 191	5 893	23 884	11 325	15 440	6 027	7 958	32 363	13 026	14 474
November	15 574	6 059	24 091	11 414	15 540	6 315	7 863	32 329	13 282	14 332
December	15 763	6 094	24 255	11 507	15 346	5 896	7 851	31 912	13 084	14 089

1. Also includes iron and steel foundries not shown separately.

Table 16-9. Primary Metals—Producer Prices

(1982=100, except as noted; not seasonally adjusted.)

Year and month	Primary metal industries (December 1984=100)	Intermediate materials						Crude materials				
		Foundry and forge shop products	Steel mill products	Primary nonferrous metals	Aluminum mill shapes	Copper and brass mill shapes	Nonferrous wire and cable	Iron ore	Iron and steel scrap	Nonferrous metal ores (December 1983=100)	Copper base scrap	Aluminum base scrap
1970	...	32.4	32.7	44.9	36.7	63.4	62.6	35.9	59.6	...	100.9	34.4
1971	...	34.6	35.2	40.2	36.4	57.5	57.2	37.0	49.1	...	80.7	32.7
1972	...	36.0	37.3	40.7	36.9	60.3	57.4	37.0	52.3	...	79.3	31.1
1973	...	38.1	38.4	48.9	37.9	68.8	61.5	38.3	80.7	...	120.1	46.8
1974	...	46.7	48.6	69.5	50.1	88.7	84.0	44.2	151.6	...	138.0	70.9
1975	...	56.2	56.4	65.0	54.9	72.8	75.2	55.4	105.4	...	87.3	44.4
1976	...	63.3	60.0	67.4	59.4	79.6	74.7	61.3	111.2	...	96.1	74.0
1977	...	66.7	65.8	72.4	67.7	80.8	77.1	66.8	99.2	...	90.1	90.2
1978	...	72.2	72.8	76.8	75.9	83.3	76.6	69.9	113.6	...	100.3	117.1
1979	...	80.2	80.2	103.9	82.8	105.0	92.1	77.8	146.8	...	129.3	169.6
1980	...	89.7	86.6	132.7	89.3	112.6	107.5	87.8	140.9	...	138.9	183.9
1981	...	95.4	96.6	114.7	98.3	107.8	102.5	96.3	140.6	...	126.3	141.7
1982	...	100.0	100.0	100.0	100.0	100.0	100.0	100.0	100.0	...	100.0	100.0
1983	...	101.6	100.9	106.8	102.2	105.7	100.7	101.2	107.4	...	110.2	142.3
1984	...	104.4	104.7	101.3	112.0	106.9	99.9	101.2	123.7	103.5	101.5	167.6
1985	99.4	105.2	104.7	93.6	107.8	106.9	100.9	97.5	112.6	73.2	95.4	123.4
1986	97.0	105.2	99.8	93.8	102.6	106.9	101.8	91.5	109.6	75.7	93.6	124.5
1987	101.0	105.7	102.3	109.3	105.6	121.8	107.0	84.2	128.4	106.0	113.0	156.4
1988	113.0	109.6	110.7	144.3	130.9	162.7	129.6	82.8	177.1	108.1	157.9	219.5
1989	118.8	114.6	114.5	149.2	135.4	182.0	146.1	82.8	173.7	109.6	179.8	204.4
1990	116.5	117.2	112.1	133.4	127.9	174.6	142.6	83.3	166.0	98.3	181.3	172.6
1991	113.1	119.0	109.5	114.0	123.2	160.5	139.2	83.6	147.6	82.6	170.0	143.1
1992	111.7	120.1	106.4	108.1	121.9	166.0	136.7	83.7	139.2	75.4	162.9	137.6
1993	111.4	121.3	108.2	98.1	120.4	150.7	133.1	82.7	172.5	67.2	136.1	129.2
1994	117.0	123.9	113.4	115.7	127.7	167.3	139.8	82.7	192.9	81.4	155.5	172.9
1995	128.2	129.3	120.1	146.8	160.4	195.2	151.5	91.8	202.7	101.6	193.5	209.4
1996	123.7	132.6	115.6	126.2	144.8	179.0	147.5	96.7	191.1	90.2	166.3	173.4
1997	124.7	134.1	116.4	126.2	147.5	177.3	148.1	96.3	188.9	82.2	157.7	195.1
1998	120.9	135.0	113.8	106.7	142.0	153.0	141.1	95.4	165.0	66.6	116.2	162.5
1999	115.8	135.1	105.3	101.5	138.1	151.2	135.6	94.9	139.2	63.1	108.2	161.7
1996												
January	125.7	131.6	116.6	137.5	150.8	188.8	150.0	97.6	199.7	97.9	181.1	179.3
February	124.4	132.1	115.2	131.8	148.0	183.8	148.6	97.6	201.4	96.7	176.7	178.6
March	124.2	132.5	114.7	132.4	148.3	186.3	148.3	97.6	197.8	95.9	179.9	179.3
April	124.1	132.4	114.9	132.4	147.3	182.4	148.6	97.7	197.8	95.5	180.0	183.8
May	124.6	132.6	115.2	135.2	145.3	191.4	150.8	94.8	199.5	97.2	182.9	179.9
June	124.6	132.7	115.6	136.9	147.1	180.9	149.3	94.6	194.8	92.4	167.8	174.6
July	123.2	132.7	115.5	122.4	145.7	172.3	145.9	96.7	190.5	86.6	157.9	167.2
August	122.8	132.8	115.9	117.2	143.2	170.0	145.0	96.7	191.6	84.3	153.2	168.1
September	122.7	132.7	116.3	116.5	142.0	169.6	145.0	96.7	191.7	83.5	151.9	168.4
October	122.7	133.0	116.0	114.4	140.3	169.6	145.6	96.7	183.4	83.2	151.8	160.0
November	122.6	133.0	115.7	115.9	139.0	175.2	145.6	96.7	172.4	85.3	154.5	166.7
December	123.0	133.0	115.6	121.5	140.3	177.1	147.4	96.7	172.2	83.9	157.9	174.8
1997												
January	123.6	133.6	115.9	125.4	141.8	179.0	147.7	99.7	182.2	86.4	163.6	188.3
February	124.0	134.0	116.1	127.6	144.1	178.5	147.9	99.7	191.1	84.8	164.6	195.5
March	124.8	134.3	116.1	130.3	147.6	183.5	149.4	99.7	186.0	87.8	167.7	202.2
April	125.0	134.2	116.4	129.0	147.2	181.0	149.6	95.2	181.6	84.8	165.4	195.9
May	125.0	134.2	116.2	129.7	146.3	180.6	150.3	95.2	185.4	87.4	170.3	198.9
June	125.4	134.3	116.3	131.6	148.0	184.8	150.2	95.2	185.1	87.0	174.0	196.8
July	125.2	134.4	116.6	126.8	147.3	181.1	149.4	95.2	189.4	82.5	161.9	193.3
August	125.2	134.1	116.6	127.6	148.1	179.0	148.4	95.2	191.7	83.1	156.3	198.1
September	125.2	134.2	116.8	126.6	150.1	173.8	148.3	95.2	189.7	80.2	150.2	193.6
October	124.8	134.1	116.6	122.6	149.7	172.4	146.6	95.2	191.2	79.0	146.6	194.2
November	124.5	134.0	116.6	120.4	149.7	168.3	145.3	95.2	196.0	73.9	140.6	193.0
December	123.9	134.1	116.2	117.2	149.8	165.5	144.1	95.2	197.1	68.8	130.7	191.5
1998												
January	123.3	134.7	115.9	113.7	147.5	159.7	143.2	95.2	197.3	67.2	122.7	185.8
February	123.0	134.9	115.9	113.8	146.4	159.5	142.0	95.2	193.5	67.9	123.3	184.6
March	122.7	135.0	115.5	111.3	145.3	157.4	142.5	95.2	186.4	68.3	123.6	181.6
April	122.6	135.2	115.4	113.1	144.2	158.4	142.5	95.2	184.1	70.8	124.9	176.8
May	122.1	135.2	115.1	109.4	144.1	156.0	141.3	95.6	184.5	69.4	123.8	171.7
June	121.6	135.2	115.1	106.7	141.2	151.2	141.7	95.5	182.0	67.4	119.0	164.0
July	120.9	134.9	114.8	104.6	139.2	149.0	141.8	95.5	175.7	68.6	114.0	150.5
August	120.6	135.0	114.3	103.0	140.8	149.5	141.3	95.5	162.5	64.5	111.8	149.9
September	120.1	135.0	113.3	103.5	140.7	151.6	140.8	95.6	147.5	65.7	113.1	149.7
October	119.1	134.9	111.8	102.6	139.0	148.8	140.2	95.6	129.1	63.8	111.2	148.8
November	118.0	134.9	110.2	100.6	138.0	149.0	138.3	95.6	119.2	63.8	106.6	145.5
December	116.9	135.0	108.7	97.6	137.1	146.4	137.4	95.2	118.5	61.9	100.5	144.6
1999												
January	115.9	135.1	107.1	95.8	135.9	144.8	136.3	95.2	124.4	60.4	99.9	143.2
February	115.1	135.2	105.7	94.2	135.1	144.4	134.4	95.2	132.7	61.9	98.4	145.4
March	114.8	135.2	105.4	92.9	134.4	142.9	133.3	95.2	125.4	60.4	99.9	145.7
April	114.7	135.1	105.3	94.0	133.8	144.2	133.1	94.9	126.2	62.4	101.6	148.8
May	114.9	135.1	104.6	99.7	135.4	149.3	134.2	94.9	134.4	62.1	104.6	158.1
June	115.0	135.1	105.2	97.1	136.9	147.2	132.2	94.8	138.2	59.4	103.1	161.2
July	115.4	135.1	104.7	103.1	137.2	154.6	134.7	94.8	137.3	61.4	113.3	167.4
August	115.7	135.1	104.7	104.1	139.4	155.1	135.3	94.8	143.4	62.1	115.3	171.1
September	116.4	135.1	104.7	106.7	140.9	158.0	137.6	94.8	143.0	63.6	116.0	172.8
October	117.1	135.1	105.0	109.1	142.7	157.1	139.3	94.8	145.0	70.3	114.1	171.6
November	117.1	135.0	105.4	109.7	142.7	158.1	138.6	94.8	154.7	66.9	114.3	174.2
December	117.4	135.2	106.1	111.3	142.8	159.0	137.8	94.8	165.9	66.0	117.5	180.7

Table 16-10. Primary Metals—Employment, Hours, and Earnings

Year and month	Primary metals						Blast furnaces and basic steel					
	Employment (thousands, seasonally adjusted)		Production workers				Seasonally adjusted		Not seasonally adjusted			
							Production workers				Average earnings (dollars)	
	Total payroll employees	Production workers	Average weekly hours (seasonally adjusted)	Aggregate weekly hours index (1982=100, seasonally adjusted)	Average earnings (dollars, not seasonally adjusted)		Average weekly hours	Aggregate weekly hours index (1982=100)	Total payroll employees (thousands)	Production workers (thousands)		
					Hourly	Weekly					Hourly	Weekly
1970	1,260	1,000	40.4	152.9	3.93	158.77	40.0	179.5	627	500	4.16	166.40
1971	1,171	923	40.1	140.5	4.23	169.62	39.6	161.5	574	455	4.49	177.80
1972	1,173	933	41.4	146.3	4.66	192.92	40.6	165.1	568	453	5.08	206.25
1973	1,259	1,011	42.3	161.8	5.04	213.19	41.7	181.5	605	485	5.51	229.77
1974	1,289	1,030	41.6	162.4	5.60	232.96	41.3	180.7	610	487	6.27	258.95
1975	1,139	887	40.0	134.3	6.18	247.20	39.5	151.8	548	428	6.94	274.13
1976	1,155	904	40.8	140.0	6.77	276.22	40.3	155.6	549	431	7.59	305.88
1977	1,182	922	41.3	144.2	7.40	305.62	40.5	157.2	554	433	8.36	338.58
1978	1,215	954	41.8	151.3	8.20	342.76	41.5	164.6	561	442	9.39	389.69
1979	1,254	986	41.4	154.8	8.98	371.77	41.2	167.0	571	451	10.41	428.89
1980	1,142	878	40.1	133.4	9.77	391.78	39.4	139.8	512	396	11.39	448.77
1981	1,122	862	40.5	132.5	10.81	437.81	40.4	141.9	506	392	12.60	509.04
1982	922	683	38.6	100.0	11.33	437.34	37.9	100.0	396	294	13.35	505.97
1983	832	620	40.5	95.2	11.35	459.68	39.5	90.8	341	256	12.89	509.16
1984	857	651	41.7	102.9	11.47	478.30	40.7	93.7	334	257	12.98	528.29
1985	808	611	41.5	96.1	11.67	484.31	41.1	85.3	303	232	13.33	547.86
1986	751	565	41.9	89.8	11.86	496.93	41.7	78.2	273	209	13.73	572.54
1987	746	562	43.1	91.8	11.94	514.61	43.4	79.0	268	203	13.77	597.62
1988	770	589	43.5	97.2	12.16	528.96	44.0	85.1	278	215	13.98	615.12
1989	772	589	43.0	96.0	12.43	534.49	43.4	83.9	279	215	14.25	618.45
1990	756	574	42.7	93.0	12.92	551.68	43.4	82.6	276	212	14.82	643.19
1991	723	545	42.2	87.2	13.33	562.53	42.7	76.4	263	200	15.36	655.87
1992	695	525	43.0	85.6	13.66	587.38	43.5	73.7	250	189	15.87	690.35
1993	683	520	43.7	86.2	13.99	611.36	44.1	72.6	240	183	16.36	721.48
1994	698	537	44.7	90.9	14.34	641.00	44.9	73.4	239	182	16.85	756.57
1995	712	553	44.0	92.1	14.62	643.28	44.4	73.6	242	185	17.33	769.45
1996	711	553	44.2	92.6	14.97	661.67	44.5	73.6	240	185	17.80	792.10
1997	711	555	44.9	94.5	15.22	683.38	44.9	72.9	235	181	18.03	809.55
1998	715	560	44.2	93.7	15.48	684.22	44.6	72.1	233	180	18.42	821.53
1999	700	546	44.2	91.6	15.83	699.69	44.8	70.9	228	176	18.81	842.69
1996												
January	713	554	43.3	90.9	14.84	644.06	44.3	73.6	242	185	17.62	780.57
February	712	554	44.0	92.4	14.70	648.27	44.8	74.4	241	185	17.46	778.72
March	711	554	43.8	92.0	14.73	645.17	44.3	73.6	241	185	17.57	778.35
April	709	551	43.9	91.7	14.99	653.56	43.8	72.7	240	184	17.88	786.72
May	711	554	44.2	92.8	14.82	653.56	44.3	74.0	241	186	17.52	776.14
June	712	555	44.3	93.2	14.91	660.51	44.4	74.1	242	187	17.65	785.43
July	706	549	44.3	92.2	15.08	657.49	44.6	74.1	241	186	17.97	797.87
August	713	555	44.3	93.2	15.02	662.38	44.3	73.6	242	186	17.85	785.40
September	713	555	44.5	93.6	15.18	680.06	44.4	73.7	240	186	18.11	807.71
October	708	552	44.4	92.9	15.09	670.00	44.5	73.1	236	182	17.96	797.42
November	708	552	44.0	92.1	15.18	675.51	44.6	72.9	237	182	18.07	814.96
December	707	552	44.5	93.1	15.15	686.30	44.7	73.0	237	182	17.94	809.09
1997												
January	708	552	44.4	92.9	15.12	672.84	44.5	72.7	236	182	17.73	792.53
February	708	553	44.7	93.7	15.09	673.01	44.6	72.9	236	181	17.76	788.54
March	708	552	44.8	93.7	15.16	679.17	44.7	72.6	235	181	17.89	799.68
April	708	553	45.1	94.5	15.15	677.21	44.7	72.6	234	180	17.92	804.61
May	708	553	44.8	93.9	15.09	674.52	44.7	72.2	234	180	17.87	798.79
June	708	553	44.7	93.7	15.16	679.17	44.5	71.9	236	181	18.03	804.14
July	707	553	44.8	93.9	15.28	670.79	44.6	72.1	234	180	18.13	803.16
August	712	557	44.9	94.8	15.16	677.65	45.1	72.9	234	180	18.00	806.40
September	713	557	45.0	95.0	15.27	691.73	45.1	72.9	235	181	18.30	827.16
October	714	559	45.2	95.8	15.33	691.38	45.5	73.9	235	181	18.26	821.70
November	716	561	45.1	95.9	15.38	699.79	45.5	74.3	235	182	18.28	831.74
December	717	562	45.2	96.3	15.43	711.32	45.5	73.9	235	182	18.15	834.90
1998												
January	720	565	45.4	97.2	15.48	702.79	46.0	75.1	235	182	18.33	846.85
February	719	565	44.8	95.9	15.46	691.06	45.4	74.2	234	181	18.34	828.97
March	719	565	44.6	95.5	15.53	691.09	45.3	74.0	234	181	18.32	828.06
April	719	565	44.1	94.5	15.66	679.64	44.6	72.9	233	181	18.66	835.97
May	718	563	44.3	94.5	15.55	691.98	45.2	73.4	234	181	18.55	842.17
June	718	563	44.3	94.5	15.54	689.98	44.8	73.2	236	183	18.53	833.85
July	708	553	44.0	92.2	15.56	670.64	44.3	72.0	234	182	18.47	810.83
August	717	562	44.0	93.7	15.44	676.27	44.3	71.6	234	180	18.44	815.05
September	717	561	43.8	93.1	15.60	683.28	44.2	71.0	233	180	18.73	829.74
October	711	556	43.8	92.3	15.31	667.52	43.8	70.0	232	178	18.18	785.38
November	706	552	43.9	91.9	15.34	678.03	43.7	69.4	230	177	18.27	798.40
December	706	552	43.7	91.4	15.35	684.61	43.3	69.2	231	178	18.13	792.28
1999												
January	704	550	43.7	91.1	15.38	673.64	43.9	69.7	228	176	18.36	807.84
February	704	550	43.8	91.3	15.39	672.54	43.9	69.7	228	176	18.45	806.27
March	703	548	44.0	91.4	15.51	680.89	44.1	70.1	228	177	18.50	812.15
April	701	547	44.0	91.2	15.60	687.96	44.5	70.7	227	176	18.53	826.44
May	699	546	44.2	91.5	15.74	698.86	44.6	70.9	227	177	18.73	840.98
June	698	544	44.3	91.3	15.90	707.55	44.9	70.5	227	176	18.99	858.35
July	701	548	44.4	92.2	16.02	698.47	45.0	71.1	228	177	19.06	850.08
August	699	547	44.4	92.1	15.98	704.72	45.0	71.5	228	177	18.93	849.96
September	697	545	44.5	91.9	16.18	716.77	45.0	71.5	227	176	18.99	852.65
October	697	546	44.3	91.7	16.01	709.24	45.2	72.2	227	177	18.90	848.61
November	698	545	44.3	91.5	16.12	720.56	45.3	72.0	228	177	19.11	865.68
December	698	546	44.4	91.9	16.17	732.50	45.4	72.1	228	177	19.09	878.14

Table 16-11. Fabricated Metal Products—Production, Capacity Utilization, Shipments, Inventories, and Orders

(Seasonally adjusted.)

Year and month	Industrial production (1992=100)							Capacity utilization (output as a percent of capacity)	Manufacturers' shipments, inventories, and orders (millions of dollars)			
	Total	Metal containers	Hardware, tools, and cutlery		Structural metal products	Other fabricated metal products			Shipments	Inventories (book value, end of period)	New orders (net)	Unfilled orders (end of period)
			Total	Hardware and tools		Total	Fasteners, stampings, etc.					
1970	77.7	84.4	83.7	84.4	85.8	70.9	75.3	75.0	44 210	7 907	43 990	14 877
1971	77.3	81.7	88.0	89.5	84.6	69.8	72.1	73.7	45 478	8 098	44 305	13 688
1972	84.8	84.4	98.4	99.7	93.0	76.8	79.3	79.9	51 487	8 408	52 879	15 077
1973	94.3	93.4	105.6	107.3	103.7	86.3	89.5	86.8	58 804	9 864	64 733	21 019
1974	90.5	94.0	101.1	100.4	99.2	83.3	84.4	80.9	67 212	13 387	74 281	28 100
1975	78.4	90.1	87.5	87.4	85.3	71.0	69.8	68.6	68 411	13 091	64 349	24 008
1976	86.9	93.1	102.5	102.4	91.6	79.9	81.2	74.6	77 560	14 304	76 372	22 810
1977	94.7	98.1	110.7	111.0	98.9	88.8	91.2	79.9	89 938	15 527	92 028	25 152
1978	98.2	97.8	109.7	109.8	101.8	93.8	96.4	81.0	101 245	17 296	105 182	29 137
1979	101.6	100.8	115.8	117.9	107.0	96.0	96.8	82.0	113 494	19 145	117 428	33 131
1980	94.4	94.3	99.0	100.2	104.2	88.6	86.1	74.9	116 071	19 532	116 195	33 296
1981	93.0	93.2	100.0	101.6	101.8	87.5	84.5	73.2	123 535	20 209	123 245	33 036
1982	84.9	94.5	85.4	85.3	94.1	79.0	72.8	66.9	119 236	21 440	113 399	27 117
1983	87.2	95.1	91.5	92.0	91.4	82.7	80.3	68.4	123 083	21 752	122 760	26 752
1984	95.2	94.3	99.5	100.8	94.6	93.8	93.9	74.3	138 107	23 330	141 650	30 254
1985	96.5	91.8	100.1	101.1	99.0	94.3	93.1	74.9	143 268	22 880	142 300	29 197
1986	95.6	88.0	100.3	101.7	97.5	93.7	91.4	73.6	143 063	22 094	143 541	29 633
1987	101.9	92.1	105.4	107.8	105.5	99.9	97.9	78.1	147 367	22 920	150 716	32 973
1988	106.1	95.4	107.2	108.9	106.8	106.0	104.3	81.1	159 505	24 950	158 170	31 661
1989	104.8	97.5	107.6	109.2	106.2	103.7	102.4	80.0	164 073	25 427	160 037	27 629
1990	101.2	100.2	102.2	102.6	103.5	99.8	98.0	77.3	165 064	25 044	163 285	25 859
1991	96.2	100.0	96.6	96.8	99.1	94.2	91.4	73.4	159 760	23 922	158 401	24 516
1992	100.0	100.0	100.0	100.0	100.0	100.0	100.0	76.9	166 532	23 815	165 793	23 725
1993	104.4	98.4	105.1	105.1	102.9	105.3	109.0	79.7	175 118	23 838	172 121	20 731
1994	112.2	104.4	116.4	117.2	110.9	112.3	118.5	83.1	190 544	25 597	191 099	21 290
1995	116.4	100.8	117.1	117.7	114.0	118.8	125.8	82.8	204 384	27 003	205 388	22 329
1996	120.1	103.5	122.4	122.8	118.3	121.5	129.7	80.4	214 007	27 894	215 791	24 159
1997	126.1	105.2	126.2	125.0	123.9	129.0	138.4	80.1	226 078	29 579	228 567	26 649
1998	128.8	105.7	127.3	126.0	127.6	131.8	141.5	76.8	239 667	30 855	238 751	25 894
1999	128.7	105.2	127.2	126.7	129.1	130.6	140.8	74.9	245 517	31 401	244 831	25 204
1996												
January	117.4	104.5	119.7	120.1	114.4	119.7	128.8	80.4	17 391	27 092	17 327	22 265
February	118.8	105.1	122.7	123.4	115.2	120.9	129.3	81.0	17 248	27 386	17 365	22 382
March	118.4	101.5	118.3	117.8	116.8	120.3	128.2	80.4	17 084	27 236	17 223	22 521
April	118.3	103.0	119.4	119.2	117.1	119.6	127.2	80.0	17 794	27 188	17 843	22 570
May	119.0	104.4	120.4	120.3	117.2	120.2	127.8	80.1	18 159	27 132	18 507	22 918
June	120.0	101.4	122.0	122.5	118.7	121.2	128.9	80.5	17 861	26 958	18 045	23 102
July	120.6	103.4	122.1	122.5	118.5	122.5	131.0	80.6	17 864	27 378	17 959	23 197
August	121.7	102.2	126.1	127.1	119.5	122.8	131.6	81.0	18 215	27 592	18 299	23 281
September	121.9	103.7	124.7	125.5	120.0	123.2	131.6	80.8	18 122	27 528	18 442	23 601
October	121.7	105.8	124.5	124.9	120.2	122.7	131.0	80.4	18 051	27 643	18 264	23 814
November	121.7	103.6	123.7	124.3	120.9	122.6	130.6	80.1	18 302	27 746	18 444	23 956
December	121.6	103.8	125.4	125.2	120.8	122.2	130.6	79.6	17 846	27 894	18 049	24 159
1997												
January	122.6	103.9	126.8	126.7	120.0	124.1	133.7	79.9	18 297	28 124	18 435	24 297
February	124.1	103.6	128.7	129.0	122.5	125.4	135.1	80.6	18 491	28 340	18 863	24 669
March	124.3	106.6	123.5	122.6	123.5	126.2	134.8	80.3	18 255	28 595	18 419	24 833
April	125.3	106.5	124.5	123.6	123.9	127.6	137.5	80.6	18 953	28 747	19 360	25 240
May	125.6	104.8	125.6	124.8	123.6	128.2	137.6	80.4	18 401	28 771	18 433	25 272
June	125.0	103.9	124.2	122.2	123.4	127.7	136.2	79.6	18 755	29 012	19 225	25 742
July	126.3	108.9	126.7	125.1	123.0	129.4	139.8	80.0	18 932	29 089	19 205	26 015
August	127.0	103.7	126.0	124.5	124.5	130.6	140.6	80.1	18 995	29 132	19 038	26 058
September	127.1	106.1	126.2	124.2	125.0	130.1	138.6	79.7	19 283	29 360	19 559	26 334
October	128.1	104.9	127.7	126.3	124.9	131.8	141.3	79.8	19 274	29 480	19 521	26 581
November	128.6	102.4	126.6	125.0	125.7	132.8	142.1	79.7	19 143	29 590	19 320	26 758
December	130.0	106.8	127.9	126.6	126.6	134.0	143.7	80.1	19 299	29 579	19 190	26 649
1998												
January	129.4	106.7	128.0	126.6	127.5	133.0	141.5	79.3	19 109	29 775	19 328	26 868
February	129.3	104.0	128.2	126.5	127.7	133.0	141.9	78.8	19 766	30 069	19 774	26 876
March	129.2	103.7	127.7	126.5	127.4	132.9	141.8	78.3	19 742	30 405	19 704	26 838
April	129.4	107.3	126.2	125.0	126.6	133.6	143.7	78.0	19 570	30 580	20 001	27 269
May	129.9	105.2	128.7	128.0	127.8	133.5	143.5	77.9	19 745	30 460	19 630	27 154
June	129.2	105.6	126.8	125.9	127.8	132.6	142.2	77.1	19 755	30 749	19 722	27 121
July	127.7	103.3	126.2	125.6	127.5	130.1	137.8	75.8	20 309	30 939	20 132	26 944
August	127.2	104.8	124.8	123.3	127.0	129.9	138.5	75.2	20 114	30 944	19 693	26 523
September	127.7	106.1	128.7	126.7	126.5	130.2	139.7	75.3	20 235	31 050	19 930	26 218
October	128.1	106.5	127.9	126.2	127.7	130.3	140.9	75.2	20 176	31 093	20 095	26 137
November	128.6	107.1	128.5	127.2	128.3	130.8	142.5	75.3	20 415	31 134	20 235	25 957
December	129.8	107.9	126.2	124.9	129.7	132.1	144.6	75.9	20 523	30 855	20 460	25 894
1999												
January	129.0	102.6	124.7	123.5	128.8	131.9	144.6	75.3	20 520	30 920	20 735	26 109
February	128.4	105.6	123.5	123.0	128.9	130.6	142.4	74.8	20 391	30 849	20 421	26 139
March	128.5	106.4	126.9	126.7	129.1	130.1	141.4	74.9	20 416	30 819	20 391	26 114
April	128.0	102.1	124.9	124.1	129.0	129.7	139.6	74.5	20 416	30 887	20 071	25 769
May	127.2	102.8	124.6	123.4	128.3	129.1	138.9	74.1	20 411	31 006	20 210	25 568
June	128.3	106.0	126.1	125.1	127.8	130.4	141.1	74.7	20 544	30 740	20 284	25 308
July	128.6	104.4	126.0	125.7	128.3	131.4	141.8	74.9	20 394	31 005	20 286	25 200
August	128.5	106.0	128.2	127.5	128.1	130.7	140.3	74.9	20 781	31 028	20 814	25 233
September	128.4	104.4	131.3	131.3	128.4	130.0	138.9	74.9	20 377	31 182	20 168	25 024
October	128.8	101.1	129.6	129.2	129.8	130.2	138.8	75.1	20 281	31 359	20 060	24 803
November	129.7	111.0	129.0	129.3	130.1	130.9	140.1	75.7	20 713	31 378	20 619	24 709
December	129.0	109.5	130.2	130.2	129.9	129.8	138.8	75.3	20 385	31 401	20 880	25 204

Table 16-12. Fabricated Metal Products—Prices, Employment, Hours, and Earnings

Year and month	Fabricated metal products industry (December 1984=100)	Producer prices (1982=100, except as noted; not seasonally adjusted) — Intermediate materials					Employment (thousands, seasonally adjusted)		Production workers			
		Metal containers	Hardware	Plumbing fixtures and brass fittings	Heating equipment	Fabricated structural metal products	Total payroll employees	Production workers	Average weekly hours, seasonally adjusted	Aggregate weekly hours index (1982=100), seasonally adjusted	Average earnings (dollars, not seasonally adjusted) — Hourly	Weekly
1970	. . .	34.3	39.8	39.9	46.6	36.7	1 559	1 188	40.7	120.3	3.53	143.67
1971	. . .	37.1	41.7	41.8	48.6	38.8	1 479	1 128	40.4	113.2	3.77	152.31
1972	. . .	39.2	42.9	43.0	49.8	40.2	1 541	1 189	41.2	121.9	4.05	166.86
1973	. . .	41.0	44.5	45.1	50.8	41.8	1 645	1 277	41.6	131.8	4.29	178.46
1974	. . .	50.1	50.2	53.5	56.9	52.9	1 632	1 256	40.8	127.4	4.61	188.09
1975	. . .	58.5	58.2	58.2	63.5	62.0	1 453	1 090	40.1	108.4	5.05	202.51
1976	. . .	61.5	61.8	62.5	66.6	63.6	1 505	1 138	40.8	115.3	5.50	224.40
1977	. . .	66.4	66.2	67.0	69.8	67.8	1 577	1 198	41.0	121.9	5.91	242.31
1978	. . .	74.1	71.5	71.4	73.5	74.3	1 667	1 269	41.0	129.3	6.35	260.35
1979	. . .	81.9	78.0	77.9	78.9	81.6	1 713	1 298	40.7	131.4	6.85	278.80
1980	. . .	90.9	85.8	88.5	87.0	88.8	1 609	1 194	40.4	119.8	7.45	300.98
1981	. . .	96.1	93.9	96.0	94.5	96.9	1 586	1 171	40.3	117.1	8.20	330.46
1982	. . .	100.0	100.0	100.0	100.0	100.0	1 424	1 028	39.2	100.0	8.77	343.78
1983	. . .	102.1	103.7	103.8	102.7	99.6	1 368	994	40.6	100.3	9.12	370.27
1984	. . .	106.5	105.9	108.6	106.6	101.9	1 462	1 078	41.4	111.0	9.40	389.16
1985	100.6	109.0	109.1	111.9	109.5	103.2	1 464	1 083	41.3	111.2	9.71	401.02
1986	101.0	110.2	109.5	115.5	113.0	103.6	1 422	1 051	41.3	107.8	9.89	408.46
1987	102.1	109.5	109.6	119.7	115.5	105.4	1 399	1 038	41.6	107.1	10.01	416.42
1988	107.4	110.2	113.7	128.7	119.2	114.3	1 428	1 062	41.9	110.5	10.29	431.15
1989	112.6	111.5	120.4	137.7	125.1	120.3	1 445	1 070	41.6	110.6	10.57	439.71
1990	115.1	114.0	125.9	144.3	131.6	121.8	1 419	1 045	41.3	107.1	10.83	447.28
1991	116.6	115.5	130.2	149.7	134.1	122.4	1 355	991	41.2	101.4	11.19	461.03
1992	117.2	113.9	132.7	153.1	137.3	122.1	1 329	975	41.6	100.7	11.42	475.07
1993	118.2	109.7	135.2	155.9	140.4	123.2	1 339	988	42.1	103.3	11.69	492.15
1994	120.3	108.1	137.5	159.6	142.5	127.3	1 388	1 037	42.9	110.5	11.93	511.80
1995	124.8	117.2	141.1	166.0	147.5	135.1	1 437	1 080	42.4	113.6	12.13	514.31
1996	126.2	110.0	143.8	171.1	151.2	137.8	1 449	1 088	42.4	114.5	12.50	530.00
1997	127.6	108.1	145.6	174.5	152.4	140.3	1 479	1 115	42.6	118.1	12.78	544.43
1998	128.7	108.3	147.0	175.1	153.3	142.5	1 509	1 137	42.3	119.5	13.07	552.86
1999	129.1	106.4	148.7	176.7	154.0	143.3	1 517	1 139	42.2	119.5	13.48	568.86
1996												
January	125.9	115.1	142.8	167.6	150.1	136.8	1 440	1 080	41.0	110.0	12.38	506.34
February	125.7	110.5	143.1	170.2	150.5	136.9	1 442	1 080	42.2	113.2	12.32	517.44
March	125.9	110.5	143.5	170.9	150.5	137.1	1 440	1 080	42.1	112.9	12.32	516.21
April	126.0	110.5	143.5	171.0	150.6	137.2	1 438	1 078	42.4	113.5	12.46	520.83
May	126.0	109.7	143.6	171.5	150.8	137.5	1 442	1 082	42.5	114.2	12.45	526.64
June	126.2	109.5	143.7	171.8	151.1	138.0	1 447	1 087	42.6	115.0	12.51	535.43
July	126.2	109.6	143.7	171.6	151.5	138.0	1 450	1 093	42.6	115.6	12.50	520.00
August	126.4	109.6	144.2	171.5	151.8	138.2	1 454	1 093	42.6	115.6	12.52	533.35
September	126.4	109.5	144.2	171.6	151.8	138.4	1 456	1 095	42.5	115.6	12.65	543.95
October	126.5	108.5	144.6	171.6	151.8	138.6	1 458	1 096	42.4	115.4	12.53	535.03
November	126.5	108.4	144.1	171.8	151.8	138.6	1 460	1 098	42.4	115.6	12.59	541.37
December	126.6	109.1	144.2	171.4	151.9	138.6	1 461	1 098	42.4	115.6	12.76	556.34
1997												
January	126.8	108.0	144.9	171.9	152.0	139.0	1 462	1 099	42.4	115.7	12.72	535.51
February	127.0	108.0	144.7	174.3	152.0	139.1	1 463	1 101	42.5	116.2	12.71	537.63
March	127.1	108.2	145.2	174.5	152.0	139.2	1 466	1 103	42.7	117.0	12.74	541.45
April	127.2	107.9	145.4	174.7	152.2	139.8	1 470	1 106	43.0	118.1	12.75	540.60
May	127.4	107.9	145.5	175.0	151.7	140.2	1 474	1 110	42.6	117.4	12.74	541.45
June	127.5	107.8	145.7	175.1	152.1	140.4	1 477	1 113	42.5	117.5	12.72	541.87
July	127.7	107.6	145.2	174.8	152.7	140.6	1 474	1 115	42.5	117.7	12.65	526.24
August	127.9	107.8	145.9	174.9	152.8	140.8	1 484	1 120	42.5	118.2	12.75	541.88
September	128.0	107.7	145.9	174.6	152.9	141.0	1 487	1 122	42.5	118.4	12.80	550.40
October	128.1	108.9	146.0	174.9	152.9	141.2	1 492	1 126	42.5	118.9	12.85	551.27
November	128.2	108.9	146.0	174.7	153.0	141.3	1 497	1 129	42.7	119.7	12.92	559.44
December	128.1	108.9	146.3	174.3	152.9	141.2	1 501	1 134	42.8	120.5	13.02	572.88
1998												
January	128.3	109.1	146.5	174.2	152.8	141.4	1 506	1 137	42.9	121.1	12.98	552.95
February	128.4	109.2	147.2	175.6	153.2	141.4	1 507	1 140	42.6	120.6	12.97	548.63
March	128.5	109.3	146.8	175.7	153.1	141.6	1 508	1 139	42.4	119.9	12.99	548.18
April	128.6	108.6	146.9	175.8	153.4	141.9	1 510	1 140	42.4	120.1	12.88	526.79
May	128.8	108.6	146.9	176.1	153.4	142.6	1 512	1 139	42.4	119.9	13.03	553.78
June	128.9	108.5	147.1	175.7	153.0	143.1	1 510	1 136	42.4	119.6	13.01	554.23
July	128.8	108.5	147.3	175.4	153.2	143.0	1 493	1 130	42.3	118.7	12.89	536.22
August	128.8	108.5	147.1	175.2	153.2	142.9	1 513	1 138	42.2	119.3	13.05	550.71
September	128.9	108.5	147.1	174.6	153.2	143.2	1 514	1 140	42.1	119.2	13.18	548.29
October	128.7	107.1	147.2	174.4	153.5	143.2	1 514	1 139	42.3	119.7	13.19	561.89
November	128.8	107.2	147.2	174.5	153.5	143.1	1 511	1 137	42.2	119.2	13.23	566.24
December	128.7	107.1	147.2	174.0	154.0	142.8	1 513	1 138	42.3	119.6	13.36	581.16
1999												
January	128.8	107.1	147.4	175.3	153.9	142.7	1 518	1 142	42.1	119.4	13.31	556.36
February	128.8	107.0	147.2	175.7	153.4	142.6	1 516	1 139	42.0	118.8	13.31	556.36
March	128.7	107.0	147.4	176.2	153.6	142.8	1 516	1 138	42.1	119.0	13.36	558.45
April	128.9	106.3	147.8	176.7	153.6	142.8	1 516	1 137	42.1	118.9	13.39	563.72
May	128.9	106.3	147.9	176.1	154.0	142.9	1 515	1 137	42.1	118.9	13.47	567.09
June	129.1	106.0	149.1	177.0	153.8	143.0	1 515	1 136	42.2	119.1	13.49	571.98
July	129.1	106.0	149.1	176.8	154.2	143.1	1 517	1 147	42.3	120.5	13.47	560.35
August	129.1	105.9	149.7	176.7	154.3	143.2	1 515	1 137	42.3	119.5	13.52	571.90
September	129.2	106.0	149.7	176.9	154.5	143.4	1 518	1 138	42.3	119.6	13.64	571.52
October	129.4	106.5	149.8	177.0	154.4	143.7	1 519	1 140	42.2	119.5	13.52	574.60
November	129.6	106.5	149.8	177.4	154.2	144.3	1 520	1 141	42.1	119.3	13.59	580.29
December	129.7	106.5	150.0	178.3	154.1	144.4	1 521	1 142	42.1	119.4	13.72	594.08

Table 16-13. Industrial Machinery and Equipment—Production and Capacity Utilization

(Seasonally adjusted.)

Year and month	Industrial production (1992=100)								Capacity utilization (output as a percent of capacity)	
	Total	Engines and turbines	Construction and allied	Metal-working	Special industry	General industrial	Computer and office equipment	Service industry machines	Total	Computer and office equipment
1970	41.1	95.9	114.6	99.7	100.1	83.8	2.3	57.7	81.3	90.9
1971	38.2	102.7	114.5	82.9	88.5	76.9	2.0	60.4	73.0	70.9
1972	44.3	109.9	131.6	96.9	98.8	86.9	2.4	74.2	82.5	79.2
1973	51.8	120.9	151.0	116.0	112.2	101.8	2.9	89.1	93.0	86.3
1974	55.2	132.8	168.3	118.7	115.4	106.7	3.5	81.9	94.6	91.7
1975	47.8	110.3	150.9	96.5	98.2	95.7	3.2	60.0	78.4	74.0
1976	50.2	120.6	140.9	95.6	97.0	97.4	3.9	74.1	78.8	75.6
1977	56.6	129.1	163.6	106.0	96.2	105.4	5.1	81.8	83.9	78.1
1978	63.3	138.5	181.8	111.1	102.0	109.1	7.5	89.3	88.2	87.3
1979	70.2	139.7	184.8	120.5	103.4	117.2	10.3	90.9	91.6	89.3
1980	70.5	127.0	176.5	119.0	100.8	111.1	13.9	78.6	85.9	88.2
1981	74.7	127.5	189.0	116.3	94.8	109.9	18.4	82.5	84.8	85.7
1982	65.8	101.5	145.2	87.3	88.0	93.5	21.3	73.7	70.5	74.3
1983	65.2	90.1	101.2	74.2	81.7	89.6	29.5	79.7	66.2	78.7
1984	78.9	115.8	115.8	90.4	90.5	101.3	42.0	89.2	75.7	86.1
1985	81.2	108.2	113.4	92.3	90.4	96.3	50.3	86.3	72.8	80.0
1986	81.8	104.7	105.4	98.2	88.9	92.8	53.7	91.4	70.3	72.5
1987	86.0	97.9	101.4	97.0	96.5	92.9	62.2	96.7	72.1	74.6
1988	97.1	107.6	114.8	106.3	105.5	102.2	74.6	103.3	79.6	79.5
1989	103.0	107.2	121.8	114.0	110.7	103.3	83.0	108.0	83.4	81.2
1990	100.1	100.5	117.6	109.4	107.5	104.0	81.4	97.6	79.4	73.7
1991	95.4	98.4	104.4	98.8	102.1	100.1	82.3	91.9	74.2	68.8
1992	100.0	100.0	100.0	100.0	100.0	100.0	100.0	100.0	75.4	75.1
1993	110.1	109.7	110.4	106.3	107.7	104.8	121.2	107.1	78.7	76.7
1994	125.6	125.0	121.8	115.9	122.2	110.6	152.9	119.8	83.1	77.7
1995	143.7	120.5	133.2	127.4	146.2	117.1	208.8	126.9	86.5	85.3
1996	159.6	125.3	140.9	128.8	151.7	119.3	296.0	133.6	86.1	85.6
1997	178.3	128.3	150.8	133.8	156.2	124.4	403.9	136.5	84.6	79.4
1998	206.4	134.8	170.2	132.8	152.9	126.3	675.1	149.1	84.9	84.5
1999	230.1	145.6	168.1	126.7	146.7	122.5	1 061.4	159.7	82.1	83.3
1996										
January	150.2	120.5	137.1	126.7	150.5	117.9	238.0	130.3	85.6	81.7
February	151.8	118.1	140.2	129.8	152.8	121.2	238.6	132.4	85.7	79.7
March	152.8	120.5	140.1	129.1	152.7	119.2	248.5	132.4	85.4	80.7
April	154.8	121.7	141.4	128.4	152.7	118.1	264.0	129.9	85.7	83.3
May	158.1	124.1	142.5	128.7	153.7	118.8	278.9	131.2	86.6	85.4
June	159.6	126.3	141.6	128.1	152.9	118.2	288.9	140.3	86.5	85.9
July	160.1	125.2	141.0	128.5	153.2	119.2	297.3	130.4	86.0	85.7
August	162.4	128.7	137.8	128.7	150.6	119.6	309.5	136.4	86.4	86.5
September	163.5	128.7	142.2	129.1	151.1	118.6	327.9	136.2	86.1	88.8
October	165.4	130.3	141.8	128.9	151.6	119.8	346.8	130.5	86.2	91.0
November	167.5	129.9	144.2	128.7	150.6	120.3	357.7	136.2	86.4	90.9
December	168.5	129.3	141.1	130.4	151.6	120.7	355.9	137.2	86.0	87.6
1997										
January	168.9	130.7	146.1	131.1	152.2	121.0	348.9	133.7	85.3	83.1
February	169.9	129.6	146.2	132.8	153.8	122.4	347.8	138.0	84.9	80.1
March	171.7	126.5	148.8	132.9	156.1	122.0	359.0	141.0	84.8	80.0
April	175.9	126.6	149.5	133.5	156.4	124.4	378.9	139.2	85.9	81.6
May	178.0	129.9	151.1	133.5	156.7	124.0	398.8	135.3	85.9	83.0
June	178.4	127.8	149.0	133.5	156.2	122.8	412.1	135.0	85.1	82.9
July	179.0	127.3	144.9	132.2	156.9	125.4	417.5	133.4	84.5	81.1
August	180.4	126.6	154.2	134.4	156.9	123.9	415.4	137.0	84.3	77.9
September	180.1	129.2	152.4	134.8	157.0	125.7	413.0	133.0	83.2	74.8
October	182.6	128.9	154.1	135.1	157.7	127.4	418.7	134.5	83.4	73.1
November	185.5	128.0	155.9	135.8	157.8	125.6	445.3	141.8	83.8	75.0
December	189.0	128.2	157.4	136.2	157.4	128.1	491.1	136.3	84.4	79.7
1998										
January	193.5	131.0	155.9	135.9	157.7	127.0	533.9	138.6	85.3	83.5
February	196.3	130.0	157.3	135.3	156.6	124.6	574.6	141.0	85.5	86.5
March	199.1	134.4	161.2	135.3	156.0	127.1	585.1	140.7	85.6	84.8
April	199.2	133.9	161.2	134.3	155.0	127.4	584.5	146.4	84.5	81.6
May	201.1	134.1	163.1	133.0	152.1	126.6	589.8	157.3	84.2	79.2
June	205.9	130.7	180.2	133.3	154.2	127.7	625.8	146.5	85.1	80.8
July	209.9	131.0	180.6	132.2	153.0	126.7	681.5	149.9	85.7	84.7
August	211.7	138.4	183.7	132.5	152.3	124.2	734.5	154.6	85.5	87.7
September	213.0	138.8	175.7	129.3	150.0	127.4	767.4	152.9	85.0	88.1
October	215.0	136.9	177.0	130.6	151.6	126.7	786.8	153.1	84.8	86.9
November	215.3	138.9	171.1	131.0	150.8	124.7	805.3	152.8	84.0	85.4
December	216.6	139.0	175.6	130.5	149.4	124.9	832.2	155.4	83.5	84.8
1999										
January	217.5	139.5	173.7	128.2	148.7	123.0	868.1	154.8	82.8	85.0
February	221.7	140.8	170.8	128.1	148.4	121.0	907.1	158.3	83.4	85.3
March	224.6	142.1	166.6	127.3	147.9	122.0	947.6	155.9	83.5	85.6
April	227.0	144.2	170.2	127.6	147.3	121.1	987.5	160.7	83.4	85.7
May	228.4	144.4	166.5	127.9	146.0	121.7	1 021.6	157.6	82.9	85.2
June	228.2	144.2	158.8	127.1	147.0	121.2	1 048.2	162.0	81.8	83.9
July	230.0	142.8	167.8	126.6	148.3	122.3	1 075.1	163.4	81.5	82.7
August	231.4	148.7	160.4	126.0	147.4	122.7	1 123.7	156.7	81.1	83.0
September	235.5	149.3	166.4	124.1	146.3	122.3	1 167.5	160.9	81.6	82.9
October	238.3	151.3	170.6	124.8	145.8	122.8	1 196.6	160.4	81.6	81.6
November	239.7	148.4	166.3	124.8	144.5	124.1	1 222.8	158.7	81.1	80.1
December	241.8	148.9	170.7	124.5	143.3	123.7	1 244.6	158.5	80.7	78.3

Table 16-14. Industrial Machinery and Equipment—Shipments, Inventories, Orders, and Prices

Year and month	Manufacturers' shipments, inventories, and orders (millions of dollars, seasonally adjusted)				Producer prices (1982=100, except as noted, not seasonally adjusted)				
					Industry groups			Commodity groups	
					(December 1984=100)		Electronic computers (December 1998 =100)	Metalworking machinery and equpment	General purpose machinery and equipment
	Shipments	Inventories (book value, end of period)	New orders (net)	Unfilled orders (end of period)	Machinery, except electrical, total	Office, computing, and accounting machines			
1970	56 893	14 500	55 322	21 737	. . .	. . .	. . .	35.6	37.4
1971	56 445	14 344	55 886	21 170	. . .	. . .	. . .	36.7	39.2
1972	66 156	15 142	70 941	25 968	. . .	. . .	. . .	37.5	40.3
1973	78 207	18 411	89 162	36 959	. . .	. . .	. . .	39.1	41.8
1974	93 041	24 189	106 101	50 084	. . .	. . .	. . .	45.8	49.7
1975	96 354	24 156	92 863	46 580	. . .	. . .	. . .	53.5	58.7
1976	105 847	25 245	107 595	48 321	. . .	. . .	. . .	56.9	62.4
1977	122 749	27 282	126 235	52 026	. . .	. . .	. . .	61.9	66.4
1978	143 919	32 086	154 051	62 233	. . .	. . .	. . .	67.6	71.2
1979	167 014	37 464	174 660	69 844	. . .	. . .	. . .	75.2	77.8
1980	180 564	40 958	179 750	68 979	. . .	. . .	. . .	85.5	87.0
1981	201 102	43 652	201 576	69 405	. . .	. . .	. . .	93.9	95.0
1982	186 773	47 908	169 274	51 864	. . .	. . .	. . .	100.0	100.0
1983	178 446	44 586	178 879	52 351	. . .	. . .	. . .	101.7	101.4
1984	211 075	48 760	212 109	53 466	. . .	. . .	. . .	104.1	103.3
1985	218 408	46 526	218 395	53 516	101.0	. . .	. . .	106.6	105.7
1986	213 574	42 409	208 567	48 416	102.0	. . .	. . .	108.4	107.2
1987	217 671	43 141	221 171	48 416	103.2	. . .	. . .	110.1	108.3
1988	244 365	47 707	250 055	57 583	106.4	. . .	. . .	113.5	112.8
1989	256 212	50 342	257 051	58 369	110.7	. . .	. . .	118.2	119.0
1990	259 367	49 673	258 894	57 872	113.9	. . .	. . .	123.0	123.7
1991	247 508	47 880	243 450	53 812	116.4	. . .	334.3	127.6	127.8
1992	258 662	47 075	258 608	53 651	116.7	. . .	280.0	130.9	129.9
1993	278 063	48 602	277 416	52 952	116.8	. . .	245.8	133.5	132.2
1994	313 047	52 905	325 788	65 608	117.5	. . .	225.9	136.5	134.8
1995	353 338	59 158	358 910	71 179	119.0	70.5	202.1	139.8	139.1
1996	381 795	57 944	383 749	73 042	119.2	63.4	169.9	143.1	142.5
1997	408 860	60 304	409 215	73 419	118.5	55.9	137.1	145.3	145.0
1998	442 316	60 532	443 332	74 458	117.7	48.8	109.1	147.2	147.2
1999	455 140	60 406	461 926	81 298	117.3	44.0	91.1	148.1	149.3
1996									
January	30 678	60 045	31 612	72 113	119.7	67.6	186.8	142.0	141.6
February	32 109	60 046	32 943	72 947	119.7	66.4	182.0	142.2	141.9
March	31 379	59 851	30 709	72 277	119.7	65.8	178.9	142.5	142.2
April	31 189	60 061	31 310	72 398	119.3	64.5	175.1	142.7	142.3
May	31 656	59 749	32 034	72 776	119.3	64.2	173.1	143.1	142.3
June	31 696	58 917	31 508	72 588	119.1	63.6	171.3	143.3	142.4
July	31 431	59 172	32 293	73 450	119.1	62.6	167.2	143.3	142.6
August	32 116	59 309	32 549	73 883	119.1	62.4	165.6	143.4	142.7
September	32 371	58 849	32 075	73 587	119.1	62.1	164.7	143.5	142.7
October	32 024	58 708	31 936	73 499	118.9	61.2	161.1	143.6	143.0
November	32 172	58 884	32 007	73 334	118.9	60.6	158.4	144.0	143.3
December	32 690	57 944	32 398	73 042	118.7	60.0	155.0	144.1	143.4
1997									
January	32 400	58 425	32 911	73 553	119.1	59.7	153.1	144.3	143.8
February	32 565	58 512	33 468	74 456	119.0	59.1	150.6	144.6	144.0
March	32 862	58 503	32 862	74 456	119.1	58.7	148.8	144.7	144.5
April	33 688	59 268	34 184	74 952	119.1	58.3	147.8	145.0	144.9
May	33 401	59 462	33 279	74 830	118.5	56.3	138.3	145.3	144.9
June	34 360	59 426	32 985	73 455	118.3	55.5	135.0	145.4	145.0
July	35 124	59 808	35 411	73 742	118.4	55.0	133.4	145.5	145.2
August	34 116	59 842	34 420	74 046	118.3	54.4	130.5	145.7	145.3
September	35 234	59 658	35 499	74 311	118.2	54.1	129.5	145.8	145.4
October	35 090	60 075	34 991	74 212	118.1	53.6	127.5	145.8	145.4
November	34 343	60 093	34 395	74 264	118.0	53.2	125.6	145.8	145.5
December	35 698	60 304	34 853	73 419	118.0	53.0	124.8	145.9	145.5
1998									
January	35 936	60 135	35 766	73 249	118.1	52.0	121.0	146.5	146.1
February	36 209	61 122	36 552	73 592	118.0	51.2	117.4	146.9	146.3
March	36 864	61 011	37 448	74 176	117.9	50.7	116.5	147.2	146.5
April	36 898	61 247	36 889	74 167	117.8	49.7	113.0	147.2	146.7
May	36 561	61 081	36 244	73 850	117.7	49.3	111.0	147.3	146.8
June	37 915	60 900	36 922	72 857	117.7	49.0	110.1	147.1	147.1
July	37 810	60 903	37 636	72 683	117.7	48.6	108.7	147.2	147.5
August	36 711	60 958	37 450	73 422	117.5	47.8	104.6	147.3	147.5
September	36 775	60 938	38 983	75 630	117.6	47.6	103.8	147.3	147.9
October	37 011	60 811	35 503	74 122	117.4	47.0	102.5	147.5	147.9
November	36 623	60 974	35 593	73 092	117.4	46.7	101.2	147.5	148.1
December	36 880	60 532	38 246	74 458	117.3	46.1	100.0	147.5	148.3
1999									
January	36 513	60 658	37 164	75 109	117.4	45.5	97.4	147.5	148.8
February	36 756	60 673	37 037	75 390	117.4	45.3	96.5	147.6	148.9
March	36 972	60 817	38 338	76 756	117.4	45.1	95.9	147.7	149.0
April	37 464	60 483	39 556	78 848	117.5	44.6	93.5	148.0	149.4
May	37 519	60 331	37 780	79 109	117.5	44.6	92.7	148.1	149.3
June	37 308	59 867	36 435	78 236	117.5	44.5	92.0	148.2	149.5
July	39 434	59 791	40 257	79 059	117.3	43.6	89.7	148.2	149.6
August	38 691	59 990	39 110	79 478	117.2	43.2	88.0	148.3	149.6
September	37 742	60 139	39 077	80 813	117.1	43.1	87.7	148.3	149.3
October	39 471	59 936	39 666	81 008	117.1	42.9	86.9	148.4	149.3
November	39 075	60 495	39 347	81 280	117.1	42.8	86.7	148.5	149.4
December	38 698	60 406	38 716	81 298	117.0	42.6	85.6	148.5	149.6

Table 16-15. Industrial Machinery and Equipment—Employment, Hours, and Earnings

Year and month	Industrial machinery and equipment						Computer and office equipment (not seasonally adjusted)				
	Employment (thousands, seasonally adjusted)		Production workers				Employment (thousands)		Production workers		
	Total payroll employees	Production workers	Average weekly hours, seasonally adjusted	Aggregate weekly hours index (1982= 100), seasonally adjusted	Average earnings (dollars, not seasonally adjusted)		Total payroll employees	Production workers	Average weekly hours	Average earnings (dollars)	
					Hourly	Weekly				Hourly	Weekly
1970	2 003	1 336	41.1	...	3.77	154.95	281	138	41.0	3.69	151.30
1971	1 834	1 195	40.6	...	4.02	163.21	257	116	41.4	3.85	159.40
1972	1 909	1 258	42.1	...	4.32	181.87	252	112	42.1	3.94	165.90
1973	2 111	1 416	42.8	...	4.60	196.88	276	127	41.3	4.12	170.20
1974	2 230	1 494	42.1	...	4.94	207.97	296	137	40.9	4.37	178.70
1975	2 076	1 350	40.8	...	5.37	219.10	278	119	40.3	4.82	194.30
1976	2 085	1 352	41.2	...	5.79	238.55	278	119	41.6	5.15	214.20
1977	2 195	1 435	41.5	...	6.26	259.79	303	136	40.9	5.36	219.20
1978	2 347	1 540	42.0	...	6.78	284.76	340	154	41.4	5.62	232.70
1979	2 508	1 648	41.7	...	7.32	305.24	386	173	41.6	6.10	253.80
1980	2 517	1 614	41.0	...	8.00	328.00	420	181	41.4	6.75	279.50
1981	2 521	1 592	40.9	...	8.81	360.33	447	182	41.2	7.46	307.40
1982	2 264	1 367	39.7	...	9.26	367.62	460	184	41.1	7.93	325.90
1983	2 053	1 207	40.5	...	9.56	387.18	474	190	41.5	8.52	353.60
1984	2 218	1 342	41.9	...	9.97	417.74	515	205	42.2	8.94	377.30
1985	2 195	1 320	41.5	...	10.30	427.45	500	184	41.6	9.34	388.50
1986	2 074	1 234	41.6	...	10.58	440.13	469	163	42.1	9.97	419.70
1987	2 028	1 203	42.2	93.8	10.73	452.81	461	155	42.6	10.28	437.90
1988	2 089	1 256	42.7	98.8	11.08	473.12	459	148	41.7	10.65	444.11
1989	2 125	1 282	42.4	100.3	11.40	483.36	459	145	42.3	10.99	464.88
1990	2 095	1 260	41.9	97.5	11.77	493.16	438	137	42.0	11.51	483.42
1991	2 000	1 193	41.7	91.8	12.15	506.66	415	135	41.5	12.13	503.40
1992	1 929	1 152	42.2	89.6	12.41	523.70	391	128	42.0	12.33	517.86
1993	1 931	1 170	43.0	92.7	12.73	547.39	363	121	41.9	12.54	525.43
1994	1 990	1 233	43.7	99.3	13.00	568.10	354	123	42.7	13.08	558.52
1995	2 067	1 295	43.4	103.5	13.24	574.62	352	123	43.0	13.59	584.37
1996	2 115	1 321	43.1	105.0	13.59	585.73	362	127	42.2	13.87	585.31
1997	2 168	1 364	43.6	109.6	14.07	613.45	376	140	42.2	14.31	603.88
1998	2 206	1 392	42.8	109.9	14.47	619.32	382	147	41.8	15.37	642.47
1999	2 140	1 349	42.2	105.0	15.02	633.84	370	149	40.9	16.49	674.44
1996											
January	2 106	1 319	42.0	102.2	13.44	568.51	360	129	41.7	13.42	559.61
February	2 106	1 318	43.1	104.8	13.40	580.22	359	128	42.9	13.65	585.59
March	2 112	1 318	43.1	104.8	13.36	578.49	361	127	43.4	13.61	590.67
April	2 111	1 317	43.2	104.9	13.44	573.89	361	127	42.1	13.70	576.77
May	2 113	1 318	43.2	105.0	13.45	578.35	362	127	42.0	13.76	577.92
June	2 115	1 318	43.2	105.0	13.52	585.42	365	128	42.7	13.99	597.37
July	2 116	1 321	43.1	105.0	13.55	574.52	363	128	41.4	13.93	576.70
August	2 116	1 321	43.1	105.0	13.64	582.43	363	127	41.0	13.96	572.36
September	2 115	1 321	43.2	105.2	13.77	596.24	361	126	42.4	14.06	596.14
October	2 119	1 323	43.0	104.9	13.71	588.16	362	127	41.5	13.95	578.93
November	2 120	1 326	43.1	105.4	13.81	597.97	362	127	42.0	14.08	591.36
December	2 125	1 329	43.3	106.1	13.98	620.71	363	128	43.2	14.33	619.06
1997											
January	2 132	1 336	43.3	106.7	13.92	602.74	364	129	41.8	14.10	589.38
February	2 139	1 341	43.4	107.3	13.90	606.04	365	130	42.7	14.10	602.07
March	2 145	1 347	43.6	108.3	13.95	611.01	368	135	42.6	14.15	602.79
April	2 152	1 355	44.0	109.9	13.96	608.66	370	137	42.4	14.13	599.11
May	2 156	1 356	43.7	109.3	13.94	606.39	374	140	42.3	13.97	590.93
June	2 162	1 361	43.4	108.9	13.97	606.30	378	142	42.3	14.18	599.81
July	2 169	1 365	43.5	109.5	14.03	600.48	381	142	41.8	14.18	592.72
August	2 177	1 371	43.5	110.0	14.04	605.12	382	143	41.3	14.26	588.94
September	2 181	1 376	43.5	110.4	14.20	620.54	380	143	41.8	14.49	605.68
October	2 193	1 381	43.5	110.8	14.24	616.59	383	145	41.7	14.64	610.49
November	2 200	1 387	43.7	111.8	14.31	629.64	382	144	42.8	14.74	630.87
December	2 206	1 391	43.7	112.1	14.42	646.02	384	145	42.8	14.73	630.44
1998											
January	2 214	1 397	43.6	112.3	14.35	627.10	384	145	41.9	14.78	619.28
February	2 216	1 399	43.4	112.0	14.38	625.53	383	146	42.5	15.08	640.90
March	2 219	1 399	43.3	111.7	14.38	625.53	383	147	42.5	14.87	631.98
April	2 218	1 399	42.8	110.4	14.34	600.85	381	146	41.4	15.10	625.14
May	2 219	1 399	43.0	110.9	14.38	619.78	382	147	41.1	15.15	622.67
June	2 218	1 400	43.2	111.5	14.42	622.94	384	148	40.7	15.13	615.79
July	2 210	1 394	42.9	110.3	14.43	610.81	384	147	40.9	15.46	632.31
August	2 208	1 394	42.8	110.0	14.46	616.00	382	146	41.7	15.51	646.77
September	2 202	1 392	42.6	109.4	14.55	608.19	381	147	42.9	15.47	663.66
October	2 194	1 387	42.5	108.7	14.57	617.77	380	147	42.3	15.80	668.34
November	2 183	1 379	42.4	107.8	14.64	625.13	378	148	42.4	16.07	681.37
December	2 173	1 372	42.1	106.5	14.73	636.34	377	149	41.7	15.94	664.70
1999											
January	2 156	1 360	42.1	105.6	14.70	620.34	369	147	41.1	15.97	656.37
February	2 155	1 359	42.1	105.5	14.73	620.13	368	147	41.2	16.00	659.20
March	2 149	1 357	42.0	105.1	14.82	623.92	368	148	40.9	15.96	652.76
April	2 144	1 353	42.0	104.8	14.86	627.09	368	148	40.5	16.07	650.84
May	2 141	1 352	42.1	105.0	14.97	631.73	372	151	40.8	16.63	678.50
June	2 139	1 349	42.1	104.7	14.99	631.08	375	151	41.0	16.57	679.37
July	2 142	1 355	42.3	105.7	15.08	628.84	372	149	40.8	16.73	682.58
August	2 135	1 343	42.3	104.8	15.14	637.39	371	148	41.0	16.87	691.67
September	2 133	1 341	42.4	104.9	15.24	635.51	370	146	40.9	17.10	699.39
October	2 130	1 340	42.3	104.5	15.18	640.60	370	147	40.9	16.52	675.67
November	2 131	1 342	42.2	104.4	15.22	646.85	370	151	40.3	16.71	673.41
December	2 132	1 343	42.2	104.5	15.36	663.55	371	153	40.9	16.80	687.12

Table 16-16. Electronic and Electric Equipment—Industrial Production

(1992=100, seasonally adjusted.)

| Year and month | Electrical machinery | Major electrical equipment and parts | | Household appliances | | | | | | | Audio and video equipment |
| | | Total | Electric distribution equipment | Total | Cooking equipment | Refrigerators and freezers | Laundry | Miscellaneous | | | |
								Total	Electrical housewares	Appliances, not elsewhere classified	
1970	26.2	82.5	98.8	57.2	45.0	70.6	67.0	53.1	73.7	48.1	39.0
1971	26.3	83.3	98.2	60.2	50.2	73.8	72.0	55.0	75.1	49.5	43.9
1972	30.1	91.4	106.7	70.6	60.0	86.2	82.4	65.2	91.9	54.6	49.3
1973	34.3	106.2	121.2	79.3	68.1	91.3	88.8	76.1	102.0	65.7	54.1
1974	33.9	107.2	116.3	75.6	60.0	89.2	75.7	76.1	105.3	61.8	47.6
1975	29.2	84.6	91.5	63.1	56.8	69.8	63.6	63.2	92.0	50.1	41.0
1976	32.8	91.0	95.2	70.3	73.9	63.6	68.4	73.3	105.7	59.0	44.6
1977	38.1	99.3	108.0	78.9	80.0	75.9	75.7	80.8	117.2	68.2	51.6
1978	42.2	108.4	115.5	79.1	87.8	77.1	73.7	79.0	112.4	67.4	58.2
1979	46.9	112.6	120.3	81.4	83.9	76.9	74.1	85.4	118.5	74.4	56.7
1980	48.6	105.0	115.6	77.6	88.7	66.6	67.1	82.9	125.7	66.3	57.8
1981	51.0	105.5	110.7	76.9	98.9	69.2	65.3	77.9	111.0	67.7	58.4
1982	51.7	91.8	99.4	68.2	83.2	57.5	58.0	72.2	105.4	59.2	51.8
1983	55.9	87.8	97.3	82.4	121.3	69.2	71.0	81.0	106.0	75.5	69.6
1984	66.7	100.6	106.1	90.3	119.9	83.8	75.1	90.7	107.1	87.1	83.0
1985	68.4	96.9	102.6	83.5	94.1	72.2	79.1	87.9	102.7	88.6	74.8
1986	71.0	96.6	100.8	89.9	104.7	84.6	88.3	88.3	97.9	93.9	77.9
1987	75.6	97.0	101.5	93.6	104.8	88.4	92.6	93.1	100.7	97.9	80.0
1988	82.5	105.8	114.1	96.9	110.6	96.1	94.1	94.2	100.3	94.8	86.8
1989	85.8	105.3	108.8	97.2	101.2	98.5	94.6	96.6	105.3	94.1	93.7
1990	87.7	103.6	107.1	95.3	97.0	87.1	96.1	98.0	104.6	91.7	92.8
1991	89.6	98.4	99.5	92.1	94.2	88.5	92.1	92.9	100.4	87.6	95.9
1992	100.0	100.0	100.0	100.0	100.0	100.0	100.0	100.0	100.0	100.0	100.0
1993	109.4	106.6	99.2	110.5	101.9	105.4	120.8	111.3	106.1	121.4	107.6
1994	130.5	113.0	108.2	122.6	127.4	122.4	142.8	112.1	106.3	128.6	122.7
1995	165.7	123.8	116.4	114.7	128.4	121.5	127.5	101.2	114.8	94.8	138.2
1996	206.6	125.3	116.5	116.1	113.3	129.1	130.3	104.9	107.0	95.8	113.7
1997	260.0	124.7	117.4	112.2	116.5	117.1	119.0	105.1	108.6	94.8	88.6
1998	315.1	125.0	117.5	118.8	121.6	130.0	132.4	107.0	101.2	97.6	67.5
1999	390.2	125.8	121.7	125.1	129.1	137.2	142.8	111.4	91.8	102.3	90.1
1996											
January	185.1	126.4	119.4	108.8	90.6	129.8	126.4	98.5	107.4	87.9	115.0
February	191.5	127.4	120.9	111.5	104.5	125.9	126.2	101.1	109.1	90.0	121.7
March	193.7	126.2	116.4	114.9	121.7	129.2	116.9	104.6	106.9	95.6	105.8
April	196.4	128.1	117.9	114.1	108.1	125.9	126.2	105.3	103.9	95.9	124.7
May	200.4	126.3	116.5	116.0	108.1	126.5	126.9	108.6	107.3	100.3	123.9
June	205.5	124.9	115.1	123.0	124.5	137.7	137.7	109.4	110.3	101.5	123.4
July	208.2	124.0	116.2	117.2	112.0	125.6	140.4	105.2	114.0	92.5	112.3
August	212.9	124.5	114.9	121.6	121.3	143.9	141.0	103.7	112.1	91.8	108.3
September	216.6	124.9	114.3	119.0	123.0	126.1	136.6	106.9	108.1	100.6	107.7
October	219.5	122.8	116.2	115.4	109.5	123.0	132.0	106.4	105.4	99.3	111.4
November	223.3	124.6	115.6	115.3	116.5	127.3	126.0	104.6	104.0	95.1	109.8
December	226.0	123.2	114.3	116.3	120.2	128.5	126.9	104.8	99.3	98.7	99.9
1997											
January	229.1	126.2	116.8	110.1	111.2	120.1	116.0	102.0	101.0	93.0	84.2
February	236.4	125.8	116.3	109.5	116.8	114.9	109.6	103.7	106.0	95.0	93.1
March	242.8	123.6	117.1	114.5	126.3	119.5	123.5	104.2	108.9	94.7	86.1
April	245.7	124.2	115.8	111.4	103.9	119.7	121.7	104.9	109.8	95.8	87.0
May	251.6	124.4	115.2	111.3	117.5	114.7	119.3	103.8	110.9	93.8	92.2
June	259.7	124.4	117.6	114.4	120.1	119.1	126.7	105.0	113.3	97.4	82.3
July	266.6	124.2	117.7	112.9	121.9	115.0	132.1	101.3	108.5	94.1	89.2
August	270.6	123.5	117.5	109.0	121.4	119.0	106.2	100.8	110.6	90.7	89.3
September	274.4	122.9	118.4	109.7	115.5	114.0	107.2	105.5	108.4	96.1	87.1
October	277.1	124.8	117.2	113.9	120.1	117.7	119.1	107.1	111.4	91.2	92.3
November	282.2	126.4	118.9	116.2	118.8	118.1	120.6	111.5	108.2	98.1	88.1
December	284.4	126.4	120.0	113.6	102.7	113.5	126.0	110.8	108.7	98.2	91.9
1998											
January	287.4	125.4	116.2	119.5	126.0	123.4	136.8	108.5	108.6	98.4	88.4
February	289.6	124.8	117.4	118.4	123.6	129.2	133.2	105.7	108.1	96.9	76.9
March	291.9	125.5	115.5	118.3	119.3	129.3	137.2	105.3	105.8	98.3	85.3
April	298.0	124.6	117.1	117.2	122.0	128.4	131.6	104.6	107.0	95.0	78.6
May	303.5	124.8	118.3	119.2	125.2	127.9	134.9	106.8	104.1	99.2	59.9
June	311.7	125.0	115.9	116.1	121.6	126.5	126.5	105.1	102.6	95.9	57.2
July	319.0	124.2	118.5	117.6	122.8	129.4	129.4	105.6	99.6	98.1	59.6
August	323.3	123.9	116.5	117.0	124.0	125.2	124.3	107.3	100.7	99.7	53.9
September	331.9	127.3	118.2	116.8	118.0	127.7	128.0	106.4	98.9	95.8	65.1
October	338.2	124.7	117.6	121.5	129.6	133.8	133.6	108.3	96.1	97.1	58.8
November	341.7	125.3	117.9	122.4	120.6	137.0	137.6	109.9	95.9	98.1	61.4
December	344.8	124.6	121.1	121.1	105.0	122.8	141.8	136.1	110.1	95.7	98.4	64.6
1999											
January	346.7	125.2	119.7	124.6	127.6	136.0	143.5	110.8	95.3	101.5	70.7
February	347.5	124.4	116.1	128.6	132.2	141.2	152.9	112.4	96.1	105.9	80.2
March	354.0	124.5	118.7	121.9	127.0	127.2	136.7	111.4	98.9	103.2	81.8
April	366.4	125.4	122.7	127.4	133.6	135.0	152.9	112.1	93.2	107.3	85.0
May	373.3	123.7	122.7	123.2	135.0	137.0	137.3	107.8	89.4	100.0	77.9
June	384.2	125.2	124.1	120.4	126.0	130.0	137.5	107.3	86.8	99.5	80.8
July	399.2	125.4	121.5	124.5	131.0	139.2	139.5	109.8	91.8	101.7	95.2
August	401.3	128.1	120.5	123.3	117.4	139.5	146.7	108.6	89.5	100.5	80.4
September	402.1	127.8	121.2	117.4	120.1	121.4	133.9	107.7	89.1	98.5	99.4
October	412.6	126.9	123.0	127.6	143.9	140.9	145.1	110.1	87.8	103.1	133.6
November	418.1	126.2	124.4	132.0	124.5	151.5	148.2	118.8	93.6	103.2	86.3
December	426.4	128.7	125.2	130.6	132.3	148.6	136.9	118.6	91.4	103.6	101.3

Table 16-17. Electronic and Electric Equipment—Production, Capacity Utilization, Shipments, Inventories, and Orders

(Seasonally adjusted.)

| Year and month | Industrial production—Continued | | | | Capacity utilization— Electrical machinery (output as a percent of capacity) | Manufacturers' shipments, inventories, and orders (millions of dollars) | | | |
| | Communication equipment | Electronic componenets | Miscellaneous electrical supplies | | | Shipments | Inventories (book value, end of period) | New orders (net) | Unfilled orders (end of period) |
			Total	Storage batteries					
1970	31.8	4.4	47.0	51.4	76.6	41 408	8 410	41 117	11 881
1971	29.0	4.7	48.9	52.2	73.5	42 377	8 058	42 639	12 148
1972	31.8	5.9	53.8	60.5	81.1	47 502	8 528	48 702	13 376
1973	34.6	7.4	60.6	65.7	88.0	54 569	10 532	58 275	17 111
1974	35.7	7.3	60.5	66.9	81.9	58 684	12 231	58 884	17 319
1975	34.8	6.0	54.7	64.4	67.0	56 068	11 110	54 610	15 857
1976	34.8	7.8	64.6	75.8	72.8	65 151	12 594	66 864	17 584
1977	38.9	9.9	78.6	86.2	80.1	77 845	13 922	80 010	19 999
1978	43.8	12.0	82.2	91.0	83.9	88 679	16 163	92 781	24 219
1979	51.2	15.3	80.9	89.4	87.7	102 361	19 566	107 314	29 261
1980	56.8	18.1	71.3	78.5	84.0	112 864	21 838	115 335	31 751
1981	57.9	21.5	74.4	80.1	81.2	122 084	23 608	123 053	32 718
1982	60.7	25.6	74.1	76.0	76.7	125 728	25 100	127 630	34 639
1983	62.1	29.8	80.9	86.0	77.8	136 138	26 922	142 131	40 794
1984	70.4	40.6	99.3	101.1	85.8	162 362	31 636	165 541	43 967
1985	78.1	41.2	95.8	97.9	80.5	163 951	30 549	163 352	43 366
1986	80.5	44.2	96.9	104.1	77.8	164 811	28 632	164 282	42 793
1987	82.9	51.9	101.4	107.2	78.7	171 287	29 859	173 210	44 741
1988	90.0	58.5	109.3	104.9	82.3	187 301	31 645	189 211	46 702
1989	91.4	65.2	108.1	104.2	81.3	194 598	33 623	192 482	44 616
1990	94.7	72.1	97.3	104.6	78.9	195 898	32 913	195 748	44 501
1991	90.6	80.9	102.5	98.7	76.3	199 278	30 981	197 659	42 988
1992	100.0	100.0	100.0	100.0	79.7	216 764	30 722	217 966	44 348
1993	107.1	114.3	107.7	109.7	81.8	233 622	31 863	233 991	44 784
1994	126.3	151.6	115.8	123.3	86.4	266 405	35 847	266 386	44 941
1995	145.4	241.0	117.4	121.3	87.7	301 447	39 413	307 634	51 470
1996	170.0	359.3	124.9	119.5	82.7	320 616	39 335	319 157	49 943
1997	204.6	540.8	129.1	128.1	83.5	351 554	40 488	356 557	55 174
1998	231.1	768.6	132.8	142.2	78.9	375 970	39 786	380 470	60 530
1999	260.8	1 127.8	134.1	145.5	78.8	413 204	43 611	439 085	85 466
1996									
January	156.4	299.1	117.7	115.7	84.4	26 038	39 776	25 968	51 400
February	162.2	309.9	124.3	131.4	85.1	25 996	39 377	25 401	50 805
March	164.9	318.1	123.1	126.9	83.9	26 375	39 099	26 594	51 024
April	165.6	325.3	120.9	103.1	83.0	26 424	39 322	26 221	50 821
May	165.5	337.8	122.9	115.7	82.5	26 456	39 135	25 506	49 871
June	169.5	349.6	127.6	130.5	82.6	26 583	39 331	26 315	49 603
July	171.3	362.6	126.5	114.8	82.0	26 474	39 098	27 701	50 830
August	171.8	379.1	126.1	115.1	82.3	26 228	39 206	26 122	50 724
September	174.0	391.4	127.2	118.7	82.1	26 715	39 367	26 104	50 113
October	177.0	403.5	127.1	116.1	81.7	27 209	39 428	30 268	53 172
November	178.9	413.3	128.0	125.2	81.6	28 185	39 636	28 414	53 401
December	183.4	422.3	128.1	122.5	81.1	27 370	39 335	23 912	49 943
1997									
January	187.3	433.2	127.0	128.3	80.9	27 031	39 024	28 241	51 153
February	191.2	456.8	127.1	127.6	82.1	28 076	39 064	30 792	53 869
March	194.9	479.8	128.9	128.9	82.9	29 456	38 942	29 140	53 553
April	198.2	487.2	127.8	127.5	82.5	28 345	39 422	27 419	52 627
May	199.4	508.6	128.5	129.5	83.1	28 464	39 610	30 276	54 439
June	204.6	537.6	126.9	125.5	84.3	29 329	39 532	30 269	55 379
July	208.7	559.8	130.2	126.5	85.2	29 104	40 120	25 247	51 522
August	206.7	585.7	131.0	132.7	85.1	29 736	40 088	34 068	55 854
September	212.6	596.9	130.0	124.9	84.8	30 809	39 950	31 118	56 163
October	214.2	603.3	127.7	121.0	84.1	29 855	40 052	29 718	56 026
November	219.1	614.9	133.9	146.5	84.0	29 842	40 278	29 227	55 411
December	218.6	625.8	130.5	121.7	82.9	30 495	40 488	30 258	55 174
1998									
January	220.6	637.2	130.7	124.8	81.9	29 532	40 801	31 417	57 059
February	222.5	646.9	132.8	128.1	80.6	30 714	41 250	30 714	57 059
March	219.9	658.7	134.7	142.4	79.4	30 838	41 364	30 850	57 071
April	226.4	681.9	135.1	140.1	79.0	30 056	41 378	31 707	58 722
May	228.5	708.2	135.3	146.7	78.4	29 767	41 236	29 144	58 099
June	232.7	746.0	133.2	147.5	78.5	30 882	40 818	30 072	57 289
July	233.9	782.0	132.5	142.0	78.6	31 216	40 345	32 840	58 913
August	235.7	809.3	132.1	146.2	78.1	31 228	40 526	31 116	58 801
September	238.1	844.7	132.7	148.1	78.6	32 422	40 172	32 870	59 249
October	239.2	882.5	134.1	153.5	78.5	32 219	40 589	33 348	60 378
November	237.7	908.2	130.0	141.1	77.9	32 634	40 315	31 933	59 677
December	238.6	917.9	130.4	140.9	77.2	33 006	39 786	33 859	60 530
1999									
January	239.6	918.8	136.3	178.4	76.3	32 830	39 581	34 895	62 595
February	239.8	924.3	132.4	146.2	75.2	32 235	40 133	32 651	63 011
March	242.6	964.0	130.4	133.7	75.5	33 032	40 356	34 264	64 243
April	250.6	1 014.9	132.8	148.1	77.0	33 655	40 542	34 364	64 952
May	257.6	1 043.6	133.9	148.2	77.4	33 836	40 825	34 067	65 183
June	260.0	1 102.7	132.8	138.9	78.7	34 196	40 997	35 158	66 145
July	271.6	1 158.5	139.0	165.4	80.9	35 373	41 221	37 976	68 748
August	275.5	1 169.4	132.0	140.2	80.5	35 339	41 204	38 616	72 025
September	272.0	1 186.3	132.7	140.4	79.8	35 307	41 518	38 734	75 452
October	272.6	1 234.5	135.8	151.5	81.1	34 860	42 091	35 884	76 476
November	268.5	1 309.4	134.3	138.6	81.3	35 605	42 665	39 352	80 223
December	272.0	1 350.6	134.7	130.3	82.0	36 281	43 611	41 524	85 466

Table 16-18. Electronic and Electric Equipment—Prices, Employment, Hours, and Earnings

| Year and month | Producer prices (1982=100, except as noted; not seasonally adjusted) | | | | | Employment (thousands, seasonally adjusted) | | Production workers | | | | |
| | Industry groups (December 1984=100) | | Finished goods: Communication and related equipment (December 1985=100) | Intermediate materials | | Total payroll employees | Production workers | Average weekly hours, seasonally adjusted | Aggregate weekly hours index (1982=100), seasonally adjusted | Average earnings (dollars, not seasonally adjusted) | |
	Electrical and electronic machinery, equipment and supplies	Electronic components and accessories		Switchgear, switchboard, etc.	Electronic components and accessories					Hourly	Weekly
1970	...	...	...	40.5	57.4	1 584	...	...	...	...	...
1971	...	...	...	42.3	58.2	1 477	...	...	...	...	...
1972	...	...	...	42.2	58.7	1 535	...	...	...	...	...
1973	...	...	...	42.9	59.3	1 667	...	...	...	...	...
1974	...	...	...	50.3	63.3	1 666	...	...	...	...	...
1975	...	...	...	58.6	65.6	1 442	...	...	...	...	...
1976	...	...	...	61.9	65.8	1 503	...	...	...	...	...
1977	...	...	...	65.9	67.9	1 591	...	...	...	...	...
1978	...	...	...	69.8	72.1	1 699	...	...	...	...	...
1979	...	...	...	75.8	77.1	1 793	...	...	...	...	...
1980	...	...	...	88.4	88.8	1 771	...	...	...	...	...
1981	...	...	...	95.1	95.5	1 774	...	...	...	...	...
1982	...	...	...	100.0	100.0	1 701	...	...	...	...	...
1983	...	...	...	103.3	104.3	1 704	...	...	...	...	...
1984	...	...	...	105.0	109.8	1 869	...	...	...	...	...
1985	...	100.5	...	106.7	112.4	1 859	...	...	...	...	...
1986	102.1	102.5	101.2	108.1	114.5	1 790	...	...	...	...	...
1987	103.3	102.6	102.5	110.1	115.0	1 750	...	...	...	...	...
1988	104.6	104.0	102.8	113.2	117.5	1 764	1 112	41.0	113.1	9.79	401.39
1989	107.1	105.1	104.7	119.0	119.4	1 744	1 102	40.8	111.5	10.05	410.04
1990	108.9	104.9	106.1	124.4	118.4	1 673	1 055	40.8	106.5	10.30	420.24
1991	110.1	104.9	107.4	128.5	118.6	1 591	999	40.7	100.7	10.70	435.49
1992	110.8	104.6	107.9	131.5	117.5	1 528	971	41.2	99.1	11.00	453.20
1993	112.0	105.3	109.1	134.6	117.7	1 526	975	41.8	100.9	11.24	469.83
1994	112.7	104.8	110.8	136.8	116.6	1 571	1 010	42.2	105.7	11.50	485.30
1995	113.3	102.5	112.1	140.3	113.6	1 625	1 045	41.6	107.8	11.69	486.30
1996	113.2	99.3	113.0	142.6	108.9	1 661	1 056	41.5	108.5	12.18	505.47
1997	111.6	95.1	114.0	145.6	104.0	1 689	1 069	42.0	111.1	12.70	533.40
1998	110.4	91.9	114.1	148.4	100.0	1 707	1 071	41.4	109.9	13.10	542.34
1999	109.5	90.1	112.7	151.0	98.2	1 670	1 043	41.4	107.0	13.46	557.24
1996											
January	113.8	102.0	112.9	142.0	112.5	1 648	1 052	40.1	104.5	11.95	482.78
February	113.9	101.8	113.1	142.0	112.2	1 651	1 053	41.7	108.8	11.88	494.21
March	113.5	100.6	113.0	142.3	110.8	1 651	1 053	41.6	108.5	11.91	494.27
April	113.3	99.7	113.0	141.7	109.4	1 655	1 055	41.2	107.7	12.01	490.01
May	113.1	99.1	112.7	142.1	108.5	1 658	1 056	41.5	108.6	12.09	496.90
June	113.0	98.7	112.6	142.6	107.9	1 661	1 057	41.6	108.9	12.19	507.10
July	113.0	98.7	112.9	142.1	108.0	1 664	1 059	41.4	108.6	12.25	497.35
August	113.1	98.7	113.1	142.7	108.0	1 665	1 057	41.7	109.2	12.28	510.85
September	113.0	98.8	113.1	142.6	108.1	1 667	1 058	41.7	109.3	12.35	518.70
October	112.7	98.0	113.2	142.7	107.3	1 668	1 057	41.5	108.7	12.33	514.16
November	112.8	97.8	113.0	144.8	107.3	1 669	1 057	41.6	108.9	12.35	519.94
December	112.7	97.8	113.9	144.0	107.2	1 670	1 055	41.8	109.3	12.54	537.97
1997											
January	112.5	97.2	113.9	144.0	106.7	1 670	1 056	41.4	108.3	12.46	513.35
February	112.2	96.6	114.0	144.6	106.0	1 672	1 058	42.0	110.1	12.41	518.74
March	112.2	96.6	113.4	144.8	105.8	1 674	1 059	42.3	111.0	12.49	527.08
April	112.0	96.2	113.5	145.0	105.4	1 675	1 059	42.4	111.2	12.55	525.85
May	111.8	95.4	113.7	145.6	104.5	1 676	1 059	42.1	110.5	12.55	524.59
June	111.8	95.5	113.6	145.7	104.5	1 683	1 063	42.1	110.9	12.59	528.78
July	111.7	95.5	114.4	145.7	104.4	1 691	1 068	42.1	111.4	12.68	522.42
August	111.1	94.2	114.2	145.7	103.0	1 696	1 073	41.9	111.4	12.74	531.26
September	111.1	94.2	114.1	145.5	102.9	1 700	1 076	41.8	111.4	12.84	540.56
October	110.8	93.6	114.1	146.0	101.9	1 707	1 080	41.9	112.1	12.90	540.51
November	110.8	93.3	114.8	147.1	101.6	1 713	1 084	41.9	112.5	12.98	554.25
December	110.8	93.3	114.8	146.9	101.4	1 718	1 089	42.0	113.3	13.11	566.35
1998											
January	110.8	92.9	114.8	147.8	101.1	1 725	1 091	41.9	113.3	12.98	542.56
February	110.6	92.6	114.8	147.3	100.7	1 725	1 089	41.8	112.8	12.95	538.72
March	110.7	92.5	114.6	147.9	100.7	1 725	1 086	41.4	111.4	13.04	538.55
April	110.5	92.4	114.4	148.1	100.4	1 723	1 083	41.3	110.8	13.06	527.62
May	110.4	92.1	114.1	147.9	100.1	1 720	1 080	41.3	110.5	13.03	536.84
June	110.4	92.0	114.1	148.3	100.0	1 718	1 078	41.4	110.6	13.06	540.68
July	110.4	91.7	113.7	148.3	99.7	1 709	1 070	41.3	109.5	13.13	533.08
August	110.3	91.5	113.6	148.3	99.6	1 702	1 064	41.5	109.4	13.10	543.65
September	110.2	91.3	113.6	148.3	99.5	1 697	1 061	41.3	108.6	13.24	542.84
October	110.0	91.2	113.7	149.0	99.4	1 689	1 055	41.4	108.2	13.13	544.90
November	110.1	91.0	113.7	150.0	99.2	1 681	1 050	41.5	108.0	13.18	554.88
December	110.0	91.0	113.5	149.8	99.1	1 677	1 047	41.2	106.9	13.27	561.32
1999											
January	110.0	90.8	114.3	150.5	98.8	1 672	1 044	41.1	106.3	13.26	543.66
February	109.9	90.7	114.2	150.5	98.6	1 668	1 039	41.3	106.3	13.26	544.99
March	109.8	90.7	114.1	150.1	98.6	1 668	1 043	40.9	105.7	13.29	542.23
April	109.7	90.5	114.0	150.6	98.3	1 667	1 044	41.2	106.6	13.32	547.45
May	109.7	90.4	113.0	150.8	98.1	1 666	1 042	41.4	106.9	13.39	553.01
June	109.5	89.9	112.8	151.5	97.8	1 667	1 040	41.5	106.9	13.42	556.93
July	109.5	89.7	112.6	151.0	97.6	1 675	1 053	41.5	108.3	13.49	550.39
August	109.5	89.9	112.1	151.1	97.7	1 669	1 045	41.6	107.7	13.52	562.43
September	109.2	90.0	111.2	150.8	98.1	1 670	1 043	41.6	107.5	13.64	563.33
October	109.1	89.7	111.4	151.7	98.3	1 672	1 042	41.6	107.4	13.60	568.48
November	109.1	89.5	111.3	152.0	98.2	1 670	1 041	41.4	106.8	13.61	572.98
December	108.9	89.3	111.3	151.9	97.9	1 673	1 039	41.5	106.8	13.73	582.15

Table 16-19. Transportation Equipment—Industrial Production

(1992 = 100, seasonally adjusted.)

Year and month	Total	Motor vehicles and parts								Aerospace and miscellaneous transportation equipment			
		Total	Autos	Trucks and truck trailers				Motor vehicle parts	Motor homes	Total	Aircraft and parts	Ships and boats	Railroad and miscellaneous
				Total	Trucks and buses								
					Total	Consumer Trucks	Business trucks						
1970	54.1	52.0	63.4	25.0	24.1	14.2	48.0	61.8	...	62.3	57.1	90.5	53.2
1971	58.5	65.2	86.9	30.5	30.3	20.0	57.1	71.8	...	55.9	47.9	88.3	59.8
1972	62.4	71.1	90.5	36.2	34.9	25.8	61.2	79.6	...	57.7	47.6	102.3	65.2
1973	71.1	82.8	100.5	45.2	44.0	33.6	72.1	92.9	...	63.8	52.7	115.0	71.4
1974	64.6	71.4	78.4	42.8	40.8	31.5	65.5	82.9	...	62.0	51.2	116.2	68.0
1975	58.2	61.0	74.6	35.3	35.8	28.5	52.8	65.8	...	59.3	48.1	120.9	65.0
1976	66.3	80.0	96.4	47.9	48.6	40.1	65.0	86.1	...	56.6	43.9	124.6	63.6
1977	71.9	92.4	107.3	59.5	59.2	50.1	73.2	98.3	...	55.6	45.0	127.4	58.3
1978	77.5	96.8	108.0	65.2	64.2	55.7	76.4	103.7	...	62.2	52.8	131.4	62.6
1979	78.7	89.0	102.8	57.0	54.8	45.8	66.6	95.1	...	71.1	64.2	129.8	68.6
1980	70.3	65.8	82.5	33.6	31.5	24.6	42.3	72.3	...	74.3	69.7	135.8	65.9
1981	66.9	62.8	82.7	34.5	32.8	26.8	41.6	65.1	...	70.5	65.1	142.8	61.4
1982	63.0	56.9	68.8	37.9	37.3	34.0	42.3	58.7	...	68.3	61.9	131.0	63.6
1983	70.5	72.1	95.2	48.9	48.3	45.9	52.4	69.3	...	69.3	63.7	109.6	68.9
1984	80.5	87.3	111.7	67.0	64.5	60.8	70.6	81.3	...	75.1	66.7	113.6	81.0
1985	88.8	95.0	120.8	75.1	73.6	68.2	82.2	87.9	...	83.7	73.8	109.1	96.9
1986	94.1	94.2	118.9	77.3	76.5	70.8	85.2	85.9	...	94.2	86.4	103.9	107.7
1987	96.1	94.9	111.0	86.2	85.2	80.1	92.9	87.1	114.2	97.5	92.9	107.3	104.2
1988	101.1	100.2	113.7	93.3	92.5	87.0	100.9	92.9	122.7	102.1	95.7	111.2	113.0
1989	105.1	101.2	115.6	96.4	95.7	92.5	100.4	91.9	108.8	109.4	103.9	112.9	120.1
1990	102.3	95.3	106.1	90.9	90.9	88.4	94.6	88.9	89.4	109.8	105.1	113.0	119.0
1991	96.5	88.5	95.7	83.5	83.6	83.4	83.9	85.8	80.3	105.0	105.4	101.3	105.7
1992	100.0	100.0	100.0	100.0	100.0	100.0	100.0	100.0	100.0	100.0	100.0	100.0	100.0
1993	103.5	113.0	104.0	122.2	122.6	123.3	121.6	114.3	106.9	93.9	91.0	95.4	99.7
1994	107.5	130.6	115.9	143.6	143.7	141.2	147.1	134.5	111.2	84.9	80.9	94.2	90.5
1995	106.7	133.2	110.1	148.8	148.0	142.6	155.9	142.7	98.6	81.0	76.5	90.4	87.7
1996	107.6	131.8	103.6	146.5	147.7	149.4	144.3	146.1	107.5	83.9	81.6	91.4	85.7
1997	117.1	140.6	102.1	164.1	165.4	167.0	162.2	157.9	103.5	94.2	96.2	90.9	88.4
1998	121.6	141.7	97.6	175.9	175.8	175.7	175.2	155.7	119.4	101.7	106.9	94.8	88.5
1999	122.4	151.0	96.7	200.7	201.8	202.4	199.9	162.4	137.5	94.9	97.9	91.9	86.3
1996													
January	104.0	128.6	95.7	137.9	138.2	136.6	140.3	151.1	102.9	79.9	76.4	86.9	85.3
February	106.0	131.5	103.0	145.2	145.9	144.9	146.9	146.7	107.0	81.2	78.4	87.1	85.0
March	95.9	110.5	79.4	131.1	131.5	130.2	133.2	122.0	118.3	81.5	78.2	90.7	85.3
April	108.8	136.6	109.3	148.3	149.7	149.9	148.8	152.3	109.3	81.7	78.2	91.7	85.7
May	109.9	138.2	111.6	145.5	146.8	146.8	146.2	156.4	115.4	82.3	79.1	91.9	85.7
June	110.3	138.6	115.1	151.7	152.4	153.4	150.2	149.7	116.0	82.8	79.5	94.6	85.3
July	111.6	139.8	115.0	159.2	160.9	166.7	151.1	148.2	96.3	84.2	81.3	91.5	87.5
August	110.6	137.3	110.4	149.1	150.5	154.7	143.1	152.9	102.3	84.6	81.8	94.0	86.7
September	109.0	132.4	110.0	145.8	147.0	150.2	141.3	142.3	112.1	86.1	84.3	93.2	86.3
October	105.7	125.2	92.5	143.0	144.5	149.1	136.5	140.9	108.9	86.7	85.8	91.6	85.5
November	109.4	131.9	102.1	146.3	147.7	150.4	142.9	147.9	108.8	87.5	87.4	91.5	84.5
December	109.6	131.2	99.5	155.2	157.0	160.5	150.9	142.5	89.8	88.4	88.3	92.2	85.5
1997													
January	112.4	136.6	101.6	157.9	159.8	162.7	154.4	152.7	99.3	88.7	88.5	92.5	86.2
February	112.9	136.6	104.6	157.8	159.5	161.3	156.2	149.8	101.7	89.8	89.3	92.8	88.4
March	113.9	137.1	104.4	163.0	164.6	166.4	161.1	147.9	93.1	91.2	91.3	92.7	88.5
April	112.6	133.0	98.7	146.5	147.1	147.8	145.3	153.9	100.3	92.5	93.4	93.8	88.0
May	113.5	134.2	101.5	152.4	152.9	152.8	152.5	150.3	100.7	93.1	94.2	93.9	88.4
June	116.7	140.6	102.3	165.0	166.1	168.1	162.4	157.3	101.2	93.4	95.3	89.4	88.2
July	114.1	135.3	97.3	147.3	148.0	145.4	151.5	160.4	99.5	93.2	94.7	90.9	88.5
August	119.8	144.1	105.3	168.7	169.7	170.8	167.3	161.1	105.2	96.0	99.0	88.7	89.4
September	122.1	147.4	105.2	176.0	177.9	180.5	173.2	164.2	110.7	97.3	101.2	88.3	88.9
October	120.7	144.4	100.0	174.3	176.0	177.3	173.3	162.5	104.4	97.5	101.2	89.7	89.0
November	123.2	148.9	104.4	182.3	184.2	187.5	178.2	163.8	122.2	98.1	102.7	88.9	87.6
December	123.8	148.7	99.4	177.6	178.8	183.2	171.2	171.5	111.7	99.4	103.8	89.6	89.7
1998													
January	121.7	143.7	102.4	173.7	174.8	178.2	168.6	158.7	109.6	100.0	104.1	93.2	89.9
February	120.8	141.9	96.3	174.3	174.9	177.8	169.6	159.3	97.1	100.0	104.0	93.2	90.0
March	120.4	140.6	94.5	176.2	177.1	179.6	172.4	155.5	115.0	100.3	104.5	92.9	90.1
April	121.9	143.3	96.7	179.8	180.7	183.4	175.7	157.9	117.6	100.8	105.5	92.5	89.7
May	124.1	146.6	97.6	180.0	180.5	181.9	177.5	165.9	112.9	101.8	106.8	94.0	89.6
June	113.2	123.2	83.4	155.7	154.9	150.2	162.0	134.4	114.5	102.6	107.9	93.9	90.0
July	105.6	106.9	64.7	127.1	123.8	117.2	134.0	128.2	118.5	102.8	108.3	97.8	88.1
August	129.1	155.8	109.5	189.9	189.9	190.3	188.5	171.5	139.0	103.1	108.8	96.8	88.3
September	126.9	152.4	113.3	177.4	176.7	174.4	179.6	168.6	127.6	102.0	108.1	93.4	87.3
October	127.1	151.1	107.0	192.4	191.9	191.9	191.1	159.7	131.6	103.6	109.9	97.6	86.9
November	124.9	148.0	103.1	194.7	194.3	193.3	195.2	153.6	124.9	102.3	108.4	96.7	86.3
December	123.9	147.1	102.2	190.3	189.9	190.2	188.8	154.8	134.3	101.2	106.9	95.5	86.3
1999													
January	122.7	146.5	98.7	195.4	195.8	195.9	194.9	152.3	138.4	99.4	105.0	92.3	85.5
February	123.2	147.8	94.5	197.2	198.1	198.5	196.9	158.5	130.8	99.3	104.0	94.4	86.6
March	122.6	148.1	95.8	193.0	194.7	194.1	195.0	161.2	132.6	97.9	102.2	93.5	86.2
April	122.1	148.4	96.4	197.3	198.1	197.3	198.8	158.4	129.8	96.5	100.9	88.9	86.2
May	122.8	150.6	94.2	205.2	206.5	207.4	204.2	160.0	138.1	96.0	100.4	86.2	86.5
June	123.5	152.9	95.9	209.5	210.6	214.2	204.0	161.3	141.4	95.2	98.6	87.9	87.1
July	122.9	152.2	96.6	199.5	198.5	197.2	200.0	166.3	137.9	94.7	98.0	88.6	86.6
August	122.9	152.2	99.0	214.4	216.4	221.6	207.3	153.3	142.7	94.7	97.4	93.5	86.1
September	123.1	155.6	99.5	199.0	200.2	201.9	196.7	172.7	147.0	92.2	93.9	91.9	86.1
October	122.3	155.7	97.9	205.0	206.6	207.8	203.9	170.1	145.4	90.6	91.7	90.9	86.0
November	121.8	155.8	101.0	200.7	202.5	203.6	200.1	171.7	126.9	89.5	89.8	94.4	85.3
December	120.4	152.7	94.1	196.0	197.6	199.0	194.8	172.0	147.5	89.7	89.8	94.5	86.3

Table 16-20. Transportation Equipment—Capacity Utilization, Shipments, Inventories, and Orders

(Seasonally adjusted.)

Year and month	Capacity utilization (output as a percent of capacity)				Manufacturers' shipments, inventories, and orders (millions of dollars)							
	Total	Motor vehicles and parts		Aerospace and miscellaneous	Shipments		Inventories (book value, end of period)		New orders (net)		Unfilled orders (end of period)	
		Total	Autos and light trucks		Total	Motor vehicles and parts	Total	Motor vehicles and parts	Total	Aircraft, missiles, and parts	Total	Aircraft, missiles, and parts
1970	70.5	66.6	. . .	76.7	74 539	42 538	14 648	4 178	67 380	17 417	34 720	26 198
1971	74.2	79.5	. . .	68.7	88 857	58 247	13 799	4 173	89 900	22 459	35 793	26 259
1972	76.8	82.5	. . .	70.6	94 706	63 923	14 775	4 670	96 501	20 963	37 627	26 151
1973	84.7	91.6	. . .	77.3	110 587	74 799	16 458	5 708	118 194	26 669	45 248	27 842
1974	75.0	76.4	. . .	73.9	108 244	68 631	19 197	6 688	114 081	29 934	51 118	30 506
1975	65.8	63.1	. . .	69.6	113 503	70 033	19 620	6 101	109 050	26 869	46 633	28 244
1976	72.7	80.2	. . .	65.3	141 028	95 380	20 886	7 814	143 502	31 851	49 078	29 421
1977	76.4	90.3	89.8	63.2	166 954	117 747	22 423	9 078	175 446	40 625	57 101	37 325
1978	80.7	91.0	88.3	70.2	188 773	131 999	26 170	10 357	213 539	54 600	81 782	54 417
1979	80.2	82.0	78.3	78.4	201 623	131 378	31 638	10 978	223 226	67 818	103 555	74 034
1980	70.9	61.3	57.8	79.1	186 516	104 560	35 900	9 864	202 584	72 514	119 700	88 051
1981	66.1	59.3	60.3	72.2	205 223	116 981	37 527	9 047	203 482	63 530	118 008	86 794
1982	60.9	52.8	53.5	67.8	201 347	112 270	43 005	8 534	209 325	73 365	125 879	93 703
1983	66.7	66.2	71.9	67.2	245 392	148 296	43 791	10 433	261 359	86 952	141 637	105 504
1984	74.1	79.0	81.6	70.0	284 593	181 993	50 770	11 680	295 202	91 620	152 189	117 923
1985	77.9	83.1	81.5	73.8	307 380	193 445	52 634	11 809	311 482	100 889	156 155	127 282
1986	78.6	78.7	76.7	78.5	322 688	198 811	53 363	11 445	327 541	107 993	161 145	133 565
1987	77.5	76.8	74.7	78.1	332 936	205 923	56 461	11 937	348 224	114 835	176 588	144 987
1988	80.6	81.2	79.2	80.0	354 849	222 353	63 202	12 310	389 635	137 443	211 575	174 721
1989	81.8	79.5	79.8	84.4	369 675	233 232	70 968	12 503	411 434	153 430	253 517	217 557
1990	77.7	71.6	71.0	84.0	370 328	217 295	77 640	13 504	395 737	150 329	279 082	242 208
1991	71.8	64.1	64.6	80.8	367 235	209 210	73 019	13 163	363 366	132 645	275 260	242 798
1992	73.8	70.7	71.2	77.2	399 270	238 384	63 290	13 081	377 147	110 830	253 076	222 194
1993	75.7	77.6	78.6	73.5	414 694	267 365	60 950	14 099	386 643	88 070	225 256	194 154
1994	76.9	85.5	86.7	67.2	450 809	314 637	61 354	15 692	440 817	90 217	215 171	180 969
1995	73.4	80.9	80.4	64.1	461 806	327 908	59 735	16 293	465 839	106 062	219 101	186 848
1996	73.0	76.4	80.5	68.3	465 173	329 155	64 596	16 369	495 239	129 688	249 119	215 171
1997	78.3	79.5	84.0	76.8	502 301	346 606	69 323	16 145	507 667	124 151	254 579	217 998
1998	78.9	77.3	80.8	81.1	536 896	359 560	75 701	17 419	524 963	124 111	243 205	204 434
1999	78.9	82.0	88.1	74.9	583 559	399 807	69 069	17 982	567 357	128 172	227 461	191 416
1996												
January	70.6	75.0	72.2	64.8	36 997	27 170	60 633	16 537	43 577	12 550	225 681	192 279
February	72.0	76.6	77.5	65.9	37 850	27 190	61 056	16 366	38 151	8 597	225 982	193 115
March	65.1	64.3	64.8	66.2	35 525	24 361	61 740	16 740	43 753	16 791	234 210	201 821
April	73.9	79.4	82.1	66.4	38 430	27 702	61 574	16 489	36 960	6 919	232 740	200 862
May	74.6	80.3	82.6	67.0	40 578	28 646	61 778	16 327	42 770	11 705	234 932	203 497
June	74.9	80.4	86.1	67.5	39 002	27 690	62 407	16 175	41 891	9 549	237 821	204 867
July	75.7	81.1	89.9	68.6	39 028	28 728	63 016	16 483	40 788	9 514	239 581	206 685
August	75.0	79.5	85.2	69.0	39 600	27 894	63 093	16 311	37 359	6 909	237 340	204 607
September	73.9	76.6	84.1	70.3	40 866	28 670	63 384	16 334	44 565	12 659	241 039	208 275
October	71.6	72.3	76.9	70.8	38 581	27 284	64 217	16 513	41 009	11 792	243 467	211 491
November	74.1	76.1	81.3	71.4	39 759	27 771	64 721	16 219	42 246	11 322	245 954	213 658
December	74.1	75.6	82.9	72.2	38 704	26 350	64 596	16 369	41 869	10 904	249 119	215 171
1997												
January	76.0	78.5	84.3	72.5	40 687	29 411	65 808	16 317	42 548	10 530	250 980	216 913
February	76.2	78.3	85.1	73.4	40 442	28 202	66 796	16 547	40 362	9 845	250 900	217 447
March	76.7	78.4	86.2	74.5	40 211	27 447	66 827	16 477	39 289	8 812	249 978	216 300
April	75.7	75.9	78.7	75.6	41 809	28 491	67 771	16 657	39 251	8 494	247 420	214 262
May	76.2	76.3	80.9	76.1	40 515	27 390	68 298	16 943	38 590	8 494	245 495	212 481
June	78.2	79.7	84.8	76.2	41 641	28 281	68 637	16 553	41 800	10 703	245 654	212 954
July	76.3	76.4	76.5	76.1	43 673	30 472	69 174	16 610	41 606	8 457	243 587	210 968
August	79.9	81.1	85.8	78.3	42 022	29 318	69 677	16 246	42 280	10 746	243 845	211 773
September	81.2	82.7	87.8	79.2	42 379	29 126	69 534	16 671	41 445	8 479	242 911	210 030
October	80.1	80.7	84.5	79.2	42 289	29 936	70 761	16 341	44 351	10 429	244 973	210 861
November	81.5	82.9	88.3	79.6	43 285	29 240	71 183	16 163	53 485	20 719	255 173	220 532
December	81.6	82.4	84.8	80.5	43 558	30 002	69 323	16 145	42 964	8 043	254 579	217 998
1998												
January	80.0	79.4	84.3	80.8	41 542	28 133	70 371	16 259	44 520	13 720	257 557	220 894
February	79.2	78.1	81.4	80.6	43 577	29 678	70 844	16 281	42 431	9 986	256 411	219 861
March	78.7	77.2	80.9	80.6	45 208	30 607	70 958	16 721	42 204	8 527	253 407	217 113
April	79.5	78.5	82.4	80.8	43 863	29 730	72 542	16 450	44 431	12 827	253 975	218 831
May	80.7	80.1	82.2	81.4	43 562	29 461	73 398	16 686	42 422	10 760	252 835	218 389
June	73.4	67.2	68.8	81.8	40 857	26 760	74 597	17 046	39 349	8 480	251 327	216 211
July	68.3	58.1	53.5	81.8	40 556	27 092	75 032	16 790	39 768	10 172	250 539	215 817
August	83.4	84.6	88.5	81.8	44 403	30 017	75 812	16 511	46 745	13 106	252 881	217 854
September	81.8	82.7	86.1	80.8	46 588	31 061	75 702	16 701	45 101	9 109	251 394	215 042
October	81.9	81.9	88.0	81.9	48 017	31 586	76 999	16 755	44 870	9 637	248 247	211 882
November	80.4	80.1	87.0	80.8	48 324	31 581	76 452	17 240	45 024	9 962	244 947	208 629
December	79.7	79.6	86.0	79.9	47 908	32 169	75 701	17 419	46 166	7 848	243 205	204 434
1999												
January	78.9	79.3	86.2	78.4	47 236	31 970	73 852	17 101	52 396	15 535	248 365	207 714
February	79.2	80.0	85.4	78.3	47 502	32 118	73 972	16 978	45 421	10 978	246 284	206 485
March	78.8	80.1	84.9	77.2	49 267	33 281	73 415	17 424	47 558	10 369	244 575	204 756
April	78.5	80.3	86.1	76.2	47 755	32 209	72 458	17 082	41 616	7 219	238 436	199 727
May	79.0	81.5	88.0	75.8	48 891	32 717	71 788	17 233	45 728	10 377	235 273	197 363
June	79.4	82.7	90.5	75.2	49 781	34 813	71 596	17 597	46 253	9 117	231 745	195 163
July	79.1	82.3	86.6	74.9	48 816	34 550	72 403	17 677	47 235	10 302	230 164	194 586
August	79.1	82.3	93.8	75.0	50 980	34 669	70 868	17 569	49 000	11 415	228 184	193 193
September	79.3	84.1	89.1	73.1	48 555	33 908	70 749	17 420	46 593	9 480	226 222	191 783
October	78.8	84.2	90.1	71.9	47 659	32 898	70 411	17 638	46 800	10 408	225 363	190 698
November	78.5	84.2	90.3	71.2	48 326	33 239	70 417	17 916	44 899	8 629	221 936	187 850
December	77.6	82.5	86.5	71.4	50 125	34 189	69 069	17 982	55 650	15 354	227 461	191 416

Table 16-21. Transportation Equipment—Motor Vehicle Sales and Inventories

Year and month	Retail sales of new passenger cars						Retail inventories of new domestic passenger cars (thousands of units, end of period)		
	Thousands of units, not seasonally adjusted			Millions of units, seasonally adjusted annual rate			Not seasonally adjusted	Seasonally adjusted	Inventory to sales ratio
	Total	Domestic	Imports	Total	Domestic	Imports			
1970	8 403	7 119	1 283	8.4	7.1	1.3	1 220	1 294	2.4
1971	10 228	8 662	1 566	10.2	8.7	1.6	1 447	1 512	2.1
1972	10 873	9 253	1 621	10.9	9.3	1.6	1 311	1 379	1.7
1973	11 350	9 589	1 762	11.4	9.6	1.8	1 600	1 654	2.5
1974	8 774	7 362	1 412	8.8	7.4	1.4	1 672	1 730	3.4
1975	8 538	6 951	1 587	8.5	7.0	1.6	1 419	1 468	2.2
1976	9 994	8 492	1 502	10.0	8.5	1.5	1 465	1 494	1.9
1977	11 046	8 971	2 075	11.1	9.0	2.1	1 731	1 743	2.3
1978	11 164	9 164	2 000	11.2	9.2	2.0	1 729	1 731	2.3
1979	10 559	8 230	2 329	10.6	8.2	2.3	1 691	1 667	2.4
1980	8 982	6 581	2 400	9.0	6.6	2.4	1 448	1 440	2.6
1981	8 534	6 209	2 326	8.5	6.2	2.3	1 471	1 495	3.6
1982	7 979	5 758	2 221	8.0	5.8	2.2	1 126	1 127	2.2
1983	9 179	6 793	2 386	9.2	6.8	2.4	1 352	1 350	2.0
1984	10 390	7 952	2 439	10.4	8.0	2.4	1 415	1 411	2.1
1985	10 978	8 205	2 774	11.0	8.2	2.8	1 630	1 619	2.5
1986	11 406	8 215	3 191	11.4	8.2	3.2	1 499	1 515	2.0
1987	10 171	7 081	3 090	10.2	7.1	3.1	1 680	1 716	2.8
1988	10 546	7 539	3 006	10.6	7.5	3.0	1 601	1 601	2.3
1989	9 777	7 078	2 699	9.8	7.1	2.7	1 669	1 687	3.1
1990	9 300	6 897	2 403	9.3	6.9	2.4	1 408	1 418	2.6
1991	8 175	6 137	2 038	8.2	6.1	2.0	1 283	1 296	2.6
1992	8 214	6 277	1 938	8.2	6.3	1.9	1 276	1 288	2.3
1993	8 518	6 734	1 784	8.5	6.7	1.8	1 365	1 378	2.4
1994	8 990	7 255	1 735	9.0	7.3	1.7	1 437	1 449	2.3
1995	8 636	7 129	1 507	8.6	7.1	1.5	1 619	1 582	2.5
1996	8 527	7 254	1 273	8.5	7.3	1.3	1 363	1 354	2.3
1997	8 273	6 906	1 366	8.3	6.9	1.4	1 330	1 264	2.3
1998	8 142	6 764	1 378	8.1	6.8	1.4	1 324	1 288	2.1
1999	8 697	6 982	1 715	8.7	7.0	1.7	1 368	1 332	2.3
1996									
January	567	479	88	8.2	6.9	1.2	1 661	1 566	2.7
February	691	596	95	8.7	7.5	1.2	1 683	1 529	2.4
March	793	674	119	8.8	7.5	1.3	1 514	1 380	2.2
April	761	657	104	8.8	7.6	1.2	1 493	1 364	2.2
May	871	753	118	9.0	7.7	1.3	1 461	1 350	2.1
June	792	677	115	8.5	7.2	1.3	1 473	1 398	2.3
July	732	624	109	8.4	7.2	1.2	1 277	1 451	2.4
August	750	621	129	8.5	7.3	1.3	1 299	1 468	2.4
September	697	593	104	8.8	7.5	1.3	1 326	1 454	2.4
October	678	576	102	8.1	6.9	1.3	1 329	1 398	2.5
November	590	496	95	8.1	6.8	1.3	1 417	1 422	2.5
December	605	508	97	8.2	6.9	1.3	1 363	1 354	2.3
1997									
January	612	513	99	8.7	7.4	1.4	1 404	1 306	2.1
February	648	550	98	8.4	7.1	1.3	1 443	1 298	2.2
March	766	641	125	8.6	7.3	1.4	1 380	1 236	2.0
April	699	592	106	8.1	6.8	1.3	1 413	1 254	2.2
May	771	653	118	8.0	6.8	1.2	1 384	1 256	2.2
June	740	625	115	8.1	6.7	1.3	1 350	1 243	2.2
July	740	616	124	8.4	7.1	1.4	1 134	1 265	2.2
August	740	601	140	8.4	7.0	1.5	1 166	1 259	2.2
September	669	553	116	8.2	6.8	1.4	1 172	1 244	2.2
October	665	556	109	8.0	6.7	1.3	1 262	1 247	2.2
November	564	469	95	8.1	6.7	1.4	1 363	1 253	2.2
December	658	537	121	8.2	6.7	1.4	1 330	1 264	2.3
1998									
January	526	432	94	7.9	6.6	1.4	1 390	1 254	2.3
February	615	511	104	7.9	6.5	1.4	1 442	1 249	2.3
March	724	604	120	8.1	6.7	1.3	1 454	1 279	2.3
April	711	598	113	8.2	6.8	1.4	1 412	1 259	2.2
May	793	670	124	8.4	7.0	1.3	1 421	1 237	2.1
June	819	694	125	8.6	7.2	1.3	1 165	1 083	1.8
July	636	510	126	7.2	5.8	1.4	961	1 121	2.3
August	675	539	136	7.6	6.2	1.4	1 037	1 189	2.3
September	685	584	101	8.2	7.0	1.3	1 114	1 229	2.1
October	712	599	114	8.6	7.2	1.3	1 208	1 251	2.1
November	562	464	98	8.1	6.7	1.4	1 318	1 287	2.3
December	684	558	125	9.0	7.3	1.6	1 324	1 288	2.1
1999									
January	546	444	102	8.0	6.5	1.5	1 426	1 332	2.5
February	671	557	114	8.6	7.1	1.6	1 444	1 308	2.2
March	788	646	142	8.5	6.9	1.6	1 468	1 330	2.3
April	737	602	135	8.7	7.0	1.7	1 455	1 293	2.2
May	830	671	159	8.9	7.1	1.8	1 384	1 276	2.2
June	832	678	154	8.8	7.1	1.7	1 354	1 269	2.2
July	771	608	163	8.8	7.0	1.8	1 124	1 294	2.2
August	799	639	160	9.0	7.3	1.7	1 092	1 273	2.1
September	716	574	142	8.6	6.9	1.7	1 125	1 298	2.3
October	689	533	156	8.7	6.8	1.9	1 237	1 317	2.3
November	639	498	141	9.0	7.1	1.9	1 340	1 315	2.2
December	680	532	148	8.9	7.1	1.8	1 368	1 332	2.3

Table 16-22. Transportation Equipment—Motor Vehicle Sales

Year and month	Retail sales of new trucks and buses								Unit sales of cars and light trucks (millions of units, seasonally adjusted annual rate)		
	Thousands of units, not seasonally adjusted				Millions of units, seasonally adjusted annual rate						
	Total	0–10,000 pounds		10,001 pounds and over	Total	0–10,000 pounds		10,001 pounds and over	Total	Domestic	Imports
		Domestic	Imports			Domestic	Imports				
1970	. . .	1 408.5	. . .	337.3	. . .	1.4	. . .	0.3	. . .	8.5	. . .
1971	. . .	1 592.5	. . .	338.9	. . .	1.7	. . .	0.3	. . .	10.4	. . .
1972	. . .	2 122.5	. . .	437.4	. . .	2.1	. . .	0.4	. . .	11.4	. . .
1973	. . .	2 509.4	. . .	495.7	. . .	2.5	. . .	0.5	. . .	12.1	. . .
1974	. . .	2 180.1	. . .	423.9	. . .	2.2	. . .	0.4	. . .	9.6	. . .
1975	. . .	2 052.6	. . .	298.3	. . .	2.1	. . .	0.3	. . .	9.1	. . .
1976	3 300.5	2 738.3	237.5	324.7	3.3	2.7	0.2	0.3	12.9	11.2	1.7
1977	3 813.0	3 112.8	323.1	377.1	3.8	3.1	0.3	0.4	14.5	12.1	2.4
1978	4 256.8	3 481.1	335.9	439.8	4.3	3.5	0.3	0.4	15.0	12.7	2.3
1979	3 589.7	2 730.2	469.4	390.1	3.6	2.7	0.5	0.4	13.7	10.9	2.8
1980	2 487.4	1 731.1	484.6	271.7	2.5	1.7	0.5	0.3	11.2	8.3	2.9
1981	2 255.6	1 581.7	447.6	226.3	2.3	1.6	0.4	0.2	10.6	7.8	2.8
1982	2 562.8	1 967.5	410.4	184.9	2.6	2.0	0.4	0.2	10.4	7.8	2.6
1983	3 117.3	2 465.2	463.3	188.8	3.1	2.5	0.5	0.2	12.1	9.3	2.8
1984	4 093.1	3 207.2	607.7	278.2	4.1	3.2	0.6	0.3	14.2	11.2	3.0
1985	4 741.7	3 618.4	828.3	295.0	4.8	3.6	0.8	0.3	15.4	11.8	3.6
1986	4 811.8	3 671.4	866.9	273.5	4.9	3.7	1.0	0.3	16.1	11.9	4.2
1987	5 000.6	3 786.1	912.2	302.3	5.0	3.8	0.9	0.3	14.9	10.9	4.0
1988	5 242.4	4 195.8	697.9	348.7	5.2	4.2	0.7	0.4	15.4	11.7	3.7
1989	5 067.8	4 107.0	630.3	330.5	5.1	4.1	0.6	0.3	14.5	11.2	3.3
1990	4 848.4	3 947.4	602.7	298.3	4.9	4.0	0.6	0.3	13.9	10.9	3.0
1991	4 365.8	3 594.8	528.8	242.2	4.4	3.6	0.5	0.2	12.3	9.7	2.6
1992	4 903.3	4 232.7	395.9	274.7	4.9	4.2	0.4	0.3	12.8	10.5	2.3
1993	5 681.1	4 980.9	364.5	335.7	5.7	5.0	0.4	0.3	13.8	11.7	2.1
1994	6 422.4	5 638.0	396.3	388.1	6.4	5.6	0.4	0.4	15.0	12.9	2.1
1995	6 481.4	5 662.7	390.5	428.2	6.5	5.7	0.4	0.4	14.7	12.8	1.9
1996	6 929.3	6 087.6	430.9	410.8	6.9	6.1	0.4	0.4	15.0	13.3	1.7
1997	7 225.8	6 225.7	571.2	428.9	7.2	6.2	0.6	0.4	15.1	13.1	1.9
1998	7 821.6	6 651.0	646.2	524.4	7.8	6.6	0.6	0.5	15.4	13.4	2.0
1999	8 717.1	7 309.6	762.8	644.7	8.7	7.3	0.8	0.6	16.8	14.3	2.5
1996											
January	483.6	428.9	25.1	29.6	6.8	6.0	0.4	0.4	14.5	12.9	1.6
February	547.4	487.0	28.2	32.2	7.2	6.4	0.4	0.4	15.5	13.9	1.6
March	611.4	537.8	37.6	36.0	6.9	6.0	0.4	0.4	15.3	13.5	1.7
April	598.4	526.6	34.1	37.7	6.8	6.0	0.4	0.4	15.2	13.6	1.7
May	651.8	572.9	40.6	38.3	6.8	5.9	0.5	0.4	15.4	13.7	1.7
June	611.9	535.4	37.1	39.4	6.7	5.9	0.4	0.4	14.8	13.1	1.7
July	584.8	513.9	35.1	35.8	6.7	5.9	0.4	0.4	14.6	13.0	1.6
August	583.6	505.1	44.6	33.9	7.0	6.1	0.5	0.4	15.1	13.4	1.7
September	534.8	470.9	31.9	32.0	7.0	6.3	0.4	0.4	15.5	13.8	1.7
October	618.7	546.1	37.1	35.5	7.3	6.4	0.4	0.4	15.0	13.3	1.7
November	555.8	487.0	40.7	28.1	7.1	6.2	0.5	0.4	14.8	13.0	1.8
December	547.1	476.0	38.8	32.3	6.9	6.1	0.5	0.4	14.8	13.0	1.8
1997											
January	502.6	435.7	37.5	29.4	7.0	6.1	0.5	0.4	15.3	13.4	1.9
February	529.2	461.5	37.0	30.7	7.0	6.1	0.5	0.4	15.0	13.1	1.8
March	659.8	567.8	53.2	38.8	7.4	6.4	0.6	0.4	15.7	13.7	2.0
April	611.6	528.4	43.9	39.3	7.0	6.0	0.6	0.4	14.6	12.8	1.9
May	664.4	571.6	55.1	37.7	7.0	6.0	0.6	0.4	14.6	12.8	1.8
June	614.9	532.6	45.9	36.4	6.8	5.8	0.5	0.4	14.4	12.6	1.9
July	637.0	547.6	52.4	37.0	7.3	6.3	0.6	0.4	15.3	13.4	2.0
August	607.7	513.6	59.5	34.6	7.4	6.3	0.6	0.4	15.4	13.3	2.1
September	569.5	486.9	48.3	34.3	7.3	6.3	0.6	0.4	15.0	13.0	2.0
October	616.7	529.3	48.3	39.1	7.2	6.2	0.6	0.4	14.8	12.9	1.9
November	582.4	508.4	41.8	32.2	7.7	6.7	0.5	0.5	15.3	13.5	1.9
December	630.0	542.3	48.3	39.4	7.6	6.6	0.6	0.5	15.3	13.3	2.0
1998											
January	518.0	447.3	38.9	31.8	7.4	6.4	0.5	0.5	14.8	12.9	1.9
February	557.5	480.1	42.8	34.6	7.3	6.3	0.6	0.5	14.8	12.8	2.0
March	680.9	588.3	48.6	44.0	7.6	6.6	0.6	0.5	15.2	13.3	1.9
April	679.9	584.2	48.8	46.9	7.8	6.7	0.6	0.5	15.5	13.5	2.0
May	748.6	649.2	55.3	44.1	8.1	7.0	0.6	0.5	16.0	14.0	1.9
June	787.7	688.2	53.7	45.8	8.5	7.3	0.6	0.5	16.5	14.6	2.0
July	628.9	526.3	58.2	44.4	7.2	6.0	0.7	0.5	13.9	11.8	2.1
August	589.7	480.9	63.8	45.0	7.2	6.0	0.6	0.6	14.3	12.2	2.0
September	629.3	525.9	58.4	45.0	7.8	6.6	0.7	0.6	15.5	13.6	2.0
October	693.8	582.3	62.3	49.2	8.3	7.0	0.7	0.6	16.3	14.2	2.1
November	613.9	518.1	51.7	44.1	8.1	6.8	0.7	0.6	15.6	13.5	2.1
December	693.4	580.2	63.7	49.5	8.4	7.1	0.7	0.6	16.8	14.4	2.4
1999											
January	576.3	481.3	54.2	40.8	8.4	7.0	0.8	0.6	15.7	13.5	2.2
February	655.1	551.4	55.4	48.3	8.6	7.2	0.8	0.7	16.6	14.2	2.3
March	791.6	670.1	62.3	59.2	8.4	7.1	0.7	0.6	16.3	13.9	2.3
April	714.8	599.1	57.3	58.4	8.4	7.1	0.7	0.6	16.5	14.1	2.4
May	802.6	679.6	67.2	55.8	8.8	7.4	0.7	0.6	17.0	14.5	2.5
June	820.4	702.4	58.7	59.3	8.7	7.4	0.7	0.6	16.9	14.4	2.4
July	758.1	638.7	66.5	52.9	8.8	7.4	0.8	0.6	16.9	14.4	2.5
August	725.1	601.9	70.5	52.7	8.9	7.5	0.7	0.6	17.3	14.9	2.4
September	726.6	608.6	62.7	55.3	9.1	7.6	0.8	0.7	17.0	14.6	2.5
October	708.2	587.6	65.7	54.9	8.7	7.2	0.8	0.7	16.7	14.0	2.7
November	677.8	559.6	67.2	51.0	8.7	7.2	0.9	0.7	17.0	14.3	2.7
December	760.5	629.3	75.1	56.1	9.1	7.6	0.9	0.7	17.3	14.6	2.7

Table 16-23. Transportation Equipment—Producer and Consumer Prices

Year and month	Producer prices (1982=100, except as noted, not seasonally adjusted)											Consumer prices (1982-84=100, seasonally adjusted)		
	Transportation equipment industry (December 1984=100)	Finished goods							Intermediate materials		Commodity group: Motor vehicles and equipment	New vehicles		Used cars and trucks
		Passenger cars	Light motor trucks	Heavy motor trucks	Truck trailers	Civilian aircraft (December 1985=100)	Ships (December 1985=100)	Railroad equipment	Aircraft engines (December 1985=100)	Aircraft parts (June 1985=100)		Total	New cars	
1970	...	50.0	42.0	36.3	...	...	...	33.2	...	...	43.3	53.1	53.0	31.2
1971	...	52.6	45.3	38.4	...	...	...	34.9	...	...	45.7	55.3	55.2	33.0
1972	...	54.0	46.2	39.3	...	...	...	37.1	...	...	47.0	54.8	54.7	33.1
1973	...	54.2	47.0	39.8	...	...	...	38.9	...	...	47.4	54.8	54.8	35.2
1974	...	57.8	52.3	44.5	...	...	...	47.3	...	...	51.4	58.0	57.9	36.7
1975	...	63.0	56.9	50.7	...	...	...	58.1	...	...	57.6	63.0	62.9	43.8
1976	...	66.8	60.4	56.1	...	...	...	62.5	...	...	61.2	67.0	66.9	50.3
1977	...	70.7	64.8	61.2	...	...	...	67.4	...	...	65.2	70.5	70.4	54.7
1978	...	75.9	70.5	66.8	...	...	...	73.0	...	...	70.0	75.9	75.8	55.8
1979	...	81.9	76.4	73.4	...	...	...	80.0	...	...	75.8	81.9	81.8	60.2
1980	...	88.9	83.3	82.3	...	...	...	90.4	...	...	83.1	88.5	88.4	62.3
1981	...	96.2	95.0	92.9	96.9	...	...	97.0	...	...	94.6	93.9	93.7	76.9
1982	...	100.0	100.0	100.0	100.0	...	...	100.0	...	...	100.0	97.5	97.4	88.8
1983	...	102.2	102.6	103.6	100.6	...	...	101.1	...	...	102.2	99.9	99.9	98.7
1984	...	104.0	106.7	108.0	104.0	...	...	102.6	...	...	104.1	102.6	102.8	112.5
1985	...	106.9	112.2	108.8	106.2	...	...	104.9	...	...	106.4	106.1	106.1	113.7
1986	104.4	110.2	117.7	113.4	104.3	100.9	100.5	105.4	99.7	103.4	109.1	110.6	110.6	108.8
1987	105.9	112.9	121.1	111.8	103.4	102.9	100.7	104.7	99.7	105.8	111.7	114.4	114.6	113.1
1988	107.8	113.0	125.0	112.4	106.6	104.5	101.0	107.5	103.2	110.3	113.1	116.5	116.9	118.0
1989	112.1	115.5	129.5	117.2	110.4	108.8	105.4	114.0	106.7	114.5	116.2	119.2	119.2	120.4
1990	115.6	118.3	130.0	120.3	110.8	115.3	110.1	118.6	113.5	117.7	118.2	121.4	121.0	117.6
1991	119.8	124.1	135.5	123.6	112.1	123.0	114.6	122.2	119.2	121.8	122.1	126.0	125.3	118.1
1992	123.0	126.9	142.4	128.6	115.1	128.8	122.1	123.7	125.0	128.0	124.9	129.2	128.4	123.2
1993	126.3	129.8	150.3	133.9	118.2	131.5	129.1	125.2	127.7	131.2	128.0	132.7	131.5	133.9
1994	130.1	133.9	157.1	138.7	122.2	135.4	131.1	129.2	130.7	134.0	131.4	137.6	136.0	141.7
1995	132.2	134.1	159.0	144.1	131.7	141.8	132.8	134.8	132.8	135.7	133.0	141.0	139.0	156.5
1996	134.2	135.4	160.3	144.5	130.7	147.3	138.7	137.2	134.7	139.3	134.1	143.7	141.4	157.0
1997	134.1	133.6	158.9	140.4	130.3	150.0	143.7	134.7	135.7	141.3	132.7	144.3	141.7	151.1
1998	133.6	131.9	155.2	142.4	135.0	150.2	145.7	135.0	137.1	142.9	131.4	143.4	140.7	150.6
1999	134.5	131.3	157.5	146.5	136.3	151.7	145.8	135.2	138.5	143.7	131.7	142.9	139.6	152.0
1996														
January	134.2	136.2	161.2	145.7	132.1	145.2	135.3	136.7	135.0	139.3	134.5	142.3	140.2	157.9
February	134.2	136.1	160.8	146.6	132.1	145.4	135.3	137.7	134.8	139.6	134.5	142.7	140.5	157.5
March	134.3	136.1	160.6	147.3	132.0	145.6	135.3	137.6	135.5	139.5	134.5	142.9	140.8	157.3
April	134.1	135.2	160.4	147.2	130.5	146.1	138.8	137.8	133.9	139.4	134.1	143.0	140.8	157.4
May	134.1	135.4	159.8	147.9	130.4	146.3	138.3	137.7	134.0	139.4	134.1	143.2	141.0	157.6
June	134.3	135.9	160.1	145.4	130.6	146.9	138.3	137.3	134.1	139.4	134.2	143.6	141.4	157.2
July	133.8	134.1	159.3	145.4	130.6	147.4	138.6	137.3	134.4	139.0	134.5	143.9	141.7	156.9
August	133.8	133.9	158.9	145.7	130.0	148.2	139.6	137.2	134.6	139.1	133.3	144.1	141.9	156.6
September	132.1	130.4	154.1	142.6	130.0	148.5	139.2	137.0	134.7	139.3	131.0	144.5	142.4	157.0
October	135.4	137.3	163.2	142.3	130.0	148.8	144.7	137.0	134.8	139.3	135.2	144.5	142.2	157.0
November	135.2	137.3	162.7	139.5	130.2	149.4	140.7	136.5	135.0	139.3	134.9	144.5	142.1	156.5
December	135.1	136.9	162.4	138.9	130.2	149.3	141.0	136.3	135.6	139.5	134.8	144.7	142.2	155.6
1997														
January	135.4	136.5	163.0	140.3	130.2	149.4	142.7	142.4	137.7	141.4	134.6	144.5	142.1	154.7
February	135.4	136.7	162.0	140.0	130.2	149.7	142.6	136.6	136.9	141.4	134.5	144.6	142.1	154.4
March	135.3	136.3	161.6	140.5	130.3	149.7	142.6	132.2	137.6	141.7	134.3	144.7	142.2	154.4
April	134.8	135.2	161.0	140.6	130.4	149.7	145.5	131.6	135.7	141.6	133.7	144.7	142.1	154.3
May	133.9	133.0	158.8	140.5	130.4	150.0	141.4	134.2	135.8	141.8	132.5	144.4	141.9	153.9
June	133.8	132.7	158.7	140.6	130.7	150.4	141.3	134.3	135.9	141.5	132.3	144.3	141.8	151.8
July	132.8	130.2	155.7	143.0	129.8	150.5	143.1	133.8	135.2	140.9	131.0	144.4	141.8	149.9
August	132.8	130.0	156.5	141.6	129.7	150.2	144.8	133.5	135.3	141.0	131.0	144.2	141.6	148.5
September	131.8	127.7	154.0	139.9	129.8	150.0	144.9	134.2	134.2	141.0	129.6	144.0	141.3	148.2
October	135.0	136.4	160.4	139.2	129.8	150.1	144.7	134.7	134.1	141.1	133.9	143.9	141.3	147.9
November	134.4	134.8	159.2	139.2	129.9	150.1	145.3	134.2	134.8	141.2	133.1	143.8	141.1	147.6
December	133.7	133.4	156.6	139.8	132.8	150.0	145.3	134.3	134.9	141.2	132.2	143.4	140.7	147.9
1998														
January	133.8	133.3	156.3	139.8	133.7	150.1	145.4	134.6	136.2	141.7	132.0	143.5	140.9	148.1
February	134.0	133.6	156.4	139.6	133.8	150.1	145.5	134.5	136.3	142.0	132.1	143.6	140.9	148.4
March	133.9	133.2	156.0	141.0	135.0	150.1	145.6	134.5	137.2	141.9	132.0	143.7	141.0	147.3
April	133.8	132.2	156.0	141.5	135.0	150.4	145.8	135.5	137.2	142.2	131.7	143.8	141.0	148.2
May	133.0	130.4	153.7	141.6	135.3	150.2	145.8	135.3	137.6	142.3	130.6	143.1	140.4	150.0
June	132.5	129.3	151.8	141.9	135.6	150.5	145.8	135.6	137.4	142.4	129.9	142.7	140.1	150.9
July	132.7	130.1	152.0	142.0	135.6	150.2	145.8	135.2	136.6	142.6	130.2	143.4	140.8	151.3
August	132.2	128.4	152.4	141.6	135.3	149.8	145.8	135.3	136.6	142.8	129.6	144.0	141.2	151.1
September	131.8	127.0	150.3	144.7	135.1	150.0	145.8	135.3	136.5	144.2	128.8	143.6	140.7	151.9
October	135.4	135.4	160.1	145.0	134.6	150.2	145.8	134.5	138.0	144.6	133.7	143.1	140.4	153.0
November	135.4	135.6	159.3	145.0	135.3	150.5	145.8	134.3	138.1	144.4	133.6	143.3	140.4	154.0
December	134.9	134.1	158.1	145.3	135.3	150.8	145.8	135.2	137.4	143.7	132.9	143.4	140.5	153.1
1999														
January	134.5	132.0	158.2	145.4	135.3	150.9	145.8	134.6	139.0	144.4	132.0	143.5	140.5	150.6
February	134.8	132.6	158.7	145.5	135.2	151.0	145.8	134.6	139.3	144.5	132.4	143.0	140.0	148.3
March	134.4	131.3	157.8	145.8	135.3	150.9	145.8	134.6	139.3	143.7	131.7	142.7	139.6	147.4
April	134.5	131.4	158.8	145.7	135.9	151.0	145.8	134.5	139.2	143.7	131.9	142.8	139.6	148.3
May	134.1	130.2	158.2	146.7	136.0	151.4	145.8	134.5	137.6	143.6	131.4	142.8	139.4	149.6
June	133.6	128.7	156.9	146.7	135.9	151.3	145.8	135.8	137.6	144.0	130.6	142.7	139.3	150.9
July	133.0	127.4	155.0	146.9	136.0	151.2	145.8	135.9	137.6	144.0	129.8	142.7	139.3	152.3
August	132.9	127.4	154.4	146.8	136.1	151.1	145.8	135.9	138.1	143.0	129.7	142.6	139.2	153.8
September	132.6	127.0	151.8	147.1	137.3	151.7	145.8	135.8	137.8	143.3	129.1	142.9	139.5	155.7
October	136.7	136.5	162.4	147.3	137.4	152.3	145.8	135.7	138.4	143.3	134.5	142.9	139.5	156.4
November	136.2	135.7	159.5	147.4	137.5	153.2	145.8	135.3	138.6	143.5	133.7	142.9	139.4	156.1
December	136.2	135.7	158.6	147.3	137.6	154.0	145.8	135.5	139.1	143.4	133.5	142.9	139.3	155.0

Table 16-24. Transportation Equipment—Employment, Hours, and Earnings

Year and month	Employment (thousands, seasonally adjusted)					Production workers							
	Total payroll employees			Production workers		Average weekly hours (seasonally adjusted)		Aggregate weekly hours index (1982=100), seasonally adjusted		Average earnings (dollars, not seasonally adjusted)			
										Hourly		Weekly	
	Total transportation equipment	Motor vehicles and equipment	Aircraft and parts	Total transportation equipment	Motor vehicles and equipment	Total transportation equipment	Motor vehicles and equipment	Total transportation equipment	Motor vehicles and equipment	Total transportation equipment	Motor vehicles and equipment	Total transportation equipment	Motor vehicles and equipment
1970	1 833	799	644	1 223	605	40.3	40.3	114.1	117.7	4.06	4.22	163.62	170.07
1971	1 743	849	509	1 196	655	40.7	41.2	112.6	130.3	4.45	4.72	181.12	194.46
1972	1 777	875	481	1 226	676	41.7	43.0	118.4	140.5	4.81	5.13	200.58	220.59
1973	1 915	977	510	1 324	755	42.1	43.5	129.1	158.5	5.15	5.46	216.82	237.51
1974	1 853	908	524	1 256	688	40.5	40.6	117.9	134.9	5.54	5.87	224.37	238.32
1975	1 700	792	499	1 142	602	40.4	40.3	106.8	117.3	6.07	6.44	245.23	259.53
1976	1 785	881	473	1 223	682	41.7	42.9	117.9	141.2	6.62	7.09	276.05	304.16
1977	1 857	947	467	1 277	735	42.5	44.0	125.6	156.0	7.29	7.85	309.83	345.40
1978	1 987	1 005	511	1 370	782	42.2	43.3	133.6	163.3	7.91	8.50	333.80	368.05
1979	2 059	990	593	1 409	764	41.1	41.1	134.1	151.8	8.53	9.06	350.58	372.37
1980	1 881	789	633	1 220	575	40.6	40.0	114.6	111.0	9.35	9.85	379.61	394.00
1981	1 879	789	626	1 207	586	40.9	40.9	114.2	115.7	10.39	11.02	424.95	450.72
1982	1 718	699	584	1 068	512	40.5	40.5	100.0	100.0	11.11	11.62	449.96	470.61
1983	1 730	754	562	1 085	568	42.1	43.3	105.7	118.9	11.67	12.14	491.31	525.66
1984	1 883	862	575	1 203	664	42.7	43.8	118.9	140.2	12.20	12.73	520.94	557.57
1985	1 960	883	616	1 244	685	42.6	43.5	122.7	143.6	12.71	13.39	541.45	582.47
1986	2 003	872	656	1 258	670	42.3	42.6	123.3	137.7	12.81	13.45	541.86	572.97
1987	2 028	866	678	1 278	673	42.0	42.2	124.3	137.2	12.94	13.53	543.48	570.97
1988	2 036	856	684	1 273	667	42.7	43.5	125.8	140.0	13.29	13.99	567.48	608.57
1989	2 052	859	711	1 278	664	42.4	43.1	125.3	138.0	13.67	14.25	579.61	614.18
1990	1 989	812	712	1 224	617	42.0	42.4	119.1	126.2	14.08	14.56	591.36	617.34
1991	1 890	789	669	1 169	602	41.9	42.3	113.3	122.9	14.75	15.23	618.03	644.23
1992	1 830	813	612	1 147	622	41.8	42.4	110.9	127.3	15.20	15.45	635.36	655.08
1993	1 756	837	542	1 120	642	43.0	44.3	111.4	137.4	15.80	16.10	679.40	713.23
1994	1 761	909	482	1 154	704	44.3	46.0	118.5	156.2	16.51	17.02	731.39	782.92
1995	1 790	971	451	1 200	761	43.8	44.9	121.6	164.9	16.74	17.34	733.21	778.57
1996	1 785	967	458	1 210	764	44.0	44.9	123.1	165.5	17.19	17.74	756.36	796.53
1997	1 845	986	501	1 256	779	44.5	45.0	129.2	169.2	17.55	18.04	780.98	811.80
1998	1 893	995	525	1 264	764	43.4	43.5	127.0	160.5	17.51	17.84	759.93	776.04
1999	1 884	1 019	495	1 251	776	43.8	45.0	126.8	168.4	18.04	18.41	790.15	828.45
1996													
January	1 773	964	449	1 201	764	42.5	43.6	118.1	160.8	16.88	17.42	714.02	756.03
February	1 778	968	451	1 204	766	43.2	44.0	120.4	162.7	16.95	17.47	733.94	770.43
March	1 745	933	451	1 173	734	42.1	41.9	114.3	148.4	16.64	17.04	703.87	720.79
April	1 783	969	453	1 209	768	44.1	45.3	123.4	167.9	17.22	17.89	757.68	812.21
May	1 786	971	455	1 211	768	44.2	45.4	123.9	168.3	17.19	17.84	764.96	818.86
June	1 787	977	450	1 214	772	44.4	45.6	124.8	169.9	17.22	17.83	766.29	814.83
July	1 786	969	457	1 212	765	44.4	45.6	124.5	168.4	17.28	17.88	737.86	775.99
August	1 791	972	457	1 214	766	44.5	45.8	125.0	169.3	17.27	17.78	765.06	808.99
September	1 792	973	459	1 216	768	44.6	45.6	125.5	169.0	17.43	18.03	786.09	832.99
October	1 795	968	468	1 219	765	44.0	44.8	124.1	165.4	17.23	17.71	761.57	795.18
November	1 798	967	472	1 218	761	44.1	44.9	124.3	164.9	17.32	17.83	770.74	804.13
December	1 804	971	475	1 225	766	44.3	44.8	125.6	165.6	17.55	18.09	800.28	841.19
1997													
January	1 811	976	479	1 233	771	44.8	45.9	127.8	170.8	17.43	17.99	777.38	818.55
February	1 815	976	483	1 233	769	44.4	45.1	126.7	167.4	17.36	17.85	769.05	801.47
March	1 824	982	486	1 237	772	44.8	45.4	128.3	169.2	17.48	17.98	786.60	823.48
April	1 821	973	491	1 235	765	44.8	45.4	128.1	167.6	17.44	17.97	779.57	815.84
May	1 826	974	494	1 242	769	44.4	45.0	127.6	167.0	17.43	17.93	779.12	815.82
June	1 835	980	500	1 248	776	44.5	45.2	128.5	169.3	17.41	17.87	774.75	807.72
July	1 844	982	506	1 254	779	44.2	44.5	128.3	167.3	17.19	17.49	728.86	736.33
August	1 864	996	509	1 270	790	44.5	45.1	130.8	172.0	17.42	17.80	771.71	795.66
September	1 860	988	511	1 270	786	43.8	43.9	128.7	166.5	17.55	17.98	777.47	801.91
October	1 868	992	513	1 276	788	44.2	44.7	130.5	170.0	17.86	18.42	794.77	828.90
November	1 887	1 005	517	1 287	795	44.0	44.3	131.1	170.0	17.91	18.47	797.00	827.46
December	1 888	1 003	520	1 285	791	44.3	44.5	131.8	169.9	18.05	18.59	823.08	860.72
1998													
January	1 889	1 002	522	1 284	787	44.0	44.1	130.8	167.5	17.72	18.17	776.14	794.03
February	1 895	1 005	524	1 288	788	43.6	43.6	130.0	165.8	17.74	18.23	771.69	793.01
March	1 897	1 004	525	1 285	784	43.5	43.6	129.4	165.0	17.88	18.42	781.36	808.64
April	1 902	1 007	526	1 284	784	42.9	42.9	127.5	162.3	17.67	18.26	731.54	752.31
May	1 902	1 005	526	1 279	778	43.4	43.5	128.5	163.3	17.60	18.06	769.12	796.45
June	1 897	999	527	1 272	774	42.9	42.6	126.3	159.1	17.40	17.73	746.46	757.07
July	1 795	890	527	1 153	649	42.9	42.1	114.5	131.9	16.84	16.77	690.44	664.09
August	1 903	1 001	527	1 257	756	43.0	42.9	125.1	156.5	17.27	17.49	739.16	743.33
September	1 907	1 004	527	1 264	764	43.6	44.1	127.6	162.6	17.46	17.73	754.27	776.57
October	1 912	1 011	526	1 273	772	43.8	44.1	129.0	164.3	17.43	17.59	770.41	782.76
November	1 908	1 009	523	1 265	766	44.1	44.7	129.1	165.3	17.48	17.63	779.61	795.11
December	1 905	1 008	522	1 263	766	44.2	44.9	129.2	166.0	17.52	17.69	798.91	827.89
1999													
January	1 903	1 010	520	1 259	764	43.4	44.3	126.5	163.4	17.42	17.59	754.29	772.20
February	1 892	1 005	514	1 253	759	43.9	45.0	127.3	164.8	17.45	17.65	764.31	792.49
March	1 898	1 012	516	1 258	770	43.7	44.7	127.2	166.1	17.60	17.91	772.64	805.95
April	1 889	1 015	508	1 251	772	43.9	45.1	127.1	168.0	17.82	18.24	785.86	829.92
May	1 883	1 016	503	1 247	774	43.6	44.5	125.8	166.2	17.92	18.33	786.69	826.68
June	1 878	1 018	496	1 244	776	44.1	45.3	127.0	169.7	18.14	18.61	798.16	843.03
July	1 890	1 029	493	1 252	784	44.2	45.5	128.1	172.2	17.88	18.16	754.54	777.25
August	1 887	1 026	488	1 256	785	43.9	45.1	127.6	170.9	18.17	18.53	794.03	828.29
September	1 880	1 025	483	1 252	785	44.0	45.4	127.5	172.0	18.50	18.96	812.15	860.78
October	1 873	1 022	478	1 247	783	43.8	45.0	126.4	170.1	18.41	18.85	810.04	852.02
November	1 870	1 022	473	1 244	781	43.6	44.7	125.5	168.5	18.39	18.80	811.00	849.76
December	1 867	1 023	470	1 244	782	43.4	44.5	125.0	168.0	18.72	19.22	838.66	887.96

Table 16-25. Instruments and Related Products—Production, Capacity Utilization, Shipments, Inventories, Prices, Employment, Hours, and Earnings

Year and month	Industrial production (1992=100, seasonally adjusted)			Capacity utilization (output as a percent of capacity, seasonally adjusted)	Manufacturers' shipments, inventories, and orders (millions of dollars, seasonally adjusted)		Producer prices (December 1984=100, not seasonally adjusted)	Employment (thousands)		Production workers			
	Total	Scientific and medical						Total payroll employees (seasonally adjusted)	Production workers (not seasonally adjusted)	Average weekly hours, seasonally adjusted	Aggregate weekly hours index (1982=100), seasonally adjusted	Average earnings (dollars, not seasonally adjusted)	
		Total	Medical		Shipments	Inventories (book value, end of period)						Hourly	Weekly
1970	36.2	32.2	23.6	77.4	18 367	4 196	...	804	...	...	...	...	...
1971	37.9	33.3	26.0	76.3	18 613	4 201	...	753	...	...	...	...	...
1972	42.5	36.6	27.9	81.4	21 043	4 435	...	786	...	...	...	...	...
1973	48.5	41.6	30.0	87.6	23 627	5 233	...	851	...	...	...	...	...
1974	51.4	43.5	30.6	86.5	27 454	6 486	...	885	...	...	...	...	...
1975	48.9	43.0	32.9	77.1	29 547	6 547	...	804	...	...	...	...	...
1976	53.7	46.1	34.5	80.5	33 238	7 214	...	840	...	...	...	...	...
1977	60.1	52.6	36.3	86.1	38 803	8 185	...	895	...	...	...	...	...
1978	66.2	57.2	38.5	89.5	44 655	9 682	...	952	...	...	...	...	...
1979	71.7	62.5	41.3	90.6	50 702	11 415	...	1 006	...	...	...	...	...
1980	73.6	67.9	42.4	87.2	59 825	13 376	...	1 022	...	...	...	...	...
1981	75.4	69.8	46.0	84.8	66 613	14 760	...	1 041	...	...	...	...	...
1982	76.3	72.2	52.3	81.7	74 918	17 038	...	1 013	...	...	...	...	...
1983	77.7	72.6	53.2	79.7	79 637	17 769	...	990	...	...	...	...	...
1984	86.0	80.8	57.8	84.6	89 398	20 206	...	1 040	...	...	...	...	...
1985	89.3	84.3	62.0	83.6	96 207	21 569	101.0	1 045	...	...	...	...	...
1986	88.8	85.7	64.2	79.1	100 798	22 461	102.0	1 018	...	...	...	...	...
1987	93.8	92.9	72.3	80.2	107 325	23 692	105.0	1 011	...	...	...	...	...
1988	97.2	95.4	76.3	80.8	116 009	25 346	107.0	1 031	508	41.4	89.9	10.60	438.84
1989	98.2	96.2	79.0	79.8	121 523	26 541	110.8	1 026	509	41.1	89.6	10.83	445.11
1990	98.4	99.2	87.8	78.5	127 978	26 552	114.6	1 006	499	41.1	87.6	11.29	464.02
1991	99.8	99.8	94.7	78.7	132 836	25 778	116.8	974	479	41.0	84.0	11.64	477.24
1992	100.0	100.0	100.0	77.4	134 941	24 685	118.7	929	457	41.1	80.2	11.89	488.68
1993	100.8	99.8	104.7	77.0	137 387	23 211	120.8	896	438	41.1	77.0	12.23	502.65
1994	99.8	98.5	102.4	75.4	138 400	22 965	122.1	861	422	41.7	75.2	12.47	520.00
1995	103.6	104.0	105.7	76.6	144 719	24 990	124.0	843	417	41.4	73.7	12.71	526.19
1996	107.6	108.4	115.3	78.6	151 017	25 266	125.1	855	423	41.7	75.4	13.13	547.52
1997	109.6	110.5	119.3	79.7	162 981	25 903	125.6	866	427	42.0	76.7	13.52	567.84
1998	112.6	114.0	121.8	80.6	168 952	26 515	126.0	873	434	41.3	76.7	13.81	570.35
1999	116.5	117.5	127.5	80.7	174 661	27 180	125.7	856	432	41.5	76.5	14.17	588.06
1996													
January	106.0	106.5	112.7	77.5	12 297	25 083	125.1	849	419	40.2	72.2	13.00	525.20
February	107.8	108.8	115.8	78.8	12 396	25 203	125.3	851	420	41.7	74.9	12.94	540.89
March	108.2	109.3	115.1	79.0	12 360	25 331	125.2	853	422	41.7	75.1	12.96	543.02
April	107.7	108.4	115.3	78.6	12 270	25 422	125.1	854	422	41.6	75.1	13.03	538.14
May	107.5	108.3	115.1	78.5	12 759	25 449	125.1	857	424	41.7	75.6	13.03	540.75
June	108.2	109.1	116.8	79.0	12 543	25 212	124.9	857	425	42.0	76.0	13.08	549.36
July	107.0	107.8	113.8	78.1	12 688	25 538	125.2	856	419	41.6	74.9	13.17	539.97
August	107.2	108.0	113.7	78.3	12 797	25 632	125.0	857	424	41.7	75.6	13.15	547.04
September	108.1	109.1	117.9	78.9	12 482	25 624	125.0	857	424	41.9	76.0	13.29	558.18
October	107.9	108.9	117.6	78.8	12 616	25 845	125.1	859	426	41.8	76.1	13.24	552.11
November	107.0	107.7	114.2	78.2	13 006	25 373	124.7	859	425	41.8	76.1	13.30	561.26
December	108.3	109.1	115.3	79.1	12 852	25 266	125.2	860	427	42.2	77.0	13.36	574.48
1997													
January	107.3	108.2	116.5	78.4	12 827	25 483	125.5	858	425	41.7	75.8	13.35	556.70
February	108.3	109.3	118.4	79.1	13 323	25 493	125.4	859	426	42.0	76.5	13.35	560.70
March	107.8	108.6	115.3	78.6	13 242	25 386	125.5	859	426	42.0	76.3	13.42	566.32
April	108.7	109.9	119.7	79.3	13 414	25 566	125.7	862	425	42.0	76.3	13.43	560.03
May	108.8	109.7	117.6	79.3	13 081	25 578	125.7	862	426	42.0	76.3	13.48	562.12
June	109.7	110.7	119.4	79.9	13 642	25 811	125.3	865	429	41.9	76.5	13.52	566.49
July	109.7	110.7	119.9	79.8	13 777	25 959	125.7	868	425	41.8	76.3	13.51	556.61
August	110.6	111.5	120.9	80.4	13 473	26 026	125.8	868	427	42.1	76.7	13.50	568.35
September	110.1	110.9	119.9	80.0	14 172	25 929	125.8	869	428	42.0	76.9	13.65	574.67
October	111.7	112.8	124.3	81.1	14 101	25 909	125.7	871	428	42.0	76.9	13.62	570.68
November	111.4	112.4	120.9	80.7	13 712	26 180	125.8	873	429	42.2	77.4	13.69	583.19
December	110.7	111.3	118.2	80.1	14 100	25 903	125.8	875	431	42.1	77.6	13.71	588.16
1998													
January	111.1	111.8	118.3	80.3	13 760	26 047	125.6	876	433	41.9	77.8	13.67	572.77
February	111.2	111.7	116.8	80.3	14 025	26 113	125.9	873	434	42.0	77.9	13.71	577.19
March	111.9	112.5	118.8	80.6	14 137	26 363	126.1	877	436	41.6	77.4	13.76	573.79
April	111.7	112.4	117.8	80.4	13 836	26 530	126.3	877	436	41.4	77.2	13.78	560.85
May	112.8	114.3	122.7	81.1	13 787	26 797	126.2	877	436	41.4	77.2	13.78	569.11
June	112.0	113.3	119.8	80.3	14 209	26 676	126.2	876	437	41.4	77.0	13.75	569.25
July	112.2	113.9	121.3	80.3	14 042	26 659	125.8	875	434	41.3	76.6	13.78	560.85
August	113.3	115.1	122.5	80.9	13 749	26 651	125.9	873	434	41.3	76.8	13.79	568.15
September	114.3	116.6	126.1	81.5	14 298	26 577	125.9	872	435	41.1	76.4	13.89	563.93
October	114.4	116.9	127.5	81.4	14 040	26 667	125.8	869	433	41.2	76.3	13.87	570.06
November	113.0	115.2	124.5	80.2	14 517	26 679	126.1	866	431	41.1	75.9	13.91	577.27
December	112.8	115.0	124.0	79.8	14 371	26 515	125.9	864	432	41.1	75.9	14.01	588.42
1999													
January	113.3	115.9	124.6	79.9	14 011	26 443	126.6	864	432	41.2	76.3	13.92	573.50
February	112.9	115.1	122.0	79.4	14 046	26 757	126.6	864	433	41.4	76.6	13.94	578.51
March	113.7	116.3	124.1	79.7	14 553	26 706	126.4	862	433	41.3	76.5	13.98	578.77
April	115.1	117.4	126.3	80.4	14 210	26 810	126.4	860	434	41.5	76.8	14.07	583.91
May	116.7	117.8	126.6	81.3	14 309	26 644	125.9	857	433	41.5	76.8	14.11	584.15
June	117.0	118.3	128.6	81.2	14 611	26 587	125.3	856	434	41.5	76.7	14.13	586.40
July	117.2	117.9	126.0	81.1	14 340	26 930	125.1	859	432	41.6	76.8	14.25	584.25
August	117.7	118.1	128.1	81.1	14 474	27 060	125.0	854	431	41.5	76.5	14.28	591.19
September	117.2	118.0	128.9	80.5	14 797	27 098	124.9	852	428	41.5	76.1	14.29	587.32
October	118.3	117.9	129.7	81.0	14 834	27 058	125.2	849	430	41.5	76.3	14.36	594.50
November	118.9	118.5	131.0	81.1	14 992	27 062	125.3	850	429	41.5	76.3	14.34	600.85
December	119.7	119.5	132.9	81.4	15 169	27 180	125.6	849	428	41.5	75.8	14.41	612.43

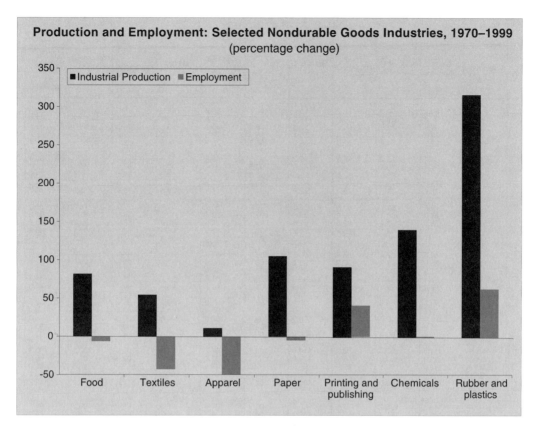

- Among the nondurable goods industries, rubber and plastics products had the most rapid increase in production, rising fourfold from 1970 to 1999. Chemicals was second, growing 140.7 percent. Paper and paper products and printing and publishing followed, doubling and nearly doubling, respectively.

- Leather and leather products (not shown in the above graph) was the only nondurable goods industry to show a drop in production (70 percent) from 1970 to 1999.

- Employment increased in rubber and plastics (63.1 percent) and in printing and publishing (40.7 percent) from 1970 to 1999, but fell in every other nondurable goods industry. Leather goods (not shown) had the largest drop of all industries in nondurables (75.6 percent), followed by tobacco (54.2 percent, also not shown).

- Food and food products remained the largest industry in nondurables measured by employment, with 1,677,000 workers in 1999. Printing and publishing, with 1,553,000 workers, was the second-largest industry.

Table 17-1. Food and Food Products—Production, Capacity Utilization, Shipments, and Inventories

(Seasonally adjusted.)

Year and month	Industrial production (1992=100)										Capacity utiliza-tion—total foods (output as a percent of capacity)	Manufacturers' shipments and inventories (millions of dollars)	
	Total foods	Meat products	Dairy products	Canned and frozen foods	Grain mill products	Bakery products	Sugar and confec-tionery	Fats and oils	Beverages	Coffee and miscella-neous		Shipments	Inventories (book value, end of period)
1970	60.6	60.5	66.2	58.2	50.4	94.6	66.4	65.8	49.5	56.6	83.6	98 535	8 738
1971	62.5	62.8	67.5	61.2	51.0	93.7	67.8	70.5	52.7	56.2	83.6	103 637	9 258
1972	65.8	67.8	72.3	66.1	53.3	98.0	69.8	66.5	55.2	58.8	85.5	115 054	9 673
1973	67.1	63.9	72.7	68.8	55.1	98.0	72.3	67.0	57.9	63.3	85.0	135 585	11 627
1974	68.0	67.3	74.5	69.3	55.0	96.8	73.7	71.7	59.7	59.4	83.6	161 884	14 625
1975	67.5	64.0	75.0	69.3	56.2	97.5	64.5	70.3	61.4	60.0	80.4	172 054	14 467
1976	71.4	71.8	76.3	72.9	58.9	97.7	68.4	75.3	65.1	65.1	82.4	180 830	15 695
1977	74.6	75.1	78.0	80.5	62.5	98.8	78.4	72.5	69.1	64.6	83.5	192 913	16 329
1978	77.2	75.5	78.1	85.1	62.9	98.2	79.5	78.6	73.0	72.2	83.6	215 989	18 073
1979	77.9	76.2	78.8	83.0	62.8	99.1	79.1	79.6	75.4	75.2	82.0	235 976	19 879
1980	79.7	79.2	81.8	83.6	65.5	96.2	80.7	81.7	77.2	78.3	81.6	256 191	21 710
1981	81.4	81.0	86.8	80.9	67.6	97.7	83.6	83.2	79.3	81.0	81.2	272 140	21 483
1982	82.4	78.8	90.1	83.5	71.6	99.4	79.6	85.6	80.0	80.4	80.2	280 529	23 016
1983	84.6	82.4	94.1	85.4	74.2	97.7	82.9	85.4	82.0	83.1	80.9	289 314	23 609
1984	86.4	83.1	90.1	87.6	77.8	99.7	85.4	85.9	84.4	86.5	81.5	304 584	24 182
1985	88.9	84.4	97.4	88.1	83.5	102.9	83.9	91.7	86.6	86.8	82.2	308 606	24 015
1986	91.2	85.6	98.6	90.9	85.2	106.1	87.1	89.6	89.3	90.2	82.9	318 203	23 884
1987	93.5	87.2	96.7	92.8	91.6	107.3	89.9	90.9	91.7	94.0	84.1	329 725	24 860
1988	94.9	90.1	100.3	94.0	90.8	103.0	91.6	94.7	94.6	96.6	84.4	354 084	27 122
1989	95.9	92.4	97.0	97.8	94.2	101.3	93.1	98.4	94.3	97.0	84.3	380 160	28 459
1990	97.0	93.2	95.9	100.9	97.3	100.6	94.0	99.2	94.9	98.3	83.9	391 728	29 714
1991	98.4	96.1	96.1	104.6	97.6	98.7	95.2	104.4	96.2	100.0	83.4	397 893	30 099
1992	100.0	100.0	100.0	100.0	100.0	100.0	100.0	100.0	100.0	100.0	83.0	406 964	30 996
1993	102.0	101.6	101.0	101.7	103.5	102.3	102.5	98.5	100.2	105.2	83.2	422 220	31 201
1994	103.7	107.4	99.9	103.4	105.2	105.6	102.1	95.4	104.1	101.7	83.3	430 963	32 332
1995	105.8	111.0	103.4	103.3	110.4	105.7	103.2	99.3	105.6	103.2	83.3	446 961	34 527
1996	105.4	112.0	100.2	101.9	100.6	103.5	107.4	97.5	109.6	107.7	80.8	461 297	35 697
1997	107.8	113.9	102.8	103.5	103.8	103.5	109.0	100.2	113.6	110.8	80.8	470 447	37 026
1998	109.3	117.6	103.6	103.5	102.8	104.2	109.9	105.2	116.9	112.7	80.1	490 365	37 299
1999	110.1	121.8	109.0	100.1	100.3	104.7	109.2	106.0	119.4	113.2	79.2	500 901	39 033
1996													
January	104.7	112.3	102.2	102.6	100.6	104.3	101.9	95.9	106.8	106.3	81.1	38 360	34 524
February	105.2	115.1	101.7	100.5	102.7	104.1	105.3	94.7	108.3	103.8	81.3	37 868	34 707
March	105.6	113.0	100.9	102.0	101.3	104.4	107.1	94.7	111.2	104.4	81.5	37 723	34 842
April	105.2	114.2	100.8	100.5	102.5	102.2	106.4	97.9	108.9	105.4	81.0	38 237	35 154
May	104.6	113.0	99.5	99.1	100.1	101.6	109.0	98.1	108.3	106.9	80.4	38 332	35 028
June	105.0	111.6	98.5	99.3	100.0	104.0	107.0	97.7	110.1	108.8	80.6	37 639	35 084
July	104.9	111.8	98.2	101.6	101.0	104.2	104.6	100.3	107.4	109.5	80.4	38 669	35 198
August	104.6	111.9	97.8	101.4	98.3	103.3	106.3	97.4	108.6	108.6	80.0	38 721	35 175
September	106.0	109.9	99.3	103.1	99.0	104.9	109.1	96.3	110.9	111.8	80.9	38 601	35 496
October	105.8	111.0	100.0	102.8	99.6	104.0	109.4	98.3	111.9	106.9	80.6	39 372	35 573
November	106.3	110.1	102.0	104.9	100.3	101.9	110.2	97.7	111.8	109.5	80.9	39 312	35 756
December	106.7	110.3	101.4	104.4	101.4	103.0	112.3	100.9	111.2	110.8	81.0	38 524	35 697
1997													
January	106.3	112.2	99.5	102.1	102.4	103.5	109.3	101.5	109.7	111.8	80.6	38 858	35 422
February	107.6	112.8	101.9	106.5	102.6	103.6	110.1	100.9	113.2	108.8	81.4	38 854	35 737
March	107.7	114.0	102.5	105.3	103.5	102.4	111.6	99.5	112.1	110.6	81.3	39 006	35 866
April	107.2	112.3	101.8	104.3	102.6	102.3	111.0	97.4	112.2	111.7	80.8	39 084	36 038
May	107.4	113.2	102.7	104.6	103.6	102.1	109.0	96.6	113.4	110.1	80.8	39 276	36 097
June	107.4	113.0	104.0	104.9	103.8	101.7	108.1	99.6	112.1	111.6	80.7	38 960	36 248
July	108.8	114.4	105.2	108.3	105.0	105.9	105.6	97.8	112.1	112.6	81.5	39 164	36 136
August	108.0	114.8	104.2	102.3	104.0	103.0	108.1	99.1	115.3	111.0	80.8	39 310	36 179
September	107.9	113.6	104.6	101.9	104.5	102.2	108.8	99.3	115.7	110.6	80.5	38 970	36 331
October	107.6	115.4	102.8	97.3	103.9	105.2	109.2	103.0	114.9	110.8	80.1	39 315	36 742
November	108.6	115.5	103.2	101.6	103.4	105.7	109.7	103.3	117.7	108.6	80.7	39 763	36 940
December	108.7	115.3	101.3	105.1	106.3	104.6	107.3	104.7	114.7	111.7	80.7	40 116	37 026
1998													
January	109.9	117.0	103.5	107.9	104.5	104.3	112.5	104.4	115.3	113.3	81.4	40 821	37 359
February	109.3	118.1	103.7	104.8	103.8	103.1	111.6	108.5	115.1	111.8	80.8	40 556	37 647
March	109.4	116.6	102.6	109.1	104.0	102.8	109.7	106.8	114.4	112.9	80.7	40 669	37 512
April	109.4	117.3	103.2	106.6	105.0	102.8	111.5	106.3	114.8	112.4	80.6	40 604	37 488
May	109.5	116.5	103.3	102.9	104.4	104.6	111.0	105.7	117.6	112.8	80.5	40 143	37 503
June	108.9	114.2	102.8	104.4	102.1	105.9	110.7	105.1	115.9	113.0	79.9	40 645	37 427
July	108.4	117.4	102.1	103.6	103.8	104.3	109.1	107.3	113.7	111.0	79.4	40 562	37 424
August	107.7	117.4	103.1	97.6	101.9	101.7	110.5	102.6	116.8	111.2	78.8	41 117	37 115
September	108.4	117.0	102.1	101.5	99.7	104.2	109.2	106.2	117.0	112.9	79.1	41 272	37 112
October	109.5	118.8	104.9	101.8	102.0	105.0	108.1	105.3	118.4	113.0	79.8	41 351	37 459
November	110.9	120.2	105.6	100.6	102.2	105.6	108.3	104.5	123.6	114.7	80.6	41 387	37 264
December	110.3	120.7	106.2	104.1	100.7	106.1	107.0	99.6	120.2	113.1	80.1	41 585	37 299
1999													
January	111.0	122.4	106.4	103.7	100.5	105.4	108.5	101.2	123.0	112.5	80.4	41 319	37 658
February	111.4	120.1	108.0	102.9	101.4	106.7	109.7	102.8	123.4	114.4	80.6	41 479	37 773
March	110.9	121.1	107.4	100.5	99.3	107.8	109.1	104.0	121.7	115.6	80.1	41 659	37 699
April	110.6	121.5	107.6	99.8	102.4	106.3	109.5	105.1	119.7	115.1	79.8	40 733	37 978
May	110.6	120.6	107.3	97.3	102.2	105.0	116.3	107.3	120.5	115.2	79.7	41 494	38 182
June	110.0	122.4	107.1	100.3	99.9	103.5	114.1	106.3	117.8	114.0	79.1	42 055	38 037
July	108.9	122.1	106.8	98.4	100.8	103.6	111.2	108.7	115.5	111.8	78.1	41 309	38 019
August	108.9	121.5	110.2	99.1	98.7	103.8	107.2	111.5	116.4	111.1	78.0	41 767	38 018
September	109.6	122.2	111.0	98.5	98.6	104.4	106.3	112.3	117.8	113.6	78.4	42 142	38 139
October	110.1	123.1	112.3	101.4	99.6	102.9	106.1	108.0	119.8	111.4	78.7	42 292	38 769
November	110.3	121.8	114.2	100.9	98.9	104.3	106.0	105.0	119.8	112.5	78.7	42 363	38 797
December	110.0	120.2	110.9	99.2	100.4	104.3	109.5	103.2	119.3	114.1	78.3	42 176	39 033

Table 17-2. Food and Food Products—Prices, Employment, Hours, and Earnings

Year and month	Producer prices (1982=100, except as noted, not seasonally adjusted)				Consumer prices—Food and beverages (1982–1984=100, seasonally adjusted)				Employment (thousands, seasonally adjusted)		Production workers			
	Food and food products industry (December 1984=100)	Finished consumer foods	Intermediate materials for food manufacturing	Crude foodstuffs and feedstuffs	Total	Food			Total payroll employees	Production workers	Average weekly hours, seasonally adjusted	Aggregate weekly hours index (1982=100), seasonally adjusted	Average earnings (dollars, not seasonally adjusted)	
						Total	Food at home	Food away from home					Hourly	Weekly
1970	. . .	43.8	44.3	45.2	40.1	39.2	39.9	37.5	1 786	1 207	40.5	110.2	3.16	127.98
1971	. . .	44.5	45.7	46.1	41.4	40.4	40.9	39.4	1 766	1 203	40.3	109.3	3.38	136.21
1972	. . .	46.9	47.0	51.5	43.1	42.1	42.7	41.0	1 745	1 192	40.5	108.7	3.60	145.80
1973	. . .	56.5	57.2	72.6	48.8	48.2	49.7	44.2	1 715	1 167	40.4	106.3	3.85	155.54
1974	. . .	64.4	82.0	76.4	55.5	55.1	57.1	49.8	1 707	1 164	40.4	106.0	4.19	169.28
1975	. . .	69.8	82.1	77.4	60.2	59.8	61.8	54.5	1 658	1 120	40.3	101.8	4.61	185.78
1976	. . .	69.6	70.6	76.8	62.1	61.6	63.1	58.2	1 689	1 145	40.5	104.4	4.98	201.69
1977	. . .	73.3	71.9	77.5	65.8	65.5	66.8	62.6	1 711	1 161	40.0	104.6	5.37	214.80
1978	. . .	79.9	81.0	87.3	72.2	72.0	73.8	68.3	1 724	1 174	39.7	105.1	5.80	230.26
1979	. . .	87.3	89.9	100.0	79.9	79.9	81.8	75.9	1 733	1 191	39.9	107.0	6.27	250.17
1980	. . .	92.4	103.7	104.6	86.7	86.8	88.4	83.4	1 708	1 175	39.7	105.1	6.85	271.95
1981	. . .	97.8	102.1	103.9	93.5	93.6	94.8	90.9	1 671	1 150	39.7	102.8	7.44	295.37
1982	. . .	100.0	100.0	100.0	97.3	97.4	98.1	95.8	1 636	1 126	39.4	100.0	7.92	312.05
1983	. . .	101.0	101.3	101.8	99.5	99.4	99.1	100.0	1 614	1 114	39.5	99.1	8.19	323.51
1984	. . .	105.4	106.3	104.7	103.2	103.2	102.8	104.2	1 611	1 119	39.8	100.3	8.39	333.92
1985	99.0	104.6	101.5	94.8	105.6	105.6	104.3	108.3	1 601	1 117	40.0	100.6	8.57	342.80
1986	100.3	107.3	98.4	93.2	109.1	109.0	107.3	112.5	1 607	1 129	40.0	101.7	8.75	350.00
1987	102.6	109.5	100.8	96.2	113.5	113.5	111.9	117.0	1 617	1 145	40.2	103.7	8.93	358.99
1988	107.1	112.6	106.0	106.1	118.2	118.2	116.6	121.8	1 626	1 155	40.3	105.0	9.12	367.54
1989	112.2	118.7	112.7	111.2	124.9	125.1	124.2	127.4	1 644	1 176	40.7	107.8	9.38	381.77
1990	116.2	124.4	117.9	113.1	132.1	132.4	132.3	133.4	1 661	1 194	40.8	109.7	9.62	392.50
1991	116.5	124.1	115.3	105.5	136.8	136.3	135.8	137.9	1 667	1 205	40.6	110.2	9.90	401.94
1992	116.9	123.3	113.9	105.1	138.7	137.9	136.8	140.7	1 663	1 212	40.6	110.9	10.20	414.12
1993	118.7	125.7	115.6	108.4	141.6	140.9	140.1	143.2	1 680	1 228	40.7	112.6	10.45	425.32
1994	120.1	126.8	118.5	106.5	144.9	144.3	144.1	145.7	1 678	1 231	41.3	114.6	10.66	440.26
1995	121.7	129.0	119.5	105.8	148.9	148.4	148.8	149.0	1 692	1 248	41.1	115.5	10.93	449.22
1996	127.1	133.6	125.3	121.5	153.7	153.3	154.3	152.7	1 692	1 254	41.0	115.9	11.20	459.20
1997	127.9	134.5	123.2	112.2	157.7	157.3	158.1	157.0	1 685	1 252	41.3	116.6	11.48	474.12
1998	126.3	134.3	123.2	103.9	161.1	160.7	161.1	161.1	1 683	1 251	41.7	117.5	11.80	492.06
1999	126.3	135.1	120.8	98.7	164.6	164.1	164.2	165.1	1 677	1 252	41.8	117.9	12.09	505.36
1996														
January	124.2	130.7	120.7	114.7	150.7	150.5	150.7	150.6	1 701	1 258	39.7	112.5	11.08	435.44
February	124.4	130.7	121.0	115.0	151.2	150.9	151.2	150.9	1 702	1 259	41.1	116.6	11.03	445.61
March	124.3	132.0	120.6	116.2	151.9	151.5	152.1	151.2	1 705	1 260	41.1	116.7	11.10	449.55
April	124.6	131.2	121.6	119.6	152.5	152.2	152.9	151.6	1 696	1 255	41.1	116.2	11.19	449.84
May	126.3	131.5	126.6	127.7	152.5	152.2	152.6	152.0	1 696	1 257	41.0	116.1	11.18	455.03
June	127.6	133.6	128.2	129.0	153.5	153.2	154.1	152.3	1 688	1 250	41.1	115.8	11.22	458.90
July	128.3	133.9	128.5	130.9	154.0	153.7	154.7	152.8	1 687	1 250	40.9	115.2	11.25	459.00
August	129.7	135.3	129.4	129.5	154.4	154.1	155.1	153.1	1 688	1 252	40.9	115.4	11.16	463.14
September	129.7	135.6	129.2	124.9	155.1	154.8	156.0	153.5	1 685	1 250	41.1	115.8	11.19	472.22
October	129.8	136.6	129.2	119.6	155.9	155.7	157.0	154.2	1 688	1 253	41.2	116.3	11.16	464.26
November	128.5	136.1	124.8	117.7	156.4	156.3	157.6	154.7	1 687	1 252	41.2	116.2	11.38	475.68
December	128.2	135.5	123.8	113.6	156.6	156.4	157.6	155.0	1 686	1 254	41.2	116.4	11.45	480.90
1997														
January	127.4	134.1	122.9	112.2	156.2	155.9	156.7	155.3	1 688	1 255	41.0	116.0	11.41	464.39
February	127.1	133.8	122.9	111.0	156.9	156.6	157.5	155.6	1 687	1 252	41.3	116.5	11.32	460.72
March	128.1	135.2	124.1	114.1	156.9	156.7	157.4	156.0	1 690	1 253	41.3	116.6	11.40	463.98
April	128.3	134.3	123.8	116.7	156.9	156.7	157.3	156.2	1 688	1 254	41.3	116.7	11.45	462.58
May	128.9	135.2	123.9	117.4	157.2	156.9	157.6	156.3	1 685	1 250	41.3	116.3	11.47	470.27
June	128.3	134.0	122.7	111.3	157.5	157.2	157.9	156.6	1 686	1 252	41.0	115.7	11.44	466.75
July	128.0	134.0	122.3	112.0	157.8	157.5	158.1	157.1	1 683	1 250	41.2	116.1	11.52	473.47
August	128.6	134.9	122.9	111.6	158.3	158.0	158.7	157.4	1 679	1 247	41.3	116.1	11.51	481.12
September	127.9	134.7	123.1	110.6	158.5	158.2	158.8	157.8	1 682	1 250	41.2	116.1	11.51	486.87
October	127.5	135.1	122.4	110.1	158.8	158.6	159.1	158.2	1 682	1 252	41.4	116.8	11.45	478.61
November	127.5	134.6	124.2	110.4	159.1	158.9	159.4	158.6	1 684	1 251	41.5	117.0	11.59	487.94
December	127.1	134.4	123.2	109.0	159.2	158.9	159.2	159.0	1 685	1 251	41.6	117.3	11.71	496.50
1998														
January	125.8	133.1	119.9	105.5	159.7	159.4	159.9	159.2	1 684	1 252	41.7	117.6	11.66	482.72
February	126.0	133.6	121.6	105.1	159.7	159.4	159.7	159.6	1 683	1 252	41.5	117.1	11.63	475.67
March	125.5	133.4	121.0	106.3	159.9	159.7	159.9	159.9	1 682	1 250	41.6	117.2	11.69	478.12
April	125.5	133.8	121.7	105.8	160.0	159.7	159.8	160.2	1 684	1 252	41.4	116.8	11.74	474.30
May	125.9	133.6	123.7	106.2	160.7	160.4	160.7	160.6	1 685	1 253	41.7	117.7	11.77	488.46
June	126.4	133.8	123.0	106.2	160.7	160.4	160.7	160.7	1 686	1 255	41.7	117.9	11.76	488.04
July	126.6	134.7	122.9	103.7	161.1	160.8	161.1	161.1	1 684	1 246	41.7	117.1	11.80	490.88
August	127.4	135.2	124.6	103.3	161.5	161.3	161.5	161.5	1 679	1 244	41.7	116.9	11.75	492.33
September	127.1	135.4	125.1	101.3	161.6	161.3	161.3	162.1	1 684	1 252	41.8	117.9	11.95	507.88
October	126.6	135.5	125.4	103.7	162.5	162.2	162.6	162.3	1 679	1 250	41.6	117.2	11.81	496.02
November	126.6	134.9	125.5	102.4	162.8	162.5	162.9	162.6	1 683	1 253	41.7	117.7	11.95	506.68
December	126.1	134.5	124.0	97.0	162.8	162.6	162.7	163.0	1 685	1 254	42.0	118.7	12.01	514.03
1999														
January	126.6	135.6	124.3	101.2	163.4	163.1	163.2	163.5	1 692	1 261	41.9	119.1	11.93	496.29
February	125.8	134.1	122.2	98.2	163.7	163.4	163.5	163.8	1 684	1 257	41.8	118.4	11.90	489.09
March	125.6	134.7	121.4	98.8	163.5	163.3	163.1	164.2	1 682	1 256	41.8	118.3	11.92	489.91
April	124.3	133.4	118.1	95.4	163.7	163.4	163.1	164.5	1 679	1 253	41.8	118.0	12.06	496.87
May	125.3	134.5	119.6	99.6	164.1	163.9	163.8	164.6	1 677	1 252	41.8	117.9	12.10	503.36
June	126.0	135.1	120.0	99.5	164.2	163.9	163.8	164.6	1 674	1 249	41.8	117.6	12.15	506.66
July	125.9	134.6	119.0	96.2	164.4	164.1	163.9	165.1	1 674	1 249	41.9	117.9	12.15	507.87
August	126.8	135.9	121.1	100.1	164.8	164.4	164.2	165.6	1 667	1 240	41.7	116.5	12.07	506.94
September	127.5	136.7	122.0	100.1	165.2	164.9	164.7	165.8	1 673	1 249	41.7	117.4	12.18	512.78
October	127.5	135.8	122.2	98.8	165.6	165.3	165.2	166.2	1 673	1 250	41.9	118.0	12.09	512.62
November	127.1	135.4	120.9	99.5	166.0	165.6	165.5	166.5	1 675	1 252	41.8	117.9	12.11	518.08
December	126.7	135.6	118.2	96.9	166.1	165.8	165.6	166.8	1 674	1 253	41.7	117.7	12.28	520.67

Table 17-3. Tobacco Products—Production, Shipments, Inventories, Price, Employment, Hours, and Earnings

Year and month	Industrial production (1992=100), seasonally adjusted	Manufacturers' shipments and inventories (millions of dollars, seasonally adjusted)		Producer prices (not seasonally adjusted)			Employment (thousands, seasonally adjusted)		Production workers			
		Shipments	Inventories (book value, end of period)	Tobacco manufactures (December 1984=100)	Cigarette manufacture (December 1982=100)	Leaf tobacco (1982=100)	Total payroll employees	Production workers	Average weekly hours, not seasonally adjusted	Aggregate weekly hours index (1982=100) seasonally adjusted	Average earnings (dollars, not seasonally adjusted)	
											Hourly	Weekly
1970	94.3	5 350	2 052	...	28.1	40.3	83	69	37.8	129.2	2.91	110.00
1971	93.1	5 528	2 099	...	28.8	41.9	77	63	37.8	118.7	3.16	119.45
1972	96.6	5 919	2 355	...	29.0	45.7	75	62	37.6	115.9	3.47	130.47
1973	101.7	6 341	2 426	...	30.2	47.7	78	65	38.6	124.0	3.76	145.14
1974	99.4	7 139	3 024	...	33.1	54.7	77	64	38.3	120.9	4.12	157.80
1975	101.7	8 058	3 290	...	37.4	...	76	62	38.2	118.1	4.55	173.81
1976	106.8	8 786	3 416	...	41.0	60.6	77	64	37.5	118.2	4.98	186.75
1977	102.8	9 051	3 511	...	45.5	65.1	71	57	37.8	106.8	5.54	209.41
1978	107.4	9 951	3 669	...	50.2	70.8	71	56	38.1	106.1	6.13	233.55
1979	106.9	10 602	3 517	...	55.2	76.7	70	56	38.0	104.4	6.67	253.46
1980	108.5	12 194	3 721	...	62.5	82.1	69	54	38.1	101.2	7.74	294.89
1981	109.9	13 130	4 436	...	68.2	91.2	70	55	38.8	105.1	8.88	344.54
1982	106.2	16 061	6 873	...	83.1	100.0	69	53	37.8	100.0	9.79	370.06
1983	101.6	16 268	6 746	...	93.5	101.3	68	52	37.4	96.3	10.38	388.21
1984	101.7	17 473	6 533	...	102.3	101.5	64	49	38.9	93.5	11.22	436.46
1985	101.8	18 559	5 943	106.6	110.7	101.2	64	48	37.2	88.4	11.96	444.91
1986	100.3	19 146	5 449	115.5	120.9	89.8	59	44	37.4	81.6	12.88	481.71
1987	104.7	20 757	5 331	126.5	133.5	85.8	55	42	39.0	80.1	14.07	548.73
1988	106.5	23 809	5 286	141.8	150.8	87.2	54	41	39.8	80.1	14.67	583.87
1989	105.4	25 875	5 570	161.4	173.1	93.8	50	37	38.6	70.6	15.31	590.97
1990	105.4	29 856	5 974	183.2	197.6	95.8	49	36	39.2	70.6	16.23	636.22
1991	98.9	31 943	6 342	207.5	225.0	101.1	49	36	39.1	70.2	16.77	655.71
1992	100.0	35 198	6 668	230.2	250.5	101.0	48	36	38.6	68.2	16.92	653.11
1993	84.1	28 383	6 322	218.0	235.2	100.3	44	33	37.4	60.7	16.89	631.69
1994	104.4	30 021	5 782	187.8	198.9	100.2	43	33	39.3	64.1	19.07	749.45
1995	111.8	32 984	5 775	193.2	204.3	102.5	42	32	39.6	62.8	19.41	768.64
1996	113.5	34 482	5 904	199.1	210.5	105.1	41	32	40.0	63.3	19.35	774.00
1997	112.9	38 693	5 797	210.8	223.3	...	41	32	38.9	61.4	19.24	748.44
1998	106.2	41 625	5 867	243.1	260.4	105.1	41	32	38.3	59.7	18.56	710.85
1999	94.3	50 551	5 101	325.7	356.7	101.6	38	28	40.0	55.8	19.07	762.80
1996												
January	108.5	2 799	5 776	195.1	205.9	111.4	42	32	35.8	58.5	18.38	658.00
February	112.3	2 788	5 725	195.0	205.9	118.8	42	32	38.7	62.6	18.13	701.63
March	116.7	2 807	5 716	195.1	205.9	102.6	41	32	39.4	63.9	19.34	762.00
April	113.2	2 887	5 612	195.1	205.9	94.4	42	32	39.3	63.5	20.40	801.72
May	111.5	2 741	5 604	201.1	213.0	...	41	32	39.9	63.2	21.06	840.29
June	118.2	2 846	5 616	201.0	212.8	...	41	32	41.0	63.4	21.40	877.40
July	113.0	2 971	5 502	201.1	212.7	94.1	41	32	38.6	63.2	20.98	809.83
August	113.3	2 982	5 608	201.4	212.9	102.6	41	32	40.0	63.9	20.24	809.60
September	119.7	2 854	5 713	201.0	212.8	110.5	42	32	42.0	64.7	18.39	772.38
October	110.3	2 966	5 783	201.1	212.6	112.6	42	32	41.2	63.2	17.75	731.30
November	113.3	2 823	5 871	201.1	212.7	112.9	42	33	41.2	65.9	18.65	768.38
December	111.6	3 027	5 904	201.2	212.6	113.2	42	33	41.9	66.9	18.68	782.69
1997												
January	117.3	3 397	5 829	201.4	212.4	118.2	42	32	39.2	63.1	18.58	728.34
February	112.3	2 870	5 796	201.2	212.1	120.8	42	32	39.1	64.0	18.59	726.87
March	120.2	3 146	5 770	203.3	214.5	111.7	42	32	39.1	63.5	19.46	760.89
April	109.1	3 116	5 835	208.4	220.6	...	41	31	38.4	60.2	20.34	781.06
May	106.7	3 167	5 836	209.2	221.4	...	41	32	38.7	61.2	20.75	803.03
June	108.9	3 215	5 790	209.6	221.8	...	41	31	39.2	58.8	21.12	827.90
July	107.2	3 225	5 814	209.4	221.6	93.2	42	32	35.3	57.7	20.93	738.83
August	107.9	3 194	5 779	209.4	221.5	94.1	41	32	37.8	60.2	19.79	748.06
September	112.6	3 358	5 680	219.4	233.7	103.2	41	32	39.4	60.9	18.26	719.44
October	129.4	3 346	5 798	219.4	233.6	105.5	41	32	39.6	61.3	18.00	712.80
November	113.8	3 399	5 890	219.3	233.4	108.5	41	32	39.5	61.5	17.80	703.10
December	109.7	3 252	5 797	219.3	233.2	112.9	41	32	40.1	62.0	18.63	747.06
1998												
January	118.6	3 260	5 962	219.6	233.1	112.9	41	32	37.8	61.2	18.36	694.01
February	111.8	3 474	5 864	223.7	237.9	112.9	41	32	37.4	61.3	18.12	677.69
March	106.2	3 336	5 882	223.7	237.7	106.7	42	33	37.1	62.1	18.42	683.38
April	110.3	3 393	5 772	231.0	246.2	99.6	42	33	37.0	62.8	18.84	697.08
May	111.2	3 421	5 779	237.7	254.0	...	41	32	39.0	61.7	20.23	788.97
June	109.6	3 561	5 716	237.9	254.3	...	40	31	39.9	59.9	20.81	830.32
July	116.1	3 444	5 665	237.9	254.3	95.8	40	31	39.3	60.2	20.53	806.83
August	107.2	3 479	5 563	246.4	264.7	95.2	40	31	39.4	60.0	18.95	746.63
September	95.0	3 523	5 783	247.0	265.3	105.2	40	31	37.4	57.8	17.94	670.96
October	100.7	3 466	6 020	247.7	266.0	109.6	40	31	39.1	58.6	16.98	663.92
November	96.0	3 398	5 939	248.4	266.0	112.0	40	31	38.9	58.2	17.32	673.75
December	91.1	3 817	5 867	316.0	345.9	112.3	40	31	37.4	55.7	17.07	638.42
1999												
January	94.8	4 017	5 682	316.5	346.4	112.4	40	31	37.3	58.5	17.15	639.70
February	99.2	4 088	5 513	316.3	346.1	112.6	40	30	37.1	57.1	17.84	661.86
March	95.4	4 149	5 363	315.8	345.5	115.5	38	29	38.1	56.2	19.39	738.76
April	94.2	4 071	5 343	316.0	345.6	88.5	38	29	38.4	56.2	19.91	764.54
May	95.4	4 063	5 308	316.1	345.7	...	38	29	39.8	57.0	20.47	814.71
June	94.5	4 230	5 208	316.2	345.8	...	39	29	40.1	56.5	20.69	829.67
July	96.0	4 265	5 160	316.1	345.6	88.2	38	28	40.3	55.6	21.09	849.93
August	94.8	4 257	5 149	316.5	346.0	96.4	36	25	40.1	49.3	20.86	836.49
September	90.9	4 275	5 177	344.5	378.5	102.9	38	27	39.9	53.7	18.90	754.11
October	91.9	4 500	5 164	344.4	378.5	106.4	38	27	42.3	54.6	17.82	753.79
November	93.1	4 475	5 075	344.5	378.6	107.3	38	27	43.0	56.0	18.02	774.86
December	94.7	4 324	5 101	345.0	378.7	112.0	38	27	44.0	56.6	18.03	793.32

Table 17-4. Textile Mill Products—Production, Capacity Utilization, Shipments, and Inventories

(Seasonally adjusted.)

Year and month	Industrial production (1992=100)					Capacity utilization (output as a percent of capacity)	Manufacturers' shipments and inventories (millions of dollars)	
	Total	Fabrics	Knit goods	Carpeting	Yarns and miscellaneous		Shipments	Inventories (book value, end of period
1970	71.8	105.9	60.4	52.4	60.3	83.5	22 614	3 676
1971	75.8	103.7	63.9	57.6	67.2	84.7	24 034	3 866
1972	83.1	101.6	75.7	66.9	74.8	88.6	28 065	4 056
1973	86.5	108.4	79.4	73.2	73.7	89.7	31 073	4 592
1974	78.7	101.3	69.7	63.2	67.4	80.5	32 790	5 044
1975	75.0	92.5	68.7	58.1	66.5	76.1	31 065	4 794
1976	83.3	106.5	71.8	67.3	75.2	83.6	36 387	5 232
1977	88.3	107.5	76.0	82.8	78.8	87.2	40 550	5 649
1978	88.6	100.3	78.5	87.0	82.7	86.0	42 281	5 935
1979	91.5	107.2	78.5	96.5	83.8	87.7	45 137	6 148
1980	89.0	107.7	79.5	84.8	77.4	84.8	47 256	6 648
1981	86.3	105.3	76.3	79.2	76.1	81.6	50 260	6 896
1982	80.1	92.2	76.7	75.8	69.7	75.5	47 516	6 723
1983	89.9	102.5	82.6	91.0	80.4	85.3	53 733	7 514
1984	90.4	100.1	81.9	99.6	82.0	85.8	56 336	7 827
1985	86.5	91.9	80.9	99.5	79.4	81.5	54 605	7 439
1986	90.5	95.0	82.2	104.7	86.6	85.4	57 188	7 191
1987	96.3	100.6	85.6	105.2	96.6	90.5	62 787	7 939
1988	95.0	102.4	82.0	106.7	95.7	88.0	64 627	8 384
1989	96.5	100.1	88.8	105.2	97.9	87.9	67 265	8 721
1990	93.2	94.4	87.7	100.9	96.4	83.5	65 533	8 732
1991	92.7	96.3	92.6	88.0	92.7	81.7	65 440	8 484
1992	100.0	100.0	100.0	100.0	100.0	87.3	70 753	8 710
1993	105.3	104.6	107.0	105.9	103.9	89.6	73 955	9 264
1994	110.6	111.1	111.0	107.4	111.4	91.2	78 027	9 804
1995	110.2	113.3	110.5	107.4	111.7	88.5	79 874	10 308
1996	108.7	108.8	110.6	108.8	110.4	85.3	80 243	9 915
1997	111.9	108.9	116.0	110.6	118.0	86.0	83 871	10 184
1998	110.9	103.5	116.9	116.5	116.1	84.4	80 624	10 180
1999	110.9	96.3	126.0	124.7	114.6	84.3	78 357	10 163
1996								
January	103.3	107.2	105.5	98.0	102.4	81.8	6 330	10 226
February	105.7	107.1	108.8	102.2	108.0	83.6	6 538	10 202
March	109.5	109.0	109.7	121.3	109.4	86.5	6 604	10 102
April	107.4	110.3	109.3	103.5	107.9	84.7	6 538	10 042
May	108.7	111.0	111.5	104.0	108.9	85.6	6 680	9 992
June	111.0	109.3	111.1	125.4	110.1	87.2	6 965	9 916
July	109.0	109.3	113.8	101.8	109.9	85.6	6 737	9 899
August	110.2	109.3	113.2	107.6	112.4	86.4	6 695	9 948
September	109.7	109.6	109.9	111.2	111.8	85.8	6 753	9 908
October	110.0	109.0	111.7	107.3	113.7	85.9	6 683	9 907
November	110.3	109.4	110.9	110.7	114.3	86.0	6 764	9 941
December	109.2	104.9	111.1	113.1	116.1	85.0	6 909	9 915
1997								
January	108.9	109.3	113.0	97.5	115.4	84.6	6 883	9 956
February	110.3	108.9	113.8	105.6	115.3	85.6	7 054	9 911
March	110.7	106.3	113.1	116.5	115.9	85.7	6 971	9 967
April	111.6	111.6	115.5	107.4	116.3	86.2	7 020	10 060
May	109.6	105.6	114.9	108.1	116.4	84.4	6 969	10 048
June	111.2	106.0	114.3	116.8	117.1	85.5	6 842	10 105
July	113.2	110.4	119.4	106.5	118.7	86.9	7 117	10 121
August	112.2	106.5	118.2	116.2	118.5	86.0	6 959	10 178
September	112.9	109.6	116.1	111.5	121.5	86.4	7 031	10 197
October	113.2	111.3	117.0	110.5	119.3	86.6	6 998	10 213
November	114.6	110.6	116.7	122.4	119.1	87.5	7 050	10 138
December	114.1	110.5	119.6	107.9	122.2	87.1	7 012	10 184
1998								
January	114.7	106.1	120.2	123.3	119.8	87.4	7 254	10 172
February	112.2	108.6	115.7	114.1	116.7	85.5	6 962	10 217
March	112.5	107.6	117.8	113.2	117.8	85.7	6 891	10 219
April	112.7	107.0	120.0	114.4	115.6	85.8	6 806	10 224
May	113.6	106.6	118.4	122.8	117.2	86.5	6 745	10 254
June	112.2	106.4	120.5	113.9	115.0	85.4	6 640	10 253
July	112.0	105.2	116.2	121.8	116.4	85.2	6 940	10 285
August	110.6	101.6	115.6	120.7	116.4	84.2	6 694	10 245
September	109.9	104.1	115.4	112.4	114.5	83.7	6 491	10 307
October	106.6	93.8	113.3	120.2	116.5	81.2	6 551	10 286
November	107.0	98.5	113.2	114.2	112.9	81.5	6 498	10 194
December	106.4	97.1	116.2	107.3	114.3	81.0	6 472	10 180
1999								
January	108.0	90.5	122.1	131.6	112.4	82.2	6 581	10 078
February	110.6	95.3	124.4	129.2	113.0	84.1	6 426	10 025
March	110.1	97.7	125.1	119.4	112.8	83.8	6 363	10 080
April	111.4	97.4	125.6	125.8	114.9	84.8	6 561	10 086
May	110.9	96.7	123.8	126.0	114.9	84.4	6 533	10 051
June	110.8	96.9	125.4	124.3	114.2	84.2	6 447	10 107
July	112.3	97.0	126.6	132.3	114.2	85.3	6 540	10 026
August	111.7	97.2	129.8	122.2	113.8	84.8	6 514	10 030
September	110.8	94.8	127.2	124.2	114.8	84.1	6 502	10 112
October	112.7	96.0	125.6	133.1	117.8	85.5	6 638	10 071
November	111.4	100.7	132.6	105.1	114.9	84.5	6 545	10 101
December	110.1	95.0	126.2	118.9	115.0	83.5	6 615	10 163

Table 17-5. Textile Mill Products—Prices, Employment, Hours, and Earnings

Year and month	Producer prices (1982=100, except as noted, not seasonally adjusted)							Employment (thousands, seasonally adjusted)		Production workers			
	Textile mill products (December 1984=100)	Intermediate materials					Crude materials: Raw cotton	Total payroll employees	Production workers	Average weekly hours, seasonally adjusted	Aggregate weekly hours index (1982=100), seasonally adjusted	Average earnings (dollars, not seasonally adjusted)	
		Synthetic fibers	Processed yarns and thread	Gray fabrics	Finished fabrics	Industrial textile products						Hourly	Weekly
1970	. . .	. . .	. . .	. . .	. . .	. . .	43.6	975	855	39.9	141.8	2.45	97.76
1971	. . .	. . .	. . .	. . .	. . .	. . .	47.2	955	837	40.6	141.3	2.57	104.34
1972	. . .	. . .	. . .	. . .	. . .	. . .	57.0	986	867	41.3	148.9	2.75	113.58
1973	. . .	. . .	. . .	. . .	. . .	. . .	93.4	1 010	886	40.9	150.7	2.95	120.66
1974	. . .	. . .	. . .	. . .	. . .	. . .	96.4	965	843	39.5	138.5	3.20	126.40
1975	. . .	. . .	. . .	. . .	. . .	. . .	75.1	868	752	39.3	122.9	3.42	134.41
1976	. . .	63.2	71.9	73.0	81.2	. . .	113.3	919	800	40.1	133.3	3.69	147.97
1977	. . .	66.2	73.0	72.1	83.3	. . .	101.1	910	792	40.4	132.9	3.99	161.20
1978	. . .	67.6	74.0	81.6	83.3	77.7	96.0	899	783	40.4	131.6	4.30	173.72
1979	. . .	73.4	78.9	87.5	86.2	82.4	104.2	885	771	40.4	129.3	4.66	188.26
1980	. . .	83.1	88.6	95.0	92.9	91.7	135.7	848	737	40.1	122.7	5.07	203.31
1981	. . .	96.5	99.8	101.0	100.5	98.5	120.0	823	713	39.6	117.3	5.52	218.59
1982	. . .	100.0	100.0	100.0	100.0	100.0	100.0	749	642	37.5	100.0	5.83	218.63
1983	. . .	96.7	100.1	101.2	98.9	99.9	114.0	741	639	40.4	107.4	6.18	249.67
1984	. . .	98.5	103.2	105.8	101.7	100.2	113.5	746	646	39.9	107.0	6.46	257.75
1985	99.7	95.5	102.1	104.4	101.4	102.5	97.7	702	606	39.7	100.1	6.70	265.99
1986	100.3	92.5	101.7	103.7	101.4	106.5	88.0	703	608	41.1	103.8	6.93	284.82
1987	102.6	91.8	103.8	107.2	104.2	106.1	105.8	725	630	41.8	109.4	7.17	299.71
1988	106.8	97.3	108.0	114.0	109.4	107.7	95.5	728	632	41.0	107.7	7.38	302.58
1989	109.3	104.8	110.4	115.2	113.6	109.2	105.6	720	622	40.9	105.6	7.67	313.70
1990	111.6	106.7	112.6	117.2	116.0	112.0	118.2	691	593	39.9	98.4	8.02	320.00
1991	112.5	105.3	112.6	117.4	117.5	113.8	116.2	670	574	40.6	97.0	8.30	336.98
1992	113.6	103.4	110.8	120.6	118.8	114.7	89.8	674	577	41.1	98.6	8.60	353.46
1993	113.6	103.6	107.8	118.6	119.5	115.5	91.9	675	575	41.4	98.9	8.88	367.63
1994	113.6	104.1	108.4	116.8	119.2	116.6	121.3	676	575	41.6	99.4	9.13	379.81
1995	116.5	109.4	112.8	121.2	121.7	119.0	156.2	663	560	40.8	94.9	9.41	383.93
1996	118.2	111.3	114.7	121.4	123.6	125.6	130.0	627	529	40.6	89.2	9.69	393.41
1997	118.8	111.1	114.0	121.9	123.8	127.9	116.5	616	522	41.4	89.8	10.03	415.24
1998	118.6	109.9	112.7	121.6	123.9	130.2	111.0	598	506	41.0	86.3	10.39	425.99
1999	116.3	103.8	108.6	114.4	122.6	129.2	87.4	560	474	40.9	80.6	10.71	438.04
1996													
January	117.4	111.0	114.4	120.8	123.1	121.7	137.0	631	531	36.3	80.1	9.56	344.16
February	117.5	111.2	114.5	120.8	123.2	121.5	136.0	635	536	40.5	90.2	9.55	383.91
March	117.7	111.2	114.1	121.9	123.1	121.5	133.0	631	533	40.7	90.1	9.55	388.69
April	118.1	111.2	114.7	122.4	123.6	121.6	143.5	627	529	40.2	88.4	9.65	386.97
May	118.3	111.0	114.5	121.6	123.5	127.4	138.2	627	529	40.8	89.7	9.62	390.57
June	118.0	109.5	114.6	120.9	123.7	127.3	136.5	627	529	41.0	90.1	9.68	400.75
July	118.3	111.7	114.5	121.1	123.7	127.4	128.8	626	528	41.0	89.9	9.69	389.54
August	118.4	111.8	114.3	121.4	123.9	127.8	128.9	625	528	41.0	89.9	9.72	401.44
September	118.5	112.1	116.4	121.3	123.8	128.1	123.2	622	526	41.0	89.6	9.78	404.89
October	118.6	112.0	114.9	121.6	123.7	128.1	120.3	624	530	40.9	90.1	9.73	399.90
November	118.6	111.7	114.8	121.2	123.9	127.1	113.3	621	525	41.2	89.9	9.78	407.83
December	118.6	111.6	114.6	121.5	123.6	127.5	120.8	621	525	41.5	90.5	9.93	417.06
1997													
January	118.6	112.7	114.2	121.4	123.7	126.2	116.6	621	526	41.1	89.8	9.94	407.54
February	118.8	111.4	114.4	121.7	123.8	126.1	116.7	619	524	40.7	88.6	9.90	399.96
March	118.8	111.4	114.4	121.6	123.6	127.7	122.5	621	526	41.3	90.3	9.93	410.11
April	118.2	111.5	114.0	121.4	123.9	127.7	114.7	618	524	41.5	90.4	9.95	411.93
May	118.5	111.3	113.9	121.8	124.0	127.8	115.5	616	523	41.4	90.0	9.95	409.94
June	118.6	111.0	113.7	121.9	123.9	127.9	116.8	617	522	41.3	89.6	9.98	416.17
July	118.8	110.9	113.5	121.9	123.9	127.7	119.4	616	523	41.4	90.0	10.02	406.81
August	118.8	111.0	113.6	121.7	123.8	127.5	120.5	614	519	41.3	89.1	10.02	416.83
September	118.9	110.5	113.7	122.4	123.9	127.8	117.6	613	520	41.6	89.9	10.10	424.20
October	119.1	110.5	114.0	122.1	124.1	127.7	116.0	612	520	41.4	89.4	10.11	418.55
November	119.0	110.4	114.2	121.7	123.7	130.6	114.6	612	519	41.5	89.5	10.16	425.70
December	119.2	110.4	114.6	122.7	123.6	130.6	107.3	612	520	41.6	89.9	10.25	431.53
1998													
January	119.0	111.2	113.3	123.4	123.6	130.3	103.3	610	517	41.7	89.6	10.26	426.82
February	119.3	111.2	113.4	123.4	123.9	130.2	108.0	608	516	41.5	89.0	10.26	421.69
March	119.2	110.9	113.3	123.0	124.5	130.2	110.1	607	514	41.3	88.2	10.29	423.95
April	119.1	111.0	113.3	123.2	124.6	130.5	101.2	606	514	40.9	87.3	10.39	417.68
May	119.1	110.9	113.2	123.0	124.7	130.4	108.0	605	513	41.1	87.6	10.37	426.21
June	119.0	110.7	113.3	122.8	124.2	130.3	118.7	601	510	41.2	87.3	10.36	429.94
July	118.7	110.8	113.0	121.6	124.0	130.4	121.8	595	504	41.0	85.9	10.36	418.54
August	118.7	110.8	112.8	121.4	124.2	130.2	116.6	594	502	41.0	85.5	10.38	427.66
September	118.3	109.5	112.7	120.6	123.7	130.3	119.4	593	501	40.7	84.7	10.48	424.44
October	117.8	107.9	111.9	118.7	123.5	130.4	114.0	589	498	41.0	84.8	10.45	429.50
November	117.8	107.2	111.3	118.9	122.7	130.4	112.3	584	494	40.8	83.7	10.52	432.37
December	117.6	106.9	111.3	118.8	122.5	128.7	98.7	580	491	40.9	83.4	10.56	437.18
1999													
January	117.1	105.5	110.4	117.8	122.3	128.5	94.4	578	489	40.8	82.9	10.63	432.64
February	116.6	105.5	109.5	116.6	122.5	128.9	91.7	573	484	40.5	81.4	10.60	426.12
March	117.0	104.7	108.9	117.6	123.0	128.9	97.4	569	482	40.4	80.9	10.63	428.39
April	116.4	104.0	108.7	116.0	122.8	129.0	95.5	565	478	40.8	81.0	10.69	437.22
May	116.4	103.5	108.5	115.5	122.6	129.0	94.9	562	475	40.9	80.7	10.69	437.22
June	116.3	103.7	108.4	114.1	122.6	129.3	90.3	560	472	40.7	79.8	10.76	442.24
July	115.9	103.2	108.1	113.4	122.5	129.4	80.0	557	472	41.1	80.6	10.71	434.83
August	116.0	103.0	108.9	112.2	122.8	129.3	83.4	556	470	41.0	80.1	10.72	440.59
September	115.9	102.9	108.7	112.0	123.1	129.6	80.7	552	468	40.9	79.5	10.78	438.75
October	116.1	103.6	107.9	113.3	123.0	129.5	81.7	550	467	41.2	79.9	10.73	445.30
November	115.9	103.4	107.8	112.4	121.9	129.7	80.3	552	466	41.3	80.0	10.80	449.28
December	116.1	103.4	107.6	111.8	121.9	129.4	78.2	549	465	41.2	79.6	10.84	453.11

Table 17-6. Apparel—Production, Capacity Utilization, Prices, Employment, Hours, and Earnings

Year and month	Apparel products (seasonally adjusted)		Producer prices (1982=100, except as noted; not seasonally adjusted)				Consumer prices: Apparel (1982-1984=100, seasonally adjusted)	Employment (thousands, seasonally adjusted)		Production workers			
	Industrial production (1992=100)	Capacity utilization (output as a percent of capacity)	Apparel industry (December 1984=100)	Finished apparel				Total payroll employees	Production workers	Average weekly hours, seasonally adjusted	Aggregate weekly hours index (1982=100), seasonally adjusted	Average earnings (dollars, not seasonally adjusted)	
				Women's	Men's and boys'	Girls', children's and infants'						Hourly	Weekly
1970	81.8	78.9	...	62.8	51.2	58.8	59.2	1 364	1 196	35.3	123.9	2.39	84.37
1971	82.9	78.6	...	64.1	52.7	60.3	61.1	1 343	1 178	35.6	122.9	2.49	88.64
1972	87.9	82.0	...	64.6	53.6	60.7	62.3	1 383	1 208	36.0	127.8	2.60	93.60
1973	88.5	81.4	...	66.7	56.1	61.9	64.6	1 438	1 250	35.9	131.7	2.76	99.08
1974	84.5	76.5	...	70.0	63.4	68.9	69.4	1 363	1 175	35.2	121.3	2.97	104.54
1975	77.4	69.3	...	71.3	66.3	70.0	72.5	1 243	1 067	35.2	110.2	3.17	111.58
1976	91.1	80.3	...	73.5	71.1	72.1	75.2	1 318	1 134	35.8	119.3	3.40	121.72
1977	98.0	84.8	...	75.6	77.1	73.2	78.6	1 316	1 129	35.6	117.9	3.62	128.87
1978	100.4	85.9	...	77.4	80.2	76.6	81.4	1 332	1 145	35.6	119.5	3.94	140.26
1979	95.3	80.5	...	81.1	84.7	81.0	84.9	1 304	1 117	35.3	115.6	4.23	149.32
1980	95.4	79.4	...	86.9	91.3	87.1	90.9	1 264	1 079	35.4	112.2	4.56	161.42
1981	97.3	80.6	...	95.0	96.0	97.1	95.3	1 244	1 060	35.7	111.0	4.97	177.43
1982	96.3	79.7	...	100.0	100.0	100.0	97.8	1 161	981	34.7	100.0	5.20	180.44
1983	100.3	82.6	...	102.1	101.3	100.5	100.2	1 163	984	36.2	104.5	5.38	194.76
1984	102.2	84.1	...	103.7	103.5	103.2	102.1	1 185	1 002	36.4	107.2	5.55	202.02
1985	98.6	80.4	101.1	105.4	105.0	103.1	105.0	1 120	944	36.4	100.7	5.73	208.57
1986	101.8	82.3	102.3	106.8	106.4	103.8	105.9	1 100	926	36.7	99.7	5.84	214.33
1987	105.5	85.2	103.9	108.4	108.6	106.7	110.6	1 097	922	37.0	100.1	5.94	219.78
1988	103.6	83.6	107.2	111.3	113.0	107.5	115.4	1 085	912	37.0	99.0	6.12	226.44
1989	100.3	80.9	110.2	113.5	116.8	110.5	118.6	1 076	907	36.9	98.3	6.35	234.32
1990	97.2	78.3	113.3	116.1	120.2	115.3	124.1	1 036	869	36.4	92.9	6.57	239.15
1991	97.8	78.7	116.0	117.9	122.7	117.8	128.7	1 006	841	37.0	91.3	6.77	250.49
1992	100.0	80.1	118.0	119.9	126.0	119.0	131.9	1 007	844	37.2	92.2	6.95	258.54
1993	102.4	81.3	119.2	120.2	127.7	120.1	133.7	989	829	37.2	90.4	7.09	263.75
1994	106.3	83.4	119.7	119.7	128.5	119.9	133.4	974	815	37.5	89.7	7.34	275.25
1995	107.1	82.5	120.6	119.6	130.3	121.6	132.0	936	776	37.0	84.2	7.64	282.68
1996	104.1	79.9	122.3	119.9	132.1	122.4	131.7	868	711	37.0	77.2	7.96	294.52
1997	102.1	78.0	123.4	120.5	132.7	122.9	132.9	824	673	37.3	73.7	8.25	307.73
1998	96.6	73.3	124.8	122.3	133.2	121.8	133.0	766	616	37.3	67.4	8.52	317.80
1999	90.7	68.9	125.3	123.9	133.1	118.2	131.3	692	551	37.5	60.7	8.86	332.25
1996													
January	101.5	78.0	121.4	119.7	131.7	122.4	132.7	884	728	33.7	72.0	7.87	262.07
February	104.7	80.4	121.6	119.9	132.1	121.7	132.1	888	729	36.9	79.0	7.82	287.78
March	103.7	79.6	121.6	119.9	132.2	121.8	132.7	881	723	36.9	78.3	7.86	290.82
April	104.6	80.3	121.5	118.9	132.2	121.8	131.9	877	720	36.8	77.8	7.95	289.38
May	104.8	80.4	122.2	119.5	132.2	121.8	131.8	872	715	37.3	78.3	7.94	296.16
June	104.7	80.3	122.5	120.2	132.3	121.8	131.6	868	712	37.5	78.4	7.99	302.82
July	104.2	79.9	122.6	120.2	132.4	121.8	131.3	867	711	37.3	77.8	7.95	292.56
August	105.6	81.0	122.5	119.4	132.0	121.8	130.5	861	705	37.5	77.6	7.94	299.34
September	104.9	80.5	123.0	120.4	131.9	123.1	131.3	859	703	37.4	77.2	7.99	300.42
October	104.1	79.8	123.1	120.6	132.2	123.5	131.4	856	700	37.4	76.8	8.02	301.55
November	103.9	79.7	122.9	120.0	132.4	123.5	131.6	852	696	37.4	76.4	8.01	301.18
December	103.1	79.1	123.1	120.1	132.3	123.9	131.9	848	693	37.4	76.1	8.14	308.51
1997													
January	102.6	78.7	122.9	120.0	132.4	124.0	132.2	844	691	37.2	75.4	8.12	299.63
February	102.2	78.3	122.9	120.2	132.3	124.0	132.8	843	690	37.0	74.9	8.18	301.02
March	103.5	79.3	123.2	120.2	132.7	124.0	132.4	838	686	37.4	75.3	8.23	308.63
April	102.6	78.6	122.9	119.8	132.4	124.0	133.1	833	681	37.5	75.0	8.21	304.59
May	102.8	78.7	123.3	120.4	132.5	122.6	133.3	830	679	37.2	74.1	8.22	305.78
June	102.6	78.5	123.4	120.4	132.7	122.6	133.1	826	676	37.3	74.0	8.25	311.03
July	101.9	77.9	123.4	120.4	132.8	122.6	133.3	820	671	37.1	73.1	8.19	299.75
August	101.7	77.7	123.5	120.7	133.0	122.6	132.5	819	667	37.1	72.6	8.23	307.80
September	101.7	77.6	123.7	120.8	133.0	122.2	133.0	813	662	37.3	72.5	8.33	312.38
October	101.6	77.6	123.4	120.6	133.1	122.2	132.8	812	661	37.3	72.4	8.33	313.21
November	100.9	76.9	124.2	121.3	132.6	122.2	132.8	807	657	37.3	71.9	8.33	313.21
December	100.8	76.8	124.2	121.2	132.5	122.3	133.1	803	652	37.5	71.8	8.42	320.80
1998													
January	100.4	76.4	124.4	122.2	133.1	122.6	133.0	799	647	37.6	71.4	8.42	314.07
February	98.9	75.2	124.3	122.2	132.9	122.6	132.9	791	641	37.3	70.2	8.38	310.90
March	98.7	75.0	124.5	121.9	132.9	122.4	132.9	789	637	37.2	69.5	8.43	313.60
April	97.7	74.2	124.7	121.9	133.0	122.2	132.5	781	629	37.4	69.0	8.48	309.52
May	96.8	73.5	124.9	121.9	133.1	122.1	132.8	774	621	37.3	68.0	8.47	316.78
June	97.0	73.5	124.9	121.8	133.3	122.2	133.1	770	619	37.3	67.8	8.50	321.30
July	96.9	73.4	124.9	121.7	133.6	122.2	132.7	766	616	37.4	67.6	8.48	312.91
August	96.3	72.9	124.9	121.7	133.5	121.2	134.3	759	610	37.5	67.1	8.54	321.10
September	95.8	72.6	125.1	122.7	133.5	120.5	133.0	755	607	37.3	66.5	8.63	316.72
October	94.8	71.8	125.3	123.2	133.5	121.2	133.0	743	595	37.4	65.3	8.65	325.24
November	93.3	70.7	125.0	123.0	133.2	121.0	132.9	734	586	37.4	64.3	8.64	325.73
December	93.2	70.6	124.9	123.1	133.3	121.0	132.1	731	584	37.3	63.9	8.71	330.11
1999													
January	92.3	70.0	125.0	123.7	133.6	121.2	131.1	725	579	37.1	63.0	8.68	319.42
February	92.2	69.9	125.1	123.6	133.1	121.1	130.7	713	570	37.5	62.7	8.64	322.27
March	91.8	69.6	125.2	123.5	133.5	118.9	130.7	710	566	37.4	62.1	8.78	328.37
April	92.4	70.2	125.3	124.0	133.1	117.6	131.9	705	563	37.5	62.0	8.83	332.01
May	91.2	69.3	125.3	124.2	133.5	117.8	131.8	699	558	37.7	61.7	8.81	333.02
June	90.7	68.9	125.1	123.9	133.1	117.7	131.4	693	552	37.6	60.9	8.89	338.71
July	89.8	68.3	125.1	123.8	132.8	117.8	130.4	688	547	37.5	60.2	8.83	326.71
August	89.2	68.0	125.5	123.9	132.9	117.8	130.0	681	542	37.4	59.5	8.88	333.00
September	89.0	67.9	125.6	123.9	132.9	116.9	131.2	678	538	37.4	59.1	9.01	331.57
October	89.1	68.0	125.6	123.7	132.9	116.9	132.0	674	535	37.5	58.9	8.99	338.92
November	89.1	68.1	125.4	123.8	132.7	117.3	131.5	672	534	37.4	58.6	8.98	337.65
December	89.1	68.2	125.3	124.9	132.9	117.2	131.5	669	533	37.5	58.7	9.04	343.52

Table 17-7. Paper and Paper Products—Production, Capacity Utilization, Shipments, and Inventories

(Seasonally adjusted.)

| Year and month | Industrial production (1992=100) | | | | | | | | Capacity utilization (output as a percent of capacity) | | Manufacturers' shipments and inventories (millions of dollars) | |
| | Total | Pulp and paper | | | | Paper products | | | Total | Pulp and paper | Shipments | Inventories (book value, end of period) |
		Total	Wood pulp	Paper	Paper-board	Total	Paper-board containers	Converted paper products				
1970	56.7	60.3	63.9	57.3	61.9	54.3	55.7	51.8	86.5	92.2	24 573	2 735
1971	59.1	62.8	67.2	59.1	64.8	56.7	57.9	54.2	87.4	93.3	25 182	2 828
1972	64.3	67.2	71.1	63.0	70.8	62.6	64.1	60.0	91.9	95.8	28 004	2 896
1973	68.8	69.7	73.8	65.7	73.0	68.3	68.4	67.0	95.4	96.1	32 495	3 317
1974	68.2	69.1	73.0	66.4	71.0	67.7	64.6	69.1	91.9	93.5	41 514	4 816
1975	59.4	59.4	62.4	58.1	60.1	59.5	57.9	60.0	78.1	79.4	41 497	4 849
1976	67.4	67.8	71.6	65.6	69.0	67.2	65.0	68.3	87.0	89.8	47 939	5 299
1977	70.1	68.6	71.6	67.9	69.0	71.5	68.1	72.3	90.1	90.8	51 881	5 667
1978	73.4	70.7	71.9	69.7	72.2	75.6	73.1	75.8	92.5	92.4	56 777	6 114
1979	76.0	74.4	76.0	74.2	74.4	77.4	74.9	77.5	92.6	94.6	64 957	6 926
1980	75.2	74.7	77.6	74.2	74.6	75.8	72.0	77.0	88.4	92.2	72 553	7 802
1981	76.6	76.4	79.1	76.2	75.8	76.9	73.6	77.8	87.2	91.3	79 970	8 593
1982	74.3	73.6	75.4	75.1	69.4	75.0	70.4	77.0	83.1	86.2	79 698	9 022
1983	81.0	79.8	80.3	81.1	76.9	82.1	75.7	85.4	89.5	91.7	84 817	9 192
1984	85.0	83.7	84.6	85.0	80.5	86.2	80.0	89.3	92.1	93.4	95 525	10 299
1985	83.8	82.4	82.7	84.0	78.6	85.1	80.0	87.7	88.2	90.4	94 679	10 140
1986	88.3	86.8	87.1	87.8	84.5	89.6	84.9	92.2	90.3	94.0	99 865	10 254
1987	90.9	90.6	91.0	91.1	89.5	91.3	89.1	92.5	90.8	95.7	108 989	11 163
1988	93.8	93.4	93.3	94.5	91.3	94.1	92.1	95.3	92.2	95.6	122 882	12 495
1989	95.4	94.3	94.9	95.3	92.1	96.6	94.0	97.9	91.1	93.9	131 896	13 404
1990	96.0	96.7	96.9	97.8	94.2	95.5	95.1	95.7	88.9	93.9	132 424	13 640
1991	96.8	97.3	97.6	97.6	96.6	96.4	95.7	96.8	86.7	91.7	130 131	13 796
1992	100.0	100.0	100.0	100.0	100.0	100.0	100.0	100.0	87.5	92.1	133 201	14 010
1993	104.0	103.3	98.6	104.0	103.3	104.6	105.8	103.9	88.9	93.2	133 263	13 972
1994	108.4	107.1	101.1	106.8	109.3	109.3	112.2	107.7	90.8	94.9	143 649	14 463
1995	109.6	108.8	103.0	108.3	111.5	110.0	111.8	109.1	90.1	94.2	173 716	17 352
1996	108.8	107.5	100.3	105.1	114.1	109.7	112.6	108.1	87.5	91.1	160 661	16 032
1997	114.3	113.1	102.7	110.8	120.2	115.2	116.7	114.3	89.9	94.2	161 992	16 240
1998	114.9	113.0	100.5	111.5	119.0	116.3	118.2	115.2	87.3	92.3	165 429	16 362
1999	116.2	114.4	98.6	112.6	122.0	117.5	120.5	115.8	86.1	92.5	164 558	16 068
1996												
January	106.2	104.5	99.7	104.0	106.8	107.4	110.0	106.1	85.9	89.0	13 829	17 307
February	104.6	103.6	97.5	101.5	109.6	105.2	109.1	103.1	84.5	88.1	13 841	17 316
March	106.2	104.5	99.0	103.0	109.1	107.4	111.9	105.0	85.7	88.8	13 582	17 241
April	108.4	107.3	99.0	106.0	112.3	109.1	111.2	108.0	87.3	91.1	13 589	16 943
May	108.3	106.8	100.9	104.3	113.6	109.3	112.3	107.8	87.2	90.7	13 489	16 633
June	109.2	106.8	100.8	105.5	111.0	111.0	114.8	109.0	87.8	90.5	13 310	16 485
July	110.0	108.7	101.6	105.8	116.6	110.9	113.9	109.3	88.4	92.1	13 436	16 429
August	108.9	108.3	102.3	104.4	118.2	110.4	112.6	107.6	87.5	91.7	13 227	16 457
September	109.7	108.1	101.7	104.5	117.3	110.8	116.7	107.7	88.0	91.4	13 090	16 369
October	109.7	109.0	101.0	105.8	118.0	110.1	112.2	109.0	87.9	92.1	13 096	16 257
November	111.6	110.3	102.2	107.7	118.0	112.5	114.5	111.5	89.4	93.1	13 101	16 144
December	112.6	111.9	99.2	108.9	121.6	113.1	113.4	113.0	90.0	94.3	13 089	16 032
1997												
January	111.4	110.3	99.2	108.2	117.7	112.2	113.5	111.5	88.9	92.9	13 148	15 926
February	113.2	112.6	105.7	110.1	119.7	113.7	115.0	113.1	90.2	94.6	13 216	15 812
March	113.7	113.0	105.8	111.0	119.1	114.1	114.8	113.9	90.4	94.8	12 968	15 918
April	113.4	111.8	102.4	110.4	117.1	114.6	116.4	113.7	89.9	93.6	13 455	15 797
May	113.9	112.4	100.0	111.0	118.5	114.9	115.4	114.8	90.0	93.9	13 168	15 829
June	113.0	111.3	101.3	109.8	117.1	114.3	118.2	112.2	89.1	92.8	13 248	15 682
July	114.3	112.7	101.5	110.7	119.8	115.4	116.5	114.9	89.8	93.8	13 464	15 728
August	114.9	113.8	102.9	111.4	121.8	115.7	118.1	114.5	90.0	94.5	13 408	15 794
September	116.2	115.1	103.4	112.9	122.9	116.9	117.9	116.5	90.7	95.4	13 733	16 016
October	115.3	114.5	103.1	111.8	123.1	115.9	116.3	115.7	89.7	94.7	13 987	15 982
November	116.3	114.4	103.8	110.8	124.7	117.7	122.3	115.2	90.2	94.4	13 847	16 054
December	115.9	114.8	104.1	112.3	123.0	116.6	117.7	116.2	89.6	94.6	14 364	16 240
1998												
January	115.2	114.4	102.9	111.4	123.7	115.8	116.7	115.4	88.8	94.1	14 105	16 351
February	115.4	113.9	103.0	111.5	121.5	116.5	117.4	116.1	88.6	93.5	13 880	16 317
March	114.5	113.0	101.8	110.8	120.4	115.6	117.9	114.5	87.7	92.7	13 957	16 320
April	115.5	114.0	102.5	112.2	120.8	116.5	117.5	116.0	88.2	93.4	13 937	16 363
May	115.1	113.1	103.8	111.5	118.8	116.4	118.9	115.2	87.7	92.6	13 938	16 388
June	114.7	113.4	100.8	111.2	121.3	115.6	117.9	114.3	87.2	92.7	13 879	16 498
July	115.9	114.4	102.0	112.1	122.5	117.0	118.4	116.4	87.9	93.4	13 929	16 584
August	114.7	112.7	99.5	112.3	116.9	116.1	117.8	115.4	86.8	92.0	13 761	16 643
September	114.2	112.1	98.3	111.8	116.4	115.7	117.6	114.7	86.2	91.4	13 518	16 527
October	115.8	112.9	97.9	112.8	116.8	117.9	118.3	117.9	87.3	92.0	13 421	16 511
November	112.8	110.0	97.8	109.2	114.9	114.7	119.8	111.9	84.8	89.5	13 489	16 483
December	114.9	111.6	96.5	111.6	115.3	117.3	122.5	114.4	86.3	90.7	13 669	16 362
1999												
January	115.7	112.9	96.6	112.3	118.2	117.8	122.1	115.5	86.7	91.7	13 443	16 180
February	115.9	112.9	98.4	111.8	118.8	118.1	122.8	115.5	86.7	91.6	13 662	16 078
March	115.9	113.6	101.3	111.6	120.8	117.5	121.3	115.5	86.5	92.1	13 404	16 073
April	115.0	114.4	95.0	111.1	126.0	115.5	118.8	113.8	85.7	92.6	13 387	15 994
May	114.6	113.2	99.0	110.9	121.4	115.7	119.0	113.9	85.2	91.6	13 394	16 023
June	115.7	114.5	101.6	112.6	121.5	116.7	117.1	116.6	85.9	92.5	13 460	16 070
July	115.0	113.6	97.2	111.7	121.6	116.0	119.1	114.4	85.2	91.7	13 575	16 009
August	115.8	114.4	98.9	112.3	122.5	116.8	119.8	115.2	85.6	92.3	13 949	15 928
September	117.2	115.6	97.8	115.4	120.5	118.3	117.2	119.2	86.4	93.1	13 777	16 133
October	118.0	116.2	98.7	113.3	126.5	119.3	122.9	117.3	86.9	93.5	13 781	16 125
November	118.1	116.1	99.6	114.9	122.5	119.5	121.9	118.2	86.7	93.3	14 268	16 137
December	117.7	116.5	100.6	113.9	125.7	118.7	127.1	113.9	86.3	93.5	14 376	16 068

Table 17-8. Paper and Paper Products—Prices, Employment, Hours, and Earnings

Year and month	Producer prices (1992=100, except as noted, not seasonally adjusted)							Employment (thousands, seasonally adjusted)		Production workers			
	Paper and paper products (December 1984=100)	Intermediate materials					Crude materials: waste paper	Total payroll employees	Production workers	Average weekly hours, seasonally adjusted	Aggregate weekly hours index (1982=100), seasonally adjusted	Average earnings (dollars, not seasonally adjusted)	
		Woodpulp	Paper	Paper-board	Paper boxes and containers	Building paper and board						Hourly	Weekly
1970	. . .	28.9	38.8	39.7	43.3	42.2	103.2	701	540	41.9	110.2	3.44	144.14
1971	. . .	29.6	39.9	40.2	44.7	42.9	92.5	677	518	42.1	106.4	3.67	154.51
1972	. . .	29.4	40.6	41.4	46.4	44.4	110.3	679	528	42.8	110.3	3.95	169.06
1973	. . .	33.8	42.4	45.2	49.9	47.1	162.9	694	540	42.9	112.7	4.20	180.18
1974	. . .	57.5	51.9	59.7	58.5	51.6	219.2	696	541	42.2	111.2	4.53	191.17
1975	. . .	74.8	60.4	66.8	63.3	53.1	90.9	633	477	41.6	96.8	5.01	208.42
1976	. . .	75.5	63.7	69.1	66.0	57.9	152.6	666	505	42.5	104.7	5.47	232.48
1977	. . .	74.2	67.8	69.1	67.1	65.6	154.6	682	515	42.9	107.6	5.96	255.68
1978	. . .	70.3	72.0	70.5	69.9	78.2	157.8	689	521	42.9	109.0	6.52	279.71
1979	. . .	82.9	80.2	79.3	79.1	76.2	170.5	697	532	42.6	110.5	7.13	303.74
1980	. . .	100.3	89.7	92.0	89.4	86.1	172.2	685	519	42.2	106.9	7.84	330.85
1981	. . .	104.8	97.7	101.2	97.7	96.7	145.0	681	515	42.5	106.8	8.60	365.50
1982	. . .	100.0	100.0	100.0	100.0	100.0	100.0	655	491	41.8	100.0	9.32	389.58
1983	. . .	91.5	98.5	98.4	99.5	104.4	. . .	654	491	42.6	102.1	9.93	423.02
1984	. . .	104.8	105.8	110.4	105.7	108.2	198.2	674	508	43.1	106.8	10.41	448.67
1985	98.8	91.4	106.0	107.7	108.8	107.4	122.9	671	508	43.1	106.8	10.83	466.77
1986	99.5	94.7	107.0	106.6	107.8	108.8	142.6	667	507	43.2	106.9	11.18	482.98
1987	104.9	111.5	111.5	118.1	115.4	111.2	181.4	674	512	43.4	108.5	11.43	496.06
1988	113.7	136.7	123.2	133.2	123.5	113.3	183.6	689	516	43.3	108.9	11.69	506.18
1989	120.8	157.4	129.6	140.1	129.8	115.6	157.1	696	521	43.3	109.9	11.96	517.87
1990	121.9	151.3	128.8	135.7	129.9	112.2	138.9	697	522	43.3	110.4	12.31	533.02
1991	121.1	119.2	126.9	130.2	128.6	111.8	121.4	688	517	43.3	109.3	12.72	550.78
1992	121.2	118.9	123.2	134.3	130.6	119.6	117.5	690	520	43.6	110.5	13.07	569.85
1993	120.2	104.2	123.8	130.0	129.9	132.7	117.4	692	522	43.6	110.9	13.42	585.11
1994	123.7	115.9	126.0	140.5	136.1	144.1	209.5	692	524	43.9	112.3	13.77	604.50
1995	146.7	183.2	159.0	183.1	163.8	144.9	371.1	693	525	43.1	110.5	14.23	613.31
1996	138.6	133.1	149.4	155.1	153.9	137.2	141.6	684	519	43.3	109.5	14.67	635.21
1997	133.5	128.6	143.9	144.4	144.7	129.6	163.3	683	521	43.7	111.0	15.05	657.69
1998	136.2	122.6	145.4	151.6	154.7	132.9	145.4	677	516	43.4	109.3	15.50	672.70
1999	136.4	119.7	141.8	153.2	158.0	141.6	183.6	668	506	43.5	107.3	15.94	693.39
1996													
January	147.8	176.6	163.1	175.7	165.3	138.5	163.4	687	521	41.6	105.7	14.58	607.99
February	146.1	160.4	160.9	172.6	163.9	138.2	163.0	685	519	43.2	109.3	14.43	617.60
March	143.0	141.4	157.5	166.6	161.1	136.3	142.0	684	518	43.1	108.8	14.44	618.03
April	140.5	120.3	152.6	161.8	157.6	136.2	123.1	681	516	43.4	109.2	14.61	626.77
May	138.2	114.1	149.4	154.0	155.3	137.9	124.1	682	516	43.4	109.2	14.58	626.94
June	137.2	120.0	148.4	150.6	152.3	135.9	128.6	683	517	43.5	109.6	14.63	634.94
July	136.3	125.5	146.4	148.0	151.1	137.4	134.9	682	516	43.4	109.2	14.78	638.50
August	135.3	127.3	144.5	145.5	148.5	137.3	136.9	681	518	43.5	109.9	14.69	637.55
September	135.1	127.8	143.5	145.6	148.6	140.5	142.2	683	520	43.4	110.0	14.73	648.12
October	134.9	128.2	142.3	146.6	148.0	138.7	146.2	683	521	43.4	110.2	14.73	642.23
November	134.6	127.6	141.7	146.9	147.3	136.2	147.8	685	522	43.5	110.7	14.85	654.89
December	134.7	128.2	142.1	147.6	147.4	133.7	146.6	685	522	43.7	111.2	14.93	664.39
1997													
January	134.5	127.4	141.7	147.1	148.1	132.4	150.3	684	521	43.7	111.0	14.82	649.12
February	133.5	125.2	140.9	144.2	146.3	130.9	157.5	684	522	43.7	111.2	14.76	637.63
March	132.5	124.5	140.8	139.7	144.6	130.9	155.9	685	522	43.9	111.7	14.92	649.02
April	131.5	121.9	141.8	137.2	142.8	129.1	151.0	684	522	43.9	111.7	14.98	650.13
May	131.5	123.5	142.8	136.8	142.0	128.1	154.0	684	522	43.8	111.5	14.97	649.70
June	131.7	125.5	143.3	137.5	141.4	128.7	154.6	683	521	43.5	110.5	14.97	649.70
July	132.0	130.0	144.4	137.8	141.5	127.4	165.4	683	520	43.5	110.3	15.16	656.43
August	132.8	132.7	145.2	143.8	140.2	127.0	192.3	681	519	43.5	110.1	15.11	655.77
September	134.1	133.3	145.5	148.4	144.1	128.4	182.1	682	519	43.6	110.3	15.17	669.00
October	134.6	133.2	146.1	150.1	145.2	127.9	168.4	682	520	43.7	110.8	15.18	664.88
November	135.9	132.8	146.5	154.4	148.2	133.8	164.8	682	520	43.9	111.3	15.22	675.77
December	137.3	133.4	147.5	156.1	151.9	131.0	163.6	682	520	43.8	111.0	15.28	683.02
1998													
January	137.7	130.7	147.9	155.9	154.9	127.3	163.5	682	522	43.7	111.2	15.19	663.80
February	137.8	127.8	147.8	156.1	156.0	128.6	164.4	681	520	43.5	110.3	15.21	654.03
March	137.5	126.4	147.6	156.0	155.5	128.2	162.4	681	520	43.5	110.3	15.28	658.57
April	137.0	121.5	146.9	155.2	154.7	131.0	153.7	680	519	42.6	107.8	15.45	656.63
May	137.0	120.8	146.4	154.2	156.3	132.0	151.8	679	518	43.5	109.9	15.50	671.15
June	136.7	123.9	145.6	153.7	155.9	131.6	149.6	678	517	43.5	109.6	15.46	672.51
July	136.7	126.1	145.5	152.2	155.8	136.2	146.7	676	515	43.6	109.5	15.63	672.09
August	136.3	123.3	145.3	150.9	154.6	141.9	145.5	676	515	43.4	109.0	15.53	669.34
September	135.5	121.1	144.2	149.0	154.7	142.8	140.5	676	514	43.6	109.3	15.82	697.66
October	134.6	116.9	143.5	146.9	153.1	134.6	132.8	675	513	43.5	108.8	15.58	679.29
November	134.0	116.1	142.6	144.7	153.0	131.3	117.3	672	511	43.5	108.4	15.62	685.72
December	133.5	116.7	141.4	143.6	151.9	129.3	116.3	672	510	43.4	107.9	15.76	698.17
1999													
January	133.0	112.7	141.4	142.2	151.3	131.5	126.6	671	509	43.5	108.0	15.70	682.95
February	132.6	112.3	140.4	142.3	150.8	131.1	138.3	672	508	43.4	107.5	15.67	672.24
March	133.3	113.8	139.9	146.4	151.3	137.8	142.2	671	508	43.7	108.2	15.75	683.55
April	134.2	113.0	140.2	148.1	155.0	138.3	142.3	670	508	43.7	108.2	15.80	688.88
May	134.8	114.1	140.3	149.3	156.8	141.6	147.4	669	507	43.4	107.3	15.88	686.02
June	135.8	116.0	140.6	149.5	157.7	145.9	171.7	668	506	43.6	107.6	15.95	693.83
July	136.3	121.6	140.5	154.5	157.6	149.6	207.4	668	505	43.5	107.1	16.02	688.86
August	137.3	123.7	141.7	158.6	159.9	150.5	208.5	667	505	43.6	107.3	15.95	690.64
September	138.7	125.1	142.5	161.0	163.3	146.5	215.5	666	505	43.4	106.9	16.24	709.69
October	139.9	125.8	144.3	162.1	164.0	142.7	223.2	665	503	43.5	106.7	16.09	704.74
November	140.2	128.1	144.7	162.2	164.3	141.2	234.6	665	504	43.4	106.6	16.08	704.30
December	140.4	130.8	145.4	162.3	164.0	142.6	244.8	665	504	43.3	106.4	16.12	712.50

Table 17-9. Printing and Publishing—Production, Capacity Utilization, Prices, Employment, Hours, and Earnings

Year and month	Industrial production (1982=100, seasonally adjusted)			Capacity utilization (output as a percent of capacity, seasonally adjusted)	Producer prices (December 1984=100, not seasonally adjusted)	Employment (thousands, seasonally adjusted)		Production workers			
								Average weekly hours, seasonally adjusted	Aggregate weekly hours index (1982=100), seasonally adjusted	Average earnings (dollars, not seasonally adjusted)	
	Total	Newspapers	Job printing			Total payroll employees	Production workers			Hourly	Weekly
1970	54.4	89.8	38.9	86.9	...	1 104	679	37.7	98.9	3.92	147.78
1971	54.8	90.2	38.7	85.3	...	1 081	658	37.5	95.3	4.20	157.50
1972	58.5	95.9	43.7	88.3	...	1 094	664	37.7	96.5	4.51	170.03
1973	60.1	98.4	46.0	87.7	...	1 111	670	37.7	97.4	4.75	179.08
1974	59.1	98.6	44.2	83.9	...	1 111	660	37.5	95.5	5.03	188.63
1975	55.4	92.8	41.2	77.0	...	1 083	624	36.9	88.9	5.38	198.52
1976	60.5	95.0	46.8	82.6	...	1 099	625	37.5	90.3	5.71	214.13
1977	66.3	97.6	52.2	89.4	...	1 141	647	37.7	94.1	6.12	230.72
1978	70.1	103.6	54.3	91.7	...	1 192	672	37.6	97.5	6.51	244.78
1979	72.0	107.3	56.3	89.5	...	1 235	697	37.5	101.0	6.94	260.25
1980	72.4	105.8	56.8	85.8	...	1 252	699	37.1	100.1	7.53	279.36
1981	74.3	106.9	58.0	83.9	...	1 266	699	37.3	100.6	8.19	305.49
1982	77.5	106.4	63.0	83.8	...	1 272	699	37.1	100.0	8.74	324.25
1983	81.4	111.3	66.9	85.2	...	1 298	712	37.6	103.3	9.11	342.54
1984	87.0	119.8	71.7	87.7	...	1 375	758	37.9	110.9	9.41	356.64
1985	90.2	121.7	75.6	86.4	103.6	1 426	788	37.8	114.9	9.71	367.04
1986	93.4	125.3	78.5	85.6	107.8	1 456	816	38.0	119.6	9.99	379.62
1987	102.5	129.3	93.3	91.0	112.2	1 503	839	38.0	123.2	10.28	390.64
1988	103.4	124.9	95.5	89.5	118.2	1 543	864	38.0	126.7	10.53	400.14
1989	103.5	121.9	96.8	87.7	124.7	1 556	863	37.9	126.2	10.88	412.35
1990	103.1	116.0	97.8	85.2	130.5	1 569	871	37.9	127.5	11.24	426.00
1991	99.1	105.9	95.2	80.8	136.4	1 536	847	37.7	123.3	11.48	432.80
1992	100.0	100.0	100.0	81.4	140.8	1 507	833	38.1	122.3	11.74	447.29
1993	100.7	98.4	100.6	81.7	145.6	1 517	839	38.3	123.9	11.93	456.92
1994	100.7	98.7	101.5	81.2	149.7	1 537	846	38.6	125.9	12.14	468.60
1995	101.4	97.2	102.1	81.2	159.0	1 546	848	38.2	125.0	12.33	471.01
1996	101.3	94.2	102.8	81.1	165.6	1 540	841	38.2	124.0	12.65	483.23
1997	105.2	97.1	106.3	83.1	169.1	1 552	847	38.5	126.0	13.06	502.81
1998	105.1	98.4	108.0	81.5	174.0	1 565	845	38.3	124.8	13.46	515.52
1999	104.4	99.3	108.9	80.5	177.6	1 553	827	38.2	122.1	13.84	528.69
1996											
January	99.0	92.2	101.0	79.6	164.5	1 542	843	37.1	120.7	12.49	458.38
February	100.2	91.0	102.6	80.5	164.8	1 541	843	38.2	124.3	12.49	473.37
March	100.1	91.6	102.3	80.4	164.8	1 543	844	38.2	124.5	12.53	478.65
April	100.4	93.3	101.6	80.5	165.1	1 539	841	38.2	124.0	12.53	474.89
May	101.2	93.7	103.0	81.1	165.3	1 538	840	38.3	124.2	12.54	476.52
June	100.5	94.9	101.6	80.6	165.4	1 538	840	38.3	124.2	12.54	475.27
July	101.2	95.9	101.9	81.1	165.2	1 539	840	38.3	124.2	12.63	479.94
August	102.1	95.8	103.1	81.7	165.5	1 540	841	38.3	124.3	12.70	490.22
September	102.1	95.5	103.4	81.6	166.1	1 541	840	38.3	124.2	12.82	497.42
October	102.6	95.5	104.2	82.0	166.4	1 543	841	38.2	124.0	12.81	493.19
November	102.9	95.0	104.6	82.1	166.7	1 541	840	38.2	123.9	12.82	496.13
December	103.1	95.7	104.5	82.2	166.9	1 541	841	38.4	124.7	12.90	503.10
1997											
January	103.2	95.5	106.3	82.2	168.0	1 541	839	38.3	124.0	12.86	486.11
February	103.8	97.1	105.2	82.6	168.1	1 543	840	38.4	124.5	12.89	491.11
March	104.0	97.3	104.5	82.6	168.0	1 545	841	38.7	125.6	13.01	503.49
April	104.6	97.6	105.3	83.0	168.5	1 551	846	38.5	125.7	12.98	497.13
May	105.1	97.3	105.9	83.2	168.2	1 553	852	38.5	126.6	12.93	492.63
June	104.6	96.8	104.6	82.7	168.4	1 556	852	38.4	126.3	12.90	490.20
July	105.7	96.6	107.0	83.4	168.7	1 555	851	38.4	126.1	13.01	495.68
August	105.3	97.1	105.8	82.9	168.9	1 555	849	38.4	125.8	13.07	504.50
September	105.7	98.0	106.2	83.1	169.2	1 555	847	38.6	126.2	13.22	518.22
October	107.1	98.1	108.6	84.0	170.7	1 556	849	38.7	126.8	13.20	513.48
November	107.0	97.2	108.1	83.9	171.1	1 558	850	38.7	127.0	13.25	520.73
December	106.5	96.9	108.3	83.3	171.3	1 561	851	38.6	126.8	13.31	521.75
1998											
January	106.0	97.3	107.5	82.8	173.2	1 563	849	38.5	126.2	13.28	504.64
February	105.8	98.2	107.4	82.4	173.0	1 564	849	38.5	126.2	13.34	509.59
March	105.5	98.8	107.7	82.1	173.1	1 563	847	38.5	125.9	13.38	515.13
April	105.5	99.0	108.5	82.0	174.0	1 565	847	38.2	124.9	13.34	504.25
May	105.5	99.3	108.2	81.8	173.9	1 566	847	38.4	125.6	13.33	507.87
June	104.2	98.7	106.4	80.7	173.6	1 568	847	38.4	125.6	13.34	506.92
July	104.4	98.2	106.6	80.8	173.7	1 567	845	38.3	124.9	13.45	512.45
August	104.5	98.0	106.3	80.8	173.7	1 565	844	38.5	125.4	13.48	520.33
September	104.4	98.4	106.9	80.6	174.3	1 565	843	38.2	124.3	13.66	527.28
October	105.1	98.1	109.5	81.1	174.9	1 565	842	38.1	123.8	13.62	523.01
November	105.1	98.3	110.0	81.1	175.2	1 563	839	38.1	123.4	13.57	525.16
December	105.3	98.5	111.1	81.2	175.2	1 560	836	38.1	123.0	13.69	531.17
1999											
January	104.3	99.7	109.3	80.4	176.4	1 560	837	38.2	123.4	13.67	515.36
February	104.3	99.9	110.2	80.4	176.5	1 558	834	38.1	122.7	13.68	517.10
March	103.7	99.7	110.0	79.9	177.0	1 556	831	38.0	121.9	13.74	520.75
April	104.2	99.0	110.8	80.3	177.1	1 554	828	38.1	121.8	13.73	523.11
May	104.1	98.5	110.8	80.3	177.2	1 551	827	38.2	121.9	13.75	522.50
June	103.5	98.3	108.5	79.9	177.2	1 551	826	38.3	122.1	13.74	520.75
July	102.8	98.1	106.4	79.4	177.4	1 552	825	38.3	122.0	13.81	526.16
August	103.6	98.7	106.8	80.0	177.7	1 552	825	38.3	122.0	13.83	531.07
September	104.6	98.9	107.6	80.8	178.1	1 551	824	38.3	121.8	13.98	539.63
October	106.0	99.3	109.2	81.9	178.6	1 551	825	38.3	122.0	13.98	539.63
November	105.7	100.2	109.1	81.7	179.1	1 549	824	38.3	121.8	14.02	543.98
December	105.3	101.2	109.3	81.5	179.2	1 548	824	38.3	121.8	14.12	550.68

Table 17-10. Chemicals and Chemical Products—Production and Capacity Utilization

(Seasonally adjusted.)

| Year and month | Industrial production (1992=100) | | | | | | | | Capacity utilization (output as a percent of capacity) | | |
| | Total | Basic chemicals | | Industrial organic chemicals | Synthetic materials | Drugs and medicines | Soap and toiletries | Agricultural chemicals | Total | Plastics materials | Synthetic fibers |
		Basic chemicals	Inorganic chemicals, not elsewhere classified								
1970	48.8	69.4	81.1	. . .	35.9	36.0	62.2	43.5	77.7	82.3	81.9
1971	51.9	71.9	74.8	. . .	40.0	40.0	62.1	45.2	77.5	81.3	87.6
1972	58.4	81.4	81.5	49.1	42.0	71.0	63.0	50.6	82.3	98.5	87.6
1973	63.9	85.0	83.5	55.6	45.7	75.4	73.5	58.0	85.5	98.5	91.5
1974	66.2	89.1	88.8	59.0	48.3	78.5	74.0	63.4	84.4	93.8	89.9
1975	60.3	74.4	72.3	50.0	49.0	72.4	61.4	66.5	73.3	64.8	76.3
1976	67.5	79.6	77.3	57.7	53.4	79.1	75.2	67.8	78.4	74.5	77.7
1977	72.4	83.9	84.2	64.3	55.7	82.1	85.1	73.2	80.8	80.6	81.1
1978	76.4	85.6	84.9	71.2	59.0	87.7	86.5	74.4	82.7	85.3	86.5
1979	79.2	88.1	86.4	77.5	60.4	89.4	89.5	77.7	83.7	86.7	91.4
1980	75.9	83.1	81.0	64.0	62.8	94.5	81.5	80.4	78.4	75.2	65.3
1981	77.3	83.6	82.2	71.9	63.4	89.2	85.2	85.8	78.1	76.9	81.2
1982	71.0	75.0	74.6	64.5	64.8	81.5	71.2	74.6	70.7	71.2	68.6
1983	76.0	79.8	78.8	75.7	67.4	83.4	79.0	73.6	75.2	82.3	84.9
1984	79.3	84.0	81.9	80.1	68.1	82.7	82.1	85.7	77.4	86.3	85.4
1985	79.4	83.3	81.1	78.7	69.4	83.4	82.7	80.7	75.6	85.7	78.4
1986	82.4	81.8	78.0	82.9	75.8	88.3	83.5	74.8	77.6	89.4	86.3
1987	87.0	85.4	81.7	90.7	78.4	91.3	87.9	84.6	81.3	98.7	92.1
1988	92.2	89.4	84.6	94.5	82.2	97.2	98.1	90.0	84.0	95.5	91.7
1989	95.1	92.6	88.0	97.5	85.1	98.0	103.5	97.2	83.7	90.3	94.8
1990	97.3	101.2	101.1	95.9	88.3	99.9	104.9	100.4	83.0	87.1	86.7
1991	96.4	97.7	97.4	92.9	93.2	98.7	99.9	97.6	80.1	81.4	85.6
1992	100.0	100.0	100.0	100.0	100.0	100.0	100.0	100.0	80.2	89.0	86.0
1993	101.5	96.0	92.5	100.9	100.5	107.1	99.7	100.8	78.7	86.7	87.7
1994	104.7	91.3	86.1	108.7	104.5	106.4	107.2	100.5	78.9	95.9	85.8
1995	107.3	93.3	90.0	109.4	108.6	112.2	109.8	100.3	79.0	91.7	86.1
1996	109.8	94.7	92.2	111.1	109.8	113.1	115.5	102.3	78.6	90.7	87.3
1997	114.6	98.7	92.8	118.8	111.8	119.5	119.4	106.0	79.7	91.9	81.8
1998	115.1	92.5	83.3	118.4	112.0	120.8	120.9	110.9	77.8	89.4	81.2
1999	117.5	97.3	90.9	125.4	116.3	122.3	120.4	111.7	78.2	91.2	81.1
1996											
January	107.7	92.1	89.8	108.0	106.8	108.8	119.1	101.9	78.3	90.0	83.8
February	107.6	91.5	89.6	108.4	106.8	109.8	117.0	102.0	78.0	90.5	83.6
March	107.6	90.4	88.9	108.9	107.7	110.9	115.0	102.0	77.8	90.8	83.9
April	106.8	92.1	89.5	109.4	107.8	108.9	111.6	99.4	76.9	90.4	83.9
May	107.9	93.9	90.7	109.8	109.5	109.0	115.3	98.4	77.5	91.8	87.0
June	107.9	94.2	92.2	110.1	110.5	108.6	113.1	101.6	77.3	92.0	87.4
July	110.4	95.0	93.7	110.6	110.6	114.3	115.0	102.1	78.8	90.7	89.7
August	110.8	96.0	94.3	111.3	110.6	113.6	116.8	104.6	79.0	91.3	88.9
September	111.5	96.7	94.9	112.4	110.7	117.1	113.2	103.6	79.3	91.2	88.0
October	112.9	98.3	94.3	113.7	113.6	117.9	116.9	104.5	80.0	90.9	93.1
November	112.6	97.3	94.2	114.9	110.9	118.3	115.5	103.8	79.6	89.4	89.7
December	113.6	98.4	93.9	115.9	111.7	118.6	117.2	104.1	80.2	89.8	89.0
1997											
January	114.1	98.5	94.8	116.5	112.6	118.0	118.9	104.5	80.4	90.9	90.0
February	113.8	99.3	95.1	117.1	110.9	118.1	119.3	103.1	80.0	91.3	83.1
March	112.7	99.3	94.9	117.5	111.1	117.0	114.4	103.7	79.1	92.2	82.4
April	114.6	99.8	95.4	117.8	113.0	119.2	118.1	105.4	80.2	91.3	88.0
May	113.7	99.2	95.1	117.5	109.5	119.0	117.3	107.4	79.4	91.2	78.9
June	113.9	99.3	94.6	116.8	108.8	119.8	119.2	106.1	79.4	91.4	77.2
July	114.5	99.2	91.7	116.3	112.8	119.3	120.1	106.5	79.6	92.8	82.0
August	115.1	98.7	92.8	117.1	111.2	122.4	120.2	106.4	79.9	91.7	79.4
September	115.4	101.0	93.4	119.5	113.3	119.2	119.6	107.7	79.8	92.5	80.6
October	116.1	97.7	89.8	122.5	111.9	121.5	121.3	107.4	80.1	91.8	79.7
November	115.4	96.7	88.9	124.2	112.1	119.3	120.4	106.5	79.4	92.9	78.5
December	116.4	97.4	88.5	123.5	113.8	119.4	122.9	107.4	79.9	92.6	81.8
1998											
January	116.3	97.5	87.3	121.4	113.3	122.0	119.8	109.4	79.6	92.0	82.0
February	115.7	97.2	86.5	119.8	111.3	121.0	121.4	107.9	78.9	88.5	83.7
March	115.5	95.4	85.6	119.5	111.8	121.0	118.4	108.3	78.6	88.5	84.0
April	116.2	95.2	85.5	119.9	113.6	123.0	119.7	107.7	78.9	90.5	84.7
May	115.6	93.2	84.4	119.9	112.5	121.7	119.8	111.5	78.3	89.2	82.7
June	114.9	91.1	81.3	118.8	109.1	120.5	120.5	111.4	77.6	85.7	81.5
July	115.5	88.5	77.6	117.1	113.0	122.7	122.8	115.2	77.8	90.4	81.8
August	114.0	87.0	76.2	116.0	108.9	120.1	121.6	114.1	76.6	85.6	81.4
September	113.9	88.4	78.3	116.1	111.9	118.5	120.1	110.4	76.4	87.1	81.7
October	114.4	89.6	81.2	116.9	111.8	118.0	121.4	112.6	76.7	89.5	79.1
November	116.2	91.2	83.5	117.6	114.9	121.5	122.9	111.4	77.7	93.9	78.2
December	114.7	90.7	84.2	117.5	111.7	120.5	119.4	110.6	76.6	91.8	73.7
1999											
January	114.5	91.7	85.3	117.1	111.8	120.2	118.3	111.1	76.4	89.0	78.3
February	116.6	93.3	88.0	117.1	115.6	124.0	119.9	110.9	77.7	92.0	80.9
March	116.8	97.8	92.2	117.8	114.4	122.8	118.8	113.1	77.8	90.2	80.9
April	115.6	99.5	95.8	119.5	114.5	119.4	117.0	113.0	76.9	90.1	81.3
May	117.0	101.2	98.1	121.9	115.6	120.5	120.1	113.1	77.8	90.5	81.5
June	116.3	92.5	83.4	124.7	115.6	119.0	122.4	112.6	77.3	89.5	83.5
July	115.8	89.4	79.5	127.4	116.0	118.5	120.9	110.9	76.9	90.9	81.0
August	117.7	89.5	77.8	128.9	114.4	122.5	122.8	110.0	78.1	87.8	82.0
September	117.4	92.3	82.5	129.9	114.5	121.8	118.8	111.8	77.8	90.5	77.3
October	119.8	100.7	94.5	132.2	119.5	125.2	118.2	110.3	79.4	94.0	79.7
November	122.7	107.4	100.5	134.0	123.8	127.2	123.0	111.7	81.3	95.4	86.8
December	122.9	106.5	101.9	135.4	120.5	127.7	123.7	113.2	81.3	94.9	80.2

Table 17-11. Chemicals and Chemical Products—Shipments, Inventories, Prices, Employment, Hours, and Earnings

Year and month	Manufacturers' shipments and inventories (millions of dollars, seasonally adjusted)		Producer prices (1982=100, except as noted, not seasonally adjusted)			Employment (thousands, seasonally adjusted)		Production workers			
			Chemical industry (December 1984=100)	Commodity groups		Total payroll employees	Production workers	Average weekly hours, seasonally adjusted	Aggregate weekly hours index (1982=100), seasonally adjusted	Average earnings (dollars, not seasonally adjusted)	
	Shipments	Inventories (book value, end of period)		Drugs and pharmaceuticals	Agricultural chemicals					Hourly	Weekly
1970	49 195	6 749	...	48.2	30.3	1 049	604	41.6	102.5	3.69	153.50
1971	51 681	6 923	...	48.8	31.5	1 011	588	41.6	99.8	3.97	165.15
1972	58 130	7 079	...	49.0	31.4	1 009	593	41.7	100.9	4.26	177.64
1973	66 003	7 553	...	49.6	33.0	1 038	611	41.8	104.2	4.51	188.52
1974	85 387	11 579	...	53.6	47.1	1 061	623	41.5	105.7	4.88	202.52
1975	91 710	12 073	...	60.3	69.6	1 015	580	41.0	97.1	5.39	220.99
1976	106 467	13 319	...	63.8	64.4	1 043	600	41.6	102.0	5.91	245.86
1977	120 905	14 633	...	66.9	64.2	1 074	616	41.7	105.0	6.43	268.13
1978	132 262	16 018	...	70.5	67.8	1 096	628	41.9	107.4	7.02	294.14
1979	151 887	17 690	...	75.9	73.3	1 109	633	41.9	108.3	7.60	318.44
1980	168 220	20 066	...	83.0	87.9	1 107	626	41.5	106.0	8.30	344.45
1981	186 909	22 438	...	92.1	97.4	1 109	628	41.6	106.8	9.12	379.39
1982	176 254	24 448	...	100.0	100.0	1 075	599	40.9	100.0	9.96	407.36
1983	189 552	24 698	...	107.6	95.9	1 043	579	41.6	98.3	10.58	440.13
1984	205 963	26 420	...	114.2	97.4	1 049	583	41.9	99.8	11.07	463.83
1985	204 790	26 119	100.7	122.0	96.2	1 044	577	41.9	98.9	11.56	484.36
1986	205 711	25 743	100.5	130.1	94.2	1 021	568	41.9	97.3	11.98	501.96
1987	229 546	26 585	103.6	139.1	96.4	1 025	575	42.3	99.3	12.37	523.25
1988	261 238	29 792	113.0	148.4	104.5	1 057	596	42.2	102.9	12.71	536.36
1989	283 196	31 725	119.6	160.0	108.7	1 074	603	42.4	104.5	13.09	555.02
1990	292 802	34 001	121.0	170.8	107.4	1 086	600	42.6	104.3	13.54	576.80
1991	298 545	34 529	124.4	182.6	111.7	1 076	580	42.9	101.6	14.04	602.32
1992	305 420	35 720	125.8	192.2	110.3	1 084	567	43.1	100.0	14.51	625.38
1993	314 907	35 771	127.2	200.9	109.9	1 081	573	43.1	100.9	14.82	638.74
1994	333 905	37 024	130.0	206.0	119.9	1 057	578	43.2	102.0	15.13	653.62
1995	361 391	39 913	143.4	210.9	130.1	1 038	580	43.2	102.5	15.62	674.78
1996	367 674	41 110	145.8	214.7	133.7	1 034	575	43.2	101.5	16.17	698.54
1997	389 189	44 249	147.1	219.1	132.7	1 036	573	43.2	101.2	16.57	715.82
1998	391 700	46 217	148.7	242.6	128.5	1 043	587	43.2	103.4	17.09	738.29
1999	413 277	47 603	149.7	251.5	123.6	1 034	585	43.0	102.7	17.38	747.34
1996											
January	29 969	39 985	144.6	213.5	135.2	1 035	582	42.5	101.1	16.08	681.79
February	29 802	39 945	144.5	213.4	136.3	1 035	581	43.2	102.6	15.96	687.88
March	29 633	40 202	145.0	214.4	138.2	1 037	580	43.1	102.1	16.00	689.60
April	30 190	40 377	145.3	214.1	136.9	1 035	578	43.0	101.6	16.15	691.22
May	30 861	40 228	146.0	214.8	134.9	1 034	575	43.2	101.5	16.04	689.72
June	30 256	40 319	146.0	215.0	132.9	1 033	576	43.4	102.1	16.11	699.17
July	31 038	40 157	145.9	215.4	129.9	1 034	574	43.3	101.6	16.16	691.65
August	30 972	40 293	146.1	215.1	129.9	1 034	575	43.2	101.5	16.22	695.84
September	30 747	40 569	146.8	215.1	131.1	1 033	573	43.1	100.9	16.26	704.06
October	31 636	40 670	146.8	215.4	132.2	1 032	571	43.1	100.6	16.29	702.10
November	31 451	40 654	146.3	214.8	132.7	1 032	570	43.3	100.8	16.38	715.81
December	31 191	41 110	146.4	215.4	133.7	1 032	570	43.5	101.3	16.45	730.38
1997											
January	32 025	41 105	146.8	217.4	134.1	1 033	569	43.1	100.2	16.37	705.55
February	32 167	41 328	146.8	218.2	133.8	1 033	569	43.3	100.7	16.49	710.72
March	31 695	41 389	146.9	218.6	134.1	1 035	569	43.2	100.4	16.42	709.34
April	32 547	41 778	147.0	217.7	134.6	1 035	570	43.3	100.8	16.42	706.06
May	32 460	41 883	147.0	218.3	134.3	1 036	570	43.3	100.8	16.48	710.29
June	32 365	42 151	147.0	218.6	132.7	1 036	571	43.1	100.6	16.53	712.44
July	32 513	42 365	147.1	219.1	132.0	1 034	571	43.1	100.6	16.58	707.97
August	32 220	42 471	147.2	219.3	132.0	1 033	573	43.2	101.1	16.57	712.51
September	32 662	43 101	147.1	219.3	131.7	1 037	575	43.2	101.5	16.62	722.97
October	32 695	43 673	147.3	220.4	131.3	1 038	577	43.3	102.1	16.64	720.51
November	32 469	44 324	147.3	221.2	131.2	1 040	579	43.3	102.4	16.84	735.91
December	33 092	44 249	147.3	221.4	130.4	1 041	580	43.2	102.4	16.91	744.04
1998											
January	32 697	44 797	147.3	221.6	130.7	1 040	582	43.5	103.4	16.88	732.59
February	32 514	45 310	147.1	224.5	129.9	1 041	584	43.4	103.6	16.92	732.64
March	32 717	45 368	149.2	243.3	130.0	1 042	586	43.4	103.9	16.96	736.06
April	32 380	45 611	149.8	243.4	129.0	1 042	587	43.2	103.6	17.13	733.16
May	32 501	45 821	149.7	244.1	129.7	1 044	588	43.1	103.6	17.09	733.16
June	32 981	46 061	149.5	245.9	129.8	1 045	589	43.2	104.0	17.02	733.56
July	32 468	46 382	149.5	247.7	129.1	1 045	589	43.1	103.7	17.15	732.31
August	32 204	46 535	149.1	247.2	128.9	1 045	588	43.1	103.6	17.10	735.30
September	32 616	46 313	148.5	247.2	126.2	1 043	587	43.1	103.4	17.25	748.65
October	31 960	46 356	148.3	248.6	127.2	1 043	586	43.1	103.2	17.16	741.31
November	32 533	46 875	148.1	248.5	126.3	1 042	586	42.9	102.7	17.21	743.47
December	33 581	46 217	147.9	249.1	125.5	1 042	586	42.7	102.2	17.24	749.94
1999											
January	32 305	46 425	147.5	247.6	125.4	1 040	585	42.8	102.3	17.16	734.45
February	33 196	46 295	147.3	248.0	124.2	1 040	585	42.9	102.5	17.11	730.60
March	33 577	45 918	147.5	249.0	125.0	1 036	584	42.8	102.1	17.09	731.45
April	33 575	46 362	147.7	249.4	125.3	1 037	585	43.0	102.8	17.17	731.44
May	33 580	46 929	148.2	249.8	123.0	1 035	584	43.0	102.6	17.30	740.44
June	34 483	46 581	149.0	251.6	123.9	1 033	583	43.0	102.4	17.26	742.18
July	34 569	46 848	149.9	252.9	122.9	1 032	583	43.1	102.7	17.39	742.55
August	35 028	46 619	150.0	252.7	123.3	1 030	581	43.2	102.6	17.41	750.37
September	35 040	46 546	151.0	253.6	123.2	1 031	585	43.2	103.3	17.67	765.11
October	35 552	46 903	152.8	254.1	124.0	1 032	586	43.0	103.0	17.61	758.99
November	35 937	47 421	153.0	254.3	121.7	1 031	589	43.0	103.5	17.64	765.58
December	35 636	47 603	152.9	254.5	121.8	1 030	589	43.0	103.5	17.67	772.18

Table 17-12. Petroleum and Coal Products—Production, Capacity Utilization, Shipments, and Inventories

(Seasonally adjusted.)

Year and month	Industrial production–Petroleum products (1992=100)								Capacity utilization: Petroleum products (output as a percent of capacity)	Manufacturers' shipments and inventories (millions of dollars)	
	Total	Petroleum refining and miscellaneous						Paving and roofing materials		Shipments	Inventories (book value, end of period)
		Total	Miscellaneous petroleum products	Distillate fuel oil	Residual fuel oil	Aviation fuel and kerosene	Automotive gasoline				
1970	80.8	80.8	79.9	82.5	79.2	78.6	80.7	74.8	93.9	24 200	2 161
1971	83.5	83.5	82.0	83.9	84.1	77.2	84.6	78.2	91.8	26 198	2 260
1972	87.4	87.3	86.2	88.3	89.3	76.2	88.9	82.0	92.8	27 918	2 142
1973	92.2	92.3	92.0	94.9	109.3	77.0	92.4	85.7	94.2	33 903	2 476
1974	89.0	89.9	90.4	89.5	120.7	71.1	90.0	79.2	87.1	57 229	3 945
1975	88.0	89.9	83.4	89.0	138.8	72.7	92.0	71.8	83.7	67 496	4 426
1976	93.6	95.6	87.6	98.2	154.6	75.8	96.8	76.0	85.2	80 022	4 711
1977	101.5	103.3	97.3	110.5	196.9	81.1	99.6	83.4	87.6	94 702	5 439
1978	104.9	105.9	109.9	106.5	186.9	79.6	101.5	94.0	87.6	100 967	5 330
1979	103.9	104.9	112.7	106.1	188.8	84.1	96.9	93.2	84.1	144 156	7 458
1980	95.9	97.2	105.6	89.6	177.1	80.0	92.1	81.8	74.7	192 969	9 693
1981	91.2	92.3	95.0	88.0	148.0	76.4	90.7	78.0	70.7	217 681	10 420
1982	86.6	87.5	80.7	87.6	120.2	76.3	89.7	76.5	70.1	203 404	17 009
1983	86.9	86.0	81.7	82.5	95.6	78.9	89.8	95.0	73.4	187 788	14 843
1984	89.9	89.5	83.4	90.2	99.8	86.9	91.5	95.0	77.8	184 488	14 260
1985	89.5	89.7	84.7	90.1	98.7	88.7	90.9	90.2	78.4	176 574	13 975
1986	95.7	94.9	92.0	94.0	99.6	96.9	95.6	103.3	83.7	122 605	8 791
1987	97.0	95.8	94.6	91.7	99.2	99.0	96.9	107.0	83.5	130 414	9 973
1988	98.8	97.9	95.5	96.1	103.8	100.9	98.5	106.9	85.3	131 682	9 196
1989	99.3	98.5	95.6	97.5	106.9	102.8	98.6	106.0	87.0	146 487	10 743
1990	100.3	99.6	98.7	98.3	106.5	106.5	98.6	106.5	87.6	173 389	13 432
1991	99.1	99.2	97.2	99.6	104.8	102.6	98.8	98.4	86.6	159 144	11 671
1992	100.0	100.0	100.0	100.0	100.0	100.0	100.0	100.0	88.6	150 227	11 350
1993	102.9	102.0	101.7	105.3	93.6	102.1	101.4	109.1	92.1	144 834	10 265
1994	102.7	101.9	102.5	107.8	92.6	104.5	99.7	107.5	91.1	143 328	11 121
1995	104.5	103.6	104.6	106.1	88.3	102.0	103.6	111.2	91.9	151 439	11 304
1996	106.8	105.4	103.3	111.5	81.3	109.4	105.0	117.7	93.4	174 284	12 520
1997	110.8	108.6	110.2	114.1	78.9	111.7	107.6	128.0	94.9	177 314	12 218
1998	113.3	110.1	112.4	115.1	85.3	110.8	109.0	138.4	94.5	145 673	10 254
1999	114.7	110.4	111.9	114.6	78.5	113.1	110.2	148.4	93.7	171 149	12 247
1996											
January	105.1	104.0	100.0	109.0	83.1	112.7	103.8	112.4	92.5	13 151	11 490
February	106.0	105.3	99.8	112.3	86.6	109.7	105.5	110.4	93.2	13 366	11 594
March	105.7	105.0	101.1	109.1	80.7	108.9	106.3	109.5	92.9	14 097	11 959
April	105.3	104.5	101.3	111.3	79.2	108.6	104.4	110.5	92.4	15 103	12 044
May	106.0	104.7	103.0	108.4	84.0	104.4	105.7	115.1	93.0	14 697	11 991
June	106.4	105.3	104.2	109.3	85.1	107.7	105.3	114.4	93.2	14 136	11 942
July	105.5	104.1	102.6	106.3	74.9	106.1	105.9	115.7	92.3	14 264	12 077
August	107.6	105.7	104.7	110.2	82.6	108.4	105.6	122.7	94.0	14 319	12 015
September	108.0	106.2	105.6	112.0	80.1	118.1	103.8	121.7	94.1	14 729	12 252
October	109.1	107.1	106.3	118.0	82.2	111.2	104.3	124.6	94.9	15 247	12 289
November	108.7	106.4	104.7	116.7	77.7	106.6	105.4	126.4	94.4	15 388	12 344
December	108.5	106.3	106.4	114.5	79.0	109.5	104.5	126.1	94.0	15 484	12 520
1997											
January	107.4	105.6	107.3	109.6	83.4	107.4	104.5	122.1	93.0	15 879	13 039
February	108.7	106.7	108.4	110.5	85.0	109.8	105.4	124.3	93.9	15 504	12 858
March	109.0	106.8	105.5	113.1	74.1	110.2	106.7	126.4	94.0	14 946	12 923
April	110.5	108.3	111.2	112.1	73.9	109.9	107.8	128.8	95.2	14 532	12 656
May	112.6	110.3	114.2	117.0	71.2	111.9	108.7	130.8	96.7	14 701	12 919
June	112.7	110.3	111.6	117.0	84.1	113.1	108.6	132.2	96.7	14 518	12 623
July	110.4	107.8	109.6	114.1	74.3	115.4	105.8	131.1	94.6	14 614	12 338
August	110.6	108.8	109.2	114.8	72.4	113.5	108.3	125.2	94.5	15 311	12 657
September	112.1	110.0	109.9	114.3	77.1	114.3	110.1	129.3	95.6	14 791	12 621
October	112.6	110.5	111.9	114.6	81.7	112.2	110.2	129.2	95.8	14 638	12 559
November	110.1	108.4	111.5	113.9	86.0	113.1	105.7	124.0	93.5	14 139	12 489
December	112.4	109.9	112.4	115.9	81.8	110.2	108.6	132.5	95.2	13 836	12 218
1998											
January	112.1	109.9	113.1	117.0	79.9	107.4	108.6	129.6	94.7	13 198	11 449
February	111.1	108.8	111.2	118.0	72.1	107.2	107.4	129.9	93.7	12 883	11 478
March	113.9	111.1	112.6	118.7	92.1	113.8	108.5	136.2	95.8	12 913	11 405
April	113.2	110.8	109.9	116.2	102.8	111.6	109.4	132.4	95.0	12 782	11 400
May	112.0	109.5	109.2	116.6	89.2	111.3	108.2	131.6	93.7	12 599	11 169
June	112.6	110.1	109.5	117.3	86.4	111.8	109.0	132.4	93.9	12 416	10 936
July	114.5	111.5	113.2	121.2	89.7	107.7	109.5	137.8	95.3	12 153	10 906
August	115.0	111.6	113.5	116.0	87.9	116.7	110.9	141.8	95.6	11 759	10 759
September	113.0	108.9	113.2	112.9	83.9	106.4	107.9	144.2	93.7	11 885	10 770
October	112.5	108.2	113.5	104.7	79.1	108.1	109.5	145.0	93.0	11 500	10 832
November	114.8	110.5	116.7	110.6	81.0	114.7	109.3	147.7	94.8	11 043	10 965
December	114.8	110.1	113.5	111.2	81.8	112.5	110.0	150.2	94.6	11 060	10 254
1999											
January	117.2	112.8	118.4	113.0	81.3	116.1	112.1	150.5	96.4	11 040	10 239
February	117.0	112.8	115.4	117.5	79.6	115.6	112.0	148.5	96.0	11 262	10 040
March	114.9	110.3	113.6	112.1	79.9	115.5	110.4	150.0	94.3	12 380	10 545
April	114.6	111.1	111.1	114.6	82.3	119.1	110.5	142.1	93.9	13 042	10 688
May	114.2	110.2	110.4	114.2	83.5	114.6	109.8	144.6	93.4	13 045	10 706
June	113.4	108.9	109.1	112.6	82.0	111.2	109.0	147.6	92.6	13 703	10 814
July	115.1	110.4	112.5	119.1	83.7	111.4	108.0	150.6	93.9	14 563	11 144
August	114.1	109.7	112.7	114.5	79.3	112.6	108.4	147.5	93.0	15 218	11 588
September	114.6	110.3	108.6	116.0	78.6	115.1	110.5	147.3	93.3	15 663	11 887
October	114.5	110.4	109.7	114.0	78.1	110.9	111.9	145.4	93.2	15 627	12 052
November	112.8	108.4	111.4	116.3	65.3	107.1	107.8	146.1	91.7	16 634	12 174
December	114.9	110.1	111.8	110.5	69.9	112.7	112.1	151.3	93.3	17 414	12 247

Table 17-13. Petroleum and Coal Products—Prices, Employment, Hours, and Earnings

Year and month	Producer prices (1982=100, except as noted, not seasonally adjusted)								Consumer prices: Motor fuel (1982–1984=100, seasonally adjusted)		Employment (thousands, seasonally adjusted)		Production workers			
	Petroleum refining and related industries, (December 1984=100)	Intermediate materials				Finished goods		Petroleum refining industry (June 1985=100)					Average weekly hours, not seasonally adjusted	Aggregate weekly hours index (1982=100), seasonally adjusted	Average earnings (dollars, not seasonally adjusted)	
		Liquefied petroleum gas	Jet fuels	Number 2 diesel fuel	Residual fuel	Gasoline	Number 2 fuel oil		Total	Gasoline	Total payroll employees	Production workers			Hourly	Weekly
1970	...	...	...	...	10.6	14.4	...	...	27.9	27.9	191	118	42.8	96.2	4.28	183.18
1971	...	15.2	...	...	14.0	15.1	...	...	28.1	28.1	194	124	42.8	100.9	4.57	195.60
1972	...	14.9	...	...	13.4	15.5	...	...	28.4	28.4	195	125	42.7	101.5	4.96	211.79
1973	...	18.0	...	14.3	16.1	18.2	13.9	...	31.2	31.2	193	124	42.4	99.9	5.28	223.87
1974	...	29.2	...	27.7	41.1	29.2	26.3	...	42.2	42.2	197	126	42.1	100.9	5.68	239.13
1975	...	35.2	28.4	31.2	41.9	34.5	30.1	...	45.1	45.1	194	123	41.2	96.3	6.48	266.98
1976	...	45.8	31.1	34.1	38.3	38.0	32.7	...	47.0	47.0	199	128	42.1	102.3	7.21	303.54
1977	...	57.3	35.7	38.5	44.2	41.3	37.6	47.9	49.7	49.7	202	131	42.7	106.6	7.83	334.34
1978	...	54.7	39.6	39.7	42.1	43.4	39.0	50.3	51.8	51.8	208	136	43.6	112.2	8.63	376.27
1979	...	64.7	53.7	57.1	57.9	60.0	56.4	68.8	70.1	70.2	210	137	43.8	114.0	9.36	409.97
1980	...	102.3	87.5	85.8	81.3	93.3	82.8	104.6	97.4	97.5	198	125	41.8	99.1	10.10	422.18
1981	...	112.0	104.5	105.0	104.8	108.0	104.1	123.9	108.5	108.5	214	134	43.2	110.0	11.38	491.62
1982	...	100.0	100.0	100.0	100.0	100.0	100.0	117.1	102.8	102.8	201	120	43.9	100.0	12.46	546.99
1983	...	113.5	91.5	87.9	89.6	90.2	87.8	106.8	99.4	99.4	196	118	43.9	98.4	13.28	582.99
1984	...	99.1	87.0	86.3	94.7	84.6	87.3	103.7	97.9	97.8	189	111	43.7	92.5	13.44	587.33
1985	...	86.3	81.0	81.2	83.2	83.3	81.6	98.3	98.7	98.6	179	109	43.0	88.7	14.06	604.58
1986	66.6	61.0	53.8	48.6	44.5	54.7	50.5	64.3	77.1	77.0	169	106	43.8	88.1	14.19	621.52
1987	70.5	57.4	54.2	55.4	53.1	58.8	55.9	68.6	80.2	80.1	164	107	44.0	89.4	14.58	641.52
1988	67.7	51.6	52.1	49.7	41.1	57.3	49.5	65.4	80.9	80.8	160	104	44.4	88.1	14.97	664.67
1989	75.7	52.7	58.1	58.9	47.6	65.1	58.0	73.6	88.5	88.5	156	102	44.3	85.7	15.41	682.66
1990	91.4	77.4	76.0	74.1	57.7	78.7	73.3	90.1	101.2	101.0	157	103	44.6	87.2	16.24	724.30
1991	83.1	75.4	66.4	65.6	49.1	69.9	65.2	80.9	99.4	99.2	160	103	44.1	86.7	17.04	751.46
1992	80.3	65.8	61.9	61.9	45.9	68.1	61.7	78.3	99.0	99.0	158	103	43.8	86.0	17.90	784.02
1993	77.6	63.6	59.0	60.5	49.6	63.9	59.1	75.2	98.0	97.7	152	99	44.2	83.1	18.53	819.03
1994	74.8	58.2	53.9	56.0	48.2	61.7	56.0	72.2	98.5	98.2	149	97	44.4	81.4	19.07	846.71
1995	77.2	65.1	55.0	57.0	52.6	63.7	56.6	74.5	100.0	99.8	145	94	43.7	77.9	19.36	846.03
1996	87.4	84.7	66.7	70.0	59.8	72.8	69.5	85.3	106.3	105.9	142	92	43.6	76.3	19.32	842.35
1997	85.6	84.5	62.9	64.5	59.5	71.9	64.8	83.1	106.2	105.8	141	93	43.1	76.1	20.20	870.62
1998	66.3	60.1	46.1	47.4	43.8	53.4	48.1	62.3	92.2	91.6	139	92	43.6	76.0	20.91	911.68
1999	76.8	73.7	52.5	57.3	51.5	64.7	56.1	73.6	100.7	100.1	134	88	43.1	72.2	21.39	921.91
1996																
January	79.4	73.0	62.8	62.2	55.8	64.1	64.3	76.7	100.7	100.5	143	92	43.1	75.6	19.41	836.57
February	77.3	76.0	57.0	59.4	57.1	62.2	61.1	74.5	101.3	101.0	143	92	42.8	75.4	19.54	836.31
March	81.8	77.4	58.9	62.6	56.8	68.0	65.9	79.2	104.4	104.2	143	92	42.9	75.7	19.21	824.11
April	90.5	81.0	66.7	75.4	56.2	76.4	75.6	88.6	109.9	109.5	142	91	43.3	75.6	19.32	836.56
May	92.8	76.3	68.8	74.5	61.9	80.1	69.4	91.0	110.7	110.3	142	92	42.6	75.2	18.98	808.55
June	87.3	74.7	62.1	64.9	61.0	75.8	60.1	85.2	108.6	108.5	142	92	44.7	78.5	18.88	843.94
July	86.3	76.0	62.0	66.1	61.5	73.6	62.6	84.1	106.8	106.5	142	92	44.3	77.1	19.01	842.14
August	86.9	80.8	66.0	66.6	61.6	72.6	67.2	84.7	105.0	104.6	142	92	43.9	76.8	18.98	833.22
September	89.9	88.4	73.0	74.7	58.4	73.6	72.8	87.9	104.7	104.1	142	92	44.2	76.6	19.34	854.83
October	92.0	95.4	75.5	80.2	61.7	74.1	80.6	90.2	105.3	104.5	141	92	43.6	75.6	19.34	843.22
November	92.5	102.5	72.6	77.0	61.7	76.6	77.1	90.7	107.5	106.8	142	92	43.9	75.9	19.61	860.88
December	92.5	114.7	75.0	76.0	64.4	76.0	77.5	90.7	110.0	109.4	141	92	43.9	76.3	20.25	888.98
1997																
January	92.9	114.8	75.1	73.2	64.6	76.6	75.8	91.1	110.8	110.3	141	92	44.9	77.3	20.11	902.94
February	91.2	103.1	74.8	73.1	61.4	75.0	72.4	89.3	111.6	111.1	141	93	43.4	77.1	20.39	884.93
March	87.3	86.0	66.7	66.5	57.6	73.5	64.0	85.0	109.7	109.1	140	93	43.0	76.4	20.48	880.64
April	85.8	79.9	60.9	66.1	56.8	72.7	64.9	83.4	107.3	106.7	141	93	42.4	76.0	19.94	845.46
May	85.5	73.8	58.7	63.6	56.2	72.8	66.2	83.1	103.0	102.5	141	94	42.4	76.7	19.96	846.30
June	83.6	76.9	59.5	61.0	57.0	71.2	60.9	80.9	103.6	103.2	141	93	42.9	76.2	19.92	854.57
July	81.3	73.0	57.6	57.7	53.1	69.3	58.8	78.5	102.1	101.6	141	93	42.8	75.2	20.02	856.86
August	85.3	75.8	59.7	62.1	55.4	73.7	61.6	82.8	106.1	105.8	141	93	43.0	76.0	19.99	859.57
September	86.1	80.4	58.4	61.3	59.8	75.3	60.2	83.7	107.8	107.6	141	93	43.3	75.9	20.27	877.69
October	84.8	83.6	62.1	64.7	69.2	70.5	66.0	82.3	105.7	105.5	141	93	43.3	75.9	20.32	879.86
November	83.6	85.2	63.7	65.8	62.9	67.9	66.5	81.0	104.0	103.5	141	93	43.3	76.6	20.42	884.19
December	79.1	81.1	58.3	58.9	59.5	64.6	60.7	76.2	103.1	102.5	142	94	42.2	74.9	20.58	868.48
1998																
January	73.8	74.6	54.8	53.9	51.5	59.4	55.1	70.4	99.9	99.3	140	92	44.5	76.4	20.66	919.37
February	70.1	70.5	52.1	51.3	47.3	55.8	54.1	66.4	97.3	96.8	140	92	42.2	74.2	20.95	884.09
March	65.6	66.0	47.2	47.6	42.6	51.7	49.7	61.5	93.7	93.1	141	92	43.1	75.6	21.20	913.72
April	67.9	62.4	47.3	50.0	49.3	54.0	51.2	64.0	92.9	92.3	140	92	42.8	75.2	21.01	899.23
May	70.2	63.4	47.9	50.0	47.1	58.3	50.6	66.6	92.5	92.0	140	92	42.9	76.1	20.81	892.75
June	68.0	59.2	43.5	45.8	46.3	57.4	46.5	64.1	93.0	92.6	141	93	43.2	76.6	20.72	895.10
July	67.0	55.7	42.9	44.7	47.7	56.0	45.5	63.1	92.3	91.7	139	91	44.8	77.0	20.81	932.29
August	63.6	54.5	43.5	44.4	38.2	51.6	43.1	59.4	90.1	89.5	138	91	44.0	76.3	20.78	914.32
September	64.2	52.5	43.1	48.1	39.0	51.0	48.0	60.0	88.7	88.1	138	91	43.2	75.8	20.81	898.99
October	65.5	52.8	47.6	47.3	41.7	52.5	47.9	61.5	89.6	89.1	137	91	44.0	75.6	21.04	925.76
November	63.3	55.2	46.2	46.1	39.0	49.8	46.3	59.1	88.9	88.4	137	91	43.9	75.8	20.92	918.39
December	56.3	54.7	37.4	39.0	35.8	43.2	38.8	51.6	87.1	86.7	138	91	44.7	76.6	21.19	947.19
1999																
January	58.6	47.2	37.5	40.2	36.0	46.4	42.6	54.0	86.9	86.4	136	90	43.9	73.9	21.18	929.80
February	56.2	48.9	37.0	38.1	30.7	44.2	38.9	51.5	86.5	86.2	136	90	43.3	74.4	21.38	925.75
March	59.9	49.8	38.0	43.2	33.9	48.1	42.9	55.5	89.1	88.6	135	90	43.7	74.6	21.53	940.86
April	73.7	52.7	48.9	53.1	39.5	64.4	51.6	70.4	102.2	101.7	135	89	42.8	72.9	21.42	916.78
May	75.4	66.0	48.3	53.0	50.8	65.6	52.2	72.2	99.3	98.7	134	88	42.6	72.3	20.98	893.75
June	74.2	67.9	48.7	53.5	52.0	63.5	50.8	70.9	97.5	96.9	133	88	43.0	72.3	21.06	905.58
July	79.6	69.0	51.0	59.8	52.3	68.9	58.2	76.6	101.0	100.3	134	88	43.4	72.1	21.28	923.55
August	85.3	82.0	57.0	65.6	56.2	75.0	60.1	82.8	105.9	105.2	132	88	42.6	71.4	21.21	903.55
September	90.2	95.3	63.3	68.8	65.8	78.4	67.1	88.0	108.6	107.9	133	87	43.2	71.3	21.55	930.96
October	87.0	100.3	63.6	67.5	65.2	73.0	63.6	84.5	108.3	107.7	133	87	43.2	71.3	21.62	933.98
November	89.5	103.4	65.6	71.9	67.2	73.8	71.4	87.2	108.0	107.4	132	86	43.0	70.1	21.76	935.68
December	91.8	102.3	71.4	72.7	68.4	75.5	73.5	89.5	113.4	112.7	132	84	43.1	69.1	21.76	937.86

Table 17-14. Rubber and Plastics Products—Production, Capacity Utilization, Shipments, and Inventories

(Seasonally adjusted.)

Year and month	Industrial production (1992=100)				Capacity utilization (output as a percent of capacity)	Manufacturers' shipments and inventories	
	Total	Tires	Other rubber products	Plastics products, not elsewhere classified		Shipments	Inventories (book value, end of period)
1970	33.0	41.7	69.5	23.8	81.2	16 754	2 386
1971	35.9	48.1	70.1	26.1	82.6	18 409	2 453
1972	43.7	54.5	79.4	33.6	91.6	21 662	2 695
1973	49.0	55.9	87.4	39.6	93.3	25 191	3 103
1974	47.9	59.1	86.2	37.3	84.9	28 828	4 023
1975	41.6	54.5	74.0	31.7	70.1	28 128	4 085
1976	48.1	54.0	80.4	40.0	78.5	32 880	4 581
1977	56.0	70.2	85.1	47.1	88.3	40 944	5 116
1978	59.3	69.9	88.0	51.4	89.2	44 823	5 801
1979	58.7	68.9	88.6	50.7	84.2	48 694	6 399
1980	53.3	55.3	78.0	48.1	73.9	49 157	6 435
1981	57.5	64.2	82.0	51.1	77.9	55 178	6 968
1982	56.8	63.4	73.1	52.0	74.4	57 307	7 748
1983	64.0	68.2	77.1	60.3	79.2	62 870	8 070
1984	72.1	78.8	85.7	67.9	84.3	72 938	8 904
1985	73.8	76.8	85.3	70.6	82.1	75 590	9 213
1986	78.2	75.0	86.6	76.8	82.9	78 379	9 285
1987	86.0	83.3	93.5	84.7	89.0	86 634	10 065
1988	88.2	88.2	98.3	85.8	87.8	95 485	11 367
1989	91.2	91.8	97.2	89.6	87.4	101 236	11 533
1990	92.2	91.0	97.6	91.1	84.6	105 250	12 292
1991	90.7	87.3	92.9	90.8	80.3	105 804	12 121
1992	100.0	100.0	100.0	100.0	84.7	113 593	12 541
1993	106.9	105.3	106.2	107.4	86.2	122 777	12 821
1994	116.5	110.0	112.7	118.5	89.6	135 145	14 232
1995	119.7	117.1	118.5	120.4	88.0	145 739	15 220
1996	123.3	116.8	120.1	125.0	87.5	150 467	15 728
1997	128.4	122.3	123.2	130.5	86.8	156 599	16 455
1998	133.2	127.7	125.6	135.8	85.6	158 156	16 766
1999	137.7	128.9	127.6	141.3	84.1	164 654	17 589
1996							
January	120.3	118.7	118.2	121.0	87.0	11 875	15 198
February	120.4	114.4	119.5	121.5	86.8	12 276	15 217
March	121.2	118.4	118.9	122.2	87.1	12 394	15 294
April	120.5	113.7	118.1	122.1	86.4	12 576	15 206
May	122.6	112.6	120.4	124.6	87.6	12 761	15 138
June	124.1	117.6	120.1	126.0	88.3	12 659	15 240
July	124.1	114.4	119.2	126.7	88.1	12 743	15 286
August	125.3	115.7	120.8	127.7	88.6	12 693	15 335
September	125.9	122.2	119.7	128.0	88.7	12 586	15 493
October	124.3	120.1	121.9	125.6	87.2	12 585	15 580
November	124.5	117.5	120.8	126.5	87.0	12 741	15 619
December	125.9	116.2	123.0	128.0	87.6	12 518	15 728
1997							
January	125.0	117.8	121.0	127.0	86.6	12 904	15 855
February	126.8	122.0	123.3	128.4	87.5	12 946	15 917
March	127.2	125.7	119.8	129.3	87.4	12 823	16 031
April	126.2	114.3	121.7	128.9	86.3	13 321	16 085
May	127.1	115.5	121.4	130.1	86.6	12 811	16 269
June	127.8	125.2	122.3	129.6	86.7	12 791	16 281
July	128.1	124.4	123.0	129.9	86.5	13 078	16 305
August	130.2	128.3	123.9	132.0	87.5	12 880	16 395
September	130.1	123.8	124.9	132.3	87.1	13 155	16 348
October	129.8	121.0	126.3	131.9	86.5	13 301	16 386
November	131.2	125.8	126.2	133.2	87.0	13 118	16 466
December	131.0	123.2	124.3	133.7	86.5	13 536	16 455
1998							
January	131.8	122.4	126.5	134.4	86.7	13 119	16 562
February	131.7	125.9	124.1	134.3	86.2	13 185	16 587
March	132.1	126.2	125.9	134.5	86.2	13 190	16 509
April	133.5	128.4	126.5	135.9	86.7	13 203	16 484
May	133.3	132.9	125.4	135.3	86.2	13 045	16 571
June	132.8	122.6	125.9	135.9	85.6	13 001	16 697
July	132.8	125.4	123.6	136.0	85.2	13 104	16 650
August	132.7	132.5	122.1	135.3	84.8	13 196	16 699
September	133.2	126.2	125.2	136.1	84.8	13 282	16 607
October	133.6	127.1	124.5	136.7	84.7	13 249	16 678
November	134.9	130.7	127.9	137.2	85.2	13 209	16 857
December	135.6	131.7	129.5	137.8	85.3	13 400	16 766
1999							
January	135.4	129.4	129.3	137.8	84.8	13 207	16 780
February	135.6	125.2	127.7	138.9	84.5	13 718	16 710
March	135.8	121.3	126.1	140.1	84.3	13 708	16 659
April	136.2	126.3	123.7	140.5	84.2	13 442	16 794
May	137.4	134.5	125.4	140.8	84.5	13 484	16 902
June	136.4	123.4	124.1	141.0	83.5	13 609	16 902
July	138.0	125.8	128.2	141.9	84.1	13 376	17 050
August	137.6	127.0	126.7	141.7	83.6	13 839	17 261
September	139.3	126.6	129.7	143.3	84.2	13 701	17 492
October	138.9	138.2	126.4	142.3	83.6	13 811	17 714
November	139.3	129.9	129.9	142.9	83.4	14 339	17 769
December	141.4	142.0	132.2	143.8	84.3	14 400	17 589

Table 17-15. Rubber and Plastics Products—Prices, Employment, Hours, and Earnings

Year and month	Producer prices (1982=100, except as noted, not seasonally adjusted)						Employment (thousands, seasonally adjusted)		Production workers			
	Rubber and plastics products (December 1984=100)	Finished tires and tubes	Intermediate materials				Total payroll employees	Production workers	Average hours, seasonally adjusted	Aggregate hours index (1982=100), seasonally adjusted	Average earnings (dollars, not seasonally adjusted)	
			Synthetic rubber	Plastic construction products	Plastic film and sheet	Plastic parts for manufacturing					Hourly	Weekly
1970	. . .	42.7	34.0	65.5	. . .	. . .	617	473	40.3	86.3	3.21	129.36
1971	. . .	42.8	34.0	63.7	47.3	. . .	617	479	40.4	87.5	3.41	137.76
1972	. . .	42.8	34.1	62.9	46.2	. . .	667	525	41.2	97.8	3.63	149.56
1973	. . .	43.7	34.3	63.4	46.9	. . .	731	579	41.2	107.9	3.84	158.21
1974	. . .	52.3	44.1	80.1	61.6	. . .	733	577	40.6	105.8	4.09	166.05
1975	. . .	58.2	49.3	83.5	69.6	. . .	643	493	39.9	89.0	4.42	176.36
1976	. . .	63.3	52.6	85.7	72.5	. . .	675	522	40.7	96.1	4.71	191.70
1977	. . .	66.6	56.1	89.7	75.0	. . .	750	588	41.1	109.2	5.21	214.13
1978	. . .	70.2	60.4	91.8	76.2	. . .	793	622	40.9	115.3	5.57	227.81
1979	. . .	80.7	70.3	99.4	81.4	82.5	821	643	40.6	118.2	6.02	244.41
1980	. . .	92.8	85.3	103.9	89.3	90.8	764	588	40.0	106.7	6.58	263.20
1981	. . .	98.2	98.0	104.3	95.7	96.6	772	597	40.3	109.0	7.22	290.97
1982	. . .	100.0	100.0	100.0	100.0	100.0	729	558	39.6	100.0	7.70	304.92
1983	. . .	96.1	97.0	110.1	102.4	101.8	743	574	41.2	107.2	8.06	332.07
1984	. . .	94.9	96.8	115.5	106.6	103.5	813	632	41.7	119.6	8.35	348.20
1985	100.0	93.0	96.8	108.6	106.1	103.5	818	632	41.1	117.6	8.60	353.46
1986	100.3	91.7	91.5	106.4	105.1	107.9	823	639	41.4	119.6	8.79	363.91
1987	100.9	91.0	98.0	108.4	106.8	108.1	842	653	41.6	123.1	8.98	373.57
1988	106.7	94.0	108.9	121.1	113.9	110.0	866	674	41.7	127.3	9.19	383.22
1989	110.2	97.2	108.5	120.1	119.9	111.3	888	692	41.4	129.6	9.46	391.64
1990	111.3	96.8	111.9	117.2	119.0	112.9	888	687	41.1	127.9	9.76	401.14
1991	113.7	98.2	106.1	115.1	120.6	113.5	862	662	41.1	123.2	10.07	413.88
1992	114.2	98.9	103.8	112.7	120.3	113.3	878	677	41.7	127.8	10.36	432.01
1993	115.4	98.9	105.7	116.6	121.4	113.9	909	703	41.8	133.2	10.57	441.83
1994	117.1	98.6	108.9	122.9	122.8	113.5	953	742	42.2	141.9	10.70	451.54
1995	123.3	100.2	126.3	133.8	135.6	115.9	980	763	41.5	143.4	10.91	452.77
1996	123.1	97.0	122.2	130.9	132.7	117.5	983	762	41.5	143.2	11.24	466.46
1997	122.8	95.2	119.3	128.2	131.7	117.2	996	773	41.8	146.4	11.57	483.63
1998	122.1	94.0	117.2	126.2	128.0	117.1	1 005	779	41.7	147.3	11.89	495.81
1999	122.2	92.9	113.9	128.0	127.5	117.4	1 006	780	41.7	147.4	12.36	515.41
1996												
January	123.0	98.4	124.5	130.5	133.8	117.0	976	757	40.4	138.5	11.13	448.54
February	122.9	97.7	123.0	130.9	133.6	117.6	975	755	41.3	141.2	11.14	460.08
March	122.8	97.2	123.2	129.8	133.5	117.7	975	755	41.4	141.6	11.15	460.50
April	122.6	96.9	122.3	130.7	131.3	117.7	976	756	41.5	142.1	11.20	460.32
May	123.0	97.4	122.0	130.6	131.6	117.7	978	757	41.6	142.6	11.20	465.92
June	123.0	96.2	122.0	131.7	132.0	117.7	982	761	41.6	143.4	11.16	465.37
July	123.2	96.3	122.1	131.8	133.3	117.6	985	764	41.5	143.6	11.25	459.00
August	123.4	97.2	122.0	131.9	132.4	117.4	988	766	41.7	144.7	11.23	467.17
September	123.5	97.3	121.4	131.2	132.8	117.4	988	766	41.8	145.0	11.30	475.73
October	123.1	96.2	121.5	130.5	132.5	117.4	989	767	41.5	144.2	11.28	469.25
November	123.3	95.9	120.8	131.4	133.1	117.4	992	770	41.4	144.4	11.33	471.33
December	123.3	97.2	121.2	130.3	133.0	117.4	989	767	41.7	144.9	11.51	490.33
1997												
January	122.9	96.7	121.2	127.7	132.3	117.5	988	765	41.5	143.8	11.48	475.27
February	122.8	95.7	121.1	128.1	132.3	117.5	990	768	41.7	145.1	11.45	475.18
March	122.4	95.6	120.7	127.4	131.2	117.4	992	769	41.8	145.6	11.50	480.70
April	122.8	96.4	119.3	128.6	131.2	117.3	993	770	42.1	146.8	11.53	480.80
May	122.9	95.8	120.2	128.4	131.8	117.3	994	771	41.7	145.6	11.52	479.55
June	122.9	95.1	119.4	128.0	131.8	117.1	995	772	41.5	145.1	11.52	480.38
July	123.0	94.8	117.6	128.7	132.0	117.1	994	772	41.7	145.8	11.57	474.37
August	123.1	94.8	118.1	129.2	132.2	117.2	997	773	41.8	146.3	11.57	482.47
September	122.9	95.5	118.3	127.9	131.7	117.1	1 000	775	41.7	146.4	11.64	488.88
October	122.7	94.1	118.5	128.1	131.3	117.1	1 002	777	41.9	147.5	11.64	487.72
November	122.8	94.3	118.4	128.1	131.3	117.1	1 003	778	42.1	148.4	11.64	494.70
December	122.8	94.1	118.9	127.7	131.5	117.1	1 004	778	42.0	148.0	11.76	505.68
1998												
January	122.7	94.0	118.7	127.6	130.1	117.3	1 007	780	42.0	148.4	11.74	491.91
February	122.6	94.5	118.6	127.1	129.8	117.3	1 008	782	41.8	148.1	11.77	489.63
March	122.5	94.5	117.7	127.3	128.5	117.3	1 010	784	41.6	147.7	11.78	488.87
April	122.5	94.2	117.4	127.4	128.6	117.2	1 009	784	41.7	148.1	11.84	485.44
May	122.3	93.8	117.4	127.5	128.8	117.2	1 007	782	41.8	148.1	11.86	496.93
June	122.1	94.0	117.2	126.0	128.4	117.0	1 006	781	41.9	148.2	11.82	496.44
July	121.9	93.7	117.4	125.6	127.6	117.0	999	773	41.8	146.3	11.92	489.91
August	121.9	93.7	117.3	125.7	127.9	117.0	1 003	778	41.7	146.9	11.86	492.19
September	121.9	94.0	116.8	125.6	126.6	117.1	1 004	778	41.6	146.6	12.00	498.00
October	121.6	94.0	116.4	125.0	126.7	117.1	1 002	776	41.8	146.9	11.91	497.84
November	121.7	94.0	115.8	125.1	126.3	117.1	1 002	776	41.7	146.6	12.00	505.20
December	121.8	93.9	115.8	124.9	126.9	117.2	1 002	776	41.8	146.9	12.11	517.10
1999												
January	121.5	93.4	114.1	124.5	126.4	117.2	1 005	779	41.4	146.1	12.24	505.51
February	121.4	92.4	114.4	124.7	126.3	117.3	1 003	777	41.7	146.8	12.20	506.30
March	121.3	92.3	113.9	124.5	125.7	117.2	1 003	776	41.9	147.3	12.25	512.05
April	121.7	93.6	113.1	125.5	126.0	117.5	1 006	780	41.7	147.3	12.28	513.30
May	121.6	93.3	113.0	126.0	125.4	117.6	1 006	778	41.8	147.3	12.27	515.34
June	121.9	93.4	112.7	126.8	126.8	117.6	1 003	776	41.8	146.9	12.30	516.60
July	122.1	92.1	113.0	129.0	127.2	117.7	1 008	780	41.7	147.3	12.41	510.05
August	122.5	92.8	113.4	130.2	127.8	117.3	1 008	782	41.7	147.7	12.37	512.12
September	122.8	92.8	113.7	130.7	127.9	117.4	1 005	780	41.8	147.7	12.51	520.42
October	122.9	91.8	114.5	130.9	129.3	117.3	1 008	784	41.5	147.4	12.42	516.67
November	123.3	93.4	115.0	132.0	130.3	117.1	1 009	785	41.5	147.6	12.46	523.32
December	123.4	93.4	115.6	131.9	130.6	117.1	1 011	787	41.5	147.9	12.57	532.97

Table 17-16. Leather and Leather Products—Production, Capacity Utilization, Prices, Employment, Hours, and Earnings

Year and month	Industrial production (1992=100, seasonally adjusted)		Capacity utilization (output as a percent of capacity, seasonally adjusted)	Producer prices (1982=100, except as noted, not seasonally adjusted)				Employment (thousands, seasonally adjusted)		Production workers			
	Total	Shoes		Leather and leather products (December 1984 =100)	Finished footwear	Leather	Cattle hides	Total payroll employees	Production workers	Average weekly hours, seasonally adjusted	Aggregate weekly hours index (1982=100), seasonally adjusted	Average earnings (dollars, not seasonally adjusted)	
												Hourly	Weekly
1970	235.0	296.8	81.8	. . .	46.2	34.6	30.4	320	273	37.2	156.4	2.49	92.63
1971	225.7	283.1	79.9	. . .	47.7	36.2	32.3	299	257	37.7	148.7	2.59	97.64
1972	234.2	280.2	84.2	. . .	50.8	45.1	69.4	296	256	38.3	150.7	2.68	102.64
1973	217.9	258.9	79.6	. . .	53.3	51.4	76.9	284	245	37.8	142.3	2.79	105.46
1974	207.2	235.1	77.4	. . .	57.1	49.6	55.1	271	232	36.9	131.8	2.99	110.33
1975	206.6	230.9	79.7	. . .	60.3	48.7	51.8	248	213	37.1	121.3	3.21	119.09
1976	205.1	223.2	81.7	. . .	64.8	60.4	78.1	263	227	37.4	130.6	3.40	127.16
1977	200.6	223.1	83.3	. . .	68.8	64.6	85.8	255	218	36.9	123.9	3.61	133.21
1978	201.6	223.4	86.8	. . .	74.7	76.6	111.2	257	220	37.1	125.5	3.89	144.32
1979	184.4	211.2	82.2	. . .	89.0	114.6	169.3	246	209	36.5	117.1	4.22	154.03
1980	181.6	204.0	84.1	. . .	95.2	99.8	104.6	233	197	36.7	110.7	4.58	168.09
1981	176.0	197.3	83.9	. . .	98.3	102.7	104.5	238	201	36.7	113.6	4.99	183.13
1982	163.1	190.5	80.7	. . .	100.0	100.0	100.0	219	183	35.6	100.0	5.33	189.75
1983	158.3	180.4	82.8	. . .	102.1	106.2	109.8	205	171	36.8	96.8	5.54	203.87
1984	141.9	160.4	78.6	. . .	102.7	119.6	143.8	189	158	36.8	89.3	5.71	210.13
1985	126.1	140.5	74.1	101.3	104.8	113.4	126.1	165	137	37.2	78.1	5.83	216.88
1986	115.0	128.0	71.9	103.0	106.9	122.9	147.7	149	123	36.9	69.5	5.92	218.45
1987	112.4	120.0	74.7	106.6	109.4	140.9	179.9	143	120	38.2	70.3	6.08	232.26
1988	112.0	121.6	78.7	113.4	115.1	167.5	205.8	143	118	37.5	67.9	6.28	235.50
1989	111.9	117.0	82.5	118.0	120.8	170.4	213.1	138	114	37.9	66.4	6.59	249.76
1990	107.8	112.2	82.7	122.6	125.6	177.5	217.8	133	109	37.4	62.8	6.91	258.43
1991	98.4	96.4	78.8	124.8	128.6	168.4	173.4	124	100	37.5	57.7	7.18	269.25
1992	100.0	100.0	83.0	127.0	132.0	163.7	171.4	120	97	38.0	56.6	7.42	281.96
1993	101.0	100.1	86.1	129.0	134.4	168.6	180.2	117	94	38.6	55.6	7.63	294.52
1994	93.6	97.8	81.4	130.6	135.5	179.6	200.9	113	90	38.5	53.0	7.97	306.85
1995	86.9	92.2	74.6	134.1	139.2	191.4	209.9	106	83	38.0	48.3	8.17	310.46
1996	87.5	83.3	78.9	134.7	141.6	177.9	186.5	96	74	38.1	43.3	8.57	326.52
1997	83.6	78.3	76.7	137.1	143.7	182.7	196.1	91	69	38.4	40.6	8.97	344.45
1998	77.1	69.9	72.4	137.1	144.7	178.4	153.6	84	63	37.6	36.5	9.35	351.56
1999	69.8	62.3	68.4	136.5	144.5	176.3	141.9	78	58	37.8	33.6	9.77	369.31
1996													
January	85.7	85.5	76.9	134.6	140.6	182.3	172.7	99	77	35.2	41.6	8.51	294.45
February	86.9	84.7	78.0	134.6	141.1	181.0	175.7	99	77	37.6	44.5	8.41	312.01
March	87.3	84.6	78.4	134.8	141.3	181.2	177.1	98	76	37.9	44.2	8.46	319.79
April	87.5	83.4	78.7	134.1	141.2	176.1	175.6	97	75	37.9	43.7	8.40	315.00
May	87.2	83.2	78.6	134.5	141.2	178.1	178.1	97	74	38.4	43.7	8.43	322.03
June	88.7	84.2	80.0	134.4	141.6	175.2	181.2	96	74	38.6	43.9	8.48	331.57
July	88.2	82.5	79.6	134.1	141.7	172.7	186.0	96	73	38.4	43.1	8.44	318.19
August	88.3	82.3	79.8	134.2	142.0	173.4	190.7	95	73	38.6	43.3	8.63	335.71
September	88.3	82.6	79.9	135.3	142.0	176.0	186.3	94	72	38.7	42.8	8.71	341.43
October	87.4	83.2	79.2	135.1	142.2	177.4	204.8	94	72	38.7	42.8	8.73	341.34
November	86.9	82.4	78.8	135.2	142.2	179.4	204.4	92	71	38.9	42.4	8.74	343.48
December	87.5	83.0	79.4	136.0	142.3	182.5	205.4	94	73	38.7	43.4	8.85	347.81
1997													
January	87.5	83.3	79.6	136.8	143.1	183.2	207.5	93	72	38.4	42.5	8.86	334.02
February	85.5	81.7	77.9	137.3	143.3	185.3	209.4	93	71	38.5	42.0	8.94	337.93
March	86.7	82.5	79.1	137.2	143.5	185.5	211.7	93	71	38.7	42.2	8.89	342.27
April	85.6	80.6	78.2	137.4	143.5	188.1	211.9	92	70	38.6	41.5	8.89	338.71
May	85.0	80.5	77.7	136.9	143.7	183.6	208.9	92	70	38.4	41.3	8.92	340.74
June	83.9	77.9	76.9	136.2	142.2	180.2	198.8	91	69	38.3	40.6	8.94	346.87
July	84.3	78.2	77.4	136.9	144.1	179.7	180.1	90	68	38.5	40.2	8.77	331.51
August	81.2	77.1	74.7	136.9	144.3	178.0	186.2	90	68	38.0	39.7	8.89	341.38
September	80.9	76.4	74.5	137.0	144.4	178.4	180.3	89	67	38.5	39.6	9.11	356.20
October	81.9	76.5	75.6	137.5	144.2	182.1	183.0	89	67	38.4	39.5	9.15	353.19
November	80.8	74.0	74.7	137.9	144.1	185.2	190.3	88	67	38.0	39.1	9.13	351.51
December	80.4	73.1	74.4	137.4	144.2	182.4	185.5	88	66	38.3	38.8	9.21	357.35
1998													
January	79.8	72.8	74.0	137.4	144.5	180.5	156.0	87	66	38.5	39.0	9.31	350.99
February	80.7	74.1	75.0	137.4	144.7	179.3	154.6	87	66	38.5	39.0	9.28	351.71
March	80.0	72.8	74.5	137.4	144.7	178.9	145.8	86	65	37.8	37.7	9.30	350.61
April	78.8	70.4	73.5	137.1	144.7	176.6	152.2	85	64	37.3	36.7	9.27	338.36
May	78.2	69.9	73.1	137.2	144.6	177.4	153.1	85	64	37.2	36.6	9.33	348.94
June	76.4	70.1	71.6	137.2	144.7	177.2	175.3	84	64	37.5	36.9	9.35	356.24
July	77.0	70.3	72.4	137.3	144.5	179.7	160.6	84	63	37.2	36.0	9.16	337.09
August	76.0	68.6	71.5	137.1	144.6	179.5	164.4	83	62	37.6	35.8	9.30	356.19
September	75.7	68.2	71.5	137.2	144.7	179.0	162.0	82	61	37.5	35.2	9.39	349.31
October	75.0	66.7	71.0	137.1	144.7	178.0	142.6	82	61	37.5	35.2	9.48	356.45
November	75.1	68.5	71.4	136.5	144.7	177.1	133.1	82	61	37.6	35.2	9.49	360.62
December	73.2	67.0	69.8	136.7	144.9	177.9	143.7	81	61	37.6	35.2	9.48	361.19
1999													
January	71.9	65.0	68.8	135.8	143.8	176.1	143.3	81	60	37.5	34.6	9.69	355.62
February	71.5	65.9	68.7	136.1	144.6	176.0	128.9	80	60	37.8	34.8	9.62	358.83
March	71.3	64.6	68.8	136.1	144.6	175.5	132.8	79	59	37.7	34.2	9.61	362.30
April	70.6	65.9	68.4	136.1	144.6	175.9	133.1	79	59	37.9	34.4	9.66	366.11
May	70.9	64.9	69.0	136.0	144.4	175.1	137.5	78	59	38.2	34.6	9.67	370.36
June	71.3	63.9	69.6	136.5	144.5	175.0	136.3	78	58	37.9	33.8	9.65	371.53
July	69.1	58.7	67.8	136.7	144.6	175.6	136.3	76	56	37.9	32.6	9.69	363.38
August	70.2	61.9	69.2	136.7	144.6	176.1	143.0	77	58	37.9	33.8	9.86	381.58
September	69.5	59.4	68.8	136.9	144.6	176.7	151.1	77	57	37.5	32.8	9.95	372.13
October	68.2	59.1	67.9	137.0	144.7	177.8	156.8	77	57	37.6	32.9	9.91	374.60
November	67.7	60.1	67.7	137.0	144.6	177.8	143.0	76	56	37.7	32.4	9.93	378.33
December	65.4	57.2	65.6	137.0	144.5	177.9	160.7	76	56	37.4	32.2	10.02	375.75

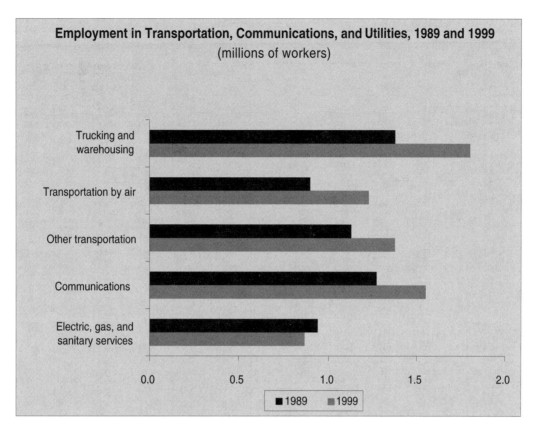

Employment in Transportation, Communications, and Utilities, 1989 and 1999
(millions of workers)

- From 1989 to 1999, employment in air transportation and in trucking and warehousing grew 37 percent and 31 percent, respectively, with both well above the average for all private nonfarm employment.

- Employment rose at a fairly steady rate from 1970 to 1999 in the communications and transportation industries. In electric, gas, and sanitary services, however, employment increased from 1970 to 1991, but (with the exception of 1999) has fallen thereafter.

- Electricity generation more than doubled between 1970 and 1999, with even greater growth in nuclear and hydro production.

- Output of gas utilities, on the other hand, has declined 20 percent since 1970.

Table 18-1. Electric and Gas Utilities—Industrial Production

(1992=100.)

Year and month	Total	Seasonally adjusted												Not seasonally adjusted	
		Electric								Gas				Electric	Gas
		Total	Generation			Sales				Total	Residential	Commercial and other	Gas transmission		
			Total	Fossil fuel	Hydro and nuclear	Total	Residential	Nonresidential							
								Total	Industrial						
1970	66.5	51.1	53.4	65.1	31.4	49.4	49.8	49.0	130.4	130.5	104.1	90.0	169.6	51.1	130.4
1971	69.6	54.0	56.3	67.5	35.5	52.3	53.2	51.5	134.4	134.4	106.6	94.2	175.2	54.0	134.4
1972	74.1	58.4	61.0	73.3	38.1	56.7	57.6	55.8	136.4	136.5	108.8	94.6	177.8	58.4	136.4
1973	77.0	62.4	63.6	76.1	41.3	61.2	62.0	60.3	134.2	134.4	106.0	97.8	176.7	62.4	134.2
1974	76.1	61.9	62.6	73.3	47.1	61.0	62.0	60.1	131.1	131.2	106.3	97.6	169.5	61.9	131.1
1975	76.8	64.0	65.0	74.5	54.6	62.9	65.5	60.9	125.2	125.2	108.8	95.0	158.6	64.0	125.2
1976	79.9	67.1	69.8	80.8	55.3	65.2	64.5	65.5	127.0	127.1	111.9	100.9	157.6	67.1	127.0
1977	82.0	70.7	73.9	85.6	55.1	68.7	68.6	68.7	120.7	120.7	102.3	92.4	156.9	70.7	120.7
1978	84.4	73.3	76.0	84.9	65.4	71.5	71.7	71.4	122.6	122.6	105.1	93.8	158.8	73.3	122.6
1979	86.8	75.2	77.8	88.5	62.6	73.6	73.0	73.9	126.6	126.6	105.6	99.1	166.5	75.2	126.6
1980	87.3	76.4	78.9	90.6	61.5	74.8	76.5	73.6	124.8	124.8	103.2	94.2	166.5	76.4	124.8
1981	85.0	78.0	79.5	91.1	62.4	77.0	77.3	76.7	109.3	109.3	97.9	91.5	127.1	78.0	109.3
1982	82.3	76.7	78.3	85.8	69.2	75.6	78.0	74.0	102.4	102.4	98.8	92.7	115.7	76.7	102.4
1983	83.7	79.2	80.4	86.9	73.1	78.3	80.7	76.5	100.4	100.4	94.4	87.2	124.2	79.2	100.4
1984	86.7	82.4	83.8	91.1	75.5	81.5	82.6	81.0	102.6	102.6	97.2	90.6	118.9	82.4	102.6
1985	88.8	84.6	85.9	93.3	77.6	83.7	84.7	83.0	104.3	104.3	93.6	86.1	130.0	84.6	104.3
1986	86.4	86.2	87.1	92.2	82.4	85.5	87.5	84.2	83.8	87.0	92.2	83.4	86.7	86.2	87.0
1987	89.4	89.4	89.5	96.5	82.4	89.3	90.9	88.2	87.5	89.0	92.1	86.7	87.4	89.4	89.0
1988	93.9	93.6	94.1	100.8	87.4	93.2	95.5	91.7	92.8	94.5	98.9	95.4	91.8	93.6	94.5
1989	97.1	96.8	97.9	102.9	92.7	96.0	96.7	95.5	95.9	98.1	102.1	97.1	96.2	96.8	98.1
1990	98.3	99.2	100.5	100.9	100.1	98.2	98.6	98.0	97.0	94.4	93.8	93.6	94.6	99.2	94.4
1991	100.4	101.2	101.9	100.1	103.7	100.6	102.5	99.3	97.8	97.3	97.3	97.5	97.3	101.2	97.3
1992	100.0	100.0	100.0	100.0	100.0	100.0	100.0	100.0	100.0	100.0	100.0	100.0	100.0	100.0	100.0
1993	103.9	103.8	103.0	103.8	102.3	104.3	106.5	102.9	102.0	104.3	105.9	102.4	103.5	103.8	104.3
1994	105.3	105.5	104.1	104.8	103.3	106.5	107.7	105.6	102.8	104.6	103.4	103.3	106.2	105.5	104.6
1995	109.0	109.5	108.9	104.8	113.0	110.0	111.6	108.9	104.9	107.2	103.4	108.2	110.5	109.5	107.2
1996	112.6	112.7	111.9	107.1	116.8	113.3	115.9	111.5	106.7	112.3	111.7	112.7	112.5	112.7	112.3
1997	112.7	113.3	112.2	111.5	112.9	114.0	114.5	113.6	107.0	110.6	106.7	115.2	112.5	113.3	110.6
1998	114.4	116.9	114.9	115.5	114.3	118.2	120.3	116.7	108.5	103.2	95.7	108.5	109.0	116.9	103.2
1999	115.6	118.2	115.4	112.2	118.4	120.0	122.0	118.6	108.8	104.8	98.3	110.3	109.0	118.2	104.8
1996															
January	113.1	112.8	112.2	106.9	117.5	113.3	117.2	110.5	106.2	114.1	112.1	113.4	114.0	119.7	201.2
February	114.7	114.3	112.8	107.3	118.5	115.3	118.8	112.8	108.0	116.0	114.2	115.7	115.1	113.7	181.2
March	114.6	114.4	113.4	106.8	120.2	115.1	119.2	112.1	107.6	115.6	113.5	115.2	114.8	108.8	160.0
April	113.7	113.2	113.3	105.0	122.0	113.2	117.7	110.0	104.8	115.8	113.0	116.3	114.2	100.9	117.7
May	114.6	114.8	114.8	108.8	121.1	114.8	117.9	112.5	106.7	114.0	111.7	110.2	112.6	105.8	81.8
June	113.1	113.7	112.3	108.3	116.6	114.6	118.4	111.9	106.2	110.7	106.1	105.7	112.5	117.5	63.2
July	109.2	110.2	108.9	104.0	114.2	111.1	112.5	110.1	106.8	105.3	100.1	102.6	107.1	125.0	58.0
August	110.7	111.4	110.6	106.8	114.7	112.0	113.3	111.1	106.1	107.9	104.2	104.4	107.9	125.8	57.9
September	110.9	111.0	109.9	106.1	113.9	111.7	112.3	111.3	106.6	110.6	108.7	105.2	109.6	114.2	58.5
October	111.4	111.4	111.1	107.9	114.5	111.8	112.2	111.5	107.5	111.5	108.8	107.3	111.3	103.8	76.8
November	112.9	112.7	112.1	111.2	113.2	113.2	114.9	112.0	107.2	113.9	111.7	112.2	112.5	104.7	123.8
December	112.5	112.7	111.3	107.0	115.8	113.6	115.6	112.3	107.5	112.1	108.6	114.1	111.3	112.8	167.3
1997															
January	113.3	113.6	113.4	111.3	115.6	113.9	114.5	113.4	107.5	112.1	108.8	112.8	112.3	120.1	196.7
February	111.7	112.0	111.6	108.7	114.6	112.4	112.3	112.5	106.5	110.7	105.6	111.9	113.0	110.8	169.9
March	110.0	111.4	111.4	109.2	113.7	111.5	111.3	111.7	105.7	104.1	95.5	106.4	110.3	105.7	148.7
April	113.0	113.4	112.2	110.5	114.0	114.2	115.3	113.4	107.0	111.7	107.8	115.5	112.5	101.1	111.4
May	112.1	110.8	109.4	107.8	110.9	111.7	111.9	111.6	106.2	118.0	118.4	123.0	114.1	102.2	84.9
June	110.9	110.7	110.5	108.2	112.9	110.9	108.7	112.5	107.0	111.9	107.3	121.7	112.1	114.5	64.6
July	112.6	113.4	112.7	112.2	113.2	114.0	114.2	113.8	106.7	108.9	102.6	115.8	113.0	129.1	61.9
August	111.5	112.0	111.7	108.6	114.9	112.3	113.2	111.6	106.6	109.0	103.9	117.6	111.2	126.8	60.0
September	113.8	114.9	114.4	115.8	113.1	115.3	115.7	115.0	108.5	108.7	102.0	120.0	112.0	118.4	59.4
October	115.4	116.7	114.1	116.7	111.6	118.3	120.1	117.0	107.7	109.9	105.4	118.9	112.0	109.1	76.9
November	114.2	115.0	113.1	113.8	112.5	116.2	117.4	115.3	107.3	111.1	109.5	115.3	111.8	106.6	124.0
December	114.3	115.2	112.1	116.8	107.6	117.1	118.8	115.9	107.1	110.5	106.9	114.4	113.8	114.9	168.5
1998															
January	109.4	110.9	109.3	109.0	109.8	112.0	111.0	112.6	106.3	102.9	97.9	106.8	107.5	116.9	182.0
February	109.8	111.6	112.1	111.2	113.1	111.4	108.4	113.5	108.1	102.0	96.8	105.3	107.4	109.8	156.4
March	113.8	115.8	114.6	115.5	113.8	116.6	118.5	115.2	107.7	105.2	100.3	108.6	110.6	109.7	150.3
April	113.0	115.2	113.3	114.3	112.4	116.5	117.7	115.7	107.8	102.9	97.8	106.6	108.2	102.3	105.8
May	116.0	119.2	117.6	120.2	115.1	120.3	122.9	118.4	110.2	101.8	94.3	106.8	109.4	109.7	74.2
June	117.8	120.3	118.0	121.9	114.4	121.8	127.4	117.8	108.6	106.6	99.7	112.3	113.3	124.5	62.9
July	117.0	118.7	116.1	118.1	114.3	120.3	125.3	116.6	107.5	110.0	103.5	119.3	114.5	135.6	63.2
August	117.3	119.0	114.9	119.3	110.8	121.6	126.3	118.2	109.3	109.8	101.0	125.9	114.6	135.3	61.4
September	119.1	122.0	119.1	121.9	116.6	123.9	130.2	119.3	108.2	106.1	95.1	123.8	113.1	125.6	58.9
October	115.6	119.0	115.1	112.4	119.1	121.0	126.0	117.0	106.8	100.1	90.1	111.1	108.6	111.2	70.7
November	110.8	114.7	113.1	108.9	116.8	115.7	112.6	117.8	110.3	93.3	85.5	98.3	100.5	106.3	104.3
December	112.5	115.9	114.5	111.9	116.9	116.8	115.1	117.8	111.2	97.5	89.4	102.5	105.2	115.3	148.1
1999															
January	114.5	115.8	115.2	111.7	118.4	116.3	116.9	115.7	106.4	108.8	104.4	114.9	112.9	122.0	193.9
February	112.6	114.9	115.7	113.3	118.0	114.4	113.1	115.2	105.7	102.5	96.2	107.9	108.7	112.9	156.4
March	116.8	119.1	117.0	115.0	118.9	120.5	123.3	118.3	108.7	106.4	102.1	110.7	110.6	113.0	153.5
April	116.3	118.6	115.3	120.5	110.4	120.8	123.3	118.9	108.9	105.7	99.5	109.9	112.3	105.1	108.8
May	116.1	118.4	114.5	114.7	114.3	120.8	122.8	119.3	109.5	105.8	99.9	111.3	111.3	108.8	76.4
June	117.4	119.6	116.8	114.1	119.2	121.5	123.7	119.7	109.3	107.5	102.0	116.3	111.3	123.9	62.9
July	119.8	122.6	118.7	116.4	120.7	125.1	129.4	122.0	111.6	107.4	103.0	115.3	109.9	140.2	61.4
August	117.8	120.0	116.8	113.6	119.7	122.0	126.7	118.6	108.0	108.2	101.3	121.0	112.1	136.3	60.1
September	117.7	119.8	115.5	109.8	120.6	122.5	127.2	119.1	108.9	108.5	101.5	124.4	111.3	123.0	59.1
October	115.2	116.9	112.5	108.8	115.8	119.6	120.1	119.1	108.2	107.9	102.1	119.8	111.0	109.3	75.4
November	110.9	115.8	114.0	104.7	122.0	117.0	114.7	118.5	111.0	88.2	79.1	91.6	97.6	107.2	99.0
December	113.5	116.9	113.9	105.0	121.5	118.9	118.7	118.8	109.4	98.1	94.3	101.3	101.5	116.3	151.1

Table 18-2. Transportation, Communications, and Utilities—Capacity Utilization and Prices

Year and month	Capacity utilization—Electric and gas utilities (percent of capacity, seasonally adjusted)			Producer prices (not seasonally adjusted)							
				Industries				Commodities			
								Electric (1982=100)		Natural gas (December 1990=100)	
	Total	Electric	Gas	Motor freight transportation and warehousing (June 1993=100)	Water transportation (December 1992=100)	Transportation by air (December 1992=100)	Pipelines, except natural gas (December 1986=100)	Commercial	Industrial	Commercial	Industrial
1970	96.2	98.9	91.9	...	...	...	...	30.8	22.5	...	...
1971	94.6	96.5	92.3	...	...	...	...	33.7	24.8	...	...
1972	95.2	97.0	92.5	...	...	...	...	34.8	26.2	...	...
1973	93.5	95.4	90.7	...	...	...	...	36.8	28.0	...	...
1974	87.3	87.3	88.6	...	...	...	...	44.8	36.4	...	...
1975	84.4	84.8	84.8	...	...	...	...	51.4	44.3	...	...
1976	85.2	85.1	86.6	...	...	...	...	54.7	47.9	...	...
1977	85.0	86.0	83.2	...	...	...	...	60.7	54.3	...	...
1978	85.4	85.3	85.5	...	...	...	...	64.6	59.1	...	...
1979	86.6	85.3	89.5	...	...	...	...	68.7	64.5	...	...
1980	85.9	84.7	89.3	...	...	...	...	80.6	77.8	...	...
1981	82.5	84.3	79.1	...	...	...	...	91.6	89.2	...	...
1982	79.3	81.3	74.9	...	...	...	...	100.0	100.0	...	...
1983	79.7	82.3	74.4	...	...	...	...	102.5	103.1	...	...
1984	81.9	84.0	77.1	...	...	...	...	108.0	108.4	...	...
1985	83.5	84.7	79.8	...	...	...	...	110.3	112.8	...	...
1986	80.6	84.9	67.6	...	...	...	...	110.5	114.5	...	...
1987	82.5	86.1	69.9	...	...	...	97.9	108.9	111.9	...	...
1988	84.9	87.8	73.7	...	...	...	94.8	109.5	112.6	...	...
1989	86.3	89.4	75.7	...	...	...	94.4	113.0	116.2	...	...
1990	85.7	89.6	72.9	...	...	...	95.8	115.3	119.6	...	...
1991	86.3	89.1	75.1	...	...	...	96.1	122.3	128.1	95.9	93.6
1992	84.5	86.8	77.2	...	...	...	96.4	124.4	129.6	96.7	94.2
1993	87.2	88.8	80.4	...	99.7	105.6	96.6	127.2	130.6	102.7	101.6
1994	87.4	89.2	80.4	101.9	100.0	108.5	102.6	128.8	129.2	103.7	99.5
1995	89.2	91.1	82.0	104.5	103.0	113.7	110.8	131.7	130.8	96.5	90.9
1996	90.4	91.6	84.8	106.3	103.7	121.1	104.6	131.6	131.6	103.2	98.9
1997	89.7	91.6	82.1	108.9	104.2	125.3	98.8	131.7	130.8	109.8	109.3
1998	90.8	94.4	75.7	111.6	105.6	124.5	99.2	130.4	130.0	106.4	103.6
1999	90.7	94.3	75.9	114.8	113.0	130.8	98.3	129.1	128.9	108.1	103.3
1996											
January	91.5	92.5	86.9	105.1	103.9	117.2	110.6	127.6	127.9	101.8	95.4
February	92.6	93.5	88.3	105.9	103.8	119.1	110.6	126.0	127.1	103.0	96.8
March	92.5	93.4	87.9	105.8	104.2	119.9	110.6	126.8	127.8	104.2	98.0
April	91.6	92.3	87.8	105.9	103.8	120.2	103.7	126.6	129.1	102.6	96.6
May	92.1	93.4	86.3	106.0	103.0	120.8	103.7	129.6	135.0	100.3	97.0
June	90.7	92.3	83.7	106.9	102.9	121.4	103.7	138.4	137.5	100.5	97.2
July	87.5	89.4	79.4	106.2	103.0	122.5	104.0	139.1	136.0	101.2	98.0
August	88.6	90.3	81.3	106.4	103.0	121.8	104.0	139.6	136.2	102.3	99.0
September	88.6	89.8	83.2	106.6	103.8	121.9	101.0	139.5	136.2	99.7	96.9
October	88.9	90.1	83.7	106.9	104.6	122.4	100.9	131.3	131.2	99.4	96.1
November	90.1	91.1	85.4	107.1	104.5	123.5	100.9	126.8	127.1	108.3	103.5
December	89.7	91.0	83.9	107.2	104.2	122.7	100.9	127.5	127.7	115.0	112.9
1997											
January	90.2	91.8	83.8	108.0	104.1	128.8	98.8	127.7	128.3	121.2	130.2
February	88.9	90.5	82.6	108.5	104.2	128.9	98.8	127.7	128.1	119.1	121.9
March	87.5	90.0	77.6	108.6	104.1	124.6	98.8	127.6	128.2	110.3	107.3
April	89.9	91.6	83.1	108.8	104.2	125.1	98.8	127.1	127.3	103.0	100.4
May	89.2	89.5	87.8	108.8	104.3	125.1	98.9	129.2	129.7	102.3	99.9
June	88.2	89.5	83.1	109.0	104.8	126.2	98.9	138.6	135.1	103.3	100.5
July	89.6	91.8	80.8	109.1	104.4	126.5	98.7	139.2	135.9	104.5	100.4
August	88.7	90.7	80.8	109.3	104.7	125.4	98.7	138.1	134.7	103.7	100.6
September	90.6	93.0	80.5	109.4	103.8	122.5	98.7	139.4	136.0	105.7	102.7
October	91.9	94.5	81.3	109.3	104.6	123.7	98.7	131.2	130.1	110.0	111.0
November	90.9	93.1	82.1	109.0	104.1	123.4	98.7	127.0	127.9	118.5	120.3
December	91.0	93.3	81.6	109.4	103.3	123.3	98.7	127.5	128.3	116.0	116.4
1998											
January	87.1	89.8	75.9	110.5	103.0	122.6	99.3	126.8	127.4	112.0	111.4
February	87.4	90.4	75.1	110.6	102.7	123.7	99.3	126.4	127.2	108.4	108.2
March	90.6	93.7	77.4	110.7	102.3	123.7	99.3	125.7	126.7	108.1	106.6
April	89.8	93.3	75.6	110.9	102.2	124.3	99.3	125.7	126.4	106.2	103.3
May	92.2	96.4	74.8	111.3	105.3	124.3	99.3	128.0	129.2	105.8	103.3
June	93.6	97.2	78.3	111.5	106.1	124.2	99.3	136.3	133.8	102.9	100.3
July	92.9	95.8	80.6	111.9	107.9	124.2	99.2	137.6	134.8	103.8	100.7
August	93.0	96.0	80.5	112.1	108.1	124.3	99.2	137.8	135.2	103.7	99.6
September	94.4	98.4	77.7	112.4	108.9	125.2	99.2	137.7	135.2	102.9	98.7
October	91.5	95.9	73.2	112.6	108.4	125.4	99.2	130.7	130.4	104.5	100.4
November	87.6	92.2	68.2	112.5	107.3	126.1	99.2	127.1	127.6	108.1	105.1
December	88.9	93.1	71.2	112.7	105.7	126.5	99.2	125.2	126.6	110.6	105.1
1999											
January	90.3	93.0	79.4	113.6	106.0	126.6	98.4	124.9	126.1	109.7	103.9
February	88.7	92.1	74.7	113.9	106.0	128.4	98.2	124.7	125.5	106.8	100.3
March	91.9	95.4	77.4	114.1	105.8	128.9	98.2	124.7	125.5	105.1	99.0
April	91.4	94.9	76.9	114.2	106.0	129.6	98.4	124.2	125.2	102.8	95.8
May	91.1	94.6	76.9	114.3	114.4	130.0	98.5	126.2	127.4	103.1	97.7
June	92.1	95.5	78.1	114.6	116.8	130.9	98.6	134.5	131.6	103.5	99.5
July	93.9	97.7	77.9	114.8	117.4	131.4	98.2	136.2	133.9	105.0	101.6
August	92.2	95.5	78.4	115.1	117.2	131.7	98.2	136.2	133.9	107.0	100.8
September	92.0	95.2	78.6	115.8	117.3	131.8	98.3	136.1	134.1	110.7	106.6
October	89.9	92.8	78.1	115.5	116.7	133.1	98.3	129.0	129.5	109.9	105.7
November	86.5	91.8	63.8	115.5	116.7	133.4	98.2	126.3	127.5	118.9	116.0
December	88.4	92.6	70.9	115.8	116.1	134.2	98.2	125.9	126.5	115.1	112.9

Table 18-3. Transportation, Communications, and Utilities—Employment, Hours, and Earnings

Year and month	Total payroll employment (thousands, seasonally adjusted)						Nonsupervisory workers				
		Transportation			Commu-nications	Electric, gas, and sanitary services	Seasonally adjusted			Average earnings (dollars, not seasonally adjusted)	
	Total	Total	Trucking and warehousing	Transpor-tation by air			Employment	Average weekly hours	Aggregate weekly hours index (1982=100)	Hourly	Weekly
1970	4 515	2 694	...	...	1 129	692	3 914	40.5	96.9	3.85	155.93
1971	4 476	2 639	...	...	1 143	698	3 872	40.1	95.1	4.21	168.82
1972	4 541	2 676	...	...	1 152	713	3 943	40.4	97.3	4.65	187.86
1973	4 656	2 746	...	...	1 180	731	4 034	40.5	99.9	5.02	203.31
1974	4 725	2 779	...	...	1 203	744	4 079	40.2	100.4	5.41	217.48
1975	4 542	2 634	...	...	1 176	733	3 894	39.7	94.6	5.88	233.44
1976	4 582	2 678	...	...	1 169	735	3 918	39.8	95.5	6.45	256.71
1977	4 713	2 781	...	...	1 185	747	4 008	39.9	97.9	6.99	278.90
1978	4 923	2 905	...	...	1 240	778	4 142	40.0	101.3	7.57	302.80
1979	5 136	3 019	...	...	1 309	807	4 299	39.9	104.9	8.16	325.58
1980	5 146	2 960	...	...	1 357	829	4 293	39.6	104.1	8.87	351.25
1981	5 165	2 920	...	...	1 391	854	4 283	39.4	103.3	9.70	382.18
1982	5 081	2 787	...	...	1 417	877	4 190	39.0	100.0	10.32	402.48
1983	4 952	2 742	...	...	1 324	886	4 072	39.0	97.3	10.79	420.81
1984	5 156	2 914	...	...	1 340	902	4 258	39.4	102.8	11.12	438.13
1985	5 233	2 997	...	...	1 319	916	4 335	39.5	104.6	11.40	450.30
1986	5 247	3 051	...	...	1 275	921	4 339	39.2	104.0	11.70	458.64
1987	5 362	3 156	...	...	1 282	925	4 446	39.2	106.5	12.03	471.58
1988	5 512	3 301	1 351	850	1 280	931	4 555	38.2	108.2	12.24	467.57
1989	5 614	3 404	1 379	897	1 272	938	4 655	38.3	111.1	12.57	481.43
1990	5 777	3 511	1 395	968	1 309	957	4 781	38.4	114.5	12.92	496.13
1991	5 755	3 495	1 378	962	1 299	961	4 774	38.1	113.4	13.20	502.92
1992	5 718	3 495	1 385	964	1 269	954	4 768	38.3	113.6	13.43	514.37
1993	5 811	3 598	1 444	988	1 269	944	4 862	39.3	118.2	13.55	532.52
1994	5 984	3 761	1 526	1 023	1 295	928	5 012	39.7	122.4	13.78	547.07
1995	6 132	3 904	1 587	1 068	1 318	911	5 140	39.4	123.9	14.13	556.72
1996	6 253	4 019	1 637	1 107	1 351	884	5 260	39.6	127.5	14.45	572.22
1997	6 408	4 123	1 677	1 134	1 419	866	5 366	39.7	130.5	14.92	592.32
1998	6 611	4 273	1 744	1 181	1 477	861	5 481	39.5	132.3	15.31	604.75
1999	6 826	4 409	1 805	1 227	1 552	865	5 660	38.7	134.1	15.69	607.20
1996											
January	6 189	3 966	1 617	1 091	1 326	897	5 202	39.1	124.4	14.32	551.32
February	6 203	3 983	1 621	1 101	1 326	894	5 221	39.6	126.5	14.34	563.56
March	6 207	3 989	1 623	1 104	1 327	891	5 224	39.8	127.2	14.33	564.60
April	6 227	4 006	1 630	1 112	1 332	889	5 238	39.4	126.3	14.40	563.04
May	6 239	4 015	1 636	1 110	1 338	886	5 250	39.5	126.9	14.35	563.96
June	6 264	4 032	1 646	1 111	1 348	884	5 270	39.6	127.7	14.41	577.84
July	6 282	4 047	1 653	1 116	1 355	880	5 287	39.5	127.8	14.45	573.67
August	6 283	4 041	1 649	1 113	1 363	879	5 283	39.7	128.3	14.50	581.45
September	6 281	4 035	1 642	1 110	1 368	878	5 286	39.8	128.7	14.59	587.98
October	6 280	4 037	1 641	1 110	1 367	876	5 286	39.8	128.7	14.51	576.05
November	6 288	4 035	1 636	1 111	1 377	876	5 294	39.8	128.9	14.59	580.68
December	6 299	4 045	1 643	1 111	1 380	874	5 291	39.7	128.5	14.63	583.74
1997											
January	6 332	4 074	1 645	1 133	1 385	873	5 324	39.5	128.7	14.75	573.78
February	6 354	4 086	1 651	1 136	1 396	872	5 343	39.5	129.1	14.69	580.26
March	6 379	4 102	1 658	1 141	1 405	872	5 366	39.9	131.0	14.74	583.70
April	6 397	4 116	1 664	1 143	1 411	870	5 384	39.6	130.4	14.80	581.64
May	6 407	4 123	1 670	1 142	1 416	868	5 391	39.6	130.6	14.76	580.07
June	6 417	4 132	1 673	1 144	1 419	866	5 394	39.4	130.0	14.81	590.92
July	6 422	4 134	1 679	1 142	1 422	866	5 394	39.3	129.7	14.98	591.71
August	6 280	3 990	1 688	985	1 428	862	5 213	40.1	127.9	15.03	608.72
September	6 454	4 164	1 696	1 153	1 427	863	5 390	40.0	131.9	15.04	606.11
October	6 478	4 178	1 699	1 161	1 439	861	5 396	39.9	131.7	15.07	599.79
November	6 481	4 180	1 699	1 161	1 442	859	5 394	39.9	131.7	15.17	612.87
December	6 489	4 185	1 704	1 158	1 446	858	5 388	39.9	131.5	15.15	602.97
1998											
January	6 504	4 194	1 708	1 161	1 451	859	5 398	39.9	131.8	15.24	598.93
February	6 528	4 214	1 717	1 163	1 455	859	5 400	39.9	131.8	15.25	608.48
March	6 546	4 228	1 722	1 167	1 459	859	5 412	39.7	131.4	15.21	599.27
April	6 560	4 232	1 730	1 170	1 469	859	5 423	39.6	131.4	15.24	595.88
May	6 584	4 253	1 738	1 174	1 471	860	5 450	39.7	132.4	15.18	599.61
June	6 597	4 261	1 744	1 177	1 478	858	5 459	39.5	131.9	15.20	601.92
July	6 620	4 278	1 748	1 181	1 482	860	5 489	39.5	132.6	15.28	606.62
August	6 641	4 302	1 757	1 187	1 478	861	5 519	39.3	132.7	15.31	610.87
September	6 654	4 308	1 758	1 191	1 485	861	5 524	39.3	132.8	15.43	606.40
October	6 675	4 319	1 765	1 192	1 495	861	5 545	39.4	133.7	15.40	605.22
November	6 692	4 328	1 767	1 195	1 499	865	5 560	39.3	133.7	15.50	615.35
December	6 725	4 350	1 776	1 205	1 509	866	5 583	39.1	133.6	15.52	606.83
1999											
January	6 736	4 351	1 783	1 198	1 520	865	5 603	39.3	134.7	15.59	603.33
February	6 755	4 360	1 787	1 205	1 529	866	5 618	39.2	134.7	15.58	607.62
March	6 772	4 371	1 791	1 211	1 532	869	5 625	39.1	134.6	15.53	602.56
April	6 782	4 381	1 795	1 213	1 536	865	5 631	39.0	134.4	15.60	602.16
May	6 797	4 392	1 798	1 218	1 541	864	5 637	38.9	134.2	15.57	604.12
June	6 817	4 408	1 803	1 224	1 544	865	5 652	38.9	134.5	15.59	608.01
July	6 834	4 420	1 808	1 230	1 551	863	5 659	38.8	134.3	15.69	610.34
August	6 848	4 426	1 810	1 234	1 558	864	5 670	38.8	134.6	15.69	618.19
September	6 866	4 436	1 816	1 238	1 565	865	5 687	38.6	134.3	15.80	608.30
October	6 875	4 441	1 818	1 241	1 572	862	5 694	38.4	133.8	15.78	605.95
November	6 898	4 453	1 823	1 246	1 581	864	5 709	38.3	133.8	15.90	608.97
December	6 911	4 459	1 818	1 253	1 588	864	5 721	38.4	134.4	15.96	612.86

Table 18-3. Transportation, Communications, and Utilities—Employment, Hours, and Earnings—*Continued*

Year and month	Nonsupervisory workers—*Continued* (not seasonally adjusted)											
	Trucking and warehousing				Communications				Electric, gas, and sanitary services			
	Employ-ment (thousands)	Average weekly hours	Average earnings		Employ-ment (thousands)	Average weekly hours	Average earnings		Employ-ment (thousands)	Average weekly hours	Average earnings	
			Hourly	Weekly			Hourly	Weekly			Hourly	Weekly
1970	. . .	. . .	. . .	. . .	886	39.3	3.41	134.01	. . .	. . .	. . .	. . .
1971	. . .	. . .	. . .	. . .	896	38.1	3.69	140.59	. . .	. . .	. . .	. . .
1972	. . .	. . .	. . .	. . .	909	39.3	4.15	163.10	609	41.5	4.82	200.03
1973	. . .	. . .	. . .	. . .	934	39.6	4.48	177.41	620	41.8	5.13	214.43
1974	. . .	. . .	. . .	. . .	943	39.6	4.91	194.44	628	41.5	5.52	229.08
1975	. . .	. . .	. . .	. . .	911	38.9	5.54	215.51	614	41.1	6.03	247.83
1976	. . .	. . .	. . .	. . .	902	38.9	6.19	240.79	611	41.2	6.58	271.10
1977	. . .	. . .	. . .	. . .	907	39.6	6.74	266.90	618	41.3	7.11	293.64
1978	. . .	. . .	. . .	. . .	939	39.9	7.33	292.47	637	41.8	7.65	319.77
1979	. . .	. . .	. . .	. . .	987	39.8	7.85	312.43	660	41.7	8.25	344.03
1980	. . .	. . .	. . .	. . .	1 014	39.9	8.50	339.15	678	41.7	8.90	371.13
1981	. . .	. . .	. . .	. . .	1 040	39.8	9.48	377.30	699	41.4	9.89	409.45
1982	. . .	. . .	. . .	. . .	1 072	39.5	10.19	402.51	711	41.4	10.78	446.29
1983	. . .	. . .	. . .	. . .	996	39.4	10.77	424.34	712	41.4	11.50	476.10
1984	. . .	. . .	. . .	. . .	1 018	39.9	11.26	449.27	719	41.5	12.20	506.30
1985	. . .	. . .	. . .	. . .	1 005	40.2	11.75	472.35	730	41.7	12.83	535.01
1986					972	40.1	12.15	487.22	733	41.8	13.39	559.70
1987	. . .	. . .	. . .		972	40.0	12.45	498.00	733	41.5	13.79	572.29
1988	1 176	38.3	10.95	419.39	951	39.8	12.85	511.43	736	41.5	14.27	592.21
1989	1 203	38.4	11.35	435.84	950	39.4	13.18	519.29	742	41.9	14.72	616.77
1990	1 215	38.5	11.68	449.68	978	39.4	13.51	532.29	759	41.6	15.23	633.57
1991	1 197	38.4	11.83	454.27	986	39.2	13.96	547.23	762	41.6	15.69	652.70
1992	1 205	38.7	12.07	467.11	981	39.4	14.42	568.15	753	41.9	16.08	673.75
1993	1 254	39.5	12.26	484.27	985	39.6	14.91	590.44	744	42.3	16.71	706.83
1994	1 328	39.9	12.50	498.75	993	39.6	15.24	603.50	734	42.4	17.24	730.98
1995	1 382	39.6	12.73	504.11	1 017	39.8	15.56	619.29	719	42.4	17.68	749.63
1996	1 426	39.8	12.95	515.41	1 058	40.4	16.03	647.61	699	42.2	18.26	770.57
1997	1 467	40.2	13.23	531.85	1 090	40.2	16.92	680.18	689	42.1	19.10	804.11
1998	1 528	40.0	13.62	544.80	1 076	40.8	17.31	706.25	689	42.2	19.97	842.73
1999	1 582	40.2	13.95	560.79	1 124	40.5	17.35	702.68	695	42.3	20.55	869.27
1996												
January	1 377	37.7	12.75	480.68	1 021	39.9	15.80	630.42	705	42.0	17.98	755.16
February	1 382	39.1	12.82	501.26	1 031	39.9	15.77	629.22	701	42.4	18.09	767.02
March	1 385	39.5	12.88	508.76	1 035	39.8	15.82	629.64	698	42.2	18.06	762.13
April	1 396	39.4	12.89	507.87	1 038	39.9	15.90	634.41	697	42.1	18.11	762.43
May	1 420	39.7	12.94	513.72	1 046	40.1	15.88	636.79	699	41.9	18.11	758.81
June	1 447	40.4	12.87	519.95	1 059	41.2	16.00	659.20	704	42.2	18.02	760.44
July	1 456	39.9	12.86	513.11	1 067	40.9	15.99	653.99	704	41.9	18.01	754.62
August	1 460	40.4	12.97	523.99	1 074	41.0	16.11	660.51	702	41.9	18.13	759.65
September	1 453	40.4	13.09	528.84	1 077	41.5	16.25	674.38	695	42.5	18.53	787.53
October	1 452	40.3	13.12	528.74	1 078	40.3	16.17	651.65	695	42.2	18.52	781.54
November	1 446	40.2	13.11	527.02	1 082	40.1	16.23	650.82	694	42.5	18.81	799.43
December	1 436	40.1	13.07	524.11	1 080	40.5	16.44	665.82	693	42.1	18.73	788.53
1997												
January	1 401	38.8	12.99	504.01	1 075	40.1	16.67	668.47	690	41.8	18.76	784.17
February	1 408	39.4	13.04	513.78	1 083	40.0	16.54	661.60	688	41.8	18.76	784.17
March	1 416	39.8	13.07	520.19	1 092	40.1	16.69	669.27	689	41.9	18.92	792.75
April	1 428	39.9	13.14	524.29	1 095	40.0	16.66	666.40	688	42.4	19.00	805.60
May	1 455	40.1	13.18	528.52	1 098	39.8	16.60	660.68	692	42.0	18.95	795.90
June	1 476	40.7	13.15	535.21	1 102	40.5	16.90	684.45	696	42.2	19.00	801.80
July	1 486	40.3	13.16	530.35	1 100	40.5	17.04	690.12	696	42.0	19.04	799.68
August	1 505	41.2	13.30	547.96	1 099	40.5	17.15	694.58	693	42.1	19.07	802.85
September	1 513	40.7	13.36	543.75	1 090	40.5	17.18	695.79	687	42.0	19.25	808.50
October	1 516	40.5	13.37	541.49	1 085	39.9	17.17	685.08	684	42.2	19.31	814.88
November	1 504	40.4	13.41	541.76	1 082	40.6	17.21	698.73	681	42.7	19.60	836.92
December	1 497	40.3	13.47	542.84	1 075	40.4	17.22	695.69	681	41.8	19.51	815.52
1998												
January	1 460	39.0	13.47	525.33	1 067	40.6	17.42	707.25	681	42.1	19.81	834.00
February	1 467	39.3	13.53	531.73	1 056	41.2	17.31	713.17	680	42.0	19.83	832.86
March	1 476	39.3	13.55	532.52	1 051	40.7	17.17	698.82	680	41.9	19.76	827.94
April	1 494	39.2	13.59	532.73	1 050	40.3	17.00	685.10	682	41.6	19.86	826.18
May	1 516	40.0	13.61	544.40	1 064	40.5	17.03	689.72	687	42.0	19.89	835.38
June	1 542	40.4	13.59	549.04	1 073	41.0	17.14	702.74	694	42.2	19.77	834.29
July	1 553	40.4	13.58	548.63	1 082	41.3	17.18	709.53	698	42.0	19.80	831.60
August	1 569	40.7	13.58	552.71	1 085	40.4	17.35	700.94	696	42.3	19.94	843.46
September	1 569	40.1	13.66	547.77	1 084	41.0	17.45	715.45	691	42.8	20.23	865.84
October	1 572	40.7	13.68	556.78	1 093	40.6	17.45	708.47	690	42.6	20.12	857.11
November	1 562	40.3	13.74	553.72	1 101	40.9	17.51	716.16	694	43.3	20.42	884.19
December	1 558	40.4	13.78	556.71	1 108	40.6	17.63	715.78	695	42.1	20.19	850.00
1999												
January	1 525	39.1	13.76	538.02	1 122	40.8	17.53	715.22	693	43.0	20.44	878.92
February	1 526	39.1	13.76	538.02	1 133	40.8	17.44	711.55	693	42.7	20.30	866.81
March	1 535	39.3	13.81	542.73	1 121	40.5	17.28	699.84	695	42.4	20.40	864.96
April	1 548	39.9	13.87	553.41	1 107	40.3	17.38	700.41	694	42.5	20.45	869.13
May	1 569	40.2	13.94	560.39	1 116	40.6	17.31	702.79	695	42.6	20.41	869.47
June	1 598	40.6	13.93	565.56	1 121	40.6	17.34	704.00	702	42.4	20.27	859.45
July	1 610	40.3	13.89	559.77	1 120	40.6	17.35	704.41	701	42.4	20.66	875.98
August	1 616	40.9	13.91	568.92	1 119	40.9	17.30	707.57	701	42.2	20.56	867.63
September	1 619	40.3	14.05	566.22	1 116	40.8	17.30	705.84	694	42.1	20.79	875.26
October	1 622	40.8	14.07	574.06	1 130	40.3	17.22	693.97	688	42.0	20.68	868.56
November	1 614	40.8	14.17	578.14	1 134	40.0	17.37	694.80	690	41.8	20.76	867.77
December	1 606	40.7	14.22	578.75	1 144	39.7	17.41	691.18	692	41.2	20.91	861.49

CHAPTER 19: RETAIL AND WHOLESALE TRADE

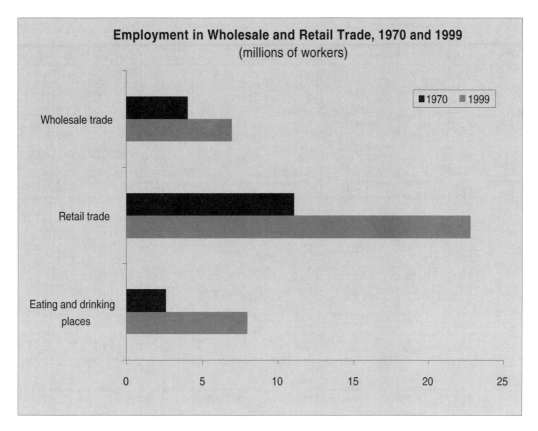

Employment in Wholesale and Retail Trade, 1970 and 1999
(millions of workers)

- The 1970 to 1999 time period saw employment in retail trade more than double and employment in wholesale grow by 73 percent. In 1999 employment in retail trade increased by 2.2 percent to 22.8 million. Employment in wholesale trade grew by 1.8 percent to 6.9 million. Fully a third of the increase in retail in 1999 came from eating and drinking establishments, reflecting a long-standing trend of much more rapid growth in this sector.

- Average weekly earnings of nonsupervisory workers in retail trade averaged $263.32 in 1999, up 3.9 percent from 1998, reflecting a 3.6 percent increase in hourly wages. Low weekly earnings in this industry reflect both low hourly wages and a short average workweek.

- Average weekly earnings of nonsupervisory workers in wholesale trade grew to $558.41, reflecting a 3.6 percent increase in average hourly earnings.

- The value of retail sales increased by 9.1 percent in 1999. Durable goods sales increased by more than 10 percent, with particularly strong growth for automotive dealers. Sales of nondurable goods increased by 8.1 percent. Though most nondurable goods stores recorded larger increases, food stores, with over 25 percent of the nondurable total, only grew by 5.3 percent in 1999. This was the smallest increase in retail sales registered by a category of nondurable goods store. Drug and proprietary stores registered the largest increase with retail sales of 13 percent.

- Beginning in 1999, total retail sales as reported by the Census Bureau included e-commerce sales of goods but not services. Although such sales are a small segment of total retail sales, they have increased over the past year with e-commerce accounting for 0.78 percent of total retail sales in the third quarter of 2000, compared with 0.63 percent in the fourth quarter of 1999.

Table 19-1. Retail and Wholesale Trade—Employment

(Total payroll employment; thousands, seasonally adjusted.)

Year and month	Wholesale trade			Retail trade						Nonsupervisory workers	
	Total	Durable goods	Nondurable goods	Total	General merchandise stores	Food stores	Auto dealers and service stations	Apparel and accessory stores	Eating and drinking places	Wholesale trade	Retail trade
1970	4 006	...	...	11 034	...	1 731	1 617	761	2 575	3 340	10 034
1971	4 014	...	...	11 338	...	1 752	1 642	779	2 700	3 327	10 288
1972	4 127	2 336	1 791	11 822	2 149	1 805	1 723	784	2 860	3 418	10 717
1973	4 291	2 457	1 835	12 315	2 229	1 856	1 778	795	3 054	3 560	11 155
1974	4 447	2 578	1 869	12 539	2 210	1 948	1 666	811	3 231	3 683	11 316
1975	4 430	2 539	1 891	12 630	2 113	2 007	1 677	806	3 380	3 650	11 373
1976	4 562	2 615	1 946	13 193	2 155	2 039	1 744	842	3 656	3 759	11 890
1977	4 723	2 732	1 991	13 792	2 204	2 106	1 801	870	3 949	3 892	12 424
1978	4 985	2 917	2 068	14 556	2 308	2 199	1 861	909	4 277	4 109	13 110
1979	5 221	3 098	2 123	14 972	2 287	2 297	1 812	949	4 513	4 290	13 458
1980	5 292	3 139	2 153	15 018	2 245	2 384	1 689	957	4 626	4 328	13 484
1981	5 375	3 182	2 193	15 171	2 230	2 448	1 653	968	4 749	4 375	13 582
1982	5 295	3 107	2 188	15 158	2 184	2 477	1 632	942	4 829	4 261	13 594
1983	5 283	3 087	2 197	15 587	2 165	2 556	1 674	963	5 038	4 239	13 989
1984	5 568	3 291	2 277	16 512	2 267	2 636	1 798	1 008	5 381	4 466	14 736
1985	5 727	3 402	2 325	17 315	2 323	2 774	1 889	1 039	5 699	4 607	15 421
1986	5 761	3 395	2 365	17 880	2 365	2 896	1 941	1 075	5 902	4 623	15 925
1987	5 848	3 437	2 411	18 422	2 411	2 958	2 001	1 123	6 086	4 685	16 378
1988	6 030	3 564	2 466	19 023	2 472	3 074	2 071	1 165	6 258	4 858	16 869
1989	6 187	3 653	2 534	19 475	2 544	3 164	2 092	1 197	6 402	4 981	17 262
1990	6 173	3 614	2 559	19 601	2 540	3 215	2 063	1 183	6 509	4 959	17 358
1991	6 081	3 531	2 550	19 284	2 453	3 204	1 984	1 151	6 476	4 872	17 006
1992	5 997	3 446	2 552	19 356	2 451	3 180	1 966	1 131	6 609	4 817	17 048
1993	5 981	3 433	2 549	19 773	2 488	3 224	2 014	1 144	6 821	4 823	17 428
1994	6 162	3 559	2 604	20 507	2 583	3 291	2 116	1 144	7 078	4 972	18 056
1995	6 378	3 715	2 663	21 187	2 681	3 366	2 190	1 125	7 354	5 163	18 639
1996	6 482	3 805	2 677	21 597	2 702	3 436	2 267	1 098	7 517	5 238	19 002
1997	6 648	3 927	2 721	21 966	2 701	3 478	2 311	1 109	7 646	5 355	19 337
1998	6 800	4 043	2 757	22 295	2 730	3 484	2 332	1 141	7 768	5 449	19 592
1999	6 924	4 120	2 804	22 788	2 771	3 495	2 369	1 174	7 940	5 538	20 046
1996											
January	6 420	3 757	2 663	21 345	2 675	3 404	2 226	1 099	7 441	5 193	18 753
February	6 423	3 763	2 660	21 398	2 685	3 407	2 234	1 099	7 455	5 194	18 821
March	6 431	3 771	2 660	21 441	2 689	3 410	2 241	1 099	7 474	5 201	18 869
April	6 440	3 780	2 660	21 448	2 678	3 410	2 249	1 094	7 483	5 206	18 880
May	6 456	3 791	2 665	21 532	2 708	3 424	2 258	1 097	7 495	5 217	18 948
June	6 474	3 803	2 671	21 572	2 710	3 431	2 269	1 098	7 501	5 231	18 977
July	6 476	3 808	2 668	21 625	2 710	3 439	2 278	1 099	7 524	5 232	19 028
August	6 500	3 816	2 684	21 658	2 704	3 444	2 282	1 096	7 539	5 250	19 051
September	6 518	3 829	2 689	21 687	2 705	3 451	2 286	1 097	7 538	5 267	19 083
October	6 542	3 840	2 702	21 774	2 717	3 459	2 290	1 097	7 582	5 286	19 179
November	6 551	3 850	2 701	21 806	2 712	3 465	2 294	1 102	7 586	5 295	19 190
December	6 557	3 859	2 698	21 861	2 719	3 469	2 297	1 101	7 596	5 295	19 224
1997											
January	6 565	3 866	2 699	21 842	2 688	3 471	2 299	1 099	7 609	5 303	19 232
February	6 582	3 880	2 702	21 833	2 674	3 472	2 301	1 096	7 616	5 314	19 232
March	6 600	3 893	2 707	21 892	2 698	3 479	2 305	1 098	7 626	5 332	19 276
April	6 613	3 904	2 709	21 905	2 698	3 475	2 306	1 100	7 631	5 332	19 288
May	6 624	3 914	2 710	21 911	2 692	3 476	2 307	1 100	7 632	5 340	19 297
June	6 636	3 922	2 714	21 937	2 697	3 479	2 306	1 102	7 641	5 348	19 310
July	6 656	3 936	2 720	21 938	2 699	3 481	2 309	1 103	7 628	5 361	19 310
August	6 670	3 945	2 725	21 990	2 704	3 479	2 315	1 110	7 654	5 370	19 353
September	6 682	3 951	2 731	22 022	2 701	3 478	2 318	1 115	7 671	5 375	19 387
October	6 706	3 961	2 745	22 061	2 711	3 482	2 320	1 123	7 672	5 387	19 427
November	6 715	3 971	2 744	22 119	2 722	3 481	2 322	1 126	7 690	5 393	19 463
December	6 726	3 980	2 746	22 146	2 735	3 476	2 322	1 131	7 690	5 405	19 479
1998											
January	6 755	3 992	2 763	22 145	2 711	3 481	2 322	1 138	7 704	5 422	19 478
February	6 761	4 004	2 757	22 140	2 708	3 477	2 319	1 135	7 716	5 424	19 480
March	6 774	4 014	2 760	22 154	2 705	3 477	2 321	1 135	7 721	5 429	19 478
April	6 786	4 024	2 762	22 163	2 709	3 473	2 321	1 141	7 719	5 437	19 486
May	6 797	4 035	2 762	22 240	2 723	3 480	2 328	1 142	7 745	5 445	19 566
June	6 799	4 047	2 752	22 261	2 724	3 479	2 332	1 143	7 749	5 447	19 566
July	6 798	4 054	2 744	22 306	2 729	3 490	2 334	1 143	7 762	5 437	19 605
August	6 809	4 060	2 749	22 345	2 737	3 485	2 334	1 144	7 782	5 453	19 625
September	6 821	4 068	2 753	22 391	2 752	3 490	2 338	1 145	7 797	5 461	19 665
October	6 821	4 068	2 753	22 414	2 756	3 489	2 342	1 135	7 815	5 464	19 681
November	6 833	4 070	2 763	22 466	2 761	3 492	2 344	1 142	7 836	5 472	19 718
December	6 850	4 079	2 771	22 509	2 760	3 492	2 348	1 143	7 858	5 495	19 753
1999											
January	6 847	4 071	2 776	22 560	2 771	3 485	2 352	1 148	7 871	5 481	19 810
February	6 870	4 089	2 781	22 662	2 778	3 495	2 361	1 161	7 904	5 508	19 917
March	6 877	4 091	2 786	22 702	2 790	3 497	2 361	1 161	7 909	5 508	19 954
April	6 892	4 097	2 795	22 744	2 793	3 497	2 363	1 159	7 930	5 518	20 007
May	6 898	4 102	2 796	22 763	2 781	3 496	2 364	1 168	7 932	5 520	20 030
June	6 905	4 102	2 803	22 810	2 777	3 494	2 365	1 172	7 965	5 529	20 072
July	6 927	4 118	2 809	22 833	2 774	3 495	2 368	1 184	7 958	5 540	20 096
August	6 946	4 132	2 814	22 841	2 768	3 498	2 369	1 181	7 958	5 551	20 107
September	6 962	4 143	2 819	22 844	2 757	3 495	2 372	1 183	7 956	5 558	20 104
October	6 973	4 155	2 818	22 863	2 752	3 496	2 377	1 186	7 950	5 569	20 124
November	6 989	4 165	2 824	22 893	2 752	3 498	2 380	1 190	7 966	5 580	20 140
December	7 002	4 173	2 829	22 936	2 766	3 501	2 386	1 182	7 986	5 593	20 193

Table 19-2. Retail and Wholesale Trade—Hours and Earnings

(Nonsupervisory workers.)

Year and month	Average weekly hours (seasonally adjusted)		Aggregate weekly hours index (1982=100, seasonally adjusted)		Average earnings (dollars, not seasonally adjusted)								
					Hourly							Weekly	
	Wholesale trade	Retail trade	Wholesale trade	Retail trade	Wholesale trade	Retail trade	General merchandise stores	Food stores	Auto dealer and service stations	Apparel and accessory stores	Eating and drinking places	Wholesale trade	Retail trade
1970	39.9	33.8	81.7	83.4	3.43	2.44	. . .	2.71	. . .	2.26	1.86	136.86	82.47
1971	39.4	33.7	80.4	85.3	3.64	2.60	. . .	2.94	. . .	2.36	1.96	143.42	87.62
1972	39.4	33.4	82.5	88.2	3.85	2.75	2.62	3.18	3.18	2.52	2.07	151.69	91.85
1973	39.2	33.1	85.6	90.9	4.07	2.91	2.76	3.38	3.38	2.63	2.18	159.54	96.32
1974	38.8	32.7	87.6	91.0	4.38	3.14	2.98	3.74	3.64	2.83	2.37	169.94	102.68
1975	38.6	32.4	86.4	90.6	4.72	3.36	3.21	4.08	3.84	3.03	2.55	182.19	108.86
1976	38.7	32.1	89.1	93.9	5.02	3.57	3.41	4.41	4.14	3.26	2.69	194.27	114.60
1977	38.8	31.6	92.5	96.5	5.39	3.85	3.71	4.77	4.49	3.45	2.93	209.13	121.66
1978	38.8	31.0	97.7	100.0	5.88	4.20	4.05	5.23	4.93	3.72	3.22	228.14	130.20
1979	38.8	30.6	102.0	101.5	6.39	4.53	4.38	5.67	5.31	4.01	3.45	247.93	138.62
1980	38.4	30.2	101.9	100.1	6.95	4.88	4.77	6.24	5.66	4.30	3.69	266.88	147.38
1981	38.5	30.1	103.3	100.6	7.55	5.25	5.15	6.85	6.07	4.65	3.95	290.68	158.03
1982	38.3	29.9	100.0	100.0	8.08	5.48	5.39	7.22	6.31	4.85	4.09	309.46	163.85
1983	38.5	29.8	99.9	102.7	8.54	5.74	5.61	7.51	6.76	5.02	4.27	328.79	171.05
1984	38.5	29.8	105.3	108.2	8.88	5.85	5.64	7.64	7.13	5.11	4.26	341.88	174.33
1985	38.4	29.4	108.4	111.7	9.15	5.94	5.92	7.35	7.41	5.25	4.33	351.36	174.64
1986	38.3	29.2	108.5	114.3	9.34	6.03	6.30	7.06	7.68	5.37	4.35	357.72	176.08
1987	38.1	29.2	109.4	117.9	9.59	6.12	6.47	6.95	7.81	5.56	4.42	365.38	178.70
1988	38.1	29.1	113.3	121.0	9.98	6.31	6.45	7.01	8.24	5.79	4.57	380.24	183.62
1989	38.0	28.9	116.1	122.9	10.39	6.53	6.64	7.15	8.57	6.01	4.75	394.82	188.72
1990	38.1	28.8	115.7	123.0	10.79	6.75	6.83	7.31	8.92	6.25	4.97	411.10	194.40
1991	38.1	28.6	113.7	119.5	11.15	6.94	7.04	7.33	9.07	6.60	5.18	424.82	198.48
1992	38.2	28.8	112.8	120.6	11.39	7.12	7.18	7.56	9.34	6.88	5.29	435.10	205.06
1993	38.2	28.8	112.8	123.4	11.74	7.29	7.29	7.80	9.66	7.01	5.35	448.47	209.95
1994	38.4	28.9	116.9	128.6	12.06	7.49	7.44	7.94	10.09	7.17	5.47	463.10	216.46
1995	38.3	28.8	121.1	132.2	12.43	7.69	7.53	8.15	10.41	7.47	5.59	476.07	221.47
1996	38.3	28.8	122.9	134.6	12.87	7.99	7.86	8.40	10.90	7.74	5.79	492.92	230.11
1997	38.4	28.9	126.1	137.7	13.45	8.33	8.16	8.68	11.41	8.07	6.06	516.48	240.74
1998	38.3	29.0	127.9	140.0	14.07	8.74	8.59	9.04	12.08	8.48	6.35	538.88	253.46
1999	38.3	29.0	129.9	143.1	14.58	9.08	8.96	9.27	12.63	8.86	6.62	558.41	263.32
1996													
January	38.0	28.5	120.9	131.5	12.66	7.89	7.73	8.38	10.38	7.73	5.69	476.02	216.98
February	38.2	28.8	121.6	133.4	12.68	7.87	7.74	8.38	10.53	7.73	5.69	481.84	221.93
March	38.3	28.9	122.1	134.2	12.69	7.90	7.81	8.38	10.77	7.71	5.69	483.49	225.15
April	38.2	28.7	121.9	133.3	12.78	7.92	7.91	8.40	10.80	7.74	5.70	486.92	224.93
May	38.3	28.8	122.5	134.3	12.75	7.92	7.88	8.37	10.88	7.73	5.72	487.05	227.30
June	38.4	28.8	123.1	134.5	12.88	7.98	7.89	8.30	11.20	7.77	5.76	499.74	234.61
July	38.2	28.7	122.5	134.4	12.83	7.93	7.86	8.28	10.89	7.66	5.76	488.82	233.14
August	38.3	28.8	123.2	135.0	12.85	7.95	7.87	8.31	10.97	7.62	5.78	493.44	234.53
September	38.4	28.9	124.0	135.7	13.04	8.06	7.93	8.44	11.08	7.77	5.82	503.34	234.55
October	38.3	28.8	124.1	135.9	12.95	8.11	7.93	8.51	11.03	7.80	5.92	495.99	232.76
November	38.3	28.9	124.3	136.5	13.07	8.13	7.86	8.53	11.13	7.78	5.92	500.58	232.52
December	38.4	28.9	124.6	136.7	13.21	8.15	7.92	8.52	11.11	7.77	5.97	511.23	238.80
1997													
January	38.2	28.9	124.2	136.8	13.19	8.24	7.97	8.61	11.00	7.96	5.95	499.90	229.90
February	38.4	28.9	125.1	136.8	13.27	8.24	8.07	8.61	11.22	7.95	5.93	510.90	236.49
March	38.4	29.0	125.5	137.6	13.29	8.26	8.15	8.65	11.33	7.97	5.95	511.67	237.06
April	38.4	28.9	125.5	137.2	13.35	8.27	8.12	8.71	11.35	8.01	5.96	511.31	236.52
May	38.5	28.9	126.0	137.2	13.34	8.27	8.08	8.66	11.39	8.09	5.99	513.59	238.18
June	38.4	28.8	125.9	136.9	13.38	8.27	8.12	8.61	11.44	8.09	5.98	517.81	243.14
July	38.4	28.9	126.2	137.3	13.39	8.26	8.10	8.61	11.44	7.98	5.98	512.84	244.50
August	38.4	29.0	126.4	138.1	13.50	8.29	8.10	8.59	11.55	7.95	6.04	519.75	246.21
September	38.4	28.9	126.5	137.9	13.55	8.44	8.25	8.75	11.59	8.17	6.18	520.32	244.76
October	38.4	29.0	126.8	138.6	13.59	8.46	8.30	8.78	11.47	8.20	6.22	521.86	243.65
November	38.5	29.0	127.3	138.9	13.79	8.50	8.27	8.79	11.65	8.21	6.21	533.67	244.80
December	38.3	28.9	126.9	138.5	13.76	8.50	8.29	8.81	11.52	8.18	6.28	528.38	248.20
1998													
January	38.4	29.0	127.6	139.0	13.81	8.61	8.43	8.93	11.56	8.30	6.24	526.16	241.94
February	38.4	29.0	127.7	139.0	13.89	8.60	8.44	8.93	11.71	8.39	6.23	534.77	246.82
March	38.3	29.0	127.4	139.0	13.90	8.64	8.58	8.97	11.82	8.41	6.26	533.76	247.97
April	38.3	29.0	127.6	139.1	13.93	8.69	8.72	8.97	12.02	8.42	6.29	527.95	249.40
May	38.4	29.1	128.2	140.1	14.00	8.69	8.66	9.01	12.13	8.49	6.31	534.80	252.01
June	38.3	29.0	127.9	139.6	13.95	8.68	8.58	8.95	12.20	8.50	6.33	534.29	254.32
July	38.3	29.1	127.6	140.4	14.07	8.69	8.53	8.96	12.23	8.41	6.33	536.07	258.96
August	38.4	29.0	128.3	140.1	14.19	8.72	8.60	8.99	12.30	8.39	6.37	549.15	260.73
September	38.2	29.1	127.9	140.8	14.17	8.88	8.72	9.39	12.22	8.58	6.43	538.46	258.41
October	38.3	29.1	128.3	140.9	14.23	8.84	8.61	9.14	12.19	8.61	6.46	543.59	255.48
November	38.4	29.1	128.8	141.2	14.36	8.86	8.55	9.16	12.29	8.61	6.45	557.17	256.05
December	38.3	29.0	129.0	141.0	14.32	8.88	8.62	9.12	12.26	8.61	6.53	548.46	259.30
1999													
January	38.3	29.0	128.7	141.4	14.42	9.00	8.72	9.25	12.29	8.75	6.51	545.08	252.90
February	38.3	29.2	129.3	143.1	14.44	8.98	8.77	9.25	12.43	8.74	6.52	548.72	256.83
March	38.2	29.0	129.0	142.4	14.37	8.99	8.83	9.26	12.43	8.73	6.52	543.19	257.11
April	38.4	29.1	129.9	143.3	14.49	9.03	8.94	9.28	12.60	8.79	6.55	552.07	259.16
May	38.3	29.0	129.6	142.9	14.58	9.03	8.88	9.26	12.66	8.84	6.57	562.79	262.77
June	38.3	29.1	129.8	143.7	14.45	9.02	8.95	9.26	12.64	8.90	6.58	553.44	265.19
July	38.4	29.1	130.4	143.9	14.57	9.03	8.90	9.22	12.76	8.76	6.58	556.57	270.00
August	38.3	29.0	130.3	143.5	14.65	9.05	8.99	9.19	12.72	8.78	6.62	565.49	270.60
September	38.4	28.8	130.8	142.5	14.68	9.19	9.14	9.36	12.77	8.98	6.68	560.78	264.67
October	38.6	29.0	131.8	143.6	14.74	9.21	9.09	9.30	12.74	9.02	6.71	567.49	266.17
November	38.4	29.0	131.3	143.7	14.76	9.22	9.07	9.29	12.73	9.02	6.74	566.78	264.61
December	38.5	29.1	132.0	144.6	14.85	9.26	9.18	9.28	12.73	8.99	6.81	570.24	271.32

Table 19-3. Retail Sales

(All retail stores; millions of dollars, not seasonally adjusted.)

Year and month	Total	Durable goods stores				Nondurable goods stores							
		Total	Building materials group [1]	Automotive group	Furniture group	Total	General merchandise group stores	Food stores	Gasoline service stations	Apparel and accessory stores	Eating and drinking places	Drug and proprietary stores	Liquor stores
1970	374 989	114 586	18 080	65 241	17 043	260 403	49 163	89 990	28 903	22 095	30 476	14 567	8 412
1971	413 969	135 113	20 924	80 718	18 183	278 856	54 365	94 002	30 620	24 178	32 321	15 143	9 294
1972	458 267	155 937	24 123	92 335	21 199	302 330	59 656	100 589	33 072	26 367	35 738	16 139	9 814
1973	511 570	176 817	27 466	104 893	24 244	334 753	65 825	111 817	36 942	29 109	40 290	17 190	10 288
1974	541 686	172 497	27 347	97 551	25 982	369 189	69 540	126 312	43 054	30 077	44 606	18 595	11 087
1975	587 704	185 479	27 299	107 348	27 046	402 225	73 759	138 665	47 603	32 398	51 067	19 995	11 896
1976	655 859	219 908	33 259	130 169	30 300	435 951	79 500	148 218	52 037	34 706	57 331	21 710	12 442
1977	722 109	249 078	38 913	150 129	33 308	473 031	87 824	158 444	56 638	37 165	63 370	23 381	13 031
1978	804 019	280 899	45 170	168 065	36 832	523 120	97 215	175 425	59 889	42 649	71 828	25 607	13 630
1979	896 561	306 561	51 016	178 641	42 417	590 000	103 817	197 985	73 521	46 070	82 110	28 455	15 194
1980	956 921	298 618	50 794	164 149	44 238	658 303	108 955	220 224	94 093	49 296	90 058	30 951	16 882
1981	1 038 163	324 211	52 230	181 903	46 900	713 952	120 534	236 188	103 072	53 998	98 118	33 999	17 702
1982	1 068 747	335 587	50 994	192 440	46 761	733 160	124 624	246 122	97 440	55 570	104 593	36 440	18 146
1983	1 170 163	390 849	58 739	229 979	54 691	779 314	135 959	256 018	102 927	60 192	113 281	40 591	19 121
1984	1 286 914	454 481	67 077	273 320	61 432	832 433	150 283	271 909	107 565	64 341	121 321	44 011	18 273
1985	1 375 027	498 125	71 196	303 199	68 287	876 902	158 636	285 062	113 341	70 195	127 949	46 994	19 532
1986	1 449 636	540 688	77 104	326 138	75 714	908 948	169 397	297 019	102 093	75 626	139 415	50 546	19 929
1987	1 541 299	575 863	83 454	342 896	78 072	965 436	181 970	309 461	104 769	79 322	153 461	54 142	19 826
1988	1 656 202	629 154	91 056	372 570	85 390	1 027 048	192 521	325 493	110 341	85 307	167 993	57 842	19 638
1989	1 758 971	657 154	92 379	386 011	91 301	1 101 817	206 306	347 045	122 882	92 341	177 829	63 343	20 099
1990	1 844 611	668 835	94 640	387 605	91 545	1 175 776	215 514	368 333	138 504	95 819	190 149	70 558	21 722
1991	1 855 937	649 974	91 496	372 647	91 676	1 205 963	226 730	374 523	137 295	97 441	194 424	75 540	22 454
1992	1 951 589	703 604	100 838	406 935	96 947	1 247 985	246 420	377 099	136 950	104 212	200 164	77 788	21 698
1993	2 082 112	781 921	110 704	459 302	105 507	1 300 191	264 049	382 709	141 697	107 403	212 778	79 704	21 551
1994	2 248 198	886 653	125 195	525 305	119 077	1 361 545	282 088	394 216	148 867	110 355	222 075	81 991	22 115
1995	2 359 013	947 347	130 616	562 719	128 283	1 411 666	297 578	402 479	157 245	111 404	229 841	85 837	22 022
1996	2 502 365	1 018 994	140 366	608 533	134 952	1 483 371	312 729	414 325	168 750	115 338	238 918	91 809	23 173
1997	2 610 562	1 063 229	148 397	632 511	140 173	1 547 333	329 394	423 725	172 081	119 605	254 124	98 822	24 092
1998	2 745 593	1 136 387	162 570	670 129	150 525	1 609 206	349 592	435 383	163 199	126 980	266 410	108 340	25 510
1999	2 994 929	1 254 996	179 735	749 030	161 453	1 739 933	378 925	458 269	180 973	135 087	285 371	120 733	28 034
1996													
January	176 968	70 493	8 387	43 418	10 063	106 475	18 662	32 881	12 456	6 600	17 400	7 133	1 680
February	184 189	75 386	8 569	48 045	9 794	108 803	20 579	31 887	12 203	7 497	18 172	7 189	1 652
March	203 811	84 718	10 194	54 155	10 789	119 093	23 344	34 226	13 518	8 971	19 958	7 509	1 837
April	203 176	85 289	12 480	52 507	10 328	117 887	23 482	33 283	13 998	9 153	19 536	7 426	1 799
May	218 545	92 686	13 948	56 506	10 782	125 859	25 911	35 549	15 258	9 562	20 823	7 755	1 958
June	209 430	88 379	13 509	53 363	10 661	121 051	24 881	34 532	14 840	9 065	20 379	7 264	1 958
July	209 582	88 325	13 292	53 403	10 794	121 257	23 721	35 492	14 839	8 760	20 706	7 484	2 034
August	217 191	89 566	12 874	53 800	11 450	127 625	26 417	35 928	15 034	10 559	21 533	7 629	2 064
September	200 631	82 658	12 183	49 647	10 851	117 973	23 805	33 376	13 885	9 199	19 569	7 207	1 782
October	213 035	87 075	12 849	52 472	11 319	125 960	25 981	34 762	14 488	9 716	20 447	7 811	1 862
November	215 495	82 612	11 329	46 556	12 484	132 883	31 055	35 163	14 007	10 936	20 064	7 700	1 994
December	250 312	91 807	10 752	44 661	15 637	158 505	44 891	37 246	14 224	15 320	20 331	9 702	2 553
1997													
January	191 130	75 879	9 153	46 747	10 411	115 251	20 768	34 473	13 732	7 091	19 127	7 889	1 710
February	188 463	77 233	9 185	48 483	9 923	111 230	21 315	31 733	12 863	7 354	18 914	7 614	1 624
March	215 391	88 631	11 448	55 915	10 937	126 760	25 417	35 754	14 240	9 559	21 164	8 328	1 856
April	210 088	88 507	13 346	54 404	10 583	121 581	24 196	33 842	14 163	8 793	20 888	7 884	1 820
May	224 372	93 019	14 636	56 111	11 125	131 353	27 193	36 737	14 912	9 831	22 430	8 299	2 064
June	217 421	91 864	14 035	55 655	10 875	125 557	26 059	34 674	14 786	9 243	21 633	7 967	2 004
July	221 551	93 215	13 944	56 614	11 318	128 336	25 523	36 552	15 077	9 338	22 431	8 064	2 099
August	225 563	92 846	12 925	56 244	11 855	132 717	27 810	36 420	15 348	11 030	23 049	7 997	2 081
September	212 529	88 535	13 241	53 017	11 319	123 994	24 578	34 301	14 547	9 529	21 103	7 930	1 892
October	221 614	89 905	13 383	53 681	11 683	131 709	27 564	35 703	14 827	10 163	21 763	8 310	2 049
November	219 590	84 150	11 514	46 862	13 020	135 440	32 658	35 389	13 685	11 353	20 375	8 148	2 079
December	262 850	99 445	11 551	48 778	17 124	163 405	46 313	38 147	13 901	16 321	21 247	10 392	2 814
1998													
January	198 262	79 975	9 853	48 085	11 599	118 287	21 861	34 955	12 945	7 630	20 044	8 530	1 839
February	194 928	80 370	9 833	49 227	10 911	114 558	22 750	32 075	11 982	7 924	19 707	8 190	1 761
March	220 258	93 177	12 456	58 165	11 776	127 081	25 768	35 014	13 088	9 549	21 898	8 715	1 886
April	224 912	95 340	14 563	58 424	11 198	129 572	27 278	35 538	13 394	10 389	21 779	8 858	1 956
May	236 260	100 165	15 824	60 661	11 664	136 095	29 062	37 340	14 366	10 414	23 397	8 971	2 135
June	234 703	103 416	15 747	63 375	11 868	131 287	27 477	35 961	14 412	9 846	22 725	8 785	2 060
July	232 508	97 987	15 194	58 258	12 254	134 521	27 055	38 039	14 820	10 129	23 302	8 893	2 215
August	231 665	95 667	14 083	56 240	12 640	135 998	28 740	37 081	14 393	11 432	23 444	8 878	2 129
September	222 124	93 241	14 306	55 143	12 076	128 883	26 344	35 711	13 505	9 787	21 955	8 719	2 048
October	235 049	97 119	14 631	57 971	12 468	137 930	29 096	37 126	13 947	10 838	23 360	9 214	2 190
November	233 002	91 508	12 961	51 195	13 800	141 494	34 592	36 145	12 943	11 890	21 724	9 121	2 192
December	281 922	108 422	13 119	53 385	18 271	173 500	49 569	40 398	13 404	17 152	23 075	11 466	3 099
1999													
January	209 566	84 699	10 715	51 229	11 961	124 867	23 958	36 158	12 624	8 032	21 208	9 365	1 935
February	212 599	89 904	11 455	55 675	11 599	122 695	24 874	33 893	11 924	8 457	21 153	9 199	1 885
March	244 511	105 375	14 272	66 245	12 812	139 136	28 984	37 420	13 700	10 609	23 322	10 113	2 081
April	242 761	103 816	16 505	63 376	12 029	138 945	28 861	36 905	14 633	10 871	23 747	9 824	2 208
May	254 557	109 323	17 613	66 422	12 460	145 234	31 044	38 971	15 185	11 231	24 789	9 995	2 334
June	252 350	110 776	17 225	67 882	12 759	141 574	29 982	37 714	15 289	10 584	24 257	9 914	2 274
July	254 576	109 354	16 555	67 004	13 107	145 222	29 432	39 982	16 325	10 783	25 307	9 820	2 485
August	256 859	110 628	15 749	68 164	13 501	146 231	30 652	38 254	16 622	12 023	24 861	9 785	2 280
September	245 799	104 113	15 275	63 300	13 247	141 686	29 071	37 972	15 938	10 754	23 445	9 679	2 268
October	250 793	102 741	15 288	61 296	13 240	148 052	31 148	38 525	16 339	11 233	25 067	10 050	2 369
November	257 707	104 063	14 942	58 943	14 919	153 644	36 590	38 256	15 657	12 397	23 421	10 128	2 428
December	312 851	120 204	14 141	59 494	19 819	192 647	54 329	44 219	16 737	18 113	24 794	12 861	3 487

1. Includes building materials; hardware; plants and garden supplies; and manufactured (mobile) homes.

Table 19-3. Retail Sales—Continued

(All retail stores; millions of dollars, not seasonally adjusted.)

Year and month	Total	Durable goods stores										Nondurable goods stores, total
		Total	Building materials group[1]			Automotive group			Furniture group			
			Total	Building materials and supply stores	Hardware stores	Total	Motor vehicle and miscellaneous automotive dealers	Auto and home supply stores	Total	Furniture and home furnishings	Household appliances and electronics	
1970	374 989	114 586	18 080	11 343	2 979	65 241	59 243	5 998	17 043	10 442	5 571	260 403
1971	413 969	135 113	20 924	13 070	3 230	80 718	73 747	6 971	18 183	11 439	5 634	278 856
1972	458 267	155 937	24 123	15 112	3 620	92 335	84 477	7 858	21 199	13 480	6 274	302 330
1973	511 570	176 817	27 466	17 314	4 187	104 893	96 121	8 772	24 244	15 430	7 210	334 753
1974	541 686	172 497	27 347	17 874	4 604	97 551	88 310	9 241	25 982	18 544	7 427	369 189
1975	587 704	185 479	27 299	17 947	5 165	107 348	97 275	10 073	27 046	16 460	8 218	402 225
1976	655 859	219 908	33 259	22 484	5 591	130 169	119 063	11 116	30 300	18 383	9 129	435 951
1977	722 109	249 078	38 913	27 123	6 139	150 129	150 129	13 095	33 308	20 384	10 046	473 031
1978	804 019	280 899	45 170	31 910	6 652	168 065	168 065	14 165	36 832	22 538	10 780	523 120
1979	896 561	306 561	51 016	36 245	7 937	178 641	152 458	16 183	42 417	25 642	12 936	590 000
1980	956 921	298 618	50 794	34 997	8 349	164 149	146 190	17 959	44 238	26 332	14 010	658 303
1981	1 038 163	324 211	52 230	35 738	8 475	181 903	162 271	19 632	46 900	27 499	15 402	713 952
1982	1 068 747	335 587	50 994	35 144	8 727	192 440	172 359	20 081	46 761	27 093	15 774	733 160
1983	1 170 163	390 849	58 739	41 256	9 140	229 979	207 871	22 108	54 691	31 296	19 280	779 314
1984	1 286 914	454 481	67 077	47 127	10 354	273 320	250 193	23 127	61 432	35 587	21 474	832 433
1985	1 375 027	498 125	71 196	50 766	10 471	303 199	277 995	25 204	68 287	38 270	25 147	876 902
1986	1 449 636	540 688	77 104	56 510	10 734	326 138	301 083	25 055	75 714	43 030	27 037	908 948
1987	1 541 299	575 863	83 454	61 302	11 036	342 896	316 274	26 622	78 072	44 477	27 121	965 436
1988	1 656 202	629 154	91 056	66 796	11 894	372 570	343 217	29 353	85 390	47 617	30 608	1 027 048
1989	1 758 971	657 154	92 379	67 457	12 637	386 011	356 485	29 526	91 301	51 202	32 666	1 101 817
1990	1 844 611	668 835	94 640	70 341	12 524	387 605	356 764	30 841	91 545	50 524	33 035	1 175 776
1991	1 855 937	649 974	91 496	68 196	12 148	372 647	343 018	29 629	91 676	49 469	33 569	1 205 963
1992	1 951 589	703 604	100 838	75 358	12 729	406 935	377 118	29 817	96 947	52 348	35 802	1 247 985
1993	2 082 112	781 921	110 704	83 144	13 060	459 302	428 519	30 783	105 507	54 819	41 289	1 300 191
1994	2 248 198	886 653	125 195	94 572	13 840	525 305	492 380	32 925	119 077	59 174	49 508	1 361 545
1995	2 359 013	947 347	130 616	98 141	13 773	562 719	528 664	34 055	128 283	61 046	56 191	1 411 666
1996	2 502 365	1 018 994	140 366	105 367	13 963	608 533	572 856	35 677	134 952	64 247	59 274	1 483 371
1997	2 610 562	1 063 229	148 397	112 199	14 006	632 511	596 115	36 396	140 173	68 019	60 699	1 547 333
1998	2 745 593	1 136 387	162 570	123 455	14 788	670 129	631 977	38 152	150 525	72 348	65 904	1 609 206
1999	2 994 929	1 254 996	179 735	138 379	15 725	749 030	708 971	40 059	161 453	77 283	71 561	1 739 933
1996												
January	201 391	81 369	10 951	8 218	1 167	48 972	46 047	2 925	10 850	5 057	4 842	120 022
February	203 647	82 990	10 991	8 281	1 176	50 542	47 608	2 934	10 895	5 166	4 771	120 657
March	205 534	84 213	11 024	8 392	1 133	50 885	47 945	2 940	11 254	5 324	4 956	121 321
April	206 506	83 864	11 473	8 544	1 199	49 877	46 913	2 964	11 295	5 350	4 965	122 642
May	207 519	84 726	11 522	8 743	1 170	50 377	47 425	2 952	11 296	5 329	4 988	122 793
June	207 920	85 003	12 004	8 976	1 164	50 421	47 459	2 962	11 268	5 345	4 946	122 917
July	208 293	85 098	11 954	8 955	1 155	50 537	47 567	2 970	11 213	5 408	4 839	123 195
August	207 754	84 264	11 890	8 937	1 136	49 880	46 923	2 957	11 276	5 371	4 958	123 490
September	210 545	86 240	11 880	8 897	1 122	51 626	48 640	2 986	11 511	5 420	5 152	124 305
October	212 290	86 614	11 978	8 918	1 161	51 801	48 782	3 019	11 418	5 455	5 049	125 676
November	212 197	85 954	12 004	9 003	1 171	51 133	48 146	2 987	11 300	5 443	4 923	126 243
December	212 907	85 852	11 997	8 927	1 192	51 035	48 036	2 999	11 243	5 411	4 894	127 055
1997												
January	214 362	86 774	12 009	8 957	1 194	52 080	49 067	3 013	11 143	5 471	4 753	127 588
February	216 017	88 195	12 273	9 221	1 170	52 902	49 910	2 992	11 375	5 505	4 931	127 822
March	216 289	88 320	12 402	9 390	1 132	52 830	49 798	3 032	11 429	5 524	4 957	127 969
April	215 573	87 688	12 255	9 321	1 140	52 183	49 193	2 990	11 542	5 576	5 044	127 885
May	212 634	85 152	12 200	9 389	1 143	50 200	47 232	2 968	11 571	5 633	5 008	127 482
June	216 262	87 931	12 353	9 275	1 168	52 134	49 085	3 049	11 613	5 641	5 038	128 331
July	218 834	89 284	12 393	9 362	1 191	53 327	50 257	3 070	11 653	5 631	5 093	129 550
August	220 112	90 069	12 384	9 307	1 195	53 935	50 787	3 148	11 833	5 758	5 124	130 043
September	220 354	90 005	12 568	9 454	1 197	53 475	50 424	3 051	11 813	5 718	5 139	130 349
October	219 836	89 580	12 603	9 490	1 208	52 978	49 934	3 044	11 897	5 755	5 154	130 256
November	220 905	90 469	12 551	9 478	1 161	53 598	50 566	3 032	12 033	5 829	5 224	130 436
December	221 753	91 348	12 706	9 607	1 116	54 298	51 270	3 028	12 180	5 928	5 235	130 405
1998												
January	222 108	91 443	13 049	9 795	1 144	53 627	50 637	2 990	12 281	5 925	5 331	130 665
February	222 574	91 185	13 136	9 860	1 179	53 274	50 167	3 107	12 366	5 969	5 384	131 389
March	223 975	92 117	13 110	9 801	1 215	54 278	51 182	3 096	12 310	5 925	5 385	131 858
April	226 183	94 050	13 267	10 034	1 213	56 138	53 000	3 138	12 223	5 952	5 241	132 133
May	227 791	94 334	13 406	10 095	1 216	56 250	53 081	3 169	12 367	5 961	5 378	133 457
June	230 046	96 195	13 441	10 206	1 236	57 495	54 281	3 214	12 462	5 992	5 436	133 851
July	228 231	93 746	13 576	10 370	1 229	54 660	51 437	3 223	12 596	6 054	5 516	134 485
August	228 078	93 384	13 568	10 337	1 256	54 046	50 811	3 235	12 660	5 986	5 631	134 694
September	230 610	95 330	13 680	10 534	1 290	55 985	52 773	3 212	12 589	5 972	5 573	135 280
October	233 751	97 530	13 925	10 614	1 249	57 875	54 625	3 250	12 718	6 078	5 579	136 221
November	235 251	98 112	14 016	10 744	1 257	58 136	54 909	3 227	12 929	6 202	5 714	137 139
December	237 116	99 247	14 301	10 971	1 290	58 994	55 745	3 249	12 966	6 303	5 668	137 869
1999												
January	239 154	99 641	14 593	11 129	1 349	59 091	55 800	3 291	12 842	6 101	5 706	139 513
February	241 580	101 280	15 278	11 499	1 345	59 792	56 494	3 298	13 032	6 271	5 700	140 300
March	242 316	101 367	14 680	11 299	1 318	60 214	56 904	3 310	13 133	6 307	5 786	140 949
April	244 556	101 905	15 014	11 432	1 347	60 391	57 027	3 364	13 137	6 298	5 810	142 651
May	247 325	103 821	14 934	11 389	1 321	62 198	58 874	3 324	13 285	6 318	5 922	143 504
June	247 995	104 059	14 837	11 407	1 296	62 326	59 027	3 299	13 434	6 408	5 984	143 936
July	250 003	105 383	15 032	11 480	1 301	63 509	60 200	3 309	13 486	6 374	6 056	144 620
August	253 458	107 252	14 996	11 646	1 301	64 926	61 581	3 345	13 637	6 557	6 031	146 206
September	253 910	106 505	14 823	11 430	1 303	64 029	60 681	3 348	13 889	6 703	6 122	147 405
October	255 263	107 081	15 084	11 767	1 290	63 869	60 577	3 292	13 839	6 655	6 135	148 182
November	257 489	108 640	15 670	12 155	1 321	64 823	61 394	3 429	13 819	6 636	6 078	148 849
December	261 628	109 545	15 526	12 185	1 294	65 438	61 975	3 463	14 043	6 709	6 296	152 083

1. Includes building materials; hardware; plants and garden supplies; and manufactured (mobile) homes.

Table 19-3. Retail Sales—Continued

(All retail stores; millions of dollars, seasonally adjusted.)

Year and month	General merchandise group stores			Food stores		Gasoline service stations	Apparel and accessory stores				Eating and drinking places	Drug and proprietary stores	Liquor stores
	Total	Department stores [1]	Variety stores	Total	Grocery stores		Total	Men's and boys' clothing and furnishings	Women's clothing and accessories	Shoe stores			
1970	49 163	36 187	6 082	89 990	82 558	28 903	22 095	4 544	8 239	4 458	30 476	14 567	8 412
1971	54 365	40 472	6 111	94 002	86 419	30 620	24 178	4 903	9 222	4 524	32 321	15 143	9 294
1972	59 656	44 451	6 598	100 589	92 856	33 072	26 367	5 684	9 739	4 884	35 738	16 139	9 814
1973	65 825	49 342	7 207	111 817	103 555	36 942	29 109	6 193	10 732	5 600	40 290	17 190	10 288
1974	69 540	52 059	7 594	126 312	117 182	43 054	30 077	6 190	11 338	5 405	44 606	18 595	11 087
1975	73 759	55 702	7 893	138 665	129 087	47 603	32 398	6 619	12 438	5 751	51 067	19 995	11 896
1976	79 500	61 500	7 101	148 218	137 992	52 037	34 706	6 815	13 426	8 249	57 331	21 710	12 442
1977	87 824	68 856	6 987	158 444	148 116	56 638	37 165	7 042	12 537	7 058	63 370	23 381	13 031
1978	97 215	76 137	7 176	175 425	164 234	59 889	42 649	7 537	15 995	8 305	71 828	25 607	13 630
1979	103 817	81 161	7 770	197 985	185 318	73 521	46 070	7 763	17 030	9 693	82 110	28 455	15 194
1980	108 955	85 464	7 791	220 224	205 630	94 093	49 296	7 664	17 592	10 530	90 058	30 951	16 882
1981	120 534	95 638	8 202	236 188	220 580	103 072	53 998	7 910	19 060	11 821	98 118	33 999	17 702
1982	124 624	99 841	8 211	246 122	230 696	97 440	55 570	7 803	20 017	11 419	104 593	36 440	18 146
1983	135 959	108 637	8 367	256 018	240 402	102 927	60 192	7 958	21 847	11 949	113 281	40 591	19 121
1984	150 283	120 487	8 700	271 909	258 465	107 565	64 341	8 206	23 764	12 306	121 321	44 011	18 273
1985	158 636	126 412	8 459	285 062	269 546	113 341	70 195	8 458	26 149	13 054	127 949	46 994	19 532
1986	169 397	134 486	7 447	297 019	280 833	102 093	75 626	8 646	28 600	13 947	139 415	50 546	19 929
1987	181 970	144 017	7 134	309 461	290 979	104 769	79 322	9 017	29 208	14 594	153 461	54 142	19 826
1988	192 521	151 523	7 458	325 493	307 173	110 341	85 307	9 826	30 567	15 444	167 993	57 842	19 638
1989	206 306	160 524	7 936	347 045	328 072	122 882	92 341	10 507	32 231	17 290	177 829	63 343	20 099
1990	215 514	165 808	8 306	368 333	348 243	138 504	95 819	10 450	32 812	18 043	190 149	70 558	21 722
1991	226 730	172 922	8 341	374 523	354 331	137 295	97 441	10 435	32 865	17 504	194 424	75 540	22 454
1992	246 420	186 423	9 516	377 099	358 148	136 950	104 212	10 197	35 750	18 122	200 164	77 788	21 698
1993	264 049	199 876	9 745	382 709	363 583	141 697	107 403	9 980	36 275	18 502	212 778	79 704	21 551
1994	282 088	217 534	9 498	394 216	374 645	148 867	110 355	10 052	34 810	19 335	222 075	81 991	22 115
1995	297 578	231 320	9 801	402 479	382 246	157 245	111 404	9 335	33 378	19 733	229 841	85 837	22 022
1996	312 729	244 765	10 552	414 325	393 389	168 750	115 338	9 568	33 451	20 578	238 918	91 809	23 173
1997	329 394	259 920	11 213	423 725	402 310	172 081	119 605	10 092	33 466	20 763	254 124	98 822	24 092
1998	349 592	275 993	11 787	435 383	412 720	163 199	126 980	10 638	34 640	21 518	266 410	108 340	25 510
1999	378 925	296 646	14 307	458 269	434 695	180 973	135 087	11 063	36 758	21 593	285 371	120 733	28 034
1996													
January	25 172	19 675	842	34 162	32 420	13 422	9 394	792	2 694	1 685	19 290	7 293	1 953
February	25 355	19 787	840	33 955	32 240	13 425	9 620	819	2 792	1 684	19 415	7 373	1 914
March	25 303	19 671	867	34 097	32 360	13 865	9 492	799	2 694	1 705	19 548	7 479	1 926
April	25 801	20 176	877	34 269	32 539	14 197	9 658	786	2 784	1 770	19 674	7 486	1 928
May	25 979	20 324	883	34 202	32 447	14 313	9 615	800	2 798	1 735	19 737	7 544	1 912
June	25 857	20 182	876	34 392	32 627	14 283	9 592	784	2 861	1 710	19 690	7 559	1 956
July	26 046	20 346	896	34 531	32 790	13 933	9 561	788	2 754	1 733	19 871	7 676	1 961
August	26 239	20 518	895	34 575	32 832	13 856	9 534	785	2 751	1 723	19 920	7 745	1 955
September	26 366	20 665	871	34 637	32 912	13 983	9 735	822	2 837	1 692	20 050	7 708	1 916
October	26 627	20 873	895	34 875	33 134	14 204	9 807	800	2 863	1 719	20 245	7 906	1 912
November	26 605	20 919	861	34 999	33 240	14 322	9 639	795	2 815	1 703	20 600	7 849	1 912
December	26 814	21 071	922	34 956	33 200	14 544	9 665	810	2 801	1 704	20 516	7 985	1 908
1997													
January	27 054	21 251	930	35 196	33 424	14 609	9 800	834	2 828	1 687	20 858	7 985	1 945
February	27 002	21 189	945	35 159	33 384	14 684	9 768	835	2 816	1 756	20 899	8 091	1 947
March	26 911	21 161	932	35 317	33 546	14 726	9 710	819	2 782	1 710	20 954	8 101	1 964
April	27 025	21 276	897	35 234	33 476	14 364	9 680	799	2 724	1 707	21 014	8 128	1 965
May	27 044	21 309	881	35 091	33 340	14 041	9 738	821	2 700	1 698	21 002	8 128	1 979
June	27 279	21 504	917	35 067	33 296	14 136	9 906	827	2 760	1 731	21 167	8 213	2 045
July	27 710	21 799	956	35 262	33 484	14 183	10 043	856	2 776	1 732	21 383	8 296	2 024
August	27 857	21 971	1 025	35 482	33 658	14 304	10 132	862	2 782	1 735	21 501	8 244	2 011
September	27 652	21 824	996	35 416	33 598	14 503	10 114	857	2 822	1 735	21 600	8 409	2 017
October	27 995	22 168	945	35 501	33 695	14 339	10 109	863	2 780	1 738	21 378	8 310	2 059
November	28 039	22 215	938	35 628	33 827	14 360	10 199	860	2 823	1 758	21 136	8 479	2 060
December	27 966	22 197	912	35 475	33 664	14 084	10 332	869	2 897	1 799	21 505	8 442	2 054
1998													
January	28 163	22 242	932	35 515	33 701	13 845	10 380	867	2 932	1 769	21 576	8 686	2 066
February	28 495	22 574	937	35 566	33 712	13 678	10 461	869	2 835	1 848	21 704	8 685	2 109
March	28 599	22 613	942	35 808	33 932	13 451	10 534	891	2 825	1 800	21 789	8 759	2 070
April	28 760	22 717	939	35 841	33 944	13 516	10 494	881	2 874	1 768	21 845	8 788	2 063
May	28 987	22 957	948	36 067	34 180	13 682	10 485	875	2 847	1 776	22 010	8 917	2 081
June	29 027	22 903	955	36 253	34 356	13 700	10 524	889	2 840	1 768	22 192	8 955	2 083
July	29 005	22 888	977	36 383	34 466	13 735	10 675	893	2 918	1 805	22 108	9 047	2 100
August	29 107	22 971	971	36 500	34 590	13 540	10 573	895	2 872	1 794	22 243	9 181	2 140
September	29 488	23 229	993	36 617	34 692	13 478	10 420	894	2 857	1 750	22 495	9 236	2 151
October	29 602	23 327	1 009	36 682	34 768	13 554	10 681	896	2 886	1 825	22 658	9 298	2 162
November	30 039	23 610	1 060	36 825	34 936	13 525	10 845	894	2 950	1 817	22 795	9 413	2 203
December	29 928	23 684	1 049	37 232	35 334	13 594	10 851	896	2 996	1 825	23 168	9 391	2 234
1999													
January	30 812	24 165	1 081	37 280	35 362	13 677	11 147	916	3 094	1 858	22 903	9 675	2 229
February	30 864	24 285	1 118	37 576	35 641	13 596	11 107	904	3 053	1 833	23 245	9 765	2 257
March	31 155	24 506	1 126	37 375	35 450	13 923	11 087	910	3 111	1 747	23 206	9 771	2 235
April	31 114	24 451	1 155	37 560	35 612	14 604	11 303	970	3 117	1 816	23 442	9 913	2 319
May	30 994	24 249	1 159	38 014	36 029	14 657	11 391	931	3 116	1 823	23 654	9 926	2 315
June	31 496	24 711	1 201	37 728	35 766	14 519	11 349	948	3 084	1 832	23 712	10 085	2 299
July	31 450	24 661	1 165	37 997	36 057	15 060	11 241	909	3 047	1 800	23 718	10 061	2 318
August	31 709	24 776	1 206	38 114	36 183	15 652	11 360	927	3 071	1 801	23 859	10 108	2 331
September	31 981	25 008	1 216	38 666	36 716	15 843	11 232	899	2 997	1 772	23 948	10 199	2 375
October	32 034	24 994	1 267	38 589	36 642	16 019	11 287	912	3 021	1 782	24 432	10 276	2 388
November	32 176	25 118	1 259	38 819	36 800	16 242	11 273	932	3 042	1 778	24 525	10 356	2 404
December	32 524	25 377	1 267	40 370	38 313	16 737	11 338	912	3 027	1 793	24 671	10 422	2 442

1. Excluding leased departments.

Table 19-4. Retail Inventories [1]

(All retail stores; book value, end of period, millions of dollars, not seasonally adjusted.)

Year and month	Total	Durable goods stores				Nondurable goods stores				
		Total	Building materials group [2]	Automotive group	Furniture group	Total	General merchandise group stores		Food stores	Apparel and accessory stores
							Total	Department stores [3]		
1970	42 808	17 482	2 877	8 410	3 330	25 326	8 834	6 283	5 166	4 245
1971	48 895	21 273	3 547	11 136	3 546	27 622	10 013	6 997	5 685	4 618
1972	53 791	23 820	4 097	11 665	4 379	29 971	10 928	7 639	6 071	4 976
1973	61 835	28 065	4 641	14 270	4 776	33 770	12 173	8 349	7 050	5 530
1974	69 644	32 590	4 910	16 770	5 428	37 054	12 595	8 890	8 164	5 798
1975	70 273	33 130	5 239	16 478	5 711	37 143	12 426	9 070	8 190	5 758
1976	77 617	37 607	6 215	18 623	6 115	40 010	13 643	10 143	8 840	6 229
1977	87 411	42 742	7 179	22 142	6 511	44 669	15 821	12 067	9 474	7 340
1978	100 242	49 717	8 036	25 490	7 750	50 525	18 110	13 598	10 305	8 566
1979	108 408	53 630	8 604	27 256	8 533	54 778	19 139	14 353	11 456	9 143
1980	117 857	55 084	9 307	25 667	9 097	62 773	20 984	15 301	13 589	10 383
1981	129 073	60 261	9 793	28 137	9 687	68 812	23 509	17 544	14 866	11 598
1982	130 797	60 492	9 805	28 437	9 607	70 305	24 068	17 897	15 473	11 698
1983	143 513	67 921	11 224	33 030	11 105	75 592	25 996	19 331	16 488	12 658
1984	162 773	78 125	12 310	39 280	12 334	84 648	31 236	23 510	17 826	13 675
1985	176 941	87 630	13 054	46 399	13 693	89 311	31 517	23 330	19 480	14 575
1986	181 651	89 586	13 373	46 190	14 297	92 065	32 528	24 167	19 772	14 830
1987	203 210	105 654	14 184	57 800	15 005	97 556	34 874	26 032	20 019	15 880
1988	214 824	112 970	15 462	60 915	16 295	101 854	35 768	27 468	21 812	16 524
1989	233 143	122 220	16 437	66 436	17 297	110 923	39 487	30 916	23 821	17 713
1990	236 152	122 141	16 368	65 517	17 477	114 011	38 969	30 716	25 402	17 957
1991	239 478	119 977	16 099	63 134	17 737	119 501	42 168	33 257	26 045	18 500
1992	248 198	124 046	16 596	66 501	18 077	124 152	44 938	35 104	26 275	20 336
1993	264 835	135 792	18 167	72 177	20 364	129 043	48 441	38 017	26 641	20 491
1994	289 205	153 704	20 438	82 691	23 007	135 501	51 191	40 456	27 425	21 288
1995	304 896	165 583	21 762	90 317	24 259	139 313	53 975	43 032	28 192	20 730
1996	314 819	171 195	22 739	93 865	24 444	143 624	54 837	44 329	29 177	20 843
1997	324 222	176 778	23 884	97 587	23 885	147 444	54 933	45 320	29 469	22 252
1998	337 861	184 111	25 885	99 778	24 893	153 750	55 862	45 476	30 339	23 252
1999	367 062	203 192	28 205	111 901	25 899	163 870	58 451	47 446	32 600	23 617
1996										
January	302 278	164 328	21 824	90 354	23 325	137 950	53 620	42 737	27 603	20 293
February	306 653	166 868	22 458	91 853	23 478	139 785	54 767	44 026	27 232	21 374
March	308 481	166 734	23 511	89 918	23 710	141 747	56 244	45 238	27 397	22 247
April	310 297	167 926	23 781	89 277	24 339	142 371	56 695	45 640	27 478	21 799
May	309 489	168 036	23 815	89 522	24 330	141 453	56 320	45 304	27 317	21 301
June	306 026	166 104	23 646	88 588	23 890	139 922	55 507	44 591	27 172	21 111
July	305 594	161 644	23 258	83 525	24 120	143 950	56 983	45 736	27 355	22 378
August	308 388	161 655	22 687	82 778	24 775	146 733	58 927	47 497	27 232	23 149
September	318 751	165 744	22 638	84 759	25 973	153 007	62 912	50 605	27 761	23 828
October	339 607	175 935	22 944	89 101	28 291	163 672	68 622	55 281	29 080	25 611
November	343 696	178 060	22 848	91 072	28 267	165 636	69 939	56 657	29 769	26 042
December	314 819	171 195	22 739	93 865	24 444	143 624	54 837	44 329	29 177	20 843
1997										
January	311 024	168 956	22 662	92 843	24 027	142 068	53 794	43 609	28 594	20 491
February	317 162	173 097	23 297	95 621	23 733	144 065	55 398	45 141	28 051	21 701
March	320 165	174 563	24 492	96 023	23 713	145 602	56 368	46 159	28 347	22 194
April	323 871	176 698	24 933	96 582	23 674	147 173	57 514	47 092	28 100	22 830
May	320 931	174 908	25 042	94 201	23 846	146 023	56 986	46 636	28 012	22 542
June	317 862	173 059	24 646	93 108	23 562	144 803	56 018	45 798	28 063	22 367
July	315 523	167 555	24 173	87 050	23 942	147 968	56 856	46 392	27 954	23 621
August	315 222	165 340	23 818	85 274	23 784	149 882	57 849	47 308	28 145	24 222
September	328 151	170 342	24 263	87 159	24 803	157 809	62 358	50 987	28 708	25 580
October	347 226	179 919	24 445	91 895	27 158	167 307	67 607	55 645	29 664	27 175
November	352 348	183 368	24 032	94 673	27 716	168 980	68 957	56 986	30 370	26 952
December	324 222	176 778	23 884	97 587	23 885	147 444	54 933	45 320	29 469	22 252
1998										
January	321 626	173 931	24 226	96 006	23 137	147 695	54 849	45 188	29 179	22 097
February	326 764	177 266	25 498	97 712	23 115	149 498	56 284	46 481	28 592	23 135
March	334 503	181 172	26 415	99 051	23 729	153 331	57 787	47 770	29 060	24 420
April	337 968	183 569	26 773	99 826	24 262	154 399	58 368	48 167	29 105	24 508
May	330 466	178 218	26 228	95 527	23 779	152 248	56 981	46 943	28 853	24 072
June	326 605	174 161	26 052	91 361	23 662	152 444	56 641	46 517	29 108	24 252
July	323 348	167 962	25 668	84 438	24 160	155 386	57 856	47 715	29 141	25 522
August	325 275	167 152	25 826	82 741	24 339	158 123	59 339	48 888	28 910	26 259
September	338 672	172 996	25 782	86 669	25 268	165 676	64 104	52 561	29 275	27 630
October	358 224	183 644	26 047	91 639	27 633	174 580	69 960	57 298	30 428	28 812
November	366 381	190 186	25 942	96 278	28 692	176 195	71 092	58 320	31 250	28 448
December	337 861	184 111	25 885	99 778	24 893	153 750	55 862	45 476	30 339	23 252
1999										
January	336 512	182 932	26 322	99 026	24 307	153 580	55 496	45 453	30 264	23 253
February	342 856	187 516	27 675	102 696	24 204	155 340	56 940	46 496	29 833	24 685
March	353 713	194 654	28 942	107 537	24 347	159 059	58 899	48 264	30 165	25 410
April	358 384	198 818	29 564	109 550	25 034	159 566	59 535	48 739	29 772	25 390
May	354 644	196 646	29 493	107 365	24 450	157 998	58 959	48 270	29 842	24 945
June	353 723	196 112	28 876	107 284	24 547	157 611	57 650	46 971	30 044	25 043
July	347 208	187 271	28 406	98 296	24 973	159 937	58 439	47 685	30 055	25 842
August	350 417	186 535	28 239	96 582	25 155	163 882	60 472	49 259	30 172	26 301
September	362 926	191 201	27 998	98 762	26 199	171 725	65 217	52 982	31 086	27 067
October	383 076	201 155	28 439	101 934	28 563	181 921	71 269	58 160	32 518	28 417
November	394 282	208 040	28 204	107 986	29 541	186 242	73 850	60 674	33 228	28 524
December	367 062	203 192	28 205	111 901	25 899	163 870	58 451	47 446	32 600	23 617

1. Data prior to 1980 are not comparable to subsequent periods due to changed inventory valuation methods; see Notes.
2. Includes building materials; hardware; plants and garden supplies; and manufactured (mobile) homes.
3. Excluding leased departments.

Table 19-4. Retail Inventories [1]—*Continued*

(All retail stores; book value, end of period, millions of dollars, seasonally adjusted.)

Year and month	Total	Durable goods stores				Nondurable goods stores				
		Total	Building materials [2]	Automotive group	Furniture group	Total	General merchandise group stores		Food stores	Apparel and accessory stores
							Total	Department stores [3]		
1970	43 867	17 908	2 981	8 679	3 374	25 959	9 438	6 713	5 095	4 422
1971	50 063	21 687	3 683	11 363	3 585	28 376	10 728	7 499	5 601	4 820
1972	55 079	24 238	4 268	11 855	4 414	30 841	11 743	8 214	5 981	5 200
1973	63 237	28 418	4 844	14 356	4 800	34 819	13 137	9 016	6 946	5 791
1974	71 067	32 861	5 131	16 737	5 439	38 206	13 647	9 632	8 043	6 071
1975	71 744	33 356	5 474	16 347	5 717	38 388	13 521	9 848	8 069	6 029
1976	79 273	37 841	6 481	18 420	6 115	41 432	14 886	11 037	8 709	6 516
1977	89 444	43 071	7 502	21 879	6 610	46 373	17 307	13 145	9 362	7 646
1978	102 694	50 136	8 397	25 188	7 876	52 558	19 853	14 829	10 193	8 914
1979	111 098	54 108	8 981	26 933	8 681	56 990	21 033	15 686	11 343	9 514
1980	121 078	55 799	9 685	25 553	9 207	65 279	23 171	16 814	13 390	10 929
1981	132 719	61 050	10 180	28 026	9 795	71 669	25 951	19 279	14 649	12 234
1982	134 628	61 316	10 203	28 352	9 714	73 312	26 548	19 645	15 248	12 392
1983	147 833	68 856	11 716	32 919	11 217	78 977	28 651	21 196	16 282	13 466
1984	167 812	79 074	12 890	39 004	12 433	88 738	34 392	25 750	17 624	14 641
1985	181 881	88 315	13 683	45 798	13 762	93 566	34 683	25 525	19 283	15 689
1986	186 510	89 983	14 033	45 246	14 340	96 527	35 743	26 412	19 612	16 067
1987	207 836	105 481	14 868	56 161	15 050	102 355	38 285	28 450	19 898	17 280
1988	219 047	112 453	16 157	58 907	16 311	106 594	39 179	29 987	21 601	18 079
1989	237 234	121 347	17 122	64 072	17 280	115 887	43 107	33 678	23 543	19 422
1990	239 815	121 194	17 015	63 107	17 442	118 621	42 377	33 387	25 038	19 690
1991	243 389	119 189	16 718	60 881	17 649	124 200	45 764	36 110	25 580	20 263
1992	252 185	123 152	17 234	64 134	17 934	129 033	48 630	38 033	25 738	22 249
1993	268 932	135 056	18 845	69 730	20 243	133 876	52 119	40 922	26 030	22 419
1994	293 605	152 996	21 201	79 967	22 961	140 609	55 054	43 548	26 750	23 291
1995	309 718	164 999	22 598	87 414	24 332	144 719	58 087	46 371	27 499	22 730
1996	319 985	170 775	23 613	90 953	24 641	149 210	59 046	47 820	28 456	22 879
1997	329 542	176 349	24 827	94 537	24 151	153 193	59 137	48 889	28 739	24 426
1998	343 197	183 630	26 935	96 572	25 170	159 567	60 053	49 004	29 587	25 524
1999	372 252	202 474	29 380	108 251	26 187	169 778	62 797	51 127	31 791	25 924
1996										
January	311 076	165 914	22 545	88 468	24 171	145 162	58 396	46 605	27 426	22 674
February	311 360	165 945	22 503	88 132	24 636	145 415	58 163	46 638	27 568	22 666
March	308 750	163 913	22 716	85 554	24 621	144 837	58 150	46 733	27 530	22 655
April	308 847	163 714	22 757	84 746	24 963	145 133	58 087	46 667	27 757	22 176
May	311 246	165 791	22 833	86 752	25 186	145 455	58 204	46 753	27 789	22 074
June	311 887	166 561	23 182	87 739	24 860	145 326	58 443	47 037	27 603	22 129
July	315 792	168 678	23 281	89 272	25 073	147 114	59 075	47 444	27 873	22 311
August	317 499	170 175	23 032	90 686	25 229	147 324	59 511	47 977	27 899	22 431
September	318 049	170 779	23 100	91 224	25 266	147 270	59 299	47 786	27 979	22 269
October	320 678	172 242	23 223	91 644	25 419	148 436	59 363	47 862	28 253	22 605
November	319 248	170 354	23 434	90 400	24 774	148 894	59 407	48 055	28 358	23 128
December	319 985	170 775	23 613	90 953	24 641	149 210	59 046	47 820	28 456	22 879
1997										
January	319 929	170 836	23 460	90 912	25 028	149 093	58 440	47 453	28 386	22 869
February	321 834	172 197	23 320	91 695	24 930	149 637	58 726	47 768	28 401	23 013
March	319 982	171 311	23 641	91 282	24 624	148 671	58 308	47 685	28 473	22 555
April	321 523	171 621	23 791	91 430	24 182	149 902	58 918	48 151	28 382	23 225
May	322 784	172 546	24 010	91 374	24 660	150 238	58 959	48 178	28 524	23 360
June	324 100	173 655	24 163	92 391	24 544	150 445	59 051	48 361	28 538	23 421
July	326 268	175 048	24 197	93 316	24 785	151 220	59 006	48 174	28 519	23 527
August	324 792	174 249	24 181	93 513	24 220	150 543	58 481	47 834	28 838	23 494
September	327 606	175 633	24 758	93 777	24 198	151 973	58 763	48 146	28 941	23 907
October	328 313	176 197	24 767	94 445	24 379	152 116	58 507	48 177	28 796	24 027
November	327 947	175 689	24 699	94 060	24 291	152 258	58 551	48 293	28 897	24 000
December	329 542	176 349	24 827	94 537	24 151	153 193	59 137	48 889	28 739	24 426
1998										
January	330 854	176 009	25 105	94 066	24 151	154 845	59 516	49 117	28 971	24 634
February	331 537	176 466	25 498	93 781	24 306	155 071	59 563	49 134	28 953	24 507
March	333 756	177 445	25 448	93 898	24 615	156 311	59 681	49 247	29 179	24 817
April	334 933	177 852	25 498	94 228	24 682	157 081	59 727	49 200	29 425	24 907
May	332 404	175 676	25 147	92 588	24 590	156 728	59 023	48 545	29 410	24 945
June	333 131	174 760	25 541	90 671	24 648	158 371	59 773	49 172	29 628	25 342
July	334 043	175 248	25 719	90 517	24 907	158 795	60 131	49 600	29 735	25 395
August	334 878	175 992	26 246	90 783	24 785	158 886	60 099	49 532	29 621	25 469
September	337 819	178 277	26 308	93 227	24 724	159 542	60 428	49 680	29 488	25 822
October	338 726	179 702	26 417	94 186	24 850	159 024	60 615	49 652	29 507	25 543
November	341 165	182 257	26 717	95 647	25 168	158 908	60 355	49 382	29 702	25 377
December	343 197	183 630	26 935	96 572	25 170	159 567	60 053	49 004	29 587	25 524
1999										
January	346 158	185 402	27 305	97 119	25 426	160 756	60 128	49 352	30 042	25 894
February	347 792	186 926	27 620	98 747	25 478	160 866	60 150	49 098	30 180	26 122
March	352 287	190 241	27 856	101 822	25 178	162 046	60 847	49 757	30 284	25 797
April	354 556	192 171	28 049	103 122	25 441	162 385	60 914	49 784	30 127	25 803
May	355 826	193 264	28 196	103 698	25 311	162 562	61 075	49 917	30 415	25 796
June	359 298	195 621	28 282	105 611	25 490	163 677	60 916	49 757	30 619	26 086
July	359 023	195 391	28 463	105 234	25 666	163 632	60 868	49 724	30 755	25 662
August	361 420	196 562	28 611	105 823	25 642	164 858	61 398	50 060	30 983	25 461
September	363 200	197 500	28 599	106 115	25 837	165 700	61 671	50 268	31 358	25 249
October	363 553	197 333	28 872	104 976	25 756	166 220	61 749	50 399	31 536	25 260
November	368 079	199 811	29 076	107 380	25 913	168 268	62 671	51 332	31 578	25 468
December	372 252	202 474	29 380	108 251	26 187	169 778	62 797	51 127	31 791	25 924

1. Data prior to 1980 are not comparable to subsequent periods due to changed inventory valuation methods; see Notes.
2. Includes building materials; hardware; plants and garden supplies; and manufactured (mobile) homes.
3. Excluding leased departments.

Table 19-5. Merchant Wholesalers—Sales and Inventories

(Millions of dollars.)

Year and month	Not seasonally adjusted						Seasonally adjusted					
	Sales			Inventories (book value, end of period)			Sales			Inventories (book value, end of period)		
	Total	Durable goods establishments	Nondurable goods establishments	Total	Durable goods establishments	Nondurable goods establishments	Total	Durable goods establishments	Nondurable goods establishments	Total	Durable goods establishments	Nondurable goods establishments
1970	289 999	133 778	156 221	...	...	...	289 999	133 778	156 221	...	...	...
1971	317 899	147 761	170 138	...	...	...	317 899	147 761	170 138	...	...	...
1972	358 388	168 879	189 509	...	...	...	358 388	168 879	189 509	...	...	...
1973	457 378	208 554	248 824	...	...	...	457 378	208 554	248 824	...	...	...
1974	575 786	255 863	319 923	...	...	...	575 786	255 863	319 923	...	...	...
1975	559 606	235 723	323 883	...	...	...	559 606	235 723	323 883	...	...	...
1976	608 381	263 605	344 776	...	...	...	608 381	263 605	344 776	...	...	...
1977	673 633	304 721	368 912	...	...	...	673 633	304 721	368 912	...	...	...
1978	796 961	372 176	424 785	...	...	...	796 961	372 176	424 785	...	...	...
1979	948 614	436 254	512 360	...	...	...	948 614	436 254	512 360	...	...	...
1980	1 117 187	486 509	630 678	124 015	78 849	45 166	1 117 187	486 509	630 678	122 631	79 372	43 259
1981	1 214 156	525 607	688 549	130 709	85 371	45 338	1 214 156	525 607	688 549	129 654	85 856	43 798
1982	1 142 535	480 318	662 217	128 514	84 806	43 708	1 142 535	480 318	662 217	127 428	85 222	42 206
1983	1 190 705	523 080	667 625	131 306	84 709	46 597	1 190 705	523 080	667 625	130 075	85 180	44 895
1984	1 346 392	622 361	724 031	143 458	94 895	48 563	1 346 392	622 361	724 031	142 452	95 474	46 978
1985	1 361 507	651 864	709 643	148 403	96 659	51 744	1 361 507	651 864	709 643	147 409	97 371	50 038
1986	1 379 514	681 691	697 823	154 081	101 369	52 712	1 379 514	681 691	697 823	153 574	102 349	51 225
1987	1 475 613	730 592	745 021	164 310	106 820	57 490	1 475 613	730 592	745 021	163 903	108 112	55 791
1988	1 614 249	801 751	812 498	179 828	115 613	64 215	1 614 249	801 751	812 498	178 801	117 045	61 756
1989	1 725 123	851 550	873 573	187 897	120 701	67 196	1 725 123	851 550	873 573	187 009	122 237	64 772
1990	1 794 072	880 767	913 305	196 881	124 839	72 042	1 794 072	880 767	913 305	195 833	126 461	69 372
1991	1 779 673	860 138	919 535	201 777	125 921	75 856	1 779 673	860 138	919 535	200 448	127 399	73 049
1992	1 849 798	908 917	940 881	209 675	130 044	79 631	1 849 798	908 917	940 881	208 302	131 509	76 793
1993	1 937 803	993 449	944 354	218 819	135 880	82 939	1 937 803	993 449	944 354	217 425	137 516	79 909
1994	2 073 734	1 098 457	975 277	237 592	149 903	87 689	2 073 734	1 098 457	975 277	236 287	151 853	84 434
1995	2 266 109	1 207 906	1 058 203	256 347	162 551	93 796	2 266 109	1 207 906	1 058 203	254 844	164 938	89 906
1996	2 399 532	1 262 698	1 136 834	258 490	165 643	92 847	2 399 532	1 262 698	1 136 834	257 626	168 163	89 463
1997	2 501 356	1 334 672	1 166 684	277 229	177 708	99 521	2 501 356	1 334 672	1 166 684	276 140	180 391	95 749
1998	2 555 117	1 381 930	1 173 187	291 478	188 341	103 137	2 555 117	1 381 930	1 173 187	290 171	191 054	99 117
1999	2 742 482	1 481 780	1 260 702	309 445	199 537	109 908	2 742 482	1 481 780	1 260 702	307 925	202 274	105 651
1996												
January	187 066	96 566	90 500	262 000	165 582	96 418	193 955	102 879	91 076	256 392	165 956	90 436
February	184 868	96 752	88 116	259 878	165 952	93 926	194 126	102 697	91 429	256 059	165 726	90 333
March	198 572	106 349	92 223	257 138	164 992	92 146	196 706	104 227	92 479	255 528	165 163	90 365
April	199 592	104 372	95 220	261 776	167 919	93 857	197 051	103 509	93 542	259 725	166 502	93 223
May	205 510	107 181	98 329	257 668	167 442	90 226	197 797	104 509	93 288	260 020	166 172	93 848
June	194 967	103 726	91 241	254 451	166 022	88 429	198 049	104 342	93 707	259 070	165 978	93 092
July	203 118	105 581	97 537	257 335	168 997	88 338	200 718	104 317	96 401	259 513	166 842	92 671
August	206 245	108 102	98 143	253 355	167 881	85 474	201 898	104 746	97 152	258 883	167 439	91 444
September	200 572	107 807	92 765	251 912	166 894	85 018	201 267	105 804	95 463	256 666	167 946	88 720
October	219 884	116 770	103 114	259 608	167 199	92 409	202 622	106 309	96 313	257 531	167 617	89 914
November	198 464	104 643	93 821	260 220	167 079	93 141	204 161	107 998	96 163	257 877	168 299	89 578
December	200 674	104 849	95 825	258 490	165 643	92 847	202 609	106 658	95 951	257 626	168 163	89 463
1997												
January	196 609	100 222	96 387	265 011	168 839	96 172	205 080	107 587	97 493	260 241	169 323	90 918
February	191 069	99 799	91 270	263 647	169 777	93 870	209 510	110 819	98 691	260 265	169 481	90 784
March	210 768	111 482	99 286	263 219	170 938	92 281	207 656	108 845	98 811	261 668	170 927	90 741
April	209 445	111 097	98 348	264 279	173 365	90 914	207 255	110 686	96 569	262 157	171 724	90 433
May	211 140	110 829	100 311	261 937	174 602	87 335	207 834	110 355	97 479	263 836	173 240	90 596
June	210 558	114 060	96 498	264 740	177 593	87 147	208 114	111 287	96 827	268 530	177 363	91 167
July	211 189	114 161	97 028	265 815	177 846	87 969	208 078	112 421	95 657	267 618	175 749	91 869
August	205 745	110 723	95 022	263 632	176 389	87 243	207 855	111 016	96 839	268 712	176 052	92 660
September	216 973	119 552	97 421	266 364	177 211	89 153	210 780	113 525	97 255	271 254	178 386	92 868
October	226 376	122 975	103 401	274 238	177 211	97 027	209 932	113 018	96 914	272 027	177 758	94 269
November	197 644	105 920	91 724	276 838	177 081	99 757	208 823	112 658	96 165	274 001	178 409	95 592
December	213 840	113 852	99 988	277 229	177 708	99 521	209 934	112 814	97 120	276 140	180 391	95 749
1998												
January	197 371	104 114	93 257	280 994	180 852	100 142	211 302	114 336	96 966	276 198	181 479	94 719
February	192 724	103 276	89 448	282 529	183 928	98 601	211 224	114 511	96 713	279 301	183 693	95 608
March	222 104	121 983	100 121	282 669	185 401	97 268	212 602	115 408	97 194	280 760	185 010	95 750
April	215 508	116 452	99 056	282 251	187 031	95 220	213 153	116 092	97 061	280 035	185 164	94 871
May	209 576	112 056	97 520	280 550	187 564	92 986	212 522	115 051	97 471	282 556	186 163	96 393
June	221 841	122 547	99 294	278 918	185 992	92 926	212 009	115 176	96 833	282 633	185 543	97 090
July	215 758	117 564	98 194	281 037	187 770	93 267	213 458	116 026	97 432	282 949	185 723	97 226
August	209 756	114 814	94 942	280 628	188 144	92 484	211 667	115 262	96 405	285 778	187 912	97 866
September	218 554	120 068	98 486	282 651	187 755	94 896	212 841	114 842	97 999	287 616	188 868	98 748
October	223 994	121 534	102 460	290 044	189 102	100 942	213 114	114 427	98 687	287 820	189 767	98 053
November	207 104	110 340	96 764	291 696	188 197	103 499	213 758	114 630	99 128	288 984	189 706	99 278
December	220 827	117 182	103 645	291 478	188 341	103 137	216 449	116 027	100 422	290 171	191 054	99 117
1999												
January	194 483	102 614	91 869	294 880	190 678	104 202	215 176	116 397	98 779	290 107	191 543	98 564
February	198 872	107 752	91 120	295 429	192 768	102 661	218 269	119 570	98 699	291 961	192 456	99 505
March	237 380	129 916	107 464	294 867	193 227	101 640	220 801	119 826	100 975	292 784	192 781	100 003
April	224 110	120 887	103 223	295 224	193 944	101 280	221 975	119 882	102 093	292 966	191 947	101 019
May	223 453	118 971	104 482	291 946	194 998	96 948	225 938	121 964	103 974	294 356	193 404	100 952
June	239 371	130 686	108 685	291 524	195 306	96 218	229 134	123 265	105 869	295 593	194 756	100 837
July	226 836	123 381	103 455	296 015	198 395	97 620	229 508	124 172	105 336	298 467	196 441	102 026
August	235 596	127 866	107 730	293 920	196 108	97 812	231 625	124 485	107 140	299 906	196 166	103 740
September	239 219	130 668	108 551	296 371	196 461	99 910	232 968	125 303	107 665	301 510	197 549	103 961
October	239 483	130 196	109 287	306 039	198 391	107 648	235 226	126 603	108 623	303 570	199 080	104 490
November	238 548	127 595	110 953	309 909	200 322	109 587	238 540	128 091	110 449	306 900	201 858	105 042
December	245 131	131 248	113 883	309 445	199 537	109 908	241 672	130 720	110 952	307 925	202 274	105 651

CHAPTER 20: FINANCE, INSURANCE, REAL ESTATE, AND PRIVATE SERVICES

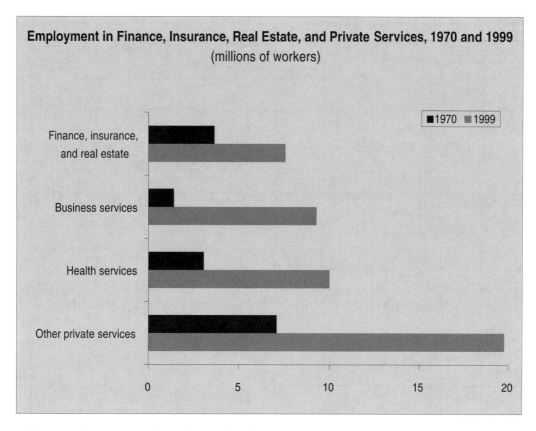

Employment in Finance, Insurance, Real Estate, and Private Services, 1970 and 1999
(millions of workers)

- Finance, insurance, and real estate; business services; health services; and other private services all grew strongly from 1970 to 1999. The strongest employment growth was in business services, a large and heterogeneous category that ranges from janitors and temporary help ("help supply") to computer and data processing services.

- Since the last business cycle employment peak in 1989, total finance, insurance and real estate payroll employment rose, but employment in the subindustry of depository institutions fell by 9.3 percent.

- From 1989 to 1999 the fastest-growing service industry continued to be business services. In total, employment in the industry grew 87.6 percent in the period, buoyed by growth in help supply of 165 percent and computer and data processing services of 149 percent.

- Hourly earnings for those employed in help supply averaged $10.56 per hour in 1999, 20 percent below the average for all private nonfarm industries. Hourly earnings for nonsupervisory workers in computer services, on the other hand, averaged $22.38 in 1999.

Table 20-1. Finance, Insurance, and Real Estate—Employment, Hours, and Earnings

Year and month	Payroll employment (thousands, seasonally adjusted)					Nonsupervisory workers			Average earnings (dollars, not seasonally adjusted)			
	Total	Finance		Insurance	Real estate	Employment (thousands, seasonally adjusted)	Average weekly hours, not seasonally adjusted	Aggregate hours index (1982=100, seasonally adjusted)	Hourly		Weekly	
		Total	Depository institutions						Total	Depository institutions	Total	Depository institutions
1970	3 645	...	...	...	...	2 879	36.7	73.0	3.07	...	112.67	...
1971	3 772	...	...	...	...	2 936	36.6	74.3	3.22	...	117.85	...
1972	3 908	1 778	...	1 373	756	3 024	36.6	76.5	3.36	...	122.98	...
1973	4 046	1 866	...	1 401	778	3 121	36.6	78.9	3.53	...	129.20	...
1974	4 148	1 936	...	1 434	778	3 169	36.5	79.8	3.77	...	137.61	...
1975	4 165	1 964	...	1 442	760	3 173	36.5	79.9	4.06	...	148.19	...
1976	4 271	2 026	...	1 468	776	3 243	36.4	81.5	4.27	...	155.43	...
1977	4 467	2 113	...	1 528	826	3 397	36.4	85.4	4.54	...	165.26	...
1978	4 724	2 233	...	1 591	900	3 593	36.4	90.3	4.89	...	178.00	...
1979	4 975	2 369	...	1 643	963	3 776	36.2	94.4	5.27	...	190.77	...
1980	5 160	2 483	...	1 688	989	3 907	36.2	97.8	5.79	...	209.60	...
1981	5 298	2 593	...	1 713	992	3 999	36.3	105.5	6.31	...	229.05	...
1982	5 340	2 647	...	1 723	970	3 996	36.2	100.0	6.78	...	245.44	...
1983	5 466	2 741	...	1 728	997	4 066	36.2	101.6	7.29	...	263.90	...
1984	5 684	2 852	...	1 765	1 067	4 226	36.5	106.4	7.63	...	278.50	...
1985	5 948	2 974	...	1 840	1 135	4 410	36.4	110.9	7.94	...	289.02	...
1986	6 273	3 145	...	1 944	1 184	4 637	36.4	116.7	8.36	...	304.30	...
1987	6 533	3 264	...	2 027	1 242	4 797	36.3	120.1	8.73	...	316.90	...
1988	6 630	3 274	2 255	2 075	1 280	4 811	35.9	119.2	9.06	7.77	325.25	277.39
1989	6 668	3 283	2 273	2 090	1 296	4 829	35.8	119.5	9.53	8.13	341.17	289.43
1990	6 709	3 268	2 251	2 126	1 315	4 860	35.8	120.2	9.97	8.43	356.93	300.11
1991	6 646	3 187	2 164	2 161	1 299	4 795	35.7	118.3	10.39	8.70	370.92	307.98
1992	6 602	3 160	2 096	2 152	1 290	4 772	35.8	118.1	10.82	8.90	387.36	315.06
1993	6 757	3 238	2 089	2 197	1 322	4 908	35.8	121.2	11.35	9.10	406.33	320.32
1994	6 896	3 299	2 066	2 236	1 361	5 018	35.8	124.0	11.83	9.37	423.51	329.82
1995	6 806	3 231	2 025	2 225	1 351	4 961	35.9	122.9	12.32	9.62	442.29	341.51
1996	6 911	3 303	2 019	2 226	1 382	5 043	35.9	125.0	12.80	9.92	459.52	349.18
1997	7 109	3 424	2 027	2 264	1 421	5 193	36.1	129.6	13.34	10.29	481.57	363.24
1998	7 389	3 588	2 046	2 335	1 465	5 429	36.4	136.3	14.07	10.83	512.15	384.47
1999	7 569	3 691	2 061	2 371	1 507	5 546	36.2	138.6	14.62	11.27	529.24	400.09
1996												
January	6 831	3 256	2 020	2 217	1 358	4 981	35.5	122.8	12.61	9.77	447.66	340.00
February	6 851	3 265	2 020	2 217	1 369	4 995	35.7	123.5	12.69	9.84	453.03	344.40
March	6 857	3 269	2 017	2 216	1 372	5 003	35.7	124.0	12.73	9.86	454.46	344.11
April	6 870	3 280	2 017	2 217	1 373	5 014	35.6	124.0	12.75	9.84	453.90	343.42
May	6 889	3 289	2 017	2 223	1 377	5 029	35.6	124.3	12.74	9.86	453.54	343.13
June	6 906	3 301	2 019	2 225	1 380	5 040	36.5	125.3	12.76	9.89	465.74	358.02
July	6 919	3 307	2 017	2 228	1 384	5 052	35.6	124.9	12.69	9.85	451.76	345.74
August	6 936	3 320	2 017	2 228	1 388	5 063	35.8	125.5	12.72	9.89	455.38	348.13
September	6 948	3 324	2 018	2 234	1 390	5 074	36.5	126.8	12.91	10.02	471.22	361.72
October	6 964	3 335	2 020	2 234	1 395	5 086	35.7	126.1	12.88	9.99	459.82	347.65
November	6 975	3 340	2 018	2 237	1 398	5 091	35.8	126.6	12.99	10.08	465.04	352.80
December	6 989	3 350	2 018	2 238	1 401	5 101	36.7	127.2	13.04	10.13	478.57	365.69
1997												
January	7 000	3 357	2 018	2 240	1 403	5 110	35.7	127.0	13.02	10.12	464.81	353.19
February	7 016	3 366	2 019	2 243	1 407	5 124	36.7	127.4	13.17	10.27	483.34	367.67
March	7 033	3 376	2 021	2 246	1 411	5 133	36.5	127.6	13.22	10.23	482.53	362.14
April	7 057	3 390	2 022	2 251	1 416	5 152	35.9	128.4	13.12	10.10	471.01	354.51
May	7 074	3 403	2 025	2 252	1 419	5 168	35.9	128.8	13.21	10.27	474.24	358.42
June	7 087	3 412	2 026	2 258	1 417	5 175	36.7	129.0	13.26	10.19	486.64	367.86
July	7 113	3 425	2 028	2 264	1 424	5 195	35.9	129.5	13.21	10.18	474.24	358.34
August	7 137	3 441	2 029	2 269	1 427	5 212	36.1	130.3	13.38	10.32	483.02	364.30
September	7 154	3 452	2 028	2 273	1 429	5 229	35.8	130.4	13.48	10.32	482.58	361.20
October	7 183	3 469	2 032	2 281	1 433	5 250	35.9	130.9	13.56	10.36	486.80	360.53
November	7 207	3 485	2 036	2 288	1 434	5 273	36.7	131.8	13.73	10.53	503.89	380.13
December	7 236	3 505	2 041	2 299	1 432	5 296	35.9	131.3	13.64	10.55	489.68	368.20
1998												
January	7 257	3 513	2 036	2 304	1 440	5 320	36.1	133.4	13.71	10.56	494.93	370.66
February	7 281	3 527	2 038	2 309	1 445	5 343	37.1	133.9	13.95	10.74	517.55	388.79
March	7 317	3 546	2 041	2 318	1 453	5 375	36.8	134.7	13.98	10.76	514.46	385.21
April	7 342	3 559	2 043	2 324	1 459	5 393	36.1	135.2	13.98	10.70	504.68	375.57
May	7 365	3 572	2 046	2 331	1 462	5 409	36.1	136.0	13.99	10.73	505.04	375.55
June	7 384	3 585	2 047	2 335	1 464	5 429	36.0	136.1	13.94	10.74	501.84	379.12
July	7 408	3 600	2 048	2 340	1 468	5 444	36.1	136.5	13.94	10.73	503.23	379.84
August	7 425	3 612	2 049	2 344	1 469	5 456	36.9	136.8	14.12	10.90	521.03	395.67
September	7 439	3 617	2 047	2 348	1 474	5 467	36.0	137.0	14.11	10.88	507.96	384.06
October	7 461	3 635	2 052	2 351	1 475	5 486	36.1	137.5	14.20	10.95	512.62	385.44
November	7 481	3 642	2 052	2 357	1 482	5 501	36.9	137.9	14.43	11.10	532.47	404.04
December	7 497	3 652	2 056	2 358	1 487	5 510	36.2	138.1	14.41	11.13	521.64	391.78
1999												
January	7 518	3 662	2 059	2 361	1 495	5 528	36.0	138.2	14.48	11.19	521.28	395.01
February	7 524	3 666	2 061	2 362	1 496	5 529	36.3	138.6	14.56	11.30	528.53	400.02
March	7 536	3 675	2 063	2 366	1 495	5 532	36.0	138.3	14.54	11.27	523.44	394.45
April	7 546	3 681	2 062	2 367	1 498	5 536	35.9	138.4	14.62	11.22	524.86	394.94
May	7 559	3 689	2 061	2 370	1 500	5 542	36.4	138.2	14.73	11.31	536.17	403.77
June	7 573	3 693	2 060	2 373	1 507	5 548	36.0	138.7	14.51	11.21	522.36	396.83
July	7 583	3 700	2 060	2 374	1 509	5 554	36.3	140.0	14.54	11.17	527.80	398.77
August	7 590	3 704	2 063	2 375	1 511	5 554	37.0	139.2	14.62	11.29	540.94	413.21
September	7 589	3 702	2 063	2 376	1 511	5 553	36.1	139.6	14.64	11.23	528.50	397.54
October	7 599	3 704	2 063	2 378	1 517	5 555	36.1	139.6	14.69	11.27	530.31	398.96
November	7 604	3 707	2 061	2 375	1 522	5 558	36.0	138.9	14.74	11.40	530.64	400.14
December	7 613	3 710	2 059	2 378	1 525	5 560	36.2	139.4	14.76	11.38	534.31	400.58

Table 20-2. Private Services—Prices and Employment

Year and month	Producer prices (not seasonally adjusted)			Employment (thousands, seasonally adjusted)											
	Hotels and motels (June 1993 = 100)	Health services (Dec. 1994 = 100)	Legal services (Dec. 1996 = 100)	Total		By industry group									
				All workers	Nonsupervisory workers	Agricultural services	Hotels and other lodging places	Personal services	Business services				Auto repair, services, and parking	Miscellaneous repair services	Motion pictures
									Total	Personnel supply services		Computer and data processing			
										Total	Help supply				
1970	...	...	...	11 548	10 481	...	...	898	1 397	...	...	...	...	189	...
1971	...	...	...	11 797	10 655	...	...	848	1 402	...	...	...	...	193	...
1972	...	...	...	12 276	11 059	...	813	828	1 491	214	...	107	399	199	...
1973	...	...	...	12 857	11 606	...	854	823	1 610	247	...	120	422	205	...
1974	...	...	...	13 441	12 100	...	878	807	1 686	257	...	135	430	217	...
1975	...	...	...	13 892	12 479	...	898	782	1 697	242	...	143	439	218	...
1976	...	...	...	14 551	13 043	184	929	790	1 806	293	...	159	466	227	...
1977	...	...	...	15 302	13 683	197	956	806	1 958	357	...	187	498	241	...
1978	...	...	...	16 252	14 476	217	988	827	2 181	438	...	224	549	261	...
1979	...	...	...	17 112	15 193	234	1 060	821	2 410	508	...	271	575	282	...
1980	...	...	...	17 890	15 921	246	1 076	818	2 564	543	...	304	571	289	...
1981	...	...	...	18 615	16 562	258	1 119	828	2 700	585	...	337	574	293	...
1982	...	...	...	19 021	16 867	267	1 133	844	2 722	541	417	365	589	287	...
1983	...	...	...	19 664	17 429	287	1 172	869	2 948	619	488	416	619	287	...
1984	...	...	...	20 746	18 284	328	1 263	918	3 353	797	643	474	682	310	...
1985	...	...	...	21 927	19 305	361	1 331	957	3 679	891	732	542	730	319	...
1986	...	...	...	22 957	20 163	389	1 378	991	3 957	990	837	588	762	322	...
1987	...	...	...	24 110	21 132	411	1 464	1 027	4 278	1 177	989	629	794	321	...
1988	...	...	...	25 504	22 323	447	1 540	1 056	4 638	1 350	1 126	673	834	350	341
1989	...	...	...	26 907	23 532	465	1 596	1 086	4 941	1 455	1 216	736	884	374	375
1990	...	...	...	27 934	24 387	490	1 631	1 104	5 139	1 535	1 288	772	914	374	408
1991	...	...	...	28 336	24 712	487	1 589	1 112	5 086	1 485	1 268	797	882	341	411
1992	...	...	...	29 052	25 347	490	1 576	1 116	5 315	1 629	1 411	836	881	347	401
1993	...	...	...	30 197	26 380	519	1 596	1 137	5 735	1 906	1 669	893	925	349	412
1994	102.6	...	...	31 579	27 632	564	1 631	1 140	6 281	2 272	2 017	959	968	338	441
1995	106.1	102.4	...	33 117	28 979	582	1 668	1 163	6 812	2 476	2 189	1 090	1 020	359	488
1996	110.1	104.6	...	34 454	30 144	627	1 715	1 180	7 293	2 654	2 352	1 228	1 080	372	525
1997	115.6	106.1	102.5	36 040	31 518	678	1 746	1 186	7 988	2 985	2 656	1 409	1 120	374	550
1998	119.9	107.7	106.1	37 533	32 786	708	1 789	1 201	8 618	3 278	2 926	1 615	1 145	376	576
1999	124.9	109.9	108.7	39 027	34 027	766	1 848	1 233	9 267	3 601	3 228	1 831	1 184	377	610
1996															
January	107.4	104.0	...	33 695	29 475	608	1 681	1 169	6 988	2 489	2 196	1 162	1 052	368	510
February	108.3	104.2	...	33 937	29 702	616	1 691	1 173	7 102	2 555	2 258	1 175	1 060	370	509
March	109.8	104.2	...	34 083	29 830	617	1 701	1 176	7 143	2 573	2 274	1 187	1 066	372	519
April	110.1	104.3	...	34 174	29 906	615	1 706	1 178	7 184	2 596	2 298	1 198	1 070	373	520
May	110.0	104.3	...	34 300	30 021	620	1 714	1 182	7 221	2 625	2 324	1 206	1 073	373	526
June	110.6	104.5	...	34 440	30 126	628	1 733	1 182	7 266	2 655	2 355	1 212	1 078	373	526
July	110.7	104.6	...	34 536	30 217	631	1 719	1 181	7 318	2 678	2 376	1 229	1 084	372	530
August	110.9	104.7	...	34 666	30 342	635	1 717	1 182	7 384	2 709	2 404	1 243	1 090	372	525
September	110.7	104.8	...	34 729	30 387	635	1 720	1 183	7 413	2 725	2 419	1 257	1 092	372	531
October	111.1	105.2	...	34 819	30 467	639	1 723	1 185	7 418	2 692	2 391	1 274	1 097	372	533
November	110.4	105.2	...	34 994	30 592	644	1 731	1 186	7 514	2 755	2 449	1 289	1 099	374	532
December	110.9	105.3	100.0	35 093	30 685	644	1 735	1 184	7 568	2 775	2 469	1 306	1 102	373	533
1997															
January	112.5	105.7	101.6	35 237	30 805	649	1 738	1 184	7 632	2 807	2 503	1 323	1 104	371	537
February	113.7	105.8	101.9	35 402	30 950	654	1 742	1 185	7 722	2 851	2 538	1 341	1 110	370	537
March	116.3	105.9	102.0	35 553	31 078	660	1 744	1 184	7 801	2 894	2 576	1 359	1 114	371	539
April	117.3	105.9	102.0	35 739	31 253	669	1 748	1 182	7 878	2 932	2 609	1 377	1 119	372	539
May	115.1	105.9	102.1	35 896	31 392	679	1 746	1 189	7 939	2 959	2 634	1 392	1 121	373	542
June	115.8	106.0	102.2	35 998	31 483	679	1 740	1 184	7 991	2 987	2 655	1 406	1 116	374	546
July	116.7	106.2	102.3	36 167	31 661	683	1 738	1 184	8 049	3 023	2 690	1 418	1 121	375	549
August	116.0	106.2	102.5	36 216	31 697	686	1 735	1 186	8 045	3 007	2 670	1 430	1 121	376	555
September	115.9	106.3	102.6	36 372	31 826	691	1 744	1 187	8 123	3 045	2 707	1 446	1 124	376	558
October	116.2	106.3	102.8	36 484	31 919	692	1 755	1 190	8 146	3 062	2 721	1 460	1 126	376	560
November	115.8	106.2	103.7	36 607	32 011	690	1 754	1 194	8 220	3 110	2 767	1 471	1 128	376	563
December	115.5	106.4	104.1	36 781	32 148	689	1 757	1 186	8 304	3 150	2 803	1 492	1 131	375	571
1998															
January	116.8	107.0	105.1	36 905	32 245	688	1 768	1 183	8 369	3 181	2 827	1 506	1 132	376	570
February	117.7	107.1	105.6	37 002	32 337	685	1 765	1 189	8 404	3 197	2 844	1 521	1 128	376	576
March	119.7	107.3	105.9	37 104	32 406	690	1 767	1 192	8 435	3 203	2 849	1 538	1 130	376	574
April	120.6	107.4	106.0	37 190	32 478	695	1 775	1 195	8 465	3 215	2 862	1 558	1 131	375	574
May	119.9	107.5	106.1	37 351	32 618	696	1 783	1 207	8 531	3 241	2 889	1 580	1 138	375	574
June	119.5	107.5	106.1	37 480	32 734	700	1 790	1 202	8 609	3 289	2 933	1 603	1 144	377	562
July	120.3	107.8	106.2	37 604	32 866	706	1 796	1 203	8 645	3 281	2 932	1 630	1 148	376	575
August	120.6	107.9	106.4	37 678	32 935	713	1 799	1 206	8 687	3 306	2 956	1 647	1 153	375	578
September	120.1	108.0	106.5	37 800	33 023	717	1 803	1 205	8 704	3 305	2 953	1 664	1 156	376	580
October	121.8	108.3	106.5	37 929	33 127	720	1 806	1 207	8 776	3 334	2 978	1 687	1 157	376	580
November	120.8	108.3	106.5	38 071	33 235	731	1 808	1 212	8 841	3 366	3 014	1 710	1 162	376	580
December	120.4	108.4	106.7	38 218	33 350	746	1 815	1 216	8 910	3 400	3 046	1 730	1 165	376	584
1999															
January	122.9	109.2	107.4	38 330	33 429	753	1 826	1 221	8 970	3 441	3 086	1 752	1 169	376	580
February	123.0	109.4	107.9	38 483	33 568	757	1 830	1 218	9 032	3 478	3 121	1 772	1 176	375	592
March	125.1	109.4	108.2	38 589	33 647	754	1 835	1 220	9 081	3 507	3 149	1 786	1 179	374	591
April	126.3	109.4	108.3	38 718	33 747	757	1 838	1 225	9 133	3 530	3 169	1 800	1 183	376	600
May	125.5	109.5	108.4	38 821	33 840	756	1 837	1 223	9 183	3 554	3 189	1 815	1 185	378	613
June	125.4	109.6	108.7	38 970	33 954	761	1 845	1 228	9 242	3 585	3 216	1 831	1 185	375	614
July	125.1	110.0	108.8	39 070	34 034	765	1 851	1 233	9 303	3 618	3 244	1 846	1 185	375	617
August	125.5	110.0	108.9	39 191	34 159	764	1 857	1 237	9 339	3 626	3 251	1 857	1 185	376	618
September	124.9	110.1	109.2	39 291	34 266	770	1 863	1 243	9 404	3 678	3 298	1 866	1 186	377	619
October	126.3	110.5	109.3	39 482	34 448	774	1 863	1 247	9 465	3 712	3 327	1 874	1 191	379	624
November	125.3	110.6	109.5	39 606	34 538	782	1 868	1 252	9 502	3 734	3 343	1 880	1 191	379	625
December	123.8	110.8	109.8	39 707	34 624	782	1 868	1 257	9 538	3 748	3 358	1 888	1 192	382	624

Table 20-2. Private Services—Prices and Employment—*Continued*

(Thousands, seasonally adjusted.)

Year and month	By industry group—*Continued*							Health services				
	Amusement and recreation	Legal services	Educational services	Social services	Museums, botanical gardens, and zoos	Membership organizations	Engineering and management	Total	Hospitals	Offices and clinics of medical doctors	Nursing and personal care facilities	Home healthcare services
1970	. . .	. . .	940	. . .	. . .	. . .	. . .	3 053	1 863	. . .	. . .	. . .
1971	. . .	. . .	948	. . .	. . .	. . .	. . .	3 239	1 935	. . .	. . .	. . .
1972	. . .	271	958	553	. . .	1 403	. . .	3 412	1 980	467	591	. . .
1973	. . .	296	975	552	. . .	1 410	. . .	3 641	2 051	519	659	. . .
1974	. . .	326	990	625	. . .	1 438	. . .	3 887	2 160	567	708	. . .
1975	. . .	341	1 001	690	. . .	1 452	. . .	4 134	2 274	608	759	. . .
1976	. . .	364	1 013	763	. . .	1 487	. . .	4 350	2 363	644	809	. . .
1977	. . .	394	1 031	855	. . .	1 495	. . .	4 584	2 465	681	860	. . .
1978	. . .	427	1 062	991	. . .	1 502	. . .	4 792	2 538	720	911	. . .
1979	. . .	460	1 090	1 081	. . .	1 516	. . .	4 993	2 608	761	951	. . .
1980	. . .	498	1 138	1 134	. . .	1 539	. . .	5 278	2 750	802	997	. . .
1981	. . .	532	1 179	1 149	. . .	1 527	. . .	5 562	2 904	845	1 029	. . .
1982	. . .	565	1 199	1 149	. . .	1 526	. . .	5 811	3 014	887	1 067	. . .
1983	. . .	602	1 225	1 188	. . .	1 510	. . .	5 986	3 037	934	1 106	. . .
1984	. . .	645	1 270	1 222	. . .	1 504	. . .	6 118	3 004	977	1 147	. . .
1985	. . .	692	1 359	1 325	. . .	1 517	. . .	6 293	2 997	1 028	1 198	. . .
1986	. . .	747	1 421	1 406	. . .	1 536	. . .	6 528	3 037	1 081	1 245	. . .
1987	. . .	801	1 449	1 454	. . .	1 614	. . .	6 794	3 142	1 139	1 283	. . .
1988	977	845	1 567	1 552	58	1 740	2 230	7 105	3 294	1 200	1 311	216
1989	1 033	880	1 647	1 644	62	1 836	2 389	7 463	3 439	1 268	1 356	244
1990	1 076	908	1 661	1 734	66	1 946	2 478	7 814	3 549	1 338	1 415	291
1991	1 122	912	1 710	1 845	69	1 982	2 433	8 183	3 655	1 405	1 493	345
1992	1 188	914	1 678	1 959	73	1 973	2 471	8 490	3 750	1 463	1 533	398
1993	1 258	924	1 711	2 070	76	2 035	2 521	8 756	3 779	1 506	1 585	469
1994	1 334	924	1 850	2 200	79	2 082	2 579	8 992	3 763	1 545	1 649	559
1995	1 417	921	1 965	2 336	80	2 146	2 731	9 230	3 772	1 609	1 691	629
1996	1 476	928	2 030	2 413	85	2 201	2 844	9 478	3 812	1 678	1 730	675
1997	1 552	944	2 104	2 518	90	2 277	2 988	9 703	3 860	1 739	1 756	710
1998	1 594	971	2 178	2 646	94	2 372	3 139	9 852	3 930	1 806	1 772	666
1999	1 660	997	2 276	2 800	98	2 425	3 254	9 989	3 982	1 877	1 784	636
1996												
January	1 435	921	1 988	2 370	82	2 172	2 790	9 351	3 791	1 647	1 713	654
February	1 446	924	2 002	2 385	83	2 178	2 798	9 388	3 798	1 655	1 717	659
March	1 458	924	2 009	2 390	83	2 181	2 815	9 414	3 803	1 661	1 722	662
April	1 471	924	2 014	2 398	84	2 184	2 810	9 430	3 804	1 668	1 724	666
May	1 469	926	2 018	2 408	85	2 195	2 831	9 448	3 808	1 672	1 728	671
June	1 474	927	2 030	2 415	85	2 199	2 843	9 472	3 808	1 678	1 732	674
July	1 479	928	2 044	2 422	86	2 199	2 845	9 491	3 811	1 683	1 734	675
August	1 488	930	2 045	2 429	86	2 213	2 858	9 506	3 811	1 689	1 734	679
September	1 481	929	2 038	2 431	86	2 217	2 870	9 527	3 820	1 692	1 736	683
October	1 497	931	2 051	2 438	87	2 221	2 878	9 548	3 823	1 695	1 739	687
November	1 501	933	2 060	2 445	87	2 227	2 891	9 571	3 829	1 700	1 741	692
December	1 506	933	2 063	2 448	88	2 231	2 901	9 587	3 833	1 703	1 743	695
1997												
January	1 520	936	2 070	2 459	89	2 235	2 904	9 613	3 835	1 711	1 745	703
February	1 528	936	2 074	2 469	89	2 238	2 925	9 629	3 841	1 720	1 747	703
March	1 535	939	2 079	2 481	89	2 245	2 933	9 646	3 848	1 720	1 748	708
April	1 541	942	2 089	2 494	89	2 256	2 954	9 667	3 849	1 726	1 753	713
May	1 557	942	2 092	2 504	90	2 265	2 963	9 686	3 853	1 735	1 758	712
June	1 563	943	2 099	2 517	90	2 272	2 976	9 692	3 856	1 736	1 756	712
July	1 566	945	2 109	2 542	90	2 283	2 992	9 716	3 862	1 741	1 758	715
August	1 556	945	2 114	2 544	90	2 291	3 011	9 728	3 866	1 742	1 760	714
September	1 558	949	2 123	2 549	91	2 296	3 023	9 739	3 871	1 747	1 760	714
October	1 559	950	2 128	2 557	91	2 305	3 044	9 757	3 876	1 755	1 762	713
November	1 558	952	2 131	2 560	91	2 309	3 054	9 771	3 883	1 761	1 764	710
December	1 568	955	2 134	2 568	91	2 324	3 071	9 792	3 888	1 771	1 766	707
1998												
January	1 565	957	2 143	2 577	91	2 335	3 085	9 794	3 895	1 773	1 763	701
February	1 569	959	2 149	2 586	92	2 344	3 098	9 802	3 897	1 778	1 766	695
March	1 572	961	2 156	2 598	92	2 354	3 111	9 808	3 902	1 782	1 766	689
April	1 577	964	2 159	2 609	93	2 359	3 118	9 816	3 912	1 788	1 769	677
May	1 582	967	2 165	2 626	93	2 364	3 133	9 837	3 921	1 794	1 771	673
June	1 581	970	2 171	2 646	93	2 369	3 141	9 848	3 929	1 800	1 772	670
July	1 594	974	2 177	2 666	93	2 374	3 149	9 856	3 937	1 806	1 772	660
August	1 600	976	2 174	2 656	94	2 381	3 150	9 867	3 943	1 814	1 773	654
September	1 615	979	2 191	2 682	95	2 387	3 159	9 885	3 950	1 823	1 776	650
October	1 613	983	2 210	2 689	94	2 395	3 164	9 897	3 957	1 830	1 777	645
November	1 627	983	2 215	2 700	96	2 399	3 176	9 906	3 959	1 836	1 778	641
December	1 632	985	2 224	2 712	96	2 405	3 181	9 917	3 962	1 839	1 778	639
1999												
January	1 632	986	2 223	2 724	97	2 413	3 189	9 920	3 963	1 847	1 782	630
February	1 633	989	2 242	2 738	97	2 420	3 198	9 939	3 971	1 853	1 783	636
March	1 637	991	2 250	2 750	98	2 428	3 205	9 953	3 975	1 859	1 785	636
April	1 639	994	2 260	2 764	97	2 423	3 219	9 967	3 978	1 865	1 783	637
May	1 640	995	2 270	2 775	97	2 419	3 232	9 975	3 980	1 871	1 785	635
June	1 649	997	2 278	2 799	98	2 427	3 246	9 983	3 983	1 875	1 785	635
July	1 650	996	2 285	2 790	98	2 419	3 265	9 994	3 983	1 880	1 784	635
August	1 664	999	2 292	2 808	98	2 426	3 276	10 008	3 987	1 885	1 786	636
September	1 672	1 000	2 294	2 823	98	2 430	3 283	10 015	3 989	1 888	1 785	635
October	1 691	1 003	2 299	2 845	99	2 431	3 300	10 027	3 992	1 893	1 785	636
November	1 701	1 005	2 305	2 868	99	2 434	3 310	10 041	3 992	1 898	1 785	637
December	1 703	1 007	2 309	2 884	99	2 438	3 327	10 053	3 997	1 903	1 787	637

Table 20-3. Private Services—Hours and Earnings

(Nonsupervisory workers.)

Year and month	Average weekly hours (seasonally adjusted)	Aggregate weekly hours index (1982=100, seasonally adjusted)	Average hourly earnings (dollars, not seasonally adjusted)											
					Business services			Auto repair services parking	Amusement and recreation	Social services	Engineering and management	Health services		
			All private services	Hotels and motels	Total	Help supply	Computer and data processing					Hospitals	Offices and clinics of doctors	Nursing and personal care facilities
1970	34.4	65.3	2.81	1.97	...	...	...	...	...	...	...	...	2.79	...
1971	33.9	65.6	3.04	2.13	...	...	...	...	...	...	...	...	3.01	...
1972	33.9	68.0	3.27	2.28	...	...	4.53	3.26	...	2.46	...	...	3.22	2.28
1973	33.8	71.3	3.47	2.41	...	...	4.79	3.47	...	2.62	...	...	3.40	2.35
1974	33.6	73.9	3.75	2.61	...	...	5.02	3.75	...	2.82	...	...	3.66	2.58
1975	33.5	76.0	4.02	2.79	...	...	5.26	3.99	...	3.26	...	...	4.02	2.84
1976	33.3	78.8	4.31	3.06	...	...	5.18	4.31	...	3.58	...	...	4.35	3.07
1977	33.0	82.0	4.65	3.31	...	...	5.32	4.61	...	3.77	...	...	4.66	3.27
1978	32.8	86.3	4.99	3.64	...	...	5.76	5.03	...	3.93	...	...	5.05	3.57
1979	32.7	90.2	5.36	4.00	...	...	6.35	5.59	...	3.97	...	...	5.48	3.85
1980	32.6	94.3	5.85	4.45	...	...	7.16	6.10	...	4.26	...	...	6.06	4.17
1981	32.6	98.2	6.41	4.85	...	...	7.92	6.44	...	4.62	...	...	6.80	4.54
1982	32.6	100.0	6.92	5.04	...	...	9.00	6.76	...	4.92	...	6.92	7.56	4.89
1983	32.7	103.6	7.31	5.27	...	...	10.10	6.94	...	5.13	...	7.41	8.12	5.20
1984	32.6	108.2	7.59	5.46	...	...	10.50	7.21	...	5.46	...	7.68	8.55	5.42
1985	32.5	114.0	7.90	5.83	...	...	10.98	7.40	...	5.63	...	8.02	9.00	5.61
1986	32.5	119.2	8.18	5.97	...	...	11.63	7.55	...	5.81	...	8.35	9.36	5.80
1987	32.5	124.9	8.49	6.17	...	...	12.29	7.78	...	6.11	...	8.61	9.84	6.00
1988	32.6	132.2	8.88	6.42	8.61	7.41	13.21	8.16	7.39	6.36	12.36	9.07	10.51	6.33
1989	32.6	139.3	9.38	6.69	9.08	7.73	14.19	8.47	7.82	6.74	13.00	9.78	11.21	6.80
1990	32.5	144.2	9.83	6.98	9.48	8.09	15.11	8.77	8.11	7.11	13.56	10.58	11.79	7.24
1991	32.4	145.3	10.23	7.14	9.76	8.31	15.57	8.96	8.04	7.43	14.08	11.14	12.51	7.56
1992	32.5	149.3	10.54	7.38	9.97	8.29	15.81	9.16	8.08	7.64	14.60	11.42	13.03	7.86
1993	32.5	155.4	10.78	7.57	10.12	8.24	16.46	9.33	8.32	7.86	15.01	11.89	13.46	8.17
1994	32.5	162.9	11.04	7.75	10.31	8.38	17.17	9.58	8.49	8.12	15.36	12.26	13.83	8.50
1995	32.4	170.5	11.39	7.93	10.71	8.80	17.79	9.92	8.74	8.33	15.79	12.54	14.30	8.77
1996	32.4	177.4	11.79	8.16	11.23	9.20	18.78	10.20	8.83	8.55	16.37	14.70	13.17	9.01
1997	32.6	186.6	12.28	8.55	11.83	9.65	20.13	10.60	9.18	8.82	17.14	15.03	13.79	9.34
1998	32.6	194.2	12.84	8.94	12.59	10.18	21.34	11.08	9.58	9.18	17.88	15.46	14.31	9.77
1999	32.6	201.3	13.36	9.25	13.26	10.56	22.38	11.45	9.81	9.54	18.52	14.85	15.96	10.17
1996														
January	32.2	172.4	11.73	8.15	11.08	9.07	18.15	10.05	9.09	8.52	16.04	14.65	12.90	8.97
February	32.3	174.3	11.72	8.04	11.09	9.15	18.25	10.07	9.13	8.46	16.07	14.61	12.95	8.93
March	32.4	175.6	11.72	8.02	11.08	9.13	18.32	10.12	9.05	8.48	16.12	14.59	12.99	8.94
April	32.3	175.5	11.71	8.08	11.13	9.13	18.35	10.12	8.90	8.47	16.20	14.64	13.01	8.98
May	32.4	176.7	11.67	8.10	11.10	9.12	18.45	10.18	8.80	8.46	16.17	14.61	13.08	8.94
June	32.5	177.9	11.66	8.04	11.20	9.14	18.80	10.14	8.38	8.52	16.35	14.63	13.15	8.94
July	32.3	177.3	11.61	7.96	11.16	9.16	18.68	10.17	8.26	8.47	16.24	14.71	13.13	9.02
August	32.4	178.6	11.63	7.95	11.17	9.09	18.87	10.18	8.25	8.49	16.34	14.67	13.19	8.99
September	32.5	179.4	11.90	8.26	11.33	9.18	19.16	10.27	8.88	8.67	16.70	14.81	13.33	9.05
October	32.4	179.3	11.94	8.36	11.30	9.24	19.15	10.30	9.07	8.63	16.55	14.77	13.35	9.09
November	32.4	180.1	12.04	8.39	11.43	9.39	19.32	10.37	9.31	8.65	16.66	14.80	13.44	9.11
December	32.5	181.2	12.16	8.58	11.59	9.53	19.65	10.45	9.44	8.74	16.91	14.87	13.53	9.11
1997														
January	32.4	181.3	12.19	8.49	11.68	9.62	19.54	10.51	9.35	8.73	16.82	14.90	13.56	9.20
February	32.6	183.3	12.24	8.49	11.76	9.60	19.87	10.44	9.43	8.76	17.03	14.92	13.60	9.20
March	32.6	184.1	12.24	8.49	11.75	9.59	19.86	10.48	9.41	8.76	17.05	14.92	13.67	9.20
April	32.6	185.1	12.19	8.48	11.72	9.58	19.76	10.48	9.30	8.74	16.96	14.94	13.64	9.24
May	32.6	185.9	12.16	8.47	11.76	9.69	19.86	10.48	9.11	8.73	16.99	14.93	13.70	9.28
June	32.5	185.9	12.14	8.43	11.80	9.62	20.13	10.49	8.73	8.80	17.09	14.95	13.68	9.25
July	32.6	187.5	12.06	8.40	11.72	9.55	19.97	10.50	8.49	8.73	16.96	15.04	13.74	9.38
August	32.6	187.7	12.12	8.38	11.78	9.56	20.16	10.61	8.78	8.78	17.02	15.00	14.00	9.00
September	32.6	188.5	12.36	8.63	11.87	9.58	20.34	10.69	9.31	8.92	17.23	15.11	13.95	9.46
October	32.6	189.0	12.41	8.66	11.91	9.67	20.47	10.76	9.46	8.91	17.33	15.19	13.95	9.50
November	32.6	189.6	12.57	8.82	12.10	9.77	20.73	10.87	9.81	8.98	17.65	15.21	14.02	9.50
December	32.6	190.4	12.61	8.96	12.11	9.87	20.67	10.88	9.82	8.98	17.56	15.26	14.13	9.54
1998														
January	32.7	191.6	12.66	8.87	12.26	10.02	20.61	10.94	9.75	9.03	17.54	15.27	14.14	9.62
February	32.6	191.5	12.75	8.91	12.41	10.08	21.02	10.91	9.81	9.09	17.75	15.28	14.20	9.62
March	32.6	191.9	12.77	8.91	12.44	10.11	21.08	10.91	9.82	9.09	17.77	15.30	14.22	9.64
April	32.6	192.4	12.77	8.91	12.48	10.14	21.06	10.99	9.65	9.08	17.72	15.37	14.24	9.71
May	32.7	193.8	12.75	8.93	12.50	10.19	21.14	11.04	9.56	9.09	17.76	15.35	14.29	9.70
June	32.6	193.9	12.70	8.87	12.52	10.16	21.24	11.05	9.18	9.11	17.68	15.37	14.24	9.72
July	32.7	195.2	12.67	8.74	12.59	10.22	21.27	11.09	9.05	9.12	17.73	15.44	14.22	9.78
August	32.7	195.7	12.75	8.75	12.62	10.13	21.53	11.12	9.12	9.20	17.95	15.50	14.31	9.77
September	32.6	195.6	12.97	8.99	12.80	10.23	21.54	11.15	9.65	9.30	18.02	15.67	14.35	9.91
October	32.7	196.8	13.00	9.07	12.71	10.20	21.65	11.20	9.80	9.28	18.13	15.63	14.43	9.89
November	32.6	196.8	13.13	9.14	12.87	10.28	21.93	11.24	10.05	9.35	18.28	15.65	14.49	9.87
December	32.7	198.1	13.16	9.25	12.85	10.35	21.77	11.31	10.13	9.36	18.20	15.71	14.58	9.94
1999														
January	32.6	198.0	13.29	9.20	13.15	10.61	21.86	11.33	10.05	9.44	18.27	15.79	14.61	9.99
February	32.6	198.8	13.30	9.22	13.15	10.53	22.08	11.32	10.09	9.43	18.27	15.83	14.59	10.00
March	32.6	199.3	13.31	9.21	13.15	10.56	22.01	11.32	10.11	9.43	18.26	15.83	14.65	10.00
April	32.6	199.9	13.30	9.18	13.20	10.54	22.20	11.37	9.97	9.45	18.35	15.84	14.77	10.04
May	32.6	200.4	13.32	9.20	13.27	10.54	22.47	11.40	9.79	9.49	18.56	15.85	14.76	10.04
June	32.6	201.1	13.21	9.13	13.20	10.50	22.36	11.39	9.34	9.47	18.30	15.89	14.73	10.11
July	32.6	201.6	13.18	9.05	13.21	10.48	22.33	11.45	9.17	9.48	18.42	15.96	14.81	10.21
August	32.6	202.3	13.23	9.09	13.24	10.47	22.48	11.45	9.28	9.54	18.59	15.94	14.88	10.19
September	32.6	202.9	13.45	9.28	13.40	10.63	22.48	11.54	9.80	9.66	18.69	16.14	14.97	10.33
October	32.7	204.6	13.51	9.42	13.32	10.58	22.68	11.55	10.09	9.67	18.80	16.14	15.13	10.35
November	32.7	205.2	13.57	9.49	13.35	10.57	22.74	11.60	10.27	9.67	18.85	16.14	15.09	10.39
December	32.7	205.7	13.65	9.59	13.43	10.70	22.82	11.70	10.49	9.74	18.88	16.19	15.16	10.44

Table 20-3. Private Services—Hours and Earnings—*Continued*

(Nonsupervisory workers.)

Year and month	Average weekly earnings (dollars, not seasonally adjusted)											
			Business services							Health services		
	All private services	Hotels and motels	Total	Help supply	Computer and data processing	Auto repair, services, and parking	Amusement and recreation	Social services	Engineering and management	Hospitals	Offices and clinics of doctors	Nursing and personal care facilities
1970	96.66	68.16	...	...	...	...	...	...	...	95.42	...	...
1971	103.06	72.42	...	...	...	...	...	...	...	103.24	...	...
1972	110.85	75.47	...	...	163.53	122.25	...	80.44	...	111.73	...	72.73
1973	117.29	79.53	...	...	173.88	130.13	...	84.36	...	117.98	...	73.79
1974	126.00	84.56	...	...	184.74	140.25	...	86.57	...	127.00	...	80.50
1975	134.67	88.44	...	...	196.20	150.02	...	98.13	...	139.49	...	88.61
1976	143.52	97.92	...	...	190.62	163.35	...	109.55	...	150.08	...	95.78
1977	153.45	103.27	...	...	197.90	172.41	...	113.10	...	158.44	...	101.37
1978	163.67	113.93	...	...	211.39	188.12	...	115.15	...	172.21	...	111.38
1979	175.27	124.00	...	...	231.78	209.63	...	120.29	...	187.42	...	119.35
1980	190.71	135.73	...	...	260.62	229.36	...	130.36	...	206.65	...	128.85
1981	208.97	148.41	...	...	294.62	244.08	...	141.37	...	231.20	...	141.19
1982	225.59	153.22	...	161.79	338.40	254.85	...	150.06	...	260.82	221.44	153.55
1983	239.04	161.79	...	171.57	387.84	260.94	...	160.57	...	276.89	233.42	162.76
1984	247.43	167.62	...	185.63	400.05	270.38	...	168.17	...	291.56	237.31	168.56
1985	256.75	176.07	...	198.25	422.73	276.76	...	173.40	...	308.70	247.82	175.03
1986	265.85	183.28	...	206.82	444.27	282.37	...	179.53	...	320.11	260.52	182.12
1987	275.93	190.04	...	218.15	460.88	285.53	...	190.02	...	335.54	267.77	189.60
1988	289.49	200.95	286.71	231.93	499.34	299.47	201.01	199.70	462.26	357.34	286.61	200.03
1989	305.79	208.73	301.46	237.31	539.22	310.85	214.27	211.64	486.20	381.14	311.98	216.92
1990	319.48	214.98	313.79	249.17	575.69	320.98	220.59	223.25	505.79	403.22	336.44	232.40
1991	331.45	217.06	322.08	256.78	591.66	326.14	215.47	232.56	525.18	427.84	355.37	242.68
1992	342.55	226.57	329.01	257.82	602.36	333.42	218.16	239.90	544.58	448.23	367.72	253.88
1993	350.35	234.67	333.96	257.91	627.13	338.68	227.97	244.45	556.87	465.72	382.86	263.07
1994	358.80	240.25	341.26	266.48	649.03	347.75	228.38	252.53	571.39	478.52	397.22	274.55
1995	369.04	245.83	354.50	279.84	672.46	356.13	235.98	259.90	587.39	494.78	407.55	285.03
1996	382.00	251.33	372.84	295.32	708.01	368.22	238.41	265.91	607.33	505.68	433.29	291.92
1997	400.33	264.20	396.31	312.66	770.98	383.72	246.94	276.07	641.04	524.55	457.83	302.62
1998	418.58	279.82	421.77	329.83	821.59	397.77	255.79	287.33	668.71	541.10	472.23	318.50
1999	435.54	285.83	446.86	341.09	861.63	407.62	259.97	297.65	690.80	553.81	488.57	329.51
1996												
January	373.01	241.24	356.78	279.36	675.18	354.77	236.34	261.56	583.86	505.43	417.96	292.42
February	377.38	243.61	363.75	286.40	686.20	361.51	241.03	261.41	597.80	502.58	423.47	286.65
March	377.38	243.81	367.86	293.99	688.83	365.33	236.21	261.18	601.28	500.44	426.07	285.19
April	377.06	244.82	366.18	289.42	691.80	363.31	237.63	260.88	602.64	500.69	424.13	289.16
May	375.77	247.86	367.41	292.75	691.88	366.48	229.68	261.41	596.67	499.66	426.41	286.08
June	382.45	253.26	376.32	297.05	720.04	371.12	232.96	268.38	614.76	503.27	435.27	293.23
July	377.33	249.15	369.40	294.95	694.90	369.17	234.58	262.57	597.63	504.55	428.04	294.95
August	380.30	252.02	373.08	295.43	711.40	373.61	235.13	264.04	606.21	504.65	432.63	291.28
September	387.94	258.54	378.42	294.68	733.83	372.80	233.54	273.11	627.92	507.98	445.22	298.65
October	386.86	259.16	376.29	298.45	721.96	373.89	240.36	267.53	612.35	506.61	440.55	290.88
November	390.10	255.06	380.62	304.24	730.30	375.39	247.65	269.02	616.42	509.12	446.21	292.43
December	397.63	263.41	388.27	307.82	750.63	376.20	254.88	275.31	632.43	514.50	453.26	297.90
1997												
January	390.08	249.61	383.10	303.03	734.70	375.21	242.17	268.88	620.66	515.54	447.48	295.32
February	400.25	263.19	393.96	311.04	765.00	376.88	251.78	275.06	645.44	516.23	454.24	298.08
March	399.02	264.04	394.80	312.63	762.62	378.33	249.37	274.19	646.20	517.72	455.21	297.16
April	394.96	259.49	391.45	309.43	754.83	376.23	243.66	270.94	639.39	518.42	451.48	296.60
May	393.98	260.88	392.78	313.96	756.67	378.33	239.59	271.50	630.33	518.07	452.10	296.96
June	398.19	264.70	395.30	307.84	777.02	383.93	240.08	277.20	642.58	521.76	456.91	302.48
July	395.57	262.92	390.28	309.42	756.86	384.30	241.12	273.25	629.22	524.90	454.79	308.60
August	398.75	266.48	396.99	314.52	772.13	389.39	243.66	275.69	634.85	525.00	458.16	304.20
September	401.70	266.67	396.46	310.39	776.99	386.98	242.06	279.20	640.96	527.34	461.75	308.40
October	404.57	270.19	398.99	314.28	784.00	389.51	249.74	277.99	641.21	530.13	463.14	306.85
November	412.30	276.07	407.77	317.53	808.47	390.23	262.91	283.77	663.64	535.39	471.07	310.65
December	411.09	270.59	406.90	321.76	793.73	389.50	261.21	280.18	649.72	535.65	467.70	309.10
1998												
January	410.18	263.44	409.48	326.65	787.30	387.28	256.43	279.93	650.73	537.50	468.03	311.69
February	418.20	278.88	416.98	327.60	815.58	389.49	259.97	285.43	670.95	539.38	477.12	311.69
March	416.30	278.88	416.74	327.56	811.58	389.49	256.30	284.52	673.48	537.03	472.10	312.34
April	413.75	277.10	413.09	320.42	804.49	390.15	252.83	282.39	662.73	536.41	469.92	314.60
May	414.38	279.51	420.00	333.21	809.66	396.34	249.52	282.70	658.90	535.72	468.71	312.34
June	415.29	279.41	421.92	333.25	817.74	396.70	246.94	284.23	659.46	536.41	468.50	315.90
July	416.84	280.55	423.02	333.17	814.64	404.79	256.12	285.46	659.56	538.86	463.57	321.76
August	423.30	287.00	429.08	334.29	841.82	406.99	259.01	291.64	676.72	542.50	472.23	321.43
September	418.93	285.88	413.44	304.85	827.14	399.17	248.97	290.16	666.74	545.32	469.25	327.03
October	423.80	286.61	428.33	333.54	833.53	403.20	255.78	289.54	672.62	543.92	473.30	320.44
November	430.66	286.08	435.01	334.10	857.46	400.14	265.32	295.46	687.33	546.19	481.07	323.74
December	429.02	277.50	435.62	341.55	833.79	402.64	266.42	292.03	675.22	548.28	478.22	323.05
1999												
January	429.27	275.08	439.21	342.70	832.87	402.22	258.29	292.64	681.47	551.07	476.29	323.68
February	432.25	281.21	441.84	343.28	850.08	402.99	263.35	293.27	688.78	552.47	480.01	321.00
March	431.24	279.98	441.84	344.26	847.39	400.73	258.82	290.44	682.92	552.47	479.06	320.00
April	430.92	280.91	443.52	340.44	852.48	404.77	257.23	292.95	688.13	549.65	482.98	322.28
May	435.56	287.96	449.85	341.50	871.84	408.12	256.50	297.99	694.14	548.41	488.56	325.30
June	430.65	283.94	444.84	340.20	858.62	408.90	253.11	295.46	677.10	549.79	481.67	327.56
July	432.30	285.98	443.86	336.41	855.24	412.20	259.51	296.72	685.22	552.22	484.29	334.89
August	439.24	292.70	451.48	342.37	883.46	415.64	262.62	302.42	700.84	551.52	492.53	334.23
September	434.44	287.68	438.18	322.09	867.73	406.21	251.86	301.39	693.40	555.22	491.02	336.76
October	441.78	293.90	450.22	342.79	877.72	408.87	263.35	301.70	699.36	560.06	508.37	334.31
November	443.74	291.34	451.23	345.64	873.22	410.64	268.05	301.70	699.34	560.06	496.46	336.64
December	444.99	286.74	455.28	353.10	876.29	410.67	270.64	302.91	700.45	563.41	497.25	339.30

Table 20-4. Selected Service Industries—Receipts of Taxable Firms

(By kind of business and SIC code, millions of dollars.)

Year	Arrangement of passenger transportation (472)	Real estate agents and managers (653)	Hotels, rooming houses, camps and other lodging places, except on membership basis (70, ex. 704)	Personal services (72)	Business services (73)	Automotive repair, services, and parking (75)	Miscellaneous repair services (76)	Motion pictures (78)
1986	7 465	48 360	47 634	39 587	170 250	53 867	22 478	23 740
1987	8 196	52 919	53 630	43 247	188 856	58 278	24 599	27 754
1988	9 521	58 980	58 637	48 329	223 369	66 053	27 659	31 746
1989	11 041	62 325	61 229	51 832	251 648	70 961	30 064	36 173
1990	12 276	63 023	64 225	54 736	280 699	73 722	32 848	39 982
1991	11 438	63 180	65 284	54 620	287 214	71 542	32 401	42 838
1992	11 926	73 115	71 038	59 597	309 439	78 511	35 238	45 662
1993	12 396	79 206	74 149	62 597	337 403	84 324	36 772	49 799
1994	13 125	80 947	79 555	66 105	375 067	91 865	40 683	53 504
1995	14 192	82 667	84 093	70 607	425 075	99 227	44 870	57 184
1996	15 354	90 186	88 961	73 905	484 242	106 638	46 101	60 279
1997	16 461	99 854	94 139	77 712	548 434	111 444	47 895	62 865
1998	17 038	108 639	100 650	82 798	638 500	119 978	52 365	66 229

Year	Amusement and recreation services (79)	Health services (80)	Legal services (81)	Vocational schools (824)	Social services (83)	Museums, art galleries, and botanical and zoological gardens (84)	Engineering, accounting, research, management and related services (87)
1986	33 984	173 885	63 390	3 327	. . .	. . .	127 885
1987	36 646	196 212	72 115	3 400	. . .	. . .	139 897
1988	41 272	221 741	81 636	4 263	. . .	. . .	160 446
1989	44 539	241 558	89 144	4 577	. . .	. . .	183 528
1990	50 126	271 212	97 640	4 519	15 509	144	198 395
1991	51 654	293 907	100 027	4 183	16 365	154	202 696
1992	57 699	321 653	108 443	4 429	18 201	192	215 624
1993	63 651	335 108	112 145	4 507	20 146	222	222 853
1994	68 453	351 419	114 603	4 710	22 498	231	235 447
1995	77 452	376 279	116 000	5 285	24 858	247	263 835
1996	85 733	398 353	124 659	6 190	27 694	273	292 260
1997	92 837	420 361	133 015	7 031	30 150	322	321 679
1998	97 512	444 727	141 827	8 268	31 970	388	360 823

Table 20-5. Selected Service Industries—Revenue of Tax-Exempt Firms

(By kind of business and SIC code, millions of dollars.)

Year	Camps and member-ship lodging (703, 704)	Selected amuse-ment and recreation services (792, 7991, 7997, 7999)	Health services (80)	Legal aid societies and similar legal services (81)	Libraries (823)	Vocational schools (824)	Social services (83)	Museums, art galleries, and botanical and zoological gardens (84)	Selected membership organizations (86 [pt])	Research, develop-ment, and testing services (873)	Commer-cial, physical, and biological research (8731)	Non-commercial research organizations (8733)	Manage-ment and public relations services (874, ex. 8744)
1986	...	5 070	...	563	...	...	...	...	...	7 125	...	...	791
1987	...	5 858	...	665	...	...	...	...	...	8 304	...	...	902
1988	...	6 506	...	775	...	...	...	...	...	9 014	...	...	1 201
1989	...	7 163	...	944	...	...	...	...	...	9 975	...	...	1 494
1990	798	7 922	267 858	1 088	476	507	45 255	2 871	31 458	11 035	...	...	1 933
1991	782	8 160	298 168	1 162	481	486	49 055	3 048	33 288	11 463	...	...	2 150
1992	808	8 993	324 416	1 161	527	549	53 673	3 199	36 256	12 534	...	...	2 246
1993	817	10 279	345 081	1 190	606	569	59 052	3 615	39 426	13 180	...	...	2 588
1994	836	11 560	363 112	1 241	655	612	63 493	3 972	41 907	13 919	...	...	3 119
1995	846	12 778	385 210	1 278	730	696	70 303	4 295	45 873	14 493	5 951	7 688	3 732
1996	877	13 299	401 047	1 259	754	772	75 240	4 729	48 897	14 906	5 703	8 293	4 821
1997	929	14 600	414 990	1 446	850	871	83 235	6 231	51 098	16 839	5 950	9 953	6 583
1998	993	15 360	436 078	1 599	934	943	90 458	6 566	55 955	18 732	6 770	10 753	7 761

CHAPTER 21: GOVERNMENT

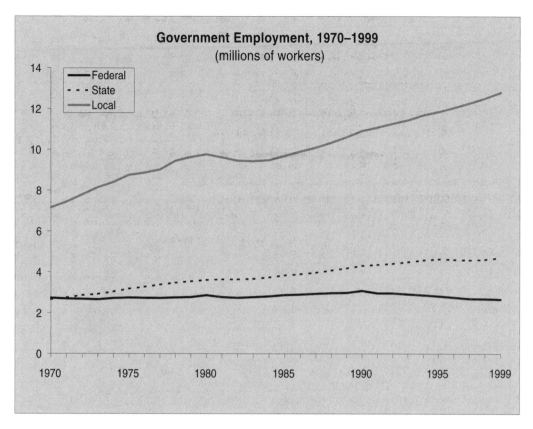

Government Employment, 1970–1999
(millions of workers)

- Federal government employment declined slightly in 1999 and was lower than it had been in 1970. Job growth continued at the state and local levels. Local governments added 5.6 million jobs over the 1970–1999 period, 58 percent of which were accounted for by education. State governments added over 2 million jobs from 1970 to 1999, 42 percent of which were due to education.

- In 1999, for the second consecutive year and the second time since 1969, the federal government achieved a budget surplus. The surplus of $124.4 billion for FY 1999 exceeded the surplus of $69.2 billion in 1998. The surplus was used mainly to repay debt held by the public—also the second time since 1969—and the ratio of debt to GDP dropped to 39.9 percent. Even excluding the "off-budget" (Social Security) surplus, the budget still registered a small surplus in FY 1999. On the national income and product accounts (NIPA) basis, the federal government displayed a similar swing to surplus in calendar 1999.

- State and local governments have had substantial and growing surpluses of receipts over current expenditures for almost the entire 1970–1999 period. Their investment spending, which is outside their NIPA current budget, also has grown; it greatly exceeds their current surplus and is substantially greater than federal investment.

Table 21-1. Federal Government Current Receipts and Expenditures

(Calendar years, billions of dollars, quarterly data are at seasonally adjusted annual rates.)

Year and quarter	Current receipts					Current expenditures						Current surplus or deficit (—), national income and product accounts		
	Total	Personal tax and nontax receipts	Corporate profits tax accruals	Indirect business tax and nontax accruals	Contributions for social insurance	Total	Consumption expenditures	Transfer payments (net)	Grants in-aid to state and local governments	Net interest paid	Subsidies less surplus of government enterprises	Total	Social insurance funds	Other
1970	184.3	88.9	30.6	19.5	45.3	198.6	100.4	57.4	19.3	15.3	6.2	-14.4	1.6	-16.0
1971	189.8	85.9	33.5	20.5	50.0	216.6	103.7	68.2	23.2	15.3	6.3	-26.8	-2.3	-24.5
1972	217.5	102.9	36.6	20.1	57.9	240.0	109.9	75.1	31.7	16.1	7.7	-22.5	0.1	-22.6
1973	248.5	109.7	43.3	21.5	74.0	259.7	111.6	86.4	34.8	19.9	7.0	-11.2	6.9	-18.1
1974	277.3	126.6	45.1	22.1	83.5	291.2	120.4	106.2	36.3	22.9	5.0	-13.9	4.0	-17.8
1975	276.1	120.9	43.6	24.2	87.5	345.4	131.2	135.6	45.1	25.6	7.9	-69.3	-15.4	-53.9
1976	318.9	141.4	54.6	23.8	99.1	371.9	138.0	146.3	50.7	29.9	7.1	-53.0	-14.4	-38.6
1977	359.9	162.3	61.6	25.6	110.3	405.0	151.3	155.0	56.6	32.5	9.8	-45.2	-12.6	-32.5
1978	417.3	189.1	71.4	28.9	127.9	444.2	164.3	165.3	65.5	38.5	10.7	-26.9	-3.0	-24.0
1979	478.3	224.8	74.4	30.1	148.9	489.6	180.0	185.9	66.3	47.0	10.3	-11.4	1.8	-13.2
1980	522.8	250.2	70.3	39.7	162.6	576.6	209.0	223.8	72.3	58.5	12.9	-53.8	-13.8	-40.0
1981	605.6	290.8	65.7	57.3	191.8	659.3	239.9	254.7	72.5	79.1	13.3	-53.7	-12.4	-41.3
1982	599.5	295.7	49.0	49.9	204.9	732.1	265.3	287.3	69.5	93.9	16.1	-132.6	-32.5	-100.1
1983	623.9	287.2	61.3	53.5	221.8	797.8	288.0	309.5	71.6	104.6	23.7	-173.9	-35.4	-138.5
1984	688.1	302.5	75.2	57.6	252.8	856.1	312.0	316.2	76.7	127.5	24.0	-168.1	-5.4	-162.7
1985	747.4	337.2	76.3	57.5	276.5	924.6	339.0	336.9	80.9	144.4	23.3	-177.1	2.6	-179.7
1986	786.4	351.4	83.8	53.7	297.5	978.5	358.3	356.0	87.6	150.5	26.1	-192.1	7.7	-199.9
1987	870.5	394.5	103.2	56.8	315.9	1 018.4	374.6	367.2	83.9	159.8	32.9	-147.9	16.4	-164.3
1988	928.9	405.7	111.1	58.9	353.1	1 066.2	382.8	387.9	91.6	172.1	31.9	-137.4	41.2	-178.6
1989	1 010.3	454.6	117.2	62.3	376.3	1 140.3	399.6	420.1	98.3	193.5	28.7	-130.0	45.6	-175.6
1990	1 055.7	473.6	118.1	63.9	400.1	1 228.7	419.9	455.3	111.4	210.5	31.6	-173.0	44.9	-217.9
1991	1 072.3	465.2	109.9	78.5	418.6	1 287.6	439.1	463.4	131.6	225.2	28.2	-215.3	27.4	-242.8
1992	1 121.3	479.4	118.8	81.3	441.8	1 418.9	445.8	565.2	149.1	229.2	29.6	-297.5	9.1	-306.7
1993	1 197.3	509.9	138.5	85.3	463.7	1 471.5	442.6	597.9	162.6	230.2	38.2	-274.1	6.9	-281.1
1994	1 293.7	547.8	156.7	95.2	493.9	1 506.0	439.7	618.6	174.5	239.6	33.6	-212.3	22.8	-235.1
1995	1 383.7	591.8	179.3	93.0	519.6	1 575.7	439.2	652.1	184.5	267.5	32.4	-192.0	19.9	-211.9
1996	1 499.1	670.0	190.6	95.1	543.3	1 635.9	445.3	691.6	190.4	273.6	35.1	-136.8	16.7	-153.5
1997	1 625.5	751.9	203.0	93.7	577.0	1 678.8	456.9	717.5	196.8	276.2	31.5	-53.3	30.5	-83.8
1998	1 754.0	836.0	209.5	96.4	612.1	1 705.0	453.7	731.0	209.1	278.8	32.4	49.0	56.9	-7.9
1999	1 874.6	902.2	219.3	100.5	652.5	1 750.2	470.8	746.1	229.3	264.7	39.3	124.4	90.7	33.7
1991														
1st quarter	1 057.5	461.0	107.1	75.9	413.4	1 217.5	443.8	401.2	122.8	220.0	29.9	-160.1	31.3	-191.3
2nd quarter	1 066.2	463.1	109.0	77.8	416.4	1 279.7	441.5	456.8	128.1	225.4	27.5	-213.5	26.4	-239.9
3rd quarter	1 077.2	465.8	111.9	78.9	420.6	1 311.8	437.8	486.6	134.9	224.8	27.7	-234.6	28.3	-262.9
4th quarter	1 088.1	471.0	111.8	81.5	423.8	1 341.3	433.4	509.0	140.6	230.8	27.5	-253.2	23.7	-276.9
1992														
1st quarter	1 100.0	463.1	120.1	80.8	436.0	1 388.3	439.5	548.9	143.2	229.2	27.5	-288.3	11.0	-299.3
2nd quarter	1 117.3	472.1	124.6	79.9	440.7	1 409.2	441.6	562.4	146.2	230.5	28.4	-291.8	8.0	-299.9
3rd quarter	1 111.9	481.4	107.0	79.1	444.4	1 428.4	451.1	565.1	152.4	230.1	29.7	-316.5	9.2	-325.8
4th quarter	1 156.0	501.0	123.4	85.5	446.2	1 449.6	450.9	584.5	154.6	226.8	32.8	-293.5	8.3	-301.8
1993														
1st quarter	1 149.0	486.0	126.7	81.7	454.6	1 449.8	442.1	584.4	155.5	228.7	39.1	-300.8	4.2	-305.0
2nd quarter	1 191.8	507.1	138.6	83.9	462.1	1 458.9	439.6	593.5	157.8	230.3	37.8	-267.2	7.0	-274.2
3rd quarter	1 201.2	515.8	135.9	83.8	465.7	1 476.7	444.4	599.4	163.4	231.0	38.5	-275.5	6.1	-281.6
4th quarter	1 247.3	530.8	152.8	91.5	472.2	1 500.4	444.4	614.0	173.7	230.8	37.4	-253.1	10.3	-263.4
1994														
1st quarter	1 243.7	526.8	138.9	94.4	483.6	1 481.2	437.6	608.1	171.3	229.3	34.9	-237.5	16.3	-253.8
2nd quarter	1 297.6	558.1	153.4	94.5	491.6	1 488.2	435.3	611.6	171.2	236.2	33.8	-190.5	22.3	-212.8
3rd quarter	1 303.5	548.0	163.1	96.1	496.4	1 515.5	447.2	618.0	175.1	242.7	32.4	-212.0	24.8	-236.8
4th quarter	1 329.9	558.4	171.5	95.9	504.1	1 539.3	438.7	636.6	180.4	250.2	33.3	-209.4	27.6	-237.0
1995														
1st quarter	1 348.2	569.4	172.6	94.6	511.6	1 556.4	439.2	641.8	185.1	259.2	31.1	-208.3	21.0	-229.3
2nd quarter	1 385.7	596.3	177.5	95.3	516.6	1 574.6	441.3	648.8	186.3	266.4	31.9	-188.9	19.0	-207.9
3rd quarter	1 391.7	593.3	185.9	90.0	522.5	1 589.3	444.6	655.4	185.2	271.1	32.9	-197.6	19.6	-217.2
4th quarter	1 409.2	608.3	181.3	92.0	527.7	1 582.4	431.8	662.5	181.3	273.3	33.6	-173.2	20.1	-193.3
1996														
1st quarter	1 446.9	637.5	187.3	90.4	531.8	1 623.4	441.8	686.9	185.5	273.9	35.4	-176.5	11.2	-187.6
2nd quarter	1 495.6	674.4	192.0	89.0	540.2	1 632.6	447.0	684.7	194.0	271.5	35.4	-137.0	15.0	-151.9
3rd quarter	1 503.4	675.6	190.9	89.7	547.2	1 633.5	442.9	689.2	193.0	273.7	34.7	-130.1	19.1	-149.2
4th quarter	1 550.5	692.6	192.3	111.3	554.2	1 654.2	449.4	705.8	189.2	275.1	34.8	-103.7	21.6	-125.3
1997														
1st quarter	1 572.7	724.9	194.3	88.5	565.0	1 659.2	451.3	709.3	191.1	273.8	33.7	-86.5	21.3	-107.7
2nd quarter	1 607.8	741.5	198.4	95.6	572.2	1 675.8	461.5	714.1	193.8	274.8	31.7	-68.0	25.8	-93.8
3rd quarter	1 645.5	759.6	209.8	95.9	580.2	1 679.2	457.5	717.1	196.7	277.5	30.4	-33.7	32.1	-65.8
4th quarter	1 676.0	781.3	209.5	94.7	590.5	1 701.0	457.2	729.4	205.6	278.5	30.3	-25.0	42.7	-67.8
1998														
1st quarter	1 711.8	807.0	209.1	95.1	600.5	1 685.9	445.5	726.9	205.0	279.6	28.7	25.9	45.7	-19.8
2nd quarter	1 740.3	826.2	210.6	95.8	607.7	1 698.4	457.5	726.6	205.4	280.2	28.7	41.9	52.9	-11.0
3rd quarter	1 772.6	845.9	213.3	97.5	615.9	1 700.6	451.0	730.9	209.9	280.0	28.8	71.9	59.0	12.9
4th quarter	1 791.5	864.8	205.1	97.3	624.2	1 735.1	460.7	739.6	216.1	275.4	43.2	56.4	70.1	-13.7
1999														
1st quarter	1 817.4	868.7	212.3	97.9	638.6	1 727.8	464.5	738.6	223.0	267.7	33.9	89.7	78.6	11.1
2nd quarter	1 849.6	888.5	214.9	98.9	647.4	1 732.2	460.2	742.8	221.4	267.1	40.7	117.5	86.1	31.4
3rd quarter	1 890.3	913.7	217.8	101.4	657.4	1 743.1	471.3	745.0	234.0	262.2	30.5	147.3	94.8	52.5
4th quarter	1 941.0	938.2	232.3	103.9	666.6	1 797.7	487.0	757.7	238.8	261.8	52.3	143.3	103.3	40.0

Table 21-2. State and Local Government Current Receipts and Expenditures

(Calendar years, billions of dollars, quarterly data are at seasonally adjusted annual rates.)

Year and quarter	Current receipts						Current expenditures						Current surplus or deficit (—), national income and product accounts		
	Total	Personal tax and nontax receipts	Corporate profits tax accruals	Indirect business tax and nontax accruals	Contributions for social insurance	Federal grants-in-aid	Total	Consumption expenditures	Transfer payments to persons	Net interest paid	Less: dividends received by government	Subsidies less surplus of government enterprises	Total	Social insurance funds	Other
1970	114.6	15.7	3.7	74.8	1.1	19.3	107.5	92.0	16.1	0.9	0.0	-1.5	7.1	0.2	6.9
1971	129.3	17.5	4.3	83.1	1.2	23.2	122.9	103.4	19.3	1.7	0.0	-1.3	6.4	0.2	6.2
1972	152.3	22.8	5.3	91.2	1.3	31.7	136.7	113.8	22.0	2.3	0.0	-1.5	15.6	0.3	15.3
1973	166.6	24.7	6.0	99.5	1.5	34.8	150.9	126.9	24.1	1.3	0.0	-1.4	15.7	0.3	15.4
1974	178.5	26.7	6.7	107.2	1.7	36.3	169.2	144.5	25.3	0.2	0.0	-0.8	9.3	0.4	8.9
1975	199.6	29.5	7.3	115.8	1.8	45.1	197.2	165.4	30.8	1.3	0.0	-0.2	2.4	0.5	1.9
1976	224.5	34.1	9.6	127.8	2.2	50.7	217.2	180.1	34.1	3.2	0.0	-0.2	7.3	0.6	6.7
1977	249.5	38.8	11.4	139.9	2.8	56.6	236.4	196.5	37.0	3.0	0.0	-0.1	13.1	1.0	12.1
1978	274.3	44.3	12.1	148.9	3.4	65.5	255.6	214.3	40.8	0.8	0.1	0.0	18.7	1.5	17.2
1979	290.8	48.4	13.6	158.6	3.9	66.3	277.8	235.0	44.3	-2.2	0.1	0.6	13.0	1.8	11.3
1980	316.6	53.9	14.5	172.3	3.6	72.3	307.8	260.5	51.2	-5.4	0.1	1.6	8.8	1.3	7.5
1981	344.4	60.6	15.4	192.0	3.9	72.5	336.9	284.6	57.1	-7.5	0.1	2.8	7.5	1.3	6.2
1982	360.3	65.9	14.0	206.8	4.0	69.5	362.5	306.8	61.2	-7.3	0.2	2.1	-2.3	1.2	-3.5
1983	392.1	73.7	15.9	226.8	4.1	71.6	387.3	325.1	66.9	-5.2	0.2	0.7	4.8	1.2	3.6
1984	436.4	84.8	18.8	251.5	4.7	76.7	412.6	349.5	71.2	-6.7	0.2	-1.1	23.8	1.4	22.4
1985	469.2	91.3	20.2	272.0	4.9	80.9	447.0	380.5	77.3	-7.9	0.2	-2.8	22.3	1.3	21.0
1986	507.9	98.6	22.7	293.1	6.0	87.6	487.2	410.8	84.4	-5.5	0.2	-2.5	20.8	1.9	18.9
1987	536.0	108.5	23.9	312.4	7.2	83.9	523.8	439.0	90.8	-3.1	0.2	-2.8	12.2	2.2	10.0
1988	573.7	114.0	26.0	333.7	8.4	91.6	558.1	467.9	98.6	-3.8	0.2	-4.5	15.6	2.5	13.1
1989	618.9	128.9	24.2	358.5	9.0	98.3	599.6	503.0	109.5	-6.6	0.2	-6.1	19.3	2.3	17.0
1990	663.4	136.0	22.5	383.4	10.0	111.4	660.8	545.8	127.8	-6.3	0.2	-6.3	2.6	2.0	0.7
1991	716.0	145.3	23.6	403.8	11.6	131.6	723.8	576.1	156.6	-2.1	0.2	-6.6	-7.8	2.4	-10.2
1992	772.2	156.4	24.4	429.2	13.1	149.1	777.2	601.6	180.1	2.8	0.2	-7.2	-4.9	3.1	-8.1
1993	823.2	164.7	26.9	454.8	14.1	162.6	821.7	629.5	195.4	5.6	0.2	-8.6	1.5	4.2	-2.7
1994	873.8	174.8	30.0	480.1	14.5	174.5	865.2	662.6	206.9	4.4	0.2	-8.5	8.6	4.6	4.0
1995	917.9	186.5	31.7	501.6	13.6	184.5	902.5	694.7	217.8	0.5	0.3	-10.2	15.3	4.0	11.4
1996	960.4	199.6	33.0	524.9	12.5	190.4	939.0	726.5	224.3	0.9	0.3	-12.5	21.4	2.7	18.7
1997	1 011.0	216.9	34.2	552.5	10.8	196.8	980.0	766.4	227.5	-0.9	0.3	-12.4	31.0	1.1	29.9
1998	1 072.0	234.9	35.1	583.1	10.0	209.1	1 031.0	808.4	234.1	-0.6	0.4	-10.9	41.7	0.4	41.3
1999	1 143.0	249.7	36.6	617.5	9.6	229.3	1 093.0	855.0	252.0	-3.0	0.4	-11.0	50.0	-0.4	50.4
1991															
1st quarter	688.6	139.7	22.7	392.4	11.0	122.8	704.2	568.4	146.6	-4.1	0.2	-6.5	-15.6	2.1	-17.7
2nd quarter	705.7	143.5	23.4	399.4	11.4	128.1	716.3	572.7	153.2	-2.9	0.2	-6.6	-10.6	2.3	-12.9
3rd quarter	725.7	145.8	24.2	409.0	11.8	134.9	730.4	578.6	160.1	-1.5	0.2	-6.6	-4.7	2.4	-7.1
4th quarter	743.8	152.2	24.3	414.4	12.2	140.6	744.1	584.5	166.7	-0.1	0.2	-6.8	-0.3	2.6	-2.9
1992															
1st quarter	751.9	151.6	24.4	420.0	12.6	143.2	757.0	590.8	172.3	1.1	0.2	-6.9	-5.1	2.8	-7.9
2nd quarter	763.2	155.2	25.5	423.3	13.0	146.2	771.7	598.8	177.7	2.4	0.2	-7.0	-8.5	3.0	-11.5
3rd quarter	776.9	156.6	21.8	432.8	13.3	152.4	785.4	605.4	184.0	3.4	0.2	-7.3	-8.5	3.3	-11.8
4th quarter	796.9	162.1	25.8	440.8	13.6	154.6	794.6	611.6	186.5	4.3	0.2	-7.6	2.3	3.5	-1.2
1993															
1st quarter	794.5	158.1	24.3	442.8	13.8	155.5	806.9	619.8	190.4	5.1	0.2	-8.2	-12.4	3.8	-16.3
2nd quarter	814.0	163.9	26.9	451.3	14.1	157.8	818.0	627.1	193.9	5.6	0.2	-8.4	-4.0	4.1	-8.1
3rd quarter	828.2	166.0	26.4	458.2	14.2	163.4	825.8	631.6	197.3	5.9	0.2	-8.8	2.4	4.3	-1.9
4th quarter	856.0	170.9	30.0	467.0	14.4	173.7	836.1	639.5	199.9	5.7	0.2	-8.9	19.9	4.5	15.4
1994															
1st quarter	852.0	168.6	26.5	470.9	14.6	171.3	851.4	650.0	203.2	5.7	0.2	-7.3	0.6	4.6	-4.0
2nd quarter	867.0	174.0	29.4	477.7	14.6	171.2	860.1	658.6	205.3	5.1	0.2	-8.7	6.9	4.7	2.2
3rd quarter	879.8	176.3	31.3	482.6	14.5	175.1	870.6	667.6	208.1	3.9	0.2	-8.8	9.2	4.6	4.6
4th quarter	896.6	180.1	32.6	489.0	14.4	180.4	878.7	674.2	210.9	2.9	0.2	-9.1	17.8	4.5	13.3
1995															
1st quarter	906.8	182.4	30.5	494.7	14.0	185.1	890.8	685.0	214.1	1.3	0.2	-9.4	15.9	4.3	11.6
2nd quarter	914.3	184.2	31.2	498.8	13.8	186.3	899.7	692.6	216.7	0.6	0.2	-9.9	14.6	4.1	10.4
3rd quarter	923.4	188.3	32.9	503.5	13.5	185.2	905.8	697.3	219.1	0.1	0.3	-10.4	17.5	3.9	13.7
4th quarter	927.0	191.3	32.1	509.3	13.2	181.3	913.8	703.8	221.3	0.0	0.3	-11.1	13.3	3.5	9.7
1996															
1st quarter	940.4	193.2	32.4	516.4	12.9	185.5	923.4	712.5	222.6	0.8	0.3	-12.1	17.0	3.2	13.8
2nd quarter	962.2	198.1	33.3	524.2	12.6	194.0	935.0	723.0	223.9	1.0	0.3	-12.6	27.2	2.9	24.3
3rd quarter	966.1	201.7	33.1	526.0	12.3	193.0	943.8	730.6	225.3	1.0	0.3	-12.7	22.3	2.6	19.6
4th quarter	972.9	205.5	33.3	533.0	11.9	189.2	953.6	740.0	225.6	0.8	0.3	-12.5	19.3	2.2	17.1
1997															
1st quarter	988.9	210.2	32.8	543.5	11.4	191.1	965.4	751.9	226.6	-0.2	0.3	-12.5	23.5	1.6	21.9
2nd quarter	999.7	213.4	33.4	548.2	11.0	193.8	973.1	760.0	227.0	-1.0	0.3	-12.5	26.6	1.2	25.4
3rd quarter	1 020.0	219.2	35.4	558.2	10.6	196.7	984.6	770.7	227.9	-1.1	0.3	-12.5	35.5	0.8	34.7
4th quarter	1 037.0	225.0	35.2	560.3	10.4	205.6	998.3	783.2	228.7	-1.2	0.4	-12.1	38.3	0.6	37.6
1998															
1st quarter	1 049.0	228.8	35.1	569.3	10.3	205.0	1 010.0	792.2	229.8	-0.4	0.4	-10.9	38.1	0.6	37.5
2nd quarter	1 057.0	230.2	35.3	576.1	10.1	205.4	1 024.0	803.5	232.1	-0.4	0.4	-10.9	33.4	0.5	32.9
3rd quarter	1 075.0	238.1	35.8	581.7	9.9	209.9	1 038.0	814.5	235.2	-0.6	0.4	-10.9	37.5	0.3	37.2
4th quarter	1 108.0	242.7	34.3	605.3	9.8	216.1	1 051.0	823.4	239.3	-1.0	0.4	-10.8	57.7	0.1	57.6
1999															
1st quarter	1 112.0	244.5	35.5	599.3	9.6	223.0	1 064.0	832.1	245.4	-2.1	0.4	-11.0	47.9	-0.2	48.1
2nd quarter	1 121.0	244.9	35.9	609.1	9.6	221.4	1 083.0	847.2	249.7	-2.7	0.4	-11.0	38.0	-0.4	38.3
3rd quarter	1 150.0	250.3	36.3	620.2	9.5	234.0	1 103.0	863.1	254.5	-3.3	0.4	-11.0	47.4	-0.5	47.9
4th quarter	1 188.0	259.2	38.5	641.6	9.5	238.8	1 121.0	877.4	258.5	-3.6	0.4	-10.9	66.6	-0.6	67.2

Table 21-3. Government Consumption Expenditures and Gross Investment [1]

(Calendar years, billions of dollars, quarterly data are at seasonally adjusted annual rates.)

Year and quarter	Total	Federal									
		Total	Defense	Nondefense							
				Total	Consumption expenditures						
					Total	Durable [2]	Nondurable	Services			
								Total	Compensation of general government employees	Capital consumption [3]	Other services
1970	237.1	116.4	90.9	25.5	21.7	-0.2	1.9	20.0	11.5	2.1	6.3
1971	251.0	117.6	89.0	28.6	24.4	-0.2	2.0	22.7	13.2	2.3	7.1
1972	270.1	125.6	93.5	32.2	27.6	-0.3	2.3	25.7	14.6	2.4	8.6
1973	287.9	127.8	93.9	33.9	29.0	-0.5	1.8	27.7	15.8	2.6	9.3
1974	322.4	138.2	99.7	38.5	32.9	-0.5	2.5	31.0	17.8	2.9	10.3
1975	361.1	152.1	107.9	44.2	37.7	-0.4	2.7	35.4	20.3	3.3	11.9
1976	384.5	160.6	113.2	47.4	40.1	-0.6	3.3	37.4	22.9	3.5	11.0
1977	415.3	176.0	122.6	53.5	45.5	-0.7	3.8	42.4	26.1	3.7	12.5
1978	455.6	191.9	132.0	59.8	50.1	-0.8	3.9	47.0	28.1	4.0	14.9
1979	503.5	211.6	146.7	65.0	54.7	-1.0	3.9	51.8	29.9	4.6	17.4
1980	569.7	245.3	169.6	75.6	63.6	-0.4	5.6	58.4	33.7	5.2	19.5
1981	631.4	281.8	197.8	84.0	71.0	-0.2	9.4	61.9	36.0	6.1	19.8
1982	684.4	312.8	228.3	84.5	71.7	0.1	7.3	64.3	37.5	6.8	20.0
1983	735.9	344.4	252.5	92.0	77.4	0.1	8.8	68.5	39.5	7.3	21.7
1984	800.8	376.4	283.5	92.8	77.1	0.1	5.0	72.1	41.4	8.0	22.6
1985	878.3	413.4	312.4	101.0	84.1	0.0	8.2	75.9	43.2	8.7	24.1
1986	942.3	438.7	332.2	106.5	89.0	-0.2	11.7	77.5	43.9	9.4	24.2
1987	997.0	460.4	351.2	109.3	89.9	-0.2	6.0	84.0	46.3	10.1	27.7
1988	1 036.9	462.6	355.9	106.8	88.2	-0.5	-0.9	89.5	50.5	10.9	28.1
1989	1 100.2	482.6	363.2	119.3	99.1	-0.4	4.8	94.6	53.3	11.8	29.5
1990	1 181.4	508.4	374.9	133.6	111.0	-0.1	4.6	106.4	58.6	12.7	35.1
1991	1 235.5	527.4	384.5	142.9	118.1	0.0	5.2	112.9	63.2	13.7	35.9
1992	1 270.5	534.5	378.5	156.0	128.8	0.3	6.1	122.4	66.8	14.2	41.4
1993	1 293.0	527.3	364.9	162.4	133.4	0.5	6.6	126.3	72.4	14.9	39.0
1994	1 327.9	521.1	355.1	165.9	138.6	1.0	6.6	131.0	74.3	15.7	41.0
1995	1 372.0	521.5	350.6	170.9	141.8	0.9	6.5	134.3	75.0	16.8	42.5
1996	1 421.9	531.6	357.0	174.6	142.9	1.1	6.1	135.7	76.4	18.0	41.3
1997	1 487.9	538.2	352.6	185.6	152.7	1.2	7.9	143.6	79.1	19.4	45.1
1998	1 540.9	540.6	349.2	191.4	154.0	-0.2	8.9	145.3	82.3	21.2	41.8
1999	1 634.4	568.6	365.0	203.5	159.6	1.3	9.4	148.9	87.2	24.2	37.5
1991											
1st quarter	1 228.6	530.3	390.7	139.6	116.6	0.5	6.2	109.9	62.6	13.4	33.8
2nd quarter	1 235.5	532.2	389.7	142.5	117.9	0.2	6.0	111.7	62.7	13.6	35.4
3rd quarter	1 238.4	526.9	383.5	143.4	118.5	-0.8	4.9	114.4	63.3	13.8	37.4
4th quarter	1 239.5	520.1	374.1	146.0	119.2	0.2	3.5	115.4	64.3	13.9	37.2
1992											
1st quarter	1 257.3	527.1	373.8	153.4	126.2	0.5	4.7	121.0	66.0	14.0	41.0
2nd quarter	1 265.1	530.5	376.9	153.6	127.0	0.2	6.2	120.6	66.2	14.1	40.3
3rd quarter	1 277.8	540.6	384.8	155.7	129.1	-0.2	6.5	122.8	66.8	14.2	41.8
4th quarter	1 281.8	539.9	378.5	161.4	133.0	0.6	7.1	125.3	68.4	14.4	42.5
1993											
1st quarter	1 279.5	528.9	367.4	161.5	131.6	0.4	6.5	124.7	71.1	14.6	38.9
2nd quarter	1 289.1	525.3	364.3	161.0	131.6	0.6	6.3	124.7	71.8	14.8	38.0
3rd quarter	1 296.2	526.9	363.9	163.0	133.9	0.5	6.2	127.2	73.2	15.0	39.1
4th quarter	1 307.1	528.0	364.1	164.0	136.7	0.7	7.3	128.7	73.4	15.2	40.1
1994											
1st quarter	1 303.3	515.8	349.4	166.3	139.5	1.0	6.9	131.5	75.1	15.4	41.0
2nd quarter	1 316.1	515.9	353.9	162.0	135.6	0.8	6.9	127.9	75.3	15.6	37.0
3rd quarter	1 348.1	532.5	366.9	165.6	138.5	1.0	5.7	131.8	73.5	15.8	42.5
4th quarter	1 344.0	520.0	350.4	169.7	140.9	1.1	7.1	132.7	73.1	16.0	43.6
1995											
1st quarter	1 360.6	523.4	352.2	171.2	141.0	1.2	6.9	132.9	74.4	16.3	42.1
2nd quarter	1 374.9	525.5	353.9	171.6	142.0	1.1	6.0	135.0	74.9	16.7	43.4
3rd quarter	1 378.3	525.0	352.7	172.3	143.3	0.8	6.6	135.9	75.4	17.0	43.6
4th quarter	1 374.5	512.3	343.6	168.7	140.6	0.5	6.5	133.6	75.2	17.4	41.0
1996											
1st quarter	1 402.6	530.6	356.1	174.5	143.4	1.3	6.4	135.6	76.5	17.6	41.5
2nd quarter	1 423.0	537.2	361.3	175.9	142.9	1.2	6.0	135.7	76.7	17.8	41.2
3rd quarter	1 423.4	529.1	355.6	173.5	141.5	1.0	5.8	134.8	76.3	18.1	40.3
4th quarter	1 438.9	529.4	355.0	174.5	143.8	0.7	6.3	136.7	75.9	18.4	42.4
1997											
1st quarter	1 459.2	529.2	346.4	182.8	150.2	1.2	7.4	141.7	78.7	18.8	44.1
2nd quarter	1 486.3	543.4	355.0	188.4	153.5	1.4	7.7	144.4	79.5	19.2	45.7
3rd quarter	1 498.0	541.3	354.7	186.6	153.3	1.0	7.9	144.4	79.4	19.6	45.4
4th quarter	1 508.2	538.9	354.4	184.5	153.6	1.1	8.6	144.0	78.9	20.0	45.1
1998											
1st quarter	1 507.6	528.0	338.6	189.3	153.7	1.3	8.3	144.0	80.5	20.4	43.1
2nd quarter	1 538.6	544.9	349.3	195.6	156.3	1.3	8.6	146.3	81.6	20.9	43.8
3rd quarter	1 550.3	541.4	355.0	186.4	149.4	-4.7	9.0	145.1	82.4	21.4	41.2
4th quarter	1 567.2	548.0	353.8	194.2	156.6	1.2	9.7	145.7	84.6	22.1	39.0
1999											
1st quarter	1 595.5	554.1	356.5	197.6	158.8	1.3	9.2	148.3	88.0	22.9	37.4
2nd quarter	1 610.9	558.3	355.3	203.0	158.0	1.3	9.0	147.7	86.7	23.7	37.2
3rd quarter	1 642.4	570.4	367.5	202.8	159.1	1.2	9.0	149.0	86.5	24.6	38.0
4th quarter	1 688.8	591.6	380.8	210.7	162.3	1.3	10.4	150.7	87.8	25.5	37.4

1. Gross government investment consists of general government and government enterprise expenditures for fixed assets; inventory investment is included in government consumption expenditures.
2. Consumption expenditures for durable goods excludes expenditures classified as investment, except for goods transferred to foreign countries by the federal government. Total includes items not shown separately.
3. Consumption of general government fixed capital, or depreciation, is a partial measure of the value of the services of general government fixed assets; a zero net rate of return on these assets is assumed.

Table 21-3. Government Consumption Expenditures and Gross Investment [1]—*Continued*

(Calendar years, billions of dollars, quarterly data are at seasonally adjusted annual rates.)

Year and quarter	Federal—*Continued*			State and local						
	Nondefense—*Continued*				Consumption expenditures			Gross investment		
	Gross investment			Total	Total [2]	Compensation of general government employees	Capital consumption [3]	Total	Structures	Equipment and software
	Total	Structures	Equipment and software							
1970	3.8	2.1	1.7	120.7	92.0	70.3	8.4	28.7	25.8	3.0
1971	4.2	2.5	1.7	133.5	103.4	78.4	9.4	30.1	27.0	3.1
1972	4.5	2.7	1.8	144.4	113.8	86.9	10.2	30.6	27.1	3.5
1973	4.9	3.1	1.8	160.1	126.9	97.1	11.3	33.2	29.1	4.1
1974	5.6	3.4	2.2	184.2	144.5	106.7	14.1	39.6	34.7	4.9
1975	6.5	4.1	2.4	209.0	165.4	120.2	16.0	43.6	38.1	5.5
1976	7.3	4.6	2.7	223.9	180.1	132.1	16.6	43.8	38.1	5.7
1977	8.0	5.0	3.0	239.3	196.5	144.1	17.5	42.8	36.9	5.9
1978	9.8	6.1	3.7	263.8	214.3	157.9	18.8	49.5	42.8	6.6
1979	10.2	6.3	4.0	291.8	235.0	173.0	21.0	56.8	49.0	7.8
1980	12.0	7.1	4.9	324.4	260.5	191.5	24.3	64.0	55.1	8.9
1981	13.0	7.7	5.3	349.6	284.6	208.6	27.8	65.0	55.4	9.5
1982	12.7	6.8	6.0	371.6	306.8	225.9	30.3	64.8	54.2	10.6
1983	14.5	6.7	7.8	391.5	325.1	241.5	31.2	66.4	54.2	12.2
1984	15.7	7.0	8.7	424.4	349.5	259.4	32.0	75.0	60.5	14.4
1985	16.9	7.3	9.6	464.9	380.5	282.7	33.7	84.4	67.6	16.8
1986	17.5	8.0	9.5	503.6	410.8	305.2	36.2	92.8	74.2	18.6
1987	19.4	9.0	10.4	537.5	439.0	326.6	39.0	98.4	78.8	19.6
1988	18.6	6.8	11.7	574.3	467.9	351.3	41.6	106.3	84.8	21.5
1989	20.3	6.9	13.4	617.7	503.0	377.7	44.4	114.7	88.7	26.0
1990	22.6	8.0	14.6	673.0	545.8	411.2	48.1	127.2	98.5	28.7
1991	24.8	9.2	15.7	708.1	576.1	434.6	51.2	132.1	103.2	28.9
1992	27.2	10.3	16.9	736.0	601.6	456.3	53.4	134.3	104.2	30.1
1993	28.9	11.2	17.7	765.7	629.5	478.9	56.4	136.2	104.5	31.7
1994	27.3	10.5	16.8	806.8	662.6	501.7	60.0	144.2	108.7	35.5
1995	29.2	10.8	18.4	850.5	694.7	523.1	64.4	155.8	117.3	38.6
1996	31.7	11.1	20.5	890.4	726.5	542.3	68.2	163.8	122.5	41.3
1997	32.9	9.7	23.2	949.7	766.4	569.8	72.4	183.3	139.3	44.0
1998	37.4	11.1	26.3	1 000.3	808.4	596.4	76.9	191.9	144.0	48.0
1999	44.0	11.0	33.0	1 065.8	855.0	624.1	83.0	210.9	157.5	53.4
1991										
1st quarter	23.1	7.7	15.3	698.3	568.4	427.7	50.2	129.9	101.0	28.9
2nd quarter	24.6	9.1	15.5	703.3	572.7	432.2	51.0	130.6	101.9	28.7
3rd quarter	24.9	9.1	15.8	711.5	578.6	436.6	51.5	132.8	104.1	28.7
4th quarter	26.8	10.8	16.0	719.4	584.5	441.8	52.1	134.9	105.7	29.1
1992										
1st quarter	27.1	10.3	16.8	730.2	590.8	448.2	52.5	139.4	110.0	29.5
2nd quarter	26.6	10.2	16.4	734.5	598.8	454.1	53.2	135.7	105.7	30.0
3rd quarter	26.7	9.7	17.0	737.2	605.4	458.7	53.7	131.8	101.5	30.3
4th quarter	28.4	11.0	17.4	741.9	611.6	464.3	54.4	130.4	99.7	30.6
1993										
1st quarter	29.9	11.5	18.4	750.5	619.8	471.3	55.3	130.8	99.9	30.9
2nd quarter	29.4	10.9	18.5	763.9	627.1	476.8	56.1	136.8	105.6	31.2
3rd quarter	29.0	11.3	17.7	769.3	631.6	480.6	56.8	137.8	105.6	32.1
4th quarter	27.3	11.2	16.1	779.1	639.5	486.8	57.5	139.6	106.9	32.7
1994										
1st quarter	26.8	10.3	16.5	787.5	650.0	493.0	58.5	137.5	103.2	34.3
2nd quarter	26.4	9.7	16.7	800.2	658.6	499.6	59.4	141.6	106.4	35.2
3rd quarter	27.1	9.9	17.2	815.6	667.6	504.8	60.5	148.0	112.1	35.9
4th quarter	28.8	11.9	16.9	824.0	674.2	509.3	61.6	149.8	113.2	36.6
1995										
1st quarter	30.2	11.4	18.8	837.1	685.0	517.7	62.8	152.1	115.0	37.2
2nd quarter	29.6	10.7	18.9	849.4	692.6	520.9	63.9	156.8	118.6	38.2
3rd quarter	28.9	11.0	17.9	853.3	697.3	524.3	64.9	156.0	117.1	38.9
4th quarter	28.1	10.1	17.9	862.2	703.8	529.6	65.9	158.4	118.5	39.9
1996										
1st quarter	31.1	11.2	19.8	872.0	712.5	534.2	67.0	159.5	119.1	40.5
2nd quarter	33.1	12.0	21.1	885.7	723.0	540.1	67.7	162.7	121.8	41.0
3rd quarter	31.9	11.4	20.5	894.3	730.6	545.2	68.7	163.7	122.1	41.6
4th quarter	30.6	10.0	20.7	909.4	740.0	549.8	69.6	169.4	127.1	42.3
1997										
1st quarter	32.6	10.2	22.4	930.0	751.9	559.5	70.7	178.2	135.4	42.7
2nd quarter	34.9	9.9	25.0	942.9	760.0	566.3	71.9	183.0	139.4	43.6
3rd quarter	33.3	10.4	22.8	956.6	770.7	573.3	72.9	186.0	141.6	44.4
4th quarter	30.9	8.4	22.5	969.3	783.2	580.1	74.3	186.1	141.0	45.1
1998										
1st quarter	35.7	10.8	24.9	979.6	792.2	586.0	75.1	187.4	141.1	46.3
2nd quarter	39.3	10.8	28.5	993.7	803.5	593.1	76.1	190.2	142.8	47.5
3rd quarter	37.1	11.5	25.6	1 008.9	814.5	600.2	77.5	194.4	145.7	48.7
4th quarter	37.7	11.5	26.2	1 019.2	823.4	606.4	79.0	195.8	146.2	49.6
1999										
1st quarter	38.8	11.4	27.4	1 041.4	832.1	613.2	80.4	209.3	158.3	50.9
2nd quarter	45.0	10.5	34.5	1 052.6	847.2	620.0	82.1	205.4	153.0	52.4
3rd quarter	43.7	10.6	33.1	1 072.1	863.1	627.9	83.7	209.0	154.8	54.2
4th quarter	48.5	11.6	36.8	1 097.3	877.4	635.4	85.7	219.8	163.9	56.0

1. Gross government investment consists of general government and government enterprise expenditures for fixed assets; inventory investment is included in government consumption expenditures.
2. Consumption expenditures for durable goods excludes expenditures classified as investment, except for goods transferred to foreign countries by the federal government. Total includes items not shown separately.
3. Consumption of general government fixed capital, or depreciation, is a partial measure of the value of the services of general government fixed assets; a zero net rate of return on these assets is assumed.

Table 21-4. Real Government Consumption Expenditures and Gross Investment [1]

(Calendar years, billions of chained [1996] dollars, quarterly data are at seasonally adjusted annual rates.)

Year and quarter	Total	Federal			Nondefense							
		Total	Defense	Total	Consumption expenditures					Services		
					Total	Total	Durable [2]	Nondurable	Total	Compensation of general government employees	Capital consumption [3]	Other services
1970	...	...	...	...	...	...	...	...	...	...	...	...
1971	...	...	...	...	...	...	...	...	...	...	...	...
1972	...	...	...	...	...	...	...	...	...	...	...	...
1973	...	...	...	...	...	...	...	...	...	...	...	...
1974	...	...	...	...	...	...	...	...	...	...	...	...
1975	...	...	...	...	...	...	...	...	...	...	...	...
1976	...	...	...	...	...	...	...	...	...	...	...	...
1977	...	...	...	...	...	...	...	...	...	...	...	...
1978	...	...	...	...	...	...	...	...	...	...	...	...
1979	...	...	...	...	...	...	...	...	...	...	...	...
1980	...	...	...	...	...	...	...	...	...	...	...	...
1981	...	...	...	...	...	...	...	...	...	...	...	...
1982	...	...	...	...	...	...	...	...	...	...	...	...
1983	...	...	...	...	...	...	...	...	...	...	...	...
1984	...	...	...	...	...	...	...	...	...	...	...	...
1985	...	...	...	...	...	...	...	...	...	...	...	...
1986	...	...	...	...	...	...	...	...	...	...	...	...
1987	1 292.5	597.8	450.2	146.5	125.4	-0.9	2.9	121.5	77.0	11.2	34.6
1988	1 307.5	586.9	446.8	138.9	119.2	-1.1	-4.6	123.5	79.0	11.8	34.1
1989	1 343.5	594.7	443.3	150.5	129.6	-1.0	4.5	125.1	79.3	12.5	34.6
1990	1 387.3	606.8	443.2	163.0	140.1	-0.7	4.6	135.6	83.2	13.3	39.9
1991	1 403.4	604.9	438.4	166.0	140.9	-0.5	5.1	136.1	83.0	14.0	39.7
1992	1 410.0	595.1	417.1	177.9	150.0	-0.1	6.1	143.6	84.5	14.6	44.7
1993	1 398.8	572.0	394.7	177.3	147.8	0.5	6.4	140.5	84.1	15.2	41.5
1994	1 400.1	551.3	375.9	175.5	148.0	1.0	6.2	140.4	81.8	15.9	42.9
1995	1 406.4	536.5	361.9	174.6	145.7	0.8	6.4	138.5	78.5	16.7	43.3
1996	1 421.9	531.6	357.0	174.6	142.9	1.1	6.1	135.7	76.4	18.0	41.3
1997	1 455.4	529.6	347.7	181.8	148.6	1.3	7.9	139.4	75.9	19.6	44.0
1998	1 486.4	526.9	341.7	185.2	147.2	0.0	9.3	138.2	76.7	21.5	40.0
1999	1 536.1	540.1	348.5	191.5	147.5	1.5	10.0	136.9	77.2	24.4	35.5
1991												
1st quarter	1 404.7	612.6	449.2	162.7	139.7	0.0	6.5	133.2	82.6	13.7	37.7
2nd quarter	1 408.9	613.4	447.1	165.7	140.9	-0.3	6.0	134.9	82.2	14.0	39.3
3rd quarter	1 403.0	602.7	436.0	166.2	141.0	-1.6	4.9	137.5	82.6	14.1	41.2
4th quarter	1 397.0	591.0	421.2	169.5	142.1	-0.2	2.9	138.8	84.5	14.3	40.7
1992												
1st quarter	1 407.6	591.8	414.9	176.8	149.0	0.1	4.4	143.9	85.1	14.4	44.6
2nd quarter	1 405.7	591.1	414.9	176.1	148.9	-0.2	6.2	142.5	84.4	14.6	43.8
3rd quarter	1 413.1	598.3	420.9	177.2	150.0	-0.6	6.4	143.7	84.3	14.7	44.8
4th quarter	1 413.7	599.1	417.6	181.4	152.3	0.3	7.3	144.4	84.1	14.8	45.5
1993												
1st quarter	1 396.4	579.6	400.7	179.0	148.3	0.3	6.5	141.1	84.9	15.0	41.7
2nd quarter	1 398.0	572.2	395.0	177.2	147.1	0.5	6.3	140.0	84.8	15.1	40.5
3rd quarter	1 398.4	568.9	392.3	176.6	147.0	0.4	5.2	140.3	83.9	15.3	41.4
4th quarter	1 402.2	567.3	391.0	176.3	148.7	0.7	7.4	140.6	83.0	15.4	42.3
1994												
1st quarter	1 388.0	550.9	373.3	177.5	150.5	1.0	6.8	142.4	83.7	15.6	43.3
2nd quarter	1 390.4	545.2	374.5	170.7	144.1	0.8	6.4	136.4	82.1	15.8	38.8
3rd quarter	1 417.5	563.2	387.8	175.4	148.1	1.0	4.6	141.5	81.3	16.0	44.3
4th quarter	1 404.5	546.1	367.8	178.3	149.4	1.1	6.9	141.2	79.9	16.2	45.1
1995												
1st quarter	1 407.3	544.1	366.9	177.2	147.1	1.1	6.9	139.2	79.7	16.4	43.2
2nd quarter	1 414.0	544.3	367.0	177.3	147.9	1.0	5.6	141.2	80.4	16.6	44.2
3rd quarter	1 410.4	540.4	363.3	177.1	148.5	0.8	6.5	141.3	80.2	16.9	44.2
4th quarter	1 393.5	517.1	350.4	166.8	139.2	0.4	6.4	132.3	73.6	17.2	41.6
1996												
1st quarter	1 404.8	529.1	356.4	172.7	141.9	1.3	6.4	134.3	74.9	17.5	41.9
2nd quarter	1 430.4	540.2	363.0	177.2	144.1	1.2	6.0	136.9	77.8	17.8	41.3
3rd quarter	1 422.0	529.5	355.4	174.1	142.0	1.0	5.7	135.3	77.0	18.2	40.2
4th quarter	1 430.6	527.6	353.3	174.4	143.6	0.8	6.4	136.4	75.9	18.5	41.9
1997												
1st quarter	1 434.6	521.7	341.6	180.1	147.3	1.3	7.5	138.6	76.1	18.9	43.5
2nd quarter	1 457.0	534.8	350.3	184.5	149.3	1.5	7.7	140.1	76.5	19.3	44.3
3rd quarter	1 464.8	533.4	350.4	182.9	149.3	1.2	7.9	140.2	76.2	19.8	44.4
4th quarter	1 465.3	528.4	348.5	179.8	148.4	1.2	8.6	138.8	74.9	20.2	43.8
1998												
1st quarter	1 461.6	515.9	332.0	183.8	147.6	1.5	8.4	137.8	75.6	20.7	41.6
2nd quarter	1 487.6	531.8	342.4	189.3	149.5	1.5	8.8	139.3	76.4	21.2	41.8
3rd quarter	1 492.9	527.5	347.2	180.3	142.7	-4.4	9.6	137.8	76.7	21.8	39.4
4th quarter	1 503.3	532.4	345.1	187.2	148.9	1.4	10.5	137.8	78.3	22.5	37.2
1999												
1st quarter	1 517.1	529.5	342.4	187.0	147.7	1.5	9.9	137.1	78.5	23.2	35.5
2nd quarter	1 519.9	532.1	340.3	191.6	146.6	1.6	9.4	136.2	77.0	24.0	35.4
3rd quarter	1 537.8	541.0	350.4	190.5	146.8	1.4	9.5	136.6	76.3	24.8	35.9
4th quarter	1 569.5	558.1	360.9	197.1	148.9	1.5	11.4	137.6	77.2	25.6	35.1

1. Gross government investment consists of general government and government enterprise expenditures for fixed assets; inventory investment is included in government consumption expenditures.
2. Consumption expenditures for durable goods excludes expenditures classified as investment, except for goods transferred to foreign countries by the federal government. Total includes items not shown separately.
3. Consumption of general government fixed capital, or depreciation, is a partial measure of the value of the services of general government fixed assets; a zero net rate of return on these assets is assumed.

Table 21-4. Real Government Consumption Expenditures and Gross Investment [1]—*Continued*

(Calendar years, billions of chained [1996] dollars, quarterly data are at seasonally adjusted annual rates.)

Year and quarter	Federal			Total	State and local					
	Nondefense				Consumption expenditures			Gross investment		
	Gross investment									
	Total	Structures	Equipment and software		Total [2]	Compensation of general government employees	Capital consumption [3]	Total	Structures	Equipment and software
1970	...	...	...	...	...	...	...	...	...	...
1971	...	...	...	...	...	...	...	...	...	...
1972	...	...	...	...	...	...	...	...	...	...
1973	...	...	...	...	...	...	...	...	...	...
1974	...	...	...	...	...	...	...	...	...	...
1975	...	...	...	...	...	...	...	...	...	...
1976	...	...	...	...	...	...	...	...	...	...
1977	...	...	...	...	...	...	...	...	...	...
1978	...	...	...	...	...	...	...	...	...	...
1979	...	...	...	...	...	...	...	...	...	...
1980	...	...	...	...	...	...	...	...	...	...
1981	...	...	...	...	...	...	...	...	...	...
1982	...	...	...	...	...	...	...	...	...	...
1983	...	...	...	...	...	...	...	...	...	...
1984	...	...	...	...	...	...	...	...	...	...
1985	...	...	...	...	...	...	...	...	...	...
1986	...	...	...	...	...	...	...	...	...	...
1987	21.5	11.6	10.6	695.6	577.3	465.0	45.8	118.8	99.9	20.3
1988	20.1	8.6	11.7	721.4	596.8	480.5	47.7	125.0	104.3	21.9
1989	21.5	8.3	13.2	749.5	617.9	493.9	50.0	131.8	106.5	26.0
1990	23.5	9.3	14.2	781.1	638.9	507.1	52.7	142.2	114.5	28.4
1991	25.4	10.4	15.0	798.9	653.4	510.7	55.2	145.5	118.3	28.1
1992	28.0	11.6	16.5	815.3	667.8	516.5	57.6	147.4	118.7	29.4
1993	29.5	12.4	17.2	827.0	680.4	521.6	60.0	146.6	116.1	31.0
1994	27.6	11.2	16.5	848.9	697.5	527.9	62.5	151.4	117.0	34.6
1995	29.0	11.1	17.9	869.9	711.3	536.5	65.3	158.6	120.9	37.8
1996	31.7	11.1	20.5	890.4	726.5	542.3	68.2	163.8	122.5	41.3
1997	33.3	9.4	23.9	925.8	745.7	550.9	71.7	180.2	134.7	45.4
1998	38.2	10.5	27.8	959.2	772.6	559.6	75.8	186.7	135.5	51.6
1999	44.7	10.1	35.0	995.6	794.6	567.5	80.6	201.2	143.2	58.9
1991										
1st quarter	23.5	8.9	14.6	792.6	648.9	510.0	54.3	143.7	116.4	28.1
2nd quarter	25.1	10.3	14.9	796.0	652.3	510.7	54.9	143.8	116.6	28.0
3rd quarter	25.5	10.3	15.2	800.6	654.7	510.7	55.6	145.9	118.8	28.0
4th quarter	27.4	12.2	15.4	806.3	657.7	511.4	56.2	148.5	121.2	28.3
1992										
1st quarter	27.9	11.7	16.4	816.1	662.1	513.8	56.8	153.9	126.3	28.8
2nd quarter	27.4	11.5	16.0	814.9	665.8	515.7	57.3	149.1	120.6	29.3
3rd quarter	27.5	10.9	16.7	815.1	670.7	518.3	57.9	144.5	115.3	29.7
4th quarter	29.3	12.3	17.1	814.9	672.7	518.2	58.5	142.3	112.7	30.0
1993										
1st quarter	30.6	12.8	17.9	817.1	675.5	519.6	59.1	141.6	112.0	30.1
2nd quarter	30.1	12.1	18.1	826.1	678.7	521.6	59.7	147.3	117.4	30.5
3rd quarter	29.6	12.5	17.3	829.7	681.6	521.8	60.3	148.1	117.3	31.3
4th quarter	27.8	12.2	15.7	835.1	685.7	523.5	60.9	149.4	117.7	32.1
1994										
1st quarter	27.2	11.2	16.1	837.3	691.4	524.5	61.5	146.0	112.7	33.5
2nd quarter	26.7	10.4	16.3	845.4	695.8	527.2	62.2	149.5	115.4	34.3
3rd quarter	27.4	10.6	16.9	854.4	699.6	529.0	62.8	154.8	120.0	35.0
4th quarter	29.0	12.5	16.6	858.5	703.2	531.0	63.5	155.4	119.7	35.8
1995										
1st quarter	30.2	11.9	18.3	863.3	707.1	534.7	64.2	156.2	119.9	36.4
2nd quarter	29.4	11.1	18.4	869.7	709.7	535.8	64.9	160.0	122.7	37.4
3rd quarter	28.7	11.2	17.5	870.4	712.1	536.5	65.6	158.3	120.2	38.2
4th quarter	27.7	10.3	17.4	876.4	716.4	538.8	66.4	159.9	120.7	39.3
1996										
1st quarter	30.8	11.3	19.5	875.7	715.5	535.4	67.1	160.2	120.2	40.0
2nd quarter	33.1	12.0	21.1	890.2	727.0	544.3	67.8	163.3	122.4	40.8
3rd quarter	32.0	11.4	20.6	892.5	729.2	543.7	68.6	163.4	121.6	41.8
4th quarter	30.8	9.9	20.9	903.0	734.5	545.8	69.4	168.5	125.7	42.7
1997										
1st quarter	32.8	10.0	22.8	912.8	736.6	546.9	70.3	176.3	132.7	43.5
2nd quarter	35.2	9.7	25.6	922.2	742.2	549.6	71.2	180.0	135.2	44.8
3rd quarter	33.7	10.1	23.6	931.4	748.7	552.4	72.1	182.8	136.6	46.2
4th quarter	31.3	8.0	23.5	936.8	755.2	554.7	73.1	181.6	134.4	47.3
1998										
1st quarter	36.3	10.3	26.1	945.5	762.6	556.2	74.1	183.0	134.1	49.1
2nd quarter	40.1	10.2	30.1	955.7	769.9	558.7	75.2	185.8	135.3	50.9
3rd quarter	37.9	10.8	27.1	965.1	776.4	561.0	76.3	188.8	136.7	52.5
4th quarter	38.5	10.7	27.9	970.7	781.6	562.5	77.5	189.1	135.8	53.9
1999										
1st quarter	39.5	10.6	29.1	987.2	786.0	564.7	78.7	201.4	146.0	55.8
2nd quarter	45.7	9.7	36.6	987.5	791.2	566.3	80.0	196.4	139.6	57.7
3rd quarter	44.4	9.7	35.1	996.4	797.6	568.6	81.3	199.0	140.2	60.0
4th quarter	49.1	10.5	39.1	1 011.2	803.7	570.2	82.6	207.9	146.9	62.1

1. Gross government investment consists of general government and government enterprise expenditures for fixed assets; inventory investment is included in government consumption expenditures.
2. Consumption expenditures for durable goods excludes expenditures classified as investment, except for goods transferred to foreign countries by the federal government. Total includes items not shown separately.
3. Consumption of general government fixed capital, or depreciation, is a partial measure of the value of the services of general government fixed assets; a zero net rate of return on these assets is assumed.

Table 21-5. National Defense Consumption Expenditures and Gross Investment [1]

(Calendar years, billions of dollars, quarterly data are at seasonally adjusted annual rates.)

Year and quarter	Total	Consumption expenditures												
		Total	Durable goods [2]						Nondurable goods			Services		
			Aircraft	Missiles	Ships	Vehicles	Electronics	Other durable goods	Petroleum products	Ammunition	Other nondurable goods	Employee compensation	Capital consumption [3]	Research and development
1970	...	...	...	...	...	...	...	...	...	...	...	...	...	...
1971	...	...	...	...	...	...	...	...	...	...	...	...	...	...
1972	93.5	82.3	3.0	1.2	0.2	0.4	0.8	0.2	1.8	2.0	0.9	40.5	15.8	5.1
1973	93.9	82.6	2.8	1.2	0.2	0.4	0.8	-0.1	1.7	1.7	0.9	41.4	16.4	5.3
1974	99.7	87.5	2.2	1.4	0.2	0.5	0.8	-0.5	2.8	1.4	1.1	44.0	16.7	5.7
1975	107.9	93.4	2.3	1.6	0.3	0.8	0.9	0.6	2.9	1.1	1.1	47.8	17.5	5.9
1976	113.2	97.9	2.2	1.3	0.3	0.6	0.7	0.9	2.5	0.6	1.4	50.2	18.8	6.4
1977	122.6	105.8	3.3	1.5	0.5	0.8	0.8	0.9	2.4	0.8	1.3	53.5	19.9	6.8
1978	132.0	114.2	3.6	2.3	0.7	1.1	1.0	1.0	2.5	1.0	1.3	57.4	21.2	7.1
1979	146.7	125.3	4.9	2.2	0.9	1.2	1.1	1.3	3.6	1.2	1.5	61.5	22.3	7.7
1980	169.6	145.3	5.6	2.3	0.7	1.5	1.4	1.3	6.8	1.4	1.9	68.4	24.4	10.2
1981	197.8	168.9	7.8	2.7	0.6	1.7	1.7	1.5	7.7	1.6	2.6	78.6	27.2	12.4
1982	228.3	193.6	10.3	3.0	0.4	1.7	2.0	1.7	6.8	2.1	2.7	87.2	31.0	14.1
1983	252.5	210.6	13.6	3.7	1.2	2.3	2.4	1.9	6.4	2.5	2.5	92.2	33.4	14.5
1984	283.5	234.9	14.0	4.0	1.0	2.8	2.7	2.4	5.9	2.2	2.3	107.3	36.6	16.2
1985	312.4	254.9	15.4	3.9	0.8	2.9	3.2	3.0	5.8	1.3	2.9	115.0	38.6	21.7
1986	332.2	269.3	17.2	4.6	0.8	3.2	3.3	2.7	3.6	3.6	3.1	118.4	41.5	23.8
1987	351.2	284.8	18.2	4.7	1.0	3.1	3.7	3.0	3.9	2.8	3.6	123.2	44.1	27.0
1988	355.9	294.6	17.9	5.0	1.1	2.5	3.7	3.3	3.5	3.5	3.6	126.5	47.0	31.5
1989	363.2	300.5	16.4	5.0	1.0	1.9	3.8	3.9	4.2	3.1	3.6	131.2	50.1	28.6
1990	374.9	308.9	14.8	5.2	1.7	1.7	3.8	3.6	5.3	2.8	2.9	134.0	53.2	26.1
1991	384.5	321.1	13.8	5.3	1.9	1.9	3.5	4.8	4.7	2.7	3.4	141.3	56.3	21.9
1992	378.5	316.9	12.6	4.7	2.2	1.5	3.3	4.7	3.5	2.6	3.4	142.5	57.9	23.7
1993	364.9	309.2	11.3	4.3	2.3	1.3	3.5	4.5	3.2	2.4	2.8	138.1	60.2	23.1
1994	355.1	301.1	9.5	3.5	1.6	0.9	3.0	4.6	3.0	1.8	2.8	134.2	61.8	22.3
1995	350.6	297.5	9.0	2.8	1.2	1.1	2.5	4.5	2.8	1.1	2.4	130.4	63.0	20.3
1996	357.0	302.4	9.0	2.6	0.9	0.9	2.5	5.0	3.4	1.4	2.9	133.1	63.0	22.3
1997	352.6	304.2	9.7	2.3	1.0	1.1	2.5	4.6	2.9	1.6	3.0	132.5	62.8	23.2
1998	349.2	299.7	10.2	2.3	0.9	1.0	2.3	4.6	2.1	1.8	3.1	131.1	62.3	20.7
1999	365.0	311.2	10.9	2.2	1.0	0.8	2.6	4.9	2.6	1.9	3.7	133.2	63.1	19.0
1991														
1st quarter	390.7	327.2	14.3	5.0	1.7	1.7	3.7	5.4	6.6	2.8	3.8	143.1	55.3	22.7
2nd quarter	389.7	323.6	13.7	5.7	2.0	2.5	4.0	4.2	3.9	2.7	3.2	141.9	55.9	20.7
3rd quarter	383.5	319.2	13.6	5.6	2.2	1.7	3.3	4.7	4.5	2.4	3.0	140.8	56.7	20.6
4th quarter	374.1	314.2	13.6	5.0	1.9	1.5	2.9	4.9	3.6	2.7	3.5	139.4	57.1	23.6
1992														
1st quarter	373.8	313.3	13.0	4.6	2.0	1.4	3.2	4.9	3.3	1.8	3.6	143.8	57.2	23.1
2nd quarter	376.9	314.6	12.7	4.6	2.0	1.5	3.1	4.3	3.6	3.4	3.3	144.8	57.7	21.3
3rd quarter	384.8	322.0	12.1	5.1	2.2	1.5	3.6	4.8	4.0	2.5	3.6	143.5	58.0	23.4
4th quarter	378.5	317.9	12.5	4.5	2.4	1.6	3.4	4.9	3.1	2.4	3.3	137.8	58.6	27.2
1993														
1st quarter	367.4	310.5	10.5	4.5	2.0	1.4	3.6	4.5	3.0	2.4	2.7	140.7	59.4	23.4
2nd quarter	364.3	308.0	13.3	3.8	3.6	1.6	3.9	4.7	3.5	2.6	2.8	138.7	59.8	22.1
3rd quarter	363.9	310.5	10.5	4.7	1.7	1.2	3.5	4.4	3.4	2.6	3.1	137.7	60.6	22.8
4th quarter	364.1	307.7	10.7	3.9	1.8	1.0	3.0	4.4	2.9	2.1	2.6	135.3	60.9	24.1
1994														
1st quarter	349.4	298.1	9.1	3.8	1.7	1.0	3.3	4.4	2.5	1.9	2.5	136.1	61.2	20.5
2nd quarter	353.9	299.7	8.9	3.4	1.6	0.9	3.2	4.7	3.4	1.5	2.2	135.8	61.7	22.4
3rd quarter	366.9	308.7	10.5	3.9	1.6	0.9	3.1	5.1	3.5	1.4	3.2	133.5	61.7	24.1
4th quarter	350.4	297.8	9.8	3.0	1.4	0.9	2.6	4.4	2.8	2.3	3.1	131.5	62.5	22.4
1995														
1st quarter	352.2	298.2	10.1	2.4	1.1	1.1	2.6	4.4	2.6	1.1	2.3	131.7	62.9	20.1
2nd quarter	353.9	299.3	7.1	3.0	1.3	1.1	2.4	4.7	2.8	1.3	2.5	130.3	63.1	20.2
3rd quarter	352.7	301.2	10.5	3.3	1.6	1.2	2.7	4.3	3.3	1.1	2.3	130.3	63.0	21.5
4th quarter	343.6	291.2	8.1	2.6	0.7	0.8	2.1	4.7	2.4	0.9	2.4	129.2	63.2	19.4
1996														
1st quarter	356.1	298.4	8.8	2.4	0.7	0.9	2.2	4.6	3.1	1.4	2.4	133.3	63.1	20.8
2nd quarter	361.3	304.1	9.0	2.9	1.3	0.9	2.9	5.4	3.4	1.6	3.1	133.5	63.0	21.8
3rd quarter	355.6	301.4	9.4	2.8	0.9	1.0	2.7	5.2	4.1	1.1	3.1	133.5	63.1	21.7
4th quarter	355.0	305.6	8.9	2.3	0.8	0.9	2.2	4.8	3.0	1.4	2.9	132.1	62.9	25.0
1997														
1st quarter	346.4	301.1	9.5	2.2	1.0	1.1	2.4	4.2	3.1	1.9	3.0	133.9	62.9	20.7
2nd quarter	355.0	308.0	10.6	2.4	1.0	1.2	2.5	4.5	3.0	1.4	2.7	132.8	62.8	25.8
3rd quarter	354.7	304.1	8.8	2.3	1.0	1.1	2.6	4.8	3.0	1.6	3.2	132.3	62.7	22.9
4th quarter	354.4	303.6	9.8	2.4	0.9	1.1	2.3	4.7	2.7	1.6	3.1	131.2	62.8	23.6
1998														
1st quarter	338.6	291.9	9.4	2.1	0.9	1.0	2.4	4.4	2.2	1.5	3.1	132.2	62.4	17.2
2nd quarter	349.3	301.2	9.9	2.0	0.8	1.0	2.3	4.8	2.2	1.4	3.1	130.8	62.2	21.2
3rd quarter	355.0	301.7	10.1	3.0	0.9	1.0	2.4	5.0	2.2	2.4	3.0	131.3	62.3	21.5
4th quarter	353.8	304.1	11.3	2.1	0.9	0.9	2.2	4.4	1.8	1.9	3.2	130.3	62.3	22.7
1999														
1st quarter	356.5	305.7	9.9	2.2	0.9	0.8	2.3	4.7	1.5	1.6	3.1	133.5	62.7	19.7
2nd quarter	355.3	302.2	11.2	2.1	1.0	0.9	2.7	4.8	2.4	1.8	3.4	132.9	62.9	15.0
3rd quarter	367.5	312.2	11.9	2.3	1.0	0.8	2.9	5.0	3.8	2.3	3.9	133.4	63.2	18.1
4th quarter	380.8	324.7	10.5	2.2	0.9	0.9	2.7	5.2	2.6	1.8	4.3	132.8	63.8	23.2

1. Gross government investment consists of general government and government enterprise expenditures for fixed assets; inventory investment is included in government consumption expenditures.
2. Consumption expenditures for durable goods excludes expenditures classified as investment, except for goods transferred to foreign countries by the federal government.
3. Consumption of general government fixed capital, or depreciation, is a partial measure of the value of the services of general government fixed assets; a zero net rate of return on these assets is assumed.

Table 21-5. National Defense Consumption Expenditures and Gross Investment [1]—*Continued*

(Calendar years, billions of dollars, quarterly data are at seasonally adjusted annual rates.)

Year and quarter	Consumption expenditures—*Continued* Services—*Continued*						Gross investment							
	Installa-tion support	Weapons support	Personnel support	Transpor-tation of material	Travel of persons	Other services	Total	Structures	Equipment and software					
									Aircraft	Missiles	Ships	Vehicles	Electronics and software	Other equip-ment
1970	. . .	. . .	. . .	. . .	. . .	. . .	. . .	. . .	. . .	. . .	. . .	. . .	. . .	. . .
1971	. . .	. . .	. . .	. . .	. . .	. . .	. . .	. . .	. . .	. . .	. . .	. . .	. . .	. . .
1972	4.3	1.6	1.9	1.8	0.9	-0.2	11.2	1.8	2.6	1.5	1.8	0.4	0.8	2.2
1973	4.3	1.6	1.7	1.6	1.0	-0.1	11.3	2.1	2.3	1.5	1.6	0.3	0.9	2.5
1974	4.6	1.8	2.0	1.7	1.1	-0.2	12.3	2.2	2.3	1.7	2.2	0.3	1.0	2.6
1975	4.8	1.7	2.1	1.8	1.0	-0.8	14.5	2.3	3.6	1.3	2.2	0.3	1.2	3.6
1976	5.3	1.9	2.3	1.8	1.0	-0.2	15.3	2.1	3.4	1.4	2.4	0.5	1.3	4.2
1977	6.1	2.1	2.3	1.9	1.2	-0.4	16.7	2.4	3.7	1.2	3.1	0.6	1.5	4.2
1978	6.2	2.4	2.6	1.9	1.4	-0.5	17.8	2.5	3.7	1.1	3.9	0.8	1.8	4.0
1979	7.1	2.9	2.9	2.2	1.3	-0.5	21.4	2.5	4.8	1.8	4.3	0.9	2.1	5.0
1980	8.4	4.4	3.2	2.6	1.6	-0.7	24.3	3.2	6.1	2.3	4.1	1.2	2.6	4.8
1981	9.2	5.2	4.3	2.8	2.1	-0.8	28.9	3.2	7.5	2.8	5.1	1.1	3.2	6.1
1982	13.4	6.0	6.0	3.1	2.6	-0.7	34.7	4.0	8.4	3.4	6.2	2.1	3.8	6.8
1983	15.1	7.3	6.5	3.4	2.4	-0.5	41.9	4.8	10.1	4.6	7.1	3.4	4.6	7.3
1984	16.5	8.6	6.8	3.3	2.9	-0.7	48.7	4.9	10.9	5.7	8.0	4.2	5.6	9.3
1985	16.5	9.8	8.5	3.1	3.1	-0.7	57.5	6.2	13.4	6.6	9.0	3.7	7.0	11.5
1986	17.8	10.4	9.4	3.4	3.3	-0.8	62.9	6.8	17.9	7.9	8.9	3.8	7.8	9.9
1987	18.4	11.0	10.9	3.5	3.7	-0.8	66.4	7.7	17.6	8.7	8.8	4.3	8.7	10.6
1988	18.2	9.8	11.4	3.6	3.7	-1.1	61.3	7.4	13.5	7.8	8.6	3.7	9.2	11.1
1989	18.1	10.3	12.4	4.0	4.0	-1.0	62.7	6.4	12.2	8.8	10.0	3.1	9.6	12.6
1990	21.2	11.7	13.1	4.8	4.0	-1.1	65.9	6.1	12.0	11.2	10.8	3.2	9.9	12.8
1991	22.7	10.2	12.8	8.8	6.9	-1.7	63.4	4.6	9.2	10.8	10.2	3.4	9.7	15.4
1992	22.2	8.5	14.6	5.9	5.5	-2.3	61.6	5.2	8.3	10.6	10.1	2.8	9.8	14.8
1993	23.8	7.2	14.4	4.5	4.8	-2.6	55.7	5.1	9.3	7.9	8.7	1.9	10.4	12.5
1994	24.4	8.5	15.1	3.8	4.4	-4.4	54.0	5.7	10.5	5.7	8.1	1.0	10.3	12.7
1995	24.3	9.1	16.9	4.2	4.2	-2.2	53.1	6.3	9.0	4.7	8.0	1.1	10.5	13.6
1996	24.5	7.3	17.3	4.9	3.9	-2.5	54.6	6.7	9.2	4.1	6.8	1.2	11.6	15.2
1997	23.7	8.4	18.6	4.6	3.7	-2.0	48.4	5.7	5.9	2.9	6.1	1.4	12.4	14.0
1998	23.0	8.6	19.2	4.6	3.6	-1.7	49.5	5.4	5.6	3.3	6.4	1.5	13.4	13.8
1999	25.8	8.7	24.1	4.8	3.8	-1.8	53.8	5.3	7.0	2.8	6.8	1.6	15.6	14.7
1991														
1st quarter	23.6	10.7	12.8	9.5	6.1	-1.6	63.5	4.8	8.7	11.5	9.8	2.9	9.8	15.9
2nd quarter	23.2	10.8	12.2	11.0	8.0	-1.9	66.1	4.8	10.3	11.5	10.6	4.3	10.2	14.5
3rd quarter	21.2	9.8	12.4	9.6	9.4	-2.2	64.2	4.5	9.8	10.7	10.2	4.3	9.5	15.3
4th quarter	23.0	9.6	13.8	5.1	4.1	-1.0	59.9	4.5	8.1	9.7	10.2	2.3	9.1	16.0
1992														
1st quarter	22.0	8.8	13.8	4.7	4.1	-2.1	60.5	5.2	7.5	9.3	10.7	2.4	10.1	15.2
2nd quarter	20.7	7.9	13.3	8.0	5.7	-3.1	62.3	5.5	9.6	11.2	10.4	2.2	9.3	14.0
3rd quarter	21.8	8.8	14.7	7.6	7.5	-2.8	62.8	4.8	8.6	11.1	9.9	3.4	10.1	14.9
4th quarter	24.3	8.6	16.6	3.5	4.6	-1.4	60.6	5.5	7.5	10.6	9.3	3.1	9.7	14.9
1993														
1st quarter	25.0	7.7	14.7	3.3	4.2	-2.5	56.9	4.8	8.1	8.7	9.2	3.0	10.5	12.7
2nd quarter	21.4	6.5	13.6	3.9	4.6	-2.6	56.3	4.9	7.9	8.4	9.0	1.8	10.9	13.4
3rd quarter	24.4	6.8	14.6	6.2	5.8	-3.6	53.4	5.4	9.5	6.5	8.2	1.4	10.4	12.0
4th quarter	24.4	7.9	14.8	4.8	4.8	-1.7	56.3	5.3	11.8	8.0	8.2	1.3	9.8	11.9
1994														
1st quarter	25.5	7.5	13.9	3.9	3.6	-4.1	51.3	5.4	7.9	6.6	7.6	1.1	10.4	12.3
2nd quarter	24.0	8.1	14.7	4.0	4.4	-5.2	54.2	5.5	9.9	5.8	8.7	1.2	10.3	12.8
3rd quarter	25.0	8.9	15.9	3.7	5.8	-3.2	58.1	6.1	12.6	5.8	8.8	0.8	10.7	13.5
4th quarter	23.2	9.6	16.0	3.6	3.8	-5.1	52.5	6.0	11.5	4.8	7.1	1.1	10.0	12.0
1995														
1st quarter	24.9	9.5	16.2	3.8	4.1	-2.8	54.0	6.8	9.3	4.1	8.7	1.2	10.8	13.1
2nd quarter	25.1	9.7	17.2	4.2	4.3	-1.1	54.6	6.0	9.1	5.8	8.5	1.0	10.1	14.0
3rd quarter	23.9	8.8	17.3	4.3	4.3	-2.7	51.5	5.9	8.1	5.2	7.6	1.1	10.8	12.8
4th quarter	23.4	8.1	17.0	4.5	4.2	-2.4	52.4	6.4	9.6	3.7	7.2	1.0	10.3	14.4
1996														
1st quarter	23.3	7.1	17.1	5.0	4.2	-2.0	57.7	6.7	13.7	4.3	7.0	1.3	10.9	13.8
2nd quarter	25.0	6.9	16.9	5.0	4.0	-2.4	57.2	7.2	9.9	4.2	7.2	1.1	11.8	15.7
3rd quarter	25.2	6.4	16.3	4.6	3.3	-3.0	54.3	6.5	7.6	4.2	6.6	1.1	12.0	16.3
4th quarter	24.5	8.8	18.7	4.9	4.0	-2.6	49.4	6.4	5.4	3.6	6.3	1.2	11.6	14.9
1997														
1st quarter	23.0	7.6	18.0	4.6	3.8	-1.8	45.3	5.9	4.4	2.7	5.6	1.3	12.4	13.1
2nd quarter	24.1	8.3	18.7	4.6	3.7	-2.3	47.0	5.6	3.6	2.7	6.7	1.4	12.6	14.3
3rd quarter	24.2	8.6	18.9	4.6	3.6	-2.0	50.6	5.7	7.1	3.0	6.4	1.5	12.5	14.4
4th quarter	23.3	8.9	19.0	4.7	3.5	-1.9	50.8	5.7	8.4	3.0	5.8	1.4	12.2	14.4
1998														
1st quarter	21.9	7.7	17.6	4.7	3.5	-2.3	46.8	5.6	4.2	2.9	6.3	1.3	13.1	13.3
2nd quarter	23.5	8.6	19.9	4.7	3.5	-0.6	48.1	5.0	5.0	2.8	6.0	1.7	13.6	13.9
3rd quarter	23.7	8.6	19.0	4.6	3.6	-2.7	53.3	5.9	6.2	4.4	6.5	1.5	13.7	15.1
4th quarter	22.9	9.4	20.5	4.6	3.8	-1.0	49.7	5.1	7.2	3.0	6.9	1.4	13.2	12.9
1999														
1st quarter	23.9	8.7	22.5	4.7	3.9	-0.8	50.8	5.4	5.9	2.7	6.8	1.4	13.5	15.0
2nd quarter	24.1	8.4	21.1	5.2	3.9	-1.5	53.1	5.4	6.7	2.7	6.6	1.7	16.0	14.0
3rd quarter	25.1	8.6	24.0	4.6	3.8	-2.7	55.4	5.3	9.1	2.8	6.5	1.4	16.5	13.8
4th quarter	30.1	9.1	28.9	4.5	3.5	-2.0	56.1	5.2	6.5	2.9	7.1	2.0	16.3	16.0

1. Gross government investment consists of general government and government enterprise expenditures for fixed assets; inventory investment is included in government consumption expenditures.

Table 21-6. Federal Government Receipts and Outlays by Fiscal Year [1]

(Millions of dollars.)

Year and month	Total receipts (net)	Total outlays (net)	Budget surplus or deficit (-)			Sources of financing, total		Individual income taxes	Corporate income taxes	Social insurance taxes and contributions		
			Total	On-budget	Off-budget	Borrowing from the public	Other financing			Employment taxes and contributions	Unemployment insurance	Other retirement contributions
1950	39 443	42 562	-3 119	-4 702	1 583	4 701	-1 582	15 755	10 449	2 648	1 332	358
1951	51 616	45 514	6 102	4 259	1 843	-4 697	-1 405	21 616	14 101	3 688	1 609	377
1952	66 167	67 686	-1 519	-3 383	1 864	432	1 087	27 934	21 226	4 315	1 712	418
1953	69 608	76 101	-6 493	-8 259	1 766	3 625	2 868	29 816	21 238	4 722	1 675	423
1954	69 701	70 855	-1 154	-2 831	1 677	6 116	-4 962	29 542	21 101	5 192	1 561	455
1955	65 451	68 444	-2 993	-4 091	1 098	2 117	876	28 747	17 861	5 981	1 449	431
1956	74 587	70 640	3 947	2 494	1 452	-4 460	513	32 188	20 880	7 059	1 690	571
1957	79 990	76 578	3 412	2 639	773	-2 836	-576	35 620	21 167	7 405	1 950	642
1958	79 636	82 405	-2 769	-3 315	546	7 016	-4 247	34 724	20 074	8 624	1 933	682
1959	79 249	92 098	-12 849	-12 149	-700	8 365	4 484	36 719	17 309	8 821	2 131	770
1960	92 492	92 191	301	510	-209	2 139	-2 440	40 715	21 494	11 248	2 667	768
1961	94 388	97 723	-3 335	-3 766	431	1 517	1 818	41 338	20 954	12 679	2 903	857
1962	99 676	106 821	-7 146	-5 881	-1 265	9 653	-2 507	45 571	20 523	12 835	3 337	875
1963	106 560	111 316	-4 756	-3 966	-789	5 968	-1 212	47 588	21 579	14 746	4 112	946
1964	112 613	118 528	-5 915	-6 546	632	2 871	3 044	48 697	23 493	16 959	3 997	1 007
1965	116 817	118 228	-1 411	-1 605	194	3 929	-2 518	48 792	25 461	17 358	3 803	1 081
1966	130 835	134 532	-3 698	-3 068	-630	2 936	762	55 446	30 073	20 662	3 755	1 129
1967	148 822	157 464	-8 643	-12 620	3 978	2 912	5 731	61 526	33 971	27 823	3 575	1 221
1968	152 973	178 134	-25 161	-27 742	2 581	22 919	2 242	68 726	28 665	29 224	3 346	1 354
1969	186 882	183 640	3 242	-507	3 749	-11 437	8 195	87 249	36 678	34 236	3 328	1 451
1970	192 807	195 649	-2 842	-8 694	5 852	5 090	-2 248	90 412	32 829	39 133	3 464	1 765
1971	187 139	210 172	-23 033	-26 052	3 019	19 839	3 194	86 230	26 785	41 699	3 674	1 952
1972	207 309	230 681	-23 373	-26 423	3 050	19 340	4 033	94 737	32 166	46 120	4 357	2 097
1973	230 799	245 707	-14 908	-15 403	495	18 533	-3 625	103 246	36 153	54 876	6 051	2 187
1974	263 224	269 359	-6 135	-7 971	1 836	2 789	3 346	118 952	38 620	65 888	6 837	2 347
1975	279 090	332 332	-53 242	-55 260	2 018	51 001	2 241	122 386	40 621	75 199	6 771	2 565
1976	298 060	371 792	-73 732	-70 512	-3 220	82 704	-8 972	131 603	41 409	79 901	8 054	2 814
1977	355 559	409 218	-53 659	-49 760	-3 899	71 699	-18 040	157 626	54 892	92 199	11 312	2 974
1978	399 561	458 746	-59 186	-54 920	-4 266	58 022	1 164	180 988	59 952	103 881	13 850	3 237
1979	463 302	504 032	-40 729	-38 745	-1 984	33 183	7 546	217 841	65 677	120 058	15 387	3 494
1980	517 112	590 947	-73 835	-72 715	-1 120	69 530	4 305	244 069	64 600	138 748	15 336	3 719
1981	599 272	678 249	-78 976	-73 956	-5 020	75 500	3 476	285 917	61 137	162 973	15 763	3 984
1982	617 766	745 755	-127 989	-120 052	-7 937	134 447	-6 458	297 744	49 207	180 686	16 600	4 212
1983	600 562	808 385	-207 822	-208 035	212	211 811	-3 989	288 938	37 022	185 766	18 799	4 429
1984	666 486	851 874	-185 388	-185 650	262	168 902	16 486	298 415	56 893	209 658	25 138	4 580
1985	734 088	946 423	-212 334	-221 698	9 363	199 410	12 924	334 531	61 331	234 646	25 758	4 759
1986	769 215	990 460	-221 245	-237 976	16 731	236 801	-15 556	348 959	63 143	255 062	24 098	4 742
1987	854 353	1 004 122	-149 769	-169 339	19 570	151 971	-2 202	392 557	83 926	273 028	25 575	4 715
1988	909 303	1 064 489	-155 187	-193 986	38 800	162 119	-6 932	401 181	94 508	305 093	24 584	4 658
1989	991 190	1 143 671	-152 481	-205 235	52 754	139 083	13 398	445 690	103 291	332 859	22 011	4 546
1990	1 031 969	1 253 198	-221 229	-277 819	56 590	220 840	389	466 884	93 507	353 891	21 635	4 522
1991	1 055 041	1 324 403	-269 361	-321 559	52 198	277 415	-8 054	467 827	98 086	370 526	20 922	4 568
1992	1 091 279	1 381 684	-290 404	-340 492	50 087	310 696	-20 292	475 964	100 270	385 491	23 410	4 788
1993	1 154 401	1 409 512	-255 110	-300 457	45 347	248 594	6 516	509 680	117 520	396 939	26 556	4 805
1994	1 258 627	1 461 902	-203 275	-258 929	55 654	184 583	18 692	543 055	140 385	428 810	28 004	4 661
1995	1 351 830	1 515 837	-164 007	-226 422	62 415	171 363	-7 356	590 244	157 004	451 045	28 878	4 550
1996	1 453 062	1 560 572	-107 510	-174 098	66 588	129 657	-22 147	656 417	171 824	476 361	28 584	4 469
1997	1 579 292	1 601 282	-21 990	-103 354	81 364	38 171	-16 181	737 466	182 293	506 751	28 202	4 418
1998	1 721 798	1 652 611	69 187	-30 008	99 195	-51 051	-18 136	828 586	188 677	540 014	27 484	4 333
1999	1 827 454	1 703 040	124 414	724	123 690	-88 288	-36 126	879 480	184 680	580 880	26 480	4 473
1998												
January	162 610	137 231	25 379	14 524	10 855	-24 807	-572	95 798	4 407	50 395	1 036	333
February	97 952	139 701	-41 750	-44 342	2 592	30 565	11 185	42 209	829	41 825	2 589	335
March	117 930	131 743	-13 813	-21 320	7 508	20 137	-6 324	39 662	19 491	47 389	301	337
April	261 002	136 400	124 603	108 419	16 184	-60 587	-64 016	158 284	27 361	56 544	4 589	332
May	95 278	134 057	-38 779	-40 591	1 812	-8 597	47 376	29 974	3 259	42 560	8 273	406
June	187 858	136 752	51 106	19 367	31 739	-12 618	-38 488	81 587	39 785	54 807	292	369
July	119 723	143 807	-24 084	-27 894	3 809	-16 370	40 454	58 969	4 072	41 130	2 301	385
August	111 741	122 907	-11 166	-13 420	2 254	33 989	-22 823	55 300	1 468	41 973	3 502	331
September	180 995	143 569	38 222	41 826	-3 604	-46 413	8 191	90 479	36 800	42 540	206	333
October	119 974	152 413	-32 462	-33 623	1 161	15 309	17 153	60 255	1 758	39 690	1 142	405
November	113 978	130 915	-17 117	-18 242	1 125	22 313	-5 196	51 341	3 440	42 940	2 655	331
December	178 646	183 803	-5 410	-6 064	654	-5 383	10 793	75 988	42 374	47 869	315	417
1999												
January	171 728	101 223	70 505	27 542	42 963	-31 250	-39 255	99 863	5 130	53 725	873	337
February	99 502	141 847	-42 345	-45 509	3 164	1 692	40 653	42 880	1 176	43 735	2 595	353
March	130 416	152 825	-22 409	-29 662	7 253	37 073	-14 664	50 531	18 553	48 592	279	355
April	266 229	152 770	113 459	96 016	17 443	-85 211	-28 248	164 919	21 699	60 186	4 284	428
May	98 663	122 631	-23 969	-28 712	4 744	-54	24 023	30 661	3 948	45 617	7 797	350
June	199 507	145 939	53 568	20 788	32 779	-22 264	-31 304	93 020	39 264	54 380	379	393
July	121 923	147 086	-25 164	-29 693	4 530	1 193	23 971	59 992	3 405	44 392	1 597	403
August	126 324	129 127	-2 803	-6 430	3 627	26 470	-23 667	60 719	3 697	44 960	4 097	344
September	200 396	142 340	58 055	54 083	3 973	-47 683	-10 372	89 250	40 235	54 794	335	356
October	121 035	147 701	-26 667	-30 497	3 830	5 754	20 913	63 505	2 180	42 412	1 052	418
November	121 375	148 408	-27 033	-29 479	2 446	6 132	20 901	57 477	1 653	45 759	2 870	386
December	201 196	168 114	33 081	-2 732	35 813	35 749	-68 830	94 535	44 946	47 742	268	415

1. Fiscal years through 1976 are from July 1 through June 30. Beginning with October 1976 (fiscal year 1977), fiscal years are from October 1 through September 30. The period from July 1 through September 30, 1976 (not shown here) is a separate fiscal period known as the transition quarter and not included in any fiscal year.

Table 21-6. Federal Government Receipts and Outlays by Fiscal Year [1]—*Continued*

(Millions of dollars.)

Year and month	Receipts by source—*Continued*				Outlays by function						
	Excise taxes	Estate and gift taxes	Customs deposits	Miscellaneous receipts	National defense	International affairs	General science, space, and technology	Energy	Natural resources and environment	Agriculture	Commerce and housing credit
1950	7 550	698	407	247	13 724	4 673	55	327	1 308	2 049	1 035
1951	8 648	708	609	261	23 566	3 647	51	383	1 310	-323	1 228
1952	8 852	818	533	359	46 089	2 691	49	474	1 233	176	1 278
1953	9 877	881	596	379	52 802	2 119	49	425	1 289	2 253	910
1954	9 945	934	542	429	49 266	1 596	46	432	1 007	1 817	-184
1955	9 131	924	585	341	42 729	2 223	74	325	940	3 514	92
1956	9 929	1 161	682	427	42 523	2 414	79	174	870	3 486	506
1957	10 534	1 365	735	573	45 430	3 147	122	240	1 098	2 288	1 424
1958	10 638	1 393	782	787	46 815	3 364	141	348	1 407	2 411	930
1959	10 578	1 333	925	662	49 015	3 144	294	382	1 632	4 509	1 933
1960	11 676	1 606	1 105	1 212	48 130	2 988	599	464	1 559	2 623	1 618
1961	11 860	1 896	982	918	49 601	3 184	1 042	510	1 779	2 641	1 203
1962	12 534	2 016	1 142	843	52 345	5 639	1 723	604	2 044	3 562	1 424
1963	13 194	2 167	1 205	1 022	53 400	5 308	3 051	530	2 251	4 384	62
1964	13 731	2 394	1 252	1 086	54 757	4 945	4 897	572	2 364	4 609	418
1965	14 570	2 716	1 442	1 594	50 620	5 273	5 823	699	2 531	3 955	1 157
1966	13 062	3 066	1 767	1 876	58 111	5 580	6 717	612	2 719	2 447	3 245
1967	13 719	2 978	1 901	2 107	71 417	5 566	6 233	782	2 869	2 990	3 979
1968	14 079	3 051	2 038	2 491	81 926	5 301	5 524	1 037	2 988	4 545	4 280
1969	15 222	3 491	2 319	2 909	82 497	4 600	5 020	1 010	2 900	5 826	-119
1970	15 705	3 644	2 430	3 424	81 692	4 330	4 511	997	3 065	5 166	2 112
1971	16 614	3 735	2 591	3 858	78 872	4 159	4 182	1 035	3 915	4 290	2 366
1972	15 477	5 436	3 287	3 632	79 174	4 781	4 175	1 296	4 241	5 259	2 222
1973	16 260	4 917	3 188	3 920	76 681	4 149	4 032	1 237	4 775	4 854	931
1974	16 844	5 035	3 334	5 368	79 347	5 710	3 980	1 303	5 697	2 230	4 705
1975	16 551	4 611	3 676	6 712	86 509	7 097	3 991	2 916	7 346	3 036	9 947
1976	16 963	5 216	4 074	8 027	89 619	6 433	4 373	4 204	8 184	3 170	7 619
1977	17 548	7 327	5 150	6 531	97 241	6 353	4 736	5 770	10 032	6 787	3 093
1978	18 376	5 285	6 573	7 419	104 495	7 482	4 926	7 992	10 983	11 357	6 254
1979	18 745	5 411	7 439	9 252	116 342	7 459	5 235	9 180	12 135	11 236	4 686
1980	24 329	6 389	7 174	12 748	133 995	12 714	5 832	10 156	13 858	8 839	9 390
1981	40 839	6 787	8 083	13 790	157 513	13 104	6 469	15 166	13 568	11 323	8 206
1982	36 311	7 991	8 854	16 161	185 309	12 300	7 200	13 527	12 998	15 944	6 256
1983	35 300	6 053	8 655	15 600	209 903	11 848	7 935	9 353	12 672	22 901	6 681
1984	37 361	6 010	11 370	17 060	227 413	15 876	8 317	7 073	12 593	13 613	6 959
1985	35 992	6 422	12 079	18 571	252 748	16 176	8 627	5 609	13 357	25 565	4 337
1986	32 919	6 958	13 327	20 008	273 375	14 152	8 976	4 690	13 639	31 449	5 059
1987	32 457	7 493	15 085	19 518	281 999	11 649	9 216	4 072	13 363	26 606	6 435
1988	35 227	7 594	16 198	20 259	290 361	10 471	10 841	2 297	14 606	17 210	19 164
1989	34 386	8 745	16 334	23 328	303 559	9 573	12 838	2 706	16 182	16 919	29 710
1990	35 345	11 500	16 707	27 978	299 331	13 764	14 444	3 341	17 080	11 958	67 600
1991	42 402	11 138	15 949	23 623	273 292	15 851	16 111	2 436	18 559	15 183	76 271
1992	45 569	11 143	17 359	27 284	298 350	16 107	16 409	4 500	20 025	15 205	10 919
1993	48 057	12 577	18 802	19 465	291 086	17 248	17 030	4 319	20 239	20 363	-21 853
1994	55 225	15 225	20 099	23 164	281 642	17 083	16 227	5 219	21 026	15 046	-4 228
1995	57 484	14 763	19 301	28 561	272 066	16 434	16 724	4 936	21 915	9 778	-17 808
1996	54 014	17 189	18 670	25 534	265 753	13 496	16 709	2 839	21 524	9 159	-10 472
1997	56 924	19 845	17 928	25 465	270 505	15 228	17 174	1 475	21 227	9 032	-14 624
1998	57 673	24 076	18 297	32 658	268 456	13 109	18 219	1 270	22 300	12 206	1 014
1999	70 414	27 782	18 336	34 929	274 873	15 243	18 125	912	23 968	23 011	2 647
1998											
January	4 679	1 808	1 387	2 768	20 738	750	1 498	291	1 638	1 958	-403
February	4 791	1 500	1 454	2 420	20 492	364	1 404	-43	1 746	330	-1 065
March	4 499	1 845	1 412	2 994	20 326	979	1 617	40	1 556	283	-972
April	5 742	4 198	1 428	2 525	22 065	1 460	1 702	-34	1 575	119	-814
May	4 841	1 845	1 297	2 823	23 212	720	1 548	42	1 574	-451	791
June	5 370	1 775	1 568	2 307	22 329	347	1 657	661	1 964	140	-20
July	6 127	1 825	1 777	3 135	25 865	815	1 711	122	2 217	176	-1 223
August	3 181	1 718	1 732	2 535	18 502	443	1 581	-113	1 855	1 656	-1 423
September	2 961	2 356	1 701	3 572	24 748	1 123	1 824	892	2 115	2 780	8 147
October	9 630	2 089	1 776	3 228	25 730	169	1 550	-135	1 859	3 287	1 078
November	6 021	2 132	1 380	3 738	18 173	4 924	1 558	-218	2 080	5 620	-701
December	5 446	2 239	1 472	2 527	27 178	822	1 918	151	2 545	3 238	-1 821
1999											
January	4 806	2 206	1 286	3 509	19 270	1 179	1 398	-107	1 458	3 939	745
February	3 892	1 600	1 403	1 868	20 909	1 372	1 312	-189	1 919	1 074	-1 237
March	5 880	2 172	1 546	2 457	25 469	949	1 663	588	1 862	1 046	-1 474
April	5 579	5 138	1 350	2 383	25 433	1 686	1 565	-156	1 611	666	-536
May	4 978	1 942	1 256	2 181	19 211	640	1 581	104	1 595	487	989
June	5 880	1 857	1 599	2 742	24 122	1 053	1 800	557	1 906	2 591	-116
July	5 723	1 938	1 725	2 771	26 153	569	1 597	-13	1 935	489	64
August	5 397	2 175	1 814	3 131	20 867	530	1 681	26	1 961	726	-1 386
September	7 167	2 294	1 727	4 242	24 279	1 371	1 773	375	2 249	1 196	7 361
October	4 181	2 554	1 788	2 948	24 036	1 000	1 524	-311	1 528	6 759	1 698
November	6 072	2 465	1 621	3 075	23 224	1 522	1 661	-199	2 078	7 401	1 108
December	5 709	2 575	1 612	3 398	31 261	3 527	1 853	32	2 350	4 362	-696

1. Fiscal years through 1976 are from July 1 through June 30. Beginning with October 1976 (fiscal year 1977), fiscal years are from October 1 through September 30. The period from July 1 through September 30, 1976 (not shown here) is a separate fiscal period known as the transition quarter and not included in any fiscal year.

Table 21-6. Federal Government Receipts and Outlays by Fiscal Year [1]—Continued

(Millions of dollars.)

Year and month	Outlays by function—Continued										
	Transportation	Community and regional development	Education, employment, and social services	Health	Medicare	Income security	Social security	Veterans benefits and services	Administration of justice	General government	Net interest
1950	967	30	241	268	...	4 097	781	8 834	193	986	4 812
1951	956	47	235	323	...	3 352	1 565	5 526	218	1 097	4 665
1952	1 124	73	339	347	...	3 655	2 063	5 341	267	1 163	4 701
1953	1 264	117	441	336	...	3 823	2 717	4 519	243	1 209	5 156
1954	1 229	100	370	307	...	4 434	3 352	4 613	257	799	4 811
1955	1 246	129	445	291	...	5 071	4 427	4 675	256	651	4 850
1956	1 450	92	591	359	...	4 734	5 478	4 891	302	1 201	5 079
1957	1 662	135	590	479	...	5 427	6 661	5 005	303	1 360	5 354
1958	2 334	169	643	541	...	7 535	8 219	5 350	325	655	5 604
1959	3 655	211	789	685	...	8 239	9 737	5 443	356	926	5 762
1960	4 126	224	968	795	...	7 378	11 602	5 441	366	1 184	6 947
1961	3 987	275	1 063	913	...	9 683	12 474	5 705	400	1 354	6 716
1962	4 290	469	1 241	1 198	...	9 207	14 365	5 619	429	1 049	6 889
1963	4 596	574	1 458	1 451	...	9 311	15 788	5 514	465	1 230	7 740
1964	5 242	933	1 555	1 788	...	9 657	16 620	5 675	489	1 518	8 199
1965	5 763	1 114	2 140	1 791	...	9 469	17 460	5 716	535	1 499	8 591
1966	5 730	1 105	4 363	2 543	64	9 678	20 694	5 916	563	1 603	9 386
1967	5 936	1 108	6 453	3 351	2 748	10 261	21 725	6 735	618	1 719	10 268
1968	6 316	1 382	7 634	4 390	4 649	11 816	23 854	7 032	659	1 757	11 090
1969	6 526	1 552	7 548	5 162	5 695	13 076	27 298	7 631	766	1 939	12 699
1970	7 008	2 392	8 634	5 907	6 213	15 655	30 270	8 669	959	2 320	14 380
1971	8 052	2 917	9 849	6 843	6 622	22 946	35 872	9 768	1 306	2 442	14 841
1972	8 392	3 423	12 529	8 674	7 479	27 650	40 157	10 720	1 653	2 960	15 478
1973	9 066	4 605	12 745	9 356	8 052	28 276	49 090	12 003	2 141	9 774	17 349
1974	9 172	4 229	12 457	10 733	9 639	33 713	55 867	13 374	2 470	10 032	21 449
1975	10 918	4 322	16 022	12 930	12 875	50 176	64 658	16 584	2 955	10 408	23 244
1976	13 739	5 442	18 910	15 734	15 834	60 799	73 899	18 419	3 328	9 747	26 727
1977	14 829	7 021	21 104	17 302	19 345	61 060	85 061	18 022	3 605	12 833	29 901
1978	15 521	11 841	26 710	18 524	22 768	61 505	93 861	18 961	3 813	12 015	35 458
1979	18 079	10 480	30 223	20 494	26 495	66 376	104 073	19 914	4 173	12 293	42 636
1980	21 329	11 252	31 843	23 169	32 090	86 557	118 547	21 169	4 584	13 028	52 538
1981	23 379	10 568	33 709	26 866	39 149	99 742	139 584	22 973	4 769	11 429	68 774
1982	20 625	8 347	27 029	27 445	46 567	107 737	155 964	23 938	4 712	10 914	85 044
1983	21 334	7 564	26 606	28 641	52 588	122 621	170 724	24 824	5 105	11 235	89 828
1984	23 669	7 673	27 579	30 417	57 540	112 694	178 223	25 588	5 663	11 817	111 123
1985	25 838	7 680	29 342	33 542	65 822	128 230	188 623	26 262	6 270	11 588	129 504
1986	28 117	7 233	30 585	35 936	70 164	119 824	198 757	26 327	6 572	12 564	136 047
1987	26 222	5 051	29 724	39 967	75 120	123 286	207 353	26 750	7 553	7 560	138 652
1988	27 272	5 294	31 938	44 487	78 878	129 373	219 341	29 386	9 236	9 465	151 838
1989	27 608	5 362	36 674	48 390	84 964	136 082	232 542	30 031	9 474	9 249	169 018
1990	29 485	8 532	38 755	57 716	98 102	147 076	248 623	29 058	9 993	10 575	184 380
1991	31 099	6 813	43 354	71 183	104 489	170 321	269 015	31 305	12 276	11 719	194 482
1992	33 332	6 841	45 248	89 497	119 024	197 022	287 585	34 064	14 426	13 039	199 373
1993	35 004	9 149	50 012	99 415	130 552	207 297	304 585	35 671	14 955	13 086	198 736
1994	38 066	10 625	46 307	107 122	144 747	214 085	319 565	37 584	15 256	11 345	202 957
1995	39 350	10 749	54 263	115 418	159 855	220 493	335 846	37 890	16 216	13 998	232 169
1996	39 565	10 745	52 001	119 378	174 225	225 967	349 676	36 985	17 548	12 004	241 090
1997	40 767	11 055	53 008	123 843	190 016	230 899	365 257	39 313	20 173	12 891	244 016
1998	40 335	9 776	54 954	131 442	192 822	233 202	379 225	41 781	22 832	15 709	241 153
1999	42 531	11 870	56 402	141 079	190 447	237 707	390 041	43 212	25 924	15 758	229 735
1998											
January	2 762	783	5 081	11 162	15 686	20 093	31 243	3 331	1 718	836	20 570
February	2 504	669	6 535	9 735	15 539	28 194	31 271	3 386	2 026	108	19 901
March	2 734	503	2 888	10 876	14 394	22 853	31 421	1 883	1 764	1 012	20 651
April	2 511	1 121	4 428	11 259	17 016	20 757	31 335	4 056	1 757	1 178	20 961
May	2 746	873	2 798	10 419	15 341	18 705	31 490	3 604	1 781	925	20 855
June	3 127	914	4 237	11 602	16 139	14 554	35 430	3 355	2 241	2 080	19 407
July	3 327	917	3 645	11 033	19 388	21 198	31 721	4 958	2 256	308	20 791
August	3 218	770	4 708	10 704	12 817	14 281	31 423	1 749	2 012	579	21 366
September	3 997	1 115	4 455	11 293	15 758	17 309	31 797	3 432	1 675	2 199	15 976
October	3 455	1 260	4 861	12 572	18 824	20 104	31 720	5 465	1 899	2 377	19 442
November	3 447	1 405	4 111	10 477	12 088	14 644	31 640	1 841	2 067	1 418	19 350
December	3 400	1 505	5 465	11 757	17 982	21 945	61 651	5 305	2 132	2 198	20 029
1999											
January	2 558	709	5 136	10 984	12 533	17 349	2 715	1 828	2 090	188	19 947
February	2 259	720	5 429	11 100	14 560	29 856	32 167	3 574	1 832	274	18 049
March	2 636	1 148	6 641	11 988	17 474	26 749	32 372	3 693	2 180	1 130	19 970
April	2 737	684	4 202	12 284	19 503	24 420	32 313	5 498	2 625	929	20 195
May	3 010	906	4 464	10 657	12 232	12 880	32 287	1 893	1 886	621	19 976
June	3 882	1 201	4 143	12 307	16 700	14 574	36 290	3 619	2 536	3 508	18 518
July	3 375	755	3 980	11 685	18 722	20 514	32 435	5 130	1 935	1 360	19 598
August	3 838	879	4 363	11 959	13 218	16 495	32 389	1 895	2 349	200	19 931
September	4 260	1 330	5 437	13 031	16 100	16 897	32 581	3 615	2 306	1 712	15 259
October	3 750	1 627	5 175	12 229	15 449	17 607	32 730	3 657	2 127	1 117	18 894
November	3 890	1 244	4 070	12 124	16 160	18 216	32 526	3 795	2 579	646	20 410
December	3 858	1 300	5 593	13 462	19 881	23 747	32 839	5 320	2 163	1 974	18 328

1. Fiscal years through 1976 are from July 1 through June 30. Beginning with October 1976 (fiscal year 1977), fiscal years are from October 1 through September 30. The period from July 1 through September 30, 1976 (not shown here) is a separate fiscal period known as the transition quarter and not included in any fiscal year.

Table 21-7. Federal Government Debt by Fiscal Year 1; Government Employment

Year and month	Federal government debt held by the public at end of fiscal year		Government employment (calendar years), (payroll employment, thousands, seasonally adjusted, except as noted)							
				Federal		State		Local		
	Federal debt (billions of dollars)	Federal debt/GDP ratio (percent)	Total	Total	Department of Defense (not seasonally adjusted)	Total	Education	Total	Education	
1950	219	80.1	6 026	1 928	737	. . .	. . .	. . .	. . .	
1951	214	66.7	6 389	2 302	1 101	. . .	. . .	. . .	. . .	
1952	215	61.6	6 609	2 420	1 199	. . .	. . .	. . .	. . .	
1953	218	58.5	6 645	2 305	1 131	. . .	. . .	. . .	. . .	
1954	224	59.4	6 751	2 188	1 027	. . .	. . .	. . .	. . .	
1955	227	57.3	6 914	2 187	1 028	1 168	308	3 558	1 792	
1956	222	52.0	7 278	2 209	1 034	1 250	334	3 819	1 928	
1957	219	48.7	7 616	2 217	1 007	1 328	362	4 071	2 073	
1958	226	49.1	7 839	2 191	960	1 415	389	4 232	2 165	
1959	235	47.7	8 083	2 233	966	1 484	420	4 366	2 250	
1960	237	45.6	8 353	2 270	941	1 536	448	4 547	2 369	
1961	238	44.9	8 594	2 279	944	1 607	474	4 708	2 468	
1962	248	43.6	8 890	2 340	963	1 668	510	4 881	2 581	
1963	254	42.3	9 225	2 358	949	1 747	557	5 121	2 738	
1964	257	40.0	9 596	2 348	934	1 856	609	5 392	2 906	
1965	261	37.9	10 074	2 378	938	1 996	679	5 700	3 102	
1966	264	34.8	10 784	2 564	1 024	2 141	775	6 080	3 375	
1967	267	32.8	11 391	2 719	1 109	2 302	873	6 371	3 572	
1968	290	33.3	11 839	2 737	1 107	2 442	958	6 660	3 736	
1969	278	29.3	12 195	2 758	1 126	2 533	1 042	6 904	3 874	
1970	283	27.9	12 554	2 731	1 044	2 664	1 104	7 158	4 004	
1971	303	28.0	12 881	2 696	1 009	2 747	1 149	7 437	4 188	
1972	322	27.4	13 334	2 684	995	2 859	1 188	7 790	4 363	
1973	341	26.0	13 732	2 663	961	2 923	1 205	8 146	4 537	
1974	344	23.8	14 170	2 724	964	3 039	1 267	8 407	4 692	
1975	395	25.3	14 686	2 748	955	3 179	1 323	8 758	4 834	
1976	477	27.5	14 871	2 733	929	3 273	1 371	8 865	4 899	
1977	549	27.8	15 127	2 727	918	3 377	1 385	9 023	4 974	
1978	607	27.4	15 672	2 753	910	3 474	1 367	9 446	5 075	
1979	640	25.6	15 947	2 773	895	3 541	1 378	9 633	5 107	
1980	712	26.1	16 241	2 866	893	3 610	1 398	9 765	5 210	
1981	789	25.8	16 031	2 772	913	3 640	1 420	9 619	5 216	
1982	925	28.6	15 837	2 739	939	3 640	1 433	9 458	5 169	
1983	1 137	33.0	15 869	2 774	947	3 662	1 450	9 434	5 139	
1984	1 307	34.0	16 024	2 807	963	3 734	1 488	9 482	5 196	
1985	1 507	36.4	16 394	2 875	988	3 832	1 540	9 687	5 344	
1986	1 741	39.6	16 693	2 899	983	3 893	1 561	9 901	5 484	
1987	1 890	40.6	17 010	2 943	985	3 967	1 586	10 100	5 598	
1988	2 052	40.9	17 386	2 971	964	4 076	1 620	10 339	5 722	
1989	2 191	40.5	17 779	2 988	973	4 182	1 668	10 609	5 875	
1990	2 412	42.0	18 304	3 085	951	4 305	1 730	10 914	6 042	
1991	2 689	45.4	18 402	2 966	921	4 355	1 768	11 081	6 136	
1992	3 000	48.2	18 645	2 969	917	4 408	1 799	11 267	6 220	
1993	3 249	49.5	18 841	2 915	870	4 488	1 834	11 438	6 353	
1994	3 433	49.4	19 128	2 870	825	4 576	1 882	11 682	6 479	
1995	3 605	49.2	19 305	2 822	779	4 635	1 919	11 849	6 606	
1996	3 734	48.5	19 419	2 757	740	4 606	1 911	12 056	6 748	
1997	3 773	46.1	19 557	2 699	698	4 582	1 904	12 276	6 918	
1998	3 722	43.1	19 823	2 686	665	4 612	1 922	12 525	7 084	
1999	3 633	39.9	20 170	2 669	640	4 695	1 968	12 806	7 272	
1998										
January	. . .	. . .	19 658	2 678	674	4 579	1 902	12 401	6 995	
February	. . .	. . .	19 684	2 675	672	4 577	1 901	12 432	7 018	
March	. . .	. . .	19 693	2 671	669	4 581	1 903	12 441	7 024	
April	. . .	. . .	19 721	2 672	666	4 588	1 906	12 461	7 039	
May	. . .	. . .	19 775	2 674	669	4 601	1 914	12 500	7 056	
June	. . .	. . .	19 782	2 675	673	4 601	1 920	12 506	7 063	
July	. . .	. . .	19 806	2 675	672	4 624	1 928	12 507	7 080	
August	. . .	. . .	19 874	2 689	666	4 630	1 934	12 555	7 111	
September	. . .	. . .	19 898	2 694	660	4 644	1 945	12 560	7 105	
October	. . .	. . .	19 926	2 711	655	4 636	1 936	12 579	7 118	
November	. . .	. . .	19 952	2 722	654	4 635	1 933	12 595	7 138	
December	. . .	. . .	19 975	2 701	653	4 652	1 945	12 622	7 149	
1999										
January	. . .	. . .	20 002	2 700	647	4 650	1 939	12 652	7 170	
February	. . .	. . .	20 075	2 710	645	4 674	1 960	12 691	7 197	
March	. . .	. . .	20 099	2 705	645	4 678	1 963	12 716	7 216	
April	. . .	. . .	20 107	2 684	643	4 686	1 968	12 737	7 222	
May	. . .	. . .	20 103	2 664	643	4 684	1 963	12 755	7 238	
June	. . .	. . .	20 123	2 662	648	4 673	1 950	12 788	7 257	
July	. . .	. . .	20 163	2 656	646	4 691	1 967	12 816	7 273	
August	. . .	. . .	20 211	2 655	641	4 698	1 972	12 858	7 305	
September	. . .	. . .	20 223	2 655	635	4 714	1 978	12 854	7 299	
October	. . .	. . .	20 248	2 647	630	4 722	1 979	12 879	7 308	
November	. . .	. . .	20 271	2 646	630	4 723	1 980	12 902	7 323	
December	. . .	. . .	20 308	2 646	630	4 727	1 983	12 935	7 343	

1. Fiscal years through 1976 are from July 1 through June 30. Beginning with October 1976 (fiscal year 1977), fiscal years are from October 1 through September 30. The period from July 1 through September 30, 1976 (not shown here) is a separate fiscal period known as the transition quarter and not included in any fiscal year.

PART III

HISTORICAL DATA

Table 22-1. Gross Domestic Product

(Billions of dollars, quarterly data are at seasonally adjusted annual rates.)

Year and quarter	Gross domestic product	Personal consumption expenditures	Gross private domestic investment				Exports and imports of goods and services			Government consumption expenditures and gross investment			Addendum: Final sales of domestic product
			Total	Fixed investment		Change in private inventories	Net exports	Exports	Imports	Total	Federal	State and local	
				Nonresidential	Residential								
1963	618.7	383.1	93.8	56.0	32.1	5.6	3.3	29.4	26.1	138.5	78.5	59.9	613.1
1964	664.4	411.7	102.1	63.0	34.3	4.8	5.5	33.6	28.1	145.1	79.8	65.3	659.6
1965	720.1	444.3	118.2	74.8	34.2	9.2	3.9	35.4	31.5	153.7	82.1	71.6	710.9
1966	789.3	481.8	131.3	85.4	32.3	13.6	1.9	38.9	37.1	174.3	94.4	79.9	775.7
1967	834.1	508.7	128.6	86.4	32.4	9.9	1.4	41.4	39.9	195.3	106.8	88.6	824.2
1968	911.5	558.7	141.2	93.4	38.7	9.1	-1.3	45.3	46.6	212.8	114.0	98.8	902.4
1969	985.3	605.5	156.4	104.7	42.6	9.2	-1.2	49.3	50.5	224.6	116.1	108.5	976.2
1970	1 039.7	648.9	152.4	109.0	41.4	2.0	1.2	57.0	55.8	237.1	116.4	120.7	1 037.7
1971	1 128.6	702.4	178.2	114.1	55.8	8.3	-3.0	59.3	62.3	251.0	117.6	133.5	1 120.3
1972	1 240.4	770.7	207.6	128.8	69.7	9.1	-8.0	66.2	74.2	270.1	125.6	144.4	1 231.3
1973	1 385.5	852.5	244.5	153.3	75.3	15.9	0.6	91.8	91.2	287.9	127.8	160.1	1 369.7
1974	1 501.0	932.4	249.4	169.5	66.0	14.0	-3.1	124.3	127.5	322.4	138.2	184.2	1 487.0
1975	1 635.2	1 030.3	230.2	173.7	62.7	-6.3	13.6	136.3	122.7	361.1	152.1	209.0	1 641.4
1976	1 823.9	1 149.8	292.0	192.4	82.5	17.1	-2.3	148.9	151.1	384.5	160.6	223.9	1 806.8
1977	2 031.4	1 278.4	361.3	228.7	110.3	22.3	-23.7	158.8	182.4	415.3	176.0	239.3	2 009.1
1978	2 295.9	1 430.4	436.0	278.6	131.6	25.8	-26.1	186.1	212.3	455.6	191.9	263.8	2 270.1
1979	2 566.4	1 596.3	490.6	331.6	141.0	18.0	-24.0	228.7	252.7	503.5	211.6	291.8	2 548.4
1980	2 795.6	1 762.9	477.9	360.9	123.2	-6.3	-14.9	278.9	293.8	569.7	245.3	324.4	2 801.9
1981	3 131.3	1 944.2	570.8	418.4	122.6	29.8	-15.0	302.8	317.8	631.4	281.8	349.6	3 101.5
1982	3 259.2	2 079.3	516.1	425.3	105.7	-14.9	-20.5	282.6	303.2	684.4	312.8	371.6	3 274.1
1983	3 534.9	2 286.4	564.2	417.4	152.5	-5.8	-51.7	277.0	328.6	735.9	344.4	391.5	3 540.7
1984	3 932.7	2 498.4	735.5	490.3	179.8	65.4	-102.0	303.1	405.1	800.8	376.4	424.4	3 867.3
1985	4 213.0	2 712.6	736.3	527.6	186.9	21.8	-114.2	303.0	417.2	878.3	413.4	464.9	4 191.2
1986	4 452.9	2 895.2	747.2	522.5	218.1	6.6	-131.9	320.3	452.2	942.3	438.7	503.6	4 446.3
1987	4 742.5	3 105.3	781.5	526.7	227.6	27.1	-142.3	365.6	507.9	997.9	460.4	537.5	4 715.3
1988	5 108.3	3 356.6	821.1	568.4	234.2	18.5	-106.3	446.9	553.2	1 036.9	462.6	574.3	5 089.8
1989	5 489.1	3 596.7	872.9	613.4	231.8	27.7	-80.7	509.0	589.7	1 100.2	482.6	617.7	5 461.4
1990	5 803.2	3 831.5	861.7	630.3	216.8	14.5	-71.4	557.2	628.6	1 181.4	508.4	673.0	5 788.7
1963													
1st quarter	603.4	375.4	90.5	53.4	30.2	6.9	2.0	27.2	25.2	135.5	77.4	58.1	596.6
2nd quarter	612.1	379.5	92.2	55.1	32.2	4.8	3.7	29.6	25.9	136.7	77.7	59.0	607.3
3rd quarter	624.9	386.5	95.0	56.8	32.5	5.7	3.1	29.8	26.7	140.3	79.6	60.7	619.1
4th quarter	634.3	391.1	97.4	58.7	33.7	5.1	4.4	31.1	26.8	141.4	79.4	62.0	629.3
1964													
1st quarter	650.4	400.7	100.7	60.1	35.4	5.1	5.9	32.9	27.0	143.1	79.9	63.2	645.3
2nd quarter	659.6	408.6	100.6	62.0	34.2	4.5	4.9	32.6	27.7	145.5	80.5	65.0	655.2
3rd quarter	671.2	417.5	102.5	64.1	33.7	4.7	5.4	33.9	28.4	145.8	79.8	66.0	666.5
4th quarter	676.3	420.1	104.5	65.7	33.8	5.0	5.7	35.0	29.3	146.0	79.0	67.0	671.3
1965													
1st quarter	696.5	430.9	115.7	70.2	33.9	11.5	3.0	31.5	28.5	146.9	78.6	68.3	684.9
2nd quarter	709.0	437.9	115.8	73.1	34.2	8.6	4.7	36.3	31.7	150.6	80.2	70.4	700.5
3rd quarter	726.2	447.2	119.6	76.1	34.3	9.3	3.7	35.7	32.0	155.7	82.7	73.0	716.9
4th quarter	748.7	461.3	121.8	79.7	34.5	7.6	4.1	38.0	33.9	161.6	86.9	74.7	741.2
1966													
1st quarter	772.3	471.8	131.8	83.1	34.8	13.9	3.2	38.2	35.0	165.5	88.8	76.7	758.4
2nd quarter	781.5	477.0	130.7	85.2	33.2	12.3	2.0	38.2	36.2	171.8	93.2	78.6	769.2
3rd quarter	794.8	486.2	130.2	86.4	31.9	11.9	0.8	39.0	38.2	177.7	97.0	80.6	782.9
4th quarter	808.6	492.0	132.6	86.9	29.2	16.5	1.5	40.4	38.8	182.4	98.7	83.7	792.1
1967													
1st quarter	819.3	496.3	129.3	85.5	28.3	15.4	2.3	41.7	39.4	191.4	105.3	86.1	803.9
2nd quarter	823.9	505.5	123.7	85.7	31.6	6.3	2.1	41.1	39.0	192.7	105.2	87.5	817.6
3rd quarter	838.7	512.7	128.5	85.9	33.4	9.3	1.1	40.7	39.5	196.3	107.3	89.0	829.4
4th quarter	854.4	520.3	132.9	88.4	36.0	8.4	0.2	41.9	41.7	201.0	109.4	91.6	846.0
1968													
1st quarter	881.4	538.1	137.2	91.9	36.9	8.4	-1.2	43.2	44.4	207.4	112.6	94.7	873.0
2nd quarter	905.7	551.9	143.4	91.2	38.2	14.1	-0.6	44.8	45.4	211.0	113.3	97.7	891.7
3rd quarter	920.9	568.0	139.7	93.1	38.9	7.7	-1.3	47.0	48.2	214.4	114.4	100.0	913.2
4th quarter	937.8	576.9	144.4	97.5	40.9	6.0	-1.9	46.2	48.2	218.5	115.8	102.7	931.8
1969													
1st quarter	961.9	588.9	155.7	101.0	43.2	11.5	-1.9	41.9	43.8	219.1	114.3	104.8	950.4
2nd quarter	977.0	600.2	155.7	103.0	43.4	9.2	-1.8	50.9	52.7	222.9	115.2	107.7	967.8
3rd quarter	997.2	610.5	160.3	106.9	43.2	10.2	-1.3	51.0	52.4	227.6	117.8	109.8	987.0
4th quarter	1 005.3	622.5	154.1	107.6	40.7	5.8	0.1	53.2	53.1	228.7	117.1	111.6	999.5
1970													
1st quarter	1 018.2	633.7	150.6	108.1	40.7	1.8	1.1	54.7	53.5	232.7	117.5	115.2	1 016.3
2nd quarter	1 034.4	643.8	153.9	109.4	39.4	5.1	2.4	57.6	55.2	234.2	115.9	118.4	1 029.3
3rd quarter	1 051.9	655.8	156.0	110.6	40.4	5.1	0.9	57.3	56.4	239.2	115.9	123.2	1 046.9
4th quarter	1 054.2	662.5	148.9	107.9	45.0	-4.0	0.4	58.3	57.9	242.4	116.3	126.1	1 058.2
1971													
1st quarter	1 099.9	681.7	171.3	110.5	48.6	12.3	0.8	59.5	58.7	246.1	116.6	129.4	1 087.6
2nd quarter	1 120.6	695.7	178.9	113.4	54.6	10.9	-3.8	59.5	63.3	249.8	117.3	132.5	1 109.7
3rd quarter	1 140.8	708.0	183.4	114.8	58.3	10.2	-3.1	62.4	65.5	252.5	118.0	134.5	1 130.6
4th quarter	1 153.1	724.3	179.1	117.9	61.5	-0.3	-6.0	56.0	61.9	255.7	118.3	137.4	1 153.4
1972													
1st quarter	1 192.5	741.7	193.1	123.3	66.6	3.2	-8.6	63.5	72.2	266.3	125.7	140.6	1 189.2
2nd quarter	1 227.5	759.9	206.5	126.3	68.2	12.0	-8.3	63.1	71.4	269.5	127.6	141.9	1 215.5
3rd quarter	1 252.0	778.2	212.4	129.1	69.6	13.7	-7.9	66.2	74.1	269.4	124.0	145.4	1 238.3
4th quarter	1 289.7	803.1	218.5	136.7	74.3	7.5	-7.1	72.1	79.2	275.1	125.3	149.9	1 282.2
1973													
1st quarter	1 338.4	827.9	232.6	144.2	77.9	10.6	-4.4	81.0	85.4	282.4	128.2	154.2	1 327.8
2nd quarter	1 374.4	843.1	246.1	152.1	75.8	18.2	-1.1	88.3	89.5	286.4	128.8	157.6	1 356.2
3rd quarter	1 394.1	861.9	241.8	157.0	75.0	9.8	3.2	94.3	91.1	287.2	125.5	161.7	1 384.3
4th quarter	1 435.3	877.2	257.6	159.8	72.7	25.0	4.7	103.4	98.7	295.7	128.9	166.8	1 410.3

Table 22-1. Gross Domestic Product—*Continued*

(Billions of dollars, quarterly data are at seasonally adjusted annual rates.)

Year and quarter	Gross domestic product	Personal consumption expenditures	Gross private domestic investment					Exports and imports of goods and services			Government consumption expenditures and gross investment			Addendum: Final sales of domestic product
			Total	Fixed investment			Change in private inventories	Net exports	Exports	Imports	Total	Federal	State and local	
				Nonresidential	Residential									
1974														
1st quarter	1 450.0	895.4	244.1	162.6	69.0	12.5	4.3	114.6	110.3	306.2	132.5	173.7	1 437.4
2nd quarter	1 487.6	923.6	252.3	167.4	67.5	17.4	-5.6	123.8	129.4	317.4	135.6	181.8	1 470.2
3rd quarter	1 514.8	951.4	245.5	172.5	67.4	5.6	-9.1	124.5	133.6	327.0	139.2	187.9	1 509.3
4th quarter	1 551.6	959.2	255.9	175.4	60.0	20.4	-2.2	134.4	136.6	338.8	145.5	193.2	1 531.2
1975														
1st quarter	1 567.2	984.4	218.7	171.1	57.7	-10.0	13.1	138.0	124.9	350.9	148.1	202.8	1 577.2
2nd quarter	1 603.1	1 013.7	216.8	170.8	59.9	-14.0	16.6	131.8	115.2	356.1	150.6	205.5	1 617.1
3rd quarter	1 659.9	1 047.2	237.7	174.5	64.6	-1.4	11.6	133.7	122.1	363.3	152.4	210.9	1 661.3
4th quarter	1 710.5	1 076.0	247.7	178.6	68.7	0.3	12.9	141.7	128.7	373.9	157.2	216.7	1 710.2
1976														
1st quarter	1 770.3	1 111.1	274.8	183.9	76.2	14.7	4.2	143.1	138.9	380.3	157.1	223.2	1 755.6
2nd quarter	1 803.1	1 131.1	291.5	188.4	80.7	22.5	-1.1	146.0	147.1	381.5	158.6	222.9	1 780.7
3rd quarter	1 837.0	1 160.8	296.6	195.1	80.6	20.8	-5.0	150.9	155.8	384.6	160.9	223.7	1 816.2
4th quarter	1 885.3	1 196.1	305.0	202.0	92.5	10.5	-7.2	155.4	162.7	391.5	165.6	225.9	1 874.8
1977														
1st quarter	1 939.1	1 231.6	326.7	214.3	97.6	14.8	-21.6	154.8	176.4	402.4	170.3	232.1	1 924.3
2nd quarter	2 006.6	1 260.3	355.1	224.0	111.7	19.5	-21.7	161.3	183.0	413.0	175.4	237.6	1 987.2
3rd quarter	2 067.5	1 291.9	378.2	232.3	115.0	30.9	-21.1	161.8	182.9	418.5	177.1	241.4	2 036.6
4th quarter	2 112.4	1 329.9	385.4	244.3	116.9	24.1	-30.3	157.1	187.4	427.4	181.4	246.0	2 088.2
1978														
1st quarter	2 150.4	1 359.8	396.2	249.7	121.1	25.5	-39.3	164.0	203.3	433.7	184.0	249.7	2 125.0
2nd quarter	2 276.6	1 419.0	429.3	274.5	130.5	24.3	-23.3	185.6	208.8	451.6	190.0	261.6	2 252.4
3rd quarter	2 338.5	1 452.1	448.8	288.1	135.8	25.0	-24.6	190.5	215.1	462.1	193.4	268.7	2 313.5
4th quarter	2 418.0	1 490.6	469.7	302.1	139.1	28.5	-17.3	204.5	221.8	475.0	200.0	275.0	2 389.5
1979														
1st quarter	2 470.9	1 531.5	478.5	316.0	138.6	23.9	-19.2	210.7	229.8	480.1	203.0	277.1	2 447.1
2nd quarter	2 529.3	1 566.9	490.9	322.6	140.9	27.4	-23.4	219.7	243.1	494.9	208.7	286.3	2 501.9
3rd quarter	2 601.5	1 620.1	495.9	340.3	143.5	12.1	-24.4	232.9	257.3	509.9	212.7	297.2	2 589.4
4th quarter	2 663.8	1 666.5	497.3	347.5	141.2	8.6	-29.0	251.5	280.5	529.0	222.2	306.8	2 655.3
1980														
1st quarter	2 732.9	1 716.0	504.3	359.8	134.5	9.9	-37.2	267.1	304.3	549.8	232.8	317.0	2 723.0
2nd quarter	2 736.9	1 719.3	468.2	349.3	111.2	7.8	-16.7	275.9	292.6	566.2	244.4	321.8	2 729.2
3rd quarter	2 793.6	1 777.1	441.7	359.6	115.9	-33.9	3.3	282.5	279.2	571.6	245.5	326.0	2 827.5
4th quarter	2 918.8	1 839.2	497.2	375.0	131.3	-9.1	-8.9	290.3	299.2	591.3	258.4	332.9	2 927.9
1981														
1st quarter	3 052.6	1 893.1	562.4	391.7	132.0	38.8	-17.0	302.8	319.7	614.1	268.2	345.9	3 013.8
2nd quarter	3 086.2	1 926.7	549.4	408.9	128.9	11.7	-16.4	305.5	322.0	626.5	280.5	346.0	3 074.5
3rd quarter	3 183.5	1 970.5	590.7	426.6	120.2	44.0	-10.2	299.7	309.9	632.5	283.3	349.3	3 139.5
4th quarter	3 203.1	1 986.4	580.7	446.3	109.6	24.8	-16.3	303.2	319.4	652.3	295.3	357.1	3 178.3
1982														
1st quarter	3 193.8	2 023.0	525.2	441.9	104.8	-21.5	-17.2	292.3	309.5	662.7	300.6	362.1	3 215.2
2nd quarter	3 248.9	2 048.8	529.2	430.6	102.8	-4.2	-5.0	294.2	299.1	675.8	307.0	368.8	3 253.0
3rd quarter	3 278.6	2 093.7	526.3	418.2	102.3	5.8	-30.3	279.0	309.3	688.9	314.7	374.2	3 272.8
4th quarter	3 315.6	2 151.7	483.5	410.5	112.8	-39.8	-29.7	265.1	294.9	710.1	328.9	381.3	3 355.4
1983														
1st quarter	3 378.5	2 188.4	495.7	399.9	130.9	-35.1	-24.6	270.6	295.3	719.1	334.2	384.9	3 413.6
2nd quarter	3 489.6	2 260.0	543.7	403.2	148.2	-7.7	-45.5	272.5	318.0	731.3	343.4	387.9	3 497.2
3rd quarter	3 582.9	2 319.4	578.0	419.6	162.6	-4.2	-65.2	278.2	343.4	750.7	355.8	394.9	3 587.1
4th quarter	3 688.8	2 377.9	639.5	447.0	168.5	23.9	-71.3	286.7	358.0	742.7	344.4	398.3	3 664.8
1984														
1st quarter	3 813.4	2 427.1	709.3	460.7	175.6	73.0	-94.3	293.7	388.0	771.2	361.5	409.8	3 740.4
2nd quarter	3 909.4	2 481.4	736.0	485.2	181.4	69.3	-103.5	303.0	406.5	795.5	376.2	419.3	3 840.0
3rd quarter	3 974.7	2 517.1	753.2	501.1	180.8	71.3	-103.1	306.5	409.6	807.5	377.2	430.2	3 903.4
4th quarter	4 033.5	2 568.0	743.6	514.3	181.3	48.0	-107.1	309.2	416.4	829.0	390.6	438.4	3 985.5
1985														
1st quarter	4 109.7	2 632.9	721.1	521.5	183.4	16.2	-91.4	305.9	397.3	847.1	399.3	447.9	4 093.5
2nd quarter	4 170.1	2 682.1	734.2	529.8	182.8	21.7	-114.7	303.9	418.6	868.4	408.2	460.2	4 148.5
3rd quarter	4 252.9	2 749.8	727.7	523.8	187.7	16.3	-117.2	297.0	414.2	892.5	421.0	471.5	4 236.6
4th quarter	4 319.3	2 785.6	762.3	535.3	193.9	33.1	-133.6	305.3	438.9	905.1	425.1	480.0	4 286.2
1986														
1st quarter	4 375.3	2 825.1	764.0	529.1	204.5	30.3	-127.1	312.0	439.0	913.2	421.8	491.4	4 344.9
2nd quarter	4 415.2	2 857.0	754.2	520.2	218.3	15.7	-129.2	314.2	443.4	933.2	434.8	498.4	4 399.6
3rd quarter	4 483.4	2 928.6	733.6	516.6	224.1	-7.0	-138.5	320.1	458.6	959.7	452.0	507.7	4 490.4
4th quarter	4 537.5	2 970.0	737.1	524.3	225.6	-12.7	-132.8	334.9	467.7	963.2	446.1	517.1	4 550.3
1987														
1st quarter	4 612.3	3 011.4	762.6	509.3	225.3	28.0	-139.4	337.5	476.8	977.6	452.1	525.5	4 584.3
2nd quarter	4 695.8	3 081.5	766.4	520.7	229.2	16.5	-144.7	356.8	501.5	992.6	459.7	532.9	4 679.3
3rd quarter	4 770.2	3 145.5	765.3	536.9	227.4	1.0	-142.8	373.7	516.5	1 002.2	461.5	540.7	4 769.2
4th quarter	4 891.6	3 182.9	831.6	540.1	228.4	63.1	-142.2	394.5	536.7	1 019.3	468.5	550.8	4 828.5
1988														
1st quarter	4 957.0	3 259.8	797.7	551.1	229.6	17.0	-121.0	421.0	542.0	1 020.5	461.2	559.3	4 940.0
2nd quarter	5 066.5	3 319.5	819.2	566.3	233.3	19.7	-103.4	441.9	545.3	1 031.2	460.0	571.2	5 046.9
3rd quarter	5 151.5	3 387.0	825.7	571.8	235.7	18.2	-96.3	455.8	552.1	1 035.1	457.2	578.0	5 133.3
4th quarter	5 258.3	3 460.1	842.0	584.5	238.4	19.1	-104.4	469.0	573.5	1 060.7	472.2	588.5	5 239.2
1989														
1st quarter	5 379.0	3 511.8	881.2	596.0	237.0	48.2	-84.2	492.0	576.2	1 070.3	470.4	599.8	5 330.8
2nd quarter	5 461.7	3 572.9	875.4	607.1	232.3	36.0	-81.4	512.5	594.0	1 094.8	482.6	612.2	5 425.6
3rd quarter	5 527.5	3 626.9	868.3	628.1	230.2	10.0	-79.6	509.4	589.0	1 111.9	490.0	621.9	5 517.5
4th quarter	5 588.0	3 675.1	866.7	622.3	227.8	16.6	-77.6	522.0	599.6	1 123.9	487.2	636.8	5 571.4
1990														
1st quarter	5 720.8	3 754.8	881.6	633.6	234.1	13.9	-74.2	541.6	615.8	1 158.5	502.0	656.5	5 706.8
2nd quarter	5 800.0	3 806.2	883.0	625.1	224.2	33.7	-60.7	554.6	615.3	1 171.4	506.9	664.6	5 766.3
3rd quarter	5 844.9	3 871.6	869.4	635.4	212.1	21.9	-78.8	555.3	634.1	1 182.7	505.8	676.9	5 823.1
4th quarter	5 847.3	3 893.4	812.8	627.2	196.9	-11.3	-72.1	577.1	649.2	1 213.1	519.1	694.0	5 858.6

Table 22-2. Real Gross Domestic Product

(Billions of chained [1996] dollars, quarterly data are at seasonally adjusted annual rates.)

Year and quarter	Gross domestic product	Personal consumption expenditures	Gross private domestic investment				Exports and imports of goods and services			Government consumption expenditures and gross investment			Addendum: Final sales of domestic product
			Total	Fixed investment		Change in private inventories	Net exports	Exports	Imports	Total	Federal	State and local	
				Nonresidential	Residential								
1963	2 690.4	1 684.0	325.7	...	...	...	...	100.7	122.7	752.4	...	...	2 683.6
1964	2 846.5	1 784.8	352.6	...	...	...	...	114.2	129.2	767.1	...	...	2 844.1
1965	3 028.5	1 897.6	402.0	...	...	...	...	116.5	142.9	791.1	...	...	3 008.5
1966	3 227.5	2 006.1	437.3	...	...	...	...	124.3	164.2	862.1	...	...	3 191.1
1967	3 308.3	2 066.2	417.2	...	...	...	...	127.0	176.2	927.1	...	...	3 288.2
1968	3 466.1	2 184.2	441.3	...	...	...	...	136.3	202.4	956.6	...	...	3 450.0
1969	3 571.4	2 264.8	466.9	...	...	...	...	143.7	213.9	952.5	...	...	3 555.9
1970	3 578.0	2 317.5	436.2	...	...	...	...	159.3	223.1	931.1	...	...	3 588.6
1971	3 697.7	2 405.2	485.8	...	...	...	...	160.4	235.0	913.8	...	...	3 688.1
1972	3 898.4	2 550.5	543.0	...	...	...	...	173.5	261.3	914.9	...	...	3 887.7
1973	4 123.4	2 675.9	606.5	...	...	...	...	211.4	273.4	908.3	...	...	4 094.3
1974	4 099.0	2 653.7	561.7	...	...	...	...	231.6	267.2	924.8	...	...	4 080.7
1975	4 084.4	2 710.9	462.2	...	...	...	...	230.0	237.5	942.5	...	...	4 118.5
1976	4 311.7	2 868.9	555.5	...	...	...	...	243.6	284.0	943.3	...	...	4 288.8
1977	4 511.8	2 992.1	639.4	...	...	...	...	249.7	315.0	952.7	...	...	4 478.8
1978	4 760.6	3 124.7	713.0	...	...	...	...	275.9	342.3	982.2	...	...	4 722.9
1979	4 912.1	3 203.2	735.4	...	...	...	...	302.4	347.9	1 001.1	...	...	4 894.4
1980	4 900.9	3 193.0	655.3	...	...	...	...	334.8	324.8	1 020.9	...	...	4 928.1
1981	5 021.0	3 236.0	715.6	...	...	...	...	338.6	333.4	1 030.0	...	...	4 989.5
1982	4 919.3	3 275.5	615.2	...	...	...	...	314.6	329.2	1 046.0	...	...	4 954.9
1983	5 132.3	3 454.3	673.7	...	...	...	...	306.9	370.7	1 081.0	...	...	5 154.5
1984	5 505.2	3 640.6	871.5	...	...	...	...	332.6	461.0	1 118.4	...	...	5 427.9
1985	5 717.1	3 820.9	863.4	...	...	...	...	341.6	490.7	1 190.5	...	...	5 698.8
1986	5 912.4	3 981.2	857.7	...	...	...	...	366.8	531.9	1 255.2	...	...	5 912.6
1987	6 113.3	4 113.4	879.3	572.5	290.7	29.6	-156.2	408.0	564.2	1 292.5	597.8	695.6	6 088.8
1988	6 368.4	4 279.5	902.8	603.6	289.2	18.4	-112.1	473.5	585.6	1 307.5	586.9	721.4	6 352.6
1989	6 591.8	4 393.7	936.5	637.0	277.3	29.6	-79.4	529.4	608.8	1 343.5	594.7	749.5	6 565.4
1990	6 707.9	4 474.5	907.3	641.7	253.5	16.5	-56.5	575.7	632.2	1 387.3	606.8	781.1	6 695.6
1963													
1st quarter	2 634.1	1 657.1	315.4	...	...	...	...	92.8	119.1	740.0	...	...	2 619.3
2nd quarter	2 668.4	1 673.0	320.8	...	...	...	...	101.3	121.9	744.3	...	...	2 663.9
3rd quarter	2 719.6	1 695.7	331.5	...	...	...	...	102.1	125.0	765.9	...	...	2 712.0
4th quarter	2 739.4	1 710.0	335.2	...	...	...	...	106.7	124.6	759.2	...	...	2 739.6
1964													
1st quarter	2 800.5	1 743.8	348.9	...	...	...	...	112.6	124.5	763.1	...	...	2 799.3
2nd quarter	2 833.8	1 775.0	347.5	...	...	...	...	111.7	127.3	772.9	...	...	2 833.5
3rd quarter	2 872.0	1 807.8	355.7	...	...	...	...	115.0	130.7	766.4	...	...	2 868.3
4th quarter	2 879.5	1 812.8	358.3	...	...	...	...	117.4	134.3	766.1	...	...	2 875.5
1965													
1st quarter	2 950.1	1 852.5	394.9	...	...	...	...	103.2	129.4	765.5	...	...	2 920.2
2nd quarter	2 989.9	1 873.2	394.6	...	...	...	...	119.6	144.7	781.3	...	...	2 973.2
3rd quarter	3 050.7	1 905.3	408.4	...	...	...	...	117.5	145.3	800.3	...	...	3 029.4
4th quarter	3 123.6	1 959.3	410.1	...	...	...	...	125.6	152.4	817.2	...	...	3 111.4
1966													
1st quarter	3 201.1	1 988.6	444.1	...	...	...	...	124.0	156.3	832.5	...	...	3 165.1
2nd quarter	3 213.2	1 994.0	436.5	...	...	...	...	123.1	160.2	857.8	...	...	3 180.0
3rd quarter	3 233.6	2 016.6	432.7	...	...	...	...	123.9	169.2	870.1	...	...	3 205.0
4th quarter	3 261.8	2 025.1	435.8	...	...	...	...	126.1	171.1	888.0	...	...	3 214.5
1967													
1st quarter	3 291.8	2 037.3	424.9	...	...	...	...	127.9	173.5	925.6	...	...	3 246.9
2nd quarter	3 289.7	2 064.6	405.0	...	...	...	...	126.6	172.4	921.3	...	...	3 281.5
3rd quarter	3 313.5	2 075.2	415.2	...	...	...	...	125.3	174.7	926.8	...	...	3 297.4
4th quarter	3 338.3	2 087.9	423.6	...	...	...	...	128.3	184.0	934.8	...	...	3 326.9
1968													
1st quarter	3 406.2	2 136.2	433.8	...	...	...	...	131.3	194.7	951.4	...	...	3 394.2
2nd quarter	3 464.8	2 169.6	451.8	...	...	...	...	133.5	197.7	956.0	...	...	3 428.5
3rd quarter	3 489.2	2 210.7	437.3	...	...	...	...	141.8	209.5	958.3	...	...	3 478.1
4th quarter	3 504.1	2 220.4	442.2	...	...	...	...	138.7	207.7	960.5	...	...	3 499.5
1969													
1st quarter	3 558.3	2 244.8	470.8	...	...	...	...	124.1	188.2	956.9	...	...	3 535.0
2nd quarter	3 567.6	2 258.8	467.1	...	...	...	...	150.5	225.3	956.0	...	...	3 551.3
3rd quarter	3 588.3	2 269.0	477.2	...	...	...	...	148.8	222.4	954.1	...	...	3 569.0
4th quarter	3 571.4	2 286.5	452.6	...	...	...	...	151.4	219.9	943.1	...	...	3 568.3
1970													
1st quarter	3 566.5	2 300.8	438.0	...	...	...	...	155.0	219.2	936.2	...	...	3 578.9
2nd quarter	3 573.9	2 312.0	439.4	...	...	...	...	160.1	223.5	927.3	...	...	3 573.2
3rd quarter	3 605.2	2 332.2	446.5	...	...	...	...	159.9	223.0	930.9	...	...	3 605.0
4th quarter	3 566.5	2 324.9	421.0	...	...	...	...	162.1	226.5	929.9	...	...	3 597.4
1971													
1st quarter	3 666.1	2 369.8	475.9	...	...	...	...	160.7	223.8	918.6	...	...	3 643.1
2nd quarter	3 686.2	2 391.4	490.2	...	...	...	...	160.6	240.7	915.2	...	...	3 667.8
3rd quarter	3 714.5	2 409.8	496.5	...	...	...	...	169.4	246.0	911.9	...	...	3 698.9
4th quarter	3 723.8	2 449.8	480.6	...	...	...	...	151.0	229.3	909.4	...	...	3 742.5
1972													
1st quarter	3 796.9	2 482.2	513.6	...	...	...	...	168.8	262.8	920.8	...	...	3 802.2
2nd quarter	3 883.8	2 527.5	544.9	...	...	...	...	166.4	253.4	921.9	...	...	3 862.7
3rd quarter	3 922.3	2 565.9	554.1	...	...	...	...	173.8	258.7	907.6	...	...	3 897.2
4th quarter	3 990.5	2 626.3	559.4	...	...	...	...	184.9	270.3	909.1	...	...	3 988.5
1973													
1st quarter	4 092.3	2 674.2	595.2	...	...	...	...	201.8	282.8	914.5	...	...	4 075.5
2nd quarter	4 133.3	2 671.4	618.2	...	...	...	...	210.5	274.7	911.5	...	...	4 094.4
3rd quarter	4 117.0	2 682.5	597.5	...	...	...	...	212.4	267.1	898.5	...	...	4 100.7
4th quarter	4 151.1	2 675.6	615.3	...	...	...	...	221.1	269.1	908.4	...	...	4 106.3

Table 22-2. Real Gross Domestic Product—*Continued*

(Billions of chained [1996] dollars, quarterly data are at seasonally adjusted annual rates.)

Year and quarter	Gross domestic product	Personal consumption expenditures	Gross private domestic investment				Exports and imports of goods and services			Government consumption expenditures and gross investment			Addendum: Final sales of domestic product
			Total	Fixed investment		Change in private inventories	Net exports	Exports	Imports	Total	Federal	State and local	
				Nonresidential	Residential								
1974													
1st quarter	4 119.3	2 652.4	579.2	...	...	...	...	228.6	260.0	920.0	...	...	4 101.8
2nd quarter	4 130.4	2 662.0	577.3	...	...	...	...	238.4	273.8	927.8	...	...	4 105.6
3rd quarter	4 084.5	2 672.2	543.4	...	...	...	...	226.7	269.0	924.2	...	...	4 089.8
4th quarter	4 062.0	2 628.4	547.0	...	...	...	...	232.6	266.3	927.4	...	...	4 025.8
1975													
1st quarter	4 010.0	2 648.8	450.8	...	...	...	...	232.2	239.6	940.8	...	...	4 054.7
2nd quarter	4 045.2	2 695.4	436.4	...	...	...	...	222.7	220.4	938.3	...	...	4 099.2
3rd quarter	4 115.4	2 734.7	474.9	...	...	...	...	226.5	238.7	941.8	...	...	4 135.9
4th quarter	4 167.2	2 764.6	486.8	...	...	...	...	238.7	251.5	949.1	...	...	4 184.3
1976													
1st quarter	4 266.1	2 824.7	535.1	...	...	...	...	237.9	267.2	952.5			4 248.8
2nd quarter	4 301.5	2 850.9	559.8	...	...	...	...	240.1	278.8	943.3	...	...	4 264.1
3rd quarter	4 321.9	2 880.3	561.1	...	...	...	...	246.8	290.2	938.9	...	...	4 289.7
4th quarter	4 357.4	2 919.6	565.9	...	...	...	...	249.7	299.8	938.6	...	...	4 352.4
1977													
1st quarter	4 410.5	2 954.7	595.5	...	...	...	...	245.9	313.9	945.3	...	...	4 393.8
2nd quarter	4 489.8	2 970.5	635.0	...	...	...	...	252.5	316.8	955.1	...	...	4 464.0
3rd quarter	4 570.6	2 999.1	670.7	...	...	...	...	254.5	312.4	956.0	...	...	4 509.7
4th quarter	4 576.1	3 044.0	656.4	...	...	...	...	246.0	316.8	954.5	...	...	4 547.5
1978													
1st quarter	4 588.9	3 060.8	667.2	...	...	...	...	251.8	338.0	956.7	...	...	4 552.0
2nd quarter	4 765.7	3 127.0	709.7	...	...	...	...	278.2	339.1	982.1	...	...	4 730.8
3rd quarter	4 811.7	3 143.1	728.8	...	...	...	...	281.1	343.6	990.3	...	...	4 774.7
4th quarter	4 876.0	3 167.8	746.3	...	...	...	...	292.3	348.3	999.6	...	...	4 834.2
1979													
1st quarter	4 888.3	3 188.6	746.0	...	...	...	...	292.3	347.3	990.6	...	...	4 855.1
2nd quarter	4 891.4	3 184.3	745.7	...	...	...	...	292.9	349.2	1 000.5	...	...	4 852.9
3rd quarter	4 926.2	3 213.9	732.1	...	...	...	...	303.1	343.9	1 002.4	...	...	4 921.9
4th quarter	4 942.6	3 225.7	717.8	...	...	...	...	321.2	351.3	1 010.8	...	...	4 947.7
1980													
1st quarter	4 958.9	3 222.4	711.7	...	...	...	...	331.3	351.7	1 025.6	...	...	4 961.4
2nd quarter	4 857.8	3 149.2	647.4	...	...	...	...	337.5	326.1	1 028.7	...	...	4 861.6
3rd quarter	4 850.3	3 181.2	599.8	...	...	...	...	336.2	302.6	1 015.4	...	...	4 923.9
4th quarter	4 936.6	3 219.4	662.2	...	...	...	...	334.3	318.9	1 013.9	...	...	4 965.2
1981													
1st quarter	5 032.5	3 233.1	726.3	...	...	...	...	340.2	332.5	1 027.5	...	...	4 985.6
2nd quarter	4 997.3	3 235.5	693.4	...	...	...	...	342.0	333.0	1 030.1	...	...	4 995.9
3rd quarter	5 056.8	3 250.5	733.9	...	...	...	...	334.8	329.3	1 027.8	...	...	5 003.5
4th quarter	4 997.1	3 225.0	708.8	...	...	...	...	337.5	338.7	1 034.8	...	...	4 972.9
1982													
1st quarter	4 914.3	3 244.3	634.8	...	...	...	...	323.8	329.1	1 033.6	...	...	4 959.7
2nd quarter	4 935.5	3 253.4	631.6	...	...	...	...	326.0	323.7	1 039.5	...	...	4 954.2
3rd quarter	4 912.1	3 274.6	623.5	...	...	...	...	311.3	338.7	1 046.8	...	...	4 916.8
4th quarter	4 915.6	3 329.6	571.1	...	...	...	...	297.5	325.4	1 064.0	...	...	4 989.1
1983													
1st quarter	4 972.4	3 360.1	590.7	...	...	...	...	302.4	332.8	1 069.8	...	...	5 036.1
2nd quarter	5 089.8	3 430.1	650.7	...	...	...	...	303.4	358.4	1 078.2	...	...	5 113.1
3rd quarter	5 180.4	3 484.7	691.4	...	...	...	...	307.9	386.3	1 097.0	...	...	5 200.3
4th quarter	5 286.8	3 542.2	762.2	...	...	...	...	314.1	405.3	1 078.8	...	...	5 268.5
1984													
1st quarter	5 402.3	3 579.7	845.0	...	...	...	...	321.4	437.8	1 091.0	...	...	5 313.9
2nd quarter	5 493.8	3 628.3	873.2	...	...	...	...	329.4	456.2	1 115.2	...	...	5 410.8
3rd quarter	5 541.3	3 653.5	890.7	...	...	...	...	336.5	468.0	1 123.1	...	...	5 456.0
4th quarter	5 583.1	3 700.9	876.9	...	...	...	...	343.1	481.8	1 144.2	...	...	5 531.0
1985													
1st quarter	5 629.7	3 756.8	848.9	...	...	...	...	342.8	471.1	1 157.6	...	...	5 619.8
2nd quarter	5 673.8	3 791.5	862.8	...	...	...	...	341.3	494.2	1 180.5	...	...	5 657.0
3rd quarter	5 758.6	3 860.9	854.1	...	...	...	...	336.2	489.3	1 209.2	...	...	5 746.0
4th quarter	5 806.0	3 874.2	887.8	...	...	...	...	346.2	508.3	1 214.7	...	...	5 772.5
1986													
1st quarter	5 858.9	3 907.9	886.2	...	...	...	...	355.9	507.3	1 224.0	...	...	5 828.7
2nd quarter	5 883.3	3 950.4	868.3	...	...	...	...	360.0	528.8	1 248.0	...	...	5 872.6
3rd quarter	5 937.9	4 019.7	838.0	...	...	...	...	368.6	543.6	1 277.4	...	...	5 956.0
4th quarter	5 969.5	4 046.8	838.2	...	...	...	...	382.6	548.1	1 271.5	...	...	5 993.1
1987													
1st quarter	6 013.3	4 049.7	863.4	554.0	291.3	33.9	-161.3	383.6	544.9	1 278.4	588.6	690.7	5 985.4
2nd quarter	6 077.2	4 101.5	863.9	566.8	294.1	17.3	-159.5	399.3	558.9	1 289.1	597.3	692.8	6 066.8
3rd quarter	6 128.1	4 147.0	860.5	585.1	289.3	-2.1	-153.2	416.7	569.9	1 292.4	598.2	695.1	6 138.7
4th quarter	6 234.4	4 155.3	929.3	584.0	288.0	69.3	-150.8	432.2	583.0	1 310.0	607.0	704.0	6 164.1
1988													
1st quarter	6 275.9	4 228.0	884.6	590.5	287.0	17.2	-124.2	456.1	580.3	1 300.1	589.6	711.3	6 263.0
2nd quarter	6 349.8	4 256.8	902.5	603.4	289.0	18.9	-104.4	468.8	573.2	1 302.4	583.2	720.0	6 334.0
3rd quarter	6 382.3	4 291.6	907.5	606.7	290.2	18.5	-108.8	477.3	586.1	1 300.3	578.3	722.8	6 365.9
4th quarter	6 465.2	4 341.4	916.7	613.8	290.8	18.9	-111.2	491.8	603.0	1 327.2	596.5	731.5	6 447.5
1989													
1st quarter	6 543.8	4 357.1	952.7	623.1	287.0	51.5	-85.2	510.5	595.7	1 319.3	583.0	737.1	6 492.7
2nd quarter	6 579.4	4 374.8	941.1	632.2	277.9	38.9	-76.2	530.8	606.9	1 340.6	596.0	745.3	6 542.8
3rd quarter	6 610.6	4 413.4	929.3	651.1	274.5	10.2	-81.5	530.8	612.3	1 353.5	601.7	752.7	6 605.8
4th quarter	6 633.5	4 429.4	922.9	641.6	269.9	17.9	-74.7	545.5	620.2	1 360.4	598.3	762.9	6 620.4
1990													
1st quarter	6 716.3	4 466.0	934.0	650.0	275.2	15.7	-62.3	565.8	628.1	1 381.2	607.8	774.1	6 705.8
2nd quarter	6 731.7	4 478.8	933.0	639.4	262.5	36.3	-61.7	577.6	639.3	1 384.7	608.7	776.7	6 697.6
3rd quarter	6 719.4	4 495.6	912.6	645.4	247.2	24.1	-67.6	572.8	640.4	1 384.8	603.1	782.2	6 699.2
4th quarter	6 664.2	4 457.7	849.6	632.1	229.2	-9.9	-34.6	586.5	621.0	1 398.6	607.8	791.3	6 680.0

Table 22-3. Chain-type Price Indexes for Gross Domestic Product and Domestic Purchases

(Index numbers, 1996=100; quarterly data are seasonally adjusted.)

Year and quarter	Gross domestic product	Personal consumption expenditures		Private fixed investment			Exports and imports of goods and services		Government consumption expenditures and gross investment			Gross domestic purchases
		Total	Excluding food and energy	Total	Nonresidential	Residential	Exports	Imports	Total	Federal	State and local	
1963	23.0	22.8	23.3	27.7	32.4	19.0	29.2	21.3	18.4	19.1	17.7	22.5
1964	23.3	23.1	23.6	27.9	32.6	19.2	29.4	21.8	18.9	19.8	18.1	22.8
1965	23.8	23.4	23.9	28.4	33.0	19.7	30.4	22.1	19.4	20.3	18.6	23.3
1966	24.5	24.0	24.4	29.0	33.5	20.4	31.3	22.6	20.2	21.0	19.5	23.9
1967	25.2	24.6	25.1	29.8	34.4	21.2	32.6	22.7	21.1	21.6	20.6	24.6
1968	26.3	25.6	26.2	31.0	35.6	22.3	33.2	23.0	22.2	22.9	21.7	25.7
1969	27.6	26.7	27.4	32.6	37.1	23.8	34.3	23.6	23.6	24.1	23.1	26.9
1970	29.1	28.0	28.6	34.0	38.8	24.6	35.8	25.0	25.4	26.0	25.0	28.4
1971	30.5	29.2	30.0	35.7	40.7	26.0	37.0	26.5	27.4	28.2	26.8	29.8
1972	31.8	30.2	30.9	37.2	42.1	27.6	38.2	28.4	29.5	30.8	28.4	31.2
1973	33.6	31.9	32.0	39.3	43.7	30.0	43.4	33.3	31.7	33.0	30.6	33.0
1974	36.6	35.1	34.4	43.2	48.0	33.1	53.7	47.7	34.8	35.8	33.9	36.4
1975	40.0	38.0	37.2	48.6	54.6	36.2	59.2	51.7	38.3	39.4	37.3	39.7
1976	42.3	40.1	39.4	51.4	57.6	38.5	61.1	53.2	40.7	42.1	39.5	41.9
1977	45.0	42.7	42.0	55.5	61.5	42.4	63.6	57.9	43.6	45.3	42.1	44.8
1978	48.2	45.8	44.8	60.2	65.7	47.6	67.5	62.0	46.4	48.2	44.8	48.0
1979	52.2	49.8	48.0	65.7	71.1	53.0	75.6	72.6	50.3	51.9	48.8	52.3
1980	57.1	55.2	52.4	71.8	77.4	58.7	83.3	90.5	55.8	57.5	54.3	57.8
1981	62.4	60.1	56.9	78.6	84.9	63.5	89.4	95.3	61.3	63.1	59.7	63.0
1982	66.3	63.5	60.8	82.9	89.7	66.9	89.8	92.1	65.4	67.5	63.6	66.7
1983	68.9	66.2	63.9	82.8	88.9	68.4	90.2	88.7	68.1	70.0	66.4	69.0
1984	71.4	68.6	66.5	83.4	88.8	70.4	91.1	87.9	71.6	74.1	69.4	71.5
1985	73.7	71.0	69.2	84.5	89.6	72.2	88.7	85.0	73.8	75.7	72.1	73.6
1986	75.3	72.7	71.8	86.5	91.2	75.2	87.3	85.0	75.1	76.1	74.1	75.2
1987	77.6	75.5	74.8	88.1	92.0	78.3	89.6	90.0	77.2	77.0	77.3	77.7
1988	80.2	78.4	77.9	90.5	94.2	81.0	94.4	94.5	79.3	78.8	79.6	80.4
1989	83.3	81.9	81.2	92.8	96.3	83.6	96.2	96.9	81.9	81.1	82.4	83.4
1990	86.5	85.6	84.6	94.7	98.2	85.5	96.8	99.4	85.2	83.8	86.2	86.8
1963												
1st quarter	22.9	22.7	23.2	27.8	32.4	19.2	29.3	21.1	18.3	19.0	17.6	22.4
2nd quarter	23.0	22.7	23.2	27.8	32.4	19.1	29.2	21.2	18.4	19.1	17.7	22.4
3rd quarter	23.0	22.8	23.3	27.6	32.4	18.9	29.2	21.4	18.3	19.0	17.7	22.5
4th quarter	23.1	22.9	23.4	27.7	32.4	19.0	29.2	21.5	18.6	19.4	17.8	22.6
1964												
1st quarter	23.2	23.0	23.5	27.6	32.4	18.8	29.2	21.7	18.7	19.6	17.9	22.7
2nd quarter	23.3	23.0	23.6	27.9	32.6	19.1	29.2	21.8	18.8	19.6	18.0	22.8
3rd quarter	23.4	23.1	23.6	27.9	32.6	19.2	29.4	21.8	19.0	19.9	18.1	22.9
4th quarter	23.5	23.2	23.7	28.2	32.8	19.6	29.8	21.8	19.0	19.9	18.2	23.0
1965												
1st quarter	23.6	23.3	23.8	28.2	32.8	19.6	30.5	22.0	19.2	20.0	18.4	23.1
2nd quarter	23.7	23.4	23.9	28.3	32.9	19.6	30.4	21.9	19.3	20.1	18.5	23.2
3rd quarter	23.8	23.5	24.0	28.3	33.0	19.6	30.4	22.0	19.4	20.3	18.6	23.3
4th quarter	24.0	23.5	24.0	28.7	33.2	20.1	30.3	22.3	19.8	20.8	18.8	23.5
1966												
1st quarter	24.1	23.7	24.1	28.5	33.1	19.8	30.8	22.4	19.9	20.7	19.0	23.6
2nd quarter	24.3	23.9	24.3	29.0	33.5	20.6	31.0	22.6	20.0	20.7	19.4	23.8
3rd quarter	24.6	24.1	24.5	29.0	33.5	20.4	31.4	22.6	20.4	21.2	19.6	24.0
4th quarter	24.8	24.3	24.7	29.4	33.8	20.9	32.0	22.7	20.5	21.2	19.9	24.2
1967												
1st quarter	24.9	24.4	24.8	29.5	34.0	20.9	32.6	22.7	20.7	21.2	20.2	24.3
2nd quarter	25.1	24.5	25.0	29.7	34.2	21.0	32.5	22.6	20.9	21.4	20.4	24.5
3rd quarter	25.3	24.7	25.2	29.8	34.4	21.1	32.5	22.6	21.2	21.7	20.7	24.7
4th quarter	25.6	24.9	25.4	30.2	34.8	21.5	32.6	22.6	21.5	22.1	20.9	25.0
1968												
1st quarter	25.9	25.2	25.8	30.5	35.0	21.9	32.9	22.8	21.8	22.4	21.3	25.2
2nd quarter	26.2	25.4	26.0	30.8	35.4	22.1	33.6	23.0	22.0	22.6	21.5	25.5
3rd quarter	26.4	25.7	26.3	31.0	35.7	22.1	33.1	23.0	22.4	23.0	21.7	25.8
4th quarter	26.8	26.0	26.6	31.7	36.2	23.0	33.4	23.2	22.7	23.4	22.2	26.1
1969												
1st quarter	27.0	26.2	26.9	32.1	36.5	23.4	33.8	23.3	22.9	23.4	22.5	26.4
2nd quarter	27.4	26.6	27.2	32.4	36.8	23.8	33.8	23.4	23.3	23.8	22.9	26.7
3rd quarter	27.8	26.9	27.5	32.7	37.2	23.8	34.3	23.6	23.8	24.4	23.3	27.1
4th quarter	28.2	27.2	27.8	33.1	37.7	24.2	35.2	24.2	24.2	24.8	23.8	27.5
1970												
1st quarter	28.5	27.5	28.1	33.4	38.1	24.2	35.3	24.4	24.8	25.5	24.3	27.8
2nd quarter	28.9	27.8	28.4	34.1	38.7	25.1	36.0	24.7	25.2	25.7	24.8	28.2
3rd quarter	29.2	28.1	28.7	34.0	39.0	24.4	35.8	25.3	25.7	26.2	25.2	28.5
4th quarter	29.6	28.5	29.2	34.4	39.5	24.6	36.0	25.6	26.0	26.4	25.7	28.9
1971												
1st quarter	30.0	28.8	29.5	35.0	40.0	25.3	37.0	26.2	26.8	27.4	26.2	29.3
2nd quarter	30.4	29.1	29.9	35.5	40.6	25.8	37.0	26.3	27.3	28.0	26.7	29.7
3rd quarter	30.7	29.4	30.1	36.0	40.9	26.3	36.8	26.6	27.7	28.4	27.0	30.0
4th quarter	31.0	29.6	30.3	36.3	41.2	26.7	37.0	27.0	28.1	29.1	27.2	30.3
1972												
1st quarter	31.4	29.9	30.6	36.7	41.7	27.0	37.6	27.5	28.9	30.2	27.8	30.8
2nd quarter	31.6	30.1	30.8	37.0	42.0	27.2	37.9	28.2	29.2	30.5	28.1	31.0
3rd quarter	31.9	30.3	31.0	37.3	42.2	27.6	38.1	28.6	29.6	30.9	28.6	31.3
4th quarter	32.3	30.6	31.2	37.9	42.5	28.5	39.0	29.3	30.2	31.6	29.0	31.7
1973												
1st quarter	32.7	31.0	31.5	38.2	42.8	28.8	40.2	30.2	30.8	32.1	29.7	32.1
2nd quarter	33.3	31.6	31.9	38.9	43.4	29.6	42.0	32.5	31.4	32.6	30.3	32.7
3rd quarter	33.9	32.1	32.2	39.8	44.1	30.6	44.5	34.1	31.9	33.3	30.8	33.3
4th quarter	34.5	32.8	32.6	40.3	44.5	31.1	46.9	36.6	32.5	33.9	31.4	33.9

Table 22-3. Chain-type Price Indexes for Gross Domestic Product and Domestic Purchases—*Continued*

(Index numbers, 1996=100; quarterly data are seasonally adjusted.)

Year and quarter	Gross domestic product	Personal consumption expenditures		Private fixed investment			Exports and imports of goods and services		Government consumption expenditures and gross investment			Gross domestic purchases
		Total	Excluding food and energy	Total	Nonresidential	Residential	Exports	Imports	Total	Federal	State and local	
1974												
1st quarter	35.2	33.8	33.2	41.0	45.3	31.8	50.2	42.4	33.3	34.4	32.3	34.8
2nd quarter	36.0	34.7	34.0	42.2	46.8	32.6	51.9	47.3	34.2	35.1	33.4	35.8
3rd quarter	37.1	35.6	34.9	43.9	48.7	33.6	54.9	49.7	35.4	36.2	34.6	36.9
4th quarter	38.2	36.5	35.7	45.6	51.0	34.5	57.8	51.4	36.5	37.6	35.6	37.9
1975												
1st quarter	39.1	37.2	36.4	47.3	53.0	35.4	59.4	52.1	37.3	38.4	36.3	38.8
2nd quarter	39.6	37.6	36.9	48.4	54.4	36.0	59.2	52.3	37.9	38.9	37.0	39.3
3rd quarter	40.4	38.3	37.5	49.0	55.0	36.4	59.0	51.1	38.6	39.6	37.6	40.0
4th quarter	41.0	38.9	38.0	49.7	55.8	37.0	59.4	51.2	39.4	40.7	38.2	40.7
1976												
1st quarter	41.5	39.3	38.6	50.2	56.5	37.2	60.2	52.0	39.9	41.1	38.8	41.1
2nd quarter	41.9	39.7	39.1	51.1	57.2	38.3	60.8	52.8	40.4	41.6	39.4	41.6
3rd quarter	42.5	40.3	39.7	51.8	57.9	38.9	61.2	53.8	40.9	42.2	39.7	42.2
4th quarter	43.2	41.0	40.4	52.6	58.8	39.6	62.3	54.3	41.7	43.3	40.2	42.9
1977												
1st quarter	44.0	41.7	41.0	53.8	60.0	40.6	63.0	56.2	42.5	44.4	41.0	43.7
2nd quarter	44.7	42.4	41.7	54.8	61.0	41.7	63.9	57.8	43.2	45.0	41.7	44.4
3rd quarter	45.3	43.1	42.4	56.0	62.0	43.0	63.6	58.6	43.7	45.2	42.4	45.1
4th quarter	46.1	43.7	43.0	57.2	63.1	44.4	63.9	59.2	44.8	46.7	43.1	45.9
1978												
1st quarter	46.9	44.4	43.7	58.3	64.0	45.7	65.2	60.2	45.3	47.2	43.8	46.7
2nd quarter	47.8	45.4	44.5	59.6	65.1	47.0	66.8	61.6	46.0	47.7	44.5	47.6
3rd quarter	48.6	46.2	45.2	60.8	66.2	48.2	67.9	62.6	46.7	48.4	45.2	48.4
4th quarter	49.6	47.1	46.0	62.0	67.4	49.5	70.1	63.7	47.5	49.5	45.8	49.4
1979												
1st quarter	50.6	48.0	46.7	63.3	68.8	50.5	72.2	66.2	48.5	50.2	46.9	50.4
2nd quarter	51.7	49.2	47.5	64.9	70.4	52.2	75.1	69.6	49.5	51.1	48.0	51.6
3rd quarter	52.8	50.4	48.4	66.5	71.9	53.9	76.9	74.8	50.9	52.1	49.7	52.9
4th quarter	53.9	51.7	49.4	67.9	73.2	55.2	78.4	79.8	52.3	54.3	50.7	54.2
1980												
1st quarter	55.1	53.3	50.7	69.4	74.8	56.6	80.7	86.5	53.6	55.2	52.1	55.7
2nd quarter	56.4	54.6	51.9	71.1	76.6	58.0	81.8	89.6	55.0	56.6	53.6	57.1
3rd quarter	57.6	55.9	53.0	72.6	78.2	59.3	84.0	92.1	56.3	57.5	55.1	58.4
4th quarter	59.2	57.1	54.2	74.2	79.9	60.8	86.8	93.6	58.3	60.4	56.5	59.9
1981												
1st quarter	60.7	58.6	55.3	76.2	82.2	62.1	89.0	96.1	59.8	61.5	58.2	61.4
2nd quarter	61.8	59.6	56.3	77.9	84.2	63.1	89.3	96.7	60.8	62.4	59.4	62.5
3rd quarter	63.0	60.6	57.5	79.2	85.8	63.9	89.5	94.2	61.6	63.1	60.2	63.6
4th quarter	64.1	61.6	58.6	80.8	87.6	64.8	89.8	94.4	63.0	65.3	61.0	64.7
1982												
1st quarter	65.0	62.4	59.4	81.8	88.6	65.8	90.3	94.0	64.1	66.4	62.1	65.6
2nd quarter	65.8	63.0	60.3	82.9	89.7	66.8	90.3	92.4	65.0	67.2	63.1	66.3
3rd quarter	66.8	64.0	61.2	83.4	90.2	67.3	89.6	91.3	65.8	67.7	64.1	67.2
4th quarter	67.4	64.6	62.1	83.5	90.2	67.6	89.1	90.6	66.8	68.8	64.9	67.8
1983												
1st quarter	68.0	65.1	62.9	83.1	89.5	68.0	89.5	88.7	67.2	69.3	65.4	68.2
2nd quarter	68.6	65.9	63.6	82.8	89.0	68.1	89.8	88.7	67.8	69.8	66.1	68.8
3rd quarter	69.2	66.6	64.3	82.6	88.7	68.5	90.4	88.9	68.4	70.3	66.7	69.4
4th quarter	69.8	67.2	65.0	82.8	88.6	69.1	91.3	88.3	68.8	70.5	67.3	69.8
1984												
1st quarter	70.6	67.8	65.6	82.9	88.5	69.5	91.4	88.6	70.7	73.4	68.4	70.7
2nd quarter	71.2	68.4	66.2	83.3	88.8	70.0	92.0	89.1	71.4	73.9	69.0	71.2
3rd quarter	71.7	68.9	66.8	83.5	88.9	70.7	91.1	87.5	71.9	74.4	69.7	71.7
4th quarter	72.2	69.4	67.4	83.8	89.0	71.2	90.1	86.4	72.5	74.9	70.3	72.2
1985												
1st quarter	73.0	70.1	68.2	84.0	89.2	71.6	89.2	84.4	73.2	75.5	71.1	72.8
2nd quarter	73.5	70.8	68.9	84.2	89.3	71.8	89.0	84.7	73.6	75.6	71.8	73.3
3rd quarter	73.9	71.2	69.5	84.5	89.7	72.3	88.3	84.7	73.8	75.4	72.4	73.7
4th quarter	74.4	71.9	70.2	85.0	90.0	73.1	88.2	86.3	74.5	76.2	73.0	74.4
1986												
1st quarter	74.7	72.3	70.8	85.4	90.2	74.0	87.6	86.5	74.6	76.0	73.3	74.7
2nd quarter	75.0	72.3	71.4	86.1	90.9	74.7	87.3	83.8	74.8	76.1	73.6	74.8
3rd quarter	75.5	72.9	72.1	87.0	91.6	75.6	86.8	84.4	75.1	76.1	74.2	75.4
4th quarter	76.0	73.4	72.8	87.5	92.0	76.5	87.6	85.3	75.8	76.2	75.3	75.9
1987												
1st quarter	76.7	74.4	73.6	87.8	91.9	77.3	88.0	87.5	76.5	76.8	76.1	76.8
2nd quarter	77.3	75.1	74.4	87.9	91.9	77.9	89.4	89.8	77.0	77.0	76.9	77.4
3rd quarter	77.8	75.9	75.1	88.1	91.8	78.6	89.7	90.7	77.6	77.2	77.8	78.0
4th quarter	78.5	76.6	76.0	88.8	92.5	79.3	91.3	92.1	77.8	77.2	78.2	78.6
1988												
1st quarter	79.0	77.1	76.6	89.6	93.3	80.0	92.3	93.4	78.5	78.2	78.6	79.2
2nd quarter	79.8	78.0	77.5	90.2	93.9	80.7	94.3	95.1	79.2	78.9	79.4	80.0
3rd quarter	80.7	78.9	78.4	90.6	94.3	81.2	95.5	94.2	79.6	79.0	80.0	80.8
4th quarter	81.4	79.7	79.2	91.5	95.2	82.0	95.4	95.1	79.9	79.1	80.5	81.5
1989												
1st quarter	82.2	80.6	80.1	92.0	95.7	82.6	96.4	96.7	81.1	80.7	81.4	82.4
2nd quarter	83.0	81.7	80.8	92.6	96.0	83.6	96.6	97.9	81.7	81.0	82.2	83.3
3rd quarter	83.6	82.2	81.4	93.0	96.5	83.9	96.0	96.2	82.2	81.4	82.6	83.7
4th quarter	84.2	83.0	82.3	93.5	97.0	84.4	95.7	96.7	82.6	81.4	83.5	84.4
1990												
1st quarter	85.2	84.1	83.2	94.0	97.5	85.0	95.7	98.0	83.9	82.6	84.8	85.5
2nd quarter	86.2	85.0	84.2	94.3	97.8	85.4	96.0	96.2	84.6	83.3	85.6	86.3
3rd quarter	87.0	86.1	85.2	94.9	98.4	85.8	97.0	99.0	85.4	83.9	86.5	87.3
4th quarter	87.8	87.3	86.0	95.5	99.2	85.9	98.4	104.5	86.7	85.4	87.7	88.4

Table 22-4. Per Capita Product and Income and U.S. Population

(Dollars, except as noted; quarterly data are seasonally adjusted at annual rates.)

| Year and quarter | Current dollars | | | | | | | Chained (1996) dollars | | | | | | Population (mid-period, thousands) |
| | Gross domestic product | Personal income | Disposable personal income | Personal consumption expenditures | | | | Gross domestic product | Disposable personal income | Personal consumption expenditures | | | | |
				Total	Durable goods	Nondurable goods	Services			Total	Durable goods	Nondurable goods	Services	
1963	3 268	2 541	2 249	2 024	273	888	863	14 212	9 886	8 896	646	3 472	4 775	189 300
1964	3 462	2 688	2 412	2 145	295	931	919	14 831	10 456	9 300	696	3 592	4 997	191 927
1965	3 705	2 868	2 567	2 286	325	986	975	15 583	10 965	9 764	774	3 735	5 198	194 347
1966	4 015	3 085	2 742	2 451	347	1 062	1 041	16 416	11 417	10 204	830	3 895	5 398	196 599
1967	4 197	3 272	2 899	2 559	354	1 092	1 113	16 646	11 776	10 396	834	3 914	5 602	198 752
1968	4 540	3 559	3 119	2 783	402	1 174	1 207	17 266	12 196	10 881	917	4 052	5 832	200 745
1969	4 860	3 851	3 329	2 987	424	1 249	1 314	17 616	12 451	11 171	940	4 118	6 048	202 736
1970	5 069	4 101	3 591	3 164	414	1 326	1 424	17 446	12 823	11 300	899	4 169	6 220	205 089
1971	5 434	4 358	3 860	3 382	467	1 375	1 541	17 804	13 218	11 581	977	4 191	6 376	207 692
1972	5 909	4 736	4 138	3 671	526	1 467	1 678	18 570	13 692	12 149	1 089	4 329	6 656	209 924
1973	6 537	5 254	4 619	4 022	583	1 619	1 821	19 456	14 496	12 626	1 190	4 428	6 904	211 939
1974	7 017	5 730	5 013	4 359	572	1 798	1 989	19 163	14 268	12 407	1 098	4 299	6 989	213 898
1975	7 571	6 166	5 470	4 771	618	1 948	2 205	18 911	14 393	12 551	1 087	4 320	7 157	215 981
1976	8 363	6 765	5 960	5 272	728	2 102	2 442	19 771	14 873	13 155	1 214	4 487	7 423	218 086
1977	9 221	7 432	6 519	5 803	823	2 257	2 724	20 481	15 256	13 583	1 314	4 550	7 674	220 289
1978	10 313	8 302	7 253	6 425	906	2 472	3 047	21 383	15 845	14 035	1 369	4 670	7 954	222 629
1979	11 401	9 247	8 033	7 091	952	2 774	3 365	21 821	16 120	14 230	1 349	4 742	8 121	225 106
1980	12 276	10 205	8 869	7 741	940	3 057	3 744	21 521	16 063	14 021	1 229	4 680	8 161	227 726
1981	13 614	11 301	9 773	8 453	1 006	3 299	4 148	21 830	16 265	14 069	1 232	4 688	8 200	230 008
1982	14 035	11 922	10 364	8 954	1 034	3 392	4 528	21 184	16 328	14 105	1 221	4 688	8 261	232 218
1983	15 085	12 576	11 036	9 757	1 200	3 547	5 010	21 902	16 673	14 741	1 389	4 801	8 589	234 332
1984	16 636	13 853	12 215	10 569	1 383	3 742	5 444	23 288	17 799	15 401	1 579	4 948	8 873	236 394
1985	17 664	14 738	12 941	11 373	1 523	3 894	5 956	23 970	18 229	16 020	1 719	5 038	9 254	238 506
1986	18 501	15 425	13 555	12 029	1 667	3 982	6 379	24 565	18 641	16 541	1 859	5 171	9 478	240 682
1987	19 529	16 317	14 246	12 787	1 728	4 181	6 878	25 174	18 870	16 938	1 874	5 248	9 798	242 842
1988	20 845	17 433	15 312	13 697	1 837	4 419	7 441	25 987	19 522	17 463	1 965	5 367	10 109	245 061
1989	22 188	18 593	16 235	14 539	1 891	4 711	7 937	26 646	19 833	17 760	1 987	5 461	10 291	247 387
1990	23 215	19 614	17 176	15 327	1 871	4 985	8 472	26 834	20 058	17 899	1 948	5 479	10 466	249 981
1963														
1st quarter	3 205	2 503	2 212	1 994	266	883	845	13 989	9 766	8 801	632	3 465	4 698	188 299
2nd quarter	3 240	2 521	2 230	2 009	271	884	854	14 125	9 831	8 856	644	3 468	4 734	188 906
3rd quarter	3 295	2 550	2 259	2 038	274	893	870	14 342	9 910	8 942	649	3 483	4 810	189 631
4th quarter	3 332	2 589	2 296	2 055	279	893	883	14 390	10 036	8 983	658	3 472	4 858	190 362
1964														
1st quarter	3 406	2 629	2 344	2 098	289	912	898	14 666	10 199	9 132	681	3 526	4 915	190 954
2nd quarter	3 444	2 667	2 403	2 133	295	926	912	14 793	10 438	9 266	696	3 580	4 972	191 560
3rd quarter	3 491	2 708	2 436	2 172	304	941	926	14 939	10 547	9 403	717	3 631	5 023	192 256
4th quarter	3 505	2 745	2 465	2 177	292	945	941	14 925	10 638	9 396	691	3 630	5 075	192 938
1965														
1st quarter	3 600	2 789	2 491	2 227	320	956	951	15 249	10 709	9 575	755	3 662	5 109	193 467
2nd quarter	3 655	2 831	2 526	2 257	318	973	966	15 412	10 807	9 656	755	3 693	5 167	193 994
3rd quarter	3 731	2 896	2 599	2 297	327	989	981	15 673	11 073	9 788	779	3 734	5 221	194 647
4th quarter	3 834	2 955	2 653	2 362	337	1 024	1 001	15 996	11 268	10 034	809	3 851	5 293	195 279
1966														
1st quarter	3 945	3 009	2 690	2 410	352	1 044	1 014	16 352	11 337	10 158	847	3 877	5 331	195 763
2nd quarter	3 982	3 050	2 711	2 430	338	1 059	1 033	16 371	11 334	10 159	809	3 901	5 380	196 277
3rd quarter	4 037	3 110	2 760	2 470	350	1 072	1 048	16 425	11 449	10 243	834	3 915	5 410	196 877
4th quarter	4 094	3 169	2 806	2 492	350	1 072	1 069	16 517	11 548	10 255	832	3 888	5 468	197 481
1967														
1st quarter	4 139	3 211	2 846	2 507	342	1 080	1 085	16 628	11 682	10 291	814	3 908	5 522	197 967
2nd quarter	4 152	3 238	2 874	2 547	358	1 087	1 103	16 576	11 740	10 403	848	3 917	5 576	198 455
3rd quarter	4 214	3 296	2 919	2 576	357	1 095	1 123	16 650	11 816	10 428	838	3 909	5 639	199 012
4th quarter	4 281	3 343	2 957	2 607	361	1 107	1 139	16 727	11 865	10 462	837	3 920	5 669	199 572
1968														
1st quarter	4 407	3 434	3 035	2 691	386	1 140	1 164	17 032	12 048	10 681	888	3 997	5 721	199 995
2nd quarter	4 518	3 524	3 111	2 753	394	1 164	1 195	17 285	12 228	10 824	903	4 039	5 808	200 452
3rd quarter	4 582	3 605	3 142	2 826	415	1 191	1 221	17 359	12 228	10 999	942	4 091	5 870	200 997
4th quarter	4 653	3 672	3 190	2 862	415	1 201	1 247	17 387	12 277	11 017	933	4 079	5 928	201 538
1969														
1st quarter	4 763	3 733	3 218	2 916	424	1 220	1 272	17 619	12 267	11 115	948	4 109	5 975	201 955
2nd quarter	4 827	3 812	3 284	2 965	424	1 241	1 300	17 625	12 358	11 159	943	4 120	6 024	202 419
3rd quarter	4 912	3 900	3 380	3 008	424	1 257	1 326	17 677	12 563	11 178	938	4 116	6 065	202 986
4th quarter	4 938	3 960	3 434	3 058	423	1 277	1 357	17 543	12 614	11 231	931	4 128	6 128	203 584
1970														
1st quarter	4 989	4 004	3 484	3 105	416	1 304	1 385	17 475	12 651	11 274	912	4 161	6 173	204 086
2nd quarter	5 053	4 095	3 572	3 145	420	1 318	1 406	17 457	12 827	11 293	918	4 156	6 190	204 721
3rd quarter	5 121	4 140	3 643	3 193	423	1 332	1 437	17 551	12 954	11 353	918	4 170	6 246	205 419
4th quarter	5 114	4 165	3 665	3 214	398	1 351	1 465	17 302	12 860	11 279	849	4 188	6 269	206 130
1971														
1st quarter	5 320	4 244	3 761	3 297	448	1 356	1 493	17 731	13 075	11 461	941	4 189	6 304	206 763
2nd quarter	5 404	4 341	3 848	3 355	461	1 370	1 524	17 777	13 226	11 532	960	4 192	6 349	207 362
3rd quarter	5 484	4 388	3 888	3 404	470	1 378	1 555	17 858	13 235	11 586	982	4 180	6 386	208 000
4th quarter	5 527	4 456	3 942	3 471	487	1 395	1 590	17 848	13 334	11 742	1 023	4 202	6 465	208 642
1972														
1st quarter	5 702	4 579	3 997	3 546	502	1 415	1 630	18 155	13 376	11 868	1 045	4 218	6 552	209 142
2nd quarter	5 855	4 646	4 048	3 625	516	1 452	1 657	18 527	13 466	12 057	1 068	4 311	6 608	209 637
3rd quarter	5 957	4 762	4 161	3 702	530	1 482	1 690	18 661	13 720	12 208	1 093	4 361	6 675	210 181
4th quarter	6 120	4 956	4 343	3 811	555	1 521	1 735	18 936	14 202	12 463	1 149	4 425	6 788	210 737
1973														
1st quarter	6 337	5 053	4 444	3 920	593	1 564	1 763	19 377	14 356	12 662	1 221	4 463	6 840	211 192
2nd quarter	6 493	5 182	4 562	3 983	586	1 592	1 804	19 528	14 455	12 621	1 199	4 415	6 899	211 663
3rd quarter	6 570	5 304	4 663	4 062	583	1 638	1 840	19 402	14 512	12 642	1 186	4 430	6 927	212 191
4th quarter	6 748	5 474	4 807	4 124	569	1 680	1 875	19 515	14 660	12 579	1 154	4 403	6 948	212 708

Table 22-4. Per Capita Product and Income and U.S. Population—*Continued*

(Dollars, except as noted; quarterly data are seasonally adjusted at annual rates.)

Year and quarter	Current dollars							Chained (1996) dollars						Population (mid-period, thousands)
	Gross domestic product	Personal income	Disposable personal income	Personal consumption expenditures				Gross domestic product	Disposable personal income	Personal consumption expenditures				
				Total	Durable goods	Nondurable goods	Services			Total	Durable goods	Nondurable goods	Services	
1974														
1st quarter	6 803	5 546	4 865	4 201	558	1 732	1 911	19 326	14 413	12 444	1 120	4 336	6 941	213 144
2nd quarter	6 964	5 654	4 947	4 324	576	1 781	1 967	19 337	14 258	12 462	1 128	4 312	6 984	213 602
3rd quarter	7 074	5 811	5 077	4 443	601	1 829	2 012	19 073	14 258	12 478	1 134	4 310	6 995	214 147
4th quarter	7 227	5 907	5 161	4 467	553	1 848	2 067	18 919	14 144	12 242	1 011	4 238	7 036	214 700
1975														
1st quarter	7 285	5 955	5 208	4 576	573	1 880	2 123	18 639	14 014	12 312	1 033	4 247	7 070	215 135
2nd quarter	7 434	6 079	5 505	4 700	595	1 927	2 179	18 758	14 638	12 499	1 052	4 328	7 145	215 652
3rd quarter	7 674	6 234	5 515	4 842	638	1 978	2 226	19 027	14 402	12 644	1 116	4 351	7 172	216 289
4th quarter	7 888	6 394	5 650	4 962	666	2 007	2 290	19 217	14 515	12 749	1 147	4 353	7 242	216 848
1976														
1st quarter	8 146	6 555	5 795	5 113	709	2 050	2 354	19 631	14 734	12 998	1 205	4 430	7 330	217 314
2nd quarter	8 280	6 673	5 883	5 194	718	2 079	2 398	19 752	14 827	13 091	1 205	4 480	7 372	217 776
3rd quarter	8 413	6 837	6 017	5 317	731	2 119	2 467	19 795	14 930	13 192	1 214	4 506	7 442	218 338
4th quarter	8 612	6 993	6 145	5 464	755	2 159	2 550	19 904	14 999	13 337	1 232	4 533	7 545	218 917
1977														
1st quarter	8 837	7 154	6 279	5 613	791	2 205	2 616	20 100	15 064	13 466	1 280	4 549	7 593	219 427
2nd quarter	9 123	7 321	6 417	5 730	813	2 238	2 679	20 412	15 125	13 505	1 308	4 530	7 618	219 956
3rd quarter	9 373	7 509	6 594	5 857	830	2 261	2 765	20 722	15 308	13 597	1 322	4 525	7 711	220 573
4th quarter	9 549	7 740	6 782	6 012	855	2 323	2 834	20 688	15 524	13 761	1 344	4 594	7 773	221 201
1978														
1st quarter	9 699	7 918	6 946	6 133	843	2 365	2 925	20 697	15 634	13 805	1 305	4 613	7 867	221 719
2nd quarter	10 242	8 192	7 172	6 384	921	2 442	3 021	21 440	15 804	14 068	1 404	4 651	7 959	222 281
3rd quarter	10 490	8 430	7 353	6 514	920	2 505	3 089	21 583	15 915	14 099	1 380	4 686	7 988	222 933
4th quarter	10 815	8 664	7 540	6 667	940	2 573	3 154	21 809	16 024	14 168	1 386	4 729	8 002	223 583
1979														
1st quarter	11 023	8 908	7 758	6 833	944	2 649	3 240	21 808	16 153	14 225	1 368	4 741	8 083	224 152
2nd quarter	11 255	9 082	7 898	6 972	936	2 717	3 319	21 765	16 050	14 169	1 334	4 710	8 120	224 737
3rd quarter	11 541	9 354	8 115	7 187	971	2 820	3 396	21 854	16 098	14 257	1 368	4 746	8 117	225 418
4th quarter	11 781	9 639	8 357	7 370	959	2 908	3 502	21 859	16 177	14 266	1 327	4 769	8 162	226 117
1980														
1st quarter	12 052	9 914	8 639	7 568	970	2 997	3 600	21 869	16 222	14 211	1 306	4 745	8 167	226 754
2nd quarter	12 036	9 977	8 673	7 561	879	3 020	3 663	21 364	15 885	13 849	1 156	4 670	8 088	227 389
3rd quarter	12 249	10 256	8 910	7 792	934	3 067	3 790	21 267	15 950	13 948	1 208	4 647	8 154	228 070
4th quarter	12 763	10 669	9 252	8 042	978	3 142	3 922	21 586	16 196	14 078	1 244	4 659	8 233	228 689
1981														
1st quarter	13 321	10 956	9 489	8 261	1 019	3 255	3 988	21 961	16 205	14 109	1 279	4 694	8 164	229 155
2nd quarter	13 437	11 101	9 584	8 389	994	3 292	4 102	21 758	16 095	14 087	1 224	4 697	8 222	229 674
3rd quarter	13 823	11 517	9 942	8 556	1 039	3 314	4 204	21 958	16 400	14 114	1 261	4 684	8 213	230 301
4th quarter	13 872	11 629	10 075	8 603	972	3 336	4 295	21 641	16 358	13 967	1 165	4 679	8 201	230 903
1982														
1st quarter	13 802	11 709	10 158	8 743	1 011	3 354	4 377	21 238	16 290	14 021	1 203	4 676	8 208	231 395
2nd quarter	14 009	11 876	10 295	8 835	1 020	3 357	4 457	21 282	16 349	14 029	1 204	4 672	8 220	231 906
3rd quarter	14 102	11 985	10 448	9 005	1 029	3 411	4 566	21 127	16 342	14 085	1 210	4 686	8 255	232 498
4th quarter	14 226	12 115	10 554	9 232	1 078	3 444	4 710	21 090	16 331	14 286	1 265	4 720	8 360	233 074
1983														
1st quarter	14 466	12 219	10 684	9 370	1 095	3 452	4 823	21 291	16 404	14 387	1 276	4 734	8 440	233 546
2nd quarter	14 911	12 431	10 861	9 657	1 179	3 521	4 957	21 749	16 484	14 657	1 370	4 771	8 560	234 028
3rd quarter	15 272	12 654	11 146	9 887	1 229	3 591	5 067	22 082	16 746	14 854	1 421	4 830	8 633	234 603
4th quarter	15 687	12 997	11 448	10 112	1 296	3 624	5 192	22 482	17 053	15 063	1 489	4 867	8 723	235 153
1984														
1st quarter	16 185	13 378	11 808	10 302	1 344	3 677	5 280	22 929	17 415	15 194	1 545	4 884	8 769	235 605
2nd quarter	16 559	13 724	12 116	10 511	1 381	3 744	5 386	23 271	17 716	15 369	1 577	4 961	8 823	236 082
3rd quarter	16 795	14 061	12 398	10 636	1 380	3 760	5 496	23 415	17 996	15 438	1 573	4 965	8 902	236 657
4th quarter	17 002	14 246	12 537	10 825	1 425	3 788	5 612	23 534	18 067	15 600	1 620	4 981	8 996	237 232
1985														
1st quarter	17 292	14 504	12 643	11 078	1 480	3 831	5 767	23 687	18 040	15 807	1 675	5 000	9 126	237 673
2nd quarter	17 508	14 650	12 975	11 261	1 497	3 880	5 884	23 822	18 342	15 919	1 689	5 029	9 195	238 176
3rd quarter	17 810	14 775	12 964	11 516	1 587	3 907	6 022	24 116	18 203	16 169	1 793	5 047	9 306	238 789
4th quarter	18 043	15 019	13 180	11 636	1 527	3 958	6 151	24 254	18 331	16 184	1 720	5 074	9 389	239 387
1986														
1st quarter	18 241	15 221	13 395	11 778	1 554	3 991	6 233	24 426	18 530	16 292	1 750	5 130	9 402	239 861
2nd quarter	18 369	15 344	13 508	11 886	1 611	3 955	6 320	24 476	18 677	16 435	1 805	5 174	9 432	240 368
3rd quarter	18 606	15 504	13 630	12 154	1 762	3 971	6 420	24 642	18 708	16 708	1 957	5 173	9 496	240 962
4th quarter	18 786	15 628	13 687	12 296	1 741	4 012	6 543	24 714	18 649	16 754	1 923	5 208	9 580	241 539
1987														
1st quarter	19 058	15 918	14 002	12 443	1 642	4 109	6 693	24 848	18 830	16 734	1 798	5 231	9 697	242 009
2nd quarter	19 362	16 144	13 980	12 706	1 720	4 172	6 814	25 058	18 608	16 912	1 871	5 257	9 763	242 520
3rd quarter	19 621	16 421	14 354	12 938	1 801	4 204	6 934	25 206	18 924	17 057	1 945	5 248	9 833	243 120
4th quarter	20 070	16 782	14 645	13 060	1 750	4 239	7 071	25 580	19 119	17 049	1 883	5 256	9 896	243 721
1988														
1st quarter	20 298	17 022	14 915	13 348	1 828	4 297	7 223	25 699	19 345	17 313	1 973	5 306	10 007	244 208
2nd quarter	20 704	17 276	15 165	13 565	1 833	4 374	7 358	25 948	19 447	17 395	1 968	5 343	10 060	244 716
3rd quarter	20 996	17 561	15 446	13 804	1 815	4 464	7 526	26 013	19 571	17 491	1 936	5 386	10 155	245 354
4th quarter	21 378	17 869	15 720	14 067	1 872	4 539	7 656	26 285	19 724	17 650	1 984	5 431	10 212	245 966
1989														
1st quarter	21 825	18 330	16 036	14 249	1 868	4 603	7 778	26 551	19 896	17 679	1 970	5 441	10 248	246 460
2nd quarter	22 111	18 515	16 171	14 464	1 892	4 701	7 870	26 635	19 800	17 710	1 994	5 432	10 263	247 017
3rd quarter	22 315	18 641	16 266	14 643	1 933	4 740	7 970	26 688	19 793	17 818	2 029	5 469	10 292	247 698
4th quarter	22 498	18 885	16 465	14 797	1 870	4 799	8 128	26 708	19 844	17 834	1 957	5 501	10 362	248 374
1990														
1st quarter	22 981	19 285	16 892	15 083	1 954	4 908	8 222	26 980	20 092	17 940	2 036	5 504	10 376	248 936
2nd quarter	23 237	19 548	17 114	15 249	1 880	4 941	8 428	26 969	20 138	17 960	1 960	5 499	10 476	249 607
3rd quarter	23 349	19 780	17 313	15 466	1 853	5 027	8 586	26 842	20 104	17 959	1 931	5 496	10 530	250 330
4th quarter	23 291	19 842	17 381	15 509	1 797	5 062	8 650	26 545	19 900	17 756	1 867	5 417	10 480	251 052

Table 22-5. Gross Private Fixed Investment by Type

(Billions of dollars, quarterly data are at seasonally adjusted annual rates.)

Year and quarter	Total	Nonresidential											Residential			
		Structures				Equipment and software							Structures			Equipment
		Total	Nonresidential buildings, incl. farm	Utilities	Mining exploration, shafts and wells	Total	Information processing equipment and software			Industrial equipment	Transportation equipment	Other	Total [2]	Single family	Multi-family	
							Computers [1]	Software	Other							
1963	88.1	21.2	13.9	5.0	2.3	34.8	0.7	0.4	5.3	10.0	9.4	8.9	31.5	16.0	6.4	0.6
1964	97.2	23.7	15.8	5.4	2.4	39.2	0.9	0.5	5.8	11.4	10.6	10.0	33.6	17.6	6.4	0.6
1965	109.0	28.3	19.5	6.1	2.4	46.5	1.2	0.7	6.6	13.6	13.2	11.2	33.5	17.8	6.0	0.7
1966	117.7	31.3	21.3	7.1	2.5	54.0	1.7	1.0	7.9	16.1	14.5	12.9	31.6	16.6	5.2	0.7
1967	118.7	31.5	20.6	7.8	2.4	54.9	1.9	1.2	8.1	16.8	14.3	12.6	31.6	16.8	4.7	0.7
1968	132.1	33.6	21.1	9.2	2.6	59.9	1.9	1.3	8.6	17.2	17.6	13.1	37.9	19.5	7.2	0.9
1969	147.3	37.7	24.4	9.6	2.8	67.0	2.4	1.8	10.4	18.9	18.9	14.5	41.6	19.7	9.5	1.0
1970	150.4	40.3	25.4	11.1	2.8	68.7	2.7	2.3	11.6	20.2	16.2	15.6	40.2	17.5	9.5	1.1
1971	169.9	42.7	27.1	11.9	2.7	71.5	2.8	2.4	12.1	19.4	18.4	16.4	54.5	25.8	12.9	1.3
1972	198.5	47.2	30.1	13.1	3.1	81.7	3.5	2.8	13.1	21.3	21.8	19.2	68.1	32.8	17.2	1.5
1973	228.6	55.0	35.5	15.0	3.5	98.3	3.5	3.2	16.3	25.9	26.6	22.8	73.6	35.2	19.4	1.7
1974	235.4	61.2	38.3	16.5	5.2	108.2	3.9	3.9	19.0	30.5	26.3	24.6	64.1	29.7	13.7	1.9
1975	236.5	61.4	35.6	17.1	7.4	112.4	3.6	4.8	19.9	31.1	25.2	27.9	60.8	29.6	6.7	1.9
1976	274.8	65.9	35.9	20.0	8.6	126.4	4.4	5.2	22.8	33.9	30.0	30.1	80.4	43.9	6.9	2.1
1977	339.0	74.6	39.9	21.5	11.5	154.1	5.7	5.5	27.5	39.2	39.3	37.1	107.9	62.2	10.0	2.4
1978	410.2	91.4	49.7	24.1	15.4	187.2	7.6	6.6	34.2	47.4	47.3	44.1	128.9	72.8	12.8	2.7
1979	472.7	114.9	65.7	27.5	19.0	216.7	10.2	8.7	39.8	55.9	53.6	48.6	137.9	72.3	17.0	3.2
1980	484.2	133.9	73.7	30.2	27.4	227.0	12.5	10.7	46.4	60.4	48.4	48.6	119.9	53.0	16.7	3.4
1981	541.0	164.6	86.3	33.0	42.5	253.8	17.1	12.9	52.3	65.2	50.6	55.6	119.0	52.0	17.5	3.6
1982	531.0	175.0	94.5	32.5	44.8	250.3	18.9	15.4	54.6	62.3	46.8	52.3	102.0	41.5	15.5	3.7
1983	570.0	152.7	90.5	28.7	30.0	264.7	23.9	18.0	58.9	58.4	53.7	51.8	148.3	72.2	22.4	4.2
1984	670.1	176.0	110.0	30.0	31.3	314.3	31.6	22.1	68.0	67.6	64.8	60.2	175.1	85.6	28.2	4.7
1985	714.5	193.3	128.0	30.6	27.9	334.3	33.7	25.6	71.5	71.9	69.7	61.8	181.9	86.1	28.5	5.1
1986	740.7	175.8	123.3	31.2	15.7	346.8	33.4	27.8	76.4	74.8	71.8	62.6	212.6	102.8	31.0	5.5
1987	754.3	172.1	126.0	26.5	13.1	354.7	35.8	31.4	74.8	76.1	70.4	66.2	221.8	114.5	25.5	5.8
1988	802.7	181.6	133.8	26.6	15.7	386.8	38.0	36.7	81.2	83.5	76.1	71.3	228.2	116.6	22.3	6.1
1989	845.2	193.4	142.7	29.5	14.9	420.0	43.1	44.4	85.5	92.7	71.4	83.0	225.7	116.9	22.3	6.1
1990	847.2	202.5	149.1	28.4	17.9	427.8	38.6	50.2	87.3	91.5	75.7	84.5	210.8	108.7	19.3	6.0
1963																
1st quarter	83.6	20.2	13.2	4.7	2.3	33.2	0.6	0.3	5.1	9.3	9.5	8.4	29.6	15.2	5.8	0.6
2nd quarter	87.3	21.2	13.9	5.0	2.3	33.9	0.7	0.4	5.3	9.8	9.0	8.7	31.6	15.9	6.4	0.6
3rd quarter	89.3	21.4	14.1	5.0	2.3	35.4	0.8	0.5	5.4	10.2	9.3	9.1	31.9	16.0	6.6	0.6
4th quarter	92.3	21.9	14.5	5.2	2.2	36.8	0.8	0.5	5.4	10.5	9.9	9.5	33.1	16.8	6.9	0.6
1964																
1st quarter	95.6	22.4	14.8	5.3	2.3	37.7	1.0	0.5	5.6	10.8	10.2	9.6	34.8	18.4	6.8	0.6
2nd quarter	96.1	23.4	15.5	5.4	2.4	38.5	0.9	0.6	5.7	10.8	10.6	9.9	33.5	17.5	6.5	0.6
3rd quarter	97.8	24.3	16.2	5.4	2.4	39.8	0.9	0.5	5.7	11.4	11.3	9.9	33.1	17.2	6.3	0.6
4th quarter	99.5	24.8	16.6	5.5	2.5	40.9	0.9	0.5	6.2	12.4	10.3	10.5	33.2	17.5	6.1	0.6
1965																
1st quarter	104.1	26.1	17.7	5.8	2.4	44.1	1.0	0.6	6.2	12.6	12.9	10.8	33.2	17.2	6.2	0.7
2nd quarter	107.3	28.2	19.3	6.0	2.6	44.9	1.1	0.6	6.5	13.3	12.8	10.6	33.5	17.5	6.1	0.7
3rd quarter	110.4	28.5	19.7	6.1	2.4	47.5	1.2	0.7	6.8	14.1	13.3	11.4	33.6	18.1	5.9	0.7
4th quarter	114.2	30.4	21.2	6.4	2.3	49.3	1.3	0.8	7.0	14.4	13.8	11.9	33.8	18.5	5.8	0.7
1966																
1st quarter	117.9	31.1	21.2	6.7	2.5	52.0	1.4	0.9	7.5	15.0	14.7	12.5	34.1	18.7	5.9	0.7
2nd quarter	118.4	31.2	21.1	7.1	2.4	54.0	1.6	1.0	7.8	16.0	14.7	12.8	32.5	17.7	5.6	0.7
3rd quarter	118.3	31.9	21.6	7.3	2.5	54.5	1.8	1.1	8.0	16.4	14.2	12.9	31.2	15.8	5.1	0.7
4th quarter	116.1	31.2	21.1	7.2	2.4	55.7	2.0	1.2	8.2	16.7	14.4	13.2	28.5	14.0	4.4	0.7
1967																
1st quarter	113.8	31.7	21.4	7.3	2.4	53.8	1.9	1.2	8.0	17.1	13.3	12.4	27.7	14.3	4.1	0.7
2nd quarter	117.4	30.9	20.2	7.7	2.5	54.8	1.9	1.2	8.1	17.0	14.0	12.7	31.0	15.8	4.2	0.7
3rd quarter	119.3	31.5	20.4	7.9	2.4	54.4	1.8	1.2	8.0	16.3	14.7	12.4	32.7	17.9	4.9	0.7
4th quarter	124.5	32.0	20.5	8.4	2.4	56.5	1.9	1.2	8.5	16.9	15.1	12.9	35.2	19.2	5.7	0.8
1968																
1st quarter	128.8	33.1	20.9	8.8	2.5	58.8	1.9	1.2	8.7	17.2	17.2	12.6	36.1	19.0	6.3	0.8
2nd quarter	129.3	33.2	21.0	9.0	2.5	58.0	1.9	1.3	8.5	17.0	16.6	12.7	37.3	19.6	6.9	0.8
3rd quarter	132.0	33.2	20.6	9.4	2.6	59.9	2.0	1.3	8.7	17.0	17.7	13.2	38.0	19.3	7.5	0.9
4th quarter	138.4	34.8	21.8	9.5	2.7	62.7	1.9	1.4	8.7	17.6	19.0	14.1	40.0	20.2	8.0	0.9
1969																
1st quarter	144.2	35.8	23.1	9.5	2.6	65.2	2.1	1.5	9.4	18.2	19.4	14.5	42.3	21.0	9.0	0.9
2nd quarter	146.4	36.7	23.6	9.4	2.8	66.4	2.4	1.7	10.1	18.7	19.1	14.4	42.4	20.2	9.7	1.0
3rd quarter	150.2	38.9	25.2	9.6	2.9	68.0	2.6	1.9	10.8	19.4	19.0	14.4	42.2	19.2	9.7	1.0
4th quarter	148.3	39.4	25.4	10.1	2.9	68.3	2.7	2.1	11.3	19.4	18.1	14.7	39.6	18.3	9.7	1.1
1970																
1st quarter	148.8	39.5	25.5	10.2	2.8	68.6	3.1	2.3	11.4	20.1	16.8	15.0	39.6	17.0	9.4	1.1
2nd quarter	148.8	40.3	25.7	10.9	2.8	69.1	3.0	2.4	11.7	20.2	16.5	15.4	38.3	16.5	9.2	1.1
3rd quarter	151.0	40.6	25.2	11.6	2.7	70.0	2.4	2.4	11.6	20.4	17.1	16.2	39.3	17.4	9.4	1.1
4th quarter	152.9	40.8	25.1	11.6	2.8	67.2	2.4	2.3	11.8	20.0	14.6	16.1	43.8	19.3	10.1	1.2
1971																
1st quarter	159.1	41.5	25.8	11.8	2.7	69.0	2.3	2.2	11.6	19.2	17.7	15.9	47.4	22.0	11.0	1.2
2nd quarter	168.0	42.3	26.7	12.1	2.5	71.1	2.8	2.3	12.2	19.1	18.3	16.4	53.3	25.3	12.2	1.3
3rd quarter	173.2	43.1	27.5	12.0	2.7	71.7	2.9	2.5	12.2	19.3	18.2	16.7	57.1	27.1	13.7	1.3
4th quarter	179.4	43.8	28.2	11.9	2.8	74.1	3.1	2.6	12.5	19.9	19.5	16.5	60.2	28.7	14.6	1.4
1972																
1st quarter	189.9	45.8	29.0	12.8	2.9	77.5	3.7	2.7	12.6	19.9	21.0	17.7	65.1	31.4	16.2	1.5
2nd quarter	194.5	46.6	29.5	13.0	3.0	79.7	3.4	2.8	12.7	20.9	21.2	18.6	66.7	32.2	17.1	1.5
3rd quarter	198.7	47.3	30.3	13.1	3.1	81.8	3.5	2.8	13.0	21.8	21.0	19.6	68.0	33.0	17.2	1.6
4th quarter	211.0	49.0	31.4	13.5	3.2	87.7	3.2	2.8	13.9	22.6	24.2	20.9	72.7	34.9	18.5	1.6
1973																
1st quarter	222.0	51.3	33.3	13.9	3.2	92.8	3.4	3.0	15.1	23.6	25.2	22.5	76.1	36.9	19.3	1.7
2nd quarter	227.8	54.1	35.2	14.6	3.3	98.0	3.7	3.1	15.9	25.3	26.9	23.1	74.0	36.9	19.6	1.7
3rd quarter	232.0	56.8	36.6	15.5	3.6	100.1	3.4	3.3	16.6	26.5	27.1	23.2	73.3	35.1	20.1	1.7
4th quarter	232.6	57.7	36.9	15.9	3.8	102.1	3.7	3.5	17.5	28.1	27.0	22.3	71.0	31.8	18.7	1.8

1. New computers and peripheral equipment.
2. Includes other structures, not shown separately.

Table 22-5. Gross Private Fixed Investment by Type—*Continued*

(Billions of dollars, quarterly data are at seasonally adjusted annual rates.)

Year and quarter	Total	Nonresidential											Residential			
		Structures				Equipment and software							Structures			Equipment
		Total	Nonresidential buildings, incl. farm	Utilities	Mining exploration, shafts and wells	Total	Information processing equipment and software			Industrial equipment	Transportation equipment	Other	Total [2]	Single family	Multi-family	
							Computers [1]	Software	Other							
1974																
1st quarter	231.5	59.0	37.6	16.2	4.1	103.6	3.5	3.6	18.0	29.1	26.8	22.7	67.1	29.7	16.8	1.9
2nd quarter	234.9	61.3	38.7	16.3	5.1	106.0	3.2	3.7	18.6	30.3	26.8	23.5	65.6	30.5	14.8	1.9
3rd quarter	239.9	61.4	37.8	16.8	5.5	111.1	4.4	4.0	19.3	31.1	27.4	24.9	65.4	30.3	13.0	1.9
4th quarter	235.4	63.2	39.1	16.8	5.9	112.2	4.4	4.4	20.3	31.5	24.2	27.4	58.2	28.3	10.3	1.8
1975																
1st quarter	228.7	61.7	37.2	16.6	6.6	109.4	4.1	4.8	20.0	30.3	24.0	26.2	55.8	26.4	8.5	1.8
2nd quarter	230.7	60.4	35.1	16.9	7.1	110.4	3.5	4.8	19.8	30.7	23.9	27.7	58.0	27.3	6.4	1.9
3rd quarter	239.1	61.3	35.0	17.1	7.6	113.2	3.3	4.7	19.8	31.5	25.8	27.9	62.7	30.8	5.8	1.9
4th quarter	247.3	62.0	34.9	17.7	8.1	116.6	3.5	4.7	19.8	31.9	27.0	29.7	66.7	34.0	6.0	2.0
1976																
1st quarter	260.1	64.1	36.5	17.8	8.4	119.8	3.7	4.8	20.6	33.1	28.3	29.3	74.1	38.2	6.0	2.0
2nd quarter	269.1	65.1	35.7	19.8	8.2	123.4	4.4	5.1	21.9	33.6	29.0	29.5	78.6	42.8	6.3	2.1
3rd quarter	275.8	66.7	35.6	21.2	8.7	128.5	4.5	5.3	23.5	34.0	30.2	30.9	78.5	45.6	7.1	2.2
4th quarter	294.5	67.8	35.9	21.3	9.2	134.1	5.0	5.6	25.2	35.0	32.4	30.9	90.3	48.8	8.3	2.2
1977																
1st quarter	311.9	69.7	37.3	20.7	10.2	144.6	5.2	5.5	25.9	36.6	36.9	34.6	95.5	53.7	8.9	2.1
2nd quarter	335.6	73.6	39.2	21.8	11.2	150.3	5.6	5.5	27.0	37.6	38.4	36.2	109.4	62.8	10.1	2.3
3rd quarter	347.3	76.4	40.9	21.6	12.0	155.9	5.8	5.5	27.7	40.1	39.3	37.6	112.5	65.0	10.6	2.5
4th quarter	361.3	78.5	42.1	21.7	12.5	165.8	6.1	5.5	29.2	42.5	42.6	39.9	114.3	67.3	10.5	2.7
1978																
1st quarter	370.8	79.2	43.3	22.2	11.8	170.5	6.3	5.9	31.0	44.0	43.1	40.2	118.5	68.3	10.8	2.6
2nd quarter	405.0	88.6	47.9	23.7	14.7	185.9	7.3	6.3	33.7	46.5	48.4	43.7	127.8	71.5	12.6	2.7
3rd quarter	423.9	95.8	52.4	24.7	16.4	192.3	8.0	6.8	35.3	49.0	48.3	45.0	133.0	75.1	13.8	2.8
4th quarter	441.2	102.0	55.2	25.9	18.8	200.2	8.7	7.4	36.7	50.2	49.6	47.7	136.2	76.3	14.1	2.9
1979																
1st quarter	454.6	104.8	57.5	26.2	18.9	211.3	9.3	7.9	38.3	53.7	54.1	48.0	135.6	73.8	14.6	2.9
2nd quarter	463.5	110.0	63.6	27.2	16.7	212.7	9.8	8.4	38.5	54.6	52.5	48.9	137.7	72.8	16.5	3.1
3rd quarter	483.8	119.1	68.7	28.3	19.3	221.1	10.4	8.9	40.2	56.0	55.4	50.3	140.2	73.3	17.9	3.3
4th quarter	488.7	125.7	73.2	28.4	21.2	221.8	11.1	9.5	42.1	59.1	52.6	47.4	137.9	69.3	19.0	3.3
1980																
1st quarter	494.4	130.3	75.3	29.7	22.4	229.5	10.9	9.9	45.1	60.0	51.7	51.9	131.2	60.7	18.9	3.4
2nd quarter	460.5	129.8	73.5	30.1	23.4	219.5	11.9	10.3	45.4	59.5	45.6	46.8	107.9	46.5	16.2	3.3
3rd quarter	475.5	133.6	71.6	30.2	29.3	226.0	13.5	10.9	47.3	59.7	48.1	46.5	112.5	47.2	15.2	3.4
4th quarter	506.4	141.9	74.3	30.9	34.4	233.2	13.8	11.5	47.9	62.5	48.1	49.4	127.9	57.5	16.6	3.5
1981																
1st quarter	523.7	147.5	81.2	32.4	31.5	244.2	15.4	12.1	50.1	63.9	50.5	52.3	128.4	59.6	18.7	3.6
2nd quarter	537.7	158.3	84.4	32.7	38.5	250.6	15.9	12.5	52.1	64.6	50.0	55.5	125.3	56.6	18.5	3.6
3rd quarter	546.8	166.8	89.1	33.4	41.2	259.8	17.2	13.1	53.4	66.0	52.0	58.0	116.5	49.7	17.0	3.7
4th quarter	555.9	185.7	90.3	33.6	58.6	260.6	20.0	14.0	53.7	66.4	49.8	56.7	105.9	42.3	15.7	3.7
1982																
1st quarter	546.7	183.8	92.6	34.0	54.1	258.1	20.8	15.1	55.0	64.3	49.5	53.3	101.2	39.0	15.6	3.6
2nd quarter	533.4	179.6	95.1	33.2	48.1	251.0	18.1	15.5	54.5	63.7	46.8	52.3	99.1	38.9	14.9	3.7
3rd quarter	520.5	170.4	94.9	32.1	40.1	247.8	18.3	15.6	55.0	62.0	43.9	53.0	98.6	39.6	15.5	3.7
4th quarter	523.3	166.2	95.3	30.8	36.7	244.3	18.2	15.4	53.8	59.2	47.1	50.5	109.0	48.3	16.2	3.8
1983																
1st quarter	530.8	156.7	90.2	28.8	34.2	243.2	21.3	16.3	55.2	56.4	47.2	46.7	126.9	59.1	18.8	4.0
2nd quarter	551.4	147.8	86.7	29.2	28.2	255.3	23.3	17.3	57.5	56.9	49.6	50.8	144.1	70.3	21.2	4.1
3rd quarter	582.2	151.0	92.2	26.9	28.4	268.6	25.2	18.7	58.1	59.3	55.1	52.2	158.2	78.7	23.7	4.3
4th quarter	615.6	155.5	92.9	30.1	29.2	291.6	25.8	19.6	64.7	61.1	63.1	57.3	164.1	80.7	26.1	4.5
1984																
1st quarter	636.3	164.5	101.5	29.0	30.5	296.2	27.7	20.4	64.0	64.8	60.8	58.5	171.0	85.1	26.8	4.6
2nd quarter	666.6	174.4	109.5	30.1	30.6	310.8	30.1	21.3	67.9	67.0	64.8	59.7	176.7	87.9	27.2	4.7
3rd quarter	681.9	181.0	112.6	30.9	32.3	320.1	32.9	22.6	68.7	68.4	66.5	61.1	176.1	85.5	29.4	4.7
4th quarter	695.7	184.2	116.4	30.1	31.7	330.2	35.7	23.9	71.4	70.4	67.2	61.5	176.5	83.9	29.4	4.8
1985																
1st quarter	704.9	193.5	123.7	30.9	32.3	328.0	33.3	24.8	71.2	69.7	67.1	61.8	178.5	86.1	29.1	4.9
2nd quarter	712.6	194.1	128.2	30.7	28.1	335.7	35.0	25.6	71.3	72.1	69.6	62.1	177.8	83.8	28.5	5.0
3rd quarter	711.4	191.0	128.5	30.2	25.9	332.8	32.4	25.7	71.0	71.4	71.4	60.8	182.6	85.7	28.4	5.1
4th quarter	729.2	194.6	131.5	30.4	25.4	340.7	34.2	26.4	72.4	74.5	70.7	62.5	188.6	88.9	28.2	5.3
1986																
1st quarter	733.6	190.9	128.3	31.7	23.4	338.2	33.7	26.8	73.0	74.1	68.1	62.4	199.2	94.0	29.9	5.4
2nd quarter	738.5	173.9	121.9	32.1	14.6	346.3	34.3	27.6	75.0	74.0	72.0	63.3	212.9	100.1	32.2	5.4
3rd quarter	740.6	168.3	120.1	31.2	12.2	348.3	32.3	28.0	77.0	75.6	74.0	61.4	218.5	106.7	31.2	5.6
4th quarter	749.8	170.1	122.8	29.7	12.6	354.2	33.3	28.6	80.5	75.5	73.0	63.3	219.9	107.8	30.9	5.6
1987																
1st quarter	734.6	165.4	120.5	27.6	11.8	343.9	35.0	29.6	73.8	75.3	67.3	63.0	219.7	110.9	27.7	5.6
2nd quarter	749.9	167.3	123.1	26.3	11.1	353.3	35.1	30.7	74.0	75.1	73.6	64.8	223.5	114.0	25.5	5.7
3rd quarter	764.3	175.3	128.7	26.0	13.8	361.6	36.3	32.0	76.0	76.4	72.6	68.2	221.5	115.6	24.1	5.9
4th quarter	768.5	180.3	131.8	26.0	15.5	359.8	36.7	33.2	75.5	77.4	68.3	68.8	222.4	117.3	24.6	6.0
1988																
1st quarter	780.7	177.5	130.9	25.8	15.3	373.6	36.6	34.5	78.5	78.8	74.9	70.3	223.7	114.5	23.1	5.9
2nd quarter	799.5	182.8	135.0	25.8	16.5	383.5	37.7	35.9	80.9	82.5	75.7	70.7	227.2	116.1	21.7	6.1
3rd quarter	807.5	182.3	134.2	27.1	15.8	389.5	38.6	37.5	81.7	85.2	74.8	71.7	229.6	116.2	21.9	6.1
4th quarter	822.9	184.0	135.3	27.7	15.3	400.5	38.9	39.1	83.5	87.4	78.9	72.7	232.2	119.8	22.4	6.2
1989																
1st quarter	833.0	189.0	140.2	29.4	13.6	406.9	41.0	40.9	82.9	90.9	72.0	79.2	230.8	121.3	22.6	6.2
2nd quarter	839.4	189.0	138.3	29.7	14.9	418.1	43.7	43.2	85.3	92.4	71.9	81.6	226.1	117.7	23.1	6.2
3rd quarter	858.4	197.6	146.5	29.3	15.6	430.6	44.3	45.7	86.8	94.7	73.1	86.0	224.2	114.5	22.8	6.1
4th quarter	850.1	197.9	145.7	29.7	15.5	424.4	43.3	47.7	86.9	92.9	68.3	85.2	221.6	114.2	20.7	6.2
1990																
1st quarter	867.7	203.7	151.6	27.5	17.0	429.9	40.9	48.4	88.4	93.3	74.2	84.7	227.9	120.2	20.0	6.2
2nd quarter	849.3	204.2	151.7	27.7	17.8	420.9	38.6	49.6	87.0	90.5	71.5	83.7	218.2	113.5	19.5	6.1
3rd quarter	847.6	205.2	151.5	28.5	18.0	430.2	36.6	50.5	86.8	92.1	79.1	85.2	206.2	104.7	19.2	5.9
4th quarter	824.2	197.0	141.6	29.7	18.9	430.2	38.5	52.2	86.9	90.1	78.1	84.4	191.1	96.6	18.3	5.9

1. New computers and peripheral equipment.
2. Includes other structures, not shown separately.

Table 22-6. Gross Real Private Fixed Investment by Type

(Billions of chained [1996] dollars, quarterly data are at seasonally adjusted annual rates.)

Year and quarter	Total	Nonresidential											Residential			
		Structures				Equipment and software							Structures			
		Total	Nonresidential buildings, incl. farm	Utilities	Mining exploration, shafts and wells	Total	Information processing equipment and software			Industrial equipment	Transportation equipment	Other	Total 2	Single family	Multi-family	Equipment
							Computers 1	Software	Other							
1987	856.0	224.3	162.6	34.9	18.6	360.0	10.3	27.9	78.0	99.9	88.0	83.8	284.7	149.5	29.3	6.1
1988	887.1	227.1	166.5	33.6	20.4	386.9	11.8	32.4	83.5	104.9	93.6	87.7	283.0	146.9	25.0	6.3
1989	911.2	232.7	171.4	35.4	18.4	414.0	14.4	40.1	86.8	112.4	84.9	98.1	271.0	142.0	24.9	6.4
1990	894.6	236.1	173.6	33.0	21.3	415.7	14.2	45.9	87.6	105.8	87.4	96.2	247.3	128.6	21.7	6.2
1987																
1st quarter	837.2	217.3	157.4	36.7	16.3	348.1	9.4	26.4	77.2	100.1	84.0	80.1	285.5	146.6	31.8	6.0
2nd quarter	853.1	219.0	159.5	34.9	15.9	358.8	10.1	27.4	77.3	98.9	91.9	82.0	288.3	149.4	29.3	6.0
3rd quarter	868.0	228.3	165.5	34.3	20.0	368.7	10.9	28.5	79.4	100.5	90.7	86.3	283.2	150.6	27.8	6.2
4th quarter	865.6	232.5	168.0	33.8	22.1	364.3	11.0	29.4	78.0	100.1	85.5	86.6	281.8	151.4	28.2	6.3
1988																
1st quarter	871.5	225.4	164.7	33.4	20.6	376.0	11.1	30.4	80.4	100.6	93.8	87.6	280.9	145.5	26.0	6.2
2nd quarter	886.7	229.6	168.7	32.7	21.4	384.7	11.7	31.6	83.5	103.9	93.8	87.3	282.7	146.9	24.4	6.3
3rd quarter	891.2	226.9	166.4	34.0	20.2	390.1	12.1	33.0	84.5	107.1	91.6	88.0	283.9	146.1	24.5	6.4
4th quarter	899.2	226.6	166.2	34.2	19.3	397.0	12.3	34.5	85.5	108.0	95.2	87.9	284.4	149.1	25.0	6.4
1989																
1st quarter	905.5	230.8	170.8	36.0	16.9	402.4	13.1	36.5	84.4	111.5	86.8	95.0	280.7	149.4	25.3	6.4
2nd quarter	906.7	228.0	166.5	35.8	18.5	413.2	14.5	38.8	86.5	112.8	85.9	97.1	271.5	142.8	25.7	6.4
3rd quarter	923.3	236.7	175.3	34.8	19.2	424.1	14.9	41.4	88.2	114.4	87.0	101.1	268.3	138.4	25.5	6.3
4th quarter	909.3	235.2	173.1	35.0	19.0	416.3	15.0	43.5	88.0	110.9	79.8	99.2	263.6	137.4	23.3	6.4
1990																
1st quarter	922.8	240.0	178.2	32.2	20.9	420.3	14.8	44.2	88.8	109.7	86.4	97.4	268.8	143.0	22.6	6.4
2nd quarter	900.3	238.9	177.2	32.3	21.5	411.1	14.2	45.4	87.6	105.5	83.2	96.0	256.3	134.4	22.1	6.2
3rd quarter	892.7	238.2	175.6	33.1	21.2	417.4	13.4	46.2	87.1	106.0	91.3	96.7	241.1	123.2	21.6	6.1
4th quarter	862.7	227.3	163.5	34.4	21.6	413.9	14.3	47.6	86.9	102.2	88.5	94.7	223.1	113.8	20.6	6.0

1. New computers and peripheral equipment.
2. Includes other structures, not shown separately.

Table 22-7. Federal Government Current Receipts and Expenditures

(Calendar years; billions of dollars, quarterly data are at seasonally adjusted annual rates.)

Year and quarter	Current receipts					Current expenditures						Current surplus or deficit (-), national income and product accounts		
	Total	Personal tax and nontax receipts	Corporate profits tax accruals	Indirect business tax and nontax accruals	Contributions for social insurance	Total	Consumption expenditures	Transfer payments (net)	Grants-in-aid to state and local governments	Net interest paid	Subsidies less surplus of government enterprises	Total	Social insurance funds	Other
1963	110.2	49.2	24.6	15.4	21.0	105.0	62.4	26.7	5.6	7.7	2.5	5.2	1.1	4.1
1964	110.2	46.0	26.1	16.3	21.7	109.3	64.2	27.2	6.5	8.4	3.0	0.8	1.5	-0.7
1965	119.3	51.1	28.9	16.6	22.7	116.1	67.4	29.3	7.2	8.9	3.3	3.2	0.8	2.4
1966	136.3	58.7	31.4	15.7	30.5	133.6	77.2	32.0	10.1	9.8	4.5	2.7	6.4	-3.6
1967	144.9	64.4	30.0	16.5	34.0	153.2	88.3	38.3	11.7	10.5	4.4	-8.3	4.9	-13.2
1968	168.5	76.5	36.1	18.2	37.8	169.8	97.0	43.5	12.7	12.1	4.5	-1.3	3.8	-5.1
1969	190.1	91.8	36.1	19.2	43.1	180.5	100.0	47.4	14.6	13.6	5.0	9.6	6.2	3.4
1970	184.3	88.9	30.6	19.5	45.3	198.6	100.4	57.4	19.3	15.3	6.2	-14.4	1.6	-16.0
1971	189.8	85.9	33.5	20.5	50.0	216.6	103.7	68.2	23.2	15.3	6.3	-26.8	-2.3	-24.5
1972	217.5	102.9	36.6	20.1	57.9	240.0	109.9	75.1	31.7	16.1	7.7	-22.5	0.1	-22.6
1973	248.5	109.7	43.3	21.5	74.0	259.7	111.6	86.4	34.8	19.9	7.0	-11.2	6.9	-18.1
1974	277.3	126.6	45.1	22.1	83.5	291.2	120.4	106.2	36.3	22.9	5.0	-13.9	4.0	-17.8
1975	276.1	120.9	43.6	24.2	87.5	345.4	131.2	135.6	45.1	25.6	7.9	-69.3	-15.4	-53.9
1976	318.9	141.4	54.6	23.8	99.1	371.9	138.0	146.3	50.7	29.9	7.1	-53.0	-14.4	-38.6
1977	359.9	162.3	61.6	25.6	110.3	405.0	151.3	155.0	56.6	32.5	9.8	-45.2	-12.6	-32.5
1978	417.3	189.1	71.4	28.9	127.9	444.2	164.3	165.3	65.5	38.5	10.7	-26.9	-3.0	-24.0
1979	478.5	224.8	74.4	30.1	148.9	489.6	180.0	185.9	66.3	47.0	10.3	-11.4	1.8	-13.2
1980	522.8	250.2	70.3	39.7	162.6	576.6	209.0	223.8	72.3	58.5	12.9	-53.8	-13.8	-40.0
1981	605.6	290.8	65.7	57.3	191.8	659.3	239.9	254.7	72.5	79.1	13.3	-53.7	-12.4	-41.3
1982	599.5	295.7	49.0	49.9	204.9	732.1	265.3	287.3	69.5	93.9	16.1	-132.6	-32.5	-100.1
1983	623.9	287.2	61.3	53.5	221.8	797.8	288.0	309.5	71.6	104.6	23.7	-173.9	-35.4	-138.5
1984	688.1	302.5	75.2	57.6	252.8	856.1	312.0	316.2	76.7	127.5	24.0	-168.1	-5.4	-162.7
1985	747.4	337.2	76.3	57.5	276.5	924.6	339.0	336.9	80.9	144.4	23.3	-177.1	2.6	-179.7
1986	786.4	351.4	83.8	53.7	297.5	978.5	358.3	356.0	87.6	150.5	26.1	-192.1	7.7	-199.9
1987	870.5	394.5	103.2	56.8	315.9	1 018.4	374.6	367.2	83.9	159.8	32.9	-147.9	16.4	-164.3
1988	928.9	405.7	111.1	58.9	353.1	1 066.2	382.8	387.9	91.6	172.1	31.9	-137.4	41.2	-178.6
1989	1 010.3	454.6	117.2	62.3	376.3	1 140.3	399.6	420.1	98.3	193.5	28.7	-130.0	45.6	-175.6
1990	1 055.7	473.6	118.1	63.9	400.1	1 228.7	419.9	455.3	111.4	210.5	31.6	-173.0	44.9	-217.9
1963														
1st quarter	107.6	48.9	22.9	15.0	20.7	103.6	61.4	27.1	5.3	7.5	2.3	4.0	0.1	3.9
2nd quarter	109.8	49.1	24.5	15.4	20.9	103.7	61.9	26.2	5.5	7.6	2.5	6.2	1.4	4.8
3rd quarter	110.9	49.2	25.2	15.4	21.1	105.2	62.6	26.4	5.8	7.8	2.6	5.7	1.4	4.3
4th quarter	112.4	49.7	25.8	15.6	21.4	107.4	63.7	27.0	6.1	8.0	2.6	5.0	1.4	3.6
1964														
1st quarter	111.0	48.1	25.9	15.7	21.4	109.1	64.0	27.5	6.5	8.2	2.9	1.9	0.8	1.1
2nd quarter	107.3	43.8	26.0	16.0	21.6	110.1	65.0	27.1	6.5	8.3	3.1	-2.7	1.6	-4.3
3rd quarter	110.3	45.4	26.5	16.5	21.8	109.1	64.3	27.1	6.2	8.4	3.2	1.1	1.8	-0.6
4th quarter	112.0	46.9	26.1	17.0	22.0	108.9	63.3	27.3	6.6	8.8	2.8	3.1	2.0	1.1
1965														
1st quarter	117.7	50.6	27.5	17.5	22.2	110.3	63.8	28.1	6.5	8.6	3.2	7.4	1.1	6.3
2nd quarter	119.6	51.9	28.4	16.8	22.4	112.9	65.8	28.0	7.1	8.8	3.2	6.6	2.2	4.5
3rd quarter	118.0	50.4	28.9	15.9	22.8	118.6	67.8	31.2	7.5	8.8	3.3	-0.6	-0.9	0.4
4th quarter	121.8	51.6	30.8	16.2	23.2	122.5	72.1	29.9	7.6	9.3	3.6	-0.7	0.8	-1.6
1966														
1st quarter	130.8	54.4	31.7	15.1	29.6	125.5	72.1	31.2	9.0	9.2	4.0	5.3	6.7	-1.4
2nd quarter	135.7	58.0	31.7	15.9	30.0	131.4	76.8	30.4	10.1	9.6	4.5	4.3	7.0	-2.7
3rd quarter	138.2	59.9	31.4	15.8	31.1	136.6	79.5	31.8	10.5	9.9	4.8	1.6	6.7	-5.0
4th quarter	140.6	62.2	30.9	16.2	31.4	140.9	80.4	34.7	10.7	10.3	4.9	-0.3	5.0	-5.3
1967														
1st quarter	141.5	62.9	29.7	16.1	32.8	150.3	86.7	37.4	11.1	10.5	4.6	-8.8	4.3	-13.1
2nd quarter	142.2	62.7	29.4	16.4	33.7	151.5	87.5	37.8	11.6	10.2	4.4	-9.3	4.9	-14.2
3rd quarter	145.7	65.2	29.6	16.5	34.4	153.2	88.1	38.9	11.6	10.4	4.2	-7.5	5.0	-12.4
4th quarter	150.2	67.0	31.4	16.8	35.1	157.9	90.9	38.9	12.7	10.9	4.5	-7.7	5.4	-13.1
1968														
1st quarter	158.3	68.9	35.2	17.5	36.7	163.1	95.1	40.5	11.8	11.3	4.4	-4.8	5.4	-10.2
2nd quarter	162.9	71.4	35.9	18.1	37.5	169.4	96.2	43.4	13.3	12.0	4.5	-6.5	3.6	-10.0
3rd quarter	173.8	81.1	36.1	18.6	38.1	171.4	97.5	44.6	12.6	12.3	4.5	2.4	3.3	-0.9
4th quarter	178.9	84.5	37.0	18.7	38.7	175.2	99.2	45.6	13.2	12.7	4.6	3.7	3.1	0.6
1969														
1st quarter	188.7	90.8	37.4	18.6	41.9	173.8	96.8	46.1	13.1	13.0	4.8	14.9	5.5	9.5
2nd quarter	191.7	93.4	36.5	19.2	42.7	179.4	99.5	47.5	14.0	13.4	4.9	12.3	5.9	6.5
3rd quarter	189.3	90.8	35.3	19.6	43.6	182.6	101.3	47.5	15.1	13.7	5.1	6.7	6.6	0.1
4th quarter	190.6	92.0	35.1	19.3	44.2	186.1	102.3	48.4	16.1	14.5	5.0	4.5	6.9	-2.4
1970														
1st quarter	185.2	90.6	30.4	19.2	44.9	186.9	101.5	49.8	17.5	14.9	5.7	-1.8	7.2	-8.9
2nd quarter	186.7	91.5	30.5	19.5	45.2	201.4	99.8	59.1	18.8	15.1	6.4	-14.7	-0.7	-14.0
3rd quarter	183.0	86.4	31.5	19.5	45.6	201.6	100.3	58.8	20.1	15.7	6.2	-18.5	1.1	-19.6
4th quarter	182.2	87.2	30.1	19.5	45.4	204.7	99.9	61.8	20.8	15.6	6.6	-22.4	-1.1	-21.3
1971														
1st quarter	187.2	83.7	33.3	20.8	49.3	208.8	102.4	62.8	21.6	15.5	6.6	-21.6	2.0	-23.6
2nd quarter	189.2	85.2	33.9	20.2	49.9	217.6	103.5	69.9	23.2	15.0	6.0	-28.4	-4.4	-24.0
3rd quarter	190.0	86.4	33.1	20.4	50.1	218.5	104.1	69.5	23.5	15.4	6.1	-28.6	-3.3	-25.2
4th quarter	192.9	88.3	33.5	20.5	50.7	221.5	104.7	70.5	24.7	15.5	6.3	-28.6	-3.5	-25.1
1972														
1st quarter	212.0	100.4	35.0	19.8	56.9	231.2	110.2	72.6	25.7	15.7	7.0	-19.2	0.9	-20.1
2nd quarter	215.1	102.5	35.2	19.9	57.5	241.1	111.3	72.4	33.9	15.9	7.4	-26.0	1.6	-27.6
3rd quarter	217.8	103.2	36.3	20.2	58.2	232.2	108.4	72.7	26.8	16.0	8.4	-14.4	2.5	-16.9
4th quarter	225.0	105.5	39.9	20.6	59.0	255.4	109.9	82.6	40.4	16.6	7.9	-30.4	-4.6	-25.8
1973														
1st quarter	241.2	104.7	43.1	21.3	72.2	255.8	111.3	83.6	35.6	18.1	7.2	-14.6	7.2	-21.7
2nd quarter	245.5	107.0	43.5	21.8	73.3	259.4	112.1	86.0	34.7	19.4	7.2	-13.9	6.9	-20.8
3rd quarter	249.1	111.1	42.2	21.2	74.5	258.5	110.5	86.9	33.9	20.7	6.6	-9.5	7.0	-16.4
4th quarter	258.1	116.1	44.3	21.7	76.0	265.0	112.6	89.1	34.9	21.5	7.0	-6.9	6.7	-13.6

Table 22-7. Federal Government Current Receipts and Expenditures—*Continued*

(Calendar years; billions of dollars, quarterly data are at seasonally adjusted annual rates.)

Year and quarter	Current receipts					Current expenditures						Current surplus or deficit (-), national income and product accounts		
	Total	Personal tax and nontax receipts	Corporate profits tax accruals	Indirect business tax and nontax accruals	Contributions for social insurance	Total	Consumption expenditures	Transfer payments (net)	Grants-in-aid to state and local governments	Net interest paid	Subsidies less surplus of government enterprises	Total	Social insurance funds	Other
1974														
1st quarter	265.3	119.6	42.5	21.6	81.5	274.4	116.7	96.4	34.6	21.7	4.9	-9.1	9.8	-18.9
2nd quarter	274.8	124.9	44.8	22.1	83.1	284.1	117.3	104.1	35.4	22.4	4.3	-9.3	5.0	-14.2
3rd quarter	286.2	129.9	49.3	22.3	84.7	297.3	121.3	109.2	36.8	23.5	5.0	-11.1	2.6	-13.7
4th quarter	283.0	132.1	43.8	22.3	84.8	308.9	126.2	115.1	38.2	23.9	5.6	-25.9	-1.4	-24.5
1975														
1st quarter	277.0	132.4	36.9	21.9	85.9	324.0	127.9	124.1	40.7	24.2	7.2	-47.0	-8.3	-38.7
2nd quarter	243.9	94.7	39.5	23.4	86.2	346.2	130.3	137.8	45.8	24.8	7.5	-102.3	-14.2	-88.1
3rd quarter	287.5	125.8	48.4	25.4	87.9	351.2	131.3	139.4	46.5	25.9	8.3	-63.7	-20.3	-43.3
4th quarter	295.9	130.5	49.4	26.1	89.9	360.1	135.2	141.1	47.5	27.6	8.8	-64.2	-18.6	-45.6
1976														
1st quarter	308.5	132.8	55.7	23.1	96.9	362.3	135.0	143.2	48.7	28.6	6.9	-53.8	-13.8	-40.0
2nd quarter	315.3	138.5	54.8	23.7	98.3	364.6	137.3	141.8	49.5	29.4	6.8	-49.3	-11.2	-38.1
3rd quarter	322.7	144.3	54.4	24.1	100.0	375.7	137.6	150.6	50.4	30.1	7.1	-53.0	-16.0	-36.9
4th quarter	328.9	149.9	53.4	24.2	101.4	385.0	142.1	149.4	54.4	31.6	7.5	-56.1	-16.6	-39.5
1977														
1st quarter	343.3	155.1	56.9	24.5	106.8	389.6	145.8	152.1	52.5	31.2	8.1	-46.3	-13.2	-33.1
2nd quarter	357.1	160.8	61.7	25.2	109.4	397.5	150.0	151.9	55.5	31.8	8.3	-40.4	-10.9	-29.5
3rd quarter	364.0	162.4	63.8	26.3	111.5	410.2	152.1	157.4	59.1	32.4	9.3	-46.2	-13.5	-32.7
4th quarter	375.1	171.0	64.0	26.4	113.6	422.8	157.3	158.5	59.2	34.5	13.4	-47.7	-12.9	-34.8
1978														
1st quarter	384.4	173.3	60.8	27.3	123.0	431.6	159.3	161.2	63.5	36.1	11.5	-47.2	-4.1	-43.1
2nd quarter	411.3	182.9	72.9	28.9	126.7	437.3	162.9	160.8	66.1	37.2	10.5	-26.0	0.0	-26.0
3rd quarter	427.6	195.3	73.9	29.2	129.2	447.4	165.0	168.4	65.5	39.3	9.4	-19.8	-4.7	-15.2
4th quarter	445.8	205.0	78.0	30.2	132.5	460.5	169.8	170.8	67.1	41.5	11.3	-14.7	-3.1	-11.5
1979														
1st quarter	461.1	211.5	75.1	29.9	144.6	467.6	173.9	175.3	64.4	44.2	9.6	-6.5	6.1	-12.6
2nd quarter	472.7	219.9	75.4	30.2	147.1	478.9	178.7	178.7	65.0	46.2	10.3	-6.2	6.2	-12.4
3rd quarter	484.4	229.4	74.7	29.9	150.4	496.4	178.1	193.0	67.6	47.4	10.3	-12.1	-2.4	-9.7
4th quarter	494.9	238.5	72.5	30.5	153.3	515.6	189.2	196.7	68.4	50.2	11.1	-20.8	-2.6	-18.1
1980														
1st quarter	508.9	237.9	78.7	32.8	159.5	539.3	196.9	206.2	69.3	55.4	11.6	-30.4	-0.6	-29.9
2nd quarter	505.3	243.8	62.1	39.1	160.4	560.0	208.5	209.2	70.8	59.1	12.5	-54.7	-5.9	-48.9
3rd quarter	524.1	252.4	67.1	41.9	162.7	593.2	210.0	237.9	73.4	58.3	13.6	-69.0	-26.0	-43.1
4th quarter	552.9	266.9	73.4	44.8	167.8	613.7	220.6	241.9	75.8	61.4	13.9	-60.8	-22.7	-38.1
1981														
1st quarter	595.4	278.0	71.9	57.8	187.7	634.8	229.8	243.6	74.4	73.4	13.7	-39.4	-5.9	-33.5
2nd quarter	601.8	288.7	64.1	58.8	190.2	646.1	238.9	244.9	74.5	75.9	12.0	-44.3	-4.9	-39.4
3rd quarter	618.5	301.1	67.2	56.6	193.7	670.3	240.1	263.9	71.9	80.8	13.9	-51.8	-18.5	-33.3
4th quarter	606.8	295.6	59.6	55.9	195.8	686.0	250.8	266.4	69.2	86.1	13.6	-79.2	-20.2	-59.0
1982														
1st quarter	599.2	295.2	48.9	52.0	203.1	700.2	257.1	270.9	68.8	89.1	14.1	-101.0	-17.8	-83.2
2nd quarter	605.4	301.7	50.4	49.0	204.4	712.8	258.3	276.7	70.4	92.6	14.9	-107.4	-24.2	-83.2
3rd quarter	595.8	289.9	50.9	49.2	205.9	740.5	267.4	292.0	69.0	96.8	15.4	-144.7	-37.4	-107.3
4th quarter	597.6	296.0	46.0	49.5	206.1	774.8	278.4	309.6	69.8	97.1	19.9	-177.2	-50.5	-126.6
1983														
1st quarter	603.7	289.9	47.5	49.9	216.4	777.7	281.8	306.4	70.6	97.9	20.9	-173.9	-40.3	-133.6
2nd quarter	629.4	295.7	59.9	54.2	219.6	800.4	288.6	312.3	72.7	101.5	24.1	-170.9	-42.5	-128.4
3rd quarter	623.4	277.8	68.0	54.5	223.0	809.2	297.9	307.0	71.8	107.2	24.9	-185.8	-31.5	-154.3
4th quarter	639.0	285.4	70.0	55.3	228.3	803.9	283.9	312.5	71.2	111.7	24.7	-164.9	-27.4	-137.5
1984														
1st quarter	672.8	288.4	80.7	57.2	246.4	829.9	299.3	310.1	75.4	117.8	27.4	-157.1	-9.7	-147.4
2nd quarter	683.6	295.2	79.4	57.9	251.2	847.2	312.6	312.2	77.4	121.7	23.4	-163.6	-5.8	-157.8
3rd quarter	690.9	307.9	70.0	57.8	255.2	860.9	315.2	315.9	75.1	132.2	22.4	-170.0	-1.9	-168.1
4th quarter	705.0	318.3	70.8	57.5	258.4	886.5	320.8	326.6	78.8	138.1	22.7	-181.5	-4.2	-177.4
1985														
1st quarter	756.7	353.7	75.5	56.7	270.8	904.5	330.4	331.8	79.1	140.8	22.5	-147.8	-0.2	-147.5
2nd quarter	717.9	308.3	74.1	61.4	274.1	917.4	335.0	334.2	80.0	144.7	22.3	-199.5	2.0	-201.4
3rd quarter	754.0	340.8	78.5	56.7	277.9	930.9	342.4	339.7	81.2	144.1	23.5	-177.0	2.1	-179.1
4th quarter	761.2	346.0	76.9	55.2	283.1	945.5	348.1	341.7	83.1	147.8	24.8	-184.3	6.4	-190.8
1986														
1st quarter	771.7	342.4	82.2	54.6	292.5	954.0	347.5	346.9	84.8	149.6	25.2	-182.3	7.9	-190.2
2nd quarter	774.3	345.1	81.2	53.1	294.9	978.4	357.0	355.1	89.0	151.2	26.1	-204.1	7.3	-211.4
3rd quarter	786.3	352.7	81.8	52.9	298.9	994.5	365.7	361.3	91.8	149.2	26.5	-208.2	5.9	-214.0
4th quarter	813.2	365.3	90.1	54.2	303.6	987.2	362.9	360.8	84.9	152.1	26.6	-174.0	9.9	-183.8
1987														
1st quarter	815.4	359.6	91.1	55.1	309.6	997.9	369.8	361.8	82.1	153.9	30.2	-182.5	12.4	-194.8
2nd quarter	884.9	411.6	102.5	57.6	313.3	1 013.7	372.9	366.3	85.8	155.9	32.9	-128.8	12.8	-141.6
3rd quarter	880.5	396.7	109.3	56.9	317.7	1 017.2	372.7	366.7	83.9	160.4	33.7	-136.7	17.4	-154.1
4th quarter	901.1	410.4	109.9	57.8	323.1	1 044.7	383.1	373.8	83.8	168.9	34.8	-143.6	22.8	-166.4
1988														
1st quarter	908.8	404.2	102.3	58.2	344.0	1 056.2	381.8	384.3	89.5	165.0	35.5	-147.4	31.7	-179.2
2nd quarter	920.6	402.5	109.5	57.8	350.8	1 055.0	380.2	383.1	90.0	170.7	30.9	-134.4	39.4	-173.8
3rd quarter	933.5	404.5	113.6	59.5	355.9	1 064.3	377.3	387.7	93.1	174.9	31.3	-130.7	44.0	-174.7
4th quarter	952.6	411.6	119.1	60.2	361.7	1 089.5	391.8	396.3	93.8	177.7	30.0	-136.9	49.7	-186.6
1989														
1st quarter	1 000.9	440.9	126.7	62.2	371.1	1 109.7	389.4	408.3	94.9	187.7	29.4	-108.9	46.7	-155.6
2nd quarter	1 004.3	449.9	119.2	61.3	374.0	1 131.7	400.9	413.0	95.6	193.5	28.7	-127.4	46.1	-173.5
3rd quarter	1 009.8	458.6	110.3	63.4	377.4	1 150.3	403.3	423.9	101.4	193.4	28.4	-140.5	44.3	-184.9
4th quarter	1 026.3	469.0	112.7	62.0	382.6	1 169.6	404.8	435.4	101.4	199.5	28.6	-143.3	45.0	-188.3
1990														
1st quarter	1 033.7	464.5	112.2	62.4	394.5	1 205.7	415.5	448.5	106.5	204.7	30.5	-172.0	43.0	-215.0
2nd quarter	1 053.5	473.5	118.5	63.0	398.5	1 224.5	418.2	454.5	110.3	210.0	31.6	-171.0	46.8	-217.8
3rd quarter	1 070.9	478.6	124.4	64.1	403.9	1 235.7	416.4	457.2	112.6	217.6	31.8	-164.8	48.6	-213.4
4th quarter	1 064.8	477.9	117.4	66.2	403.4	1 249.0	429.6	461.0	116.3	209.9	32.3	-184.1	41.1	-225.2

Table 22-8. State and Local Government Current Receipts and Expenditures

(Calendar years; billions of dollars, quarterly data are at seasonally adjusted annual rates.)

Year and quarter	Current receipts						Current expenditures						Surplus or deficit (-), national income and product accounts		
	Total	Personal tax and nontax receipts	Corporate profits tax accruals	Indirect business tax and nontax accruals	Contributions to social insurance	Federal grants-in-aid	Total	Consumption expenditures	Transfer payments to persons	Net interest paid	Less: dividends received by government	Subsidies less surplus of government enterprises	Total	Social insurance funds	Other
1963	53.4	6.1	1.7	39.4	0.6	5.6	47.7	42.4	5.7	1.2	...	-1.6	5.7	0.0	5.7
1964	58.4	6.8	1.8	42.6	0.7	6.5	52.0	46.3	6.2	1.2	...	-1.6	6.4	0.0	6.3
1965	63.3	7.3	2.0	46.1	0.8	7.2	56.8	50.8	6.7	1.1	...	-1.7	6.5	0.1	6.4
1966	71.5	8.7	2.2	49.7	0.8	10.1	63.8	56.8	7.6	1.0	...	-1.6	7.7	0.1	7.6
1967	78.9	9.7	2.6	53.9	0.9	11.7	71.9	63.2	9.2	1.0	...	-1.5	7.0	0.1	6.8
1968	89.5	11.8	3.3	60.8	0.9	12.7	82.1	71.1	11.4	1.0	0.0	-1.5	7.5	0.1	7.3
1969	100.7	14.1	3.6	67.4	1.0	14.6	92.8	80.2	13.2	0.8	0.0	-1.4	8.0	0.2	7.8
1970	114.6	15.7	3.7	74.8	1.1	19.3	107.5	92.0	16.1	0.9	0.0	-1.5	7.1	0.2	6.9
1971	129.3	17.5	4.3	83.1	1.2	23.2	122.9	103.4	19.3	1.7	0.0	-1.3	6.4	0.2	6.2
1972	152.3	22.8	5.3	91.2	1.3	31.7	136.7	113.8	22.0	2.3	0.0	-1.5	15.6	0.3	15.3
1973	166.6	24.7	6.0	99.5	1.5	34.8	150.9	126.9	24.1	1.3	0.0	-1.4	15.7	0.3	15.4
1974	178.5	26.7	6.7	107.2	1.7	36.3	169.2	144.5	25.3	0.2	0.0	-0.8	9.3	0.4	8.9
1975	199.6	29.5	7.3	115.8	1.8	45.1	197.2	165.4	30.8	1.3	0.0	-0.2	2.4	0.5	1.9
1976	224.5	34.1	9.6	127.8	2.2	50.7	217.2	180.1	34.1	3.2	0.0	-0.2	7.3	0.6	6.7
1977	249.5	38.8	11.4	139.9	2.8	56.6	236.4	196.5	37.0	3.0	0.0	-0.1	13.1	1.0	12.1
1978	274.3	44.3	12.1	148.9	3.4	65.5	255.6	214.3	40.8	0.8	0.1	0.0	18.7	1.5	17.2
1979	290.8	48.4	13.6	158.6	3.9	66.3	277.8	235.0	44.3	-2.2	0.1	0.6	13.0	1.8	11.3
1980	316.6	53.9	14.5	172.3	3.6	72.3	307.8	260.5	51.2	-5.4	0.1	1.6	8.8	1.3	7.5
1981	344.4	60.6	15.4	192.0	3.9	72.5	336.9	284.6	57.1	-7.5	0.1	2.8	7.5	1.3	6.2
1982	360.3	65.9	14.0	206.8	4.0	69.5	362.5	306.8	61.2	-7.3	0.2	2.1	-2.3	1.2	-3.5
1983	392.1	73.7	15.9	226.8	4.1	71.6	387.3	325.1	66.9	-5.2	0.2	0.7	4.8	1.2	3.6
1984	436.4	84.8	18.8	251.5	4.7	76.7	412.6	349.5	71.2	-6.7	0.2	-1.1	23.8	1.4	22.4
1985	469.2	91.3	20.2	272.0	4.9	80.9	447.0	380.5	77.3	-7.9	0.2	-2.8	22.3	1.3	21.0
1986	507.9	98.6	22.7	293.1	6.0	87.6	487.2	410.8	84.4	-5.5	0.2	-2.5	20.8	1.9	18.9
1987	536.0	108.5	23.9	312.4	7.2	83.9	523.8	439.0	90.8	-3.1	0.2	-2.8	12.2	2.2	10.0
1988	573.7	114.0	26.0	333.7	8.4	91.6	558.1	467.9	98.6	-3.8	0.2	-4.5	15.6	2.5	13.1
1989	618.9	128.9	24.2	358.5	9.0	98.3	599.6	503.0	109.5	-6.6	0.2	-6.1	19.3	2.3	17.0
1990	663.4	136.0	22.5	383.4	10.0	111.4	660.8	545.8	127.8	-6.3	0.2	-6.3	2.6	2.0	0.7
1963															
1st quarter	51.5	5.9	1.5	38.2	0.6	5.3	46.2	41.1	5.6	1.1	...	-1.6	5.3	0.0	5.3
2nd quarter	52.6	5.9	1.6	38.9	0.6	5.5	47.1	42.0	5.7	1.1	...	-1.6	5.5	0.0	5.4
3rd quarter	54.1	6.1	1.7	39.8	0.6	5.8	48.1	42.8	5.7	1.2	...	-1.6	6.0	0.0	6.0
4th quarter	55.2	6.3	1.7	40.5	0.7	6.1	49.3	43.8	5.8	1.3	...	-1.6	5.9	0.0	5.9
1964															
1st quarter	56.9	6.5	1.8	41.4	0.7	6.5	50.5	44.9	6.0	1.2	...	-1.6	6.3	0.0	6.3
2nd quarter	57.8	6.7	1.8	42.1	0.7	6.5	51.6	45.8	6.1	1.2	...	-1.6	6.3	0.0	6.2
3rd quarter	58.8	6.9	1.9	43.2	0.7	6.2	52.4	46.7	6.2	1.1	...	-1.7	6.5	0.1	6.4
4th quarter	59.9	7.1	1.8	43.7	0.7	6.6	53.5	47.8	6.4	1.1	...	-1.7	6.4	0.1	6.3
1965															
1st quarter	60.9	7.2	1.9	44.6	0.7	6.5	54.7	48.9	6.5	1.1	...	-1.7	6.2	0.1	6.1
2nd quarter	62.5	7.2	1.9	45.5	0.8	7.1	56.0	50.1	6.6	1.1	...	-1.7	6.5	0.1	6.4
3rd quarter	64.2	7.3	2.0	46.6	0.8	7.5	57.6	51.5	6.7	1.1	...	-1.6	6.5	0.1	6.5
4th quarter	65.6	7.5	2.1	47.7	0.8	7.6	58.9	52.7	6.8	1.0	...	-1.6	6.8	0.1	6.7
1966															
1st quarter	68.4	8.0	2.3	48.4	0.8	9.0	60.8	54.3	7.0	1.0	...	-1.6	7.7	0.1	7.6
2nd quarter	70.8	8.5	2.3	49.1	0.8	10.1	62.8	55.9	7.5	1.0	...	-1.6	8.0	0.1	7.9
3rd quarter	72.7	9.0	2.2	50.2	0.8	10.5	64.7	57.6	7.7	1.0	...	-1.6	8.0	0.1	7.8
4th quarter	74.2	9.4	2.2	51.1	0.8	10.7	66.9	59.4	8.2	0.9	...	-1.6	7.3	0.1	7.2
1967															
1st quarter	75.7	9.4	2.6	51.8	0.9	11.1	68.3	60.7	8.4	0.8	...	-1.6	7.4	0.1	7.3
2nd quarter	77.2	9.4	2.6	52.8	0.9	11.6	70.4	62.2	8.9	0.9	...	-1.6	6.8	0.1	6.7
3rd quarter	79.6	9.8	2.6	54.7	0.9	11.6	73.3	64.2	9.5	1.0	...	-1.4	6.4	0.1	6.2
4th quarter	83.0	10.2	2.7	56.4	0.9	12.7	75.8	66.0	10.1	1.2	...	-1.5	7.2	0.1	7.1
1968															
1st quarter	85.3	10.9	3.2	58.4	0.9	11.8	78.2	68.2	10.6	1.0	0.0	-1.6	7.1	0.1	6.9
2nd quarter	89.0	11.5	3.3	60.0	0.9	13.3	80.9	69.9	11.4	1.0	0.0	-1.5	8.1	0.1	8.0
3rd quarter	90.6	12.1	3.3	61.7	1.0	12.6	83.3	72.0	11.7	1.0	0.0	-1.5	7.4	0.1	7.2
4th quarter	93.2	12.6	3.4	63.1	1.0	13.2	86.0	74.3	12.1	1.0	0.0	-1.4	7.3	0.2	7.1
1969															
1st quarter	95.7	13.1	3.8	64.6	1.0	13.1	88.3	76.3	12.6	0.9	0.0	-1.4	7.4	0.1	7.2
2nd quarter	98.7	13.6	3.7	66.4	1.0	14.0	91.0	78.8	12.8	0.8	0.0	-1.4	7.7	0.2	7.6
3rd quarter	102.7	14.7	3.5	68.4	1.0	15.1	94.2	81.4	13.4	0.8	0.0	-1.4	8.4	0.2	8.3
4th quarter	105.8	15.0	3.4	70.2	1.1	16.1	97.6	84.2	14.0	0.8	0.0	-1.5	8.3	0.2	8.1
1970															
1st quarter	109.7	15.4	3.8	72.0	1.1	17.5	101.6	87.6	14.7	0.8	0.0	-1.5	8.1	0.2	7.9
2nd quarter	113.1	15.6	3.7	73.9	1.1	18.8	105.4	90.4	15.6	0.8	0.0	-1.5	7.7	0.2	7.5
3rd quarter	116.7	15.8	3.8	75.8	1.1	20.1	109.5	93.5	16.6	0.9	0.0	-1.5	7.1	0.2	6.9
4th quarter	118.9	15.9	3.6	77.5	1.1	20.8	113.5	96.3	17.5	1.1	0.0	-1.4	5.4	0.2	5.2
1971															
1st quarter	122.8	16.2	4.1	79.8	1.1	21.6	118.0	99.7	18.3	1.3	0.0	-1.4	4.8	0.2	4.6
2nd quarter	127.5	17.2	4.2	81.8	1.2	23.2	121.6	102.3	19.1	1.6	0.0	-1.3	5.9	0.2	5.7
3rd quarter	131.1	17.7	4.4	84.5	1.2	23.5	124.7	104.8	19.6	1.8	0.0	-1.3	6.5	0.2	6.2
4th quarter	135.8	19.0	4.5	86.4	1.2	24.7	127.3	106.7	20.3	2.0	0.0	-1.3	8.5	0.2	8.2
1972															
1st quarter	141.3	21.3	5.0	88.1	1.3	25.7	132.4	109.8	21.2	2.3	0.0	-1.4	8.9	0.2	8.7
2nd quarter	153.4	22.8	5.0	90.3	1.3	33.9	134.8	112.2	21.6	2.4	0.0	-1.5	18.6	0.3	18.3
3rd quarter	148.6	23.1	5.2	92.2	1.3	26.8	138.5	115.3	22.5	2.4	0.0	-1.6	10.1	0.3	9.9
4th quarter	165.8	23.8	5.7	94.4	1.4	40.4	141.1	118.0	22.5	2.2	0.0	-1.6	24.7	0.3	24.4
1973															
1st quarter	163.9	23.8	6.0	97.0	1.4	35.6	145.1	121.5	23.2	1.9	0.0	-1.5	18.8	0.3	18.5
2nd quarter	164.8	24.2	6.1	98.4	1.5	34.7	149.2	125.1	24.0	1.5	0.0	-1.4	15.7	0.3	15.4
3rd quarter	167.1	25.0	5.9	100.8	1.5	33.9	152.5	128.6	24.2	1.2	0.0	-1.4	14.6	0.3	14.3
4th quarter	170.4	25.9	6.1	101.9	1.6	34.9	156.7	132.3	25.0	0.8	0.0	-1.3	13.7	0.3	13.3

Table 22-8. State and Local Government Current Receipts and Expenditures—*Continued*

(Calendar years; billions of dollars, quarterly data are at seasonally adjusted annual rates.)

Year and quarter	Current receipts						Current expenditures						Surplus or deficit (-), national income and product accounts		
	Total	Personal tax and nontax receipts	Corporate profits tax accruals	Indirect business tax and nontax accruals	Contributions to social insurance	Federal grants-in-aid	Total	Consumption expenditures	Transfer payments to persons	Net interest paid	Less: dividends received by government	Subsidies less surplus of government enterprises	Total	Social insurance funds	Other
1974															
1st quarter	171.2	25.3	6.3	103.3	1.6	34.6	159.5	136.9	23.4	0.4	0.0	-1.1	11.7	0.4	11.3
2nd quarter	176.3	26.2	6.6	106.3	1.6	35.4	165.7	141.8	24.7	0.1	0.0	-0.9	10.6	0.4	10.2
3rd quarter	182.4	27.4	7.3	109.2	1.7	36.8	172.4	147.0	25.9	0.1	0.0	-0.6	10.0	0.4	9.6
4th quarter	184.3	27.9	6.5	110.0	1.7	38.2	179.4	152.4	27.1	0.3	0.0	-0.4	4.9	0.4	4.5
1975															
1st quarter	188.2	28.1	6.1	111.5	1.8	40.7	187.8	158.2	29.2	0.6	0.0	-0.2	0.5	0.4	0.0
2nd quarter	197.5	29.0	6.6	114.2	1.8	45.8	195.0	163.8	30.5	1.0	0.0	-0.2	2.5	0.5	2.0
3rd quarter	203.9	29.8	8.2	117.5	1.9	46.5	200.4	168.1	31.0	1.5	0.0	-0.2	3.6	0.5	3.1
4th quarter	208.8	30.9	8.5	119.9	2.0	47.5	205.6	171.4	32.6	2.0	0.0	-0.4	3.2	0.5	2.7
1976															
1st quarter	216.3	32.4	9.7	123.6	2.0	48.7	210.8	175.0	33.4	2.7	0.0	-0.3	5.6	0.5	5.0
2nd quarter	221.1	33.6	9.6	126.3	2.1	49.5	214.7	178.4	33.4	3.1	0.0	-0.2	6.5	0.6	5.9
3rd quarter	225.9	34.7	9.7	128.9	2.2	50.4	219.6	181.6	34.7	3.4	0.0	-0.1	6.3	0.6	5.7
4th quarter	234.7	35.9	9.6	132.5	2.3	54.4	223.7	185.3	35.0	3.5	0.0	-0.1	11.0	0.7	10.3
1977															
1st quarter	238.1	36.9	10.5	135.7	2.5	52.5	228.6	189.7	35.7	3.4	0.0	-0.1	9.5	0.8	8.7
2nd quarter	246.1	38.1	11.4	138.4	2.7	55.5	234.4	193.9	37.5	3.2	0.0	-0.1	11.7	0.9	10.8
3rd quarter	254.6	39.4	11.9	141.3	2.9	59.1	238.9	198.8	37.3	2.9	0.0	-0.1	15.7	1.1	14.7
4th quarter	259.2	40.9	11.9	144.1	3.0	59.2	243.6	203.6	37.7	2.5	0.0	-0.1	15.6	1.2	14.4
1978															
1st quarter	265.5	42.3	10.5	146.0	3.2	63.5	248.8	208.0	39.2	1.9	0.1	-0.2	16.8	1.3	15.4
2nd quarter	276.7	44.0	12.4	150.9	3.3	66.1	253.7	211.7	41.0	1.2	0.1	-0.1	23.0	1.4	21.5
3rd quarter	273.9	44.9	12.5	147.6	3.5	65.5	257.8	216.4	41.3	0.5	0.1	0.0	16.1	1.5	14.6
4th quarter	281.1	46.2	13.0	151.2	3.6	67.1	262.1	221.0	41.7	-0.2	0.1	0.1	19.0	1.7	17.3
1979															
1st quarter	282.4	46.2	13.7	154.3	3.8	64.4	268.4	227.1	42.4	-1.0	0.1	0.3	14.0	1.7	12.3
2nd quarter	285.6	46.4	13.8	156.5	3.9	65.0	273.9	230.8	43.5	-1.8	0.1	0.6	11.7	1.8	9.9
3rd quarter	294.9	49.9	13.6	159.9	3.9	67.6	280.8	238.1	44.5	-2.6	0.1	0.8	14.1	1.8	12.3
4th quarter	300.5	51.3	13.2	163.7	4.0	68.4	288.2	244.1	46.9	-3.4	0.1	0.9	12.3	1.8	10.5
1980															
1st quarter	307.3	51.3	16.1	167.0	3.6	69.3	297.1	251.2	49.1	-4.3	0.1	1.0	10.2	1.4	8.8
2nd quarter	308.3	52.9	12.7	168.9	2.9	70.8	302.9	257.8	49.0	-5.0	0.1	1.3	5.4	0.7	4.7
3rd quarter	319.7	54.5	14.0	174.0	3.8	73.4	312.0	263.7	52.4	-5.7	0.1	1.7	7.7	1.5	6.2
4th quarter	331.2	57.0	15.1	179.4	4.0	75.8	319.3	269.2	54.3	-6.4	0.1	2.2	11.9	1.6	10.3
1981															
1st quarter	339.5	58.2	16.9	186.3	3.7	74.4	327.9	276.7	55.6	-6.9	0.1	2.7	11.5	1.3	10.2
2nd quarter	343.0	59.6	15.1	189.9	3.8	74.5	335.0	282.2	57.4	-7.4	0.1	3.0	8.0	1.3	6.7
3rd quarter	347.8	61.7	15.7	194.7	3.9	71.9	340.0	287.2	57.7	-7.7	0.1	3.0	7.7	1.3	6.4
4th quarter	347.5	63.1	14.1	197.2	4.0	69.2	344.7	292.3	57.7	-7.8	0.1	2.6	2.9	1.3	1.6
1982															
1st quarter	351.3	63.8	14.2	200.4	4.0	68.8	352.3	298.9	59.0	-7.9	0.1	2.4	-1.0	1.3	-2.3
2nd quarter	358.3	64.8	14.3	204.9	4.0	70.4	360.0	304.7	61.0	-7.7	0.2	2.2	-1.7	1.2	-3.0
3rd quarter	363.3	67.3	14.4	208.6	4.1	69.0	365.9	309.2	62.1	-7.2	0.2	1.9	-2.6	1.2	-3.8
4th quarter	368.1	67.9	13.3	213.1	4.1	69.8	371.9	314.3	62.6	-6.5	0.2	1.7	-3.8	1.2	-5.0
1983															
1st quarter	372.9	68.5	12.6	217.1	4.0	70.6	380.7	319.4	65.8	-5.5	0.2	1.2	-7.8	1.2	-9.0
2nd quarter	387.8	71.8	15.6	223.8	4.1	72.7	385.0	323.0	66.3	-5.0	0.2	0.8	2.9	1.2	1.7
3rd quarter	399.4	75.9	17.5	230.1	4.1	71.8	389.5	327.0	67.2	-4.9	0.2	0.4	9.9	1.2	8.7
4th quarter	408.4	78.7	17.9	236.3	4.3	71.2	394.0	330.8	68.3	-5.2	0.2	0.2	14.4	1.3	13.1
1984															
1st quarter	425.1	81.6	20.2	243.4	4.5	75.4	402.5	339.0	69.9	-5.9	0.2	-0.3	22.6	1.4	21.2
2nd quarter	435.6	84.4	19.8	249.3	4.7	77.4	409.1	345.8	70.6	-6.5	0.2	-0.8	26.6	1.5	25.1
3rd quarter	436.9	85.6	17.5	253.9	4.8	75.1	416.0	353.2	71.3	-7.0	0.2	-1.3	20.9	1.5	19.5
4th quarter	448.1	87.3	17.7	259.6	4.8	78.8	422.9	359.9	72.8	-7.5	0.2	-2.1	25.3	1.4	23.9
1985															
1st quarter	456.5	88.7	19.9	264.1	4.7	79.1	431.8	367.6	74.9	-8.0	0.2	-2.5	24.7	1.3	23.4
2nd quarter	464.7	90.7	19.5	269.7	4.8	80.0	440.7	375.4	76.4	-8.1	0.2	-2.8	24.0	1.2	22.7
3rd quarter	473.7	91.6	21.0	275.1	4.9	81.2	452.2	385.2	78.1	-7.9	0.2	-3.1	21.5	1.3	20.2
4th quarter	482.0	94.2	20.6	278.9	5.2	83.1	463.1	393.8	79.8	-7.5	0.2	-3.0	18.9	1.5	17.5
1986															
1st quarter	499.3	95.4	21.5	292.1	5.5	84.8	472.7	400.7	81.6	-6.7	0.2	-2.7	26.6	1.6	25.0
2nd quarter	501.1	96.3	22.0	288.1	5.8	89.0	480.7	405.7	83.7	-5.9	0.1	-2.6	20.4	1.8	18.6
3rd quarter	513.2	99.0	22.4	294.0	6.1	91.8	490.6	412.9	85.3	-5.1	0.1	-2.4	22.6	2.0	20.7
4th quarter	518.0	103.5	24.8	298.4	6.4	84.9	504.6	424.1	87.0	-4.2	0.2	-2.2	13.4	2.1	11.3
1987															
1st quarter	517.0	104.1	21.0	303.1	6.7	82.1	511.4	429.0	88.4	-3.5	0.2	-2.4	5.7	2.1	3.6
2nd quarter	539.3	113.3	23.7	309.5	7.0	85.8	520.3	436.0	90.0	-3.0	0.2	-2.5	19.0	2.1	16.8
3rd quarter	539.4	106.1	25.4	316.7	7.3	83.9	527.4	441.5	91.6	-2.8	0.2	-2.8	12.0	2.2	9.8
4th quarter	548.1	110.5	25.5	320.5	7.7	83.8	536.0	449.6	93.2	-3.0	0.2	-3.6	12.1	2.3	9.8
1988															
1st quarter	556.8	110.3	23.9	325.1	8.0	89.5	545.7	457.2	95.4	-2.8	0.2	-3.8	11.1	2.4	8.7
2nd quarter	569.0	114.1	25.8	330.7	8.3	90.0	554.3	464.7	97.4	-3.4	0.2	-4.2	14.6	2.5	12.1
3rd quarter	578.5	114.5	26.6	335.7	8.5	93.1	562.1	471.5	99.6	-4.1	0.2	-4.7	16.4	2.6	13.8
4th quarter	590.4	116.9	27.8	343.3	8.7	93.8	570.2	478.5	102.0	-4.9	0.2	-5.2	20.2	2.6	17.7
1989															
1st quarter	602.5	124.4	26.7	347.7	8.8	94.9	582.1	489.8	104.4	-6.0	0.2	-5.9	20.5	2.5	17.9
2nd quarter	614.1	129.1	24.7	355.9	8.9	95.6	593.3	498.8	107.4	-6.5	0.2	-6.3	20.8	2.4	18.4
3rd quarter	625.9	129.8	22.6	363.0	9.0	101.4	604.2	506.4	111.1	-6.7	0.2	-6.4	21.7	2.3	19.4
4th quarter	633.1	132.3	23.0	367.2	9.3	101.4	618.8	516.9	114.9	-7.0	0.2	-5.8	14.4	2.1	12.2
1990															
1st quarter	643.3	131.2	21.5	374.6	9.5	106.5	636.1	530.6	118.9	-6.8	0.2	-6.4	7.2	2.0	5.2
2nd quarter	654.3	134.1	22.7	377.4	9.9	110.3	650.5	539.5	124.3	-6.9	0.2	-6.3	3.9	2.0	1.9
3rd quarter	672.8	138.8	23.6	387.5	10.2	112.6	668.3	550.4	130.4	-6.2	0.2	-6.2	4.5	2.0	2.6
4th quarter	683.2	140.1	22.2	394.0	10.5	116.3	688.3	562.5	137.6	-5.3	0.2	-6.3	-5.0	2.0	-7.0

Table 22-9. U.S. International Transactions

(Millions of dollars, seasonally adjusted.)

Year and quarter	Exports of goods, services, and income				Imports of goods, services, and income [1]				Unilateral current transfers, net [2]	U.S.-owned assets abroad, net [3]					
													U.S. private assets, net		
	Total	Goods	Services	Income receipts	Total	Goods	Services	Income payments		Total	U.S. official reserve assets, net	U.S. government assets, other than official reserve assets, net	Total	Direct investment	Foreign securities
1963	35 776	22 272	7 348	6 157	-26 970	-17 048	-8 362	-1 560	-4 392	-7 270	378	-1 662	-5 986	-3 483	-1 105
1964	40 165	25 501	7 840	6 824	-29 102	-18 700	-8 619	-1 783	-4 240	-9 560	171	-1 680	-8 050	-3 760	-677
1965	42 722	26 461	8 824	7 437	-32 708	-21 510	-9 111	-2 088	-4 583	-5 716	1 225	-1 605	-5 336	-5 011	-759
1966	46 454	29 310	9 616	7 528	-38 468	-25 493	-10 494	-2 481	-4 955	-7 321	570	-1 543	-6 347	-5 418	-720
1967	49 353	30 666	10 667	8 021	-41 476	-26 866	-11 863	-2 747	-5 294	-9 757	53	-2 423	-7 386	-4 805	-1 308
1968	54 911	33 626	11 917	9 367	-48 671	-32 991	-12 302	-3 378	-5 629	-10 977	-870	-2 274	-7 833	-5 295	-1 569
1969	60 132	36 414	12 806	10 913	-53 998	-35 807	-13 322	-4 869	-5 735	-11 585	-1 179	-2 200	-8 206	-5 960	-1 549
1970	68 387	42 469	14 171	11 748	-59 901	-39 866	-14 520	-5 515	-6 156	-8 470	3 348	-1 589	-10 229	-7 590	-1 076
1971	72 384	43 319	16 358	12 707	-66 414	-45 579	-15 400	-5 435	-7 402	-11 758	3 066	-1 884	-12 940	-7 618	-1 113
1972	81 986	49 381	17 841	14 765	-79 237	-55 797	-16 868	-6 572	-8 544	-13 787	706	-1 568	-12 925	-7 747	-618
1973	113 050	71 410	19 832	21 808	-98 997	-70 499	-18 843	-9 655	-6 913	-22 874	158	-2 644	-20 388	-11 353	-671
1974	148 484	98 306	22 591	27 587	-137 274	-103 811	-21 379	-12 084	-9 249	-34 745	-1 467	366	-33 643	-9 052	-1 854
1975	157 936	107 088	25 497	25 351	-132 745	-98 185	-21 996	-12 564	-7 075	-39 703	-849	-3 474	-35 380	-14 244	-6 247
1976	172 090	114 745	27 971	29 375	-162 109	-124 228	-24 570	-13 311	-5 686	-51 269	-2 558	-4 214	-44 498	-11 949	-8 885
1977	184 655	120 816	31 485	32 354	-193 764	-151 907	-27 640	-14 217	-5 226	-34 785	-375	-3 693	-30 717	-11 890	-5 460
1978	220 516	142 075	36 353	42 088	-229 870	-176 002	-32 189	-21 680	-5 788	-61 130	732	-4 660	-57 202	-16 056	-3 626
1979	287 965	184 439	39 692	63 834	-281 657	-212 007	-36 689	-32 961	-6 593	-64 915	6	-3 746	-61 176	-25 222	-4 726
1980	344 440	224 250	47 584	72 606	-333 774	-249 750	-41 491	-42 532	-8 349	-85 815	-7 003	-5 162	-73 651	-19 222	-3 568
1981	380 928	237 044	57 354	86 529	-364 196	-265 067	-45 503	-53 626	-11 702	-113 054	-4 082	-5 097	-103 875	-9 624	-5 699
1982	366 983	211 157	64 079	91 747	-355 975	-247 642	-51 749	-56 583	-16 544	-127 882	-4 965	-6 131	-116 786	-4 556	-7 983
1983	356 106	201 799	64 307	90 000	-377 488	-268 901	-54 973	-53 614	-17 310	-66 373	-1 196	-5 006	-60 172	-12 528	-6 762
1984	399 913	219 926	71 168	108 819	-473 923	-332 418	-67 748	-73 756	-20 335	-40 376	-3 131	-5 489	-31 757	-16 407	-4 756
1985	387 612	215 915	73 155	98 542	-483 769	-338 088	-72 862	-72 819	-21 998	-44 752	-3 858	-2 821	-38 074	-18 927	-7 481
1986	407 098	223 344	86 689	97 064	-530 142	-368 425	-80 147	-81 571	-24 132	-111 723	312	-2 022	-110 014	-23 995	-4 271
1987	457 053	250 208	98 661	108 184	-594 443	-409 765	-90 787	-93 891	-23 265	-79 296	9 149	1 006	-89 450	-35 034	-5 251
1988	567 862	320 230	110 919	136 713	-663 741	-447 189	-98 526	-118 026	-25 274	-106 573	-3 912	2 967	-105 628	-22 528	-7 980
1989	650 494	362 120	127 087	161 287	-721 307	-477 365	-102 479	-141 463	-26 169	-175 383	-25 293	1 233	-151 323	-43 447	-22 070
1990	708 881	389 307	147 832	171 742	-759 189	-498 337	-117 659	-143 192	-26 654	-81 234	-2 158	2 317	-81 393	-37 183	-28 765
1963															
1st quarter	8 428	5 063	1 849	1 516	-6 478	-4 064	-2 057	-357	-1 107	-1 922	32	-482	-1 472	-980	-522
2nd quarter	9 244	5 599	2 150	1 495	-6 674	-4 226	-2 066	-382	-1 371	-2 631	124	-654	-2 101	-874	-536
3rd quarter	8 832	5 671	1 620	1 541	-6 893	-4 372	-2 122	-399	-918	-887	227	-86	-1 028	-721	-100
4th quarter	9 275	5 939	1 731	1 605	-6 926	-4 386	-2 118	-422	-999	-1 831	-5	-440	-1 386	-908	53
1964															
1st quarter	9 885	6 242	1 922	1 721	-6 982	-4 416	-2 140	-426	-993	-2 086	-51	-288	-1 747	-822	20
2nd quarter	9 975	6 199	2 088	1 688	-7 179	-4 598	-2 142	-439	-1 269	-2 018	303	-386	-1 935	-970	-206
3rd quarter	10 009	6 423	1 851	1 735	-7 349	-4 756	-2 153	-440	-935	-2 255	70	-414	-1 911	-1 018	2
4th quarter	10 299	6 637	1 982	1 680	-7 594	-4 930	-2 186	-478	-1 043	-3 200	-151	-592	-2 457	-949	-494
1965															
1st quarter	9 689	5 768	2 047	1 874	-7 395	-4 711	-2 187	-497	-1 037	-1 576	843	-374	-2 045	-1 606	-198
2nd quarter	11 263	6 876	2 448	1 939	-8 208	-5 428	-2 269	-511	-1 478	-1 270	69	-536	-803	-1 250	-147
3rd quarter	10 625	6 643	2 120	1 862	-8 307	-5 516	-2 263	-528	-1 013	-1 454	42	-254	-1 242	-1 030	-209
4th quarter	11 149	7 174	2 212	1 763	-8 802	-5 855	-2 393	-554	-1 058	-1 416	271	-441	-1 246	-1 125	-205
1966															
1st quarter	11 190	7 242	2 124	1 824	-9 068	-6 012	-2 483	-573	-1 140	-1 465	424	-321	-1 568	-1 115	-437
2nd quarter	11 726	7 169	2 705	1 852	-9 390	-6 195	-2 601	-594	-1 547	-1 967	68	-504	-1 531	-1 373	-115
3rd quarter	11 470	7 290	2 301	1 879	-9 505	-6 169	-2 693	-643	-1 073	-1 681	83	-339	-1 425	-1 314	-115
4th quarter	12 068	7 609	2 487	1 972	-10 098	-6 710	-2 717	-671	-1 194	-2 208	-5	-380	-1 823	-1 616	-53
1967															
1st quarter	12 439	7 751	2 731	1 957	-10 248	-6 708	-2 866	-674	-1 315	-1 203	1 027	-643	-1 587	-1 186	-265
2nd quarter	12 275	7 693	2 666	1 916	-10 136	-6 475	-2 986	-675	-1 472	-2 339	-419	-543	-1 377	-964	-261
3rd quarter	12 134	7 530	2 540	2 064	-10 262	-6 526	-3 059	-677	-1 309	-3 155	-375	-551	-2 229	-1 359	-419
4th quarter	12 506	7 692	2 731	2 083	-10 833	-7 157	-2 955	-721	-1 199	-3 060	-180	-685	-2 195	-1 297	-363
1968															
1st quarter	13 016	7 998	2 816	2 202	-11 571	-7 796	-2 997	-778	-1 249	-1 299	912	-706	-1 505	-981	-449
2nd quarter	13 577	8 324	2 936	2 317	-11 885	-8 051	-2 990	-844	-1 363	-2 427	-135	-632	-1 660	-1 172	-283
3rd quarter	14 195	8 745	3 039	2 411	-12 611	-8 612	-3 129	-870	-1 445	-3 447	-572	-568	-2 307	-1 573	-318
4th quarter	14 126	8 559	3 129	2 438	-12 604	-8 532	-3 185	-887	-1 573	-3 803	-1 075	-368	-2 360	-1 568	-519
1969															
1st quarter	12 921	7 468	2 884	2 569	-11 622	-7 444	-3 174	-1 004	-1 177	-2 595	-45	-406	-2 144	-1 556	-366
2nd quarter	15 492	9 536	3 283	2 673	-13 978	-9 527	-3 303	-1 148	-1 645	-3 428	-298	-632	-2 498	-1 663	-498
3rd quarter	15 439	9 400	3 245	2 794	-14 072	-9 380	-3 368	-1 324	-1 319	-3 361	-685	-703	-1 973	-1 548	-546
4th quarter	16 279	10 010	3 394	2 875	-14 329	-9 456	-3 481	-1 392	-1 593	-2 199	-151	-459	-1 589	-1 192	-139
1970															
1st quarter	16 461	10 258	3 235	2 968	-14 458	-9 587	-3 449	-1 422	-1 383	-2 611	481	-399	-2 693	-1 958	-306
2nd quarter	17 419	10 744	3 645	3 030	-14 861	-9 766	-3 690	-1 405	-1 586	-1 725	1 025	-348	-2 402	-2 144	80
3rd quarter	17 267	10 665	3 625	2 977	-15 141	-10 049	-3 715	-1 377	-1 611	-2 146	802	-423	-2 525	-1 718	-517
4th quarter	17 241	10 802	3 666	2 773	-15 443	-10 464	-3 668	-1 311	-1 576	-1 989	1 040	-419	-2 610	-1 771	-333
1971															
1st quarter	17 980	10 920	4 048	3 012	-15 551	-10 600	-3 724	-1 227	-1 746	-2 747	868	-573	-3 042	-2 033	-408
2nd quarter	18 163	10 878	4 087	3 198	-16 764	-11 614	-3 867	-1 283	-1 808	-2 534	839	-567	-2 806	-1 949	-368
3rd quarter	18 676	11 548	3 972	3 156	-17 460	-12 171	-3 861	-1 428	-1 752	-3 390	1 377	-387	-4 380	-2 308	-346
4th quarter	17 564	9 973	4 251	3 340	-16 639	-11 194	-3 948	-1 497	-2 098	-3 084	-18	-355	-2 711	-1 327	9
1972															
1st quarter	19 757	11 833	4 473	3 451	-19 153	-13 501	-4 173	-1 479	-2 297	-3 585	620	-212	-3 993	-2 187	-476
2nd quarter	19 427	11 618	4 233	3 576	-19 105	-13 254	-4 228	-1 623	-2 011	-2 125	-60	-271	-1 794	-1 481	-318
3rd quarter	20 788	12 351	4 634	3 803	-19 767	-14 022	-4 095	-1 650	-2 306	-3 952	96	-518	-3 530	-2 435	203
4th quarter	22 015	13 579	4 503	3 933	-21 212	-15 020	-4 371	-1 821	-1 933	-4 125	50	-566	-3 609	-1 644	-28
1973															
1st quarter	24 681	15 474	4 579	4 628	-23 000	-16 285	-4 613	-2 102	-1 536	-7 886	213	-572	-7 527	-3 785	55
2nd quarter	27 127	17 112	4 828	5 187	-24 301	-17 168	-4 741	-2 392	-1 953	-4 154	11	-423	-3 742	-2 691	-86
3rd quarter	29 329	18 271	5 145	5 913	-24 841	-17 683	-4 640	-2 518	-1 751	-3 189	-23	-608	-2 558	-2 159	-196
4th quarter	31 912	20 553	5 279	6 080	-26 855	-19 363	-4 849	-2 643	-1 674	-7 646	-43	-1 042	-6 561	-2 718	-445

1. A minus sign indicates imports of goods or services or income payments.
2. A minus sign indicates net unilateral transfers to foreigners.
3. A minus sign indicates capital outflow or an increase in official reserve assets.

Table 22-9. U.S. International Transactions—*Continued*

(Millions of dollars, seasonally adjusted.)

Year and quarter	U.S. claims on unaffiliated foreigners reported by U.S. nonbanking concerns	U.S. claims reported by U.S. banks, not included elsewhere	Foreign-owned assets, Total	Foreign official assets in the U.S., net	Other foreign assets, Total	Direct investment	U.S. Treasury securities and U.S. currency flows	U.S. securities other than U.S. Treasury securities	U.S. liabilities to unaffiliated foreigners reported by U.S. nonbanking concerns	U.S. liabilities reported by U.S. banks, not included elsewhere	Statistical discrepancy [2]	Balance on Goods and services	Balance on Current account
1963	157	-1 556	3 217	1 986	1 231	231	-149	287	-37	898	-360	4 210	4 414
1964	-1 108	-2 505	3 643	1 660	1 983	322	-146	-85	75	1 818	-907	6 022	6 823
1965	341	93	742	134	607	415	-131	-358	178	503	-457	4 664	5 431
1966	-442	233	3 661	-672	4 333	425	-356	906	476	2 882	629	2 940	3 031
1967	-779	-495	7 379	3 451	3 928	698	-135	1 016	584	1 765	-205	2 604	2 583
1968	-1 203	233	9 928	-774	10 703	807	136	4 414	1 475	3 871	438	250	611
1969	-126	-570	12 702	-1 301	14 002	1 263	-68	3 130	792	8 886	-1 516	91	399
1970	-596	-967	6 359	6 908	-550	1 464	81	2 189	2 014	-6 298	-219	2 254	2 331
1971	-1 229	-2 980	22 970	26 879	-3 909	367	-24	2 289	369	-6 911	-9 779	-1 303	-1 433
1972	-1 054	-3 506	21 461	10 475	10 986	949	-39	4 507	815	4 754	-1 879	-5 443	-5 795
1973	-2 383	-5 980	18 388	6 026	12 362	2 800	-216	4 041	1 035	4 702	-2 654	1 900	7 140
1974	-3 221	-19 516	35 341	10 546	24 796	4 760	1 797	378	1 844	16 017	-2 558	-4 292	1 962
1975	-1 357	-13 532	17 170	7 027	10 143	2 603	4 090	2 503	319	628	4 417	12 404	18 116
1976	-2 296	-21 368	38 018	17 693	20 326	4 347	4 283	1 284	-578	10 990	8 955	-6 082	4 295
1977	-1 940	-11 427	53 219	36 816	16 403	3 728	2 434	2 437	1 086	6 719	-4 099	-27 246	-14 335
1978	-3 853	-33 667	67 036	33 678	33 358	7 897	5 178	2 254	1 889	16 141	9 236	-29 763	-15 143
1979	-5 014	-26 213	40 852	-13 665	54 516	11 877	7 060	1 351	1 621	32 607	24 349	-24 565	-285
1980	-4 023	-46 838	62 612	15 497	47 115	16 918	7 145	5 457	6 852	10 743	20 886	-19 407	2 317
1981	-4 377	-84 175	86 232	4 960	81 272	25 195	6 127	6 905	917	42 128	21 792	-16 172	5 030
1982	6 823	-111 070	96 589	3 593	92 997	12 635	11 027	6 085	-2 383	65 633	36 630	-24 156	-5 536
1983	-10 954	-29 928	88 694	5 845	82 849	10 372	14 089	8 164	-118	50 342	16 162	-57 767	-38 691
1984	533	-11 127	117 752	3 140	114 612	24 468	27 101	12 568	16 626	33 849	16 733	-109 073	-94 344
1985	-10 342	-1 323	146 115	-1 119	147 233	19 742	25 633	50 962	9 851	41 045	16 478	-121 880	-118 155
1986	-21 773	-59 975	230 009	35 648	194 360	35 420	7 909	70 969	3 325	76 737	28 590	-138 538	-147 177
1987	-7 046	-42 119	248 634	45 387	203 247	58 470	-2 243	42 120	18 363	86 537	-9 048	-151 684	-160 655
1988	-21 193	-53 927	246 522	39 758	206 764	57 735	26 039	26 353	32 893	63 744	-19 289	-114 566	-121 153
1989	-27 646	-58 160	224 928	8 503	216 425	68 274	35 518	38 767	22 086	51 780	47 101	-90 638	-96 982
1990	-27 824	12 379	141 571	33 910	107 661	48 494	16 266	1 592	45 133	-3 824	23 204	-78 857	-76 961
1963													
1st quarter	-27	57	1 191	946	245	40	25	14	-36	202	-112	791	843
2nd quarter	-108	-583	1 527	910	617	108	-109	119	69	430	-95	1 457	1 199
3rd quarter	47	-254	205	56	149	105	1	52	11	-20	-339	797	1 021
4th quarter	245	-776	295	75	220	-22	-66	102	-80	286	186	1 166	1 350
1964													
1st quarter	-206	-739	462	393	69	87	32	-42	0	-8	-286	1 608	1 910
2nd quarter	-166	-593	630	227	403	109	-108	14	19	369	-139	1 547	1 527
3rd quarter	-532	-363	769	275	494	56	-65	-30	37	496	-239	1 365	1 725
4th quarter	-204	-810	1 781	763	1 018	70	-5	-27	19	961	-243	1 503	1 662
1965													
1st quarter	286	-527	208	-202	410	184	60	57	3	106	111	917	1 257
2nd quarter	165	429	-330	-194	-136	-21	64	-243	63	1	23	1 627	1 577
3rd quarter	-19	16	587	115	472	147	-149	-227	49	652	-438	984	1 305
4th quarter	-91	175	280	421	-141	104	-106	54	63	-256	-153	1 138	1 289
1966													
1st quarter	-159	143	458	-164	622	143	-102	173	68	340	25	871	982
2nd quarter	-68	25	961	-57	1 018	133	-316	518	78	605	217	1 078	789
3rd quarter	-105	109	909	-342	1 251	-37	66	107	195	920	287	322	485
4th quarter	-110	-44	1 332	-111	1 443	187	-4	108	135	1 017	100	669	776
1967													
1st quarter	-107	-29	401	708	-307	169	-6	133	219	-822	-74	908	876
2nd quarter	-69	-83	1 884	1 100	784	174	-61	329	66	276	-212	898	667
3rd quarter	-40	-411	2 513	548	1 965	127	-36	520	164	1 190	79	485	563
4th quarter	-563	28	2 584	1 098	1 486	228	-32	34	135	1 121	2	311	474
1968													
1st quarter	-231	156	1 374	-533	1 907	367	22	855	207	456	-271	21	196
2nd quarter	-567	362	2 192	-2 007	4 199	133	86	1 122	478	2 380	-94	219	329
3rd quarter	-213	-203	2 809	442	2 367	148	-8	1 124	315	788	499	43	139
4th quarter	-191	-82	3 550	1 321	2 229	160	36	1 312	474	247	304	-29	-51
1969													
1st quarter	-132	-90	3 664	-1 117	4 781	359	-125	1 388	90	3 069	-1 191	-266	122
2nd quarter	-21	-316	3 896	-766	4 662	267	-35	365	181	3 884	-337	-11	-131
3rd quarter	141	-20	3 833	1 256	2 577	261	79	396	345	1 496	-520	-103	48
4th quarter	-114	-144	1 311	-672	1 983	376	13	981	176	437	531	467	357
1970													
1st quarter	-366	-63	2 160	2 830	-670	592	16	304	222	-1 804	-169	457	620
2nd quarter	-73	-265	848	694	154	212	-35	374	534	-931	-95	933	972
3rd quarter	-157	-133	1 940	1 411	529	357	1	720	510	-1 059	-309	526	515
4th quarter	0	-506	1 413	1 975	-562	303	99	792	748	-2 504	354	336	222
1971													
1st quarter	-355	-246	3 092	5 178	-2 086	196	179	559	-62	-2 958	-1 028	644	683
2nd quarter	-131	-358	5 154	5 630	-476	140	1 862	196	-34	-2 640	-2 211	-516	-409
3rd quarter	-337	-1 389	8 726	10 367	-1 641	-293	-795	626	79	-1 258	-4 800	-512	-536
4th quarter	-406	-987	5 997	5 704	293	324	-1 270	908	386	-55	-1 740	-918	-1 173
1972													
1st quarter	-248	-1 082	4 367	2 762	1 605	-136	-3	1 059	-14	699	911	-1 368	-1 693
2nd quarter	-185	190	4 277	1 103	3 174	373	-83	961	250	1 673	-463	-1 631	-1 689
3rd quarter	-241	-1 057	6 382	4 740	1 642	310	-12	718	216	410	-1 145	-1 132	-1 285
4th quarter	-380	-1 557	6 437	1 871	4 566	403	59	1 769	363	1 972	-1 182	-1 309	-1 130
1973													
1st quarter	-809	-2 988	10 743	9 937	806	631	-119	1 718	246	-1 670	-3 002	-845	145
2nd quarter	-202	-763	3 056	-403	3 458	835	-185	489	54	2 265	225	31	873
3rd quarter	-502	299	2 168	-772	2 940	539	-205	1 173	454	979	-1 716	1 093	2 737
4th quarter	-870	-2 528	2 423	-2 736	5 159	795	293	662	281	3 128	1 840	1 620	3 383

1. A minus sign indicates capital outflow or decrease in foreign official assets in the United States.
2. Sum of credits and debits with the signs reversed.

Table 22-9. U.S. International Transactions—*Continued*

(Millions of dollars, seasonally adjusted.)

Year and quarter	Exports of goods, services, and income				Imports of goods, services, and income [1]				Unilateral current transfers, net [2]	U.S.-owned assets abroad, net [3]			U.S. private assets, net		
	Total	Goods	Services	Income receipts	Total	Goods	Services	Income payments		Total	U.S. official reserve assets, net	U.S. government assets, other than official reserve assets, net	Total	Direct investment	Foreign securities
1974															
1st quarter	34 698	22 614	5 189	6 895	-29 643	-21 952	-4 985	-2 706	-3 443	-5 914	-246	1 389	-7 057	900	-600
2nd quarter	37 295	24 500	5 691	7 104	-34 710	-26 346	-5 359	-3 005	-2 475	-10 318	-358	267	-10 227	-1 790	-272
3rd quarter	37 385	24 629	5 633	7 123	-36 004	-27 368	-5 360	-3 276	-1 676	-7 694	-1 002	-354	-6 338	-4 385	-282
4th quarter	39 105	26 563	6 078	6 464	-36 918	-28 145	-5 675	-3 098	-1 656	-10 818	139	-938	-10 019	-3 776	-699
1975															
1st quarter	40 047	27 480	6 454	6 113	-33 797	-24 980	-5 580	-3 237	-2 043	-10 576	-327	-877	-9 372	-4 022	-1 931
2nd quarter	38 675	25 866	6 807	6 002	-31 284	-22 832	-5 309	-3 143	-2 377	-9 591	-28	-875	-8 688	-3 990	-985
3rd quarter	38 347	26 109	5 886	6 352	-33 078	-24 487	-5 379	-3 212	-1 189	-5 099	-333	-745	-4 021	-1 495	-938
4th quarter	40 868	27 633	6 351	6 884	-34 588	-25 886	-5 729	-2 973	-1 467	-14 436	-161	-977	-13 298	-4 736	-2 393
1976															
1st quarter	41 183	27 575	6 556	7 052	-37 464	-28 176	-5 883	-3 405	-1 153	-12 364	-777	-749	-10 838	-3 923	-2 467
2nd quarter	42 309	28 256	6 660	7 393	-39 494	-30 182	-5 980	-3 332	-1 167	-11 701	-1 580	-914	-9 207	-2 017	-1 405
3rd quarter	43 818	29 056	7 311	7 451	-41 737	-32 213	-6 231	-3 293	-2 165	-10 618	-408	-1 428	-8 782	-3 327	-2 751
4th quarter	44 780	29 858	7 444	7 478	-43 416	-33 657	-6 478	-3 281	-1 201	-16 588	207	-1 124	-15 671	-2 682	-2 262
1977															
1st quarter	44 916	29 668	7 494	7 754	-46 360	-36 585	-6 676	-3 099	-1 243	-1 198	-420	-1 062	284	-1 880	-749
2nd quarter	46 796	30 852	7 901	8 043	-48 401	-38 063	-6 940	-3 398	-1 426	-12 182	-24	-885	-11 273	-3 783	-1 784
3rd quarter	47 125	30 752	7 991	8 382	-48 511	-38 005	-6 894	-3 612	-1 371	-6 297	112	-1 001	-5 408	-2 762	-2 177
4th quarter	45 818	29 544	8 098	8 176	-50 495	-39 254	-7 133	-4 108	-1 185	-15 109	-43	-746	-14 320	-3 466	-749
1978															
1st quarter	48 847	30 470	8 704	9 673	-54 471	-42 487	-7 612	-4 372	-1 396	-15 219	187	-1 009	-14 397	-4 771	-1 115
2nd quarter	54 213	35 674	8 772	9 767	-56 513	-43 419	-7 768	-5 326	-1 477	-5 606	248	-1 257	-4 597	-3 720	-1 094
3rd quarter	56 058	36 523	9 203	10 332	-58 300	-44 422	-8 248	-5 630	-1 425	-9 703	115	-1 394	-8 424	-2 753	-510
4th quarter	61 399	39 408	9 673	12 318	-60 587	-45 674	-8 561	-6 352	-1 491	-30 601	182	-999	-29 784	-4 812	-907
1979															
1st quarter	64 530	41 475	9 664	13 391	-63 492	-47 582	-8 649	-7 261	-1 462	-7 841	-2 446	-1 094	-4 301	-5 465	-908
2nd quarter	68 445	43 885	9 713	14 847	-67 584	-50 778	-8 960	-7 846	-1 552	-15 565	322	-970	-14 917	-7 220	-492
3rd quarter	74 411	47 104	9 936	17 371	-71 856	-54 002	-9 329	-8 525	-1 632	-27 156	2 779	-779	-29 156	-7 166	-2 331
4th quarter	80 577	51 975	10 378	18 224	-78 726	-59 645	-9 751	-9 330	-1 949	-14 353	-649	-904	-12 800	-5 370	-995
1980															
1st quarter	85 274	54 237	10 997	20 040	-86 559	-65 815	-10 335	-10 409	-2 174	-12 662	-2 116	-1 441	-9 105	-5 188	-787
2nd quarter	83 441	55 967	11 491	15 983	-82 734	-62 274	-10 106	-10 354	-1 648	-24 724	502	-1 159	-24 067	-2 659	-1 387
3rd quarter	86 148	55 830	12 543	17 775	-79 906	-59 010	-10 292	-10 604	-1 909	-19 666	-1 109	-1 382	-17 175	-4 156	-944
4th quarter	89 578	58 216	12 554	18 808	-84 577	-62 651	-10 760	-11 166	-2 618	-28 761	-4 279	-1 178	-23 304	-7 219	-450
1981															
1st quarter	94 665	60 317	13 684	20 664	-91 024	-67 004	-11 360	-12 660	-2 678	-21 922	-3 436	-1 361	-17 125	-2 044	-473
2nd quarter	96 294	60 141	14 392	21 761	-92 303	-67 181	-11 447	-13 675	-2 763	-24 158	-905	-1 491	-21 762	-5 709	-1 564
3rd quarter	95 013	58 031	14 835	22 147	-89 787	-64 407	-11 236	-14 144	-3 145	-17 945	-4	-1 268	-16 673	-1 124	-697
4th quarter	94 958	58 555	14 446	21 957	-91 082	-66 475	-11 460	-13 147	-3 117	-49 028	262	-976	-48 314	-745	-2 966
1982															
1st quarter	94 006	55 163	16 032	22 811	-90 336	-63 502	-12 749	-14 085	-3 955	-36 335	-1 089	-800	-34 446	-2 695	-628
2nd quarter	96 060	55 344	16 187	24 529	-88 318	-60 580	-13 096	-14 642	-3 953	-42 754	-1 132	-1 727	-39 895	1 074	-471
3rd quarter	90 925	52 089	16 003	22 833	-90 938	-63 696	-12 794	-14 448	-4 027	-23 547	-794	-2 524	-20 229	903	-3 397
4th quarter	85 993	48 561	15 857	21 575	-86 379	-59 864	-13 109	-13 406	-4 611	-25 246	-1 950	-1 080	-22 217	-3 838	-3 488
1983															
1st quarter	86 146	49 198	16 239	20 709	-85 097	-59 757	-12 951	-12 389	-3 566	-28 890	-787	-1 136	-26 967	-862	-1 549
2nd quarter	87 214	49 340	16 093	21 781	-91 096	-64 783	-13 557	-12 756	-3 951	-2 974	16	-1 263	-1 727	-1 842	-2 813
3rd quarter	89 919	50 324	16 308	23 287	-98 901	-70 370	-14 133	-13 978	-4 339	-12 191	529	-1 171	-11 549	-4 861	-1 308
4th quarter	92 831	52 937	15 671	24 223	-102 822	-73 991	-14 337	-14 494	-5 453	-22 318	-953	-1 436	-19 929	-4 962	-1 093
1984															
1st quarter	96 000	52 991	17 353	25 656	-112 576	-79 740	-16 131	-16 705	-4 354	-8 338	-657	-2 033	-5 648	-1 837	758
2nd quarter	100 257	54 626	18 045	27 586	-119 220	-83 798	-16 885	-18 537	-4 445	-25 718	-566	-1 342	-23 811	-1 967	-764
3rd quarter	102 296	55 893	17 936	28 467	-120 533	-83 918	-17 168	-19 447	-5 147	15 298	-799	-1 392	17 489	-3 209	-1 106
4th quarter	101 361	56 416	17 834	27 111	-121 591	-84 962	-17 564	-19 065	-6 359	-21 618	-1 110	-720	-19 789	-9 396	-3 644
1985															
1st quarter	97 794	54 866	18 227	24 701	-116 249	-80 319	-17 707	-18 223	-5 064	-5 491	-233	-760	-4 498	-2 783	-2 474
2nd quarter	97 437	54 154	18 214	25 069	-120 891	-84 565	-18 276	-18 050	-5 235	-2 340	-356	-1 053	-931	-4 374	-2 219
3rd quarter	94 771	52 836	17 961	23 974	-120 285	-83 909	-18 151	-18 225	-5 789	-5 776	-121	-453	-5 202	-4 698	-1 572
4th quarter	97 612	54 059	18 756	24 797	-126 349	-89 295	-18 732	-18 322	-5 911	-31 146	-3 148	-555	-27 444	-7 073	-1 217
1986															
1st quarter	100 332	53 536	21 052	25 744	-129 342	-89 220	-19 855	-20 267	-5 199	-17 406	-115	-266	-17 025	-9 781	-5 930
2nd quarter	102 206	56 828	20 912	24 466	-131 690	-91 743	-19 066	-20 881	-6 208	-24 945	16	-230	-24 731	-7 298	-1 051
3rd quarter	101 288	55 645	21 969	23 674	-132 879	-92 801	-20 448	-19 630	-6 458	-32 615	280	-1 554	-31 341	-4 975	181
4th quarter	103 275	57 335	22 761	23 179	-136 232	-94 661	-20 778	-20 793	-6 269	-36 753	132	29	-36 914	-1 938	2 529
1987															
1st quarter	104 750	56 696	23 602	24 452	-138 887	-96 023	-21 273	-21 591	-5 496	8 177	1 956	-5	6 226	-6 547	-1 749
2nd quarter	111 642	60 202	24 740	26 700	-146 125	-100 648	-22 537	-22 940	-5 502	-26 738	3 419	-168	-29 989	-7 541	-287
3rd quarter	116 688	64 217	24 986	27 485	-151 111	-104 412	-22 833	-23 866	-5 706	-27 791	32	310	-28 133	-8 795	-1 159
4th quarter	123 968	69 093	25 329	29 546	-158 324	-108 682	-24 146	-25 496	-6 926	-32 943	3 742	868	-37 553	-12 150	-2 056
1988															
1st quarter	134 932	75 655	26 598	32 679	-161 810	-109 963	-24 503	-27 344	-6 074	2 892	1 502	-1 597	2 987	-5 037	-4 504
2nd quarter	139 984	79 542	27 567	32 875	-163 265	-110 836	-24 282	-28 147	-5 615	-23 428	39	-854	-22 613	-2 594	1 318
3rd quarter	143 879	80 941	28 453	34 485	-165 901	-110 901	-24 588	-30 412	-5 872	-49 965	-7 380	1 960	-44 545	-7 791	-1 500
4th quarter	149 068	84 092	28 302	36 674	-172 770	-115 489	-25 157	-32 124	-7 685	-36 074	1 925	3 457	-41 456	-7 105	-3 294
1989															
1st quarter	156 957	87 426	30 576	38 955	-176 065	-116 477	-25 140	-34 448	-6 048	-53 703	-4 000	961	-50 664	-12 136	-2 225
2nd quarter	164 161	92 208	31 110	40 843	-182 745	-120 907	-25 241	-36 597	-5 753	-8 202	-12 095	-306	4 199	-7 686	-6 192
3rd quarter	162 980	90 163	32 316	40 501	-180 394	-118 873	-25 792	-35 729	-6 630	-51 678	-5 996	489	-46 171	-8 704	-9 149
4th quarter	166 398	92 323	33 087	40 988	-182 103	-121 108	-26 306	-34 689	-7 739	-61 803	-3 202	87	-58 688	-14 922	-4 504
1990															
1st quarter	172 087	95 301	35 016	41 770	-186 462	-122 447	-28 173	-35 842	-6 540	37 828	-3 177	-756	41 761	-10 391	-8 580
2nd quarter	175 566	97 573	35 988	42 005	-186 533	-122 169	-28 764	-35 600	-7 644	-37 204	371	-796	-36 779	-4 651	-11 037
3rd quarter	175 578	96 339	37 402	41 837	-191 921	-125 389	-29 923	-36 609	-7 339	-43 716	1 739	-338	-45 117	-17 898	-1 037
4th quarter	185 652	100 094	39 428	46 130	-194 269	-128 332	-30 795	-35 142	-5 133	-38 142	-1 091	4 205	-41 255	-4 240	-8 111

1. A minus sign indicates imports of goods or services or income payments.
2. A minus sign indicates net unilateral transfers to foreigners.
3. A minus sign indicates capital outflow or an increase in official reserve assets.

Table 22-9. U.S. International Transactions—*Continued*

(Millions of dollars, seasonally adjusted.)

Year and quarter	U.S.-owned assets abroad, net[1] —Continued / U.S. private assets, net—Continued / U.S. claims — on unaffiliated foreigners reported by U.S. non-banking concerns	reported by U.S. banks, not included elsewhere	Foreign-owned assets in the United States, net[1] — Total	Foreign official assets in the United States, net	Other foreign assets in the United States, net — Total	Direct invest-ment	U.S. Treasury securities and U.S. currency flows	U.S. securities other than U.S. Treasury securities	U.S. liabilities — to unaffiliated foreigners reported by U.S. nonbanking concerns	reported by U.S. banks, not included elsewhere	Statistical discrepancy[2]	Balance on — Goods and services	Current account
1974													
1st quarter	-2 113	-5 244	6 514	-1 138	7 652	1 784	336	712	354	4 466	-2 212	866	1 612
2nd quarter	-588	-7 577	9 962	4 434	5 528	539	60	363	390	4 176	246	-1 514	110
3rd quarter	273	-1 944	9 303	3 062	6 241	1 610	400	227	239	3 765	-1 314	-2 466	-295
4th quarter	-793	-4 751	9 563	4 188	5 375	828	1 001	-925	861	3 610	724	-1 179	531
1975													
1st quarter	353	-3 772	2 788	3 419	-631	278	892	344	359	-2 504	3 581	3 374	4 207
2nd quarter	112	-3 825	4 371	2 244	2 127	870	10	385	55	807	206	4 532	5 014
3rd quarter	-939	-649	2 991	-1 731	4 722	86	2 424	737	-163	1 638	-1 972	2 129	4 080
4th quarter	-883	-5 286	7 021	3 095	3 926	1 369	764	1 038	68	687	2 602	2 369	4 813
1976													
1st quarter	-747	-3 701	7 769	3 699	4 070	1 471	737	1 036	154	672	2 029	72	2 566
2nd quarter	-999	-4 786	8 453	4 039	4 414	1 086	-91	134	-231	3 516	1 600	-1 246	1 648
3rd quarter	616	-3 320	9 120	2 958	6 162	999	3 325	64	-184	1 958	1 582	-2 077	-84
4th quarter	-1 166	-9 561	12 677	6 997	5 680	790	312	51	-317	4 844	3 748	-2 833	163
1977													
1st quarter	-771	3 684	3 062	5 554	-2 492	980	1 181	749	-98	-5 304	823	-6 099	-2 687
2nd quarter	-1 124	-4 582	14 781	7 888	6 893	965	-799	589	-102	6 240	4 250	-6 250	-3 031
3rd quarter	1 310	-1 779	14 676	8 257	6 419	1 023	1 651	337	768	2 640	-5 622	-6 156	-2 757
4th quarter	-1 355	-8 750	20 703	15 117	5 586	761	401	763	518	3 143	268	-8 745	-5 862
1978													
1st quarter	-2 241	-6 270	18 684	15 448	3 236	1 356	1 381	396	507	-404	3 555	-10 925	-7 020
2nd quarter	315	-98	1 551	-5 113	6 664	2 313	1 493	1 082	304	1 472	7 832	-6 741	-3 777
3rd quarter	-29	-5 132	17 582	4 903	12 679	2 620	-368	296	912	9 219	-4 212	-6 944	-3 667
4th quarter	-1 898	-22 167	29 220	18 440	10 780	1 608	2 672	480	166	5 854	2 060	-5 154	-679
1979													
1st quarter	-3 854	5 926	2 707	-8 697	11 404	1 554	2 964	409	-296	6 773	5 558	-5 092	-424
2nd quarter	716	-7 921	7 663	-9 775	17 438	3 354	743	524	799	12 018	8 593	-6 140	-691
3rd quarter	-1 826	-17 833	25 349	6 036	19 313	3 382	2 402	166	210	13 153	884	-6 291	923
4th quarter	-50	-6 385	5 134	-1 228	6 362	3 588	951	252	908	663	9 317	-7 043	-98
1980													
1st quarter	-1 927	-1 203	9 582	-7 413	16 995	3 321	4 300	2 435	340	6 599	6 539	-10 916	-3 459
2nd quarter	144	-20 165	11 373	7 731	3 643	5 756	229	496	1 671	-4 509	14 292	-4 922	-941
3rd quarter	365	-12 440	14 930	7 564	7 366	4 713	222	263	1 252	916	403	-929	4 333
4th quarter	-2 605	-13 030	26 726	7 614	19 112	3 128	2 394	2 263	3 590	7 737	-348	-2 641	2 383
1981													
1st quarter	-2 944	-11 664	9 819	5 502	4 317	3 146	2 486	2 357	121	-3 793	11 140	-4 363	963
2nd quarter	513	-15 002	15 364	-3 159	18 523	5 294	1 641	3 512	13	8 063	7 566	-4 095	1 228
3rd quarter	458	-15 310	17 531	-5 992	23 523	5 505	-248	704	1 084	16 478	-1 667	-2 777	2 081
4th quarter	-2 404	-42 199	43 519	8 609	34 910	11 251	2 248	332	-301	21 380	4 750	-4 934	759
1982													
1st quarter	2 220	-33 343	27 240	-3 265	30 505	2 154	1 297	1 263	-65	25 856	9 325	-5 056	-285
2nd quarter	-1 095	-39 403	35 260	1 534	33 726	2 945	4 193	2 486	-2 023	26 125	3 653	-2 145	3 789
3rd quarter	3 670	-21 405	18 663	2 694	15 969	2 849	2 091	555	-282	10 756	8 876	-8 398	-4 040
4th quarter	2 028	-16 919	15 424	2 629	12 795	4 685	3 446	1 781	-13	2 896	14 775	-8 555	-4 997
1983													
1st quarter	-4 253	-20 303	16 266	-38	16 304	1 254	3 713	2 873	-2 763	11 227	15 090	-7 271	-2 517
2nd quarter	-590	3 518	16 325	1 612	14 713	3 287	4 616	2 470	-64	4 404	-5 570	-12 907	-7 833
3rd quarter	-1 764	-3 616	20 420	-2 689	23 109	4 059	2 308	1 777	1 311	13 654	4 619	-17 871	-12 901
4th quarter	-4 347	-9 527	35 682	6 960	28 722	1 771	3 452	1 044	1 398	21 057	2 027	-19 720	-15 444
1984													
1st quarter	-3 012	-1 557	23 302	-2 956	26 258	4 858	2 450	1 333	6 092	11 525	5 910	-25 527	-20 930
2nd quarter	-934	-20 146	42 689	-156	42 845	8 625	8 036	362	4 232	21 590	6 411	-28 012	-23 439
3rd quarter	3 987	17 817	7 568	-884	8 452	4 432	6 103	1 447	1 662	-5 192	458	-27 257	-23 384
4th quarter	492	-7 241	44 192	7 136	37 056	6 552	10 512	9 426	4 640	5 926	3 953	-28 276	-26 589
1985													
1st quarter	475	284	18 342	-10 962	29 304	4 913	3 390	9 615	-720	12 106	10 597	-24 933	-23 519
2nd quarter	2 337	3 325	29 334	8 502	20 832	4 376	6 888	7 194	1 724	650	1 619	-30 473	-28 689
3rd quarter	-2 779	3 847	38 263	2 506	35 757	4 839	9 136	11 669	2 801	7 312	-1 265	-31 263	-31 303
4th quarter	-10 375	-8 779	60 179	-1 165	61 344	5 618	6 219	22 484	6 046	20 977	5 528	-35 212	-34 648
1986													
1st quarter	-6 230	4 916	41 489	2 712	38 777	3 431	6 420	18 730	696	9 500	10 042	-34 487	-34 209
2nd quarter	-2 722	-13 660	53 710	15 918	37 792	5 520	4 620	22 752	1 635	3 265	6 851	-33 069	-35 692
3rd quarter	-7 638	-18 909	70 876	15 789	55 087	8 746	-854	17 107	1 947	28 141	-282	-35 635	-38 049
4th quarter	-5 183	-32 322	63 933	1 229	62 704	17 723	-2 277	12 380	-953	35 831	11 975	-35 343	-39 226
1987													
1st quarter	-5 715	20 237	42 247	14 199	28 048	12 883	-2 326	18 372	6 151	-7 032	-11 246	-36 998	-39 265
2nd quarter	712	-22 873	57 331	10 444	46 887	8 593	-731	15 960	5 595	17 470	9 301	-38 243	-39 985
3rd quarter	-1 319	-16 860	83 145	764	82 381	20 763	-1 835	12 676	6 656	44 121	-15 319	-38 042	-40 129
4th quarter	-724	-22 623	65 910	19 980	45 930	16 230	2 649	-4 888	-39	31 978	8 222	-38 406	-41 282
1988													
1st quarter	-3 454	15 982	32 028	24 925	7 103	8 425	6 511	2 423	12 593	-22 849	-2 077	-32 213	-32 952
2nd quarter	-9 954	-11 383	74 531	6 006	68 525	13 717	7 673	9 702	6 742	30 691	-22 325	-28 009	-28 896
3rd quarter	-5 217	-30 037	52 797	-1 974	54 771	13 778	4 743	7 464	6 399	22 387	24 962	-26 095	-27 924
4th quarter	-2 568	-28 489	87 166	10 801	76 365	21 815	7 112	6 764	7 159	33 515	-19 841	-28 252	-31 387
1989													
1st quarter	-9 293	-27 010	66 666	7 700	58 966	18 584	10 961	8 544	6 637	14 240	12 065	-23 615	-25 156
2nd quarter	-5 767	23 844	10 980	-5 115	16 094	15 325	4 789	9 365	12 000	-25 385	21 426	-22 830	-24 337
3rd quarter	-5 924	-22 394	74 068	13 060	61 008	11 519	12 744	10 270	-1 121	27 596	1 515	-22 186	-24 044
4th quarter	-6 662	-32 600	73 215	-7 142	80 357	22 846	7 024	10 588	4 570	35 329	12 096	-22 004	-23 444
1990													
1st quarter	3 019	57 713	-22 824	-6 421	-16 403	15 774	1 709	1 311	12 904	-48 101	5 930	-20 303	-20 915
2nd quarter	-5 069	-16 022	41 215	6 207	35 008	13 773	6 257	2 114	6 713	6 151	14 443	-17 372	-18 611
3rd quarter	-15 514	-10 668	63 231	13 937	49 294	8 313	6 044	-2 874	16 838	20 973	4 002	-21 571	-23 682
4th quarter	-10 260	-18 644	59 949	20 186	39 763	10 635	2 256	1 041	8 678	17 153	-1 175	-19 605	-13 750

1. A minus sign indicates capital outflow or decrease in foreign official assets in the United States.
2. Sum of credits and debits with the signs reversed.

Table 22-10. Productivity and Related Data

(1992=100, seasonally adjusted.)

Year and quarter	Business sector								Nonfarm business sector							
	Output per hour of all persons	Output	Hours of all persons	Compensation per hour	Real compensation per hour	Unit labor costs	Unit nonlabor payments	Implicit price deflator	Output per hour of all persons	Output	Hours of all persons	Compensation per hour	Real compensation per hour	Unit labor costs	Unit nonlabor payments	Implicit price deflator
1963	55.0	36.8	67.0	15.4	65.4	28.0	26.9	27.6	58.1	36.6	63.1	16.0	67.8	27.5	26.5	27.1
1964	57.5	39.2	68.1	16.2	67.9	28.2	27.5	27.9	60.6	39.1	64.6	16.7	69.9	27.6	27.3	27.5
1965	59.6	41.9	70.4	16.8	69.4	28.2	28.6	28.4	62.4	41.9	67.1	17.2	71.1	27.6	28.2	27.8
1966	62.0	44.8	72.3	17.9	71.9	28.9	29.3	29.1	64.6	44.9	69.5	18.2	73.2	28.2	28.9	28.5
1967	63.4	45.6	72.0	19.0	73.8	29.9	29.7	29.9	65.8	45.7	69.4	19.3	75.1	29.4	29.4	29.4
1968	65.4	47.9	73.4	20.4	76.3	31.3	30.6	31.0	67.8	48.1	70.9	20.7	77.5	30.6	30.4	30.5
1969	65.7	49.4	75.2	21.9	77.4	33.3	30.9	32.4	67.9	49.5	72.9	22.2	78.5	32.6	30.5	31.9
1970	67.0	49.4	73.7	23.5	78.9	35.1	31.6	33.9	68.9	49.5	71.8	23.7	79.5	34.4	31.3	33.3
1971	69.9	51.3	73.3	25.0	80.4	35.8	34.4	35.3	71.8	51.4	71.5	25.3	81.1	35.2	33.9	34.7
1972	72.2	54.7	75.7	26.6	82.7	36.8	35.8	36.5	74.2	54.9	73.9	26.9	83.6	36.2	34.9	35.8
1973	74.5	58.5	78.5	28.9	84.5	38.8	37.7	38.4	76.6	58.9	76.9	29.1	85.1	38.0	35.3	37.0
1974	73.2	57.6	78.6	31.7	83.5	43.2	40.0	42.1	75.4	58.0	77.0	32.0	84.2	42.4	38.0	40.8
1975	75.8	57.0	75.2	34.9	84.4	46.1	46.1	46.1	77.4	57.0	73.6	35.2	85.0	45.5	44.6	45.1
1976	78.5	60.9	77.6	38.0	86.8	48.4	48.6	48.5	80.3	61.1	76.1	38.2	87.3	47.6	47.5	47.6
1977	79.8	64.3	80.6	41.0	87.9	51.4	51.5	51.4	81.5	64.6	79.2	41.3	88.5	50.7	50.6	50.6
1978	80.7	68.3	84.7	44.6	89.5	55.3	54.8	55.1	82.6	68.8	83.3	45.0	90.2	54.5	53.4	54.1
1979	80.7	70.6	87.5	48.9	89.7	60.7	58.3	59.8	82.3	70.9	86.3	49.3	90.3	59.9	56.5	58.7
1980	80.4	69.8	86.8	54.2	89.5	67.4	61.5	65.2	82.0	70.2	85.6	54.6	90.0	66.5	60.5	64.3
1981	82.0	71.7	87.4	59.4	89.5	72.4	69.2	71.2	83.0	71.6	86.2	59.9	90.3	72.1	67.7	70.5
1982	81.7	69.6	85.2	63.8	90.9	78.2	70.3	75.3	82.5	69.4	84.1	64.3	91.6	77.9	69.4	74.8
1983	84.6	73.3	86.6	66.5	91.0	78.6	76.4	77.8	86.3	73.8	85.6	67.1	91.8	77.8	76.2	77.2
1984	87.0	79.7	91.6	69.5	91.3	79.8	80.4	80.0	88.1	80.0	90.7	70.0	92.0	79.4	79.3	79.4
1985	88.7	83.1	93.6	72.9	92.7	82.1	82.2	82.2	89.3	83.0	93.0	73.2	93.2	82.0	81.6	81.9
1986	91.4	86.1	94.2	76.7	95.8	83.9	82.8	83.5	92.0	86.2	93.8	77.0	96.3	83.7	82.4	83.2
1987	91.9	89.2	97.0	79.7	96.3	86.7	83.6	85.6	92.3	89.3	96.7	80.0	96.6	86.6	83.2	85.4
1988	93.0	92.9	100.0	83.5	97.3	89.8	85.7	88.3	93.5	93.3	99.8	83.6	97.5	89.4	85.4	87.9
1989	93.9	96.2	102.4	85.8	95.9	91.3	91.8	91.5	94.2	96.5	102.4	85.8	95.9	91.1	91.3	91.2
1990	95.2	97.6	102.6	90.7	96.5	95.3	93.9	94.8	95.3	97.8	102.7	90.5	96.3	95.0	93.6	94.5
1963																
1st quarter	54.1	36.0	66.6	15.2	64.8	28.1	26.5	27.5	57.1	35.7	62.5	15.8	67.3	27.6	26.1	27.1
2nd quarter	54.5	36.5	67.0	15.3	65.0	28.0	26.7	27.6	57.6	36.3	63.0	15.8	67.4	27.5	26.4	27.1
3rd quarter	55.6	37.3	67.0	15.5	65.5	27.9	27.2	27.6	58.8	37.1	63.2	16.0	67.7	27.2	26.8	27.1
4th quarter	55.8	37.6	67.3	15.7	66.1	28.1	27.2	27.8	58.8	37.4	63.6	16.2	68.3	27.5	26.7	27.2
1964																
1st quarter	57.2	38.5	67.3	16.0	67.2	27.9	27.6	27.8	60.2	38.5	64.0	16.4	69.0	27.3	27.3	27.3
2nd quarter	57.3	39.0	68.0	16.1	67.4	28.0	27.5	27.8	60.6	39.0	64.4	16.6	69.5	27.4	27.4	27.4
3rd quarter	57.9	39.6	68.3	16.3	68.2	28.1	27.6	27.9	61.1	39.5	64.7	16.8	70.4	27.5	27.5	27.5
4th quarter	57.5	39.6	68.9	16.4	68.4	28.6	27.2	28.1	60.3	39.5	65.4	16.9	70.4	28.0	26.9	27.6
1965																
1st quarter	58.6	40.8	69.6	16.6	68.9	28.3	28.0	28.2	61.3	40.7	66.4	17.0	70.6	27.7	27.8	27.7
2nd quarter	58.7	41.4	70.5	16.7	68.9	28.4	28.1	28.3	61.7	41.3	67.0	17.1	70.7	27.8	27.8	27.8
3rd quarter	60.1	42.3	70.3	16.9	69.6	28.1	28.8	28.4	62.8	42.2	67.1	17.3	71.2	27.6	28.4	27.9
4th quarter	60.9	43.4	71.2	17.1	69.8	28.0	29.4	28.5	63.9	43.3	67.9	17.5	71.7	27.4	28.9	28.0
1966																
1st quarter	62.0	44.6	71.9	17.5	70.9	28.2	29.6	28.7	64.8	44.6	68.9	17.8	72.3	27.5	29.0	28.0
2nd quarter	61.8	44.7	72.3	17.8	71.6	28.8	29.1	28.9	64.5	44.8	69.5	18.1	72.9	28.1	28.7	28.3
3rd quarter	61.8	44.8	72.5	18.1	72.0	29.2	29.1	29.2	64.4	45.0	69.8	18.4	73.2	28.5	28.7	28.6
4th quarter	62.4	45.1	72.4	18.4	72.6	29.5	29.4	29.4	64.8	45.2	69.7	18.6	73.6	28.7	29.2	28.9
1967																
1st quarter	63.1	45.5	72.2	18.6	73.2	29.4	29.7	29.5	65.5	45.5	69.4	18.9	74.5	28.9	29.4	29.1
2nd quarter	63.5	45.4	71.5	18.9	74.0	29.8	29.5	29.7	65.7	45.4	69.1	19.2	75.2	29.2	29.2	29.2
3rd quarter	63.4	45.7	72.0	19.1	74.1	30.1	29.8	30.0	65.9	45.7	69.4	19.4	75.4	29.5	29.4	29.5
4th quarter	63.5	46.0	72.5	19.3	74.1	30.4	30.0	30.2	66.0	46.1	69.8	19.7	75.6	29.8	29.6	29.7
1968																
1st quarter	64.9	47.1	72.5	19.9	75.6	30.6	30.4	30.6	67.5	47.2	69.9	20.2	76.9	30.0	30.2	30.1
2nd quarter	65.6	48.0	73.1	20.2	76.2	30.9	30.9	30.9	68.1	48.1	70.7	20.6	77.4	30.2	30.7	30.4
3rd quarter	65.5	48.3	73.7	20.6	76.4	31.4	30.6	31.1	67.9	48.4	71.3	20.9	77.5	30.7	30.3	30.6
4th quarter	65.4	48.5	74.1	21.0	77.0	32.1	30.6	31.5	67.8	48.6	71.7	21.3	78.1	31.4	30.3	31.0
1969																
1st quarter	65.7	49.3	75.1	21.1	76.4	32.1	31.3	31.8	68.4	49.5	72.3	21.6	78.2	31.6	30.9	31.3
2nd quarter	65.6	49.4	75.2	21.7	77.2	33.0	31.0	32.3	67.9	49.5	73.0	21.9	78.3	32.3	30.6	31.7
3rd quarter	65.7	49.6	75.4	22.1	77.8	33.6	30.9	32.6	67.8	49.8	73.4	22.3	78.5	32.9	30.5	32.0
4th quarter	65.6	49.2	75.1	22.6	78.3	34.4	30.6	33.0	67.5	49.4	73.1	22.8	78.9	33.7	30.0	32.4
1970																
1st quarter	65.9	49.2	74.7	23.0	78.5	34.9	30.5	33.3	67.7	49.3	72.9	23.2	79.0	34.2	30.1	32.7
2nd quarter	66.6	49.3	74.0	23.3	78.4	35.0	31.7	33.7	68.7	49.4	72.0	23.5	79.2	34.3	31.4	33.2
3rd quarter	68.0	49.9	73.3	23.8	79.2	35.0	32.1	33.9	70.0	50.0	71.4	24.0	80.0	34.3	31.7	33.4
4th quarter	67.5	49.1	72.7	24.1	79.1	35.7	32.2	34.4	69.3	49.2	70.9	24.3	79.6	35.0	31.9	33.9
1971																
1st quarter	69.6	50.8	72.9	24.6	79.9	35.3	33.9	34.8	71.5	50.9	71.2	24.8	80.6	34.6	33.5	34.2
2nd quarter	69.7	51.1	73.4	24.9	80.1	35.7	34.4	35.2	71.7	51.2	71.4	25.1	81.1	35.1	33.9	34.6
3rd quarter	70.6	51.6	73.1	25.3	80.8	35.9	34.9	35.5	72.4	51.7	71.3	25.5	81.5	35.3	34.5	35.0
4th quarter	69.8	51.6	74.0	25.5	80.7	36.5	34.4	35.7	71.6	51.7	72.3	25.7	81.4	35.9	33.8	35.1
1972																
1st quarter	70.7	53.0	74.9	26.1	82.0	36.9	34.7	36.1	72.9	53.2	73.1	26.3	82.8	36.1	34.3	35.5
2nd quarter	72.2	54.5	75.4	26.4	82.4	36.5	35.8	36.3	74.2	54.7	73.7	26.6	83.2	35.9	35.1	35.6
3rd quarter	72.5	55.1	75.9	26.7	82.7	36.8	36.2	36.6	74.7	55.3	74.1	27.0	83.7	36.2	35.2	35.8
4th quarter	73.4	56.2	76.7	27.3	83.6	37.2	36.5	36.9	75.2	56.4	74.9	27.6	84.5	36.6	35.1	36.1
1973																
1st quarter	74.9	58.1	77.6	28.1	84.9	37.6	36.9	37.3	77.0	58.5	75.9	28.3	85.5	36.8	35.5	36.3
2nd quarter	74.9	58.7	78.4	28.5	84.4	38.1	37.7	37.9	77.0	59.1	76.8	28.8	85.1	37.3	35.5	36.7
3rd quarter	74.0	58.3	78.8	29.1	84.5	39.4	37.5	38.7	76.4	59.0	77.2	29.3	85.1	38.4	34.9	37.1
4th quarter	74.2	58.8	79.4	29.7	84.0	40.0	38.7	39.5	75.8	58.9	77.7	29.9	84.7	39.5	35.4	38.0

Table 22-10. Productivity and Related Data—*Continued*

(1992=100, seasonally adjusted.)

Year and quarter	Nonfinancial corporations										Manufacturing					
	Output per hour of all employees	Output	Employee hours	Compensation per hour	Real compensation per hour	Unit costs			Unit profits	Implicit price deflator	Output per hour of all persons	Output	Hours of all persons	Compensation per hour	Real compensation per hour	Unit labor costs
						Total	Labor costs	Nonlabor or costs								
1963	61.8	34.4	55.8	17.2	73.2	26.7	27.9	23.3	57.8	29.3	45.8	43.2	94.4	16.4	69.5	35.7
1964	64.1	36.9	57.5	18.0	75.3	26.7	28.0	23.3	60.2	29.6	47.5	45.8	96.4	17.0	71.5	35.9
1965	65.8	39.9	60.7	18.5	76.3	26.8	28.1	23.1	64.8	30.0	48.7	49.6	102.0	17.4	71.8	35.8
1966	66.7	42.7	64.0	19.5	78.2	27.6	29.2	23.2	64.7	30.7	49.2	53.4	108.6	18.2	73.0	37.0
1967	67.7	43.8	64.7	20.6	80.0	28.8	30.4	24.6	60.5	31.5	51.0	55.1	108.0	19.2	74.7	37.6
1968	70.0	46.6	66.5	22.1	82.6	30.2	31.6	26.2	60.3	32.7	52.8	57.8	109.6	20.7	77.2	39.1
1969	70.1	48.4	69.1	23.6	83.7	32.3	33.7	28.3	54.4	34.1	53.7	59.6	110.9	22.2	78.5	41.3
1970	70.4	48.0	68.1	25.3	84.7	34.8	35.9	31.9	44.4	35.6	54.3	56.7	104.4	23.7	79.5	43.7
1971	73.3	49.9	68.0	26.9	86.3	35.8	36.7	33.4	50.2	37.0	58.0	58.3	100.5	25.2	80.8	43.4
1972	75.3	53.8	71.5	28.4	88.4	36.6	37.8	33.5	54.1	38.1	60.5	63.5	105.1	26.5	82.3	43.8
1973	76.1	57.0	74.9	30.7	89.9	38.9	40.4	35.1	55.5	40.3	61.7	68.1	110.4	28.5	83.4	46.2
1974	74.5	56.0	75.2	33.7	88.7	43.9	45.2	40.5	49.2	44.4	61.5	66.3	107.9	31.6	83.4	51.5
1975	77.3	55.1	71.3	37.0	89.3	47.3	47.9	45.9	64.1	48.8	64.5	62.7	97.2	35.5	85.6	55.0
1976	79.8	59.5	74.6	40.0	91.4	49.0	50.2	45.9	72.3	51.0	67.2	68.4	101.9	38.4	87.8	57.2
1977	81.6	63.8	78.2	43.2	92.5	51.4	52.9	47.4	79.4	53.8	69.9	74.2	106.1	41.8	89.6	59.8
1978	82.1	68.1	82.9	46.8	93.9	55.1	57.0	50.0	82.5	57.4	70.6	78.1	110.6	45.2	90.6	64.0
1979	81.5	70.2	86.1	51.1	93.8	60.7	62.7	55.1	76.7	62.0	70.0	79.0	112.7	49.6	90.9	70.8
1980	81.1	69.2	85.3	56.4	93.1	68.4	69.6	65.1	68.8	68.4	70.3	75.5	107.5	55.6	91.7	79.1
1981	82.6	71.5	86.5	61.6	92.9	74.6	74.6	74.8	82.4	75.3	70.9	75.8	107.0	61.1	92.1	86.1
1982	83.4	70.0	83.9	66.1	94.1	80.0	79.2	82.3	75.0	79.6	74.4	72.9	97.9	67.0	95.4	89.9
1983	85.9	73.3	85.3	68.4	93.6	80.1	79.6	81.5	91.2	81.1	76.9	76.1	98.9	68.8	94.2	89.5
1984	88.2	80.2	91.0	71.2	93.6	80.9	80.7	81.1	108.6	83.2	79.7	83.9	105.3	71.2	93.6	89.4
1985	89.9	83.8	93.2	74.4	94.7	82.7	82.7	82.4	104.2	84.5	82.5	86.3	104.6	75.1	95.6	91.0
1986	91.6	85.9	93.7	78.0	97.5	85.3	85.1	85.7	88.0	85.5	86.3	88.9	103.0	78.5	98.1	91.0
1987	94.7	90.7	95.8	81.7	98.7	86.0	86.2	85.3	98.1	87.0	88.6	91.9	103.8	80.7	97.5	91.1
1988	95.5	95.8	100.0	383.8	97.7	87.6	87.7	87.4	108.0	89.4	90.3	96.2	106.6	84.0	97.9	93.0
1989	94.6	97.4	102.0	986.2	96.3	92.0	91.1	94.6	97.3	92.5	90.5	96.9	107.1	86.6	96.8	95.8
1990	95.4	98.3	103.0	90.8	96.6	95.9	95.2	98.0	94.3	95.8	92.9	97.4	104.8	90.8	96.6	97.7
1963																
1st quarter	60.8	33.5	55.1	17.0	72.7	26.8	28.0	23.5	55.4	29.2	45.1	42.3	93.7	16.2	68.9	35.9
2nd quarter	61.5	34.3	55.7	17.1	72.8	26.6	27.8	23.2	58.0	29.2	45.9	43.2	94.3	16.3	69.2	35.4
3rd quarter	62.1	34.8	56.0	17.3	73.1	26.6	27.8	23.3	58.5	29.3	45.9	43.4	94.6	16.4	69.3	35.7
4th quarter	62.5	35.2	56.3	17.5	73.8	26.7	28.0	23.3	59.2	29.4	46.5	44.1	94.9	16.6	70.2	35.8
1964																
1st quarter	63.8	36.0	56.4	17.7	74.5	26.5	27.8	23.1	61.3	29.5	47.0	44.7	95.0	16.8	70.6	35.7
2nd quarter	63.9	36.6	57.2	17.9	74.9	26.6	27.9	23.2	60.3	29.5	47.5	45.6	96.1	17.0	71.2	35.7
3rd quarter	64.6	37.3	57.8	18.1	75.6	26.7	28.0	23.2	60.1	29.5	47.7	46.2	97.0	17.2	71.8	36.0
4th quarter	64.1	37.5	58.5	18.1	75.6	27.0	28.3	23.5	58.9	29.7	48.0	46.8	97.5	17.2	71.7	35.9
1965																
1st quarter	65.3	38.9	59.5	18.3	75.8	26.7	27.9	23.3	64.1	29.8	48.3	48.4	100.3	17.3	71.7	35.7
2nd quarter	65.5	39.4	60.2	18.4	75.8	26.8	28.1	23.2	64.8	30.0	48.8	49.3	101.0	17.4	71.6	35.6
3rd quarter	65.9	40.1	60.9	18.6	76.4	26.8	28.2	23.1	64.7	30.0	48.9	50.1	102.4	17.4	71.8	35.6
4th quarter	66.5	41.2	62.0	18.8	76.9	26.8	28.3	23.0	65.8	30.1	48.7	50.8	104.2	17.6	72.0	36.1
1966																
1st quarter	66.6	42.0	63.1	19.0	77.1	27.0	28.5	22.7	67.1	30.4	48.8	52.1	106.7	17.8	72.3	36.5
2nd quarter	66.7	42.6	63.8	19.4	77.8	27.4	29.0	23.0	65.2	30.6	48.9	53.1	108.6	18.1	72.6	36.9
3rd quarter	66.6	42.9	64.4	19.7	78.3	27.8	29.5	23.3	63.1	30.8	49.3	53.9	109.4	18.3	73.0	37.2
4th quarter	66.9	43.3	64.7	19.9	78.8	28.1	29.8	23.6	63.4	31.1	49.7	54.6	109.8	18.6	73.4	37.4
1967																
1st quarter	67.1	43.3	64.6	20.2	79.5	28.4	30.1	24.0	61.0	31.2	50.1	54.6	108.8	18.8	74.1	37.5
2nd quarter	67.6	43.5	64.3	20.4	80.1	28.7	30.2	24.4	59.9	31.3	50.7	54.4	107.5	19.0	74.6	37.6
3rd quarter	67.7	43.8	64.7	20.7	80.3	29.0	30.6	24.9	59.9	31.6	51.0	54.8	107.4	19.4	75.1	38.0
4th quarter	68.3	44.6	65.3	21.0	80.4	29.2	30.7	25.2	61.2	31.9	52.2	56.5	108.2	19.6	75.2	37.6
1968																
1st quarter	69.2	45.3	65.5	21.6	82.0	29.7	31.2	25.7	60.1	32.3	52.5	57.1	108.7	20.1	76.5	38.3
2nd quarter	70.0	46.3	66.2	21.9	82.6	29.9	31.3	26.0	61.1	32.5	52.9	57.7	109.2	20.6	77.4	38.9
3rd quarter	70.3	47.0	67.0	22.3	82.6	30.3	31.7	26.4	59.9	32.8	52.7	57.9	109.9	20.8	77.1	39.4
4th quarter	70.5	47.6	67.5	22.7	83.3	30.8	32.2	26.8	60.0	33.2	53.1	58.7	110.4	21.2	77.7	39.9
1969																
1st quarter	70.2	48.0	68.4	23.0	83.2	31.2	32.7	27.3	58.7	33.6	53.7	59.5	110.8	21.6	78.2	40.1
2nd quarter	70.2	48.4	69.0	23.4	83.5	31.9	33.4	28.0	56.1	33.9	53.5	59.5	111.2	21.9	78.2	41.0
3rd quarter	70.1	48.8	69.6	23.8	83.9	32.6	34.0	28.6	53.5	34.3	53.8	59.9	111.4	22.4	78.7	41.6
4th quarter	69.8	48.6	69.6	24.3	84.3	33.4	34.8	29.4	49.5	34.7	53.8	59.3	110.2	22.8	79.0	42.4
1970																
1st quarter	69.3	47.9	69.2	24.7	84.2	34.3	35.7	30.6	44.2	35.1	53.0	57.5	108.4	23.1	78.9	43.6
2nd quarter	70.1	48.0	68.5	25.1	84.3	34.6	35.8	31.5	46.6	35.6	54.0	57.0	105.6	23.6	79.4	43.7
3rd quarter	71.2	48.4	68.0	25.6	85.1	34.8	35.9	32.1	45.1	35.7	54.8	56.8	103.6	24.0	79.8	43.8
4th quarter	71.0	47.5	67.0	25.9	84.8	35.6	36.4	33.3	41.8	36.1	55.6	55.6	99.9	24.3	79.7	43.6
1971																
1st quarter	72.8	49.1	67.4	26.3	85.7	35.3	36.2	33.1	49.5	36.5	56.9	57.3	100.6	24.8	80.7	43.6
2nd quarter	72.9	49.5	67.8	26.7	86.2	35.7	36.6	33.3	49.9	36.9	57.7	58.0	100.5	25.1	80.8	43.5
3rd quarter	73.7	50.0	67.9	27.1	86.6	36.0	36.8	33.7	50.1	37.2	58.3	58.3	100.0	25.3	80.8	43.5
4th quarter	73.9	50.9	68.9	27.3	86.6	36.1	37.0	33.6	51.3	37.4	59.3	59.8	100.9	25.5	80.9	43.1
1972																
1st quarter	74.4	52.2	70.1	27.9	87.6	36.3	37.4	33.2	52.9	37.7	60.0	61.8	102.9	26.0	81.7	43.3
2nd quarter	74.9	53.3	71.2	28.2	88.0	36.6	37.6	33.8	51.9	37.9	60.1	63.0	104.7	26.3	82.0	43.7
3rd quarter	75.4	54.1	71.7	28.5	88.4	36.7	37.9	33.5	54.3	38.2	60.4	63.5	105.2	26.6	82.4	44.0
4th quarter	76.3	55.6	72.9	29.2	89.4	36.9	38.2	33.5	57.0	38.6	61.3	65.8	107.4	27.0	82.9	44.1
1973																
1st quarter	77.0	56.9	73.9	29.8	90.0	37.3	38.7	33.7	58.2	39.1	61.5	67.3	109.4	27.7	83.8	45.1
2nd quarter	76.1	56.9	74.7	30.3	89.8	38.5	39.9	34.7	54.7	39.8	61.6	68.0	110.4	28.2	83.4	45.8
3rd quarter	75.8	56.9	75.0	31.0	90.0	39.5	40.9	35.6	53.8	40.7	62.1	68.6	110.4	28.7	83.4	46.3
4th quarter	75.4	57.1	75.8	31.6	89.5	40.5	42.0	36.3	55.4	41.7	61.5	68.5	111.4	29.3	82.9	47.6

Table 22-10. Productivity and Related Data—Continued

(1992=100, seasonally adjusted.)

Year and quarter	Business sector								Nonfarm business sector							
	Output per hour of all persons	Output	Hours of all persons	Com-pensa-tion per hour	Real com-pensa-tion per hour	Unit labor costs	Unit nonlabor pay-ments	Implicit price deflator	Output per hour of all persons	Output	Hours of all persons	Com-pensa-tion per hour	Real com-pensa-tion per hour	Unit labor costs	Unit nonlabor pay-ments	Implicit price deflator
1974																
1st quarter	73.3	58.1	79.3	30.3	83.2	41.3	38.6	40.3	75.7	58.6	77.3	30.7	84.2	40.5	35.9	38.8
2nd quarter	73.7	58.2	79.0	31.3	83.7	42.5	39.3	41.3	75.7	58.6	77.4	31.5	84.4	41.7	37.8	40.3
3rd quarter	72.9	57.3	78.6	32.2	83.9	44.2	39.9	42.7	74.7	57.7	77.2	32.4	84.4	43.4	38.2	41.5
4th quarter	73.2	56.8	77.6	32.9	83.2	45.0	42.3	44.0	75.3	57.2	76.0	33.2	83.9	44.1	40.3	42.7
1975																
1st quarter	74.4	55.8	75.0	34.0	84.0	45.7	43.9	45.0	76.0	55.9	73.5	34.2	84.6	45.0	42.6	44.1
2nd quarter	75.7	56.3	74.4	34.7	84.6	45.8	45.4	45.6	77.3	56.3	72.8	34.9	85.2	45.1	44.1	44.8
3rd quarter	76.5	57.5	75.2	35.1	84.2	45.9	47.3	46.4	78.1	57.4	73.5	35.5	85.0	45.4	45.5	45.5
4th quarter	76.6	58.4	76.3	35.9	84.4	46.9	47.7	47.2	78.1	58.4	74.8	36.1	85.0	46.2	45.9	46.1
1976																
1st quarter	77.9	60.2	77.2	36.8	85.6	47.3	48.2	47.6	79.6	60.4	75.8	37.0	86.0	46.5	46.8	46.6
2nd quarter	78.5	60.8	77.4	37.6	86.6	47.9	48.3	48.0	80.4	61.0	75.9	37.8	87.1	47.0	47.3	47.1
3rd quarter	78.6	61.1	77.7	38.4	87.0	48.8	48.5	48.7	80.5	61.3	76.1	38.7	87.7	48.0	47.5	47.8
4th quarter	79.0	61.7	78.0	39.2	87.7	49.6	49.4	49.5	80.7	61.9	76.7	39.4	88.1	48.8	48.4	48.7
1977																
1st quarter	79.5	62.6	78.8	39.9	87.6	50.2	50.4	50.3	81.1	62.8	77.5	40.1	88.0	49.5	49.3	49.4
2nd quarter	79.5	64.0	80.6	40.5	87.4	51.0	51.3	51.1	81.5	64.3	79.0	40.9	88.2	50.2	50.4	50.3
3rd quarter	80.5	65.4	81.2	41.4	88.1	51.4	52.1	51.7	82.3	65.7	79.8	41.7	88.7	50.7	51.5	51.0
4th quarter	79.8	65.4	81.9	42.1	88.4	52.8	52.4	52.7	81.2	65.4	80.5	42.5	89.0	52.3	51.2	51.9
1978																
1st quarter	79.3	65.4	82.4	43.3	89.4	54.6	51.6	53.5	81.2	65.7	81.0	43.7	90.2	53.8	50.2	52.5
2nd quarter	80.8	68.5	84.8	44.0	89.0	54.5	54.8	54.6	82.7	69.0	83.4	44.4	89.8	53.7	53.2	53.5
3rd quarter	81.1	69.2	85.3	45.0	89.4	55.4	55.8	55.6	82.9	69.5	83.9	45.3	90.1	54.7	54.3	54.6
4th quarter	81.4	70.2	86.2	46.1	89.8	56.6	56.9	56.7	83.4	70.8	84.9	46.4	90.5	55.7	55.5	55.6
1979																
1st quarter	80.8	70.3	87.0	47.3	90.1	58.5	56.7	57.8	82.5	70.7	85.7	47.6	90.7	57.7	54.7	56.6
2nd quarter	80.7	70.3	87.2	48.4	89.8	60.0	58.1	59.3	82.3	70.7	85.9	48.7	90.4	59.2	56.3	58.1
3rd quarter	80.6	70.9	87.9	49.4	89.5	61.3	59.0	60.5	82.1	71.2	86.7	49.8	90.0	60.6	57.1	59.3
4th quarter	80.5	71.0	88.2	50.6	89.4	62.9	59.4	61.6	82.1	71.3	86.8	51.0	90.1	62.2	57.7	60.5
1980																
1st quarter	80.8	71.0	87.9	52.1	89.2	64.5	60.6	63.1	82.3	71.4	86.8	52.4	89.7	63.7	59.6	62.2
2nd quarter	80.0	69.0	86.2	53.6	89.6	67.0	60.2	64.5	81.5	69.3	85.1	53.9	90.1	66.2	60.1	64.0
3rd quarter	80.1	68.8	85.9	54.9	89.7	68.6	61.4	65.9	81.8	69.2	84.7	55.3	90.3	67.6	60.3	65.0
4th quarter	80.7	70.4	87.2	56.2	89.6	69.6	63.9	67.5	82.4	70.8	85.9	56.6	90.3	68.7	62.0	66.3
1981																
1st quarter	82.0	72.0	87.8	57.5	89.2	70.1	67.8	69.3	83.5	72.3	86.5	58.0	90.0	69.5	66.3	68.3
2nd quarter	81.6	71.3	87.4	58.8	89.5	72.1	67.9	70.5	82.6	71.3	86.3	59.2	90.2	71.7	66.3	69.7
3rd quarter	82.7	72.3	87.4	60.1	89.8	72.7	70.7	72.0	83.5	72.0	86.3	60.6	90.5	72.6	69.0	71.3
4th quarter	81.6	71.1	87.1	61.0	89.6	74.8	70.2	73.1	82.5	70.8	85.9	61.5	90.3	74.6	69.2	72.6
1982																
1st quarter	80.8	69.5	86.0	62.3	90.4	77.1	68.6	74.0	81.7	69.3	84.8	62.8	91.1	76.9	67.6	73.5
2nd quarter	81.6	69.9	85.6	63.4	91.1	77.7	70.0	74.9	82.4	69.7	84.5	63.8	91.7	77.4	69.1	74.4
3rd quarter	81.7	69.4	84.9	64.5	91.0	78.9	70.6	75.8	82.7	69.2	83.8	65.0	91.8	78.6	69.6	75.3
4th quarter	82.4	69.5	84.3	65.2	91.1	79.0	72.0	76.4	83.3	69.2	83.1	65.7	91.8	78.9	71.2	76.1
1983																
1st quarter	83.2	70.4	84.7	65.7	91.3	79.0	73.3	76.9	84.3	70.4	83.6	66.3	92.2	78.7	72.5	76.4
2nd quarter	84.7	72.6	85.6	66.2	91.0	78.1	76.3	77.5	86.3	73.0	84.6	66.8	91.8	77.4	76.0	76.9
3rd quarter	84.9	74.1	87.3	66.6	90.6	78.4	77.5	78.1	87.0	75.0	86.2	67.2	91.5	77.2	77.7	77.4
4th quarter	85.6	76.0	88.8	67.5	91.1	78.9	78.4	78.7	87.3	76.8	87.9	68.0	91.7	77.8	78.3	78.0
1984																
1st quarter	86.3	78.0	90.4	68.2	90.8	79.0	79.6	79.3	87.5	78.4	89.6	68.7	91.4	78.5	78.5	78.5
2nd quarter	87.1	79.7	91.5	69.1	91.1	79.3	80.6	79.8	88.2	79.9	90.6	69.6	91.7	78.9	79.4	79.1
3rd quarter	87.2	80.3	92.1	69.9	91.5	80.1	80.5	80.3	88.3	80.5	91.2	70.4	92.2	79.7	79.6	79.7
4th quarter	87.5	80.9	92.5	70.6	91.8	80.8	80.8	80.8	88.4	81.0	91.6	71.1	92.4	80.4	79.8	80.2
1985																
1st quarter	87.6	81.7	93.3	71.4	91.9	81.5	81.5	81.5	88.4	81.7	92.5	71.8	92.5	81.3	80.6	81.0
2nd quarter	88.1	82.3	93.5	72.2	92.2	82.0	82.0	82.0	88.7	82.4	92.8	72.6	92.7	81.8	81.4	81.7
3rd quarter	89.5	83.8	93.6	73.3	93.0	82.0	82.8	82.3	89.8	83.6	93.1	73.6	93.4	82.0	82.6	82.2
4th quarter	89.8	84.5	94.1	74.6	93.6	83.0	82.4	82.8	90.2	84.5	93.7	74.8	93.9	82.9	81.9	82.6
1986																
1st quarter	90.8	85.3	94.0	75.4	94.3	83.1	82.7	83.0	91.3	85.4	93.5	75.8	94.7	83.0	82.5	82.8
2nd quarter	91.4	85.7	93.7	76.2	95.7	83.3	83.0	83.2	92.1	85.8	93.2	76.5	96.1	83.1	82.8	83.0
3rd quarter	91.8	86.5	94.3	76.9	96.0	83.7	83.2	83.5	92.4	86.6	93.8	77.2	96.5	83.6	82.6	83.3
4th quarter	91.6	86.9	94.9	78.1	96.9	85.3	82.2	84.2	92.2	87.1	94.5	78.5	97.4	85.2	81.6	83.9
1987																
1st quarter	91.2	87.6	96.1	78.4	96.0	85.9	82.4	84.6	91.7	87.7	95.7	78.7	96.4	85.8	82.0	84.4
2nd quarter	91.8	88.7	96.6	79.2	96.1	86.3	83.6	85.3	92.4	88.9	96.2	79.5	96.5	86.1	83.2	85.0
3rd quarter	91.7	89.3	97.4	79.9	96.0	87.1	83.9	85.9	92.1	89.4	97.1	80.2	96.4	87.1	83.4	85.7
4th quarter	92.7	91.0	98.1	81.1	96.7	87.5	84.5	86.4	93.1	91.1	97.9	81.4	97.0	87.4	84.0	86.2
1988																
1st quarter	92.7	91.5	98.7	81.8	96.9	88.2	84.5	86.9	93.0	91.6	98.5	82.0	97.1	88.2	84.0	86.7
2nd quarter	92.9	92.8	99.9	83.2	97.4	89.5	84.7	87.8	93.4	93.1	99.7	83.3	97.6	89.2	84.5	87.5
3rd quarter	93.0	93.1	100.1	84.1	97.4	90.4	86.1	88.8	93.5	93.6	100.0	84.2	97.5	90.0	85.6	88.4
4th quarter	93.2	94.4	101.2	84.7	97.1	90.8	87.3	89.5	94.1	95.2	101.1	84.8	97.3	90.1	87.4	89.1
1989																
1st quarter	93.7	95.7	102.1	84.8	96.4	90.5	90.2	90.4	94.0	95.9	102.0	84.9	96.5	90.3	89.3	90.0
2nd quarter	93.9	96.1	102.3	85.3	95.5	90.8	92.2	91.3	94.1	96.3	102.4	85.2	95.4	90.6	91.7	91.0
3rd quarter	93.8	96.4	102.7	85.9	95.5	91.5	92.5	91.9	94.2	96.6	102.6	85.9	95.5	91.2	92.2	91.6
4th quarter	94.3	96.8	102.7	87.2	96.1	92.5	92.6	92.5	94.6	97.0	102.6	87.2	96.1	92.2	92.0	92.2
1990																
1st quarter	95.0	98.2	103.4	88.5	96.0	93.2	93.8	93.4	95.1	98.4	103.4	88.4	95.9	92.9	93.3	93.0
2nd quarter	95.4	98.2	103.0	90.2	96.9	94.6	94.0	94.4	95.5	98.5	103.1	90.1	96.8	94.3	93.7	94.1
3rd quarter	95.6	97.7	102.3	91.6	96.8	95.9	94.1	95.2	95.6	97.9	102.4	91.4	96.6	95.6	93.7	94.9
4th quarter	94.8	96.5	101.8	92.4	96.1	97.4	93.7	96.1	94.9	96.6	101.8	92.3	96.0	97.2	93.6	95.9

Table 22-10. Productivity and Related Data—*Continued*

(1992=100, seasonally adjusted.)

Year and quarter	Nonfinancial corporations										Manufacturing					
	Output per hour of all employees	Output	Employee hours	Compensation per hour	Real compensation per hour	Unit costs Total	Labor costs	Nonlabor costs	Unit profits	Implicit price deflator	Output per hour of all persons	Output	Hours of all persons	Compensation per hour	Real compensation per hour	Unit labor costs
1974																
1st quarter	74.7	56.6	75.7	32.3	88.7	41.7	43.2	37.8	50.5	42.5	60.2	66.3	110.0	30.1	82.7	50.0
2nd quarter	75.1	56.7	75.5	33.2	88.9	42.9	44.3	39.3	49.9	43.5	61.3	66.7	108.8	31.2	83.4	50.9
3rd quarter	74.3	56.0	75.4	34.2	88.9	44.7	46.0	41.3	48.2	45.0	61.9	67.2	108.4	32.1	83.5	51.8
4th quarter	73.8	54.6	74.0	35.0	88.3	46.5	47.4	43.8	48.1	46.6	62.5	65.3	104.5	33.3	84.0	53.3
1975																
1st quarter	75.0	53.3	71.1	36.0	89.0	47.4	48.0	45.7	51.6	47.7	62.4	60.7	97.3	34.4	85.1	55.1
2nd quarter	77.1	54.2	70.3	36.6	89.5	47.1	47.5	46.1	60.3	48.3	63.9	61.1	95.6	35.2	85.9	55.0
3rd quarter	78.5	56.0	71.3	37.3	89.3	47.0	47.5	45.8	71.4	49.1	65.6	63.6	96.9	35.8	85.8	54.6
4th quarter	78.4	56.8	72.5	38.0	89.4	47.8	48.5	46.0	72.4	49.9	66.0	65.5	99.2	36.4	85.6	55.2
1976																
1st quarter	79.5	58.7	73.9	38.8	90.2	47.7	48.8	44.9	76.8	50.2	66.3	67.2	101.3	37.2	86.6	56.2
2nd quarter	79.6	59.2	74.4	39.6	91.1	48.6	49.7	45.6	72.1	50.6	66.7	67.8	101.7	38.0	87.6	57.0
3rd quarter	80.0	59.8	74.8	40.5	91.7	49.3	50.6	46.0	71.1	51.2	67.4	68.7	102.0	38.8	88.0	57.6
4th quarter	79.9	60.1	75.2	41.3	92.3	50.4	51.7	46.9	69.4	52.0	68.4	70.0	102.4	39.6	88.6	58.0
1977																
1st quarter	80.2	61.1	76.2	41.9	91.9	51.0	52.2	47.7	71.4	52.7	69.2	71.8	103.8	40.5	89.0	58.6
2nd quarter	81.5	63.4	77.8	42.7	92.2	51.0	52.4	47.1	79.9	53.4	70.0	74.2	106.1	41.3	89.1	59.0
3rd quarter	82.9	65.3	78.8	43.6	92.7	51.0	52.5	46.8	84.9	53.9	70.4	75.2	106.9	42.3	89.9	60.1
4th quarter	81.9	65.3	79.8	44.4	93.1	52.6	54.2	48.2	81.0	55.0	70.0	75.5	107.8	43.0	90.2	61.4
1978																
1st quarter	81.3	65.3	80.3	45.3	93.6	54.1	55.7	49.5	74.2	55.8	69.8	75.5	108.2	43.9	90.7	62.9
2nd quarter	82.4	68.2	82.8	46.2	93.4	54.3	56.1	49.4	85.3	56.9	70.6	78.1	110.6	44.5	90.0	63.0
3rd quarter	82.2	68.8	83.7	47.2	93.7	55.4	57.4	50.0	84.4	57.9	70.9	78.9	111.4	45.5	90.3	64.1
4th quarter	82.5	69.9	84.8	48.4	94.2	56.6	58.6	51.0	85.6	59.0	70.9	79.7	112.5	46.6	90.9	65.8
1979																
1st quarter	82.0	70.2	85.7	49.4	94.1	58.1	60.3	52.4	80.4	60.0	70.2	79.7	113.6	47.6	90.8	67.9
2nd quarter	81.7	70.1	85.8	50.6	93.9	59.9	61.9	54.3	78.2	61.4	70.4	79.3	112.6	49.1	91.1	69.7
3rd quarter	81.2	70.1	86.4	51.7	93.5	61.6	63.6	56.0	74.7	62.7	69.6	78.6	112.9	50.1	90.7	72.0
4th quarter	81.2	70.3	86.7	52.9	93.3	63.1	65.1	57.7	73.4	64.0	69.8	78.2	112.0	51.5	90.8	73.7
1980																
1st quarter	81.1	70.2	86.6	54.3	92.9	65.2	66.9	60.5	71.7	65.7	70.3	78.3	111.4	52.9	90.6	75.3
2nd quarter	80.5	68.3	84.8	55.8	93.2	68.0	69.3	64.5	61.2	67.4	69.8	74.5	106.7	54.8	91.6	78.5
3rd quarter	81.1	68.3	84.3	57.2	93.3	69.5	70.5	66.7	66.7	69.2	70.0	73.4	105.0	56.5	92.2	80.7
4th quarter	81.7	70.0	85.7	58.6	93.3	70.9	71.7	68.6	75.1	71.2	70.8	76.0	107.3	58.0	92.5	82.0
1981																
1st quarter	82.0	70.9	86.5	59.7	92.7	72.6	72.9	71.7	80.3	73.2	70.4	75.9	107.7	58.9	91.4	83.7
2nd quarter	82.3	71.3	86.6	61.0	93.0	74.0	74.1	73.7	80.2	74.5	70.8	76.5	107.9	60.4	92.0	85.3
3rd quarter	83.5	72.5	86.8	62.3	93.1	74.9	74.6	75.6	89.1	76.1	71.3	76.6	107.4	61.7	92.2	86.5
4th quarter	82.6	71.3	86.3	63.3	93.0	77.1	76.7	78.2	80.0	77.3	70.9	74.4	105.0	63.1	92.6	88.9
1982																
1st quarter	82.7	70.5	85.2	64.6	93.8	78.8	78.2	80.3	74.2	78.4	72.5	73.8	101.8	64.9	94.2	89.5
2nd quarter	83.6	70.4	84.3	65.7	94.4	79.5	78.6	81.8	77.9	79.3	74.6	73.8	98.9	66.8	95.9	89.5
3rd quarter	83.7	69.9	83.5	66.7	94.1	80.5	79.7	82.7	77.7	80.2	75.5	72.9	96.5	67.9	95.9	89.9
4th quarter	83.5	69.1	82.7	67.2	93.9	81.5	80.5	84.2	70.0	80.5	75.1	71.1	94.7	68.3	95.4	90.9
1983																
1st quarter	84.6	70.3	83.1	67.6	93.9	80.7	79.9	82.8	78.5	80.5	76.0	72.5	95.4	68.6	95.3	90.2
2nd quarter	85.9	72.4	84.3	68.1	93.6	79.9	79.3	81.7	89.7	80.8	76.5	74.7	97.7	68.6	94.3	89.7
3rd quarter	86.5	74.3	85.9	68.5	93.2	79.7	79.2	81.2	96.7	81.2	77.4	77.5	100.1	68.8	93.6	88.8
4th quarter	86.7	76.2	87.8	69.4	93.6	80.2	80.0	80.6	98.9	81.8	77.6	79.6	102.6	69.3	93.4	89.3
1984																
1st quarter	87.5	78.4	89.5	69.9	93.1	79.9	79.9	80.2	109.6	82.5	78.8	82.3	104.5	69.9	93.0	88.7
2nd quarter	88.2	80.0	90.7	70.8	93.4	80.4	80.3	80.7	110.7	83.0	79.4	83.8	105.6	70.6	93.2	89.0
3rd quarter	88.3	80.8	91.5	71.7	93.9	81.3	81.2	81.7	106.9	83.5	80.2	84.7	105.6	71.7	93.8	89.4
4th quarter	88.7	81.8	92.2	72.4	94.0	81.7	81.6	81.9	107.2	83.8	80.3	84.7	105.6	72.6	94.3	90.4
1985																
1st quarter	88.8	82.4	92.8	73.1	94.1	82.3	82.3	82.1	105.3	84.2	80.9	85.2	105.4	73.8	95.0	91.3
2nd quarter	89.4	83.2	93.1	73.9	94.3	82.7	82.6	82.9	102.3	84.4	82.5	86.2	104.5	74.5	95.1	90.3
3rd quarter	90.8	84.8	93.3	74.8	94.8	82.2	82.3	81.9	109.3	84.5	83.1	86.6	104.2	75.4	95.7	90.8
4th quarter	90.7	85.0	93.7	75.9	95.3	83.5	83.7	82.8	100.0	84.9	83.7	87.1	104.1	76.6	96.2	91.6
1986																
1st quarter	91.3	85.8	93.9	76.7	95.8	84.2	84.0	85.1	93.0	85.0	85.1	88.3	103.8	77.4	96.7	91.0
2nd quarter	91.2	85.3	93.6	77.4	97.2	85.0	84.8	85.4	88.5	85.3	86.0	88.6	103.0	77.9	97.9	90.6
3rd quarter	91.5	85.7	93.7	78.3	97.8	85.7	85.6	86.2	85.4	85.7	86.5	88.8	102.7	78.8	98.4	91.1
4th quarter	92.5	86.8	93.8	79.6	98.8	86.1	86.1	86.1	85.1	86.0	87.4	89.8	102.7	79.7	98.8	91.2
1987																
1st quarter	93.3	88.2	94.5	80.6	98.7	86.1	86.4	85.4	90.1	86.5	87.6	90.1	103.0	80.2	98.3	91.6
2nd quarter	94.6	90.0	95.1	81.3	98.6	85.8	86.0	85.4	97.0	86.7	88.6	91.2	103.0	80.4	97.5	90.7
3rd quarter	95.3	91.7	96.2	81.9	98.4	85.6	85.9	84.9	103.9	87.2	88.7	92.3	104.0	80.9	97.2	91.2
4th quarter	95.6	93.0	97.2	82.9	98.8	86.4	86.7	85.6	101.1	87.6	89.3	94.0	105.3	81.3	96.9	91.0
1988																
1st quarter	95.7	94.3	98.5	82.8	98.0	86.3	86.5	85.9	106.2	88.0	89.6	94.9	105.9	82.7	97.9	92.3
2nd quarter	96.0	95.4	99.4	83.9	98.3	87.2	87.5	86.5	106.5	88.8	90.2	95.9	106.4	83.5	97.7	92.5
3rd quarter	95.7	95.8	100.1	84.7	98.2	88.4	88.6	87.9	107.3	90.0	90.6	96.7	106.7	84.3	97.7	93.0
4th quarter	96.4	97.7	101.3	85.2	97.8	88.6	88.4	89.1	112.1	90.6	90.9	97.5	107.3	85.5	98.1	94.1
1989																
1st quarter	95.2	97.4	102.3	85.5	97.2	90.4	89.9	91.8	101.2	91.3	90.7	97.9	107.8	86.0	97.7	94.8
2nd quarter	94.4	97.0	102.7	85.8	96.0	91.7	90.8	94.1	98.7	92.3	90.6	97.3	107.4	85.8	96.1	94.7
3rd quarter	94.7	97.4	102.9	86.4	96.0	92.5	91.2	96.0	97.2	92.9	89.9	96.2	107.0	86.7	96.4	96.5
4th quarter	94.7	97.7	103.2	87.6	96.6	93.6	92.5	96.4	92.1	93.4	90.7	96.1	106.0	88.0	97.0	97.1
1990																
1st quarter	94.6	98.1	103.7	88.7	96.2	94.5	93.8	96.5	94.7	94.5	92.0	97.3	105.7	88.8	96.3	96.5
2nd quarter	95.6	99.0	103.5	90.4	97.1	95.1	94.5	96.5	100.2	95.5	92.3	97.6	105.8	90.4	97.1	98.0
3rd quarter	95.6	98.4	102.9	91.8	97.0	96.7	96.0	98.6	92.5	96.3	93.6	98.1	104.7	91.4	96.6	97.6
4th quarter	96.1	97.8	101.8	92.6	96.3	97.5	96.4	100.4	89.9	96.9	93.7	96.5	103.0	92.5	96.2	98.7

Table 23-1. New Plant and Equipment Spending [1]

(Billions of dollars, seasonally adjusted annual rates.)

Year and quarter	Mining	Manufacturing Total	Durables Total	Stone, clay and glass products	Primary metals	Blast furnaces and steel mills	Non-ferrous metals	Fabricated metals	Machinery except electrical	Electrical machinery
1961	1.26	15.53	7.43	0.70	1.28	0.86	0.29	0.52	1.11	1.05
1962	1.41	16.03	7.81	0.72	1.25	0.76	0.34	0.59	1.26	0.99
1963	1.26	17.27	8.64	0.70	1.51	0.88	0.46	0.69	1.24	1.02
1964	1.33	21.23	10.98	0.81	2.22	1.44	0.56	0.85	1.61	1.17
1965	1.36	25.41	13.49	0.86	2.57	1.59	0.71	0.86	2.24	1.69
1966	1.42	31.37	17.23	1.13	3.06	1.72	1.01	1.14	2.91	2.51
1967	1.38	32.25	17.83	0.92	3.31	1.90	1.11	1.29	3.02	3.13
1968	1.44	32.34	17.93	0.89	3.45	2.01	1.11	1.36	2.90	3.16
1969	1.77	36.27	19.97	1.12	3.29	1.83	1.06	1.34	3.63	3.27
1970	2.02	36.99	19.80	1.06	3.24	1.63	1.18	1.22	3.78	3.49
1971	2.67	33.60	16.78	0.94	2.69	1.27	1.02	1.20	3.15	3.03
1972	2.88	35.42	18.22	1.34	2.44	1.07	0.97	1.43	3.23	2.83
1973	3.30	42.35	22.63	1.58	2.94	1.25	1.22	1.81	3.95	3.48
1974	4.58	52.48	26.77	1.65	4.27	1.97	1.77	1.93	5.13	3.80
1975	6.12	53.66	25.37	1.67	5.43	3.08	1.72	1.96	4.86	3.08
1976	7.63	58.53	27.50	1.91	5.32	3.13	1.42	2.20	5.43	3.61
1977	9.81	67.48	32.77	2.30	4.97	2.88	1.30	2.45	6.35	4.61
1978	10.55	78.13	39.02	3.05	5.07	2.65	1.45	2.93	7.19	5.92
1979	11.05	95.13	47.72	3.69	5.96	3.36	1.60	3.17	9.80	7.69
1980	12.71	112.60	54.82	3.69	6.65	3.70	2.02	3.26	10.68	10.20
1981	15.81	128.68	58.93	3.03	7.19	3.87	2.34	3.42	12.39	11.41
1982	14.11	123.97	54.58	2.70	6.78	4.27	1.72	2.81	12.28	12.21
1983	10.64	117.35	51.61	2.62	5.89	3.66	1.57	2.56	11.98	12.68
1984	11.86	139.61	64.57	3.13	6.83	3.99	1.96	3.14	13.62	16.22
1985	12.00	152.88	70.87	3.58	7.45	4.66	1.75	3.25	13.83	17.09
1986	8.15	137.95	65.68	3.13	6.74	3.76	1.75	3.61	11.36	15.64
1987	8.28	141.06	68.03	3.32	8.59	5.30	1.98	3.62	11.87	16.84
1988	9.29	163.45	77.04	3.63	10.99	7.01	2.51	3.91	13.70	20.84
1989	9.21	183.80	82.56	4.00	12.03	7.87	2.64	4.17	14.58	20.46
1990	9.88	192.61	82.58	3.29	12.16	7.78	2.88	4.39	13.66	22.04
1991	10.02	182.81	77.64	2.89	10.74	6.53	2.81	4.03	12.68	20.97
1992	8.88	174.02	73.32	3.36	9.76	5.64	2.67	3.67	10.64	20.42
1993	10.08	179.47	81.45	4.31	9.87	5.64	2.59	3.92	9.71	24.41
1985										
1st quarter	12.13	147.69	68.84	3.36	7.22	4.34	1.87	3.13	13.87	17.66
2nd quarter	12.56	155.97	72.87	3.77	7.33	4.61	1.71	3.03	14.69	18.73
3rd quarter	12.14	154.76	70.77	3.69	7.46	4.68	1.73	3.38	13.65	16.78
4th quarter	11.19	151.98	70.61	3.47	7.69	4.88	1.72	3.44	13.20	15.72
1986										
1st quarter	9.71	142.28	65.33	3.18	7.19	4.29	1.71	3.65	12.02	14.42
2nd quarter	8.16	138.09	65.38	2.81	6.57	3.42	1.82	3.62	11.07	16.26
3rd quarter	7.35	133.95	65.53	2.95	6.29	3.61	1.55	3.52	11.25	14.97
4th quarter	7.52	138.07	66.31	3.51	6.95	3.75	1.89	3.64	11.18	16.55
1987										
1st quarter	7.49	135.22	67.34	3.07	7.47	4.57	1.59	3.57	11.12	16.51
2nd quarter	7.86	137.20	66.48	3.18	8.17	4.95	1.94	3.51	11.00	16.35
3rd quarter	8.60	142.75	68.57	3.57	8.81	5.44	2.09	3.61	12.29	17.07
4th quarter	9.03	146.91	69.43	3.42	9.53	5.94	2.24	3.79	12.72	17.29
1988										
1st quarter	9.29	155.63	73.68	3.44	10.29	6.35	2.49	3.86	13.68	19.40
2nd quarter	9.59	159.99	76.04	3.71	10.66	6.80	2.41	4.05	13.45	21.05
3rd quarter	9.25	165.72	77.43	3.53	11.61	7.48	2.59	3.88	13.01	21.04
4th quarter	9.01	169.85	80.02	3.78	11.22	7.21	2.57	3.87	14.48	21.60
1989										
1st quarter	8.99	173.07	79.84	4.03	11.10	7.15	2.48	4.00	14.26	20.46
2nd quarter	9.18	180.51	82.14	4.13	11.88	7.72	2.61	4.10	14.77	19.95
3rd quarter	9.22	185.92	83.80	4.12	12.17	7.97	2.67	4.38	14.49	21.14
4th quarter	9.39	191.98	83.86	3.78	12.66	8.40	2.78	4.19	14.77	20.36
1990										
1st quarter	9.70	191.73	85.75	3.61	12.60	8.23	2.90	4.52	14.64	23.07
2nd quarter	9.76	194.70	83.74	3.32	12.32	7.92	2.87	4.43	14.50	22.09
3rd quarter	9.89	195.06	83.16	3.26	11.91	7.46	2.91	4.44	13.85	22.15
4th quarter	10.13	189.25	79.01	3.02	11.94	7.63	2.84	4.20	12.16	21.25
1991										
1st quarter	10.05	190.50	80.31	2.92	11.91	7.54	2.92	4.18	13.12	21.18
2nd quarter	10.09	187.18	78.89	2.78	11.03	6.79	2.88	4.05	12.67	20.81
3rd quarter	9.97	178.24	75.54	2.82	10.75	6.70	2.69	4.01	12.59	21.08
4th quarter	9.98	178.33	76.85	3.02	9.72	5.53	2.75	3.89	12.49	20.95
1992										
1st quarter	8.99	173.14	73.26	3.00	9.82	5.76	2.67	3.65	10.31	20.27
2nd quarter	9.20	172.52	73.74	3.13	10.01	5.92	2.54	3.62	11.46	20.93
3rd quarter	8.96	173.05	72.63	3.32	9.58	5.58	2.64	3.49	10.54	20.55
4th quarter	8.43	176.74	73.64	3.83	9.67	5.41	2.80	3.88	10.29	20.08
1993										
1st quarter	8.98	173.99	78.19	4.16	8.94	5.22	2.26	3.54	10.39	24.04
2nd quarter	9.10	177.55	80.33	4.32	9.62	5.52	2.58	3.95	8.48	24.30
3rd quarter	11.09	182.48	82.74	4.27	10.16	5.80	2.64	4.02	9.93	23.91
4th quarter	10.92	182.15	83.64	4.44	10.53	5.88	2.81	4.12	10.05	25.20
1994										
1st quarter	11.43	185.04	86.03	5.03	11.28	6.93	2.31	3.99	9.10	25.33
2nd quarter	10.70	193.99	91.71	5.42	12.08	7.26	2.55	3.92	9.17	28.36

1. These series were discontinued in mid-1994; see Notes.

Table 23-1. New Plant and Equipment Spending [1]—Continued

(Billions of dollars, seasonally adjusted annual rates.)

| Year and quarter | Manufacturing—Continued | | | | | | | | | |
| | Durables—Continued | | | Nondurables | | | | | | |
	Transportation equipment	Motor vehicles	Aircraft	Total	Food and beverages	Textiles	Paper	Chemicals	Petroleum	Rubber
1961	1.78	1.38	0.30	8.10	1.50	0.35	0.62	1.60	2.97	0.36
1962	1.98	1.45	0.40	8.22	1.45	0.39	0.62	1.58	3.08	0.38
1963	2.37	1.82	0.44	8.63	1.50	0.43	0.70	1.72	3.10	0.39
1964	3.08	2.48	0.41	10.25	1.75	0.59	0.91	2.10	3.51	0.47
1965	3.74	3.00	0.53	11.92	1.87	0.79	1.07	2.82	3.88	0.59
1966	4.61	3.13	1.17	14.15	2.11	0.96	1.32	3.35	4.48	0.65
1967	4.44	2.85	1.25	14.42	2.05	0.77	1.49	3.08	4.84	0.67
1968	4.25	2.67	1.23	14.40	2.20	0.65	1.27	2.80	4.96	0.96
1969	4.80	2.99	1.29	16.31	2.76	0.86	1.62	3.01	5.26	1.07
1970	4.65	3.05	0.88	17.19	3.32	0.80	1.74	3.38	5.16	0.92
1971	3.54	2.42	0.63	16.82	3.35	0.90	1.29	3.27	5.21	0.79
1972	4.41	3.00	0.68	17.20	3.28	1.06	1.46	3.38	4.79	1.03
1973	5.60	3.83	0.79	19.72	3.74	1.02	1.99	4.17	4.61	1.56
1974	6.60	4.29	1.21	25.71	4.25	1.06	2.88	6.18	7.04	1.61
1975	5.46	3.33	1.19	28.28	4.38	0.86	2.93	7.12	9.07	1.20
1976	5.79	3.60	1.02	31.03	5.39	0.98	2.99	7.37	10.02	1.37
1977	8.32	5.82	1.14	34.71	5.72	1.18	3.48	7.35	11.82	1.77
1978	10.97	7.10	1.77	39.10	6.59	1.32	3.78	7.58	13.68	2.22
1979	13.47	8.06	2.71	47.41	7.42	1.45	5.18	9.24	16.77	2.18
1980	16.10	8.54	3.60	57.77	8.51	1.60	6.39	10.62	22.75	1.68
1981	16.91	9.10	3.40	69.75	10.13	1.76	5.95	11.99	31.94	1.77
1982	13.55	7.13	3.45	69.39	9.43	1.55	5.47	11.44	33.50	1.72
1983	11.86	6.56	2.95	65.74	8.46	1.63	5.73	11.59	29.47	2.05
1984	16.63	10.17	3.63	75.04	9.71	2.00	6.90	13.46	32.56	2.62
1985	19.61	13.39	3.51	82.01	11.35	1.82	8.14	14.35	34.06	3.34
1986	18.86	12.79	3.86	72.28	11.62	1.71	8.26	14.54	23.05	3.30
1987	16.73	10.88	3.60	73.03	12.10	2.00	8.54	13.92	22.06	2.94
1988	15.76	9.75	3.49	86.41	14.16	2.18	10.92	16.62	26.03	3.26
1989	18.71	11.49	4.17	101.24	15.89	2.25	15.58	18.47	30.08	3.79
1990	17.89	11.28	4.02	110.04	16.36	2.18	16.53	20.63	34.79	3.48
1991	17.19	10.20	4.05	105.17	17.43	1.96	11.50	21.52	35.59	3.43
1992	16.06	8.67	4.36	100.69	18.95	2.05	10.53	23.15	29.59	3.85
1993	19.16	12.28	3.23	98.02	18.78	2.27	10.31	21.83	28.71	3.32
1985										
1st quarter	17.87	11.32	3.59	78.85	10.70	2.06	7.58	14.28	32.98	2.99
2nd quarter	19.32	13.16	3.46	83.10	11.45	1.87	7.74	14.70	35.72	3.03
3rd quarter	19.59	12.97	3.79	83.99	11.46	1.78	8.23	14.45	35.10	3.34
4th quarter	20.89	15.26	3.22	81.37	11.62	1.55	8.75	14.00	32.34	3.89
1986										
1st quarter	18.73	12.67	3.87	76.95	10.62	1.54	8.52	13.85	29.34	3.92
2nd quarter	18.59	12.60	3.89	72.71	11.47	1.77	8.50	14.26	23.59	3.46
3rd quarter	20.46	14.62	3.69	68.41	11.96	1.58	8.35	14.07	19.50	3.16
4th quarter	17.85	11.43	3.98	71.76	12.26	1.92	7.77	15.67	20.79	2.81
1987										
1st quarter	18.93	13.27	3.57	67.88	12.13	1.94	7.79	12.78	19.43	2.71
2nd quarter	17.49	11.47	3.71	70.72	11.85	2.10	8.14	13.76	20.47	3.03
3rd quarter	15.88	9.92	3.69	74.17	12.09	1.91	8.56	14.33	23.05	3.03
4th quarter	15.32	9.54	3.45	77.48	12.36	2.03	9.35	14.54	24.14	2.94
1988										
1st quarter	15.25	9.47	3.32	81.95	13.80	2.11	9.60	15.53	25.19	3.25
2nd quarter	15.26	9.35	3.44	83.95	13.84	2.14	10.48	16.54	25.42	2.82
3rd quarter	16.02	10.01	3.57	88.28	14.04	2.26	11.10	18.02	25.89	3.53
4th quarter	16.36	10.04	3.60	89.83	14.83	2.19	12.01	16.29	26.95	3.43
1989										
1st quarter	17.39	9.93	4.49	93.23	14.91	2.16	13.81	17.46	26.58	3.40
2nd quarter	18.54	11.62	3.95	98.37	16.26	2.20	14.39	17.90	28.31	3.82
3rd quarter	18.65	11.75	3.74	102.12	15.73	2.29	15.67	18.35	30.52	3.96
4th quarter	19.83	12.27	4.50	108.12	16.45	2.33	17.75	19.75	33.26	3.90
1990										
1st quarter	18.80	12.03	4.30	105.98	15.98	2.23	17.30	20.08	31.50	3.52
2nd quarter	18.19	11.33	4.12	110.95	16.89	2.17	18.53	20.24	33.80	3.59
3rd quarter	18.28	11.63	4.03	111.90	16.36	2.21	16.72	20.40	36.01	3.50
4th quarter	16.63	10.43	3.69	110.24	16.21	2.10	14.20	21.44	36.61	3.33
1991										
1st quarter	17.50	10.99	3.63	110.19	17.21	2.09	12.85	20.97	39.34	3.52
2nd quarter	17.86	11.23	3.84	108.29	16.82	1.95	11.64	21.51	38.74	3.34
3rd quarter	16.09	8.97	4.07	102.70	17.69	1.85	11.39	21.75	33.80	3.26
4th quarter	17.56	9.89	4.66	101.48	18.02	1.95	10.57	21.61	32.17	3.58
1992										
1st quarter	17.02	9.26	4.93	99.87	18.65	1.94	11.01	22.02	30.15	3.73
2nd quarter	15.42	7.96	4.52	98.78	18.59	2.17	9.84	22.75	29.01	3.64
3rd quarter	15.69	8.23	4.46	100.42	18.72	2.12	10.25	23.31	29.56	3.81
4th quarter	16.16	9.28	3.56	103.09	19.81	1.98	10.94	24.05	29.67	4.15
1993										
1st quarter	17.23	10.22	3.51	95.80	19.79	2.05	10.60	21.42	26.07	3.00
2nd quarter	19.95	13.02	3.40	97.22	19.24	2.16	10.37	21.57	28.38	3.24
3rd quarter	20.27	13.68	3.00	99.74	18.99	2.37	9.79	22.10	30.44	3.41
4th quarter	18.86	11.89	3.02	98.51	17.29	2.50	10.45	22.09	29.30	3.54
1994										
1st quarter	21.49	15.16	2.52	99.02	17.01	2.20	10.01	21.93	29.60	3.44
2nd quarter	21.07	14.10	2.81	102.28	18.77	2.41	10.35	22.91	28.83	4.30

1. These series were discontinued in mid-1994; see Notes.

Table 23-1. New Plant and Equipment Spending [1]—*Continued*

(Billions of dollars, seasonally adjusted annual rates.)

Year and quarter	Transportation				Public utilities			Communica-tions	Wholesale and retail trade	Finance and insurance	Personal and business services
	Total	Railroads	Air	Other	Total	Electric	Gas and other				
1961	3.14	1.19	0.73	1.22	5.20	3.78	1.42	3.59	4.14	1.39	4.08
1962	3.59	1.43	0.53	1.63	5.12	3.76	1.36	4.02	4.53	1.46	4.69
1963	3.64	1.72	0.35	1.57	5.33	4.01	1.32	4.19	4.91	1.68	5.39
1964	4.71	2.20	0.92	1.60	5.80	4.27	1.53	4.75	5.72	1.90	5.84
1965	5.66	2.60	1.08	1.98	6.49	4.76	1.73	5.47	6.51	2.21	6.41
1966	6.68	3.09	1.66	1.93	7.82	5.73	2.09	6.23	7.09	2.23	7.57
1967	6.57	2.50	2.28	1.79	9.33	7.30	2.03	6.61	6.88	2.46	7.27
1968	6.91	2.15	2.54	2.23	10.52	7.97	2.54	7.07	7.04	3.03	8.09
1969	7.23	2.61	2.28	2.34	11.70	9.05	2.65	8.57	7.62	3.62	8.96
1970	7.17	2.48	2.50	2.18	13.03	10.56	2.46	10.40	8.78	3.91	9.62
1971	6.42	2.39	1.33	2.71	14.70	12.28	2.42	10.96	9.32	4.66	10.58
1972	7.14	2.35	1.93	2.86	16.26	13.60	2.66	12.27	10.95	6.37	12.11
1973	8.00	2.91	1.89	3.21	17.99	15.07	2.92	13.30	13.18	7.75	14.16
1974	9.16	3.63	1.80	3.73	19.96	16.85	3.11	14.46	15.02	8.45	15.56
1975	9.95	3.88	1.54	4.53	20.23	16.94	3.29	12.90	14.77	9.96	14.83
1976	11.10	4.25	1.13	5.72	22.90	19.29	3.61	13.66	17.61	9.19	17.83
1977	12.20	4.67	2.15	5.38	27.83	23.24	4.58	16.27	20.84	10.13	20.28
1978	12.07	4.93	3.00	4.14	32.10	26.70	5.40	19.79	26.14	13.52	24.52
1979	13.91	5.86	3.73	4.32	37.53	30.78	6.75	23.55	30.81	18.23	25.06
1980	13.56	5.91	3.66	3.98	41.32	33.30	8.01	26.80	31.95	22.57	24.89
1981	12.67	5.03	3.48	4.15	47.17	37.37	9.80	30.09	35.68	28.38	26.26
1982	11.75	4.28	3.61	3.86	53.58	43.65	9.93	30.06	36.78	30.35	25.58
1983	10.81	3.85	3.38	3.57	52.95	44.87	8.08	27.85	44.45	32.04	25.08
1984	13.44	5.32	3.31	4.81	57.53	45.18	12.35	31.60	53.39	37.89	28.52
1985	14.57	5.65	4.11	4.81	59.58	44.01	15.58	37.08	60.10	45.15	28.76
1986	15.05	5.33	5.17	4.55	56.61	41.03	15.58	38.22	65.37	49.57	28.44
1987	15.07	4.72	5.34	5.01	56.26	39.10	17.17	37.17	68.53	54.06	30.07
1988	16.63	5.52	5.63	5.48	60.37	40.90	19.47	37.24	76.37	59.22	32.93
1989	18.84	6.26	6.73	5.85	66.28	44.81	21.47	39.83	84.52	70.30	34.62
1990	21.47	6.40	8.87	6.20	67.21	44.10	23.11	43.13	95.63	68.96	33.72
1991	22.66	5.95	10.17	6.54	66.57	43.76	22.82	42.68	104.99	63.98	34.67
1992	22.64	6.67	8.93	7.04	72.21	48.22	23.99	41.53	116.23	72.76	38.32
1993	21.77	6.14	6.42	9.22	75.98	52.55	23.43	45.02	131.37	80.47	42.57
1985											
1st quarter	13.50	5.35	3.40	4.75	59.17	44.80	14.37	36.07	58.32	41.74	28.61
2nd quarter	14.29	5.79	3.33	5.17	59.52	44.13	15.39	37.56	60.57	43.31	28.54
3rd quarter	14.86	5.86	4.60	4.39	59.50	43.48	16.02	38.50	60.24	46.41	27.96
4th quarter	15.35	5.47	5.00	4.88	59.66	43.51	16.15	36.08	61.01	48.07	29.89
1986											
1st quarter	14.82	5.25	5.31	4.26	57.86	42.31	15.55	39.33	62.15	49.84	28.17
2nd quarter	15.28	5.38	5.50	4.39	56.98	41.26	15.72	40.24	64.68	46.18	28.04
3rd quarter	14.77	5.50	4.69	4.58	56.30	40.85	15.46	36.33	66.13	50.92	28.54
4th quarter	15.11	5.16	5.10	4.84	55.44	39.78	15.66	37.17	67.97	50.86	29.00
1987											
1st quarter	14.70	4.49	5.58	4.64	54.52	38.59	15.93	36.26	66.16	52.40	28.88
2nd quarter	14.53	4.66	4.94	4.93	54.49	39.03	15.46	36.15	67.72	51.78	29.72
3rd quarter	15.27	4.84	5.14	5.29	57.47	38.97	18.50	37.87	67.72	54.23	30.39
4th quarter	15.58	4.84	5.64	5.11	57.76	39.47	18.29	38.08	71.96	56.84	31.25
1988											
1st quarter	15.97	5.32	5.32	5.33	57.43	38.86	18.56	36.25	73.68	56.20	32.06
2nd quarter	16.50	5.54	5.44	5.52	58.67	39.62	19.05	37.81	74.84	61.36	33.27
3rd quarter	16.65	5.43	5.74	5.48	61.08	41.54	19.54	37.44	77.50	59.51	32.83
4th quarter	17.26	5.73	5.94	5.58	63.21	42.77	20.44	37.22	79.05	59.28	33.55
1989											
1st quarter	17.60	6.10	5.56	5.94	65.92	43.86	22.06	39.46	81.63	65.46	35.07
2nd quarter	18.42	5.81	6.79	5.83	68.74	46.70	22.05	38.16	83.71	68.10	35.05
3rd quarter	20.68	6.29	8.44	5.96	65.30	44.62	20.67	39.77	86.33	71.07	35.43
4th quarter	18.69	6.81	6.22	5.66	65.23	43.91	21.33	41.49	85.97	75.21	33.10
1990											
1st quarter	21.74	6.51	9.07	6.16	65.45	43.68	21.77	42.41	94.11	71.68	34.33
2nd quarter	21.72	6.64	9.23	5.85	65.05	42.96	22.09	43.44	94.63	72.39	33.93
3rd quarter	20.47	5.55	9.08	5.85	67.96	44.12	23.84	42.78	94.42	68.82	33.98
4th quarter	22.06	6.95	8.25	6.85	69.39	45.18	24.21	43.55	99.10	64.32	32.68
1991											
1st quarter	23.00	5.74	10.88	6.39	67.15	43.56	23.59	43.14	100.80	65.82	33.19
2nd quarter	22.79	6.29	9.93	6.57	65.02	43.09	21.93	41.84	104.36	60.86	33.25
3rd quarter	21.93	6.49	8.99	6.45	67.10	43.67	23.43	42.54	107.29	64.88	35.13
4th quarter	23.13	5.18	11.23	6.73	66.76	44.37	22.39	43.13	106.65	64.88	37.01
1992											
1st quarter	21.82	6.79	8.73	6.30	69.09	46.06	23.03	39.26	110.90	73.49	37.54
2nd quarter	23.32	6.40	9.77	7.15	72.56	48.45	24.12	41.35	113.18	71.61	37.55
3rd quarter	23.66	6.87	9.36	7.43	72.48	48.37	24.11	42.18	117.79	72.02	37.68
4th quarter	21.66	6.64	7.80	7.22	73.79	49.37	24.42	42.72	121.83	73.87	40.35
1993											
1st quarter	22.38	6.16	7.26	8.96	73.78	49.98	23.79	43.79	124.11	77.60	38.84
2nd quarter	21.50	5.94	6.63	8.92	74.45	50.61	23.83	45.68	127.91	79.13	43.63
3rd quarter	21.32	5.89	6.70	8.74	75.94	52.96	22.98	45.06	133.21	82.46	43.01
4th quarter	21.84	6.55	5.06	10.23	78.87	55.60	23.27	45.28	138.74	82.29	44.42
1994											
1st quarter	22.47	7.46	4.23	10.77	73.20	48.68	24.51	43.56	145.46	88.51	49.67
2nd quarter	19.59	5.36	4.53	9.70	76.51	53.55	22.96	42.97	152.63	91.53	49.16

1. These series were discontinued in mid-1994; see Notes.

Because the following table is designed to be viewed as facing pages, please turn to page 312 for Table 24-1.

Table 24-1. Personal Income and Its Disposition

(Billions of dollars, seasonally adjusted annual rate.)

Year and month	Personal income	Wage and salary disburse-ments	Other labor income	Proprietors' income [1] Farm	Proprietors' income [1] Nonfarm	Rental income of persons [2]	Personal dividend income	Personal interest income	Transfer payments to persons	Less: Personal contributions for social insurance	Personal tax and nontax payments	Disposable personal income
1972												
January	948.1	613.4	51.9	14.8	75.7	21.8	26.1	79.7	92.1	27.3	118.6	829.5
February	959.2	620.5	52.6	15.0	75.0	21.9	26.2	80.3	95.4	27.6	121.8	837.4
March	965.6	624.0	53.2	15.4	75.7	22.0	26.1	80.9	95.9	27.6	124.6	841.0
April	972.0	627.9	53.8	16.6	77.0	22.2	26.2	81.6	94.4	27.7	126.6	845.4
May	978.1	630.5	54.4	17.2	77.5	22.4	26.5	82.4	95.0	27.8	124.7	853.5
June	971.9	633.9	55.0	17.9	75.1	12.7	26.6	83.3	95.2	27.8	124.9	847.1
July	989.8	636.1	55.6	18.7	78.2	22.6	27.0	84.4	95.8	28.7	125.0	864.8
August	1 002.4	642.8	56.2	19.7	80.1	22.7	27.1	85.5	96.3	28.1	126.5	875.9
September	1 010.5	648.6	56.8	20.8	79.6	22.8	27.2	86.5	96.3	28.2	127.5	883.0
October	1 032.6	656.2	57.4	22.5	82.6	22.8	27.5	87.8	104.3	28.4	128.7	903.9
November	1 046.5	661.9	58.0	23.2	84.6	22.8	27.6	88.7	108.2	28.6	129.4	917.1
December	1 054.4	668.2	58.6	23.6	85.6	22.9	28.0	89.6	106.6	28.7	129.6	924.8
1973												
January	1 056.7	676.1	59.0	22.4	84.9	23.0	28.0	90.2	107.7	34.7	130.6	926.1
February	1 067.6	684.2	59.6	23.0	84.7	23.2	28.4	91.1	108.3	34.9	128.1	939.5
March	1 076.9	689.2	60.2	24.3	84.1	23.4	28.7	92.2	109.9	35.0	126.7	950.2
April	1 085.0	695.3	60.9	27.3	82.9	21.8	29.1	93.1	109.7	35.2	128.4	956.6
May	1 098.0	699.9	61.6	28.9	83.8	24.3	29.2	94.4	111.4	35.4	132.1	965.9
June	1 107.3	705.5	62.3	30.1	84.1	24.0	29.6	96.1	111.2	35.5	133.1	974.2
July	1 114.9	711.4	63.0	29.7	84.8	22.7	29.9	98.5	110.9	36.0	134.4	980.4
August	1 125.0	715.1	63.8	31.5	84.6	22.4	30.5	100.3	112.9	36.1	135.9	989.1
September	1 136.7	721.7	64.5	33.3	84.8	22.4	30.7	101.8	113.6	36.3	138.0	998.6
October	1 153.5	728.5	65.3	39.1	84.9	23.3	30.9	102.9	114.7	36.3	139.7	1 013.7
November	1 166.6	736.7	66.2	40.0	85.5	23.5	31.2	104.3	115.9	36.6	142.2	1 024.3
December	1 173.3	740.7	67.0	38.8	85.5	23.6	32.3	105.8	116.2	36.6	144.1	1 029.2
1974												
January	1 175.9	744.1	67.9	33.8	86.4	23.5	32.2	107.3	120.1	39.3	142.9	1 033.0
February	1 182.3	748.3	68.8	30.7	87.8	23.5	32.4	108.9	121.3	39.5	145.3	1 037.0
March	1 187.8	751.8	69.7	27.7	89.1	23.5	32.9	110.6	122.3	39.7	146.7	1 041.2
April	1 194.3	756.6	70.7	23.2	88.7	21.7	33.0	112.5	127.8	39.9	147.8	1 046.5
May	1 209.0	766.0	71.7	21.4	90.0	23.4	33.3	114.2	129.4	40.3	151.5	1 057.5
June	1 220.1	774.6	72.7	20.7	90.0	23.3	33.6	115.7	130.1	40.5	154.2	1 065.9
July	1 236.5	780.9	73.7	22.4	91.8	23.1	33.5	116.9	135.1	40.9	156.1	1 080.4
August	1 243.3	783.3	74.8	22.9	92.6	23.0	33.4	118.4	135.9	41.0	157.1	1 086.2
September	1 253.4	789.1	75.8	23.6	92.4	22.9	33.6	119.9	137.3	41.3	158.6	1 094.8
October	1 265.6	795.1	77.0	25.4	91.5	22.8	33.6	121.8	139.9	41.4	160.2	1 105.4
November	1 266.0	790.6	78.1	25.4	91.3	22.7	33.5	123.1	142.2	41.0	159.8	1 106.2
December	1 273.0	791.2	79.3	24.7	92.2	22.6	33.2	124.2	146.7	41.0	160.1	1 112.9
1975												
January	1 276.8	792.3	80.5	21.6	94.3	22.4	33.0	125.1	149.7	42.1	160.6	1 116.2
February	1 281.2	790.0	81.7	20.7	94.5	22.3	32.9	125.7	155.1	41.8	160.2	1 121.0
March	1 285.2	792.7	82.9	20.4	93.4	22.2	32.8	126.0	156.6	41.8	160.8	1 124.5
April	1 291.8	793.5	84.2	21.0	94.6	22.2	32.7	125.4	160.0	41.8	141.6	1 150.3
May	1 304.6	800.6	85.5	21.6	95.9	22.1	32.6	125.7	162.6	42.1	81.3	1 223.3
June	1 336.1	806.3	86.8	22.6	97.0	22.1	32.6	126.4	184.7	42.2	148.2	1 187.9
July	1 333.8	810.9	88.2	24.9	98.5	22.1	32.5	127.6	171.4	42.4	153.3	1 180.4
August	1 350.2	823.1	89.5	25.8	99.1	22.0	32.7	128.6	172.3	42.9	156.2	1 194.0
September	1 361.3	829.1	90.9	26.2	100.4	21.9	33.2	129.7	172.9	43.1	157.2	1 204.1
October	1 376.4	837.8	92.3	26.5	101.8	21.7	33.4	130.9	175.2	43.3	159.6	1 216.8
November	1 386.3	846.1	93.8	26.0	103.1	21.7	33.8	131.9	173.6	43.7	161.5	1 224.8
December	1 396.9	852.6	95.2	24.9	104.6	21.6	32.7	132.9	176.2	43.9	163.2	1 233.7
1976												
January	1 414.2	864.9	96.6	22.2	106.6	21.8	35.2	133.5	179.1	45.6	164.6	1 249.6
February	1 426.0	871.7	98.1	20.9	108.9	21.7	36.5	134.6	179.5	45.9	165.3	1 260.7
March	1 433.5	876.2	99.6	19.8	111.0	21.7	36.7	135.9	178.6	46.0	165.5	1 268.0
April	1 443.8	883.3	101.2	19.2	111.9	21.4	37.3	137.9	177.9	46.3	169.9	1 274.0
May	1 453.8	890.7	102.8	18.6	113.0	21.3	38.2	139.3	176.5	46.6	172.4	1 281.5
June	1 462.0	893.3	104.4	18.1	114.7	20.4	38.6	140.4	178.7	46.6	174.1	1 287.9
July	1 480.7	900.6	106.0	17.8	117.0	21.4	39.3	141.2	184.5	47.1	176.7	1 304.0
August	1 493.6	909.4	107.6	17.6	118.0	21.4	39.9	142.2	184.9	47.4	179.2	1 314.4
September	1 504.0	914.6	109.3	17.4	119.8	21.5	40.4	143.4	185.3	47.6	181.3	1 322.8
October	1 511.8	920.1	110.9	17.3	119.4	21.7	41.1	144.2	184.8	47.7	184.1	1 327.7
November	1 533.5	930.9	112.6	17.4	123.1	21.8	41.9	145.8	188.2	48.1	186.3	1 347.3
December	1 547.3	938.0	114.4	17.6	124.1	21.8	42.4	147.7	189.7	48.4	186.8	1 360.5
1977												
January	1 553.0	939.3	116.3	18.6	124.8	22.0	42.0	150.9	188.8	49.8	183.1	1 370.0
February	1 570.6	950.5	118.1	18.5	125.6	21.9	42.6	153.0	190.6	50.3	202.1	1 368.5
March	1 585.4	959.5	119.8	18.0	126.6	21.7	43.2	154.9	192.3	50.6	190.6	1 394.8
April	1 597.8	968.9	121.4	16.3	128.2	20.0	43.6	156.2	193.3	51.0	196.5	1 401.3
May	1 611.1	981.5	123.0	15.7	129.3	20.8	43.5	158.0	191.0	51.5	201.3	1 409.9
June	1 622.2	990.6	124.6	15.2	128.7	20.4	44.6	159.9	190.1	51.9	199.0	1 423.3
July	1 641.6	999.5	126.2	14.5	132.1	19.9	45.3	161.7	194.7	52.3	199.8	1 441.8
August	1 655.6	1 005.4	127.8	14.7	132.8	19.7	45.6	163.9	198.1	52.5	201.3	1 454.3
September	1 671.7	1 016.8	129.4	16.2	132.8	19.6	45.9	166.5	197.5	53.0	204.5	1 467.2
October	1 691.6	1 030.5	131.0	19.2	132.9	19.3	46.3	170.0	196.0	53.5	209.3	1 482.2
November	1 714.9	1 038.5	132.5	21.1	136.5	19.5	46.8	172.6	201.1	53.7	212.0	1 502.8
December	1 730.0	1 044.7	133.9	21.6	139.9	20.0	47.3	175.0	201.5	53.8	214.4	1 515.7

1. Includes inventory valuation and capital consumption adjustments.
2. Includes capital consumption adjustment.

Table 24-1. Personal Income and Its Disposition—*Continued*

(Billions of dollars, seasonally adjusted annual rate.)

Year and month	Personal outlays — Total	Personal consumption expenditures — Total	Durable goods	Nondurable goods	Services	Personal saving — Billions of dollars	Percent of disposable personal income	Disposable personal income	Personal consumption expenditures — Total	Durable goods	Nondurable goods	Services
1972												
January	754.4	734.4	104.7	291.5	338.2	75.1	9.1	2 784.7	...	...	...	...
February	759.0	738.9	103.5	295.0	340.3	78.4	9.4	2 800.1	...	...	...	...
March	772.2	751.9	106.4	301.1	344.3	68.8	8.2	2 807.8	...	...	...	...
April	775.7	755.1	106.9	301.8	346.5	69.7	8.2	2 817.8	...	...	...	...
May	781.2	760.5	108.5	305.4	346.6	72.3	8.5	2 838.4	...	...	...	...
June	785.0	764.0	108.8	305.9	349.3	62.1	7.3	2 812.6	...	...	...	...
July	793.4	772.3	110.5	309.2	352.6	71.4	8.3	2 861.4	...	...	...	...
August	800.0	778.7	112.1	310.9	355.7	75.9	8.7	2 889.5	...	...	...	...
September	805.0	783.5	111.7	314.3	357.5	78.0	8.8	2 900.0	...	...	...	...
October	819.2	797.5	115.7	319.8	362.0	84.7	9.4	2 965.0	...	...	...	...
November	824.9	803.1	117.0	320.2	365.9	92.1	10.0	2 999.4	...	...	...	...
December	830.9	808.8	118.4	321.5	368.9	93.9	10.2	3 014.5	...	...	...	...
1973												
January	841.6	819.3	122.9	327.0	369.5	84.5	9.1	3 009.1	...	...	...	...
February	851.2	828.7	125.2	331.3	372.2	88.3	9.4	3 037.2	...	...	...	...
March	858.3	835.5	127.6	332.8	375.2	91.9	9.7	3 049.4	...	...	...	...
April	861.3	838.2	125.4	334.6	378.2	95.2	10.0	3 046.6	...	...	...	...
May	867.4	844.1	126.1	336.3	381.7	98.5	10.2	3 061.8	...	...	...	...
June	870.5	846.9	120.9	340.1	385.9	103.8	10.6	3 070.4	...	...	...	...
July	880.8	856.9	123.0	346.7	387.2	99.7	10.2	3 079.2	...	...	...	...
August	880.3	856.2	121.7	344.9	389.6	108.8	11.0	3 070.6	...	...	...	...
September	896.7	872.5	126.7	351.2	394.7	101.9	10.2	3 088.2	...	...	...	...
October	897.2	871.5	122.3	352.9	396.3	116.5	11.5	3 117.1	...	...	...	...
November	906.1	880.2	121.9	359.1	399.2	118.2	11.5	3 124.3	...	...	...	...
December	906.0	880.0	119.0	360.3	400.7	123.2	12.0	3 113.5	...	...	...	...
1974												
January	913.1	888.1	119.0	365.1	404.0	119.9	11.6	3 096.0	...	...	...	...
February	918.3	893.2	117.0	369.3	406.8	118.7	11.4	3 071.7	...	...	...	...
March	930.0	904.8	120.6	373.0	411.2	111.2	10.7	3 049.0	...	...	...	...
April	939.4	914.1	121.4	377.3	415.4	107.1	10.2	3 043.9	...	...	...	...
May	951.0	925.6	124.3	380.7	420.5	106.4	10.1	3 046.9	...	...	...	...
June	956.6	931.0	123.3	383.1	424.7	109.3	10.3	3 045.6	...	...	...	...
July	966.3	940.7	126.1	387.6	427.0	114.1	10.6	3 065.7	...	...	...	...
August	983.0	957.2	133.4	393.0	430.7	103.2	9.5	3 050.1	...	...	...	...
September	982.4	956.5	126.8	394.5	435.2	112.5	10.3	3 044.2	...	...	...	...
October	985.7	959.8	122.6	396.8	440.5	119.8	10.8	3 051.9	...	...	...	...
November	982.0	956.2	116.8	397.7	441.8	124.2	11.2	3 031.8	...	...	...	...
December	987.2	961.4	116.5	396.1	448.8	125.7	11.3	3 026.6	...	...	...	...
1975												
January	1 000.5	974.7	121.0	402.2	451.6	115.7	10.4	3 016.8	...	...	...	...
February	1 014.3	988.6	126.2	404.8	457.6	106.7	9.5	3 014.0	...	...	...	...
March	1 015.6	990.0	122.5	406.4	461.0	108.9	9.7	3 014.4	...	...	...	...
April	1 020.4	994.9	123.8	405.5	465.7	129.9	11.3	3 072.5	...	...	...	...
May	1 044.6	1 019.1	129.6	419.5	469.9	178.7	14.6	3 255.6	...	...	...	...
June	1 052.2	1 027.1	131.4	421.7	473.9	135.7	11.4	3 142.0	...	...	...	...
July	1 065.6	1 039.9	136.2	424.9	478.8	114.8	9.7	3 095.9	...	...	...	...
August	1 073.0	1 047.0	136.5	429.4	481.1	121.1	10.1	3 118.8	...	...	...	...
September	1 080.9	1 054.8	141.1	429.1	484.6	123.2	10.2	3 129.8	...	...	...	...
October	1 086.7	1 060.6	139.2	429.8	491.6	130.1	10.7	3 144.9	...	...	...	...
November	1 101.8	1 075.6	144.1	436.4	495.1	123.0	10.0	3 146.6	...	...	...	...
December	1 118.5	1 092.0	149.9	439.3	502.9	115.1	9.3	3 151.6	...	...	...	...
1976												
January	1 134.7	1 107.9	152.1	447.1	508.6	114.9	9.2	3 181.5	...	...	...	...
February	1 135.9	1 108.9	155.0	443.6	510.3	124.8	9.9	3 204.9	...	...	...	...
March	1 143.6	1 116.4	155.3	445.6	515.5	124.4	9.8	3 219.0	...	...	...	...
April	1 154.2	1 126.9	158.1	450.2	518.5	119.7	9.4	3 226.4	...	...	...	...
May	1 151.8	1 124.3	152.7	449.9	521.6	129.7	10.1	3 229.4	...	...	...	...
June	1 170.0	1 142.2	158.1	457.9	526.2	117.9	9.2	3 231.0	...	...	...	...
July	1 179.4	1 151.3	159.6	459.3	532.3	124.7	9.6	3 254.5	...	...	...	...
August	1 188.2	1 160.0	158.4	463.1	538.5	126.2	9.6	3 261.4	...	...	...	...
September	1 199.7	1 171.2	160.8	465.4	544.9	123.1	9.3	3 263.5	...	...	...	...
October	1 209.0	1 180.1	160.7	470.1	549.4	118.7	8.9	3 257.3	...	...	...	...
November	1 221.8	1 192.7	163.1	470.7	558.8	125.5	9.3	3 290.0	...	...	...	...
December	1 244.7	1 215.4	172.1	476.9	566.4	115.8	8.5	3 303.3	...	...	...	...
1977												
January	1 248.3	1 218.4	167.9	479.7	570.8	121.7	8.9	3 309.3	...	...	...	...
February	1 264.8	1 234.6	173.7	486.5	574.4	103.8	7.6	3 280.3	...	...	...	...
March	1 272.3	1 241.7	179.4	485.4	576.9	122.6	8.8	3 326.7	...	...	...	...
April	1 282.0	1 251.1	178.4	490.1	582.6	119.3	8.5	3 321.7	...	...	...	...
May	1 292.9	1 261.5	178.2	493.8	589.5	117.0	8.3	3 323.3	...	...	...	...
June	1 300.0	1 268.3	179.8	492.8	595.7	123.2	8.7	3 335.6	...	...	...	...
July	1 317.2	1 285.1	181.1	499.0	605.0	124.6	8.6	3 361.0	...	...	...	...
August	1 323.2	1 290.7	183.3	497.7	609.6	131.1	9.0	3 375.5	...	...	...	...
September	1 332.7	1 299.8	185.1	499.5	615.3	134.5	9.2	3 393.0	...	...	...	...
October	1 349.8	1 316.4	185.8	507.6	622.9	132.4	8.9	3 411.7	...	...	...	...
November	1 366.1	1 332.1	189.4	517.4	625.3	136.8	9.1	3 438.7	...	...	...	...
December	1 375.6	1 341.3	192.4	516.4	632.4	140.1	9.2	3 451.1	...	...	...	...

Table 24-1. Personal Income and Its Disposition—*Continued*

(Billions of dollars, seasonally adjusted annual rate.)

Year and month	Personal income	Sources of personal income									Disposition of personal income	
		Wage and salary disburse-ments	Other labor income	Proprietors' income [1]		Rental income of persons [2]	Personal dividend income	Personal interest income	Transfer payments to persons	Less: Personal contributions for social insurance	Personal tax and nontax payments	Disposable personal income
				Farm	Nonfarm							
1978												
January	1 736.4	1 051.5	135.2	20.8	137.4	21.3	47.9	176.8	202.4	56.9	216.3	1 520.0
February	1 753.4	1 062.2	136.7	20.3	139.6	21.7	48.2	179.1	202.9	57.3	216.0	1 537.3
March	1 777.2	1 078.0	138.1	20.3	142.3	21.8	48.6	181.6	204.4	57.9	214.5	1 562.7
April	1 803.2	1 096.3	139.7	21.9	146.7	20.8	48.9	184.2	203.3	58.7	221.0	1 582.1
May	1 820.3	1 104.0	141.1	22.7	148.4	20.9	49.3	186.8	206.1	59.0	225.7	1 594.6
June	1 839.4	1 118.2	142.6	22.9	150.0	21.3	50.0	189.4	204.6	59.6	233.8	1 605.7
July	1 861.9	1 128.1	144.1	22.6	149.8	22.7	50.7	191.7	212.2	60.1	237.2	1 624.7
August	1 880.3	1 136.3	145.7	22.2	152.9	23.2	51.8	194.5	214.1	60.4	240.0	1 640.3
September	1 896.1	1 147.4	147.2	21.9	153.5	23.6	52.5	197.6	213.2	60.9	243.3	1 652.8
October	1 918.9	1 164.7	148.8	20.1	154.9	23.4	53.0	201.0	214.4	61.6	247.8	1 671.1
November	1 935.8	1 174.8	150.3	20.9	153.1	23.8	53.5	204.6	216.7	62.0	251.0	1 684.7
December	1 956.4	1 187.4	151.8	21.9	153.5	24.4	54.2	208.3	217.5	62.5	254.8	1 701.6
1979												
January	1 977.1	1 198.0	153.1	24.8	154.0	26.0	54.6	212.6	221.4	67.5	255.1	1 722.0
February	1 994.9	1 208.6	154.7	25.4	155.9	26.2	55.5	216.4	220.3	68.0	257.4	1 737.5
March	2 018.6	1 223.2	156.3	25.5	158.0	25.8	55.9	219.9	222.7	68.7	260.8	1 757.8
April	2 022.6	1 225.0	158.0	23.2	157.5	22.1	56.3	222.9	226.3	68.8	261.8	1 760.8
May	2 041.5	1 235.8	159.7	23.4	158.7	23.1	56.9	226.3	226.9	69.3	265.6	1 775.9
June	2 059.4	1 250.1	161.5	23.4	159.7	22.7	57.3	229.7	224.8	69.9	271.4	1 787.9
July	2 090.0	1 261.1	163.3	24.2	159.5	22.5	57.6	232.2	240.1	70.5	276.1	1 813.9
August	2 109.7	1 269.3	165.1	23.9	162.9	22.9	57.9	236.5	242.1	70.8	278.9	1 830.9
September	2 125.9	1 281.9	167.0	23.6	161.3	20.9	58.4	241.6	242.7	71.4	282.8	1 843.2
October	2 154.5	1 292.5	168.8	23.7	163.3	25.7	59.0	248.1	245.2	71.8	286.1	1 868.4
November	2 178.5	1 305.2	170.7	22.6	163.4	27.0	59.6	254.5	247.8	72.3	289.7	1 888.9
December	2 205.3	1 318.6	172.8	20.8	165.5	28.5	60.1	261.2	250.8	72.9	293.5	1 911.8
1980												
January	2 234.8	1 326.4	175.1	17.5	169.0	31.3	61.3	271.1	258.6	75.6	285.8	1 949.1
February	2 248.8	1 338.0	177.2	14.7	166.1	31.8	61.3	276.6	259.0	75.9	288.9	1 959.9
March	2 260.7	1 350.6	179.2	11.7	161.9	33.2	62.4	280.4	257.2	75.8	292.8	1 967.9
April	2 258.4	1 349.5	181.0	5.4	159.9	33.2	63.4	281.3	259.9	75.3	293.9	1 964.5
May	2 265.4	1 353.2	182.8	4.2	158.5	31.6	64.2	282.8	263.4	75.4	296.5	1 968.9
June	2 282.5	1 361.1	184.7	5.0	160.1	31.9	64.9	283.5	267.3	76.0	299.7	1 982.8
July	2 314.9	1 364.2	186.5	10.8	162.2	30.5	64.6	279.2	293.5	76.6	301.8	2 013.0
August	2 336.2	1 381.7	188.2	13.4	162.7	28.2	64.5	281.7	293.6	77.8	307.3	2 028.9
September	2 366.1	1 395.0	190.0	15.7	166.0	27.1	64.5	286.6	299.5	78.4	311.7	2 054.4
October	2 409.8	1 420.1	191.7	18.5	169.0	28.5	64.8	298.0	298.5	79.4	318.7	2 091.1
November	2 439.6	1 438.7	193.4	20.0	168.1	32.7	65.4	304.9	296.6	80.2	324.2	2 115.3
December	2 470.0	1 450.9	194.9	20.6	169.8	35.5	66.2	311.2	301.5	80.7	328.6	2 141.4
1981												
January	2 491.7	1 465.5	196.3	19.4	173.7	39.9	67.4	317.0	302.0	89.5	332.5	2 159.2
February	2 508.7	1 473.2	197.8	19.3	173.3	39.6	68.6	322.3	304.4	89.8	335.9	2 172.9
March	2 531.4	1 484.8	199.4	19.3	174.2	39.2	69.7	327.2	308.1	90.3	340.3	2 191.1
April	2 530.0	1 493.7	201.0	18.7	164.0	38.3	71.3	327.3	306.6	90.7	343.6	2 186.4
May	2 547.1	1 500.7	202.6	19.3	162.2	38.0	72.6	334.4	308.4	91.1	348.8	2 198.3
June	2 571.4	1 512.0	204.1	20.4	160.9	38.0	73.8	344.1	309.5	91.6	352.4	2 219.0
July	2 629.0	1 522.5	205.7	24.5	164.9	38.2	75.2	364.4	326.2	92.5	358.1	2 270.9
August	2 656.7	1 537.6	207.2	24.9	165.7	38.7	75.6	373.6	326.8	93.3	363.8	2 292.9
September	2 671.3	1 543.9	208.7	24.1	165.3	39.5	76.5	379.6	327.1	93.5	366.3	2 304.9
October	2 675.1	1 554.0	210.2	19.7	162.8	41.5	77.2	377.3	326.6	94.1	355.2	2 319.9
November	2 689.3	1 560.1	211.8	18.0	163.1	42.1	77.7	380.6	330.2	94.4	359.1	2 330.3
December	2 690.9	1 558.7	213.4	16.6	160.6	42.4	78.0	384.5	331.1	94.3	361.8	2 329.2
1982												
January	2 695.4	1 567.2	215.2	16.2	153.9	42.1	77.0	389.7	331.9	97.8	355.1	2 340.3
February	2 712.8	1 575.7	216.7	15.4	155.3	41.7	76.4	394.2	335.7	98.3	361.2	2 351.6
March	2 720.0	1 576.6	218.2	14.7	156.2	41.0	76.0	398.8	336.8	98.3	360.7	2 359.3
April	2 739.5	1 577.3	219.6	14.2	164.1	38.9	75.2	406.2	342.2	98.2	356.3	2 383.2
May	2 758.0	1 590.0	220.9	14.0	166.6	38.4	74.7	408.8	343.5	98.9	368.3	2 389.7
June	2 764.6	1 593.0	222.3	13.6	165.8	38.4	74.4	409.4	346.9	99.1	374.8	2 389.9
July	2 780.2	1 600.5	223.6	13.8	163.7	39.9	74.7	405.3	358.3	99.7	355.1	2 425.0
August	2 786.9	1 603.6	224.9	13.1	166.0	40.2	75.1	404.0	359.9	99.9	357.8	2 429.0
September	2 792.1	1 601.6	226.2	12.4	168.2	40.2	75.8	402.7	364.7	99.6	358.5	2 433.7
October	2 807.6	1 602.2	227.6	14.1	173.4	40.0	76.8	399.5	369.6	99.7	361.3	2 446.3
November	2 825.4	1 609.4	228.8	16.0	174.8	38.7	77.9	399.7	379.8	99.8	363.5	2 461.9
December	2 838.2	1 619.7	229.8	15.8	177.0	35.3	78.8	401.4	380.7	100.3	366.7	2 471.4
1983												
January	2 843.7	1 628.6	230.3	10.8	176.6	38.0	79.5	406.6	376.7	103.4	356.6	2 487.2
February	2 849.2	1 624.1	231.4	15.6	174.4	37.5	80.2	409.6	379.3	103.0	358.2	2 491.0
March	2 867.9	1 635.0	232.7	15.6	174.0	37.3	80.7	412.4	383.7	103.5	360.5	2 507.4
April	2 884.7	1 647.3	234.3	10.2	182.4	37.5	81.2	412.6	383.4	104.1	359.0	2 525.7
May	2 914.5	1 666.0	235.8	9.5	184.1	37.5	82.1	417.0	387.6	104.9	370.0	2 544.5
June	2 928.5	1 674.8	237.3	7.2	186.0	37.4	82.7	423.1	385.6	105.5	373.4	2 555.1
July	2 955.0	1 690.4	239.0	3.7	192.8	37.1	83.8	433.9	380.7	106.3	351.2	2 603.8
August	2 958.4	1 696.8	240.7	-0.2	191.0	30.1	84.8	441.1	380.5	106.5	353.6	2 604.8
September	2 992.4	1 710.1	242.5	-0.1	197.5	37.2	85.7	447.6	379.1	107.3	356.2	2 636.2
October	3 026.1	1 738.2	244.2	0.0	197.1	37.9	86.4	453.4	377.8	108.9	362.0	2 664.1
November	3 055.4	1 745.2	246.2	4.2	200.1	38.0	87.0	458.7	385.1	109.2	363.7	2 691.6
December	3 087.3	1 760.1	248.4	9.5	203.5	37.9	87.5	463.5	387.1	110.0	366.8	2 720.4

1. Includes inventory valuation and capital consumption adjustments.
2. Includes capital consumption adjustment.

Table 24-1. Personal Income and Its Disposition—*Continued*

(Billions of dollars, seasonally adjusted annual rate.)

Year and month	Personal outlays	Personal consumption expenditures				Personal saving		Disposable personal income	Constant (1996) dollars			
	Total	Total	Durable goods	Nondurable goods	Services	Billions of dollars	Percent of disposable personal income		Personal consumption expenditures			
									Total	Durable goods	Nondurable goods	Services
1978												
January	1 370.2	1 335.0	180.3	515.2	639.5	149.8	9.9	3 439.7	...	...	...	...
February	1 397.1	1 361.1	187.2	524.2	649.7	140.3	9.1	3 462.4	...	...	...	...
March	1 420.1	1 383.5	193.4	533.8	656.3	142.6	9.1	3 497.1	...	...	...	...
April	1 440.0	1 402.7	202.1	535.9	664.7	142.2	9.0	3 512.7	...	...	...	...
May	1 457.6	1 419.5	205.5	543.3	670.8	137.0	8.6	3 513.3	...	...	...	...
June	1 473.5	1 434.7	206.5	549.5	678.8	132.2	8.2	3 513.3	...	...	...	...
July	1 475.7	1 436.3	203.6	552.4	680.3	149.0	9.2	3 535.3	...	...	...	...
August	1 497.1	1 457.0	210.2	557.2	689.7	143.2	8.7	3 551.3	...	...	...	...
September	1 503.7	1 463.1	201.3	565.9	695.9	149.0	9.0	3 557.7	...	...	...	...
October	1 517.7	1 476.4	208.6	566.3	701.6	153.4	9.2	3 570.0	...	...	...	...
November	1 531.2	1 489.3	210.0	575.4	703.8	153.6	9.1	3 580.5	...	...	...	...
December	1 548.7	1 506.2	212.0	584.0	710.1	152.9	9.0	3 597.5	...	...	...	...
1979												
January	1 558.0	1 514.9	208.8	585.5	720.6	164.0	9.5	3 610.2	...	...	...	...
February	1 576.7	1 533.4	212.4	592.9	728.1	160.8	9.3	3 618.4	...	...	...	...
March	1 590.1	1 546.4	213.4	603.2	729.8	167.6	9.5	3 633.5	...	...	...	...
April	1 594.5	1 550.1	211.0	599.4	739.7	166.3	9.4	3 609.8	...	...	...	...
May	1 612.3	1 567.3	212.6	609.3	745.3	163.6	9.2	3 608.2	...	...	...	...
June	1 628.9	1 583.2	207.4	622.9	753.0	159.1	8.9	3 603.5	...	...	...	...
July	1 640.0	1 593.6	214.0	623.0	756.6	173.9	9.6	3 627.9	...	...	...	...
August	1 670.9	1 623.9	219.3	637.8	766.9	160.0	8.7	3 633.3	...	...	...	...
September	1 690.4	1 642.9	223.4	646.5	773.0	152.7	8.3	3 625.7	...	...	...	...
October	1 700.0	1 651.8	216.4	649.4	786.1	168.4	9.0	3 644.6	...	...	...	...
November	1 717.7	1 668.7	216.7	660.3	791.7	171.2	9.1	3 658.3	...	...	...	...
December	1 729.2	1 678.9	217.5	663.3	798.1	182.6	9.5	3 670.4	...	...	...	...
1980												
January	1 762.4	1 711.7	227.5	675.7	808.5	186.7	9.6	3 700.1	...	...	...	...
February	1 766.0	1 715.3	220.9	678.4	816.0	193.9	9.9	3 681.6	...	...	...	...
March	1 771.7	1 721.1	211.7	685.0	824.4	196.2	10.0	3 653.5	...	...	...	...
April	1 760.2	1 709.7	200.2	685.4	824.1	204.3	10.4	3 625.5	...	...	...	...
May	1 765.3	1 714.8	196.3	687.0	831.4	203.5	10.3	3 604.1	...	...	...	...
June	1 784.2	1 733.4	202.8	687.4	843.1	198.7	10.0	3 607.0	...	...	...	...
July	1 812.4	1 761.4	214.4	692.2	854.8	200.7	10.0	3 633.8	...	...	...	...
August	1 828.9	1 777.6	211.6	702.4	863.6	200.0	9.9	3 632.5	...	...	...	...
September	1 843.7	1 792.3	213.2	704.0	875.1	210.6	10.3	3 646.5	...	...	...	...
October	1 877.9	1 826.2	223.8	713.8	888.6	213.2	10.2	3 685.3	...	...	...	...
November	1 886.1	1 834.0	224.4	715.4	894.2	229.2	10.8	3 700.8	...	...	...	...
December	1 911.1	1 857.4	223.1	726.2	908.1	230.3	10.8	3 725.0	...	...	...	...
1981												
January	1 933.1	1 876.2	227.4	741.0	907.7	226.1	10.5	3 721.7	...	...	...	...
February	1 948.7	1 891.6	234.8	745.5	911.3	224.2	10.3	3 707.2	...	...	...	...
March	1 969.0	1 911.4	238.2	750.8	922.4	222.1	10.1	3 711.7	...	...	...	...
April	1 971.3	1 912.9	229.0	754.7	929.1	215.1	9.8	3 688.5	...	...	...	...
May	1 981.7	1 922.6	227.3	753.9	941.5	216.6	9.9	3 691.4	...	...	...	...
June	2 004.2	1 944.6	228.7	760.0	955.9	214.8	9.7	3 709.9	...	...	...	...
July	2 013.5	1 953.1	232.5	759.7	960.8	257.4	11.3	3 772.0	...	...	...	...
August	2 039.5	1 978.7	247.8	763.6	967.3	253.4	11.1	3 783.2	...	...	...	...
September	2 041.5	1 979.7	237.4	766.1	976.1	263.5	11.4	3 775.8	...	...	...	...
October	2 039.4	1 977.2	224.7	768.4	984.1	280.5	12.1	3 783.8	...	...	...	...
November	2 045.3	1 982.6	224.5	767.6	990.5	285.0	12.2	3 780.1	...	...	...	...
December	2 063.0	1 999.3	223.9	774.7	1 000.7	266.2	11.4	3 767.8	...	...	...	...
1982												
January	2 070.0	2 006.1	228.7	770.9	1 006.5	270.3	11.5	3 764.4	...	...	...	...
February	2 094.1	2 030.5	236.6	781.6	1 012.3	257.5	11.0	3 769.8	...	...	...	...
March	2 095.8	2 032.3	236.7	775.9	1 019.7	263.5	11.2	3 774.1	...	...	...	...
April	2 099.5	2 035.4	232.3	776.1	1 027.1	283.6	11.9	3 808.7	...	...	...	...
May	2 118.2	2 053.6	244.1	778.6	1 030.9	271.4	11.4	3 796.4	...	...	...	...
June	2 122.3	2 057.4	233.3	781.1	1 042.9	267.5	11.2	3 769.3	...	...	...	...
July	2 146.8	2 081.5	234.7	795.6	1 051.2	278.2	11.5	3 802.5	...	...	...	...
August	2 153.3	2 087.6	235.7	790.5	1 061.4	275.8	11.4	3 799.5	...	...	...	...
September	2 178.1	2 112.0	247.0	792.9	1 072.1	255.6	10.5	3 796.5	...	...	...	...
October	2 198.8	2 132.7	241.0	802.2	1 089.5	247.5	10.1	3 794.5	...	...	...	...
November	2 222.2	2 155.3	255.1	800.8	1 099.5	239.7	9.7	3 807.9	...	...	...	...
December	2 235.8	2 167.2	257.5	805.1	1 104.6	235.6	9.5	3 816.9	...	...	...	...
1983												
January	2 246.1	2 177.8	255.1	803.7	1 119.1	241.1	9.7	3 824.6	...	...	...	...
February	2 247.8	2 179.7	253.8	801.7	1 124.3	243.2	9.8	3 825.8	...	...	...	...
March	2 276.1	2 207.6	258.3	813.4	1 136.0	231.3	9.2	3 843.1	...	...	...	...
April	2 304.9	2 235.7	268.3	815.2	1 152.2	220.8	8.7	3 847.7	...	...	...	...
May	2 327.7	2 257.9	275.3	823.8	1 158.9	216.8	8.5	3 861.3	...	...	...	...
June	2 357.0	2 286.4	284.4	833.1	1 168.9	198.1	7.8	3 864.6	...	...	...	...
July	2 380.1	2 308.0	289.5	840.0	1 178.6	223.7	8.6	3 924.4	...	...	...	...
August	2 391.6	2 318.7	287.0	841.4	1 190.3	213.2	8.2	3 913.7	...	...	...	...
September	2 405.1	2 331.6	288.4	845.6	1 197.5	231.0	8.8	3 947.7	...	...	...	...
October	2 433.0	2 358.5	299.3	849.8	1 209.4	231.0	8.7	3 978.1	...	...	...	...
November	2 447.9	2 372.1	301.3	854.0	1 216.8	243.7	9.1	4 007.5	...	...	...	...
December	2 481.2	2 403.1	313.9	852.6	1 236.6	239.2	8.8	4 044.8	...	...	...	...

Table 24-1. Personal Income and Its Disposition—*Continued*

(Billions of dollars, seasonally adjusted annual rate.)

Year and month	Personal income	Sources of personal income									Disposition of personal income	
		Wage and salary disburse-ments	Other labor income	Proprietors' income [1]		Rental income of persons [2]	Personal dividend income	Personal interest income	Transfer payments to persons	Less: Personal contributions for social insurance	Personal tax and nontax payments	Disposable personal income
				Farm	Nonfarm							
1984												
January	3 116.9	1 781.1	251.2	16.7	204.9	37.5	87.7	465.4	387.2	114.6	366.7	2 750.1
February	3 155.2	1 793.3	253.4	21.3	218.8	37.1	89.1	470.8	386.9	115.3	370.7	2 784.5
March	3 184.0	1 805.9	255.5	23.4	222.3	36.6	90.2	477.4	388.8	116.0	372.7	2 811.3
April	3 220.4	1 828.3	257.4	22.0	227.2	35.0	90.9	485.9	391.0	117.2	375.3	2 845.0
May	3 233.4	1 832.7	259.4	22.3	225.8	35.1	90.9	494.3	390.4	117.4	378.8	2 854.6
June	3 266.0	1 851.2	261.3	22.2	228.0	36.0	91.0	503.3	391.4	118.4	384.7	2 881.3
July	3 294.4	1 866.4	263.2	21.2	225.4	38.4	90.7	516.5	391.6	119.2	389.9	2 904.5
August	3 328.1	1 873.8	265.1	21.1	238.4	40.1	90.5	523.9	394.6	119.4	392.8	2 935.3
September	3 360.3	1 891.4	267.0	21.4	244.9	41.8	91.5	529.2	393.6	120.3	397.9	2 962.4
October	3 350.1	1 893.6	268.8	22.3	222.9	43.9	92.0	529.8	397.2	120.3	400.1	2 950.0
November	3 377.3	1 909.8	270.6	22.7	224.9	46.2	92.5	532.5	399.2	121.1	405.5	2 971.8
December	3 411.7	1 927.6	272.3	23.0	227.4	46.0	93.0	534.9	409.4	121.9	411.3	3 000.5
1985												
January	3 426.6	1 932.8	274.0	23.4	241.0	42.6	94.6	536.5	411.8	130.2	410.6	3 016.0
February	3 444.9	1 942.2	275.6	23.3	244.3	41.6	95.2	538.7	414.5	130.5	443.2	3 001.7
March	3 470.2	1 963.0	277.2	22.9	244.2	40.9	95.9	540.9	416.9	131.7	473.3	2 996.9
April	3 475.3	1 964.4	278.8	21.5	243.6	40.4	96.4	544.5	417.3	131.6	417.1	3 058.2
May	3 486.5	1 974.2	280.3	20.9	242.7	40.2	96.9	545.8	417.8	132.3	350.2	3 136.3
June	3 506.2	1 992.5	281.8	20.4	242.5	40.2	97.6	546.0	418.5	133.4	429.7	3 076.6
July	3 515.9	1 994.0	283.2	19.8	245.8	41.1	98.0	541.5	425.8	133.4	429.1	3 086.8
August	3 527.5	2 008.2	284.6	19.9	245.3	41.1	98.3	542.7	421.7	134.3	432.4	3 095.1
September	3 540.9	2 024.6	286.0	20.2	245.3	31.5	98.7	545.7	424.3	135.3	435.7	3 105.2
October	3 576.8	2 035.6	287.5	21.9	250.6	39.5	99.1	552.8	425.9	136.0	437.7	3 139.1
November	3 585.8	2 044.6	288.7	22.1	250.6	31.1	99.7	557.9	427.5	136.6	439.4	3 146.4
December	3 623.6	2 068.8	289.8	21.9	250.2	38.8	99.8	563.3	429.2	138.3	443.5	3 180.1
1986												
January	3 630.1	2 065.1	290.6	20.3	248.2	37.4	101.8	571.0	437.9	142.1	436.9	3 193.2
February	3 647.7	2 073.1	291.7	19.9	251.5	36.5	103.4	575.3	439.1	142.7	438.0	3 209.7
March	3 674.8	2 089.1	293.0	19.7	255.9	35.8	104.5	578.3	442.5	143.9	438.7	3 236.1
April	3 674.3	2 084.9	294.5	19.3	255.5	35.7	105.6	579.0	443.5	143.7	438.0	3 236.3
May	3 686.6	2 092.2	295.9	20.0	254.8	34.8	106.3	580.3	446.4	144.3	440.1	3 246.5
June	3 703.7	2 103.2	297.4	21.3	256.2	33.7	107.1	581.0	448.7	145.0	446.0	3 257.7
July	3 721.3	2 111.8	298.9	24.9	255.3	32.0	107.3	580.8	455.9	145.6	447.6	3 273.7
August	3 734.6	2 126.1	300.5	26.1	257.5	30.7	107.4	581.0	451.8	146.5	452.2	3 282.4
September	3 752.0	2 133.0	302.1	26.8	265.2	29.3	107.5	581.1	453.8	146.9	455.4	3 296.7
October	3 756.6	2 151.7	303.6	25.8	254.1	26.6	107.5	580.0	455.4	148.0	461.1	3 295.6
November	3 770.6	2 167.5	305.5	26.0	251.2	25.4	107.6	580.7	455.7	148.9	467.6	3 303.1
December	3 797.0	2 175.0	307.4	26.2	261.6	28.3	107.4	582.2	458.1	149.2	478.0	3 319.1
1987												
January	3 823.8	2 189.7	310.0	26.6	265.1	30.9	108.8	584.7	460.6	152.6	463.4	3 360.4
February	3 854.0	2 208.1	311.9	27.1	268.1	33.0	108.5	587.5	463.4	153.6	460.3	3 393.8
March	3 878.7	2 223.4	313.8	27.7	270.3	34.2	108.6	590.9	464.2	154.4	467.3	3 411.4
April	3 886.7	2 228.8	315.3	28.7	269.5	30.2	108.6	595.0	465.3	154.8	596.4	3 290.2
May	3 922.0	2 247.3	317.0	29.2	272.6	30.5	109.7	599.5	472.0	155.7	487.5	3 434.5
June	3 937.2	2 256.5	318.6	29.4	274.1	31.9	110.5	604.4	467.9	156.1	490.6	3 446.7
July	3 961.6	2 264.7	320.1	28.8	277.2	35.9	111.7	609.9	469.7	156.7	496.0	3 465.6
August	3 998.9	2 291.5	321.7	29.0	278.5	37.9	113.0	615.7	469.8	158.2	503.8	3 495.1
September	4 016.6	2 297.4	323.1	29.4	278.7	39.6	114.4	621.9	470.4	158.4	508.4	3 508.3
October	4 057.6	2 320.9	324.7	30.1	279.7	40.7	115.7	632.3	472.7	159.3	512.9	3 544.7
November	4 082.4	2 338.2	326.1	29.8	280.7	41.9	117.1	636.5	472.4	160.2	518.3	3 564.1
December	4 130.4	2 375.9	327.3	32.4	283.4	43.0	117.9	638.2	474.4	162.2	531.4	3 598.9
1988												
January	4 132.5	2 363.1	328.0	33.2	292.9	44.8	120.7	633.4	487.8	171.5	515.5	3 617.0
February	4 155.3	2 381.1	329.2	32.9	296.5	45.1	121.3	633.2	488.4	172.5	514.3	3 641.0
March	4 182.6	2 394.7	330.6	32.6	300.4	44.7	122.6	633.6	496.8	173.4	513.8	3 668.9
April	4 206.5	2 420.4	332.2	29.7	306.5	42.4	124.4	632.9	492.9	174.9	517.9	3 688.6
May	4 223.1	2 432.4	333.7	25.8	309.8	41.5	126.2	635.6	493.6	175.5	515.8	3 707.3
June	4 253.6	2 451.3	335.3	24.8	315.0	40.7	128.2	640.0	495.0	176.7	516.2	3 737.4
July	4 288.6	2 470.7	337.0	30.3	315.3	38.8	130.1	647.8	496.7	177.9	518.6	3 770.0
August	4 305.4	2 472.0	338.7	29.3	318.3	39.0	132.5	654.5	499.0	177.9	518.0	3 787.4
September	4 332.2	2 486.5	340.5	24.4	321.3	42.1	134.3	661.7	500.3	178.8	520.5	3 811.7
October	4 368.6	2 517.1	342.3	13.5	322.4	47.7	136.3	668.0	502.2	180.8	526.7	3 841.9
November	4 385.2	2 513.7	344.2	12.8	324.4	51.0	137.9	677.3	504.5	180.6	526.9	3 858.2
December	4 431.4	2 529.5	346.1	23.1	329.9	51.4	138.7	688.3	506.2	181.7	531.8	3 899.6
1989												
January	4 493.2	2 552.2	348.2	31.4	333.2	47.5	143.6	704.9	520.6	188.6	563.0	3 930.2
February	4 511.8	2 550.4	350.3	38.5	329.5	46.5	145.9	716.1	523.2	188.6	564.5	3 947.3
March	4 547.7	2 565.0	352.5	37.3	329.7	45.8	148.5	725.8	532.9	189.7	568.5	3 979.2
April	4 566.3	2 580.8	354.6	32.7	325.6	45.8	151.0	735.1	531.4	190.7	578.9	3 987.5
May	4 564.9	2 569.5	356.8	31.5	325.3	45.0	152.8	741.1	532.7	189.9	577.7	3 987.1
June	4 589.2	2 581.6	359.1	30.5	328.1	43.8	154.6	744.9	537.4	190.7	580.2	4 009.0
July	4 607.1	2 603.4	361.4	29.2	323.1	41.6	156.0	744.1	540.4	192.0	585.8	4 021.3
August	4 616.5	2 599.9	363.8	29.0	328.2	40.4	157.2	745.1	544.7	191.8	587.4	4 029.1
September	4 628.6	2 613.4	366.2	29.4	327.7	30.2	159.1	745.6	549.6	192.6	591.9	4 036.7
October	4 659.2	2 644.1	368.5	31.4	329.5	21.8	161.8	743.1	553.5	194.5	598.8	4 060.4
November	4 695.7	2 644.7	371.1	32.2	336.5	38.3	163.9	744.5	559.0	194.4	600.5	4 095.2
December	4 717.1	2 657.2	373.8	32.8	339.1	39.2	163.6	747.3	559.3	195.0	604.6	4 112.6

1. Includes inventory valuation and capital consumption adjustments.
2. Includes capital consumption adjustment.

Table 24-1. Personal Income and Its Disposition—*Continued*

(Billions of dollars, seasonally adjusted annual rate.)

Year and month	Personal outlays					Personal saving		Disposable personal income	Constant (1996) dollars			
	Total	Personal consumption expenditures				Billions of dollars	Percent of disposable personal income		Personal consumption expenditures			
		Total	Durable goods	Nondurable goods	Services				Total	Durable goods	Nondurable goods	Services
1984												
January	2 511.0	2 433.3	321.9	870.6	1 240.8	239.2	8.7	4 071.8	. . .	. . .	. . .	. . .
February	2 490.1	2 411.2	314.0	861.8	1 235.4	294.5	10.6	4 104.0	. . .	. . .	. . .	. . .
March	2 516.8	2 437.0	314.2	866.7	1 256.0	294.5	10.5	4 133.2	. . .	. . .	. . .	. . .
April	2 543.1	2 462.2	321.1	877.3	1 263.8	301.9	10.6	4 166.9	. . .	. . .	. . .	. . .
May	2 561.9	2 480.0	326.5	880.7	1 272.8	292.7	10.3	4 174.7	. . .	. . .	. . .	. . .
June	2 585.0	2 502.0	330.7	893.6	1 277.7	296.3	10.3	4 205.5	. . .	. . .	. . .	. . .
July	2 581.1	2 497.6	326.4	883.8	1 287.5	323.4	11.1	4 227.1	. . .	. . .	. . .	. . .
August	2 599.2	2 515.2	324.5	887.4	1 303.3	336.1	11.5	4 259.2	. . .	. . .	. . .	. . .
September	2 623.1	2 538.4	329.2	898.0	1 311.2	339.3	11.5	4 289.9	. . .	. . .	. . .	. . .
October	2 624.1	2 538.7	327.5	891.5	1 319.6	325.9	11.0	4 259.1	. . .	. . .	. . .	. . .
November	2 665.2	2 579.2	342.4	903.4	1 333.3	306.6	10.3	4 283.4	. . .	. . .	. . .	. . .
December	2 673.0	2 586.2	343.9	901.1	1 341.2	327.5	10.9	4 315.7	. . .	. . .	. . .	. . .
1985												
January	2 703.6	2 615.9	349.7	902.9	1 363.4	312.4	10.4	4 322.5	. . .	. . .	. . .	. . .
February	2 726.2	2 637.8	348.8	914.2	1 374.7	275.5	9.2	4 282.4	. . .	. . .	. . .	. . .
March	2 734.1	2 644.9	357.1	914.3	1 373.5	262.8	8.8	4 257.9	. . .	. . .	. . .	. . .
April	2 748.2	2 658.4	349.2	924.5	1 384.7	310.0	10.1	4 335.8	. . .	. . .	. . .	. . .
May	2 787.3	2 696.7	367.6	925.5	1 403.6	349.0	11.1	4 434.1	. . .	. . .	. . .	. . .
June	2 782.2	2 691.1	353.0	922.5	1 415.7	294.4	9.6	4 336.2	. . .	. . .	. . .	. . .
July	2 804.7	2 713.0	359.3	926.9	1 426.8	282.1	9.1	4 344.0	. . .	. . .	. . .	. . .
August	2 836.8	2 744.7	372.7	933.0	1 439.0	258.3	8.3	4 346.5	. . .	. . .	. . .	. . .
September	2 885.0	2 791.7	405.2	938.6	1 447.9	220.2	7.1	4 349.5	. . .	. . .	. . .	. . .
October	2 853.0	2 759.6	361.4	940.5	1 457.7	286.1	9.1	4 381.8	. . .	. . .	. . .	. . .
November	2 872.8	2 778.8	362.6	949.9	1 466.3	273.6	8.7	4 375.1	. . .	. . .	. . .	. . .
December	2 913.0	2 818.3	372.7	952.1	1 493.5	267.1	8.4	4 408.2	. . .	. . .	. . .	. . .
1986												
January	2 926.1	2 829.3	382.7	961.0	1 485.6	267.1	8.4	4 412.6	. . .	. . .	. . .	. . .
February	2 918.9	2 821.4	370.6	954.3	1 496.5	290.8	9.1	4 437.4	. . .	. . .	. . .	. . .
March	2 922.6	2 824.6	364.9	956.5	1 503.2	313.5	9.7	4 483.7	. . .	. . .	. . .	. . .
April	2 937.0	2 838.6	384.3	943.7	1 510.6	299.3	9.2	4 489.2	. . .	. . .	. . .	. . .
May	2 962.0	2 863.1	393.9	952.5	1 516.6	284.5	8.8	4 491.4	. . .	. . .	. . .	. . .
June	2 968.6	2 869.4	383.5	955.7	1 530.1	289.1	8.9	4 487.5	. . .	. . .	. . .	. . .
July	2 990.9	2 891.0	395.3	956.4	1 539.3	282.9	8.6	4 504.8	. . .	. . .	. . .	. . .
August	3 010.0	2 909.9	413.4	954.6	1 541.9	272.5	8.3	4 508.1	. . .	. . .	. . .	. . .
September	3 085.8	2 984.8	465.3	959.5	1 559.9	210.9	6.4	4 511.2	. . .	. . .	. . .	. . .
October	3 049.5	2 947.5	414.0	967.3	1 566.2	246.1	7.5	4 501.7	. . .	. . .	. . .	. . .
November	3 047.2	2 945.6	399.6	963.8	1 582.2	255.9	7.7	4 500.0	. . .	. . .	. . .	. . .
December	3 118.3	3 016.9	447.9	976.2	1 592.7	200.7	6.0	4 511.8	. . .	. . .	. . .	. . .
1987												
January	3 064.2	2 963.7	379.1	978.0	1 606.6	296.3	8.8	4 536.9	4 001.2	415.9	1 252.9	2 335.0
February	3 130.4	3 030.1	405.4	1 005.1	1 619.7	263.3	7.8	4 562.3	4 073.4	444.3	1 277.4	2 347.3
March	3 140.7	3 040.4	407.5	1 000.0	1 632.9	270.7	7.9	4 571.8	4 074.6	445.6	1 267.5	2 358.1
April	3 167.3	3 066.3	416.0	1 007.4	1 642.9	122.9	3.7	4 393.3	4 094.3	453.4	1 273.3	2 362.5
May	3 177.3	3 076.4	412.3	1 011.8	1 652.3	257.1	7.5	4 573.3	4 096.5	448.8	1 275.9	2 368.0
June	3 203.1	3 101.9	423.3	1 016.4	1 662.2	243.6	7.1	4 571.0	4 113.7	459.3	1 275.9	2 372.8
July	3 224.3	3 122.1	429.9	1 017.7	1 674.5	241.3	7.0	4 587.4	4 132.6	465.2	1 275.4	2 385.9
August	3 261.7	3 159.3	446.1	1 023.9	1 689.2	233.4	6.7	4 607.0	4 164.3	481.9	1 277.6	2 395.5
September	3 257.3	3 155.2	437.5	1 024.3	1 693.3	251.0	7.2	4 607.8	4 144.1	471.3	1 275.0	2 390.5
October	3 268.2	3 166.4	420.1	1 027.4	1 719.0	276.5	7.8	4 637.9	4 143.0	451.9	1 276.0	2 413.7
November	3 277.8	3 176.1	424.0	1 031.8	1 720.3	286.2	8.0	4 651.6	4 145.3	455.8	1 279.0	2 407.6
December	3 308.0	3 206.2	435.5	1 040.0	1 730.7	290.9	8.1	4 689.2	4 177.5	469.2	1 288.2	2 414.4
1988												
January	3 345.0	3 242.8	446.4	1 041.1	1 755.2	272.0	7.5	4 700.1	4 213.8	481.9	1 285.5	2 439.9
February	3 351.2	3 248.8	444.8	1 042.7	1 761.2	289.7	8.0	4 726.1	4 217.1	480.5	1 289.3	2 440.9
March	3 390.2	3 287.7	448.3	1 064.5	1 774.9	278.6	7.6	4 746.2	4 253.0	482.8	1 312.6	2 450.2
April	3 394.2	3 291.5	443.3	1 063.7	1 784.5	294.4	8.0	4 746.8	4 235.7	476.7	1 302.7	2 450.7
May	3 424.5	3 321.6	449.8	1 071.2	1 800.6	282.9	7.6	4 756.3	4 261.4	483.1	1 309.2	2 462.7
June	3 448.7	3 345.5	452.5	1 076.0	1 817.1	288.7	7.7	4 773.6	4 273.1	484.8	1 310.3	2 471.8
July	3 471.9	3 368.8	447.3	1 086.4	1 835.1	298.1	7.9	4 792.8	4 282.8	478.4	1 313.8	2 486.3
August	3 496.3	3 392.9	445.0	1 096.8	1 851.1	291.1	7.7	4 802.4	4 302.1	474.7	1 325.6	2 498.3
September	3 502.8	3 399.2	443.5	1 102.4	1 853.3	308.9	8.1	4 810.3	4 289.8	471.6	1 324.8	2 490.0
October	3 544.9	3 440.0	452.3	1 112.0	1 875.6	297.0	7.7	4 833.4	4 327.7	479.9	1 333.2	2 510.5
November	3 560.4	3 455.2	455.6	1 118.7	1 880.9	297.9	7.7	4 842.5	4 336.6	482.8	1 339.4	2 509.4
December	3 590.5	3 485.1	473.6	1 118.9	1 892.6	309.1	7.9	4 878.5	4 360.0	501.5	1 335.2	2 515.4
1989												
January	3 617.0	3 505.9	469.7	1 136.2	1 900.0	313.2	8.0	4 892.3	4 364.2	495.0	1 349.1	2 512.5
February	3 620.9	3 509.6	455.5	1 130.0	1 924.0	326.4	8.3	4 898.7	4 355.5	479.8	1 337.1	2 535.7
March	3 632.0	3 519.8	456.1	1 136.8	1 926.9	347.2	8.7	4 919.5	4 351.6	481.9	1 336.9	2 529.2
April	3 678.1	3 563.1	474.3	1 152.9	1 935.9	309.4	7.8	4 897.8	4 376.5	500.3	1 337.2	2 532.5
May	3 687.8	3 571.3	462.0	1 164.1	1 945.2	299.3	7.5	4 879.8	4 370.9	486.9	1 343.0	2 536.5
June	3 701.8	3 584.2	466.1	1 166.9	1 951.2	307.2	7.7	4 895.6	4 376.9	490.2	1 345.3	2 536.4
July	3 720.7	3 602.3	471.1	1 168.4	1 962.7	300.6	7.5	4 899.1	4 388.7	494.8	1 345.1	2 543.3
August	3 757.6	3 638.0	491.9	1 172.1	1 974.0	271.5	6.7	4 907.3	4 431.0	516.6	1 355.5	2 549.7
September	3 761.4	3 640.5	473.2	1 181.5	1 985.7	275.2	6.8	4 901.6	4 420.6	496.5	1 363.3	2 554.7
October	3 778.2	3 655.3	466.7	1 183.3	2 005.3	282.2	6.9	4 907.7	4 418.0	488.9	1 358.0	2 567.3
November	3 788.9	3 665.2	462.8	1 189.6	2 012.8	306.3	7.5	4 936.9	4 418.5	483.6	1 364.3	2 567.2
December	3 828.9	3 704.8	463.6	1 202.9	2 038.3	283.7	6.9	4 941.7	4 451.7	485.4	1 376.8	2 586.3

Table 24-1. Personal Income and Its Disposition—*Continued*

(Billions of dollars, seasonally adjusted annual rate.)

Year and month	Personal income	Sources of personal income									Disposition of personal income	
		Wage and salary disburse-ments	Other labor income	Proprietors' income [1]		Rental income of persons [2]	Personal dividend income	Personal interest income	Transfer payments to persons	Less: Personal contributions for social insurance	Personal tax and nontax payments	Disposable personal income
				Farm	Nonfarm							
1990												
January	4 766.4	2 676.0	376.9	33.2	345.2	41.1	165.6	753.7	576.5	201.7	590.3	4 176.2
February	4 807.4	2 705.4	379.6	33.3	344.0	42.0	166.0	757.7	578.9	199.5	596.9	4 210.5
March	4 828.7	2 723.4	382.1	33.0	340.7	43.1	166.6	761.4	580.4	202.0	599.9	4 228.8
April	4 865.1	2 745.9	384.4	31.9	344.2	43.5	167.4	764.7	583.3	200.2	603.5	4 261.6
May	4 869.6	2 741.9	386.8	31.5	348.4	45.1	164.7	768.2	584.4	201.4	606.6	4 263.1
June	4 903.1	2 763.3	389.1	31.1	349.1	47.3	165.8	771.7	590.5	204.7	612.6	4 290.5
July	4 935.0	2 780.1	391.4	31.2	352.0	51.3	166.6	775.7	592.4	205.7	616.2	4 318.9
August	4 943.9	2 773.0	393.6	30.9	358.3	53.4	166.8	778.8	594.5	205.3	615.8	4 328.1
September	4 975.4	2 792.1	395.8	30.4	357.6	54.8	166.0	781.4	603.6	206.3	620.1	4 355.3
October	4 967.8	2 776.1	398.1	29.7	352.8	55.6	164.2	785.8	610.7	205.2	616.6	4 351.1
November	4 977.3	2 778.8	400.1	29.1	355.4	56.0	162.9	786.0	614.3	205.3	616.9	4 360.4
December	4 999.3	2 798.7	401.9	28.3	350.9	55.8	162.5	784.4	623.3	206.5	620.4	4 378.9
1991												
January	4 987.9	2 786.4	403.0	26.8	344.4	53.9	168.9	776.5	640.4	212.5	601.8	4 386.1
February	4 999.4	2 784.7	404.8	26.4	347.3	53.7	173.9	774.1	646.9	212.3	599.7	4 399.8
March	5 012.3	2 788.3	406.8	26.4	348.5	54.1	175.3	772.7	652.8	212.6	600.8	4 411.5
April	5 038.6	2 795.1	409.3	28.0	352.7	55.8	176.5	774.2	659.9	212.9	604.3	4 434.2
May	5 059.0	2 804.7	411.6	27.9	355.4	56.5	178.2	774.1	664.2	213.5	605.2	4 453.8
June	5 094.6	2 833.4	414.0	27.1	357.9	57.1	179.4	773.8	667.3	215.4	610.0	4 484.6
July	5 089.8	2 822.3	416.4	24.0	360.5	57.0	180.4	774.5	670.0	215.3	608.0	4 481.8
August	5 105.3	2 831.7	418.9	23.5	360.2	57.6	180.9	773.5	674.6	215.6	609.9	4 495.4
September	5 135.3	2 853.2	421.5	23.9	363.0	58.3	181.9	771.6	679.2	217.3	616.9	4 518.3
October	5 135.4	2 845.1	424.1	26.3	363.5	53.8	181.6	767.5	690.1	216.6	618.8	4 516.6
November	5 156.5	2 858.8	427.0	27.5	365.9	59.6	181.4	765.3	688.5	217.4	622.2	4 534.3
December	5 210.2	2 887.1	429.9	28.8	374.2	60.1	180.6	763.3	705.2	219.1	628.7	4 581.5
1992												
January	5 241.1	2 885.6	433.3	30.9	387.1	58.8	179.2	762.1	726.1	221.9	607.8	4 633.3
February	5 284.5	2 922.2	436.4	32.0	389.4	59.1	178.5	760.7	730.4	224.2	616.0	4 668.5
March	5 304.8	2 932.3	439.4	31.4	391.2	60.0	178.1	759.3	737.7	224.7	620.4	4 684.3
April	5 330.0	2 938.8	442.2	32.2	397.4	62.4	178.2	759.3	744.5	225.0	624.4	4 705.6
May	5 355.3	2 955.3	445.2	32.6	400.4	63.8	178.9	757.1	748.1	226.0	627.6	4 727.7
June	5 371.3	2 963.2	448.1	35.8	399.7	65.2	180.8	753.9	751.0	226.5	629.9	4 741.4
July	5 383.5	2 969.3	451.1	33.4	404.8	65.8	183.4	747.7	755.0	226.9	633.3	4 750.2
August	5 373.4	2 991.6	454.0	33.2	403.7	28.7	186.6	744.3	759.6	228.3	639.5	4 733.9
September	5 415.2	2 991.2	456.9	33.0	402.1	65.0	189.5	741.6	764.2	228.2	641.1	4 774.1
October	5 464.0	3 009.2	459.9	33.1	415.1	73.7	192.8	739.8	769.5	229.2	646.2	4 817.8
November	5 484.3	3 027.4	462.7	32.6	417.6	76.7	196.4	738.4	763.0	230.5	652.4	4 831.9
December	5 677.1	3 204.7	465.4	31.8	412.0	80.1	201.3	737.5	771.6	227.3	690.6	4 986.5
1993												
January	5 461.7	2 973.9	467.8	29.3	427.2	84.7	190.5	738.7	782.5	232.9	641.5	4 820.2
February	5 470.9	2 976.2	470.5	29.2	427.8	87.3	192.1	737.6	783.6	233.4	644.9	4 826.0
March	5 464.8	2 967.9	473.2	29.9	424.2	82.1	194.0	735.8	790.6	233.0	645.7	4 819.1
April	5 575.0	3 060.5	476.2	33.7	429.9	89.3	195.8	732.6	793.2	235.9	666.3	4 908.8
May	5 607.5	3 088.2	478.9	34.6	431.7	90.3	198.0	729.9	793.5	237.7	673.7	4 933.8
June	5 603.2	3 077.4	481.7	34.9	428.4	91.2	200.8	727.1	798.8	237.0	673.1	4 930.1
July	5 609.2	3 091.4	484.4	25.5	433.5	85.0	203.4	723.5	800.5	238.0	677.7	4 931.6
August	5 640.1	3 112.7	487.0	20.8	434.4	93.0	206.2	720.8	804.6	239.4	683.5	4 956.7
September	5 641.6	3 111.1	489.6	22.5	429.7	94.4	209.4	718.3	805.8	239.3	684.2	4 957.4
October	5 669.0	3 124.6	491.8	27.4	434.8	95.6	212.8	715.3	807.0	240.3	688.3	4 980.7
November	5 693.2	3 132.2	494.5	35.7	436.5	97.5	215.6	713.8	808.2	240.9	690.5	5 002.6
December	5 883.4	3 306.0	497.5	38.0	442.5	99.8	216.9	713.2	815.4	245.8	726.3	5 157.1
1994												
January	5 656.4	3 133.0	501.6	40.9	398.4	78.9	217.8	712.5	822.0	248.7	695.3	4 961.1
February	5 725.4	3 123.8	504.1	41.0	440.8	105.9	219.4	714.0	824.6	248.1	693.4	5 032.1
March	5 759.4	3 144.6	506.1	39.9	444.4	109.3	222.2	716.8	825.7	249.5	697.7	5 061.6
April	5 832.1	3 211.5	507.1	36.1	442.8	110.3	226.1	721.3	828.6	251.7	761.3	5 070.8
May	5 870.6	3 238.9	508.2	33.9	446.8	112.0	229.5	726.7	828.2	253.4	717.6	5 153.1
June	5 879.5	3 235.8	509.0	31.8	447.2	113.6	233.0	733.2	829.4	253.4	717.6	5 162.0
July	5 904.8	3 252.5	509.4	29.2	443.1	114.0	236.8	741.8	832.6	254.6	721.4	5 183.5
August	5 932.2	3 258.3	509.6	27.6	448.5	116.3	240.4	750.1	836.5	255.0	723.3	5 209.0
September	5 968.7	3 278.2	509.5	26.4	452.8	118.3	243.8	758.8	837.3	256.3	728.1	5 240.6
October	6 026.8	3 316.0	509.5	26.5	454.1	116.0	246.9	771.9	844.7	258.8	736.4	5 290.4
November	6 034.9	3 313.4	508.6	25.6	457.0	115.2	249.8	778.8	845.4	258.7	736.9	5 298.0
December	6 065.5	3 334.3	507.1	24.4	459.8	114.3	251.0	783.4	851.3	260.1	742.3	5 323.2
1995												
January	6 095.0	3 353.0	503.9	22.4	465.7	116.9	248.5	782.5	865.9	264.0	748.2	5 346.8
February	6 109.6	3 363.9	502.2	21.3	467.0	117.0	248.0	784.8	870.3	264.8	752.2	5 357.4
March	6 125.1	3 372.8	500.6	20.4	468.8	116.8	248.6	787.1	875.3	265.4	755.0	5 370.1
April	6 148.4	3 396.1	499.7	19.8	467.9	115.2	249.6	790.1	876.9	267.0	809.4	5 339.0
May	6 157.8	3 392.3	498.5	19.6	471.9	115.0	250.8	792.0	884.4	266.7	762.2	5 395.6
June	6 183.6	3 414.2	497.3	19.6	475.6	115.1	252.0	793.4	884.5	268.2	769.9	5 413.8
July	6 203.7	3 434.0	496.1	19.3	476.5	115.1	250.2	793.6	888.2	269.4	776.0	5 427.7
August	6 223.4	3 444.9	495.0	20.3	480.6	116.4	250.5	794.7	891.2	270.1	781.0	5 442.3
September	6 250.7	3 462.7	493.9	21.9	480.4	118.3	254.8	795.9	894.0	271.2	787.6	5 463.1
October	6 278.2	3 477.3	492.9	25.5	481.7	118.2	257.7	798.2	898.9	272.1	793.7	5 484.5
November	6 304.4	3 488.8	492.0	27.4	484.0	124.7	263.5	798.9	897.9	272.8	799.6	5 504.7
December	6 331.3	3 496.2	491.2	29.0	485.9	126.6	273.1	799.0	903.5	273.3	805.3	5 526.0

1. Includes inventory valuation and capital consumption adjustments.
2. Includes capital consumption adjustment.

Table 24-1. Personal Income and Its Disposition—*Continued*

(Billions of dollars, seasonally adjusted annual rate.)

Year and month	Personal outlays					Personal saving		Constant (1996) dollars				
	Total	Personal consumption expenditures				Billions of dollars	Percent of disposable personal income	Disposable personal income	Personal consumption expenditures			
		Total	Durable goods	Nondurable goods	Services				Total	Durable goods	Nondurable goods	Services
1990												
January	3 871.2	3 747.5	507.4	1 210.4	2 029.7	305.0	7.3	4 988.3	4 476.3	529.6	1 364.9	2 572.1
February	3 868.5	3 744.2	477.1	1 222.9	2 044.1	341.9	8.1	5 008.3	4 453.6	496.4	1 369.8	2 583.0
March	3 897.9	3 772.7	474.7	1 231.7	2 066.3	330.8	7.8	5 008.0	4 467.9	494.2	1 375.8	2 594.0
April	3 916.9	3 791.6	477.2	1 228.4	2 086.0	344.7	8.1	5 032.0	4 477.1	497.0	1 370.7	2 606.0
May	3 924.5	3 798.5	466.0	1 228.7	2 103.8	338.6	7.9	5 019.6	4 472.6	485.5	1 369.7	2 616.2
June	3 955.7	3 828.6	464.4	1 242.6	2 121.5	334.8	7.8	5 028.1	4 486.8	485.2	1 377.5	2 622.7
July	3 975.1	3 846.4	466.4	1 247.0	2 132.9	343.7	8.0	5 047.4	4 495.2	486.6	1 377.7	2 629.7
August	4 002.1	3 872.8	459.6	1 259.3	2 153.9	326.0	7.5	5 025.3	4 496.7	479.3	1 377.6	2 640.0
September	4 025.9	3 895.6	465.1	1 269.2	2 161.2	329.5	7.6	5 025.4	4 495.0	484.4	1 372.4	2 638.0
October	4 024.8	3 893.9	455.9	1 269.4	2 168.6	326.3	7.5	4 990.7	4 466.2	473.1	1 359.8	2 635.2
November	4 028.4	3 897.3	453.0	1 276.4	2 167.9	332.0	7.6	4 992.3	4 462.0	470.7	1 366.3	2 626.2
December	4 020.3	3 889.2	444.2	1 266.8	2 178.2	358.6	8.2	5 004.5	4 444.8	462.7	1 353.4	2 631.8
1991												
January	4 004.8	3 873.6	423.7	1 263.7	2 186.1	381.2	8.7	4 990.3	4 407.2	437.7	1 350.2	2 624.6
February	4 029.4	3 898.2	435.2	1 265.9	2 197.0	370.4	8.4	4 999.0	4 429.1	447.6	1 357.0	2 628.6
March	4 073.6	3 942.0	459.1	1 273.8	2 209.1	337.9	7.7	5 009.5	4 476.3	472.5	1 369.4	2 635.6
April	4 070.9	3 939.3	441.2	1 274.1	2 223.9	363.3	8.2	5 023.8	4 463.1	453.4	1 365.2	2 648.6
May	4 097.2	3 965.3	439.3	1 286.0	2 240.0	356.6	8.0	5 024.9	4 473.8	451.3	1 372.9	2 653.6
June	4 103.3	3 971.1	443.6	1 283.0	2 244.5	381.3	8.5	5 051.3	4 472.9	457.5	1 368.0	2 651.1
July	4 124.4	3 992.7	450.2	1 286.6	2 255.9	357.4	8.0	5 040.9	4 490.8	461.3	1 374.7	2 658.0
August	4 126.0	3 994.1	444.4	1 287.5	2 262.1	369.4	8.2	5 044.2	4 481.6	456.3	1 371.8	2 657.3
September	4 140.1	4 008.0	452.1	1 280.7	2 275.2	378.2	8.4	5 051.1	4 480.5	463.1	1 361.6	2 659.5
October	4 131.4	3 999.1	440.4	1 278.2	2 280.5	385.2	8.5	5 038.7	4 461.4	450.3	1 359.7	2 656.2
November	4 161.3	4 028.9	442.7	1 283.8	2 302.4	373.1	8.2	5 043.6	4 481.4	452.2	1 360.3	2 674.3
December	4 175.4	4 042.7	444.4	1 282.7	2 315.6	406.1	8.9	5 079.0	4 481.7	455.9	1 356.6	2 674.3
1992												
January	4 240.4	4 108.5	458.7	1 307.4	2 342.4	392.9	8.5	5 122.7	4 542.4	469.6	1 385.6	2 690.7
February	4 254.1	4 121.7	463.4	1 306.8	2 351.5	414.3	8.9	5 145.2	4 542.6	472.7	1 383.3	2 689.8
March	4 271.5	4 139.2	454.8	1 301.6	2 382.7	412.9	8.8	5 148.7	4 549.4	463.9	1 374.5	2 716.3
April	4 280.7	4 149.0	453.1	1 306.1	2 389.9	424.9	9.0	5 160.1	4 549.8	461.5	1 378.7	2 714.7
May	4 305.8	4 174.4	464.2	1 313.0	2 397.1	421.9	8.9	5 176.6	4 570.8	471.8	1 383.9	2 719.4
June	4 322.3	4 191.0	472.5	1 308.3	2 410.3	419.1	8.8	5 180.8	4 579.5	480.8	1 374.5	2 728.5
July	4 348.7	4 218.4	469.5	1 317.5	2 431.4	401.5	8.5	5 172.0	4 593.0	476.9	1 381.3	2 739.5
August	4 323.4	4 192.9	473.8	1 327.8	2 391.2	410.5	8.7	5 167.1	4 576.5	481.6	1 389.9	2 708.0
September	4 396.6	4 265.8	479.4	1 332.7	2 453.7	377.5	7.9	5 183.6	4 631.8	487.8	1 393.1	2 754.8
October	4 427.6	4 296.7	485.6	1 347.2	2 463.8	390.2	8.1	5 213.7	4 649.7	492.9	1 407.3	2 752.5
November	4 443.5	4 312.9	478.3	1 349.6	2 484.9	388.4	8.0	5 220.1	4 659.4	484.6	1 409.1	2 769.7
December	4 476.2	4 345.4	496.0	1 357.2	2 492.2	510.3	10.2	5 380.3	4 688.6	504.0	1 414.5	2 772.8
1993												
January	4 478.3	4 346.8	499.3	1 357.7	2 489.8	341.8	7.1	5 188.7	4 679.1	506.7	1 414.9	2 759.6
February	4 493.8	4 362.5	483.6	1 363.7	2 515.2	332.2	6.9	5 185.8	4 687.7	491.3	1 416.8	2 783.2
March	4 473.2	4 342.7	479.9	1 345.8	2 517.1	345.9	7.2	5 169.0	4 658.0	488.1	1 398.9	2 775.2
April	4 532.1	4 402.0	502.9	1 369.6	2 529.5	376.7	7.7	5 251.7	4 709.6	508.7	1 423.4	2 779.9
May	4 546.7	4 417.9	508.8	1 371.1	2 538.0	387.2	7.8	5 264.0	4 713.5	514.8	1 425.3	2 775.4
June	4 572.8	4 443.8	510.6	1 370.5	2 562.7	357.3	7.2	5 260.3	4 741.5	516.4	1 428.0	2 799.3
July	4 599.3	4 470.6	521.6	1 377.2	2 571.8	332.3	6.7	5 255.7	4 764.4	526.6	1 435.3	2 804.2
August	4 614.4	4 485.7	519.3	1 377.5	2 588.8	342.2	6.9	5 274.6	4 773.4	523.2	1 434.1	2 818.3
September	4 637.4	4 508.3	521.4	1 384.1	2 602.8	319.9	6.5	5 270.1	4 792.7	524.2	1 445.0	2 825.5
October	4 668.7	4 539.0	532.4	1 392.0	2 614.6	312.0	6.3	5 275.6	4 807.8	534.3	1 445.6	2 829.4
November	4 689.2	4 559.6	538.6	1 395.3	2 625.7	313.4	6.3	5 289.3	4 820.9	540.2	1 446.7	2 835.3
December	4 707.8	4 577.6	542.8	1 397.8	2 637.0	449.3	8.7	5 450.7	4 838.2	545.2	1 449.9	2 844.4
1994												
January	4 688.5	4 558.5	535.3	1 389.5	2 633.7	272.6	5.5	5 245.3	4 819.6	536.9	1 444.1	2 840.2
February	4 763.8	4 633.8	550.0	1 414.1	2 669.7	268.3	5.3	5 307.6	4 887.6	550.8	1 470.3	2 867.4
March	4 779.7	4 649.0	553.3	1 425.5	2 670.2	282.0	5.6	5 326.8	4 892.6	553.1	1 481.4	2 858.6
April	4 789.9	4 659.1	560.1	1 418.3	2 680.7	280.9	5.5	5 331.1	4 898.2	560.2	1 471.9	2 866.5
May	4 803.2	4 671.6	548.7	1 422.8	2 700.1	349.9	6.8	5 409.0	4 903.6	546.5	1 476.8	2 881.7
June	4 834.2	4 701.8	552.1	1 434.2	2 715.5	327.8	6.3	5 403.5	4 921.8	548.4	1 484.1	2 890.6
July	4 850.7	4 718.3	556.3	1 439.7	2 722.4	332.7	6.4	5 404.7	4 919.7	551.0	1 483.8	2 886.0
August	4 897.6	4 763.9	567.0	1 453.2	2 743.6	311.3	6.0	5 416.5	4 953.7	561.5	1 492.9	2 900.0
September	4 912.4	4 776.8	566.4	1 456.9	2 753.4	328.2	6.3	5 441.8	4 960.2	560.7	1 495.9	2 904.4
October	4 943.7	4 806.8	575.6	1 463.9	2 767.3	346.7	6.6	5 486.4	4 984.8	570.5	1 504.1	2 910.6
November	4 962.3	4 823.9	583.5	1 467.2	2 773.2	335.6	6.3	5 486.1	4 995.3	577.4	1 506.4	2 911.5
December	4 973.0	4 833.2	581.0	1 470.6	2 781.6	350.3	6.6	5 507.7	5 000.7	575.0	1 509.1	2 916.8
1995												
January	5 006.8	4 864.7	587.2	1 485.0	2 792.5	340.0	6.4	5 515.3	5 018.0	579.7	1 524.0	2 914.2
February	4 996.9	4 853.7	565.6	1 468.0	2 820.1	360.5	6.7	5 513.6	4 995.2	558.0	1 505.9	2 932.4
March	5 032.7	4 887.5	581.6	1 474.5	2 831.4	337.4	6.3	5 517.2	5 021.5	573.6	1 513.0	2 935.3
April	5 042.9	4 897.3	569.5	1 482.7	2 845.0	296.1	5.5	5 471.5	5 018.8	561.0	1 516.9	2 941.9
May	5 092.9	4 945.4	585.4	1 493.9	2 866.1	302.7	5.6	5 521.3	5 060.7	578.5	1 526.7	2 955.9
June	5 138.2	4 988.3	598.4	1 500.0	2 890.0	275.5	5.1	5 534.2	5 099.3	592.7	1 532.3	2 974.3
July	5 125.8	4 974.4	587.7	1 494.8	2 891.9	301.8	5.6	5 538.8	5 076.2	582.1	1 525.1	2 969.4
August	5 178.5	5 026.0	608.4	1 502.2	2 915.4	263.9	4.8	5 542.2	5 118.1	602.5	1 531.0	2 984.5
September	5 171.0	5 015.3	592.6	1 510.9	2 911.8	292.1	5.3	5 559.0	5 103.3	587.3	1 539.1	2 977.1
October	5 177.3	5 018.4	591.3	1 506.0	2 921.1	307.2	5.6	5 568.9	5 095.6	586.4	1 531.3	2 978.1
November	5 220.1	5 059.3	597.8	1 518.3	2 943.1	284.6	5.2	5 587.4	5 135.3	594.3	1 546.2	2 995.0
December	5 259.0	5 097.6	610.8	1 531.3	2 955.5	267.0	4.8	5 599.7	5 165.6	606.3	1 556.5	3 002.8

Table 24-2. Industrial Production and Capacity Utilization

(Seasonally adjusted.)

Year and month	Total industrial production	Industrial production indexes (1992=100)										Capacity utilization (output as a percent of capacity)					
		Major market groups					Major industry groups					Total industry	Manufacturing			Mining	Utilities
		Products				Materials	Manufacturing			Mining	Utilities		Total	Primary process-ing	Ad-vanced process-ing		
		Total	Con-sumer goods	Business equip-ment	Construc-tion supplies		Total	Durables	Non-durables								
1972																	
January	62.7	61.0	67.6	45.9	79.1	64.9	58.9	55.5	63.9	100.3	71.7	82.3	81.2	82.8	80.7	88.8	94.3
February	63.2	61.5	67.8	46.5	79.5	65.1	59.4	56.1	64.0	100.1	73.0	82.6	81.5	82.7	81.1	88.7	95.7
March	63.7	61.9	68.1	47.3	80.2	65.7	59.9	56.6	64.6	100.7	73.0	83.1	82.0	83.5	81.2	89.3	95.2
April	64.7	62.9	69.4	48.3	81.4	66.8	60.9	57.7	65.4	102.0	74.4	84.2	83.1	84.5	82.3	90.6	96.6
May	64.5	62.6	68.7	48.4	81.8	66.9	60.7	57.7	65.1	100.5	73.1	83.8	82.7	84.9	81.4	89.4	94.5
June	64.7	62.9	69.0	48.6	82.3	66.9	60.9	57.7	65.6	101.1	73.0	83.8	82.7	84.7	81.5	90.0	94.0
July	64.6	62.8	68.7	48.4	82.8	67.0	60.9	57.9	65.4	101.7	73.1	83.5	82.5	84.9	81.0	90.6	93.7
August	65.5	63.6	69.9	49.1	83.7	68.0	61.8	58.6	66.3	101.4	74.0	84.4	83.4	85.8	81.8	90.5	94.4
September	66.2	64.2	70.2	50.2	84.8	68.9	62.3	59.4	66.4	102.7	74.5	85.1	83.9	86.4	82.3	91.8	94.7
October	67.2	65.0	71.1	51.2	85.8	70.0	63.3	60.8	66.9	102.4	76.1	86.1	85.0	87.8	83.4	91.6	96.2
November	68.0	65.7	71.4	52.5	87.0	70.9	64.1	61.9	67.2	101.9	76.7	86.9	85.9	88.8	84.2	91.2	96.6
December	68.6	66.3	72.2	53.0	86.4	71.8	64.9	62.6	68.0	101.4	76.8	87.5	86.7	89.3	85.3	90.9	96.3
1973																	
January	68.7	66.3	71.5	54.1	86.8	71.9	65.0	63.2	67.5	101.3	76.1	87.3	86.6	89.1	85.2	90.9	95.0
February	69.7	67.2	72.5	55.0	89.8	72.8	65.9	64.2	68.2	101.9	77.4	88.3	87.6	90.6	85.9	91.6	96.2
March	69.6	67.2	72.6	55.3	88.7	72.7	66.1	64.2	68.6	100.3	75.5	88.0	87.5	90.4	86.0	90.2	93.3
April	69.9	67.4	72.4	56.1	88.1	73.2	66.3	64.4	68.7	100.1	76.4	88.1	87.5	90.3	86.0	90.2	93.9
May	70.2	67.6	72.5	56.8	88.6	73.6	66.5	64.8	68.8	100.8	76.6	88.3	87.6	90.5	86.1	90.9	93.7
June	70.7	68.1	72.7	57.6	88.8	74.2	67.0	65.5	68.9	101.8	77.7	88.7	87.9	90.4	86.6	91.9	94.6
July	71.2	68.3	72.6	58.0	88.7	75.0	67.3	65.8	69.3	103.4	77.9	89.0	88.1	91.1	86.6	93.4	94.3
August	71.1	68.2	72.5	58.2	88.9	75.1	67.4	65.7	69.6	103.6	77.6	88.7	88.0	91.0	86.5	93.7	93.5
September	71.7	69.1	73.8	59.5	89.1	75.0	67.8	66.5	69.4	103.3	79.6	89.2	88.2	90.5	87.1	93.5	95.3
October	71.9	69.2	73.4	60.0	89.1	75.6	68.2	66.8	70.0	103.5	78.1	89.2	88.5	90.9	87.2	93.8	93.2
November	72.0	69.2	73.3	60.1	89.5	75.7	68.3	67.1	69.9	103.4	76.7	89.0	88.5	91.2	87.0	93.8	91.0
December	70.8	67.8	71.2	58.7	88.9	75.1	67.1	65.7	68.8	103.8	74.5	87.4	86.6	90.2	84.7	94.3	88.0
1974																	
January	69.8	66.9	70.2	58.4	86.7	74.0	66.3	64.3	68.9	103.0	74.5	85.9	85.3	88.4	83.6	93.6	87.5
February	69.6	66.7	69.7	58.6	86.2	73.5	66.0	63.9	68.9	103.4	74.0	85.4	84.7	87.7	83.1	94.0	86.5
March	69.9	67.3	70.6	59.1	86.4	73.4	66.3	63.9	69.7	102.7	75.4	85.5	84.8	87.4	83.4	93.3	87.8
April	69.8	67.5	70.4	59.7	86.8	72.7	66.0	63.8	69.0	102.6	75.9	85.1	84.2	87.0	82.7	93.1	88.0
May	70.6	68.1	71.0	60.8	86.6	73.9	66.8	64.9	69.5	103.5	77.5	85.8	85.0	87.3	83.8	93.9	89.5
June	70.8	68.4	71.5	61.0	85.9	73.9	67.1	65.2	69.6	102.4	77.8	85.8	85.1	87.1	84.0	92.9	89.5
July	70.5	68.0	71.0	61.1	83.6	73.8	66.7	64.7	69.5	103.6	75.4	85.2	84.3	86.4	83.2	94.0	86.4
August	70.2	67.8	71.4	60.1	82.7	73.4	66.7	64.7	69.4	100.7	76.7	84.7	84.1	85.9	83.1	91.3	87.4
September	70.5	68.1	71.2	61.6	81.9	73.7	66.8	65.0	69.1	102.0	77.3	84.8	83.9	85.3	83.2	92.5	87.7
October	70.0	67.6	70.9	61.4	79.5	73.1	66.2	64.6	68.3	103.2	77.0	83.9	83.0	83.5	82.6	93.6	87.1
November	68.0	66.4	69.0	60.9	77.3	69.8	64.4	62.8	66.5	96.8	75.8	81.3	80.4	80.1	80.6	87.8	85.3
December	65.2	64.1	67.1	57.4	73.6	66.1	61.3	59.5	63.8	97.1	75.9	77.7	76.3	74.9	77.2	88.0	85.0
1975																	
January	63.5	62.2	64.3	56.4	71.7	64.7	59.5	57.5	62.2	101.3	74.5	75.5	73.9	72.7	74.5	91.7	83.3
February	62.5	61.7	64.4	55.2	71.3	62.8	58.3	56.0	61.5	101.1	75.6	74.1	72.3	71.0	73.0	91.5	84.2
March	61.3	60.9	64.0	53.7	69.7	61.2	57.0	54.9	59.9	99.9	77.6	72.6	70.5	68.2	71.8	90.3	86.2
April	61.9	61.5	65.7	53.5	69.7	61.6	57.6	55.1	61.2	99.2	78.7	73.1	71.1	68.9	72.3	89.6	87.1
May	61.7	61.5	66.1	52.9	69.3	61.1	57.5	54.6	61.7	98.7	76.3	72.7	70.8	69.0	71.8	89.0	84.2
June	62.5	62.3	67.4	52.6	69.7	62.0	58.4	54.6	63.8	100.0	76.7	73.5	71.7	70.2	72.4	90.2	84.3
July	62.9	62.8	68.8	52.4	70.3	62.1	58.9	54.9	64.8	97.9	76.6	73.8	72.3	71.2	72.7	88.2	84.0
August	64.0	63.4	69.3	52.9	72.1	64.1	59.9	56.0	65.7	98.3	77.9	75.0	73.3	73.1	73.4	88.5	85.2
September	64.7	63.7	70.0	52.9	72.9	65.3	60.7	56.7	66.6	98.2	77.4	75.6	74.1	74.9	73.6	88.3	84.4
October	65.0	63.8	69.9	53.1	73.4	66.0	61.1	57.0	67.2	99.2	76.3	75.8	74.5	75.0	74.1	89.1	83.0
November	65.6	64.4	70.7	53.5	73.5	66.7	61.6	57.4	67.9	100.2	77.5	76.4	74.9	75.5	74.5	89.9	84.0
December	66.1	64.8	71.3	53.6	73.3	67.5	62.2	58.1	68.4	99.9	76.7	76.8	75.5	76.1	75.2	89.6	82.9
1976																	
January	66.8	65.4	72.0	53.5	75.9	68.4	62.9	58.9	68.8	100.3	78.4	77.5	76.2	77.2	75.6	89.9	84.6
February	68.0	66.6	73.5	54.7	77.9	69.4	64.3	60.5	70.0	99.8	77.1	78.7	77.7	78.8	77.2	89.4	83.0
March	67.9	66.3	72.9	54.5	77.5	69.7	64.1	60.3	69.6	99.0	78.0	78.3	77.2	78.5	76.6	88.7	83.8
April	68.1	66.3	73.1	54.5	77.9	70.2	64.3	60.6	69.7	98.8	78.9	78.4	77.2	78.5	76.7	88.5	84.6
May	68.9	67.1	74.0	55.0	79.0	71.0	65.1	61.8	69.9	100.1	79.3	79.1	78.1	78.9	77.7	89.6	84.8
June	69.0	67.0	74.0	54.8	79.3	71.3	65.0	61.6	70.0	100.0	79.3	79.0	77.8	79.1	77.2	89.5	84.6
July	69.4	67.6	74.3	55.4	80.5	71.5	65.6	62.3	70.6	99.3	79.7	79.3	78.3	79.3	77.8	88.9	84.8
August	69.8	67.8	74.7	55.5	81.2	72.1	65.9	63.0	70.2	99.8	79.8	79.6	78.5	79.5	78.0	89.3	84.8
September	70.0	68.0	74.4	55.6	81.4	72.4	66.2	62.3	71.8	101.6	79.5	79.7	78.6	80.2	77.6	90.9	84.3
October	70.2	68.4	74.7	56.0	82.0	72.4	66.4	62.4	72.4	101.5	80.8	79.8	78.7	80.2	77.7	90.8	85.6
November	71.4	69.8	76.7	57.9	82.8	73.1	67.3	63.8	72.5	101.6	84.0	80.9	79.6	80.0	79.2	90.9	88.8
December	72.0	70.4	77.4	58.9	81.9	73.7	68.0	64.5	73.1	101.6	83.9	81.4	80.2	80.5	79.8	90.8	88.4
1977																	
January	72.4	70.9	78.1	59.1	81.6	73.8	68.5	64.9	73.8	100.3	83.0	81.6	80.6	80.5	80.5	89.6	87.3
February	72.4	70.6	77.3	59.1	81.9	74.5	68.7	65.2	73.7	102.1	79.9	81.5	80.6	81.5	79.9	91.0	83.7
March	73.3	71.2	78.0	59.3	84.0	75.8	69.6	65.9	74.9	103.6	78.8	82.3	81.4	82.8	80.5	92.0	82.4
April	74.3	72.3	78.7	60.9	86.2	76.5	70.6	67.3	75.3	104.4	79.9	83.3	82.3	83.8	81.5	92.5	83.4
May	75.0	72.9	79.2	61.1	87.5	77.5	71.2	67.9	76.0	104.7	81.9	83.9	82.9	84.7	81.8	92.4	85.2
June	75.6	73.5	79.7	61.8	88.5	78.0	71.8	68.6	76.3	105.4	82.7	84.3	83.3	85.2	82.2	92.7	85.8
July	75.6	73.8	80.0	62.4	89.3	77.7	71.8	68.9	75.9	104.5	83.7	84.2	83.2	84.7	82.2	91.7	86.7
August	75.9	74.3	80.7	62.8	89.4	77.8	72.4	69.4	76.7	101.9	83.1	84.3	83.6	85.0	82.8	89.1	85.8
September	76.3	74.5	80.4	64.4	88.8	78.4	72.5	69.8	76.2	106.8	82.8	84.6	83.5	84.2	83.1	93.2	85.4
October	76.2	74.4	80.7	64.0	89.0	78.2	72.4	69.7	76.2	105.5	83.0	84.2	83.2	84.4	82.5	91.7	85.4
November	76.2	74.5	80.8	64.4	88.7	78.2	72.5	69.5	76.8	105.0	81.9	84.1	83.2	84.2	82.6	91.0	84.1
December	75.9	75.0	81.0	65.1	89.0	76.7	72.8	70.2	76.5	96.8	82.8	83.5	83.4	84.0	83.0	83.6	84.8

Table 24-2. Industrial Production and Capacity Utilization—*Continued*

(Seasonally adjusted.)

Year and month	Total industrial production	Industrial production indexes (1992=100)										Capacity utilization (output as a percent of capacity)					
		Major market groups					Major industry groups					Total industry	Manufacturing			Mining	Utilities
		Products				Materials	Manufacturing			Mining	Utilities		Total	Primary processing	Advanced processing		
		Total	Consumer goods	Business equipment	Construction supplies		Total	Durables	Non-durables								
1978																	
January	75.7	74.4	79.6	64.6	89.2	76.9	72.6	69.5	77.0	96.0	83.0	83.0	82.9	84.2	82.1	82.7	84.9
February	75.7	74.8	80.6	65.0	89.4	76.3	72.6	69.5	76.9	95.9	83.5	82.8	82.6	83.4	82.2	82.5	85.2
March	76.4	75.7	81.4	65.8	89.3	76.9	73.1	70.2	77.1	100.3	83.7	83.4	83.0	82.9	83.0	86.1	85.3
April	79.0	77.5	83.1	67.9	92.0	80.7	75.2	72.6	78.9	109.9	83.6	86.0	85.2	85.7	84.9	94.1	85.0
May	79.1	77.2	82.4	67.9	91.8	81.1	75.3	72.7	78.8	109.4	84.5	85.8	85.0	86.3	84.2	93.6	85.7
June	79.9	78.5	83.8	69.1	93.1	81.5	76.2	73.6	79.8	110.0	84.7	86.6	85.8	86.4	85.4	93.9	85.8
July	80.2	78.5	83.5	69.6	92.7	82.0	76.4	74.3	79.4	110.4	84.5	86.6	85.8	86.2	85.6	94.1	85.3
August	80.4	78.7	83.3	70.9	92.2	82.2	76.8	74.9	79.3	109.3	84.5	86.6	85.9	86.5	85.6	93.0	85.3
September	80.8	79.1	83.7	71.1	93.0	82.7	77.2	75.4	79.7	109.0	85.3	86.7	86.2	86.8	85.8	92.6	85.9
October	81.2	79.2	83.4	72.1	93.3	83.4	77.6	76.0	79.6	109.9	85.5	86.9	86.3	87.3	85.8	93.2	85.8
November	81.7	79.8	83.2	73.6	94.1	83.7	78.2	76.8	80.1	109.4	84.9	87.2	86.8	87.6	86.3	92.6	85.1
December	82.0	80.1	83.4	73.8	95.0	84.1	78.6	77.4	80.2	108.7	85.3	87.3	86.9	88.1	86.3	91.9	85.3
1979																	
January	81.6	80.1	82.8	75.7	93.5	83.1	78.3	77.4	79.4	106.7	85.5	86.7	86.4	86.2	86.5	90.1	85.4
February	82.2	80.5	82.7	76.6	94.3	84.0	78.9	78.2	79.6	106.4	88.5	87.1	86.7	87.0	86.6	89.8	88.4
March	82.4	80.7	82.8	77.3	94.1	84.3	79.2	78.5	80.0	106.2	87.8	87.1	86.9	87.1	86.7	89.6	87.6
April	81.6	79.6	81.1	76.4	93.3	83.9	78.0	76.5	80.0	108.2	89.3	86.1	85.3	86.6	84.6	91.3	89.1
May	82.6	80.8	82.4	78.1	93.7	84.5	79.2	78.3	80.3	107.7	88.6	86.9	86.4	86.8	86.1	90.9	88.4
June	82.6	80.6	82.2	78.2	93.4	84.8	79.3	78.7	80.0	108.0	86.7	86.7	86.3	87.0	85.8	91.1	86.5
July	82.0	80.1	80.9	77.9	93.9	84.2	78.9	78.0	80.0	106.4	85.2	85.9	85.6	87.0	84.6	89.8	85.0
August	81.7	79.7	80.3	77.3	92.3	83.9	78.1	76.8	79.8	109.3	85.9	85.4	84.5	85.8	83.7	92.2	85.6
September	81.7	79.9	80.5	77.8	92.4	83.7	78.1	77.1	79.4	110.1	85.8	85.3	84.3	85.1	83.8	92.9	85.5
October	82.1	80.4	80.9	78.3	92.7	83.9	78.5	77.2	80.2	110.0	86.2	85.5	84.5	85.0	84.2	92.8	85.8
November	81.7	79.9	80.5	77.2	92.2	83.5	77.9	76.4	79.9	110.6	86.8	84.9	83.6	84.2	83.3	93.3	86.4
December	81.5	79.9	81.0	76.5	91.6	83.2	77.8	76.3	79.9	109.9	86.0	84.5	83.3	83.7	83.1	92.7	85.5
1980																	
January	81.9	79.7	80.3	76.9	90.9	84.4	78.0	76.1	80.5	113.9	84.2	84.7	83.3	83.9	82.9	96.0	83.6
February	81.9	80.4	80.7	78.3	91.2	83.6	78.2	76.7	80.0	112.0	85.2	84.6	83.3	82.9	83.5	94.3	84.5
March	81.9	80.4	81.0	77.8	90.4	83.5	77.9	76.5	79.6	113.0	87.8	84.4	82.7	82.1	83.1	95.0	86.9
April	80.3	78.9	79.6	77.3	84.2	81.8	76.2	74.5	78.6	111.7	86.1	82.6	80.8	79.2	81.8	93.8	85.0
May	78.3	77.4	77.8	75.9	80.9	79.2	73.9	71.7	76.8	112.4	85.6	80.4	78.1	74.8	80.0	94.3	84.4
June	77.3	77.0	77.7	75.2	79.8	77.4	72.8	70.3	76.2	111.5	86.0	79.2	76.7	72.8	79.0	93.4	84.6
July	76.8	77.2	78.1	75.2	79.1	76.0	72.2	69.6	75.9	109.8	88.1	78.5	75.9	71.0	78.9	91.9	86.5
August	77.7	78.2	79.0	75.5	82.7	76.8	73.4	70.9	76.9	108.5	88.8	79.3	77.0	72.7	79.6	90.7	87.1
September	78.9	78.9	80.1	75.7	83.9	78.5	74.5	71.9	78.2	110.5	89.3	80.3	77.9	74.5	79.9	92.2	87.4
October	79.5	79.3	80.3	76.7	84.4	79.3	75.4	73.2	78.4	109.7	88.8	80.7	78.6	75.7	80.3	91.4	86.8
November	80.7	79.9	80.4	77.5	85.8	81.4	76.7	75.0	78.8	111.4	89.3	81.8	79.7	78.3	80.5	92.8	87.2
December	81.1	80.1	80.5	78.2	85.7	82.0	76.9	74.9	79.5	113.6	88.9	82.1	79.7	78.4	80.4	94.4	86.7
1981																	
January	80.4	79.6	80.2	76.5	85.6	81.1	76.4	74.2	79.4	113.0	84.6	81.2	79.0	78.6	79.2	93.8	82.5
February	80.8	80.2	80.6	78.0	84.6	81.3	76.9	74.7	79.8	114.1	83.0	81.4	79.2	78.9	79.4	94.3	80.8
March	81.2	80.4	80.4	78.2	85.6	80.9	77.1	75.1	79.8	115.2	84.1	81.6	79.3	78.8	79.6	94.9	81.9
April	80.6	80.5	80.3	78.1	85.4	80.5	77.2	75.2	79.9	109.6	82.9	80.9	79.3	78.8	79.5	90.0	80.7
May	81.3	81.2	81.0	79.2	85.1	81.1	77.8	76.0	80.2	110.3	85.2	81.4	79.6	78.8	80.1	90.3	82.8
June	81.8	81.2	80.3	80.0	83.3	82.3	77.7	75.9	80.0	115.0	86.6	81.8	79.3	78.3	79.9	93.7	84.1
July	82.6	81.6	81.1	79.8	83.0	83.4	78.2	76.3	80.7	117.8	86.9	82.3	79.6	78.8	80.1	95.6	84.4
August	82.2	81.0	80.4	78.4	83.0	83.4	77.5	75.8	79.9	119.4	85.6	81.8	78.8	78.9	78.8	96.6	83.1
September	81.5	80.5	79.8	78.0	80.4	82.5	76.9	74.9	79.7	118.6	84.5	80.9	78.0	77.4	78.4	95.5	82.0
October	80.9	80.2	79.4	77.9	79.0	81.5	76.1	74.1	78.7	118.7	85.6	80.1	77.0	75.4	77.8	95.2	82.9
November	79.8	79.5	78.9	76.0	77.2	79.8	74.9	72.4	78.3	117.3	85.2	78.8	75.6	73.5	76.8	93.7	82.5
December	78.9	79.1	78.2	75.6	74.9	78.3	73.7	71.1	77.3	117.7	85.5	77.7	74.2	70.7	76.1	93.7	82.8
1982																	
January	77.6	78.1	77.8	72.9	74.0	76.7	72.2	68.8	76.9	116.8	86.3	76.3	72.6	69.3	74.3	92.6	83.5
February	79.3	80.0	79.4	75.0	77.3	78.1	74.3	71.1	78.7	117.7	84.2	77.8	74.6	71.5	76.2	92.9	81.4
March	78.7	79.5	78.9	74.8	75.8	77.5	73.8	70.6	78.3	116.8	83.8	77.1	73.9	70.4	75.7	91.9	81.0
April	78.0	78.7	78.7	73.5	75.4	76.5	73.1	69.9	77.6	115.1	83.8	76.2	73.1	69.3	75.1	90.2	80.9
May	77.4	78.4	78.8	72.3	76.5	75.9	72.8	69.6	77.4	113.1	82.0	75.4	72.7	68.7	74.7	88.3	79.1
June	77.1	78.2	79.4	71.7	76.4	75.5	72.8	69.5	77.5	111.1	81.6	75.0	72.6	68.9	74.4	86.3	78.7
July	76.5	77.7	79.1	70.9	76.3	74.7	72.2	68.8	77.0	109.7	81.6	74.2	71.8	68.0	73.8	85.0	78.6
August	76.1	77.2	79.5	68.9	76.6	74.4	71.9	68.1	77.8	108.4	81.8	73.7	71.4	68.4	72.9	83.6	78.7
September	75.5	76.7	78.9	68.3	76.0	73.8	71.5	67.0	77.9	106.9	80.7	73.0	70.9	68.2	72.2	82.1	77.6
October	74.9	76.0	78.7	66.6	75.2	73.3	70.7	65.6	78.0	107.0	81.1	72.2	69.9	67.5	71.2	81.8	77.9
November	74.7	75.9	78.7	65.8	75.9	72.9	70.5	65.2	77.9	106.4	81.7	71.9	69.6	67.2	70.8	81.0	78.4
December	74.1	75.7	77.8	66.4	73.7	71.9	70.0	65.1	77.0	105.9	79.2	71.1	69.0	66.2	70.4	80.3	75.9
1983																	
January	75.7	76.7	79.6	65.6	77.8	74.1	71.8	66.8	78.9	107.1	79.4	72.5	70.6	69.0	71.4	81.0	76.1
February	75.5	76.5	79.8	65.1	79.0	74.0	72.1	67.4	78.8	104.4	77.6	72.3	70.8	69.9	71.3	79.0	74.2
March	76.2	77.1	80.1	65.7	79.6	75.0	73.1	68.6	79.6	103.1	78.7	72.9	71.8	71.2	72.0	77.9	75.2
April	77.2	78.0	81.4	65.8	82.1	75.9	74.0	69.5	80.3	104.2	81.1	73.7	72.5	72.3	72.5	78.7	77.4
May	78.1	78.8	82.3	66.1	83.0	77.0	75.0	70.5	81.4	104.0	82.7	74.5	73.4	73.9	73.1	78.6	78.9
June	78.6	79.6	83.1	66.6	84.2	77.0	75.6	71.2	81.9	104.1	81.8	74.8	73.9	74.1	73.7	78.6	77.9
July	80.0	80.5	83.9	67.3	86.6	79.0	76.7	72.7	82.4	106.2	85.5	76.1	74.8	75.5	74.5	80.1	81.3
August	81.0	81.6	85.1	68.3	86.5	80.1	77.6	73.6	83.2	107.9	88.0	77.0	75.6	76.1	75.4	81.3	83.6
September	82.4	83.2	86.3	71.1	87.1	81.2	79.3	75.7	84.4	109.1	86.2	78.2	77.2	77.4	77.0	82.2	81.8
October	83.1	83.3	85.5	71.7	88.5	82.6	79.8	76.6	84.3	110.4	87.4	78.7	77.6	78.4	77.2	83.2	82.9
November	83.0	83.4	85.2	72.7	88.0	82.2	80.1	77.0	84.3	109.8	84.5	78.6	77.7	78.2	77.5	82.7	80.1
December	83.4	84.2	85.7	73.6	87.3	82.1	80.0	77.5	83.5	109.0	91.9	78.9	77.5	77.8	77.4	82.0	87.0

Table 24-2. Industrial Production and Capacity Utilization—*Continued*

(Seasonally adjusted.)

Year and month	Total industrial production	Industrial production indexes (1992=100)										Capacity utilization (output as a percent of capacity)					
		Major market groups					Major industry groups					Total industry	Manufacturing			Mining	Utilities
		Products				Materials	Manufacturing			Mining	Utilities		Total	Primary processing	Advanced processing		
		Total	Consumer goods	Business equipment	Construction supplies		Total	Durables	Non-durables								
1984																	
January	85.1	85.4	86.9	76.0	89.0	84.6	82.0	80.1	84.6	112.9	88.0	80.4	79.3	79.5	79.2	84.9	83.3
February	85.0	85.3	86.5	75.6	90.3	84.4	82.4	80.5	85.1	111.6	83.3	80.1	79.5	80.2	79.2	84.0	78.8
March	85.9	85.9	86.6	77.1	90.9	85.7	83.0	81.3	85.4	112.3	88.5	80.8	79.8	80.7	79.4	84.5	83.7
April	86.4	86.5	87.5	77.4	91.0	86.0	83.4	81.9	85.5	113.7	88.3	81.0	80.0	80.5	79.8	85.6	83.4
May	86.9	86.8	86.8	78.2	90.4	86.7	83.7	82.4	85.6	115.6	88.8	81.3	80.1	80.9	79.7	87.1	83.9
June	87.3	87.5	87.2	79.5	90.6	86.7	84.3	83.0	86.0	116.0	87.5	81.5	80.3	81.0	80.1	87.5	82.6
July	87.5	87.8	87.1	80.6	90.6	86.8	84.5	83.6	85.8	117.0	85.8	81.5	80.4	80.3	80.4	88.4	81.1
August	87.5	87.5	86.0	81.2	90.2	87.1	84.6	84.2	85.2	115.6	86.8	81.3	80.2	80.2	80.2	87.4	82.0
September	87.3	87.4	86.2	80.8	90.0	87.0	84.4	83.9	85.2	116.1	86.3	81.0	79.8	80.1	79.7	87.9	81.4
October	86.9	87.6	86.6	81.1	90.1	85.8	84.5	83.8	85.4	112.3	86.0	80.5	79.6	79.4	79.8	85.1	81.1
November	87.0	87.9	86.8	81.2	90.9	85.5	84.5	83.9	85.4	112.0	86.4	80.4	79.5	79.2	79.6	85.0	81.5
December	86.6	87.5	86.4	81.4	90.4	85.2	84.3	83.8	85.0	111.2	85.0	79.8	79.0	78.2	79.4	84.6	80.2
1985																	
January	86.9	87.6	86.4	81.4	89.4	85.7	84.4	84.1	84.7	110.0	89.8	79.9	78.9	78.5	79.1	83.7	84.6
February	87.7	88.3	87.0	81.9	90.8	86.6	84.9	84.6	85.2	112.1	91.5	80.4	79.1	79.2	79.0	85.4	86.3
March	87.9	88.7	87.2	82.3	92.0	86.6	85.4	85.2	85.7	112.1	88.7	80.4	79.3	79.3	79.4	85.4	83.6
April	88.0	88.9	86.8	83.2	93.3	86.6	85.6	85.5	85.7	112.1	89.1	80.3	79.2	79.6	79.1	85.4	83.9
May	88.2	89.6	87.5	83.4	94.1	86.2	86.0	85.7	86.3	112.1	87.2	80.3	79.4	79.2	79.5	85.5	82.1
June	88.0	89.3	87.6	82.1	94.0	86.1	85.7	85.6	86.0	112.2	86.9	79.9	78.9	79.2	78.7	85.5	81.8
July	87.6	88.8	87.0	82.5	93.8	85.9	85.4	85.4	85.5	110.7	87.4	79.4	78.3	79.0	78.0	84.2	82.2
August	88.2	89.6	87.9	82.9	95.0	86.0	86.1	86.2	86.1	110.0	87.2	79.6	78.8	79.4	78.5	83.6	82.0
September	88.7	90.1	88.6	83.0	95.1	86.6	86.4	86.0	87.0	110.8	89.7	79.9	78.8	79.4	78.5	84.1	84.2
October	87.9	89.2	88.1	81.3	94.4	86.0	85.7	85.3	86.4	109.8	88.5	79.0	77.9	79.0	77.4	83.2	83.1
November	88.4	90.1	88.3	83.4	95.4	86.0	86.7	86.7	86.7	108.1	87.3	79.2	78.5	79.0	78.3	81.8	81.8
December	89.0	90.3	88.6	82.8	94.3	87.1	86.6	86.5	86.8	111.2	92.0	79.5	78.2	78.9	77.9	83.9	86.2
1986																	
January	89.6	91.4	90.0	83.5	97.8	87.0	87.9	87.4	88.4	111.0	86.9	79.8	79.1	79.5	79.0	83.6	81.3
February	89.0	90.4	89.7	82.5	96.8	86.8	87.4	87.0	88.0	108.8	86.3	79.2	78.6	79.3	78.2	81.9	80.7
March	88.1	89.6	88.7	82.0	96.1	85.9	86.6	86.3	87.0	106.5	85.7	78.2	77.8	78.3	77.5	80.2	80.1
April	88.7	90.7	90.8	82.2	97.3	86.0	87.8	87.3	88.6	103.3	85.3	78.7	78.7	79.1	78.5	77.8	79.7
May	88.6	90.3	90.4	81.9	97.0	86.0	87.7	87.1	88.6	102.2	85.4	78.4	78.5	79.1	78.1	77.0	79.7
June	88.2	90.0	90.7	80.3	96.9	85.7	87.5	86.4	88.9	100.7	85.9	78.1	78.1	78.9	77.7	75.9	80.1
July	88.5	90.4	90.8	81.6	97.3	85.8	87.7	86.9	88.8	100.6	87.0	78.2	78.2	78.5	78.0	75.9	81.2
August	88.8	90.7	90.9	81.9	98.1	86.0	88.2	87.3	89.5	99.7	85.5	78.3	78.6	79.6	78.0	75.4	79.7
September	88.7	90.7	90.5	82.3	99.1	85.8	88.2	87.8	88.9	98.2	85.8	78.2	78.4	79.6	77.8	74.5	80.0
October	89.5	91.6	91.3	82.2	100.4	86.5	88.9	87.9	90.3	99.4	87.3	78.8	78.9	79.9	78.4	75.5	81.3
November	89.9	91.9	91.6	81.4	101.8	87.2	89.3	88.2	90.6	100.6	88.0	79.1	79.1	80.7	78.2	76.7	82.0
December	90.8	93.1	93.0	82.3	102.5	87.5	90.3	89.1	91.8	100.0	87.9	79.7	79.9	81.2	79.2	76.5	81.9
1987																	
January	90.2	92.1	91.5	81.4	101.5	87.4	89.6	88.5	91.0	100.6	87.6	79.1	79.1	80.6	78.3	77.3	81.5
February	91.2	93.3	92.8	83.2	102.3	88.2	91.0	90.2	92.0	100.5	86.2	80.0	80.2	81.5	79.5	77.6	80.1
March	91.6	93.7	93.3	83.0	102.4	88.5	91.2	90.3	92.4	100.4	88.4	80.2	80.3	81.9	79.4	78.0	82.0
April	92.0	93.9	92.8	83.4	103.4	89.1	91.6	90.8	92.8	100.5	88.2	80.5	80.6	82.7	79.4	78.4	81.7
May	92.4	94.3	93.2	83.3	103.6	89.5	91.9	90.8	93.3	100.9	89.8	80.7	80.7	83.0	79.4	79.1	83.1
June	93.2	95.3	93.9	85.3	106.0	90.1	92.8	91.9	94.1	101.0	89.9	81.4	81.4	83.5	80.2	79.5	83.0
July	93.7	95.7	94.1	85.4	105.9	90.9	93.4	92.1	95.2	100.4	90.9	81.8	81.8	84.7	80.2	79.4	83.8
August	93.8	95.8	94.4	85.0	106.5	91.0	93.3	92.2	94.7	103.1	91.7	81.5	81.5	84.3	80.0	81.7	84.5
September	93.7	95.6	93.6	86.0	105.3	91.1	93.4	92.5	94.6	103.1	89.3	81.6	81.5	84.4	79.9	81.9	82.2
October	95.0	96.8	94.7	87.8	106.9	92.4	94.6	94.6	94.8	104.3	91.1	82.6	82.5	85.4	80.8	83.1	83.7
November	95.3	96.9	94.8	88.1	106.8	92.9	95.1	94.9	95.3	105.0	89.4	82.8	82.8	86.0	80.9	83.8	82.0
December	95.9	97.2	95.0	89.1	106.3	93.8	95.6	95.6	95.8	105.3	90.1	83.2	83.1	86.6	81.2	84.2	82.5
1988																	
January	95.9	97.7	95.9	89.4	105.2	93.4	95.4	95.6	95.3	104.1	94.0	83.2	82.9	85.4	81.4	83.4	85.9
February	96.2	98.1	96.0	90.2	106.1	93.6	95.8	95.9	95.8	104.4	93.9	83.4	83.1	85.7	81.6	83.8	85.7
March	96.3	97.9	95.6	90.0	106.2	93.9	95.7	95.8	95.7	105.6	93.9	83.3	82.9	85.8	81.2	85.0	85.6
April	96.8	98.6	96.6	91.9	106.7	94.2	96.7	97.2	96.2	104.7	91.4	83.7	83.7	86.1	82.2	84.5	83.2
May	96.9	98.5	96.2	92.9	106.9	94.5	96.6	97.7	95.3	105.6	92.7	83.7	83.5	86.0	82.0	85.4	84.1
June	97.0	98.3	96.0	93.1	106.2	94.9	96.6	97.8	95.1	105.6	93.5	83.6	83.4	85.9	81.9	85.7	84.7
July	97.6	98.9	96.3	94.1	106.9	95.7	97.3	98.4	96.0	105.2	94.7	84.1	83.8	86.3	82.4	85.6	85.6
August	98.1	99.6	97.3	95.1	105.9	95.9	97.5	98.5	96.4	105.7	98.0	84.5	84.0	86.0	82.8	86.3	88.4
September	97.8	99.3	96.8	95.3	106.1	95.5	97.7	99.3	96.0	104.0	93.0	84.1	84.0	86.1	82.8	85.2	83.7
October	98.0	99.6	97.5	95.2	106.3	95.7	97.9	99.3	96.4	104.0	93.9	84.2	84.1	86.2	82.8	85.6	84.4
November	98.8	100.2	97.9	97.1	106.2	96.6	98.9	100.7	96.7	103.7	93.6	84.8	84.8	86.9	83.5	86.1	83.9
December	99.3	100.8	98.5	97.9	107.2	97.0	99.4	101.2	97.4	103.9	93.7	85.1	85.1	87.4	83.8	86.1	83.8
1989																	
January	99.8	101.4	98.8	98.5	109.3	97.5	100.3	102.4	97.9	103.4	91.7	85.4	85.7	88.3	84.2	86.0	81.9
February	99.0	100.5	98.0	97.6	106.7	96.9	99.1	101.0	97.0	101.9	95.6	84.6	84.5	86.5	83.4	85.0	85.3
March	100.0	101.5	99.1	98.5	106.4	97.7	99.9	101.3	98.4	102.3	98.4	85.3	85.0	87.1	83.8	85.4	87.7
April	100.2	101.8	98.8	100.5	106.2	97.9	100.0	101.9	97.9	104.9	98.0	85.3	85.0	86.5	84.1	87.9	87.2
May	99.6	100.9	98.0	99.2	105.1	97.6	99.4	101.0	97.6	104.8	97.2	84.7	84.2	85.8	83.3	88.0	86.5
June	99.4	101.1	97.6	100.9	104.8	97.0	99.4	101.1	97.5	103.4	96.0	84.4	84.1	85.4	83.3	87.0	85.3
July	98.4	99.7	96.0	99.4	104.9	96.5	98.3	100.0	96.5	102.8	95.6	83.4	83.0	84.7	82.0	86.7	84.8
August	98.8	100.2	96.6	99.6	104.5	96.8	98.7	100.4	96.8	103.8	96.1	83.6	83.1	84.6	82.2	87.7	85.2
September	98.6	100.2	96.6	99.2	104.3	96.3	98.4	100.1	96.5	103.7	96.6	83.3	82.7	83.9	82.0	87.8	85.6
October	98.2	99.3	97.1	96.1	104.2	96.5	97.9	98.4	97.3	102.8	97.6	82.8	82.1	84.1	80.9	87.2	86.4
November	98.6	99.9	97.2	97.1	104.7	96.6	98.2	98.7	97.7	103.5	98.1	83.0	82.2	84.0	81.2	88.0	86.7
December	99.0	100.9	98.4	99.5	105.1	96.3	98.3	99.6	96.9	101.2	104.8	83.2	82.1	82.9	81.7	86.2	92.6

Table 24-2. Industrial Production and Capacity Utilization—Continued

(Seasonally adjusted.)

Year and month	Total industrial production	Industrial production indexes (1992=100)										Capacity utilization (output as a percent of capacity)					
		Major market groups					Major industry groups					Total industry	Manufacturing			Mining	Utilities
		Products				Materials	Manufacturing			Mining	Utilities		Total	Primary processing	Advanced processing		
		Total	Consumer goods	Business equipment	Construction supplies		Total	Durables	Non-durables								
1990																	
January	98.6	100.2	96.8	97.7	105.6	96.2	98.1	98.0	98.3	105.2	97.3	82.7	81.8	83.3	81.0	89.7	85.8
February	99.1	100.6	97.7	98.1	105.7	96.9	99.0	99.4	98.6	104.6	94.8	83.0	82.5	84.0	81.5	89.2	83.4
March	99.6	101.1	98.2	98.5	105.5	97.3	99.3	100.2	98.4	104.4	97.6	83.3	82.6	83.9	81.8	89.2	85.7
April	99.0	100.0	97.4	96.8	104.6	97.4	98.6	99.2	97.8	104.9	97.9	82.7	81.8	83.7	80.7	89.6	85.8
May	99.4	100.5	97.5	98.4	103.6	97.6	99.0	99.9	97.9	104.7	98.6	82.9	82.0	83.6	81.1	89.5	86.2
June	99.3	100.3	98.2	97.8	103.2	97.8	98.9	100.0	97.6	104.5	99.8	82.7	81.8	83.4	80.8	89.5	87.0
July	99.3	100.4	97.6	98.9	102.5	97.7	98.8	99.8	97.8	104.9	99.0	82.6	81.6	83.1	80.8	89.9	86.2
August	99.5	100.4	97.8	99.7	101.5	98.0	99.1	100.1	98.0	104.4	99.3	82.6	81.7	83.3	80.8	89.5	86.3
September	99.6	100.6	98.4	99.4	101.7	98.0	99.0	100.1	97.9	105.4	100.6	82.6	81.5	83.0	80.7	90.4	87.3
October	99.1	100.0	97.2	99.2	101.0	97.6	98.4	99.1	97.8	105.9	99.5	82.0	80.9	82.2	80.1	91.0	86.2
November	97.7	98.7	95.9	97.3	100.0	96.4	97.2	96.8	97.5	105.1	97.3	80.8	79.7	81.0	79.0	90.4	84.1
December	97.2	98.2	95.3	96.2	99.2	95.6	96.6	95.7	97.5	103.7	97.8	80.2	79.0	80.0	78.5	89.2	84.5
1991																	
January	96.7	97.6	95.9	95.9	95.5	95.3	95.8	94.7	96.9	104.0	100.4	79.6	78.2	78.6	78.0	89.5	86.6
February	95.9	96.8	94.8	95.8	94.6	94.6	95.1	93.9	96.4	105.3	97.0	78.9	77.5	77.9	77.3	90.6	83.6
March	95.0	96.0	94.8	94.8	93.9	93.5	94.1	93.1	95.1	104.1	97.6	78.1	76.6	76.7	76.6	89.6	84.1
April	95.4	96.4	95.0	95.3	95.0	93.8	94.4	93.7	95.2	103.5	98.9	78.2	76.8	76.9	76.7	89.1	85.2
May	96.1	97.1	96.7	94.9	94.8	94.6	95.0	94.0	96.2	103.0	102.2	78.7	77.1	77.2	77.1	88.7	87.9
June	97.2	98.5	98.1	96.1	98.2	95.3	96.3	95.7	97.0	103.0	102.1	79.6	78.1	78.4	78.0	88.7	87.8
July	97.3	97.9	97.9	95.1	96.8	96.4	96.6	95.9	97.3	101.8	101.7	79.5	78.2	79.1	77.7	87.7	87.4
August	97.4	97.7	97.4	95.2	97.1	97.1	96.8	96.1	97.5	101.4	101.5	79.5	78.2	79.6	77.5	87.4	87.1
September	98.4	98.9	98.9	97.1	97.7	97.5	97.8	97.5	98.2	101.6	101.4	80.2	79.0	80.0	78.5	87.6	86.9
October	98.3	98.5	98.6	96.7	96.3	97.9	97.8	97.3	98.3	101.5	100.9	80.0	78.9	80.0	78.2	87.6	86.3
November	98.1	98.5	98.6	96.6	97.6	97.5	97.6	97.4	97.7	100.8	102.3	79.8	78.6	79.6	77.9	87.0	87.4
December	97.5	97.7	97.9	95.5	96.4	97.2	97.1	96.5	97.7	100.9	99.3	79.2	78.1	79.4	77.3	87.2	84.7
1992																	
January	97.6	97.4	97.2	95.0	97.5	98.0	97.3	96.4	98.3	100.4	98.3	79.1	78.1	80.5	76.8	86.7	83.8
February	98.1	98.1	97.9	97.3	99.0	98.1	97.9	97.8	98.0	99.4	98.9	79.4	78.5	80.5	77.3	85.8	84.1
March	99.0	98.9	99.0	97.3	99.4	99.1	98.9	98.5	99.4	99.5	99.1	79.9	79.1	81.4	77.8	86.0	84.2
April	99.7	99.7	99.8	99.1	99.8	99.6	99.5	99.3	99.8	100.5	100.6	80.4	79.5	81.6	78.3	86.8	85.3
May	100.0	100.0	100.0	99.4	101.1	99.9	99.9	100.2	99.6	100.4	99.6	80.4	79.6	81.7	78.5	86.8	84.4
June	99.7	99.4	99.2	99.6	99.7	100.2	99.9	99.9	100.0	99.5	98.1	80.1	79.4	81.8	78.0	85.9	83.0
July	100.4	100.3	100.3	100.6	100.9	100.6	100.6	100.5	100.7	100.6	98.8	80.5	79.8	82.2	78.5	86.9	83.5
August	100.2	100.4	100.5	100.8	101.0	99.7	100.4	100.2	100.5	99.1	98.6	80.2	79.5	81.5	78.4	85.6	83.2
September	100.5	100.6	100.4	101.4	99.9	100.5	100.6	100.6	100.7	99.9	100.0	80.3	79.6	82.1	78.2	86.2	84.3
October	101.3	101.4	101.6	102.3	100.5	101.1	101.3	101.7	100.9	100.5	101.4	80.8	79.9	82.5	78.6	86.7	85.4
November	101.8	101.9	101.9	103.3	100.6	101.7	101.9	102.3	101.3	100.3	102.2	81.0	80.2	82.9	78.8	86.5	86.0
December	101.8	102.0	102.1	103.8	100.4	101.4	101.7	102.6	100.7	99.9	104.3	80.9	79.9	82.2	78.7	86.1	87.7
1993																	
January	102.2	102.3	102.4	104.4	101.3	102.0	102.5	103.5	101.3	99.8	100.9	81.1	80.4	83.1	78.9	86.1	84.7
February	102.7	102.7	103.0	103.9	102.3	102.7	102.8	103.9	101.5	99.3	104.7	81.3	80.4	83.5	78.8	85.7	87.9
March	102.9	102.8	103.0	105.1	101.0	102.9	103.0	104.5	101.3	98.8	105.2	81.3	80.4	83.2	78.9	85.2	88.2
April	103.2	103.1	103.1	105.5	101.4	103.4	103.5	105.2	101.6	98.8	103.6	81.4	80.7	83.6	79.1	85.2	86.9
May	102.7	102.7	102.5	105.8	102.5	102.7	103.1	105.0	101.0	98.9	101.4	80.9	80.2	82.9	78.7	85.3	84.9
June	102.9	102.5	102.7	105.1	101.6	103.7	103.1	105.0	101.1	100.2	103.2	80.9	80.1	83.5	78.2	86.4	86.4
July	103.2	103.1	103.8	104.8	102.6	103.3	103.4	104.9	101.7	99.1	104.6	81.0	80.1	83.0	78.5	85.4	87.5
August	103.0	103.0	103.6	103.6	103.6	103.1	103.1	104.3	101.8	99.3	105.2	80.7	79.7	82.6	78.2	85.5	88.0
September	104.1	104.1	104.4	106.0	104.6	104.2	104.4	106.5	102.0	100.2	104.5	81.4	80.6	83.5	78.9	86.3	87.4
October	104.4	104.1	104.2	106.7	105.5	104.9	104.6	107.5	101.5	101.8	104.5	81.5	80.6	84.0	78.7	87.6	87.3
November	104.9	104.2	104.2	107.1	105.7	105.8	105.1	108.2	101.8	101.7	104.6	81.6	80.7	84.4	78.7	87.5	87.4
December	105.7	104.9	104.8	108.0	108.1	107.0	106.1	109.6	102.2	101.6	105.1	82.1	81.3	85.1	79.1	87.5	87.7
1994																	
January	105.9	105.4	105.4	109.6	107.1	106.6	106.1	109.8	102.1	101.0	107.9	82.1	81.1	84.9	79.0	86.9	90.0
February	106.2	105.5	106.0	109.3	105.9	107.3	106.5	110.0	102.7	101.5	107.2	82.1	81.1	84.8	79.1	87.3	89.4
March	107.1	106.1	106.4	110.0	106.6	108.6	107.6	110.9	103.9	103.1	105.1	82.5	81.7	85.5	79.6	88.6	87.6
April	107.6	106.5	106.8	110.6	109.0	109.4	108.4	112.3	104.1	102.1	103.7	82.7	82.1	86.2	79.8	87.7	86.3
May	108.5	107.1	107.9	111.2	109.7	110.7	109.4	113.4	105.0	102.6	103.5	83.2	82.6	86.9	80.1	88.1	86.1
June	109.0	107.6	108.3	112.1	110.5	111.3	109.6	113.9	104.9	102.8	107.6	83.3	82.5	86.5	80.2	88.3	89.4
July	109.6	107.8	108.2	113.3	112.3	112.5	110.5	115.6	104.9	102.7	106.1	83.5	82.8	87.5	80.1	88.2	88.1
August	110.0	108.0	109.1	113.4	111.6	113.1	111.0	115.9	105.7	102.6	105.3	83.5	82.9	87.3	80.4	88.1	87.3
September	110.2	107.9	108.2	113.9	112.3	113.7	111.3	116.7	105.3	100.2	104.9	83.3	82.8	87.4	80.1	87.5	86.9
October	110.7	108.9	108.8	115.5	113.8	113.7	111.9	117.5	105.8	101.6	105.1	83.5	83.0	87.1	80.5	87.2	86.9
November	111.5	109.2	109.0	116.3	113.2	115.2	112.9	118.6	106.7	102.4	103.7	83.7	83.3	87.6	80.8	87.9	85.6
December	112.6	110.0	109.6	117.5	115.9	116.8	114.1	120.6	107.0	103.8	104.3	84.3	83.8	88.6	81.0	89.1	85.9
1995																	
January	113.3	110.4	109.8	119.6	114.4	117.8	114.8	121.9	107.2	102.8	104.9	84.4	84.0	88.7	81.3	88.2	86.3
February	113.2	110.3	109.8	119.7	113.5	117.8	114.6	121.9	106.7	102.6	106.5	84.0	83.5	88.1	80.8	88.1	87.5
March	113.4	110.4	109.9	120.6	112.4	118.1	114.9	122.5	106.7	101.4	106.7	83.8	83.3	87.6	80.8	87.1	87.4
April	113.1	110.0	109.6	120.1	111.9	118.2	114.6	122.1	106.5	101.4	106.9	83.3	82.7	86.8	80.3	87.1	87.4
May	113.6	110.1	109.8	119.7	110.5	119.0	114.9	122.5	106.6	101.8	109.0	83.3	82.5	86.6	80.1	87.6	89.0
June	114.0	110.7	110.6	120.9	110.9	119.2	115.4	123.5	106.8	101.8	108.4	83.2	82.6	86.0	80.5	87.6	88.4
July	113.6	110.3	110.2	119.5	111.3	118.7	114.8	122.5	106.4	102.4	109.8	82.5	81.7	84.9	79.7	88.2	89.4
August	115.1	111.8	111.8	122.4	111.5	120.2	116.2	125.0	106.7	101.3	114.1	83.3	82.3	85.0	80.7	87.3	92.7
September	115.8	112.4	112.0	124.0	113.2	121.0	117.3	127.0	106.9	102.5	109.7	83.4	82.7	85.5	81.0	88.4	89.1
October	115.3	111.5	110.9	123.0	113.1	121.4	116.9	126.6	106.6	101.4	109.2	82.8	82.0	85.1	80.2	87.5	88.6
November	115.7	111.8	111.4	123.6	113.0	122.0	117.1	127.4	106.1	102.3	111.5	82.7	81.7	84.6	80.0	88.3	90.3
December	115.9	112.0	111.1	124.3	115.5	122.0	117.3	128.1	105.7	101.6	112.4	82.4	81.4	84.4	79.6	87.7	91.0

Table 24-3. Civilian Population, Labor Force, Employment, and Unemployment

(Thousands of persons, 16 years of age and over; seasonally adjusted, except as noted)

Year and month	Noninsti-tutional population (Not seasonally adjusted)	Labor force — Thousands of persons	Labor force — Participa-tion rate [1]	Employed — Thousands of persons	Employed — Ratio: Employ-ment to population [2]	Unemployed — Total	Unemployed — Long-term [3]	Men 20 years and over — Employed	Men 20 years and over — Unem-ployed	Women 20 years and over — Employed	Women 20 years and over — Unem-ployed	Both sexes, 16 to 19 years — Employed	Both sexes, 16 to 19 years — Unem-ployed
1972													
January	142 736	85 978	60.2	80 959	56.7	5 019	1 257	46 471	2 071	27 956	1 624	6 532	1 324
February	143 017	86 036	60.2	81 108	56.7	4 928	1 292	46 600	1 993	28 016	1 506	6 492	1 429
March	143 263	86 611	60.5	81 573	56.9	5 038	1 232	46 821	2 034	28 126	1 625	6 626	1 379
April	143 483	86 614	60.4	81 655	56.9	4 959	1 203	46 863	2 019	28 114	1 619	6 678	1 321
May	143 760	86 809	60.4	81 887	57.0	4 922	1 168	46 950	2 006	28 184	1 698	6 753	1 218
June	144 033	87 006	60.4	82 083	57.0	4 923	1 141	47 147	1 981	28 175	1 666	6 761	1 276
July	144 285	87 143	60.4	82 230	57.0	4 913	1 154	47 244	1 960	28 225	1 702	6 761	1 251
August	144 522	87 517	60.6	82 578	57.1	4 939	1 156	47 321	1 898	28 382	1 684	6 875	1 357
September	144 761	87 392	60.4	82 543	57.0	4 849	1 131	47 394	1 878	28 417	1 657	6 732	1 314
October	144 988	87 491	60.3	82 616	57.0	4 875	1 123	47 354	1 910	28 438	1 689	6 824	1 276
November	145 211	87 592	60.3	82 990	57.2	4 602	1 040	47 529	1 791	28 567	1 523	6 894	1 288
December	145 446	87 943	60.5	83 400	57.3	4 543	1 006	47 747	1 742	28 698	1 512	6 955	1 289
1973													
January	145 720	87 487	60.0	83 161	57.1	4 326	947	47 701	1 688	28 596	1 552	6 864	1 086
February	145 943	88 364	60.5	83 912	57.5	4 452	894	47 884	1 693	28 995	1 492	7 033	1 267
March	146 230	88 846	60.8	84 452	57.8	4 394	889	48 117	1 695	29 110	1 498	7 225	1 201
April	146 459	89 018	60.8	84 559	57.7	4 459	809	48 098	1 670	29 304	1 480	7 157	1 309
May	146 719	88 977	60.6	84 648	57.7	4 329	816	48 068	1 671	29 432	1 403	7 148	1 255
June	146 981	89 548	60.9	85 185	58.0	4 363	779	48 244	1 628	29 505	1 541	7 436	1 194
July	147 233	89 604	60.9	85 299	57.9	4 305	756	48 452	1 566	29 592	1 532	7 255	1 207
August	147 471	89 509	60.7	85 204	57.8	4 305	788	48 353	1 575	29 578	1 546	7 273	1 184
September	147 731	89 838	60.8	85 488	57.9	4 350	785	48 408	1 543	29 710	1 539	7 370	1 268
October	147 980	90 131	60.9	85 987	58.1	4 144	793	48 631	1 467	29 885	1 416	7 471	1 261
November	148 219	90 716	61.2	86 320	58.2	4 396	832	48 764	1 560	30 071	1 518	7 485	1 318
December	148 479	90 890	61.2	86 401	58.2	4 489	767	48 902	1 628	29 991	1 573	7 508	1 288
1974													
January	148 753	91 199	61.3	86 555	58.2	4 644	799	49 107	1 755	29 893	1 598	7 555	1 291
February	148 982	91 485	61.4	86 754	58.2	4 731	829	49 057	1 809	30 146	1 600	7 551	1 322
March	149 225	91 453	61.3	86 819	58.2	4 634	849	48 986	1 735	30 293	1 581	7 540	1 318
April	149 478	91 287	61.1	86 669	58.0	4 618	889	48 853	1 796	30 376	1 579	7 440	1 243
May	149 750	91 596	61.2	86 891	58.0	4 705	880	49 039	1 736	30 424	1 618	7 428	1 351
June	150 012	91 868	61.2	86 941	58.0	4 927	926	48 946	1 800	30 512	1 670	7 483	1 457
July	150 248	92 212	61.4	87 149	58.0	5 063	924	48 883	1 833	30 869	1 733	7 397	1 497
August	150 493	92 059	61.2	87 037	57.8	5 022	960	48 950	1 957	30 662	1 764	7 425	1 301
September	150 753	92 488	61.4	87 051	57.7	5 437	1 021	48 978	1 978	30 569	1 918	7 504	1 541
October	151 009	92 518	61.3	86 995	57.6	5 523	1 072	48 959	2 129	30 570	1 846	7 466	1 548
November	151 256	92 766	61.3	86 626	57.3	6 140	1 128	48 833	2 380	30 424	2 166	7 369	1 594
December	151 494	92 780	61.2	86 144	56.9	6 636	1 326	48 458	2 727	30 431	2 295	7 255	1 614
1975													
January	151 755	93 128	61.4	85 627	56.4	7 501	1 555	48 086	3 127	30 343	2 629	7 198	1 745
February	151 990	92 776	61.0	85 256	56.1	7 520	1 841	47 927	3 214	30 215	2 595	7 114	1 711
March	152 217	93 165	61.2	85 187	56.0	7 978	2 074	47 776	3 476	30 334	2 742	7 077	1 760
April	152 443	93 399	61.3	85 189	55.9	8 210	2 442	47 759	3 632	30 410	2 831	7 020	1 747
May	152 704	93 884	61.5	85 451	56.0	8 433	2 643	47 835	3 772	30 483	2 838	7 133	1 823
June	152 976	93 575	61.2	85 355	55.8	8 220	2 843	47 754	3 627	30 618	2 753	6 983	1 840
July	153 309	94 021	61.3	85 894	56.0	8 127	2 943	48 050	3 611	30 794	2 679	7 050	1 837
August	153 580	94 162	61.3	86 234	56.1	7 928	2 862	48 239	3 453	30 966	2 643	7 029	1 832
September	153 848	94 202	61.2	86 279	56.1	7 923	2 906	48 126	3 585	30 979	2 600	7 174	1 738
October	154 082	94 267	61.2	86 370	56.1	7 897	2 689	48 165	3 489	31 121	2 657	7 084	1 751
November	154 338	94 250	61.1	86 456	56.0	7 794	2 789	48 203	3 497	31 135	2 624	7 118	1 673
December	154 589	94 409	61.1	86 665	56.1	7 744	2 868	48 266	3 346	31 268	2 638	7 131	1 760
1976													
January	154 853	94 934	61.3	87 400	56.4	7 534	2 713	48 592	3 161	31 595	2 619	7 213	1 754
February	155 066	94 998	61.3	87 672	56.5	7 326	2 519	48 721	3 041	31 680	2 575	7 271	1 710
March	155 306	95 215	61.3	87 985	56.7	7 230	2 441	48 836	3 012	31 842	2 518	7 307	1 700
April	155 529	95 746	61.6	88 416	56.8	7 330	2 210	49 097	3 002	31 951	2 545	7 368	1 783
May	155 765	95 847	61.5	88 794	57.0	7 053	2 115	49 193	2 968	32 147	2 384	7 454	1 701
June	156 027	95 885	61.5	88 563	56.8	7 322	2 332	49 010	3 167	32 267	2 498	7 286	1 657
July	156 276	96 583	61.8	89 093	57.0	7 490	2 316	49 236	3 136	32 334	2 673	7 523	1 681
August	156 525	96 741	61.8	89 223	57.0	7 518	2 378	49 417	3 046	32 437	2 673	7 369	1 799
September	156 779	96 553	61.6	89 173	56.9	7 380	2 296	49 485	3 075	32 390	2 635	7 298	1 670
October	156 993	96 704	61.6	89 274	56.9	7 430	2 292	49 524	3 076	32 412	2 638	7 338	1 716
November	157 235	97 254	61.9	89 634	57.0	7 620	2 354	49 561	3 241	32 753	2 644	7 320	1 735
December	157 438	97 348	61.8	89 803	57.0	7 545	2 375	49 599	3 227	32 914	2 597	7 290	1 721
1977													
January	157 688	97 208	61.6	89 928	57.0	7 280	2 200	49 738	3 046	32 872	2 527	7 318	1 707
February	157 913	97 785	61.9	90 342	57.2	7 443	2 174	49 838	3 136	32 997	2 616	7 507	1 691
March	158 131	98 115	62.0	90 808	57.4	7 307	2 057	50 031	2 939	33 246	2 642	7 531	1 726
April	158 371	98 330	62.1	91 271	57.6	7 059	1 936	50 185	2 824	33 470	2 562	7 616	1 673
May	158 657	98 665	62.2	91 754	57.8	6 911	1 928	50 280	2 847	33 851	2 408	7 623	1 656
June	158 929	99 093	62.4	91 959	57.9	7 134	1 918	50 544	2 769	33 678	2 577	7 737	1 788
July	159 185	98 913	62.1	92 084	57.8	6 829	1 907	50 597	2 698	33 749	2 492	7 738	1 639
August	159 430	99 366	62.3	92 441	58.0	6 925	1 836	50 745	2 720	33 809	2 542	7 887	1 663
September	159 674	99 453	62.3	92 702	58.1	6 751	1 853	50 825	2 532	34 218	2 538	7 659	1 681
October	159 915	99 815	62.4	93 052	58.2	6 763	1 789	51 046	2 679	34 187	2 462	7 819	1 622
November	160 129	100 576	62.8	93 761	58.6	6 815	1 804	51 316	2 584	34 536	2 589	7 909	1 642
December	160 377	100 491	62.7	94 105	58.7	6 386	1 717	51 492	2 509	34 668	2 416	7 945	1 461

1. Civilian labor force as a percent of the civilian noninstitutional population.
2. Civilian employment as a percent of the civilian population.
3. Fifteen weeks and over.

Table 24-3. Civilian Population, Labor Force, Employment, and Unemployment—*Continued*

(Thousands of persons, 16 years of age and over; seasonally adjusted, except as noted)

Year and month	Noninstitutional population (Not seasonally adjusted)	Labor force — Thousands of persons	Labor force — Participation rate [1]	Employed — Thousands of persons	Employed — Ratio: Employment to population [2]	Unemployed — Total	Unemployed — Long-term [3]	Men 20 years and over — Employed	Men 20 years and over — Unemployed	Women 20 years and over — Employed	Women 20 years and over — Unemployed	Both sexes, 16 to 19 years — Employed	Both sexes, 16 to 19 years — Unemployed
1978													
January	160 617	100 873	62.8	94 384	58.8	6 489	1 643	51 542	2 535	34 948	2 375	7 894	1 579
February	160 831	100 837	62.7	94 519	58.8	6 318	1 584	51 578	2 483	35 118	2 210	7 823	1 625
March	161 038	101 092	62.8	94 755	58.8	6 337	1 531	51 635	2 468	35 310	2 238	7 810	1 631
April	161 263	101 574	63.0	95 394	59.2	6 180	1 502	51 912	2 335	35 546	2 263	7 936	1 582
May	161 518	101 896	63.1	95 769	59.3	6 127	1 420	52 050	2 298	35 597	2 283	8 122	1 546
June	161 795	102 371	63.3	96 343	59.5	6 028	1 352	52 240	2 200	35 828	2 322	8 275	1 506
July	162 034	102 399	63.2	96 090	59.3	6 309	1 373	52 190	2 232	35 764	2 464	8 136	1 613
August	162 259	102 511	63.2	96 431	59.4	6 080	1 242	52 228	2 229	35 856	2 295	8 347	1 556
September	162 502	102 795	63.3	96 670	59.5	6 125	1 308	52 284	2 229	36 274	2 308	8 112	1 588
October	162 783	103 080	63.3	97 133	59.7	5 947	1 319	52 448	2 222	36 525	2 158	8 160	1 567
November	163 017	103 562	63.5	97 485	59.8	6 077	1 242	52 802	2 216	36 559	2 281	8 124	1 580
December	163 272	103 809	63.6	97 581	59.8	6 228	1 269	52 807	2 330	36 686	2 278	8 088	1 620
1979													
January	163 516	104 057	63.6	97 948	59.9	6 109	1 250	53 072	2 277	36 697	2 262	8 179	1 570
February	163 726	104 502	63.8	98 329	60.1	6 173	1 297	53 233	2 291	36 904	2 312	8 192	1 570
March	164 027	104 589	63.8	98 480	60.0	6 109	1 365	53 120	2 270	37 159	2 289	8 201	1 550
April	164 162	104 172	63.5	98 103	59.8	6 069	1 272	53 085	2 253	36 944	2 238	8 074	1 578
May	164 459	104 171	63.3	98 331	59.8	5 840	1 239	53 178	2 117	37 134	2 189	8 019	1 534
June	164 721	104 638	63.5	98 679	59.9	5 959	1 171	53 309	2 193	37 221	2 251	8 149	1 515
July	164 970	105 002	63.6	99 006	60.0	5 996	1 123	53 384	2 302	37 514	2 196	8 108	1 498
August	165 198	105 096	63.6	98 776	59.8	6 320	1 203	53 336	2 350	37 548	2 406	7 892	1 564
September	165 431	105 530	63.8	99 340	60.0	6 190	1 172	53 510	2 345	37 798	2 254	8 032	1 591
October	165 813	105 700	63.7	99 404	59.9	6 296	1 219	53 478	2 417	37 931	2 300	7 995	1 579
November	166 051	105 812	63.7	99 574	60.0	6 238	1 239	53 435	2 449	38 065	2 264	8 074	1 525
December	166 300	106 258	63.9	99 933	60.1	6 325	1 277	53 555	2 435	38 259	2 319	8 119	1 571
1980													
January	166 544	106 562	64.0	99 879	60.0	6 683	1 353	53 501	2 724	38 367	2 380	8 011	1 579
February	166 759	106 697	64.0	99 995	60.0	6 702	1 358	53 686	2 726	38 389	2 395	7 920	1 581
March	166 984	106 442	63.7	99 713	59.7	6 729	1 457	53 353	2 842	38 406	2 341	7 954	1 546
April	167 197	106 591	63.8	99 233	59.4	7 358	1 694	53 035	3 292	38 427	2 565	7 771	1 501
May	167 407	106 929	63.9	98 945	59.1	7 984	1 740	52 915	3 598	38 335	2 624	7 695	1 762
June	167 643	106 780	63.7	98 682	58.9	8 098	1 760	52 712	3 662	38 312	2 656	7 658	1 780
July	167 932	107 159	63.8	98 796	58.8	8 363	1 995	52 733	3 820	38 374	2 733	7 689	1 810
August	168 103	107 105	63.7	98 824	58.8	8 281	2 162	52 815	3 770	38 511	2 762	7 498	1 749
September	168 297	107 098	63.6	99 077	58.9	8 021	2 309	52 866	3 747	38 595	2 601	7 616	1 673
October	168 503	107 405	63.7	99 317	58.9	8 088	2 306	53 094	3 584	38 620	2 788	7 603	1 716
November	168 695	107 568	63.8	99 545	59.0	8 023	2 329	53 210	3 550	38 795	2 767	7 540	1 706
December	168 883	107 352	63.6	99 634	59.0	7 718	2 406	53 333	3 332	38 737	2 775	7 564	1 611
1981													
January	169 104	108 026	63.9	99 955	59.1	8 071	2 389	53 392	3 468	39 042	2 824	7 521	1 779
February	169 280	108 242	63.9	100 191	59.2	8 051	2 344	53 445	3 483	39 280	2 777	7 466	1 791
March	169 453	108 553	64.1	100 571	59.4	7 982	2 276	53 662	3 445	39 464	2 770	7 445	1 767
April	169 641	108 925	64.2	101 056	59.6	7 869	2 231	53 886	3 350	39 628	2 772	7 542	1 747
May	169 829	109 222	64.3	101 048	59.5	8 174	2 221	53 879	3 580	39 759	2 844	7 410	1 750
June	170 042	108 396	63.7	100 298	59.0	8 098	2 250	53 576	3 526	39 682	2 832	7 040	1 740
July	170 246	108 556	63.8	100 693	59.1	7 863	2 166	53 814	3 365	39 683	2 855	7 196	1 643
August	170 399	108 725	63.8	100 689	59.1	8 036	2 241	53 718	3 519	39 723	2 834	7 248	1 683
September	170 593	108 294	63.5	100 064	58.7	8 230	2 261	53 625	3 550	39 342	2 942	7 097	1 738
October	170 809	109 024	63.8	100 378	58.8	8 646	2 303	53 482	3 819	39 843	3 029	7 053	1 798
November	170 996	109 236	63.9	100 207	58.6	9 029	2 345	53 335	4 026	39 908	3 115	6 964	1 888
December	171 166	108 912	63.6	99 645	58.2	9 267	2 374	53 149	4 280	39 708	3 173	6 788	1 814
1982													
January	171 335	109 089	63.7	99 692	58.2	9 397	2 409	53 103	4 358	39 821	3 131	6 768	1 908
February	171 489	109 467	63.8	99 762	58.2	9 705	2 758	53 172	4 435	39 859	3 304	6 731	1 966
March	171 667	109 567	63.8	99 672	58.1	9 895	2 965	53 054	4 624	39 936	3 403	6 682	1 868
April	171 844	109 820	63.9	99 576	57.9	10 244	3 086	53 081	4 742	39 848	3 544	6 647	1 958
May	172 026	110 451	64.2	100 116	58.2	10 335	3 276	53 234	4 788	40 121	3 555	6 761	1 992
June	172 190	110 081	63.9	99 543	57.8	10 538	3 451	52 933	5 072	40 219	3 564	6 391	1 902
July	172 364	110 342	64.0	99 493	57.7	10 849	3 555	52 896	5 183	40 228	3 655	6 369	2 011
August	172 511	110 514	64.1	99 633	57.8	10 881	3 696	52 797	5 240	40 336	3 627	6 500	2 014
September	172 690	110 721	64.1	99 504	57.6	11 217	3 889	52 760	5 536	40 275	3 681	6 469	2 000
October	172 881	110 744	64.1	99 215	57.4	11 529	4 185	52 624	5 711	40 105	3 805	6 486	2 013
November	173 058	111 050	64.2	99 112	57.3	11 938	4 485	52 537	5 853	40 111	4 029	6 464	2 056
December	173 199	111 083	64.1	99 032	57.2	12 051	4 662	52 497	5 903	40 164	4 122	6 371	2 026
1983													
January	173 354	110 695	63.9	99 161	57.2	11 534	4 668	52 487	5 618	40 268	3 987	6 406	1 929
February	173 505	110 634	63.8	99 089	57.1	11 545	4 641	52 453	5 738	40 336	3 948	6 300	1 859
March	173 656	110 587	63.7	99 179	57.1	11 408	4 612	52 615	5 630	40 368	3 876	6 196	1 902
April	173 794	110 828	63.8	99 560	57.3	11 268	4 370	52 814	5 643	40 542	3 735	6 204	1 890
May	173 953	110 796	63.7	99 642	57.3	11 154	4 538	52 922	5 609	40 538	3 721	6 182	1 824
June	174 125	111 879	64.3	100 633	57.8	11 246	4 470	53 515	5 347	40 695	3 874	6 423	2 025
July	174 306	111 756	64.1	101 208	58.1	10 548	4 329	53 835	5 170	41 041	3 503	6 332	1 875
August	174 440	112 231	64.3	101 608	58.2	10 623	4 070	53 837	5 162	41 314	3 539	6 457	1 922
September	174 602	112 298	64.3	102 016	58.4	10 282	3 854	53 983	5 036	41 650	3 482	6 383	1 764
October	174 779	111 926	64.0	102 039	58.4	9 887	3 648	54 146	4 817	41 597	3 356	6 296	1 714
November	174 951	112 228	64.1	102 729	58.7	9 499	3 535	54 499	4 605	41 788	3 261	6 442	1 633
December	175 121	112 327	64.1	102 996	58.8	9 331	3 379	54 662	4 422	41 852	3 302	6 482	1 607

1. Civilian labor force as a percent of the civilian noninstitutional population.
2. Civilian employment as a percent of the civilian population.
3. Fifteen weeks and over.

Table 24-3. Civilian Population, Labor Force, Employment, and Unemployment—*Continued*

(Thousands of persons, 16 years of age and over; seasonally adjusted, except as noted)

Year and month	Noninstitutional population (Not seasonally adjusted)	Labor force		Employed		Unemployed		By age and sex					
								Men 20 years and over		Women 20 years and over		Both sexes, 16 to 19 years	
		Thousands of persons	Participa-tion rate [1]	Thousands of persons	Ratio: Employ-ment to population [2]	Total	Long-term [3]	Employed	Unem-ployed	Employed	Unem-ployed	Employed	Unem-ployed
1984													
January	175 533	112 209	63.9	103 201	58.8	9 008	3 254	54 975	4 275	41 812	3 182	6 414	1 551
February	175 679	112 615	64.1	103 824	59.1	8 791	2 991	55 213	4 128	42 196	3 120	6 415	1 543
March	175 824	112 713	64.1	103 967	59.1	8 746	2 881	55 281	4 052	42 328	3 126	6 358	1 568
April	175 969	113 098	64.3	104 336	59.3	8 762	2 858	55 373	4 077	42 512	3 148	6 451	1 537
May	176 123	113 649	64.5	105 193	59.7	8 456	2 884	55 661	3 879	43 071	3 094	6 461	1 483
June	176 284	113 817	64.6	105 591	59.9	8 226	2 612	55 996	3 754	42 944	2 992	6 651	1 480
July	176 440	113 972	64.6	105 435	59.8	8 537	2 638	55 921	3 869	42 979	3 158	6 535	1 510
August	176 583	113 682	64.4	105 163	59.6	8 519	2 604	55 930	3 876	42 885	3 182	6 348	1 461
September	176 763	113 857	64.4	105 490	59.7	8 367	2 538	56 095	3 851	42 967	2 993	6 428	1 523
October	176 956	114 019	64.4	105 638	59.7	8 381	2 526	56 183	3 745	43 052	3 177	6 403	1 459
November	177 135	114 170	64.5	105 972	59.8	8 198	2 438	56 274	3 734	43 244	3 074	6 454	1 390
December	177 306	114 581	64.6	106 223	59.9	8 358	2 401	56 313	3 812	43 472	3 051	6 438	1 495
1985													
January	177 384	114 725	64.7	106 302	59.9	8 423	2 284	56 184	3 765	43 589	3 151	6 529	1 507
February	177 516	114 876	64.7	106 555	60.0	8 321	2 389	56 216	3 739	43 787	3 114	6 552	1 468
March	177 667	115 328	64.9	106 989	60.2	8 339	2 394	56 356	3 715	44 035	3 160	6 598	1 464
April	177 799	115 331	64.9	106 936	60.1	8 395	2 393	56 374	3 812	44 000	3 187	6 562	1 396
May	177 944	115 234	64.8	106 932	60.1	8 302	2 292	56 531	3 640	43 905	3 192	6 496	1 470
June	178 096	114 965	64.6	106 505	59.8	8 460	2 310	56 288	3 861	43 958	3 178	6 259	1 421
July	178 263	115 320	64.7	106 807	59.9	8 513	2 329	56 435	3 757	43 975	3 140	6 397	1 616
August	178 405	115 291	64.6	107 095	60.0	8 196	2 258	56 655	3 675	44 103	3 144	6 337	1 377
September	178 572	115 905	64.9	107 657	60.3	8 248	2 242	56 845	3 694	44 395	3 153	6 417	1 401
October	178 770	116 145	65.0	107 847	60.3	8 298	2 295	56 969	3 678	44 565	3 044	6 313	1 576
November	178 940	116 135	64.9	108 007	60.4	8 128	2 207	56 972	3 642	44 617	3 052	6 418	1 434
December	179 112	116 354	65.0	108 216	60.4	8 138	2 208	56 995	3 606	44 889	3 038	6 332	1 494
1986													
January	179 670	116 682	64.9	108 887	60.6	7 795	2 089	57 637	3 489	44 944	2 908	6 306	1 398
February	179 821	116 882	65.0	108 480	60.3	8 402	2 308	57 269	3 758	44 804	3 156	6 407	1 488
March	179 985	117 220	65.1	108 837	60.5	8 383	2 261	57 353	3 766	44 960	3 164	6 524	1 453
April	180 148	117 316	65.1	108 952	60.5	8 364	2 162	57 358	3 700	45 081	3 119	6 513	1 545
May	180 311	117 528	65.2	109 089	60.5	8 439	2 232	57 287	3 836	45 289	3 119	6 513	1 484
June	180 503	118 084	65.4	109 576	60.7	8 508	2 320	57 471	3 832	45 621	3 136	6 484	1 540
July	180 682	118 129	65.4	109 810	60.8	8 319	2 269	57 514	3 859	45 837	3 005	6 459	1 455
August	180 828	118 150	65.3	110 015	60.8	8 135	2 276	57 597	3 701	45 926	3 006	6 492	1 428
September	180 997	118 395	65.4	110 085	60.8	8 310	2 318	57 630	3 862	45 972	2 986	6 483	1 462
October	181 186	118 516	65.4	110 273	60.9	8 243	2 188	57 660	3 823	46 046	3 010	6 567	1 410
November	181 363	118 634	65.4	110 475	60.9	8 159	2 202	57 941	3 775	46 070	2 957	6 464	1 427
December	181 547	118 611	65.3	110 728	61.0	7 883	2 161	58 185	3 713	46 132	2 812	6 411	1 358
1987													
January	181 827	118 845	65.4	110 953	61.0	7 892	2 168	58 264	3 635	46 219	2 866	6 470	1 391
February	181 998	119 122	65.5	111 257	61.1	7 865	2 117	58 279	3 596	46 444	2 834	6 534	1 435
March	182 179	119 270	65.5	111 408	61.2	7 862	2 070	58 362	3 539	46 549	2 907	6 497	1 416
April	182 344	119 336	65.4	111 794	61.3	7 542	2 091	58 503	3 415	46 746	2 756	6 545	1 371
May	182 533	120 008	65.7	112 434	61.6	7 574	2 104	58 713	3 462	47 052	2 706	6 669	1 406
June	182 703	119 644	65.5	112 246	61.4	7 398	2 087	58 581	3 477	47 102	2 627	6 563	1 294
July	182 885	119 902	65.6	112 634	61.6	7 268	1 921	58 740	3 380	47 229	2 642	6 665	1 246
August	183 002	120 318	65.7	113 057	61.8	7 261	1 878	58 810	3 294	47 322	2 660	6 925	1 307
September	183 161	120 011	65.5	112 909	61.6	7 102	1 866	58 964	3 147	47 285	2 670	6 660	1 285
October	183 311	120 509	65.7	113 282	61.8	7 227	1 794	59 073	3 200	47 533	2 629	6 676	1 398
November	183 470	120 540	65.7	113 505	61.9	7 035	1 797	59 210	3 102	47 622	2 604	6 673	1 329
December	183 620	120 729	65.7	113 793	62.0	6 936	1 767	59 217	3 051	47 781	2 588	6 795	1 297
1988													
January	183 822	120 969	65.8	114 016	62.0	6 953	1 714	59 346	3 077	47 862	2 574	6 808	1 302
February	183 969	121 156	65.9	114 227	62.1	6 929	1 738	59 535	3 049	47 919	2 628	6 773	1 252
March	184 111	120 913	65.7	114 037	61.9	6 876	1 744	59 393	3 086	48 090	2 490	6 554	1 300
April	184 232	121 251	65.8	114 650	62.2	6 601	1 563	59 832	2 869	48 147	2 466	6 671	1 266
May	184 374	121 071	65.7	114 292	62.0	6 779	1 647	59 644	3 080	47 946	2 489	6 702	1 210
June	184 562	121 473	65.8	114 927	62.3	6 546	1 531	59 751	2 930	48 146	2 453	7 030	1 163
July	184 729	121 665	65.9	115 060	62.3	6 605	1 601	59 888	2 876	48 186	2 517	6 986	1 212
August	184 830	122 125	66.1	115 282	62.4	6 843	1 639	59 877	3 117	48 467	2 463	6 938	1 263
September	184 962	121 960	65.9	115 356	62.4	6 604	1 569	59 980	2 877	48 511	2 468	6 865	1 259
October	185 114	122 206	66.0	115 638	62.5	6 568	1 562	60 023	2 932	48 859	2 431	6 756	1 205
November	185 244	122 637	66.2	116 100	62.7	6 537	1 468	60 042	2 989	49 254	2 448	6 804	1 100
December	185 402	122 622	66.1	116 104	62.6	6 518	1 490	60 059	2 945	49 257	2 395	6 788	1 178
1989													
January	185 644	123 390	66.5	116 708	62.9	6 682	1 480	60 477	2 898	49 529	2 467	6 702	1 317
February	185 777	123 135	66.3	116 776	62.9	6 359	1 304	60 588	2 838	49 497	2 341	6 691	1 180
March	185 897	123 227	66.3	117 022	62.9	6 205	1 353	60 795	2 710	49 503	2 410	6 724	1 085
April	186 024	123 565	66.4	117 097	62.9	6 468	1 397	60 764	2 864	49 565	2 443	6 768	1 161
May	186 181	123 474	66.3	117 099	62.9	6 375	1 348	60 795	2 720	49 583	2 486	6 721	1 169
June	186 329	123 995	66.5	117 418	63.0	6 577	1 300	61 054	2 787	49 542	2 518	6 822	1 272
July	186 483	123 967	66.5	117 472	63.0	6 495	1 435	60 947	2 804	49 693	2 562	6 832	1 129
August	186 598	124 166	66.5	117 655	63.1	6 511	1 302	60 915	2 849	49 804	2 472	6 936	1 190
September	186 726	123 944	66.4	117 354	62.8	6 590	1 360	60 668	3 002	50 015	2 389	6 671	1 199
October	186 871	124 211	66.5	117 581	62.9	6 630	1 392	60 958	2 935	49 871	2 507	6 752	1 188
November	187 017	124 637	66.6	117 912	63.0	6 725	1 418	60 958	2 992	50 221	2 502	6 733	1 231
December	187 165	124 497	66.5	117 830	63.0	6 667	1 375	61 068	2 962	50 116	2 500	6 646	1 205

1. Civilian labor force as a percent of the civilian noninstitutional population.
2. Civilian employment as a percent of the civilian population.
3. Fifteen weeks and over.

Table 24-3. Civilian Population, Labor Force, Employment, and Unemployment—*Continued*

(Thousands of persons, 16 years of age and over; seasonally adjusted, except as noted)

Year and month	Noninstitutional population (Not seasonally adjusted)	Labor force		Employed		Unemployed		By age and sex					
								Men 20 years and over		Women 20 years and over		Both sexes, 16 to 19 years	
		Thousands of persons	Participation rate [1]	Thousands of persons	Ratio: Employment to population [2]	Total	Long-term [3]	Employed	Unemployed	Employed	Unemployed	Employed	Unemployed
1990													
January	188 413	125 833	66.8	119 081	63.2	6 752	1 412	61 742	3 063	50 436	2 489	6 903	1 200
February	188 516	125 710	66.7	119 059	63.2	6 651	1 350	61 805	2 946	50 438	2 506	6 816	1 199
March	188 630	125 801	66.7	119 203	63.2	6 598	1 331	61 832	2 974	50 463	2 471	6 908	1 153
April	188 778	125 649	66.6	118 852	63.0	6 797	1 376	61 579	3 107	50 457	2 519	6 816	1 171
May	188 913	125 893	66.6	119 151	63.1	6 742	1 415	61 778	3 043	50 646	2 515	6 727	1 184
June	189 058	125 573	66.4	118 983	62.9	6 590	1 436	61 762	3 066	50 550	2 412	6 671	1 112
July	189 188	125 732	66.5	118 810	62.8	6 922	1 534	61 683	3 183	50 514	2 575	6 613	1 164
August	189 342	125 990	66.5	118 802	62.7	7 188	1 607	61 715	3 291	50 635	2 641	6 452	1 256
September	189 528	125 892	66.4	118 524	62.5	7 368	1 695	61 608	3 387	50 587	2 735	6 329	1 246
October	189 710	125 995	66.4	118 536	62.5	7 459	1 689	61 606	3 487	50 616	2 721	6 314	1 251
November	189 872	126 070	66.4	118 306	62.3	7 764	1 831	61 545	3 700	50 541	2 778	6 220	1 286
December	190 017	126 142	66.4	118 241	62.2	7 901	1 804	61 506	3 794	50 530	2 796	6 205	1 311
1991													
January	190 163	125 955	66.2	117 940	62.0	8 015	1 866	61 383	3 766	50 472	2 856	6 085	1 393
February	190 271	126 020	66.2	117 755	61.9	8 265	1 955	61 117	4 051	50 523	2 924	6 115	1 290
March	190 381	126 238	66.3	117 652	61.8	8 586	2 137	61 144	4 206	50 422	3 019	6 086	1 361
April	190 517	126 548	66.4	118 109	62.0	8 439	2 206	61 280	4 183	50 760	2 944	6 069	1 312
May	190 650	126 176	66.2	117 440	61.6	8 736	2 252	61 052	4 168	50 457	3 196	5 931	1 372
June	190 800	126 331	66.2	117 639	61.7	8 692	2 533	61 147	4 229	50 585	3 122	5 907	1 341
July	190 946	126 154	66.1	117 568	61.6	8 586	2 388	61 179	4 245	50 636	2 956	5 753	1 385
August	191 116	126 150	66.0	117 484	61.5	8 666	2 460	61 122	4 235	50 601	3 087	5 761	1 344
September	191 302	126 650	66.2	117 928	61.6	8 722	2 497	61 279	4 307	50 864	3 077	5 785	1 338
October	191 497	126 642	66.1	117 800	61.5	8 842	2 638	61 174	4 276	50 811	3 196	5 815	1 370
November	191 657	126 701	66.1	117 770	61.4	8 931	2 718	61 201	4 332	50 759	3 240	5 810	1 359
December	191 798	126 664	66.0	117 466	61.2	9 198	2 892	61 074	4 453	50 728	3 305	5 664	1 440
1992													
January	191 953	127 261	66.3	117 978	61.5	9 283	3 060	61 116	4 651	51 095	3 261	5 767	1 371
February	192 067	127 207	66.2	117 753	61.3	9 454	3 182	61 062	4 657	51 033	3 372	5 658	1 425
March	192 204	127 604	66.4	118 144	61.5	9 460	3 196	61 363	4 650	51 204	3 389	5 577	1 421
April	192 354	127 841	66.5	118 426	61.6	9 415	3 130	61 468	4 699	51 323	3 441	5 635	1 275
May	192 503	128 119	66.6	118 375	61.5	9 744	3 444	61 513	4 859	51 245	3 474	5 617	1 411
June	192 663	128 459	66.7	118 419	61.5	10 040	3 758	61 537	4 890	51 383	3 512	5 499	1 638
July	192 826	128 563	66.7	118 713	61.6	9 850	3 614	61 641	4 779	51 458	3 598	5 614	1 473
August	193 018	128 613	66.6	118 826	61.6	9 787	3 579	61 681	4 768	51 386	3 584	5 759	1 435
September	193 229	128 501	66.5	118 720	61.4	9 781	3 504	61 663	4 723	51 359	3 540	5 698	1 518
October	193 442	128 026	66.2	118 628	61.3	9 398	3 505	61 550	4 709	51 373	3 409	5 705	1 280
November	193 621	128 441	66.3	118 876	61.4	9 565	3 397	61 644	4 666	51 535	3 432	5 697	1 467
December	193 784	128 554	66.3	118 997	61.4	9 557	3 651	61 721	4 529	51 524	3 606	5 752	1 422
1993													
January	193 962	128 400	66.2	119 075	61.4	9 325	3 346	61 895	4 434	51 505	3 477	5 675	1 414
February	194 108	128 458	66.2	119 275	61.4	9 183	3 190	61 963	4 400	51 573	3 378	5 739	1 405
March	194 248	128 598	66.2	119 542	61.5	9 056	3 115	62 007	4 489	51 808	3 162	5 727	1 405
April	194 398	128 584	66.1	119 474	61.5	9 110	3 014	62 032	4 397	51 732	3 332	5 710	1 381
May	194 549	129 264	66.4	120 115	61.7	9 149	3 101	62 309	4 367	51 996	3 348	5 810	1 434
June	194 719	129 411	66.5	120 290	61.8	9 121	3 141	62 409	4 392	52 183	3 313	5 698	1 416
July	194 882	129 397	66.4	120 467	61.8	8 930	3 046	62 497	4 349	52 088	3 258	5 882	1 323
August	195 063	129 619	66.4	120 856	62.0	8 763	3 026	62 634	4 230	52 294	3 197	5 928	1 336
September	195 259	129 268	66.2	120 554	61.7	8 714	3 042	62 437	4 188	52 241	3 222	5 876	1 304
October	195 444	129 573	66.3	120 823	61.8	8 750	3 029	62 614	4 140	52 379	3 269	5 830	1 341
November	195 625	129 711	66.3	121 169	61.9	8 542	2 986	62 732	3 949	52 531	3 251	5 906	1 342
December	195 794	129 941	66.4	121 464	62.0	8 477	2 968	62 760	3 941	52 813	3 249	5 891	1 287
1994													
January	195 953	130 596	66.6	121 966	62.2	8 630	3 060	62 798	3 990	53 052	3 270	6 116	1 370
February	196 090	130 669	66.6	122 086	62.3	8 583	3 118	62 708	4 001	53 266	3 237	6 112	1 345
March	196 213	130 400	66.5	121 930	62.1	8 470	3 055	62 780	3 844	53 099	3 296	6 051	1 330
April	196 363	130 621	66.5	122 290	62.3	8 331	2 921	62 906	3 726	53 274	3 164	6 110	1 441
May	196 510	130 779	66.6	122 864	62.5	7 915	2 836	63 116	3 511	53 624	3 062	6 124	1 342
June	196 693	130 561	66.4	122 634	62.3	7 927	2 735	63 041	3 553	53 393	3 047	6 200	1 327
July	196 859	130 652	66.4	122 706	62.3	7 946	2 822	63 034	3 679	53 531	2 955	6 141	1 312
August	197 043	131 275	66.6	123 342	62.6	7 933	2 750	63 294	3 591	53 744	3 027	6 304	1 315
September	197 248	131 421	66.6	123 687	62.7	7 734	2 746	63 631	3 402	53 991	3 045	6 065	1 287
October	197 430	131 744	66.7	124 112	62.9	7 632	2 955	63 818	3 450	54 071	2 862	6 223	1 320
November	197 607	131 891	66.7	124 516	63.0	7 375	2 666	64 080	3 336	54 168	2 884	6 268	1 155
December	197 765	131 951	66.7	124 721	63.1	7 230	2 488	64 359	3 202	54 054	2 737	6 308	1 291
1995													
January	197 753	132 038	66.8	124 663	63.0	7 375	2 396	64 185	3 323	54 087	2 793	6 391	1 259
February	197 886	132 115	66.8	124 928	63.1	7 187	2 345	64 378	3 096	54 226	2 756	6 324	1 335
March	198 007	132 108	66.7	124 955	63.1	7 153	2 287	64 321	3 149	54 141	2 755	6 493	1 249
April	198 148	132 590	66.9	124 945	63.1	7 645	2 473	64 165	3 299	54 366	2 986	6 414	1 360
May	198 286	131 851	66.5	124 421	62.7	7 430	2 577	63 829	3 356	54 272	2 730	6 320	1 344
June	198 453	131 949	66.5	124 522	62.7	7 427	2 266	63 992	3 236	54 020	2 851	6 510	1 340
July	198 615	132 343	66.6	124 816	62.8	7 527	2 311	63 962	3 222	54 476	2 885	6 378	1 420
August	198 801	132 336	66.6	124 852	62.8	7 484	2 391	63 875	3 277	54 434	2 840	6 543	1 367
September	199 005	132 611	66.6	125 133	62.9	7 478	2 306	64 179	3 266	54 507	2 834	6 447	1 378
October	199 192	132 716	66.6	125 388	62.9	7 328	2 272	64 272	3 073	54 692	2 905	6 424	1 350
November	199 355	132 614	66.5	125 188	62.8	7 426	2 339	63 931	3 313	54 850	2 755	6 407	1 358
December	199 508	132 511	66.4	125 088	62.7	7 423	2 331	64 041	3 274	54 674	2 754	6 373	1 395

1. Civilian labor force as a percent of the civilian noninstitutional population.
2. Civilian employment as a percent of the civilian population.
3. Fifteen weeks and over.

Table 24-4. Civilian Employment and Selected Unemployment Rates

(Seasonally adjusted.)

Year and month	Employment by industry (thousands of persons)		Unemployment rates (percent of civilian labor force in group)													
	Agricul-tural	Nonagri-cultural	All civilian workers	20 years and over		Both sexes, 16 to 19 years	By race		Persons of Hispanic origin	By marital or family status			Wage and salary workers, by industry of last job			
				Men	Women		White	Black		Married men, spouse present	Married women, spouse present	Women who maintain families	Private nonagricultural			Agricul-tural
													Total	Construc-tion	Manufac-turing	
1972																
January	3 366	77 593	5.8	4.3	5.5	16.9	5.2	11.2	...	3.0	5.3	7.2	6.0	10.3	6.1	8.6
February	3 358	77 750	5.7	4.1	5.1	18.0	5.1	11.2	...	2.9	5.3	7.0	6.0	10.8	6.0	8.1
March	3 438	78 135	5.8	4.2	5.5	17.2	5.2	10.7	...	2.8	5.4	7.0	6.0	10.3	6.0	6.9
April	3 382	78 273	5.7	4.1	5.4	16.5	5.3	9.8	...	2.8	5.5	7.2	5.9	10.5	5.8	6.3
May	3 412	78 475	5.7	4.1	5.7	15.3	5.1	10.2	...	2.8	5.6	7.0	5.9	10.9	5.9	8.0
June	3 402	78 681	5.7	4.0	5.6	15.9	5.1	10.2	...	2.8	5.6	7.7	5.7	9.7	5.7	7.6
July	3 461	78 769	5.6	4.0	5.7	15.6	5.1	10.5	...	2.8	5.7	7.3	5.9	10.4	5.9	6.7
August	3 603	78 975	5.6	3.9	5.6	16.5	5.1	10.6	...	2.7	5.6	7.3	5.9	11.3	5.6	6.7
September	3 568	78 975	5.5	3.8	5.5	16.3	5.0	10.4	...	2.8	5.3	7.2	5.6	8.9	5.3	8.9
October	3 634	78 982	5.6	3.9	5.6	15.8	5.1	10.6	...	2.8	5.2	8.3	5.8	10.1	5.4	9.9
November	3 517	79 473	5.3	3.6	5.1	15.7	4.7	10.0	...	2.5	5.0	6.5	5.3	10.1	4.8	8.2
December	3 596	79 804	5.2	3.5	5.0	15.6	4.6	9.4	...	2.4	5.0	6.3	5.1	9.7	4.6	7.1
1973																
January	3 456	79 705	4.9	3.4	5.1	13.7	4.5	9.1	...	2.4	4.9	7.1	5.0	9.4	4.8	6.8
February	3 415	80 497	5.0	3.4	4.9	15.3	4.5	9.5	...	2.4	4.8	6.6	5.1	9.3	4.4	7.3
March	3 469	80 983	4.9	3.4	4.9	14.3	4.4	9.4	7.3	2.4	4.6	7.0	4.9	8.9	4.4	6.6
April	3 407	81 152	5.0	3.4	4.8	15.5	4.5	9.9	7.9	2.4	4.6	6.9	4.9	9.1	4.3	7.4
May	3 376	81 272	4.9	3.4	4.6	14.9	4.3	9.6	8.1	2.3	4.6	6.7	4.8	8.8	4.5	8.9
June	3 509	81 676	4.9	3.3	5.0	13.8	4.3	9.8	7.9	2.2	4.7	8.0	4.8	8.0	4.4	7.0
July	3 540	81 759	4.8	3.1	4.9	14.3	4.2	9.8	7.2	2.1	4.7	7.0	4.8	9.1	4.0	5.7
August	3 425	81 779	4.8	3.2	5.0	14.0	4.3	9.2	7.4	2.2	5.0	6.5	4.9	8.4	4.2	7.5
September	3 342	82 146	4.8	3.1	4.9	14.7	4.3	9.7	7.7	2.1	4.7	6.8	4.8	9.0	4.4	6.4
October	3 424	82 563	4.6	2.9	4.5	14.4	4.1	8.8	8.0	2.2	4.3	7.0	4.6	8.9	4.1	6.8
November	3 593	82 727	4.8	3.1	4.8	15.0	4.3	9.3	8.1	2.2	4.6	8.0	4.9	9.0	4.4	7.4
December	3 658	82 743	4.9	3.2	5.0	14.6	4.4	9.0	7.6	2.3	4.7	7.1	5.0	8.4	4.4	6.7
1974																
January	3 756	82 799	5.1	3.5	5.1	14.6	4.6	9.5	7.6	2.4	4.8	6.7	5.1	9.5	4.8	6.7
February	3 824	82 930	5.2	3.6	5.0	14.9	4.6	9.8	7.8	2.4	5.0	6.4	5.3	8.5	5.1	6.9
March	3 726	83 093	5.1	3.4	5.0	14.9	4.5	9.8	7.6	2.3	4.7	6.5	5.1	8.6	5.0	7.0
April	3 582	83 087	5.1	3.5	4.9	14.3	4.5	9.5	7.0	2.4	4.5	6.6	5.2	9.9	4.9	7.3
May	3 529	83 362	5.1	3.4	5.0	15.4	4.6	9.7	7.3	2.2	4.7	7.0	5.2	9.5	4.8	7.0
June	3 386	83 555	5.4	3.5	5.2	16.3	4.8	10.1	8.6	2.5	4.8	6.7	5.5	9.9	5.2	7.4
July	3 436	83 713	5.5	3.6	5.3	16.8	4.9	10.4	8.8	2.7	5.1	6.2	5.6	10.2	5.4	8.3
August	3 429	83 608	5.5	3.8	5.4	14.9	5.0	9.9	8.1	2.8	5.3	6.6	5.7	10.9	5.7	7.4
September	3 460	83 591	5.9	3.9	5.9	17.0	5.4	10.8	8.1	2.8	5.8	7.4	6.1	11.6	6.0	7.3
October	3 431	83 564	6.0	4.2	5.7	17.2	5.4	11.5	8.2	3.0	5.3	7.3	6.2	12.1	6.5	8.3
November	3 405	83 221	6.6	4.6	6.6	17.8	6.0	12.4	8.6	3.4	6.5	8.5	6.9	13.6	7.5	7.6
December	3 361	82 783	7.2	5.3	7.0	18.2	6.4	13.1	9.1	3.8	7.0	8.3	7.7	15.3	8.7	7.7
1975																
January	3 401	82 226	8.1	6.1	8.0	19.5	7.4	14.1	10.7	4.6	8.1	9.0	8.7	15.7	10.4	10.7
February	3 361	81 895	8.1	6.3	7.9	19.4	7.4	14.4	11.2	4.7	8.0	9.7	8.7	16.3	10.7	9.1
March	3 358	81 829	8.6	6.8	8.3	19.9	7.8	15.1	12.1	5.1	8.4	9.9	9.3	17.8	11.3	10.6
April	3 315	81 874	8.8	7.1	8.5	19.9	8.0	15.3	12.4	5.5	8.7	9.6	9.8	19.2	12.0	11.3
May	3 560	81 891	9.0	7.3	8.5	20.4	8.4	15.1	14.3	5.7	8.7	10.5	10.1	21.5	12.3	9.4
June	3 368	81 987	8.8	7.1	8.2	20.9	8.1	15.0	11.7	5.5	8.2	10.2	9.8	19.8	12.1	10.4
July	3 457	82 437	8.6	7.0	8.0	20.7	8.0	14.1	11.6	5.4	7.6	10.4	9.5	19.5	11.4	9.0
August	3 429	82 805	8.4	6.7	7.9	20.7	7.7	15.2	12.1	5.2	7.6	9.8	9.2	19.1	10.7	11.3
September	3 508	82 771	8.4	6.9	7.7	19.5	7.7	15.4	12.7	5.3	7.6	9.8	9.1	18.5	10.5	11.1
October	3 397	82 973	8.4	6.8	7.9	19.8	7.7	14.9	13.0	5.2	7.5	10.4	9.0	17.8	10.1	10.8
November	3 331	83 125	8.3	6.8	7.8	19.0	7.6	14.6	12.4	4.9	7.3	10.1	8.9	17.4	9.9	10.3
December	3 259	83 406	8.2	6.5	7.8	19.8	7.4	14.5	12.1	4.7	7.2	10.4	8.7	16.8	9.2	11.7
1976																
January	3 387	84 013	7.9	6.1	7.7	19.6	7.2	14.3	11.4	4.4	7.2	10.6	8.3	15.5	8.5	11.4
February	3 304	84 368	7.7	5.9	7.5	19.0	6.9	14.4	10.7	4.2	7.2	10.2	8.0	15.4	8.2	10.6
March	3 296	84 689	7.6	5.8	7.3	18.9	6.9	13.5	11.0	4.2	6.9	9.5	7.8	15.7	7.7	10.9
April	3 438	84 978	7.7	5.8	7.4	19.5	6.9	13.8	11.7	4.1	7.0	9.6	7.7	15.6	7.8	11.5
May	3 367	85 427	7.4	5.7	6.9	18.6	6.7	13.2	10.5	4.1	6.8	9.2	7.7	14.7	7.7	12.9
June	3 310	85 253	7.6	6.1	7.2	18.5	6.9	14.3	11.1	4.4	7.0	9.6	7.9	16.3	7.8	11.5
July	3 358	85 735	7.8	6.0	7.6	18.3	7.1	13.9	11.7	4.4	7.3	10.1	8.1	16.8	7.7	11.7
August	3 380	85 843	7.8	5.8	7.6	19.6	7.1	14.3	12.4	4.1	7.4	10.5	8.1	16.6	7.8	11.0
September	3 278	85 895	7.6	5.9	7.5	18.6	7.0	13.7	11.8	4.4	7.2	10.6	8.0	15.7	7.7	11.3
October	3 316	85 958	7.7	5.8	7.5	19.0	7.0	13.9	11.6	4.2	7.2	10.5	7.9	14.7	7.8	11.2
November	3 263	86 371	7.8	6.1	7.5	19.2	7.1	14.0	11.7	4.3	7.0	9.8	8.0	15.4	7.7	13.5
December	3 251	86 552	7.8	6.1	7.3	19.1	7.0	14.1	11.7	4.2	6.9	10.3	7.9	14.3	8.1	13.6
1977																
January	3 185	86 743	7.5	5.8	7.1	18.9	6.8	13.8	11.2	4.1	6.6	9.5	7.6	14.8	7.3	13.0
February	3 222	87 120	7.6	5.9	7.3	18.4	6.9	14.2	11.4	4.1	6.9	9.5	7.7	14.7	7.5	12.8
March	3 212	87 596	7.4	5.5	7.4	18.6	6.7	13.9	11.2	3.8	7.0	9.7	7.6	13.9	7.0	12.7
April	3 313	87 958	7.2	5.3	7.1	18.0	6.4	12.8	9.6	3.7	6.7	9.3	7.1	12.5	6.9	12.5
May	3 432	88 322	7.0	5.4	6.6	17.8	6.3	13.5	9.9	3.6	6.5	8.9	7.2	13.4	6.5	11.6
June	3 340	88 619	7.2	5.2	7.1	18.8	6.4	13.9	10.1	3.5	6.7	9.4	7.0	12.6	6.5	11.8
July	3 247	88 837	6.9	5.1	6.9	17.5	6.0	13.9	9.5	3.4	6.5	9.2	6.9	12.0	6.5	9.4
August	3 260	89 181	7.0	5.1	7.0	17.4	6.0	15.1	9.4	3.4	6.4	9.9	6.9	11.5	6.6	10.1
September	3 201	89 501	6.8	4.7	6.9	18.0	6.0	14.5	9.7	3.3	6.4	10.4	6.7	10.5	6.7	10.5
October	3 272	89 780	6.8	5.0	6.7	17.2	5.9	14.5	9.4	3.6	6.2	9.3	6.8	11.8	6.6	10.0
November	3 375	90 386	6.8	4.8	7.0	17.2	5.8	14.7	9.3	3.3	6.4	9.4	6.7	11.4	6.4	9.6
December	3 320	90 785	6.4	4.6	6.5	15.5	5.5	13.6	8.8	3.2	6.0	8.1	6.3	10.8	5.8	10.0

Table 24-4. Civilian Employment and Selected Unemployment Rates—*Continued*

(Seasonally adjusted.)

Year and month	Employment by industry (thousands of persons)		Unemployment rates (percent of civilian labor force in group)													
			All civilian workers	20 years and over		Both sexes, 16 to 19 years	By race		Persons of Hispanic origin	By marital or family status			Wage and salary workers, by industry of last job			
	Agricultural	Nonagricultural		Men	Women		White	Black		Married men, spouse present	Married women, spouse present	Women who maintain families	Private nonagricultural			Agricultural
													Total	Construction	Manufacturing	
1978																
January	3 434	90 950	6.4	4.7	6.4	16.7	5.5	13.9	9.3	3.1	5.8	8.3	6.4	11.6	5.9	9.4
February	3 320	91 199	6.3	4.6	5.9	17.2	5.5	13.1	9.9	3.0	5.5	7.8	6.3	11.1	6.0	9.8
March	3 351	91 404	6.3	4.6	6.0	17.3	5.4	13.1	9.5	3.1	5.4	8.7	6.2	11.0	5.7	10.1
April	3 349	92 045	6.1	4.3	6.0	16.6	5.3	12.9	8.5	2.8	5.1	9.9	6.0	9.8	5.4	8.2
May	3 325	92 444	6.0	4.2	6.0	16.0	5.2	13.0	9.6	2.8	5.8	9.1	5.9	9.7	5.6	8.0
June	3 483	92 860	5.9	4.0	6.1	15.4	5.0	12.8	9.1	2.8	5.5	8.7	5.7	9.6	5.6	8.9
July	3 441	92 649	6.2	4.1	6.4	16.5	5.3	13.0	9.5	2.6	5.6	9.9	5.9	9.8	5.4	9.2
August	3 401	93 030	5.9	4.1	6.0	15.7	5.1	12.3	9.1	2.7	5.6	8.2	5.7	9.2	5.4	8.5
September	3 400	93 270	6.0	4.1	6.0	16.4	5.2	11.9	8.9	2.7	5.7	8.4	5.9	10.9	5.3	8.7
October	3 409	93 724	5.8	4.1	5.6	16.1	5.0	11.8	8.5	2.6	5.2	7.6	5.6	11.2	5.1	9.4
November	3 284	94 201	5.9	4.0	5.9	16.3	5.0	12.7	8.4	2.5	5.5	7.8	5.7	10.8	5.2	8.2
December	3 396	94 185	6.0	4.2	5.8	16.7	5.2	12.4	8.7	2.7	5.6	8.0	5.9	12.2	5.3	8.3
1979																
January	3 305	94 643	5.9	4.1	5.8	16.1	5.1	12.4	8.2	2.7	5.4	7.9	5.8	10.8	5.2	7.5
February	3 373	94 956	5.9	4.1	5.9	16.1	5.1	13.1	7.7	2.8	5.3	8.5	5.8	11.5	5.1	9.0
March	3 368	95 112	5.8	4.1	5.8	15.9	5.1	12.5	7.9	2.7	5.3	8.3	5.8	10.3	5.4	8.1
April	3 291	94 812	5.8	4.1	5.7	16.3	5.0	12.9	8.2	2.7	5.2	8.1	5.7	10.3	5.5	8.9
May	3 272	95 059	5.6	3.8	5.6	16.1	4.8	12.4	7.9	2.4	5.0	8.6	5.6	9.5	5.3	9.3
June	3 331	95 348	5.7	4.0	5.7	15.7	4.9	12.2	8.4	2.6	5.1	9.0	5.6	9.7	5.3	8.3
July	3 335	95 671	5.7	4.1	5.5	15.6	4.9	12.1	8.1	2.8	4.9	8.1	5.7	9.7	5.6	9.9
August	3 374	95 402	6.0	4.2	6.0	16.5	5.3	12.4	8.7	2.9	5.4	8.2	6.0	9.1	6.0	9.6
September	3 371	95 969	5.9	4.2	5.6	16.5	5.2	11.7	7.6	2.8	5.0	8.1	5.9	9.1	6.1	10.4
October	3 325	96 079	6.0	4.3	5.7	16.5	5.2	12.3	8.7	2.9	5.2	8.4	5.9	10.0	6.0	9.5
November	3 436	96 138	5.9	4.4	5.6	15.9	5.2	11.9	9.2	3.0	4.8	8.4	5.9	10.5	6.0	10.6
December	3 400	96 533	6.0	4.3	5.7	16.2	5.2	12.2	9.1	2.9	5.1	8.4	5.9	11.1	6.0	9.7
1980																
January	3 316	96 563	6.3	4.8	5.8	16.5	5.5	13.0	8.7	3.5	5.3	8.9	6.3	11.7	6.8	10.1
February	3 397	96 598	6.3	4.8	5.9	16.6	5.5	12.9	8.9	3.3	5.4	8.8	6.3	11.4	6.8	9.6
March	3 418	96 295	6.3	5.1	5.7	16.3	5.6	12.9	9.2	3.5	5.3	8.8	6.4	13.2	6.7	10.3
April	3 326	95 907	6.9	5.8	6.3	16.2	6.1	13.8	10.4	4.1	5.7	9.0	7.1	14.6	8.2	12.0
May	3 382	95 563	7.5	6.4	6.4	18.6	6.6	14.4	10.1	4.5	5.9	8.3	7.9	16.1	9.6	11.4
June	3 296	95 386	7.6	6.5	6.5	18.9	6.7	14.6	10.1	4.7	6.1	8.4	8.0	15.4	9.5	10.1
July	3 319	95 477	7.8	6.8	6.6	19.1	6.9	15.3	10.8	4.9	6.2	8.9	8.2	15.8	9.9	11.6
August	3 234	95 590	7.7	6.7	6.7	18.9	6.9	14.6	10.8	4.9	6.2	9.4	8.1	16.5	9.5	13.2
September	3 443	95 634	7.5	6.6	6.3	18.0	6.6	14.8	11.4	4.7	5.9	9.1	7.9	15.5	9.2	11.7
October	3 372	95 945	7.5	6.3	6.7	18.4	6.6	15.1	10.6	4.5	6.0	10.1	7.8	14.1	9.1	11.3
November	3 396	96 149	7.5	6.3	6.7	18.5	6.5	15.1	9.9	4.3	5.8	9.8	7.8	14.5	8.8	10.1
December	3 492	96 142	7.2	5.9	6.7	17.6	6.3	15.0	10.3	4.1	5.8	10.2	7.5	13.6	8.5	10.5
1981																
January	3 429	96 526	7.5	6.1	6.7	19.1	6.7	14.6	10.6	4.2	6.1	10.3	7.6	13.7	8.4	10.8
February	3 345	96 846	7.4	6.1	6.6	19.3	6.6	14.7	11.3	4.2	5.8	10.0	7.6	13.8	8.5	12.4
March	3 365	97 206	7.4	6.0	6.6	19.2	6.5	15.1	10.2	4.2	5.9	9.7	7.4	14.9	8.2	12.1
April	3 529	97 527	7.2	5.9	6.5	18.8	6.4	14.7	9.5	3.8	5.8	9.8	7.3	14.5	7.7	9.5
May	3 369	97 679	7.5	6.2	6.7	19.1	6.6	14.8	10.0	4.0	5.7	10.4	7.6	15.9	7.8	10.9
June	3 334	96 964	7.5	6.2	6.7	19.8	6.5	15.7	10.3	4.3	5.7	10.5	7.4	16.3	7.5	12.6
July	3 296	97 397	7.2	5.9	6.7	18.6	6.3	15.0	10.0	4.0	5.7	11.3	7.3	15.3	7.5	11.4
August	3 379	97 310	7.4	6.1	6.7	18.8	6.3	16.3	10.0	4.1	5.5	10.3	7.4	16.1	7.3	12.4
September	3 361	96 703	7.6	6.2	7.0	19.7	6.6	15.9	9.6	4.3	6.0	10.6	7.7	15.8	7.9	11.7
October	3 412	96 966	7.9	6.7	7.1	20.3	6.9	16.7	10.7	4.6	6.1	10.6	8.0	17.4	8.5	13.3
November	3 415	96 792	8.3	7.0	7.2	21.3	7.3	16.8	11.2	4.9	6.5	10.9	8.3	17.6	9.3	13.8
December	3 227	96 418	8.5	7.5	7.4	21.1	7.5	17.2	11.7	5.4	6.5	10.4	8.9	17.6	10.5	14.0
1982																
January	3 393	96 299	8.6	7.6	7.3	22.0	7.6	17.3	11.7	5.4	6.3	10.4	8.8	18.8	10.4	15.0
February	3 375	96 387	8.9	7.7	7.7	22.6	7.8	17.7	12.1	5.4	6.9	10.4	9.1	18.3	10.6	13.4
March	3 372	96 300	9.0	8.0	7.9	21.8	8.0	18.1	12.2	5.7	7.0	10.6	9.4	18.3	10.8	13.9
April	3 351	96 225	9.3	8.2	8.2	22.8	8.3	18.2	12.9	6.0	7.7	11.3	9.8	19.3	11.3	14.8
May	3 434	96 682	9.4	8.3	8.1	22.8	8.2	18.5	13.9	6.1	7.2	11.9	9.9	18.8	11.6	18.0
June	3 331	96 212	9.6	8.7	8.1	22.9	8.5	18.5	13.8	6.5	7.0	12.1	10.0	19.5	12.4	15.2
July	3 402	96 091	9.8	8.9	8.3	24.0	8.7	18.8	14.2	6.7	7.3	12.3	10.3	20.4	12.4	14.6
August	3 408	96 225	9.8	9.0	8.3	23.7	8.7	18.9	14.8	6.8	7.2	11.8	10.2	20.4	12.4	14.7
September	3 385	96 119	10.1	9.5	8.4	23.6	9.0	19.7	14.4	7.1	7.5	12.2	10.6	21.7	13.6	13.4
October	3 489	95 726	10.4	9.8	8.7	23.7	9.2	20.1	15.0	7.4	7.9	11.3	10.9	22.6	13.8	12.5
November	3 510	95 602	10.8	10.0	9.1	24.1	9.6	20.2	15.2	7.5	8.5	12.6	11.4	21.7	14.5	15.7
December	3 414	95 618	10.8	10.1	9.3	24.1	9.7	20.9	15.7	7.5	8.2	13.5	11.5	21.5	14.3	16.2
1983																
January	3 439	95 722	10.4	9.7	9.0	23.1	9.1	21.2	15.3	7.2	7.8	13.3	10.9	20.4	13.0	15.6
February	3 382	95 707	10.4	9.9	8.9	22.8	9.3	19.9	15.5	7.2	7.6	13.0	10.9	19.8	13.3	16.3
March	3 360	95 819	10.3	9.7	8.8	23.5	9.1	20.1	15.6	7.2	7.5	13.2	10.8	20.5	12.9	16.1
April	3 341	96 219	10.2	9.7	8.4	23.4	8.9	20.4	14.8	7.1	7.3	13.0	10.5	20.4	12.4	17.6
May	3 328	96 314	10.1	9.6	8.4	22.8	8.8	20.3	14.0	7.0	7.4	12.8	10.5	20.2	12.4	17.2
June	3 462	97 171	10.1	9.1	8.7	24.0	8.7	20.7	14.3	6.6	7.8	12.6	10.1	18.2	11.6	17.3
July	3 481	97 727	9.4	8.8	7.9	22.8	8.2	19.4	12.4	6.1	6.9	12.1	9.6	17.8	10.8	14.5
August	3 502	98 106	9.5	8.7	7.9	22.9	8.2	19.7	13.0	6.4	6.8	11.6	9.7	18.0	11.1	15.0
September	3 347	98 669	9.2	8.5	7.7	21.7	8.0	18.8	12.9	6.0	6.7	11.8	9.2	17.9	10.0	15.8
October	3 303	98 736	8.8	8.2	7.5	21.4	7.7	18.2	12.1	5.7	6.3	11.3	9.0	15.6	9.5	16.0
November	3 291	99 438	8.5	7.8	7.2	20.2	7.4	17.5	12.3	5.5	6.2	10.4	8.6	15.2	8.9	15.6
December	3 332	99 664	8.3	7.5	7.3	19.9	7.1	17.8	11.6	5.2	6.3	11.2	8.4	16.3	8.5	15.7

Table 24-4. Civilian Employment and Selected Unemployment Rates—*Continued*

(Seasonally adjusted.)

| Year and month | Employment by industry (thousands of persons) | | Unemployment rates (percent of civilian labor force in group) | | | | | | | | | | | | | |
	Agricultural	Nonagricultural	All civilian workers	20 years and over Men	20 years and over Women	Both sexes, 16 to 19 years	By race White	By race Black	Persons of Hispanic origin	Married men, spouse present	Married women, spouse present	Women who maintain families	Private nonagricultural Total	Private nonagricultural Construction	Private nonagricultural Manufacturing	Agricultural
1984																
January	3 293	99 908	8.0	7.2	7.1	19.5	6.9	17.3	11.4	5.0	5.9	10.9	8.0	15.3	8.2	15.4
February	3 353	100 471	7.8	7.0	6.9	19.4	6.8	16.2	10.4	4.8	5.9	10.7	7.8	14.9	7.7	13.8
March	3 233	100 734	7.8	6.8	6.9	19.8	6.7	16.6	11.5	4.7	5.8	10.8	7.7	13.5	7.6	15.1
April	3 291	101 045	7.7	6.9	6.9	19.2	6.7	16.5	11.6	4.7	5.8	10.5	7.8	14.6	7.6	13.0
May	3 343	101 850	7.4	6.5	6.7	18.7	6.4	15.7	10.6	4.6	5.7	9.9	7.2	14.9	7.1	13.9
June	3 383	102 208	7.2	6.3	6.5	18.2	6.2	15.6	10.3	4.5	5.7	9.7	7.0	14.7	7.3	12.8
July	3 344	102 091	7.5	6.5	6.8	18.8	6.3	16.7	10.4	4.5	5.8	10.0	7.4	14.6	7.5	13.9
August	3 286	101 877	7.5	6.5	6.9	18.7	6.4	16.0	10.7	4.6	5.9	10.1	7.5	14.2	7.4	12.5
September	3 393	102 097	7.3	6.4	6.5	19.2	6.4	15.0	10.5	4.6	5.7	9.7	7.2	13.8	7.3	13.9
October	3 194	102 444	7.4	6.2	6.9	18.6	6.3	15.3	10.8	4.5	5.8	10.4	7.3	13.4	7.3	13.6
November	3 394	102 578	7.2	6.2	6.6	17.7	6.2	15.0	10.2	4.4	5.5	10.9	7.2	13.9	7.2	11.3
December	3 385	102 838	7.3	6.3	6.6	18.8	6.3	15.2	10.4	4.5	5.5	10.1	7.3	13.7	7.4	12.9
1985																
January	3 317	102 985	7.3	6.3	6.7	18.8	6.3	15.2	10.5	4.5	5.7	10.2	7.3	13.5	7.5	15.9
February	3 317	103 238	7.2	6.2	6.6	18.3	6.2	15.8	9.8	4.4	5.3	10.9	7.2	13.3	7.6	13.2
March	3 250	103 739	7.2	6.2	6.7	18.2	6.2	15.1	10.5	4.2	5.8	10.2	7.2	13.3	7.6	12.8
April	3 306	103 630	7.3	6.3	6.8	17.5	6.3	15.1	10.4	4.3	5.8	10.9	7.3	13.7	8.0	13.5
May	3 280	103 652	7.2	6.0	6.8	18.5	6.2	15.2	10.6	4.0	5.7	10.6	7.1	10.5	7.7	11.3
June	3 161	103 344	7.4	6.4	6.7	18.5	6.5	14.4	10.7	4.6	5.9	9.7	7.3	13.9	7.7	12.9
July	3 143	103 664	7.4	6.2	6.7	20.2	6.4	15.2	11.2	4.4	5.6	10.4	7.2	13.5	8.0	13.9
August	3 121	103 974	7.1	6.1	6.7	17.9	6.2	14.3	10.4	4.3	5.4	10.7	7.2	13.3	7.9	13.3
September	3 064	104 593	7.1	6.1	6.6	17.9	6.1	15.2	10.4	4.4	5.7	11.1	7.2	13.7	7.7	12.8
October	3 051	104 796	7.1	6.1	6.4	20.0	6.1	15.0	11.1	4.1	5.4	10.5	7.1	13.2	7.6	13.0
November	3 062	104 945	7.0	6.0	6.4	18.3	5.9	15.6	10.6	4.2	5.4	10.1	7.1	13.2	7.7	13.1
December	3 141	105 075	7.0	6.0	6.3	19.1	6.0	15.0	10.5	4.3	5.3	9.7	7.0	12.5	7.3	11.0
1986																
January	3 287	105 600	6.7	5.7	6.1	18.1	5.7	14.5	10.2	4.3	5.0	9.9	6.7	12.8	6.9	11.2
February	3 083	105 397	7.2	6.2	6.6	18.8	6.3	14.4	11.9	4.4	5.4	9.9	7.2	13.2	7.2	13.8
March	3 200	105 637	7.2	6.2	6.6	18.2	6.2	14.6	10.7	4.5	5.5	10.1	7.1	13.0	7.1	12.2
April	3 153	105 799	7.1	6.1	6.5	19.2	6.1	14.8	10.3	4.2	5.3	9.6	7.2	12.4	6.9	13.9
May	3 150	105 939	7.2	6.3	6.4	18.6	6.2	14.6	10.8	4.5	5.5	9.9	7.2	12.9	7.3	15.1
June	3 193	106 383	7.2	6.3	6.4	19.2	6.2	15.1	10.6	4.5	5.4	9.9	7.2	12.5	7.5	13.7
July	3 141	106 669	7.0	6.3	6.2	18.4	6.1	14.4	10.7	4.5	5.2	9.3	7.2	13.3	7.0	11.5
August	3 082	106 933	6.9	6.0	6.1	18.0	5.9	14.8	10.9	4.3	5.1	10.1	7.0	12.2	7.0	12.9
September	3 171	106 914	7.0	6.3	6.1	18.4	6.0	14.9	11.1	4.3	5.1	9.8	7.0	12.9	7.0	12.7
October	3 128	107 145	7.0	6.2	6.1	17.7	6.0	14.6	10.4	4.5	5.0	8.9	7.1	13.5	7.4	11.7
November	3 220	107 255	6.9	6.1	6.0	18.1	6.0	14.3	9.3	4.4	4.9	9.9	7.0	14.9	7.2	9.9
December	3 148	107 580	6.6	6.0	5.7	17.5	5.8	13.7	10.5	4.3	4.7	9.9	6.7	13.5	6.9	12.0
1987																
January	3 143	107 810	6.6	5.9	5.8	17.7	5.7	14.0	10.6	4.2	4.7	9.7	6.6	12.2	6.6	11.3
February	3 208	108 049	6.6	5.8	5.8	18.0	5.7	13.8	9.8	4.1	4.7	9.6	6.6	11.6	6.7	11.3
March	3 214	108 194	6.6	5.7	5.9	17.9	5.7	13.8	9.3	4.1	4.5	9.7	6.6	12.5	6.8	10.9
April	3 246	108 548	6.3	5.5	5.6	17.3	5.4	12.9	8.9	4.0	4.5	9.4	6.3	12.1	6.3	9.4
May	3 345	109 089	6.3	5.6	5.4	17.4	5.4	13.6	8.6	4.0	4.2	9.4	6.3	12.2	6.3	8.3
June	3 216	109 030	6.2	5.6	5.3	16.5	5.4	12.9	8.5	4.1	4.1	9.6	6.2	11.8	5.8	9.2
July	3 235	109 399	6.1	5.4	5.3	15.8	5.2	12.9	8.1	3.9	4.2	9.1	6.1	10.9	6.0	11.5
August	3 112	109 945	6.0	5.3	5.3	15.9	5.1	12.6	7.9	3.7	4.2	9.1	5.9	11.1	5.5	10.4
September	3 189	109 720	5.9	5.1	5.3	16.2	5.1	12.6	8.3	3.7	4.2	8.8	5.9	12.3	5.7	8.2
October	3 219	110 063	6.0	5.1	5.2	17.3	5.2	12.3	8.4	3.7	4.2	8.9	5.9	11.3	5.8	10.8
November	3 145	110 360	5.8	5.0	5.2	16.6	5.0	12.1	8.8	3.5	4.2	8.6	5.8	10.5	5.5	11.6
December	3 213	110 580	5.7	4.9	5.1	16.0	4.9	12.1	8.1	3.4	4.3	8.2	5.6	10.6	5.1	11.6
1988																
January	3 247	110 769	5.7	4.9	5.1	16.1	5.0	12.0	7.6	3.5	4.1	8.9	5.7	11.8	5.4	11.4
February	3 201	111 026	5.7	4.9	5.2	15.6	4.9	12.4	8.5	3.4	4.0	8.4	5.7	10.9	5.6	10.7
March	3 169	110 868	5.7	4.9	4.9	16.6	4.8	12.7	8.4	3.4	4.0	7.6	5.6	10.8	5.3	11.0
April	3 224	111 426	5.4	4.6	4.9	16.0	4.6	12.2	8.8	3.0	3.8	8.6	5.3	10.6	5.2	10.4
May	3 121	111 171	5.6	4.9	4.9	15.3	4.7	12.3	8.8	3.3	3.9	8.3	5.6	10.7	5.4	12.0
June	3 111	111 816	5.4	4.7	4.8	14.2	4.6	11.5	8.8	3.2	3.8	7.9	5.4	10.3	4.9	9.6
July	3 060	112 000	5.4	4.6	5.0	14.8	4.7	11.6	7.9	3.1	4.0	8.1	5.4	10.4	5.2	11.1
August	3 119	112 163	5.6	4.9	4.8	15.4	4.8	11.4	8.1	3.4	4.0	7.5	5.6	10.7	5.5	11.1
September	3 165	112 191	5.4	4.6	4.8	15.5	4.8	11.0	7.4	3.1	3.8	8.1	5.5	9.6	5.6	11.1
October	3 231	112 407	5.4	4.7	4.7	15.1	4.7	11.1	7.8	3.1	3.7	7.9	5.5	10.1	5.3	10.2
November	3 241	112 859	5.3	4.7	4.7	13.9	4.6	11.0	7.9	3.3	3.8	7.7	5.5	10.6	5.2	9.5
December	3 194	112 910	5.3	4.7	4.6	14.8	4.6	11.3	7.6	3.1	3.6	8.2	5.3	10.2	5.1	8.8
1989																
January	3 287	113 421	5.4	4.6	4.7	16.4	4.6	11.8	8.6	3.1	3.7	8.1	5.5	10.3	5.2	9.5
February	3 234	113 542	5.2	4.5	4.5	15.0	4.3	11.9	7.0	3.1	3.4	8.1	5.2	10.1	4.8	9.2
March	3 198	113 824	5.0	4.3	4.6	13.9	4.2	11.1	6.6	2.9	3.5	7.9	5.1	9.7	4.8	8.8
April	3 162	113 935	5.2	4.5	4.7	14.6	4.5	11.1	8.1	3.1	4.1	7.7	5.2	9.7	4.8	10.1
May	3 125	113 974	5.2	4.3	4.8	14.8	4.4	11.2	7.9	2.9	3.8	8.4	5.2	9.5	5.0	10.1
June	3 068	114 350	5.3	4.4	4.8	15.7	4.5	11.7	8.2	2.8	3.8	8.0	5.3	10.0	5.1	10.2
July	3 227	114 245	5.2	4.4	4.9	14.2	4.5	11.0	8.8	3.0	3.9	8.2	5.4	10.2	5.1	8.5
August	3 284	114 371	5.2	4.5	4.7	14.6	4.5	11.1	8.8	3.1	3.8	7.9	5.3	10.3	5.2	8.8
September	3 219	114 135	5.3	4.7	4.6	15.2	4.5	11.7	8.1	3.3	3.8	7.7	5.5	10.4	5.3	8.0
October	3 215	114 366	5.3	4.6	4.8	15.0	4.5	11.7	8.0	3.1	4.0	7.7	5.4	9.1	5.4	10.1
November	3 132	114 780	5.4	4.7	4.7	15.5	4.6	11.7	7.9	3.1	3.7	8.2	5.5	9.8	5.4	12.0
December	3 188	114 642	5.4	4.6	4.8	15.3	4.6	11.6	8.3	3.1	3.8	8.0	5.4	9.7	5.6	9.5

Table 24-4. Civilian Employment and Selected Unemployment Rates—*Continued*

(Seasonally adjusted.)

Year and month	Employment by industry (thousands of persons)		Unemployment rates (percent of civilian labor force in group)													
			All civilian workers	20 years and over		Both sexes, 16 to 19 years	By race		Persons of Hispanic origin	By marital or family status			Wage and salary workers, by industry of last job			
	Agricultural	Nonagricultural		Men	Women		White	Black		Married men, spouse present	Married women, spouse present	Women who maintain families	Private nonagricultural			Agricultural
													Total	Construction	Manufacturing	
1990																
January	3 210	115 871	5.4	4.7	4.7	14.8	4.6	11.1	7.3	3.4	3.7	7.9	5.5	9.2	6.0	8.9
February	3 188	115 871	5.3	4.5	4.7	15.0	4.6	11.0	7.5	3.1	3.7	7.8	5.4	9.2	5.6	9.1
March	3 260	115 943	5.2	4.6	4.7	14.3	4.5	10.9	7.4	3.1	3.6	8.2	5.3	10.0	5.5	9.3
April	3 231	115 621	5.4	4.8	4.8	14.7	4.7	10.7	8.5	3.3	3.6	7.6	5.6	10.3	5.6	12.3
May	3 266	115 885	5.4	4.7	4.7	15.0	4.6	10.6	7.9	3.2	3.6	7.9	5.5	11.4	5.6	8.8
June	3 245	115 738	5.2	4.7	4.6	14.3	4.5	10.5	7.7	3.1	3.6	8.2	5.3	9.8	5.0	9.4
July	3 192	115 618	5.5	4.9	4.9	15.0	4.7	11.4	8.0	3.4	3.8	8.4	5.6	10.5	5.8	9.8
August	3 197	115 605	5.7	5.1	5.0	16.3	4.9	11.7	8.3	3.5	4.0	8.3	5.8	11.6	5.9	9.9
September	3 206	115 318	5.9	5.2	5.1	16.4	5.0	12.1	8.3	3.5	4.0	9.0	6.0	12.1	6.1	10.0
October	3 270	115 266	5.9	5.4	5.1	16.5	5.1	12.1	8.5	3.7	4.1	8.7	6.1	13.0	5.9	9.3
November	3 189	115 117	6.2	5.7	5.2	17.1	5.3	12.4	8.9	3.9	4.2	9.0	6.4	13.8	6.3	9.6
December	3 245	114 996	6.3	5.8	5.2	17.4	5.4	12.4	9.9	3.9	4.1	9.0	6.5	14.2	6.8	11.9
1991																
January	3 208	114 732	6.4	5.8	5.4	18.6	5.6	11.9	9.1	4.1	4.1	9.3	6.5	14.4	6.9	12.0
February	3 270	114 485	6.6	6.2	5.5	17.4	5.8	12.2	9.2	4.3	4.4	9.2	6.9	15.4	7.2	11.2
March	3 177	114 475	6.8	6.4	5.6	18.3	6.0	12.5	9.8	4.4	4.7	9.0	7.0	14.1	7.6	13.0
April	3 241	114 868	6.7	6.4	5.5	17.8	5.9	12.7	9.8	4.5	4.6	9.5	7.0	14.8	7.5	11.7
May	3 275	114 165	6.9	6.4	6.0	18.8	6.1	12.8	10.0	4.4	4.7	9.5	7.1	14.9	7.5	12.2
June	3 300	114 339	6.9	6.5	5.8	18.5	6.2	12.5	10.1	4.5	4.6	9.2	7.2	15.2	7.7	11.7
July	3 319	114 249	6.8	6.5	5.5	19.4	6.2	11.9	9.6	4.3	4.5	8.3	7.2	16.4	7.0	10.8
August	3 313	114 171	6.9	6.5	5.7	18.9	6.2	12.4	10.5	4.4	4.5	9.5	7.1	15.4	7.3	11.8
September	3 319	114 609	6.9	6.6	5.7	18.8	6.2	12.3	10.9	4.5	4.6	9.4	7.1	15.9	7.0	11.9
October	3 289	114 511	7.0	6.5	5.9	19.1	6.2	13.3	10.7	4.3	4.5	9.7	7.1	16.2	6.9	12.4
November	3 296	114 474	7.0	6.6	6.0	19.0	6.3	12.5	10.4	4.7	4.6	9.5	7.4	16.9	7.2	12.0
December	3 146	114 320	7.3	6.8	6.1	20.3	6.5	12.9	10.2	4.9	4.9	9.2	7.6	16.8	7.5	11.2
1992																
January	3 155	114 823	7.3	7.1	6.0	19.2	6.4	13.5	11.0	4.9	4.8	9.2	7.5	17.1	7.5	11.2
February	3 239	114 514	7.4	7.1	6.2	20.1	6.5	14.2	11.3	5.1	5.0	9.6	7.7	17.9	7.7	11.2
March	3 236	114 908	7.4	7.0	6.2	20.3	6.5	14.1	11.2	4.8	5.0	10.0	7.7	17.2	7.5	10.1
April	3 245	115 181	7.4	7.1	6.3	18.5	6.5	14.1	11.0	4.9	5.1	10.0	7.7	16.5	7.7	11.9
May	3 213	115 162	7.6	7.3	6.3	20.1	6.6	14.7	11.7	5.1	5.1	10.1	7.9	16.8	7.9	14.6
June	3 297	115 122	7.8	7.4	6.4	23.0	6.9	14.6	12.1	5.2	5.2	10.2	7.9	17.1	8.2	13.0
July	3 285	115 428	7.7	7.2	6.5	20.8	6.7	14.4	11.7	5.2	5.2	10.4	7.9	16.5	8.1	13.9
August	3 279	115 547	7.6	7.2	6.5	19.9	6.7	14.2	11.7	5.3	5.0	10.7	8.0	16.8	7.9	11.1
September	3 274	115 446	7.6	7.1	6.4	21.0	6.7	13.9	11.8	5.3	5.0	9.6	7.9	17.4	8.0	16.0
October	3 254	115 374	7.3	7.1	6.2	18.3	6.5	14.3	11.8	5.2	5.0	9.4	7.8	16.0	8.1	13.1
November	3 207	115 669	7.4	7.0	6.2	20.5	6.5	14.1	12.0	5.0	5.0	11.0	7.6	15.4	7.9	14.2
December	3 259	115 738	7.4	6.8	6.5	19.8	6.5	14.3	11.5	4.9	5.0	10.1	7.7	16.3	7.5	12.3
1993																
January	3 222	115 853	7.3	6.7	6.3	19.9	6.3	14.1	11.3	4.6	5.0	10.4	7.4	14.5	7.5	11.4
February	3 125	116 150	7.1	6.6	6.1	19.7	6.2	13.5	11.5	4.6	4.6	10.2	7.3	14.3	7.4	12.2
March	3 119	116 423	7.0	6.8	5.8	19.7	6.1	13.7	11.3	4.6	4.4	9.2	7.2	14.9	7.4	11.6
April	3 074	116 400	7.1	6.6	6.1	19.5	6.1	14.0	11.0	4.6	5.0	9.6	7.3	14.6	7.4	12.3
May	3 100	117 015	7.1	6.5	6.0	19.8	6.2	13.1	10.2	4.6	4.7	10.0	7.3	15.2	7.2	11.3
June	3 108	117 182	7.0	6.6	6.0	19.9	6.2	13.4	10.4	4.5	4.7	9.9	7.2	15.0	7.5	11.9
July	3 126	117 341	6.9	6.5	5.9	18.4	6.1	12.7	10.7	4.5	4.7	9.7	7.1	16.2	7.2	12.0
August	3 026	117 830	6.8	6.3	5.8	18.4	6.0	12.3	9.8	4.4	4.4	9.2	7.0	14.8	7.4	12.4
September	3 174	117 380	6.7	6.3	5.8	18.2	5.9	12.5	10.0	4.3	4.6	9.2	7.0	14.2	7.2	10.8
October	3 084	117 739	6.8	6.2	5.9	18.7	6.2	11.8	11.4	4.4	4.7	9.4	7.0	13.9	6.8	12.3
November	3 157	118 012	6.6	5.9	5.8	18.5	5.7	12.6	10.5	4.1	4.5	9.6	6.8	12.8	6.6	11.0
December	3 116	118 348	6.5	5.9	5.8	17.9	5.8	11.7	10.6	4.0	4.5	10.0	6.7	13.1	6.7	11.5
1994																
January	3 302	118 664	6.6	6.0	5.8	18.3	5.7	13.1	10.5	4.1	4.4	9.1	6.9	13.3	6.2	13.0
February	3 339	118 747	6.6	6.0	5.7	18.0	5.7	12.8	10.1	4.4	4.4	9.6	6.9	13.2	6.3	13.8
March	3 354	118 576	6.5	5.8	5.8	18.0	5.7	12.4	9.9	4.1	4.4	9.4	6.7	13.3	6.1	13.0
April	3 428	118 862	6.4	5.6	5.6	19.1	5.6	11.9	10.8	3.9	4.1	9.4	6.5	12.3	5.8	10.6
May	3 409	119 455	6.1	5.3	5.4	18.0	5.2	11.7	9.6	3.7	4.1	9.0	6.2	11.5	5.4	8.8
June	3 299	119 335	6.1	5.3	5.4	17.6	5.3	11.3	10.3	3.6	4.2	8.8	6.2	12.2	5.3	8.5
July	3 333	119 373	6.1	5.5	5.2	17.6	5.3	10.9	10.1	3.6	4.0	7.7	6.2	11.4	5.5	13.4
August	3 451	119 891	6.0	5.4	5.3	17.3	5.2	11.2	9.8	3.5	4.2	8.9	6.1	10.7	5.4	12.7
September	3 430	120 257	5.9	5.1	5.3	17.5	5.1	10.6	10.1	3.3	4.1	8.9	6.0	10.6	5.4	10.8
October	3 490	120 622	5.8	5.1	5.0	17.5	5.0	11.3	9.5	3.3	3.9	8.8	5.9	10.6	5.2	9.9
November	3 574	120 942	5.6	4.9	5.1	15.6	4.8	10.8	8.9	3.3	3.9	8.5	5.8	10.5	4.8	9.7
December	3 577	121 144	5.5	4.7	4.8	17.0	4.8	9.9	9.3	3.2	3.7	9.0	5.6	11.1	4.9	9.8
1995																
January	3 519	121 144	5.6	4.9	4.9	16.5	4.8	10.3	10.2	3.3	3.7	8.7	5.7	11.4	4.8	10.9
February	3 620	121 308	5.4	4.6	4.8	17.4	4.7	10.1	9.0	3.2	3.7	8.3	5.6	10.6	4.5	9.8
March	3 634	121 321	5.4	4.7	4.8	16.1	4.7	9.7	8.9	3.2	3.9	7.6	5.6	11.0	4.6	10.1
April	3 566	121 379	5.8	4.9	5.2	17.5	5.0	10.7	8.9	3.4	4.1	9.4	5.9	11.7	4.8	11.0
May	3 349	121 072	5.6	5.0	4.8	17.5	5.0	10.0	9.8	3.4	3.8	8.1	6.0	12.4	5.3	12.1
June	3 461	121 061	5.6	4.8	5.0	17.1	4.9	10.7	9.1	3.4	3.8	8.5	5.7	11.2	5.0	11.7
July	3 379	121 437	5.7	4.8	5.0	18.2	4.9	10.9	8.8	3.4	4.0	8.2	5.9	11.3	5.2	11.1
August	3 374	121 478	5.7	4.9	5.0	17.3	4.9	11.1	9.6	3.3	4.2	7.0	5.8	12.1	4.9	10.1
September	3 285	121 848	5.6	4.8	4.9	17.6	4.9	11.1	9.1	3.4	4.0	8.1	5.9	12.6	4.9	11.3
October	3 438	121 950	5.5	4.6	5.0	17.4	4.9	10.0	9.4	3.1	3.9	7.9	5.8	11.5	4.9	12.0
November	3 338	121 850	5.6	4.9	4.8	17.5	5.0	9.7	9.5	3.3	3.7	7.6	5.8	11.9	5.1	11.3
December	3 352	121 736	5.6	4.9	4.8	18.0	4.9	10.2	9.3	3.1	3.8	6.9	5.8	11.1	4.9	11.7

Table 24-5. Nonfarm Employment

(Wage and salary workers on nonfarm payrolls; thousands, seasonally adjusted.)

Year and month	Total	Goods-producing industries [1]					Service-producing industries							
		Total	Construc-tion	Manufacturing			Total	Transpor-tation and public utilities	Wholesale trade	Retail trade	Finance insurance, and real estate	Services (private)	Government	
				Total	Durable goods	Nondur-able goods							Total	Federal
1972														
January	72 303	23 210	3 852	18 730	10 691	8 039	49 093	4 485	4 059	11 585	3 848	11 990	13 126	2 703
February	72 525	23 260	3 810	18 824	10 762	8 062	49 265	4 497	4 067	11 653	3 854	12 024	13 170	2 698
March	72 808	23 384	3 847	18 909	10 822	8 087	49 424	4 527	4 090	11 677	3 865	12 065	13 200	2 691
April	73 061	23 487	3 877	18 989	10 883	8 106	49 574	4 519	4 102	11 703	3 878	12 133	13 239	2 695
May	73 341	23 590	3 897	19 069	10 942	8 127	49 751	4 522	4 108	11 745	3 886	12 201	13 289	2 691
June	73 643	23 677	3 911	19 139	10 985	8 154	49 966	4 543	4 132	11 791	3 914	12 330	13 256	2 676
July	73 636	23 586	3 878	19 086	10 972	8 114	50 050	4 535	4 129	11 805	3 917	12 320	13 344	2 645
August	73 929	23 700	3 911	19 161	11 039	8 122	50 229	4 533	4 142	11 852	3 926	12 367	13 409	2 666
September	74 115	23 797	3 918	19 244	11 101	8 143	50 318	4 564	4 151	11 871	3 933	12 362	13 437	2 671
October	74 527	24 003	3 951	19 418	11 247	8 171	50 524	4 578	4 161	11 943	3 945	12 440	13 457	2 674
November	74 881	24 121	3 930	19 558	11 353	8 205	50 760	4 584	4 181	12 035	3 959	12 499	13 502	2 678
December	75 235	24 179	3 848	19 703	11 470	8 233	51 056	4 611	4 200	12 174	3 967	12 562	13 542	2 684
1973														
January	75 474	24 368	3 932	19 808	11 555	8 253	51 106	4 598	4 216	12 139	3 976	12 630	13 547	2 673
February	75 908	24 610	4 020	19 957	11 677	8 280	51 298	4 605	4 241	12 176	4 000	12 689	13 587	2 665
March	76 137	24 690	4 027	20 031	11 734	8 297	51 447	4 623	4 249	12 211	4 015	12 730	13 619	2 664
April	76 312	24 754	4 045	20 077	11 769	8 308	51 558	4 630	4 258	12 226	4 021	12 759	13 664	2 667
May	76 516	24 814	4 078	20 104	11 811	8 293	51 702	4 644	4 261	12 295	4 033	12 773	13 696	2 670
June	76 738	24 928	4 125	20 167	11 863	8 304	51 810	4 643	4 290	12 314	4 045	12 793	13 725	2 655
July	76 758	24 940	4 154	20 145	11 887	8 258	51 818	4 645	4 300	12 314	4 059	12 779	13 721	2 624
August	77 018	24 992	4 143	20 202	11 925	8 277	52 026	4 663	4 319	12 324	4 064	12 885	13 771	2 645
September	77 164	24 978	4 145	20 185	11 921	8 264	52 186	4 693	4 318	12 372	4 072	12 981	13 750	2 654
October	77 502	25 113	4 138	20 323	12 024	8 299	52 389	4 711	4 335	12 413	4 075	13 021	13 834	2 659
November	77 833	25 214	4 147	20 408	12 081	8 327	52 619	4 703	4 350	12 483	4 089	13 099	13 895	2 668
December	77 992	25 264	4 168	20 431	12 102	8 329	52 728	4 716	4 360	12 500	4 100	13 133	13 919	2 680
1974														
January	77 953	25 175	4 144	20 359	12 043	8 316	52 778	4 737	4 399	12 420	4 113	13 172	13 937	2 683
February	78 177	25 211	4 251	20 284	11 986	8 298	52 966	4 738	4 419	12 431	4 131	13 239	14 008	2 699
March	78 177	25 134	4 216	20 242	11 958	8 284	53 043	4 737	4 422	12 437	4 133	13 280	14 034	2 705
April	78 261	25 102	4 156	20 260	12 004	8 256	53 159	4 731	4 430	12 479	4 137	13 303	14 079	2 711
May	78 407	25 067	4 131	20 244	11 987	8 257	53 340	4 733	4 441	12 529	4 145	13 390	14 102	2 719
June	78 434	25 017	4 064	20 258	12 017	8 241	53 417	4 734	4 455	12 541	4 157	13 444	14 086	2 723
July	78 517	24 925	3 975	20 250	12 035	8 215	53 592	4 740	4 461	12 563	4 158	13 515	14 155	2 729
August	78 478	24 833	3 966	20 157	11 951	8 206	53 645	4 734	4 468	12 542	4 158	13 533	14 210	2 732
September	78 498	24 721	3 921	20 089	11 915	8 174	53 777	4 713	4 463	12 608	4 161	13 552	14 280	2 739
October	78 569	24 582	3 882	19 978	11 874	8 104	53 987	4 716	4 476	12 685	4 164	13 616	14 330	2 737
November	78 238	24 216	3 827	19 663	11 666	7 997	54 022	4 704	4 481	12 647	4 164	13 646	14 380	2 738
December	77 565	23 653	3 774	19 185	11 345	7 840	53 912	4 688	4 459	12 574	4 158	13 636	14 397	2 738
1975														
January	77 145	23 266	3 757	18 769	11 076	7 693	53 879	4 645	4 438	12 478	4 151	13 649	14 518	2 735
February	76 742	22 781	3 641	18 397	10 831	7 566	53 961	4 596	4 418	12 500	4 144	13 696	14 607	2 736
March	76 419	22 481	3 522	18 216	10 716	7 500	53 938	4 565	4 402	12 491	4 141	13 722	14 617	2 737
April	76 298	22 335	3 461	18 134	10 617	7 517	53 963	4 548	4 405	12 443	4 149	13 769	14 649	2 737
May	76 459	22 359	3 471	18 139	10 581	7 558	54 100	4 543	4 402	12 524	4 150	13 813	14 668	2 739
June	76 388	22 291	3 454	18 091	10 524	7 567	54 097	4 519	4 400	12 595	4 151	13 792	14 640	2 738
July	76 626	22 254	3 447	18 060	10 455	7 605	54 372	4 521	4 416	12 636	4 157	13 947	14 695	2 750
August	76 980	22 448	3 484	18 205	10 529	7 676	54 532	4 519	4 427	12 696	4 169	14 018	14 703	2 750
September	77 188	22 607	3 508	18 350	10 613	7 737	54 581	4 522	4 449	12 717	4 178	14 001	14 714	2 756
October	77 499	22 723	3 516	18 447	10 638	7 809	54 776	4 520	4 456	12 772	4 192	14 058	14 778	2 757
November	77 619	22 765	3 527	18 473	10 640	7 833	54 854	4 519	4 469	12 805	4 194	14 103	14 764	2 754
December	77 915	22 891	3 547	18 567	10 700	7 867	55 024	4 496	4 482	12 883	4 207	14 159	14 797	2 753
1976														
January	78 326	23 070	3 588	18 703	10 793	7 910	55 256	4 539	4 497	12 934	4 211	14 242	14 833	2 750
February	78 606	23 165	3 589	18 798	10 856	7 942	55 441	4 550	4 516	13 029	4 218	14 293	14 835	2 744
March	78 819	23 237	3 572	18 907	10 929	7 958	55 582	4 559	4 528	13 051	4 228	14 367	14 849	2 739
April	79 134	23 360	3 587	18 999	11 005	7 994	55 774	4 568	4 549	13 137	4 240	14 435	14 845	2 736
May	79 192	23 320	3 564	18 985	11 050	7 935	55 872	4 568	4 560	13 177	4 250	14 481	14 836	2 733
June	79 258	23 315	3 555	18 992	11 069	7 923	55 943	4 575	4 562	13 168	4 262	14 541	14 835	2 723
July	79 485	23 359	3 564	19 015	11 078	7 937	56 126	4 595	4 569	13 207	4 266	14 622	14 867	2 723
August	79 581	23 356	3 567	19 031	11 117	7 914	56 225	4 595	4 570	13 261	4 275	14 639	14 885	2 724
September	79 842	23 498	3 565	19 152	11 177	7 975	56 344	4 615	4 587	13 307	4 300	14 665	14 870	2 727
October	79 842	23 406	3 571	19 049	11 094	7 955	56 436	4 597	4 592	13 315	4 319	14 708	14 905	2 726
November	80 141	23 555	3 601	19 161	11 196	7 965	56 586	4 605	4 600	13 341	4 330	14 775	14 935	2 732
December	80 338	23 580	3 590	19 186	11 218	7 968	56 758	4 631	4 611	13 386	4 347	14 836	14 947	2 728
1977														
January	80 517	23 628	3 542	19 276	11 276	8 000	56 889	4 647	4 624	13 441	4 363	14 893	14 921	2 723
February	80 794	23 803	3 665	19 321	11 288	8 033	56 991	4 656	4 633	13 475	4 375	14 939	14 913	2 724
March	81 221	24 000	3 739	19 436	11 381	8 055	57 221	4 657	4 653	13 580	4 401	15 014	14 916	2 729
April	81 610	24 186	3 813	19 546	11 446	8 100	57 424	4 678	4 675	13 634	4 422	15 086	14 929	2 723
May	81 977	24 308	3 843	19 639	11 520	8 119	57 669	4 701	4 692	13 704	4 437	15 147	14 988	2 724
June	82 381	24 431	3 879	19 723	11 582	8 141	57 950	4 707	4 713	13 762	4 454	15 232	15 082	2 724
July	82 760	24 515	3 908	19 799	11 658	8 141	58 245	4 725	4 735	13 806	4 469	15 336	15 174	2 720
August	82 974	24 508	3 911	19 796	11 656	8 140	58 466	4 727	4 754	13 872	4 484	15 411	15 218	2 726
September	83 431	24 612	3 935	19 851	11 704	8 147	58 819	4 766	4 776	13 942	4 513	15 529	15 293	2 731
October	83 661	24 656	3 944	19 878	11 731	8 147	59 005	4 747	4 787	13 998	4 538	15 600	15 335	2 729
November	84 031	24 739	3 967	19 926	11 762	8 164	59 292	4 764	4 809	14 091	4 565	15 693	15 370	2 731
December	84 271	24 746	3 991	20 057	11 868	8 189	59 525	4 784	4 831	14 169	4 581	15 750	15 410	2 746

1. Includes mining, not shown seperately.

Table 24-5. Nonfarm Employment—*Continued*

(Wage and salary workers on nonfarm payrolls; thousands, seasonally adjusted.)

Year and month	Total	Goods-producing industries [1]					Service-producing industries							
		Total	Construc-tion	Manufacturing			Total	Transportation and public utilities	Wholesale trade	Retail trade	Finance insurance, and real estate	Services (private)	Government	
				Total	Durable goods	Nondurable goods							Total	Federal
1978														
January	84 464	24 780	3 941	20 145	11 942	8 203	59 684	4 804	4 848	14 222	4 600	15 745	15 465	2 739
February	84 808	24 870	3 968	20 203	11 987	8 216	59 938	4 825	4 872	14 249	4 631	15 837	15 524	2 740
March	85 338	25 055	4 065	20 277	12 034	8 243	60 283	4 858	4 898	14 338	4 650	15 947	15 592	2 740
April	86 083	25 458	4 220	20 358	12 100	8 258	60 625	4 896	4 930	14 402	4 666	16 066	15 665	2 748
May	86 404	25 507	4 211	20 413	12 153	8 260	60 897	4 908	4 956	14 485	4 688	16 153	15 707	2 752
June	86 811	25 656	4 283	20 491	12 212	8 279	61 155	4 938	4 983	14 560	4 718	16 237	15 719	2 757
July	87 037	25 717	4 304	20 523	12 258	8 265	61 320	4 906	4 991	14 613	4 740	16 330	15 740	2 760
August	87 324	25 778	4 310	20 570	12 308	8 262	61 546	4 929	5 020	14 651	4 755	16 435	15 756	2 761
September	87 434	25 820	4 311	20 616	12 363	8 253	61 614	4 953	5 039	14 688	4 772	16 475	15 687	2 764
October	87 797	25 972	4 336	20 729	12 462	8 267	61 825	4 993	5 069	14 752	4 794	16 496	15 721	2 764
November	88 249	26 116	4 347	20 851	12 548	8 303	62 133	5 021	5 095	14 835	4 827	16 612	15 743	2 764
December	88 559	26 235	4 352	20 956	12 624	8 332	62 324	5 044	5 122	14 860	4 845	16 691	15 762	2 746
1979														
January	88 728	26 264	4 309	21 019	12 677	8 342	62 464	5 062	5 148	14 914	4 871	16 692	15 777	2 757
February	88 985	26 319	4 326	21 043	12 717	8 326	62 666	5 082	5 160	14 938	4 891	16 799	15 796	2 757
March	89 426	26 511	4 456	21 102	12 768	8 334	62 915	5 101	5 182	15 004	4 907	16 908	15 813	2 754
April	89 363	26 462	4 423	21 092	12 766	8 326	62 901	5 005	5 188	14 968	4 924	16 955	15 861	2 758
May	89 681	26 527	4 467	21 110	12 781	8 329	63 154	5 109	5 206	14 958	4 952	17 042	15 887	2 769
June	89 955	26 599	4 493	21 162	12 828	8 334	63 356	5 166	5 230	14 931	4 971	17 120	15 938	2 776
July	90 019	26 606	4 505	21 148	12 819	8 329	63 413	5 163	5 235	14 881	4 986	17 148	16 000	2 782
August	90 159	26 474	4 506	21 003	12 698	8 305	63 685	5 188	5 242	14 901	5 015	17 221	16 118	2 811
September	90 149	26 471	4 495	21 012	12 745	8 267	63 678	5 178	5 247	14 945	5 014	17 261	16 033	2 776
October	90 360	26 467	4 496	20 998	12 705	8 293	63 893	5 183	5 264	15 033	5 039	17 337	16 037	2 775
November	90 466	26 383	4 497	20 908	12 631	8 277	64 083	5 198	5 280	15 098	5 055	17 390	16 062	2 778
December	90 617	26 451	4 533	20 929	12 655	8 274	64 166	5 196	5 266	15 083	5 068	17 471	16 082	2 785
1980														
January	90 729	26 448	4 570	20 892	12 614	8 278	64 281	5 195	5 290	15 095	5 092	17 506	16 103	2 790
February	90 876	26 386	4 550	20 834	12 611	8 223	64 490	5 186	5 310	15 125	5 108	17 617	16 144	2 820
March	90 995	26 307	4 461	20 833	12 617	8 216	64 688	5 182	5 315	15 142	5 122	17 703	16 224	2 881
April	90 780	25 979	4 380	20 573	12 384	8 189	64 801	5 165	5 296	15 025	5 125	17 746	16 444	3 111
May	90 316	25 630	4 333	20 258	12 117	8 141	64 686	5 151	5 280	14 986	5 139	17 804	16 326	2 958
June	89 974	25 331	4 287	20 003	11 925	8 078	64 643	5 126	5 266	14 942	5 152	17 847	16 310	2 946
July	89 676	25 042	4 246	19 777	11 761	8 016	64 634	5 120	5 263	14 921	5 161	17 919	16 250	2 891
August	89 964	25 197	4 259	19 929	11 852	8 077	64 767	5 118	5 270	14 955	5 173	17 990	16 261	2 829
September	90 046	25 254	4 271	19 959	11 894	8 065	64 792	5 120	5 288	14 967	5 184	18 051	16 182	2 783
October	90 334	25 371	4 286	20 048	11 974	8 074	64 963	5 136	5 297	14 992	5 211	18 095	16 232	2 794
November	90 550	25 485	4 282	20 146	12 066	8 080	65 065	5 130	5 310	15 019	5 223	18 156	16 227	2 797
December	90 774	25 585	4 306	20 199	12 112	8 087	65 189	5 139	5 325	15 045	5 230	18 240	16 210	2 799
1981														
January	91 003	25 594	4 265	20 236	12 151	8 085	65 409	5 150	5 347	15 096	5 261	18 357	16 198	2 797
February	91 095	25 575	4 272	20 197	12 105	8 092	65 520	5 159	5 358	15 146	5 271	18 400	16 186	2 789
March	91 206	25 654	4 306	20 227	12 132	8 095	65 552	5 163	5 365	15 163	5 277	18 439	16 145	2 781
April	91 219	25 567	4 313	20 274	12 173	8 101	65 652	5 161	5 381	15 208	5 290	18 487	16 125	2 780
May	91 142	25 511	4 240	20 277	12 167	8 110	65 631	5 157	5 376	15 204	5 297	18 533	16 064	2 774
June	91 285	25 634	4 194	20 286	12 174	8 112	65 651	5 163	5 380	15 185	5 298	18 581	16 044	2 780
July	91 410	25 630	4 168	20 278	12 151	8 127	65 780	5 180	5 381	15 170	5 305	18 624	16 120	2 787
August	91 320	25 559	4 144	20 219	12 104	8 115	65 761	5 184	5 381	15 199	5 310	18 682	16 005	2 772
September	91 191	25 564	4 119	20 240	12 120	8 120	65 627	5 176	5 380	15 217	5 311	18 725	15 818	2 752
October	91 216	25 443	4 117	20 119	12 048	8 071	65 773	5 169	5 385	15 203	5 315	18 805	15 896	2 756
November	91 014	25 264	4 092	19 960	11 916	8 044	65 750	5 170	5 388	15 135	5 316	18 848	15 893	2 751
December	90 831	25 044	4 075	19 756	11 751	8 005	65 787	5 151	5 382	15 145	5 318	18 896	15 895	2 743
1982														
January	90 448	24 695	3 930	19 555	11 621	7 934	65 753	5 147	5 368	15 090	5 325	18 945	15 878	2 740
February	90 474	24 709	4 014	19 479	11 553	7 926	65 765	5 139	5 358	15 128	5 327	18 964	15 849	2 738
March	90 337	24 544	3 981	19 344	11 467	7 877	65 793	5 128	5 353	15 134	5 333	18 977	15 868	2 736
April	90 031	24 292	3 953	19 136	11 308	7 828	65 739	5 108	5 333	15 140	5 331	18 954	15 873	2 737
May	89 965	24 165	3 977	19 013	11 211	7 802	65 800	5 113	5 324	15 177	5 332	18 984	15 870	2 724
June	89 703	23 898	3 919	18 828	11 075	7 753	65 805	5 095	5 303	15 175	5 342	18 996	15 894	2 742
July	89 380	23 670	3 888	18 663	10 967	7 696	65 710	5 079	5 288	15 172	5 341	19 025	15 805	2 749
August	89 177	23 479	3 867	18 519	10 807	7 712	65 698	5 065	5 272	15 182	5 341	19 035	15 803	2 743
September	88 995	23 396	3 853	18 471	10 761	7 710	65 599	5 043	5 254	15 191	5 345	19 040	15 726	2 718
October	88 787	23 126	3 837	18 242	10 558	7 684	65 661	5 033	5 241	15 175	5 348	19 059	15 805	2 740
November	88 649	22 964	3 844	18 095	10 446	7 649	65 685	5 023	5 231	15 139	5 356	19 118	15 818	2 748
December	88 675	22 894	3 840	18 047	10 412	7 635	65 781	5 016	5 220	15 209	5 360	19 152	15 824	2 746
1983														
January	88 826	22 930	3 877	18 062	10 424	7 638	65 896	4 977	5 214	15 254	5 375	19 202	15 874	2 772
February	88 758	22 846	3 820	18 060	10 427	7 633	65 912	4 969	5 213	15 264	5 389	19 217	15 860	2 766
March	88 946	22 826	3 793	18 077	10 435	7 642	66 120	4 977	5 209	15 333	5 398	19 337	15 866	2 765
April	89 211	22 911	3 808	18 159	10 495	7 664	66 300	4 989	5 225	15 383	5 421	19 430	15 852	2 763
May	89 497	23 041	3 841	18 260	10 575	7 685	66 456	4 995	5 239	15 427	5 432	19 496	15 867	2 768
June	89 886	23 172	3 902	18 330	10 620	7 710	66 714	4 994	5 263	15 505	5 444	19 622	15 886	2 769
July	90 313	23 334	3 946	18 443	10 712	7 731	66 979	4 999	5 278	15 608	5 470	19 729	15 895	2 775
August	89 973	23 430	3 993	18 495	10 750	7 745	66 543	4 366	5 299	15 687	5 494	19 819	15 878	2 775
September	91 088	23 628	4 031	18 654	10 868	7 786	67 460	5 045	5 325	15 781	5 517	19 922	15 870	2 784
October	91 408	23 809	4 069	18 788	10 978	7 810	67 599	5 047	5 349	15 846	5 529	19 976	15 852	2 786
November	91 727	23 961	4 108	18 901	11 069	7 832	67 766	5 034	5 377	15 910	5 548	20 048	15 849	2 778
December	92 110	24 058	4 132	18 972	11 130	7 842	68 052	5 037	5 406	16 024	5 571	20 150	15 864	2 781

1. Includes mining, not shown seperately.

Table 24-5. Nonfarm Employment—*Continued*

(Wage and salary workers on nonfarm payrolls; thousands, seasonally adjusted.)

Year and month	Total	Goods-producing industries [1]					Service-producing industries							
		Total	Construc-tion	Manufacturing			Total	Transpor-tation and public utilities	Wholesale trade	Retail trade	Finance insurance, and real estate	Services (private)	Government	
				Total	Durable goods	Nondur-able goods							Total	Federal
1984														
January	92 524	24 199	4 174	19 066	11 202	7 864	68 325	5 087	5 443	16 121	5 585	20 221	15 868	2 778
February	93 043	24 430	4 296	19 172	11 287	7 885	68 613	5 103	5 480	16 201	5 603	20 337	15 889	2 784
March	93 312	24 496	4 269	19 263	11 360	7 903	68 816	5 117	5 500	16 258	5 624	20 422	15 895	2 788
April	93 650	24 586	4 294	19 329	11 403	7 926	69 064	5 127	5 521	16 325	5 634	20 520	15 937	2 794
May	93 952	24 675	4 334	19 372	11 446	7 926	69 277	5 144	5 536	16 353	5 651	20 627	15 966	2 802
June	94 325	24 783	4 387	19 420	11 498	7 922	69 542	5 164	5 555	16 447	5 670	20 718	15 988	2 806
July	94 647	24 865	4 405	19 484	11 554	7 930	69 782	5 166	5 587	16 522	5 685	20 768	16 054	2 813
August	94 885	24 897	4 421	19 498	11 584	7 914	69 988	5 186	5 602	16 568	5 705	20 825	16 102	2 817
September	95 186	24 893	4 455	19 462	11 580	7 882	70 293	5 184	5 626	16 663	5 725	20 986	16 109	2 817
October	95 499	24 909	4 467	19 480	11 598	7 882	70 590	5 196	5 642	16 768	5 752	21 082	16 150	2 824
November	95 829	24 917	4 495	19 467	11 596	7 871	70 912	5 196	5 656	16 929	5 773	21 181	16 177	2 831
December	95 997	24 963	4 535	19 483	11 614	7 869	71 034	5 200	5 671	16 958	5 798	21 257	16 150	2 834
1985														
January	96 249	24 968	4 550	19 472	11 616	7 856	71 281	5 213	5 687	16 972	5 817	21 391	16 201	2 834
February	96 397	24 914	4 549	19 420	11 580	7 840	71 483	5 223	5 689	17 034	5 836	21 477	16 224	2 835
March	96 734	24 953	4 615	19 393	11 568	7 825	71 781	5 204	5 707	17 150	5 859	21 598	16 263	2 846
April	96 896	24 918	4 640	19 328	11 520	7 808	71 978	5 220	5 710	17 209	5 884	21 670	16 285	2 856
May	97 163	24 893	4 664	19 285	11 497	7 788	72 270	5 231	5 717	17 291	5 907	21 795	16 329	2 868
June	97 280	24 843	4 659	19 246	11 469	7 777	72 437	5 232	5 725	17 343	5 928	21 858	16 351	2 878
July	97 465	24 786	4 659	19 200	11 428	7 772	72 679	5 241	5 728	17 353	5 950	21 915	16 492	2 888
August	97 696	24 795	4 688	19 186	11 407	7 779	72 901	5 227	5 737	17 413	5 978	22 055	16 491	2 896
September	97 878	24 761	4 724	19 124	11 358	7 766	73 117	5 243	5 745	17 443	6 008	22 186	16 492	2 894
October	98 098	24 768	4 740	19 124	11 365	7 759	73 330	5 253	5 756	17 475	6 038	22 287	16 521	2 895
November	98 286	24 754	4 750	19 108	11 351	7 757	73 532	5 254	5 761	17 511	6 071	22 405	16 530	2 903
December	98 500	24 765	4 765	19 110	11 342	7 768	73 735	5 257	5 762	17 579	6 103	22 482	16 552	2 910
1986														
January	98 599	24 787	4 793	19 105	11 341	7 764	73 812	5 260	5 756	17 584	6 116	22 527	16 569	2 914
February	98 718	24 738	4 789	19 077	11 313	7 764	73 980	5 255	5 755	17 618	6 150	22 588	16 614	2 914
March	98 796	24 679	4 795	19 039	11 283	7 756	74 117	5 246	5 744	17 684	6 174	22 663	16 606	2 914
April	98 974	24 651	4 823	19 016	11 266	7 750	74 323	5 242	5 755	17 734	6 208	22 762	16 622	2 911
May	99 096	24 567	4 800	18 986	11 238	7 748	74 529	5 251	5 763	17 801	6 235	22 833	16 646	2 901
June	98 973	24 472	4 784	18 924	11 177	7 747	74 501	5 148	5 730	17 836	6 262	22 895	16 630	2 885
July	99 276	24 431	4 792	18 883	11 152	7 731	74 845	5 250	5 779	17 903	6 294	22 978	16 641	2 879
August	99 435	24 429	4 811	18 881	11 148	7 733	75 006	5 222	5 767	17 985	6 320	23 061	16 651	2 888
September	99 747	24 415	4 812	18 879	11 130	7 749	75 332	5 261	5 767	18 051	6 343	23 153	16 757	2 896
October	99 980	24 407	4 827	18 860	11 105	7 755	75 573	5 259	5 768	18 092	6 365	23 255	16 834	2 895
November	100 145	24 407	4 831	18 860	11 097	7 763	75 738	5 285	5 770	18 111	6 383	23 334	16 855	2 895
December	100 394	24 446	4 868	18 867	11 093	7 774	75 948	5 290	5 776	18 159	6 419	23 431	16 873	2 901
1987														
January	100 543	24 444	4 884	18 852	11 080	7 772	76 099	5 297	5 786	18 139	6 434	23 554	16 889	2 909
February	100 772	24 512	4 916	18 890	11 109	7 781	76 260	5 310	5 802	18 197	6 453	23 620	16 878	2 913
March	101 005	24 517	4 911	18 899	11 108	7 791	76 488	5 314	5 809	18 247	6 474	23 737	16 907	2 922
April	101 367	24 542	4 925	18 909	11 101	7 808	76 825	5 342	5 822	18 325	6 507	23 861	16 968	2 932
May	101 564	24 586	4 951	18 924	11 109	7 815	76 978	5 343	5 827	18 342	6 524	23 973	16 969	2 938
June	101 713	24 584	4 951	18 920	11 103	7 817	77 129	5 343	5 834	18 394	6 534	24 047	16 977	2 945
July	102 047	24 643	4 951	18 976	11 107	7 869	77 404	5 351	5 844	18 438	6 555	24 186	17 030	2 945
August	102 266	24 706	4 965	19 021	11 159	7 862	77 560	5 367	5 858	18 455	6 566	24 296	17 018	2 948
September	102 430	24 761	4 962	19 072	11 194	7 878	77 669	5 394	5 874	18 500	6 573	24 350	16 978	2 953
October	102 980	24 856	5 007	19 117	11 225	7 892	78 124	5 410	5 891	18 627	6 590	24 472	17 134	2 962
November	103 200	24 933	5 020	19 183	11 261	7 922	78 267	5 429	5 902	18 666	6 584	24 539	17 147	2 971
December	103 544	24 992	5 047	19 216	11 287	7 929	78 552	5 439	5 923	18 722	6 599	24 669	17 200	2 976
1988														
January	103 623	24 910	4 979	19 204	11 266	7 938	78 713	5 450	5 918	18 747	6 608	24 779	17 211	2 972
February	104 046	24 990	5 022	19 240	11 294	7 946	79 056	5 458	5 944	18 875	6 608	24 920	17 251	2 973
March	104 311	25 057	5 073	19 261	11 308	7 953	79 254	5 476	5 964	18 867	6 619	25 026	17 302	2 973
April	104 537	25 098	5 092	19 285	11 334	7 951	79 439	5 482	5 983	18 906	6 620	25 145	17 303	2 967
May	104 811	25 111	5 091	19 302	11 340	7 962	79 700	5 496	6 003	18 962	6 623	25 275	17 341	2 963
June	105 132	25 156	5 118	19 325	11 363	7 962	79 976	5 506	6 027	19 010	6 630	25 440	17 363	2 962
July	105 400	25 170	5 125	19 333	11 385	7 948	80 230	5 519	6 048	19 062	6 634	25 591	17 376	2 961
August	105 599	25 136	5 125	19 300	11 362	7 938	80 463	5 535	6 058	19 102	6 633	25 715	17 420	2 964
September	105 814	25 157	5 132	19 321	11 384	7 937	80 657	5 537	6 076	19 121	6 632	25 846	17 445	2 976
October	106 091	25 193	5 128	19 363	11 410	7 953	80 898	5 544	6 094	19 165	6 639	25 962	17 494	2 983
November	106 368	25 236	5 131	19 410	11 445	7 965	81 132	5 562	6 108	19 202	6 648	26 085	17 527	2 986
December	106 691	25 265	5 135	19 437	11 469	7 968	81 426	5 573	6 135	19 283	6 651	26 218	17 566	2 985
1989														
January	106 993	25 340	5 182	19 466	11 485	7 981	81 653	5 578	6 160	19 336	6 649	26 334	17 596	2 982
February	107 244	25 303	5 143	19 471	11 486	7 985	81 941	5 607	6 185	19 414	6 656	26 448	17 631	2 985
March	107 438	25 308	5 134	19 483	11 482	8 001	82 130	5 581	6 205	19 448	6 658	26 586	17 652	2 986
April	107 637	25 323	5 159	19 472	11 477	7 995	82 314	5 610	6 199	19 467	6 659	26 708	17 681	2 986
May	107 738	25 303	5 160	19 453	11 453	8 000	82 435	5 610	6 194	19 469	6 662	26 767	17 733	3 000
June	107 838	25 254	5 153	19 421	11 420	8 001	82 584	5 618	6 186	19 470	6 668	26 878	17 764	3 000
July	107 933	25 222	5 170	19 382	11 380	8 002	82 711	5 627	6 190	19 480	6 672	26 951	17 791	3 001
August	108 048	25 251	5 181	19 374	11 370	8 004	82 797	5 526	6 190	19 441	6 679	27 039	17 872	2 994
September	108 178	25 200	5 177	19 327	11 330	7 997	82 978	5 614	6 183	19 489	6 680	27 144	17 868	2 984
October	108 290	25 183	5 201	19 284	11 290	7 994	83 107	5 629	6 183	19 522	6 676	27 213	17 884	2 984
November	108 571	25 216	5 226	19 290	11 287	8 003	83 355	5 649	6 185	19 564	6 683	27 347	17 927	2 983
December	108 692	25 137	5 170	19 268	11 269	7 999	83 555	5 734	6 182	19 571	6 685	27 433	17 950	2 978

1. Includes mining, not shown seperately.

Table 24-5. Nonfarm Employment—*Continued*

(Wage and salary workers on nonfarm payrolls; thousands, seasonally adjusted.)

| Year and month | Total | Goods-producing industries [1] | | | | | Service-producing industries | | | | | | Government | |
| | | Total | Construction | Manufacturing | | | Total | Transportation and public utilities | Wholesale trade | Retail trade | Finance insurance, and real estate | Services (private) | Total | Federal |
				Total	Durable goods	Nondurable goods								
1990														
January	108 946	25 114	5 270	19 140	11 139	8 001	83 832	5 741	6 191	19 626	6 687	27 549	18 038	3 002
February	109 263	25 267	5 307	19 254	11 259	7 995	83 996	5 760	6 177	19 617	6 699	27 670	18 073	3 007
March	109 461	25 212	5 269	19 238	11 244	7 994	84 249	5 762	6 168	19 622	6 694	27 801	18 202	3 093
April	109 499	25 123	5 194	19 220	11 219	8 001	84 376	5 770	6 173	19 631	6 701	27 811	18 290	3 155
May	109 790	25 074	5 183	19 181	11 196	7 985	84 716	5 785	6 173	19 623	6 708	27 898	18 529	3 349
June	109 869	25 031	5 159	19 159	11 181	7 978	84 838	5 788	6 184	19 635	6 716	27 958	18 557	3 340
July	109 707	24 950	5 120	19 118	11 148	7 970	84 757	5 781	6 185	19 638	6 719	28 008	18 426	3 168
August	109 543	24 861	5 085	19 067	11 096	7 971	84 682	5 773	6 183	19 621	6 726	28 048	18 331	3 042
September	109 457	24 783	5 056	19 016	11 051	7 965	84 674	5 783	6 176	19 605	6 723	28 075	18 312	2 992
October	109 274	24 657	4 993	18 955	11 012	7 943	84 617	5 787	6 163	19 559	6 718	28 084	18 306	2 981
November	109 074	24 460	4 953	18 797	10 884	7 913	84 614	5 780	6 154	19 538	6 709	28 125	18 308	2 964
December	108 965	24 375	4 909	18 754	10 860	7 894	84 590	5 799	6 148	19 499	6 702	28 138	18 304	2 943
1991														
January	108 759	24 175	4 805	18 660	10 783	7 877	84 584	5 812	6 121	19 423	6 707	28 203	18 318	2 952
February	108 500	24 058	4 799	18 549	10 688	7 861	84 442	5 774	6 106	19 362	6 699	28 169	18 332	2 951
March	108 330	23 926	4 744	18 473	10 633	7 840	84 404	5 758	6 093	19 336	6 699	28 172	18 346	2 950
April	108 145	23 822	4 685	18 432	10 613	7 819	84 323	5 757	6 084	19 271	6 680	28 165	18 366	2 954
May	108 107	23 791	4 677	18 413	10 597	7 816	84 316	5 753	6 077	19 249	6 665	28 200	18 372	2 957
June	108 200	23 741	4 661	18 383	10 562	7 821	84 459	5 742	6 078	19 275	6 651	28 278	18 435	2 973
July	108 131	23 688	4 634	18 365	10 552	7 813	84 443	5 754	6 081	19 254	6 631	28 297	18 426	2 970
August	108 215	23 687	4 619	18 384	10 543	7 841	84 528	5 756	6 070	19 265	6 619	28 384	18 434	2 973
September	108 223	23 648	4 612	18 360	10 519	7 841	84 575	5 746	6 076	19 256	6 610	28 469	18 418	2 979
October	108 209	23 574	4 578	18 326	10 487	7 839	84 635	5 744	6 069	19 237	6 605	28 535	18 445	2 984
November	108 115	23 467	4 520	18 285	10 447	7 838	84 648	5 738	6 060	19 223	6 598	28 549	18 480	2 983
December	108 121	23 409	4 522	18 229	10 395	7 834	84 712	5 725	6 055	19 233	6 594	28 604	18 501	2 981
1992														
January	108 084	23 317	4 513	18 151	10 324	7 827	84 767	5 706	6 045	19 245	6 578	28 670	18 523	2 978
February	108 077	23 263	4 489	18 125	10 315	7 810	84 814	5 709	6 038	19 253	6 583	28 681	18 550	2 982
March	108 119	23 239	4 488	18 103	10 295	7 808	84 880	5 708	6 036	19 253	6 575	28 726	18 582	2 984
April	108 301	23 258	4 482	18 133	10 306	7 827	85 043	5 711	6 024	19 319	6 583	28 807	18 599	2 983
May	108 495	23 274	4 493	18 140	10 310	7 830	85 221	5 709	6 016	19 362	6 593	28 917	18 624	2 984
June	108 541	23 247	4 481	18 132	10 298	7 834	85 294	5 715	6 005	19 353	6 599	28 996	18 626	2 976
July	108 595	23 227	4 473	18 123	10 290	7 833	85 368	5 712	5 985	19 362	6 593	29 072	18 644	2 965
August	108 741	23 209	4 487	18 097	10 268	7 829	85 532	5 718	5 975	19 373	6 601	29 149	18 716	2 962
September	108 807	23 178	4 483	18 074	10 247	7 827	85 629	5 726	5 964	19 380	6 613	29 236	18 710	2 969
October	108 941	23 179	4 493	18 064	10 234	7 830	85 762	5 732	5 965	19 423	6 622	29 333	18 687	2 949
November	109 119	23 182	4 500	18 060	10 233	7 827	85 937	5 732	5 965	19 471	6 631	29 433	18 705	2 944
December	109 266	23 209	4 518	18 069	10 230	7 839	86 057	5 738	5 948	19 463	6 648	29 541	18 719	2 945
1993														
January	109 502	23 240	4 520	18 098	10 246	7 852	86 262	5 763	5 957	19 509	6 658	29 648	18 727	2 944
February	109 816	23 323	4 605	18 104	10 248	7 856	86 493	5 773	5 951	19 576	6 670	29 767	18 756	2 942
March	109 749	23 259	4 550	18 093	10 236	7 857	86 490	5 773	5 944	19 534	6 675	29 809	18 755	2 935
April	110 055	23 261	4 574	18 072	10 215	7 857	86 794	5 780	5 954	19 640	6 695	29 954	18 771	2 923
May	110 398	23 324	4 643	18 067	10 202	7 865	87 074	5 795	5 974	19 711	6 719	30 069	18 806	2 915
June	110 539	23 306	4 650	18 049	10 186	7 863	87 233	5 812	5 968	19 744	6 741	30 152	18 816	2 906
July	110 744	23 312	4 678	18 030	10 187	7 843	87 432	5 823	5 984	19 790	6 766	30 250	18 819	2 904
August	110 957	23 344	4 700	18 044	10 190	7 854	87 613	5 820	5 982	19 853	6 781	30 337	18 840	2 907
September	111 204	23 383	4 715	18 066	10 211	7 855	87 821	5 834	5 998	19 893	6 807	30 420	18 869	2 903
October	111 525	23 441	4 757	18 081	10 230	7 851	88 084	5 848	6 010	19 967	6 833	30 529	18 897	2 901
November	111 780	23 480	4 781	18 097	10 246	7 851	88 300	5 864	6 022	19 988	6 857	30 650	18 919	2 897
December	112 034	23 536	4 808	18 112	10 265	7 847	88 498	5 847	6 036	20 056	6 877	30 731	18 951	2 895
1994														
January	112 302	23 583	4 815	18 155	10 305	7 850	88 719	5 894	6 054	20 088	6 892	30 817	18 974	2 897
February	112 532	23 606	4 832	18 167	10 316	7 851	88 926	5 914	6 067	20 165	6 909	30 883	18 988	2 896
March	112 982	23 700	4 898	18 198	10 341	7 857	89 282	5 938	6 088	20 266	6 927	31 042	19 021	2 888
April	113 350	23 785	4 949	18 234	10 372	7 862	89 565	5 906	6 109	20 347	6 927	31 218	19 058	2 884
May	113 697	23 834	4 971	18 264	10 397	7 867	89 863	5 972	6 130	20 393	6 918	31 350	19 100	2 872
June	113 980	23 890	4 986	18 305	10 437	7 868	90 090	5 982	6 145	20 454	6 917	31 498	19 094	2 862
July	114 333	23 935	5 005	18 333	10 449	7 884	90 398	5 998	6 161	20 535	6 908	31 687	19 109	2 857
August	114 673	23 995	5 015	18 383	10 493	7 890	90 678	6 013	6 195	20 604	6 901	31 818	19 147	2 861
September	114 980	24 056	5 050	18 406	10 520	7 886	90 924	6 021	6 220	20 680	6 885	31 935	19 183	2 866
October	115 235	24 090	5 057	18 437	10 548	7 889	91 145	6 034	6 240	20 743	6 865	32 063	19 200	2 861
November	115 641	24 179	5 097	18 485	10 592	7 893	91 462	6 055	6 258	20 845	6 853	32 230	19 221	2 852
December	115 918	24 220	5 112	18 513	10 609	7 904	91 698	6 087	6 285	20 894	6 836	32 361	19 235	2 848
1995														
January	116 235	24 269	5 128	18 549	10 634	7 915	91 966	6 082	6 310	21 012	6 824	32 487	19 251	2 840
February	116 523	24 273	5 134	18 552	10 661	7 891	92 250	6 107	6 336	21 067	6 813	32 659	19 268	2 837
March	116 679	24 266	5 124	18 555	10 674	7 881	92 413	6 114	6 354	21 045	6 811	32 812	19 277	2 831
April	116 864	24 291	5 137	18 568	10 690	7 878	92 573	6 119	6 363	21 118	6 800	32 880	19 293	2 827
May	116 830	24 237	5 113	18 541	10 683	7 858	92 593	6 108	6 367	21 119	6 792	32 929	19 278	2 829
June	117 024	24 248	5 136	18 531	10 673	7 858	92 776	6 110	6 383	21 185	6 790	33 021	19 287	2 832
July	117 138	24 239	5 153	18 505	10 676	7 829	92 899	6 106	6 388	21 214	6 794	33 109	19 288	2 828
August	117 444	24 278	5 180	18 521	10 691	7 830	93 166	6 135	6 396	21 253	6 802	33 283	19 297	2 826
September	117 664	24 302	5 212	18 514	10 698	7 816	93 362	6 141	6 400	21 284	6 806	33 431	19 300	2 814
October	117 789	24 305	5 239	18 491	10 692	7 799	93 484	6 182	6 404	21 279	6 812	33 490	19 317	2 804
November	117 946	24 291	5 242	18 477	10 695	7 782	93 655	6 192	6 410	21 317	6 821	33 590	19 325	2 795
December	118 118	24 298	5 223	18 502	10 740	7 762	93 820	6 206	6 417	21 347	6 827	33 693	19 330	2 787

1. Includes mining, not shown seperately.

Table 24-6. Average Hours and Earnings

(Production or nonsupervisory workers on private nonfarm payrolls; seasonally adjusted, except as noted.)

Year and month	Average weekly hours					Indexes of aggregate weekly hours (1982=100)		Average hourly earnings (Dollars)					Average weekly earnings (Dollars)			
			Manufacturing					All industries [1]						Not seasonally adjusted		
	All industries [1]	Construction	Average weekly hours	Overtime hours	Retail trade	All industries [1]	Manufacturing	Current dollars	1982 dollars	Construction	Manufacturing	Retail trade	All industries [1]	Construction	Manufacturing	Retail trade
1972																
January	36.9	37.0	40.2	3.1	33.7	87.4	111.0	3.61	8.43	5.91	3.71	2.69	133.21	211.23	148.06	89.70
February	37.0	36.9	40.4	3.2	33.5	87.7	112.2	3.61	8.41	5.93	3.73	2.70	133.57	211.46	149.20	89.43
March	37.0	36.8	40.4	3.3	33.6	88.3	112.9	3.64	8.47	5.96	3.75	2.71	134.68	215.49	151.13	90.03
April	37.1	36.5	40.7	3.6	33.6	88.8	114.3	3.66	8.51	6.00	3.78	2.72	135.79	215.39	153.09	90.64
May	36.9	36.2	40.5	3.4	33.4	88.6	114.2	3.67	8.52	6.03	3.79	2.72	135.42	217.80	153.50	90.36
June	37.0	36.4	40.6	3.5	33.5	89.2	114.9	3.67	8.50	6.02	3.80	2.74	135.79	219.78	155.04	92.89
July	36.9	36.4	40.5	3.4	33.4	88.9	114.2	3.69	8.50	6.03	3.81	2.75	136.16	223.05	153.52	94.88
August	36.9	36.6	40.6	3.5	33.3	89.3	114.9	3.72	8.55	6.07	3.85	2.77	137.27	228.09	155.09	94.33
September	37.0	36.7	40.6	3.5	33.3	89.6	115.5	3.74	8.56	6.10	3.87	2.78	138.38	231.99	158.69	92.85
October	37.1	36.7	40.7	3.6	33.4	90.5	117.0	3.77	8.59	6.17	3.89	2.79	139.87	234.00	158.30	92.63
November	37.0	36.0	40.8	3.7	33.3	90.9	118.3	3.78	8.59	6.21	3.91	2.81	139.86	221.25	159.92	92.40
December	36.8	35.3	40.5	3.7	33.3	90.8	118.6	3.81	8.62	6.27	3.95	2.83	140.21	220.92	163.58	94.42
1973																
January	36.8	36.0	40.4	3.9	33.3	91.4	118.8	3.83	8.63	6.37	3.98	2.82	140.94	221.15	159.60	92.87
February	37.0	35.8	40.9	4.0	33.3	92.3	121.5	3.84	8.61	6.29	3.99	2.85	142.08	218.61	161.60	93.81
March	37.1	36.6	40.8	3.8	33.3	92.8	121.7	3.86	8.58	6.31	4.00	2.86	143.21	226.07	162.80	94.14
April	37.1	36.8	40.9	4.1	33.1	93.0	122.1	3.89	8.59	6.33	4.03	2.88	144.32	228.86	164.02	94.79
May	37.0	36.9	40.7	3.9	33.2	93.0	121.7	3.90	8.55	6.34	4.05	2.89	144.30	233.10	164.84	95.08
June	37.0	36.9	40.6	3.8	33.2	93.3	121.8	3.92	8.56	6.35	4.06	2.91	145.04	236.88	166.05	97.78
July	37.0	36.8	40.7	3.8	33.2	93.2	121.7	3.96	8.63	6.39	4.10	2.92	146.52	239.02	166.05	99.86
August	36.9	36.8	40.5	3.7	33.0	93.3	121.4	3.96	8.46	6.40	4.12	2.93	146.12	241.16	165.65	98.94
September	36.9	36.7	40.7	3.8	33.0	93.4	121.8	3.99	8.51	6.46	4.14	2.95	147.23	244.60	170.15	97.65
October	36.8	36.5	40.6	3.8	32.9	93.6	122.4	4.01	8.48	6.50	4.17	2.96	147.57	246.09	169.31	96.79
November	37.0	37.8	40.7	3.9	33.0	94.5	123.2	4.04	8.47	6.54	4.19	2.98	149.48	245.15	171.37	97.12
December	36.8	36.7	40.6	3.7	32.9	94.1	123.1	4.06	8.46	6.56	4.21	3.01	149.41	239.94	174.69	98.94
1974																
January	36.7	36.1	40.5	3.6	32.9	93.8	122.0	4.07	8.39	6.55	4.22	3.01	149.37	227.01	169.60	97.57
February	36.8	37.2	40.4	3.5	32.8	94.1	121.2	4.10	8.35	6.60	4.24	3.02	150.88	237.60	170.02	97.87
March	36.7	36.5	40.4	3.5	32.8	93.8	120.7	4.12	8.31	6.62	4.26	3.04	151.20	237.83	171.25	98.82
April	36.4	35.9	39.3	2.8	33.0	93.1	117.4	4.13	8.29	6.65	4.27	3.05	150.33	234.60	166.96	100.06
May	36.7	36.4	40.3	3.5	32.7	93.9	120.4	4.19	8.31	6.69	4.36	3.11	153.77	242.36	175.71	101.08
June	36.6	36.7	40.2	3.4	32.7	93.9	120.0	4.24	8.35	6.75	4.42	3.14	155.18	249.83	178.16	103.93
July	36.6	36.7	40.2	3.4	32.6	93.7	119.8	4.25	8.30	6.76	4.45	3.16	155.55	252.30	177.60	106.18
August	36.5	36.4	40.2	3.3	32.7	93.5	119.0	4.29	8.28	6.92	4.50	3.19	156.59	257.74	179.25	106.51
September	36.6	36.8	40.0	3.2	32.7	93.4	118.1	4.33	8.25	7.00	4.54	3.21	158.48	264.79	183.37	104.97
October	36.4	36.8	40.0	3.2	32.5	93.1	117.0	4.36	8.24	7.00	4.60	3.22	158.70	266.92	184.06	104.01
November	36.2	36.8	39.5	2.8	32.5	91.7	113.4	4.36	8.15	7.04	4.61	3.23	157.83	258.08	183.02	103.68
December	36.1	37.0	39.3	2.7	32.5	90.4	109.2	4.40	8.16	7.09	4.64	3.25	158.84	262.41	186.73	105.62
1975																
January	36.1	37.1	39.2	2.5	32.4	89.7	105.9	4.41	8.12	7.13	4.66	3.26	159.20	253.46	181.12	104.29
February	35.9	35.9	38.9	2.4	32.4	88.3	102.3	4.43	8.11	7.11	4.70	3.29	159.04	248.86	180.95	105.27
March	35.8	35.2	38.8	2.4	32.4	87.4	101.0	4.45	8.12	7.29	4.74	3.30	159.31	256.16	183.44	105.92
April	35.9	36.1	39.2	2.4	32.2	87.4	101.6	4.46	8.11	7.26	4.76	3.32	160.11	259.56	184.78	106.23
May	35.9	36.5	39.0	2.3	32.4	87.7	101.2	4.48	8.13	7.28	4.78	3.34	160.83	264.97	186.03	107.55
June	36.0	35.8	39.2	2.5	32.4	87.8	101.4	4.51	8.13	7.35	4.81	3.35	162.36	263.90	189.60	109.88
July	36.0	36.2	39.4	2.6	32.3	88.2	101.8	4.53	8.09	7.36	4.83	3.36	163.08	271.57	188.94	111.89
August	36.2	36.8	39.7	2.8	32.5	89.2	103.8	4.57	8.13	7.34	4.87	3.38	165.43	275.98	192.15	112.22
September	36.2	36.9	39.9	2.8	32.3	89.5	105.3	4.60	8.11	7.36	4.90	3.39	166.52	272.28	197.38	109.50
October	36.2	36.3	39.8	2.8	32.3	89.8	105.9	4.61	8.09	7.33	4.92	3.41	166.88	276.02	196.80	109.46
November	36.2	36.4	39.9	2.9	32.4	90.1	106.2	4.66	8.12	7.41	4.96	3.43	168.69	269.31	198.90	109.78
December	36.3	36.6	40.2	3.0	32.3	90.7	107.9	4.67	8.09	7.44	4.99	3.45	169.52	273.39	205.73	111.83
1976																
January	36.3	37.7	40.5	3.1	32.5	91.5	109.5	4.70	8.10	7.44	5.02	3.47	170.61	268.17	201.60	111.30
February	36.3	37.1	40.3	3.1	32.4	91.8	109.8	4.73	8.16	7.48	5.06	3.47	171.70	269.69	202.40	111.33
March	36.1	36.1	40.2	3.2	32.2	91.6	110.1	4.75	8.18	7.53	5.10	3.49	171.48	265.19	204.11	111.30
April	36.1	36.6	39.6	2.6	32.4	92.0	109.2	4.77	8.18	7.59	5.11	3.50	172.20	275.23	199.92	112.67
May	36.2	36.6	40.3	3.3	32.2	92.4	110.9	4.81	8.22	7.68	5.16	3.53	174.12	280.42	207.55	112.96
June	36.2	36.9	40.2	3.2	32.1	92.3	110.6	4.84	8.23	7.65	5.19	3.54	175.21	284.25	209.79	115.05
July	36.2	36.6	40.3	3.2	32.0	92.7	111.0	4.87	8.24	7.73	5.23	3.55	176.29	288.75	209.32	117.15
August	36.1	36.6	40.1	3.1	31.9	92.5	110.3	4.91	8.27	7.77	5.28	3.60	177.25	290.60	210.53	117.10
September	36.0	36.2	39.8	3.2	31.9	92.6	110.5	4.94	8.26	7.80	5.32	3.64	177.84	289.14	214.13	116.12
October	36.0	37.1	40.0	3.1	31.8	92.6	109.9	4.97	8.27	7.86	5.32	3.67	178.92	302.48	213.33	115.66
November	36.0	37.0	40.1	3.2	31.8	92.8	110.9	5.01	8.31	7.88	5.38	3.69	180.36	290.24	216.81	115.61
December	36.0	36.8	40.0	3.2	31.8	93.0	110.8	5.04	8.32	7.91	5.42	3.72	181.44	291.77	222.22	118.50
1977																
January	35.8	35.6	39.7	3.3	31.7	92.8	110.5	5.06	8.30	7.99	5.48	3.71	181.15	271.88	215.05	116.25
February	36.1	37.5	40.3	3.3	31.7	94.0	112.4	5.10	8.29	7.99	5.48	3.75	184.11	289.38	218.65	117.94
March	36.0	36.9	40.2	3.3	31.7	94.5	113.3	5.13	8.30	8.01	5.52	3.77	184.68	289.38	221.90	118.63
April	36.0	36.7	40.4	3.6	31.6	95.2	114.5	5.17	8.31	8.03	5.58	3.79	186.12	291.77	222.96	118.94
May	36.1	36.7	40.4	3.5	31.7	95.7	115.1	5.20	8.32	8.03	5.61	3.82	187.72	294.09	226.24	120.33
June	36.0	36.3	40.5	3.5	31.5	96.1	116.0	5.23	8.31	8.08	5.66	3.84	188.28	296.37	230.52	122.50
July	36.0	36.4	40.3	3.5	31.6	96.4	115.8	5.27	8.34	8.07	5.70	3.87	189.72	300.27	228.17	125.45
August	36.0	36.1	40.4	3.5	31.5	96.5	115.7	5.28	8.33	8.10	5.73	3.88	190.08	299.26	229.31	124.74
September	36.0	36.2	40.4	3.5	31.5	97.0	116.2	5.32	8.35	8.15	5.77	3.91	191.52	303.14	235.65	122.85
October	36.0	36.3	40.5	3.5	31.6	97.4	116.4	5.36	8.39	8.20	5.82	3.93	192.96	308.39	236.29	123.09
November	35.9	36.5	40.4	3.6	31.3	97.7	116.7	5.39	8.38	8.22	5.85	3.96	193.50	298.19	238.10	122.53
December	35.9	36.2	40.4	3.5	31.3	97.8	117.3	5.41	8.37	8.26	5.88	3.99	194.22	299.27	243.72	124.90

1. Includes industries not shown seperately.

Table 24-6. Average Hours and Earnings—*Continued*

(Production or nonsupervisory workers on private nonfarm payrolls; seasonally adjusted, except as noted.)

Year and month	Average weekly hours					Indexes of aggregate weekly hours (1982=100)		Average hourly earnings (Dollars)					Average weekly earnings (Dollars)			
	All indus- tries [1]	Con- struction	Manufacturing		Retail trade	All indus- tries [1]	Manufac- turing	All industries [1]					All indus- tries [1]	Not seasonally adjusted		
			Average weekly hours	Overtime hours				Current dollars	1982 dollars	Con- struction	Manufac- turing	Retail trade		Con- struction	Manufac- turing	Retail trade
1978																
January	35.5	34.7	39.6	3.4	31.0	97.0	115.8	5.47	8.42	8.32	5.95	4.05	194.19	275.55	234.02	124.23
February	35.6	35.7	39.9	3.7	30.9	97.7	117.0	5.50	8.42	8.37	5.98	4.06	195.80	288.22	236.81	124.64
March	35.9	36.6	40.5	3.5	31.2	99.1	118.9	5.54	8.42	8.45	6.01	4.09	198.89	304.08	242.80	126.59
April	36.0	36.9	40.8	3.9	31.1	100.4	120.3	5.60	8.45	8.48	6.05	4.13	201.60	309.96	244.02	127.82
May	35.9	36.6	40.4	3.5	31.1	100.3	119.6	5.63	8.42	8.57	6.09	4.16	202.12	312.68	245.23	128.54
June	35.9	37.2	40.5	3.6	31.1	101.1	120.2	5.67	8.41	8.63	6.12	4.18	203.55	324.80	249.29	130.94
July	35.9	37.3	40.6	3.6	31.1	101.3	120.6	5.71	8.41	8.67	6.18	4.21	204.99	330.05	249.05	134.40
August	35.8	37.2	40.5	3.5	31.0	101.4	120.4	5.74	8.40	8.73	6.21	4.23	205.49	331.25	249.27	133.56
September	35.8	37.0	40.6	3.6	30.9	101.6	121.1	5.79	8.42	8.78	6.27	4.27	207.28	333.38	256.00	131.63
October	35.9	37.1	40.5	3.6	30.9	102.1	121.6	5.84	8.39	8.81	6.33	4.30	209.66	337.31	257.00	132.13
November	35.8	36.9	40.6	3.7	30.8	102.6	122.7	5.87	8.39	8.87	6.39	4.33	210.15	324.85	261.35	131.89
December	35.8	37.1	40.6	3.6	30.9	103.0	123.4	5.91	8.38	8.91	6.43	4.36	211.58	331.67	268.27	134.90
1979																
January	35.7	36.5	40.5	3.6	30.6	102.9	123.5	5.95	8.38	8.95	6.47	4.42	212.42	311.95	260.65	133.95
February	35.7	36.7	40.5	3.6	30.7	103.3	123.6	6.00	8.36	9.06	6.53	4.43	214.20	320.57	262.51	134.55
March	35.8	37.4	40.6	3.7	30.7	104.2	124.0	6.03	8.32	9.03	6.56	4.45	215.87	333.53	266.34	135.74
April	35.4	35.7	39.2	2.9	30.9	102.6	119.9	6.03	8.22	9.12	6.56	4.48	213.46	321.82	254.80	137.70
May	35.7	37.2	40.2	3.4	30.6	103.9	122.9	6.09	8.21	9.20	6.65	4.49	217.41	341.30	265.86	136.50
June	35.7	37.2	40.2	3.4	30.7	104.4	123.1	6.13	8.17	9.21	6.68	4.51	218.84	347.32	269.47	139.50
July	35.7	36.9	40.2	3.4	30.7	104.3	123.0	6.18	8.14	9.29	6.72	4.53	220.63	350.03	268.13	142.38
August	35.7	37.4	40.1	3.2	30.6	104.2	121.4	6.21	8.11	9.33	6.75	4.56	221.70	355.85	268.00	142.24
September	35.7	37.4	40.2	3.2	30.6	104.3	121.6	6.27	8.10	9.42	6.79	4.59	223.84	361.76	274.04	140.61
October	35.6	36.9	40.2	3.2	30.5	104.3	121.4	6.28	8.04	9.40	6.82	4.61	223.57	357.77	274.85	139.54
November	35.6	37.0	40.1	3.2	30.6	104.5	120.4	6.32	8.01	9.48	6.87	4.64	224.99	348.07	277.55	140.45
December	35.6	37.2	40.2	3.2	30.6	104.8	120.7	6.38	7.99	9.54	6.93	4.67	227.13	356.00	285.48	142.91
1980																
January	35.5	36.4	40.0	3.1	30.5	104.7	120.0	6.40	7.90	9.42	6.94	4.73	227.84	334.29	277.41	142.44
February	35.5	36.9	40.1	3.0	30.4	104.7	119.4	6.45	7.88	9.61	7.00	4.74	228.98	342.72	278.60	142.44
March	35.3	36.4	39.8	3.1	30.3	104.1	118.4	6.51	7.82	9.70	7.07	4.79	229.80	349.69	281.39	143.82
April	35.2	36.9	39.5	2.9	29.9	103.1	116.1	6.54	7.79	9.77	7.11	4.79	230.86	355.62	279.74	142.56
May	35.1	36.8	39.3	2.6	30.1	102.1	112.5	6.57	7.75	9.83	7.16	4.82	231.26	361.86	280.60	144.12
June	35.2	37.4	39.2	2.4	30.2	101.5	110.1	6.63	7.74	9.89	7.22	4.85	232.71	372.78	284.07	147.14
July	35.0	36.9	39.1	2.5	30.0	100.9	108.4	6.66	7.76	9.95	7.29	4.91	233.10	374.98	282.85	150.61
August	35.2	36.9	39.4	2.6	30.1	101.6	110.3	6.71	7.77	10.05	7.36	4.93	235.52	376.24	288.01	151.41
September	35.2	37.2	39.6	2.7	30.1	102.2	111.1	6.76	7.76	10.10	7.42	4.96	237.95	387.60	295.71	149.49
October	35.3	37.5	39.8	2.8	30.2	102.7	111.9	6.83	7.76	10.18	7.51	4.99	241.10	390.26	298.50	149.90
November	35.4	37.6	40.0	3.0	30.2	103.1	113.2	6.90	7.75	10.26	7.60	5.02	243.57	378.96	305.52	150.60
December	35.4	37.3	40.3	3.1	30.0	103.5	114.1	6.94	7.73	10.33	7.64	5.03	244.98	385.39	314.16	152.20
1981																
January	35.5	37.5	40.1	3.1	30.3	104.2	114.3	6.99	7.72	10.37	7.69	5.13	248.15	381.79	308.43	152.52
February	35.4	36.5	40.0	3.0	30.3	104.1	113.6	7.05	7.71	10.41	7.75	5.16	249.57	366.80	306.13	153.62
March	35.4	37.5	40.0	3.0	30.3	104.3	113.8	7.11	7.74	10.48	7.81	5.18	251.69	390.90	311.62	154.96
April	35.4	37.2	40.1	2.9	30.2	104.3	114.4	7.14	7.72	10.54	7.87	5.21	252.76	387.76	312.84	156.60
May	35.3	36.6	40.1	3.0	30.0	103.7	114.3	7.18	7.71	10.64	7.93	5.21	253.45	391.46	317.59	156.08
June	35.2	36.6	39.9	2.9	30.0	103.8	113.8	7.22	7.70	10.77	7.97	5.23	254.14	396.55	320.39	158.17
July	35.3	36.8	39.9	2.9	30.1	104.1	113.4	7.26	7.65	10.88	8.01	5.26	256.28	408.62	317.59	161.92
August	35.3	36.7	39.9	2.9	30.2	104.0	113.1	7.34	7.67	10.97	8.09	5.29	259.10	409.16	320.40	162.23
September	35.1	36.8	39.7	2.7	30.1	103.7	112.6	7.39	7.66	11.02	8.16	5.36	259.39	397.38	322.32	161.87
October	35.1	37.2	39.7	2.6	29.9	103.7	111.5	7.41	7.65	11.10	8.19	5.30	260.09	419.63	323.95	157.64
November	35.2	37.8	39.5	2.6	30.1	103.4	109.8	7.46	7.67	11.26	8.22	5.30	262.59	414.77	325.94	158.24
December	35.0	37.3	39.4	2.5	29.6	102.4	107.7	7.46	7.65	11.21	8.23	5.35	261.10	418.86	329.97	160.89
1982																
January	34.4	34.2	38.0	2.3	29.8	100.2	102.5	7.52	7.69	11.57	8.38	5.38	258.69	388.61	312.38	157.18
February	35.2	37.2	39.6	2.5	30.1	102.6	106.5	7.54	7.69	11.36	8.33	5.38	265.41	408.12	326.93	159.35
March	34.9	37.2	39.1	2.4	29.8	101.6	104.2	7.57	7.72	11.42	8.37	5.40	264.19	422.17	327.27	159.35
April	34.8	36.9	38.9	2.2	29.9	100.8	102.3	7.59	7.72	11.43	8.41	5.43	264.13	417.28	325.85	161.02
May	34.9	37.1	39.0	2.4	29.9	100.8	101.7	7.65	7.71	11.57	8.46	5.45	266.99	431.63	329.55	162.71
June	34.9	36.9	39.1	2.3	29.8	100.3	100.7	7.67	7.64	11.60	8.51	5.48	267.68	430.50	334.05	164.65
July	34.8	37.0	39.2	2.3	29.8	99.9	99.8	7.71	7.64	11.68	8.54	5.49	268.31	441.18	332.60	167.38
August	34.8	36.9	39.0	2.3	29.9	99.6	98.6	7.75	7.66	11.72	8.56	5.51	269.70	439.17	331.50	167.38
September	34.8	37.0	39.0	2.3	30.0	99.3	98.2	7.75	7.66	11.67	8.58	5.51	269.70	433.94	333.76	165.85
October	34.7	36.8	38.9	2.3	29.9	98.7	96.5	7.78	7.65	11.80	8.58	5.55	269.97	441.49	333.45	165.09
November	34.8	36.9	39.1	2.3	29.9	98.6	96.0	7.80	7.68	11.78	8.61	5.57	271.44	423.45	337.98	165.17
December	34.8	37.0	39.1	2.4	29.8	98.6	95.8	7.83	7.74	11.88	8.63	5.59	272.48	440.13	344.60	169.28
1983																
January	35.0	37.9	39.4	2.4	30.1	99.5	96.7	7.88	7.78	11.85	8.66	5.63	275.80	439.39	341.04	166.13
February	34.6	36.8	39.3	2.4	29.4	98.4	96.5	7.91	7.81	11.95	8.72	5.67	273.69	424.80	338.72	163.88
March	34.8	36.7	39.6	2.5	29.7	99.1	97.6	7.92	7.80	11.95	8.72	5.67	275.62	434.62	345.71	166.72
April	34.9	36.7	39.8	2.7	29.8	99.8	98.6	7.95	7.77	11.95	8.74	5.69	277.46	435.17	348.25	168.15
May	35.0	37.0	40.0	2.8	29.8	100.4	99.7	7.99	7.78	11.89	8.78	5.72	279.65	442.44	349.92	169.88
June	35.0	37.2	40.1	2.9	29.8	101.1	100.7	8.01	7.78	11.91	8.80	5.74	280.35	446.84	354.24	172.47
July	35.0	37.2	40.3	3.0	29.9	101.9	101.9	8.04	7.79	11.91	8.83	5.76	281.40	451.91	353.60	175.34
August	35.0	37.2	40.3	3.1	29.8	101.0	102.4	8.01	7.72	11.93	8.84	5.77	280.35	451.82	352.96	174.46
September	35.1	37.1	40.6	3.3	29.8	103.3	104.3	8.09	7.79	11.97	8.90	5.78	283.96	457.45	362.71	172.82
October	35.2	37.0	40.7	3.3	30.0	104.1	105.4	8.14	7.81	11.99	8.94	5.80	286.53	450.96	362.23	173.12
November	35.1	37.1	40.7	3.3	29.9	104.4	106.2	8.14	7.80	12.00	8.98	5.80	285.71	433.79	366.38	172.56
December	35.2	37.1	40.6	3.4	30.1	104.9	106.5	8.16	7.81	11.99	9.00	5.81	287.23	444.18	372.86	177.45

1. Includes industries not shown seperately.

Table 24-6. Average Hours and Earnings—*Continued*

(Production or nonsupervisory workers on private nonfarm payrolls; seasonally adjusted, except as noted.)

Year and month	Average weekly hours					Indexes of aggregate weekly hours (1982=100)		Average hourly earnings (Dollars) All industries [1]					Average weekly earnings (Dollars)			
	All indus- tries [1]	Con- struction	Manufacturing		Retail trade	All indus- tries [1]	Manufac- turing	Current dollars	1982 dollars	Con- struction	Manufac- turing	Retail trade	All indus- tries [1]	Not seasonally adjusted		
			Average weekly hours	Overtime hours										Con- struction	Manufac- turing	Retail trade
1984																
January	35.2	37.4	40.7	3.5	30.0	105.4	107.4	8.21	7.81	12.08	9.05	5.82	288.99	441.41	369.05	171.70
February	35.3	38.4	41.1	3.5	30.0	106.5	109.0	8.21	7.80	12.03	9.06	5.82	289.81	446.59	369.15	171.70
March	35.1	37.1	40.7	3.5	29.9	106.2	108.6	8.23	7.82	12.07	9.09	5.83	288.87	442.60	370.37	172.58
April	35.3	37.6	40.9	3.5	30.0	107.1	109.6	8.28	7.85	12.10	9.11	5.85	292.28	451.88	373.01	174.04
May	35.2	37.6	40.7	3.4	29.9	107.2	109.2	8.27	7.82	12.14	9.13	5.84	291.10	460.63	371.18	174.03
June	35.2	38.0	40.7	3.4	29.9	107.6	109.3	8.31	7.84	12.15	9.16	5.85	292.51	464.74	373.32	176.95
July	35.1	37.5	40.6	3.4	29.8	107.9	109.4	8.34	7.83	12.17	9.19	5.85	292.73	465.08	370.36	177.51
August	35.1	37.6	40.5	3.3	29.8	107.9	109.3	8.34	7.77	12.15	9.23	5.84	292.73	465.02	370.06	176.60
September	35.1	37.6	40.5	3.3	29.7	108.5	109.0	8.38	7.77	12.16	9.26	5.84	294.14	472.01	377.40	174.33
October	35.0	37.6	40.5	3.3	29.6	108.5	108.8	8.38	7.75	12.15	9.29	5.86	293.30	465.50	374.63	172.58
November	35.1	38.1	40.5	3.4	29.6	109.1	108.6	8.41	7.78	12.15	9.32	5.89	295.19	452.08	379.32	173.46
December	35.1	38.0	40.6	3.4	29.7	109.4	108.8	8.44	7.79	12.21	9.36	5.87	296.24	461.73	387.69	177.26
1985																
January	35.0	37.6	40.4	3.3	29.6	109.4	108.4	8.44	7.77	12.26	9.39	5.88	295.40	448.81	380.43	171.09
February	34.9	37.9	40.1	3.3	29.6	109.3	107.0	8.47	7.76	12.33	9.43	5.90	295.60	452.74	375.17	171.67
March	35.0	38.2	40.5	3.2	29.6	110.1	107.8	8.50	7.76	12.27	9.45	5.91	297.50	461.83	382.18	173.16
April	34.9	37.9	40.3	3.3	29.3	109.8	106.8	8.52	7.76	12.30	9.49	5.91	297.35	464.28	380.95	172.27
May	34.9	37.6	40.4	3.1	29.6	110.4	106.8	8.52	7.75	12.29	9.50	5.93	297.35	466.73	382.45	174.94
June	34.9	37.5	40.5	3.2	29.5	110.5	106.7	8.57	7.77	12.28	9.53	5.93	299.09	464.06	387.46	176.71
July	34.9	37.7	40.4	3.2	29.4	110.2	106.3	8.57	7.76	12.31	9.55	5.94	299.09	471.69	382.96	177.59
August	34.9	37.6	40.6	3.3	29.4	110.8	106.7	8.59	7.77	12.33	9.57	5.95	299.79	471.94	384.75	177.29
September	34.9	37.7	40.6	3.3	29.4	111.0	106.3	8.63	7.80	12.38	9.58	5.97	301.19	481.73	390.46	175.81
October	34.9	37.8	40.7	3.3	29.3	111.3	106.5	8.63	7.76	12.34	9.60	5.96	301.19	476.45	390.05	174.03
November	34.9	37.4	40.7	3.4	29.3	111.4	106.3	8.65	7.74	12.32	9.63	5.97	301.89	451.41	394.28	174.02
December	34.9	37.4	41.0	3.6	29.2	111.9	107.2	8.71	7.76	12.44	9.70	6.02	303.98	462.50	406.58	178.80
1986																
January	35.1	38.5	40.8	3.5	29.4	112.5	106.9	8.68	7.71	12.32	9.66	6.00	304.67	461.77	394.79	173.35
February	34.8	36.5	40.6	3.4	29.2	111.7	106.2	8.71	7.76	12.37	9.69	6.01	303.11	436.13	391.31	173.03
March	34.9	36.9	40.8	3.5	29.3	112.1	106.2	8.73	7.82	12.29	9.72	6.01	304.68	447.49	396.01	174.27
April	34.8	37.5	40.6	3.4	29.1	111.9	105.7	8.72	7.85	12.37	9.70	6.01	303.46	462.38	393.26	173.98
May	34.8	37.4	40.7	3.5	29.2	112.1	105.8	8.74	7.85	12.42	9.73	6.01	304.15	469.20	394.63	174.89
June	34.7	37.2	40.6	3.4	29.1	111.6	105.2	8.75	7.83	12.45	9.73	6.02	303.63	467.21	396.17	177.00
July	34.7	37.4	40.6	3.5	29.1	112.0	104.8	8.75	7.83	12.45	9.74	6.02	303.63	472.15	391.55	178.20
August	34.8	37.6	40.8	3.5	29.2	112.5	105.4	8.77	7.84	12.50	9.75	6.03	305.20	476.44	393.98	178.50
September	34.7	37.7	40.7	3.5	29.1	112.6	105.3	8.77	7.81	12.52	9.74	6.04	304.32	485.87	399.34	176.35
October	34.6	37.2	40.6	3.5	29.1	112.6	104.9	8.80	7.83	12.60	9.76	6.06	304.48	481.33	396.58	175.74
November	34.7	37.1	40.8	3.5	29.2	113.1	105.4	8.85	7.85	12.68	9.78	6.07	307.10	462.82	401.39	176.32
December	34.7	37.3	40.9	3.6	28.9	113.2	105.7	8.85	7.83	12.74	9.80	6.08	307.10	471.04	409.76	178.46
1987																
January	34.7	38.5	40.9	3.6	29.0	113.7	105.8	8.87	7.80	12.58	9.81	6.05	307.79	469.84	401.88	172.35
February	34.9	38.2	41.2	3.7	29.3	114.5	106.7	8.89	7.78	12.55	9.83	6.05	310.26	463.10	401.88	174.50
March	34.8	37.8	41.0	3.7	29.3	114.5	106.3	8.91	7.77	12.67	9.85	6.06	310.07	472.74	403.27	175.42
April	34.7	37.3	40.9	3.7	29.3	114.6	106.4	8.92	7.74	12.66	9.86	6.08	309.52	471.99	398.75	177.83
May	34.8	38.2	41.0	3.7	29.3	115.4	106.7	8.95	7.75	12.71	9.88	6.09	311.46	489.06	403.68	177.83
June	34.8	37.7	41.0	3.7	29.3	115.4	106.6	8.95	7.72	12.76	9.88	6.10	311.46	483.99	405.66	179.97
July	34.7	37.8	41.0	3.8	29.2	115.6	107.0	8.96	7.70	12.69	9.87	6.12	310.91	486.75	400.72	182.40
August	34.9	37.8	41.0	3.8	29.4	116.4	107.3	9.02	7.72	12.73	9.93	6.13	314.80	489.83	403.27	183.31
September	34.8	37.7	40.9	3.8	29.5	116.3	107.5	9.03	7.70	12.71	9.99	6.18	314.24	467.57	407.59	182.90
October	34.8	37.9	41.1	3.8	29.2	116.8	108.3	9.06	7.70	12.74	9.98	6.15	315.29	498.19	410.94	179.26
November	34.8	37.6	41.1	3.9	29.2	117.2	108.7	9.10	7.72	12.85	10.00	6.16	316.68	477.11	414.41	179.22
December	34.7	38.1	41.1	3.9	28.8	117.1	108.8	9.12	7.72	12.79	10.02	6.19	316.46	482.78	420.93	181.37
1988																
January	34.7	37.7	41.1	3.9	29.1	117.2	108.7	9.14	7.72	13.02	10.05	6.21	317.16	468.50	413.28	177.22
February	34.7	37.4	41.0	3.8	29.1	118.0	108.8	9.13	7.70	12.92	10.05	6.22	316.81	446.44	409.44	178.46
March	34.6	37.8	41.0	3.8	29.1	117.8	108.6	9.15	7.69	12.86	10.07	6.24	316.59	481.50	412.27	178.46
April	34.6	37.6	40.8	3.7	29.1	118.2	108.3	9.20	7.70	12.99	10.12	6.26	318.32	491.18	415.33	181.83
May	34.6	37.7	41.0	3.8	29.1	118.5	108.9	9.24	7.71	12.99	10.15	6.28	319.70	466.73	416.15	182.12
June	34.6	37.9	41.0	3.8	29.1	118.9	109.2	9.26	7.69	13.04	10.17	6.30	320.40	501.94	419.00	184.97
July	34.7	37.6	41.0	3.8	29.2	119.4	109.2	9.28	7.67	13.09	10.18	6.32	322.02	502.43	414.33	189.03
August	34.5	37.6	40.9	3.8	29.0	119.0	108.7	9.30	7.65	13.11	10.21	6.32	320.85	503.58	414.73	186.55
September	34.6	37.5	40.9	3.8	29.1	119.5	108.9	9.35	7.66	13.15	10.24	6.36	323.51	508.24	423.74	185.66
October	34.7	37.8	41.0	3.9	29.2	120.3	109.5	9.40	7.67	13.17	10.28	6.38	326.18	517.92	424.15	186.59
November	34.6	37.9	41.1	3.9	29.1	120.3	110.1	9.40	7.65	13.15	10.31	6.41	325.24	467.57	428.70	185.18
December	34.6	37.6	41.0	3.9	29.2	120.8	109.9	9.44	7.67	13.27	10.33	6.41	326.62	495.13	432.22	190.67
1989																
January	34.6	37.5	41.1	3.9	29.1	121.1	110.5	9.49	7.67	13.37	10.37	6.43	328.35	487.64	425.99	184.40
February	34.6	37.3	41.2	4.0	29.0	121.4	110.7	9.53	7.68	13.37	10.41	6.46	329.74	481.21	424.32	183.10
March	34.6	37.8	41.1	3.9	29.0	121.7	110.6	9.55	7.65	13.41	10.43	6.46	330.43	500.41	427.22	184.40
April	34.6	37.9	41.3	4.0	28.9	122.0	110.9	9.58	7.62	13.47	10.42	6.48	331.47	509.38	427.22	188.14
May	34.5	37.4	40.9	3.7	28.9	121.7	109.7	9.59	7.59	13.46	10.42	6.48	330.86	506.31	426.59	186.62
June	34.5	37.1	40.9	3.7	28.9	121.5	109.2	9.62	7.59	13.49	10.45	6.50	331.89	507.86	429.50	188.92
July	34.5	38.2	40.9	3.7	28.9	121.7	108.8	9.66	7.60	13.53	10.48	6.52	333.27	525.15	424.85	193.10
August	34.5	38.0	40.9	3.7	28.9	121.7	108.7	9.68	7.62	13.53	10.52	6.55	333.96	526.32	427.41	191.81
September	34.5	37.7	40.8	3.6	28.8	121.9	108.3	9.72	7.63	13.55	10.53	6.57	335.34	528.05	435.07	190.45
October	34.5	38.1	40.7	3.7	28.9	122.1	107.8	9.75	7.62	13.62	10.56	6.59	336.38	538.61	430.68	190.74
November	34.5	38.1	40.8	3.6	28.8	122.4	108.0	9.79	7.62	13.72	10.58	6.60	337.76	522.73	433.78	189.33
December	34.4	37.6	40.6	3.6	28.8	122.2	107.5	9.83	7.63	13.79	10.62	6.65	338.15	514.95	440.67	193.89

1. Includes industries not shown seperately.

Table 24-6. Average Hours and Earnings—*Continued*

(Production or nonsupervisory workers on private nonfarm payrolls; seasonally adjusted, except as noted.)

Year and month	Average weekly hours					Indexes of aggregate weekly hours (1982=100)		Average hourly earnings (Dollars)					Average weekly earnings (Dollars)			
	All indus-tries [1]	Con-struction	Manufacturing		Retail trade	All indus-tries [1]	Manufac-turing	All industries [1]					All indus-tries [1]	Not seasonally adjusted		
			Average weekly hours	Overtime hours				Current dollars	1982 dollars	Con-struction	Manufac-turing	Retail trade		Con-struction	Manufac-turing	Retail trade
1990																
January	34.5	38.7	40.7	3.7	28.9	122.9	106.7	9.83	7.56	13.65	10.57	6.67	339.14	512.86	429.95	188.55
February	34.5	38.4	40.8	3.6	28.9	123.2	107.8	9.88	7.57	13.69	10.68	6.69	340.86	508.77	431.07	188.94
March	34.6	38.4	40.9	3.7	28.9	123.5	107.9	9.92	7.56	13.72	10.75	6.71	343.23	518.85	437.12	190.85
April	34.5	38.1	40.8	3.5	28.9	123.1	107.6	9.93	7.56	13.66	10.74	6.71	342.59	508.40	427.45	194.79
May	34.5	38.0	40.9	3.7	28.8	123.2	107.5	9.97	7.58	13.75	10.79	6.73	343.97	525.86	441.72	193.15
June	34.5	38.3	40.9	3.7	28.9	123.4	107.4	10.01	7.57	13.77	10.83	6.76	345.35	534.89	445.52	196.52
July	34.4	37.6	40.9	3.7	28.7	122.8	106.9	10.03	7.55	13.77	10.86	6.76	345.03	528.00	440.24	199.58
August	34.4	38.1	40.8	3.6	28.7	122.8	106.3	10.05	7.49	13.78	10.87	6.77	345.72	537.42	441.05	197.57
September	34.4	38.4	40.8	3.7	28.7	122.7	106.2	10.08	7.46	13.84	10.91	6.78	346.75	545.84	451.41	196.13
October	34.3	37.0	40.7	3.6	28.6	121.9	105.5	10.11	7.43	13.83	10.97	6.80	346.77	531.50	447.45	193.40
November	34.3	38.3	40.5	3.5	28.6	121.8	103.9	10.13	7.43	13.85	10.96	6.81	347.46	529.45	447.17	193.29
December	34.4	39.0	40.6	3.5	28.6	121.8	103.9	10.15	7.43	13.82	10.99	6.81	349.16	534.14	456.37	198.85
1991																
January	34.2	37.3	40.4	3.4	28.5	120.8	102.7	10.18	7.43	14.03	11.02	6.83	348.16	506.80	443.81	189.61
February	34.3	38.2	40.3	3.3	28.6	120.6	101.6	10.19	7.43	13.96	11.03	6.84	349.52	515.69	439.30	191.12
March	34.2	37.9	40.3	3.3	28.6	120.2	101.1	10.22	7.44	13.93	11.07	6.85	349.52	528.07	443.51	193.05
April	34.1	37.8	40.4	3.4	28.5	119.7	101.2	10.26	7.46	14.01	11.11	6.90	349.87	528.07	445.51	195.14
May	34.2	38.0	40.4	3.4	28.6	120.0	101.2	10.30	7.46	13.98	11.15	6.92	352.26	533.90	449.35	196.94
June	34.3	38.0	40.8	3.6	28.6	120.2	102.0	10.32	7.46	13.97	11.18	6.94	353.98	537.77	457.26	202.06
July	34.2	37.9	40.7	3.6	28.6	120.0	102.0	10.35	7.47	13.97	11.22	6.96	353.97	538.86	453.29	202.76
August	34.3	37.9	40.9	3.6	28.6	120.3	102.5	10.37	7.47	14.01	11.23	6.97	355.69	544.36	457.26	202.46
September	34.3	38.3	40.9	3.7	28.6	120.4	102.5	10.39	7.46	14.01	11.26	6.98	356.38	552.87	466.99	201.19
October	34.3	38.2	40.9	3.7	28.6	120.3	102.4	10.39	7.45	14.01	11.29	6.99	356.38	553.90	462.79	198.80
November	34.3	37.9	41.0	3.7	28.7	120.1	102.3	10.42	7.44	13.99	11.32	7.01	357.41	529.20	467.10	199.65
December	34.3	38.5	41.0	3.7	28.6	120.1	102.0	10.45	7.44	14.05	11.32	7.03	358.44	535.15	474.55	204.28
1992																
January	34.3	38.5	40.9	3.5	28.6	120.0	101.2	10.45	7.43	14.07	11.29	7.03	358.44	516.37	458.78	195.84
February	34.3	38.1	41.1	3.7	28.6	120.0	101.6	10.47	7.43	14.02	11.34	7.04	359.12	510.50	460.00	199.80
March	34.3	38.0	41.0	3.7	28.6	120.1	101.5	10.50	7.43	14.12	11.38	7.07	360.15	524.81	465.03	200.36
April	34.4	38.8	41.1	3.8	28.9	120.9	101.9	10.52	7.43	14.11	11.41	7.08	361.89	537.09	461.37	202.35
May	34.5	38.4	41.2	3.9	28.8	121.3	102.2	10.54	7.42	14.12	11.44	7.09	363.63	548.49	470.60	203.48
June	34.3	38.1	41.1	3.8	28.6	120.8	102.0	10.57	7.42	14.23	11.46	7.11	362.55	551.07	473.30	204.90
July	34.4	38.2	41.1	3.8	28.6	121.1	102.0	10.59	7.42	14.14	11.48	7.13	364.30	548.49	466.42	207.74
August	34.4	38.2	41.1	3.8	28.8	121.3	101.9	10.62	7.42	14.20	11.52	7.15	365.33	556.78	470.60	209.57
September	34.4	37.8	41.0	3.7	29.0	121.5	101.6	10.62	7.40	14.09	11.51	7.19	365.33	527.93	472.73	209.09
October	34.4	38.2	41.1	3.8	28.8	121.8	101.7	10.65	7.40	14.20	11.51	7.18	366.36	559.52	474.54	205.35
November	34.4	37.9	41.2	3.8	28.8	122.0	102.0	10.67	7.39	14.22	11.54	7.19	367.05	534.38	480.48	205.92
December	34.4	37.8	41.2	3.9	28.8	122.1	102.1	10.69	7.39	14.23	11.57	7.20	367.74	531.59	487.30	209.95
1993																
January	34.5	38.1	41.4	4.0	28.8	122.8	102.9	10.72	7.39	14.22	11.60	7.22	369.84	514.40	477.17	202.55
February	34.5	38.1	41.4	4.2	28.9	123.4	103.1	10.73	7.38	14.25	11.62	7.24	370.19	518.57	477.17	204.73
March	34.3	38.2	41.1	3.9	28.3	122.5	102.2	10.78	7.41	14.34	11.64	7.26	369.75	535.68	475.67	202.11
April	34.5	38.5	41.6	4.4	28.7	123.8	103.5	10.78	7.39	14.33	11.68	7.25	371.91	539.41	479.70	206.18
May	34.5	38.6	41.3	4.1	28.8	124.2	102.8	10.80	7.38	14.36	11.70	7.28	372.60	561.74	483.62	210.10
June	34.4	38.5	41.3	4.1	28.7	124.2	102.5	10.82	7.39	14.35	11.72	7.28	372.21	560.03	484.79	210.54
July	34.5	38.8	41.4	4.1	28.8	124.9	102.9	10.84	7.39	14.41	11.74	7.29	373.98	569.45	480.52	214.60
August	34.5	38.7	41.5	4.1	28.8	125.1	103.0	10.86	7.39	14.41	11.77	7.31	374.67	574.06	485.55	215.33
September	34.6	38.8	41.7	4.3	28.8	125.6	103.8	10.89	7.40	14.38	11.82	7.31	376.79	556.88	491.78	211.55
October	34.6	38.4	41.6	4.3	29.0	126.1	103.7	10.91	7.38	14.43	11.84	7.34	377.49	574.06	493.24	211.68
November	34.6	39.0	41.6	4.3	28.8	126.3	104.0	10.93	7.39	14.45	11.87	7.35	378.18	559.31	498.54	210.50
December	34.6	38.8	41.7	4.4	28.9	126.7	104.3	10.96	7.39	14.48	11.92	7.37	379.22	556.03	508.80	215.65
1994																
January	34.6	38.4	41.7	4.4	28.8	127.0	104.6	10.99	7.41	14.49	11.93	7.40	380.25	535.35	496.34	210.09
February	34.4	37.6	41.2	4.5	28.7	126.7	103.7	11.02	7.42	14.62	12.01	7.42	379.09	524.18	490.80	209.35
March	34.7	38.9	42.1	4.7	28.9	128.5	106.1	11.03	7.40	14.55	11.99	7.43	382.74	553.14	502.38	212.33
April	34.7	38.4	41.9	4.4	29.0	128.9	106.0	11.05	7.41	14.60	12.00	7.46	383.44	557.57	504.42	214.39
May	34.7	39.2	42.0	4.6	28.9	129.4	106.7	11.07	7.41	14.66	12.01	7.47	384.13	562.86	504.84	215.88
June	34.7	38.9	42.0	4.7	29.0	129.9	107.0	11.09	7.39	14.68	12.04	7.49	384.82	579.62	507.67	218.58
July	34.7	38.8	42.1	4.7	29.0	130.4	107.4	11.12	7.38	14.75	12.05	7.50	385.86	587.45	501.28	222.31
August	34.6	38.8	42.0	4.7	29.0	130.5	107.5	11.14	7.37	14.74	12.08	7.51	385.44	589.44	504.42	220.97
September	34.6	38.7	41.9	4.6	28.9	130.8	107.6	11.17	7.37	14.82	12.11	7.53	386.48	599.60	515.16	218.66
October	34.7	38.6	42.1	4.8	29.0	131.5	108.3	11.21	7.39	14.92	12.15	7.55	388.99	597.17	512.25	220.29
November	34.6	38.9	42.1	4.8	28.9	131.8	108.6	11.22	7.38	14.85	12.17	7.56	388.21	573.65	517.65	217.26
December	34.6	39.1	42.1	4.8	28.9	132.4	108.8	11.25	7.39	14.85	12.18	7.59	389.25	576.96	526.38	222.39
1995																
January	34.6	39.1	42.1	4.8	28.8	132.7	109.1	11.27	7.38	14.78	12.21	7.58	389.94	556.04	514.50	215.17
February	34.5	37.8	41.9	4.7	28.7	132.6	108.7	11.30	7.38	14.96	12.26	7.61	389.85	550.19	511.24	214.40
March	34.5	38.9	41.8	4.6	28.7	132.9	108.5	11.33	7.38	14.98	12.26	7.61	390.89	568.42	511.66	215.93
April	34.5	38.8	41.6	4.4	28.8	133.0	108.0	11.35	7.37	15.01	12.29	7.63	391.58	562.86	496.92	221.09
May	34.3	38.0	41.5	4.3	28.8	132.5	107.4	11.37	7.37	15.05	12.30	7.65	389.99	577.89	509.22	219.27
June	34.5	38.9	41.5	4.3	28.8	133.3	107.4	11.41	7.38	15.11	12.34	7.68	393.65	595.58	512.51	222.62
July	34.4	38.9	41.4	4.3	28.7	133.2	106.9	11.45	7.40	15.12	12.41	7.71	393.88	606.00	505.92	227.50
August	34.4	38.8	41.5	4.4	28.8	133.7	107.4	11.47	7.40	15.13	12.42	7.73	394.57	604.96	512.53	225.68
September	34.4	38.7	41.5	4.4	28.8	134.1	107.3	11.50	7.41	15.16	12.43	7.76	395.60	612.47	523.74	224.55
October	34.4	39.1	41.5	4.4	28.7	134.0	107.1	11.53	7.41	15.18	12.47	7.75	396.63	615.54	518.33	223.78
November	34.4	38.8	41.5	4.4	28.8	134.3	106.9	11.56	7.42	15.24	12.49	7.77	397.66	590.56	523.33	222.51
December	34.3	38.6	41.2	4.3	28.7	134.2	106.3	11.58	7.42	15.10	12.52	7.80	397.19	577.22	529.20	226.20

1. Includes industries not shown seperately.

Table 24-7. Consumer Price Indexes

(All urban consumers; 1982–1984=100, seasonally adjusted)

Year and month	All items	Food	Housing					Apparel	Transportation			Medical care	Energy	All items less food and energy
			Total	Shelter		Fuels and utilities	House-hold furnish-ings and operations		Total	New vehicles	Motor fuel			
				Total	Rent of primary residence									
1972														
January	41.2	41.1	38.9	38.0	...	32.0	49.2	61.7	39.7	54.7	28.2	36.8	27.0	43.5
February	41.4	41.7	39.0	38.1	...	32.1	49.2	61.9	39.6	54.7	28.1	36.9	26.8	43.6
March	41.4	41.6	39.0	38.2	...	32.2	49.4	61.9	39.6	54.9	28.1	37.0	26.9	43.6
April	41.5	41.6	39.1	38.3	...	32.3	49.4	62.1	39.6	55.0	27.8	37.1	26.9	43.8
May	41.6	41.7	39.2	38.4	...	32.4	49.6	62.2	39.7	55.0	28.0	37.2	27.0	43.9
June	41.7	41.9	39.4	38.6	...	32.5	49.6	62.2	39.7	55.0	27.7	37.3	27.0	44.0
July	41.8	42.1	39.6	38.8	...	32.6	49.7	62.2	39.8	55.1	28.0	37.3	27.1	44.1
August	41.9	42.2	39.7	39.0	...	32.7	49.8	62.0	40.0	55.3	28.4	37.4	27.3	44.3
September	42.1	42.5	39.8	39.0	...	32.8	49.9	62.5	40.2	55.6	29.0	37.4	27.6	44.3
October	42.2	42.8	39.8	39.1	...	32.9	49.9	62.8	40.1	54.1	29.1	37.8	27.7	44.4
November	42.4	43.0	39.9	39.2	...	33.0	50.0	63.0	40.3	54.0	29.3	37.8	27.9	44.4
December	42.5	43.2	40.1	39.3	...	33.0	50.2	63.2	40.4	54.2	29.3	37.9	27.8	44.6
1973														
January	42.7	44.0	40.1	39.4	...	33.1	50.2	63.2	40.4	54.1	29.4	38.0	27.9	44.6
February	43.0	44.6	40.2	39.5	...	33.4	50.3	63.4	40.6	54.3	29.6	38.1	28.2	44.8
March	43.4	45.8	40.4	39.6	...	33.5	50.4	63.8	40.7	54.5	29.7	38.2	28.3	45.0
April	43.7	46.5	40.5	39.7	...	33.7	50.6	64.2	41.0	54.7	30.2	38.3	28.6	45.1
May	43.9	47.1	40.6	39.9	...	33.8	50.7	64.4	41.0	54.8	30.4	38.5	28.8	45.3
June	44.2	47.6	40.9	40.0	...	34.0	51.0	64.6	41.2	54.8	31.0	38.6	29.2	45.4
July	44.2	47.7	41.0	40.1	...	34.1	51.1	64.6	41.2	55.1	31.0	38.6	29.2	45.5
August	45.0	50.5	41.3	40.5	...	34.4	51.3	64.9	41.2	55.2	31.0	38.7	29.4	45.7
September	45.2	50.4	41.7	41.0	...	34.5	51.5	65.2	41.1	55.2	30.8	38.9	29.4	46.0
October	45.6	50.7	42.1	41.6	...	35.1	51.7	65.4	41.4	55.0	32.2	39.6	30.3	46.3
November	45.9	51.4	42.5	41.8	...	35.8	52.0	65.7	41.8	55.0	33.7	39.7	31.5	46.5
December	46.3	51.9	42.8	42.1	...	36.7	52.2	66.0	42.2	54.8	35.2	39.9	32.5	46.7
1974														
January	46.8	52.5	43.3	42.4	...	37.9	52.7	66.3	42.8	55.1	37.2	40.1	34.1	46.9
February	47.3	53.6	43.6	42.7	...	38.6	53.1	67.0	43.4	55.2	39.3	40.3	35.4	47.2
March	47.8	54.2	44.1	43.0	...	38.9	53.9	67.5	44.2	55.5	42.1	40.7	36.9	47.6
April	48.1	54.1	44.4	43.2	...	39.6	54.4	68.2	44.7	55.8	42.7	41.0	37.6	47.9
May	48.6	54.5	44.9	43.5	...	40.1	55.5	68.7	45.3	56.6	43.6	41.4	38.3	48.5
June	49.0	54.5	45.4	43.9	...	40.5	56.3	69.2	45.9	57.5	43.6	42.1	38.6	49.0
July	49.3	54.3	45.9	44.4	...	41.0	57.1	69.5	46.4	58.6	43.7	42.6	38.9	49.5
August	49.9	55.1	46.5	44.9	...	41.6	58.1	70.8	46.6	59.0	43.4	43.2	39.2	50.2
September	50.6	56.2	47.1	45.5	...	42.0	59.0	71.0	47.0	59.8	43.2	43.7	39.3	50.7
October	51.0	56.8	47.7	46.0	...	42.3	59.8	71.2	47.3	60.9	42.6	44.1	39.2	51.2
November	51.5	57.5	48.1	46.3	...	42.6	60.6	71.7	47.6	61.0	42.4	44.4	39.4	51.6
December	51.9	58.2	48.6	'46.9	...	42.8	61.2	71.7	47.9	61.0	42.5	44.8	39.6	52.0
1975														
January	52.3	58.4	49.0	47.3	...	43.4	61.6	71.8	48.0	60.3	42.8	45.3	40.0	52.3
February	52.6	58.5	49.4	47.7	...	43.8	62.1	72.0	48.3	61.1	42.8	45.8	40.3	52.8
March	52.8	58.4	49.7	47.9	...	44.0	62.4	72.1	48.7	62.7	43.0	46.3	40.6	53.0
April	53.0	58.3	50.0	48.2	...	44.5	62.8	72.1	48.8	63.0	43.0	46.7	41.0	53.3
May	53.1	58.6	50.2	48.3	...	44.8	63.1	72.2	48.9	62.7	43.5	47.0	41.3	53.5
June	53.5	59.2	50.5	48.7	...	45.2	63.4	72.2	49.4	62.9	44.5	47.4	41.7	53.8
July	54.0	60.3	50.7	48.9	...	45.4	63.6	72.6	50.2	62.9	46.1	47.8	42.5	54.0
August	54.2	60.3	51.0	49.0	...	45.8	63.8	72.6	50.6	63.3	46.5	48.1	42.8	54.2
September	54.6	60.7	51.3	49.3	...	46.4	64.1	72.7	51.4	63.7	46.9	48.5	43.2	54.5
October	54.9	61.3	51.5	49.6	...	46.7	64.4	73.0	51.7	64.0	47.3	48.9	43.5	54.8
November	55.3	61.7	52.0	50.0	...	47.4	64.6	73.2	52.4	64.2	47.3	48.8	43.9	55.2
December	55.6	62.1	52.3	50.3	...	47.7	64.8	73.4	52.6	65.3	47.2	49.3	44.1	55.5
1976														
January	55.8	61.9	52.6	50.5	...	48.0	65.7	73.7	53.0	65.5	47.1	49.7	44.5	55.9
February	55.9	61.3	52.8	50.6	...	48.3	66.1	74.0	53.3	65.8	46.7	50.2	44.4	56.2
March	56.0	60.9	52.9	50.7	...	48.4	66.5	74.2	53.8	66.1	46.3	50.7	44.1	56.5
April	56.1	60.9	53.1	50.7	...	48.6	66.7	74.3	54.0	66.3	45.7	51.0	43.9	56.7
May	56.4	61.1	53.2	50.9	...	48.7	66.8	74.6	54.3	66.4	46.1	51.4	44.1	57.0
June	56.7	61.3	53.5	51.2	...	48.8	67.1	74.9	54.8	66.5	46.7	51.8	44.4	57.2
July	57.0	61.6	53.8	51.6	...	49.1	67.4	75.3	55.1	66.7	46.8	52.3	44.8	57.6
August	57.3	61.8	54.1	51.9	...	49.6	67.6	75.8	55.4	67.1	46.9	52.6	45.2	57.9
September	57.6	62.1	54.4	52.2	...	50.0	67.8	76.1	56.0	67.6	47.2	53.0	45.7	58.2
October	57.9	62.4	54.6	52.3	...	50.5	68.1	76.2	56.6	68.7	47.8	53.2	46.1	58.5
November	58.1	62.3	54.8	52.4	...	51.4	68.4	76.5	57.0	68.4	48.2	53.9	46.8	58.7
December	58.4	62.5	55.1	52.4	...	52.3	68.6	76.8	57.3	68.6	48.3	54.2	47.5	58.9
1977														
January	58.7	62.7	55.6	52.9	...	53.3	68.9	77.2	57.8	68.8	48.5	54.6	48.1	59.3
February	59.3	63.9	55.9	53.2	...	53.5	69.2	77.6	58.2	68.9	49.2	54.9	48.1	59.7
March	59.6	64.2	56.2	53.5	...	53.9	69.4	77.5	58.7	69.3	49.7	55.5	48.4	60.0
April	60.0	65.0	56.5	54.0	...	54.1	69.5	77.6	59.0	69.4	49.7	56.0	48.6	60.3
May	60.2	65.3	56.8	54.3	...	54.0	69.8	78.1	59.1	69.7	50.0	56.5	48.9	60.6
June	60.5	65.7	57.1	54.7	...	54.1	70.2	78.5	59.1	70.0	49.7	57.0	48.9	61.0
July	60.8	65.9	57.6	55.2	...	54.5	70.5	79.1	59.0	70.3	49.4	57.3	49.1	61.2
August	61.1	66.2	57.9	55.5	...	55.0	70.8	79.2	58.9	70.6	49.4	57.7	49.5	61.5
September	61.3	66.4	58.3	55.9	...	55.4	71.0	79.1	59.1	70.9	49.6	58.2	49.8	61.8
October	61.6	66.6	58.6	56.2	...	55.7	71.3	79.3	59.3	72.1	50.1	58.4	50.5	62.0
November	62.0	67.1	59.0	56.6	...	56.8	71.5	79.8	59.5	72.6	50.5	58.6	51.3	62.3
December	62.3	67.4	59.4	57.0	...	56.8	71.9	80.1	59.8	73.6	50.9	59.0	51.6	62.7

Table 24-7. Consumer Price Indexes—*Continued*

(All urban consumers; 1982–1984=100, seasonally adjusted)

Year and month	All items	Food	Housing Total	Shelter Total	Rent of primary residence	Fuels and utilities	House-hold furnish-ings and operations	Apparel	Transportation Total	New vehicles	Motor fuel	Medical care	Energy	All items less food and energy
1978														
January	62.7	67.9	59.7	57.5	...	56.7	72.2	80.1	60.1	74.2	50.9	59.3	51.1	63.1
February	63.0	68.6	60.1	57.8	...	57.1	72.3	79.5	60.2	74.5	50.6	59.9	50.6	63.4
March	63.4	69.5	60.5	58.3	...	57.5	72.8	79.9	60.3	74.8	50.7	60.2	51.0	63.8
April	63.9	70.6	61.0	58.8	...	58.0	73.3	80.7	60.4	74.7	50.4	60.7	51.4	64.3
May	64.5	71.6	61.6	59.4	...	58.3	73.8	81.3	60.7	74.9	50.5	61.1	51.7	64.7
June	65.0	72.7	62.1	60.0	...	58.4	74.4	81.6	61.1	75.4	50.7	61.5	51.9	65.2
July	65.5	73.0	62.7	60.7	...	58.4	74.8	81.5	61.6	75.7	51.1	61.9	52.1	65.6
August	65.9	73.3	63.1	61.3	...	58.6	75.3	81.7	62.0	76.0	51.8	62.4	52.6	66.1
September	66.5	73.6	63.8	62.1	...	58.8	75.8	81.9	62.6	76.6	52.5	62.8	53.2	66.7
October	67.1	74.2	64.5	62.8	...	59.4	76.4	82.4	63.3	77.3	53.5	63.3	54.1	67.2
November	67.5	74.7	64.9	63.3	...	59.6	76.9	82.6	63.9	77.9	54.4	63.8	54.9	67.6
December	67.9	75.1	65.2	63.5	...	60.0	77.4	82.6	64.5	78.6	55.4	64.1	55.9	68.0
1979														
January	68.5	76.4	65.7	64.0	...	60.4	77.9	83.0	64.6	79.0	56.0	64.8	55.8	68.5
February	69.2	77.7	66.5	64.9	...	60.8	78.2	83.3	65.2	79.8	56.4	65.2	55.9	69.2
March	69.9	78.4	67.0	65.5	...	61.3	78.6	83.6	66.4	80.3	59.0	65.7	57.4	69.8
April	70.6	79.0	67.7	66.3	...	61.9	79.0	84.0	67.8	81.2	62.1	66.1	59.5	70.3
May	71.4	79.7	68.4	67.1	...	62.7	79.3	84.5	69.1	81.6	65.2	66.6	62.0	70.8
June	72.2	80.0	69.3	68.0	...	64.0	79.7	84.7	70.5	81.9	69.1	67.1	64.7	71.3
July	73.0	80.5	70.2	69.0	...	65.1	80.0	84.8	71.7	82.4	72.7	67.7	67.3	71.9
August	73.7	80.4	71.2	70.1	...	66.4	80.4	85.0	72.7	82.7	75.9	68.2	69.7	72.7
September	74.4	80.9	72.1	71.1	...	67.4	80.7	85.6	73.5	82.9	78.8	68.7	71.9	73.3
October	75.2	81.5	73.1	72.3	...	68.2	81.2	86.1	74.0	83.2	80.4	69.2	73.5	74.0
November	76.0	82.0	74.2	73.5	...	68.8	82.0	86.6	74.7	83.8	81.7	69.8	74.8	74.8
December	76.9	82.8	75.2	74.6	...	69.6	82.5	87.3	75.8	84.2	83.8	70.6	76.8	75.7
1980														
January	78.0	83.3	76.2	75.9	...	70.4	83.0	88.1	78.0	85.2	89.8	71.4	79.1	76.7
February	79.0	83.4	77.2	76.8	...	71.5	83.6	88.7	79.8	86.3	94.1	72.3	81.9	77.5
March	80.1	84.1	78.3	78.1	...	72.6	84.4	89.7	81.8	86.5	99.6	73.0	84.5	78.6
April	80.9	84.7	79.4	79.3	...	73.7	84.9	90.1	82.2	87.4	98.7	73.6	85.4	79.5
May	81.7	85.2	80.5	80.5	...	74.5	85.5	90.3	82.8	88.0	98.7	74.2	86.4	80.1
June	82.5	85.7	82.0	82.3	...	75.5	86.1	90.6	82.7	87.9	98.1	74.7	86.5	81.0
July	82.6	86.6	81.5	81.3	...	76.3	86.6	90.9	83.1	88.5	97.9	75.2	86.7	80.8
August	83.2	88.0	81.8	81.4	...	76.9	87.2	91.4	83.7	89.8	97.8	75.6	87.2	81.3
September	83.9	89.1	82.3	82.0	...	77.3	87.9	92.0	84.6	90.5	97.7	76.3	87.5	82.1
October	84.7	89.8	83.4	83.4	...	77.5	88.3	92.7	85.3	90.3	98.5	76.9	88.0	83.0
November	85.6	90.8	84.4	84.7	...	78.1	88.6	93.1	86.1	90.6	98.7	77.3	88.8	83.9
December	86.4	91.3	85.5	85.8	...	79.2	89.1	93.3	86.8	90.6	99.4	77.8	90.7	84.9
1981														
January	87.2	91.6	86.1	86.3	84.7	80.7	89.6	93.4	88.5	90.9	103.5	78.6	92.1	85.4
February	88.0	92.1	86.6	86.3	85.2	82.7	90.3	93.9	90.7	90.9	109.9	79.2	95.2	85.9
March	88.6	92.6	87.1	86.7	85.9	83.8	90.9	94.3	91.8	90.4	113.0	79.9	97.4	86.4
April	89.1	92.8	87.8	87.3	86.5	84.8	91.7	94.7	91.7	91.9	110.6	80.7	97.6	87.0
May	89.7	92.8	88.8	88.6	87.1	85.2	92.1	94.8	92.2	93.9	109.0	81.4	97.9	87.8
June	90.5	93.2	89.8	89.9	87.6	85.7	92.7	95.0	92.7	94.7	107.8	82.3	97.3	88.6
July	91.5	93.9	91.3	91.5	87.9	87.0	93.3	95.4	93.5	95.1	107.2	83.4	97.3	89.8
August	92.2	94.4	92.2	92.5	88.8	87.9	93.9	95.9	93.9	94.8	107.2	84.3	97.8	90.7
September	93.1	94.8	93.4	93.9	89.5	88.8	94.4	96.1	94.6	95.1	107.7	85.1	98.6	91.8
October	93.4	95.0	93.4	93.8	90.0	88.9	94.8	96.4	95.5	95.6	108.3	85.9	99.2	92.1
November	93.8	95.1	93.8	94.0	90.6	89.9	95.5	96.4	96.2	96.1	108.9	86.8	100.5	92.5
December	94.1	95.3	94.1	94.3	91.3	90.4	95.8	96.7	96.4	96.8	108.6	87.5	101.5	93.0
1982														
January	94.4	95.6	94.4	94.4	91.9	91.3	96.2	96.7	96.7	96.9	108.1	88.2	100.6	93.3
February	94.7	96.3	94.7	94.7	92.3	91.7	96.7	97.0	96.2	96.3	106.0	88.8	98.0	93.8
March	94.7	96.2	94.6	94.2	92.9	92.6	97.1	97.3	95.8	96.0	103.6	89.6	96.6	93.9
April	95.0	96.4	95.4	95.3	93.2	93.1	97.3	97.5	94.5	96.8	97.3	90.5	94.2	94.7
May	95.9	97.2	96.7	96.8	93.8	93.8	97.8	97.6	95.1	97.2	97.8	91.3	95.7	95.4
June	97.0	98.1	97.7	98.0	94.3	94.5	98.0	97.7	97.2	97.7	102.8	92.2	98.4	96.1
July	97.5	98.2	98.1	98.5	95.0	94.9	98.3	98.1	98.1	98.1	104.3	93.0	99.3	96.7
August	97.7	98.0	98.4	98.9	95.5	95.4	98.3	98.1	98.2	98.3	104.1	93.9	99.8	97.1
September	97.7	98.2	98.2	98.4	95.7	96.1	98.5	98.1	98.0	98.3	103.2	94.7	100.3	97.2
October	98.1	98.2	98.6	98.4	96.5	97.7	98.9	98.3	98.2	98.0	103.2	95.5	101.7	97.5
November	98.0	98.2	98.3	97.9	97.0	98.4	98.8	98.3	98.2	97.9	102.8	96.5	102.5	97.3
December	97.7	98.2	97.5	96.5	97.4	98.9	99.1	98.2	97.7	98.3	100.4	97.2	102.8	97.2
1983														
January	97.9	98.1	98.0	97.2	98.0	99.4	99.3	98.6	97.6	98.6	99.0	97.9	99.6	97.6
February	98.0	98.2	98.2	97.5	98.5	99.2	99.4	99.1	96.9	98.9	95.9	98.8	97.7	98.0
March	98.1	98.8	98.3	97.6	98.8	99.0	99.6	99.1	96.5	99.0	94.2	99.0	96.8	98.2
April	98.8	99.2	98.9	98.4	99.3	99.5	100.0	99.3	97.8	99.2	98.0	99.4	98.9	98.6
May	99.2	99.5	99.1	98.7	99.5	99.9	99.9	99.9	98.6	99.5	100.5	99.9	100.4	98.9
June	99.4	99.6	99.3	99.0	99.9	99.9	100.1	100.3	99.0	99.7	101.0	100.4	100.6	99.2
July	99.8	99.6	99.7	99.4	100.2	100.3	100.3	100.9	99.6	99.8	101.3	100.8	100.9	99.8
August	100.1	99.7	99.8	99.6	100.6	100.2	100.3	101.0	100.4	100.3	102.1	101.4	101.2	100.1
September	100.4	100.0	100.1	100.1	101.1	100.6	100.3	100.8	100.7	100.6	101.2	101.8	101.0	100.5
October	100.8	100.3	100.4	100.3	101.3	100.8	100.6	100.6	101.1	100.8	100.7	102.3	100.8	101.0
November	101.1	100.3	100.8	100.7	101.7	101.3	100.9	100.9	101.5	101.0	99.5	102.8	100.5	101.5
December	101.4	100.6	101.0	101.1	102.1	101.2	101.2	101.1	101.5	101.3	98.6	103.4	100.0	101.8

Table 24-7. Consumer Price Indexes—*Continued*

(All urban consumers; 1982–1984=100, seasonally adjusted)

Year and month	All items	Food	Housing Total	Shelter Total	Shelter Rent of primary residence	Fuels and utilities	Household furnishings and operations	Apparel	Transportation Total	New vehicles	Motor fuel	Medical care	Energy	All items less food and energy
1984														
January	102.1	102.0	101.5	101.4	102.5	102.4	101.2	101.5	102.0	101.4	98.9	104.0	100.2	102.5
February	102.6	102.7	102.1	101.8	102.9	104.2	101.0	101.2	102.2	101.6	99.4	105.0	101.4	102.8
March	102.9	102.9	102.3	102.3	103.5	103.6	101.2	101.3	102.9	101.9	100.1	105.2	101.4	103.2
April	103.3	102.9	102.9	103.0	104.3	104.3	101.4	101.2	103.3	102.1	99.9	105.8	101.7	103.7
May	103.5	102.7	103.1	103.2	104.6	104.4	101.6	101.4	103.7	102.3	99.5	106.2	101.6	104.1
June	103.7	103.1	103.3	103.6	105.1	104.3	101.7	101.3	103.9	102.5	98.3	106.7	100.8	104.5
July	104.1	103.3	103.9	104.3	105.6	105.3	101.5	101.9	103.7	102.8	96.4	107.2	100.5	105.0
August	104.4	103.9	104.2	104.7	106.1	105.6	102.0	102.5	103.8	103.0	95.4	107.7	100.1	105.4
September	104.7	103.8	104.7	105.1	106.5	106.0	102.5	102.7	104.1	103.3	96.1	108.1	100.6	105.8
October	105.1	104.0	104.9	105.5	107.0	105.8	102.6	103.0	104.8	103.5	97.4	108.7	101.1	106.2
November	105.3	104.1	105.1	105.8	107.4	105.9	102.6	103.0	104.9	103.6	97.0	109.3	100.8	106.4
December	105.5	104.5	105.3	106.4	108.1	105.4	102.7	103.1	104.7	103.7	96.0	109.8	100.1	106.8
1985														
January	105.7	104.7	105.5	106.7	108.5	105.6	102.5	103.2	105.1	104.4	96.4	110.2	100.3	107.1
February	106.3	105.2	106.0	107.4	109.2	105.3	103.3	104.1	105.6	104.9	96.5	110.8	100.3	107.7
March	106.8	105.5	106.4	107.8	109.7	106.0	103.6	104.5	106.3	105.3	98.1	111.4	101.3	108.1
April	107.0	105.4	106.7	108.1	110.2	106.3	104.0	104.5	106.8	105.5	99.8	112.0	102.3	108.4
May	107.2	105.2	107.4	109.2	111.0	106.4	103.9	104.4	106.5	105.7	99.4	112.6	102.2	108.8
June	107.5	105.5	107.6	109.6	111.6	106.6	103.7	105.1	106.5	106.0	99.8	113.3	102.2	109.1
July	107.7	105.5	107.9	110.1	112.0	106.7	103.5	105.2	106.6	106.2	100.0	113.9	102.2	109.4
August	107.9	105.6	108.3	110.8	112.6	106.4	103.7	105.3	106.2	106.4	98.7	114.6	101.2	109.8
September	108.1	105.8	108.5	111.0	113.0	106.8	103.8	105.5	106.2	106.8	98.2	115.2	101.2	110.0
October	108.5	105.8	108.9	111.5	113.8	106.8	104.4	105.7	106.5	106.8	98.2	115.8	101.2	110.5
November	109.0	106.5	109.5	112.3	114.6	107.3	104.6	106.0	107.0	107.3	98.9	116.5	101.8	111.1
December	109.5	107.3	109.8	112.7	115.0	107.7	104.5	106.1	107.5	107.4	99.7	117.1	102.4	111.4
1986														
January	109.9	107.5	110.1	113.2	115.4	107.8	104.5	106.1	108.0	107.8	100.1	118.0	102.6	111.9
February	109.7	107.3	110.0	113.5	115.6	106.4	104.6	105.4	107.0	108.1	95.9	118.8	99.5	112.2
March	109.1	107.5	110.3	114.3	116.4	105.3	104.9	105.0	103.6	108.4	83.5	119.7	92.6	112.5
April	108.7	107.7	110.4	115.0	117.6	104.4	104.9	105.0	101.0	109.0	74.3	120.4	87.2	112.9
May	109.0	108.2	110.4	115.2	117.8	103.7	105.0	104.9	101.4	109.9	75.5	121.2	87.2	113.1
June	109.4	108.3	110.9	115.6	118.2	104.7	105.1	104.9	102.3	110.7	77.9	121.8	88.8	113.4
July	109.5	109.1	110.9	115.9	118.9	103.6	105.2	105.5	101.1	111.3	72.9	122.5	85.6	113.8
August	109.6	110.1	111.1	116.3	119.0	103.6	105.2	106.4	100.1	111.6	69.0	123.2	83.6	114.2
September	110.0	110.2	111.5	116.9	119.4	103.4	105.7	106.9	100.6	111.8	70.8	124.0	84.4	114.6
October	110.2	110.5	111.6	117.5	120.0	102.4	105.7	106.6	100.5	112.3	69.2	124.7	82.8	115.0
November	110.4	111.1	111.6	117.8	120.4	101.7	105.5	106.9	100.8	113.1	68.6	125.5	82.1	115.3
December	110.8	111.4	111.9	118.1	120.7	101.8	106.1	107.2	101.1	113.4	69.1	126.2	82.5	115.6
1987														
January	111.5	111.9	112.2	118.4	121.2	102.2	106.3	108.0	102.7	113.9	74.1	126.8	85.1	116.1
February	111.9	112.3	112.6	118.9	121.6	102.2	106.5	108.6	103.6	112.9	78.4	127.3	87.1	116.4
March	112.3	112.5	112.9	119.3	122.0	102.4	106.8	109.2	103.9	112.9	78.7	127.9	87.3	116.8
April	112.8	112.7	113.4	120.1	122.2	102.3	107.2	109.8	104.4	113.3	79.3	128.7	87.3	117.5
May	113.1	113.3	113.7	120.5	122.5	102.5	107.1	110.3	104.5	113.8	77.8	129.3	86.8	117.9
June	113.6	114.0	114.0	120.8	122.5	103.1	107.1	110.3	105.2	114.3	79.5	130.1	88.2	118.1
July	113.9	113.8	114.2	120.9	123.0	103.3	107.2	110.3	106.0	114.9	81.2	130.7	88.9	118.5
August	114.4	114.0	114.8	121.7	123.8	104.0	107.3	111.0	106.7	115.0	83.1	131.3	90.2	118.9
September	114.8	114.5	115.1	122.2	124.2	104.0	107.5	111.6	107.0	115.3	82.7	132.0	90.0	119.4
October	115.1	114.7	115.4	122.9	124.6	103.3	107.4	112.3	107.1	115.4	82.6	132.5	89.3	120.0
November	115.5	114.7	115.7	123.2	124.6	103.7	107.4	113.0	107.4	115.8	82.7	133.1	89.7	120.3
December	115.7	115.3	116.0	123.9	125.5	103.4	107.3	112.7	107.3	115.4	82.1	133.6	89.2	120.6
1988														
January	116.1	115.8	116.3	124.4	125.9	103.2	107.5	113.2	107.1	115.1	81.2	134.6	88.5	121.1
February	116.2	115.8	116.7	124.9	126.2	103.5	107.7	112.1	107.1	115.1	80.8	135.4	88.4	121.3
March	116.6	116.0	117.1	125.3	126.6	103.5	108.3	113.4	107.1	115.1	80.0	136.0	88.1	121.9
April	117.2	116.6	117.6	125.8	126.9	103.9	109.1	115.1	107.5	115.4	80.6	136.8	88.5	122.5
May	117.6	117.0	117.8	126.1	127.2	103.7	109.3	115.1	108.0	115.8	80.3	137.7	88.2	122.9
June	118.1	117.7	118.2	126.6	127.6	104.2	109.6	115.5	108.4	116.3	80.2	138.4	88.6	123.4
July	118.6	118.9	118.5	127.0	127.9	104.3	109.8	115.9	108.9	116.6	81.2	139.3	89.1	123.8
August	119.0	119.6	118.9	127.6	128.4	104.4	109.7	114.5	109.7	117.1	82.5	139.9	89.8	124.1
September	119.6	120.2	119.4	128.1	128.9	105.0	110.1	116.3	110.0	117.9	81.4	140.7	89.5	124.8
October	120.0	120.5	119.8	128.4	129.1	105.7	110.3	117.5	110.0	117.9	80.8	141.6	89.5	125.3
November	120.4	120.7	120.1	129.0	129.5	105.6	110.6	117.7	110.3	118.0	80.8	142.1	89.5	125.8
December	120.8	121.2	120.5	129.4	129.9	106.2	110.6	118.2	110.4	118.0	80.3	142.9	89.3	126.2
1989														
January	121.3	121.8	120.8	129.6	130.4	106.6	111.0	118.4	111.0	118.3	81.1	144.0	89.9	126.7
February	121.7	122.6	121.1	130.1	130.9	106.4	110.7	117.1	111.7	118.5	82.6	145.1	90.5	127.0
March	122.3	123.4	121.4	130.8	131.2	106.7	110.3	118.1	112.5	118.7	84.4	145.9	91.5	127.5
April	123.2	124.1	121.8	131.1	131.6	107.1	110.5	118.6	115.1	118.9	93.8	146.8	96.2	128.0
May	123.8	124.9	122.2	131.8	132.0	107.4	110.6	118.9	115.9	119.1	95.7	147.6	97.0	128.5
June	124.1	125.3	122.6	132.2	132.6	107.5	111.0	118.7	115.8	119.1	94.4	148.8	96.5	128.9
July	124.6	125.8	123.3	133.0	133.0	108.1	111.1	118.3	115.4	119.1	93.2	149.7	96.3	129.4
August	124.6	126.1	123.6	133.4	133.5	108.3	111.4	117.1	114.5	119.0	89.1	150.8	94.6	129.7
September	124.9	126.5	123.8	133.7	133.7	108.3	111.5	118.7	114.0	118.8	86.9	151.9	93.4	130.1
October	125.5	127.0	124.4	134.6	134.4	108.4	111.9	119.6	114.6	119.3	87.8	152.9	94.1	130.8
November	125.9	127.5	124.8	135.2	135.0	108.8	111.9	120.0	114.5	120.3	86.2	154.2	93.6	131.3
December	126.4	128.0	125.3	135.7	135.3	109.3	112.0	119.8	114.8	120.9	86.1	155.1	93.9	131.8

Table 24-7. Consumer Price Indexes—*Continued*

(All urban consumers; 1982–1984=100, seasonally adjusted)

Year and month	All items	Food	Housing Total	Shelter Total	Shelter Rent of primary residence	Fuels and utilities	House-hold furnish-ings and operations	Apparel	Transportation Total	Transportation New vehicles	Transportation Motor fuel	Medical care	Energy	All items less food and energy
1990														
January	127.6	129.8	126.0	136.1	135.8	111.1	112.4	119.9	117.1	121.3	93.5	156.2	98.6	132.3
February	128.1	131.0	126.1	136.4	136.1	110.7	112.6	122.0	117.3	121.2	93.3	157.2	97.8	132.9
March	128.6	131.2	126.7	137.4	136.7	110.7	112.6	123.8	117.3	120.9	92.5	158.5	97.2	133.7
April	129.0	131.0	127.0	138.0	137.2	110.5	112.6	124.1	117.8	120.8	92.9	159.8	97.2	134.2
May	129.2	131.3	127.3	138.4	137.6	110.2	112.8	124.0	117.6	120.9	91.8	161.0	96.4	134.6
June	130.0	132.3	128.0	139.4	138.2	110.7	113.0	124.2	118.1	120.8	92.7	162.2	97.0	135.3
July	130.6	133.0	128.6	140.5	138.7	109.9	113.2	124.2	118.5	120.8	93.1	163.6	96.8	136.0
August	131.7	133.4	129.6	141.6	139.3	111.4	113.3	124.5	120.8	121.1	101.2	165.0	101.3	136.8
September	132.6	133.7	130.1	141.9	139.7	112.6	113.8	125.4	123.3	121.2	109.6	166.1	106.2	137.3
October	133.5	134.3	130.5	142.2	140.2	113.7	114.3	125.4	125.7	121.8	117.2	167.4	110.5	137.8
November	133.8	134.7	130.7	142.4	140.5	114.1	114.0	125.4	126.2	122.5	117.4	168.9	110.8	138.2
December	134.3	134.8	130.9	143.0	141.0	113.4	114.0	126.2	126.9	123.4	117.8	170.0	110.6	138.8
1991														
January	134.8	135.2	131.9	143.9	141.2	115.0	114.4	126.9	125.6	124.2	110.9	171.2	108.1	139.7
February	134.9	135.3	132.3	144.2	141.6	115.1	115.4	127.3	123.9	124.8	102.6	172.3	104.2	140.4
March	134.9	135.5	132.5	144.6	142.1	114.9	115.5	127.0	122.8	125.3	97.7	173.4	101.5	140.7
April	135.2	136.3	132.6	145.0	142.6	114.2	115.6	127.5	122.6	125.5	97.6	174.5	100.8	141.1
May	135.7	136.8	133.0	145.3	143.0	114.7	116.0	128.0	123.3	125.7	99.4	175.4	101.8	141.5
June	136.1	137.6	133.1	145.7	143.2	114.4	115.8	127.9	123.5	126.0	98.2	176.6	100.8	142.0
July	136.3	136.8	133.5	146.1	143.7	115.0	116.0	128.7	123.4	126.3	96.4	177.6	100.3	142.5
August	136.7	136.3	133.7	146.4	143.7	115.0	116.2	129.9	124.1	126.4	97.7	179.0	100.8	143.1
September	137.1	136.5	134.2	146.9	144.4	115.5	116.4	130.0	124.1	126.4	97.8	180.1	101.1	143.6
October	137.3	136.4	134.6	147.4	144.4	116.0	116.4	130.1	124.0	126.7	97.3	181.0	101.2	143.9
November	137.9	136.9	135.1	148.0	144.8	116.5	116.6	131.0	124.5	127.0	98.4	182.1	102.0	144.4
December	138.3	137.2	135.5	148.6	145.1	116.8	116.6	130.7	125.2	127.5	99.5	183.3	102.7	144.9
1992														
January	138.4	136.7	135.8	149.1	145.4	116.4	117.0	130.9	124.6	127.6	97.1	184.5	101.2	145.3
February	138.7	137.3	136.0	149.3	145.7	116.4	117.1	131.0	124.6	127.9	96.7	185.8	100.8	145.6
March	139.2	137.7	136.3	149.8	146.5	116.4	117.4	131.3	125.1	128.3	97.0	187.0	100.8	146.1
April	139.5	137.6	136.6	150.0	146.2	117.0	117.7	130.7	125.6	128.6	96.8	188.1	101.1	146.5
May	139.8	137.4	136.8	150.3	146.5	117.2	117.6	131.6	126.0	129.0	97.6	188.9	101.6	147.0
June	140.2	137.7	137.3	150.9	146.7	117.5	118.1	132.1	126.5	129.3	99.8	189.8	102.9	147.3
July	140.6	137.6	137.6	151.1	147.0	117.9	118.2	132.7	126.9	129.3	100.4	190.8	103.3	147.8
August	140.9	138.5	137.8	151.5	147.0	118.1	118.2	132.3	127.0	129.8	99.8	191.7	103.1	148.1
September	141.2	139.1	138.0	151.6	147.1	118.4	118.2	132.2	127.1	130.0	99.5	192.6	103.2	148.3
October	141.8	139.1	138.5	152.3	147.9	118.7	118.4	132.5	128.2	130.0	100.8	193.7	103.9	149.0
November	142.2	138.9	138.9	152.7	148.4	119.5	118.6	132.7	128.7	130.4	101.2	194.7	104.7	149.4
December	142.4	139.0	139.1	152.9	148.5	119.5	118.5	132.8	128.9	130.5	101.7	195.5	104.9	149.8
1993														
January	142.8	139.3	139.5	153.6	148.9	119.6	118.4	132.8	129.3	130.9	101.5	196.6	104.7	150.3
February	143.2	139.8	139.5	153.8	149.1	118.9	118.5	134.0	129.7	131.1	101.6	197.6	104.0	150.8
March	143.4	139.7	139.9	154.0	149.1	120.3	118.4	134.0	129.4	131.3	100.8	198.3	104.5	151.0
April	143.9	140.2	140.5	154.7	149.7	120.7	118.9	134.0	129.7	131.7	100.1	199.3	104.5	151.6
May	144.3	141.2	140.7	155.0	150.0	121.0	118.9	133.5	129.9	132.2	98.1	200.7	103.9	152.0
June	144.4	140.8	141.1	155.5	150.4	121.4	119.0	133.0	129.9	132.3	96.8	201.6	103.5	152.3
July	144.6	140.8	141.2	155.6	150.4	121.7	118.6	132.8	130.1	132.9	95.6	202.4	103.1	152.5
August	144.9	141.3	141.6	156.0	150.8	122.0	119.1	134.0	130.5	133.4	95.3	203.0	103.0	153.0
September	145.1	141.6	141.9	156.3	151.0	122.4	119.5	133.7	130.4	133.6	94.2	203.8	102.6	153.1
October	145.7	142.2	142.2	156.6	151.3	122.6	120.0	133.8	132.0	134.2	99.2	204.7	105.0	153.6
November	146.0	142.5	142.5	157.0	151.5	122.3	120.4	134.4	132.3	134.6	97.8	205.3	104.0	154.1
December	146.4	143.0	142.9	157.6	151.9	122.5	120.6	134.1	132.2	134.9	96.3	206.0	103.3	154.5
1994														
January	146.4	143.1	143.1	157.9	152.2	122.2	120.7	133.3	131.8	135.3	94.8	206.6	102.4	154.7
February	146.8	142.9	143.6	158.6	152.7	123.0	120.3	133.2	132.3	135.7	96.7	207.4	103.8	155.0
March	147.2	142.9	143.9	159.1	153.2	123.4	120.3	133.8	132.7	136.1	96.3	208.1	103.9	155.5
April	147.3	143.2	143.9	159.2	153.3	122.8	120.3	133.5	132.9	136.4	96.1	209.2	103.4	155.8
May	147.6	143.5	144.3	159.7	153.4	122.8	121.0	134.0	132.5	137.0	94.5	209.9	102.4	156.2
June	148.0	144.0	144.5	159.9	153.5	122.7	121.4	134.8	133.3	137.5	95.3	210.7	102.7	156.7
July	148.5	144.8	144.7	160.1	154.0	122.8	121.4	134.2	134.5	138.1	98.1	211.5	104.1	156.9
August	149.1	145.3	145.2	161.0	154.5	123.0	121.3	133.2	136.1	138.4	102.6	212.4	106.3	157.4
September	149.4	145.5	145.4	161.4	155.0	122.7	121.3	133.6	136.2	138.9	102.0	213.3	105.7	157.7
October	149.5	145.5	145.6	161.8	155.1	122.5	121.3	133.0	136.3	139.2	101.4	214.3	105.3	158.0
November	149.9	145.8	145.9	162.3	155.5	122.7	121.2	132.5	136.8	139.2	102.1	215.2	105.7	158.4
December	150.2	147.0	145.9	162.3	155.7	122.6	121.0	132.1	137.2	139.4	102.0	216.1	105.5	158.6
1995														
January	150.6	146.9	146.5	162.8	156.1	123.5	121.9	132.2	137.5	139.8	100.9	216.8	105.3	159.2
February	151.0	147.5	146.8	163.2	156.3	123.3	122.3	131.9	137.9	139.9	101.0	217.6	105.4	159.6
March	151.3	147.3	147.1	163.7	156.6	123.3	122.4	132.3	138.5	140.0	100.4	218.3	105.1	160.1
April	151.9	148.3	147.5	164.3	157.0	123.4	122.4	131.9	139.3	140.6	100.7	218.9	105.2	160.6
May	152.2	148.4	147.8	164.8	157.3	123.1	122.5	131.6	139.7	140.9	101.7	219.4	105.4	160.9
June	152.5	148.5	148.1	165.3	157.6	123.4	122.4	131.3	140.7	141.1	103.4	220.1	106.3	161.3
July	152.7	148.7	148.5	165.7	158.0	123.5	122.9	131.4	140.0	141.0	101.3	220.9	105.4	161.6
August	153.0	148.8	148.9	166.0	158.2	124.1	123.3	132.5	139.5	141.1	99.8	221.8	105.2	162.0
September	153.2	149.3	149.1	166.6	158.5	123.4	123.6	132.3	139.2	141.3	98.2	222.6	103.7	162.4
October	153.7	149.7	149.7	167.2	158.8	124.0	123.8	132.4	139.5	141.6	97.9	223.2	104.0	162.9
November	153.8	149.8	149.9	167.6	159.2	124.0	123.7	132.0	139.2	141.9	96.2	223.9	103.1	163.2
December	154.1	150.1	150.2	167.9	159.6	124.4	124.0	132.2	139.2	142.1	97.8	224.6	104.1	163.3

Table 24-8. Producer Price Indexes

(By stage of processing, 1982=100; seasonally adjusted.)

Year and month	Finished goods								Intermediate materials, supplies, and components			Crude materials for further processing			
			Consumer goods												
					Consumer goods, except foods										
	Total	Total less food and energy	Total	Foods	Total	Nondurable goods, except food	Durable goods	Capital equipment	Total	Processed fuels and lubricants	Intermediate materials less food and energy	Total	Foodstuffs and feedstuffs	Nonfood materials	Crude nonfood materials less energy
1972															
January	41.0	...	40.7	45.5	39.0	33.6	49.6	42.3	37.5	...	...	37.8	48.4	25.8	...
February	41.3	...	40.9	45.9	39.1	33.6	49.8	42.5	37.7	...	...	38.1	48.9	26.0	...
March	41.3	...	40.9	45.7	39.2	33.7	49.9	42.6	37.8	...	...	38.1	48.4	26.4	...
April	41.3	...	40.9	45.7	39.2	33.8	49.9	42.7	37.9	...	...	38.7	49.4	26.6	...
May	41.5	...	41.1	46.3	39.3	33.9	49.9	42.8	38.0	...	...	39.3	50.1	26.9	...
June	41.7	...	41.4	46.8	39.4	33.9	50.0	42.8	38.0	...	...	39.4	50.4	27.0	...
July	41.8	...	41.6	47.1	39.5	34.0	50.1	42.9	38.1	...	...	40.0	51.5	27.1	...
August	42.0	...	41.7	47.3	39.6	34.1	50.4	42.9	38.2	...	...	40.3	52.2	27.2	...
September	42.2	...	42.0	47.8	39.8	34.3	50.6	43.0	38.5	...	...	40.5	52.4	27.1	...
October	42.0	...	41.9	47.6	39.6	34.4	49.7	42.8	38.7	...	...	40.9	53.0	27.3	...
November	42.3	...	42.1	48.3	39.7	34.6	49.7	42.9	39.0	...	...	42.0	54.6	28.1	...
December	42.7	...	42.6	49.3	39.8	34.6	50.0	43.0	39.6	...	...	43.8	57.7	28.6	...
1973															
January	43.0	...	43.0	50.5	39.9	34.7	49.8	43.0	39.8	...	...	45.0	59.3	29.1	...
February	43.5	...	43.5	51.2	40.3	35.2	50.0	43.3	40.4	...	...	47.1	62.5	30.0	...
March	44.4	...	44.7	53.9	40.5	35.4	50.2	43.6	41.1	...	...	49.3	66.1	30.6	...
April	44.7	...	45.0	54.5	40.8	35.6	50.6	43.8	41.3	...	...	50.1	67.3	31.0	...
May	45.0	...	45.3	55.0	40.9	35.8	50.9	44.1	42.2	...	...	52.5	70.5	32.6	...
June	45.5	...	45.9	56.2	41.1	36.0	51.0	44.2	43.0	...	...	55.0	74.0	34.0	...
July	45.4	...	45.7	55.7	41.2	36.0	51.2	44.3	42.3	...	...	52.5	69.7	33.4	...
August	47.0	...	47.7	61.0	41.4	36.1	51.4	44.4	43.5	...	...	64.1	89.9	35.9	...
September	46.9	...	47.5	60.3	41.5	36.3	51.4	44.6	43.0	...	...	60.9	81.3	38.2	...
October	46.8	...	47.4	59.6	41.7	36.8	51.0	44.7	43.4	...	...	58.5	76.9	38.0	...
November	47.2	...	47.9	59.8	42.2	37.4	51.4	44.9	43.8	...	...	59.0	77.4	38.6	...
December	47.6	...	48.3	60.1	42.8	38.1	51.7	45.3	44.8	...	...	59.1	75.7	40.4	...
1974															
January	48.8	49.7	49.6	62.2	43.7	39.2	52.4	45.8	45.9	26.4	47.5	63.3	82.3	42.0	86.3
February	49.7	50.0	50.7	63.8	44.6	40.2	52.7	46.2	46.8	28.6	48.1	64.3	83.5	42.8	86.5
March	50.2	50.5	51.1	63.5	45.5	41.3	53.1	46.8	48.1	30.5	49.5	62.3	78.9	43.4	88.3
April	50.7	51.1	51.5	63.0	46.4	42.3	53.6	47.4	49.0	31.6	50.9	60.6	74.7	44.2	89.7
May	51.3	52.2	52.0	62.9	47.2	43.2	54.4	48.7	50.6	33.1	52.5	58.3	71.8	42.6	83.8
June	51.3	53.1	51.8	60.8	48.0	44.2	55.0	49.7	51.5	33.8	53.7	55.4	65.8	43.0	82.9
July	52.7	54.0	53.2	63.1	49.0	45.0	55.9	50.7	53.4	35.7	55.2	59.8	72.4	45.0	84.2
August	53.7	55.0	54.1	64.6	49.6	45.7	56.4	52.1	55.8	36.7	57.0	62.9	78.1	45.3	85.5
September	54.3	55.7	54.6	65.1	50.1	46.2	56.9	53.1	55.9	35.9	57.6	60.9	74.3	45.3	82.5
October	55.3	56.7	55.6	66.3	50.9	46.7	58.3	54.2	57.2	36.9	58.2	63.2	78.6	45.6	80.6
November	56.4	57.4	56.7	69.1	51.2	47.0	58.8	55.0	57.8	37.0	58.8	64.2	80.4	45.7	77.6
December	56.4	57.9	56.6	68.0	51.6	47.3	59.3	55.5	57.8	37.3	59.1	61.5	76.8	44.1	71.6
1975															
January	56.7	58.3	56.8	68.0	51.9	47.6	59.6	56.2	58.0	38.1	59.6	59.6	74.0	43.0	69.8
February	56.6	58.7	56.6	67.3	52.0	47.6	60.0	56.7	57.8	37.5	59.8	57.9	70.9	42.9	69.2
March	56.6	59.0	56.4	66.7	52.1	47.6	60.3	57.2	57.4	37.9	59.7	57.1	70.0	42.2	68.2
April	57.1	59.2	56.9	67.8	52.3	47.8	60.5	57.5	57.5	38.3	59.7	59.5	74.4	42.5	67.7
May	57.4	59.3	57.3	68.5	52.5	48.1	60.5	57.8	57.3	38.2	59.7	61.2	76.8	43.4	68.8
June	57.9	59.5	57.8	69.5	52.7	48.4	60.7	58.0	57.3	38.5	59.8	61.5	77.4	43.3	66.5
July	58.4	59.8	58.4	70.5	53.1	48.8	60.7	58.4	57.5	38.9	59.9	62.4	79.3	43.3	66.5
August	58.9	59.9	59.0	71.3	53.5	49.3	61.1	58.5	58.0	39.9	60.1	63.0	80.2	43.6	67.7
September	59.3	60.2	59.4	71.8	53.9	49.7	61.3	58.9	58.2	40.5	60.3	64.5	81.9	44.7	71.2
October	59.8	60.6	59.9	72.4	54.3	50.1	61.8	59.3	58.8	41.0	61.0	65.1	83.0	44.8	71.5
November	60.0	61.0	60.1	72.3	54.8	50.5	62.4	59.7	59.0	41.8	61.4	64.4	81.6	44.8	71.9
December	60.1	61.4	60.1	71.9	55.1	50.8	62.5	60.0	59.2	41.8	61.8	64.0	80.1	45.7	73.1
1976															
January	60.0	61.7	59.9	70.9	55.2	51.0	62.7	60.4	59.4	41.6	62.1	63.0	78.4	45.5	72.4
February	59.9	61.9	59.6	69.7	55.4	51.1	63.0	60.7	59.6	41.5	62.3	62.1	77.2	44.8	73.8
March	60.0	62.2	59.6	69.5	55.5	51.2	63.1	61.1	59.8	41.4	62.6	61.5	75.8	45.3	74.5
April	60.3	62.3	60.0	70.7	55.5	51.3	62.9	61.3	60.0	41.5	62.8	63.9	79.0	46.5	78.1
May	60.4	62.4	60.0	70.6	55.5	51.3	62.9	61.5	60.3	41.3	63.2	63.6	77.8	47.4	80.6
June	60.5	62.8	60.1	69.8	56.0	51.9	63.3	61.8	60.8	41.5	63.6	65.2	79.9	48.3	82.8
July	60.7	63.1	60.3	69.5	56.4	52.4	63.4	62.1	61.1	41.9	63.9	64.8	77.7	50.0	87.3
August	60.9	63.5	60.4	68.9	56.8	52.9	63.8	62.5	61.3	42.3	64.3	63.6	76.1	49.4	84.1
September	61.1	63.9	60.5	68.5	57.2	53.1	64.4	62.9	61.9	42.9	64.7	63.4	75.6	49.5	84.4
October	61.4	64.1	60.9	68.7	57.7	53.7	64.7	63.1	62.0	43.2	65.0	63.0	74.0	50.5	82.2
November	61.9	64.6	61.4	68.6	58.4	54.6	65.2	63.4	62.4	43.9	65.3	63.4	73.9	51.3	81.8
December	62.4	64.9	61.9	70.1	58.4	54.5	65.3	64.0	62.8	44.2	65.6	64.5	76.8	50.3	81.1
1977															
January	62.5	65.1	62.1	70.2	58.6	54.7	65.6	64.0	63.0	44.8	65.8	64.3	77.6	49.1	78.7
February	63.2	65.4	62.8	71.5	59.2	55.4	65.9	64.3	63.3	46.0	65.9	65.7	78.6	50.9	79.7
March	63.7	65.7	63.4	72.6	59.5	55.8	66.2	64.7	63.9	46.6	66.4	66.6	79.9	51.4	81.5
April	64.0	65.9	63.7	72.8	59.9	56.2	66.3	65.0	64.4	47.2	66.7	67.3	82.6	51.9	82.1
May	64.4	66.1	64.2	73.7	60.1	56.5	66.6	65.3	64.9	47.5	67.1	67.6	81.0	52.4	82.5
June	64.6	66.5	64.2	73.2	60.4	56.7	67.0	65.7	64.9	47.8	67.4	65.5	77.6	51.5	79.7
July	64.8	66.8	64.5	73.7	60.6	56.9	67.2	66.0	65.1	48.2	67.9	64.7	76.4	51.3	78.8
August	65.2	67.3	64.8	74.1	60.9	57.1	67.8	66.6	65.4	48.5	68.2	63.9	74.3	51.8	79.2
September	65.5	67.8	65.0	73.7	61.4	57.5	68.4	67.0	65.7	48.7	68.7	63.7	73.8	52.1	79.2
October	65.9	68.2	65.3	73.9	61.7	57.7	68.9	67.6	65.8	49.1	68.8	64.0	74.4	52.1	78.5
November	66.4	68.8	65.8	74.6	62.2	58.1	69.4	68.1	66.3	49.2	69.1	65.4	76.6	52.5	78.4
December	66.7	69.0	66.1	74.9	62.4	58.3	69.6	68.6	66.6	49.3	69.4	66.4	77.7	53.5	80.1

Table 24-8. Producer Price Indexes—*Continued*

(By stage of processing, 1982=100; seasonally adjusted.)

Year and month	Finished goods								Intermediate materials, supplies, and components			Crude materials for further processing			
	Total	Total less food and energy	Consumer goods					Capital equipment	Total	Processed fuels and lubricants	Intermediate materials less food and energy	Total	Foodstuffs and feedstuffs	Nonfood materials	Crude nonfood materials less energy
			Total	Foods	Consumer goods, except foods										
					Total	Nondurable goods, except food	Durable goods								
1978															
January	67.0	69.2	66.4	75.6	62.6	58.4	70.0	68.8	66.9	49.5	69.8	67.3	79.3	53.6	80.3
February	67.5	69.5	66.9	77.1	62.6	58.4	70.3	69.1	67.4	49.4	70.3	68.4	81.2	53.7	80.6
March	67.8	69.9	67.3	77.6	63.0	58.6	70.8	69.6	67.8	49.3	70.6	69.8	83.5	54.1	80.3
April	68.6	70.6	68.2	79.1	63.6	58.8	72.3	69.9	68.1	49.1	71.1	72.1	86.9	55.3	82.2
May	69.1	71.1	68.6	79.4	64.1	59.0	73.0	70.5	68.7	49.6	71.6	72.8	87.4	56.2	84.6
June	69.7	71.7	69.3	80.5	64.6	59.5	73.5	71.0	69.2	50.2	72.2	74.6	89.8	57.4	87.4
July	70.3	72.3	69.9	80.7	65.2	60.0	74.5	71.5	69.4	49.6	72.5	74.2	88.1	58.3	89.6
August	70.4	72.8	69.9	80.0	65.6	60.2	75.2	72.0	69.9	49.5	73.2	73.7	86.8	58.6	90.4
September	71.1	73.5	70.6	80.8	66.3	60.7	76.1	72.6	70.5	49.8	73.7	75.1	88.7	59.5	92.3
October	71.4	73.4	71.0	82.2	66.3	61.3	75.3	72.8	71.3	50.4	74.5	77.0	91.4	60.4	94.7
November	72.0	74.1	71.5	82.4	66.9	62.0	75.6	73.5	71.9	51.0	75.2	77.4	91.6	61.1	96.3
December	72.8	74.7	72.5	83.6	67.7	62.7	76.6	74.0	72.4	51.5	75.6	78.0	92.4	61.7	96.8
1979															
January	73.7	75.3	73.3	85.0	68.4	63.3	77.4	74.5	73.1	51.8	76.3	80.1	95.8	62.0	96.4
February	74.4	75.9	74.2	86.5	69.0	63.8	78.2	75.2	73.7	52.0	77.0	82.1	98.4	63.5	99.6
March	75.0	76.4	74.8	87.2	69.6	64.4	78.8	75.7	74.6	52.9	77.8	83.8	100.0	65.2	104.2
April	75.8	77.0	75.6	87.6	70.5	65.5	79.2	76.4	75.7	54.7	78.9	84.4	100.7	65.7	105.1
May	76.2	77.4	75.9	86.8	71.4	66.6	79.7	76.8	76.6	57.1	79.6	84.7	99.8	67.4	106.7
June	76.6	78.0	76.4	85.9	72.4	67.9	80.4	77.3	77.5	59.5	80.1	85.6	99.1	70.0	111.6
July	77.4	78.5	77.3	86.2	73.6	69.5	80.9	77.8	78.7	61.9	81.1	86.5	100.5	70.3	109.4
August	78.2	78.8	78.3	86.7	74.7	71.4	80.7	77.8	79.8	65.2	81.8	85.5	98.6	70.6	106.4
September	79.5	79.7	79.8	87.8	76.4	73.1	82.4	78.7	81.1	68.3	82.7	87.9	100.9	73.0	106.5
October	80.4	80.4	80.6	87.8	77.7	74.6	83.2	79.2	82.4	70.8	83.9	88.8	101.1	74.6	108.9
November	81.4	81.0	81.8	89.5	78.6	75.6	84.1	79.8	83.2	72.4	84.5	90.0	102.0	76.1	111.3
December	82.2	81.7	82.6	90.0	79.5	76.6	84.8	80.6	84.0	73.4	85.2	91.2	102.9	77.7	111.3
1980															
January	83.4	83.3	83.9	89.5	81.6	78.3	87.6	81.7	86.0	76.8	87.2	90.9	100.0	80.2	112.6
February	84.6	84.2	85.2	89.3	83.6	80.6	89.0	82.3	87.6	80.0	88.2	92.6	101.8	81.9	115.3
March	85.5	84.7	86.1	90.0	84.7	82.4	88.7	83.1	88.2	82.5	88.6	90.8	99.1	81.2	111.7
April	86.2	85.5	86.7	88.6	86.1	84.6	89.1	84.4	88.5	84.0	88.8	88.3	94.0	81.7	109.9
May	86.6	85.7	87.1	89.1	86.4	85.0	89.0	84.6	89.0	84.2	89.1	89.5	96.3	81.5	107.2
June	87.3	86.6	87.9	89.8	87.2	85.6	90.3	85.1	89.8	84.7	89.8	90.1	97.1	81.8	106.1
July	88.7	87.7	89.4	92.8	88.1	86.2	91.7	86.2	90.5	86.2	90.3	94.6	104.2	83.4	109.6
August	89.7	88.4	90.5	95.2	88.6	86.7	92.2	87.0	91.5	86.4	91.1	99.0	110.9	85.3	112.4
September	90.1	88.8	90.8	95.3	89.0	87.0	92.8	87.5	91.9	87.3	91.4	100.4	111.9	87.1	116.2
October	90.8	89.6	91.3	96.1	89.5	87.4	93.5	88.8	92.8	87.4	92.1	102.2	113.9	88.6	118.2
November	91.4	90.1	92.0	96.5	90.2	88.3	93.7	89.3	93.5	88.9	92.6	103.5	114.6	90.6	119.8
December	91.8	90.4	92.4	96.6	90.7	89.3	93.7	89.7	94.4	91.5	93.7	102.7	111.7	92.3	119.3
1981															
January	92.8	91.4	93.3	96.8	92.0	91.0	93.9	90.8	95.6	94.0	94.7	103.4	111.1	94.4	113.3
February	93.6	92.0	94.1	96.5	93.1	92.5	94.4	91.7	96.1	96.7	94.9	104.2	107.6	100.1	106.2
March	94.7	92.6	95.3	97.2	94.6	94.6	94.6	92.4	97.1	100.6	95.6	103.8	106.0	101.1	108.9
April	95.7	93.5	96.4	97.2	96.1	96.4	95.5	93.1	98.3	103.1	96.6	104.2	105.6	102.4	111.9
May	96.0	94.0	96.6	97.4	96.2	96.2	96.2	93.8	98.7	103.3	97.1	103.8	103.8	103.7	113.7
June	96.5	94.6	97.0	98.0	96.6	96.5	96.6	94.4	99.0	102.4	97.7	104.9	105.8	103.8	115.5
July	96.7	94.8	97.1	99.0	96.4	96.3	96.4	95.0	99.2	100.9	98.4	105.0	105.6	104.0	116.4
August	96.8	95.3	97.1	98.9	96.4	96.3	96.7	95.4	99.7	101.6	98.9	104.0	104.6	103.1	115.5
September	97.2	95.9	97.5	98.7	97.1	97.0	97.2	96.1	99.7	101.2	99.3	102.7	102.2	103.1	112.6
October	97.6	96.5	97.8	98.5	97.5	97.1	98.1	96.9	99.8	101.1	99.5	101.2	100.5	101.8	110.8
November	97.9	97.0	98.0	98.1	98.0	97.6	98.7	97.5	99.9	101.1	99.7	99.7	98.2	101.3	107.5
December	98.3	97.6	98.4	98.1	98.5	98.3	98.9	98.1	100.0	101.3	99.8	98.8	96.1	101.7	106.0
1982															
January	98.9	98.1	99.0	98.9	99.0	98.9	99.1	98.6	100.4	102.7	99.9	99.7	99.2	100.4	101.2
February	98.8	98.1	99.0	99.2	98.8	99.0	98.4	98.2	100.3	101.2	100.0	100.0	100.1	99.8	100.7
March	98.8	98.7	98.8	99.0	98.7	98.5	98.9	98.7	99.9	99.7	99.9	99.7	100.4	98.9	100.0
April	99.0	99.0	98.9	100.2	98.4	98.1	98.9	99.0	99.7	98.6	99.8	100.2	101.9	98.4	101.1
May	99.0	99.4	98.8	100.9	98.0	97.3	99.3	99.5	99.7	97.3	100.1	101.9	104.4	99.2	102.2
June	99.8	99.9	99.8	101.6	99.0	98.5	99.9	100.0	99.8	98.4	100.0	101.8	104.0	99.5	101.0
July	100.2	100.1	100.1	100.1	100.1	100.1	100.2	100.3	100.0	100.6	99.8	100.7	101.1	100.3	101.4
August	100.6	100.6	100.5	100.1	100.7	100.8	100.7	100.7	99.9	100.9	99.7	99.8	99.6	100.0	100.0
September	100.7	100.8	100.7	100.1	100.9	101.1	100.6	101.0	100.0	99.5	100.2	99.2	98.1	100.3	98.9
October	101.0	101.3	101.0	100.0	101.3	101.6	100.9	101.1	99.9	99.7	100.2	98.7	97.1	100.5	97.7
November	101.4	102.0	101.4	100.0	102.0	102.4	101.4	101.3	100.1	100.2	100.2	99.2	97.2	101.3	96.3
December	101.8	102.2	101.7	100.1	102.4	102.8	101.7	101.9	100.1	100.5	100.3	98.8	97.3	100.4	95.9
1983															
January	101.0	101.8	100.8	99.6	101.2	101.1	101.7	101.8	99.8	98.3	100.3	98.8	97.7	100.1	97.3
February	101.1	102.2	100.8	100.3	100.9	100.2	102.4	102.1	100.0	96.1	100.8	100.0	100.2	99.8	99.8
March	101.0	102.5	100.7	100.5	100.5	99.6	102.5	102.2	99.7	95.1	100.8	100.5	100.4	100.7	102.2
April	101.1	102.4	100.7	101.1	100.3	99.3	102.5	102.3	99.5	92.7	100.9	101.2	102.2	99.9	102.1
May	101.4	102.6	101.0	101.1	100.8	99.8	102.8	102.5	99.8	93.7	101.0	100.9	101.6	100.1	103.4
June	101.6	102.8	101.3	100.7	101.4	100.8	102.9	102.6	100.2	95.2	101.3	100.5	100.3	100.6	104.8
July	101.6	103.1	101.3	100.2	101.5	100.8	103.1	102.8	100.5	95.0	101.8	99.5	98.5	100.6	106.2
August	101.9	103.5	101.6	100.6	101.8	101.2	103.3	103.1	100.9	95.5	102.0	102.2	103.1	101.2	108.4
September	102.2	103.5	101.8	101.5	101.8	101.1	103.3	103.3	101.6	96.3	102.3	103.3	104.9	101.6	109.0
October	102.2	103.6	101.9	102.4	101.5	101.0	102.8	103.4	101.7	97.0	102.5	103.2	105.2	101.0	109.1
November	102.0	103.8	101.5	101.6	101.3	100.5	103.2	103.5	101.8	95.6	102.8	102.3	103.2	101.3	109.9
December	102.3	104.1	101.9	102.3	101.5	100.6	103.5	103.8	101.9	94.8	103.1	103.5	104.9	101.9	111.2

Table 24-8. Producer Price Indexes—*Continued*

(By stage of processing, 1982=100; seasonally adjusted.)

Year and month	Finished goods								Intermediate materials, supplies, and components			Crude materials for further processing			
			Consumer goods												
					Consumer goods, except foods										
	Total	Total less food and energy	Total	Foods	Total	Nondurable goods, except food	Durable goods	Capital equipment	Total	Processed fuels and lubricants	Intermediate materials less food and energy	Total	Foodstuffs and feedstuffs	Nonfood materials	Crude nonfood materials less energy
1984															
January	103.0	104.5	102.7	104.8	101.6	100.6	103.7	104.1	102.1	94.6	103.4	104.6	106.8	102.2	111.5
February	103.4	104.7	103.1	105.3	101.9	101.0	103.9	104.5	102.5	95.5	103.8	103.8	104.5	103.0	113.8
March	103.8	105.2	103.6	106.2	102.2	101.1	104.5	104.6	103.0	95.8	104.4	105.7	108.4	102.8	114.8
April	103.9	105.3	103.5	105.2	102.5	101.6	104.4	105.3	103.2	96.2	104.5	105.2	107.0	103.1	115.1
May	103.8	105.3	103.5	104.7	102.7	102.0	104.4	105.1	103.4	97.2	104.6	104.5	105.3	103.6	115.7
June	103.8	105.5	103.4	104.5	102.6	101.9	104.4	105.2	103.6	97.5	104.8	103.3	103.3	103.2	114.1
July	104.0	105.7	103.6	105.9	102.3	101.3	104.6	105.5	103.4	96.4	104.9	104.0	105.2	102.8	112.0
August	103.8	105.9	103.3	105.8	102.0	100.7	104.7	105.6	103.2	95.0	105.1	103.3	104.0	102.4	109.6
September	103.8	106.2	103.2	105.5	101.9	100.4	105.0	105.9	103.1	94.9	105.0	102.8	103.5	102.1	110.5
October	103.6	105.9	103.1	105.2	101.9	100.9	104.2	105.6	103.2	95.2	105.1	101.5	101.5	101.4	108.5
November	104.0	106.2	103.4	105.6	102.2	101.1	104.7	105.8	103.3	95.2	105.3	101.9	103.3	100.4	107.7
December	104.0	106.3	103.5	105.6	102.3	101.0	105.0	105.6	103.2	94.7	105.3	101.4	102.9	99.8	107.3
1985															
January	104.0	106.9	103.4	105.4	102.3	100.6	105.7	106.3	103.1	94.5	105.3	99.9	101.2	98.5	107.4
February	104.1	107.3	103.4	106.0	102.0	100.0	105.9	106.9	102.8	92.9	105.3	99.4	100.5	98.1	107.2
March	104.1	107.6	103.3	105.4	102.1	100.2	106.0	107.1	102.7	92.5	105.2	97.6	97.8	97.4	107.0
April	104.6	107.6	103.9	104.8	103.3	101.9	106.1	107.1	102.9	94.4	105.2	96.7	95.8	97.8	107.4
May	104.9	107.8	104.2	103.8	104.1	103.0	106.5	107.4	103.2	95.6	105.3	95.8	93.6	98.1	105.3
June	104.6	108.2	103.8	103.7	103.6	102.0	106.8	107.6	102.6	91.7	105.5	95.2	93.5	97.1	103.6
July	104.7	108.4	103.8	104.3	103.4	101.6	106.9	107.7	102.3	90.6	105.3	94.9	92.9	97.1	104.3
August	104.5	108.5	103.6	103.8	103.3	101.4	107.1	107.9	102.3	90.4	105.3	92.9	89.9	96.1	103.6
September	103.8	107.9	102.9	102.5	102.9	101.6	106.5	107.2	102.2	90.5	105.2	91.8	87.9	96.0	103.3
October	104.9	108.9	103.9	103.9	103.7	102.1	107.0	108.3	102.3	91.3	105.1	94.1	92.2	96.1	103.7
November	105.5	109.1	104.6	105.3	104.1	102.5	107.3	108.5	102.5	92.5	105.1	95.7	96.0	95.4	103.0
December	106.0	109.1	105.3	106.1	104.6	103.4	107.4	108.6	102.9	94.3	105.1	95.5	95.9	95.1	102.4
1986															
January	105.5	109.3	104.6	105.8	103.8	102.2	107.1	108.6	102.4	92.0	105.0	94.2	93.3	95.2	103.6
February	104.1	109.5	102.8	104.8	101.6	98.8	107.4	108.7	101.2	85.5	104.9	90.5	91.8	89.2	103.5
March	102.8	109.6	101.0	104.8	99.1	94.9	107.6	108.9	99.9	77.6	105.0	88.2	91.0	85.1	103.8
April	102.3	110.1	100.3	105.0	97.9	92.7	108.4	109.2	98.9	73.0	104.7	85.6	89.0	82.0	103.9
May	102.8	110.2	101.0	106.1	98.4	93.4	108.4	109.3	98.7	71.7	104.6	86.5	91.2	81.5	104.1
June	103.1	110.5	101.2	106.2	98.7	93.8	108.6	109.6	98.6	71.2	104.7	86.2	90.9	81.1	104.7
July	102.3	110.7	100.2	107.6	96.5	90.3	108.9	109.7	98.0	66.7	104.8	86.4	93.5	78.3	105.3
August	102.7	110.8	100.7	109.5	96.4	90.2	108.9	109.8	98.0	65.7	104.9	86.7	96.3	75.8	99.7
September	102.9	110.7	100.9	109.0	97.0	91.3	108.4	109.7	98.5	68.1	105.1	86.6	94.9	77.1	100.3
October	103.5	111.8	101.5	109.8	97.4	90.7	110.7	110.6	98.3	66.8	105.1	87.4	95.9	77.7	102.0
November	103.4	112.0	101.4	109.5	97.4	90.6	110.9	110.8	98.3	66.7	105.2	87.6	96.0	78.2	102.8
December	103.6	112.1	101.5	109.3	97.7	91.0	111.1	110.9	98.5	67.5	105.3	86.9	94.4	78.3	104.1
1987															
January	104.1	112.5	102.1	108.0	99.2	92.7	111.5	111.3	99.0	69.5	105.6	89.3	92.6	83.2	105.4
February	104.4	112.3	102.5	108.6	99.5	93.5	110.5	111.1	99.8	71.7	105.9	90.2	93.6	84.1	106.2
March	104.5	112.4	102.6	108.3	99.8	94.0	110.7	111.1	99.9	71.5	106.2	90.5	93.1	84.8	106.5
April	105.1	112.9	103.3	109.6	100.2	94.3	111.4	111.6	100.3	72.0	106.5	92.5	97.4	85.4	107.5
May	105.2	113.0	103.4	110.5	100.0	94.0	111.3	111.6	100.8	72.8	107.0	93.8	99.1	86.3	110.0
June	105.5	113.1	103.8	110.4	100.5	94.7	111.3	111.5	101.4	73.7	107.5	94.5	98.2	87.9	113.2
July	105.7	113.3	104.0	110.2	100.9	95.3	111.5	111.7	101.9	75.1	107.9	95.6	97.1	90.3	115.9
August	105.9	113.6	104.2	109.4	101.4	96.2	111.6	112.0	102.4	76.2	108.3	96.5	96.8	91.9	119.1
September	106.2	113.9	104.5	110.3	101.0	96.0	112.0	112.0	102.6	74.7	108.9	96.0	97.4	90.8	122.8
October	106.0	114.0	104.4	109.9	102.1	96.0	112.0	112.0	103.1	74.5	109.6	95.8	97.3	90.6	126.6
November	106.0	114.2	104.3	109.9	101.8	95.9	112.0	112.1	103.5	74.3	110.1	95.1	96.2	90.1	127.5
December	105.8	114.3	104.1	109.1	101.8	96.1	111.6	112.2	103.8	73.3	110.7	94.9	96.9	89.3	127.9
1988															
January	106.4	115.0	104.6	110.7	101.6	95.8	112.4	112.8	104.1	70.6	111.8	94.2	98.5	87.3	129.4
February	106.3	115.3	104.4	110.9	101.8	95.9	112.6	113.0	104.4	70.7	112.2	95.2	100.7	87.5	131.7
March	106.6	115.6	104.7	110.3	102.0	96.1	112.7	113.2	104.8	70.4	112.8	94.1	99.8	86.3	133.0
April	107.0	115.9	105.2	110.4	102.7	97.1	112.8	113.5	105.5	70.8	113.6	95.4	100.9	87.8	132.1
May	107.2	116.2	105.4	110.7	102.8	97.1	113.2	113.8	106.2	71.4	114.3	95.8	101.3	88.1	130.7
June	107.5	116.6	105.7	111.7	102.8	97.0	113.3	114.0	107.4	74.1	114.9	97.0	106.3	87.0	131.1
July	108.4	117.2	106.6	113.0	103.5	97.9	113.9	114.4	108.3	74.1	115.8	96.7	108.4	85.2	133.2
August	108.8	117.7	107.1	113.7	103.8	97.9	114.6	114.9	108.5	73.6	116.3	97.0	110.5	84.5	134.3
September	109.0	118.1	107.3	115.3	103.4	97.3	114.8	115.2	108.7	72.4	116.8	97.0	112.9	83.0	133.3
October	109.2	118.4	107.5	114.9	103.8	97.8	115.0	115.5	108.6	69.3	117.3	96.6	113.6	82.0	133.6
November	109.6	118.7	107.9	115.1	104.3	98.5	115.1	115.7	108.8	68.1	118.0	95.2	109.7	82.1	136.0
December	110.0	119.2	108.3	115.7	104.7	98.8	115.5	116.1	109.4	69.2	118.6	98.1	111.3	85.6	137.6
1989															
January	111.1	119.9	109.5	116.9	105.9	100.2	116.3	116.9	110.8	72.6	119.5	102.0	114.1	90.1	140.6
February	111.9	120.5	110.5	117.6	106.9	101.4	116.7	117.3	111.3	73.6	119.9	101.7	112.2	90.7	140.3
March	112.3	120.7	110.9	118.2	107.4	102.1	116.6	117.5	111.9	75.2	120.2	102.9	113.2	92.0	140.6
April	113.1	120.8	111.9	117.8	109.0	104.5	116.5	117.6	112.5	78.4	120.5	104.1	111.2	95.1	140.3
May	114.0	121.6	112.9	118.3	110.3	105.9	117.2	118.3	112.6	78.5	120.6	104.5	110.9	95.9	139.8
June	114.0	122.2	112.7	118.0	110.1	105.5	117.7	118.9	112.5	78.2	120.6	103.2	109.4	94.7	137.9
July	113.8	122.1	112.4	118.4	109.5	104.8	117.2	118.9	112.2	77.2	120.3	103.5	108.9	95.5	135.9
August	113.4	122.7	111.7	118.7	108.3	102.9	117.9	119.3	111.8	75.5	120.2	101.2	110.1	91.2	136.8
September	114.0	123.1	112.5	118.7	109.4	104.1	118.7	119.7	112.1	76.4	120.2	102.5	109.6	93.5	137.5
October	114.6	123.5	113.1	119.9	109.8	104.6	118.6	120.0	112.2	76.8	120.3	102.7	109.3	94.0	137.9
November	114.8	123.9	113.2	120.5	109.6	104.4	118.7	120.4	112.0	76.1	120.0	103.5	112.2	93.6	134.9
December	115.5	124.2	114.1	121.8	110.3	105.2	119.1	120.6	112.2	78.0	119.8	105.1	114.6	94.5	132.8

Table 24-8. Producer Price Indexes—*Continued*

(By stage of processing, 1982=100; seasonally adjusted.)

Year and month	Finished goods								Intermediate materials, supplies, and components			Crude materials for further processing			
	Total	Total less food and energy	Consumer goods					Capital equipment	Total	Processed fuels and lubricants	Intermediate materials less food and energy	Total	Foodstuffs and feedstuffs	Nonfood materials	Crude nonfood materials less energy
			Total	Foods	Consumer goods, except foods										
					Total	Nondurable goods, except food	Durable goods								
1990															
January	117.7	124.5	116.9	124.2	113.3	109.5	118.7	121.0	113.7	85.9	120.0	106.7	114.6	97.0	132.7
February	117.6	124.9	116.7	124.9	112.7	108.5	119.0	121.4	112.8	81.5	119.9	106.8	114.6	97.2	131.6
March	117.5	125.3	116.3	124.5	112.4	108.0	119.1	121.8	112.9	80.4	120.2	105.1	114.1	94.8	133.9
April	117.4	125.5	116.1	123.3	112.6	108.2	119.4	122.1	113.1	80.3	120.5	102.7	114.3	91.1	137.0
May	117.5	126.0	116.3	123.8	112.5	108.1	119.5	122.1	113.1	79.0	120.6	103.1	113.4	92.3	138.0
June	117.6	126.4	116.3	123.6	112.8	108.0	120.5	122.5	112.9	78.4	120.4	100.6	113.5	88.2	137.3
July	117.9	126.6	116.6	124.5	112.7	107.9	120.7	122.9	112.8	76.9	120.6	101.0	114.4	88.3	138.0
August	119.2	127.1	118.2	124.7	115.0	111.0	120.8	123.3	114.0	83.5	120.8	110.5	113.1	103.9	140.1
September	120.7	127.7	120.0	124.3	117.9	114.5	121.9	123.8	115.8	90.9	121.5	115.8	111.7	113.1	139.9
October	121.9	128.0	121.5	124.7	120.0	117.6	121.5	124.1	117.4	97.7	122.1	125.8	112.3	128.3	138.4
November	122.6	128.4	122.3	125.4	120.7	118.4	122.0	124.5	117.7	98.2	122.3	117.8	111.3	116.4	135.7
December	122.0	128.6	121.4	124.7	119.8	117.0	122.4	124.8	116.9	94.3	122.1	110.8	109.5	106.6	133.8
1991															
January	122.6	129.5	122.0	125.0	120.5	117.8	123.0	125.6	116.9	93.7	122.4	113.3	108.3	110.9	134.2
February	121.8	129.8	120.8	124.7	118.9	115.5	123.4	125.8	115.9	89.8	122.1	104.1	107.3	98.0	133.7
March	121.3	130.1	120.2	125.0	117.9	114.0	123.7	126.0	114.7	85.1	121.7	100.5	108.0	92.3	131.8
April	121.3	130.4	120.2	125.2	117.8	114.0	123.7	126.1	114.2	83.7	121.5	100.2	107.7	92.0	131.7
May	121.6	130.6	120.4	125.3	118.1	114.5	123.4	126.5	114.1	84.0	121.3	100.9	105.8	94.0	130.4
June	121.4	130.7	120.1	124.9	117.8	114.1	123.4	126.6	113.9	83.4	121.3	99.2	105.9	91.3	126.1
July	121.1	131.0	119.6	124.3	117.4	113.5	123.4	126.7	113.6	82.5	121.1	99.4	104.7	92.3	125.4
August	121.3	131.3	119.9	123.0	118.3	114.7	123.6	126.8	113.8	83.7	121.0	99.1	102.7	93.0	125.8
September	121.5	131.8	120.1	122.8	118.7	115.0	124.2	127.2	114.0	84.7	121.0	98.4	104.1	91.2	125.7
October	121.9	132.3	120.5	123.1	119.2	115.4	124.9	127.6	114.0	84.1	121.1	100.8	104.9	94.3	125.4
November	122.4	132.5	121.0	123.4	119.8	116.2	124.9	127.8	114.1	84.7	121.1	100.7	103.9	94.7	124.4
December	122.3	132.6	120.8	122.8	119.8	116.1	125.0	128.0	114.0	84.7	121.1	98.2	102.6	91.6	123.4
1992															
January	122.0	133.0	120.4	122.8	119.1	115.2	125.2	128.2	113.4	81.5	121.0	97.2	104.5	88.9	123.4
February	122.3	133.1	120.8	123.5	119.4	115.7	124.9	128.3	113.8	82.6	121.3	98.6	106.1	90.1	125.2
March	122.4	133.4	120.8	123.1	119.6	115.7	125.4	128.6	113.9	82.0	121.5	97.1	105.4	88.1	127.7
April	122.5	133.8	120.9	122.6	119.9	116.2	125.6	129.0	114.1	82.5	121.7	98.1	104.1	90.5	128.4
May	122.9	134.3	121.4	122.5	120.7	117.2	125.7	129.0	114.5	83.9	121.8	100.3	106.2	92.6	129.1
June	123.4	134.1	121.9	122.9	121.3	118.1	125.5	129.0	115.1	86.4	122.0	101.6	106.4	94.7	128.8
July	123.3	134.3	121.9	122.7	121.3	118.0	125.8	129.1	115.2	86.6	122.1	101.6	105.0	95.6	129.6
August	123.4	134.3	121.9	123.3	121.1	117.6	126.0	129.4	115.1	86.0	122.3	100.7	103.9	94.7	130.4
September	123.7	134.6	122.3	123.5	121.5	118.3	125.8	129.4	115.3	86.2	122.4	102.8	103.9	98.0	130.4
October	124.2	134.9	122.8	123.9	122.0	119.0	126.0	129.7	115.3	86.6	122.4	102.8	105.8	96.9	128.9
November	124.1	135.1	122.6	123.8	121.9	118.6	126.3	129.9	115.1	85.3	122.4	102.5	104.3	97.4	128.2
December	124.2	135.2	122.7	124.7	121.7	118.3	126.4	130.1	115.1	84.8	122.5	101.3	105.4	94.8	130.5
1993															
January	124.4	135.6	122.9	124.8	121.9	118.5	126.6	130.4	115.4	84.6	122.9	101.7	106.2	95.0	135.0
February	124.7	135.9	123.2	124.7	122.3	118.9	127.0	130.7	115.9	85.2	123.5	101.2	105.8	94.5	136.8
March	125.0	136.1	123.4	124.5	122.7	119.4	127.3	130.9	116.3	86.0	123.8	101.7	106.5	94.7	137.0
April	125.7	136.5	124.3	126.5	123.1	119.8	127.9	131.1	116.6	86.3	124.0	103.4	109.4	95.3	138.4
May	125.7	136.6	124.4	126.8	123.1	119.8	127.9	131.2	116.3	85.7	123.7	105.6	110.6	98.4	140.3
June	125.2	136.4	123.7	125.3	122.7	119.1	128.0	131.1	116.3	86.4	123.7	103.8	106.5	98.0	140.3
July	125.1	136.6	123.4	125.0	122.5	118.7	128.3	131.5	116.3	85.3	123.7	101.6	107.8	93.7	142.1
August	123.9	134.9	121.9	125.0	120.4	115.6	128.6	131.6	116.2	84.0	123.9	100.8	108.1	92.2	140.4
September	124.1	134.9	122.1	125.5	120.4	115.6	128.5	131.7	116.3	84.3	124.0	101.2	108.0	93.0	140.7
October	124.2	135.0	122.3	125.4	120.7	116.1	128.2	131.8	116.4	84.8	124.0	103.7	107.2	97.4	142.6
November	124.4	135.3	122.3	126.8	120.3	115.2	128.9	132.2	116.5	83.7	124.3	103.0	111.3	93.7	144.1
December	124.4	135.7	122.3	127.5	119.9	114.5	129.2	132.4	116.2	81.0	124.5	101.7	113.3	90.5	145.3
1994															
January	124.8	136.3	122.6	127.4	120.4	115.0	129.9	132.9	116.5	81.1	124.7	103.8	113.6	93.6	148.3
February	125.0	136.3	122.9	126.9	121.0	115.9	129.9	133.1	116.9	83.1	124.9	102.1	114.3	90.5	151.0
March	125.1	136.4	122.9	127.3	120.9	115.6	130.1	133.3	117.1	83.0	125.1	103.8	114.0	93.3	151.5
April	125.1	136.6	122.9	127.2	120.9	115.4	130.3	133.7	117.1	82.3	125.3	103.8	113.4	93.8	150.7
May	125.1	137.0	122.7	126.5	120.8	115.1	130.9	134.1	117.2	81.5	125.6	102.2	108.4	94.3	149.7
June	125.2	137.2	122.8	126.0	121.2	115.6	131.1	134.3	117.8	82.4	126.3	102.7	106.8	96.1	151.2
July	125.7	137.3	123.4	126.3	121.9	116.5	131.4	134.4	118.3	84.0	126.7	101.7	102.6	97.2	155.5
August	126.2	137.6	124.0	126.1	122.9	117.7	131.8	134.6	119.1	85.3	127.4	101.6	100.7	98.2	158.8
September	125.9	137.7	123.5	126.0	122.2	116.7	131.7	134.9	119.6	84.0	128.4	99.7	100.7	95.1	160.5
October	125.5	137.4	123.1	126.0	121.7	116.2	131.2	134.4	120.1	82.9	129.3	98.6	99.1	94.5	161.3
November	126.1	137.6	123.9	126.8	122.4	117.2	131.4	134.5	121.0	83.9	130.3	99.8	101.1	95.0	166.6
December	126.6	137.9	124.4	128.7	122.4	117.1	131.7	134.9	121.5	83.7	131.0	101.1	102.6	96.3	169.9
1995															
January	126.9	138.4	124.6	128.2	122.9	117.6	132.1	135.6	122.8	83.8	132.6	102.1	103.5	97.3	174.5
February	127.2	138.7	124.9	128.4	123.2	117.9	132.1	135.8	123.7	84.3	133.7	102.9	105.0	97.6	176.5
March	127.4	139.0	125.1	128.7	123.4	118.3	132.0	135.9	124.3	84.7	134.3	102.3	103.7	97.5	177.8
April	127.7	139.3	125.4	128.9	123.7	118.7	132.3	136.2	125.0	85.1	135.2	103.7	102.5	100.4	180.2
May	127.8	139.7	125.5	127.8	124.3	119.5	132.4	136.5	125.2	85.5	135.5	102.4	99.0	100.6	179.6
June	127.8	139.8	125.5	127.5	124.4	119.6	132.3	136.6	125.5	85.6	135.7	103.0	101.7	99.9	179.5
July	128.0	140.2	125.6	128.6	124.2	119.1	132.6	136.9	125.6	84.5	136.1	101.6	103.5	96.5	176.4
August	127.9	140.2	125.5	128.3	124.1	119.0	132.7	137.0	125.6	84.1	136.1	99.7	103.2	93.7	173.4
September	128.1	140.2	125.8	129.9	123.9	118.8	132.3	136.8	125.5	82.8	136.2	102.0	107.6	94.5	170.9
October	128.4	141.0	126.0	129.9	124.2	118.9	133.2	137.6	125.4	83.0	135.8	101.9	109.6	93.1	166.6
November	128.7	141.3	126.2	131.1	123.9	118.2	133.9	138.0	125.2	82.6	135.5	104.1	114.5	93.5	163.6
December	129.3	141.5	127.0	131.0	125.1	119.9	134.0	138.0	125.4	84.4	135.2	106.5	115.7	96.6	162.3

Table 24-9. Money Stock and Selected Components

(Averages of daily figures; billions of dollars, seasonally adjusted.)

Year and month	Money stock measures [1]			Selected components					
	M1	M2	M3	Currency	Demand deposits	Other checkable deposits	Savings deposits	Small time deposits	Large time deposits
1972									
January	230.0	717.6	783.7	52.3	176.6	0.2	292.5	192.5	59.1
February	232.2	725.6	792.8	52.6	178.4	0.2	295.7	197.6	59.1
March	234.2	733.4	800.5	53.0	180.1	0.2	300.7	201.4	58.3
April	235.4	738.3	807.7	53.1	181.2	0.2	303.6	203.3	60.3
May	235.8	743.3	816.0	53.4	181.2	0.2	304.6	205.7	63.8
June	236.8	749.8	824.7	53.7	181.6	0.2	308.1	209.0	64.1
July	239.1	759.8	835.9	54.0	183.5	0.2	310.3	213.6	64.6
August	241.2	769.0	846.9	54.4	185.2	0.2	311.3	217.0	68.4
September	243.3	778.5	856.6	54.8	187.0	0.2	312.9	220.4	69.9
October	245.0	786.9	865.8	55.3	188.4	0.2	315.5	223.9	70.4
November	246.3	793.8	875.7	55.7	189.3	0.2	316.2	226.2	71.2
December	249.1	802.1	885.8	56.2	191.6	0.2	318.7	228.3	73.3
1973									
January	251.3	810.2	896.2	56.6	193.4	0.2	320.0	235.8	74.9
February	252.0	814.0	906.0	56.9	193.8	0.3	321.4	240.5	79.0
March	251.5	815.2	914.8	57.2	193.0	0.3	324.9	241.9	86.3
April	252.6	819.6	922.3	57.8	193.4	0.3	326.7	244.8	89.7
May	254.8	826.7	932.2	58.1	195.2	0.3	327.2	247.8	92.7
June	256.9	833.4	940.9	58.5	196.6	0.3	330.1	250.7	91.9
July	257.9	836.9	950.6	58.8	197.1	0.3	330.4	252.2	96.3
August	258.1	839.1	959.4	59.1	197.0	0.3	326.2	255.5	105.4
September	258.0	839.4	966.0	59.6	196.7	0.3	323.6	255.9	111.3
October	259.1	842.7	972.0	59.9	197.5	0.3	324.3	256.8	112.0
November	260.9	848.7	977.2	60.3	199.0	0.3	322.8	259.9	109.4
December	262.7	855.3	984.9	60.8	200.3	0.3	323.8	262.4	111.2
1974									
January	263.6	859.5	993.8	61.3	200.7	0.3	324.7	268.0	115.6
February	265.1	864.1	1 002.2	61.8	201.7	0.3	325.8	272.7	117.9
March	266.5	870.0	1 010.5	62.3	202.5	0.4	330.1	276.3	119.0
April	267.0	872.8	1 020.7	63.0	202.3	0.4	332.5	277.5	125.9
May	267.4	874.4	1 029.1	63.4	202.3	0.4	331.9	278.1	132.5
June	268.6	878.0	1 037.9	63.7	202.9	0.4	333.9	279.3	134.9
July	269.7	881.9	1 044.4	64.1	203.3	0.4	334.9	280.6	137.7
August	270.5	884.6	1 049.1	64.7	203.5	0.4	332.5	281.7	142.4
September	271.3	888.4	1 053.3	65.2	203.8	0.4	331.3	283.1	143.8
October	272.4	893.6	1 058.8	65.8	204.4	0.4	333.0	284.7	143.7
November	273.6	898.7	1 063.8	66.5	205.1	0.4	333.1	285.4	141.0
December	274.0	902.2	1 070.0	67.0	205.1	0.4	335.4	284.8	145.4
1975									
January	273.7	906.4	1 076.1	67.4	204.3	0.5	338.0	289.7	147.9
February	274.8	914.2	1 082.7	67.8	204.9	0.5	341.9	294.7	145.0
March	276.2	925.2	1 090.0	68.4	205.6	0.6	349.7	299.3	142.1
April	275.9	935.3	1 095.9	68.5	205.2	0.6	356.6	304.1	137.1
May	279.1	948.1	1 106.6	69.1	207.6	0.6	361.1	308.0	135.3
June	282.7	963.6	1 119.1	70.0	209.8	0.7	369.3	312.7	131.5
July	284.3	976.1	1 129.2	70.5	210.5	0.7	374.1	318.7	128.8
August	284.7	984.0	1 135.6	71.0	210.5	0.7	374.9	322.3	129.4
September	286.0	992.2	1 146.3	71.2	211.7	0.7	376.5	325.1	130.4
October	285.4	998.3	1 153.9	71.7	210.8	0.8	379.8	328.6	131.1
November	286.6	1 007.2	1 163.8	72.3	211.5	0.8	381.4	331.2	130.9
December	286.8	1 016.4	1 171.7	72.8	211.3	0.9	385.4	334.9	131.1
1976									
January	288.2	1 026.9	1 182.2	73.2	212.0	1.0	390.7	342.2	128.3
February	290.5	1 040.6	1 193.7	73.9	213.5	1.1	400.0	346.6	124.4
March	292.5	1 050.2	1 204.6	74.7	214.5	1.2	409.8	348.0	125.3
April	294.4	1 061.1	1 217.0	75.5	215.5	1.4	417.2	351.4	124.1
May	295.8	1 072.5	1 228.3	76.1	215.9	1.5	420.6	356.2	121.2
June	296.4	1 078.4	1 236.6	76.6	215.6	1.7	423.8	359.4	123.3
July	297.9	1 087.6	1 246.8	77.1	215.9	1.8	427.2	364.1	124.1
August	299.7	1 099.4	1 260.0	77.6	216.9	2.0	429.5	369.0	122.8
September	300.0	1 111.7	1 268.7	78.1	216.8	2.2	433.0	375.0	121.2
October	302.1	1 125.7	1 281.1	78.6	218.6	2.3	439.7	380.6	119.2
November	303.4	1 138.7	1 294.6	79.1	219.4	2.5	443.5	384.0	118.2
December	305.9	1 152.3	1 311.9	79.5	221.5	2.7	449.2	388.1	120.0
1977									
January	307.9	1 165.5	1 323.1	80.2	222.6	2.8	454.9	397.3	118.9
February	311.2	1 177.9	1 335.9	80.8	225.1	3.0	460.0	403.2	118.5
March	313.6	1 188.9	1 348.7	81.3	226.8	3.1	467.1	408.1	118.9
April	315.7	1 200.0	1 360.9	82.1	228.1	3.1	473.1	413.2	117.7
May	317.0	1 209.5	1 374.7	82.5	228.7	3.2	474.6	417.7	119.0
June	319.0	1 218.7	1 388.3	83.1	229.6	3.3	478.1	422.5	121.8
July	321.0	1 228.3	1 401.6	83.9	230.0	3.5	481.8	427.5	124.8
August	323.0	1 238.5	1 416.3	84.5	231.4	3.6	483.3	430.4	129.3
September	324.9	1 247.4	1 428.8	85.2	232.7	3.7	485.1	434.3	132.1
October	326.4	1 254.8	1 442.4	85.9	233.8	3.9	488.2	438.2	136.6
November	328.4	1 262.9	1 457.5	86.6	235.1	4.0	487.1	440.1	142.0
December	330.5	1 270.7	1 472.3	87.4	236.4	4.2	488.2	443.3	148.1

1. See Notes for definitions of M1, M2, and M3.

Table 24-9. Money Stock and Selected Components—*Continued*

(Averages of daily figures; billions of dollars, seasonally adjusted.)

Year and month	Money stock measures [1]			Selected components					
	M1	M2	M3	Currency	Demand deposits	Other checkable deposits	Savings deposits	Small time deposits	Large time deposits
1978									
January	334.1	1 280.2	1 486.9	88.0	239.1	4.3	490.4	450.8	150.8
February	335.0	1 286.0	1 498.5	88.7	239.1	4.4	492.5	454.4	153.9
March	336.6	1 292.7	1 513.5	89.4	240.0	4.6	498.0	457.2	159.5
April	339.6	1 300.9	1 529.0	90.0	242.2	4.7	501.2	460.5	163.0
May	344.7	1 311.2	1 545.0	90.8	246.1	4.9	501.0	462.9	168.8
June	347.1	1 319.6	1 556.4	91.5	247.3	4.9	501.5	469.3	171.1
July	348.5	1 325.9	1 568.6	92.0	247.5	5.0	498.8	478.5	174.8
August	350.4	1 335.2	1 584.7	92.7	248.6	5.1	496.0	484.5	180.4
September	352.7	1 346.4	1 598.2	93.6	250.3	5.2	495.8	492.4	182.6
October	353.4	1 353.4	1 612.0	94.4	250.4	5.3	494.9	501.2	184.9
November	355.1	1 359.9	1 630.9	95.2	250.2	6.7	485.3	509.6	193.8
December	356.9	1 366.5	1 646.1	96.0	249.5	8.5	478.1	519.3	199.2
1979									
January	358.2	1 372.2	1 657.5	96.8	248.5	10.0	469.4	535.7	200.5
February	359.6	1 378.5	1 669.8	97.4	248.1	11.1	463.0	546.0	202.4
March	362.1	1 388.5	1 683.8	98.0	248.8	12.3	463.3	554.3	202.7
April	367.7	1 402.9	1 701.5	98.8	252.4	13.4	461.4	563.9	198.6
May	369.4	1 411.1	1 711.9	99.5	252.7	14.0	456.7	570.0	198.7
June	373.6	1 424.3	1 729.3	100.3	254.7	14.9	458.8	576.0	196.4
July	378.1	1 436.6	1 745.1	101.2	257.0	15.7	460.9	581.7	198.6
August	379.7	1 448.5	1 763.4	102.1	257.1	16.1	458.3	588.0	204.1
September	379.7	1 455.6	1 784.3	103.1	256.2	16.4	452.9	597.6	211.1
October	380.9	1 461.5	1 797.8	103.9	256.9	16.5	442.7	611.7	218.3
November	380.5	1 466.7	1 799.8	104.3	256.5	16.5	425.9	626.3	222.7
December	381.4	1 474.3	1 809.7	104.8	256.6	16.8	420.6	633.1	226.2
1980									
January	385.4	1 483.4	1 823.7	106.0	258.9	17.4	415.1	644.2	227.1
February	389.7	1 495.5	1 842.7	106.7	261.7	18.0	407.4	653.9	231.2
March	388.1	1 500.8	1 851.1	107.5	258.9	18.5	400.3	667.6	234.2
April	383.4	1 503.5	1 855.5	107.7	253.4	19.0	388.3	685.9	235.0
May	384.6	1 513.4	1 868.1	108.7	253.4	19.2	383.1	693.8	237.0
June	389.5	1 530.7	1 886.0	109.6	255.3	20.6	393.1	692.4	230.5
July	394.9	1 547.6	1 905.3	110.5	257.8	22.0	407.1	689.2	226.5
August	400.1	1 563.6	1 923.1	111.6	260.6	23.2	415.2	687.0	229.7
September	405.4	1 575.7	1 936.9	112.4	264.2	24.5	418.7	689.7	234.1
October	409.1	1 586.0	1 954.9	113.4	266.1	25.7	420.0	697.6	239.5
November	410.4	1 596.6	1 976.3	114.8	264.2	27.9	411.3	711.2	249.3
December	408.1	1 600.4	1 996.3	115.3	261.2	28.1	397.1	728.0	262.9
1981									
January	410.8	1 607.7	2 021.3	115.3	248.2	43.8	380.8	751.0	272.7
February	414.4	1 619.7	2 040.3	116.2	241.3	53.3	372.5	761.0	277.9
March	418.7	1 637.7	2 059.2	117.0	238.8	59.3	372.3	767.0	275.6
April	427.0	1 661.0	2 088.1	117.9	239.5	66.0	374.6	765.8	270.1
May	424.4	1 665.4	2 103.5	118.3	236.3	66.0	368.4	772.0	278.6
June	425.5	1 672.0	2 120.2	118.7	234.6	67.9	363.4	781.0	283.0
July	427.9	1 684.2	2 140.3	119.5	233.7	69.8	363.9	784.1	288.4
August	427.8	1 696.6	2 159.6	119.9	232.2	70.7	354.1	795.7	297.0
September	427.5	1 707.8	2 181.0	120.1	230.5	72.3	347.2	804.7	300.9
October	428.5	1 723.2	2 203.7	120.5	230.4	73.4	343.1	819.3	301.0
November	430.9	1 737.0	2 225.4	121.4	229.8	76.0	340.4	824.0	302.6
December	436.2	1 756.1	2 254.9	122.5	231.4	78.7	341.2	823.1	306.0
1982									
January	442.1	1 771.2	2 278.6	123.2	233.6	81.8	345.4	826.7	307.4
February	441.5	1 775.6	2 287.0	123.9	231.3	82.6	343.1	835.3	313.6
March	442.4	1 787.7	2 305.6	124.5	229.8	84.4	344.7	844.2	316.2
April	446.8	1 806.2	2 333.4	125.5	229.9	87.6	346.6	849.7	315.5
May	446.5	1 816.7	2 344.8	126.7	228.8	87.1	345.6	855.7	316.8
June	447.9	1 827.9	2 362.1	127.4	227.6	88.3	346.2	861.5	318.2
July	449.1	1 836.9	2 374.7	128.1	226.8	88.9	345.9	872.0	322.2
August	452.5	1 851.9	2 399.7	129.0	227.3	91.0	344.0	876.9	327.8
September	457.5	1 865.4	2 415.7	129.9	229.0	93.9	345.1	879.2	328.2
October	464.6	1 876.2	2 436.2	130.8	230.8	98.6	354.4	875.2	331.4
November	471.1	1 889.4	2 449.5	131.6	233.2	102.5	360.1	871.1	332.2
December	474.3	1 911.2	2 460.9	132.5	234.1	104.1	397.2	851.4	326.1
1983									
January	476.7	1 964.3	2 490.9	133.6	233.6	106.0	521.6	796.6	302.2
February	483.8	2 001.9	2 519.2	135.0	234.1	111.0	600.3	756.2	290.1
March	490.2	2 020.1	2 536.0	136.4	235.5	114.4	641.4	735.8	285.1
April	492.8	2 034.0	2 555.8	137.4	234.5	116.9	663.4	728.2	283.5
May	499.8	2 048.1	2 570.7	138.7	236.9	120.0	679.2	721.9	282.7
June	504.3	2 058.9	2 588.1	139.6	237.7	122.3	690.3	722.5	286.5
July	509.0	2 070.9	2 598.6	140.5	238.3	124.6	692.4	732.6	287.8
August	511.6	2 079.9	2 612.7	141.4	238.9	125.8	686.4	743.3	296.4
September	513.4	2 088.6	2 629.3	142.7	238.7	126.9	684.0	752.4	302.4
October	517.2	2 104.1	2 648.2	144.1	238.8	129.7	684.2	767.5	304.6
November	518.5	2 116.8	2 675.9	145.3	238.2	130.8	682.3	779.4	310.3
December	520.8	2 127.8	2 699.2	146.2	238.5	132.1	682.3	784.8	316.8

1. See Notes for definitions of M1, M2, and M3.

Table 24-9. Money Stock and Selected Components—*Continued*

(Averages of daily figures; billions of dollars, seasonally adjusted.)

Year and month	Money stock measures [1]			Selected components					
	M1	M2	M3	Currency	Demand deposits	Other checkable deposits	Savings deposits	Small time deposits	Large time deposits
1984									
January	524.4	2 142.5	2 716.8	147.4	240.2	132.7	686.4	795.4	321.9
February	527.0	2 162.8	2 745.0	148.0	240.5	134.2	690.5	803.0	327.1
March	530.8	2 179.8	2 773.2	149.1	241.0	136.3	699.6	806.2	333.5
April	534.0	2 196.2	2 802.9	150.1	242.3	137.2	704.8	809.8	338.2
May	536.6	2 209.4	2 830.6	150.7	241.8	139.4	702.3	816.5	352.2
June	540.5	2 220.9	2 852.6	151.9	242.6	140.8	700.9	828.0	363.4
July	542.1	2 230.1	2 874.8	152.7	242.0	141.2	696.3	842.7	374.0
August	542.4	2 237.1	2 889.0	153.5	241.4	141.3	685.2	859.1	383.3
September	543.9	2 250.4	2 908.1	154.4	241.3	142.7	682.3	870.8	388.2
October	543.9	2 264.6	2 933.5	154.7	240.9	143.4	684.7	882.3	398.1
November	547.3	2 286.9	2 961.4	155.5	242.3	145.1	692.2	887.9	399.6
December	551.2	2 311.8	2 992.8	156.1	243.4	147.4	702.2	889.7	403.1
1985									
January	555.7	2 336.9	3 018.7	156.8	245.0	149.5	721.1	890.9	402.2
February	562.5	2 358.6	3 042.5	157.9	247.5	152.7	735.6	886.0	403.4
March	565.8	2 370.9	3 058.1	158.5	247.6	155.1	747.1	882.6	407.3
April	569.4	2 380.1	3 063.4	159.4	248.4	156.9	750.8	882.6	407.9
May	575.2	2 395.5	3 080.8	160.5	251.1	158.6	755.5	884.3	409.8
June	582.9	2 419.3	3 106.3	161.7	252.9	162.4	770.6	887.4	406.8
July	590.7	2 436.9	3 116.5	162.8	255.5	165.5	783.2	888.7	402.5
August	598.0	2 451.6	3 134.7	164.3	257.6	169.1	790.7	885.1	407.2
September	604.6	2 463.5	3 153.3	165.2	261.3	171.8	795.6	883.6	413.2
October	608.0	2 474.1	3 169.7	166.2	261.6	174.6	804.3	884.8	417.2
November	611.9	2 483.3	3 184.6	167.1	262.1	177.7	810.9	884.3	419.3
December	619.3	2 497.6	3 209.7	167.8	266.8	179.8	813.0	886.4	422.1
1986									
January	620.5	2 507.1	3 233.4	168.5	265.4	181.8	818.1	893.0	431.2
February	624.2	2 517.7	3 252.2	169.5	265.8	183.9	818.8	893.5	435.0
March	632.8	2 538.0	3 278.3	170.8	269.8	186.9	826.6	894.3	435.0
April	640.2	2 562.7	3 308.5	171.5	272.6	190.8	836.9	892.9	431.3
May	652.0	2 590.9	3 333.3	172.8	277.3	196.5	849.0	886.9	429.2
June	661.5	2 612.0	3 355.7	173.7	279.8	201.4	865.3	883.5	426.9
July	672.1	2 634.9	3 386.9	174.8	283.4	206.3	878.5	885.1	427.1
August	680.7	2 655.1	3 412.1	176.0	284.9	212.0	889.4	881.8	430.9
September	688.5	2 675.7	3 439.7	177.0	287.6	216.9	901.4	877.8	431.6
October	695.4	2 695.0	3 458.4	178.4	288.1	222.7	918.3	871.7	426.8
November	705.2	2 708.1	3 469.8	179.5	291.4	228.8	930.4	863.2	422.3
December	724.2	2 734.5	3 501.2	180.6	302.8	235.6	938.9	858.3	419.8
1987									
January	729.4	2 749.8	3 526.4	182.1	299.3	242.6	952.4	858.9	422.5
February	730.0	2 753.6	3 535.7	183.5	295.9	245.0	956.8	854.4	424.3
March	733.1	2 759.6	3 543.8	184.2	295.0	248.0	966.4	850.2	427.4
April	743.4	2 773.8	3 564.6	185.6	299.2	252.9	972.0	846.6	426.9
May	745.9	2 779.8	3 581.4	186.6	298.7	254.6	970.2	843.9	434.5
June	743.6	2 781.7	3 596.3	187.8	294.1	254.8	971.6	851.2	438.7
July	745.0	2 788.0	3 604.0	188.9	292.4	255.6	969.8	862.8	439.2
August	746.9	2 796.9	3 626.1	190.2	290.9	257.5	963.9	870.2	445.2
September	748.6	2 807.4	3 649.7	191.6	290.3	259.3	958.8	877.4	450.5
October	756.5	2 821.8	3 672.3	193.3	295.3	261.3	952.7	890.5	457.4
November	753.0	2 825.9	3 684.6	195.5	291.2	260.3	941.9	908.5	463.9
December	749.6	2 833.4	3 692.2	196.8	287.5	259.5	936.0	920.1	466.3
1988									
January	755.5	2 854.5	3 715.4	198.1	289.0	262.6	935.9	935.8	464.8
February	757.2	2 877.7	3 743.0	199.1	287.5	264.5	934.9	952.0	469.7
March	761.2	2 898.1	3 767.6	200.4	287.8	266.7	942.8	961.4	475.1
April	767.4	2 917.9	3 795.4	202.0	289.1	270.1	946.6	968.1	473.9
May	771.6	2 933.7	3 821.7	203.4	288.5	273.3	946.1	972.0	478.6
June	779.1	2 946.8	3 842.8	204.8	291.0	275.9	953.3	977.1	483.2
July	783.3	2 957.6	3 860.5	206.2	289.6	278.9	955.0	986.5	489.2
August	785.1	2 962.5	3 872.8	207.4	290.2	279.0	947.6	993.7	499.1
September	785.0	2 967.1	3 884.1	208.8	289.2	279.0	937.6	1 005.1	508.7
October	783.6	2 975.0	3 899.7	209.9	287.2	279.4	933.9	1 019.2	514.5
November	784.4	2 989.1	3 919.1	211.0	287.0	280.1	933.4	1 027.7	515.8
December	786.3	2 996.9	3 935.5	212.2	287.0	280.9	925.6	1 035.0	517.6
1989									
January	785.0	3 000.2	3 942.4	213.1	284.9	280.7	915.0	1 052.4	522.4
February	783.4	3 001.1	3 949.7	213.6	283.3	280.2	901.1	1 064.5	530.4
March	782.9	3 008.6	3 970.6	214.9	283.0	278.6	895.8	1 074.5	538.8
April	778.7	3 014.5	3 981.9	215.4	279.5	277.4	882.9	1 091.3	543.3
May	774.6	3 020.5	3 987.9	216.4	279.2	272.5	862.4	1 108.4	549.0
June	774.1	3 037.6	4 009.6	217.4	277.0	272.4	861.7	1 122.4	548.5
July	779.5	3 062.8	4 033.2	218.2	278.9	274.1	865.6	1 134.6	547.3
August	781.0	3 085.1	4 043.3	218.8	278.2	275.6	868.9	1 140.3	548.8
September	782.2	3 103.1	4 051.2	219.4	277.1	278.0	872.4	1 141.9	547.5
October	786.9	3 124.3	4 063.0	220.1	279.1	280.8	879.5	1 145.7	545.7
November	788.1	3 143.0	4 078.9	221.0	278.2	282.5	889.4	1 146.4	545.2
December	792.5	3 161.3	4 091.4	222.6	278.6	285.1	893.7	1 148.1	540.5

1. See Notes for definitions of M1, M2, and M3.

Table 24-9. Money Stock and Selected Components—*Continued*

(Averages of daily figures; billions of dollars, seasonally adjusted.)

Year and month	Money stock measures [1]			Selected components					
	M1	M2	M3	Currency	Demand deposits	Other checkable deposits	Savings deposits	Small time deposits	Large time deposits
1990									
January	794.8	3 175.1	4 099.8	224.3	278.2	286.1	897.2	1 152.8	534.8
February	797.7	3 187.3	4 102.9	225.9	278.1	287.1	900.8	1 153.7	530.3
March	801.1	3 198.8	4 106.2	228.0	277.3	289.3	910.5	1 154.5	527.3
April	805.9	3 210.9	4 110.9	229.9	276.9	292.5	914.7	1 156.3	518.4
May	804.4	3 209.3	4 111.7	231.6	274.7	291.1	910.9	1 156.5	518.6
June	810.1	3 223.3	4 121.1	233.8	275.3	293.2	917.0	1 159.5	514.4
July	811.7	3 234.1	4 132.1	235.9	275.5	291.4	919.9	1 166.1	510.9
August	818.0	3 253.3	4 147.5	238.8	278.1	291.8	921.9	1 166.9	508.4
September	821.6	3 264.9	4 153.9	241.7	278.5	292.7	921.5	1 167.7	499.8
October	820.4	3 268.9	4 156.6	243.9	277.0	291.5	922.0	1 170.6	494.4
November	822.2	3 272.9	4 151.8	245.5	276.8	292.5	924.4	1 170.1	491.0
December	824.4	3 281.0	4 155.8	247.0	276.8	293.7	922.0	1 171.1	479.8
1991									
January	826.7	3 296.7	4 179.6	251.1	273.9	294.6	923.0	1 176.0	479.3
February	832.5	3 314.6	4 197.7	254.1	274.6	296.7	930.5	1 175.2	482.0
March	838.5	3 331.4	4 204.9	256.1	274.8	300.6	947.9	1 168.6	478.1
April	842.5	3 340.9	4 210.6	256.3	275.6	303.6	960.6	1 160.5	470.3
May	849.3	3 352.0	4 212.0	257.0	277.8	307.3	970.3	1 149.5	469.4
June	858.1	3 362.1	4 212.8	258.2	280.3	311.7	985.6	1 138.0	464.6
July	863.1	3 366.6	4 208.5	259.5	280.4	314.5	995.6	1 130.4	454.6
August	868.7	3 365.6	4 201.7	261.4	280.3	318.3	1 001.2	1 121.1	450.3
September	871.7	3 365.0	4 194.0	262.6	279.6	321.3	1 005.9	1 111.1	442.9
October	878.6	3 369.1	4 197.0	264.2	282.6	324.1	1 018.5	1 097.7	432.6
November	887.6	3 374.7	4 202.0	265.9	285.6	329.0	1 033.4	1 080.4	424.2
December	896.3	3 381.0	4 208.2	267.5	289.5	332.3	1 043.2	1 063.2	415.7
1992									
January	910.4	3 390.7	4 217.1	269.1	296.4	337.9	1 059.5	1 044.5	408.4
February	925.2	3 409.9	4 235.4	270.8	302.7	344.5	1 082.0	1 020.6	404.4
March	936.3	3 413.9	4 236.1	271.9	308.6	348.7	1 104.4	1 000.8	401.0
April	943.7	3 410.4	4 224.3	273.6	311.8	351.3	1 119.1	982.1	393.6
May	950.8	3 409.3	4 219.2	275.1	313.3	355.1	1 125.7	963.4	391.5
June	954.9	3 405.8	4 217.5	276.7	313.4	356.8	1 135.7	950.1	385.4
July	965.0	3 407.4	4 219.3	279.4	317.4	359.2	1 144.0	938.9	378.4
August	975.7	3 412.4	4 228.6	282.4	320.5	363.7	1 153.1	923.8	376.8
September	988.9	3 422.5	4 234.6	285.4	327.4	367.2	1 162.9	910.9	371.6
October	1 004.5	3 436.0	4 232.3	287.8	334.3	374.0	1 174.4	895.6	363.7
November	1 016.0	3 437.9	4 228.2	289.9	337.2	381.1	1 185.4	878.6	358.4
December	1 024.3	3 435.7	4 219.2	292.6	339.8	384.3	1 185.3	866.1	353.0
1993									
January	1 030.3	3 431.8	4 203.3	294.6	340.0	388.2	1 181.9	858.1	343.6
February	1 033.4	3 427.7	4 203.0	296.7	341.7	387.5	1 182.7	850.6	342.5
March	1 038.4	3 425.0	4 204.0	298.8	343.2	388.8	1 188.6	843.0	339.1
April	1 047.5	3 425.5	4 209.5	301.4	349.0	389.6	1 193.5	835.2	341.6
May	1 066.3	3 452.0	4 238.6	304.2	357.9	396.3	1 200.0	826.9	346.8
June	1 075.8	3 457.7	4 238.8	306.8	361.5	399.0	1 208.7	819.4	343.9
July	1 086.0	3 458.4	4 237.5	309.7	364.8	402.4	1 209.5	812.6	337.6
August	1 095.7	3 462.7	4 239.3	312.4	369.7	404.5	1 211.5	804.6	340.1
September	1 105.7	3 470.2	4 249.5	315.5	374.7	406.8	1 211.1	798.6	337.8
October	1 113.8	3 473.8	4 254.8	317.7	377.8	410.1	1 212.5	792.7	337.7
November	1 123.9	3 486.0	4 271.1	319.8	384.0	412.5	1 219.1	785.6	335.7
December	1 129.7	3 490.8	4 280.0	322.1	385.5	414.6	1 217.7	780.1	333.5
1994									
January	1 131.9	3 493.8	4 282.9	325.4	386.3	412.6	1 217.9	775.9	334.5
February	1 136.3	3 496.5	4 266.6	328.7	388.4	411.7	1 219.6	770.4	332.1
March	1 140.4	3 500.3	4 274.6	331.7	387.9	413.1	1 227.4	766.5	330.6
April	1 141.1	3 503.5	4 281.9	334.1	387.6	411.8	1 228.1	764.5	330.0
May	1 143.1	3 511.3	4 290.4	337.2	385.4	412.5	1 220.7	765.0	337.3
June	1 146.1	3 500.8	4 289.6	340.1	384.9	412.4	1 215.1	768.3	339.1
July	1 151.4	3 507.8	4 308.8	343.1	385.6	413.1	1 209.3	773.5	339.8
August	1 151.5	3 505.4	4 310.3	345.4	385.6	411.0	1 200.4	779.2	346.3
September	1 152.6	3 505.5	4 318.4	347.6	386.9	408.9	1 190.2	785.3	352.3
October	1 150.7	3 504.1	4 327.4	350.3	385.9	405.9	1 177.7	795.2	357.0
November	1 150.4	3 505.5	4 341.2	352.9	384.5	404.8	1 167.4	804.7	361.8
December	1 150.1	3 505.4	4 354.1	354.4	383.6	404.1	1 148.5	814.7	363.6
1995									
January	1 150.6	3 510.3	4 377.7	357.3	384.4	401.0	1 129.2	832.4	362.9
February	1 146.9	3 509.2	4 380.4	358.4	383.5	397.0	1 111.4	852.7	371.8
March	1 146.9	3 510.6	4 397.4	362.1	381.7	394.7	1 100.6	875.5	378.0
April	1 149.3	3 518.2	4 418.5	365.4	380.3	394.8	1 090.9	892.4	380.7
May	1 144.7	3 542.3	4 457.7	368.0	381.3	386.4	1 087.8	905.6	389.2
June	1 144.5	3 569.6	4 495.7	367.8	384.6	382.5	1 099.7	913.2	391.5
July	1 146.6	3 589.3	4 524.5	367.9	386.7	381.7	1 099.7	919.5	394.6
August	1 146.3	3 609.8	4 556.2	368.9	388.5	378.6	1 105.8	922.0	399.7
September	1 142.4	3 621.9	4 575.6	369.7	388.6	374.2	1 111.2	923.6	404.5
October	1 137.3	3 632.6	4 594.0	370.9	391.0	366.3	1 117.9	926.0	415.5
November	1 134.1	3 641.3	4 608.2	371.5	390.5	363.4	1 124.3	928.2	421.6
December	1 126.8	3 650.1	4 617.5	372.5	389.2	356.6	1 133.3	929.7	420.0

1. See Notes for definitions of M1, M2, and M3.

Table 24-10. Interest Rates, Bond Yields, and Stock Price Indexes

(Not seasonally adjusted.)

Year and month	Short-term rates					U.S. Treasury securites			Bond yields				Stock price indexes	
	Federal funds	Federal Reserve discount [1]	U.S. Treasury bills, 3-month	U.S. Treasury bills, 6-month	Bank prime rate	One-year	Ten-year	Long-term composite [2]	Domestic corporate (Moody's)		State and local bonds (Bond Byer)	Fixed-rate first mortgages	Dow Jones industrials (30 stocks)	Standard and Poor's composite (500 stocks) [3]
									Aaa	Baa				
1972														
January	3.50	4.50	3.41	3.66	5.18	4.28	5.95	5.62	7.19	8.23	5.12	7.44	904.65	103.30
February	3.29	4.50	3.18	3.59	4.75	4.27	6.08	5.67	7.27	8.23	5.28	7.33	914.37	105.24
March	3.83	4.50	3.72	4.09	4.75	4.67	6.07	5.66	7.24	8.24	5.31	7.30	939.23	107.69
April	4.17	4.50	3.72	4.22	4.97	4.96	6.19	5.74	7.30	8.24	5.43	7.29	958.16	108.81
May	4.27	4.50	3.65	4.07	5.00	4.64	6.13	5.64	7.30	8.23	5.30	7.37	948.22	107.65
June	4.46	4.50	3.87	4.27	5.04	4.93	6.11	5.59	7.23	8.20	5.33	7.37	943.43	108.01
July	4.55	4.50	4.06	4.59	5.25	4.96	6.11	5.57	7.21	8.23	5.41	7.40	925.92	107.21
August	4.80	4.50	4.01	4.53	5.27	4.98	6.21	5.54	7.19	8.19	5.30	7.40	958.34	111.01
September	4.87	4.50	4.65	5.09	5.50	5.52	6.55	5.70	7.22	8.09	5.36	7.42	950.58	109.39
October	5.04	4.50	4.72	5.12	5.73	5.52	6.48	5.69	7.21	8.06	5.18	7.42	944.10	109.56
November	5.06	4.50	4.78	5.08	5.75	5.27	6.28	5.50	7.12	7.99	5.02	7.43	1 001.19	115.05
December	5.33	4.50	5.06	5.29	5.79	5.52	6.36	5.63	7.08	7.93	5.05	7.44	1 020.32	117.50
1973														
January	5.94	4.77	5.31	5.53	6.00	5.89	6.46	5.94	7.15	7.90	5.05	7.44	1 026.82	118.42
February	6.58	5.05	5.56	5.75	6.02	6.19	6.64	6.14	7.22	7.97	5.13	7.44	974.04	114.16
March	7.09	5.50	6.05	6.43	6.30	6.85	6.71	6.20	7.29	8.03	5.29	7.46	957.35	112.42
April	7.12	5.50	6.29	6.53	6.61	6.85	6.67	6.11	7.26	8.09	5.15	7.54	944.10	110.27
May	7.84	5.90	6.35	6.62	7.01	6.89	6.85	6.22	7.29	8.06	5.15	7.65	922.41	107.22
June	8.49	6.33	7.19	7.24	7.49	7.31	6.90	6.32	7.37	8.13	5.17	7.73	893.90	104.75
July	10.40	6.98	8.02	8.08	8.30	8.39	7.13	6.53	7.45	8.24	5.40	8.05	903.61	105.83
August	10.50	7.29	8.67	8.70	9.23	8.82	7.40	6.81	7.68	8.53	5.48	8.50	883.73	103.80
September	10.78	7.50	8.48	8.54	9.86	8.31	7.09	6.42	7.63	8.63	5.10	8.82	909.98	105.61
October	10.01	7.50	7.16	7.26	9.94	7.40	6.79	6.26	7.60	8.41	5.05	8.77	967.62	109.84
November	10.03	7.50	7.87	7.82	9.75	7.57	6.73	6.31	7.67	8.42	5.18	8.58	878.98	102.03
December	9.95	7.50	7.37	7.45	9.75	7.27	6.74	6.35	7.68	8.48	5.12	8.54	824.08	94.78
1974														
January	9.65	7.50	7.76	7.63	9.73	7.42	6.99	6.56	7.83	8.48	5.22	8.54	857.24	96.11
February	8.97	7.50	7.06	6.88	9.21	6.88	6.96	6.54	7.85	8.53	5.20	8.46	831.34	93.45
March	9.35	7.50	7.99	7.83	8.85	7.76	7.21	6.81	8.01	8.62	5.40	8.41	874.00	97.44
April	10.51	7.60	8.23	8.17	10.02	8.62	7.51	7.04	8.25	8.87	5.73	8.58	847.79	92.46
May	11.31	8.00	8.43	8.50	11.25	8.78	7.58	7.07	8.37	9.05	6.02	8.97	829.84	89.67
June	11.93	8.00	8.15	8.23	11.54	8.67	7.54	7.03	8.47	9.27	6.13	9.09	831.43	89.79
July	12.92	8.00	7.75	8.03	11.97	8.80	7.81	7.18	8.72	9.48	6.68	9.28	783.00	82.82
August	12.01	8.00	8.75	8.85	12.00	9.36	8.04	7.33	9.00	9.77	6.71	9.59	729.30	76.03
September	11.34	8.00	8.37	8.60	12.00	8.87	8.04	7.30	9.24	10.18	6.76	9.96	651.28	68.12
October	10.06	8.00	7.24	7.56	11.68	8.05	7.90	7.22	9.27	10.48	6.57	9.98	638.62	69.44
November	9.45	8.00	7.59	7.55	10.83	7.66	7.68	6.93	8.89	10.60	6.61	9.79	642.10	71.74
December	8.53	7.81	7.18	7.09	10.50	7.31	7.43	6.78	8.89	10.63	7.05	9.62	596.50	67.07
1975														
January	7.13	7.40	6.49	6.53	10.05	6.83	7.50	6.68	8.83	10.81	6.82	9.43	659.09	72.56
February	6.24	6.82	5.59	5.68	8.96	5.98	7.39	6.61	8.62	10.65	6.39	9.11	724.89	80.10
March	5.54	6.40	5.55	5.64	7.93	6.11	7.73	6.73	8.67	10.48	6.73	8.90	765.06	83.78
April	5.49	6.25	5.69	6.01	7.50	6.90	8.23	7.03	8.95	10.58	6.95	8.82	790.93	84.72
May	5.22	6.12	5.32	5.65	7.40	6.39	8.06	6.99	8.90	10.69	6.97	8.91	836.56	90.10
June	5.55	6.00	5.20	5.47	7.07	6.29	7.86	6.86	8.77	10.62	6.94	8.89	845.70	92.40
July	6.10	6.00	6.17	6.49	7.15	7.11	8.06	6.89	8.84	10.55	7.07	8.89	856.28	92.49
August	6.14	6.00	6.46	6.94	7.66	7.70	8.40	7.06	8.95	10.59	7.17	8.94	815.51	85.71
September	6.24	6.00	6.38	6.87	7.88	7.75	8.43	7.29	8.95	10.61	7.44	9.13	818.28	84.67
October	5.82	6.00	6.08	6.38	7.96	6.95	8.14	7.29	8.86	10.62	7.39	9.22	831.26	88.57
November	5.22	6.00	5.47	5.75	7.53	6.49	8.05	7.21	8.78	10.56	7.43	9.15	845.51	90.07
December	5.20	6.00	5.50	5.93	7.26	6.60	8.00	7.17	8.79	10.56	7.31	9.10	840.80	88.70
1976														
January	4.87	5.79	4.96	5.24	7.00	5.81	7.74	6.94	8.60	10.41	7.07	9.02	929.34	96.86
February	4.77	5.50	4.85	5.14	6.75	5.91	7.79	6.92	8.55	10.24	6.94	8.81	971.70	100.64
March	4.84	5.50	5.05	5.49	6.75	6.21	7.73	6.87	8.52	10.12	6.91	8.76	988.55	101.08
April	4.82	5.50	4.88	5.20	6.75	5.92	7.56	6.73	8.40	9.94	6.60	8.73	992.51	101.93
May	5.29	5.50	5.19	5.60	6.75	6.40	7.90	6.99	8.58	9.86	6.87	8.77	988.82	101.16
June	5.48	5.50	5.45	5.79	7.20	6.52	7.86	6.92	8.62	9.89	6.87	8.85	985.59	101.77
July	5.31	5.50	5.28	5.60	7.25	6.20	7.83	6.85	8.56	9.82	6.79	8.93	993.20	104.20
August	5.29	5.50	5.15	5.42	7.01	6.00	7.77	6.79	8.45	9.64	6.61	9.00	981.63	103.29
September	5.25	5.50	5.08	5.31	7.00	5.84	7.59	6.70	8.38	9.40	6.51	8.98	994.37	105.45
October	5.02	5.50	4.93	5.07	6.77	5.50	7.41	6.65	8.32	9.29	6.30	8.93	951.95	101.89
November	4.95	5.43	4.81	4.94	6.50	5.29	7.29	6.62	8.25	9.23	6.29	8.81	944.58	101.19
December	4.65	5.25	4.36	4.51	6.35	4.89	6.87	6.39	7.98	9.12	5.94	8.79	976.86	104.66
1977														
January	4.61	5.25	4.60	4.79	6.25	5.29	7.21	6.68	7.96	9.08	5.87	8.72	970.62	103.81
February	4.68	5.25	4.66	4.90	6.25	5.47	7.39	7.15	8.04	9.12	5.88	8.67	941.77	100.96
March	4.69	5.25	4.61	4.88	6.25	5.50	7.46	7.20	8.10	9.12	5.89	8.69	946.11	100.57
April	4.73	5.25	4.54	4.79	6.25	5.44	7.37	7.13	8.04	9.07	5.72	8.75	929.10	99.05
May	5.35	5.25	4.94	5.19	6.41	5.84	7.46	7.17	8.05	9.01	5.75	8.82	926.31	98.76
June	5.39	5.25	5.00	5.20	6.75	5.80	7.28	6.99	7.95	8.91	5.62	8.86	916.56	99.29
July	5.42	5.25	5.14	5.35	6.75	5.94	7.33	6.97	7.94	8.87	5.63	8.94	908.20	100.18
August	5.90	5.27	5.50	5.81	6.83	6.37	7.40	7.00	7.98	8.82	5.62	8.94	872.26	97.75
September	6.14	5.75	5.77	5.99	7.13	6.53	7.34	6.94	7.92	8.80	5.51	8.90	853.30	96.23
October	6.47	5.80	6.19	6.41	7.52	6.97	7.52	7.08	8.04	8.89	5.64	8.92	823.96	93.74
November	6.51	6.00	6.16	6.43	7.75	6.95	7.58	7.14	8.08	8.95	5.49	8.92	828.51	94.28
December	6.56	6.00	6.06	6.38	7.75	6.96	7.69	7.23	8.19	8.99	5.57	8.96	818.80	93.82

1. Discount window borrowing, Federal Reserve Bank of New York.
2. Maturities of more than ten years.
3. 1941–1943=10.

Table 24-10. Interest Rates, Bond Yields, and Stock Price Indexes—*Continued*

(Not seasonally adjusted.)

Year and month	Short-term rates					U.S. Treasury securites			Bond yields				Stock price indexes	
	Federal funds	Federal Reserve discount[1]	U.S. Treasury bills, 3-month	U.S. Treasury bills, 6-month	Bank prime rate	One-year	Ten-year	Long-term composite[2]	Domestic corporate (Moody's)		State and local bonds (Bond Byer)	Fixed-rate first mortgages	Dow Jones industrials (30 stocks)	Standard and Poor's composite (500 stocks)[3]
									Aaa	Baa				
1978														
January	6.70	6.37	6.45	6.69	7.93	7.28	7.96	7.50	8.41	9.17	5.71	9.02	781.09	90.25
February	6.78	6.50	6.46	6.74	8.00	7.34	8.03	7.60	8.47	9.20	5.62	9.16	763.57	88.98
March	6.79	6.50	6.32	6.65	8.00	7.31	8.04	7.63	8.47	9.22	5.61	9.20	756.37	88.82
April	6.89	6.50	6.31	6.70	8.00	7.45	8.15	7.74	8.56	9.32	5.79	9.36	794.66	92.71
May	7.36	6.84	6.43	7.02	8.27	7.82	8.35	7.87	8.69	9.49	6.03	9.58	838.56	97.41
June	7.60	7.00	6.71	7.20	8.63	8.09	8.46	7.94	8.76	9.60	6.22	9.71	840.26	97.66
July	7.81	7.23	7.08	7.48	9.00	8.39	8.64	8.09	8.88	9.60	6.28	9.74	831.71	97.19
August	8.04	7.43	7.04	7.36	9.01	8.31	8.41	7.87	8.69	9.48	6.12	9.79	887.93	103.92
September	8.45	7.83	7.84	7.95	9.41	8.64	8.42	7.82	8.69	9.42	6.09	9.76	878.64	103.86
October	8.96	8.26	8.13	8.49	9.94	9.14	8.64	8.07	8.89	9.59	6.13	9.86	857.69	100.58
November	9.76	9.50	8.79	9.20	10.94	10.01	8.81	8.16	9.03	9.83	6.19	10.11	804.29	94.71
December	10.03	9.50	9.12	9.40	11.55	10.30	9.01	8.35	9.16	9.94	6.50	10.35	807.94	96.11
1979														
January	10.07	9.50	9.35	9.50	11.75	10.41	9.10	8.43	9.25	10.13	6.46	10.39	837.39	99.71
February	10.06	9.50	9.27	9.35	11.75	10.24	9.10	8.43	9.26	10.08	6.31	10.41	825.18	98.23
March	10.09	9.50	9.46	9.46	11.75	10.25	9.12	8.45	9.37	10.26	6.33	10.43	847.84	100.11
April	10.01	9.50	9.49	9.50	11.75	10.12	9.18	8.44	9.38	10.33	6.28	10.50	864.96	102.07
May	10.24	9.50	9.58	9.53	11.75	10.12	9.25	8.55	9.50	10.47	6.25	10.69	837.41	99.73
June	10.29	9.50	9.05	9.06	11.65	9.57	8.91	8.32	9.29	10.38	6.12	11.04	838.65	101.73
July	10.47	9.69	9.27	9.19	11.54	9.64	8.95	8.35	9.20	10.29	6.13	11.09	836.95	102.71
August	10.94	10.24	9.45	9.45	11.91	9.98	9.03	8.42	9.23	10.35	6.20	11.09	873.55	107.36
September	11.43	10.70	10.18	10.13	12.90	10.84	9.33	8.68	9.44	10.54	6.52	11.30	878.50	108.60
October	13.77	11.77	11.47	11.34	14.39	12.44	10.30	9.44	10.13	11.40	7.08	11.64	840.39	104.47
November	13.18	12.00	11.87	11.86	15.55	12.39	10.65	9.80	10.76	11.99	7.30	12.83	815.78	103.66
December	13.78	12.00	12.07	11.85	15.30	11.98	10.39	9.59	10.74	12.06	7.22	12.90	836.14	107.78
1980														
January	13.82	12.00	12.04	11.85	15.25	12.06	10.80	10.03	11.09	12.42	7.35	12.88	860.74	110.87
February	14.13	12.52	12.82	12.72	15.63	13.92	12.41	11.55	12.38	13.57	8.16	13.04	878.22	115.34
March	17.19	13.00	15.53	15.10	18.31	15.82	12.75	11.87	12.96	14.45	9.16	15.28	803.56	104.69
April	17.61	13.00	14.00	13.62	19.77	13.30	11.47	10.83	12.04	14.19	8.63	16.33	786.33	102.97
May	10.98	12.94	9.15	9.15	16.57	9.39	10.18	9.82	10.99	13.17	7.59	14.26	828.19	107.69
June	9.47	11.40	7.00	7.22	12.63	8.16	9.78	9.40	10.58	12.71	7.63	12.71	869.86	114.55
July	9.03	10.87	8.13	8.10	11.48	8.65	10.25	9.83	11.07	12.65	8.13	12.19	909.79	119.83
August	9.61	10.00	9.26	9.45	11.12	10.24	11.10	10.53	11.64	13.15	8.67	12.56	947.33	123.50
September	10.87	10.17	10.32	10.55	12.23	11.52	11.51	10.94	12.02	13.70	8.94	13.20	946.67	126.51
October	12.81	11.00	11.58	11.57	13.79	12.49	11.75	11.20	12.31	14.23	9.11	13.79	949.17	130.22
November	15.85	11.47	13.89	13.61	16.06	14.15	12.68	11.83	12.97	14.64	9.56	14.21	971.08	135.65
December	18.90	12.87	15.66	14.77	20.35	14.88	12.84	11.89	13.21	15.14	10.20	14.79	945.96	133.48
1981														
January	19.08	13.00	14.73	13.88	20.16	14.08	12.57	11.65	12.81	15.03	9.66	14.90	962.13	132.97
February	15.93	13.00	14.91	14.14	19.43	14.57	13.19	12.23	13.35	15.37	10.09	15.13	945.50	128.40
March	14.70	13.00	13.48	12.98	18.05	13.71	13.12	12.15	13.33	15.34	10.16	15.40	987.18	133.19
April	15.72	13.00	13.63	13.43	17.15	14.32	13.68	12.62	13.88	15.56	10.62	15.58	1 004.86	134.43
May	18.52	13.87	16.29	15.34	19.61	16.20	14.10	12.96	14.32	15.95	10.77	16.40	979.52	131.73
June	19.10	14.00	14.56	13.95	20.03	14.86	13.47	12.39	13.75	15.80	10.67	16.70	996.27	132.28
July	19.04	14.00	14.70	14.40	20.39	15.72	14.28	13.05	14.38	16.17	11.14	16.83	947.94	129.13
August	17.82	14.00	15.61	15.55	20.50	16.72	14.94	13.78	14.89	16.34	12.26	17.29	926.25	129.63
September	15.87	14.00	14.95	15.06	20.08	16.52	15.32	14.14	15.49	16.92	12.92	18.16	853.38	118.27
October	15.08	14.00	13.87	14.01	18.45	15.38	15.15	14.13	15.40	17.11	12.83	18.45	853.24	119.80
November	13.31	13.03	11.27	11.53	16.84	12.41	13.39	12.68	14.22	16.39	11.89	17.83	860.44	122.92
December	12.37	12.10	10.93	11.47	15.75	12.85	13.72	12.88	14.23	16.55	12.91	16.92	878.28	123.79
1982														
January	13.22	12.00	12.41	12.93	15.75	14.32	14.59	13.73	15.18	17.10	13.28	17.40	853.41	117.28
February	14.78	12.00	13.78	13.71	16.56	14.73	14.43	13.63	15.27	17.18	12.97	17.60	833.15	114.50
March	14.68	12.00	12.49	12.62	16.50	13.95	13.86	12.98	14.58	16.82	12.82	17.16	812.33	110.84
April	14.94	12.00	12.82	12.86	16.50	13.98	13.87	12.84	14.46	16.78	12.58	16.89	844.96	116.31
May	14.45	12.00	12.15	12.22	16.50	13.34	13.62	12.67	14.26	16.64	11.95	16.68	846.72	116.35
June	14.15	12.00	12.11	12.31	16.50	14.07	14.30	13.32	14.81	16.92	12.44	16.70	804.37	109.70
July	12.59	11.81	11.92	12.24	16.26	13.24	13.95	12.97	14.61	16.80	12.28	16.82	818.41	109.38
August	10.12	10.68	9.01	10.11	14.39	11.43	13.06	12.15	13.71	16.32	11.23	16.27	832.11	109.65
September	10.31	10.00	8.20	9.54	13.50	10.85	12.34	11.48	12.94	15.63	10.66	15.43	917.27	122.43
October	9.71	9.68	7.75	8.30	12.52	9.32	10.91	10.51	12.12	14.73	9.68	14.61	988.71	132.66
November	9.20	9.35	8.04	8.32	11.85	9.16	10.55	10.18	11.68	14.30	10.06	13.83	1 027.76	138.10
December	8.95	8.73	8.02	8.22	11.50	8.91	10.54	10.33	11.83	14.14	9.96	13.62	1 033.08	139.37
1983														
January	8.68	8.50	7.81	7.90	11.16	8.62	10.46	10.37	11.79	13.94	9.50	13.25	1 064.29	144.27
February	8.51	8.50	8.13	8.24	10.98	8.92	10.72	10.60	12.01	13.95	9.58	13.04	1 087.43	146.80
March	8.77	8.50	8.30	8.33	10.50	9.04	10.51	10.34	11.73	13.61	9.20	12.80	1 129.58	151.88
April	8.80	8.50	8.25	8.35	10.50	8.98	10.40	10.19	11.51	13.29	9.04	12.78	1 168.43	157.71
May	8.63	8.50	8.19	8.20	10.50	8.90	10.38	10.21	11.46	13.09	9.11	12.63	1 212.86	164.10
June	8.98	8.50	8.82	8.89	10.50	9.66	10.85	10.64	11.74	13.37	9.52	12.87	1 221.47	166.39
July	9.37	8.50	9.12	9.29	10.50	10.20	11.38	11.10	12.15	13.39	9.53	13.42	1 213.93	166.96
August	9.56	8.50	9.39	9.53	10.89	10.53	11.85	11.42	12.51	13.64	9.72	13.81	1 189.21	162.42
September	9.45	8.50	9.05	9.19	11.00	10.16	11.65	11.26	12.37	13.55	9.58	13.73	1 237.04	167.16
October	9.48	8.50	8.71	8.90	11.00	9.81	11.54	11.21	12.25	13.46	9.66	13.54	1 252.20	167.65
November	9.34	8.50	8.71	8.89	11.00	9.94	11.69	11.32	12.41	13.61	9.74	13.44	1 250.00	165.23
December	9.47	8.50	8.96	9.14	11.00	10.11	11.83	11.44	12.57	13.75	9.89	13.42	1 257.64	164.36

1. Discount window borrowing, Federal Reserve Bank of New York.
2. Maturities of more than ten years.
3. 1941–1943=10.

Table 24-10. Interest Rates, Bond Yields, and Stock Price Indexes—*Continued*

(Not seasonally adjusted.)

| Year and month | Short-term rates | | | | | U.S. Treasury securites | | | Bond yields | | | | Stock price indexes | |
	Federal funds	Federal Reserve discount [1]	U.S. Treasury bills, 3-month	U.S. Treasury bills, 6-month	Bank prime rate	One-year	Ten-year	Long-term composite [2]	Domestic corporate (Moody's) Aaa	Baa	State and local bonds (Bond Byer)	Fixed-rate first mortgages	Dow Jones industrials (30 stocks)	Standard and Poor's composite (500 stocks) [3]
1984														
January	9.56	8.50	8.93	9.06	11.00	9.90	11.67	11.29	12.20	13.65	9.63	13.37	1 258.89	166.39
February	9.59	8.50	9.03	9.13	11.00	10.04	11.84	11.44	12.08	13.59	9.64	13.23	1 164.46	157.25
March	9.91	8.50	9.08	9.32	11.21	10.59	12.32	11.90	12.57	13.99	9.94	13.39	1 161.97	157.44
April	10.29	8.87	9.69	9.83	11.93	10.90	12.63	12.17	12.81	14.31	9.96	13.65	1 152.71	157.60
May	10.32	9.00	9.90	10.31	12.39	11.66	13.41	12.89	13.28	14.74	10.49	13.94	1 143.42	156.55
June	11.06	9.00	9.94	10.55	12.60	12.08	13.56	13.04	13.55	15.05	10.67	14.42	1 121.14	153.12
July	11.23	9.00	10.13	10.58	13.00	12.03	13.36	12.82	13.44	15.15	10.42	14.67	1 113.27	151.08
August	11.64	9.00	10.49	10.65	13.00	11.82	12.72	12.23	12.87	14.63	9.99	14.47	1 212.82	164.42
September	11.30	9.00	10.41	10.51	12.97	11.58	12.52	11.97	12.66	14.35	10.10	14.35	1 213.51	166.11
October	9.99	9.00	9.97	10.05	12.58	10.90	12.16	11.66	12.63	13.94	10.25	14.13	1 199.30	164.82
November	9.43	8.83	8.79	8.99	11.77	9.82	11.57	11.25	12.29	13.48	10.17	13.64	1 211.30	166.27
December	8.38	8.37	8.16	8.36	11.06	9.33	11.50	11.21	12.13	13.40	9.95	13.18	1 188.96	164.48
1985														
January	8.35	8.00	7.76	8.03	10.61	9.02	11.38	11.15	12.08	13.26	9.51	13.08	1 238.16	171.61
February	8.50	8.00	8.17	8.28	10.50	9.29	11.51	11.35	12.13	13.23	9.65	12.92	1 283.23	180.88
March	8.58	8.00	8.57	8.92	10.50	9.86	11.86	11.78	12.56	13.69	9.77	13.17	1 268.83	179.42
April	8.27	8.00	8.00	8.31	10.50	9.14	11.43	11.42	12.23	13.51	9.42	13.20	1 266.36	180.62
May	7.97	7.81	7.56	7.75	10.31	8.46	10.85	10.96	11.72	13.15	9.01	12.91	1 279.40	184.90
June	7.53	7.50	7.01	7.16	9.78	7.80	10.16	10.36	10.94	12.40	8.69	12.22	1 314.00	188.89
July	7.88	7.50	7.05	7.16	9.50	7.86	10.31	10.51	10.97	12.43	8.81	12.03	1 343.17	192.54
August	7.90	7.50	7.18	7.35	9.50	8.05	10.33	10.59	11.05	12.50	9.08	12.19	1 326.18	188.31
September	7.92	7.50	7.08	7.27	9.50	8.07	10.37	10.67	11.07	12.48	9.27	12.19	1 317.95	184.06
October	7.99	7.50	7.17	7.32	9.50	8.01	10.24	10.56	11.02	12.36	9.08	12.14	1 351.58	186.18
November	8.05	7.50	7.20	7.26	9.50	7.88	9.78	10.08	10.55	11.99	8.54	11.78	1 432.88	197.45
December	8.27	7.50	7.07	7.09	9.50	7.67	9.26	9.59	10.16	11.58	8.42	11.26	1 517.02	207.26
1986														
January	8.14	7.50	7.04	7.13	9.50	7.73	9.19	9.51	10.05	11.44	8.08	10.88	1 534.86	208.19
February	7.86	7.50	7.03	7.08	9.50	7.61	8.70	9.07	9.67	11.11	7.44	10.71	1 652.73	219.37
March	7.48	7.10	6.59	6.60	9.10	7.03	7.78	8.13	9.00	10.50	7.08	10.08	1 757.35	232.33
April	6.99	6.83	6.06	6.07	8.83	6.44	7.30	7.59	8.79	10.19	7.19	9.94	1 807.05	237.98
May	6.85	6.50	6.12	6.16	8.50	6.65	7.71	8.02	9.09	10.29	7.54	10.14	1 801.80	238.46
June	6.92	6.50	6.21	6.28	8.50	6.73	7.80	8.23	9.13	10.34	7.87	10.68	1 867.70	245.30
July	6.56	6.16	5.84	5.85	8.16	6.27	7.30	7.86	8.88	10.16	7.51	10.51	1 809.92	240.18
August	6.17	5.82	5.57	5.58	7.90	5.93	7.17	7.72	8.72	10.18	7.21	10.20	1 843.45	245.00
September	5.89	5.50	5.19	5.31	7.50	5.77	7.45	8.08	8.89	10.20	7.11	10.01	1 813.47	238.27
October	5.85	5.50	5.18	5.26	7.50	5.72	7.43	8.04	8.86	10.24	7.08	9.97	1 817.04	237.36
November	6.04	5.50	5.35	5.42	7.50	5.80	7.25	7.81	8.68	10.07	6.84	9.70	1 883.65	245.09
December	6.91	5.50	5.49	5.53	7.50	5.87	7.11	7.67	8.49	9.97	6.87	9.31	1 924.07	248.61
1987														
January	6.43	5.50	5.45	5.47	7.50	5.78	7.08	7.60	8.36	9.72	6.66	9.20	2 065.13	264.51
February	6.10	5.50	5.59	5.60	7.50	5.96	7.25	7.69	8.38	9.65	6.61	9.08	2 202.34	280.93
March	6.13	5.50	5.56	5.56	7.50	6.03	7.25	7.62	8.36	9.61	6.65	9.04	2 292.61	292.47
April	6.37	5.50	5.76	5.93	7.75	6.50	8.02	8.31	8.85	10.04	7.55	9.83	2 302.64	289.32
May	6.85	5.50	5.75	6.11	8.14	7.00	8.61	8.79	9.33	10.51	8.00	10.60	2 291.11	289.12
June	6.73	5.50	5.69	5.99	8.25	6.80	8.40	8.63	9.32	10.52	7.79	10.54	2 384.02	301.38
July	6.58	5.50	5.78	5.86	8.25	6.68	8.45	8.70	9.42	10.61	7.72	10.28	2 481.72	310.09
August	6.73	5.50	6.00	6.14	8.25	7.03	8.76	8.97	9.67	10.80	7.82	10.33	2 655.01	329.36
September	7.22	5.95	6.32	6.57	8.70	7.67	9.42	9.58	10.18	11.31	8.26	10.89	2 570.80	318.66
October	7.29	6.00	6.40	6.86	9.07	7.59	9.52	9.61	10.52	11.62	8.70	11.26	2 224.59	280.16
November	6.69	6.00	5.81	6.23	8.78	6.96	8.86	8.99	10.01	11.23	7.95	10.65	1 931.86	245.01
December	6.77	6.00	5.80	6.36	8.75	7.17	8.99	9.12	10.11	11.29	7.96	10.65	1 910.07	240.96
1988														
January	6.83	6.00	5.90	6.31	8.75	6.99	8.67	8.82	9.88	11.07	7.69	10.43	1 947.35	250.48
February	6.58	6.00	5.69	5.96	8.51	6.64	8.21	8.41	9.40	10.62	7.49	9.89	1 980.65	258.13
March	6.58	6.00	5.69	5.91	8.50	6.71	8.37	8.61	9.39	10.57	7.74	9.93	2 044.31	265.74
April	6.87	6.00	5.92	6.21	8.50	7.01	8.72	8.91	9.67	10.90	7.81	10.20	2 036.13	262.61
May	7.09	6.00	6.27	6.53	8.84	7.40	9.09	9.24	9.90	11.04	7.91	10.46	1 988.91	256.12
June	7.51	6.00	6.50	6.76	9.00	7.49	8.92	9.04	9.86	11.00	7.78	10.46	2 104.94	270.68
July	7.75	6.00	6.73	6.97	9.29	7.75	9.06	9.20	9.96	11.11	7.76	10.43	2 104.22	269.05
August	8.01	6.37	7.02	7.36	9.84	8.17	9.26	9.33	10.11	11.21	7.79	10.60	2 051.29	263.73
September	8.19	6.50	7.23	7.43	10.00	8.09	8.98	9.06	9.82	10.90	7.66	10.48	2 080.06	267.97
October	8.30	6.50	7.34	7.50	10.00	8.11	8.80	8.89	9.51	10.41	7.46	10.30	2 144.31	277.40
November	8.35	6.50	7.68	7.76	10.05	8.48	8.96	9.07	9.45	10.48	7.46	10.27	2 099.04	271.02
December	8.76	6.50	8.09	8.24	10.50	8.99	9.11	9.13	9.57	10.65	7.61	10.61	2 148.58	276.51
1989														
January	9.12	6.50	8.29	8.38	10.50	9.05	9.09	9.07	9.62	10.65	7.35	10.73	2 234.68	285.41
February	9.36	6.59	8.48	8.49	10.93	9.25	9.17	9.16	9.64	10.61	7.44	10.65	2 304.30	294.01
March	9.85	7.00	8.83	8.87	11.50	9.57	9.36	9.33	9.80	10.67	7.59	11.03	2 283.11	292.71
April	9.84	7.00	8.70	8.73	11.50	9.36	9.18	9.18	9.79	10.61	7.49	11.05	2 348.91	302.25
May	9.81	7.00	8.40	8.39	11.50	8.98	8.86	8.95	9.57	10.46	7.25	10.77	2 439.55	313.93
June	9.53	7.00	8.22	8.00	11.07	8.44	8.28	8.40	9.10	10.03	7.02	10.20	2 494.90	323.73
July	9.24	7.00	7.92	7.63	10.98	7.89	8.02	8.19	8.93	9.87	6.96	9.88	2 554.03	331.93
August	8.99	7.00	7.91	7.72	10.50	8.18	8.11	8.26	8.96	9.88	7.06	9.99	2 691.11	346.61
September	9.02	7.00	7.72	7.74	10.50	8.22	8.19	8.31	9.01	9.91	7.26	10.13	2 693.41	347.33
October	8.84	7.00	7.63	7.61	10.50	7.99	8.01	8.15	8.92	9.81	7.22	9.95	2 692.01	347.40
November	8.55	7.00	7.65	7.46	10.50	7.77	7.87	8.03	8.89	9.81	7.14	9.77	2 642.49	340.22
December	8.45	7.00	7.64	7.45	10.50	7.72	7.84	8.02	8.86	9.82	6.98	9.74	2 728.47	348.57

1. Discount window borrowing, Federal Reserve Bank of New York.
2. Maturities of more than ten years.
3. 1941–1943=10.

Table 24-10. Interest Rates, Bond Yields, and Stock Price Indexes—*Continued*

(Not seasonally adjusted.)

Year and month	Short-term rates					U.S. Treasury securites			Bond yields					
									Domestic corporate (Moody's)		State and local bonds (Bond Byer)	Fixed-rate first mortgages	Stock price indexes	
	Federal funds	Federal Reserve discount [1]	U.S. Treasury bills, 3-month	U.S. Treasury bills, 6-month	Bank prime rate	One-year	Ten-year	Long-term composite [2]	Aaa	Baa			Dow Jones industrials (30 stocks)	Standard and Poor's composite (500 stocks) [3]
1990														
January	8.23	7.00	7.64	7.52	10.11	7.92	8.21	8.39	8.99	9.94	7.10	9.90	2 679.24	339.97
February	8.24	7.00	7.76	7.72	10.00	8.11	8.47	8.66	9.22	10.14	7.22	10.20	2 614.18	330.45
March	8.28	7.00	7.87	7.83	10.00	8.35	8.59	8.74	9.37	10.21	7.29	10.27	2 700.13	338.47
April	8.26	7.00	7.78	7.82	10.00	8.40	8.79	8.92	9.46	10.30	7.39	10.37	2 708.26	338.18
May	8.18	7.00	7.78	7.82	10.00	8.32	8.76	8.90	9.47	10.41	7.35	10.48	2 793.81	350.25
June	8.29	7.00	7.74	7.64	10.00	8.10	8.48	8.62	9.26	10.22	7.24	10.16	2 894.82	360.39
July	8.15	7.00	7.66	7.57	10.00	7.94	8.47	8.64	9.24	10.20	7.19	10.04	2 934.23	360.03
August	8.13	7.00	7.44	7.36	10.00	7.78	8.75	8.97	9.41	10.41	7.32	10.10	2 681.89	330.75
September	8.20	7.00	7.38	7.33	10.00	7.76	8.89	9.11	9.56	10.64	7.43	10.18	2 550.69	315.41
October	8.11	7.00	7.19	7.20	10.00	7.55	8.72	8.93	9.53	10.74	7.49	10.18	2 460.54	307.12
November	7.81	7.00	7.07	7.04	10.00	7.31	8.39	8.60	9.30	10.62	7.18	10.01	2 518.56	315.29
December	7.31	6.79	6.81	6.76	10.00	7.05	8.08	8.31	9.05	10.43	7.09	9.67	2 610.92	328.75
1991														
January	6.91	6.50	6.30	6.34	9.52	6.64	8.09	8.33	9.04	10.45	7.08	9.64	2 587.60	325.49
February	6.25	6.00	5.95	5.93	9.05	6.27	7.85	8.12	8.83	10.07	6.91	9.37	2 863.04	362.26
March	6.12	6.00	5.91	5.91	9.00	6.40	8.11	8.38	8.93	10.09	7.10	9.50	2 920.11	372.28
April	5.91	5.98	5.67	5.73	9.00	6.24	8.04	8.29	8.86	9.94	7.02	9.49	2 925.53	379.68
May	5.78	5.50	5.51	5.65	8.50	6.13	8.07	8.33	8.86	9.86	6.95	9.47	2 928.42	377.99
June	5.90	5.50	5.60	5.76	8.50	6.36	8.28	8.54	9.01	9.96	7.13	9.62	2 968.13	378.29
July	5.82	5.50	5.58	5.71	8.50	6.31	8.27	8.50	9.00	9.89	7.05	9.58	2 978.18	380.23
August	5.66	5.50	5.39	5.47	8.50	5.78	7.90	8.17	8.75	9.65	6.90	9.24	3 006.08	389.40
September	5.45	5.20	5.25	5.29	8.20	5.57	7.65	7.96	8.61	9.51	6.80	9.01	3 010.35	387.20
October	5.21	5.00	5.03	5.08	8.00	5.33	7.53	7.88	8.55	9.49	6.68	8.86	3 019.73	386.88
November	4.81	4.58	4.60	4.66	7.58	4.89	7.42	7.83	8.48	9.45	6.73	8.71	2 986.12	385.92
December	4.43	4.11	4.12	4.16	7.21	4.38	7.09	7.58	8.31	9.26	6.69	8.50	2 958.64	388.51
1992														
January	4.03	3.50	3.84	3.88	6.50	4.15	7.03	7.48	8.20	9.13	6.54	8.43	3 227.06	416.08
February	4.06	3.50	3.84	3.94	6.50	4.29	7.34	7.78	8.29	9.23	6.74	8.76	3 257.27	412.56
March	3.98	3.50	4.05	4.19	6.50	4.63	7.54	7.93	8.35	9.25	6.76	8.94	3 247.41	407.36
April	3.73	3.50	3.81	3.93	6.50	4.30	7.48	7.88	8.33	9.21	6.67	8.85	3 294.08	407.41
May	3.82	3.50	3.66	3.78	6.50	4.19	7.39	7.80	8.28	9.13	6.57	8.67	3 376.78	414.81
June	3.76	3.50	3.70	3.81	6.50	4.17	7.26	7.72	8.22	9.05	6.49	8.51	3 337.79	408.27
July	3.25	3.02	3.28	3.36	6.02	3.60	6.84	7.40	8.07	8.84	6.13	8.13	3 329.40	415.05
August	3.30	3.00	3.14	3.23	6.00	3.47	6.59	7.19	7.95	8.65	6.16	7.98	3 307.45	417.93
September	3.22	3.00	2.97	3.01	6.00	3.18	6.42	7.08	7.92	8.62	6.25	7.92	3 293.92	418.48
October	3.10	3.00	2.84	2.98	6.00	3.30	6.59	7.26	7.99	8.84	6.41	8.09	3 198.69	412.50
November	3.09	3.00	3.14	3.35	6.00	3.68	6.87	7.43	8.10	8.96	6.36	8.31	3 238.49	422.84
December	2.92	3.00	3.25	3.39	6.00	3.71	6.77	7.30	7.98	8.81	6.22	8.22	3 303.15	435.64
1993														
January	3.02	3.00	3.06	3.17	6.00	3.50	6.60	7.17	7.91	8.67	6.16	8.02	3 277.71	435.23
February	3.03	3.00	2.95	3.08	6.00	3.39	6.26	6.89	7.71	8.39	5.87	7.68	3 367.26	441.70
March	3.07	3.00	2.97	3.08	6.00	3.33	5.98	6.65	7.58	8.15	5.64	7.50	3 440.73	450.16
April	2.96	3.00	2.89	3.00	6.00	3.24	5.97	6.64	7.46	8.14	5.76	7.47	3 423.62	443.08
May	3.00	3.00	2.96	3.07	6.00	3.36	6.04	6.68	7.43	8.21	5.73	7.47	3 478.17	445.25
June	3.04	3.00	3.10	3.23	6.00	3.54	5.96	6.55	7.33	8.07	5.63	7.42	3 513.81	448.06
July	3.06	3.00	3.05	3.15	6.00	3.47	5.81	6.34	7.17	7.93	5.57	7.21	3 529.43	447.29
August	3.03	3.00	3.05	3.17	6.00	3.44	5.68	6.18	6.85	7.60	5.45	7.11	3 597.01	454.13
September	3.09	3.00	2.96	3.06	6.00	3.36	5.36	5.94	6.66	7.34	5.29	6.92	3 592.28	459.24
October	2.99	3.00	3.04	3.13	6.00	3.39	5.33	5.90	6.67	7.31	5.25	6.83	3 625.80	463.90
November	3.02	3.00	3.12	3.27	6.00	3.58	5.72	6.25	6.93	7.66	5.47	7.16	3 674.69	462.89
December	2.96	3.00	3.08	3.25	6.00	3.61	5.77	6.27	6.93	7.69	5.35	7.17	3 743.62	465.95
1994														
January	3.05	3.00	3.02	3.19	6.00	3.54	5.75	6.24	6.92	7.65	5.31	7.06	3 868.36	472.99
February	3.25	3.00	3.21	3.38	6.00	3.87	5.97	6.44	7.08	7.76	5.40	7.15	3 905.62	471.58
March	3.34	3.00	3.52	3.79	6.06	4.32	6.48	6.90	7.48	8.13	5.91	7.68	3 816.98	463.81
April	3.56	3.00	3.74	4.13	6.45	4.82	6.97	7.32	7.88	8.52	6.23	8.32	3 661.48	447.23
May	4.01	3.24	4.19	4.64	6.99	5.31	7.18	7.47	7.99	8.62	6.19	8.60	3 707.99	450.90
June	4.25	3.50	4.18	4.58	7.25	5.27	7.10	7.43	7.97	8.65	6.11	8.40	3 737.58	454.83
July	4.26	3.50	4.39	4.81	7.25	5.48	7.30	7.61	8.11	8.80	6.23	8.61	3 718.30	451.40
August	4.47	3.76	4.50	4.91	7.51	5.56	7.24	7.55	8.07	8.74	6.21	8.51	3 797.48	464.24
September	4.73	4.00	4.64	5.02	7.75	5.76	7.46	7.81	8.34	8.98	6.28	8.64	3 880.60	466.96
October	4.76	4.00	4.96	5.39	7.75	6.11	7.74	8.02	8.57	9.20	6.52	8.93	3 868.10	463.81
November	5.29	4.40	5.25	5.69	8.15	6.54	7.96	8.16	8.68	9.32	6.97	9.17	3 792.43	461.01
December	5.45	4.75	5.64	6.21	8.50	7.14	7.81	7.97	8.46	9.10	6.80	9.20	3 770.31	455.19
1995														
January	5.53	4.75	5.81	6.31	8.50	7.05	7.78	7.93	8.46	9.08	6.53	9.15	3 872.46	465.25
February	5.92	5.25	5.80	6.10	9.00	6.70	7.47	7.69	8.26	8.85	6.22	8.83	3 953.72	481.92
March	5.98	5.25	5.73	5.91	9.00	6.43	7.20	7.52	8.12	8.70	6.10	8.46	4 062.78	493.15
April	6.05	5.25	5.67	5.80	9.00	6.27	7.06	7.41	8.03	8.60	6.02	8.32	4 230.66	507.91
May	6.01	5.25	5.70	5.73	9.00	6.00	6.63	6.99	7.65	8.20	5.95	7.96	4 391.57	523.81
June	6.00	5.25	5.50	5.46	9.00	5.64	6.17	6.59	7.30	7.90	5.84	7.57	4 510.76	539.35
July	5.85	5.25	5.47	5.41	8.80	5.59	6.28	6.71	7.41	8.04	5.92	7.61	4 684.76	557.37
August	5.74	5.25	5.41	5.40	8.75	5.75	6.49	6.90	7.57	8.19	6.06	7.86	4 639.27	559.11
September	5.80	5.25	5.26	5.28	8.75	5.62	6.20	6.63	7.32	7.93	5.91	7.64	4 746.76	578.77
October	5.76	5.25	5.30	5.34	8.75	5.59	6.04	6.43	7.12	7.75	5.80	7.48	4 760.46	582.92
November	5.80	5.25	5.35	5.29	8.75	5.43	5.93	6.31	7.02	7.68	5.64	7.38	4 935.81	595.53
December	5.60	5.25	5.16	5.15	8.65	5.31	5.71	6.11	6.82	7.49	5.45	7.20	5 136.10	614.57

1. Discount window borrowing, Federal Reserve Bank of New York.
2. Maturities of more than ten years.
3. 1941–1943=10.

PART IV

STATE AND REGIONAL DATA

CHAPTER 25: STATE AND REGIONAL DATA, ANNUAL, 1970–1999

Table 25-1. Personal Income and Employment

(Millions of dollars, except as noted.)

Year	Total	Nonfarm	Farm	Earnings by place of work	Less: Personal contributions for social insurance	Plus: Adjustment for residence	Equals: Net earnings by place of residence	Dividends, interest, and rent	Transfer payments	Per capita Total	Per capita Disposable	Population (thousands)	Total employment (thousands)
UNITED STATES													
1970	834 455	815 830	18 625	666 477	22 345	-175	643 957	116 085	74 413	4 095	3 584	203 799	91 282
1971	899 249	880 065	19 184	712 000	24 570	-198	687 232	123 658	88 359	4 348	3 851	206 818	91 586
1972	988 362	965 175	23 187	785 638	27 892	-229	757 517	132 683	98 162	4 723	4 125	209 275	94 317
1973	1 107 992	1 072 094	35 898	881 106	35 555	-244	845 307	150 538	112 147	5 242	4 609	211 349	98 433
1974	1 220 181	1 189 050	31 131	955 807	40 331	-264	915 212	172 277	132 692	5 720	5 003	213 334	100 118
1975	1 326 214	1 296 261	29 953	1 018 049	42 417	-313	975 319	182 921	167 974	6 155	5 460	215 457	98 907
1976	1 469 752	1 443 832	25 920	1 133 101	46 761	-339	1 086 001	200 924	182 827	6 756	5 951	217 554	101 597
1977	1 630 901	1 605 707	25 194	1 260 972	51 791	-377	1 208 804	226 977	195 120	7 421	6 508	219 761	105 049
1978	1 841 340	1 812 135	29 205	1 426 887	59 514	-410	1 366 963	264 398	209 979	8 291	7 242	222 098	109 689
1979	2 072 839	2 041 891	30 948	1 592 777	69 923	-398	1 522 456	315 322	235 061	9 230	8 017	224 569	113 289
1980	2 313 921	2 292 617	21 304	1 729 911	76 988	-454	1 652 469	381 662	279 790	10 183	8 848	227 225	114 231
1981	2 588 335	2 560 348	27 987	1 896 642	91 773	-443	1 804 426	465 884	318 025	11 280	9 752	229 466	115 304
1982	2 756 954	2 732 508	24 446	1 984 358	98 765	-520	1 885 073	517 181	354 700	11 901	10 344	231 664	114 557
1983	2 935 040	2 918 117	16 923	2 106 552	105 667	-508	2 000 377	551 913	382 750	12 554	11 014	233 792	116 057
1984	3 260 064	3 228 886	31 178	2 349 155	117 982	-579	2 230 594	635 439	394 031	13 824	12 186	235 825	121 091
1985	3 498 662	3 467 624	31 038	2 528 400	133 141	-603	2 394 656	682 691	421 315	14 705	12 908	237 924	124 512
1986	3 697 359	3 665 380	31 979	2 676 617	145 041	-575	2 531 001	717 155	449 203	15 397	13 528	240 133	126 981
1987	3 945 515	3 907 792	37 723	2 876 817	156 295	-608	2 719 914	757 070	468 531	16 284	14 213	242 289	130 416
1988	4 255 000	4 218 399	36 601	3 111 553	176 235	-651	2 934 667	823 435	496 898	17 403	15 282	244 499	134 518
1989	4 582 429	4 539 071	43 358	3 302 615	190 911	-664	3 111 040	931 066	540 323	18 566	16 207	246 819	137 241
1990	4 885 525	4 841 640	43 885	3 508 380	202 934	-737	3 304 709	986 055	594 761	19 584	17 146	249 464	139 427
1991	5 065 416	5 026 507	38 909	3 605 195	214 239	-788	3 390 168	1 005 433	669 815	20 089	17 673	252 153	138 664
1992	5 376 622	5 331 348	45 274	3 853 906	225 952	-797	3 627 157	997 830	751 635	21 082	18 594	255 030	139 305
1993	5 598 446	5 554 845	43 601	4 019 490	237 265	-798	3 781 427	1 018 460	798 559	21 718	19 104	257 783	141 996
1994	5 878 362	5 832 931	45 431	4 212 378	253 544	-860	3 957 974	1 086 612	833 776	22 581	19 808	260 327	145 572
1995	6 192 235	6 155 539	36 696	4 412 022	268 271	-893	4 142 858	1 163 537	885 840	23 562	20 604	262 803	149 359
1996	6 538 103	6 488 613	49 490	4 653 407	279 891	-914	4 372 602	1 236 804	928 697	24 651	21 375	265 229	152 607
1997	6 928 762	6 881 919	46 843	4 938 711	297 384	-969	4 640 358	1 326 244	962 160	25 874	22 260	267 784	156 228
1998	7 383 687	7 339 276	44 411	5 291 148	315 714	-1 012	4 974 422	1 426 300	982 965	27 322	23 363	270 248	160 242
1999	7 783 152	7 738 227	44 925	5 629 596	337 942	-1 021	5 290 633	1 476 316	1 016 203	28 542	24 322	272 691	163 760
ALABAMA													
1970	10 276	9 997	279	8 302	301	135	8 136	1 048	1 092	2 979	2 670	3 450	1 413
1971	11 279	10 967	312	9 028	326	143	8 845	1 147	1 287	3 225	2 901	3 497	1 423
1972	12 544	12 162	382	10 076	378	171	9 869	1 243	1 432	3 544	3 163	3 540	1 471
1973	14 181	13 616	565	11 378	484	188	11 081	1 429	1 671	3 960	3 538	3 581	1 526
1974	15 786	15 416	370	12 477	559	198	12 115	1 676	1 995	4 351	3 880	3 628	1 552
1975	17 537	17 101	436	13 519	603	203	13 119	1 860	2 558	4 765	4 292	3 681	1 543
1976	19 893	19 397	496	15 474	693	217	14 998	2 083	2 812	5 323	4 769	3 737	1 594
1977	22 005	21 607	397	17 191	777	246	16 661	2 341	3 003	5 817	5 207	3 783	1 651
1978	24 923	24 399	524	19 564	888	269	18 945	2 720	3 258	6 500	5 803	3 834	1 714
1979	27 855	27 314	541	21 559	1 020	296	20 835	3 235	3 784	7 199	6 395	3 869	1 739
1980	30 781	30 549	232	23 068	1 117	327	22 278	4 048	4 455	7 892	6 996	3 900	1 736
1981	34 137	33 630	507	25 036	1 307	425	24 155	4 996	4 987	8 712	7 702	3 919	1 724
1982	36 052	35 637	414	25 782	1 384	446	24 844	5 688	5 520	9 185	8 197	3 925	1 692
1983	38 487	38 198	290	27 539	1 523	440	26 456	6 063	5 968	9 783	8 728	3 934	1 722
1984	42 681	42 202	479	30 601	1 681	492	29 412	7 042	6 227	10 800	9 689	3 952	1 787
1985	46 015	45 550	465	33 056	1 890	503	31 670	7 735	6 611	11 583	10 329	3 973	1 831
1986	48 704	48 256	448	34 948	1 956	526	33 518	8 253	6 933	12 202	10 884	3 992	1 868
1987	51 846	51 334	513	37 380	2 083	535	35 832	8 856	7 159	12 912	11 457	4 015	1 923
1988	55 699	54 911	788	40 252	2 345	531	38 437	9 779	7 482	13 842	12 380	4 024	1 982
1989	60 044	59 119	926	42 638	2 554	550	40 634	11 187	8 224	14 899	13 241	4 030	2 019
1990	64 095	63 267	828	45 311	2 719	529	43 121	11 722	9 252	15 832	14 097	4 049	2 062
1991	67 650	66 526	1 123	47 736	2 915	536	45 356	12 094	10 199	16 536	14 758	4 091	2 074
1992	72 282	71 304	978	51 127	3 098	574	48 602	12 105	11 575	17 462	15 618	4 139	2 113
1993	75 439	74 441	999	53 380	3 287	600	50 693	12 370	12 376	17 991	16 063	4 193	2 176
1994	79 832	78 775	1 057	56 165	3 534	647	53 279	13 511	13 042	18 860	16 779	4 233	2 200
1995	83 903	83 131	772	58 317	3 755	680	55 242	14 575	14 087	19 683	17 473	4 263	2 263
1996	87 221	86 375	846	60 577	3 870	674	57 381	14 935	14 906	20 329	17 965	4 290	2 298
1997	91 283	90 352	931	63 185	4 055	717	59 847	15 763	15 673	21 129	18 596	4 320	2 346
1998	96 257	95 207	1 051	66 427	4 215	817	63 028	17 186	16 043	22 123	19 456	4 351	2 388
1999	100 452	99 135	1 317	69 580	4 438	884	66 026	17 908	16 519	22 987	20 170	4 370	2 410

Table 25-1. Personal Income and Employment—Continued

(Millions of dollars, except as noted.)

Year	Total	Nonfarm	Farm	Earnings by place of work	Less: Personal contributions for social insurance	Plus: Adjustment for residence	Equals: Net earnings by place of residence	Dividends, interest, and rent	Transfer payments	Total	Disposable	Population (thousands)	Total employment (thousands)
ALASKA													
1970	1 595	1 594	2	1 501	43	-47	1 411	113	72	5 243	4 534	304	149
1971	1 766	1 765	2	1 657	47	-61	1 549	126	91	5 581	4 862	316	153
1972	1 939	1 937	2	1 822	52	-76	1 694	142	103	5 939	5 103	326	158
1973	2 266	2 264	2	2 011	65	-94	1 852	169	246	6 801	5 931	333	167
1974	2 795	2 793	2	2 689	97	-210	2 383	205	207	8 108	6 891	345	189
1975	3 932	3 928	4	4 223	162	-613	3 448	252	233	10 600	8 932	371	227
1976	4 736	4 732	4	5 294	203	-884	4 206	299	231	12 048	10 151	393	243
1977	4 906	4 901	5	4 918	180	-454	4 285	342	279	12 346	10 437	397	237
1978	5 013	5 008	5	4 803	171	-325	4 307	407	299	12 464	10 695	402	237
1979	5 328	5 325	4	5 021	186	-290	4 545	492	291	13 204	11 162	404	241
1980	6 002	5 998	4	5 621	212	-329	5 080	578	343	14 807	12 738	405	244
1981	6 902	6 900	2	6 542	270	-471	5 802	695	405	16 492	13 862	418	253
1982	8 263	8 261	2	7 567	312	-562	6 693	847	723	18 379	15 699	450	278
1983	9 302	9 299	2	8 458	354	-620	7 483	1 030	789	19 045	16 569	488	298
1984	9 958	9 956	2	9 084	373	-638	8 074	1 214	671	19 385	17 091	514	310
1985	10 756	10 754	2	9 541	401	-631	8 509	1 371	876	20 200	17 903	532	318
1986	10 721	10 714	7	9 290	399	-570	8 321	1 410	991	19 699	17 673	544	311
1987	10 427	10 417	10	8 795	374	-533	7 888	1 499	1 039	19 334	17 206	539	312
1988	10 776	10 765	11	9 030	412	-557	8 061	1 598	1 117	19 882	17 827	542	318
1989	11 778	11 772	6	9 856	474	-619	8 763	1 786	1 230	21 526	19 003	547	331
1990	12 566	12 559	8	10 445	504	-654	9 287	1 923	1 356	22 719	19 937	553	341
1991	13 243	13 235	8	11 006	538	-696	9 772	2 008	1 463	23 264	20 650	569	349
1992	14 039	14 031	8	11 598	555	-726	10 317	2 092	1 629	23 913	21 234	587	353
1993	14 789	14 776	12	12 054	586	-738	10 730	2 244	1 815	24 772	22 037	597	361
1994	15 168	15 152	15	12 219	615	-755	10 849	2 454	1 865	25 253	22 381	601	367
1995	15 513	15 497	17	12 333	632	-758	10 943	2 623	1 948	25 798	22 874	601	368
1996	15 762	15 745	17	12 389	639	-772	10 979	2 695	2 088	26 057	23 010	605	372
1997	16 465	16 444	20	12 699	659	-767	11 272	2 930	2 262	27 042	23 772	609	378
1998	17 167	17 147	20	13 170	684	-812	11 675	3 041	2 451	27 904	24 441	615	387
1999	17 704	17 679	25	13 362	701	-812	11 849	3 185	2 669	28 577	25 022	620	390
ARIZONA													
1970	6 897	6 708	189	5 321	180	-29	5 112	1 195	590	3 843	3 385	1 795	747
1971	7 860	7 647	213	6 054	211	-28	5 814	1 334	712	4 145	3 696	1 896	786
1972	9 013	8 793	220	7 002	254	-32	6 716	1 479	817	4 487	3 958	2 009	850
1973	10 476	10 223	253	8 134	338	-31	7 765	1 733	977	4 929	4 400	2 125	925
1974	11 854	11 450	404	9 086	387	-41	8 659	2 016	1 179	5 329	4 729	2 224	955
1975	12 640	12 410	229	9 294	398	-47	8 849	2 155	1 636	5 528	5 016	2 286	935
1976	14 262	13 914	348	10 544	439	-47	10 059	2 396	1 807	6 074	5 474	2 348	976
1977	16 122	15 840	282	12 008	508	-56	11 443	2 750	1 929	6 642	5 944	2 427	1 048
1978	19 100	18 764	336	14 240	613	-69	13 558	3 374	2 168	7 586	6 734	2 518	1 149
1979	22 702	22 291	412	16 892	767	-71	16 054	4 189	2 459	8 604	7 591	2 639	1 241
1980	26 255	25 761	494	19 034	875	-80	18 078	5 205	2 972	9 590	8 493	2 738	1 285
1981	29 950	29 516	434	21 113	1 063	-16	20 034	6 440	3 476	10 658	9 348	2 810	1 317
1982	31 629	31 217	412	21 840	1 132	-9	20 699	7 047	3 883	10 945	9 634	2 890	1 320
1983	34 601	34 271	330	23 778	1 249	2	22 531	7 825	4 245	11 654	10 346	2 969	1 383
1984	39 521	38 965	556	27 374	1 434	7	25 946	9 088	4 487	12 885	11 471	3 067	1 511
1985	43 957	43 436	521	30 519	1 677	20	28 862	10 068	5 027	13 808	12 232	3 184	1 632
1986	47 848	47 349	499	33 232	1 869	40	31 403	10 934	5 512	14 463	12 826	3 308	1 712
1987	52 003	51 368	635	36 052	2 010	68	34 109	11 867	6 027	15 130	13 404	3 437	1 778
1988	55 837	55 066	771	38 781	2 258	110	36 633	12 648	6 556	15 795	14 073	3 535	1 848
1989	60 011	59 326	685	40 496	2 431	169	38 234	14 254	7 523	16 568	14 677	3 622	1 881
1990	63 319	62 678	641	42 618	2 558	231	40 291	14 694	8 335	17 211	15 247	3 679	1 910
1991	66 077	65 349	729	44 521	2 734	221	42 007	14 699	9 371	17 563	15 566	3 762	1 918
1992	70 120	69 479	641	47 612	2 909	239	44 942	14 339	10 839	18 131	16 127	3 867	1 942
1993	74 900	74 105	795	51 170	3 151	252	48 272	14 954	11 674	18 756	16 640	3 993	2 029
1994	82 014	81 497	517	55 942	3 508	259	52 693	16 779	12 542	19 774	17 498	4 148	2 163
1995	88 870	88 116	754	61 136	3 850	273	57 559	17 958	13 353	20 634	18 217	4 307	2 282
1996	95 787	95 145	642	66 330	4 146	299	62 482	19 232	14 073	21 611	18 890	4 432	2 414
1997	103 704	103 086	618	71 851	4 474	320	67 697	21 193	14 814	22 781	19 819	4 552	2 526
1998	112 635	111 878	757	79 272	4 873	357	74 756	22 639	15 240	24 133	20 860	4 667	2 636
1999	120 360	119 562	798	85 339	5 272	406	80 473	23 851	16 036	25 189	21 721	4 778	2 725

Table 25-1. Personal Income and Employment—*Continued*

(Millions of dollars, except as noted.)

Year	Total	Nonfarm	Farm	Derivation of personal income — Earnings by place of work	Less: Personal contributions for social insurance	Plus: Adjustment for residence	Equals: Net earnings by place of residence	Dividends, interest, and rent	Transfer payments	Per capita (dollars) — Total	Per capita — Disposable	Population (thousands)	Total employment (thousands)
ARKANSAS													
1970	5 500	5 067	433	4 293	149	21	4 165	654	681	2 849	2 548	1 930	805
1971	6 105	5 682	423	4 729	169	19	4 579	723	803	3 096	2 802	1 972	831
1972	6 893	6 388	505	5 393	198	18	5 214	786	893	3 415	3 076	2 018	867
1973	8 203	7 270	934	6 435	254	15	6 196	931	1 077	3 985	3 581	2 058	902
1974	9 191	8 339	851	7 037	294	8	6 751	1 134	1 306	4 376	3 904	2 100	927
1975	10 047	9 240	807	7 432	310	8	7 130	1 273	1 644	4 655	4 227	2 158	905
1976	11 179	10 531	648	8 311	349	-2	7 959	1 413	1 807	5 155	4 620	2 169	941
1977	12 514	11 786	729	9 348	395	-6	8 947	1 628	1 939	5 670	5 100	2 207	981
1978	14 587	13 392	1 196	11 017	458	-12	10 548	1 915	2 125	6 509	5 858	2 241	1 022
1979	16 084	15 073	1 011	11 906	528	-12	11 366	2 289	2 429	7 088	6 333	2 269	1 033
1980	17 363	16 978	385	12 231	577	-1	11 653	2 824	2 885	7 586	6 741	2 289	1 035
1981	19 638	18 767	871	13 577	677	-18	12 882	3 491	3 265	8 564	7 616	2 293	1 030
1982	20 539	19 897	642	13 776	722	-14	13 040	3 947	3 551	8 952	7 905	2 294	1 014
1983	21 848	21 455	393	14 661	779	-42	13 840	4 172	3 836	9 476	8 466	2 306	1 043
1984	24 496	23 638	858	16 761	865	-63	15 833	4 692	3 971	10 560	9 512	2 320	1 084
1985	26 211	25 373	838	17 804	965	-66	16 773	5 181	4 257	11 264	10 121	2 327	1 104
1986	27 364	26 593	770	18 601	1 046	-88	17 467	5 390	4 507	11 734	10 567	2 332	1 116
1987	28 540	27 608	932	19 708	1 113	-106	18 489	5 387	4 664	12 184	10 925	2 342	1 143
1988	30 493	29 221	1 272	21 207	1 252	-140	19 816	5 788	4 889	13 016	11 696	2 343	1 177
1989	32 410	31 243	1 167	22 240	1 372	-141	20 727	6 366	5 317	13 813	12 372	2 346	1 197
1990	34 159	33 276	883	23 372	1 458	-207	21 707	6 696	5 756	14 509	12 988	2 354	1 212
1991	36 164	35 181	983	24 879	1 567	-221	23 091	6 746	6 327	15 255	13 682	2 371	1 238
1992	39 322	38 052	1 270	27 311	1 703	-259	25 350	6 889	7 084	16 425	14 754	2 394	1 264
1993	41 190	39 979	1 212	28 582	1 806	-270	26 506	7 101	7 584	16 995	15 255	2 424	1 311
1994	43 498	42 165	1 333	30 335	1 964	-292	28 079	7 530	7 889	17 750	15 842	2 451	1 340
1995	45 995	44 576	1 419	31 917	2 064	-270	29 583	7 934	8 478	18 546	16 509	2 480	1 394
1996	48 700	46 885	1 815	33 559	2 137	-263	31 179	8 586	8 935	19 442	17 258	2 505	1 418
1997	51 059	49 352	1 707	34 938	2 259	-260	32 419	9 254	9 386	20 229	17 855	2 524	1 441
1998	53 962	52 447	1 515	36 813	2 368	-259	34 186	10 141	9 635	21 260	18 706	2 538	1 461
1999	56 752	55 032	1 720	38 907	2 508	-263	36 136	10 747	9 869	22 244	19 532	2 551	1 484
CALIFORNIA													
1970	96 421	94 685	1 735	75 208	2 530	-102	72 576	14 579	9 265	4 815	4 272	20 023	9 057
1971	102 416	100 681	1 735	79 018	2 720	-110	76 188	15 528	10 700	5 034	4 516	20 346	9 036
1972	112 211	109 995	2 216	87 368	3 109	-113	84 146	16 546	11 518	5 451	4 801	20 585	9 369
1973	124 102	121 139	2 963	96 657	3 897	-97	92 663	18 761	12 678	5 947	5 291	20 868	9 844
1974	138 734	135 063	3 672	106 884	4 423	-109	102 351	21 364	15 019	6 553	5 809	21 173	10 163
1975	152 721	149 424	3 297	115 984	4 718	2	111 268	22 707	18 746	7 091	6 360	21 537	10 287
1976	171 412	167 924	3 488	130 732	5 242	103	125 593	25 007	20 813	7 815	6 945	21 935	10 633
1977	191 536	187 973	3 563	146 803	5 963	-50	140 790	28 438	22 308	8 570	7 571	22 350	11 120
1978	219 674	216 166	3 508	168 168	6 911	-61	161 196	34 436	24 042	9 618	8 450	22 839	11 803
1979	252 213	247 568	4 645	191 708	8 314	-35	183 359	42 511	26 343	10 846	9 479	23 255	12 462
1980	286 289	280 549	5 739	213 877	8 969	-84	204 824	50 770	30 695	12 029	10 497	23 801	12 777
1981	320 691	316 238	4 453	233 668	10 981	256	222 943	61 712	36 035	13 205	11 541	24 286	12 970
1982	341 872	337 183	4 689	247 494	12 026	260	235 727	66 588	39 557	13 774	12 119	24 820	12 899
1983	367 505	363 219	4 286	267 409	13 203	267	254 472	70 854	42 178	14 491	12 769	25 360	13 219
1984	411 616	406 613	5 002	300 918	15 056	240	286 102	82 098	43 416	15 927	14 032	25 844	13 852
1985	447 103	442 074	5 029	327 930	16 947	186	311 169	88 236	47 698	16 909	14 815	26 441	14 360
1986	477 762	472 269	5 494	352 886	19 008	126	334 005	92 316	51 441	17 628	15 442	27 102	14 789
1987	517 348	510 718	6 631	385 758	21 248	43	364 552	98 827	53 969	18 625	16 142	27 777	15 396
1988	561 121	554 136	6 985	419 509	24 067	1	395 443	108 090	57 588	19 713	17 239	28 464	16 134
1989	606 701	599 896	6 806	449 232	25 825	-19	423 388	120 813	62 501	20 765	17 985	29 218	16 556
1990	655 567	648 561	7 006	482 926	27 681	-76	455 169	130 572	69 826	21 889	19 027	29 950	16 970
1991	669 842	663 950	5 893	490 699	29 099	-40	461 560	130 471	77 811	22 024	19 303	30 414	16 878
1992	701 572	694 997	6 574	512 714	30 163	8	482 560	128 721	90 291	22 722	20 069	30 876	16 527
1993	714 107	706 788	7 319	520 223	30 828	78	489 473	129 798	94 836	22 927	20 227	31 147	16 506
1994	735 104	727 891	7 214	533 114	32 081	119	501 152	136 049	97 903	23 473	20 646	31 317	16 692
1995	771 470	764 482	6 988	553 877	33 346	144	520 675	148 704	102 091	24 496	21 431	31 494	17 093
1996	812 404	804 819	7 586	584 012	34 494	161	549 679	156 465	106 260	25 563	22 085	31 781	17 505
1997	862 114	853 866	8 248	625 526	36 392	121	589 256	166 163	106 696	26 759	22 836	32 218	17 841
1998	924 253	916 005	8 248	677 510	39 030	132	638 612	176 327	109 314	28 280	23 937	32 683	18 498
1999	991 382	983 112	8 270	736 215	42 777	100	693 539	183 792	114 051	29 910	25 195	33 145	19 029

Table 25-1. Personal Income and Employment—Continued

(Millions of dollars, except as noted.)

Year	Total	Nonfarm	Farm	Derivation of personal income						Per capita (dollars)		Population (thousands)	Total employment (thousands)
				Earnings by place of work	Less: Personal contributions for social insurance	Plus: Adjustment for residence	Equals: Net earnings by place of residence	Dividends, interest, and rent	Transfer payments	Total	Disposable		
COLORADO													
1970	9 018	8 716	302	7 160	213	2	6 949	1 342	727	4 055	3 559	2 224	1 032
1971	10 166	9 848	318	8 087	245	3	7 844	1 470	851	4 413	3 896	2 304	1 072
1972	11 520	11 167	352	9 268	292	4	8 979	1 597	944	4 791	4 170	2 405	1 149
1973	13 252	12 794	458	10 671	386	3	10 287	1 864	1 101	5 310	4 643	2 496	1 243
1974	14 901	14 344	558	11 903	441	4	11 467	2 162	1 273	5 864	5 103	2 541	1 276
1975	16 347	15 860	486	12 914	469	8	12 454	2 311	1 582	6 321	5 573	2 586	1 285
1976	18 148	17 794	354	14 362	518	9	13 853	2 556	1 740	6 895	6 050	2 632	1 340
1977	20 400	20 119	281	16 206	592	12	15 626	2 903	1 871	7 567	6 597	2 696	1 411
1978	23 625	23 407	218	18 821	701	20	18 140	3 456	2 029	8 539	7 423	2 767	1 505
1979	27 342	27 124	217	21 722	866	20	20 877	4 195	2 270	9 596	8 295	2 849	1 594
1980	31 442	31 153	289	24 624	1 003	28	23 648	5 152	2 642	10 809	9 347	2 909	1 654
1981	36 154	35 883	271	27 965	1 250	5	26 720	6 345	3 089	12 141	10 430	2 978	1 722
1982	39 632	39 467	164	30 407	1 402	1	29 006	7 120	3 506	12 945	11 098	3 062	1 765
1983	42 523	42 180	343	32 436	1 487	-2	30 948	7 706	3 868	13 570	11 928	3 134	1 794
1984	46 762	46 335	427	35 686	1 648	7	34 045	8 705	4 012	14 751	13 028	3 170	1 892
1985	49 467	49 075	391	37 727	1 841	16	35 901	9 350	4 215	15 416	13 575	3 209	1 926
1986	51 062	50 670	393	38 719	1 951	22	36 790	9 705	4 568	15 772	13 922	3 237	1 925
1987	53 528	53 044	484	40 364	2 005	34	38 394	10 153	4 980	16 417	14 452	3 260	1 915
1988	56 387	55 814	573	42 425	2 196	49	40 278	10 858	5 251	17 285	15 250	3 262	1 981
1989	60 760	60 146	614	44 900	2 380	66	42 586	12 435	5 739	18 548	16 261	3 276	2 017
1990	65 095	64 182	912	48 307	2 565	91	45 833	13 046	6 216	19 703	17 251	3 304	2 055
1991	68 992	68 343	649	51 230	2 818	91	48 503	13 482	7 007	20 487	17 942	3 368	2 102
1992	74 207	73 582	625	55 690	3 037	93	52 747	13 590	7 870	21 447	18 753	3 460	2 152
1993	80 212	79 370	842	60 643	3 318	93	57 417	14 281	8 515	22 526	19 636	3 561	2 253
1994	85 860	85 378	482	64 425	3 617	97	60 906	16 028	8 926	23 498	20 398	3 654	2 368
1995	92 947	92 434	512	69 305	3 904	104	65 505	17 572	9 870	24 865	21 595	3 738	2 448
1996	100 012	99 402	610	74 738	4 181	106	70 664	18 976	10 373	26 231	22 585	3 813	2 545
1997	108 763	108 146	617	81 592	4 524	109	77 177	20 800	10 786	27 950	23 880	3 891	2 657
1998	118 514	117 716	798	89 950	4 966	111	85 096	22 670	10 748	29 860	25 346	3 969	2 756
1999	127 955	127 027	928	98 324	5 468	106	92 961	23 770	11 224	31 546	26 674	4 056	2 846
CONNECTICUT													
1970	15 468	15 389	79	11 401	375	719	11 744	2 583	1 141	5 090	4 414	3 039	1 414
1971	16 227	16 149	77	11 765	403	742	12 104	2 698	1 425	5 300	4 666	3 061	1 388
1972	17 488	17 412	76	12 790	455	781	13 115	2 869	1 505	5 697	4 941	3 070	1 416
1973	19 154	19 067	87	14 154	579	803	14 378	3 158	1 618	6 241	5 450	3 069	1 480
1974	20 955	20 865	90	15 360	660	836	15 536	3 516	1 904	6 813	5 949	3 076	1 511
1975	22 329	22 248	81	15 987	679	911	16 219	3 600	2 510	7 239	6 409	3 085	1 468
1976	24 334	24 246	88	17 464	730	1 006	17 740	3 910	2 684	7 885	6 895	3 086	1 493
1977	26 909	26 821	88	19 401	807	1 115	19 709	4 364	2 836	8 712	7 622	3 089	1 546
1978	30 081	29 996	85	21 819	923	1 267	22 163	5 003	2 915	9 720	8 428	3 095	1 616
1979	34 008	33 927	81	24 550	1 098	1 441	24 894	5 880	3 234	10 971	9 448	3 100	1 675
1980	38 726	38 641	85	27 432	1 245	1 685	27 872	7 122	3 731	12 439	10 655	3 113	1 709
1981	43 380	43 296	84	29 972	1 484	1 868	30 356	8 719	4 305	13 865	11 817	3 129	1 732
1982	46 782	46 672	110	31 979	1 626	2 024	32 376	9 604	4 801	14 903	12 678	3 139	1 731
1983	49 963	49 852	111	34 508	1 751	2 146	34 903	9 893	5 166	15 799	13 776	3 162	1 749
1984	55 906	55 774	132	38 654	1 966	2 295	38 984	11 582	5 340	17 580	15 411	3 180	1 831
1985	60 063	59 931	132	42 235	2 238	2 431	42 427	11 932	5 704	18 763	16 298	3 201	1 890
1986	64 598	64 453	145	45 769	2 482	2 588	45 875	12 664	6 059	20 038	17 305	3 224	1 949
1987	71 099	70 955	144	51 011	2 763	2 719	50 967	13 822	6 309	21 895	18 742	3 247	1 997
1988	78 551	78 393	158	56 521	3 130	2 902	56 293	15 454	6 804	24 007	20 815	3 272	2 054
1989	84 703	84 558	145	59 621	3 335	2 797	59 083	18 050	7 569	25 797	22 364	3 283	2 048
1990	87 935	87 751	185	61 622	3 465	2 768	60 925	18 466	8 543	26 736	23 279	3 289	2 019
1991	88 344	88 181	164	61 792	3 591	2 820	61 021	17 734	9 588	26 863	23 376	3 289	1 937
1992	93 779	93 588	191	64 965	3 704	3 461	64 722	17 795	11 263	28 635	24 603	3 275	1 918
1993	96 866	96 652	215	67 239	3 839	3 466	66 866	18 279	11 721	29 602	25 317	3 272	1 939
1994	99 788	99 598	190	69 332	4 031	3 505	68 806	18 865	12 117	30 532	26 139	3 268	1 923
1995	104 315	104 139	176	72 132	4 269	4 119	71 983	19 333	12 999	31 947	27 082	3 265	1 961
1996	109 354	109 174	180	75 317	4 448	4 892	75 761	20 248	13 344	33 472	28 018	3 267	1 992
1997	116 347	116 173	174	80 955	4 808	4 845	80 992	21 410	13 946	35 596	29 264	3 269	2 020
1998	122 564	122 354	210	86 075	5 059	4 742	85 757	22 690	14 117	37 452	30 365	3 273	2 059
1999	128 983	128 735	248	91 257	5 394	5 123	90 987	23 545	14 451	39 300	31 697	3 282	2 093

Table 25-1. Personal Income and Employment—*Continued*

(Millions of dollars, except as noted.)

Year	Total	Nonfarm	Farm	Derivation of personal income						Per capita (dollars)		Population (thousands)	Total employment (thousands)
				Earnings by place of work	Less: Personal contributions for social insurance	Plus: Adjustment for residence	Equals: Net earnings by place of residence	Dividends, interest, and rent	Transfer payments	Total	Disposable		
DELAWARE													
1970	2 536	2 499	37	2 093	72	-47	1 975	397	164	4 608	3 814	550	275
1971	2 765	2 725	40	2 298	81	-58	2 159	411	194	4 892	4 091	565	280
1972	3 043	2 992	51	2 553	92	-65	2 395	432	215	5 303	4 425	574	293
1973	3 400	3 302	98	2 891	119	-93	2 679	475	247	5 871	4 895	579	305
1974	3 701	3 617	85	3 107	134	-104	2 869	531	301	6 347	5 315	583	302
1975	3 962	3 867	95	3 280	139	-105	3 035	525	401	6 729	5 709	589	292
1976	4 356	4 270	87	3 603	151	-116	3 337	586	434	7 349	6 147	593	296
1977	4 707	4 649	58	3 860	163	-127	3 570	660	478	7 913	6 632	595	296
1978	5 179	5 116	63	4 278	184	-156	3 939	741	499	8 658	7 266	598	304
1979	5 718	5 663	56	4 686	213	-176	4 297	851	570	9 549	7 950	599	312
1980	6 427	6 413	14	5 155	239	-222	4 694	1 040	693	10 803	8 984	595	312
1981	7 076	7 034	42	5 547	281	-240	5 026	1 261	789	11 873	9 799	596	314
1982	7 626	7 559	66	5 962	309	-260	5 392	1 394	839	12 727	10 657	599	317
1983	8 191	8 111	80	6 433	332	-305	5 796	1 506	889	13 529	11 487	605	326
1984	9 061	8 964	97	7 082	363	-342	6 377	1 750	934	14 816	12 668	612	341
1985	9 927	9 823	105	7 754	413	-381	6 961	1 961	1 006	16 056	13 749	618	359
1986	10 531	10 384	147	8 196	446	-382	7 368	2 072	1 090	16 781	14 330	628	372
1987	11 423	11 308	114	8 973	488	-436	8 049	2 231	1 142	17 933	15 391	637	389
1988	12 507	12 322	184	9 880	558	-492	8 830	2 418	1 259	19 312	16 675	648	405
1989	13 778	13 584	194	10 750	621	-586	9 543	2 874	1 360	20 930	18 015	658	418
1990	14 476	14 338	138	11 368	658	-682	10 027	2 986	1 462	21 636	18 612	669	423
1991	15 204	15 075	129	11 781	696	-679	10 406	3 157	1 640	22 342	19 361	680	417
1992	15 939	15 827	112	12 319	713	-668	10 938	3 155	1 845	23 094	20 078	690	416
1993	16 663	16 553	110	13 027	743	-831	11 454	3 250	1 959	23 823	20 670	699	424
1994	17 378	17 257	121	13 587	795	-862	11 930	3 327	2 121	24 530	21 156	708	428
1995	18 237	18 145	92	14 140	850	-888	12 402	3 555	2 280	25 391	21 839	718	447
1996	19 369	19 259	110	14 703	903	-788	13 012	3 873	2 485	26 640	22 758	727	458
1997	20 143	20 062	81	15 572	956	-994	13 622	4 032	2 489	27 405	23 109	735	470
1998	22 003	21 872	131	16 855	1 023	-867	14 965	4 420	2 618	29 571	24 997	744	484
1999	23 192	23 061	132	17 881	1 093	-930	15 858	4 642	2 692	30 778	26 021	754	498
DISTRICT OF COLUMBIA													
1970	3 789	3 789	0	6 571	130	-3 503	2 938	551	300	5 018	4 313	755	674
1971	4 162	4 162	0	7 140	138	-3 818	3 184	603	375	5 545	4 827	751	669
1972	4 517	4 517	0	7 724	155	-4 150	3 419	651	447	6 073	5 254	744	671
1973	4 785	4 785	0	8 208	189	-4 435	3 585	691	510	6 522	5 628	734	664
1974	5 266	5 266	0	9 022	213	-4 894	3 915	760	592	7 306	6 332	721	676
1975	5 731	5 731	0	9 974	228	-5 505	4 240	758	732	8 068	7 026	710	680
1976	6 110	6 110	0	10 850	242	-6 075	4 532	815	762	8 775	7 523	696	677
1977	6 615	6 615	0	11 916	259	-6 720	4 937	890	788	9 702	8 411	682	683
1978	7 001	7 001	0	12 987	287	-7 503	5 197	996	808	10 448	8 963	670	696
1979	7 432	7 432	0	14 188	335	-8 458	5 394	1 138	900	11 336	9 591	656	709
1980	7 881	7 881	0	15 624	377	-9 696	5 550	1 310	1 021	12 347	10 480	638	707
1981	8 617	8 617	0	16 955	452	-10 637	5 866	1 620	1 131	13 530	11 328	637	696
1982	9 389	9 389	0	18 048	496	-11 296	6 257	1 871	1 261	14 805	12 471	634	681
1983	9 823	9 823	0	18 875	606	-11 669	6 600	1 906	1 317	15 532	13 202	632	677
1984	10 847	10 847	0	20 516	677	-12 593	7 246	2 213	1 389	17 126	14 571	633	700
1985	11 534	11 534	0	21 899	801	-13 385	7 712	2 438	1 385	18 177	15 443	635	714
1986	12 146	12 146	0	23 300	903	-14 218	8 179	2 513	1 455	19 030	16 192	638	734
1987	12 898	12 898	0	25 090	993	-15 286	8 811	2 581	1 506	20 251	17 100	637	747
1988	14 147	14 147	0	27 631	1 156	-16 805	9 670	2 863	1 614	22 440	19 196	630	770
1989	15 174	15 174	0	29 369	1 285	-17 925	10 159	3 405	1 610	24 311	20 769	624	778
1990	16 078	16 078	0	31 517	1 422	-19 101	10 993	3 341	1 743	26 627	22 921	604	789
1991	16 651	16 651	0	33 118	1 511	-20 262	11 345	3 349	1 957	28 068	24 396	593	775
1992	17 533	17 533	0	35 000	1 587	-21 503	11 910	3 388	2 236	30 013	26 305	584	768
1993	18 251	18 251	0	36 395	1 675	-22 372	12 348	3 467	2 435	31 665	27 796	576	768
1994	18 499	18 499	0	37 252	1 767	-23 050	12 435	3 591	2 474	32 743	28 510	565	747
1995	18 217	18 217	0	37 588	1 826	-23 401	12 362	3 462	2 393	33 045	28 734	551	740
1996	18 517	18 517	0	37 872	1 866	-23 489	12 517	3 402	2 599	34 401	29 468	538	722
1997	19 081	19 081	0	39 034	1 908	-24 379	12 748	3 765	2 568	36 087	30 384	529	718
1998	19 665	19 665	0	40 578	2 004	-25 459	13 114	3 976	2 575	37 714	31 300	521	724
1999	20 686	20 686	0	43 882	2 203	-27 791	13 888	4 192	2 607	39 858	32 905	519	741

Table 25-1. Personal Income and Employment—*Continued*

(Millions of dollars, except as noted.)

Year	Total	Nonfarm	Farm	Derivation of personal income						Per capita (dollars)		Population (thousands)	Total employment (thousands)
				Earnings by place of work	Less: Personal contributions for social insurance	Plus: Adjustment for residence	Equals: Net earnings by place of residence	Dividends, interest, and rent	Transfer payments	Total	Disposable		
FLORIDA													
1970	27 419	26 850	570	19 551	657	-20	18 874	5 914	2 631	4 006	3 560	6 845	2 966
1971	30 701	30 029	672	21 684	759	-14	20 911	6 603	3 187	4 286	3 833	7 163	3 082
1972	35 365	34 591	774	25 182	914	-11	24 257	7 357	3 750	4 703	4 136	7 520	3 338
1973	41 495	40 628	866	29 519	1 229	-10	28 280	8 690	4 525	5 235	4 633	7 927	3 666
1974	46 712	45 773	939	32 589	1 422	-1	31 166	10 091	5 456	5 616	4 989	8 317	3 766
1975	50 353	49 315	1 038	34 046	1 456	-10	32 580	10 691	7 082	5 895	5 334	8 542	3 676
1976	55 438	54 365	1 073	37 241	1 574	10	35 677	11 877	7 884	6 376	5 732	8 695	3 730
1977	62 309	61 234	1 075	41 674	1 774	21	39 921	13 673	8 715	7 010	6 285	8 889	3 929
1978	72 332	71 047	1 285	48 257	2 100	25	46 182	16 497	9 653	7 921	7 058	9 132	4 235
1979	84 094	82 728	1 366	55 147	2 537	21	52 631	20 305	11 158	8 879	7 864	9 471	4 457
1980	98 882	97 127	1 755	63 416	2 967	15	60 464	25 110	13 308	10 049	8 857	9 840	4 695
1981	114 110	112 640	1 469	70 995	3 638	114	67 471	31 114	15 525	11 195	9 839	10 193	4 881
1982	123 450	121 545	1 905	76 007	4 033	136	72 110	33 740	17 600	11 789	10 278	10 471	4 970
1983	135 842	133 174	2 668	84 369	4 445	161	80 085	36 551	19 206	12 637	11 276	10 750	5 185
1984	151 952	150 010	1 941	94 549	5 054	212	89 707	42 053	20 191	13 764	12 395	11 040	5 529
1985	166 919	164 967	1 952	103 855	5 841	257	98 271	46 596	22 052	14 705	13 085	11 351	5 809
1986	179 952	177 853	2 098	112 331	6 498	313	106 146	49 921	23 885	15 423	13 666	11 668	6 056
1987	196 939	194 689	2 251	124 217	7 086	374	117 505	53 936	25 498	16 415	14 540	11 997	6 141
1988	216 505	213 633	2 871	136 719	8 092	451	129 079	59 530	27 895	17 593	15 650	12 306	6 444
1989	240 687	238 064	2 623	145 630	8 922	531	137 239	72 268	31 180	19 045	16 919	12 638	6 657
1990	258 479	256 251	2 228	155 631	9 462	639	146 809	76 991	34 679	19 855	17 731	13 018	6 802
1991	268 304	265 582	2 722	160 515	9 988	660	151 186	77 963	39 155	20 189	18 148	13 289	6 778
1992	279 028	276 490	2 538	171 411	10 610	697	161 498	73 012	44 518	20 661	18 517	13 505	6 829
1993	296 927	294 321	2 606	182 048	11 346	723	171 425	77 661	47 841	21 652	19 379	13 714	7 073
1994	311 909	309 683	2 225	190 871	12 200	754	179 426	81 453	51 030	22 340	19 939	13 962	7 314
1995	333 525	331 269	2 256	202 726	13 021	782	190 487	88 225	54 813	23 512	20 936	14 185	7 576
1996	355 136	353 157	1 979	215 167	13 646	807	202 328	94 832	57 976	24 616	21 682	14 427	7 831
1997	377 683	375 459	2 222	227 683	14 412	841	214 112	102 608	60 962	25 722	22 453	14 683	8 103
1998	401 474	398 824	2 650	245 917	15 379	895	231 433	107 432	62 609	26 930	23 352	14 908	8 351
1999	419 792	416 428	3 365	261 020	16 397	959	245 583	110 470	63 740	27 780	23 981	15 111	8 634
GEORGIA													
1970	15 630	15 205	425	13 195	431	-69	12 695	1 642	1 293	3 394	3 000	4 605	2 121
1971	17 268	16 783	485	14 458	488	-65	13 905	1 814	1 549	3 666	3 274	4 710	2 167
1972	19 411	18 906	505	16 298	571	-58	15 669	2 000	1 742	4 038	3 556	4 807	2 253
1973	22 064	21 245	819	18 513	736	-56	17 722	2 345	1 998	4 497	3 992	4 907	2 356
1974	24 312	23 608	704	19 954	832	-56	19 066	2 757	2 490	4 867	4 319	4 995	2 374
1975	26 061	25 403	658	20 806	855	-47	19 905	2 887	3 269	5 152	4 657	5 059	2 313
1976	29 189	28 545	644	23 597	961	-78	22 558	3 120	3 511	5 694	5 101	5 126	2 399
1977	32 423	32 052	371	26 394	1 074	-98	25 222	3 510	3 691	6 221	5 541	5 212	2 503
1978	36 945	36 367	578	30 154	1 246	-81	28 827	4 119	4 000	6 989	6 186	5 286	2 622
1979	41 633	41 017	617	33 755	1 462	-99	32 194	4 900	4 539	7 722	6 756	5 391	2 705
1980	46 489	46 430	59	36 736	1 644	-117	34 975	6 066	5 448	8 474	7 442	5 486	2 747
1981	52 536	52 018	518	40 868	1 973	-29	38 866	7 487	6 183	9 435	8 247	5 568	2 785
1982	56 801	56 121	680	43 789	2 170	-71	41 548	8 488	6 766	10 054	8 838	5 650	2 802
1983	62 145	61 682	463	47 900	2 411	-114	45 383	9 427	7 335	10 849	9 514	5 728	2 886
1984	71 100	70 149	951	55 221	2 766	-180	52 275	11 100	7 725	12 185	10 748	5 835	3 081
1985	78 364	77 592	772	60 998	3 215	-199	57 585	12 373	8 407	13 143	11 518	5 963	3 224
1986	85 126	84 315	811	66 557	3 611	-243	62 703	13 402	9 021	13 990	12 269	6 085	3 354
1987	92 007	91 141	867	72 059	3 896	-244	67 919	14 535	9 554	14 820	12 930	6 208	3 455
1988	100 277	99 141	1 136	78 216	4 361	-237	73 617	16 358	10 302	15 876	13 931	6 316	3 568
1989	107 725	106 392	1 334	82 675	4 685	-202	77 788	18 612	11 326	16 803	14 687	6 411	3 634
1990	115 414	114 223	1 191	87 892	5 001	-117	82 775	20 009	12 630	17 738	15 537	6 507	3 691
1991	121 094	119 580	1 515	91 213	5 269	-123	85 821	20 706	14 567	18 289	16 109	6 621	3 647
1992	130 684	129 116	1 568	99 152	5 637	-158	93 356	21 098	16 230	19 333	17 064	6 759	3 727
1993	138 771	137 343	1 427	105 345	6 058	-155	99 132	22 002	17 637	20 129	17 688	6 894	3 899
1994	149 165	147 275	1 890	112 808	6 585	-195	106 028	24 272	18 866	21 170	18 574	7 046	4 058
1995	159 800	158 103	1 697	120 919	7 118	-240	113 561	26 066	20 174	22 230	19 430	7 189	4 229
1996	172 935	171 133	1 802	130 414	7 594	-293	122 527	28 749	21 660	23 586	20 482	7 332	4 379
1997	183 762	181 952	1 811	139 478	8 142	-330	131 006	30 621	22 135	24 547	21 153	7 486	4 499
1998	199 576	197 762	1 815	151 754	8 780	-431	142 543	34 226	22 807	26 134	22 420	7 637	4 641
1999	212 929	210 942	1 987	163 810	9 536	-514	153 760	35 610	23 558	27 340	23 378	7 788	4 781

Table 25-1. Personal Income and Employment—*Continued*

(Millions of dollars, except as noted.)

Year	Total	Nonfarm	Farm	Earnings by place of work	Less: Personal contributions for social insurance	Plus: Adjustment for residence	Equals: Net earnings by place of residence	Dividends, interest, and rent	Transfer payments	Total	Disposable	Population (thousands)	Total employment (thousands)
HAWAII													
1970	3 888	3 753	135	3 258	92	0	3 166	516	206	5 096	4 382	763	434
1971	4 221	4 088	133	3 477	101	0	3 375	575	271	5 332	4 663	792	437
1972	4 660	4 527	134	3 831	115	0	3 715	623	323	5 697	4 918	818	453
1973	5 178	5 040	138	4 246	151	0	4 095	716	368	6 151	5 325	842	473
1974	5 965	5 608	357	4 881	175	0	4 706	819	441	6 952	6 052	858	485
1975	6 465	6 255	210	5 213	190	0	5 022	875	568	7 388	6 578	875	499
1976	7 032	6 857	175	5 632	204	0	5 427	936	668	7 880	6 964	892	505
1977	7 652	7 465	187	6 133	224	0	5 908	1 034	709	8 356	7 351	916	509
1978	8 497	8 328	169	6 770	259	0	6 512	1 226	759	9 148	7 993	929	527
1979	9 679	9 482	197	7 647	304	0	7 343	1 501	835	10 188	8 881	950	556
1980	11 140	10 750	390	8 744	342	0	8 401	1 776	962	11 512	10 054	968	575
1981	12 041	11 835	206	9 204	402	0	8 802	2 113	1 126	12 309	10 748	978	569
1982	12 846	12 604	242	9 847	434	0	9 413	2 212	1 221	12 927	11 514	994	568
1983	14 056	13 712	344	10 654	470	0	10 184	2 531	1 341	13 880	12 354	1 013	579
1984	15 328	15 095	234	11 524	506	0	11 018	2 914	1 397	14 912	13 322	1 028	585
1985	16 316	16 101	214	12 325	571	0	11 754	3 070	1 491	15 693	13 959	1 040	602
1986	17 259	16 998	260	13 113	626	0	12 487	3 208	1 564	16 409	14 560	1 052	616
1987	18 574	18 343	231	14 228	692	0	13 536	3 407	1 631	17 392	15 242	1 068	647
1988	20 399	20 145	254	15 704	805	0	14 899	3 754	1 746	18 891	16 536	1 080	674
1989	22 483	22 246	237	17 216	912	0	16 303	4 273	1 907	20 540	17 758	1 095	702
1990	24 915	24 670	245	19 154	1 017	0	18 137	4 514	2 263	22 391	19 428	1 113	731
1991	26 198	25 995	203	20 264	1 100	0	19 164	4 705	2 328	23 155	20 179	1 131	752
1992	27 859	27 671	188	21 785	1 157	0	20 628	4 518	2 713	24 227	21 272	1 150	754
1993	29 068	28 887	181	22 184	1 181	0	21 003	5 072	2 992	25 026	22 024	1 162	750
1994	29 740	29 563	177	22 300	1 211	0	21 088	5 406	3 245	25 335	22 351	1 174	745
1995	30 202	30 040	161	22 244	1 223	0	21 020	5 539	3 643	25 584	22 596	1 180	742
1996	30 393	30 233	160	22 303	1 216	0	21 087	5 584	3 723	25 661	22 568	1 184	741
1997	31 209	31 045	164	22 699	1 235	0	21 464	5 980	3 765	26 241	23 006	1 189	742
1998	31 815	31 642	173	23 069	1 250	0	21 819	6 178	3 818	26 725	23 368	1 190	745
1999	32 653	32 462	192	23 663	1 297	0	22 365	6 355	3 933	27 544	24 075	1 185	750
IDAHO													
1970	2 552	2 272	280	2 041	64	14	1 991	333	228	3 558	3 194	717	324
1971	2 778	2 514	264	2 187	71	15	2 131	378	270	3 761	3 376	739	332
1972	3 168	2 829	339	2 521	83	16	2 454	407	307	4 150	3 750	763	347
1973	3 683	3 215	467	2 931	110	19	2 840	494	348	4 709	4 222	782	365
1974	4 349	3 702	647	3 466	129	22	3 360	571	418	5 382	4 788	808	381
1975	4 635	4 233	402	3 609	145	28	3 492	629	514	5 571	4 996	832	393
1976	5 241	4 884	357	4 078	163	35	3 950	706	585	6 116	5 476	857	419
1977	5 751	5 500	251	4 446	181	36	4 300	823	629	6 510	5 814	883	435
1978	6 668	6 343	325	5 189	208	43	5 024	975	669	7 319	6 522	911	460
1979	7 363	7 128	235	5 603	246	48	5 405	1 180	778	7 894	7 023	933	470
1980	8 280	7 873	407	6 133	267	62	5 928	1 419	933	8 735	7 779	948	466
1981	9 050	8 655	395	6 517	312	54	6 260	1 718	1 072	9 405	8 286	962	463
1982	9 368	8 982	386	6 495	325	63	6 234	1 904	1 231	9 621	8 557	974	453
1983	10 128	9 541	586	7 174	346	65	6 893	1 935	1 300	10 315	9 240	982	464
1984	10 968	10 466	501	7 741	377	78	7 443	2 193	1 332	11 069	9 956	991	474
1985	11 577	11 119	458	8 131	417	86	7 799	2 338	1 440	11 647	10 452	994	476
1986	11 851	11 377	474	8 269	434	101	7 936	2 393	1 522	11 968	10 799	990	476
1987	12 422	11 838	584	8 750	454	110	8 406	2 444	1 572	12 611	11 356	985	490
1988	13 354	12 721	633	9 485	525	127	9 087	2 587	1 680	13 548	12 175	986	512
1989	14 721	13 863	857	10 442	587	142	9 997	2 912	1 812	14 803	13 152	994	529
1990	16 054	15 081	974	11 448	641	154	10 961	3 122	1 971	15 866	14 071	1 012	553
1991	16 825	16 026	799	11 914	704	168	11 379	3 254	2 192	16 195	14 357	1 039	570
1992	18 382	17 581	801	13 157	756	173	12 574	3 367	2 441	17 236	15 189	1 066	590
1993	20 105	19 040	1 065	14 560	817	182	13 926	3 554	2 626	18 258	16 116	1 101	617
1994	21 399	20 706	694	15 393	900	204	14 697	3 925	2 777	18 846	16 609	1 135	653
1995	22 869	22 073	796	16 199	949	230	15 480	4 377	3 012	19 630	17 283	1 165	673
1996	24 173	23 298	876	16 966	987	260	16 238	4 650	3 285	20 353	17 856	1 188	695
1997	25 217	24 548	669	17 542	1 044	292	16 789	5 034	3 394	20 830	18 201	1 211	715
1998	26 986	26 067	919	18 877	1 099	320	18 099	5 350	3 537	21 923	19 138	1 231	737
1999	28 582	27 633	950	20 266	1 188	341	19 418	5 493	3 671	22 835	19 883	1 252	756

Table 25-1. Personal Income and Employment—*Continued*

(Millions of dollars, except as noted.)

Year	Total	Nonfarm	Farm	Derivation of personal income						Per capita (dollars)		Population (thousands)	Total employment (thousands)
				Earnings by place of work	Less: Personal contributions for social insurance	Plus: Adjustment for residence	Equals: Net earnings by place of residence	Dividends, interest, and rent	Transfer payments	Total	Disposable		
ILLINOIS													
1970	50 948	50 171	777	41 489	1 367	14	40 136	6 993	3 820	4 580	3 930	11 125	5 144
1971	54 617	53 682	935	44 206	1 488	-27	42 691	7 328	4 598	4 874	4 251	11 206	5 105
1972	59 280	58 241	1 040	47 978	1 668	-46	46 264	7 846	5 170	5 266	4 534	11 258	5 156
1973	66 471	64 615	1 856	53 558	2 113	-65	51 379	8 981	6 111	5 903	5 122	11 260	5 351
1974	72 877	71 179	1 698	58 155	2 398	-79	55 678	10 239	6 960	6 464	5 584	11 274	5 442
1975	78 990	76 534	2 456	61 955	2 477	-105	59 373	10 761	8 856	6 986	6 113	11 306	5 342
1976	86 598	84 877	1 721	67 915	2 716	-86	65 113	11 658	9 828	7 623	6 609	11 360	5 458
1977	95 637	93 882	1 755	75 188	2 974	-20	72 194	13 053	10 391	8 385	7 256	11 406	5 587
1978	106 079	104 523	1 556	83 415	3 366	65	80 115	14 947	11 018	9 277	8 008	11 434	5 748
1979	117 000	115 189	1 811	91 249	3 871	148	87 526	17 508	11 966	10 243	8 784	11 423	5 811
1980	126 662	126 335	327	95 059	4 152	247	91 154	20 940	14 567	11 077	9 519	11 435	5 688
1981	140 177	138 494	1 683	102 778	4 823	184	98 138	25 315	16 724	12 250	10 502	11 443	5 684
1982	145 889	145 067	822	104 636	5 067	111	99 679	27 807	18 403	12 771	11 108	11 423	5 583
1983	151 615	152 144	-529	107 666	5 272	74	102 468	29 465	19 681	13 289	11 630	11 409	5 542
1984	167 548	166 503	1 045	120 277	5 841	-31	114 405	33 365	19 779	14 682	12 925	11 412	5 746
1985	176 786	175 288	1 499	127 583	6 496	-102	120 986	34 770	21 030	15 508	13 610	11 400	5 815
1986	185 432	184 229	1 203	134 620	7 041	-162	127 417	36 089	21 925	16 284	14 304	11 387	5 928
1987	196 947	195 728	1 218	144 350	7 550	-251	136 549	37 849	22 549	17 289	15 038	11 391	6 073
1988	210 272	209 751	521	155 127	8 492	-346	146 288	40 682	23 302	18 461	16 141	11 390	6 233
1989	224 024	222 205	1 819	163 526	9 194	-381	153 951	45 225	24 848	19 634	17 054	11 410	6 344
1990	237 593	236 206	1 387	173 203	9 786	-287	163 131	47 603	26 859	20 756	18 042	11 447	6 442
1991	245 952	245 383	569	178 159	10 350	-315	167 494	49 229	29 229	21 320	18 649	11 536	6 418
1992	264 869	263 399	1 470	192 446	10 867	-386	181 194	50 349	33 326	22 764	20 016	11 635	6 403
1993	274 221	272 937	1 284	200 606	11 473	-396	188 736	50 813	34 672	23 386	20 472	11 726	6 496
1994	288 509	286 768	1 741	210 738	12 281	-449	198 008	54 744	35 758	24 440	21 292	11 805	6 672
1995	304 767	304 404	364	220 715	13 029	-548	207 139	59 424	38 205	25 643	22 282	11 885	6 838
1996	322 790	320 789	2 001	233 061	13 566	-652	218 843	63 968	39 978	27 005	23 295	11 953	6 944
1997	340 490	338 707	1 783	246 655	14 427	-700	231 528	67 814	41 147	28 347	24 260	12 012	7 055
1998	361 775	360 623	1 152	262 936	15 236	-947	246 753	73 396	41 626	29 974	25 491	12 070	7 215
1999	377 744	377 052	692	277 451	16 184	-1 004	260 263	75 426	42 054	31 145	26 384	12 128	7 319
INDIANA													
1970	19 827	19 376	451	16 407	570	57	15 893	2 441	1 493	3 810	3 333	5 204	2 291
1971	21 549	20 872	677	17 634	628	117	17 123	2 632	1 794	4 105	3 628	5 250	2 290
1972	23 593	23 010	583	19 385	721	149	18 812	2 808	1 972	4 455	3 896	5 296	2 367
1973	27 177	25 887	1 290	22 332	925	193	21 599	3 258	2 320	5 100	4 504	5 329	2 483
1974	29 103	28 307	796	23 396	1 043	254	22 607	3 762	2 734	5 440	4 729	5 350	2 493
1975	31 197	30 040	1 157	24 423	1 062	299	23 660	4 086	3 451	5 830	5 159	5 351	2 405
1976	35 002	33 863	1 139	27 710	1 189	350	26 870	4 506	3 626	6 516	5 710	5 372	2 489
1977	38 910	38 104	805	30 859	1 326	412	29 945	5 105	3 860	7 199	6 286	5 405	2 578
1978	43 602	42 794	808	34 604	1 521	466	33 549	5 822	4 231	8 006	6 964	5 446	2 671
1979	48 256	47 564	691	37 817	1 749	544	36 612	6 801	4 843	8 814	7 637	5 475	2 713
1980	51 881	51 495	386	38 730	1 823	667	37 574	8 230	6 077	9 449	8 246	5 491	2 632
1981	56 752	56 422	330	41 401	2 127	713	39 987	9 991	6 774	10 355	8 990	5 480	2 611
1982	58 494	58 215	279	41 325	2 184	778	39 918	11 018	7 558	10 698	9 362	5 468	2 530
1983	61 063	61 323	-261	42 944	2 290	826	41 479	11 464	8 119	11 203	9 865	5 450	2 550
1984	67 928	67 255	674	48 187	2 529	985	46 643	12 883	8 403	12 445	11 006	5 458	2 653
1985	71 752	71 177	575	50 987	2 813	1 070	49 243	13 655	8 854	13 143	11 578	5 459	2 709
1986	75 382	74 925	457	53 530	3 031	1 167	51 666	14 284	9 432	13 821	12 199	5 454	2 770
1987	80 258	79 620	638	57 682	3 244	1 241	55 679	14 867	9 712	14 664	12 896	5 473	2 866
1988	85 759	85 606	153	61 852	3 651	1 332	59 533	15 921	10 305	15 616	13 742	5 492	2 954
1989	92 630	91 798	832	66 313	3 969	1 415	63 760	17 763	11 106	16 770	14 625	5 524	3 031
1990	97 907	97 196	712	69 646	4 195	1 486	66 936	18 836	12 135	17 625	15 398	5 555	3 091
1991	101 147	101 033	114	71 741	4 464	1 510	68 787	18 852	13 508	18 055	15 831	5 602	3 093
1992	108 845	108 264	581	77 566	4 746	1 646	74 466	19 052	15 327	19 269	16 917	5 649	3 143
1993	114 675	113 978	697	82 092	5 064	1 725	78 752	19 579	16 344	20 112	17 588	5 702	3 221
1994	121 537	120 927	610	87 089	5 494	1 870	83 465	21 125	16 947	21 153	18 402	5 746	3 315
1995	126 525	126 305	220	90 449	5 774	2 056	86 730	22 590	17 204	21 845	18 968	5 792	3 409
1996	132 890	131 910	980	94 568	5 967	2 210	90 810	23 985	18 094	22 775	19 680	5 835	3 450
1997	139 454	138 464	990	99 124	6 313	2 438	95 249	25 483	18 722	23 748	20 404	5 872	3 511
1998	148 767	148 196	571	105 620	6 672	2 782	101 730	27 754	19 284	25 182	21 544	5 908	3 580
1999	155 365	155 154	211	110 519	7 036	2 959	106 443	28 922	20 001	26 143	22 279	5 943	3 646

Table 25-1. Personal Income and Employment—*Continued*

(Millions of dollars, except as noted.)

Year	Total	Nonfarm	Farm	Earnings by place of work	Less: Personal contributions for social insurance	Plus: Adjustment for residence	Equals: Net earnings by place of residence	Dividends, interest, and rent	Transfer payments	Per capita (dollars) Total	Per capita (dollars) Disposable	Population (thousands)	Total employment (thousands)
IOWA													
1970	10 924	9 702	1 223	8 453	299	89	8 244	1 693	988	3 862	3 419	2 829	1 295
1971	11 421	10 405	1 016	8 720	328	88	8 480	1 813	1 128	4 005	3 584	2 852	1 297
1972	12 796	11 323	1 473	9 870	370	94	9 594	1 986	1 216	4 473	3 937	2 861	1 316
1973	15 460	12 747	2 712	12 115	472	88	11 731	2 335	1 394	5 398	4 796	2 864	1 374
1974	16 050	14 349	1 701	12 244	554	84	11 774	2 662	1 613	5 596	4 840	2 868	1 407
1975	17 841	15 892	1 949	13 440	597	100	12 944	2 913	1 984	6 192	5 438	2 881	1 407
1976	19 106	17 905	1 201	14 263	650	92	13 704	3 209	2 193	6 580	5 729	2 904	1 455
1977	21 225	19 999	1 226	15 815	700	66	15 181	3 698	2 346	7 283	6 351	2 914	1 488
1978	24 630	22 199	2 431	18 538	792	62	17 808	4 246	2 576	8 438	7 389	2 919	1 514
1979	26 584	25 036	1 548	19 579	941	72	18 710	4 996	2 878	9 114	7 906	2 917	1 557
1980	28 181	27 560	621	19 787	1 003	93	18 877	5 905	3 400	9 671	8 366	2 914	1 541
1981	31 894	30 174	1 720	21 928	1 131	120	20 917	7 118	3 860	10 968	9 496	2 908	1 513
1982	32 425	31 691	734	20 916	1 159	193	19 951	8 067	4 407	11 227	9 797	2 888	1 476
1983	32 967	33 037	-70	20 931	1 181	209	19 959	8 295	4 713	11 485	10 105	2 871	1 479
1984	36 586	35 320	1 266	23 906	1 281	242	22 867	8 954	4 766	12 798	11 431	2 859	1 506
1985	37 903	36 387	1 516	24 890	1 396	283	23 778	9 055	5 070	13 395	11 974	2 830	1 503
1986	39 144	37 240	1 905	25 880	1 479	275	24 677	9 180	5 288	14 020	12 568	2 792	1 501
1987	41 225	38 911	2 313	27 961	1 616	272	26 617	9 173	5 435	14 899	13 238	2 767	1 523
1988	42 399	41 067	1 333	28 871	1 816	310	27 365	9 373	5 661	15 315	13 574	2 768	1 567
1989	45 888	43 793	2 094	31 333	1 981	319	29 671	10 197	6 019	16 562	14 601	2 771	1 611
1990	48 313	46 343	1 970	32 907	2 100	325	31 132	10 712	6 469	17 380	15 295	2 780	1 646
1991	49 849	48 443	1 405	33 730	2 214	351	31 868	10 941	7 040	17 859	15 744	2 791	1 666
1992	53 161	51 000	2 161	36 675	2 314	376	34 737	10 810	7 614	18 939	16 766	2 807	1 681
1993	53 391	52 849	542	36 683	2 422	345	34 606	10 702	8 084	18 929	16 679	2 821	1 705
1994	57 999	55 627	2 371	40 724	2 608	342	38 458	11 218	8 323	20 498	18 096	2 829	1 740
1995	60 171	58 582	1 589	41 682	2 760	385	39 308	12 111	8 752	21 181	18 663	2 841	1 800
1996	64 696	61 383	3 313	45 155	2 856	413	42 712	12 858	9 127	22 713	19 974	2 848	1 832
1997	67 930	64 798	3 132	47 130	3 017	462	44 575	13 889	9 466	23 798	20 770	2 854	1 859
1998	71 080	69 284	1 797	48 986	3 187	484	46 284	15 087	9 710	24 844	21 664	2 861	1 900
1999	73 499	72 424	1 076	50 713	3 367	522	47 869	15 686	9 945	25 615	22 296	2 869	1 929
KANSAS													
1970	8 577	7 972	605	6 405	230	438	6 614	1 164	799	3 816	3 363	2 248	1 017
1971	9 309	8 606	703	6 960	254	430	7 136	1 257	916	4 145	3 706	2 246	1 022
1972	10 405	9 428	977	7 886	293	453	8 046	1 375	984	4 613	4 085	2 256	1 048
1973	11 943	10 553	1 390	9 114	373	468	9 209	1 591	1 143	5 274	4 662	2 264	1 090
1974	12 965	11 898	1 068	9 722	430	483	9 775	1 877	1 313	5 717	4 996	2 268	1 122
1975	14 097	13 281	816	10 419	471	497	10 444	2 065	1 587	6 186	5 470	2 279	1 133
1976	15 448	14 853	595	11 448	521	514	11 441	2 245	1 763	6 721	5 935	2 299	1 169
1977	16 937	16 426	511	12 463	556	560	12 467	2 540	1 930	7 307	6 410	2 318	1 208
1978	18 853	18 556	297	13 853	648	605	13 811	2 945	2 097	8 082	7 065	2 333	1 252
1979	21 690	20 960	730	16 018	765	654	15 907	3 476	2 307	9 240	8 003	2 347	1 298
1980	23 781	23 677	104	16 887	847	731	16 771	4 266	2 744	10 038	8 674	2 369	1 312
1981	26 824	26 546	278	18 601	997	759	18 362	5 299	3 163	11 248	9 614	2 385	1 326
1982	28 789	28 231	558	19 519	1 065	782	19 236	5 986	3 566	11 989	10 273	2 401	1 310
1983	29 888	29 580	308	20 275	1 102	760	19 933	6 163	3 792	12 373	10 825	2 416	1 327
1984	32 971	32 266	706	22 699	1 208	804	22 294	6 824	3 853	13 602	12 035	2 424	1 370
1985	34 784	34 022	763	23 891	1 329	850	23 413	7 303	4 069	14 330	12 635	2 427	1 375
1986	36 256	35 372	885	25 027	1 419	835	24 443	7 497	4 316	14 904	13 244	2 433	1 375
1987	38 107	36 964	1 143	26 475	1 495	911	25 892	7 721	4 494	15 583	13 749	2 445	1 428
1988	40 207	39 133	1 074	27 941	1 662	925	27 204	8 264	4 740	16 331	14 427	2 462	1 440
1989	42 267	41 525	742	29 050	1 784	972	28 238	8 868	5 161	17 093	14 973	2 473	1 463
1990	45 104	43 749	1 354	31 089	1 882	982	30 189	9 346	5 569	18 182	16 009	2 481	1 484
1991	46 990	46 011	979	32 040	2 005	961	30 996	9 866	6 128	18 832	16 651	2 495	1 499
1992	50 407	49 037	1 370	34 840	2 112	994	33 722	9 877	6 808	19 955	17 715	2 526	1 512
1993	52 250	50 950	1 301	36 352	2 211	1 010	35 151	9 974	7 126	20 510	18 130	2 548	1 536
1994	54 857	53 528	1 329	38 116	2 359	960	36 718	10 663	7 475	21 352	18 834	2 569	1 564
1995	56 627	55 898	729	39 310	2 472	974	37 811	11 097	7 718	21 889	19 184	2 587	1 613
1996	60 074	58 650	1 423	41 726	2 585	1 131	40 273	11 873	7 928	23 121	20 154	2 598	1 646
1997	63 721	62 343	1 378	44 420	2 765	1 046	42 702	12 681	8 338	24 355	21 062	2 616	1 692
1998	67 780	66 587	1 193	47 420	2 932	1 269	45 757	13 642	8 381	25 687	22 185	2 639	1 740
1999	71 194	69 867	1 326	50 082	3 106	1 298	48 273	14 219	8 701	26 824	23 146	2 654	1 762

Table 25-1. Personal Income and Employment—*Continued*

(Millions of dollars, except as noted.)

Year	Total	Nonfarm	Farm	Derivation of personal income						Per capita (dollars)		Population (thousands)	Total employment (thousands)
				Earnings by place of work	Less: Personal contributions for social insurance	Plus: Adjustment for residence	Equals: Net earnings by place of residence	Dividends, interest, and rent	Transfer payments	Total	Disposable		

KENTUCKY

Year	Total	Nonfarm	Farm	Earnings by place of work	Less: Personal contributions for social insurance	Plus: Adjustment for residence	Equals: Net earnings by place of residence	Dividends, interest, and rent	Transfer payments	Total	Disposable	Population (thousands)	Total employment (thousands)
1970	10 287	9 854	433	8 161	274	165	8 051	1 136	1 100	3 184	2 812	3 231	1 336
1971	11 185	10 737	449	8 851	305	109	8 656	1 230	1 300	3 391	3 023	3 298	1 360
1972	12 394	11 837	557	9 859	349	103	9 613	1 340	1 442	3 715	3 265	3 336	1 392
1973	13 974	13 349	625	11 127	445	61	10 744	1 520	1 710	4 145	3 686	3 372	1 461
1974	15 741	15 037	704	12 434	513	29	11 950	1 754	2 036	4 607	4 018	3 417	1 496
1975	17 113	16 600	513	13 171	546	15	12 640	1 929	2 544	4 933	4 397	3 469	1 465
1976	19 283	18 700	583	14 964	610	-19	14 335	2 151	2 797	5 462	4 848	3 530	1 523
1977	21 788	21 076	712	17 018	682	5	16 341	2 480	2 966	6 095	5 365	3 575	1 579
1978	24 501	23 863	638	19 103	783	18	18 338	2 994	3 169	6 784	5 957	3 611	1 645
1979	27 838	27 134	705	21 332	909	10	20 432	3 723	3 683	7 640	6 714	3 644	1 668
1980	30 159	29 588	572	22 455	976	34	21 513	4 197	4 449	8 231	7 267	3 664	1 646
1981	33 439	32 460	978	24 479	1 144	-2	23 333	5 102	5 004	9 110	7 996	3 670	1 639
1982	35 319	34 429	890	25 240	1 214	-11	24 015	5 832	5 471	9 589	8 429	3 683	1 621
1983	36 423	36 201	222	25 589	1 260	19	24 348	6 159	5 916	9 859	8 708	3 694	1 629
1984	40 877	39 793	1 084	29 180	1 399	-56	27 725	7 035	6 117	11 062	9 869	3 695	1 683
1985	42 703	41 878	825	30 391	1 550	-66	28 775	7 542	6 386	11 558	10 266	3 695	1 706
1986	44 234	43 651	582	31 334	1 658	-38	29 639	7 890	6 705	11 995	10 665	3 688	1 742
1987	47 081	46 392	689	33 776	1 787	-66	31 923	8 196	6 962	12 782	11 317	3 683	1 775
1988	49 939	49 278	661	35 791	2 001	-75	33 715	8 865	7 358	13 570	12 033	3 680	1 827
1989	53 696	52 661	1 034	38 146	2 190	-116	35 840	9 823	8 033	14 602	12 852	3 677	1 877
1990	57 175	56 213	963	40 269	2 338	-66	37 866	10 486	8 823	15 484	13 623	3 693	1 919
1991	60 329	59 336	992	41 806	2 490	-97	39 220	10 990	10 119	16 241	14 360	3 715	1 916
1992	65 060	63 842	1 218	45 748	2 675	-326	42 748	11 139	11 173	17 320	15 309	3 756	1 964
1993	67 559	66 521	1 038	47 690	2 822	-352	44 516	11 286	11 757	17 815	15 718	3 792	2 009
1994	70 781	69 719	1 063	50 078	3 045	-440	46 593	11 947	12 242	18 514	16 275	3 823	2 053
1995	74 080	73 428	652	51 781	3 222	-491	48 068	12 870	13 141	19 215	16 818	3 855	2 129
1996	78 221	77 215	1 006	54 446	3 352	-596	50 499	13 816	13 906	20 155	17 562	3 881	2 162
1997	82 905	81 816	1 089	57 595	3 564	-664	53 367	14 773	14 764	21 215	18 397	3 908	2 212
1998	87 945	86 992	953	60 818	3 736	-645	56 437	16 412	15 096	22 353	19 329	3 934	2 253
1999	92 036	91 519	518	64 063	3 986	-724	59 353	17 141	15 542	23 237	20 033	3 961	2 301

LOUISIANA

Year	Total	Nonfarm	Farm	Earnings by place of work	Less: Personal contributions for social insurance	Plus: Adjustment for residence	Equals: Net earnings by place of residence	Dividends, interest, and rent	Transfer payments	Total	Disposable	Population (thousands)	Total employment (thousands)
1970	11 336	11 040	296	9 193	296	3	8 899	1 288	1 149	3 106	2 796	3 650	1 429
1971	12 348	12 016	333	9 967	327	-10	9 630	1 397	1 321	3 328	2 999	3 711	1 445
1972	13 515	13 149	366	10 951	370	-22	10 559	1 505	1 452	3 593	3 214	3 762	1 488
1973	15 132	14 539	593	12 255	469	-38	11 748	1 709	1 676	3 994	3 587	3 789	1 550
1974	17 233	16 611	622	13 817	550	-56	13 212	2 063	1 958	4 510	4 015	3 821	1 598
1975	19 263	18 838	425	15 341	610	-84	14 647	2 221	2 396	4 956	4 458	3 887	1 641
1976	21 960	21 505	455	17 655	696	-115	16 844	2 454	2 662	5 557	4 950	3 952	1 702
1977	24 636	24 184	453	19 872	768	-141	18 962	2 771	2 903	6 135	5 449	4 016	1 756
1978	28 314	27 941	373	22 952	902	-189	21 862	3 305	3 148	6 951	6 131	4 073	1 848
1979	32 342	31 831	511	26 118	1 072	-235	24 811	3 961	3 570	7 813	6 842	4 139	1 899
1980	37 301	37 119	182	29 591	1 239	-340	28 013	5 017	4 272	8 833	7 709	4 223	1 968
1981	42 990	42 742	248	33 816	1 533	-367	31 917	6 318	4 756	10 037	8 686	4 283	2 036
1982	45 955	45 702	253	35 324	1 631	-345	33 348	7 110	5 497	10 558	9 269	4 353	2 029
1983	47 754	47 537	216	35 710	1 617	-326	33 767	7 741	6 246	10 865	9 647	4 395	1 990
1984	51 171	50 861	309	38 028	1 714	-319	35 995	8 759	6 417	11 628	10 388	4 400	2 032
1985	53 432	53 211	221	38 906	1 828	-288	36 790	9 538	7 104	12 121	10 820	4 408	2 020
1986	53 005	52 793	212	37 660	1 805	-233	35 622	9 592	7 792	12 028	10 867	4 407	1 939
1987	53 287	52 919	368	37 872	1 806	-197	35 869	9 515	7 903	12 266	11 061	4 344	1 915
1988	56 239	55 678	561	40 179	2 002	-178	37 999	10 019	8 222	13 113	11 876	4 289	1 947
1989	59 528	59 132	396	41 883	2 163	-142	39 578	11 014	8 936	13 997	12 586	4 253	1 966
1990	64 229	63 884	345	45 303	2 337	-120	42 845	11 575	9 809	15 223	13 681	4 219	2 020
1991	68 179	67 760	419	47 823	2 528	-128	45 167	11 743	11 269	16 076	14 483	4 241	2 045
1992	72 466	72 000	466	50 650	2 633	-116	47 900	11 606	12 960	16 968	15 337	4 271	2 055
1993	75 911	75 434	478	52 497	2 779	-109	49 609	11 991	14 311	17 717	15 993	4 285	2 104
1994	80 872	80 324	547	55 472	3 019	-120	52 333	12 797	15 741	18 779	16 922	4 307	2 147
1995	84 573	83 997	576	58 116	3 184	-137	54 795	13 832	15 946	19 541	17 559	4 328	2 217
1996	87 879	87 131	747	60 434	3 302	-143	56 989	14 595	16 294	20 254	17 996	4 339	2 265
1997	92 290	91 724	566	63 627	3 512	-144	59 970	15 559	16 761	21 209	18 715	4 351	2 319
1998	97 516	97 176	341	67 416	3 692	-141	63 583	16 932	17 001	22 352	19 758	4 363	2 371
1999	99 887	99 367	520	68 762	3 777	-93	64 892	17 576	17 418	22 847	20 171	4 372	2 388

Table 25-1. Personal Income and Employment—*Continued*

(Millions of dollars, except as noted.)

Year	Total	Nonfarm	Farm	Derivation of personal income						Per capita (dollars)		Population (thousands)	Total employment (thousands)
				Earnings by place of work	Less: Personal contributions for social insurance	Plus: Adjustment for residence	Equals: Net earnings by place of residence	Dividends, interest, and rent	Transfer payments	Total	Disposable		
MAINE													
1970	3 412	3 332	81	2 678	87	-18	2 573	470	369	3 423	3 075	997	446
1971	3 650	3 580	70	2 816	94	-17	2 705	506	439	3 594	3 276	1 016	443
1972	3 999	3 930	69	3 088	105	-20	2 963	546	490	3 864	3 500	1 035	453
1973	4 520	4 368	151	3 476	132	-11	3 334	606	580	4 319	3 876	1 046	470
1974	5 050	4 850	200	3 813	149	-6	3 658	694	698	4 764	4 281	1 060	478
1975	5 386	5 304	82	3 948	157	-19	3 772	728	887	5 019	4 553	1 073	475
1976	6 222	6 056	166	4 649	179	-22	4 447	808	966	5 708	5 159	1 090	498
1977	6 789	6 658	131	5 050	196	-25	4 829	920	1 040	6 142	5 557	1 105	513
1978	7 531	7 440	90	5 613	225	-23	5 366	1 052	1 113	6 751	6 075	1 115	532
1979	8 434	8 357	76	6 218	258	-16	5 943	1 235	1 255	7 497	6 711	1 125	546
1980	9 474	9 428	46	6 815	289	-14	6 512	1 493	1 469	8 408	7 502	1 127	555
1981	10 459	10 341	118	7 359	338	-51	6 970	1 817	1 672	9 231	8 166	1 133	554
1982	11 223	11 119	104	7 792	370	-50	7 372	2 015	1 836	9 873	8 657	1 137	556
1983	12 078	12 007	71	8 415	400	-41	7 974	2 125	1 980	10 551	9 373	1 145	568
1984	13 480	13 364	117	9 376	445	-31	8 900	2 517	2 063	11 665	10 423	1 156	591
1985	14 575	14 473	102	10 232	505	-11	9 717	2 686	2 173	12 533	11 143	1 163	610
1986	15 754	15 662	92	11 093	565	28	10 557	2 930	2 267	13 463	11 895	1 170	635
1987	17 289	17 156	133	12 273	626	47	11 695	3 260	2 335	14 595	12 779	1 185	658
1988	19 036	18 922	114	13 628	722	61	12 967	3 594	2 475	15 813	13 887	1 204	692
1989	20 600	20 472	128	14 616	797	60	13 879	4 053	2 667	16 886	14 827	1 220	708
1990	21 521	21 365	156	15 101	824	59	14 337	4 204	2 981	17 479	15 414	1 231	707
1991	21 820	21 716	104	14 940	846	50	14 145	4 218	3 458	17 662	15 661	1 235	683
1992	22 676	22 506	169	15 581	894	66	14 753	4 102	3 820	18 350	16 347	1 236	686
1993	23 292	23 137	155	15 984	944	103	15 143	4 125	4 024	18 810	16 759	1 238	698
1994	24 174	24 028	145	16 496	1 000	140	15 637	4 347	4 191	19 531	17 323	1 238	709
1995	25 046	24 932	114	16 821	1 051	183	15 954	4 691	4 402	20 240	17 919	1 237	711
1996	26 434	26 289	145	17 586	1 085	209	16 710	5 037	4 687	21 293	18 734	1 241	721
1997	27 774	27 679	95	18 416	1 145	240	17 511	5 360	4 903	22 305	19 435	1 245	735
1998	29 353	29 226	127	19 540	1 201	279	18 618	5 690	5 046	23 529	20 327	1 248	753
1999	30 828	30 679	149	20 807	1 287	301	19 821	5 854	5 153	24 603	21 165	1 253	771
MARYLAND													
1970	18 010	17 866	143	12 704	396	2 503	14 811	2 078	1 121	4 573	3 866	3 938	1 702
1971	19 684	19 566	118	13 754	442	2 755	16 066	2 242	1 376	4 894	4 194	4 023	1 729
1972	21 593	21 438	154	15 115	503	2 991	17 603	2 415	1 575	5 291	4 457	4 081	1 781
1973	23 923	23 690	233	16 830	647	3 192	19 375	2 743	1 805	5 822	4 933	4 109	1 846
1974	26 378	26 190	188	18 386	734	3 466	21 118	3 173	2 087	6 382	5 368	4 133	1 868
1975	28 592	28 364	228	19 538	775	3 851	22 614	3 378	2 601	6 878	5 887	4 157	1 846
1976	31 442	31 244	197	21 562	842	4 166	24 887	3 734	2 820	7 536	6 455	4 172	1 866
1977	34 360	34 213	147	23 487	914	4 574	27 146	4 169	3 045	8 191	6 960	4 195	1 919
1978	38 168	37 964	204	26 127	1 040	4 939	30 026	4 798	3 345	9 062	7 688	4 212	2 003
1979	42 381	42 209	172	28 775	1 216	5 372	32 931	5 668	3 782	10 035	8 467	4 223	2 061
1980	47 475	47 411	64	31 444	1 351	5 945	36 038	6 916	4 521	11 230	9 530	4 228	2 075
1981	52 861	52 720	140	34 546	1 615	6 405	39 337	8 353	5 171	12 403	10 405	4 262	2 102
1982	56 730	56 584	146	36 339	1 742	6 983	41 581	9 381	5 768	13 246	11 167	4 283	2 090
1983	61 372	61 285	87	39 535	1 944	7 358	44 948	10 151	6 273	14 228	12 173	4 313	2 158
1984	68 506	68 236	270	44 271	2 187	8 048	50 132	11 855	6 519	15 693	13 413	4 365	2 253
1985	74 852	74 570	282	48 590	2 551	8 693	54 731	13 207	6 913	16 961	14 573	4 413	2 357
1986	80 612	80 320	291	52 655	2 845	9 315	59 125	14 075	7 411	17 966	15 447	4 487	2 444
1987	87 731	87 435	297	57 800	3 085	10 102	64 817	15 170	7 745	19 216	16 337	4 566	2 572
1988	96 072	95 717	355	63 397	3 572	11 175	71 000	16 840	8 232	20 626	17 767	4 658	2 669
1989	104 005	103 653	352	67 886	3 909	12 033	76 009	19 065	8 931	22 001	18 767	4 727	2 727
1990	110 450	110 114	336	72 024	4 182	12 522	80 364	20 265	9 821	23 023	19 712	4 797	2 761
1991	114 466	114 177	290	73 219	4 354	13 210	82 074	21 309	11 083	23 571	20 304	4 856	2 684
1992	119 417	119 092	326	76 257	4 484	14 051	85 824	21 185	12 409	24 358	21 080	4 903	2 659
1993	124 076	123 767	309	79 204	4 677	14 522	89 049	22 086	12 941	25 104	21 675	4 943	2 683
1994	129 849	129 561	287	82 622	4 977	14 950	92 595	23 545	13 709	26 046	22 408	4 985	2 733
1995	135 115	134 897	219	86 111	5 215	15 013	95 909	24 835	14 371	26 896	23 104	5 024	2 796
1996	140 809	140 442	367	89 354	5 416	15 291	99 228	26 301	15 280	27 844	23 680	5 057	2 837
1997	148 826	148 585	241	94 782	5 738	15 452	104 496	28 406	15 924	29 222	24 661	5 093	2 904
1998	158 264	157 944	320	101 150	6 066	16 594	111 677	30 249	16 338	30 850	25 849	5 130	2 972
1999	167 895	167 531	364	107 700	6 511	18 138	119 327	31 609	16 959	32 465	27 116	5 172	3 047

Table 25-1. Personal Income and Employment—*Continued*

(Millions of dollars, except as noted.)

Year	Total	Nonfarm	Farm	Derivation of personal income						Per capita (dollars)		Population (thousands)	Total employment (thousands)
				Earnings by place of work	Less: Personal contributions for social insurance	Plus: Adjustment for residence	Equals: Net earnings by place of residence	Dividends, interest, and rent	Transfer payments	Total	Disposable		
MASSACHUSETTS													
1970	25 589	25 513	76	19 957	623	-109	19 225	3 824	2 539	4 486	3 866	5 704	2 679
1971	27 244	27 174	70	21 052	679	-111	20 262	3 962	3 020	4 748	4 147	5 739	2 644
1972	29 420	29 350	70	22 826	753	-110	21 963	4 146	3 311	5 106	4 385	5 762	2 697
1973	32 108	32 031	77	24 958	946	-134	23 879	4 540	3 689	5 551	4 804	5 784	2 787
1974	34 802	34 726	76	26 564	1 048	-149	25 366	5 059	4 376	6 024	5 202	5 777	2 811
1975	37 100	37 025	75	27 529	1 063	-154	26 313	5 124	5 663	6 439	5 645	5 762	2 728
1976	40 208	40 125	83	30 118	1 147	-181	28 790	5 530	5 887	6 994	6 101	5 749	2 756
1977	43 863	43 778	85	33 113	1 254	-222	31 637	6 122	6 104	7 636	6 633	5 744	2 833
1978	48 698	48 588	110	37 087	1 424	-285	35 378	6 866	6 454	8 480	7 343	5 743	2 959
1979	54 427	54 333	94	41 410	1 684	-357	39 369	7 931	7 127	9 472	8 134	5 746	3 079
1980	61 329	61 219	110	46 010	1 905	-479	43 626	9 546	8 157	10 673	9 121	5 746	3 142
1981	68 242	68 124	118	50 252	2 283	-598	47 371	11 622	9 249	11 830	10 013	5 769	3 155
1982	73 889	73 756	133	54 043	2 536	-728	50 778	13 096	10 015	12 803	10 935	5 771	3 157
1983	80 376	80 207	170	59 610	2 804	-904	55 901	13 878	10 597	13 859	11 896	5 799	3 230
1984	90 815	90 626	189	67 780	3 224	-1 176	63 381	16 436	10 999	15 549	13 415	5 841	3 422
1985	98 329	98 160	169	74 427	3 719	-1 360	69 348	17 576	11 405	16 720	14 336	5 881	3 533
1986	105 976	105 792	184	80 751	4 133	-1 497	75 121	18 727	12 128	17 954	15 316	5 903	3 630
1987	115 761	115 605	156	88 921	4 555	-1 679	82 687	20 447	12 627	19 504	16 557	5 935	3 661
1988	127 580	127 401	178	98 108	5 133	-1 923	91 053	22 846	13 681	21 334	18 370	5 980	3 771
1989	135 096	134 931	165	101 884	5 442	-2 047	94 396	25 182	15 518	22 458	19 248	6 015	3 744
1990	139 772	139 621	151	103 656	5 568	-2 099	95 988	26 457	17 327	23 223	19 915	6 019	3 647
1991	142 464	142 291	173	103 382	5 709	-2 152	95 520	26 942	20 002	23 749	20 482	5 999	3 480
1992	149 096	148 921	174	109 642	5 965	-2 263	101 414	26 774	20 907	24 876	21 525	5 993	3 512
1993	154 262	154 092	170	114 052	6 258	-2 413	105 381	27 380	21 501	25 664	22 126	6 011	3 579
1994	161 886	161 731	155	119 718	6 684	-2 598	110 437	28 656	22 793	26 841	23 050	6 031	3 651
1995	170 052	169 901	151	125 641	7 148	-2 703	115 789	30 199	24 063	28 051	23 901	6 062	3 686
1996	180 237	180 070	167	133 668	7 522	-2 936	123 209	32 300	24 727	29 618	24 961	6 085	3 752
1997	191 613	191 439	173	141 988	8 099	-3 169	130 720	34 994	25 898	31 332	26 112	6 115	3 845
1998	205 189	205 079	110	153 065	8 644	-3 506	140 915	37 722	26 551	33 394	27 600	6 144	3 948
1999	219 533	219 416	117	165 786	9 420	-3 872	152 493	39 712	27 328	35 551	29 294	6 175	4 018
MICHIGAN													
1970	37 310	36 924	385	30 198	1 020	111	29 290	4 817	3 203	4 194	3 641	8 897	3 558
1971	40 381	40 023	358	32 743	1 136	103	31 710	4 827	3 844	4 501	3 942	8 972	3 571
1972	44 815	44 335	480	36 545	1 299	111	35 356	5 139	4 319	4 966	4 272	9 025	3 687
1973	50 370	49 761	609	41 310	1 700	137	39 747	5 727	4 896	5 552	4 815	9 072	3 858
1974	53 984	53 288	696	43 078	1 841	139	41 376	6 496	6 112	5 926	5 165	9 109	3 854
1975	57 191	56 576	615	43 988	1 852	152	42 288	6 932	7 972	6 279	5 554	9 108	3 695
1976	64 588	64 079	509	50 635	2 112	195	48 718	7 629	8 241	7 084	6 175	9 117	3 844
1977	72 863	72 269	594	57 945	2 396	221	55 770	8 544	8 549	7 957	6 874	9 157	4 016
1978	81 287	80 739	548	65 130	2 745	268	62 652	9 575	9 060	8 834	7 562	9 202	4 188
1979	89 727	89 151	576	71 023	3 132	308	68 199	11 109	10 419	9 701	8 310	9 249	4 234
1980	95 967	95 415	553	71 910	3 183	353	69 080	13 095	13 792	10 369	9 009	9 256	4 039
1981	102 455	101 940	515	75 458	3 671	381	72 168	15 679	14 609	11 125	9 621	9 209	3 992
1982	104 477	104 058	419	74 572	3 714	390	71 248	16 912	16 317	11 462	10 027	9 115	3 837
1983	110 771	110 571	200	78 959	3 977	424	75 406	18 120	17 245	12 243	10 675	9 048	3 881
1984	122 857	122 340	517	88 148	4 480	487	84 155	21 424	17 279	13 576	11 876	9 049	4 059
1985	133 728	133 106	622	96 939	5 185	507	92 261	23 417	18 051	14 734	12 804	9 076	4 257
1986	142 146	141 705	441	103 186	5 667	490	98 009	25 128	19 009	15 573	13 550	9 128	4 373
1987	148 191	147 616	575	107 467	5 937	509	102 039	26 466	19 685	16 130	13 998	9 187	4 511
1988	158 529	158 023	506	115 954	6 646	517	109 825	28 202	20 502	17 198	15 010	9 218	4 612
1989	169 113	168 217	896	122 567	7 200	513	115 880	31 387	21 846	18 276	15 850	9 253	4 744
1990	177 103	176 436	667	127 387	7 498	458	120 347	33 089	23 668	19 022	16 589	9 310	4 826
1991	181 495	180 944	552	128 886	7 805	475	121 556	33 227	26 712	19 318	16 895	9 395	4 755
1992	192 038	191 471	566	138 147	8 225	532	130 454	33 413	28 171	20 278	17 873	9 470	4 787
1993	203 828	203 211	617	147 527	8 735	639	139 431	34 288	30 109	21 390	18 703	9 529	4 850
1994	219 121	218 658	463	159 335	9 614	697	150 418	38 485	30 217	22 862	19 954	9 584	5 027
1995	231 594	230 890	705	169 934	10 226	702	160 410	39 496	31 688	23 975	20 821	9 660	5 188
1996	238 095	237 575	520	172 677	10 629	741	162 789	42 298	33 008	24 447	21 044	9 739	5 298
1997	250 211	249 682	529	179 934	11 226	794	169 502	45 142	35 567	25 570	21 920	9 785	5 385
1998	263 252	262 768	484	190 184	11 765	904	179 323	48 971	34 957	26 807	22 803	9 820	5 459
1999	277 296	276 567	729	200 874	12 479	944	189 338	50 792	37 166	28 113	23 836	9 864	5 573

Table 25-1. Personal Income and Employment—*Continued*

(Millions of dollars, except as noted.)

Year	Total	Nonfarm	Farm	Earnings by place of work	Less: Personal contributions for social insurance	Plus: Adjustment for residence	Equals: Net earnings by place of residence	Dividends, interest, and rent	Transfer payments	Per capita Total	Per capita Disposable	Population (thousands)	Total employment (thousands)
MINNESOTA													
1970	15 463	14 544	919	12 427	420	-28	11 979	2 118	1 366	4 053	3 557	3 815	1 699
1971	16 467	15 626	841	13 104	461	-28	12 615	2 257	1 595	4 275	3 790	3 852	1 706
1972	17 898	16 887	1 010	14 289	517	-30	13 742	2 393	1 762	4 628	4 038	3 867	1 780
1973	21 099	18 882	2 218	16 995	662	-37	16 296	2 752	2 051	5 431	4 807	3 885	1 878
1974	22 757	21 073	1 684	17 972	761	-33	17 179	3 174	2 405	5 838	5 065	3 898	1 921
1975	24 404	23 102	1 302	18 919	806	-33	18 080	3 445	2 879	6 216	5 429	3 926	1 920
1976	26 623	25 807	816	20 578	896	-42	19 640	3 804	3 179	6 729	5 841	3 957	1 977
1977	30 085	28 550	1 535	23 406	977	-54	22 375	4 327	3 382	7 559	6 552	3 980	2 034
1978	33 924	32 271	1 653	26 574	1 141	-69	25 364	4 942	3 618	8 471	7 311	4 005	2 123
1979	37 996	36 721	1 276	29 589	1 358	-87	28 144	5 819	4 034	9 409	8 050	4 038	2 222
1980	42 157	41 236	921	31 830	1 497	-90	30 242	7 062	4 853	10 320	8 867	4 085	2 254
1981	46 546	45 568	978	34 293	1 753	-130	32 411	8 581	5 554	11 320	9 685	4 112	2 241
1982	49 546	48 750	796	35 550	1 877	-153	33 520	9 780	6 247	11 992	10 309	4 131	2 201
1983	52 158	52 090	68	37 185	2 010	-182	34 992	10 435	6 731	12 594	10 866	4 141	2 228
1984	59 267	57 904	1 363	43 055	2 269	-237	40 550	11 718	6 999	14 255	12 431	4 158	2 336
1985	63 152	61 924	1 228	46 020	2 558	-286	43 176	12 444	7 532	15 093	13 168	4 184	2 399
1986	66 784	65 264	1 520	48 815	2 774	-327	45 713	13 169	7 902	15 881	13 899	4 205	2 432
1987	71 570	69 588	1 982	52 882	3 002	-379	49 501	13 837	8 232	16 899	14 671	4 235	2 526
1988	75 578	74 437	1 141	56 093	3 394	-460	52 239	14 638	8 702	17 592	15 308	4 296	2 599
1989	82 277	80 306	1 971	60 566	3 700	-444	56 422	16 535	9 321	18 966	16 459	4 338	2 654
1990	87 795	85 928	1 867	64 363	3 954	-476	59 933	17 764	10 099	20 011	17 328	4 387	2 712
1991	90 714	89 643	1 071	66 220	4 212	-484	61 524	18 219	10 971	20 489	17 809	4 427	2 737
1992	97 025	95 867	1 158	71 956	4 511	-519	66 927	18 099	11 999	21 698	18 808	4 472	2 783
1993	99 787	99 716	72	73 757	4 746	-523	68 488	18 559	12 740	22 068	19 033	4 522	2 840
1994	107 152	105 988	1 163	79 052	5 118	-564	73 369	20 417	13 365	23 467	20 241	4 566	2 930
1995	113 217	112 607	610	82 439	5 413	-603	76 423	22 676	14 118	24 583	21 107	4 605	3 022
1996	122 080	120 228	1 852	89 159	5 736	-681	82 742	24 689	14 648	26 267	22 288	4 648	3 086
1997	129 136	128 272	864	93 598	6 096	-774	86 728	27 401	15 007	27 548	23 316	4 688	3 141
1998	139 442	138 162	1 280	101 633	6 516	-888	94 229	29 806	15 406	29 503	24 847	4 726	3 224
1999	147 050	145 969	1 081	107 991	6 973	-952	100 066	31 033	15 951	30 793	26 113	4 776	3 298
MISSISSIPPI													
1970	5 866	5 448	417	4 714	157	36	4 594	586	686	2 641	2 385	2 221	917
1971	6 495	6 040	455	5 155	175	58	5 038	642	816	2 867	2 631	2 266	939
1972	7 403	6 886	516	5 918	208	73	5 784	700	919	3 208	2 900	2 307	979
1973	8 489	7 779	711	6 779	264	94	6 608	822	1 059	3 613	3 287	2 350	1 019
1974	9 362	8 830	532	7 261	303	123	7 081	978	1 302	3 936	3 544	2 379	1 031
1975	10 093	9 706	387	7 595	322	150	7 422	1 066	1 604	4 205	3 846	2 400	1 001
1976	11 562	10 980	582	8 807	363	182	8 627	1 174	1 761	4 757	4 315	2 430	1 039
1977	12 937	12 322	615	9 884	403	223	9 704	1 325	1 908	5 259	4 785	2 460	1 071
1978	14 445	13 985	459	10 972	461	279	10 790	1 562	2 093	5 806	5 226	2 488	1 102
1979	16 425	15 707	719	12 383	535	337	12 186	1 858	2 382	6 549	5 877	2 508	1 117
1980	17 868	17 660	209	12 808	584	426	12 649	2 357	2 862	7 076	6 347	2 525	1 114
1981	20 061	19 703	358	14 109	692	456	13 873	2 951	3 236	7 901	7 034	2 539	1 110
1982	21 223	20 803	420	14 525	740	475	14 259	3 399	3 566	8 301	7 524	2 557	1 082
1983	22 120	22 031	90	14 894	780	531	14 645	3 554	3 921	8 615	7 772	2 568	1 091
1984	24 397	23 927	470	16 616	852	595	16 359	4 034	4 003	9 463	8 589	2 578	1 121
1985	25 679	25 248	431	17 551	947	625	17 229	4 191	4 259	9 922	8 998	2 588	1 129
1986	26 695	26 515	180	18 016	1 022	611	17 605	4 565	4 525	10 293	9 376	2 594	1 136
1987	28 249	27 718	531	19 217	1 076	650	18 791	4 723	4 735	10 913	9 906	2 589	1 147
1988	30 177	29 517	660	20 588	1 214	690	20 064	5 086	5 026	11 695	10 657	2 580	1 176
1989	32 281	31 780	501	21 652	1 330	733	21 054	5 762	5 464	12 540	11 364	2 574	1 196
1990	33 928	33 599	329	22 750	1 397	757	22 109	5 856	5 963	13 164	11 927	2 577	1 210
1991	35 775	35 323	452	23 900	1 494	787	23 193	5 965	6 618	13 806	12 554	2 591	1 218
1992	38 398	37 865	533	25 778	1 586	806	24 999	6 011	7 388	14 711	13 388	2 610	1 242
1993	40 768	40 304	464	27 622	1 717	830	26 735	6 178	7 855	15 468	14 028	2 636	1 297
1994	44 077	43 381	697	30 065	1 897	863	29 031	6 714	8 332	16 549	14 953	2 663	1 347
1995	46 242	45 669	573	31 167	2 012	939	30 094	7 062	9 086	17 185	15 497	2 691	1 379
1996	48 898	47 973	925	32 752	2 076	987	31 663	7 538	9 696	18 044	16 215	2 710	1 404
1997	51 589	50 748	842	34 371	2 186	1 106	33 290	8 148	10 151	18 885	16 925	2 732	1 432
1998	55 063	54 209	854	36 688	2 308	1 255	35 635	9 053	10 375	20 013	17 900	2 751	1 465
1999	57 278	56 412	866	38 237	2 422	1 321	37 135	9 512	10 630	20 688	18 467	2 769	1 493

Table 25-1. Personal Income and Employment—Continued

(Millions of dollars, except as noted.)

Year	Total	Nonfarm	Farm	Derivation of personal income						Per capita (dollars)		Population (thousands)	Total employment (thousands)
				Earnings by place of work	Less: Personal contributions for social insurance	Plus: Adjustment for residence	Equals: Net earnings by place of residence	Dividends, interest, and rent	Transfer payments	Total	Disposable		
MISSOURI													
1970	18 003	17 456	547	15 062	515	-701	13 846	2 474	1 684	3 843	3 364	4 685	2 203
1971	19 396	18 806	590	16 066	567	-682	14 817	2 627	1 952	4 107	3 629	4 723	2 200
1972	21 120	20 376	745	17 519	632	-702	16 185	2 824	2 111	4 443	3 877	4 753	2 242
1973	23 574	22 331	1 242	19 505	794	-734	17 977	3 165	2 432	4 937	4 358	4 775	2 325
1974	25 277	24 609	668	20 411	886	-760	18 766	3 642	2 869	5 282	4 626	4 785	2 341
1975	27 494	26 777	717	21 685	925	-769	19 991	3 904	3 599	5 733	5 090	4 795	2 291
1976	30 416	29 933	483	24 132	1 021	-846	22 265	4 295	3 856	6 306	5 556	4 824	2 365
1977	33 874	33 153	721	27 040	1 120	-986	24 933	4 869	4 071	6 991	6 162	4 845	2 424
1978	37 933	36 996	937	30 338	1 290	-1 139	27 909	5 612	4 411	7 787	6 818	4 871	2 513
1979	42 601	41 394	1 208	33 794	1 487	-1 302	31 005	6 621	4 976	8 713	7 598	4 889	2 580
1980	46 217	45 979	238	35 187	1 606	-1 516	32 064	8 086	6 067	9 390	8 195	4 922	2 554
1981	51 576	50 751	825	38 403	1 872	-1 661	34 869	9 895	6 812	10 457	9 082	4 932	2 549
1982	54 396	54 078	318	39 615	2 011	-1 728	35 875	11 081	7 439	11 035	9 515	4 929	2 525
1983	57 919	58 058	-138	42 105	2 152	-1 757	38 197	11 748	7 975	11 716	10 321	4 944	2 571
1984	64 479	64 125	354	47 164	2 397	-1 884	42 883	13 385	8 212	12 960	11 479	4 975	2 679
1985	69 342	68 641	701	50 941	2 702	-2 002	46 237	14 212	8 893	13 868	12 240	5 000	2 753
1986	72 859	72 401	457	53 526	2 931	-2 050	48 545	14 903	9 411	14 505	12 814	5 023	2 817
1987	77 115	76 472	643	57 059	3 124	-2 180	51 755	15 597	9 762	15 250	13 440	5 057	2 855
1988	81 744	81 171	573	60 653	3 463	-2 263	54 927	16 533	10 284	16 086	14 221	5 082	2 905
1989	87 050	86 215	835	63 872	3 753	-2 397	57 722	18 260	11 068	17 083	15 026	5 096	2 960
1990	91 000	90 420	579	66 331	3 937	-2 637	59 756	19 325	11 919	17 751	15 611	5 126	2 994
1991	95 730	95 270	460	68 084	4 130	-2 623	61 331	20 308	14 091	18 560	16 432	5 158	2 963
1992	101 493	100 839	655	72 577	4 334	-2 697	65 545	20 998	14 950	19 542	17 343	5 194	2 980
1993	106 298	105 925	373	75 875	4 555	-2 781	68 539	21 593	16 166	20 295	17 996	5 238	3 066
1994	112 314	111 746	568	80 497	4 915	-2 795	72 787	22 828	16 699	21 267	18 781	5 281	3 142
1995	117 640	117 475	165	84 421	5 236	-2 893	76 292	23 471	17 877	22 094	19 431	5 325	3 227
1996	123 992	123 065	926	89 105	5 445	-3 070	80 590	24 671	18 730	23 099	20 187	5 368	3 288
1997	131 131	130 146	985	94 275	5 766	-3 225	85 284	26 099	19 747	24 252	21 081	5 407	3 363
1998	138 128	137 653	476	98 941	6 017	-3 554	89 370	28 526	20 232	25 403	21 974	5 438	3 421
1999	144 235	144 100	136	103 762	6 362	-3 692	93 708	29 562	20 965	26 376	22 745	5 468	3 478
MONTANA													
1970	2 527	2 228	299	1 960	67	-1	1 892	395	240	3 625	3 221	697	301
1971	2 694	2 434	260	2 071	72	-1	1 998	415	281	3 789	3 410	711	307
1972	3 132	2 716	416	2 451	84	0	2 367	455	310	4 355	3 874	719	319
1973	3 646	3 059	587	2 854	108	0	2 746	542	358	5 012	4 444	727	333
1974	3 966	3 491	475	3 035	123	1	2 914	633	420	5 380	4 755	737	344
1975	4 341	3 933	408	3 268	132	2	3 138	697	506	5 794	5 166	749	344
1976	4 703	4 473	230	3 499	145	3	3 357	783	563	6 200	5 485	759	359
1977	5 119	5 049	70	3 755	165	4	3 595	909	615	6 636	5 833	771	372
1978	6 053	5 742	312	4 507	194	3	4 317	1 063	673	7 721	6 837	784	390
1979	6 549	6 435	115	4 734	222	6	4 518	1 275	756	8 299	7 248	789	397
1980	7 211	7 095	116	5 036	242	14	4 808	1 512	892	9 143	8 009	789	394
1981	8 147	7 943	204	5 535	284	26	5 277	1 840	1 030	10 244	8 999	795	396
1982	8 580	8 418	162	5 629	300	18	5 346	2 077	1 157	10 672	9 473	804	392
1983	8 991	8 876	115	5 879	312	10	5 577	2 149	1 265	11 045	9 842	814	400
1984	9 609	9 565	44	6 204	332	6	5 878	2 397	1 334	11 705	10 478	821	410
1985	9 785	9 857	-72	6 258	358	4	5 904	2 482	1 399	11 900	10 657	822	409
1986	10 143	9 905	238	6 516	369	-1	6 146	2 496	1 501	12 465	11 269	814	404
1987	10 463	10 189	274	6 743	380	-3	6 361	2 521	1 581	12 996	11 652	805	409
1988	10 693	10 609	83	6 866	430	-1	6 435	2 596	1 662	13 362	11 916	800	419
1989	11 693	11 293	400	7 523	467	-2	7 054	2 843	1 796	14 623	12 946	800	427
1990	12 416	12 049	367	7 939	499	-4	7 435	2 983	1 998	15 524	13 785	800	437
1991	13 337	12 797	540	8 684	547	-14	8 123	3 090	2 124	16 509	14 733	808	447
1992	14 076	13 649	426	9 233	597	-6	8 631	3 128	2 317	17 114	15 253	822	459
1993	15 178	14 411	767	10 189	641	-5	9 543	3 147	2 488	18 072	16 124	840	474
1994	15 499	15 149	350	10 269	684	-1	9 584	3 334	2 581	18 129	16 082	855	499
1995	16 297	15 938	359	10 600	717	1	9 885	3 628	2 784	18 764	16 686	869	508
1996	16 992	16 714	279	10 984	748	3	10 240	3 857	2 895	19 383	17 153	877	524
1997	17 721	17 515	206	11 339	776	-7	10 556	4 229	2 936	20 167	17 771	879	531
1998	18 755	18 494	261	12 027	808	-4	11 215	4 488	3 052	21 324	18 749	880	544
1999	19 438	19 074	364	12 652	849	-3	11 801	4 616	3 021	22 019	19 303	883	552

Table 25-1. Personal Income and Employment—*Continued*

(Millions of dollars, except as noted.)

Year	Total	Nonfarm	Farm	Derivation of personal income						Per capita (dollars)		Population (thousands)	Total employment (thousands)
				Earnings by place of work	Less: Personal contributions for social insurance	Plus: Adjustment for residence	Equals: Net earnings by place of residence	Dividends, interest, and rent	Transfer payments	Total	Disposable		
NEBRASKA													
1970	5 648	5 109	540	4 535	163	-106	4 267	886	495	3 796	3 358	1 488	715
1971	6 200	5 512	688	4 986	178	-109	4 699	938	563	4 121	3 712	1 504	728
1972	6 873	6 059	814	5 530	198	-118	5 214	1 040	619	4 527	4 001	1 518	748
1973	8 054	6 825	1 229	6 486	255	-121	6 110	1 208	735	5 269	4 674	1 529	775
1974	8 404	7 634	770	6 611	292	-130	6 189	1 376	840	5 465	4 787	1 538	793
1975	9 507	8 395	1 112	7 441	311	-137	6 992	1 496	1 018	6 168	5 508	1 541	790
1976	9 996	9 404	592	7 770	342	-145	7 283	1 622	1 091	6 453	5 740	1 549	811
1977	10 870	10 337	533	8 353	367	-143	7 843	1 850	1 177	6 993	6 140	1 554	831
1978	12 674	11 566	1 108	9 859	423	-166	9 269	2 104	1 301	8 120	7 178	1 561	855
1979	13 742	12 985	756	10 529	495	-195	9 839	2 459	1 444	8 784	7 668	1 564	877
1980	14 578	14 482	96	10 689	542	-211	9 936	2 951	1 691	9 272	8 099	1 572	879
1981	16 866	16 016	851	12 207	625	-251	11 332	3 592	1 942	10 685	9 410	1 579	874
1982	17 761	17 034	727	12 512	670	-258	11 584	4 033	2 143	11 228	9 709	1 582	864
1983	18 379	17 910	470	12 831	698	-272	11 861	4 205	2 313	11 601	10 299	1 584	870
1984	20 601	19 505	1 095	14 720	773	-322	13 625	4 584	2 392	12 968	11 662	1 589	889
1985	21 778	20 385	1 393	15 754	861	-347	14 546	4 696	2 537	13 743	12 356	1 585	902
1986	22 379	21 029	1 350	16 167	915	-345	14 907	4 798	2 674	14 215	12 776	1 574	902
1987	23 553	21 911	1 642	17 241	983	-342	15 916	4 872	2 765	15 035	13 473	1 567	930
1988	25 119	23 161	1 958	18 527	1 098	-374	17 055	5 168	2 896	15 984	14 314	1 571	953
1989	26 581	24 806	1 776	19 316	1 186	-383	17 747	5 742	3 092	16 878	15 011	1 575	971
1990	28 591	26 438	2 154	20 855	1 264	-382	19 210	6 039	3 342	18 088	16 071	1 581	995
1991	29 853	27 872	1 982	21 589	1 337	-400	19 851	6 383	3 618	18 766	16 716	1 591	999
1992	31 548	29 484	2 064	22 972	1 396	-436	21 139	6 462	3 947	19 688	17 557	1 602	1 006
1993	32 513	30 832	1 681	23 644	1 472	-444	21 728	6 535	4 249	20 167	17 951	1 612	1 029
1994	34 325	32 664	1 662	25 035	1 580	-457	22 998	6 917	4 411	21 168	18 799	1 622	1 070
1995	36 293	35 024	1 270	26 163	1 646	-484	24 033	7 576	4 684	22 196	19 584	1 635	1 081
1996	39 618	37 097	2 521	28 900	1 726	-518	26 657	7 988	4 973	24 045	21 201	1 648	1 107
1997	40 722	39 056	1 666	29 528	1 824	-565	27 139	8 397	5 186	24 590	21 455	1 656	1 122
1998	42 949	41 393	1 557	31 125	1 916	-594	28 615	8 863	5 472	25 861	22 432	1 661	1 149
1999	45 065	43 584	1 480	32 816	2 039	-630	30 147	9 240	5 678	27 049	23 370	1 666	1 170
NEVADA													
1970	2 440	2 403	37	2 052	60	-39	1 953	339	147	4 946	4 360	493	256
1971	2 718	2 680	38	2 263	68	-41	2 154	379	185	5 227	4 660	520	267
1972	3 038	2 993	46	2 520	79	-45	2 397	423	219	5 557	4 924	547	280
1973	3 478	3 419	59	2 891	105	-54	2 731	495	252	6 114	5 425	569	304
1974	3 873	3 836	37	3 153	119	-57	2 977	582	313	6 490	5 735	597	317
1975	4 345	4 310	35	3 483	129	-58	3 296	618	431	7 009	6 353	620	326
1976	4 993	4 955	38	4 011	147	-67	3 796	712	484	7 719	6 893	647	349
1977	5 798	5 769	29	4 703	175	-83	4 446	817	535	8 550	7 588	678	384
1978	7 035	7 012	24	5 742	217	-116	5 408	1 024	603	9 780	8 595	719	432
1979	8 237	8 226	11	6 634	270	-131	6 234	1 295	708	10 765	9 389	765	468
1980	9 544	9 485	60	7 587	313	-158	7 116	1 566	862	11 780	10 348	810	490
1981	10 833	10 807	26	8 430	382	-167	7 881	1 901	1 050	12 780	11 187	848	502
1982	11 448	11 408	40	8 733	401	-168	8 165	2 112	1 171	12 986	11 449	882	497
1983	12 145	12 114	31	9 197	428	-176	8 594	2 274	1 278	13 465	11 959	902	502
1984	13 351	13 310	41	10 064	475	-188	9 402	2 598	1 352	14 435	12 848	925	528
1985	14 581	14 546	35	10 911	541	-196	10 174	2 907	1 501	15 332	13 573	951	551
1986	15 716	15 684	32	11 739	602	-214	10 923	3 111	1 682	16 027	14 141	981	577
1987	17 281	17 236	44	12 995	673	-239	12 083	3 387	1 810	16 886	14 833	1 023	623
1988	19 544	19 483	62	14 827	791	-278	13 758	3 803	1 984	18 180	15 905	1 075	670
1989	22 256	22 179	77	16 675	910	-325	15 440	4 538	2 278	19 568	17 144	1 137	720
1990	25 194	25 114	80	18 852	1 023	-384	17 445	5 127	2 622	20 674	18 112	1 219	767
1991	27 349	27 276	73	19 895	1 094	-391	18 410	5 692	3 248	21 283	18 797	1 285	780
1992	30 199	30 146	53	21 868	1 173	-412	20 283	6 195	3 722	22 694	19 989	1 331	788
1993	32 386	32 291	94	23 655	1 285	-465	21 905	6 534	3 947	23 465	20 563	1 380	831
1994	35 878	35 812	65	26 160	1 451	-513	24 196	7 568	4 114	24 635	21 670	1 456	913
1995	39 377	39 325	52	28 742	1 617	-561	26 563	8 374	4 440	25 808	22 692	1 526	968
1996	43 331	43 282	49	31 671	1 779	-631	29 261	9 318	4 752	27 142	23 573	1 596	1 041
1997	47 254	47 206	48	34 298	1 906	-632	31 759	10 441	5 054	28 201	24 542	1 676	1 108
1998	51 976	51 902	74	37 401	2 051	-681	34 669	11 948	5 358	29 806	25 726	1 744	1 151
1999	56 127	56 061	67	40 897	2 251	-751	37 895	12 627	5 606	31 022	26 685	1 809	1 212

Table 25-1. Personal Income and Employment—*Continued*

(Millions of dollars, except as noted.)

Year	Total	Nonfarm	Farm	Derivation of personal income						Per capita (dollars)		Population (thousands)	Total employment (thousands)
				Earnings by place of work	Less: Personal contributions for social insurance	Plus: Adjustment for residence	Equals: Net earnings by place of residence	Dividends, interest, and rent	Transfer payments	Total	Disposable		
NEW HAMPSHIRE													
1970	2 890	2 871	19	2 067	70	220	2 217	433	240	3 896	3 424	742	334
1971	3 126	3 109	18	2 212	78	230	2 364	470	293	4 102	3 670	762	336
1972	3 457	3 438	20	2 459	90	252	2 621	514	322	4 423	3 893	782	350
1973	3 913	3 889	24	2 793	116	283	2 960	575	378	4 880	4 350	802	374
1974	4 313	4 297	16	3 012	132	329	3 209	653	452	5 279	4 685	817	381
1975	4 642	4 622	19	3 158	137	359	3 379	686	576	5 592	5 030	830	370
1976	5 301	5 280	21	3 656	154	410	3 911	772	618	6 258	5 584	847	394
1977	6 009	5 989	20	4 153	176	480	4 457	891	661	6 892	6 118	872	418
1978	6 960	6 939	21	4 845	205	572	5 212	1 026	722	7 786	6 852	894	446
1979	8 007	7 984	23	5 538	248	680	5 970	1 214	823	8 781	7 727	912	469
1980	9 164	9 150	14	6 136	280	849	6 705	1 492	968	9 915	8 757	924	483
1981	10 377	10 353	24	6 760	337	958	7 381	1 841	1 155	11 079	9 753	937	494
1982	11 284	11 266	18	7 287	376	1 048	7 959	2 063	1 261	11 906	10 583	948	500
1983	12 495	12 480	15	8 169	422	1 173	8 920	2 234	1 342	13 041	11 596	958	520
1984	14 198	14 177	21	9 237	480	1 387	10 145	2 658	1 396	14 534	12 969	977	556
1985	15 767	15 742	25	10 430	570	1 510	11 370	2 938	1 459	15 819	13 999	997	590
1986	17 399	17 373	26	11 669	651	1 594	12 611	3 243	1 544	16 974	14 916	1 025	622
1987	19 369	19 325	44	13 208	738	1 721	14 191	3 587	1 591	18 371	16 144	1 054	640
1988	21 390	21 343	48	14 589	841	1 882	15 630	4 032	1 729	19 759	17 493	1 083	665
1989	22 792	22 744	48	15 208	889	1 974	16 293	4 585	1 914	20 635	18 279	1 105	665
1990	23 029	22 987	42	15 115	899	2 013	16 228	4 642	2 159	20 713	18 450	1 112	648
1991	23 609	23 566	43	14 961	920	2 055	16 096	4 627	2 885	21 326	19 106	1 107	621
1992	24 652	24 596	56	16 010	978	2 123	17 155	4 411	3 086	22 154	19 863	1 113	634
1993	25 273	25 233	40	16 682	1 021	2 181	17 841	4 449	2 982	22 521	20 078	1 122	647
1994	26 990	26 949	40	17 663	1 106	2 262	18 819	4 762	3 410	23 820	21 260	1 133	672
1995	28 650	28 618	32	18 650	1 188	2 297	19 758	5 235	3 656	25 008	22 250	1 146	686
1996	30 228	30 192	36	19 838	1 248	2 446	21 036	5 606	3 587	26 042	22 924	1 161	703
1997	32 389	32 353	36	21 358	1 343	2 630	22 645	6 002	3 743	27 607	24 030	1 173	724
1998	35 194	35 156	38	23 213	1 441	2 868	24 639	6 685	3 869	29 679	25 778	1 186	746
1999	37 372	37 329	43	24 721	1 543	3 109	26 288	7 107	3 977	31 114	26 973	1 201	765
NEW JERSEY													
1970	34 763	34 649	114	25 154	895	3 056	27 315	4 771	2 677	4 835	4 233	7 190	3 125
1971	37 335	37 228	107	26 793	991	3 139	28 940	5 114	3 281	5 127	4 549	7 282	3 119
1972	40 507	40 404	103	29 132	1 104	3 335	31 364	5 479	3 665	5 521	4 828	7 337	3 184
1973	44 327	44 188	139	32 020	1 379	3 489	34 130	6 089	4 108	6 043	5 331	7 335	3 288
1974	48 236	48 084	152	34 450	1 537	3 678	36 592	6 829	4 815	6 576	5 779	7 335	3 301
1975	51 658	51 546	112	35 924	1 599	3 960	38 284	7 120	6 254	7 037	6 269	7 341	3 191
1976	56 572	56 455	118	39 500	1 715	4 303	42 088	7 700	6 784	7 703	6 797	7 344	3 248
1977	62 004	62 004	126	43 504	1 881	4 695	46 318	8 584	7 228	8 462	7 386	7 342	3 325
1978	69 206	69 063	143	48 695	2 163	5 273	51 805	9 732	7 669	9 408	8 193	7 356	3 464
1979	77 188	77 053	134	53 850	2 511	6 019	57 357	11 323	8 508	10 469	9 030	7 373	3 555
1980	86 877	86 753	125	59 123	2 806	7 111	63 428	13 698	9 751	11 778	10 137	7 376	3 608
1981	96 717	96 559	158	64 451	3 297	7 747	68 901	16 891	10 924	13 057	11 198	7 407	3 643
1982	104 023	103 853	171	68 896	3 610	8 281	73 566	18 449	12 008	13 999	12 004	7 431	3 651
1983	112 284	112 082	202	75 020	3 978	8 515	79 556	19 793	12 935	15 036	13 036	7 468	3 752
1984	124 377	124 176	201	83 243	4 507	8 900	87 636	23 420	13 321	16 549	14 414	7 515	3 933
1985	133 549	133 317	232	90 530	5 112	9 260	94 678	24 940	13 932	17 652	15 227	7 566	4 049
1986	142 617	142 382	235	97 739	5 729	9 838	101 847	26 084	14 686	18 711	16 105	7 622	4 146
1987	155 179	154 916	263	107 638	6 380	10 384	111 641	28 234	15 304	20 230	17 272	7 671	4 249
1988	170 764	170 506	257	119 472	7 262	10 658	122 868	31 570	16 326	22 142	19 129	7 712	4 349
1989	182 298	182 047	250	125 672	7 749	10 192	128 115	36 521	17 661	23 595	20 391	7 726	4 388
1990	192 117	191 892	226	132 044	8 106	10 515	134 453	38 211	19 453	24 766	21 503	7 757	4 346
1991	195 796	195 579	216	133 440	8 486	10 328	135 283	38 159	22 353	25 153	21 870	7 784	4 206
1992	208 197	207 983	214	142 158	8 944	11 632	144 847	37 714	25 637	26 597	23 163	7 828	4 205
1993	213 419	213 172	247	147 545	9 128	11 557	149 973	36 673	26 773	27 101	23 489	7 875	4 233
1994	220 817	220 554	263	153 208	9 689	11 424	154 943	38 561	27 314	27 885	24 104	7 919	4 272
1995	233 209	232 941	268	160 833	10 188	12 103	162 748	41 463	28 997	29 277	25 255	7 966	4 339
1996	246 659	246 377	282	169 602	10 590	13 116	172 128	44 525	30 005	30 795	26 385	8 010	4 397
1997	260 727	260 482	245	178 234	11 093	15 008	182 149	47 637	30 940	32 372	27 437	8 054	4 461
1998	277 757	277 490	267	190 301	11 858	16 945	195 388	51 144	31 224	34 310	28 786	8 096	4 581
1999	289 503	289 231	272	199 972	12 488	18 627	206 111	51 540	31 852	35 551	29 683	8 143	4 652

Table 25-1. Personal Income and Employment—*Continued*

(Millions of dollars, except as noted.)

Year	Total	Nonfarm	Farm	Earnings by place of work	Less: Personal contributions for social insurance	Plus: Adjustment for residence	Equals: Net earnings by place of residence	Dividends, interest, and rent	Transfer payments	Per capita Total	Per capita Disposable	Population (thousands)	Total employment (thousands)
NEW MEXICO													
1970	3 271	3 130	142	2 646	80	-22	2 544	404	324	3 197	2 850	1 023	399
1971	3 613	3 471	142	2 900	92	-22	2 786	448	379	3 431	3 110	1 053	416
1972	4 054	3 904	150	3 259	106	-20	3 133	498	423	3 761	3 381	1 078	440
1973	4 568	4 376	193	3 656	137	-17	3 502	569	497	4 137	3 722	1 104	461
1974	5 160	4 999	161	4 071	159	-16	3 897	668	596	4 568	4 091	1 130	478
1975	5 866	5 675	191	4 597	176	-13	4 408	733	725	5 045	4 597	1 163	491
1976	6 606	6 471	135	5 175	197	-13	4 965	824	817	5 527	4 991	1 195	512
1977	7 459	7 311	147	5 881	226	-11	5 644	943	872	6 087	5 494	1 225	539
1978	8 571	8 389	182	6 761	265	-11	6 486	1 132	954	6 847	6 121	1 252	568
1979	9 756	9 538	218	7 618	314	-10	7 294	1 365	1 096	7 619	6 805	1 281	593
1980	11 002	10 811	190	8 367	353	-4	8 011	1 683	1 308	8 402	7 520	1 309	598
1981	12 440	12 315	126	9 297	429	-12	8 857	2 090	1 494	9 334	8 253	1 333	613
1982	13 493	13 372	122	9 899	468	-15	9 416	2 434	1 643	9 894	8 716	1 364	621
1983	14 455	14 326	130	10 512	496	-11	10 004	2 661	1 790	10 367	9 346	1 394	633
1984	15 889	15 739	149	11 565	546	-4	11 015	2 991	1 882	11 215	10 151	1 417	658
1985	17 259	17 045	214	12 496	616	3	11 883	3 340	2 036	11 999	10 827	1 438	678
1986	17 883	17 686	197	12 787	652	10	12 145	3 541	2 197	12 226	11 083	1 463	684
1987	18 756	18 525	231	13 356	681	24	12 699	3 723	2 334	12 686	11 382	1 479	703
1988	19 854	19 540	314	14 147	761	35	13 420	3 945	2 489	13 322	11 959	1 490	739
1989	21 183	20 804	378	14 942	827	42	14 156	4 304	2 722	14 085	12 585	1 504	755
1990	22 739	22 325	413	16 008	884	48	15 172	4 579	2 988	14 960	13 396	1 520	767
1991	24 358	23 944	413	17 099	968	51	16 181	4 822	3 355	15 744	14 126	1 547	790
1992	25 964	25 496	468	18 334	1 022	55	17 368	4 841	3 755	16 425	14 723	1 581	803
1993	27 819	27 286	533	19 792	1 109	61	18 744	5 005	4 069	17 226	15 380	1 615	832
1994	29 670	29 213	457	20 955	1 211	72	19 816	5 464	4 390	17 946	15 983	1 653	865
1995	31 716	31 333	383	22 146	1 311	74	20 909	5 936	4 870	18 852	16 815	1 682	907
1996	33 232	32 846	386	22 809	1 349	82	21 541	6 426	5 264	19 478	17 291	1 706	918
1997	34 861	34 338	523	23 934	1 405	88	22 617	6 827	5 416	20 233	17 853	1 723	933
1998	36 712	36 103	609	25 273	1 469	93	23 897	7 170	5 645	21 178	18 663	1 734	948
1999	38 020	37 327	693	26 164	1 532	116	24 748	7 380	5 892	21 853	19 229	1 740	958
NEW YORK													
1970	89 292	88 834	458	72 372	2 599	-3 308	66 465	13 951	8 876	4 887	4 188	18 272	8 468
1971	95 115	94 665	449	76 318	2 825	-3 416	70 077	14 287	10 752	5 179	4 500	18 365	8 348
1972	101 636	101 237	399	81 551	3 107	-3 672	74 772	14 871	11 993	5 538	4 757	18 352	8 350
1973	108 803	108 294	508	87 114	3 843	-3 892	79 379	16 209	13 215	5 980	5 164	18 195	8 468
1974	117 323	116 839	484	92 307	4 238	-4 118	83 951	18 035	15 337	6 492	5 586	18 073	8 395
1975	125 420	125 009	410	96 585	4 399	-4 467	87 718	18 398	19 304	6 955	6 068	18 032	8 175
1976	134 395	133 969	426	103 472	4 637	-4 913	93 923	19 842	20 631	7 477	6 499	17 975	8 128
1977	145 544	145 195	349	112 044	4 958	-5 468	101 618	22 162	21 764	8 153	7 063	17 852	8 202
1978	159 114	158 663	451	123 050	5 506	-6 120	111 424	24 948	22 742	8 979	7 750	17 720	8 381
1979	175 040	174 490	550	135 126	6 321	-6 972	121 833	28 965	24 242	9 927	8 514	17 634	8 591
1980	194 906	194 372	534	148 641	6 983	-8 186	133 472	33 508	27 926	11 095	9 480	17 567	8 622
1981	217 203	216 659	544	162 990	8 295	-8 947	145 748	40 024	31 430	12 364	10 459	17 568	8 700
1982	234 717	234 201	516	175 264	9 074	-9 815	156 375	43 898	34 444	13 344	11 252	17 590	8 710
1983	250 945	250 588	357	186 818	9 736	-10 286	166 796	46 892	37 257	14 188	12 154	17 687	8 772
1984	279 294	278 840	454	206 812	10 774	-10 937	185 101	55 149	39 044	15 739	13 531	17 746	9 058
1985	297 729	297 215	513	222 806	12 253	-11 573	198 979	57 863	40 886	16 734	14 278	17 792	9 293
1986	317 914	317 295	619	239 999	13 482	-12 467	214 050	60 372	43 492	17 827	15 191	17 833	9 495
1987	340 068	339 380	688	259 231	14 497	-13 287	231 446	63 852	44 770	19 031	16 060	17 869	9 553
1988	369 668	369 086	582	281 706	16 384	-14 012	251 310	70 792	47 566	20 604	17 583	17 941	9 769
1989	395 022	394 312	710	293 378	17 492	-13 654	262 232	81 365	51 425	21 966	18 582	17 983	9 844
1990	419 743	419 033	710	309 976	18 476	-14 036	277 464	85 320	56 959	23 315	19 899	18 003	9 819
1991	431 672	431 072	599	312 257	19 011	-13 895	279 350	87 391	64 930	23 942	20 585	18 030	9 570
1992	455 657	455 017	641	334 208	19 944	-15 964	298 301	84 547	72 809	25 199	21 735	18 082	9 501
1993	464 201	463 489	712	340 317	20 474	-15 887	303 955	82 924	77 322	25 589	21 948	18 141	9 527
1994	478 586	478 028	559	347 730	21 321	-15 864	310 544	86 970	81 072	26 359	22 555	18 157	9 570
1995	503 163	502 686	477	363 361	22 461	-17 340	323 559	93 271	86 333	27 721	23 703	18 151	9 621
1996	530 990	530 356	634	386 538	23 353	-19 443	343 742	97 209	90 039	29 266	24 804	18 144	9 711
1997	553 004	552 653	351	405 524	24 657	-21 295	359 572	102 486	90 945	30 480	25 570	18 143	9 857
1998	585 372	584 825	547	431 822	25 948	-22 844	383 031	108 798	93 543	32 236	26 801	18 159	10 088
1999	616 678	615 968	710	461 170	27 821	-24 908	408 442	111 373	96 863	33 890	28 020	18 197	10 343

Table 25-1. Personal Income and Employment—*Continued*

(Millions of dollars, except as noted.)

Year	Total	Nonfarm	Farm	Derivation of personal income						Per capita (dollars)		Population (thousands)	Total employment (thousands)
				Earnings by place of work	Less: Personal contributions for social insurance	Plus: Adjustment for residence	Equals: Net earnings by place of residence	Dividends, interest, and rent	Transfer payments	Total	Disposable		
NORTH CAROLINA													
1970	16 748	16 020	728	14 129	481	13	13 661	1 757	1 330	3 285	2 891	5 099	2 469
1971	18 255	17 565	690	15 305	541	10	14 774	1 908	1 573	3 510	3 117	5 201	2 490
1972	20 647	19 826	821	17 422	633	4	16 793	2 096	1 759	3 899	3 417	5 296	2 602
1973	23 492	22 264	1 229	19 856	818	2	19 039	2 428	2 025	4 365	3 853	5 382	2 720
1974	25 904	24 732	1 172	21 504	931	9	20 582	2 812	2 510	4 743	4 162	5 461	2 743
1975	27 889	26 779	1 110	22 339	968	14	21 386	3 043	3 460	5 039	4 524	5 535	2 647
1976	31 233	30 047	1 186	25 129	1 081	15	24 063	3 427	3 743	5 584	4 960	5 593	2 754
1977	34 339	33 452	888	27 583	1 188	22	26 417	3 918	4 004	6 058	5 358	5 668	2 851
1978	38 921	37 749	1 172	31 414	1 377	21	30 058	4 563	4 300	6 780	5 972	5 740	2 948
1979	43 288	42 511	777	34 558	1 607	18	32 969	5 419	4 899	7 461	6 519	5 802	3 051
1980	48 648	47 989	659	37 700	1 783	23	35 941	6 846	5 862	8 247	7 208	5 899	3 060
1981	54 704	53 642	1 061	41 662	2 124	-27	39 511	8 461	6 732	9 184	8 007	5 957	3 082
1982	58 324	57 269	1 055	43 641	2 286	-36	41 320	9 502	7 503	9 690	8 562	6 019	3 051
1983	63 685	63 064	621	47 674	2 514	-54	45 106	10 514	8 065	10 480	9 231	6 077	3 138
1984	72 659	71 370	1 289	54 757	2 847	-90	51 820	12 450	8 390	11 788	10 432	6 164	3 305
1985	79 105	77 949	1 156	59 636	3 249	-153	56 234	13 875	8 995	12 649	11 159	6 254	3 410
1986	84 988	83 855	1 132	64 056	3 585	-214	60 257	15 102	9 628	13 444	11 847	6 322	3 512
1987	91 734	90 651	1 083	69 718	3 900	-295	65 522	16 116	10 095	14 325	12 518	6 404	3 631
1988	100 196	98 791	1 405	76 054	4 420	-350	71 284	18 007	10 905	15 461	13 596	6 481	3 774
1989	108 585	106 935	1 650	81 331	4 827	-401	76 104	20 399	12 082	16 539	14 435	6 565	3 864
1990	115 609	113 504	2 104	85 831	5 110	-446	80 275	21 855	13 478	17 367	15 257	6 657	3 929
1991	120 648	118 262	2 386	88 399	5 390	-450	82 560	22 573	15 515	17 879	15 749	6 748	3 891
1992	130 627	128 321	2 307	96 804	5 806	-499	90 500	22 885	17 242	19 120	16 898	6 832	3 993
1993	139 239	136 622	2 617	102 719	6 205	-539	95 975	24 049	19 215	20 042	17 680	6 947	4 119
1994	147 793	144 946	2 847	108 925	6 708	-601	101 616	26 288	19 888	20 931	18 367	7 061	4 238
1995	157 634	154 951	2 683	115 043	7 181	-678	107 184	28 250	22 199	21 938	19 207	7 185	4 392
1996	167 638	164 684	2 953	121 409	7 524	-742	113 143	30 570	23 925	22 940	19 970	7 308	4 501
1997	179 688	176 704	2 984	129 676	8 075	-818	120 784	33 574	25 329	24 188	20 907	7 429	4 650
1998	192 070	189 851	2 218	138 121	8 566	-815	128 740	37 230	26 099	25 454	21 903	7 546	4 749
1999	198 943	197 052	1 891	146 473	9 184	-873	136 415	35 327	27 201	26 003	22 227	7 651	4 853
NORTH DAKOTA													
1970	1 989	1 697	292	1 600	62	-54	1 484	294	211	3 214	2 892	619	281
1971	2 299	1 883	416	1 851	67	-57	1 726	325	248	3 669	3 360	627	284
1972	2 761	2 100	661	2 263	75	-61	2 128	357	276	4 377	4 002	631	288
1973	3 903	2 392	1 511	3 321	99	-64	3 158	438	308	6 172	5 659	632	300
1974	3 881	2 733	1 148	3 205	117	-77	3 011	518	353	6 120	5 438	634	308
1975	4 044	3 118	926	3 258	133	-83	3 042	590	413	6 334	5 650	638	314
1976	3 990	3 527	463	3 125	147	-98	2 880	651	459	6 184	5 513	645	326
1977	4 172	3 914	258	3 151	143	-105	2 903	762	507	6 427	5 762	649	331
1978	5 294	4 447	847	4 147	166	-117	3 864	878	552	8 136	7 278	651	346
1979	5 477	4 982	495	4 187	195	-135	3 857	1 011	610	8 398	7 491	652	354
1980	5 297	5 644	-347	3 675	213	-152	3 309	1 266	722	8 095	7 085	654	356
1981	6 820	6 513	308	4 791	252	-174	4 365	1 628	828	10 342	9 056	660	360
1982	7 352	7 080	272	5 000	272	-177	4 551	1 870	930	10 990	9 831	669	361
1983	7 704	7 384	320	5 267	284	-180	4 803	1 869	1 032	11 386	10 263	677	367
1984	8 375	7 831	544	5 776	301	-186	5 290	1 993	1 092	12 307	11 149	680	368
1985	8 673	8 044	629	5 990	326	-185	5 479	2 029	1 165	12 811	11 623	677	366
1986	8 788	8 155	634	6 001	342	-181	5 478	2 030	1 280	13 126	11 965	670	360
1987	8 968	8 331	638	6 195	358	-182	5 655	1 963	1 351	13 565	12 297	661	365
1988	8 352	8 508	-156	5 597	392	-187	5 018	1 977	1 357	12 745	11 438	655	369
1989	9 280	8 962	318	6 271	422	-192	5 657	2 154	1 468	14 357	12 916	646	373
1990	10 121	9 509	612	6 896	448	-190	6 257	2 270	1 595	15 880	14 320	637	376
1991	10 318	9 893	426	7 054	482	-202	6 370	2 296	1 653	16 270	14 639	634	385
1992	11 242	10 423	819	7 896	507	-223	7 166	2 276	1 800	17 692	16 001	635	390
1993	11 362	10 962	400	7 913	539	-241	7 133	2 300	1 928	17 830	16 015	637	400
1994	12 177	11 465	712	8 638	574	-255	7 809	2 401	1 967	19 033	17 142	640	415
1995	12 243	12 016	227	8 497	588	-274	7 635	2 563	2 045	19 084	17 084	642	421
1996	13 607	12 705	902	9 640	613	-301	8 726	2 727	2 154	21 166	19 018	643	430
1997	13 330	13 363	-33	9 099	642	-322	8 135	2 939	2 257	20 798	18 491	641	434
1998	14 521	13 939	581	10 175	667	-321	9 188	3 042	2 291	22 767	20 311	638	440
1999	14 773	14 566	207	10 225	700	-330	9 196	3 244	2 333	23 313	20 692	634	444

Table 25-1. Personal Income and Employment—*Continued*

(Millions of dollars, except as noted.)

| Year | Total | Nonfarm | Farm | Derivation of personal income | | | | | | Per capita (dollars) | | Population (thousands) | Total employment (thousands) |
				Earnings by place of work	Less: Personal contributions for social insurance	Plus: Adjustment for residence	Equals: Net earnings by place of residence	Dividends, interest, and rent	Transfer payments	Total	Disposable		
OHIO													
1970	43 748	43 246	502	35 983	1 143	-179	34 660	5 710	3 378	4 101	3 591	10 669	4 683
1971	46 461	45 973	488	37 751	1 235	-129	36 386	6 056	4 019	4 328	3 849	10 735	4 627
1972	50 410	49 829	580	41 040	1 379	-126	39 534	6 437	4 439	4 691	4 106	10 747	4 710
1973	56 188	55 456	732	45 785	1 776	-154	43 855	7 202	5 131	5 218	4 576	10 767	4 902
1974	61 722	60 864	858	49 524	1 988	-131	47 406	8 163	6 153	5 733	5 015	10 766	4 964
1975	65 556	64 692	864	51 232	2 019	-77	49 136	8 614	7 807	6 087	5 368	10 770	4 809
1976	72 611	71 779	833	57 104	2 231	-87	54 785	9 422	8 403	6 753	5 926	10 753	4 889
1977	80 906	80 179	727	63 948	2 477	-100	61 370	10 605	8 931	7 511	6 555	10 771	5 034
1978	89 887	89 209	677	71 092	2 816	-119	68 158	12 162	9 567	8 326	7 251	10 795	5 207
1979	99 899	99 097	802	78 144	3 263	-141	74 740	14 271	10 889	9 251	8 008	10 799	5 298
1980	109 120	108 528	592	81 735	3 448	-156	78 130	17 261	13 728	10 103	8 797	10 801	5 215
1981	118 479	118 335	144	86 828	3 996	-467	82 365	20 842	15 272	10 982	9 502	10 788	5 151
1982	123 547	123 292	255	87 662	4 106	-588	82 969	22 812	17 766	11 485	10 048	10 757	4 983
1983	130 647	130 741	-94	91 901	4 317	-709	86 875	24 782	18 991	12 167	10 658	10 738	4 978
1984	144 407	143 600	807	102 544	4 835	-841	96 868	28 179	19 360	13 449	11 856	10 738	5 183
1985	153 456	152 669	787	109 303	5 410	-929	102 964	29 738	20 754	14 295	12 566	10 735	5 316
1986	160 236	159 646	590	113 930	5 793	-964	107 174	31 034	22 029	14 933	13 152	10 730	5 431
1987	168 668	168 019	648	120 556	6 158	-1 005	113 393	32 318	22 957	15 675	13 701	10 760	5 583
1988	180 757	180 093	664	130 177	6 819	-1 060	122 297	34 509	23 950	16 739	14 707	10 799	5 721
1989	193 035	191 992	1 042	136 988	7 360	-1 101	128 526	38 654	25 854	17 825	15 565	10 829	5 845
1990	204 114	203 062	1 052	144 263	7 740	-1 091	135 432	40 762	27 920	18 792	16 442	10 862	5 911
1991	210 117	209 586	531	147 150	8 103	-1 127	137 920	41 264	30 933	19 217	16 854	10 934	5 888
1992	222 812	221 863	948	157 194	8 502	-1 181	147 511	41 223	34 078	20 242	17 810	11 008	5 903
1993	232 463	231 702	761	164 589	8 965	-1 261	154 363	42 645	35 455	20 999	18 388	11 070	6 011
1994	245 156	244 172	984	173 959	9 711	-1 313	162 935	45 286	36 936	22 063	19 277	11 111	6 195
1995	255 313	254 546	767	180 582	10 228	-1 299	169 055	47 440	38 818	22 887	19 892	11 155	6 363
1996	264 162	263 110	1 052	186 222	10 548	-1 301	174 373	49 601	40 187	23 613	20 358	11 187	6 462
1997	279 342	277 799	1 543	196 810	11 180	-1 358	184 271	53 370	41 701	24 913	21 393	11 212	6 573
1998	294 027	292 971	1 056	207 680	11 691	-1 717	194 272	57 711	42 044	26 164	22 389	11 238	6 691
1999	305 643	305 070	573	216 692	12 295	-1 790	202 606	60 248	42 788	27 152	23 150	11 257	6 791
OKLAHOMA													
1970	8 925	8 555	370	6 958	229	64	6 793	1 155	977	3 477	3 095	2 566	1 120
1971	9 716	9 367	349	7 493	255	63	7 301	1 284	1 132	3 711	3 344	2 618	1 132
1972	10 682	10 243	440	8 316	289	72	8 100	1 343	1 240	4 020	3 567	2 657	1 183
1973	12 188	11 435	754	9 495	375	82	9 202	1 590	1 397	4 524	4 055	2 694	1 221
1974	13 623	13 154	469	10 451	440	106	10 116	1 855	1 651	4 986	4 399	2 732	1 256
1975	15 176	14 759	417	11 492	481	140	11 151	2 005	2 020	5 475	4 904	2 772	1 269
1976	16 867	16 519	347	12 777	528	175	12 425	2 218	2 224	5 974	5 322	2 823	1 305
1977	18 874	18 689	185	14 394	601	151	13 944	2 538	2 393	6 586	5 835	2 866	1 359
1978	21 518	21 336	182	16 500	709	147	15 938	3 012	2 567	7 387	6 477	2 913	1 428
1979	25 200	24 534	666	19 334	847	161	18 648	3 614	2 938	8 485	7 425	2 970	1 483
1980	29 131	28 819	312	22 003	994	169	21 178	4 548	3 405	9 580	8 329	3 041	1 551
1981	34 067	33 707	360	25 509	1 245	192	24 456	5 753	3 857	11 003	9 422	3 096	1 630
1982	37 887	37 406	481	28 027	1 391	197	26 833	6 696	4 358	11 817	10 036	3 206	1 678
1983	38 579	38 398	181	27 824	1 373	235	26 686	7 120	4 774	11 725	10 285	3 290	1 642
1984	41 683	41 309	374	30 004	1 472	285	28 817	7 981	4 885	12 687	11 244	3 286	1 672
1985	43 396	43 012	384	30 943	1 590	326	29 678	8 558	5 160	13 265	11 767	3 271	1 655
1986	43 222	42 580	642	30 500	1 601	374	29 273	8 426	5 523	13 288	12 038	3 253	1 595
1987	43 221	42 651	569	30 384	1 612	422	29 193	8 236	5 791	13 464	12 034	3 210	1 607
1988	45 153	44 379	774	31 703	1 779	469	30 393	8 634	6 126	14 257	12 748	3 167	1 617
1989	48 090	47 264	826	33 509	1 927	493	32 076	9 494	6 520	15 265	13 576	3 150	1 632
1990	51 027	50 205	822	35 596	2 047	560	34 109	9 900	7 017	16 214	14 264	3 147	1 665
1991	52 947	52 300	648	36 833	2 190	590	35 233	10 020	7 695	16 721	14 839	3 166	1 678
1992	56 155	55 347	808	39 214	2 302	627	37 540	9 997	8 619	17 526	15 618	3 204	1 692
1993	58 395	57 507	888	41 071	2 390	650	39 331	9 993	9 070	18 085	16 117	3 229	1 729
1994	60 800	59 937	862	42 403	2 526	699	40 575	10 624	9 600	18 730	16 647	3 246	1 763
1995	63 333	62 999	334	43 409	2 632	727	41 505	11 364	10 464	19 394	17 233	3 266	1 815
1996	66 289	65 893	395	45 321	2 736	745	43 330	11 992	10 967	20 151	17 775	3 290	1 866
1997	69 952	69 166	786	48 283	2 896	800	46 188	12 512	11 252	21 106	18 472	3 314	1 915
1998	74 133	73 518	615	51 162	3 045	828	48 946	13 643	11 544	22 199	19 395	3 339	1 966
1999	77 077	76 071	1 006	53 502	3 181	876	51 197	13 906	11 975	22 953	20 023	3 358	1 989

Table 25-1. Personal Income and Employment—*Continued*

(Millions of dollars, except as noted.)

Year	Total	Nonfarm	Farm	Derivation of personal income						Per capita (dollars)		Population (thousands)	Total employment (thousands)
				Earnings by place of work	Less: Personal contributions for social insurance	Plus: Adjustment for residence	Equals: Net earnings by place of residence	Dividends, interest, and rent	Transfer payments	Total	Disposable		
OREGON													
1970	8 276	8 038	238	6 492	225	-68	6 199	1 275	802	3 940	3 431	2 100	926
1971	9 056	8 825	231	7 045	251	-56	6 738	1 384	933	4 212	3 700	2 150	951
1972	10 153	9 862	291	7 975	295	-50	7 631	1 499	1 023	4 625	4 023	2 195	1 001
1973	11 497	11 099	397	9 018	381	-55	8 582	1 710	1 205	5 135	4 487	2 239	1 058
1974	13 062	12 558	504	10 088	439	-61	9 588	1 988	1 486	5 726	4 969	2 281	1 089
1975	14 367	13 954	414	10 810	467	-29	10 313	2 180	1 874	6 181	5 446	2 325	1 105
1976	16 398	16 010	388	12 427	526	-13	11 888	2 461	2 049	6 913	6 039	2 372	1 156
1977	18 431	18 096	335	14 021	602	-70	13 348	2 843	2 239	7 556	6 511	2 439	1 223
1978	21 272	20 935	336	16 248	708	-128	15 412	3 421	2 438	8 476	7 285	2 510	1 297
1979	24 275	23 875	399	18 380	835	-199	17 346	4 203	2 726	9 415	8 068	2 578	1 352
1980	26 930	26 449	481	19 738	906	-246	18 587	5 099	3 244	10 196	8 788	2 641	1 353
1981	28 981	28 592	389	20 365	1 024	-259	19 082	6 153	3 746	10 862	9 395	2 668	1 324
1982	29 654	29 377	277	20 127	1 054	-245	18 827	6 597	4 230	11 128	9 644	2 665	1 274
1983	31 392	31 112	280	21 150	1 108	-229	19 813	7 040	4 539	11 832	10 352	2 653	1 300
1984	34 309	33 903	406	23 277	1 216	-276	21 785	7 893	4 631	12 866	11 320	2 667	1 348
1985	36 205	35 777	428	24 730	1 348	-311	23 071	8 259	4 876	13 547	11 876	2 673	1 379
1986	38 003	37 450	554	26 084	1 456	-355	24 273	8 730	5 000	14 162	12 345	2 684	1 414
1987	40 274	39 783	491	27 861	1 567	-416	25 878	9 169	5 227	14 911	13 004	2 701	1 464
1988	44 030	43 363	667	30 788	1 813	-487	28 488	9 840	5 702	16 062	14 190	2 741	1 532
1989	48 060	47 447	613	33 243	2 021	-540	30 683	11 212	6 165	17 222	14 933	2 791	1 587
1990	52 178	51 530	648	36 333	2 179	-609	33 544	11 890	6 743	18 253	16 003	2 859	1 639
1991	54 891	54 243	648	38 030	2 354	-649	35 027	12 390	7 474	18 806	16 387	2 919	1 648
1992	58 163	57 534	629	40 655	2 495	-705	37 455	12 389	8 319	19 558	17 023	2 974	1 666
1993	61 916	61 151	766	43 357	2 658	-772	39 927	13 072	8 917	20 404	17 707	3 034	1 711
1994	66 130	65 475	654	46 291	2 890	-847	42 554	14 297	9 279	21 421	18 506	3 087	1 796
1995	71 209	70 628	581	49 033	3 121	-1 010	44 902	16 268	10 039	22 668	19 603	3 141	1 861
1996	75 561	74 844	717	52 841	3 333	-1 219	48 290	16 858	10 413	23 649	20 281	3 195	1 937
1997	80 578	79 758	820	56 626	3 573	-1 423	51 630	18 178	10 770	24 845	21 134	3 243	2 004
1998	85 197	84 473	724	59 685	3 730	-1 710	54 245	19 514	11 439	25 958	22 105	3 282	2 043
1999	89 614	88 956	658	63 185	3 978	-1 792	57 416	20 159	12 038	27 023	23 003	3 316	2 082
PENNSYLVANIA													
1970	48 153	47 724	429	38 735	1 333	-378	37 023	6 224	4 905	4 077	3 568	11 812	5 226
1971	51 036	50 656	380	40 496	1 448	-360	38 687	6 559	5 790	4 294	3 801	11 884	5 159
1972	55 755	55 358	397	44 238	1 621	-370	42 248	6 968	6 539	4 683	4 058	11 905	5 247
1973	61 420	60 892	528	48 715	2 035	-333	46 347	7 799	7 274	5 168	4 509	11 885	5 402
1974	67 674	67 162	512	52 997	2 300	-339	50 359	8 819	8 496	5 704	4 952	11 864	5 419
1975	73 412	72 940	472	56 156	2 396	-371	53 388	9 320	10 703	6 170	5 438	11 898	5 302
1976	80 837	80 278	558	61 571	2 588	-359	58 624	10 279	11 934	6 800	5 975	11 887	5 353
1977	89 035	88 527	508	67 852	2 820	-357	64 675	11 563	12 796	7 493	6 549	11 882	5 429
1978	98 539	97 988	551	75 271	3 169	-367	71 735	13 104	13 701	8 305	7 234	11 865	5 564
1979	109 533	108 843	690	82 906	3 657	-390	78 859	15 287	15 387	9 225	7 996	11 874	5 672
1980	120 478	120 013	465	88 494	3 982	-424	84 088	18 720	17 670	10 151	8 817	11 868	5 638
1981	132 632	131 960	672	94 889	4 644	-411	89 835	22 928	19 870	11 184	9 642	11 859	5 605
1982	140 802	140 231	571	97 006	4 876	-243	91 887	26 118	22 797	11 887	10 323	11 845	5 495
1983	147 437	147 064	372	100 501	5 088	-82	95 332	27 592	24 513	12 455	10 944	11 838	5 455
1984	159 652	158 819	833	109 375	5 639	109	103 844	31 434	24 375	13 512	11 880	11 815	5 606
1985	170 034	169 204	830	115 971	6 305	258	109 924	34 150	25 960	14 445	12 689	11 771	5 714
1986	178 938	178 064	874	122 132	6 828	371	115 675	35 844	27 419	15 186	13 360	11 783	5 809
1987	190 657	189 805	852	132 000	7 405	472	125 067	37 481	28 109	16 142	14 123	11 811	5 999
1988	205 200	204 507	693	142 998	8 353	704	135 349	40 391	29 460	17 323	15 203	11 846	6 166
1989	222 195	221 260	935	152 870	9 002	893	144 761	45 753	31 681	18 725	16 401	11 866	6 267
1990	235 802	234 903	900	162 095	9 527	957	153 525	48 112	34 166	19 823	17 433	11 896	6 344
1991	244 892	244 290	603	165 912	10 024	947	156 835	49 204	38 853	20 505	18 095	11 943	6 261
1992	258 186	257 138	1 048	176 607	10 606	1 075	167 076	48 214	42 897	21 550	18 984	11 981	6 268
1993	267 020	266 065	956	182 992	11 207	1 266	173 051	48 759	45 211	22 211	19 579	12 022	6 311
1994	275 337	274 547	790	189 064	11 862	1 414	178 616	50 650	46 071	22 864	20 090	12 043	6 384
1995	285 923	285 347	576	195 616	12 388	1 654	184 883	53 053	47 988	23 738	20 773	12 045	6 487
1996	299 001	298 006	995	203 510	12 679	1 828	192 659	55 587	50 755	24 838	21 568	12 038	6 545
1997	313 523	312 871	653	213 083	13 333	2 022	201 772	59 164	52 587	26 092	22 507	12 016	6 659
1998	328 364	327 621	743	225 667	13 973	1 539	213 234	62 146	52 985	27 358	23 456	12 002	6 778
1999	343 088	342 386	702	236 726	14 730	1 627	223 624	64 372	55 093	28 605	24 456	11 994	6 897

Table 25-1. Personal Income and Employment—*Continued*

(Millions of dollars, except as noted.)

Year	Total	Nonfarm	Farm	Earnings by place of work	Less: Personal contributions for social insurance	Plus: Adjustment for residence	Equals: Net earnings by place of residence	Dividends, interest, and rent	Transfer payments	Per capita Total	Per capita Disposable	Population (thousands)	Total employment (thousands)
RHODE ISLAND													
1970	3 910	3 900	10	2 996	113	66	2 949	540	421	4 114	3 661	951	440
1971	4 140	4 131	9	3 139	122	61	3 078	565	497	4 295	3 824	964	436
1972	4 515	4 507	9	3 454	136	55	3 374	596	546	4 625	4 067	976	447
1973	4 863	4 856	7	3 674	172	70	3 573	669	621	4 972	4 379	978	452
1974	5 154	5 144	10	3 765	187	88	3 665	759	729	5 405	4 753	954	439
1975	5 531	5 521	10	3 902	191	81	3 793	777	961	5 844	5 240	946	424
1976	6 093	6 083	10	4 382	209	89	4 261	847	985	6 411	5 697	950	442
1977	6 690	6 681	9	4 821	229	103	4 696	953	1 041	7 004	6 238	955	459
1978	7 364	7 354	10	5 342	258	102	5 186	1 069	1 109	7 693	6 753	957	475
1979	8 222	8 214	8	5 938	299	110	5 750	1 243	1 229	8 595	7 468	957	484
1980	9 243	9 235	8	6 483	330	124	6 276	1 546	1 421	9 742	8 520	949	486
1981	10 306	10 298	9	6 976	376	154	6 754	1 918	1 634	10 815	9 465	953	486
1982	11 073	11 045	29	7 349	407	208	7 149	2 129	1 795	11 605	10 207	954	477
1983	11 896	11 857	39	7 926	443	264	7 747	2 240	1 909	12 439	10 977	956	482
1984	13 194	13 160	34	8 793	497	333	8 630	2 628	1 936	13 717	12 171	962	507
1985	14 229	14 184	45	9 553	547	393	9 398	2 734	2 098	14 685	13 011	969	522
1986	15 233	15 186	47	10 322	609	418	10 131	2 912	2 190	15 587	13 724	977	541
1987	16 478	16 434	44	11 219	667	488	11 040	3 171	2 266	16 651	14 524	990	550
1988	18 205	18 157	48	12 404	756	564	12 211	3 577	2 417	18 271	16 052	996	564
1989	19 670	19 635	35	13 076	808	627	12 895	4 153	2 622	19 657	17 249	1 001	566
1990	20 287	20 255	33	13 361	842	669	13 188	4 185	2 915	20 194	17 795	1 005	555
1991	20 444	20 409	35	13 063	867	701	12 897	4 009	3 537	20 363	17 980	1 004	528
1992	21 269	21 232	38	13 859	927	727	13 659	3 925	3 685	21 257	18 848	1 001	534
1993	22 090	22 057	32	14 323	969	771	14 125	3 972	3 992	22 137	19 582	998	538
1994	22 612	22 584	28	14 729	1 017	848	14 561	4 079	3 972	22 762	20 075	993	538
1995	23 787	23 759	27	15 408	1 058	869	15 219	4 371	4 196	24 046	21 219	989	541
1996	24 818	24 793	26	15 934	1 080	929	15 783	4 768	4 267	25 123	22 048	988	545
1997	26 284	26 267	17	16 766	1 141	976	16 601	5 083	4 601	26 631	23 144	987	552
1998	27 667	27 650	18	17 728	1 223	1 051	17 556	5 451	4 661	28 012	24 188	988	561
1999	29 107	29 088	19	18 633	1 286	1 159	18 506	5 789	4 813	29 377	25 342	991	571
SOUTH CAROLINA													
1970	7 961	7 758	203	6 635	217	116	6 534	761	666	3 064	2 745	2 598	1 196
1971	8 715	8 496	219	7 208	243	128	7 092	841	781	3 274	2 938	2 662	1 215
1972	9 795	9 563	232	8 127	283	145	7 990	927	878	3 603	3 172	2 718	1 262
1973	11 181	10 864	317	9 268	369	159	9 058	1 085	1 038	4 029	3 567	2 775	1 328
1974	12 678	12 322	356	10 383	429	174	10 128	1 244	1 307	4 459	3 940	2 843	1 365
1975	13 689	13 404	286	10 795	442	185	10 538	1 370	1 782	4 720	4 277	2 900	1 326
1976	15 462	15 223	239	12 309	505	221	12 025	1 538	1 899	5 257	4 702	2 941	1 376
1977	16 990	16 800	190	13 537	555	244	13 225	1 753	2 013	5 684	5 070	2 989	1 411
1978	19 264	19 014	249	15 395	643	261	15 014	2 046	2 204	6 334	5 635	3 041	1 467
1979	21 744	21 476	268	17 246	749	286	16 784	2 427	2 533	7 044	6 198	3 087	1 510
1980	24 429	24 386	43	18 809	835	320	18 294	3 051	3 084	7 794	6 880	3 135	1 527
1981	27 504	27 321	182	20 818	997	352	20 173	3 778	3 553	8 651	7 597	3 179	1 541
1982	29 096	28 905	190	21 565	1 064	385	20 886	4 298	3 911	9 071	8 041	3 208	1 518
1983	31 614	31 569	45	23 392	1 180	399	22 611	4 838	4 165	9 775	8 661	3 234	1 552
1984	35 696	35 433	264	26 592	1 339	448	25 700	5 666	4 331	10 910	9 727	3 272	1 631
1985	38 536	38 349	187	28 387	1 506	505	27 386	6 347	4 803	11 666	10 376	3 303	1 663
1986	40 974	40 899	76	30 108	1 664	569	29 012	6 860	5 102	12 258	10 901	3 343	1 706
1987	44 136	43 896	240	32 656	1 785	614	31 485	7 359	5 293	13 056	11 563	3 381	1 748
1988	47 923	47 593	330	35 605	2 029	633	34 209	8 076	5 638	14 045	12 512	3 412	1 820
1989	51 276	50 933	343	38 081	2 236	588	36 434	8 487	6 356	14 834	13 082	3 457	1 871
1990	56 158	55 890	269	40 906	2 396	508	39 019	9 971	7 168	16 050	14 199	3 499	1 926
1991	58 406	58 038	368	41 931	2 511	509	39 929	10 339	8 138	16 409	14 610	3 559	1 899
1992	61 803	61 455	348	44 333	2 631	548	42 251	10 437	9 115	17 165	15 313	3 601	1 912
1993	64 711	64 387	325	46 361	2 783	570	44 149	10 816	9 746	17 805	15 856	3 635	1 948
1994	68 511	68 048	463	48 526	2 974	654	46 206	11 811	10 494	18 686	16 578	3 666	1 998
1995	72 050	71 692	358	50 842	3 171	753	48 423	12 431	11 196	19 473	17 191	3 700	2 057
1996	76 287	75 865	422	53 331	3 281	862	50 912	13 375	12 000	20 403	17 916	3 739	2 102
1997	81 049	80 599	451	56 329	3 485	989	53 834	14 516	12 700	21 385	18 702	3 790	2 165
1998	86 560	86 253	307	60 102	3 688	1 048	57 462	15 905	13 193	22 544	19 671	3 840	2 222
1999	91 490	91 115	375	63 750	3 930	1 126	60 945	16 768	13 777	23 545	20 555	3 886	2 272

Table 25-1. Personal Income and Employment—*Continued*

(Millions of dollars, except as noted.)

Year	Total	Nonfarm	Farm	Derivation of personal income						Per capita (dollars)		Population (thousands)	Total employment (thousands)
				Earnings by place of work	Less: Personal contributions for social insurance	Plus: Adjustment for residence	Equals: Net earnings by place of residence	Dividends, interest, and rent	Transfer payments	Total	Disposable		
SOUTH DAKOTA													
1970	2 171	1 802	369	1 691	57	6	1 641	309	221	3 256	2 982	667	305
1971	2 376	1 977	399	1 845	62	6	1 789	331	255	3 538	3 283	671	306
1972	2 754	2 188	566	2 167	69	7	2 105	366	282	4 065	3 776	677	309
1973	3 505	2 479	1 027	2 835	92	7	2 750	430	325	5 163	4 767	679	323
1974	3 520	2 834	687	2 716	106	8	2 618	523	379	5 178	4 711	680	326
1975	3 862	3 156	706	2 925	115	10	2 820	593	448	5 667	5 232	681	326
1976	3 840	3 562	279	2 804	124	12	2 692	652	496	5 591	5 093	687	336
1977	4 376	3 936	440	3 204	127	13	3 090	756	530	6 351	5 867	689	342
1978	5 064	4 446	618	3 762	146	15	3 631	860	573	7 347	6 747	689	355
1979	5 621	4 965	656	4 117	175	16	3 959	1 017	645	8 158	7 476	689	360
1980	5 625	5 510	115	3 808	187	18	3 639	1 230	756	8 142	7 362	691	354
1981	6 517	6 116	401	4 308	211	15	4 111	1 534	872	9 451	8 570	690	349
1982	6 847	6 539	308	4 331	224	12	4 119	1 757	970	9 915	8 936	691	346
1983	7 066	6 889	176	4 483	239	6	4 250	1 776	1 040	10 195	9 346	693	354
1984	8 101	7 483	618	5 369	264	-1	5 104	1 913	1 084	11 619	10 772	697	364
1985	8 340	7 798	542	5 518	293	-4	5 221	1 969	1 150	11 942	11 047	698	367
1986	8 691	8 107	583	5 754	316	-11	5 428	2 057	1 207	12 486	11 560	696	368
1987	9 199	8 442	757	6 232	347	-18	5 866	2 073	1 260	13 217	12 174	696	383
1988	9 639	8 963	676	6 558	389	-25	6 144	2 176	1 319	13 807	12 711	698	390
1989	10 288	9 617	672	6 916	429	-35	6 452	2 405	1 431	14 767	13 531	697	398
1990	11 312	10 354	958	7 742	464	-54	7 224	2 557	1 531	16 238	14 846	697	412
1991	11 897	11 052	845	8 143	501	-65	7 577	2 661	1 658	16 961	15 524	701	423
1992	12 732	11 793	939	8 853	533	-81	8 239	2 687	1 806	17 966	16 420	709	434
1993	13 297	12 453	845	9 279	564	-96	8 619	2 755	1 924	18 565	16 874	716	445
1994	14 177	13 194	983	9 972	612	-120	9 240	2 921	2 016	19 607	17 894	723	467
1995	14 454	13 931	523	9 902	638	-143	9 121	3 162	2 171	19 848	18 016	728	475
1996	15 883	14 676	1 207	10 993	661	-171	10 160	3 430	2 292	21 736	19 784	731	483
1997	16 280	15 449	831	11 089	696	-172	10 222	3 687	2 370	22 275	20 034	731	488
1998	17 391	16 373	1 018	11 930	731	-197	11 001	3 969	2 420	23 797	21 402	731	497
1999	18 361	17 361	1 001	12 699	787	-212	11 700	4 184	2 477	25 045	22 463	733	509
TENNESSEE													
1970	12 557	12 254	302	10 514	351	-154	10 008	1 357	1 192	3 189	2 840	3 937	1 785
1971	13 839	13 541	299	11 508	397	-165	10 946	1 494	1 399	3 451	3 097	4 010	1 817
1972	15 569	15 203	366	13 044	464	-191	12 389	1 640	1 540	3 808	3 413	4 088	1 924
1973	17 786	17 256	530	14 842	596	-181	14 065	1 916	1 806	4 298	3 853	4 138	2 025
1974	19 732	19 376	356	16 147	684	-191	15 273	2 256	2 202	4 696	4 210	4 202	2 055
1975	21 378	21 099	279	16 917	708	-189	16 020	2 473	2 885	5 017	4 542	4 261	1 983
1976	24 132	23 734	398	19 217	788	-184	18 245	2 724	3 162	5 574	5 027	4 329	2 052
1977	26 887	26 562	325	21 566	887	-240	20 440	3 084	3 363	6 108	5 513	4 402	2 135
1978	30 761	30 414	347	24 824	1 017	-307	23 499	3 602	3 660	6 895	6 189	4 462	2 228
1979	34 535	34 152	383	27 527	1 183	-358	25 986	4 301	4 247	7 618	6 829	4 533	2 282
1980	38 268	38 028	240	29 537	1 292	-424	27 822	5 315	5 130	8 319	7 449	4 600	2 264
1981	42 556	42 149	406	32 241	1 532	-460	30 249	6 507	5 799	9 196	8 227	4 628	2 263
1982	45 043	44 751	292	33 338	1 644	-417	31 278	7 392	6 373	9 695	8 709	4 646	2 224
1983	47 884	47 921	-37	35 497	1 780	-430	33 287	7 767	6 830	10 276	9 251	4 660	2 247
1984	53 675	53 291	384	40 043	2 002	-431	37 610	9 011	7 054	11 453	10 376	4 687	2 354
1985	57 750	57 442	307	43 169	2 268	-447	40 454	9 766	7 530	12 247	11 055	4 715	2 411
1986	61 581	61 392	189	46 071	2 497	-488	43 086	10 346	8 149	12 995	11 742	4 739	2 490
1987	66 524	66 279	245	50 161	2 731	-523	46 908	10 949	8 667	13 909	12 512	4 783	2 593
1988	71 901	71 603	297	54 086	3 066	-536	50 484	12 093	9 324	14 910	13 470	4 822	2 680
1989	77 105	76 751	354	57 355	3 358	-564	53 433	13 492	10 180	15 883	14 295	4 854	2 754
1990	82 267	81 926	342	60 668	3 568	-602	56 497	14 364	11 405	16 821	15 193	4 891	2 797
1991	86 583	86 181	402	63 348	3 822	-579	58 947	14 632	13 004	17 503	15 842	4 947	2 796
1992	94 465	93 931	534	69 564	4 104	-441	65 019	14 750	14 696	18 840	17 052	5 014	2 858
1993	100 394	99 886	508	74 342	4 415	-563	69 365	15 105	15 925	19 741	17 857	5 086	2 965
1994	106 855	106 302	553	79 588	4 826	-636	74 127	16 158	16 570	20 696	18 658	5 163	3 087
1995	114 260	113 895	365	84 702	5 181	-715	78 806	17 316	18 138	21 800	19 613	5 241	3 172
1996	119 287	119 028	259	87 890	5 366	-662	81 862	18 395	19 030	22 450	20 056	5 314	3 225
1997	125 449	125 161	288	92 616	5 693	-797	86 126	19 432	19 891	23 324	20 754	5 378	3 303
1998	133 514	133 387	127	98 134	5 984	-992	91 159	21 735	20 620	24 576	21 834	5 433	3 372
1999	140 234	140 259	-25	103 499	6 351	-1 078	96 070	22 655	21 510	25 574	22 674	5 484	3 437

Table 25-1. Personal Income and Employment—Continued

(Millions of dollars, except as noted.)

Year	Total	Nonfarm	Farm	Derivation of personal income: Earnings by place of work	Less: Personal contributions for social insurance	Plus: Adjustment for residence	Equals: Net earnings by place of residence	Dividends, interest, and rent	Transfer payments	Per capita (dollars): Total	Per capita (dollars): Disposable	Population (thousands)	Total employment (thousands)
TEXAS													
1970	40 969	39 771	1 197	33 751	1 081	-97	32 572	5 275	3 121	3 646	3 227	11 237	5 045
1971	44 434	43 377	1 057	36 324	1 200	-102	35 021	5 740	3 672	3 861	3 457	11 510	5 123
1972	49 287	47 966	1 321	40 358	1 366	-128	38 864	6 307	4 117	4 192	3 711	11 759	5 334
1973	56 283	54 077	2 206	45 985	1 782	-155	44 048	7 324	4 911	4 683	4 158	12 019	5 608
1974	63 719	62 513	1 207	51 454	2 101	-132	49 221	8 650	5 849	5 194	4 570	12 268	5 822
1975	72 117	70 770	1 347	58 057	2 326	-130	55 600	9 281	7 236	5 738	5 112	12 568	5 938
1976	82 087	80 778	1 309	66 672	2 635	-95	63 942	10 191	7 954	6 362	5 632	12 903	6 207
1977	92 059	90 768	1 291	75 298	2 996	-308	71 994	11 479	8 587	6 979	6 128	13 192	6 521
1978	106 800	105 762	1 038	87 307	3 537	-429	83 341	13 931	9 528	7 912	6 960	13 498	6 898
1979	124 003	122 220	1 784	100 905	4 302	-436	96 167	17 010	10 826	8 929	7 763	13 887	7 222
1980	142 772	142 089	683	114 532	5 048	-544	108 940	21 130	12 703	9 957	8 616	14 338	7 511
1981	167 976	165 913	2 063	133 967	6 366	-352	127 248	26 357	14 371	11 391	9 753	14 746	7 925
1982	183 378	182 082	1 296	143 994	7 058	-425	136 511	30 477	16 390	11 961	10 344	15 331	8 098
1983	193 793	192 133	1 660	150 691	7 267	-408	143 016	32 320	18 457	12 303	10 832	15 752	8 087
1984	214 431	212 822	1 609	165 744	7 981	-470	157 293	37 843	19 295	13 396	11 871	16 007	8 468
1985	231 003	229 498	1 505	177 720	8 932	-499	168 289	42 035	20 679	14 196	12 584	16 273	8 720
1986	234 594	233 379	1 215	178 130	9 151	-459	168 520	43 191	22 883	14 165	12 681	16 561	8 561
1987	240 782	238 844	1 938	182 466	9 263	-458	172 744	43 724	24 314	14 486	12 926	16 622	8 773
1988	255 402	253 543	1 859	193 727	10 268	-461	182 997	46 831	25 573	15 324	13 751	16 667	8 935
1989	274 343	272 454	1 889	206 201	11 207	-470	194 525	51 701	28 117	16 323	14 579	16 807	9 066
1990	297 569	294 850	2 719	224 620	12 235	-504	211 881	54 357	31 332	17 458	15 600	17 045	9 307
1991	314 726	312 044	2 681	237 542	13 319	-577	223 647	55 688	35 390	18 150	16 307	17 340	9 469
1992	337 934	334 869	3 065	255 454	14 225	-589	240 640	55 616	41 678	19 146	17 239	17 650	9 557
1993	356 784	353 022	3 762	271 857	15 198	-597	256 061	55 945	44 778	19 825	17 824	17 997	9 863
1994	377 583	374 448	3 135	286 929	16 402	-648	269 878	59 840	47 864	20 590	18 495	18 338	10 192
1995	402 097	399 618	2 479	304 128	17 656	-714	285 758	64 296	52 043	21 526	19 289	18 680	10 539
1996	428 726	426 754	1 972	324 926	18 805	-771	305 349	68 149	55 228	22 557	20 054	19 006	10 847
1997	469 205	466 362	2 843	357 429	20 476	-886	336 067	74 783	58 355	24 242	21 421	19 355	11 288
1998	508 636	506 054	2 582	391 487	22 205	-947	368 334	80 882	59 420	25 803	22 674	19 712	11 690
1999	538 345	533 946	4 399	418 392	23 762	-999	393 630	83 329	61 386	26 858	23 544	20 044	11 939
UTAH													
1970	3 614	3 531	83	2 945	95	2	2 852	465	297	3 391	3 026	1 066	455
1971	4 026	3 943	83	3 255	108	3	3 150	523	354	3 658	3 291	1 101	467
1972	4 514	4 417	97	3 649	127	5	3 528	584	403	3 979	3 558	1 135	494
1973	5 057	4 919	138	4 103	165	8	3 946	642	469	4 326	3 865	1 169	523
1974	5 686	5 582	104	4 589	192	11	4 408	745	533	4 743	4 228	1 199	545
1975	6 355	6 282	73	5 062	209	14	4 867	828	659	5 150	4 647	1 234	553
1976	7 302	7 222	80	5 834	237	17	5 614	966	722	5 739	5 118	1 272	580
1977	8 331	8 261	69	6 675	270	22	6 426	1 115	790	6 328	5 629	1 316	613
1978	9 606	9 528	78	7 681	313	27	7 394	1 335	876	7 041	6 254	1 364	651
1979	11 026	10 935	92	8 705	380	35	8 361	1 673	993	7 786	6 891	1 416	679
1980	12 464	12 400	64	9 600	426	52	9 226	2 064	1 174	8 464	7 515	1 473	689
1981	14 078	14 038	40	10 702	519	54	10 237	2 474	1 368	9 290	8 204	1 515	699
1982	15 282	15 237	45	11 358	565	54	10 847	2 859	1 576	9 807	8 640	1 558	709
1983	16 481	16 445	36	12 064	602	43	11 505	3 264	1 712	10 333	9 218	1 595	721
1984	18 223	18 163	61	13 444	674	38	12 807	3 681	1 735	11 233	10 075	1 622	764
1985	19 462	19 401	62	14 364	756	40	13 648	3 950	1 865	11 846	10 594	1 643	793
1986	20 367	20 276	91	14 956	804	35	14 187	4 142	2 039	12 248	10 943	1 663	805
1987	21 208	21 085	123	15 615	842	25	14 799	4 198	2 211	12 638	11 245	1 678	835
1988	22 225	22 017	208	16 601	939	24	15 687	4 238	2 300	13 156	11 706	1 689	870
1989	23 843	23 641	202	17 723	1 021	21	16 723	4 604	2 515	13 977	12 448	1 706	903
1990	25 939	25 693	246	19 394	1 105	17	18 306	4 821	2 812	14 996	13 219	1 730	945
1991	27 750	27 526	224	20 823	1 207	10	19 626	4 978	3 146	15 661	13 853	1 772	967
1992	29 788	29 526	262	22 590	1 294	6	21 302	4 979	3 508	16 354	14 452	1 821	986
1993	31 950	31 641	309	24 338	1 396	8	22 951	5 180	3 819	17 031	15 000	1 876	1 034
1994	34 579	34 366	212	26 394	1 532	7	24 869	5 802	3 908	17 912	15 685	1 930	1 112
1995	37 278	37 116	162	28 445	1 673	6	26 778	6 293	4 206	18 858	16 454	1 977	1 160
1996	40 354	40 192	162	30 777	1 793	17	29 000	6 909	4 445	19 955	17 308	2 022	1 228
1997	43 696	43 511	185	33 342	1 938	19	31 422	7 579	4 695	21 156	18 261	2 065	1 282
1998	46 831	46 591	240	35 745	2 054	23	33 714	8 241	4 875	22 294	19 294	2 101	1 321
1999	49 600	49 336	264	38 017	2 198	30	35 849	8 711	5 040	23 288	20 222	2 130	1 355

Table 25-1. Personal Income and Employment—*Continued*

(Millions of dollars, except as noted.)

Year	Total	Nonfarm	Farm	Earnings by place of work	Less: Personal contributions for social insurance	Plus: Adjustment for residence	Equals: Net earnings by place of residence	Dividends, interest, and rent	Transfer payments	Total	Disposable	Population (thousands)	Total employment (thousands)
						Derivation of personal income					Per capita (dollars)		

VERMONT

Year	Total	Nonfarm	Farm	Earnings	Less SI	Plus Adj	Net earnings	Div/int/rent	Transfer	Per cap Total	Disposable	Population	Total emp
1970	1 622	1 555	67	1 276	45	-26	1 205	246	171	3 634	3 161	446	205
1971	1 752	1 685	67	1 353	49	-24	1 280	267	205	3 856	3 449	454	206
1972	1 934	1 859	75	1 486	54	-21	1 411	293	230	4 176	3 667	463	211
1973	2 131	2 053	78	1 633	68	-20	1 545	325	261	4 548	4 041	469	220
1974	2 304	2 240	64	1 721	76	-17	1 629	362	313	4 869	4 325	473	222
1975	2 492	2 426	65	1 809	79	-11	1 719	377	396	5 192	4 631	480	220
1976	2 791	2 710	81	2 042	87	-5	1 949	414	428	5 753	5 164	485	228
1977	3 041	2 972	69	2 224	96	-2	2 127	472	442	6 179	5 500	492	236
1978	3 506	3 408	98	2 611	114	-1	2 496	544	466	7 036	6 257	498	252
1979	3 972	3 863	108	2 926	133	6	2 798	646	528	7 853	6 939	506	261
1980	4 460	4 349	111	3 181	147	14	3 048	786	626	8 702	7 663	513	266
1981	5 010	4 885	125	3 481	175	18	3 324	965	720	9 717	8 520	516	271
1982	5 340	5 218	122	3 643	190	24	3 477	1 060	803	10 287	9 091	519	272
1983	5 740	5 656	83	3 937	206	23	3 754	1 126	859	10 968	9 717	523	279
1984	6 345	6 265	80	4 345	229	29	4 145	1 327	873	12 048	10 706	527	290
1985	6 887	6 789	98	4 809	265	30	4 574	1 410	903	12 994	11 484	530	302
1986	7 392	7 296	96	5 219	296	34	4 958	1 495	939	13 842	12 168	534	313
1987	8 100	7 982	118	5 805	327	42	5 519	1 616	964	14 992	13 084	540	323
1988	8 905	8 783	121	6 392	376	49	6 065	1 817	1 023	16 197	14 218	550	337
1989	9 769	9 642	127	6 877	415	52	6 514	2 137	1 118	17 517	15 315	558	344
1990	10 193	10 087	106	7 102	430	52	6 723	2 213	1 257	18 055	15 838	565	344
1991	10 332	10 238	95	7 126	446	52	6 732	2 224	1 376	18 218	16 062	567	337
1992	10 999	10 834	165	7 653	468	53	7 239	2 201	1 560	19 293	17 083	570	344
1993	11 357	11 238	119	7 963	488	55	7 530	2 195	1 632	19 785	17 496	574	352
1994	11 898	11 779	119	8 270	517	62	7 815	2 359	1 724	20 553	18 192	579	362
1995	12 449	12 349	100	8 520	555	69	8 034	2 553	1 862	21 359	18 906	583	365
1996	13 073	12 939	133	8 959	575	76	8 459	2 704	1 909	22 295	19 550	586	371
1997	13 752	13 654	98	9 351	606	86	8 831	2 909	2 013	23 362	20 310	589	376
1998	14 648	14 524	124	9 960	636	100	9 423	3 146	2 079	24 803	21 456	591	384
1999	15 371	15 213	158	10 602	679	114	10 037	3 139	2 195	25 889	22 318	594	393

VIRGINIA

Year	Total	Nonfarm	Farm	Earnings	Less SI	Plus Adj	Net earnings	Div/int/rent	Transfer	Per cap Total	Disposable	Population	Total emp
1970	17 685	17 440	245	14 045	436	847	14 456	2 056	1 174	3 795	3 264	4 660	2 158
1971	19 448	19 220	227	15 376	492	872	15 755	2 275	1 417	4 092	3 556	4 753	2 196
1972	21 657	21 362	294	17 175	571	928	17 532	2 501	1 624	4 486	3 842	4 828	2 263
1973	24 396	24 007	390	19 325	736	1 000	19 589	2 882	1 926	4 972	4 293	4 907	2 384
1974	27 300	26 946	354	21 373	843	1 129	21 658	3 361	2 281	5 484	4 701	4 978	2 451
1975	30 005	29 706	299	22 937	891	1 388	23 434	3 680	2 891	5 934	5 209	5 056	2 425
1976	33 538	33 273	266	25 591	991	1 611	26 211	4 143	3 184	6 534	5 704	5 133	2 501
1977	37 439	37 246	193	28 534	1 099	1 851	29 285	4 689	3 464	7 192	6 242	5 206	2 585
1978	42 483	42 167	317	32 271	1 254	2 185	33 202	5 468	3 813	8 040	6 940	5 284	2 697
1979	47 894	47 715	179	35 863	1 475	2 583	36 971	6 563	4 360	8 995	7 760	5 325	2 769
1980	54 627	54 538	89	39 767	1 655	3 159	41 271	8 153	5 202	10 176	8 784	5 368	2 802
1981	61 470	61 166	303	44 179	1 987	3 385	45 576	9 910	5 984	11 291	9 681	5 444	2 820
1982	66 326	66 211	115	47 319	2 187	3 460	48 592	11 178	6 556	12 075	10 419	5 493	2 832
1983	71 985	71 941	44	51 501	2 449	3 440	52 492	12 421	7 072	12 936	11 284	5 565	2 905
1984	80 697	80 385	312	58 462	2 787	3 553	59 228	14 101	7 367	14 298	12 562	5 644	3 054
1985	87 362	87 149	212	63 953	3 238	3 674	64 389	15 210	7 762	15 286	13 348	5 715	3 198
1986	94 364	94 107	257	69 424	3 632	3 825	69 617	16 479	8 268	16 237	14 184	5 812	3 335
1987	102 817	102 457	360	76 261	4 008	4 043	76 296	17 878	8 643	17 332	15 028	5 932	3 502
1988	112 022	111 526	496	82 813	4 552	4 445	82 706	20 110	9 207	18 556	16 181	6 037	3 582
1989	121 058	120 441	616	88 602	4 992	4 682	88 292	22 769	9 996	19 780	17 162	6 120	3 683
1990	127 614	126 978	636	92 362	5 273	5 405	92 493	24 147	10 974	20 538	17 899	6 214	3 727
1991	132 536	131 954	582	94 729	5 537	5 866	95 059	25 284	12 193	21 092	18 447	6 284	3 667
1992	140 207	139 570	636	100 526	5 804	6 203	100 925	25 514	13 768	21 965	19 254	6 383	3 689
1993	147 223	146 708	515	105 252	6 130	6 565	105 687	26 832	14 704	22 773	19 915	6 465	3 765
1994	154 982	154 363	618	110 255	6 552	6 702	110 404	28 996	15 582	23 709	20 633	6 537	3 852
1995	161 442	160 895	546	114 656	6 876	6 929	114 708	30 092	16 642	24 456	21 216	6 601	3 943
1996	169 938	169 415	524	120 820	7 211	6 675	120 283	31 843	17 813	25 495	21 977	6 665	4 026
1997	180 226	179 821	405	128 877	7 720	7 263	128 420	33 330	18 476	26 768	22 882	6 733	4 129
1998	192 429	192 026	403	138 220	8 231	7 131	137 120	36 369	18 941	28 343	24 040	6 789	4 219
1999	204 736	204 433	303	148 217	8 907	7 783	147 093	37 972	19 671	29 789	25 139	6 873	4 324

Table 25-1. Personal Income and Employment—*Continued*

(Millions of dollars, except as noted.)

Year	Total	Nonfarm	Farm	Derivation of personal income — Earnings by place of work	Less: Personal contributions for social insurance	Plus: Adjustment for residence	Equals: Net earnings by place of residence	Dividends, interest, and rent	Transfer payments	Per capita (dollars) — Total	Per capita (dollars) — Disposable	Population (thousands)	Total employment (thousands)
WASHINGTON													
1970	14 372	14 008	364	11 199	381	63	10 882	2 060	1 430	4 205	3 754	3 417	1 491
1971	15 100	14 690	410	11 572	408	62	11 226	2 201	1 673	4 381	3 948	3 447	1 457
1972	16 307	15 775	531	12 565	456	72	12 180	2 342	1 785	4 731	4 217	3 447	1 481
1973	18 473	17 693	780	14 287	590	88	13 785	2 688	2 000	5 312	4 723	3 477	1 558
1974	20 999	20 087	912	16 132	687	131	15 576	3 087	2 336	5 919	5 268	3 548	1 622
1975	23 641	22 714	927	18 007	764	197	17 439	3 335	2 866	6 533	5 834	3 619	1 659
1976	26 502	25 734	769	20 283	858	244	19 668	3 704	3 130	7 181	6 398	3 691	1 739
1977	29 544	28 928	616	22 750	963	223	22 011	4 222	3 312	7 832	6 961	3 772	1 815
1978	34 536	33 762	774	26 788	1 150	266	25 904	5 052	3 580	8 887	7 823	3 886	1 939
1979	39 987	39 233	755	30 887	1 384	318	29 821	6 171	3 995	9 965	8 699	4 013	2 061
1980	45 338	44 447	891	34 127	1 539	383	32 971	7 478	4 889	10 913	9 544	4 155	2 110
1981	50 418	49 573	845	37 022	1 835	428	35 615	9 127	5 676	11 903	10 378	4 236	2 126
1982	53 161	52 395	766	38 301	1 950	460	36 811	9 951	6 399	12 431	11 038	4 277	2 101
1983	56 435	55 346	1 089	40 392	2 052	480	38 820	10 628	6 987	13 124	11 769	4 300	2 148
1984	60 901	59 863	1 038	43 166	2 206	538	41 498	12 142	7 261	14 021	12 630	4 344	2 224
1985	64 847	64 100	746	45 836	2 482	581	43 934	12 954	7 958	14 738	13 241	4 400	2 290
1986	69 114	68 049	1 065	49 204	2 741	601	47 064	13 607	8 443	15 522	13 969	4 453	2 365
1987	73 872	72 816	1 055	52 794	2 948	653	50 499	14 458	8 915	16 300	14 572	4 532	2 486
1988	80 130	79 188	943	57 527	3 369	740	54 899	15 630	9 601	17 270	15 494	4 640	2 618
1989	88 616	87 562	1 054	63 039	3 772	824	60 090	18 068	10 458	18 670	16 583	4 746	2 738
1990	98 143	97 071	1 072	70 240	4 157	926	67 009	19 550	11 584	20 026	17 761	4 901	2 864
1991	104 786	103 651	1 135	74 962	4 554	970	71 377	20 273	13 136	20 901	18 618	5 013	2 898
1992	112 634	111 258	1 375	81 775	4 926	1 036	77 884	20 225	14 525	21 917	19 541	5 139	2 930
1993	117 621	116 046	1 575	85 122	5 085	1 099	81 136	20 790	15 694	22 414	20 023	5 248	2 975
1994	123 337	122 138	1 199	88 442	5 409	1 162	84 195	22 742	16 400	23 119	20 566	5 335	3 087
1995	129 681	128 420	1 260	92 096	5 721	1 294	87 670	24 409	17 603	23 878	21 192	5 431	3 128
1996	139 328	137 642	1 686	98 912	6 070	1 474	94 316	26 618	18 393	25 287	22 240	5 510	3 220
1997	150 283	148 924	1 359	107 273	6 638	1 643	102 279	28 967	19 037	26 817	23 397	5 604	3 328
1998	162 855	161 375	1 481	117 482	7 194	1 925	112 213	31 014	19 628	28 632	24 645	5 688	3 417
1999	174 948	173 817	1 131	127 897	7 903	2 002	121 996	32 515	20 437	30 392	26 041	5 756	3 489
WEST VIRGINIA													
1970	5 444	5 410	34	4 386	158	-82	4 147	578	719	3 117	2 757	1 747	660
1971	5 981	5 947	34	4 756	177	-99	4 480	629	872	3 378	3 004	1 770	670
1972	6 617	6 576	41	5 250	202	-113	4 935	684	998	3 682	3 259	1 797	684
1973	7 268	7 214	54	5 669	248	-116	5 305	782	1 181	4 026	3 590	1 805	700
1974	8 085	8 046	40	6 249	281	-130	5 838	912	1 336	4 457	3 929	1 814	711
1975	9 154	9 131	23	7 036	311	-157	6 568	1 008	1 579	4 974	4 399	1 841	717
1976	10 287	10 275	11	7 966	351	-193	7 422	1 125	1 740	5 479	4 823	1 877	739
1977	11 535	11 530	5	8 994	387	-225	8 382	1 278	1 875	6 053	5 339	1 906	758
1978	12 872	12 853	19	10 038	437	-262	9 339	1 455	2 078	6 703	5 930	1 920	781
1979	14 411	14 384	27	11 061	509	-272	10 281	1 705	2 426	7 432	6 532	1 939	791
1980	15 947	15 931	15	11 866	552	-299	11 015	2 106	2 826	8 172	7 162	1 951	784
1981	17 325	17 341	-16	12 462	633	-277	11 552	2 577	3 196	8 866	7 779	1 954	764
1982	18 403	18 430	-27	12 812	672	-232	11 909	2 979	3 515	9 439	8 328	1 950	743
1983	18 723	18 741	-19	12 548	664	-189	11 694	3 148	3 881	9 626	8 534	1 945	724
1984	20 081	20 062	19	13 445	719	-137	12 589	3 575	3 918	10 417	9 279	1 928	735
1985	20 853	20 837	16	13 885	782	-115	12 987	3 694	4 172	10 936	9 736	1 907	735
1986	21 578	21 542	36	14 135	817	-89	13 229	3 921	4 428	11 464	10 258	1 882	735
1987	22 198	22 195	2	14 522	852	-23	13 647	3 998	4 553	11 950	10 688	1 858	742
1988	23 259	23 231	28	15 194	940	8	14 262	4 233	4 764	12 708	11 429	1 830	755
1989	24 440	24 386	55	15 694	1 005	87	14 776	4 628	5 037	13 529	12 059	1 807	762
1990	26 133	26 096	37	16 897	1 060	68	15 905	4 878	5 350	14 579	12 997	1 792	783
1991	27 367	27 346	21	17 463	1 125	68	16 407	4 938	6 022	15 219	13 606	1 798	784
1992	29 101	29 049	52	18 493	1 182	80	17 392	4 940	6 770	16 118	14 459	1 805	795
1993	30 375	30 317	58	19 145	1 235	91	18 000	4 945	7 430	16 724	15 007	1 816	807
1994	31 666	31 611	55	20 210	1 322	132	19 020	5 144	7 502	17 413	15 565	1 818	829
1995	32 611	32 596	15	20 710	1 385	165	19 489	5 408	7 714	17 913	15 968	1 821	846
1996	33 771	33 773	-2	21 201	1 409	190	19 981	5 788	8 001	18 566	16 493	1 819	855
1997	35 200	35 205	-5	21 917	1 447	306	20 776	6 078	8 346	19 388	17 174	1 816	867
1998	36 679	36 681	-2	22 732	1 482	431	21 681	6 516	8 482	20 246	17 902	1 812	879
1999	37 884	37 898	-14	23 441	1 539	505	22 407	6 894	8 583	20 966	18 498	1 807	883

Table 25-1. Personal Income and Employment—*Continued*

(Millions of dollars, except as noted.)

Year	Total	Nonfarm	Farm	Derivation of personal income						Per capita (dollars)		Population (thousands)	Total employment (thousands)
				Earnings by place of work	Less: Personal contributions for social insurance	Plus: Adjustment for residence	Equals: Net earnings by place of residence	Dividends, interest, and rent	Transfer payments	Total	Disposable		
WISCONSIN													
1970	17 629	16 948	680	13 581	480	252	13 353	2 684	1 591	3 983	3 457	4 426	1 954
1971	18 901	18 161	740	14 432	525	263	14 170	2 859	1 872	4 238	3 727	4 460	1 957
1972	20 670	19 885	785	15 843	599	286	15 530	3 060	2 080	4 595	3 996	4 498	2 014
1973	23 182	22 215	966	17 847	767	312	17 392	3 440	2 349	5 130	4 472	4 518	2 116
1974	25 512	24 655	857	19 344	880	338	18 803	3 919	2 791	5 622	4 876	4 538	2 159
1975	27 697	26 787	910	20 578	930	343	19 992	4 230	3 475	6 061	5 315	4 570	2 148
1976	30 578	29 777	801	22 871	1 022	388	22 237	4 558	3 783	6 670	5 824	4 585	2 211
1977	34 218	33 028	1 189	25 864	1 128	429	25 166	4 995	4 057	7 417	6 438	4 613	2 293
1978	38 408	37 223	1 185	29 049	1 296	484	28 237	5 707	4 465	8 292	7 142	4 632	2 382
1979	43 302	41 847	1 455	32 460	1 519	523	31 463	6 730	5 109	9 281	8 028	4 666	2 465
1980	47 881	46 402	1 479	34 536	1 633	547	33 449	8 191	6 241	10 161	8 811	4 712	2 449
1981	52 018	50 848	1 170	36 317	1 886	597	35 028	9 909	7 081	11 006	9 482	4 726	2 424
1982	54 819	53 794	1 025	37 141	1 972	618	35 787	11 123	7 909	11 592	10 073	4 729	2 382
1983	56 873	56 441	432	38 462	2 039	673	37 096	11 298	8 479	12 046	10 562	4 721	2 385
1984	62 423	61 485	938	42 670	2 234	789	41 225	12 596	8 603	13 182	11 589	4 736	2 478
1985	65 733	64 805	928	44 997	2 455	877	43 420	13 140	9 173	13 845	12 170	4 748	2 510
1986	69 101	67 894	1 207	47 577	2 633	959	45 903	13 685	9 513	14 530	12 761	4 756	2 552
1987	73 378	72 141	1 237	50 971	2 815	1 067	49 224	14 362	9 792	15 358	13 456	4 778	2 621
1988	78 126	77 395	730	54 667	3 189	1 228	52 706	15 281	10 138	16 201	14 180	4 822	2 702
1989	84 013	82 466	1 548	58 482	3 486	1 265	56 261	16 953	10 799	17 299	15 074	4 857	2 760
1990	89 025	87 887	1 139	61 930	3 713	1 361	59 577	17 815	11 632	18 160	15 817	4 902	2 835
1991	92 669	91 966	703	64 143	3 951	1 398	61 590	18 322	12 758	18 711	16 310	4 953	2 861
1992	99 454	98 620	834	69 647	4 234	1 491	66 904	18 730	13 819	19 872	17 332	5 005	2 916
1993	104 337	103 772	565	73 544	4 469	1 584	70 659	19 207	14 471	20 639	17 959	5 055	2 974
1994	110 570	109 902	668	78 106	4 827	1 691	74 971	20 716	14 883	21 699	18 802	5 096	3 067
1995	115 960	115 505	455	81 482	5 105	1 751	78 127	22 104	15 728	22 573	19 516	5 137	3 148
1996	121 864	121 023	841	85 206	5 304	1 927	81 828	23 838	16 198	23 554	20 196	5 174	3 201
1997	128 912	128 472	440	89 686	5 656	2 116	86 146	25 923	16 842	24 790	21 100	5 200	3 258
1998	137 056	136 245	812	95 466	5 938	2 412	91 941	28 031	17 085	26 245	22 226	5 222	3 322
1999	143 811	143 029	782	100 628	6 313	2 538	96 853	29 310	17 648	27 390	23 163	5 250	3 395
WYOMING													
1970	1 308	1 225	84	1 032	36	0	996	210	102	3 919	3 476	334	159
1971	1 451	1 358	93	1 138	41	-1	1 097	236	119	4 269	3 812	340	165
1972	1 633	1 500	134	1 304	47	-3	1 253	251	130	4 709	4 251	347	172
1973	1 912	1 752	159	1 533	63	-7	1 463	298	151	5 410	4 814	353	182
1974	2 250	2 133	117	1 813	76	-13	1 723	356	171	6 172	5 393	365	194
1975	2 550	2 479	71	2 053	87	-16	1 950	396	204	6 701	5 945	380	203
1976	2 852	2 802	50	2 299	100	-23	2 176	448	229	7 212	6 342	395	214
1977	3 355	3 309	46	2 728	116	-30	2 582	518	255	8 152	7 169	412	231
1978	4 044	3 974	69	3 313	144	-39	3 130	628	286	9 384	8 225	431	250
1979	4 777	4 678	99	3 916	178	-56	3 682	766	329	10 572	9 122	452	267
1980	5 573	5 487	86	4 537	208	-77	4 253	929	392	11 753	10 166	474	280
1981	6 333	6 282	51	5 075	257	-87	4 731	1 132	470	12 879	11 051	492	290
1982	6 710	6 678	33	5 138	268	-83	4 787	1 383	541	13 251	11 545	506	288
1983	6 493	6 450	43	4 897	247	-61	4 589	1 265	638	12 723	11 229	510	275
1984	6 812	6 795	18	5 103	257	-55	4 791	1 400	621	13 493	12 020	505	277
1985	7 117	7 096	21	5 331	282	-54	4 995	1 463	659	14 242	12 704	500	278
1986	6 941	6 900	41	5 094	278	-42	4 774	1 439	727	14 004	12 616	496	265
1987	6 770	6 712	57	4 868	270	-27	4 570	1 460	740	14 194	12 757	477	260
1988	6 962	6 914	48	4 989	296	-22	4 670	1 526	765	14 968	13 467	465	265
1989	7 510	7 429	81	5 286	313	-16	4 957	1 733	820	16 383	14 612	458	267
1990	8 159	8 014	145	5 716	337	-12	5 367	1 907	885	17 996	16 077	453	272
1991	8 636	8 421	215	6 021	362	-4	5 655	1 995	986	18 867	16 929	458	279
1992	9 061	8 861	200	6 301	381	-13	5 907	2 062	1 092	19 550	17 516	463	282
1993	9 515	9 271	244	6 708	398	-17	6 293	2 047	1 176	20 287	18 102	469	287
1994	9 954	9 856	98	6 911	423	-20	6 468	2 245	1 241	20 957	18 663	475	300
1995	10 293	10 204	90	7 034	437	-20	6 577	2 404	1 312	21 514	19 145	478	303
1996	10 609	10 545	64	7 116	447	-19	6 650	2 567	1 393	22 098	19 178	480	306
1997	11 434	11 259	175	7 574	464	-17	7 093	2 899	1 442	23 820	20 597	480	309
1998	11 966	11 898	68	7 847	483	-19	7 345	3 142	1 479	24 927	21 452	480	316
1999	12 660	12 509	151	8 372	513	-22	7 838	3 305	1 517	26 396	22 654	480	322

Table 25-1. Personal Income and Employment—*Continued*

(Millions of dollars, except as noted.)

Year	Total	Nonfarm	Farm	Derivation of personal income						Per capita (dollars)		Population (thousands)	Total employment (thousands)
				Earnings by place of work	Less: Personal contributions for social insurance	Plus: Adjustment for residence	Equals: Net earnings by place of residence	Dividends, interest, and rent	Transfer payments	Total	Disposable		
NEW ENGLAND													
1970	52 892	52 559	333	40 375	1 313	852	39 914	8 097	4 881	4 453	3 869	11 878	5 518
1971	56 140	55 828	312	42 338	1 425	880	41 793	8 469	5 878	4 680	4 123	11 996	5 454
1972	60 814	60 496	318	46 102	1 593	936	45 446	8 964	6 404	5 031	4 366	12 088	5 573
1973	66 688	66 264	423	50 689	2 013	993	49 668	9 874	7 145	5 490	4 794	12 148	5 783
1974	72 577	72 122	455	54 235	2 251	1 079	53 063	11 043	8 472	5 970	5 206	12 157	5 843
1975	77 479	77 146	333	56 334	2 307	1 166	55 194	11 291	10 994	6 363	5 629	12 176	5 685
1976	84 948	84 498	449	62 310	2 507	1 296	61 099	12 280	11 568	6 959	6 113	12 207	5 811
1977	93 301	92 899	402	68 762	2 757	1 449	67 454	13 723	12 124	7 612	6 672	12 257	6 007
1978	104 140	103 725	415	77 318	3 149	1 632	75 802	15 560	12 778	8 465	7 376	12 303	6 280
1979	117 069	116 679	390	86 580	3 720	1 864	84 724	18 147	14 197	9 483	8 204	12 345	6 515
1980	132 395	132 022	373	96 056	4 196	2 179	94 039	21 984	16 372	10 701	9 226	12 372	6 641
1981	147 774	147 297	477	104 799	4 992	2 350	102 156	26 883	18 735	11 883	10 175	12 436	6 692
1982	159 591	159 075	515	112 092	5 507	2 527	109 112	29 967	20 512	12 800	11 007	12 468	6 694
1983	172 548	172 059	489	122 565	6 026	2 660	119 199	31 496	21 853	13 755	11 956	12 544	6 828
1984	193 939	193 366	573	138 186	6 840	2 838	134 184	37 148	22 607	15 341	13 402	12 642	7 198
1985	209 851	209 280	571	151 686	7 844	2 993	146 834	39 276	23 741	16 471	14 292	12 741	7 447
1986	226 352	225 762	590	164 823	8 737	3 166	159 253	41 972	25 127	17 638	15 220	12 833	7 688
1987	248 095	247 457	638	182 438	9 677	3 338	176 099	45 903	26 093	19 156	16 426	12 951	7 829
1988	273 667	273 000	667	201 642	10 957	3 535	194 219	51 318	28 129	20 915	18 145	13 085	8 082
1989	292 630	291 981	648	211 282	11 686	3 463	203 059	58 162	31 408	22 200	19 216	13 182	8 075
1990	302 739	302 066	673	215 956	12 028	3 461	207 390	60 167	35 182	22 900	19 874	13 220	7 920
1991	307 013	306 401	612	215 264	12 379	3 526	206 412	59 755	40 846	23 257	20 256	13 201	7 586
1992	322 471	321 678	793	227 711	12 935	4 167	218 942	59 208	44 320	24 452	21 269	13 188	7 628
1993	333 140	332 409	731	236 243	13 519	4 163	226 887	60 401	45 852	25 208	21 846	13 216	7 754
1994	347 347	346 670	677	246 210	14 355	4 219	236 073	63 068	48 206	26 229	22 688	13 243	7 854
1995	364 297	363 698	599	257 171	15 269	4 835	246 737	66 382	51 178	27 426	23 565	13 283	7 950
1996	384 144	383 456	687	271 302	15 958	5 615	260 959	70 663	52 522	28 820	24 499	13 329	8 085
1997	408 160	407 566	594	288 834	17 141	5 608	277 300	75 757	55 103	30 510	25 604	13 378	8 252
1998	434 615	433 988	628	309 580	18 206	5 534	296 909	81 383	56 324	32 365	26 916	13 429	8 451
1999	461 194	460 461	734	331 807	19 609	5 934	318 132	85 145	57 917	34 173	28 320	13 496	8 611
MIDEAST													
1970	196 543	195 362	1 181	157 629	5 425	-1 677	150 527	27 972	18 044	4 623	3 991	42 517	19 469
1971	210 097	209 003	1 094	166 798	5 926	-1 759	159 113	29 216	21 768	4 901	4 286	42 870	19 304
1972	227 051	225 946	1 105	180 314	6 582	-1 931	171 800	30 816	24 435	5 281	4 551	42 992	19 526
1973	246 658	245 151	1 507	195 779	8 212	-2 072	185 495	34 005	27 157	5 758	4 993	42 837	19 973
1974	268 578	267 157	1 421	210 268	9 155	-2 310	198 803	38 148	31 628	6 289	5 431	42 709	19 960
1975	288 774	287 457	1 317	221 455	9 538	-2 638	209 279	39 499	39 996	6 758	5 921	42 728	19 485
1976	313 712	312 326	1 385	240 559	10 174	-2 994	227 391	42 956	43 365	7 352	6 412	42 667	19 568
1977	342 391	341 203	1 189	262 663	10 995	-3 404	248 265	48 027	46 099	8 047	6 981	42 547	19 855
1978	377 206	375 794	1 412	290 408	12 349	-3 934	274 125	54 318	48 733	8 892	7 689	42 421	20 411
1979	417 293	415 690	1 603	319 530	14 253	-4 605	300 672	63 233	53 388	9 852	8 462	42 358	20 900
1980	464 044	462 844	1 201	348 481	15 739	-5 473	327 269	75 193	61 582	10 978	9 421	42 272	20 962
1981	515 105	513 548	1 557	379 378	18 582	-6 082	354 713	91 078	69 314	12 169	10 357	42 329	21 061
1982	553 286	551 817	1 470	401 514	20 106	-6 350	375 058	101 111	77 117	13 055	11 125	42 382	20 946
1983	590 053	588 954	1 099	427 182	21 683	-6 470	399 029	107 841	83 183	13 869	11 980	42 544	21 141
1984	651 738	649 883	1 855	471 299	24 147	-6 816	440 336	125 820	85 582	15 268	13 221	42 687	21 891
1985	697 625	695 663	1 962	507 549	27 436	-7 129	472 985	134 559	90 081	16 302	14 049	42 794	22 486
1986	742 758	740 592	2 166	544 020	30 233	-7 543	506 244	140 960	95 554	17 277	14 880	42 991	22 999
1987	797 956	795 743	2 213	590 732	32 850	-8 052	549 830	149 549	98 576	18 476	15 780	43 190	23 509
1988	868 357	866 285	2 073	645 084	37 286	-8 772	599 026	164 872	104 459	19 992	17 238	43 435	24 127
1989	932 472	930 030	2 442	679 925	40 057	-9 048	630 820	188 984	112 669	21 394	18 352	43 585	24 421
1990	988 666	986 357	2 309	719 024	42 372	-9 826	666 827	198 234	123 605	22 611	19 514	43 726	24 482
1991	1 018 680	1 016 844	1 836	729 727	44 083	-10 351	675 293	202 569	140 818	23 211	20 137	43 887	23 912
1992	1 074 930	1 072 589	2 341	776 549	46 277	-11 377	718 895	198 203	157 832	24 393	21 202	44 068	23 816
1993	1 103 630	1 101 296	2 334	799 480	47 904	-11 746	739 830	197 158	166 642	24 937	21 604	44 256	23 946
1994	1 140 466	1 138 446	2 020	823 463	50 412	-11 988	761 064	206 642	172 760	25 700	22 200	44 377	24 134
1995	1 193 865	1 192 233	1 632	857 650	52 928	-12 858	791 864	219 638	182 363	26 856	23 151	44 454	24 430
1996	1 255 345	1 252 958	2 388	901 579	54 807	-13 486	833 286	230 897	191 162	28 201	24 109	44 514	24 670
1997	1 315 305	1 313 734	1 571	946 230	57 684	-14 186	874 360	245 491	195 454	29 511	24 995	44 570	25 068
1998	1 391 425	1 389 417	2 008	1 006 373	60 872	-14 091	931 409	260 732	199 283	31 161	26 175	44 653	25 626
1999	1 461 043	1 458 863	2 181	1 067 332	64 846	-15 237	987 249	267 729	206 065	32 628	27 286	44 778	26 180

Table 25-1. Personal Income and Employment—*Continued*

(Millions of dollars, except as noted.)

| Year | Total | Nonfarm | Farm | Derivation of personal income | | | | | | Per capita (dollars) | | Population (thousands) | Total employment (thousands) |
				Earnings by place of work	Less: Personal contributions for social insurance	Plus: Adjustment for residence	Equals: Net earnings by place of residence	Dividends, interest, and rent	Transfer payments	Total	Disposable		
GREAT LAKES													
1970	169 462	166 666	2 796	137 658	4 581	255	133 332	22 644	13 485	4 203	3 648	40 320	17 630
1971	181 909	178 710	3 199	146 765	5 012	325	142 079	23 702	16 128	4 478	3 939	40 622	17 549
1972	198 768	195 300	3 468	160 791	5 667	373	155 497	25 290	17 981	4 869	4 221	40 824	17 933
1973	223 387	217 934	5 453	180 831	7 281	422	173 973	28 608	20 807	5 456	4 758	40 947	18 710
1974	243 198	238 293	4 904	193 498	8 150	521	185 869	32 579	24 750	5 926	5 152	41 037	18 911
1975	260 632	254 629	6 002	202 175	8 340	613	194 448	34 623	31 561	6 341	5 581	41 105	18 399
1976	289 377	284 375	5 002	226 235	9 271	760	217 724	37 773	33 881	7 026	6 130	41 187	18 891
1977	322 534	317 463	5 071	253 804	10 301	942	244 445	42 300	35 788	7 799	6 771	41 353	19 508
1978	359 263	354 489	4 774	283 289	11 744	1 165	272 710	48 213	38 340	8 655	7 479	41 510	20 196
1979	398 184	392 849	5 335	310 693	13 535	1 381	298 539	56 419	43 226	9 569	8 241	41 611	20 521
1980	431 511	428 174	3 337	321 969	14 239	1 657	309 387	67 718	54 405	10 350	8 971	41 694	20 024
1981	469 882	466 040	3 842	342 782	16 503	1 409	327 688	81 737	60 458	11 282	9 733	41 648	19 862
1982	487 227	484 426	2 801	345 336	17 044	1 309	329 601	89 672	67 953	11 743	10 248	41 492	19 316
1983	510 969	511 221	-252	359 931	17 895	1 288	343 323	95 130	72 516	12 352	10 814	41 366	19 336
1984	565 164	561 183	3 981	401 826	19 920	1 390	383 295	108 446	73 423	13 654	12 012	41 393	20 120
1985	601 455	597 045	4 410	429 809	22 359	1 424	408 873	114 720	77 861	14 522	12 730	41 418	20 607
1986	632 297	628 399	3 898	452 844	24 165	1 490	430 168	120 220	81 909	15 253	13 386	41 455	21 053
1987	667 441	663 124	4 317	481 026	25 703	1 561	456 884	125 863	84 694	16 048	13 999	41 590	21 654
1988	713 443	710 869	2 574	517 776	28 797	1 671	490 650	134 595	88 197	17 100	14 978	41 721	22 222
1989	762 815	756 678	6 137	547 876	31 208	1 711	518 378	149 984	94 454	18 218	15 853	41 873	22 724
1990	805 743	800 787	4 956	576 428	32 932	1 928	545 424	158 105	102 214	19 149	16 699	42 077	23 105
1991	831 381	828 912	2 469	590 079	34 673	1 942	557 347	160 894	113 140	19 599	17 152	42 419	23 016
1992	888 017	883 617	4 400	635 000	36 574	2 103	600 529	162 767	124 721	20 764	18 250	42 766	23 152
1993	929 524	925 601	3 923	668 357	38 706	2 291	631 942	166 532	131 050	21 575	18 868	43 083	23 552
1994	984 893	980 427	4 466	709 226	41 925	2 496	669 797	180 355	134 741	22 724	19 804	43 342	24 277
1995	1 034 159	1 031 650	2 510	743 162	44 362	2 662	701 462	191 054	141 643	23 703	20 582	43 629	24 945
1996	1 079 799	1 074 406	5 393	771 735	46 015	2 924	728 644	203 690	147 465	24 604	21 201	43 888	25 355
1997	1 138 409	1 133 124	5 285	812 209	48 801	3 289	766 697	217 732	153 980	25 825	22 125	44 082	25 783
1998	1 204 878	1 200 803	4 075	861 885	51 301	3 434	814 019	235 863	154 996	27 224	23 195	44 257	26 267
1999	1 259 859	1 256 872	2 987	906 163	54 307	3 647	855 503	244 698	159 658	28 348	24 070	44 442	26 723
PLAINS													
1970	62 776	58 281	4 494	50 173	1 744	-355	48 074	8 938	5 763	3 840	3 384	16 350	7 506
1971	67 468	62 815	4 653	53 532	1 918	-351	51 263	9 547	6 658	4 095	3 652	16 475	7 516
1972	74 607	68 361	6 246	59 525	2 154	-357	57 014	10 342	7 252	4 505	3 965	16 563	7 544
1973	87 538	76 209	11 329	70 369	2 746	-393	67 230	11 919	8 389	5 264	4 675	16 628	7 731
1974	92 855	85 130	7 725	72 882	3 145	-425	69 312	13 770	9 772	5 570	4 865	16 672	8 065
1975	101 249	93 722	7 527	78 086	3 358	-415	74 313	15 007	11 929	6 047	5 347	16 743	8 219
1976	109 419	104 990	4 429	84 120	3 703	-512	79 905	16 478	13 036	6 488	5 701	16 864	8 181
1977	121 538	116 314	5 223	93 431	3 989	-650	88 792	18 803	13 942	7 171	6 291	16 950	8 439
1978	138 372	130 481	7 891	107 071	4 607	-808	101 656	21 588	15 129	8 126	7 114	17 028	8 657
1979	153 711	147 042	6 669	117 812	5 416	-975	111 420	25 398	16 893	8 990	7 810	17 097	8 958
1980	165 837	164 088	1 749	121 862	5 896	-1 128	114 838	30 767	20 232	9 637	8 365	17 208	9 248
1981	187 045	181 684	5 361	134 531	6 841	-1 323	126 367	37 647	23 031	10 834	9 377	17 264	9 251
1982	197 115	193 403	3 713	137 443	7 277	-1 329	128 837	42 575	25 703	11 399	9 864	17 292	9 212
1983	206 081	204 948	1 133	143 077	7 666	-1 417	133 995	44 490	27 596	11 895	10 442	17 325	9 083
1984	230 380	224 434	5 946	162 690	8 494	-1 585	152 612	49 370	28 398	13 254	11 752	17 382	9 196
1985	243 973	237 200	6 773	173 003	9 463	-1 691	161 849	51 708	30 415	14 020	12 414	17 402	9 513
1986	254 901	247 568	7 333	181 170	10 175	-1 804	169 191	53 633	32 078	14 656	13 011	17 393	9 664
1987	269 737	260 619	9 118	194 045	10 924	-1 919	181 202	55 235	33 300	15 477	13 660	17 428	9 755
1988	283 039	276 440	6 599	204 239	12 213	-2 075	189 951	58 129	34 959	16 143	14 258	17 533	10 011
1989	303 631	295 224	8 407	217 324	13 254	-2 160	201 910	64 162	37 560	17 256	15 167	17 595	10 223
1990	322 236	312 741	9 494	230 182	14 050	-2 432	213 700	68 011	40 524	18 217	16 007	17 689	10 430
1991	335 351	328 184	7 167	236 861	14 880	-2 464	219 517	70 675	45 159	18 842	16 623	17 798	10 619
1992	357 609	348 443	9 166	255 768	15 707	-2 586	237 475	71 208	48 925	19 928	17 605	17 945	10 670
1993	368 899	363 685	5 213	263 503	16 510	-2 730	244 264	72 417	52 217	20 389	17 950	18 093	10 787
1994	393 000	384 212	8 788	282 034	17 766	-2 889	261 378	77 366	54 256	21 558	18 957	18 230	11 021
1995	410 645	405 532	5 113	292 414	18 754	-3 037	270 623	82 657	57 364	22 363	19 573	18 363	11 328
1996	439 948	427 804	12 144	314 677	19 621	-3 196	291 860	88 237	59 852	23 802	20 712	18 484	11 640
1997	462 250	453 428	8 822	329 139	20 806	-3 550	304 783	95 094	62 373	24 861	21 497	18 593	11 871
1998	491 292	483 390	7 901	350 209	21 965	-3 801	324 444	102 936	63 912	26 282	22 644	18 693	12 101
1999	514 176	507 870	6 306	368 288	23 334	-3 995	340 958	107 169	66 050	27 350	23 564	18 800	12 370

Table 25-1. Personal Income and Employment—*Continued*

(Millions of dollars, except as noted.)

Year	Total	Nonfarm	Farm	Derivation of personal income — Earnings by place of work	Less: Personal contributions for social insurance	Plus: Adjustment for residence	Equals: Net earnings by place of residence	Dividends, interest, and rent	Transfer payments	Per capita (dollars) — Total	Disposable	Population (thousands)	Total employment (thousands)
SOUTHEAST													
1970	146 709	142 345	4 365	117 117	3 908	1 011	114 221	18 776	13 712	3 336	2 956	43 974	19 254
1971	161 619	157 021	4 598	128 025	4 400	986	124 611	20 703	16 305	3 590	3 205	45 013	19 635
1972	181 809	176 449	5 360	144 697	5 141	1 046	140 602	22 778	18 429	3 951	3 484	46 019	20 523
1973	207 663	200 031	7 632	164 967	6 650	1 117	159 434	26 539	21 690	4 419	3 920	46 992	21 636
1974	232 035	225 036	6 999	181 226	7 642	1 235	174 819	31 037	26 179	4 839	4 275	47 955	22 069
1975	252 583	246 321	6 262	191 935	8 023	1 476	185 387	33 500	33 695	5 177	4 654	48 788	21 642
1976	283 155	276 573	6 582	216 260	8 963	1 666	208 963	37 231	36 961	5 719	5 103	49 514	22 351
1977	315 802	309 850	5 952	241 594	9 988	1 901	233 507	42 451	39 844	6 277	5 585	50 312	23 208
1978	360 348	353 191	7 157	275 962	11 567	2 208	266 603	50 246	43 499	7 050	6 243	51 113	24 309
1979	408 144	401 042	7 102	308 456	13 586	2 576	297 446	60 687	50 012	7 852	6 915	51 977	25 020
1980	460 761	456 322	4 439	337 984	15 221	3 125	325 888	75 091	59 782	8 713	7 666	52 881	25 378
1981	520 469	513 582	6 887	374 242	18 237	3 553	359 558	92 690	68 221	9 705	8 505	53 627	25 676
1982	556 531	549 701	6 829	393 118	19 745	3 777	377 149	103 552	75 829	10 259	9 028	54 249	25 577
1983	598 511	593 514	4 996	421 282	21 401	3 835	403 716	112 354	82 441	10 911	9 674	54 856	26 111
1984	669 482	661 122	8 361	474 255	24 026	4 025	454 254	129 517	85 711	12 060	10 768	55 515	27 394
1985	722 928	715 546	7 382	511 589	27 278	4 230	488 541	142 049	92 338	12 864	11 419	56 199	28 241
1986	768 564	761 773	6 791	543 241	29 790	4 450	517 901	151 720	98 943	13 517	12 002	56 861	28 986
1987	825 358	817 279	8 079	587 548	32 122	4 761	560 187	161 446	103 725	14 345	12 684	57 536	29 715
1988	894 629	884 124	10 505	636 703	36 272	5 241	605 672	177 944	111 013	15 393	13 676	58 120	30 733
1989	968 835	957 836	10 999	675 927	39 632	5 603	641 898	204 806	122 131	16 495	14 585	58 733	31 480
1990	1 035 261	1 025 106	10 155	717 193	42 120	6 348	681 421	218 552	135 288	17 408	15 443	59 470	32 078
1991	1 083 034	1 071 067	11 967	743 742	44 635	6 828	705 935	223 972	153 127	17 974	16 015	60 256	31 954
1992	1 153 443	1 140 995	12 448	800 898	47 467	7 109	760 539	220 385	172 519	18 887	16 840	61 070	32 440
1993	1 218 508	1 206 260	12 248	844 983	50 584	7 393	801 792	230 336	186 380	19 690	17 523	61 886	33 474
1994	1 289 941	1 276 593	13 347	893 298	54 626	7 469	846 141	246 622	197 178	20 563	18 237	62 730	34 464
1995	1 366 116	1 354 202	11 913	940 896	58 170	7 715	890 441	264 061	211 614	21 500	19 014	63 539	35 597
1996	1 445 912	1 432 636	13 276	992 020	60 767	7 494	938 747	283 021	224 144	22 477	19 734	64 329	36 465
1997	1 532 182	1 518 892	13 290	1 050 294	64 550	8 208	993 952	303 655	234 576	23 518	20 508	65 150	37 466
1998	1 633 047	1 620 815	12 231	1 123 142	68 429	8 294	1 063 007	329 138	240 902	24 780	21 518	65 901	38 372
1999	1 712 414	1 699 590	12 824	1 189 760	72 976	9 032	1 125 816	338 581	248 017	25 703	22 238	66 622	39 260
SOUTHWEST													
1970	60 062	58 164	1 898	48 675	1 570	-85	47 021	8 028	5 012	3 614	3 201	16 621	7 311
1971	65 623	63 863	1 761	52 770	1 759	-89	50 922	8 807	5 894	3 843	3 445	17 077	7 457
1972	73 036	70 905	2 131	58 935	2 015	-108	56 813	9 626	6 597	4 173	3 697	17 503	7 807
1973	83 516	80 110	3 406	67 270	2 633	-121	64 517	11 217	7 782	4 655	4 145	17 943	8 215
1974	94 357	92 116	2 241	75 063	3 087	-82	71 893	13 188	9 275	5 141	4 535	18 354	8 511
1975	105 799	103 614	2 185	83 439	3 381	-50	80 009	14 174	11 616	5 631	5 037	18 789	8 633
1976	119 822	117 682	2 140	95 168	3 799	21	91 391	15 629	12 803	6 218	5 528	19 270	9 001
1977	134 513	132 608	1 905	107 580	4 331	-225	103 024	17 709	13 781	6 825	6 023	19 710	9 467
1978	155 988	154 250	1 738	124 809	5 123	-363	119 323	21 449	15 216	7 730	6 810	20 180	10 043
1979	181 662	178 582	3 080	144 749	6 229	-356	138 164	26 178	17 320	8 744	7 634	20 777	10 539
1980	209 160	207 480	1 680	163 935	7 270	-459	156 206	32 565	20 388	9 762	8 493	21 426	10 944
1981	244 433	241 451	2 982	189 886	9 102	-188	180 596	40 640	23 198	11 118	9 564	21 985	11 485
1982	266 387	264 076	2 311	203 760	10 049	-252	193 459	46 654	26 274	11 688	10 113	22 791	11 717
1983	281 428	279 127	2 301	212 804	10 386	-182	202 237	49 925	29 266	12 024	10 605	23 405	11 746
1984	311 524	308 835	2 688	234 687	11 433	-183	223 071	57 903	30 549	13 102	11 631	23 776	12 309
1985	335 615	332 990	2 625	251 678	12 815	-150	238 713	64 000	32 902	13 888	12 322	24 166	12 685
1986	343 547	340 994	2 553	254 649	13 272	-36	241 341	66 092	36 114	13 974	12 520	24 585	12 552
1987	354 762	351 389	3 373	262 257	13 566	55	248 746	67 550	38 467	14 335	12 785	24 748	12 861
1988	376 245	372 527	3 717	278 357	15 066	153	263 443	72 058	40 744	15 135	13 562	24 860	13 138
1989	403 626	399 848	3 778	295 149	16 392	234	278 991	79 753	44 882	16 092	14 348	25 083	13 334
1990	434 654	430 059	4 595	318 842	17 725	336	301 453	83 530	49 671	17 119	15 251	25 391	13 650
1991	458 108	453 637	4 471	335 995	19 211	284	317 068	85 228	55 811	17 745	15 888	25 816	13 856
1992	490 173	485 190	4 983	360 614	20 457	332	340 489	84 793	64 891	18 636	16 727	26 303	13 994
1993	517 898	511 920	5 978	383 890	21 849	367	362 408	85 897	69 592	19 300	17 295	26 834	14 453
1994	550 067	545 095	4 971	406 229	23 648	381	382 963	92 708	74 396	20 086	17 973	27 385	14 984
1995	586 017	582 066	3 950	430 820	25 449	360	405 731	99 555	80 731	20 978	18 734	27 935	15 543
1996	624 034	620 638	3 396	459 386	27 037	354	432 703	105 799	85 532	21 946	19 443	28 434	16 046
1997	677 722	672 952	4 770	501 498	29 251	323	472 570	115 315	89 837	23 414	20 619	28 945	16 662
1998	732 117	727 553	4 563	547 194	31 592	331	515 933	124 335	91 849	24 857	21 779	29 453	17 240
1999	773 803	766 907	6 896	583 396	33 747	399	550 048	128 466	95 289	25 862	22 606	29 920	17 612

Table 25-1. Personal Income and Employment—Continued

(Millions of dollars, except as noted.)

Year	Total	Nonfarm	Farm	Derivation of personal income						Per capita (dollars)		Population (thousands)	Total employment (thousands)
				Earnings by place of work	Less: Personal contributions for social insurance	Plus: Adjustment for residence	Equals: Net earnings by place of residence	Dividends, interest, and rent	Transfer payments	Total	Disposable		
ROCKY MOUNTAIN													
1970	19 020	17 972	1 048	15 138	475	16	14 679	2 746	1 594	3 775	3 342	5 038	2 271
1971	21 116	20 097	1 019	16 739	537	19	16 220	3 021	1 875	4 065	3 622	5 194	2 343
1972	23 967	22 629	1 338	19 193	634	22	18 582	3 293	2 093	4 464	3 946	5 368	2 482
1973	27 549	25 739	1 810	22 092	831	22	21 283	3 839	2 427	4 984	4 404	5 527	2 646
1974	31 152	29 252	1 900	24 807	961	25	23 872	4 466	2 814	5 514	4 846	5 650	2 740
1975	34 227	32 787	1 441	26 906	1 041	36	25 901	4 861	3 465	5 920	5 264	5 782	2 778
1976	38 246	37 175	1 072	30 072	1 164	42	28 950	5 458	3 838	6 465	5 714	5 916	2 912
1977	42 955	42 237	718	33 809	1 324	44	32 529	6 267	4 159	7 066	6 215	6 079	3 060
1978	49 995	48 994	1 001	39 511	1 560	54	38 005	7 458	4 533	7 990	7 019	6 257	3 257
1979	57 057	56 299	758	44 681	1 892	55	42 843	9 088	5 126	8 861	7 732	6 439	3 406
1980	64 971	64 009	962	49 930	2 146	78	47 862	11 076	6 033	9 856	8 611	6 592	3 482
1981	73 763	72 801	961	55 794	2 620	51	53 225	13 509	7 029	10 940	9 500	6 743	3 571
1982	79 572	78 782	790	59 026	2 859	53	56 220	15 342	8 010	11 526	10 028	6 904	3 608
1983	84 615	83 493	1 122	62 451	2 994	55	59 513	16 319	8 784	12 028	10 646	7 035	3 654
1984	92 374	91 323	1 051	68 178	3 288	74	64 964	18 376	9 034	12 994	11 560	7 109	3 817
1985	97 408	96 548	860	71 811	3 654	91	68 248	19 583	9 577	13 590	12 063	7 168	3 882
1986	100 364	99 128	1 236	73 554	3 836	114	69 832	20 175	10 358	13 940	12 415	7 200	3 876
1987	104 390	102 868	1 523	76 341	3 950	139	72 530	20 776	11 084	14 487	12 857	7 206	3 909
1988	109 620	108 076	1 544	80 366	4 386	177	76 157	21 805	11 659	15 220	13 512	7 203	4 047
1989	118 525	116 372	2 153	85 873	4 768	211	81 317	24 527	12 682	16 384	14 463	7 234	4 143
1990	127 663	125 019	2 645	92 804	5 148	246	87 903	25 878	13 882	17 491	15 402	7 299	4 261
1991	135 540	133 113	2 427	98 671	5 637	252	93 285	26 800	15 455	18 208	16 058	7 444	4 365
1992	145 514	143 199	2 315	106 971	6 065	254	101 160	27 126	17 228	19 062	16 777	7 634	4 469
1993	156 962	153 734	3 227	116 438	6 570	262	110 130	28 208	18 623	20 003	17 566	7 847	4 664
1994	167 291	165 456	1 835	123 392	7 155	287	116 524	31 334	19 433	20 782	18 172	8 050	4 931
1995	179 684	177 765	1 919	131 583	7 680	322	124 225	34 274	21 184	21 841	19 088	8 227	5 093
1996	192 141	190 151	1 990	140 581	8 156	367	132 791	36 959	22 391	22 930	19 878	8 379	5 299
1997	206 831	204 980	1 852	151 388	8 747	396	143 037	40 541	23 253	24 259	20 898	8 526	5 494
1998	223 051	220 765	2 285	164 447	9 410	432	155 469	43 891	23 691	25 756	22 110	8 660	5 674
1999	238 235	235 579	2 656	177 631	10 216	452	167 867	45 895	24 473	27 072	23 188	8 800	5 831
FAR WEST													
1970	126 992	124 481	2 511	99 710	3 330	-192	96 188	18 883	11 921	4 686	4 149	27 101	12 313
1971	135 277	132 729	2 549	105 032	3 594	-207	101 231	20 193	13 854	4 907	4 392	27 570	12 301
1972	148 309	145 089	3 220	116 081	4 106	-212	111 763	21 575	14 971	5 312	4 677	27 918	12 742
1973	164 994	160 655	4 339	129 109	5 190	-212	123 707	24 538	16 749	5 824	5 169	28 328	13 405
1974	185 428	179 944	5 484	143 828	5 940	-307	137 581	28 045	19 802	6 438	5 694	28 801	13 865
1975	205 471	200 585	4 887	157 719	6 431	-501	150 787	29 966	24 718	7 002	6 262	29 346	14 103
1976	231 073	226 212	4 861	178 378	7 181	-618	170 579	33 119	27 375	7 721	6 847	29 929	14 625
1977	257 866	253 132	4 734	199 327	8 106	-434	190 788	37 697	29 382	8 440	7 442	30 553	15 287
1978	296 027	291 211	4 816	228 519	9 415	-365	218 739	45 567	31 721	9 462	8 297	31 285	16 235
1979	339 719	333 708	6 011	260 277	11 292	-338	248 648	56 173	34 898	10 628	9 268	31 965	17 141
1980	385 242	377 678	7 564	289 693	12 281	-434	276 979	67 268	40 995	11 752	10 250	32 780	17 549
1981	429 865	423 945	5 920	315 231	14 894	-212	300 124	81 702	48 039	12 857	11 219	33 434	17 744
1982	457 245	451 227	6 017	332 069	16 178	-255	315 636	88 307	53 301	13 414	11 802	34 086	17 618
1983	490 834	484 801	6 033	357 260	17 616	-278	339 366	94 357	57 112	14 138	12 481	34 716	18 045
1984	545 463	538 740	6 723	398 033	19 832	-323	377 878	108 858	58 727	15 443	13 648	35 321	18 848
1985	589 808	583 353	6 456	431 274	22 292	-370	408 613	116 796	64 399	16 367	14 393	36 037	19 499
1986	628 576	621 164	7 412	462 317	24 832	-412	437 073	122 383	69 120	17 074	15 011	36 815	20 072
1987	677 776	669 314	8 462	502 431	27 502	-492	474 436	130 748	72 591	18 006	15 682	37 641	20 929
1988	736 000	727 078	8 922	547 385	31 257	-580	515 548	142 715	77 738	19 096	16 763	38 542	21 946
1989	799 895	791 101	8 793	589 259	33 914	-678	554 667	160 690	84 538	20 233	17 585	39 534	22 634
1990	868 563	859 505	9 058	637 951	36 562	-797	600 592	173 577	94 394	21 396	18 657	40 594	23 312
1991	896 310	888 350	7 960	654 856	38 740	-806	615 310	175 539	105 460	21 686	19 041	41 332	23 305
1992	944 465	935 637	8 828	690 395	40 469	-799	649 127	174 139	121 199	22 457	19 836	42 057	23 019
1993	969 886	959 940	9 947	706 595	41 623	-798	664 174	177 510	128 202	22 784	20 107	42 568	23 134
1994	1 005 357	996 031	9 326	728 526	43 657	-834	684 034	188 517	132 805	23 397	20 588	42 970	23 600
1995	1 057 453	1 048 393	9 060	758 325	45 660	-891	711 774	205 915	139 763	24 380	21 365	43 374	24 161
1996	1 116 779	1 106 564	10 215	802 129	47 530	-986	753 613	217 538	145 629	25 456	22 053	43 872	24 817
1997	1 187 903	1 177 243	10 660	859 120	50 403	-1 058	807 660	232 659	147 584	26 671	22 864	44 539	25 401
1998	1 273 263	1 262 544	10 719	928 318	53 940	-1 145	873 233	248 022	152 008	28 168	23 954	45 202	26 242
1999	1 362 427	1 352 086	10 341	1 005 219	58 907	-1 252	945 060	258 633	158 734	29 727	25 170	45 832	26 952

NOTES

NOTES

These notes pertain to the data in Tables 1-1 through 25-1. The notes are arranged by table number, with the tables to which they pertain and the general subject heading shown at the top of each group of notes. The notes provide information about data sources, definitions, methodology, revisions, and sources of additional information.

The tables are divided into four main parts.

PART I (Tables 1-1 through 12-5) pertains to the U.S. economy as a whole.

PART II (Tables 13-1 through 21-7) presents data by industry or industry group, arranged in accordance with the 1987 U.S. Standard Industrial Classification (SIC). The SIC classifies economic activity into divisions such as mining, manufacturing, retail trade, etc. and into a hierarchy of more detailed industry groups within each division. The tables in Part II present data for each SIC division and within manufacturing, for each major ("two-digit") industry group. Some of these data are repeated from the tables in Part I, giving the user the convenience of a profile of the industry in a single location. Where data are repeated in this way, these notes will normally cross reference earlier discussions of the data, rather than repeat the discussion.

The 1987 SIC is published in the Standard Industrial Classification Manual, 1987, Executive Office of the President, Office of Management and Budget (Washington, DC: U.S. Government Printing Office, 1988). Brief descriptions adapted from the SIC Manual are provided in these notes for the industry groups in Part II. These descriptions list only the main activities for each industry group; the SIC Manual should be consulted for complete details.

For industry data to be collected and published in the future, the SIC is being replaced by the North American Industry Classification System (NAICS) as the official U.S. system for the classification of data. However, as few data using the new system have been published, this edition of Business Statistics continues to present data on an SIC basis. A description of the NAICS and agency plans for its implementation is given in a lead article in the 1998 edition of Business Statistics. Additional information is available on the Census Bureau Internet site at http://www.census.gov.

PART III (Tables 22-1 through 24-10) contains additional historical data for selected quarterly and monthly series. In most cases, quarterly data are shown beginning with 1963 and monthly data beginning with 1972.

PART IV (Table 25-1) contains data on personal income, population, and employment by state and region. The data are annual and cover 1970 through 1999.

The table subtitles or column headings for the data tables normally indicate that the data are "seasonally adjusted" or "not seasonally adjusted" or "at a seasonally adjusted annual rate." These headings refer to the monthly or quarterly, rather than the annual, data.

Seasonal adjustment removes from the time series the average impact of variations that normally occur at about the same time each year due to, for example, weather, holidays, and tax payment dates.

A simplified example of the process of seasonal adjustment, or deseasonalizing, can indicate why it is so important for the interpretation of economic time series. Statisticians compare actual monthly data for a number of years with "moving average" trends of the monthly data for the 12 months centered on each month's data. For example, they may find that in November, sales values are usually about 95 percent of the moving average, while in December, usual sales values are 110 percent of the average. Suppose that actual November sales in the current year are $100 and December sales are $105. The seasonally adjusted value for November will be $105 ($100/0.95) while the value for December will be $95 ($105/1.10). Thus, an apparent increase in the unadjusted data turns out to be a decrease when adjusted for the usual seasonal pattern.

The statistical method used to achieve the seasonal adjustment may vary from one data set to another. Many of the data are adjusted by a method known as X-12-ARIMA, developed by the Bureau of the Census. A description of the method is found in "New Capabilities and Methods of the X-12-ARIMA Seasonal Adjustment Program," David F. Findley, Brian C. Monsell, William R. Bell, Mark C. Otto and Bor-Chung Chen, *Journal of Business and Economic Statistics*, April 1998. A preprint version of this article can be downloaded from the Bureau of the Census web site.

Data that are presented at annual rates show values at their annual equivalents—the values that would be registered if the rate of activity measured during a particular month or quarter were maintained for a full year.

Most of the data in this volume are from federal government sources and may be reproduced freely. A few are from private sources and are used with permission; further use may be subject to copyright restrictions. A list of data sources, including addresses, phone numbers,

Email addresses, Internet addresses, and complete citations for the government periodicals cited may be found at the end of these Notes.

The tables in this volume incorporate data revisions and corrections released by the source agencies through September 2000.

TABLES 1-1 THROUGH 1-9 AND 22-1 THROUGH 22-4 NATIONAL INCOME AND PRODUCT

SOURCE: U.S. DEPARTMENT OF COMMERCE, BUREAU OF ECONOMIC ANALYSIS (BEA).

All data on these pages are from the national income and product accounts (NIPAs). The data are as published in the 1999 comprehensive NIPA revisions and as subsequently updated and revised through September 2000.

Revisions

NIPA data normally undergo revision at the end of July each year. Typically these annual revisions cover annual and quarterly data for the previous three years, but may also include more limited revisions to data for earlier years. Approximately once every five years the NIPA data undergo "benchmark" revision, on which occasions some definitional or other comprehensive changes may affect data back to 1929—the earliest year for which official national account data are available.

Results of the latest comprehensive revision of the NIPAs were released beginning in October 1999, concluding in April 2000. These results are incorporated in the current and historical pages of Business Statistics 2000.

The 1999 comprehensive revision embodied all the possible sources of revision. Some definitions and classifications were changed; measurement methods were improved; and new data were incorporated. As a result, all data have been completely revised back to 1929.

The changes are described in detail in articles in the *Survey of Current Business* in August through December 1999 and April 2000. (See References at the end of this section of Notes for citations.) The most salient changes are as follows:

Business and government expenditures for computer software, beginning in 1959, are now recognized as fixed investment. Previously, the treatment had been inconsistent: the value of the software "embedded in" (bundled with) computer hardware was included in the business fixed investment totals, but software sold separately or created by a firm's own employees was not. In the case of federal, state, and local governments, both purchases and production of software were classified as government consumption, not government investment. Because software is not used up in a single year but has an average service life of 3 to 5 years, the previous treatment understated the level and growth of GDP. The new treatment of software was a major factor in the upward revision in real GDP growth rates in the period since 1977.

Consistent with the new treatment, capital consumption allowances for software are now entered in the government consumption accounts, representing a partial measure of the services of the stock of government software. Business capital consumption now includes allowances for the using-up of software.

Government employee retirement plans have been reclassified. Previously, retirement plans for state and local government employees as well as for federal employees, both civilian and military, were treated the same as Social Security and other social insurance programs. The surpluses of the plans were included in the government surplus (or offset part of a larger government deficit). Now, they are being treated like private pension plans, and included in the personal income and saving accounts. This change does not affect GDP or total national saving, but it reallocates measured saving from the government to the personal sector. Social Security, Medicare, unemployment insurance, and workers' compensation remain in the government sector.

Reflecting this and other revisions, personal saving in 1998, which was previously shown (as in *Business Statistics 1999*) to have been 0.5 percent of disposable personal income, is now shown as 3.7 percent. But the personal saving rate is higher than previously estimated in other years as well, so that the significant downtrend in the saving rate over the period since 1982 is still apparent. It should be noted, however, that disposable personal income is not a complete measure of the resources accruing to individuals. By definition the NIPAs exclude capital gains. If capital gains are included in income, current household saving rates become the highest in 40 years or more. See "Current Issues in Economic Measurement" in *Business Statistics 1999*.

Also reflecting the reclassification of these retirement plans, the current surplus of the federal government for 1998 is now shown as $46.9 billion, versus $72.8 billion as calculated last year, and the state and local surplus as $41.7 billion instead of $150.2 billion.

Improvements in the measurement of real output for a number of GDP components, principally improved consumer price measures and improved estimates for banking services, also contributed to the upward revision in real growth rates.

Definitions and notes on the data

The NIPAs show the composition of production and the distribution to labor and capital of the income resulting from production.

Gross domestic product (GDP), the featured measure of U.S. output, is the market value of the goods and services produced by labor and property located in the United States. Market values include indirect business taxes, such as taxes on sales and property, and represent the values paid by the final consumer. GDP is "gross" product in the sense that capital consumption allowances (i.e. economic depreciation) have not been deducted. GDP is the sum of personal consumption expenditures, gross private domestic investment (including change in private inventories and before deduction of charges for consumption of fixed capital), net exports of goods and services, and government consumption expenditures and gross investment. GDP excludes intermediate purchases of goods and services by business, because their value is already included in the value of the final products of business.

GDP, rather than gross national product (GNP), has been the featured measure of U.S. production since the comprehensive NIPA revisions in 1991. GDP refers to production taking place within the geographic boundaries of the United States, including production from capital and labor supplied by nonresidents; GNP refers to production by labor and property supplied by U.S. residents, whether located in the United States or abroad. GDP is consistent in coverage with other national economic indicators such as employment and productivity. It also is the measure used by almost all other countries and thus facilitates comparison of economic activity in the United States with that of other countries. GNP, however, provides a better comparison base for national saving.

Personal consumption expenditures (PCE) is goods and services purchased by persons residing in the United States. PCE consists mainly of purchases of new goods and services by individuals from business. It includes purchases that are financed by insurance, e.g. medical insurance. In addition, PCE includes purchases of new goods and services by nonprofit institutions, net purchases of used goods ("net" here meaning purchases of used goods from business less sales of used goods to business) by individuals and nonprofit institutions, and purchases

abroad of goods and services by U.S. residents traveling or working in foreign countries. PCE also includes purchases for certain goods and services provided by government agencies. (See the notes for Tables 3-1 through 3-4 for additional information).

Gross private domestic investment consists of private fixed investment and change in private inventories.

Private fixed investment consists of both nonresidential and residential fixed investment. The term "residential" refers to the construction and equipping of living quarters for permanent occupancy; as will be seen below, hotels and motels are included in nonresidential fixed investment. Private fixed investment consists of purchases of fixed assets, which are commodities that will be used in a production process for more than one year, including replacements and additions to the capital stock, and it is measured "gross," before a deduction for consumption of fixed capital. It covers all investment by private businesses and nonprofit institutions in the United States, regardless of whether the investment is owned by U.S. residents. It does not include purchases of the same types of equipment and structures by government agencies, which are included in government gross investment, or investment by U.S. residents in other countries.

Nonresidential fixed investment is the total of nonresidential structures and nonresidential equipment and software.

Nonresidential structures consists of new construction, brokers' commissions on sales of structures, and net purchases of used structures by private business and by nonprofit institutions from government agencies (i.e., purchases of used structures from government minus sales of used structures to government). New construction also includes hotels, motels, and mining exploration, shafts, and wells.

Nonresidential equipment and software consists of private business purchases, on capital account, of new machinery, equipment, and vehicles; purchases and in-house production of software; dealers' margins on sales of used equipment; and net purchases of used equipment from government agencies, persons, and the rest of the world, i.e., purchases of such equipment minus sales of such equipment. It does not, however, include the estimated personal-use portion of equipment purchased for both business and personal use, which is included in PCE.

Residential private fixed investment consists of both residential structures and residential producers' durable equipment, i.e. equipment such as appliances owned by landlords and rented to tenants. Investment in structures consists of new units, improvements to existing units, manufactured homes, brokers' commissions on the sale of residential property, and net purchases of used residential structures from government agencies, i.e., purchases of such structures from government minus sales of such structures to government.

Change in private inventories is the change in the physical volume of inventories held by businesses, valued at the average price of the period. It differs from the change in the book value of inventories reported by most businesses; an *inventory valuation adjustment* converts historical cost valuations of inventories to replacement cost.

Net exports of goods and services is exports of goods and services less imports of goods and services. It does not include income payments or receipts or transfer payments to and from the rest of the world.

Government consumption expenditures is purchases by governments (federal, state, and local) of goods and services for current consumption. It includes compensation of general government employees and an allowance for consumption of general government fixed capital including software (i.e., depreciation). Receipts for certain services provided by government-primarily tuition payments for higher education and charges for medical care-are defined as government sales, which are treated as deductions from government purchases.

Gross government investment consists of general government and government enterprise expenditures for fixed assets (structures and equipment and software). Government inventory investment is included in government consumption expenditures.

Real, or chained (1996) dollar, estimates are estimates from which the effect of price change has been removed. Prior to the 1996 comprehensive revision, constant-dollar measures were obtained by combining real output measures for different goods and services using the relative prices of a single year as weights for the entire time span of the series. In the recent environment of rapid technological change, which has caused the prices of computers and electronic components to decline dramatically relative to other prices, this method distorted the measurement of economic growth and caused excessive revisions of growth rates at each benchmark revision. The current, chained-dollar measure changes the relative price weights each year as relative prices shift over time.

Chained-dollar estimates, although expressed for continuity's sake as if they had occurred according to the prices of a single year (currently, 1996) are usually not additive; that is, because of the changes in price weights over the years, the 1996-dollar components in any given table usually do not add to the 1996-dollar total. In time periods close to the base year, the difference between the sum of components and the total is usually quite small. In earlier periods, the differences become much larger. For this reason, the BEA no longer publishes chained-dollar estimates prior to 1987, except for selected aggregate series. (For the more detailed components, quantity trends are represented by indexes, which can be obtained from BEA.)

GDP price indexes measure price changes between any two adjacent years for a fixed "market basket" of goods and services—the average quantities in those two years. The annual measures are chained together to form an index with prices in 1996 set to equal 100. This avoids the substitution bias, overstating price increase, that arises when the quantity weights are held constant over longer periods of time while the composition of output is changing.

Implicit price deflators are GDP price measures, 1996=100, consisting of the ratios of current-dollar to real GDP components (multiplied by 100). Because the price indexes now use the chain-type formula, they differ little from the implicit price deflators and are preferred for price measurement.

Final sales of domestic product is GDP minus change in private inventories. Thus, it is the sum of personal consumption expenditures, gross private domestic fixed investment, government consumption expenditures and gross investment, and net exports of goods and services.

Gross domestic purchases is the market value of goods and services purchased by U.S. residents, regardless of where those goods and services were produced. It is GDP minus net exports (i.e., minus exports plus imports) of goods and services; equivalently, it is the sum of personal consumption expenditures, gross private domestic investment, and government consumption expenditures and gross investment. The price index for gross domestic purchases is therefore a measure of price change for goods and services purchased by (rather than produced by) U.S. residents.

Final sales to domestic purchasers is gross domestic purchases minus change in private inventories.

Gross national product (GNP) refers to all goods and services produced by labor and property supplied by U.S. residents, whether located in the United States or abroad, expressed at market prices. It is equal to gross domestic product (GDP) plus income receipts from the rest of the world less income payments to the rest of the world. More information is given above under gross domestic product.

Net national product is the net (of depreciation) market value of goods and services attributable to the labor and property supplied by U.S. residents and is equal to GNP less the consumption of fixed capital. The measure of fixed capital consumption used relates only to fixed capital located in the United States. Investment in that capital is measured by private fixed investment and government gross investment.

National income is the income received by labor and capital as a result of their participation in the production process. It is expressed at factor cost—the remuneration paid to the labor and capital factors of production—rather than at market value. It consists of compensation of employees; proprietors' income with inventory valuation and capital consumption adjustments; rental income of persons with capital consumption adjustment; corporate profits with inventory valuation and capital consumption adjustments; and net interest. Conceptually, national income can be derived from net national product by deducting indirect business tax and nontax liability and business transfer payments and adding subsidies less current surplus of government enterprises. In practice, the product and income sides of the national accounts are estimated separately from different source data and there is always some statistical discrepancy between the two sides of the accounts.

Compensation of employees is the income accruing to employees as remuneration for their work. It is the sum of wage and salary accruals and supplements to wages and salaries.

Wage and salary accruals consists of the monetary remuneration of employees, including the compensation of corporate officers; corporate directors' fees paid to directors who are also employees of the corporation; commissions, tips, and bonuses; voluntary employee contributions to certain deferred compensation plans, such as 401(k) plans; and receipts in kind that represent income. *Wage and salary disbursements* is wages and salaries as just defined except that retroactive wage payments are recorded when paid, rather than when earned. In the NIPAs, wages accrued is the appropriate measure for national income, and wages disbursed is the appropriate measure for personal income.

Supplements to wages and salaries consists of employer contributions for social insurance and other labor income. Employer contributions for social insurance consists of employer payments under the following federal, state, and local government programs: Old-age, survivors, and disability insurance (Social Security); hospital insurance (Medicare); unemployment insurance; railroad retirement; pension benefit guaranty; veterans life insurance; publicly administered workers' compensation; military medical insurance; and temporary disability insurance. Other labor income consists of employer payments (including payments in kind) to private pension and profit-sharing plans; private group health and life insurance plans; privately administered workers' compensation plans; government employee retirement plans; supplemental unemployment benefit plans; and several minor categories of employee compensation, including judicial fees to jurors and witnesses, compensation of prison inmates, and marriage fees to justices of the peace.

In the national accounts, all capital income—corporate profits, proprietors' income, and rental income—is converted from the basis usually shown in the books of business and reported to the Internal Revenue Service to a basis that more closely represents income from current production. In the source data, depreciation of structures and equipment will probably reflect a historical cost basis and a possibly arbitrary service life used for tax purposes. These values are adjusted to reflect the average actual life of the capital good and the cost of replacing it in the current period's prices. This conversion is done for all three forms of capital income. In addition, the measurement of income from current production is defined to exclude any element of capital gains, so corporate and proprietors' income also require an adjustment for inventory valuation to exclude any profits or losses that might appear in the books if the cost of inventory acquisition is not valued in the current period's prices. These two adjustments are called the *inventory valuation adjustment (IVA)* and the *capital consumption adjustment (CCAdj)*. They will be described in more detail below.

Proprietors' income with inventory valuation and capital consumption adjustments is the current-production income (including income in kind) of sole proprietorships and partnerships and of tax-exempt cooperatives. The imputed net rental income of owner-occupants of farm dwellings is included, but the imputed net rental income of owner-occupants of nonfarm dwellings is included in rental income of persons. Fees paid to outside directors of corporations are included. Proprietors' income excludes dividends and monetary interest received by nonfinancial business and rental incomes received by persons not primarily engaged in the real estate business; these incomes are included in dividends, net interest, and rental income of persons.

Rental income of persons with capital consumption adjustment is the net current-production income of persons from the rental of real property (except for the income of persons primarily engaged in the real estate business); the imputed net rental income of owner-occupants of nonfarm dwellings; and the royalties received by persons from patents, copyrights, and rights to natural resources.

Corporate profits with inventory valuation and capital consumption adjustments (often referred to as "economic profits") is the current-production income, net of economic depreciation, of organizations treated as corporations in the NIPAs. These organizations consist of all entities required to file federal corporate tax returns, including mutual financial institutions and cooperatives subject to federal income tax; private noninsured pension funds; nonprofit institutions that primarily serve business; Federal Reserve Banks; and federally sponsored credit agencies. With several differences, this income is measured as receipts less expenses as defined in federal tax law. Among these differences: receipts exclude capital gains and dividends received; expenses exclude depletion and capital losses and losses resulting from bad debts; inventory withdrawals are valued at replacement cost; and depreciation is on a consistent accounting basis and is valued at replacement cost. Because national income is defined as the income of U.S. residents, its profits component includes income earned abroad by U.S. corporations and excludes income earned in the United States by the rest of the world.

Profits before tax is also the net-of-depreciation income of organizations treated as corporations in the NIPAs, except that it reflects the inventory- and depreciation-accounting practices used for federal income tax returns. As a result, it includes gains or losses associated with price changes for inventory and fixed capital, rather than measuring profits from current production only. It consists of profits tax liability, dividends, and undistributed corporate profits.

Profits tax liability is the sum of federal, state, and local income taxes on all income subject to taxes; this income includes capital gains and other income excluded from profits before tax. The taxes are measured on an accrual basis, net of applicable tax credits.

Profits after tax is profits before tax less profits tax liability. It consists of dividends and undistributed corporate profits.

Dividends is payments in cash or other assets, excluding the corporations' own stock, that are made by corporations located in the United States and abroad to stockholders who are U.S. residents. The payments are measured net of dividends received by U.S. corporations. Dividends paid to state and local government social insurance funds and general government are included.

Undistributed profits is corporate profits after tax less dividends.

Inventory valuation adjustment (IVA) for corporations is the difference between the cost of inventory withdrawals as valued in the source data used to determine profits before tax and the cost of withdrawals valued at replacement cost. In the NIPAs, inventory profits or losses are shown as adjustments to business income (corporate profits and nonfarm proprietors' income); they are shown as the IVA with the sign reversed. No adjustment is needed to farm proprietors' income because farm inventories are measured on a current-market-cost basis.

Consumption of fixed capital is a charge for the using up of private and government fixed capital located in the United States. It is based on studies of prices of used equipment and structures in resale markets. For general government and for nonprofit institutions that primarily serve individuals, it is recorded in government consumption expenditures and in personal consumption expenditures, respectively, as the value of the current services of the fixed capital assets owned and used by these entities.

Private capital consumption allowances consists of tax-return-based depreciation charges for corporations and nonfarm proprietorships and of historical-cost depreciation (calculated by BEA using a geometric pattern of price declines) for farm proprietorships, rental income of persons, and nonprofit institutions.

The private capital consumption adjustment (CCAdj) is the difference between private capital consumption allowances and private consumption of fixed capital, and therefore reflects the net effect of the two adjustments made to reported nonfarm business profits that convert historical to replacement costs and incorporate actual, rather than tax-based, service lives. In the latest comprehensive revision, the CCAdj has changed markedly as a result of the inclusion of software in fixed investment.

Net interest is the interest paid by private business less the interest received by private business, plus the interest received from the rest of the world less the interest paid to the rest of the world. Interest payments on mortgage and home improvement loans and on home equity loans are counted as interest paid by business because home ownership is treated as a business in the NIPAs. In addition to monetary interest, net interest includes imputed interest, which is paid by corporate financial business and is measured as the difference between the income received from the investment of depositors' or beneficiaries' funds and the amount of income paid out explicitly. The imputed interest paid by life insurance carriers and noninsured pension plans attributes their investment income to persons in the period it is earned. The remaining imputed interest payments have counter-entries on the product side of the accounts representing imputed service charges paid back to the financial institutions by persons and governments.

Gross product and domestic income of nonfinancial corporate business provide consistent information for the nonfinancial corporate sector of the economy on gross product, income, and the distribution of the total value of output among capital consumption, employee compensation, profits, and interest. Excluded from nonfinancial corporate business are households, institutions, general government, all noncorporate business, and financial business.

Data availability

Annual data are available beginning with 1929; quarterly data begin with 1946. Not all data are available for all time periods.

New data normally are released toward the end of each month. The first estimates for each calendar quarter are released in the month after the quarter's end. Revisions for the most recent quarter are released in the second and third months after the quarter's end.

The most recent data are published each month in the *Survey of Current Business;* current and historical data may be obtained from the BEA internet site (http://www.bea.doc.gov) and the STAT-USA subscription internet site (http://www.stat-usa.gov). BEA plans to make the data available on a CD-ROM, which will be announced on the Web site.

References

For information about the 1999 comprehensive revisions, see various issues of the *Survey of Current Business,* available by subscription and on the BEA Web site. Relevant *Survey* articles describe definitional and classificational changes (August 1999); new and redesigned tables (September 1999); statistical changes (October 1999); improved estimates of the NIPAs (December 1999); real inventories, sales, and inventory-sales ratios (January 2000); comparison of personal income and IRS adjusted gross income (February 2000); and improved NIPA estimates for 1929–1999 (April 2000).

For summaries of BEA's definitions, methodology, and principal source data, also see *Survey of Current Business:* "Updated Summary NIPA Methodologies," September 1998, and "A Guide to the NIPA's," March 1998.

More detailed, but less recent, information on BEA methodology is found in the following methodology papers available on the BEA internet site or by purchase from the National Technical Information Service: *MP-1: Introduction to National Economic Accounting* (March 1985); *MP-2: Corporate Profits: Profits Before Tax, Profits Tax Liability, and Dividends* (May 1985); *MP-3: Foreign Transactions* (May 1987); *MP-5: Government Transactions* (November 1988); *MP-6: Personal Consumption Expenditures* (June 1990).

For discussion of alternative measures of change in output and prices, see *Survey of Current Business:* "BEA's Chain Indexes, Time Series, and Measures of Long-Term Economic Growth," May 1997; "Alternative Measures of Change in Real Output and Prices, Quarterly Estimates for 1959–1992," March 1993; "Alternative Measures of Change in Real Output and Prices," April 1992.

TABLE 1-10
COMPOSITE INDEXES OF ECONOMIC ACTIVITY

SOURCE: THE CONFERENCE BOARD.

The composite indexes of leading, coincident, and lagging indicators are intended to help predict or identify peaks and troughs in the business cycle. They are calculated from sets of component series selected for their utility as indicators of stages of the business cycle. The component series originate from a variety of sources, as indicated below. Several of the component series appear on the page with the composites; other components (or variations of them) can be found in various tables in *Business Statistics,* as indicated.

The classification of indicators into leading, coincident, and lagging series grows out of an approach to the study of economic fluctuations pioneered by Wesley C. Mitchell and Arthur F. Burns early in the 20th century. It was observed that indicators of business activity tended to move up and down over periods that were longer than a year and therefore were not accounted for by seasonal variation. Although these periods of expansion and contraction were not uniform in length, their recurrent nature has caused them to be called "business cycles."

Furthermore, researchers found that some indicators that described the general state of business activity, such as different measures of production and income, tended to move together, with their peaks occurring within a few months of each other and their low points, or troughs, also tending to occur at about the same time. These are the *coincident indicators*. Other indicators also moved cyclically, but their peaks and troughs came noticeably before the peaks and troughs in the coincident indicators; these are the *leading indicators,* which of course are of great interest to anyone with a stake in the future performance of the economy. Finally, still other indicators had peaks and troughs noticeably later than those in the coincident indicators; these are the *lagging indicators*. Lagging indicators can be valuable in observing whether cyclical imbalances have been corrected and preconditions exist for a new cycle phase.

The composites were originally compiled and published by the Commerce Department, Bureau of Economic Analysis. In 1995, responsibility for compilation and publication was transferred to The Conference Board, a not-for-profit business research organization.

It is frequently said that the leading indicator index is designed to predict turning points in business activity six months in advance. However, the actual leads over the last six business cycles have varied between 3 and 15 months, and the index has sometimes turned down without a corresponding recession, so it is important not to rely solely on these composites.

Index components

The *index of leading economic indicators* consists of the following ten components, with monthly data seasonally adjusted except as noted:

Average weekly hours are average hours worked per week by production workers in manufacturing. Source: Bureau of Labor Statistics. (See Table 8-6.)

Initial claims, unemployment insurance are average weekly claims for unemployment insurance under state programs. For inclusion in the leading index, the signs of the month-to-month changes are reversed, because claims increase when employment conditions worsen. Source: U.S. Department of Labor, Employment and Training Administration. (See Table 8-4.)

Manufacturers' new orders, consumer goods and materials are new orders, net of order cancellations, in billions of 1996 dollars. Source: Bureau of the Census,

with inflation adjustment by The Conference Board. (See Table 15-6 for current-dollar data.)

Vendor performance, slower deliveries diffusion index tracks the relative speed with which goods-producing companies receive deliveries from their suppliers. An increase in this series indicates a slowdown in deliveries and is generally caused by increased demand for manufacturing materials. The survey asks purchasing managers if their suppliers' deliveries were obtained faster, slower, or the same as the previous month's deliveries. The index records the percentage reporting slower deliveries plus one-half of the percentage reporting no change in delivery speed. Source: National Association of Purchasing Managers.

Manufacturers' new orders, nondefense capital goods are in billions of 1996 dollars. Source: Bureau of the Census, with inflation adjustment by The Conference Board. (See Table 15-6 for new orders for nondefense capital goods in current dollars.)

Building permits, new private housing units is the number of new private housing units authorized by local building permits. Source: Bureau of the Census. (See Table 14-4.)

Stock prices: 500 common stocks is an index based on 1941–1943=10. Source: Standard and Poor's Corporation. (See Table 10-8.)

Money supply (M2) is in billions of 1996 dollars. Source: Federal Reserve Board of Governors, with inflation adjustment by The Conference Board. (See Table 10-1 for the M2 money supply in current dollars.)

Interest rate spread is equal to the rate on 10-year treasury bonds less the rate on federal funds. The interest rate series are not seasonally adjusted. Source: Federal Reserve Board of Governors.

Index of consumer expectations is based on the first quarter of 1966=100. The monthly data are not seasonally adjusted. Source: University of Michigan, Survey Research Center. This is a copyrighted series used by permission; it may not be reproduced without written permission from the source.

The *index of coincident economic indicators* consists of the following four components, with monthly data seasonally adjusted:

Employees on nonagricultural payrolls are total wage and salary employees, in thousands. Source: Bureau of Labor Statistics. (See Table 8-5.)

Personal income less transfer payments is in billions of chained 1996 dollars (seasonally adjusted annual rate). Source: Bureau of Economic Analysis, with inflation adjustment by The Conference Board. (See Table 3-1 for total personal income and transfer payments in current dollars.)

Index of industrial production is an index of the output of the mining, manufacturing, and utility sectors of the U.S. economy. The index is based on 1992=100. Source: Federal Reserve, Board of Governors. (See Table 4-1.)

Manufacturing and trade sales are in millions of 1996 dollars. Source: Bureau of Economic Analysis. (See Table 5-8.)

The *index of lagging economic indicators* consists of the following seven components, with monthly data seasonally adjusted except as noted.

Average duration of unemployment is in weeks. As with initial claims, the signs of the month-to-month changes are reversed. Source: Bureau of Labor Statistics. (See Table 8-2.)

Ratio: manufacturing and trade inventories to sales is calculated from sales and inventories in chained 1996 dollars. Source: Bureau of Economic Analysis. (See Table 5-8.)

Manufacturing labor cost per unit of output is the percent change over a six-month span in this monthly index, which is constructed by The Conference Board. (For the Bureau of Labor Statistics quarterly index of manufacturing labor cost, see Table 7-3.)

Average prime interest rate is an average percentage rate per annum used by banks to price short-term business loans; not seasonally adjusted. Source: Federal Reserve Board of Governors. (See Table 10-7.)

Commercial and industrial loans outstanding is in billions of 1996 dollars. Sources: Federal Reserve Board of Governors, with inflation adjustment by The Conference Board. (See Table 10-4 for current-dollar data.)

Consumer installment credit outstanding is expressed as a percent of personal income. Sources: Bureau of Economic Analysis (see Table 3-1) and Federal Reserve Board of Governors (see Table 10-6).

Consumer price index for services is the annual rate of change in the services component of the Consumer Price Index. Source: Bureau of Labor Statistics. (See Table 6-1.)

Notes on the data

Each composite index is scaled so that its average monthly value equals 100 in a base year, currently 1996. Changes in the components are calculated and standardized to equalize the volatility of each component in an index and to equalize the volatility across indexes.

A benchmark revision of the indexes was made in March 2000, incorporating data revisions and updating the base year to 1996. The most recent comprehensive revisions, which included addition and deletion of components, were introduced in 1996.

Data availability

Data are published each month by The Conference Board. The monthly report *Business Cycle Indicators* is available by subscription from The Conference Board, 845 Third Avenue, New York, NY 10022. A monthly press release from The Conference Board, with recent monthly data and information about the indexes and their components, is available at http://www.tcb-indicators.org. The full historical database (with monthly data back to 1959) is available by subscription from the same internet site.

References

In addition to The Conference Board's *Business Cycle Indicators* (referenced above), see the *Survey of Current Business:* "Business Cycle Indicators: Upcoming Revision of the Composite Indexes" (October 1993).

TABLE 2-1 THROUGH 2-9
INCOME DISTRIBUTION AND POVERTY

SOURCE: U.S. DEPARTMENT OF COMMERCE, BUREAU OF THE CENSUS.

All data in this chapter are derived from the Current Population Survey (CPS), which is also the source of data on labor force, employment, and unemployment (see the notes for Tables 8-1 through 8-3). In March of each year, the 50,000 households in this monthly survey are asked questions about earnings and other income in the previous year. The latest data available are data for 1999 collected in March 2000.

The population covered by the survey is the civilian non-institutional population of the United States and members of the Armed Forces in the United States living off post or with their families on post, but excluding all other members of the Armed Forces. Because it is a survey of households, homeless persons are not included.

Definitions

Households consist of all persons who occupy a housing unit. A household includes the related family members and all the unrelated persons, if any, such as lodgers, foster children, wards, or employees who share the housing unit. A person living alone in a housing unit or a group of unrelated persons sharing a housing unit as partners is also counted as a household. The count of households excludes group quarters.

A *family* is a group of two or more persons related by birth, marriage, or adoption who reside together.

Median income is the amount that divides the income distribution into two equal groups, half having incomes above the median, half having incomes below the median. The medians for persons are based on persons 15 years old and over with income.

All historical income figures are shown in constant 1999 dollars. They are converted from current-dollar values using the *CPI-U-X1*. This index uses a historically consistent method of measuring changes in the cost of home ownership, and is similar in concept and behavior to the deflators used in the NIPAs for consumer income and spending. See the notes for Table 6-1 for further explanation of this price index.

Mean income is the amount obtained by dividing the total aggregate income of a group by the number of units in that group.

Earnings include wages, salaries, armed forces pay, commissions, tips, piece-rate payments, and cash bonuses before deductions such as taxes, bonds, pensions, and union dues; net income from nonfarm self-employment; and net income from farm self-employment.

Income, in the official definition used in the survey, is money income including earnings as defined above; unemployment compensation; workers' compensation; Social Security; Supplemental Security Income; cash public assistance (welfare payments); veterans' payments; survivor benefits; disability benefits; pension or retirement income; interest income; dividends (but not capital gains); rents, royalties, and payments from estates or trusts; educational assistance, such as scholarships or grants; child support; alimony; financial assistance from outside of the household; and other cash income regularly received, such as foster child payments, military family allotments, and foreign government pensions. Receipts not counted as income include capital gains or losses, withdrawals of bank deposits, money borrowed, tax refunds, gifts, and lump-sum inheritances or insurance payments.

The *Gini coefficient* (also known as Gini ratio or index of income concentration) is a statistical measure of income inequality ranging from 0 to 1. A measure of 1 indicates "perfect" inequality; i.e., one household having all the income and the rest having none. A measure of 0 indicates "perfect" equality; i.e., all households having equal shares of income. For more detailed discussion, see *Current Population Reports,* Series P-60, No. 123. There are small differences between the Gini coefficients presented in the report's main tables and those presented in the tables comparing alternative definitions of income. In the latter, the coefficients were recalculated, for comparability with the other income definitions, using a slightly different method.

The *poverty population* is the number of persons with family or individual incomes below a specified level intended to measure the cost of a minimum standard of living. These minimum levels vary by size and composition of family and are known as poverty thresholds. The poverty thresholds are based on a definition developed by Mollie Orshansky of the Social Security Administration in 1964 and are adjusted each year for price increase, using the percent change in the Consumer Price Index for all urban consumers (CPI-U). For more detail and further references, see Bureau of the Census, *Current Population Reports: Consumer Income, P60-210,* "Poverty in the United States: 1999," pp. A2-A4. The *poverty rate* for a demographic group is the number of poor persons or families in that group expressed as a percentage of the total number of persons or families in the group.

Unrelated individuals are persons 15 years and over who are not living with any relatives. The poverty status of unrelated individuals is determined independently of income of other persons with whom they may share a household.

A person with *work experience* is one who, during the preceding calendar year, did any work for pay or profit or worked without pay on a family-operated farm or business at any time during the year, on a part-time or full-time basis. A year-round worker is one who worked for 50 weeks or more during the preceding calendar year. A person is classified as having worked full time if he or she worked 35 hours or more per week during a majority of the weeks worked. A year-round, full-time worker is a person who worked 35 or more hours per week and 50 or more weeks during the previous calendar year.

Notes on the data

The following are the principal changes that may affect year-to-year comparability of income and poverty data from the CPS.

With 1972 data, 1970 census sample design and population controls were introduced; previous data used 1960.

With 1984 data, 1980 census sample design was introduced; 1980 population controls were introduced, and were extended back to 1979 data.

With 1993 data, there was a major redesign of the CPS, including computer-assisted interviewing. The limits used to code income amounts were changed, resulting in reporting of higher income values for the highest income families and, consequently, an exaggerated year-to-year increase in income inequality. In addition, 1990 Census population controls were introduced, and were extended back to the 1992 data.

For more information on these and other changes that could affect comparability, see "Money Income in the United States: 1999", P60–209, Appendix B.

Alternative definitions of income

In June 1999, the Census Bureau published a report on "Experimental Poverty Measures, 1990 to 1997." This report is discussed in the article "Current Issues in Economic Measurement" at the beginning of the 1999 edition of *Business Statistics*. The experimental measures are still under development and encompass significant revisions of both the concept of the poverty threshold and the resources with which that threshold is compared. They are not included in this chapter.

The Census Bureau also calculates "alternative" income and poverty measures based on a number of different definitions of income, but the same concept of the poverty threshold, as the official measure. These measures in many cases require simulation—use of data from sources other than the CPS to estimate elements of family and individual income as reported in the CPS. *Business Statistics* shows median household income and poverty rates according to three of these alternative definitions, with the official definition also shown for comparison in the same table (Table 2-8).

Definition 1 is the official Census definition of money income described above.

Definition 4 is Definition 1 income minus government cash transfers (Social Security, unemployment compensation, workers' compensation, veteran's payments, railroad retirement, Black Lung payments, government education assistance, Supplemental Security Income, and welfare payments), plus realized capital gains and employers' payments for health insurance coverage. Capital gains and health insurance are not collected in the CPS but are simulated using statistical data from the Internal Revenue Service and the National Medical Care Expenditure Survey. Definition 4 is, in effect, the income generated by the workings of the economy before government interventions in the form of taxes and transfer payments.

Definition 14 is income after all government tax and transfer interventions. It consists of Definition 4 income *minus* payroll taxes and federal and state income taxes, plus the Earned Income Credit; all of the cash transfers listed above as being subtracted in Definition 4; the "fungible" value of Medicare and Medicaid; the value of regular-price school lunches provided by government; and the value of noncash transfers, including food stamps, rent subsidies, and free and reduced-price school lunches. The tax information is not collected in the CPS but is simulated using statistical data from the Internal Revenue Service, Social Security payroll tax formulas, and a model of each state's income tax regulations. The "fungible" value approach to medical benefits counts such benefits as income only to the extent that they free up resources that could have been spent on medical care; if family income is not sufficient to cover the family's basic food and housing requirements, Medicare and Medicaid are treated as having no income value. Data on average Medicare and Medicaid outlays per enrollee were used in the valuation process. Food stamp values are reported in the March CPS. Estimates of other government subsidy payments used data from the Department of Agriculture (for school lunches) and the 1985 American Housing Survey.

Definition 15 is Definition 14 income plus the net imputed return on equity in owner-occupied housing—the calculated annual benefit of converting one's home equity into an annuity, net of property taxes. (It also can be thought of as measuring the extent to which home ownership relieves the owner of the need for rental or mortgage payments.) Information from the 1987 American Housing Survey was used to assign values of home equity and amounts of property taxes. Because disposable personal income in the NIPAs includes the imputed rent on owner-occupied housing plus most of the cash and in-kind transfers included in Definitions 14 and 15, Definition 15 is the Census income definition closest to the NIPA concept.

Alternative poverty rates are also calculated and shown in this table using poverty thresholds that have been adjusted for price increase using the CPI-U-X1, instead of the CPI-U, which is used in the official thresholds.

The *standard error* is a measure of the variability that arises from the use of a sample to estimate data for an entire population. The sample estimate and its standard error can be used to construct a "confidence interval." For example, if all possible samples were surveyed, the average result from about 90 percent of samples would fall within the interval from 1.645 standard errors below the estimate to 1.645 standard errors above the estimate. Standard errors are shown for the estimates of median income and poverty by state to indicate the necessary degree of caution in making comparisons among states or over time.

Data availability

Data are published annually, in September or October, by the Bureau of the Census, in a series with the general title *Current Population Reports: Consumer Income, P60.* Data in this report were derived from P60–209, "Money Income in the United States: 1999," and P60–210, "Poverty in the United States: 1999," issued in September 2000. These reports also contain extensive explanations and references to other relevant sources.

Data are available on the Census internet site at http://www.census.gov.

TABLES 3-1 THROUGH 3-4 AND 24-1 SOURCES AND DISPOSITION OF PERSONAL INCOME; PERSONAL CONSUMPTION EXPENDITURE BY MAJOR TYPE OF PRODUCT

SOURCE: U.S. DEPARTMENT OF COMMERCE, BUREAU OF ECONOMIC ANALYSIS.

All personal income and personal consumption expenditure series are from the national income and product accounts (NIPAs). All series are shown at a seasonally adjusted annual rate and, except for the per capita series and the saving rate, are in billions of dollars.

Revisions

Data in this book reflect revisions to the NIPAs available through September 2000. An important revision has been made in the concepts of personal income and saving, in that the retirement plans of federal, state, and local employees are now treated like private pensions; formerly they were treated as government social insurance programs. The most significant differences are that employer contributions to, and the dividends and interest received by, these retirement funds are now treated as a component of personal income; but benefits paid by the plans are treated as transactions within the personal sector rather than transfer payments. In other words, this conceptual revision raises "Other labor income" and dividends and interest, while reducing transfer payments received and personal contributions for social insurance. The effect is to move the accumulation of assets in these pension funds from the government surplus to the personal saving sector. (See the notes for Tables 1-1 through 1-9 for additional information.)

Definitions

Personal income is the income received by persons from participation in production; from government and business transfer payments; and from government interest, which is treated like a transfer payment. Persons refers to individuals, nonprofit institutions that primarily serve individuals, private noninsured welfare funds, and private trust funds. Proprietors' income is treated in its entirety as received by individuals. Life insurance carriers and private noninsured pension funds are not counted as persons, but their saving is credited to persons.

Personal income is the sum of wage and salary disbursements, other labor income, proprietors' income with inventory valuation and capital consumption adjustments, rental income of persons with capital consumption adjustment, personal dividend income, personal interest income, and transfer payments to persons, less personal contributions for social insurance.

Personal income differs from national income in that it includes transfer payments and interest received by persons, regardless of source, while it excludes both employee and employer contributions for social insurance, business interest paid (other than to persons), and undistributed corporate profits.

Wage and salary disbursements consists of the monetary remuneration of employees, including the compensation of corporate officers; commissions, tips, and bonuses; voluntary employee contributions to certain deferred compensation plans such as 401(k) plans; and receipts in kind that represent income. As explained in the notes to Tables 1-1 through 1-9, wage and salary disbursements are the appropriate concept for personal income whereas wage and salary accruals are used in computing national income.

Commodity-producing industries consists of the following Standard Industrial Classification (SIC) divisions: Agriculture, forestry, and fishing; mining; construction; and manufacturing. Distributive industries consists of the following SIC divisions: Transportation (excluding the U.S. Postal Service); communications; electric, gas, and sanitary services; wholesale trade; and retail trade. Service industries consists of the rest-of-the-world sector and the following SIC divisions: Finance, insurance, real estate, and services. Government consists of federal, state, and local general government and government enterprises.

Other labor income consists of employer payments to private pension and profit-sharing plans, private group health and life insurance plans, privately administered workers' compensation plans, supplemental unemployment benefit plans, and government employee retirement plans, along with several minor categories of employee compensation, including judicial fees to jurors and witnesses, compensation of prison inmates, and marriage fees to justices of the peace.

Proprietors' income with inventory valuation and capital consumption adjustments is the current-production income (including income-in-kind) of sole proprietors and partnerships and of tax-exempt cooperatives. The imputed net rental income of owner-occupants of farm dwellings is included. Dividends and monetary interest received by proprietors of nonfinancial business and rental incomes received by persons not primarily engaged in the real estate business are excluded; these incomes are included in dividends, net interest, and rental income of persons. Fees paid to outside directors of corporations are included. The two valuation adjustments are designed to obtain income measures in which inventory withdrawals are valued at replacement, rather than historical, cost and charges for depreciation are on a consistent accounting basis and are valued at replacement cost.

Rental income of persons with capital consumption adjustment is the net current-production income of persons from the rental of real property, except income of persons primarily engaged in the real estate business; the imputed net rental income of owner-occupants of non-farm dwellings; and the royalties received by persons from patents, copyrights, and rights to natural resources. The capital consumption adjustment converts charges for depreciation to a consistent accounting basis valued at replacement cost.

Personal dividend income is the dividend income of persons from all sources, excluding capital gains distributions. It equals net dividends paid by corporations (i.e., dividends paid by corporations less dividends received by corporations) less a small amount of corporate dividends received by general government. Dividends received by government employee retirement systems are now included in personal dividend income.

Personal interest income is the interest income (monetary and imputed) of persons from all sources, including interest paid by government to government employee retirement plans.

Transfer payments to persons is income payments to persons for which no current services are performed. It consists of business transfer payments to persons and government transfer payments. Government transfer payments consists of benefits from the following social insurance funds: Old-age, survivors, and disability insurance (Social Security); hospital insurance and supplementary medical insurance (Medicare); unemployment insurance; railroad retirement; pension benefit guaranty; veterans' life insurance; workers' compensation; military medical insurance; and temporary disability insurance. Government transfer payments also includes benefits from certain other programs, including the value of benefits received in-kind as well as cash transfers. Among the programs included are veterans' benefits, in addition to veterans' life insurance; food stamps; black lung; supplemental security income; public assistance (including Medicaid); and educational assistance. Government payments to nonprofit institutions, other than for work under research and development contracts, also are included. Payments from government employee retirement plans are no longer included (see above).

Personal contributions for social insurance, which is subtracted to arrive at personal income, includes payments by employees, self-employed, and other individuals who participate in the following programs: Old-age, survivors, and disability insurance (Social Security); hospital insurance and supplementary medical insurance (Medicare); unemployment insurance; railroad retirement; veterans' life insurance; and temporary disability insurance.

Contributions to government employee retirement plans are no longer included (see above).

Personal tax and nontax payments is tax payments (net of refunds) by persons residing in the United States that are not chargeable to business expense and certain other personal payments to government agencies (except government enterprises) that are treated like taxes. Personal taxes includes taxes on income, including taxes on realized net capital gains, and on personal property. Nontaxes includes donations and fees, fines, and forfeitures. Personal contributions for social insurance is not included. As of the 1999 revisions, estate and gift taxes are now classified as capital transfers and are no longer included in personal tax and nontax payments.

Disposable personal income is personal income less personal tax and nontax payments. It is the income available to persons for spending or saving. Disposable personal income in chained (1996) dollars represents the inflation-adjusted value of disposable personal income.

Personal outlays is the sum of personal consumption expenditures, interest paid by persons, and personal transfer payments to the rest of the world (net). The last item is personal remittances in cash and in kind to the rest of the world less such remittances from the rest of the world.

Personal saving is derived by subtracting personal outlays and personal tax and nontax payments from personal income. It is the current saving of individuals (including proprietors), nonprofit institutions that primarily serve individuals, life insurance carriers, retirement funds (now including those of government employees), private non-insured welfare funds, and private trust funds. Conceptually, personal saving may also be viewed as the sum of the net acquisition of financial assets and the change in physical assets less the sum of net borrowing and consumption of fixed capital. In either case, it is defined to exclude capital gains.

Personal consumption expenditures is goods and services purchased by persons residing in the United States. Persons are defined as individuals and nonprofit institutions that primarily serve individuals. Most of personal consumption expenditures (PCE) consists of purchases of new goods and services by individuals from business, including purchases financed by insurance (e.g. medical insurance). In addition, PCE includes purchases of new goods and services by nonprofit institutions, net purchases of used goods by individuals and nonprofit institutions, and purchases abroad of goods and services by U.S. residents traveling or working in foreign countries. PCE also includes purchases for certain goods and services provided by the government, primarily tuition payments for higher education, charges for medical care, and charges for water and sanitary services. Finally, PCE includes imputed purchases that keep PCE invariant to changes in the way that certain activities are carried out. For example, to take account of the value of the services provided by owner-occupied housing, PCE includes an imputation equal to the estimated rent homeowners would pay if they rented their houses from themselves. (Actual purchases of residential structures by individuals are classified as gross private domestic investment.)

In general, *durable goods* are commodities that can be stored or inventoried and that have an average life of at least 3 years. *Nondurable goods* are all other commodities that can be stored or inventoried.

Data availability

Data are released monthly in a BEA press release, normally the first business day following the monthly release of the latest national income and product account (NIPA) estimates. Data are subsequently published each month in the *Survey of Current Business*. Current and historical data are available on the BEA internet site (http://www.bea.doc.gov), and may also be obtained from the STAT-USA subscription internet site (http://www.stat-usa.gov).

References

A discussion of monthly estimates of personal income and its disposition appears in the November 1979 *Survey of Current Business*. A more detailed description of concepts, sources, and methods used in estimating personal consumption expenditures appears in *Personal Consumption Expenditures* (NIPA Methodology Paper No. 6, 1990), available on the BEA internet site from the National Technical Information Service (NTIS Accession No. PB 90-254244). Additional and more recent information can be found in the articles listed in the Notes for Tables 1-1 through 1-9.

TABLES 4-1 THROUGH 4-4 AND 24-2 INDUSTRIAL PRODUCTION AND CAPACITY UTILIZATION

Source: Board of Governors of the Federal Reserve System.

The industrial production index measures changes in the physical volume or quantity of output of manufacturing, mining, and electric and gas utilities. Capacity utilization is calculated by dividing a seasonally adjusted industrial production index for an industry or group of industries by a related index of productive capacity.

Around the 15th day of each month, the Federal Reserve issues estimates of industrial production and capacity utilization for the previous month. The production estimates are in the form of index numbers (currently 1992=100) reflecting the monthly levels of total output of the nation's factories, mines, and gas and electric utilities. Capacity estimates are expressed as index numbers, 1992 output=100, and capacity utilization represents the production index as a percent of the capacity index. Monthly estimates are subject to revision in each of the three subsequent months, as well as annual and comprehensive revisions in subsequent years.

Definitions and notes on the data

The index of industrial production measures a large portion of the goods output of the national economy on a monthly basis. That portion, together with construction, accounts for the bulk of the variation in output over the course of the business cycle. The index, with its substantial industrial detail, also is helpful in illuminating structural developments in the economy.

The total industrial production index and indexes for its major components are constructed from individual industry series (267 series for data from 1992 forward) based on the 1987 Standard Industrial Classification (SIC). The individual series are grouped in two ways: market groups and industry groups.

Market groups. For analyzing market trends and product flows, the individual series are grouped into final products, intermediate products, and materials. Final products are assumed to be purchased by consumers, businesses, or government for final use. Intermediate products are expected to become inputs in nonindustrial sectors, such as construction, agriculture, and services. Materials are industrial output requiring further processing within the industrial sector. Total products comprise final and intermediate products, and final products are divided into consumer goods and equipment.

Industry groups typically are groupings by 2-digit SIC and major aggregates of these industries—for example, durable and nondurable manufacturing, mining, and utilities. Indexes are also calculated for primary processing and advanced processing. *Primary processing* manufacturing includes textile mill products, paper and products, industrial chemicals, synthetic materials and fertilizers, petroleum products, rubber and plastic products, lumber and products, primary metals, fabricated metals, and stone, clay, and glass products. *Advanced processing* manufacturing includes foods, tobacco products, apparel products, printing and publishing, chemical products and other agricultural chemicals, leather and products, furniture and fixtures, industrial machinery and equipment, electrical machinery, transportation equipment, instruments, and miscellaneous manufactures.

The index of industrial production is constructed with data from a variety of sources. Current monthly estimates of production in some industries are based on measures of physical output. For industries in which direct measurement is not possible, output is inferred from production-worker hours or the use of electric power, adjusted for trends in output relative to input derived from annual and benchmark revisions. In annual and benchmark revisions, the individual indexes are revised using data from the quinquennial Censuses of Manufactures and Mineral Industries and the Annual Survey of Manufactures, prepared by the Bureau of the Census; the Minerals Yearbook, prepared by the Department of the Interior; publications of the Department of Energy, and other sources.

The weights used in computing the indexes are based on value added—the difference between the value of production and the cost of materials and supplies consumed. Important changes in weighting methods were introduced during 1997 (See Revisions below).

To separate seasonal movements from cyclical patterns and underlying trends, components of the index are adjusted for two kinds of short-time recurring fluctuations, differences in the number of working days from month to month and seasonal variation. Individual series are seasonally adjusted by the X-11 ARIMA method.

The index does not cover production on farms, in the construction industry, in transportation, or in various trade and service industries. A number of groups and subgroups include data for individual series not published separately.

Capacity utilization is calculated for the manufacturing, mining, and electric and gas utilities industries. Output is measured by seasonally-adjusted indexes of industrial production. The capacity indexes attempt to capture the concept of sustainable practical capacity, which is defined as the greatest level of output that a plant can maintain within the framework of a realistic work schedule, taking account of normal downtime, and assuming sufficient availability of inputs to operate the machinery and equipment in place. The 76 individual capacity indexes are based on a variety of data, including capacity data measured in physical units compiled by trade associations, Census Bureau surveys of utilization rates and investment, and estimates of growth of the capital stock.

Revisions

Revisions to data for recent years normally occur annually, taking into account additional source data that have become available. The latest annual revisions were introduced in November 1999. A subsequent revision is expected in November 2000, too late for inclusion in this volume.

Comprehensive revisions introduced in 1997 moved the reference year from 1987 to 1992=100 and introduced new aggregation methods beginning with the data for 1977. Under the new aggregation methods, the value-added weights for each industry are updated annually, rather than quinquennially. The more frequent updating takes more accurate account of changes in the relative valuations of the individual industry series and thus provides a more accurate overall index, eliminating an upward bias.

Data availability

Data are available monthly in Federal Reserve release G.17. Selected data are subsequently published monthly in the *Federal Reserve Bulletin.* Historical data may be purchased on diskette from Publications Services, Board of Governors of the Federal Reserve System. Current and historical data are available on the Federal Reserve internet site (http://www.bog.frb.fed.us/releases/).

References

Descriptions of recent revisions are found in *Federal Reserve Bulletin:* "Industrial Production and Capacity Utilization: 1999 Annual Revision," (March 2000) and "Industrial Production and Capacity Utilization: Historical Revision and Recent Developments" (February 1997). For information on seasonal adjustment methods, see "A Revision to Industrial Production and Capacity Utilization, 1991–1995" (January 1996). A detailed description of the industrial production index, together with a history of the index, a glossary of terms, and a bibliography is presented in *Industrial Production-1986 Edition,* available from the Publication Services, Board of Governors of the Federal Reserve System.

TABLES 5-1 THROUGH 5-4 AND 22-5 THROUGH 22-6 GROSS SAVING AND INVESTMENT ACCOUNT

SOURCES: U.S. DEPARTMENT OF COMMERCE, BUREAU OF ECONOMIC ANALYSIS.

Revisions

Data in this book reflect revisions to the NIPAs available through September 2000. The comprehensive revision introduced late in 1999 included major conceptual changes affecting the estimates of saving and investment. The redefinition of fixed investment to include computer software affected investment, capital consumption, and the capital consumption adjustment, while the reclassification of government employee retirement funds affected personal saving and government surpluses. See the notes for Tables 1-1 through 1-9 and Tables 3-1 through 3-4 for additional information.

Definitions

Personal saving is derived by subtracting personal outlays and personal tax and nontax payments from personal income. It is the current saving of individuals (including proprietors), nonprofit institutions that primarily serve individuals, life insurance carriers, retirement funds, private noninsured welfare funds, and private trust funds. Conceptually, personal saving may also be viewed as the sum of the net acquisition of financial assets and the change in physical assets less the sum of net borrowing and consumption of fixed capital. In either case, it is defined to exclude capital gains, i.e., it includes the noncorporate inventory valuation and capital consumption adjustments. (See Notes to Tables 1-1 through 1-9.)

Undistributed profits is corporate profits after tax less dividends; in the saving and investment account table, it also includes the corporate inventory valuation adjustment (IVA) and corporate capital consumption adjustment (CCAdj). (See Notes to Tables 1-1 through 1-9.)

Consumption of fixed capital is a charge for the using up of private and government fixed capital, including software, located in the United States. It is based on studies of prices of used equipment and structures in resale markets. For general government and for nonprofit institutions that primarily serve individuals, it is recorded in government consumption expenditures and in personal consumption expenditures, respectively, as the value of the current services of the fixed capital assets owned and used by these entities. *Private consumption of fixed capital* consists of tax-return-based depreciation charges for corporations and nonfarm proprietorships and of historical-cost depreciation (calculated by BEA using a geometric pattern of price declines) for farm proprietorships, rental income of persons, and nonprofit institutions, *minus* the capital consumption adjustments. (In other words, from the point of view of saving, the CCAdj is taken out of book depreciation and added to income and profits—it is a reallocation from one form of gross saving to another.)

Gross private domestic investment consists of private fixed investment and change in private inventories.

Private fixed investment consists of both nonresidential and residential fixed investment. It consists of purchases of fixed assets, which are commodities that will be used in a production process for more than one year, including replacements and additions to the capital stock, and it is measured before a deduction for consumption of fixed capital. It covers all investment by private businesses and nonprofit institutions in the United States, regardless of whether the investment is owned by U.S. residents. It does not include purchases of the same types of equipment and structures by government agencies, which are included in government gross investment, or investment by U.S. residents in other countries.

Nonresidential fixed investment consists of structures, equipment and software not related to personal residences.

Nonresidential structures consists of new construction, brokers' commissions on sales of structures, and net purchases (purchases less sales) of used structures by private business and by nonprofit institutions from government agencies. New construction also includes hotels, motels and mining exploration, shafts, and wells.

Nonresidential equipment and software consists of private business purchases, on capital account, of new machinery, equipment, and vehicles; purchases and in-house production of software; dealers' margins on sales of used equipment; and net purchases (purchases less sales) of used equipment from government agencies, persons, and the rest of the world. (It does not, however, include the personal-use portion of equipment purchased for both business and personal use, which is included in PCE.)

Residential private fixed investment consists of both structures and residential producers' durable equipment, i.e. equipment owned by landlords and rented to tenants.

Investment in structures consists of new units, improvements to existing units, manufactured homes, brokers' commissions on the sale of residential property, and net purchases (purchases less sales) of used structures from government agencies.

Data availability

Current data are included in the monthly release of the latest national income and product account (NIPA) estimates and are subsequently published each month in the *Survey of Current Business.* Current and historical data may be obtained from the BEA internet site (http://www.bea.doc.gov) or the STAT-USA subscription internet site (http://www.stat-usa.gov).

References

Sources of information about the NIPAs are listed in the notes for Tables 1-1 through 1-9.

TABLES 5-5 THROUGH 5-8
MANUFACTURING AND TRADE SALES AND INVENTORIES

SOURCES: U.S. DEPARTMENT OF COMMERCE, BUREAU OF THE CENSUS (CURRENT DOLLAR SERIES) AND U.S. DEPARTMENT OF COMMERCE, BUREAU OF ECONOMIC ANALYSIS (CONSTANT DOLLAR SERIES).

The current dollar data on these pages draw together summary data from the separate series on manufacturers' shipments, inventories, and orders; merchant wholesalers' sales and inventories; and retail sales and inventories included in Part II of this book. See the notes to Tables 15-4, 15-5, and 19-3 through 19-5 for information about these data.

Estimates of real sales, inventories, and inventory-sales ratios are published by the Bureau of Economic Analysis.

Annual values for monthly inventory-sales ratios are averages of monthly data.

Data availability

Sales, inventories and inventory-sales ratios for manufacturers, merchant wholesalers, and retailers are published monthly by the Bureau of the Census in a press release entitled "Manufacturing and Trade Inventories and Sales"; recent data are available on the web (http://www.census.gov/mtis/www/mtis.html). Sales and inventories in constant dollars are published regularly by the Bureau of Economic Analysis in the *Survey of Current Business;* recent data are available on the BEA internet site (http://www.bea.doc.gov) or from the STAT-USA subscription internet site (http://www.stat-usa.gov).

References

For information about the 1996 historical revisions to sales and inventories in constant dollars, see "Real Inventories, Sales, and Inventory-Sales Ratios for Manufacturing and Trade, 1977–1995," *Survey of Current Business,* May 1996.

TABLES 5-9 AND 5-10
ANNUAL CAPITAL EXPENDITURES

SOURCE: *U.S. DEPARTMENT OF COMMERCE, BUREAU OF THE CENSUS.*

These data are from the Census Bureau's Annual Capital Expenditures Survey (ACES). The survey provides detailed information on capital investment in new and used structures and equipment by nonfarm businesses. The program was initiated with a small test survey in 1992 and currently provides data for the latest three years (1996 through 1998).

In the 1998 survey, data were collected from a sample of approximately 34,000 companies with employees and 12,000 non-employer businesses (businesses with an owner but no employees). For companies with employees, the data are reported for 97 separate industry categories based on two-digit and selected three-digit Standard Industrial Classification (SIC) codes. Total capital expenditures, with no industry detail, are shown for the nonemployer businesses.

Capital expenditures include all capitalized costs during the year for both new and used structures and equipment, including software, chargeable to fixed asset accounts for which depreciation or amortization accounts are ordinarily maintained. For projects lasting longer than one year, this definition includes gross additions to construction-in-progress accounts, even if the asset was not in use and not yet depreciated. For capital leases, the company using the asset (lessee) is asked to include the cost or present value of the leased assets in the year in which the lease was entered into. Also included in capital expenditures are capitalized leasehold improvements and capitalized interest charges on loans used to finance capital projects.

Data availability

The "Annual Capital Expenditure Survey: 1998" was published by the Census Bureau in May 2000 and contains data for 1998 and revised data for 1997. Revised 1996 data are found on the 1997 survey. Current and past surveys are available on the Census internet site, http://www.census.gov/csd/ace.

TABLES 6-1 AND 24-7
CONSUMER PRICE INDEXES

SOURCE: *U.S. DEPARTMENT OF LABOR, BUREAU OF LABOR STATISTICS (BLS).*

The Consumer Price Index (CPI) is a statistical measure of the average change in the cost to consumers of a fixed market basket of goods and services purchased by urban consumers. The reference base for most indexes currently is 1982–1984=100. Except as noted, the indexes in this volume are for all urban consumers (CPI-U); recent data represent the 1993–1995 buying habits of about 87 percent of the noninstitutional population of the United States at that time. An alternative index, the CPI-W, represents the buying habits only of urban wage earners and clerical workers. Revisions in the calculation of the CPI, introduced in January 1998 and subsequent months, were discussed in "Current Issues in Economic Measurement" in the 1999 edition of *Business Statistics.*

The CPI-U was introduced in 1978. Before that time, only CPI-W data are available. The movements of the CPI-U before 1978 are based on the changes in the CPI-W. The index levels are different, however, because the two indexes differed in the 1982–1984 base period.

Users should note an important difference between the CPI and measures such as those in the National Income and Product Accounts. Because the official CPI-U and CPI-W are so widely used in the calculation of cost-of-living adjustments to wages and to government payments and tax variables, these indexes are not retrospectively revised to incorporate new information and methods. (An exception is occasionally made for outright mathematical error.) Instead, the new information and methods of calculation are introduced in the current index and affect future index changes only. See below for information on special CPI indexes that can be used to provide more consistent historical information.

Notes on the data

The CPI is based on prices of food, clothing, shelter, fuel, utilities, transportation, medical care, and other goods and services that people buy for day-to-day living. The quantity and quality of these items are kept essentially constant between major revisions so that only price changes will be measured. All taxes directly associated with the purchase and use of items are included in the index.

As of 1999, data collected from more than 23,000 retail establishments and about 5,800 housing units in 87 urban areas across the country are used to develop the U.S. city average.

Periodic major revisions of the indexes update the content and weights of the market basket of goods and services priced for the CPI; update the statistical sample of urban areas, outlets, and unique items used in calculating the CPI; and improve the statistical methods used. In addition, retail outlets and items are resampled on a rotating five-year basis; adjustments for changing quality are made at times of major product changes, such as the annual auto model changeover; and other methodological changes are introduced from time to time.

The most basic aspect of the 1998 revision was the incorporation of a new set of expenditure weights. Consumer Expenditure Survey data from 1993–1995 were used to calculate a new expenditure weight for each item strata category in every CPI index area. These new market baskets took effect with the index for January 1998. At the same time, many of the samples underlying the CPI were replaced. These samples include geographic areas, items selected for pricing, and outlets in which items are priced.

CPI weights for 1964–1977 were derived from reported expenditures of a sample of wage-earner and clerical-worker families and individuals in 1960–1961 and adjusted for price changes between the survey dates and 1963. Weights for 1978–86 were derived from a consumer expenditure survey (CES) undertaken over the 1972–1974 period and adjusted for price change between the survey dates and December 1977. For 1987–1997, the spending patterns reflected in the CPI were derived from a CES undertaken over the 1982–1984 period. The reported expenditures were adjusted for price change between the survey dates and December 1986.

The CES is composed of two separate surveys: an interview survey and a diary survey, both conducted by the Bureau of the Census for BLS. Each expenditure reported in the two surveys is coded to detailed categories, which are then combined in expenditure classes and ultimately into major expenditure groups. Data as of 1998 are grouped into eight such groups: (1) food and beverages, (2) housing, (3) apparel, (4) transportation, (5) medical care, (6) recreation, (7) education and communication, and (8) other goods and services. Education and communication and recreation are new groups, and several subcategories have been rearranged as well.

The expenditure base of the CPI that is established by the CES encompasses only out-of-pocket consumer spending. Consumers also benefit from goods and services that are financed by government and private insurance, particularly in the medical care area. In the NIPAs, personal consumption expenditures (PCE) includes all spending whether purchased out of pocket or financed by government or employer-financed insurance, whereas the CES includes only out-of-pocket spending and payment of insurance premiums by individuals. For this reason, there is a large difference between the relatively small weight of medical care spending in the CPI and the markedly greater percentage of PCE accounted for by total medical care spending.

Seasonally adjusted national CPI indexes are published for selected series for which there is a significant seasonal pattern of price change. The factors currently in use were derived by the X-12-ARIMA seasonal adjustment method. Seasonally adjusted indexes and seasonal factors for the preceding five years are updated annually based on data through the previous December. Detailed descriptions of BLS seasonal adjustment procedures are available upon request from the Bureau of Labor Statistics.

Definitions

Definitions of the major CPI groupings were modified beginning with the data for January 1998 and carried back to 1993. The definitions below are these current definitions.

The *food and beverage index* includes both food at home and food away from home (restaurant meals and other food bought and eaten away from home).

The *housing index* measures changes in rental costs and in expenses connected with the acquisition and operation of a home. The CPI-U, beginning with data for January 1983, and the CPI-W, beginning with data for January 1985, reflect a change in the methodology used to compute the homeownership component. A rental equivalence measure replaced the asset-price approach. The central purpose of the change was to separate shelter costs from the investment component of home-ownership so that the index would reflect only the cost of shelter services provided by owner-occupied homes. In addition to these measures of the cost of shelter, the housing category includes insurance, fuel, utilities, and household furnishings and operations.

The *apparel index* includes the purchase of apparel and footwear.

The *private transportation index* includes prices paid by urban consumers on such items as new and used automobiles and other vehicles, gasoline, motor oil, tires, repairs and maintenance, insurance, registration fees, driver's licenses, parking fees, etc. Auto finance charges are no longer included in the CPI. City bus, streetcar, subway, taxicab, intercity bus, airplane, and railroad coach fares are some of the components of the *public transportation index*.

The *medical care index* includes prices for professional medical services; hospital and related services; prescription and nonprescription drugs; and other medical care commodities. The portion of health insurance premiums used to cover the costs of these medical goods and services is distributed among the items; the portion of health insurance costs attributable to administrative expenses and profits of insurance providers constitutes a separate health insurance item. Effective with the January 1997 data, the method of calculating the hospital cost component was changed from the pricing of individual commodities and services to a more comprehensive cost-of-treatment approach.

Recreation includes components formerly in housing, apparel, entertainment, and "other".

Education and communication is a new group including components formerly in housing and "other", such as telephone services and computers.

Other goods and services now includes tobacco, personal care, and miscellaneous.

The *CPI-U-X1* is a special version of the CPI that is used by many researchers to provide a more historically consistent series. As explained above, the official CPI-U treated homeownership on an asset price basis until January 1983 and then changed to a rental equivalence method. The CPI-U-X1 incorporates a rental equivalence approach to homeowners' costs for the years 1967–1982 as well. It is rebased to the December 1982 value of the CPI-U (1982–1984=100); thus it is identical to the CPI-U in December 1982 and all subsequent periods.

The *CPI-U-RS* is a research series CPI that retroactively incorporates all methodological changes implemented between 1978 and 1999, including rental equivalence method, new or improved quality adjustments, and improvement of formulas to eliminate bias and allow for some consumer substitution within categories. This index is calculated from 1977 forward. Unlike the official CPIs and the CPI-U-X1, its historical values will be revised each time that a significant change is made in the calculation of the current index.

Data availability

The indexes are initially issued in a press release about two weeks following the month to which the data pertain. The *CPI Detailed Report* is issued about a month after the press release. Selected CPI data are published monthly in the *Monthly Labor Review,* which also contains periodic articles analyzing price developments. Complete historical data are available on the BLS internet site (http://stats.bls.gov).

References

Two special issues of the *Monthly Labor Review* cover the CPI in detail. The December 1996 issue describes the subsequently-implemented 1997 and 1998 revisions in a series of articles, and the December 1993 issue on "The Anatomy of Price Change" includes: "The Consumer Price Index: Underlying Concepts and Caveats"; "Basic Components of the CPI: Estimation of Price Changes"; "The Commodity Substitution Effect in CPI Data, 1982–1991"; and "Quality Adjustment of Price Indexes." A new formula for calculating basic components is described in "Incorporating a geometric mean formula into the CPI", *Monthly Labor Review,* October 1998. The CPI-U-RS is described in "Consumer Price Index research series using current methods, 1978–1998," *Monthly Labor Review,* June 1999.

For a detailed discussion of the treatment of homeownership, see "Changing the Homeownership Component of the Consumer Price Index to Rental Equivalence," *CPI Detailed Report* (January 1983).

BLS Handbook of Methods Bulletin 2490 (April 1997), Chapter 17 "Consumer Price Indexes" describes the methodology used in computing the CPI.

General discussions of the nature and quality of the CPI include: "Using Survey Data to Assess Bias in the Consumer Price Index," *Monthly Labor Review* (April 1998); Joel Popkin, "Improving the CPI: The Record and Suggested Next Steps," *Business Economics,* Vol. XXXII,

No. 3 (July 1997), pages 42–47; *Measurement Issues in the Consumer Price Index,* Bureau of Labor Statistics, U.S. Department of Labor, June 1997; *Toward a More Accurate Measure of the Cost of Living,* Final Report to the Senate Finance Committee from the Advisory Commission to Study the Consumer Price Index, December 4, 1996 (the "Boskin Commission" report); and *Government Price Statistics,* U.S. Congress Joint Economic Committee, 87th Congress, 1st Session, January 24, 1961 (the "Stigler Committee" report).

TABLES 6-2 AND 24-8
PRODUCER PRICE INDEXES

SOURCE: *U.S. DEPARTMENT OF LABOR, BUREAU OF LABOR STATISTICS.*

Producer Price Indexes (PPI) measure average changes in prices received by domestic producers of commodities by stage of processing, by industry, and by product. Most of the indexes currently are published on a base of 1982=100, but there are a number of exceptions for products introduced since 1982, identified in this book in the column headings for the individual series. Table 6-2 presents data by stage of processing. The industry tables in Part II of this book present a number of additional PPI series by commodity, industry, or product.

Definitions

The *stage-of-processing* PPI indexes organize products by class of buyer and degree of fabrication. These have been the featured measures since 1978. The three major indexes are (1) *finished goods,* commodities that will not undergo further processing and are ready for sale to the ultimate user (e.g., automobiles, meats, apparel, machine tools); (2) *intermediate materials, supplies, and components,* commodities that have been processed but require further processing before they become finished goods (e.g., steel mill products, cotton yarns, lumber, flour), as well as physically complete goods that are purchased by business firms as inputs for their operations (e.g., diesel fuel and paper boxes); and (3) *crude materials* for further processing, products entering the market for the first time which have not been manufactured or fabricated but which will be processed before becoming finished goods (e.g., scrap metals, crude petroleum, raw cotton, livestock).

Notes on the data

The probability sample used for calculating the PPI provides over 100,000 price quotations per month, selected to represent the movement of prices of all commodities produced in the manufacturing; agriculture, forestry, and fishing; mining; and gas and electricity and public utility sectors. In addition, new PPIs are gradually being introduced for the products of industries in the transportation, trade, finance, and services sectors.

To the extent possible, prices used in calculating the PPI represent prices received by domestic producers in the first important commercial transaction for each commodity. These indexes attempt to measure only price changes; i.e., price changes not influenced by changes in quality, quantity, terms of sale, or level of distribution. Most quotations are the selling prices of selected manufacturers or other producers, although a few prices are those quoted on organized exchanges or markets. Transaction prices are sought instead of list or book prices.

Price data are generally collected monthly, primarily by mail questionnaire. Most prices are obtained directly from producing companies on a voluntary and confidential basis. Prices generally are reported for the Tuesday of the week containing the 13th day of the month.

The name "Producer Price Index" became effective with the release of March 1978 data, replacing the term "Wholesale Price Index." The change was made to reflect the coverage of the data more accurately. At the same time, there was a shift in analytical emphasis from the All Commodities Index and other traditional commodity grouping indexes to the Finished Goods Index and other stage-of-processing indexes.

For analysis of general price trends, stage-of-processing indexes are more useful than commodity grouping indexes. Commodity grouping indexes sometimes produce exaggerated or misleading signals of price changes by reflecting the same price movement through various stages of processing.

The BLS revises the Producer Price Index weighting structure periodically when data from economic censuses become available. Beginning with data for January 1996, the weights used to construct the PPI reflect 1992 shipment values as measured by the 1992 Economic Censuses and other sources. Data for 1992 through 1995 reflect 1987 shipment values; 1987 through 1991 reflect 1982 values; 1976 through 1986 reflect 1972 values; and 1967 through 1975 reflect 1963 values.

BLS has been working for a number of years on a comprehensive overhaul of the theory, methods, and procedures used to construct the PPI. One aspect of this overhaul was the already mentioned shift in emphasis beginning in 1978 to the stage-of-processing measures. Other changes that have been phased in since 1978 include the replacement of judgment sampling with probability sampling techniques; expansion to systematic coverage of the net output of virtually all industries in the mining and manufacturing sectors; introduction of measures for selected service industries; a shift from a commodity to an industry orientation; the exclusion of imports from, and the inclusion of exports in, the survey universe. These changes have resulted in a system of indexes that is easier to use in conjunction with data on wages, productivity, employment, and other series that are organized in terms of the SIC and the Bureau of the Census product class designations.

Seasonal factors for the PPI are revised annually to take into account the most recent 12 months of data. Seasonally adjusted data for the previous five years are subject to these annual revisions.

Data availability

The indexes are initially issued in a press release about two weeks following the month to which the data pertain and subsequently are published in greater detail in the monthly BLS publication, PPI Detailed Report. Selected PPI data also are published monthly in the *Monthly Labor Review,* which also contains periodic articles analyzing price developments. Historical data tables providing annual and monthly data for all available periods for all published series are available on request from BLS. Complete historical data are available on the BLS internet site (http://stats.bls.gov).

References

The following *Monthly Labor Review* articles and technical notes contain background information: "Comparing PPI Energy Indexes to Alternative Data Sources" (December 1998); "Are Producer Prices Good Proxies for Export Prices" (October 1997); "Effect of 1992 Weights on Producer Price Indexes" (July 1996); "Hospital Price Inflation: What Does the PPI Tell Us?" (July 1996); "Seasonal Adjustment of Producer Price

Index for Passenger Cars" (June 1996); "Effect of Updated Weights on Producer Price Indexes" (March 1993); "Milestones in the Producer Price Index Methodology and Presentation" (August 1989); "New Stage of Process Price System Developed for the Producer Price Index" (April 1988); "Improving the Measurement of Producer Price Changes" (April 1977).

BLS Handbook of Methods Bulletin 2490 (April 1997), Chapter 14, "Producer Prices" describes the methodology used in computing the PPI.

TABLE 6-2
PURCHASING POWER OF THE DOLLAR

SOURCE: U.S. DEPARTMENT OF LABOR, BUREAU OF LABOR STATISTICS; CALCULATIONS BY EDITORS.

The purchasing power of the dollar measures changes in the quantity of goods and services a dollar will buy at a particular date compared with a selected base date. It must be defined in terms of: (1) The specific commodities and services that are to be purchased with the dollar; (2) the market level (producer, retail, etc.) at which they are purchased; and (3) the dates for which the comparison is to be made. Thus, the purchasing power of the dollar for a selected period, compared with another period, may be measured in terms of a single commodity or a large group of commodities; for example, all goods and services purchased by consumers at retail, or all finished commodities sold in primary markets.

The BLS publishes two basic price indexes that may be used to calculate the purchasing power of the dollar in the United States: (1) The Producer Price Index (PPI) for Finished Goods, which relates to prices received by the producers of finished commodities at the primary market level, and (2) the Consumer Price Index (CPI-W, through 1977; CPI-U, beginning 1978), which measures average changes in retail prices of goods and services. These indexes are described in the sections of the notes pertaining to the Producer Price Index and the Consumer Price Index, respectively.

The purchasing power of the dollar is computed by dividing the price index number for the base period by the price index number for the date to be compared, and expressing the result in dollars and cents. The base period is the period in which the price index equals 100 (and the purchasing power is $1.00). In this book, 1982 through 1984 is used as the base period for the two indexes shown so that they can be readily compared. The purchasing power in terms of the CPI is calculated by

BLS and published in the CPI press release. The comparable purchasing power in terms of the PPI is calculated by the editors of Business Statistics.

TABLE 6-3
PRICES RECEIVED AND PAID BY FARMERS

SOURCE: U.S. DEPARTMENT OF AGRICULTURE, NATIONAL AGRICULTURAL STATISTICS SERVICE (NASS).

The data on prices received and paid by farmers represent prices farmers received for commodities sold and prices paid for production input goods and services. Prices are weighted and aggregated into price indexes. These indexes provide measures of relative price changes for agricultural outputs and inputs. These price measures are based on voluntary reports from agribusiness firms, merchants, dealers, and farmers. Data are collected at regular intervals using mailed inquiries, telephone, and personal enumeration. In January 1995, these data were converted to a reference base of 1990–1992=100. Prices-paid indexes were available only quarterly for several years but have been published monthly beginning with January 1996, with monthly indexes for 1995 constructed for historical comparison.

Definitions

Prices received by farmers represent sales from producers to first buyers. They include all grades and qualities. The average commodity price from the survey multiplied by the total quantity marketed theoretically should give the total cash receipts for the commodity.

Prices paid by farmers represent the average costs of inputs purchased by farmers and ranchers to produce agricultural commodities. Conceptually, the average price when multiplied by quantity purchased should equal total producer expenditures for the item.

Ratio of prices received to prices paid is the ratio of the index of prices received for all farm products to the index of prices paid for all commodities and services. (For some years, prices paid are available only for the first month of each quarter. Each month's ratio of prices received to prices paid is based on the latest data available.)

Notes on the data

In 1995, NASS reweighted and reconstructed the prices paid and received indexes. The indexes are now based on five-year moving average weights compared with fixed weights previously. The changes in the construction of the indexes simplified updating component items and reference periods while maintaining appropriate weights. The overall changes to the weighting and construction of the indexes did not have a significant effect on the index levels and therefore had little effect on the level of parity prices. Indexes are now published on a 1990–1992=100 base. As required by law, the parity ratio (ratio of prices received to prices paid) also continues to be published on a base of 1910–1914=100.

Prices paid. Since 1995, the Prices Paid Survey of items purchased by farm establishments has been conducted annually in April. Surveys are conducted for feed, seed, fertilizer, agricultural chemicals, fuel, and farm machinery. About 135 selected items are priced to represent groups of similar items purchased which make up the major production expenditure categories. The number of input items consumed on farms is so extensive that it is not feasible to collect price data for all of the inputs. Items on the questionnaire are described in the simplest way consistent with definite identification. Firms are requested to report the prices for the most commonly sold item that meets the general specification on the questionnaire.

Reported data are summarized to regional estimates and then weighted to U.S. prices. Weights are based on available consumption or expenditure information. Average prices, including state and local taxes, are used in computing the indexes and are published in *Agricultural Prices* for the same month as the survey. Regional prices are published for feed, fuel, and fertilizer. U.S. prices are published for the remaining items surveyed.

Bureau of Labor Statistics (BLS) indexes are used to measure price change for the months when no survey data are collected. The BLS indexes measure price changes for farm supplies and repairs, autos and trucks, building materials, and marketing containers. Before 1995, quarterly prices-paid surveys were conducted by NASS. Quarterly feeder livestock surveys still are conducted.

Revisions: prices paid. Any revisions are published in the monthly and in annual issues of "Agricultural Prices". The basis for revision must be supported by additional data that directly affect the level of the estimate. More revisions are likely in April when separate prices paid surveys are conducted.

Survey procedures: prices received: Primary sales data used to determine grain prices are obtained from probability samples of mills and elevators. These procedures ensure that virtually all grain moving into commercial channels has a chance of being included in the survey. Livestock prices are obtained from packers, stockyards, auctions, dealers, and market check data. Inter-farm sales of grain and livestock are not included since they represent very small percentages of total marketings. Grain marketed for seed is also excluded. Fruit and vegetable prices are obtained from sample surveys and market check data.

Summary and estimation procedures: prices received: Survey quantities sold are expanded by strata to state levels and used to weight average strata prices to a state average. State prices are then weighted to a U.S. price.

Revisions: prices received: For most items, the current month's price represents a three- to five-day period around the mid-month. Previous month's prices represent actual dollars received for quantities sold during the entire month. Revisions are published in monthly issues of *Agricultural Prices* and in the annual summary published in July. A schedule of monthly revisions is published in the December issue of *Agricultural Prices* and in the July annual summary.

Reliability: prices received: U.S. price estimates generally have a sampling error of less than one-half percent for the major commodities such as corn, wheat, soybeans, cotton, and rice.

Data availability

Prices paid and received by farmers are available each month in a press release issued around the end of the month. Data are subsequently published monthly in *Agricultural Prices.* Data also are available on the NASS internet site (http://www.usda.gov/nass/).

Reference

"Revised Prices Received and Paid Indexes, United States, 1975–1993 for Base Periods 1910–1914=100 and 1990–1992=100," Statistical Bulletin number 917 (National Agricultural Statistics Service, February 1995).

TABLES 7-1 AND 7-2
EMPLOYMENT COST INDEXES

SOURCE: U.S. DEPARTMENT OF LABOR, BUREAU OF LABOR STATISTICS (BLS).

The Employment Cost Index (ECI) is a quarterly measure of the change in the cost of labor, free from the influence of employment shifts among occupations and indus-

tries. It uses a fixed market basket of labor, similar in concept to the Consumer Price Index's fixed market basket of goods and services, to measure changes over time in employer costs of employing labor. Data are quarterly in all cases; in most cases, index levels have a base period of June 1989=100.

Definitions

Total compensation includes wages, salaries, and the employer's costs for employee benefits. Excluded from wages and salaries and employee benefits are such items as payment-in-kind, free room and board, and tips. *Wages and salaries* consist of earnings before payroll deductions, including production bonuses, incentive earnings, commissions, and cost-of-living adjustments.

Benefits include the cost to employers for paid leave, supplemental pay (including nonproduction bonuses), insurance, retirement and savings plans, and legally required benefits (such as Social Security, workers' compensation, and unemployment insurance).

Private industry workers are workers in private nonfarm industry excluding proprietors, the self-employed, and household workers.

Civilian workers includes private nonfarm industry workers and workers in state and local government. Federal workers are not included.

Notes on the data

Employee benefit costs are calculated as cents per hour worked for benefits ranging from employer payments for Social Security to paid time off for holidays.

The data are collected from a probability sample of approximately 25,100 occupational observations in about 6,000 sample establishments in private industry, and about 4,000 occupations within about 800 establishments in state and local governments. The sample establishments are classified in industry categories based on the 1987 Standard Industrial Classification (SIC). Within an establishment, specific job categories are selected to represent broader occupational definitions. On average, each reporting unit provides wage and compensation information on five well-specified occupations. Data are collected each quarter for the pay period including the 12th day of March, June, September, and December.

Beginning with March 1995, ECI measures are based on 1990 fixed employment counts. From June 1986 through December 1994, ECI measures were based on 1980 fixed employment counts, while prior to June 1986, they were base on 1970 employment counts. Use of fixed weights ensures that changes in the indexes reflect only changes in compensation, not employment shifts among industries or occupations with different levels of wages and compensation.

Data availability

Data for wages and salaries for the private nonfarm economy are available beginning with data for 1975; data for compensation begin with 1980. The series for state and local government and the civilian nonfarm economy begin with 1981. Historical data are published in the March issue of the BLS periodical *Compensation and Working Conditions.* Complete historical data are available on the BLS internet site (http://stats.bls.gov).

Wage and salary change and compensation cost change data also are available from BLS by major occupational and industry groups, as well as by region and bargaining status. Wage and salary change information is available from 1975 to the present for most of these series. Compensation cost change data are available from 1980 to the present for most series. For 10 occupational and industry series, benefit cost change data are available from the early 1980s to the present. For state and local governments and the civilian economy (state and local governments plus private industry), wage and salary change and compensation cost change data are available for major occupational and industry series. The data for all these series are provided from June 1981 to present.

Updates are available about four weeks following the end of the reference quarter. Reference quarters end in March, June, September, and December.

References

Chapter 8 "National Compensation Measures" *BLS Handbook of Methods* Bulletin 2490 (April 1997); *Employment Cost Indexes and Levels,* 1975–1997, BLS Bulletin 2504 (1998); and the following *Monthly Labor Review* articles: "Is the ECI Sensitive to the Method of Aggregation" (June 1997); "Employment Cost Index Rebased to June 1989" (April 1990); "Measuring the Precision of the Employment Cost Index" (March 1989); "Employment Cost Index to Replace Hourly Earnings Index" (July 1988).

TABLES 7-3 AND 22-10
PRODUCTIVITY AND RELATED DATA

SOURCE: U.S. DEPARTMENT OF LABOR, BUREAU OF LABOR STATISTICS (BLS).

Productivity measures relate real physical output to real input. As such, they encompass a family of measures that includes single-factor input measures, such as output per unit of labor input or output per unit of capital input, as well as measures of multifactor productivity (output per unit of combined labor and capital inputs). The indexes published in this book are indexes of labor productivity expressed in terms of output per hour. Data are provided for four sectors of the economy: Business, nonfarm business, the nonfinancial corporate sector, and manufacturing. All data are presented as indexes, 1992=100.

Definitions

Output per hour of all persons (labor productivity) is the value of goods and services in constant prices produced per hour of labor input.

Compensation per hour is the wages and salaries of employees plus employers' contributions for social insurance and private benefit plans, and the wages, salaries, and supplementary payments for the self-employed-the sum of these divided by hours at work.

Real compensation per hour is compensation per hour deflated by the change in the CPI-U-RS for the period 1978 to 1999. (See Notes for Table 6-1.) The CPI-U is used for more recent data, and the CPI-W for data before 1978.

Unit labor costs are the labor costs expended in the production of a unit of output and are derived by dividing compensation by output.

Unit nonlabor payments include profits, depreciation, interest, and indirect taxes per unit of output. They are computed by subtracting compensation of all persons from current-dollar value of output and dividing by output.

Unit nonlabor costs contain all the components of unit nonlabor payments except unit profits.

Hours of all persons are the total hours at work of payroll workers, self-employed persons, and unpaid family workers.

Notes on the data

The output for the business sector is equal to constant-dollar gross domestic product less the following: the rental value of owner-occupied dwellings; the output of nonprofit institutions; the output of paid employees of private households; and general government output. The measures are derived from data supplied by the U.S. Department of Commerce, Bureau of Economic Analysis (BEA). For manufacturing, annual estimates of sectoral output are produced by the BLS. Quarterly manufacturing output indexes from the Federal Reserve Board of Governors are adjusted to these annual measures by the BLS.

Nonfinancial corporate output excludes unincorporated businesses and financial corporations from business sector output. It accounted for about 54 percent of the value of GDP in 1996. For this sector, it is possible to calculate unit profits and unit nonlabor costs separately. Compensation and hours data are developed from BLS and BEA data. The primary source for hours and employment is the BLS Current Employment Statistics (CES) program (see Notes for Tables 8-5 through 8-9). The CES provides data on hours paid for production or nonsupervisory workers. Paid hours of nonproduction and supervisory workers are estimated by the BLS Office of Productivity and Technology. Weekly paid hours are adjusted to hours at work using the annual BLS Hours at Work survey, conducted for this purpose. For paid employees, hours at work differs from hours paid in that it excludes paid vacation and holidays, paid sick leave, and other paid personal or administrative leave.

Although the labor productivity measures relate output to labor input, they do not measure the contribution of labor or any other specific factor of production. Rather, they reflect the joint effect of many influences, including changes in technology; capital investment; level of output; utilization of capacity, energy, and materials; the organization of production; managerial skill; and the characteristics and efforts of the work force.

Revisions

Data for recent years are revised frequently to take account of revisions in the output and labor input measures that underlie the estimates. Customarily, all revisions to source data are reflected in the release following the source data revision.

Data availability

Most of the series begin in 1959. Series are available quarterly and annually. Quarterly measures are based entirely on seasonally adjusted data. For some manufacturing series, only annual averages are available. Updates are performed near the end of each of the first two months of each quarter, reflecting new data for the preceding quarter. Complete historical data are available on the BLS internet site (http://stats.bls.gov).

BLS also publishes productivity estimates for a number of individual industries. A listing is given in *Productivity Measures for Selected Industries and Government Services,* BLS Bulletin 2440.

References

Chapter 10 "Productivity Measures: Business Sector and Major Subsectors" *BLS Handbook of Methods* Bulletin 2490 (April 1997), and the following *Monthly Labor Review* articles: "Possible measurement bias in aggregate productivity growth" (February 1999); "Improvements to the Quarterly Productivity Measures" (October 1995); "Hours of Work: A New Base for BLS Productivity Statistics" (February 1990); and "New Sector Definitions for Productivity Series" (October 1976).

TABLE 7-4
CORPORATE PROFITS AND DIVIDENDS

Source: U.S. Department of Commerce, Bureau of the Census (since 1983); Federal Trade Commission (prior to 1983); and Securities and Exchange Commission (prior to 1972).

The corporate profits and dividend data are taken from the Quarterly Financial Report (QFR) data set. The QFR, which is based on an extensive sample survey, provides estimates of income and retained earnings, balance sheets, and related financial and operating ratios for industry groups, classified according to the SIC.

Notes on the data

Purpose of the QFR: The QFR provides data on business financial conditions for use by government and private sector organizations and individuals. Among its users, the Commerce Department regularly employs QFR data as an important component in determining corporate profits for the national income and product accounts (NIPAs), and the Treasury Department estimates aggregate corporate tax liability through use of QFR data.

The QFR program designs and maintains probability samples of corporate enterprises; collects, analyzes, and summarizes periodic confidential reports from those corporations; estimates national aggregates based upon the individual company reports; and publishes the resulting aggregates.

Classification by industry: The industry combinations used in the QFR are based on the 1987 SIC. A reporting corporation is initially classified into the SIC division accounting for more gross receipts than any other SIC division. To be in scope for the QFR, more gross receipts of the reporting corporation must be accounted for by either (not a combination of) SIC Division B (Mining), Division D (Manufacturing), Division F (Wholesale Trade), or Division G (Retail Trade) than by any other SIC division.

For the most part, after a corporation is assigned to a division, it is further classified by the 2-digit SIC major group accounting for more gross receipts than any other 2-digit group within the division. In certain cases, corporations are further classified into 3-digit SIC groups. QFR data are published for these major groups when precision criteria are satisfied.

Note that these procedures may lead to a conglomerate corporation being assigned to a major group from which only a small proportion of its receipts are obtained. For example, if a corporation obtains 25 percent of its gross receipts from mining activities, 30 percent from manufacturing, 20 percent from wholesale, and 25 percent from retail, it would be classified in the Manufacturing Division. Furthermore, if the 30 percent of manufacturing activity was conducted in two major groups, 20 percent in one and 10 percent in the other, the activities of the corporation as a whole would be classified in the major group accounting for 20 percent of total receipts.

Sample. Nearly all corporations whose operations are within the scope of the QFR and which have total assets greater than $250 million are included in the sample. They are permanent sample members. For smaller corporations (as measured by asset size), a replacement scheme is used which provides that one-eighth of the sample be replaced each quarter. Corporations removed are those that have been in the reporting group the longest (usually eight quarters). Therefore, samples of small corporations for adjacent quarters are seven-eighths identical. The composition of the sample changes each quarter to reflect the effects of corporate births, deaths, acquisitions, divestitures, mergers, consolidations, and the like.

Comparisons with other statistics: QFR estimates will not necessarily agree with other financial and industrial statistics compilations whether based upon a sample or complete canvass. For example:

- The QFR eliminates multiple counting of interplant and other intra-company transfers included in census establishment statistics.

- The conventional accounting concept of profits is used in the QFR estimates. This differs from the concept of profits employed in the national income and product accounts.

- Corporations' QFR submissions generally embody the accounting conventions adopted for financial reporting purposes. As such, they may differ from those used by corporations for reporting income to the IRS.

- QFR estimates by corporation size are based upon the total assets of consolidated corporate enterprises. They differ from estimates based upon other criteria such as value of shipments or number of employees. They differ also from estimates based upon other reporting units such as establishments, nonconsolidated corporations, or enterprises consolidated differently than in the QFR.

- QFR estimates are based upon a changing sample of audited, unaudited, and estimated reports required to be submitted within 25 days after the end of each quarterly reporting period by corporations. Aggregated for any four consecutive quarters, the QFR estimates will differ from similar aggregations of finalized and audited annual reports.

Changes in the series. A number of changes in accounting, industry classification, and sample design affect the comparability of the QFR data over time. When the QFR series began in 1947, corporations were instructed to consolidate all of their subsidiaries that were taxable under the U.S. Internal Revenue Code and that were fully consolidated in their latest report to stockholders. The income tax liability rule was expected to eliminate most foreign operations. However, as the number of multinational corporations increased between 1947 and 1973, foreign operations gradually became more significant in the QFR data. New consolidation rules were put into effect in the fourth quarter of 1973 to maximize coverage and minimize the impact of foreign operations on QFR statistics. As a result of these changes, foreign operations are included on an investment basis. The change in consolidation rules and the creation of a line item to

reflect equity in earnings from nonconsolidated subsidiaries significantly lessened the comparability of pre-
and post-fourth quarter 1973 reports. There was a net
decrease in sales and in net income before taxes. The net
effect of the rule changes on net income after taxes was
small, as, under both rules, foreign activity should be
included above the net income after tax line.

Industry classification from 1959 through the third quarter of 1972 was based on the 1957 SIC (the 1967 SIC
revision did not affect the level of aggregation used in
the QFR); from the fourth quarter of 1972 through 1987,
on the 1972 SIC; and from 1988 forward, on the 1987
SIC. Prior to the first quarter of 1974, a corporation was
classified as a manufacturer only if 50 percent or more of
its gross receipts were derived from manufacturing operations. The new classification rules are more inclusive.

Data availability

QFR data are scheduled for release approximately 75 days
after the end of the first, second, and third calendar quarters
and approximately 95 days after the end of the fourth calendar quarter. The QFR publishes information on the most
recently closed quarter for manufacturing, mining, and
wholesaling and the preceding quarter's data for retailing
except in the fourth quarter, when the 95-day publication
lag permits synchronized presentation. Current data are
available in press releases and on the Bureau of the Census
internet site (http://www.census.gov). Historical data may
be purchased on diskette from the Bureau of the Census.

The QFR is prepared by the Bureau of the Census. The
Federal Trade Commission had been responsible for the
program from inception in 1947 until December 1982.
That responsibility was shared with the Securities and
Exchange Commission until 1971.

TABLES 8-1 THROUGH 8-3, 24-3 AND 24-4
LABOR FORCE, EMPLOYMENT, AND
UNEMPLOYMENT

SOURCE: U.S. DEPARTMENT OF LABOR, BUREAU OF LABOR
STATISTICS (BLS).

The labor force, employment and unemployment data
are derived from the Current Population Survey (CPS), a
sample survey of households conducted each month by
the Bureau of the Census for the Bureau of Labor
Statistics. The data pertain to the U.S. civilian noninstitutional population (i.e., population not in institutions)16
years of age and over.

Due to changes in questionnaire design and survey
methodology, data for 1994 and subsequent years are not
fully comparable with data for 1993 and earlier years. In
addition, data beginning with 1990 incorporate 1990 census-based population controls adjusted for the estimated
undercount. Other discontinuities have been introduced
in various years, usually with January data. See "Notes
on the Data" below for additional information.

Definitions

The *civilian noninstitutional population* comprises all
civilians 16 years of age and older who are not inmates of
penal or mental institutions, sanitariums, or homes for the
aged, infirm, or needy.

Civilian employment includes those civilians who (1)
worked for pay or profit at any time during the week that
includes the 12th day of the month (the survey week) or
who worked unpaid for 15 hours or more in a family-
operated enterprise or (2) were temporarily absent from
regular jobs because of vacation, illness, industrial dis-
pute, bad weather, or similar reasons. Each employed
person is counted only once; those who hold more than
one job are counted in the job at which they worked the
greatest number of hours during the survey week.

Unemployed persons are all civilians who were not
employed (according to the above definition) during the
survey week, but were available for work, except for temporary illness, and had made specific efforts to find
employment sometime during the prior 4 weeks. Persons
who did not look for work because they were on layoff
are also counted as unemployed.

The *civilian labor force* comprises all civilians classified
as employed or unemployed.

Civilians in the noninstitutional population, 16 years of
age and over, who are not classified as employed or
unemployed are defined as "not in the labor force." This
group includes those engaged in own-home housework,
in school, unable to work because of long-term illness,
retired, too old, seasonal workers for whom the survey
week fell in an "off" season (not reported as unemployed), persons who became discouraged and gave up
the search for work, and the voluntarily idle. Also
included are those doing only incidental work (less than
15 hours) in a family business during the survey week.

Not in the labor force, want a job consists of persons who
are not employed; are not counted as unemployed under
the criteria given above; but who did want a job at the
time of the survey.

The civilian *labor force participation rate* represents the percent of the civilian noninstitutional population (age 16 and over) that is in the civilian labor force.

The *employment to population ratio* represents the percent of the civilian noninstitutional population (age 16 and over) that is employed.

The *long-term unemployed* are persons currently unemployed (searching or on layoff) who have been unemployed for 15 consecutive weeks or longer. If a person ceases to look for work for 2 weeks or more, or is temporarily employed, the continuity of long-term unemployment is broken. If he or she starts searching for work or is laid off again, the monthly CPS will record the length of his or her unemployment as the time since the search was recommenced or since the latest layoff.

Median and average weeks unemployed are summary measures of the length of time that persons classified as unemployed have been looking for work. For persons on layoff, the duration represents the number of full weeks they have been on layoff. Mean number of weeks is the arithmetic average computed by aggregating all the weeks of unemployment experienced by all unemployed persons (during their current spell of unemployment) and dividing by the number of unemployed. Median number of weeks unemployed is the number of weeks of unemployment experienced by the person at the midpoint of the distribution of all unemployed persons, ranked by duration of unemployment.

The civilian *unemployment rate* is the number of unemployed as a percent of the civilian labor force. The unemployment rates for groups within the civilian population (such as, for example, males 20 years and over) are the number of unemployed in a group as a percent of the labor force in that group. The unemployment rates by industry and occupation refer to experienced wage and salary workers and are based on industry or occupation of the last job held.

The *augmented unemployment rate* is a broader measure of potential labor availability used by the Federal Reserve Board, based on BLS data. The numbers shown here, as percentages, are calculated by the editors of *Business Statistics* using the Federal Reserve definition: the numerator, augmented unemployment, is the number of unemployed plus those who are not in the labor force and want a job; the denominator, the augmented labor force, is the number in the civilian labor force plus the number of those who are not in the labor force and want a job.

Notes on the data

The CPS data are collected monthly by trained interviewers from sample households selected to represent the U.S. population 16 years of age and older. Sample size was about 60,000 households from mid-1989 to mid-1995 but has since been reduced in two stages to about 50,000 households beginning in January 1996. The data collected are based on the activity or status reported for the calendar week, Sunday through Saturday, that includes the 12th day of the month. Households are interviewed on a rotating basis so that three-fourths of the sample is the same for any two consecutive months.

Data relating to 1994 and subsequent years are not fully comparable with data for 1993 and earlier years because of the introduction of a major redesign of the survey questionnaire and collection methodology. The redesign includes new and revised questions for the classification of individuals as employed or unemployed, the collection of new data on multiple job holding, a change in the definition of discouraged workers, and the implementation of more completely automated data collection.

The 1994 redesign of the CPS was the most extensive in many years. However, there are also several earlier periods of noncomparability in the labor force data, which resulted from the introduction of new decennial census data into the CPS estimation procedures, expansions of the sample, and other improvements made to increase the reliability of the estimates. Each change introduces a discontinuity, usually between December of the previous year and January of the newly altered year. The discontinuities are usually minor or negligible with respect to figures expressed as percents (e.g., labor force participation rate), but can be significant with respect to levels (e.g., labor force in thousands of persons). For strict comparability, the following allowances should be made when making certain data comparisons. More detailed explanations of the changes listed below can be found in the February issue of the BLS publication *Employment and Earnings* for the year in which the change was introduced.

(1) Beginning in 1953, the introduction of the 1950 census data added about 600,000 to the population and about 350,000 to the labor force, total employment, and agricultural employment.

(2) Beginning in 1960, the inclusion of Alaska and Hawaii (on their admission as states) added an estimated 500,000 to the population, about 300,000 to the labor force, and about 240,000 to nonagricultural employment.

(3) Beginning in 1962, the introduction of the 1960 census data for the 50 states reduced the population including Alaska and Hawaii by about 50,000 and the labor force and total employment by about 200,000.

(4) Beginning in 1972, the introduction of the 1970 census data added about 800,000 to the population, and a little over 300,000 to the labor force and total employment. A subsequent adjustment in March 1973, also based on 1970 census data, which substantially affected major categories for white and black and other workers, resulted in a net increase of 60,000 in the labor force and total employment.

(5) Beginning in 1978, an expansion in the sample and changes in the estimation procedures added about 250,000 to the labor force and total employment.

(6) Beginning in 1982, changes in the estimation procedures and the introduction of the 1980 census data caused substantial increases in the population and estimates of persons in all labor force categories. Rates on labor force characteristics, however, were essentially unchanged. In order to avoid major breaks, all of the survey data were adjusted back to 1970. These revisions did not, however, smooth out the breaks in series occurring between 1972 and 1979 that are described above.

(7) Beginning in 1986, the population controls used in the estimation procedures were revised to reflect an explicit estimate of the number of undocumented immigrants (largely Hispanic) since 1980 and an improved estimate of the number of emigrants among legal foreign-born residents for the same time period. As a result, the Hispanic-origin civilian population and labor force estimates were raised by about 425,000 and 305,000 respectively, and Hispanic civilian employment by 270,000. There were smaller, partly offsetting changes in non-Hispanic categories, and the total civilian population and labor force estimates were raised by nearly 400,000 and total civilian employment by about 350,000. Total and subgroup unemployment levels and rates were not significantly affected. Because of the magnitude of the adjustments for Hispanics, data were revised back to January 1980 to the extent possible.

(8) Effective February 1996, 1990 census-based population controls, adjusted for the estimated undercount, were introduced into estimates for 1990 through 1993. (They already had been introduced in January 1994 for the data beginning with that month.) The new controls raised the estimate of the civilian non-

institutional population for 1990 by about 1.1 million; employment by about 880,000; and unemployment by about 175,000. The overall unemployment rate was increased by about 0.1 percentage point.

(9) Beginning in January 1997, the population controls were revised to reflect updated information on immigrants to, and emigrants from, the United States. These revisions raised the estimate of the civilian noninstitutional population by about 470,000; the civilian labor force by about 320,000; and employment by about 290,000.

(10) Effective with the data for January 1998, new composite estimation procedures and minor revisions in the population controls were introduced, resulting in relatively minor changes in the civilian labor force, employment, and unemployment estimates.

(11) Effective in January 1999, population controls were again revised to reflect new information on immigration. The total civilian noninstutional population was raised by about 310,000, with an upward revision for women that more than offset a downward revision for men. An upward revision for the non-Hispanic population more than offset a downward revision for Hispanics. Effects on rates were small.

(12) Effective in January 2000, the population controls were revised to reflect new information on immigration and deaths, lowering the population by about 215,000, labor force by 125,000, and employment by 120,000. Rates were not significantly affected.

Nonagricultural employment estimates from the CPS differ in level and trend from estimates compiled from establishment payrolls (Table 8-5). The differences are attributable in part to differences in definitions and coverage and in part to differences in sample design, collection methodology, and the sampling variability inherent in the surveys.

• The CPS data include domestics and other private household workers, self-employed persons, and unpaid family workers who worked 15 hours or more in the survey week in family-operated enterprises. The payroll or establishment survey, on the other hand, covers only employees on payrolls of nonfarm establishments.

• Persons holding more than one job during the survey week are counted once in the household survey, but multiple jobholders are counted each time (i.e., on each payroll) in the establishment survey.

• Persons with a job but not at work (i.e., absent because of bad weather, work stoppages, personal reasons, etc.) are included in the household survey but are excluded from the payroll survey if on leave without pay for the entire payroll period.

See "Current Issues in Economic Measurement" in *Business Statistics 1999*.

The monthly labor force, employment and unemployment data are seasonally adjusted by an extension of the X-11-ARIMA method. All seasonally adjusted civilian labor force and unemployment rate statistics, as well as the major employment and unemployment estimates, are computed by aggregating independently adjusted series. For example, the seasonally adjusted level of total unemployment is the sum of the seasonally adjusted levels of unemployment for the four sex-age groups (men and women 16 to 19, and men and women 20 years and over). Seasonally adjusted employment is the sum of the seasonally adjusted level of employment for eight sex-age-industry groups (men and women 16 to 19, and men and women 20 years and over, employed in nonagricultural and agricultural industries). The seasonally adjusted civilian labor force is the sum of all 12 components. Finally, the seasonally adjusted civilian worker unemployment rate is calculated by taking total seasonally adjusted unemployment as a percent of the total seasonally adjusted civilian labor force. Seasonal adjustment factors are revised at the end of each year to reflect recent experience, and the revisions affect the preceding three years as well.

Data availability

Data for each month usually are released on the first Friday of the following month in a press release that also contains data from the establishment survey (Tables 8-5 through 8-9). Data are subsequently published in the BLS monthly periodical *Employment and Earnings*, which also contains detailed explanatory notes. Selected data are published each month in the *Monthly Labor Review*, which also contains frequent articles analyzing labor force, employment, and unemployment developments.

Monthly and annual data beginning with 1948 are available. Historical unadjusted data are published in *Labor Force Statistics Derived from the Current Population Survey*, BLS Bulletin 2307. Historical seasonally-adjusted data are available from BLS upon request. Complete historical data are available on the BLS internet site (http://stats.bls.gov).

References

Historical background on the CPS, as well as a description of the 1994 redesign, are found in three articles in the September 1993 *Monthly Labor Review*: "Why Is It Necessary to Change"; "Redesigning the Questionnaire"; and "Evaluating Changes in the Estimates." The redesign also is described in the February 1994 issue of *Employment and Earnings*. Information on the latest revision of population controls is found in the February 2000 issue of *Employment and Earnings*. See also Chapter 1, "Labor Force Data Derived from the Current Population Survey," *BLS Handbook of Methods*, Bulletin 2490 (April 1997).

TABLE 8-4
INSURED UNEMPLOYMENT

SOURCE: U.S. DEPARTMENT OF LABOR, EMPLOYMENT AND TRAINING ADMINISTRATION.

State programs of unemployment insurance cover operations of regular programs under state unemployment insurance laws. In 1976, the law was amended to extend coverage (effective January 1, 1978) to include virtually all state and local government employees plus many agricultural and domestic workers.

The federal civilian employees unemployment insurance program (UCFE) provides unemployment insurance protection to civilian employees of the federal government or of wholly or partially owned instrumentalities, with the following exceptions: Elective officers in the executive and legislative branches of government, certain foreign service personnel, temporary emergency workers, and other small groups.

Unemployment compensation for ex-service members (UCX) provides unemployment insurance protection to veterans under the law of the state in which the claim for compensation is filed.

An *initial claim* is the first claim in a benefit year filed by a worker after losing his job, or the first claim filed at the beginning of a subsequent period of unemployment in the same benefit year. The initial claim establishes the starting date for any insured unemployment that may result if the claimant is unemployed for one week or longer. Transitional claims (filed by persons as they start a new benefit year in a continuing spell of unemployment) are excluded; therefore, the data more closely represent instances of new unemployment.

Monthly averages in this book are averages of the weekly data published by the Employment and Training Administration. Annual data are averages of the monthly data.

Data availability

Data are published in weekly press releases from the Employment and Training Administration. These releases are available on their internet site

(http://www.doleta.gov). Also, historical data on weekly claims is available at the Department of Labor's Information Technology Support Center (http://www.itsc.state.md.us).

TABLES 8-5 AND 24-5
NONAGRICULTURAL EMPLOYMENT

SOURCE: U.S. DEPARTMENT OF LABOR, BUREAU OF LABOR STATISTICS *(BLS).*

The nonagricultural employment data, as well as the hours and earnings data in Tables 8-6 through 8-9 and Table 24-6, are compiled from payroll records. Information is reported monthly on a voluntary basis to the BLS and its cooperating state agencies by a large sample of establishments representing all industries except agriculture. In most industries, the sampling probabilities are based on the size of the establishment; most large establishments are therefore in the sample. In June 2000, the sample included about 300,000 establishments employing about 48 million people. These data often are referred to as the "establishment data" or the "payroll data." The data by industry conform to the definitions in the 1987 Standard Industrial Classification (SIC).

Definitions

An establishment is an economic unit that produces goods or services (such as a factory or store) at a single location and is engaged in one type of economic activity.

Employed persons are all persons who received pay (including holiday and sick pay) for any part of the payroll period including the 12th day of the month (except in government—see below). Included are all full-time and part-time workers in nonfarm establishments. Persons holding more than one job are counted in each establishment that reports them. Not covered are proprietors, the self-employed, unpaid volunteer or family workers, farm workers, domestic workers in households, and military personnel; salaried officers of corporations are included.

Persons on an establishment payroll who are on paid sick leave (when pay is received directly from the employer), on paid holiday or vacation, or who work during a portion of the pay period even though they are unemployed or on strike during the rest of the period are counted as employed. Not counted as employed are persons who are laid off, on leave without pay, or on strike for the entire period, or who are hired but have not been paid during the period.

Intermittent workers are counted if they performed any service during the month. BLS considers regular full-time teachers (private and governmental) to be employed during the summer vacation period whether or not they are specifically paid in those months.

The government division of the SIC includes federal, state, and local activities such as legislative, executive, and judicial functions, as well as all government-owned and government-operated business enterprises, establishments, and institutions (arsenals, navy yards, hospitals, etc.), and government force account construction. Federal government employment is civilian employment only and pertains to an individual's employment status on the last day of the month. Employees of the Central Intelligence Agency and the National Security Agency are not included in these statistics.

Nonagricultural employment in these series differs from the measures in the household survey (Tables 8-1 through 8-3) in that, among other factors, it excludes domestics and other private household workers, self-employed persons, and unpaid family workers. Persons holding more than one job during the survey week are counted once in the household survey, but multiple job-holders are counted each time (i.e., on each payroll) in the establishment survey. Persons with a job but not at work (i.e., absent because of bad weather, work stoppages, personal reasons, etc.) are included in the household survey but are excluded from the payroll survey if on leave without pay for the entire payroll period. See "Current Issues in Economic Measurement" in *Business Statistics,* 1999 edition.

The *diffusion index of employment change,* for 356 nonagricultural industries, represents the percent of industries in which employment was rising over a six-month span, plus one-half of the industries with unchanged employment. It is based on seasonally adjusted data and centered within the span; i.e., the diffusion index reported for June represents the change from March to September. *Business Statistics* uses the June value to represent the year. Diffusion indexes measure the dispersion of economic gains and losses, with values below 50 percent associated with recessions.

Production or nonsupervisory workers. The data refer to the private, nonfarm sector and cover all production and related workers in mining and manufacturing; construction workers in construction; and nonsupervisory workers in transportation, communication, electric, gas, and sanitary services; wholesale and retail trade; finance, insurance, and real estate; and services. These groups account for about four-fifths of the total employment on private nonagricultural payrolls.

Production and related workers include working supervisors and all nonsupervisory workers (including group leaders and trainees) engaged in fabricating, processing, assembling, inspecting, receiving, storing, handling, packing, warehousing, shipping, trucking, hauling, maintenance, repair, janitorial, guard services, product development, auxiliary production for plant's own use (e.g., power plant), record keeping, and other services closely associated with these production operations.

Construction workers include the following employees in the construction division of the SIC: Working supervisors, qualified craft workers, mechanics, apprentices, laborers, etc., engaged in new work, alterations, demolition, repair, maintenance, etc., whether working at the site of construction or working in shops or yards at jobs (such as precutting and preassembling) ordinarily performed by members of the construction trades.

Nonsupervisory employees include employees (not above the working supervisory level) such as office and clerical workers, repairers, salespersons, operators, drivers, physicians, lawyers, accountants, nurses, social workers, research aides, teachers, drafters, photographers, beauticians, musicians, restaurant workers, custodial workers, attendants, line installers and repairers, laborers, janitors, guards, and other employees at similar occupational levels whose services are closely associated with those of the employees listed.

Notes on the data

Benchmark adjustments. The establishment survey data are adjusted annually to comprehensive counts of employment (called "benchmarks"). Benchmark information on employment, by industry, is compiled by state agencies from reports of establishments covered under state unemployment insurance laws. These tabulations cover about 98 percent of all employees on nonfarm payrolls. Benchmark data for the residual are obtained from the records of the Social Security Administration and a

number of other agencies in private industry or government.

The estimates for the benchmark month are compared with new benchmark levels, industry by industry. If revisions are necessary, the monthly series of estimates between benchmark periods are adjusted by graduated amounts between the new benchmark and the preceding one, and the new benchmark for each industry is then carried forward progressively to the current month by use of the sample trends. Thus, under this procedure, the benchmark is used to establish the level of employment; the sample is used to measure the month-to-month changes in the level. Data for all months since the last benchmark to which the series has been adjusted are subject to revision.

Seasonal adjustment. The seasonal movements that recur periodically (such as warm and cold weather, holidays, vacations, etc.) are generally the largest single component of month-to-month changes in employment. After adjusting the data to remove such seasonal variation, the basic trends are more evident. Since the early 1980s the BLS has used the X-11-ARIMA procedure to seasonally adjust the establishment-based series. Seasonal adjustment factors are directly applied to the component levels. Seasonally adjusted totals for employment series are then obtained by aggregating seasonally adjusted components directly, while hours and earnings series represent weighted averages of the seasonally adjusted component series. Seasonally adjusted data are not published for a small number of series characterized by small seasonal components relative to their trend and/or irregular components. Theses series, however, are used in aggregating to broader seasonally adjusted levels.

Seasonal adjustment factors for federal government employment are derived from unadjusted data that include Christmas temporary workers employed by the Postal Service. The number of temporary census workers for the decennial census is removed, however, prior to the calculation of seasonal adjustment factors.

Revisions of the seasonally adjusted data, usually for the most recent five-year period, are made once a year coincident with the benchmark revisions.

Data availability

Employment data by industry division are available beginning with 1919. Data for each month usually are released on the first Friday of the following month in a press release that also contains data from the household survey (Tables 8-1 through 8-3). Data are subsequently published in the BLS monthly periodical *Employment and Earnings,* which also contains detailed explanatory notes. Selected data are published each month in the *Monthly Labor Review,* which also contains frequent articles analyzing labor force, employment, and unemployment developments. Complete historical data are available on the BLS internet site (http://stats.bls.gov).

References

Chapter 2 "Employment, Hours, and Earnings from the Establishment Survey," *BLS Handbook of Methods,* Bulletin 2490 (April 1997).

TABLES 8-6, 8-7, AND 24-6
AVERAGE HOURS PER WEEK; AGGREGATE EMPLOYEE HOURS

SOURCE: U.S. DEPARTMENT OF LABOR, BUREAU OF LABOR STATISTICS (BLS).

The nonagricultural employment, hours, and earnings data are compiled from payroll records. Information is reported monthly on a voluntary basis to the BLS and its cooperating state agencies by a large sample of establishments representing all industries except agriculture. These data often are referred to as the "establishment data" or the "payroll data." The data by industry conform to the definitions in the 1987 Standard Industrial Classification (SIC). See the notes for Table 8-5 for a general description of the establishment survey.

Definitions

Hours represent the average weekly hours for which production or nonsupervisory workers received pay; average weekly hours are different from standard or scheduled hours. Such factors as unpaid absenteeism, labor turnover, part-time work, and work stoppages cause average weekly hours to be lower than scheduled hours of work for an establishment. These hours pertain to jobs, not to persons; thus, a person with two half-time jobs is represented as two jobs each with a 20-hour work week in this series, not as one person with a 40-hour week.

Overtime hours represent the portion of average weekly hours which was in excess of regular hours and for which overtime premiums were paid. Weekend and holiday hours are included only if overtime premiums were paid. Hours for which only shift differential, hazard, incentive, or other similar types of premiums were paid are excluded.

Production or nonsupervisory workers. See the notes to Table 8-5 for definitions.

Notes on the data

Benchmark adjustments. Independent benchmarks are not available for the hours and earnings series. At the time of the annual adjustment of the employment series to new benchmarks, the levels of hours and earnings may be affected slightly by the revised employment weights (which are used in computing the industry averages for hours and earnings), as well as by the changes in seasonal adjustment factors also introduced with the benchmark revision.

Method of computing industry series. "Average weekly hours" for individual industries are computed by dividing production or nonsupervisory worker hours (reported by establishments classified in each industry) by the number of production or nonsupervisory workers reported for the same establishments. Estimates for SIC divisions and major industry groups are averages (weighted by employment) of the figures for component industries.

Seasonal adjustment. Hours and earnings series are seasonally adjusted by applying factors directly to the corresponding unadjusted series. Data for some industries are not seasonally adjusted because the seasonal component is small relative to the trend-cycle and/or irregular components and consequently cannot be separated with sufficient precision.

Aggregate hours. These provide a partial measure of labor input to the industry. Data pertain to production and nonsupervisory workers in nonfarm establishments. The indexes are obtained by multiplying seasonally adjusted production or nonsupervisory worker employment by seasonally adjusted average weekly hours and dividing by the monthly average for the 1982 period. For total private, goods-producing, service-producing, and major industry divisions, the indexes are obtained by summing the seasonally adjusted aggregate weekly employee hours for the component industries and dividing by the monthly average for the 1982 period.

Data availability

Data for each month usually are released on the first Friday of the following month in a press release that also contains employment data from the household and establishment surveys (Tables 8-1 through 8-3 and 8-5). Data subsequently are published in the BLS monthly periodical *Employment and Earnings,* which also contains detailed explanatory notes. Selected data are published each month in the *Monthly Labor Review*. Complete historical data are available on the BLS internet site (http://stats.bls.gov).

References

Chapter 2 "Employment, Hours, and Earnings from the Establishment Survey," *BLS Handbook of Methods*, Bulletin 2490 (April 1997).

TABLES 8-8, 8-9, AND 24-6
HOURLY AND WEEKLY EARNINGS

SOURCE: U.S. DEPARTMENT OF LABOR, BUREAU OF LABOR STATISTICS (BLS).

The nonagricultural employment, hours, and earnings data are compiled from payroll records. Information is reported monthly on a voluntary basis to the BLS and its cooperating state agencies by a large sample of establishments representing all industries except agriculture. These data often are referred to as the "establishment data" or the "payroll data." The data by industry conform to the definitions in the 1987 Standard Industrial Classification (SIC). See the notes for Table 8-5 for a general description of the establishment survey.

Definitions

Earnings are the payments production or nonsupervisory workers receive during the survey period (before deductions for taxes and other items), including premium pay for overtime or late-shift work but excluding irregular bonuses, tips, and other special payments.

Real earnings are earnings adjusted to reflect the effects of changes in consumer prices as measured by the Consumer Price Index for Urban Wage Earners and Clerical Workers (CPI-W).

Production or nonsupervisory workers. See the notes to Table 8-5 for definitions.

Notes on the data

The hours and earnings series are based on reports of gross payroll and corresponding paid hours for full- and part-time production and related workers, construction workers, or nonsupervisory workers who received pay for any part of the pay period that included the 12th of the month.

Total payrolls are before deductions; e.g., for the employee share of old-age and unemployment insurance, group insurance, withholding taxes, bonds, and union dues. The payroll figures also include pay for overtime, holidays, vacations, and sick leave (paid directly by the employer for the period reported). Excluded from the payroll figures are fringe benefits (health and other types of insurance, contributions to retirement, etc., paid by the employer, and the employer share of payroll taxes); bonuses (unless earned and paid regularly each pay period); other pay not earned in the pay period reported (e.g., retroactive pay); tips; and the value of free rent, fuel, meals, or other payment in kind. The exclusion of tips is particularly significant for hotels, motels, and eating and drinking places.

Average hourly earnings data are on a "gross" basis; that is, they reflect not only changes in basic hourly and incentive wage rates but also such variable factors as premium pay for overtime and late-shift work, and changes in output of workers paid on an incentive basis. Also, shifts in the volume of employment between relatively high-paid and low-paid work affect the general average of hourly earnings.

Averages of hourly earnings should not be confused with wage rates, which represent the rates stipulated for a given unit of work or time, while earnings refer to the actual return to the worker for a stated period of time. The earnings series do not represent total labor cost to the employer because of the exclusion of irregular bonuses, retroactive items, the cost of employer-provided benefits, payroll taxes paid by employers, and earnings for those employees not covered under the production-worker or nonsupervisory-worker definition. Similarly, average weekly earnings are not the amounts available to workers for spending, since they do not reflect such deductions as those for income and social security taxes, etc.

Method of computing industry series. Average hourly earnings are obtained by dividing the reported total production or nonsupervisory worker payroll by the total production or nonsupervisory worker hours. Estimates for both hours and hourly earnings for nonfarm divisions and major industry groups are employment-weighted averages of the figures for component industries.

Average weekly earnings are computed by multiplying average hourly earnings by average weekly hours. In addition to the factors mentioned above, which exert varying influences upon average hourly earnings, average weekly earnings are affected by changes in the length of the workweek, part-time work, work stoppages, labor turnover, and absenteeism. Persistent long-term increases in the proportion of part-time workers in retail trade and many of the service industries have reduced average workweeks and have affected the average weekly earnings series.

Average weekly earnings are per job, not per person; a person with two half-time jobs will be reflected as two jobs with low weekly earnings rather than one person with the total earnings from his or her two jobs.

Independent benchmarks are not available for the hours and earnings series. At the time of the annual adjustment of the employment series to new benchmarks, the levels of hours and earnings may be affected slightly by the revised employment weights (which are used in computing the industry averages for hours and earnings), as well as by the changes in seasonal adjustment factors also introduced with the benchmark revision.

Seasonal adjustment. Hours and earnings series are seasonally adjusted by applying factors directly to the corresponding unadjusted series; seasonally adjusted average weekly earnings are the product of seasonally adjusted hourly earnings and weekly hours. Weekly earnings in constant dollars, seasonally adjusted, are obtained by dividing seasonally adjusted average weekly earnings by the seasonally adjusted Consumer Price Index for Urban Wage Earners and Clerical Workers (CPI-W).

Data availability

Data for each month usually are released on the first Friday of the following month in a press release that also contains employment data from the household and establishment surveys (Tables 8-1 through 8-3 and 8-5 through 8-7). Data subsequently are published in the BLS monthly periodical *Employment and Earnings,* which also contains detailed explanatory notes. Selected data are published each month in the *Monthly Labor Review.* Complete historical data are available on the BLS internet site (http://stats.bls.gov).

TABLES 9-1 AND 9-2
ENERGY SUPPLY AND CONSUMPTION

SOURCES: U.S. DEPARTMENT OF ENERGY, ENERGY INFORMATION ADMINISTRATION; U.S. DEPARTMENT OF COMMERCE, BUREAU OF ECONOMIC ANALYSIS.

Definitions

The *British Thermal Unit (Btu)* is a measure used to combine data for different energy sources into a consistent aggregate. It is the amount of energy required to raise the temperature of 1 pound of water 1 degree Fahrenheit when the water is near 39.2 degrees Fahrenheit.

Notes on the data

These data are published in the *Monthly Energy Review,* Tables 1.3, 2.2, and 1.9. Consumption by end-use sector is based on total, not net, consumption. The gross domestic product (GDP) data used to calculate energy consumption per dollar of GDP are from the Bureau of Economic Analysis and include revisions through August 2000.

Energy Production: Crude oil includes lease condensates. Hydroelectric power includes electrical utility and industrial generation. Other energy production includes energy generated for distribution from wood, waste, photovoltaic, and solar thermal energy.

Because of a lack of consistent monthly historical data, some renewable energy sources are not included in total consumption. In 1999, for example, 3.4 quadrillion Btu of renewable energy used by electric utilities to generate electricity for distribution and 0.1 quadrillion Btu of ethanol blended into motor gasoline are included, but an estimated 3.9 quadrillion Btu used by residential, commercial, and industrial consumers is not.

References

Energy Information Administration, *Monthly Energy Review.* Current and historical data are available on the EIA internet site (http://www.eia.doe.gov).

TABLES 10-1, 10-2 AND 24-9
MONEY STOCK, LIQUID ASSETS, AND DEBT; COMPONENTS OF THE MONEY STOCK

SOURCE: BOARD OF GOVERNORS OF THE FEDERAL RESERVE SYSTEM.

Estimates of three monetary aggregates (M1, M2, and M3), a debt aggregate, and the components of these measures are published weekly. The monthly data are averages of daily figures.

Definitions

M1 consists of (1) currency outside the U.S. Treasury, Federal Reserve Banks, and the vaults of depository institutions; (2) travelers checks of nonbank issuers; (3) demand deposits at all commercial banks other than those due to depository institutions, the U.S. government, and foreign banks and official institutions, less cash items in the process of collection and Federal Reserve float; and (4) other checkable deposits, consisting of negotiable order of withdrawal (NOW) and automatic transfer service (ATS) accounts at depository institutions, credit union share draft accounts, and demand deposits at thrift institutions.

M2 consists of M1 plus savings deposits (including money market deposit accounts), small-denomination time deposits (time deposits—including retail repurchase agreements [RPs]—in amounts of less than $100,000), and balances in retail money market mutual funds. It excludes individual retirement account (IRA) and Keogh balances at depository institutions and money market funds.

M3 consists of M2 plus large-denomination time deposits (in amounts of $100,000 or more), balances in institutional money funds, RP liabilities (overnight and term) issued by all depository institutions, and Eurodollars (overnight and term) held by U.S. residents at foreign branches of U.S. banks worldwide and at all banking offices in the United Kingdom and Canada. It excludes amounts held by depository institutions, the U.S. government, money funds, and foreign banks and official institutions.

Debt is the outstanding credit market debt of the domestic nonfinancial sectors—the federal sector (U.S. government, not including government-sponsored enterprises or federally related mortgage pools) and the nonfederal sectors (state and local governments, households and nonprofit organizations, nonfinancial corporate and nonfarm noncorporate businesses, and farms). Domestic nonfinancial debt is monitored by the Federal Reserve as an indicator of the effect of monetary policy. Nonfederal debt consists of mortgages, tax-exempt and corporate bonds, consumer credit, bank loans, commercial paper, and other loans. The data, which are derived from the Federal Reserve Board's flow of funds accounts, are break-adjusted (that is, discontinuities in the data have been smoothed into the series) and month-averaged (that is, the data have been derived by averaging adjacent month-end levels). Therefore, they cannot be derived from the data on debt levels shown in Table 10-5.

Currency consists of currency outside the U.S. Treasury, the Federal Reserve Banks and the vaults of depository institutions.

Demand deposits consists of demand deposits at commercial banks and foreign-related institutions other than those due to depository institutions, the U.S. government, and foreign banks and official institutions, less cash items in the process of collection and Federal Reserve float. *Other checkable deposits* consists of NOW and ATS balances at all depository institutions; credit union share draft balances; and demand deposits at thrift institutions.

Savings deposits includes money market deposit accounts.

Small time deposits are those issued at commercial banks and thrift institutions in amounts of less than $100,000. Retail RPs are included. All IRA and Keogh account balances at commercial banks and thrift institutions are subtracted from small time deposits.

Large time deposits are those issued in amounts of $100,000 or more at commercial banks and thrift institutions, excluding those booked at international banking facilities. Deposits held at commercial banks by money market mutual funds, depository institutions, the U.S. government, and foreign banks and official institutions also are excluded.

Notes on the data

Seasonal adjustment. Seasonally-adjusted M1 is calculated by summing currency, travelers checks, demand deposits, and other checkable deposits, each seasonally adjusted separately. Seasonally-adjusted M2 is computed by adjusting each of its non-M1 components and then adding this result to seasonally-adjusted M1. Similarly, seasonally-adjusted M3 is obtained by adjusting each of its non-M2 components and then adding this result to seasonally-adjusted M2.

Revisions. Money stock measures are revised annually, usually in February, based on a benchmark and seasonal factor review. These revisions typically extend back a number of years. The monetary aggregates were redefined in major revisions in 1980.

Data availability

Estimates are released weekly in Federal Reserve Statistical Release H.6, "Money Stock, Liquid Assets, and Debt Measures" and are subsequently published each month in the *Federal Reserve Bulletin*. Historical data beginning with 1959 are available from Publications Services, Board of Governors of the Federal Reserve System. Current and historical data are available on the Federal Reserve internet site (http://www.federalreserve.gov/releases/).

References

An explanation of the 1980 redefinition of the monetary aggregates is found in the *Federal Reserve Bulletin* for February 1980.

TABLE 10-3
AGGREGATE RESERVES OF DEPOSITORY INSTITUTIONS AND MONETARY BASE

SOURCE: BOARD OF GOVERNORS OF THE FEDERAL RESERVE SYSTEM.

The data presented here are in millions of dollars, seasonally adjusted and adjusted for changes in reserve requirements ("break-adjusted"). (For example, an observed increase in reserves will not represent an easing in monetary conditions if it is the result of an increase in reserves required by the Federal Reserve. Therefore, the mandated increases and decreases are deducted to provide the "break-adjusted" series.) Monthly data are averages of daily figures. Annual data are for December.

Definitions

Total reserves consists of reserve balances with Federal Reserve Banks plus vault cash used to satisfy reserve requirements. Seasonally-adjusted, break-adjusted total reserves equal seasonally-adjusted, break-adjusted required reserves plus unadjusted excess reserves.

Seasonally-adjusted, break-adjusted nonborrowed reserves equal seasonally adjusted, break-adjusted total reserves less unadjusted total borrowings of depository institutions from the Federal Reserve.

Extended credit consists of borrowing at the discount window under the terms and conditions established for the extended credit program to help depository institutions deal with sustained liquidity pressures. Because there is not the same need to repay such borrowing promptly as there is with traditional short-term adjustment credit, the money market impact of extended credit is similar to that of nonborrowed reserves.

To adjust *required reserves* for discontinuities due to regulatory changes in reserve requirements, a multiplicative procedure is used to estimate what required reserves would have been in past periods had current reserve requirements been in effect. Break-adjusted required reserves include required reserves against transactions deposits and personal time and savings deposits (but not reservable nondeposit liabilities).

The seasonally-adjusted, break-adjusted *monetary base* consists of (1) seasonally adjusted, break-adjusted total reserves plus (2) the seasonally-adjusted currency component of the money stock plus (3) for all quarterly reporters on the "Report of Transaction Accounts, Other Deposits and Vault Cash" and for all those weekly reporters whose vault cash exceeds their required reserves, the seasonally adjusted, break-adjusted difference between current vault cash and the amount applied to satisfy current reserve requirements.

Data availability

Data are released weekly in Federal Reserve release H.3 and subsequently published in the *Federal Reserve Bulletin.* Historical data are available from the Money and Reserves Projections Section, Division of Monetary Affairs, Board of Governors of The Federal Reserve System, Washington, D.C. 20551. Current and historical data also are available on the Federal Reserve internet site (http://www.federalreserve.gov/releases/).

TABLE 10-4
ASSETS AND LIABILITIES OF COMMERCIAL BANKS

SOURCE: BOARD OF GOVERNORS OF THE FEDERAL RESERVE SYSTEM.

These data on the assets and liabilities of commercial banks were introduced by the Federal Reserve in 1994, replacing several discontinued data sets as noted below. Weekly data are Wednesday figures; monthly data are pro rata averages of the weekly figures; annual data are for December.

Definitions and notes on the data

The current Federal Reserve data set H.8, Assets and Liabilities of Commercial Banks in the United States, was introduced in March 1994. It incorporates key items from three statistical releases that were discontinued: the previous version of the H.8, Assets and Liabilities of Insured Domestically Chartered and Foreign-Related Institutions; the G.7, Loans and Securities at Commercial Banks; and the G.10, Major Nondeposit Funds of Commercial Banks. The new data series are available beginning with 1988.

The new H.8 contains monthly and weekly balance sheets for all commercial banks, domestically chartered banks, small domestic banks, large domestic banks, and foreign-related institutions. The data are adjusted for known reclassifications between balance sheet items and are available both seasonally adjusted and not seasonally adjusted.

The data for *all commercial banks in the United States* cover the following types of institutions in the 50 states and the District of Columbia: domestically chartered commercial banks that submit a weekly report of condition (large domestic); other domestically chartered commercial banks (small domestic); branches and agencies of foreign banks, and Edge Act and Agreement corporations (foreign-related institutions). International Banking Facilities are excluded. Small domestic banks and foreign-related institutions are estimated based on weekly samples and on quarter-end condition reports. Data are adjusted for breaks caused by reclassifications of assets and liabilities.

Loans and leases in bank credit excludes federal funds sold to, reverse repurchase agreements (RPs) with, and loans to commercial banks in the United States; all of these are in interbank loans. In a reverse repurchase agreement, a bank has provided liquidity to a borrower by buying a security from him, which the borrower promises to repurchase at a certain date. The security held by the lending bank is classified in its assets accounts as a reverse RP.

Security loans consists of reverse repurchase agreements with brokers and dealers and loans to purchase and carry securities.

Interbank loans consists of federal funds sold to, reverse repurchase agreements with, and loans to commercial banks in the United States.

Cash assets includes vault cash, cash items in process of collection, balances due from depository institutions, and balances due from Federal Reserve Banks.

Other assets excludes the due-from position with related foreign offices, which has been subtracted from amounts due to related foreign offices to yield the liability item Net due foreign offices.

Total assets excludes unearned income, reserves for losses on loans and leases, and reserves for transfer risk. Loans are reported gross of these items.

Residual: Assets less liabilities. This balancing item is not intended as a measure of equity capital for use in capital adequacy analysis. On a seasonally adjusted basis this item reflects any differences in the seasonal patterns estimated for total assets and total liabilities.

Revisions

Data are revised annually to reflect new benchmark information and revised seasonal factors.

Data availability

Assets and Liabilities of Commercial Banks, Federal Reserve release H.8, is released each Friday around 4:30 p.m. eastern time. Selected data are subsequently published in the *Federal Reserve Bulletin.* Historical data may be purchased on diskette from Publications Services, Board of Governors of the Federal Reserve System. Current and historical data are available on the Federal Reserve internet site (http://www.federalreserve.gov/releases/).

TABLE 10-5
CREDIT MARKET DEBT OUTSTANDING, HOUSEHOLD DEBT BURDENS, AND DELINQUENCY RATES

SOURCE: BOARD OF GOVERNORS OF THE FEDERAL RESERVE SYSTEM.

The flow of funds accounts compiled quarterly by the Federal Reserve Board supplement the national income and product and international transactions accounts by providing a comprehensive and detailed accounting of financial transactions, with a balance sheet for each financial and nonfinancial sector of the economy. The most widely used of these data measure the debt of nonfinancial sectors, taken from the liability sides of those sectors' balance sheets. For example, aggregate domestic nonfinancial debt is used by the Federal Reserve along with the monetary aggregates as an indicator of the effects of monetary policy, and a range of growth rates for that aggregate is projected in their semiannual report. (See Notes to Tables 10-1 and 10.2.) Reproduced here are aggregate data on U.S. credit market debt outstanding owed by domestic financial and nonfinancial sectors and by foreigners. Data on the creditors who hold this debt as assets are not shown; often, multiple layers of financial intermediation or securitization are involved, and aggregates of such data over several financial sectors are not considered very meaningful.

Definitions and notes on the data

Quarterly data on debt outstanding are shown on an end-of-period basis, not adjusted for seasonal variation or for "breaks" or discontinuities in the series. For these and other reasons they differ from the monthly debt aggregates shown in Table 10-1.

Data for the current and preceding years are revised each year to reflect revisions in source data.

Domestic financial sectors:

Federal government-related sectors include federally sponsored credit agencies, federally related mortgage pools, and the monetary authority (Federal Reserve).

The private sector includes commercial banks, thrift institutions, insurance and pension funds (except federal government), mutual funds, investment trusts, and other financial institutions.

Domestic nonfinancial sectors:

Federal government consists of all federal government agencies and funds that are in the unified budget, except for the District of Columbia government, which is included in the state and local sector.

- Treasury securities as shown here exclude securities issued by the Treasury but held by agencies within the U.S. government (e.g., in the Social Security trust funds). It corresponds to the Federal "debt held by the public" shown in Table 21-7 (except that the latter table uses a fiscal year, not a calendar year, basis). Federal government debt as shown here is smaller than the official total public debt and the "debt subject to limit," both of which include the securities held by U.S. government agencies. The value shown here is considered a more accurate measure of the effect of government borrowing in relation to the economy and credit markets.

- Budget agency securities and mortgages are those issued by government-owned corporations and agencies, such as the Export-Import Bank, that issue securities individually.

Households also include personal trusts and nonprofit organizations.

State and local governments reflects general funds only; retirement funds are included in the financial sector. *Foreign credit market debt held in the United States* is included along with the debt of domestic financial and nonfinancial sectors in total credit market debt outstanding.

The *household debt service burden* is estimated debt payments as a percent of disposable personal income. Debt payments consist of the estimated required payments on outstanding mortgage and consumer debt. These payments are not based on reports from households, but are estimated in the aggregate by the Federal Reserve Board based mainly on reports by lenders.

Delinquency rates of credit card accounts held at banks are compiled from the quarterly FFIEC (Federal Financial Institutions Examination Council) Consolidated Reports of Condition and Income (FFIEC 031 through 034). Data for each calendar quarter become available approximately sixty days after the end of the quarter.

Mortgage delinquency rates of over 90 days are compiled by the Mortgage Bankers Association of America in their National Delinquency Survey.

Data availability

Debt estimates are released quarterly, about nine weeks following the end of a quarter, in Federal Reserve Statistical Release Z.1, "Flow of Funds Accounts of the United States," and are subsequently published in the *Federal Reserve Bulletin*. Releases and data on diskettes are available from Publications Services, Board of Governors of the Federal Reserve System. Current and historical data also are available on the Federal Reserve internet site (http://www.federalreserve.gov/releases).

The household debt burden data are estimated by the Federal Reserve about three months after the end of each quarter and are available on the same internet site.

Delinquency rates of credit card accounts held at banks are also available on the Federal Reserve internet site, listed under Charge-Off and Delinquency Rates on Loans at Commercial Banks.

Mortgage delinquency rates can be obtained from the Mortgage Bankers Association of America by length of delinquency (30, 60, 90 days or more) and type of loan, as well as for various levels of geography. MBAA statistical information can be found on their internet site (http://www.mbaa.org/marketdata/).

References

A *Guide to the Flow of Funds Accounts* is available from Publications Services, Board of Governors of the Federal Reserve System.

TABLE 10-6
CONSUMER INSTALLMENT CREDIT

SOURCE: BOARD OF GOVERNORS OF THE FEDERAL RESERVE SYSTEM.

The consumer installment credit series cover most short- and intermediate-term credit extended to individuals through regular business channels, excluding loans secured by real estate (e.g., first and second mortgages and home equity credit). (The household debt series presented in Table 10-5 is more comprehensive, comprising both mortgage and consumer debt.) Consumer installment credit is categorized by major holders and by major types of credit.

Definitions and notes on the data

Categories of holders include commercial banks, finance companies, credit unions, savings institutions, nonfinancial businesses, and pools of securitized assets. Retailers and gasoline companies are included in the nonfinancial businesses category. *Pools of securitized assets* comprises the outstanding balances of pools upon which securities have been issued; these balances are no longer carried on the balance sheets of the loan originators.

The major types of consumer credit are revolving and nonrevolving. *Revolving credit* includes credit arising from purchases on credit card plans of retail stores and banks, cash advances and check credit plans of banks, and some overdraft credit arrangements. *Non-revolving credit* includes automobile loans (new and passenger automobiles), mobile home loans, and all other installment loans not included in revolving credit, such as loans for education, boats, trailers, or vacations. These loans may be secured or unsecured.

Debt secured by real estate (including first liens, junior liens, and home equity loans) is excluded. Credit extended to governmental agencies and nonprofit or charitable organizations, as well as credit extended to business or to individuals exclusively for business purposes, is excluded.

The consumer credit series are based on comprehensive benchmark data that become available periodically. Current monthly estimates are brought forward from the latest benchmarks in accordance with weighted changes indicated by sample data. Classifications are made on a

"holder" basis. Thus, installment paper sold by retail outlets is included in figures for the banks and finance companies that purchased the paper.

The amount of outstanding credit represents the sum of the balances in the installment receivable accounts of financial institutions and retail outlets at the end of each month. Net change measures the change during the month in the amount of consumer installment credit outstanding. It is defined as the amount of consumer installment credit extended less the amount liquidated (including repayments, chargeoffs, and other credits) during the month. Each monthly change is computed by subtracting the seasonally-adjusted amount outstanding at the end of the previous month from the amount outstanding at the end of the current month. Information is not available to make separate estimates of the amount of extensions, liquidations, and chargeoffs of bad debts.

The estimates of the amount of credit outstanding and net change include any finance and insurance charges included as part of the installment contract. Unearned income on loans is included in some cases where lenders cannot separate the components.

The seasonally-adjusted data are adjusted for differences in the number of trading days and for seasonal influences. The seasonal factors used are derived by the X-11-ARIMA process.

Data availability

Current data are available monthly in the Federal Reserve statistical release G.19, Consumer Credit, and in the *Federal Reserve Bulletin*. The data for earlier years may be purchased on diskette from Publication Services, Board of Governors of the Federal Reserve System. Current and historical data are available on the Federal Reserve internet site (http://www.federalreserve.gov/releases/).

TABLES 10-7, 10-8 AND 24-10
INTEREST RATES, BOND YIELDS, STOCK PRICES AND YIELDS

SOURCES: BOARD OF GOVERNORS OF THE FEDERAL RESERVE SYSTEM; MOODY'S INVESTORS SERVICE; THE BOND BUYER; DOW JONES, INC.; STANDARD AND POOR'S CORPORATION; NEW YORK STOCK EXCHANGE.

Definitions and notes on the data

Interest rates and bond yields are percents per year and are averages of business day figures, except as noted.

The daily *effective federal funds rate* is a weighted average of rates on trades through New York brokers. Monthly figures include each calendar day in the month. Annualized figures use a 360-day year.

The *Federal Reserve discount rate* is the rate for discount window borrowing at the Federal Reserve Bank of New York. Annualized figures use a 360-day year.

The *Eurodollar rate* shown is the bid rate for Eurodollar deposits at 11 a.m. London time for one-month deposits.

The *U.S. Treasury bills, three-month rate and the U.S. Treasury bills, 6-month rate* shown are the auction averages; the monthly averages are computed on an issue-date basis. The rates are quoted on a discount basis, and annualized figures use a 360-day year.

Bankers' acceptances, three-month rates are representative closing yields for acceptances of the highest rated money center banks. The rates are quoted on a discount basis, and annualized figures use a 360-day year.

CDs (secondary market), three-month rates are averages of dealer offering rates on nationally traded certificates of deposit. Annualized figures use a 360-day year.

The *bank prime rate* is one of several base rates used by banks to price short-term business loans. Monthly and annual figures include each calendar day in the month or year.

U.S. Treasury securities. The rates shown for 1-year, 10-year, and 30-year securities are yields on actively traded issues adjusted to constant maturities. Yields on Treasury securities at "constant maturity" are interpolated by the U.S. Treasury from the daily yield curve. This curve, which relates the yield on a security to its time to maturity, is based on the closing market bid yields on actively traded Treasury securities in the over-the-counter market. These market yields are calculated from composites of quotations reported by five leading U.S. Government securities dealers to the Federal Reserve Bank of New York. The constant maturity yield values are read from the yield curve at fixed maturities, currently 1, 2, 3, 5, 7, 10, 20, and 30 years. This method provides a yield for a 10-year maturity, for example, even if no outstanding security has exactly 10 years remaining to maturity. The long-term composite is the unweighted average of rates on all outstanding bonds neither due nor callable in less than 10 years.

Domestic corporate bond yields. The rates shown are for general obligation bonds based on Thursday figures and

are provided by Moody's Investors Service and republished by the Federal Reserve.

The *A-rated utility bond rate* shown is an estimate compiled by the Federal Reserve of the yield on a recently offered A-rated utility bond with a maturity of 30 years and call protection of five years; Friday quotations.

The *state and local bond yields* are the Bond Buyer index as republished by the Federal Reserve. The index is based on 20 state and local government general obligation bonds maturing in 20 years or less.

The *fixed rate mortgage rates* are contract interest rates on commitments for fixed-rate first mortgages. The rates are obtained by the Federal Reserve from the Federal Home Loan Mortgage Corporation (FHLMC).

Stock price indexes. The Dow Jones industrial average is an average of 30 stocks compiled by Dow Jones, Inc. The Standard and Poor's composite is an index of 500 stocks based on 1941–1943=10 compiled by Standard and Poor's Corporation. The New York Stock Exchange indexes are compiled by the New York Stock Exchange and are based on December 31, 1965=50, except for the utility index, which is based on December 31, 1965=100. The monthly and annual data are averages of daily figures.

Data availability

Interest rates and bond yields are published weekly in the Federal Reserve's H.15 release. Most are subsequently published in the *Federal Reserve Bulletin,* as are the stock indexes. The starting dates for individual interest rate series vary; some date back to 1911, and many begin in the 1950s and 1960s. Historical data may be purchased on diskette from Publications Services, Board of Governors of the Federal Reserve System. Current and historical data are available on the Federal Reserve internet site (http://www.federalreserve.gov/releases/).

TABLES 11-1 AND 22-9
U.S. INTERNATIONAL TRANSACTIONS

SOURCE: U.S. DEPARTMENT OF COMMERCE, BUREAU OF ECONOMIC ANALYSIS.

The U.S. international transactions accounts, or "balance of payments," provide a comprehensive view of economic transactions between the United States and foreign countries. They are subdivided into three sets of accounts, comprising credit and debit items, which in concept provide a complete accounting for U.S. international transactions and should therefore sum to zero. In practice, there are substantial discrepancies due to measurement problems.

The balance on the "current account" is the most frequently quoted statistic from these accounts, and is frequently if imprecisely called the "trade balance." The current account includes estimates of exports and imports of goods and of travel, transportation, and other services; receipts and payments of income between U.S. and foreign residents; and foreign aid and other current transfers. The "financial account" covers most international flows of capital, private and official, including direct investment. A "capital account", which is small relative to the other two accounts, includes certain transactions in existing assets.

More detailed data on exports and imports of goods and services are shown in Tables 11-3 through 11-10.

Definitions

Credits (+): The following items are treated as credits in the international transactions accounts: Exports of goods and services and income receipts; unilateral current transfers to the United States; capital account transactions receipts; financial inflows, i.e. increases in foreign-owned assets (U.S. liabilities) and decreases in U.S.-owned assets (U.S. claims).

Debits (-): The following items are treated as debits in the international transactions accounts, indicated by minus signs in the data cells: Imports of goods and services and income payments; unilateral current transfers to foreigners; capital accounts transactions payments; financial outflows, i.e. decreases in foreign-owned assets (U.S. liabilities) and increases in U.S.-owned assets (U.S. claims).

The *balance on goods* is the excess of exports of goods over imports of goods. (A minus sign indicates an excess of imports over exports.)

The *balance on services* is the excess of service exports over service imports. (A minus sign indicates an excess of imports over exports.)

The *balance on goods and services* is the sum of the balance on goods and the balance on services.

The *balance on income* is the excess of income receipts from abroad over income payments to foreigners. (A minus sign indicates an excess of payments over receipts.)

The *balance on goods, services, and income* is the excess of exports of goods, services, and income over imports of goods, services, and income. It is equal to the sum of the balance on goods and services and the balance on income. (A minus sign indicates an excess of imports over exports.)

The *balance on unilateral transfers* is equal to unilateral transfers, net, i.e. transfers to the United States minus transfers from the United States.

The *balance on current account* is equal to the sum of the balance on goods, services, and income and the balance on unilateral transfers.

The *capital account* covers net capital transfers and the acquisition and disposal of nonproduced nonfinancial assets. The major types of capital transfers are debt forgiveness and assets that accompany immigrants.

Nonproduced nonfinancial assets include rights to natural resources, patents, copyrights, trademarks, franchises, and leases.

The *financial account* includes all other inflows and outflows of capital, i.e. changes in U.S.-owned assets abroad and foreign-owned assets in the United States, including official reserve assets, direct investment, securities, currency, and bank deposits.

In concept, the balance on current account is necessarily offset exactly by the net financial and capital inflow or outflow; for example, a U.S. current account deficit results in more dollars held by foreigners, which must be reflected in additional claims on the United States held by foreigners, whether in the form of U.S. currency, securities, loans, or other forms of obligation. But because of different and incomplete data sources, the financial and capital accounts do not exactly offset the current account. The *statistical discrepancy* in the U.S. international accounts-the sum of all credits and debits, with the sign reversed-measures the amount by which the net financial and capital flow would have to be augmented (or diminished, in the case of a negative entry) to offset the current account balance exactly. (In the quarterly accounts, a part of this discrepancy, the *seasonal adjustment discrepancy,* results from separate seasonal adjustment.) The statistical discrepancy in the international accounts is not the same as the statistical discrepancy in the national income and product accounts, which arises from measurement differences between domestic output and domestic income.

Notes on the data

Exports and imports of goods in the international transactions account exclude exports of goods under U.S. military agency sales contracts identified in Census Bureau export documents and imports of goods under direct defense expenditures identified in import documents. They also reflect various other adjustments (for valuation, coverage, and timing) of Census Bureau statistics to a balance-of-payments basis.

Services include some goods, mainly military equipment (included in transfers under military agency sales contracts); major equipment, other materials, supplies, and petroleum products purchased abroad by U.S. military agencies (included in direct defense expenditures abroad); and fuels purchased by airline and steamship operators (included in other transportation).

U.S. government grants include transfers of goods and services under U.S. military grant programs. The data for 1974 include extraordinary U.S. government transactions with India.

Beginning in 1982, *private remittances* and *other transfers* includes taxes paid by U.S. private residents to foreign governments and taxes paid by private nonresidents to the U.S. government.

At the present time, all U.S. Treasury-owned *gold* is held in the United States.

Beginning with the data for 1982, *direct investment income* and the reinvested earnings component of *direct investment* financial flows are measured on a current-cost (replacement-cost) basis after adjustment to reported depreciation, depletion, and expensed exploration and development costs. For prior years, depreciation is valued in terms of the historical cost of assets and reflects a mix of prices for the various years in which capital investments were made. See *Survey of Current Business*, July 1999, pp 65–67, and *Survey of Current Business*, June 1992, pages 72ff.

Repayments on U.S. credits and other long-term assets includes sales of foreign obligations to foreigners. The data for 1974 include extraordinary U.S. government transactions with India, described in "Special U.S. Government Transactions," *Survey of Current Business*, June 1974, page 27.

Foreign official assets in the United States. *U.S. Treasury securities* consists of bills, certificates, marketable bonds

and notes, and nonmarketable convertible and nonconvertible bonds and notes; *other U.S. government securities* consists of U.S. Treasury and Export-Import Bank obligations, not included elsewhere, and of debt securities of U.S. government corporations and agencies; *other U.S. government liabilities* includes, primarily, U.S. government liabilities associated with military agency sales contracts and other transactions arranged with or through foreign official agencies; other foreign official assets consists of investments in U.S. corporate stocks and in debt securities of private corporations and state and local governments.

Estimates of *U.S. currency flows* abroad were introduced for the first time as part of the July 1997 revisions. Data for 1974 and subsequent years were affected (see *Survey of Current Business,* July 1997). Beginning with the 1998 revisions, currency flows are published separately from U.S. treasury securities.

For 1978–1983, *U.S. treasury securities* includes foreign-currency-denominated notes sold to private residents abroad.

Relation of balance on current account to net foreign investment. Conceptually, "net foreign investment" in the national income and product accounts (NIPAs) should be equal to the balance on current account plus allocation of special drawing rights, aside from the fact that the NIPAs pertain only to the 50 states and the District of Columbia while the international transactions accounts also include U.S. territories and Puerto Rico. The foreign transactions account in the NIPAs includes (a) adjustments to the international transactions accounts for the treatment of gold, (b) adjustments for the different geographical treatment of transactions with U.S. territories and Puerto Rico, and (c) services furnished without payment by financial pension plans except life insurance carriers and private noninsured pension plans. A reconciliation of the balance on goods and services from the international accounts and the NIPA net exports appears periodically in the "Reconciliation and Other Special Tables" section of the *Survey of Current Business,* most recently in the July 2000 issue. A reconciliation of the other foreign transactions in the two sets of accounts appears in Table 4.5 of the NIPAs.

Revisions

The international transactions accounts are revised annually in July. Changes in definitions and methodology, as well as the incorporation of newly available source data, may be introduced in these revisions.

Data availability

Quarterly and annual data are available. Data first are reported in a press release and subsequently published in an article in the *Survey of Current Business,* which can also be found on the BEA internet site. Revisions to historical data are published annually. The most recent historical revisions also appear in the July 2000 issue of the *Survey.* Complete historical data may be purchased on diskette from BEA. Historical data also are available on the BEA internet site (http://www.bea.doc.gov).

References

Discussions of the impact of changes in methodology and incorporation of new data sources are found in the July (June for 1995 and earlier) issues of the *Survey of Current Business* each year, the most recent being "U.S. International Transactions, Revised Estimates for 1982–1999" (July 2000).

The Balance of Payments of the United States: Concepts, Data Sources, and Estimating Procedures (May 1990), available on the BEA internet site or from NTIS (Accession No. PB 90-268715) describes the methodology in detail and provides a list of data sources.

TABLE 11-2
INTERNATIONAL INVESTMENT POSITION OF THE UNITED STATES

SOURCE: U.S. DEPARTMENT OF COMMERCE, BUREAU OF ECONOMIC ANALYSIS.

The data on the international investment position of the United States measure the extent to which the United States and its residents hold claims of ownership on foreigners, or are creditors of foreigners; the extent to which foreigners, including foreign governments, hold claims of ownership on assets located in the United States or are creditors of U.S. residents and entities; and the net difference between the two amounts. This difference measures the amount by which the United States is a net creditor of the rest of the world or a net debtor to the rest of the world. A position of net U.S. indebtedness is represented by a minus sign in the net international investment position.

Changes in the net investment position can arise in two principal ways. The first way is through inflows or outflows of capital. A net inflow of capital increases U.S. indebtedness to foreigners, while a net outflow increases foreigners' indebtedness to the U.S. A deficit in the U.S.

international current account requires an equivalent inflow of foreign capital, while a surplus would require an equivalent outflow of U.S. capital; see notes on Table 11-1. The second way is through valuation adjustments, which are of several kinds: prices of assets can change; changes in exchange rates can cause revaluation of foreign-currency-denominated assets; and there can be miscellaneous other adjustments due to changes in coverage, statistical discrepancies, etc.

Definitions

Direct investment occurs when an individual or business in one country (the parent) obtains a lasting interest in, and a degree of influence over the management of, a business enterprise in another country (the affiliate). The U.S. data define this degree of interest to be ownership of at least 10 percent of the voting securities of an incorporated business enterprise or the equivalent interest in an unincorporated business enterprise.

When direct investment positions are valued at the historical costs carried on the books of the affiliated companies, much of the investment will reflect the price levels of earlier time periods. Therefore, before calculating the overall U.S. position, BEA estimates the aggregate direct investment totals using two alternative valuation bases. (Detailed direct investment data by country and industry are available only on a historical cost basis.)

At *current cost,* the portion of the direct investment position representing parents' shares of their affiliates' tangible assets (property, plant, equipment, and inventories) is revalued to replacement cost in today's money, using a perpetual inventory model, appropriate price indexes, and depreciation allowances. This is an adjustment made to the asset side of the balance sheet and reflects prices of tangible assets only.

The *market value* method revalues the owners' equity portion of the direct investment positions using general country indexes of stock market prices. This adjustment is made on the liability and owner's equity side of the balance sheet. Stock price changes reflect changes not only in the value of tangible assets but also in the value of intangible assets and in the outlook for a country or industry.

Market values are more volatile than current cost, reflecting the volatility of the stock market. Note, for example, that in some years the total market value of direct investment is greater than the current replacement cost, while in other years (e.g. 1984 and 1985) it is less.

U.S. official reserve assets include gold, valued at the current market price; special drawing rights; the U.S. reserve position in the International Monetary Fund; and official holdings of foreign currencies.

Other U.S. government assets include other U.S. government claims on foreigners and holdings of foreign currency and short-term assets.

U.S. nonbank claims are U.S. claims on affiliated foreigners reported by U.S. nonbanking concerns.

U.S. bank claims are claims on foreigners, such as loans and commercial paper, held by U.S. banks and not reported elsewhere in the accounts.

Foreign official assets include foreign government holdings of claims on the United States, including U.S. government securities and other liabilities and deposits held by such governments in U.S. banks.

Foreign-owned assets in the United States, other than official assets, also include *U.S. Treasury securities, U.S. currency, corporate and other bonds, corporate stocks, U.S. liabilities (to foreigners) reported by U.S. nonbanking concerns, and U.S. bank liabilities* (such as deposits) *to foreigners.*

Data availability

The annual (year-end) data are presented each year, along with revisions for earlier years and a descriptive article, in the July issue of the *Survey of Current Business.* The articles and the data are available on the BEA internet site (http://www.bea.doc.gov).

References

Relevant articles in the July 2000 *Survey of Current Business* are: "The International Investment Position of the United States at Yearend 1999" and "Direct Investment Positions for 1999: Country and Industry Detail." For background on the valuation of direct investment and other components, see "Valuation of the U.S. Net International Investment Position," *Survey of Current Business,* May 1991. Also see the references for Table 11-1.

TABLES 11-3 THROUGH 11-10
EXPORTS AND IMPORTS OF GOODS AND SERVICES

Sources: U.S. Department of Commerce, Bureau of the Census and Bureau of Economic Analysis (BEA).

Monthly and annual data on exports and imports of goods are compiled by the Bureau of the Census from documents collected by the U.S. Customs Service. BEA makes certain adjustments to these data (described below) to place the estimates on a "balance of payments" basis-a basis consistent with the national and international accounts. Data on exports and imports of services are prepared by BEA from a variety of sources. Monthly data on services are available from the beginning of 1992. Annual and quarterly data for earlier years are available as part of the international transactions accounts. Current data on goods and services are available each month in a joint Census-BEA press release.

Definitions: Goods

Goods: Census Basis. The Census basis goods data are compiled from the documents collected by the U.S. Customs Service and reflect the movement of goods between foreign countries and the 50 states, the District of Columbia, Puerto Rico, the U.S. Virgin Islands, and U.S. Foreign Trade Zones. They include government and non-government shipments of goods. They exclude shipments between the United States and its territories and possessions, transactions with U.S. military, diplomatic and consular installations abroad, U.S. goods returned to the United States by its Armed Forces, personal and household effects of travelers, and in-transit shipments. The general import values reflect the total arrival of merchandise from foreign countries that immediately enters consumption channels, warehouses, or Foreign Trade Zones.

For *imports,* the value reported is the U.S. Customs Service appraised value of merchandise (generally, the price paid for merchandise for export to the United States). Import duties, freight, insurance, and other charges incurred in bringing merchandise to the United States are excluded.

Exports are valued at the f.a.s. (free alongside ship) value of merchandise at the U.S. port of export, based on the transaction price including inland freight, insurance, and other charges incurred in placing the merchandise alongside the carrier at the U.S. port of exportation.

Goods: Balance of payments (BOP) basis. Goods on a Census basis are adjusted by the BEA to goods on a BOP basis to bring the data in line with the concepts and definitions used to prepare the international and national accounts. Broadly, the adjustments include changes in ownership that occur without goods passing into or out of the customs territory of the United States. These adjustments are necessary to supplement coverage of the Census basis data, to eliminate duplication of transactions recorded elsewhere in the international accounts, and to value transactions according to a standard definition.

The *export* adjustments include: (1) Deduction of *U.S. military sales contracts,* because the Census Bureau has included these contracts in the goods data, but BEA includes them in the service category "Transfers Under U.S. Military Sales Contracts." BEA's source material for these contracts is more comprehensive, but does not distinguish between goods and services. (2) Addition of *private gift parcels* mailed to foreigners by individuals through the U.S. Postal Service. (Only commercial shipments are covered in Census goods exports.) (3) Addition to *nonmonetary gold exports* of gold purchased by foreign official agencies from private dealers in the United States and held at the Federal Reserve Bank of New York. The Census data include only gold that leaves the customs territory. (4) *Smaller adjustments* include deductions for repairs of goods, exposed motion picture film, and military grant aid; and additions for sales of fish in U.S. territorial waters, exports of electricity to Mexico, and vessels and oil rigs that change ownership without export documents being filed.

The *import* adjustments include: (1) On *inland freight in Canada,* the customs value for imports for certain Canadian goods is the point of origin in Canada. The BEA makes an addition for the inland freight charges of transporting these Canadian goods to the U.S. border. (2) An addition is made to *nonmonetary gold imports* for gold sold by foreign official agencies to private purchasers out of stock held at the Federal Reserve Bank of New York. The Census Bureau data include only gold that enters the customs territory. (3) A deduction is made for *imports by U.S. military agencies* because the Census Bureau has included these contracts in the goods data, but BEA includes them in the service category "Direct Defense Expenditures." BEA's source material is more comprehensive, but does not distinguish between goods and services. (4) *Smaller adjustments* include deductions for repairs of goods and for exposed motion picture film; and additions for imported electricity from Mexico, conversion of vessels for commercial use, and repairs to U.S. vessels abroad.

Definitions: Services

The statistics are estimates of service transactions between foreign countries and the 50 states, the District of Columbia, Puerto Rico, the U.S. Virgin Islands, and other U.S. territories and possessions. Transactions with U.S. military, diplomatic, and consular installations abroad are excluded because they are considered to be

part of the U.S. economy. Services are shown in the broad categories described below. For six of these, the categories are the same for imports and exports. For the seventh, exports is "Transfers under U.S. Military Sales Contracts" while for imports the category is "Direct Defense Expenditures."

Travel—Purchases of services and goods by U.S. travelers abroad and by foreign visitors to the United States. A traveler is defined as a person who stays for a period of less than one year in a country of which the person is not a resident. Included are expenditures for food, lodging, recreation, gifts, and other items incidental to a foreign visit.

Passenger fares—Fares paid by residents of one country to residents in other countries. Receipts consist of fares received by U.S. carriers from foreign residents for travel between the United States and foreign countries and between two foreign points. Payments consist of fares paid by U.S. residents to foreign carriers for travel between the United States and foreign countries.

Break in series: Travel and passenger fares—Beginning with data for 1984, these items incorporate results from a survey administered by the U.S. Travel and Tourism Administration. See *Survey of Current Business,* June 1989, pages 57ff.

Other transportation—Charges for the transportation of goods by ocean, air, waterway, pipeline, and rail carriers to and from the United States. Includes freight charges, operating expenses that transportation companies incur in foreign ports, and payments for vessel charter and aircraft and freight car rentals. (*Break in series.* Estimates of freight charges for the transportation of goods by truck between the United States and Canada are included in the data beginning with 1986. Reliable estimates for earlier years are not available. See *Survey of Current Business,* June 1994, pages 70ff.)

Royalties and license fees—Transactions with foreign residents involving intangible assets and proprietary rights, such as the use of patents, techniques, processes, formulas, designs, know-how, trademarks, copyrights, franchises, and manufacturing rights. The term "royalties" generally refers to payments for the utilization of copyrights or trademarks, and "license fees" generally refers to payments for the use of patents or industrial processes.

Other private services—Transactions with affiliated foreigners for which no identification by type is available and transactions with unaffiliated foreigners. (The term "affiliated" refers to a direct investment relationship, which exists when a U.S. person has ownership or control, directly or indirectly, of 10 percent or more of a foreign business enterprise, or when a foreign person has a similar interest in a U.S. enterprise.) Transactions with unaffiliated foreigners consist of education services; financial services; insurance premiums and losses; telecommunications services; and business, professional, and technical services. Included in the last group are advertising services; computer and data processing services; database and other information services; research, development, and testing services; management, consulting, and public relations services; legal services; construction, engineering, architectural, and mining services; industrial engineering services; installation, maintenance and repair of equipment; and other services, including medical services and film and tape rental.

BEA conducts surveys of international transactions in financial services and "selected services" (largely business, professional, and technical services). Beginning with data for 1986, other private services includes estimates of business, professional, and technical services from the BEA surveys of selected services. (See *Survey of Current Business,* June 1989, pages 57ff.)

Breaks in series: Royalties and license fees and other private services—These items are presented on a gross basis beginning in 1982. The definition of exports is revised to exclude U.S. parents' payments to foreign affiliates and to include U.S. affiliates' receipts from foreign parents. The definition of imports is revised to include U.S. parents' payments to foreign affiliates and to exclude U.S. affiliates' receipts from foreign parents.

Transfers under U.S. military sales contracts (exports only)—Exports of goods and services in which U.S. government military agencies participate. Includes both goods, such as equipment, and services, such as repair services and training, that cannot be separately identified. Transfers of goods and services under U.S. military grant programs are included.

Direct defense expenditures (imports only)—Expenditures incurred by U.S. military agencies abroad, including expenditures by U.S. personnel, payments of wages to foreign residents, construction expenditures, payments for foreign contractual services, and procurement of foreign goods. Included are both goods and services that cannot be separately identified.

U.S. government miscellaneous services—Transactions of U.S. Government nonmilitary agencies with foreign residents. Most of these transactions involve the provision of services to, or purchases of services from, foreigners; transfers of some goods are also included.

Services estimates are based on quarterly, annual, and benchmark surveys and partial information generated from monthly reports. Service transactions are estimated at market prices. Estimates are seasonally adjusted when statistically significant seasonal patterns are present.

Definitions: Area groupings

North America—Canada, Mexico

South/Central America—Anguilla, Antigua and Barbuda, Argentina, Aruba, Bahamas, Barbados, Belize, Bermuda, Bolivia, Brazil, British Virgin Islands, Cayman Islands, Chile, Colombia, Costa Rica, Cuba, Dominica, Dominican Republic, Ecuador, El Salvador, Falkland Islands, French Guiana, Grenada, Guadeloupe, Guatemala, Guyana, Haiti, Honduras, Jamaica, Martinique, Montserrat, Netherlands Antilles, Nicaragua, Panama, Paraguay, Peru, St. Kitts and Nevis, St. Lucia, St. Vincent and the Grenadines, Suriname, Trinidad and Tobago, Turks and Caicos Islands, Uruguay, Venezuela.

Western Europe—Andorra, Austria, Belgium, Bosnia-Herzegovina, Croatia, Cyprus, Denmark, Faroe Islands, Finland, France, Germany, Gibraltar, Greece, Iceland, Ireland, Italy, Liechtenstein, Luxembourg, Malta and Gozo, Macedonia, Monaco, Netherlands, Norway, Portugal, San Marino, Slovenia, Spain, Svalbard, Sweden, Switzerland, Turkey, United Kingdom, Vatican City, Yugoslavia.

European Union—Austria, Belgium, Denmark, Finland, France, Germany, Greece, Ireland, Italy, Luxembourg, Netherlands, Portugal, Spain, Sweden, United Kingdom.

European Free Trade Association—Iceland, Liechtenstein, Norway, Sweden, Switzerland.

Eastern Europe and former Soviet Republics—Albania, Armenia, Azerbaijan, Belarus, Bulgaria, Czech Republic, Estonia, Georgia, Hungary, Kazakhstan, Kyrgyzstan, Latvia, Lithuania, Moldova, Poland, Romania, Russia, Slovakia, Tajikistan, Turkmenistan, Ukraine, Uzbekistan.

ASEAN—Association of Southeast Asian Nations: Brunei, Indonesia, Malaysia, Philippines, Singapore, Thailand.

MERCOSUR (Southern Common Market)—Argentina, Brazil, Paraguay, Uruguay.

Central American Common Market—Costa Rica, El Salvador, Guatemala, Honduras, Nicaragua.

Newly Industrialized Countries — Hong Kong, South Korea, Singapore, Taiwan.

Organization of Petroleum Exporting Countries (OPEC) — Algeria, Gabon, Indonesia, Iran, Iraq, Kuwait, Libya, Nigeria, Qatar, Saudi Arabia, United Arab Emirates, Venezuela.

Pacific Rim Countries — Australia, Brunei, China, Hong Kong, Indonesia, Japan, Korea, Macao, Malaysia, New Zealand, Papua New Guinea, Philippines, Singapore, Taiwan.

Notes on the data

U.S./Canada data exchange and substitution. The data for U.S. exports to Canada are derived from import data compiled by Canada. The use of Canada's import data to produce U.S. export data requires several alignments in order to compare the two series: Coverage: Canadian imports are based on country of origin. U.S. goods shipped from a third country are included. U.S. exports exclude these foreign shipments. U.S. export coverage also excludes certain Canadian postal shipments. *Valuation:* Canadian imports are valued at point of origin in the United States. However, U.S. exports are valued at the port of exit in the United States and include inland freight charges, making the U.S. export value slightly larger. Canada requires inland freight to be reported. *Reexports:* U.S. exports include reexports of foreign goods. Again, the aggregate U.S. export figure is slightly larger. *Exchange Rate:* Average monthly exchange rates are applied to convert the published data to U.S. currency.

End-use categories and seasonal adjustment of trade in goods. Goods are initially classified under the Harmonized System, which describes and measures the characteristics of goods traded. Combining trade into approximately 140 export and 140 import end-use categories makes it possible to examine goods according to their principal uses. These categories are used as the basis for computing the seasonal and working-day adjusted data. These adjusted data are then summed to the six end-use aggregates for publication.

The seasonal adjustment procedure is based on a model that estimates the monthly movements as percentages above or below the general level of each end-use commodity series (unlike other methods that redistribute the actual series values over the calendar year). Imports of petroleum and petroleum products are adjusted for the length of the month.

Data availability

Data are released in a monthly joint Census-BEA press release (FT-900) about six weeks after the end of the month to which the data pertain. The data on trade in goods by end-use category (BOP basis) and trade in services are subsequently published each month in the *Survey of Current Business.* Additional data and information on goods is obtainable from the Foreign Trade Division, Bureau of the Census, Washington, DC 20233. Additional data and information on services is obtainable from the Balance of Payments Division, Bureau of Economic Analysis, Washington, DC 20230. Current releases and some historical data are available on the Bureau of the Census internet site (http://www.census.gov/foreign-trade/www/).

Revisions

Data for recent years normally are revised annually. Data on trade in services may be subject to extensive revision as part of BEA's annual revision of the international transactions accounts, usually released in July.

References

Discussion of the impact of changes in methodology and incorporation of new data sources are found in discussions of annual revisions of the international transactions accounts in the June or July issue of the BEA publication, *Survey of Current Business,* the most recent being "U.S. International Transactions, Revised Estimates for 1982–1999" (July 2000).

TABLE 11-11
EXPORT AND IMPORT PRICE INDEXES

Source: U.S. Department of Labor, Bureau of Labor Statistics (BLS).

The BLS International Price Program produces monthly and quarterly export and import price indexes for non-military goods traded between the United States and the rest of the world.

Definitions

The export price index provides a measure of price change for all products sold by U.S. residents (i.e., businesses and individuals located within the geographic boundaries of the United States, whether or not owned by U.S. citizens) to foreign buyers.

The import price index provides a measure of price change for goods purchased from other countries by U.S. residents.

Notes on the data

The product universe for both the import and export indexes includes raw materials, agricultural products, and manufactures. Price data are collected primarily by mail questionnaire, in all but a few cases directly from the exporter or importer.

To the extent possible, the data refer to prices at the U.S. border for exports and at either the foreign border or the U.S. border for imports. For nearly all products, the prices refer to transactions completed during the first week of the month and represent the actual price for which the product was bought or sold, including discounts, allowances, and rebates.

The indexes are weighted indexes of the Laspeyres type. The values assigned to each weight category are based on trade value figures compiled by the Bureau of the Census. The weights currently used refer to 1990. Adjustments are made to account for changes in product characteristics in order to obtain a "pure" measure of price change.

For the export price indexes, the preferred pricing basis is f.a.s. (free alongside ship) U.S. port of exportation. Where necessary, adjustments are made to reported prices to place them on this basis. An attempt is made to collect two prices for imports: f.o.b. (free on board) at the port of exportation and c.i.f. (cost, insurance, and freight) at the U.S. port of importation.

Data availability

Indexes are published monthly in a press release and a more detailed report. Selected data subsequently are published in the *Monthly Labor Review*. Indexes are published for detailed product categories, as well as for all commodities. Aggregate import indexes by country or region of origin also are available, as are indexes for selected categories of internationally traded services. Additional information is available from the Division of International Prices, Bureau of Labor Statistics. Complete historical data are available on the BLS internet site (http://stats.bls.gov).

References

"BLS to Produce Monthly Indexes of Export and Import Prices," *Monthly Labor Review* (December 1988) and

Chapter 15 "International Price Indexes," *BLS Handbook of Methods* Bulletin 2490 (April 1997).

TABLES 12-1 THROUGH 12-4
INTERNATIONAL COMPARISONS: PRODUCTION, PRICES, LABOR FORCE, UNEMPLOYMENT RATES, AND STOCK INDEXES

SOURCES: INDUSTRIAL PRODUCTION-BOARD OF GOVERNORS OF THE FEDERAL RESERVE SYSTEM AND DEPARTMENT OF COMMERCE, INTERNATIONAL TRADE ADMINISTRATION, OFFICE OF TRADE AND ECONOMIC ANALYSIS. CONSUMER PRICE INDEXES-DEPARTMENT OF LABOR, BUREAU OF LABOR STATISTICS AND DEPARTMENT OF COMMERCE, INTERNATIONAL TRADE ADMINISTRATION, OFFICE OF TRADE AND ECONOMIC ANALYSIS. UNEMPLOYMENT RATE AND LABOR FORCE-DEPARTMENT OF LABOR, BUREAU OF LABOR STATISTICS. STOCK PRICE INDEXES-COMMODITY SYSTEMS, INC.

Industrial production. The index base is 1992=100. The German data before 1991 apply to West Germany only. The indexes for countries other than the United States are from the Office of Trade and Economic Analysis. Data for the United States are from the Federal Reserve (see the notes for Tables 4-1 through 4-4).

Consumer price indexes. The index base is 1982-1984=100. The data for Germany prior to 1991 are for West Germany only. Data for countries other than the United States are provided by the Office of Trade and Economic Analysis. Data for the United States are from the Bureau of Labor Statistics (see the notes for Table 6-1).

Unemployment rates and labor forces. These data are from the U.S. Bureau of Labor Statistics (BLS), and have been adjusted by BLS to approximate U.S. concepts and definitions. (See notes for Tables 8-1 through 8-4.) The quarterly unemployment rates for France, Germany, and the United Kingdom before 1992 should be taken as less precise approximations of the U.S. concept of unemployment than the annual data. The German data are for West Germany only and do not cover former East Germany.

No adjustment is made to unemployment rates from Canada. Slight adjustments are made to those from Japan. Substantial adjustments were made to the Italian data prior to a 1992 definitional change. For France, Germany, and the United Kingdom before 1992, unemployment adjustment factors were based on annual household labor force surveys.

The concept of "layoff" differs from country to country. In the United States and Canada, persons who are laid off are classified as unemployed. The employees do not remain on the payroll, receive no payments from their firms, and are frequently not rehired. However, in Europe and Japan, these people are classified as employed. In general, employers reduce hours or days worked, rather than letting people go for weeks without work. The workers continue to receive pay, which is supplemented by a subsidy for time not worked. Because of these differences, the strict U.S. definition of unemployment is not applied on this point.

The adjusted statistics use the age at which compulsory schooling ends in each country instead of the U.S. standard of 16 years and older. This is 16 years in France and in the United Kingdom since 1973; 15 years in Canada, Japan, Germany, Italy since 1993, and the United Kingdom before 1973; and 14 years in Italy before 1993. Data pertain to the noninstitutional population except in Japan and Germany, where the institutionalized population of working age is included.

There are several breaks in the series due to changes in methods or definitions. Among the more important of these are ones for the United States (1994), France (1992), Germany (1983), and Italy (1986, 1991, and 1993).

These data and more in-depth information on measurement procedures and standards are available from the Bureau of Labor Statistics internet site (http://stats.bls.gov).

Stock price indexes. Daily closing averages (except for the S&P 500) are provided by Commodity Systems, Inc. (CSI) and averaged by months and years by the editors. The daily data are available for a fee from CSI in a variety of forms, including electronically. CSI can be contacted at http://www.csidata.com, or by telephone at (800) 274-4727. These data cannot be reproduced without permission from the source. The Standard and Poor's composite is an index of 500 stocks based on 1941–1943=10 compiled by Standard and Poor's Corporation.

TABLE 12-5
EXCHANGE RATES

SOURCE: BOARD OF GOVERNORS OF THE FEDERAL RESERVE SYSTEM.

Definitions and notes on the data

This table shows measures of the U.S. dollar relative to foreign currencies-both to the currencies of some important individual countries and to average values for major groups of countries. All measures are defined as the foreign currency price of the U.S. dollar, so that where the value is relatively high, the dollar is relatively "strong"— but less competitive—and the other currencies in question are relatively "weak" and more competitive.

For consistency, this is done even in the case of currencies that are commonly quoted in the financial press, and elsewhere, in dollars per foreign currency unit instead of foreign currency units per dollar. Notably, this is the case for the new euro and for the British pound. Where *Business Statistics* shows the 1999 value of the dollar as .9387 euros, the more usual statement would be that during 1999 the euro on average was worth $1.0653 (one divided by .9387). Where *Business Statistics* shows the 1999 value of the dollar as 0.6184 British pounds, the more usual statement would be that the pound averaged $1.6172. The Canadian dollar is also sometimes quoted relative to the U.S. dollar, rather than as shown here.

Foreign exchange rates shown are averages of the daily noon buying rates in New York City for cable transfers payable in foreign currencies; annual figures are averages of monthly data.

The introduction in January 1999 of the euro as the common currency for 11 European countries—Austria, Belgium, Finland, France, Germany, Ireland, Italy, Luxembourg, Netherlands, Portugal, and Spain—marked a major change in the international currency system. The values of the currencies of those countries will no longer fluctuate relative to each other, but the value of the euro will still fluctuate relative to countries outside the European Monetary Union. During the current transition period, the currencies of the EMU member countries such as the German mark continue to circulate, and their values relative to the dollar continue to fluctuate-but due only to euro/dollar fluctuations.

To provide continuous series after 1998 for Germany and France, *Business Statistics* converts the euro to its equivalent for those countries, using the following fixed values for 1 euro: 1.95583 German marks and 6.55957 French francs.

There is no fully satisfactory historical equivalent to the euro. For comparisons over time, the Federal Reserve Board uses a "restated German mark," derived simply by dividing each historical value of the mark by the euro conversion factor, 1.95583. Essentially the same trends could be derived from using the values for the mark shown in this table.

Trade-weighted indexes of the value of the dollar against groups of foreign currencies also appear in this table. In each case, weighted averages of the individual currency values of the dollar are set at 100 in a base period. The weights are based on goods trade only, excluding trade in services. Base periods differ for different indexes.

The first four columns show the more familiar type of foreign exchange indexes, which use nominal values of each currency. The last two columns are price-adjusted (i.e., they are indexes of "real" exchange rates), aggregating values of the dollar in terms of each currency that have been adjusted for inflation, using each country's consumer price index. Where any currency has had an episode of hyperinflation with the consequent huge depreciation in terms of the dollar, the nominal index will not reflect the actual competitiveness of the dollar in terms of that currency over the longer term. Because there have been hyperinflations in some of the countries making up the Broad Index and its Other Important Trading Partners component (see below), price-adjusted indexes are also shown for those two groupings in the final two columns.

G-10 Index (March 1973=100): This measure is an index of the exchange value of the U.S. dollar in terms of the weighted average currencies of the G-10 (other industrialized) countries, which are Belgium, Canada, France, Germany, Italy, Japan, the Netherlands, Sweden, Switzerland, and the United Kingdom. Unlike the three indexes that follow, the weights in this index, which represented "multilateral" (world market) trade shares, were fixed. The Federal Reserve ceased to calculate this index as of December 1998.

The three newer indexes use weights that focus more directly on U.S. competitiveness and that change as trade flows shift. Each country's weight is based on an average of the country's share of U.S. imports, the country's share of U.S. exports, and the country's share of exports that go to other countries that are large importers of U.S. goods. *The Broad Index* (January 1997=100): The new overall index includes currencies of all countries that have a share of U.S. nonoil goods imports or nonagricultural goods exports of at least 0.5 percent. The list of currencies and the weights are updated each year. These countries are then classified as either Major Currencies or Other Important Trading Partners as outlined below.

Major Currency Index (March 1973=100): This index serves purposes similar to those of the discontinued G-10 index, and its level and movements are similar. It is a measure of the competitiveness of U.S. goods in the major industrial countries and a gauge of financial pres-

sure on the dollar. The index includes countries whose currencies are traded in deep and relatively liquid financial markets and circulate widely outside the country of issue, and for which information on short and long-term interest rates is readily available. As of November 1999, this index includes the currencies of the following countries: Canada, the euro countries, Japan, United Kingdom, Switzerland, Australia, and Sweden.

Other Important Trading Partners (OITP) Index (January 1997=100): This index captures the competitiveness of U.S. goods in key emerging markets in Latin America, Asia, the Middle East, and Eastern Europe, whose currencies do not circulate widely outside the country of issue. Hyperinflations and large depreciations for some of these countries have led to a persistent upward trend in the nominal version of this index. Hence, the nominal OITP index is mainly useful for analysis of short-term developments, and the price-adjusted index is shown to give a more appropriate measure of longer-term competitiveness. The countries that make up this index include, as of November 1999, Mexico, China, Taiwan, South Korea, Singapore, Hong Kong, Malaysia, Brazil, Thailand, Indonesia, Philippines, Russia, India, Saudi Arabia, Israel, Argentina, Venezuela, Chile, and Colombia.

References and data availability

More information on the dollar value indexes can be found in the article "New Summary Measures of the Foreign Exchange Value of the Dollar," *Federal Reserve Bulletin,* vol. 84 (October 1998). This is available on the Federal Reserve web site, http://www.federalreserve.gov, as are the exchange rate indexes and the H.10 and G.5 releases containing daily, weekly, and monthly data for bilateral exchange rates.

Additional information can be found on the Federal Reserve Bank of St. Louis web site, http://www.stls.frb.org/fred/data/exchange.html.

TABLES 13-1 THROUGH 13-3
MINING INDUSTRIES

Sources: Industrial production and capacity utilization: Board of Governors of the Federal Reserve System (see notes to Tables 4-1 through 4-4); producer prices and employment, hours, and earnings: U.S. Department of Labor, Bureau of Labor Statistics (see notes to Table 6-2 and Tables 8-5 through 8-9).

Mining (SIC Division B) includes all establishments primarily engaged in the extraction of naturally occurring solids (such as coals and ores), liquids (such as crude petroleum), and gases (such as natural gas). Quarrying, well operations, and other preparation customarily done at the mine site are included, as are exploration and development of mineral properties.

Oil and gas extraction (SIC Major Group 13) is classified in mining and includes producing crude petroleum and natural gas; extracting oil from oil sands and shale; producing natural gas and cycle condensate; and producing gas and hydrocarbon liquids from coal at the mine site. Petroleum refining is classified in Manufacturing, Major Group 29. Pipeline transportation of oil and gas is classified in Division E, Transportation.

Notes on the data

Industrial production and capacity utilization. These indexes are for industry groups as defined by the SIC code. The indexes for *total mining* cover SIC Division B as described above; *metal mining* covers Major Group 10, which includes mining for iron, copper, lead, zinc, gold, silver, and ferroalloy ores; *coal mining* covers SIC Major Group 12, which includes mining for bituminous coal and lignite and anthracite coal; *oil and gas extraction* covers Major Group 13, which includes extraction of crude oil and natural gas, production of natural gas liquids, and oil field services; *crude oil and natural gas* covers SIC 131, oil and gas extraction; *natural gas liquids* is SIC 132; and *oil and gas well drilling* is SIC 138, which also includes other oil and gas field services. *Stone and earth minerals* is Major Group 14, which includes mining and quarrying of stone, sand and gravel, clay, and chemical and fertilizer minerals.

The *producer price indexes and employment, hours, and earnings* data for metal mining and coal mining cover SICs 10 and 12, respectively; *oil and gas extraction* covers SIC 13; the indexes for crude materials use the stage-of-processing classification. The data for *nonmetallic minerals except fuel* cover SIC 14.

TABLE 13-4
PETROLEUM AND PETROLEUM PRODUCTS-IMPORTS AND STOCKS

SOURCES: IMPORTS: U.S. DEPARTMENT OF COMMERCE, BUREAU OF THE CENSUS (SEE NOTES TO TABLES 11-3 THROUGH 11-8); STOCKS: U.S. DEPARTMENT OF ENERGY, ENERGY INFORMATION ADMINISTRATION.

Notes on the data

The import data are published as Exhibit 17: "Imports of Energy-related Petroleum Products, including Crude Petroleum" of the monthly Census-BEA foreign trade press release. *Total energy-related petroleum products* includes the following Standard International Trade Classification (SITC) commodity groupings: crude oil, petroleum preparations, and liquefied propane and butane gas.

The data on petroleum stocks are derived from the Department of Energy's weekly petroleum supply reporting system and are published in the Energy Information Administration publication "Petroleum Supply Monthly." Stock totals are as of the end of the period. Geographic coverage includes the 50 states and the District of Columbia.

Data availability

Data on stocks are available from the Energy Information Administration internet site (http://www.eia.doe.gov). See the notes to Tables 11-3 through 11-8 for availability of import data.

TABLES 14-1 AND 14-2
CONSTRUCTION COSTS, PRICES, EMPLOYMENT, HOURS, AND EARNINGS

SOURCES: CONSTRUCTION COST INDEXES: U.S. DEPARTMENT OF COMMERCE, BUREAU OF THE CENSUS; PRODUCER PRICES, EMPLOYMENT, HOURS, AND EARNINGS: U.S. DEPARTMENT OF LABOR, BUREAU OF LABOR STATISTICS (SEE NOTES TO TABLES 6-2 AND 8-5 THROUGH 8-9).

Construction (SIC Division C) includes establishments primarily engaged in construction, including new work, additions, alterations, reconstruction, installations, and repairs. Construction of buildings and heavy construction other than buildings are included. Specialized construction activities, such as plumbing, painting, and electrical work, also are included.

General building contractors is SIC Major Group 15 and includes both residential and nonresidential building; heavy construction except building is Major Group 16 and includes highways, pipelines, power lines, water mains, and other heavy construction; special trade contractors is Major Group 17 and includes plumbing, painting, carpentry, and other specialized building trades.

The *Construction Cost Indexes* are included in the Bureau of the Census "Construction Put in Place" release (C-30 release). See the notes to Table 14-3 for additional information on availability.

TABLE 14-3
CONSTRUCTION PUT IN PLACE

SOURCE: U.S. DEPARTMENT OF COMMERCE, BUREAU OF THE CENSUS.

The Census Bureau's estimates of the value of new construction put in place are intended to provide monthly estimates of the total dollar value of construction work done in the United States.

Definitions and notes on the data

The estimates cover all construction work done each month on new residential and nonresidential buildings and structures, public construction, and improvements to existing buildings and structures. Included are the cost of labor and materials; cost of architectural and engineering work; overhead costs assigned to the project; interest and taxes paid during construction; and contractor's profits.

The total value put-in-place for a given period is the sum of the value of work done on all projects underway during this period, regardless of when work on each individual project was started or when payment was made to the contractors. For some categories, estimates are derived by distributing the total construction cost of the project by means of historic construction progress patterns.

The statistics on the value of construction put in place result from direct measurement and indirect estimation. A series results from direct measurement when it is based on reports of the actual value of construction progress or construction expenditures obtained from a complete census or a sample survey. All other series are developed by indirect estimation using related construction statistics. On an annual basis, the estimates for series directly measured monthly, quarterly, or annually accounted for about 71 percent of total construction in 1998 (private multifamily residential, private residential improvements, private nonresidential buildings, farm nonresidential construction, public utility construction, all other private construction, and virtually all of public construction). On a monthly basis, directly measured data are available for about 55 percent of the value-in-place estimates.

The data shown are divided into three categories: not seasonally adjusted, seasonally adjusted at annual rate, and constant 1996 dollars, seasonally adjusted at annual rate. The seasonally adjusted at annual rate data are obtained by removing normal seasonal movement from the unadjusted data to bring out underlying trends and

business cycles. Seasonal adjustment accounts for month-to-month variations resulting from normal or average changes in any phenomena affecting the data such as weather conditions, the differing lengths of months, and the varying number of weekdays and weekends within each month. It neither adjusts for abnormal conditions within each month nor for year-to-year variations in weather. The seasonally adjusted annual rate is the seasonally adjusted monthly rate multiplied by 12.

The constant 1996 dollar series are converted from monthly estimates in current dollars using cost indexes derived for each category of construction. The deflators for the various categories are related indexes or combinations of related indexes from private companies and federal agencies. The selection of the indexes and procedures used for developing the deflators for each category resulted primarily from recommendations made jointly by the Bureau of Economic Analysis and the Census Bureau.

New housing units includes new houses, apartments, condominiums, and town houses. The classification excludes residential units in buildings that are primarily nonresidential. It also excludes mobile homes and houseboats. *Improvements* (included in total residential but not shown separately) includes remodeling, additions, and major replacements to properties subsequent to completion of original building. It includes construction of additional housing units in existing residential structures; finishing of basements and attics; and modernization of kitchens, bathrooms, etc. Also included are improvements outside of residential structures, such as the addition of swimming pools and garages, and replacement of major equipment items such as water heaters, furnaces, and central air-conditioners. Maintenance and repair work is not included.

Nonresidential buildings includes industrial, office, hotels and motels, and other commercial buildings. It also includes categories not shown separately in this book, including religious, educational, cultural, and health care facilities.

Industrial includes all buildings and structures at manufacturing sites. *Office* includes office and professional buildings used primarily for office space. *Hotels, motels* includes hotels, motels, resort lodging, tourist courts and cabins, and similar facilities. *Other commercial* includes buildings and structures intended for use by wholesale, retail, or service trade establishments. For example, shopping centers or malls, department stores, low-rise banks and financial institutions, drug stores, parking garages, auto service stations and repair garages, beauty schools, grocery stores, restaurants, and dry cleaning stores are included in this category. Also included are warehouses and storage buildings, cold storage plants, grain elevators and silos, except such facilities at industrial sites.

Public utilities construction expenditures are classified in terms of the industry rather than the function of the building or structure. Construction expenditures made by the following types of privately owned public utility companies or cooperatives are included in this category: Railroad, telephone, telegraph, television cable, petroleum pipelines, electric light and power, and gas manufacturing, transmission, and distribution.

Also included in total private construction are farm construction and privately-built streets and bridges, dams and reservoirs, sewer and water facilities, golf courses, parks and playgrounds, and airfields.

Public construction includes both state and local construction and federal construction. State and local construction includes housing and redevelopment, educational facilities, hospitals, general administrative buildings, police and fire buildings, industrial buildings, parking and transportation facilities, highways, streets, and buildings, sewer systems, water systems, erosion control and other resource protective construction, and miscellaneous nonbuilding construction.

Housing and redevelopment includes houses, apartment buildings, and all other residential structures. *Highways and streets* includes highways, streets, bridges, overpasses, tunnels, toll facilities, street lighting, and miscellaneous road erosion control.

Federal construction in general is classified based on the agency responsible for the work; for example, Veterans Administration expenditures are classified as "hospital," and Bureau of Reclamation expenditures are classified as "conservation and development." However, the expenditures reported by a few agencies are subdivided into two or more types of construction.

Housing includes new family housing units and the rehabilitation of existing units constructed for the armed services. Military barracks, bachelor officers' quarters, and family housing for Coast Guard personnel are classified under "military facilities." Housing for forest rangers and national park employees is classified under "conservation and development."

Industrial includes construction done at Department of Energy research and development facilities. It also includes manufacturing, assembling, and processing buildings and their related facilities, such as arsenals, ordnance works, and shipyards.

Military facilities, with the specific exceptions noted below, covers construction owned by the Department of Defense and the Coast Guard. This category includes troop housing, administration and training buildings, warehouses, mess halls, recreation centers, educational facilities, airfields and airport buildings, missile sites, etc. The following specific types of construction owned by the Department of Defense are classified in other categories: Family housing for the armed services, civil works, industrial facilities, military hospitals, and soldiers' homes.

Highways and streets includes streets, bridges, vehicular tunnels, viaducts, and forest and park roads owned by federal agencies other than the Department of Defense. Also included are the following built in connection with a federal road: culverts, drainage, erosion control, lighting, guard rails, and earthwork protective structures.

The monthly and annual estimates of construction put in place are derived by combining data from sample surveys, direct reporting by federal agencies, and indirect estimates for categories not available directly. Among the sample surveys from which data are derived are the Census Bureau's Construction Progress Reporting Survey, Housing Starts Survey, and Housing Sales Survey, and the Bureau of Labor Statistics' Consumer Expenditure Survey.

Revisions

Revised data for recent years normally are published each May. The revisions incorporate data not previously available. Seasonally-adjusted statistics are also revised using newly computed seasonal factors. Extensive revisions of the data, including converting the constant-dollar data from 1992 to 1996 dollars, were published in May 2000. Information on the revisions is found in the May 2000 issue of the Bureau of the Census monthly publication "Current Construction Reports-Value of Construction Put in Place" (the C-30 Report). The full report also contains general information on the series and references to other sources, and is available on the Bureau of the Census internet site.

Data availability

The construction put in place data are first issued in a monthly press release. A full report (the C-30 report) follows. Data are shown by type of construction, seasonally-adjusted and unadjusted, and in current and constant dollars. Statistics are available monthly at the U.S. level, and, for selected categories, are available annually by the nine geographic divisions. The Census Bureau has derived monthly estimates of new construction put in place since 1960.

Press releases on expenditures for residential improvements and repairs are issued quarterly. An annual supplement shows data by specific kind of job (e.g., painting) and by region.

Current data and historical data are available on the Bureau of the Census internet site (http://www.census.gov).

TABLE 14-4
HOUSING STARTS AND BUILDING PERMITS; HOME SALES AND PRICES

SOURCES: U.S. DEPARTMENT OF COMMERCE, BUREAU OF THE CENSUS AND NATIONAL ASSOCIATION OF REALTORS.

These data are mainly from two Bureau of the Census Surveys. The *Building Permits Survey* provides current data on new residential construction authorized by building permits. The *Survey of Construction* covers housing starts and completions. A *Housing Sales Survey* is a subset of the Survey of Construction and covers new homes sold and for sale. Data on sales of existing homes are from the Existing Homes Survey of the National Association of Realtors.

Definitions and notes on the data

The *Survey of Construction* provides current data on starts and completions of new single- and multi-family housing units and sales of new one-family houses. It covers new residential buildings currently authorized by a building permit or started in areas not requiring a building permit. The data collected include start date, completion date, sale date, sales price (for single-family houses only), and physical characteristics of each housing unit, such as square footage and number of bedrooms. Data are collected through telephone or personal interviews.

A *housing unit* is a house, an apartment, a group of rooms or a single room intended for occupancy as separate living quarters, i.e., the occupants live separately from any other individuals in the building and the unit has a direct access from the outside of the building or through a common hall. As of January 2000, a previous requirement that the residents must have the capability to eat separately has been eliminated. Based on the old definition some senior housing projects were excluded

from the multifamily housing statistics because they did not have their own eating facilities. Housing starts exclude group quarters such as dormitories or rooming houses, transient accommodations such as motels, and manufactured homes. Publicly owned housing units are excluded, but units in structures built by private developers with subsidies or for sale to local public housing authorities are both classified as private housing.

The *start* of construction of a privately owned housing unit is when excavation begins for the footings or foundation of a building intended primarily as a housekeeping residential structure and designed for nontransient occupancy. All housing units in a multifamily building are defined as being started when excavation for the building has begun.

One-family structures include fully detached, semidetached, rowhouses, and townhouses. The type of ownership is not the criterion—a condominium apartment building is classified as a multifamily structure.

The *Building Permits Survey* covers all places that issue permits to authorize new private residential buildings or changes in or demolition of existing structures. Data are collected through a mail-out/mail-back monthly survey of selected permit-issuing places and an annual mail-out/mail-back census of the permit-issuing places that do not report monthly.

Data on housing units authorized by local building permits relate to the time of issuance rather than to the actual start of construction. They do, however, provide some indication of residential building activity in advance of the start of actual construction. Although construction is started on most residential buildings in the same month in which the permit is issued, several months sometimes may pass before start of construction.

The 19,000 areas with local building permit systems for which figures are currently published account for a major portion of residential building in the United States. For the country as a whole, approximately 96 percent of private housing units are now constructed in permit-issuing places. Beginning with 1994, data are based upon 19,000 places. Data for 1984 through 1993 are for 17,000 places; data for 1978 through 1983 are for 16,000 places; data for 1972 through 1977 are for 14,000 places; data for 1971 are for 13,000 places.

The statistics on shipments of manufactured homes are produced by the National Conference of States on Building Codes and Standards and published by the Manufactured Housing Institute.

A *manufactured* home is a movable dwelling, 8 feet or more wide and 40 feet or more long, designed to be towed on its own chassis, with transportation gear integral to the unit when it leaves the factory, and without need of a permanent foundation. Multiwides and expandable manufactured homes are included. Excluded are travel trailers, motor homes, and modular housing. The shipments figures are based on reports submitted by manufacturers on the number of homes actually shipped during the survey month. Shipments to dealers may not necessarily be placed for residential use in the same month as they are shipped. The number of manufactured "homes" used for nonresidential purposes (e.g., offices) is not known.

The *Housing Sales Survey* (a subset of the Survey of Construction) is conducted by the Bureau of the Census under contract with the U.S. Department of Housing and Urban Development. Statistics are estimates derived from a survey of new one-family houses sold or for sale for which building permits have been issued in permit-issuing places, or which have been started in nonpermit areas. Contractor- and owner-built houses are excluded. The information is obtained by monthly interviews with the builders or owners of the new houses in the sample. These monthly interviews continue until the house is sold or withdrawn from the sales market.

The *sales price* used in this survey is the price agreed upon between the purchaser and the seller at the time the first sales contract is signed or deposit made. It includes the price of the improved lot. The *median sales price* is the sales price of the house that falls on the middle point of the total number of houses sold. Half of the houses sold have a sales price less than the median; half have a greater price. Changes in the median sales price reflect the changing proportion of houses of different size, locations, etc., as well as any changes in the sales price of houses of identical characteristics.

Data on *sales of existing single-family* homes pertain to homes occupied prior to sale and represent closed or pending sales contracts. These data are from the National Association of Realtors.

Data availability

Housing start and building permit data have been collected by the Bureau of the Census monthly since 1959.

Housing Starts and Building Permits press releases contain the first available start and permit data and are released three weeks after the reference month. New One Family Homes Sold (C25) reports are released six

weeks after the reference month and provide data on houses sold and for sale, average and median sale prices, and sale prices by type of financing. Both releases contain national and regional data.

Housing Starts (C20) reports are available four weeks after the reference period and Housing Units Authorized by Building Permits reports six weeks after. These contain more detailed data than the earlier press releases.

These reports and the associated historical data are available on the Bureau of the Census internet site (http://www.census.gov), as are the data on manufactured homes.

Existing-homes sales data are published monthly in *Real Estate Outlook: Market Trends and Insights,* available by subscription from the National Association of Realtors, and also available on the National Association of Realtors internet site (http://nar.realtor.com).

References

Definitions and methodological descriptions for the Census Bureau surveys are provided in the January 2000 issues of the Bureau's Housing Starts (C20) and New One Family Homes Sold (C25) monthly publications; these and a description of the Manufactured Homes Survey are available on the Census internet site.

TABLES 15-1 THROUGH 15-3
TOTAL MANUFACTURING: PRODUCTION, CAPACITY, PRICES, EMPLOYMENT, HOURS, AND EARNINGS

SOURCES: INDUSTRIAL PRODUCTION AND CAPACITY UTILIZATION: BOARD OF GOVERNORS OF THE FEDERAL RESERVE SYSTEM (SEE NOTES TO TABLES 4-1 THROUGH 4-4); PRODUCER PRICES AND EMPLOYMENT, HOURS, AND EARNINGS: U.S. DEPARTMENT OF LABOR, BUREAU OF LABOR STATISTICS (SEE NOTES TO TABLE 6-2 AND TABLES 8-5 THROUGH 8-9).

Manufacturing (SIC Division D) includes establishments engaged in the mechanical or chemical transformation of materials or substances into new products. These establishments typically are described as plants, factories, or mills. The Division is subdivided into 20 Major Groups, each of which is described briefly at the beginning of the notes for the pages on which data for the group are presented.

There are numerous borderline cases between manufacturing and other divisions of the SIC. Logging, for example, is included in manufacturing, while threshing and cotton ginning fall under Agriculture, Forestry, and Fishing. Dressing of ores and crushing and grinding of sand and gravel are classified under Mining. Production of computer software is classified under Services.

Notes on the data

Many data series divide manufacturing into durable and nondurable goods. *Durable goods* include SIC Major Groups 24, 25, and 32 through 39 (lumber and wood products; furniture and fixtures; stone, clay, and glass; primary metals industries; fabricated metal products; industrial and commercial machinery and computer equipment; electronic and other electrical equipment; transportation equipment; instruments; and miscellaneous manufactures). *Nondurable goods* include Major Groups 20 through 23 and 26 through 31 (food and kindred products; tobacco products; textile mill products; apparel and related products; paper and allied products; printing and publishing; chemicals; petroleum refining; rubber and miscellaneous plastic products; and leather and leather products).

TABLES 15-4 THROUGH 15-7
MANUFACTURERS' SHIPMENTS, INVENTORIES, AND ORDERS

SOURCE: U.S. DEPARTMENT OF COMMERCE, BUREAU OF THE CENSUS.

These data are from the Bureau of the Census monthly M3 survey, a sample-based survey intended to provide measures of changes in domestic manufacturing activity and indications of future production commitments. The sample includes all larger establishments and a selection of smaller ones. Currently, reported monthly data represent approximately 55 percent of shipments at the total manufacturing level; coverage rates for the major industries vary from about 20 to 99 percent.

Definitions and notes on the data

Shipments. The value of shipments data represent net selling values, f.o.b. (free on board) plant, after discounts and allowances and excluding freight charges and excise taxes. For multi-establishment companies, the M3 reports typically are company- or division-level reports that encompass groups of plants or products. The data reported are usually net sales and receipts from customers and do not include the value of interplant transfers. The reported sales are used to calculate month-to-month changes that bring forward the estimates for the entire industry (i.e., estimates of the statistical "universe") that have been developed from the Annual Survey of Manufactures (ASM). The value of products made else-

where under contract from materials owned by the plant is also included in shipments, as well as receipts for contract work performed for others, resales, miscellaneous activities such as the sale of scrap and refuse, installation and repair work performed by employees of the plant, and the receipts for research and development performed at the plant.

Inventories. Inventories in the M3 survey are collected on a current cost or pre-LIFO basis. Because different inventory valuation methods are reflected in the reported data, the estimates differ slightly from replacement cost estimates. Companies using the LIFO (last in, first out) method for valuing inventories report their pre-LIFO value; that is, the adjustment to their base-period prices is excluded. In the ASM, inventories are collected according to this same definition. However, there are discontinuities in the historical data in both surveys. Inventory data prior to 1982 are not comparable to later years because of changes in valuation methods. Until 1982, respondents were asked in the ASM to report their inventories at book values; that is, according to whatever method they used for tax purposes (LIFO, FIFO [first in, first out], and so forth.) Because of this, the value of aggregate inventories for an industry was not precise. The change in instructions for reporting current cost inventories was carried to the monthly survey beginning in January 1987. The data for 1982 to 1987 were redefined (but not re-collected by survey) on a pre-LIFO or current cost basis.

Inventory data are requested from respondents by three stages of fabrication: finished goods, work in process, and raw materials and supplies. There are several limitations to the quality of these data for two reasons. First, response to the stage of fabrication inquiries is lower than for total inventories because not all companies keep their data monthly at this level of detail. Second, a product considered to be a finished good in one industry, such as steel mill shapes, may be reported as a raw material in another industry, such as stamping plants. (For some purposes this is an advantage rather than a problem. When a factory accumulates inventory which it considers to be raw materials, it can be expected that that accumulation is intentional. But when a factory—whether a materials-making or a final-product producer—has a buildup of finished goods inventories, it may indicate involuntary accumulation as a result of sales falling short of expectations. Hence, the two types of accumulation can have different economic interpretations.) Therefore, within the two-digit SIC major groups the same type of inventory may be included under different stage of fabrication categories. Like total inventories, stage of fabrication inventories are also benchmarked to the ASM data, but the stage of fabrication data are benchmarked at the two-digit major group level, as opposed to the level of total inventories which is benchmarked at the individual industry level.

New orders received and unfilled orders. New orders, as reported in the monthly survey, are net of order cancellations and include orders received and filled during the month as well as orders received for future delivery. They also include the value of contract changes that increase or decrease the value of the unfilled orders to which they relate. Orders are defined to include those supported by binding legal documents such as signed contracts, letters of award, or letters of intent, although in some industries this definition may not be strictly applicable. Unfilled orders include orders (as defined above) that have not been reflected as shipments. Generally, unfilled orders at the end of the reporting period are equal to unfilled orders at the beginning of the period plus net new orders received less net shipments.

Coverage. The M3 survey covers companies that have employees and are classified in SIC Division D, Manufacturing. The monthly estimates are based on information obtained from most manufacturing companies with $500 million or more in annual shipments, as well as from selected smaller companies.

Benchmarking and revisions

Data beginning with 1987 were revised in August 1998. The revisions reflected benchmarking to the 1995–1996 ASM, revision of seasonal factors, and other adjustments.

Data availability

Data have been collected monthly since 1958.

An Advance Report on Durable Goods Manufacturers' Shipments and Orders is available as a press release about 17 working days after the end of each month. Content includes seasonally and not seasonally adjusted estimates of shipments, new orders, and unfilled orders for durable goods industries.

The Manufacturers' Shipments, Inventories, and Orders reports are released about 22 working days after the end of each month. Content includes revisions to the advance report plus estimates for inventories and non-durable goods industries, tabulations by market category, and ratios of shipments to inventories and to unfilled orders. Revisions include selected data for the two previous months.

Computer diskettes, including data back to 1958, can be purchased from Manufacturing & Construction Division, Manufacturers' Shipments, Inventories, and Orders Branch, Bureau of the Census, Washington, D.C. 20233,(301)457-4804. The data also are available on the Census Bureau internet site (http://www.census.gov).

References

Bureau of the Census publication M3-1(97), "Manufacturers' Shipments, Inventories, and Orders 1987–1997" contains the 1998 revisions. Report M3-1(95), (July 1996) contains revised data beginning with 1982. These reports can be purchased from Census Bureau's customer services on (301) 457-4100.

TABLES 16-1 AND 16-2
DURABLE GOODS
LUMBER AND WOOD PRODUCTS

SOURCES: INDUSTRIAL PRODUCTION AND CAPACITY UTILIZATION: BOARD OF GOVERNORS OF THE FEDERAL RESERVE SYSTEM (SEE NOTES TO TABLES 4-1 THROUGH 4-4); PRODUCER PRICES AND EMPLOYMENT, HOURS, AND EARNINGS: U.S. DEPARTMENT OF LABOR, BUREAU OF LABOR STATISTICS (SEE NOTES TO TABLES 6-2 AND 8-5 THROUGH 8-9).

Lumber and wood products (SIC Major Group 24) includes timber and pulpwood cutting; sawmills and other mills engaged in producing basic wooden materials; and manufacture of finished articles made entirely or mostly of wood. However, furniture, office fixtures, musical instruments, toys, and some other wooden articles are classified elsewhere (SIC 25 and 39).

Industrial production: Logging (SIC 241) covers timber cutting and production of rough products in the field, including wood chips; *lumber* (SIC 242) covers sawmills and planing mills; *lumber products* includes millwork, veneer, plywood, and structural wood members (SIC 243), wood containers (SIC 244), wood buildings and mobile homes (SIC 245), and miscellaneous wood products (SIC 249); *plywood* includes hardwood and softwood veneer and plywood (SIC 2435, 2436); *manufactured homes* (SIC 245) includes manufactured homes (as distinct from motor homes, which are in SIC 371) and prefabricated wood buildings and components. (See Table 14-4 and its Notes for information on manufactured homes.)

TABLE 16-3
FURNITURE AND FIXTURES

Sources: Industrial production and capacity utilization: Board of Governors of the Federal Reserve System (see notes to Tables 4-1 through 4-4); producer prices and employment, hours, and earnings: U.S. Department of Labor, Bureau of Labor Statistics (see notes to Tables 6-2 and 8-5 through 8-9).

Furniture and fixtures (SIC Major Group 25) includes manufacture of household, office, public building, and restaurant furniture and of office and store fixtures.

Industrial production: Household furniture (SIC 251) includes household furniture, including upholstered, made of wood, metal, or other materials.

TABLES 16-4 AND 16-5
STONE, CLAY, AND GLASS

Sources: Industrial production and capacity utilization: Board of Governors of the Federal Reserve System (see notes to Tables 4-1 through 4-4); manufacturers' shipments and inventories: U.S. Department of Commerce, Bureau of the Census (see notes to Tables 15-4 through 15-7); producer prices and employment, hours, and earnings: U.S. Department of Labor, Bureau of Labor Statistics (see notes to Tables 6-2 and 8-5 through 8-9).

Stone, clay, glass, and concrete products (SIC Major Group 32) includes manufacture of flat glass and other glass products, cement, structural clay products, pottery, concrete and gypsum products, cut stone, abrasive and asbestos products, and other products from materials taken from the earth principally in the form of stone, clay, and sand. When separate reports are available, mining and quarrying are classified in Division B, Mining.

Industrial production: Pressed and blown glass (SIC 322) includes manufacture of pressed, blown, or shaped glass and glassware from glass produced in the same establishment; *glass containers* (SIC 3221) covers manufacture of glass containers for commercial packing and bottling and for home canning; *cement* (SIC 324) covers hydraulic cement, including portland, natural, masonry, and pozzolana cements; *structural clay products* (SIC 325) covers brick and structural clay tile; *concrete and miscellaneous* covers pottery and related products (SIC 326), concrete, gypsum, and plaster products (SIC 327), cut stone and stone products (SIC 328), and abrasive, asbestos, and miscellaneous nonmetallic mineral products (SIC 329).

TABLES 16-6 THROUGH 16-10
PRIMARY METALS

Sources: Industrial production and capacity utilization: Board of Governors of the Federal Reserve System (see notes to Tables 4-1 through 4-4); manufacturers' shipments, inventories, and orders: U.S. Department of Commerce, Bureau of the Census (see notes to Tables 15-4 through 15-7); producer prices and employment, hours, and earnings: U.S. Department of Labor, Bureau of Labor Statistics (see notes to Tables 6-2 and 8-5 through 8-9).

Primary metal industries (SIC Major Group 33) includes smelting and refining of ferrous and nonferrous metals from ore, pig, or scrap; rolling, drawing, and alloying metals; manufacture of castings and other basic metal products; and manufacture of nails, spikes, and insulated wire and cable. The production of coke is included. Metal forgings and stampings are classified in Major Group 34, Fabricated Metal Products.

Industrial production: iron and steel includes steel works, blast furnaces, and rolling and finishing mills (SIC 331) and iron and steel foundries (SIC 332); basic steel and mill products is SIC 331.

TABLES 16-11 AND 16-12
FABRICATED METAL PRODUCTS

Sources: Industrial production and capacity utilization: Board of Governors of the Federal Reserve System (see notes to Tables 4-1 through 4-4); manufacturers' shipments, inventories, and orders: U.S. Department of Commerce, Bureau of the Census (see notes to Tables 15-4 through 15-7); producer prices and employment, hours, and earnings: U.S. Department of Labor, Bureau of Labor Statistics (see notes to Tables 6-2 and 8-5 through 8-9).

Fabricated metal products, except machinery and transportation equipment (SIC Major Group 34) includes fabricating ferrous and nonferrous metal products, such as metal cans, tinware, hand tools, cutlery, nonelectrical heating apparatus, structural metal products, metal forgings and stampings, ordnance (except vehicles and guided missiles), and a variety of metal and wire products not elsewhere classified. Some important segments of metal fabricating industries, such as machinery, transportation equipment, scientific and controlling instruments, jewelry, and silverware, are not included.

Industrial production: metal containers (SIC 341) covers metal cans and shipping containers; *hardware, tools, and cutlery* (SIC 342) covers cutlery, handtools, and general hardware; *hardware and tools* covers hand and edge tools (SIC 3423), saw blades and handsaws (SIC 3425), and hardware, not elsewhere classified (SIC 3429); *structural metal products* (SIC 344) covers fabricated structural metal products including structural metal, doors, plate work, sheet metal work, and ornamental metal work; *other fabricated metal products* includes screw machine products and bolts, nuts, screws, rivets, and washers (SIC 345), metal forgings and stampings (SIC 346), coatings, engraving, and allied services (SIC 347), ordnance and accessories, except vehicles and guided missiles (SIC 348), and miscellaneous fabricated metal products (SIC 349); *fasteners, stampings, etc.* is SIC 345, 346, and 347.

TABLES 16-13 THROUGH 16-15
INDUSTRIAL MACHINERY AND EQUIPMENT

SOURCES: INDUSTRIAL PRODUCTION AND CAPACITY UTILIZATION: BOARD OF GOVERNORS OF THE FEDERAL RESERVE SYSTEM (SEE NOTES TO TABLES 4-1 THROUGH 4-4); MANUFACTURERS' SHIPMENTS, INVENTORIES, AND ORDERS: U.S. DEPARTMENT OF COMMERCE, BUREAU OF THE CENSUS (SEE NOTES TO TABLES 15-4 THROUGH 15-7); PRODUCER PRICES AND EMPLOYMENT, HOURS, AND EARNINGS: U.S. DEPARTMENT OF LABOR, BUREAU OF LABOR STATISTICS (SEE NOTES TO TABLES 6-2 AND 8-5 THROUGH 8-9).

Industrial and commercial machinery and computer equipment (SIC Major Group 35) includes manufacture of industrial and commercial machinery and equipment and computers. Included are manufacture of engines and turbines; farm and garden machinery; construction, mining, and oil field machinery; elevators and conveying equipment; hoists and cranes; metalworking machinery; computer and peripheral equipment; office machinery; and refrigeration machinery. Motor-powered machines ordinarily are included, except for electrical household appliances. Equipment for the generation and transmission of electricity is not included. Hand tools are not included unless powered.

Industrial production: engines and turbines (SIC 351) includes steam, gas, and hydraulic turbines and turbine generator set units and internal combustion engines, not elsewhere classified (aircraft engines and automotive engines, except diesel, are classified in SIC 37); *construction and allied machinery* (SIC 353) includes construction, mining, and materials handling machinery and equipment; *metalworking machinery* (SIC 354) includes machine tools and accessories, power-driven handtools,

rolling mill machinery, and welding and soldering equipment; *special industry machinery* (SIC 355) includes textile machinery, woodworking machinery, paper industries machinery, printing machinery, food products machinery, and others; *general industrial machinery* (SIC 356) includes pumps, bearings, compressors, fans, industrial process furnaces, and others; *computer and office equipment* (SIC 357) includes electronic computers (mainframe, micro, mini, and personal), computer storage devices and peripheral equipment, and calculating machines; *service industry machines* (SIC 358) includes automatic vending machines, commercial laundry machines, air-conditioning and warm air heating equipment, commercial refrigeration equipment, and others.

TABLES 16-16 THROUGH 16-18
ELECTRONIC AND ELECTRIC EQUIPMENT

SOURCES: INDUSTRIAL PRODUCTION AND CAPACITY UTILIZATION: BOARD OF GOVERNORS OF THE FEDERAL RESERVE SYSTEM (SEE NOTES TO TABLES 4-1 THROUGH 4-4); MANUFACTURERS' SHIPMENTS, INVENTORIES, AND ORDERS: U.S. DEPARTMENT OF COMMERCE, BUREAU OF THE CENSUS (SEE NOTES TO TABLES 15-4 THROUGH 15-7); PRODUCER PRICES AND EMPLOYMENT, HOURS, AND EARNINGS: U.S. DEPARTMENT OF LABOR, BUREAU OF LABOR STATISTICS (SEE NOTES TO TABLES 6-2 AND 8-5 THROUGH 8-9).

Electronic and other electrical equipment and components, except computer equipment (SIC Major Group 36) includes manufacture of machinery, apparatus, and supplies for the generation, storage, transmission, transformation, and utilization of electrical energy. Included are electricity distribution equipment; electrical industrial apparatus; household appliances; electrical lighting and wiring equipment; radio and television receiving equipment; communications equipment; electronic components, which include transistors; and other electrical equipment and supplies. Industrial machinery and equipment powered by electric motors are not included, nor are measuring and controlling instruments.

Industrial production: electrical machinery is SIC Major Group 36; *major electrical equipment and parts* includes electric transmission and distribution equipment (SIC 361) and electrical industrial apparatus (SIC 362); *electric distribution equipment* is SIC 361; *household appliances* (SIC 363) includes cooking equipment (SIC 3631); *refrigerators and freezers* (SIC 3632); *household laundry equipment* (SIC 3633) and *miscellaneous household appliances* (SIC 3634, 3635, and 3639); *audio and video equipment* (SIC 365) includes household radios, TV, tape players, and phonograph records, tapes, and disks; *communica-*

tions equipment (SIC 366) includes telephone and telegraph apparatus and broadcasting and communications equipment; *electronic components* (SIC 367) includes tubes, circuit boards, semiconductors, capacitors, resistors, coils, and connectors; *miscellaneous electrical supplies* (SIC 369) includes *storage batteries* (SIC 3691), magnetic and optical recording media (such as blank computer diskettes), and electrical machinery, not elsewhere classified.

TABLES 16-19 THROUGH 16-24
TRANSPORTATION EQUIPMENT, INCLUDING MOTOR VEHICLES

SOURCES: INDUSTRIAL PRODUCTION AND CAPACITY UTILIZATION: BOARD OF GOVERNORS OF THE FEDERAL RESERVE SYSTEM (SEE NOTES TO TABLES 4-1 THROUGH 4-4); MANUFACTURERS' SHIPMENTS, INVENTORIES, AND ORDERS: U.S. DEPARTMENT OF COMMERCE, BUREAU OF THE CENSUS (SEE NOTES TO TABLES 15-4 THROUGH 15-7); RETAIL SALES OF CARS AND TRUCKS: U.S. DEPARTMENT OF COMMERCE, BUREAU OF ECONOMIC ANALYSIS; PRODUCER PRICES, CONSUMER PRICES, AND EMPLOYMENT, HOURS, AND EARNINGS: U.S. DEPARTMENT OF LABOR, BUREAU OF LABOR STATISTICS (SEE NOTES TO TABLES 6-2, 6-1, AND 8-5 THROUGH 8-9).

Transportation equipment (SIC Major Group 37) includes manufacture of equipment for transportation of passengers and cargo by land, air, and water, including motor vehicles, aircraft, guided missiles and space vehicles, ships, boats, and railroad equipment. Manufacture of equipment for moving materials on farms and work sites is included in Major Group 35, industrial machinery and equipment.

Industrial production and capacity utilization: Motor vehicles and parts (SIC 371) includes *motor vehicles, motor vehicle parts and accessories* (SIC 3714), *truck trailers, and motor homes* (SIC 3716); *aerospace and miscellaneous transportation equipment* includes *aircraft and parts* (SIC 372), *ships and boats* (SIC 373), and *railroad and miscellaneous* (SIC 374–railroad equipment, 375–motorcycles, bicycles, and parts, 376–guided missiles, space vehicles, and parts, and 379–miscellaneous transportation equipment, including travel trailers, tanks, golf cars, and snowmobiles).

Retail sales and inventories of cars, trucks, and buses. These estimates are prepared by the Bureau of Economic Analysis based on data from the American Automobile Manufacturers Association, Ward's Automotive Reports, and other sources. Data are available in BEA press releases and on the STAT-USA subscription internet site (http://www.stat-usa.gov).

TABLE 16-25
INSTRUMENTS AND RELATED PRODUCTS

SOURCES: INDUSTRIAL PRODUCTION AND CAPACITY UTILIZATION: BOARD OF GOVERNORS OF THE FEDERAL RESERVE SYSTEM (SEE NOTES TO TABLES 4-1 THROUGH 4-4); MANUFACTURERS' SHIPMENTS AND INVENTORIES: U.S. DEPARTMENT OF COMMERCE, BUREAU OF THE CENSUS (SEE NOTES TO TABLES 15-4 THROUGH 15-7); PRODUCER PRICES AND EMPLOYMENT, HOURS, AND EARNINGS: U.S. DEPARTMENT OF LABOR, BUREAU OF LABOR STATISTICS (SEE NOTES TO TABLES 6-2 AND 8-5 THROUGH 8-9).

Measuring, analyzing, and controlling instruments; photographic, medical and optical goods; watches and clocks (SIC Major Group 38) includes manufacture of instruments (including professional and scientific) for measuring, testing, analyzing, and controlling, and their associated sensors and accessories; hydrological, hydrographic, meteorological, and geophysical equipment; navigation and guidance systems; surgical and medical instruments, equipment, and supplies; photographic equipment and supplies; and watches and clocks.

Industrial production: Scientific and medical instruments includes search, detection, navigation, guidance, aeronautical, and nautical systems, instruments, and equipment (SIC 381); laboratory apparatus and analytical, optical, measuring, and controlling instruments (SIC 382); and surgical, medical, and dental instruments and supplies (SIC 384); *medical instruments* is SIC 384.

TABLES 17-1 AND 17-2
FOOD AND FOOD PRODUCTS

SOURCES: INDUSTRIAL PRODUCTION AND CAPACITY UTILIZATION: BOARD OF GOVERNORS OF THE FEDERAL RESERVE SYSTEM (SEE NOTES TO TABLES 4-1 THROUGH 4-4); MANUFACTURERS' SHIPMENTS AND INVENTORIES: U.S. DEPARTMENT OF COMMERCE, BUREAU OF THE CENSUS (SEE NOTES TO TABLES 15-4 THROUGH 15-7); PRODUCER PRICES, CONSUMER PRICES, AND EMPLOYMENT, HOURS, AND EARNINGS: U.S. DEPARTMENT OF LABOR, BUREAU OF LABOR STATISTICS (SEE NOTES TO TABLES 6-2, 6-1, AND 8-5 THROUGH 8-9).

Food and kindred products (SIC Major Group 20) includes manufacture or processing of foods for human consumption and prepared feeds for animals.

Industrial production: meat products (SIC 201) includes meat packing plants, production of sausages and other prepared meat products, and poultry slaughtering and processing; *dairy products* (SIC 202) includes manufacture of creamery butter, cheese, dry and condensed dairy products, and ice cream and frozen desserts and processing of fluid milk; *canned and frozen foods* (SIC 203) includes canning, freezing, drying, dehydrating, and pickling of fruits, vegetables, and specialty foods; *grain mill products* (SIC 204) includes flour milling, breakfast cereal manufacture, rice milling, prepared mixes and doughs, wet corn milling, and dog and cat food; *bakery products* (SIC 205) includes bread, cookies, crackers, and frozen bakery products; *sugar and confectionery* (SIC 206) includes manufacture and refining of sugar and syrup from cane and sugar beets, candy and confectionery, chocolate and cocoa products, chewing gum, and salted and roasted nuts; *fats and oils* (SIC 207) includes cottonseed, soybean, and vegetable oil mills and manufacture of animal and marine fats and oils; *beverages* (SIC 208) includes alcoholic and nonalcoholic beverages and flavoring extracts and syrups; *coffee and miscellaneous* includes roasted coffee, seafoods, snack foods, macaroni and spaghetti, and miscellaneous food preparations.

TABLE 17-3
TOBACCO PRODUCTS

Sources: Industrial production: Board of Governors of the Federal Reserve (see notes to Tables 4-1 through 4-4); manufacturers' shipments and inventories: U.S. Department of Commerce, Bureau of the Census (see notes to 15-4 through 15-7); producer prices and employment, hours, and earnings: U.S. Department of Labor, Bureau of Labor Statistics (see notes to Tables 6-2 and 8-5 through 8-9).

Tobacco products (SIC Major Group 21) includes manufacture of cigarettes, cigars, smoking and chewing tobacco, and snuff and stemming and redrying of tobacco. It also includes manufacture of nontobacco cigarettes.

TABLES 17-4 AND 17-5
TEXTILE MILL PRODUCTS

Sources: Industrial production and capacity utilization: Board of Governors of the Federal Reserve System (see notes to Tables 4-1 through 4-4); manufacturers' shipments and inventories: U.S. Department of Commerce, Bureau of the Census (see notes to Tables 15-4 through 15-7); producer prices and employment, hours, and earnings: U.S. Department of Labor, Bureau of Labor Statistics (see notes to Tables 6-2 and 8-5 through 8-9).

Textile mill products (SIC Major Group 22) includes (1) preparation of fiber and manufacture of yarn, thread, twine, and cordage; (2) manufacture of broad woven, nar-

row woven, and knit fabrics and carpet and rugs from yarn; (3) dyeing and finishing fiber, yarn, fabrics, and knit apparel; (4) coating, waterproofing, or otherwise treating fabrics; (5) integrated manufacture of finished articles from yarn; and (6) manufacture of felt goods, lace, nonwoven fabrics, and miscellaneous textiles.

Industrial production: Fabrics (SIC 221, 222, 223, and 224) includes broadwoven and narrow woven fabrics of cotton, wool, silk, and manmade fiber; *knit goods* (SIC 225) includes knitting of hosiery, underwear, and outerwear; *carpeting* (SIC 227) includes manufacture of carpets and rugs from textile materials and from materials such as reeds, sisal, or jute; *yarns and miscellaneous* (SIC 228 and 229) includes yarn and thread mills, coated fabrics (not rubberized), tire cord, nonwoven fabrics, cordage and twine, linen goods, and textiles not elsewhere classified.

TABLE 17-6
APPAREL

Sources: Industrial production and capacity utilization: Board of Governors of the Federal Reserve System (see notes to Tables 4-1 through 4-4); producer prices, consumer prices, and employment, hours, and earnings: U.S. Department of Labor, Bureau of Labor Statistics (see notes to Tables 6-2, 6-1, and 8-5 through 8-9).

Apparel and other finished products made from fabrics and similar materials (SIC Major Group 23) includes production of clothing and other products by cutting and sewing purchased woven or knit fabrics, leather, rubberized fabrics, plastics, and furs. Also includes manufacture of clothing by cutting and joining (for example, by adhesives) materials such as paper and nonwoven fabrics.

TABLES 17-7 AND 17-8
PAPER AND ALLIED PRODUCTS

Sources: Industrial production and capacity utilization: Board of Governors of the Federal Reserve System (see notes to Tables 4-1 through 4-4); manufacturers' shipments and inventories: U.S. Department of Commerce, Bureau of the Census (see notes to Tables 15-4 through 15-7); producer prices and employment, hours, and earnings: U.S. Department of Labor, Bureau of Labor Statistics (see notes to Tables 6-2 and 8-5 through 8-9).

Paper and allied products (SIC Major Group 26) includes manufacture of pulps from wood and other cellulose fibers and rags; manufacture of paper and paperboard and paper products such as bags, boxes, and envelopes. Also included is manufacture of plastic bags.

Industrial production and capacity utilization: Pulp and paper includes pulp mills (SIC 261), paper mills (SIC 262), and paperboard mills (SIC 263); *paper products* includes paperboard containers and boxes (SIC 265) and converted paper and paperboard products, except containers and boxes (SIC 267).

TABLE 17-9
PRINTING AND PUBLISHING

SOURCES: INDUSTRIAL PRODUCTION AND CAPACITY UTILIZATION: BOARD OF GOVERNORS OF THE FEDERAL RESERVE SYSTEM (SEE NOTES TO TABLES 4-1 THROUGH 4-4); PRODUCER PRICES AND EMPLOYMENT, HOURS, AND EARNINGS: U.S. DEPARTMENT OF LABOR, BUREAU OF LABOR STATISTICS (SEE NOTES TO TABLES 6-2 AND 8-5 THROUGH 8-9).

Printing, publishing, and allied industries (SIC Major Group 27) includes printing, lithography, and services performed for the printing trade, such as bookbinding and plate making. Also included are publishers of newspapers, books, and periodicals.

Industrial production: Newspapers (SIC 271) includes publishing and printing of newspapers; *commercial printing* (SIC 275) includes lithographic, offset, and gravure printing.

TABLES 17-10 AND 17-11
CHEMICALS AND CHEMICAL PRODUCTS

SOURCES: INDUSTRIAL PRODUCTION AND CAPACITY UTILIZATION: BOARD OF GOVERNORS OF THE FEDERAL RESERVE SYSTEM (SEE NOTES TO TABLES 4-1 THROUGH 4-4); MANUFACTURERS' SHIPMENTS AND INVENTORIES: U.S. DEPARTMENT OF COMMERCE, BUREAU OF THE CENSUS (SEE NOTES TO TABLES 15-4 THROUGH 15-7); PRODUCER PRICES AND EMPLOYMENT, HOURS, AND EARNINGS: U.S. DEPARTMENT OF LABOR, BUREAU OF LABOR STATISTICS (SEE NOTES TO TABLES 6-2 AND 8-5 THROUGH 8-9).

Chemicals and allied products (SIC Major Group 28) includes production of basic chemicals and manufacture of products by predominantly chemical processes. Three general classes of products are included: (1) basic chemicals; (2) chemical products to be used in further manufacture,

including synthetic fibers and plastic materials; (3) finished chemical products, including drugs, cosmetics, paints, fertilizers, and explosives. The mining of natural chemicals and fertilizers is classified in Division B, Mining.

Industrial production and capacity utilization: Basic chemicals (SIC 281–Industrial Inorganic Chemicals) includes alkalies, chlorine, industrial gases, inorganic pigments, and industrial organic chemicals not elsewhere classified (SIC 2819); *synthetic materials* (SIC 282) includes plastic materials, synthetic resins, and nonvulcanizable elastomers (SIC 2821), synthetic fibers (SIC 2823 and 2824), and synthetic rubber (vulcanizable elastomers); *drugs and medicines* (SIC 283) includes medicinal chemicals and pharmaceutical products; *soaps and toiletries* (SIC 284) includes soap, detergents, cleaning preparations, perfumes, cosmetics, and other toiletries; *industrial organic chemicals* (SIC 286) includes noncyclic organic chemicals, solvents, polyhydric alcohols, synthetic perfumes and flavorings, rubber processing chemicals, plasticizers, synthetic tanning agents, and others; *agricultural chemicals* (SIC 287) includes nitrogenous and phosphatic fertilizers, pesticides, and agricultural chemicals not elsewhere classified.

TABLES 17-12 AND 17-13
PETROLEUM AND COAL PRODUCTS

SOURCES: INDUSTRIAL PRODUCTION AND CAPACITY UTILIZATION: BOARD OF GOVERNORS OF THE FEDERAL RESERVE SYSTEM (SEE NOTES TO TABLES 4-1 THROUGH 4-4); MANUFACTURERS' SHIPMENTS AND INVENTORIES: U.S. DEPARTMENT OF COMMERCE, BUREAU OF THE CENSUS (SEE NOTES TO TABLES 15-4 THROUGH 15-7); PRODUCER PRICES, CONSUMER PRICES, AND EMPLOYMENT, HOURS, AND EARNINGS: U.S. DEPARTMENT OF LABOR, BUREAU OF LABOR STATISTICS (SEE NOTES TO TABLES 6-2, 6-1, AND 8-5 THROUGH 8-9).

Petroleum refining and related industries (SIC Major Group 29) includes refining petroleum, manufacturing paving and roofing materials, and compounding lubricating oils and greases from purchased materials. Producing coke and byproducts is classified in Major Group 33, Primary Metals. Gas distribution is classified in public utilities.

Industrial production: Petroleum refining and miscellaneous (SIC 291, 299) includes petroleum refining, blending and compounding lubricating oils and greases, and production of petroleum and coal products not elsewhere classified; *paving and roofing materials* (SIC 295) includes manufacture of asphalt and tar paving materials and asphalt roofing materials.

TABLES 17-14 AND 17-15
RUBBER AND PLASTICS PRODUCTS

SOURCES: INDUSTRIAL PRODUCTION AND CAPACITY UTILIZATION: BOARD OF GOVERNORS OF THE FEDERAL RESERVE SYSTEM (SEE NOTES TO TABLES 4-1 THROUGH 4-4); MANUFACTURERS' SHIPMENTS AND INVENTORIES: U.S. DEPARTMENT OF COMMERCE, BUREAU OF THE CENSUS (SEE NOTES TO TABLES 15-4 THROUGH 15-7); PRODUCER PRICES AND EMPLOYMENT, HOURS, AND EARNINGS: U.S. DEPARTMENT OF LABOR, BUREAU OF LABOR STATISTICS (SEE NOTES TO TABLES 6-2 AND 8-5 THROUGH 8-9).

Rubber and miscellaneous plastics products (SIC Major Group 30) includes manufacturing products, not elsewhere classified, from plastic resins and from natural, synthetic, or reclaimed rubber. Many products made from these materials, including boats, toys, buckles, and buttons, are classified elsewhere (SIC 37 and 39). Tire manufacture is included, but recapping and retreading are classified in Services. Manufacture of synthetic rubber and synthetic plastic resins is classified in Chemicals, Major Group 28.

Industrial production: Tires (SIC 301) includes manufacture of pneumatic casings, inner tubes, and solid and cushion tires for all types of vehicles, airplanes, and farm equipment and of tire repair and retreading materials; *other rubber products* includes manufacture of rubber and plastics footwear (SIC 302), gaskets, packing, and sealing devices and rubber and plastic hosing and belting (SIC 305), and fabricated rubber products not elsewhere classified (SIC 306); *plastics products, not elsewhere classified* (SIC 308) includes manufacture of unsupported and laminated plastic film, sheet, and profile shapes, plastics pipe, plastics bottles, plastics foam products, and plastics plumbing fixtures.

TABLE 17-16
LEATHER AND LEATHER PRODUCTS

SOURCES: INDUSTRIAL PRODUCTION AND CAPACITY UTILIZATION: BOARD OF GOVERNORS OF THE FEDERAL RESERVE SYSTEM (SEE NOTES TO TABLES 4-1 THROUGH 4-4); PRODUCER PRICES AND EMPLOYMENT, HOURS, AND EARNINGS: U.S. DEPARTMENT OF LABOR, BUREAU OF LABOR STATISTICS (SEE NOTES TO TABLES 6-2 AND 8-5 THROUGH 8-9).

Leather and leather products (SIC Major Group 31) includes tanning, currying, and finishing hides and skins and manufacturing finished leather and artificial leather products and some similar products made of other materials.

Industrial production: Shoes (SIC 314) includes manufacture of footwear, except rubber or plastic footwear.

TABLES 18-1 THROUGH 18-3
TRANSPORTATION, COMMUNICATIONS, AND UTILITIES

SOURCES: INDUSTRIAL PRODUCTION AND CAPACITY UTILIZATION: BOARD OF GOVERNORS OF THE FEDERAL RESERVE SYSTEM (SEE NOTES TO TABLES 4-1 THROUGH 4-4); PRODUCER PRICES AND EMPLOYMENT, HOURS, AND EARNINGS: U.S. DEPARTMENT OF LABOR, BUREAU OF LABOR STATISTICS (SEE NOTES TO TABLES 6-2 AND 8-5 THROUGH 8-9).

Transportation, communications, and electric, gas, and sanitary services (SIC Division E) includes establishments providing to the general public or to other business enterprises passenger and freight transportation, communications services, or electricity, gas, steam, water or sanitary services. Private courier and delivery services are included. The U.S. Postal Service is classified in this group in the SIC, but postal service employment is counted by BLS in the government sector and is not included in the employment data in this chapter.

Industrial production: Electric utilities includes the generation, transmission, and/or distribution of electric energy for sale (SIC 491) and part of SIC 493–combination electric, gas, and other utility services; *gas utilities* includes natural gas transmission and distribution and manufacture and distribution of liquefied petroleum gas (SIC 493) and part of SIC 493.

Employment, hours, and earnings: Trucking and warehousing (SIC Major Group 42) includes local and long-distance trucking, warehousing and storage, and courier services (except by air); *communications* (SIC Major Group 48) includes telephone, telegraph, radio and television, and other communications services; *electric, gas, and sanitary services* (SIC Major Group 49) includes electricity and gas production and distribution, water supply, sewerage systems, and refuse systems.

TABLES 19-1 AND 19-2
RETAIL AND WHOLESALE TRADE: EMPLOYMENT, HOURS, AND EARNINGS

SOURCES: EMPLOYMENT, HOURS, AND EARNINGS: U.S. DEPARTMENT OF LABOR, BUREAU OF LABOR STATISTICS (SEE NOTES TO TABLES 8-5 THROUGH 8-9).

Wholesale trade (SIC Division F) includes establishments primarily engaged in selling merchandise to retailers; to commercial, professional, or institutional purchasers; or to other wholesalers. Certain establishments that sell merchandise to both businesses and consumers, such as paint stores and gasoline service stations, are classified in Retail Trade. Wholesale trade includes merchant wholesalers-wholesalers who take title to the goods they sell-as well as sales branches of manufacturing or mining enterprises (apart from their plants or mines) and commodity brokers and commission merchants. However, the data in this book pertain to merchant wholesalers only.

Retail trade (SIC Division G) includes establishments primarily engaged in selling merchandise for personal or household consumption and rendering services incidental to the sales of the goods. However, establishments engaged in selling such merchandise as plumbing equipment, electrical supplies, and office furniture are classified in Wholesale Trade, even if a higher proportion of their sales is made to individuals for personal or household use.

General merchandise stores (SIC Major Group 53) includes department stores, variety stores, and general stores; food stores (SIC Major Group 54) includes grocery stores, meat markets, bakeries, and other food specialty stores; auto dealers and service stations (SIC Major Group 55) includes new and used motor vehicle dealers, auto supply stores, and gasoline service stations; apparel and accessory stores (SIC Major Group 56) includes men's, women's, and children's clothing stores, shoe stores, and accessory stores; eating and drinking places (SIC Major Group 58) includes restaurant, carry-outs, institutional food service, bars, and taverns.

TABLES 19-3 AND 19-4
RETAIL SALES AND INVENTORIES

SOURCE: U.S. DEPARTMENT OF COMMERCE, BUREAU OF THE CENSUS.

Each month the Bureau of the Census prepares estimates of retail sales and inventories by kind of business based on a mail-out/mail-back survey of a sample of companies with one or more establishments that sell merchandise and related services to final consumers.

E-commerce sales of the goods included in retail trade are included in the retail sales data; these data do not, consequently, include online sales of services such as travel services, financial brokerages, and ticket sales agencies. Firms are now asked to report e-commerce sales separately, and these sales data are now published quarterly; the sample is not of sufficient size to warrant monthly publication. Also, these sales have not been collected long enough to allow calculation of seasonal adjustments.

In the second quarter of 2000, e-commerce sales were $5,518 million, compared with $5,240 million in the first quarter of 2000 and $5,198 million in the fourth quarter of 1999. E-commerce accounted for 0.68 percent of total retail sales in the second quarter, compared with 0.70 percent in the first quarter and 0.63 percent in the fourth quarter of 1999.

Notes on the data

Inventory data prior to 1980 are not comparable to later years due to changes in valuation methods. Prior to 1980, inventories are book values of merchandise on hand at the end of the period and are valued according to the valuation method used by each respondent. Thus the aggregates are a mixture of LIFO (last-in-first-out) and non-LIFO values. Beginning with 1980, inventories are valued using methods other than LIFO in order to better reflect the current costs of goods held as inventory.

The survey sample is stratified by kind of business and estimated sales. All firms with sales above an applicable size cutoff are included. Firms are selected randomly from the remaining strata. To reduce reporting burden, only specially selected panels report each month, with the remainder reporting quarterly in three rotating panels.

New samples are drawn every five years, and the samples are updated every quarter to add new businesses and drop companies that are no longer active.

Data availability

An Advance Monthly Retail Sales report is released about nine working days after the close of the reference month, based on responses from a sub-sample of the complete retail sample.

Revised and more complete monthly *Retail Trade, Sales, and Inventories* reports are released six weeks after the close of the reference month. They contain preliminary figures for the current month and final figures for the prior 12 months. Statistics include retail sales, inventories, and ratios of inventories to sales. Data are both seasonally adjusted and unadjusted.

The *Annual Benchmark Report for Retail Trade* is released annually each spring. It includes updated seasonal adjustment factors; revised and benchmarked monthly estimates of sales and inventories; monthly data for the most recent 10 years; detailed annual estimates and ratios for the United States by kind of business; and comparable prior-year statistics and year-to-year changes. Data are available on the Bureau of the Census internet site (http://www.census.gov).

TABLE 19-5
MERCHANT WHOLESALERS: SALES AND INVENTORIES

SOURCE: *U.S. DEPARTMENT OF COMMERCE, BUREAU OF THE CENSUS.*

These data pertain to merchant wholesalers and are based on a monthly survey conducted by the Bureau of the Census.

Notes on the data

Inventory data prior to 1980 are not comparable to later years because of changes in valuation methods and are not included in this book. Prior to 1980, inventories are book values of stocks on hand at the end of the period and are valued according to the valuation method used by each respondent. Thus the aggregates are a mixture of LIFO (last-in-first-out) and non-LIFO values. Beginning with 1980 inventories are valued using methods other than LIFO in order to better reflect the current costs of goods held as inventory.

The survey covers wholesale companies with employment that are primarily engaged in merchant wholesale trade in the United States (SIC Division F). These include merchant wholesalers that take title of the goods they sell, and jobbers, industrial distributors, exporters, and importers. Excluded are non-merchant wholesalers such as manufacturers' sales branches and offices; agents, mer-

chandise or commodity brokers, and commission merchants; and other businesses whose primary activities are other than wholesale trade.

Companies provide data on dollar values of merchant wholesale sales, end-of-month inventories, and methods of inventory valuation.

A survey has been conducted monthly since 1946. A mail-out/mail-back survey of selected wholesale firms is used. Firms are first stratified by merchant wholesale sales, inventories and major kind of business (determined from the latest census of wholesale trade). All firms with wholesale sales or inventories above applicable size cut-offs for each major kind of business are included in the survey. Remaining firms are stratified by major kind of business and estimated sales, and a simple random sample is selected from each stratum. Companies selected with certainty report each month. To minimize reporting burden, randomly selected firms are put in one of three rotating panels and report once each quarter for the two preceding months.

New samples are drawn every five years, and the samples are updated every quarter to add new businesses and drop companies that are no longer active.

Data availability

Monthly Wholesale Trade, Sales and Inventories reports are released 6 weeks after the close of the reference month. They contain preliminary current-month figures and final figures for the previous month. Statistics include sales, inventories, and stock/sale ratios by 3-digit SIC code, along with standard errors. Data are both seasonally adjusted and unadjusted.

The *Annual Benchmark Report for Wholesale Trade* is released annually each spring. It contains estimated annual sales, monthly and year-end inventories, inventory/sales ratios, purchases, gross margins, and gross margin/sales ratios by kind of business. Annual estimates are benchmarked to the most recent census of wholesale trade. These reports also present the results of a benchmarking operation that revises monthly sales and inventories estimates. Estimates are both seasonally adjusted and unadjusted.

Data are available on the Bureau of the Census internet site (http://www.census.gov).

TABLE 20-1
FINANCE, INSURANCE, AND REAL ESTATE

SOURCES: EMPLOYMENT, HOURS, AND EARNINGS: U.S.
DEPARTMENT OF LABOR, BUREAU OF LABOR STATISTICS (SEE
NOTES TO TABLES 8-5 THROUGH 8-9).

Finance, insurance, and real estate (SIC Division H)
includes establishments operating primarily in these
fields. *Finance* includes *depository institutions* (SIC
Major Group 60), nondepository credit institutions
(Major Group 61), and securities brokers and dealers and
exchanges (Major Groups 62 and 67). *Insurance* (SIC
Major Groups 63 and 64) covers carriers, agents, and brokers of all types of insurance. *Real estate* (SIC Major
Group 65) includes buyers, sellers, agents, developers, and
owners of real estate.

TABLES 20-2 AND 20-3
PRIVATE SERVICES

SOURCES: PRODUCER PRICES, EMPLOYMENT, HOURS, AND EARN-
INGS: U.S. DEPARTMENT OF LABOR, BUREAU OF LABOR
STATISTICS (SEE NOTES TO TABLES 6-2 AND 8-5 THROUGH 8-9).

Services (SIC Division I) includes establishments
engaged in providing a wide variety of services to individuals, businesses, government, and other organizations.
Personal, business, repair, health, amusement, legal, and
engineering services and hotels and other lodging places
are among the categories included.

The SIC Division definition includes both governmental
and private activities, classified according to the type of
service provided. However, the employment, hours, and
earnings data shown on these pages pertain only to the
private economy.

The data presented here on employment, hours, and
earnings include one industry—agricultural services—
which the SIC places in Division A (agriculture, forestry,
and fishing).

Agricultural services (SIC Major Group 7) includes soil
preparation and crop services, veterinary services, and
landscape services, whether provided to farmers or to
consumers.

Hotels and other lodging places (SIC Major Group 70)
includes hotels, motels, rooming houses, and RV camps;
personal services (SIC Major Group 72) includes laundry,
photography, hair care, shoe repair, and funeral services;
business services (SIC Major Group 73) includes *person-*

nel supply services (SIC 736), *computer and data processing services* (SIC 737), and also advertising, equipment
rental, and other business services. Personnel supply
services includes employment agencies and *help supply
services* (SIC 7363), which supply temporary or continuing help on a contract or fee basis.

Auto repair, services, and parking (SIC Major Group 75)
includes auto rental, parking, and repair; *miscellaneous
repair services* (SIC Major Group 76) includes electrical
and watch and clock repair, reupholstery and furniture
repair, and other repair services.

Motion pictures (SIC Major Group 78) includes motion
picture production and distribution, motion picture theaters, and video tape rental; *amusement and recreation*
(SIC Major Group 79) includes theaters, sports events,
and sports facilities, such as golf courses and health clubs;
legal services (SIC Major Group 81) includes establishments headed by attorneys; *educational services* (SIC
Major Group 82) includes private schools and colleges,
libraries, and vocational schools; *social services* (SIC
Major Group 83) includes private family services, day
care, and job training.

Museums, botanical gardens, and zoos (SIC Major Group
84) includes private museums, galleries, botanical gardens, and zoos; *membership organizations* (SIC Major
Group 86) includes business and professional associations, labor unions, and civic, religious, and political
organizations; *engineering and management* (SIC Major
Group 87) includes engineering, accounting, research,
and management services.

Health services (SIC Major Group 80) includes *hospitals*
(SIC 806), *offices and clinics of medical doctors* (SIC
801), *nursing and personal care facilities* (SIC 805), *home
health care services* (SIC 808), and also dental offices,
medical and dental laboratories, and other health care
practitioners.

TABLES 20-4 AND 20-5
**SELECTED SERVICE INDUSTRIES-RECEIPTS AND
REVENUE**

SOURCE: U.S. DEPARTMENT OF COMMERCE, BUREAU OF THE
CENSUS.

The Census Service Annual Survey provides, for selected
service industries, annual estimates of operating receipts
of taxable firms, and revenues of private, nonprofit firms
that are exempt from federal income taxation. The survey is based on a sample of establishments.

Definitions and notes on the data

Many of the service industries covered are described in the preceding section of the Notes. In addition to those, the survey includes *arrangement of passenger transportation* (SIC 472) and *real estate agents and managers* (SIC 653). It excludes elementary and secondary schools (SIC 821); colleges, universities, professional schools, and junior colleges (SIC 822); miscellaneous educational services (SIC 829); labor unions and similar labor organizations (SIC 863); political organizations (SIC 865); religious organizations (SIC 866); private households (SIC 881); and services not elsewhere classified (SIC 899).

Separate estimates were developed for taxable and non-taxable firms in camps and membership lodging; selected amusement and recreation services; selected health services; legal services; libraries; vocational schools; social services; museums, art galleries, botanical gardens, and zoos; research, development, and testing services; and selected management and public relations services. Firms considered tax-exempt include membership lodging, membership organizations, and noncommercial research organizations. Firms in all remaining SICs were defined to be taxable. For tax-exempt firms, employer firms only were sampled; for all other kinds of business, data represent combined estimates for employer and nonemployer firms. Government-operated hospitals were included, while all other government establishments were excluded.

Data availability

Data are published annually as *Current Business Reports, Service Annual Survey*. They are available on the Bureau of the Census internet site (http://www.census.gov).

TABLES 21-1 THROUGH 21-5 AND 22-7 THROUGH 22-8 GOVERNMENT RECEIPTS AND EXPENDITURES

SOURCE: U.S. DEPARTMENT OF COMMERCE, BUREAU OF ECONOMIC ANALYSIS.

These data are from the national income and product accounts (NIPAs), as published in the 1999 comprehensive NIPA revisions and as subsequently revised and updated through September 2000. For more information on the 1999 comprehensive revision, see the notes for Tables 1-1 through 1-9.

Notes on the data

The data on government receipts and expenditures record transactions of governments (federal, state, and local) with other U.S. residents and foreigners. Each entry in the government receipts and expenditures account has a corresponding entry elsewhere in the NIPAs. Thus, for example, the sum of personal tax and nontax receipts by federal and state and local governments is equal to personal tax and nontax payments as shown in the personal income table.

The government receipts and expenditures estimates are derived primarily from financial statements for federal, state, and local governments. However, a number of adjustments are made to place the data on the basis required for the NIPAs. Annual data are placed on a calendar year basis. Data are converted from the cash basis usually found in financial statements to the timing bases required for the NIPAs. In the NIPAs, receipts from businesses generally are on an accrual basis, purchases of goods and services are recorded when delivered, and receipts from and transfer payments to persons are on a cash basis.

The federal receipts and expenditure data from the NIPAs in Tables 21-1 through 21-5 thus differ from the federal receipts and outlay data in Tables 21-6 and 21-7 in that, among other differences, the latter are by fiscal year and are on a modified cash basis.

Definitions

Personal tax and nontax receipts is personal tax payments that are not chargeable to business expense and certain other personal payments to government agencies (except government enterprises) that are treated like taxes. Personal taxes includes taxes on income, including on realized net capital gains, and on personal property. Nontaxes includes donations and fees, fines, and forfeitures. Personal contributions for social insurance are not included. As of the 1999 revisions, estate and gift taxes are classified as capital transfers and are no longer included in personal tax and nontax payments. However, estate and gift taxes continue to be included in federal government receipts in Table 21-6.

Corporate profits tax accruals is the sum of federal, state, and local income taxes on all corporate earnings, including realized net capital gains. These taxes are net of refunds and applicable tax credits.

Indirect business tax and nontax accruals is tax liabilities that are chargeable to business expense in the calculation of profit-type incomes and certain other business liabilities to government agencies (except government enterprises) that are treated like taxes. Examples are sales and property taxes and regulatory and inspection fees. Employer contributions for social insurance are not included.

Contributions for social insurance includes employer and personal contributions for Social Security, Medicare, unemployment insurance, and other government social insurance programs. As of the 1999 revisions, contributions to government employee retirement plans are no longer included in this category, as these plans are now treated the same as private pension plans. See the Notes to Tables 1-1 through 1-9.

Government consumption expenditures is purchases by governments (federal, state, and local) of goods and services for current consumption. It includes compensation of general government employees (including employer contributions to retirement plans, as of the 1999 revision) and an allowance for consumption of general government fixed capital, including software (i.e., depreciation). Receipts for certain services provided by government-primarily tuition payments for higher education and charges for medical care-are defined as government sales, which are treated as deductions from government purchases.

Transfer payments includes payments to persons for which they do not render current services. Examples are Social Security benefits, Medicare, Medicaid, unemployment benefits, and public assistance. Retirement payments to retired government employees from their pension plans are no longer included. U.S. government nonmilitary grants to other countries are included.

Federal grants-in-aid are net payments from federal to state and local governments to help finance programs such as health (Medicaid), public assistance (e.g., the old Aid to Families with Dependent Children and the new Temporary Assistance for Needy Families), and education. Investment grants to state and local governments for highways, transit, air transportation, and water treatment plants are now classified as capital transfers and no longer included in this category. However, such investment grants continue to be included as federal government outlays in Table 21-6.

Net interest paid is interest paid to U.S. and foreign persons and businesses and to foreign governments less interest received from business and from foreigners. Interest paid consists of monetary interest paid on public debt and other financial obligations. Interest received consists of monetary and imputed interest received on loans and investments; in the NIPAs it no longer includes interest received by government employee retirement plans, which is now credited to personal income. However, such interest received is still deducted from interest paid in Table 21-6.

Subsidies less current surplus of government enterprises. Subsidies are the monetary grants paid by government to business, including to government enterprises at another level of government. Subsidies no longer include federal maritime construction subsidies, which are now classified as a capital transfer. The current surplus of government enterprises is their current operating revenue and subsidies received from other levels of government less their current expenses. No deduction is made for depreciation charges and net interest paid.

Surplus or deficit(-), national income and product accounts is the sum of government receipts less the sum of current government expenditures. As of the 1999 revisions, these surpluses-particularly those of state and local governments-are significantly smaller than they were before the revisions, because the net accumulations of employee retirement plans are now classified as personal saving rather than in the government sector.

Gross government investment consists of general government and government enterprise expenditures for fixed assets (structures, equipment, and software). Government inventory investment is included in government consumption expenditures.

Capital consumption. Consumption of fixed capital, or depreciation, is included in government consumption expenditures as a partial measure of the value of the services of general government fixed assets, including structures, equipment, and software. Because this depreciation allowance is the only entry on the product side of the accounts measuring the output associated with such capital, a zero net return on these assets is implicitly assumed.

Data availability

The most recent data are published each month in the Survey of Current Business. Current and historical data may be obtained from the BEA internet site (http://www.bea.doc.gov) and the STAT-USA subscription internet site (http://www.stat-usa.gov).

References

For information on the classification of government expenditures into current consumption and gross investment, first undertaken in the 1996 comprehensive revisions, see the Survey of Current Business article "Preview of the Comprehensive Revision of the National Income and Product Accounts: Recognition of Government Investment and Incorporation of a New Methodology for

Calculating Depreciation," September 1995. Other sources of information about the NIPAs are listed in the Notes for Tables 1-1 through 1-9.

TABLES 21-6 AND 21-7
FEDERAL GOVERNMENT RECEIPTS AND OUTLAYS AND FEDERAL DEBT BY FISCAL YEAR

SOURCE: U.S. DEPARTMENT OF THE TREASURY; U.S. OFFICE OF MANAGEMENT AND BUDGET.

The monthly data on federal government receipts and outlays are from the *Monthly Treasury Statement* and are on a modified cash basis. Annual data, also on a modified cash basis, are from the *Budget of the United States Government: Historical Tables* and are by federal fiscal years: July 1 to June 30 through 1976 and October 1 to September 30 for subsequent years. There are numerous differences in both timing and definition between these estimates and the NIPA estimates in Tables 21-1 and 21-3 through 21-5; see the Notes for those tables above for definitional differences that were introduced with the 1999 comprehensive revision.

Definitions

The definitions in these tables are not affected by the changes in government accounts that have been made in the National Income and Product Accounts.

Receipts are composed of taxes or other compulsory payments to the government and gifts. Other types of payments to government are netted against outlays.

Outlays occur when the federal government liquidates an obligation through a cash payment or when interest accrues on public debt issues. Beginning in 1992, outlays include the subsidy cost of direct and guaranteed loans made. Before 1992, the costs and repayments associated with such loans are recorded on a cash basis. As noted above, various types of nontax receipts are netted against cash outlays. These accounts do not distinguish between investment outlays and current consumption, and do not include allowances for depreciation.

The total surplus (deficit-) is receipts minus outlays.

On-budget and off-budget. By law, two government programs that are included in the federal receipts and outlays totals are "off-budget"-old age, survivors, and disability insurance (Social Security) and the Postal Service. The former accounts for nearly all of the off-budget activity. The surplus (deficit-) not accounted for by these two programs is the on-budget surplus or deficit.

Sources of financing are the means by which the total deficit is financed, and by definition sum to the total deficit with the sign reversed. The principal source is *borrowing from the public,* shown as a positive number, i.e. the increase in the debt held by the public. When there is a budget surplus, as in Fiscal Years 1998 and 1999, debt can be reduced, indicated by a minus sign in this column. *Other financing* includes drawdown (or buildup, shown here with a minus sign) in Treasury cash balances, seigniorage on coins, direct and guaranteed loan account cash transactions, and miscellaneous other transactions.

Outlays by function present outlays according to the major purpose of the spending. Functional classifications cut across departmental and agency lines. Most categories of offsetting receipts are netted against cash outlays in the appropriate function, but there is also a category of *undistributed offsetting receipts,* which includes proceeds from the sale or lease of assets and payments from federal agencies to federal retirement funds and the Social Security and Medicare trust funds.

Federal debt held by the public consists of all Federal debt held outside the federal government accounts—by individuals, financial institutions including the Federal Reserve Banks, and foreign individuals, businesses, and central banks. It does not include federal debt held by federal government trust funds such as the Social Security trust fund. The level and change of the ratio of this debt to the value of GDP provide proportional measures of the impact of federal borrowing on credit markets.

References

Differences between the federal government accounts in the NIPAs and in the budget presentations are discussed in *Budget of the United States: Analytical Perspectives,* available from the Government Printing Office and on the internet site listed below. Definitions and budget concepts are discussed in that volume and also in the *Historical Tables,* referenced below.

Data availability

The monthly data are published in the *Monthly Treasury Statement* prepared by the Financial Management Service, U.S. Department of the Treasury. The publication is available on the Financial Management Service internet site (http://www.fms.treas.gov).

These monthly data are only shown for the most recent two years. The annual data are from the *Budget of the United States Government: Historical Tables* and are available on the internet site http://www.gpo.gov/usbudget. These annual data include revisions that have not been allocated to the monthly data.

TABLE 21-7
GOVERNMENT EMPLOYMENT

SOURCE: U.S. DEPARTMENT OF LABOR, BUREAU OF LABOR STATISTICS (SEE NOTES TO TABLE 8-5).

The government division of the SIC includes federal, state, and local activities such as legislative, executive, and judicial functions, as well as all government-owned and government-operated business enterprises, establishments, and institutions (arsenals, navy yards, hospitals, etc.), and government force account construction. The figures relate to civilian employment only. BLS considers regular full-time teachers (private and governmental) to be employed during the summer vacation period whether or not they are specifically paid in those months.

Employment in federal government establishments represents those who occupied positions the last day of the month. Intermittent workers are counted if they performed any service during the month. Federal government employment excludes employees of the Central Intelligence Agency and the National Security Agency.

TABLES 22-1 THROUGH 22-4
SELECTED NATIONAL INCOME AND PRODUCT ACCOUNT DATA
SEE THE NOTES FOR TABLES 1-1 THROUGH 1-10.

TABLES 22-5 AND 22-6
PRIVATE FIXED INVESTMENT
SEE THE NOTES FOR TABLES 5-1 THROUGH 5-3.

TABLES 22-7 AND 22-8
GOVERNMENT RECEIPTS AND EXPENDITURES
SEE THE NOTES FOR TABLES 21-1 AND 21-2.

TABLE 22-9
U.S. INTERNATIONAL TRANSACTIONS
SEE THE NOTES FOR TABLE 11-1.

TABLE 22-10
PRODUCTIVITY AND RELATED DATA
SEE THE NOTES FOR TABLE 7-3.

TABLE 23-1
NEW PLANT AND EQUIPMENT SPENDING

SOURCE: U.S. BUREAU OF ECONOMIC ANALYSIS AND BUREAU OF THE CENSUS.

The data on new plant and equipment spending are from the *Plant and Equipment Survey*. This survey program, which began in 1947, was concluded with the data released in September 1994 and was replaced by a new semi-annual Investment Plans Survey (IPS). The IPS was, in turn, discontinued as of March 1996, due to budgetary limitations at the Bureau of the Census. Although an annual capital expenditure survey (ACES) now provides annual data (see notes for Tables 5-9 and 5-10), there is no longer any official survey of capital spending by industry on a less-than-annual basis. There is also no survey by industry of future investment plans. The ACES differs significantly in survey design, scope, and publication detail from the former Plant and Equipment Survey.

To provide a historical time series on new investment by U.S. businesses, the back data from the Plant and Equipment Survey are included in the historical statistics section of this book.

Coverage. The Plant and Equipment Survey covered businesses classified in SIC Divisions A (excluding agricultural producers), B through H, and I (except private households).

Content. Basic data on spending for plant and equipment were collected for each quarter, with additional data obtained for the 3rd and 4th quarters. Quarterly data included actual expenditures for the prior quarter and planned spending for each of the next three quarters.

Methods. The Census Bureau conducted this survey from the third quarter of 1988 through 1994; the Bureau of Economic Analysis conducted it for prior periods. A mail-out/mail-back quarterly survey of selected large companies, and a mail-out/mail-back annual survey of additional companies in selected industries was used. The survey panels were benchmarked in 1982. Beginning in 1989, a survey panel maintenance program was used to assess and improve industry coverage based on information from other censuses and surveys. Beginning with 1991, companies not responding to voluntary quarterly survey requests received mandatory annual requests for comparable information.

Data availability

Quarterly and annual data from the Plant and Equipment Survey covering 1947 through mid-1994 are available from the Bureau of the Census.

TABLE 24-1
PERSONAL INCOME

See the notes for Tables 3-1 through 3-4.

TABLE 24-2
INDUSTRIAL PRODUCTION AND CAPACITY UTILIZATION

See the notes for Tables 4-1 through 4-4.

TABLES 24-3 AND 24-4
CIVILIAN POPULATION, LABOR FORCE, EMPLOYMENT, AND UNEMPLOYMENT

See the notes for Tables 8-1 through 8-3.

TABLES 24-5 AND 24-6
NONAGRICULTURAL EMPLOYMENT, HOURS, AND EARNINGS

See the notes for Tables 8-5 through 8-9.

TABLE 24-7
CONSUMER PRICE INDEXES

See the notes for Table 6-1.

TABLE 24-8
PRODUCER PRICE INDEXES

See the notes for Table 6-2.

TABLE 24-9
MONEY STOCK AND SELECTED COMPONENTS

See the notes for Tables 10-1 and 10-2.

TABLE 24-10
INTEREST RATE, BOND YIELDS, AND STOCK PRICES

See the notes for Tables 10-7 and 10-8.

TABLE 25-1
STATE AND REGIONAL DATA, ANNUAL, 1970–1999

This appendix contains annual time-series data on personal income and employment for the United States, each state, the District of Columbia and eight geographic regions. All data are from the Bureau of Economic Analysis, U.S. Department of Commerce. All revisions available through September 2000 are included. With one significant exception concerning U.S. residents working abroad and foreign residents working in the United States, which will be discussed below, these data utilize the same concepts and definitions as the personal income estimates contained in the national income and product accounts (NIPAs). Summaries of these definitions can be found in the Notes for Table 3-1. In particular, it should be noted that these state data all incorporate the definitional changes adopted in 1999 affecting government employee retirement plans. These changes affect total personal income, personal contributions for social insurance, dividends, and interest.

Additional Notes on the State and Regional Data

The U.S. data that accompany the state data represent the total of the state data. They differ from those in the NIPAs mainly in that the state data consist of only the income earned by persons who live within the United States, but include in that total all foreign residents working in the United States. NIPA totals include the labor earnings and retirement fund revenues of Federal civilian and military personnel abroad and U.S. residents on foreign assignment for less than a year. However, earnings of foreign residents are included in the NIPA totals only if they live and work in the United States for a year or more.

The population estimates shown are the ones used in the calculation of per capita amounts. These are midyear estimates from the Bureau of the Census.

The dividends, interest, and rent total includes the capital consumption adjustment for rental income of persons.

Total employment is the average annual number of jobs, full-time plus part-time; each job that a person holds is counted at full weight. The estimates are on a place-of-work basis. Both wage and salary employment and self-employment are included. The main source for the wage and salary employment estimates is Bureau of Labor Statistics estimates from unemployment insurance data (the ES-202 data). Self-employment is estimated mainly from individual and partnership federal income tax returns.

The employment estimates correspond closely in coverage to the earnings estimates. However, the earnings estimates include the income of limited partnerships and of tax-exempt cooperatives, for which there are no corresponding employment estimates.

The BEA state-level earnings estimates included in Business Statistics are adjusted to a place-of-residence basis to adjust for interstate and international commuting. The difference between earnings by place of residence and earnings by place of work is shown in the "Adjustment for residence" column. This adjustment is a net figure: income received by state (or area) residents from employment outside the state, minus income paid to persons residing outside the state but working in the state. Compared with previous estimates, the "Adjustment for Residence" for the United States as a whole is now a smaller negative adjustment. This is because in the 2000 comprehensive revision, the wages and salaries of foreign residents temporarily working in the United States are now included, i.e. treated as income of residents, in the state personal income figures and in the U.S. total of those figures.

The states are divided into regions as follows:

- **New England:** Connecticut, Maine, Massachusetts, New Hampshire, Rhode Island, Vermont

- **Mideast:** Delaware, District of Columbia, Maryland, New Jersey, New York, Pennsylvania

- **Great Lakes:** Illinois, Indiana, Michigan, Ohio, Wisconsin

- **Plains:** Iowa, Kansas, Minnesota, Missouri, Nebraska, North Dakota, South Dakota

- **Southeast:** Alabama, Arkansas, Florida, Georgia, Kentucky, Louisiana, Mississippi, North Carolina, South Carolina, Tennessee, Virginia, West Virginia

- **Southwest:** Arizona, New Mexico, Oklahoma, Texas

- **Rocky Mountain:** Colorado, Idaho, Montana, Utah, Wyoming

- **Far West:** Alaska, California, Hawaii, Nevada, Oregon, Washington

These regional groupings are the ones used by the Bureau of Economic Analysis. They differ from the region and division definitions used by the U.S. Bureau of the Census.

The data provided here are from a larger data set maintained by the Bureau of Economic Analysis. The latest revisions are described in "Comprehensive Revision of State Personal Income: Revised Estimates for 1969–98, Preliminary Estimates for 1999," *Survey of Current Business,* June 2000.

DATA SOURCES

Most of the data in this volume are from the government agencies and private sources listed below. The specific source(s) for the individual data sets are identified at the beginning of the notes for the relevant data pages.

Board of Governors of the Federal Reserve System
20th Street and Constitution Ave., NW Washington, DC 20551

Data Inquiries and Publication Sales:
   Publications Services
   Mail Stop 127
   Board of Governors of the
   Federal Reserve System
   Washington, DC 20551
   Telephone: (202) 452-3244

Monthly Publication:
   Federal Reserve Bulletin

Internet Address:
   http://www.federalreserve.gov/

BUREAU OF THE CENSUS, U.S. DEPARTMENT OF COMMERCE
Washington, DC 20233

Data Inquiries:
   General Information: (301) 457-4100
   Foreign Trade Information: (301) 457-3041

Internet Address:
   http://www.census.gov

BUREAU OF ECONOMIC ANALYSIS, U.S. DEPARTMENT OF COMMERCE
Washington, DC 20230

Data Inquiries:
  Public Information Office:
  (202) 606-9900

Monthly Publication:
  Survey of Current Business
  Available by subscription from the Superintendent of Documents

Internet Address:
  http://www.bea.doc.gov

BUREAU OF LABOR STATISTICS, U.S. DEPARTMENT OF LABOR
2 Massachusetts Ave., NE
Washington, DC 20212

Data Inquiries:
  General: (202) 606-5886
  24-Hour Hotline: (202) 606-7828

Monthly Publications:
  Monthly Labor Review
  Employment and Earnings
  Compensation and Working Conditions
  Producer Price Indexes
  CPI Detailed Report
  Available by subscription from the Superintendent of Documents

Internet Address:
  http://stats.bls.gov

COMMODITY SYSTEMS, INC. (CSI)
200 West Palmetto Park Road, Suite 200
Boca Raton, FL 33432

Data Orders:
  (800) 274-4727
  (561) 392-8663

Internet Address:
  http://www.csidata.com

CONFERENCE BOARD, THE
845 Third Avenue, New York, NY 10022

Data Inquiries:
  Michael Boldin
  Email: lei@conference-board.org

Publication Sales:
  Customer Service: (212) 339-0345

Monthly Publication:
  Business Cycle Indicators

Internet Address:
  http://www.tcb-indicators.org

FINANCIAL MANAGEMENT SERVICE, U.S. DEPARTMENT OF THE TREASURY
401 14th Street, SW,
Washington, DC 20227

Data Inquiries:
  Budget Reports Branch:
  (202) 874 -9880

Monthly Publication:
  Monthly Treasury Statement
  Available by subscription from the Superintendent of Documents

Internet Address:
  http://www.fms.treas.gov

EMPLOYMENT AND TRAINING ADMINISTRATION, U.S. DEPARTMENT OF LABOR
200 Constitution Avenue, NW
Washington, DC 20210

Data Inquiries:
  (202) 219-6871

Internet Address:
  http://www.doleta.gov

**ENERGY INFORMATION ADMINISTRATION, U.S.
DEPARTMENT OF ENERGY**
1000 Independence Ave., SW
Washington, DC 20585

Data Inquiries and Publications:
    National Energy Information Center
    Phone: (202) 586-8800
    Email: infoctr@eia.doe.gov

Monthly Publication:
    Monthly Energy Review

Internet Address:
    http://www.eia.doe.gov

MORTGAGE BANKERS ASSOCIATION OF AMERICA
1125 15th Street NW
Washington, DC 20005

Data Inquiries:
    (202) 861-6500

Internet Address:
    http://www.mbaa.org

**NATIONAL AGRICULTURAL STATISTICS SERVICE, U.S.
DEPARTMENT OF AGRICULTURE**
14th & Independence Ave., SW
Washington, DC 20250

Data Inquiries:
    Information Hotline: (800) 727-9540

Publication Sales:
    Telephone: (800) 999-6779
    Fax: (703) 834-0110

Internet Address:
    http://www.usda.gov/nass/

To order government publications:
    Superintendent of Documents
    P.O. Box 371954
    Pittsburgh, PA 15250-7954
    (202) 512-1800

INDEX

INDEX